BECK

Racing Price Guide and Alphabetical Checklist

Number 4

Edited by

DR. JAMES BECKETT & STEVEN JUDD

Beckett Publications • Dallas, Texas

 Prices in this guide reflect current retail rates determined just prior to printing. They do not reflect for-sale prices by the author, publisher, distributors, advertisers, or any card dealers associated with this guide. Every effort has been made to eliminate errors. Readers are invited to write us noting any errors which may be researched and corrected in subsequent printings. The publisher will not be held responsible for losses which may occur in the sale or purchase of cards because of information contained herein.

Manufactured in the United States of America
First Printing
ISBN 1-887432-71-X

Beckett Racing Price Guide
Table of Contents

Racing Price Guide

Drag Racing

Indy & Formula 1

Dirt, Sprint & Modified

Promo Cards & Collectibles

Die-Cast

Drag Racing Die-Cast

Indy & Formula One Die-Cast

Dirt & Sprint Die-Cast

Alphabetical Checklist

Index to Advertisers

About the Author

Jim Beckett, the leading authority on sport card values in the United States, maintains a wide range of activities in the world of sports. He possesses one of the finest collections of sports cards and autographs in the world, has made numerous appearances on radio and television, and has been frequently cited in many national publications. He was awarded the first "Special Achievement Award" for Contributions to the Hobby by the National Sports Collectors Convention in 1980, the "Jock-Jaspersen Award" for Hobby Dedication in 1983, and the "Buck Barker, Spirit of the Hobby" Award in 1991.

Dr. Beckett is the author of *Beckett Baseball Card Price Guide, The Official Price Guide to Baseball Cards, The Sport Americana Price Guide to Baseball Collectibles, The Sport Americana Baseball Memorabilia and Autograph Price Guide, Beckett Football Card Price Guide, The Official Price Guide to Football Cards, Beckett Hockey Card Price Guide, The Official Price Guide to Hockey Cards, Beckett Basketball Card Price Guide, The Official Price Guide to Basketball Cards, and The Sport Americana Baseball Card Alphabetical Checklist.* In addition, he is the founder, publisher, and editor of *Beckett Baseball Card Monthly, Beckett Basketball Monthly, Beckett Football Card Monthly, Beckett Hockey Collector, Beckett Racing Monthly, Beckett Sports Collectibles and Autographs, Beckett Hot Toys and Beckett SciFi Collector* magazines.

Jim Beckett received his Ph.D. in Statistics from Southern Methodist University in 1975. Prior to starting Beckett Publications in 1984, Dr. Beckett served as an Associate Professor of Statistics at Bowling Green State University and as a vice president of a consulting firm in Dallas, Texas. He currently resides in Dallas with his wife, Patti, and their daughters, Christina, Rebecca, and Melissa.

How To Use This Book

Isn't it great? A book that is geared toward every type of racing collector. From the individual driver collectors to the set collectors to the die-cast collectors this book has something for each to enjoy. The second Beckett Racing Price Guide and Alphabetical Checklist has been arranged to fit the collector's needs with the inclusion of a comprehensive card price guide, die-cast price guide and an alphabetical checklist. The cards and die-cast you collect – who appears on them, what they look like, where they are from, and (most important to most of you) what their current values are – enumerated within. Many of the features contained in the other Beckett Price Guides have been incorporated into this volume since condition grading, terminology, and many other aspects of collecting are common to the card hobby in general. We hope you find the book both interesting and useful in your collecting pursuits.

The *Beckett Guide* has been successful where other attempts have failed because it is complete, current, and valid. This Price Guide contains two prices by condition for all the racing cards listed. Since the condition that most die-cast pieces are commonly sold in is Near Mint-Mint, the die-cast price guide has been arranged to provide two pricing columns. The prices for each piece reflects the current selling range for that piece. The HI column generally represents full retail selling price. The LO column generally represents the lowest price one could expect to find with extensive shopping. The prices for both the cards and die-cast were added to the listings just prior to printing and reflect not the author's opinions or desires but the going retail prices for each card or die-cast, based on the marketplace (racing shows and events, sports card shops, ads from racing publications, current mail-order catalogs, local club meetings, auction results, on-line networks, and other first-hand reportings of actually realized prices).

What is the best price guide available on the market today? Of course, card sellers prefer the price guide with the highest prices, while card buyers naturally prefer the one with the lowest prices. Accuracy, however, is the true test. Use the price guide trusted by more collectors and dealers than all the others combined. Look for the *Beckett*® name. I won't put my name on anything I won't stake my reputation on. Not the lowest and not the highest — but the most accurate, with integrity.

To facilitate your use of this book, read the complete introductory section on the following pages before going to the pricing pages. Every collectible field has its own terminology; we've tried to capture most of these terms and definitions in our glossary. Please read carefully the section on grading and the condition of your cards, as you cannot determine which price column is appropriate for a given card without first knowing its condition.

Welcome to the world of racing cards and die-cast.

Jim Beckett

Introduction

Welcome to the exciting world of racing card and die-cast collecting, America's fastest-growing avocation. You have made a good choice in buying this book, since it will open up to you the entire panorama of this field in the simplest, most concise way.

The growth of *Beckett Baseball Card Monthly, Beckett Basketball Monthly, Beckett Football Card Monthly, Beckett Hockey Monthly, Beckett Future Stars and Beckett Racing Monthly* is an indication of the unprecedented popularity of sports cards. Founded in 1984 by Dr. James Beckett, the author of this Price Guide, *Beckett Baseball Card Monthly* contains the most extensive and accepted monthly Price Guide, collectible glossy superstar covers, colorful feature articles, "Short Prints," Convention Calendar, tips for beginners, "Readers Write" letters to and responses from the editor, information on errors and varieties, autograph collecting tips and profiles of the sport's Hottest stars. Published every month, *BBCM* is the hobby's largest paid circulation periodical. The other five magazines were built on the success of *BBCM*.

So collecting racing cards — while still pursued as a hobby with youthful exuberance by kids in the neighborhood — has also taken on the trappings of an industry, with thousands of full- and part-time card dealers, as well as vendors of supplies, clubs and conventions. In fact, each year since 1980 thousands of hobbyists have assembled for a National Sports Collectors Convention, at which hundreds of dealers have displayed their wares, seminars have been conducted, autographs penned by sports notables, and millions of cards changed hands. The Beckett Guide is the best annual guide available to the exciting world of racing cards and die-cast. Read it and use it. May your enjoyment and your card collection increase in the coming months and years.

How to Collect

Each collection is personal and reflects the individuality of its owner. There are no set rules on how to collect cards. Since card collecting is a hobby or leisure pastime, what you collect, how much you collect, and how much time and money you spend collecting are entirely up to you. The funds you have available for collecting and your own personal taste should determine how you collect. Information and ideas presented here are intended to help you get the most enjoyment from this hobby.

It is impossible to collect every card ever produced. Therefore, beginners as well as intermediate and advanced collectors usually specialize in some way. One of the reasons this hobby is popular is that individual collectors can define and tailor their collecting methods to match their own tastes. To give you some ideas of the various approaches to collecting, we will list some of the more popular areas of specialization.

Many collectors select complete sets from particular years. For example, they may concentrate on assembling complete sets from all the years since their birth or since they became avid racing fans. They may try to collect a card for every driver during that specified period of time.

Many collectors wish to acquire only certain drivers. Usually such drivers are the superstars of the sport, but typically collectors will specialize in all the cards of a driver who has become their favorite for various reasons. Racing fans are a loyal group and they will stick with their favorites through thick and thin. The Alphabetical Checklist that is a part of this book will be extremely useful for those who collect their favorites.

Some collectors only collect cards, while some only collect die-cast. There are those who collect by sponsor and those who collect by car number. In all, there is no right or wrong way to collect. It is up to you to decide what you want to buy and how you want to build your collection. We only insist that you have fun in your collecting.

Obtaining Cards

Several avenues are open to card collectors. Cards still can be purchased in the traditional way: by the pack at the local candy, grocery, drug or major discount stores.

But there are also thousands of card shops across the country that specialize in selling cards individually or by the pack, box, or set. Another alternative is the thousands of card shows held each month around the country, which feature anywhere from

eight to 800 tables of sports cards and memorabilia for sale.

Since the beginning of the modern era of racing card collecting in 1988, it has been possible to purchase complete sets of racing cards and die-cast pieces through mail-order advertisers found in traditional racing media publications, such as *Winston Cup Scene, Circle Track, Stock Car Racing* and others. These sets also are advertised in the card and die-cast collecting periodicals. Many collectors will begin by subscribing to at least one of the hobby periodicals, all with good up-to-date information. In fact, subscription offers can be found in the advertising section of this book.

Most serious card and die-cast collectors obtain old (and new) cards from one or more of several main sources: (1) trading or buying from other collectors or dealers; (2) responding to sale or auction ads in publications or dealer catalogs; (3) buying at a local hobby store; (4) attending a race event and buying from a souvenir trailer or vendor set up at the track; (5) attending collectibles shows or conventions; and/or (6) trading or buying on-line.

We advise that you try all six methods since each has its own distinct advantages: (1) trading is a great way to make new friends; (2) hobby periodicals and dealer catalogs can help you keep up with what's going on in the hobby (including when and where the conventions are happening); (3) stores provide the opportunity to enjoy personalized service and consider a great diversity of material in a relaxed sports-oriented atmosphere; and (4) & (5) racing events and shows allow you to choose from multiple dealers and thousands of cards in one area or under one roof in a competitive situation, and (6) the internet has brought a whole new experience to collecting.

Preserving Your Cards

Cards are fragile. They must be handled properly in order to retain their value. Careless handling can easily result in creased or bent cards. It is, however, not recommended that tweezers or tongs be used to pick up your cards since such utensils might mar or indent card surfaces and thus reduce those cards' conditions and values.

In general, your cards should be handled directly as little as possible. This is sometimes easier to say than to do.

Although there are still many who use custom boxes, storage trays, or even shoe boxes, plastic sheets are the preferred method of many collectors for storing cards.

A collection stored in plastic pages in a three-ring album allows you to view your collection at any time without the need to touch the card itself. Cards can also be kept in single holders (of various types and thickness) designed for the enjoyment of each card individually.

For a large collection, some collectors may use a combination of the above methods. When purchasing plastic sheets for your cards, be sure that you find the pocket size that fits the cards snugly. Don't put your 1995 Optima XL cards in a sheet designed to fit 1995 Maxx.

Most hobby and collectibles shops and virtually all collectors' conventions will have these plastic pages available in quantity for the various sizes offered, or you can purchase them directly from the advertisers in this book.

Also, remember that pocket size isn't the only factor to consider when looking for plastic sheets. Other factors such as safety, economy, appearance, availability, or personal preference also may indicate which types of sheets a collector may want to buy.

Damp, sunny and/or hot conditions — no, this is not a weather forecast — are three elements to avoid in extremes if you are interested in preserving your collection. Too much (or too little) humidity can cause the gradual deterioration of a card. Direct, bright sun (or fluorescent light) over time will bleach out the color of a card. Extreme heat accelerates the decomposition of the card. On the other hand, many cards have lasted more than 75 years without much scientific intervention. So be cautious, even if the above factors typically present a problem only when present in the extreme. It never hurts to be prudent.

Collecting vs. Investing

Collecting individual players and collecting complete sets are both popular vehicles for investment and speculation.

Most investors and speculators stock up on complete sets, on quantities of drivers, or on specific cards they think have good investment potential.

There is obviously no guarantee in this book, or anywhere else for that matter, that cards will outperform the stock market or other investment alternatives in the future. After all, racing cards do not pay quarterly dividends and cards cannot be sold at their "current values" as easily as stocks or bonds.

Many hobbyists maintain that the best investment is and always will be the building of a collection, which traditionally has held up better than outright speculation.

Some of the obvious questions are: Which cards? When to buy? When to sell? The best investment you can make is in your own education.

The more you know about your collection and the hobby, the more informed the decisions you will be able to make. We're not selling investment tips. We're selling information about the current value of racing cards and die-cast. It's up to you to use that information to your best advantage.

Terminology

Each hobby has its own language to describe its area of interest. With racing being relatively new to the card collecting hobby it has adapted many of the terms and phrases used in other areas of sports card collecting. Most sets are usually referred to by year, by maker, and sometimes by title or theme of the set.

Glossary/Legend

Our glossary defines terms used in the card and die-cast collecting hobby and in this book. Many of these terms are also common to other types of sports memorabilia collecting. Some terms may have several meanings depending on use and context.

ACETATE - A transparent plastic.

ACR- AC Racing.

AM - American Miniatures.

ANN - Announcer.

AP - All-Pro.

ART - Art card.

AUTO - Autograph.

AW - Award Winners.

B - Brothers.

BB - Back to Back.

BC - Busch Clash.

BD - Burning Desire

BF - Buck Fever.

BGN - Busch Grand National.

BL - Blister Pack.

BR - Braille.

BRICK - A group of 50 or more cards having common characteristics that is intended to be bought, sold or traded as a unit.

BT - Breaking Through.

BX - Boxed.

BY - Brickyard 400.

BYS - Brickyard Special.

C - Classics, Conquerors.

CC - Cup Contenders.

CHECKLIST - A list of the cards contained in a particular set. The list is always in numerical order if the cards are numbered. Some unnumbered sets are artificially numbered in alphabetical order, by team and alphabetically within the team, or by uniform number for convenience.

CJT - Crown Jewel Times.

CL - Checklist card. A card that lists in order the cards and drivers in the set or series.

CLEARCHROME - A method of card manufacturing technology patented by MAXX. It involves the production of a card using an acetate material.

CO - Club Only.

COIN - A small disc of metal or plastic portraying a player in its center.

COLLECTOR ISSUE - A set produced for the sake of the card itself with no product or service sponsor. It derives its name from the fact that most of these sets are produced for sale directly to the hobby market.

COMMON CARD - A typical card of any set; it has no premium value accruing from subject matter, numerical scarcity, popular demand, or anomaly.

COMMON DRIVER - A typical driver card of any set; it has no premium value accruing from subject matter, numerical scarcity, popular demand, or anomaly.

CONVENTION - A gathering of dealers and collectors at a single location for the purpose of buying, selling, and trading sports memorabilia items. Conventions are open to the public and sometimes feature autograph guests, door prizes, contests, seminars, etc. They are frequently referred to simply as "shows."

COR - Corrected card.

COUPON - See Tab.

CPC - Championship Pit Crew.

DB - Daytona Beach.

DD - Double Duty, Driving with Dale.

DEALER - A person who engages in buying, selling, and trading sports collectibles or supplies. A dealer may also be a collector, but as a dealer, his main goal is to earn a profit.

DEI - Dale Earnhardt Inc.

DIE - CUT - A card with part of its stock partially cut, allowing one or more parts to be folded or removed. After removal or appropriate folding, the remaining part of the card can frequently be made to stand up.

DISPLAY CARD - A sheet, usually containing three to nine cards, that is printed and used by the manufacturer to advertise and/or display the packages containing his products and cards. The backs of display cards are blank or contain advertisements.

DOY - Driver of the Year.

DP - Double Print (a card that was printed in double the quantity compared to the other cards in the same series).

DR - Daytona Review, Delco Remy.

DT - Double Trouble.

DUFEX - A method of card manufacturing technology patented by Pinnacle Brands, Inc. It involves a refractive quality to a card with a foil coating.

DW - Daytona Winner.

DYK - Did You Know.

D93 - Daytona 1993.

EMBOSSED - A raised surface; features of a card that are projected from a flat background. (i.e. Action Packed cards).

EOD - End of the Day.

ERR - Error card. A card with erroneous information, spelling, or depiction on either side of the card. Most errors are not corrected by the producing card company.

ETCHED - Impressions within the surface of a card.

EY - Early Years

FB - Fastback.

FCS - Future Cup Stars.

FF - Fan Favorite.

FOIL - Foil embossed stamp on card.

FOLD - Foldout.

F.Q.S. - Fastest Qualifying Speed.

FS - Father/son card.

FULL BLEED - A borderless card; a card containing a photo that encompasses the entire card.

FULL SHEET - A complete sheet of cards that has not been cut up into individual cards by the manufacturer. Also called an uncut sheet.

GLOSS - A card with luster; a shiny finish as in a card with UV coating.

GMP - Georgia Marketing and Promotions.

HB - History Book.

HG - Hot Guns.

HO - Hood Open.

HOLO - Hologram.

HOLOGRAM - A three-dimensional photographic image.

HR - Heroes of Racing.

HV - Heavenly Views

I - Idols.

IB - In the Blood.

IMHOF - International Motorsports Hall of Fame.

INSERT - A card of a different type or any other sports collectible (typically a poster or sticker) contained and sold in the same package along with a card or cards of a major set. An insert card is either unnumbered or not numbered in the same sequence as the major set. Sometimes the inserts are randomly distributed and are not found in every pack.

INTERACTIVE - A concept that involves collector participation.

IROC - International Race of Champions

ISSUE - Synonymous with set, but usually used in conjunction with a manufacturer, e.g., a MAXX issue.

K - Knights.

KARAT - A unit of measure for the fineness of gold; i.e. 24K.

LAYERING - The separation or peeling of one or more layers of the card stock, usually at the corner of the card.

LEGITIMATE ISSUE - A set produced to promote or boost sales of a product or service, e.g., bubblegum, cereal, cigarettes, etc. Most collector issues are not legitimate issues in this sense.

LUM - Lumina.

MAJOR SET - A set produced by a national manufacturer of cards containing a large number of cards. Usually 50 or more different cards comprise a major set.

MB - Matchbox.

MC - Monte Carlo.

MEM - Memorial card. For example 1993 Finish Line NNO Alan Kulwicki.

METALLIC - A glossy design method that enhances card features.

MM - Memorable Moment.

MO - Members Only

MRO- Motor Racing Outreach.

MT - Mac Tools.

MULTI-DRIVER CARD - A single card depicting two or more drivers.

NASCAR - The National Association for Stock Car Auto Racing.

NB - Notchback.

NDA - No Driver Associated.

NL - Next in Line.

NM - Newsmakers.

NMC - New Monte Carlo for 1995.

NNO - No Number on Card.

NITROKROME - A method of card manufacturing technology patented by Press Pass. It involves the use of etched technology to bring out color in the card.

NON-SPORT CARD - A card from a set whose major theme is a subject other than a sports subject. A card of a sports figure or event that is part of a non-sport set is still a non-sport card.

NOTCHING - The grooving of the card, usually caused by fingernails, rubber bands, or bumping card edges against other objects.

NP - NASCAR Properties on Stand.

NS - No Sponsor.

NTB - New Thunderbird Mold for 1995.

OC - Out of the Chute.

OTM - On the mark

OWN - Owner.

P - Promo or Prototype.

PACKS - A means with which cards are issued in terms of pack type (wax, cello, foil, rack, blister, etc.) and channels of distribution (hobby, retail, etc.).

PARALLEL- A card that is similar in design to its counterpart from the basic set, but offers a distinguishing quality.

PB - Petty Back.

PBC - Polybag.

PLASTIC SHEET - A clear, plastic page that is punched for insertion into a binder (with standard three-ring spacing) containing pockets for displaying cards. Many different styles of sheets exist with pockets of varying sizes to hold the many differing card formats. Also called a display sheet or storage sheet.

PLATINUM - A metallic element used in the process of creating a glossy card.

PLS - Platinum Series.

PO - Power Owners.

PP - Power Prospects, Precision Performers, Past & Present.

PPGC - PPG Champs.

PR - Personal Rides.

PRE - Preview.

PREMIUM - A card, sometimes on photographic stock, that is purchased or obtained in conjunction with, or redemption for another card or product. the premium is not packaged in the same unit as the primary item.

PRISMATIC/PRISM - A glossy or bright design that refracts or disperses light.

PROMO/PROTOTYPE - A card or die-cast issued to preview a set or a release in special association with a racing sponsor. Promo cards are usually issued to the dealers purchasing the cards.

PS - Pole Sitters, Peachstate.

PVC - Polyvinyl Chloride, a substance used to make many of the popular card display protective sheets. Non-PVC sheets are considered preferable for long-term storage of cards by many.

PW - Pole Winner, Power Winner.

RARE - A card or series of cards of very limited availability. Unfortunately, "rare" is a subjective term frequently used indiscriminately to hype value. "Rare" cards are harder to obtain than "scarce" cards.

RCCA - Racing Collectibles Club of America.

RCI - Racing Collectibles, Inc.

REDEMPTION- A program established by multiple card manufacturers that allows collectors to mail in a special card (usually a random insert) in return for special cards, sets or other prizes not available through conventional channels.

REGIONAL - A card or set of cards issued and distributed only in a limited geographical area of the country.

REPLICA - An identical copy or reproduction.

REV - Revell.

RET - Retro

ROY - Rookie of the Year.

RQ - Rookie Qualifier.

RR - Race Review

RS - Riding Shotgun.

RW - Race Winner.

S - SportsKings, Shades, Shattered.

SASE - Self-Addressed, Stamped Envelope.

SB - Scrapbook.

SCARCE - A card or series of cards of limited availability. This subjective term is sometimes used indiscriminately to hype value. "Scarce" cards are not as difficult to obtain as "rare" cards.

SD - Season Debut.

SET - One each of the entire run of cards of the same type produced by a particular manufacturer during a single year.

SHEEN - Brightness or luster emitted by a card.

SI - Sports Image.

SKIP-NUMBERED - A set that has many unissued card numbers between the lowest number in the set and the highest number in the set; e.g., the 1987 World of Outlaw set. A major set in which a few numbers were not printed is not considered to be skip-numbered.

SL - Stat Leaders.

SM - Speed Machines

SP - Single or Short Print (a card which was printed in lesser quantity compared to the other cards in the same series; see also DP and TP).

SPECIAL CARD - A card that portrays something other than a single driver or team; for example, a card that portrays the previous year's winner of the Daytona 500.

SR - Star Rookie.

SS - Split Shift.

SSA - Super Star Awards.

ST - Small Town. Saturday Night

STANDARD SIZE - Most modern sports cards measure 2-1/2 by 3-1/2 inches. Exceptions are noted in card descriptions throughout this book.

STAR CARD - A card that portrays a driver of some repute, usually determined by his ability, however, sometimes referring to sheer popularity.

STICKER - A card with removable layer that can be affixed to (stuck on) another surface.

STC - Seven-Time Champion

STO - SuperTruck Owner.

STOCK - The cardboard or paper on which the card is printed.

SUPERIMPOSED - To be affixed on top of something, i.e., a driver photo over a solid background.

SUPERSTAR CARD - A card that portrays a superstar.

T - Tribute

T4 - Turn Four

T10 - Top Ten.

TA - The Allisons.

TB - Thunderbird.

TC - Trophy Case.

TD - Track Dominators.

TEST SET - A set, usually containing a small number of cards, issued by a national card producer and distributed in a limited section or sections of the country. Presumably, the purpose of a test set is to test market appeal for a particular type of card.

THREE-DIMENSIONAL (3D) - A visual image that provides an illusion of depth and perspective.

TOPICAL - a subset or group of cards that have a common theme.

TP - Triple Print (a card that was printed in triple the quantity compared to the other cards in the same series.).

TRAN - Transporter.

TRANSPARENT - Clear, see through.

TRIMMED - A card cut down from its original size. Trimmed cards are undesirable to most collectors.

TT - Texas Tornado

TT - Top Team.

TTM - To the Maxx.

TW - Team Work.

UER - Uncorrected Error.

UV - Ultraviolet, a glossy coating used in producing cards.

VAR - Variation card. One of two or more cards from the same series with the same number (or player with identical pose if the series is unnumbered) differing from one another by some aspect, the different feature stemming from the printing or stock of the card. This can be caused when the manufacturer of the cards notices an error in one or more of the cards, makes the changes, and then resumes the print run. In this case there will be two versions or variations of the same card. Sometimes one of the variations is relatively scarce.

VL - Victory Lane.

VT - Valvoline Team.

WC - Winston Cup, Winner's Circle.

WCA - Wives, Camera, Action

WCC - Winston Cup Champion.

WCS - Winston Cup Scene.

WD - Winston Decal.

WIN - Winner Insert, Winners.

WP - War Paint

WRC - White Rose Collectibles.

WS - Winston Select.

YB - Yellow & Black Box.

YBH - Yellow Box Hobby Only.

YG - Young Guns.

YR - Year in Review.

YS - Young Stars.

Understanding Card Values

Determining Value

Why are some cards more valuable than others? Obviously, the economic laws of supply and demand are applicable to card collecting just as they are to any other field where a commodity is bought, sold or traded in a free, unregulated market.

Supply (the number of cards available on the market) is less than the total number of cards originally produced since attrition diminishes that original quantity. Each year a percentage of cards is typically thrown away, destroyed or otherwise lost to collectors. This percentage is much, much smaller today than it was in the past because more and more people have become increasingly aware of the value of their cards.

For those who collect only Mint condition cards, the supply of older cards can be quite small indeed. Until recently, collectors were not so conscious of the need to preserve the condition of their cards. For this reason, it is difficult to know exactly how many 1972 STP cards are currently available, Mint or otherwise. It is generally accepted that there are fewer 1972 STP cards available than 1988 Maxx. If demand were equal for each of these sets, the law of supply and demand would increase the price for the least available set. Demand, however, is never equal for all sets, so price correlations can be complicated. The demand for a card is influenced by many factors. These include: (1) the age of the card; (2) the number of cards printed; (3) the driver(s) portrayed on the card; (4) the attractiveness and popularity of the set; and (5) the physical condition of the card.

In general, (1) the older the card, (2) the fewer the number of the cards printed, (3) the more famous, popular and talented the driver, (4) the more attractive and popular the set, and (5) the better the condition of the card, the higher the value of the card will be. There are exceptions to all but one of these factors: the condition of the card. Given two cards similar in all respects except condition, the one in the best condition will always be valued higher.

While those guidelines help to establish the value of a card, the countless exceptions and peculiarities make any simple, direct mathematical formula to determine card values impossible.

Regional Variation

Since the market varies from region to region, card prices of local drivers may be higher. This is known as a regional premium. How significant the premium is — and if there is any premium at all — depends on the local popularity of the driver.

The largest regional premiums usually do not apply to superstars, who often are so well-known nationwide that the prices of their key cards are too high for local dealers to realize a premium.

Lesser stars often command the strongest premiums. Their popularity is concentrated in their home region, creating local demand that greatly exceeds overall demand.

Regional premiums can apply to popular retired drivers and sometimes can be found in the areas where the drivers grew up or started racing.

A regional discount is the converse of a regional premium. Regional discounts occur when a driver has been so popular in his region for so long that local collectors and dealers have accumulated quantities of his key cards. The abundant supply may make the cards available in that area at the lowest prices anywhere.

Set Prices

A somewhat paradoxical situation exists in the price of a complete set vs. the combined cost of the individual cards in the set. In nearly every case, the sum of the prices for the individual cards is higher than the cost for the complete set. This is prevalent especially in the cards of the last few years. The reasons for this apparent anomaly stem from the habits of collectors and from the carrying costs to dealers. Today, each card in a set normally is produced in the same quantity as all other cards in its set.

Many collectors pick up only stars, superstars and particular teams. As a result, the dealer is left with a shortage of certain driver cards and an abundance of others. He therefore incurs an expense in simply "carrying" these less desirable cards in stock. On the other hand, if he sells a complete set, he gets rid of large numbers of cards at one time. For this reason, he generally is willing to receive less money for a complete set. By doing this, he recovers all of his costs and also makes a profit.

The disparity between the price of the complete set and the sum of the individual cards also has been influenced by the fact that some of the major manufacturers now are pre-collating card sets. Since "pulling" individual cards from the sets involves a specific type of labor (and cost), the singles or star card market is not affected significantly by pre-collation.

Set prices also do not include rare card varieties, unless specifically stated. Of course, the prices for sets do include one example of each type for the given set, but this is the least expensive variety.

Distribution Info

We are always looking for information or photographs of printing sheets of cards for research. Each year, we try to update the hobby's knowledge of distribution anomalies. Please let us know at the address in this book if you have first-hand knowledge that would be helpful in this pursuit.

Grading Your Cards

Each hobby has its own grading terminology — stamps, coins, comic books, record collecting, etc. Collectors of sports cards are no exception. The one invariable criterion for determining the value of a card is its condition: The better the condition of the card, the more valuable it is. Condition grading, however, is subjective. Individual card dealers and collectors differ in the strictness of their grading, but the stated condition of a card should be determined without regard to whether it is being bought or sold.

No allowance is made for age. A 1960 card is judged by the same standards as a 1992 card. But there are specific sets and cards that are condition sensitive (marked with "!" in the Price Guide) because of their border color, consistently poor centering, etc. Such cards and sets sometimes command premiums above the listed percentages in Mint condition.

Centering

Current centering terminology uses numbers representing the percentage of border on either side of the main design. Obviously, centering is diminished in importance for borderless cards such as 1995 Traks.

Slightly Off-Center (60/40): A slightly off-center card is one that, upon close inspection, is found to have one border bigger than the opposite border. This degree once was offensive to only purists, but now some hobbyists try to avoid cards that are anything other than perfectly centered.

Off-Center (70/30): An off-center card has one border that is noticeably more than twice as wide as the opposite border.

Badly Off-Center (80/20 or worse): A badly off-center card has virtually no border on one side of the card.

Miscut: A miscut card actually shows part of the adjacent card in its larger border and consequently a corresponding amount of its card is cut off.

Corner Wear

Corner wear is the most scrutinized grading criteria in the hobby. These are the major categories of corner wear:

Corner with a slight touch of wear: The corner still is sharp, but there is a slight touch of wear showing. On a dark-bordered card, this shows as a dot of white.

Fuzzy corner: The corner still comes to a point, but the point has just begun to fray. A slightly "dinged" corner is considered the same as a fuzzy corner.

Slightly rounded corner: The fraying of the corner has increased to where there is only a hint of a point. Mild layering may be evident. A "dinged" corner is considered the same as a slightly rounded corner.

Rounded corner: The point is completely gone. Some layering is noticeable.

Badly rounded corner: The corner is completely round and rough. Severe layering is evident.

Creases

A third common defect is the crease. The degree of creasing in a card is difficult to show in a drawing or picture. On giving the specific condition of an expensive card for sale, the seller should note any creases additionally. Creases can be categorized as to severity according to the following scale:

Light Crease: A light crease is a crease that is barely noticeable upon close inspection. In fact, when cards are in plastic sheets or holders, a light crease may not be seen (until the card is taken out of the holder). A light crease on the front is much more serious than a light crease on the card back only.

Medium Crease: A medium crease is noticeable when held and studied at arm's length by the naked eye, but does not overly detract from the appearance of the card. It is an obvious crease, but not one that breaks the picture surface of the card.

Heavy Crease: A heavy crease is one that has torn or broken through the card's picture surface, e.g., puts a tear in the photo surface.

Alterations

Deceptive Trimming: This occurs when someone alters the card in order (1) to shave off edge wear, (2) to improve the sharpness of the corners, or (3) to improve centering — obviously their objective is to falsely increase the perceived value of the card to an unsuspecting buyer. The shrinkage usually is evident only if the trimmed card is compared to an adjacent full-sized card or if the trimmed card is itself measured.

Obvious Trimming: Obvious trimming is noticeable and unfortunate. It is usually performed by non-collectors who give no thought to the present or future value of their cards.

Deceptively Retouched Borders: This occurs when the borders (especially on those cards with dark borders) are touched up on the edges and corners with magic marker or crayons of appropriate color in order to make the card appear Mint.

Categorization of Defects

Miscellaneous Flaws

The following are common minor flaws that, depending on severity, lower a card's condition by one to four grades and often render it no better than Excellent-Mint: bubbles (lumps in surface), gum and wax stains, diamond cutting (slanted borders), notching, off-centered backs, paper wrinkles, scratched-off cartoons or puzzles on back, rubber band marks, scratches, surface impressions and warping.

The following are common serious flaws that, depending on severity, lower a card's condition at least four grades and often render it no better than Good: chemical or sun fading, erasure marks, mildew, miscutting (severe off-centering), holes, bleached or re-touched borders, tape marks, tears, trimming, water or coffee stains and writing.

Condition Guide

Grades

Mint (Mt) - A card with no flaws or wear. The card has four perfect corners, 60/40 or better centering from top to bottom and from left to right, original gloss, smooth edges and original color borders. A Mint card does not have print spots, color or focus imperfections.

Near Mint-Mint (NrMt-Mt) - A card with one minor flaw. Any one of the following would lower a Mint card to Near Mint-Mint: one corner with a slight touch of wear, barely noticeable print spots, color or focus imperfections. The card must have 60/40 or better centering in both directions, original gloss, smooth edges and original color borders.

Near Mint (NrMt) - A card with one minor flaw. Any one of the following would lower a Mint card to Near Mint: one fuzzy corner or two to four corners with slight touches of wear, 70/30 to 60/40 centering, slightly rough edges, minor print spots, color or focus imperfections. The card must have original gloss and original color borders.

Excellent-Mint (ExMt) - A card with two or three fuzzy, but not rounded, corners and centering no worse than 80/20. The card may have no more than two of the following: slightly rough edges, very slightly discolored borders, minor print spots, color or focus imperfections. The card must have original gloss.

Excellent (Ex) - A card with four fuzzy but definitely not rounded corners and centering no worse than 80/20. The card may have a small amount of original gloss lost, rough edges, slightly discolored borders and minor print spots, color or focus imperfections.

Very Good (Vg) - A card that has been handled but not abused: slightly rounded corners with slight layering, slight notching on edges, a significant amount of gloss lost from the surface but no scuffing and moderate discoloration of borders. The card may have a few light creases.

Good (G), Fair (F), Poor (P) - A well-worn, mishandled or abused card: badly rounded and layered corners, scuffing, most or all original gloss missing, seriously discolored borders, moderate or heavy creases, and one or more serious flaws. The grade of Good, Fair or Poor depends on the severity of wear and flaws. Good, Fair and Poor cards generally are used only as fillers.

The most widely used grades are defined above. Obviously, many cards will not perfectly fit one of the definitions.

Therefore, categories between the major grades known as in-between grades are used, such as Good to Very Good (G-Vg), Very Good to Excellent (VgEx), and Excellent-Mint to Near Mint (ExMt-NrMt). Such grades indicate a card with all qualities of the lower category but with at least a few qualities of the higher category.

Beckett Racing Price Guide lists each card and set in three grades, with the middle grade valued at about 40-45% of the top grade, and the bottom grade valued at about 10-15% of the top grade.

The value of cards that fall between the listed columns can also be calculated using a percentage of the top grade. For example, a card that falls between the top and middle grades (Ex, ExMt or NrMt in most cases) will generally be valued at anywhere from 50% to 90% of the top grade.

Similarly, a card that falls between the middle and bottom grades (G-Vg, Vg or VgEx in most cases) will generally be valued at anywhere from 20% to 40% of the top grade.

There are also cases where cards are in better condition than the top grade or worse than the bottom grade. Cards that grade worse than the lowest grade are generally valued at 5-10% of the top grade.

When a card exceeds the top grade by one — such as NrMt-Mt when the top grade is NrMt, or Mint when the top grade is NrMt-Mt — a premium of up to 50% is possible, with 10-20% the usual norm.

When a card exceeds the top grade by two — such as Mint when the top grade is NrMt, or NrMt-Mt when the top grade is ExMt — a premium of 25-50% is the usual norm. But certain condition sensitive cards or sets, particularly those from the pre-war era, can bring premiums of up to 100% or even more.

Unopened packs, boxes and factory-collated sets are considered Mint in their unknown (and presumed perfect) state. Once opened, however, each card can be graded (and valued) in its own right by taking into account any defects that may be present in spite of the fact that the card has never been handled.

Selling Your Cards

Just about every collector sells cards or will sell cards eventually. Someday you may be interested in selling your duplicates or maybe even your whole collection. You may sell to other collectors, friends or dealers. You may even sell cards you purchased from a certain dealer back to that same dealer. In any event, it helps to know some of the mechanics of the typical transaction between buyer and seller.

Dealers will buy cards in order to resell them to other collectors who are interested in the cards. Dealers will always pay a higher percentage for items that (in their opinion) can be resold quickly, and a much lower percentage for those items that are perceived as having low demand and hence are slow moving. In either case, dealers must buy at a price that allows for the expense of doing business and a margin for profit.

If you have cards for sale, the best advice we can give is that you get several offers for your cards either from card shops or at a card show and take the best offer, all things considered. Note, the "best" offer may not be the one for the highest amount. And remember, if a dealer really wants your cards, he won't let you get away without making his best competitive offer. Another alternative is to place your cards in an auction as one or several lots.

Many people think nothing of going into a department store and paying $15 for an item of clothing for which the store paid $5. But if you were selling your $15 card to a dealer and he offered you $5 for it, you might consider his mark-up unreasonable. To complete the analogy: Most department stores (and card dealers) that consistently pay $10 for $15 items eventually go out of business. An exception is when the dealer has lined up a willing buyer for the item(s) you are attempting to sell, or if the cards are so Hot that it's likely he'll likely have to hold the cards for just a short period of time.

In those cases, an offer of up to 75 percent of book value still will allow the dealer to make a reasonable profit considering the short time he will need to hold the merchandise. In general, however, most cards and collections will bring offers in the range of 25 to 50 percent of retail price. Also consider that most material from the last five to 10 years is plentiful. If that's what you're selling, don't be surprised if your best offer is well below that range.

Interesting Notes

The first card numerically of an issue is the single card most likely to obtain excessive wear.

Consequently, you typically will find the price on the #1 card (in NrMt or Mint condition) somewhat higher than might otherwise be the case.

Similarly, but to a lesser extent (because normally the less important, reverse side of the card is the one exposed), the last card numerically in an issue also is prone to abnormal wear. This extra wear and tear occurs because the first and last cards are exposed to the elements (human element included) more than any of the other cards. They are generally end cards in any brick formations, rubber bandings, stackings on wet surfaces and like activities.

Sports cards have no intrinsic value. The value of a card, like the value of other collectibles, can be determined only by you and your enjoyment in viewing and possessing these cardboard treasures.

Remember, the buyer ultimately determines the price of each racing card. You are the determining price factor because you have the ability to say "No" to the price of any card by not exchanging your hard-earned money for a given issue. When the cost of a trading card exceeds the enjoyment you will receive from it, your answer should be "No." We assess and report the prices. You set them!

We are always interested in receiving the price input of collectors and dealers. We happily credit major contributors.

We welcome your opinions, since your contributions assist us in ensuring a better guide each year.

If you would like to join our survey list for the next editions of this book and others authored by Dr. Beckett, please send your name and address to Dr. James Beckett, 15850 Dallas Parkway, Dallas, TX 75248.

History of Racing Cards

The history of racing cards is not an extensive story like with the other major sports. For the modern era of the racing card market only began in 1988. Before that time there were only a few sets produced and the majority of those sets were about forms of racing other than NASCAR. The early cards, 1960-1980, mainly paid tribute to Indy and Drag Racing. While the racing card market may have lagged behind the other sports in early history, it has more than kept up with them in terms of growth since 1988. In just a few short years racing cards have grown from plain photos on plain cardboard to colorful, high-tech works of art.

One of the earliest known racing card set that features racing drivers is the 1911 American Auto Drivers set. The cards were produced for the American Tobacco Company and were inserted in packs of cigarettes. Each of the 25 cards was available with a small ad for either Hassan or Mecca Cigarettes on the cardback. The unnumbered cards feature top race car drivers of the day from both North America and Europe. They represented all types of auto racing events.

There were also a few other racing or automobile focused sets produced during the first half of this century. Sets like the 1911 Turkey Reds and the 1931 Ogden's Motor Races featured the cars and events of that time period. The drivers of the cars were secondary. Other sets issued in Europe like the 1939 Churchman's King of Speed and the Will's Cigarette set featured a few racing cards but those cards were only part of multisport set. These few sets represent the trend for the majority of automobile related issues prior to World War II.

It wasn't until the post World War II era that more driver focused racing sets were introduced to the market. From 1954-1966 racing saw the production of only six sets. Three of the sets, 1954 Stark and Wetzel Meats, 1960 Hawes Wax and the 1962 Marhoefer Meats, focused on the most popular form of racing at the time, Indy Car. As you can see from the set names, each was a promotional type set. The cards of the two meat products sets were distributed in various meat products. This makes it difficult to find Near Mint or better copies of these cards. The Hawes set was made for the Hawes Furniture Wax company by Canadian card manufacturer Parkhurst. This is the same company that produced the majority of Hockey cards issued during the 50's and early 60's. Topps and Donruss also issued a set each focused on Hot Rods and Drag racing in 1965. Donruss' issue of the 1965 Spec Sheet set comes well before the beginning of their regular production of baseball cards in 1981.

The decade of the 70's saw the production of primarily drag racing sets. More than half of the few racing sets produced during that time had a drag racing theme. All the drag racing sets were produced by Fleer and each focused on drivers of the American Hot Rod Association.

The first NASCAR related set was produced in 1972. The eleven card STP set featured full-bleed photos and unnumbered card backs that contained some biographical information on each of the drivers and the STP name and address. This set was a promotion of the STP corporation and features some of the top names in NASCAR at that time. The cards are tough to come by and usually are found in conditions less than Near Mint. This set is the only full NASCAR card set until the 1983 UNO set and the 1986 SportStars Photo-Graphics set.

Centering

50/50

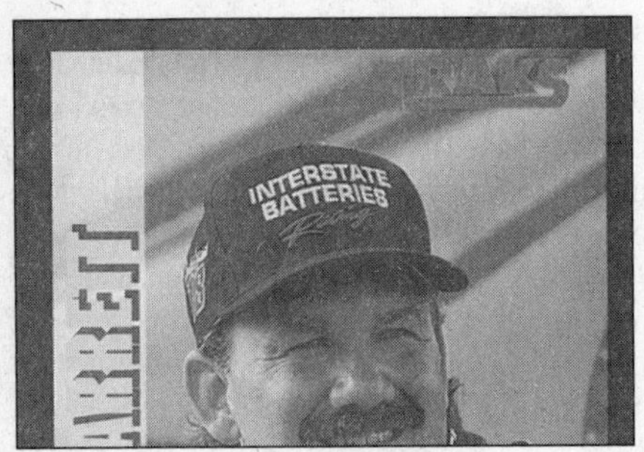

60/40

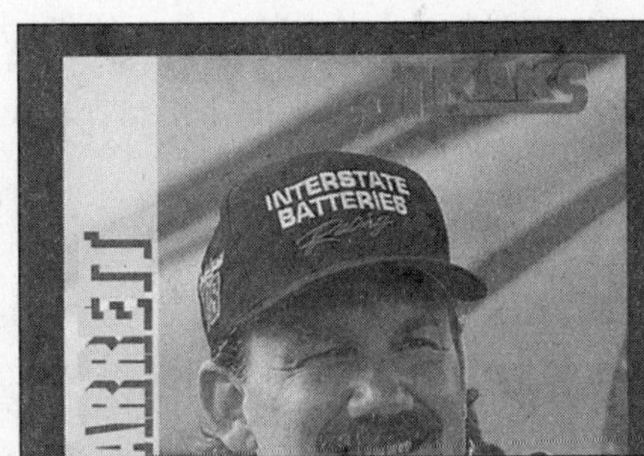

70/30

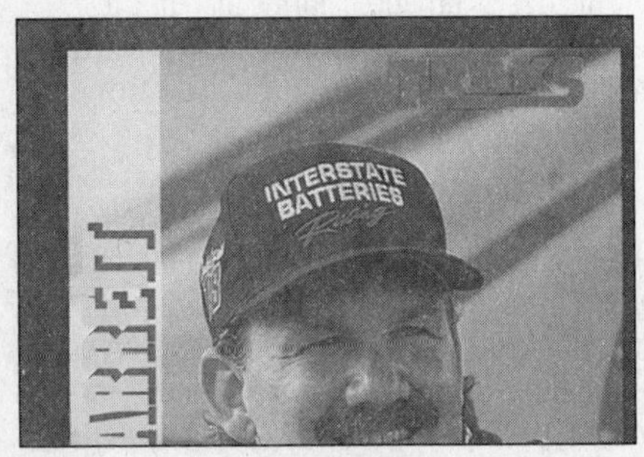

80/20

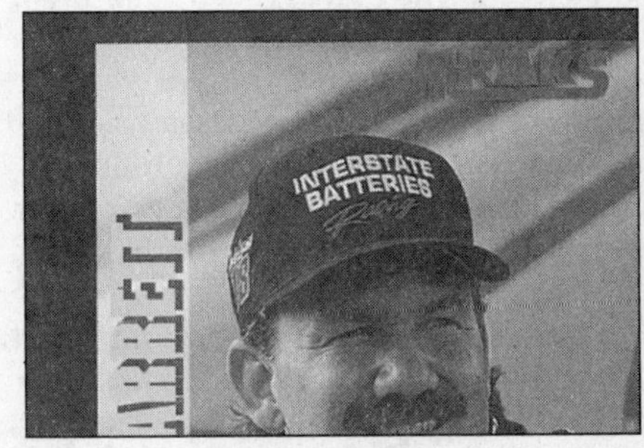

Miscut

Corner Wear

The partial cards shown at right have been photographed at 300%. This was done in order to magnify each card's corner wear to such a degree that differences could be shown on a printed page.

Corner with a slight touch of wear: The corner still is sharp, but there is a slight touch of wear showing. On a dark-bordered card, this shows as a dot of white.

Fuzzy corner: The corner still comes to a point, but the point has just begun to fray. A slightly "dinged" corner is considered the same as a fuzzy corner.

Slightly rounded corner: The fraying of the corner has increased to where there is only a hint of a point. Mild layering may be evident. A "dinged" corner is considered the same as a slightly rounded corner.

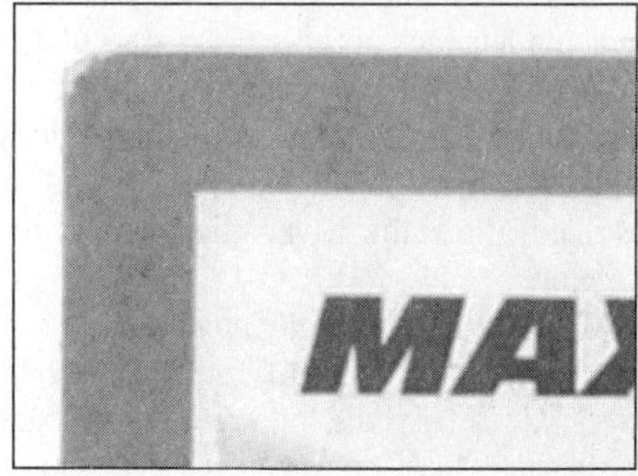

Rounded corner: The point is completely round and rough. Serious layering is evident.

From 1980 to the beginning of the modern racing card collecting era (1988), IndyCar sets dominated the market. This was primarily due to the introduction of the A & S Racing Collectables company. This manufacturer produced IndyCar sets from 1983-87. Another form of open-wheel racing also saw its first regular issued set, the 1987 World of Outlaw set. This set features the first card of NASCAR superstar Jeff Gordon.

The Modern Era

In 1988, the racing card market changed. The J.R. Maxx company decided to produce a 100-card racing set that focused on the drivers and cars of NASCAR racing. It was just part of the evolution that NASCAR was going through. The sport itself was growing in popularity and it made common sense for there to be trading cards of these growing heroes of racing. The set was to be the first mass marketed NASCAR trading card set ever issued. Maxx also signed an agreement to be the only licensed card of NASCAR. The issue of this set is considered to be the start of the modern era of racing cards. Through the marketing of these cards, racing fans became aware that there were now racing cards available of their favorite drivers.

During the period of time from 1988-1991, other forms of racing were also flourishing from a card standpoint. There were a couple drag racing sets each of those years, a regular manufacturer of World of Outlaw cards, All World Indy began producing Indy sets and local small tracks started seeing the sale of racing cards that featured the drivers that were racing in that region.

Maxx was the only major producer of NASCAR cards from 1988-90. They were not only making a base set of cards, but were also contracting with companies like Crisco and Holly Farms to make promotional sets that featured those companies logos.

In 1991, the NASCAR card market saw the introduction to two new companies Traks and Pro Set. Pro Set was a major sports card manufacturer of the time but Traks was just getting started. Traks first set in 1991 would include the first NASCAR card of a young driver named Jeff Gordon. They would also go on to produce two promotional Dale Earnhardt sets, a Kyle Petty set and a Richard Petty set that year. Pro Set entered the racing card market from two ways NASCAR and NHRA. They produced full sets for each form of racing.

In 1993, the market would see a dramatic expansion with five new card companies coming jumping into hobby. Action Packed, Finish Line, Hi-Tech, Press Pass, and Wheels all started issuing racing sets in 1993. Action Packed not only brought its embossed printing process to racing cards but also brought the first high end retail product that racing had seen. Prior to this time boxes were generally retailed for $10-$20, but Action Packed's cost was nearly double the highest retail box prices. This did not discourage fans and collectors who were willing to purchase this new high end product. That year also saw the introduction of the parallel insert cards. The 1993 Finish Line set had a silver foil parallel version for each card. This silver parallel set was one of the most sought after and very few collectors were not working on the set at the time.

With greater competition, companies were looking for that edge that would separate their products from the rest. Many new innovations in racing cards hit the market in 1994. Finish Line introduced Phone Cards to racing collectors through inserts in their Finish Line Gold product. Press Pass introduced the first interactive game, with their Cup Chase insert cards. SkyBox introduced the first single race interactive game with their Brickyard winner redemption card. Press Pass with its VIP brand introduced signature redemption cards with its 24K Gold exchange cards. Maxx introduced the first ClearChrome cards with the 20-card subset in their Maxx Medallion product. So from nearly every manufacturer, the collectors were getting something new and different than they had ever seen before.

The market continued to grow in 1996. The hobby saw a total of 30 base brand products produced from nine different manufacturers. The market also saw the lose of Maxx in 1996. The grandfather of the moden racing card era filed bankruptcy and went out of business in the summer. Parallel inserts, Phone Cards and interactive games and race used equipment inserts were also the trend. There were very few products issued in 1996 that didn't include at least one of those four types of cards.

The year of 1997 in racing collectibles was one of both growth and decline. The die cast market exhibited growth while trying to reach more collectors with product and product line variations. The big 3 (Action/RCCA, Racing Champions and Ravell) each debuted new premium lines. Action, in conjunction with Hasbro, started its Winner's Circle line to establish a presence in the mass market, Revelll also established its Revell Racing line to serve the same function. Racing Champions, through its merger with Wheels, that established a foundation that has helped to launch a new premium line in conjunction with the 50th anniversary of NASCAR.

The card market exhibited slight growth in 1997. Maxx rejoined the market after being resurrected by Upper Deck. Press Pass was bought by Wheels. Finish Line shut its doors and shutdown it's phone cards. An emphasis was placed again on high-end inserts whether it be autographed cards or cards containing "race-used" items.

The current market in not unlike each of the sports card markets and it is incurring similar problems. The largest industry problem seems to be that their are simply too many products for the market to bear. The high dollar insert cards and the multiple levels of parallel cards that are being produced have stopped the collector from being able to afford everything that is made. They could afford everything made as recently as 1992. So what is the result? A buyer's market in which new products usually are available cheaper to the consumer than they originally cost the dealer from the factory. The hobby is still facing this very complex problem with no easy solutions.

Finding Out More

The above has been a thumbnail sketch of racing card collecting from its inception to the present. It is difficult to tell the whole story in just a few pages. Serious collectors should subscribe to at least one of the excellent hobby periodicals. We also suggest that collectors visit their local card shop(s), attend local racing shows or events in their area and sign up for any dealer's catalogs that are available. Card collecting is still a young and informal hobby. You can learn more about it at shops and shows and reading periodicals and catalogs. After all, smart dealers realize that spending a few minutes to teach and educate the beginners about the hobby often pays off in the long run.

Additional Reading

Each year Beckett Publications produces comprehensive annual price guides for each of the four major sports: *Beckett Baseball Card Price Guide, Beckett Football Card Price Guide, Beckett Basketball Card Price Guide,* and *Beckett Hockey Card Price Guide.* The aim of these annual guides is to provide information and accurate pricing on a wide array of sports cards, ranging from main issues by the major card manufacturers to various regional, promotional, and food issues. Also alphabetical checklists, such as *Sport Americana Baseball Card Alphabetical Checklist #6,* are published to assist the collector in identifying all the cards of any particular player. The seasoned collector will find these tools valuable sources of information that will enable him to pursue his hobby interests.

In addition, abridged editions of the Beckett Price Guides have been published for each of the four major sports as part of the House of Collectibles series: *The Official Price Guide to Baseball Cards, The Official Price Guide to Football Cards, The Official Price Guide to Basketball Cards,* and *The Official Price Guide to Hockey Cards.* Published in a convenient mass-market paperback format, these price guides provide information and accurate pricing on all the main issues by the major card manufacturers.

Advertising

Within this Price Guide you will find advertisements for sports memorabilia material, mail order, and retail sports collectibles establishments. All advertisements were accepted in good faith based on the reputation of the advertiser; however, neither the author, the publisher, the distributors, nor the other advertisers in this Price Guide accept any responsibility for any particular advertiser not complying with the terms of his or her ad.

Readers also should be aware that prices in advertisements are subject to change over the annual period before a new edition of this volume is issued each spring. When replying to an advertisement late in the year, the reader should take this into account, and contact the dealer by phone or in writing for up-to-date price information. Should you come into contact with any of the advertisers in this guide as a result of their advertisement herein, please mention this source as your contact.

Prices in this Guide

Prices found in this guide reflect current retail rates just prior to the printing of this book. They do not reflect the FOR SALE prices of the author, the publisher, the distributors, the advertisers, or any card dealers associated with this guide. No one is obligated in any way to buy, sell or trade his or her cards based on these prices. The price listings were compiled by the author from actual buy/sell transactions at sports conventions, sports card shops, buy/sell advertisements in the hobby papers, for sale prices from dealer catalogs and price lists, and discussions with leading hobbyists in the U.S. and Canada. All prices are in U.S. dollars.

Acknowledgments

A great deal of diligence, hard work, and dedicated effort went into this third volume. However, the high standards to which we hold ourselves could not have been met without the expert input and generous amount of time contributed by many people. Our sincere thanks are extended to each and every one of you.

A complete list of these invaluable contributors appears after the Price Guide section.

1990 AC Racing Proven Winners

-card black-bordered set features drivers sponsored e AC Racing team. The cards were given away as lete sets and include six top drivers and one nbered checklist card. The Proven Winners name is ed on the back of the checklist card. The cards were uted as a promotion given out at many of NASCAR ways.

	MINT	NRMT
'LETE SET (7)	60.00	27.00
ION CARD (1-6)	4.00	1.80
usty Wallace	12.00	5.50
arrell Waltrip	6.00	2.70
ale Earnhardt	25.00	11.00
en Schrader	4.00	1.80
cky Rudd	6.00	2.70
obby Hillin	4.00	1.80
) Cover/Checklist Card	4.00	1.80

1991 AC Racing

0-card set was given away as a promotion at many AR speedways. The cards feature some of the top s in racing that carried the AC Racing logo on their

	MINT	NRMT
LETE SET (10)	30.00	13.50
ION CARD (1-9)	1.00	.45
ale Earnhardt	12.00	5.50
usty Wallace	6.00	2.70
arrell Waltrip	2.00	.90
nie Irvan	4.00	1.80
cky Rudd	2.00	.90
n Schrader	1.00	.45
le Petty	2.00	.90
ck Wilson	1.00	.45
ıt Stricklin	1.00	.45
Cover Card Checklist	1.00	.45

1992 AC-Delco

0-card set was produced and distributed by AC- and GM Service Parts in 1992. The cards feature a ordered design and include drivers of the 1992 AC eam.

	MINT	NRMT
.ETE SET (10)	10.00	4.50
ON CARD (1-10)	.50	.23
sty Wallace	3.00	1.35
ky Rudd	1.25	.55
e Petty	1.25	.55
rrell Waltrip	1.25	.55
ie Irvan	2.00	.90
n Schrader	.75	.35
ve Marcis	.75	.35
t Stricklin	.75	.35
Delco 500 Race	.50	.23
over/Checklist Card	.50	.23

992 AC Racing Postcards

-card set was produced and distributed by AC in 1992. The unnumbered cards are postcard sized mately 3-3/4" by 5-1/4") and feature an artist's ng of a top AC Racing sponsored driver on the acks are primarily black in color and include the ing logo. The cards were sold as a complete set ed in a black wrap-around cardboard package. ere also given away at the AC suite at Michigan ay.

	MINT	NRMT
ETE SET (8)	15.00	6.75
ON CARD (1-8)	.75	.35

	MINT	NRMT
❑ 1 Dale Earnhardt	6.00	2.70
❑ 2 Ernie Irvan	2.00	.90
❑ 3 Kyle Petty	1.00	.45
❑ 4 Ricky Rudd	1.00	.45
❑ 5 Ken Schrader	.75	.35
❑ 6 Hut Stricklin	.75	.35
❑ 7 Rusty Wallace	3.00	1.35
❑ 8 Darrell Waltrip	1.00	.45

1993 AC Racing Foldouts

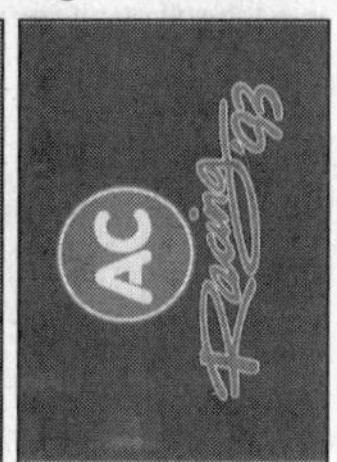

This 10-card set features drivers sponsored by the AC Racing team. The cards are bi-fold and measure approximately 3-1/2" by 4-5/8" when fully unfolded. Numbering was done according to the driver's car number. The cards were sold as complete sets and packaging included a gray AC Racing 1:64 scale die cast car as well.

	MINT	NRMT
COMPLETE SET (10)	10.00	4.50
COMMON CARD	.30	.14
❑ 2 Rusty Wallace	1.50	.70
❑ 3 Dale Earnhardt	3.00	1.35
❑ 4 Ernie Irvan	1.00	.45
❑ 17 Darrell Waltrip	.50	.23
❑ 24 Jeff Gordon	3.00	1.35
❑ 25 Ken Schrader	.30	.14
❑ 40 Kenny Wallace	.30	.14
❑ 41 Phil Parsons	.30	.14
❑ 42 Kyle Petty	.50	.23
❑ NNO Cover/Checklist Card	.30	.14

1992 Action Packed Allison Family

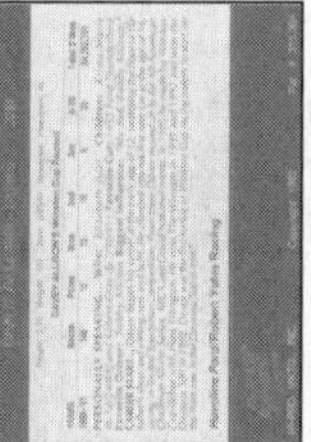

Produced by Action Packed to honor the career of the late Clifford Allison, this set was distributed in factory set form. The cards included Clifford's father Bobby and brother Davey and were sold packaged in a black folding binder with proceeds going to help The Children of Clifford Allison Trust Fund. Production was limited to 5000 numbered sets. The sets were donated by Action Packed to the Allison family. Also, there was one set of 24K gold cards done. This set was originally bought in an auction by Hank Jones.

	MINT	NRMT
COMPLETE SET (3)	40.00	18.00
COMMON CARD	10.00	4.50
❑ NNO Bobby Allison	10.00	4.50
❑ NNO Clifford Allison	10.00	4.50
❑ NNO Davey Allison	20.00	9.00

1993 Action Packed

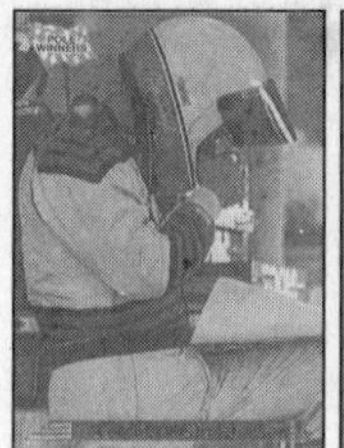

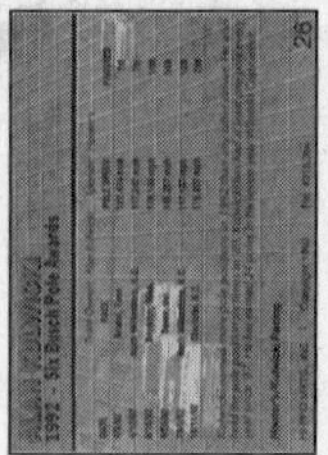

This is the first Action Packed racing release, issued in three seperate series, and features the now standard raised embossed printing process. Twenty-four pack boxes with seven cards per pack housed the first series, while series two and three contained 6-cards per pack. The series one set was released in early 1993 and includes five different subsets: 92 Race Winners, 92 Pole Winners, Top Ten Points, Young Guns, and King Richard Petty. Series two, released in mid-1993, is highlighted by the first Dale Earnhardt Action Packed cards. A four card sub-set of Dale Earnhardt featured braile on the back of the cards. The series two includes six different subsets: Daytona '93 (90-95), Back in Black (120-123), Back in Black Braile (124-127), The Allisons (140-149), Young Guns (150-156), and Brothers (161-164). Fall 1993 saw the release of series three featuring Rusty Wallace and Race Week in Charlotte subsets, along with 6-card memorial insert sets of both Davey Allison and Alan Kulwicki. 24K Gold insert cards were also distributed throughout packs of all three series.

	MINT	NRMT
COMPLETE SET (207)	100.00	45.00
COMP.SERIES 1 SET (84)	60.00	27.00
COMP.SERIES 2 SET (84)	30.00	13.50
COMP.SERIES 3 SET (39)	15.00	6.75
COMMON CARD (1-84)	.50	.23
COMMON CARD (85-168)	.30	.14
COMMON CARD (169-207)	.20	.09
COMMON DRIVER (1-84)	1.00	.45
COMMON DRIVER (85-168)	.60	.25
COMMON DRIVER (169-207)	.40	.18
❑ 1 Alan Kulwicki WIN	6.00	2.70
❑ 2 Kyle Petty WIN Pattie Petty	2.00	.90
❑ 3 Darrell Waltrip's Car WIN	1.00	.45
❑ 4 Geoff Bodine WIN	1.00	.45
❑ 5 Davey Allison WIN	4.00	1.80
❑ 6 Rusty Wallace WIN	2.00	.90
❑ 7 Harry Gant WIN	1.00	.45
❑ 8 Ernie Irvan WIN	2.00	.90
❑ 9 Mark Martin WIN	2.00	.90
❑ 10 Richard Petty Braille	2.00	.90
❑ 11 Terry Labonte's Car	2.00	.90
❑ 12 Bobby Labonte	2.50	1.10
❑ 13 Kyle Petty's Car	1.00	.45
❑ 14 Kyle Petty	2.00	.90
❑ 15 Dale Jarrett	2.50	1.10
❑ 16 Darrell Waltrip	2.00	.90
❑ 17 Darrell Waltrip's Car	1.00	.45
❑ 18 Ken Schrader's Car	.50	.23
❑ 19 Ken Schrader	1.00	.45
❑ 20 Ken Schrader PW	1.00	.45
❑ 21 Davey Allison PW	4.00	1.80
❑ 22 Mark Martin PW	2.00	.90
❑ 23 Kyle Petty PW	2.00	.90
❑ 24 Darrell Waltrip PW	1.00	.45
❑ 25 Ernie Irvan PW	2.00	.90
❑ 26 Alan Kulwicki PW	3.00	1.35
❑ 27 Brett Bodine PW	1.00	.45
❑ 28 Rusty Wallace PW	2.00	.90
❑ 29 Rick Mast PW	1.00	.45
❑ 30 Sterling Marlin's Car PW	1.00	.45
❑ 31 Richard Petty's Car BR	2.00	.90
❑ 32 Jeff Gordon	8.00	3.60
❑ 33 Ernie Irvan's Car	2.00	.90
❑ 34 Ernie Irvan	2.00	.90
❑ 35 Kenny Wallace	1.00	.45
❑ 36 Terry Labonte	3.00	1.35
❑ 37 Geoff Bodine's Car	.50	.23
❑ 38 Geoff Bodine	1.00	.45
❑ 39 Geoff Bodine	1.00	.45
❑ 40 Alan Kulwicki T10	2.50	1.10
❑ 41 Darrell Waltrip T10	1.00	.45
❑ 42 Kyle Petty T10	2.00	.90
❑ 43 Davey Allison T10	4.00	1.80

❑ 44 Mark Martin T10	2.00	.90
❑ 45 Harry Gant T10	1.00	.45
❑ 46 Terry Labonte T10	2.00	.90
❑ 47 Sterling Marlin T10	1.00	.45
❑ 48 Rick Mast	1.00	.45
❑ 49 Rick Mast w/Car	1.00	.45
❑ 50 Richard Petty's Car KR	1.25	.55
❑ 51 Richard Petty KR Lynda Petty	1.25	.55
❑ 52 Richard Petty KR	1.25	.55
❑ 53 Richard Petty KR	1.25	.55
❑ 54 Richard Petty KR	1.25	.55
❑ 55 Sterling Marlin	2.00	.90
❑ 56 Sterling Marlin's Car	1.00	.45
❑ 57 Brett Bodine	1.00	.45
❑ 58 Morgan Shepherd	1.00	.45
❑ 59 Morgan Shepherd's Car	.50	.23
❑ 60 Kenny Wallace YG	1.00	.45
❑ 61 Jeff Gordon YG	6.00	2.70
❑ 62 Bobby Labonte YG	2.50	1.10
❑ 63 Jeff Gordon YG Kenny Wallace Bobby Labonte	6.00	2.70
❑ 64 Alan Kulwicki	3.00	1.35
❑ 65 Wally Dallenbach Jr.'s Car	.50	.23
❑ 66 Wally Dallenbach Jr.	1.00	.45
❑ 67 Michael Waltrip	1.00	.45
❑ 68 Michael Waltrip's Car	.50	.23
❑ 69 Hut Stricklin	1.00	.45
❑ 70 Richard Petty's Car Braille	1.25	.55
❑ 71 Richard Petty Braille	1.25	.55
❑ 72 Richard Petty Braille	1.25	.55
❑ 73 Harry Gant	2.00	.90
❑ 74 Harry Gant's Car	1.00	.45
❑ 75 Richard Petty Braille	1.25	.55
❑ 76 Richard Petty Braille	1.25	.55
❑ 77 Mark Martin	3.00	1.35
❑ 78 Mark Martin's Car	2.00	.90
❑ 79 Davey Allison's Car	2.00	.90
❑ 80 Davey Allison	4.00	1.80
❑ 81 Richard Petty	2.00	.90
❑ 82 Richard Petty's Car	2.00	.90
❑ 83 Rusty Wallace	3.00	1.35
❑ 84 Rusty Wallace's Car	2.00	.90
❑ 85 Alan Kulwicki	2.00	.90
❑ 86 Jeff Gordon	4.00	1.80
❑ 87 Jeff Gordon's Car	2.00	.90
❑ 88 Dale Earnhardt	4.00	1.80
❑ 89 Dale Earnhardt's Car	2.00	.90
❑ 90 Dale Jarrett D93	1.25	.55
❑ 91 Kyle Petty D93	1.25	.55
❑ 92 Richard Petty D93	1.25	.55
❑ 93 Jeff Gordon D93	4.00	1.80
❑ 94 Dale Earnhardt D93	4.00	1.80
❑ 95 Dale Earnhardt D93	4.00	1.80
❑ 96 Brett Bodine	.60	.25
❑ 97 Davey Allison	2.50	1.10
❑ 98 Davey Allison's Car	1.25	.55
❑ 99 Kyle Petty	1.25	.55
❑ 100 Kyle Petty's Car	.60	.25
❑ 101 Kenny Wallace	.60	.25
❑ 102 Kenny Wallace's Car	.30	.14
❑ 103 Darrell Waltrip	1.25	.55
❑ 104 Darrell Waltrip's Car	.60	.25
❑ 105 Rick Mast	.60	.25
❑ 106 Rick Mast's Car	.30	.14
❑ 107 Rusty Wallace	2.00	.90
❑ 108 Rusty Wallace's Car	1.50	.70
❑ 109 Mark Martin	2.00	.90
❑ 110 Mark Martin's Car	1.50	.70
❑ 111 Geoff Bodine	.60	.25
❑ 112 Geoff Bodine's Car	.30	.14
❑ 113 Wally Dallenbach Jr.	.60	.25
❑ 114 Wally Dallenbach Jr.'s Car	.30	.14
❑ 115 Dale Jarrett	1.50	.70
❑ 116 Morgan Shepherd	.60	.25
❑ 117 Morgan Shepherd's Car	.30	.14
❑ 118 Rick Wilson	.60	.25
❑ 119 Rick Wilson's Car	.30	.14
❑ 120 Dale Earnhardt BB	2.00	.90
❑ 121 Dale Earnhardt BB	2.00	.90
❑ 122 Dale Earnhardt BB	2.00	.90
❑ 123 Dale Earnhardt BB	2.00	.90
❑ 124 Dale Earnhardt Braille	2.00	.90
❑ 125 Dale Earnhardt Braille	2.00	.90
❑ 126 Dale Earnhardt Braille	2.00	.90
❑ 127 Dale Earnhardt Braille	2.00	.90
❑ 128 Ernie Irvan	1.50	.70
❑ 129 Ernie Irvan's Car	1.25	.55
❑ 130 Sterling Marlin	1.25	.55
❑ 131 Sterling Marlin's Car	.60	.25
❑ 132 Jimmy Spencer	.60	.25
❑ 133 Jimmy Spencer's Car	.30	.14
❑ 134 Ken Schrader	.60	.25
❑ 135 Ken Schrader's Car	.30	.14
❑ 136 Michael Waltrip	.60	.25
❑ 137 Michael Waltrip's Car	.30	.14
❑ 138 Dale Earnhardt PW	4.00	1.80
❑ 139 Dale Earnhardt WIN	4.00	1.80
❑ 140 Bobby Allison TA Davey Allison Liz Allison Katherine Patton Allison	2.00	.90
❑ 141 Donnie Allison TA	.60	.25
❑ 142 Clifford Allison TA	1.50	.70
❑ 143 Donnie Allison TA Bobby Allison	.60	.25
❑ 144 Davey Allison TA Liz Allison Robbie Allison Krista Allison	2.00	.90
❑ 145 Donnie Allison TA Kenny Allison Donald Allison Ronald Allison	.60	.25
❑ 146 Davey Allison TA Clifford Allison Bobby Allison	2.00	.90
❑ 147 Bobby Allison TA Judy Allison	.60	.25
❑ 148 Donnie Allison TA Pat Allison	.60	.25
❑ 149 Hut Stricklin TA Pam Stricklin Taylor Stricklin	.60	.25
❑ 150 Jeff Gordon YG	4.00	1.80
❑ 151 Kenny Wallace YG	.60	.25
❑ 152 Bobby Labonte YG	1.50	.70
❑ 153 Jeff Gordon YG	4.00	1.80
❑ 154 Kenny Wallace YG	.60	.25
❑ 155 Bobby Labonte YG	1.50	.70
❑ 156 Jeff Gordon YG Kenny Wallace Bobby Labonte	4.00	1.80
❑ 157 Harry Gant	1.25	.55
❑ 158 Harry Gant's Car	.60	.25
❑ 159 Hut Stricklin	.60	.25
❑ 160 Richard Petty Kyle Petty	1.00	.45
❑ 161 Geoff Bodine B Brett Bodine	.60	.25
❑ 162 Terry Labonte B Bobby Labonte	1.50	.70
❑ 163 Rusty Wallace B Kenny Wallace	1.50	.70
❑ 164 Michael Waltrip B Darrell Waltrip	.60	.25
❑ 165 Ned Jarrett Dale Jarrett	1.25	.55
❑ 166 Bobby Labonte	1.50	.70
❑ 167 Terry Labonte	2.00	.90
❑ 168 Terry Labonte's Car	1.50	.70
❑ 169 Geoff Bodine	.40	.18
❑ 170 Wally Dallenbach Jr.	.40	.18
❑ 171 Dale Earnhardt	2.50	1.10
❑ 172 Harry Gant	.75	.35
❑ 173 Jeff Gordon	2.50	1.10
❑ 174 Bobby Hillin	.20	.09
❑ 175 Sterling Marlin	.75	.35
❑ 176 Mark Martin	1.00	.45
❑ 177 Morgan Shepherd	.40	.18
❑ 178 Kenny Wallace	.40	.18
❑ 179 Michael Waltrip	.40	.18
❑ 180 Brett Bodine	.40	.18
❑ 181 Derrike Cope	.40	.18
❑ 182 Ernie Irvan	.75	.35
❑ 183 Dale Jarrett	1.00	.45
❑ 184 Bobby Labonte	1.25	.55
❑ 185 Terry Labonte	1.00	.45
❑ 186 Kyle Petty	.75	.35
❑ 187 Ken Schrader	.40	.18
❑ 188 Jimmy Spencer	.40	.18
❑ 189 Hut Stricklin	.40	.18
❑ 190 Darrell Waltrip	.75	.35
❑ 191 Rusty Wallace RW	.75	.35
❑ 192 Rusty Wallace RW	.75	.35
❑ 193 Rusty Wallace RW	.75	.35
❑ 194 Rusty Wallace's Car RW	.75	.35
❑ 195 Rusty Wallace's Car RW	.75	.35
❑ 196 Rusty Wallace in Pits RW	.75	.35
❑ 197 Rusty Wallace RW	.75	.35
❑ 198 Dale Earnhardt WIN	2.00	.90
❑ 199 Ernie Irvan WIN	.75	.35
❑ 200 Rick Mast WIN	.20	.09
❑ 201 Ernie Irvan PS	.75	.35
❑ 202 Dale Earnhardt WIN	2.00	.90
❑ 203 Ken Schrader PS	.20	.09
❑ 204 Sterling Marlin WIN	.75	.35
❑ 205 Jeff Gordon PS	2.00	.90
❑ 206 Michael Waltrip WIN	.20	.09
❑ 207 Dale Earnhardt WIN	2.00	.90
❑ AKDA Alan Kulwicki Davey Allison	20.00	9.00
❑ AKDAG Alan Kulwicki Davey Allison 24K Gold	75.00	34.00

1993 Action Packed 24K G

These insert cards were randomly distributed in a series of 1993 Action Packed cards. Th distinguishable from the regular issue cards by suffix on the card numbers as well as the 24Kt. Go on the card fronts. There was a 73G card of Rusty pit stop action done but was never released.

	MINT
COMPLETE SET (72)	2000.00
COMPLETE SERIES 1 (17)	1000.00
COMPLETE SERIES 2 (21)	500.00
COMPLETE SERIES 3 (34)	500.00
COMMON CARD (1G-17G)	20.00
COMMON CARD (18G-38G)	15.00
COMMON CARD (39G-72G)	12.00

❑ 1G Alan Kulwicki T10	100.00
❑ 2G Darrell Waltrip T10	40.00
❑ 3G Kyle Petty T10	40.00
❑ 4G Davey Allison T10	120.00
❑ 5G Mark Martin T10	60.00
❑ 6G Harry Gant T10	40.00
❑ 7G Terry Labonte T10	60.00
❑ 8G Sterling Marlin T10	40.00
❑ 9G Kenny Wallace YG	20.00
❑ 10G Jeff Gordon YG	120.00
❑ 11G Bobby Labonte YG	50.00
❑ 12G Jeff Gordon YG Kenny Wallace YG Bobby Labonte YG	100.00
❑ 13G Richard Petty KR	50.00
❑ 14G Richard Petty KR	50.00
❑ 15G Richard Petty KR	50.00
❑ 16G Richard Petty KR	50.00
❑ 17G Richard Petty KR	50.00
❑ 18G Dale Earnhardt BB	100.00
❑ 19G Dale Earnhardt BB	100.00
❑ 20G Dale Earnhardt BB	100.00
❑ 21G Dale Earnhardt BB	100.00
❑ 22G Dale Earnhardt BB Braille	100.00
❑ 23G Dale Earnhardt BB Braille	100.00
❑ 24G Dale Earnhardt BB Braille	100.00
❑ 25G Dale Earnhardt BB Braille	100.00
❑ 26G Jeff Gordon YG	100.00
❑ 27G Kenny Wallace YG	15.00
❑ 28G Bobby Labonte YG	30.00
❑ 29G Jeff Gordon YG	100.00
❑ 30G Kenny Wallace YG	15.00
❑ 31G Bobby Labonte YG	30.00
❑ 32G Jeff Gordon YG Kenny Wallace YG Bobby Labonte YG	80.00
❑ 33G Dale Jarrett D93	40.00
❑ 34G Kyle Petty D93	30.00
❑ 35G Richard Petty D93	40.00
❑ 36G Jeff Gordon D93	100.00
❑ 37G Dale Earnhardt D93	100.00
❑ 38G Dale Earnhardt D93	100.00
❑ 39G Alan Kulwicki	50.00
❑ 40G Alan Kulwicki	50.00
❑ 41G Alan Kulwicki	50.00
❑ 42G Alan Kulwicki	50.00
❑ 43G Alan Kulwicki	50.00
❑ 44G Alan Kulwicki	50.00
❑ 45G Davey Allison	60.00
❑ 46G Davey Allison	60.00
❑ 47G Davey Allison	60.00
❑ 48G Davey Allison	60.00
❑ 49G Davey Allison	60.00
❑ 50G Davey Allison	60.00
❑ 51G Geoff Bodine	12.00
❑ 52G Wally Dallenbach Jr.	12.00
❑ 53G Dale Earnhardt	80.00
❑ 54G Harry Gant	25.00
❑ 55G Jeff Gordon	80.00
❑ 56G Bobby Hillin	12.00
❑ 57G Sterling Marlin	25.00
❑ 58G Mark Martin	50.00
❑ 59G Morgan Shepherd	12.00
❑ 60G Kenny Wallace	12.00
❑ 61G Michael Waltrip	12.00

Brett Bodine	12.00	5.50
Derrike Cope	12.00	5.50
Ernie Irvan	25.00	11.00
Dale Jarrett	40.00	18.00
Bobby Labonte	30.00	13.50
Terry Labonte	50.00	22.00
Kyle Petty	25.00	11.00
Ken Schrader	12.00	5.50
Jimmy Spencer	12.00	5.50
Hut Stricklin	12.00	5.50
Darrell Waltrip	25.00	11.00

1993 Action Packed Davey Allison

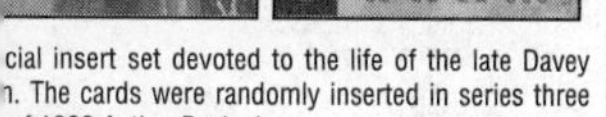

cial insert set devoted to the life of the late Davey
n. The cards were randomly inserted in series three
of 1993 Action Packed.

	MINT	NRMT
LETE SET (6)	8.00	3.60
MON CARD (DA1-DA6)	1.50	.70
Davey Allison	1.50	.70
Davey Allison Judy Allison	1.50	.70
Davey Allison Bobby Allison	1.50	.70
Davey Allison Robbie Allison	1.50	.70
Davey Allison	1.50	.70
Davey Allison	1.50	.70

1993 Action Packed Alan Kulwicki

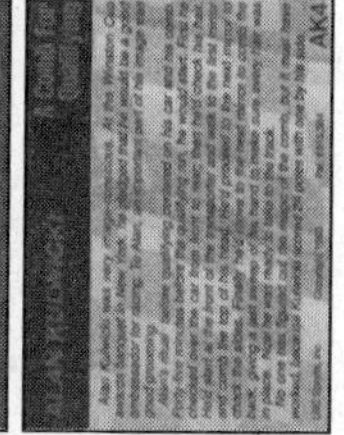

cial insert set devoted to the life of the late Alan
ki. The cards were randomly inserted in series three
of 1993 Action Packed.

	MINT	NRMT
LETE SET (6)	8.00	3.60
ON CARD (AK1-AK6)	1.50	.70
Alan Kulwicki	1.50	.70
Alan Kulwicki	1.50	.70
Alan Kulwicki Richard Petty	1.50	.70
Alan Kulwicki	1.50	.70
Alan Kulwicki	1.50	.70
Alan Kulwicki	1.50	.70

1994 Action Packed

94 Action Packed set was released in three series ch pack containing six cards. Wax boxes contained ks per box and color photos of popular drivers atured on the wrapper fronts. The standard Action 24K Gold insert was distributed throughout all series with series three also including a Richard ss Racing insert. Series one is highlighted by Race s, Top Ten, Young Guns, Two Timers and Pit Crew s subsets. Series two features Neil Bonnett and tty subsets along with a Daytona Review. A special etty Diamond card (#92D) was also inserted in wo, at a rate of approximatey 1:1,650, that features

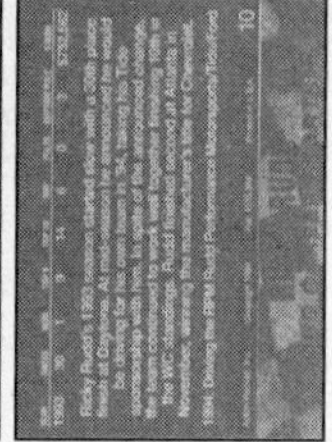

an authentic diamond embedded in the card front. The diamond earring Kyle Petty card is numbered of 1000. The third series is highlighted by a Rest and Relaxation subset (139-167) and a Winner subset (179-193).

	MINT	NRMT
COMPLETE SET (209)	75.00	34.00
COMPLETE SERIES 1 (66)	25.00	11.00
COMPLETE SERIES 2 (72)	25.00	11.00
COMPLETE SERIES 3 (71)	25.00	11.00
COMMON CARD (1-209)	.15	.07
COMMON DRIVER (1-209)	.30	.14
❑ 1 Dale Earnhardt	3.00	1.35
❑ 2 Rusty Wallace	1.50	.70
❑ 3 Mark Martin	1.50	.70
❑ 4 Dale Jarrett	1.25	.55
❑ 5 Kyle Petty	.60	.25
❑ 6 Ernie Irvan	.75	.35
❑ 7 Morgan Shepherd	.30	.14
❑ 8 Dale Earnhardt Winston Cup Champion	3.00	1.35
❑ 9 Ken Schrader	.30	.14
❑ 10 Ricky Rudd	.60	.25
❑ 11 Harry Gant	.60	.25
❑ 12 Jimmy Spencer	.30	.14
❑ 13 Darrell Waltrip Sarah Waltrip	.60	.25
❑ 14 Jeff Gordon	3.00	1.35
❑ 15 Sterling Marlin	.60	.25
❑ 16 Geoff Bodine	.30	.14
❑ 17 Michael Waltrip	.30	.14
❑ 18 Terry Labonte	1.50	.70
❑ 19 Bobby Labonte	1.00	.45
❑ 20 Brett Bodine	.30	.14
❑ 21 Rick Mast	.30	.14
❑ 22 Wally Dallenbach Jr.	.30	.14
❑ 23 Kenny Wallace	.30	.14
❑ 24 Hut Stricklin	.30	.14
❑ 25 Derrike Cope	.30	.14
❑ 26 Bobby Hillin	.30	.14
❑ 27 Rick Wilson	.30	.14
❑ 28 Lake Speed	.30	.14
❑ 29 Alan Kulwicki	1.25	.55
❑ 30 Jeff Gordon Rookie of the Year	3.00	1.35
❑ 31 Rusty Wallace's Car WIN	.75	.35
❑ 32 Dale Earnhardt WIN	2.50	1.10
❑ 33 Mark Martin WIN	1.00	.45
❑ 34 Ernie Irvan w/Crew WIN	.75	.35
❑ 35 Dale Jarrett WIN Joe Gibbs	.75	.35
❑ 36 Morgan Shepherd WIN	.15	.07
❑ 37 Kyle Petty WIN	.30	.14
❑ 38 Ricky Rudd WIN	.30	.14
❑ 39 Geoff Bodine WIN	.15	.07
❑ 40 Davey Allison WIN	1.50	.70
❑ 41 Dale Earnhardt's Car	.75	.35
❑ 42 Rusty Wallace's Car	.75	.35
❑ 43 Mark Martin's Car	.75	.35
❑ 44 Dale Jarrett Kyle Petty with Car	.60	.25
❑ 45 Kyle Petty's Car	.30	.14
❑ 46 Ernie Irvan's Car	.60	.25
❑ 47 Morgan Shepherd's Car	.15	.07
❑ 48 Bill Elliott's Car	.75	.35
❑ 49 Ken Schrader's Car	.15	.07
❑ 50 Ricky Rudd's Car	.30	.14
❑ 51 John Andretti R	.15	.07
❑ 52 Ward Burton R	.15	.07
❑ 53 Steve Grissom R	.15	.07
❑ 54 Joe Nemechek R	.15	.07
❑ 55 Jeff Burton R	.15	.07
❑ 56 Loy Allen Jr. R	.15	.07
❑ 57 Lake Speed TC	.15	.07
❑ 58 Ernie Irvan with Car TC	.75	.35
❑ 59 Geoff Bodine TC	.15	.07
❑ 60 Dick Trickle TC	.30	.14
❑ 61 Jimmy Hensley TC	.15	.07
❑ 62 Buddy Parrott	.15	.07
❑ 63 Donnie Richeson	.15	.07
❑ 64 Steve Hmiel	.15	.07
❑ 65 Mike Hill	.15	.07
❑ 66 Doug Hewitt	.15	.07
❑ 67 Rusty Wallace	1.50	.70
❑ 68 Dale Earnhardt	3.00	1.35
❑ 69 Mark Martin	1.50	.70
❑ 70 Darrell Waltrip	.60	.25
❑ 71 Dale Jarrett	1.25	.55
❑ 72 Morgan Shepherd	.30	.14
❑ 73 Jeff Gordon	3.00	1.35
❑ 74 Ken Schrader	.30	.14
❑ 75 Brett Bodine	.30	.14
❑ 76 Harry Gant	.60	.25
❑ 77 Sterling Marlin	.60	.25
❑ 78 Terry Labonte	1.50	.70
❑ 79 Ricky Rudd	.60	.25
❑ 80 Geoff Bodine	.30	.14
❑ 81 Ernie Irvan	.75	.35
❑ 82 Kyle Petty	.60	.25
❑ 83 Jimmy Spencer	.30	.14
❑ 84 Hut Stricklin	.30	.14
❑ 85 Bobby Labonte	1.00	.45
❑ 86 Derrike Cope	.30	.14
❑ 87 Loy Allen Jr.	.30	.14
❑ 88 Michael Waltrip	.30	.14
❑ 89 Ted Musgrave	.30	.14
❑ 90 Lake Speed	.30	.14
❑ 91 Todd Bodine	.30	.14
❑ 92 Kyle Petty KPS	.60	.25
❑ 93 Kyle Petty BR KPS	.60	.25
❑ 94 Kyle Petty KPS	.60	.25
❑ 95 Kyle Petty KPS Aerosmith	.60	.25
❑ 96 Kyle Petty KPS Pattie Petty Austin Petty Montgomery Petty	.60	.25
❑ 97 Kyle Petty KPS Michael Waltrip	.60	.25
❑ 98 Neil Bonnett David Bonnett	.60	.25
❑ 99 Neil Bonnett Dale Earnhardt	2.50	1.10
❑ 100 Neil Bonnett Darrell Waltrip	.60	.25
❑ 101 Neil Bonnett	.75	.35
❑ 102 Neil Bonnett	.75	.35
❑ 103 Jeff Gordon DR	2.50	1.10
❑ 104 Dale Earnhardt DR	2.50	1.10
❑ 105 Ernie Irvan DR Kim Irvan Jordan Irvan	.75	.35
❑ 106 Loy Allen Jr. DR	.15	.07
❑ 107 Sterling Marlin DR	.60	.25
❑ 108 Rusty Wallace's Car	.75	.35
❑ 109 Sterling Marlin's Car	.30	.14
❑ 110 Terry Labonte's Car	.75	.35
❑ 111 Geoff Bodine's Car	.15	.07
❑ 112 Ricky Rudd's Car	.30	.14
❑ 113 Lake Speed's Car	.15	.07
❑ 114 Ted Musgrave's Car	.15	.07
❑ 115 Mark Martin's Car	.75	.35
❑ 116 Hut Stricklin's Car	.15	.07
❑ 117 Ken Schrader's Car	.15	.07
❑ 118 Jimmy Spencer's Car	.15	.07
❑ 119 Kyle Petty's Car	.30	.14
❑ 120 Wally Dallenbach Jr.'s Car	.15	.07
❑ 121 John Andretti's Car	.15	.07
❑ 122 Steve Grissom's Car	.15	.07
❑ 123 Ward Burton's Car	.15	.07
❑ 124 Joe Nemechek's Car	.15	.07
❑ 125 Jeff Burton's Car	.15	.07
❑ 126 Dale Earnhardt's Car	.75	.35
❑ 127 Darrell Waltrip's Car	.30	.14
❑ 128 Dale Jarrett's Car	.60	.25
❑ 129 Morgan Shepherd's Car	.15	.07
❑ 130 Bobby Labonte's Car	.30	.14
❑ 131 Jeff Gordon's Car	.75	.35
❑ 132 Brett Bodine's Car	.15	.07
❑ 133 Michael Waltrip's Car	.15	.07
❑ 134 Todd Bodine's Car	.15	.07
❑ 135 Ernie Irvan's Car	.60	.25
❑ 136 Harry Gant's Car	.30	.14
❑ 137 Rick Mast's Car	.15	.07
❑ 138 Bill Elliott's Car	.75	.35
❑ 139 Brett Bodine RR Diane Bodine	.15	.07
❑ 140 Geoff Bodine RR	.30	.14
❑ 141 Todd Bodine RR	.15	.07
❑ 142 Jeff Burton RR	.30	.14
❑ 143 Derrike Cope RR	.30	.14
❑ 144 Wally Dallenbach Jr. RR	.15	.07
❑ 145 Harry Gant RR	.30	.14
❑ 146 Jeff Gordon RR	3.00	1.35
❑ 147 Steve Grissom RR Kyle Grissom	.15	.07
❑ 148 Ernie Irvan RR	.60	.25
❑ 149 Dale Jarrett RR	1.25	.55
❑ 150 Bobby Labonte RR	1.00	.45
❑ 151 Terry Labonte RR Justin Labonte	1.50	.70

❑ 152 Sterling Marlin RR	.30	.14
❑ 153 Mark Martin RR	1.50	.70
❑ 154 Rick Mast RR Ricky Mast	.15	.07
❑ 155 Ted Musgrave RR Brittany Musgrave	.15	.07
❑ 156 Joe Nemechek RR	.15	.07
❑ 157 Kyle Petty RR	.30	.14
❑ 158 Ricky Rudd RR Linda Rudd	.30	.14
❑ 159 Greg Sacks RR	.30	.14
❑ 160 Ken Schrader RR	.30	.14
❑ 161 Morgan Shepherd RR	.15	.07
❑ 162 Lake Speed RR	.15	.07
❑ 163 Jimmy Spencer RR	.15	.07
❑ 164 Hut Stricklin RR	.15	.07
❑ 165 Mike Wallace RR	.15	.07
❑ 166 Darrell Waltrip RR Stevie Waltrip Jessica Waltrip Sarah Waltrip	.30	.14
❑ 167 Michael Waltrip RR	.15	.07
❑ 168 Roger Penske Don Miller	.15	.07
❑ 169 Junior Johnson	.30	.14
❑ 170 Robert Yates	.15	.07
❑ 171 Joe Gibbs	.30	.14
❑ 172 Ricky Rudd	.60	.25
❑ 173 Glen Wood Len Wood Eddie Wood Kim Wood	.15	.07
❑ 174 Jack Roush	.15	.07
❑ 175 Joe Hendrick(Papa) Rick Hendrick	.15	.07
❑ 176 Felix Sabates	.15	.07
❑ 177 Richard Childress	.15	.07
❑ 178 Richard Petty	.75	.35
❑ 179 Dale Earnhardt WIN	2.50	1.10
❑ 180 Dale Earnhardt WIN	2.50	1.10
❑ 181 Ernie Irvan WIN	.75	.35
❑ 182 Ernie Irvan WIN	.75	.35
❑ 183 Rusty Wallace WIN	1.00	.45
❑ 184 Terry Labonte WIN	1.00	.45
❑ 185 Sterling Marlin WIN	.30	.14
❑ 186 Rusty Wallace WIN	1.00	.45
❑ 187 Dale Earnhardt WIN	2.50	1.10
❑ 188 Ernie Irvan WIN	.75	.35
❑ 189 Jeff Gordon WIN	2.50	1.10
❑ 190 Rusty Wallace WIN	1.00	.45
❑ 191 Rusty Wallace WIN	1.00	.45
❑ 192 Rusty Wallace WIN	1.00	.45
❑ 193 Jimmy Spencer WIN	.15	.07
❑ 194 Ernie Irvan Kim Irvan Jordan Irvan	1.00	.45
❑ 195 Ernie Irvan	1.00	.45
❑ 196 Ernie Irvan	1.00	.45
❑ 197 Ernie Irvan	1.00	.45
❑ 198 Ernie Irvan	1.00	.45
❑ 199 Mark Martin	1.50	.70
❑ 200 Mark Martin	1.50	.70
❑ 201 Mark Martin	1.50	.70
❑ 202 Mark Martin	1.50	.70
❑ 203 Mark Martin	1.50	.70
❑ 204 Rusty Wallace Kenny Wallace Mike Wallace	1.00	.45
❑ 205 Todd Bodine Brett Bodine Geoff Bodine	.15	.07
❑ 206 Rusty Wallace WS	1.00	.45
❑ 207 Geoff Bodine WS	.15	.07
❑ 208 Joe Nemechek WS	.15	.07
❑ 209 Jeff Gordon WS	2.50	1.10
❑ 92D Kyle Petty/1000 Diamond Earring	250.00	110.00

1994 Action Packed 24K Gold

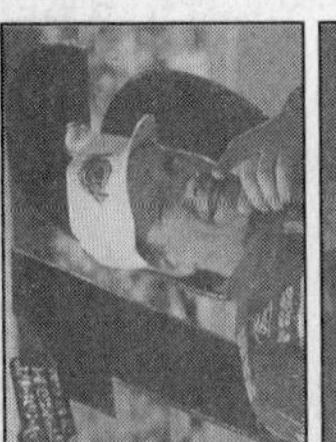

Randomly inserted in packs over all three 1994 Action Packed series, each card includes the 24Kt. Gold logo on the card front. There were 1,000 of the Jeff Gordon card (#189G) inserted in series three. The only way the card came was autographed and the card is not included in the complete set price. Many cards in the set were also used in subsets in the regular issue. Wrapper stated odds for pulling a 24K Gold card are 1:96 packs.

	MINT	NRMT
COMPLETE SET (60)	1500.00	700.00
COMPLETE SERIES 1 (20)	500.00	220.00
COMPLETE SERIES 2 (25)	500.00	220.00
COMPLETE SERIES 3 (15)	500.00	220.00
COMMON CAR (11G-20G)	10.00	4.50
COMMON DRIVER (1G-10G)	15.00	6.75
COMMON DRIVER (21G-45G)	15.00	6.75
COMMON DRIVER (179G-193G)	15.00	6.75
❑ 1G Rusty Wallace WIN	50.00	22.00
❑ 2G Dale Earnhardt WIN	100.00	45.00
❑ 3G Mark Martin WIN	50.00	22.00
❑ 4G Ernie Irvan with Crew WIN	35.00	16.00
❑ 5G Dale Jarrett WIN	40.00	18.00
❑ 6G Morgan Shepherd WIN	15.00	6.75
❑ 7G Kyle Petty WIN	30.00	13.50
❑ 8G Ricky Rudd WIN	30.00	13.50
❑ 9G Geoff Bodine WIN	15.00	6.75
❑ 10G Davey Allison WIN	50.00	22.00
❑ 11G Dale Earnhardt's Car	50.00	22.00
❑ 12G Rusty Wallace's Car	35.00	16.00
❑ 13G Mark Martin's Car	35.00	16.00
❑ 14G Dale Jarrett Kyle Petty with Car	30.00	13.50
❑ 15G Kyle Petty's Car	10.00	4.50
❑ 16G Ernie Irvan's Car	30.00	13.50
❑ 17G Morgan Shepherd's Car	10.00	4.50
❑ 18G Bill Elliott's Car	35.00	16.00
❑ 19G Ken Schrader's Car	10.00	4.50
❑ 20G Ricky Rudd's Car	10.00	4.50
❑ 21G Rusty Wallace	50.00	22.00
❑ 22G Dale Earnhardt	100.00	45.00
❑ 23G Mark Martin	50.00	22.00
❑ 24G Darrell Waltrip	30.00	13.50
❑ 25G Dale Jarrett	40.00	18.00
❑ 26G Morgan Shepherd	15.00	6.75
❑ 27G Jeff Gordon	100.00	45.00
❑ 28G Ken Schrader	15.00	6.75
❑ 29G Brett Bodine	15.00	6.75
❑ 30G Harry Gant	30.00	13.50
❑ 31G Sterling Marlin	30.00	13.50
❑ 32G Terry Labonte	50.00	22.00
❑ 33G Ricky Rudd	30.00	13.50
❑ 34G Geoff Bodine	15.00	6.75
❑ 35G Ernie Irvan	35.00	16.00
❑ 36G Kyle Petty	30.00	13.50
❑ 37G Jimmy Spencer	15.00	6.75
❑ 38G Hut Stricklin	15.00	6.75
❑ 39G Bobby Labonte	35.00	16.00
❑ 40G Derrike Cope	15.00	6.75
❑ 41G Loy Allen Jr.	15.00	6.75
❑ 42G Michael Waltrip	15.00	6.75
❑ 43G Ted Musgrave	15.00	6.75
❑ 44G Lake Speed	15.00	6.75
❑ 45G Todd Bodine	15.00	6.75
❑ 179G Dale Earnhardt WIN	80.00	36.00
❑ 180G Dale Earnhardt WIN	80.00	36.00
❑ 181G Ernie Irvan WIN	30.00	13.50
❑ 182G Ernie Irvan WIN	30.00	13.50
❑ 183G Rusty Wallace WIN	50.00	22.00
❑ 184G Terry Labonte WIN	50.00	22.00
❑ 185G Sterling Marlin WIN	30.00	13.50
❑ 186G Rusty Wallace WIN	50.00	22.00
❑ 187G Dale Earnhardt WIN	80.00	36.00
❑ 188G Ernie Irvan WIN	30.00	13.50
❑ 189G Jeff Gordon WIN AUTO	350.00	160.00
❑ 190G Rusty Wallace WIN	50.00	22.00
❑ 191G Rusty Wallace WIN	50.00	22.00
❑ 192G Rusty Wallace WIN	50.00	22.00
❑ 193G Jimmy Spencer WIN	15.00	6.75

1994 Action Packed Champ and Challenger

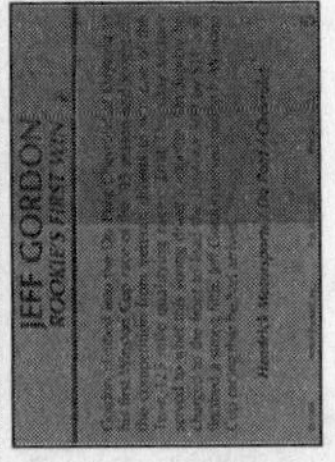

Action Packed issued this special set to highlight the careers of two of NASCAR's most popular drivers of -- the 1993 "Champ" Dale Earnhardt and "Challenger Gordon. The cards were distributed in 6-card packs 24 packs per box. Cards #1-20 have green and borders and focus on Gordon, while cards #21-40 fe black and white borders and highlight Earnhardt's Championship season. The last two cards (#41 featured both Gordon and Earnhardt. Complete fa sets were sold through both the Action Packed c network and the Action Packed Club.

	MINT	N
COMPLETE SET (42)	15.00	
COMPLETE FACT. SET (42)	20.00	
COMMON CARD (1-42)	.50	
❑ 1 Jeff Gordon	.60	
❑ 2 Ray Evernham	.50	
❑ 3 Jeff Gordon	.60	
❑ 4 Jeff Gordon	.60	
❑ 5 Jeff Gordon	.60	
❑ 6 Jeff Gordon	.60	
❑ 7 Jeff Gordon in Pits	.50	
❑ 8 Jeff Gordon in Pits	.50	
❑ 9 Jeff Gordon	.60	
❑ 10 Jeff Gordon	.60	
❑ 11 Jeff Gordon	.60	
❑ 12 Jimmy Johnson	.50	
❑ 13 Jeff Gordon	.60	
❑ 14 Jeff Gordon	.60	
❑ 15 Jeff Gordon	.60	
❑ 16 Jeff Gordon's Car	.50	
❑ 17 Jeff Gordon's Car	.50	
❑ 18 Jeff Gordon	.60	
❑ 19 Jeff Gordon	.60	
❑ 20 Jeff Gordon	.60	
❑ 21 Dale Earnhardt	.60	
❑ 22 Dale Earnhardt	.60	
❑ 23 Dale Earnhardt	.60	
❑ 24 Dale Earnhardt	.60	
❑ 25 Dale Earnhardt	.60	
❑ 26 Dale Earnhardt	.60	
❑ 27 Dale Earnhardt	.60	
❑ 28 Dale Earnhardt	.60	
❑ 29 Dale Earnhardt	.60	
❑ 30 Dale Earnhardt	.60	
❑ 31 Dale Earnhardt Neil Bonnett	.60	
❑ 32 Dale Earnhardt's Car	.50	
❑ 33 Dale Earnhardt's Car	.50	
❑ 34 Dale Earnhardt Alan Kulwicki Cars	.60	
❑ 35 Dale Earnhardt's Car	.50	
❑ 36 Dale Earnhardt's Car	.50	
❑ 37 Dale Earnhardt Rusty Wallace Cars	.60	
❑ 38 Dale Earnhardt	.60	
❑ 39 Dale Earnhardt	.60	
❑ 40 Dale Earnhardt	.60	
❑ 41 Dale Earnhardt Jeff Gordon Cars	.50	
❑ 42 Dale Earnhardt Jeff Gordon	.60	

1994 Action Packed Cham and Challenger 24K Gold

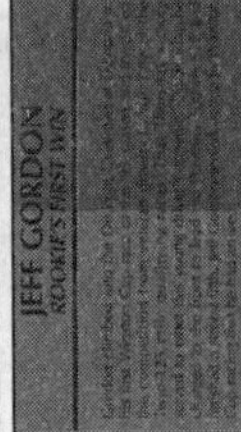

This insert set is basically a parallel to 12-cards fr regular issue 1994 Action Packed Champ and Cha issue. As with all Action Packed Gold cards, the Gold stamp appears on the card fronts, while the include a "G" suffix on the card numbers. Wrapper odds for pulling one of the popular inserts is 1:96.

	MINT
COMPLETE SET (12)	500.00
COMMON CARD	50.00
❑ 1G Jeff Gordon	50.00
❑ 5G Jeff Gordon	50.00
❑ 9G Jeff Gordon	50.00
❑ 17G Jeff Gordon's Car	50.00
❑ 20G Jeff Gordon	50.00

Dale Earnhardt	50.00	22.00
Dale Earnhardt	50.00	22.00
Dale Earnhardt	50.00	22.00
Dale Earnhardt's Car	50.00	22.00
Dale Earnhardt	50.00	22.00
Dale Earnhardt's Car	50.00	22.00
Jeff Gordon's Car		
Dale Earnhardt	50.00	22.00
Jeff Gordon		

1994 Action Packed Richard Childress Racing

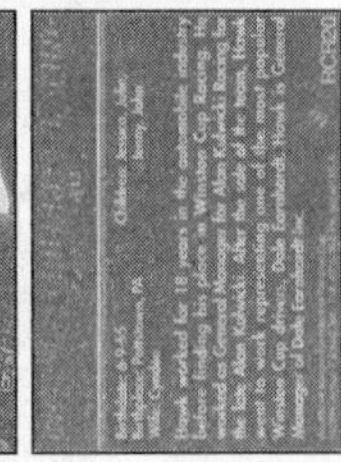

'd Childress, Dale Earnhardt and the Goodwrench Team are the focus of this insert set from series packs of 1994 Action Packed. The cards were issued same pack ratio as the regular series cards, except #18 and #20 which are considered tougher to find the rest of the set.

	MINT	NRMT
LETE SET (20)	12.00	5.50
ION CARD (1-20)	.40	.18
1 Richard Childress	.40	.18
2 Dale Earnhardt's Car	.75	.35
3 Dale Earnhardt	1.50	.70
4 Dale Earnhardt	1.50	.70
5 Dale Earnhardt's Car	.75	.35
6 Dale Earnhardt's Car	.75	.35
7 Andy Petree	.40	.18
8 Eddie Lanier	.40	.18
9 David Smith	.40	.18
10 Jimmy Elledge	.40	.18
11 Cecil Gordon	.40	.18
12 Danny Lawrence	.40	.18
13 Danny Myers	.40	.18
14 Joe Dan Bailey	.40	.18
15 Gene DeHart	.40	.18
16 John Mulloy	.40	.18
17 Hank Jones	.40	.18
18 Craig Donley SP	3.00	1.35
19 Jim Baldwin	.40	.18
20 Don Hawk SP	3.00	1.35

94 Action Packed Coastars

Packed produced these cards in 1994 as 6-card ready to be punched-out from their backing. The were intended to be used as drink coasters and the driver's photo on front and his car on back. re most often found intact in the original 6-card The cards were distributed through the Action dealer network and were also made available to Packed Club members.

	MINT	NRMT
LETE SET (18)	12.00	5.50
ON CARD (1-18)	.50	.23
off Bodine	.50	.23
le Earnhardt	2.50	1.10
Elliott	1.25	.55
rry Gant	.75	.35
f Gordon	2.50	1.10
ie Irvan	.75	.35
e Jarrett	1.00	.45
bby Labonte	1.00	.45
rry Labonte	1.25	.55
terling Marlin	.75	.35
ark Martin	1.25	.55
e Nemechek	.50	.23
yle Petty	.75	.35

❏ 14 Ricky Rudd	.75	.35
❏ 15 Ken Schrader	.50	.23
❏ 16 Rusty Wallace	1.25	.55
❏ 17 Darrell Waltrip	.75	.35
❏ 18 Michael Waltrip	.50	.23

1994 Action Packed Mint Collection Jeff Gordon

This four-card set was originally done for distribution through the Home Shopping Network. Two of the cards are regular cards from the 1994 Action Packed Champ and Challenger set. The other two cards were produced with a gold leaf coating. The sets are numbered of 1,000 and come in a black slip cover case. The sets are sold and priced below as complete sets only.

	MINT	NRMT
COMPLETE SET (4)	40.00	18.00

1994 Action Packed Select 24K Gold

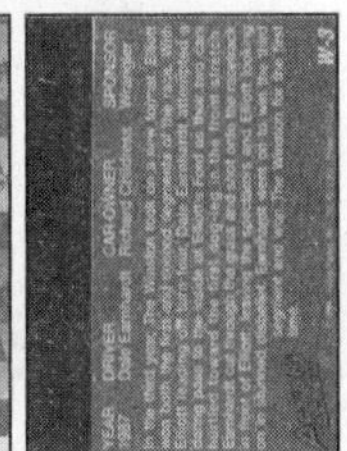

This 10-card set was produced by Action Packed and was distributed through the Winston Cup Catalog in a seperate black card display box with each card placed in a black felt inset slot. It focuses on the 1985-1994 winners of the Winston Select. It features the first Action Packed card of Bill Elliott. We have received recent reports that some of these cards have shown up in packs. The reports have not been overwhelming enough to confirm if the cards are being pulled out of original 1994 Action Packed boxes or the repackaged retail boxes available from some of the larger national retailers. We would suspect the latter of the two.

	MINT	NRMT
COMPLETE SET (10)	110.00	50.00
COMMON CARD (W1-W10)	5.00	2.20
❏ W1 Darrell Waltrip	6.00	2.70
❏ W2 Bill Elliott	10.00	4.50
❏ W3 Dale Earnhardt	20.00	9.00
❏ W4 Terry Labonte	10.00	4.50
❏ W5 Rusty Wallace	10.00	4.50
❏ W6 Dale Earnhardt	20.00	9.00
❏ W7 Davey Allison	15.00	6.75
❏ W8 Davey Allison	15.00	6.75
❏ W9 Dale Earnhardt	20.00	9.00
❏ W10 Geoff Bodine	5.00	2.20

1994 Action Packed Smokin' Joes

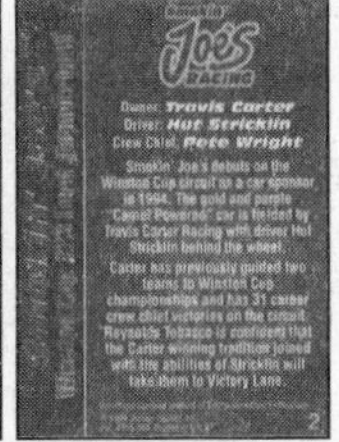

This 13-card set was produced by Action Packed and was distributed through the Winston Cup Catalog. It features members of the Smokin' Joe's racing teams in the NASCAR, NHRA, and AMA circuits. The set includes a 24K Gold checklist.

	MINT	NRMT
COMPLETE SET (13)	15.00	6.75
COMMON CARDS (1-13)	1.00	.45
❏ 1 Hut Stricklin	2.00	.90
❏ 2 Hut Stricklin's Car	1.50	.70

❏ 3 Jim Head	1.50	.70
❏ 4 Jim Head's Car	1.00	.45
❏ 5 Gordie Bonin	1.50	.70
❏ 6 Gordie Bonin's Car	1.00	.45
❏ 7 Mike Hale	1.50	.70
❏ 8 Mike Hale's Bike	1.00	.45
❏ 9 Kevin Magee	1.50	.70
❏ 10 Kevin Magee's Bike	1.00	.45
❏ 11 Mike Smith	1.50	.70
❏ 12 Mike Smith's Bike	1.00	.45
❏ 13 Checklist Card	1.50	.70

1995 Action Packed Country

Action Packed's third Winston Cup card release for 1995 was entitled Winston Cup Country and was produced by Pinnacle Brands. The set is comprised of several series of subsets: Riding Shotgun (1-10), Shades (11-20), Motor Racing Outreach (21-25) Now and Then (26-43), Winners (44-56), Crew Chiefs (57-61), Drivers (62-85), SuperTruck Drivers (86-91), SuperTrucks (92-98) and SuperTruck Owners (99-101). The embossed cards were packed 24-foil packs to a box with 6-cards per pack and distributed to both hobby and retail outlets. Insert sets include: Silver Speed parallel, 24KT Team, 2nd Career Choice, and Team Rainbow.

	MINT	NRMT
COMPLETE SET (101)	20.00	9.00
COMMON CARD (1-101)	.10	.05
COMMON DRIVER (1-101)	.20	.09
❏ 1 Bobby Labonte RS	.40	.18
❏ 2 Jeremy Mayfield RS	.20	.09
❏ 3 Bill Elliott RS	.75	.35
❏ 4 Darrell Waltrip RS	.40	.18
❏ 5 Dale Earnhardt RS	1.25	.55
❏ 6 Jeff Gordon RS	1.25	.55
❏ 7 Ricky Rudd RS	.40	.18
❏ 8 John Andretti RS	.20	.09
❏ 9 Kenny Wallace RS	.20	.09
❏ 10 Sterling Marlin RS	.40	.18
❏ 11 Dale Earnhardt S	1.25	.55
❏ 12 Rusty Wallace S	.60	.25
❏ 13 Dale Jarrett S	.40	.18
❏ 14 Jeff Gordon S	1.25	.55
❏ 15 Sterling Marlin S	.40	.18
❏ 16 Ricky Rudd S	.40	.18
❏ 17 Dale Earnhardt Taylor Nicole Earnhardt S	1.25	.55
❏ 18 Darrell Waltrip S	.40	.18
❏ 19 Terry Labonte S	.60	.25
❏ 20 Richard Petty S	.75	.35
❏ 21 Stevie Waltrip Darrell Waltrip MRO	.40	.18
❏ 22 Jeff Gordon Brooke Gordon MRO	1.25	.55
❏ 23 Rice Speed Lake Speed MRO	.20	.09
❏ 24 Bill Elliott Cindy Elliott MRO	.75	.35
❏ 25 Dale Earnhardt Teresa Earnhardt Max Helton	1.25	.55
❏ 26 Dale Earnhardt NT	1.25	.55
❏ 27 Dale Earnhardt NT	1.25	.55
❏ 28 Dale Earnhardt NT	1.25	.55
❏ 29 Dale Earnhardt NT	1.25	.55
❏ 30 Dale Earnhardt NT	1.25	.55
❏ 31 Dale Earnhardt NT	1.25	.55
❏ 32 Darrell Waltrip NT	.40	.18
❏ 33 Darrell Waltrip NT	.40	.18
❏ 34 Darrell Waltrip NT	.40	.18
❏ 35 Darrell Waltrip NT	.40	.18
❏ 36 Darrell Waltrip NT	.40	.18
❏ 37 Darrell Waltrip NT	.40	.18
❏ 38 Rusty Wallace NT	.60	.25
❏ 39 Rusty Wallace NT	.60	.25
❏ 40 Rusty Wallace NT	.60	.25
❏ 41 Rusty Wallace NT	.60	.25
❏ 42 Rusty Wallace NT	.60	.25
❏ 43 Rusty Wallace NT	.60	.25
❏ 44 Mark Martin WIN	.60	.25

❑ 45 Dale Earnhardt WIN Teresa Earnhardt	1.25	.55
❑ 46 Bobby Labonte WIN	.40	.18
❑ 47 Kyle Petty WIN	.40	.18
❑ 48 Terry Labonte WIN	.60	.25
❑ 49 Bobby Labonte WIN	.40	.18
❑ 50 Jeff Gordon WIN	1.25	.55
❑ 51 Jeff Gordon WIN	1.25	.55
❑ 52 Dale Jarrett WIN	.75	.35
❑ 53 Sterling Marlin WIN	.40	.18
❑ 54 Dale Earnhardt WIN	1.25	.55
❑ 55 Mark Martin WIN	.60	.25
❑ 56 Bobby Labonte WIN Joe Gibbs	.40	.18
❑ 57 Andy Petree	.10	.05
❑ 58 Steve Hmiel	.10	.05
❑ 59 Ray Evernham	.10	.05
❑ 60 Tony Glover	.10	.05
❑ 61 Robin Pemberton	.10	.05
❑ 62 Dale Earnhardt	2.00	.90
❑ 63 Jeff Gordon	2.00	.90
❑ 64 Ted Musgrave	.20	.09
❑ 65 Dale Jarrett	.75	.35
❑ 66 Bobby Hamilton	.20	.09
❑ 67 Morgan Shepherd	.20	.09
❑ 68 Bobby Labonte	.75	.35
❑ 69 Michael Waltrip	.20	.09
❑ 70 Ricky Rudd	.40	.18
❑ 71 Ken Schrader	.20	.09
❑ 72 Bill Elliott	1.00	.45
❑ 73 Steve Grissom	.20	.09
❑ 74 Derrike Cope	.20	.09
❑ 75 Brett Bodine	.20	.09
❑ 76 John Andretti	.20	.09
❑ 77 Rick Mast	.20	.09
❑ 78 Dick Trickle	.20	.09
❑ 79 Ricky Craven	.40	.18
❑ 80 Todd Bodine	.20	.09
❑ 81 Robert Pressley	.20	.09
❑ 82 Kenny Wallace	.20	.09
❑ 83 Jeff Burton	.20	.09
❑ 84 Jimmy Spencer	.20	.09
❑ 85 Geoff Bodine	.20	.09
❑ 86 Ron Hornaday Jr. STD	.20	.09
❑ 87 Butch Miller STD	.10	.05
❑ 88 Ken Schrader STD	.20	.09
❑ 89 Tobey Butler STD	.10	.05
❑ 90 Rick Carelli STD	.10	.05
❑ 91 Scott Lagasse STD	.20	.09
❑ 92 Sammy Swindell's SuperTruck	.10	.05
❑ 93 Scott Lagasse's SuperTruck	.10	.05
❑ 94 Mike Bliss' SuperTruck	.10	.05
❑ 95 Mike Chase's SuperTruck	.10	.05
❑ 96 Geoff Bodine's SuperTruck	.10	.05
❑ 97 Ken Schrader's SuperTruck	.10	.05
❑ 98 Ron Hornaday Jr.'s SuperTruck	.10	.05
❑ 99 Jeff Gordon Rick Hendrick STO	1.25	.55
❑ 100 Jim Venable STO	.10	.05
❑ 101 Ken Schrader STO	.20	.09

1995 Action Packed Country Silver Speed

This 84-card set is a parallel to the base set. The cards were randomly inserted in 1995 Action Packed Country packs at the rate of approximately one card every six foil packs. The cards were printed with a silver foil background on the driver photo and the Silver Streak logo on the card back.

	MINT	NRMT
COMPLETE SET (84)	60.00	27.00
COMMON CARD (1-84)	.60	.25
COMMON DRIVER (1-84)	1.20	.55

*SILVER SPEEDS: 3X TO 6X BASIC CARDS

1995 Action Packed Country 24KT Team

The 24KT, Micro-Etched cards feature 10 of Winston Cup's best drivers in the 14-card set. Three Dale Earnhardt and three Jeff Gordon cards highlight a new design for Action Packed's 24K insert line. The cards were seeded at a rate of one per 72 packs.

	MINT	NRMT
COMPLETE SET (14)	300.00	135.00
COMMON CARD (1-14)	6.00	2.70
❑ 1 Jeff Gordon	60.00	27.00
❑ 2 Jeff Gordon	60.00	27.00
❑ 3 Jeff Gordon	60.00	27.00
❑ 4 Mark Martin	30.00	13.50
❑ 5 Dale Earnhardt	60.00	27.00
❑ 6 Dale Earnhardt	60.00	27.00
❑ 7 Dale Earnhardt	60.00	27.00
❑ 8 Rusty Wallace	30.00	13.50
❑ 9 Sterling Marlin	12.00	5.50
❑ 10 Bobby Labonte	25.00	11.00
❑ 11 Bill Elliott	30.00	13.50
❑ 12 Ricky Rudd	12.00	5.50
❑ 13 Ken Schrader	6.00	2.70
❑ 14 Ted Musgrave	6.00	2.70

1995 Action Packed Country 2nd Career Choice

This 9-card insert set features some of the top Winston Cup drivers identifing what they would be doing if they weren't racing. The cards utilize holographic gold-foil printing technology. The cards were seeded at a rate of one per 24 packs.

	MINT	NRMT
COMPLETE SET (9)	50.00	22.00
COMMON CARD (1-9)	2.00	.90
❑ 1 Bobby Hillin	2.00	.90
❑ 2 Kenny Wallace	2.00	.90
❑ 3 Rusty Wallace	10.00	4.50
❑ 4 Dale Jarrett	10.00	4.50
❑ 5 Derrike Cope	2.00	.90
❑ 6 Dale Earnhardt	20.00	9.00
❑ 7 Bobby Labonte	8.00	3.60
❑ 8 Sterling Marlin	2.00	.90
❑ 9 Terry Labonte	10.00	4.50

1995 Action Packed Country Team Rainbow

This 12-card insert set takes a look at Jeff Gordon and the DuPont Rainbow Warrior team. The cards use lenticular printing technolgy to bring them to life. The cards were randomly inserted in hobby packs only at a rate of one per 36 packs.

	MINT	NRMT
COMPLETE SET (12)	150.00	70.00
COMMON CARD (1-12)	10.00	4.50
❑ 1 Jeff Gordon Brooke Gordon	20.00	9.00
❑ 2 Jeff Gordon's Car	10.00	4.50

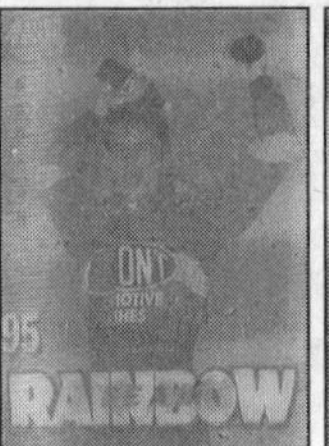

❑ 3 Jeff Gordon w/Crew Refuse To Lose	20.00
❑ 4 Ray Evernham	10.00
❑ 5 Jeff Gordon Brooke Gordon	20.00
❑ 6 Pit Stop	10.00
❑ 7 Jeff Gordon's Car	10.00
❑ 8 Jeff Gordon Ray Evernham Rick Hendrick	20.00
❑ 9 Jeff Gordon's Helmet	10.00
❑ 10 Victory Shout	20.00
❑ 11 Interview	20.00
❑ 12 Jeff Gordon Ray Evernham	20.00

1995 Action Packed Hendrick Motorsports

This eight-card set was distributed through Her Motorsport's merchandising trailers, as well as som Hendrick's car dealerships.

	MINT
COMPLETE SET (8)	5.00
COMMON CARD (1-8)	.30
COMMON DRIVER (1-8)	.50
❑ 1 Jeff Gordon	2.00
❑ 2 Ken Schrader	.50
❑ 3 Terry Labonte	1.00
❑ 4 Scott Lagasse	.50
❑ 5 Ricky Hendrick Jr.	.30
❑ 6 Rick Hendrick/Cover Card	.30
❑ 7 Papa Joe Hendrick	.30
❑ 8 Jimmy Johnson	.30

1995 Action Packed McDonald's Bill Elliott

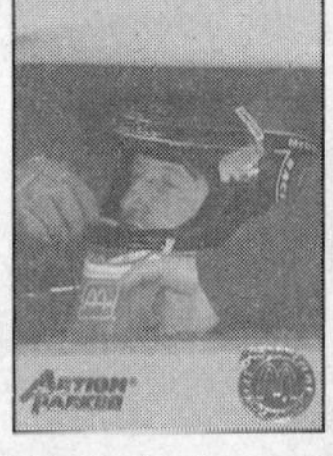

Originally offered during 1995 Speedweeks at Da these cards were distributed through participating and North Carolina area McDonald's restaurants. card cello packs, as well as 21-card factory sets produced. The set features Bill Elliott's life in and from racing. Approximately one autograph certifica distributed one per case.

	MINT
COMPLETE SET (21)	16.00
COMPLETE FACT. SET (21)	20.00
COMMON CARD (MC1-MC21)	1.00
AUTO. CERTIFICATE	100.00

995 Action Packed Preview

n Packed's first racing issue for 1995 is also only called Action Packed Winston Cup Preview as rapper states. The cards were packaged in 6-card with 24 packs per box. A new Driving With Dale was included featuring popular drivers discussing t's like to race against Earnhardt. The now standard Packed subsets of Race Winners, Pole Winners op Ten were also part of the regular issue. This set the first regular issue Bill Elliott Action Packed There was also a Dale Earnhardt Big Picture ption card randomly inserted in packs. The card out to make a big picture of Dale Earnhardt. There reported 2,500 cards produced.

	MINT	NRMT
LETE SET (78)	20.00	9.00
ON CARD (1-78)	.10	.05
ON DRIVER (1-78)	.20	.09
hn Andretti	.20	.09
ett Bodine	.20	.09
off Bodine	.20	.09
dd Bodine	.20	.09
ff Burton	.40	.18
rrike Cope	.20	.09
le Earnhardt	2.00	.90
l Elliott	1.00	.45
ff Gordon	2.00	.90
teve Grissom	.20	.09
Dale Jarrett	1.00	.45
teve Kinser	.20	.09
Bobby Labonte	.75	.35
erry Labonte	1.00	.45
Mark Martin	1.00	.45
Kyle Petty	.40	.18
Ricky Rudd	.40	.18
Ken Schrader	.20	.09
immy Spencer	.20	.09
Dick Trickle	.20	.09
Kenny Wallace	.20	.09
Mike Wallace	.20	.09
Rusty Wallace	1.00	.45
Darrell Waltrip	.40	.18
Michael Waltrip	.20	.09
Ricky Craven	.20	.09
Steve Kinser	.20	.09
Robert Pressley	.20	.09
oy Allen Jr. PW	.10	.05
Geoff Bodine PW	.10	.05
Chuck Bown PW	.10	.05
Ward Burton PW	.10	.05
Dale Earnhardt PW	1.00	.45
Bill Elliott PW	.50	.23
Harry Gant PW	.20	.09
eff Gordon PW	1.00	.45
David Green PW	.10	.05
rnie Irvan PW	.20	.09
Sterling Marlin PW	.20	.09
Mark Martin PW	.50	.23
Rick Mast PW	.10	.05
ed Musgrave PW	.10	.05
Ricky Rudd PW	.20	.09
Greg Sacks PW	.10	.05
immy Spencer PW	.10	.05
Rusty Wallace PW	.50	.23
Geoff Bodine WIN	.10	.05
Dale Earnhardt WIN	1.00	.45
Bill Elliott WIN	.50	.23
eff Gordon WIN	1.00	.45
rnie Irvan WIN	.20	.09
Dale Jarrett WIN	.40	.18
erry Labonte WIN	.50	.23
Sterling Marlin WIN	.20	.09
Mark Martin WIN	.50	.23
Ricky Rudd WIN	.20	.09
immy Spencer WIN	.10	.05
Rusty Wallace WIN	.50	.23
Dale Earnhardt WC Champ	1.00	.45
Mark Martin T10	.50	.23
Rusty Wallace T10	.50	.23
Ken Schrader T10	.10	.05
❏ 63 Ricky Rudd T10	.20	.09
❏ 64 Morgan Shepherd T10	.10	.05
❏ 65 Terry Labonte T10	.50	.23
❏ 66 Jeff Gordon T10	1.00	.45
❏ 67 Darrell Waltrip T10	.20	.09
❏ 68 Bill Elliott T10	.50	.23
❏ 69 Bill Elliott DD	.50	.23
❏ 70 Jeff Gordon DD	1.00	.45
❏ 71 Ernie Irvan DD	.20	.09
❏ 72 Mark Martin DD	.50	.23
❏ 73 Richard Petty DD	.40	.18
❏ 74 Robert Pressley DD	.10	.05
❏ 75 Ricky Rudd DD	.20	.09
❏ 76 Ken Schrader DD	.10	.05
❏ 77 Rusty Wallace DD	.50	.23
❏ 78 Darrell Waltrip DD	.20	.09
❏ BP1 Dale Earnhardt	20.00	9.00

1995 Action Packed Preview 24K Gold

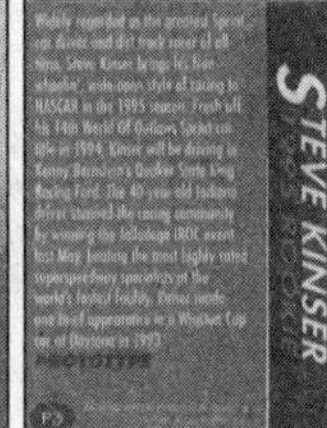

Randomly inserted in 1995 Action Packed Preview packs, each card includes the now standard 24Kt. Gold logo on the card front. These Gold cards are essentially parallel versions of the corresponding driver's Driving With Dale subset card. Wrapper stated odds for pulling a 24K Gold card are 1:96.

	MINT	NRMT
COMPLETE SET (10)	200.00	90.00
COMMON CARD (1G-10G)	8.00	3.60
❏ 1G Bill Elliott	40.00	18.00
❏ 2G Jeff Gordon	80.00	36.00
❏ 3G Ernie Irvan	15.00	6.75
❏ 4G Mark Martin	40.00	18.00
❏ 5G Richard Petty	20.00	9.00
❏ 6G Robert Pressley	8.00	3.60
❏ 7G Ricky Rudd	15.00	6.75
❏ 8G Ken Schrader	8.00	3.60
❏ 9G Rusty Wallace	40.00	18.00
❏ 10G Darrell Waltrip	15.00	6.75

1995 Action Packed Preview Bill Elliott

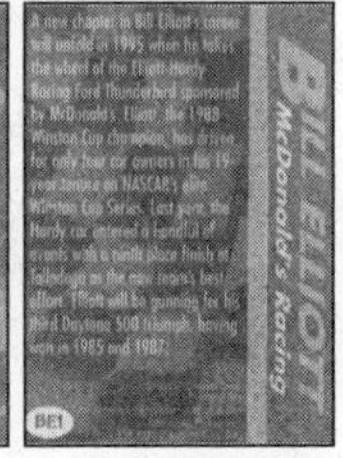

Action Packed added Bill Elliott to its stable of featured drivers in 1995. This special 6-card insert was distributed in 1995 Action Packed foil packs and includes cards of Elliott's life away from auto racing. There was also a Bill Elliott promo card issued through the Elliott Fan Club.

	MINT	NRMT
COMPLETE SET (6)	8.00	3.60
COMMON CARD (BE1-BE6)	1.50	.70
❏ BE1 Bill Elliott with Car	1.50	.70
❏ BE2 Bill Elliott in Helmet	1.50	.70
❏ BE3 Bill Elliott with brothers	1.50	.70
❏ BE4 Bill Elliott's Airplane	1.50	.70
❏ BE5 Bill Elliott's Car	1.50	.70
❏ BE6 Bill Elliott Skiing	1.50	.70
❏ BEFC1 Bill Elliott Club Promo Elliott Fan Club issue	8.00	3.60

1995 Action Packed Stars

Action Packed's second Winston Cup card release for 1995 was entitled Winston Cup Stars and was Pinnacle Brands' first NASCAR release after acquiring the rights to the Action Packed name. The set is comprised of several series of subsets: Out of the Chute (1-30), Mean Rides (31-45), Race Winners (46-53), Picture Perfect (54-59), Settles In (60-65), Cope With It (66-70), On The Other Side (71-75), Winning The War (76-81), and McDonald's Bill Elliott (82-86) featuring two cards using Pinnacle's patented lenticular printing technology. These two cards (84-85) showing Bill Elliott "morphing" into the Batman logo and the Thunderbat race car, were produced in fewer numbers than the other regular issue cards. Cards were packed 24-foil packs to a box with 6-cards per pack and distributed to both hobby and retail outlets. Insert sets include: Silver Speed parallel, 24K Gold, Dale Earnhardt Race For Eight, and Trucks That Haul (hobby pack exclusive).

	MINT	NRMT
COMPLETE SET (86)	35.00	16.00
COMP.SET (84) W/O 84,85	20.00	9.00
COMMON CARD (1-86)	.10	.05
COMMON DRIVER (1-86)	.20	.09
❏ 1 Sterling Marlin OC	.40	.18
❏ 2 Terry Labonte OC	1.00	.45
❏ 3 Mark Martin OC	1.00	.45
❏ 4 Geoff Bodine OC	.20	.09
❏ 5 Jeff Burton OC	.40	.18
❏ 6 Ricky Rudd OC	.40	.18
❏ 7 Brett Bodine OC	.20	.09
❏ 8 Derrike Cope OC	.20	.09
❏ 9 Ted Musgrave OC	.20	.09
❏ 10 Darrell Waltrip OC	.40	.18
❏ 11 Bobby Labonte OC	.75	.35
❏ 12 Morgan Shepherd OC	.20	.09
❏ 13 Jimmy Spencer OC	.20	.09
❏ 14 Ken Schrader OC	.20	.09
❏ 15 Dale Jarrett OC	.60	.25
❏ 16 Kyle Petty OC	.40	.18
❏ 17 Michael Waltrip OC	.20	.09
❏ 18 Robert Pressley OC	.20	.09
❏ 19 John Andretti OC	.20	.09
❏ 20 Todd Bodine OC	.20	.09
❏ 21 Joe Nemechek OC	.20	.09
❏ 22 Bill Elliott OC	1.00	.45
❏ 23 Dale Earnhardt OC	2.00	.90
❏ 24 Jeff Gordon OC	2.00	.90
❏ 25 Rusty Wallace OC	1.00	.45
❏ 26 Rick Mast OC	.20	.09
❏ 27 Dick Trickle OC	.20	.09
❏ 28 Randy LaJoie OC	.20	.09
❏ 29 Steve Grissom OC	.20	.09
❏ 30 Ricky Craven OC	.20	.09
❏ 31 Dale Earnhardt's Car	1.00	.45
❏ 32 Rusty Wallace's Car	.50	.23
❏ 33 Sterling Marlin's Car	.20	.09
❏ 34 Terry Labonte's Car	.50	.23
❏ 35 Mark Martin's Car	.50	.23
❏ 36 Bill Elliott's Car	.50	.23
❏ 37 Ricky Rudd's Car	.20	.09
❏ 38 Joe Nemechek's Car	.10	.05
❏ 39 Darrell Waltrip's Car	.20	.09
❏ 40 Jeff Gordon's Car	1.00	.45
❏ 41 Jimmy Spencer's Car	.10	.05
❏ 42 Ken Schrader's Car	.10	.05
❏ 43 Dale Jarrett's Car	.40	.18
❏ 44 Steve Kinser's Car	.10	.05
❏ 45 Bobby Hamilton's Car	.10	.05
❏ 46 Sterling Marlin RW	.40	.18
❏ 47 Jeff Gordon RW	2.00	.90
❏ 48 Terry Labonte RW	1.00	.45
❏ 49 Jeff Gordon RW	2.00	.90
❏ 50 Sterling Marlin RW	.40	.18
❏ 51 Jeff Gordon RW	2.00	.90
❏ 52 Dale Earnhardt RW	2.00	.90
❏ 53 Rusty Wallace RW	1.00	.45
❏ 54 Sterling Marlin OC	.40	.18
❏ 55 Sterling Marlin OC	.40	.18

❑ 56 Sterling Marlin OC	.40	.18
❑ 57 Sterling Marlin OC	.40	.18
❑ 58 Sterling Marlin OC	.40	.18
❑ 59 Sterling Marlin OC	.40	.18
❑ 60 Jeff Gordon PP	1.00	.45
❑ 61 Jeff Gordon PP	1.00	.45
❑ 62 Jeff Gordon PP	1.00	.45
❑ 63 Jeff Gordon PP	1.00	.45
❑ 64 Jeff Gordon PP	1.00	.45
❑ 65 Jeff Gordon PP	1.00	.45
❑ 66 Derrike Cope CWI	.20	.09
❑ 67 Derrike Cope CWI	.20	.09
❑ 68 Derrike Cope CWI	.20	.09
❑ 69 Derrike Cope CWI	.20	.09
❑ 70 Derrike Cope CWI	.20	.09
❑ 71 Ernie Irvan OOS	.40	.18
❑ 72 Ernie Irvan OOS	.40	.18
❑ 73 Ernie Irvan OOS	.40	.18
❑ 74 Ernie Irvan OOS	.40	.18
❑ 75 Ernie Irvan OOS	.40	.18
❑ 76 Rusty Wallace WW	.50	.23
❑ 77 Rusty Wallace WW	.50	.23
❑ 78 Rusty Wallace WW	.50	.23
❑ 79 Rusty Wallace WW	.50	.23
❑ 80 Rusty Wallace WW	.50	.23
❑ 81 Rusty Wallace WW	.50	.23
❑ 82 Bill Elliott's Thunderbat Car	.50	.23
❑ 83 Bill Elliott's Car	.50	.23
❑ 84 Bill Elliott Magic Motion SP	8.00	3.60
❑ 85 Bill Elliott Magic Motion SP	8.00	3.60
❑ 86 Jeff Gordon. Bobby Labonte Terry Labonte	1.50	.70

1995 Action Packed Stars Silver Speed

With the change to Pinnacle Brands, Action Packed changed to include its first full parallel set -- Silver Speed. The cards were inserted in 1995 Action Packed Stars packs at the rate of approximately one card every six foil packs. The cards were printed with a silver foil background on the driver photo and a Silver Speed logo on the card back. Only 84 of 86 of the regular cards were produced with the two Bill Elliott lenticular cards (84-85) being left out.

	MINT	NRMT
COMPLETE SET (84)	100.00	45.00
COMMON CARD (1-86)	.60	.25
COMMON DRIVER (1-86)	1.20	.55

*SILVER SPEEDS: 3X TO 6X BASIC CARDS

1995 Action Packed Stars 24K Gold

Randomly inserted in 1995 Action Packed Stars packs, each card includes the now standard 24Kt. Gold logo on the card front. These Gold cards are essentially parallel versions of the corresponding driver's regular cards with an emphasis on Jeff Gordon and Dale Earnhardt. Wrapper stated odds for pulling a 24K Gold card are 1:72.

	MINT	NRMT
COMPLETE SET (21)	600.00	275.00
COMMON CARD (1G-21G)	10.00	4.50

*SINGLES: 10X TO 25X BASE CARD HI

❑ 1G Sterling Marlin	10.00	4.50
❑ 2G Jeff Gordon	75.00	34.00
❑ 3G Terry Labonte	35.00	16.00
❑ 4G Jeff Gordon	75.00	34.00
❑ 5G Sterling Marlin	10.00	4.50
❑ 6G Jeff Gordon	75.00	34.00
❑ 7G Dale Earnhardt	75.00	34.00
❑ 8G Rusty Wallace	35.00	16.00
❑ 9G Dale Earnhardt	75.00	34.00
❑ 10G Dale Earnhardt	75.00	34.00
❑ 11G Dale Earnhardt	75.00	34.00
❑ 12G Dale Earnhardt	75.00	34.00
❑ 13G Dale Earnhardt	75.00	34.00
❑ 14G Dale Earnhardt	75.00	34.00
❑ 15G Dale Earnhardt	75.00	34.00
❑ 16G Dale Earnhardt	75.00	34.00
❑ 17G Rusty Wallace	35.00	16.00
❑ 18G Rusty Wallace	35.00	16.00
❑ 19G Jeff Gordon	75.00	34.00
❑ 20G Jeff Gordon	75.00	34.00
❑ 21G Ernie Irvan	10.00	4.50

1995 Action Packed Stars Dale Earnhardt Race for Eight

Using Pinnacle Brands' micro-etching printing technology, Action Packed produced this 8-card Dale Earnhardt insert set distributed through 1995 Action Packed Stars packs. The cards were inserted at the ratio of 1:24 packs.

	MINT	NRMT
COMPLETE SET (8)	80.00	36.00
COMMON CARD (DE1-DE8)	10.00	4.50

❑ DE1 Dale Earnhardt	10.00	4.50
❑ DE2 Dale Earnhardt	10.00	4.50
❑ DE3 Dale Earnhardt	10.00	4.50
❑ DE4 Dale Earnhardt	10.00	4.50
❑ DE5 Dale Earnhardt Teresa Earnhardt	10.00	4.50
❑ DE6 Dale Earnhardt	10.00	4.50
❑ DE7 Dale Earnhardt	10.00	4.50
❑ DE8 Dale Earnhardt's Car	10.00	4.50

1995 Action Packed Stars Dale Earnhardt Silver Salute

The set consists of four oversized (approximately 5" by 7") cards distributed in both 1995 Action Packed Stars (1,3) and Action Packed Country (2,4). The cards commemorate Earnhardt's silver car used in the 1995 Winston Select. Two cards (1,2) were inserted at the rate of one per box, with the other two (3,4) inserted about one per case.

	MINT	NRMT
COMPLETE SET (4)	150.00	70.00
COMMON CARD (1-4)	10.00	4.50

❑ 1 Dale Earnhardt w/Silver Car	10.00	4.50
❑ 2 Dale Earnhardt Richard Childress	10.00	4.50
❑ 3 Dale Earnhardt's Silver Car	70.00	32.00
❑ 4 Dale Earnhardt Teresa Earnhardt	70.00	32.00

1995 Action Packed Stars Trucks That Haul

NASCAR's SuperTrucks is the feature of this hobby only insert in 1995 Action Packed Stars foil packs. The cards use Pinnacle's micro-etching printing process and were inserted at the average rate of 1:36 packs.

	MINT	NRMT
COMPLETE SET (6)	50.00	22.00
COMMON CARD (1-6)	5.00	2.20

❑ 1 Jeff Gordon and Rick Hendrick's Truck	20.00	9.00
❑ 2 Teresa Earnhardt's Truck	10.00	
❑ 3 Frank Vessels' Truck	5.00	
❑ 4 Geoff Bodine's Truck	5.00	
❑ 5 Richard Childress' Truck	5.00	
❑ 6 Ken Schrader's Truck	5.00	

1995 Action Packed Mamm

This six-card set features the top names in NASCAR cards are approximately 7.5" X 10.5" in size. They distributed through Action Packed dealer network cards came in clear poly pag packs with each pack h one card.

	MINT
COMPLETE SET (6)	15.00
COMMON CARD (MM1-MM6)	2.00

❑ MM1 Dale Earnhardt	4.00
❑ MM2 Bill Elliott	2.00
❑ MM3 Rusty Wallace	2.00
❑ MM4 Jeff Gordon	4.00
❑ MM5 Mark Martin	2.00
❑ MM6 Dale Earnhardt	4.00

1995 Action Packed Sundro Dale Earnhardt

One card was inserted in each specially marked 12- of Sundrop citrus soda. 500 signed copies of each three cards were also randomly inserted in the soft packages. However, the autographed cards we certified in any way and are otherwise indistinguis from the unsigned regular cards. Autographed car commonly found for $25-$50.

	MINT
COMPLETE SET (3)	15.00
COMMON CARD (SD1-SD3)	5.00

❑ SD1 Dale Earnhardt	5.00
❑ SD2 Dale Earnhardt	5.00
❑ SD3 Dale Earnhardt Kelly Earnhardt Kerry Earnhardt Dale Earnhardt Jr.	8.00

1996 Action Packed Credentials

This 105-card set was released by Pinnacle Brands. the first Action Packed regular issue set to feature s, instead of the normal rounded corners. The cards atured the embossed technology that Action Packed wn for. The set features nine topical subsets; Jeff n Defending Champion (1-5), Dale Earnhardt Seven-;hampion (6-10), Mark Martin On the Mark (11-15), na Winners (16-19), Drivers (20-54), Speed nes (55-64), Crew Chiefs (65-69), Owners (70-83), d the Scenes (84-93), and Wives, Camera, Action 1). Cards were distributed in six card packs with 24 per box and 10 boxes per case. The packs carried a sted retail price of $2.99.

	MINT	NRMT
LETE SET (105)	12.00	5.50
ION CARD (1-105)	.10	.05
ION DRIVER (1-105)	.20	.09
ff Gordon DC	1.00	.45
ff Gordon DC	1.00	.45
ff Gordon DC	1.00	.45
ff Gordon DC	1.00	.45
ff Gordon DC	1.00	.45
le Earnhardt STC	1.00	.45
le Earnhardt STC	1.00	.45
le Earnhardt STC	1.00	.45
le Earnhardt STC	1.00	.45
ale Earnhardt STC	1.00	.45
ark Martin OTM	.50	.23
ark Martin OTM	.50	.23
ark Martin OTM	.50	.23
ark Martin OTM	.50	.23
ark Martin OTM	.50	.23
ale Jarrett DW	.40	.18
ale Earnhardt DW	1.00	.45
rnie Irvan DW	.20	.09
ale Jarrett DW	.40	.18
eff Gordon	2.00	.90
ale Earnhardt	2.00	.90
terling Marlin	.40	.18
ark Martin	1.00	.45
usty Wallace	1.00	.45
erry Labonte	1.00	.45
ed Musgrave	.20	.09
ill Elliott	1.00	.45
icky Rudd	.40	.18
obby Labonte	.75	.35
organ Shepherd	.20	.09
ichael Waltrip	.20	.09
ale Jarrett	.75	.35
obby Hamilton	.20	.09
errike Cope	.20	.09
rnie Irvan	.40	.18
en Schrader	.20	.09
ohn Andretti	.20	.09
arrell Waltrip	.40	.18
rett Bodine	.20	.09
ick Mast	.20	.09
ard Burton	.20	.09
ake Speed	.20	.09
oy Allen	.20	.09
ut Stricklin	.20	.09
immy Spencer	.20	.09
ike Wallace	.20	.09
oe Nemechek	.20	.09
obert Pressley	.20	.09
eoff Bodine	.20	.09
eremy Mayfield	.60	.25
eff Burton	.40	.18
enny Wallace	.20	.09
obby Hillin	.20	.09
ohnny Benson	.20	.09
usty Wallace SM	.50	.23
erry Labonte SM	.50	.23
ale Earnhardt SM	1.00	.45
ichael Waltrip SM	.10	.05
obby Hamilton SM	.10	.05
obby Labonte SM	.40	.18
arrell Waltrip SM	.20	.09
ark Martin SM	.50	.23
ichard Childress SM	.10	.05
en Schrader SM	.10	.05
avid Smith	.10	.05
ay Evernham	.20	.09
immy Makar	.10	.05
arry McReynolds	.10	.05
odd Parrott	.10	.05
oger Penske Don Miller OWN	.10	.05
ichard Childress OWN	.10	.05
arry McClure OWN	.10	.05
ick Hendrick OWN	.10	.05
ack Roush OWN	.10	.05
ale Yarborough OWN	.10	.05
icky Rudd OWN	.20	.09
obby Allison OWN	.10	.05
ichard Petty OWN	.50	.23
arrell Waltrip OWN	.20	.09
oe Gibbs OWN	.20	.09
❑ 81 Bill Elliott Charles Hardy OWN	.50	.23
❑ 82 Robert Yates OWN	.10	.05
❑ 83 Michael Kranefuss Carl Haas OWN	.10	.05
❑ 84 Andrea Nemechek BTS	.10	.05
❑ 85 Kim Wallace BTS	.10	.05
❑ 86 Buffy Waltrip BTS	.10	.05
❑ 87 Kim Irvan BTS	.10	.05
❑ 88 Kim Burton Paige Burton BTS	.10	.05
❑ 89 Rice Speed BTS	.10	.05
❑ 90 Stevie Waltrip Darrell Waltrip BTS	.20	.09
❑ 91 Cindy Elliott Bill Elliott BTS	.50	.23
❑ 92 Brooke Gordon BTS	.75	.35
❑ 93 Donna Labonte BTS	.20	.09
❑ 94 Darrell Waltrip WCA	.20	.09
❑ 95 Sterling Marlin WCA	.20	.09
❑ 96 Michael Waltrip WCA	.10	.05
❑ 97 Kenny Wallace with Brandy Brittany Brooke WCA	.10	.05
❑ 98 Bobby Labonte WCA	.40	.18
❑ 99 Jeff Gordon WCA	1.00	.45
❑ 100 Jeremy Mayfield WCA	.40	.18
❑ 101 Bill Elliott WCA	.50	.23
❑ 102 Johnny Benson	.20	.09
❑ 103 Ricky Craven Travis Roy	.20	.09
❑ 104 Dale Earnhardt CL	1.00	.45
❑ 105 Jeff Gordon CL	1.00	.45

1996 Action Packed Credentials Silver Speed

This 42-card set is a partial parallel to the Credentials base set. The Silver Speed cards took the best cards from the 105 card set and prints them on a silver holographic stock. The cards were randomly inserted in packs at a ratio of 1:6.

	MINT	NRMT
COMPLETE SET (42)	60.00	27.00
COMMON CARD	.60	.25
COMMON DRIVER	1.20	.55

*SILVER SPEED CARD: 3X TO 6X BASIC CARD

1996 Action Packed Credentials Fan Scan

This 9-card insert set allowed collectors to go inside a race car during a NASCAR race. Each card back included a 1-800 phone number along with a personal identification number. During selected NASCAR races, the collector could phone the number, enter the PIN, and listen to the sounds the driver is hearing inside his helmet. Advanced broadcast electronics made the technology possilbe. The cards were seeded one in 72 packs.

	MINT	NRMT
COMPLETE SET (9)	150.00	70.00
COMMON CARD (1-9)	5.00	2.20

*SINGLES: 10X TO 25X BASE CARD HI

	MINT	NRMT
❑ 1 Dale Earnhardt	75.00	34.00
❑ 2 Dale Earnhardt's Car	60.00	27.00
❑ 3 Mark Martin	30.00	13.50
❑ 4 Jeff Gordon	75.00	34.00
❑ 5 Ted Musgrave	5.00	2.20
❑ 6 Ernie Irvan	10.00	4.50
❑ 7 Bobby Hamilton	5.00	2.20
❑ 8 Dale Jarrett	25.00	11.00
❑ 9 Jeff Burton	10.00	4.50

1996 Action Packed Credentials Leaders of the Pack

This 10-card insert set features the top Winston Cup drivers. The cards were printed on rainbow holographic foil with holographic and gold foil stamping. The cards were available in hobby only packs at a rate of one in 35.

	MINT	NRMT
COMPLETE SET (10)	100.00	45.00
COMMON CARD (1-10)	3.00	1.35

*SINGLES: 3X TO 8X BASE CARD HI

	MINT	NRMT
❑ 1 Dale Earnhardt	25.00	11.00
❑ 2 Dale Earnhardt	25.00	11.00
❑ 3 Dale Earnhardt	25.00	11.00
❑ 4 Dale Earnhardt	25.00	11.00
❑ 5 Jeff Gordon	25.00	11.00
❑ 6 Jeff Gordon	25.00	11.00
❑ 7 Jeff Gordon	25.00	11.00
❑ 8 Jeff Gordon	25.00	11.00
❑ 9 Sterling Marlin	3.00	1.35
❑ 10 Sterling Marlin	3.00	1.35

1996 Action Packed Credentials Oversized

This four-card series feature the top drivers in Winston Cup. The cards measure 5" X 7" and were available one per special retail box.

	MINT	NRMT
COMPLETE SET (4)	20.00	9.00
COMMON CARD (1-4)	2.50	1.10
❑ 1 Dale Earnhardt	8.00	3.60
❑ 2 Jeff Gordon	8.00	3.60
❑ 3 Dale Jarrett	2.50	1.10
❑ 4 Bill Elliott	4.00	1.80

1996 Action Packed McDonald's

For the second year, McDonald's distributed a small card set produced by Action Packed. The 1996 set features square corners instead of Action Packed's traditional rounded ones. While the set has a strong Bill Elliott focus, like the 1995 issue, it also includes cards of other top Winston Cup drivers and their rides. The set was distributed through 4-card packs with one unnumbered checklist card per pack. Packs originally sold for 99-cents from participating McDonald's stores.

	MINT	NRMT
COMPLETE SET (29)	12.00	5.50
COMMON CARD (1-28)	.15	.07
❑ 1 Bill Elliott	.75	.35
❑ 2 Dale Earnhardt	1.50	.70
❑ 3 Jeff Gordon	1.50	.70
❑ 4 Sterling Marlin	.25	.11
❑ 5 Mark Martin	.75	.35
❑ 6 Bobby Labonte	.60	.25
❑ 7 Terry Labonte	.75	.35
❑ 8 Ernie Irvan	.25	.11

	MINT	NRMT
❑ 9 Kenny Wallace	.15	.07
❑ 10 Dale Jarrett	.60	.25
❑ 11 Bill Elliott's Car	.40	.18
❑ 12 Dale Earnhardt's Car	.75	.35
❑ 13 Jeff Gordon's Car	.75	.35
❑ 14 Sterling Marlin's Car	.15	.07
❑ 15 Mark Martin's Car	.40	.18
❑ 16 Bobby Labonte's Car	.40	.18
❑ 17 Terry Labonte's Car	.40	.18
❑ 18 Ernie Irvan's Car	.15	.07
❑ 19 Kenny Wallace's Car	.15	.07
❑ 20 Dale Jarrett's Car	.40	.18
❑ 21 Bill Elliott	.50	.23
❑ 22 Bill Elliott	.50	.23
❑ 23 Bill Elliott	.50	.23
❑ 24 Bill Elliott	.50	.23
❑ 25 Bill Elliott	.50	.23
❑ 26 Bill Elliott	.50	.23
❑ 27 Bill Elliott	.50	.23
❑ 28 Bill Elliott	.50	.23
❑ NNO Bill Elliott Checklist Card DP	.15	.07

1997 Action Packed

This 86-card set was released by Pinnacle Brands. The cards still feature the embossed technology that Action Packed is known for. The set features three topical subsets; Championship Drive (53-56), 1996 A Look Back (57-68), and Orient Express (71-84). Cards were distributed in six card packs with 24 packs per box and 10 boxes per case. The packs carried a suggested retail price of $2.99.

	MINT	NRMT
COMPLETE SET (86)	15.00	6.75
COMMON CARD (1-86)	.10	.05
COMMON DRIVER (1-86)	.20	.09

	MINT	NRMT
❑ 1 Bobby Hamilton	.20	.09
❑ 2 Rusty Wallace	1.00	.45
❑ 3 Dale Earnhardt	2.00	.90
❑ 4 Sterling Marlin	.40	.18
❑ 5 Terry Labonte	1.00	.45
❑ 6 Mark Martin	1.00	.45
❑ 7 Jeremy Mayfield	.60	.25
❑ 8 Jeff Gordon	2.00	.90
❑ 9 Ernie Irvan	.40	.18
❑ 10 Ricky Rudd	.40	.18
❑ 11 Bill Elliott	1.00	.45
❑ 12 Jimmy Spencer	.20	.09
❑ 13 Dale Jarrett	.75	.35
❑ 14 Ward Burton	.20	.09
❑ 15 Michael Waltrip	.20	.09
❑ 16 Ted Musgrave	.20	.09
❑ 17 Darrell Waltrip	.40	.18
❑ 18 Bobby Labonte	.75	.35
❑ 19 John Andretti	.20	.09
❑ 20 Robert Pressley	.20	.09
❑ 21 Chad Little	.20	.09
❑ 22 Geoff Bodine	.20	.09
❑ 23 Morgan Shepherd	.20	.09
❑ 24 Mike Skinner	.20	.09
❑ 25 Ricky Craven	.20	.09
❑ 26 Robby Gordon	.20	.09
❑ 27 Mark Martin's Car	.50	.23
❑ 28 Jeremy Mayfield's Car	.40	.18
❑ 29 Jeff Gordon's Car	1.00	.45
❑ 30 Ernie Irvan's Car	.20	.09
❑ 31 Ricky Rudd's Car	.20	.09
❑ 32 Bill Elliott's Car	.50	.23
❑ 33 Jimmy Spencer's Car	.10	.05
❑ 34 Dale Jarrett's Car	.40	.18
❑ 35 Ward Burton's Car	.10	.05
❑ 36 Michael Waltrip's Car	.10	.05
❑ 37 Ted Musgrave's Car	.10	.05
❑ 38 Darrell Waltrip's Car	.20	.09
❑ 39 Bobby Labonte's Car	.40	.18
❑ 40 John Andretti's Car	.10	.05
❑ 41 Robert Pressley's Car	.10	.05
❑ 42 Chad Little's Car	.10	.05
❑ 43 Morgan Shepherd's Car	.10	.05
❑ 44 Rusty Wallace's Car	.50	.23
❑ 45 Dale Earnhardt's Car	1.00	.45
❑ 46 Sterling Marlin's Car	.20	.09
❑ 47 Terry Labonte's Car	.50	.23
❑ 48 Geoff Bodine's Car	.10	.05
❑ 49 Bobby Hamilton's Car	.10	.05
❑ 50 Mike Skinner's Car	.10	.05
❑ 51 Ricky Craven's Car	.10	.05
❑ 52 Robby Gordon's Car	.10	.05
❑ 53 Terry Labonte	1.00	.45
❑ 54 Dale Jarrett	.75	.35
❑ 55 Randy LaJoie	.20	.09
❑ 56 David Green	.20	.09
❑ 57 Randy LaJoie	.20	.09
❑ 58 Bill Elliott	1.00	.45
❑ 59 Michael Waltrip	.20	.09
❑ 60 Hut Stricklin	.20	.09
❑ 61 Johnny Benson	.20	.09
❑ 62 Carl Hill	.10	.05
❑ 63 Dale Jarrett	.75	.35
❑ 64 Bill Elliott	1.00	.45
❑ 65 Elmo Langley	.20	.09
❑ 66 Harry Hyde	.20	.09
❑ 67 Richard Petty	.50	.23
❑ 68 Johnny Benson	.20	.09
❑ 69 Rusty Wallace	1.00	.45
❑ 70 David Green	.20	.09
❑ 71 Michael Waltrip	.20	.09
❑ 72 Dale Jarrett	.75	.35
❑ 73 Rusty Wallace's Car	.50	.23
❑ 74 Michael Waltrip's Car	.10	.05
❑ 75 Robby Gordon's Car	.10	.05
❑ 76 Sterling Marlin's Car	.20	.09
❑ 77 Ernie Irvan's Car	.20	.09
❑ 78 Dale Jarrett's Car	.40	.18
❑ 79 David Green	.20	.09
❑ 80 Ernie Irvan	.40	.18
❑ 81 Johnny Benson's Car	.10	.05
❑ 82 Robin Pemberton	.10	.05
❑ 83 Terry Labonte's Car	.50	.23
❑ 84 Dale Earnhardt's Car	1.00	.45
❑ 85 Darrell Waltrip CL	.20	.09
❑ 86 Bobby Hamilton CL	.10	.05

1997 Action Packed First Impressions

This 86-card set is a parallel to the base set. These cards a marked on the backs by a sillouette First Impressions logo. The cards were randomly inserted in packs at a ratio of 1:7.

	MINT	NRMT
COMPLETE SET (86)	60.00	27.00
COMMON CARD (1-86)	.40	.18
COMMON DRIVER (1-86)	.75	.35

1997 Action Packed 24KT Gold

Each card from this 14-card set is marked with the now standard 24Kt. Gold logo on the card front. The cards were randomly inserted in hobby packs at a ratio of 1:71 and inserted in retail packs at a ratio of 1:86.

	MINT	NRMT
COMPLETE SET (14)	350.00	160.00
COMMON CARD (1-14)	8.00	3.60
*SINGLES: 15X TO 40X BASE CARD HI		

	MINT	NRMT
❑ 1 Rusty Wallace	50.00	22.00
❑ 2 Dale Earnhardt	90.00	40.00
❑ 3 Jeff Gordon	90.00	40.00
❑ 4 Ernie Irvan	15.00	6.75
❑ 5 Terry Labonte	50.00	22.00
❑ 6 Johnny Benson	8.00	3.60
❑ 7 David Green	8.00	3.60
❑ 8 Dale Jarrett	40.00	18.00
❑ 9 Sterling Marlin	15.00	6.75
❑ 10 Michael Waltrip	8.00	3.60
❑ 11 Mark Martin	50.00	22.00
❑ 12 Bobby Hamilton	8.00	3.60
❑ 13 Ted Musgrave	8.00	3.60
❑ 14 Randy LaJoie	20.00	9.00

1997 Action Packed Chevy Madness

This 6-card set is actually the beginning of a 15-ca that was distributed in 1997 Pinnacle(13-15) and Racer's Choice(7-12). The cards feature the top drivers from the Winston Cup Series. The cards randomly inserted into hobby packs at a ratio of 1:1 inserted into retail packs at a ratio of 1:12.

	MINT
COMPLETE SET (6)	20.00
COMMON CARD (1-6)	1.25
*SINGLES: 2.5X TO 6X BASE CARD HI	

	MINT
❑ 1 Dale Earnhardt's Car	12.00
❑ 2 Darrell Waltrip's Car	2.50
❑ 3 Dave Marcis' Car	2.50
❑ 4 Jeff Gordon's Car	12.00
❑ 5 Sterling Marlin's Car	2.50
❑ 6 Steve Grissom's Car	1.25

1997 Action Packed Fifth Anniversary

This 12-card set celebrates five years of NASCAR production by Action Packed. The set includes curre retired NASCAR stars. The cards were randomly ins into hobby packs at a ratio of 1:128 and inserted into packs at a ratio of 1:153.

	MINT
COMPLETE SET (12)	400.00
COMMON CARD (1-12)	20.00

	MINT
❑ 1 Richard Petty	30.00
❑ 2 Cale Yarborough	20.00
❑ 3 Bobby Allison	20.00
❑ 4 Ned Jarrett	20.00
❑ 5 Benny Parsons	20.00
❑ 6 Dale Earnhardt	120.00
❑ 7 Rusty Wallace	60.00
❑ 8 Jeff Gordon	120.00
❑ 9 Terry Labonte	60.00
❑ 10 Dale Jarrett	50.00
❑ 11 Mark Martin	60.00
❑ 12 Bill Elliott	60.00

1997 Action Packed Fifth Anniversary Autograph

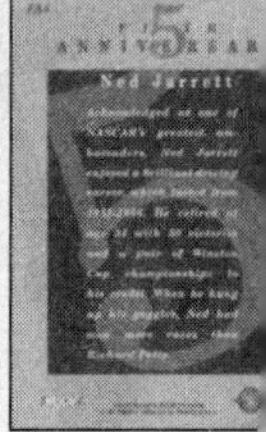

This 5-card set is a partial parallel to the Fifth Anniv set. It contains the first five cards from that set fea autographs from retired NASCAR legends. The card randomly inserted into hobby packs at a ratio of and inserted into retail packs at a ratio of 1:198.

	MINT
COMPLETE SET (5)	150.00
COMMON CARD (1-5)	40.00

	MINT
❑ 1 Richard Petty	60.00
❑ 2 Cale Yarborough	40.00
❑ 3 Bobby Allison	40.00
❑ 4 Ned Jarrett	40.00
❑ 5 Benny Parsons	40.00

1997 Action Packed Ironman Champion

card set higlights Terry Labonte's run for the 1997 on Cup Points Championship. The cards were nly inserted into hobby packs at a ratio of 1:192 serted into retail packs at a ratio of 1:230.

	MINT	NRMT
LETE SET (2)	60.00	27.00
ON CARD (1-2)	30.00	13.50
ry Labonte	40.00	18.00
rry Labonte Bobby Labonte	30.00	13.50

1997 Action Packed Rolling Thunder

4-card set features some of the top stars from R. The cards were randomly inserted into hobby at a ratio of 1:23 and inserted into retail packs at a f 1:28.

	MINT	NRMT
LETE SET (14)	100.00	45.00
ON CARD (1-14)	2.50	1.10
LES: 5X TO 12X BASE CARD HI		
rk Martin	25.00	11.00
le Earnhardt	40.00	18.00
f Gordon	40.00	18.00
nie Irvan	5.00	2.20
rry Labonte	25.00	11.00
le Petty	5.00	2.20
rrell Waltrip	5.00	2.20
ke Skinner	2.50	1.10
cky Craven	2.50	1.10
ale Jarrett	20.00	9.00
terling Marlin	5.00	2.20
teve Grissom	2.50	1.10
ill Elliott	25.00	11.00
icky Rudd	5.00	2.20

1997 ActionVision

12-card set utilizes Kodak's KODAMOTION ology to provide race action replay cards. This t marks the first time that NASCAR trading cards been marketed in this fashion. Cards were uted in one card packs with 18 packs per box and es per case.

	MINT	NRMT
LETE SET (12)	60.00	27.00
ON CARD (1-12)	5.00	2.20
rry Labonte	6.00	2.70
ff Gordon Victory Lane	8.00	3.60
le Earnhardt Qualifying	8.00	3.60
le Jarrett Victory Lane	6.00	2.70
f Gordon Rusty Wallace Terry Labonte	8.00	3.60
f Gordon Terry Labonte Ricky Craven	8.00	3.60
sty Wallace Pit Stop	5.00	2.20
le Earnhardt Pit Stop	8.00	3.60
rry Labonte Pit Stop	5.00	2.20
eff Gordon Pit Stop	8.00	3.60
ale Jarrett Pit Stop	5.00	2.20
ill Elliott Talladega Crash	6.00	2.70

1997 ActionVision Precious Metal

-card series is the last section of a 9-card set that arted in 1997 VIP. The cards from this set contain a of sheet metal along with a picture of the driver and r which is in cased in a polyurethane card. Cards with multi-colored pieces of sheet metal often carry a 25% premium over those that do not. Each of the four cards inserted into ActionVision was limited in production to 350 of each driver. The cards were randomly inserted into packs at a ratio of 1:160.

	MINT	NRMT
COMPLETE SET	700.00	325.00
COMMON CARD (6-9)	120.00	55.00
❑ 6 Dale Earnhardt	350.00	160.00
❑ 7 Dale Jarrett	175.00	80.00
❑ 8 Ernie Irvan	120.00	55.00
❑ 9 Mark Martin	200.00	90.00

1997 Alka-Seltzer Terry Labonte

This three card Terry Labonte set was available through a mail-in offer from Alka-Seltzer. The offer was posted on Alka-Seltzer's home page on the internet. (http://www.alka-seltzer.com) The collector had to fill out a form on-line and in return would receive a free sample of cherry flavored Alka-Seltzer along with one Terry Labonte trading card.

	MINT	NRMT
COMPLETE SET (3)	2.00	.90
COMMON CARD (1-3)	1.00	.45
❑ 1 Terry Labonte with Car	1.00	.45
❑ 2 Terry Labonte with Car	1.00	.45
❑ 3 Terry Labonte	1.00	.45

1993-94 Alliance Robert Pressley/Dennis Setzer

The Alliance Racing Team set was released two consecutive years by D and D Racing Images. The cards in both sets are identical except for the driver card #11. The 1993 release features Robert Pressley (#11A), while the 1994 set includes Dennis Setzer (#11B). Either set carries the same value.

	MINT	NRMT
COMPLETE SET (12)	6.00	2.70
COMMON CARD (1-11)	.50	.23
❑ 1 Barbara Welch	.50	.23
❑ 2 Ricky Pearson	.50	.23
❑ 3 Ricky Case	.50	.23
❑ 4 Jeff Fender	.50	.23
❑ 5 Dick Boles	.50	.23
❑ 6 Chris McPherson	.50	.23
❑ 7 Clarence Ogle	.50	.23
❑ 8 Eddie Pearson	.50	.23
❑ 9 Owen Edwards	.50	.23
❑ 10 Dennis McCarson	.50	.23
❑ 11A Robert Pressley	1.00	.45
❑ 11B Dennis Setzer	1.00	.45
❑ NNO Alliance Transporter Checklist back	.50	.23

1992 Arena Joe Gibbs Racing

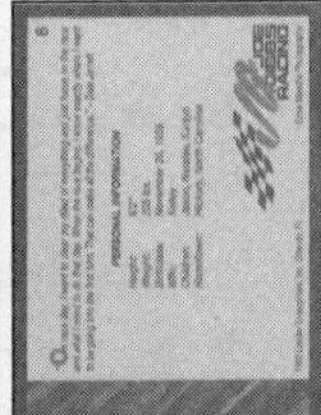

Arena Trading Cards Inc. produced this set honoring the Interstate Batteries Joe Gibbs Racing Team. The cards were sold in complete set form and included a Hologram card featuring Dale Jarrett's Interstate Batteries car along with an unnumbered cover/checklist card

	MINT	NRMT
COMPLETE SET (12)	3.00	1.35
COMMON CARD (1-10)	.25	.11
❑ 1 Joe Gibbs	.30	.14
❑ 2 Dale Jarrett	.50	.23
❑ 3 Jimmy Makar	.25	.11
❑ 4 Dale Jarrett's Crew	.25	.11
❑ 5 Dale Jarrett's Car	.25	.11
❑ 6 Dale Jarrett's Car	.25	.11
❑ 7 Dale Jarrett Jimmy Makar Teamwork	.25	.11
❑ 8 Dale Jarrett Race Day	.25	.11
❑ 9 Joe Gibbs Jimmy Makar	.25	.11
❑ 10 Dale Jarrett's Transporter	.25	.11
❑ NNO Dale Jarrett's Car HOLO	1.00	.45
❑ NNO Cover Card Checklist	.20	.09

1995 Assets

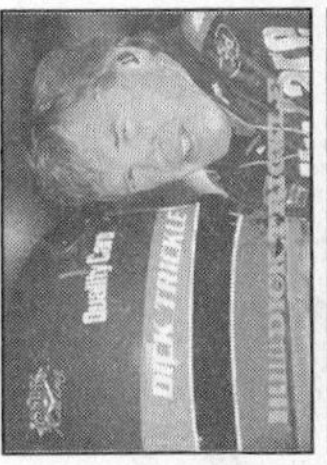

This 50-card set features the top names in racing in Classic's first racing issue under the Assets brand. The cards are printed on 18pt. stock and use full-bleed printing. There are three topical subsets; Drivers (1-28),Winners (29-44), and Cars (45-50). The cards came six cards per pack, 18 packs per box and 16 boxes per case.

	MINT	NRMT
COMPLETE SET (50)	12.00	5.50
COMMON CARD (1-50)	.20	.09
❑ 1 Dale Earnhardt	2.00	.90
❑ 2 Rusty Wallace	.75	.35
❑ 3 Jeff Gordon	2.00	.90
❑ 4 Kyle Petty	.30	.14
❑ 5 Brett Bodine	.20	.09
❑ 6 Sterling Marlin	.30	.14
❑ 7 Darrell Waltrip	.30	.14
❑ 8 Sterling Marlin	.30	.14
❑ 9 Geoff Bodine	.20	.09
❑ 10 Ricky Craven	.20	.09
❑ 11 Robert Pressley	.20	.09
❑ 12 Bobby Labonte	.30	.14
❑ 13 Dale Jarrett	.50	.23
❑ 14 Dick Trickle	.20	.09
❑ 15 Jeff Burton	.30	.14
❑ 16 John Andretti	.20	.09
❑ 17 Ken Schrader	.20	.09
❑ 18 Ernie Irvan	.30	.14
❑ 19 Michael Waltrip	.20	.09
❑ 20 Morgan Shepherd	.20	.09
❑ 21 Ricky Rudd	.30	.14
❑ 22 Steve Kinser	.20	.09
❑ 23 Ted Musgrave	.20	.09
❑ 24 Terry Labonte	.75	.35
❑ 25 Todd Bodine	.20	.09
❑ 26 Ward Burton	.20	.09
❑ 27 Mark Martin	.75	.35
❑ 28 Bobby Hamilton	.20	.09
❑ 29 Dale Earnhardt	2.00	.90
❑ 30 Rusty Wallace	.75	.35
❑ 31 Jeff Gordon	2.00	.90
❑ 32 Kyle Petty	.30	.14
❑ 33 Geoff Bodine	.20	.09
❑ 34 Sterling Marlin	.30	.14
❑ 35 Darrell Waltrip	.30	.14
❑ 36 Dale Jarrett	.50	.23
❑ 37 Ken Schrader	.20	.09
❑ 38 Ernie Irvan	.30	.14
❑ 39 Ricky Rudd	.30	.14
❑ 40 Terry Labonte	.75	.35
❑ 41 Mark Martin	.75	.35
❑ 42 Morgan Shepherd	.20	.09
❑ 43 Ward Burton	.20	.09
❑ 44 Dale Earnhardt	2.00	.90
❑ 45 Morgan Shepherd's Car	.20	.09

❑ 46 Dale Earnhardt's Car	1.00	.45
❑ 47 Rusty Wallace's Car	.50	.23
❑ 48 Mark Martin's Car	.50	.23
❑ 49 Jeff Gordon's Car	1.00	.45
❑ 50 Checklist	.20	.09

1995 Assets Gold Signature

This 50-card set is a parallel version of the base set. Each card features a gold facsimile signature across the front of the card to differentiate them from the base cards. The odds of pulling a gold signature card were one per 10 packs. Complete sets were also one of the prize levels offered in the Assets Coca-Cola 600 Die Cut redemption game.

	MINT	NRMT
COMPLETE SET (50)	100.00	45.00
COMMON CARD (1-50)	2.00	.90
*GOLD SIG: 5X TO 10X BASIC CARDS		

1995 Assets 1-Minute/$2 Phone Cards

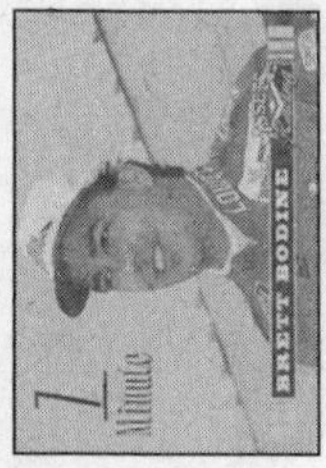

This 20-card insert set features Winston Cup personalities on 1-minute phone cards. The cards were inserted at a rate of one per pack. The cards expired 12/31/95. There were three parallel versions of the 1-minute set: the 1-minute signature set, the $2 set and the $2 signature set. The cards in the 1-minute gold signature set expired on 12/31/95 and were inserted at a rate of one per 26 packs. The cards in both the $2 set and the $2 signature set expired on 5/1/96. The $2 cards were inserted one per six packs, while the $2 signature cards were inserted one per 58 packs.

	MINT	NRMT
COMPLETE 1MIN SET (20)	20.00	9.00
COMMON 1MIN CARD (1-20)	.50	.23
COMP. 1MIN GOLD SIG.(20)	90.00	40.00
1 MIN GOLD SIG: 2X TO 4X 1MIN CARDS		
COMP. 2.00 PHONE SET (20)	50.00	22.00
*2.00 PHONE CARDS: 1.25X TO 2X 1MIN CARDS		
COMP. 2.00 PHONE SIG (20)	300.00	135.00
*2.00 PHONE SIG.: 5X TO 10X 1MIN CARDS		

❑ 1 Dick Trickle	.50	.23
❑ 2 Bobby Labonte		
❑ 3 Brett Bodine	.50	.23
❑ 4 Dale Earnhardt		
❑ 5 Dale Jarrett		
❑ 6 Darrell Waltrip		
❑ 7 Ernie Irvan		
❑ 8 Geoff Bodine	.50	.23
❑ 9 Jeff Gordon		
❑ 10 John Andretti	.50	.23
❑ 11 Ken Schrader	.50	.23
❑ 12 Kyle Petty		
❑ 13 Mark Martin		
❑ 14 Michael Waltrip	.50	.23
❑ 15 Morgan Shepherd	.50	.23
❑ 16 Ward Burton	.50	.23
❑ 17 Ricky Rudd		
❑ 18 Rusty Wallace		
❑ 19 Sterling Marlin		
❑ 20 Terry Labonte		

1995 Assets $5/$25 Phone Cards

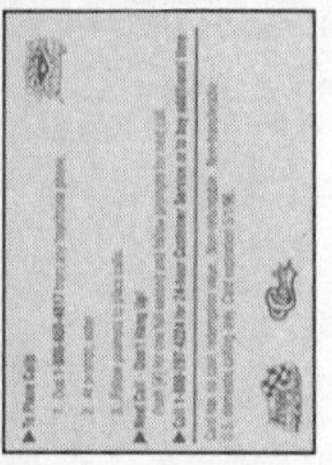

This 10-card insert set features the top Winston Cup personalities on $5 phone cards. Each card was useable for $5 worth of phone time. The expiration date of the cards was 5/1/96 and the odds of pulling one from a pack were one in 18. There is also a $25 denomination that was a parallel to the $5 set. The $25 denomination also expired on 5/1/96 and they were randomly inserted at a rate of one per 288 packs.

	MINT	NRMT
COMPLETE 5.00 SET (10)	50.00	22.00
COMMON 5.00 CARD (1-10)	4.00	1.80
COMPLETE 25.00 SET (10)	250.00	110.00
*25.00 PHONE CARDS: 1.75X TO 3.5X 5.00 CARDS		

❑ 1 Sterling Marlin	4.00	1.80
❑ 2 Dale Earnhardt	4.00	1.80
❑ 3 Darrell Waltrip	4.00	1.80
❑ 4 Jeff Gordon	4.00	1.80
❑ 5 Ken Schrader	4.00	1.80
❑ 6 Kyle Petty	4.00	1.80
❑ 7 Mark Martin	4.00	1.80
❑ 8 Richard Petty	4.00	1.80
❑ 9 Rusty Wallace	4.00	1.80
❑ 10 Terry Labonte	4.00	1.80

1995 Assets $100/$1000 Phone Cards

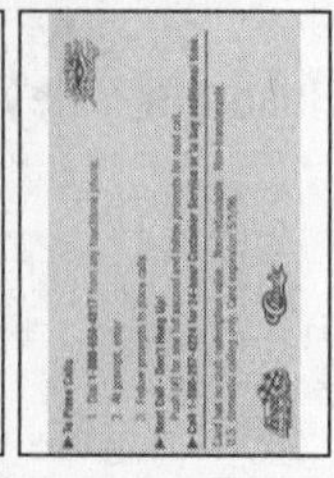

This 5-card insert set features five of the top Winston Cup personalities on $100 phone cards. The cards were inserted at a rate of one per 3,200 packs. Each card has a covered pin number on the back that must be revealed to use the card. The cards have an expiration date of 5/1/96. There is also a 5-card parallel version of this set in the amount of $1,000. The cards are indentical to the $100 except for the dollor denomination. The odds of finding a $1,000 card were one per 28,800 packs. There was a $1000 Dale Earnhardt promo phone card that was distributed to dealers and the media. The card is identical to the regular issue except for it doesn't have a pin number to make it valid.

	MINT	NRMT
COMPLETE SET (5)	450.00	200.00
COMMON 100.00 CARD (1-5)	75.00	34.00
*1000.00 PHONE CARD SINGLES	700.00	325.00

❑ 1 Ricky Rudd	75.00	34.00
❑ 2 Dale Earnhardt	75.00	34.00
❑ 3 Jeff Gordon	75.00	34.00
❑ 4 Mark Martin	75.00	34.00
❑ 5 Rusty Wallace	75.00	34.00

1995 Assets Coca-Cola 600 Die Cuts

This 10-card insert set was an interactive game for the 1995 Coca-Cola 600 race. The cards were die-cut phone cards and if you held the winner of the race, Bobby Labonte, you could then call the 800 number on the back of the card and enter that cards pin number. You would

then hear what you won for that card and would h send that card in for the redemption for those prize grand prize was a trip for two to the 1996 Coca-Col There were 3,000 special 10-card winner sets pro and numerous bonus prizes offered. The expiration game was 12/1/95.

	MINT
COMPLETE SET (10)	60.00
COMMON CARD (1-10)	4.00
*SINGLES: 2X TO 5X BASE CARD HI..	4.00

❑ 1 Dale Earnhardt	5.00
❑ 2 Rusty Wallace	5.00
❑ 3 Jeff Gordon	5.00
❑ 4 Bobby Labonte	5.00
❑ 5 Terry Labonte	6.00
❑ 6 Geoff Bodine	4.00
❑ 7 Dale Jarrett	5.00
❑ 8 Mark Martin	5.00
❑ 9 Ricky Rudd	4.00
❑ 10 Field Card	4.00

1995 Assets Images Previe

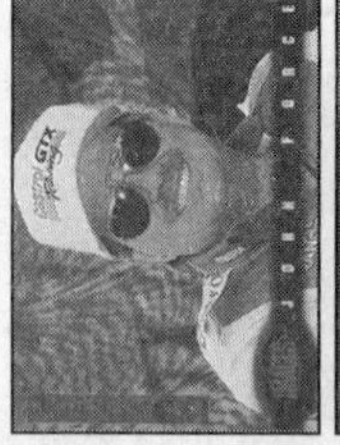

This 5-card insert set was a preview for Classic's I racing product. The cards feature micro-foil techr and could be found at a rate of one per 18 Assets pa

	MINT
COMPLETE SET (5)	80.00
COMMON CARD (RI1-RI5)	8.00

❑ RI1 Dale Earnhardt	8.00
❑ RI2 Al Unser Jr.	8.00
❑ RI3 Rick Mears	8.00
❑ RI4 Jeff Gordon	8.00
❑ RI5 John Force	15.00

1996 Assets

This 50-card set was produced by Classic. The card printed on 18-point stock and each card front featu stamping and dual photos. The cards were distribu six card packs (5 regular cards + 1 phone card) w packs per box and 12 boxes per case.

	MINT
COMPLETE SET (50)	12.00
COMMON CARD (1-50)	.05
COMMON DRIVER (1-50)	.10

❑ 1 Dale Earnhardt	2.00
❑ 2 Jeff Gordon	2.00
❑ 3 Ricky Rudd	.20
❑ 4 Geoff Bodine	.10

ıie Irvan	.20	.09
ın Andretti	.10	.05
le Petty	.20	.09
rrell Waltrip	.20	.09
le Jarrett	.30	.14
terling Marlin	.20	.09
immy Spencer	.10	.05
oy Allen Jr.	.10	.05
ichard Childress	.05	.02
en Schrader	.10	.05
ed Jarrett	.05	.02
/ard Burton	.10	.05
odd Bodine	.10	.05
lark Martin	.75	.35
lorgan Shepherd	.10	.05
obby Labonte	.20	.09
obert Pressley	.10	.05
ut Stricklin	.10	.05
erry Punch	.05	.02
icky Rudd	.20	.09
/ard Burton	.10	.05
obby Hamilton	.10	.05
ohnny Benson	.10	.05
lichael Waltrip	.10	.05
lark Martin	.75	.35
ndy Petree	.05	.02
ed Musgrave	.10	.05
like Wallace	.10	.05
rnie Irvan	.20	.09
eff Burton	.20	.09
obert Yates	.05	.02
ick Trickle	.10	.05
enny Wallace	.10	.05
ale Earnhardt	2.00	.90
rett Bodine	.10	.05
icky Craven	.10	.05
yle Petty	.20	.09
ale Jarrett	.30	.14
arrell Waltrip	.20	.09
ale Earnhardt	2.00	.90
ohn Andretti	.10	.05
erry Labonte	.75	.35
ichard Petty	.30	.14
rnie Irvan	.20	.09
ark Martin	.75	.35
icky Rudd	.20	.09

96 Assets $2 Phone Cards

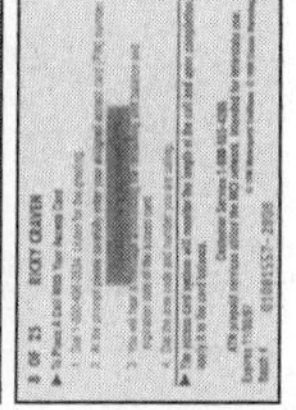

-card set features top drivers on $2 phone cards. orizontally designed card featured a driver or car n the front and usage instruction on the back. The on date for the use of the cards was 11/30/97. The were randomly inserted in packs at approximately pack.

	MINT	NRMT
ETE SET (25)	40.00	18.00
ON CARD (1-25)	1.50	.70
ES: .75X TO 2X BASE CARD HI		1.50

e Earnhardt	6.00	2.70
rd Burton	1.50	.70
my Spencer	1.50	.70
ff Bodine	1.50	.70
e Jarrett	2.50	1.10
e Irvan	2.00	.90
Schrader	1.50	.70
ky Craven	1.50	.70
k Martin	3.00	1.35
le Earnhardt's Car	1.50	.70
rrell Waltrip	2.00	.90
erling Marlin	2.00	.90
cky Rudd	2.00	.90
l Elliott	3.00	1.35
sty Wallace's Car	2.00	.90
hn Andretti	1.50	.70
ie Irvan	2.00	.90
chael Waltrip	1.50	.70
le Petty	2.00	.90
ke Wallace	1.50	.70
bby Hamilton	1.50	.70

❑ 22 Dale Jarrett's Car	2.00	.90
❑ 23 Ted Musgrave	1.50	.70
❑ 24 Jeremy Mayfield	1.50	.70
❑ 25 Ernie Irvan's Car	1.50	.70

1996 Assets $5 Phone Cards

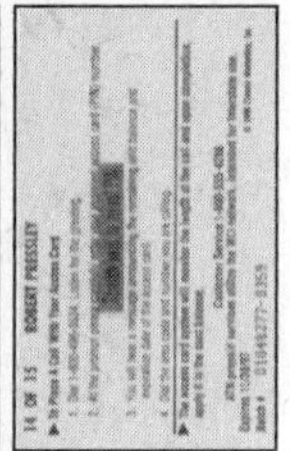

This 15-card set features top drivers from the Winston Cup series. Each card carried $5 in phone time. The cards feature a horizontal design on the front and dialing instructions on the back. The phone time expired 11/30/97. The cards were seeded one in five packs.

	MINT	NRMT
COMPLETE SET (15)	80.00	36.00
COMMON CARD (1-15)	4.00	1.80
*SINGLES: 2X TO 5X BASE CARD HI..	4.00	1.80

❑ 1 Ricky Rudd	5.00	2.20
❑ 2 Jeff Burton	5.00	2.20
❑ 3 Mark Martin	8.00	3.60
❑ 4 Darrell Waltrip	5.00	2.20
❑ 5 Bill Elliott	8.00	3.60
❑ 6 Dale Earnhardt	15.00	6.75
❑ 7 Brett Bodine	4.00	1.80
❑ 8 Ted Musgrave	4.00	1.80
❑ 9 Michael Waltrip	4.00	1.80
❑ 10 Ernie Irvan	5.00	2.20
❑ 11 Dale Earnhardt's Car	4.00	1.80
❑ 12 Kyle Petty	5.00	2.20
❑ 13 Jimmy Spencer	4.00	1.80
❑ 14 Robert Pressley	4.00	1.80
❑ 15 John Andretti	4.00	1.80

1996 Assets $10 Phone Cards

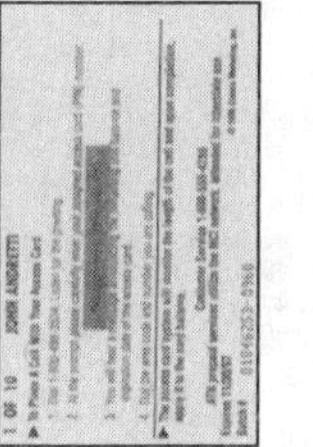

Each card in the 10-card insert set features $10 in phone time. The cards carry a hortizontal design on the front and dialing instructions on the back. The phone time expired 11/30/97. The cards were inserted one in 15 packs.

	MINT	NRMT
COMPLETE SET (10)	100.00	45.00
COMMON CARD (1-10)	8.00	3.60
*SINGLES: 5X TO 12X BASE CARD HI	8.00	3.60

❑ 1 John Andretti	8.00	3.60
❑ 2 Bobby Hamilton	8.00	3.60
❑ 3 Robert Pressley	8.00	3.60
❑ 4 Dale Earnhardt	30.00	13.50
❑ 5 Ernie Irvan	10.00	4.50
❑ 6 Jimmy Spencer	8.00	3.60
❑ 7 Kyle Petty	10.00	4.50
❑ 8 Mark Martin	15.00	6.75
❑ 9 Dale Earnhardt's Car	10.00	4.50
❑ 10 Ricky Rudd	10.00	4.50

1996 Assets $100 Cup Champion Interactive Phone Cards

This 20-card set was an interactive game. Each card from this set carried a minimum $5 phone time value. Because the game rewarded the card that featured the 1996 Winston Cup Champion and Terry Labonte was not on a regular card in the set, the field card was the winning card in the set. The field card was activated for an additional

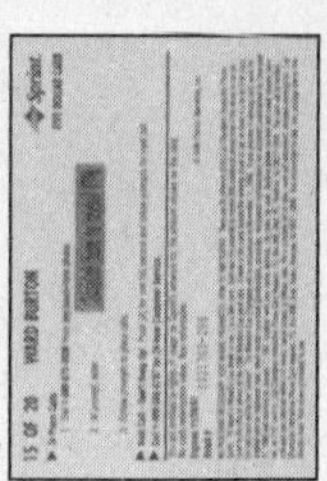

$95 worth of phone time. The $100 phone cards were randomly seeded one in 15 packs. The phone time on each of the cards expired 11/30/97.

	MINT	NRMT
COMPLETE SET (20)	175.00	80.00
COMMON CARD (1-20)	5.00	2.20

❑ 1 Dale Earnhardt	20.00	9.00
❑ 2 Jeff Gordon	20.00	9.00
❑ 3 Jeff Burton	7.00	3.10
❑ 4 Dale Jarrett	8.00	3.60
❑ 5 Kyle Petty	7.00	3.10
❑ 6 Darrell Waltrip	7.00	3.10
❑ 7 Ernie Irvan	8.00	3.60
❑ 8 Sterling Marlin	7.00	3.10
❑ 9 Ricky Rudd	7.00	3.10
❑ 10 Rusty Wallace's Car	7.00	3.10
❑ 11 Mark Martin	10.00	4.50
❑ 12 Ken Schrader	5.00	2.20
❑ 13 Ted Musgrave	5.00	2.20
❑ 14 Michael Waltrip	5.00	2.20
❑ 15 Ward Burton	5.00	2.20
❑ 16 Bobby Labonte	8.00	3.60
❑ 17 Kenny Wallace	5.00	2.20
❑ 18 Ricky Craven	5.00	2.20
❑ 19 Bobby Hamilton	5.00	2.20
❑ 20 Field Card WIN	50.00	22.00

1996 Assets $1,000 Cup Champion Interactive Phone Cards

This 20-card set was an interactive game. Each card from this set carried a minimum $10 phone time value. Because the game rewarded the card that featured the 1996 Winston Cup Champion and Terry Labonte was not on a regular card in the set, the field card was the winning card in the set. The field card was activated for an additional $990 worth of phone time. The $1000 phone cards were randomly seeded one in 432 packs. The phone time on each of the cards expired 11/30/97.

	MINT	NRMT
COMPLETE SET (20)	400.00	180.00
COMMON CARD (1-20)	12.00	5.50

❑ 1 Dale Earnhardt	40.00	18.00
❑ 2 Rick Mast	12.00	5.50
❑ 3 Ricky Craven	12.00	5.50
❑ 4 Ward Burton	12.00	5.50
❑ 5 Ricky Rudd	14.00	6.25
❑ 6 Dale Jarrett	15.00	6.75
❑ 7 Michael Waltrip	12.00	5.50
❑ 8 Jeff Burton	14.00	6.25
❑ 9 Ken Schrader	12.00	5.50
❑ 10 Mark Martin	20.00	9.00
❑ 11 Darrell Waltrip	14.00	6.25
❑ 12 Kyle Petty	14.00	6.25
❑ 13 Ernie Irvan	14.00	6.25
❑ 14 Bobby Hamilton	12.00	5.50
❑ 15 Ted Musgrave	12.00	5.50
❑ 16 Kenny Wallace	12.00	5.50
❑ 17 Rusty Wallace's Car	14.00	6.25
❑ 18 Bobby Labonte	15.00	6.75
❑ 19 Sterling Marlin	14.00	6.25
❑ 20 Field Card WIN	200.00	90.00

1996 Assets Competitor's License

Each card from this 20-card insert set features a custom holographic overlay and simulate a driver's license. The cards were randomly inserted one in 15 packs.

	MINT	NRMT
COMPLETE SET (20)	120.00	55.00
COMMON CARD (CL1-CL20)	5.00	2.20
*SINGLES: 4X TO 10X BASE CARD HI	5.00	2.20

❑ CL1 Ernie Irvan	6.00	2.70
❑ CL2 Kyle Petty	6.00	2.70

Card	MINT	NRMT
❑ CL3 Mark Martin	15.00	6.75
❑ CL4 Dale Earnhardt	25.00	11.00
❑ CL5 Brett Bodine	5.00	2.20
❑ CL6 Ward Burton	5.00	2.20
❑ CL7 Sterling Marlin	6.00	2.70
❑ CL8 Ricky Craven	5.00	2.20
❑ CL9 Ted Musgrave	5.00	2.20
❑ CL10 Darrell Waltrip	6.00	2.70
❑ CL11 Ricky Rudd	6.00	2.70
❑ CL12 Dale Jarrett	10.00	4.50
❑ CL13 Geoff Bodine	5.00	2.20
❑ CL14 Michael Waltrip	5.00	2.20
❑ CL15 Ken Schrader	5.00	2.20
❑ CL16 Bobby Hamilton	5.00	2.20
❑ CL17 Bobby Labonte	6.00	2.70
❑ CL18 Jimmy Spencer	5.00	2.20
❑ CL19 Jeff Burton	6.00	2.70
❑ CL20 Terry Labonte	12.00	5.50

1996 Assets Race Day

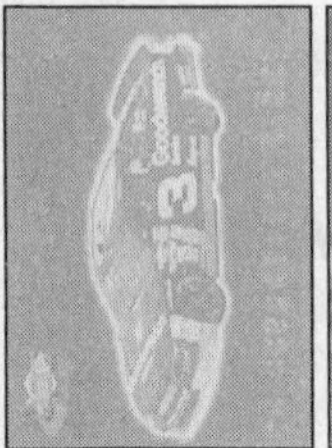

Randomly inserted one in 40 packs are these Race Day insert cards. The 10-card set features topics such as a typical day for a crew chief to an in-depth look at the superstitions and strategies behind 10 top racing teams. These cards are textrued to give them a road-surface look and feel.

	MINT	NRMT
COMPLETE SET (10)	80.00	36.00
COMMON CARD (RD1-RD10)	5.00	2.20
*SINGLES: 4X TO 10X BASE CARD HI	5.00	2.20
❑ RD1 Morgan Shepherd's Car	5.00	2.20
❑ RD2 Rusty Wallace's Car	10.00	4.50
❑ RD3 Dale Earnhardt's Car	20.00	9.00
❑ RD4 Sterling Marlin's Car	6.00	2.70
❑ RD5 Bobby Labonte's Car	6.00	2.70
❑ RD6 Mark Martin's Car	10.00	4.50
❑ RD7 Ernie Irvan's Car	6.00	2.70
❑ RD8 Dale Jarrett's Car	6.00	2.70
❑ RD9 Michael Waltrip's Car	5.00	2.20
❑ RD10 Ricky Rudd's Car	6.00	2.70

1996 Autographed Racing

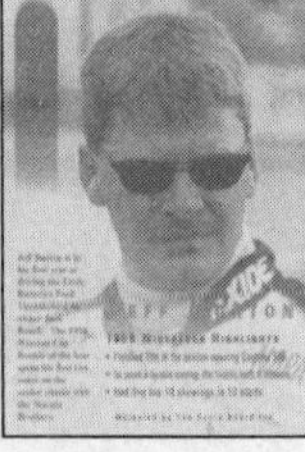

This 50-card set was the first issue by Score Board of the Autographed Racing brand. The product was packaged 5-cards per pack, 24 packs per box and 12 boxes per case. Original suggested retail on the packs was $4.99 each. The complete set consist of the top drivers on both the Winston Cup and Busch circuits. Also included were special redemption cards for officially licensed racing memorabilia at a rate of one per box. These cards can be redeemed for authentic autographed items from all the top names in racing. The memorabilia redemption cards will feature a special scratch-off area, which when removed, indicates for which specific memorabilia item the card can be redeemed.

	MINT	NRMT
COMPLETE SET (50)	10.00	4.50
COMMON CARD (1-50)	.10	.05
COMMON DRIVER (1-50)	.20	.09
❑ 1 Dale Earnhardt	2.00	.90
❑ 2 Jeff Gordon	2.00	.90
❑ 3 Kyle Petty	.40	.18
❑ 4 Rick Mast	.20	.09
❑ 5 Richard Childress	.10	.05
❑ 6 Terry Labonte	1.00	.45
❑ 7 Rusty Wallace's Car	.50	.23
❑ 8 Ken Schrader	.20	.09
❑ 9 Geoff Bodine	.20	.09
❑ 10 Richard Petty	.50	.23
❑ 11 Mike Skinner	.20	.09
❑ 12 Kenny Wallace	.20	.09
❑ 13 Sterling Marlin	.40	.18
❑ 14 Robert Pressley	.20	.09
❑ 15 Dale Jarrett	1.00	.45
❑ 16 Ted Musgrave	.20	.09
❑ 17 Ricky Rudd	.40	.18
❑ 18 Joe Gibbs	.20	.09
❑ 19 Morgan Shepherd	.20	.09
❑ 20 Mark Martin's Car	.50	.23
❑ 21 Hut Stricklin	.20	.09
❑ 22 Larry McReynolds	.10	.05
❑ 23 Brett Bodine	.20	.09
❑ 24 Mark Martin	1.00	.45
❑ 25 Dale Earnhardt's Car	1.00	.45
❑ 26 Elton Sawyer	.20	.09
❑ 27 Jeff Burton	.40	.18
❑ 28 Wood Brothers	.10	.05
❑ 29 David Smith	.10	.05
❑ 30 Ernie Irvan	.40	.18
❑ 31 Steve Hmiel	.10	.05
❑ 32 Mike Wallace	.20	.09
❑ 33 Dave Marcis	.40	.18
❑ 34 Michael Waltrip	.20	.09
❑ 35 Darrell Waltrip	.40	.18
❑ 36 Robin Pemberton	.10	.05
❑ 37 Loy Allen Jr.	.20	.09
❑ 38 Dick Trickle	.20	.09
❑ 39 Robert Yates	.10	.05
❑ 40 Randy Lajoie	.20	.09
❑ 41 John Andretti	.20	.09
❑ 42 Larry McClure	.10	.05
❑ 43 Bobby Labonte	.75	.35
❑ 44 Ward Burton	.20	.09
❑ 45 Jeremy Mayfield	.60	.25
❑ 46 Ricky Craven	.20	.09
❑ 47 Jimmy Spencer	.20	.09
❑ 48 Todd Bodine	.20	.09
❑ 49 Jack Roush	.10	.05
❑ 50 Bobby Hamilton	.20	.09

1996 Autographed Racing Autographs

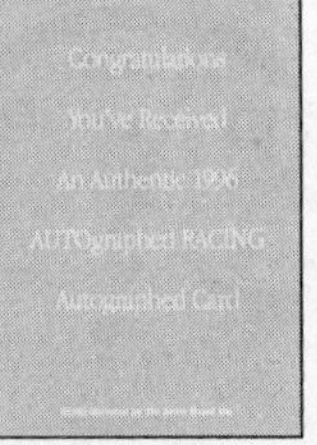

This 65-card insert set features hand-signed cards of the top names in racing. The cards were inserted at a rate of one in 12 packs. The cards featured red foil on the front along with the autograph. The backs carry the statement, "Congratulations. You've received an authentic 1996 Autographed Racing Autographed Card. There is also a "Certified" parallel version to the 65-card set. The parallel Certified version cards feature gold foil stamping on the front. In addition to the difference in foil color, each autographed is numbered. The backs of the Certified cards feature the same statement as the regular autographs. Certified autographs were inserted in packs at a rate of one in 24 packs.

	MINT	NRMT
COMPLETE SET (65)	800.00	350.00

Card	Price
COMMON CARD (1-65)	8.00
COMMON DRIVER (1-65)	15.00
COMP.CERT.AUTO SET (65)	1500.00
*CERT.AUTO CARD: 1.25X TO 2X BASIC AUTO	
❑ 1 Loy Allen Jr.	15.00
❑ 2 John Andretti	15.00
❑ 3 Paul Andrews	8.00
❑ 4 Johnny Benson	15.00
❑ 5 Brett Bodine	15.00
❑ 6 Geoff Bodine	15.00
❑ 7 Todd Bodine	15.00
❑ 8 Jeff Burton	30.00
❑ 9 Ward Burton	15.00
❑ 10 Richard Childress	8.00
❑ 11 Ricky Craven	15.00
❑ 12 Barry Dodson	8.00
❑ 13 Dale Earnhardt	150.00
❑ 14 Joe Gibbs	15.00
❑ 15 Tony Glover	8.00
❑ 16 Jeff Gordon	150.00
❑ 17 David Green	15.00
❑ 18 Bobby Hamilton	15.00
❑ 19 Doug Hewitt	8.00
❑ 20 Steve Hmiel	8.00
❑ 21 Ernie Irvan	30.00
❑ 22 Dale Jarrett	50.00
❑ 23 Ned Jarrett	8.00
❑ 24 Jason Keller	15.00
❑ 25 Bobby Labonte	50.00
❑ 26 Terry Labonte	60.00
❑ 27 Randy Lajoie	15.00
❑ 28 Jimmy Makar	8.00
❑ 29 Dave Marcis	30.00
❑ 30 Sterling Marlin	30.00
❑ 31 Mark Martin	60.00
❑ 32 Rick Mast	15.00
❑ 33 Jeremy Mayfield	40.00
❑ 34 Larry McClure	8.00
❑ 35 Mike McLaughlin	15.00
❑ 36 Larry McReynolds	8.00
❑ 37 Patty Moise	15.00
❑ 38 Brad Parrott	8.00
❑ 39 Buddy Parrott	8.00
❑ 40 Todd Parrott	8.00
❑ 41 Robin Pemberton	8.00
❑ 42 Runt Pittman	8.00
❑ 43 Charley Pressley	8.00
❑ 44 Robert Pressley	15.00
❑ 45 Dr. Jerry Punch	8.00
❑ 46 Chuck Rider	8.00
❑ 47 Jack Roush	8.00
❑ 48 Ricky Rudd	30.00
❑ 49 Elton Sawyer	15.00
❑ 50 Ken Schrader	15.00
❑ 51 Morgan Shepherd	15.00
❑ 52 Mike Skinner	15.00
❑ 53 David Smith	8.00
❑ 54 Jimmy Spencer	15.00
❑ 55 Hut Stricklin	15.00
❑ 56 Dick Trickle	15.00
❑ 57 Kenny Wallace	15.00
❑ 58 Mike Wallace	15.00
❑ 59 Darrell Waltrip	30.00
❑ 60 Michael Waltrip	15.00
❑ 61 Eddie Wood	8.00
❑ 62 Glen Wood	8.00
❑ 63 Kim Wood	8.00
❑ 64 Len Wood	8.00
❑ 65 Robert Yates	8.00

1996 Autographed Racin Front Runners

This 89-card set features a double-front design. E has basically two front sides. Many cards fea same photo only paired up with a different ph Front Runners logo on each side is stamped in s The cards are unnumbered and checklisted b alphabetical order by the best driver to appear card. Odds of finding a Front Runners card was o cks.

	MINT	NRMT
LETE SET (89)	25.00	11.00
ON CARD	.20	.09
ett Bodine	.20	.09
Todd Bodine		
off Bodine	.20	.09
Paul Andrews		
off Bodine	.20	.09
Brett Bodine		
off Bodine	.20	.09
Todd Bodine		
ff Burton	.20	.09
Jeff Burton's Car		
ff Burton	.20	.09
Ward Burton		
ff Burton	.20	.09
Ted Musgrave		
ff Burton	.20	.09
Jack Roush		
ff Burton's Car	.20	.09
Jack Roush		
icky Craven	.30	.14
Ricky Craven DuPont Uniform		
icky Craven	.30	.14
Charley Pressley		
icky Craven DuPont Uniform	.30	.14
Charley Pressley		
ale Earnhardt	1.00	.45
wearing helmet		
Richard Childress		
ale Earnhardt	1.00	.45
wearing helmet		
Dale Earnhardt celebrating		
ale Earnhardt	1.00	.45
wearing helmet		
Dale Earnhardt's car		
ale Earnhardt	1.00	.45
wearing helmet		
Dale Earnhardt's Olympic car		
ale Earnhardt	1.00	.45
wearing helmet		
Richard Petty		
ale Earnhardt's Car	.75	.35
Richard Childress		
rnie Irvan profile shot	.30	.14
Ernie Irvan front shot		
rnie Irvan profile shot	.30	.14
Ernie Irvan's car		
rnie Irvan profile shot	.30	.14
Dale Jarrett Victory Lane at Daytona		
rnie Irvan profile shot	.30	.14
Dale Jarrett with shades		
rnie Irvan profile shot	.30	.14
Larry McReynolds		
rnie Irvan profile shot	.30	.14
Robert Yates		
rnie Irvan front shot	.30	.14
Ernie Irvan's car		
nie Irvan front shot	.30	.14
Dale Jarrett Victory Lane at Daytona		
nie Irvan front shot	.30	.14
Dale Jarrett with shades		
nie Irvan front shot	.30	.14
Larry McReynolds		
nie Irvan front shot	.30	.14
Robert Yates		
nie Irvan's car	.30	.14
Dale Jarrett's car		
nie Irvan's car	.30	.14
Robert Yates		
ale Jarrett Victory Lane	.50	.23
Dale Jarrett with shades		
ale Jarrett Victory Lane	.50	.23
Dale Jarrett's car		
ale Jarrett Victory Lane	.50	.23
Ned Jarrett		
ale Jarrett Victory Lane	.50	.23
Todd Parrott		
ale Jarrett Victory Lane	.50	.23
Robert Yates		
ale Jarrett with shades	.50	.23
Dale Jarrett's car		
ale Jarrett with shades	.50	.23
Robert Yates		
ale Jarrett's car	.50	.23
Robert Yates		
obby Labonte with shades	.50	.23
Joe Gibbs		
obby Labonte with shades	.50	.23
Bobby Labonte w/o shades		
obby Labonte with shades	.50	.23
Jimmy Makar		
obby Labonte w/o shades	.50	.23
Joe Gibbs		
obby Labonte w/o shades	.50	.23
Bobby Labonte's car		

❑ 45 Bobby Labonte w/o shades	.50	.23
Bobby Labonte's car		
❑ 46 Bobby Labonte w/o shades	.50	.23
Jimmy Makar		
❑ 47 Bobby Labonte's car	.50	.23
Joe Gibbs		
❑ 48 Sterling Marlin with shades	.30	.14
Tony Glover		
❑ 49 Sterling Marlin with shades	.30	.14
Sterling Marlin's car		
❑ 50 Sterling Marlin with shades	.30	.14
Larry McClure		
❑ 51 Sterling Marlin with shades	.30	.14
Runt Pittman		
❑ 52 Sterling Marlin w/o shades	.30	.14
Tony Glover		
❑ 53 Sterling Marlin w/o shades	.30	.14
Sterling Marlin with shades		
❑ 54 Sterling Marlin w/o shades	.30	.14
Sterling Marlin's car		
❑ 55 Sterling Marlin w/o shades	.30	.14
Larry McClure		
❑ 56 Sterling Marlin w/o shades	.30	.14
Runt Pittman		
❑ 57 Sterling Marlin's car	.30	.14
Tony Glover		
❑ 58 Sterling Marlin's car	.30	.14
Runt Pittman		
❑ 59 Mark Martin with hat	.60	.25
Jeff Burton		
❑ 60 Mark Martin with hat	.60	.25
Steve Hmiel		
❑ 61 Mark Martin with hat	.60	.25
Mark Martin w/o hat		
❑ 62 Mark Martin with hat	.60	.25
Mark Martin's car		
❑ 63 Mark Martin with hat	.60	.25
Ted Musgrave		
❑ 64 Mark Martin with hat	.60	.25
Jack Roush		
❑ 65 Mark Martin w/o hat	.60	.25
Jeff Burton		
❑ 66 Mark Martin w/o hat	.60	.25
Steve Hmiel		
❑ 67 Mark Martin w/o hat	.60	.25
Mark Martin's car		
❑ 68 Mark Martin w/o hat	.60	.25
Ted Musgrave		
❑ 69 Mark Martin w/o hat	.60	.25
Jack Roush		
❑ 70 Mark Martin's car	.60	.25
Jeff Burton's Car		
❑ 71 Mark Martin's car	.60	.25
Jack Roush		
❑ 72 Ted Musgrave	.20	.09
Jack Roush		
❑ 73 Richard Petty	.60	.25
Richard Childress		
❑ 74 Richard Petty	.60	.25
Bobby Hamilton profile shot		
❑ 75 Richard Petty	.60	.25
Bobby Hamilton		
❑ 76 Richard Petty	.60	.25
Kyle Petty		
❑ 77 Robert Pressley	.20	.09
Charley Pressley		
❑ 78 Elton Sawyer	.20	.09
Patty Moise		
❑ 79 Kenny Wallace	.20	.09
Mike Wallace		
❑ 80 Rusty Wallace's Car	.30	.14
Robin Pemberton		
❑ 81 Darrell Waltrip with helmet	.30	.14
Darrell Waltrip w/o helmet		
❑ 82 Darrell Waltrip with helmet	.30	.14
Michael Waltrip with shades		
❑ 83 Darrell Waltrip with helmet	.30	.14
Michael Waltrip w/o shades		
❑ 84 Darrell Waltrip w/o helmet	.30	.14
Michael Waltrip with shades		
❑ 85 Darrell Waltrip w/o helmet	.30	.14
Michael Waltrip w/o shades		
❑ 86 Michael Waltrip w/o shades	.20	.09
Michael Waltrip's car		
❑ 87 Michael Waltrip w/o shades	.20	.09
Michael Waltrip with shades		
❑ 88 Michael Waltrip w/o shades	.20	.09
The Wood Brothers		
❑ 89 Michael Waltrip's car	.20	.09
The Wood Brothers		

1996 Autographed Racing High Performance

This 20-card insert set includes the top names in racing on foil-stamped cards. The card fronts feature a driver's

photo framed by a wood and marble design. The cards were inserted at a rate of one in eight packs.

	MINT	NRMT
COMPLETE SET (20)	60.00	27.00
COMMON CARD (HP1-HP20)	1.50	.70
*SINGLES: 2.5X TO 6X BASE CARD HI		

❑ HP1 Dale Earnhardt	15.00	6.75
❑ HP2 Kyle Petty	3.00	1.35
❑ HP3 Jeremy Mayfield	2.00	.90
❑ HP4 Sterling Marlin	3.00	1.35
❑ HP5 Ward Burton	1.50	.70
❑ HP6 Mark Martin	8.00	3.60
❑ HP7 Bobby Labonte	3.00	1.35
❑ HP8 Ricky Craven	1.50	.70
❑ HP9 Michael Waltrip	1.50	.70
❑ HP10 Ricky Rudd	3.00	1.35
❑ HP11 Ted Musgrave	1.50	.70
❑ HP12 Ken Schrader	1.50	.70
❑ HP13 Dale Jarrett	6.00	2.70
❑ HP14 Brett Bodine	1.50	.70
❑ HP15 Jimmy Spencer	1.50	.70
❑ HP16 Bobby Hamilton	1.50	.70
❑ HP17 Darrell Waltrip	3.00	1.35
❑ HP18 Robert Pressley	1.50	.70
❑ HP19 Ernie Irvan	3.00	1.35
❑ HP20 Geoff Bodine	1.50	.70

1996 Autographed Racing Kings of the Circuit $5 Phone Cards

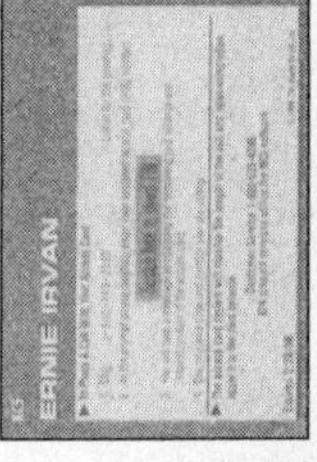

This 10-card insert set highlights the careers of racing legends. Each card carries a $5 phone time value. The cards are printed on silver foil board. The backs feature dialing instructions for the phone time. The phone time on the cards expired 2/28/98. Odds of finding a Kings of the Circuit card are one in 30 packs.

	MINT	NRMT
COMPLETE SET (10)	80.00	36.00
COMMON CARD (KC1-KC10)	4.00	1.80
CARD CARDS HALF VALUE		
*SINGLES: 4X TO 10X BASE CARD HI		

❑ KC1 Dale Jarrett	10.00	4.50
❑ KC2 Mark Martin	12.00	5.50
❑ KC3 Sterling Marlin	5.00	2.20
❑ KC4 Bill Elliott	12.00	5.50
❑ KC5 Ernie Irvan	10.00	4.50
❑ KC6 Dale Earnhardt	20.00	9.00
❑ KC7 Bill Elliott	12.00	5.50
❑ KC8 Dale Earnhardt's Car	12.00	5.50
❑ KC9 Rusty Wallace's Car	4.00	1.80
❑ KC10 Dale Earnhardt	20.00	9.00

1997 Autographed Racing

This 50-card set wasthe second issue by Score Board of the Autographed Racing brand. The product was packaged 5 cards per pack, 24 packs per box, and 10 boxes per case. The complete set consists of drivers from the Winston Cup and Busch circuits.

	MINT	NRMT
COMPLETE SET (50)	10.00	4.50
COMMON CARD (1-50)	.10	.05
COMMON DRIVER (1-50)	.20	.09

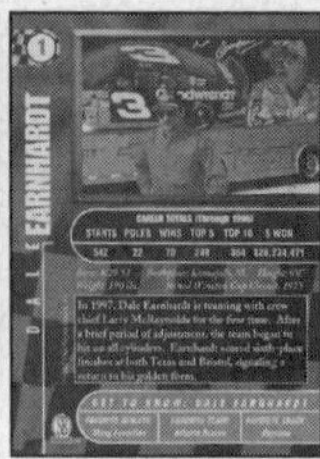

❑ 1 Dale Earnhardt	1.50	.70
❑ 2 Kyle Petty	.40	.18
❑ 3 Terry Labonte	.75	.35
❑ 4 Jeff Gordon	1.50	.70
❑ 5 Michael Waltrip	.20	.09
❑ 6 Dale Jarrett	.60	.25
❑ 7 Lake Speed	.20	.09
❑ 8 Bobby Labonte	.60	.25
❑ 9 Robby Gordon	.20	.09
❑ 10 Rick Mast	.20	.09
❑ 11 Geoff Bodine	.20	.09
❑ 12 Sterling Marlin	.40	.18
❑ 13 Jeff Burton	.40	.18
❑ 14 Steve Park	1.50	.70
❑ 15 Darrell Waltrip	.40	.18
❑ 16 Randy LaJoie	.20	.09
❑ 17 Mark Martin	.75	.35
❑ 18 Bobby Hamilton	.20	.09
❑ 19 Ernie Irvan	.40	.18
❑ 20 Steve Grissom	.20	.09
❑ 21 Ted Musgrave	.20	.09
❑ 22 Jeremy Mayfield	.50	.23
❑ 23 Ricky Rudd	.40	.18
❑ 24 Ricky Craven	.20	.09
❑ 25 Hut Stricklin	.20	.09
❑ 26 Morgan Shepherd	.20	.09
❑ 27 Brett Bodine	.20	.09
❑ 28 John Andretti	.20	.09
❑ 29 Robert Pressley	.20	.09
❑ 30 Dick Trickle	.20	.09
❑ 31 Ernie Irvan's Car	.20	.09
❑ 32 Robby Gordon's Car	.10	.05
❑ 33 Bobby Hamilton's Car	.10	.05
❑ 34 Dale Jarrett's Car	.30	.14
❑ 35 Rusty Wallace's Car	.40	.18
❑ 36 Dale Earnhardt's Car	.75	.35
❑ 37 Sterling Marlin's Car	.20	.09
❑ 38 Mark Martin's Car	.40	.18
❑ 39 Bobby Labonte's Car	.40	.18
❑ 40 Michael Waltrip's Car	.10	.05
❑ 41 Dale Earnhardt Jeff Gordon	1.50	.70
❑ 42 Dale Jarrett Ernie Irvan	.40	.18
❑ 43 Jeff Burton Ricky Craven	.20	.09
❑ 44 Mark Martin Sterling Marlin	.40	.18
❑ 45 Micahel Waltrip Bobby Labonte	.20	.09
❑ 46 Bobby Hamilton Kyle Petty	.10	.05
❑ 47 Dale Earnhardt Dale Jarrett	1.00	.45
❑ 48 Darrell Waltrip Geoff Bodine	.10	.05
❑ 49 Dale Earnhardt's car Rusty Wallace's car	.60	.25
❑ 50 Bobby Labonte Terry Labonte	.60	.25

1997 Autographed Racing Autographs

This insert set features hand-signed cards from the top names in racing. It is important to note that the 56-card checklist presented below may not be complete. Some of the autographed cards distributed in this product are in the form of redemption cards and cards from the 1996 Autographed Racing product. Due to the bankruptcy of Score Board this year all redemption cards are unredeemable. The same driver may have two or possibly three different autograph cards in this product. The cards were randomly inserted into packs at a ratio of 5:24.

	MINT	NRMT
COMMON CARD	4.00	1.80
COMMON DRIVER	8.00	3.60
❑ 1 John Andretti	8.00	3.60
❑ 2 Tommy Baldwin	8.00	3.60
❑ 3 Brett Bodine	8.00	3.60
❑ 4 Geoff Bodine	8.00	3.60
❑ 5 Todd Bodine	8.00	3.60
❑ 6 Jeff Burton	15.00	6.75
❑ 7 Richard Childress	4.00	1.80
❑ 8 Ricky Craven	8.00	3.60
❑ 9 Wally Dallenbach Jr.	8.00	3.60
❑ 10 Gary DeHart	4.00	1.80
❑ 11 Randy Dorton	4.00	1.80
❑ 12 Dale Earnhardt	200.00	90.00
❑ 13 Ray Evernham	8.00	3.60
❑ 14 Joe Gibbs	15.00	6.75
❑ 15 Tony Glover	4.00	1.80
❑ 16 Jeff Gordon	200.00	90.00
❑ 17 Robby Gordon	8.00	3.60
❑ 18 Andy Graves	4.00	1.80
❑ 19 Steve Grissom	8.00	3.60
❑ 20 Bobby Hamilton	8.00	3.60
❑ 21 Rick Hendrick	4.00	1.80
❑ 22 Steve Hmiel	4.00	1.80
❑ 23 Ron Hornaday Jr.	8.00	3.60
❑ 24 Ernie Irvan	15.00	6.75
❑ 25 Dale Jarrett	60.00	27.00
❑ 26 Jimmy Johnson	4.00	1.80
❑ 27 Terry Labonte	75.00	34.00
❑ 28 Bobby Labonte	60.00	27.00
❑ 29 Randy LaJoie	8.00	3.60
❑ 30 Jimmy Makar	4.00	1.80
❑ 31 Sterling Marlin	15.00	6.75
❑ 32 Dave Marcis	15.00	6.75
❑ 33 Mark Martin	75.00	34.00
❑ 34 Rick Mast	8.00	3.60
❑ 35 Jeremy Mayfield	50.00	22.00
❑ 36 Kenny Mayne	15.00	6.75
❑ 37 Larry McReynolds	4.00	1.80
❑ 38 Ted Musgrave	8.00	3.60
❑ 39 Buddy Parrott	4.00	1.80
❑ 40 Todd Parrott	4.00	1.80
❑ 41 Robin Pemberton	4.00	1.80
❑ 42 Kyle Petty	15.00	6.75
❑ 43 Shelton Pittman	4.00	1.80
❑ 44 Robert Pressley	8.00	3.60
❑ 45 Dr. Jerry Punch	8.00	3.60
❑ 46 Harry Raimer	4.00	1.80
❑ 47 Dave Rezendes	8.00	3.60
❑ 48 Greg Sacks	8.00	3.60
❑ 49 Morgan Shepherd	8.00	3.60
❑ 50 Hut Stricklin	8.00	3.60
❑ 51 Dick Trickle	8.00	3.60
❑ 52 Kenny Wallace	8.00	3.60
❑ 53 Mike Wallace	8.00	3.60
❑ 54 Darrell Waltrip	15.00	6.75
❑ 55 Michael Waltrip	8.00	3.60
❑ 56 Wood Brothers	4.00	1.80

1997 Autographed Racing Mayne Street

This 30-card insert set is named for ESPN annoucer Kenny Mayne. The card backs features his commentary on each driver. The cards were randomly inserted into hobby packs at a ratio of 1:4.

	MINT	NRMT
COMPLETE SET (30)	40.00	18.00
COMMON CARD (KM1-KM30)	1.00	.45
*SINGLES: 2.5X TO 6X BASE CARD HI		
❑ KM1 Dale Earnhardt	12.00	5.50
❑ KM2 Kyle Petty	2.00	
❑ KM3 Terry Labonte	6.00	
❑ KM4 Jeff Gordon	12.00	
❑ KM5 Michael Waltrip	1.00	
❑ KM6 Dale Jarrett	5.00	
❑ KM7 Lake Speed	1.00	
❑ KM8 Bobby Labonte	3.00	
❑ KM9 Robby Gordon	1.00	
❑ KM10 Rick Mast	1.00	
❑ KM11 Geoff Bodine	1.00	
❑ KM12 Sterling Marlin	2.00	
❑ KM13 Jeff Burton	2.00	
❑ KM14 Steve Park	4.00	
❑ KM15 Darrell Waltrip	2.00	
❑ KM16 Randy LaJoie	1.00	
❑ KM17 Mark Martin	6.00	
❑ KM18 Bobby Hamilton	1.00	
❑ KM19 Ernie Irvan	2.00	
❑ KM20 Steve Grissom	1.00	
❑ KM21 Ted Musgrave	1.00	
❑ KM22 Jeremy Mayfield	2.00	
❑ KM23 Ricky Rudd	2.00	
❑ KM24 Ricky Craven	1.00	
❑ KM25 Hut Stricklin	1.00	
❑ KM26 Morgan Shepherd	1.00	
❑ KM27 Brett Bodine	1.00	
❑ KM28 John Andretti	1.00	
❑ KM29 Robert Pressley	1.00	
❑ KM30 Dick Trickle	1.00	

1997 Autographed Racing Take the Checkered Flag

The 2-card set features hand-numbered commemorating the winner of each leg of the W Million. Each card contains a portion of a real che flag. The cards were randomly inserted into hobby at a ratio of 1:240.

	MINT
COMPLETE SET (2)	60.00
COMMON CARD (TF1-TF2)	25.00
❑ TF1 Jeff Gordon	50.00
❑ TF2 Mark Martin	25.00

1992 Bikers of the Racing Scen

Eagle Productions produced this set featuring parti and other personalities associated with the First Winston Cup Harley Ride in September 1992. The feature the Winston Cup personality with their f Harley motorcyle. Each checklist card carries production number which was limited to 90,000.

	MINT
COMPLETE SET (34)	10.00
COMMON CARD (1-34)	.25
❑ 1 Richard Petty The King	.75
❑ 2 Pre-Dawn	.25
❑ 3 Richard Childress	.25
❑ 4 Spook Caspers	.25
❑ 5 Kirk Shelmerdine	.25
❑ 6 Danny Myers	.25
❑ 7 Paul Andrews	.25
❑ 8 Will Lind	.25
❑ 9 Jerry Huskins Randy Butner	.25
❑ 10 Jimmy Cox	.25
❑ 11 Danny Culler	.25
❑ 12 Dennis Dawson	.25
❑ 13 Bryan Dorsey	.25
❑ 14 Dan Gatewood	.25
❑ 15 Kevin Youngblood	.25
❑ 16 John Hall	.25
❑ 17 Jimmy Means	.25
❑ 18 Robin Metdepenningen	.25
❑ 19 Gary Nelson	.25
❑ 20 Tommy Rigsbee	.25

Jimmy Shore	.25	.11
Marty Tharpe	.25	.11
Danny West	.25	.11
Mike McQueen	.25	.11
Darren Jolly		
Kyle Petty	.50	.23
Waddell Wilson	.25	.11
Steve Barkdoll	.25	.11
Dick Brooks	.25	.11
Tracy Leslie	.25	.11
Michael Waltrip	.50	.23
Beth Bruce	.40	.18
Michael Waltrip		
Rick Wilson		
Richard Childress		
Danny Culler		
Don Tilley		
Rick Wilson	.25	.11
Harry Gant	.50	.23
Checklist Card	.25	.11

1998 Burger King Dale Earnhardt

-card set was distributed at participating Burger s in the south east section of the country.

	MINT	NRMT
LETE SET (4)	10.00	4.50
ON CARD (1-4)	2.00	.90
ale Earnhardt's Car	2.00	.90
ale Earnhardt	3.00	1.35
ale Earnhardt's Car	2.00	.90
ale Earnhardt	3.00	1.35

1992 Card Dynamics Davey Allison

ve-card set was issued in a display box and has five ed aluminum cards that feature Davey Allison. The were distributed by Card Dynamics and 4,000 sets produced. There is a numbered certificate of nticity that comes with each set.

	MINT	NRMT
LETE SET (5)	70.00	32.00
ON CARD (1-5)	15.00	6.75

1992 Card Dynamics Harry Gant

ve-card set was issued in a display box and has five ed aluminum cards that feature Harry Gant. The sets distributed by Card Dynamics and 4,000 sets were ced. There is a numbered certificate of authenticity omes with each set. The set was not produced in the al quantities stated on the certificate.

	MINT	NRMT
LETE SET (5)	25.00	11.00
ON CARD (1-5)	5.00	2.20

92 Card Dynamics Gant Oil

992 Gant Oil cards were produced as promotional tising for Gant Oil Company. The cards could be ased for $6.00 when you bought gas at one of the rticipating Gant Oil stations through out North na. There was one driver available every month over ourse of the 10 month long NASCAR season uary to November). Each card has a production number and are made on polished aluminum. Cards numbered but have been numbered below in order ase with number of cards produced following each name.

	MINT	NRMT
LETE SET (10)	300.00	135.00
ON CARD	25.00	11.00
arrell Waltrip/4000	30.00	13.50
❑ 2 Harry Gant/4000	30.00	13.50
❑ 3 Sterling Marlin/4000	30.00	13.50
❑ 4 Rusty Wallace/4000	40.00	18.00
❑ 5 Davey Allison/5000	50.00	22.00
❑ 6 Mark Martin/4000	40.00	18.00
❑ 7 Ernie Irvan/4000	40.00	18.00
❑ 8 Kyle Petty/4000	25.00	11.00
❑ 9 Bill Elliott/5000	40.00	18.00
❑ 10 Alan Kulwicki/5000	40.00	18.00

1992 Card Dynamics Jerry Glanville

This five-card set was issued in a display box and has five polished aluminum cards that feature Jerry Glanville. The sets were distributed by Card Dynamics and 5,000 sets were produced. There is a numbered certificate of authenticity that comes with each set.

	MINT	NRMT
COMPLETE SET (5)	25.00	11.00
COMMON CARD (1-5)	5.00	2.20

1992 Card Dynamics Ernie Irvan

This five-card set was issued in a display box and has five polished aluminum cards that feature Ernie Irvan. The sets were distributed by Card Dynamics and 2,000 sets were produced. There is a numbered certificate of authenticity that comes with each set. The set was not produced in the oirginal quantities stated on the certificate.

	MINT	NRMT
COMPLETE SET (5)	30.00	13.50
COMMON CARD (1-5)	6.00	2.70

1992 Card Dynamics Alan Kulwicki

This five-card set was issued in a display box and has five polished aluminum cards that feature Alan Kulwicki. The sets were distributed by Card Dynamics and 4,000 sets were produced. There is a numbered certificate of authenticity that comes with each set. The set was not produced in the original quantities stated on the certificate.

	MINT	NRMT
COMPLETE SET (5)	70.00	32.00
COMMON CARD (1-5)	15.00	6.75

1992 Card Dynamics Kyle Petty

This five-card set was issued in a display box and has five polished aluminum cards that feature Kyle Petty. The sets were distributed by Card Dynamics and 4,000 sets were produced. There is a numbered certificate of authenticity that comes with each set. The set was not produced in the original quantities stated on the certificate.

	MINT	NRMT
COMPLETE SET (5)	25.00	11.00
COMMON CARD (1-5)	5.00	2.20

1992 Card Dynamics Ricky Rudd

This five-card set was issued in a display box and has five polished aluminum cards that feature Ricky Rudd. The sets were distributed by Card Dynamics and 4,000 sets were produced. There is a numbered certificate of authenticity that comes with each set. The set was not produced in the original quantities stated on the certificate.

	MINT	NRMT
COMPLETE SET (5)	25.00	11.00
COMMON CARD (1-5)	5.00	2.20

1992 Card Dynamics Rusty Wallace

This five-card set was issued in a display box and has five polished aluminum cards that feature Rusty Wallace. The sets were distributed by Card Dynamics and 2,000 sets were produced. There is a numbered certificate of authenticity that comes with each set. The set was not produced in the original quantities stated on the certificate.

	MINT	NRMT
COMPLETE SET (5)	40.00	18.00
COMMON CARD (1-5)	8.00	3.60

1992 Card Dynamics Darrell Waltrip

This five-card set was issued in a display box and has five polished aluminum cards that feature Darrell Waltrip. The sets were distributed by Card Dynamics and 4,000 sets were produced. There is a numbered certificate of authenticity that comes with each set.

	MINT	NRMT
COMPLETE SET (5)	25.00	11.00
COMMON CARD (1-5)	5.00	2.20

1992 Card Dynamics Michael Waltrip

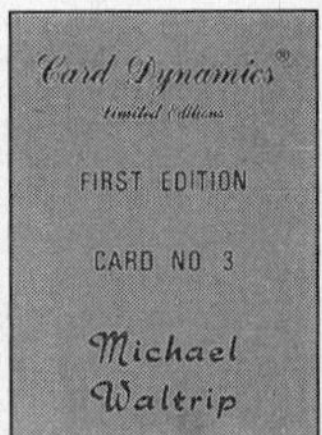

This five-card set was issued in a display box and has five polished aluminum cards that feature Michael Waltrip. The sets were distributed by Card Dynamics and 2,000 sets were produced. There is a numbered certificate of authenticity that comes with each set. The sets were not produced in the original quantities (15,000) stated on the certificate.

	MINT	NRMT
COMPLETE SET (5)	25.00	11.00
COMMON CARD (1-5)	5.00	2.20

1994 Card Dynamics Black Top Busch Series

This 10-card set was made exclusively for Black Top Racing in King, North Carolina. The set features some of the best NASCAR Winston Cup drivers to race in the Busch series. 5,000 of each card was made. The cards are unnumbered and are listed below numbered in alphabetical order.

	MINT	NRMT
COMPLETE SET (10)	80.00	36.00
COMMON CARD	4.00	1.80
❑ 1 Dale Earnhardt	15.00	6.75
❑ 2 Harry Gant	5.00	2.20
❑ 3 Jeff Gordon	15.00	6.75
❑ 4 Steve Grissom	4.00	1.80
❑ 5 Ernie Irvan	7.50	3.40
❑ 6 Alan Kulwicki	7.50	3.40
❑ 7 Bobby Labonte	8.00	3.60
❑ 8 Terry Labonte	10.00	4.50
❑ 9 Mark Martin	10.00	4.50
❑ 10 Robert Pressley	4.00	1.80

1993 Card Dynamics Alliance Racing Daytona

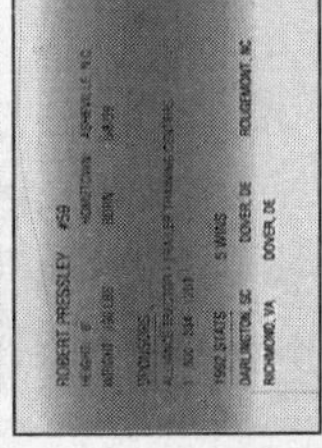

This three-card set was sold to dealers who attended the Alliance Racing dealers meeting at Daytona Beach on February 11, 1993, during SpeedWeek. There were 999 of the sets produced with each one coming in a blue display box. There was a sequentially numbered certificate in each set. The promo cards were given away as door prizes at the meeting. Only 99 promo sets were produced.

	MINT	NRMT
COMPLETE SET (3)	60.00	27.00

COMMON CARD	20.00	9.00
❑ 1 Robert Pressley	30.00	13.50
❑ 2 Robert Pressley's Car	20.00	9.00
❑ 3 Ricky Pearson	20.00	9.00

1993-95 Card Dynamics Double Eagle Postcards

This nine-card postcard size set is a continuing production. The cards have released in separate series. The first series consisted of five cards and was released in 1993, the second series consisted of two cards and was released in 1994. The third series consisted of two cards and was released in 1995. Each card was produced in quantities of 500 each. The cards were made exclusively for Double Eagle Racing of Asheboro, North Carolina. The cards are unnumbered and are in order of release below. Cards 1-5 are series one cards, 6 and 7 are series two and cards 8 and 9 are series three.

	MINT	NRMT
COMPLETE SET (9)	750.00	350.00
COMMON CARD	40.00	18.00
❑ 1 Jeff Gordon Baby Ruth	150.00	70.00
❑ 2 Rusty Wallace	75.00	34.00
❑ 3 Dale Earnhardt	150.00	70.00
❑ 4 Alan Kulwicki	75.00	34.00
❑ 5 Ernie Irvan	60.00	27.00
❑ 6 Harry Gant	40.00	18.00
❑ 7 Jeff Gordon DuPont	150.00	70.00
❑ 8 Mark Martin	75.00	34.00
❑ 9 Geoff Bodine	40.00	18.00

1993 Card Dynamics Gant Oil

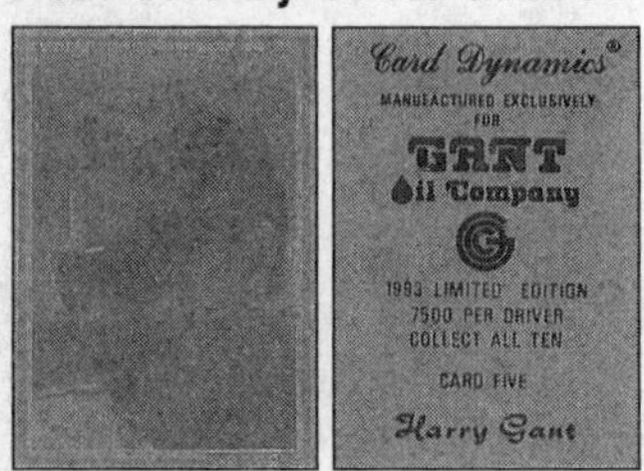

The 1993 Gant Oil cards were produced as promotional advertising for Gant Oil Company. The cards could be purchased for $8.00 when you bought gas at one of the participating Gant Oil stations throughout North Carolina. There was one driver available every month over the course of the 10 month long NASCAR season (February to November). Each card has a production serial number and is made of polished aluminum. There were 6,000 of each card produced.

	MINT	NRMT
COMPLETE SET (10)	110.00	50.00
COMMON CARD	6.00	2.70
❑ 1 Richard Petty	10.00	4.50
❑ 2 Bill Elliott	12.00	5.50
❑ 3 Rusty Wallace	12.00	5.50
❑ 4 Geoff Bodine	6.00	2.70
❑ 5 Harry Gant	8.00	3.60
❑ 6 Jeff Gordon	20.00	9.00
❑ 7 Kyle Petty	8.00	3.60
❑ 8 Dale Earnhardt	20.00	9.00
❑ 9 Dale Jarrett	10.00	4.50
❑ 10 Alan Kulwicki	12.00	5.50

1993-95 Card Dynamics North State Chevrolet

This three-card set was issued over three consecutive years, 1993-1995. The cards were made specifically for North State Chevrolet in Greensboro, North Carolina. The Dale Earnhardt card was produced in shorter quantities due to distribution through a competitior of Dale Earnhardt Chevrolet. There are 2,000 of each of the Ernie Irvan and Harry Gant. There are 650 of the Dale Earnhardt card. The cards are unnumbered, but are numbered and listed below in the order of year they were released.

	MINT	NRMT
COMPLETE SET (3)	175.00	80.00
COMMON CARD	20.00	9.00
❑ 1 Ernie Irvan	40.00	18.00
❑ 2 Dale Earnhardt	125.00	55.00
❑ 3 Harry Gant	20.00	9.00

1993 Card Dynamics Robert Pressley

This one-card and die-cast combination piece was sold to Alliance Fan Club members. There were 2,759 sets produced. Each piece comes in a display box and with a certificate of authenticity.

	MINT	NRMT
COMPLETE SET (1)	15.00	6.75
COMMON CARD	15.00	6.75
❑ 1 Robert Pressley with die-cast car	15.00	6.75

1993 Card Dynamics Robert Pressley Postcard

This postcard was sold to Alliance Fan Club members at an open house meeting in Arden, North Carolina. There were 500 produced.

	MINT	NRMT
COMPLETE SET (1)	25.00	11.00
COMMON CARD	25.00	11.00
❑ 1 Robert Pressley	25.00	11.00

1993 Card Dynamics Quik Chek

The 1993 Quik Chek cards were produced as promotional advertising for Quik Chek Food and Gas Marts. The cards could be purchased for $6.00 when you bought gas at a Quik Chek. There was one driver available every month over the course of the 10 month long NASCAR season (February to November). Each card has a production serial number and was made on polished aluminum. Cards are unnumbered, but have been numbered below in order of release with number of cards produced following each drivers name.

	MINT	NRMT
COMPLETE SET (10)	100.00	45.00
COMMON CARD	6.00	2.70
❑ 1 Alan Kulwicki/7000	14.00	6.25
❑ 2 Harry Gant/5000	8.00	3.60
❑ 3 Richard Petty/5000	12.00	5.50
❑ 4 Bill Elliott/5000	14.00	6.25
❑ 5 Rusty Wallace/5000	14.00	6.25
❑ 6 Geoff Bodine/5000	6.00	2.70
❑ 7 Kyle Petty/5000	8.00	3.60
❑ 8 Dale Earnhardt/7000	18.00	8.00
❑ 9 Jeff Gordon/7000	18.00	8.00
❑ 10 Mark Martin/5000	14.00	6.25

1994 Card Dynamics Double Eagle Dale Earnhardt

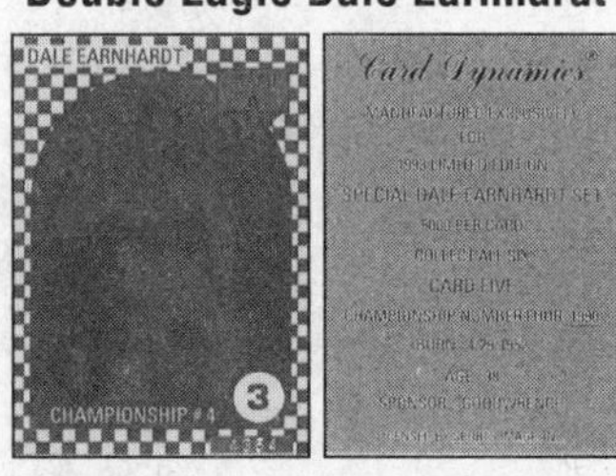

This six-card set was made by Card Dynamics exclusively for Double Eagle Racing in Asheboro, North Carolina. The set features Dale's career from his 1979 Rookie of the Year award to his 1991 Winston Cup title. There were 5,000 of each polished aluminum card made. The cards are unnumbered but arranged below in order of the year they feature.

	MINT	NRMT
COMPLETE SET (6)	75.00	34.00
COMMON CARD	15.00	6.75
❑ 1 Dale Earnhardt 1979 Rookie of the Year	15.00	6.75
❑ 2 Dale Earnhardt 1980 Winston Cup Champion	15.00	6.75
❑ 3 Dale Earnhardt 1986 Winston Cup Champion	15.00	6.75
❑ 4 Dale Earnhardt 1987 Winston Cup Champion	15.00	
❑ 5 Dale Earnhardt 1990 Winston Cup Champion	15.00	
❑ 6 Dale Earnhardt 1991 Winston Cup Champion	15.00	

1994 Card Dynamics Gant (

The 1994 Gant Oil cards were produced as promo advertising for Gant Oil Company. The cards cou purchased for $8.00 when you bought gas at one participating Gant Oil stations throughout North Car There was one driver available every month ove course of the 10 month long NASCAR season (Febru November). Each card has a production serial numbe is made of polished aluminum. There were 6,000 of card produced. Cards are unnumbered, but have numbered below in order of release with number of produced following each drivers name.

	MINT
COMPLETE SET (10)	80.00
COMMON CARD	6.00
❑ 1 Harry Gant	8.00
❑ 2 Rusty Wallace	10.00
❑ 3 Ernie Irvan	8.00
❑ 4 Jeff Gordon	15.00
❑ 5 Hut Stricklin	6.00
❑ 6 Darrell Waltrip	8.00
❑ 7 Morgan Shepherd	6.00
❑ 8 Mark Martin	10.00
❑ 9 Bobby Labonte	8.00
❑ 10 Ken Schrader	6.00

1994 Card Dynamics Jeff Gordon Fan Club

This three-card set features Jeff's younger years three cards are made of polished aluminum and com display box. There were 1,200 sets made and they sold by the Jeff Gordon Fan Club.

	MINT
COMPLETE SET (3)	50.00
COMMON CARD	20.00

1994 Card Dynamics Montgomery Motors

This six-card set was available through Montgo Motors located in Troy, North Carolina. The cards given away free to any person who test drove a new Lincoln or Mercury. You could also purchase the car $30.00 from the dealership. There were 1,000 silve versions of each card made. A gold leaf parallel vers each card was also made. There were 200 of each of and they were signed by the drivers.

	MINT
COMPLETE SET (3)	90.00
COMMON CARD	30.00
❑ 1 Ernie Irvan	30.00
❑ 2 Mark Martin	30.00
❑ 3 Rusty Wallace	30.00

1994 Card Dynamics Texas Pete Joe Nemeche

This one-card and die-cast combination piec produced in a quantity of 15,000. The pieces available to those who sent in labels from cans of Pete's Chili No Beans. The item comes in a white c box with each box sequentially numbered of 15,0 the front. A letter of authenticity also accompani piece and can be found inside the box.

	MINT
COMPLETE SET (1)	10.00

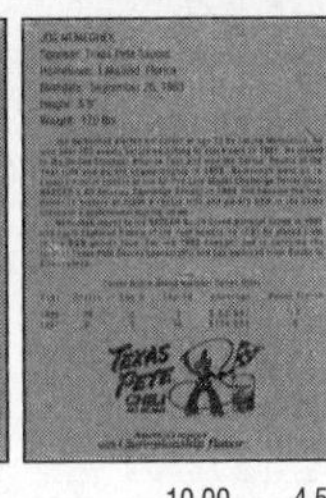

ION CARD	10.00	4.50
e Nemechek with die-cast car	10.00	4.50

1995 Card Dynamics Allsports Postcards

two postcards were issued through the featured 's fan club. Your club membership was free when rdered the postcard. There were 500 of each ard produced. Each card was hand signed and dually numbered.

	MINT	NRMT
PLETE SET (2)	70.00	32.00
ION CARD	35.00	16.00
teve Grissom	35.00	16.00
hawna Robinson	35.00	16.00

1996 Classic

60-card set features the top drivers and crew bers and contains many of the car and sponsor es for the 1996 season. The first 50 cards in the set packaged like a regular set would be. The last 10 in the set (51-60) were more like inserts. The SP were reported to come anywhere from one every 9 to one every 36 packs. There were no stated odds e SP cards. The set is commonly sold without the 10 cards in the set due to the difficulty in finding short printed cards. There were 10 cards in each 36 packs per box and 12 boxes per case. There also Hot Boxes of Classic produced. A Hot Box d at least 5 inserts per pack.

	MINT	NRMT
PLETE SET (60)	30.00	13.50
PLETE SET (50)	5.00	2.20
PLETE SP SET (10)	25.00	11.00
ION CARD (1-50)	.10	.05
ION DRIVER (1-50)	.20	.09
ION DRIVER (51-60)	1.00	.45
terling Marlin	.40	.18
odd Bodine	.20	.09
ed Musgrave	.20	.09
ick Trickle	.20	.09
ack Roush	.10	.05
icky Rudd	.40	.18
ike Wallace	.20	.09
ave Marcis	.40	.18
obert Pressley	.20	.09
Ned Jarrett	.10	.05
Jeremy Mayfield	.50	.23
Richard Petty	.40	.18
Kyle Petty	.40	.18
Mark Martin	.75	.35
Steve Hmiel	.10	.05
Kenny Wallace	.20	.09
Elton Sawyer	.20	.09
Jason Keller	.20	.09
Larry McClure	.10	.05
Ward Burton	.20	.09
Shelton Pittman	.10	.05
Larry McReynolds	.10	.05
Robert Yates	.10	.05
❑ 24 Darrell Waltrip	.40	.18
❑ 25 Tony Glover	.10	.05
❑ 26 Michael Waltrip	.20	.09
❑ 27 Len Wood Glen Wood	.10	.05
❑ 28 Morgan Shepherd	.20	.09
❑ 29 Brett Bodine	.20	.09
❑ 30 Mark Martin's Car	.40	.18
❑ 31 Sterling Marlin's Car	.20	.09
❑ 32 Dale Earnhardt's Car	.75	.35
❑ 33 Dale Jarrett's Car	.40	.18
❑ 34 Bobby Hamilton's Car	.10	.05
❑ 35 Michael Waltrip's Car	.10	.05
❑ 36 Rusty Wallace's Car	.40	.18
❑ 37 Ernie Irvan	.40	.18
❑ 38 Rick Mast	.20	.09
❑ 39 David Green	.20	.09
❑ 40 Joe Gibbs	.20	.09
❑ 41 Michael Waltrip	.20	.09
❑ 42 Ted Musgrave	.20	.09
❑ 43 Bobby Labonte	.60	.25
❑ 44 Ward Burton	.20	.09
❑ 45 Ricky Craven	.20	.09
❑ 46 Ken Schrader	.20	.09
❑ 47 Geoff Bodine	.20	.09
❑ 48 Johnny Benson	.20	.09
❑ 49 Dale Jarrett	.60	.25
❑ 50 Robin Pemberton	.10	.05
❑ 51 Mark Martin SP	5.00	2.20
❑ 52 Sterling Marlin SP	2.00	.90
❑ 53 Dale Earnhardt SP	10.00	4.50
❑ 54 Michael Waltrip SP	1.00	.45
❑ 55 Ricky Rudd SP	2.00	.90
❑ 56 Ernie Irvan SP	2.00	.90
❑ 57 Dale Jarrett SP	4.00	1.80
❑ 58 Bobby Labonte SP	4.00	1.80
❑ 59 Kyle Petty SP	2.00	.90
❑ 60 Darrell Waltrip SP	2.00	.90

1996 Classic Printer's Proof

This 50-card set is a parallel to the base set. Each card features a red foil "Printers Proof 1 of 498" logo on the front to differentiate them from the base cards. The cards are inserted one per 60 packs.

	MINT	NRMT
COMPLETE SET (50)	200.00	90.00
COMMON CARD (1-50)	2.00	.90
COMMON DRIVER (1-50)	4.00	1.80

*STARS: 12X TO 30X BASIC CARDS

1996 Classic Silver

This 50-card set is a parallel to the base brand. The cards feature a "Sliver 96" logo on the front that differentiates them from the base cards. The cards were inserted one per pack.

	MINT	NRMT
COMPLETE SET (50)	16.00	7.25
COMMON CARD (1-50)	.20	.09
COMMON DRIVER (1-50)	.30	.14

*STARS: .6X TO 1.5X BASIC CARDS

1996 Classic Images Preview

This five-card set is a preview of the '96 Images set. The cards feature top names in racing in micro-foil printing.

The odds of pulling a Images Preview card was one per 30 Classic packs.

	MINT	NRMT
COMPLETE SET (5)	20.00	9.00
COMMON CARD (RP1-RP5)	4.00	1.80
❑ RP1 Sterling Marlin	4.00	1.80
❑ RP2 Mark Martin	8.00	3.60
❑ RP3 Bobby Labonte	6.00	2.70
❑ RP4 Ricky Rudd	4.00	1.80
❑ RP5 Dale Earnhardt's Car Richard Childress	12.00	5.50

1996 Classic Innerview

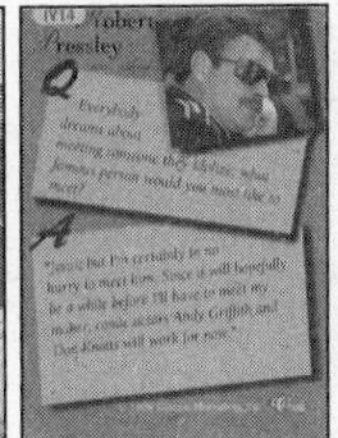

This 15-card insert set gives fans a look at the top drivers. The double foil stamped cards feature a gold facsimile signature of each driver on the front of their card. The backs feature a driver's answer to a specific question to give the fan more insight to what goes on behind-the-scenes. The cards are randomly inserted in packs at a rate of one per 50 packs.

	MINT	NRMT
COMPLETE SET (15)	50.00	22.00
COMMON CARD (IV1-IV15)	1.50	.70
❑ IV1 Mark Martin	8.00	3.60
❑ IV2 Ted Musgrave	1.50	.70
❑ IV3 Dale Earnhardt	15.00	6.75
❑ IV4 Sterling Marlin	3.00	1.35
❑ IV5 Kyle Petty	3.00	1.35
❑ IV6 Mark Martin	8.00	3.60
❑ IV7 Dale Earnhardt	15.00	6.75
❑ IV8 Brett Bodine	1.50	.70
❑ IV9 Geoff Bodine	1.50	.70
❑ IV10 Ricky Rudd	3.00	1.35
❑ IV11 Sterling Marlin	3.00	1.35
❑ IV12 Bobby Labonte	6.00	2.70
❑ IV13 Morgan Shepherd	1.50	.70
❑ IV14 Robert Pressley	1.50	.70
❑ IV15 Michael Waltrip	1.50	.70

1996 Classic Mark Martin's Challengers

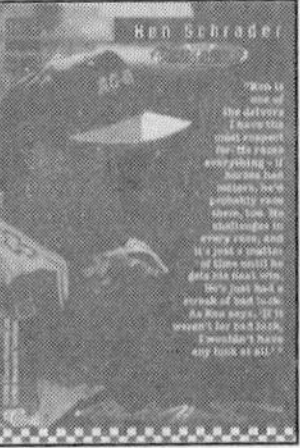

This 10-card set features some of Mark's toughest competitors. Each card has Mark's comments on the back telling what makes each driver a good competitor. The cards feature micro-foil technology and were inserted in packs at a rate of one per 15 packs.

	MINT	NRMT
COMPLETE SET (10)	12.00	5.50

COMMON CARD (MC1-MC10)	.75	.35
❑ MC1 Ted Musgrave	.75	.35
❑ MC2 Michael Waltrip	.75	.35
❑ MC3 Dale Earnhardt's Car	4.00	1.80
❑ MC4 Dale Jarrett	3.00	1.35
❑ MC5 Sterling Marlin	1.50	.70
❑ MC6 Ken Schrader	.75	.35
❑ MC7 Geoff Bodine	.75	.35
❑ MC8 Rusty Wallace's Car	1.00	.45
❑ MC9 Bobby Labonte	3.00	1.35
❑ MC10 Mark Martin	4.00	1.80

1996 Classic Race Chase

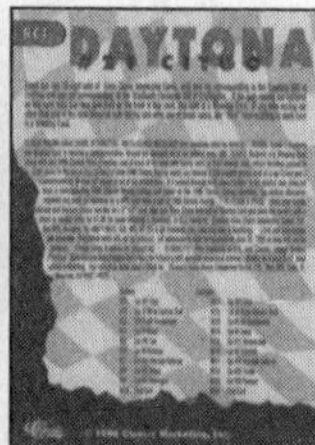

This 20-card insert set was an interactive game for two specific races in the 1996 season. The set is divided into subsets; cards 1-10 were for the '96 Daytona 500 and cards 11-20 were for the '96 TranSouth Financial 400. If you held the winning card for either of those two races, Dale Jarrett and Jeff Gordon respectively, you could redeem that card for a 10-card foil stamped set of the related race. You could also redeem the winning card along with a regular Classic drivers card for each of the second through tenth place finishers for a $50 phone card of a top driver and the 10-card foil stamped set. Since the winners of each of the two races were not represented in the set, the Field Card was the winner in both interactive race games. The expiration for the redemption cards was June 30, 1996.

	MINT	NRMT
COMPLETE SET (20)	40.00	18.00
COMMON CARD (RC1-RC20)	1.25	.55
❑ RC1 Michael Waltrip's Car	1.25	.55
❑ RC2 Rusty Wallace's Car	3.00	1.35
❑ RC3 Dale Earnhardt's Car	6.00	2.70
❑ RC4 Sterling Marlin's Car	2.50	1.10
❑ RC5 Ricky Rudd's Car	2.50	1.10
❑ RC6 Mark Martin's Car	3.00	1.35
❑ RC7 Bobby Labonte's Car	2.50	1.10
❑ RC8 Ernie Irvan's Car	2.50	1.10
❑ RC9 Morgan Shepherd's Car	1.25	.55
❑ RC10 Field Card WIN	1.25	.55
❑ RC11 Michael Waltrip's Car	1.25	.55
❑ RC12 Rusty Wallace's Car	3.00	1.35
❑ RC13 Dale Earnhardt's Car	6.00	2.70
❑ RC14 Sterling Marlin's Car	2.50	1.10
❑ RC15 Darrell Waltrip's Car	2.50	1.10
❑ RC16 Mark Martin's Car	3.00	1.35
❑ RC17 Bobby Labonte's Car	2.50	1.10
❑ RC18 Ernie Irvan's Car	2.50	1.10
❑ RC19 Johnny Benson's Car	1.25	.55
❑ RC20 Field Card WIN	1.25	.55

1992 Clevite Engine Builders

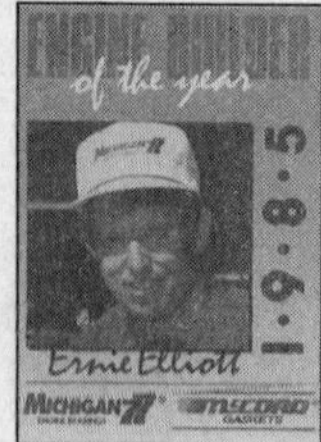

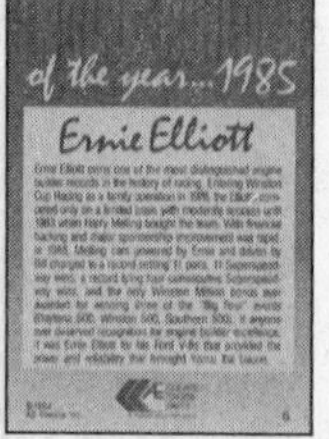

This 12-card promotional set features the top Winston Cup engine builders from 1985-91. The Engine Builder Award is given out each year to the engine builder who has accumulated the most points over the year. The cards are silver bordered and have a color photo on the front. Starting with Ernie Elliott in 1985, the cards are in order of the year that engine builder won the award.

	MINT	NRMT
COMPLETE SET (12)	15.00	6.75
COMMON CARD (1-12)	1.00	.45
❑ 1 A.E.Clevite Co.	1.00	.45
❑ 2 A.E.Clevite Co.	1.00	.45
❑ 3 Michigan Bearings	1.00	.45
❑ 4 McCord gaskets	1.00	.45
❑ 5 A.E.Clevite Timing	1.00	.45
❑ 6 Ernie Elliott	1.50	.70
❑ 7 Randy Dorton	1.50	.70
❑ 8 Lou LaRosa	1.50	.70
❑ 9 David Evans	1.50	.70
❑ 10 Rick Wetzel	1.50	.70
❑ 11 Eddie Lanier	1.50	.70
❑ 12 Shelton Pittman	1.50	.70

1991 CM Handsome Harry

This 14-card set features one of the most popular drivers in Winston Cup history, Harry Gant. The cards feature a combination of shots of Harry in his early days and at home. Reportedly there were 25,000 sets produced. Also included is a Harry Gant promo card. The card is a cartoon and has the word PROMO in the upper right corner of the front of the card.

	MINT	NRMT
COMPLETE SET (14)	4.00	1.80
COMMON CARD (1-14)	.30	.14

1997 Collector's Choice

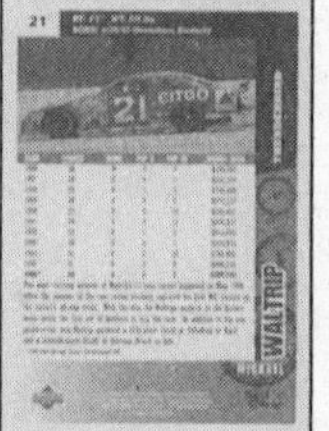

The 1997 Collector's Choice set was issued in one series totaling 155 cards and featured the top names in NASCAR. The set contains the subsets: Drivers (1-50), Maximum MPH (51-100), Speedway Challenge (101-126), Team 3 (127-144) and Transitions (145-153). The cards were packaged 10 cards per pack, 36 packs per box and 12 boxes per case. Suggested retail price on a pack was 99 cents. This was the premiere issue of the Collector's Choice brand in racing by Upper Deck. Also included as an insert in packs (1:4 packs) was a game piece for Upper Deck's Meet the Stars promotion. Each game piece was a multiple choice trivia card about racing. The collector would scratch of the box next to the answer that they felt best matched the question to determine if they won. Instant win game pieces were also inserted one in 72 packs. Winning game pieces could be sent into Upper Deck for a prize drawing. The Grand Prize was a chance to meet Jeff Gordon. Prizes for 2nd through 4th were for Upper Deck Authenticated shopping sprees. The 5th prize was two special Jeff Gordon Meet the Stars cards. The blank back cards measure 5" X 7"and are titled Dynamic Debut and Magic Memories. These two cards are priced at the bottom of the base set.

	MINT	NRMT
COMPLETE SET (155)	12.00	5.50
COMMON CARD (1-155)	.10	.05
COMMON DRIVER (1-155)	.20	.09
❑ 1 Rick Mast	.20	.09
❑ 2 Rusty Wallace	.75	.35
❑ 3 Dale Earnhardt	1.50	.70
❑ 4 Sterling Marlin	.40	.18
❑ 5 Terry Labonte	.75	.35
❑ 6 Mark Martin	.75	.35
❑ 7 Geoff Bodine	.20	.09
❑ 8 Hut Stricklin	.20	.09
❑ 9 Lake Speed	.20	.09
❑ 10 Ricky Rudd	.40	.18
❑ 11 Brett Bodine	.20	.09
❑ 12 Derrike Cope	.20	.09
❑ 13 Bill Elliott	.75	.35
❑ 14 Bobby Hamilton	.20	.09
❑ 15 Wally Dallenbach	.20	.09
❑ 16 Ted Musgrave	.20	.09
❑ 17 Darrell Waltrip	.40	.18
❑ 18 Bobby Labonte	.60	.25
❑ 19 Loy Allen	.20	.09
❑ 20 Morgan Shepherd	.20	.09
❑ 21 Michael Waltrip	.20	.09
❑ 22 Ward Burton	.20	.09
❑ 23 Jimmy Spencer	.20	
❑ 24 Jeff Gordon	1.50	
❑ 25 Ken Schrader	.20	
❑ 26 Kyle Petty	.40	
❑ 27 Bobby Hillin	.20	
❑ 28 Ernie Irvan	.40	
❑ 29 Jeff Purvis	.20	
❑ 30 Johnny Benson	.20	
❑ 31 Dave Marcis	.40	
❑ 32 Jeremy Mayfield	.50	
❑ 33 Robert Pressley	.20	
❑ 34 Jeff Burton	.40	
❑ 35 Joe Nemechek	.20	
❑ 36 Dale Jarrett	.60	
❑ 37 John Andretti	.20	
❑ 38 Kenny Wallace	.20	
❑ 39 Elton Sawyer	.20	
❑ 40 Dick Trickle	.20	
❑ 41 Ricky Craven	.20	
❑ 42 Chad Little	.20	
❑ 43 Todd Bodine	.20	
❑ 44 David Green	.20	
❑ 45 Randy Lajoie	.20	
❑ 46 Larry Pearson	.20	
❑ 47 Jason Keller	.20	
❑ 48 Hermie Sadler	.20	
❑ 49 Mike McLaughlin	.20	
❑ 50 Tim Fedewa	.20	
❑ 51 Rick Mast's Car MM	.10	
❑ 52 Rusty Wallace's Car MM	.40	
❑ 53 Ricky Craven's Car MM	.10	
❑ 54 Sterling Marlin's Car MM	.20	
❑ 55 Terry Labonte's Car MM	.40	
❑ 56 Mark Martin's Car MM	.40	
❑ 57 Geoff Bodine's Car MM	.10	
❑ 58 Hut Stricklin's Car MM	.10	
❑ 59 Lake Speed's Car MM	.10	
❑ 60 Ricky Rudd's Car MM	.20	
❑ 61 Brett Bodine's Car MM	.10	
❑ 62 Derrike Cope's Car MM	.10	
❑ 63 Bill Elliott's Car MM	.40	
❑ 64 Bobby Hamilton's Car MM	.10	
❑ 65 Wally Dallenbach's Car MM	.10	
❑ 66 Ted Musgrave's Car MM	.10	
❑ 67 Darrell Waltrip's Car MM	.20	
❑ 68 Bobby Labonte's Car MM	.10	
❑ 69 Loy Allen's Car MM	.10	
❑ 70 Morgan Shepherd's Car MM	.10	
❑ 71 Michael Waltrip's Car MM	.10	
❑ 72 Ward Burton's Car MM	.10	
❑ 73 Jimmy Spencer's Car MM	.10	
❑ 74 Jeff Gordon's Car MM	.75	
❑ 75 Ken Schrader's Car MM	.10	
❑ 76 Kyle Petty's Car MM	.20	
❑ 77 Bobby Hillin's Car MM	.10	
❑ 78 Ernie Irvan's Car MM	.20	
❑ 79 Jeff Purvis's Car MM	.10	
❑ 80 Johnny Benson's Car MM	.10	
❑ 81 Dave Marcis's Car MM	.20	
❑ 82 Jeremy Mayfield's Car MM	.30	
❑ 83 Robert Pressley's Car MM	.10	
❑ 84 Jeff Burton's Car MM	.20	
❑ 85 Joe Nemechek's Car MM	.10	
❑ 86 Dale Jarrett's Car MM	.20	
❑ 87 John Andretti's Car MM	.10	
❑ 88 Kenny Wallace's Car MM	.10	
❑ 89 Elton Sawyer's Car MM	.10	
❑ 90 Dick Trickle's Car MM	.10	
❑ 91 Chad Little's Car MM	.10	
❑ 92 Todd Bodine's Car MM	.10	
❑ 93 David Green's Car MM	.10	
❑ 94 Randy Lajoie's Car MM	.10	
❑ 95 Larry Pearson's Car MM	.10	
❑ 96 Jason Keller's Car MM	.10	
❑ 97 Hermie Sadler's Car MM	.10	
❑ 98 Mike McLaughlin's Car MM	.10	
❑ 99 Tim Fedewa's Car MM	.10	
❑ 100 Patty Moise's Car MM	.10	
❑ 101 Jeff Gordon SC	.75	
❑ 102 Rusty Wallace SC	.40	
❑ 103 Sterling Marlin SC	.20	
❑ 104 Terry Labonte SC	.40	
❑ 105 Mark Martin SC	.40	
❑ 106 Ricky Rudd SC	.20	
❑ 107 Ted Musgrave SC	.10	
❑ 108 Michael Waltrip SC	.10	
❑ 109 Dale Jarrett SC	.40	
❑ 110 Ernie Irvan SC	.20	
❑ 111 Bill Elliott SC	.40	
❑ 112 Ken Schrader SC	.10	
❑ 113 Bobby Labonte SC	.40	
❑ 114 Kyle Petty SC	.20	
❑ 115 Ricky Craven SC	.10	
❑ 116 Bobby Hamilton SC	.10	
❑ 117 Johnny Benson SC	.10	
❑ 118 Jeremy Mayfield SC	.30	
❑ 119 Darrell Waltrip SC	.20	
❑ 120 Junior Johnson SC	.10	

Glen Wood SC	.10	.05
Benny Parsons SC	.20	.09
Bobby Allison SC	.20	.09
Ned Jarrett SC	.20	.09
Cale Yarborough SC	.20	.09
Richard Petty SC	.40	.18
Jeff Gordon T3	.75	.35
Jeff Gordon T3	.75	.35
Jeff Gordon's Car T3	.75	.35
Terry Labonte T3	.40	.18
Terry Labonte T3	.40	.18
Terry Labonte's Car T3	.40	.18
Ken Schrader T3	.10	.05
Ken Schrader T3	.10	.05
Ken Schrader's Car T3	.10	.05
Mark Martin T3	.40	.18
Mark Martin T3	.40	.18
Mark Martin's Car T3	.40	.18
Ted Musgrave T3	.10	.05
Ted Musgrave T3	.10	.05
Ted Musgrave's Car T3	.10	.05
Jeff Burton T3	.20	.09
Jeff Burton T3	.20	.09
Jeff Burton's Car T3	.10	.05
Rusty Wallace TRA	.40	.18
Ricky Craven TRA	.10	.05
Ricky Rudd TRA	.20	.09
Bill Elliott TRA	.40	.18
Joe Nemechek TRA	.10	.05
Brett Bodine TRA	.10	.05
Darrell Waltrip TRA	.20	.09
Geoff Bodine TRA	.10	.05
Dave Marcis TRA	.20	.09
Jeff Gordon CL	.75	.35
Rusty Wallace CL	.40	.18
) Jeff Gordon 5X7 DD	5.00	2.20
) Jeff Gordon 5X7 MM	5.00	2.20

1997 Collector's Choice Speedecals

'8-card insert set features driver's cars on stickers. ickers were randomly inserted one in three packs.

	MINT	NRMT
LETE SET (48)	20.00	9.00
ION CARD (S1-S48)	.20	.09
LES: .6X TO 1.5X BASE CARD HI		

Rick Mast's Car	.20	.09
Joe Nemechek's Car	.20	.09
Rusty Wallace's Car	1.00	.45
Rusty Wallace's Helmet	1.00	.45
Bill Elliott's Car	1.00	.45
Bill Elliott's Helmet	1.00	.45
Sterling Marlin's Car	.40	.18
Sterling Marlin's Helmet	.40	.18
Terry Labonte's Car	1.00	.45
Terry Labonte's Helmet	1.00	.45
Mark Martin's Car	1.00	.45
Mark Martin's Helmet	1.00	.45
Bobby Hamilton's Car	.20	.09
Derrike Cope's Car	.20	.09
Ricky Craven's Car	.20	.09
Ricky Craven's Helmet	.20	.09
Lake Speed's Car	.20	.09
Morgan Shepherd's Car	.20	.09
Ricky Rudd's Car	.40	.18
Ricky Rudd's Helmet	.40	.18
Kyle Petty's Car	.40	.18
Kyle Petty's Helmet	.40	.18
Johnny Benson's Car	.20	.09
Johnny Benson's Helmet	.20	.09
Ernie Irvan's Car	.40	.18
Kenny Wallace's Car	.20	.09
Jeff Burton's Car	.40	.18
Jeff Burton's Helmet	.40	.18
Ken Schrader's Car	.20	.09
Dave Marcis's Car	.40	.18
Ted Musgrave's Car	.20	.09
Ted Musgrave's Helmet	.20	.09
Darrell Waltrip's Car	.40	.18
Darrell Waltrip's Helmet	.40	.18
❑ S35 Bobby Labonte's Car	.40	.18
❑ S36 Bobby Labonte's Helmet	.40	.18
❑ S37 Dale Jarrett's Car	.75	.35
❑ S38 Dale Jarrett's Helmet	.75	.35
❑ S39 Jeremy Mayfield's Car	.60	.25
❑ S40 Jeremy Mayfield's Car	.60	.25
❑ S41 Michael Waltrip's Car	.20	.09
❑ S42 Michael Waltrip's Helmet	.20	.09
❑ S43 Ward Burton's Car	.20	.09
❑ S44 Wally Dallenbach's Car	.20	.09
❑ S45 Wally Dallenbach's Helmet	.20	.09
❑ S46 Jimmy Spencer's Car	.20	.09
❑ S47 Jeff Gordon's Car	2.00	.90
❑ S48 Jeff Gordon's Helmet	2.00	.90

1997 Collector's Choice Triple Force

This 30-card insert set features 10 groups of three cards. Each group of three cards was given a letter designation. Taking each of the three interlocking die-cut cards a collector could put them together like a puzzle. The cards together formed a photo across all three cards. The odds of pulling a Triple Force card were one in eleven packs.

	MINT	NRMT
COMPLETE SET (30)	80.00	36.00
COMMON CARD (A1-J3)	1.25	.55
*SINGLES: 3X TO 8X BASE CARD HI		

❑ A1 Dale Jarrett	4.00	1.80
❑ A2 Ernie Irvan	2.50	1.10
❑ A3 Dale Jarrett	4.00	1.80
❑ B1 Ted Musgrave	1.25	.55
❑ B2 Jeff Burton	1.25	.55
❑ B3 Mark Martin	6.00	2.70
❑ C1 Johnny Benson	1.25	.55
❑ C2 Ricky Craven	1.25	.55
❑ C3 Jeremy Mayfield	1.50	.70
❑ D1 Terry Labonte	6.00	2.70
❑ D2 Terry Labonte	6.00	2.70
❑ D3 Terry Labonte	6.00	2.70
❑ E1 Jimmy Spencer	1.25	.55
❑ E2 Dale Jarrett	4.00	1.80
❑ E3 Michael Waltrip	1.25	.55
❑ F1 Jeff Gordon	12.00	5.50
❑ F2 Terry Labonte	6.00	2.70
❑ F3 Ken Schrader	1.25	.55
❑ G1 Terry Labonte	6.00	2.70
❑ G2 Jeff Gordon	12.00	5.50
❑ G3 Jeff Gordon	12.00	5.50
❑ H1 Bobby Hamilton	1.25	.55
❑ H2 Rusty Wallace	6.00	2.70
❑ H3 Geoff Bodine	1.25	.55
❑ I1 Ricky Craven	1.25	.55
❑ I2 Ernie Irvan	2.50	1.10
❑ I3 Dale Jarrett	4.00	1.80
❑ J1 Mark Martin	6.00	2.70
❑ J2 Rusty Wallace	6.00	2.70
❑ J3 Johnny Benson	1.25	.55

1997 Collector's Choice Upper Deck 500

The cards from this 90-card insert set make up pieces to a game. The cards carry driver or car photos. Each card is given a value of laps, track position, or penalty. Similar to a card game the collector plays their cards until one player has accumulated 500 laps. The cards were inserted one per pack.

	MINT	NRMT
COMPLETE SET (90)	15.00	6.75
COMMON CARD (UD1-UD90)	.20	.09
*SINGLES: .4X TO 1X BASE CARD HI		

❑ UD1 Dale Earnhardt	2.00	.90
❑ UD2 Rusty Wallace	1.00	.45
❑ UD3 Rusty Wallace's Car	.50	.23
❑ UD4 Robin Pemberton	.20	.09
❑ UD5 Sterling Marlin	.40	.18
❑ UD6 Sterling Marlin's Car	.20	.09
❑ UD7 Terry Labonte	1.00	.45
❑ UD8 Terry Labonte's Car	.50	.23
❑ UD9 Mark Martin	1.00	.45
❑ UD10 Mark Martin's Car	.50	.23
❑ UD11 Steve Hmiel	.20	.09
❑ UD12 Geoff Bodine	.20	.09
❑ UD13 Geoff Bodine's Car	.20	.09
❑ UD14 Hut Stricklin	.20	.09
❑ UD15 Hut Stricklin's Car	.20	.09
❑ UD16 Lake Speed	.20	.09
❑ UD17 Lake Speed's Car	.20	.09
❑ UD18 Ricky Rudd	.40	.18
❑ UD19 Ricky Rudd's Car	.20	.09
❑ UD20 Brett Bodine	.20	.09
❑ UD21 Brett Bodine's Car	.20	.09
❑ UD22 Derrike Cope	.20	.09
❑ UD23 Derrike Cope's Car	.20	.09
❑ UD24 Bobby Allison	.20	.09
❑ UD25 Bill Elliott	1.00	.45
❑ UD26 Bill Elliott's Car	.50	.23
❑ UD27 Bobby Hamilton	.20	.09
❑ UD28 Bobby Hamilton's Car	.20	.09
❑ UD29 Richard Petty	.40	.18
❑ UD30 Wally Dallenbach	.20	.09
❑ UD31 Wally Dallenbach's Car	.20	.09
❑ UD32 Ted Musgrave	.20	.09
❑ UD33 Ted Musgrave's Car	.20	.09
❑ UD34 Darrell Waltrip	.40	.18
❑ UD35 Darrell Waltrip's Car	.20	.09
❑ UD36 Bobby Labonte	.30	.14
❑ UD37 Bobby Labonte's Car	.40	.18
❑ UD38 Loy Allen	.20	.09
❑ UD39 Loy Allen's Car	.20	.09
❑ UD40 Morgan Shepherd	.20	.09
❑ UD41 Morgan Shepherd's Car	.20	.09
❑ UD42 Michael Waltrip	.20	.09
❑ UD43 Michael Waltrip's Car	.20	.09
❑ UD44 Ward Burton	.20	.09
❑ UD45 Ward Burton's Car	.20	.09
❑ UD46 Jimmy Spencer	.20	.09
❑ UD47 Jimmy Spencer's Car	.20	.09
❑ UD48 Jeff Gordon	2.00	.90
❑ UD49 Jeff Gordon's Car	1.00	.45
❑ UD50 Ray Evernham	.20	.09
❑ UD51 Rick Hendrick	.20	.09
❑ UD52 Ken Schrader	.20	.09
❑ UD53 Ken Schrader's Car	.20	.09
❑ UD54 Kyle Petty	.40	.18
❑ UD55 Kyle Petty's Car	.20	.09
❑ UD56 Bobby Hillin	.20	.09
❑ UD57 Bobby Hillin's Car	.20	.09
❑ UD58 Ernie Irvan		
❑ UD59 Ernie Irvan's Car	.40	.18
❑ UD60 Jeff Purvis	.20	.09
❑ UD61 Jeff Purvis's Car	.20	.09
❑ UD62 Johnny Benson	.20	.09
❑ UD63 Johnny Benson's Car	.20	.09
❑ UD64 Dave Marcis	.40	.18
❑ UD65 Dave Marcis's Car	.20	.09
❑ UD66 Jeremy Mayfield	.20	.09
❑ UD67 Jeremy Mayfield's Car	.40	.18
❑ UD68 Cale Yarborough	.20	.09
❑ UD69 Robert Pressley	.20	.09
❑ UD70 Robert Pressley's Car	.20	.09
❑ UD71 Jeff Burton	.40	.18
❑ UD72 Jeff Burton's Car	.20	.09
❑ UD73 Joe Nemechek	.20	.09
❑ UD74 Joe Nemechek's Car	.20	.09
❑ UD75 Dale Jarrett	.50	.23
❑ UD76 Dale Jarrett's Car	.40	.18
❑ UD77 John Andretti	.20	.09
❑ UD78 John Andretti's Car	.20	.09
❑ UD79 Kenny Wallace	.20	.09
❑ UD80 Kenny Wallace's Car	.20	.09
❑ UD81 Elton Sawyer	.20	.09
❑ UD82 Elton Sawyer's Car	.20	.09
❑ UD83 Dick Trickle	.20	.09
❑ UD84 Dick Trickle's Car	.20	.09
❑ UD85 Ricky Craven	.20	.09
❑ UD86 Ricky Craven's Car	.20	.09
❑ UD87 Chad Little	.20	.09
❑ UD88 Chad Little's Car	.20	.09

❑ UD89 Rick Mast	.20	.09
❑ UD90 Rick Mast's Car	.20	.09

1997 Collector's Choice Victory Circle

The top 10 active career victory leaders was the focus of this 10-card insert set. The cards feature red foil stamping on the front and were inserted one in fifty packs.

	MINT	NRMT
COMPLETE SET (10)	120.00	55.00
COMMON CARD (VC1-VC10)	3.00	1.35
*SINGLES: 8X TO 20X BASE CARD HI		

	MINT	NRMT
❑ VC1 Darrell Waltrip	3.00	1.35
❑ VC2 Dale Earnhardt	30.00	13.50
❑ VC3 Rusty Wallace	15.00	6.75
❑ VC4 Bill Elliott	15.00	6.75
❑ VC5 Mark Martin	15.00	6.75
❑ VC6 Geoff Bodine	3.00	1.35
❑ VC7 Terry Labonte	15.00	6.75
❑ VC8 Ricky Rudd	6.00	2.70
❑ VC9 Jeff Gordon	30.00	13.50
❑ VC10 Ernie Irvan	6.00	2.70

1998 Collector's Choice

The 1998 Collector's Choice set was issued in one series totaling 117 cards and featured the top names in NASCAR. The set consists of five topical subsets: Speed Merchants (1-36), Rollin' Thunder (37-72), Future Stock (73-87), Perils of the Pits (88-98), and Trophy Dash (99-112). The cards were packaged 14 cards per pack and 36 packs per box. Suggested retail price on a pack was $1.29.

	MINT	NRMT
COMPLETE SET (117)	12.00	5.50
COMMON CARD (1-117)	.10	.05
COMMON DRIVER (1-117)	.20	.09

	MINT	NRMT
❑ 1 Morgan Shepherd	.20	.09
❑ 2 Rusty Wallace	.75	.35
❑ 3 Dale Earnhardt	1.50	.70
❑ 4 Sterling Marlin	.40	.18
❑ 5 Terry Labonte	.75	.35
❑ 6 Mark Martin	.75	.35
❑ 7 Geoff Bodine	.20	.09
❑ 8 Hut Stricklin	.20	.09
❑ 9 Lake Speed	.20	.09
❑ 10 Ricky Rudd	.40	.18
❑ 11 Brett Bodine	.20	.09
❑ 12 Dale Jarrett	.60	.25
❑ 13 Bill Elliott	.75	.35
❑ 14 Bobby Hamilton	.20	.09
❑ 15 Wally Dallenbach	.20	.09
❑ 16 Ted Musgrave	.20	.09
❑ 17 Darrell Waltrip	.40	.18
❑ 18 Bobby Labonte	.60	.25
❑ 19 Steve Grissom	.20	.09
❑ 20 Rick Mast	.20	.09
❑ 21 Michael Waltrip	.20	.09
❑ 22 Ward Burton	.20	.09
❑ 23 Jimmy Spencer	.20	.09
❑ 24 Jeff Gordon	1.50	.70
❑ 25 Ricky Craven	.40	.18
❑ 26 Kyle Petty	.40	.18
❑ 27 Kenny Wallace	.20	.09
❑ 28 Ernie Irvan	.40	.18
❑ 29 David Green	.20	.09
❑ 30 Johnny Benson	.20	.09
❑ 31 Mike Skinner	.20	.09
❑ 32 Jeremy Mayfield	.50	.23
❑ 33 Ken Schrader	.20	.09
❑ 34 Jeff Burton	.40	.18
❑ 35 Robby Gordon	.20	.09
❑ 36 Derrike Cope	.20	.09
❑ 37 Morgan Shepherd's Car	.10	.05
❑ 38 Rusty Wallace's Car	.40	.18
❑ 39 Dale Earnhardt's Car	.10	.05
❑ 40 Sterling Marlin's Car	.10	.05
❑ 41 Terry Labonte's Car	.40	.18
❑ 42 Mark Martin's Car	.40	.18
❑ 43 Geoff Bodine's Car	.10	.05
❑ 44 Hut Stricklin's Car	.10	.05
❑ 45 Lake Speed's Car	.10	.05
❑ 46 Ricky Rudd's Car	.20	.09
❑ 47 Brett Bodine's Car	.10	.05
❑ 48 Dale Jarrett's Car	.40	.18
❑ 49 Bill Elliott's Car	.40	.18
❑ 50 Bobby Hamilton's Car	.10	.05
❑ 51 Wally Dallenbach's Car	.10	.05
❑ 52 Ted Musgrave's Car	.10	.05
❑ 53 Darrell Waltrip's Car	.20	.09
❑ 54 Bobby Labonte's Car	.30	.14
❑ 55 Steve Grissom's Car	.10	.05
❑ 56 Rick Mast's Car	.10	.05
❑ 57 Michael Waltrip's Car	.10	.05
❑ 58 Ward Burton's Car	.10	.05
❑ 59 Jimmy Spencer's Car	.10	.05
❑ 60 Jeff Gordon's Car	.75	.35
❑ 61 Ricky Craven's Car	.10	.05
❑ 62 Kyle Petty's Car	.20	.09
❑ 63 Kenny Wallace's Car	.10	.05
❑ 64 Ernie Irvan's Car	.20	.09
❑ 65 David Green's Car	.10	.05
❑ 66 Johnny Benson's Car	.10	.05
❑ 67 Mike Skinner's Car	.10	.05
❑ 68 Jeremy Mayfield's Car	.20	.09
❑ 69 Ken Schrader's Car	.10	.05
❑ 70 Jeff Burton's Car	.20	.09
❑ 71 Robby Gordon's Car	.10	.05
❑ 72 Derrike Cope's Car	.10	.05
❑ 73 Jeff Burton FS	.20	.09
❑ 74 Robby Gordon FS	.10	.05
❑ 75 Mike Skinner FS	.10	.05
❑ 76 Johnny Benson FS	.10	.05
❑ 77 Ricky Craven FS	.10	.05
❑ 78 Ward Burton FS	.10	.05
❑ 79 Jeremy Mayfield FS	.25	.11
❑ 80 Steve Grissom FS	.10	.05
❑ 81 John Andretti FS	.10	.05
❑ 82 David Green FS	.10	.05
❑ 83 Bobby Labonte FS	.30	.14
❑ 84 Kenny Wallace FS	.10	.05
❑ 85 Mike Wallace FS	.10	.05
❑ 86 Joe Nemechek FS	.10	.05
❑ 87 Chad Little FS	.10	.05
❑ 88 Jeff Gordon PP	.75	.35
❑ 89 Terry Labonte PP	.40	.18
❑ 90 Ricky Craven PP	.10	.05
❑ 91 Kyle Petty PP	.20	.09
❑ 92 Dale Jarrett PP	.30	.14
❑ 93 Rusty Wallace PP	.40	.18
❑ 94 Ricky Rudd PP	.20	.09
❑ 95 Bobby Labonte PP	.30	.14
❑ 96 Bobby Hamilton PP	.10	.05
❑ 97 Mark Martin PP	.40	.18
❑ 98 Jeff Gordon TD	.75	.35
❑ 99 Mark Martin TD	.40	.18
❑ 100 Terry Labonte TD	.40	.18
❑ 101 Dale Jarrett TD	.30	.14
❑ 102 Jeff Burton TD	.20	.09
❑ 103 Dale Earnhardt TD	.75	.35
❑ 104 Bobby Hamilton TD	.10	.05
❑ 105 Ricky Rudd TD	.20	.09
❑ 106 Michael Waltrip TD	.10	.05
❑ 107 Jeremy Mayfield TD	.25	.11
❑ 108 Ted Musgrave TD	.10	.05
❑ 109 Bill Elliott TD	.40	.18
❑ 110 Johnny Benson TD	.10	.05
❑ 111 Rusty Wallace TD	.40	.18
❑ 112 Darrell Waltrip TD	.20	.09
❑ 113 Checklist	.10	.05
❑ 114 Checklist	.10	.05
❑ 115 Checklist	.10	.05
❑ 116 Checklist	.10	.05
❑ 117 Checklist	.10	.05

1998 Collector's Choice Star Quest

This 50-card set is a four-tier insert set that features

autographed cards in its fourth tier. The Qua Tier(first)cards were inserted into packs at a ratio c The Pole Tier(second)cards were inserted into pack ratio of 1:11. The Win Tier(third) cards were inserte packs at a ratio of 1:71. The Championship Tier(f autographed cards were inserted into packs at a ra 1:250.

	MINT	N
COMPLETE SET (50)	15.00	
COMPLETE 1-STAR SET (20)	15.00	
COMMON 1-STAR (SQ1 - SQ20)	.25	
COMMON 1-STAR DRIVER	.50	
COMPLETE 2-STAR SET (10)	25.00	
COMMON 2-STAR (SQ21 - SQ30)	.60	
COMMON 2-STAR DRIVER	1.25	
COMPLETE 3-STAR SET (10)	175.00	
COMMON 3-STAR (SQ31 - SQ40)	5.00	
COMPLETE 4-STAR SET (10)	500.00	2
COMMON 4-STAR (SQ41 - SQ50)	30.00	

	MINT
❑ SQ1 Brett Bodine	.50
❑ SQ2 Jimmy Spencer's Car	.25
❑ SQ3 Mike Wallace	.50
❑ SQ4 Bobby Labonte	2.00
❑ SQ5 Morgan Shepherd	.50
❑ SQ6 Derrike Cope's Car	.25
❑ SQ7 Kenny Wallace	.50
❑ SQ8 Chad Little	.50
❑ SQ9 Hut Stricklin	.50
❑ SQ10 Lake Speed's Car	.25
❑ SQ11 Ricky Craven	1.00
❑ SQ12 Steve Grissom	.50
❑ SQ13 Dick Trickle's Car	.25
❑ SQ14 Rick Mast	.50
❑ SQ15 David Green's Car	.25
❑ SQ16 Wally Dallenbach	.50
❑ SQ17 Joe Nemechek	.50
❑ SQ18 Ken Schrader's Car	.25
❑ SQ19 Geoff Bodine's Car	.25
❑ SQ20 Bobby Hamilton's Car	.25
❑ SQ21 Mike Skinner	1.25
❑ SQ22 Michael Waltrip	1.25
❑ SQ23 Johnny Benson	1.25
❑ SQ24 Ward Burton	1.25
❑ SQ25 Robby Gordon's Car	.60
❑ SQ26 Dale Earnhardt	12.00
❑ SQ27 Ted Musgrave's Car	.60
❑ SQ28 Jeremy Mayfield's Car	2.00
❑ SQ29 Mark Martin's Car	3.00
❑ SQ30 Sterling Marlin	2.50
❑ SQ31 Ernie Irvan	10.00
❑ SQ32 Ricky Rudd	10.00
❑ SQ33 Jeff Burton	10.00
❑ SQ34 Rusty Wallace	25.00
❑ SQ35 Darrell Waltrip	10.00
❑ SQ36 Jeff Gordon	50.00
❑ SQ37 Terry Labonte	25.00
❑ SQ38 Bill Elliott	25.00
❑ SQ39 Dale Jarrett	20.00
❑ SQ40 Kyle Petty	10.00
❑ SQ41 Jeff Gordon Auto	150.00
❑ SQ42 Bill Elliott Auto	75.00
❑ SQ43 Dale Jarrett Auto	60.00
❑ SQ44 Kyle Petty Auto	40.00
❑ SQ45 Bobby Labonte Auto	60.00
❑ SQ46 Mark Martin Auto	75.00
❑ SQ47 Geoff Bodine Auto	30.00
❑ SQ48 Rusty Wallace Auto	75.00
❑ SQ49 Robby Gordon Auto	30.00
❑ SQ50 Ted Musgrave Auto	30.00

1998 Collector's Choice CC

The cards from this 90-card insert set make up piec game. The cards carry driver or car photos. Each given a value of laps, track position, or penalty. Sin a card game the collector plays their cards until one has accumulated 600 laps. The cards were insert per pack.

	MINT
COMPLETE SET (90)	15.00
COMMON CARD (CC1-CC90)	.10

ION DRIVER (CC1-CC90)	.20	.09
LES: .5X TO 1.25X BASE CARD HI		
Play Card	.10	.05
Play Card	.10	.05
Play Card	.10	.05
Play Card	.10	.05
Play Card	.10	.05
Morgan Shepherd	.20	.09
Rusty Wallace	1.00	.45
Sterling Marlin	.40	.18
Terry Labonte	1.00	.45
0 Mark Martin	1.00	.45
1 Geoff Bodine	.20	.09
2 Hut Stricklin	.20	.09
3 Lake Speed	.20	.09
4 Ricky Rudd	.40	.18
5 Brett Bodine	.20	.09
6 Dale Jarrett	.75	.35
7 Bill Elliott	1.00	.45
8 Bobby Hamilton	.20	.09
9 Wally Dallenbach	.20	.09
0 Ted Musgrave	.20	.09
1 Darrell Waltrip	.40	.18
2 Bobby Labonte	.60	.25
3 Steve Grissom	.20	.09
4 Rick Mast	.20	.09
5 Michael Waltrip	.20	.09
6 Ward Burton	.20	.09
7 Jimmy Spencer	.20	.09
8 Ricky Craven	.20	.09
9 Kyle Petty	.40	.18
0 Kenny Wallace	.20	.09
1 Ernie Irvan	.40	.18
2 David Green	.20	.09
3 Johnny Benson	.20	.09
4 Mike Skinner	.20	.09
5 Jeremy Mayfield	.40	.18
6 Ken Schrader	.20	.09
7 Jeff Burton	.40	.18
8 Robby Gordon	.20	.09
9 Derrike Cope	.20	.09
0 Morgan Shepherd's Car	.10	.05
1 Rusty Wallace's Car	.50	.23
2 Sterling Marlin	.40	.18
3 Mark Martin	1.00	.45
4 Geoff Bodine	.20	.09
5 Hut Stricklin	.20	.09
6 Lake Speed's Car	.10	.05
7 Ricky Rudd's Car	.20	.09
8 Brett Bodine	.20	.09
9 Dale Jarrett's Car	.40	.18
0 Bill Elliott's Car	.50	.23
1 Bobby Hamilton	.20	.09
2 Wally Dallenbach	.20	.09
3 Ted Musgrave's Car	.10	.05
4 Darrell Waltrip	.40	.18
5 Bobby Labonte's Car	.40	.18
6 Steve Grissom's Car	.10	.05
7 Rick Mast's Car	.10	.05
8 Michael Waltrip	.20	.09
9 Ward Burton	.20	.09
0 Jimmy Spencer's Car	.10	.05
1 Ricky Craven's Car	.10	.05
2 Kyle Petty	.40	.18
3 Kenny Wallace	.20	.09
4 Ernie Irvan's Car	.20	.09
5 David Green's Car	.10	.05
6 Johnny Benson's Car	.10	.05
7 Mike Skinner	.20	.09
8 Jeremy Mayfield's Car	.30	.14
9 Ken Schrader's Car	.10	.05
0 Jeff Burton's Car	.20	.09
1 Robby Gordon	.20	.09
2 Derrike Cope	.20	.09
3 Morgan Shepherd	.20	.09
4 Rusty Wallace's Car	.50	.23
5 Sterling Marlin's Car	.20	.09
6 Mark Martin	1.00	.45
7 Geoff Bodine's Car	.10	.05
8 Hut Stricklin	.20	.09
9 Lake Speed	.20	.09
0 Ricky Rudd's Car	.20	.09
❑ CC82 Dale Jarrett	1.00	.45
❑ CC83 Bill Elliott's Car	.50	.23
❑ CC84 Bobby Hamilton	.20	.09
❑ CC85 Wally Dallenbach	.20	.09
❑ CC86 Ted Musgrave's Car	.10	.05
❑ CC87 Darrell Waltrip	.40	.18
❑ CC88 Bobby Labonte's Car	.40	.18
❑ CC89 Steve Grissom	.20	.09
❑ CC90 Rick Mast	.20	.09

1992 Coyote Rookies

This 14-card set features Winston Cup Rookies of the Year from 1980-1991. The first card is a checklist, then the next 12 cards are in order of ROY winner starting with Jody Ridley in 1980 and finishing with Bobby Hamilton in 1991. The final card in the set is a promo/checklist card with Jody Ridley on the front.

	MINT	NRMT
COMPLETE SET (14)	8.00	3.60
COMMON CARD (1-14)	.25	.11
❑ 1 Checklist Card	.25	.11
❑ 2 Jody Ridley	.25	.11
❑ 3 Ron Bouchard	.25	.11
❑ 4 Geoff Bodine	.40	.18
❑ 5 Sterling Marlin	.60	.25
❑ 6 Rusty Wallace	1.50	.70
❑ 7 Ken Schrader	.40	.18
❑ 8 Alan Kulwicki	1.50	.70
❑ 9 Davey Allison	1.75	.80
❑ 10 Ken Bouchard	.40	.18
❑ 11 Dick Trickle	.25	.11
❑ 12 Rob Moroso	.40	.18
❑ 13 Bobby Hamilton	.40	.18
❑ 14 Jody Ridley Promo/CL	.25	.11

1998 Creative Images

This 10-card promotional set was produced and distributed by Creative Images. Reportedly, only 3,000 sets were produced. These sets were recently offered in a mail-order advertisment for $29.95 per set.

	MINT	NRMT
COMPLETE SET (10)	30.00	13.50
COMMON CARD	4.00	1.80
❑ 10 Dale Jarrett	5.00	2.20
❑ 11 Bill Elliott	6.00	2.70
❑ 12 Terry Labonte	6.00	2.70
❑ 13 Ricky Rudd	4.00	1.80
❑ 13 Rusty Wallace	6.00	2.70
❑ 29 Dale Earnhardt	8.00	3.60
❑ 30 Jeff Gordon	8.00	3.60
❑ 07 Darrell Waltrip	4.00	1.80
❑ 08 Ernie Irvan	4.00	1.80
❑ 09 Mark Martin	6.00	2.70

1995 Crown Jewels

The 80-card Ruby base set is Wheels Race Cards inaugural Crown Jewels brand issue. The cards, printed on 24 pt. paper stock, came five cards per pack, 24 packs per box and 12 boxes per case. There were two methods of distribution of the product; a hobby only version, that was limited to 2200 cases and a special retail version. The set includes subsets of Winston Cup Drivers (1-30), Winston Cup Driver/Owners (31-35), Winston Cup Crew Chiefs (36-40), Winston Cup Cars (41-53), Busch Drivers (54-63), Headliners (64-73) and Win Cards (74-80). Three redemption programs were included as inserts. All of them are priced in the set headers. All three, the Gemstone game cards, the Dual Jewels redemption game and the E-Race to win cards expired 12/31/95. There were also three individual inserts randomly seeded in packs. Sterling Marlin Back-to-Back Daytona winner could be found one in 288 packs. The Chad Little Goody's 300 winner autographed card was seeded one in 576. Finally a two sided card that featured Jeff Gordon on one side and Terry Labonte on the other was randomly inserted at a rate of one in 288 packs.

	MINT	NRMT
COMPLETE RUBY SET (80)	12.00	5.50
COMMON RUBY CARD (1-80)	.15	.07
COMMON RUBY DRIVER (1-80)	.30	.14
COMP.E-RACE TO WIN SET (10)	.50	.23
❑ 1 Dale Earnhardt	2.50	1.10
❑ 2 Jeff Gordon	2.50	1.10
❑ 3 Mark Martin	1.25	.55
❑ 4 Rusty Wallace	1.25	.55
❑ 5 Ricky Rudd	.60	.25
❑ 6 Terry Labonte	1.25	.55
❑ 7 Bobby Labonte	1.00	.45
❑ 8 Ken Schrader	.30	.14
❑ 9 Sterling Marlin	.60	.25
❑ 10 Darrell Waltrip	.60	.25
❑ 11 Geoff Bodine	.30	.14
❑ 12 Kyle Petty	.60	.25
❑ 13 Dale Jarrett	1.00	.45
❑ 14 Ernie Irvan	.60	.25
❑ 15 Bill Elliott	1.25	.55
❑ 16 Morgan Shepherd	.30	.14
❑ 17 Michael Waltrip	.30	.14
❑ 18 Ted Musgrave	.30	.14
❑ 19 Lake Speed	.30	.14
❑ 20 Jimmy Spencer	.30	.14
❑ 21 Brett Bodine	.30	.14
❑ 22 Joe Nemechek	.30	.14
❑ 23 Steve Grissom	.30	.14
❑ 24 Derrike Cope	.30	.14
❑ 25 John Andretti	.30	.14
❑ 26 Kenny Bernstein	.30	.14
❑ 27 Joe Gibbs	.30	.14
❑ 28 Larry McClure	.15	.07
❑ 29 Travis Carter	.15	.07
❑ 30 Junior Johnson	.30	.14
❑ 31 Geoff Bodine	.30	.14
❑ 32 Ricky Rudd	.60	.25
❑ 33 Darrell Waltrip	.60	.25
❑ 34 Joe Nemechek	.30	.14
❑ 35 Bill Elliott	1.25	.55
❑ 36 Robin Pemberton	.15	.07
❑ 37 Jimmy Makar	.15	.07
❑ 38 Bill Ingle	.15	.07
❑ 39 Robbie Loomis	.15	.07
❑ 40 Buddy Parrott	.15	.07
❑ 41 Ken Schrader's Car	.15	.07
❑ 42 Bobby Labonte's Car	.25	.11
❑ 43 Joe Nemechek's Car	.15	.07
❑ 44 Derrike Cope's Car	.15	.07
❑ 45 Brett Bodine's Car	.15	.07
❑ 46 Kyle Petty's Car	.30	.14
❑ 47 Hut Stricklin's Car	.15	.07
❑ 48 Jimmy Spencer's Car	.15	.07
❑ 49 Ricky Rudd's Transporter	.15	.07
❑ 50 Kyle Petty's Transporter	.15	.07
❑ 51 Darrell Waltrip's Transporter	.15	.07
❑ 52 Terry Labonte's Transporter	.30	.14
❑ 53 Geoff Bodine's Transporter	.15	.07
❑ 54 David Green	.30	.14
❑ 55 Tommy Houston	.30	.14
❑ 56 Johnny Benson	.30	.14
❑ 57 Chad Little	.30	.14
❑ 58 Kenny Wallace	.30	.14
❑ 59 Hermie Sadler	.30	.14
❑ 60 Jason Keller	.30	.14
❑ 61 Bobby Dotter	.30	.14
❑ 62 Stevie Reeves	.30	.14
❑ 63 Mike McLaughlin	.30	.14
❑ 64 Dale Earnhardt's Car Darrell Waltrip's Cars CJT	.75	.35
❑ 65 Bill Elliott w/Car CJT	.60	.25
❑ 66 Sterling Marlin CJT	.60	.25
❑ 67 Chad Little CJT Mark Rypien	.30	.14
❑ 68 Jeff Gordon CJT Terry Labonte	.75	.35
❑ 69 Ernie Irvan CJT	.30	.14
❑ 70 Dale Jarrett CJT	.60	.25
❑ 71 Bobby Labonte CJT	.40	.18
❑ 72 Kyle Petty CJT	.40	.18
❑ 73 Jeff Gordon CJT Terry Labonte's Car	1.00	.45
❑ 74 Sterling Marlin RW	.60	.25
❑ 75 Jeff Gordon RW	2.00	.90
❑ 76 Terry Labonte RW	1.00	.45
❑ 77 Jeff Gordon RW	2.00	.90
❑ 78 Sterling Marlin RW	.60	.25
❑ 79 Checklist (1-73)	.15	.07
❑ 80 Checklist (74-80/Inserts)	.15	.07
❑ DT1 Jeff Gordon DT Terry Labonte DT	70.00	32.00
❑ GS1 Chad Little AUTO	50.00	22.00
❑ SM1 Sterling Marlin BB	25.00	11.00

1995 Crown Jewels Diamond

The Crown Jewels Diamond cards are a parallel of the 80-card Ruby base set. These cards were randomly inserted at a rate of one per 13 hobby packs. The cards are sequentially numbered to 599 and feature all-foil and embossed technology.

	MINT	NRMT
COMPLETE SET (80)	400.00	180.00
COMMON CARD (1-80)	4.00	1.80
COMMON DRIVER (1-80)	8.00	3.60
*DIAMOND STARS: 20X TO 35X RUBYS		

1995 Crown Jewels Emerald

The Crown Jewels Emerald cards are a parallel of the 80-card Ruby base set. These cards were randomly inserted at a rate of one per 9 packs of Crown Jewels. The cards are sequentially numbered to 1199 and feature all-foil technology.

	MINT	NRMT
COMPLETE SET (80)	300.00	135.00
COMMON CARD (1-80)	2.00	.90
COMMON DRIVER (1-80)	4.00	1.80
*EMERALD STARS: 10X TO 16X RUBYS		

1995 Crown Jewels Sapphire

The Crown Jewels Sapphire cards are an embossed parallel of the 80-card Ruby base set. Sapphire sets were available through the Gemstones interactive redemption game. Collectors who found the 11 letters that spelled C-R-O-W-N J-E-W-E-L-S were able to send those letters in for one of the 2,500 Sapphire sets. Each Sapphire set came in a felt-lined black "Jewel" box. The game expired March 31, 1996.

	MINT	NRMT
COMPLETE SET (80)	50.00	22.00
COMMON CARD (1-80)	.60	.25
COMMON DRIVER (1-80)	1.25	.55
*SAPPHIRE CARDS: 2X TO 4X RUBYS		

1995 Crown Jewels Dual Jewels

The six-card Ruby insert set features double-sided pairings of the top Winston Cup drivers. The Ruby Dual Jewel cards were inserted one per 48 packs in Crown Jewels. Emerald and Diamond parallels were produced as well and randomly inserted in packs. There was also Dual Jewels redemption game. If you had 2 Ruby, 2 Emerald, and 2 Diamond Dual Jewels redemption cards, you could redeem them for an uncut sheet of the six Dual Jewels cards in Sapphire foil stamping. The expiration of the cards was 12/31/95.

	MINT	NRMT
COMPLETE RUBY SET (6)	100.00	45.00
COMMON CARD (DJ1-DJ6)	8.00	3.60
COMP.EMERALD SET (6)	120.00	55.00
*EMERALD CARDS: .5X TO 1.25X RUBYS		
COMP.DIAMOND SET (6)	250.00	110.00
*DIAMOND CARDS: 1X TO 2.5X RUBYS		
UNCUT SAPPHIRE SHEET	40.00	18.00

	MINT	NRMT
❑ DJ1 Dale Earnhardt Jeff Gordon	40.00	18.00
❑ DJ2 Rusty Wallace Dale Jarrett	15.00	6.75
❑ DJ3 Bill Elliott Terry Labonte	15.00	6.75
❑ DJ4 Mark Martin Ernie Irvan	8.00	3.60
❑ DJ5 Kyle Petty Ricky Rudd	8.00	3.60
❑ DJ6 Dale Earnhardt Dave Marcis	30.00	13.50

1995 Crown Jewels Signature Gems

Each of the seven die-cut, micro-etched insert cards feature a top Winston Cup star. The Signature Gems cards were inserted at a rate of one per 48 packs in Crown Jewels.

	MINT	NRMT
COMPLETE SET (7)	100.00	45.00
COMMON CARD (SG1-SG7)	6.00	2.70
*SINGLES: 4X TO 10X BASE CARD HI		
UNCUT SIG.SERIES SHEET	60.00	27.00

	MINT	NRMT
❑ SG1 Jeff Gordon		
❑ SG2 Rusty Wallace		
❑ SG3 Dale Earnhardt		
❑ SG4 Ernie Irvan	12.00	5.50
❑ SG5 Ricky Rudd	6.00	2.70
❑ SG6 Mark Martin		
❑ SG7 Bill Elliott		

1996 Crown Jewels Elite

The 1996 Crown Jewels Elite set was issued in one series totalling 78 cards. The set contains the topical subsets: Winston Cup Drivers (1-25), Victories (26-34), Ov (35-39), Crew Chiefs (40-47), Driver/Crew Chief (4 Car/Hauler (57-66) and BGN Drivers (67-78). Each c printed on 24-point paper and comes with a red m foil stamping. There were 1,125 hobby cases each 16 boxes per case, 24 packs per box and 5 card pack. There were also 375 cases of the parallel Tre Chest version. Treasure Chest cards are differen from the base elite card by a foil stamped treasure on the front of the card. Another parallel version wa Diamond Tribute cards. These cards were from a s 300 case press run that were sold only to W distributor network.

	MINT	N
COMPLETE RUBY SET (78)	12.00	
COMMON CARD (1-78)	.10	
COMMON DRIVER (1-78)	.20	
COMP. T.CHEST SET (78)	15.00	
*TREASURE CHEST CARDS: .5X TO 1.25X BASE CA		
COMP. DIAM.TRIBUTE SET (78)	15.00	
*DIAMOND TRIBUTE CARDS: .5X TO 1.25X BASE CA		

	MINT
❑ 1 Dale Earnhardt	2.00
❑ 2 Jeff Gordon	2.00
❑ 3 Terry Labonte	1.00
❑ 4 Mark Martin	1.00
❑ 5 Sterling Marlin	.40
❑ 6 Rusty Wallace	1.00
❑ 7 Bill Elliott	1.00
❑ 8 Bobby Labonte	.75
❑ 9 Dale Jarrett	.75
❑ 10 Bobby Hamilton	.20
❑ 11 Ted Musgrave	.20
❑ 12 Darrell Waltrip	.40
❑ 13 Kyle Petty	.40
❑ 14 Ken Schrader	.20
❑ 15 Michael Waltrip	.20
❑ 16 Derrike Cope	.20
❑ 17 Jeff Burton	.40
❑ 18 Ricky Craven	.20
❑ 19 Steve Grissom	.20
❑ 20 Robert Pressley	.20
❑ 21 Joe Nemechek	.20
❑ 22 Brett Bodine	.20
❑ 23 Jimmy Spencer	.20
❑ 24 Ward Burton	.20
❑ 25 Jeremy Mayfield	.60
❑ 26 Dale Jarrett	.75
❑ 27 Dale Earnhardt	2.00
❑ 28 Jeff Gordon	2.00
❑ 29 Jeff Gordon	2.00
❑ 30 Jeff Gordon	2.00
❑ 31 Terry Labonte	1.00
❑ 32 Rusty Wallace	1.00
❑ 33 Sterling Marlin	.40
❑ 34 Rusty Wallace	1.00
❑ 35 Travis Carter	.10
❑ 36 Bobby Allison	.10
❑ 37 Robert Yates	.10
❑ 38 Larry Hedrick	.10
❑ 39 Cale Yarborough	.10
❑ 40 Bill Ingle	.10
❑ 41 David Smith	.10
❑ 42 Todd Parrott	.10
❑ 43 Charlie Pressley	.10
❑ 44 Donnie Wingo	.10
❑ 45 Eddie Wood	.10
❑ 46 Len Wood	.10
❑ 47 Donnie Richeson	.10
❑ 48 Joe Nemechek Jeff Buice	.10
❑ 49 Charley Pressley Ricky Craven	.10
❑ 50 Donnie Richeson Brett Bodine	.10
❑ 51 Jimmy Fennig Derrike Cope	.10
❑ 52 Todd Parrott Dale Jarrett	.20
❑ 53 Steve Hmiel Mark Martin	.40
❑ 54 Robin Pemberton Rusty Wallace	.40
❑ 55 Bobby Labonte Jimmy Makar	.20
❑ 56 David Smith Dale Earnhardt	1.00
❑ 57 Dale Earnhardt's Transporter	1.00
❑ 58 Kyle Petty's Transporter	.20
❑ 59 Derrike Cope's Transporter	.10
❑ 60 Rusty Wallace's Transporter	.50
❑ 61 Bill Elliott's Transporter	.50
❑ 62 Dale Jarrett's Transporter	.40
❑ 63 Terry Labonte's Transporter	.50
❑ 64 Bobby Labonte's Transporter	.40
❑ 65 Joe Nemechek's Transporter	.10
❑ 66 Steve Grissom's Transporter	.10

Dавid Green.................... .20 .09
Randy Lajoie.................... .20 .09
Curtis Markham.................... .20 .09
Phil Parsons.................... .20 .09
Chad Little.................... .20 .09
Jason Keller.................... .20 .09
Jeff Green.................... .20 .09
Mark Martin.................... 1.00 .45
Steve Grissom.................... .20 .09
Bobby Labonte.................... .75 .35
Checklist.................... .10 .05
Checklist.................... .10 .05

1996 Crown Jewels Elite Emerald

'8-card set is a parallel version of the base Elite set. ards carry an emerald (green) colored foil stamping lifferentiates them from the base Elite cards. The were randomly inserted 1 in 13 packs in regular packs. There is also a Emerald Treasure Chest n. This version is only available in Treasure Chest at a rate of 1 in 13 packs. These cards carry a green amped treasure chest on the front and have been with a multiplier below.

	MINT	NRMT
LETE SET (78)....................	250.00	110.00
ION CARD (1-78)....................	1.25	.55
ION DRIVER (1-78)....................	2.50	1.10

RALD CARDS: 5X TO 12X BASE ELITE CARDS
. T.CHEST SET (78).................... 300.00 135.00
SURE CHEST CARDS: 6X TO 15X BASE ELITE
S

1996 Crown Jewels Elite Sapphire

8-card set is a parallel version of the base Elite set. ards carry a sapphire (blue) colored foil stamping ifferentiates them from the base Elite cards. The were randomly inserted one in seven packs in the r Elite product. There is also a Sapphire Treasure version. This version is only available in Treasure boxes at a rate of one in seven packs. These cards a blue foil stamped treasure chest on the front and een priced with a multiplier below. Another parallel Citrine cards from Diamond Tribute boxes. The carry a yellow foil stamping and were available in nd Tribute packs at a rate of one in seven.

	MINT	NRMT
LETE SET (78)....................	100.00	45.00
ION CARD (1-78)....................	.60	.25
ION DRIVER (1-78)....................	1.25	.55

HIRE CARDS: 2.5X TO 6X BASE ELITE CARDS
T.CHEST SET (78).................... 125.00 55.00
SURE CHEST CARDS: 3X TO 8X BASE ELITE
S
DIAM.TRIB.CITRINE SET (78).. 100.00 45.00
.TRIBUTE CITRINE CARDS: 2.5X TO 6X BASE

1996 Crown Jewels Elite thstones of the Champions

nly inserted in packs at a rate of one in 192, this d set features the active Winston Cup Champions. ard carries the actual birthstone for that driver. The vere seeded in packs of the regular Elite product 1 packs. 375 of each of the base Birthstone of ions were released. There is a Treasure Chest version of each card. The cards carry a treasure ogo and were randomly seeded in Elite Treasure acks at a rate of one in 192. There are 125 of each reasure chest versions.

	MINT	NRMT
ETE SET (6)....................	250.00	110.00
ON CARD (BC1-BC6)....................	15.00	6.75

*SINGLES: 15X TO 40X BASE CARD HI
COMP. T.CHEST SET (6).................... 300.00 135.00
*TREASURE CHEST CARDS: 20X TO 50X BASIC CARDS

❑ BC1 Dale Earnhardt....................	90.00	40.00
❑ BC2 Jeff Gordon....................	90.00	40.00
❑ BC3 Rusty Wallace....................	60.00	27.00
❑ BC4 Darrell Waltrip....................	18.00	8.00
❑ BC5 Bill Elliott....................	60.00	27.00
❑ BC6 Terry Labonte....................	60.00	27.00

1996 Crown Jewels Elite Dual Jewels Amethyst

Randomly inserted in packs at a rate of one in 96, this eight-card set features the top NASCAR drivers on dual sided cards. Each card has basically two front sides. The cards carry an amethyst or purple color foil stamping. There was also a Treasure Chest parallel version of each card. The parallels have a treasure chest logo on them to differentiate them from the base dual jewels cards. These cards were seeded one in 96 Treasure Chest packs.

	MINT	NRMT
COMPLETE SET (8)....................	80.00	36.00
COMMON CARD (DJ1-DJ8)....................	3.00	1.35
COMP. T.CHEST SET (8)....................	100.00	45.00

*TREASURE CHEST CARDS: .5X TO 1.25X BASIC CARD

❑ DJ1 Dale Earnhardt.................... Jeff Gordon	30.00	13.50
❑ DJ2 Dale Jarrett.................... Sterling Marlin	15.00	6.75
❑ DJ3 Terry Labonte.................... Bobby Labonte	15.00	6.75
❑ DJ4 Bill Elliott.................... Mark Martin	15.00	6.75
❑ DJ5 Darrell Waltrip.................... Michael Waltrip	6.00	2.70
❑ DJ6 Bobby Hamilton.................... Richard Petty	6.00	2.70
❑ DJ7 Rusty Wallace.................... Kenny Wallace	15.00	6.75
❑ DJ8 Ward Burton.................... Jeff Burton	6.00	2.70

1996 Crown Jewels Elite Dual Jewels Garnet

Randomly inserted in packs at a rate of one in 48, this eight-card set features the top NASCAR drivers on dual sided cards. Each card has basically two front sides. The cards carry an garnet or reddish brown color foil stamping. There was also a Treasure Chest parallel version of each card. The parallels have a treasure chest logo on them to differentiate them from the base dual jewels cards. These cards were seeded one in 48 Treasure Chest packs.

	MINT	NRMT
COMPLETE SET (8)....................	60.00	27.00
COMMON CARD (DJ1-DJ8)....................	2.00	.90
COMP. T.CHEST SET (8)....................	80.00	36.00

*TREASURE CHEST CARDS: .5X TO 1.25X BASIC CARD

❑ DJ1 Dale Earnhardt.................... Jeff Gordon	20.00	9.00
❑ DJ2 Dale Jarrett.................... Sterling Marlin	10.00	4.50
❑ DJ3 Terry Labonte.................... Bobby Labonte	10.00	4.50
❑ DJ4 Bill Elliott.................... Mark Martin	10.00	4.50
❑ DJ5 Darrell Waltrip.................... Michael Waltrip	4.00	1.80
❑ DJ6 Bobby Hamilton.................... Kyle Petty	4.00	1.80
❑ DJ7 Rusty Wallace.................... Kenny Wallace	10.00	4.50
❑ DJ8 Ward Burton.................... Jeff Burton	4.00	1.80

1996 Crown Jewels Elite Dual Jewels Sapphire

Randomly inserted in packs at a rate of one in 192, this eight-card set features the top NASCAR drivers on dual sided cards. Each card has basically two front sides. The cards carry a sapphire or deep blue color foil stamping. There was also a Treasure Chest parallel version of each card. The parallels have a treasure chest logo on them to differentiate them from the base dual jewels cards. These cards were seeded one in 192 Treasure Chest packs.

	MINT	NRMT
COMPLETE SET (8)....................	150.00	70.00

COMMON CARD (DJ1-DJ8)....................	5.00	2.20
COMP. T. CHEST SET (8)....................	200.00	90.00

*TREASURE CHEST CARDS: .5X TO 1.25X BASIC CARDS

❑ DJ1 Dale Earnhardt.................... Jeff Gordon	50.00	22.00
❑ DJ2 Dale Jarrett.................... Sterling Marlin	25.00	11.00
❑ DJ3 Terry Labonte.................... Bobby Labonte	25.00	11.00
❑ DJ4 Bill Elliott.................... Mark Martin	25.00	11.00
❑ DJ5 Darrell Waltrip.................... Michael Waltrip	10.00	4.50
❑ DJ6 Bobby Hamilton.................... Richard Petty	10.00	4.50
❑ DJ7 Rusty Wallace.................... Kenny Wallace	25.00	11.00
❑ DJ8 Ward Burton.................... Jeff Burton	10.00	4.50

1996 Crown Jewels Elite Earnhardt 7 Gems

Randomly inserted in packs at a rate of one in 384, this card salutes Dale Earnhardt's seven Winston Cup Championships with seven different gemstones. The stones are amethyst, citrine, emerald, peridot, ruby, sapphire, and topaz. The card was available in base elite boxes at a rate of one in 384 packs. There was Treasure Chest parallel version. The only difference in this card is the the treasure chest logo on the front of the card. This card was available in Elite Treasure Chest wax boxes at a rate of one in 384 packs. Finally there is also a seven diamonds version of this card. This card carries seven actual diamonds. The card was only available in Elite Diamond Tribute boxes at a rate of one in 384 packs. There were 300 of this card made.

	MINT	NRMT
Dale Earnhardt Card....................	80.00	36.00
Dale Earnhardt Treasure Chest Card ...	100.00	45.00
Dale Earnhardt 7 Diamonds Card........	250.00	110.00

1996 Crown Jewels Elite Diamond Tribute Crown Signature Amethyst

This 10-card set features the top Winston Cup drivers. The cards carry a facsimile signature across the front and carry an amethyst or purple logo. There were 480 of each card available only in Diamond Tribute boxes at a rate of one in 24 packs. There were also 480 of each card done in two parallel versions, Garnet and Peridot. These cards were randomly inserted in retail boxes at a rate of one in 30 packs.

	MINT	NRMT
COMPLETE SET (10)....................	80.00	36.00
COMMON CARD (CS1-CS10)....................	2.00	.90

*SINGLES: 4X TO 10X BASE CARD HI
COMP. GARNET SET (10).................... 50.00 22.00
*GARNET CARDS: 3X TO 6X BASE CARDS
COMP.PERIDOT SET (10).................... 50.00 22.00
*PERIDOT CARDS: 3X TO 6X BASE CARDS

❑ CS1 Dale Earnhardt....................	25.00	11.00
❑ CS2 Jeff Gordon....................	25.00	11.00
❑ CS3 Rusty Wallace....................	15.00	6.75
❑ CS4 Bill Elliott....................	15.00	6.75
❑ CS5 Terry Labonte....................	15.00	6.75
❑ CS6 Bobby Labonte....................	5.00	2.20
❑ CS7 Ricky Craven....................	2.00	.90
❑ CS8 Sterling Marlin....................	4.00	1.80
❑ CS9 Dale Jarrett....................	12.00	5.50
❑ CS10 Mark Martin....................	15.00	6.75

1996 Crown Jewels Elite Diamond Tribute Diamonds in the Rough Sapphire

This five-card set pays tribute to some of the best up and coming young drivers on the Winston Cup circuit. The cards were available in Diamond Tribute boxes only at a rate of one in 48 packs. There were also two parallel versions, Ruby and Citrine. The parallel versions were available via retail boxes at a rate of one in 60 packs. There are 480 of each version of the Diamonds in the Rough cards.

	MINT	NRMT
COMPLETE SAPPHIRE SET (5)	15.00	6.75
COMMON CARD (DR1-DR5)	3.00	1.35
COMP.RUBY SET (5)	10.00	4.50
*RUBY CARDS: .3X TO .6X BASE CARDS		
COMP.CITRINE SET (5)	10.00	4.50
*CITRINE CARDS: .3X TO .6X BASE CARDS		

❑ DR1 Jeff Burton	6.00	2.70
❑ DR2 Steve Grissom	3.00	1.35
❑ DR3 Ricky Craven	3.00	1.35
❑ DR4 Robert Pressley	3.00	1.35
❑ DR5 Jeremy Mayfield	6.00	2.70

1992 Dayco Series 1

The 1992 set was the first of three releases sponsored by Dayco. The cards in each set are numbered consecutively, although they are most often sold as separate series. The 1992 release features nine drivers pictured with their cars at Daytona. An unnumbered checklist/cover card rounds out the set as the tenth card.

	MINT	NRMT
COMPLETE SET (10)	10.00	4.50
COMMON DRIVER (1-9)	.75	.35

❑ 1 Davey Allison	2.00	.90
❑ 2 Rusty Wallace	2.00	.90
❑ 3 Derrike Cope	.75	.35
❑ 4 Ernie Irvan	.75	.35
❑ 5 Dale Jarrett	1.50	.70
❑ 6 Hut Stricklin	.75	.35
❑ 7 Sterling Marlin	1.00	.45
❑ 8 Morgan Shepherd	.75	.35
❑ 9 Bobby Hamilton	.75	.35
❑ NNO Cover Card Checklist	.75	.35

1993 Dayco Series 2 Rusty Wallace

The 1993 Dayco set highlights the career of Rusty Wallace. The cards are numbered as a continuation of the 1992 Dayco release. Two foil cards are included as well as a checklist on the back of card #11.

	MINT	NRMT
COMPLETE SET (15)	8.00	3.60
COMMON DRIVER (11-25)	.60	.25

❑ 11 Rusty Wallace checklist back	.60	.25
❑ 12 Rusty Wallace's Car Dale Earnhardt's Car	1.00	.45
❑ 13 Rusty Wallace's Car Rick Mears' Car	.60	.25
❑ 14 Rusty Wallace Roger Penske	.60	.25
❑ 15 Rusty Wallace	.60	.25
❑ 16 Mike Wallace Kenny Wallace Rusty Wallace	.60	.25
❑ 17 Rusty Wallace	.60	.25
❑ 18 Rusty Wallace	.60	.25
❑ 19 Rusty Wallace	.60	.25
❑ 20 Rusty Wallace in Pits	.60	.25
❑ 21 Rusty Wallace Buddy Parrott	.60	.25
❑ 22 Rusty Wallace	.60	.25
❑ 23 Rusty Wallace Buddy Parrott Don Miller	.60	.25
❑ 24 Rusty Wallace FOIL	.60	.25
❑ 25 Rusty Wallace's Car FOIL	.60	.25

1994 Dayco Series 3

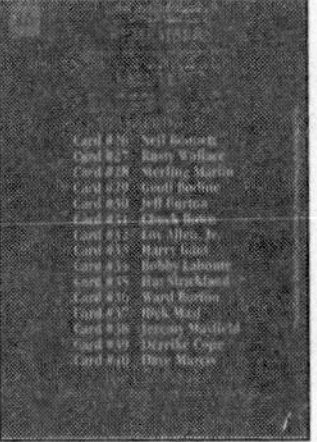

The 1994 set was the last of three releases sponsored by Dayco. The cards are numbered consecutively from series two, although they are most often sold as a separate set. The 1994 release is very similar in design to the 1992 first series and features 14-drivers pictured with their cars at Daytona. Neil Bonnett's card begins the set and includes a checklist cardback.

	MINT	NRMT
COMPLETE SET (15)	10.00	4.50
COMMON CARD (26-40)	.75	.35

❑ 26 Neil Bonnett CL	1.00	.45
❑ 27 Rusty Wallace	1.25	.55
❑ 28 Sterling Marlin	1.00	.45
❑ 29 Geoff Bodine	.75	.35
❑ 30 Jeff Burton	.75	.35
❑ 31 Chuck Bown	.75	.35
❑ 32 Loy Allen Jr.	.75	.35
❑ 33 Harry Gant	1.00	.45
❑ 34 Bobby Labonte	1.00	.45
❑ 35 Hut Stricklin	.75	.35
❑ 36 Ward Burton	.75	.35
❑ 37 Rick Mast	.75	.35
❑ 38 Jeremy Mayfield	.75	.35
❑ 39 Derrike Cope	.75	.35
❑ 40 Dave Marcis	.75	.35

1992 Erin Maxx Trans-Am

This 100-card set was produced by Erin Maxx and features top drivers and cars of SCCA Trans-Am racing. The cards feature color photos of the driver or car on the cardfront with a small driver photo on the cardback.

	MINT	NRMT
COMPLETE SET (100)	18.00	8.00
COMMON CARD (1-100)	.15	.07

❑ 1 Wayne Akers' Car	.15	.07
❑ 2 Wayne Akers	.25	.11
❑ 3 Bobby Archer's Car	.15	.07
❑ 4 Bobby Archer	.25	.11
❑ 5 Tommy Archer's Car	.15	.07
❑ 6 Tommy Archer	.25	.11
❑ 7 Jack Baldwin's Car		.25
❑ 8 Jack Baldwin		.50
❑ 9 Jerry Clinton's Car		.15
❑ 10 Jerry Clinton		.25
❑ 11 Jim Derhaag's Car		.15
❑ 12 Jim Derhaag		.25
❑ 13 Michael Dingman's Car		.15
❑ 14 Michael Dingman		.25
❑ 15 Ron Fellows' Car		.25
❑ 16 Ron Fellows		.50
❑ 17 Paul Gentilozzi's Car		.25
❑ 18 Paul Gentilozzi		.50
❑ 19 Scott Sharp's Car		.25
❑ 20 Scott Sharp		.50
❑ 21 Stuart Hayner's Car		.15
❑ 22 Stuart Hayner		.25
❑ 23 Phil Mahre's Car		.15
❑ 24 Phil Mahre		.25
❑ 25 Steve Mahre's Car		.15
❑ 26 Steve Mahre		.25
❑ 27 Deborah Gregg's Car		.15
❑ 28 Deborah Gregg		.25
❑ 29 Greg Pickett's Car		.15
❑ 30 Greg Pickett		.25
❑ 31 George Robinson's Car		.15
❑ 32 George Robinson		.25
❑ 33 Randy Ruhlman's Car		.15
❑ 34 Randy Ruhlman		.25
❑ 35 Trois-Rivieres		.15
❑ 36 Trois-Rivieres Winners		.15
❑ 37 R.J. Valentine's Car		.15
❑ 38 R.J. Valentine		.25
❑ 39 Tech Inspection		.15
❑ 40 Scott Sharp's Car Wet Racing		.25
❑ 41 Tech Pix		.15
❑ 42 Scott Sharp's Car Series Champion		.25
❑ 43 Wally Owens' Car		.15
❑ 44 Kenwood's Tour De Force		.15
❑ 45 Glenn Fox's Car		.15
❑ 46 Glenn Fox		.25
❑ 47 Courtney Smith's Car		.15
❑ 48 Courtney Smith		.25
❑ 49 Checklist 1-50		.15
❑ 50 Checklist 51-100		.15
❑ 51 John Anderson's Car		.15
❑ 52 Glenn Andrew's Car		.15
❑ 53 Jeff Davis' Car		.15
❑ 54 Peter De Man's Car		.15
❑ 55 Rick Dittman's Car		.15
❑ 56 Mike Downs' Car		.15
❑ 57 Bill Gray's Car		.15
❑ 58 Ed Hinchliff's Car		.15
❑ 59 Steve Anderson's Car		.15
❑ 60 Les Lindley's Car		.15
❑ 61 Bruce Nesbitt's Car		.15
❑ 62 Frank Panzarella's Car		.15
❑ 63 Bob Patch's Car		.15
❑ 64 Mark Pielsticker's Car		.15
❑ 65 Andy Porterfield's Car		.15
❑ 66 Brian Richards' Car		.15
❑ 67 Don Sak's Car		.15
❑ 68 Craig Shafer's Car		.15
❑ 69 Jerry Simmons' Car		.15
❑ 70 Rich Sloma's Car		.15
❑ 73 Scott Sharp Ron Fellows Greg Pickett Mexico Winners		.15
❑ 74 Irv Hoerr Darin Brassfield Greg Pickett Dallas Winners		.15
❑ 75 Scott Sharp Paul Gentilozzi Irv Hoerr George Robinson Les Lindley Dallas Fast Five		.15
❑ 76 Scott Sharp Greg Pickett Paul Gentilozzi Detroit Winners		.15
❑ 77 Scott Sharp Irv Hoerr Jack Baldwin George Robinson Tom Gloy Detroit Fast Five		.15
❑ 78 Irv Hoerr Scott Sharp Stuart Hayner Portland Winners		.15
❑ 79 Irv Hoerr Stuart Hayner Paul Gentilozzi Phil Mahre		.15

Jack Baldwin
Portland Fast Five
Darin Brassfield .... .15 .07
Scott Sharp
Jack Baldwin
Cleveland Winners
Darin Brassfield .... .15 .07
Ron Fellows
Irv Hoerr
Scott Sharp
Jack Baldwin
Cleveland Fast Five
George Robinson .... .15 .07
Jack Baldwin
Les Lindley
Des Moines Winners
Scott Sharp .... .15 .07
Jack Baldwin
Irv Hoerr
Ron Fellows
Darin Brassfield
Des Moines Fast Five
Scott Sharp .... .15 .07
Jack Baldwin
Les Lindley
Watkins Glen Winners
Scott Sharp .... .15 .07
Darin Brassfield
Jack Baldwin
Paul Gentilozzi
Scott Pruett
Watkins Glen Fast Five
Scott Sharp .... .15 .07
Les Lindley
Darin Brassfield
Mosport Winners
Will Moody .... .15 .07
Darin Brassfield .... .15 .07
Paul Gentilozzi
Scott Sharp
Mid Ohio Winners
Scott Sharp .... .15 .07
Ron Fellows
Paul Gentilozzi
Jack Baldwin
Irv Hoerr
Denver Fast Five
Scott Sharp .... .15 .07
Chris Kneifel
Irv Hoerr
R.A. Winners
Scott Sharp .... .15 .07
Chris Kneifel
Bob Sobey
Les Lindley
Darin Brassfield
R.A. Fast Five
ack Baldwin .... .15 .07
Ron Fellows
Scott Sharp
Texas World Winners
aul Gentilozzi .... .15 .07
Steve Petty
Scott Sharp
Darin Brassfield
Irv Hoerr
Texas World Fast Five
ast Five Alumni .... .15 .07
cott Sharp .... .15 .07
Ron Fellows
Jack Baldwin
Fast Five Shootout
uz McCall .... .15 .07
92 Class Picture .... .15 .07
92 Grid .... .15 .07
92 Long Beach Start .... .15 .07
Scott Sharp's Car .... .15 .07
Mosport Win

994 Ernie Irvan Fan Club

e card set was distributed exclusively to members Ernie Irvan Fan Club. The black-bordered cards feature Irvan and family and were sold for $5.00 each through the Club in complete set form. Each card back contains either statistical or biographical information and are unnumbered.

	MINT	NRMT
COMPLETE SET (5)	8.00	3.60
COMMON CARD	1.00	.45
❑ 1 Ernie Irvan	2.00	.90
❑ 2 Ernie Irvan	2.00	.90
❑ 3 Ernie Irvan	2.00	.90
❑ 4 Ernie Irvan	2.00	.90
❑ 5 Ernie Irvan's Car	1.00	.45

1993 Finish Line

Pro Set produced this 180-card set for Finish Line. The set features star drivers, cars and crew members of the top Winston Cup teams from the previous season. Cards were packaged 12 per foil pack with 36 packs per box and in 23-card jumbo packs. Inserts included a Silver parallel set (one per foil pack/two per jumbo), an unnumbered Alan Kulwicki memorial card, as well as a 15-card Davey Allison set (jumbo packs only). A special hologram card featuring Davey Allison (numbered of 5000) was also produced and randomly distributed through foil packs. A factory set was also available through the Finsh Line Racing Club. Each factory set came with a Finish Line binder and sheets and the Davey Allison set was also included.

	MINT	NRMT
COMPLETE SET (180)	10.00	4.50
COMMON CARD (1-180)	.10	.05
COMMON DRIVER (1-180)	.20	.09
❑ 1 Alan Kulwicki	.75	.35
❑ 2 Harry Gant	.40	.18
❑ 3 Ricky Rudd	.40	.18
❑ 4 Darrell Waltrip	.40	.18
❑ 5 Rusty Wallace	1.00	.45
❑ 6 Brett Bodine	.20	.09
❑ 7 Ted Musgrave	.20	.09
❑ 8 Rick Mast	.20	.09
❑ 9 Hut Stricklin	.20	.09
❑ 10 Todd Bodine	.20	.09
❑ 11 Bobby Hillin	.20	.09
❑ 12 Mark Martin's Car	.50	.23
❑ 13 Wally Dallenbach Jr.'s Car	.10	.05
❑ 14 Jeff Gordon's Car	.75	.35
❑ 15 Michael Waltrip's Car	.10	.05
❑ 16 Richard Jackson	.10	.05
❑ 17 Jack Roush	.10	.05
❑ 18 Junior Johnson	.20	.09
❑ 19 Glen Wood	.10	.05
❑ 20 Leo Jackson	.10	.05
❑ 21 George Bradshaw	.10	.05
❑ 22 Rick Mast's Car	.10	.05
❑ 23 Ken Wilson	.10	.05
❑ 24 Don Miller	.10	.05
❑ 25 Donnie Richeson	.10	.05
❑ 26 Doug Richert	.10	.05
❑ 27 Terry Labonte Bobby Labonte	.75	.35
❑ 28 Robert Pressley	.20	.09
❑ 29 Jeff Burton	.20	.09
❑ 30 Chuck Bown	.20	.09
❑ 31 Mike Wallace	.20	.09
❑ 32 Derrike Cope's Car	.10	.05
❑ 33 Gary Nelson	.10	.05
❑ 34 Winston Kelley Dick Brooks Jim Phillips	.10	.05
❑ 35 Danny Myers	.10	.05
❑ 36 Waddell Wilson	.10	.05
❑ 37 Alan Kulwicki	.75	.35
❑ 38 Kyle Petty	.40	.18
❑ 39 Terry Labonte	1.00	.45
❑ 40 Ernie Irvan	.60	.25
❑ 41 Geoff Bodine	.20	.09
❑ 42 Dale Jarrett	.75	.35
❑ 43 Wally Dallenbach Jr.	.20	.09
❑ 44 Jimmy Means	.20	.09
❑ 45 Rusty Wallace's Car	.30	.14
❑ 46 Sterling Marlin's Car	.20	.09
❑ 47 Morgan Shepherd's Car	.10	.05
❑ 48 Davey Allison's Car	.50	.23
❑ 49 Phil Parsons	.20	.09
❑ 50 Bill Stavola	.10	.05
❑ 51 Darrell Waltrip	.40	.18
❑ 52 Chuck Rider	.10	.05
❑ 53 Junie Donlavey	.10	.05
❑ 54 Gary DeHart	.10	.05
❑ 55 Donnie Wingo	.10	.05
❑ 56 Ken Howes	.10	.05
❑ 57 Robin Pemberton	.10	.05
❑ 58 Jeff Hammond	.10	.05
❑ 59 Butch Miller	.20	.09
❑ 60 Ricky Craven	.40	.18
❑ 61 Richard Petty	.50	.23
❑ 62 Joey Knuckles	.10	.05
❑ 63 Donnie Allison	.20	.09
❑ 64 Joe Moore Allen Bestwick	.10	.05
❑ 65 Jim Bown	.10	.05
❑ 66 Davey Allison	1.00	.45
❑ 67 Ricky Rudd	.40	.18
❑ 68 Ernie Irvan	.60	.25
❑ 69 Geoff Bodine	.20	.09
❑ 70 Dick Trickle	.20	.09
❑ 71 Dave Marcis	.20	.09
❑ 72 Rick Wilson	.20	.09
❑ 73 Jimmy Spencer's Car	.10	.05
❑ 74 Ken Schrader's Car	.10	.05
❑ 75 Rick Wilson's Car	.10	.05
❑ 76 Alan Kulwicki	.75	.35
❑ 77 Joe Gibbs	.20	.09
❑ 78 Felix Sabates	.10	.05
❑ 79 Buddy Parrott	.10	.05
❑ 80 Mike Beam	.10	.05
❑ 81 Mike Hill	.10	.05
❑ 82 David Green	.20	.09
❑ 83 Jeff Gordon	2.00	.90
❑ 84 Tom Peck	.20	.09
❑ 85 Richard Petty	.50	.23
❑ 86 Dale Inman	.10	.05
❑ 87 Barney Hall Eli Gold	.10	.05
❑ 88 Pete Wright	.10	.05
❑ 89 Davey Allison	.50	.23
❑ 90 Terry Labonte	1.00	.45
❑ 91 Morgan Shepherd	.20	.09
❑ 92 Ted Musgrave	.20	.09
❑ 93 Jimmy Hensley	.20	.09
❑ 94 Geoff Bodine's Bobsled	.10	.05
❑ 95 Darrell Waltrip's Car	.20	.09
❑ 96 Harry Gant's Car	.10	.05
❑ 97 Rick Hendrick	.10	.05
❑ 98 Bill Davis	.10	.05
❑ 99 Cale Yarborough	.20	.09
❑ 100 Paul Andrews	.10	.05
❑ 101 Ray Evernham	.10	.05
❑ 102 David Fuge	.10	.05
❑ 103 Ward Burton	.20	.09
❑ 104 Jimmy Spencer	.20	.09
❑ 105 Danny Glad	.10	.05
❑ 106 David Smith	.10	.05
❑ 107 Darrell Waltrip	.40	.18
❑ 108 Brett Bodine	.20	.09
❑ 109 Michael Waltrip	.20	.09
❑ 110 Jeff Gordon	2.00	.90
❑ 111 Dale Jarrett's Car	.30	.14
❑ 112 Kenny Wallace's Car	.10	.05
❑ 113 Bobby Allison	.20	.09
❑ 114 Richard Petty	.50	.23
❑ 115 Barry Dodson	.10	.05
❑ 116 Doug Hewitt	.10	.05
❑ 117 Bobby Labonte	.60	.25
❑ 118 Bobby Dotter	.10	.05
❑ 119 Neil Bonnett	.50	.23
❑ 120 Jimmy Fennig	.10	.05
❑ 121 Kyle Petty	.40	.18
❑ 122 Rusty Wallace	1.00	.45
❑ 123 Michael Waltrip	.20	.09
❑ 124 Ernie Irvan's Car	.30	.14
❑ 125 Brett Bodine's Car	.10	.05
❑ 126 Bobby Hamilton's Car	.10	.05
❑ 127 Larry Hedrick	.10	.05
❑ 128 Howard Comstock	.10	.05
❑ 129 Robbie Loomis	.10	.05
❑ 130 Steve Grissom	.20	.09
❑ 131 Shelton Pittman	.10	.05
❑ 132 Jimmy Johnson	.10	.05
❑ 133 Mark Martin	1.00	.45
❑ 134 Ken Schrader	.20	.09
❑ 135 Bobby Labonte	.60	.25
❑ 136 Hut Stricklin's Car	.10	.05
❑ 137 Walter Bud Moore	.10	.05
❑ 138 Tony Glover	.10	.05
❑ 139 Troy Beebe	.10	.05
❑ 140 Tracy Leslie	.10	.05

❑ 141 Will Lind	.10	.05
❑ 142 Harry Gant	.40	.18
❑ 143 Ken Schrader	.20	.09
❑ 144 Ricky Rudd's Car	.20	.09
❑ 145 Bobby Hillin's Car	.10	.05
❑ 146 Billy Hagan	.10	.05
❑ 147 Larry McReynolds	.10	.05
❑ 148 Richard Lasater	.10	.05
❑ 149 Eddie Wood	.10	.05
❑ 150 Sterling Marlin	.40	.18
❑ 151 Kenny Wallace	.20	.09
❑ 152 Larry McClure	.10	.05
❑ 153 Steve Hmiel	.10	.05
❑ 154 Kenny Wallace	.20	.09
❑ 155 Andy Petree	.10	.05
❑ 156 Morgan Shepherd	.20	.09
❑ 157 Geoff Bodine's Car	.10	.05
❑ 158 Robert Yates	.10	.05
❑ 159 Joe Nemechek	.20	.09
❑ 160 Jack Sprague	.10	.05
❑ 161 Kenny Bernstein	.20	.09
❑ 162 Glen Wood Family	.10	.05
❑ 163 Tommy Houston	.20	.09
❑ 164 Mark Martin	1.00	.45
❑ 165 Bobby Labonte's Car	.20	.09
❑ 166 Leonard Wood	.10	.05
❑ 167 Ted Musgrave's Car	.10	.05
❑ 168 Sterling Marlin	.40	.18
❑ 169 Dale Jarrett	.75	.35
❑ 170 Alan Kulwicki's Car	.50	.23
❑ 171 Kyle Petty's Car	.20	.09
❑ 172 Junior Johnson	.20	.09
❑ 173 Joe Gibbs Dale Jarrett	.40	.18
❑ 174 Jimmy Makar	.10	.05
❑ 175 Tim Brewer	.10	.05
❑ 176 Len Wood	.10	.05
❑ 177 Ned Jarrett	.20	.09
❑ 178 Roger Penske	.10	.05
❑ 179 Doug Williams	.10	.05
❑ 180 Hut Stricklin	.20	.09
❑ NNO Alan Kulwicki Memorial	4.00	1.80
❑ NNO Davey Allison HOLO/5000	100.00	45.00

1993 Finish Line Silver

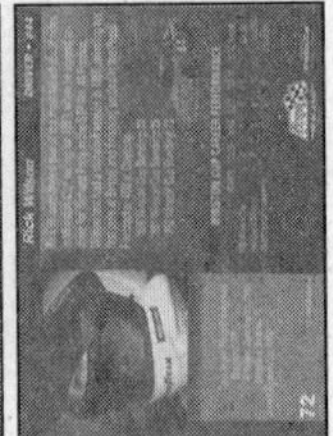

A parallel set to the regular issue 1993 Finish Line set, these cards feature a "Silver Series '93" logo on the front. Cards were packaged one per foil pack and two per jumbo pack.

	MINT	NRMT
COMPLETE SET (180)	70.00	32.00
COMMON CARD (1-180)	.20	.09
COMMON DRIVER (1-180)	.40	.18

*STARS: 1.25X TO 3X BASIC CARDS

1993 Finish Line Davey Allison

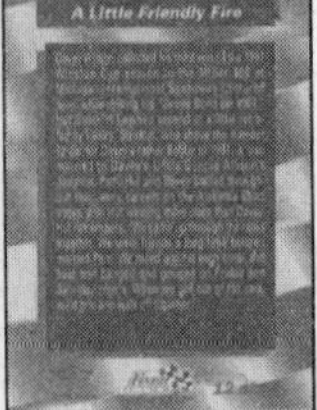

Pro Set produced this 15-card set for Finish Line to honor the 1992 Driver of the Year, Davey Allison. The cards were packaged one per 1993 Finish Line jumbo pack.

	MINT	NRMT
COMPLETE SET (15)	12.00	5.50
COMMON CARD (1-15)	1.00	.45

1993 Finish Line Commemorative Sheets

Produced by Pro Set for Finish Line Racing Club, this 30-sheet, blank backed set features the fronts of six 1993 Finish Line cards. The sheets measure approximately 8-1/2" by 11" and include the Finish Line logo along with sheet number. Although the sheets are individually numbered of 10,000, reportedly less than 2500 sets were actually distributed.

	MINT	NRMT
COMPLETE SET	75.00	34.00
COMMON SHEET (1-30)	2.00	.90
❑ 1 Daytona Dale Jarrett/Joe Gibbs Dale Jarrett's Car Jim Phillips/Dick Brooks/Winston Kelley Jeff Burton Jimmy Makar Mike Wallace	2.00	.90
❑ 2 Rockingham Rusty Wallace Barney Hall/Eli Gold Ernie Irvan UER misspelled Irvin Ward Burton Tony Glover Ray Evernham	4.00	1.80
❑ 3 Richmond Davey Allison Ken Schrader's Car Tom Peck Paul Andrews Ken Schrader Neil Bonnett	4.00	1.80
❑ 4 Atlanta Morgan Shepherd Ricky Rudd's Car Junior Johnson Barry Dodson Glen Wood Family Robert Pressley	2.00	.90
❑ 5 Darlington Dave Marcis Dave Marcis' Car Jimmy Hensley Jack Roush Mark Martin Billy Hagan	4.00	1.80
❑ 6 Bristol Alan Kulwicki Sterling Marlin's Car Joey Knuckles Gary Nelson Roger Penske Chuck Rider	2.50	1.10
❑ 7 North Wilkesboro Donnie Richeson Rick Mast's Car Butch Miller Ricky Rudd Brett Bodine Don Miller	2.50	1.10
❑ 8 Martinsville Geoff Bodine Davey Allison's Car Doug Hewitt Bill Davis Darrell Waltrip Howard Comstock	2.50	1.10
❑ 9 Talladega Harry Gant Rusty Wallace's Car Todd Bodine Bobby Hillin Jr. Bobby Hillin Jr.'s Car Walter Bud Moore	2.50	1.10
❑ 10 Sonoma Dave Fuge Wally Dallenbach Jr.'s Car Jeff Gordon Wally Dallenbach Jr. Bobby Hamilton's Car Danny Myers	5.00	2.20
❑ 11 Charlotte Mark Martin's Car Chuck Bown Jeff Gordon's Car Terry Labonte Bill Stavola Rick Mast	4.00	
❑ 12 Dover Richard Petty Jimmy Spencer's Car Steve Grissom Dale Inman David Smith Jimmy Spencer	2.50	
❑ 13 Pocono Dale Jarrett Michael Waltrip's Car Gary DeHart Dick Trickle Michael Waltrip Ted Musgrave	2.50	
❑ 14 Michigan Kyle Petty Alan Kulwicki's Car Junie Donlavey Robin Pemberton Alan Kulwicki Mike Beam	4.00	
❑ 15 Daytona Felix Sabates Kenny Wallace's Car Mike Hill Joe Gibbs Joe Moore/Allen Bestwick Hut Stricklin	2.00	
❑ 16 New Hampshire Ricky Craven Morgan Shepherd Bobby Labonte Glen Wood Jimmy Means Bobby Labonte's Car	2.50	
❑ 17 Pocono Kenny Wallace Troy Beebe Junior Johnson Richard Jackson Will Lind Ricky Rudd	2.50	
❑ 18 Talladega Darrell Waltrip Leonard Wood Ken Schrader Tim Brewer Geoff Bodine's Car Ned Jarrett	2.00	
❑ 19 Watkins Glen George Bradshaw Bobby Labonte/Terry Labonte Robbie Loomis Waddell Wilson Rick Wilson's Car Sterling Marlin	2.50	
❑ 20 Michigan Phil Parsons Derrike Cope's Car Bobby Allison Larry McClure Andy Petree Davey Allison	4.00	
❑ 21 Bristol Brett Bodine Brett Bodine's Car Rusty Wallace Buddy Parrott Jimmy Johnson Tracy Leslie	4.00	
❑ 22 Darlington Kyle Petty Kyle Petty's Car Cale Yarborough Pete Wright Jeff Hammond Danny Glad	2.50	
❑ 23 Richmond Robert Yates Jeff Gordon Shelton Pittman Michael Waltrip Kenny Bernstein Ken Wilson	5.00	
❑ 24 Dover Ernie Irvan Ernie Irvan's Car Donnie Allison David Green Leo Jackson Bobby Dotter	2.50	

Martinsville	2.00	.90
Ted Musgrave		
Geoff Bodine		
Len Wood		
Donnie Wingo		
Geoff Bodine's Bobsled		
Morgan Shepherd		
North Wilkesboro	2.50	1.10
Harry Gant		
Harry Gant's Car		
Jack Sprague		
Richard Lasater		
Sterling Marlin		
Larry McReynolds		
Charlotte	4.00	1.80
Steve Hmiel		
Mark Martin		
Richard Petty		
Eddie Wood		
Larry Hedrick		
Joe Nemechek		
Rockingham	2.50	1.10
Terry Labonte		
Hut Stricklin's Car		
Dale Jarrett		
Bobby Labonte		
Hut Stricklin		
Doug Williams		
Phoenix	2.50	1.10
Richard Petty		
Rick Wilson		
Ken Howes		
Jim Bown		
Jimmy Fennig		
Kenny Wallace		
Atlanta	4.00	1.80
Alan Kulwicki		
Darrell Waltrip's Car		
Rick Hendrick		
Darrell Waltrip		
Doug Richert		
Tommy Houston		

1994 Finish Line

e first time Finish Line produced their own NASCAR 1994. The 150-card set was packaged in 12-card and retail foil packs and 23-card jumbo packs. included a Silver parallel set, along with six other inish Line once again included unnumbered tribute that featured Jeff Gordon, Hermie Sadler, Harry nd a large (5" by 7") Sterling Marlin card.

	MINT	NRMT
LETE SET (150)	10.00	4.50
ON CARD (1-150)	.10	.05
ON DRIVER (1-150)	.20	.09

rry Gant	.40	.18
ck Mast	.20	.09
ally Dallenbach Jr.'s Car	.10	.05
off Bodine's Car	.10	.05
ddy Parrott	.10	.05
rney Hall	.10	.05
ark Martin	1.00	.45
avis Carter	.10	.05
d Jarrett	.10	.05
rnie Irvan	.40	.18
yle Petty	.40	.18
ut Stricklin	.20	.09
mmy Makar	.10	.05
ohn Andretti	.20	.09
obby Hillin	.20	.09
mmy Hensley	.20	.09
erry Labonte's Car	.50	.23
enny Wallace	.20	.09
ed Musgrave's Car	.10	.05
ale Jarrett	.75	.35
terling Marlin	.40	.18
i Gold	.10	.05
ave Marcis	.40	.18
ake Speed	.20	.09
ary DeHart	.10	.05

❑ 26 Bobby Labonte	.60	.25
❑ 27 Ken Schrader	.20	.09
❑ 28 Kyle Petty's Car	.20	.09
❑ 29 Rusty Wallace	1.00	.45
❑ 30 Steve Grissom	.20	.09
❑ 31 Ernie Irvan	.40	.18
❑ 32 Michael Waltrip	.20	.09
❑ 33 Doug Hewitt	.10	.05
❑ 34 Jimmy Means	.20	.09
❑ 35 Hut Stricklin	.20	.09
❑ 36 Jeff Gordon	2.00	.90
❑ 37 Morgan Shepherd's Car	.10	.05
❑ 38 Terry Labonte	1.00	.45
❑ 39 Geoff Bodine	.20	.09
❑ 40 Darrell Waltrip's Car	.20	.09
❑ 41 Pete Wright	.10	.05
❑ 42 Morgan Shepherd	.20	.09
❑ 43 Michael Waltrip's Car	.10	.05
❑ 44 Bobby Hillin	.20	.09
❑ 45 Jeff Burton's Car	.20	.09
❑ 46 Ken Wilson	.10	.05
❑ 47 Donnie Wingo	.10	.05
❑ 48 Greg Sacks	.20	.09
❑ 49 Junior Johnson	.20	.09
❑ 50 Rick Mast	.20	.09
❑ 51 Lake Speed's Car	.10	.05
❑ 52 Ernie Irvan's Car	.20	.09
❑ 53 Rick Hendrick	.10	.05
❑ 54 Leo Jackson	.10	.05
❑ 55 Ray Evernham	.40	.18
❑ 56 Ken Schrader's Car	.10	.05
❑ 57 Neil Bonnett	.50	.23
❑ 58 Richard Petty OWN	.50	.23
❑ 59 Chuck Rider	.10	.05
❑ 60 Kyle Petty	.40	.18
❑ 61 Brett Bodine	.20	.09
❑ 62 Jimmy Spencer	.20	.09
❑ 63 Bobby Labonte's Car	.40	.18
❑ 64 Richard Petty	.50	.23
❑ 65 Ricky Rudd	.40	.18
❑ 66 Steve Hmiel	.10	.05
❑ 67 Dale Jarrett	.75	.35
❑ 68 Brett Bodine's Car	.10	.05
❑ 69 Lake Speed	.20	.09
❑ 70 Kenny Bernstein	.20	.09
❑ 71 Larry McReynolds	.10	.05
❑ 72 Robin Pemberton	.10	.05
❑ 73 Ricky Rudd	.40	.18
❑ 74 Rusty Wallace	1.00	.45
❑ 75 Jeff Gordon	2.00	.90
❑ 76 Loy Allen Jr.	.20	.09
❑ 77 Loy Allen Jr.'s Car	.10	.05
❑ 78 Dale Jarrett	.75	.35
❑ 79 Harry Gant	.40	.18
❑ 80 Morgan Shepherd	.20	.09
❑ 81 Mike Beam	.10	.05
❑ 82 Sterling Marlin's Car	.20	.09
❑ 83 Glen Wood	.10	.05
❑ 84 Kyle Petty	.40	.18
❑ 85 Mark Martin	1.00	.45
❑ 86 Joe Nemechek	.20	.09
❑ 87 Mike Wallace	.20	.09
❑ 88 Barry Dodson	.10	.05
❑ 89 Wally Dallenbach Jr.	.20	.09
❑ 90 Rusty Wallace	1.00	.45
❑ 91 Ricky Rudd's Car	.20	.09
❑ 92 Jack Roush	.10	.05
❑ 93 Ken Schrader	.20	.09
❑ 94 Len Wood	.10	.05
Eddie Wood		
❑ 95 Dale Inman	.10	.05
❑ 96 Roger Penske	.10	.05
❑ 97 Donnie Richeson	.10	.05
❑ 98 Mike Hill	.10	.05
❑ 99 Mark Martin's Car	.50	.23
❑ 100 Jerry Punch	.10	.05
❑ 101 Jimmy Hensley	.20	.09
❑ 102 Darrell Waltrip	.40	.18
❑ 103 Brett Bodine	.20	.09
❑ 104 Rusty Wallace's Car	.50	.23
❑ 105 Tony Glover	.10	.05
❑ 106 Ward Burton's Car	.10	.05
❑ 107 Ted Musgrave	.20	.09
❑ 108 Todd Bodine	.20	.09
❑ 109 Dale Jarrett's Car	.40	.18
❑ 110 Leonard Wood	.10	.05
❑ 111 Jimmy Spencer	.20	.09
❑ 112 Ernie Irvan	.40	.18
❑ 113 Jeff Burton	.20	.09
❑ 114 Jeff Hammond	.10	.05
❑ 115 Ward Burton	.20	.09
❑ 116 Ken Schrader	.20	.09
❑ 117 Butch Mock	.10	.05
❑ 118 Derrike Cope	.20	.09
❑ 119 Robert Yates	.10	.05
❑ 120 Benny Parsons	.10	.05
❑ 121 Jimmy Spencer's Car	.10	.05
❑ 122 Morgan Shepherd	.20	.09
❑ 123 Jeff Gordon 's Car	1.00	.45
❑ 124 Terry Labonte	1.00	.45
❑ 125 Joe Gibbs	.20	.09
❑ 126 Mark Martin	1.00	.45
❑ 127 Hut Stricklin's Car	.10	.05
❑ 128 Bobby Labonte	.60	.25
❑ 129 Darrell Waltrip	.40	.18
❑ 130 Walter Bud Moore	.10	.05
❑ 131 Robbie Loomis	.20	.09
❑ 132 Bobby Allison	.20	.09
❑ 133 Ken Howes	.10	.05
❑ 134 Michael Waltrip	.20	.09
❑ 135 Ricky Rudd	.40	.18
❑ 136 Jimmy Johnson	.10	.05
❑ 137 Jimmy Spencer	.20	.09
❑ 138 Harry Gant	.40	.18
❑ 139 Jimmy Fennig	.10	.05
❑ 140 Derrike Cope	.20	.09
❑ 141 Geoff Bodine	.20	.09
❑ 142 Felix Sabates	.10	.05
❑ 143 Cale Yarborough	.20	.09
❑ 144 Junie Donlavey	.10	.05
❑ 145 Sterling Marlin	.40	.18
❑ 146 Richard Broome	.10	.05
❑ 147 Chuck Bown	.20	.09
❑ 148 Larry McClure	.10	.05
❑ 149 Ted Musgrave	.10	.05
❑ 150 Wally Dallenbach Jr.	.20	.09
❑ NNO Jeff Gordon ROY	5.00	2.20
❑ NNO Hermie Sadler ROY	2.00	.90
❑ NNO Harry Gant Last Ride	3.00	1.35
❑ NNO Sterling Marlin 5X7	3.00	1.35

1994 Finish Line Silver

A parallel set to the regular issue 1994 Finish Line set, these cards feature a "94 Silver" logo on the front printed in silver foil. Cards were packaged one per foil pack and two per jumbo pack.

	MINT	NRMT
COMPLETE SET (150)	60.00	27.00
COMMON CARD (1-150)	.25	.11
COMMON DRIVER (1-150)	.50	.23

*STARS: 2.5X TO 5X BASIC CARDS

1994 Finish Line Neil Bonnett

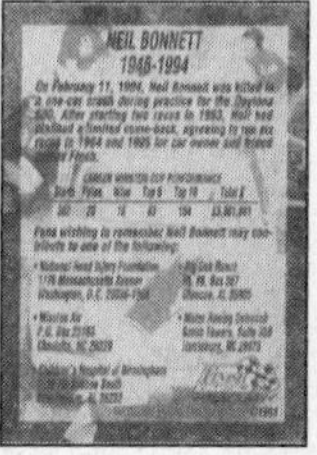

Neil Bonnett is the focus of this five-card set randomly inserted in 1994 Finish Line retail packs. All five cards are unnumbered.

	MINT	NRMT
COMPLETE SET (5)	6.00	2.70
COMMON CARD	1.50	.70

1994 Finish Line Busch Grand National

Finish Line produced this 15-card insert set that focuses on up-and-coming drivers from Busch Series racing. The cards were randomly packed in all types of 1994 Finish Line racing packs. The odds of pulling a BGN card from a regular pack or a jumbo pack was one in eight packs.

	MINT	NRMT
COMPLETE SET (15)	12.00	5.50
COMMON CARD (BGN1-BGN15)	.75	.35

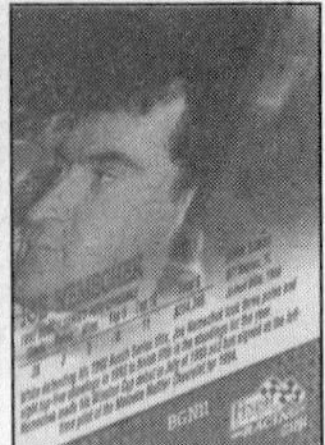

❑ BGN1 David Green	.75	.35
❑ BGN2 Jeff Burton	1.25	.55
❑ BGN3 Bobby Dotter	.75	.35
❑ BGN4 Todd Bodine	.75	.35
❑ BGN5 Hermie Sadler	.75	.35
❑ BGN6 Tom Peck	.75	.35
❑ BGN7 Tracy Leslie	.75	.35
❑ BGN8 Ricky Craven	1.50	.70
❑ BGN9 Chuck Bown	.75	.35
❑ BGN10 Steve Grissom	1.25	.55
❑ BGN11 Joe Nemechek	1.25	.55
❑ BGN12 Robert Pressley	1.25	.55
❑ BGN13 Rodney Combs	.75	.35
❑ BGN14 Ward Burton	1.25	.55
❑ BGN15 Mike Wallace	.75	.35

1994 Finish Line Down Home

This 10-card set was produced by Finish Line for insertion in its 1994 racing product. The cards focus on drivers from small towns with information about the driver as well as their hometown. The cards were randomly inserted in all types of 1994 Finish Line racing packs. The cards were seeded in packs at a rate of one in eight packs.

	MINT	NRMT
COMPLETE SET (10)	12.00	5.50
COMMON CARD (1-10)	.60	.25

*SINGLES: 1.25X TO 3X BASE CARD HI

❑ 1 Harry Gant	1.25	.55
❑ 2 Ernie Irvan	1.25	.55
❑ 3 Dale Jarrett	1.25	.55
❑ 4 Mark Martin	1.25	.55
❑ 5 Kyle Petty	1.25	.55
❑ 6 Ricky Rudd	1.25	.55
❑ 7 Ken Schrader	.60	.25
❑ 8 Morgan Shepherd	.60	.25
❑ 9 Jimmy Spencer	.60	.25
❑ 10 Rusty Wallace	1.25	.55

1994 Finish Line Gold Signature

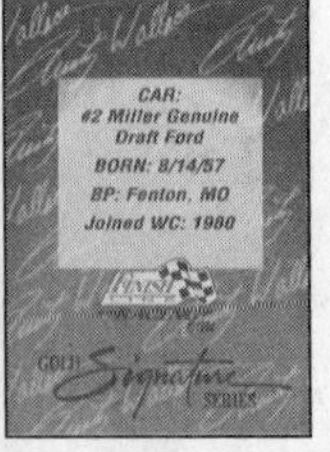

Gold foil signatures adorn the fronts of these 5 cards randomly inserted in 1994 Finish Line hobby packs. Backs feature a short driver bio and the set title "Gold Signature Series." Odds of finding a Gold Signature card was one in 20 packs. The cards are unnumbered and have been listed below in alphabetical order.

	MINT	NRMT
COMPLETE SET (5)	30.00	13.50
COMMON CARD	4.00	1.80

*SINGLES: 4X TO 10X BASE CARD HI

❑ NNO Ernie Irvan	4.00	1.80
❑ NNO Dale Jarrett	4.00	1.80
❑ NNO Mark Martin	4.00	1.80
❑ NNO Kyle Petty	4.00	1.80
❑ NNO Rusty Wallace	4.00	1.80

1994 Finish Line New Stars on the Horizon

Finish Line produced this eight-card insert set that focuses on 1994 Winston Cup rookies. The cards were randomly packed in all types of 1994 Finish Line racing packs. The cards could be pulled at a rate of one in eight packs.

	MINT	NRMT
COMPLETE SET (8)	8.00	3.60
COMMON CARD (1-8)	.75	.35

❑ 1 John Andretti	1.50	.70
❑ 2 Todd Bodine	.75	.35
❑ 3 Chuck Bown	.75	.35
❑ 4 Jeff Burton	1.50	.70
❑ 5 Ward Burton	1.50	.70
❑ 6 Steve Grissom	1.50	.70
❑ 7 Joe Nemechek	1.50	.70
❑ 8 Loy Allen Jr.	.75	.35

1994 Finish Line Victory Lane

Finish Line produced this 18-card insert set that focuses on 1993 race winners. The cards were inserted one per 1994 Finish Line special retail jumbo pack and one every eight regular packs. The cards were printed on silver foil card stock.

	MINT	NRMT
COMPLETE SET (18)	30.00	13.50
COMMON CARD (VL1-VL18)	1.00	.45

*SINGLES: 2X TO 5X BASE CARD HI

❑ VL1 Davey Allison VL	2.00	.90
❑ VL2 Geoff Bodine	1.00	.45
❑ VL3 Ernie Irvan VL	2.00	.90
❑ VL4 Dale Jarrett	2.00	.90
❑ VL5 Mark Martin VL	2.00	.90
❑ VL6 Kyle Petty	2.00	.90
❑ VL7 Morgan Shepherd	1.00	.45
❑ VL8 Ricky Rudd	2.00	.90
❑ VL9 Rusty Wallace VL	2.00	.90
❑ VL10 Rusty Wallace	2.00	.90
❑ VL11 Ricky Rudd	2.00	.90
❑ VL12 Morgan Shepherd	1.00	.45
❑ VL13 Kyle Petty	2.00	.90
❑ VL14 Mark Martin	2.00	.90
❑ VL15 Dale Jarrett	2.00	.90
❑ VL16 Davey Allison	2.00	.90
❑ VL17 Geoff Bodine	1.00	.45
❑ VL18 Ernie Irvan	2.00	.90

1994 Finish Line Gold

Finish Line produced their first premium NASCAR set in 1994 -- Finish Line Gold. The 100-card set was packaged in 8-card packs with 32 packs per box in 2,500 numbered

12 box cases. Inserts included an Autograph se
Calling Cards and a Teamwork set. Finish Line produ
special Ernie Irvan hologram card (numbered of 3
randomly inserted in packs. The three promo cards
at the end of the set came packaged in together in a
pack. They were distributed to dealers and membe
the media.

	MINT	N
COMPLETE SET (100)	15.00	
COMMON CARD (1-100)	.10	
COMMON DRIVER (1-100)	.20	

❑ 1 Joe Gibbs	.20
❑ 2 Hut Stricklin's Car	.10
❑ 3 Ricky Rudd's Car	.20
❑ 4 Sterling Marlin	.40
❑ 5 Hut Stricklin	.20
❑ 6 Lake Speed	.20
❑ 7 Kyle Petty	.40
❑ 8 Ernie Irvan	.40
❑ 9 Dale Jarrett	.75
❑ 10 Rusty Wallace	1.00
❑ 11 Jeff Gordon	2.00
❑ 12 Michael Waltrip	.20
❑ 13 Darrell Waltrip	.40
❑ 14 Mark Martin	1.00
❑ 15 Morgan Shepherd	.20
❑ 16 Rusty Wallace's Car	.50
❑ 17 Robert Pressley	.20
❑ 18 Ted Musgrave	.20
❑ 19 Ken Schrader	.20
❑ 20 Wally Dallenbach Jr.'s Car	.10
❑ 21 Geoff Bodine	.20
❑ 22 Kyle Petty	.40
❑ 23 Brett Bodine's Car	.10
❑ 24 Rusty Wallace	1.00
❑ 25 Brett Bodine	.20
❑ 26 Robert Yates	.10
❑ 27 Morgan Shepherd	.20
❑ 28 Jeff Gordon	2.00
❑ 29 Terry Labonte	1.00
❑ 30 Darrell Waltrip's Car	.20
❑ 31 Darrell Waltrip	.40
❑ 32 Bobby Labonte's Car	.40
❑ 33 Terry Labonte	1.00
❑ 34 Ricky Rudd	.40
❑ 35 Ken Schrader	.20
❑ 36 Harry Gant	.40
❑ 37 Kenny Wallace	.20
❑ 38 Dale Jarrett	.75
❑ 39 Geoff Bodine	.20
❑ 40 Morgan Shepherd's Car	.10
❑ 41 Harry Gant	.40
❑ 42 Jimmy Spencer	.20
❑ 43 Ernie Irvan	.40
❑ 44 Ricky Craven	.40
❑ 45 Lake Speed	.20
❑ 46 Ernie Irvan's Car	.20
❑ 47 Terry Labonte's Car	.50
❑ 48 Mark Martin	1.00
❑ 49 Ricky Rudd	.40
❑ 50 Ted Musgrave	.20
❑ 51 Sterling Marlin's Car	.20
❑ 52 Harry Gant	.40
❑ 53 Jimmy Spencer	.20
❑ 54 Geoff Bodine	.20
❑ 55 Ted Musgrave	.20
❑ 56 Felix Sabates Chany Sabates	.10
❑ 57 Ricky Rudd	.40
❑ 58 Kyle Petty's Car	.20
❑ 59 Rusty Wallace	1.00
❑ 60 Jeff Gordon	2.00
❑ 61 Jack Roush	.10
❑ 62 Michael Waltrip	.20
❑ 63 Geoff Bodine's Car	.10
❑ 64 Darrell Waltrip	.40
❑ 65 Jeff Gordon 's Car	1.00
❑ 66 Darrell Waltrip	.40
❑ 67 Hut Stricklin	.20
❑ 68 Rusty Wallace	1.00
❑ 69 Morgan Shepherd	.20
❑ 70 Sterling Marlin	.40

<yle Petty	.40	.18
Mark Martin	1.00	.45
Hut Stricklin	.20	.09
Michael Waltrip's Car	.10	.05
)ale Jarrett	.75	.35
<en Schrader	.20	.09
Terry Labonte	1.00	.45
Hermie Sadler	.20	.09
Mark Martin's Car	.50	.23
Ernie Irvan	.40	.18
Mark Martin	1.00	.45
3rett Bodine	.20	.09
Richard Petty	.75	.35
Michael Waltrip	.20	.09
<yle Petty	.40	.18
.ake Speed's Car	.10	.05
<en Schrader's Car	.10	.05
Jeff Gordon	2.00	.90
)ale Jarrett	.75	.35
Jimmy Spencer	.20	.09
Harry Gant	.40	.18
)avid Green	.20	.09
Ernie Irvan	.40	.18
Ricky Rudd	.40	.18
)ale Jarrett's Car	.40	.18
.ake Speed	.20	.09
Jimmy Spencer's Car	.10	.05
Morgan Shepherd	.20	.09
Brett Bodine	.20	.09
Sterling Marlin	.40	.18
Ernie Irvan Hologram	60.00	27.00

numbered of 3000

1994 Finish Line Gold Autographs

en drivers and crew members signed copies of their r 1994 Finish Line Gold cards to be randomly d into packs (approximately one per box). The aphs were signed using a gold paint pen and to less than 2000 copies of each card.

	MINT	NRMT
.ETE SET (19)	300.00	135.00
ON AUTO	8.00	3.60
ON DRIVER	15.00	6.75
ke Speed	15.00	6.75
organ Shepherd	15.00	6.75
uddy Parrott	8.00	3.60
obert Pressley	15.00	6.75
erry Labonte	50.00	22.00
enny Wallace	15.00	6.75
ale Jarrett	40.00	18.00
icky Craven	30.00	13.50
ony Glover	8.00	3.60
ay Evernham	8.00	3.60
en Schrader	15.00	6.75
ermie Sadler	15.00	6.75
rnie Irvan	30.00	13.50
ark Martin	50.00	22.00
ichael Waltrip	15.00	6.75
avid Green	15.00	6.75
icky Rudd	30.00	13.50
mmy Makar	8.00	3.60
rett Bodine	15.00	6.75

1994 Finish Line Gold Calling Cards

first time in racing, prepaid calling cards were d in card packs with this set. Each card had a value of $2.50 and was printed on the usual plastic imilar to a credit card. The cards are numbered of and carried an expiration date of 12/31/95. Phone with the pin number revealed are generally worth .50X of a Mint unscratched cards.

	MINT	NRMT
ETE SET (9)	12.00	5.50
ON CARD	.60	.25

ES: 1.25X TO 3X BASE CARD HI

❑ NNO Geoff Bodine	.60	.25
❑ NNO Jeff Gordon	1.25	.55
❑ NNO Ernie Irvan	1.25	.55
❑ NNO Dale Jarrett	1.25	.55
❑ NNO Kyle Petty	1.25	.55
❑ NNO Ricky Rudd	1.25	.55
❑ NNO Darrell Waltrip	1.25	.55
❑ NNO Mark Martin	1.25	.55
❑ NNO Rusty Wallace	1.25	.55

1994 Finish Line Gold Teamwork

Teamwork cards were randomly inserted in 1994 Finish Line Gold at a rate of one per eight packs. Each card features a top Winston Cup NASCAR driver along with their crew chief and were printed on gold foil stock.

	MINT	NRMT
COMPLETE SET (10)	20.00	9.00
COMMON CARD (TG1-TG10)	.75	.35

*SINGLES: 1.5X TO 4X BASE CARD HI

❑ TG1 Rusty Wallace Buddy Parrott	.75	.35
❑ TG2 Mark Martin Steve Hmiel	.75	.35
❑ TG3 Ricky Rudd Bill Ingle	.75	.35
❑ TG4 Dale Jarrett Jimmy Makar	.75	.35
❑ TG5 Morgan Shepherd Leonard Wood	.75	.35
❑ TG6 Jeff Gordon Ray Evernham	.75	.35
❑ TG7 Ernie Irvan Larry McReynolds	.75	.35
❑ TG8 Brett Bodine Donnie Richeson	.75	.35
❑ TG9 Geoff Bodine Paul Andrews	.75	.35
❑ TG10 Darrell Waltrip Barry Dodson	.75	.35

1995 Finish Line

Classic produced this 1995 set for Finish Line. The 120-card set was packaged in 10-card hobby and 10-card retail foil packs with 36-packs per box. Hobby cases were numbered sequentially to 1995. Inserts included Silver foil and Printer's Proof parallel sets, along with four others. Hobby and retail pack versions differed according to which inserts could be found. Two different Dale Earnhardt autographed cards, one for hobby and one for retail packs, were also randomly inserted. Each signed card was numbered of 250. Other than the signature the cards are the same as card #89 in the set. There have also been reports that Sam's Club got some of the autographed cards in 1996.

	MINT	NRMT
COMPLETE SET (120)	12.00	5.50
COMMON CARD (1-120)	.10	.05
COMMON DRIVER (1-120)	.20	.09

❑ 1 Dale Earnhardt	2.00	.90
❑ 2 Rusty Wallace	1.00	.45
❑ 3 Darrell Waltrip	.40	.18
❑ 4 Sterling Marlin	.40	.18
❑ 5 Terry Labonte	1.00	.45
❑ 6 Mark Martin	1.00	.45
❑ 7 Geoff Bodine	.20	.09
❑ 8 Jeff Burton	.20	.09
❑ 9 Jimmy Spencer	.20	.09
❑ 10 Ricky Rudd	.40	.18
❑ 11 Brett Bodine	.20	.09
❑ 12 Bobby Allison	.20	.09
❑ 13 John Andretti Nancy Andretti	.20	.09
❑ 14 Rick Hendrick	.10	.05
❑ 15 Robert Gee	.10	.05
❑ 16 Ted Musgrave	.20	.09
❑ 17 Darrell Waltrip	.40	.18
❑ 18 Dale Jarrett	.75	.35
❑ 19 Kenny Wallace	.20	.09
❑ 20 David Green	.20	.09
❑ 21 Morgan Shepherd	.20	.09
❑ 22 Rick Mast	.20	.09
❑ 23 Chad Little	.20	.09
❑ 24 Jeff Gordon Brooke Sealy	2.00	.90
❑ 25 Ken Schrader	.20	.09
❑ 26 Steve Kinser Kenny Bernstein	.20	.09
❑ 27 Sterling Marlin	.40	.18
❑ 28 Ernie Irvan	.30	.14
❑ 29 Geoff Bodine	.20	.09
❑ 30 Michael Waltrip Elizabeth Waltrip	.20	.09
❑ 31 Ward Burton	.20	.09
❑ 32 Jeremy Mayfield	.60	.25
❑ 33 Robert Pressley	.20	.09
❑ 34 Rusty Wallace	1.00	.45
❑ 35 Todd Bodine	.20	.09
❑ 36 Paul Andrews	.10	.05
❑ 37 Dale Jarrett	.75	.35
❑ 38 Morgan Shepherd	.20	.09
❑ 39 Joe Nemechek Andrea Nemechek	.20	.09
❑ 40 Felix Sabates	.10	.05
❑ 41 Ricky Craven	.40	.18
❑ 42 Kyle Petty	.40	.18
❑ 43 Richard Petty	.50	.23
❑ 44 Robert Yates	.10	.05
❑ 45 Hermie Sadler	.20	.09
❑ 46 Johnny Benson	.20	.09
❑ 47 Ken Schrader	.20	.09
❑ 48 Steve Grissom	.20	.09
❑ 49 Bobby Dotter	.20	.09
❑ 50 Dick Trickle	.20	.09
❑ 51 Ernie Irvan Jordan Irvan	.40	.18
❑ 52 Kyle Petty	.40	.18
❑ 53 Jeff Gordon	2.00	.90
❑ 54 Mark Martin	1.00	.45
❑ 55 Morgan Shepherd	.20	.09
❑ 56 Ward Burton	.20	.09
❑ 57 Jimmy Makar	.10	.05
❑ 58 Darrell Waltrip	.40	.18
❑ 59 Walter Bud Moore	.10	.05
❑ 60 Rick Mast	.20	.09
❑ 61 Michael Waltrip	.20	.09
❑ 62 Derrike Cope	.20	.09
❑ 63 Buddy Parrott	.10	.05
❑ 64 Lake Speed	.20	.09
❑ 65 Ray Evernham	.10	.05
❑ 66 Steve Hmiel	.10	.05
❑ 67 Jeff Gordon Ray Evernham	1.00	.45
❑ 68 Brett Bodine	.20	.09
❑ 69 Terry Labonte	1.00	.45
❑ 70 Rusty Wallace	1.00	.45
❑ 71 Larry Pearson	.10	.05
❑ 72 Ted Musgrave	.20	.09
❑ 73 Kyle Petty	.40	.18
❑ 74 John Andretti	.20	.09
❑ 75 Todd Bodine Lynn Bodine	.20	.09
❑ 76 Joe Nemechek	.20	.09
❑ 77 Jimmy Spencer	.20	.09
❑ 78 Brett Bodine	.20	.09

❑ 79 Mark Martin	1.00	.45
❑ 80 Harry Gant	.40	.18
❑ 81 Lake Speed	.20	.09
❑ 82 Larry McReynolds	.10	.05
❑ 83 Ricky Rudd	.40	.18
❑ 84 Loy Allen Jr.	.20	.09
❑ 85 Travis Carter	.10	.05
❑ 86 Mike Wallace	.20	.09
❑ 87 Geoff Bodine	.20	.09
❑ 88 Dennis Setzer	.20	.09
❑ 89 Dale Earnhardt	2.00	.90
❑ 90 Mike Wallace	.20	.09
❑ 91 Bobby Labonte	.75	.35
❑ 92 Ernie Irvan	.40	.18
❑ 93 Jeff Burton	.20	.09
❑ 94 Sterling Marlin	.40	.18
❑ 95 Michael Waltrip	.20	.09
❑ 96 Tim Fedewa	.20	.09
❑ 97 Terry Labonte	1.00	.45
❑ 98 Jeremy Mayfield	.60	.25
❑ 99 Bill Ingle	.10	.05
❑ 100 Ken Schrader	.20	.09
❑ 101 Tony Glover	.10	.05
❑ 102 Todd Bodine	.20	.09
❑ 103 Bobby Labonte	.75	.35
❑ 104 Richard Petty	.50	.23
❑ 105 Jeff Gordon	2.00	.90
❑ 106 Ricky Rudd	.40	.18
❑ 107 A.G. Dillard	.10	.05
❑ 108 Junior Johnson	.20	.09
❑ 109 Steve Grissom	.20	.09
❑ 110 Dale Jarrett	.75	.35
❑ 111 Dale Earnhardt	2.00	.90
❑ 112 Kenny Wallace	.20	.09
❑ 113 Jimmy Johnson	.10	.05
❑ 114 Dave Marcis	.40	.18
❑ 115 Kenny Bernstein	.20	.09
❑ 116 Bobby Hamilton	.20	.09
❑ 117 Steve Kinser	.20	.09
❑ 118 John Andretti	.20	.09
❑ 119 Derrike Cope	.20	.09
❑ 120 Ricky Craven	.40	.18
❑ 89AUH Dale Earnhardt AU/250 Red Hobby	250.00	110.00
❑ 89AUR Dale Earnhardt AU/250 Blue Retail	250.00	110.00

1995 Finish Line Printer's Proof

A parallel to the regular 1995 Finish Line set, these cards feature a red foil "Printer's Proof" logo on the cardfront along with the numbering "One of 398." The cards were inserted in hobby packs only with wrapper stated odds of 1:18 packs.

	MINT	NRMT
COMPLETE SET (120)	600.00	275.00
COMMON CARD (1-120)	2.00	.90
COMMON DRIVER (1-120)	4.00	1.80

*STARS 15X TO X BASIC CARDS

1995 Finish Line Silver

A parallel set to the regular issue 1995 Finish Line set, these cards feature a "95 Silver" logo on the front printed in silver foil. Cards were packaged one per foil pack in both hobby and retail versions.

	MINT	NRMT
COMPLETE SET (120)	30.00	13.50
COMMON CARD (1-120)	.20	.09
COMMON DRIVER (1-120)	.40	.18

*STARS 2.5X TO 4X BASIC CARDS

1995 Finish Line Dale Earnhardt

Randomly inserted in 1995 Finish Line packs, these 10 cards feaured Dale Earnhardt and were printed using Classic's micro-lined printing technology. Wrapper stated odds for pulling one of the cards was 1:18.

	MINT	NRMT
COMPLETE SET (10)	80.00	36.00
COMMON CARD (DE1-DE10)	8.00	3.60

1995 Finish Line Gold Signature

Cards from this 16-card set were randomly inserted in 1995 Finish Line retail packs. Each card was numbered one of 1995. The cards could be found at a rate of one per nine retail packs.

	MINT	NRMT
COMPLETE SET (16)	200.00	90.00
COMMON CARD (GS1-GS16)	6.00	2.70

*SINGLES: 12X TO 30X BASE CARD HI

❑ GS1 Jeff Gordon	12.00	5.50
❑ GS2 Rusty Wallace	12.00	5.50
❑ GS3 Dale Earnhardt	12.00	5.50
❑ GS4 Sterling Marlin	12.00	5.50
❑ GS5 Terry Labonte	12.00	5.50
❑ GS6 Mark Martin	12.00	5.50
❑ GS7 Geoff Bodine	6.00	2.70
❑ GS8 Ken Schrader	6.00	2.70
❑ GS9 Kyle Petty	12.00	5.50
❑ GS10 Ricky Rudd	12.00	5.50
❑ GS11 Michael Waltrip	6.00	2.70
❑ GS12 Darrell Waltrip	12.00	5.50
❑ GS13 Dale Jarrett	15.00	6.75
❑ GS14 Morgan Shepherd	6.00	2.70
❑ GS15 Lake Speed	6.00	2.70
❑ GS16 Ted Musgrave	6.00	2.70

1995 Finish Line Standout Cars

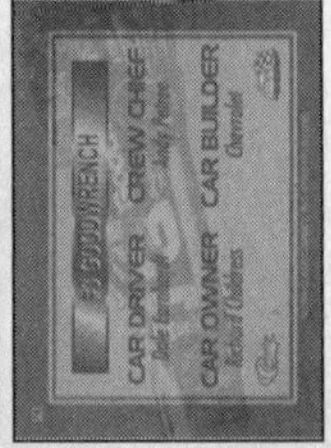

Randomly inserted in hobby only packs, these 10 cards feature top driver's cars in a "Standout" format. The c background could actually be folded to allow the ca stand-up by itself. Wrapper stated odds for pulling c the cards is 1:9 packs.

	MINT
COMPLETE SET (10)	30.00
COMMON CARD (SC1-SC10)	1.00

*SINGLES: 2X TO 5X BASE CARD HI

❑ SC1 Dale Earnhardt's Car	2.00
❑ SC2 Mark Martin's Car	2.00
❑ SC3 Rusty Wallace's Car	2.00
❑ SC4 Ricky Rudd's Car	2.00
❑ SC5 Morgan Shepherd's Car	1.00
❑ SC6 Terry Labonte's Car	5.00
❑ SC7 Jeff Gordon's Car	2.00
❑ SC8 Darrell Waltrip's Car	2.00
❑ SC9 Geoff Bodine's Car	1.00
❑ SC10 Michael Waltrip's Car	1.00

1995 Finish Line Standout Drivers

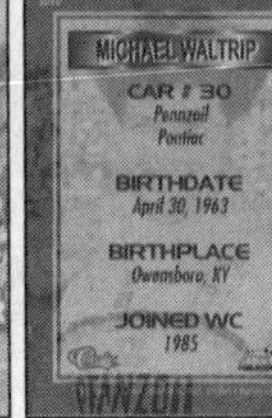

Randomly inserted in retail only packs, these 10 feature top drivers in a "Standout" format. The background could actually be folded to allow the c stand-up by itself. The same ten drivers were us both the Standout Cars and Standout Drivers inser Wrapper stated odds for pulling one of the cards packs.

	MINT
COMPLETE SET (10)	40.00
COMMON CARD (SD1-SD10)	1.50

*SINGLES: 3X TO 8X BASE CARD HI

❑ SD1 Dale Earnhardt	3.00
❑ SD2 Mark Martin	3.00
❑ SD3 Rusty Wallace	3.00
❑ SD4 Ricky Rudd	3.00
❑ SD5 Morgan Shepherd	1.50
❑ SD6 Terry Labonte	3.00
❑ SD7 Jeff Gordon	3.00
❑ SD8 Darrell Waltrip	3.00
❑ SD9 Geoff Bodine	1.50
❑ SD10 Michael Waltrip	1.50

1995 Finish Line Coca-Cola 600

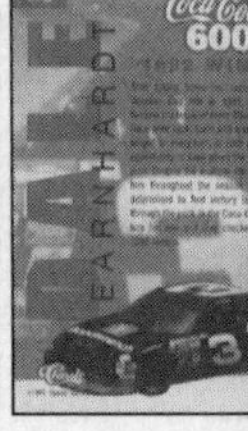

Although packaged and distributed separately, the Cola 600 set is simply a parallel version of the 5 1995 Assets racing release. Each card features spe foil lettering on the cardfront commemorating th Speed Street Festival in conjunction with the Co 600 in Charlotte. The cards were packaged in fact form only. Two insert sets were also included i factory set: Die-Cuts and Coca-Cola 600 race W The sets were sold during the Speed Street Festi on a live QVC broadcast from the festival.

	MINT
COMPLETE SET (50)	8.00
COMPLETE FACT.SET (65)	15.00
COMMON CARD (1-50)	.20

*STARS: .4X TO .65X ASSETS CARDS

1995 Finish Line Coca-Cola 600 Die-Cuts

cards were packaged one complete set per 1995 Line Coca-Cola 600 factory set. They are essentially llel to the 1995 Assets Coca-Cola 600 Die-Cuts ssue except for a different cardback and smaller r of cards -- five instead of ten.

	MINT	NRMT
.ETE SET (5)	3.00	1.35
ON CARD (C1-C5)	.30	.14
ale Earnhardt	1.00	.45
usty Wallace	.50	.23
eff Gordon	1.00	.45
ale Jarrett	.30	.14
ark Martin	.50	.23

1995 Finish Line Coca-Cola 600 Winners

nplete set was included in each 1995 Finish Line ola 600 factory set. The ten cards feature former s of the Coca-Cola 600 printed on reflective foil ck.

	MINT	NRMT
ETE SET (10)	5.00	2.20
N CARD (CC1-CC10)	.30	.14
Darrell Waltrip	.30	.14
Dale Earnhardt	1.00	.45
Kyle Petty	.30	.14
Darrell Waltrip	.30	.14
Darrell Waltrip	.30	.14
Rusty Wallace	.50	.23
Davey Allison's Car	.50	.23
Dale Earnhardt	1.00	.45
Dale Earnhardt	1.00	.45
Jeff Gordon	1.00	.45

5 Finish Line SuperTrucks

gural 1995 Finish Line SuperTrucks set features s that were packaged in 10-card foil packs with s per box. Sixteen-box case production was to 650 cases. Inserts include a Rainbow foil set, along with Calling Cards, Champion's Choice, gnatures and Winter Heat Hot Shoes.

	MINT	NRMT
TE SET (80)	10.00	4.50
COMMON CARD (1-80)	.10	.05
COMMON DRIVER (1-80)	.15	.07
COMMON WC DRIVER (1-80)	.50	.23
❑ 1 Mike Skinner	.30	.14
❑ 2 Butch Gilliland	.15	.07
❑ 3 Rick Carelli	.30	.14
❑ 4 Walker Evans' Truck	.10	.05
❑ 5 Joe Bessey	.15	.07
❑ 6 Ken Schrader	.50	.23
❑ 7 Scott Lagasse	.30	.14
❑ 8 Bob Keselowski's Truck	.10	.05
❑ 9 Butch Gilliland's Truck	.10	.05
❑ 10 Mike Hulbert	.15	.07
❑ 11 Kerry Teague	.15	.07
❑ 12 Troy Beebe	.15	.07
❑ 13 Walker Evans	.15	.07
❑ 14 Joe Ruttman	.15	.07
❑ 15 P.J. Jones	.15	.07
❑ 16 Jack Sprague's Truck	.10	.05
❑ 17 Jeff Gordon	1.50	.70
❑ 18 Tobey Butler	.15	.07
❑ 19 Jerry Glanville's Truck	.10	.05
❑ 20 Roger Mears	.15	.07
❑ 21 Bill Sedgewick	.15	.07
❑ 22 Gary Collins	.15	.07
❑ 23 Walker Evans	.15	.07
❑ 24 Sammy Swindell	.30	.14
❑ 25 Steve McEachern's Truck	.10	.05
❑ 26 Geoff Bodine	.50	.23
❑ 27 Terry Labonte	.75	.35
❑ 28 Butch Miller	.15	.07
❑ 29 Geoff Bodine's Truck	.15	.07
❑ 30 Mike Skinner. Richard Childress	.30	.14
❑ 31 Tommy Archer	.15	.07
❑ 32 Steve McEachern	.15	.07
❑ 33 Tobey Butler	.15	.07
❑ 34 Bob Strait	.15	.07
❑ 35 Jerry Glanville	.15	.07
❑ 36 Mike Skinner's Truck	.15	.07
❑ 37 Joe Bessey	.15	.07
❑ 38 P.J. Jones	.15	.07
❑ 39 Jack Sprague	.15	.07
❑ 40 Tommy Archer's Truck	.10	.05
❑ 41 Kerry Teague	.15	.07
❑ 42 Roger Mears	.15	.07
❑ 43 Ron Hornaday	.30	.14
❑ 44 Tommy Archer	.15	.07
❑ 45 Scott Lagasse	.30	.14
❑ 46 Walker Evans	.15	.07
❑ 47 Gary Collins' Truck	.10	.05
❑ 48 Jack Sprague	.15	.07
❑ 49 Bob Keselowski	.15	.07
❑ 50 Geoff Bodine	.50	.23
❑ 51 Ken Schrader	.50	.23
❑ 52 Tobey Butler's Truck	.10	.05
❑ 53 Kerry Teague's Truck	.10	.05
❑ 54 Mike Skinner	.30	.14
❑ 55 Terry Labonte	.75	.35
❑ 56 Troy Beebe	.15	.07
❑ 57 Richard Childress	.10	.05
❑ 58 Jerry Glanville	.15	.07
❑ 59 Butch Miller	.15	.07
❑ 60 Terry Labonte's Truck	.15	.07
❑ 61 T.J. Clark	.15	.07
❑ 62 Butch Gilliland	.15	.07
❑ 63 Joe Ruttman	.15	.07
❑ 64 Scott Lagasse's Truck	.15	.07
❑ 65 Steve McEachern	.15	.07
❑ 66 Gary Collins	.15	.07
❑ 67 Bob Strait	.15	.07
❑ 68 Rick Carelli's Truck	.10	.05
❑ 69 Sammy Swindell	.30	.14
❑ 70 Ken Schrader's Truck	.10	.05
❑ 71 Ron Hornaday	.30	.14
❑ 72 T.J. Clark	.15	.07
❑ 73 Geoff Bodine	.50	.23
❑ 74 Mike Hulbert	.15	.07
❑ 75 Ken Schrader	.50	.23
❑ 76 P.J. Jones' Truck	.10	.05
❑ 77 Roger Mears' Truck	.10	.05
❑ 78 Bob Keselowski	.15	.07
❑ 79 Rick Carelli	.30	.14
❑ 80 Checklist	.10	.05

1995 Finish Line SuperTrucks Rainbow Foil

A parallel set to the regular issue 1995 Finish Line SuperTrucks set, these cards feature a rainbow foil logo on the cardfront. The cards were packaged one per foil pack.

	MINT	NRMT
COMPLETE SET (80)	50.00	22.00
COMMON CARD (1-80)	.20	.09
COMMON DRIVER (1-80)	.50	.23

*STARS: 2X TO 4X BASIC CARDS

1995 Finish Line SuperTrucks Calling Cards

Randomly packed at the rate of approximately 1:18 packs, these Calling Cards carry a phone time value of three minutes with an expiration date of 12/31/96. Each card features a gold foil Finish Line logo on the cardfront and a serial number of 2,100 on the card back. Phone cards with the pin numbered revealed are generally worth .25X to .50X of Mint cards.

	MINT	NRMT
COMPLETE SET (10)	25.00	11.00
COMMON CARD (1-10)	2.50	1.10
❑ 1 Geoff Bodine	4.00	1.80
❑ 2 Rick Carelli	2.50	1.10
❑ 3 Walker Evans	2.50	1.10
❑ 4 Jerry Glanville	2.50	1.10
❑ 5 Ron Hornaday	2.50	1.10
❑ 6 P.J. Jones	2.50	1.10
❑ 7 Terry Labonte	5.00	2.20
❑ 8 Roger Mears	2.50	1.10
❑ 9 Ken Schrader	4.00	1.80
❑ 10 Mike Skinner	4.00	1.80

1995 Finish Line SuperTrucks Champion's Choice

Champion's Choice cards were randomly inserted in 1995 Finish Line SuperTrucks packs at the wrapper stated odds of 1:9 packs. The cards feature favorites to win SuperTrucks racing events in 1995.

	MINT	NRMT
COMPLETE SET (6)	10.00	4.50
COMMON CARD (CC1-CC6)	1.00	.45
COM.WC DRIVER (CC1-CC6)	2.50	1.10
❑ CC1 Roger Mears	1.00	.45
❑ CC2 Terry Labonte	3.00	1.35
❑ CC3 Rick Carelli	1.00	.45
❑ CC4 Ron Hornaday	1.50	.70
❑ CC5 Sammy Swindell	1.50	.70
❑ CC6 Geoff Bodine	2.50	1.10

1995 Finish Line SuperTrucks Super Signature Series

Super Signature Series cards were randomly inserted in 1995 Finish Line SuperTrucks packs at the wrapper stated odds of 1:9 packs. The 10-cards feature top SuperTrucks drivers printed with a gold foil signature on the cardfront.

	MINT	NRMT
COMPLETE SET (10)	20.00	9.00
COMMON CARD (SS1-SS10)	1.50	.70
COM.WC DRIV. (SS1-SS10)	4.00	1.80
❑ SS1 Jeff Gordon	10.00	4.50
❑ SS2 Richard Childress	1.50	.70
❑ SS3 Ken Schrader	4.00	1.80
❑ SS4 Jerry Glanville	1.50	.70
❑ SS5 Mike Skinner	2.50	1.10
❑ SS6 Tobey Butler	1.50	.70
❑ SS7 Joe Bessey	1.50	.70
❑ SS8 Scott Lagasse	2.50	1.10
❑ SS9 P.J. Jones	1.50	.70
❑ SS10 Terry Labonte	6.00	2.70

1995 Finish Line SuperTrucks Winter Heat Hot Shoes

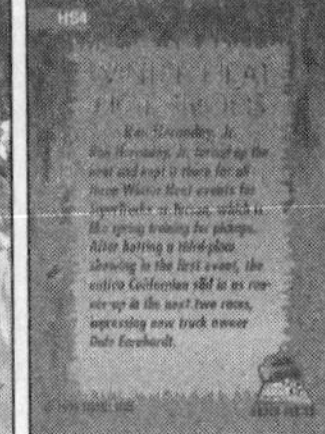

Winter Heat Hot Shoes cards are randomly inserted in 1995 Finish Line SuperTrucks packs at the wrapper stated odds of 1:9 packs. The four-cards feature top performers from the SuperTrucks Winter Heat events held in Tucson. The cards are printed with gold foil layering on the cardfront.

	MINT	NRMT
COMPLETE SET (4)	5.00	2.20
COMMON CARD (HS1-HS4)	1.25	.55
❑ HS1 Mike Skinner	1.50	.70
❑ HS2 P.J. Jones	1.25	.55
❑ HS3 Rick Carelli	1.25	.55
❑ HS4 Ron Hornaday	1.50	.70

1996 Finish Line

This 100-card set features new looks for '96 of the top Winston Cup drivers and their cars. After teaming up with Classic to produce their '95 line, Finish Line returned to making their own cards in '96. The cards were packaged 10 cards per pack, 36 packs per box and 16 boxes per case. The packs had a suggested retail price of $1.99. There were a total of 1,500 cases produced. The product was distributed through both hobby and retail channels.

	MINT	NRMT
COMPLETE SET (100)	10.00	4.50
COMMON CARD (1-100)	.10	.05
COMMON DRIVER (1-100)	.20	.09
❑ 1 Jeff Gordon	2.00	.90
❑ 2 Ted Musgrave	.20	.09
❑ 3 Rusty Wallace	1.00	.45
❑ 4 Ward Burton's Car	.10	.05
❑ 5 Terry Labonte	1.00	.45
❑ 6 Derrike Cope	.20	.09
❑ 7 Steve Grissom	.20	.09
❑ 8 Mark Martin	1.00	.45
❑ 9 Mark Martin's Car	.50	.23
❑ 10 Ricky Rudd	.40	.18
❑ 11 Darrell Waltrip	.40	.18
❑ 12 Jeff Burton	.40	.18
❑ 13 Ernie Irvan	.40	.18
❑ 14 Jeremy Mayfield	.60	.25
❑ 15 Michael Waltrip's Car	.10	.05
❑ 16 Hut Stricklin	.20	.09
❑ 17 Brett Bodine	.20	.09
❑ 18 Gary DeHart	.10	.05
❑ 19 Bobby Hamilton	.20	.09
❑ 20 Kyle Petty	.40	.18
❑ 21 Derrike Cope's Car	.10	.05
❑ 22 Dick Trickle	.20	.09
❑ 23 Sterling Marlin	.40	.18
❑ 24 Joe Gibbs	.20	.09
❑ 25 Bobby Allison	.20	.09
❑ 26 Bobby Labonte	.75	.35
❑ 27 Rusty Wallace	1.00	.45
❑ 28 Rusty Wallace's Car	.50	.23
❑ 29 Morgan Shepherd	.20	.09
❑ 30 Geoff Bodine	.20	.09
❑ 31 Ricky Craven	.20	.09
❑ 32 Jimmy Spencer	.20	.09
❑ 33 Ernie Irvan's Car	.20	.09
❑ 34 Michael Waltrip	.20	.09
❑ 35 Joe Nemechek	.20	.09
❑ 36 Ward Burton	.20	.09
❑ 37 John Andretti	.20	.09
❑ 38 Ken Schrader	.20	.09
❑ 39 Mike Wallace	.20	.09
❑ 40 Bill Elliott's Car	.50	.23
❑ 41 Sterling Marlin	.40	.18
❑ 42 Bill Elliott	1.00	.45
❑ 43 Dale Jarrett	.75	.35
❑ 44 Morgan Shepherd	.20	.09
❑ 45 Jimmy Spencer's Car	.10	.05
❑ 46 Mike Wallace	.20	.09
❑ 47 Chad Little	.20	.09
❑ 48 Todd Bodine	.20	.09
❑ 49 Bobby Hamilton	.20	.09
❑ 50 Larry McReynolds	.10	.05
❑ 51 Kenny Wallace	.20	.09
❑ 52 Ricky Rudd	.40	.18
❑ 53 Steve Grissom	.20	.09
❑ 54 Derrike Cope	.20	.09
❑ 55 Brett Bodine	.20	.09
❑ 56 Darrell Waltrip	.40	.18
❑ 57 Ted Musgrave	.20	.09
❑ 58 Johnny Benson	.20	.09
❑ 59 Geoff Bodine	.20	.09
❑ 60 Mark Martin	1.00	.45
❑ 61 Michael Waltrip	.20	.09
❑ 62 Sterling Marlin's Car	.20	.09
❑ 63 Larry McClure	.10	.05
❑ 64 Jeff Burton	.40	.18
❑ 65 Ward Burton	.20	.09
❑ 66 Rick Mast	.20	.09
❑ 67 Darrell Waltrip's Car	.20	.09
❑ 68 Darrell Waltrip	.40	.18
❑ 69 Bobby Labonte	.75	.35
❑ 70 Johnny Benson	.20	.09
❑ 71 Todd Bodine	.20	.09
❑ 72 Jimmy Makar	.10	.05
❑ 73 Hut Stricklin	.20	.09
❑ 74 Terry Labonte's Car	.50	.23
❑ 75 Joe Nemechek	.20	.09
❑ 76 Ricky Craven	.20	.09
❑ 77 Bill Elliott	1.00	.45
❑ 78 Terry Labonte	1.00	.45
❑ 79 Robert Yates	.10	.05
❑ 80 Ricky Rudd's Car	.20	.09
❑ 81 Robin Pemberton	.10	.05
❑ 82 Ray Evernham	.10	.05
❑ 83 Tony Glover	.10	.05
❑ 84 David Green	.20	.09
❑ 85 Bobby Labonte's Car	.40	.18
❑ 86 Kyle Petty	.40	.18
❑ 87 Jeff Gordon	2.00	.90
❑ 88 Rick Hendrick	.10	.05
❑ 89 Ken Schrader	.20	.09
❑ 90 Dale Jarrett's Car	.40	.18
❑ 91 Felix Sabates	.10	.05
❑ 92 Ernie Irvan Jordan Irvan	.40	.18
❑ 93 Bill Ingle	.10	.05
❑ 94 Jimmy Spencer	.20	.09
❑ 95 Jeff Gordon's Car	1.00	.45
❑ 96 Jack Roush	.10	.05
❑ 97 Steve Hmiel	.10	.05
❑ 98 Johnny Benson's Car	.10	.05
❑ 99 John Andretti	.20	.09
❑ 100 Dale Jarrett	.75	.35

1996 Finish Line Printer's Proof

This 100-card set is a parallel to the base set. Each card features a Printer's Proof logo on the front to differentiate it from the base card. Each card is also stamped "one of

500" on the front. The cards were inserted at a rate per 18 packs.

	MINT
COMPLETE SET (100)	300.00
COMMON CARD (1-100)	2.50
COMMON DRIVER (1-100)	5.00

*STARS: 20X TO X BASIC CARDS

1996 Finish Line Silver

This 100-card set is a parallel to the base set. The feature a "Silver 96 Series" logo on the fr differentiate them from the regular cards. The Silve were inserted one per pack.

	MINT
COMPLETE SET (100)	30.00
COMMON CARD (1-100)	.30
COMMON DRIVER (1-100)	.60

*STARS: 2X TO X BASIC CARDS

1996 Finish Line Comin' Back Ernie Irvan

This five-card insert set features Ernie Irvan's cor from his near fatal accident at Michigan in 199 return to the Winston Cup circuit. The cards use m technology and are inserted at a rate of one per 18

	MINT
COMPLETE SET (5)	12.00
COM.E.IRVAN CARD (EI1-EI5)	3.00

1996 Finish Line Gold Signature

This 18-card insert set features the top names in Cup racing. Each card has a facsimile gold sigr

ecific driver across the front. The back of the card uentially numbered of 1,996. The cards are nly inserted in packs at a rate of one per 36.

	MINT	NRMT
LETE SET (18)	100.00	45.00
ON CARD (GS1-GS18)	3.00	1.35
LES: 6X TO 15X BASE CARD HI		
Jeff Gordon	40.00	18.00
Sterling Marlin	6.00	2.70
Mark Martin	20.00	9.00
Rusty Wallace	20.00	9.00
Terry Labonte	20.00	9.00
Bill Elliott	20.00	9.00
Bobby Labonte	12.00	5.50
Ted Musgrave	3.00	1.35
Geoff Bodine	3.00	1.35
) Bobby Hamilton	3.00	1.35
1 Darrell Waltrip	6.00	2.70
2 Michael Waltrip	3.00	1.35
3 Ernie Irvan	6.00	2.70
4 Dale Jarrett	6.00	2.70
5 Ken Schrader	3.00	1.35
6 Ricky Craven	3.00	1.35
7 Ricky Rudd	6.00	2.70
3 Kyle Petty	6.00	2.70

1996 Finish Line Man and Machine

the 10 cards from the Man and Machine insert set ed on 16pt. stock and are fully embossed. Each atures the driver, the owner and the car for the ve 10 teams in the set. The cards were inserted at one per nine packs.

	MINT	NRMT
ETE SET (10)	15.00	6.75
N CARD (MM1-MM10)	.50	.23
ES: 1X TO 2.5X BASE CARD HI		
Jeff Gordon's Car	10.00	4.50
Mark Martin's Car	5.00	2.20
Rusty Wallace's Car	5.00	2.20
Sterling Marlin's Car	1.00	.45
Terry Labonte's Car	5.00	2.20
Ernie Irvan's Car	1.00	.45
Bobby Labonte's Car	2.50	1.10
Bill Elliott's Car	5.00	2.20
Derrike Cope's Car	.50	.23
) Johnny Benson's Car	.50	.23

1996 Finish Line ga-Phone XL Redemption

r-card insert set offers four $25 dollar oversized ırds. Each card is die-cut and measures 4" by 7" ws a horizontal picture of the driver and his car. s were made available through redemption cards y inserted in packs at a rate of one per 36 packs. ere 8,000 of each card made. Also, you only ne redemption card and $60 to send in to Finish btain the complete four card set.

	MINT	NRMT
TE SET (4)	50.00	22.00
COMMON CARD	12.00	5.50
*SINGLES: 5X TO 12X BASE CARD HI		
❑ NNO Bill Elliott	12.00	5.50
❑ NNO Jeff Gordon	40.00	18.00
❑ NNO Mark Martin	12.00	5.50
❑ NNO Rusty Wallace	12.00	5.50

1996 Finish Line Rise To The Top Jeff Gordon

This 10-card insert set features Jeff Gordon's "Rise to the Top" to win the 1995 Winston Cup Championship. Each card features micro-foil technology and was randomly inserted at a rate of one per 18 packs.

	MINT	NRMT
COMPLETE SET (10)	40.00	18.00
COMMON GORDON (JG1-JG10)	5.00	2.20

1996 Finish Line Black Gold

The 1996 Finish Line Black Gold Limited set was issued in one series totalling 30 cards. The one-card packs carried a suggested retail of $6.00 each. There were 16 boxes per case, 12 packs per box and one card per pack. The cards feature a driver or his car micro photo-etched onto a metal card front. The back is comprised of a 24pt. stock paper. The two pieces, metal front and paper back, were attached to make one card. There was an interactive game that involved one of the cards in the set. The DE - Designated Entry card allowed collectors a chance to win a 1997 Chevy Monte Carlo. By sending in that card or a scratch off BGL card (1:3 packs) that had Bobby Labonte's name on it, they were automatically entered in the drawing. Bobby Labonte was the winner of the NAPA 500 November 8th which was the qualifier for the BGL cards to be winners. There was also to special gold inserts, a Jeff Gordon and a Bill Elliott card. These cards were randomly seeded 1:192 packs. A $25 Black Gold Megaphone XL Jumbo Die-Cut Phone card was randomly seeded 1:12 boxes. The four jumbo die-cut phone cards were printed in quantities of 2,750 each and have been priced at the bottom of the set. Each of the jumbo phone cards carries an expiration date for the phone time of 1/1/2000.

	MINT	NRMT
COMPLETE SET (30)	160.00	70.00
COMMON CARD (C1-C14)	4.00	1.80
COMMON CARD (D1-D16)	5.00	2.20
❑ C1 Jeff Gordon's Car	10.00	4.50
❑ C2 Rusty Wallace's Car	7.00	3.10
❑ C3 Sterling Marlin's Car	5.00	2.20
❑ C4 Terry Labonte's Car	7.00	3.10
❑ C5 Mark Martin's Car	7.00	3.10
❑ C6 Ernie Irvan's Car	5.00	2.20
❑ C7 Bobby Labonte's Car	6.00	2.70
❑ C8 Kyle Petty's Car	5.00	2.20
❑ C9 Ricky Rudd's Car	5.00	2.20
❑ C10 Bill Elliott's Car	7.00	3.10
❑ C11 Dale Jarrett's Car	6.00	2.70
❑ C12 Darrell Waltrip's Car	5.00	2.20
❑ C13 Johnny Benson's Car	4.00	1.80
❑ C14 Michael Waltrip's Car	4.00	1.80
❑ D1 Jeff Gordon	12.00	5.50
❑ D2 Rusty Wallace	8.00	3.60
❑ D3 DE- Designated Entry	5.00	2.20
❑ D4 Sterling Marlin	6.00	2.70
❑ D5 Terry Labonte	8.00	3.60
❑ D6 Mark Martin	8.00	3.60
❑ D7 Ernie Irvan	6.00	2.70
❑ D8 Bobby Labonte	7.00	3.10
❑ D9 Kyle Petty	6.00	2.70
❑ D10 Ricky Rudd	6.00	2.70
❑ D11 Bill Elliott	8.00	3.60
❑ D12 Ted Musgrave	5.00	2.20
❑ D13 Darrell Waltrip	6.00	2.70
❑ D14 Dale Jarrett	7.00	3.10
❑ D15 Johnny Benson	5.00	2.20
❑ D16 Michael Waltrip	5.00	2.20
❑ SG1 Jeff Gordon Special Gold	40.00	18.00
❑ SG2 Bill Elliott Special Gold	25.00	11.00
❑ JPC1 Bill Elliott	4.00	1.80
❑ JPC2 Jeff Gordon	4.00	1.80
❑ JPC3 Ernie Irvan	4.00	1.80
❑ JPC4 Terry Labonte	4.00	1.80

1996 Flair

This 100-card set is the inagural issue of the Flair brand by Fleer/SkyBox. The cards printed on double thick board feature top drivers from both the Winston Cup and Busch circuits. Cards also featured 100 percent etched-foil and three photos on every basic card. The cards were available through both hobby and retail outlets. The product was distributed via six box cases, with 24 packs per box and five cards per pack. Each pack carried a suggested retail of $4.99.

	MINT	NRMT
COMPLETE SET (100)	30.00	13.50
COMMON CARD (1-100)	.15	.07
COMMON DRIVER (1-100)	.30	.14
❑ 1 John Andretti	.30	.14
❑ 2 Johnny Benson	.30	.14
❑ 3 Brett Bodine	.30	.14
❑ 4 Geoff Bodine	.30	.14
❑ 5 Jeff Burton	.60	.25
❑ 6 Ward Burton	.30	.14
❑ 7 Derrike Cope	.30	.14
❑ 8 Ricky Craven	.30	.14
❑ 9 Wally Dallenbach	.30	.14
❑ 10 Dale Earnhardt	3.00	1.35
❑ 11 Bill Elliott	1.50	.70
❑ 12 Jeff Gordon	3.00	1.35
❑ 13 Steve Grissom	.30	.14
❑ 14 Bobby Hamilton	.30	.14
❑ 15 Ernie Irvan	.60	.25
❑ 16 Dale Jarrett	1.25	.55
❑ 17 Bobby Labonte	1.25	.55
❑ 18 Terry Labonte	1.50	.70
❑ 19 Dave Marcis	.60	.25
❑ 20 Sterling Marlin	.60	.25
❑ 21 Mark Martin	1.50	.70
❑ 22 Rick Mast	.30	.14
❑ 23 Jeremy Mayfield	1.00	.45
❑ 24 Ted Musgrave	.30	.14
❑ 25 Joe Nemechek	.30	.14
❑ 26 Kyle Petty	.60	.25
❑ 27 Robert Pressley	.30	.14
❑ 28 Ricky Rudd	.60	.25
❑ 29 Ken Schrader	.30	.14
❑ 30 Lake Speed	.30	.14
❑ 31 Jimmy Spencer	.30	.14
❑ 32 Hut Stricklin	.30	.14
❑ 33 Kenny Wallace	.30	.14
❑ 34 Mike Wallace	.30	.14
❑ 35 Rusty Wallace	1.50	.70
❑ 36 Michael Waltrip	.30	.14
❑ 37 Glenn Allen Jr.	.30	.14
❑ 38 Rodney Combs	.30	.14
❑ 39 David Green	.30	.14
❑ 40 Randy LaJoie	.30	.14
❑ 41 Chad Little	.30	.14
❑ 42 Curtis Markham	.30	.14
❑ 43 Mike McLaughlin	.30	.14
❑ 44 Patty Moise	.30	.14

❑ 45 Phil Parsons	.30	.14
❑ 46 Jeff Purvis	.30	.14
❑ 47 Bobby Allison	.15	.07
❑ 48 Richard Childress	.15	.07
❑ 49 Joe Gibbs	.30	.14
❑ 50 Rick Hendrick	.15	.07
❑ 51 Richard Petty	.75	.35
❑ 52 Jack Roush	.15	.07
❑ 53 Ray Evernham	.60	.25
❑ 54 Todd Parrott	.15	.07
❑ 55 Robin Pemberton	.15	.07
❑ 56 David Smith	.15	.07
❑ 57 John Andretti's Car	.15	.07
❑ 58 Johnny Benson's Car	.15	.07
❑ 59 Brett Bodine's Car	.15	.07
❑ 60 Geoff Bodine's Car	.15	.07
❑ 61 Jeff Burton's Car	.30	.14
❑ 62 Ward Burton's Car	.15	.07
❑ 63 Derrike Cope's Car	.15	.07
❑ 64 Ricky Craven's Car	.15	.07
❑ 65 Wally Dallenbach's Car	.15	.07
❑ 66 Dale Earnhardt's Car	1.50	.70
❑ 67 Bill Elliott's Car	.75	.35
❑ 68 Jeff Gordon's Car	1.50	.70
❑ 69 Steve Grissom's Car	.15	.07
❑ 70 Bobby Hamilton's Car	.15	.07
❑ 71 Ernie Irvan's Car	.30	.14
❑ 72 Dale Jarrett's Car	.60	.25
❑ 73 Bobby Labonte's Car	.60	.25
❑ 74 Terry Labonte's Car	.75	.35
❑ 75 Dave Marcis' Car	.30	.14
❑ 76 Sterling Marlin's Car	.30	.14
❑ 77 Mark Martin's Car	.75	.35
❑ 78 Rick Mast's Car	.15	.07
❑ 79 Jeremy Mayfield's Car	.50	.23
❑ 80 Ted Musgrave's Car	.15	.07
❑ 81 Joe Nemechek's Car	.15	.07
❑ 82 Kyle Petty's Car	.30	.14
❑ 83 Robert Pressley's Car	.15	.07
❑ 84 Ricky Rudd's Car	.30	.14
❑ 85 Ken Schrader's Car	.15	.07
❑ 86 Lake Speed's Car	.15	.07
❑ 87 Jimmy Spencer's Car	.15	.07
❑ 88 Hut Stricklin's Car	.15	.07
❑ 89 Kenny Wallace's Car	.15	.07
❑ 90 Mike Wallace's Car	.15	.07
❑ 91 Rusty Wallace's Car	.75	.35
❑ 92 Michael Waltrip's Car	.15	.07
❑ 93 Dale Jarrett Ernie Irvin	.75	.35
❑ 94 Dale Jarrett	1.25	.55
❑ 95 Bobby Labonte	1.25	.55
❑ 96 Terry Labonte	1.50	.70
❑ 97 Mark Martin	1.50	.70
❑ 98 Mike Wallace	.30	.14
❑ 99 Jeff Gordon CL (1-67)	1.50	.70
❑ 100 Rusty Wallace CL (68-100/inserts)	.75	.35

1996 Flair Autographs

This 12-card insert set consist of the top names in NASCAR. Autograph redemption cards were randomly inserted in packs at a rate of one in 100. The redemption card featured one of the 12 drivers on the front and instructions on how and where to redeem it.

	MINT	NRMT
COMPLETE SET (12)	900.00	400.00
COMMON CARD (1-12)	20.00	9.00

❑ 1 Ricky Craven	20.00	9.00
❑ 2 Dale Earnhardt	250.00	110.00
❑ 3 Bill Elliott	90.00	40.00
❑ 4 Jeff Gordon	250.00	110.00
❑ 5 Ernie Irvan	40.00	18.00
❑ 6 Dale Jarrett	75.00	34.00
❑ 7 Bobby Labonte	60.00	27.00
❑ 8 Terry Labonte	90.00	40.00
❑ 9 Sterling Marlin	40.00	18.00
❑ 10 Mark Martin	90.00	40.00
❑ 11 Ted Musgrave	20.00	9.00
❑ 12 Rusty Wallace	90.00	40.00

1996 Flair Center Spotlight

A card from this 10-card insert set was randomly inserted one in five packs. The cards show the cars of leading drivers with 100 percent foil designs and a glittering UV coating. Each card front shows a car with two spotlight type effects in the backgound.

	MINT	NRMT
COMPLETE SET (10)	50.00	22.00
COMMON CARD (1-10)	1.25	.55
*SINGLES: 1.5X TO 4X BASE CARD HI		

❑ 1 Johnny Benson	1.25	.55
❑ 2 Dale Earnhardt	15.00	6.75

❑ 3 Bill Elliott	8.00	3.60
❑ 4 Jeff Gordon	15.00	6.75
❑ 5 Bobby Hamilton	1.25	.55
❑ 6 Bobby Labonte	5.00	2.20
❑ 7 Terry Labonte	8.00	3.60
❑ 8 Mark Martin	8.00	3.60
❑ 9 Ricky Rudd	2.50	1.10
❑ 10 Rusty Wallace	8.00	3.60

1996 Flair Hot Numbers

This 10-card insert set featues holofoil stamping and embossed printing to showcase NASCAR's top drivers. The card fronts feature a driver's photo, the driver's car number in holofoil and a facsimile of the driver's signature. Hot Number cards were inserted one in 24 packs.

	MINT	NRMT
COMPLETE SET (10)	200.00	90.00
COMMON CARD (1-10)	8.00	3.60
*SINGLES: 8X TO 20X BASE CARD HI		

❑ 1 Dale Earnhardt	60.00	27.00
❑ 2 Bill Elliott	35.00	16.00
❑ 3 Jeff Gordon	60.00	27.00
❑ 4 Ernie Irvan	25.00	11.00
❑ 5 Dale Jarrett	25.00	11.00
❑ 6 Bobby Labonte	10.00	4.50
❑ 7 Terry Labonte	35.00	16.00
❑ 8 Mark Martin	35.00	16.00
❑ 9 Ricky Rudd	10.00	4.50
❑ 10 Rusty Wallace	35.00	16.00

1996 Flair Power Performance

Cards from this uniquely die-cut 10-card set were seeded one in 12 packs. The card fronts feature a driver's photo imposed over a tachometer. The words Power Performance and the driver's name also appear on the front in holofoil stamping.

	MINT	NRMT
COMPLETE SET (10)	80.00	36.00
COMMON CARD (1-10)	2.00	.90
*SINGLES: 3X TO 8X BASE CARD HI		

❑ 1 Ricky Craven	2.00	.90
❑ 2 Dale Earnhardt	25.00	11.00
❑ 3 Bill Elliott	15.00	6.75
❑ 4 Jeff Gordon	25.00	11.00
❑ 5 Dale Jarrett	12.00	5.50
❑ 6 Terry Labonte	15.00	6.75
❑ 7 Sterling Marlin	4.00	1.80
❑ 8 Mark Martin	15.00	
❑ 9 Ricky Rudd	4.00	
❑ 10 Rusty Wallace	15.00	

1992 Food Lion Richard Pe

2,300 factory sets were produced and packaged in boxes with the Food Lion logo on each box. Thes were offered and sold to Food Lion employees a corporate headquarters and warehouses. In the su of 1993, the remaining 400 sets were offered to the at the cost of $34.

	MINT
COMPLETE SET (116)	15.00
COMMON PETTY (1-116)	.30

❑ 1 Daytona, FL February	.10
❑ 2 Richard Petty 1964	.30
❑ 3 Richard Petty w/Car	.30
❑ 4 Richard Petty 1981	.30
❑ 5 Rockingham, NC March	.10
❑ 6 Richard Petty 1971	.30
❑ 7 Richard Petty 1974	.30
❑ 8 Richard Petty's Car	.30
❑ 9 Richmond, VA March	.10
❑ 10 Richard Petty's Car	.30
❑ 11 Richard Petty	.30
❑ 12 Richard Petty	.30
❑ 13 Atlanta, GA March	.10
❑ 14 Richard Petty's Car	.30
❑ 15 Richard Petty	.30
❑ 16 Richard Petty's Car	.30
❑ 17 Darlington, SC March	.10
❑ 18 Richard Petty	.30
❑ 19 Richard Petty's Car	.30
❑ 20 Richard Petty's Car	.30
❑ 21 Bristol, TN April	.10
❑ 22 Richard Petty	.30
❑ 23 Richard Petty in Car	.30
❑ 24 Richard Petty w/Car	.30
❑ 25 N. Wilkesboro, NC April	.10
❑ 26 Richard Petty w/Dad	.30
❑ 27 Richard Petty's Car	.30
❑ 28 Richard Petty's Car	.30
❑ 29 Martinsville, VA April	.10
❑ 30 Richard Petty	.30
❑ 31 Richard Petty	.30
❑ 32 Richard Petty	.30
❑ 33 Talladega, AL May	.10
❑ 34 Richard Petty w/Car	.30
❑ 35 Richard Petty's Trailer	.30
❑ 36 Richard Petty 1983	.30
❑ 37 Charlotte, NC May	.10
❑ 38 Richard Petty w/Car	.30
❑ 39 Richard Petty on Car	.30
❑ 40 Richard Petty 1977	.30
❑ 41 Dover, DE May	.10
❑ 42 Richard Petty in Car	.30
❑ 43 Richard Petty	.30
❑ 44 Richard Petty 1984	.30
❑ 45 Sonoma, CA June	.10
❑ 46 Richard Petty w/Car	.30
❑ 47 Richard Petty w/Car	.30
❑ 48 Richard Petty w/Car	.30
❑ 49 Pocono, PA June	.10
❑ 50 Richard Petty	.30
❑ 51 Richard Petty	.30
❑ 52 Richard Petty w/Brother	.30
❑ 53 Brooklyn, MI June	.10
❑ 54 Richard Petty	.30
❑ 55 Richard Petty 1981	.30
❑ 56 Richard Petty w/Car	.30
❑ 57 Daytona, FL July	.10
❑ 58 Richard Petty's Car	.30
❑ 59 Richard Petty 1975	.30
❑ 60 Richard Petty 1984	.30
❑ 61 Pocono, PA July	.10
❑ 62 Richard Petty's Car	.30
❑ 63 Richard Petty	.30
❑ 64 Richard Petty's Car	.30
❑ 65 Talladega, AL July	.10
❑ 66 Richard Petty on Bike	.30

ichard Petty 1984	.30	.14
ichard Petty's Car	.30	.14
Vatkins Glen, NY Aug.	.10	.05
ichard Petty w/Car	.30	.14
ichard Petty	.30	.14
ichard Petty	.30	.14
rooklyn, MI August	.10	.05
ichard Petty w/Brother	.30	.14
ichard Petty 1974	.30	.14
ichard Petty	.30	.14
ristol, TN August	.10	.05
ichard Petty's Car	.30	.14
ichard Petty	.30	.14
ichard Petty in Car	.30	.14
arlington, SC Sept.	.10	.05
ichard Petty's Car	.30	.14
ichard Petty	.30	.14
ichard Petty	.30	.14
ichmond, VA September	.10	.05
ichard Petty 1970	.30	.14
ichard Petty's Car	.30	.14
ichard Petty w/Dodge	.30	.14
over, DE September	.10	.05
ichard Petty	.30	.14
ichard Petty	.30	.14
ichard Petty	.30	.14
artinsville, VA Sept.	.10	.05
ichard Petty 1970	.30	.14
ichard Petty 1969	.30	.14
ichard Petty	.30	.14
. Wilkesboro, NC Oct.	.10	.05
ichard Petty w/Brother	.30	.14
ichard Petty	.30	.14
Richard Petty	.30	.14
Charlotte, NC October	.10	.05
Richard Petty	.30	.14
Richard Petty w/Car	.30	.14
Richard Petty	.30	.14
Rockingham, NC October	.10	.05
Richard Petty's Car	.30	.14
Richard Petty's Car	.30	.14
Richard Petty Pit Stop	.30	.14
Phoenix, AZ November	.10	.05
Richard Petty	.30	.14
Richard Petty	.30	.14
Richard Petty	.30	.14
Atlanta, GA November	.10	.05
Richard Petty's Car	.30	.14
Richard Petty's Transporter	.30	.14
Richard Petty's Car	.30	.14
Richard Petty HOLO	300.00	135.00

1991 Galfield Press Pioneers of Racing

edly 3,077 sets were produced. This set was issued oneers of Racing binder, and produced by noted R historian Greg Fielden. Greg personally signed the binders the set came in.

	MINT	NRMT
LETE SET (107)	100.00	45.00
ON CARD (1-107)	.75	.35
eball Roberts	2.00	.90
Tim Flock		
rb Thomas	1.00	.45
Tim Flock		
yd Seay	.75	.35
ur Abreast Start	.75	.35
n Flock	1.00	.45
Barney Smith		
rol Tillman	.75	.35
rshall Teague	1.00	.45
Herb Thomas		
il Orr	.75	.35
rtis Turner	2.00	.90
Fireball Roberts		
00,000 at 105 MPH	.75	.35
ill Holland	.75	.35
ack Smith	.75	.35
onty Flock	1.00	.45
ob Flock	.75	.35
urtis Turner	1.00	.45
reball Roberts	4.00	1.80
onty Flock	1.00	.45
aytona Beach	.75	.35
m Reed	2.00	.90
Lee Petty		
ohn Fish	.75	.35
urtis Turner	1.00	.45
Sara Christian		
m Flock	1.00	.45
unior Johnson	5.00	2.20
ex White	2.00	.90
Fireball Roberts		
oe Weatherly	1.00	.45
Marvin Panch		
Eduardo Dibos		
❑ 26 Eddie Skinner	.75	.35
❑ 27 Iggy Katona	.75	.35
Johnny Mantz		
❑ 28 Bill Widenhouse	.75	.35
❑ 29 Buck Baker	1.00	.45
Jimmie Lewallen		
❑ 30 Bobby Johns	.75	.35
Joe Weatherly		
❑ 31 Banjo Matthews	.75	.35
❑ 32 Fonty Flock	1.00	.45
Jimmie Lewallen		
❑ 33 Joe Guide, Jr.	.75	.35
❑ 34 Larry Flynn	.75	.35
❑ 35 Lakewood Speedway	.75	.35
❑ 36 North Wilkesboro Speedway	.75	.35
❑ 37 Fonty Flock	1.00	.45
Marvin Panch		
❑ 38 Herb Thomas	1.00	.45
Frank Mundy		
❑ 39 Bill O'Dell	.75	.35
❑ 40 Jimmy Florian	.75	.35
❑ 41 1959 Daytona	.75	.35
❑ 42 Paul Goldsmith	1.00	.45
❑ 43 Louise Smith	2.00	.90
❑ 44 Frank Mundy	.75	.35
❑ 45 Doug Cooper	.75	.35
❑ 46 Red Vogt	.75	.35
❑ 47 Raleigh Speedway	.75	.35
❑ 48 Gober Sosebee	.75	.35
Tommy Moon		
Swayne Pritchett		
❑ 49 Curtis Turner	1.00	.45
❑ 50 Dick Bailey	.75	.35
❑ 51 Don Kimberling	1.00	.45
Joe Weatherly		
Eddie Pagan		
Fireball Roberts		
Joe Eubanks		
❑ 52 Pee Wee Jones	.75	.35
Jim Reed		
❑ 53 Checklist Card	.75	.35
❑ 54 Marion Cox	.75	.35
❑ 55 Benny Georgeson	.75	.35
❑ 57 Cotton Owens	.75	.35
❑ 58 Harold Nash	1.00	.45
Bucky Sager		
Ted Rambo		
Mike Brown		
Joe Guide Jr.		
Fireball Roberts		
Dick Rathmann		
❑ 59 Danny Letner	.75	.35
❑ 60 Bob Flock	.75	.35
❑ 61 Tim Flock	1.00	.45
❑ 62 Tim Flock	1.00	.45
Herb Thomas		
❑ 63 Red Byron	.75	.35
Mickey Rhodes		
❑ 64 Tim Flock	1.00	.45
Jim Paschal		
Fonty Flock		
❑ 65 Larry Frank	1.00	.45
❑ 66 Herb Thomas	1.00	.45
❑ 67 Hershel McGriff	.75	.35
❑ 68 Fireball Roberts	4.00	1.80
❑ 69 Curtis Turner	1.00	.45
❑ 70 Marshall Teague	.75	.35
❑ 71 Hershel McGriff	.75	.35
Frankie Schneider		
❑ 72 Bobby Myers	.75	.35
❑ 73 Paul Goldsmith	1.00	.45
❑ 74 Herschel Buchanan	.75	.35
Joe Guide Jr.		
❑ 75 Buddy Shuman	.75	.35
Mickey Fenn		
❑ 76 Bob Welborn	.75	.35
❑ 77 Axel Anderson	.75	.35
❑ 78 Marvin Panch	1.00	.45
Tiny Lund		
Bob Pronger		
Bob Welborn		
❑ 79 June Cleveland	.75	.35
❑ 80 Tim Flock	1.00	.45
❑ 81 Dick Rathmann	.75	.35
❑ 82 Glenn Dunnaway	.75	.35
❑ 83 Herb Thomas	1.00	.45
❑ 84 Cotton Owens	.75	.35
❑ 85 Red Byron	.75	.35
❑ 86 Fireball Roberts	4.00	1.80
❑ 87 Joe Weatherly	1.00	.45
❑ 88 Tim Flock	1.00	.45
❑ 89 Herb Thomas	1.00	.45
❑ 90 Gwyn Staley	.75	.35
Charlie Scott		
❑ 91 Curtis Turner	2.00	.90
Bobby Isaac		
❑ 92 Paul Goldsmith	1.00	.45
Jimmy Thompson		
❑ 93 Fireball Roberts	2.00	.90
Roy Jones		
❑ 94 Junior Johnson	5.00	2.20
❑ 95 Lloyd Seay	.75	.35
❑ 96 Jimmy Thompson	.75	.35
❑ 97 Eduardo Dibos	.75	.35
❑ 98 Raymond Parks	.75	.35
❑ 99 Daytona Speedweek	.75	.35
❑ 100 Tim Flock	1.00	.45
❑ 101 Tim Flock	1.00	.45
Joe Lee Johnson		
Spud Murphy		
❑ 102 Tim Flock	1.00	.45
Ted Chester		
❑ 103 Joe Weatherly	1.00	.45
❑ 104 Red Byron	.75	.35
❑ 105 Ed Livingston	.75	.35
Friday Hassler		
❑ 106 Doug Yates	.75	.35
❑ 107 Checklist Card	.75	.35

1992 Hilton G. Hill Gold True Legend

The 16-card set features drivers who raced from 1949-1971. The set includes such greats as Curtis Turner, Tiny Lund and Tim Flock. There was also approximately 20 uncut sheets produced.

	MINT	NRMT
COMPLETE SET (16)	12.00	5.50
COMMON CARD (1-16)	.60	.25
❑ 1 Checklist	.60	.25
❑ 2 Bowman Gray Stadium	.60	.25
❑ 3 Bob Welborn	.75	.35
❑ 4 Tim Flock	1.00	.45
❑ 5 Curtis Turner	1.00	.45
❑ 6 Bob McGinnis	.75	.35
❑ 7 Tiny Lund	1.00	.45
❑ 8 Bobby Myers	.75	.35
❑ 9 E.H. Weddle	.75	.35
❑ 10 PeeWee Jones	.75	.35
❑ 11 Johnny Dodson	.75	.35
❑ 12 Whitey Norman	.75	.35
❑ 13 Jimmie Lewallen	.75	.35
❑ 14 Jack Holloway	.75	.35
❑ 15 Billy Myers	.75	.35
❑ 16 Phillip Smith	.75	.35

1993 Hi-Tech Tire Test

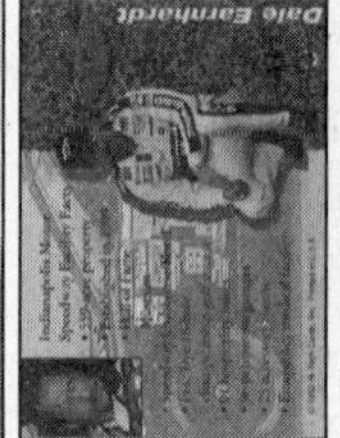

Hi-Tech produced this set commemorating the 1992 NASCAR tire tests at the Indianapolis Motor Speedway. The ten-card set was distributed in two 5-card packs each packed 36 per box. Reportedly, production was limited to 1000 cases.

	MINT	NRMT
COMPLETE SET (10)	5.00	2.20
COMMON CARD (1-10)	.30	.14
❑ 1 Dale Earnhardt's Car	.50	.23
❑ 2 Darrell Waltrip's Car	.40	.18
❑ 3 Davey Allison's car	.50	.23
❑ 4 Rusty Wallace's Car	.50	.23
❑ 5 Ernie Irvan's Car	.40	.18
❑ 6 Mark Martin's Car	.50	.23
❑ 7 Kyle Petty's Car	.40	.18
❑ 8 Land Speed Record at IMS	.30	.14
❑ 9 Bill Elliott's Car	.50	.23
❑ 10 Brickyard 400 Logo	.30	.14

1994 Hi-Tech Brickyard 400

For the second year, Hi-Tech produced a set commemorating the Brickyard 400. The 1994 set was expanded to 70-cards featuring action from the 1993 tire tests at IMS. The cards were packaged 8-cards per pack with 24-packs per box. Reportedly, production was limited to 2,500 12-box cases. Inserts included a Richard

Petty set as well as Metamorphosis cards. The Metamorphosis card shows an IndyCar transforming into a stock car racer. It was packed approximately one per box. There was also a 70-card Artist Proof parallel version of the base set. The cards feature a 1 of 200 logo on the front to differentiate them from the base cards. The Artist Proof cards were inserted at a rate of one per box.

	MINT	NRMT
COMPLETE SET (70)	10.00	4.50
COMMON CARD (1-70)	.05	.02
COMMON DRIVER (1-70)	.10	.05

	MINT	NRMT
❑ 1 Track Action	.05	.02
❑ 2 Rusty Wallace's Car	.50	.23
❑ 3 Bobby Hillin's Car	.05	.02
❑ 4 Morgan Shepherd's Car	.10	.05
❑ 5 Dave Marcis' Car	.05	.02
❑ 6 Brett Bodine in Pits	.05	.02
❑ 7 Morgan Shepherd's Car	.05	.02
❑ 8 Geoff Bodine's Car	.05	.02
❑ 9 Dale Earnhardt's Car	1.00	.45
❑ 10 Bill Elliott's Car	.50	.23
❑ 11 Kenny Wallace's Car	.05	.02
❑ 12 Bobby Labonte's Car	.20	.09
❑ 13 Geoff Bodine's Car	.05	.02
❑ 14 Mark Martin's Car	.50	.23
❑ 15 Bill Elliott's Car	.50	.23
❑ 16 P.J. Jones' Car	.05	.02
❑ 17 John Andretti's Car	.05	.02
❑ 18 Darrell Waltrip's Car	.10	.05
❑ 19 Mark Martin's Car	.50	.23
❑ 20 Jeff Gordon's Car	1.00	.45
❑ 21 Greg Sacks' Car	.05	.02
❑ 22 Terry Labonte's Car	.50	.23
❑ 23 Lake Speed's Car	.05	.02
❑ 24 Greg Sacks' Car	.05	.02
❑ 25 Geoff Bodine's Car	.05	.02
❑ 26 Kenny Wallace's Car	.05	.02
❑ 27 Mark Martin's Car	.50	.23
Jimmy Spencer's Car		
❑ 28 Rusty Wallace's Car	.50	.23
❑ 29 Mark Martin's Car	.50	.23
❑ 30 Lake Speed in Car	.05	.02
❑ 31 Mark Martin's Car	.50	.23
❑ 32 Geoff Bodine's Car	.05	.02
Brett Bodine's Car		
❑ 33 Race Action	.05	.02
❑ 34 Pit Action	.05	.02
❑ 35 Action	.05	.02
❑ 36 Rick Mast	.10	.05
❑ 37 Rusty Wallace	1.00	.45
❑ 38 Dale Earnhardt	2.00	.90
❑ 39 Terry Labonte	1.00	.45
❑ 40 Mark Martin	1.00	.45
❑ 41 Geoff Bodine	.05	.02
Todd Bodine		
Brett Bodine		
❑ 42 Sterling Marlin	.20	.09
❑ 43 D.K. Ulrich	.05	.02
❑ 44 Bill Elliott's Car	.50	.23
❑ 45 Jimmy Spencer	.10	.05
❑ 46 John Andretti	.10	.05
❑ 47 Geoff Bodine	.10	.05
❑ 48 Darrell Waltrip	.20	.09
❑ 49 Dale Jarrett	.75	.35
❑ 50 Morgan Shepherd	.10	.05
❑ 51 Bobby Labonte	.75	.35
❑ 52 Jeff Gordon	2.00	.90
❑ 53 Ken Schrader	.10	.05
❑ 54 Brett Bodine	.10	.05
❑ 55 Lake Speed	.10	.05
❑ 56 Michael Waltrip	.10	.05
❑ 57 Jimmy Horton	.10	.05
❑ 58 Harry Gant	.20	.09
❑ 59 Kenny Wallace	.10	.05
❑ 60 Kyle Petty	.20	.09
❑ 61 Rick Wilson	.10	.05
❑ 62 Ted Musgrave	.10	.05
❑ 63 Greg Sacks	.10	.05
❑ 64 Dave Marcis	.20	.09
❑ 65 Todd Bodine	.10	.05
❑ 66 Bobby Hillin	.10	.05
❑ 67 Derrike Cope	.10	.05
❑ 68 Performance History	.05	.02
❑ 69 Jeff Gordon	1.00	.45
❑ 70 Checklist Card	.05	.02
❑ BYSE1 Metamorphosis Card	2.50	1.10

1994 Hi-Tech Brickyard 400 Richard Petty

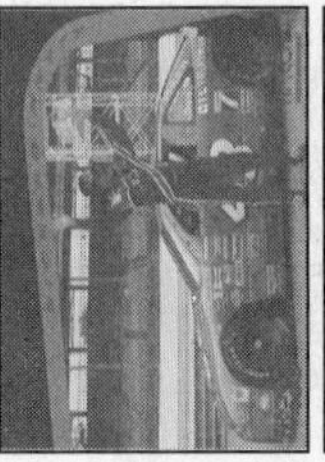

Richard Petty is the focus of this Hi-Tech issue. The cards were randomly inserted in 1994 Hi-Tech Brickyard 400 packs and highlight Petty's involvement with the historic race at IMS. The cards were randomly inserted at a rate of one per 20 Hi-Tech Brickyard 400 packs.

	MINT	NRMT
COMPLETE SET (6)	8.00	3.60
COMMON CARD (1-6)	1.00	.45

	MINT	NRMT
❑ 1 Richard Petty w/Car	2.50	1.10
Becomes King Richard		
❑ 2 Richard Petty's Car	1.00	.45
Ceremonial Laps at IMS		
❑ 3 Richard Petty's Car	1.00	.45
Thoughts on IMS		
❑ 4 Richard Petty w/Car	1.00	.45
❑ 5 Richard Petty w/Car	1.00	.45
❑ 6 Richard Petty's Car	1.00	.45

1995 Hi-Tech Brickyard 400

In 1995, Hi-Tech again produced a card set commemorating the 1994 Brickyard 400. The cards were released in two seperate complete factory sets. The tin box version contained 90 regular cards, 10 Top Ten cards and one Jeff Gordon 23K Gold card. The 90 regular cards were printed on 18 point card stock with gold foil layering. Production was limited to 10,000 factory sets. Hi-Tech also produced the set for distribution in a wooden factory set box with a special Jeff Gordon Gold and Silver card (numbered of 1000). The wooden box version was limited to 1000 sets. Although the cards carry the year 1994 on the copyright line, it's considered a 1995 release.

	MINT	NRMT
COMPLETE FACT.SET (101)	50.00	22.00
COMP.WOOD BOX (101)	200.00	90.00
COMPLETE SET (90)	25.00	11.00
COMMON CARD (1-90)	.15	.07
COMMON DRIVER (1-90)	.30	.14

	MINT	NRMT
❑ 1 Rick Mast's Car	.15	.07
❑ 2 Dale Earnhardt's Car	.75	.35
❑ 3 Jeff Gordon's Car UER	.75	.35
card numbered 00		
❑ 4 Geoff Bodine's Car	.15	.07
❑ 5 Bobby Labonte's Car	.30	.14
❑ 6 Bill Elliott's Car	.75	.35
❑ 7 Brett Bodine's Car	.15	.07
❑ 8 Sterling Marlin's Car	.30	.14
❑ 9 Mark Martin's Car	.75	.35
❑ 10 Morgan Shepherd's Car	.15	.07
❑ 11 Rusty Wallace's Car	.75	.35
❑ 12 Greg Sacks' Car	.15	.07
❑ 13 Dale Jarrett's Car	.50	.23
❑ 14 Michael Waltrip's Car	.15	.07
❑ 15 Dave Marcis' Car	.15	.07
❑ 16 Ernie Irvan's Car	.50	.23
❑ 17 Rich Bickle's Car	.15	.07
❑ 18 Hut Stricklin's Car	.15	
❑ 19 Terry Labonte's Car	.75	
❑ 20 Wally Dallenbach Jr.'s Car	.15	
❑ 21 Ken Schrader's Car	.15	
❑ 22 Jimmy Hensley's Car	.15	
❑ 23 Todd Bodine's Car	.15	
❑ 24 Danny Sullivan's Car	.15	
❑ 25 Darrell Waltrip's Car	.30	
❑ 26 John Andretti's Car	.15	
❑ 27 Jeff Purvis' Car	.15	
❑ 28 Joe Nemechek's Car	.15	
❑ 29 Jeremy Mayfield's Car	.15	
❑ 30 Bobby Hamilton's Car	.15	
❑ 31 Ward Burton's Car	.15	
❑ 32 Jimmy Spencer's Car	.15	
❑ 33 Bobby Hillin's Car	.15	
❑ 34 Kyle Petty's Car	.30	
❑ 35 Ted Musgrave's Car	.15	
❑ 36 Jeff Burton's Car	.15	
❑ 37 Derrike Cope's Car	.15	
❑ 38 Lake Speed's Car	.15	
❑ 39 Harry Gant's Car	.30	
❑ 40 Jeff Gordon Race Action	.75	
❑ 41 Dale Earnhardt	.75	
❑ 42 Hut Stricklin's Car	.15	
❑ 43 Wally Dallenbach Jr.'s Car	.15	
❑ 44 Joe Nemechek	.30	
❑ 45 Rick Mast	.30	
❑ 46 Richard Jackson Team	.15	
Rick Mast's Crew		
❑ 47 Terry Labonte	.75	
❑ 48 Jeremy Mayfield	.30	
❑ 49 Bobby Hamilton	.30	
❑ 50 Bobby Hillin	.30	
❑ 51 Jeff Burton	.30	
❑ 52 Kyle Petty	.50	
❑ 53 Jeff Gordon's Car	.75	
Geoff Bodine's Car		
Ken Schrader's Car		
❑ 54 Checklist	.15	
❑ 55 John Andretti	.30	
❑ 56 Dale Earnhardt	.75	
❑ 57 Danny Sullivan	.30	
❑ 58 Jimmy Spencer	.30	
❑ 59 Michael Waltrip	.30	
❑ 60 Ken Schrader	.30	
❑ 61 Bobby Labonte	.50	
❑ 62 Early-Race	.15	
Race Action		
❑ 63 Bill Elliott's Car	.75	
❑ 64 Todd Bodine	.30	
❑ 65 Ted Musgrave	.30	
❑ 66 Lake Speed	.30	
❑ 67 Harry Gant	.50	
❑ 68 Greg Sacks	.30	
❑ 69 Jeff Purvis	.30	
❑ 70 Mark Martin	.75	
❑ 71 Rich Bickle	.30	
❑ 72 Dave Marcis	.30	
❑ 73 Brett Bodine	.30	
❑ 74 Geoff Bodine	.30	
❑ 75 Dale Jarrett	.50	
❑ 76 Ward Burton	.30	
❑ 77 Dale Earnhardt's Car	.75	
❑ 78 Darrell Waltrip	.50	
❑ 79 Ernie Irvan	.75	
❑ 80 Morgan Shepherd	.30	
❑ 81 Jimmy Hensley	.30	
❑ 82 Derrike Cope	.30	
❑ 83 Rusty Wallace	.75	
❑ 84 Sterling Marlin	.50	
❑ 85 Hut Stricklin	.30	
❑ 86 Ernie Irvan's Car	.75	
❑ 87 Dale Earnhardt	.75	
❑ 88 Jeff Gordon	.75	
❑ 89 Jeff Gordon's Car	.75	
❑ 90 Indianapolis Motor Speedway	.15	
❑ NNO Jeff Gordon Gold/10000	.75	
tin box insert		
❑ NNO Jeff Gordon Gold/Silver	100.00	
numbered of 1000		
wooden box insert		

1995 Hi-Tech Brickyard 4[cut off] Top Ten

The Top Ten set was issued as an insert into facto[cut off] of 1994 Hi-Tech Brickyard 400. The 10-cards distributed in both the tin and wooden box versions set and were printed on holographic foil stock. Eac[cut off] was produced with three different background de[cut off] stars, doughnut shaped, and raindrop shaped. Th[cut off] background version seems to be the toughest to fi[cut off] cards carrying a 25% premium.

	MINT
COMPLETE SET (10)	15.00

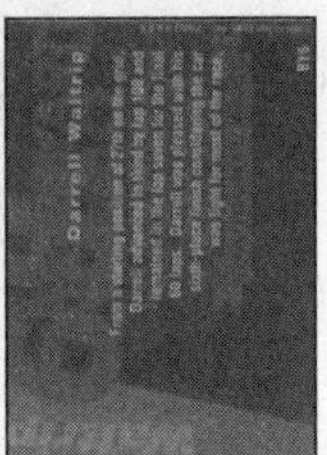

ION CARD (BY1-BY10)	.75	.35
1 Jeff Gordon	.75	.35
2 Brett Bodine	.75	.35
3 Bill Elliott's Car	.75	.35
4 Rusty Wallace	.75	.35
5 Dale Earnhardt	.75	.35
6 Darrell Waltrip	.75	.35
7 Ken Schrader	.75	.35
8 Michael Waltrip	.75	.35
9 Todd Bodine	.75	.35
10 Morgan Shepherd	.75	.35

91 Hickory Motor Speedway

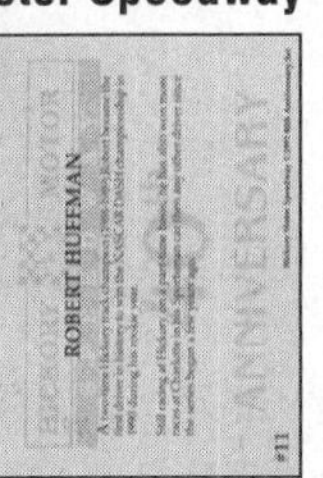

set was produced to honor the 40th Anniversary of ry Motor Speedway. Color and black and white s of the short track's most famous events are ed. The cards were released in complete set form old at the track.

	MINT	NRMT
PLETE SET (12)	5.00	2.20
ION CARD (1-11)	.30	.14
pening Day Traffic	.30	.14
oe Littlejohn	.30	.14
Ribbon Cutting		
he First Race	.30	.14
ickory Today	.30	.14
ack Ingram's Car	.40	.18
Jack's Last Race		
ale Earnhardt	2.00	.90
Harry Gant		
Tommy Houston		
Morgan Shepherd		
Dale Jarrett		
Homecoming at Hickory		
ax Prestwood Jr.	.30	.14
Packed House	.30	.14
ale Fischlein's Car	.30	.14
Action on the Track		
Dale Earnhardt's Car	1.00	.45
Joe Nemechek's Car		
Busch Action		
Robert Huffman w/Car	.50	.23
O Cover Card	.30	.14

1994 High Gear

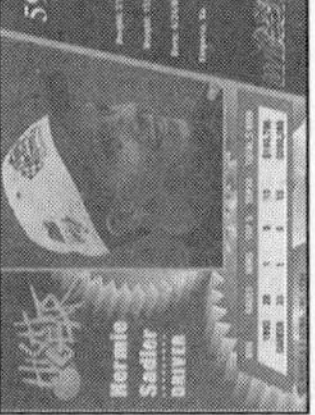

00-card set was issued in two 100-card series. The are printed on 24-pt paper stock, and use UV g and silver foil stamping. The set features top on Cup and Busch Grand National drivers along with crew chiefs, owner, and mechanics. There are five topical subsets; Awards (70-74), Winners (75-87), Busch Clash (88-99), Earnhardt Family (179-186), Winners (187-200). There were 3,000 numbered cases of the first series and 1,000 numbered cases of the second series. Cards came packaged six cards per pack; 24 packs per box and 24 boxes per case. In series one High Gear boxes there was a possibility of pulling a Jeff Gordon Busch Clash signature card. There were 1,500 of these cards and each was individually numbered of 1,500 on the back in black pen. They were randomly inserted in packs of series one at a rate of 1:1152 packs. In series two boxes and boxes of High Gear Day One, there was a Mark Martin "Feel the Heat" autographed card. There were 1,000 of these cards, inserted in packs at a rate of one per 1152 packs.

	MINT	NRMT
COMPLETE SET (200)	22.00	10.00
COMPLETE SERIES 1 (100)	10.00	4.50
COMPLETE SERIES 2 (100)	12.00	5.50
COMMON CARD (1-200)	.10	.05
COMMON DRIVER (1-200)	.20	.09
❑ 1 Dale Earnhardt	2.00	.90
❑ 2 Rusty Wallace	1.00	.45
❑ 3 Mark Martin	1.00	.45
❑ 4 Ken Schrader	.20	.09
❑ 5 Ernie Irvan	.40	.18
❑ 6 Geoff Bodine	.20	.09
❑ 7 Harry Gant	.40	.18
❑ 8 Ricky Rudd	.40	.18
❑ 9 Sterling Marlin	.40	.18
❑ 10 Rick Mast	.20	.09
❑ 11 Michael Waltrip	.20	.09
❑ 12 Terry Labonte	1.00	.45
❑ 13 Bobby Labonte	.60	.25
❑ 14 Dick Trickle	.20	.09
❑ 15 Rick Wilson	.20	.09
❑ 16 Kenny Wallace	.20	.09
❑ 17 Hut Stricklin	.20	.09
❑ 18 Wally Dallenbach, Jr.	.20	.09
❑ 19 Jimmy Hensley	.20	.09
❑ 20 Ted Musgrave	.20	.09
❑ 21 Bobby Hillin	.20	.09
❑ 22 Dave Marcis	.40	.18
❑ 23 Derrike Cope	.20	.09
❑ 24 Neil Bonnett	.50	.23
❑ 25 Lake Speed	.20	.09
❑ 26 Robert Yates	.10	.05
❑ 27 Leo Jackson	.10	.05
❑ 28 Richard Petty	.50	.23
❑ 29 Junior Johnson	.20	.09
❑ 30 Rick Hendrick	.10	.05
❑ 31 Bobby Allison	.20	.09
❑ 32 Felix Sabates	.10	.05
❑ 33 Richard Childress	.10	.05
❑ 34 Bill Davis	.10	.05
❑ 35 Cale Yarborough	.20	.09
❑ 36 Jack Roush	.10	.05
❑ 37 Chuck Rider	.10	.05
❑ 38 Andy Petree	.10	.05
❑ 39 Buddy Parrott	.10	.05
❑ 40 Jimmy Makar	.10	.05
❑ 41 Mike Hill	.10	.05
❑ 42 Mike Beam	.10	.05
❑ 43 Charley Pressley	.10	.05
❑ 44 Ray Evernham	.10	.05
❑ 45 Larry McReynolds	.10	.05
❑ 46 Steve Hmiel	.10	.05
❑ 47 Ricky Craven	.20	.09
❑ 48 David Green	.20	.09
❑ 49 Bobby Dotter	.20	.09
❑ 50 Robert Pressley	.20	.09
❑ 51 Joe Bessey	.20	.09
❑ 52 Tim Fedewa	.20	.09
❑ 53 Mike McLaughlin	.20	.09
❑ 54 Roy Payne	.20	.09
❑ 55 Larry Pearson	.20	.09
❑ 56 Mike Wallace	.20	.09
❑ 57 Tracy Leslie	.20	.09
❑ 58 Tom Peck	.20	.09
❑ 59 Hermie Sadler	.20	.09
❑ 60 Chuck Bown	.20	.09
❑ 61 Todd Bodine	.20	.09
❑ 62 Shawna Robinson	.20	.09
❑ 63 Randy LaJoie	.20	.09
❑ 64 Ward Burton	.20	.09
❑ 65 Jeff Burton	.20	.09
❑ 66 Joe Nemechek	.20	.09
❑ 67 Steve Grissom	.20	.09
❑ 68 Harry Gant	.40	.18
❑ 69 Tommy Houston	.20	.09
❑ 70 Rusty Wallace's Pit Crew	.50	.23
❑ 71 Rusty Wallace	.50	.23
Driver of the Year		
❑ 72 Steve Grissom	.10	.05
BGN Champion		
❑ 73 Jeff Gordon	2.00	.90
Winston Cup Rookie of the Year		
❑ 74 Hermie Sadler	.20	.09
BGN Rookie of the Year		
❑ 75 Dale Jarrett WIN	.40	.18
❑ 76 Rusty Wallace WIN	.50	.23
❑ 77 Davey Allison WIN	.40	.18
❑ 78 Morgan Shepherd WIN	.10	.05
❑ 79 Dale Earnhardt WIN	1.00	.45
❑ 80 Rusty Wallace WIN	.50	.23
❑ 81 Rusty Wallace WIN	.50	.23
❑ 82 Rusty Wallace WIN	.50	.23
❑ 83 Ernie Irvan WIN	.20	.09
❑ 84 Geoff Bodine WIN	.10	.05
❑ 85 Dale Earnhardt BB WIN	1.00	.45
❑ 86 Kyle Petty WIN	.20	.09
❑ 87 Ricky Rudd WIN	.20	.09
❑ 88 Kyle Petty BC	.20	.09
❑ 89 Mark Martin BC	.50	.23
❑ 90 Ken Schrader BC	.10	.05
❑ 91 Rusty Wallace BC	.50	.23
❑ 92 Dale Earnhardt BC	1.00	.45
❑ 93 Brett Bodine BC	.10	.05
❑ 94 Geoff Bodine BC	.10	.05
❑ 95 Ernie Irvan BC	.20	.09
❑ 96 Bobby Labonte BC	.40	.18
❑ 97 Jeff Gordon BC	1.00	.45
❑ 98 Harry Gant BC	.20	.09
❑ 99 P.J. Jones BC	.10	.05
❑ 100 Davey Allison's Car	1.00	.45
Alan Kulwicki's Car		
❑ 101 Jeff Gordon	2.00	.90
❑ 102 Todd Bodine	.20	.09
❑ 103 Wally Dallenbach Jr.	.20	.09
❑ 104 Sterling Marlin	.40	.18
❑ 105 Terry Labonte	1.00	.45
❑ 106 Mark Martin	1.00	.45
❑ 107 Geoff Bodine	.20	.09
❑ 108 Jeff Burton	.40	.18
❑ 109 Ward Burton	.20	.09
❑ 110 Mike Wallace	.20	.09
❑ 111 Derrike Cope	.20	.09
❑ 112 Chuck Bown	.20	.09
❑ 113 Robert Pressley	.20	.09
❑ 114 John Andretti	.20	.09
❑ 115 Lake Speed	.20	.09
❑ 116 Ted Musgrave	.20	.09
❑ 117 Darrell Waltrip	.40	.18
❑ 118 Dale Jarrett	.75	.35
❑ 119 Loy Allen Jr.	.20	.09
❑ 120 Bobby Hamilton	.20	.09
❑ 121 Morgan Shepherd	.20	.09
❑ 122 Kyle Petty	.40	.18
❑ 123 Hut Stricklin	.20	.09
❑ 124 Joe Nemechek	.20	.09
❑ 125 Jimmy Hensley	.20	.09
❑ 126 Brett Bodine	.20	.09
❑ 127 Jimmy Spencer	.20	.09
❑ 128 Ernie Irvan	.40	.18
❑ 129 Steve Grissom	.20	.09
❑ 130 Greg Sacks	.20	.09
❑ 131 Tony Glover	.10	.05
❑ 132 Barry Dodson	.10	.05
❑ 133 Pete Wright	.10	.05
❑ 134 Chris Hussey	.10	.05
❑ 135 Gary DeHart	.10	.05
❑ 136 Doug Hewitt	.10	.05
❑ 137 Paul Andrews	.10	.05
❑ 138 Bill Ingle	.10	.05
❑ 139 Jimmy Fennig	.10	.05
❑ 140 Jeff Hammond	.10	.05
❑ 141 Donnie Richeson	.10	.05
❑ 142 Leonard Wood	.10	.05
❑ 143 Robbie Loomis	.10	.05
❑ 144 Larry Hedrick	.10	.05
❑ 145 Billy Hagan	.10	.05
❑ 146 Travis Carter	.10	.05
❑ 147 Roger Penske	.10	.05
❑ 148 Richard Jackson	.10	.05
❑ 149 Larry McClure	.10	.05
❑ 150 Bill Stavola	.10	.05
❑ 151 Mickey Stavola	.10	.05
❑ 152 Eddie Wood	.10	.05
❑ 153 Glen Wood	.10	.05
❑ 154 Len Wood	.10	.05
❑ 155 Ricky Rudd	.40	.18
❑ 156 Butch Mock	.10	.05
❑ 157 D.K. Ulrich	.10	.05
❑ 158 Joe Gibbs	.20	.09
❑ 159 Don Miller	.10	.05
❑ 160 Eddie Masencup	.10	.05
❑ 161 Mike Colyer	.10	.05
❑ 162 Hank Jones	.10	.05
❑ 163 Harry Gant	.40	.18
❑ 164 Kenny Wallace	.20	.09
❑ 165 Terry Labonte	1.00	.45
❑ 166 Morgan Shepherd	.20	.09
❑ 167 Chad Little	.20	.09
❑ 168 Ernie Irvan	.40	.18

❑ 169 Shawna Robinson	.20	.09
❑ 170 Mike McLaughlin	.20	.09
❑ 171 Elton Sawyer	.20	.09
❑ 172 Dirk Stephens	.10	.05
❑ 173 Ken Schrader	.20	.09
❑ 174 Dennis Setzer	.20	.09
❑ 175 Mark Martin	1.00	.45
❑ 176 Jim Bown	.20	.09
❑ 177 Bobby Labonte	.60	.25
❑ 178 Ed Whitaker	.10	.05
❑ 179 Tony Eury	.10	.05
❑ 180 Kelley Earnhardt Kerry Earnhardt Dale Earnhardt Jr	2.00	.90
❑ 181 Kelley Earnhardt	.40	.18
❑ 182 Kerry Earnhardt	.40	.18
❑ 183 Dale Earnhardt Jr.	8.00	3.60
❑ 184 Teresa Earnhardt	.40	.18
❑ 185 Don Hawk	.10	.05
❑ 186 Dale Earnhardt WIN	1.00	.45
❑ 187 Rusty Wallace WIN	.50	.23
❑ 188 Dale Earnhardt BB WIN	1.00	.45
❑ 189 Mark Martin WIN	.50	.23
❑ 190 Mark Martin WIN	.50	.23
❑ 191 Mark Martin WIN	.50	.23
❑ 192 Mark Martin WIN	.50	.23
❑ 193 Rusty Wallace WIN	.50	.23
❑ 194 Rusty Wallace WIN	.50	.23
❑ 195 Ernie Irvan WIN	.20	.09
❑ 196 Rusty Wallace WIN	.50	.23
❑ 197 Ernie Irvan WIN	.20	.09
❑ 198 Rusty Wallace WIN	.50	.23
❑ 199 Mark Martin WIN	.50	.23
❑ 200 Rusty Wallace WIN	.50	.23
❑ MMS1 Mark Martin AUTO Feel The Heat	80.00	36.00
❑ NNO Jeff Gordon BC AUTO/1500	120.00	55.00

1994 High Gear Gold

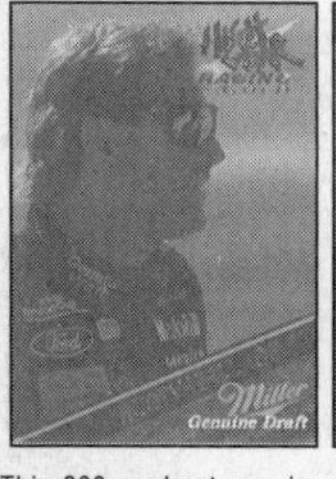

This 200-card set was issued in two series and is a parallel to the base High Gear cards. The cards featured gold foil stamping and the word "GOLD" appears below the High Gear logo on the front. There were 20 cards in the first series that were produced in shorter quantity than the other 80 in that series. Due to a UV coating problem cards 1, 6, 11, 16, 25, 30, 35, 40, 41, 46, 51, 56, 61, 66, 71, 76, 81, 86, 91, 96 were produced in smaller quantities. The majority of these cards were produced in 15-35% less quantities. Cards 1, 6, 71, 81, and 91 were the shortest at 40-50% less quantites. Those five cards appear with the SP distinction in the checklist below.

	MINT	NRMT
COMPLETE SET (200)	200.00	90.00
COMPLETE SERIES 1 (100)	100.00	45.00
COMPLETE SERIES 2 (100)	100.00	45.00
COMMON CARD (1-100)	.40	.18
COMMON CARD (101-200)	.50	.23
COMMON DRIVER (1-100)	.75	.35
COMMON DRIVER (101-200)	1.00	.45

*GOLD CARDS: 3X TO 6X BASIC CARDS

❑ 1 Dale Earnhardt SP	15.00	6.75
❑ 6 Geoff Bodine SP	2.00	.90
❑ 71 Rusty Wallace DOY SP	8.00	3.60
❑ 81 Rusty Wallace WIN SP	8.00	3.60
❑ 91 Rusty Wallace BC SP	8.00	3.60

1994 High Gear Dominators

This 7-card insert set features Jumbo size cards (4" by 6") of the top drivers in Winston Cup racing. The cards were distributed as box inserts in High Gear series one and two, along with High Gear Day One. Cards D1-D3 were available in series one boxes at a rate of one in six. Card D4 was available in High Gear Day One boxes at a rate of one in eight. Cards D5-D7 were available in series two boxes at a rate of one in six. There are 3,000 of each of the cards D1-D3, while there are 1,750 of the cards D4-D7.

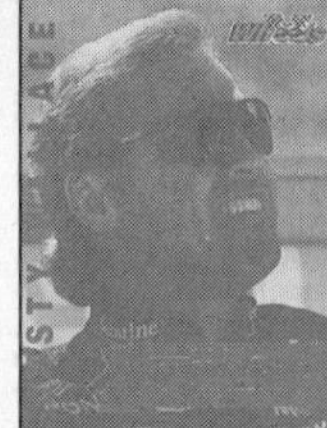

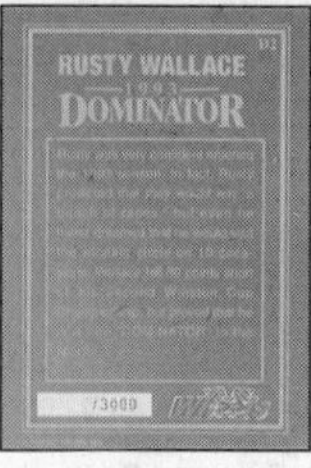

	MINT	NRMT
COMPLETE SET (7)	150.00	70.00
COMPLETE SERIES 1 (3)	75.00	34.00
COMPLETE SERIES 2 (3)	75.00	34.00
COMMON CARD (D1-D4)	15.00	6.75
COMMON CARD (D5-D7)	15.00	6.75

❑ D1 Mark Martin	15.00	6.75
❑ D2 Rusty Wallace	15.00	6.75
❑ D3 Dale Earnhardt	30.00	13.50
❑ D4 Ernie Irvan	15.00	6.75
❑ D5 Jeff Gordon	40.00	18.00
❑ D6 Mark Martin	20.00	9.00
❑ D7 Harry Gant	15.00	6.75

1994 High Gear Legends

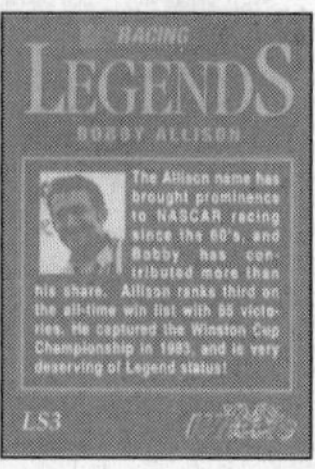

This six-card insert set features some of the greatest names in racing history. The cards were issued in series one, series two and High Gear Day One boxes. Series one boxes offered cards LS1-LS3 at an average of one Legends card per box. Series two and High Gear Day One boxes offered cards LS4-LS6 at a rate of one per box (24 packs).

	MINT	NRMT
COMPLETE SET (6)	25.00	11.00
COMPLETE SERIES 1 (3)	10.00	4.50
COMPLETE SERIES 2 (3)	15.00	6.75
COMMON CARD (LS1-LS3)	4.00	1.80
COMMON CARD (LS4-LS6)	4.00	1.80

❑ LS1 Cale Yarborough	4.00	1.80
❑ LS2 David Pearson	4.00	1.80
❑ LS3 Bobby Allison	4.00	1.80
❑ LS4 Richard Petty	8.00	3.60
❑ LS5 Benny Parsons	4.00	1.80
❑ LS6 Ned Jarrett	4.00	1.80

1994 High Gear Mega Gold

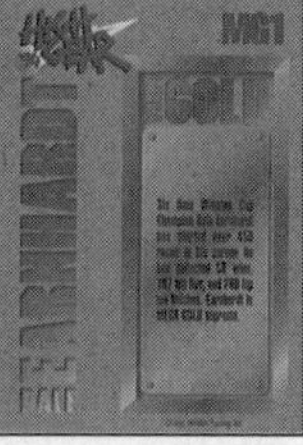

This 12-card insert set features 12 of the best drivers in Winston Cup. Cards are on all gold board and could be found at a rate of one per 12 packs. There was also a special Dale Earnhardt 7-Time Champion card. This card is the same as the regular card except that the entire card is embossed and comes with a 7-Time Champion seal on the front. The sets were also sold on QVC. There were 3,900 sets offered, including the 7-time Dale Earnhardt card for $99. An uncut sheet of all 13 cards was available. There are two different versions of uncut sheets also. The common version is a blank back sheet. The more difficult verions has complete card backs.

	MINT
COMPLETE SET (12)	60.00
COMMON CARD (MG1-MG12)	2.00

*SINGLES: 4X TO 10X BASE CARD HI

❑ MG1 Dale Earnhardt	4.00
❑ MG2 Ernie Irvan	4.00
❑ MG3 Rusty Wallace	4.00
❑ MG4 Mark Martin	4.00
❑ MG5 Jeff Gordon	4.00
❑ MG6 Ken Schrader	2.00
❑ MG7 Geoff Bodine	2.00
❑ MG8 Ricky Rudd	4.00
❑ MG9 Kyle Petty	4.00
❑ MG10 Terry Labonte	5.00
❑ MG11 Darrell Waltrip	4.00
❑ MG12 Michael Waltrip	2.00
❑ SMG1 Dale Earnhardt MG1S	50.00

1994 High Gear Rookie Shootout Autographs

This seven-card insert set features seven of the d that were competing for the '94 Winston Cup Roo the Year. Cards RS1-RS3 were available in serie boxes. There were 1,500 of each of the three card they were randomly seeded at one card per 384 p Cards RS4-RS7 were available in series two High boxes and series two High Gear Day One boxes. were 1,000 of each of the four cards and they randomly inserted at a rate of one card per 288 packs

	MINT
COMPLETE SET (7)	300.00
COMPLETE SERIES 1 (3)	125.00
COMPLETE SERIES 2 (4)	180.00
COMMON AUTO (RS1-RS3)	40.00
COMMON AUTO (RS4-RS7)	50.00

❑ RS1 Steve Grissom AUTO/1500	40.00
❑ RS2 Ward Burton AUTO/1500	40.00
❑ RS3 Jeff Burton AUTO/1500	40.00
❑ RS4 Joe Nemechek AUTO/1000	50.00
❑ RS5 Mike Wallace AUTO/1000	50.00
❑ RS6 Loy Allen Jr. AUTO/1000	50.00
❑ RS7 John Andretti AUTO/1000	50.00

1994 High Gear Rookie Thunder Update

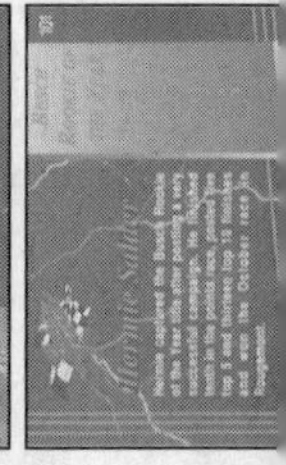

This 5-card insert set features four former Rookies Year. The cards were an update to the 93 Wheels R Thunder set. The cards were packaged in three cellophane packs and you got one pack in the top o High Gear series one boxes. There was one checkli two cards in each pack. The four driver cards came versions, a base version and a platinum parallel vers

	MINT
COMPLETE SET (5)	14.00
COMMON CARD (101-104)	2.00

*PLATINUM CARDS 1.5X TO 3X BASIC CARDS

❑ 101 Hermie Sadler	2.00
❑ 102 Jeff Gordon	6.00

Bobby Hamilton	2.00	.90
Dale Earnhardt	6.00	2.70
) Checklist Card	.50	.23

1994 High Gear Day One

100-card set is a parallel to the 1994 High Gear two set. The cards were packaged separately in six packs. There were 24 packs per box and 24 boxes ase. The cards that went into the first 500 cases of Gear series two off the press were stamped with a foil "Day 1" logo to differentiate them from the r series two cards.

	MINT	NRMT
'LETE SET (100)	18.00	8.00
ION CARD (101-200)	.15	.07
ION DRIVER (101-200)	.25	.11
NES: .6X to 1.25X SERIES 2 BASE CARDS		

94 High Gear Day One Gold

00-card set is a parallel to the base Day One set. ards feature a gold foil stamped "Day 1" logo to ntiate them from the base Day One cards. The gold were randomly inserted in packs of Day One at a one card per two packs.

	MINT	NRMT
LETE SET (100)	100.00	45.00
ION CARD (101-200)	.75	.35
ION DRIVER (101-200)	1.50	.70
) CARDS: 4X TO X BASIC CARDS		

994 High Gear Power Pak Teams

are three individually boxed driver's team sets that rt of the Power Pak Teams: 21-card Dale Earnhardt, 'd Harry Gant and 41-card Rusty Wallace sets. Each set is individually boxed and features that driver and eam. There was also a gold parallel version of each sets. There were 800 cases produced. There were s in each case and the cases were packaged in the ing ratios: 15 Dale Earnhardt sets, 10 Rusty Wallace 5 Harry Gant sets, 3 Gold Dale Earnhardt sets, 2 Rusty Wallace sets and 1 Gold Harry Gant set.

	MINT	NRMT
LETE EARNHARDT (21)	15.00	6.75
LETE GANT (34)	15.00	6.75
LETE WALLACE (41)	15.00	6.75
ION EARN.TEAM (1-20)	.75	.35
ION GANT TEAM (1-33)	.60	.25
COMMON WALL.TEAM (1-40)	.60	.25
COMP.GOLD EARNHARDT (21)	30.00	13.50
COMP.GOLD GANT (34)	30.00	13.50
COMP.GOLD WALLACE (41)	30.00	13.50
*GOLD CARDS: 1.25X TO X BASIC CARDS		
❑ E1 Richard Childress	.75	.35
❑ E2 Andy Petree	.75	.35
❑ E3 Dale Earnhardt	2.50	1.10
❑ E4 Dale Earnhardt Richard Childress	2.50	1.10
❑ E5 Dale Earnhardt Andy Petree	2.50	1.10
❑ E6 David Smith	.75	.35
❑ E7 Danny Meyers	.75	.35
❑ E8 Danny Lawrence	.75	.35
❑ E9 Eddie Lanier	.75	.35
❑ E10 Jimmy Elledge	.75	.35
❑ E11 Joe Dan Bailey	.75	.35
❑ E12 Jim Baldwin	.75	.35
❑ E13 Craig Donley	.75	.35
❑ E14 John Mulloy	.75	.35
❑ E15 Gene Dehart	.75	.35
❑ E16 Jim Cook Hal Carter	.75	.35
❑ E17 RCR Enterprises Office	.75	.35
❑ E18 Dale Earnhardt in Pits	.75	.35
❑ E19 Dale Earnhardt w/Crew	.75	.35
❑ E20 Dale Earnhardt's Car	2.50	1.10
❑ E21 Dale Earnhardt's Car checklist card numbered CL	1.50	.70
❑ G1 Harry Gant	1.00	.45
❑ G2 Leo Jackson	.60	.25
❑ G3 Charley Pressley	.60	.25
❑ G4 Billy Abernathy	.60	.25
❑ G5 Ricky Viers	.60	.25
❑ G6 David Rogers	.60	.25
❑ G7 Jimmy Penland	.60	.25
❑ G8 Allen Hester	.60	.25
❑ G9 Jay Guy	.60	.25
❑ G10 Ellis Frazier	.60	.25
❑ G11 Hoss Berry	.60	.25
❑ G12 Eddie Masencup	.60	.25
❑ G13 Shaun Woods	.60	.25
❑ G14 Renee Forrest	.60	.25
❑ G15 Phil Banks	.60	.25
❑ G16 Joe Schmaling	.60	.25
❑ G17 Bruce Morris	.60	.25
❑ G18 Dean Johnson	.60	.25
❑ G19 DeWayne Felkel	.60	.25
❑ G20 Jim Presnell	.60	.25
❑ G21 Jan McDougald	.60	.25
❑ G22 Marc Parks	.60	.25
❑ G23 Jerry Vess	.60	.25
❑ G24 Teddy Blackwell	.60	.25
❑ G25 Roger Chastain	.60	.25
❑ G26 Brad Turner	.60	.25
❑ G27 Kent Mashburn	.60	.25
❑ G28 Harry Gant in Pits	.60	.25
❑ G29 Harry Gant	1.00	.45
❑ G30 Harry Gant in Pits	.60	.25
❑ G31 Harry Gant's Car	.60	.25
❑ G32 Harry Gant's Car	.60	.25
❑ G33 Harry Gant's Car	.60	.25
❑ G34 Harry Gant's Car checklist card numbered CL	.60	.25
❑ W1 Roger Penske	.60	.25
❑ W2 Rusty Wallace	1.25	.55
❑ W3 Don Miller	.60	.25
❑ W4 Dick Paysor	.60	.25
❑ W5 Buddy Parrott	.60	.25
❑ W6 Todd Parrott	.60	.25
❑ W7 Brad Parrott	.60	.25
❑ W8 Bill Wilburn	.60	.25
❑ W9 Scott Robinson	.60	.25
❑ W10 Paul VanderLaan	.60	.25
❑ W11 Gary Brooks	.60	.25
❑ W12 Earl Barban Jr.	.60	.25
❑ W13 Jeff Thousand	.60	.25
❑ W14 Nick Ollila	.60	.25
❑ W15 Angela Crawford	.60	.25
❑ W16 Stella Paysor	.60	.25
❑ W17 Lori Wetzel	.60	.25
❑ W18 Dave Hoffert	.60	.25
❑ W19 Robert Pressley	.60	.25
❑ W20 Dennis Beaver	.60	.25
❑ W21 Jerry Branz	.60	.25
❑ W22 David Munari	.60	.25
❑ W23 Rocky Owenby Barry Poovey	.60	.25
❑ W24 Jamie Freeze Mike Wingate	.60	.25
❑ W25 Steve Triplett James Shoffner	.60	.25
❑ W26 Phil Ditmars Eric Durchman	.60	.25
❑ W27 Ronnie Phillips Billy Woodruff	.60	.25
❑ W28 Matt King Jimmy Zamrzla	.60	.25
❑ W29 Mark Campbell	.60	.25
❑ W30 David Evans	.60	.25
❑ W31 Tony Lambert David Little	.60	.25
❑ W32 David Kenny Dave Roberts	.60	.25
❑ W33 Bo Schlager Mark Armstrong	.60	.25
❑ W34 Rusty Wallace Buddy Parrott	1.25	.55
❑ W35 Rusty Wallace	1.25	.55
❑ W36 Rusty Wallace in Pits	.60	.25
❑ W37 Rusty Wallace	1.25	.55
❑ W38 Rusty Wallace w/Car	.60	.25
❑ W39 Rusty Wallace	1.25	.55
❑ W40 Rusty Wallace's Car	.60	.25
❑ W41 Rusty Wallace's Car checklist card numbered CL	.75	.35

1995 High Gear

This 100-card set features top drivers from both Winston Cup and Busch Circuits. The cards are printed on 24-point paper and display silver foil stamping and UV coating. There were 1,000 cases produced. Each case contained 20 boxes, with 24 packs per box and six cards per pack. There were also two randomly inserted autograph cards. Terry Labonte was featured on an "IceMan" card and Steve Kinser was featured on "The Outlaw" card. The autograph cards were randomly inserted at a rate of one per 480 packs. The set also included two subsets; Split Shift (61-68), and Race Winner (86-97).

	MINT	NRMT
COMPLETE SET (100)	12.00	5.50
COMMON CARD (1-100)	.10	.05
COMMON DRIVER (1-100)	.20	.09
COMP.E-RACE TO WIN SET (10)	1.00	.45
❑ 1 Dale Earnhardt	2.00	.90
❑ 2 Rusty Wallace	1.00	.45
❑ 3 Mark Martin	1.00	.45
❑ 4 Ricky Rudd	.40	.18
❑ 5 Morgan Shepherd	.20	.09
❑ 6 Jeff Gordon	2.00	.90
❑ 7 Darrell Waltrip	.40	.18
❑ 8 Terry Labonte	1.00	.45
❑ 9 Michael Waltrip	.20	.09
❑ 10 Ted Musgrave	.20	.09
❑ 11 Geoff Bodine	.20	.09
❑ 12 Ken Schrader	.20	.09
❑ 13 Bill Elliott	1.00	.45
❑ 14 Lake Speed	.20	.09
❑ 15 Sterling Marlin	.40	.18
❑ 16 Rick Mast	.20	.09
❑ 17 Kyle Petty	.40	.18
❑ 18 Ernie Irvan	.40	.18
❑ 19 Dale Jarrett	.75	.35
❑ 20 Brett Bodine	.20	.09
❑ 21 Bobby Labonte	.75	.35
❑ 22 Todd Bodine	.20	.09
❑ 23 Jeff Burton	.40	.18
❑ 24 Joe Nemechek	.20	.09
❑ 25 Steve Grissom	.20	.09
❑ 26 Derrike Cope	.20	.09
❑ 27 John Andretti	.20	.09
❑ 28 Mike Wallace	.20	.09
❑ 29 Ward Burton	.20	.09
❑ 30 Loy Allen Jr.	.20	.09
❑ 31 Richard Childress	.10	.05
❑ 32 Roger Penske	.10	.05
❑ 33 Jack Roush	.10	.05
❑ 34 Rick Hendrick	.10	.05
❑ 35 Ricky Rudd OWN	.40	.18
❑ 36 Robert Yates	.10	.05
❑ 37 Junior Johnson	.20	.09
❑ 38 Bobby Allison	.20	.09
❑ 39 Felix Sabates	.10	.05
❑ 40 Cale Yarborough	.20	.09
❑ 41 Andy Petree	.10	.05
❑ 42 Charlie Pressley	.10	.05

❑ 43 Ray Evernham	.20	.09
❑ 44 Larry McReynolds	.10	.05
❑ 45 Steve Hmiel	.10	.05
❑ 46 Robbie Loomis	.10	.05
❑ 47 Paul Andrews	.10	.05
❑ 48 Jeff Hammond	.10	.05
❑ 49 Doug Hewitt	.10	.05
❑ 50 Gary Dehart	.10	.05
❑ 51 Kenny Wallace	.20	.09
❑ 52 Ricky Craven	.20	.09
❑ 53 Dennis Setzer	.20	.09
❑ 54 Johnny Benson	.20	.09
❑ 55 David Green	.20	.09
❑ 56 Hermie Sadler	.20	.09
❑ 57 Elton Sawyer	.20	.09
❑ 58 Chad Little	.20	.09
❑ 59 Larry Pearson	.20	.09
❑ 60 Mike McLaughlin	.20	.09
❑ 61 Terry Labonte SS	.50	.23
❑ 62 Mike Wallace SS	.10	.05
❑ 63 Mark Martin SS	.50	.23
❑ 64 Kenny Wallace SS	.10	.05
❑ 65 Ken Schrader SS	.10	.05
❑ 66 Bobby Labonte SS	.40	.18
❑ 67 Joe Nemechek SS	.10	.05
❑ 68 Harry Gant SS	.20	.09
❑ 69 Johnny Benson Jr. BGN ROY	.10	.05
❑ 70 David Green BGN Champ	.10	.05
❑ 71 Dale Earnhardt's Car	1.00	.45
❑ 72 Rusty Wallace's Car	.50	.23
❑ 73 Mark Martin's Car	.50	.23
❑ 74 Ken Schrader's Car	.10	.05
❑ 75 Ricky Rudd's Car	.20	.09
❑ 76 Morgan Shepherd's Car	.10	.05
❑ 77 Terry Labonte's Car	.50	.23
❑ 78 Jeff Gordon's Car	1.00	.45
❑ 79 Darrell Waltrip's Car	.20	.09
❑ 80 Bill Elliott's Car	.50	.23
❑ 81 Sterling Marlin's Car	.20	.09
❑ 82 Lake Speed's Car	.10	.05
❑ 83 Ted Musgrave's Car	.10	.05
❑ 84 Michael Waltrip's Car	.10	.05
❑ 85 Geoff Bodine's Car	.10	.05
❑ 86 Dale Earnhardt RW	1.00	.45
❑ 87 Rusty Wallace RW	.50	.23
❑ 88 Mark Martin RW	.50	.23
❑ 89 Ricky Rudd RW	.20	.09
❑ 90 Terry Labonte RW	.50	.23
❑ 91 Jeff Gordon RW	1.00	.45
❑ 92 Bill Elliott RW	.50	.23
❑ 93 Sterling Marlin RW	.20	.09
❑ 94 Geoff Bodine RW	.10	.05
❑ 95 Dale Jarrett RW	.40	.18
❑ 96 Ernie Irvan RW	.20	.09
❑ 97 Jimmy Spencer RW	.10	.05
❑ 98 Jeff Gordon in Pits	1.00	.45
❑ 99 Jeff Burton ROY	.20	.09
❑ 100 Bill Elliott FF	.50	.23
❑ SKS1 Steve Kinser AU/1500	40.00	18.00
❑ TLS1 Terry Labonte AU/1500	60.00	27.00

1995 High Gear Gold

This 100-card set is a parallel to the base High Gear set. The cards feature gold foil stamping and the word "gold" appears under the High Gear logo on the fronts of the cards. The cards were found one per pack.

	MINT	NRMT
COMPLETE SET (100)	40.00	18.00
COMMON CARD (1-100)	.30	.14
COMMON DRIVER (1-100)	.60	.25

*STARS: 2X TO 4X BASIC CARDS

1995 High Gear Busch Clash

This 16-card insert set features the 16 drivers who qualified for the 1995 Busch Clash. Each card was printed in silver foil as well as a gold foil parallel. The silver cards use MicroEtch printing technology and were inserted at the ratio of 1:8 packs. Gold cards were inserted at the wrapper stated odds of 1:24 packs.

	MINT	NRMT
COMPLETE SET (16)	40.00	18.00
COMMON CARD (BC1-BC16)	1.25	.55
*SINGLES: 2.5X TO 6X BASE CARD HI		
COMPLETE GOLD SET (16)	70.00	32.00
*GOLD CARDS: 5X TO 12X BASIC CARDS		
UNCUT GOLD SHEET	40.00	18.00

❑ BC1 Loy Allen Jr.	1.25	.55
❑ BC2 Geoff Bodine	1.25	.55
❑ BC3 Ted Musgrave	1.25	.55
❑ BC4 Bill Elliott	2.50	1.10
❑ BC5 Ernie Irvan	2.50	1.10
❑ BC6 Rusty Wallace	2.50	1.10
❑ BC7 Jeff Gordon	2.50	1.10
❑ BC8 Dale Earnhardt	2.50	1.10
❑ BC9 Rick Mast	1.25	.55
❑ BC10 Mark Martin	2.50	1.10
❑ BC11 Jimmy Spencer	1.25	.55
❑ BC12 Ward Burton	1.25	.55
❑ BC13 Ricky Rudd	2.50	1.10
❑ BC14 Sterling Marlin	2.50	1.10
❑ BC15 Greg Sacks	1.25	.55
❑ BC16 David Green	1.25	.55

1995 High Gear Dominators

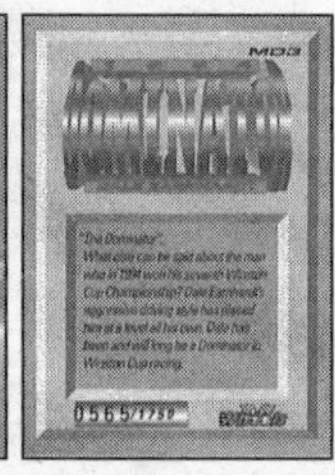

This four-card insert set feaures top Winston Cup drivers on 3 1/2" by 5" cards. The cards are numbered of 1,750 on the backs of the card. They came in a white envelope and were inserted in boxes at a rate of one per seven boxes. The Rusty Wallace (D1) was available in Day One boxes and the other three (D2-D4) were found in regular High Gear boxes. A four card uncut sheet of the Dominators was also produced. There was also a Mini-Dominator version of each of the four cards. These cards were a standard size replica of the jumbo card. The cards were distributed the same as their larger versions and were inserted 1:168 packs. The four Mini-Dominator cards sell for the same price as the large versions.

	MINT	NRMT
COMPLETE SET (4)	100.00	45.00
COMMON CARD (D1-D4)	6.00	2.70
*SINGLES: 12X TO 30X BASE CARD HI		
UNCUT 4 CARD SHEET	100.00	45.00

❑ D1 Rusty Wallace/1750	6.00	2.70
❑ D2 Terry Labonte/1750	6.00	2.70
❑ D3 Dale Earnhardt/1750	6.00	2.70
❑ D4 Geoff Bodine/1750	6.00	2.70

1995 High Gear Legends

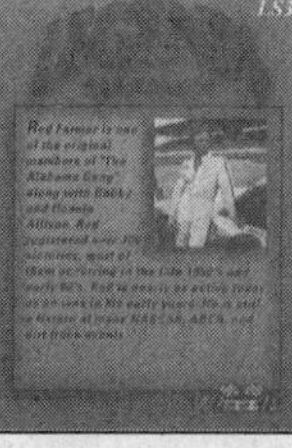

This three-card insert set features three of the al legends of Stock Car racing. The cards are print silver foil board and were inserted one per 24 packs.

	MINT
COMPLETE SET (3)	10.00
COMMON CARD (L1-L3)	4.00

❑ L1 Junior Johnson	4.00
❑ L2 Fred Lorenzen	4.00
❑ L3 Red Farmer	4.00

1995 High Gear Day One

This 100-card set is a separately packaged version base '95 High Gear set. The cards feature a silv stamped "Day 1" logo to distinguish them from the cards. The cards in the first 500 cases off the press stamped with this "Day 1" logo. There were two su Split Shift (61-68), and Race Winner (86-97). They packaged six cards to a pack, 24 packs to a box a boxes per case.

	MINT
COMPLETE SET (100)	20.00
COMMON CARD (1-100)	.10
COMMON DRIVER (1-100)	.20

*DAY ONE CARDS: .75X TO 1.5X BASE HIGH GEAR CARDS

1995 High Gear Day One G

This 100-card set is a parallel to the base Day On The cards feature a gold foil stamping on the Da logo on the front of the card. The cards were inserte per High Gear Day One pack.

	MINT
COMPLETE SET (100)	60.00
COMMON CARD (1-100)	.50
COMMON DRIVER (1-100)	1.00

*STARS: 2.5X TO 5X DAY ONE CARDS

1998 High Gear

The 1998 High Gear set was issued in one series to 72 cards. The cards feature color photos printed on board with multi-level foil stamping. The set contai topical subsets: NASCAR Winston Cup Drivers (NASCAR Winston Cup Cars (28-36), NASCAR Series Drivers (37-41), NASCAR Craftsman Truck D (42-45), Awards (46-54), '98 Preview (55-63 Carmeleon (64-71).

	MINT	NRMT
'LETE SET (72)	20.00	9.00
ION CARD (1-72)	.10	.05
ION DRIVER (1-72)	.20	.09
eff Gordon	2.00	.90
ale Jarrett	.75	.35
lark Martin	1.00	.45
eff Burton	.40	.18
ale Earnhardt	2.00	.90
erry Labonte	1.00	.45
obby Labonte	.75	.35
ll Elliott	1.00	.45
usty Wallace	1.00	.45
Ken Schrader	.20	.09
Johnny Benson	.20	.09
Ted Musgrave	.20	.09
Jeremy Mayfield	.60	.25
Ernie Irvan	.40	.18
Kyle Petty	.40	.18
Bobby Hamilton	.20	.09
Ricky Rudd	.40	.18
Michael Waltrip	.20	.09
Ricky Craven	.20	.09
Jimmy Spencer	.20	.09
Ward Burton	.20	.09
Sterling Marlin	.40	.18
Darrell Waltrip	.40	.18
Joe Nemechek	.20	.09
Mike Skinner	.20	.09
David Green	.20	.09
Wally Dallenbach	.20	.09
Rusty Wallace's Car	.50	.23
Dale Earnhardt's Car	1.00	.45
Terry Labonte's Car	.50	.23
Mark Martin's Car	.50	.23
Bobby Labonte's Car	.40	.18
Jeff Gordon's Car	1.00	.45
Dale Jarrett's Car	.40	.18
Bill Elliott's Car	.50	.23
Jeff Burton's Car	.20	.09
Randy LaJoie	.20	.09
Todd Bodine	.20	.09
Steve Park	.75	.35
Phil Parsons	.20	.09
Elliott Sadler	.20	.09
Rich Bickle	.20	.09
Jack Sprague	.20	.09
Joe Ruttman	.20	.09
Ron Hornaday Jr.	.20	.09
Mark Martin	1.00	.45
Brian Whitesell	.10	.05
Dale Earnhardt's Car	1.00	.45
Mike Skinner	.20	.09
Jeff Gordon	2.00	.90
Jeff Burton	.40	.18
Jimmy Fenning	.10	.05
Charlie Siegars	.10	.05
Dale Jarrett	.75	.35
Johnny Benson	.20	.09
Todd Bodine	.20	.09
Robert Pressley	.20	.09
Bobby Hamilton	.20	.09
Ernie Irvan	.40	.18
Kenny Irwin	.60	.25
Sterling Marlin	.40	.18
Steve Park	.75	.35
John Andretti	.20	.09
Dale Earnhardt's Car	1.00	.45
Terry Labonte's Car	.50	.23
Ricky Rudd's Car	.20	.09
Bobby Labonte's Car	.40	.18
Michael Waltrip's Car	.10	.05
Jeff Gordon's Car	1.00	.45
Darrell Waltrip's Car	.20	.09
Bill Elliott's Car	.50	.23
Checklist	.10	.05

1998 High Gear First Gear

ed one per pack, this 72-card set is an all-foil micro-
d parallel version of the base set.

	MINT	NRMT
'LETE SET (72)	30.00	13.50
ION CARD (1-72)	.15	.07
ION DRIVER (1-72)	.30	.14

1998 High Gear MPH

mly inserted in hobby only packs at the rate of one this 72-card set is parallel to the base set with al foil-stamping. Only 100 of each card were ced and individually numbered.

	MINT	NRMT
'LETE SET (72)	600.00	275.00
ION CARD (1-72)	3.00	1.35
ION DRIVER (1-72)	6.00	2.70

1998 High Gear Autographs

Randomly inserted in packs at the rate of one in 192, this 20-card set features autographed color photos of top NASCAR Winston Cup drivers with a certificate of authenticity. The cards are checklisted below in alphabetical order.

	MINT	NRMT
COMPLETE SET (20)	1200.00	550.00
COMMON CARD (1-20)	15.00	6.75
❑ 1 Johnny Benson/250	15.00	6.75
❑ 2 Jeff Burton/250	30.00	13.50
❑ 3 Ward Burton/250	15.00	6.75
❑ 4 Ricky Craven/200	15.00	6.75
❑ 5 Wally Dallenbach/250	15.00	6.75
❑ 6 Dale Earnhardt/50	300.00	135.00
❑ 7 Bill Elliott/250	90.00	40.00
❑ 8 Jeff Gordon/50	300.00	135.00
❑ 9 Bobby Hamilton/250	15.00	6.75
❑ 10 Ernie Irvan/225	30.00	13.50
❑ 11 Dale Jarrett/200	60.00	27.00
❑ 12 Bobby Labonte/250	50.00	22.00
❑ 13 Terry Labonte/150	100.00	45.00
❑ 14 Mark Martin/100	125.00	55.00
❑ 15 Jeremy Mayfield/250	40.00	18.00
❑ 16 Ted Musgrave/250	15.00	6.75
❑ 17 Joe Nemechek/250	15.00	6.75
❑ 18 Kyle Petty/200	30.00	13.50
❑ 19 Ken Schrader/250	15.00	6.75
❑ 20 Mike Skinner/250	15.00	6.75
❑ 21 Darrell Waltrip/250	30.00	13.50
❑ 22 Michael Waltrip/250	15.00	6.75

1998 High Gear Custom Shop Redemption

Randomly inserted in packs at the rate of one in 192, redemption cards for this five-card set allowed the collector to customize his own card by selecting one of three fronts and three backs for each card. The collector then received his custom-made card by return mail with his chosen front and back selection.

	MINT	NRMT
COMPLETE SET (5)	400.00	180.00
COMMON CARD (CS1-CS5)	80.00	36.00
*SINGLES: 30X TO 75X BASE CARD HI		
❑ CS1 Dale Earnhardt	150.00	70.00
❑ CS2 Jeff Gordon	150.00	70.00
❑ CS3 Mark Martin	100.00	45.00
❑ CS4 Terry Labonte	100.00	45.00
❑ CS5 Dale Jarrett	80.00	36.00

1998 High Gear Gear Jammers

Randomly inserted in packs at the rate of one in two, this 27-card set features color photos printed on die-cut, foil stamped cards.

	MINT	NRMT
COMPLETE SET (27)	25.00	11.00
COMMON CARD (GJ1-GJ27)	.60	.25
*SINGLES: 1.25X TO 3X BASE CARD HI		
❑ GJ1 Rusty Wallace	3.00	1.35
❑ GJ2 Dale Earnhardt's Car	3.00	1.35
❑ GJ3 Sterling Marlin	1.25	.55
❑ GJ4 Terry Labonte	3.00	1.35
❑ GJ5 Mark Martin	3.00	1.35
❑ GJ6 Ricky Rudd	1.25	.55
❑ GJ7 Ted Musgrave	.60	.25
❑ GJ8 Darrell Waltrip	1.25	.55
❑ GJ9 Bobby Labonte	2.50	1.10
❑ GJ10 Michael Waltrip	.60	.25
❑ GJ11 Ward Burton	.60	.25
❑ GJ12 Jeff Gordon	6.00	2.70
❑ GJ13 Bobby Hamilton	.60	.25
❑ GJ14 Kyle Petty	1.25	.55
❑ GJ15 Dale Jarrett	2.50	1.10
❑ GJ16 Bill Elliott	3.00	1.35
❑ GJ17 Jeff Burton	1.25	.55
❑ GJ18 Wally Dallenbach	.60	.25
❑ GJ19 Jimmy Spencer	.60	.25
❑ GJ20 Ken Schrader	.60	.25
❑ GJ21 Johnny Benson	.60	.25
❑ GJ22 David Green	.60	.25
❑ GJ23 Mike Skinner	.60	.25
❑ GJ24 Joe Nemechek	.60	.25
❑ GJ25 Jeremy Mayfield	2.00	.90
❑ GJ26 Ricky Craven	.60	.25
❑ GJ27 Morgan Shepherd	.60	.25

1998 High Gear High Groove

Randomly inserted in packs at the rate of one in 10, this nine-card set features color photos of cars belonging to top drivers printed on die-cut, foil stamped cards.

	MINT	NRMT
COMPLETE SET (9)	30.00	13.50
COMMON CARD (HG1-HG9)	1.50	.70
*SINGLES: 1.5X TO 4X BASE CARD HI		
❑ HG1 Rusty Wallace's Car	4.00	1.80
❑ HG2 Dale Earnhardt's Car	8.00	3.60
❑ HG3 Terry Labonte's Car	4.00	1.80
❑ HG4 Mark Martin's Car	4.00	1.80
❑ HG5 Jeff Gordon's Car	8.00	3.60
❑ HG6 Bobby Labonte's Car	3.00	1.35
❑ HG7 Dale Jarrett's Car	3.00	1.35
❑ HG8 Bill Elliott's Car	4.00	1.80
❑ HG9 Jeff Burton's Car	1.50	.70

1998 High Gear Man and Machine - Car

Randomly inserted in retail packs at the rate of one in 20, this nine-card set features color portraits of top drivers' cars printed on interlocking all-foil cards made to be matched with the hobby only version of this set containing color photos of the drivers.

	MINT	NRMT
COMPLETE SET (9)	40.00	18.00
COMMON CARD (1-9)	1.25	.55
*SINGLES: 2.5X TO 6X BASE CARD HI		
❑ 1 Jeff Gordon's Car	12.00	5.50
❑ 2 Mark Martin's Car	6.00	2.70
❑ 3 Dale Jarrett's Car	5.00	2.20
❑ 4 Jeff Burton's Car	1.25	.55
❑ 5 Terry Labonte's Car	6.00	2.70
❑ 6 Bobby Labonte's Car	5.00	2.20
❑ 7 Dale Earnhardt's Car	12.00	5.50

❑ 8 Bill Elliott's Car	6.00	2.70
❑ 9 Rusty Wallace's Car	6.00	2.70

1998 High Gear Man and Machine - Driver

Randomly inserted in hobby packs only at the rate of one in 20, this nine-card set features color portraits of top drivers printed on interlocking all-foil cards made to be matched with the retail only version of this set containing color photos of their cars.

	MINT	NRMT
COMPLETE SET (9)	75.00	34.00
COMMON CARD (MM1-MM9)	4.00	1.80
*SINGLES: 4X TO 10X BASE CARD HI		
❑ MM1 Jeff Gordon	20.00	9.00
❑ MM2 Mark Martin	10.00	4.50
❑ MM3 Dale Jarrett	8.00	3.60
❑ MM4 Jeff Burton	4.00	1.80
❑ MM5 Terry Labonte	10.00	4.50
❑ MM6 Bobby Labonte	8.00	3.60
❑ MM7 Dale Earnhardt	20.00	9.00
❑ MM8 Bill Elliott	10.00	4.50
❑ MM9 Rusty Wallace	10.00	4.50

1998 High Gear Pure Gold

Randomly inserted in packs at the rate of one in six, this nine-card set commemorates NASCAR's 50th anniversary and features color photos of the best all-time drivers printed on all-foil cards.

	MINT	NRMT
COMPLETE SET (9)	30.00	13.50
COMMON CARD (PG1-PG9)	.75	.35
*SINGLES: 1.5X TO 4X BASE CARD HI		
❑ PG1 Dale Earnhardt	8.00	3.60
❑ PG2 Richard Petty	2.00	.90
❑ PG3 Jeff Gordon	8.00	3.60
❑ PG4 Terry Labonte	4.00	1.80
❑ PG5 Mark Martin	4.00	1.80
❑ PG6 Darrell Waltrip	1.50	.70
❑ PG7 Ned Jarrett	.75	.35
❑ PG8 Bill Elliott	4.00	1.80
❑ PG9 Rusty Wallace	4.00	1.80

1998 High Gear Top Tier

Randomly inserted in packs, this eight-card set features color photos of the top eight 1997 NASCAR Winston Cup finishers printed on all-foil cards. The insertion ratios are printed after the driver's name.

	MINT	NRMT
COMPLETE SET (8)	200.00	90.00
COMMON CARD (TT1-TT8)	6.00	2.70
❑ TT1 Jeff Gordon 1:384	100.00	45.00
❑ TT2 Dale Jarrett 1:192	40.00	18.00
❑ TT3 Mark Martin 1:100	30.00	13.50
❑ TT4 Jeff Burton 1:60	12.00	5.50
❑ TT5 Dale Earnhardt 1:40	25.00	11.00
❑ TT6 Terry Labonte 1:40	12.00	5.50
❑ TT7 Bobby Labonte 1:20	6.00	2.70
❑ TT8 Bill Elliott 1:20	8.00	3.60

1994-95 Highland Mint/VIP

The 1994-95 Highland Mint cards are replicas of the 1994 VIP series cards. The silver and bronze cards contain 4.25 ounces of metal. Each card is individually numbered, packaged in a lucite display holder and accompanied by a certificate of authenticity. The production mintage according to Highland Mint is listed below parenthetically referencing silver/bronze. The actual card numbering follows that of the original cards, but we have listed and numbered them below alphabetically for convenience. A 24-karat gold-plated on silver version of the Dale Earnhardt card (numbered of 500) was also produced. Prices below reflect that of the Bronze version cards. Silver cards generally sell for four to five times that of the Bronze. The Gold Earnhardt card is valued at approximately $500.

	MINT	NRMT
COMPLETE SET (6)	275.00	125.00
COMMON CARD	40.00	18.00
❑ 1B Dale Earnhardt (1,000/5,000)	60.00	27.00
❑ 1G Dale Earnhardt/500	40.00	18.00
❑ 1S Dale Earnhardt/1000	40.00	18.00
❑ 2B Bill Elliott (500/2,500)	40.00	18.00
❑ 2S Bill Elliott/500	40.00	18.00
❑ 3B Jeff Gordon (1,000/5,000)	60.00	27.00
❑ 3S Jeff Gordon/1000	40.00	18.00
❑ 4B Ernie Irvan (1,000/5,000)	40.00	18.00
❑ 4S Ernie Irvan/1000	40.00	18.00
❑ 5B Mark Martin (1,000/5,000)	40.00	18.00
❑ 5S Mark Martin/1000	40.00	18.00
❑ 6B Rusty Wallace (1,000/5,000)	40.00	18.00
❑ 6S Rusty Wallace/1000	40.00	18.00

1992 Hooters Alan Kulwicki

This 15-card set is a promotional issue by the restaurant chain Hooters. The cards were sold in complete set form at many of the restaurants as well as given away at some racing events. The cards feature Alan Kulwicki and his Hooters sponsored #7 Ford Thunderbird.

	MINT	NRMT
COMPLETE SET (15)	10.00	4.50
COMMON CARD (1-14)	.75	.35

1993 Hoyle Playing Cards

Hoyle produced these three decks of playing cards in early 1993. Each deck features racing stats or race action photos from the era highlighted. All three sets are packaged in similar boxes that differ according to box color: 1947-59 (green), 1960-79 (orange) and 1980-91 (yellow). Although drivers in some photos can be specifically identified, the cards are seldom sold as singles. Therefore, we list only complete set prices for the three card decks.

	MINT	NRMT
COMPLETE SET 1947-1959 (54)	3.00	1.35

COMPLETE SET 1960-1979 (54)	3.00
COMPLETE SET 1980-1991 (54)	3.00

1995 Images

This 100-card set is the inaugural issue for this b
The product was a joint effort between manufac
Classic and Finish Line. The set features the top d
from NASCAR, NHRA, Indy Car and World of Outlaws
cards have action photography and are printed o
point micro-lined foil board. The product came six-
per pack, 24-packs per box and 16 boxes per case.
case consisted of 8 red boxes and 8 black boxes. C
inserts were only available in one color box and n
other. There was also Hot Boxes in which half of
pack would consist of insert cards. A Hot Box cou
found 1 in every 4 cases. Two known uncorrected e
exsist in this set. card # 36 Ray Evernham doesn't h
card number on the back of the card and card #7
Burton is misnumbered #4.

	MINT	N
COMPLETE SET (100)	12.00	
COMMON CARD (1-100)	.10	
COMMON DRIVER (1-100)	.20	
❑ 1 Al Unser Jr.	.40	
❑ 2 Rusty Wallace	1.00	
❑ 3 Dale Earnhardt	2.00	
❑ 4 Sterling Marlin	.40	
❑ 5 Terry Labonte	1.00	
❑ 6 Mark Martin	1.00	
❑ 7 Geoff Bodine	.20	
❑ 8 Jeff Burton	.20	
❑ 9 Lake Speed	.20	
❑ 10 Ricky Rudd	.40	
❑ 11 Brett Bodine	.20	
❑ 12 Derrike Cope	.20	
❑ 13 John Force	.75	
❑ 14 Robby Gordon	.20	
❑ 15 Dick Trickle	.20	
❑ 16 Ted Musgrave	.20	
❑ 17 Darrell Waltrip	.40	
❑ 18 Bobby Labonte	.75	
❑ 19 Loy Allen Jr.	.20	
❑ 20 Walker Evans	.10	
❑ 21 Morgan Shepherd	.20	
❑ 22 Joe Amato	.20	
❑ 23 Jimmy Spencer	.20	
❑ 24 Jeff Gordon	2.00	
❑ 25 Ken Schrader	.20	
❑ 26 Hut Stricklin	.20	
❑ 27 Steve Kinser	.20	
❑ 28 Dale Jarrett	.75	
❑ 29 Steve Grissom	.20	
❑ 30 Michael Waltrip	.20	
❑ 31 Ward Burton	.20	
❑ 32 Roger Mears	.20	
❑ 33 Robert Pressley	.20	
❑ 34 Bill Seebold	.10	
❑ 35 Mike Skinner	.20	
❑ 36 Ray Evernham UER Unnumbered	.10	
❑ 37 John Andretti	.20	
❑ 38 Sammy Swindell	.20	
❑ 39 Larry McReynolds	.10	
❑ 40 Tony Glover	.10	
❑ 41 Ricky Craven	.40	

Kyle Petty	.40	.18
Bobby Hamilton	.20	.09
David Green	.20	.09
Steve Hmiel	.10	.05
Bobby Labonte	.75	.35
Darrell Waltrip	.40	.18
Jeff Gordon	2.00	.90
Al Unser Jr.	.40	.18
Dale Earnhardt	2.00	.90
P.J. Jones	.20	.09
Ken Schrader	.20	.09
Geoff Bodine	.20	.09
Sterling Marlin	.40	.18
Terry Labonte	1.00	.45
Morgan Shepherd	.20	.09
Robert Pressley	.20	.09
Ricky Rudd	.40	.18
Ward Burton	.20	.09
Rick Carelli	.20	.09
Ted Musgrave	.20	.09
Kenny Bernstein	.20	.09
Jimmy Spencer	.20	.09
Brett Bodine	.20	.09
Mark Martin	1.00	.45
Rusty Wallace	1.00	.45
Lake Speed	.20	.09
Rick Mast	.20	.09
Dick Trickle	.20	.09
Michael Waltrip	.20	.09
Dave Marcis	.20	.09
Jeff Gordon	2.00	.90
John Andretti	.20	.09
Derrike Cope	.20	.09
Todd Bodine	.20	.09
Kyle Petty	.40	.18
Dale Jarrett	.75	.35
Jeff Burton UER Numbered 4	.20	.09
Steve Grissom	.20	.09
Ernie Irvan	.75	.35
Bobby Labonte	.75	.35
Ernie Irvan	.75	.35
Bobby Hamilton	.20	.09
Sterling Marlin	.40	.18
Robby Gordon	.20	.09
Todd Bodine	.20	.09
Joe Nemechek	.20	.09
Mark Martin	1.00	.45
Ricky Rudd	.40	.18
Mike Wallace	.20	.09
Terry Labonte	1.00	.45
Geoff Bodine	.20	.09
Ernie Irvan	.75	.35
Rusty Wallace	1.00	.45
Ricky Craven	.40	.18
John Force	.75	.35
Dale Earnhardt	2.00	.90
Jeremy Mayfield	.60	.25
Dale Earnhardt CL	1.00	.45
Jeff Gordon CL	1.00	.45

1995 Images Gold

)0-card set is a parallel of the base Images set. The are printed on Gold foil board and could be found r pack.

	MINT	NRMT
.ETE SET (100)	40.00	18.00
ON CARD (1-100)	.30	.14
ON DRIVER (1-100)	.60	.25

S: 1.5X TO X BASIC CARDS

1995 Images Circuit Champions

)-card insert set features eight Champions from a of racing circuits along with two all-time greats. etate cards are sequentially number to 675 and d at a rate of one per 192 packs. The cards were d in both the Red and Black boxes.

	MINT	NRMT
COMPLETE SET (10)	150.00	70.00
COMMON CARD (1-10)	8.00	3.60

*SINGLES: 15X TO 40X BASE CARD HI

❑ 1 Al Unser Jr.	15.00	6.75
❑ 2 Roger Mears	8.00	3.60
❑ 3 Bill Seebold	8.00	3.60
❑ 4 John Force	15.00	6.75
❑ 5 Steve Kinser	15.00	6.75
❑ 6 Mike Skinner	8.00	3.60
❑ 7 David Green	8.00	3.60
❑ 8 Dale Earnhardt	15.00	6.75
❑ 9 Glen Wood Leonard Wood	8.00	3.60
❑ 10 Joe Amato	15.00	6.75

1995 Images Driven

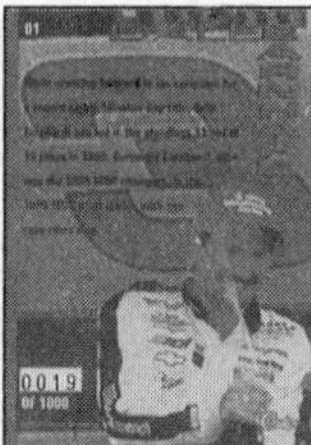

This 15-card insert set features some of the top drivers in NASCAR, NHRA, and IndyCar racing. The cards use holographic foil technology and are sequentially numbered to 1,800. The cards can be found one per 24 packs in the Red Images boxes only.

	MINT	NRMT
COMPLETE SET (15)	50.00	22.00
COMMON CARD (D1-D15)	1.50	.70

*SINGLES: 2.5X TO 6X BASE CARD HI

❑ D1 Dale Earnhardt	3.00	1.35
❑ D2 Jeff Gordon	3.00	1.35
❑ D3 Bobby Labonte	3.00	1.35
❑ D4 Sterling Marlin	3.00	1.35
❑ D5 Mark Martin	3.00	1.35
❑ D6 Kyle Petty	3.00	1.35
❑ D7 Ricky Rudd	3.00	1.35
❑ D8 Rusty Wallace	3.00	1.35
❑ D9 Ken Schrader	1.50	.70
❑ D10 John Force	3.00	1.35
❑ D11 Michael Waltrip	1.50	.70
❑ D12 Robby Gordon	1.50	.70
❑ D13 Terry Labonte	3.00	1.35
❑ D14 Al Unser Jr.	3.00	1.35
❑ D15 Darrell Waltrip	3.00	1.35

1995 Images Hard Chargers

This 10-card insert set uses holographic foil technology to bring the top NASCAR drivers to life. The cards come sequentially number to 2,500 and are inserted one per 24 packs in the Black Images boxes only.

	MINT	NRMT
COMPLETE SET (10)	40.00	18.00
COMMON CARD (HC1-HC10)	1.25	.55

*SINGLES: 2.5X TO 6X BASE CARD HI

❑ HC1 Bobby Labonte	2.50	1.10
❑ HC2 Sterling Marlin	2.50	1.10
❑ HC3 Mark Martin	2.50	1.10
❑ HC4 Ricky Rudd	2.50	1.10
❑ HC5 Ken Schrader	1.25	.55
❑ HC6 Rusty Wallace	2.50	1.10
❑ HC7 Michael Waltrip	1.25	.55
❑ HC8 Jeff Gordon	2.50	1.10
❑ HC9 Dale Earnhardt	2.50	1.10
❑ HC10 Terry Labonte	2.50	1.10

1995 Images Owner's Pride

Owners of some of the top teams in racing are featured in this 15-card insert set. The fronts of the micro-lined, foil-board cards feature a photo of the car. The backs contain a large photo of the owner. Each card is numbered 1 of 5,000 and could be found one per 18 packs. The Owner's Pride cards could be found in both the Red and Black boxes.

	MINT	NRMT
COMPLETE SET (15)	25.00	11.00
COMMON CARD (OP1-OP15)	.50	.23
COMMON DRIVER (OP1-OP15)	1.00	.45

*SINGLES: 2X TO 5X BASE CARD HI

❑ OP1 Travis Carter	.50	.23
❑ OP2 Richard Childress	.50	.23
❑ OP3 A.G. Dillard	.50	.23
❑ OP4 Joe Gibbs	1.00	.45
❑ OP5 Jeff Gordon	2.00	.90
❑ OP6 Junior Johnson	1.00	.45
❑ OP7 Larry McClure	.50	.23
❑ OP8 Jack Roush	.50	.23
❑ OP9 Ricky Rudd	2.00	.90
❑ OP10 Felix Sabates Chaney Sabates	.50	.23
❑ OP11 Robert Yates	.50	.23
❑ OP12 Kenny Bernstein	1.00	.45
❑ OP13 Dale Earnhardt	2.00	.90
❑ OP14 Rick Hendrick	.50	.23
❑ OP15 Roger Penske Don Miller	.50	.23

1995 Images Race Reflections Dale Earnhardt

The 10-card insert set is a tribute to racing great Dale Earnhardt. The innovative double foil-board cards are randomly inserted in Black boxes only at a rate of one every 32 packs. There is also a parallel version of each card that has a facsimile signature on the front. The signature cards were inserted at a rate of one per 96 packs.

	MINT	NRMT
COMPLETE SET (10)	100.00	45.00
COMMON CARD (DE1-DE10)	10.00	4.50

*SIGNATURE CARDS: 1X TO 2X BASIC CARDS

1995 Images Race Reflections Jeff Gordon

This 10-card insert set highlights much of the success Jeff Gordon enjoyed in his career through the middle of 1995. The innovative double foil-board cards are randomly inserted in Red boxes only at a rate of one every 32 packs. There is also a parallel version of each of the ten cards. The parallel features a facsimile signature on the fronts of the cards. The signature cards were randomly inserted at a rate of one every 96 packs.

	MINT	NRMT
COMPLETE SET (10)	100.00	45.00
COMMON CARD (JG1-JG10)	10.00	4.50

*SIGNATURE CARDS: 1X TO 2X BASIC CARDS

1991 IROC

The 1991 IROC set was produced by Dodge and included a short sales brochure covering the Daytona IROC automobile and the 1991 IROC race schedule. Each cardback contains an action photo along with the set title 1991 IROC. Cardfronts contain the driver's photo and career highlights surrounded by a checkered flag border. Distribution was by complete set only sealed in a cello wrapper. The cards later were illegally reprinted. The counterfeits can be distinguished by an incomplete checkered flag design along the card border. One side of the border will be missing approximately 1/4 of the checkered flag.

	MINT	NRMT
COMPLETE SET (12)	500.00	220.00
COMMON CARD (1-12)	25.00	11.00
❑ 1 Al Unser	30.00	13.50
❑ 2 Tom Kendall	25.00	11.00
❑ 3 Bob Wollek	25.00	11.00
❑ 4 Mark Martin	70.00	32.00
❑ 5 Bill Elliott	70.00	32.00
❑ 6 Al Unser Jr.	40.00	18.00
❑ 7 Scott Pruett	25.00	11.00
❑ 8 Geoff Bodine	30.00	13.50
❑ 9 Geoff Brabham	25.00	11.00
❑ 10 Rusty Wallace	70.00	32.00
❑ 11 Dorsey Schroeder	25.00	11.00
❑ 12 Dale Earnhardt	150.00	70.00

1997 Jurassic Park

This 61-card set is another uniquely themed set from Wheels. The cards feature the top names in racing and are printed on 24 point stock. Each card has a jungle-like background and is stamped in silver foil. The cards were packed 6 cards per pack and 24 packs per box.

	MINT	NRMT
COMPLETE SET (61)	20.00	9.00
COMMON CARD (1-61)	.15	.07
COMMON DRIVER (1-61)	.30	.14
❑ 1 Jeff Gordon	2.50	1.10
❑ 2 Dale Jarrett	1.00	.45
❑ 3 Terry Labonte	1.25	.55
❑ 4 Mark Martin	1.25	.55
❑ 5 Rusty Wallace	1.25	.55
❑ 6 Bobby Labonte	1.00	.45
❑ 7 Sterling Marlin	.60	.25
❑ 8 Jeff Burton	.60	.25
❑ 9 Ted Musgrave	.30	.14
❑ 10 Michael Waltrip	.30	.14
❑ 11 David Green	.30	.14
❑ 12 Ricky Craven	.30	.14
❑ 13 Johnny Benson	.30	.14
❑ 14 Jeremy Mayfield	.75	.35
❑ 15 Bobby Hamilton	.30	.14
❑ 16 Kyle Petty	.60	.25
❑ 17 Darrell Waltrip	.60	.25
❑ 18 Wally Dallenbach	.30	.14
❑ 19 Bill Elliott	1.25	.55
❑ 20 Jeff Green	.30	.14
❑ 21 Joe Nemechek	.30	.14
❑ 22 Derrike Cope	.30	.14
❑ 23 Ward Burton	.30	.14
❑ 24 Chad Little	.30	.14
❑ 25 Mike Skinner	.30	.14
❑ 26 Todd Bodine	.30	.14
❑ 27 Hut Stricklin	.30	.14
❑ 28 Ken Schrader	.30	.14
❑ 29 Steve Grissom	.30	.14
❑ 30 Robby Gordon	.30	.14
❑ 31 Kenny Wallace	.30	.14
❑ 32 Bobby Hillin	.30	.14
❑ 33 Jimmy Spencer	.30	.14
❑ 34 John Andretti	.30	.14
❑ 35 Steve Park	2.50	1.10
❑ 36 Michael Waltrip	.30	.14
❑ 37 Dale Jarrett	1.00	.45
❑ 38 Mike McLaughlin	.30	.14
❑ 39 Todd Bodine	.30	.14
❑ 40 Terry Labonte	1.50	.70
❑ 41 Jeff Fuller	.30	.14
❑ 42 Phil Parsons	.30	.14
❑ 43 Jason Keller	.30	.14
❑ 44 Mark Martin	1.25	.55
❑ 45 Randy Lajoie	.30	.14
❑ 46 Joe Nemechek	.30	.14
❑ 47 Loy Allen	.30	.14
❑ 48 Jeff Gordon	2.50	1.10
❑ 49 Mark Martin	1.25	.55
❑ 50 Mark Martin	1.25	.55
❑ 51 Jeff Gordon	2.50	1.10
❑ 52 John Andretti	.30	.14
❑ 53 Jimmy Makar	.15	.07
❑ 54 Robert Pressley	.30	.14
❑ 55 Donnie Wingo	.15	.07
❑ 56 Richard Childress	.15	.07
❑ 57 Andy Petree	.15	.07
❑ 58 Travis Carter	.15	.07
❑ 59 Joe Gibbs	.30	.14
❑ 60 Checklist	.15	.07
❑ 61 Checklist	.15	.07

1997 Jurassic Park Triceratops

This 61-card set is a parallel to the base set. These cards are diecut and features the image of a triceratops in the background. The cards were randomly inserted in packs at a ratio of 1:2.

	MINT	NRMT
COMPLETE SET (1-61)	40.00	18.00
COMMON CARD (1-61)	.30	.14
COMMON DRIVER (1-61)	.60	.25

1997 Jurassic Park Carnivore

This 12-card insert set features the top drivers from the NASCAR circuit. The cards are horizontal and feature the drivers' numbers in the background. The cards were randomly inserted in packs at a ratio of 1:15.

	MINT	NRMT
COMPLETE SET (12)	80.00	36.00
COMMON CARD (C1-C12)	2.00	.90

*SINGLES: 3X TO 8X BASE CARD HI

❑ C1 Dale Earnhardt	25.00	11.00
❑ C2 Jeff Gordon	25.00	11.00
❑ C3 Dale Jarrett	12.00	5.50
❑ C4 Bobby Labonte	8.00	3.60

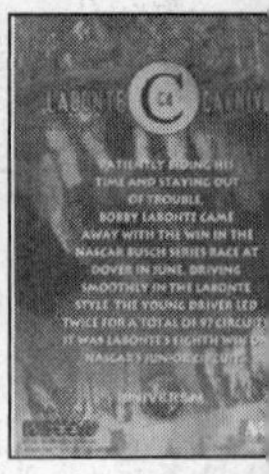

❑ C5 Jimmy Spencer	2.00
❑ C6 Bill Elliott	15.00
❑ C7 Terry Labonte	15.00
❑ C8 Rusty Wallace	15.00
❑ C9 Ward Burton	2.00
❑ C10 Mark Martin	15.00
❑ C11 Todd Bodine	2.00
❑ C12 Sterling Marlin	4.00

1997 Jurassic Park Pterano

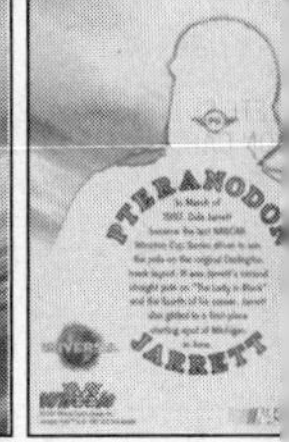

This 10-card insert set is printed on clear plasti contains portrait shots of the top drivers on the NA circuit. The cards were randomly inserted in pack ratio of 1:30.

	MINT
COMPLETE SET (10)	100.00
COMMON CARD (P1-P10)	3.00

*SINGLES: 5X TO 12X BASE CARD HI

❑ P1 Dale Earnhardt	35.00
❑ P2 Jeff Gordon	35.00
❑ P3 Bobby Labonte	10.00
❑ P4 Terry Labonte	20.00
❑ P5 Rusty Wallace	20.00
❑ P6 Ward Burton	3.00
❑ P7 Sterling Marlin	6.00
❑ P8 Mark Martin	20.00
❑ P9 Dale Jarrett	16.00
❑ P10 Kyle Petty	6.00

1997 Jurassic Park Rapto

This 16-card insert set features drivers on micro-cards. The cards were randomly inserted in pac ratio of 1:6.

	MINT
COMPLETE SET (16)	40.00
COMMON CARD (R1-R16)	1.25

*SINGLES: 2X TO 5X BASE CARD HI

❑ R1 Terry Labonte	10.00
❑ R2 Jeff Gordon	18.00
❑ R3 Johnny Benson	1.25
❑ R4 Jeff Burton	2.50
❑ R5 Bobby Hamilton	1.25
❑ R6 Rickey Craven	1.25
❑ R7 Michael Waltrip	1.25
❑ R8 Bobby Labonte	5.00
❑ R9 Dale Jarrett	8.00
❑ R10 Bill Elliott	10.00
❑ R11 Rusty Wallace	10.00
❑ R12 Jimmy Spencer	1.25

Sterling Marlin	2.50	1.10
Kyle Petty	2.50	1.10
Ken Schrader	1.25	.55
Robby Gordon	1.25	.55

1997 Jurassic Park Thunder Lizard

0-card set once again features the innovations that ors have come to expect from Wheels. Each card is ed with actual lizard skin. The cards were randomly ed in packs at a ratio of 1:90.

	MINT	NRMT
LETE SET (10)	300.00	135.00
ION CARD (TL1-TL10)	8.00	3.60
LES: 12X TO 30X BASE CARD HI		
Jeff Gordon	100.00	45.00
Dale Jarrett	50.00	22.00
Bobby Labonte	30.00	13.50
Rusty Wallace	60.00	27.00
Bill Elliott	60.00	27.00
Ward Burton	8.00	3.60
Mark Martin	60.00	27.00
Dale Earnhardt	100.00	45.00
Mike Skinner	8.00	3.60
0 Robbie Gordon	8.00	3.60

1997 Jurassic Park T-Rex

0-card insert set features cards that are diecut, sed and micro-etched. The cards were randomly d in packs at a ratio of 1:60.

	MINT	NRMT
LETE SET (10)	225.00	100.00
ON CARD (TR1-TR10)	5.00	2.20
LES: 8X TO 20X BASE CARD HI		
Terry Labonte	25.00	11.00
Jeff Gordon	50.00	22.00
Dale Jarrett	25.00	11.00
Bobby Labonte	12.00	5.50
Dale Earnhardt	50.00	22.00
Rusty Wallace	30.00	13.50
Mike Skinner	5.00	2.20
Joe Nemechek	5.00	2.20
Jermey Mayfield	8.00	3.60
0 Bill Elliott	30.00	13.50

997 Jurrasic Park the Ride Jeff Gordon

ecast/card set was available through a redemption am by Wheels and through RCCA(Racing bles Club of America). The set consists of five Jeff n cards, one cover card, and a 1:64 Action/RCCA ff Gordon Jurrasic Park Hood Opened car.

	MINT	NRMT
LETE SET (5)	50.00	22.00
ON CARD (1-5)	5.00	2.20
ST CAR	25.00	11.00
f Gordon	5.00	2.20
f Gordon	5.00	2.20
f Gordon	5.00	2.20
❑ 4 Jeff Gordon	5.00	2.20
❑ 5 Jeff Gordon	5.00	2.20
❑ NNO Cover Card	1.00	.45

1992 Just Racing Larry Caudill

This 30-card set features NASCAR driver Larry Caudill. The sets were sold in complete set form. Each set was boxed and sealed and came with a numbered certificate of authenticity. There was also a 100 signed and numbered cards randomly inserted in the sets. The signed cards are usually sold for $5-$10.

	MINT	NRMT
COMPLETE SET (30)	6.00	2.70
COMMON CARD (1-30)	.25	.11

1996 KnightQuest

This 45-card set takes the angle of King Arthur's time. The drivers are the Knights and the track is their battle field. Each card is printed on 24-pt paper stock with UV coating and foil stamped in silver holographic foil. The set is made up of three subsets: Armor Knights (1-20), Conquerors (21-33) and Wizards (34-45). The cards are packaged four cards per pack, 24 cards per box and 20 boxes per case. There were 999 Hobby cases and 609 Retail cases produced. Wheels also continued its E-Race to Win redemption game for KnightQuest. The expiration of both game cards was 5/31/96.

	MINT	NRMT
COMPLETE SET (45)	12.00	5.50
COMMON CARD (1-45)	.10	.05
COMMON DRIVER (1-45)	.20	.09
❑ 1 Dale Earnhardt K	2.00	.90
❑ 2 Jeff Gordon K	2.00	.90
❑ 3 Sterling Marlin K	.40	.18
❑ 4 Ted Musgrave K	.20	.09
❑ 5 Mark Martin K	1.00	.45
❑ 6 Terry Labonte K	1.00	.45
❑ 7 Rusty Wallace K	1.00	.45
❑ 8 Morgan Shepherd K	.20	.09
❑ 9 Bobby Labonte K	.75	.35
❑ 10 Ricky Rudd K	.40	.18
❑ 11 Bill Elliott K	1.00	.45
❑ 12 Ernie Irvan K	.60	.25
❑ 13 Ken Schrader K	.20	.09
❑ 14 Derrike Cope K	.20	.09
❑ 15 Dale Jarrett K	.75	.35
❑ 16 Geoff Bodine K	.20	.09
❑ 17 Darrell Waltrip K	.40	.18
❑ 18 Kyle Petty K	.40	.18
❑ 19 Michael Waltrip K	.20	.09
❑ 20 Brett Bodine K	.20	.09
❑ 21 Jeff Gordon C	2.00	.90
❑ 22 Dale Earnhardt C	2.00	.90
❑ 23 Rusty Wallace C	1.00	.45
❑ 24 Mark Martin C	1.00	.45
❑ 25 Dale Earnhardt C	2.00	.90
❑ 26 Bobby Labonte C	.75	.35
❑ 27 Kyle Petty C	.40	.18
❑ 28 Terry Labonte C	1.00	.45
❑ 29 Bobby Labonte C	.75	.35
❑ 30 Jeff Gordon C	2.00	.90
❑ 31 Jeff Gordon C	2.00	.90
❑ 32 Dale Jarrett C	.75	.35
❑ 33 Sterling Marlin C	.40	.18
❑ 34 Junior Johnson W	.20	.09
❑ 35 Travis Carter W	.10	.05
❑ 36 Bob Brannan W	.10	.05
❑ 37 Tony Glover W	.10	.05
❑ 38 Don Miller W	.10	.05
❑ 39 Larry McReynolds W	.10	.05
❑ 40 Ray Evernham W	.10	.05
❑ 41 Steve Hmiel W	.10	.05
❑ 42 Cecil Gordon W	.10	.05
❑ 43 Andy Petree W	.10	.05
❑ 44 Richard Childress W	.10	.05
❑ 45 Don Hawk W	.10	.05

1996 KnightQuest Black Knights

This 45-card set is a parallel to the base set. The cards have a silver and holographic laser gold foil stamping and are printed on 24-pt UV coated paper stock. The cards come sequentially numbered of 899. The odds of pulling a Black Knight card are one per 13 packs. The Black Knight cards were inserted only in hobby packs.

	MINT	NRMT
COMPLETE SET (45)	200.00	90.00
COMMON CARD (1-45)	1.50	.70
COMMON DRIVER (1-45)	3.00	1.35
*STARS: 6X TO 15X BASIC CARDS		

1996 KnightQuest Red Knight Preview

This 45-card set is a parallel to the base KnightQuest set. The set was originially distributed at the Winston Cup preview show in Winston-Salem, North Carolina January 20, 1996. It was later made available through a mail order offer. The set comes in a black padded watch style box. The inside is lined in red felt and a logo of Preview Edition January 20, 1996 1 of 1,996 can be found on the inside lid of the box. Each card is identical to the base KnightQuest cards except for the special red foil preview edition logo that appears on each of the Red Knight cards.

	MINT	NRMT
COMPLETE SET (45)	35.00	16.00
COMMON CARD (1-45)	.40	.18
COMMON DRIVER (1-45)	.60	.25
*RED KNIGHT CARDS: 1.5X TO 2X BASE KNIGHTQUEST CARDS		

1996 KnightQuest Royalty

This 45-card set parallel set features 24-pt UV coated paper stock and rich purple foil stamping. The cards are sequentially numbered of 2299. The Royalty cards were seeded one per seven packs. The cards were available in both hobby and retail packs.

	MINT	NRMT
COMPLETE SET (45)	150.00	70.00
COMMON CARD (1-45)	2.00	.90
COMMON DRIVER (1-45)	3.00	1.35
*STARS: 4X TO 8X BASIC CARDS		

1996 KnightQuest White Knights

This 45-card set is parallel to the base set. The cards have a silver and holographic, laser gold foil stamping and are printed on 24-pt UV coated paper stock. The cards come sequentially numbered of 499. White Knight cards were available only in retail packs and inserted at a rate of one per 13 packs.

	MINT	NRMT
COMPLETE SET (45)	250.00	110.00
COMMON CARD (1-45)	1.50	.70
COMMON DRIVER (1-45)	3.00	1.35
*STARS: 6X TO 15X BASIC CARDS		

1996 KnightQuest First Knights

This 10-card insert set features some of the drivers who won Poles in 1995. The cards are printed on foil board and are die-cut. Each card is sequentially numbered of 1,499 and can be found one per 36 packs. The First Knight cards were available in hobby packs.

	MINT	NRMT
COMPLETE SET (10)	80.00	36.00
COMMON CARD (FK1-FK10)	2.00	.90
*SINGLES: 4X TO 10X BASE CARD HI		
❑ FK1 Dale Earnhardt	30.00	13.50
❑ FK2 Dale Jarrett	12.00	5.50

❑ FK3 Jeff Gordon	30.00	13.50
❑ FK4 Mark Martin	15.00	6.75
❑ FK5 Bobby Labonte	10.00	4.50
❑ FK6 Terry Labonte	15.00	6.75
❑ FK7 Ricky Rudd	4.00	1.80
❑ FK8 Ken Schrader	2.00	.90
❑ FK9 Bill Elliott	15.00	6.75
❑ FK10 Sterling Marlin	4.00	1.80

1996 KnightQuest Knights of the Round Table

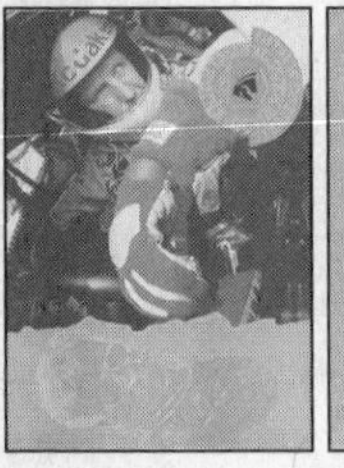

The 10-card insert set features the top 10 drivers in Winston Cup. The cards use a gold embossed printing process on 1/4 of the card to show a silhouette of the driver. The other 3/4 of the card show the driver in the car, belted up and ready to go. There are 1,199 of each card and they can be found in both hobby and retail packs at a rate of one per 72 packs.

	MINT	NRMT
COMPLETE SET (10)	150.00	70.00
COMMON CARD (KT1-KT10)	4.00	1.80
*SINGLES: 8X TO 20X BASE CARD HI		
❑ KT1 Jeff Gordon	50.00	22.00
❑ KT2 Dale Earnhardt	50.00	22.00
❑ KT3 Darrell Waltrip	8.00	3.60
❑ KT4 Mark Martin	20.00	9.00
❑ KT5 Terry Labonte	20.00	9.00
❑ KT6 Sterling Marlin	8.00	3.60
❑ KT7 Bill Elliott	20.00	9.00
❑ KT8 Rusty Wallace	20.00	9.00
❑ KT9 Michael Waltrip	4.00	1.80
❑ KT10 Ernie Irvan	8.00	3.60

1996 KnightQuest Kenji Momota

This four-card set features the first Japanese driver to ever race in the SuperTruck series. The cards are printed on 24-pt, UV coated paper stock. They can be found one per 48 packs. There is also two different signature versions of card # KMS1. There were 1,500 signature cards produced with an English signature and 1,000 with a Japanese signature. The odds of finding a signature card was one in 480 packs. The Kenji Momota cards were available in both hobby and retail packs.

	MINT	NRMT
COMPLETE SET (4)	10.00	4.50
COMMON CARD (KM1-KM4)	4.00	1.80
❑ KM1 Kenji Momota	4.00	1.80
❑ KM2 Kenji Momota	4.00	1.80
❑ KM3 Kenji Momota	4.00	1.80
❑ KM4 Kenji Momota	4.00	1.80
❑ KMS1 Kenji Momota AUTO American 1500 signed	15.00	6.75
❑ KMS1 Kenji Momota AUTO Japanese 1000 signed	15.00	6.75

1996 KnightQuest Protectors of the Crown

This six-card set features the active Winston Cup Champions. The cards are printed on foil board using embossed technology. Each card is numbered sequentially of 899 and can be found one per hobby 98 packs. There was also an uncut sheet available through the E-Race to Win redemption game. By being unnumbered, the cards on the uncut sheet are different than the regular Protectors of the Crown inserts.

	MINT	NRMT
COMPLETE SET (6)	200.00	90.00
COMMON CARD (PC1-PC6)	12.00	5.50
*SINGLES: 12X TO 30X BASE CARD HI		
❑ PC1 Darrell Waltrip	20.00	9.00
❑ PC2 Dale Earnhardt	80.00	36.00
❑ PC3 Terry Labonte	40.00	18.00
❑ PC4 Rusty Wallace	40.00	18.00
❑ PC5 Bill Elliott	40.00	18.00
❑ PC6 Jeff Gordon	80.00	36.00

1996 KnightQuest Redemption Game

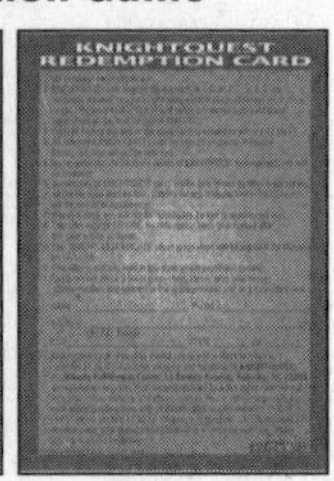

This is the game where you try to spell KNIGHTQUEST. Winners receive a special 20-card uncut press sheet. The letter game cards were randomly inserted at a rate of one per 12 packs.

	MINT	NRMT
COMPLETE SET (11)	30.00	13.50
COMMON LETTER	3.00	1.35
UNCUT SHEET PRIZE	40.00	18.00

1996 KnightQuest Santa Claus

This 5-card set features four of the top names in Winston Cup and Santa Claus. Each card has Merry Christmas on the front and wish you a Merry Christmas on the back. Each card is numbered 1 of 1,499. There is also parallel green version of each card available in hobby packs.

	MINT	NRMT
COMPLETE RED SET (5)	80.00	36.00
COMMON CARD (SC1-SC5)	10.00	4.50
COMPLETE GREEN SET (5)	80.00	36.00
*SINGLES: 8X TO 20X BASE CARD HI		
*GREEN CARDS: 1X TO 1.5X RED CARDS		
❑ SC1 Dale Earnhardt	50.00	22.00
❑ SC2 Bobby Labonte		15.00
❑ SC3 Rusty Wallace		20.00
❑ SC4 Mark Martin		20.00
❑ SC5 Santa Claus		15.00

1991 Langenberg ARCA/Hot Stuff

M.B. Langenberg (H.S.Promotions) produced th under the name Hot Stuff in 1991. The cards fe drivers of the ARCA PermaTex Supercar Series and printed on thin white stock. They were originally s complete set form.

	MINT	N
COMPLETE SET (68)	10.00	
COMMON CARD (1-68)	.20	
❑ 1 Bob Brevak	.20	
❑ 2 Lee Raymond	.20	
❑ 3 Carl Miskotten III	.20	
❑ 4 Mike Fry	.20	
❑ 5 Scott Stovall	.20	
❑ 6 Bobby Bowsher	.40	
❑ 7 Brian Jaeger	.20	
❑ 8 Bob Dotter Sr.	.40	
❑ 9 Eric Smith	.20	
❑ 10 Glenn Brewer	.20	
❑ 11 Mike Wallace	.75	
❑ 12 Roger Blackstock	.20	
❑ 13 Glenn Sullivan	.20	
❑ 14 Roger Otto	.20	
❑ 15 Craig Rubright	.20	
❑ 16 Roy Payne	.40	
❑ 17 Billy Simmons	.20	
❑ 18 Graham Taylor	.20	
❑ 19 Chris Gehrke	.20	
❑ 20 Keith Waid	.20	
❑ 21 Bobby Bowsher	.40	
❑ 22 Billy Thomas	.20	
❑ 23 Chet Blanton	.20	
❑ 24 Dave Jensen	.20	
❑ 25 Bill Venturini	.40	
❑ 26 Mike Davis	.20	
❑ 27 Ken Rowley	.20	
❑ 28 Charlie Glotzbach	.20	
❑ 29 Bob Keselowski	.40	
❑ 30 Wayne Dellinger	.20	
❑ 31 Cecil Eunice	.20	
❑ 32 Mark Gibson	.20	
❑ 33 Dale McDowell	.20	
❑ 34 Bob Brevak	.20	
❑ 35 Bobby Gerhart	.20	
❑ 36 Frank Kimmel	.20	
❑ 37 Jerry Cook	.20	
❑ 38 Jerry Hufflin	.20	
❑ 39 Brad Holman	.20	
❑ 40 Ben Hess	.40	
❑ 41 Jimmy Horton	.40	
❑ 42 Richard Hinds	.20	
❑ 43 Bill Flowers	.20	
❑ 44 Ferrel Harris	.20	
❑ 45 Mark Gibson	.20	
❑ 46 Joe Booher	.20	
❑ 47 Ken Ragan	.20	
❑ 48 Donnie Moran	.20	
❑ 49 Bobby Massey	.20	
❑ 50 Checklist	.20	
❑ 51 Dave Simko	.20	
❑ 52 David Boggs	.20	
❑ 53 Larry Couch	.20	
❑ 54 Dorsey Schroeder	.40	
❑ 55 Mark Thompson	.20	
❑ 56 Jerry Hill	.20	
❑ 57 Gary Weinbroer	.20	
❑ 58 Scott Hansen	.20	
❑ 59 Gary Hawes	.20	
❑ 60 Tom Bigelow	.20	
❑ 61 David Elliott	.20	
❑ 62 '91 Daytona Action	.20	
❑ 63 '91 Daytona Action	.20	
❑ 64 '91 Atlanta Action	.20	

	MINT	NRMT
'88 Dayton Pit Stop	.20	.09
Goodyear Tire	.20	.09
Hoosier Tire	.20	.09
'91 ARCA Schedule	.20	.09

1991 Langenberg ARTGO

36-card set was produced by Hot Stuff Promotions ckford, Illinois. The cards were sold at the ARTGO tar 100 race, at Rockford Speedway on July 23,

	MINT	NRMT
PLETE SET (36)	8.00	3.60
MON CARD (1-36)	.25	.11
Matt Kenseth	4.00	1.80
obbie Reiser	.25	.11
arry Schuler	.25	.11
d Holmes	.25	.11
l Schill	.25	.11
erry Wood	.25	.11
odd Coon	.25	.11
ryan Refner	.25	.11
oe Shear	.25	.11
John Zeigler	.25	.11
Scott Hansen	.25	.11
Kregg Hurlbert	.25	.11
John Knaus	.25	.11
Bill Venturini	.40	.18
Johnny Spaw	.25	.11
Nolan McBride	.25	.11
Monte Gress	.25	.11
Tom Carlson	.25	.11
David Anspaugh	.25	.11
John Loehman	.25	.11
Keith Nelson	.25	.11
Dennis Berry	.25	.11
Dick Harrington	.25	.11
Dave Weltmeyer	.25	.11
Kevin Cywinski	.25	.11
Tony Strupp	.25	.11
Jim Weber	.25	.11
Steve Carlson	.25	.11
Tracy Schuler	.25	.11
Al Schill, Jr.	.25	.11
M.G. Gajewski	.25	.11
Bob Brownell	.25	.11
Joe Shear	.25	.11
Dennis Lampman	.25	.11
Conrad Morgan	.25	.11
Checklist Card	.25	.11

1991 Langenberg Stock Car Champions

30-card set features track champions from around ountry. Each card in the set carries a Say NO! To logo on the front to each drivers name.

	MINT	NRMT
PLETE SET (30)	8.00	3.60
MON CARD (1-30)	.30	.14
ohn Knaus	.30	.14
teve Fraise	.30	.14
eith Berner	.30	.14
rian Ater	.30	.14
om Rients	.30	.14
evin Nuttleman	.30	.14
el Walen	.30	.14
Humphrey	.30	.14
hris Harat	.30	.14
Brad Denney	.30	.14
Richie Jensen	.30	.14
Jay Stuart	.30	.14
Jeff Martin	.30	.14
Howard Willis	.30	.14
Ronnie Thomas	.30	.14
Babe Branscombe	.30	.14
Tom Guithues	.30	.14
Randy Olson	.30	.14
Dennis Setzer	.50	.23
Charlie Williamson	.30	.14
Bryan Refner	.30	.14
Fred Joehnck	.30	.14
Roger Otto	.30	.14
Terry Cook	.30	.14
Roger Avants	.30	.14
Larry Mosher	.30	.14
Nick Kuipers	.30	.14
Terry Lackey	.30	.14
Vinny Annarummo	.30	.14
Checklist Card	.30	.14

1992 Langenberg ARCA/Flash

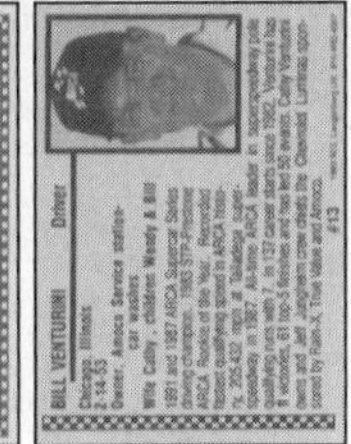

M.B. Langenberg produced this set under the name '92 Flash. The cards feature drivers of the ARCA Supercar Series and were printed on slightly thicker card stock than the 1991 release. They were originally sold in complete set form and included an unnumbered Clifford Allison card. Reportedly there were 5,000 sets produced.

	MINT	NRMT
COMPLETE SET (111)	18.00	8.00
COMMON CARD (1-110)	.10	.05
COMMON DRIVER (1-110)	.15	.07
❑ 1 Bill Venturini	.40	.18
❑ 2 Bobby Bowsher	.40	.18
❑ 3 Bob Keselowski	.25	.11
❑ 4 Bob Dotter Sr.	.25	.11
❑ 5 Bobby Gerhart	.15	.07
❑ 6 Bob Brevak	.15	.07
❑ 7 Ben Hess	.15	.07
❑ 8 Glenn Brewer	.15	.07
❑ 9 Mark Gibson	.15	.07
❑ 10 Roy Payne	.25	.11
❑ 11 Checklist	.10	.05
❑ 12 Jim Clarke	.15	.07
❑ 13 Bill Venturini's Car	.25	.11
❑ 14 Bobby Bowsher's Car	.25	.11
❑ 15 Bob Keselowski	.25	.11
❑ 16 Bob Dotter Sr.	.25	.11
❑ 17 Bobby Gerhart	.15	.07
❑ 18 Bob Brevak	.15	.07
❑ 19 Ben Hess	.15	.07
❑ 20 Glenn Brewer	.15	.07
❑ 21 Mark Gibson	.15	.07
❑ 22 Roy Payne	.25	.11
❑ 23 Bob Strait	.15	.07
❑ 24 Billy Thomas	.15	.07
❑ 25 Jerry Huffman	.15	.07
❑ 26 Gary Hawes	.15	.07
❑ 27 Keith Waid	.15	.07
❑ 28 Clay Young's Car Craig Rubright's Car Bob Keselowski's Car '91 Atlanta	.10	.05
❑ 29 Jerry Hill	.15	.07
❑ 30 Randy Huffman's Car	.10	.05
❑ 31 Dale McDowell	.15	.07
❑ 32 Roger Blackstock's Car	.10	.05
❑ 33 Red Farmer	.40	.18
❑ 34 Dave Weltmeyer	.15	.07
❑ 35 H.B. Bailey	.25	.11
❑ 36 Loy Allen Jr.	1.00	.45
❑ 37 Bill Venturini Champion	.40	.18
❑ 38 Jeff McClure	.15	.07
❑ 39 Lee Raymond	.15	.07
❑ 40 Dave Mader	.15	.07
❑ 41 Andy Genzman	.15	.07
❑ 42 Rich Bickle	.40	.18
❑ 43 Alan Pruitt	.15	.07
❑ 44 Bob Schacht's Car Bill Venturini's Car Bob Keselowski's Car '91 Michigan	.15	.07
❑ 45 David Hall	.15	.07
❑ 46 Jerry Hufflin	.15	.07
❑ 47 Thad Coleman	.15	.07
❑ 48 Mike Wren	.15	.07
❑ 49 Eddie Bierschwale	.25	.11
❑ 50 Tom Sherrill	.15	.07
❑ 51 Scotty Sands	.15	.07
❑ 52 '92 Daytona Race Action	.10	.05
❑ 53 Stan Fox	.40	.18
❑ 54 Jimmy Horton	.40	.18
❑ 55 Gary Weinbroer's Car	.15	.07
❑ 56 Craig Rubright	.15	.07
❑ 57 Jerry Churchill	.15	.07
❑ 58 Clifford Allison	1.50	.70
❑ 59 Rich Bickle's Car Roulo Brothers	.15	.07
❑ 60 Mike Fry's Car	.15	.07
❑ 61 Jeff Purvis	.75	.35
❑ 62 Ron Burchette	.15	.07
❑ 63 T.W. Taylor	.25	.11
❑ 64 Bob Denny	.15	.07
❑ 65 Billy Bigley Jr.	.15	.07
❑ 66 Charlie Baker	.15	.07
❑ 67 Bobby Massey	.15	.07
❑ 68 Mike Davis	.15	.07
❑ 69 Graham Taylor's Car	.10	.05
❑ 70 Tim Fedewa	.40	.18
❑ 71 Andy Hillenburg	.40	.18
❑ 72 Mark Gibson Pit Stop	.10	.05
❑ 73 Frank Kimmel	.15	.07
❑ 74 Frank Kimmel Pit Stop	.10	.05
❑ 75 David Elliott	.15	.07
❑ 76 Clay Young	.15	.07
❑ 77 Scott Bloomquist's Car	.25	.11
❑ 78 Dennis Setzer	.40	.18
❑ 79 Dave Jensen	.15	.07
❑ 80 Brad Smith's Car	.10	.05
❑ 81 Bob Keselowski w/Car Tech Inspection	.10	.05
❑ 82 Wayne Dellinger	.15	.07
❑ 83 Bobby Woods	.15	.07
❑ 84 Paul Holt Jr.	.15	.07
❑ 85 Mark Thompson	.15	.07
❑ 86 Tim Porter	.15	.07
❑ 87 Ken Rowley's Car	.10	.05
❑ 88 Jody Gara's Car	.10	.05
❑ 89 Mark Harding	.15	.07
❑ 90 Tim Priebe's Car	.10	.05
❑ 91 James Elliott	.15	.07
❑ 92 Wally Finney	.15	.07
❑ 93 Richard Hampton's Car	.10	.05
❑ 94 T.W. Taylor Pit Stop	.10	.05
❑ 95 James Hylton's Car	.10	.05
❑ 96 Rich Hayes	.15	.07
❑ 97 Joe Booher	.15	.07
❑ 98 Eric Smith's Car	.10	.05
❑ 99 Ron Otto's Car	.10	.05
❑ 100 Bob Williams	.15	.07
❑ 101 Tony Schwengel's Car	.10	.05
❑ 102 Dave Simko	.15	.07
❑ 103 Ben Hess Pit Stop	.10	.05
❑ 104 Ken Ragan	.15	.07
❑ 105 Maurice Randall's Car	.10	.05
❑ 106 Bob Schacht	.15	.07
❑ 107 Robbie Cowart	.15	.07
❑ 108 Checklist	.10	.05
❑ 109 Arca Officials & Sched	.10	.05
❑ 110 Hoosier Tire Midwest	.10	.05
❑ NNO Clifford Allison	1.50	.70

1993 Langenberg ARCA/Flash Prototype

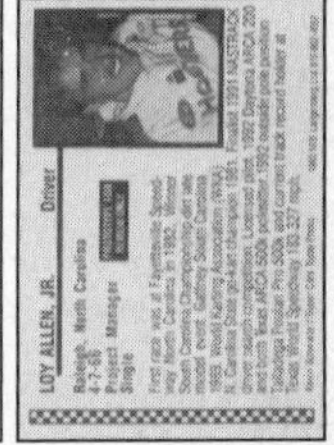

M.B. Langenberg produced this prototype card under the name '93 Flash. The Loy Allen card was made as a preview to the 1993 ARCA set that was never produced.

	MINT	NRMT
COMPLETE SET (1)	2.00	.90
COMMON CARD (PR1)	2.00	.90
❑ PR1 Loy Allen Jr.	2.00	.90

1994 Langenberg ARCA/Flash

M.B. Langenberg produced this set under the name '94

M.B.L. Flash. The cards feature drivers of the ARCA Supercar Series and were printed on thin card stock with a blue-green cardback. They were originally sold in complete set form. Two promo cards were produced and distributed to advertise the series, but are not considered part of the complete regular set.

	MINT	NRMT
COMPLETE SET (100)	20.00	9.00
COMMON CARD (1-100)	.20	.09

❑ 1 ARCA Cover Card	.20	.09
❑ 2 Tim Steele	.45	.20
❑ 3 Bob Keselowski	.45	.20
❑ 4 Bobby Bowsher	.45	.20
❑ 5 Frank Kimmel	.20	.09
❑ 6 Bob Brevak	.20	.09
❑ 7 Bob Strait	.20	.09
❑ 8 Robert Ham	.20	.09
❑ 9 Glenn Brewer	.20	.09
❑ 10 Ken Allen	.20	.09
❑ 11 Bob Dotter Sr.	.20	.09
❑ 12 L.W. Miller	.20	.09
❑ 13 Rick Sheppard	.20	.09
❑ 14 Eric Smith	.20	.09
❑ 15 Dave Weltmeyer	.20	.09
❑ 16 Craig Rubright	.20	.09
❑ 17 Roger Blackstock	.20	.09
❑ 18 Jeff Purvis	.75	.35
❑ 19 Randy Churchill	.20	.09
❑ 20 Mark Thompson	.20	.09
❑ 21 Jeep Pflum	.20	.09
❑ 22 Curt Dickie	.20	.09
❑ 23 Gary Hawes	.20	.09
❑ 24 Loy Allen Jr.	.75	.35
❑ 25 Brigette Anne Shirley	.20	.09
❑ 26 ARCA Officials	.20	.09
❑ 27 Jerry Huffman	.20	.09
❑ 28 Jimmy Horton	.45	.20
❑ 29 Jerry Foyt	.20	.09
❑ 30 Todd Coon	.20	.09
❑ 31 Ken Rowley	.20	.09
❑ 32 Dave Jensen	.20	.09
❑ 33 Joe Niemiroski	.20	.09
❑ 34 Tony Schwengel	.20	.09
❑ 35 Rick Heuser	.20	.09
❑ 36 Laura Lane	.20	.09
❑ 37 Gary Bradberry	.45	.20
❑ 38 Alan Pruitt	.20	.09
❑ 39 Danny Kelley	.20	.09
❑ 40 Wally Finney	.20	.09
❑ 41 Billy Bigley Jr.	.45	.20
❑ 42 Bob Schacht	.20	.09
❑ 43 Ken Schrader	1.00	.45
❑ 44 John Wilkinson	.20	.09
❑ 45 Billy Thomas	.20	.09
❑ 46 Donny Paul	.20	.09
❑ 47 David Hall	.20	.09
❑ 48 Andy Stone	.20	.09
❑ 49 Bob Hill	.20	.09
❑ 50 Ron Burchette	.20	.09
❑ 51 Red Farmer	.45	.20
❑ 52 James Hylton	.45	.20
❑ 53 Mike Wallace	1.00	.45
❑ 54 Tom Bigelow	.20	.09
❑ 55 Wayne Larson	.20	.09
❑ 56 Peter Gibbons	.20	.09
❑ 57 Jeff McClure	.45	.20
❑ 58 Andy Farr	.20	.09
❑ 59 Kerry Teague	.45	.20
❑ 60 Bob Williams	.20	.09
❑ 61 Bobby Gerhart	.20	.09
❑ 62 Jerry Glanville	.45	.20
❑ 63 Marvin Smith	.20	.09
❑ 64 Dale Fischlein	.20	.09
❑ 65 Rich Bickle	.45	.20
❑ 66 Greg Caver	.20	.09
❑ 67 Randy Huffman	.20	.09
❑ 68 Bill Venturini	.45	.20
❑ 69 Dave Simko	.20	.09
❑ 70 Tim Porter	.20	.09
❑ 71 Jody Gara	.20	.09
❑ 72 Perry Tripp	.20	.09
❑ 73 Bill Venturini	.45	.20
❑ 74 John Stradtman	.20	.09
❑ 75 Scotty Sands	.20	.09
❑ 76 Rich Hayes	.20	.09
❑ 77 Tim Fedewa	.45	.20
❑ 78 Joey Sonntag	.20	.09
❑ 79 Tom Sherrill	.20	.09
❑ 80 Delma Cowart	.45	.20
❑ 81 Jerry Hill	.20	.09
❑ 82 David Boggs	.20	.09
❑ 83 Greg Roe	.20	.09
❑ 84 Bobby Coyle	.20	.09
❑ 85 Mark Gibson	.20	.09
❑ 86 Gary Weinbroer	.20	.09
❑ 87 1994 ARCA Schedule	.20	.09
❑ 88 ARCA Pace Car CL	.20	.09
❑ 89 Checklist 21-60	.20	.09
❑ 90 Checklist 61-100	.20	.09
❑ 91 Tim Steele's Car	.20	.09
❑ 92 Bob Keselowski's Car	.20	.09
❑ 93 Bobby Bowsher's Car	.20	.09
❑ 94 Frank Kimmel's Car	.20	.09
❑ 95 Bob Brevak's Car	.20	.09
❑ 96 Bob Strait's Car	.20	.09
❑ 97 Robert Ham's Car	.20	.09
❑ 98 Glenn Brewer's Car	.20	.09
❑ 99 Ken Allen's Car	.20	.09
❑ 100 Jeff McClure's Car	.20	.09

1992 Limited Editions Chuck Bown

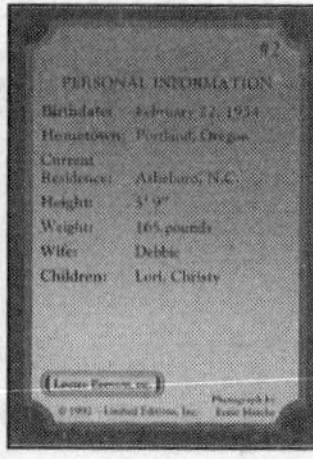

This is one of six Busch series driver sets produced by Limited Editions and distributed in complete set form. Each of the black bordered issues looks similar, but features a different driver. Chuck Bown is the focus of this set. Promo complete sets were also produced with the word "PROMO" on the card fronts. There is no price differnce for the promo version.

	MINT	NRMT
COMPLETE SET (15)	4.00	1.80
COMMON CARD (1-15)	.30	.14

1992 Limited Editions Harry Gant

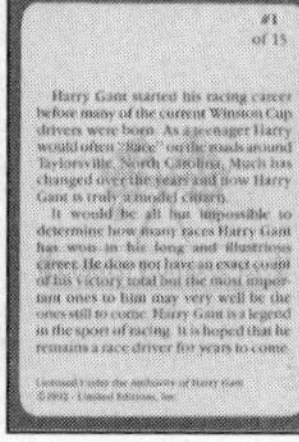

This set is the first in a continuing series of driver sets produced by Limited Editions. The Harry Gant issue differs from the others in that it contains a green border as opposed to black. The cards were distributed in a white box picturing Gant and were individually numbered of 25,000. Uncut sheets of the sets were also made available to members of the Limited Editions Collector Club -- 500 numbered and signed by Gant and 2000 unsigned.

	MINT	NRMT
COMPLETE SET (15)	5.00	2.20
HARRY GANT'S CAR (1-15)	.30	.14
HARRY GANT (1-15)	.40	.18

1992 Limited Editions Jerry Glanville

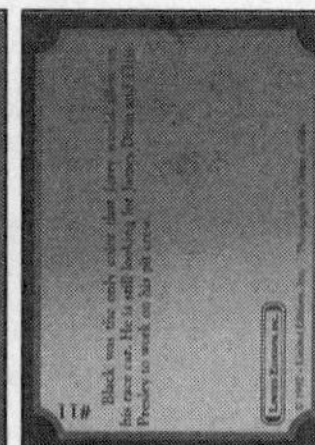

This set is issue #5 in a line of Busch series driver sets produced by Limited Editions. Each of the black bordered issues looks similar, but features a different driver. Glanville is the focus of this set.

	MINT	N
COMPLETE SET (12)	4.00	
JERRY GLANVILLE'S CAR (1-12)	.30	
JERRY GLANVILLE (1-12)	.40	

1992 Limited Editions Jeff Gordon

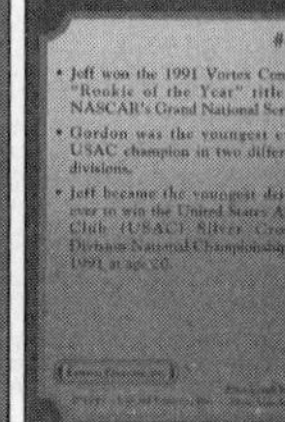

This set is issue #6 in a line of Busch series driver produced by Limited Editions. Each of the issues similar, but features a different driver. Jeff Gordon an Baby Ruth Race Team are the focus of this set. T were 300 Jeff Gordon autographed cards rand inserted in the sets. The card he signed was card # is valued at approximately $150. There was also a fa binder. Inside each binder was a promo card o Gordon, each stamped 1 of 1,000. There were unstamped versions of the promo card. The 1 indicated how many binders there were.

	MINT	N
COMPLETE SET (12)	7.00	
COMMON CARD (1-12)	.30	

❑ 1 Cover Card	.30	
❑ 2 Jeff Gordon	.75	
❑ 3 Jeff Gordon's Car	.30	
❑ 4 Jeff Gordon	.75	
❑ 5 Jeff Gordon	.75	
❑ 6 Jeff Gordon	.75	
❑ 7 Jeff Gordon's Car	.30	
❑ 8 Jeff Gordon	.75	
❑ 9 Jeff Gordon	.75	
❑ 10 Jeff Gordon Race Action	.30	
❑ 11 Jeff Gordon	.75	
❑ 12 Jeff Gordon	.75	

1992 Limited Editions Jimmy Hensley

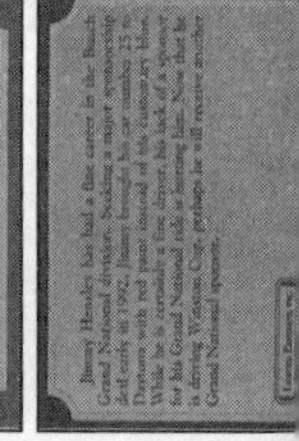

This is one of six Busch series driver sets produc Limited Editions and distributed in complete set Each of the black bordered issues looks simila focuses on a different driver. Jimmy Hensley is the of this set.

	MINT	N
COMPLETE SET (15)	4.00	
JIMMY HENSLEY'S CAR (1-15)	.30	
JIMMY HENSLEY (1-15)	.35	

1992 Limited Editions Tommy Houston

This is one of six Busch series driver sets produc Limited Editions and distributed in complete set Each of the black bordered issues looks simila features a different driver. Tommy Houston is the fo this set.

	MINT	N
COMPLETE SET (15)	4.00	
TOMMY HOUSTON'S CAR (1-15)	.30	
TOMMY HOUSTON (1-15)	.35	

1992 Limited Editions Kenny Wallace

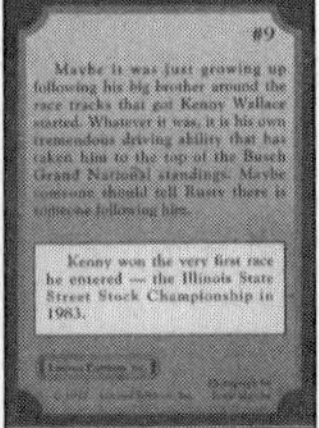

s one of six Busch series driver sets produced by ed Editions and distributed in complete set form. of the black bordered issues looks similar, but es on a different driver. Kenny Wallace is the focus set.

	MINT	NRMT
·LETE SET (15)	4.00	1.80
Y WALLACE'S CAR (1-15)	.30	.14
Y WALLACE (1-15)	.35	.16

1995 Lipton Tea Johnny Benson Jr.

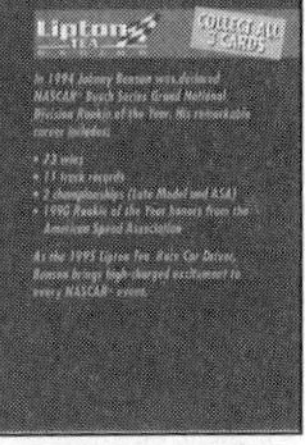

ages of Lipton Tea included one of three Johnny on Jr. cards produced in 1995. Each of the three features an artist's rendering of a Lipton Tea Racing action scene. The cards are unnumbered.

	MINT	NRMT
·LETE SET (3)	6.00	2.70
MON CARD	2.00	.90
❏ Johnny Benson Jr. w/Car	2.00	.90
Rookie of the Year		
❏ Johnny Benson Jr.	2.00	.90
❏ Johnny Benson Jr. in Pits	2.00	.90
20 Seconds and Counting		

92 Mac Tools Winner's Cup

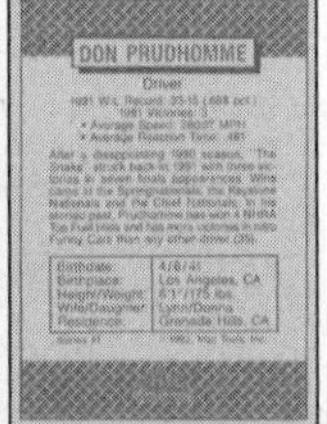

Tools produced this set honoring top performers of ASCAR, Indycar and NHRA racing circuits. The set is Winners' Cup Series and mentions it as a series one issue. There was no series two set produced. The cards were packaged in two different packs. Each pack contained 10 cards and a cover card. The cards are unnumbered and have been arranged below alphabetically.

	MINT	NRMT
COMPLETE SET (21)	16.00	7.25
COMMON CARD	.50	.23
❏ 1 Bobby Allison	.75	.35
Hut Stricklin		
❏ 2 Davey Allison	2.00	.90
❏ 3 Dale Armstrong	.50	.23
❏ 4 Ron Ayers	.50	.23
❏ 5 Kenny Bernstein	.75	.35
❏ 6 Michael Brotherton	.50	.23
❏ 7 Jim Crawford	.50	.23
❏ 8 Mike Dunn	.50	.23
❏ 9 Harry Gant	.75	.35
❏ 10 Darrell Gwynn	.50	.23
❏ 11 Jerry Gwynn	.50	.23
❏ 12 Ernie Irvan	.75	.35
❏ 13 Lori Johns	.50	.23
❏ 14 Bobby Labonte	2.00	.90
❏ 15 Mark Martin	2.50	1.10
❏ 16 Tom McEwen	.50	.23
❏ 17 Richard Petty	1.25	.55
❏ 18 Don Prudhomme	.75	.35
❏ 19 Kenny Wallace	.50	.23
❏ 20 Rusty Wallace	2.50	1.10
❏ 21 Cover/Checklist Card UER	.25	.11
Hut Stricklin misspelled Strickland		

1993 Maxwell House

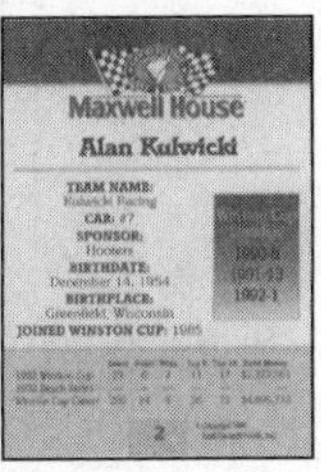

The 1993 Maxwell House set was produced by Kraft General Foods for distribution in Maxwell House coffee products. The cards were released in two series of 15-driver cards and one cover card each. Series one features a solid blue border, while the border on series two is a mix of light and dark blue. The cards are often sold in separate series in their original cello wrappers.

	MINT	NRMT
COMPLETE SET (32)	20.00	9.00
COMPLETE SERIES 1 (16)	10.00	4.50
COMPLETE SERIES 2 (16)	10.00	4.50
COMMON CARD (1-15)	.40	.18
COMMON CARD (16-30)	.40	.18
❏ 1 Bobby Labonte	1.00	.45
❏ 2 Alan Kulwicki	.75	.35
❏ 3 Davey Allison	1.00	.45
❏ 4 Harry Gant	.60	.25
❏ 5 Kyle Petty	.60	.25
❏ 6 Mark Martin	1.25	.55
❏ 7 Ricky Rudd	.60	.25
❏ 8 Darrell Waltrip	.60	.25
❏ 9 Ernie Irvan	.75	.35
❏ 10 Rusty Wallace	1.25	.55
❏ 11 Morgan Shepherd	.40	.18
❏ 12 Brett Bodine	.40	.18
❏ 13 Ken Schrader	.40	.18
❏ 14 Dale Jarrett	.75	.35
❏ 15 Richard Petty	.75	.35
❏ 16 Bobby Labonte	.75	.35
Terry Labonte		
❏ 17 Davey Allison	1.00	.45
Bobby Allison		
❏ 18 Richard Petty	.75	.35
Kyle Petty		
❏ 19 Rusty Wallace	1.00	.45
Kenny Wallace		
❏ 20 Geoff Bodine	.40	.18
Brett Bodine		
❏ 21 Darrell Waltrip	.60	.25
Michael Waltrip		
❏ 22 Dale Jarrett	.75	.35
Ned Jarrett		
❏ 23 Sterling Marlin	.60	.25
Coo Coo Marlin		
❏ 24 Jeff Gordon	2.00	.90
Kenny Wallace		
Bobby Labonte		
❏ 25 Jeff Gordon	4.00	1.80
❏ 26 Kenny Wallace	.40	.18
❏ 27 Hut Stricklin	.40	.18
❏ 28 Geoff Bodine	.40	.18
❏ 29 Terry Labonte	1.25	.55
❏ 30 Bobby Hillin	.40	.18
❏ NNO Cover Card 1	.40	.18
❏ NNO Cover Card 2	.40	.18

1988 Maxx Charlotte

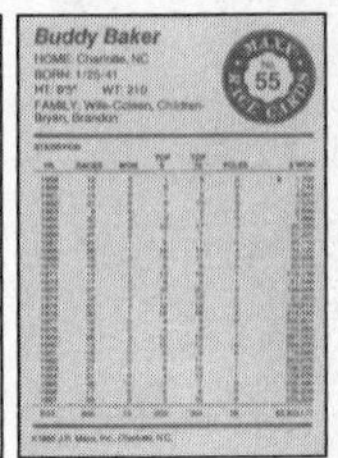

This set contains cards from the second and third printings of 1988 Maxx. The Charlotte name refers to the what was believed to be the location of the second and third printings. Actually, the second and third printings took place at the same location as the first printing. The set is often called the "First Annual Edition" by collectors. It contains numerous variations from the Myrtle Beach set. The cover cards were printed with two different starburst descriptions (pack versus factory set) in both the Charlotte and Myrtle Beach versions. During the second printing, 10 cards including the two variations of the cover card were changed. The Myrtle Beach notation was removed from the four checklist cards. The special offer price ($19.95) was changed prior to the second printing to $21.45 on the Cover Cards.The Talladega Streaks #10 card was eliminated to make room for Darrell Waltrip. Checklist #19 was changed to reflect this move. On card #26 Phil Parsons, his wife's name was included in the family section on the back of the card. It was excluded in the first printing Myrtle Beach. During the third printing of this set six cards were changed. The #59 1988 Begins card was eliminated to make room for the #59 Brett Bodine card. Checklist #69 was changed to reflect this move. The #43 Daytona International Speedway card was changed to card #47. The #47 Single File card was eliminated. Richard Petty was included in the set on, of course, card #43. Checklist #36 was updated to reflect the changes on cards #43 and #47. On the #88 Ken Bouchard card, the family section was changed to reflect the fact that he and his fiancee, Heidi, were married during the season. There was also a card #99 of Dale Earnhardt that originally wasn't released due to Maxx not getting approval from Dale. The card was later issued with a sticker on it via an insert redemption in the 1994 Maxx Medallion set. (See that set for more on the stickered version.) Then in 1996, as Maxx was going out of business, a signed version of this card was supposed to be released through a product called Maxx Made in America. The only reports we have of this card being in the Made in America product are that the cards are unsigned and carry no distinguishing marks that would differentiate that card from any other 1988 Maxx card. There were a few of the original #99 card released in 1988 and now appears to be some more released through other means in 1996. For more on the varitions in the 1988 Maxx set and a photo of an uncut sheet with the #99 Dale Earnhardt card please refer to Beckett Racing Monthly October 1996 issue #26. We have received reported prices on the original #99 card without any sticker or other distinguishing marks between $75 - $150.

	MINT	NRMT
COMPLETE SET (100)	100.00	45.00
COMPLETE FACT.SET (100)	120.00	55.00
COMMON CARD (1-100)	.75	.35
COMMON DRIVER (1-100)	1.50	.70
❏ 1A Cover Card	.50	.23
mentions 10 cards		
❏ 1B Cover Card	60.00	27.00
mentions 100 cards		
❏ 2 Richard Petty's Car	3.00	1.35
❏ 3 J.D. McDuffie	2.50	1.10
❏ 4 Cale Yarborough's Car	1.50	.70
❏ 5 Davey Allison	12.00	5.50
❏ 6 Rodney Combs	1.50	.70
❏ 7 Bobby Allison's Car	1.50	.70
Neil Bonnett's Car		

Geoff Bodine's Car		
Buddy Baker's Car		
❑ 8 Mickey Gibbs	1.50	.70
❑ 9 Atlanta International	4.00	1.80
with Dale Earnhardt's Car		
❑ 10 Darrell Waltrip	3.00	1.35
❑ 11 Sterling Marlin's Car	1.50	.70
❑ 12 Brad Teague	1.50	.70
❑ 13 Alabama Thunder	4.00	1.80
with Dale Earnhardt's Car		
❑ 14 Rusty Wallace	8.00	3.60
❑ 15 Pit Row Action	.75	.35
❑ 16 Larry Pollard	1.50	.70
❑ 17 The Winston	8.00	3.60
with Dale Earnhardt's Car		
❑ 18 Benny Parsons' Car	1.50	.70
❑ 19 Checklist 1	.25	.11
no Myrtle Beach line		
❑ 20 Neil Bonnett	4.00	1.80
❑ 21 Martinsville Speedway	1.25	.55
❑ 22 Bill Elliott's Car	2.50	1.10
❑ 23 Michael Waltrip's Car	.75	.35
❑ 24 Trevor Boys	1.50	.70
❑ 25 Morgan Shepherd	2.50	1.10
❑ 26 Phil Parsons	2.25	1.00
mentions wife Marcia		
❑ 27 Darrell Waltrip In Pits	1.50	.70
❑ 28 Hut Stricklin	1.50	.70
❑ 29 Richard Childress	.75	.35
❑ 30 Bobby Allison	3.00	1.35
❑ 31 Richard Petty's Car	2.50	1.10
Ricky Rudd's Car		
❑ 32 Richmond Fairgrounds	120.00	55.00
❑ 33 Derrike Cope	2.50	1.10
❑ 34 Neil Bonnett's Car	1.50	.70
❑ 35 Geoff Bodine's Car	.75	.35
Benny Parsons' Car		
❑ 36A Checklist 2	10.00	4.50
no Myrtle Beach line		
card #43 Daytona Int.		
❑ 36B Checklist 2	1.00	.45
no Myrtle Beach line		
card #43 Richard Petty		
❑ 37 Larry Pearson	1.50	.70
❑ 38 Dale Earnhardt in Pits	8.00	3.60
Wrangler		
❑ 39 Dave Pletcher	1.50	.70
❑ 40 Davey Allison ROY	20.00	9.00
❑ 41 Alan Kulwicki's Car	3.00	1.35
❑ 42 Jimmy Means	1.50	.70
❑ 43 Richard Petty	6.00	2.70
❑ 44 Dave Marcis	3.00	1.35
❑ 45 Tire Wars	.75	.35
Dale Earnhardt's Trailer		
❑ 46 Lake Speed	1.50	.70
❑ 47 Daytona Int. Speedway	.75	.35
❑ 48 Mark Martin	8.00	3.60
❑ 49 Dale Earnhardt's Car	5.00	2.20
Davey Allison's Car		
❑ 50 Bill Elliott	8.00	3.60
❑ 51 Ken Ragan	1.50	.70
❑ 52 Bobby Hillin	1.50	.70
❑ 53 Alabama Int. Speedway	.75	.35
❑ 54 Dale Earnhardt's Car	10.00	4.50
Goodwrench		
❑ 55 Buddy Baker	3.00	1.35
❑ 56 Charlotte Motor Speedway	.75	.35
❑ 57 Rick Wilson Crash	.75	.35
❑ 58 Alan Kulwicki	6.00	2.70
❑ 59 Brett Bodine	1.50	.70
❑ 60 Richard Petty's Car	3.00	1.35
❑ 61 Dale Jarrett	6.00	2.70
❑ 62 Rusty Wallace's Car	3.00	1.35
Geoff Bodine's Car		
❑ 63 Terry Labonte	8.00	3.60
❑ 64 Dave Marcis' Car	1.50	.70
❑ 65 Greg Sacks	1.50	.70
❑ 66 Jimmy Horton	1.50	.70
❑ 67 Geoff Bodine	1.50	.70
❑ 68 Rick Wilson	1.50	.70
❑ 69A Checklist 3	10.00	4.50
no Myrtle Beach line		
card 59 1988 Begins		
❑ 69B Checklist 3	1.00	.45
no Myrtle Beach line		
card 59 Brett Bodine		
❑ 70 Bill Elliott	4.00	1.80
Fan's Favorite Driver		
❑ 71 Mark Stahl	1.50	.70
❑ 72 Harry Ranier/Lundy Shop	.75	.35
❑ 73 Phoenix Int. Raceway	1.25	.55
❑ 74 Ken Schrader	1.50	.70
❑ 75 Darrell Waltrip's Car	1.50	.70
❑ 76 Benny Parsons	3.00	1.35
❑ 77 Watkins Glen Int.	.75	.35
❑ 78 Phil Barkdoll	1.50	.70
❑ 79 Speedway Club	.75	.35
Charlotte Motor Speedway		
❑ 80 Sterling Marlin	3.00	1.35
❑ 81 Ken Schrader's Car	.75	.35
❑ 82 Riverside International	.75	.35
with Richard Petty's Car		
❑ 83 Buddy Arrington	1.50	.70
❑ 84 Dale Earnhardt's Car	4.00	1.80
Richard Petty's Car		
Bill Elliott's Car		
Double Pleasure		
❑ 85 Connie Saylor	.75	.35
❑ 86 North Wilkesboro Speedway	.75	.35
❑ 87 Dale Earnhardt w/Crew	70.00	32.00
Winston Cup Champion		
❑ 88 Ken Bouchard	1.50	.70
mentions Ken being married		
❑ 89 Davey Allison's Car	4.00	1.80
❑ 90 Cale Yarborough	3.00	1.35
❑ 91 Michigan Int. Speedway	.75	.35
❑ 92 Eddie Bierschwale	.75	.35
❑ 93 Jim Sauter	1.50	.70
❑ 94 Bobby Allison's Car	1.50	.70
Benny Parsons' Car		
❑ 95 Ernie Irvan	6.00	2.70
❑ 96 Buddy Baker's Car	1.50	.70
❑ 97 Filling the Stands	.75	.35
Charlotte Motor Speedway		
❑ 98 Michael Waltrip	1.50	.70
❑ 99 Great Body	.75	.35
Pit Row Scene		
❑ 100 Checklist 4	.25	.11
no Myrtle Beach line		

1988 Maxx Myrtle Beach

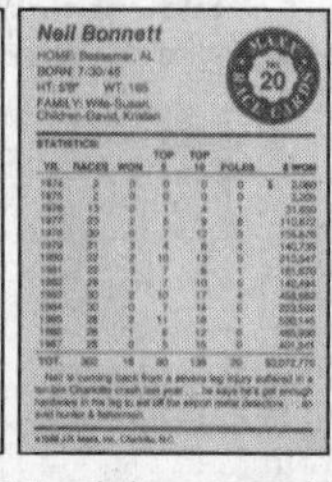

This was Maxx's first attempt at producing a mass-market racing product. The Myrtle Beach (First Edition) set contains 100 cards including a Cover Card and four checklists. The set was initially introduced at the 1988 Coca Cola 600 in Charlotte. The Myrtle Beach name was attached to this set due to the printer's notation on the four checklists. The 100 standard sized cards comprising this set were issued in complete factory sets which were made available to collectors for the price of $19.95 through an offer on the cover cards. Ten-card shrink-wrapped packs were packaged in 44-count boxes and in 1989 Maxx Combo packs which contained three 10-card '88 packs. It is important to note the combo packs contain cards from all three printings of this set. The Cover Card from this set was produced with two different descriptions located in the yellow starburst on the front of the card. The cover card in the factory sets reads "100 Collector cards...", while the cover card in the shrink-wrapped packs shows "10 Collector cards...". The scarce nature of this set is attributable to the ten variations which it contains. Reportedly 10,000 of the Myrtle Beach sets were produced. The cards listed below are the ten Myrtle Beach variations.

	MINT	NRMT
COMPLETE SET (100)	400.00	180.00
COMPLETE FACT.SET (100)	500.00	220.00
❑ 1A Cover Card	6.00	2.70
mentions 10 cards		
❑ 1B Cover Card	125.00	55.00
mentions 100 cards		
❑ 10 Talladega Streaks	100.00	45.00
❑ 19 Checklist 1	14.00	6.25
with Myrtle Beach line		
❑ 26 Phil Parsons	100.00	45.00
does not mention wife Marcia		
❑ 36 Checklist 2	14.00	6.25
with Myrtle Beach line		
❑ 43 Daytona Int. Speedway	15.00	6.75
❑ 47 Single File	15.00	6.75
with Davey Allison's Car		
❑ 59 1988 Begins	15.00	6.75
Daytona Int. Speedway		
❑ 69 Checklist 3	14.00	6.25
with Myrtle Beach line		
❑ 88 Ken Bouchard	15.00	6.75
mentions Ken being engaged		
❑ 100 Checklist 4	14.00	
with Myrtle Beach line		

1989 Maxx Previews

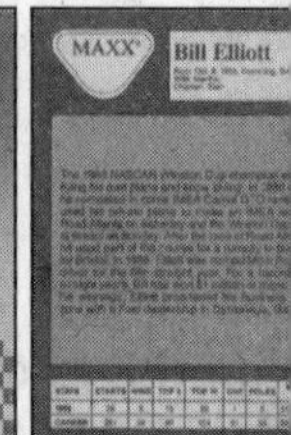

This ten-card set was produced by Maxx to give colle a preview of the '89 Maxx release. It consists of two cards and eight unnumbered driver cards. These were available in '89 Maxx Combo packs. Each c pack contained three ten-card packs of '88 Maxx an '89 Preview cards, one of which was a cover card. cards were collated so one pack contained one half Preview set and the other pack contained the other h the set. The first Cover card features a starburst d and is considered the toughest of the two. The se Cover card features Bill Elliott's car and can be found either a checklist back or coupon back good for 10(toward the 500 needed for a subscription to G National Scene.

	MINT	N
COMPLETE SET (10)	20.00	
COMMON CARD	1.00	
❑ NNO Geoff Bodine	1.00	
❑ NNO Bill Elliott	3.00	
❑ NNO Bobby Hillin	1.00	
❑ NNO Sterling Marlin	2.00	
❑ NNO Mark Martin	3.00	
❑ NNO Richard Petty	2.50	
❑ NNO Rusty Wallace	3.00	
❑ NNO Michael Waltrip	1.00	
❑ NNO Cover Card A	6.00	
Explosion Art Logo		
❑ NNO Cover Card B1	1.50	
Bill Elliott's Car		
Checklist Back		
❑ NNO Cover Card B2	1.50	
Bill Elliott's Car		
100 Laps Back		

1989 Maxx

This set consists of 220 cards featuring drivers, their team owners, crew chiefs, All-Pro crew members all-time greats from the NASCAR circuit. It was available as a mail order set, commonly refered to a Toolbox set, as a hobby set, and through wax boxes 48 12-card wax packs, containing ten regular cards cover card, and two sticker cards. The set price inc the corrected version of card #5, Geoff Bodine. A Wi Cup set containing the first one hundred cards of th was also produced. It was packaged in a yellow box red checkerboard squares. This set is commonly k as the "Peak" set since it features a picture of Kyle P Peak Antifreeze sponsored car on the box.

	MINT	
COMPLETE SET (220)	250.00	1
COMPLETE FACT.SET (220)	250.00	1
COMPLETE TOOLBOX SET (220)	250.00	1
COMPLETE PEAK SET (100)	125.00	
COMMON CARD (1-220)	1.00	
COMMON DRIVER (1-220)	2.00	
❑ 1 Ken Bouchard	2.00	
Rookie of the Year		
❑ 2 Ernie Irvan	4.00	

Dale Earnhardt 80.00 36.00
Rick Wilson 2.00 .90
Geoff Bodine ERR 12.00 5.50
last line of text incomplete
Geoff Bodine COR 10.00 4.50
text complete on last line
Mark Martin 12.00 5.50
Alan Kulwicki 10.00 4.50
Bobby Hillin 2.00 .90
Bill Elliott 12.00 5.50
Ken Bouchard 2.00 .90
Terry Labonte 10.00 4.50
Bobby Allison 4.00 1.80
Robert Gee 1.00 .45
Harry Hyde 1.00 .45
Brett Bodine 2.00 .90
Larry Pearson 2.00 .90
Darrell Waltrip 4.00 1.80
Barry Dodson 1.00 .45
Bill Stavola 1.00 .45
Mickey Stavola
James Lewter 1.00 .45
Neil Bonnett 6.00 2.70
Tim Brewer 1.00 .45
Eddie Bierschwale 1.00 .45
Travis Carter 1.00 .45
Ken Schrader 2.00 .90
Ricky Rudd 4.00 1.80
Rusty Wallace 12.00 5.50
Davey Allison 30.00 13.50
Dale Jarrett 8.00 3.60
Michael Waltrip 2.00 .90
Jim Sauter 1.00 .45
Todd Parrott 1.00 .45
Harry Gant 4.00 1.80
Rodney Combs 2.00 .90
Tony Glover 1.00 .45
Will Lind 1.00 .45
Cale Yarborough 4.00 1.80
Kirk Shelmerdine 1.00 .45
Ted Conder 1.00 .45
Felix Sabates
Raymond Beadle 1.00 .45
Jim Bown 1.00 .45
Kyle Petty 4.00 1.80
Richard Petty 10.00 4.50
Jeff Hammond 1.00 .45
Harry Melling 1.00 .45
Butch Mock 1.00 .45
Bob Rahilly
Doug Williams 1.00 .45
Mickey Gibbs 1.00 .45
Darrell Bryant 1.00 .45
Bill Elliott 10.00 4.50
Winston Cup Champion
Walter Bud Moore 1.00 .45
Jimmy Means 2.00 .90
Billy Woodruff 1.00 .45
Rusty Wallace 12.00 5.50
Phil Parsons 2.00 .90
Leonard Wood 1.00 .45
Hut Stricklin 2.00 .90
Ken Thompson 1.00 .45
Gary Nelson 1.00 .45
Dale Earnhardt w/Crew 10.00 4.50
Pit Crew Champs
Rick Hendrick 1.00 .45
Barry Dodson 1.00 .45
Roland Wlodyka 1.00 .45
Danny Schiff 2.00 .90
Buddy Baker
Gale Wilson 1.00 .45
Rick Mast 4.00 1.80
Brad Teague 1.00 .45
Derrike Cope 2.00 .90
Checklist 1-100 1.00 .45
J.D. McDuffie 4.00 1.80
Dave Marcis 4.00 1.80
David Evans 1.00 .45
Phil Barkdoll 2.00 .90
Ernie Elliott 2.00 .90
Morgan Shepherd 2.00 .90
Dale Inman 1.00 .45
Junior Johnson 4.00 1.80
David Smith 1.00 .45
Jimmy Fennig 1.00 .45
Jimmy Horton 2.00 .90
Mike Beam 1.00 .45
Jimmy Makar 1.00 .45
Lake Speed 2.00 .90
Mike Alexander 1.00 .45
Dennis Connor 1.00 .45
Mike Hill 1.00 .45
Richard Childress 4.00 1.80
Greg Sacks 2.00 .90
Waddell Wilson 1.00 .45
Chad Little 2.00 .90
Norman Koshimizu 1.00 .45

❑ 92 Harold Elliott 1.00 .45
❑ 93 Cliff Champion 1.00 .45
❑ 94 Sterling Marlin 4.00 1.80
❑ 95 Trevor Boys 1.00 .45
❑ 96 Howard Poston (Slick) 1.00 .45
❑ 97 Jake Elder 1.00 .45
❑ 98 Chuck Rider 1.00 .45
❑ 99 Connie Saylor 1.00 .45
❑ 100 Bill Elliott 10.00 4.50
Fan's Favorite Driver
❑ 101 Richard Petty's Car 4.00 1.80
Year in Review
❑ 102 Dale Earnhardt's Car 12.00 5.50
Neil Bonnett's Car
Year in Review
❑ 103 Neil Bonnett's Car 4.00 1.80
Alan Kulwicki's Car
Year in Review
❑ 104 Motorcraft Quality Parts 500 1.00 .45
Year in Review
❑ 105 Lake Speed in Pits 1.00 .45
Year in Review
❑ 106 Bill Elliott in Pits 4.00 1.80
Year in Review
❑ 107 First Union 400 1.00 .45
Year in Review
❑ 108 Dale Earnhardt's Car 6.00 2.70
Year in Review
❑ 109 Winston 500 1.00 .45
Year in Review
❑ 110 Coca Cola 400 1.00 .45
Year in Review
❑ 111 Harry Gant in Pits 2.00 .90
Year in Review
❑ 112 Budweiser 400 1.00 .45
Year in Review
❑ 113 Davey Allison's Car 4.00 1.80
Year in Review
❑ 114 Alan Kulwicki's Car 4.00 1.80
Rusty Wallace's Car
Year in Review
❑ 115 Bill Elliott's Car 4.00 1.80
Rick Wilson's Car
Year in Review
❑ 116 Sterling Marlin's Car 2.00 .90
Year in Review
❑ 117 Talladega Diehard 500 1.00 .45
Year in Review
❑ 118 Neil Bonnett's Car 2.00 .90
Year in Review
❑ 119 Davey Allison's Car 4.00 1.80
Year in Review
❑ 120 Busch 500 1.00 .45
Year in Review
❑ 121 Dale Earnhardt's Car 6.00 2.70
Year in Review
❑ 122 Geoff Bodine's Car 1.00 .45
Year in Review
❑ 123 Bill Elliott in Pits 4.00 1.80
Year in Review
❑ 124 Davey Allison's Car 4.00 1.80
Phil Parson's Car
Dale Jarrett's Car
Year in Review
❑ 125 Darrell Waltrip's Car 2.00 .90
Sterling Marlin's Car
Bill Elliott's Car
Rusty Wallace's Car
Year in Review
❑ 126 Holly Farms 400 1.00 .45
Year in Review
❑ 127 Alan Kulwicki's Car 4.00 1.80
Bill Elliott's Car
Rusty Wallace's Car
Davey Allison's Car
Mark Martin's Car
Year in Review
❑ 128 Checker 500 1.00 .45
Year in Review
❑ 129 Bill Elliott in Pits 4.00 1.80
Year in Review
❑ 130 The Winston 1.00 .45
Year in Review
❑ 131 Benny Parsons 2.00 .90
Phil Parsons
❑ 132 Tommy Houston 2.00 .90
❑ 133 Kenny Bernstein 2.00 .90
❑ 134 Jack Roush 1.00 .45
❑ 135 Rob Moroso 2.00 .90
❑ 136 Les Richter 1.00 .45
❑ 137 Dick Beaty 1.00 .45
❑ 138 Harold Kinder 1.00 .45
❑ 139 Checklist 101-160 1.00 .45
❑ 140 Darrell Waltrip 4.00 1.80
Michael Waltrip
❑ 141 Bobby Allison 4.00 1.80
Victory Lane
❑ 142 Neil Bonnett 4.00 1.80
Victory Lane
❑ 143 Neil Bonnett 4.00 1.80
Victory Lane
❑ 144 Dale Earnhardt w/Crew 15.00 6.75
Victory Lane
❑ 145 Lake Speed 2.00 .90
Victory Lane
❑ 146 Bill Elliott 4.00 1.80
Victory Lane
❑ 147 Terry Labonte 4.00 1.80
Victory Lane
❑ 148 Dale Earnhardt 15.00 6.75
Teresa Earnhardt
Victory Lane
❑ 149 Phil Parsons 2.00 .90
Victory Lane
❑ 150 Darrell Waltrip 4.00 1.80
Victory Lane
❑ 151 Bill Elliott 4.00 1.80
Victory Lane
❑ 152 Rusty Wallace 4.00 1.80
Victory Lane
❑ 153 Geoff Bodine 2.00 .90
Victory Lane
❑ 154 Rusty Wallace 4.00 1.80
Victory Lane
❑ 155 Bill Elliott 4.00 1.80
Victory Lane
❑ 156 Bill Elliott 4.00 1.80
Victory Lane
❑ 157 Ken Schrader 2.00 .90
Victory Lane
❑ 158 Ricky Rudd 2.00 .90
Victory Lane
❑ 159 Davey Allison 4.00 1.80
Victory Lane
❑ 160 Dale Earnhardt 15.00 6.75
Victory Lane
❑ 161 Bill Elliott w/Crew 4.00 1.80
Victory Lane
❑ 162 Davey Allison 4.00 1.80
Victory Lane
❑ 163 Bill Elliott 4.00 1.80
Victory Lane
❑ 164 Darrell Waltrip 2.00 .90
Victory Lane
❑ 165 Rusty Wallace 4.00 1.80
Victory Lane
❑ 166 Rusty Wallace 4.00 1.80
Victory Lane
❑ 167 Rusty Wallace 4.00 1.80
Victory Lane
❑ 168 Alan Kulwicki 4.00 1.80
Victory Lane
❑ 169 Rusty Wallace 4.00 1.80
Victory Lane
❑ 170 Terry Labonte 4.00 1.80
Junior Johnson
Victory Lane
❑ 171 Sterling Marlin 4.00 1.80
Victory Lane
❑ 172 Tommy Ellis 1.00 .45
❑ 173 Billy Hagan 1.00 .45
❑ 174 Rod Osterlund 1.00 .45
❑ 175 Elton Sawyer 2.00 .90
❑ 176 Robert Yates 2.00 .90
❑ 177 Ed Berrier 1.00 .45
❑ 178 Kenny Wallace 2.00 .90
❑ 179 Joe Thurman 1.00 .45
❑ 180 Davey Allison 14.00 6.25
Bobby Allison
❑ 181 Richard Petty's Car 4.00 1.80
Classic
❑ 182 Smokey Yunick 2.00 .90
Classic
❑ 183 Ralph Moody's Car 1.00 .45
Classic
❑ 184 Donnie Allison 2.00 .90
Classic
❑ 185 Marvin Panch's Car 1.00 .45
Johnny Allen's Car
Classic
❑ 186 Fred Lorenzen 4.00 1.80
Classic
❑ 187 Wendell Scott's Car 2.00 .90
Classic
❑ 188 Curtis Turner 2.00 .90
Classic
❑ 189 Asheville-Weaverville track 1.00 .45
Classic
❑ 190 Junior Johnson 4.00 1.80
Chris Economaki
Classic
❑ 191 Darel Dieringer's Car 1.00 .45
Classic
❑ 192 Marvin Panch 2.00 .90
Classic
❑ 193 Richard Petty's Car 4.00 1.80

Jack Smith's Car		
Classic		
❑ 194 David Pearson	2.00	.90
Classic		
❑ 195 Talladega 1970	1.00	.45
Classic		
❑ 196 Tim Flock In Car	2.00	.90
Classic		
❑ 197 Glenn Fireball Roberts' Car	2.00	.90
Classic		
❑ 198 Bobby Isaac	4.00	1.80
Classic		
❑ 199 Wood Brothers 1967	2.00	.90
Classic		
❑ 200 Ned Jarrett	2.00	.90
Classic		
❑ 201 Jack Ingram	2.00	.90
❑ 202 Brett Bodine	4.00	1.80
Geoff Bodine		
❑ 203 Elmo Langley	2.00	.90
❑ 204 Steve Grissom	4.00	1.80
❑ 205 Ronald Cooper	1.00	.45
❑ 206 Tim Morgan	1.00	.45
Larry McClure Team		
❑ 207 Ronnie Silver	1.00	.45
❑ 208 Jimmy Spencer	4.00	1.80
❑ 209 Ben Hess	1.00	.45
❑ 210 Rusty Wallace	6.00	2.70
Kenny Wallace		
❑ 211 Bob Whitcomb	1.00	.45
❑ 212 Billy Standridge	1.00	.45
❑ 213 Glen Wood	1.00	.45
❑ 214 L.D. Ottinger	1.00	.45
❑ 215 David Pearson	2.00	.90
❑ 216 Patty Moise	2.00	.90
❑ 217 Checklist 162-220	1.00	.45
❑ 218 Chuck Bown	2.00	.90
❑ 219 Jimmy Hensley	2.00	.90
❑ 220 Richard Petty	14.00	6.25
Kyle Petty		

1989 Maxx Stickers

Inserted two per pack in 1989 Maxx, each sticker card features two removable sticker flags. Each flag contains a colored number representing a race car number. The sticker cards are not numbered individually, but have been assigned card numbers below in the order of the left flag number.

	MINT	NRMT
COMPLETE SET (20)	50.00	22.00
COMMON STICKER (1-20)	3.00	1.35
❑ 1 2/33	3.00	1.35
❑ 2 3/52	3.00	1.35
❑ 3 4/42	3.00	1.35
❑ 4 5/43	3.00	1.35
❑ 5 6/84	3.00	1.35
❑ 6 7/55	3.00	1.35
❑ 7 8/57	3.00	1.35
❑ 8 9/71	3.00	1.35
❑ 9 11/88	3.00	1.35
❑ 10 12/68	3.00	1.35
❑ 11 15/3	3.00	1.35
❑ 12 16/75	3.00	1.35
❑ 13 17/83	3.00	1.35
❑ 14 21/17	3.00	1.35
❑ 15 25/33	3.00	1.35
❑ 16 26/43	3.00	1.35
❑ 17 27/94	3.00	1.35
❑ 18 28/5	3.00	1.35
❑ 19 29/27	3.00	1.35
❑ 20 30/9	3.00	1.35

1989 Maxx Crisco

This 25-card set contains one Cover card, and 24 driver cards. It was produced by Maxx and distributed by Proctor and Gamble as a complete set. They were given away with a purchase of their product in selected stores throughout the country. They were kept in a floor standup display, featuring Greg Sacks, that held 96 sets. It is

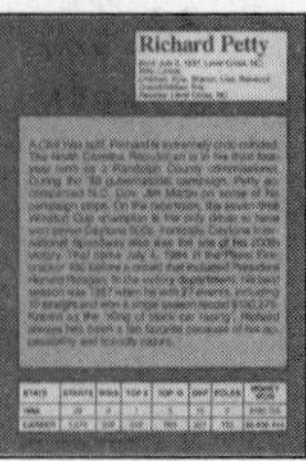

reported that one million sets were produced. Two weeks after these sets were shipped to Proctor and Gamble, Greg Sacks parted company with his car owner Buddy Baker and a large portion of these sets were destroyed. However, many of these sets found their way into the hobby through closeout sales.

	MINT	NRMT
COMPLETE SET (25)	5.00	2.20
COMMON CARD (1-24)	.20	.09
❑ 1 Greg Sacks	.20	.09
❑ 2 Darrell Waltrip	.40	.18
❑ 3 Ken Schrader	.20	.09
❑ 4 Bill Elliott	1.00	.45
❑ 5 Rusty Wallace	1.00	.45
❑ 6 Dale Earnhardt	2.00	.90
❑ 7 Terry Labonte	1.00	.45
❑ 8 Geoff Bodine	.20	.09
❑ 9 Brett Bodine	.20	.09
❑ 10 Davey Allison	.50	.23
❑ 11 Ricky Rudd	.40	.18
❑ 12 Kyle Petty	.40	.18
❑ 13 Alan Kulwicki	.50	.23
❑ 14 Neil Bonnett	.50	.23
❑ 15 Rick Wilson	.20	.09
❑ 16 Harry Gant	.40	.18
❑ 17 Richard Petty	.50	.23
❑ 18 Phil Parsons	.20	.09
❑ 19 Sterling Marlin	.40	.18
❑ 20 Bobby Hillin	.20	.09
❑ 21 Michael Waltrip	.20	.09
❑ 22 Dale Jarrett	.50	.23
❑ 23 Morgan Shepherd	.20	.09
❑ 24 Greg Sacks w/Car	.20	.09
❑ NNO Header Card	.20	.09

1990 Maxx

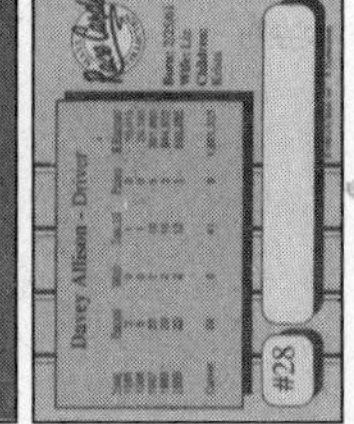

This 200-card set was produced in three different print runs. It was distributed in four different factory sets. The "tin box" set was sold by Maxx through a mail order offer for $29.95, and contains cards from the first printing. The cards from these sets have a glossy finish. The second of the sets was the white box Hobby set distributed to authorized Maxx dealers containing cards from the first printing. The third of the sets was the red/white box Hobby set which contains cards from the second printing. In the second printing four error cards were corrected: #8 Bobby Hillin, #28 Davey Allison, #39 Kirk Shelmerdine, and #97 Chuck Bown. The fourth of these sets was the red/yellow Hobby set which contains cards from the third printing. In the third printing three error cards were corrected:#13 Mickey Gibbs, #69 Checklist, and #85 Larry McClure. Cards from all three printings of this set were also distributed in wax packs. The packs are distinguishable by the lettering on the bottom of them. Packs from the first printing have white lettering, packs from the second printing have black lettering, and packs form the third printing also have black lettering and have the roman numeral three under the lettering. It is important to note that because of the black borders on these cards they are susceptible to chipping.

	MINT	NRMT
COMPLETE SET (200)	60.00	27.00
COMPLETE FACT.SET WHITE (200)	80.00	36.00
COMP.FACT.SET RED/WHITE (200)	70.00	32.00
COMP.FACT.SET RED/YELLOW (200)	60.00	
COMPLETE TIN GLOSSY SET (200)	150.00	
COMMON CARD (1-200)	.50	
COMMON DRIVER (1-200)	1.00	
GLOSSY CARDS 3X TO X BASIC CARDS		
❑ 1 Terry Labonte	6.00	
❑ 2 Ernie Irvan	2.00	
❑ 3 Dale Earnhardt	15.00	
❑ 4 Phil Parsons	1.00	
❑ 5 Ricky Rudd	2.00	
❑ 6 Mark Martin	6.00	
❑ 7 Alan Kulwicki	5.00	
❑ 8A Bobby Hillin ERR	12.00	
career totals wrong, 332 races		
❑ 8B Bobby Hillin COR	2.00	
career totals correct, 177 races		
❑ 9 Bill Elliott	6.00	
❑ 10 Derrike Cope	1.00	
❑ 11 Geoff Bodine	1.00	
❑ 12 Bobby Allison	1.00	
❑ 13A Mickey Gibbs ERR	10.00	
only one child listed		
❑ 13B Mickey Gibbs COR	2.00	
both children listed		
❑ 14 A.J. Foyt	1.00	
❑ 15 Morgan Shepherd	1.00	
❑ 16 Larry Pearson	1.00	
❑ 17 Darrell Waltrip	2.00	
❑ 18 Cale Yarborough	2.00	
❑ 19 Barry Dodson	.50	
❑ 20 Bob Whitcomb	.50	
❑ 21 Neil Bonnett	3.00	
❑ 22 Rob Moroso	1.00	
❑ 23 Eddie Bierschwale	1.00	
❑ 24 Cliff Champion	.50	
❑ 25 Ken Schrader	1.00	
❑ 26 Brett Bodine	1.00	
❑ 27 Rusty Wallace	6.00	
❑ 28A Davey Allison ERR	20.00	
1988 top tens 13		
❑ 28B Davey Allison COR	12.00	
1988 top tens 16		
❑ 29 Dale Jarrett	4.00	
❑ 30 Michael Waltrip	1.00	
❑ 31 Jim Sauter	1.00	
❑ 32 Tony Glover	.50	
❑ 33 Harry Gant	2.00	
❑ 34 Rodney Combs	1.00	
❑ 35 Jimmy Fennig	.50	
❑ 36 Raymond Beadle	.50	
❑ 37 Buddy Parrott	.50	
❑ 38 Brandon Baker	.50	
❑ 39A Kirk Shelmerdine ERR	10.00	
copyright line in autograph area		
❑ 39B Kirk Shelmerdine COR	3.00	
copyright removed from autograph area		
❑ 40 Jim Phillips	.50	
❑ 41 Jim Bown	1.00	
❑ 42 Kyle Petty	2.00	
❑ 43 Richard Petty	5.00	
❑ 44 Bob Tullius	.50	
❑ 45 Richard Childress	.50	
❑ 46 Steve Hmiel	.50	
❑ 47 Ronnie Silver	.50	
❑ 48 Greg Sacks	1.00	
❑ 49 Tony Spanos	.50	
❑ 50 Darrell Waltrip w/Crew	.50	
Pit Crew Champions		
❑ 51 Junie Donlavey	.50	
❑ 52 Jimmy Means	1.00	
❑ 53 Mike Beam	.50	
❑ 54 Jack Roush	.50	
❑ 55 Felix Sabates	.50	
❑ 56 Ted Conder	.50	
❑ 57 Hut Stricklin	1.00	
❑ 58 Ken Ragan	1.00	
❑ 59 Ronald Cooper	.50	
❑ 60 Jeff Hammond	.50	
❑ 61 Elton Sawyer	1.00	
❑ 62 Leo Jackson	.50	
❑ 63 Rick Hendrick	.50	
❑ 64 Dale Inman	.50	
❑ 65 Travis Carter	.50	
❑ 66 Dick Trickle	1.00	
❑ 67 Brad Teague	1.00	
❑ 68 Richard Broome	.50	
❑ 69A Checklist A ERR	6.00	
card 85 Tim McClure		
❑ 69B Checklist A COR	2.00	
card 85 Larry McClure		
❑ 70 J.D. McDuffie	1.00	
❑ 71 Dave Marcis	1.00	
❑ 72 Harry Melling	.50	
❑ 73 Phil Barkdoll	1.00	
❑ 74 Leonard Wood	.50	
❑ 75 Rick Wilson	1.00	
❑ 76 Gary Nelson	.50	

Card	MINT	NRMT
A Ben Hess ERR	8.00	3.60
mentions Hess as single		
B Ben Hess COR	1.25	.55
mentions Hess as engaged		
Larry McReynolds	.50	.23
Darrell Bryant	.50	.23
Jimmy Horton	1.00	.45
Kenny Bernstein	1.00	.45
Doug Richert	.50	.23
Lake Speed	1.00	.45
Mike Alexander	.50	.23
A Larry McClure ERR	3.00	1.35
Tim Morgan on front and back		
B Larry McClure COR	3.00	1.35
correct name on front and back		
Robin Pemberton	.50	.23
Waddell Wilson	.50	.23
Jimmy Spencer	1.00	.45
Rod Osterlund	.50	.23
Stan Barrett	1.00	.45
Tommy Ellis	.50	.23
Danny Schiff	.50	.23
Buddy Baker	2.00	.90
Sterling Marlin	3.00	1.35
Kenny Wallace	1.00	.45
Tim Brewer	.50	.23
A Chuck Bown ERR	12.00	5.50
name Brown on front		
B Chuck Bown COR	1.50	.70
Bown on front		
Butch Miller	.50	.23
Connie Saylor	.50	.23
Darrell Waltrip	2.00	.90
Fan's Favorite Driver		
Dan Ford	.50	.23
Howard Poston Slick	.50	.23
David Evans	.50	.23
Harold Elliott	.50	.23
Ken Thompson	.50	.23
Robert Gee	.50	.23
James Lewter	.50	.23
Will Lind	.50	.23
Jerry Schweitz	.50	.23
Eddie Wood	.50	.23
Norman Koshimizu	.50	.23
Barry Dodson	.50	.23
Mike Hill	.50	.23
Jimmy Makar	.50	.23
Barry Dodson	.50	.23
Dale Earnhardt	8.00	3.60
All Pro		
Junior Johnson	2.00	.90
Shawna Robinson	1.00	.45
Richard Jackson	.50	.23
Chad Little	1.00	.45
Chuck Rider	.50	.23
L.D. Ottinger	.50	.23
Dennis Connor	.50	.23
Ken Bouchard	1.00	.45
Jimmy Hensley	1.00	.45
Robert Yates	.50	.23
Doug Williams	.50	.23
Mark Stahl	1.00	.45
Rick Mast	1.00	.45
Walter Bud Moore	.50	.23
David Pearson	1.00	.45
Paul Andrews	.50	.23
Tommy Houston	1.00	.45
Jack Pennington	.50	.23
Billy Hagan	1.00	.45
Joe Thurman	.50	.23
A Bill Ingle ERR	10.00	4.50
Billy on front and back		
B Bill Ingle COR	1.50	.70
Bill on front and back		
Patty Moise	2.00	.90
Glen Wood	.50	.23
Billy Standridge	1.00	.45
Harry Hyde	.50	.23
Steve Grissom	1.00	.45
Bob Rahilly	.50	.23
Butch Mock	.50	.23
Ernie Elliott	.50	.23
Les Richter	.50	.23
Dick Beaty	.50	.23
Harold Kinder	.50	.23
Elmo Langley	.50	.23
Dick Trickle	1.00	.45
Rookie of the Year		
Bobby Hamilton	1.00	.45
Jack Ingram	.50	.23
Bill Stavola	.50	.23
Bob Jenkins	.50	.23
Ned Jarrett	2.00	.90
Benny Parsons	2.00	.90
Jerry Punch	.50	.23
Ken Squier	.50	.23
Chris Economaki	.50	.23

Card	MINT	NRMT
❑ 160 Jack Arute	.50	.23
❑ 161 Dick Berggren	.50	.23
❑ 162 Mike Joy	.50	.23
❑ 163 Barney Hall	.50	.23
❑ 164 Eli Gold	.50	.23
❑ 165 Dick Brooks	.50	.23
❑ 166 Winston Kelley	.50	.23
❑ 167 Darrell Waltrip	1.00	.45
Year in Review		
❑ 168 Rusty Wallace's Car	2.00	.90
Darrell Waltrip's Car		
Year in Review		
❑ 169 Sterling Marlin's Car	1.00	.45
Year in Review		
❑ 170 Pontiac 400	.50	.23
Year in Review		
❑ 171 Harry Gant	1.00	.45
Year in Review		
❑ 172 Bill Elliott's Car	2.00	.90
Bobby Hillin's Car		
Year in Review		
❑ 173 First Union 400	.50	.23
Year in Review		
❑ 174 Darrell Waltrip	1.00	.45
Year in Review		
❑ 175 Davey Allison	2.00	.90
Year in Review		
❑ 176 Sterling Marlin	1.00	.45
Year in Review		
❑ 177 Darrell Waltrip's Car	1.00	.45
Year in Review		
❑ 178 Darrell Waltrip w/Crew	1.00	.45
Year in Review		
❑ 179 Dale Earnhardt w/Crew	4.00	1.80
Teresa Earnhardt		
Year in Review		
❑ 180 Banquet Foods 300	.50	.23
Year in Review		
❑ 181 Terry Labonte	2.00	.90
Year in Review		
❑ 182 Bill Elliott	2.00	.90
Year in Review		
❑ 183 Dale Earnhardt's Car	2.00	.90
Rick Wilson's Car		
Morgan Shepherd's Car		
Ken Schrader's Car		
Year in Review		
❑ 184 Bill Elliott	2.00	.90
Year in Review		
❑ 185 Darrell Waltrip's Car	1.00	.45
Terry Labonte's Car		
Mark Martin's Car		
Dale Jarrett's Car		
Year in Review		
❑ 186 Bud At The Glen	.50	.23
Year in Review		
❑ 187 Rusty Wallace's Car	2.00	.90
Year in Review		
❑ 188 Busch 500	.50	.23
Year in Review		
❑ 189 Heinz Southern 500	.50	.23
Year in Review		
❑ 190 Rusty Wallace	2.00	.90
Year in Review		
❑ 191 Dale Earnhardt's Car	2.00	.90
Year in Review		
❑ 192 Richard Petty's Car	2.00	.90
Kyle Petty's Car		
Year in Review		
❑ 193 Richard Childress	1.00	.45
Year in Review		
❑ 194 Michael Waltrip's Car	.50	.23
Phil Parsons' Car		
Year in Review		
❑ 195 Dale Earnhardt's Car	2.00	.90
Mark Martin's Car		
Year in Review		
❑ 196 Rusty Wallace's Car	2.00	.90
Year in Review		
❑ 197 Rusty Wallace in Pits	2.00	.90
Year in Review		
❑ 198 Rusty Wallace	2.00	.90
Year in Review		
❑ 199 Checklist B	.50	.23
❑ 200 Checklist C	.50	.23
Club Maxx offer		

1990 Maxx Bill Elliott Vortex Comics

This set was actually issued as a 4-card panel inside Vortex Comics' Legends of NASCAR Bill Elliott comic book. The cards are most often found attached as a panel of four and utilize the same card design found in the regular issue 1990 Maxx set.

	MINT	NRMT
COMPLETE SET (4)	4.00	1.80
COMMON CARD (E1-E4)	1.00	.45
❑ E1 Bill Elliott	1.00	.45
❑ E2 Bill Elliott's Car	1.00	.45
❑ E3 Bill Elliott	1.00	.45
Awesome		
❑ E4 Bill Elliott	1.00	.45
1990 Season		

1990 Maxx Holly Farms

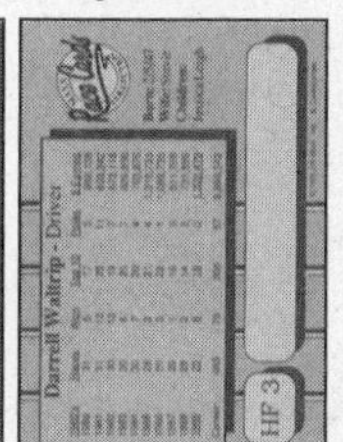

This is a 30-card set produced by Maxx and distributed by Holly Farms. It consists of 30 driver cards and one prize card, which was for a contest to win a trip to the 1991 Daytona 500. It was distributed as a 30-card set packaged in cello-wrap and given only to Holly Farms employees. As part of a Holly Farms promotion, three-card packs were produced and made available to the public in exchange for proof of purchase seals form Holly Farm products. These cards are distingushable from regular 1990 Maxx cards by a red, yellow, and black Holly Farms logo located in the upper right hand corner of the card.

	MINT	NRMT
COMPLETE SET (30)	8.00	3.60
COMPLETE FACTORY SET (30)	8.00	3.60
COMMON DRIVER (HF1-HF30)	.25	.11
❑ HF1 Dale Earnhardt	2.50	1.10
❑ HF2 Bill Elliott	1.25	.55
❑ HF3 Darrell Waltrip	.50	.23
❑ HF4 Rusty Wallace	1.25	.55
❑ HF5 Ken Schrader	.25	.11
❑ HF6 Richard Petty	1.00	.45
❑ HF7 Harry Gant	.50	.23
❑ HF8 Mark Martin	1.25	.55
❑ HF9 Davey Allison	1.25	.55
❑ HF10 Neil Bonnett	.75	.35
❑ HF11 Alan Kulwicki	1.00	.45
❑ HF12 Terry Labonte	1.25	.55
❑ HF13 Ricky Rudd	.50	.23
❑ HF14 Geoff Bodine	.25	.11
❑ HF15 Sterling Marlin	.50	.23
❑ HF16 Morgan Shepherd	.25	.11
❑ HF17 Kyle Petty	.50	.23
❑ HF18 Michael Waltrip	.25	.11
❑ HF19 Phil Parsons	.25	.11
❑ HF20 Dale Jarrett	.75	.35
❑ HF21 Brett Bodine	.25	.11
❑ HF22 Lake Speed	.25	.11
❑ HF23 Ernie Irvan	1.00	.45
❑ HF24 Junior Johnson	.50	.23
❑ HF25 Cale Yarborough	.50	.23
❑ HF26 Bobby Allison	.50	.23
❑ HF27 Derrike Cope	.25	.11
❑ HF28 Bobby Hillin	.25	.11
❑ HF29 Benny Parsons	.25	.11
❑ HF30 Ned Jarrett	.25	.11

1991 Maxx

This 240-card set was distributed in two different factory sets and in 15-card wax packs. The front of these cards have a black outer border, two shades of blue for the inner border and the drivers' name boxed in yellow at the bottom of the card. The "Deluxe" mail order set contains

240 cards from the regular set , the 20-card Winston Acrylic set, and the 48-card Maxx Update set. The standard hobby factory set is packaged in a blue, shrink-wrapped box with Richard Petty and Bill Elliott cards visible. A special version of this set containing a Bill Elliott autograph card was available through the J.C.Penney catalog. The Bill Elliott autographed card is usually found in the $40 - $60 range.

	MINT	NRMT
COMPLETE SET (240)	8.00	3.60
COMPLETE FACT.SET (240)	10.00	4.50
COMP.MAIL ORDER SET (308)	15.00	6.75
COMPLETE JC PENNEY'S SET (241)	65.00	29.00
COMMON CARD (1-240)	.10	.05
COMMON DRIVER (1-240)	.20	.09

Card	MINT	NRMT
❑ 1 Rick Mast	.20	.09
❑ 2 Rusty Wallace	1.00	.45
❑ 3 Dale Earnhardt	2.00	.90
❑ 4 Ernie Irvan	.40	.18
❑ 5 Ricky Rudd	.40	.18
❑ 6 Mark Martin	1.00	.45
❑ 7 Alan Kulwicki	.75	.35
❑ 8 Rick Wilson	.20	.09
❑ 9 Bill Elliott	1.00	.45
❑ 10 Derrike Cope	.20	.09
❑ 11 Geoff Bodine	.20	.09
❑ 12 Hut Stricklin	.20	.09
❑ 13 Ken Bouchard	.20	.09
❑ 14 A.J. Foyt	.40	.18
❑ 15 Morgan Shepherd	.20	.09
❑ 16 Joey Knuckles	.10	.05
❑ 17 Darrell Waltrip	.40	.18
❑ 18 Greg Sacks	.20	.09
❑ 19 Chad Little	.20	.09
❑ 20 Jimmy Hensley	.20	.09
❑ 21 Dale Jarrett	.75	.35
❑ 22 Sterling Marlin	.40	.18
❑ 23 Eddie Bierschwale	.10	.05
❑ 24 Mickey Gibbs	.20	.09
❑ 25 Ken Schrader	.20	.09
❑ 26 Brett Bodine	.20	.09
❑ 27 Bobby Allison	.40	.18
❑ 28 Davey Allison	1.00	.45
❑ 29 Jeff Hammond	.10	.05
❑ 30 Michael Waltrip	.20	.09
❑ 31 Jim Sauter	.20	.09
❑ 32 Cale Yarborough	.40	.18
❑ 33 Harry Gant	.40	.18
❑ 34 Jimmy Makar	.10	.05
❑ 35 Robert Yates	.40	.18
❑ 36 Neil Bonnett	.50	.23
❑ 37 Rick Hendrick	.10	.05
❑ 38 Harry Hyde	.10	.05
❑ 39 Kenny Wallace	.20	.09
❑ 40 Tom Kendall	.20	.09
❑ 41 Larry Pearson	.20	.09
❑ 42 Kyle Petty	.40	.18
❑ 43 Richard Petty	.75	.35
❑ 44 Jimmy Horton	.20	.09
❑ 45 Mike Beam	.10	.05
❑ 46 Walter Bud Moore	.10	.05
❑ 47 Jack Pennington	.10	.05
❑ 48 James Hylton	.10	.05
❑ 49 Rodney Combs	.20	.09
❑ 50 Bill Elliott w/Crew	.50	.23
Pit Crew Champs		
❑ 51 Jeff Purvis	.20	.09
❑ 52 Jimmy Means	.20	.09
❑ 53 Bobby Labonte	1.00	.45
❑ 54 Richard Childress	.20	.09
❑ 55 Billy Hagan	.10	.05
❑ 56 Bill Ingle	.10	.05
❑ 57 Jim Bown	.10	.05
❑ 58 Ken Ragan	.10	.05
❑ 59 Larry McReynolds	.10	.05
❑ 60 Jack Roush	.10	.05
❑ 61 Phil Parsons	.10	.05
❑ 62 Harry Melling	.10	.05
❑ 63 Barry Dodson	.10	.05
❑ 64 Tony Glover	.10	.05
❑ 65 Tommy Houston	.20	.09
❑ 66 Dick Trickle	.20	.09
❑ 67 Cliff Champion	.20	.09
❑ 68 Bobby Hamilton	.20	.09
❑ 69 Gary Nelson	.20	.09
❑ 70 J.D. McDuffie	.40	.18
❑ 71 Dave Marcis	.40	.18
❑ 72 Ernie Elliott	.20	.09
❑ 73 Phil Barkdoll	.20	.09
❑ 74 Junie Donlavey	.20	.09
❑ 75 Chuck Rider	.10	.05
❑ 76 Ben Hess	.20	.09
❑ 77 Steve Hmiel	.10	.05
❑ 78 Felix Sabates	.10	.05
❑ 79 Tim Brewer	.10	.05
❑ 80 Tim Morgan	.10	.05
❑ 81 Larry McClure	.10	.05
❑ 82 Mark Stahl	.10	.05
❑ 83 Lake Speed	.10	.05
❑ 84 Waddell Wilson	.10	.05
❑ 85 Mike Alexander	.10	.05
❑ 86 Robin Pemberton	.10	.05
❑ 87 Junior Johnson	.20	.09
❑ 88 Leonard Wood	.10	.05
❑ 89 Kenny Bernstein	.20	.09
❑ 90 Buddy Baker	.20	.09
❑ 91 Patty Moise	.20	.09
❑ 92 Elton Sawyer	.20	.09
❑ 93 Bob Whitcomb	.10	.05
❑ 94 Terry Labonte	1.00	.45
❑ 95 Raymond Beadle	.10	.05
❑ 96 Kirk Shelmerdine	.10	.05
❑ 97 Chuck Bown	.20	.09
❑ 98 Jimmy Spencer	.20	.09
❑ 99 Bobby Hillin	.20	.09
❑ 100 Rob Moroso	.40	.18
Rookie of the Year		
❑ 101 Rod Osterlund	.10	.05
❑ 102 Les Richter	.10	.05
❑ 103 Jimmy Fennig	.10	.05
❑ 104 Doyle Ford	.10	.05
❑ 105 Elmo Langley	.20	.09
❑ 106 Richard Jackson	.10	.05
❑ 107 Jimmy Cox	.10	.05
❑ 108 Dick Beaty	.10	.05
❑ 109 Kyle Petty's Car	.20	.09
Memorable Moments		
❑ 110 Bob Tullius	.10	.05
❑ 111 Buddy Parrott	.10	.05
❑ 112 H.B. Bailey	.10	.05
❑ 113 Mark Martin's Car	.40	.18
Geoff Bodine's Car		
Sterling Marlin's Car		
Ernie Irvan's Car		
Memorable Moments		
❑ 114 Billy Standridge	.10	.05
❑ 115 Doug Williams	.10	.05
❑ 116 Tracy Leslie	.10	.05
❑ 117 Donnie Allison	.40	.18
❑ 118 Michael Waltrip Crash	.10	.05
Memorable Moments		
❑ 119 Ed Berrier	.10	.05
❑ 120 Travis Carter	.10	.05
❑ 121 Dennis Connor	.10	.05
❑ 122 Richard Petty's Car	.40	.18
Rob Moroso's Car		
Memorable Moments		
❑ 123 Ward Burton	.40	.18
❑ 124 Bob Rahilly	.10	.05
❑ 125 Butch Mock	.10	.05
❑ 126 Robin Pemberton	.10	.05
❑ 127 Michael Waltrip's Car	.10	.05
Derrike Cope's Car		
Memorable Moments		
❑ 128 Donnie Wingo	.10	.05
❑ 129 Darrell Bryant	.10	.05
❑ 130 Mike McLaughlin	.10	.05
❑ 131 Robbie Loomis	.10	.05
❑ 132 Charlie Glotzbach	.10	.05
❑ 133 Dave Rezendes	.10	.05
❑ 134 Davey Johnson	.10	.05
❑ 135 Paul Andrews	.10	.05
❑ 136 Daytona MM	.10	.05
❑ 137 The Racestoppers	.10	.05
❑ 138 Jack Ingram	.10	.05
❑ 139 Joe Nemechek	.20	.09
❑ 140 Geoff Bodine's Car	.10	.05
Kyle Petty's Car		
Ernie Irvan's Car		
Memorable Moments		
❑ 141 Jeffrey Ellis	.10	.05
❑ 142 Butch Miller	.10	.05
❑ 143 Bill Venturini	.20	.09
❑ 144 Richard Broome	.10	.05
❑ 145 Alan Kulwicki in Pits	.40	.18
Memorable Moments		
❑ 146 Dave Mader	.10	.05
❑ 147 Robert Pressley	.40	.18
❑ 148 Steve Loyd	.10	.05
❑ 149 Ricky Pearson	.10	.05
❑ 150 Darrell Waltrip	.40	.18
Fan's Favorite Driver		
❑ 151 Don Bierschwale	.10	.05
❑ 152 Leo Jackson	.10	.05
❑ 153 Tommy Ellis	.10	.05
❑ 154 Randy Baker	.10	.05
❑ 155 Bill Stavola	.10	.05
❑ 156 D.K. Ulrich	.10	.05
❑ 157 L.D. Ottinger	.10	.05
❑ 158 Phoenix MM	.10	.05
❑ 159 Glen Wood	.10	.05
Eddie Wood		
Len Wood		
❑ 160 Andy Petree	.10	.05

Card	MINT
❑ 161 Steve Grissom	.20
❑ 162 Dale Inman	.10
❑ 163 Charlotte Motor Speedway	.10
Memorable Moments	
❑ 164 Dick Moroso	.10
❑ 165 Doug Richert	.10
❑ 166 Peter Sospenzo	.10
❑ 167 Chuck Bown	.10
Memorable Moments	
❑ 168 Sandi Fix	.10
Miss Winston	
❑ 169 David Pearson	.20
❑ 170 Derrike Cope	.10
Year in Review	
❑ 171 Mark Martin	.50
Year in Review	
❑ 172 Kyle Petty	.20
Year in Review	
❑ 173 Dale Earnhardt	1.00
Year in Review	
❑ 174 Dale Earnhardt	1.00
Year in Review	
❑ 175 Davey Allison	.40
Bobby Allison	
Year in Review	
❑ 176 Brett Bodine	.10
Year in Review	
❑ 177 Geoff Bodine	.10
Year in Review	
❑ 178 Dale Earnhardt	1.00
Year in Review	
❑ 179 Dale Earnhardt	1.00
Year in Review	
❑ 180 Rusty Wallace	.50
Year in Review	
❑ 181 Derrike Cope	.10
Year in Review	
❑ 182 Rusty Wallace	.50
Year in Review	
❑ 183 Harry Gant	.20
Year in Review	
❑ 184 Dale Earnhardt	1.00
Year in Review	
❑ 185 Dale Earnhardt	1.00
Year in Review	
❑ 186 Geoff Bodine	.10
Year in Review	
❑ 187 Dale Earnhardt	1.00
Year in Review	
❑ 188 Ricky Rudd	.20
Year in Review	
❑ 189 Mark Martin	.50
Year in Review	
❑ 190 Ernie Irvan w/Crew	.40
Year in Review	
❑ 191 Dale Earnhardt	1.00
Teresa Earnhardt	
Year in Review	
❑ 192 Dale Earnhardt	1.00
Teresa Earnhardt	
Year in Review	
❑ 193 Bill Elliott	.50
Year in Review	
❑ 194 Geoff Bodine	.10
Year in Review	
❑ 195 Mark Martin	.50
Year in Review	
❑ 196 Davey Allison w/Crew	.40
Year in Review	
❑ 197 Alan Kulwicki	.40
Year in Review	
❑ 198 Dale Earnhardt	1.00
Year in Review	
❑ 199 Morgan Shepherd	.10
Year in Review	
❑ 200 Dale Earnhardt	1.00
Teresa Earnhardt	
Year in Review	
❑ 201 Jeff Burton	.75
❑ 202 Larry Hedrick	.10
❑ 203 Todd Bodine	.20
❑ 204 Tom Peck	.20
❑ 205 Kirk Shelmerdine	.10
❑ 206 David Smith	.10
❑ 207 Darrell Andrews	.10
❑ 208 Danny Lawrence	.10
❑ 209 Mike Hill	.10
❑ 210 Norman Koshimizu	.10
❑ 211 James Lewter	.10
❑ 212 Will Lind	.10
❑ 213 Cecil Gordon	.10
❑ 214 Howard Poston	.10
❑ 215 Eddie Lanier	.10
❑ 216 Troy Martin	.10
❑ 217 Bobby Moody	.10
❑ 218 Henry Benfield	.10
❑ 219 Kirk Shelmerdine	.10
❑ 220 Dale Earnhardt	1.00

All Pro		
1 Jack Arute	.10	.05
2 Dick Berggren	.10	.05
3 Dick Brooks	.10	.05
4 Chris Economaki	.10	.05
5 Eli Gold	.10	.05
6 Barney Hall	.10	.05
7 Ned Jarrett	.20	.09
8 Bob Jenkins	.10	.05
9 Mike Joy	.10	.05
0 Winston Kelley	.10	.05
1 Benny Parsons	.20	.09
2 Jim Phillips	.10	.05
3 Jerry Punch	.10	.05
4 Ken Squier	.10	.05
5 Bobby Dotter	.10	.05
5 Jake Elder	.10	.05
7 Checklist 1-60	.10	.05
3 Checklist 61-120	.10	.05
9 Checklist 121-180	.10	.05
) Checklist 181-240	.10	.05

1991 Maxx Update

48-card set was distributed in 1991 Maxx "Deluxe" order sets and foil packs from the second printing. It lso made available for purchase individually through s mail order division. It contains 33 corrected cards the 1991 Maxx set and 15 updated cards of drivers as Dale Earnhardt, Ernie Irvan, Mark Martin, Alan cki, Richard Petty, and Bobby Labonte.

	MINT	NRMT
PLETE SET (48)	5.00	2.20
MON CARD	.20	.09
ick Mast	.20	.09
ale Earnhardt	2.00	.90
nie Irvan	.40	.18
icky Rudd	.40	.18
ark Martin	1.00	.45
an Kulwicki	.50	.23
ck Wilson	.20	.09
ll Elliott	1.00	.45
eoff Bodine	.20	.09
lut Stricklin	.20	.09
Ken Bouchard	.20	.09
Morgan Shepherd	.20	.09
Darrell Waltrip	.40	.18
Sterling Marlin	.40	.18
Ken Schrader	.20	.09
Michael Waltrip	.20	.09
Harry Gant	.40	.18
Kenny Wallace	.20	.09
om Kendall	.20	.09
Kyle Petty	.40	.18
Richard Petty	.50	.23
Rodney Combs	.20	.09
ill Elliott	.50	.23
Pit Crew Champions		
obby Labonte	1.00	.45
ichard Childress	.20	.09
im Bown	.20	.09
en Ragan	.20	.09
ick Trickle	.20	.09
obby Hamilton	.20	.09
hil Barkdoll	.20	.09
ake Speed	.20	.09
like Alexander	.20	.09
erry Labonte	1.00	.45
huck Bown	.20	.09
mmy Spencer	.20	.09
Rob Moroso	.60	.25
Rookie of the Year		
Donnie Allison	.40	.18
Robin Pemberton	.20	.09
Charlie Glotzbach	.20	.09
Joe Nemechek	.20	.09
Jeffrey Ellis	.20	.09
Robert Pressley	.60	.25
Darrell Waltrip	.40	.18
Fan's Favorite Driver		
Dick Moroso	.20	.09

❑ 165 Doug Richert	.20	.09
❑ 200 Dale Earnhardt	1.00	.45
Teresa Earnhardt		
Year in Review		
❑ 220 Dale Earnhardt	1.00	.45
All Pro		
❑ 235 Bobby Dotter	.20	.09

1991 Maxx Bill Elliott Team Coors/Melling

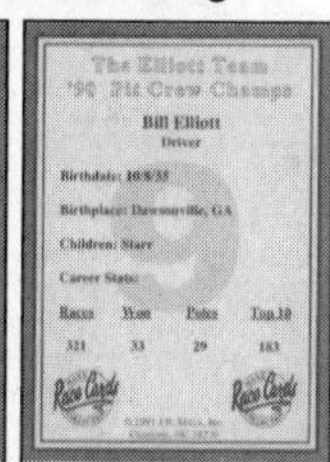

This 30-card set features Bill Elliott and members of the Coors-Melling Racing Team. Both versions of the set are virtually identical except for the set name on the cardback and that the Elliott set does not include team owner Harry Melling. His card replaced that of Teresa Alligood. Both sets were offered through Bill Elliott's souvenir program and through Maxx's mail order program. All the cards are unnumbered, but have been assigned numbers according to the listing found on the checklist card.

	MINT	NRMT
COMPLETE ELLIOTT SET (40)	10.00	4.50
COMMON CARD	.30	.14
COMP.COORS/MELLING SET (40)	10.00	4.50
COORS/MELLING VERSION: SAME PRICE		
❑ 1 Jim Waldrop	.30	.14
❑ 2 Melvin Turner	.30	.14
❑ 3 Casey Elliott	.75	.35
❑ 4 Dan Elliott	.30	.14
❑ 5 Bill Elliott	1.00	.45
❑ 6 Diana Pugh	.30	.14
❑ 7 Bill Elliott's Car	.75	.35
❑ 8 Matt Thompson	.30	.14
❑ 9 Mike Thomas	.30	.14
❑ 10 Wayne McCord	.30	.14
❑ 11 Bill Elliott's Pit Crew	.30	.14
Pit Crew Champs		
❑ 12 Charles Palmer	.30	.14
❑ 13 Jerry Seabolt	.30	.14
❑ 14 Denver Harris	.30	.14
❑ 15 Terron Carver	.30	.14
❑ 16 Mike Dalrymple	.30	.14
❑ 17 Alan Palmer	.30	.14
❑ 18 Michael Rinker	.30	.14
❑ 19 Doug Shaak	.30	.14
❑ 20 Bill Elliott	1.00	.45
❑ 21 Dave Kriska	.30	.14
❑ 22 Alexis Leras	.30	.14
❑ 23 Mike Colt	.30	.14
❑ 24 Chuck Hill	.30	.14
❑ 25 Glen Blakely	.30	.14
❑ 26 Tommy Cole	.30	.14
❑ 27 Clinton Chumbley	.30	.14
❑ 28 Mike Brandt	.30	.14
❑ 29 Phil Seabolt	.30	.14
❑ 30 Ron Brooks	.30	.14
❑ 31 Johnny Trammell	.30	.14
❑ 32 Mike Rich	.30	.14
❑ 33 Mark Gaddis	.30	.14
❑ 34 Gregory Trammell	.30	.14
❑ 35 Wayne Hamby	.30	.14
❑ 36 Dan Palmer	.30	.14
❑ 37A Teresa Alligood	.30	.14
Elliott Team only		
❑ 37B Harry Melling	.30	.14
Coors/Melling Team only		
❑ 38 Ernie Elliott	.30	.14
❑ 39 Team Shops	.30	.14
❑ 40 Cover/Checklist Card	.30	.14

1991 Maxx McDonald's

This 31-card set was produced by Maxx and distributed in over 250 McDonald's locations in North Carolina and South Carolina between August 30 and October 24, 1991. Any customer purchasing a Bacon, Egg and Cheese Value Meal or a Big Mac Extra Value Meal was given a five-card cellophane pack. Each pack contained one cover card and four driver cards. It features the top 28 finishers in the

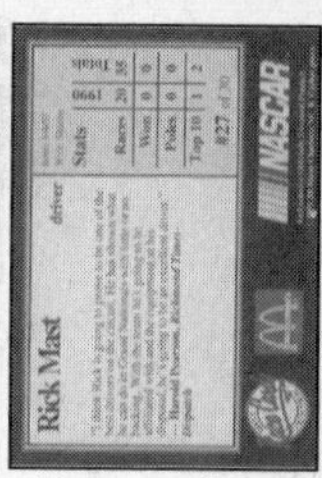

1990 NASCAR Winston Cup points race, one McDonald's All-Star Team card, and one cover card. This set contains eight error cards that were corrected in the middle of the press run. The blue portion of the McDonald's All-Star Racing Team logo is missing from the upper right hand corner of all the error cards. It is important to note that due to the nature of the distribution of these cards that a large portion became available to the hobby.

	MINT	NRMT
COMPLETE SET (31)	10.00	4.50
COMMON CARD (1-30)	.30	.14
❑ 1A Dale Earnhardt ERR	6.00	2.70
without blue part of logo		
❑ 1B Dale Earnhardt COR	3.00	1.35
with blue part of logo		
❑ 2A Mark Martin ERR	2.00	.90
without blue part of logo		
❑ 2B Mark Martin COR	1.25	.55
with blue part of logo		
❑ 3A Geoff Bodine ERR	1.25	.55
without blue part of logo		
❑ 3B Geoff Bodine COR	.75	.35
with blue part of logo		
❑ 4A Bill Elliott ERR	2.00	.90
without blue part of logo		
❑ 4B Bill Elliott COR	1.25	.55
with blue part of logo		
❑ 5 Morgan Shepherd	.30	.14
❑ 6 Rusty Wallace	1.25	.55
❑ 7 Ricky Rudd	.50	.23
❑ 8 Alan Kulwicki	1.00	.45
❑ 9 Ernie Irvan	1.00	.45
❑ 10 Ken Schrader	.30	.14
❑ 11 Kyle Petty	.50	.23
❑ 12 Brett Bodine	.30	.14
❑ 13 Davey Allison	1.25	.55
❑ 14 Sterling Marlin	.50	.23
❑ 15 Terry Labonte	1.25	.55
❑ 16 Michael Waltrip	.30	.14
❑ 17 Harry Gant	.50	.23
❑ 18 Derrike Cope	.30	.14
❑ 19 Bobby Hillin	.30	.14
❑ 20 Darrell Waltrip	.50	.23
❑ 21A Dave Marcis ERR	.50	.23
without blue part of logo		
❑ 21B Dave Marcis COR	.30	.14
with blue part of logo		
❑ 22A Dick Trickle ERR	.50	.23
without blue part of logo		
❑ 22B Dick Trickle COR	.30	.14
with blue part of logo		
❑ 23A Rick Wilson ERR	.50	.23
without blue part of logo		
❑ 23B Rick Wilson COR	.30	.14
with blue part of logo		
❑ 24A Jimmy Spencer ERR	.50	.23
without blue part of logo		
❑ 24B Jimmy Spencer COR	.30	.14
with blue part of logo		
❑ 25 Dale Jarrett	.75	.35
❑ 26 Richard Petty	.75	.35
❑ 27 Rick Mast	.30	.14
❑ 28 Hut Stricklin	.30	.14
❑ 29 Jimmy Means	.30	.14
❑ 30 Dale Earnhardt	3.00	1.35
Mark Martin		
Bill Elliott		
❑ NNO Cover Card	.30	.14

1991 Maxx Motorsport

This 40-card set was produced by Maxx for Prospective Marketing International/Ford Motorsport Sportswear. It features the top-ten 1991 Ford race teams and the 1991 Winston Legends champion. It was made available as a sequentially numbered set in orange tuck boxes through the Fall 1992 Ford Motorsport Sportswear and Accessories Catalog. 75,000 of these sets were produced.

	MINT	NRMT
COMPLETE SET (40)	6.00	2.70
COMMON CARD (1-40)	.10	.05

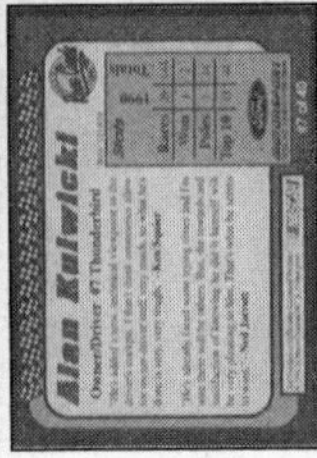

COMMON DRIVER (1-40)	.20	.09
❑ 1 Bill Elliott	1.50	.70
❑ 2 Davey Allison	1.00	.45
❑ 3 Wally Dallenbach Jr.	.20	.09
❑ 4 Sterling Marlin	.30	.14
❑ 5 Mark Martin	1.50	.70
❑ 6 Morgan Shepherd	.20	.09
❑ 7 Alan Kulwicki	1.00	.45
❑ 8 Dale Jarrett	.50	.23
❑ 9 Geoff Bodine	.20	.09
❑ 10 Chad Little	.20	.09
❑ 11 Robert Yates	.10	.05
❑ 12 Jack Roush	.10	.05
❑ 13 Walter Bud Moore	.10	.05
❑ 14 Harry Melling	.10	.05
❑ 15 Wood Brothers	.10	.05
❑ 16 Junior Johnson	.10	.05
❑ 17 Chuck Little	.10	.05
❑ 18 Junie Donlavey	.10	.05
❑ 19 Larry McReynolds	.10	.05
❑ 20 Robin Pemberton	.10	.05
❑ 21 Donnie Wingo	.10	.05
❑ 22 Mike Beam	.10	.05
❑ 23 Ernie Elliott	.10	.05
❑ 24 Paul Andrews	.10	.05
❑ 25 Leonard Wood	.10	.05
❑ 26 Harry Hyde	.10	.05
❑ 27 Tim Brewer	.10	.05
❑ 28 Davey Allison's Car	.50	.23
❑ 29 Bill Elliott's Car	.50	.23
❑ 30 Davey Allison's Car	.50	.23
❑ 31 Wally Dallenbach Jr.'s Car	.10	.05
❑ 32 Sterling Marlin's Car	.20	.09
❑ 33 Mark Martin's Car	.50	.23
❑ 34 Morgan Shepherd's Car	.10	.05
❑ 35 Alan Kulwicki's Car	.50	.23
❑ 36 Dale Jarrett's Car	.30	.14
❑ 37 Geoff Bodine's Car	.10	.05
❑ 38 Chad Little's Car	.10	.05
❑ 39 Elmo Langley's Car Cale Yarborough's Car	.10	.05
❑ 40 Wally Dallenbach Jr. w/Crew	.20	.09

1991 Maxx Racing For Kids

These three sheets feature six cards on each that are from the 1990 Maxx set. The cards came on uncut sheets and each card has a "Special Edition Racing For Kids" logo in the upper left hand corner. The cards are a parallel to the regular version. The sheets were issued as a promotional insert in Racing For Kids magazine over three months, January, February and March 1991. We've included prices for uncut sheets below with the corresponding individual card numbers after the drivers' name.

	MINT	NRMT
COMPLETE SET (3)	75.00	34.00
COMMON SHEET	20.00	9.00
❑ 1 Sheet 1 Bill Elliott Pit Champs 50 Michael Waltrip 39 Neil Bonnett 21 Mark Martin 6 Dale Earnhardt 3 Junior Johnson 117	30.00	13.50
❑ 2 Sheet 2 Bill Elliott 9 Kyle Petty 42 Derrike Cope 10 Ken Schrader 25 Ricky Rudd 5 Richard Childress 45	20.00	9.00
❑ 3 Sheet 3 Richard Petty 43 Rusty Wallace 27 Davey Allison 28 A.J. Foyt 14 Darrell Waltrip 17 Alan Kulwicki 7	25.00	11.00

1991 Maxx The Winston Acrylics

This 20-card set was distributed as a complete set in the '91 Maxx mail order set and was randomly inserted into '91 Maxx wax packs. They were produced on laser-etched acrylic and are relatively thin when compared to a standard card. Widespread reports show that many of the mail order sets did not contain all of the cards in this set. The cards are unnumbered and have been listed below in alphabetical order.

	MINT	NRMT
COMPLETE SET (20)	8.00	3.60
COMMON CARD	.25	.11
❑ 1 Davey Allison	.75	.35
❑ 2 Brett Bodine	.25	.11
❑ 3 Geoff Bodine	.25	.11
❑ 4 Derrike Cope	.25	.11
❑ 5 Dale Earnhardt	1.50	.70
❑ 6 Bill Elliott	.75	.35
❑ 7 Harry Gant	.50	.23
❑ 8 Bobby Hillin	.25	.11
❑ 9 Alan Kulwicki	.75	.35
❑ 10 Terry Labonte	.75	.35
❑ 11 Mark Martin	.75	.35
❑ 12 Phil Parsons	.25	.11
❑ 13 Kyle Petty	.50	.23
❑ 14 Ricky Rudd	.50	.23
❑ 15 Ken Schrader	.25	.11
❑ 16 Morgan Shepherd	.25	.11
❑ 17 Lake Speed	.25	.11
❑ 18 Dick Trickle	.25	.11
❑ 19 Rusty Wallace	.75	.35
❑ 20 Darrell Waltrip	.50	.23

1991 Maxx Winston 20th Anniversary Foils

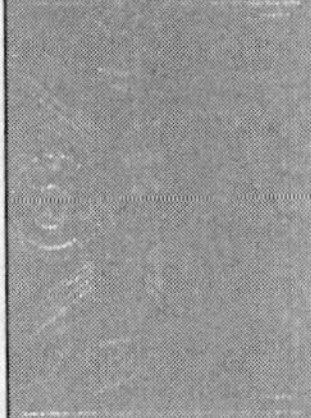

This 21-card set was produced to commemorate 20 years of involvement in the NASCAR circuit by the R.J. Reynolds Tobacco Company. It portrays the past Winston Cup Champions on foil-etched cards. This set was made available through multi-pack premium offers on Winston cigarettes and later through the Club Maxx mail order club. The cards are unnumbered and listed in order by year of Winston Cup win.

	MINT	NRMT
COMPLETE SET (21)	8.00	3.60
COMMON CARD	.25	.11
❑ 1 Richard Petty 1971 Car	.75	.35
❑ 2 Richard Petty 1972 Car	.75	.35
❑ 3 Benny Parsons 1973 Car	.25	.11
❑ 4 Richard Petty 1974 Car	.75	.35
❑ 5 Richard Petty 1975 Car	.75	.35
❑ 6 Cale Yarborough 1976 Car	.25	.11
❑ 7 Cale Yarborough 1977 Car	.25	.11
❑ 8 Cale Yarborough 1978 Car	.25	.11
❑ 9 Richard Petty 1979 Car	.75	.35
❑ 10 Dale Earnhardt 1980 Car	1.50	.70
❑ 12 Darrell Waltrip 1981 Car	.25	.11
❑ 12 Darrell Waltrip 1982 Car	.25	.11
❑ 13 Bobby Allison 1983 Car	.25	.11
❑ 14 Terry Labonte 1984 Car	.75	.35
❑ 15 Darrell Waltrip 1985 Car	.25	
❑ 16 Dale Earnhardt 1986 Car	1.50	
❑ 17 Dale Earnhardt 1987 Car	1.50	
❑ 18 Bill Elliott 1988 Car	.75	
❑ 19 Rusty Wallace 1989 Car	.75	
❑ 20 Dale Earnhardt 1990 Car	1.50	
❑ NNO Checklist	.50	

1992 Maxx All-Pro Team

This 50-card set was produced by Maxx for Garg Performance Eyewear. It features every member o 1991 All-Pro team. The set was made available thr speedway vendors and thorugh Maxx's mail o program. The set is basically a promotion for Garg Sunglasses.

	MINT	N
COMPLETE SET (50)	4.00	
COMMON CARD (1-48)	.10	
❑ 1 Dale Earnhardt	2.00	
❑ 2 Harry Gant	.20	
❑ 3 Mark Martin	1.00	
❑ 4 Larry McReynolds	.10	
❑ 5 Kirk Shelmerdine	.10	
❑ 6 Tony Glover	.10	
❑ 7 Larry Wallace	.10	
❑ 8 Leo Jackson	.10	
❑ 9 Eddie Lanier	.10	
❑ 10 Harold Stott	.10	
❑ 11 Andy Petree	.10	
❑ 12 Will Lind	.10	
❑ 13 Kirk Shelmerdine	.10	
❑ 14 Doug Richert	.10	
❑ 15 Tim Brewer	.10	
❑ 16 Scott Robinette	.10	
❑ 17 Darrell Andrews	.10	
❑ 18 Todd Parrott	.10	
❑ 19 David Smith	.10	
❑ 20 Charley Pressley	.10	
❑ 21 Gary Brooks	.10	
❑ 22 Norman Koshimizu	.10	
❑ 23 Danny Myers	.10	
❑ 24 Henry Benfield	.10	
❑ 25 Dan Ford	.10	
❑ 26 Paul Andrews	.10	
❑ 27 Mike Hill	.10	
❑ 28 Will Lind	.10	
❑ 29 Mike Thomas	.10	
❑ 30 Shorty Edwards	.10	
❑ 31 Danny Lawrence	.10	
❑ 32 Devin Barbee	.10	
❑ 33 Ronnie Reavis	.10	
❑ 34 Howard Poston (Slick)	.10	
❑ 35 Dan Ford	.10	
❑ 36 Darrell Dunn	.10	
❑ 37 Gale Wilson	.10	
❑ 38 Norman Koshimizu	.10	
❑ 39 Jerry Schweitz	.10	
❑ 40 James Lewter	.10	
❑ 41 Abbie Garwood	.10	
❑ 42 Mark Osborn	.10	
❑ 43 David Little	.10	
❑ 44 Wayne Dalton	.10	
❑ 45 Troy Martin	.10	
❑ 46 Glen Bobo	.10	
❑ 47 Bobby Moody	.10	
❑ 48 David Munari	.10	
❑ NNO Dale Inman	.10	
❑ NNO Checklist	.10	

1992 Maxx Black

This 300-card set was distributed through hobby s 14-card wax packs. The set is a parallel to the R with the cards featuring black borders instead of r considered to be the first "premium" racing card. produced to be a "hobby" only product. These card 5th Anniversary Edition theme and new logo. Cele its anniversary, Maxx inserted cards from their p sets into factory sets, four per set, and into the packs, one per pack.

	MINT	NRMT
PLETE SET (300)	20.00	9.00
PLETE FACT.SET (304)	25.00	11.00
MON CARD (1-300)	.15	.07
MON DRIVER (1-300)	.30	.14

RS: 1.5X TO 2X RED CARDS

1992 Maxx Black Update

32-card set was produced as a "hobby" only product. ntains 30 numbered cards and two unnumbered , and shows updated photos of drivers who changed ms along with a few noted personalities. It features st Maxx cards of Joe Gibbs and Jerry Glanville.

	MINT	NRMT
PLETE SET (32)	4.00	1.80
MON CARD	.10	.05
MON DRIVER (U1-U30)	.25	.11

E PRICE AS RED UPDATE CARDS

992 Maxx Bobby Hamilton

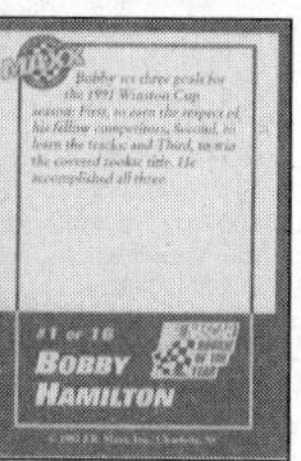

6-card set was produced to honor Bobby Hamilton Winston Cup 1992 Rookie of the Year. It was uted as a complete set in one foil pack.

	MINT	NRMT
ETE SET (16)	3.00	1.35
HAMILTON'S CAR (1-16)	.25	.11
HAMILTON (1-16)	.30	.14

1992 Maxx Craftsman

ht-card set was produced by Maxx and distributed s. It features drivers with Craftsman sponsorship. only made available to those who ordered a red set from the 1992 Sears Christmas Wish catalog.

	MINT	NRMT
ETE SET (8)	5.00	2.20
N CARD	.50	.23
Geoff Bodine	.50	.23
Bill Elliott	2.00	.90
Harry Gant	.75	.35
Bobby Hamilton	.50	.23
Sterling Marlin	.75	.35
Greg Sacks	.50	.23
Darrell Waltrip	.75	.35
Rick Wilson	.50	.23

1992 Maxx IMHOF

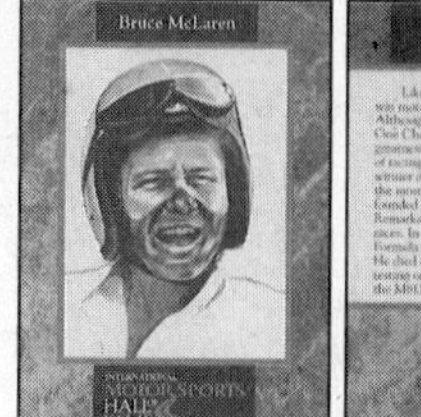

This 40-card set was produced by Maxx to honor new and previous inductees into the International Motor Sports Hall of Fame. The cards include sketches by renowed motorsports artist Jeanne Barnes.

	MINT	NRMT
COMPLETE SET (40)	8.00	3.60
COMMON CARD (1-40)	.20	.09
COMMON DRIVER (1-40)	.30	.14
❑ 1 Checklist	.20	.09
❑ 2 IMHOF Aerial View	.20	.09
❑ 3 IMHOF Rotunda	.20	.09
❑ 4 Gerald Dial Chairman	.20	.09
❑ 5 Don Naman Exec. Dir.	.20	.09
❑ 6 IMHOF Commission	.20	.09
❑ 7 Groundbreaking	.20	.09
❑ 8 Ribbon Cutting	.20	.09
❑ 9 Jenny Gilliand Miss IMHOF	.20	.09
❑ 10 Official Car Chevy	.20	.09
❑ 11 Buck Baker Art	.30	.14
❑ 12 Tony Bettenhausen Art	.30	.14
❑ 13 Jack Brabham Art	.30	.14
❑ 14 Malcolm Campbell Art	.30	.14
❑ 15 Jim Clark Art	.30	.14
❑ 16 Juan Manuel Fangio Art	.30	.14
❑ 17 Tim Flock Art	.30	.14
❑ 18 Dan Gurney Art	.30	.14
❑ 19 Anton Hulman(Tony) Art	.30	.14
❑ 20 Ned Jarrett Art	.30	.14
❑ 21 Junior Johnson Art	.30	.14
❑ 22 Parnelli Jones Art	.30	.14
❑ 23 Fred Lorenzen Art	.30	.14
❑ 24 Bruce McLaren Art	.30	.14
❑ 25 Stirling Moss Art	.30	.14
❑ 26 Barney Oldfield Art	.30	.14
❑ 27 Glenn Fireball Roberts Art	.30	.14
❑ 28 Wilbur Shaw Art	.30	.14
❑ 29 Carroll Shelby Art	.30	.14
❑ 30 Bobby Unser Art	.30	.14
❑ 31 Bill Vukovich Art	.30	.14
❑ 32 Smokey Yunick Art	.30	.14
❑ 33 Jeanne Barnes Artist	.20	.09
❑ 34 Winston Cutaway Car	.20	.09
❑ 35 1919 Indy Racer	.20	.09
❑ 36 Richard Petty's Car	.30	.14
❑ 37 Darrell Waltrip's Car	.20	.09
❑ 38 Don Garlits' Car	.20	.09
❑ 39 Glenn Fireball Roberts' Car	.20	.09
❑ 40 T.G. Shepherd	.20	.09

1992 Maxx McDonald's

This 37-card set was produced by Maxx and distributed by McDonald's. It was made available exclusively at over 1,300 McDonald's locations throughout 15 states in August 1992. Customers could obtain four-card packs for $.99 each or by purchasing an Extra Value Meal. It features members of the 1992 McDonald's All-Star Race Team and 29 other top NASCAR Winston Cup drivers, plus the respective car owners and crew chiefs of the McDonald's All-Star Racing Team. Like its predessor, a large amount of these cards found their way into the hobby. Each pack came with a cover card.

	MINT	NRMT
COMPLETE SET (37)	10.00	4.50
COMMON CARD (1-36)	.20	.09
❑ 1 Dale Earnhardt Davey Allison Bill Elliott	2.00	.90
❑ 2 Dale Earnhardt	2.00	.90
❑ 3 Davey Allison	.75	.35
❑ 4 Bill Elliott	1.00	.45
❑ 5 Richard Childress	.20	.09
❑ 6 Robert Yates	.20	.09
❑ 7 Junior Johnson	.20	.09
❑ 8 Kirk Shelmerdine	.20	.09
❑ 9 Larry McReynolds	.20	.09
❑ 10 Tim Brewer	.20	.09
❑ 11 Ricky Rudd	.40	.18
❑ 12 Harry Gant	.40	.18
❑ 13 Ernie Irvan	.40	.18
❑ 14 Mark Martin	1.00	.45
❑ 15 Sterling Marlin	.40	.18
❑ 16 Darrell Waltrip	.40	.18
❑ 17 Ken Schrader	.20	.09
❑ 18 Rusty Wallace	1.00	.45
❑ 19 Morgan Shepherd	.20	.09
❑ 20 Alan Kulwicki	.60	.25
❑ 21 Geoff Bodine	.20	.09
❑ 22 Michael Waltrip	.20	.09
❑ 23 Hut Stricklin	.20	.09
❑ 24 Dale Jarrett	.75	.35
❑ 25 Terry Labonte	1.00	.45
❑ 26 Brett Bodine	.20	.09
❑ 27 Rick Mast	.20	.09
❑ 28 Bobby Hamilton	.20	.09
❑ 29 Ted Musgrave	.20	.09
❑ 30 Richard Petty	.50	.23
❑ 31 Jimmy Spencer	.20	.09
❑ 32 Chad Little	.20	.09
❑ 33 Derrike Cope	.20	.09
❑ 34 Dave Marcis	.40	.18
❑ 35 Kyle Petty	.40	.18
❑ 36 Dick Trickle	.20	.09
❑ NNO Cover Card	.20	.09

1992 Maxx Motorsport

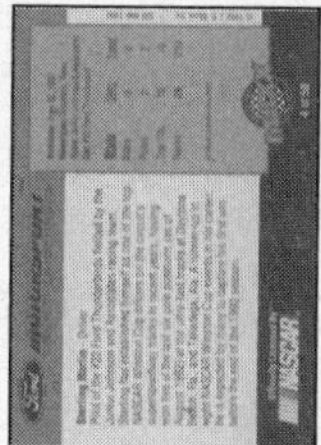

This 50-card set was produced by Maxx for Prospective Marketing International/Ford Motorsport Sportswear. It features drivers, owners, and crew chiefs from the 13 Ford race teams. This set was only made available thorugh the 1993 Ford Motorsport Sportswear and Accessories Catalog. 50,000 of these sets were made.

	MINT	NRMT
COMPLETE SET (50)	6.00	2.70
COMMON CARD (1-50)	.10	.05
COMMON DRIVER (1-50)	.20	.09
❑ 1 Bill Elliott	1.00	.45
❑ 2 Davey Allison	.75	.35
❑ 3 Alan Kulwicki	.50	.23
❑ 4 Sterling Marlin	.40	.18
❑ 5 Mark Martin	1.00	.45
❑ 6 Geoff Bodine	.20	.09
❑ 7 Brett Bodine	.20	.09
❑ 8 Morgan Shepherd	.20	.09
❑ 9 Dick Trickle	.20	.09
❑ 10 Wally Dallenbach Jr.	.20	.09
❑ 11 Jimmy Hensley	.20	.09
❑ 12 Charlie Glotzbach	.20	.09
❑ 13 Chad Little	.20	.09
❑ 14 Junior Johnson	.20	.09
❑ 15 Robert Yates	.10	.05
❑ 16 Jack Roush	.10	.05
❑ 17 Walter Bud Moore	.10	.05

- ❑ 18 Kenny Bernstein .20 .09
- ❑ 19 Eddie Wood .10 .05
- ❑ 20 Bill Stavola .10 .05
- ❑ 21 Cale Yarborough .20 .09
- ❑ 22 Junie Donlavey .10 .05
- ❑ 23 Harry Melling .10 .05
- ❑ 24 Tim Brewer .10 .05
- ❑ 25 Larry McReynolds .10 .05
- ❑ 26 Paul Andrews .10 .05
- ❑ 27 Mike Beam .10 .05
- ❑ 28 Steve Hmiel .10 .05
- ❑ 29 Donnie Wingo .10 .05
- ❑ 30 Donnie Richeson .10 .05
- ❑ 31 Leonard Wood .10 .05
- ❑ 32 Ken Wilson .10 .05
- ❑ 33 Steve Loyd .10 .05
- ❑ 34 Bob Johnson .10 .05
- ❑ 35 Gene Roberts .10 .05
- ❑ 36 Bill Elliott w/Crew .50 .23
- ❑ 37 Davey Allison w/Crew .50 .23
- ❑ 38 Alan Kulwicki w/Crew .40 .18
- ❑ 39 Sterling Marlin w/Crew .20 .09
- ❑ 40 Mark Martin w/Crew .50 .23
- ❑ 41 Geoff Bodine w/Crew .10 .05
- ❑ 42 Brett Bodine w/Crew .10 .05
- ❑ 43 Morgan Shepherd w/Crew .10 .05
- ❑ 44 Dick Trickle w/Crew .10 .05
- ❑ 45 Wally Dallenbach Jr. w/Crew .10 .05
- ❑ 46 Jimmy Hensley w/Crew .10 .05
- ❑ 47 Charlie Glotzbach w/Crew .10 .05
- ❑ 48 Chad Little w/Crew .10 .05
- ❑ 49 Mark Martin's Car .50 .23
  Alan Kulwicki's Car
  Davey Allison's Car
  Bill Elliott's Car
  Formation Flying
- ❑ 50 Mark Martin .50 .23
  Alan Kulwicki
  Davey Allison
  Bill Elliott

1992 Maxx Red

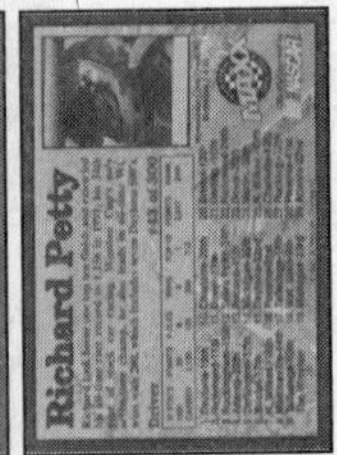

This 300-card set was made available through hobby sets and 14-card wax packs. Special versions of the hobby sets were distributed through different retail outlets. QVC sold these sets with an autographed Bill Elliott card and Sears sold a set through its catalog that contained the 16-card Bobby Hamilton 1992 Rookie of the Year set and the 8-card Craftsman set.

	MINT	NRMT
COMPLETE SET (300)	10.00	4.50
COMPLETE FACT.SET (304)	12.00	5.50
COMMON CARD (1-300)	.10	.05
COMMON DRIVER (1-300)	.20	.09

- ❑ 1 Rick Mast .20 .09
- ❑ 2 Rusty Wallace 1.00 .45
- ❑ 3 Dale Earnhardt 2.00 .90
- ❑ 4 Ernie Irvan .40 .18
- ❑ 5 Ricky Rudd .40 .18
- ❑ 6 Mark Martin 1.00 .45
- ❑ 7 Alan Kulwicki .75 .35
- ❑ 8 Rick Wilson .20 .09
- ❑ 9 Phil Parsons .20 .09
- ❑ 10 Derrike Cope .20 .09
- ❑ 11 Bill Elliott 1.00 .45
- ❑ 12 Hut Stricklin .20 .09
- ❑ 13 Bobby Dotter .20 .09
- ❑ 14 Mike Chase .20 .09
- ❑ 15 Geoff Bodine .20 .09
- ❑ 16 Wally Dallenbach Jr. .20 .09
- ❑ 17 Darrell Waltrip .40 .18
- ❑ 18 Dale Jarrett .75 .35
- ❑ 19 Randy LaJoie .20 .09
- ❑ 20 Buddy Baker .20 .09
- ❑ 21 Morgan Shepherd .20 .09
- ❑ 22 Sterling Marlin .40 .18
- ❑ 23 Mike Wallace .20 .09
- ❑ 24 Kenny Wallace .20 .09
- ❑ 25 Ken Schrader .20 .09
- ❑ 26 Brett Bodine .20 .09
- ❑ 27 Jimmy Hensley .20 .09
- ❑ 28 Davey Allison 1.00 .45
- ❑ 29 Jeff Gordon 2.50 1.10
- ❑ 30 Michael Waltrip .20 .09
- ❑ 31 Clifford Allison .40 .18
- ❑ 32 Cecil Eunice .10 .05
- ❑ 33 Harry Gant .20 .09
- ❑ 34 Chuck Bown .20 .09
- ❑ 35 Todd Bodine .20 .09
- ❑ 36 H.B. Bailey .10 .05
- ❑ 37 Joe Nemechek .20 .09
- ❑ 38 Dave Rezendes .20 .09
- ❑ 39 Tommy Houston .20 .09
- ❑ 40 Tom Kendall .20 .09
- ❑ 41 Larry Pearson .20 .09
- ❑ 42 Kyle Petty .40 .18
- ❑ 43 Richard Petty .75 .35
- ❑ 44 Bobby Labonte .60 .25
- ❑ 45 Irv Hoerr .10 .05
- ❑ 46 Dick Trickle .20 .09
- ❑ 47 Greg Sacks .20 .09
- ❑ 48 James Hylton .20 .09
- ❑ 49 Stanley Smith .10 .05
- ❑ 50 Jeff Gordon 2.50 1.10
  Rookie of the Year
- ❑ 51 Jeff Purvis .20 .09
- ❑ 52 Jimmy Means .20 .09
- ❑ 53 Bobby Hillin .20 .09
- ❑ 54 Jack Ingram .10 .05
- ❑ 55 Ted Musgrave .20 .09
- ❑ 56 Bill Sedgwick .20 .09
- ❑ 57 Jeff Burton .20 .09
- ❑ 58 Steve Grissom .20 .09
- ❑ 59 Patty Moise .20 .09
- ❑ 60 Elton Sawyer .20 .09
- ❑ 61 Bill Venturini .20 .09
- ❑ 62 Mike McLaughlin .20 .09
- ❑ 63 Ed Berrier .10 .05
- ❑ 64 Tracy Leslie .20 .09
- ❑ 65 Shawna Robinson .20 .09
- ❑ 66 Chad Little .20 .09
- ❑ 67 Ed Ferree .10 .05
- ❑ 68 Bobby Hamilton .20 .09
- ❑ 69 Peter Sospenzo .10 .05
- ❑ 70 John Paul Jr. .20 .09
- ❑ 71 Dave Marcis .20 .09
- ❑ 72 Jim Bown .20 .09
- ❑ 73 Phil Barkdoll .20 .09
- ❑ 74 Tom Peck .20 .09
- ❑ 75 Joe Ruttman .20 .09
- ❑ 76 Charlie Glotzbach .20 .09
- ❑ 77 Rich Bickle .20 .09
- ❑ 78 Larry Phillips .10 .05
- ❑ 79 David Green .20 .09
- ❑ 80 Jack Sprague .20 .09
- ❑ 81 Robert Pressley .20 .09
- ❑ 82 Mark Stahl .20 .09
- ❑ 83 Lake Speed .20 .09
- ❑ 84 Butch Miller .20 .09
- ❑ 85 Jeff Green .20 .09
- ❑ 86 Ward Burton .20 .09
- ❑ 87 Dorsey Schroeder .20 .09
- ❑ 88 Ricky Craven 1.00 .45
- ❑ 89 Jim Sauter .20 .09
- ❑ 90 Troy Beebe .10 .05
- ❑ 91 Bobby Labonte .60 .25
  BGN Champ
- ❑ 92 Dave Mader .20 .09
- ❑ 93 Mickey Gibbs .20 .09
- ❑ 94 Terry Labonte 1.00 .45
- ❑ 95 Eddie Bierschwale .20 .09
- ❑ 96 Randy Baker .10 .05
- ❑ 97 Tommy Ellis .10 .05
- ❑ 98 Jimmy Spencer .20 .09
- ❑ 99 Bobby Hamilton .20 .09
  Rookie of the Year
- ❑ 100 Bill Elliott .50 .23
  Most Popular Driver
- ❑ 101 Ed McClure .10 .05
  Teddy McClure
  Jerry McClure
- ❑ 102 Richard Childress .10 .05
- ❑ 103 Rick Hendrick .10 .05
- ❑ 104 Robert Yates .10 .05
- ❑ 105 Leo Jackson .10 .05
- ❑ 106 Larry McClure .10 .05
- ❑ 107 Tim Morgan .10 .05
- ❑ 108 Jack Roush .10 .05
- ❑ 109 Junior Johnson .20 .09
- ❑ 110 Roger Penske .10 .05
- ❑ 111 Don Miller .10 .05
- ❑ 112 Walter Bud Moore .10 .05
- ❑ 113 Chuck Rider .10 .05
- ❑ 114 Bobby Allison .20 .09
- ❑ 115 Bob Bilby .10 .05
- ❑ 116 Eddie Wood .10 .05
- ❑ 117 Len Wood .10 .05
- ❑ 118 Glen Wood .10 .05
- ❑ 119 Billy Hagan .20
- ❑ 120 Kenny Bernstein .20
- ❑ 121 Butch Mock .10
- ❑ 122 Bob Rahilly .10
- ❑ 123 Richard Jackson .10
- ❑ 124 George Bradshaw .10
- ❑ 125 David Fuge .10
- ❑ 126 Mark Smith .10
- ❑ 127 D.K. Ulrich .10
- ❑ 128 Ray DeWitt .10
  Diane DeWitt
- ❑ 129 Travis Carter .10
- ❑ 130 Bill Stavola .10
- ❑ 131 Larry Hedrick .10
- ❑ 132 Chuck Little .10
- ❑ 133 Bob Whitcomb .10
- ❑ 134 Felix Sabates .10
- ❑ 135 Cale Yarborough .20
- ❑ 136 Dick Moroso .10
- ❑ 137 Harry Melling .10
- ❑ 138 Junie Donlavey .10
- ❑ 139 Don Bierschwale .10
- ❑ 140 Sam McMahon III .10
- ❑ 141 A.J. Foyt .20
- ❑ 142 Jeffrey Ellis .10
- ❑ 143 Tony Glover .10
- ❑ 144 Ken Wilson .10
- ❑ 145 Dale Inman .10
- ❑ 146 Steve Hmiel .10
- ❑ 147 Morgan Shepherd w/Crew .10
  Pit Crew Champs
- ❑ 148 Kirk Shelmerdine .10
- ❑ 149 Waddell Wilson .10
- ❑ 150 Larry McReynolds .10
- ❑ 151 Andy Petree .10
- ❑ 152 Tony Glover .10
- ❑ 153 Robin Pemberton .10
- ❑ 154 Mike Beam .10
- ❑ 155 Jeff Hammond .10
- ❑ 156 Richard Broome .10
- ❑ 157 Eddie Dickerson .10
- ❑ 158 Ernie Elliott .10
- ❑ 159 Donnie Wingo .10
- ❑ 160 Paul Andrews .10
- ❑ 161 Tim Brewer .10
- ❑ 162 Bill Ingle .10
- ❑ 163 Jimmy Fennig .10
- ❑ 164 Dewey Livengood .10
- ❑ 165 Bob Johnson .10
- ❑ 166 Clyde McLeod .10
- ❑ 167 Buddy Parrott .10
- ❑ 168 Doug Williams .10
- ❑ 169 Steve Loyd .10
- ❑ 170 Leonard Wood .10
- ❑ 171 Gene Roberts .10
- ❑ 172 Jimmy Makar .10
- ❑ 173 Robbie Loomis .20
- ❑ 174 David Ifft .10
- ❑ 175 Steve Barkdoll .10
- ❑ 176 Donnie Allison .20
- ❑ 177 Dennis Connor .10
- ❑ 178 Barry Dodson .10
- ❑ 179 Harry Hyde .10
- ❑ 180 Bob Labonte .10
- ❑ 181 Steve Bird .10
- ❑ 182 Jeff Hensley .10
- ❑ 183 Ricky Pearson .10
- ❑ 184 Scott Houston .10
- ❑ 185 Eddie Pearson .10
- ❑ 186 Tony Eury .10
- ❑ 187 Donnie Richeson .10
- ❑ 188 Military Cars .10
  Memorable Moments
- ❑ 189 Sterling Marlin's Car .20
  Memorable Moments
- ❑ 190 Davey Allison's Car .20
  Darrell Waltrip's Car
  Memorable Moments
- ❑ 191 Geoff Bodine's Car .10
  Brett Bodine's Car
  Memorable Moments
- ❑ 192 Kyle Petty's Car .20
  Memorable Moments
- ❑ 193 Rick Mast's Car .10
  Memorable Moments
- ❑ 194 Ken Schrader's Car .10
  Memorable Moments
- ❑ 195 Darrell Waltrip's Car .20
  Memorable Moments
- ❑ 196 Talladega Speedway .10
  Memorable Moments
- ❑ 197 Bobby Hamilton's Car .10
  Ted Musgrave's Car
  Memorable Moments
- ❑ 198 Davey Allison .20
  Dale Jarrett Cars MM
- ❑ 199 Richmond International .10
  Memorable Moments

Card	MINT	NRMT
Mark Martin's Car Memorable Moments	.50	.23
1 Harry Gant's Car Memorable Moments	.20	.09
2 Rusty Wallace Memorable Moments	.50	.23
3 Dale Earnhardt's Car Memorable Moments	1.00	.45
4 Robert Black	.10	.05
5 Les Richter	.10	.05
6 Dick Beaty	.10	.05
7 Doyle Ford	.10	.05
8 Buster Auton	.10	.05
9 Bruce Roney	.10	.05
0 Mike Chaplin	.10	.05
1 Chuck Romeo	.10	.05
2 Jimmy Cox	.10	.05
3 Buddy Morrow	.10	.05
4 Tim Earp	.10	.05
5 Elmo Langley	.10	.05
6 Jack Whittemore	.10	.05
7 Carl Hill	.10	.05
8 Art Krebs	.10	.05
9 Gary Nelson	.10	.05
0 Chris Economaki	.10	.05
1 Ned Jarrett	.20	.09
2 Neil Bonnett	.50	.23
3 Mike Joy	.10	.05
Dick Berggren	.10	.05
Winston Kelley	.10	.05
Jack Arute	.10	.05
Jim Phillips	.10	.05
Ken Squier	.10	.05
Beth Bruce Miss Winston	.10	.05
Renee White Miss Winston	.10	.05
Dale Earnhardt All Pro	1.00	.45
Harry Gant All Pro	.20	.09
Mark Martin All Pro	.50	.23
Larry McReynolds All Pro	.10	.05
Kirk Shelmerdine Tony Glover All Pro	.10	.05
Larry Wallace All Pro	.10	.05
Leo Jackson Eddie Lanier All Pro	.10	.05
Harold Stott All Pro	.10	.05
Andy Petree Will Lind All Pro	.10	.05
Kirk Shelmerdine All Pro	.10	.05
Doug Richert Tim Brewer All Pro	.10	.05
Scott Robinette All Pro	.10	.05
Darrell Andrews Todd Parrott All Pro	.10	.05
David Smith All Pro	.10	.05
Charley Pressley Gary Brooks All Pro	.10	.05
Norman Koshimizu All Pro	.10	.05
Danny Myers Henry Benfield All Pro	.10	.05
Dan Ford All Pro	.10	.05
Paul Andrews Mike Hill All Pro	.10	.05
Will Lind All Pro	.10	.05
Mike Thomas Shorty Edwards All Pro	.10	.05
Danny Lawrence All Pro	.10	.05
Devin Barbee Ronnie Reavis All Pro	.10	.05
Howard Poston (Slick) All Pro	.10	.05
Dan Ford Darrell Dunn All Pro	.10	.05

Card	MINT	NRMT
❑ 256 Gale Wilson All Pro	.10	.05
❑ 257 Norman Koshimizu Jerry Schweitz All Pro	.10	.05
❑ 258 James Lewter All Pro	.10	.05
❑ 259 Abbie Garwood Mark Osborn All Pro	.10	.05
❑ 260 David Little All Pro	.10	.05
❑ 261 Wayne Dalton Troy Martin All Pro	.10	.05
❑ 262 Glen Bobo All Pro	.10	.05
❑ 263 Bobby Moody David Munari All Pro	.10	.05
❑ 264 Ernie Irvan Year in Review	.20	.09
❑ 265 Dale Earnhardt Teresa Earnhardt Year in Review	1.00	.45
❑ 266 Kyle Petty Year in Review	.20	.09
❑ 267 Ken Schrader Year in Review	.10	.05
❑ 268 Ricky Rudd Year in Review	.20	.09
❑ 269 Rusty Wallace Year in Review	.50	.23
❑ 270 Darrell Waltrip Year in Review	.20	.09
❑ 271 Dale Earnhardt Teresa Earnhardt Year in Review	1.00	.45
❑ 272 Harry Gant Year in Review	.20	.09
❑ 273 Davey Allison Year in Review	.40	.18
❑ 274 Davey Allison Deborah Allison Year in Review	.40	.18
❑ 275 Ken Schrader Year in Review	.10	.05
❑ 276 Davey Allison w/Crew Year in Review	.40	.18
❑ 277 Darrell Waltrip Year in Review	.20	.09
❑ 278 Davey Allison Robert Yates Year in Review	.40	.18
❑ 279 Bill Elliott Year in Review	.50	.23
❑ 280 Rusty Wallace Year in Review	.50	.23
❑ 281 Dale Earnhardt Teresa Earnhardt Year in Review	1.00	.45
❑ 282 Ernie Irvan Year in Review	.20	.09
❑ 283 Dale Jarrett Year in Review	.40	.18
❑ 284 Alan Kulwicki Year in Review	.40	.18
❑ 285 Harry Gant Year in Review	.20	.09
❑ 286 Harry Gant Year in Review	.20	.09
❑ 287 Harry Gant Year in Review	.20	.09
❑ 288 Harry Gant Year in Review	.20	.09
❑ 289 Dale Earnhardt Richard Childress Year in Review	1.00	.45
❑ 290 Geoff Bodine Year in Review	.10	.05
❑ 291 Davey Allison Year in Review	.40	.18
❑ 292 Davey Allison Robert Yates Year in Review	.40	.18
❑ 293 Mark Martin Year in Review	.50	.23
❑ 294 Dale Earnhardt Year in Review	1.00	.45
❑ 295 Checklist No. 1	.10	.05
❑ 296 Checklist No. 2	.10	.05
❑ 297 Checklist No. 3	.10	.05
❑ 298 Checklist No. 4	.10	.05
❑ 299 Checklist No. 5	.10	.05
❑ 300 Checklist No. 6	.10	.05

1992 Maxx Red Update

This 30-card set was produced with the intent of being distributed on the "retail" market. It contains 30 numbered cards and two unnumbered cards, shows updated photos of drivers who changed uniforms along with a few noted personalities. It features the first Maxx cards of Joe Gibbs and Jerry Glanville.

	MINT	NRMT
COMPLETE SET (32)	4.00	1.80
COMMON CARD (U1-U30)	.10	.05
COMMON DRIVER (U1-U30)	.20	.09
❑ U1 Greg Sacks	.20	.09
❑ U2 Geoff Bodine	.20	.09
❑ U3 Jeff Burton	.40	.18
❑ U4 Derrike Cope	.20	.09
❑ U5 Jerry Glanville	.10	.05
❑ U6 Jeff Gordon	2.00	.90
❑ U7 Jimmy Hensley	.20	.09
❑ U8 Ben Hess	.10	.05
❑ U9 Dale Jarrett	.75	.35
❑ U10 Chad Little	.20	.09
❑ U11 Mark Martin	1.00	.45
❑ U12 Joe Nemechek	.20	.09
❑ U13 Bob Schacht	.10	.05
❑ U14 Stanley Smith	.10	.05
❑ U15 Lake Speed	.20	.09
❑ U16 Dick Trickle	.20	.09
❑ U17 Kenny Wallace	.20	.09
❑ U18 Ron McCreary	.10	.05
❑ U19 Joe Gibbs	.20	.09
❑ U20 Dick Brooks	.10	.05
❑ U21 Bill Connell	.10	.05
❑ U22 Eli Gold	.10	.05
❑ U23 Barney Hall	.10	.05
❑ U24 Glenn Jarrett	.10	.05
❑ U25 Bob Jenkins	.10	.05
❑ U26 John Kernan	.10	.05
❑ U27 Benny Parsons	.20	.09
❑ U28 Pat Patterson	.10	.05
❑ U29 Randy Pemberton	.10	.05
❑ U30 Dr. Jerry Punch	.10	.05
❑ NNO Eddie Pearson	.10	.05
❑ NNO Geoff Bodine Make a Wish Foundation	.20	.09

1992 Maxx Sam Bass

This 11-card set was designed by noted motorsports artist Sam Bass. The set contains paintings of drivers such as Bobby Allison, Richard Petty, and Neil Bonnett. It is important to note this set also contains the only Tim Richmond card made by Maxx. This set was sent free to the buyers of the black mail order set.

	MINT	NRMT
COMPLETE SET (11)	8.00	3.60
COMMON CARD (1-10)	.75	.35
❑ 1 Richard Petty	1.50	.70
❑ 2 J.D. McDuffie	.75	.35
❑ 3 Ned Jarrett	.75	.35
❑ 4 Tim Richmond	1.00	.45
❑ 5 Harold Kinder	.75	.35
❑ 6 Rob Moroso	1.00	.45
❑ 7 Bobby Allison	1.00	.45
❑ 8 Bill Elliott	2.00	.90

❑ 9 Junior Johnson	.75	.35
❑ 10 Neil Bonnett	1.00	.45
❑ NNO Sam Bass	.75	.35

1992 Maxx Texaco Davey Allison

This 20-card set was produced by Maxx and made available at over 1,200 Texaco gas stations in the eastern and southeastern region of the country in February 1992. This set features 1992 Daytona 500 winner Davey Allison and the Robert Yates Texaco Havoline Racing Team. They were available in four-card packs and could be purchased for $.99. Full sets were made available through Club Maxx for in July of 1992. 2,000 of the cover cards in this set were autographed and randomly inserted into packs. A large number of these cards found their way into the hobby through factory closeouts.

	MINT	NRMT
COMPLETE SET (20)	5.00	2.20
COMMON CARD (1-20)	.10	.05
AUTO. COVER CARD	140.00	65.00

❑ 1 Davey Allison	.75	.35
❑ 2 Davey Allison's Car	.30	.14
❑ 3 Robert Yates	.10	.05
❑ 4 Larry McReynolds	.10	.05
❑ 5 Davey Allison's Car w/Crew	.30	.14
❑ 6 Davey Allison's Car w/Crew	.30	.14
❑ 7 Davey Allison's Transporter	.10	.05
❑ 8 Davey Allison's Car	.30	.14
❑ 9 Robert Yates Larry McReynolds	.10	.05
❑ 10 Davey Allison	.75	.35
❑ 11 Davey Allison w/Car	.30	.14
❑ 12 Davey Allison's Car Dale Earnhardt's Car Leading The Pack	.25	.11
❑ 13 Davey Allison in Pits	.30	.14
❑ 14 Davey Allison Deborah Allison Robert Yates Larry McReynolds	.25	.11
❑ 15 Davey Allison Larry McReynolds	.25	.11
❑ 16 Davey Allison	.75	.35
❑ 17 Davey Allison Robert Yates	.25	.11
❑ 18 Davey Allison Robert Yates Larry McReynolds	.25	.11
❑ 19 Davey Allison Bobby Allison Robert Yates Larry McReynolds	.25	.11
❑ 20 Davey Allison w/Crew Checklist Card	.25	.11

1992 Maxx The Winston

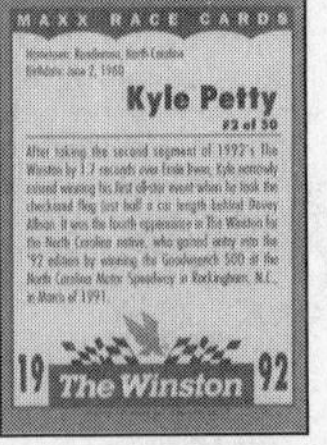

MAXX RACE CARDS
Kyle Petty
19 The Winston 92

This 50-card set was produced by Maxx and documents the first ever night running of The Winston. 50,000 sets were made and it was made available through Maxx's mail order program.

	MINT	NRMT
COMPLETE SET (50)	8.00	3.60
COMMON CARD (1-50)	.10	.05
COMMON DRIVER (1-50)	.20	.09

❑ 1 Davey Allison	.75	.35
❑ 2 Kyle Petty	.40	.18
❑ 3 Ken Schrader	.20	.09
❑ 4 Ricky Rudd	.40	.18
❑ 5 Bill Elliott	1.00	.45
❑ 6 Rusty Wallace	1.00	.45
❑ 7 Alan Kulwicki	.60	.25
❑ 8 Ernie Irvan	.40	.18
❑ 9 Richard Petty	.50	.23
❑ 10 Terry Labonte	1.00	.45
❑ 11 Darrell Waltrip	.40	.18
❑ 12 Harry Gant	.40	.18
❑ 13 Geoff Bodine	.20	.09
❑ 14 Dale Earnhardt	2.00	.90
❑ 15 Michael Waltrip	.20	.09
❑ 16 Dave Mader	.20	.09
❑ 17 Mark Martin	1.00	.45
❑ 18 Dale Jarrett	.75	.35
❑ 19 Morgan Shepherd	.20	.09
❑ 20 Hut Stricklin	.20	.09
❑ 21 Davey Allison's Car	.40	.18
❑ 22 Kyle Petty's Car	.20	.09
❑ 23 Ken Schrader's Car	.10	.05
❑ 24 Ricky Rudd's Car	.20	.09
❑ 25 Bill Elliott's Car	.50	.23
❑ 26 Rusty Wallace's Car	.50	.23
❑ 27 Alan Kulwicki's Car	.40	.18
❑ 28 Ernie Irvan's Car	.20	.09
❑ 29 Richard Petty's Car	.40	.18
❑ 30 Terry Labonte's Car	.50	.23
❑ 31 Darrell Waltrip's Car	.20	.09
❑ 32 Harry Gant's Car	.20	.09
❑ 33 Geoff Bodine's Car	.10	.05
❑ 34 Dale Earnhardt 's Car	1.00	.45
❑ 35 Michael Waltrip's Car	.10	.05
❑ 36 Dave Mader's Car	.10	.05
❑ 37 Mark Martin's Car	.50	.23
❑ 38 Dale Jarrett's Car	.40	.18
❑ 39 Morgan Shepherd's Car	.10	.05
❑ 40 Hut Stricklin's Car	.10	.05
❑ 41 Davey Allison's Car	.40	.18
❑ 42 Davey Allison's Pole Win	.40	.18
❑ 43 Michael Waltrip Win	.10	.05
❑ 44 Final Pace Lap	.10	.05
❑ 45 First Segment	.10	.05
❑ 46 Second Segment	.10	.05
❑ 47 Third Segment	.10	.05
❑ 48 Davey Allison's Car Kyle Petty's Car	.40	.18
❑ 49 Victory Lane	.10	.05
❑ 50 Davey Allison Win	.60	.25

1993 Maxx

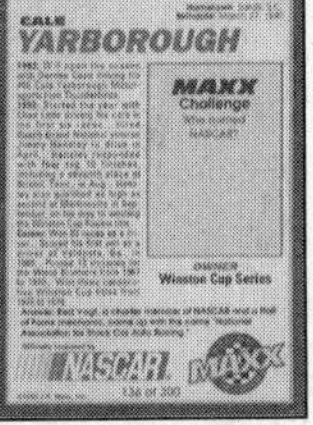

This 300-card set was distributed in complete factory set form and through 12-card wax packs. It is commonly known as the green set for the bright green border. A blue bordered parallel set was released later in the year through Club Maxx. The blue bordered set is known as the Maxx Premier Series and is priced under that title.

	MINT	NRMT
COMPLETE SET (300)	14.00	6.25
COMPLETE FACT.SET (300)	18.00	8.00
COMMON CARD (1-300)	.10	.05
COMMON DRIVER (1-300)	.20	.09

❑ 1 Rick Mast	.20	.09
❑ 2 Rusty Wallace	1.00	.45
❑ 3 Dale Earnhardt	2.00	.90
❑ 4 Ernie Irvan	.40	.18
❑ 5 Ricky Rudd	.40	.18
❑ 6 Mark Martin	1.00	.45
❑ 7 Alan Kulwicki	.75	.35
❑ 8 Sterling Marlin	.40	.18
❑ 9 Chad Little	.20	.09
❑ 10 Derrike Cope	.20	.09
❑ 11 Bill Elliott	1.00	.45
❑ 12 Jimmy Spencer	.20	.09
❑ 13 Alan Kulwicki's Car Bill Elliott's Car Memorable Moment	.40	.18
❑ 14 Terry Labonte	1.00	
❑ 15 Geoff Bodine	.20	
❑ 16 Wally Dallenbach Jr.	.20	
❑ 17 Darrell Waltrip	.40	
❑ 18 Dale Jarrett	.75	
❑ 19 Tom Peck	.20	
❑ 20 Alan Kulwicki's Car	.40	
❑ 21 Morgan Shepherd	.20	
❑ 22 Bobby Labonte	.60	
❑ 23 Eddie Bierschwale	.10	
❑ 24 Jeff Gordon	2.00	
❑ 25 Ken Schrader	.20	
❑ 26 Brett Bodine	.20	
❑ 27 Hut Stricklin	.20	
❑ 28 Davey Allison	1.00	
❑ 29 Jimmy Horton	.20	
❑ 30 Michael Waltrip	.20	
❑ 31 Steve Grissom	.20	
❑ 32 Charlie Glotzbach	.20	
❑ 33 Harry Gant	.40	
❑ 34 Todd Bodine	.20	
❑ 35 Jeff Purvis	.20	
❑ 36 Ward Burton	.20	
❑ 37 Bill Elliott's Car	.40	
❑ 38 Jerry O'Neill	.10	
❑ 39 Buddy Baker	.20	
❑ 40 Kenny Wallace	.20	
❑ 41 Phil Parsons	.20	
❑ 42 Kyle Petty	.40	
❑ 43 Richard Petty	.50	
❑ 44 Rick Wilson	.20	
❑ 45 Jeff Burton	.20	
❑ 46 Al Unser Jr.	.40	
❑ 47 Bill Venturini	.20	
❑ 48 James Hylton	.10	
❑ 49 Stanley Smith	.10	
❑ 50 Tommy Houston	.20	
❑ 51 Richard Lasater	.10	
❑ 52 Jimmy Means	.20	
❑ 53 Mike Wallace	.20	
❑ 54 Jack Sprague	.10	
❑ 55 Ted Musgrave	.20	
❑ 56 Dale Earnhardt's Car	.40	
❑ 57 Troy Beebe	.10	
❑ 58 Bill Sedgwick	.10	
❑ 59 Robert Pressley	.20	
❑ 60 Jeff Green	.20	
❑ 61 Kyle Petty's Car	.20	
❑ 62 H.B. Bailey	.10	
❑ 63 Chuck Bown	.20	
❑ 64 Dorsey Schroeder	.20	
❑ 65 Dave Mader	.10	
❑ 66 Jimmy Hensley	.20	
❑ 67 Ed Berrier	.10	
❑ 68 Bobby Hamilton	.20	
❑ 69 Greg Sacks	.20	
❑ 70 Tommy Ellis	.10	
❑ 71 Dave Marcis	.20	
❑ 72 Tracy Leslie	.10	
❑ 73 Phil Barkdoll	.20	
❑ 74 Kyle Petty's Car Memorable Moment	.20	
❑ 75 Dick Trickle	.20	
❑ 76 Butch Miller	.20	
❑ 77 Mike Potter	.10	
❑ 78 Shawna Robinson	.20	
❑ 79 Dave Rezendes	.20	
❑ 80 Bobby Dotter	.20	
❑ 81 Lonnie Rush Jr.	.10	
❑ 82 Andy Belmont	.20	
❑ 83 Lake Speed	.20	
❑ 84 Rich Bickle	.20	
❑ 85 Mark Martin's Car	.40	
❑ 86 Mickey Gibbs	.10	
❑ 87 Joe Nemechek	.20	
❑ 88 Sterling Marlin's Car	.20	
❑ 89 Jerry Hill	.10	
❑ 90 Bobby Hillin	.20	
❑ 91 Bob Schacht	.10	
❑ 92 Kerry Teague	.10	
❑ 93 Larry Pearson	.20	
❑ 94 Davey Allison's Car Bill Elliott's Car Memorable Moment	.40	
❑ 95 Jim Sauter	.10	
❑ 96 Ed Ferree	.10	
❑ 97 Bobby Hamilton's Car	.10	
❑ 98 Jim Bown	.10	
❑ 99 Ricky Craven	.40	
❑ 100 Junior Johnson	.20	
❑ 101 Robert Yates	.10	
❑ 102 Leo Jackson	.10	
❑ 103 Felix Sabates	.10	
❑ 104 Jack Roush	.10	
❑ 105 Rick Hendrick	.10	
❑ 106 Billy Hagen	.10	

7 Tim Morgan	.10	.05
8 Larry McClure	.10	.05
9 Teddy McClure	.10	.05
Jerry McClure		
Ed McClure		
0 Richard Childress	.10	.05
1 Roger Penske	.10	.05
2 Don Miller	.10	.05
3 Bobby Labonte's Car	.20	.09
4 Glen Wood	.10	.05
5 Len Wood	.10	.05
6 Eddie Wood	.10	.05
7 Kenny Bernstein	.20	.09
8 Walter Bud Moore	.10	.05
9 Ray DeWitt	.10	.05
0 D.K. Ulrich	.10	.05
1 Davey Allison's Car	.40	.18
2 Joe Gibbs	.20	.09
3 Bill Stavola	.10	.05
4 Mickey Stavola	.10	.05
5 Richard Jackson	.10	.05
6 Chuck Rider	.10	.05
7 George Bradshaw	.10	.05
8 Mark Smith	.10	.05
9 Bobby Allison	.20	.09
0 Bob Bilby	.10	.05
Davey Allison Crash	.40	.18
Memorable Moments		
2 Larry Hedrick	.10	.05
3 Harry Melling	.10	.05
4 Junie Donlavey	.10	.05
5 Bill Davis	.10	.05
6 Cale Yarborough	.20	.09
Frank Cicci	.10	.05
Scott Welliver		
Dick Moroso	.10	.05
Butch Mock	.10	.05
Bob Rahilly	.10	.05
Don Bierschwale	.10	.05
Paul Andrews	.10	.05
Mike Beam	.10	.05
Larry McReynolds	.10	.05
Steve Barkdoll	.10	.05
Robin Pemberton	.10	.05
Steve Hmiel	.10	.05
Gary DeHart	.10	.05
Pete Wright	.10	.05
Ricky Rudd's Car	.20	.09
Jake Elder	.10	.05
Mike Hill	.10	.05
Tony Glover	.10	.05
Andy Petree	.10	.05
Buddy Parrott	.10	.05
Richard Petty	.40	.18
Memorable Moment		
Leonard Wood	.10	.05
Donnie Richeson	.10	.05
Donnie Wingo	.10	.05
Ken Howes	.10	.05
Sandy Jones	.10	.05
Jimmy Makar	.10	.05
Ken Wilson	.10	.05
Barry Dodson	.10	.05
Doug Hewitt	.10	.05
Howard Comstock	.10	.05
David Fuge	.10	.05
Jeff Gordon's Car	.40	.18
Robbie Loomis	.10	.05
Jimmy Fennig	.10	.05
Bob Johnson	.10	.05
Doug Richert	.10	.05
Ernie Elliott	.10	.05
Doug Williams	.10	.05
Tim Brewer	.10	.05
Gil Martin	.10	.05
Kenny Wallace's Car	.10	.05
Ray Evernham	.10	.05
Troy Selberg	.10	.05
Dennis Connor	.10	.05
Jeff Hammond	.10	.05
Dale Inman	.10	.05
Harry Hyde	.10	.05
Vic Kangas	.10	.05
Bob Labonte	.10	.05
Ken Schrader's Car	.10	.05
Clyde McLeod	.10	.05
Ricky Pearson	.10	.05
Tony Eury	.10	.05
Alan Kulwicki	.40	.18
Winston Cup Champion		
Jimmy Hensley	.20	.09
WC Rookie of the Year		
Larry McReynolds	.10	.05
Crew Chief of the Year		
Bill Elliott	.40	.18
Fan's Favorite Driver		
Ken Schrader w/Crew	.20	.09
Pit Crew Champs		

❑ 195 Joe Nemechek	.20	.09
BGN Champion		
❑ 196 Ricky Craven	.40	.18
BGN Rookie of the Year		
❑ 197 Ricky Rudd	.40	.18
IROC Champion		
❑ 198 Dick Beaty	.10	.05
❑ 199 Davey Allison's Car	.40	.18
Richard Petty's Car		
Bobby Labonte's Car		
Mark Martin's Car		
Memorable Moment		
❑ 200 Barney Hall	.10	.05
❑ 201 Eli Gold	.10	.05
❑ 202 Ned Jarrett	.20	.09
❑ 203 Glenn Jarrett	.10	.05
❑ 204 Dick Berggren	.10	.05
❑ 205 Jack Arute	.10	.05
❑ 206 Bob Jenkins	.10	.05
❑ 207 Benny Parsons	.20	.09
❑ 208 Jerry Punch	.10	.05
❑ 209 Joe Moore	.10	.05
❑ 210 Jim Phillips	.10	.05
❑ 211 Chris Economaki	.10	.05
❑ 212 Winston Kelley	.10	.05
❑ 213 Dick Brooks	.10	.05
❑ 214 John Kernan	.10	.05
❑ 215 Mike Joy	.10	.05
❑ 216 Randy Pemberton	.10	.05
❑ 217 Allen Bestwick	.10	.05
❑ 218 Ken Squier	.10	.05
❑ 219 Neil Bonnett	.40	.18
❑ 220 Davey Allison Crash	.40	.18
Memorable Moment		
❑ 221 Larry Phillips	.10	.05
Brooke Gordon		
❑ 222 Mike Love	.10	.05
Charlie Cragen		
❑ 223 Steve Murgic	.10	.05
Ricky Icenhower		
❑ 224 Michael Ritch	.10	.05
Joe Kosiski		
❑ 225 Steve Hendren	.10	.05
Larry Phillips		
❑ 226 Darrell Waltrip	.20	.09
Memorable Moment		
❑ 227 Buster Auton	.10	.05
❑ 228 Jimmy Cox	.10	.05
❑ 229 Les Richter	.10	.05
❑ 230 Ray Hill	.10	.05
❑ 231 Doyle Ford	.10	.05
❑ 232 Chuck Romeo	.10	.05
❑ 233 Elmo Langley	.10	.05
❑ 234 Jack Whittemore	.10	.05
❑ 235 Walt Green	.10	.05
❑ 236 Mike Chaplin	.10	.05
❑ 237 Tim Earp	.10	.05
❑ 238 Bruce Roney	.10	.05
❑ 239 Carl Hill	.10	.05
❑ 240 Mark Connolly	.10	.05
❑ 241 Gary Miller	.10	.05
❑ 242 Marlin Wright	.10	.05
❑ 243 Gary Nelson	.10	.05
❑ 244 Ernie Irvan's Car	.40	.18
❑ 245 Richard Petty w/Car	.40	.18
Memorable Moment		
❑ 246 Harry Gant	.20	.09
All Pro		
❑ 247 Tony Glover	.10	.05
All Pro		
❑ 248 David Little	.10	.05
All Pro		
❑ 249 Gary Brooks	.10	.05
All Pro		
❑ 250 Bill Wilburn	.10	.05
All Pro		
❑ 251 Jeff Clark	.10	.05
All Pro		
❑ 252 Shelton Pittman	.10	.05
All Pro		
❑ 253 Scott Robinson	.10	.05
All Pro		
❑ 254 Glen Bobo	.10	.05
All Pro		
❑ 255 James Lewter	.10	.05
All Pro		
❑ 256 Jerry Schweitz	.10	.05
All Pro		
❑ 257 Harold Stott	.10	.05
All Pro		
❑ 258 Ryan Pemberton	.10	.05
All Pro		
❑ 259 Gale Wilson	.10	.05
All Pro		
❑ 260 Danny Glad	.10	.05
All Pro		
❑ 261 Howard Poston (Slick)	.10	.05
All Pro		

❑ 262 Brooke Sealy	.20	.09
Miss Winston		
❑ 263 Geoff Bodine	.20	.09
Year in Review		
❑ 264 Davey Allison	.50	.23
Robert Yates		
Larry McReynolds		
Year in Review		
❑ 265 Bill Elliott w/Crew	.50	.23
Year in Review		
❑ 266 Bill Elliott	.50	.23
Year in Review		
❑ 267 Bill Elliott	.50	.23
Junior Johnson		
Year in Review		
❑ 268 Bill Elliott	.50	.23
Year in Review		
❑ 269 Alan Kulwicki w/Crew	.40	.18
Year in Review		
❑ 270 Davey Allison	.50	.23
Robert Yates		
Larry McReynolds		
Year in Review		
❑ 271 Mark Martin	.50	.23
Jack Roush		
Steve Hmiel		
Year in Review		
❑ 272 Davey Allison w/Crew	.50	.23
Year in Review		
❑ 273 Robert Yates	.10	.05
Year in Review		
❑ 274 Dale Earnhardt	1.00	.45
Kerry Earnhardt		
Dale Earnhardt Jr.		
Year in Review		
❑ 275 Harry Gant	.20	.09
Year in Review		
❑ 276 Ernie Irvan	.40	.18
Year in Review		
❑ 277 Alan Kulwicki w/Crew	.40	.18
Year in Review		
❑ 278 Davey Allison	.50	.23
Year in Review		
❑ 279 Ernie Irvan	.40	.18
Year in Review		
❑ 280 Darrell Waltrip	.20	.09
Year in Review		
❑ 281 Ernie Irvan	.40	.18
Year in Review		
❑ 282 Kyle Petty	.40	.18
Felix Sabates		
Year in Review		
❑ 283 Harry Gant	.20	.09
Year in Review		
❑ 284 Darrell Waltrip	.20	.09
Year in Review		
❑ 285 Darrell Waltrip	.20	.09
Year in Review		
❑ 286 Rusty Wallace w/Crew	.50	.23
Year in Review		
❑ 287 Ricky Rudd w/Crew	.40	.18
Year in Review		
❑ 288 Geoff Bodine	.20	.09
Year in Review		
❑ 289 Geoff Bodine w/Crew	.20	.09
Year in Review		
❑ 290 Mark Martin	.50	.23
Year in Review		
❑ 291 Kyle Petty	.40	.18
Year in Review		
❑ 292 Davey Allison	.50	.23
Robert Yates		
Year in Review		
❑ 293 Bill Elliott	.50	.23
Year in Review		
❑ 294 Alan Kulwicki	.40	.18
Memorable Moment		
❑ 295 Checklist #1	.10	.05
❑ 296 Checklist #2	.10	.05
❑ 297 Checklist #3	.10	.05
❑ 298 Checklist #4	.10	.05
❑ 299 Checklist #5	.10	.05
❑ 300 Checklist #6	.10	.05

1993 Maxx Premier Series

This 300-card set was distributed primarily through the Maxx Club mail order program. It is commonly known as the blue set. Collectors who bought this set were also sent an 8" by 10" chromium card commemorating Dale Earnhardt's six NASCAR Winston Cup titles. The jumbo chromium card of Dale is numbered of 80,000. This card is priced under the 1993 Maxx Premier Plus Jumbo listing.

	MINT	NRMT
COMPLETE SET (300)	40.00	18.00
COMMON CARD (1-300)	.10	.05

	MINT	NRMT
COMMON DRIVER (1-300)	.25	.11
*STARS: 1.25X TO 2X GREEN CARDS		

1993 Maxx Baby Ruth Jeff Burton

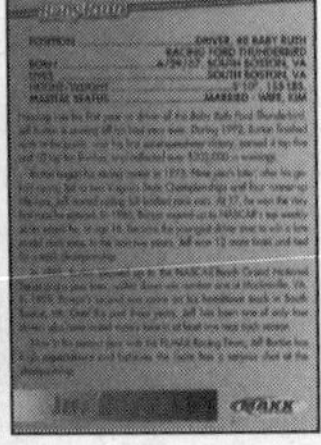

This four-card set was produced by Maxx and distributed by the Baby Ruth Race Team. It features photos of Baby Ruth driver Jeff Burton.

	MINT	NRMT
COMPLETE SET (4)	10.00	4.50
COMMON CARD	2.50	1.10

1993 Maxx Jeff Gordon

This 20-card set was produced by Maxx and was distributed only in set form through Club Maxx for $4.95 per set. It highlights his career from his early childhood to debut on the Winston Cup circuit. 1,000 Jeff Gordon autographed cards were randomly inserted into the sets at a 1:100 ratio.

	MINT	NRMT
COMPLETE SET (20)	8.00	3.60
COMMON CARD (1-20)	.50	.23
❏ NNO Jeff Gordon AUTO	140.00	65.00

1993 Maxx Lowes Foods Stickers

Maxx produced this sticker set for distribution through Lowes Foods Stores. The stickers were distributed over a 5-week period (one per week) and include three drivers per sticker strip. Sticker fronts feature a top Winston Cup driver along with the Maxx and Lowes logos. Backs include Lowes Food Stores coupons. The strips actually are three individual stickers attached together. We've listed and priced the stickers in complete three-sticker strips.

	MINT	NRMT
COMPLETE SET (5)	15.00	6.75
COMMON PANEL (1-5)	2.00	.90
❏ 1 Jimmy Spencer Ricky Rudd Kenny Wallace	2.00	.90
❏ 2 Bill Elliott Darrell Waltrip Jeff Gordon	8.00	3.60
❏ 3 Davey Allison Kyle Petty Bobby Hamilton	4.00	1.80
❏ 4 Terry Labonte Sterling Marlin Bobby Labonte	4.00	1.80
❏ 5 Morgan Shepherd Brett Bodine Ken Schrader	2.00	.90

1993 Maxx Motorsport

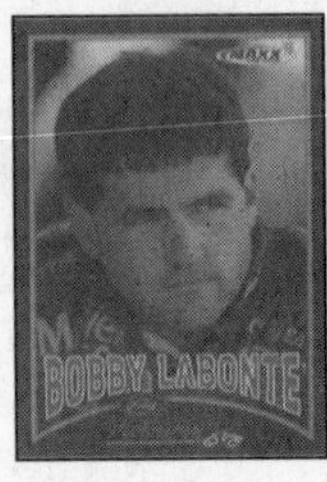

This 50-card set was produced by Maxx and distributed by Ford Motorsports. It consists of Ford's twenty drivers and their cars, plus the cards of the late Davey Allison and Alan Kulwicki.

	MINT	NRMT
COMPLETE SET (50)	6.00	2.70
COMMON CARD (1-50)	.10	.05
COMMON DRIVER (1-50)	.20	.09
❏ 1 Brett Bodine	.20	.09
❏ 2 Geoff Bodine	.20	.09
❏ 3 Todd Bodine	.20	.09
❏ 4 Derrike Cope	.20	.09
❏ 5 Wally Dallenbach Jr.	.20	.09
❏ 6 Bill Elliott	.75	.35
❏ 7 Bobby Hamilton	.20	.09
❏ 8 Jimmy Hensley	.20	.09
❏ 9 Bobby Hillin	.20	.09
❏ 10 P.J. Jones	.20	.09
❏ 11 Bobby Labonte	.60	.25
❏ 12 Sterling Marlin	.40	.18
❏ 13 Mark Martin	.75	.35
❏ 14 Rick Mast	.20	.09
❏ 15 Ted Musgrave	.20	.09
❏ 16 Greg Sacks	.20	.09
❏ 17 Morgan Shepherd	.20	.09
❏ 18 Lake Speed	.20	.09
❏ 19 Jimmy Spencer	.20	.09
❏ 20 Hut Stricklin	.20	.09
❏ 21 Brett Bodine's Car	.10	.05
❏ 22 Geoff Bodine's Car	.10	.05
❏ 23 Todd Bodine's Car	.10	.05
❏ 24 Derrike Cope's Car	.10	.05
❏ 25 Wally Dallenbach Jr.'s Car	.10	.05
❏ 26 Bill Elliott's Car	.50	.23
❏ 27 Bill Hamilton's Car	.10	.05
❏ 28 Jimmy Hensley's Car	.10	.05
❏ 29 Bobby Hillin's Car	.10	.05
❏ 30 P.J. Jones' Car	.10	.05
❏ 31 Bobby Labonte's Car	.20	.09
❏ 32 Sterling Marlin's Car	.20	.09
❏ 33 Mark Martin's Car	.50	.23
❏ 34 Rick Mast's Car	.10	.05
❏ 35 Ted Musgrave's Car	.10	.05
❏ 36 Greg Sacks' Car	.10	.05
❏ 37 Morgan Shepherd's Car	.10	.05
❏ 38 Lake Speed's Car	.10	.05
❏ 39 Jimmy Spencer's Car	.10	.05
❏ 40 Hut Stricklin's Car	.10	.05
❏ 41 Davey Allison	.75	.35
❏ 42 Davey Allison's Car	.50	.23
❏ 43 Alan Kulwicki	.50	.23
❏ 44 Alan Kulwicki's Car	.40	.18
❏ 45 Lee Morse	.10	.05
❏ 46 Michael Kranefuss	.10	.05
❏ 47 Alan Kulwicki	.50	.23
Bill Elliott		
❏ 48 Manufacturers' Champs	.10	
❏ 49 Davey Allison's Car Takes Richmond	.50	
❏ 50 Mark Martin's Car Streak Begins	.50	

1993 Maxx Premier Plus

This 212-card set was the first "super premium" racir produced. Factory sets were available through dealers and Maxx's mail order program. It was available in eight-card foil packs. Insert cards of the Mascot and the Maxx Rookie Contenders (1 of 20 were included in hobby sets and randomly inserted packs. There is also a version of the Maxx R Contenders card that doesn't have the 1 of 20,000 p on it.

	MINT
COMPLETE SET (212)	20.00
COMPLETE FACT.SET (212)	30.00
COMMON CARD (1-212)	.15
COMMON DRIVER (1-212)	.30
❏ 1 Rick Mast	.30
❏ 2 Rusty Wallace	1.50
❏ 3 Dale Earnhardt	3.00
❏ 4 Ernie Irvan	1.00
❏ 5 Ricky Rudd	.60
❏ 6 Mark Martin	1.50
❏ 7 Alan Kulwicki	1.25
❏ 8 Sterling Marlin	.60
❏ 9 Chad Little	.30
❏ 10 Derrike Cope	.30
❏ 11 Bill Elliott	1.50
❏ 12 Jimmy Spencer	.30
❏ 13 Alan Kulwicki's Car Bill Elliott's Car Memorable Moment	.60
❏ 14 Terry Labonte	1.00
❏ 15 Geoff Bodine	.30
❏ 16 Wally Dallenbach, Jr.	.30
❏ 17 Darrell Waltrip	.60
❏ 18 Dale Jarrett	1.25
❏ 19 Tom Peck	.30
❏ 20 Alan Kulwicki's Car	.60
❏ 21 Morgan Shepherd	.30
❏ 22 Bobby Labonte	1.00
❏ 23 Kyle Petty's Car Memorable Moment	.30
❏ 24 Jeff Gordon	3.00
❏ 25 Ken Schrader	.30
❏ 26 Brett Bodine	.30
❏ 27 Hut Stricklin	.30
❏ 28 Davey Allison	1.50
❏ 29 Davey Allison's Car Bill Elliott's Car Memorable Moment	1.00
❏ 30 Michael Waltrip	.30
❏ 31 Steve Grissom	.30
❏ 32 Ken Schrader's Car	.15
❏ 33 Harry Gant	.60
❏ 34 Todd Bodine	.30
❏ 35 Bobby Hamilton's Car	.15
❏ 36 Ward Burton	.30
❏ 37 Bill Elliott's Car	1.00
❏ 38 Jerry O'Neill	.15
❏ 39 Jeff Gordon's Car	1.00
❏ 40 Kenny Wallace	.30
❏ 41 Phil Parsons	.30
❏ 42 Kyle Petty	.60
❏ 43 Richard Petty	.60
❏ 44 Rick Wilson	.30
❏ 45 Jeff Burton	.30
❏ 46 Al Unser Jr.	.60
❏ 47 Bill Venturini	.15
❏ 48 Richard Petty Memorable Moment	1.00
❏ 49 Stanley Smith	.15
❏ 50 Tommy Houston	.30
❏ 51 Bobby Labonte's Car	.30
❏ 52 Jimmy Means	.30

Mike Wallace	.30	.14
Jack Sprague	.15	.07
Ted Musgrave	.30	.14
Dale Earnhardt's Car	1.00	.45
Davey Allison's Car	1.00	.45
Richard Petty's Car		
Bobby Labonte's Car		
Mark Martin's Car		
Memorable Moment		
Jim Sauter	.15	.07
Robert Pressley	.30	.14
Davey Allison's Car	1.00	.45
Kyle Petty's Car		
Memorable Moment		
Kyle Petty's Car	.30	.14
Davey Allison Crash	1.00	.45
Memorable Moment		
Chuck Bown	.30	.14
Sterling Marlin's Car	.30	.14
Darrell Waltrip	.30	.14
Memorable Moment		
Jimmy Hensley	.30	.14
Ernie Irvan's Car	.60	.25
Bobby Hamilton	.30	.14
Greg Sacks	.30	.14
Tommy Ellis	.15	.07
Dave Marcis	.30	.14
Tracy Leslie	.15	.07
Ricky Craven	.60	.25
Richard Petty w/Car	1.00	.45
Memorable Moment		
Dick Trickle	.30	.14
Butch Miller	.30	.14
Jim Bown	.15	.07
Shawna Robinson	.30	.14
Davey Allison's Car	1.00	.45
Bobby Dotter	.15	.07
Alan Kulwicki	1.00	.45
Memorable Moment		
Kenny Wallace's Car	.15	.07
ake Speed	.30	.14
Bobby Hillin	.30	.14
Mark Martin's Car	1.00	.45
ob Schacht	.15	.07
oe Nemechek	.30	.14
Ricky Rudd's Car	.30	.14
unior Johnson	.30	.14
obert Yates	.15	.07
eo Jackson	.15	.07
elix Sabates	.15	.07
ack Roush	.15	.07
ick Hendrick	.15	.07
illy Hagan	.15	.07
im Morgan	.15	.07
arry McClure	.15	.07
eddy McClure	.15	.07
Jerry McClure		
Ed McClure		
ichard Childress	.15	.07
Roger Penske	.15	.07
Don Miller	.15	.07
Glen Wood	.15	.07
Len Wood	.15	.07
Eddie Wood	.15	.07
Kenny Bernstein	.30	.14
Walter Bud Moore	.15	.07
Ray DeWitt	.15	.07
D.K. Ulrich	.15	.07
Joe Gibbs	.30	.14
Bill Stavola	.15	.07
Mickey Stavola	.15	.07
Richard Jackson	.15	.07
Chuck Rider	.15	.07
George Bradshaw	.15	.07
Mark Smith	.15	.07
Bobby Allison	.30	.14
Bob Bilby	.15	.07
Larry Hedrick	.15	.07
Harry Melling	.15	.07
Junie Donlavey	.15	.07
Bill Davis	.15	.07
Cale Yarborough	.30	.14
Frank Cicci	.15	.07
Scott Welliver		
Dick Moroso	.15	.07
Butch Mock	.15	.07
Bob Rahilly	.15	.07
Paul Andrews	.15	.07
Mike Beam	.15	.07
Larry McReynolds	.15	.07
Tim Brewer	.15	.07
Robin Pemberton	.15	.07
Steve Hmiel	.15	.07
Gary DeHart	.15	.07
Pete Wright	.15	.07
Jake Elder	.15	.07
Mike Hill	.15	.07
Tony Glover	.15	.07

❑ 138 Andy Petree	.15	.07
❑ 139 Buddy Parrott	.15	.07
❑ 140 Leonard Wood	.15	.07
❑ 141 Donnie Richeson	.15	.07
❑ 142 Donnie Wingo	.15	.07
❑ 143 Ken Howes	.15	.07
❑ 144 Sandy Jones	.15	.07
❑ 145 Jimmy Makar	.15	.07
❑ 146 Ken Wilson	.15	.07
❑ 147 Barry Dodson	.15	.07
❑ 148 Doug Hewitt	.15	.07
❑ 149 Howard Comstock	.15	.07
❑ 150 David Fuge	.15	.07
❑ 151 Robbie Loomis	.15	.07
❑ 152 Jimmy Fennig	.15	.07
❑ 153 Bob Johnson	.15	.07
❑ 154 Doug Richert	.15	.07
❑ 155 Ernie Elliott	.15	.07
❑ 156 Doug Williams	.15	.07
❑ 157 Tim Brewer	.15	.07
❑ 158 Ray Evernham	.15	.07
❑ 159 Troy Seberg	.15	.07
❑ 160 Dennis Connor	.15	.07
❑ 161 Jeff Hammond	.15	.07
❑ 162 Dale Inman	.15	.07
❑ 163 Harry Hyde	.15	.07
❑ 164 Vic Kangas	.15	.07
❑ 165 Bob Labonte	.15	.07
❑ 166 Clyde McLeod	.15	.07
❑ 167 Ricky Pearson	.15	.07
❑ 168 Tony Eury	.15	.07
❑ 169 Ricky Rudd	.60	.25
IROC Champion		
❑ 170 Dick Beaty	.15	.07
❑ 171 Ken Schrader w/Crew	.30	.14
Pit Crew Champs		
❑ 172 Alan Kulwicki	1.00	.45
WC Champion		
❑ 173 Jimmy Hensley	.30	.14
WC Rookie of the Year		
❑ 174 Larry McReynolds	.15	.07
Crew Chief of the Year		
❑ 175 Bill Elliott	1.00	.45
Fan's Favorite Driver		
❑ 176 Joe Nemechek	.30	.14
BGN Champion		
❑ 177 Ricky Craven	.60	.25
BGN Rookie of the Year		
❑ 178 Geoff Bodine	.30	.14
Year in Review		
❑ 179 Davey Allison	1.50	.70
Year in Review		
❑ 180 Bill Elliott	1.50	.70
Year in Review		
❑ 181 Bill Elliott	1.50	.70
Year in Review		
❑ 182 Bill Elliott	1.50	.70
Year in Review		
❑ 183 Bill Elliott	1.50	.70
Junior Johnson		
Year in Review		
❑ 184 Alan Kulwicki	1.00	.45
Year in Review		
❑ 185 Davey Allison	1.50	.70
Year in Review		
❑ 186 Mark Martin	1.50	.70
Year in Review		
❑ 187 Davey Allison	1.50	.70
Year in Review		
❑ 188 Bobby Allison	.30	.14
Year in Review		
❑ 189 Dale Earnhardt	3.00	1.35
Kerry Earnhardt		
Dale Earnhardt Jr.		
Year in Review		
❑ 190 Harry Gant	.30	.14
Year in Review		
❑ 191 Ernie Irvan	1.00	.45
Year in Review		
❑ 192 Alan Kulwicki	1.00	.45
Year in Review		
❑ 193 Davey Allison	1.50	.70
Robert Yates		
Larry McReynolds		
Year in Review		
❑ 194 Ernie Irvan	1.00	.45
Year in Review		
❑ 195 Darrell Waltrip	.30	.14
Year in Review		
❑ 196 Ernie Irvan w/Crew	1.00	.45
Year in Review		
❑ 197 Kyle Petty	.60	.25
Year in Review		
❑ 198 Harry Gant	.30	.14
Year in Review		
❑ 199 Darrell Waltrip	.30	.14
Year in Review		
❑ 200 Darrell Waltrip	.30	.14
Year in Review		
❑ 201 Rusty Wallace	1.50	.70
Year in Review		
❑ 202 Ricky Rudd	.60	.25
Year in Review		
❑ 203 Geoff Bodine	.30	.14
Year in Review		
❑ 204 Geoff Bodine	.30	.14
Year in Review		
❑ 205 Mark Martin	1.50	.70
Year in Review		
❑ 206 Kyle Petty	.60	.25
Year in Review		
❑ 207 Davey Allison w/Crew	1.50	.70
Year in Review		
❑ 208 Bill Elliott	1.50	.70
Year in Review		
❑ 209 Checklist #1	.15	.07
❑ 210 Checklist #2	.15	.07
❑ 211 Checklist #3	.15	.07
❑ 212 Checklist #4	.15	.07
❑ NNO Mascot Card	3.00	1.35
❑ NNO Jeff Gordon	15.00	6.75
Bobby Labonte		
Kenny Wallace		

1993 Maxx Premier Plus Jumbos

These three cards commemorate special happenings in the 1992 Winston Cup season. The Alan Kulwicki and Davey Allison cards pay tribute to the two great drivers. The Dale Earnhardt card celebrates his sixth Winston Cup championship. The cards use Maxx's Chromium technology and measure 8" X 10". The Dale Earnhardt card was sold with the 1993 Maxx Premier Series set via the Maxx Club. There were 80,000 of Earnhardt card. The other two cards were sold through the club and retail outlets.

	MINT	NRMT
COMPLETE SET (3)	35.00	16.00
COMMON CARD	10.00	4.50
❑ NNO Davey Allison	10.00	4.50
❑ NNO Dale Earnhardt	15.00	6.75
❑ NNO Alan Kulwicki	10.00	4.50

1993 Maxx Retail Jumbos

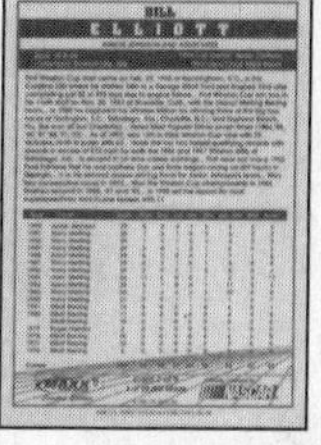

This nine-card set was inserted in special blister retail packs that were distributed in retail outlets such as K-Mart and Wal-Mart. The jumbo cards measure 3" by 5".

	MINT	NRMT
COMPLETE SET (9)	15.00	6.75
COMMON CARD (1-9)	1.00	.45
❑ 1 Darrell Waltrip	2.00	.90
❑ 2 Ken Schrader	1.00	.45
❑ 3 Phil Parsons	1.00	.45
❑ 4 Sterling Marlin	2.00	.90
❑ 5 Mark Martin	3.00	1.35
❑ 6 Dale Jarrett	2.00	.90
❑ 7 Bill Elliott	3.00	1.35
❑ 8 Derrike Cope	1.00	.45
❑ 9 Brett Bodine	1.00	.45

1993 Maxx Texaco Davey Allison

This 20-card set was produced by Maxx and made available through Texaco gas stations in the southeastern region of the country. They were distributed in four-card packs and could be purchased for $.99. 5,000 of these cards were autographed by Davey Allison and randomly inserted into packs. Like their predecessor, a large number of these cards made thier way into the hobby.

	MINT	NRMT
COMPLETE SET (20)	10.00	4.50
COMMON CARD (1-20)	.40	.18

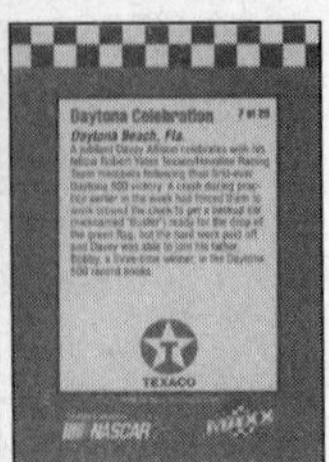

	MINT	NRMT
❑ 1 Davey Allison	1.00	.45
❑ 2 Davey Allison Clifford Allison Bobby Allison	1.00	.45
❑ 3 Robert Yates	.40	.18
❑ 4 Larry McReynolds	.40	.18
❑ 5 Davey Allison w/Crew	.40	.18
❑ 6 Davey Allison Robert Yates Larry McReynolds	.40	.18
❑ 7 Davey Allison	1.00	.45
❑ 8 Davey Allison's Car Rusty Wallace's Car The Winston Pole	.40	.18
❑ 9 Davey Allison Crash	.40	.18
❑ 10 Davey Allison Robert Yates Larry McReynolds	.40	.18
❑ 11 Davey Allison Bobby Allison Robert Yates	.40	.18
❑ 12 Davey Allison Bobby Allison	.40	.18
❑ 13 Davey Allison	1.00	.45
❑ 14 Davey Allison Larry McReynolds Robert Yates	.40	.18
❑ 15 Davey Allison in Pits	.40	.18
❑ 16 Davey Allison The Wonder Years	.40	.18
❑ 17 Davey Allison's Car	.40	.18
❑ 18 Davey Allison Bobby Hillin	.40	.18
❑ 19 Davey Allison	1.00	.45
❑ 20 Davey Allison w/Crew Checklist on back	.40	.18
❑ AU1 Davey Allison/5000	160.00	70.00

1993 Maxx Winnebago Motorsports

This 11-card set was produced by Maxx and distributed by Winnebago Motorsports. The cards feature drivers in non-racing photos using Winnebago vehicles.

	MINT	NRMT
COMPLETE SET (11)	20.00	9.00
COMMON CARD (1-10)	1.00	.45
COMMON DRIVER (1-10)	2.00	.90

	MINT	NRMT
❑ 1 Sterling Marlin	2.50	1.10
❑ 2 Jeff Gordon Bobby Labonte Rich Bickle Kenny Wallace	8.00	3.60
❑ 3 Bobby Allison	2.50	1.10
❑ 4 Winnebago Motor. Van	1.00	.45
❑ 5 Bobby Allison Judy Allison	2.00	.90
❑ 6 Bobby Allison Richard Childress Jimmy Spencer Ken Schrader Sterling Marlin Bob Keselowski Vectra & Celebrities	2.00	.90
❑ 7 Ken Schrader	2.00	.90
❑ 8 Tony Bettenhausen	2.00	.90
Stefan Johansson		
❑ 9 David Rampy's Funny Car	1.00	.45
❑ 10 Bob Keselowski's Car	1.00	.45
❑ NNO Cover Card	1.00	.45

1993 Maxx The Winston

This 51-card set was produced by Maxx and features drivers who raced in the 1993 Winston Select. Each set contains a special chromium Dale Earnhardt card and were originally available through Club Maxx at a price of $10 per set.

	MINT	NRMT
COMPLETE SET (51)	6.00	2.70
COMMON CARD (1-51)	.10	.05

	MINT	NRMT
❑ 1 Dale Earnhardt	1.00	.45
❑ 2 Mark Martin	.50	.23
❑ 3 Ernie Irvan	.40	.18
❑ 4 Ken Schrader	.10	.05
❑ 5 Geoff Bodine	.10	.05
❑ 6 Darrell Waltrip	.20	.09
❑ 7 Sterling Marlin	.20	.09
❑ 8 Rusty Wallace	.50	.23
❑ 9 Davey Allison	.50	.23
❑ 10 Brett Bodine	.10	.05
❑ 11 Rick Mast	.10	.05
❑ 12 Morgan Shepherd	.10	.05
❑ 13 Harry Gant	.20	.09
❑ 14 Bill Elliott	.50	.23
❑ 15 Terry Labonte	.50	.23
❑ 16 Ricky Rudd	.20	.09
❑ 17 Jimmy Hensley	.10	.05
❑ 18 Michael Waltrip	.10	.05
❑ 19 Dale Jarrett	.40	.18
❑ 20 Kyle Petty	.20	.09
❑ 21 Dale Earnhardt's Car	.50	.23
❑ 22 Mark Martin's Car	.40	.18
❑ 23 Ernie Irvan's Car	.20	.09
❑ 24 Ken Schrader's Car	.10	.05
❑ 25 Geoff Bodine's Car	.10	.05
❑ 26 Darrell Waltrip's Car	.10	.05
❑ 27 Sterling Marlin's Car	.10	.05
❑ 28 Rusty Wallace's Car	.40	.18
❑ 29 Davey Allison's Car	.40	.18
❑ 30 Brett Bodine's Car	.10	.05
❑ 31 Rick Mast's Car	.10	.05
❑ 32 Morgan Shepherd's Car	.10	.05
❑ 33 Harry Gant's Car	.10	.05
❑ 34 Bill Elliott's Car	.40	.18
❑ 35 Terry Labonte's Car	.40	.18
❑ 36 Ricky Rudd's Car	.10	.05
❑ 37 Jimmy Hensley's Car	.10	.05
❑ 38 Michael Waltrip's Car	.10	.05
❑ 39 Dale Jarrett's Car	.20	.09
❑ 40 Kyle Petty's Car	.10	.05
❑ 41 Ernie Irvan Pole Win	.40	.18
❑ 42 Sterling Marlin Win	.20	.09
❑ 43 Charlotte Motor Speedway	.10	.05
❑ 44 Winston Starting Lineup	.10	.05
❑ 45 First Segment	.10	.05
❑ 46 Second Segment	.10	.05
❑ 47 Third Segment	.10	.05
❑ 48 Third Segment	.10	.05
❑ 49 Dale Earnhardt's Car Win	.50	.23
❑ 50 Dale Earnhardt VL Brooke Sealy	1.00	.45
❑ 51 Dale Earnhardt Chromium	2.00	.90

1994 Maxx

The 1994 Maxx set was released in two separate series with the first series also being issued as a factory set packaged with four Rookies of the Year inserts. The sets feature the now standard Maxx subsets: Memorable Moments, Year in Review and highlight cards featuring the various NASCAR award winners from 1993. Each series also included randomly packed rookies insert cards with series two also containing an assortment of autographed insert cards. Packaging for each series was similar: 10 cards per pack with 36 packs per box. Jumbo

packs were produced for series one with 20-card pack.

	MINT	N
COMPLETE SET (340)	18.00	
COMPLETE FACT.SET (244)	18.00	
COMPLETE SERIES 1 (240)	10.00	
COMPLETE SERIES 2 (100)	8.00	
COMMON CARD (1-340)	.10	
COMMON DRIVER (1-340)	.20	

	MINT
❑ 1 Rick Mast	.20
❑ 2 Rusty Wallace	1.00
❑ 3 Dale Earnhardt	2.00
❑ 4 Jimmy Hensley	.20
❑ 5 Ricky Rudd	.40
❑ 6 Mark Martin	1.00
❑ 7 Alan Kulwicki	.50
❑ 8 Sterling Marlin	.40
❑ 9 P.J. Jones	.20
❑ 10 Geoff Bodine	.20
❑ 11 Bill Elliott	1.00
❑ 12 Jimmy Spencer	.20
❑ 13 Jeff Gordon Memorable Moment	1.00
❑ 14 Terry Labonte	1.00
❑ 15 Lake Speed	.20
❑ 16 Wally Dallenbach Jr.	.20
❑ 17 Darrell Waltrip	.40
❑ 18 Dale Jarrett	.75
❑ 19 Chad Little	.20
❑ 20 Bobby Hamilton	.20
❑ 21 Morgan Shepherd	.20
❑ 22 Bobby Labonte	.60
❑ 23 Dale Earnhardt's Car	1.00
❑ 24 Jeff Gordon	2.00
❑ 25 Ken Schrader	.20
❑ 26 Brett Bodine	.20
❑ 27 Hut Stricklin	.20
❑ 28 Davey Allison	.75
❑ 29 Ernie Irvan	.40
❑ 30 Michael Waltrip	.20
❑ 31 Neil Bonnett	.50
❑ 32 Jimmy Horton	.20
❑ 33 Harry Gant	.40
❑ 34 Rusty Wallace's Car	.50
❑ 35 Mark Martin's Car	.50
❑ 36 Dale Jarrett's Car	.40
❑ 37 Loy Allen Jr.	.10
❑ 38 Dale Jarrett's Car Memorable Moment	.40
❑ 39 Kyle Petty's Car	.20
❑ 40 Kenny Wallace	.20
❑ 41 Dick Trickle	.20
❑ 42 Kyle Petty	.40
❑ 43 Richard Petty	.50
❑ 44 Rick Wilson	.20
❑ 45 T.W. Taylor	.10
❑ 46 James Hylton	.20
❑ 47 Phil Parsons	.20
❑ 48 Ernie Irvan's Car	.20
❑ 49 Stanley Smith	.10
❑ 50 Morgan Shepherd's Car	.10
❑ 51 Joe Ruttman	.20
❑ 52 Jimmy Means	.20
❑ 53 Davey Allison's Car Memorable Moment	.40
❑ 54 Bill Elliott's Car	.50
❑ 55 Ted Musgrave	.20
❑ 56 Ken Schrader's Car	.10
❑ 57 Bob Schacht	.10
❑ 58 Jim Sauter	.10
❑ 59 Ricky Rudd w/Car	.20
❑ 60 Harry Gant's Car	.20
❑ 61 Ken Bouchard	.20
❑ 62 Dave Marcis' Car	.20
❑ 63 Rich Bickle	.20
❑ 64 Darrell Waltrip's Car	.20
❑ 65 Jeff Gordon's Car	1.00
❑ 66 Jeff Burton's Car	.20
❑ 67 Geoff Bodine's Car	.10
❑ 68 Greg Sacks	.20
❑ 69 Tom Kendall	.20
❑ 70 Michael Waltrip's Car	.10

Dave Marcis .40 .18
John Andretti .20 .09
Todd Bodine's Car .10 .05
Bobby Labonte's Car .40 .18
Todd Bodine .20 .09
Brett Bodine's Car .10 .05
Jeff Purvis .20 .09
Rick Mast's Car .10 .05
Rick Carelli .20 .09
Wally Dallenbach Jr.'s Car .10 .05
Jimmy Spencer's Car .10 .05
Bobby Hillin's Car .10 .05
Lake Speed's Car .10 .05
Richard Childress .10 .05
Roger Penske .10 .05
Don Miller .10 .05
Jack Roush .10 .05
Joe Gibbs .20 .09
Felix Sabates .10 .05
Bobby Hillin .20 .09
Tim Morgan .10 .05
Larry McClure .10 .05
Teddy McClure .10 .05
Jerry McClure
Ed McClure
Glen Wood .10 .05
Len Wood .10 .05
Eddie Wood .10 .05
Junior Johnson .20 .09
Derrike Cope .20 .09
Andy Hillenburg .20 .09
Rick Hendrick .10 .05
Leo Jackson .10 .05
Bobby Allison .20 .09
Bob Bilby .10 .05
Bill Stavola .10 .05
Mickey Stavola .10 .05
Paul Moore (Bud) .10 .05
Chuck Rider .10 .05
Billy Hagan .10 .05
Bill Davis .10 .05
Kenny Bernstein .20 .09
Richard Jackson .10 .05
Ray DeWitt .10 .05
Diane DeWitt
D.K. Ulrich .10 .05
Cale Yarborough .20 .09
Junie Donlavey .10 .05
Larry Hedrick .10 .05
Robert Yates .10 .05
George Bradshaw .10 .05
Mark Smith .10 .05
David Fuge .10 .05
Harry Melling .10 .05
Atlanta MM .10 .05
Dick Moroso .10 .05
Butch Mock .10 .05
Alan Kulwicki's Transporter .40 .18
Memorable Moment
Andy Petree .10 .05
Buddy Parrott .10 .05
Steve Hmiel .10 .05
Howard Comstock .10 .05
Jimmy Makar .10 .05
Robin Pemberton .10 .05
Jeff Hammond .10 .05
Tony Glover .10 .05
Leonard Wood .10 .05
Mike Beam .10 .05
Mike Hill .10 .05
Gary DeHart .10 .05
Ray Evernham .40 .18
Ken Howes .10 .05
Jimmy Fennig .10 .05
Larry Dodson .10 .05
Ken Wilson .10 .05
Donnie Wingo .10 .05
Doug Hewitt .10 .05
Pete Wright .10 .05
Jim Brewer .10 .05
Donnie Richeson .10 .05
Randy Jones .10 .05
Bob Johnson .10 .05
Geoff Bodine's Car .10 .05
Brett Bodine's Car
Memorable Moment
Doug Williams .10 .05
Waddell Wilson .10 .05
Doug Richert .10 .05
Larry McReynolds .10 .05
Dennis Connor .10 .05
Larry Hyde .10 .05
Paul Andrews .10 .05
Bobbie Loomis .20 .09
Troy Selberg .10 .05
Dale Inman .10 .05
Tony Eury .10 .05
Dale Fischlein .10 .05

❑ 163 Steve Grissom .20 .09
❑ 164 Ricky Craven .20 .09
❑ 165 David Green .20 .09
❑ 166 Chuck Bown .20 .09
❑ 167 Joe Nemechek .20 .09
❑ 168 Ward Burton .20 .09
❑ 169 Bobby Dotter .20 .09
❑ 170 Robert Pressley .20 .09
❑ 171 Hermie Sadler .20 .09
❑ 172 Mike Wallace .20 .09
❑ 173 Tracy Leslie .20 .09
❑ 174 Tom Peck .20 .09
❑ 175 Jeff Burton .20 .09
❑ 176 Rodney Combs .20 .09
❑ 177 Talladega Speedway .10 .05
Memorable Moments
❑ 178 Tommy Houston .20 .09
❑ 179 Joe Bessey .20 .09
❑ 180 Tim Fedewa .20 .09
❑ 181 Jack Sprague .20 .09
❑ 182 Richard Lasater .10 .05
❑ 183 Roy Payne .20 .09
❑ 184 Shawna Robinson .20 .09
❑ 185 Larry Pearson .20 .09
❑ 186 Jim Bown .20 .09
❑ 187 Nathan Buttke .10 .05
❑ 188 Butch Miller .20 .09
❑ 189 Jason Keller .20 .09
❑ 190 Randy LaJoie .20 .09
❑ 191 Dave Rezendes .20 .09
❑ 192 Jeff Green .20 .09
❑ 193 Ed Berrier .10 .05
❑ 194 Troy Beebe .10 .05
❑ 195 Dennis Setzer .20 .09
❑ 196 David Bonnett .20 .09
❑ 197 Steve Grissom .10 .05
BGN Champion
❑ 198 Hermie Sadler .10 .05
BGN Rookie of the Year
❑ 199 Rusty Wallace w/Crew .50 .23
❑ 200 Steve Hmiel .10 .05
Crew Chief of the Year
❑ 201 Jeff Gordon 1.00 .45
WC Rookie of the Year
❑ 202 Bill Elliott .50 .23
Fan's Favorite Driver
❑ 203 Davey Allison .40 .18
IROC Champion
❑ 204 Jimmy Horton Crash .10 .05
Memorable Moment
❑ 205 Dale Jarrett's Car .40 .18
Kyle Petty's Car
Memorable Moment
❑ 206 Rusty Wallace's Car .50 .23
Memorable Moments
❑ 207 Dale Jarrett .40 .18
Joe Gibbs
Year in Review
❑ 208 Rusty Wallace .50 .23
Year in Review
❑ 209 Davey Allison .40 .18
Year in Review
❑ 210 Morgan Shepherd w/Crew .10 .05
Year in Review
❑ 211 Dale Earnhardt 1.00 .45
Year in Review
❑ 212 Rusty Wallace .50 .23
Year in Review
❑ 213 Rusty Wallace w/Crew .50 .23
Year in Review
❑ 214 Rusty Wallace .50 .23
Year in Review
❑ 215 Ernie Irvan .20 .09
Year in Review
❑ 216 Geoff Bodine w/Crew .10 .05
Year in Review
❑ 217 Sterling Marlin .20 .09
Year in Review
❑ 218 Dale Earnhardt 1.00 .45
Year in Review
❑ 219 Dale Earnhardt 1.00 .45
Year in Review
❑ 220 Kyle Petty .20 .09
Year in Review
❑ 221 Ricky Rudd .20 .09
Year in Review
❑ 222 Dale Earnhardt 1.00 .45
Year in Review
❑ 223 Rusty Wallace .50 .23
Year in Review
❑ 224 Dale Earnhardt 1.00 .45
Year in Review
❑ 225 Dale Earnhardt 1.00 .45
Year in Review
❑ 226 Mark Martin .50 .23
Year in Review
❑ 227 Mark Martin .50 .23
Year in Review

❑ 228 Mark Martin .50 .23
Year in Review
❑ 229 Mark Martin .50 .23
Year in Review
❑ 230 Rusty Wallace w/Crew .50 .23
Year in Review
❑ 231 Rusty Wallace w/Crew .50 .23
Year in Review
❑ 232 Ernie Irvan .40 .18
Robert Yates
Larry McReyonlds
Year in Review
❑ 233 Rusty Wallace .50 .23
Year in Review
❑ 234 Ernie Irvan .40 .18
Year in Review
❑ 235 Rusty Wallace .50 .23
Year in Review
❑ 236 Mark Martin .50 .23
Year in Review
❑ 237 Rusty Wallace .50 .23
Year in Review
❑ 238 Dale Earnhardt 1.00 .45
WC Champion
Year in Review
❑ 239 Checklist #1 .10 .05
❑ 240 Checklist #2 .10 .05
❑ 241 Bill Elliott 1.00 .45
❑ 242 Harry Gant .40 .18
❑ 243 Harry Gant's Car .20 .09
❑ 244 Sterling Marlin .40 .18
❑ 245 Sterling Marlin's Car .20 .09
❑ 246 Terry Labonte 1.00 .45
❑ 247 Terry Labonte's Car .50 .23
❑ 248 Morgan Shepherd .20 .09
❑ 249 Morgan Shepherd's Car .10 .05
❑ 250 Ernie Irvan .40 .18
❑ 251 Ernie Irvan's Car .20 .09
❑ 252 Dale Jarrett .75 .35
❑ 253 Dale Jarrett's Car .40 .18
❑ 254 Bobby Labonte .60 .25
❑ 255 Bobby Labonte's Car .40 .18
❑ 256 Ken Schrader .20 .09
❑ 257 Ken Schrader's Car .10 .05
❑ 258 Mark Martin 1.00 .45
❑ 259 Mark Martin's Car .50 .23
❑ 260 Michael Waltrip .20 .09
❑ 261 Michael Waltrip's Car .10 .05
❑ 262 Derrike Cope .20 .09
❑ 263 Hut Stricklin .20 .09
❑ 264 Sterling Marlin .40 .18
❑ 265 Chuck Bown .20 .09
❑ 266 Ted Musgrave .20 .09
❑ 267 Jimmy Spencer .20 .09
❑ 268 Wally Dallenbach Jr. .20 .09
❑ 269 Jeff Purvis .20 .09
❑ 270 Greg Sacks .20 .09
❑ 271 Rich Bickle .20 .09
❑ 272 Bobby Hamilton .20 .09
❑ 273 Dick Trickle's Car .10 .05
❑ 274 Hut Stricklin's Car .10 .05
❑ 275 Terry Labonte's Car .50 .23
❑ 276 Ted Musgrave's Car .10 .05
❑ 277 Greg Sacks' Car .10 .05
❑ 278 Jimmy Hensley's Car .10 .05
❑ 279 Derrike Cope's Car .10 .05
❑ 280 Bobby Hamilton's Car .10 .05
❑ 281 Ricky Rudd's Car .20 .09
❑ 282 Geoff Bodine's Car .10 .05
❑ 283 Kevin Hamlin .10 .05
❑ 284 Charley Pressley .10 .05
❑ 285 Jim Long .10 .05
❑ 286 Bill Ingle .10 .05
❑ 287 Peter Sospenzo .10 .05
❑ 288 Freddy Fryar .10 .05
❑ 289 Chris Hussey .10 .05
❑ 290 Mike Hillman .10 .05
❑ 291 Gordon Gibbs .10 .05
❑ 292 Ken Glen .10 .05
❑ 293 Tony Furr .10 .05
❑ 294 Pete Wright .10 .05
❑ 295 Travis Carter .10 .05
❑ 296 Gary Bechtel .10 .05
Carolyn Bechtel
❑ 297 A.G. Dillard .20 .09
❑ 298 Kenny Wallace .20 .09
❑ 299 Elton Sawyer .20 .09
❑ 300 Rodney Combs .20 .09
❑ 301 Phil Parsons .20 .09
❑ 302 Kevin Lepage .20 .09
❑ 303 Johnny Benson, Jr. .20 .09
❑ 304 Mike McLaughlin .20 .09
❑ 305 Patty Moise .20 .09
❑ 306 Larry Pearson .20 .09
❑ 307 Robert Pressley .20 .09
❑ 308 Clyde McLeod .10 .05
❑ 309 Ricky Pearson .10 .05
❑ 310 Gil Martin .10 .05

❑ 311 Fil Martocci	.10	.05
❑ 312 Frank Cicci Scott Welliver John Gittler	.10	.05
❑ 313 John Andretti's Car Memorable Moment	.10	.05
❑ 314 Shawna Robinson's Car Memorable Moment	.10	.05
❑ 315 Mike Skinner's Car MM	.10	.05
❑ 316 Loy Allen Jr. Memorable Moment	.10	.05
❑ 317 Bob Jenkins	.10	.05
❑ 318 Buddy Baker	.10	.05
❑ 319 Checklist Card 1	.10	.05
❑ 320 Checklist Card 2	.10	.05
❑ 321 Joe Nemechek Winston Select	.10	.05
❑ 322 Rusty Wallace Winston Select Pole	.50	.23
❑ 323 Winston Select Action	.10	.05
❑ 324 Winston Select Action	.10	.05
❑ 325 Winston Select Action	.10	.05
❑ 326 Ken Schrader's Car Winston Select	.10	.05
❑ 327 Jeff Gordon's Car Winston Select	1.00	.45
❑ 328 Jeff Gordon Winston Select	1.00	.45
❑ 329 Winston Select Action	.10	.05
❑ 330 Winston Select Action	.10	.05
❑ 331 Winston Select Action	.10	.05
❑ 332 Geoff Bodine Crash Winston Select	.10	.05
❑ 333 Winston Select Action	.10	.05
❑ 334 Ernie Irvan's Car Dale Earnhardt's Car Ward Burton's Car Winston Select	.20	.09
❑ 335 Jeff Gordon's Car Rusty Wallace's Car Dale Earnhardt's Car Winston Select	1.00	.45
❑ 336 Geoff Bodine's Car Ernie Irvan's Car Winston Select	.10	.05
❑ 337 Winston Select Action	.10	.05
❑ 338 Geoff Bodine's Car Winston Select	.10	.05
❑ 339 Geoff Bodine Winston Select	.10	.05
❑ 340 Geoff Bodine Winston Select	.10	.05

1994 Maxx Autographs

Maxx packaged the 37 Autographs cards throughout the print run of 1994 series two and Medallion products. Although a few older Maxx issues were included, most of the cards signed were from series one 1994 Maxx and the Rookie Class of '94 insert sets. Wrapper stated odds for pulling an autographed card from series two was 1:200 packs. To pull a signed card from Maxx Medallion collectors faced wrapper stated odds of 1:18 packs. Each signed card was crimped with Maxx's corporate seal which reads "J.R. Maxx Inc. Corporate Seal 1988 North Carolina."

	MINT	NRMT
COMPLETE SET (16)	1000.00	450.00
COMMON CARD	10.00	4.50
COMMON DRIVER	20.00	9.00

❑ 1 Rick Mast	20.00	9.00
❑ 2 Steve Grissom Rookie Class	20.00	9.00
❑ 3 Joe Nemechek Rookie Class	20.00	9.00
❑ 4 John Andretti Rookie Class	20.00	9.00
❑ 5 Ricky Rudd	40.00	18.00
❑ 6 Mark Martin	75.00	34.00
❑ 7 Loy Allen Jr. Rookie Class	20.00	9.00
❑ 8 Jeremy Mayfield Rookie Class	50.00	22.00
❑ 9 Loy Allen Jr. Rookie Class	20.00	9.00
❑ 9 Bill Elliott '91 Maxx	100.00	45.00
❑ 11 Bill Elliott '92 Maxx Red	75.00	34.00
❑ 14 Terry Labonte	75.00	34.00
❑ 18 Dale Jarrett	60.00	27.00
❑ 20 Buddy Baker '92 Maxx Black	20.00	9.00
❑ 20 Buddy Baker '92 Maxx Red	20.00	9.00
❑ 22 Bobby Labonte	50.00	22.00
❑ 24 Jeff Gordon	250.00	110.00
❑ 25 Ken Schrader	20.00	9.00
❑ 33 Harry Gant	30.00	13.50
❑ 37 Loy Allen Jr.	20.00	9.00
❑ 42 Kyle Petty	40.00	18.00
❑ 47 Phil Parsons	20.00	9.00
❑ 63 Rich Bickle	20.00	9.00
❑ 94 Glen Wood	10.00	4.50
❑ 95 Len Wood	10.00	4.50
❑ 96 Eddie Wood	10.00	4.50
❑ 154 Larry McReynolds	10.00	4.50
❑ 163 Steve Grissom	20.00	9.00
❑ 167 Joe Nemechek	20.00	9.00
❑ 168 Ward Burton	20.00	9.00
❑ 172 Mike Wallace	20.00	9.00
❑ 175 Jeff Burton	40.00	18.00
❑ 184 Shawna Robinson	20.00	9.00
❑ 227 Mark Martin	75.00	34.00
❑ 298 Kenny Wallace	20.00	9.00
❑ 307 Robert Pressley	20.00	9.00
❑ 318 Buddy Baker	20.00	9.00

1994 Maxx Rookie Class of '94

Maxx produced this set featuring the nine candidates for the 1994 Winston Cup Rookie of the Year award. The cards were distributed in 1994 Maxx series two packs at the stated odds of 1:12.

	MINT	NRMT
COMPLETE SET (10)	20.00	9.00
COMMON CARD (1-10)	2.00	.90

❑ 1 Jeff Burton	4.00	1.80
❑ 2 Steve Grissom	4.00	1.80
❑ 3 Joe Nemechek	4.00	1.80
❑ 4 John Andretti	4.00	1.80
❑ 5 Ward Burton	4.00	1.80
❑ 6 Mike Wallace	2.00	.90
❑ 7 Loy Allen Jr.	2.00	.90
❑ 8 Jeremy Mayfield	8.00	3.60
❑ 9 Billy Standridge	2.00	.90
❑ 10 Checklist	2.00	.90

1994 Maxx Rookies of the Year

Maxx produced this set featuring various Winston Cup Rookies of the Year awarded between 1966 and 1993. The cards were distributed in 1994 Maxx series one packs at the wrapper stated odds of 1:12 packs.

	MINT	NRMT
COMPLETE SET (16)	25.00	11.00
COMMON CARD (1-16)	1.00	.45

*SINGLES: 2X TO 5X BASE CARD HI

❑ 1 James Hylton	1.00	.45
❑ 2 Ricky Rudd	2.00	.90
❑ 3 Dale Earnhardt	12.00	5.50
❑ 4 Geoff Bodine	1.00	.45
❑ 5 Sterling Marlin	2.00	.90
❑ 6 Rusty Wallace	2.00	.90
❑ 7 Ken Schrader	1.00	.45
❑ 8 Alan Kulwicki	2.00	.90
❑ 9 Davey Allison	2.00	
❑ 10 Ken Bouchard	1.00	
❑ 11 Dick Trickle	1.00	
❑ 12 Bobby Hamilton	1.00	
❑ 13 Jimmy Hensley	1.00	
❑ 14 Kenny Wallace	1.00	
❑ 15 Bobby Labonte	2.00	
❑ 16 Jeff Gordon	12.00	

1994 Maxx Medallion

Maxx released the Medallion set in late 1994. The fi cards in the set were printed on typical cardboard while the last 20 cards were produced on a clear p stock. Packs contained eight total cards; seven re issue cards and one clear card. Boxes contained 18 p Maxx also included randomly packed (approxim 1:360) certificates for the 1988 Dale Earnhardt (#99) that had been previously unreleased. Each carried a gold sticker on the front to show which nu of 999 the card was and to differentiate it from the released in 1988. Also randomly inserted in pac Medallion were autographed cards. Pricing for cards can be found under the 1994 Maxx Auto listing.

	MINT
COMPLETE SET (75)	25.00
COMPLETE REG.SET (55)	8.00
COMPLETE CLEAR SET (20)	20.00
COMMON CARD (1-55)	.15
COMMON CARD (56-75)	.75
COMMON DRIVER (1-55)	.30
COMMON DRIVER (56-75)	1.50

❑ 1 Jeff Gordon's Car	1.25
❑ 2 Brett Bodine's Car	.15
❑ 3 Bill Elliott	1.25
❑ 4 Rusty Wallace	1.25
❑ 5 Darrell Waltrip	.60
❑ 6 Ken Schrader	.30
❑ 7 Michael Waltrip's Car	.15
❑ 8 Todd Bodine's Car	.15
❑ 9 Morgan Shepherd	.30
❑ 10 Ricky Rudd	.60
❑ 11 Terry Labonte	1.25
❑ 12 Ted Musgrave's Car	.15
❑ 13 Sterling Marlin's Car	.30
❑ 14 Lake Speed	.30
❑ 15 Bobby Labonte	.75
❑ 16 Ernie Irvan's Car	.30
❑ 17 Greg Sacks' Car	.15
❑ 18 Jeff Burton	.60
❑ 19 Joe Nemechek's Car	.15
❑ 20 Bobby Hillin's Car	.15
❑ 21 Rick Mast's Car	.15
❑ 22 Wally Dallenbach Jr.'s Car	.15
❑ 23 Bobby Hamilton	.30
❑ 24 Kyle Petty	.60
❑ 25 Jeremy Mayfield's Car	.60
❑ 26 Derrike Cope's Car	.15
❑ 27 John Andretti's Car	.15
❑ 28 Rich Bickle's Car	.15
❑ 29 A.J. Foyt's Car	.30
❑ 30 Ward Burton	.30
❑ 31 Jimmy Hensley's Car	.15
❑ 32 Jeff Purvis	.30
❑ 33 Mark Martin	1.25
❑ 34 Hut Stricklin's Car	.15
❑ 35 Harry Gant	.60
❑ 36 Geoff Bodine's Car	.15
❑ 37 Dale Jarrett	1.00
❑ 38 Dave Marcis' Car	.30
❑ 39 Mike Chase	.30
❑ 40 Jimmy Spencer's Car	.15
❑ 41 NASCAR Arrives In	.15
❑ 42 A Warm Welcome	.15
❑ 43 Birthday Wishes	.15
❑ 44 Gentlemen Start Your Engines	.15
❑ 45 In Formation	.15
❑ 46 Jeff Gordon's Car Dale Earnhardt's Car A Page In History	1.25

'he Youngest Leader	.50	.23
with Jeff Gordon's Car		
Coming Off Turn One	.60	.25
with Jeff Gordon's Car		
Jeff Gordon's Car	1.00	.45
Geoff Bodine's Car		
Swapping the Lead		
Jeff Gordon's Car	1.00	.45
Just Racin'		
Dave Marcis' Car	.30	.14
Mike Chase's Car		
Hitting The Wall		
Jeff Gordon's Car	1.00	.45
Ernie Irvan's Car		
Going For The Win		
Jeff Gordon	2.50	1.10
New Kid in Town		
NASCAR World	.15	.07
Checklist Card	.15	.07
Jeff Gordon	8.00	3.60
Bobby Labonte	.75	.35
Jeff Burton's Car	1.50	.70
Wally Dallenbach Jr.'s Car	.75	.35
Brett Bodine	1.50	.70
Ernie Irvan	3.00	1.35
Morgan Shepherd	1.50	.70
Jimmy Spencer's Car	.75	.35
Bill Elliott	4.00	1.80
Mike Wallace	1.50	.70
Ricky Rudd	3.00	1.35
Ernie Irvan's Car	1.50	.70
A.J. Foyt	3.00	1.35
Rusty Wallace	4.00	1.80
Mark Martin	4.00	1.80
Ted Musgrave	1.50	.70
Ricky Rudd's Car	1.50	.70
Kyle Petty	3.00	1.35
Harry Gant	3.00	1.35
Geoff Bodine's Car	.75	.35
P Dale Earnhardt 1988 Maxx	400.00	180.00

1994 Maxx Motorsport

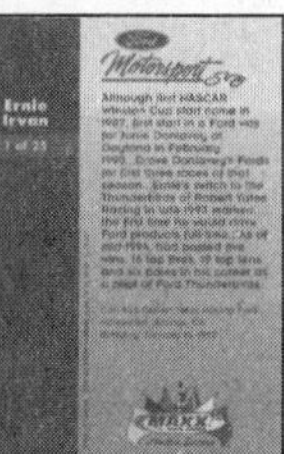

5-card set was produced by Maxx and distributed rd Motorsport and Club Maxx. This year's set s top Ford drivers on oversized (approximately 3- y 5") cards utilizing the metallic printing process only found with Maxx Premier Plus. Reportedly, sets were produced.

	MINT	NRMT
LETE SET (25)	12.00	5.50
ON CARD (1-24)	.40	.18
ie Irvan	.75	.35
sty Wallace	1.25	.55
ark Martin	1.25	.55
l Elliott	1.25	.55
nmy Spencer	.40	.18
d Musgrave	.40	.18
off Bodine	.40	.18
ett Bodine	.40	.18
dd Bodine	.40	.18
eff Burton	.40	.18
ick Mast	.40	.18
ake Speed	.40	.18
organ Shepherd	.40	.18
icky Rudd	.60	.25
errike Cope	.40	.18
ut Stricklin	.40	.18
oy Allen Jr.	.40	.18
ike Wallace	.40	.18
reg Sacks	.40	.18
mmy Hensley	.40	.18
ich Bickle	.40	.18
obby Hillin	.40	.18
eremy Mayfield	.40	.18
andy LaJoie	.40	.18
hecklist	.20	.09

1994 Maxx Premier Plus

produced the Premier Plus set for the second year

in 1994. The cards were produced using a metallic chromium printing process now standard with Premier Plus. The cards closely resemble those found in series one 1994 Maxx, except for the special printing features and card numbering. An Alan Kulwicki set was produced and randomly inserted in packs. Cards could be found in eight-card packs, 36-pack boxes and complete factory sets which also included six Alan Kulwicki insert cards per set.

	MINT	NRMT
COMPLETE SET (200)	20.00	9.00
COMPLETE FACT.SET (206)	25.00	11.00
COMMON CARD (1-200)	.15	.07
COMMON DRIVER (1-200)	.30	.14
❑ 1 Rick Mast	.30	.14
❑ 2 Rusty Wallace	1.50	.70
❑ 3 Dale Earnhardt	3.00	1.35
❑ 4 Jimmy Hensley	.30	.14
❑ 5 Ricky Rudd	.60	.25
❑ 6 Mark Martin	1.50	.70
❑ 7 Alan Kulwicki	1.25	.55
❑ 8 Sterling Marlin	.60	.25
❑ 9 Bill Elliott	.75	.35
Fan's Favorite Driver		
❑ 10 Geoff Bodine	.30	.14
❑ 11 Bill Elliott	1.50	.70
❑ 12 Jimmy Spencer	.30	.14
❑ 13 Jeff Gordon	1.50	.70
Memorable Moment		
❑ 14 Terry Labonte	1.50	.70
❑ 15 Lake Speed	.30	.14
❑ 16 Wally Dallenbach Jr.	.30	.14
❑ 17 Darrell Waltrip	.60	.25
❑ 18 Dale Jarrett	1.25	.55
❑ 19 Dale Jarrett's Car	.60	.25
Memorable Moment		
❑ 20 Bobby Hamilton	.30	.14
❑ 21 Morgan Shepherd	.30	.14
❑ 22 Bobby Labonte	1.00	.45
❑ 23 Dale Earnhardt's Car	1.50	.70
❑ 24 Jeff Gordon	3.00	1.35
❑ 25 Ken Schrader	.30	.14
❑ 26 Brett Bodine	.30	.14
❑ 27 Hut Stricklin	.30	.14
❑ 28 Davey Allison	1.50	.70
❑ 29 Ernie Irvan	.60	.25
❑ 30 Michael Waltrip	.30	.14
❑ 31 Davey Allison's Car	.60	.25
Memorable Moment		
❑ 32 Jimmy Horton	.30	.14
❑ 33 Harry Gant	.60	.25
❑ 34 Rusty Wallace's Car	.75	.35
❑ 35 Mark Martin's Car	.75	.35
❑ 36 Dale Jarrett's Car	.60	.25
❑ 37 Travis Carter	.15	.07
❑ 38 Hut Stricklin's Car	.15	.07
❑ 39 Kyle Petty's Car	.30	.14
❑ 40 Kenny Wallace	.30	.14
❑ 41 Dick Trickle	.30	.14
❑ 42 Kyle Petty	.60	.25
❑ 43 Richard Petty	.75	.35
❑ 44 Rick Wilson	.30	.14
❑ 45 Atlanta MM	.15	.07
❑ 46 Jeff Gordon	3.00	1.35
WC Rookie of the Year		
❑ 47 Phil Parsons	.30	.14
❑ 48 Ernie Irvan's Car	.30	.14
❑ 49 Alan Kulwicki's Transporter	.30	.14
Memorable Moment		
❑ 50 Morgan Shepherd's Car	.15	.07
❑ 51 Hermie Sadler	.30	.14
BGN Rookie of the Year		
❑ 52 Jimmy Means	.30	.14
❑ 53 Steve Hmiel	.15	.07
❑ 54 Bill Elliott's Car	.75	.35
❑ 55 Ted Musgrave	.30	.14
❑ 56 Ken Schrader's Car	.15	.07
❑ 57 Geoff Bodine's Car	.15	.07
Brett Bodine's Car		
Memorable Moment		
❑ 58 Davey Allison	1.50	.70
IROC Champion		
❑ 59 Ricky Rudd's Car	.30	.14
❑ 60 Harry Gant's Car	.30	.14
❑ 61 Steve Grissom	.15	.07
BGN Champion		
❑ 62 Dave Marcis' Car	.30	.14
❑ 63 New Hampshire	.15	.07
Memorable Moment		
❑ 64 Darrell Waltrip's Car	.30	.14
❑ 65 Jeff Gordon's Car	1.50	.70
❑ 66 Jeff Burton's Car	.30	.14
❑ 67 Geoff Bodine's Car	.15	.07
❑ 68 Greg Sacks	.30	.14
❑ 69 Talladega Speedway	.60	.25
Memorable Moment		
❑ 70 Michael Waltrip's Car	.15	.07
❑ 71 Dave Marcis	.60	.25
❑ 72 Jimmy Horton Crash	.15	.07
Memorable Moment		
❑ 73 Todd Bodine's Car	.15	.07
❑ 74 Bobby Labonte's Car	.60	.25
❑ 75 Todd Bodine	.30	.14
❑ 76 Brett Bodine's Car	.15	.07
❑ 77 Neil Bonnett	.75	.35
❑ 78 Rick Mast's Car	.15	.07
❑ 79 Dale Jarrett's Car	.60	.25
Kyle Petty's Car		
Memorable Moment		
❑ 80 Wally Dallenbach Jr.'s Car	.15	.07
❑ 81 Jimmy Spencer's Car	.15	.07
❑ 82 Bobby Hillin's Car	.15	.07
❑ 83 Lake Speed's Car	.15	.07
❑ 84 Richard Childress	.15	.07
❑ 85 Roger Penske	.15	.07
❑ 86 Don Miller	.15	.07
❑ 87 Jack Roush	.15	.07
❑ 88 Joe Gibbs	.30	.14
❑ 89 Felix Sabates	.15	.07
❑ 90 Bobby Hillin	.30	.14
❑ 91 Tim Morgan	.15	.07
❑ 92 Larry McClure	.15	.07
❑ 93 Teddy McClure	.15	.07
Jerry McClure		
Ed McClure		
❑ 94 Glen Wood	.15	.07
❑ 95 Len Wood	.15	.07
❑ 96 Eddie Wood	.15	.07
❑ 97 Junior Johnson	.30	.14
❑ 98 Derrike Cope	.30	.14
❑ 99 Rusty Wallace w/Crew	.75	.35
Pit Crew Champions		
❑ 100 Rick Hendrick	.15	.07
❑ 101 Leo Jackson	.15	.07
❑ 102 Bobby Allison	.30	.14
❑ 103 Bob Bilby	.15	.07
❑ 104 Bill Stavola	.15	.07
❑ 105 Mickey Stavola	.15	.07
❑ 106 Walter Bud Moore	.15	.07
❑ 107 Chuck Rider	.15	.07
❑ 108 Billy Hagan	.15	.07
❑ 109 Bill Davis	.15	.07
❑ 110 Kenny Bernstein	.30	.14
❑ 111 Richard Jackson	.15	.07
❑ 112 Ray DeWitt	.15	.07
Diane DeWitt		
❑ 113 D.K. Ulrich	.15	.07
❑ 114 Cale Yarborough	.30	.14
❑ 115 Junie Donlavey	.15	.07
❑ 116 Larry Hedrick	.15	.07
❑ 117 Robert Yates	.15	.07
❑ 118 Rusty Wallace's Car	.75	.35
Memorable Moment		
❑ 119 Andy Petree	.15	.07
❑ 120 Buddy Parrott	.15	.07
❑ 121 Steve Hmiel	.15	.07
❑ 122 Howard Comstock	.15	.07
❑ 123 Jimmy Makar	.15	.07
❑ 124 Robin Pemberton	.15	.07
❑ 125 Jeff Hammond	.15	.07
❑ 126 Tony Glover	.15	.07
❑ 127 Leonard Wood	.15	.07
❑ 128 Mike Beam	.15	.07
❑ 129 Mike Hill	.15	.07
❑ 130 Gary DeHart	.15	.07
❑ 131 Ray Evernham	.60	.25
❑ 132 Ken Howes	.15	.07
❑ 133 Jimmy Fennig	.15	.07
❑ 134 Barry Dodson	.15	.07
❑ 135 Ken Wilson	.15	.07
❑ 136 Donnie Wingo	.15	.07
❑ 137 Doug Hewitt	.15	.07
❑ 138 Pete Wright	.15	.07
❑ 139 Tim Brewer	.15	.07
❑ 140 Donnie Richeson	.15	.07
❑ 141 Sandy Jones	.15	.07
❑ 142 Bob Johnson	.15	.07
❑ 143 Doug Williams	.15	.07
❑ 144 Waddell Wilson	.15	.07
❑ 145 Doug Richert	.15	.07

❑ 146 Larry McReynolds	.15	.07
❑ 147 Paul Andrews	.15	.07
❑ 148 Robbie Loomis	.30	.14
❑ 149 Dale Inman	.15	.07
❑ 150 Steve Grissom	.30	.14
❑ 151 Ricky Craven	.30	.14
❑ 152 David Green	.30	.14
❑ 153 Chuck Bown	.30	.14
❑ 154 Joe Nemechek	.30	.14
❑ 155 Ward Burton	.30	.14
❑ 156 Bobby Dotter	.30	.14
❑ 157 Robert Pressley	.30	.14
❑ 158 Hermie Sadler	.30	.14
❑ 159 Tracy Leslie	.30	.14
❑ 160 Mike Wallace	.30	.14
❑ 161 Tom Peck	.30	.14
❑ 162 Jeff Burton	.60	.25
❑ 163 Rodney Combs	.30	.14
❑ 164 Tommy Houston	.30	.14
❑ 165 Dale Earnhardt w/Crew	1.50	.70
WC Champion		
❑ 166 Dale Jarrett	.60	.25
Year in Review		
❑ 167 Rusty Wallace	.75	.35
Year in Review		
❑ 168 Davey Allison	.75	.35
Year in Review		
❑ 169 Morgan Shepherd w/Crew	.15	.07
Year in Review		
❑ 170 Dale Earnhardt	1.50	.70
Year in Review		
❑ 171 Rusty Wallace	.75	.35
Year in Review		
❑ 172 Rusty Wallace w/Crew	.75	.35
Year in Review		
❑ 173 Rusty Wallace	.75	.35
Year in Review		
❑ 174 Ernie Irvan	.30	.14
Year in Review		
❑ 175 Geoff Bodine w/Crew	.15	.07
Year in Review		
❑ 176 Sterling Marlin	.30	.14
Year in Review		
❑ 177 Dale Earnhardt	1.50	.70
Year in Review		
❑ 178 Dale Earnhardt w/Crew	1.50	.70
Year in Review		
❑ 179 Kyle Petty	.30	.14
Year in Review		
❑ 180 Ricky Rudd	.30	.14
Year in Review		
❑ 181 Dale Earnhardt w/Crew	1.50	.70
Year in Review		
❑ 182 Rusty Wallace w/Crew	.75	.35
Year in Review		
❑ 183 Dale Earnhardt	1.50	.70
Richard Childress		
Year in Review		
❑ 184 Dale Earnhardt	1.50	.70
Year in Review		
❑ 185 Mark Martin	.75	.35
Year in Review		
❑ 186 Mark Martin	.75	.35
Year in Review		
❑ 187 Mark Martin	.75	.35
Year in Review		
❑ 188 Mark Martin w/Crew	.75	.35
Year in Review		
❑ 189 Rusty Wallace	.75	.35
Year in Review		
❑ 190 Rusty Wallace w/Crew	.75	.35
Year in Review		
❑ 191 Ernie Irvan	.60	.25
Robert Yates		
Larry McReynolds		
Year in Review		
❑ 192 Rusty Wallace	.75	.35
Year in Review		
❑ 193 Ernie Irvan	.60	.25
Year in Review		
❑ 194 Rusty Wallace	.75	.35
Year in Review		
❑ 195 Mark Martin	.75	.35
Jack Roush		
Year in Review		
❑ 196 Rusty Wallace	.75	.35
Year in Review		
❑ 197 Checklist	.15	.07
❑ 198 Checklist	.15	.07
❑ 199 Checklist	.15	.07
❑ 200 Checklist	.15	.07

1994 Maxx Premier Plus Alan Kulwicki

Maxx produced these fourteen cards honoring the late Alan Kulwicki to be random inserts in 1994 Premier Plus. Wrapper stated odds for pulling a card was 1:15 packs. Six cards could also be randomly found in each Premier Plus factory set.

	MINT	NRMT
COMPLETE SET (14)	20.00	9.00
COMMON CARD (1-14)	2.00	.90

1994 Maxx Premier Series

Maxx again offered a special Premier Series set to its Club Maxx members. The 1994 issue included 300 regular cards all featuring new photography and different card design. Eight cards that constitute the first series of the 1994 Maxx Jumbo issue were also included with each complete set.

	MINT	NRMT
COMPLETE SET (300)	30.00	13.50
COMPLETE FACT.SET (308)	40.00	18.00
COMMON CARD (1-300)	.15	.07
COMMON DRIVER (1-300)	.30	.14

❑ 1 Rick Mast	.30	.14
❑ 2 Rusty Wallace	.75	.35
❑ 3 Dale Earnhardt	.75	.35
❑ 4 Jimmy Hensley	.30	.14
❑ 5 Ricky Rudd	.50	.23
❑ 6 Mark Martin	.75	.35
❑ 7 Alan Kulwicki	.75	.35
❑ 8 Sterling Marlin	.50	.23
❑ 9 P.J. Jones	.30	.14
❑ 10 Geoff Bodine	.30	.14
❑ 11 Bill Elliott	.75	.35
❑ 12 Jimmy Spencer	.30	.14
❑ 13 Jeff Gordon	.75	.35
Memorable Moment		
❑ 14 Terry Labonte	.75	.35
❑ 15 Lake Speed	.30	.14
❑ 16 Wally Dallenbach, Jr.	.30	.14
❑ 17 Darrell Waltrip	.50	.23
❑ 18 Dale Jarrett	.75	.35
❑ 19 Chad Little	.30	.14
❑ 20 Bobby Hamilton	.30	.14
❑ 21 Morgan Shepherd	.30	.14
❑ 22 Bobby Labonte	.50	.23
❑ 23 Dale Earnhardt's Car	.75	.35
❑ 24 Jeff Gordon	.75	.35
❑ 25 Ken Schrader	.30	.14
❑ 26 Brett Bodine	.30	.14
❑ 27 Hut Stricklin	.30	.14
❑ 28 Davey Allison	.75	.35
❑ 29 Ernie Irvan	.75	.35
❑ 30 Michael Waltrip	.30	.14
❑ 31 Neil Bonnett	.50	.23
❑ 32 Jimmy Horton	.30	.14
❑ 33 Harry Gant	.50	.23
❑ 34 Rusty Wallace's Car	.75	.35
❑ 35 Mark Martin's Car	.75	.35
❑ 36 Dale Jarrett's Car	.50	.23
❑ 37 Loy Allen Jr.	.30	.14
❑ 38 Dale Jarrett's Car	.50	.23
Memorable Moment		
❑ 39 Kyle Petty's Car	.30	.14
❑ 40 Kenny Wallace	.30	.14
❑ 41 Dick Trickle	.30	.14
❑ 42 Kyle Petty	.50	.23
❑ 43 Richard Petty	.75	.35
❑ 44 Rick Wilson	.30	.14

❑ 45 T.W. Taylor	.15
❑ 46 James Hylton	.30
❑ 47 Phil Parsons	.30
❑ 48 Ernie Irvan's Car	.50
❑ 49 Stanley Smith	.15
❑ 50 Morgan Shepherd's Car	.15
❑ 51 Joe Ruttman	.30
❑ 52 Jimmy Means	.30
❑ 53 Davey Allison's Car	.75
Memorable Moment	
❑ 54 Bill Elliott's Car	.75
❑ 55 Ted Musgrave	.30
❑ 56 Ken Schrader's Car	.15
❑ 57 Bob Schacht	.15
❑ 58 Jim Sauter	.15
❑ 59 Ricky Rudd's Car	.30
❑ 60 Harry Gant's Car	.30
❑ 61 Ken Bouchard	.30
❑ 62 Dave Marcis	.30
❑ 63 Rich Bickle	.30
❑ 64 Darrell Waltrip's Car	.30
❑ 65 Jeff Gordon's Car	.75
❑ 66 Jeff Burton's Car	.15
❑ 67 Geoff Bodine's Car	.15
❑ 68 Greg Sacks	.30
❑ 69 Tom Kendall	.30
❑ 70 Michael Waltrip	.30
❑ 71 Dave Marcis	.30
❑ 72 John Andretti	.30
❑ 73 Todd Bodine's Car	.15
❑ 74 Bobby Labonte's Car	.30
❑ 75 Todd Bodine	.30
❑ 76 Brett Bodine's Car	.15
❑ 77 Jeff Purvis	.30
❑ 78 Rick Mast's Car	.15
❑ 79 Rick Carelli	.30
❑ 80 Wally Dallenbach Jr.'s Car	.15
❑ 81 Jimmy Spencer's Car	.15
❑ 82 Bobby Hillin's Car	.15
❑ 83 Lake Speed's Car	.15
❑ 84 Richard Childress	.15
❑ 85 Roger Penske	.15
❑ 86 Don Miller	.15
❑ 87 Jack Roush	.15
❑ 88 Joe Gibbs	.30
❑ 89 Felix Sabates	.15
❑ 90 Bobby Hillin	.30
❑ 91 Tim Morgan	.15
❑ 92 Larry McClure	.15
❑ 93 Teddy McClure	.15
Jerry McClure	
Ed McClure	
❑ 94 Glen Wood	.15
❑ 95 Len Wood	.15
❑ 96 Eddie Wood	.15
❑ 97 Junior Johnson	.30
❑ 98 Derrike Cope	.30
❑ 99 Andy Hillenburg	.30
❑ 100 Rick Hendrick	.15
❑ 101 Leo Jackson	.15
❑ 102 Bobby Allison	.30
❑ 103 Bob Bilby	.15
❑ 104 Bill Stavola	.15
❑ 105 Mickey Stavola	.15
❑ 106 Walter Bud Moore	.15
❑ 107 Chuck Rider	.15
❑ 108 Billy Hagan	.15
❑ 109 Bill Davis	.15
❑ 110 Kenny Bernstein	.30
❑ 111 Richard Jackson	.15
❑ 112 Ray DeWitt	.15
Diane DeWitt	
❑ 113 D.K. Ulrich	.15
❑ 114 Cale Yarborough	.30
❑ 115 Junie Donlavey	.15
❑ 116 Larry Hedrick	.15
❑ 117 Robert Yates	.15
❑ 118 George Bradshaw	.15
❑ 119 Mark Smith	.15
❑ 120 David Fuge	.15
❑ 121 Harry Melling	.15
❑ 122 Atlanta MM	.15
❑ 123 Dick Moroso	.15
❑ 124 Butch Mock	.15
❑ 125 Alan Kulwicki's Transporter	.30
Memorable Moment	
❑ 126 Andy Petree	.15
❑ 127 Buddy Parrott	.15
❑ 128 Steve Hmiel	.15
❑ 129 Howard Comstock	.15
❑ 130 Jimmy Makar	.15
❑ 131 Robin Pemberton	.15
❑ 132 Jeff Hammond	.15
❑ 133 Tony Glover	.15
❑ 134 Leonard Wood	.15
❑ 135 Mike Beam	.15
❑ 136 Mike Hill	.15
❑ 137 Gary DeHart	.15

Ray Evernham	.15	.07
Ken Howes	.15	.07
Jimmy Fennig	.15	.07
Barry Dodson	.15	.07
Ken Wilson	.15	.07
Donnie Wingo	.15	.07
Doug Hewitt	.15	.07
Pete Wright	.15	.07
Tim Brewer	.15	.07
Donnie Richeson	.15	.07
Sandy Jones	.15	.07
Bob Johnson	.15	.07
Geoff Bodine's Car Brett Bodine's Car Memorable Moment	.15	.07
Doug Williams	.15	.07
Waddell Wilson	.15	.07
Doug Richert	.15	.07
Larry McReynolds	.15	.07
Dennis Connor	.15	.07
Harry Hyde	.15	.07
Paul Andrews	.15	.07
Robbie Loomis	.15	.07
Troy Selberg	.15	.07
Dale Inman	.15	.07
Tony Eury	.15	.07
Dave Fischlein	.15	.07
Steve Grissom	.30	.14
Ricky Craven	.50	.23
David Green	.30	.14
Chuck Bown	.30	.14
Joe Nemechek	.30	.14
Ward Burton	.30	.14
Bobby Dotter	.30	.14
Robert Pressley	.30	.14
Hermie Sadler	.30	.14
Mike Wallace	.30	.14
Tracy Leslie	.30	.14
Tom Peck	.30	.14
Jeff Burton	.30	.14
Rodney Combs	.30	.14
New Hampshire Memorable Moment	.15	.07
Tommy Houston	.30	.14
Joe Bessey	.30	.14
Tim Fedewa	.30	.14
Jack Sprague	.30	.14
Richard Lasater	.15	.07
Roy Payne	.30	.14
Shawna Robinson	.30	.14
Larry Pearson	.30	.14
Jim Bown	.30	.14
Nathan Buttke	.15	.07
Butch Miller	.30	.14
Jason Keller	.30	.14
Randy LaJoie	.30	.14
Dave Rezendes	.30	.14
Jeff Green	.30	.14
Ed Berrier	.15	.07
Troy Beebe	.15	.07
Dennis Setzer	.30	.14
David Bonnett	.30	.14
Barney Hall	.15	.07
Eli Gold	.15	.07
Ned Jarrett	.15	.07
Benny Parsons	.30	.14
Jack Arute	.15	.07
Jerry Punch	.15	.07
Talladega Speedway Memorable Moment	.15	.07
Mike Joy	.15	.07
Dick Brooks	.15	.07
Winston Kelley	.15	.07
Jim Phillips	.15	.07
John Kernan	.15	.07
Randy Pemberton	.15	.07
Ken Squier	.15	.07
Joe Moore	.15	.07
Chris Economaki	.15	.07
Allen Bestwick	.15	.07
Glenn Jarrett	.15	.07
Dick Berggren	.15	.07
Les Richter	.15	.07
Gary Nelson	.15	.07
Ray Hill	.15	.07
Carl Hill	.15	.07
Chuck Romeo	.15	.07
Jack Whittemore	.15	.07
Jimmy Cox	.15	.07
Bruce Roney	.15	.07
Marlin Wright	.15	.07
Mike Chaplin	.15	.07
Tim Earp	.15	.07
Doyle Ford	.15	.07
Buster Auton	.15	.07
Elmo Langley	.15	.07
Walt Green	.15	.07
Gary Miller	.15	.07

❑ 232 Morris Metcalfe	.15	.07
❑ 233 Rich Burgdoff	.15	.07
❑ 234 Jimmy Horton Crash Memorable Moment	.15	.07
❑ 235 Steve Hmiel All Pro	.15	.07
❑ 236 Troy Martin All Pro	.15	.07
❑ 237 Gary Brooks All Pro	.15	.07
❑ 238 Eddie Wood All Pro	.15	.07
❑ 239 Raymond Fox III All Pro	.15	.07
❑ 240 David Smith All Pro	.15	.07
❑ 241 Robert Yates All Pro	.15	.07
❑ 242 Todd Parrott All Pro	.15	.07
❑ 243 David Munari All Pro	.15	.07
❑ 244 James Lewter All Pro	.15	.07
❑ 245 Norman Koshimizu All Pro	.15	.07
❑ 246 Harold Stott All Pro	.15	.07
❑ 247 Will Lind All Pro	.15	.07
❑ 248 Norman Koshimizu All Pro	.15	.07
❑ 249 Danny Lawrence All Pro	.15	.07
❑ 250 Dan Ford All Pro	.15	.07
❑ 251 Barry Beggarly	.15	.07
❑ 252 Steve Boley Jerry Williams	.15	.07
❑ 253 Mel Walen Larry Phillips	.15	.07
❑ 254 Barry Beggarly Charlie Cragen	.15	.07
❑ 255 Robert Miller Tony Ponder	.15	.07
❑ 256 Steve Grissom BGN Champion	.15	.07
❑ 257 Hermie Sadler BGN Rookie of the Year	.30	.14
❑ 258 Rusty Wallace w/Crew Pit Crew Champions	.75	.35
❑ 259 Steve Hmiel Crew Chief of the Year	.15	.07
❑ 260 Jeff Gordon WC Rookie of the Year	.75	.35
❑ 261 Bill Elliott Fan's Favorite Driver	.75	.35
❑ 262 Davey Allison IROC Champion	.75	.35
❑ 263 Dale Jarrett's Car Kyle Petty's Car Memorable Moment	.30	.14
❑ 264 Morgan Shepherd's Car Memorable Moment	.15	.07
❑ 265 Rusty Wallace's Car Memorable Moment	1.00	.45
❑ 266 Dale Jarrett Year in Review	.50	.23
❑ 267 Rusty Wallace Year in Review	1.00	.45
❑ 268 Davey Allison w/Crew Year in Review	1.00	.45
❑ 269 Morgan Shepherd Year in Review	.15	.07
❑ 270 Dale Earnhardt Year in Review	2.50	1.10
❑ 271 Rusty Wallace Year in Review	1.00	.45
❑ 272 Rusty Wallace Year in Review	1.00	.45
❑ 273 Rusty Wallace Year in Review	1.00	.45
❑ 274 Ernie Irvan Year in Review	.75	.35
❑ 275 Geoff Bodine Year in Review	.15	.07
❑ 276 Sterling Marlin Year in Review	.30	.14
❑ 277 Dale Earnhardt Year in Review	2.50	1.10
❑ 278 Dale Earnhardt Year in Review	2.50	1.10
❑ 279 Kyle Petty Year in Review	.30	.14
❑ 280 Ricky Rudd Year in Review	.30	.14
❑ 281 Dale Earnhardt Year in Review	2.50	1.10

❑ 282 Rusty Wallace Year in Review	1.00	.45
❑ 283 Dale Earnhardt Year in Review	2.50	1.10
❑ 284 Dale Earnhardt Year in Review	2.50	1.10
❑ 285 Mark Martin Year in Review	1.00	.45
❑ 286 Mark Martin Year in Review	1.00	.45
❑ 287 Mark Martin Year in Review	1.00	.45
❑ 288 Mark Martin Year in Review	1.00	.45
❑ 289 Rusty Wallace Year in Review	1.00	.45
❑ 290 Rusty Wallace Year in Review	1.00	.45
❑ 291 Ernie Irvan Robert Yates Larry McReynolds Year in Review	.75	.35
❑ 292 Rusty Wallace Year in Review	1.00	.45
❑ 293 Ernie Irvan Year in Review	.75	.35
❑ 294 Rusty Wallace Year in Review	1.00	.45
❑ 295 Mark Martin Year in Review	1.00	.45
❑ 296 Rusty Wallace Year in Review	1.00	.45
❑ 297 Dale Earnhardt Year in Review WC Champion	4.00	1.80
❑ 298 Checklist #1	.15	.07
❑ 299 Checklist #2	.15	.07
❑ 300 Checklist #3	.15	.07

1994 Maxx Premier Series Jumbos

The Maxx Premier Series Jumbos were distributed in two series; the first eight cards with Maxx Premier Plus factory sets and the second four cards with the Premier Series binder sold through Club Maxx. The twelve cards are actually enlarged (3-1/2" by 5") copies of the corresponding driver's 1994 Premier Plus issue.

	MINT	NRMT
COMPLETE SET (12)	20.00	9.00
COMPLETE SERIES 1 (8)	10.00	4.50
COMPLETE SERIES 2 (4)	10.00	4.50
COMMON CARD (1-8)	1.00	.45
COMMON CARD (9-12)	2.00	.90
❑ 1 Bill Elliott	2.50	1.10
❑ 2 Ernie Irvan's Car	1.50	.70
❑ 3 Dale Jarrett's Car	1.00	.45
❑ 4 Mark Martin	2.50	1.10
❑ 5 Darrell Waltrip	1.50	.70
❑ 6 Richard Petty	1.50	.70
❑ 7 Alan Kulwicki	1.50	.70
❑ 8 Jeff Gordon	1.50	.70
❑ 9 Rusty Wallace's Car	2.50	1.10
❑ 10 Kyle Petty	2.00	.90
❑ 11 Davey Allison	1.50	.70
❑ 12 Harry Gant	2.50	1.10

1994 Maxx The Select 25

This 25-card chromium set was produced by Maxx and features the top drivers in the 1993 Winston Cup Points standings. These cards were made available in specially marked two packs of Winston Select cigarettes and through a mail-in offer which required 20 Winston Select wrappers and $14.95. This set was closed-out by the manufacturer when the cards set aside for the mail-in offer where not redeemed.

	MINT	NRMT
COMPLETE SET (25)	15.00	6.75
COMMON CARD (1-25)	.50	.23

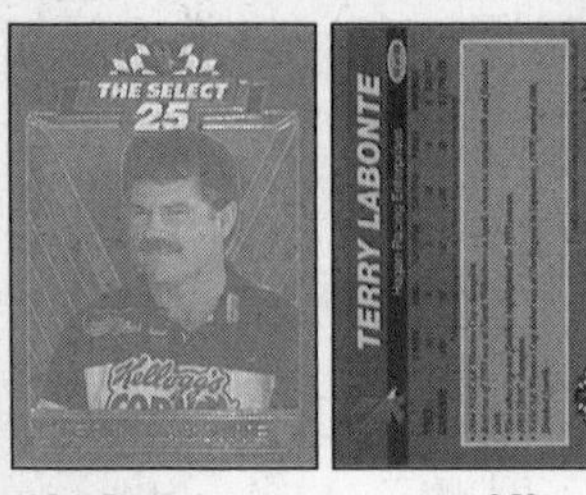

❑ 1 Dale Earnhardt	2.50	1.10
❑ 2 Rusty Wallace	1.25	.55
❑ 3 Mark Martin	1.25	.55
❑ 4 Dale Jarrett	1.00	.45
❑ 5 Kyle Petty	.75	.35
❑ 6 Ernie Irvan	.75	.35
❑ 7 Morgan Shepherd	.50	.23
❑ 8 Bill Elliott	1.25	.55
❑ 9 Ken Schrader	.50	.23
❑ 10 Ricky Rudd	.75	.35
❑ 11 Harry Gant	.75	.35
❑ 12 Jimmy Spencer	.50	.23
❑ 13 Darrell Waltrip	.75	.35
❑ 14 Jeff Gordon	2.50	1.10
❑ 15 Sterling Marlin	.75	.35
❑ 16 Geoff Bodine	.50	.23
❑ 17 Michael Waltrip	.50	.23
❑ 18 Terry Labonte	1.25	.55
❑ 19 Bobby Labonte	1.00	.45
❑ 20 Brett Bodine	.50	.23
❑ 21 Rick Mast	.50	.23
❑ 22 Wally Dallenbach Jr.	.50	.23
❑ 23 Kenny Wallace	.50	.23
❑ 24 Hut Stricklin	.50	.23
❑ 25 Ted Musgrave	.50	.23

1994 Maxx Texaco Ernie Irvan

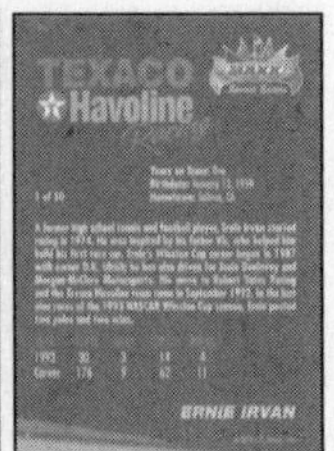

Maxx continued the line of Texaco cards in 1994, this year with new team driver Ernie Irvan. For the first time the cards were distributed through foil packs with eight cards per pack. Cards 20-24 were produced with gold foil layering.

	MINT	NRMT
COMPLETE SET (50)	6.00	2.70
COMMON CARD (1-50)	.10	.05
❑ 1 Ernie Irvan	.50	.23
❑ 2 Robert Yates	.10	.05
❑ 3 Larry McReynolds	.10	.05
❑ 4 Ernie Irvan's Car	.10	.05
❑ 5 Ernie Irvan's Car	.10	.05
❑ 6 Ernie Irvan	.50	.23
Larry McReynolds		
❑ 7 Ernie Irvan's Car	.10	.05
In the Driver's Seat		
❑ 8 On the Pole	.10	.05
Talladega race action		
❑ 9 Ernie Irvan in Pits	.10	.05
❑ 10 Ernie Irvan's Car	.10	.05
❑ 11 Ernie Irvan's Car	.10	.05
❑ 12 Ernie Irvan	.10	.05
A Career in Review		
❑ 13 Robert Yates	.10	.05
Follow the Leader		
❑ 14 Ernie Irvan's Car w/Crew	.10	.05
❑ 15 Ernie Irvan's Transporter	.10	.05
❑ 16 Ernie Irvan's Car	.10	.05
Robert Yates Racing Shop		
❑ 17 Ernie Irvan's Car	.10	.05
Robert Yates Racing Shop		
❑ 18 Ernie Irvan's Shop	.10	.05
Wave of the Future		
❑ 19 Ernie Irvan w/Car	.50	.23
❑ 20 Ernie Irvan	.50	.23
Robert Yates		
Larry McReynolds		
❑ 21 Ernie Irvan	.50	.23
❑ 22 Ernie Irvan w/Crew	.50	.23
❑ 23 Ernie Irvan	.50	.23
❑ 24 Ernie Irvan	.50	.23
❑ 25 Jeremy Anderson	.10	.05
❑ 26 Gary Beveridge	.10	.05
❑ 27 Mike Bumgarner	.10	.05
❑ 28 Gene Carrigan	.10	.05
❑ 29 Jeff Clark	.10	.05
❑ 30 Bret Conway	.10	.05
❑ 31 Steve Foster	.10	.05
❑ 32 Raymond Fox III	.10	.05
❑ 33 Libby Gant	.10	.05
❑ 34 Dennis Greene	.10	.05
❑ 35 Michael Hanson	.10	.05
❑ 36 Eric Horn	.10	.05
❑ 37 Vernon Hubbard	.10	.05
❑ 38 Gil Kerley	.10	.05
❑ 39 Joey Knuckles	.10	.05
❑ 40 Norman Koshimizu	.10	.05
❑ 41 Dave Kriska	.10	.05
❑ 42 Larry Lackey	.10	.05
❑ 43 James Lewter	.10	.05
❑ 44 Mike Long	.10	.05
❑ 45 Nick Ramey	.10	.05
❑ 46 Wade Thomas	.10	.05
❑ 47 Terry Throneburg	.10	.05
❑ 48 Doug Yates	.10	.05
❑ 49 Richard Yates	.10	.05
❑ 50 Checklist Card	.10	.05

1995 Maxx

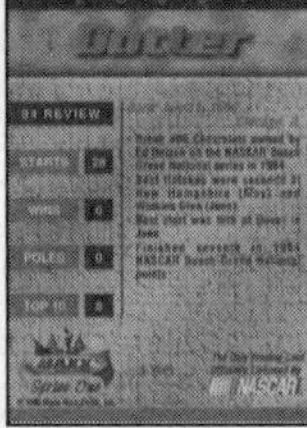

Two series were again produced for the 1995 Maxx base brand release. The cards were issued 10 per pack with 36-packs per foil box. Memorable Moments and Victory Lane subsets were included in series one. Several insert sets were distributed over the print run for each series as well. The first card of the Dale Earnhardt Chase the Champion series was included in Maxx one. The popular insert set was distributed by Maxx over the course of the year through five of its different product releases. Series two included a 10-card Bill Elliott Bat Chase insert set packaged approximately 2 cards every 36 packs. A promo card for each series was produced as well. All promo cards are priced in the promo card section of the book.

	MINT	NRMT
COMPLETE SET (270)	28.00	12.50
COMPLETE SERIES 1 (180)	18.00	8.00
COMPLETE SERIES 2 (90)	10.00	4.50
COMMON CARD (1-270)	.10	.05
COMMON DRIVER (1-270)	.20	.09
❑ 1 Rick Mast	.20	.09
❑ 2 Rusty Wallace	1.00	.45
❑ 3 Jeff Gordon's Car	1.00	.45
Memorable Moment		
❑ 4 Sterling Marlin	.40	.18
❑ 5 Terry Labonte	1.00	.45
❑ 6 Mark Martin	1.00	.45
❑ 7 Geoff Bodine	.20	.09
❑ 8 Jeff Burton	.40	.18
❑ 9 Sterling Marlin	.40	.18
Victory Lane		
❑ 10 Ricky Rudd	.40	.18
❑ 11 Bill Elliott	1.00	.45
❑ 12 Derrike Cope	.20	.09
❑ 13 Rusty Wallace	.50	.23
Victory Lane		
❑ 14 Technical Tidbit	.10	.05
❑ 15 Lake Speed	.20	.09
❑ 16 Ted Musgrave	.20	.09
❑ 17 Darrell Waltrip	.40	.18
❑ 18 Dale Jarrett	.75	.35
❑ 19 Loy Allen Jr.	.20	.09
❑ 20 Technical Tidbit	.10	.05
Roof Flaps		
❑ 21 Morgan Shepherd	.20	.09
❑ 22 Bobby Labonte	.75	.35
❑ 23 Hut Stricklin	.20	.09
❑ 24 Jeff Gordon	2.00	.90
❑ 25 Ken Schrader	.20	.09
❑ 26 Brett Bodine	.20	.09
❑ 27 Jimmy Spencer	.20	
❑ 28 Ernie Irvan	.40	
❑ 29 Steve Grissom	.20	
❑ 30 Michael Waltrip	.20	
❑ 31 Ward Burton	.20	
❑ 32 Dick Trickle	.20	
❑ 33 Harry Gant	.40	
❑ 34 Ernie Irvan's Car	.20	
Jimmy Spencer's Car		
Memorable Moment		
❑ 35 Richard Childress	.10	
❑ 36 Walter Bud Moore	.10	
❑ 37 Felix Sabates	.10	
❑ 38 Ernie Irvan	.40	
Victory Lane		
❑ 39 Kenny Wallace	.20	
❑ 40 Bobby Hamilton	.20	
❑ 41 Joe Nemechek	.20	
❑ 42 Kyle Petty	.40	
❑ 43 Richard Petty	.50	
❑ 44 John Andretti	.20	
❑ 45 Wally Dallenbach Jr.	.20	
❑ 46 Ernie Irvan	.40	
Victory Lane		
❑ 47 Steve Kinser	.20	
❑ 48 Darlington	.10	
Victory Lane		
❑ 49 Robert Yates	.10	
❑ 50 Roger Penske	.10	
❑ 51 Rusty Wallace's Car	.50	
Victory Lane		
❑ 52 Glen Wood	.10	
❑ 53 Len Wood	.10	
❑ 54 Eddie Wood	.10	
❑ 55 Jimmy Hensley	.20	
❑ 56 Don Miller	.10	
❑ 57 Tim Morgan	.10	
❑ 58 Terry Labonte	.50	
Victory Lane		
❑ 59 Larry McClure	.10	
❑ 60 Rusty Wallace	.50	
Victory Lane		
❑ 61 Jack Roush	.10	
❑ 62 Rick Hendrick	.10	
❑ 63 Talladega Speedway	.10	
Victory Lane		
❑ 64 Kenny Bernstein	.20	
❑ 65 Butch Mock	.10	
❑ 66 Chuck Rider	.10	
❑ 67 Cale Yarborough	.20	
❑ 68 Ernie Irvan	.40	
Victory Lane		
❑ 69 Teddy McClure	.10	
❑ 70 Joe Gibbs	.20	
❑ 71 Dave Marcis	.20	
❑ 72 Jeff Gordon	1.00	
Victory Lane		
❑ 73 Geoff Bodine	.20	
Victory Lane		
❑ 74 Richard Jackson	.10	
❑ 75 Todd Bodine	.20	
❑ 76 Junior Johnson	.20	
❑ 77 Greg Sacks	.20	
❑ 78 Bill Davis	.10	
❑ 79 D.K. Ulrich	.10	
❑ 80 Jeff Gordon	1.00	
Victory Lane		
❑ 81 Travis Carter	.10	
❑ 82 Bill Stavola	.10	
❑ 83 Rusty Wallace	.50	
Victory Lane		
❑ 84 Mickey Stavola	.10	
❑ 85 Leo Jackson	.10	
❑ 86 Larry Hedrick	.10	
❑ 87 Rusty Wallace	.50	
Victory Lane		
❑ 88 Gary Bechtel	.10	
Carolyn Bechtel		
❑ 89 Rusty Wallace	.50	
Victory Lane		
❑ 90 Mike Wallace	.20	
❑ 91 Bobby Allison	.20	
❑ 92 Jimmy Spencer	.20	
Victory Lane		
❑ 93 Junie Donlavey	.10	
❑ 94 A.G. Dillard	.10	
❑ 95 Ricky Rudd	.20	
Victory Lane		
❑ 96 Andy Petree	.10	
❑ 97 Larry McReynolds	.10	
❑ 98 Jeremy Mayfield	.60	
❑ 99 Geoff Bodine	.20	
Victory Lane		
❑ 100 Buddy Parrott	.10	
❑ 101 Steve Hmiel	.10	
❑ 102 Jimmy Spencer	.20	
Victory Lane		
❑ 103 Ken Howes	.10	

	MINT	NRMT
Leonard Wood	.10	.05
Jeff Gordon	1.00	.45
Victory Lane		
Bill Ingle	.10	.05
Jimmy Fennig	.10	.05
Doug Hewitt	.10	.05
Mark Martin	.50	.23
Victory Lane		
Robin Pemberton	.10	.05
Ray Evernham	.10	.05
Geoff Bodine	.20	.09
Victory Lane		
Donnie Wingo	.10	.05
Pete Peterson	.10	.05
Rusty Wallace	.50	.23
Victory Lane		
Tony Glover	.10	.05
Gary DeHart	.10	.05
Jimmy Makar	.10	.05
Bill Elliott	.50	.23
Victory Lane		
Mike Beam	.10	.05
Kevin Hamlin	.10	.05
Paul Andrews	.10	.05
Terry Labonte	.50	.23
Victory Lane		
Chris Hussey	.10	.05
Mark Martin	.50	.23
IROC Champion		
Memorable Moment		
Jim Long	.10	.05
Rusty Wallace	.50	.23
Victory Lane		
Donnie Richeson	.10	.05
Rusty Wallace	.50	.23
Victory Lane		
Troy Selberg	.10	.05
Tony Furr	.10	.05
Mike Hill	.10	.05
Geoff Bodine	.20	.09
Victory Lane		
Freddy Fryar	.10	.05
Philippe Lopez	.10	.05
Dale Jarrett	.40	.18
Victory Lane		
Jeff Hammond	.10	.05
Buddy Barnes	.10	.05
Jeff Gordon's Car	1.00	.45
Darrell Waltrip's Car		
Terry Labonte's Car		
Ken Schrader's Car		
Victory Lane		
Charley Pressley	.10	.05
Doug Richert	.10	.05
Terry Labonte	.50	.23
Victory Lane		
Mike Hillman	.10	.05
Derrike Cope's Car	.10	.05
Bobby Hillin's Car		
Billy Standridge's Car		
Memorable Moment		
Robbie Loomis	.10	.05
Mark Martin	.50	.23
Victory Lane		
Harry Gant	.20	.09
Memorable Moment		
Bobby Labonte Crash	.40	.18
Memorable Moment		
David Green	.20	.09
BGN Champion		
Memorable Moment		
David Green	.20	.09
Ricky Craven	.20	.09
Chad Little	.20	.09
Kenny Wallace	.20	.09
Robert Pressley	.20	.09
Johnny Benson	.20	.09
Bobby Dotter	.20	.09
Larry Pearson	.10	.05
Dennis Setzer	.20	.09
Tim Fedewa	.20	.09
Jeff Burton	.40	.18
Rusty Wallace's Car	.50	.23
Mark Martin's Car	.50	.23
Ernie Irvan's Car	.20	.09
Ken Schrader's Car	.10	.05
Morgan Shepherd's Car	.10	.05
Ricky Rudd's Car	.20	.09
Michael Waltrip's Car	.10	.05
Ted Musgrave's Car	.10	.05
Jeff Gordon's Car	1.00	.45
Lake Speed's Car	.10	.05
Kyle Petty's Car	.20	.09
Sterling Marlin's Car	.20	.09
Terry Labonte's Car	.50	.23
Darrell Waltrip's Car	.20	.09
Dale Jarrett's Car	.40	.18
Rick Mast's Car	.10	.05
❑ 177 Geoff Bodine's Car	.10	.05
❑ 178 Todd Bodine's Car	.10	.05
❑ 179 Hut Stricklin's Car	.10	.05
❑ 180 Checklist Card	.10	.05
❑ 181 Lake Speed	.20	.09
❑ 182 Loy Allen Jr.	.20	.09
❑ 183 Steve Grissom	.20	.09
❑ 184 Dick Trickle	.20	.09
❑ 185 Bobby Hamilton	.20	.09
❑ 186 John Andretti	.20	.09
❑ 187 Charles Hardy	.10	.05
❑ 188 Tony Gibson	.10	.05
❑ 189 Jeremy Mayfield's Car	.30	.14
❑ 190 Jeremy Mayfield	.60	.25
❑ 191 Ken Howes	.10	.05
❑ 192 Robin Pemberton	.10	.05
❑ 193 Chris Hussey	.10	.05
❑ 194 Bill Davis	.10	.05
❑ 195 Davy Jones	.20	.09
❑ 196 Randy LaJoie	.20	.09
❑ 197 Donnie Richeson	.10	.05
❑ 198 Tony Furr	.10	.05
❑ 199 Mike Hill	.10	.05
❑ 200 Elton Sawyer	.20	.09
❑ 201 Johnny Benson, Jr.	.20	.09
❑ 202 Bobby Dotter	.20	.09
❑ 203 Andy Petree	.10	.05
❑ 204 Ricky Rudd	.40	.18
❑ 205 Ricky Rudd's Car	.20	.09
❑ 206 Darrell Waltrip	.40	.18
❑ 207 Darrell Waltrip's Car	.20	.09
❑ 208 Chad Little	.20	.09
❑ 209 Hut Stricklin's Car	.10	.05
❑ 210 Hut Stricklin	.20	.09
❑ 211 Richard Broome	.10	.05
❑ 212 Geoff Bodine	.20	.09
❑ 213 Geoff Bodine's Car	.10	.05
❑ 214 Robert Pressley	.20	.09
❑ 215 Mark Martin	1.00	.45
❑ 216 Dale Jarrett	.75	.35
❑ 217 Joe Nemechek	.20	.09
❑ 218 Joe Nemechek's Car	.10	.05
❑ 219 Joe Nemechek	.20	.09
❑ 220 Joe Nemechek's Car	.10	.05
❑ 221 Bill Elliott	1.00	.45
❑ 222 Bill Elliott's Car	.50	.23
❑ 223 Brett Bodine	.20	.09
❑ 224 Brett Bodine's Car	.10	.05
❑ 225 Junior Johnson	.20	.09
❑ 226 Jimmy Spencer	.20	.09
❑ 227 Jimmy Spencer's Car	.10	.05
❑ 228 Travis Carter	.10	.05
❑ 229 Cecil Gordon	.10	.05
❑ 230 Terry Labonte	1.00	.45
❑ 231 Terry Labonte's Car	.50	.23
❑ 232 Terry Labonte	1.00	.45
❑ 233 Terry Labonte's Car	.50	.23
❑ 234 Kyle Petty	.40	.18
❑ 235 Kyle Petty's Car	.20	.09
❑ 236 Jeff Gordon	2.00	.90
❑ 237 Jeff Gordon's Car	1.00	.45
❑ 238 Scott Lagasse's Truck	.10	.05
❑ 239 Scott Lagasse	.20	.09
❑ 240 Bobby Labonte	.75	.35
❑ 241 Bobby Labonte's Car	.40	.18
❑ 242 David Green's Car	.10	.05
❑ 243 Bobby Labonte	.75	.35
❑ 244 Michael Waltrip	.20	.09
❑ 245 Michael Waltrip's Car	.10	.05
❑ 246 Michael Waltrip	.20	.09
❑ 247 Michael Waltrip's Car	.10	.05
❑ 248 Ricky Craven	.20	.09
❑ 249 Ricky Craven's Car	.10	.05
❑ 250 Ricky Craven	.20	.09
❑ 251 Ricky Craven's Car	.10	.05
❑ 252 Ken Schrader	.20	.09
❑ 253 Ken Schrader's Car	.10	.05
❑ 254 Ken Schrader	.20	.09
❑ 255 Ken Schrader's Car	.10	.05
❑ 256 Ken Schrader	.20	.09
❑ 257 Ken Schrader's Truck	.10	.05
❑ 258 Ray Evernham	.40	.18
❑ 259 Joe Gibbs	.20	.09
❑ 260 Bob Jenkins	.10	.05
❑ 261 Jeff Fuller	.20	.09
❑ 262 Mike McLaughlin	.20	.09
❑ 263 Kenny Wallace	.20	.09
❑ 264 Cale Yarborough	.20	.09
❑ 265 Chuck Bown	.20	.09
❑ 266 Dave Marcis	.40	.18
❑ 267 Howard Comstock	.10	.05
❑ 268 Jimmy Means	.10	.05
❑ 269 Chad Little's Car	.10	.05
❑ 270 Checklist Card	.10	.05

1995 Maxx Autographs

This 48-card sets features 1995 Maxx series one cards autographed by some of the top personalities in NASCAR. The cards were randomly inserted in 1995 Maxx series two packs. To guarantee its authenticity, each signed card was crimped with Maxx's corporate seal which reads "J.R. Maxx Inc. Corporate Seal 1988 North Carolina." Most of the Johnny Benson cards were signed on the back.

	MINT	NRMT
COMPLETE SET (48)	800.00	350.00
COMMON CARD	10.00	4.50
COMMON DRIVER	20.00	9.00
❑ 5 Terry Labonte	100.00	45.00
❑ 7 Geoff Bodine	20.00	9.00
❑ 16 Ted Musgrave	20.00	9.00
❑ 21 Morgan Shepherd	20.00	9.00
❑ 22 Bobby Labonte	60.00	27.00
❑ 24 Jeff Gordon	250.00	110.00
❑ 25 Ken Schrader	20.00	9.00
❑ 30 Michael Waltrip	20.00	9.00
❑ 41 Joe Nemechek	20.00	9.00
❑ 42 Kyle Petty	40.00	18.00
❑ 96 Andy Petree	10.00	4.50
❑ 97 Larry McReynolds	10.00	4.50
❑ 100 Buddy Parrott	10.00	4.50
❑ 101 Steve Hmiel	10.00	4.50
❑ 103 Ken Howes	10.00	4.50
❑ 104 Leonard Wood	10.00	4.50
❑ 106 Bill Ingle	10.00	4.50
❑ 108 Doug Hewitt	10.00	4.50
❑ 110 Robin Pemberton	10.00	4.50
❑ 113 Donnie Wingo	10.00	4.50
❑ 114 Pete Peterson	10.00	4.50
❑ 116 Tony Glover	10.00	4.50
❑ 117 Gary DeHart	10.00	4.50
❑ 118 Jimmy Makar	10.00	4.50
❑ 120 Mike Beam	10.00	4.50
❑ 121 Kevin Hamlin	10.00	4.50
❑ 122 Paul Andrews	10.00	4.50
❑ 124 Chris Hussey	10.00	4.50
❑ 126 Jim Long	10.00	4.50
❑ 128 Donnie Richeson	10.00	4.50
❑ 130 Troy Selberg	10.00	4.50
❑ 131 Tony Furr	10.00	4.50
❑ 132 Mike Hill	10.00	4.50
❑ 135 Philippe Lopez	10.00	4.50
❑ 137 Jeff Hammond	10.00	4.50
❑ 138 Buddy Barnes	10.00	4.50
❑ 140 Charley Pressley	10.00	4.50
❑ 141 Doug Richert	10.00	4.50
❑ 143 Mike Hillman	10.00	4.50
❑ 145 Robbie Loomis	10.00	4.50
❑ 151 Ricky Craven	40.00	18.00
❑ 152 Chad Little	20.00	9.00
❑ 154 Robert Pressley	20.00	9.00
❑ 155 Johnny Benson	20.00	9.00
❑ 156 Bobby Dotter	20.00	9.00
❑ 157 Larry Pearson	20.00	9.00
❑ 158 Dennis Setzer	20.00	9.00
❑ 159 Tim Fedewa	20.00	9.00

1995 Maxx Chase the Champion

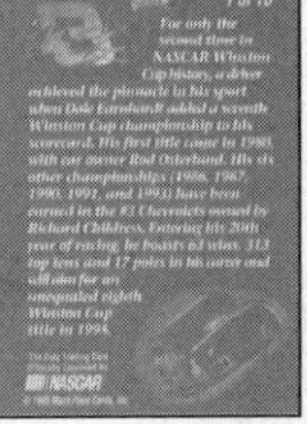

Dale Earnhardt Chase the Champion cards were distributed over Maxx's five major racing issues of 1995: series one and two Maxx (1:36), Premier Plus (1:24), Premier Series (2 per factory set) and Medallion (1:18). The cards were consecutively numbered and include silver foil layering on the cardfront. Card #1 was in series one packs, cards #2, 3 were in premier series sets, cards #4, 5 inserts in premier plus packs, cards #6, 7 inserts in series two packs, and #8-10 were inserts in medallion.

	MINT	NRMT
COMPLETE SET (10)	80.00	36.00
CARDS (1/6/7)	8.00	3.60
CARDS (2-5/8-10)	10.00	4.50
❑ 1 Dale Earnhardt	8.00	3.60
❑ 2 Dale Earnhardt	10.00	4.50
❑ 3 Dale Earnhardt	10.00	4.50
❑ 4 Dale Earnhardt's Car	10.00	4.50

❑ 5 Dale Earnhardt	10.00	4.50
❑ 6 Dale Earnhardt	8.00	3.60
❑ 7 Dale Earnhardt Teresa Earnhardt	8.00	3.60
❑ 8 Dale Earnhardt	10.00	4.50
❑ 9 Dale Earnhardt Richard Childress Teresa Earnhardt	10.00	4.50
❑ 10 Dale Earnhardt	10.00	4.50

1995 Maxx Bill Elliott Bat Chase

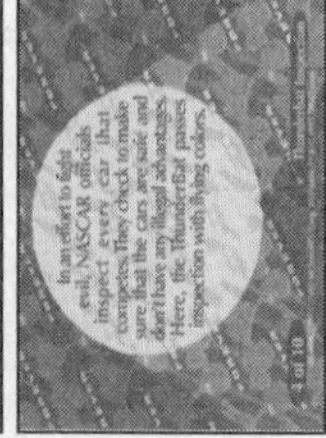

Bill Elliott's special ThunderBat paint scheme car is the focus of this ten-card set. Series two packs included two of the Bat Chase insert cards approximately every 36 packs. These sets were also made available thru Club Maxx for $5.99 in October, 1995. The sets were purchased immediately by both Club members and dealers. A glow-in-the-dark paint was used on the border of all ten cards. There was also a autographed 8" X 10" version of Bill Elliott's Thunderbat card. The card was signed in gold and was available through the Maxx Club. The card can commonly be found in the $80-150 range. Each of the autographed cards were numberd to 500.

	MINT	NRMT
COMPLETE SET (10)	30.00	13.50
COMMON CARD (1-10)	3.00	1.35

1995 Maxx License to Drive

License to Drive inserts were distributed over three products with three different insertion ratios: Maxx series one (1:40), Maxx series two (2:36) and Maxx Premier Plus (1:17). The five series two cards were numbered with an LTD prefix. Crown Chrome versions of the five Premier Plus cards were also produced and inserted in Maxx Crown Chrome packs at the rate of 1:22 packs.

	MINT	NRMT
COMPLETE SET (15)	90.00	40.00
COMP.MAXX SERIES 1 SET (5)	30.00	13.50
COMP.MAXX SERIES 2 (5)	20.00	9.00
COMP.MAXX PREM. PLUS (5)	40.00	18.00
COMMON CARD (1-5)	6.00	2.70
COMMON CARD (6-10)	8.00	3.60
COMMON CARD (11-15)	4.00	1.80
*SINGLES: 5X TO 12X BASE CARD HI		
COMP.CROWN CHROME (5)	50.00	22.00
*CROWN CHROME SAME PRICE AS PREM. PLUS		
❑ 1 Terry Labonte's Car	12.00	5.50
❑ 2 Harry Gant's Car	8.00	3.60
❑ 3 Sterling Marlin's Car	8.00	3.60
❑ 4 Dick Trickle's Car	6.00	2.70
❑ 5 Hut Stricklin's Car	6.00	2.70
❑ 6 Ted Musgrave's Car	8.00	3.60
❑ 7 Mark Martin's Car	14.00	6.25
❑ 8 Ward Burton's Car	8.00	3.60
❑ 9 Rick Mast's Car	8.00	3.60
❑ 10 Morgan Shepherd's Car	8.00	3.60
❑ 11 Michael Waltrip's Car	4.00	1.80
❑ 12 Darrell Waltrip's Car	5.00	2.20
❑ 13 Geoff Bodine's Car	4.00	1.80
❑ 14 Brett Bodine's Car	4.00	1.80
❑ 15 Todd Bodine's Car	4.00	1.80

1995 Maxx Over the Wall

Over the Wall inserts feature pit scenes of top Winston Cup race teams. The cards were randomly inserted in 1995 Maxx series one packs at the wrapper stated rate of 1:20 packs.

	MINT	NRMT
COMPLETE SET (10)	40.00	18.00
COMMON CARD (1-10)	1.00	.45
*SINGLES: 2X TO 5X BASE CARD HI		
❑ 1 Jeff Gordon in Pits	10.00	4.50
❑ 2 Brett Bodine in Pits	1.00	.45
❑ 3 Hut Stricklin in Pits	1.00	.45
❑ 4 Kyle Petty in Pits	2.00	.90
❑ 5 Darrell Waltrip in Pits	2.00	.90
❑ 6 Kenny Wallace in Pits	1.00	.45
❑ 7 Ken Schrader in Pits	1.00	.45
❑ 8 Bill Elliott in Pits	5.00	2.20
❑ 9 Geoff Bodine in Pits	1.00	.45
❑ 10 Terry Labonte in Pits	2.00	.90

1995 Maxx Stand Ups

This six-card set features drivers and cars from Winston Cup. The cards were produced using a die-cut "stand-up" card design and were issued in special retail packs at the rate of one per pack.

	MINT	NRMT
COMPLETE SET (6)	4.00	1.80
COMMON CARD (1-6)	.50	.23
❑ 1 Geoff Bodine	.50	.23
❑ 2 John Andretti's Car Sterling Marlin's Car Geoff Bodine's Car	.75	.35
❑ 3 Jeff Burton	.50	.23
❑ 4 Ernie Irvan's Car	.75	.35
❑ 5 Rusty Wallace's Car	1.00	.45
❑ 6 Richard Petty	.75	.35

1995 Maxx SuperTrucks

SuperTrucks cards were distributed over three products with three different insertion ratios: Maxx series one (1:40), Maxx Premier Plus (1:17) and Maxx Medallion (1:2). The last 15 cards were numbered with an ST prefix. Unnumbered Crown Chrome versions of the five Premier Plus cards were also produced and inserted in Maxx Crown Chrome packs at the rate of 1:22 packs.

	MINT	NRMT
COMPLETE SET (20)	55.00	25.00
COMPLETE MAXX SET (5)	20.00	
COMP.MAXX PREM. PLUS SET (5)	25.00	
COMP.MAXX MEDALLION (10)	14.00	
COMMON CARD (1-5)	4.00	
COMMON CARD (6-10)	5.00	
COMMON CARD (11-20)	1.50	
COMP.CROWN CHROME (5)	25.00	
*CROWN CHROMES:SAME PRICE AS PREM.PLUS		
❑ 1 Mike Skinner's Truck P.J.Jones' Truck	5.00	
❑ 2 Rick Carelli's Truck	4.00	
❑ 3 Tobey Butler's Truck C.Huartson's Truck	4.00	
❑ 4 Scott Lagasse's Truck T.J.Clark's Truck	5.00	
❑ 5 Rick Carelli's Truck	4.00	
❑ 6 Scott Lagasse's Trcuk	6.00	
❑ 7 Ken Schrader's Truck	10.00	
❑ 8 Geoff Bodine's Truck	10.00	
❑ 9 Jerry Glanville's Truck	5.00	
❑ 10 Rick Carelli's Truck	5.00	
❑ 11 John Nemechek's Truck	1.50	
❑ 12 Sammy Swindell's Truck	2.00	
❑ 13 Bob Strait's Truck	1.50	
❑ 14 Mike Chase's Truck	1.50	
❑ 15 Walker Evans' Truck	1.50	
❑ 16 Bob Brevak's Truck	1.50	
❑ 17 Tobey Butler's Truck	1.50	
❑ 18 Steve Portenga's Truck	1.50	
❑ 19 Jerry Churchill's Truck	1.50	
❑ 20 Butch Miller's Truck	1.50	

1995 Maxx Top 5 of 2005

Top 5 of 2005 was an exclusive insert to 1995 series two. The cards were inserted at the wrapper rate of 2:36 and featured drivers Maxx felt could b contenders ten years down the road.

	MINT
COMPLETE SET (5)	10.00
COMMON CARD (TOP1-TOP5)	1.00
*SINGLES: 1.5X TO 4X BASE CARD HI	
❑ TOP1 Ricky Craven	2.00
❑ TOP2 Bobby Labonte	4.00
❑ TOP3 Jason Keller	1.00
❑ TOP4 David Hutio	1.00
❑ TOP5 Toby Porter	1.00

1995 Maxx Medallion

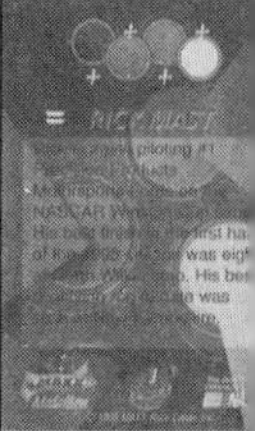

The second year of the Medallion brand featur "Colors of NASCAR" theme. The 61-card set consists of the top NASCAR drivers and their cars. Maxx prc 999 cases of this product, which came 18 packs p with 8 cards per pack. Randomly inserted in pack On the Road Again, Head-to-Head, Busch Grand Na SuperTrucks, Jeff Gordon Puzzles and the final thre Earnhardt Chase the Champion cards. Although th and Head-to-Head cards are numbered differently inserts, most consider the cards part of the regular bringing the number of cards in the set to an ev Maxx also included a special Checkered Flag Chas one per case, that contains parallel cards printed foil.

	MINT	NRMT
LETE SET (70)	20.00	9.00
ON CARD (1-61)	.10	.05
ON DRIVER (1-61)	.20	.09
GN CARD (BGN1-BGN5)	.50	.23
TH CARD (HTH1-HTH4)	.50	.23
ck Mast	.20	.09
sty Wallace	1.00	.45
erling Marlin	.40	.18
rry Labonte	1.00	.45
rk Martin	1.00	.45
off Bodine	.20	.09
ff Burton	.40	.18
ke Speed	.20	.09
cky Rudd	.40	.18
rett Bodine	.20	.09
errike Cope	.20	.09
ed Musgrave	.20	.09
arrell Waltrip	.40	.18
obby Labonte	.75	.35
organ Shepherd	.20	.09
mmy Spencer	.20	.09
eff Gordon	2.00	.90
en Schrader	.20	.09
ut Stricklin	.20	.09
ale Jarrett	.75	.35
lichael Waltrip	.20	.09
Vard Burton	.20	.09
ohn Andretti	.20	.09
yle Petty	.40	.18
obby Hamilton	.20	.09
odd Bodine	.20	.09
obby Hillin	.20	.09
oe Nemechek	.20	.09
like Wallace	.20	.09
ill Elliott	1.00	.45
ick Mast's Car	.10	.05
usty Wallace's Car	.50	.23
terling Marlin's Car	.20	.09
erry Labonte's Car	.50	.23
lark Martin's Car	.50	.23
eoff Bodine's Car	.10	.05
eff Burton's Car	.20	.09
ake Speed's Car	.10	.05
icky Rudd's Car	.20	.09
rett Bodine's Car	.10	.05
errike Cope's Car	.10	.05
ed Musgrave's Car	.10	.05
arrell Waltrip's Car	.20	.09
obby Labonte's Car	.40	.18
lorgan Shepherd's Car	.10	.05
mmy Spencer's Car	.10	.05
eff Gordon's Car	1.00	.45
en Schrader's Car	.10	.05
ut Stricklin's Car	.10	.05
ale Jarrett's Car	.40	.18
lichael Waltrip's Car	.10	.05
Vard Burton's Car	.10	.05
ohn Andretti's Car	.10	.05
yle Petty's Car	.20	.09
obby Hamilton's Car	.10	.05
odd Bodine's Car	.10	.05
obby Hillin's Car	.10	.05
oe Nemechek's Car	.10	.05
like Wallace's Car	.10	.05
ill Elliott's Car	.50	.23
hecklist Card	.10	.05
1 Johnny Benson	.50	.23
2 Chad Little	.50	.23
3 Jason Keller	.50	.23
4 Mike McLaughlin	.50	.23
5 Larry Pearson	.50	.23
1 Ricky Craven	.40	.18
2 Ricky Craven's Car	.20	.09
3 Robert Pressley	.50	.23
4 Robert Pressley's Car	.10	.05

995 Maxx Medallion Blue

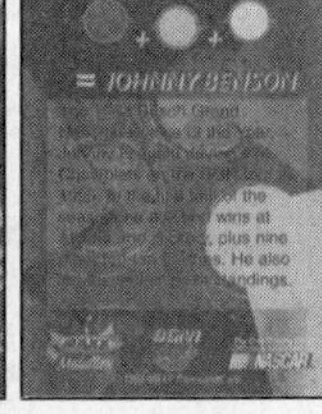

il parallel cards could be found only in Checkered hase boxes randomly packed in 1995 Maxx on cases (one box per case). All 70 regular issue cards were produced with a special blue foil layering instead of gold.

	MINT	NRMT
COMPLETE BLUE SET (70)	200.00	90.00
COMMON CARD (1-61)	1.25	.55
COMMON DRIVER (1-61)	2.50	1.10
COMMON BGN CARD (BGN1-BGN5)	2.00	.90
COMMON HTH CARD (HTH1-HTH4)	2.00	.90

*BLUE FOILS: 8X TO X BASIC CARDS

1995 Maxx Medallion Jeff Gordon Puzzle

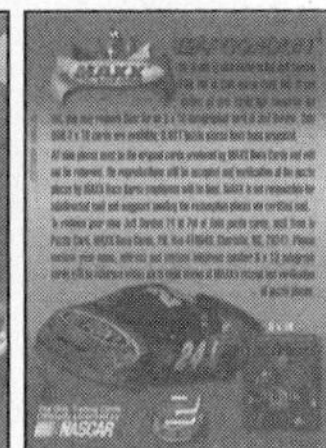

Nine Jeff Gordon puzzle cards were produced for and distributed through 1995 Maxx Medallion. Although wrapper stated odds are 1:40, most pack breakers reported much easier ratios on the eight regular cards (#1-3,5-9), about one in four packs, and a much tougher ratio on the short printed card (#4), about one per case. The #4 puzzle cards were inserted into the Checkered Flag Chase boxes. Once completed, the puzzle could be returned to Maxx in exchange for a signed 8" by 10" Jeff Gordon card. Maxx reports only 999 of the cards were signed and numbered. Since Maxx has gone out of business numerous extra signed Jeff Gordon photos have surfaced. We have had multiple reports of people having the same numbered photos of 999.

	MINT	NRMT
COMPLETE SET (9)	20.00	9.00
COMMON CARD (1-9)	2.00	.90
J.GORDON AUTO/999	200.00	90.00
❑ 1 Jeff Gordon	2.00	.90
❑ 2 Jeff Gordon	2.00	.90
❑ 3 Jeff Gordon	2.00	.90
❑ 4 Jeff Gordon SP	6.00	2.70
❑ 5 Jeff Gordon	2.00	.90
❑ 6 Jeff Gordon	2.00	.90
❑ 7 Jeff Gordon	2.00	.90
❑ 8 Jeff Gordon	2.00	.90
❑ 9 Jeff Gordon	2.00	.90

1995 Maxx Medallion On the Road Again

Unlike many of the 1995 Maxx inserts, On the Road Again was exclusive to one product -- Maxx Medallion. The cards were packaged approximately one every two foil packs and feature top Winston Cup race teams' transporters.

	MINT	NRMT
COMPLETE SET (10)	10.00	4.50
COMMON CARD (OTR1-OTR10)	1.00	.45
❑ OTR1 Ken Schrader's Trans.	1.00	.45
❑ OTR2 Jeff Gordon's Transporter	2.00	.90
❑ OTR3 Terry Labonte's Trans.	1.50	.70
❑ OTR4 Steve Grissom's Trans.	1.00	.45
❑ OTR5 Bill Elliott's Transporter	1.50	.70
❑ OTR6 Jeff Burton's Transporter	1.00	.45
❑ OTR7 Bobby Labonte's Trans.	1.50	.70
❑ OTR8 Lake Speed's Transporter	1.00	.45
❑ OTR9 Derrike Cope's Transporter	1.00	.45
❑ OTR10 Ricky Rudd's Transporter	1.00	.45

1995 Maxx Premier Plus

Maxx again used its chromium printing technology to produce a Premier Plus issue. The cards were distributed in 7-card packs with 36 packs per foil box. In additon to a few new insert sets, Premier Plus included continuations to three other Maxx insert issues. A Crown Chrome parallel release was also produced and issued in its own packs. Crown Chrome came 6-cards to a pack with 24 packs per box. A special Silver Select Dale Earnhardt card was produced and distributed only through Crown Chrome and each was numbered of 750. Maxx reportedly limited production to 9000 numbered boxes.

	MINT	NRMT
COMPLETE SET (183)	25.00	11.00
COMMON CARD (1-183)	.15	.07
COMMON DRIVER (1-183)	.30	.14
D.EARNHARDT SILVER SELECT/750	100.00	45.00
❑ 1 Rick Mast	.30	.14
❑ 2 Rusty Wallace	1.50	.70
❑ 3 Scott Lagasse	.30	.14
❑ 4 Sterling Marlin	.60	.25
❑ 5 Terry Labonte	1.50	.70
❑ 6 Mark Martin	1.50	.70
❑ 7 Geoff Bodine	.30	.14
❑ 8 Jeff Burton	.60	.25
❑ 9 Ricky Craven	.60	.25
❑ 10 Ricky Rudd	.60	.25
❑ 11 Bill Elliott	1.50	.70
❑ 12 Derrike Cope	.30	.14
❑ 13 Scott Lagasse's SuperTruck	.15	.07
❑ 14 Ken Schrader's SuperTruck	.15	.07
❑ 15 Lake Speed	.30	.14
❑ 16 Ted Musgrave	.30	.14
❑ 17 Darrell Waltrip	.60	.25
❑ 18 Dale Jarrett	1.25	.55
❑ 19 Loy Allen Jr.	.30	.14
❑ 20 Steve Kinser	.30	.14
❑ 21 Morgan Shepherd	.30	.14
❑ 22 Bobby Labonte	1.25	.55
❑ 23 Randy LaJoie	.30	.14
❑ 24 Jeff Gordon	3.00	1.35
❑ 25 Ken Schrader	.30	.14
❑ 26 Brett Bodine	.30	.14
❑ 27 Jimmy Spencer	.30	.14
❑ 28 Ernie Irvan	.60	.25
❑ 29 Steve Grissom	.30	.14
❑ 30 Michael Waltrip	.30	.14
❑ 31 Ward Burton	.30	.14
❑ 32 Dick Trickle	.30	.14
❑ 33 Harry Gant	.60	.25
❑ 34 Terry Labonte's Car	.75	.35
❑ 35 Mark Martin's Car	.75	.35
❑ 36 Bobby Labonte's Car	.60	.25
❑ 37 Rusty Wallace's Car	.75	.35
❑ 38 Sterling Marlin's Car	.30	.14
❑ 39 Kyle Petty's Car	.30	.14
❑ 40 Bobby Hamilton	.30	.14
❑ 41 Joe Nemechek	.30	.14
❑ 42 Kyle Petty	.60	.25
❑ 43 Richard Petty	.75	.35
❑ 44 Brett Bodine's Car	.15	.07
❑ 45 John Andretti	.30	.14
❑ 46 Todd Bodine's Car	.15	.07
❑ 47 Michael Waltrip's Car	.15	.07
❑ 48 Dale Jarrett's Car	.60	.25
❑ 49 Joe Nemechek's Car	.15	.07
❑ 50 Morgan Shepherd's Car	.15	.07
❑ 51 Bill Elliott's Car	.75	.35
❑ 52 Ricky Craven's Car	.15	.07
❑ 53 Kenny Wallace	.30	.14
❑ 54 Bobby Hamilton's Car	.15	.07
❑ 55 Jimmy Hensley	.30	.14
❑ 56 Ken Schrader's Car	.15	.07
❑ 57 Steve Kinser's Car	.15	.07
❑ 58 Dick Trickle's Car	.15	.07
❑ 59 Ricky Rudd's Car	.30	.14
❑ 60 Robert Pressley's Car	.15	.07
❑ 61 Ted Musgrave's Car	.15	.07
❑ 62 Rick Mast's Car	.15	.07
❑ 63 Darrell Waltrip's Car	.30	.14

Card	MINT	NRMT
❑ 64 Jeff Gordon's Car	1.50	.70
❑ 65 Jeff Burton's Car	.30	.14
❑ 66 Geoff Bodine's Car	.15	.07
❑ 67 Jimmy Spencer's Car	.15	.07
❑ 68 Roger Penske	.15	.07
❑ 69 Don Miller	.15	.07
❑ 70 Jack Roush	.15	.07
❑ 71 Dave Marcis	.60	.25
❑ 72 Joe Gibbs	.30	.14
❑ 73 Junior Johnson	.30	.14
❑ 74 Rick Hendrick	.15	.07
❑ 75 Todd Bodine	.30	.14
❑ 76 Felix Sabates	.15	.07
❑ 77 Greg Sacks	.30	.14
❑ 78 Tim Morgan	.15	.07
❑ 79 Larry McClure	.15	.07
❑ 80 Glen Wood	.15	.07
❑ 81 Len Wood	.15	.07
❑ 82 Eddie Wood	.15	.07
❑ 83 Leo Jackson	.15	.07
❑ 84 Bobby Allison	.30	.14
❑ 85 Gary Bechtel Carolyn Bechtel	.15	.07
❑ 86 Bill Stavola	.15	.07
❑ 87 Mickey Stavola	.15	.07
❑ 88 Walter Bud Moore	.15	.07
❑ 89 Chuck Rider	.15	.07
❑ 90 Mike Wallace	.30	.14
❑ 91 Bill Davis	.15	.07
❑ 92 Kenny Bernstein	.30	.14
❑ 93 Richard Jackson	.15	.07
❑ 94 D.K. Ulrich	.15	.07
❑ 95 Cale Yarborough	.30	.14
❑ 96 Junie Donlavey	.15	.07
❑ 97 Larry Hedrick	.15	.07
❑ 98 Jeremy Mayfield	1.00	.45
❑ 99 Robert Yates	.15	.07
❑ 100 Travis Carter	.15	.07
❑ 101 Butch Mock	.15	.07
❑ 102 Dick Brooks	.15	.07
❑ 103 Andy Petree	.15	.07
❑ 104 Buddy Parrott	.15	.07
❑ 105 Steve Hmiel	.15	.07
❑ 106 Jimmy Makar	.15	.07
❑ 107 Robin Pemberton	.15	.07
❑ 108 Jeff Hammond	.15	.07
❑ 109 Tony Glover	.15	.07
❑ 110 Leonard Wood	.15	.07
❑ 111 Mike Beam	.15	.07
❑ 112 Mike Hill	.15	.07
❑ 113 Gary DeHart	.15	.07
❑ 114 Ray Evernham	.15	.07
❑ 115 Ken Howes	.15	.07
❑ 116 Bill Ingle	.15	.07
❑ 117 Pete Peterson	.15	.07
❑ 118 Cecil Gordon	.15	.07
❑ 119 Donnie Wingo	.15	.07
❑ 120 Doug Hewitt	.15	.07
❑ 121 Donnie Richeson	.15	.07
❑ 122 Richard Broome	.15	.07
❑ 123 Kevin Hamlin	.15	.07
❑ 124 Charley Pressley	.15	.07
❑ 125 Larry McReynolds	.15	.07
❑ 126 Paul Andrews	.15	.07
❑ 127 Robbie Loomis	.15	.07
❑ 128 Troy Selberg	.15	.07
❑ 129 Jimmy Fennig	.15	.07
❑ 130 Barry Dodson	.15	.07
❑ 131 David Green	.30	.14
❑ 132 Ricky Craven	.30	.14
❑ 133 Chad Little	.30	.14
❑ 134 Kenny Wallace	.30	.14
❑ 135 Bobby Dotter	.30	.14
❑ 136 Tracy Leslie	.30	.14
❑ 137 Larry Pearson	.30	.14
❑ 138 Dennis Setzer	.30	.14
❑ 139 Robert Pressley	.30	.14
❑ 140 Johnny Benson Jr.	.30	.14
❑ 141 Terry Labonte	1.50	.70
❑ 142 Terry Labonte's Car	.75	.35
❑ 143 Ken Schrader	.30	.14
❑ 144 Ken Schrader's Car	.15	.07
❑ 145 Joe Nemechek	.30	.14
❑ 146 Joe Nemechek's Car	.15	.07
❑ 147 Jeff Gordon Victory Lane	1.50	.70
❑ 148 Sterling Marlin Victory Lane	.30	.14
❑ 149 Rusty Wallace Victory Lane	.75	.35
❑ 150 Ernie Irvan Victory Lane	.30	.14
❑ 151 Ernie Irvan Victory Lane	.30	.14
❑ 152 Darlington Victory Lane	.15	.07
❑ 153 Rusty Wallace in Pits Victory Lane	.75	.35
❑ 154 Terry Labonte Victory Lane	.75	.35
❑ 155 Rusty Wallace Victory Lane	.75	.35
❑ 156 Talladega Speedway Victory Lane	.15	.07
❑ 157 Ernie Irvan w/Crew Victory Lane	.30	.14
❑ 158 Jeff Gordon Victory Lane	1.50	.70
❑ 159 Geoff Bodine Victory Lane	.30	.14
❑ 160 Jeff Gordon Victory Lane	1.50	.70
❑ 161 Rusty Wallace Victory Lane	.75	.35
❑ 162 Rusty Wallace Victory Lane	.75	.35
❑ 163 Rusty Wallace Victory Lane	.75	.35
❑ 164 Jimmy Spencer Victory Lane	.30	.14
❑ 165 Ricky Rudd w/Crew Victory Lane	.60	.25
❑ 166 Geoff Bodine Victory Lane	.30	.14
❑ 167 Jimmy Spencer Victory Lane	.30	.14
❑ 168 Jeff Gordon Victory Lane	1.50	.70
❑ 169 Mark Martin Victory Lane	.75	.35
❑ 170 Geoff Bodine Victory Lane	.30	.14
❑ 171 Rusty Wallace Victory Lane	.75	.35
❑ 172 Bill Elliott Junior Johnson Victory Lane	.75	.35
❑ 173 Terry Labonte Victory Lane	.75	.35
❑ 174 Rusty Wallace Victory Lane	.75	.35
❑ 175 Rusty Wallace Victory Lane	.75	.35
❑ 176 Geoff Bodine Victory Lane	.30	.14
❑ 177 Dale Jarrett Victory Lane	.60	.25
❑ 178 Rockingham Race Action Victory Lane	.15	.07
❑ 179 Terry Labonte Victory Lane	.75	.35
❑ 180 Mark Martin Victory Lane	.75	.35
❑ 181 Jeff Burton Rookie of the Year	.60	.25
❑ 182 Checklist #1	.15	.07
❑ 183 Checklist #2	.15	.07

1995 Maxx Crown Chrome

Crown Chrome is a parallel issue to Maxx's Premier Plus chromium card series. The art used on both sets is identical, but Crown Chrome was produced on clear plastic stock. All the same inserts were produced and packaged as 1995 Premier Plus. Packaging was done 6-cards per pack with 24 packs per box. None of the cards were numbered. The two checklist cards from Premier Plus were done on four Crown Chrome cards increasing the set to 185 total cards. A special Silver Select Dale Earnhardt card was produced and distributed only through Crown Chrome and each was numbered of 750. Maxx reportedly limited production to 9000 numbered boxes.

	MINT	NRMT
COMPLETE SET (185)	55.00	25.00
COMMON CARD (1-185)	.20	.09
COMMON DRIVER (1-185)	.40	.18

CROWN CHROMES:SAME PRICE AS PREM.PLUS

1995 Maxx Premier Plus PaceSetters

PaceSetter inserts were exclusive to the Maxx Pr Plus and Crown Chrome parallel issues. The cards packaged approximately 1:17 packs in Premier Plus 1:12 in Crown Chrome.

	MINT	N
COMPLETE SET (9)	60.00	
COMMON CARD (PS1-PS9)	1.50	

*SINGLES: 2X TO 5X BASE CARD HI

COMP. CROWN CHROME (9)	60.00	

*CROWN CHROME CARDS SAME PRICE

Card	MINT
❑ PS1 Mark Martin	10.00
❑ PS2 Rusty Wallace	10.00
❑ PS3 Ken Schrader	1.50
❑ PS4 Ricky Rudd	15.00
❑ PS5 Morgan Shepherd	1.50
❑ PS6 Terry Labonte	10.00
❑ PS7 Jeff Gordon	20.00
❑ PS8 Darrell Waltrip	15.00
❑ PS9 Bill Elliott	10.00

1995 Maxx Premier Plus Series Two Previews

Five cards were produced to preview the 1995 series two set. The cards were randomly insert Premier Plus packs at the rate of 1:17 packs. A C Chrome parallel version was also produced and ins in Crown Chrome packs at the approximate rate of 1:

	MINT	N
COMPLETE SET (5)	12.00	
COMMON CARD (PRE1-PRE5)	2.00	
COMP. CROWN CHROME (5)	15.00	

*CROWN CHROME CARDS: SAME PRICE AS PREMIER PLUS

Card	MINT
❑ PRE1 Lake Speed	2.00
❑ PRE2 Jimmy Spencer	2.00
❑ PRE3 Steve Grissom	2.00
❑ PRE4 Dale Jarrett	4.00
❑ PRE5 Dick Trickle	2.00

1995 Maxx Premier Plus Top Hats

Five cards were produced by Maxx to honor top

on Cup drivers. The cards were randomly inserted in er Plus packs at the rate of 1:17 packs. A Crown ne parallel version was also produced and inserted cks at the approximate rate of 1:22. Each Top Hat s numbered 1 of 1995.

	MINT	NRMT
'LETE SET (5)	12.00	5.50
ION CARD (TH1-TH5)	2.50	1.10
'. CROWN CHROME (5)	15.00	6.75
WN CHROME CARDS: SAME PRICE		
Ted Musgrave	2.50	1.10
' Ward Burton	2.50	1.10
; Steve Grissom	2.50	1.10
' Jimmy Spencer	2.50	1.10
• Brett Bodine	2.50	1.10

1995 Maxx Premier Plus Retail Jumbos

x-card set feature jumbo sized cards (3 1/2" X 5") of of the best Winston Cup drivers. The cards use the er Plus chromium printing technology. Originally the were only available through Kmart stores but were listributed via the Maxx Club. In the blister Kmart Jumbo cards came one per along with two 1995 series one packs and one Texaco Ernie Irvan pack. ards are unnumbered and checklisted below in etical order.

	MINT	NRMT
LETE SET (6)	6.00	2.70
ION CARD (1-6)	.75	.35
eoff Bodine	.75	.35
ff Burton	1.25	.55
ark Martin	2.00	.90
cky Rudd	1.25	.55
organ Shepherd	.75	.35
usty Wallace	2.00	.90

995 Maxx Premier Series

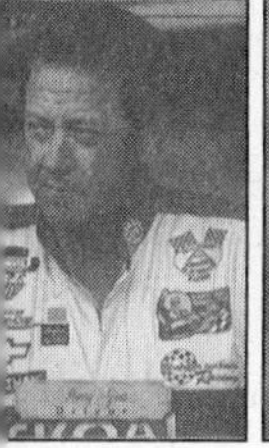

axx members had the chance to purchase the 1995 Premier Series set directly from Maxx for $64.95 hipping charges. Non-members could buy the set 9.95 plus shipping. Production was limited to numbered sets and each factory set included two arnhardt Chase the Champion cards (#2-3). These rdt cards are priced in the 1995 MAXX Chase the ion listings. A special gold foil embossed binder to the set was offered for sale as well.

	MINT	NRMT
LETE FACT. SET (302)	75.00	34.00
LETE SET (300)	60.00	27.00
ON CARD (1-300)	.20	.09
ON DRIVER (1-300)	.30	.14
k Mast	.30	.14
sty Wallace	1.00	.45
f Gordon's Car	1.00	.45
Memorable Moment		
rling Marlin	.50	.23
ry Labonte	1.00	.45
rk Martin	1.00	.45
off Bodine	.30	.14
f Burton	.50	.23
ky Craven	.30	.14
cky Rudd	.50	.23
ll Elliott	1.00	.45
errike Cope	.30	.14
odd Bodine's Car	.20	.09
Memorable Moment		
re Wars	.20	.09
Tech Card		
ke Speed	.30	.14
ed Musgrave	.30	.14
arrell Waltrip	.50	.23
ale Jarrett	.75	.35
nie Irvan	.50	.23
y Allen Jr.	.30	.14

❑ 20 Steve Kinser	.30	.14
❑ 21 Morgan Shepherd	.30	.14
❑ 22 Bobby Labonte	.75	.35
❑ 23 Randy LaJoie	.30	.14
❑ 24 Jeff Gordon	2.00	.90
❑ 25 Ken Schrader	.30	.14
❑ 26 Brett Bodine	.30	.14
❑ 27 Jimmy Spencer	.30	.14
❑ 28 Ernie Irvan	.50	.23
❑ 29 Steve Grissom	.30	.14
❑ 30 Michael Waltrip	.30	.14
❑ 31 Ward Burton	.30	.14
❑ 32 Dick Trickle	.30	.14
❑ 33 Harry Gant	.50	.23
❑ 34 Terry Labonte's Car	.50	.23
❑ 35 Mark Martin's Car	.50	.23
❑ 36 Bobby Labonte's Car	.50	.23
❑ 37 Rusty Wallace's Car	.50	.23
❑ 38 Sterling Marlin's Car	.30	.14
❑ 39 Kyle Petty's Car	.30	.14
❑ 40 Bobby Hamilton	.30	.14
❑ 41 Joe Nemechek	.30	.14
❑ 42 Kyle Petty	.50	.23
❑ 43 Richard Petty	.75	.35
❑ 44 Bobby Hillin	.30	.14
❑ 45 John Andretti	.30	.14
❑ 46 Scott Lagasse	.30	.14
❑ 47 Billy Standridge	.30	.14
❑ 48 Dale Jarrett's Car	.50	.23
❑ 49 Joe Nemechek's Car	.20	.09
❑ 50 Morgan Shepherd's Car	.20	.09
❑ 51 Bill Elliott's Car	.50	.23
❑ 52 Ricky Craven's Car	.20	.09
❑ 53 Kenny Wallace	.30	.14
❑ 54 John Andretti's Car	.20	.09
❑ 55 Jimmy Hensley	.30	.14
❑ 56 Ken Schrader's Car	.20	.09
❑ 57 Scott Lagasse's SuperTruck	.20	.09
❑ 58 Dick Trickle's Car	.20	.09
❑ 59 Ricky Rudd's Car	.30	.14
❑ 60 Robert Pressley's Car	.20	.09
❑ 61 Ted Musgrave's Car	.20	.09
❑ 62 Rick Mast's Car	.20	.09
❑ 63 Darrell Waltrip's Car	.30	.14
❑ 64 Jeff Gordon's Car	1.00	.45
❑ 65 Jeff Burton's Car	.30	.14
❑ 66 Geoff Bodine's Car	.20	.09
❑ 67 Jimmy Spencer's Car	.20	.09
❑ 68 Todd Bodine's Car	.20	.09
❑ 69 Michael Waltrip's Car	.20	.09
❑ 70 Brett Bodine's Car	.20	.09
❑ 71 Dave Marcis	.50	.23
❑ 72 Steve Kinser's Car	.20	.09
❑ 73 Mike Wallace's Car	.20	.09
❑ 74 Maxx Card's Car	.20	.09
❑ 75 Todd Bodine	.30	.14
❑ 76 Ward Burton's Car	.20	.09
❑ 77 Greg Sacks	.30	.14
❑ 78 Jeremy Mayfield's Car	.50	.23
❑ 79 Loy Allen Jr.'s Car	.20	.09
❑ 80 Roger Penske	.20	.09
❑ 81 Don Miller	.20	.09
❑ 82 Jack Roush	.20	.09
❑ 83 Joe Gibbs	.30	.14
❑ 84 Felix Sabates	.20	.09
❑ 85 Tim Morgan	.20	.09
❑ 86 Larry McClure	.20	.09
❑ 87 Teddy McClure	.20	.09
Jerry McClure		
Ed McClure		
❑ 88 Glen Wood	.20	.09
❑ 89 Len Wood	.20	.09
❑ 90 Mike Wallace	.30	.14
❑ 91 Eddie Wood	.20	.09
❑ 92 Junior Johnson	.30	.14
❑ 93 Rick Hendrick	.20	.09
❑ 94 Leo Jackson	.20	.09
❑ 95 Bobby Allison	.30	.14
❑ 96 Gary Bechtel	.20	.09
Carolyn Bechtel		
❑ 97 Bill Stavola	.20	.09
❑ 98 Jeremy Mayfield	.60	.25
❑ 99 Mickey Stavola	.20	.09
❑ 100 Walter Bud Moore	.20	.09
❑ 101 Chuck Rider	.20	.09
❑ 102 Ken Schrader's SuperTruck	.20	.09
❑ 103 Bill Davis	.20	.09
❑ 104 Kenny Bernstein	.30	.14
❑ 105 Richard Jackson	.20	.09
❑ 106 Ray DeWitt	.20	.09
Diane DeWitt		
❑ 107 D.K. Ulrich	.20	.09
❑ 108 Cale Yarborough	.30	.14
❑ 109 Junie Donlavey	.20	.09
❑ 110 Larry Hedrick	.20	.09
❑ 111 Robert Yates	.20	.09
❑ 112 George Bradshaw	.20	.09
❑ 113 Mark Smith	.20	.09
❑ 114 David Fuge	.20	.09
❑ 115 Travis Carter	.20	.09
❑ 116 A.G. Dillard	.20	.09
❑ 117 Butch Mock	.20	.09
❑ 118 Harry Melling	.20	.09
❑ 119 Dick Moroso	.20	.09
❑ 120 Dick Brooks	.20	.09
❑ 121 Roof Flaps	.20	.09
Tech Card		
❑ 122 Andy Petree	.20	.09
❑ 123 Buddy Parrott	.20	.09
❑ 124 Steve Hmiel	.20	.09
❑ 125 Jimmy Makar	.20	.09
❑ 126 Robin Pemberton	.20	.09
❑ 127 Jeff Hammond	.20	.09
❑ 128 Tony Glover	.20	.09
❑ 129 Leonard Wood	.20	.09
❑ 130 Mike Beam	.20	.09
❑ 131 Mike Hill	.20	.09
❑ 132 Gary DeHart	.20	.09
❑ 133 Ray Evernham	.50	.23
❑ 134 Ken Howes	.20	.09
❑ 135 Bill Ingle	.20	.09
❑ 136 Pete Peterson	.20	.09
❑ 137 Cecil Gordon	.20	.09
❑ 138 Donnie Wingo	.20	.09
❑ 139 Doug Hewitt	.20	.09
❑ 140 Phillipe Lopez	.20	.09
❑ 141 Chris Hussey	.20	.09
❑ 142 Donnie Richeson	.20	.09
❑ 143 Richard Broome	.20	.09
❑ 144 Kevin Hamlin	.20	.09
❑ 145 Ken Glen	.20	.09
❑ 146 Charley Pressley	.20	.09
❑ 147 Tony Furr	.20	.09
❑ 148 Larry McReynolds	.20	.09
❑ 149 Dale Fischlein	.20	.09
❑ 150 Paul Andrews	.20	.09
❑ 151 Robbie Loomis	.20	.09
❑ 152 Mike Hillman	.20	.09
❑ 153 Troy Selberg	.20	.09
❑ 154 Jimmy Fennig	.20	.09
❑ 155 Barry Dodson	.20	.09
❑ 156 Waddell Wilson	.20	.09
❑ 157 Dale Inman	.20	.09
❑ 158 Charlie Smith	.20	.09
❑ 159 David Green	.30	.14
❑ 160 David Green's Car	.20	.09
❑ 161 Ricky Craven	.30	.14
❑ 162 Ricky Craven's Car	.20	.09
❑ 163 Chad Little	.30	.14
❑ 164 Chad Little's Car	.20	.09
❑ 165 Kenny Wallace	.30	.14
❑ 166 Bobby Dotter	.30	.14
❑ 167 Tracy Leslie	.30	.14
❑ 168 Larry Pearson	.30	.14
❑ 169 Dennis Setzer	.30	.14
❑ 170 Robert Pressley	.30	.14
❑ 171 Johnny Benson Jr.	.30	.14
❑ 172 Tim Fedewa	.30	.14
❑ 173 Mike McLaughlin	.30	.14
❑ 174 Jim Bown	.30	.14
❑ 175 Elton Sawyer	.30	.14
❑ 176 Jason Keller	.30	.14
❑ 177 Rodney Combs	.30	.14
❑ 178 Doug Heveron	.30	.14
❑ 179 Tommy Houston	.30	.14
❑ 180 Kevin Lepage	.30	.14
❑ 181 Dirk Stephens	.30	.14
❑ 182 Stevie Reeves	.30	.14
❑ 183 Phil Parsons	.30	.14
❑ 184 Ernie Irvan's Car	.30	.14
Jimmy Spencer's Car		
Memorable Moment		
❑ 185 Shawna Robinson	.30	.14
❑ 186 Patty Moise	.30	.14
❑ 187 Terry Labonte	1.00	.45
❑ 188 Terry Labonte's Car	.50	.23
❑ 189 Ken Schrader	.30	.14
❑ 190 Ken Schrader's Car	.20	.09
❑ 191 Joe Nemechek	.30	.14
❑ 192 Joe Nemechek's Car	.20	.09
❑ 193 Bobby Hillin's Car	.20	.09
Billy Standridge Cars		
Memorable Moment		
❑ 194 Barney Hall	.20	.09
❑ 195 Eli Gold	.20	.09
❑ 196 Benny Parsons	.30	.14
❑ 197 Dr. Jerry Punch	.20	.09
❑ 198 Buddy Baker	.30	.14
❑ 199 Mike Joy	.20	.09
❑ 200 Winston Kelley	.20	.09
❑ 201 Jim Phillips	.20	.09
❑ 202 John Kernan	.20	.09
❑ 203 Randy Pemberton	.20	.09
❑ 204 Bill Weber	.20	.09
❑ 205 Joe Moore	.20	.09
❑ 206 Mark Garrow	.20	.09

❑ 207 Allen Bestwick .20 .09
❑ 208 Glenn Jarrett .20 .09
❑ 209 Pat Patterson .20 .09
❑ 210 Dr. Dick Berggren .20 .09
❑ 211 Harry Gant MM .30 .14
❑ 212 Ken Squier .20 .09
❑ 213 Bobby Labonte's Car .50 .23
Bobby Hamilton's Car
Rick Mast's Car
Memorable Moment
❑ 214 Mike Helton .20 .09
❑ 215 Gary Nelson .20 .09
❑ 216 Ray Hill .20 .09
❑ 217 Carl Hill .20 .09
❑ 218 Brian DeHart .20 .09
❑ 219 Jack Whittemore .20 .09
❑ 220 Jimmy Cox .20 .09
❑ 221 Bruce Roney .20 .09
❑ 222 Marlin Wright .20 .09
❑ 223 David Hoots .20 .09
❑ 224 Tim Earp .20 .09
❑ 225 Doyle Ford .20 .09
❑ 226 Buster Auton .20 .09
❑ 227 Elmo Langley .20 .09
❑ 228 Walt Green .20 .09
❑ 229 Gary Miller .20 .09
❑ 230 Morris Metcalfe .20 .09
❑ 231 Rich Burgdoff .20 .09
❑ 232 Jeff Burton .50 .23
Ward Burton
Memorable Moment
❑ 233 Larry McReynolds .20 .09
All Pro
❑ 234 Troy Martin .20 .09
All Pro
❑ 235 Dan Ford .20 .09
All Pro
❑ 236 Bill Wilburn .20 .09
All Pro
❑ 237 Raymond Fox III .20 .09
All Pro
❑ 238 David Smith .20 .09
All Pro
❑ 239 Robert Yates .20 .09
All Pro
❑ 240 Darrell Andrews .20 .09
All Pro
❑ 241 Glen Bobo .20 .09
All Pro
❑ 242 James Lewter .20 .09
All Pro
❑ 243 Norman Koshimizu .20 .09
All Pro
❑ 244 Eric Horn .20 .09
All Pro
❑ 245 Joe Dan Bailey .20 .09
All Pro
❑ 246 Joe Lewis .20 .09
All Pro
❑ 247 Danny Lawrence .20 .09
All Pro
❑ 248 Slick Poston .20 .09
All Pro
❑ 249 Derrike Cope's Car .30 .14
Terry Labonte's Car
Memorable Moment
❑ 250 David Rogers' Car .20 .09
WRS National Champion
❑ 251 Mark Burgtorf .20 .09
David Rogers
❑ 252 Dale Planck .20 .09
John Knaus
❑ 253 Barry Beggarly .20 .09
Charlie Cragen
❑ 254 Larry Phillips .20 .09
Paul Peeples Jr.
❑ 255 David Green .30 .14
BGN Champion
❑ 256 Johnny Benson Jr. .30 .14
BGN Rookie of the Year
❑ 257 Jeff Gordon w/Crew 1.00 .45
Pit Crew Champions
❑ 258 Ray Evernham .20 .09
Crew Chief of the Year
❑ 259 Jeff Burton .30 .14
WC Rookie of the Year
❑ 260 Bill Elliott .50 .23
Fans' Favorite Driver
❑ 261 Mark Martin .50 .23
IROC Champion
❑ 262 Jeff Gordon .50 .23
Year in Review
❑ 263 Sterling Marlin .30 .14
Year in Review
❑ 264 Rusty Wallace .50 .23
Year in Review
❑ 265 Ernie Irvan .30 .14
Year in Review
❑ 266 Ernie Irvan .30 .14
Year in Review
❑ 267 Darlington Speedway .20 .09
Year in Review
❑ 268 Rusty Wallace in Pits .50 .23
Year in Review
❑ 269 Terry Labonte .50 .23
Year in Review
❑ 270 Rusty Wallace .50 .23
Year in Review
❑ 271 Talladega Speedway .20 .09
Year in Review
❑ 272 Ernie Irvan w/Crew .30 .14
Year in Review
❑ 273 Jeff Gordon 1.00 .45
Year in Review
❑ 274 Geoff Bodine .30 .14
Year in Review
❑ 275 Jeff Gordon 1.00 .45
Year in Review
❑ 276 Rusty Wallace .50 .23
Year in Review
❑ 277 Rusty Wallace .50 .23
Year in Review
❑ 278 Rusty Wallace .50 .23
Year in Review
❑ 279 Jimmy Spencer .30 .14
Year in Review
❑ 280 Ricky Rudd w/ Crew .30 .14
Year in Review
❑ 281 Geoff Bodine .30 .14
Year in Review
❑ 282 Jimmy Spencer .30 .14
Year in Review
❑ 283 Jeff Gordon 1.00 .45
Year in Review
❑ 284 Mark Martin .50 .23
Jack Roush
Year in Review
❑ 285 Geoff Bodine .30 .14
Year in Review
❑ 286 Rusty Wallace .50 .23
Year in Review
❑ 287 Bill Elliott .50 .23
Junior Johnson
Year in Review
❑ 288 Terry Labonte .50 .23
Year in Review
❑ 289 Rusty Wallace w/ Crew .50 .23
Year in Review
❑ 290 Rusty Wallace .50 .23
Year in Review
❑ 291 Geoff Bodine .30 .14
Year in Review
❑ 292 Dale Jarrett .50 .23
Year in Review
❑ 293 Rockingham Speedway .20 .09
Year in Review
❑ 294 Terry Labonte .50 .23
Year in Review
❑ 295 Mark Martin .50 .23
Year in Review
❑ 296 Bobby Labonte Crash .50 .23
Memorable Moment
❑ 297 Phoenix International .20 .09
Memorable Moment
Tearin' Down The Walls
❑ 298 Checklist #1 .20 .09
❑ 299 Checklist #2 .20 .09
❑ 300 Checklist #3 .20 .09

1995 Maxx Premier Series Update

This 15-card set is an update to the regular 300 card Premier Series set. The set is packaged in a brown box and was primarily distributed through the Maxx Club.

	MINT	NRMT
COMPLETE SET (15)	6.00	2.70
COMMON CARD (1-15)	.20	.09
COMMON DRIVER (1-15)	.30	.14

❑ 1 Loy Allen .30 .14
❑ 2 Elton Sawyer .30 .14
❑ 3 Hut Stricklin .30 .14
❑ 4 Ward Burton .30 .14
❑ 5 Bobby Hillin .30 .14
❑ 6 Dave Marcis .50 .23
❑ 7 Greg Sacks .30 .14
❑ 8 Jeremy Mayfield 1.00 .45
❑ 9 Mike Beam .20 .09
❑ 10 Ricky Craven .30 .14
❑ 11 Robert Pressley .30 .14
❑ 12 Ernie Irvan .50 .23
❑ 13 Ernie Irvan in Pits .50 .23
❑ 14 Ernie Irvan's Car .30
❑ 15 Checklist .20

1995 Maxx Larger than Li
Dale Earnhardt

This seven-card set is a 8" X 10" version of cards nu 1-7 of the regular Chase the Champions set. The r size card # 8 from the Maxx Dale Earnhardt Cha Champion series came along with the seven jumbo in a large foil pack. There were a reported 20,000 produced. The cards were primarily distributed th the Maxx Club.

	MINT
COMPLETE SET (7)	25.00
COMMON CARD (1-7)	5.00

1996 Maxx

JIMMY SPENCER

The 1996 Maxx set has a total of 100 cards. The packs were distributed 36-packs per foil box. T features the topical subset Memorable Moments (# 50, 61, 70, 97 and 98) and closes with checklist (#99-100). A wide assortment of insert cards randomly packed as well. Sterling Marlin was featu the 1996 Maxx series one wrapper. There was a S Marlin redemption card randomly inserted in pac rate of one in 12. The card entiled the holder to the card for a five card Sterling Marlin set. Th expired May 1, 1996. The complete Sterling Marlin priced in the header below.

	MINT
COMPLETE SET (100)	10.00
COMMON CARD (1-100)	.10
COMMON DRIVER (1-100)	.20
S.MARLIN REDEMPTION SET (5)	5.00

❑ 1 Rick Mast .20
❑ 2 Rusty Wallace .75
❑ 3 Dale Earnhardt 1.50
❑ 4 Sterling Marlin .40
❑ 5 Terry Labonte .75
❑ 6 Mark Martin .75
❑ 7 Geoff Bodine .20
❑ 8 Jeff Burton .40
❑ 9 Lake Speed .20
❑ 10 Ricky Rudd .40
❑ 11 Brett Bodine .20
❑ 12 Derrike Cope .20
❑ 13 Joe Nemechek's Car .10
❑ 14 Jimmy Spencer's Car .10
❑ 15 Dick Trickle .20
❑ 16 Ted Musgrave .20
❑ 17 Darrell Waltrip .40
❑ 18 Bobby Labonte .60
❑ 19 Geoff Bodine's Car .10
❑ 20 Rick Mast's Car .10
❑ 21 Morgan Shepherd .20
❑ 22 Bobby Labonte's Car .40
❑ 23 Jimmy Spencer .20
❑ 24 Jeff Gordon 1.50
❑ 25 Ken Schrader .20
❑ 26 Hut Stricklin .20
❑ 27 Darrell Waltrip's Car .20
❑ 28 Dale Jarrett .60
❑ 29 Steve Grissom .20
❑ 30 Michael Waltrip .20
❑ 31 Kyle Petty's Car .20
❑ 32 Bill Elliott's Car .40
❑ 33 Robert Pressley .20
❑ 34 Jimmy Hensley's Car .10
Greg Sacks' Car
Rockingham Rumble Memorable Moment
❑ 35 Terry Labonte's Car .40
❑ 36 Ride Across America MM .10
❑ 37 John Andretti .20
❑ 38 Ricky Rudd's Car .20
❑ 39 Michael Waltrip's Car .10
❑ 40 Bobby Hamilton's Car .10
❑ 41 Ricky Craven .20

Kyle Petty	.40	.18
Richard Petty	.40	.18
Bobby Hamilton	.20	.09
Derrike Cope's Car	.10	.05
Steve Grissom's Car	.10	.05
John Andretti's Car	.10	.05
Dale Jarrett's Car	.40	.18
Ken Schrader's Car	.10	.05
Promising Pole Position MM	.10	.05
Morgan Shepherd's Car	.10	.05
Robert Yates	.10	.05
Rusty Wallace's Car	.40	.18
Mark Martin's Car	.40	.18
Roger Penske Don Miller	.10	.05
Ricky Craven's Car	.10	.05
Robert Pressley's Car	.10	.05
en Wood Kim Wood Eddie Wood Glen Wood	.10	.05
eff Burton's Car	.10	.05
Richard Jackson	.10	.05
lton Sawyer's Car Lake Speed's Car Bitten By The Monster Mile Memorable Moment	.10	.05
Brett Bodine's Car	.10	.05
ed Musgrave's Car	.10	.05
ake Speed's Car	.10	.05
ack Roush	.10	.05
Rick Hendrick	.10	.05
huck Rider	.10	.05
harles Hardy	.10	.05
oe Gibbs	.20	.09
Mark Martin's Car Testing In The Rain MM	.40	.18
unior Johnson	.20	.09
ravis Carter	.10	.05
obby Allison	.20	.09
ohnny Benson Jr.	.20	.09
had Little	.20	.09
ason Keller	.20	.09
Mike McLaughlin	.20	.09
eff Green	.20	.09
eonard Wood	.10	.05
ay Evernham	.40	.18
ill Ingle	.10	.05
oug Hewitt	.10	.05
obbie Loomis	.10	.05
ndy Petree	.10	.05
arry McReynolds	.10	.05
teve Hmiel	.10	.05
oe Nemechek	.20	.09
eff Gordon's Car	.75	.35
obin Pemberton	.10	.05
Mike Beam	.10	.05
en Howes	.10	.05
oward Comstock	.10	.05
ony Glover	.10	.05
ll Elliott	.75	.35
ary DeHart	.10	.05
mmy Makar	.10	.05
ed Musgrave's Car Riding The Wall MM	.10	.05
ale Jarrett's Car Ernie Irvan's Car On The Comeback Trail MM	.40	.18
Checklist (1-100)	.10	.05
Checklist (Chase Cards)	.10	.05

1996 Maxx Chase the Champion

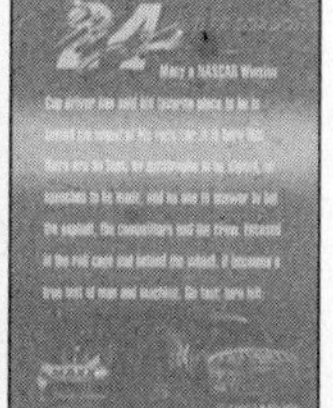

e second year, Maxx produced an insert set g the previous season's Winston Cup champion. ase the Champion cards will be distributed over the of 1996 in various Maxx racing card products. one packs contained card #1 at the wrapper stated one in 36. Cards #2 and 3 were inserted in factory '96 Maxx Premier Plus. Cards # 4, 5 and 6 were randomly inserted in packs of '96 Maxx Odyssey at a rate of one per 18 packs. Card # 8 was found in Maxx Made in America packs. Cards #7 and 9-14 were supposed to be distributed through packs of Maxx products scheduled to be released in the second half of the year. Since Maxx filed for bankruptcy those products never made it to the market. But the cards had already been printed and some decent quantities of those cards did become available in the secondary market.

	MINT	NRMT
COMPLETE SET (14)	175.00	80.00
COMMON CARD	10.00	4.50
❑ 1 Jeff Gordon	10.00	4.50
❑ 2 Jeff Gordon	15.00	6.75
❑ 3 Jeff Gordon	15.00	6.75
❑ 4 Jeff Gordon	10.00	4.50
❑ 5 Jeff Gordon	10.00	4.50
❑ 6 Jeff Gordon	15.00	6.75
❑ 7 Jeff Gordon	15.00	6.75
❑ 8 Jeff Gordon	15.00	6.75
❑ 9 Jeff Gordon	15.00	6.75
❑ 10 Jeff Gordon	15.00	6.75
❑ 11 Jeff Gordon	15.00	6.75
❑ 12 Jeff Gordon	15.00	6.75
❑ 13 Jeff Gordon	15.00	6.75
❑ 14 Jeff Gordon	15.00	6.75

1996 Maxx Family Ties

Family Ties inserts feature a famous racing family connection on silver foil card stock. The cards were randomly inserted in packs at the rate of one in 18.

	MINT	NRMT
COMPLETE SET (5)	15.00	6.75
COMMON CARD (FT1-FT5)	2.50	1.10
❑ FT1 Geoff Bodine Brett Bodine Todd Bodine	2.50	1.10
❑ FT2 Jeff Burton Ward Burton	2.50	1.10
❑ FT3 Terry Labonte Bobby Labonte	6.00	2.70
❑ FT4 Rusty Wallace Mike Wallace Kenny Wallace	6.00	2.70
❑ FT5 Darrell Waltrip Michael Waltrip	2.50	1.10

1996 Maxx On The Road Again

Transporters were again the focus of Maxx's On the Road inserts. The first five cards of the series were randomly inserted in packs at the rate of one in 18 packs.

	MINT	NRMT
COMPLETE SET (5)	4.00	1.80
COMMON CARD (OTRA1-OTRA5)	.75	.35
❑ OTRA1 Kyle Petty's Transporter	.75	.35
❑ OTRA2 Busch Grand National Transporter	.75	.35
❑ OTRA3 Rusty Wallace's Trans.	1.50	.70
❑ OTRA4 Darrell Waltrip's Trans.	.75	.35
❑ OTRA5 Winston Cup Transporter	.75	.35

1996 Maxx Over The Wall

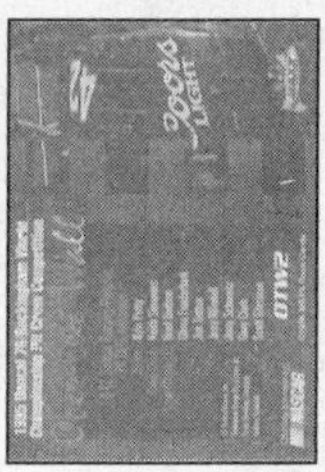

The 1995 Unocal 76/Rockingham World Championship Pit Crew Competition was the focus of this 10-card Maxx insert set. The cards included the featured pit crew's best time in the competition printed in blue foil. They were randomly inserted in Maxx packs at the rate of 1:12.

	MINT	NRMT
COMPLETE SET (10)	10.00	4.50
COMMON CARD (OTW1-OTW10)	1.25	.55
❑ OTW1 Brett Bodine's Car	1.25	.55
❑ OTW2 Kyle Petty's Car	2.50	1.10
❑ OTW3 Jeff Burton's Car	2.50	1.10
❑ OTW4 Derrike Cope's Car	1.25	.55
❑ OTW5 Terry Labonte's Car	5.00	2.20
❑ OTW6 Geoff Bodine's Car	1.25	.55
❑ OTW7 Bobby Labonte's Car	4.00	1.80
❑ OTW8 Joe Nemechek's Car	1.25	.55
❑ OTW9 Ricky Rudd's Car	2.50	1.10
❑ OTW10 Todd Bodine's Car	1.25	.55

1996 Maxx Racing Responses

These cards contain the answers to questions posed on the backs of the 1996 Maxx series one regular issue cards. The five cards were randomly inserted in packs at the rate of one in 12 packs.

	MINT	NRMT
COMPLETE SET (5)	.50	.23
COMMON CARD (1-5)	.10	.05
❑ 1 Responses 1-18	.10	.05
❑ 2 Responses 19-39	.10	.05
❑ 3 Responses 40-59	.10	.05
❑ 4 Responses 60-77	.10	.05
❑ 5 Responses 78-96	.10	.05

1996 Maxx SuperTrucks

Randomly inserted in packs at a rate of one in 12, this 10-card issue features top machines of the NASCAR SuperTrucks Series.

	MINT	NRMT
COMPLETE SET (10)	12.00	5.50
COMMON CARD (ST1-ST10)	1.25	.55
❑ ST1 Mike Bliss' Truck	1.25	.55
❑ ST2 Tommy Archer's Truck	1.25	.55
❑ ST3 Rodney Combs' Truck	1.25	.55
❑ ST4 Rodney Combs Jr.'s Truck	1.25	.55
❑ ST5 Chad Little's Truck	1.25	.55

Card	MINT	NRMT
❑ ST6 Derrike Cope's Truck	1.25	.55
❑ ST7 T.J.Clark's Truck	1.25	.55
❑ ST8 Darrell Waltrip's Truck	2.50	1.10
❑ ST9 Kenny Wallace's Truck	1.25	.55
❑ ST10 Kenji Momota's Truck	1.25	.55

1996 Maxx Made in America

This 100-card set was the last Maxx product released before they went out of business. As best as we can tell the product was actually distributed by Maxx's printer. The cards feature a car or driver photo on the front with a US flag in the background. There were eight cards per pack and 36 packs per box. The product was originally scheduled to have a special 1988 #99 Dale Earnhardt autograph card inserted one in 6,703 packs. We have received no confirmation that this card ever made it into packs. We have received a few reports of an unsigned version of this card being found in packs.

	MINT	NRMT
COMPLETE SET (100)	12.00	5.50
COMMON CARD (1-100)	.10	.05
COMMON DRIVER (1-100)	.20	.09
❑ 1 Rick Mast	.20	.09
❑ 2 Rusty Wallace	1.00	.45
❑ 3 Jeff Green	.20	.09
❑ 4 Sterling Marlin	.40	.18
❑ 5 Terry Labonte	1.00	.45
❑ 6 Mark Martin	1.00	.45
❑ 7 Geoff Bodine	.20	.09
❑ 8 Ernie Irvan's Car	.20	.09
❑ 9 Lake Speed	.20	.09
❑ 10 Ricky Rudd	.40	.18
❑ 11 Brett Bodine	.20	.09
❑ 12 Derrike Cope	.20	.09
❑ 13 Joe Nemechek's Car	.10	.05
❑ 14 Jimmy Spencer's Car	.10	.05
❑ 15 Jeff Burton's Car	.20	.09
❑ 16 Ted Musgrave	.20	.09
❑ 17 Darrell Waltrip	.40	.18
❑ 18 Bobby Labonte	.75	.35
❑ 19 Lake Speed's Car	.10	.05
❑ 20 Rick Mast's Car	.10	.05
❑ 21 Michael Waltrip	.10	.05
❑ 22 Ward Burton	.10	.05
❑ 23 Jimmy Spencer	.10	.05
❑ 24 Jeff Gordon	2.00	.90
❑ 25 Ken Schrader	.20	.09
❑ 26 Jeremy Mayfield's Car	.40	.18
❑ 27 Darrell Waltrip's Car	.20	.09
❑ 28 Ernie Irvan	.40	.18
❑ 29 Bobby Labonte	.75	.35
❑ 30 Johnny Benson's Car	.10	.05
❑ 31 Kyle Petty's Car	.20	.09
❑ 32 Bill Elliott's Car	.50	.23
❑ 33 Robert Pressley	.20	.09
❑ 34 Bobby Labonte's Car	.40	.18
❑ 35 Terry Labonte's Car	.50	.23
❑ 36 Ward Burton's Car	.10	.05
❑ 37 John Andretti	.20	.09
❑ 38 Ricky Rudd's Car	.20	.09
❑ 39 Bobby Hamilton's Car	.10	.05
❑ 40 Dale Jarrett's Car	.40	.18
❑ 41 Ricky Craven	.20	.09
❑ 42 Kyle Petty	.40	.18
❑ 43 Richard Petty	.40	.18
❑ 44 Bobby Hamilton	.20	.09
❑ 45 Derrike Cope's Car	.10	.05
❑ 46 Kenny Wallace	.20	.09
❑ 47 John Andretti's Car	.10	.05
❑ 48 Geoff Bodine's Car	.10	.05
❑ 49 Ken Schrader's Car	.10	.05
❑ 50 Morgan Shepherd's Car	.10	.05
❑ 51 Michael Waltrip's Car	.10	.05
❑ 52 Mike McLaughlin's Car	.10	.05
❑ 53 Rusty Wallace's Car	.50	.23
❑ 54 Mark Martin's Car	.50	.23
❑ 55 Tim Fedewa	.20	.09
❑ 56 Ricky Craven's Car	.10	.05
❑ 57 Robert Pressley's Car	.10	.05
❑ 58 Jason Keller's Car	.10	.05
❑ 59 Tim Fedewa's Car	.10	.05
❑ 60 Larry Pearson's Car	.10	.05
❑ 61 Hermie Sadler	.20	.09
❑ 62 Jeff Fuller's Car	.10	.05
❑ 63 Ted Musgrave's Car	.10	.05
❑ 64 David Green	.20	.09
❑ 65 Phil Parsons' Car	.10	.05
❑ 66 Sterling Marlin's Car	.20	.09
❑ 67 Steve Grissom	.20	.09
❑ 68 Chad Little's Car	.10	.05
❑ 69 Hermie Sadler's Car	.10	.05
❑ 70 Jeff Green's Car	.10	.05
❑ 71 Phil Parsons	.20	.09
❑ 72 Jeff Fuller	.20	.09
❑ 73 Jeff Fuller's Car	.10	.05
❑ 74 Chad Little	.20	.09
❑ 75 Morgan Shepherd	.20	.09
❑ 76 Jason Keller	.20	.09
❑ 77 Mike McLaughlin	.20	.09
❑ 78 Ricky Craven	.20	.09
❑ 79 Ricky Craven's Car	.10	.05
❑ 80 Michael Waltrip	.20	.09
❑ 81 Michael Waltrip's Car	.10	.05
❑ 82 Terry Labonte	1.00	.45
❑ 83 Terry Labonte's Car	.50	.23
❑ 84 Joe Nemechek	.20	.09
❑ 85 Joe Nemechek's Car	.10	.05
❑ 86 Larry Pearson	.20	.09
❑ 87 Joe Nemechek	.20	.09
❑ 88 Dale Jarrett	.75	.35
❑ 89 Rodney Combs	.20	.09
❑ 90 Bobby Labonte's Car	.40	.18
❑ 91 Steve Grissom	.20	.09
❑ 92 Steve Grissom's Car	.10	.05
❑ 93 Kenny Wallace's Car	.10	.05
❑ 94 Bill Elliott	1.00	.45
❑ 95 Kenny Wallace	.20	.09
❑ 96 Dale Jarrett	.75	.35
❑ 97 Dale Jarrett's Car	.40	.18
❑ 98 Jeremy Mayfield	.60	.25
❑ 99 Jeff Burton	.40	.18
❑ 100 Checklist	.10	.05

1996 Maxx Made in America Blue Ribbon

Each card in this 15-card insert set features a pop-up design. The car or driver photo on the front of each card can be popped out and formed into the shape of the photo. The cards were inserted one per pack.

	MINT	NRMT
COMPLETE SET (15)	5.00	2.20
COMMON CARD (BR1-BR15)	.15	.07
COMMON DRIVER (BR1-BR15)	.30	.14
❑ BR1 Derrike Cope's Car	.15	.07
❑ BR2 Ernie Irvan	1.00	.45
❑ BR3 Bill Elliott	1.25	.55
❑ BR4 Ricky Craven	.30	.14
❑ BR5 Michael Waltrip	.30	.14
❑ BR6 Rusty Wallace's Car	.60	.25
❑ BR7 Bobby Labonte's Car	.50	.23
❑ BR8 John Andretti	.30	.14
❑ BR9 Ward Burton	.30	.14
❑ BR10 Ricky Rudd's Car	.30	.14
❑ BR11 Darrell Waltrip's Car	.30	.14
❑ BR12 Johnny Benson's Car	.15	.07
❑ BR13 Sterling Marlin's Car	.30	.14
❑ BR14 Chad Little's Car	.15	.07
❑ BR15 Jeff Green	.30	.14

1996 Maxx Odyssey

This 100-card set features most of the top names from Winston Cup and Busch racing. The cards were printed on 18 point paper stock as opposed to Maxx's normal 14 point board. Each card front features a driver or car photo, gold foil stamping and the Racing Odyssey logo. Cards were packaged 10 cards per pack and 36 packs per box.

	MINT	NRMT
COMPLETE SET (100)	8.00	3.60

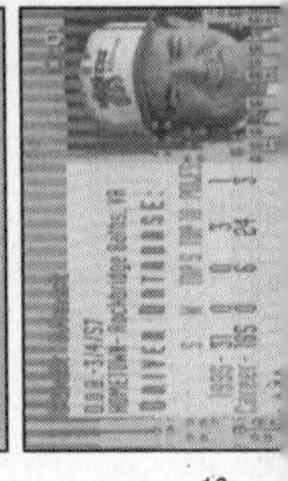

	MINT
COMMON CARD (1-100)	.10
COMMON DRIVER (1-100)	.20
❑ 1 Rick Mast	.20
❑ 2 Rusty Wallace	.75
❑ 3 Jeff Green	.20
❑ 4 Sterling Marlin	.40
❑ 5 Terry Labonte	.75
❑ 6 Mark Martin	.75
❑ 7 Geoff Bodine	.20
❑ 8 Geoff Bodine's Car	.10
❑ 9 Lake Speed	.20
❑ 10 Ricky Rudd	.40
❑ 11 Brett Bodine	.20
❑ 12 Derrike Cope	.20
❑ 13 Joe Nemechek's Car	.10
❑ 14 Jimmy Spencer's Car	.10
❑ 15 Jeff Burton's Car	.20
❑ 16 Ted Musgrave	.20
❑ 17 Darrell Waltrip	.40
❑ 18 Bobby Labonte	.60
❑ 19 Lake Speed's Car	.10
❑ 20 Rick Mast's Car	.10
❑ 21 Michael Waltrip	.20
❑ 22 Ward Burton	.20
❑ 23 Jimmy Spencer	.20
❑ 24 Jeff Gordon	1.50
❑ 25 Ken Schrader	.20
❑ 26 Jeremy Mayfield's Car	.40
❑ 27 Darrell Waltrip's Car	.20
❑ 28 Ernie Irvan	.40
❑ 29 Steve Grissom	.20
❑ 30 Johnny Benson's Car	.10
❑ 31 Kyle Petty's Car	.20
❑ 32 Bill Elliott's Car	.40
❑ 33 Robert Pressley	.20
❑ 34 Bobby Labonte's Car	.40
❑ 35 Terry Labonte's Car	.40
❑ 36 Ward Burton's Car	.10
❑ 37 John Andretti	.20
❑ 38 Ricky Rudd's Car	.20
❑ 39 Bobby Hamilton's Car	.10
❑ 40 Dale Jarrett's Car	.40
❑ 41 Ricky Craven	.20
❑ 42 Kyle Petty	.40
❑ 43 Richard Petty	.40
❑ 44 Bobby Hamilton	.20
❑ 45 Derrike Cope's Car	.10
❑ 46 Steve Grissom's Car	.10
❑ 47 John Andretti's Car	.10
❑ 48 Ernie Irvan's Car	.20
❑ 49 Ken Schrader's Car	.10
❑ 50 Morgan Shepherd's Car	.10
❑ 51 Michael Waltrip's Car	.10
❑ 52 Mike McLaughlin's Car	.10
❑ 53 Rusty Wallace's Car	.40
❑ 54 Mark Martin's Car	.40
❑ 55 Tim Fedewa	.20
❑ 56 Ricky Craven's Car	.10
❑ 57 Robert Pressley's Car	.10
❑ 58 Jason Keller's Car	.10
❑ 59 Tim Fedewa's Car	.10
❑ 60 Larry Pearson's Car	.10
❑ 61 Hermie Sadler	.20
❑ 62 Brett Bodine's Car	.10
❑ 63 Ted Musgrave's Car	.10
❑ 64 David Green	.20
❑ 65 Phil Parsons' Car	.10
❑ 66 Steve Grissom's Car	.10
❑ 67 Steve Grissom	.20
❑ 68 Chad Little's Car	.10
❑ 69 Hermie Sadler's Car	.10
❑ 70 Jeff Green's Car	.10
❑ 71 Phil Parsons	.20
❑ 72 Jeff Fuller	.20
❑ 73 Jeff Fuller's Car	.10
❑ 74 Chad Little	.20
❑ 75 Morgan Shepherd	.20
❑ 76 Jason Keller	.20
❑ 77 Mike McLaughlin	.20
❑ 78 Ricky Craven	.20
❑ 79 Ricky Craven's Car	.10
❑ 80 Michael Waltrip	.20

Michael Waltrip's Car	.10	.05
Terry Labonte	.75	.35
Terry Labonte's Car	.40	.18
Joe Nemechek	.20	.09
Joe Nemechek's Car	.10	.05
Larry Pearson	.20	.09
Joe Nemechek	.20	.09
Dale Jarrett	.60	.25
Rodney Combs	.20	.09
Mike Skinner Will Lind	.20	.09
Steve Grissom	.20	.09
Steve Grissom's Car	.10	.05
Kenny Wallace's Car	.10	.05
Bill Elliott	.75	.35
Kenny Wallace	.20	.09
Dale Jarrett	.60	.25
Dale Jarrett's Car	.40	.18
Jeremy Mayfield	.50	.23
Jeff Burton	.40	.18
Checklist	.10	.05

1996 Maxx Odyssey Millennium

0-card, holographic, die-cut set features Winston rivers and their cars. The cards were randomly ed in packs at a rate of one per three packs. The was originally intended to be the first 10 of a larger d set. The rest of the cards were not released due to s bankruptcy shortly after the release of Odyssey.

	MINT	NRMT
LETE SET (10)	12.00	5.50
ION CARD (MM1-MM10)	.40	.18
ION DRIVER (MM1-MM10)	.75	.35

1996 Maxx Odyssey On The Road Again

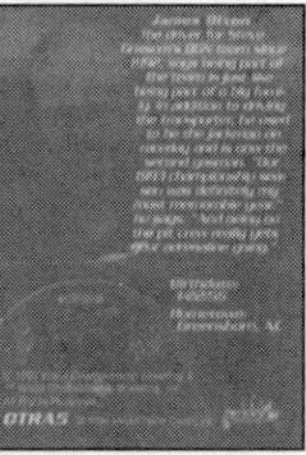

ve-card insert features the transporters that bring ce cars and equipment to and from the track. The were randomly inserted one in three packs.

	MINT	NRMT
LETE SET (5)	2.00	.90
ON CARD (OTRA1-OTRA5)	.30	.14
A1 Steve Grissom's Trans.	.30	.14
A2 Michael Waltrip's Trans.	.30	.14
A3 Sterling Marlin's Trans.	.60	.25
A4 Brett Bodine's Trans.	.30	.14
A5 Steve Grissom's Trans.	.30	.14

1996 Maxx Odyssey Radio Active

5-card set use die-cut printing to make them a pop-d. The set features drivers from Winston Cup, and the SuperTruck series. The cards were nly inserted in packs at a rate of one per two packs.

	MINT	NRMT
LETE SET (15)	8.00	3.60
ON CARD (RA1-RA15)	.20	.09
ON DRIVER (RA1-RA15)	.40	.18

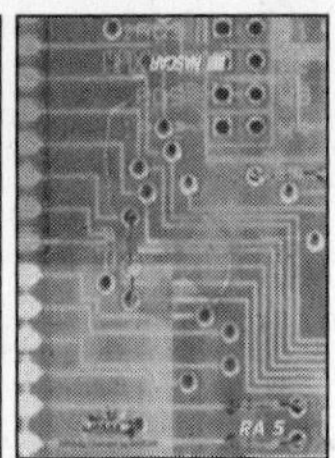

1996 Maxx Premier Series

The 1996 Maxx Premier set was issued in one series totalling 300 cards. The cards were sold via mail-order through the Maxx Club. The product was sold in complete set form only. The set features a "Year in Review" yearbook theme and contains NASCAR Winston Cup, Busch Grand National and SuperTruck drivers, owners and crew chiefs. The cards were available with a sheet and binder combination to house the set. Cards #2 and #3 of the Chase the Champion series was available as part of this set. The seven card Superlatives set was also inserted one per factory Premier Series set. Sets originally retailed to Club members for $49.99.

	MINT	NRMT
COMPLETE SET (300)	50.00	22.00
COMMON CARD (1-300)	.20	.09
COMMON DRIVER (1-300)	.30	.14
❑ 1 Rick Mast	.30	.14
❑ 2 Rusty Wallace	2.00	.90
❑ 3 Dale Earnhardt	4.00	1.80
❑ 4 Sterling Marlin	.50	.23
❑ 5 Terry Labonte	2.00	.90
❑ 6 Mark Martin	2.00	.90
❑ 7 Geoff Bodine	.30	.14
❑ 8 Jeff Burton	.50	.23
❑ 9 Lake Speed	.30	.14
❑ 10 Ricky Rudd	.50	.23
❑ 11 Brett Bodine	.30	.14
❑ 12 Derrike Cope	.30	.14
❑ 13 MM - Rockingham Rumble	.20	.09
❑ 14 MM - Rain, Rain, Go Away	.20	.09
❑ 15 Dick Trickle	.30	.14
❑ 16 Ted Musgrave	.30	.14
❑ 17 Darrell Waltrip	.50	.23
❑ 18 Bobby Labonte	1.50	.70
❑ 19 Loy Allen	.30	.14
❑ 20 Jeremy Mayfield's Car	.60	.25
❑ 21 Morgan Shepherd	.30	.14
❑ 22 Randy LaJoie	.30	.14
❑ 23 Jimmy Spencer	.30	.14
❑ 24 Jeff Gordon	4.00	1.80
❑ 25 Ken Schrader	.30	.14
❑ 26 Hut Stricklin	.30	.14
❑ 27 Elton Sawyer	.30	.14
❑ 28 Dale Jarrett	1.50	.70
❑ 29 Steve Grissom	.30	.14
❑ 30 Michael Waltrip	.30	.14
❑ 31 Ward Burton	.30	.14
❑ 32 Chuck Brown	.30	.14
❑ 33 Robert Pressley	.30	.14
❑ 34 Terry Labonte's Car	1.00	.45
❑ 35 Mark Martin's Car	1.00	.45
❑ 36 Bobby Labonte's Car	.75	.35
❑ 37 John Andretti	.30	.14
❑ 38 Rusty Wallace's Car	1.00	.45
❑ 39 Loy Allen's Car	.20	.09
❑ 40 Greg Sacks	.30	.14
❑ 41 Ricky Craven	.30	.14
❑ 42 Kyle Petty	.50	.23
❑ 43 Richard Petty	1.00	.45
❑ 44 Bobby Hamilton	.30	.14
❑ 45 Jeff Purvis	.30	.14
❑ 46 Elton Sawyer's Car	.20	.09
❑ 47 Ernie Irvan's Car	.30	.14
❑ 48 Joe Nemechek's Car	.20	.09
❑ 49 Morgan Shepherd's Car	.20	.09
❑ 50 Bill Elliott's Car	1.00	.45
❑ 51 Ricky Craven's Car	.20	.09
❑ 52 Richard Petty's Car	.50	.23
❑ 53 Ken Schrader's Car	.20	.09
❑ 54 Ward Burton's Car	.20	.09
❑ 55 Dick Trickle's Car	.20	.09
❑ 56 Ricky Rudd's Car	.30	.14
❑ 57 Robert Pressley's Car	.20	.09
❑ 58 Ted Musgrave's Car	.20	.09
❑ 59 Rick Mast's Car	.20	.09
❑ 60 Darrell Waltrip's Car	.30	.14
❑ 61 Sterling Marlin's Car	.30	.14
❑ 62 Geoff Bodine's Car	.20	.09
❑ 63 Jimmy Spencer's Car	.20	.09
❑ 64 Todd Bodine's Car	.20	.09
❑ 65 Michael Waltrip's Car	.20	.09
❑ 66 Brett Bodine's Car	.20	.09
❑ 67 Derrike Cope's Car	.20	.09
❑ 68 John Andretti's Car	.20	.09
❑ 69 Steve Grissom's Car	.20	.09
❑ 70 Lake Speed's Car	.20	.09
❑ 71 Dave Marcis	.50	.23
❑ 72 Kyle Petty's Car	.30	.14
❑ 73 Dale Earnhardt's Car	2.00	.90
❑ 74 Ward Burton's Car	.20	.09
❑ 75 Todd Bodine	.30	.14
❑ 76 Mike Skinner	.30	.14
❑ 77 Ron Hornaday Jr.	.30	.14
❑ 78 Joe Ruttman	.30	.14
❑ 79 Butch Miller	.30	.14
❑ 80 Roger Penske	.20	.09
❑ 81 Don Miller	.20	.09
❑ 82 Larry McClure	.20	.09
❑ 83 Jack Roush	.20	.09
❑ 84 Joe Gibbs	.30	.14
❑ 85 Felix Sabates	.20	.09
❑ 86 Gary Bechtel	.20	.09
❑ 87 Joe Nemechek	.30	.14
❑ 88 Ernie Irvan	.50	.23
❑ 89 Dale Jarrett's Car	.75	.35
❑ 90 Mike Wallace	.30	.14
❑ 91 Len Wood	.20	.09
❑ 92 Glen Wood	.20	.09
❑ 93 Charles Hardy	.20	.09
❑ 94 Bill Elliott	2.00	.90
❑ 95 Junior Johnson	.20	.09
❑ 96 Rick Hendrick	.20	.09
❑ 97 Leo Jackson	.20	.09
❑ 98 Jeremy Mayfield	1.25	.55
❑ 99 Bobby Allison	.20	.09
❑ 100 Carolyn Bechtel	.20	.09
❑ 101 Michael Kranefuss	.20	.09
❑ 102 Carl Haas	.20	.09
❑ 103 Bud Moore	.20	.09
❑ 104 Chuck Rider	.20	.09
❑ 105 Eddie Wood	.20	.09
❑ 106 Richard Jackson	.20	.09
❑ 107 Bill Stavola	.20	.09
❑ 108 Cale Yarborough	.20	.09
❑ 109 Junie Donlavey	.20	.09
❑ 110 Larry Hedrick	.20	.09
❑ 111 Robert Yates	.20	.09
❑ 112 Travis Carter	.20	.09
❑ 113 Alan Dillard	.20	.09
❑ 114 Butch Mock	.20	.09
❑ 115 Harry Melling	.20	.09
❑ 116 Bill Davis	.20	.09
❑ 117 Kim Wood Hall	.20	.09
❑ 118 Mike Wallace's Car	.20	.09
❑ 119 Andy Petree	.20	.09
❑ 120 Buddy Parrott	.20	.09
❑ 121 Steve Hmiel	.20	.09
❑ 122 Jimmy Makar	.20	.09
❑ 123 Robin Pemberton	.20	.09
❑ 124 Tony Glover	.20	.09
❑ 125 Leonard Wood	.20	.09
❑ 126 Larry McReynolds	.20	.09
❑ 127 Gary DeHart	.20	.09
❑ 128 Ray Evernham	.50	.23
❑ 129 Ken Howes	.20	.09
❑ 130 Bill Ingle	.20	.09
❑ 131 Pete Peterson	.20	.09
❑ 132 Cecil Gordon	.20	.09
❑ 133 Donnie Wingo	.20	.09
❑ 134 Doug Hewitt	.20	.09
❑ 135 Philippe Lopez	.20	.09
❑ 136 Donnie Richeson	.20	.09
❑ 137 Richard Broome	.20	.09
❑ 138 Kevin Hamlin	.20	.09
❑ 139 Charley Pressley	.20	.09
❑ 140 Dale Fischlein	.20	.09
❑ 141 Paul Andrews	.20	.09
❑ 142 Robbie Loomis	.20	.09
❑ 143 Troy Selberg	.20	.09
❑ 144 Jimmy Fennig	.20	.09
❑ 145 Barry Dodson	.20	.09
❑ 146 Waddell Wilson	.20	.09
❑ 147 Dale Inman	.20	.09
❑ 148 Peter Sospenzo	.20	.09
❑ 149 Tim Brewer	.20	.09
❑ 150 Rick Ren	.20	.09
❑ 151 Mike Beam	.20	.09
❑ 152 Howard Comstock	.20	.09
❑ 153 Jeff Hammond	.20	.09
❑ 154 Chris Hussey	.20	.09
❑ 155 Todd Parrott	.20	.09
❑ 156 Johnny Benson's Car	.20	.09
❑ 157 Chad Little's Car	.20	.09
❑ 158 Mike McLaughlin's Car	.20	.09
❑ 159 Jeff Green's Car	.20	.09
❑ 160 Chad Little	.30	.14

❑ 161 David Green .30 .14
❑ 162 Jeff Green .30 .14
❑ 163 Curtis Markham .30 .14
❑ 164 Hermie Sadler .30 .14
❑ 165 Jeff Fuller .30 .14
❑ 166 Bobby Dotter .30 .14
❑ 167 Tracy Leslie .30 .14
❑ 168 Larry Pearson .30 .14
❑ 169 Dennis Setzer .30 .14
❑ 170 Ricky Craven .50 .23
❑ 171 Tim Fedewa .30 .14
❑ 172 Mike McLaughlin .30 .14
❑ 173 Jim Bown .30 .14
❑ 174 Elton Sawyer .30 .14
❑ 175 Jason Keller .30 .14
❑ 176 Rodney Combs .30 .14
❑ 177 Doug Heveron .30 .14
❑ 178 Tommy Houston .30 .14
❑ 179 Kevin Lapage .30 .14
❑ 180 Maxx Car .20 .09
❑ 181 Phil Parsons .30 .14
❑ 182 Ricky Craven's Car .20 .09
❑ 183 Patty Moise .30 .14
❑ 184 Kenny Wallace .30 .14
❑ 185 Terry Labonte BGN 2.00 .90
❑ 186 Steve Grissom BGN .30 .14
❑ 187 Steve Grissom's Car .20 .09
❑ 188 Joe Nemechek BGN .30 .14
❑ 189 Joe Nemechek's Car .20 .09
❑ 190 Michael Waltrip BGN .30 .14
❑ 191 Michael Waltrip's Car .20 .09
❑ 192 Ronnie Silver .20 .09
❑ 193 Barney Hall .20 .09
❑ 194 Eli Gold .20 .09
❑ 195 Benny Parsons .20 .09
❑ 196 Dr. Jerry Punch .20 .09
❑ 197 Buddy Baker .20 .09
❑ 198 Winston Kelley .20 .09
❑ 199 Jim Phillips .20 .09
❑ 200 John Kernan .20 .09
❑ 201 Randy Pemberton .20 .09
❑ 202 Bill Weber .20 .09
❑ 203 Joe Moore .20 .09
❑ 204 Bob Jenkins .20 .09
❑ 205 Allen Bestwick .20 .09
❑ 206 Glenn Jarrett .20 .09
❑ 207 Dr. Dick Berggren .20 .09
❑ 208 Mel Walen .20 .09
❑ 209 Dale Plank .20 .09
❑ 210 Jon Compagnone .20 .09
❑ 211 Paul White .20 .09
❑ 212 Ray Guss .20 .09
❑ 213 Jeff Wildung .20 .09
❑ 214 Phil Warren .20 .09
❑ 215 Mike Helton .20 .09
❑ 216 Gary Nelson .20 .09
❑ 217 Ray Hill .20 .09
❑ 218 Carl Hill .20 .09
❑ 219 Brian DeHart .20 .09
❑ 220 Jack Whittemore .20 .09
❑ 221 Jimmy Cox .20 .09
❑ 222 Bruce Roney .20 .09
❑ 223 Marlin Wright .20 .09
❑ 224 David Hoots .20 .09
❑ 225 Tim Earp .20 .09
❑ 226 Doyle Ford .20 .09
❑ 227 Buster Auton .20 .09
❑ 228 Elmo Langley .20 .09
❑ 229 Walt Green .20 .09
❑ 230 Gary Miller .20 .09
❑ 231 Morris Metcalfe .20 .09
❑ 232 Rich Burgdoff .20 .09
❑ 233 Hoss Berry .20 .09
❑ 234 Steve Peterson .20 .09
❑ 235 Jason Keller's Car .20 .09
❑ 236 Patty Moise's Car .20 .09
❑ 237 Kenny Wallace's Car .20 .09
❑ 238 Kenny Wallace's Car .20 .09
❑ 239 Curtis Markham's Car .20 .09
❑ 240 Tim Fedewa's Car .20 .09
❑ 241 Dennis Setzer's Car .20 .09
❑ 242 Terry Labonte's Car 1.00 .45
❑ 243 Jeff Fuller's Car .20 .09
❑ 244 Hermie Sadler's Car .20 .09
❑ 245 Tommy Houston's Car .20 .09
❑ 246 Doug Heveron's Car .20 .09
❑ 247 Kevin LePage's Car .20 .09
❑ 248 Tracy Leslie's Car .20 .09
❑ 249 Dirk Stephens' Car .20 .09
❑ 250 MM - Testing in the Rain .20 .09
❑ 251 Larry Pearson's Car .20 .09
❑ 252 Phil Parson's Car .20 .09
❑ 253 Elton Sawyer's Car .20 .09
❑ 254 MM - Riding the Wall .20 .09
❑ 255 MM - On the Comeback Trail .20 .09
❑ 256 Larry Phillips .20 .09
WRS National Champion
❑ 257 Jeff Fuller .30 .14
Busch Rookie of the Year
❑ 258 Johnny Benson .30 .14
Busch Series Champion
❑ 259 Winston Cup Pit Crew Champs. .30 .14
#11 Lowe's Team
❑ 260 Ricky Craven .30 .14
Winston Cup Rookie of the Year
❑ 261 Bill Elliott 1.00 .45
Fan Favorite
❑ 262 Dale Earnhardt 2.00 .90
❑ 263 Race 1 - Daytona .20 .09
❑ 264 Race 2 - Rockingham .20 .09
❑ 265 Race 3 - Richmond .20 .09
❑ 266 Race 4 - Atlanta .20 .09
❑ 267 Race 5 - Darlington .20 .09
❑ 268 Race 6 - Bristol .20 .09
❑ 269 Race 7 - North Wilkesboro .20 .09
❑ 270 Race 8 - Martinsville .20 .09
❑ 271 Race 9 - Talladega .20 .09
❑ 272 Race 10 - Sonoma .20 .09
❑ 273 Winston Select Open .20 .09
❑ 274 Winston Select .20 .09
❑ 275 Race 11 - Charlotte .20 .09
❑ 276 Race 12 - Dover .20 .09
❑ 277 Race 13 - Pocono .20 .09
❑ 278 Race 14 - Michigan .20 .09
❑ 279 Race 15 - Daytona .20 .09
❑ 280 Race 16 - New Hampshire .20 .09
❑ 281 Race 17 - Pocono .20 .09
❑ 282 Race 18 - Talladega .20 .09
❑ 283 Race 19 - Indianapolis .20 .09
❑ 284 Race 20 - Watkins Glen .20 .09
❑ 285 Race 21 - Michigan .20 .09
❑ 286 Race 22 - Bristol .20 .09
❑ 287 Race 23 - Darlington .20 .09
❑ 288 Race 24 - Richmond .20 .09
❑ 289 Race 25 - Dover .20 .09
❑ 290 Race 26 - Martinsville .20 .09
❑ 291 Race 27 - North Wilkesboro .20 .09
❑ 292 Race 28 - Charlotte .20 .09
❑ 293 Race 29 - Rockingham .20 .09
❑ 294 Race 30 - Phoenix .20 .09
❑ 295 Race 31 - Atlanta .20 .09
❑ 296 Jeff Gordon 2.00 .90
Winston Cup Champion
❑ 297 Mike Skinner .30 .14
SuperTruck Champion
❑ 298 Checklist #1 .20 .09
❑ 299 Checklist #2 .20 .09
❑ 300 Checklist #3 .20 .09

1996 Maxx Premier Series Superlatives

This seven-card insert set was inserted one complete set per factory set of 1996 Maxx Premier Series. The cards take the theme of "the best" and "the most" of the 1995 NASCAR class. For example Ricky Craven is given the title "Most Likely to Succeed." Each card front features a driver and a car photo along with the driver's name and the title Maxx has honored them with.

	MINT	NRMT
COMPLETE SET (7)	7.00	3.10
COMMON CARD (SL1-SL7)	.50	.23
❑ SL1 Bill Elliott	1.50	.70
❑ SL2 Mark Martin	1.50	.70
❑ SL3 Bobby Labonte	1.25	.55
❑ SL4 Terry Labonte	1.50	.70
❑ SL5 Bobby Hamilton	.50	.23
❑ SL6 Ricky Craven	.50	.23
❑ SL7 Ken Schrader	.50	.23

1996 Maxx Autographs

These three cards were intended to be inserted into Maxx Signed and Sealed. Due to Maxx's bankruptcy the Signed and Sealed set was never distributed in a Maxx product. The exact distribution pattern of these cards is unknown.

	MINT	N
COMPLETE SET (3)	250.00	11
❑ 5 Terry Labonte	90.00	4
❑ 24 Jeff Gordon	150.00	7
❑ 25 Ken Schrader	50.00	2

1996 Maxx Band-Aid Dale Jarrett

This four-card set features Dale Jarrett bearing NASCAR Busch Grand National sponsor. We have received any reports as to how it was origi distributed.

	MINT	N
COMPLETE SET (4)	6.00	
COMMON CARD (1-4)	1.00	
❑ 1 Dale Jarrett	2.00	
❑ 2 Dale Jarrett	2.00	
❑ 3 Dale Jarrett's Car	1.00	
❑ 4 Dale Jarrett Zachary Jarrett	2.00	

1996 Maxx Pepsi 500

This five-card set features past winners of the Day 500. The cards were originally offered in 12 pac Pepsi during a regional promotion in the Daytona ar conjunction with the race. They were also offered thr the Maxx Club.

	MINT	N
COMPLETE SET (5)	5.00	
COMMON CARD (1-5)	.50	
❑ 1 Bobby Allison	1.00	
❑ 2 Geoff Bodine	.50	
❑ 3 Darrell Waltrip	1.00	
❑ 4 Derrike Cope	.50	
❑ 5 Sterling Marlin	2.00	

1997 Maxx

This 120-card set marks Maxx's return to the hobby a 18 month hiatus. The product was produced distributed by Upper Deck. Cards were distributed card packs with 24 packs per box. The packs car suggested retail price of $1.99. According to Upper this product contains 50 randomly inserted Earnhardt autographed 1988 Maxx cards.

	MINT	N
COMPLETE SET (120)	12.00	
COMMON CARD (1-120)	.10	
COMMON DRIVER (1-120)	.20	
CAR CARDS HALF VALUE		
❑ 1 Morgan Shepherd	.20	
❑ 2 Rusty Wallace	.75	
❑ 3 Dale Earnhardt	1.50	
❑ 4 Sterling Marlin	.40	
❑ 5 Terry Labonte	.75	
❑ 6 Mark Martin	.75	
❑ 7 Geoff Bodine	.20	
❑ 8 Hut Stricklin	.20	
❑ 9 Lake Speed	.20	
❑ 10 Ricky Rudd	.40	
❑ 11 Brett Bodine	.20	
❑ 12 Dale Jarrett	.60	
❑ 13 Bill Elliott	.75	
❑ 14 Dick Trickle	.20	
❑ 15 Wally Dallenbach	.20	
❑ 16 Ted Musgrave	.20	
❑ 17 Darrell Waltrip	.40	
❑ 18 Bobby Labonte	.60	
❑ 19 Gary Bradberry	.20	
❑ 20 Rick Mast	.20	
❑ 21 Michael Waltrip	.20	
❑ 22 Ward Burton	.20	
❑ 23 Jimmy Spencer	.20	
❑ 24 Jeff Gordon	1.50	
❑ 25 Ricky Craven	.20	

Chad Little	.20	.09
Kenny Wallace	.20	.09
Ernie Irvan	.40	.18
Jeff Green	.20	.09
Johnny Benson	.20	.09
Mike Skinner	.20	.09
Mike Wallace	.20	.09
Ken Schrader	.20	.09
Jeff Burton	.40	.18
David Green	.20	.09
Derrike Cope	.20	.09
Jeremy Mayfield	.50	.23
Dave Marcis	.40	.18
John Andretti	.20	.09
Robby Gordon	.20	.09
Steve Grissom	.20	.09
Joe Nemechek	.20	.09
Bobby Hamilton	.20	.09
Kyle Petty	.40	.18
Elliott Sadler	.40	.18
Morgan Shepherd's Car	.10	.05
Rusty Wallace's Car	.40	.18
Dale Earnhardt's Car	.75	.35
Sterling Marlin's Car	.20	.09
Terry Labonte's Car	.40	.18
Mark Martin's Car	.40	.18
Geoff Bodine's Car	.10	.05
Hut Stricklin's Car	.10	.05
Lake Speed's Car	.10	.05
Ricky Rudd's Car	.20	.09
Brett Bodine's Car	.10	.05
Dale Jarrett's Car	.40	.18
Bill Elliott's Car	.40	.18
Dick Trickle's Car	.10	.05
Wally Dallenbach's Car	.10	.05
Ted Musgrave's Car	.10	.05
Darrell Waltrip's Car	.20	.09
Bobby Labonte's Car	.40	.18
Gary Bradberry's Car	.10	.05
Rick Mast's Car	.10	.05
Michael Waltrip's Car	.10	.05
Ward Burton's Car	.10	.05
Jimmy Spencer's Car	.10	.05
Jeff Gordon's Car	.75	.35
Ricky Craven's Car	.10	.05
Chad Little's Car	.10	.05
Kenny Wallace's Car	.10	.05
Ernie Irvan's Car	.20	.09
Jeff Green's Car	.10	.05
Johnny Benson's Car	.10	.05
Mike Skinner's Car	.10	.05
Mike Wallace's Car	.10	.05
Ken Schrader's Car	.10	.05
Jeff Burton's Car	.20	.09
David Green's Car	.10	.05
Derrike Cope's Car	.10	.05
Jeremy Mayfield's Car	.30	.14
Dave Marcis's Car	.20	.09
John Andretti's Car	.10	.05
Robby Gordon's Car	.10	.05
Steve Grissom's Car	.10	.05
Joe Nemechek's Car	.10	.05
Bobby Hamilton's Car	.10	.05
Kyle Petty's Car	.20	.09
Elliott Sadler's Car	.10	.05
Terry Labonte PS	.40	.18
Robbie Gordon PS	.10	.05
Bobby Labonte PS	.40	.18
Ward Burton PS	.10	.05
Bill Elliott PS	.40	.18
Bill Elliott PS	.40	.18
Ted Musgrave PS	.10	.05
Rusty Wallace PS	.40	.18
Ricky Craven PS	.10	.05
Bobby Hamilton PS	.10	.05
Rusty Wallace PS	.40	.18
Ernie Irvan PS	.20	.09
Mark Martin PS	.40	.18
Jeff Burton PS	.20	.09
Joe Nemechek PS	.10	.05
Mark Martin MO	.40	.18
Rusty Wallace MO	.40	.18
Morgan Shepherd MO	.10	.05
Derrike Cope MO	.10	.05
Ricky Rudd MO	.20	.09
Lake Speed MO	.10	.05
Sterling Marlin MO	.20	.09
Michael Waltrip MO	.10	.05
Terry Labonte MO	.40	.18
Geoff Bodine MO	.10	.05
Ken Schrader MO	.10	.05
Dale Jarrett MO	.40	.18
Bill Elliott MO	.40	.18
Darrell Waltrip MO	.20	.09
Ernie Irvan MO	.20	.09

1997 Maxx Chase The Champion

This 10-card set features the top drivers from the NASCAR circuit on micro-etched cards. The cards were randomly inserted in packs at a ratio of 1:5.

	MINT	NRMT
COMPLETE SET (10)	25.00	11.00
COMMON CARD (C1-C10)	.75	.35
*SINGLES: 2.5X TO 6X BASE CARD HI		

❑ C1 Jeff Gordon	8.00	3.60
❑ C2 Mark Martin	5.00	2.20
❑ C3 Terry Labonte	5.00	2.20
❑ C4 Dale Jarrett	4.00	1.80
❑ C5 Jeff Burton	1.50	.70
❑ C6 Bobby Labonte	1.50	.70
❑ C7 Ricky Rudd	1.50	.70
❑ C8 Michael Waltrip	.75	.35
❑ C9 Jeremy Mayfield	1.00	.45
❑ C10 Bill Elliott	5.00	2.20

1997 Maxx Chase The Champion Gold

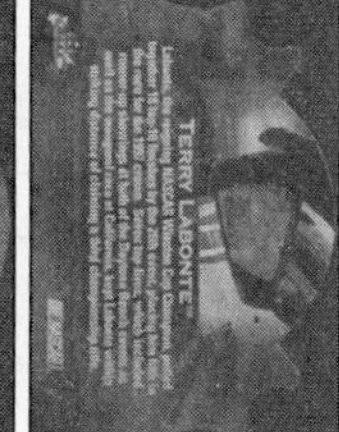

This 10-card set is a diecut parallel to the the regular set. The cards were randomly inserted in packs at a ratio of 1:21.

	MINT	NRMT
COMPLETE SET (10)	80.00	36.00
COMMON CARD (C1-C10)	2.50	1.10

1997 Maxx Flag Firsts

This 25-card set looks back at the first victories of some of today's top NASCAR drivers. The cards were randomly inserted in packs at a ratio of 1:3.

	MINT	NRMT
COMPLETE SET (25)	40.00	18.00
COMMON CARD (FF1-FF25)	1.00	.45
*SINGLES: 2.5X TO 6X BASE CARD HI		

❑ FF1 Morgan Shepherd	1.00	.45
❑ FF2 Rusty Wallace	6.00	2.70
❑ FF3 Dale Jarrett	5.00	2.20
❑ FF4 Sterling Marlin	2.00	.90
❑ FF5 Terry Labonte	6.00	2.70
❑ FF6 Mark Martin	6.00	2.70
❑ FF7 Geoff Bodine	1.00	.45
❑ FF8 Ken Schrader	1.00	.45
❑ FF9 Lake Speed	1.00	.45
❑ FF10 Ricky Rudd	2.00	.90
❑ FF11 Brett Bodine	1.00	.45
❑ FF12 Derrike Cope	1.00	.45
❑ FF13 Kyle Petty	2.00	.90
❑ FF14 Dale Earnhardt	12.00	5.50
❑ FF15 Bobby Hamilton	1.00	.45
❑ FF16 John Andretti	1.00	.45
❑ FF17 Darrell Waltrip	2.00	.90
❑ FF18 Bobby Labonte	4.00	1.80
❑ FF19 Bill Elliott	6.00	2.70
❑ FF20 Ernie Irvan	2.00	.90
❑ FF21 Jeff Burton	2.00	.90
❑ FF22 Ward Burton	1.00	.45
❑ FF23 Jimmy Spencer	1.00	.45
❑ FF24 Jeff Gordon	10.00	4.50
❑ FF25 Dave Marcis	2.00	.90

1997 Maxx Rookies of the Year

This 9-card set features eight of the past winners of the Maxx Winston Cup Rookie of the Year Award. It is important to note that card #MR9 Johnny Benson does not have the Maxx logo with the Rookie of the year logo in the bottom right corner like the other eight cards in the set. The cards were randomly inserted in packs at a ratio of 1:11.

	MINT	NRMT
COMPLETE SET (9)	20.00	9.00
COMMON CARD (MR1-MR9)	1.25	.55
*SINGLES: 3X TO 8X BASE CARD HI		

❑ MR1 Ken Bouchard	1.25	.55
❑ MR2 Dick Trickle	1.25	.55
❑ MR3 Rob Moroso	1.25	.55
❑ MR4 Bobby Hamilton	1.25	.55
❑ MR5 Jimmy Hensley	1.25	.55
❑ MR6 Jeff Gordon	15.00	6.75
❑ MR7 Jeff Burton	2.50	1.10
❑ MR8 Ricky Craven	1.25	.55
❑ MR9 Johnny Benson	1.25	.55

1998 Maxx

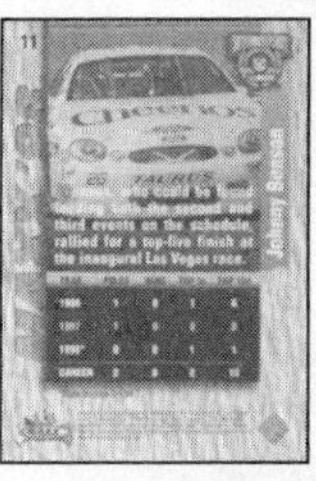

The 1998 Maxx set was issued in one series totalling 105 cards. This product features a special "Signed, Sealed & Delivered autographed insert card of Richard Petty that earns one lucky collector a free trip to the famous Richard Petty Driving Experience! The set contains the topical subsets: Home Cookin (61-75), License to Drive (76-90), and Front Runners (91-105).

	MINT	NRMT
COMPLETE SET (105)	30.00	13.50
COMMON CARD (1-105)	.10	.05
COMMON DRIVER (1-105)	.20	.09

❑ 1 Jeremy Mayfield	.60	.25
❑ 2 Rusty Wallace	1.00	.45
❑ 3 Dale Earnhardt	2.00	.90
❑ 4 Bobby Hamilton	.20	.09
❑ 5 Terry Labonte	1.00	.45
❑ 6 Mark Martin	1.00	.45
❑ 7 Geoff Bodine	.20	.09
❑ 8 Ernie Irvan	.40	.18
❑ 9 Jeff Burton	.40	.18
❑ 10 Ricky Rudd	.20	.09
❑ 11 Johnny Benson	.20	.09
❑ 12 Dale Jarrett	.75	.35

❑ 13 Jerry Nadeau	.20	.09
❑ 14 Steve Park	.75	.35
❑ 15 Bill Elliott	1.00	.45
❑ 16 Ted Musgrave	.20	.09
❑ 17 Darrell Waltrip	.40	.18
❑ 18 Bobby Labonte	.75	.35
❑ 19 Todd Bodine	.20	.09
❑ 20 Kyle Petty	.40	.18
❑ 21 Michael Waltrip	.20	.09
❑ 22 Ken Schrader	.20	.09
❑ 23 Jimmy Spencer	.20	.09
❑ 24 Jeff Gordon	2.00	.90
❑ 25 Ricky Craven	.20	.09
❑ 26 John Andretti	.20	.09
❑ 27 Sterling Marlin	.40	.18
❑ 28 Kenny Irwin	.60	.25
❑ 29 Mike Skinner	.20	.09
❑ 30 Derrike Cope	.20	.09
❑ 31 Jeremy Mayfield's Car	.30	.14
❑ 32 Rusty Wallace's Car	.50	.23
❑ 33 Dale Earnhardt's Car	1.00	.45
❑ 34 Bobby Hamilton's Car	.10	.05
❑ 35 Terry Labonte's Car	.50	.23
❑ 36 Mark Martin's Car	.50	.23
❑ 37 Geoff Bodine's Car	.10	.05
❑ 38 Ernie Irvan's Car	.20	.09
❑ 39 Jeff Burton's Car	.20	.09
❑ 40 Ricky Rudd's Car	.20	.09
❑ 41 Johnny Benson's Car	.10	.05
❑ 42 Dale Jarrett's Car	.40	.18
❑ 43 Jerry Nadeau's Car	.10	.05
❑ 44 Steve Park's Car	.40	.18
❑ 45 Bill Elliott's Car	.50	.23
❑ 46 Ted Musgrave's Car	.10	.05
❑ 47 Darrell Waltrip's Car	.20	.09
❑ 48 Bobby Labonte's Car	.40	.18
❑ 49 Todd Bodine's Car	.10	.05
❑ 50 Kyle Petty's Car	.20	.09
❑ 51 Michael Waltrip's Car	.10	.05
❑ 52 Ken Schrader's Car	.10	.05
❑ 53 Jimmy Spencer's Car	.10	.05
❑ 54 Jeff Gordon's Car	1.00	.45
❑ 55 Ricky Craven's Car	.10	.05
❑ 56 John Andretti's Car	.10	.05
❑ 57 Sterling Marlin's Car	.20	.09
❑ 58 Kenny Irwin's Car	.30	.14
❑ 59 Mike Skinner' s Car	.10	.05
❑ 60 Derrike Cope's Car	.10	.05
❑ 61 Jimmy Spencer's Car HC	.10	.05
❑ 62 Bill Elliott's Car HC	.50	.23
❑ 63 Darrell Waltrip's Car HC	.20	.09
❑ 64 Jeff Gordon's Car HC	1.00	.45
❑ 65 John Andretti's Car HC	.10	.05
❑ 66 Johnny Benson's Car HC	.10	.05
❑ 67 Jeff Burton's Car HC	.20	.09
❑ 68 Bobby Hamilton's Car HC	.10	.05
❑ 69 Ernie Irvan's Car HC	.20	.09
❑ 70 Dale Jarrett's Car HC	.40	.18
❑ 71 Bobby Labonte's Car HC	.40	.18
❑ 72 Terry Labonte's Car HC	.50	.23
❑ 73 Kyle Petty's Car HC	.20	.09
❑ 74 Ricky Rudd's Car HC	.20	.09
❑ 75 Morgan Shepherd HC	.20	.09
❑ 76 Kenny Irwin's Car LTD	.30	.14
❑ 77 Steve Park's Car LTD	.40	.18
❑ 78 Jerry Nadeau's Car LTD	.10	.05
❑ 79 Todd Bodine's Car LTD	.10	.05
❑ 80 Mike Skinner's Car LTD	.10	.05
❑ 81 Jeremy Mayfield's Car LTD	.30	.14
❑ 82 Ricky Craven's Car LTD	.10	.05
❑ 83 Steve Grissom's Car LTD	.10	.05
❑ 84 Brett Bodine's Car LTD	.10	.05
❑ 85 Jeff Burton's Car LTD	.20	.09
❑ 86 Ward Burton's Car LTD	.10	.05
❑ 87 Chad Little's Car LTD	.10	.05
❑ 88 David Green's Car LTD	.10	.05
❑ 89 John Andretti's Car LTD	.10	.05
❑ 90 Bobby Labonte's Car LTD	.40	.18
❑ 91 Jeff Gordon's Car FR	1.00	.45
❑ 92 Dale Jarrett's Car FR	.40	.18
❑ 93 Mark Martin's Car FR	.50	.23
❑ 94 Jeff Burton's Car FR	.20	.09
❑ 95 Dale Earnhardt's Car FR	1.00	.45
❑ 96 Terry Labonte's Car FR	.50	.23
❑ 97 Bobby Labonte's Car FR	.40	.18
❑ 98 Bill Elliott's Car FR	.50	.23
❑ 99 Rusty Wallace's Car FR	.50	.23
❑ 100 Ken Schrader's Car FR	.10	.05
❑ 101 Johnny Benson's Car FR	.10	.05
❑ 102 Ted Musgrave's Car FR	.10	.05
❑ 103 Ernie Irvan's Car FR	.20	.09
❑ 104 Steve Park's Car FR	.30	.14
❑ 105 Kenny Irwin's Car FR	.30	.14

1998 Maxx Focus On A Champion

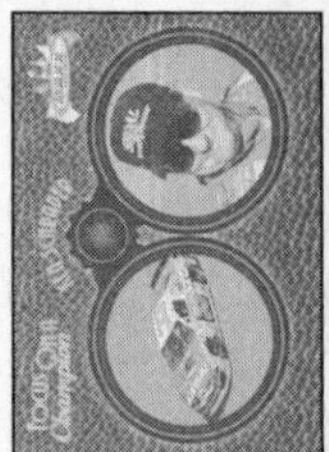

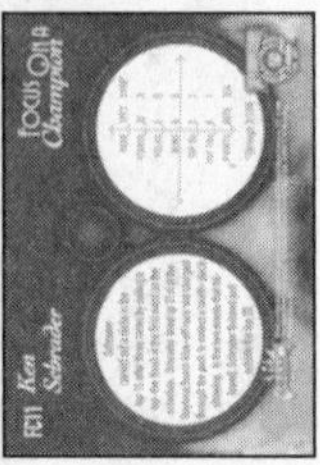

This 15-card set features the top contenders for the Winston Cup Championship. These cards are randomly inserted one per 24 packs.

	MINT	NRMT
COMPLETE SET (15)	100.00	45.00
COMMON CARD (FC1-FC15)	2.50	1.10
*SINGLES: 5X TO 12X BASE CARD HI		

❑ FC1 Jeff Gordon	25.00	11.00
❑ FC2 Dale Jarrett	10.00	4.50
❑ FC3 Dale Earnhardt	25.00	11.00
❑ FC4 Mark Martin	12.00	5.50
❑ FC5 Jeff Burton	5.00	2.20
❑ FC6 Kyle Petty	5.00	2.20
❑ FC7 Terry Labonte	10.00	4.50
❑ FC8 Bobby Labonte	6.00	2.70
❑ FC9 Bill Elliott	10.00	4.50
❑ FC10 Rusty Wallace	10.00	4.50
❑ FC11 Ken Schrader	2.50	1.10
❑ FC12 Johnny Benson	2.50	1.10
❑ FC13 Ted Musgrave	2.50	1.10
❑ FC14 Ernie Irvan	5.00	2.20
❑ FC15 Kenny Irwin	8.00	3.60

1998 Maxx Focus On A Champion Cel

This 15-card set features the top contenders for the Winston Cup Championship on acetate cards. These cards are randomly inserted one per 96 packs.

	MINT	NRMT
COMPLETE SET (15)	250.00	110.00
COMMON CARD (FC1-FC15)	6.00	2.70

1998 Maxx Swappin' Paint

This 25-card set features the cars of the top contenders for the Winston Cup Championship. These cards are randomly inserted one per three packs.

	MINT	NRMT
COMPLETE SET (25)	30.00	13.50
COMMON CARD (SW1-SW25)	.75	.35
COMMON DRIVER (SW1-SW25)	1.50	.70
*SINGLES: 3X TO 8X BASE CARD HI		

❑ SW1 Steve Park	6.00	2.70
❑ SW2 Terry Labonte's Car	4.00	1.80
❑ SW3 Ernie Irvan's Car	1.50	.70
❑ SW4 Bobby Hamilton	1.50	.70
❑ SW5 Derrike Cope's Car	.75	.35
❑ SW6 John Andretti's Car	.75	.35
❑ SW7 Geoff Bodine's Car	.75	.35
❑ SW8 Hut Stricklin's Car	.75	.35
❑ SW9 Jeff Burton's Car	1.50	.70
❑ SW10 Robert Pressley's Car	.75	.35
❑ SW11 Brett Bodine's Car	.75	.35
❑ SW12 Rick Mast's Car	.75	.35
❑ SW13 Jerry Nadeau's Car	.75	.35
❑ SW14 Sterling Marlin's Car	1.50	.70
❑ SW15 Johnny Benson's Car	.75	.35
❑ SW16 Ted Musgrave's Car	.75	.35
❑ SW17 Todd Bodine's Car	.75	.35
❑ SW18 J.Mayfield w/R.Wallace	5.00	
❑ SW19 Mark Martin's Car	4.00	
❑ SW20 Chad Little	1.50	
❑ SW21 Joe Nemechek's Car	.75	
❑ SW22 Dick Trickle	1.50	
❑ SW23 Jimmy Spencer's Car	.75	
❑ SW24 Kenny Irwin's Car	2.00	
❑ SW25 Ricky Craven's Car	.75	

1998 Maxx Teamwork

This 10-card set features the cars and pit crews of th
contenders for the Winston Cup Championship. T
cards are randomly inserted one per 11 packs.

	MINT	N
COMPLETE SET (10)	30.00	
COMMON CARD (TW1-TW10)	1.00	
*SINGLES: 2X TO 5X BASE CARD HI		

❑ TW1 Jeff Gordon's Car	10.00
❑ TW2 Terry Labonte's Car	5.00
❑ TW3 Ricky Craven's Car	1.00
❑ TW4 Mark Martin's Car	5.00
❑ TW5 Jeff Burton's Car	2.00
❑ TW6 Ted Musgrave's Car	1.00
❑ TW7 Chad Little's Car	1.00
❑ TW8 Johnny Benson's Car	1.00
❑ TW9 Dale Jarrett's Car	4.00
❑ TW10 Kenny Irwin's Car	3.00

1998 Maxx 1997 Year In Review

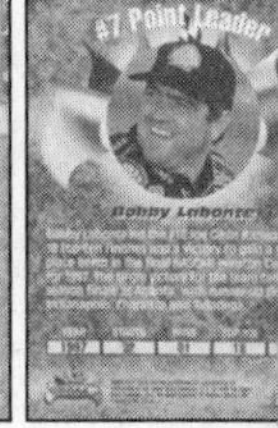

The 1997 Maxx Year in Review Boxed Set was iss
one series totalling 161 cards.

	MINT
COMPLETE FACT.SET (175)	30.00
COMMON CARD	.10
COMMON DRIVER	.20

❑ 1 Jeff Gordon	1.50
❑ 2 Mike Skinner	.20
❑ 3 Ricky Craven's Car	.10
❑ 4 Ward Burton's Car	.10
❑ 5 Hendrick Sweep	.40
❑ 6 Jeff Gordon's Car	.75
❑ 7 Mark Martin's Car	.40
❑ 8 Ernie Irvan's Car	.20
❑ 9 Dale Earnhardt's Car	.75
❑ 10 Ricky Craven's Car	.10
❑ 11 Rusty Wallace	.75
❑ 12 Terry Labonte's Car	.40
❑ 13 Kyle Petty's Car	.20
❑ 14 Ricky Rudd's Car	.20
❑ 15 Ernie Irvan's Car	.20
❑ 16 Dale Jarrett	.60
❑ 17 Robby Gordon	.20
❑ 18 Johnny Benson's Car	.10
❑ 19 Geoff Bodine's Car	.10
❑ 20 Steve Grissom's Car	.10
❑ 21 Dale Jarrett	.60
❑ 22 Dale Jarrett's Car	.30
❑ 23 Darrell Waltrip	.40
❑ 24 Michael Waltrip's Car	.10
❑ 25 Ted Musgrave's Car	.10
❑ 26 Jeff Burton	.40
❑ 27 Dale Jarrett's Car	.30

Steve Grissom's Car .10 .05
Jeff Gordon's Car .75 .35
Darrell Waltrip's Car .20 .09
Jeff Gordon's Car .75 .35
Rusty Wallace's Car .40 .18
Dale Earnhardt's Car .75 .35
Jeremy Mayfield's Car .25 .11
Ted Musgrave's Car .10 .05
Jeff Gordon's Car .75 .35
Kenny Wallace .20 .09
Mark Martin's Car .40 .18
Rusty Wallace .75 .35
Ricky Craven's Car .10 .05
Mark Martin .75 .35
John Andretti .20 .09
Jeff Burton's Car .20 .09
Bill Elliott .75 .35
Dale Jarrett's Car .30 .14
Mark Martin .75 .35
Mark Martin's Car .40 .18
Darrell Waltrip's Car .20 .09
Ernie Irvan's Car .20 .09
Alcatraz Island .10 .05
Jeff Gordon's Car .75 .35
Jeff Gordon 1.50 .70
Dale Earnhardt's Car .75 .35
Jeff Burton's Car .20 .09
Darrell Waltrip's Car .20 .09
Ricky Rudd .40 .18
Bobby Labonte .60 .25
Jeff Burton's Car .20 .09
Bobby Labonte's Car .30 .14
Dave Marcis' Car .10 .05
Jeff Gordon 1.50 .70
Bobby Hamilton's Car .10 .05
Derrike Cope's Car .10 .05
Morgan Shepherd's Car .10 .05
Ward Burton's Car .10 .05
Ernie Irvan .40 .18
Dale Jarrett .60 .25
Derrike Cope's Car .10 .05
Ted Musgrave's Car .10 .05
Bill Elliott's Car .40 .18
Jeff Gordon 1.50 .70
Joe Nemechek .20 .09
Ricky Rudd .40 .18
Jimmy Spencer's Car .10 .05
Ted Musgrave's Car .10 .05
John Andretti .20 .09
Mike Skinner .20 .09
Terry Labonte's Car .20 .09
Kyle Petty's Car .20 .09
Ward Burton's Car .10 .05
Jeff Burton .40 .18
Ken Schrader .20 .09
Hut Stricklin's Car .10 .05
Rusty Wallace's Car .40 .18
Dale Jarrett .60 .25
Dale Jarrett's Car .30 .14
Joe Nemechek .20 .09
Johnny Benson's Car .10 .05
Ted Musgrave's Car .10 .05
Bill Elliott's Car .40 .18
Ricky Rudd .40 .18
Ernie Irvan's Car .20 .09
Kyle Petty's Car .20 .09
Michael Waltrip's Car .10 .05
Darrell Waltrip's Car .20 .09
Jeff Gordon's Car .75 .35
Todd Bodine .20 .09
Steve Grissom's Car .10 .05
Ricky Rudd .40 .18
Robby Gordon's Car .10 .05
Mark Martin .75 .35
Johnny Benson's Car .10 .05
Rusty Wallace's Car .40 .18
Bill Elliott's Car .40 .18
Jeff Burton's Car .20 .09
Dale Jarrett .60 .25
Kenny Wallace .20 .09
Steve Grissom's Car .10 .05
Geoff Bodine's Car .10 .05
David Green's Car .10 .05
Jeff Gordon 1.50 .70
Bobby Labonte .60 .25
Chad Little's Car .10 .05
Dick Trickle's Car .10 .05
Jeff Burton's Car .20 .09
Dale Jarrett .60 .25
Bill Elliott's Car .40 .18
Ted Musgrave's Car .10 .05
Joe Nemechek .20 .09
Kenny Irwin .50 .23
Jeff Gordon 1.50 .70
Ken Schrader .20 .09
Ernie Irvan's Car .20 .09
John Andretti's Car .10 .05
Geoff Bodine's Car .10 .05

❑ 126 Mark Martin .75 .35
❑ 127 Mark Martin's Car .40 .18
❑ 128 Dale Earnhardt's Car .75 .35
❑ 129 Robby Gordon's Car .10 .05
❑ 130 Jeff Gordon's Car .75 .35
❑ 131 Jeff Burton .40 .18
❑ 132 Ward Burton's Car .10 .05
❑ 133 Ricky Craven's Car .10 .05
❑ 134 Bobby Hamilton's Car .10 .05
❑ 135 Rusty Wallace's Car .40 .18
❑ 136 Dale Jarrett .60 .25
❑ 137 Geoff Bodine .20 .09
❑ 138 Terry Labonte's Car .40 .18
❑ 139 Bobby Labonte's Car .30 .14
❑ 140 Darrell Waltrip's Car .20 .09
❑ 141 Terry Labonte .75 .35
❑ 142 Ernie Irvan .40 .18
❑ 143 Kyle Petty's Car .20 .09
❑ 144 Mark Martin's Car .40 .18
❑ 145 Ken Schrader's Car .10 .05
❑ 146 Bobby Hamilton .20 .09
❑ 147 Bobby Labonte .60 .25
❑ 148 Sterling Marlin's Car .20 .09
❑ 149 Bill Elliott .75 .35
❑ 150 Bobby Hamilton .20 .09
❑ 151 Dale Jarrett .60 .25
❑ 152 Bobby Hamilton's Car .10 .05
❑ 153 Kyle Petty's Car .20 .09
❑ 154 Dale Jarrett's Car .30 .14
❑ 155 Darrell Waltrip's Car .20 .09
❑ 156 Bobby Labonte .60 .25
❑ 157 Geoff Bodine .20 .09
❑ 158 Bobby Hamilton's Car .10 .05
❑ 159 Mark Martin's Car .40 .18
❑ 160 Chad Little's Car .10 .05
❑ 161 Checklist .10 .05
❑ AW1 Jeff Gordon 3.00 1.35
❑ AW2 Mike Skinner .30 .14
❑ AW3 Dale Jarrett 1.25 .55
❑ AW4 Bill Elliott 1.50 .70
❑ PO1 Jeff Gordon 3.00 1.35
❑ PO2 Dale Jarrett 1.25 .55
❑ PO3 Mark Martin 1.50 .70
❑ PO4 Jeff Burton .60 .25
❑ PO5 Dale Earnhardt 3.00 1.35
❑ PO6 Terry Labonte 1.50 .70
❑ PO7 Bobby Labonte 1.25 .55
❑ PO8 Bill Elliott 1.50 .70
❑ PO9 Rusty Wallace 1.50 .70
❑ PO10 Ken Schrader .30 .14

1998 Maxx 10th Anniversary

The 1998 Maxx 10th Anniversary set was issued in one series totalling 134 cards. The card fronts feature color photos surrounded by a white-border with the Maxx 10th Anniversary logo in the upper right corner. The set contains the topical subsets: Family Ties (91-107), Farewell Tour (108-116) and Racin' Up Wins (117-126).

	MINT	NRMT
COMPLETE SET (134)	40.00	18.00
COMMON CARD (1-134)	.15	.07
COMMON DRIVER (1-134)	.30	.14

❑ 1 Rusty Wallace 1.50 .70
❑ 2 Chad Little .30 .14
❑ 3 Bobby Hamilton .30 .14
❑ 4 Terry Labonte 1.50 .70
❑ 5 Mark Martin 1.50 .70
❑ 6 Alan Kulwicki .75 .35
❑ 7 Geoff Bodine .30 .14
❑ 8 Brett Bodine .30 .14
❑ 9 Ricky Rudd .60 .25
❑ 10 Donnie Allison .30 .14
❑ 11 Jeremy Mayfield 1.00 .45
❑ 12 Jerry Nadeau .30 .14
❑ 13 Jeff Burton .60 .25
❑ 14 Bill Elliott 1.50 .70
❑ 15 Elton Sawyer .30 .14
❑ 16 Darrell Waltrip .60 .25
❑ 17 Bobby Labonte 1.25 .55
❑ 18 Ward Burton .30 .14
❑ 19 Michael Waltrip .30 .14
❑ 20 David Pearson .60 .25
❑ 21 Bobby Allison .60 .25
❑ 22 Jimmy Spencer .30 .14
❑ 23 Dale Jarrett 1.25 .55
❑ 24 Jeff Gordon 3.00 1.35
❑ 25 Johnny Benson .30 .14
❑ 26 Kevin LePage .30 .14
❑ 27 Davey Allison 1.00 .45
❑ 28 Kenny Irwin 1.00 .45
❑ 29 Ken Schrader .30 .14
❑ 30 Harry Gant .60 .25
❑ 31 Cale Yarborough .60 .25
❑ 32 Ernie Irvan .60 .25
❑ 33 Ned Jarrett .60 .25
❑ 34 Dale Earnhardt Jr. 5.00 2.20
❑ 35 Jeff Green .30 .14
❑ 36 Sterling Marlin .60 .25
❑ 37 Steve Grissom .30 .14
❑ 38 Robert Pressley .30 .14
❑ 39 Richard Petty .60 .25
❑ 40 Kyle Petty .60 .25
❑ 41 John Andretti .30 .14
❑ 42 Benny Parsons .30 .14
❑ 43 Buddy Baker .30 .14
❑ 44 Neil Bonnett .75 .35
❑ 45 Kenny Wallace .30 .14
❑ 46 Rusty Wallace's Car .75 .35
❑ 47 Chad Little's Car .15 .07
❑ 48 Bobby Hamilton's Car .15 .07
❑ 49 Terry Labonte's Car .75 .35
❑ 50 Mark Martin's Car .75 .35
❑ 51 Alan Kulwicki's Car .40 .18
❑ 52 Geoff Bodine's Car .15 .07
❑ 53 Brett Bodine's Car .15 .07
❑ 54 Ricky Rudd's Car .30 .14
❑ 55 Donnie Allison's Car .15 .07
❑ 56 Jeremy Mayfield's Car .50 .23
❑ 57 Jerry Nadeau's Car .15 .07
❑ 58 Jeff Burton's Car .30 .14
❑ 59 Bill Elliott's Car .75 .35
❑ 60 Elton Sawyer .30 .14
❑ 61 Darrell Waltrip's Car .30 .14
❑ 62 Bobby Labonte's Car .60 .25
❑ 63 Ward Burton's Car .15 .07
❑ 64 Michael Waltrip's Car .15 .07
❑ 65 David Pearson's Car .30 .14
❑ 66 Bobby Allison's Car .30 .14
❑ 67 Jimmy Spencer's Car .15 .07
❑ 68 Dale Jarrett's Car .60 .25
❑ 69 Jeff Gordon's Car 1.50 .70
❑ 70 Johnny Benson's Car .15 .07
❑ 71 Kevin LePage's Car .15 .07
❑ 72 Davey Allison's Car .50 .23
❑ 73 Kenny Irwin's Car .50 .23
❑ 74 Ken Schrader's Car .15 .07
❑ 75 Harry Gant's Car .30 .14
❑ 76 Cale Yarborough's Car .30 .14
❑ 77 Ernie Irvan's Car .30 .14
❑ 78 Ned Jarrett's Car .15 .07
❑ 79 Dale Earnhardt Jr.'s Car 2.50 1.10
❑ 80 Jeff Green's Car .15 .07
❑ 81 Sterling Marlin's Car .30 .14
❑ 82 Steve Grissom's Car .15 .07
❑ 83 Robert Pressley's Car .15 .07
❑ 84 Richard Petty's Car .30 .14
❑ 85 Kyle Petty's Car .30 .14
❑ 86 John Andretti's Car .15 .07
❑ 87 Benny Parsons's Car .15 .07
❑ 88 Buddy Baker's Car .15 .07
❑ 89 Neil Bonnett's Car .15 .07
❑ 90 Kenny Wallace's Car .15 .07
❑ 91 Donnie Allison .15 .07
❑ 92 Bobby Allison .60 .25
❑ 93 Davey Allison 1.00 .45
❑ 94 Richard Petty .60 .25
❑ 95 Kyle Petty .60 .25
❑ 96 Dale Earnhardt 3.00 1.35
❑ 97 Dale Earnhardt Jr. 5.00 2.20
❑ 98 Darrell Waltrip .60 .25
❑ 99 Michael Waltrip .15 .07
❑ 100 Mike Wallace .15 .07
❑ 101 Rusty Wallace 1.50 .70
❑ 102 Kenny Wallace .15 .07
❑ 103 Geoff Bodine .15 .07
❑ 104 Brett Bodine .15 .07
❑ 105 Todd Bodine .15 .07
❑ 106 Terry Labonte 1.50 .70
❑ 107 Bobby Labonte 1.25 .55
❑ 108 Richard Petty .60 .25
❑ 109 Bobby Allison .15 .07
❑ 110 Cale Yarborough .60 .25
❑ 111 Benny Parsons .15 .07
❑ 112 Buddy Baker .15 .07
❑ 113 Davey Allison 1.00 .45
❑ 114 Harry Gant .60 .25
❑ 115 Neil Bonnett .75 .35
❑ 116 Alan Kulwicki .75 .35

	MINT	NRMT
❑ 117 B.Elliott/R.Wallace	1.25	.55
❑ 118 D.Waltrip/R.Wallace	1.00	.45
❑ 119 Dale Earnhardt	3.00	1.35
❑ 120 D.Allison/H.Gant	.75	.35
❑ 121 B.Elliott/D.Allison	1.25	.55
❑ 122 Rusty Wallace	1.50	.70
❑ 123 Rusty Wallace	1.50	.70
❑ 124 Jeff Gordon	3.00	1.35
❑ 125 Jeff Gordon	3.00	1.35
❑ 126 Jeff Gordon	3.00	1.35
❑ 127 Checklist	.15	.07
❑ 128 Checklist	.15	.07
❑ 129 Checklist	.15	.07
❑ 130 Checklist	.15	.07
❑ 131 Checklist	.15	.07
❑ 132 Checklist	.15	.07
❑ 133 Checklist	.15	.07
❑ 134 Checklist	.15	.07

1998 Maxx 10th Anniversary Buy-Back Autographs

Randomly inserted in packs at a rate of one in 288, this assorted insert set features some of the greatest MAXX cards of all time, complete with authentic driver autographs on each white-bordered card front. Due to the rarity of certain cards in this set, only a checklist has been provided.

	MINT	NRMT
COMMON CARD		
SEMISTARS		

❑ 1 Bobby Allison '88 #30
❑ 2 Buddy Baker '88 #55
❑ 3 Brett Bodine '88 #59
❑ 4 Geoff Bodine '88 #67
❑ 5 Harry Gant '89 #16
❑ 6 Harry Gant '90 #33
❑ 7 Harry Gant '91 #17
❑ 8 Harry Gant '91 #183
❑ 9 Harry Gant '92 NNO
❑ 10 Harry Gant '92 #33
❑ 11 Harry Gant '92 #272
❑ 12 Harry Gant '92 #285
❑ 13 Harry Gant '92 #286
❑ 14 Harry Gant '92 #287
❑ 15 Harry Gant '92 #288
❑ 16 Harry Gant '93 #33
❑ 17 Harry Gant '93 #246
❑ 18 Harry Gant '93 #275
❑ 19 Harry Gant '95 #33
❑ 20 Jeff Gordon '92 #29
❑ 21 Jeff Gordon '92 #50
❑ 22 Jeff Gordon '93 #24
❑ 23 Jeff Gordon '94 #13
❑ 24 Jeff Gordon '94 #16
❑ 25 Ernie Irvan '88 #95
❑ 26 Dale Jarrett '88 #61
❑ 28 Dave Marcis '88 #44
❑ 29 Benny Parsons '88 #76
❑ 30 Kyle Petty '89 #42
❑ 31 Kyle Petty '91 #42
❑ 32 Kyle Petty '91 #172
❑ 33 Kyle Petty '92 #35
❑ 34 Kyle Petty '92 #42
❑ 35 Kyle Petty '92 #266
❑ 36 Kyle Petty '93 #42
❑ 37 Kyle Petty '93 #291
❑ 38 Kyle Petty '95 #42
❑ 39 K.Petty/R.Petty '89 #220
❑ 40 Richard Petty '88 #43
❑ 41 Richard Petty SSD
❑ 42 Morgan Shepherd '88 #25
❑ 43 Lake Speed '88 #46
❑ 44 Hut Stricklin '88 #28
❑ 45 Rusty Wallace '88 #14
❑ 46 Darrell Waltrip '88 #10
❑ 47 Michael Waltrip '88 #98
❑ 48 Cale Yarborough '88 #90

1998 Maxx 10th Anniversary Card of the Year

Randomly inserted in packs at a rate of one in 23, these insert cards will depict, for the years 1988 through 1998.

	MINT	NRMT
COMPLETE SET (10)	80.00	36.00
COMMON CARD (C1-C10)	4.00	1.80
*SINGLES: 3X TO 8X BASE CARD HI		
❑ CY1 Davey Allison	8.00	3.60
❑ CY2 K.Petty/R.Petty	6.00	2.70
❑ CY3 Rusty Wallace	10.00	4.50
❑ CY4 Darrell Waltrip	4.00	1.80
❑ CY5 Jeff Gordon	20.00	9.00

	MINT	NRMT
❑ CY6 Richard Petty	5.00	2.20
❑ CY7 Rusty Wallace	10.00	4.50
❑ CY8 Dale Jarrett	8.00	3.60
❑ CY9 Mark Martin	10.00	4.50
❑ CY10 Jeff Gordon	20.00	9.00

1998 Maxx 10th Anniversary Champions Past

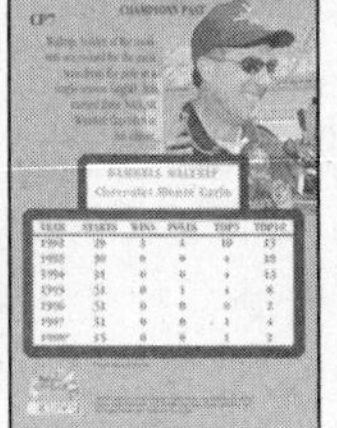

Randomly inserted in packs at a rate of one in 5, this is the first of a two-tiered insert set that features the past ten Winston Cup Champions.

	MINT	NRMT
COMPLETE SET (10)	40.00	18.00
COMMON CARD (CP1-CP10)	2.50	1.10
*SINGLES: 1.5X TO 4X BASE CARD HI		
❑ CP1 Jeff Gordon	12.00	5.50
❑ CP2 Terry Labonte	6.00	2.70
❑ CP3 Dale Earnhardt	12.00	5.50
❑ CP4 Alan Kulwicki	4.00	1.80
❑ CP5 Rusty Wallace	6.00	2.70
❑ CP6 Bill Elliott	6.00	2.70
❑ CP7 Darrell Waltrip	2.50	1.10
❑ CP8 Bobby Allison	2.50	1.10
❑ CP9 Richard Petty	3.00	1.35
❑ CP10 Cale Yarborough	2.50	1.10

1998 Maxx 10th Anniversary Champions Past Diecut

Sequentially numbered to 1,000, this limited edition die-cut insert is the second of the two-tiered collection featuring the past ten Winston Cup champions.

	MINT	NRMT
COMPLETE SET (10)	160.00	70.00
COMMON CARD (CP1-CP10)	10.00	4.50
*DIECUT CARDS: 1.5X TO 4X BASIC CARDS		10.00

4.50

1998 Maxx 10th Anniversary Maxximum Preview

Randomly inserted one in every pack, this 25-card insert set features the all-new Ionix technology with a unique design of top drivers who are also included in the Maxx Maxximum set.

	MINT	NRMT
COMPLETE SET (25)	30.00	13.50
COMMON CARD (P1-P25)	.60	
*SINGLES: .75X TO 2X BASE CARD HI		
❑ P1 Darrell Waltrip	1.25	
❑ P2 Rusty Wallace	3.00	
❑ P3 Sterling Marlin	1.25	
❑ P4 Bobby Hamilton	.60	
❑ P5 Terry Labonte	3.00	
❑ P6 Mark Martin	3.00	
❑ P7 Geoff Bodine	.60	
❑ P8 Ernie Irvan	1.25	
❑ P9 Jeff Burton	1.25	
❑ P10 Ricky Rudd	1.25	
❑ P11 Dale Jarrett	2.50	
❑ P12 Jeremy Mayfield	2.00	
❑ P13 Jerry Nadeau	.60	
❑ P14 Ken Schrader	.60	
❑ P15 Kyle Petty	1.25	
❑ P16 Chad Little	.60	
❑ P17 Todd Bodine	.60	
❑ P18 Bobby Labonte	2.50	
❑ P19 Bill Elliott	3.00	
❑ P20 Mike Skinner	.60	
❑ P21 Michael Waltrip	.60	
❑ P22 John Andretti	.60	
❑ P23 Jimmy Spencer	.60	
❑ P24 Jeff Gordon	6.00	
❑ P25 Kenny Irwin	1.50	

1998 Maxximum

The 1998 Maxximum set was issued in one s totalling 100 cards. The cards feature the new technology, Ionix, with picture-perfect full-bleed photography. The set contains the topical subsets Men (1-25), Steel Chariots (26-50), Armor Clad (5 and Heat of Battle (76-100).

	MINT
COMPLETE SET (100)	50.00
COMMON CARD (1-100)	.20
COMMON DRIVER (1-100)	.40
❑ 1 Darrell Waltrip	.75
❑ 2 Rusty Wallace	2.00
❑ 3 Dale Earnhardt	4.00
❑ 4 Bobby Hamilton	.40
❑ 5 Terry Labonte	2.00
❑ 6 Mark Martin	2.00
❑ 7 Geoff Bodine	.40
❑ 8 Ernie Irvan	.75
❑ 9 Jeff Burton	.75
❑ 10 Ricky Rudd	.75
❑ 11 Dale Jarrett	1.50
❑ 12 Jeremy Mayfield	1.25
❑ 13 Jerry Nadeau	.40
❑ 14 Ken Schrader	.40
❑ 15 Kyle Petty	.75
❑ 16 Chad Little	.40
❑ 17 Todd Bodine	.40
❑ 18 Bobby Labonte	1.50
❑ 19 Bill Elliott	2.00
❑ 20 Mike Skinner	.40
❑ 21 Michael Waltrip	.40
❑ 22 John Andretti	.40
❑ 23 Jimmy Spencer	.40
❑ 24 Jeff Gordon	4.00
❑ 25 Kenny Irwin	1.25
❑ 26 Darrell Waltrip's Car	.40
❑ 27 Rusty Wallace's Car	1.00
❑ 28 Dale Earnhardt's Car	2.00
❑ 29 Bobby Hamilton's Car	.20
❑ 30 Terry Labonte's Car	1.00
❑ 31 Mark Martin's Car	1.00
❑ 32 Geoff Bodine's Car	.20
❑ 33 Ernie Irvan's Car	.40
❑ 34 Jeff Burton's Car	.40
❑ 35 Ricky Rudd's Car	.40
❑ 36 Dale Jarrett's Car	.75
❑ 37 Jeremy Mayfield's Car	.60
❑ 38 Jerry Nadeau's Car	.20
❑ 39 Ken Schrader's Car	.20
❑ 40 Kyle Petty's Car	.40

	MINT	NRMT
Chad Little's Car	.20	.09
Todd Bodine's Car	.20	.09
Bobby Labonte's Car	.75	.35
Bill Elliott's Car	1.00	.45
Mike Skinner's Car	.20	.09
Michael Waltrip's Car	.20	.09
John Andretti's Car	.20	.09
Jimmy Spencer's Car	.20	.09
Jeff Gordon's Car	2.00	.90
Kenny Irwin's Car	.60	.25
Darrell Waltrip	.75	.35
Rusty Wallace	2.00	.90
Dale Earnhardt Jr.	5.00	2.20
Bobby Hamilton	.40	.18
Terry Labonte	2.00	.90
Mark Martin	2.00	.90
Geoff Bodine	.40	.18
Ernie Irvan	.75	.35
Jeff Burton	.75	.35
Ricky Rudd	.75	.35
Dale Jarrett	1.50	.70
Jeremy Mayfield	1.25	.55
Jerry Nadeau	.40	.18
Ken Schrader	.40	.18
Kyle Petty	.75	.35
Chad Little	.40	.18
Todd Bodine	.40	.18
Bobby Labonte	1.50	.70
Bill Elliott	2.00	.90
Mike Skinner	.40	.18
Michael Waltrip	.40	.18
John Andretti	.40	.18
Jimmy Spencer	.40	.18
Jeff Gordon	4.00	1.80
Kenny Irwin	1.25	.55
Darrell Waltrip's Car	.40	.18
Rusty Wallace	2.00	.90
Dale Earnhardt Jr.	5.00	2.20
Bobby Hamilton's Car	.20	.09
Terry Labonte's Car	1.00	.45
Mark Martin's Car	1.00	.45
Geoff Bodine's Car	.20	.09
Ernie Irvan's Car	.40	.18
Jeff Burton's Car	.40	.18
Ricky Rudd's Car	.40	.18
Dale Jarrett's Car	.75	.35
Jeremy Mayfield's Car	.60	.25
Jerry Nadeau's Car	.20	.09
Ken Schrader's Car	.20	.09
Kyle Petty's Car	.40	.18
Chad Little's Car	.20	.09
Todd Bodine's Car	.20	.09
Bobby Labonte's Car	.75	.35
Bill Elliott's Car	.75	.35
Mike Skinner's Car	.20	.09
Michael Waltrip's Car	.20	.09
John Andretti's Car	.20	.09
Jimmy Spencer's Car	.20	.09
Jeff Gordon's Car	2.00	.90
Kenny Irwin's Car	.60	.25

8 Maxximum Battle Proven

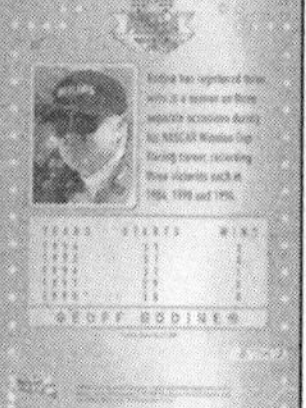

nly inserted in packs at a rate of one 4, this die-cut et highlights the top drivers in NASCAR who have sted more than one career Winston Cup victory.

	MINT	NRMT
ETE SET (15)	30.00	13.50
ON CARD (B1-B15)	.75	.35
ES: .75X TO 2X BASE CARD HI		

arrell Waltrip	1.50	.70
ale Earnhardt	.75	.35
usty Wallace	.75	.35
ll Elliott	.75	.35
ff Gordon	.75	.35
ark Martin	.75	.35
erry Labonte	.75	.35
cky Rudd	1.50	.70
eoff Bodine	.75	.35
rnie Irvan	1.50	.70
ale Jarrett	.75	.35
yle Petty	1.50	.70
❑ B13 Sterling Marlin	1.50	.70
❑ B14 Bobby Labonte	.75	.35
❑ B15 Jeff Burton	1.50	.70

1998 Maxximum Field Generals One Star

Sequentially numbered to 2,000, this die-cut insert set is the first of a four-tiered collection showcasing the best Winston Cup drivers.

	MINT	NRMT
SEMISTARS		
*SINGLES: 2.5X TO 6X BASE CARD HI		
ONE STAR PRINT RUN 2000 #'D SETS		
COMP. TWO STAR SET (15)		
COMMON TWO STAR (1-15)		
SEMISTARS TWO STAR		

1998 Maxximum Field Generals Two Star

Sequentially numbered to 1,000, this die-cut insert set is the second of a four-tiered collection showcasing the best Winston Cup drivers.

	MINT	NRMT
COMPLETE SET (15)	200.00	90.00
COMMON CARD (1-15)	4.00	1.80

1998 Maxximum Field Generals Three Star Autographs

Sequentially numbered to 100, this double die-cut autographed insert set is the third of a four-tiered collection showcasing the best Winston Cup drivers.

	MINT	NRMT
COMPLETE SET (15)	1200.00	550.00
COMMON CARD (1-15)	25.00	11.00
❑ 1 Rusty Wallace	100.00	45.00
❑ 2 Jeremy Mayfield	60.00	27.00
❑ 3 Jeff Gordon	250.00	110.00
❑ 4 Terry Labonte	100.00	45.00
❑ 5 Dale Jarrett	80.00	36.00
❑ 6 Mark Martin	100.00	45.00
❑ 7 Jeff Burton	50.00	22.00
❑ 8 Kenny Irwin	60.00	27.00
❑ 9 Darrell Waltrip	50.00	22.00
❑ 10 Dale Earnhardt	250.00	110.00
❑ 11 Ernie Irvan	50.00	22.00
❑ 12 Bobby Labonte	80.00	36.00
❑ 13 Kyle Petty	50.00	22.00
❑ 14 Jimmy Spencer	25.00	11.00
❑ 15 John Andretti	25.00	11.00

1998 Maxximum Field Generals Four Star Autographs

Sequentially numbered 1/1, this double die-cut autographed insert set is the fourth of a four-tiered collection showcasing the best Winston Cup drivers. Due to the scarcity of these cards, only a unpriced listing is provided.

MINT NRMT

❑ 1 Rusty Wallace
❑ 2 Jeremy Mayfield
❑ 3 Jeff Gordon
❑ 4 Terry Labonte
❑ 5 Dale Jarrett
❑ 6 Mark Martin
❑ 7 Jeff Burton
❑ 8 Kenny Irwin
❑ 9 Darrell Waltrip
❑ 10 Dale Earnhardt
❑ 11 Ernie Irvan
❑ 12 Bobby Labonte
❑ 13 Kyle Petty
❑ 14 Jimmy Spencer
❑ 15 John Andretti

1998 Maxximum First Class

Randomly inserted in packs at a rate of one in 3, this insert focuses on 20 drivers who have established themselves to be the most successful drivers on the current Winston Cup circuit.

	MINT	NRMT
COMPLETE SET (20)	30.00	13.50
COMMON CARD (F1-F20)	.75	.35
*SINGLES: .75X TO 2X BASE CARD HI		

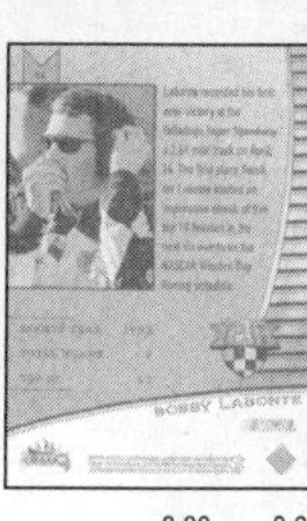

❑ F1 Jeff Gordon	8.00	3.60
❑ F2 Jimmy Spencer	.75	.35
❑ F3 John Andretti	.75	.35
❑ F4 Michael Waltrip	.75	.35
❑ F5 Bill Elliott	4.00	1.80
❑ F6 Bobby Labonte	3.00	1.35
❑ F7 Kyle Petty	1.50	.70
❑ F8 Ken Schrader	.75	.35
❑ F9 Jeremy Mayfield	2.50	1.10
❑ F10 Dale Jarrett	3.00	1.35
❑ F11 Ricky Rudd	1.50	.70
❑ F12 Jeff Burton	1.50	.70
❑ F13 Ernie Irvan	1.50	.70
❑ F14 Geoff Bodine	.75	.35
❑ F15 Mark Martin	4.00	1.80
❑ F16 Terry Labonte	4.00	1.80
❑ F17 Bobby Hamilton	.75	.35
❑ F18 Rusty Wallace	4.00	1.80
❑ F19 Darrell Waltrip	1.50	.70
❑ F20 Sterling Marlin	1.50	.70

1995 Metallic Impressions Classic Dale Earnhardt

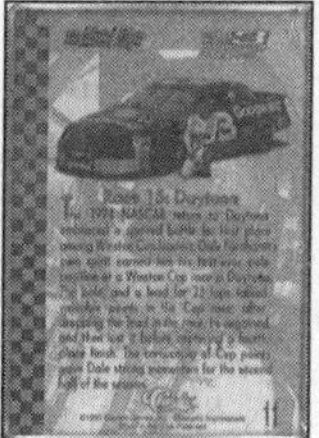

Metallic Impressions produced this 21-card Dale Earnhardt set for Classic Inc. The metal cards were distributed in complete set form in a tin box. Production was limited to 9,950 sets with each including a numbered certificate of authenticity. In the top of each tin box was a 21st card numbered E1. It featured Dale and car owner Richard Childress. Metallic Impressions also produced a five-card and a 10-card version of this set. The card fronts are the same as the ones in the larger 21 card set. The difference is the numbering on the back. For example in the ten card set card #5 is the same as card #9 in the 21 card set except for the number. The 10-card set is valued at $20 and the five-card set is valued at $10.

	MINT	NRMT
COMPLETE SET (21)	25.00	11.00
DALE EARNHARDT'S CAR	1.25	.55
DALE EARNHARDT	1.50	.70
❑ E1 Dale Earnhardt Richard Childress	1.50	.70

1995 Metallic Impressions Kyle Petty

This 10-card set from Metallic Impressions features Kyle Petty on the company's full color embossed metal cards. The backs have additional photos and commentary on Kyle and his many interest. The 10-card set was produced in a quantity of 19,950. Each set is accompanied by an individually numbered Certificate of Authenticity. There is also a five card version of this set available in a tin box. The five card set is valued at $10.

	MINT	NRMT
COMPLETE SET (10)	20.00	9.00
COMMON CARD	2.00	.90

1995 Metallic Impressions Upper Deck Rusty Wallace

This set was produced in conjunction with Upper Deck.

Card fronts show photos of Rusty in every aspect of race-day action. Cards are embossed in strudy, durable metal with card edges rooled for extra durability and safety. Full-color card backs feature an additional photo, commentary and selected race results. The 20-card set comes in a specifically designed embossed collector's tin with an individually numbered Certificate of Authenticity. There were 12,500 sets produced. There is also a five card version of this set in a tin box. The five card version is valued at $10.

	MINT	NRMT
COMPLETE SET (20)	40.00	18.00
RUSTY WALLACE'S CAR	2.00	.90
RUSTY WALLACE	2.50	1.10

1995 Metallic Impressions Winston Cup Champions

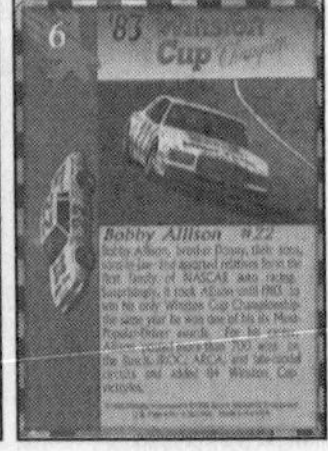

This 10-card set issued by Metallic Impressions features 10 former Winston Cup Champions. The cards are made of embossed metal and come in a tin display box. There were 49,900 sets made.

	MINT	NRMT
COMPLETE SET (10)	35.00	16.00
COMMON CARD (1-10)	2.00	.90
❑ 1 Richard Petty	4.00	1.80
❑ 2 Benny Parsons	2.00	.90
❑ 3 Cale Yarborough	2.00	.90
❑ 4 Dale Earnhardt	10.00	4.50
❑ 5 Darrell Waltrip	3.00	1.35
❑ 6 Bobby Allison	2.00	.90
❑ 7 Terry Labonte	5.00	2.20
❑ 8 Bill Elliott	5.00	2.20
❑ 9 Rusty Wallace	5.00	2.20
❑ 10 Alan Kulwicki	4.00	1.80

1996 Metallic Impressions 25th Anniversary Winston Cup Champions

This 25-card set was produced by Metallic Impressions. The cards were available through packs of Winston cigarettes. There was one card per every two pack of cigarettes. The set was also available by trading in Winston cigarette wrappers.

	MINT	NRMT
COMPLETE SET (25)	40.00	18.00
COMMON CARD (1-25)	1.00	.45
❑ 1 Richard Petty	2.00	.90
❑ 2 Richard Petty	2.00	.90
❑ 3 Benny Parsons	1.00	.45
❑ 4 Richard Petty	2.00	.90
❑ 5 Richard Petty	2.00	.90
❑ 6 Cale Yarborough	1.00	.45
❑ 7 Cale Yarborough	1.00	.45
❑ 8 Cale Yarborough	1.00	.45
❑ 9 Richard Petty	2.00	.90
❑ 10 Dale Earnhardt	4.00	1.80
❑ 11 Darrell Waltrip	1.50	.70
❑ 12 Darrell Waltrip	1.50	.70
❑ 13 Bobby Allison	1.50	.70
❑ 14 Terry Labonte	2.00	.90
❑ 15 Darrell Waltrip	1.50	.70
❑ 16 Dale Earnhardt	4.00	1.80
❑ 17 Dale Earnhardt	4.00	1.80
❑ 18 Bill Elliott	2.50	1.10
❑ 19 Rusty Wallace	2.50	1.10
❑ 20 Dale Earnhardt	4.00	1.80
❑ 21 Dale Earnhardt	4.00	1.80
❑ 22 Alan Kulwicki	2.00	.90
❑ 23 Dale Earnhardt	4.00	1.80
❑ 24 Dale Earnhardt	4.00	1.80
❑ 25 Jeff Gordon	4.00	1.80

1996 Metallic Impressions Avon All-Time Racing Greatest

This five-card sets was produced by Metallic Impressions for Avon. The set was originally sold through the May 1996 Avon catalog. The five NASCAR drivers featured in the set are all former Winston Cup champions. The cards are embossed metal and come in a metal tin.

	MINT	NRMT
COMPLETE SET (5)	20.00	9.00
COMMON CARD (1-5)	4.00	1.80
❑ 1 Dale Earnhardt	8.00	3.60
❑ 2 Darrell Waltrip	4.00	1.80
❑ 3 Bill Elliott	5.00	2.20
❑ 4 Terry Labonte	5.00	2.20
❑ 5 Rusty Wallace	5.00	2.20

1996 Metallic Impressions Jeff Gordon Winston Cup Champ

Jeff Gordon is the feature of this 10-card set produced by Metallic Impressions. The metal cards were distributed in complete set form in a tin box. Each set comes with a numbered certificate of authenticity. Metallic Impressions also produced a five-card version of this set. The five card set is valued at $12.50.

	MINT	NRMT
COMPLETE SET (10)	25.00	11.00
JEFF GORDON'S CAR	2.50	1.10
JEFF GORDON	3.00	1.35

1996 Metallic Impressions Winston Cup Top Five

This five-card set features the Top Five finishers in the 1996 Winston Cup points race. The cards are made of embossed metal and come in a colorful tin. $1.00 from each card set sold went to benefit the continued development of Brenner Childern's Hospital.

	MINT	NRMT
COMPLETE SET (5)	12.00	5.50
COMMON CARD (1-5)	2.00	.90
❑ 1 Terry Labonte	2.50	1.10
❑ 2 Jeff Gordon	4.00	1.80
❑ 3 Dale Jarrett	2.00	.90
❑ 4 Dale Earnhardt	4.00	1.80
❑ 5 Mark Martin	2.50	1.10

1996 M-Force

This 45-card set is the first issued by Press Pass under the M-Force brand name. The cards feature 38 point board, two-sided mirror foil, and a damage resistant laminent. The top drivers and cars are included in 1996 race action. The cards were packaged two cards per pack, 24 packs per box and 20 boxes per case. The product was distributed through hobby channels.

	MINT	NRMT
COMPLETE SET (45)	30.00	13.50
COMMON CARD (1-45)	.20	.09
COMMON DRIVER (1-45)	.40	.18
❑ 1 Rusty Wallace	2.00	.90
❑ 2 Rusty Wallace's Car	1.00	.45
❑ 3 Dale Earnhardt	4.00	1.80
❑ 4 Dale Earnhardt's Car	2.00	.90
❑ 5 Sterling Marlin	.75	.35
❑ 6 Sterling Marlin's Car	.40	.18
❑ 7 Terry Labonte	2.00	.90
❑ 8 Terry Labonte's Car	1.00	.45
❑ 9 Mark Martin	2.00	.90
❑ 10 Mark Martin's Car	1.00	.45
❑ 11 Ricky Rudd	.75	.35
❑ 12 Ricky Rudd's Car	.40	.18
❑ 13 Ted Musgrave	.40	
❑ 14 Richard Petty	1.00	
❑ 15 Darrell Waltrip	.75	
❑ 16 Bobby Allison	.20	
❑ 17 Bobby Labonte	1.50	
❑ 18 Michael Waltrip	.40	
❑ 19 Jeff Gordon	4.00	
❑ 20 Jeff Gordon's Car	2.00	
❑ 21 Ken Schrader in Car	.40	
❑ 22 Ernie Irvan	.75	
❑ 23 Ernie Irvan's Car	.40	
❑ 24 Steve Grissom	.40	
❑ 25 Johnny Benson	.40	
❑ 26 Bobby Hamilton	.40	
❑ 27 Bobby Hamilton's Car	.20	
❑ 28 Ricky Craven	.40	
❑ 29 Ricky Craven's Car	.20	
❑ 30 Kyle Petty	.75	
❑ 31 Kyle Petty's Car	.40	
❑ 32 David Pearson	.20	
❑ 33 Dale Jarrett	1.50	
❑ 34 Dale Jarrett's Car	.75	
❑ 35 Bill Elliott	2.00	
❑ 36 Bill Elliott's Car	1.00	
❑ 37 Jeremy Mayfield	1.25	
❑ 38 Jeff Burton	.75	
❑ 39 Cale Yarborough	.75	
❑ 40 Jeff Gordon	4.00	
❑ 41 Mark Martin	2.00	
❑ 42 Rusty Wallace	2.00	
❑ 43 Bill Elliott	2.00	
❑ 44 Ernie Irvan	2.00	
❑ 45 Dale Earnhardt's Car CL	2.00	

1996 M-Force Blacks

This 12-card insert set features the top drivers Winston Cup. The fronts of the cards are embossed or car portraits on black foil board. The backs featu same silver mirror foil as the base cards. The Blacks randomly inserted one in 96 packs.

	MINT
COMPLETE SET (12)	400.00
COMMON CARD (B1-B12)	15.00
*SINGLES: 8X TO 20X BASE CARD HI	
❑ B1 Rusty Wallace	50.00
❑ B2 Rusty Wallace's Car	20.00
❑ B3 Dale Earnhardt	100.00
❑ B4 Dale Earnhardt's Car	40.00
❑ B5 Terry Labonte	50.00
❑ B6 Mark Martin	50.00
❑ B7 Jeff Gordon	100.00
❑ B8 Jeff Gordon's Car	40.00
❑ B9 Ernie Irvan	15.00
❑ B10 Dale Jarrett	40.00
❑ B11 Bill Elliott	50.00
❑ B12 Jeff Gordon	100.00

1996 M-Force Sheet Meta

This 6-card insert set was the first to incorporate race used sheet metal into a trading card. The p sheet metal along with a photo of the dri permanently in cased in a clear polyurethane card. containing multi-colored pieces of sheet metal 25% premium oer those that do not. The card seeded one in 288 packs.

	MINT
COMPLETE SET (6)	1200.00
COMMON CARD (M1-M6)	200.00
❑ M1 Rusty Wallace	200.00
❑ M2 Dale Earnhardt	350.00
❑ M3 Terry Labonte	200.00
❑ M4 Mark Martin	200.00
❑ M5 Jeff Gordon	350.00
❑ M6 Bill Elliott	200.00

1996 M-Force Silvers

the top drivers are a part of this insert set. The card are embossed driver or car portraits on silver foil . The backs of the cards feature the same silver foil as the base cards. The Silvers were inserted eight packs.

	MINT	NRMT
'LETE SET (18)	100.00	45.00
ION CARD (S1-S18)	2.00	.90
LES: 2X TO 5X BASE CARD HI		
Rusty Wallace's Car	5.00	2.20
Dale Earnhardt	25.00	11.00
Dale Earnhardt's Car	10.00	4.50
Sterling Marlin	4.00	1.80
Terry Labonte	12.00	5.50
Terry Labonte's Car	5.00	2.20
Ricky Rudd	4.00	1.80
Richard Petty	8.00	3.60
Bobby Labonte	7.00	3.10
Jeff Gordon's Car	10.00	4.50
Bobby Hamilton's Car	2.00	.90
Ricky Craven	2.00	.90
Kyle Petty	4.00	1.80
Jeff Gordon	25.00	11.00
Mark Martin	12.00	5.50
Rusty Wallace	12.00	5.50
Bill Elliott	12.00	5.50
Ernie Irvan	10.00	4.50

992 Miller Genuine Draft Rusty Wallace

ix-card set was released by the Miller Brewing ny. The cards were inserted into twelve packs of Genuine Draft. There were three cards in a white pe glued inside the twelve packs. Each three cards nvelope is considered a "set." Each card features art y Sam Bass and measures 3 5/8" X 5 3/8". The lso carries "Miller Brewing Company Reminds You ase THINK WHEN YOU DRINK." Think when you s in a yellow triangle. The cards are blank backed.

	MINT	NRMT
.ETE SET (6)	18.00	8.00
ON CARD	3.00	1.35

993 Miller Genuine Draft Rusty Wallace Post Cards

e-card set was available as a send-away offer from Brewing Company. The cards measure 3 1/2" X 5 d came in a white envelope. There was one cover each envelope.

	MINT	NRMT
.ETE SET (5)	12.00	5.50
ON CARD	3.00	1.35
Rusty Wallace The Boss	3.00	1.35
Rusty Wallace Fire and Ice	3.00	1.35
Rusty Wallace Midnight Rider	3.00	1.35
Rusty Wallace Pocono Draft '92	3.00	1.35
Cover Card	.50	.23

1991 Motorcraft Racing

91 release features members and machines of the raft Racing teams. The cards were primarily ed through participating Ford dealerships and are bered. We have listed and numbered the cards alphabetical order.

	MINT	NRMT
ETE SET (7)	10.00	4.50
N CARD	1.50	.70

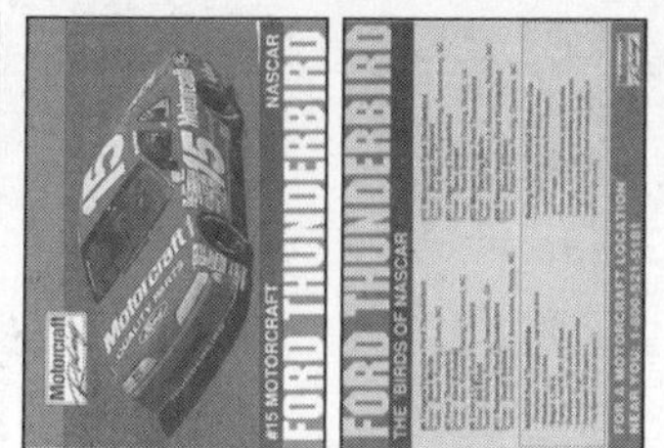

	MINT	NRMT
❑ 1 Bob Glidden's Car	1.50	.70
Morgan Shepherd's Car		
❑ 2 Bob Glidden w/Car	1.50	.70
❑ 3 Bob Glidden's Car	1.50	.70
❑ 4 Bob Glidden Family Racing	1.50	.70
❑ 5 Walter Bud Moore	1.50	.70
❑ 6 Morgan Shepherd	2.00	.90
❑ 7 Morgan Shepherd's Car	1.50	.70

1992 Motorcraft Racing

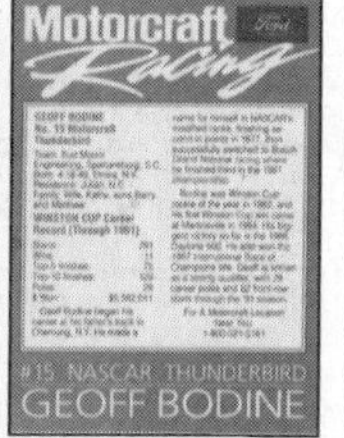

This 1992 release features members and machines of the Motorcraft Racing teams. The cards were primarily distributed in complete set form through participating Ford dealerships and are unnumbered. We have listed and numbered the cards below in alphabetical order.

	MINT	NRMT
COMPLETE SET (10)	6.00	2.70
COMMON CARD	.60	.25
❑ 1 Geoff Bodine	1.00	.45
❑ 2 Geoff Bodine's Car	.60	.25
❑ 3 Geoff Bodine's Pit Crew	.60	.25
❑ 4 Geoff Bodine	.60	.25
Bob Glidden Cars		
❑ 5 Bob Glidden	.60	.25
❑ 6 Bob Glidden's Car	.60	.25
❑ 7 Bob Glidden	.60	.25
Etta Glidden		
❑ 8 Walter Bud Moore	.60	.25
❑ 9 Cover Card	.60	.25
❑ 10 Motorcraft Special Events	.60	.25

1993 Motorcraft Decade of Champions

This 1993 release honors Motorcraft Quality Part's ten years of motorsports sponsorship. The cards were primarily distributed in complete set form through participating Ford dealerships and are unnumbered. We have listed and numbered the cards below in alphabetical order.

	MINT	NRMT
COMPLETE SET (10)	6.00	2.70
COMMON CARD	.75	.35
❑ 1 Geoff Bodine's Car	1.00	.45
❑ 2 Manny Esquerra's Truck	.75	.35
❑ 3 Bob Glidden's Car	.75	.35
❑ 4 Bob Glidden's Car	.75	.35
❑ 5 John Jones' Car	.75	.35
❑ 6 Mark Oswald's Car	.75	.35
❑ 7 Ricky Rudd's Car	1.25	.55
❑ 8 Morgan Shepherd's Car	1.00	.45
❑ 9 Rickie Smith's Car	.75	.35
❑ NNO Cover Card	.50	.23

1993 Motorcraft Manufacturers' Championship

Ford produced this set to honor its 1992 NASCAR Manufacturers' Championship. Eight car and drivers are included along with a trophy card and a cover card. As is common with Motorcraft sets, the cards are unnumbered and listed below alphabetically.

	MINT	NRMT
COMPLETE SET (10)	6.00	2.70
COMMON CARD	.50	.23
❑ 1 Davey Allison	1.50	.70
❑ 2 Geoff Bodine	.50	.23
❑ 3 Bill Elliott	1.50	.70
❑ 4 Jimmy Hensley	.50	.23
❑ 5 Alan Kulwicki	1.00	.45
❑ 6 Sterling Marlin	.75	.35
❑ 7 Mark Martin	1.00	.45
❑ 8 Morgan Shepherd	.50	.23
❑ 9 Cover Card	.50	.23
❑ 10 Trophy Card	.50	.23

1994 MW Windows

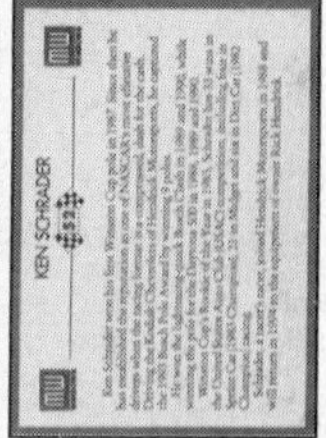

This five-card set was produced for distribution at the 1994 National Association of Homebuilders Show held in Las Vegas and was sponsored by MW Windows. The cards are called the Aces Collection and feature four drivers and one checklist card picturing the four. Reportedly, production was held to 7500 complete sets. The cards are unnumbered, but have been assigned numbers below alphabetically with the checklist card last.

	MINT	NRMT
COMPLETE SET (5)	15.00	6.75
COMMON CARD	1.50	.70
❑ 1 Jeff Gordon	4.00	1.80
❑ 2 Bobby Labonte	2.00	.90
❑ 3 Terry Labonte	2.50	1.10
❑ 4 Ken Schrader	1.50	.70
❑ 5 Jeff Gordon: Bobby Labonte Terry Labonte Ken Schrader Checklist	2.50	1.10

1995 MW Windows

This five-card set was produced for distribution at the 1995 National Association of Homebuilders Show held in Houston and was sponsored by MW Windows. The cards are titled Fast Riders and feature four drivers and one checklist card picturing the four. Reportedly, production was held to 7500 complete sets.The cards are unnumbered, but have been assigned numbers below alphabetically with the checklist card last.

	MINT	NRMT
COMPLETE SET (5)	10.00	4.50

COMMON CARD	2.00	.90
❑ 1 David Green	2.00	.90
❑ 2 Dale Jarrett	2.00	.90
❑ 3 Terry Labonte	3.00	1.35
❑ 4 Michael Waltrip	2.00	.90
❑ 5 Terry Labonte Michael Waltrip Dale Jarrett David Green Checklist	2.50	1.10

1994 Optima XL

This 64-card set was the first time Press Pass issued cards under the Optima XL brand name. The cards are larger than the standard card, measuring 2 1/2" x 4 11/16". There are seven topical subsets that combine to make up the entire set. Those subsets are, Spotlight (1-30), Double Duty (31-36), Trophy Case (37-42), Dale Earnhardt Racing Family (43-46), RCR Racing Family (47-49), Winston Cup Scene (50-58), News Makers (59-64). There is one known variation. The #43 Teresa Earnhardt card was originally printed with a picture of both Teresa and Dale. Early in the production the card was changed to be a picture of Teresa. The set price only includes the common version. The cards were packaged six card per pack and came 24 packs per box and 20 boxes per case. There was also a two-card insert set known as Chrome featuring Jeff Gordon and Ernie Irvan. The cards were printed embossed on silver foil and inserted one per 240 packs.

	MINT	NRMT
COMPLETE SET (64)	18.00	8.00
COMMON CARD (1-64)	.15	.07
COMMON DRIVER (1-64)	.30	.14
❑ 1 Brett Bodine	.30	.14
❑ 2 Geoff Bodine	.30	.14
❑ 3 Jeff Burton	.30	.14
❑ 4 Dale Earnhardt	2.50	1.10
❑ 5 Harry Gant	.60	.25
❑ 6 Jeff Gordon	2.50	1.10
❑ 7 Steve Grissom	.30	.14
❑ 8 Ernie Irvan	.60	.25
❑ 9 Dale Jarrett	1.00	.45
❑ 10 Terry Labonte	1.25	.55
❑ 11 Sterling Marlin	.60	.25
❑ 12 Mark Martin	1.25	.55
❑ 13 Joe Nemechek	.30	.14
❑ 14 Kyle Petty	.60	.25
❑ 15 Ricky Rudd	.60	.25
❑ 16 Greg Sacks	.30	.14
❑ 17 Ken Schrader	.30	.14
❑ 18 Morgan Shepherd	.30	.14
❑ 19 Lake Speed	.30	.14
❑ 20 Jimmy Spencer	.30	.14
❑ 21 Hut Stricklin	.30	.14
❑ 22 Rusty Wallace	1.25	.55
❑ 23 Darrell Waltrip	.60	.25
❑ 24 Michael Waltrip	.30	.14
❑ 25 Ernie Irvan	.60	.25
❑ 26 Jeff Gordon	2.50	1.10
❑ 27 Mark Martin	1.25	.55
❑ 28 Kyle Petty	.60	.25
❑ 29 Ken Schrader	.30	.14
❑ 30 Rusty Wallace	1.25	.55
❑ 31 Geoff Bodine DD	.15	.07
❑ 32 Ernie Irvan DD	.30	.14
❑ 33 Ricky Rudd DD	.30	.14
❑ 34 Ken Schrader DD	.15	.07
❑ 35 Rusty Wallace DD	.60	.25
❑ 36 Darrell Waltrip DD	.30	.14
❑ 37 Sterling Marlin's Car TC	.30	.14
❑ 38 Jeff Gordon TC	1.25	.55
❑ 39 Terry Labonte's Car TC	.60	.25
❑ 40 Rusty Wallace's Car TC	.60	.25
❑ 41 Dale Earnhardt's Car TC	1.25	.55
❑ 42 Ernie Irvan's Car TC	.30	.14
❑ 43A Teresa Earnhardt	.75	.35
❑ 43B Teresa Earnhardt Dale Earnhardt	120.00	55.00
❑ 44 Kerry Earnhardt	.60	.25
❑ 45 Kelley Earnhardt	.60	.25
❑ 46 Dale Earnhardt Jr.	12.00	5.50
❑ 47 Richard Childress	.15	.07
❑ 48 Hank Jones	.15	.07
❑ 49 Andy Petree	.15	.07
❑ 50 Race Day Frenzy WCS	.15	.07
❑ 51 Rusty Wallace in Pits WCS	.60	.25
❑ 52 Rusty Wallace Mark Martin Ernie Irvan WCS	.60	.25
❑ 53 Ricky Rudd's Car WCS	.30	.14
❑ 54 Charlotte Motor Speed. WCS	.15	.07
❑ 55 Steve Grissom Jeff Burton WCS	.15	.07
❑ 56 Jeff Gordon WCS	1.25	.55
❑ 57 Joe Nemechek in Pits WCS	.15	.07
❑ 58 The Duel in the Sun WCS Charlotte Motor Speed.	.15	.07
❑ 59 John Andretti NM	.15	.07
❑ 60 Shawna Robinson NM	.15	.07
❑ 61 Loy Allen Jr. NM	.15	.07
❑ 62 Jeff Gordon NM	1.25	.55
❑ 63 Tommy Houston NM	.15	.07
❑ 64 Geoff Bodine NM	.15	.07
❑ CC1 Jeff Gordon Chrome	50.00	22.00
❑ CC2 Ernie Irvan Chrome	10.00	4.50

1994 Optima XL Red Hot

This 64-card set is a parallel of the base set. It features red foil stamping on the front to set it apart from the base brand. Like with the base set, the #43 Teresa Earnhardt card has a variation. The first ones printed pictured both Teresa and Dale. The more common version features Teresa by herself. The Red Hot cards were inserted at a rate of one per three packs.

	MINT	NRMT
COMPLETE SET (64)	80.00	36.00
COMMON CARD (1-64)	.75	.35
COMMON DRIVER (1-64)	1.50	.70
TERESA EARNHARDT/DALE (43B)	135.00	60.00

*RED CARDS: 2.5X TO 5X BASIC CARDS

1994 Optima XL Double Clutch

This six-card insert set features drivers who were active on both the Winston Cup and Busch circuits. The cards were inserted at a rate of one per 48 packs. All six cards could also be found in a Super Pack. These super packs were inserted at a rate of one per 2400 packs.

	MINT	NRMT
COMPLETE SET (6)	50.00	22.00
COMMON CARD (DC1-DC6)	3.00	1.35

*SINGLES: 5X TO 12X BASE CARD HI

❑ DC1 Dale Earnhardt	3.00	1.35
❑ DC2 Ernie Irvan	3.00	1.35
❑ DC3 Terry Labonte	3.00	1.35
❑ DC4 Sterling Marlin	3.00	1.35
❑ DC5 Mark Martin	3.00	1.35
❑ DC6 Morgan Shepherd	3.00	1.35

1995 Optima XL

This 60-card set is the second edition of the oversized brand of racing cards produced by Press Pass. The cards

measure 2 1/2" X 4 11/16" and use photography fror 1995 season. The set consists of seven subsets: Wi Cup Drivers (1-24), Busch Drivers (25-30), Trophy (31-36), Team 24 (37-42), Thunderous Thunderbirds 48), Monte Carlo Assault (49-54), and Optima Re (55-59). The product was distributed to both hobby retail outlets and came six cards per pack, 36 pack box and 12 boxes per case.

	MINT	N
COMPLETE SET (60)	15.00	
COMMON CARD (1-60)	.15	
COMMON DRIVER (1-60)	.30	
❑ 1 Brett Bodine	.30	
❑ 2 Geoff Bodine	.30	
❑ 3 Todd Bodine	.30	
❑ 4 Derrike Cope	.30	
❑ 5 Ricky Craven	.30	
❑ 6 Dale Earnhardt	3.00	
❑ 7 Bill Elliott	1.50	
❑ 8 Jeff Gordon	3.00	
❑ 9 Steve Grissom	.30	
❑ 10 Dale Jarrett	1.25	
❑ 11 Bobby Labonte	1.25	
❑ 12 Terry Labonte	1.50	
❑ 13 Sterling Marlin	.60	
❑ 14 Mark Martin	1.50	
❑ 15 Ted Musgrave	.30	
❑ 16 Kyle Petty	.60	
❑ 17 Robert Pressley	.30	
❑ 18 Ricky Rudd	.60	
❑ 19 Ken Schrader	.30	
❑ 20 Morgan Shepherd	.30	
❑ 21 Hut Stricklin	.30	
❑ 22 Rusty Wallace	1.50	
❑ 23 Darrell Waltrip	.60	
❑ 24 Michael Waltrip	.30	
❑ 25 Johnny Benson Jr.	.30	
❑ 26 David Green	.30	
❑ 27 Jeff Green	.30	
❑ 28 Jason Keller	.30	
❑ 29 Chad Little	.30	
❑ 30 Larry Pearson	.30	
❑ 31 Jeff Gordon TC	1.50	
❑ 32 Bobby Labonte TC	.60	
❑ 33 Terry Labonte TC	.75	
❑ 34 Sterling Marlin TC	.30	
❑ 35 Mark Martin TC	.75	
❑ 36 Kyle Petty TC	.30	
❑ 37 Chad Knaus	.15	
❑ 38 Ray Evernham	.60	
❑ 39 Mike Belden	.15	
❑ 40 Mike Trower	.15	
❑ 41 Andy Papathanassiou	.15	
❑ 42 Barry Muse	.15	
❑ 43 Ted Musgrave's Car	.15	
❑ 44 Bill Elliott's Car	.75	
❑ 45 Rusty Wallace's Car	.75	
❑ 46 Dale Jarrett's Car	.60	
❑ 47 Ricky Rudd's Car	.30	
❑ 48 Mark Martin's Car	.75	
❑ 49 Ken Schrader's Car	.15	
❑ 50 Jeff Gordon's Car	1.50	
❑ 51 Dale Earnhardt's Car	1.50	
❑ 52 Bobby Labonte's Car	.60	
❑ 53 Terry Labonte's Car	.75	
❑ 54 Sterling Marlin's Car	.30	
❑ 55 Bill Elliott OR	.75	
❑ 56 Jeff Gordon OR	1.50	
❑ 57 Sterling Marlin OR	.30	
❑ 58 Mark Martin OR	.75	
❑ 59 Ricky Rudd OR	.30	
❑ 60 Checklist	.15	

1995 Optima XL Cool Blu

The 60-card Cool Blue set is a parallel of the base XL set. The cards feature blue foil stamping on th and could be found only in retail packs. The Co cards were inserted at a rate of one per pack.

	MINT
COMPLETE BLUE SET (60)	60.00
COMMON CARD BLUE (1-60)	.30

MON DRIVER BLUE (1-60)	.60	.25
JE STARS: 2X TO X BASIC CARDS		

1995 Optima XL Die Cut

i0-card Die Cut set is a parallel of the base Optima XL Every card is individually die cut to conform to each s unique design. The Die Cut cards could be found er 30 packs.

	MINT	NRMT
PLETE SET (60)	500.00	220.00
MON CARD (1-60)	4.00	1.80
MON DRIVER (1-60)	8.00	3.60
CUT STARS: 10X TO 25X BASIC CARDS		

1995 Optima XL Red Hot

0-card Red Hot set is a parallel of the base Optima t. The cards feature red foil stamping on the fronts vere found only in hobby packs. The Red Hot cards seeded one per pack.

	MINT	NRMT
PLETE RED SET (60)	60.00	27.00
ION CARD RED (1-60)	.30	.14
ION DRIVER RED (1-60)	.60	.25
RS: 2X TO X BASIC CARDS		

1995 Optima XL JG/XL

-card insert set featuring the 1995 Winston Cup ion, Jeff Gordon, created an interesting twist as far ls of finding the individual cards. The higher the umber the tougher the card was to pull out of a Card #1 came 1 per 36 packs, card #2 came 1 per ks, card # 3 came 1:216 packs and card # 4 came packs.

	MINT	NRMT
ETE SET (4)	200.00	90.00
ON CARD (1-4)	6.00	2.70
f Gordon	6.00	2.70
f Gordon	20.00	9.00
f Gordon	50.00	22.00
f Gordon	150.00	70.00

1995 Optima XL Stealth

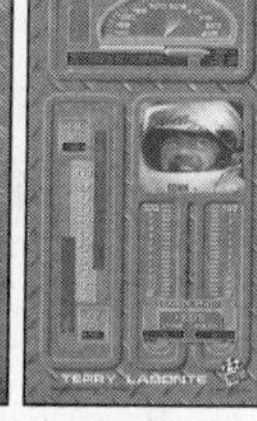

card insert set features the top drivers in Winston ing. Each of the 2 1/2" X 4 11/16" insert cards was using the embossed foil technology. There have ports that some of the cards have been found embossed printing but have shown no premium over the regular issues. The Stealth cards could be found 1 per 18 packs.

	MINT	NRMT
COMPLETE SET (18)	140.00	65.00
COMMON CARD (XLS1-XLS18)	3.00	1.35
*SINGLES: 4X TO 10X BASE CARD HI		
❑ XLS1 Ricky Craven	3.00	1.35
❑ XLS2 Dale Earnhardt	30.00	13.50
❑ XLS3 Bill Elliott	14.00	6.25
❑ XLS4 Jeff Gordon	30.00	13.50
❑ XLS5 Ernie Irvan	6.00	2.70
❑ XLS6 Bobby Labonte	6.00	2.70
❑ XLS7 Terry Labonte	14.00	6.25
❑ XLS8 Sterling Marlin	6.00	2.70
❑ XLS9 Mark Martin	14.00	6.25
❑ XLS10 Ted Musgrave	3.00	1.35
❑ XLS11 Kyle Petty	6.00	2.70
❑ XLS12 Robert Pressley	3.00	1.35
❑ XLS13 Ricky Rudd	6.00	2.70
❑ XLS14 Ken Schrader	3.00	1.35
❑ XLS15 Morgan Shepherd	3.00	1.35
❑ XLS16 Rusty Wallace	14.00	6.25
❑ XLS17 Darrell Waltrip	6.00	2.70
❑ XLS18 Michael Waltrip	3.00	1.35

1992 Pace American Canadian Tour

This 50-card set features drivers who raced in the American Canadian Tour. The cards were sold in complete set form and reportedly 30,000 sets were produced. Each set was individually numbered. The cards were produced by Pace Cards, Inc. of Stowe, Vermont.

	MINT	NRMT
COMPLETE SET (50)	12.00	5.50
COMMON CARD (1-50)	.25	.11
❑ 1 Junior Hanley	.25	.11
❑ 2 Robbie Crouch	.25	.11
❑ 3 Beaver Dragon	.25	.11
❑ 4 Kevin Lepage	.40	.18
❑ 5 Derek Lynch	.25	.11
❑ 6 Brad Leighton	.25	.11
❑ 7 Randy MacDonald	.25	.11
❑ 8 Dan Beede	.25	.11
❑ 9 Roger Laperle	.25	.11
❑ 10 Ralph Nason	.25	.11
❑ 11 Jean-Paul Cabana	.25	.11
❑ 12 Bill Zardo, Sr.	.25	.11
❑ 13 Claude Leclerc	.25	.11
❑ 14 Robbie Thompson	.25	.11
❑ 15 Danny Knoll, Jr.	.25	.11
❑ 16 Bill Zardo, Jr.	.25	.11
❑ 17 John Greedy	.25	.11
❑ 18 Blair Bessett	.25	.11
❑ 19 Buzzie Bezanson	.25	.11
❑ 20 Phil Pinkham	.25	.11
❑ 21 Sylvain Metivier	.25	.11
❑ 22 Andre Beaudoin	.25	.11
❑ 23 Gord Bennett	.25	.11
❑ 24 Donald Forte	.25	.11
❑ 25 Jeff Stevens	.25	.11
❑ 26 Yvon Bedard	.25	.11
❑ 27 Dave Dion	.25	.11
❑ 28 Rollie MacDonald	.25	.11
❑ 29 Ricky Craven	.50	.23
❑ 30 Chuck Bown	.40	.18
❑ 31 Bob Randall	.25	.11
❑ 32 Dave Moody	.25	.11
❑ 33 Stan Meserve	.25	.11
❑ 34 Tom Curley	.25	.11
❑ 35 Robbie Crouch	.25	.11
❑ 36 Dan Beede	.25	.11
❑ 37 Derek Lynch	.25	.11
❑ 38 Dan Beede Roger Laperle	.25	.11
❑ 39 Randy MacDonald Brad Leighton	.25	.11
❑ 40 Randy MacDonald	.25	.11
❑ 41 Robbie Thompson	.25	.11
❑ 42 Bill Zardo, Sr.	.25	.11
❑ 43 Claude Leclerc Brad Leighton	.25	.11
❑ 44 John Greedy	.25	.11
❑ 45 Roger Laperle Yvon Bedard	.25	.11
❑ 46 Gord Bennett	.25	.11
❑ 47 Beaver Dragon Ralph Nason	.25	.11
❑ 48 Yvon Bedard	.25	.11
❑ 49 Jean-Paul Cabana Buzzie Bezanson Sylvain Metivier	.25	.11
❑ 50 Randy MacDonald John Greedy	.25	.11

1993 Pepsi 400 Victory Lane

Produced and distributed by Pepsi, this five-card set honors past winners of the Pepsi 400. The cards are unnumbered and listed below alphabetically. Although no year is present on the cards, they can be distinguished from the 1994 Pepsi 400 release by the orange colored Victory Lane title on the cardfronts.

	MINT	NRMT
COMPLETE SET (5)	12.00	5.50
COMMON DRIVER	1.25	.55
❑ 1 Bobby Allison	3.00	1.35
❑ 2 Davey Allison	5.00	2.20
❑ 3 Buddy Baker	1.25	.55
❑ 4 Ernie Irvan	3.50	1.55
❑ 5 David Pearson	1.25	.55

1994 Pepsi 400 Victory Lane

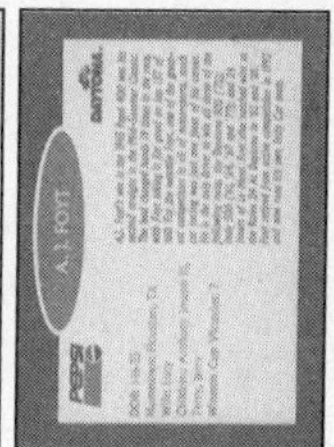

Pepsi again produced and distributed a Pepsi 400 commemorative set in 1994. The cards are very similar to the 1993 issue, except they include the year 1994 on the cardfronts, as well as a yellow colored Victory Lane title. The cards are unnumbered and listed below alphabetically.

	MINT	NRMT
COMPLETE SET (6)	8.00	3.60
COMMON DRIVER	1.25	.55
❑ 1 Donnie Allison	1.25	.55
❑ 2 A.J.Foyt	1.25	.55
❑ 3 Richard Petty	3.00	1.35
❑ 4 Greg Sacks	1.25	.55
❑ 5 Cale Yarborough	1.25	.55
❑ 6 Cover/Checklist Card	.30	.14

1992 Pepsi Richard Petty

This five-card set features the King of stock car racing, Richard Petty. The cards highlight Richard Petty's career. The cards were a promotional giveaway by Pepsi Co.

	MINT	NRMT
COMPLETE SET (5)	5.00	2.20
COMMON CARD	1.00	.45

1996 Pinnacle

The 1996 Pinnacle set was issued in one series totalling 96 cards. This is the first issue under the Pinnacle name brand. The cards features NASCAR's top drivers and their rides printed on 20 point board. Each card has gold foil stamping and UV coating. The set includes these subsets; Jeff Gordon Persistence (66-73), Sterling Marlin Sterling (74-77), Hall of Fame (78-81), and Winners (85-89). The cards come 10-cards per pack, 24 packs per box and 16 boxes per case. The packs carried a suggested retail price for $2.49 each.

	MINT	NRMT
COMPLETE SET (96)	12.00	5.50
COMMON CARD (1- 96)	.10	.05
COMMON DRIVER (1-96)	.20	.09

	MINT	NRMT
❑ 1 Rick Mast	.20	.09
❑ 2 Rusty Wallace	1.00	.45
❑ 3 Dale Earnhardt	2.00	.90
❑ 4 Sterling Marlin	.40	.18
❑ 5 Terry Labonte	1.00	.45
❑ 6 Mark Martin	1.00	.45
❑ 7 Geoff Bodine	.20	.09
❑ 8 Hut Stricklin	.20	.09
❑ 9 Lake Speed	.20	.09
❑ 10 Ricky Rudd	.40	.18
❑ 11 Brett Bodine	.20	.09
❑ 12 Derrike Cope	.20	.09
❑ 13 Dale Jarrett	.75	.35
❑ 14 Joe Nemechek	.20	.09
❑ 15 Wally Dallenbach	.20	.09
❑ 16 Ted Musgrave	.20	.09
❑ 17 Darrell Waltrip	.40	.18
❑ 18 Bobby Labonte	.75	.35
❑ 19 Kenny Wallace	.20	.09
❑ 20 Bobby Hillin Jr.	.20	.09
❑ 21 Michael Waltrip	.20	.09
❑ 22 Ward Burton	.20	.09
❑ 23 Jimmy Spencer	.20	.09
❑ 24 Jeff Gordon	2.00	.90
❑ 25 Ken Schrader	.20	.09
❑ 26 Morgan Shepherd	.20	.09
❑ 27 Bill Elliott	1.00	.45
❑ 28 Ernie Irvan	.40	.18
❑ 29 Bobby Hamilton	.20	.09
❑ 30 Johnny Benson	.20	.09
❑ 31 Kyle Petty	.40	.18
❑ 32 Ricky Craven	.20	.09
❑ 33 Robert Pressley	.20	.09
❑ 34 John Andretti	.20	.09
❑ 35 Jeremy Mayfield	.60	.25
❑ 36 Rick Mast's Car	.10	.05
❑ 37 Rusty Wallace's Car	.50	.23
❑ 38 Dale Earnhardt's Car	1.00	.45
❑ 39 Sterling Marlin's Car	.20	.09
❑ 40 Terry Labonte's Car	.50	.23
❑ 41 Mark Martin's Car	.50	.23
❑ 42 Geoff Bodine's Car	.10	.05
❑ 43 Ricky Rudd's Car	.20	.09
❑ 44 Derrike Cope's Car	.10	.05
❑ 45 Ted Musgrave's Car	.10	.05
❑ 46 Darrell Waltrip's Car	.20	.09
❑ 47 Bobby Labonte's Car	.40	.18
❑ 48 Michael Waltrip's Car	.10	.05
❑ 49 Ward Burton's Car	.10	.05
❑ 50 Jimmy Spencer's Car	.10	.05
❑ 51 Jeff Gordon's Car	1.00	.45
❑ 52 Ernie Irvan's Car	.20	.09
❑ 53 Johnny Benson's Car	.10	.05
❑ 54 Robert Pressley's Car	.10	.05
❑ 55 John Andretti's Car	.10	.05
❑ 56 Ricky Craven's Car	.10	.05
❑ 57 Kyle Petty's Car	.20	.09
❑ 58 Bobby Hamilton's Car	.10	.05
❑ 59 Dave Marcis' Car	.20	.09
❑ 60 Morgan Shepherd's Car	.10	.05
❑ 61 Bobby Hillin's Car	.10	.05
❑ 62 Kenny Wallace's Car	.10	.05
❑ 63 Joe Nemechek's Car	.10	.05
❑ 64 Dale Jarrett's Car	.40	.18
❑ 65 Hut Stricklin's Car	.10	.05
❑ 66 Jeff Gordon PER	1.00	.45
❑ 67 Jeff Gordon PER	1.00	.45
❑ 68 Jeff Gordon PER	1.00	.45
❑ 69 Jeff Gordon PER	1.00	.45
❑ 70 Jeff Gordon PER	1.00	.45
❑ 71 Jeff Gordon PER	1.00	.45
❑ 72 Jeff Gordon PER	1.00	.45
❑ 73 Jeff Gordon PER	1.00	.45
❑ 74 Sterling Marlin STE	.20	.09
❑ 75 Sterling Marlin STE	.20	.09
❑ 76 Sterling Marlin STE	.20	.09
❑ 77 Sterling Marlin STE	.20	.09
❑ 78 Joe Gibbs HOF	.20	.09
❑ 79 Bobby Labonte HOF	.20	.09
❑ 80 Jimmy Makar HOF	.10	.05
❑ 81 Bobby Labonte's Car HOF	.40	.18
❑ 82 Elmo Langley	.10	.05
❑ 83 Doyle Ford	.10	.05
❑ 84 Buster Auton	.10	.05
❑ 85 Jeff Gordon W	1.00	.45
❑ 86 Rusty Wallace W	.50	.23
❑ 87 Sterling Marlin W	.20	.09
❑ 88 Ernie Irvan W	.20	.09
❑ 89 Rusty Wallace W	.50	.23
❑ 90 Bobby Labonte's Transporter	.05	.02
❑ 91 Dale Earnhardt's Transporter	1.00	.45
❑ 92 Jeff Gordon's Transporter	1.00	.45
❑ 93 Sterling Marlin's Transporter	.20	.09
❑ 94 Rusty Wallace's Transporter	.50	.23
❑ 95 Jeff Gordon CL	1.00	.45
❑ 96 Mark Martin CL	.50	.23

1996 Pinnacle Artist's Proof

This 96-card parallel set features an Artist's Proof logo and rainbow foil stamping to differentiate each card from the base set. The cards were randomly inserted in both hobby and retail packs at a rate of one in 47 and in magazine packs at a rate of one in 75.

	MINT	NRMT
COMPLETE SET (96)	400.00	180.00
COMMON CARD (1- 96)	2.50	1.10
COMMON DRIVER (1-96)	5.00	2.20

*ARTIST PROOF CARDS: 10X TO 25X BASIC CARDS

1996 Pinnacle Winston Cup Collection

This 96-card set is a parallel version of the base Pinnacle issue. The cards use all-foil dufex printing technology to differentiate themselves from the base Pinnacle cards. The Winston Cup Collection cards were seeded in retail packs one in nine and in hobby and magazine packs at a rate of one in 14.

	MINT	NRMT
COMMON DRIVER (1-96)	1.00	.45

*WC COLLECTION CARDS: 2.5X TO 6X BASIC CARDS

1996 Pinnacle Bill's Back

Randomly inserted in hobby and retail packs at a rate of one in 360, this two-card set features NASCAR's perennial fan favorite Bill Elliott. The two card salute cpatures Bill's return to racing after a potentially career-ending crash. The cards are printed on all-foil dufex card stock.

	MINT	NRMT
COMPLETE SET (2)	60.00	27.00
COMMON CARD (1-2)	30.00	13.50

	MINT	NRMT
❑ 1 Bill Elliott	30.00	13.50
❑ 2 Bill Elliott	30.00	13.50

1996 Pinnacle Checkered Flag

This 15-card insert set featues the top names in racing. The cards were available only through magazine packs at a rate of one in 38 packs. The cards fronts feature driver photos in front of a checkered flag, rainbow hologram background. The drivers name is in a gold foil stripe across the bottom of each card..

	MINT	NRMT
COMPLETE SET (15)	125.00	55.00
COMMON CARD (1-15)	3.00	1.35

*SINGLES: 6X TO 15X BASE CARD HI

	MINT	NRMT
❑ 1 Jeff Gordon	18.00	8.00
❑ 2 Rusty Wallace	9.00	
❑ 3 Dale Earnhardt	18.00	
❑ 4 Sterling Marlin	6.00	
❑ 5 Terry Labonte	9.00	
❑ 6 Mark Martin	9.00	
❑ 7 Bobby Labonte	4.00	
❑ 8 Dale Jarrett	6.00	
❑ 9 Bill Elliott	9.00	
❑ 10 Ricky Rudd	6.00	
❑ 11 Michael Waltrip	3.00	
❑ 12 Ricky Craven	3.00	
❑ 13 Ernie Irvan	6.00	
❑ 14 Geoff Bodine	3.00	
❑ 15 Darrell Waltrip	6.00	

1996 Pinnacle Cut Above

Randomly inserted in retail and hobby packs at a r
one in 24, this 15-card insert set highlights the top d
on the circuit. The photo of the driver is impossed
background of blown up picture of that particular d
uniform. The card is die-cut and uses gold foil sta
for the drivers name.

	MINT
COMPLETE SET (15)	100.00
COMMON CARD (1-15)	2.00

*SINGLES: 4X TO 10X BASE CARD HI

	MINT
❑ 1 Jeff Gordon	30.00
❑ 2 Bill Elliott	15.00
❑ 3 Terry Labonte	15.00
❑ 4 Ernie Irvan	4.00
❑ 5 Johnny Benson	2.00
❑ 6 Ricky Rudd	4.00
❑ 7 Dale Jarrett	10.00
❑ 8 Rusty Wallace	15.00
❑ 9 Bobby Labonte	7.00
❑ 10 Mark Martin	15.00
❑ 11 Ricky Craven	2.00
❑ 12 Robert Pressley	2.00
❑ 13 Ted Musgrave	2.00
❑ 14 Sterling Marlin	4.00
❑ 15 Geoff Bodine	2.00

1996 Pinnacle Driver's Su

Bill Elliott is the focus of this one card insert set. T
incorporates a piece of Bill's driver's suit into th
The cards were seeded one per 270 packs.

	MINT
COMPLETE SET (1)	100.00
BILL ELLIOTT CARD	100.00

	MINT
❑ 1 Bill Elliott	100.00

1996 Pinnacle Team Pinna

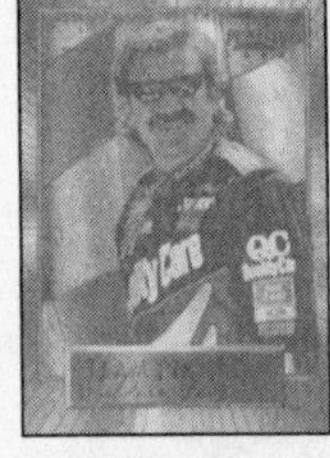

Randomly inserted in retail and hobby packs at a
one in 90 and magazine packs at a rate of one
each of the 12 cards in this set features a doub
design. The cards display one of NASCAR's top dr
one side and either their crew chief or owner
flipside. The driver's side of of each card feature
printing technology.

	MINT
COMPLETE SET (12)	400.00
COMMON CARD (1-12)	12.00

ɜLES: 12X TO 30X BASE CARD HI

eff Gordon Ray Evernham	80.00	36.00
usty Wallace Robin Pemberton	40.00	18.00
ale Earnhardt David Smith	80.00	36.00
ale Jarrett Todd Parrott	25.00	11.00
erry Labonte Gary DeHart	40.00	18.00
ark Martin Steve Hmiel	40.00	18.00
ill Elliott Mike Beam	40.00	18.00
terling Marlin Tony Glover	12.00	5.50
icky Rudd Richard Broome	12.00	5.50
Jeff Gordon Rick Hendrick	80.00	36.00
Dale Earnhardt Richard Childress	80.00	36.00
Dale Jarrett Robert Yates	25.00	11.00

996 Pinnacle Pole Position

996 Pinnacle Pole Position set was issued in one totalling 100 cards. The product was distributed ɔ K-Mart stores. The set contains the following subsets: Drivers (1-25) and The Early Years (72-ne cards were packaged seven cards per pack, and ;ks per box. The packs carried a suggested retail f $1.99.

	MINT	NRMT
LETE SET (100)	20.00	9.00
ON CARD (1-100)	.15	.07
ON DRIVER (1-100)	.30	.14

hn Andretti	.30	.14
sty Wallace	1.50	.70
le Earnhardt	3.00	1.35
erling Marlin	.60	.25
rry Labonte	1.50	.70
rk Martin	1.50	.70
off Bodine	.30	.14
t Stricklin	.30	.14
nny Wallace	.30	.14
icky Rudd	.60	.25
yle Petty	.60	.25
nie Irvan	.60	.25
ale Jarrett	1.25	.55
ll Elliott	1.50	.70
ff Burton	.60	.25
obert Pressley	.30	.14
arrell Waltrip	.60	.25
obby Labonte	1.25	.55
obby Hamilton	.30	.14
hnny Benson Jr.	.30	.14
ichael Waltrip	.30	.14
ard Burton	.30	.14
mmy Spencer	.30	.14
ff Gordon	3.00	1.35
en Schrader	.30	.14
usty Wallace's Car	.75	.35
ale Earnhardt's Car	1.50	.70
erling Marlin's Car	.30	.14
rry Labonte's Car	.75	.35
ark Martin's Car	.75	.35
cky Rudd's Car	.30	.14
ett Bodine's Car	.15	.07
errike Cope's Car	.15	.07
d Musgrave's Car	.15	.07
arrell Waltrip's Car	.30	.14
obby Labonte's Car	.60	.25
chael Waltrip's Car	.15	.07
ard Burton's Car	.15	.07
mmy Spencer's Car	.15	.07
ff Gordon's Car	1.50	.70
nie Irvan's Car	.30	.14
❑ 42 Kyle Petty's Car	.30	.14
❑ 43 Bobby Hamilton's Car	.15	.07
❑ 44 Dale Jarrett's Car	.60	.25
❑ 45 Johnny Benson's Car	.15	.07
❑ 46 Robert Pressley's Car	.15	.07
❑ 47 Ricky Craven's Car	.15	.07
❑ 48 Bobby Hillin's Car	.15	.07
❑ 49 Jeff Burton's Car	.30	.14
❑ 50 Joe Nemechek's Car	.15	.07
❑ 51 Jeff Gordon 95C	1.50	.70
❑ 52 Jeff Gordon 95C	1.50	.70
❑ 53 Jeff Gordon 95C	1.50	.70
❑ 54 Jeff Gordon 95C	1.50	.70
❑ 55 Jeff Gordon 95C	1.50	.70
❑ 56 Dale Earnhardt SE	1.50	.70
❑ 57 Dale Earnhardt SE	1.50	.70
❑ 58 Dale Earnhardt SE	1.50	.70
❑ 59 Dale Earnhardt SE	1.50	.70
❑ 60 Dale Earnhardt SE	1.50	.70
❑ 61 Johnny Benson Jr. RS	.15	.07
❑ 62 Johnny Benson Jr. RS	.15	.07
❑ 63 Johnny Benson Jr. RS	.15	.07
❑ 64 Sterling Marlin WIN	.30	.14
❑ 65 Rusty Wallace WIN	.75	.35
❑ 66 Michael Waltrip WIN	.15	.07
❑ 67 Dale Jarrett WIN	.60	.25
❑ 68 Jeff Gordon WIN	1.50	.70
❑ 69 Jeff Gordon WIN	1.50	.70
❑ 70 Rusty Wallace WIN	.75	.35
❑ 71 Sterling Marlin WIN	.30	.14
❑ 72 Dale Earnhardt EY	1.50	.70
❑ 73 Jeff Gordon EY	1.50	.70
❑ 74 Kyle Petty EY	.30	.14
❑ 75 Bobby Labonte EY	.60	.25
❑ 76 Sterling Marlin EY	.30	.14
❑ 77 Mark Martin EY	.75	.35
❑ 78 Rusty Wallace EY	.75	.35
❑ 79 Terry Labonte EY	.75	.35
❑ 80 Ricky Rudd EY	.30	.14
❑ 81 Darrell Waltrip EY	.30	.14
❑ 82 Ray Evernham	.30	.14
❑ 83 Larry McReynolds	.15	.07
❑ 84 David Smith	.15	.07
❑ 85 Andy Petree	.15	.07
❑ 86 Richard Broome	.15	.07
❑ 87 Richard Childress	.15	.07
❑ 88 Larry McClure	.15	.07
❑ 89 Rick Hendrick	.15	.07
❑ 90 Filbert Martocci	.15	.07
❑ 91 Jack Roush	.15	.07
❑ 92 Joe Gibbs	.30	.14
❑ 93 Robert Yates	.15	.07
❑ 94 John Andretti	.30	.14
❑ 95 John Andretti	.30	.14
❑ 96 John Andretti	.30	.14
❑ 97 John Andretti	.30	.14
❑ 98 John Andretti	.30	.14
❑ 99 Bill McCarthy CL	.15	.07
❑ 100 Gary Miller CL	.15	.07

1996 Pinnacle Pole Position Lightning Fast

This 100-card set is a parallel to the base Pole Position set. The cards feature foil treatments and have no copy on the front of the card to differentiate themselves from the base cards. The cards were available one in seven packs.

	MINT	NRMT
COMPLETE SET (100)	100.00	45.00
COMMON CARD (1-100)	.30	.14
COMMON DRIVER (1-100)	.50	.23

*LIGHTNING FAST CARDS: 3X TO 6X BASIC CARDS

1996 Pinnacle Pole Position Certified Strong

Randomly inserted in packs at a rate of one in 23, this 15-card set features rainbow foil hologram technology. The top drivers in NASCAR make an appearance in this set.

	MINT	NRMT
COMPLETE SET (15)	170.00	75.00
COMMON CARD (1-15)	3.00	1.35

*SINGLES: 5X TO 10X BASE CARD HI

❑ 1 Jeff Gordon	30.00	13.50
❑ 2 Rusty Wallace	15.00	6.75
❑ 3 Dale Earnhardt	30.00	13.50
❑ 4 Sterling Marlin	6.00	2.70
❑ 5 Terry Labonte	15.00	6.75
❑ 6 Mark Martin	15.00	6.75
❑ 7 Ernie Irvan	6.00	2.70
❑ 8 Dale Jarrett	12.00	5.50
❑ 9 Jeremy Mayfield	6.00	2.70
❑ 10 Ricky Rudd	6.00	2.70
❑ 11 Bobby Labonte	8.00	3.60
❑ 12 Bobby Hamilton	3.00	1.35
❑ 13 Bill Elliott	15.00	6.75
❑ 14 Kyle Petty	6.00	2.70
❑ 15 Ricky Craven	3.00	1.35

1996 Pinnacle Pole Position No Limit

This 16-card insert set features the top cars on the NASCAR circuit. Each card was printed on silver mirror foil board and the front has a shot of the car and the words "speed limit" with the international no symbol over the top of it. The cards were randomly inserted in packs at a rate of one in 37. The is also a gold parallel version of this set. The cards feature gold mirror foil board instead of the base silver. The gold cards were seeded one in 240 packs.

	MINT	NRMT
COMPLETE SET (16)	250.00	110.00
COMMON CARD (1-16)	5.00	2.20
*SINGLES: 6X TO 15X BASE CARD HI		
COMP.GOLD SET (16)	800.00	350.00

*GOLD CARDS: 30X TO 60X BASIC CARDS

❑ 1 Jeff Gordon	50.00	22.00
❑ 2 Rusty Wallace	25.00	11.00
❑ 3 Dale Earnhardt	50.00	22.00
❑ 4 Sterling Marlin	10.00	4.50
❑ 5 Terry Labonte	25.00	11.00
❑ 6 Mark Martin	25.00	11.00
❑ 7 Ernie Irvan	10.00	4.50
❑ 8 Robert Pressley	5.00	2.20
❑ 9 Dale Jarrett	20.00	9.00
❑ 10 Ricky Rudd	10.00	4.50
❑ 11 Bill Elliott	25.00	11.00
❑ 12 Darrell Waltrip	10.00	4.50
❑ 13 Jeff Burton	10.00	4.50
❑ 14 Jimmy Spencer	5.00	2.20
❑ 15 Bobby Labonte	12.00	5.50
❑ 16 Ken Schrader	5.00	2.20

1997 Pinnacle

This 96-car set was produced by Pinnacle Brands. The set features four topical subsets: Race Review (59-72), Texas Tornado (73-84), New Face (85-87), and Turn 4 (88-95). Cards were distributed in ten card packs with 18 packs per box and 24 boxes per case. The packs carried a suggested retail price of $2.99.

	MINT	NRMT
COMPLETE SET (96)	20.00	9.00
COMMON CARD (1-96)	.10	.05
COMMON DRIVER (1-96)	.20	.09
❑ 1 Kyle Petty	.40	.18
❑ 2 Rusty Wallace	1.00	.45
❑ 3 Dale Earnhardt	2.00	.90
❑ 4 Sterling Marlin	.40	.18
❑ 5 Terry Labonte	1.00	.45
❑ 6 Mark Martin	1.00	.45
❑ 7 Geoff Bodine	.20	.09
❑ 8 Bill Elliott	1.00	.45
❑ 9 David Green	.20	.09
❑ 10 Ricky Rudd	.40	.18
❑ 11 Brett Bodine	.20	.09
❑ 12 Derrike Cope	.20	.09
❑ 13 Jeremy Mayfield	.60	.25
❑ 14 Robby Gordon	.20	.09
❑ 15 Steve Grissom	.20	.09
❑ 16 Ted Musgrave	.20	.09
❑ 17 Darrell Waltrip	.40	.18
❑ 18 Bobby Labonte	.75	.35
❑ 19 Johnny Benson	.20	.09
❑ 20 Bobby Hamilton	.20	.09
❑ 21 Michael Waltrip	.20	.09
❑ 22 Ward Burton	.20	.09
❑ 23 Jimmy Spencer	.20	.09
❑ 24 Jeff Gordon	2.00	.90
❑ 25 Ricky Craven	.20	.09
❑ 26 Mike Skinner	.20	.09
❑ 27 Dale Jarrett	.75	.35
❑ 28 Ernie Irvan	.40	.18
❑ 29 Jeff Green	.20	.09
❑ 30 Kyle Petty's Car	.20	.09
❑ 31 Rusty Wallace's Car	.50	.23
❑ 32 Dale Earnhardt's Car	1.00	.45
❑ 33 Sterling Marlin's Car	.20	.09
❑ 34 Terry Labonte's Car	.50	.23
❑ 35 Mark Martin's Car	.50	.23
❑ 36 Geoff Bodine's Car	.10	.05
❑ 37 Bill Elliott's Car	.50	.23
❑ 38 David Green's Car	.10	.05
❑ 39 Ricky Rudd's Car	.20	.09
❑ 40 Brett Bodine's Car	.10	.05
❑ 41 Derrike Cope's Car	.10	.05
❑ 42 Jeremy Mayfield's Car	.40	.18
❑ 43 Robby Gordon's Car	.10	.05
❑ 44 Steve Grissom's Car	.10	.05
❑ 45 Ted Musgrave's Car	.10	.05
❑ 46 Darrell Waltrip's Car	.20	.09
❑ 47 Bobby Labonte's Car	.40	.18
❑ 48 Johnny Benson's Car	.10	.05
❑ 49 Bobby Hamilton's Car	.10	.05
❑ 50 Michael Waltrip's Car	.10	.05
❑ 51 Ward Burton's Car	.10	.05
❑ 52 Jimmy Spencer's Car	.10	.05
❑ 53 Jeff Gordon's Car	1.00	.45
❑ 54 Ricky Craven's Car	.10	.05
❑ 55 Mike Skinner's Car	.10	.05
❑ 56 Dale Jarrett's Car	.40	.18
❑ 57 Ernie Irvan's Car	.20	.09
❑ 58 Jeff Green's Car	.10	.05
❑ 59 Terry Labonte RR	.50	.23
❑ 60 Dale Jarrett RR	.40	.18
❑ 61 Mark Martin RR	.50	.23
❑ 62 Rusty Wallace RR	.50	.23
❑ 63 Bill Elliott RR	.50	.23
❑ 64 Bobby Labonte RR	.40	.18
❑ 65 Ernie Irvan RR	.20	.09
❑ 66 Dale Earnhardt's Car RR	1.00	.45
❑ 67 Ricky Rudd RR	.20	.09
❑ 68 Dale Earnhardt's Car RR	1.00	.45
❑ 69 Dale Earnhardt RR	1.00	.45
❑ 70 Dale Earnhardt's Car RR	1.00	.45
❑ 71 Sterling Marlin RR	.20	.09
❑ 72 Mike Skinner RR	.10	.05
❑ 73 Rusty Wallace TT	.50	.23
❑ 74 Dale Jarrett TT	.40	.18
❑ 75 Mark Martin TT	.50	.23
❑ 76 Terry Labonte TT	.50	.23
❑ 77 Bobby Labonte TT	.40	.18
❑ 78 Sterling Marlin TT	.20	.09
❑ 79 Kyle Petty TT	.20	.09
❑ 80 Ernie Irvan TT	.20	.09
❑ 81 Bobby Hamilton TT	.10	.05
❑ 82 Dale Earnhardt TT	1.00	.45
❑ 83 Michael Waltrip TT	.10	.05
❑ 84 Dale Earnhardt TT	1.00	.45
❑ 85 Jeff Green NF	.10	.05
❑ 86 Mike Skinner NF	.10	.05
❑ 87 David Green NF	.10	.05
❑ 88 Johnny Benson's Car T4	.10	.05
❑ 89 Dale Jarrett's Car T4	.40	.18
❑ 90 Mark Martin's Car T4	.50	.23
❑ 91 Dale Earnhardt's Car T4	1.00	.45
❑ 92 Rusty Wallace's Car T4	.50	.23
❑ 93 Terry Labonte's Car T4	.50	.23
❑ 94 Darrell Waltrip's Car T4	.20	.09
❑ 95 Dale Earnhardt's Car T4	1.00	.45
❑ 96 Rusty Wallace CL	.50	.23

1997 Pinnacle Artist's Proofs

This 96-card set is a three-tier parallel of the regular set. The tiers in this set are color coded. The first tier is red. The 50 red cards were randomly inserted in packs at a ratio of 1:33. The second tier is blue. The 36 blue cards were randomly inserted in packs at a ratio of 1:117. The third tier is purple. The 10 purple cards were randomly inserted in packs at a ratio of 1:620.

	MINT	NRMT
COMPLETE RED SET (50)	80.00	36.00
COMMON RED	1.50	.70
COMPLETE BLUE SET (36)	300.00	135.00
COMMON BLUE	4.00	1.80
COMMON BLUE DRIVER	8.00	3.60
COMP. PURPLE SET (10)	600.00	275.00
COMMON PURPLE	6.00	2.70
COMMON PURPLE DRIVER	12.00	5.50
❑ 1 Kyle Petty B	15.00	6.75
❑ 2 Rusty Wallace P	90.00	40.00
❑ 3 Dale Earnhardt P	150.00	70.00
❑ 4 Sterling Marlin B	15.00	6.75
❑ 5 Terry Labonte P	90.00	40.00
❑ 6 Mark Martin P	90.00	40.00
❑ 7 Geoff Bodine B	8.00	3.60
❑ 8 Bill Elliott P	90.00	40.00
❑ 9 David Green B	8.00	3.60
❑ 10 Ricky Rudd P	25.00	11.00
❑ 11 Brett Bodine B	8.00	3.60
❑ 12 Derrike Cope B	8.00	3.60
❑ 13 Jeremy Mayfield B	20.00	9.00
❑ 14 Robby Gordon B	8.00	3.60
❑ 15 Steve Grissom B	8.00	3.60
❑ 16 Ted Musgrave B	8.00	3.60
❑ 17 Darrell Waltrip B	15.00	6.75
❑ 18 Bobby Labonte P	60.00	27.00
❑ 19 Johnny Benson B	8.00	3.60
❑ 20 Bobby Hamilton B	8.00	3.60
❑ 21 Michael Waltrip B	8.00	3.60
❑ 22 Ward Burton B	8.00	3.60
❑ 23 Jimmy Spencer B	8.00	3.60
❑ 24 Jeff Gordon P	150.00	70.00
❑ 25 Ricky Craven B	15.00	6.75
❑ 26 Mike Skinner B	8.00	3.60
❑ 27 Dale Jarrett P	75.00	34.00
❑ 28 Ernie Irvan P	25.00	11.00
❑ 29 Jeff Green B	8.00	3.60
❑ 30 Kyle Petty's Car B	4.00	1.80
❑ 31 Rusty Wallace's Car B	15.00	6.75
❑ 32 Dale Earnhardt's Car B	35.00	16.00
❑ 33 Sterling Marlin's Car B	4.00	1.80
❑ 34 Terry Labonte's Car B	15.00	6.75
❑ 35 Mark Martin's Car B	15.00	6.75
❑ 36 Geoff Bodine's Car R	1.50	.70
❑ 37 Bill Elliott's Car B	15.00	6.75
❑ 38 David Green's Car R	1.50	.70
❑ 39 Ricky Rudd's Car B	4.00	1.80
❑ 40 Brett Bodine's Car R	1.50	.70
❑ 41 Derrike Cope's Car R	1.50	.70
❑ 42 Jeremy Mayfield's Car R	1.50	.70
❑ 43 Robby Gordon's Car R	1.50	.70
❑ 44 Steve Grissom's Car R	1.50	.70
❑ 45 Ted Musgrave's Car R	1.50	.70
❑ 46 Darrell Waltrip's Car B	4.00	1.80
❑ 47 Bobby Labonte's Car B	4.00	1.80
❑ 48 Johnny Benson's Car B	4.00	1.80
❑ 49 Bobby Hamilton's Car B	4.00	1.80
❑ 50 Michael Waltrip's Car B	4.00	1.80
❑ 51 Ward Burton's Car R	1.50	.70
❑ 52 Jimmy Spencer's Car R	1.50	.70
❑ 53 Jeff Gordon's Car B	35.00	16.00
❑ 54 Ricky Craven's Car R	1.50	.70
❑ 55 Mike Skinner's Car B	4.00	1.80
❑ 56 Dale Jarrett's Car B	15.00	6.75
❑ 57 Ernie Irvan's Car B	4.00	1.80
❑ 58 Jeff Green's Car R	1.50	.70
❑ 59 Terry Labonte RR R	8.00	3.60
❑ 60 Dale Jarrett RR R	8.00	
❑ 61 Mark Martin RR R	8.00	
❑ 62 Rusty Wallace RR R	8.00	
❑ 63 Bill Elliott RR R	8.00	
❑ 64 Bobby Labonte RR R	1.50	
❑ 65 Ernie Irvan RR R	1.50	
❑ 66 Dale Earnhardt's Car RR R	12.00	
❑ 67 Ricky Rudd RR R	1.50	
❑ 68 Dale Earnhardt's Car RR R	12.00	
❑ 69 Dale Earnhardt RR R	12.00	
❑ 70 Dale Earnhardt's Car RR R	12.00	
❑ 71 Sterling Marlin RR R	1.50	
❑ 72 Mike Skinner RR R	1.50	
❑ 73 Rusty Wallace TT R	8.00	
❑ 74 Dale Jarrett TT R	8.00	
❑ 75 Mark Martin TT R	8.00	
❑ 76 Terry Labonte TT R	8.00	
❑ 77 Bobby Labonte TT R	1.50	
❑ 78 Sterling Marlin TT R	1.50	
❑ 79 Kyle Petty TT R	1.50	
❑ 80 Ernie Irvan TT R	1.50	
❑ 81 Bobby Hamilton TT R	1.50	
❑ 82 Dale Earnhardt TT R	12.00	
❑ 83 Michael Waltrip TT R	1.50	
❑ 84 Dale Earnhardt TT R	12.00	
❑ 85 Jeff Green NF R	1.50	
❑ 86 Mike Skinner NF R	1.50	
❑ 87 David Green NF R	1.50	
❑ 88 Johnny Benson's Car T4 R	1.50	
❑ 89 Dale Jarrett's Car T4 R	8.00	
❑ 90 Mark Martin's Car T4 R	8.00	
❑ 91 Dale Earnhardt's Car T4 R	12.00	
❑ 92 Rusty Wallace's Car T4 R	8.00	
❑ 93 Terry Labonte's Car T4 R	8.00	
❑ 94 Darrell Waltrip's Car T4 R	1.50	
❑ 95 Dale Earnhardt's Car T4 R	12.00	
❑ 96 Rusty Wallace CL R	1.50	

1997 Pinnacle Press Plate

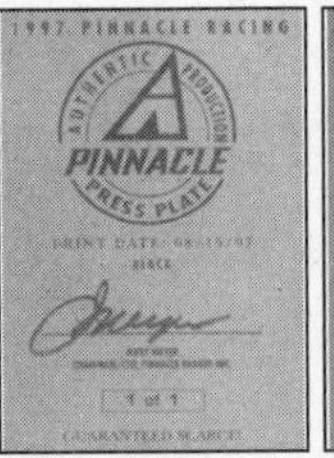

Randomly inserted in packs at the rate of one in 1
this all-aluminum set consists of the Authentic Press
that transfers the ink to the cardboard for each indi
card back and front. Each plate displays an authenti
seal on the back along with the personal signatu
Pinnacle Chairman and CEO, Jerry Meyer. Each car
eight press plates for each of the four colors us
printing the front and the back. Since supply is so li
only common card pricing is provided.

	MINT
COMMON CARD (1-96)	35.00
COMMON DRIVER (1-96)	50.00

1997 Pinnacle Trophy Collection

This 96-card set is a parallel of the regular set. The
were randomly inserted in packs at a ratio of 1:6.

	MINT
COMPLETE SET (96)	150.00
COMMON CARD (1-96)	.60
COMMON DRIVER (1-96)	1.25

1997 Pinnacle Chevy Madn

This 3-card insert set is a continuation of the set th

d in 1997 Action Packed. The cards were randomly ed in packs at a ratio of 1:23.

	MINT	NRMT
ᴾLETE SET (3)	30.00	13.50
ᴍON CARD (13-15)	1.50	.70
;LES: 3X TO 8X BASE CARD HI		
Dale Earnhardt's Car	20.00	9.00
David Green's Car	1.50	.70
Jeff Gordon's Car	20.00	9.00

1997 Pinnacle Helmets

0-card set features ten helmets worn by Bobby te during the 1997 Winston Cup season. Each card Dufex surface and features a logo from a different am. The cards were randomly inserted in hobby at a ratio of 1:89.

	MINT	NRMT
LETE SET (10)	200.00	90.00
ON HELMET (1-10)	25.00	11.00
bby Labonte Carolina Panthers	25.00	11.00
bby Labonte Jacksonville Jaguars	25.00	11.00
bby Labonte Dallas Cowboys	25.00	11.00
bby Labonte Miami Dolphins	25.00	11.00
bby Labonte New York Giants	25.00	11.00
bby Labonte Detroit Lions	25.00	11.00
bby Labonte San Francisco 49ers	25.00	11.00
bby Labonte Atlanta Falcons	25.00	11.00
bby Labonte Pittsburgh Steelers	25.00	11.00
bby Labonte Arizona Cardinals	25.00	11.00

997 Pinnacle Spellbound

-car set features 12 drivers, each of whom appears tter of the words, "NASCAR RACING". The cards ndomly inserted in packs at a ratio of 1:23.

	MINT	NRMT
ETE SET (12)	100.00	45.00
N CARD (1-12)	2.50	1.10
ES: 5X TO 12X BASE CARD HI		

❑ 1-N Terry Labonte	18.00	8.00
❑ 2-A Dale Jarrett	15.00	6.75
❑ 3-S Dale Earnhardt	30.00	13.50
❑ 4-C Rusty Wallace	18.00	8.00
❑ 5-A Mark Martin	18.00	8.00
❑ 6-R Jeff Gordon	30.00	13.50
❑ 7-R Bobby Hamilton	2.50	1.10
❑ 8-A Kyle Petty	5.00	2.20
❑ 9-C Ernie Irvan	5.00	2.20
❑ 10-I Ricky Rudd	5.00	2.20
❑ 11-N Bill Elliott	18.00	8.00
❑ 12-G Bobby Labonte	10.00	4.50

1997 Pinnacle Spellbound Autographs

This five-card set features the autographs of five drivers from the regular set. Each of the drivers signed 500 cards. The Jeff Gordon card inserted packs was actually a redemtpion that could be redemmed for an autogrpahed card. An insert ratio was not given for these cards.

	MINT	NRMT
COMPLETE SET (12)	600.00	275.00
COMMON CARD (1-12)	75.00	34.00
❑ 1-N Terry Labonte	100.00	45.00
❑ 2-A Dale Jarrett	75.00	34.00
❑ 3-S Dale Earnhardt	300.00	135.00
❑ 6-R Jeff Gordon Redemption Card	5.00	2.20
❑ 6A-R Jeff Gordon Auto'd Card	300.00	135.00
❑ 11-N Bill Elliott	100.00	45.00

1997 Pinnacle Team Pinnacle

This 10-card insert set features 10 top NASCAR drivers on double-sided cards with their crew chiefs. These cards have red and blue versions. Both colors have the same value.The cards were randomly inserted in packs at a ratio of 1:240.

	MINT	NRMT
COMPLETE SET(10)	700.00	325.00
COMMON CARD (1-10)	30.00	13.50
*SINGLES: 40X TO 75X BASE CARD HI		
❑ 1 Jeff Gordon Ray Evernham	150.00	70.00
❑ 2 Rusty Wallace Robin Pemberton	90.00	40.00
❑ 3 Dale Earnhardt Larry McReynolds	150.00	70.00
❑ 4 Darrell Waltrip Jeff Hammond	30.00	13.50
❑ 5 Terry Labonte Gary DeHart	90.00	40.00
❑ 6 Mark Martin Jimmy Fenning	90.00	40.00
❑ 7 Bobby Labonte Jimmy Makar	30.00	13.50
❑ 8 Ricky Rudd Jim Long	30.00	13.50
❑ 9 Dale Jarrett Todd Parrott	75.00	34.00
❑ 10 Bill Elliott Mike Beam	90.00	40.00

1997 Pinnacle Certified

This 100-card set was released by Pinnacle Brands. The set features two topical subsets: War Paint (69-88) and Burning Desire (89-98). Cards were distributed in six card packs with 20 packs per obox and 16 boxes per case. The packs carried a suggested retail price of $4.99.

	MINT	NRMT
COMPLETE SET (100)	40.00	18.00
COMMON CARD (1-100)	.25	.11
COMMON DRIVER (1-100)	.50	.23
❑ 1 Kyle Petty	1.00	.45
❑ 2 Rusty Wallace	2.50	1.10
❑ 3 Dale Earnhardt	5.00	2.20
❑ 4 Sterlimg Marlin	1.00	.45
❑ 5 Terry Labonte	2.50	1.10
❑ 6 Mark Martin	2.50	1.10
❑ 7 Bill Elliott	2.50	1.10
❑ 8 Jeremy Mayfield	1.50	.70
❑ 9 Ted Musgrave	.50	.23
❑ 10 Ricky Rudd	1.00	.45
❑ 11 Robby Gordon	.50	.23
❑ 12 Johnny Benson	.50	.23
❑ 13 Bobby Hamilton	.50	.23
❑ 14 Mike Skinner	.50	.23
❑ 15 Dale Jarrett	2.00	.90
❑ 16 Steve Grissom	.50	.23
❑ 17 Darrell Waltrip	1.00	.45
❑ 18 Bobby Labonte	2.00	.90
❑ 19 Ernie Irvan	1.00	.45
❑ 20 Jeff Green	.50	.23
❑ 21 Michael Waltrip	.50	.23
❑ 22 Ward Burton	.50	.23
❑ 23 Geoff Bodine	.50	.23
❑ 24 Jeff Gordon	5.00	2.20
❑ 25 Ricky Craven	.50	.23
❑ 26 Jimmy Spencer	.50	.23
❑ 27 Brett Bodine	.50	.23
❑ 28 David Green	.50	.23
❑ 29 John Andretti	.50	.23
❑ 30 Ken Schrader	.50	.23
❑ 31 Chad Little	.50	.23
❑ 32 Joe Nemecheck	.50	.23
❑ 33 Hut Stricklin	.50	.23
❑ 34 Kenny Wallace	.50	.23
❑ 35 Kyle Petty's Car	.50	.23
❑ 36 Rusty Wallace's Car	1.25	.55
❑ 37 Dale Earnhardt's Car	2.50	1.10
❑ 38 Sterling Marlin's Car	.50	.23
❑ 39 Terry Labonte's Car	1.25	.55
❑ 40 Mark Martin's Car	1.25	.55
❑ 41 Bill Elliott's Car	1.25	.55
❑ 42 Jeremy Mayfield's Car	.75	.35
❑ 43 Jeff Burton's Car	.50	.23
❑ 44 Ricky Rudd's Car	.50	.23
❑ 45 Robby Gordon's Car	.25	.11
❑ 46 Johnny Benson's Car	.25	.11
❑ 47 Bobby Hamilton's Car	.25	.11
❑ 48 Mike Skinner's Car	.25	.11
❑ 49 Dale Jarrett's Car	1.00	.45
❑ 50 Steve Grissom's Car	.25	.11
❑ 51 Darrell Waltrip's Car	.50	.23
❑ 52 Bobby Labonte's Car	1.00	.45
❑ 53 Ernie Irvan's Car	.50	.23
❑ 54 Jeff Green's Car	.25	.11
❑ 55 Michael Waltrip's Car	.25	.11
❑ 56 Ward Burton's Car	.25	.11
❑ 57 Geoff Bodine's Car	.25	.11
❑ 58 Jeff Gordon's Car	2.50	1.10
❑ 59 Terry Labonte's Car	1.25	.55
❑ 60 Jimmy Spencer's Car	.25	.11
❑ 61 Brett Bodine's Car	.25	.11
❑ 62 David Green's Car	.25	.11
❑ 63 John Andretti's Car	.25	.11
❑ 64 Ken Schrader's Car	.25	.11
❑ 65 Chad Little's Car	.25	.11
❑ 66 Joe Nemecheck's Car	.25	.11
❑ 67 Hut Stricklin's Car	.25	.11
❑ 68 Kenny Wallace's Car	.25	.11
❑ 69 Darrell Waltrip's Car WP	.50	.23
❑ 70 Darrell Waltrip's Car WP	.50	.23
❑ 71 Darrell Waltrip's Car WP	.50	.23
❑ 72 Jeremy Mayfield's Car WP	.75	.35
❑ 73 Jeremy Mayfield's Car WP	.75	.35
❑ 74 Jeff Gordon's Car WP	2.50	1.10
❑ 75 Ward Burton's Car WP	.25	.11
❑ 76 Dale Earnhardt's Car WP	2.50	1.10
❑ 77 Bobby Labonte's Car WP	1.00	.45
❑ 78 Michael Waltrip's Car WP	.25	.11
❑ 79 Robby Gordon's Car WP	.25	.11
❑ 80 Terry Labonte's Car WP	1.25	.55
❑ 81 Bill Elliott's Car WP	1.25	.55
❑ 82 Bobby Hamilton's Car WP	.25	.11
❑ 83 Chad Little's Car WP	.25	.11
❑ 84 Jeff Green's Car WP	.25	.11
❑ 85 Jeff Green's Car WP	.25	.11
❑ 86 Rick Mast's Car WP	.25	.11
❑ 87 Ernie Irvan's Car WP	.50	.23

❑ 88 Geoff Bodine's Car WP	.25	.11
❑ 89 Jeff Gordon BD	2.50	1.10
❑ 90 Terry Labonte BD	1.25	.55
❑ 91 Mark Martin BD	1.25	.55
❑ 92 Dale Jarrett BD	1.00	.45
❑ 93 Dale Earnhardt BD	2.50	1.10
❑ 94 Ricky Rudd BD	.50	.23
❑ 95 Rusty Wallace BD	1.25	.55
❑ 96 Bobby Hamilton BD	.25	.11
❑ 97 Bobby Labonte BD	1.00	.45
❑ 98 Kyle Petty BD	.50	.23
❑ NNO Checklist 2	.25	.11
❑ NNO Checklist 1	.25	.11

1997 Pinnacle Certified Mirror Blue

This 100-card set is a parallel of the base set. It is important to note that the two checklist cards in this set have a mirror-like finish, but are not labeled as a mirror cards. There is only one mirror version, rather than three of each checklist card. The cards were randomly inserted in packs at a ratio of 1:199.

	MINT	NRMT
COMMON CARD (1-100)	15.00	6.75
COMMON DRIVER (1-100)	30.00	13.50

*MIRROR BLUE CARDS: 40X TO X BASIC CARDS

1997 Pinnacle Certified Mirror Gold

This 100-card set is a parallel of the base set. It is important to note that the two checklist cards in this set have a mirror-like finish, but are not labeled as a mirror cards. There is only one mirror version, rather than three of each checklist card. The cards were randomly inserted in packs at a ratio of 1:299.

	MINT	NRMT
COMMON CARD (1-100)	40.00	18.00
COMMON DRIVER (1-100)	100.00	45.00

*MIRROR GOLD CARDS: 75X TO X BASIC CARDS

1997 Pinnacle Certified Mirror Red

This 100-card set is a parallel of the base set. It is important to note that the two checklist cards in this set have a mirror-like finish, but are not labeled as a mirror cards. There is only one mirror version, rather than three of each checklist card. The cards were randomly inserted in packs at a ratio of 1:99.

	MINT	NRMT
COMMON CARD (1-100)	8.00	3.60
COMMON DRIVER (1-100)	15.00	6.75

*MIRROR RED CARDS: 20X TO X BASIC CARDS

1997 Pinnacle Certified Red

This 100-card set is a parallel of the base set. It is important to note that the two checklist cards in this set do not have a red-bordered front, thus the standard checklist cards are considered to fit this set. The cards were randomly inserted in packs at a ratio of 1:5.

	MINT	NRMT
COMPLETE SET (100)	150.00	70.00
COMMON CARD (1-100)	1.00	.45
COMMON DRIVER (1-100)	2.00	.90

*RED CARDS: 4X TO 8X BASE CARDS

1997 Pinnacle Certified Certified Team

This 10-card insert set features some of the top stars from the Winston Cup circuit. The cards were randomly inserted in packs at a ratio of 1:19.

	MINT	NRMT
COMPLETE SET (10)	150.00	70.00
COMMON CARD (1-10)	6.00	2.70

*SINGLES: 2.5X TO 6X BASE CARD HI

❑ 1 Dale Earnhardt	40.00	18.00
❑ 2 Jeff Gordon	40.00	18.00
❑ 3 Ricky Rudd	6.00	2.70
❑ 4 Bobby Labonte	10.00	4.50
❑ 5 Terry Labonte	25.00	11.00
❑ 6 Rusty Wallace	25.00	11.00
❑ 7 Mark Martin	25.00	11.00
❑ 8 Bill Elliott	25.00	11.00
❑ 9 Dale Jarrett	12.00	5.50
❑ 10 Jeremy Mayfield	6.00	2.70

1997 Pinnacle Certified Certified Gold Team

This 10-card insert set is a parallel version of the aforementioned set. These cards can be distinguished from the base Certified Team cards by their gold borders. The cards were randomly inserted in packs at a ratio of 1:119.

	MINT	NRMT
COMPLETE SET (10)	400.00	180.00
COMMON CARD (1-10)	20.00	9.00

1997 Pinnacle Certified Epix

This 10-car insert set features some of the top drivers in NASCAR. The cards were randomly inserted in packs at a ratio of 1:15.

	MINT	NRMT
COMPLETE SET (10)	100.00	45.00
COMMON CARD (1-10)	5.00	2.20

*ORANGE CARDS: 2X TO 5X BASE CARD HI

❑ E2 Jeff Gordon	40.00	18.00
❑ E3 Ricky Rudd	5.00	2.20
❑ E4 Bobby Labonte	12.00	5.50
❑ E5 Terry Labonte	25.00	11.00
❑ E6 Rusty Wallace	25.00	11.00
❑ E7 Mark Martin	25.00	11.00
❑ E8 Darrell Waltrip	5.00	2.20
❑ E9 Dale Jarrett	20.00	9.00
❑ E10 Ernie Irvan	5.00	2.20

1997 Pinnacle Certified Epix Emerald

This 10-card insert set is a parallel to the orange Epix set. Although an exact ratio was never release by Pinnacle Brands, it is believed in hobby circles that these cards are found one per eight boxes.

	MINT	NRMT
COMPLETE SET (10)	450.00	200.00
COMMON CARD (1-10)	25.00	11.00

1997 Pinnacle Certified Epix Purple

This 10-card insert set is a parallel to the orange Epix set. Although an exact ratio was never release by Pinnacle Brands, it is believed in hobby circles that these cards are found two per five boxes.

	MINT	N
COMPLETE SET (10)	225.00	1(
COMMON CARD (1-10)	18.00	

1997 Pinnacle Checkers

This nine-card set was issued through Checkers Dr Restaurants. The cards were distributed via single packs. Each pack has one collector card and t-shirt card. You received one pack free wtih a purchase combo meal at all participating Checkers. It to Checkers Racing points to get one free t-shirt. Each offer card was worth one point.

	MINT
COMPLETE SET (9)	2.00
COMMON CARD (1-9)	.25

❑ 1 Ricky Rudd	.25
❑ 2 Sterling Marlin	.30
❑ 3 Johnny Benson	.25
❑ 4 Ricky Rudd	.30
❑ 5 Sterling Marlin	.30
❑ 6 Johnny Benson	.25
❑ 7 Ricky Rudd	.30
❑ 8 Sterling Marlin	.30
❑ 9 Johnny Benson	.25

1997 Pinnacle Mint

This product combines the collectiblility of car coins into one set. This 30-diecut card set features names from the Winston Cup circuit. This cards ca to hold the coins available in this product. Die-cu were distributed two per pack with the regular card distributed one per pack. Coins were distributed t pack. The packs carried a suggested retail price of $

	MINT
COMPLETE DIECUT SET (30)	12.00
COMMON DIECUT (1-30)	.10
COMMON DIECUT DRIVER (1-30)	.20

❑ 1 Terry Labonte	1.50
❑ 2 Jeff Gordon	3.00
❑ 3 Dale Jarrett	1.25
❑ 4 Darrell Waltrip	.40
❑ 5 Mark Martin	1.50
❑ 6 Ricky Rudd	.40
❑ 7 Rusty Wallace	1.50
❑ 8 Sterling Marlin	.40
❑ 9 Bobby Hamilton	.20
❑ 10 Ernie Irvan	.40
❑ 11 Bobby Labonte	1.25
❑ 12 Johnny Benson	.20
❑ 13 Michael Waltrip	.20
❑ 14 Jimmy Spencer	.20
❑ 15 Ted Musgrave	.20
❑ 16 Geoff Bodine	.20
❑ 17 Bill Elliott	1.50
❑ 18 John Andretti	.20
❑ 19 Ward Burton	.20
❑ 20 Randy LaJoie	.20
❑ 21 Dale Earnhardt's Car	1.50
❑ 22 Ricky Rudd's Car	.20
❑ 23 Dale Jarrett's Car	.60
❑ 24 Jeff Gordon's Car	1.50
❑ 25 Terry Labonte's Car	.75
❑ 26 Mark Martin's Car	.75

3obby Labonte's Car	.60	.25
Ernie Irvan's Car	.20	.09
3ill Elliott's Car	.75	.35
Johnny Benson's Car	.10	.05

997 Pinnacle Mint Bronze

0-card set parallels the diecut card set and has a logo containing the drivers' numbers in place of ecut area. The cards were randomly inserted in at a ratio of 1:1.

	MINT	NRMT
LETE SET (30)	40.00	18.00
ON CARD (1-30)	.50	.23
'ON DRIVER (1-30)	.75	.35

1997 Pinnacle Mint Gold

0-card set parallels the diecut card set and has a go containing the drivers' numbers in place of the area. The cards were randomly inserted in hobby at a ratio of 1:48 and in retail packs at a ratio of

	MINT	NRMT
LETE SET (30)	600.00	275.00
ON CARD (1-30)	5.00	2.20
ON DRIVER (1-30)	8.00	3.60

997 Pinnacle Mint Silver

)-card set parallels the diecut card set and has a ogo containing the drivers' numbers in place of the area. The cards were randomly inserted in hobby at a ratio of 1:20 and in retail packs at a ratio of

	MINT	NRMT
.ETE SET (30)	300.00	135.00
ON CARD (1-30)	3.00	1.35
ON DRIVER (1-30)	5.00	2.20

997 Pinnacle Mint Coins

coin set parallels the diecut card set. The drivers' s and cars are featured on the front of the coins e Pinnacle Mint logo is featured on the back. The e randomly inserted in hobby packs at a ratio of in retail packs at a ratio of 1:1.

	MINT	NRMT
ETE SET (30)	40.00	18.00
N COIN (1-30)	.30	.14
N DRIVER (1-30)	.60	.25

y Labonte	2.00	.90
Gordon	4.00	1.80
Jarrett	1.50	.70
rell Waltrip	1.25	.55
k Martin	2.00	.90
y Rudd	1.25	.55
ty Wallace	2.00	.90
ling Marlin	1.25	.55
by Hamilton	.60	.25
ie Irvan	1.25	.55
bby Labonte	1.50	.70
nny Benson	.60	.25
chael Waltrip	.60	.25
nmy Spencer	.60	.25
d Musgrave	.60	.25
off Bodine	.60	.25
Elliott	2.00	.90
n Andretti	.60	.25

❑ 19 Ward Burton	.60	.25
❑ 20 Randy LaJoie	.60	.25
❑ 21 Dale Earnhardt's Car	2.00	.90
❑ 22 Ricky Rudd's Car	.60	.25
❑ 23 Dale Jarrett's Car	.75	.35
❑ 24 Jeff Gordon's Car	2.00	.90
❑ 25 Terry Labonte's Car	1.00	.45
❑ 26 Mark Martin's Car	1.00	.45
❑ 27 Bobby Labonte's Car	.75	.35
❑ 28 Ernie Irvan's Car	.60	.25
❑ 29 Bill Elliott's Car	1.00	.45
❑ 30 Johnny Benson's Car	.30	.14

1997 Pinnacle Mint 24KT Gold-Plated Coins

This 30-coin set parallels the base coin set. The coins were randomly inserted in hobby packs at a ratio of 1:48 and in retail packs at a ratio of 1:96.

	MINT	NRMT
COMPLETE SET (30)	400.00	180.00
COMMON COIN (1-30)	4.00	1.80
COMMON DRIVER (1-30)	6.00	2.70

1997 Pinnacle Mint Nickel-Silver Coins

This 30-coin set parallels the base coin set. The coins were randomly inserted in hobby packs at a ratio of 1:20 and in retail packs at a ratio of 1:40.

	MINT	NRMT
COMPLETE SET (30)	200.00	90.00
COMMON COIN (1-30)	2.50	1.10
COMMON DRIVER (1-30)	3.50	1.55

1998 Pinnacle Mint

The 1998 Pinnacle Mint set was issued in one series totalling 30 cards. The set offers two coins and three cards per pack. Die-cut cards were also included to provide the perfect fit to make a card-and-coin collectible. The set features 30 drivers with coins that come in brass, nickel-silver, solid silver and solid gold as well as bronze-plated proof coins, silver-plated proof coins, and gold-plated proof coins.

	MINT	NRMT
COMPLETE SET (30)	20.00	9.00
COMMON CARD (1-30)	.20	.09
COMMON DRIVER (1-30)	.40	.18

❑ 1 Jeff Gordon	4.00	1.80
❑ 2 Mark Martin	2.00	.90
❑ 3 Dale Earnhardt	4.00	1.80
❑ 4 Terry Labonte	2.00	.90
❑ 5 Dale Jarrett	1.50	.70
❑ 6 Bobby Labonte	1.50	.70
❑ 7 Bill Elliott	2.00	.90
❑ 8 Ted Musgrave	.40	.18
❑ 9 Ricky Rudd	.75	.35
❑ 10 Rusty Wallace	2.00	.90
❑ 11 Jeremy Mayfield	1.25	.55
❑ 12 Michael Waltrip	.40	.18
❑ 13 Jeff Gordon's Car	2.00	.90
❑ 14 Mark Martin's Car	1.00	.45
❑ 15 Dale Jarrett's Car	.75	.35
❑ 16 Terry Labonte's Car	1.00	.45
❑ 17 Dale Earnhardt's Car	2.00	.90
❑ 18 Bobby Labonte's Car	.75	.35
❑ 19 Bill Elliott's Car	1.00	.45
❑ 20 Ted Musgrave's Car	.20	.09
❑ 21 Ricky Rudd's Car	.40	.18
❑ 22 Rusty Wallace's Car	1.00	.45
❑ 23 Jeremy Mayfield's Car	.60	.25
❑ 24 Michael Waltrip's Car	.20	.09
❑ 25 Mark Martin MM	1.00	.45
❑ 26 Rusty Wallace MM	1.00	.45
❑ 27 Jeff Gordon MM	2.00	.90
❑ 28 Dale Jarrett MM	.75	.35
❑ 29 Ricky Rudd MM	.40	.18
❑ 30 Ernie Irvan MM	.40	.18

1998 Pinnacle Mint Diecut

This 30-card set parallels the base(bronze) card set and has a diecut area in place of the bronze area containing the drivers' numbers. The cards were randomly inserted in packs at a ratio of 1:1 in hobby packs and were inserted in packs at a ratio of 2:1 in retail packs.

	MINT	NRMT
COMPLETE SET (30)	20.00	9.00
COMMON CARD (1-30)	.15	.07
COMMON DRIVER (1-30)	.30	.14

1998 Pinnacle Mint Championship Mint

This two-card set depicts Jeff Gordon and his car during his 1997 Winston Cup Championship season. These cards were randomly inserted into hobby packs at a ratio of one per 41 packs and into retail packs at a ratio of one per 71 packs.

	MINT	NRMT
COMPLETE SET (2)	40.00	18.00
COMMON CARD (1-2)	20.00	9.00
❑ 1 Jeff Gordon	20.00	9.00
❑ 2 Jeff Gordon's Car	20.00	9.00

1998 Pinnacle Mint Gold Mint Team

This 30-card set parallels the base set and was randomly inserted in both hobby and retail packs at a rate of one in 47.

	MINT	NRMT
COMPLETE SET (30)	400.00	180.00
COMMON CARD (1-30)	4.00	1.80
COMMON DRIVER (1-30)	8.00	3.60

1998 Pinnacle Mint Silver Mint Team

This 30-card set parallels the base set and was randomly inserted in both hobby and retail packs at a rate of 1:15 and 1:23 respectively.

	MINT	NRMT
COMPLETE SET (30)	250.00	110.00
COMMON CARD (1-30)	2.00	.90
COMMON DRIVER (1-30)	4.00	1.80

1998 Pinnacle Mint Coins

This 30-coin set parallels the base card set. These coins were inserted into hobby packs at a ratio of 2:1 and into retail packs at a ratio of 1:1.

	MINT	NRMT
COMPLETE SET (30)	30.00	13.50
COMMON COIN (1-30)	.25	.11
COMMON DRIVER (1-30)	.50	.23
❑ 1 Jeff Gordon	5.00	2.20
❑ 2 Mark Martin	2.50	1.10
❑ 3 Dale Earnhardt	5.00	2.20
❑ 4 Terry Labonte	2.50	1.10
❑ 5 Dale Jarrett	2.00	.90
❑ 6 Bobby Labonte	2.00	.90
❑ 7 Bill Elliott	2.50	1.10
❑ 8 Ted Musgrave	.25	.11
❑ 9 Ricky Rudd	1.00	.45
❑ 10 Rusty Wallace	2.50	1.10
❑ 11 Jeremy Mayfield	1.50	.70
❑ 12 Michael Waltrip	.50	.23
❑ 13 Jeff Gordon's Car	2.50	1.10
❑ 14 Mark Martin's Car	1.25	.55
❑ 15 Dale Jarrett's Car	1.00	.45
❑ 16 Terry Labonte's Car	1.25	.55
❑ 17 Dale Earnhardt's Car	2.50	1.10
❑ 18 Bobby Labonte's Car	1.00	.45
❑ 19 Bill Elliott's Car	1.25	.55
❑ 20 Ted Musgrave's Car	.25	.11
❑ 21 Ricky Rudd's Car	.50	.23
❑ 22 Rusty Wallace's Car	1.25	.55
❑ 23 Jeremy Mayfield's Car	.75	.35
❑ 24 Michael Waltrip's Car	.25	.11
❑ 01 Mark Martin MM	1.25	.55
❑ 02 Rusty Wallace MM	1.25	.55
❑ 03 Jeff Gordon MM	2.50	1.10
❑ 04 Dale Jarrett MM	1.00	.45
❑ 05 Ricky Rudd MM	.50	.23
❑ 06 Ernie Irvan MM	.50	.23

1998 Pinnacle Mint Bronze Plated Proof Coins

This 30-card set parallels the base coin set. The set was serially numbered to 500.

	MINT	NRMT
COMPLETE SET (30)	300.00	135.00
COMMON COIN (1-30)	2.50	1.10
COMMON DRIVER (1-30)	5.00	2.20
❑ 1 Jeff Gordon	50.00	22.00
❑ 2 Mark Martin	25.00	11.00
❑ 3 Dale Earnhardt	50.00	22.00
❑ 4 Terry Labonte	25.00	11.00
❑ 5 Dale Jarrett	20.00	9.00
❑ 6 Bobby Labonte	20.00	9.00
❑ 7 Bill Elliott	25.00	11.00
❑ 8 Ted Musgrave	5.00	2.20
❑ 9 Ricky Rudd	10.00	4.50
❑ 10 Rusty Wallace	50.00	22.00
❑ 11 Jeremy Mayfield	15.00	6.75
❑ 12 Michael Waltrip	5.00	2.20
❑ 13 Jeff Gordon's Car	25.00	11.00
❑ 14 Mark Martin's Car	12.50	5.50
❑ 15 Dale Jarrett's Car	10.00	4.50
❑ 16 Terry Labonte's Car	12.50	5.50
❑ 17 Dale Earnhardt's Car	25.00	11.00
❑ 18 Bobby Labonte's Car	10.00	4.50
❑ 19 Bill Elliott's Car	12.50	5.50
❑ 20 Ted Musgrave's Car	2.50	1.10
❑ 21 Ricky Rudd's Car	5.00	2.20
❑ 22 Rusty Wallace's Car	12.50	5.50
❑ 23 Jeremy Mayfield's Car	8.00	3.60
❑ 24 Michael Waltrip's Car	2.50	1.10
❑ 01 Mark Martin MM	12.50	5.50
❑ 02 Rusty Wallace MM	12.50	5.50
❑ 03 Jeff Gordon MM	25.00	11.00
❑ 04 Dale Jarrett MM	10.00	4.50
❑ 05 Ricky Rudd MM	5.00	2.20
❑ 06 Ernie Irvan MM	5.00	2.20

1998 Pinnacle Mint Championship Mint Coins

Randomly inserted in hobby packs and retail packs at a rate of 1:89 and 1:129 respectively, this 3-card set is a metal alloy insert made from the melted hood of Jeff Gordon's 1997 Talladega race car. The retail version contains traditional sized coins, one of Gordon and one of the car. Hobby packs contain a double-sized version of the coins.

	MINT	NRMT
COMPLETE SET (4)	250.00	110.00
COMMON COIN	40.00	18.00

❑ 1A Jeff Gordon's Car Standard	50.00	22.00
❑ 1B Jeff Gordon's Car Oversized	40.00	18.00
❑ 2A Jeff Gordon Standard Size	100.00	45.00
❑ 2B Jeff Gordon Oversized	75.00	34.00

1998 Pinnacle Mint Gold Plated Coins

This 30-card set parallels the coin base set and was randomly inserted in both hobby and retail packs at a rate of one in 199.

	MINT	NRMT
COMPLETE SET (30)	450.00	200.00
COMMON COIN (1-30)	3.75	1.70
COMMON DRIVER (1-30)	7.50	3.40

1998 Pinnacle Mint Gold Plated Proof Coins

This 30-card set paralles the base coin set and was serially numbered to 100.

	MINT	NRMT
COMPLETE SET (30)	900.00	400.00
COMMON COIN (1-30)	7.50	3.40
COMMON DRIVER (1-30)	15.00	6.75

1998 Pinnacle Mint Nickel-Silver Coins

This 30-card set parallels the base coin set and was randomly inserted in both hobby and retail packs at a rate of one in 41.

	MINT	NRMT
COMPLETE SET (30)	240.00	110.00
COMMON COIN (1-30)	1.50	.70
COMMON DRIVER (1-30)	3.00	1.35

1998 Pinnacle Mint Silver Plated Proof Coins

This 30-card set parallels the base coin set and was serially numbered to 250.

	MINT	NRMT
COMPLETE SET (30)	450.00	200.00
COMMON COIN (1-30)	4.00	1.80
COMMON DRIVER (1-30)	8.00	3.60

1998 Pinnacle Mint Solid Gold Coin

This 30-card set parallels the base coin set and was randomly inserted in both hobby and retail packs. These coins were 1 of 1's and were issued via redemption cards from Pinnacle. It is unknown how many of these coins were released by Pinnacle before their bankruptcy.

MINT NRMT

❑ 1 Jeff Gordon
❑ 2 Mark Martin
❑ 3 Dale Earnhardt
❑ 4 Terry Labonte
❑ 5 Dale Jarrett
❑ 6 Bobby Labonte
❑ 7 Bill Elliott
❑ 8 Ted Musgrave
❑ 9 Ricky Rudd
❑ 10 Rusty Wallace
❑ 11 Jeremy Mayfield
❑ 12 Michael Waltrip
❑ 13 Jeff Gordon's Car
❑ 14 Mark Martin's Car
❑ 15 Dale Jarrett's Car
❑ 16 Terry Labonte's Car
❑ 17 Dale Earnhardt's Car
❑ 18 Bobby Labonte's Car
❑ 19 Bill Elliott's Car
❑ 20 Ted Musgrave's Car
❑ 21 Ricky Rudd's Car
❑ 22 Rusty Wallace's Car
❑ 23 Jeremy Mayfield's Car
❑ 24 Michael Waltrip's Car
❑ 25 Mark Martin MM
❑ 26 Rusty Wallace MM
❑ 27 Jeff Gordon MM
❑ 28 Dale Jarrett MM
❑ 29 Ricky Rudd MM
❑ 30 Ernie Irvan MM

1998 Pinnacle Mint Solid Silver Coin

This 30-card set parallels the base coin set an[d] randomly inserted in both hobby and retail packs at of 1:288 and 1:960 respectively.

	MINT
COMPLETE SET (30)	1800.00
COMMON COIN (1-30)	10.00
❑ 1 Jeff Gordon	200.00
❑ 2 Mark Martin	100.00
❑ 3 Dale Earnhardt	200.00
❑ 4 Terry Labonte	100.00
❑ 5 Dale Jarrett	80.00
❑ 6 Bobby Labonte	80.00
❑ 7 Bill Elliott	100.00
❑ 8 Ted Musgrave	20.00
❑ 9 Ricky Rudd	40.00
❑ 10 Rusty Wallace	100.00
❑ 11 Jeremy Mayfield	60.00
❑ 12 Michael Waltrip	20.00
❑ 13 Jeff Gordon's Car	100.00
❑ 14 Mark Martin's Car	50.00
❑ 15 Dale Jarrett's Car	40.00
❑ 16 Terry Labonte's Car	50.00
❑ 17 Dale Earnhardt's Car	100.00
❑ 18 Bobby Labonte's Car	40.00
❑ 19 Bill Elliott's Car	50.00
❑ 20 Ted Musgrave's Car	10.00
❑ 21 Ricky Rudd's Car	20.00
❑ 22 Rusty Wallace's Car	50.00
❑ 23 Jeremy Mayfield's Car	30.00
❑ 24 Michael Waltrip's Car	10.00
❑ 25 Mark Martin MM	50.00
❑ 26 Rusty Wallace MM	50.00
❑ 27 Jeff Gordon MM	100.00
❑ 28 Dale Jarrett MM	40.00
❑ 29 Ricky Rudd MM	20.00
❑ 30 Ernie Irvan MM	20.00

1997 Pinnacle Precision

This 77-card set was distributed in collectibles c[ans]. The cards themselves are made of steel. Each i[ncluded] two two-card packs of steel cards, one koozie [and] static ling-on decal. The cans carried a suggest[ed] price of $9.99.

	MINT
COMPLETE SET (77)	150.00
COMMON CARD (1-77)	.50
COMMON DRIVER (1-77)	1.00
TERRY LABONTE AUTO	200.00
STATED ODDS 1:1,120	
❑ 1 Bob Brannan	.50
❑ 2 Rick Hendrick	.50
❑ 3 Jeff Gordon	10.00
❑ 4 Jeff Gordon Pit Action	5.00
❑ 5 Jeff Gordon's Car	5.00
❑ 6 Jeff Gordon	10.00
❑ 7 Ray Evernham	1.00
❑ 8 Jeff Gordon's Car	5.00
❑ 9 Jeff Gordon	10.00
❑ 10 Don Hawk	.50
❑ 11 Richard Childress	.50
❑ 12 Dale Earnhardt's Transporter	5.00
❑ 13 Dale Earnhardt Pit Action	5.00
❑ 14 Dale Earnhardt's Car	5.00
❑ 15 Dale Earnhardt	10.00
❑ 16 David Smith	.50
❑ 17 Dale Earnhardt's Car	5.00
❑ 18 Dale Earnhardt	10.00
❑ 19 Sterling Marlin's Transporter	1.00

arry McClure	.50	.23
terling Marlin	2.00	.90
terling Marlin Pit Action	1.00	.45
terling Marlin's Car	1.00	.45
terling Marlin	2.00	.90
helton Pittman	.50	.23
terling Marlin's Car	1.00	.45
terling Marlin	2.00	.90
ale Jarrett's Transporter	2.00	.90
obert Yates	.50	.23
ale Jarrett	4.00	1.80
ale Jarrett Pit Action	2.00	.90
ale Jarrett's Car	2.00	.90
ale Jarrett	4.00	1.80
odd Parrott	.50	.23
ale Jarrett's Car	2.00	.90
ale Jarrett	4.00	1.80
usty Wallace's Transporter	2.50	1.10
oger Penske	.50	.23
usty Wallace	5.00	2.20
usty Wallace Pit Action	2.50	1.10
usty Wallace's Car	2.50	1.10
usty Wallace	5.00	2.20
obin Pemberton	.50	.23
usty Wallace's Car	2.50	1.10
usty Wallace	5.00	2.20
eve Jones	.50	.23
ll Elliott	5.00	2.20
ll Elliott	5.00	2.20
ll Elliott Pit Action	2.50	1.10
ll Elliott's Car	2.50	1.10
ll Elliott	5.00	2.20
ike Beam	.50	.23
ll Elliott's Car	2.50	1.10
ll Elliott	5.00	2.20
erry Labonte's Transporter	2.50	1.10
ck Hendrick	.50	.23
erry Labonte	5.00	2.20
erry Labonte Pit Action	2.50	1.10
erry Labonte's Car	2.50	1.10
rry Labonte	5.00	2.20
ary DeHart	.50	.23
rry Labonte's Car	2.50	1.10
rry Labonte	5.00	2.20
cky Rudd's Transporter	1.00	.45
cky Rudd	2.00	.90
cky Rudd	2.00	.90
cky Rudd Pit Action	1.00	.45
cky Rudd's Car	1.00	.45
cky Rudd	2.00	.90
cky Rudd	2.00	.90
cky Rudd's Car	1.00	.45
cky Rudd	2.00	.90
bby Labonte	4.00	1.80
cky Craven	1.00	.45
nny Benson	1.00	.45
emy Mayfield	3.00	1.35
ecklist	.50	.23

997 Pinnacle Precision Bronze

card set parallels the base set and was produced ronze finish. The cards were randomly inserted s at a ratio of 1:4.

	MINT	NRMT
TE SET (77)	500.00	220.00
N CARD (1-77)	1.50	.70
N DRIVER (1-77)	3.00	1.35

E CARDS: 1.5X TO 3X BASIC CARDS

7 Pinnacle Precision Gold

card set parallels the base set and was produced old finish. The cards were randomly inserted into ratio of 1:68.

	MINT	NRMT
TE SET (77)	2500.00	1100.00
N CARD (1-77)	12.50	5.50
N DRIVER (1-77)	25.00	11.00

ARDS: 15X TO 25X BASIC CARDS

Pinnacle Precision Silver

card set parallels the base set and was produced ver finish. The cards were randomly inserted into ratio of 1:10.

	MINT	NRMT
TE SET (77)	1000.00	450.00
CARD (1-77)	3.00	1.35
DRIVER (1-77)	6.00	2.70

ARDS: 3X TO 6X BASIC CARDS

1997 Pinnacle Precision Terry Labonte Autographs

This is a 7-card Terry Labonte set that features his autograph on each card. Reportedly, only 50 of each card was signed. The cards were randomly inserted in cans at a ratio of 1:1,120.

	MINT	NRMT
COMPLETE SET (7)	1200.00	550.00
COMMON CARD	175.00	80.00
❑ 55 Terry Labonte's Transporter	175.00	80.00
❑ 57 Terry Labonte	200.00	90.00
❑ 58 Terry Labonte's Car	175.00	80.00
❑ 59 Terry Labonte's Car	175.00	80.00
❑ 60 Terry Labonte	200.00	90.00
❑ 62 Terry Labonte's Car	175.00	80.00
❑ 63 Terry Labonte	200.00	90.00

1997 Pinnacle Totally Certified Platinum Red

Randomly inserted two in every pack, this 100-card set is the base set of this product and is sequentally numbered to 2,999. The difference is found in the red design element.

	MINT	NRMT
COMPLETE SET (100)	120.00	55.00
COMMON CARD (1-100)	.50	.23
COMMON DRIVER (1-100)	1.00	.45
❑ 1 Kyle Petty	2.00	.90
❑ 2 Rusty Wallace	5.00	2.20
❑ 3 Dale Earnhardt	10.00	4.50
❑ 4 Sterling Marlin	2.00	.90
❑ 5 Terry Labonte	5.00	2.20
❑ 6 Mark Martin	5.00	2.20
❑ 7 Bill Elliott	5.00	2.20
❑ 8 Jeremy Mayfield	3.00	1.35
❑ 9 Ted Musgrave	1.00	.45
❑ 10 Ricky Rudd	2.00	.90
❑ 11 Robby Gordon	1.00	.45
❑ 12 Johnny Benson	1.00	.45
❑ 13 Bobby Hamilton	1.00	.45
❑ 14 Mike Skinner	1.00	.45
❑ 15 Dale Jarrett	4.00	1.80
❑ 16 Steve Grissom	1.00	.45
❑ 17 Darrell Waltrip	1.00	.45
❑ 18 Bobby Labonte	4.00	1.80
❑ 19 Ernie Irvan	2.00	.90
❑ 20 Jeff Green	1.00	.45
❑ 21 Michael Waltrip	1.00	.45
❑ 22 Ward Burton	1.00	.45
❑ 23 Geoff Bodine	1.00	.45
❑ 24 Jeff Gordon	10.00	4.50
❑ 25 Ricky Craven	1.00	.45
❑ 26 Jimmy Spencer	1.00	.45
❑ 27 Brett Bodine	1.00	.45
❑ 28 David Green	1.00	.45
❑ 29 John Andretti	1.00	.45
❑ 30 Ken Schrader	1.00	.45
❑ 31 Chad Little	1.00	.45
❑ 32 Joe Nemechek	1.00	.45
❑ 33 Hut Stricklin	1.00	.45
❑ 34 Kenny Wallace	1.00	.45
❑ 35 Kyle Petty's Car	1.00	.45
❑ 36 Rusty Wallace's Car	2.50	1.10
❑ 37 Dale Earnhardt's Car	5.00	2.20
❑ 38 Sterling Marlin's Car	1.00	.45
❑ 39 Terry Labonte's Car	2.50	1.10
❑ 40 Mark Martin's Car	2.50	1.10
❑ 41 Bill Elliott's Car	2.50	1.10
❑ 42 Jeremy Mayfield's Car	1.50	.70
❑ 43 Ted Musgrave's Car	.50	.23
❑ 44 Ricky Rudd's Car	1.00	.45
❑ 45 Robby Gordon's Car	.50	.23
❑ 46 Johnny Benson's Car	.50	.23
❑ 47 Bobby Hamilton's Car	.50	.23
❑ 48 Mike Skinner's Car	.50	.23
❑ 49 Dale Jarrett's Car	2.00	.90
❑ 50 Steve Grissom's Car	.50	.23
❑ 51 Darrell Waltrip's Car	1.00	.45
❑ 52 Bobby Labonte's Car	2.00	.90
❑ 53 Ernie Irvan's Car	1.00	.45
❑ 54 Jeff Green's Car	.50	.23
❑ 55 Michael Waltrip's Car	.50	.23
❑ 56 Ward Burton's Car	.50	.23
❑ 57 Geoff Bodine's Car	.50	.23
❑ 58 Jeff Gordon's Car	5.00	2.20
❑ 59 Ricky Craven's Car	.50	.23
❑ 60 Jimmy Spencer's Car	.50	.23
❑ 61 Brett Bodine's Car	.50	.23
❑ 62 David Green's Car	.50	.23
❑ 63 John Andretti's Car	.50	.23
❑ 64 Ken Schrader's Car	.50	.23
❑ 65 Chad Little's Car	.50	.23
❑ 66 Joe Nemechek's Car	.50	.23
❑ 67 Hut Stricklin's Car	.50	.23
❑ 68 Kenny Wallace's Car	.50	.23
❑ 69 Darrell Waltrip WP	1.00	.45
❑ 70 Darrell Waltrip WP	1.00	.45
❑ 71 Darrell Waltrip WP	1.00	.45
❑ 72 Jeremy Mayfield WP	1.50	.70
❑ 73 Jeremy Mayfield WP	1.50	.70
❑ 74 Jeff Gordon WP	5.00	2.20
❑ 75 Ward Burton WP	.50	.23
❑ 76 Dale Earnhardt WP	5.00	2.20
❑ 77 Bobby Labonte WP	2.00	.90
❑ 78 Michael Waltrip WP	.50	.23
❑ 79 Robby Gordon WP	.50	.23
❑ 80 Terry Labonte WP	2.50	1.10
❑ 81 Bill Elliott WP	2.50	1.10
❑ 82 Bobby Hamilton WP	.50	.23
❑ 83 Chad Little WP	.50	.23
❑ 84 Jeff Green WP	.50	.23
❑ 85 Jeff Green WP	.50	.23
❑ 86 Rick Mast WP	.50	.23
❑ 87 Ernie Irvan WP	1.00	.45
❑ 88 Geoff Bodine WP	.50	.23
❑ 89 Jeff Gordon BD	5.00	2.20
❑ 90 Terry Labonte BD	2.50	1.10
❑ 91 Mark Martin BD	2.50	1.10
❑ 92 Dale Jarrett BD	2.00	.90
❑ 93 Dale Earnhardt BD	5.00	2.20
❑ 94 Ricky Rudd BD	1.00	.45
❑ 95 Rusty Wallace BD	2.50	1.10
❑ 96 Bobby Hamilton BD	.50	.23
❑ 97 Bobby Labonte BD	2.00	.90
❑ 98 Kyle Petty BD	1.00	.45
❑ 99 Checklist 1	.50	.23
❑ 100 Checklist 2	.50	.23

1997 Pinnacle Totally Certified Platinum Blue

Randomly inserted one in every pack, this 100-card set is parallel to the base set and is sequentally numbered to 1,999. The difference is found in the blue design element.

	MINT	NRMT
COMPLETE SET (100)	250.00	110.00
COMMON CARD (1-100)	1.00	.45
COMMON DRIVER (1-100)	2.00	.90

*BLUE STARS: 1X TO 2X PLATINUM RED

1997 Pinnacle Totally Certified Platinum Gold

Randomly inserted in packs at the rate of one in 37 packs, this 100-card set is parallel to the base set and is sequentally numbered to 49. The difference is found in the gold design element.

	MINT	NRMT
COMPLETE SET (100)	6000.00	
COMMON CARD (1-100)	30.00	13.50
COMMON DRIVER (1-100)	80.00	36.00

*GOLD STARS: 30X TO 60X PLATINUM RED

1991-92 Pioneers of Stock Car Racing

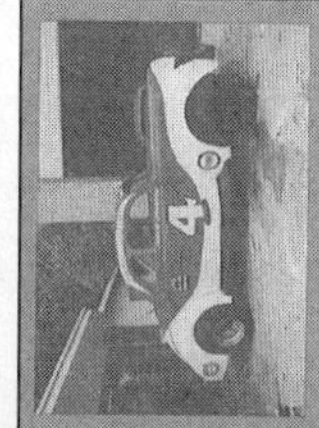

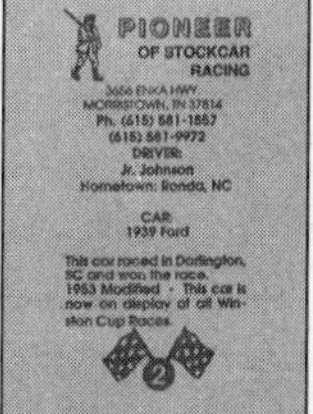

This set was issued in two series of six-cards each. Series one was released in 1991 with series two being issued in 1992.

	MINT	NRMT
COMPLETE SET (12)	5.00	2.20
COMPLETE SERIES 1 (6)	2.50	1.10
COMPLETE SERIES 2 (6)	2.50	1.10
COMMON CARD (1-5)	.50	.23
COMMON CARD (6-10)	.50	.23

❑ 1 Rod Long	.50	.23
❑ 2 Junior Johnson	.75	.35
❑ 3 Bobby Myers	.50	.23
❑ 4 Darrell Waltrip Walter Wallace Freddy Fryar P.B.Correll	.75	.35
❑ 5 Curtis Crider	.50	.23
❑ 6 Rod Long	.50	.23
❑ 7 Billy Myers	.50	.23
❑ 8 Bill Morton	.50	.23
❑ 9 Gene Glover	.50	.23
❑ 10 Tim Flock	.50	.23
❑ NNO Cover Card Series 1	.50	.23
❑ NNO Cover Card Series 2	.50	.23

1994 Power

In 1994, Pro Set produced only a Power racing set. The 150-cards include eight different subsets: Daytona Beach, Power Teams, Power Winners, Power Prospects, Stat Leaders, Power Rigs, Power Owners and MRN Radio announcers. The cards were packaged 12-cards per foil pack. A Gold parallel set was also produced and inserted one per pack along with a randomly inserted Dale Earnhardt Hologram card (numbered of 3500). Each of the last 20 cards in the set (cars subset) was also produced in a gold prism foil version inserted one per special 25-card retail blister pack.

	MINT	NRMT
COMPLETE SET (150)	8.00	3.60
COMMON CARD (1-150)	.05	.02
COMMON DRIVER (1-150)	.08	.04

❑ 1 Loy Allen Jr. DB	.08	.04
❑ 2 Dale Earnhardt DB	1.00	.45
❑ 3 Ernie Irvan DB	.25	.11
❑ 4 Sterling Marlin DB	.15	.07
❑ 5 Jeff Gordon DB	1.00	.45
❑ 6 Richard Childress PT	.05	.02
❑ 7 Roger Penske PT	.05	.02
❑ 8 Jack Roush PT	.05	.02
❑ 9 Robert Yates PT	.05	.02
❑ 10 Glen Wood PT	.05	.02
❑ 11 Joe Gibbs PT	.08	.04
❑ 12 Felix Sabates PT	.05	.02
❑ 13 Ricky Rudd PT	.15	.07
❑ 14 Junior Johnson PT	.08	.04
❑ 15 Joe Hendrick (Papa) PT	.05	.02
❑ 16 Dale Earnhardt PW	1.00	.45
❑ 17 Rusty Wallace PW	.50	.23
❑ 18 Ernie Irvan PW	.25	.11
❑ 19 Dale Jarrett PW	.25	.11
❑ 20 Mark Martin PW	.50	.23
❑ 21 Morgan Shepherd PW	.05	.02
❑ 22 Kyle Petty PW	.15	.07
❑ 23 Ricky Rudd PW	.15	.07
❑ 24 Geoff Bodine PW	.08	.04
❑ 25 Davey Allison PW	.50	.23
❑ 26 Loy Allen Jr. PP	.08	.04
❑ 27 John Andretti PP	.08	.04
❑ 28 Steve Grissom PP	.08	.04
❑ 29 Ward Burton PP	.08	.04
❑ 30 Mike Wallace PP	.08	.04
❑ 31 Joe Nemechek PP	.05	.02
❑ 32 Todd Bodine PP	.08	.04
❑ 33 Chuck Bown PP	.08	.04
❑ 34 Robert Pressley PP	.08	.04
❑ 35 Jeff Burton PP	.08	.04
❑ 36 Randy LaJoie PP	.08	.04
❑ 37 Billy Standridge PP	.05	.02
❑ 38 Dale Earnhardt SL	1.00	.45
❑ 39 Rusty Wallace SL	.50	.23
❑ 40 Terry Labonte SL	.50	.23
❑ 41 Ricky Rudd SL	.15	.07
❑ 42 Geoff Bodine SL	.08	.04
❑ 43 Harry Gant SL	.15	.07
❑ 44 Mark Martin SL	.50	.23
❑ 45 Buddy Baker SL	.05	.02
❑ 46 Darrell Waltrip SL	.15	.07
❑ 47 Leonard Wood SL	.05	.02
❑ 48 Dale Inman SL	.05	.02
❑ 49 Tim Brewer SL	.05	.02
❑ 50 Harry Hyde SL	.05	.02
❑ 51 Jeff Hammond SL	.05	.02
❑ 52 Travis Carter SL	.05	.02
❑ 53 Buddy Parrott SL	.05	.02
❑ 54 Rusty Wallace in Pits SL	.25	.11
❑ 55 Brett Bodine In Pits SL	.05	.02
❑ 56 Mark Martin in Pits SL	.25	.11
❑ 57 Bill Elliott in Pits SL	.25	.11
❑ 58 Michael Waltrip in Pits SL	.05	.02
❑ 59 Dale Earnhardt's Trans. PR	.30	.14
❑ 60 Darrell Waltrip's Trans. PR	.05	.02
❑ 61 Ernie Irvan's Trans. PR	.08	.04
❑ 62 Mark Martin's Trans. PR	.15	.07
❑ 63 Rusty Wallace's Trans. PR	.15	.07
❑ 64 Richard Petty PO	.25	.11
❑ 65 Junior Johnson PO	.08	.04
❑ 66 Richard Childress PO	.05	.02
❑ 67 Walter Bud Moore PO	.05	.02
❑ 68 Harry Melling PO	.05	.02
❑ 69 Darrell Waltrip PO	.15	.07
❑ 70 Eli Gold MR	.05	.02
❑ 71 Barney Hall MR	.05	.02
❑ 72 Dick Brooks MR Winston Kelley MR Jim Phillips MR	.05	.02
❑ 73 Joe Moore MR Allen Bestwick MR Fred Armstrong MR	.05	.02
❑ 74 Bobby Allison	.08	.04
❑ 75 Kenny Bernstein	.08	.04
❑ 76 Rich Bickle	.08	.04
❑ 77 Brett Bodine	.08	.04
❑ 78 Geoff Bodine	.08	.04
❑ 79 George Bradshaw	.05	.02
❑ 80 Travis Carter	.05	.02
❑ 81 Richard Childress	.05	.02
❑ 82 Derrike Cope	.08	.04
❑ 83 Wally Dallenbach Jr.	.08	.04
❑ 84 Bill Davis	.05	.02
❑ 85 Junie Donlavey	.05	.02
❑ 86 Harry Gant	.15	.07
❑ 87 Harry Gant	.15	.07
❑ 88 Joe Gibbs	.08	.04
❑ 89 Jeff Gordon	1.00	.45
❑ 90 Jeff Gordon	1.00	.45
❑ 91 Bobby Hamilton	.08	.04
❑ 92 Rick Hendrick	.05	.02
❑ 93 Jimmy Hensley	.08	.04
❑ 94 Jimmy Hensley	.08	.04
❑ 95 Ernie Irvan	.25	.11
❑ 96 Richard Jackson	.05	.02
❑ 97 Junior Johnson	.08	.04
❑ 98 Bobby Labonte	.15	.07
❑ 99 Chad Little	.08	.04
❑ 100 Dave Marcis	.08	.04
❑ 101 Sterling Marlin	.15	.07
❑ 102 Sterling Marlin	.15	.07
❑ 103 Rick Mast	.08	.04
❑ 104 Larry McClure	.05	.02
❑ 105 Walter Bud Moore	.05	.02
❑ 106 Ted Musgrave	.08	.04
❑ 107 Roger Penske	.05	.02
❑ 108 Kyle Petty	.15	.07
❑ 109 Kyle Petty	.15	.07
❑ 110 Richard Petty	.25	.11
❑ 111 Chuck Rider	.05	.02
❑ 112 Jack Roush	.05	.02
❑ 113 Felix Sabates	.05	.02
❑ 114 Greg Sacks	.08	.04
❑ 115 Ken Schrader	.08	.04
❑ 116 Lake Speed	.08	.04
❑ 117 Jimmy Spencer	.08	.04
❑ 118 Jimmy Spencer	.08	.04
❑ 119 Hut Stricklin	.08	.04
❑ 120 Dick Trickle	.08	.04
❑ 121 Mike Wallace	.08	.04
❑ 122 Rusty Wallace	.50	.23
❑ 123 Rusty Wallace	.50	.23
❑ 124 Roger Penske	.05	.02
❑ 125 Darrell Waltrip	.15	.07
❑ 126 Michael Waltrip	.08	.04
❑ 127 Pete Wright	.05	.02
❑ 128 Cale Yarborough	.08	.04
❑ 129 Robert Yates	.05	.02
❑ 130 Jeff Burton	.08	.04
❑ 131 Hut Stricklin's Car	.05	.02
❑ 132 Jeff Gordon's Car	.40	.18
❑ 133 Geoff Bodine's Car	.05	
❑ 134 Todd Bodine's Car	.05	
❑ 135 Randy LaJoie's Car	.05	
❑ 136 Derrike Cope's Car	.05	
❑ 137 Lake Speed's Car	.05	
❑ 138 Ward Burton's Car	.05	
❑ 139 Mike Wallace's Car	.05	
❑ 140 Terry Labonte's Car	.25	
❑ 141 Sterling Marlin's Car	.08	
❑ 142 Jimmy Spencer's Car	.05	
❑ 143 Michael Waltrip's Car	.05	
❑ 144 Brett Bodine's Car	.05	
❑ 145 Rick Mast's Car	.05	
❑ 146 Harry Gant's Car	.08	
❑ 147 Wally Dallenbach Jr.'s Car	.05	
❑ 148 Ernie Irvan's Car	.15	
❑ 149 Greg Sacks' Car	.05	
❑ 150 Darrell Waltrip's Car	.08	
❑ NNO Dale Earnhardt Hologram numbered of 3500	90.00	

1994 Power Gold

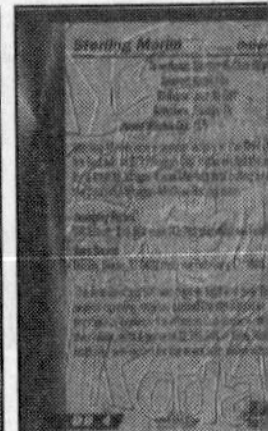

A parallel to the regular 1994 Power set, these cards feature a "Gold Cup '94" foil logo on the car The cards are identical to the regular issue, except logo, and were inserted one per foil pack.

	MINT
COMPLETE SET (150)	40.00
COMMON CARD (1-150)	.15
COMMON DRIVER (1-150)	.25

*GOLD CARDS: 1.5X TO 3X BASIC CARDS

1994 Power Preview

This 31-card set was issued as a preview to the racing set released later in the year. The card distributed to hobby outlets in factory set form o included 18 silver foil stamped driver cards, 12 pr car cards and one gold foil Dale Earnhardt tribu (#31).

	MINT
COMPLETE SET (31)	3.00
COMMON CARD (1-31)	.10
PRISM CARS (19-30)	.20

❑ 1 Geoff Bodine	.10
❑ 2 Derrike Cope	.10
❑ 3 Wally Dallenbach Jr.	.10
❑ 4 Ted Musgrave	.10
❑ 5 Jimmy Spencer	.10
❑ 6 Michael Waltrip	.10
❑ 7 Hut Stricklin	.10
❑ 8 Rusty Wallace	.50
❑ 9 Darrell Waltrip	.30
❑ 10 Dale Jarrett	.40
❑ 11 Ken Schrader	.10
❑ 12 Jeff Gordon	1.00
❑ 13 Ricky Rudd	.30
❑ 14 Kyle Petty	.30
❑ 15 Mark Martin	.50
❑ 16 Harry Gant	.30
❑ 17 Harry Gant Leo Jackson	.10
❑ 18 Bobby Hillin Junie Donlavey	.10
❑ 19 Mark Martin's Car FOIL	.30

Card	MINT	NRMT
ed Musgrave's Car FOIL	.20	.09
Vally Dallenbach's Car FOIL	.20	.09
eff Gordon's Car FOIL	.50	.23
obby Hillin's Car FOIL	.20	.09
ieoff Bodine's Car FOIL	.20	.09
arry Gant's Car FOIL	.20	.09
yle Petty's Car FOIL	.20	.09
lichael Waltrip's Car FOIL	.20	.09
lut Stricklin's Car FOIL	.20	.09
ale Jarrett's Car FOIL	.20	.09
errike Cope's Car FOIL	.20	.09
ale Earnhardt WC Champ	1.00	.45

1997 Predator

6-car set is another uniquely themed set from s. The cards feature the top names in racing. There vo Double Eagle cards in this product that erates Terry Labonte's 1984 and 1996 Winston Cup pionship winning seasons. The Gold Double Eagle vas made available only in First Slash boxes while ver Double Eagle card was made available only in bby boxes. The cards were packaged 5 cards per 20 packs per box and 16 boxes per case. The first ses off the press had the First Slash logo stamped of the cards in those cases.

	MINT	NRMT
LETE SET (66)	15.00	6.75
ON CARD (1-66)	.10	.05
ON DRIVER (1-66)	.20	.09
SLASH COMP. SET (66)	20.00	9.00

T SLASH CARDS: .75X TO 1.5X BASIC CARDS

Card	MINT	NRMT
f Gordon	2.00	.90
rry Labonte	1.00	.45
le Earnhardt	2.00	.90
le Jarrett	.75	.35
rk Martin	1.00	.45
sty Wallace	1.00	.45
erling Marlin	.40	.18
vid Green	.20	.09
f Burton	.40	.18
obby Hamilton	.20	.09
lichael Waltrip	.20	.09
obby Labonte	.75	.35
icky Craven	.20	.09
ohnny Benson	.20	.09
eremy Mayfield	.60	.25
lut Stricklin	.20	.09
yle Petty	.40	.18
arrell Waltrip	.40	.18
ohn Andretti	.20	.09
ill Elliott	1.00	.45
obert Pressley	.20	.09
oe Nemechek	.20	.09
errike Cope	.20	.09
Vard Burton	.40	.18
had Little	.20	.09
ike Skinner	.20	.09
mmy Spencer	.20	.09
ave Marcis	.40	.18
Vally Dallenbach	.20	.09
enny Wallace	.20	.09
rett Bodine	.20	.09
ed Musgrave	.20	.09
obby Gordon	.20	.09
andy Lajoie	.20	.09
eff Fuller	.20	.09
ason Keller	.20	.09
like McLaughlin	.20	.09
obby Labonte	.75	.35
ale Jarrett	.75	.35
lichael Waltrip	.20	.09
ark Martin	1.00	.45
teve Park	2.00	.90
lenn Allen	.20	.09
eff Gordon	2.00	.90
erry Labonte	1.00	.45
obby Hamilton	.20	.09
obby Labonte	.75	.35
ay Evernham	.20	.09
ary DeHart	.10	.05
❑ 50 Todd Parrott	.10	.05
❑ 51 Steve Hmiel	.10	.05
❑ 52 Robin Pemberton	.10	.05
❑ 53 Jimmy Makar	.10	.05
❑ 54 Jeff Hammond	.10	.05
❑ 55 Larry McReynolds	.10	.05
❑ 56 Kevin Hamlin	.10	.05
❑ 57 David Smith	.10	.05
❑ 58 Richard Childress	.10	.05
❑ 59 Joe Gibbs	.20	.09
❑ 60 Rick Hendrick	.10	.05
❑ 61 Robert Yates	.10	.05
❑ 62 Johnny Benson	.20	.09
❑ 63 Randy Lajoie	.20	.09
❑ 64 Bill Elliott	1.00	.45
❑ 65 Ron Hornaday	.20	.09
❑ 66 Checklist	.10	.05
❑ GD1 Terry Labonte	25.00	11.00
❑ SD1 Terry Labonte	15.00	6.75

1997 Predator Black Wolf First Strike

This set was made available by Wheels through a Collect-N-Purchase offer in which collectors had to collect 8 cards and send them to buy this set directly from Wheels. This 66-card set was packaged in a simulated gatorskin case and was reportedly limtied in production to 3,750 sets.

	MINT	NRMT
COMPLETE SET (66)	75.00	34.00
COMMON CARD (1-66)	.50	.23
COMMON DRIVER (1-66)	1.00	.45

1997 Predator Grizzly

This 66-card set is a parallel to the base set. These cards are copper foil stamped and are set against a color enhanced background. The cards were randomly inserted into packs at a ratio of 1:5.

	MINT	NRMT
COMPLETE SET (66)	80.00	36.00
COMMON CARD (1-66)	.50	.23
COMMON DRIVER (1-66)	1.00	.45
*GRIZZLY CARDS: 2X TO 5X BASIC CARDS		
FIRST SLASH COMP. SET (66)	120.00	55.00
*FIRST SLASH CARDS: .75X TO 1.5X GRIZZLY		

1997 Predator Red Wolf

This 66-card set is a parallel to the base set. These cards are red foil stamped and are set against a micro-etched background. The cards were randomly inserted into packs at a ratio of 1:10.

	MINT	NRMT
COMPLETE SET (66)	150.00	70.00
COMMON CARD (1-66)	1.50	.70
COMMON DRIVER (1-66)	3.00	1.35
*RED WOLF CARDS: 3X TO 8X BASIC CARDS		
FIRST SLASH COMP. SET (66)	250.00	110.00
*FIRST SLASH CARDS: .75X TO 1.5X RED WOLF		

1997 Predator American Eagle

This 10-card insert set features the top drivers from NASCAR. The cards are set against a background of an

eagle. The cards were randomly inserted in packs at a ratio of 1:30.

	MINT	NRMT
COMPLETE SET (10)	80.00	36.00
COMMON CARD (AE1-AE10)	4.00	1.80
*SINGLES: 8X TO 20X BASE CARD HI		
COMP. FIRST SLASH SET (10)	100.00	45.00
*FIRST SLASH CARDS: 10X TO 25X BASIC CARDS		

Card	MINT	NRMT
❑ AE1 Dale Earnhardt	25.00	11.00
❑ AE2 Jeff Gordon	25.00	11.00
❑ AE3 Rusty Wallace	15.00	6.75
❑ AE4 Terry Labonte	15.00	6.75
❑ AE5 Dale Jarrett	12.00	5.50
❑ AE6 Sterling Marlin	4.00	1.80
❑ AE7 Mark Martin	15.00	6.75
❑ AE8 Bobby Labonte	4.00	1.80
❑ AE9 Bill Elliott	15.00	6.75
❑ AE10 Darrell Waltrip	4.00	1.80

1997 Predator Eye of the Tiger

This 8-card insert set features NASCAR top stars on horizontal cards that are foil enhanced and micro-etched. The cards were randomly inserted in packs at a ratio of 1:10.

	MINT	NRMT
COMPLETE SET (8)	30.00	13.50
COMMON CARD (ET1-ET8)	1.50	.70
*SINGLES: 1.5X TO 4X BASE CARD HI		
COMP. FIRST SLASH SET(8)	40.00	18.00
*FIRST SLASH CARDS: 2X TO 5X BASIC CARDS		

Card	MINT	NRMT
❑ ET1 Dale Earnhardt	10.00	4.50
❑ ET2 Jeff Gordon	10.00	4.50
❑ ET3 Rusty Wallace	6.00	2.70
❑ ET4 Terry Labonte	6.00	2.70
❑ ET5 Dale Jarrett	5.00	2.20
❑ ET6 Mark Martin	6.00	2.70
❑ ET7 Bobby Labonte	3.00	1.35
❑ ET8 Sterling Marlin	1.50	.70

1997 Predator Gatorback

This 10-card set is a sublevel parallel of the Gatorback Authentic insert set. The cards feature a simulated crocodile hide distinguishing it from the Gatorback Authentic cards. The cards were randomly inserted in packs at a ratio of 1:40.

	MINT	NRMT
COMPLETE SET (10)	80.00	36.00
COMMON CARD (GB1-GB10)	2.50	1.10
*SINGLES: 5X TO 12X BASE CARD HI		

COMP. FIRST SLASH SET(10)	100.00	45.00
*FIRST SLASH CARDS: 6X TO 15X BASIC CARDS		
❑ GB1 Dale Earnhardt	30.00	13.50
❑ GB2 Jeff Gordon	30.00	13.50
❑ GB3 Mike Skinner	2.50	1.10
❑ GB4 Dale Jarrett	15.00	6.75
❑ GB5 Rusty Wallace	20.00	9.00
❑ GB6 Bobby Labonte	10.00	4.50
❑ GB7 Mark Martin	20.00	9.00
❑ GB8 Sterling Marlin	5.00	2.20
❑ GB9 Darrell Waltrip	5.00	2.20
❑ GB10 Bill Elliott	20.00	9.00

1997 Predator Gatorback Authentic

This 10-card set is the rarest of all Predator insert sets. The cards are highlighted by actual crocodile hide imported from Australia. There are two versions of each card; the white crocodile skin cards cards are found only in First Slash boxes and the brown crocodile skin cards are found only in Hobby boxes. The cards were randomly inserted in packs at a ratio of 1:120.

	MINT	NRMT
COMPLETE SET (10)	300.00	135.00
COMMON CARD (GBA1-GBA10)	8.00	3.60
*SINGLES: 15X TO 40X BASE CARD HI		
COMP. FIRST SLASH SET(10)	400.00	180.00
*FIRST SLASH CARDS: 20X TO 50X BASIC CARDS		
8.00	3.60	
❑ GBA1 Dale Earnhardt	120.00	55.00
❑ GBA2 Jeff Gordon	120.00	55.00
❑ GBA3 Mike Skinner	8.00	3.60
❑ GBA4 Dale Jarrett	60.00	27.00
❑ GBA5 Rusty Wallace	75.00	34.00
❑ GBA6 Bobby Labonte	30.00	13.50
❑ GBA7 Mark Martin	75.00	34.00
❑ GBA8 Sterling Marlin	15.00	6.75
❑ GBA9 Darrell Waltrip	15.00	6.75
❑ GBA10 Bill Elliott	75.00	34.00

1997 Predator Golden Eagle

This 10-card insert set features the top drivers from NASCAR. The cards are set against a background of an eagle highlighted by gold foil. The cards were randomly inserted in packs at a ratio of 1:40.

	MINT	NRMT
COMPLETE SET (10)	100.00	45.00
COMMON CARD (GE1-GE10)	2.50	1.10
*SINGLES: 5X TO 12X BASE CARD HI		
COMP. FIRST SLASH SET (10)	120.00	55.00
*FIRST SLASH CARDS: 6X TO 15X BASIC CARDS		
2.50	1.10	
❑ GE1 Dale Earnhardt	30.00	13.50
❑ GE2 Jeff Gordon	30.00	13.50
❑ GE3 Rusty Wallace	20.00	9.00
❑ GE4 Terry Labonte	20.00	9.00
❑ GE5 Dale Jarrett	15.00	6.75
❑ GE6 Sterling Marlin	5.00	2.20
❑ GE7 Mark Martin	20.00	9.00
❑ GE8 Bobby Labonte	10.00	4.50
❑ GE9 Bill Elliott	20.00	9.00
❑ GE10 Darrell Waltrip	5.00	2.20

1993 Press Pass Davey Allison

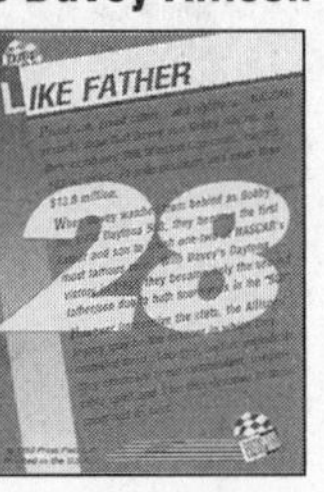

This five-card set uses prism printing technology to highlight Davey Allison's career. There were 25,000 sets produced and were distributed through a mail in offer in the '93 Press Pass Preview set. The sets could be had for $7.95 + $3.00 shipping and handling. In 1994, Press Pass also made the sets available to members of the Press Pass Club and the Press Pass Dealer Network.

	MINT	NRMT
COMPLETE SET (5)	4.00	1.80
COMMON CARD (1-5)	1.00	.45
❑ 1 Davey Allison	1.00	.45
❑ 2 Davey Allison	1.00	.45
❑ 3 Davey Allison	1.00	.45
❑ 4 Davey Allison Bobby Allison	1.00	.45
❑ 5 Davey Allison	1.00	.45

1993 Press Pass Preview

This 34-card set was the debut set from manufacturer Press Pass. The set was released in the late summer of '93 and features some of the top names in racing. The set originally retailed for $12.95.

	MINT	NRMT
COMPLETE SET (34)	8.00	3.60
COMMON CARD (1-34)	.10	.05
COMMON DRIVER (1-34)	.20	.09
CAR CARDS HALF VALUE		
❑ 1 Davey Allison Foil	1.25	.55
❑ 2 Brett Bodine	.20	.09
❑ 3 Geoff Bodine	.20	.09
❑ 4 Derrike Cope	.20	.09
❑ 5 Harry Gant	.40	.18
❑ 6 Jimmy Hensley	.20	.09
❑ 7 Dale Jarrett	.75	.35
❑ 8 Alan Kulwicki	.75	.35
❑ 9 Sterling Marlin	.40	.18
❑ 10 Mark Martin	1.00	.45
❑ 11 Kyle Petty	.40	.18
❑ 12 Ken Schrader	.20	.09
❑ 13 Morgan Shepherd	.20	.09
❑ 14 Jimmy Spencer	.20	.09
❑ 15 Rusty Wallace	1.00	.45
❑ 16 Joe Gibbs	.20	.09
❑ 17 Jeff Gordon Kenny Wallace Bobby Labonte	2.50	1.10
❑ 18A Jeff Gordon Redemption card expired	2.50	1.10
❑ 18B Jeff Gordon Foil	4.00	1.80
❑ 19 Bobby Labonte	.60	.25
❑ 20 Kenny Wallace	.20	.09
❑ 21 Alan Kulwicki	.75	.35
❑ 22 Rusty Wallace	1.00	.45
❑ 23 Bobby Allison	.20	.09
❑ 24 Morgan Shepherd's Car	.10	.05
❑ 25 Kenny Wallace's Car	.10	.05
❑ 26 Jeff Gordon's Car	1.25	.55
❑ 27 Dale Jarrett's Car	.40	.18
❑ 28 Bobby Labonte's Car	.40	.18
❑ 29 Jimmy Spencer's Car	.10	
❑ 30 Kyle Petty's Car	.20	
❑ 31 Rusty Wallace's Car	.60	
❑ 32 Sterling Marlin's Car	.20	
❑ 33 Harry Gant's Car	.20	
❑ 34 Mark Martin's Car	.60	

1994 Press Pass

This 150-card base brand set features top drivers both the Winston Cup and Busch circuits. The cards 10-cards to a pack. There were two different 36- boxes which the packs came in. There was a regul and a Race Day box. The only difference in the two was the Race Day packs gave the collector the oppo to pull a Race Day insert card. The Race Day packs easily identifiable due to the bright yellow star bu the front of the pack.

	MINT
COMPLETE SET (150)	10.00
COMMON CARD (1-150)	.10
COMMON DRIVER (1-150)	.20
❑ 1 Brett Bodine	.20
❑ 2 Geoff Bodine	.20
❑ 3 Derrike Cope	.20
❑ 4 Wally Dallenbach Jr.	.20
❑ 5 Dale Earnhardt	2.00
❑ 6 Harry Gant	.40
❑ 7 Jeff Gordon	2.00
❑ 8 Bobby Hamilton	.20
❑ 9 Jimmy Hensley	.20
❑ 10 Bobby Hillin	.20
❑ 11 Ernie Irvan	.40
❑ 12 Dale Jarrett	.75
❑ 13 Bobby Labonte	.60
❑ 14 Terry Labonte	1.00
❑ 15 Dave Marcis	.20
❑ 16 Sterling Marlin	.40
❑ 17 Mark Martin	1.00
❑ 18 Rick Mast	.20
❑ 19 Jimmy Means	.20
❑ 20 Ted Musgrave	.20
❑ 21 Kyle Petty	.40
❑ 22 Ken Schrader	.20
❑ 23 Morgan Shepherd	.20
❑ 24 Lake Speed	.20
❑ 25 Jimmy Spencer	.20
❑ 26 Hut Stricklin	.20
❑ 27 Kenny Wallace	.20
❑ 28 Rusty Wallace	2.00
❑ 29 Darrell Waltrip	.40
❑ 30 Michael Waltrip	.20
❑ 31 Rusty Wallace Kenny Wallace	.50
❑ 32 Mark Martin Jack Roush	.50
❑ 33 Darrell Waltrip Michael Waltrip	.40
❑ 34 Dale Jarrett Joe Gibbs	.40
❑ 35 Geoff Bodine Bobby Hillin	.10
❑ 36 Brett Bodine Kenny Bernstein	.10
❑ 37 Derrike Cope's Car	.10
❑ 38 Morgan Shepherd's Car	.10
❑ 39 Bobby Hamilton's Car	.10
❑ 40 Jeff Gordon's Car	1.00
❑ 41 Bobby Hillin's Car	.10
❑ 42 Dale Jarrett's Car	.40
❑ 43 Ken Schrader's Car	.10
❑ 44 Bobby Labonte's Car	.20
❑ 45 Jimmy Spencer's Car	.10
❑ 46 Kyle Petty's Car	.20
❑ 47 Rusty Wallace's Car	.50
❑ 48 Geoff Bodine's Car	.10
❑ 49 Michael Waltrip's Car	.10
❑ 50 Dick Trickle's Car	.10
❑ 51 Sterling Marlin's Car	.20
❑ 52 Harry Gant's Car	.20
❑ 53 Ernie Irvan's Car	.20

Mark Martin's Car	.50	.23
Todd Bodine	.20	.09
Chuck Bown	.20	.09
Ward Burton	.20	.09
Ricky Craven	.20	.09
Bobby Dotter	.20	.09
David Green	.20	.09
Steve Grissom	.20	.09
Joe Nemechek	.20	.09
Shawna Robinson	.20	.09
Steve Grissom's Car	.10	.05
Joe Nemechek's Car	.10	.05
Bobby Dotter's Car	.10	.05
Ricky Craven's Car	.10	.05
Todd Bodine's Car	.10	.05
Chuck Bown's Car	.10	.05
Shawna Robinson's Car	.10	.05
David Green's Car	.10	.05
Hermie Sadler's Car	.10	.05
Bobby Allison	.20	.09
Kenny Bernstein	.20	.09
Geoff Bodine	.20	.09
Bill Davis	.10	.05
Junie Donlavey	.10	.05
Joe Gibbs	.20	.09
Rick Hendrick	.10	.05
Leo Jackson	.10	.05
Walter Bud Moore	.10	.05
Roger Penske Don Miller	.10	.05
Chuck Rider	.10	.05
Jack Roush	.10	.05
Felix Sabates	.10	.05
Bill Stavola Mickey Stavola	.10	.05
Darrell Waltrip	.40	.18
Glen Wood Eddie Wood Len Wood	.10	.05
Cale Yarborough	.20	.09
Robert Yates	.10	.05
Paul Andrews	.10	.05
Barry Dodson	.10	.05
Ray Evernham	.10	.05
Jimmy Fennig	.10	.05
Jeff Hammond	.10	.05
Doug Hewitt	.10	.05
Steve Hmiel	.10	.05
Ken Howes	.10	.05
Sandy Jones	.10	.05
Jimmy Makar	.10	.05
Larry McReynolds	.10	.05
Buddy Parrott	.10	.05
Robin Pemberton	.10	.05
Donnie Richeson	.10	.05
Doug Williams	.10	.05
Ken Wilson	.10	.05
Donnie Wingo	.10	.05
Leonard Wood	.10	.05
Allen Bestwick	.10	.05
Dick Brooks	.10	.05
Eli Gold	.10	.05
Barney Hall	.10	.05
Ned Jarrett	.10	.05
Winston Kelley	.10	.05
Joe Moore	.10	.05
Benny Parsons	.20	.09
Jim Phillips	.10	.05
Rusty Wallace DOY	.50	.23
Ken Schrader Pole Win	.10	.05
Steve Hmiel	.10	.05
Mark Martin TT	.50	.23
Dale Jarrett TT	.40	.18
Rusty Wallace TT	.50	.23
Jeff Gordon ROY	1.00	.45
Steve Grissom BGN Champ	.10	.05
Joe Nemechek Pop. Driver	.10	.05
Davey Allison HR	.50	.23
Donnie Allison HR	.20	.09
Tim Flock HR	.10	.05
Alan Kulwicki HR	.40	.18
Fred Lorenzen HR	.10	.05
Tiny Lund HR	.10	.05
David Pearson HR	.10	.05
Glenn Roberts(Fireball) HR	.10	.05
Curtis Turner HR	.10	.05
Geoff Bodine Art	.10	.05
Geoff Bodine Art	.10	.05
Derrike Cope Art	.10	.05
Speed Racer Art	.10	.05
Dale Jarrett Art	.40	.18
Mark Martin Art	.50	.23
Ken Schrader Art	.10	.05
Morgan Shepherd Art	.10	.05
Rusty Wallace Art	.50	.23
Harry Gant Farewell	.20	.09
Harry Gant Farewell	.20	.09
Checklist #1	.10	.05
❑ 148 Checklist #2	.10	.05
❑ 149 Checklist #3	.10	.05
❑ 150 Checklist #4	.10	.05

1994 Press Pass Checkered Flags

This four-card insert set features 1993 multiple race winners. The cards use gold foil stamping and could be found one in every 12 packs.

	MINT	NRMT
COMPLETE SET (4)	10.00	4.50
COMMON CARD (CF1-CF4)	.60	.25
*SINGLES: 1.25X TO 3X BASE CARD HI		
❑ CF1 Dale Earnhardt	.60	.25
❑ CF2 Ernie Irvan	.60	.25
❑ CF3 Mark Martin	.60	.25
❑ CF4 Rusty Wallace	.60	.25

1994 Press Pass Cup Chase

This 30-card set was the first interactive racing game set produced. The specially stamped "Cup Chase" cards were a parallel to the first 30 cards in the set. The collector that owned the Dale Earnhardt Cup Chase card, the 1994 Winston Cup Champion, was able to redeem that card for a special Dale Earnhardt card and an uncut sheet of the 30 Cup Chase cards. An interesting note about the uncut sheet is that in the bottom right hand corner there is a black card and the sheet doesn't have the Dale Earnhardt card on it. The Cup Chase cards were inserted in packs of Press Pass at a rate of one every 18. The cards could be redeemed until March 31, 1995.

	MINT	NRMT
COMPLETE SET (30)	125.00	55.00
COMMON CARD (CC1-CC30)	2.00	.90
D.EARNHARDT PRIZE (SPCL1)	30.00	13.50
UNCUT SHEET PRIZE	100.00	45.00
❑ CC1 Brett Bodine	2.00	.90
❑ CC2 Geoff Bodine	2.00	.90
❑ CC3 Derrike Cope	2.00	.90
❑ CC4 Wally Dallenbach Jr.	2.00	.90
❑ CC5 Dale Earnhardt W1	30.00	13.50
❑ CC6 Harry Gant	4.00	1.80
❑ CC7 Jeff Gordon	20.00	9.00
❑ CC8 Bobby Hamilton	2.00	.90
❑ CC9 Jimmy Hensley	2.00	.90
❑ CC10 Bobby Hillin	2.00	.90
❑ CC11 Ernie Irvan	4.00	1.80
❑ CC12 Dale Jarrett	8.00	3.60
❑ CC13 Bobby Labonte	6.00	2.70
❑ CC14 Terry Labonte	8.00	3.60
❑ CC15 Dave Marcis	2.00	.90
❑ CC16 Sterling Marlin	4.00	1.80
❑ CC17 Mark Martin W2	15.00	6.75
❑ CC18 Rick Mast	2.00	.90
❑ CC19 Jimmy Means	2.00	.90
❑ CC20 Ted Musgrave	2.00	.90
❑ CC21 Kyle Petty	4.00	1.80
❑ CC22 Ken Schrader	2.00	.90
❑ CC23 Morgan Shepherd	2.00	.90
❑ CC24 Lake Speed	2.00	.90
❑ CC25 Jimmy Spencer	2.00	.90
❑ CC26 Hut Stricklin	2.00	.90
❑ CC27 Kenny Wallace	2.00	.90
❑ CC28 Rusty Wallace W3	15.00	6.75
❑ CC29 Darrell Waltrip	4.00	1.80
❑ CC30 Michael Waltrip	2.00	.90

1994 Press Pass Prospects

This five-card insert set uses Thermofoil printing technology to bring five of the top Busch Grand National drivers to collectors. The five drivers were in their rookie years on the Winston Cup circuit in 1994. The cards were randomly seeded at a rate of one per eight packs. The uncut sheet was the prize for returning the second place finisher in the Press Pass Cup Chase

	MINT	NRMT
COMPLETE SET (5)	6.00	2.70
COMMON CARD (PP1-PP5)	1.00	.45
UNCUT SHEET PRIZE	15.00	6.75
❑ PP1 Chuck Bown	1.00	.45
❑ PP2 Ward Burton	2.00	.90
❑ PP3 Ricky Craven	2.50	1.10
❑ PP4 Steve Grissom	2.00	.90
❑ PP5 Joe Nemechek	2.00	.90

1994 Press Pass Race Day

This 12-card insert set was issued across two Press Pass brands. The first 10 cards in the set were made available through specially marked "Race Day" boxes of Press Pass. The last two cards were randomly inserted in boxes of 1994 VIP. The cards feature drivers who took the checkered flag during 1993 and the 1994 Daytona 500 winner. The cards are printed using the holofoil technology and were randomly inserted in packs at a rate of one per 72.

	MINT	NRMT
COMPLETE SET (12)	100.00	45.00
COMPLETE SERIES 1 (10)	75.00	34.00
COMPLETE SERIES 2 (2)	25.00	11.00
COMMON CARD (RD1-RD10)	2.00	.90
COMMON CARD (RD11-RD12)	15.00	6.75
*SINGLES: 4X TO 10X BASE CARD HI		
❑ RD1 Davey Allison	4.00	1.80
❑ RD2 Geoff Bodine	2.00	.90
❑ RD3 Ernie Irvan	4.00	1.80
❑ RD4 Dale Jarrett	7.00	3.10
❑ RD5 Mark Martin	10.00	4.50
❑ RD6 Kyle Petty	4.00	1.80
❑ RD7 Jeff Gordon	4.00	1.80
❑ RD8 Morgan Shepherd	2.00	.90
❑ RD9 Rusty Wallace	4.00	1.80
❑ RD10 Dale Earnhardt	4.00	1.80
❑ RD11 Sterling Marlin	20.00	9.00
❑ NNO Cover Card	4.00	1.80

1994 Press Pass Authentics

These 8" X 10" cards are blown up versions of the five drivers' regular 1994 Press Pass cards. The cards are actually 5" X 7" and framed in a black border. The cards came in two versions: signed and unsigned. There were 1,500 cards unsigned and 1,000 cards signed. The signed cards were each signed in gold pen by the driver. All cards are numbered of 2,500 no matter if they are signed or

unsigned. The cards were made available through the Press Pass Club and to the Press Pass dealer network. The original retail for the pieces were $25 for any of the unsigned and $35 for any of the signed. The prices below refer to the unsigned versions.

	MINT	NRMT
COMPLETE SET (5)	90.00	40.00
COMMON CARD	10.00	4.50
❑ NNO Jeff Gordon	30.00	13.50
❑ NNO Ernie Irvan	15.00	6.75
❑ NNO Mark Martin	20.00	9.00
❑ NNO Kyle Petty	10.00	4.50
❑ NNO Rusty Wallace	20.00	9.00

1994 Press Pass Holofoils

Press Pass produced this Holofoils set featuring six popular Winston Cup drivers. The cards were sold directly to collectors in complete set form along with a certificate numbering the set one of 15,000 made. The cards contain a photo of the driver printed on holofoil card stock with driver stats on the backs.

	MINT	NRMT
COMPLETE SET (6)	10.00	4.50
COMMON CARD (H1-H6)	1.00	.45
❑ H1 Dale Earnhardt	3.00	1.35
❑ H2 Jeff Gordon	3.00	1.35
❑ H3 Ernie Irvan	1.25	.55
❑ H4 Mark Martin	1.50	.70
❑ H5 Kyle Petty	1.00	.45
❑ H6 Rusty Wallace	1.50	.70

1995 Press Pass

This 145-card base brand set features top drivers from the Winston Cup and Busch Grand National circuits. The cards came 10 cards per pack, 36 packs per box and 20 boxes per case. The set is broken into 10 topical subsets: Winston Cup Drivers (1-36), Winston Cup Cars (37-54), Busch Series Drivers (55-72), busch Series Cars (73-81), Winston Cup Owners (82-90), Winston Cup Crew Chiefs (91-99), Small Town Saturday Night (100-108), Award Winners (109-117), Heroes of Racing (118-123) SportsKings (124-126), Personal Rides (127-135), Breaking Through (136-143). Also randomly inserted at a rate of one per box in special retail boxes were autograph cards. The only two drivers cards that were autographed are the Sterling Marlin and David Green cards.

	MINT	NRMT
COMPLETE SET (145)	14.00	6.25
COMMON CARD (1-145)	.10	.05
COMMON DRIVER (1-145)	.20	.09
❑ 1 Loy Allen Jr.	.20	.09
❑ 2 John Andretti	.20	.09
❑ 3 Brett Bodine	.20	.09
❑ 4 Geoff Bodine	.20	.09
❑ 5 Todd Bodine	.20	.09
❑ 6 Jeff Burton	.40	.18
❑ 7 Ward Burton	.20	.09
❑ 8 Derrike Cope	.20	.09
❑ 9 Dale Earnhardt	2.00	.90
❑ 10 Jeff Gordon	2.00	.90
❑ 11 Steve Grissom	.20	.09
❑ 12 Bobby Hamilton	.20	.09
❑ 13 Ernie Irvan	.40	.18
❑ 14 Dale Jarrett	1.00	.45
❑ 15 Bobby Labonte	.75	.35
❑ 16 Terry Labonte	1.00	.45
❑ 17 Dave Marcis	.40	.18
❑ 18 Sterling Marlin	.40	.18
❑ 19 Mark Martin	1.00	.45
❑ 20 Rick Mast	.20	.09
❑ 21 Ted Musgrave	.20	.09
❑ 22 Joe Nemechek	.20	.09
❑ 23 Kyle Petty	.40	.18
❑ 24 Ricky Rudd	.40	.18
❑ 25 Greg Sacks	.20	.09
❑ 26 Ken Schrader	.20	.09
❑ 27 Morgan Shepherd	.20	.09
❑ 28 Lake Speed	.20	.09
❑ 29 Jimmy Spencer	.20	.09
❑ 30 Hut Stricklin	.20	.09
❑ 31 Dick Trickle	.20	.09
❑ 32 Kenny Wallace	.20	.09
❑ 33 Mike Wallace	.20	.09
❑ 34 Rusty Wallace	1.00	.45
❑ 35 Darrell Waltrip	.40	.18
❑ 36 Michael Waltrip Elizabeth Waltrip	.20	.09
❑ 37 Morgan Shepherd's Car	.10	.05
❑ 38 Jeff Gordon's Car	1.00	.45
❑ 39 Geoff Bodine's Car	.10	.05
❑ 40 Ted Musgrave's Car	.10	.05
❑ 41 Dale Earnhardt's Car	1.00	.45
❑ 42 Dale Jarrett's Car	.40	.18
❑ 43 Terry Labonte's Car	.50	.23
❑ 44 Sterling Marlin's Car	.20	.09
❑ 45 Ken Schrader's Car	.10	.05
❑ 46 Kyle Petty's Car	.20	.09
❑ 47 Rusty Wallace's Car	.50	.23
❑ 48 Michael Waltrip's Car	.10	.05
❑ 49 Brett Bodine's Car	.10	.05
❑ 50 John Andretti's Car	.10	.05
❑ 51 Ernie Irvan's Car	.20	.09
❑ 52 Ricky Rudd's Car	.20	.09
❑ 53 Mark Martin's Car	.50	.23
❑ 54 Darrell Waltrip's Car	.20	.09
❑ 55 Johnny Benson Jr.	.20	.09
❑ 56 Jim Bown	.20	.09
❑ 57 Ricky Craven	.40	.18
❑ 58 Bobby Dotter	.20	.09
❑ 59 Tim Fedewa	.20	.09
❑ 60 David Green	.20	.09
❑ 61 Tommy Houston	.20	.09
❑ 62 Jason Keller	.20	.09
❑ 63 Randy LaJoie	.20	.09
❑ 64 Tracy Leslie	.20	.09
❑ 65 Chad Little	.20	.09
❑ 66 Mark Martin	1.00	.45
❑ 67 Mike McLaughlin	.20	.09
❑ 68 Larry Pearson	.20	.09
❑ 69 Robert Pressley	.20	.09
❑ 70 Elton Sawyer	.20	.09
❑ 71 Dennis Setzer	.20	.09
❑ 72 Kenny Wallace	.20	.09
❑ 73 Dennis Setzer's Car	.10	.05
❑ 74 Chad Little's Car	.10	.05
❑ 75 Bobby Dotter's Car	.10	.05
❑ 76 Ricky Craven's Car	.10	.05
❑ 77 Mike McLaughlin's Car	.10	.05
❑ 78 Randy LaJoie's Car	.10	.05
❑ 79 David Green's Car	.10	.05
❑ 80 Larry Pearson's Car	.10	.05
❑ 81 Kenny Wallace's Car	.10	.05
❑ 82 Richard Childress	.10	.05
❑ 83 Rick Hendrick	.10	.05
❑ 84 Walter Bud Moore	.10	.05
❑ 85 Roger Penske Don Miller	.10	.05
❑ 86 Richard Petty	.50	.23
❑ 87 Chuck Rider	.10	.05
❑ 88 Felix Sabates	.10	.05
❑ 89 Cale Yarborough	.20	.09
❑ 90 Robert Yates	.10	.05
❑ 91 Mike Beam	.10	.05
❑ 92 Ray Evernham	.40	.18
❑ 93 Steve Hmiel	.10	.05
❑ 94 Ken Howes	.10	
❑ 95 Bill Ingle	.10	
❑ 96 Larry McReynolds	.10	
❑ 97 Buddy Parrott	.10	
❑ 98 Andy Petree	.10	
❑ 99 Leonard Wood	.10	
❑ 100 John Andretti ST	.20	
❑ 101 Geoff Bodine ST	.20	
❑ 102 Jeff Gordon ST	1.00	
❑ 103 Steve Kinser ST	.20	
❑ 104 Mark Martin ST	.50	
❑ 105 Joe Nemechek ST	.20	
❑ 106 Ken Schrader ST	.20	
❑ 107 Jimmy Spencer ST	.20	
❑ 108 Darrell Waltrip ST	.40	
❑ 109 Jeff Burton AW	.40	
❑ 110 Geoff Bodine AW	.20	
❑ 111 Ray Evernham AW	.20	
❑ 112 David Green AW	.20	
❑ 113 Johnny Benson AW	.20	
❑ 114 David Green AW	.20	
❑ 115 Dale Earnhardt's Car AW	1.00	
❑ 116 Mark Martin's Car AW	.50	
❑ 117 Michael Waltrip's Car AW	.10	
❑ 118 Buck Baker HR	.20	
❑ 119 Buddy Baker HR	.20	
❑ 120 Harry Gant HR	.40	
❑ 121 J.D. McDuffie HR	.10	
❑ 122 Marvin Panch HR	.10	
❑ 123 Lennie Ponds HR	.10	
❑ 124 Bobby Allison S	.20	
❑ 125 David Pearson S	.20	
❑ 126 Richard Petty S	.50	
❑ 127 Geoff Bodine PR	.20	
❑ 128 Harry Gant PR	.40	
❑ 129 Jeff Gordon PR	1.00	
❑ 130 Bobby Hamilton PR	.20	
❑ 131 Kyle Petty PR	.40	
❑ 132 Richard Petty PR	.50	
❑ 133 Ken Schrader PR	.20	
❑ 134 Morgan Shepherd PR	.20	
❑ 135 Rusty Wallace PR	.50	
❑ 136 Jeff Gordon BT	1.00	
❑ 137 Sterling Marlin BT	.40	
❑ 138 Jimmy Spencer BT	.20	
❑ 139 Johnny Benson BT	.20	
❑ 140 Ricky Craven BT	.40	
❑ 141 Elton Sawyer BT	.20	
❑ 142 Dennis Setzer BT	.20	
❑ 143 Mike Wallace BT	.20	
❑ 144 Checklist	.10	
❑ 145 Checklist	.10	
❑ A18 Sterling Marlin Autograghed	20.00	
❑ A60 David Green Autographed	12.00	

1995 Press Pass Red Hot

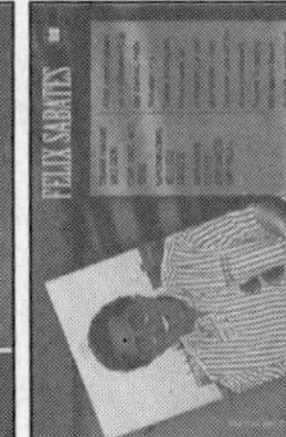

This 145-card set is a parallel of the base set. The feature a red foil stamping to differentiate them. Th Hot cards were randomly seeded at a rate of one two packs.

	MINT	N
COMPLETE SET (145)	60.00	
COMMON CARD (1-145)	.50	
COMMON DRIVER (1-145)	1.00	

*RED STARS: 5X TO 8X BASIC CARDS

1995 Press Pass Checkered Flags

This eight-card set features Winston Cup drivers wh multiple races in the 1994 season. The cards are go stamped and were inserted in packs at a rate of o nine.

	MINT	N
COMPLETE SET (8)	20.00	
COMMON CARD (CF1-CF8)	.75	

*SINGLES: 1.5X TO 4X BASE CARD HI

❑ CF1 Geoff Bodine	.75	
❑ CF2 Dale Earnhardt	8.00	

Jeff Gordon	8.00	3.60
Ernie Irvan	4.00	1.80
Terry Labonte	4.00	1.80
Mark Martin	5.00	2.20
Jimmy Spencer	.75	.35
Rusty Wallace	5.00	2.20

995 Press Pass Cup Chase

i6-card insert set is a parallel of the first 36 cards in ıse Press Pass set. The cards feature a gold foil "Cup Chase" to differentiate the cards. This is the d year of the interactive game from Press Pass. The changed in 1995 and the collector could now n a Cup Chase card of not only the Winston Cup oion but the winner of five specific races throughout ar. The five races were the Daytona 500, Winston 500, Coca-Cola 600, Brickyard 400 and the MBNA you held a Cup Chase card for the winner of any of five races, you could redeem it for a special ism card of the 1994 winning driver of that specific If you had the Winston Cup Champion card (Jeff n), you could redeem that card for the entire set of ecial holoprism cards. Odds of finding a Cup Chase vas one per 24 packs. The winning cards could be ned until January 31, 1996.

	MINT	NRMT
LETE SET (36)	100.00	45.00
ION CARD (1-36)	2.50	1.10
y Allen Jr.	2.50	1.10
hn Andretti	2.50	1.10
ett Bodine	2.50	1.10
eoff Bodine	2.50	1.10
dd Bodine	2.50	1.10
ff Burton	5.00	2.20
ard Burton	2.50	1.10
errick Cope	2.50	1.10
le Earnhardt	25.00	11.00
Winner Card Expired		
eff Gordon Winner Card Expired	25.00	11.00
Steve Grissom	2.50	1.10
Bobby Hamilton	2.50	1.10
Ernie Irvan	2.50	1.10
Dale Jarrett	6.00	2.70
Bobby Labonte Winner Card Expired	10.00	4.50
Terry Labonte	8.00	3.60
Dave Marcis	5.00	2.20
Sterling Marlin Winner Card Expired	8.00	3.60
Mark Martin Winner Card Expired	12.00	5.50
Rick Mast	2.50	1.10
Ted Musgrave	2.50	1.10
Joe Nemechek	2.50	1.10
Kyle Petty	5.00	2.20
Ricky Rudd	5.00	2.20
Greg Sacks	2.50	1.10
Ken Schrader	2.50	1.10
Morgan Shepherd	2.50	1.10
Lake Speed	2.50	1.10
Jimmy Spencer	2.50	1.10
Hut Stricklin	2.50	1.10
Dick Trickle	2.50	1.10
Kenny Wallace	2.50	1.10

❑ 33 Mike Wallace	2.50	1.10
❑ 34 Rusty Wallace	8.00	3.60
❑ 35 Darrell Waltrip	5.00	2.20
❑ 36 Michael Waltrip	2.50	1.10

1995 Press Pass Cup Chase Redemption

This five-card insert set features the winning drivers of these 1994 races: the Daytona 500, Winston Select 500, Coca-Cola 600, Brickyard 400 and the MBNA 500. The cards were printed using holoprism technology and were made available two different ways. First, the cards were inserted as chiptoppers at a rate of one per hobby case. The cards were also the redemption prizes for the Cup Chase game winners.

	MINT	NRMT
COMPLETE SET (5)	120.00	55.00
COMMON CARD (CCR1-CCR5)	8.00	3.60
*SINGLES: 8X TO 20X BASE CARD HI		
❑ CCR1 Sterling Marlin	20.00	9.00
❑ CCR2 Dale Earnhardt	40.00	18.00
❑ CCR3 Jeff Gordon	40.00	18.00
❑ CCR4 Jeff Gordon	40.00	18.00
❑ CCR5 Rusty Wallace	25.00	11.00

1995 Press Pass Race Day

This 12-card insert set features winning drivers from the 1994 Winston Cup season. The cards use holofoil technology and were inserted at a rate of one per 24 packs.

	MINT	NRMT
COMPLETE SET (12)	80.00	36.00
COMMON CARD (RD1-RD12)	2.00	.90
*SINGLES: 4X TO 10X BASE CARD HI		
❑ RD1 Cover Card	6.00	2.70
❑ RD2 Geoff Bodine	2.00	.90
❑ RD3 Dale Earnhardt	20.00	9.00
❑ RD4 Jeff Gordon	20.00	9.00
❑ RD5 Ernie Irvan	4.00	1.80
❑ RD6 Dale Jarrett	8.00	3.60
❑ RD7 Terry Labonte	10.00	4.50
❑ RD8 Sterling Marlin	4.00	1.80
❑ RD9 Mark Martin	10.00	4.50
❑ RD10 Ricky Rudd	4.00	1.80
❑ RD11 Jimmy Spencer	2.00	.90
❑ RD12 Rusty Wallace	10.00	4.50

1995 Press Pass Premium

This 36-card set features the top 36 Winston Cup drivers. The first issue of the Premium brand by Press Pass was printed in a quantity of 18,000 boxes. The cards use gold foil stamping and are printed on 24-point stock. The cards came 3 per pack, 36 packs per box and 8 boxes per case.

	MINT	NRMT
COMPLETE SET (36)	20.00	9.00
COMMON CARD (1-36)	.30	.14
❑ 1 Dale Earnhardt	3.00	1.35
❑ 2 Mark Martin	1.50	.70
❑ 3 Rusty Wallace	1.50	.70
❑ 4 Ken Schrader	.30	.14

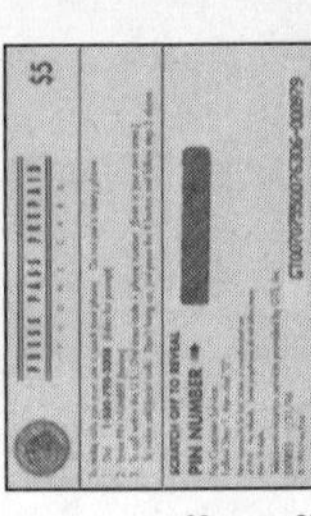

❑ 5 Ricky Rudd	.60	.25
❑ 6 Morgan Shepherd	.30	.14
❑ 7 Terry Labonte	1.50	.70
❑ 8 Jeff Gordon	3.00	1.35
❑ 9 Darrell Waltrip	.60	.25
❑ 10 Michael Waltrip	.30	.14
❑ 11 Ted Musgrave	.30	.14
❑ 12 Sterling Marlin	.60	.25
❑ 13 Kyle Petty	.60	.25
❑ 14 Dale Jarrett	1.25	.55
❑ 15 Geoff Bodine	.30	.14
❑ 16 Brett Bodine	.30	.14
❑ 17 Todd Bodine	.30	.14
❑ 18 Bobby Labonte	1.25	.55
❑ 19 Ernie Irvan	.60	.25
❑ 20 Richard Petty	.75	.35
❑ 21 Greg Sacks	.30	.14
❑ 22 Joe Nemechek	.30	.14
❑ 23 Steve Grissom	.30	.14
❑ 24 John Andretti	.30	.14
❑ 25 Ricky Craven	.30	.14
❑ 26 Steve Kinser	.30	.14
❑ 27 Robert Pressley	.30	.14
❑ 28 Randy LaJoie	.30	.14
❑ 29 Davy Jones	.30	.14
❑ 30 Mark Martin	1.50	.70
❑ 31 Rusty Wallace	1.50	.70
❑ 32 Ricky Rudd	.60	.25
❑ 33 Jeff Gordon	3.00	1.35
❑ 34 Kyle Petty	.60	.25
❑ 35 Ken Schrader	.30	.14
❑ 36 Sterling Marlin	.60	.25

1995 Press Pass Premium Holofoil

This 36-card set is a parallel to the base set. The cards feature holofoil printing technology and were inserted at a rate of one per pack.

	MINT	NRMT
COMPLETE SET (36)	40.00	18.00
COMMON CARD (1-36)	.75	.35
*HOLOFOIL STARS: 1X TO 2.5X BASIC CARDS		

1995 Press Pass Premium Red Hot

This 36-card set is a parallel of the base set. The cards are red foil stamped and inserted at a rate of one per nine packs.

	MINT	NRMT
COMPLETE SET (36)	150.00	70.00
COMMON CARD (1-36)	3.00	1.35
*RED HOTS STARS: 4X TO 10X BASIC CARDS		

1995 Press Pass Premium Hot Pursuit

This nine-card insert set features nine of the best drivers in Winston Cup. The cards use NitroKrome printing technology and were inserted at a rate of one per 18 packs.

	MINT	NRMT
COMPLETE SET (9)	80.00	36.00

COMMON CARD (HP1-HP9)	3.00	1.35
*SINGLES: 4X TO 10X BASE CARD HI		
❑ HP1 Geoff Bodine	3.00	1.35
❑ HP2 Dale Earnhardt	35.00	16.00
❑ HP3 Jeff Gordon	35.00	16.00
❑ HP4 Dale Jarrett	12.00	5.50
❑ HP5 Mark Martin	15.00	6.75
❑ HP6 Kyle Petty	6.00	2.70
❑ HP7 Ricky Rudd	6.00	2.70
❑ HP8 Ken Schrader	3.00	1.35
❑ HP9 Rusty Wallace	15.00	6.75

1995 Press Pass Premium Phone Cards

This 9-card set is the first phone card insert issued by Press Pass. The cards feature $5 worth of phone time and were inserted at the rate of one per 36 packs. There was also a parallel 9-card set of $50 phone cards. The odds of finding one of the $50 cards was one in 864 packs. Ken Schrader, Sterling Marlin and Geoff Bodine also had autographed versions of both $5 and $50 phone cards. The odds of finding a signed phone card was one every 216 packs. Finally there were 18 $1995 Jeff Gordon phone cards produced. All 18 of the cards were signed in a special white ink pen. Odds of finding one of the $1995 phone cards was one in 36,000 packs. The phone time expired 1/31/96.

	MINT	NRMT
COMPLETE 5.00 SET (9)	40.00	18.00
COMMON 5.00 CARD	1.50	.70
*AUTO. 5.00 CARDS: 2X TO 3X 5.00 CARDS		
COMPLETE 50.00 SET (9)	200.00	90.00
*50.00 PHONE CARDS: 2X TO 5X $5 CARDS		
*AUTO. 50.00 CARDS: 8X TO 12X $5 CARDS		
1995.00 JEFF GORDON AUTO	2000.00	900.00
❑ NNO Geoff Bodine	1.50	.70
❑ NNO Jeff Gordon	15.00	6.75
❑ NNO Dale Jarrett	6.00	2.70
❑ NNO Terry Labonte	8.00	3.60
❑ NNO Sterling Marlin	9.00	4.00
❑ NNO Mark Martin	8.00	3.60
❑ NNO Kyle Petty	9.00	4.00
❑ NNO Ken Schrader	1.50	.70
❑ NNO Michael Waltrip	1.50	.70

1996 Press Pass

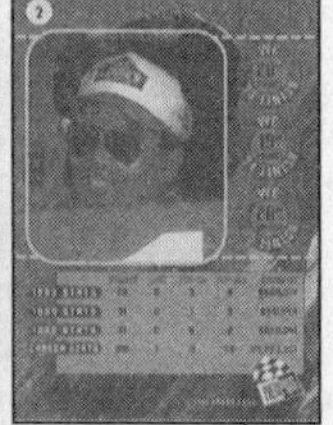

This 120-card set is the base brand from Press Pass. It features the best drivers in stock car racing. This is the first set to ever include each of NASCAR's Winston Cup Regional Series champions. The set is also the first to show many of the driver and sponsor changes for the 1996 season. The set features the following topical subsets: Winston Cup Drivers (1-36), Winston Cup Cars (37-54), Busch Grand National Drivers (55-63), SuperTrucks Drivers (64-72), Teamwork (73-81), Daytona Winner (82-90), Shattered (91-99), Champions (100-108), Winner's Circle (109-112) and '96 Preview (113-119). Hobby product was packaged eight cards per pack, 24 packs per box and 20 boxes per case. Also, included in Hobby only packs was a special Jeff Gordon Championship card. It pays tribute to the 1995 Winston Cup Champion. These cards are found one per 480 packs. Retail product was packed eight cards per pack, 36 packs per box and 20 boxes per case.

	MINT	NRMT
COMPLETE SET (120)	12.00	5.50
COMMON CARD (1-120)	.10	.05
COMMON DRIVER (1-120)	.20	.09
❑ 1 John Andretti	.20	.09
❑ 2 Brett Bodine	.20	.09
❑ 3 Geoff Bodine	.20	.09
❑ 4 Todd Bodine	.20	.09
❑ 5 Jeff Burton	.40	.18
❑ 6 Ward Burton	.20	.09
❑ 7 Derrike Cope	.20	.09
❑ 8 Ricky Craven	.20	.09
❑ 9 Dale Earnhardt	2.00	.90
❑ 10 Bill Elliott	1.00	.45
❑ 11 Jeff Gordon	2.00	.90
❑ 12 Steve Grissom	.20	.09
❑ 13 Bobby Hamilton	.20	.09
❑ 14 Ernie Irvan	.40	.18
❑ 15 Dale Jarrett	.75	.35
❑ 16 Bobby Labonte	.75	.35
❑ 17 Terry Labonte	1.00	.45
❑ 18 Dave Marcis	.40	.18
❑ 19 Sterling Marlin	.40	.18
❑ 20 Mark Martin	1.00	.45
❑ 21 Rick Mast	.20	.09
❑ 22 Jeremy Mayfield	.60	.25
❑ 23 Ted Musgrave	.20	.09
❑ 24 Joe Nemechek	.20	.09
❑ 25 Kyle Petty	.40	.18
❑ 26 Robert Pressley	.20	.09
❑ 27 Ricky Rudd	.40	.18
❑ 28 Ken Schrader	.20	.09
❑ 29 Morgan Shepherd	.20	.09
❑ 30 Lake Speed	.20	.09
❑ 31 Hut Stricklin	.20	.09
❑ 32 Dick Trickle	.20	.09
❑ 33 Mike Wallace	.20	.09
❑ 34 Rusty Wallace	1.00	.45
❑ 35 Darrell Waltrip	.40	.18
❑ 36 Michael Waltrip	.20	.09
❑ 37 Kyle Petty's Car	.20	.09
❑ 38 Jeff Gordon's Car	1.00	.45
❑ 39 Ted Musgrave's Car	.10	.05
❑ 40 Dale Earnhardt's Car	1.00	.45
❑ 41 Bobby Labonte's Car	.40	.18
❑ 42 Terry Labonte's Car	.50	.23
❑ 43 Sterling Marlin's Car	.20	.09
❑ 44 Ricky Craven's Car	.10	.05
❑ 45 Derrike Cope's Car	.10	.05
❑ 46 Bill Elliott's Car	.50	.23
❑ 47 Rusty Wallace's Car	.50	.23
❑ 48 Michael Waltrip's Car	.10	.05
❑ 49 Bobby Hamilton's Car	.10	.05
❑ 50 Dale Jarrett's Car	.40	.18
❑ 51 Ernie Irvan's Car	.20	.09
❑ 52 Ricky Rudd's Car	.20	.09
❑ 53 Mark Martin's Car	.50	.23
❑ 54 Darrell Waltrip's Car	.20	.09
❑ 55 Johnny Benson Jr.	.20	.09
❑ 56 Tim Fedewa	.20	.09
❑ 57 Jeff Fuller	.20	.09
❑ 58 Jeff Green	.20	.09
❑ 59 Jason Keller	.20	.09
❑ 60 Chad Little	.20	.09
❑ 61 Mike McLaughlin	.20	.09
❑ 62 Larry Pearson	.20	.09
❑ 63 Elton Sawyer	.20	.09
❑ 64 Mike Bliss	.20	.09
❑ 65 Rick Carelli	.20	.09
❑ 66 Ron Hornaday Jr.	.20	.09
❑ 67 Ernie Irvan	.40	.18
❑ 68 Butch Miller	.20	.09
❑ 69 Joe Ruttman	.20	.09
❑ 70 Bill Sedgwick	.20	.09
❑ 71 Mike Skinner	.20	.09
❑ 72 Bob Strait	.20	.09
❑ 73 Roger Penske TW	.20	.09
Don Miller		
Robin Pemberton		
Rusty Wallace TW		
❑ 74 Larry McClure TW	.20	
Tony Glover		
Sterling Marlin		
❑ 75 Rick Hendrick TW	.20	
Gary DeHart		
Terry Labonte		
❑ 76 Jack Roush TW	.20	
Steve Hmiel		
Mark Martin		
❑ 77 Joe Gibbs TW	.20	
Jimmy Makar		
Bobby Labonte		
❑ 78 Jeff Gordon TW	1.00	
Rick Hendrick		
Ray Evernham		
❑ 79 Robert Yates TW	.20	
Larry McReynolds		
Dale Jarrett		
❑ 80 Richard Petty TW	.40	
Robbie Loomis		
Bobby Hamilton		
❑ 81 Charles Hardy TW	.20	
Mike Beam		
Bill Elliott		
❑ 82 Bobby Allison DW	.20	
❑ 83 Geoff Bodine DW	.20	
❑ 84 Derrike Cope DW	.20	
❑ 85 Bill Elliott DW	.50	
❑ 86 Ernie Irvan DW	.20	
❑ 87 Dale Jarrett DW	.40	
❑ 88 Sterling Marlin DW	.20	
❑ 89 Richard Petty DW	.40	
❑ 90 Darrell Waltrip DW	.20	
❑ 91 Ricky Craven S	.20	
❑ 92 Bill Elliott S	.50	
❑ 93 Jeff Gordon S	1.00	
❑ 94 Bobby Labonte S	.40	
❑ 95 Sterling Marlin S	.20	
❑ 96 Mark Martin S	.50	
❑ 97 Kyle Petty S	.20	
❑ 98 Ricky Rudd S	.20	
❑ 99 Rusty Wallace S	.50	
❑ 100 Jeff Gordon WCC	1.00	
Brooke Gordon		
❑ 101 Andy Hillenburg	.20	
AACA Champion		
❑ 102 Jon Compagnone Jr.	.10	
Eastern Seaboard Champ		
❑ 103 Phil Warren	.10	
Mid-Atlantic Champion		
❑ 104 Jeff Wildung	.10	
Northwest Champion		
❑ 105 Mel Walen	.10	
Great Northern Champion		
❑ 106 Paul White	.10	
Sunbelt Champion		
❑ 107 Dale Planck	.10	
Mid-America Champion		
❑ 108 Ray Guss Jr.	.10	
Central Champion		
❑ 109 Unocal Race Stoppers WC	.10	
❑ 110 Bill Brodrick WC	.10	
❑ 111 Jeff Gordon WC	1.00	
Johnny Benson Jr.		
❑ 112 Bill Venturini WC	.10	
❑ 113 Johnny Benson PRE	.20	
❑ 114 David Green PRE	.20	
❑ 115 Dale Jarrett PRE	.40	
❑ 116 Mike McLaughlin PRE	.20	
❑ 117 Morgan Shepherd PRE	.20	
❑ 118 Michael Waltrip PRE	.20	
❑ 119 Rusty Wallace's Car PRE	.50	
❑ 120 Checklist Card	.10	
❑ 0 Jeff Gordon Championship	60.00	

1996 Press Pass Scorcher

The Scorchers sets is 120-card parallel version base set. Each card features red foil stampi differentiate them from the base cards. The car inserted in hobby packs at a rate of one per pack was also a retail 120-card set (Torquers) that is a p of the base set. Each of the Torquers features bl stamping to differentiate them from the base cards. cards are in retail packs at a rate of one per pack.

	MINT
COMPLETE SET (120)	40.00
COMMON CARD (1-120)	.30
COMMON DRIVER (1-120)	.60
*SCORCHERS: 2X TO 4X BASIC CARDS	

1996 Press Pass Torquer

This 120-card set is a parallel of the base set. Eac features blue foil stamping to differentiate them fr

:ards. The cards are in retail packs only at a rate of er pack.

	MINT	NRMT
ˈLETE SET (120)	40.00	18.00
ΛON CARD (1-120)	.30	.14
ΛON DRIVER (1-120)	.60	.25
QUERS: 1.25X TO 3X BASIC CARDS		

1996 Press Pass Burning Rubber

ɜeven-card set is the first to incorporate race used ment into trading cards. Press Pass took tires from ıg race cars in the 1995 season and had them cut ieces. These pieces were then attached to the cards ɒppear in this set. Each card is individually numbered) and the backs contain a certificate of authenticity. ards were inserted at a rate of one per 480 packs.

	MINT	NRMT
ˈLETE SET (7)	700.00	325.00
ΛON CARD (BR1-BR7)	60.00	27.00
Kyle Petty's Car	60.00	27.00
2 Jeff Gordon's Car	250.00	110.00
3 Dale Earnhardt's Car	250.00	110.00
4 Terry Labonte's Car	125.00	55.00
5 Sterling Marlin's Car	60.00	27.00
6 Bill Elliott's Car	125.00	55.00
7 Mark Martin's Car	125.00	55.00

1996 Press Pass Checkered Flags

ɜix-card set continues the insert theme started in . The cards feature some of the tops names in AR and were distributed in Wal-Mart only packs at a of 1:9 packs.

	MINT	NRMT
ˈLETE SET (6)	20.00	9.00
ΛON CARD (CF1-CF6)	1.50	.70
LES: 1.5X TO 4X BASE CARD HI		
Jeff Gordon	12.00	5.50
Bobby Labonte	2.00	.90
Terry Labonte	6.00	2.70
Sterling Marlin	1.50	.70
Mark Martin	6.00	2.70
Rusty Wallace	6.00	2.70

996 Press Pass Cup Chase

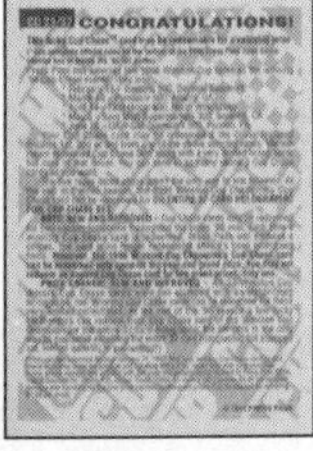

ɜ7-card set is the third year in a row for Press Pass' ctive game. This is the first year that you could n a Cup Chase driver's card for a prize if they finish top 3 in any one of the five selected races. The ctive races are the February 18th Daytona 500, 1 10th Purolator 500, April 14th First Union 400, ɜth Save Mart Supermarkets 300, and the June 16th GM Teamwork 500. The prize for having one of the ree finishers is a limited holographic foil card of that . There is also a Grand Prize awarded to those who n the 1996 Winston Cup Champion's Cup Chase t the end of the season. The Grand Prize is an entire rd holographic foil cup chase set. Prizes could be redeemed through January 31, 1997. The Cup Chase cards are seeded one per 24 packs.

	MINT	NRMT
COMPLETE SET (37)	120.00	55.00
COMMON CARD (1-37)	1.50	.70
*SINGLES: 4X TO 10X BASE CARD HI		
❑ 1 John Andretti	1.50	.70
❑ 2 Brett Bodine	1.50	.70
❑ 3 Geoff Bodine WIN	1.50	.70
❑ 4 Todd Bodine	1.50	.70
❑ 5 Jeff Burton	3.00	1.35
❑ 6 Ward Burton	1.50	.70
❑ 7 Derrike Cope	1.50	.70
❑ 8 Ricky Craven	1.50	.70
❑ 9 Dale Earnhardt WIN	25.00	11.00
❑ 10 Bill Elliott	6.00	2.70
❑ 11 Jeff Gordon WIN	25.00	11.00
❑ 12 Steve Grissom	1.50	.70
❑ 13 Bobby Hamilton	1.50	.70
❑ 14 Ernie Irvan	3.00	1.35
❑ 15 Dale Jarrett WIN	8.00	3.60
❑ 16 Bobby Labonte	4.00	1.80
❑ 17 Terry Labonte WIN	25.00	11.00
❑ 18 Dave Marcis	3.00	1.35
❑ 19 Sterling Marlin	3.00	1.35
❑ 20 Mark Martin WIN	8.00	3.60
❑ 21 Rick Mast	1.50	.70
❑ 22 Jeremy Mayfield	3.00	1.35
❑ 23 Ted Musgrave	1.50	.70
❑ 24 Joe Nemechek	1.50	.70
❑ 25 Kyle Petty	3.00	1.35
❑ 26 Robert Pressley	1.50	.70
❑ 27 Ricky Rudd WIN	3.00	1.35
❑ 28 Ken Schrader WIN	10.00	4.50
❑ 29 Morgan Shepherd	1.50	.70
❑ 30 Lake Speed	1.50	.70
❑ 31 Hut Stricklin	1.50	.70
❑ 32 Dick Trickle	1.50	.70
❑ 33 Mike Wallace	1.50	.70
❑ 34 Rusty Wallace WIN	8.00	3.60
❑ 35 Darrell Waltrip	3.00	1.35
❑ 36 Michael Waltrip	1.50	.70
❑ 37 Johnny Benson, Jr.	1.50	.70

1996 Press Pass Focused

This set is made up of ten of the top drivers in Winston Cup. Each card is produced on clear acetate stock. The cards were randomly seeded at a rate of one per 72 packs.

	MINT	NRMT
COMPLETE SET (10)	120.00	55.00
COMMON CARD (F1-F10)	6.00	2.70
*SINGLES: 6X TO 15X BASE CARD HI		
❑ F1 Dale Earnhardt	40.00	18.00
❑ F2 Bill Elliott	25.00	11.00
❑ F3 Jeff Gordon	40.00	18.00
❑ F4 Ernie Irvan	6.00	2.70
❑ F5 Terry Labonte	25.00	11.00
❑ F6 Sterling Marlin	6.00	2.70
❑ F7 Mark Martin	25.00	11.00
❑ F8 Kyle Petty	6.00	2.70
❑ F9 Ricky Rudd	6.00	2.70
❑ F10 Rusty Wallace	25.00	11.00

1996 Press Pass F.Q.S.

This 18-card set uses Nitrokrome technology to bring you nine of the fastest Winston Cup drivers and their cars. F.Q.S is an acronym for Fastest Qualifing Speed. Every driver's card number ends with the letter A, while each driver's car card number ends with the letter B. The cards were randomly inserted at a rate of one per 12 packs.

	MINT	NRMT
COMPLETE SET (18)	100.00	45.00
COMMON CAR (FQS1B-FQS9B)	1.25	.55
COM DRIVER (FQS1A-FQS9A)	2.50	1.10
*SINGLES: 2.5X TO 6X BASE CARD HI		
❑ FQS1A Dale Earnhardt	15.00	6.75
❑ FQS1B Dale Earnhardt's Car	6.00	2.70
❑ FQS2A Bill Elliott	8.00	3.60
❑ FQS2B Bill Elliott's Car	3.00	1.35
❑ FQS3A Jeff Gordon	15.00	6.75
❑ FQS3B Jeff Gordon's Car	6.00	2.70
❑ FQS4A Dale Jarrett	6.00	2.70
❑ FQS4B Dale Jarrett's Car	2.50	1.10
❑ FQS5A Bobby Labonte	6.00	2.70
❑ FQS5B Bobby Labonte's Car	2.50	1.10
❑ FQS6A Terry Labonte	8.00	3.60
❑ FQS6B Terry Labonte's Car	3.00	1.35
❑ FQS7A Sterling Marlin	2.50	1.10
❑ FQS7B Sterling Marlin's Car	1.25	.55
❑ FQS8A Mark Martin	8.00	3.60
❑ FQS8B Mark Martin's Car	3.00	1.35
❑ FQS9A Ricky Rudd	2.50	1.10
❑ FQS9B Ricky Rudd's Car	1.25	.55

1996 Press Pass/R & N China

This 26-card set was produced by R and N China. Each card is made out of porcelain and is a replica of a 1996 Press Pass card.

	MINT	NRMT
COMPLETE SET (26)	600.00	275.00
COMMON CARD	25.00	11.00
❑ 1 John Andretti	25.00	11.00
❑ 5 Jeff Burton	25.00	11.00
❑ 8 Ricky Craven	25.00	11.00
❑ 9 Dale Earnhardt	35.00	16.00
❑ 11 Jeff Gordon	35.00	16.00
❑ 13 Bobby Hamilton	25.00	11.00
❑ 14 Ernie Irvan	28.00	12.50
❑ 15 Dale Jarrett	28.00	12.50
❑ 16 Bobby Labonte	25.00	11.00
❑ 17 Terry Labonte	30.00	13.50
❑ 19 Sterling Marlin	25.00	11.00
❑ 20 Mark Martin	30.00	13.50
❑ 22 Jeremy Mayfield	25.00	11.00
❑ 23 Ted Musgrave	25.00	11.00
❑ 24 Joe Nemechek	25.00	11.00
❑ 25 Kyle Petty	25.00	11.00
❑ 28 Ken Schrader	25.00	11.00
❑ 34 Rusty Wallace	30.00	13.50
❑ 35 Darrell Waltrip	25.00	11.00
❑ 36 Michael Waltrip	25.00	11.00
❑ 38 Jeff Gordon's Car	30.00	13.50
❑ 42 Terry Labonte's Car	28.00	12.50
❑ 47 Rusty Wallace's Car	28.00	12.50
❑ 50 Dale Jarrett's Car	25.00	11.00
❑ 53 Mark Martin's Car	28.00	12.50
❑ 55 Johnny Benson	25.00	11.00

1996 Press Pass Premium

The 1996 Press Pass Premium set issued in one series totalling 45 cards. The cards came in three card packs with a holofoil card in every pack. The set contains the topical subsets: Premium Drivers (1-32) and Premium Cars (33-45).This extremely limited collection is highlighted by "Burning Rubber II", Press Pass' enhanced, second edition of its innovative race-used tire cards and valuable "Prime Time" phone cards worth $5, $10, $20 and an incredible $1,996 in phone time.

	MINT	NRMT
COMPLETE SET (45)	12.00	5.50
COMMON CARD (1-45)	.15	.07
COMMON DRIVER (1-45)	.30	.14

❑ 1 Jeff Gordon	3.00	1.35
❑ 2 Dale Earnhardt	3.00	1.35
❑ 3 Sterling Marlin	.60	.25
❑ 4 Mark Martin	1.50	.70
❑ 5 Rusty Wallace	1.50	.70
❑ 6 Terry Labonte	1.50	.70
❑ 7 Ted Musgrave	.30	.14
❑ 8 Bill Elliott	1.50	.70
❑ 9 Ricky Rudd	.60	.25
❑ 10 Bobby Labonte	1.25	.55
❑ 11 Morgan Shepherd	.30	.14
❑ 12 Michael Waltrip	.30	.14
❑ 13 Dale Jarrett	1.25	.55
❑ 14 Bobby Hamilton	.30	.14
❑ 15 Derrike Cope	.30	.14
❑ 16 Geoff Bodine	.30	.14
❑ 17 Ken Schrader	.30	.14
❑ 18 John Andretti	.30	.14
❑ 19 Darrell Waltrip	.60	.25
❑ 20 Brett Bodine	.30	.14
❑ 21 Ward Burton	.30	.14
❑ 22 Ricky Craven	.30	.14
❑ 23 Steve Grissom	.30	.14
❑ 24 Joe Nemechek	.30	.14
❑ 25 Robert Pressley	.30	.14
❑ 26 Kyle Petty	.60	.25
❑ 27 Jeremy Mayfield	1.00	.45
❑ 28 Jeff Burton	.60	.25
❑ 29 Ernie Irvan	.60	.25
❑ 30 Wally Dallenbach	.30	.14
❑ 31 Johnny Benson	.30	.14
❑ 32 Chad Little	.30	.14
❑ 33 Michael Waltrip's Car	.15	.07
❑ 34 Jeff Gordon's Car	1.50	.70
❑ 35 Dale Earnhardt's Car	1.50	.70
❑ 36 Bobby Labonte's Car	.60	.25
❑ 37 Terry Labonte's Car	.75	.35
❑ 38 Ricky Craven's Car	.15	.07
❑ 39 Bill Elliott's Car	.75	.35
❑ 40 Rusty Wallace's Car	.75	.35
❑ 41 Dale Jarrett's Car	.60	.25
❑ 42 Bobby Hamilton's Car	.15	.07
❑ 43 Ernie Irvan's Car	.30	.14
❑ 44 Ricky Rudd's Car	.30	.14
❑ 45 Mark Martin's Car Checklist	.75	.35

1996 Press Pass Premium Emerald Proofs

This 45-card set is a parallel to the base Press Pass Premium set. The card features emerald foil stamping and are individually numbered of 380. The cards were randomly inserted in packs at a rate of 1:36 packs.

	MINT	NRMT
COMPLETE SET (45)	400.00	180.00
COMMON CARD (1-45)	4.00	1.80
COMMON DRIVER (1-45)	8.00	3.60

*STARS: 10X TO 25X BASIC CARDS

1996 Press Pass Premium Holofoil

This 45-card set is a parallel of the base Press Pass Premium set. The cards feature a holofoil printing process that differentiate them from the base set. The holofoil cards were inserted one per pack.

	MINT	NRMT
COMPLETE SET (45)	30.00	13.50
COMMON CARD (1-45)	.30	.14
COMMON DRIVER (1-45)	.60	.25

*HOLOFOIL CARDS: .75X TO 2X BASIC CARDS

1996 Press Pass Premium $5 Phone Cards

Randomly inserted in packs at a rate of one in 36, this nine-card insert set features some of the best drivers in Winston Cup. Each card is worth $5 in phone time and carries an expiration of 4/30/97. There are two parallel versions of the $5 set, a $10 set and a $20 set. The cards are indentical except they carry $10 and $20 worth of phone time respectively. The $10 cards were randomly inserted in packs 1:216. The $20 cards were randomly inserted 1:864. There is also a $1,996 Mark Martin Phone Card. Any of the phone cards that have had the pin numbered scratched usually are worth .25X to .50X a mint phone card.

	MINT	NRMT
COMPLETE SET (9)	30.00	13.50
COMMON CARD (1-9)	1.50	.70
10.00 DOLLAR SET (9)	80.00	36.00
COMMON 10.00 DOLLAR CARD	4.00	1.80
*10.00 DOLLAR PHONE CARDS: 1X TO 2.5X $5 CARDS		
20.00 DOLLAR SET (9)	150.00	70.00
COMMON 20.00 DOLLAR CARD	10.00	4.50
*20.00 DOLLAR PHONE CARDS: 2.5X TO 5X $5 CARDS		
1,996 MARK MARTIN PHONE CARD	300.00	135.00

❑ 1 Johnny Benson	1.50	.70
❑ 2 Ricky Craven	1.50	.70
❑ 3 Bill Elliott	8.00	3.60
❑ 4 Dale Jarrett	6.00	2.70
❑ 5 Bobby Labonte	6.00	2.70
❑ 6 Sterling Marlin	3.00	1.35
❑ 7 Mark Martin	8.00	3.60
❑ 8 Kyle Petty	7.00	3.10
❑ 9 Michael Waltrip	1.50	.70

1996 Press Pass Premium Burning Rubber II

This seven-card set is the second edition of the race-used tire cards. The cards feature an actual tire look. There is an all-foil hub surrounded by the race-tire rubber. Tires from the 1996 Daytona race were acquired to use on the cards. The cards were inserted in both hobby and retail products. Cards BR1-BR4 could be found in hobby packs, while BR-5-BR7 could be found in retail packs. The odds of finding a Burning Rubber card were 1:288 packs.

	MINT	NRMT
COMPLETE SET (7)	800.00	350.00
COMMON CARD (BR1-BR7)	50.00	22.00

❑ BR1 Jeff Gordon	250.00	110.00
❑ BR2 Mark Martin	125.00	55.00
❑ BR3 Dale Jarrett	100.00	45.00
❑ BR4 Ken Schrader	50.00	22.00
❑ BR5 Dale Earnhardt	250.00	110.00
❑ BR6 Rusty Wallace	125.00	55.00
❑ BR7 Ernie Irvan	120.00	55.00

1996 Press Pass Premium Crystal Ball

Randomly inserted in packs at a rate of one in 18, this 12-card insert set uses die-cut printing to bring some of the top drivers into view. The cards uses a crystal ball design and feature the driver in the crystal ball with his name in script across the base.

	MINT	NRMT
COMPLETE SET (12)	100.00	45.00
COMMON CARD (CB1-CB12)	2.50	1.10

*SINGLES: 3X TO 8X BASE CARD HI

❑ CB1 Johnny Benson	2.50	
❑ CB2 Ricky Craven	2.50	
❑ CB3 Dale Earnhardt	30.00	
❑ CB4 Bill Elliott	15.00	
❑ CB5 Jeff Gordon	30.00	
❑ CB6 Ernie Irvan	5.00	
❑ CB7 Dale Jarrett	12.00	
❑ CB8 Bobby Labonte	8.00	
❑ CB9 Terry Labonte	15.00	
❑ CB10 Sterling Marlin	5.00	
❑ CB11 Mark Martin	15.00	
❑ CB12 Rusty Wallace	15.00	

1996 Press Pass Premium Hot Pursuit

Randomly inserted in packs at a rate of one in 18 nine-card insert set features Press Pass' NitroK printing technology. The cards feature the top nam Winston Cup racing.

	MINT	N
COMPLETE SET (9)	80.00	
COMMON CARD (HP1-HP9)	2.00	

*SINGLES: 2.5X TO 6X BASE CARD HI

❑ HP1 Dale Earnheardt UER Misspelled Earnheardt on the back	30.00	
❑ HP2 Bill Elliott	15.00	
❑ HP3 Jeff Gordon	30.00	
❑ HP4 Ernie Irvan	4.00	
❑ HP5 Bobby Labonte	8.00	
❑ HP6 Mark Martin	15.00	
❑ HP7 Ricky Rudd	4.00	
❑ HP8 Rusty Wallace	15.00	
❑ HP9 Michael Waltrip	2.00	

1997 Press Pass Autograph

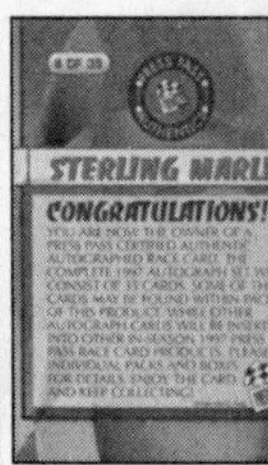

This 40-card set features autographed cards from th stars from the Winston Cup and Busch Circuits. cards were inserted in to three Press Pass prod ActionVision, Press Pass Premium, and VIP. The were randomly inserted in ActionVision packs at a ra 1:160, Press Pass Premuim packs at a ratio of 1:72 p and VIP packs at a ratio of 1:60 packs.

	MINT	N
COMPLETE SET (40)	1400.00	6
COMMON CARD (1-40)	10.00	
COMMON DRIVER (1-40)	20.00	

❑ 1 Terry Labonte ActionVision Press Pass Premuim VIP	80.00	
❑ 2 Jeff Gordon Actionvision Press Pass Premium VIP	250.00	1
❑ 3 Dale Jarrett ActionVision VIP	60.00	
❑ 4 Dale Earnhardt ActionVision Press Pass Premium	250.00	1

VIP		
teve Hmiel	10.00	4.50
Press Pass Premium		
VIP		
icky Rudd	40.00	18.00
ActionVision		
VIP		
usty Wallace	80.00	36.00
ActionVision		
VIP		
terling Marlin	40.00	18.00
ActionVision		
VIP		
obby Hamilton	20.00	9.00
Press Pass Premium		
VIP		
Bobby Labonte	60.00	27.00
Press Pass Premium		
VIP		
Ken Schrader	20.00	9.00
Press Pass Premium		
VIP		
Jeff Burton	40.00	18.00
ActionVision		
VIP		
Michael Waltrip	20.00	9.00
Press Pass Premium		
VIP		
Ted Musgrave	20.00	9.00
Press Pass Premium		
VIP		
Geoff Bodine	20.00	9.00
Press Pass Premium		
Ricky Craven	20.00	9.00
VIP		
Johnny Benson	20.00	9.00
Press Pass Premium		
Jeremy Mayfield	50.00	22.00
VIP		
Kyle Petty	40.00	18.00
ActionVision		
Press Pass Premium		
VIP		
Bill Elliott	80.00	36.00
ActionVision		
VIP		
Wood Brothers	10.00	4.50
VIP		
Joe Nemechek	20.00	9.00
Press Pass Premium		
Wally Dallenbach	20.00	9.00
Press Pass Premium		
Robby Gordon	20.00	9.00
Press Pass Premium		
VIP		
David Green	20.00	9.00
VIP		
ason Keller	20.00	9.00
Press Pass Premium		
VIP		
eff Green	20.00	9.00
Press Pass Premium		
VIP		
Robby Gordon	20.00	9.00
Jeff Green		
Mike Skinner		
VIP		
Mike McLaughlin	20.00	9.00
Press Pass Premium		
VIP		
Chad Little	20.00	9.00
VIP		
eff Fuller	20.00	9.00
Press Pass Premium		
VIP		
odd Bodine	20.00	9.00
Press Pass Premium		
VIP		
odney Combs	20.00	9.00
Press Pass Premium		
andy LaJoie	20.00	9.00
Press Pass Premium		
VIP		
ay Evernham	15.00	6.75
VIP		
arry McReynolds	10.00	4.50
Press Pass Premium		
ary DeHart	10.00	4.50
VIP		
Mike Beam	10.00	4.50
VIP		
arrell Waltrip	40.00	18.00
VIP		
Ward Burton	20.00	9.00
VIP		
Mike Skinner	20.00	9.00
VIP		

1997 Press Pass

The 1997 Press Pass set was issued in one series totalling 140 cards. The set contains the topical subsets: Winston Cup Drivers (1-30), Winston Cup Cars (31-45), SuperTruck Drivers (46-54), Japan Race (55-63), BGN Drivers (64-78), Back-to-Back (79-90), Highlights (91-109), Champions (110-120), '97 Preview (121-133), and 10 Wins (1334-138). The cards were distributed to both hobby and retail. The hobby product consisted of eight card packs, 24 packs per box and 20 boxes per case. The retail boxes consisted of eight card packs, 32 packs per box and 20 boxes per case. There are two insert cards priced at the bottom of the base set listing. One is the Jeff Gordon Sam Bass Top Flight card. The card was intended to be in the 1996 VIP Top Flight set but was inserted in '97 Press Pass packs at a rate of one in 480 packs. Also a special holofoil Terry Labonte Winston Cup Champion card could be found in packs at a rate of one in 480.

	MINT	NRMT
COMPLETE SET (140)	15.00	6.75
COMMON CARD (1-140)	.10	.05
COMMON DRIVER (1-140)	.20	.09
❑ 1 Terry Labonte	1.00	.45
❑ 2 Jeff Gordon	2.00	.90
❑ 3 Dale Jarrett	.75	.35
❑ 4 Dale Earnhardt	2.00	.90
❑ 5 Mark Martin	1.00	.45
❑ 6 Ricky Rudd	.40	.18
❑ 7 Rusty Wallace	1.00	.45
❑ 8 Sterling Marlin	.40	.18
❑ 9 Bobby Hamilton	.20	.09
❑ 10 Ernie Irvan	.40	.18
❑ 11 Bobby Labonte	.75	.35
❑ 12 Ken Schrader	.20	.09
❑ 13 Jeff Burton	.40	.18
❑ 14 Michael Waltrip	.20	.09
❑ 15 Ted Musgrave	.20	.09
❑ 16 Geoff Bodine	.20	.09
❑ 17 Rick Mast	.20	.09
❑ 18 Morgan Shepherd	.20	.09
❑ 19 Ricky Craven	.20	.09
❑ 20 Johnny Benson	.20	.09
❑ 21 Hut Stricklin	.20	.09
❑ 22 Jeremy Mayfield	.60	.25
❑ 23 Kyle Petty	.40	.18
❑ 24 Kenny Wallace	.20	.09
❑ 25 Darrell Waltrip	.40	.18
❑ 26 Bill Elliott	1.00	.45
❑ 27 Robert Pressley	.20	.09
❑ 28 Ward Burton	.20	.09
❑ 29 Joe Nemechek	.20	.09
❑ 30 Mike Skinner	.20	.09
❑ 31 Rusty Wallace's Car	.50	.23
❑ 32 Dale Earnhardt's Car	1.00	.45
❑ 33 Sterling Marlin's Car	.20	.09
❑ 34 Terry Labonte's Car	.50	.23
❑ 35 Mark Martin's Car	.50	.23
❑ 36 Ricky Rudd's Car	.20	.09
❑ 37 Bobby Labonte's Car	.40	.18
❑ 38 Michael Waltrip's Car	.10	.05
❑ 39 Jeff Gordon's Car	1.00	.45
❑ 40 Ernie Irvan's Car	.20	.09
❑ 41 Ricky Craven's Car	.10	.05
❑ 42 Kyle Petty's Car	.20	.09
❑ 43 Bobby Hamilton's Car	.10	.05
❑ 44 Dale Jarrett's Car	.40	.18
❑ 45 Bill Elliott's Car	.50	.23
❑ 46 Mike Bliss	.20	.09
❑ 47 Rick Carelli	.20	.09
❑ 48 Ron Hornaday	.20	.09
❑ 49 Butch Miller	.20	.09
❑ 50 Joe Ruttman	.20	.09
❑ 51 Bill Sedgwick	.20	.09
❑ 52 Mike Skinner	.20	.09
❑ 53 Rusty Wallace	1.00	.45
❑ 54 Darrell Waltrip	.40	.18
❑ 55 Johnny Benson's Car	.10	.05
❑ 56 Dale Earnhardt's Car	1.00	.45
❑ 57 Jeff Gordon's Car	1.00	.45
❑ 58 Ernie Irvan's Car	.20	.09
❑ 59 Dale Jarrett's Car	.40	.18
❑ 60 Terry Labonte's Car	.50	.23
❑ 61 Sterling Marlin's Car	.20	.09
❑ 62 Rusty Wallace's Car	.50	.23
❑ 63 Michael Waltrip's Car	.10	.05
❑ 64 Todd Bodine	.20	.09
❑ 65 Rodney Combs	.20	.09
❑ 66 Ricky Craven	.20	.09
❑ 67 Jeff Fuller	.20	.09
❑ 68 David Green	.20	.09
❑ 69 Jeff Green	.20	.09
❑ 70 Dale Jarrett	.75	.35
❑ 71 Jason Keller	.20	.09
❑ 72 Terry Labonte	1.00	.45
❑ 73 Randy LaJoie	.20	.09
❑ 74 Chad Little	.20	.09
❑ 75 Mark Martin	1.00	.45
❑ 76 Mike McLaughlin	.20	.09
❑ 77 Larry Pearson	.20	.09
❑ 78 Michael Waltrip	.20	.09
❑ 79 Michael Waltrip	.20	.09
❑ 80 Dale Jarrett	.75	.35
❑ 81 Bobby Labonte	.75	.35
❑ 82 Terry Labonte	1.00	.45
❑ 83 Ricky Craven	.20	.09
❑ 84 Rusty Wallace	1.00	.45
❑ 85 Ken Schrader	.20	.09
❑ 86 Mike Wallace	.20	.09
❑ 87 Jeremy Mayfield	.60	.25
❑ 88 Chad Little	.20	.09
❑ 89 Mark Martin	1.00	.45
❑ 90 Kenny Wallace	.20	.09
❑ 91 Robby Gordon	.20	.09
❑ 92 Jimmy Johnson	.10	.05
❑ 93 Michael Waltrip David Pearson	.20	.09
❑ 94 Dale Jarrett	.75	.35
❑ 95 Dale Earnhardt's Car	1.00	.45
❑ 96 Jeff Gordon Dale Jarrett's Cars	.75	.35
❑ 97 Terry Labonte Richard Petty	.40	.18
❑ 98 Sterling Marlin	.40	.18
❑ 99 Rusty Wallace's Car	.50	.23
❑ 100 Michael Waltrip	.20	.09
❑ 101 Ernie Irvan	.40	.18
❑ 102 Dale Jarrett	.75	.35
❑ 103 Geoff Bodine	.20	.09
❑ 104 Jeff Gordon's Car	1.00	.45
❑ 105 Jeff Gordon's Car	1.00	.45
❑ 106 Terry Labonte's Car	.50	.23
❑ 107 Ricky Rudd	.40	.18
❑ 108 Bobby Hamilton Richard Petty	.40	.18
❑ 109 Bobby Labonte	.75	.35
❑ 110 Terry Labonte	1.00	.45
❑ 111 Randy LaJoie	.20	.09
❑ 112 Mark Martin	1.00	.45
❑ 113 Ron Hornaday	.20	.09
❑ 114 Kelly Tanner	.20	.09
❑ 115 Joe Kosiski	.20	.09
❑ 116 Lyndon Amick	.20	.09
❑ 117 Dave Dion	.20	.09
❑ 118 Tony Hirschman	.20	.09
❑ 119 Chris Raudman	.10	.05
❑ 120 Mike Cope	.20	.09
❑ 121 Kyle Petty	.40	.18
❑ 122 Rusty Wallace's Car	.50	.23
❑ 123 Michael Waltrip	.20	.09
❑ 124 Dale Jarrett	.75	.35
❑ 125 Chad Little	.20	.09
❑ 126 Joe Nemechek	.20	.09
❑ 127 Steve Grissom	.20	.09
❑ 128 Robby Gordon	.20	.09
❑ 129 Mike Wallace	.20	.09
❑ 130 Bill Elliott's Car	.50	.23
❑ 131 Ken Schrader	.20	.09
❑ 132 Wally Dallenbach	.20	.09
❑ 133 Derrike Cope	.20	.09
❑ 134 Jeff Gordon W	1.00	.45
❑ 135 Jeff Gordon W	1.00	.45
❑ 136 Jeff Gordon W	1.00	.45
❑ 137 Jeff Gordon W	1.00	.45
❑ 138 Jeff Gordon W	1.00	.45
❑ 139 Checklist	.10	.05
❑ 140 Checklist	.10	.05
❑ SB1 Jeff Gordon - Sam Bass	75.00	34.00
❑ 0 Terry Labonte WC Champ	40.00	18.00

1997 Press Pass Lasers

This 140-card set is a parallel version of the base Press Pass set. The cards feature silver foil and were available only in hobby product. The cards were inserted one per pack.

	MINT	NRMT
COMPLETE SET (140)	50.00	22.00
COMMON CARD (1-140)	.30	.14
COMMON DRIVER (1-140)	.60	.25

*LASERS CARDS: 1.25X TO 3X BASIC CARDS

1997 Press Pass Oil Slicks

This 140-card set is the top end parallel version in the Press Pass product. The cards feature holographic foil and 100 of each card was produced. The Oil Slicks were only available in the hobby product at a rate of one in 36 packs.

	MINT	NRMT
COMPLETE SET (140)	600.00	275.00
COMMON CARD (1-140)	4.00	1.80
COMMON DRIVER (1-140)	8.00	3.60

*OIL SLICK CARDS: 15X TO 40X BASIC CARD

1997 Press Pass Torquers

This 140-card set is the retail only parallel version of the Press Pass base set. The cards feature blue foil stamping and were inserted in retail packs at a rate of one per pack.

	MINT	NRMT
COMPLETE SET (140)	50.00	22.00
COMMON CARD (1-140)	.30	.14
COMMON DRIVER (1-140)	.60	.25

TORQUERS CARDS: 2X TO X BASIC CARDS

1997 Press Pass Banquet Bound

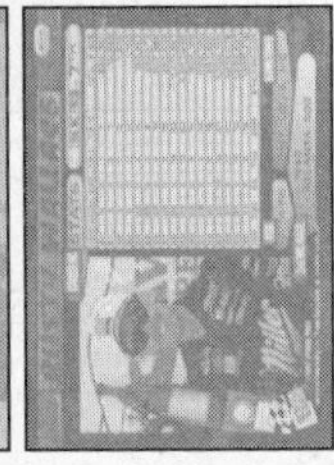

This 10-card insert set features the top drivers from 1996. The cards are printed on rainbow holofoil board and were inserted one in 12 packs.

	MINT	NRMT
COMPLETE SET (10)	40.00	18.00
COMMON CARD (BB1-BB10)	1.00	.45

*SINGLES: 2X TO 5X BASE CARD HI

	MINT	NRMT
❑ BB1 Terry Labonte	6.00	2.70
❑ BB2 Jeff Gordon	12.00	5.50
❑ BB3 Dale Jarrett	4.00	1.80
❑ BB4 Dale Earnhardt	12.00	5.50
❑ BB5 Mark Martin	6.00	2.70
❑ BB6 Ricky Rudd	2.00	.90
❑ BB7 Rusty Wallace	6.00	2.70
❑ BB8 Sterling Marlin	2.00	.90
❑ BB9 Bobby Hamilton	1.00	.45
❑ BB10 Ernie Irvan	2.00	.90

1997 Press Pass Burning Rubber

Authentic race-used tires from the top drivers are incorporated in this seven-card insert set. The cards feature an acetate, die-cut design with a photo of the driver in the center with a tire shaped piece of race used rubber surrounding it. The cards were seeded in packs at a rate of one in 480.

	MINT	NRMT
COMPLETE SET (7)	800.00	350.00
COMMON CARD (BR1-BR7)	50.00	22.00
❑ BR1 Rusty Wallace	120.00	55.00
❑ BR2 Dale Earnhardt	250.00	110.00
❑ BR3 Terry Labonte	120.00	55.00
❑ BR4 Michael Waltrip	50.00	22.00
❑ BR5 Jeff Gordon	250.00	110.00
❑ BR6 Ernie Irvan	80.00	36.00
❑ BR7 Dale Jarrett	80.00	36.00

1997 Press Pass Clear Cut

Randomly inserted in packs at a rate of one in 18, this 10-card set features drivers who won races in 1996. The cards feature a clear die-cut acetate design.

	MINT	NRMT
COMPLETE SET (10)	60.00	27.00
COMMON CARD (C1-C10)	1.50	.70

*SINGLES: 3X TO 8X BASE CARD HI

	MINT	NRMT
❑ C1 Dale Earnhardt	18.00	8.00
❑ C2 Jeff Gordon	18.00	8.00
❑ C3 Ernie Irvan	3.00	1.35
❑ C4 Dale Jarrett	8.00	3.60
❑ C5 Bobby Labonte	4.00	1.80
❑ C6 Terry Labonte	10.00	4.50
❑ C7 Mark Martin	10.00	4.50
❑ C8 Ricky Rudd	3.00	1.35
❑ C9 Rusty Wallace	10.00	4.50
❑ C10 Michael Waltrip	1.50	.70

1997 Press Pass Cup Chase

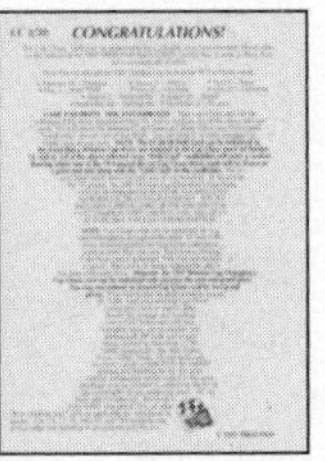

This was the fourth consecutive year of the popular Press Pass' interactive game. This year if the collector owned a Cup Chase card of one of the three top finishers from any one of the 10 selected Winston Cup race events, the card could be redeemed for a limited gold NitroKrome die-cut card of that driver. Card number CC 20 is a Field Card. In the event that a Winston Cup driver not featured in the Cup Chase set finishes 1st, 2nd, or 3rd at one of the 10 selected races, the Field Card can be redeemed. The prize for the Field Card is one of the 19 featured drivers gold NitroKrome die-cut cards drawn at random. At the end of the '97 season, the '97 Winston Cup Champion's Cup Chase card can be redeemed for the entire 20-card gold NitroKrome die-cut Cup Chase set. This set includeds a special card of the 1996 Winston Cup Champion Terry Labonte that is available only through this redemption. Each Cup Chase card can be redeemed for two uses throuhout the entire '97 season. Each time the card is redeemed Press Pass embossed one of the corners. After the card has been embossed twice it is no longer redeemable. The Cup Chase card of the '97 WC Champion can only be redeemed once. Deadline to claim prizes was January 31, 1998. The 10 eligible races are Feb.16 - Daytona, March 9- Atlanta, April 6 - Texas, May 4 - Sears Point, May 25 - Charlotte, June 22- California, August 2 - Indianapolis, August 23 - Bristol, September 28 - Martinsville, November 2 - Phoenix. There is also a die-cut parallel version of the 20 card set. The die-cut cards were inserted as chip toppers in each case.

	MINT	NRMT
COMPLETE SET (20)	120.00	55.00
COMMON CARD (CC1-CC20)	2.00	.90

*DC CARDS: 1X TO 2X WINNER CARDS
*DC CARDS: 1.5X TO 4X NON-WINNER CARDS

	MINT
❑ CC1 Johnny Benson	2.00
❑ CC2 Jeff Burton WIN	8.00
❑ CC3 Ward Burton	2.00
❑ CC4 Ricky Craven WIN	8.00
❑ CC5 Dale Earnhardt	20.00
❑ CC6 Bill Elliott	12.00
❑ CC7 Jeff Gordon WIN	20.00
❑ CC8 Bobby Hamilton WIN	6.00
❑ CC9 Ernie Irvan WIN	8.00
❑ CC10 Dale Jarrett WIN	10.00
❑ CC11 Bobby Labonte WIN	8.00
❑ CC12 Terry Labonte WIN	12.00
❑ CC13 Sterling Marlin	4.00
❑ CC14 Mark Martin WIN	12.00
❑ CC15 Kyle Petty	4.00
❑ CC16 Ricky Rudd	8.00
❑ CC17 Ken Schrader	2.00
❑ CC18 Rusty Wallace	12.00
❑ CC19 Michael Waltrip	2.00
❑ CC20 Field Card WIN	12.00

1997 Press Pass Victory La

Randomly inserted in packs at a rate of one in 18, th card set was divided with nine cards being driver nine cards being driver's cars. The cards are numb with an a or b extension after the number. All the A were shots of the driver while all the B cards were of their cars. The A cards were available in hobby and the B cards were available in retail packs.

	MINT
COMPLETE SET (18)	100.00
COMP.DRIVER SET (9)	75.00
COMP.CAR SET (9)	30.00
COMMON CAR (VL1B-VL9B)	.75
COMMON DRIVER (VL1A-VL9A)	1.50

*SINGLES: 3X TO 8X BASE CARD HI

	MINT
❑ VL1A Dale Earnhardt	20.00
❑ VL1B Dale Earnhardt's Car	7.50
❑ VL2A Jeff Gordon	20.00
❑ VL2B Jeff Gordon's Car	7.50
❑ VL3A Ernie Irvan	3.00
❑ VL3B Ernie Irvan's Car	1.50
❑ VL4A Dale Jarrett	8.00
❑ VL4B Dale Jarrett's Car	3.00
❑ VL5A Terry Labonte	10.00
❑ VL5B Terry Labonte's Car	4.00
❑ VL6A Sterling Marlin	3.00
❑ VL6B Sterling Marlin's Car	1.50
❑ VL7A Ricky Rudd	3.00
❑ VL7B Ricky Rudd's Car	1.50
❑ VL8A Rusty Wallace	10.00
❑ VL8B Rusty Wallace's Car	4.00
❑ VL9A Michael Waltrip	1.50
❑ VL9B Michael Waltrip's Car	.75

1997 Press Pass Premiu

The 1997 Press Pass Premium set was issued series totalling 45 cards. Cards were distributed in packs with 36 packs per box. The packs ca suggested retail price of $3.29.

	MINT
COMPLETE SET (45)	20.00
COMMON CARD (1-45)	.15
COMMON DRIVER (1-45)	.30

erry Labonte	1.50	.70
ff Gordon	3.00	1.35
ale Jarrett	1.25	.55
ale Earnhardt	3.00	1.35
ark Martin	1.50	.70
cky Rudd	.60	.25
usty Wallace	1.50	.70
erling Marlin	.60	.25
obby Hamilton	.30	.14
rnie Irvan	.60	.25
Bobby Labonte	1.25	.55
Ken Schrader	.30	.14
eff Burton	.60	.25
Michael Waltrip	.30	.14
ed Musgrave	.30	.14
Ricky Craven	.30	.14
ohnny Benson	.30	.14
Wally Dallenbach	.30	.14
eremy Mayfield	1.00	.45
Kyle Petty	.60	.25
Bill Elliott	1.50	.70
Ward Burton	.30	.14
oe Nemechek	.30	.14
Chad Little	.30	.14
Darrell Waltrip	.60	.25
Robby Gordon	.30	.14
Mike Skinner	.30	.14
Robby Gordon David Green		
Rusty Wallace's Car	.75	.35
Dale Earnhardt's Car	1.50	.70
erry Labonte's Car	.75	.35
Mark Martin's Car	.75	.35
Ricky Rudd's Car	.30	.14
eff Gordon's Car	1.50	.70
obby Hamilton's Car	.15	.07
ale Jarrett's Car	.60	.25
ill Elliott's Car	.75	.35
ill Elliott	1.50	.70
eff Gordon	3.00	1.35
rnie Irvan	.60	.25
ale Jarrett	1.25	.55
obby Labonte	1.25	.55
terling Marlin	.60	.25
Mark Martin	1.50	.70
Rusty Wallace	1.50	.70
hecklist	.15	.07

997 Press Pass Premium Emerald Proofs

-card set is a parallel to the base Press Pass m set. The cards features emerald foil stamping e individually numbered of 380. The cards were ly inserted in packs at a ratio of 1:45.

	MINT	NRMT
ETE SET (45)	500.00	220.00
ON CARD (1-45)	4.00	1.80
ON DRIVER (1-45)	8.00	3.60

ALD PROOF CARDS: 25X TO X BASIC CARDS

997 Press Pass Premium Mirrors

-card set is a parallel to the base Press Pass m set. The cards features a foil background. The vere randomly inserted in packs at a ratio of 1:1.

	MINT	NRMT
ETE SET (45)	40.00	18.00
ON CARD (1-45)	.30	.14
ON DRIVER (1-45)	.60	.25

997 Press Pass Premium Oil Slicks

-card set is a parallel to the base Press Pass m set. The cards features a rainbow foil Press Pass m logo and are individually numbered of 100. The vere randomly inserted in packs at a ratio of 1:96.

	MINT	NRMT
COMPLETE SET (45)	900.00	400.00
COMMON CARD (1-45)	6.00	2.70
COMMON DRIVER (1-45)	12.00	5.50

*OIL SLICKS: 15X TO 40X BASIC CARDS

1997 Press Pass Premium Crystal Ball

This 12-card insert set features some of the top names from NASCAR. The cards use a crystal ball design and feature the driver in the crystal ball with his name across the base. The cards were randomly inserted in packs at a ratio of 1:18.

	MINT	NRMT
COMPLETE SET (12)	80.00	36.00
COMMON CARD (CB1-CB12)	2.00	.90

*SINGLES: 2.5X TO 6X BASE CARD HI

❑ CB1 Ricky Craven	2.00	.90
❑ CB2 Dale Earnhardt's Car	15.00	6.75
❑ CB3 Bill Elliott	12.00	5.50
❑ CB4 Jeff Gordon	25.00	11.00
❑ CB5 Ernie Irvan	4.00	1.80
❑ CB6 Dale Jarrett	8.00	3.60
❑ CB7 Bobby Labonte	6.00	2.70
❑ CB8 Terry Labonte	12.00	5.50
❑ CB9 Sterling Marlin	4.00	1.80
❑ CB10 Mark Martin	12.00	5.50
❑ CB11 Ricky Rudd	4.00	1.80
❑ CB12 Rusty Wallace	12.00	5.50

1997 Press Pass Premium Crystal Ball Die-Cut

This 12-card insert set is a parallel of the standard Crystal Ball set. There cards are distinguished by their die-cut design.The cards use a crystal ball design and feature the driver in the crystal ball with his name across the base. The cards were randomly inserted in packs at a ratio of 1:36.

	MINT	NRMT
COMPLETE SET (12)	120.00	55.00
COMMON CARD (CB1-CB12)	3.00	1.35

*CRYSTAL BALL DIECUTS; .6X TO 1.5X BASIC CARDS
3.00...1.35

1997 Press Pass Premium Double Burners

This five-card insert set features pieces of race-used tire rubber and race-used driver uniforms on the same card. The piece of the driver's uniform appears on the front of the card while the piece of the driver's tire appears on the back. Cards that contain multi-colored pieces of cloth carry a 25% premium over those that do not. The cards were randomly inserted in packs at a ratio of 1:432 and are individually numnered of 350.

	MINT	NRMT
COMPLETE SET (5)	900.00	400.00
COMMON CARD (DB1-DB5)	75.00	34.00
❑ DB1 Dale Earnhardt	300.00	135.00
❑ DB2 Jeff Gordon	300.00	135.00
❑ DB3 Terry Labonte	150.00	70.00

❑ DB4 Rusty Wallace	150.00	70.00
❑ DB5 Michael Waltrip	75.00	34.00

1997 Press Pass Premium Lap Leaders

This 12-card insert set features cel cards that are printed on acetate. The cards are randomly inserted in packs at a ratio of 1:12.

	MINT	NRMT
COMPLETE SET (12)	50.00	22.00
COMMON CARD (LL1-LL12)	1.50	.70

*SINGLES: 2X TO 5X BASE CARD HI

❑ LL1 Dale Earnhardt	15.00	6.75
❑ LL2 Bill Elliott	8.00	3.60
❑ LL3 Jeff Gordon	15.00	6.75
❑ LL4 Ernie Irvan	3.00	1.35
❑ LL5 Dale Jarrett	6.00	2.70
❑ LL6 Bobby Labonte	6.00	2.70
❑ LL7 Terry Labonte	8.00	3.60
❑ LL8 Mark Martin	8.00	3.60
❑ LL9 Kyle Petty	3.00	1.35
❑ LL10 Ricky Rudd	3.00	1.35
❑ LL11 Rusty Wallace	8.00	3.60
❑ LL12 Michael Waltrip	1.50	.70

1998 Press Pass Gold Signings

This 9-card set is a partial parallel of the Press Pass signings set. Each driver signed 100 cards for this set. These cards were inserted into 1998 Press Pass Premium and into 1998 VIP. Insert ratios are not known at this time.

	MINT	NRMT
COMPLETE SET (9)	1000.00	450.00
COMMON CARD	25.00	11.00

❑ 1 Jeff Gordon Press Pass Premium VIP	300.00	135.00
❑ 2 Dale Jarrett Press Pass Premium VIP	100.00	45.00
❑ 3 Dale Earnhardt Press Pass Premium VIP	300.00	135.00
❑ 4 Terry Labonte Press Pass Premium VIP	125.00	55.00
❑ 10 Bobby Labonte VIP	75.00	34.00
❑ 12 Jeff Burton Press Pass Premium VIP	50.00	22.00
❑ 13 Michael Waltrip Press Pass Premium VIP	25.00	11.00
❑ 22 Bill Elliott Press Pass Premium VIP	125.00	55.00
❑ 40 Jimmy Spencer VIP	25.00	11.00

1998 Press Pass Signings

This 39-card set contains the autographs of the top drivers and crew chiefs on the Winston Cup and Busch circuits. These cards were inserted into 1998 Press Pass Premium, 1998 Press Pass Stealth and 1998 VIP. These cards were inserted into 1998 Press Pass Premium at a ratio of one per 48 packs, 1998 Press Pass Stealth at a ratio of one per 72 packs and 1998 VIP at a ratio of one per 60 packs.

	MINT	NRMT
COMPLETE SET (39)	1200.00	550.00
COMMON CARD (1-40)	8.00	3.60
COMMON DRIVER (1-40)	15.00	6.75
❑ 1 Jeff Gordon	175.00	80.00
Press Pass Premium		
Press Pass Stealth		
VIP		
❑ 2 Dale Jarrett	60.00	27.00
Press Pass Premium		
Press Pass Stealth		
VIP		
❑ 3 Dale Earnhardt	175.00	80.00
Press Pass Premium		
Press Pass Stealth		
VIP		
❑ 4 Terry Labonte	75.00	34.00
Press Pass Premium		
Press Pass Stealth		
VIP		
❑ 5 Ricky Rudd	30.00	13.50
Press Pass Premium		
Press Pass Stealth		
VIP		
❑ 6 John Andretti	15.00	6.75
Press Pass Stealth		
VIP		
❑ 7 Sterling Marlin	30.00	13.50
Press Pass Stealth		
VIP		
❑ 8 Bobby Hamilton	15.00	6.75
Press Pass Stealth		
VIP		
❑ 9 Ernie Irvan	30.00	13.50
Press Pass Stealth		
VIP		
❑ 10 Bobby Labonte	50.00	22.00
Press Pass Stealth		
VIP		
❑ 11 Ken Schrader	15.00	6.75
Press Pass Premium		
❑ 12 Jeff Burton	30.00	13.50
Press Pass Premium		
VIP		
❑ 13 Michael Waltrip	15.00	6.75
Press Pass Premium		
Press Pass Stealth		
❑ 14 Ted Musgrave	15.00	6.75
Press Pass Stealth		
VIP		
❑ 15 Geoff Bodine	15.00	6.75
Press Pass Stealth		
VIP		
❑ 16 Ward Burton	15.00	6.75
Press Pass Stealth		
VIP		
❑ 17 Ricky Craven	15.00	6.75
Press Pass Premium		
❑ 18 Johnny Benson	15.00	6.75
Press Pass Premium		
VIP		
❑ 20 Wally Dallenbach	15.00	6.75
VIP		
❑ 21 Tony Stewart	50.00	22.00
Press Pass Stealth		
❑ 22 Bill Elliott	75.00	34.00
Press Pass Premium		
Press Pass Stealth		
VIP		
❑ 23 Mike Skinner	15.00	6.75
Press Pass Premium		
Press Pass Stealth		
VIP		
❑ 24 David Green	15.00	6.75
Press Pass Premium		
❑ 25 Joe Nemechek	15.00	6.75
Press Pass Premium		
VIP		
❑ 26 Kenny Irwin	40.00	18.00
Press Pass Stealth		
❑ 27 Steve Park	50.00	22.00
Press Pass Premium		
Press Pass Stealth		
VIP		
❑ 28 Robin Pemberton	8.00	3.60
Press Pass Premium		
VIP		
❑ 29 Larry McReynolds	8.00	3.60
Press Pass Premium		
Press Pass Stealth		
VIP		
❑ 30 Jimmy Makar	8.00	3.60
Press Pass Premium		
VIP		
❑ 31 Ray Evernham	15.00	6.75
Press Pass Premium		
Press Pass Stealth		
VIP		
❑ 32 Todd Parrott	8.00	3.60
Press Pass Premium		
Press Pass Stealth		
VIP		
❑ 33 Randy Lajoie	15.00	6.75
Press Pass Premium		
VIP		
❑ 34 Robert Pressley	15.00	6.75
Press Pass Stealth		
VIP		
❑ 35 Tim Fedewa	15.00	6.75
Press Pass Premium		
VIP		
❑ 36 Kevin LePage	15.00	6.75
Press Pass Premium		
VIP		
❑ 37 Mike McLaughlin	15.00	6.75
Press Pass Stealth		
VIP		
❑ 38 Jason Keller	15.00	6.75
Press Pass Premium		
VIP		
❑ 39 Dale Earnhardt,Jr.	200.00	90.00
Press Pass Premium		
Press Pass Stealth		
VIP		
❑ 40 Jimmy Spencer	15.00	6.75
Press Pass Stealth		
VIP		

1998 Press Pass

The 1998 Press Pass set was issued in one series totalling 150 cards and was distributed in eight-card packs. The fronts feature color photos with silver-etched foil highlights. The set contains the topical subsets: NASCAR Winston Cup Drivers (1-27), NASCAR Winston Cup Cars (28-36), NASCAR Busch Series Drivers (37-49), NASCAR Craftsman Truck Series (50-54), 1998 NASCAR Winston Cup Previews (55-63), Teammates (64-81), Champions (82-93), NASCAR Winston Cup Crew Chiefs (94-100), and NASCAR's 50 Greatest Drivers of All-Time (101-150). A special all foil Jeff Gordon Winston Cup Champion card can be found in hobby packs at the rate of one in 480.

	MINT	NRMT
COMPLETE SET (150)	30.00	13.50
COMP. REGULAR SET (1-100)	15.00	6.75
COMP. RETRO SET (101-150)	15.00	6.75
COMMON CARD (1-100)	.10	.05
COMMON DRIVER (1-100)	.20	.09
COMMON CARD (101-150)	.25	.11
❑ 1 Jeff Gordon	2.00	.90
❑ 2 Mark Martin	1.00	.45
❑ 3 Dale Jarrett	.75	.35
❑ 4 Dale Earnhardt	2.00	.90
❑ 5 Terry Labonte	1.00	.45
❑ 6 Ricky Rudd	.40	.18
❑ 7 Rusty Wallace	1.00	.45
❑ 8 Sterling Marlin	.40	.18
❑ 9 Bobby Hamilton	.20	.09
❑ 10 Ernie Irvan	.40	.18
❑ 11 Bobby Labonte	.75	.35
❑ 12 Ken Schrader	.20	.09
❑ 13 Jeff Burton	.40	.18
❑ 14 Michael Waltrip	.20	.09
❑ 15 Ted Musgrave	.20	.09
❑ 16 Geoff Bodine	.20	.09
❑ 17 Ward Burton	.20	.09
❑ 18 Ricky Craven	.40	.18
❑ 19 Johnny Benson	.20	
❑ 20 Jeremy Mayfield	.60	
❑ 21 Kyle Petty	.40	
❑ 22 Darrell Waltrip	.40	
❑ 23 Bill Elliott	1.00	
❑ 24 Mike Skinner	.20	
❑ 25 David Green	.20	
❑ 26 Joe Nemechek	.20	
❑ 27 Wally Dallenbach	.20	
❑ 28 Rusty Wallace's Car	.40	
❑ 29 Dale Earnhardt's Car	1.00	
❑ 30 Terry Labonte's Car	.40	
❑ 31 Mark Martin's Car	.40	
❑ 32 Ricky Rudd's Car	.10	
❑ 33 Bobby Labonte's Car	.10	
❑ 34 Jeff Gordon's Car	1.00	
❑ 35 Dale Jarrett's Car	.40	
❑ 36 Bill Elliott's Car	.40	
❑ 37 Randy LaJoie	.20	
❑ 38 Todd Bodine	.20	
❑ 39 Tim Fedewa	.20	
❑ 40 Kevin LePage	.20	
❑ 41 Mark Martin	1.00	
❑ 42 Mike McLaughlin	.20	
❑ 43 Jason Keller	.20	
❑ 44 Steve Park	.75	
❑ 45 Dale Jarrett	.75	
❑ 46 Dale Earnhardt,Jr.	4.00	
❑ 47 Ricky Craven	.40	
❑ 48 Elliott Sadler	.40	
❑ 49 Hermie Sadler	.20	
❑ 50 Rich Bickle	.20	
❑ 51 Jack Sprague	.20	
❑ 52 Joe Ruttman	.20	
❑ 53 Mike Bliss	.20	
❑ 54 Ron Hornaday	.20	
❑ 55 Ernie Irvan	.40	
❑ 56 Kenny Irwin	.40	
❑ 57 Sterling Marlin	.40	
❑ 58 Steve Park	.40	
❑ 59 Johnny Benson	.20	
❑ 60 Todd Bodine	.20	
❑ 61 Bobby Hamilton	.20	
❑ 62 Ted Musgrave	.20	
❑ 63 Jimmy Spencer	.20	
❑ 64 Darren Jolly	.10	
❑ 65 Jeff Knight	.10	
❑ 66 Barry Muse	.10	
❑ 67 Mike Belden	.10	
❑ 68 Mike Trower	.10	
❑ 69 Chris Anderson	.10	
❑ 70 Patrick Donahue	.10	
❑ 71 Brian Whitesell	.10	
❑ 72 Ray Evernham	.10	
❑ 73 J.J. Clodfelter	.10	
❑ 74 Ben Leslie	.10	
❑ 75 Dennis Ritchie	.10	
❑ 76 Mitch Williams	.10	
❑ 77 Lonnie Dubay	.10	
❑ 78 Luke Shimp	.10	
❑ 79 Butch Hylton	.10	
❑ 80 Steve Spahr	.10	
❑ 81 Jimmy Fennig	.10	
❑ 82 Randy LaJoie	.20	
❑ 83 Jack Sprague	.20	
❑ 84 Mike Stefanik	.20	
❑ 85 Butch Gilliland	.20	
❑ 86 Mike Swaim Jr.	.20	
❑ 87 Hal Goodson	.20	
❑ 88 Bryan Germone	.20	
❑ 89 Joe Kosiski	.20	
❑ 90 Kelly Tanner	.20	
❑ 91 Gary Scelzi	.20	
❑ 92 Mark Martin IROC	.50	
❑ 93 Andy Green	.10	
❑ 94 Jimmy Makar	.10	
❑ 95 Ray Evernham	.10	
❑ 96 Jimmy Fennig	.10	
❑ 97 Larry McReynolds	.10	
❑ 98 Todd Parrott	.10	
❑ 99 Robin Pemberton	.10	
❑ 100 1998 NASCAR Winston Cup Schedule CL	.10	
❑ 101 Jeff Gordon RET	3.00	
❑ 102 Mark Martin RET	1.50	
❑ 103 Dale Jarrett RET	1.25	
❑ 104 Dale Earnhardt RET	3.00	
❑ 105 Rusty Wallace RET	1.50	
❑ 106 Ricky Rudd RET	.50	
❑ 107 Bill Elliott RET	1.50	
❑ 108 Terry Labonte RET	1.50	
❑ 109 Ralph Earnhardt RET	.50	
❑ 110 Richie Evans RET	.25	
❑ 111 Red Farmer RET	.25	
❑ 112 Ray Hendrick RET	.25	
❑ 113 Darrell Waltrip RET	.50	
❑ 114 Tiny Lund RET	.25	
❑ 115 Jerry Cook RET	.25	

Geoff Bodine RET	.25	.11
Bob Welborn RET	.25	.11
Fred Lorenzen RET	.50	.23
Herb Thomas RET	.25	.11
Tim Flock RET	.50	.23
Lee Petty RET	.50	.23
Buck Baker RET	.25	.11
Rex White RET	.25	.11
Ned Jarrett RET	.50	.23
Benny Parsons RET	.50	.23
Joe Weatherly RET	.25	.11
David Pearson RET	.50	.23
Bobby Isaac RET	.25	.11
Tim Richmond RET	.50	.23
Curtis Turner RET	.25	.11
Alan Kulwicki RET	.60	.25
Bobby Allison RET	.50	.23
Cale Yarborough RET	.50	.23
Richard Petty RET	.60	.25
Davey Allison RET	.60	.25
Glen Wood RET	.25	.11
Harry Gant RET	.50	.23
Junior Johnson RET	.50	.23
Fireball Roberts RET	.50	.23
Neil Bonnett RET	.60	.25
LeeRoy Yarborough RET	.25	.11
Buddy Baker RET	.25	.11
A.J. Foyt RET	.50	.23
Red Byron RET	.25	.11
Cotton Owens RET	.25	.11
Hershel McGriff RET	.25	.11
Marvin Panch RET	.25	.11
Jack Ingram RET	.25	.11
Marshall Teague RET	.25	.11
Ernie Irvan CL	.25	.11
ff Gordon 1997 Champion	75.00	34.00

998 Press Pass Oil Slicks

mly inserted in hobby packs only at the rate of one this 100-card set is a partial parallel version of the set with an all new custom made foil and typography n. Only 100 of each card were produced and are dually numbered.

	MINT	NRMT
ION CARD (1-100)	4.00	1.80
ION DRIVER (1-100)	8.00	3.60

998 Press Pass Autographs

mly inserted in hobby packs at the rate of one in his 14-card set features autographed color photos NASCAR drivers. Only 200 of each card were ced and are individually numbered.

	MINT	NRMT
LETE SET (14)	800.00	
ION CARD (1-14)	15.00	6.75
ale Earnhardt	250.00	110.00
ff Gordon	250.00	110.00
ale Jarrett	75.00	34.00
erry Labonte	100.00	45.00
ark Martin	100.00	45.00
obby Labonte	80.00	36.00
ff Burton	30.00	13.50
usty Wallace	100.00	45.00
ichael Waltrip	15.00	6.75
Ricky Craven	15.00	6.75
Ricky Rudd	30.00	13.50
Mike Skinner	15.00	6.75
Darrell Waltrip	30.00	13.50
ohnny Benson	15.00	6.75

998 Press Pass Cup Chase

as the fifth consecutive year of the popular Press nteractive game. This year if the collector owned a hase card of one of the three top finishers from any the 11 selected Winston Cup race events, the card be redeemed for a all-foil embossed die-cut card f that driver. Card number CC 20 is a Field Card. In ent that a Winston Cup driver not featured in the

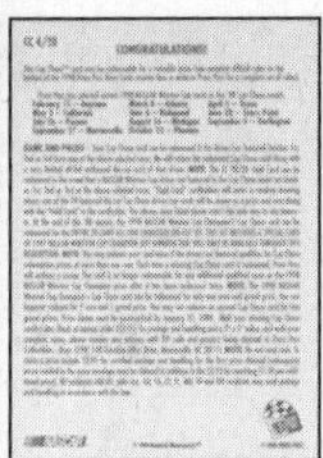

Cup Chase set finishes 1st, 2nd, or 3rd at one of the 11 selected races, the Field Card can be redeemed. The prize for the Field Card is one of the 19 featured drivers die-cut cards drawn at random. At the end of the '98 season, the '98 Winston Cup Champion's Cup Chase card can be redeemed for a special 20-card Cup Chase set. Each Cup Chase card can be redeemed for two uses throuhout the entire '98 season. Each time the card is redeemed Press Pass embossed one of the corners. After the card has been embossed twice it is no longer redeemable. The Cup Chase card of the '97 WC Champion can only be redeemed once. Deadline to claim prizes is January 31, 1999. The 11 eligible races are February 15 - Daytona, March 8- Atlanta, April 5 - Texas, May 3 - California, June 6 - Richmond, June 28 - Sears Point, July 26 - Pocono, August 16 - Michigan, September 6 - Darlington, September 27 - Martinsville, October 25 - Phoenix.

	MINT	NRMT
COMPLETE SET (20)	200.00	90.00
COMMON CARD (CC1-CC20)	5.00	2.20
❑ CC1 Johnny Benson	5.00	2.20
❑ CC2 Jeff Burton WIN 2	8.00	3.60
❑ CC3 Ward Burton	5.00	2.20
❑ CC4 Ricky Craven	8.00	3.60
❑ CC5 Dale Earnhardt's Car WIN 2	30.00	13.50
❑ CC6 Bill Elliott	25.00	11.00
❑ CC7 Jeff Gordon WIN 2 CHAMP	40.00	18.00
❑ CC8 Bobby Hamilton WIN	10.00	4.50
❑ CC9 Ernie Irvan	8.00	3.60
❑ CC10 Dale Jarrett WIN 2	30.00	13.50
❑ CC11 Bobby Labonte WIN 2	20.00	9.00
❑ CC12 Terry Labonte WIN 2	30.00	13.50
❑ CC13 Sterling Marlin	8.00	3.60
❑ CC14 Mark Martin WIN 2	30.00	13.50
❑ CC15 Kyle Petty	8.00	3.60
❑ CC16 Ricky Rudd WIN	10.00	4.50
❑ CC17 Ken Schrader	5.00	2.20
❑ CC18 Rusty Wallace WIN 2	25.00	11.00
❑ CC19 Michael Waltrip	5.00	2.20
❑ CC20 Field Card WIN 2	20.00	9.00

1998 Press Pass Oil Cans

Randomly inserted in packs at the rate of one in 18, this nine-card set features color photos of top NASCAR Winston Cup drivers on all foil embossed cards.

	MINT	NRMT
COMPLETE SET (9)	60.00	27.00
COMMON CARD (OC1-OC9)	4.00	1.80
*SINGLES: 4X TO 10X BASE CARD HI		
❑ OC1 Jeff Burton	4.00	1.80
❑ OC2 Dale Earnhardt's Car	15.00	6.75
❑ OC3 Jeff Gordon	20.00	9.00
❑ OC4 Dale Jarrett	10.00	4.50
❑ OC5 Bobby Labonte	4.00	1.80
❑ OC6 Terry Labonte	12.00	5.50
❑ OC7 Mark Martin	12.00	5.50
❑ OC8 Ricky Rudd	4.00	1.80
❑ OC9 Rusty Wallace	12.00	5.50

1998 Press Pass Pit Stop

Randomly inserted in packs at the rate of one in 12, this 18-card set features color photos of the hottest teams as

they make their record pit stops printed on die-cut cards with intricate foil stamping.

	MINT	NRMT
COMPLETE SET (18)	60.00	27.00
COMMON CARD (PS1-PS18)	1.50	.70
*SINGLES: 2.5X TO 6X BASE CARD HI		
❑ PS1 Rusty Wallace's Car	10.00	4.50
❑ PS2 Dale Earnhardt's Car	18.00	8.00
❑ PS3 Sterling Marlin's Car	3.00	1.35
❑ PS4 Terry Labonte's Car	10.00	4.50
❑ PS5 Mark Martin's Car	10.00	4.50
❑ PS6 Ricky Rudd's Car	3.00	1.35
❑ PS7 Ted Musgrave's Car	1.50	.70
❑ PS8 Darrell Waltrip's Car	3.00	1.35
❑ PS9 Bobby Labonte's Car	4.00	1.80
❑ PS10 Michael Waltrip's Car	1.50	.70
❑ PS11 Ward Burton's Car	1.50	.70
❑ PS12 Jeff Gordon's Car	18.00	8.00
❑ PS13 Kenny Irwin's Car	1.50	.70
❑ PS14 John Andretti's Car	1.50	.70
❑ PS15 Kyle Petty's Car	3.00	1.35
❑ PS16 Dale Jarrett's Car	8.00	3.60
❑ PS17 Bill Elliott's Car	10.00	4.50
❑ PS18 Jeff Burton's Car	3.00	1.35

1998 Press Pass Shockers

Randomly inserted in hobby packs only at the rate of one in 12, this 15-card set features color photos of the best NASCAR Winston Cup drivers printed on extra thick die-cut cards.

	MINT	NRMT
COMPLETE SET (15)	100.00	45.00
COMMON CARD (ST1A-ST15A)	2.50	1.10
*SINGLES: 5X TO 12X BASE CARD HI		
❑ ST1A Terry Labonte	15.00	6.75
❑ ST2A Jeff Gordon	25.00	11.00
❑ ST3A Dale Earnhardt	25.00	11.00
❑ ST4A Dale Jarrett	12.00	5.50
❑ ST5A Mark Martin	15.00	6.75
❑ ST6A Ricky Rudd	5.00	2.20
❑ ST7A Rusty Wallace	15.00	6.75
❑ ST8A Bill Elliott	15.00	6.75
❑ ST9A Bobby Labonte	6.00	2.70
❑ ST10A Kyle Petty	5.00	2.20
❑ ST11A Jeff Burton	5.00	2.20
❑ ST12A Michael Waltrip	2.50	1.10
❑ ST13A Ted Musgrave	2.50	1.10
❑ ST14A Mike Skinner	2.50	1.10
❑ ST15A Ward Burton	2.50	1.10

1998 Press Pass Torpedoes

Randomly inserted in packs at the rate of one in 12, this 15-card set features color photos of the hot cars of the best NASCAR Winston Cup drivers printed on extra thick die-cut cards.

	MINT	NRMT
COMPLETE SET (15)	50.00	22.00
COMMON CARD (ST1B-ST15B)	1.50	.70
*SINGLES: 2.5X TO 6X BASE CARD HI		
❑ ST1B Terry Labonte's Car	8.00	3.60
❑ ST2B Jeff Gordon's Car	15.00	6.75
❑ ST3B Dale Earnhardt's Car	15.00	6.75
❑ ST4B Dale Jarrett's Car	6.00	2.70

❑ ST5B Mark Martin's Car	8.00	3.60
❑ ST6B Ricky Rudd's Car	1.50	.70
❑ ST7B Rusty Wallace's Car	8.00	3.60
❑ ST8B Bill Elliott's Car	8.00	3.60
❑ ST9B Bobby Labonte's Car	6.00	2.70
❑ ST10B Kyle Petty's Car	1.50	.70
❑ ST11B Jeff Burton's Car	1.50	.70
❑ ST12B Michael Waltrip's Car	1.50	.70
❑ ST13B Ted Musgrave's Car	1.50	.70
❑ ST14B Mike Skinner's Car	1.50	.70
❑ ST15B Ward Burton's Car	1.50	.70

1998 Press Pass Triple Gear "3 in 1" Redemption

This nine-card set features actual pieces of race-used tires, firesuits and sheet metal from the pictured driver's car. 33 redemption cards for each driver was produced. 11 cards for each driver were inserted in the following products: 1998 Press Pass, 1998 Press Pass Premium, and 1998 VIP.

	MINT	NRMT
COMPLETE SET (9)	4500.00	
COMMON CARD (STG1-STG9)	150.00	70.00
❑ STG1 Rusty Wallace	500.00	220.00
❑ STG2 Dale Earnhardt	800.00	350.00
❑ STG3 Terry Labonte	500.00	220.00
❑ STG4 Mark Martin	500.00	220.00
❑ STG5 Bobby Labonte	350.00	160.00
❑ STG6 Jeff Gordon	800.00	350.00
❑ STG7 Mike Skinner	125.00	55.00
❑ STG8 Dale Jarrett	400.00	180.00
❑ STG9 Jeff Burton	300.00	135.00

1998 Press Pass Triple Gear "Burning Rubber"

Randomly inserted in packs at the rate of one in 480, this nine-card set features actual pieces of race-used tires from NASCAR Winston Cup's top drivers. Each card is individually numbered to 250.

	MINT	NRMT
COMPLETE SET (9)	900.00	400.00
COMMON CARD (TG1-TG9)	50.00	22.00
❑ TG1 Rusty Wallace	120.00	55.00
❑ TG2 Dale Earnhardt	225.00	100.00
❑ TG3 Terry Labonte	120.00	55.00
❑ TG4 Mark Martin	120.00	55.00
❑ TG5 Bobby Labonte	100.00	45.00
❑ TG6 Jeff Gordon	225.00	100.00
❑ TG7 Mike Skinner	50.00	22.00
❑ TG8 Dale Jarrett	100.00	45.00
❑ TG9 Jeff Burton	75.00	34.00

1998 Press Pass Premium

The 1998 Press Pass Premium set was issued in one series totalling 54 cards. The 3-card packs retail for $3.49 each. The set contains the topical subsets: NASCAR Busch Series (1-13), NASCAR Winston Cup Cars (14-27), and NASCAR Winston Cup Drivers (28-53).

	MINT	NRMT
COMPLETE SET (54)	30.00	13.50

COMMON CARD (1-54)	.20	.09
COMMON DRIVER (1-54)	.40	.18
❑ 1 Randy LaJoie	.40	.18
❑ 2 Tim Fedewa	.40	.18
❑ 3 Mike McLaughlin	.40	.18
❑ 4 Elliott Sadler	.40	.18
❑ 5 Tony Stewart	2.50	1.10
❑ 6 Jeff Burton	.75	.35
❑ 7 Michael Waltrip	.40	.18
❑ 8 Dale Jarrett	1.50	.70
❑ 9 Mark Martin	2.00	.90
❑ 10 Jason Keller	.40	.18
❑ 11 Hermie Sadler	.40	.18
❑ 12 Dale Earnhardt,Jr.	5.00	2.20
❑ 13 Joe Nemechek	.40	.18
❑ 14 Rusty Wallace's Car	1.00	.45
❑ 15 Dale Earnhardt's Car	2.00	.90
❑ 16 Bobby Hamilton's Car	.20	.09
❑ 17 Terry Labonte's Car	1.00	.45
❑ 18 Mark Martin's Car	1.00	.45
❑ 19 Ricky Rudd's Car	.40	.18
❑ 20 Bobby Labonte's Car	.75	.35
❑ 21 Jeff Gordon's Car	2.00	.90
❑ 22 Johnny Benson's Car	.20	.09
❑ 23 Kenny Irwin's Car	.60	.25
❑ 24 John Andretti's Car	.20	.09
❑ 25 Dale Jarrett's Car	.75	.35
❑ 26 Bill Elliott's Car	1.00	.45
❑ 27 Jeff Burton's Car	.40	.18
❑ 28 Jeff Gordon	4.00	1.80
❑ 29 Dale Jarrett	1.50	.70
❑ 30 Mark Martin	2.00	.90
❑ 31 Jeff Burton	.75	.35
❑ 32 Dale Earnhardt	4.00	1.80
❑ 33 Terry Labonte	2.00	.90
❑ 34 Bobby Labonte	1.50	.70
❑ 35 Bill Elliott	2.00	.90
❑ 36 Rusty Wallace	2.00	.90
❑ 37 Ken Schrader	.40	.18
❑ 38 Johnny Benson	.40	.18
❑ 39 Ted Musgrave	.40	.18
❑ 40 Jeremy Mayfield	1.25	.55
❑ 41 Ernie Irvan	.75	.35
❑ 42 John Andretti	.40	.18
❑ 43 Bobby Hamilton	.40	.18
❑ 44 Ricky Rudd	.75	.35
❑ 45 Michael Waltrip	.40	.18
❑ 46 Ricky Craven	.40	.18
❑ 47 Jimmy Spencer	.40	.18
❑ 48 Geoff Bodine	.40	.18
❑ 49 Ward Burton	.40	.18
❑ 50 Sterling Marlin	.75	.35
❑ 51 Todd Bodine	.40	.18
❑ 52 Joe Nemechek	.40	.18
❑ 53 Mike Skinner	.40	.18
❑ 54 Kenny Irwin CL	.75	.35
❑ 0 Dale Earnhardt Daytona	100.00	45.00

1998 Press Pass Premium Reflectors

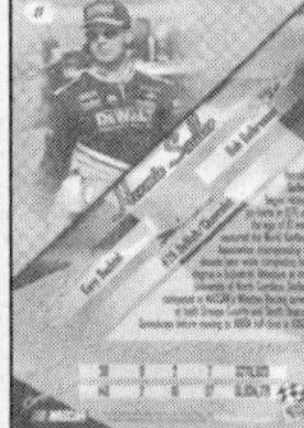

This 54-card set is a parallel of regular base set. These cards were randomly inserted at a ratio of one in 8 packs.

	MINT	NRMT
COMPLETE SET (54)	150.00	70.00
COMMON CARD (1-54)	1.00	
COMMON DRIVER (1-54)	2.00	

1998 Press Pass Premium Flag Chasers

Randomly inserted in packs at a rate of one in 2, thi card insert set features multi-dimensional all-foil, di cards with intricate micro-etching of the top NAS Winston Cup drivers and cars.

	MINT	N
COMPLETE SET (27)	40.00	
COMMON CARD (FC1-FC27)	.75	
*SINGLES: .75X TO 2X BASE CARD HI		
❑ FC1 Jeff Gordon	8.00	
❑ FC2 Steve Park	3.00	
❑ FC3 Dale Jarrett	3.00	
❑ FC4 Mark Martin	4.00	
❑ FC5 Jeff Burton	.75	
❑ FC6 Rusty Wallace	4.00	
❑ FC7 Ricky Rudd	.75	
❑ FC8 Terry Labonte	4.00	
❑ FC9 Bobby Labonte	3.00	
❑ FC10 Ernie Irvan	.75	
❑ FC11 Johnny Benson	.75	
❑ FC12 Michael Waltrip	.75	
❑ FC13 Bill Elliott	4.00	
❑ FC14 Ken Schrader	.75	
❑ FC15 Wally Dallenbach	.75	
❑ FC16 Kenny Irwin	2.50	
❑ FC17 Ricky Craven	.75	
❑ FC18 Mike Skinner	.75	
❑ FC19 Rusty Wallace's Car	2.00	
❑ FC20 Dale Earnhardt's Car	4.00	
❑ FC21 Terry Labonte's Car	2.00	
❑ FC22 Ricky Rudd's Car	.75	
❑ FC23 Bobby Labonte's Car	1.50	
❑ FC24 Jeff Gordon's Car	4.00	
❑ FC25 Dale Jarrett's Car	1.50	
❑ FC26 Bill Elliott's Car	2.00	
❑ FC27 Jeff Burton's Car	.75	

1998 Press Pass Premium Flag Chasers Reflectors

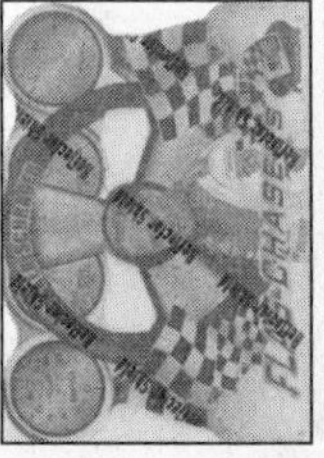

Randomly inserted in packs at a rate of one in 2, th card insert set features multi-dimensional all-foil, c cards with intricate micro-etching of the top NA Winston Cup drivers and cars.

	MINT
COMPLETE SET (27)	300.00
COMMON CARD (FC1-FC27)	3.00
COMMON DRIVER (FC1-FC27)	6.00

1998 Press Pass Premium Rivalries

Randomly inserted in packs at a rate of one in 6, th card insert set celebrates NASCAR's 50th anniversar inter-locking die-cut cards that depict the top six duels from NASCAR's premier division.

	MINT
COMPLETE SET (12)	50.00

ION CARD (1A - 6B)	1.00	.45
LES: 1X TO 2.5X BASE CARD HI		
Jeff Burton	2.00	.90
Jeff Gordon	10.00	4.50
David Pearson	1.00	.45
Richard Petty	2.50	1.10
Dale Earnhardt	10.00	4.50
Rusty Wallace	5.00	2.20
Cale Yarborough	2.00	.90
Bobby Allison	2.00	.90
Mark Martin	5.00	2.20
Dale Jarrett	4.00	1.80
Jeff Gordon's Car	5.00	2.20
Dale Earnhardt's Car	5.00	2.20

998 Press Pass Premium Steel Horses

mly inserted in packs at a rate of one in 12, this 12-nsert set highlights the top NASCAR Winston Cup an all-foil, die-cut, embossed and etched set.

	MINT	NRMT
LETE SET (12)	50.00	22.00
ION CARD (SH1-SH12)	2.50	1.10
LES: 1.25X TO 3X BASE CARD HI		
Rusty Wallace's Car	6.00	2.70
Dale Earnhardt's Car	12.00	5.50
Terry Labonte's Car	6.00	2.70
Mark Martin's Car	6.00	2.70
Ricky Rudd's Car	2.50	1.10
Bobby Labonte's Car	5.00	2.20
Jeff Gordon's Car	12.00	5.50
Kenny Irwin's Car	4.00	1.80
Sterling Marlin's Car	2.50	1.10
0 Dale Jarrett's Car	5.00	2.20
1 Bill Elliott's Car	6.00	2.70
2 Jeff Burton's Car	2.50	1.10

998 Press Pass Premium Triple Gear "Firesuit"

mly inserted in packs at a rate of one in 432, this 9-nsert set features authentic pieces of the drivers' s. These cards are numbered to 150.

	MINT	NRMT
ON CARD (TGF1-TGF9)	60.00	27.00
1 Rusty Wallace	175.00	80.00
2 Dale Earnhardt	300.00	135.00
3 Terry Labonte	175.00	80.00
4 Mark Martin	175.00	80.00
5 Bobby Labonte	100.00	45.00
6 Jeff Gordon	300.00	135.00
7 Mike Skinner	60.00	27.00
8 Dale Jarrett	150.00	70.00
9 Jeff Burton	90.00	40.00

1998 Press Pass Stealth

98 Press Pass Stealth set was issued in one series g 60 cards. The set features silver foil stamping coating and highlighted with a shimmering metal specially produced on the NASCAR Winston Cup

Series. The set contains the topical subset: Teammates (45-59).

	MINT	NRMT
COMPLETE SET (60)	30.00	13.50
COMMON CARD (1-60)	.15	.07
COMMON DRIVER (1-60)	.30	.14
❑ 1 Dale Earnhardt's Car	1.50	.70
❑ 2 Dale Earnhardt's Car	1.50	.70
❑ 3 Richard Childress	.15	.07
❑ 4 Jeff Burton	.60	.25
❑ 5 Jeff Burton's Car	.30	.14
❑ 6 Jack Roush	.30	.14
❑ 7 Bill Elliott	1.50	.70
❑ 8 Bill Elliott's Car	.75	.35
❑ 9 Joe Garone	.15	.07
❑ 10 Jeff Gordon	3.00	1.35
❑ 11 Jeff Gordon's Car	1.50	.70
❑ 12 Ray Evernham	.30	.14
❑ 13 Kenny Irwin	1.00	.45
❑ 14 Kenny Irwin's Car	.50	.23
❑ 15 Robert Yates	.30	.14
❑ 16 Dale Jarrett	1.25	.55
❑ 17 Dale Jarrett's Car	.60	.25
❑ 18 Todd Parrott	.15	.07
❑ 19 Bobby Labonte	1.25	.55
❑ 20 Bobby Labonte's Car	.60	.25
❑ 21 Jimmy Makar	.15	.07
❑ 22 Terry Labonte	1.50	.70
❑ 23 Terry Labonte's Car	.75	.35
❑ 24 Andy Graves	.15	.07
❑ 25 Mark Martin	1.50	.70
❑ 26 Mark Martin's Car	.75	.35
❑ 27 Jimmy Fennig	.15	.07
❑ 28 Ricky Rudd	.60	.25
❑ 29 Ricky Rudd's Car	.30	.14
❑ 30 Bill Ingle	.15	.07
❑ 31 Rusty Wallace	1.50	.70
❑ 32 Rusty Wallace's Car	.75	.35
❑ 33 Robin Pemberton	.15	.07
❑ 34 Michael Waltrip	.30	.14
❑ 35 Michael Waltrip's Car	.15	.07
❑ 36 Glen Wood	.15	.07
❑ 37 Dale Earnhardt Jr.	4.00	1.80
❑ 38 Jason Keller	.30	.14
❑ 39 Randy LaJoie	.30	.14
❑ 40 Mark Martin	1.50	.70
❑ 41 Mike McLaughlin	.30	.14
❑ 42 Elliott Sadler	.30	.14
❑ 43 Hermie Sadler	.30	.14
❑ 44 Tony Stewart	2.00	.90
❑ 45 Dale Jarrett TM	1.25	.55
❑ 46 Kenny Irwin TM	1.00	.45
❑ 47 Jeff Gordon TM	3.00	1.35
❑ 48 Terry Labonte TM	1.50	.70
❑ 49 Jeremy Mayfield TM	1.00	.45
❑ 50 Rusty Wallace TM	1.50	.70
❑ 51 Jeff Burton TM	.60	.25
❑ 52 Ted Musgrave TM	.30	.14
❑ 53 Chad Little TM	.30	.14
❑ 54 Johnny Benson TM	.30	.14
❑ 55 Mark Martin TM	1.50	.70
❑ 56 Sterling Marlin TM	.60	.25
❑ 57 Joe Nemechek TM	.30	.14
❑ 58 Mike Skinner TM	.30	.14
❑ 59 Dale Earnhardt's Car TM	1.50	.70
❑ 60 Dale Earnhardt Jr. CL	1.50	.70
❑ 0 Jeff Gordon Champ Bronze 1:110	20.00	9.00
❑ 0 Jeff Gordon Champ Silver 1:220	40.00	18.00
❑ 0 Jeff Gordon Champ Gold 1:440	60.00	27.00

1998 Press Pass Stealth Awards

Randomly inserted in progressive odds at a rate of 1:22 through 1:420, this insert set honors those drivers who have proven their excellence and risen to the top in 6 key categories: Most Laps Completed (1:22), All Charged Up (1:68), Top Rookie (1:90), Most Money Won (1:120), Most Poles (1:200), and Most Wins (1:420).

	MINT	NRMT
COMPLETE SET (7)	200.00	90.00

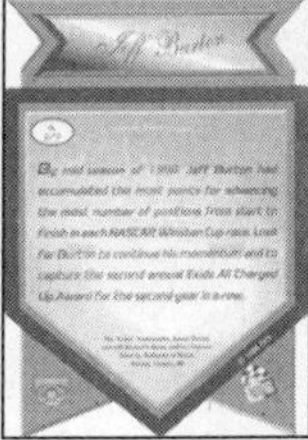

COMMON CARD (1-7)	5.00	2.20
❑ 1 Jeremy Mayfield 1:22	5.00	2.20
❑ 2 Jeff Burton 1:68	10.00	4.50
❑ 3 Kenny Irwin 1:90	12.00	5.50
❑ 4 Mark Martin 1:120	20.00	9.00
❑ 5 Jeff Gordon 1:200	60.00	27.00
❑ 6 Mark Martin 1:420	60.00	27.00
❑ 7 Jeff Gordon 1:420	100.00	45.00

1998 Press Pass Stealth Fan Talk

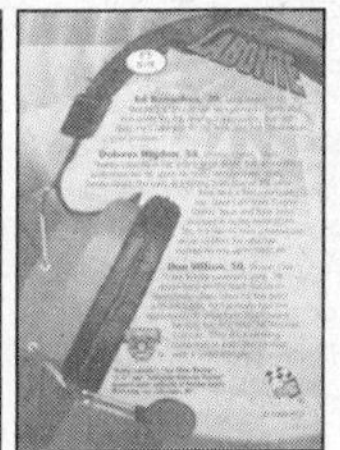

Randomly inserted in packs at a rate of one in 10, this all-foil, micro-etched insert set gives fans their chance to say why their favorite driver is the best in the business.

	MINT	NRMT
COMPLETE SET (9)	50.00	22.00
COMMON CARD (1-9)	2.50	1.10
*SINGLES: 1.25X TO 3X BASE CARD HI		
❑ 1 Dale Earnhardt	12.00	5.50
❑ 2 Bill Elliott	6.00	2.70
❑ 3 Jeff Gordon	12.00	5.50
❑ 4 Dale Jarrett	5.00	2.20
❑ 5 Bobby Labonte	5.00	2.20
❑ 6 Terry Labonte	6.00	2.70
❑ 7 Mark Martin	6.00	2.70
❑ 8 Ricky Rudd	2.50	1.10
❑ 9 Rusty Wallace	6.00	2.70

1998 Press Pass Stealth Fan Talk Diecut

Randomly inserted in packs at a rate of one in 30, this special die-cut insert version gives fans their chance to say why their favorite driver is the best in the business.

	MINT	NRMT
COMPLETE SET (9)	80.00	36.00
COMMON CARD (1-9)	5.00	2.20

1998 Press Pass Stealth Fusion

Randomly inserted one in every pack, this special fiery red foil is a parallel of the base set.

	MINT	NRMT
COMPLETE SET (60)	80.00	36.00

COMMON CARD (1-60)	.50	.23
COMMON DRIVER (1-60)	1.00	.45
*FUSION CARDS: 1.5X TO 3X	.50	.23

1998 Press Pass Stealth Octane

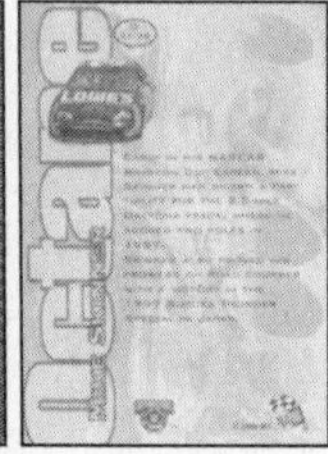

Randomly inserted in packs at a rate of one in 2, this insert offers a "set within a set" that features the top 18 NASCAR Winston Cup drivers and their rides on all-foil, micro-etched cards.

	MINT	NRMT
COMPLETE SET (36)	40.00	18.00
COMMON CARD (1-36)	.30	.14
COMMON DRIVER (1-36)	.60	.25
*SINGLES: .75X TO 2X BASE CARD HI		
❑ 1 John Andretti	.60	.25
❑ 2 John Andretti's Car	.30	.14
❑ 3 Johnny Benson	.60	.25
❑ 4 Johnny Benson's Car	.30	.14
❑ 5 Jeff Burton	1.25	.55
❑ 6 Jeff Burton's Car	.60	.25
❑ 7 Ward Burton	.60	.25
❑ 8 Ward Burton's Car	.30	.14
❑ 9 Dale Earnhardt's Car	3.00	1.35
❑ 10 Dale Earnhardt's Car	3.00	1.35
❑ 11 Bill Elliott	3.00	1.35
❑ 12 Bill Elliott's Car	1.50	.70
❑ 13 Jeff Gordon	6.00	2.70
❑ 14 Jeff Gordon's Car	3.00	1.35
❑ 15 Ernie Irvan	1.25	.55
❑ 16 Ernie Irvan's Car	.60	.25
❑ 17 Dale Jarrett	2.50	1.10
❑ 18 Dale Jarrett's Car	1.25	.55
❑ 19 Bobby Labonte	2.50	1.10
❑ 20 Bobby Labonte's Car	1.25	.55
❑ 21 Terry Labonte	3.00	1.35
❑ 22 Terry Labonte's Car	1.50	.70
❑ 23 Sterling Marlin	1.25	.55
❑ 24 Sterling Marlin's Car	.60	.25
❑ 25 Mark Martin	3.00	1.35
❑ 26 Mark Martin's Car	1.50	.70
❑ 27 Jeremy Mayfield	2.00	.90
❑ 28 Jeremy Mayfield's Car	1.00	.45
❑ 29 Ricky Rudd	1.25	.55
❑ 30 Ricky Rudd's Car	.60	.25
❑ 31 Mike Skinner	.60	.25
❑ 32 Mike Skinner's Car	.30	.14
❑ 33 Jimmy Spencer	.60	.25
❑ 34 Jimmy Spencer's Car	.30	.14
❑ 35 Rusty Wallace	3.00	1.35
❑ 36 Rusty Wallace's Car	1.50	.70

1998 Press Pass Stealth Octane Diecut

Randomly inserted in packs at a rate of one in 11, this special die-cut insert version offers a "set within a set" that features the top 18 NASCAR Winston Cup drivers and their rides on all-foil, micro-etched cards.

	MINT	NRMT
COMPLETE SET (36)	120.00	55.00
COMMON CARD (1-36)	1.00	.45
COMMON DRIVER (1-36)	2.00	.90

1998 Press Pass Stealth Race-Used Gloves

Randomly inserted in packs at a rate of one in 400, this 8-card insert set features a piece of race-used gloves from top NASCAR Winston Cup drivers like Jeff Gordon, and Mark Martin. These cards are numbered to 205. Cards with multi-colored cloth carry a 25% premium over those that do not.

	MINT	NRMT
COMPLETE SET (8)	1200.00	550.00
COMMON CARD (1-8)	100.00	45.00
❑ G1 Rusty Wallace	175.00	80.00
❑ G2 Jeff Burton	100.00	45.00
❑ G3 Terry Labonte	175.00	80.00
❑ G4 Mark Martin	175.00	80.00
❑ G5 Bobby Labonte	150.00	70.00
❑ G6 Jeff Gordon	250.00	110.00
❑ G7 Dale Jarrett	150.00	70.00
❑ G8 Dale Earnhardt	250.00	110.00

1998 Press Pass Stealth Stars

Randomly inserted in packs at a rate of one in 6, this 18-card insert set features NASCAR Winston Cup superstars on all-foil.

	MINT	NRMT
COMPLETE SET (18)	60.00	27.00
COMMON CARD (1-18)	1.25	.55
*SINGLES: 1.5X TO 4X BASE CARD HI		
❑ 1 Johnny Benson	1.25	.55
❑ 2 Jeff Burton	2.50	1.10
❑ 3 Dale Earnhardt,Jr.	15.00	6.75
❑ 4 Bill Elliott	6.00	2.70
❑ 5 Jeff Gordon	12.00	5.50
❑ 6 Bobby Hamilton	1.25	.55
❑ 7 Kenny Irwin	4.00	1.80
❑ 8 Dale Jarrett	5.00	2.20
❑ 9 Bobby Labonte	5.00	2.20
❑ 10 Terry Labonte	6.00	2.70
❑ 11 Sterling Marlin	2.50	1.10
❑ 12 Mark Martin	6.00	2.70
❑ 13 Jeremy Mayfield	4.00	1.80
❑ 14 Ted Musgrave	1.25	.55
❑ 15 Ricky Rudd	2.50	1.10
❑ 16 Jimmy Spencer	1.25	.55
❑ 17 Rusty Wallace	6.00	2.70
❑ 18 Michael Waltrip	1.25	.55

1998 Press Pass Stealth Stars Diecut

This 18-card set parallels the regular Stars set. These cards are randomly inserted into packs at a ratio of one per 30 packs.

	MINT	NRMT
COMPLETE SET (18)	200.00	90.00
COMMON CARD (1-18)	5.00	2.20

1991 Pro Set

This was Pro Set's first NASCAR release in a run of sets produced by the company from 1991-1994. The set

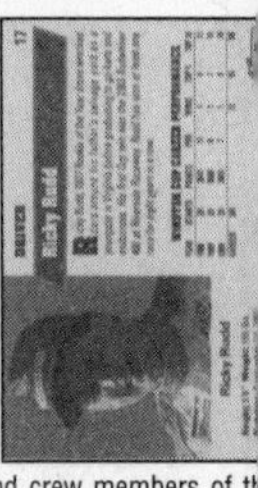

features star drivers, cars and crew members of th Winston Cup teams. Three cards containing errors corrected in a later printing and a 37-card Legends was also included with the release. The cards packaged 12 per foil pack with 36 packs per box thousand signed cards of Bobby Allison (#38) wer randomly inserted as was a special hologram featuring the Winston Cup Trophy (numbered of 5 The Allison cards were signed using a black fin Sharpie pen.

	MINT
COMPLETE SET (143)	10.00
COMMON CARD (1-143)	.10
COMMON DRIVER (1-143)	.20
❑ 1 Rick Mast	.20
❑ 2 Richard Jackson	.10
❑ 3 Bob Johnson	.10
❑ 4 Rick Mast w/Car	.20
❑ 5 Rusty Wallace	1.00
❑ 6 Rusty Wallace	1.00
❑ 7 Jimmy Makar	.10
❑ 8 Rusty Wallace's Car	.50
❑ 9 Ernie Irvan's Car	.20
❑ 10 Don Miller	.10
❑ 11 Bill Venturini	.20
❑ 12 Roger Penske	.10
❑ 13 Ernie Irvan	.40
❑ 14 Ernie Irvan	.40
❑ 15 Larry McClure	.10
❑ 16 Tony Glover	.10
❑ 17 Ricky Rudd	.40
❑ 18A Rick Hendrick ERR	.50
pictured in dark sweater and white shirt	
❑ 18B Rick Hendrick COR	.50
updated photo	
❑ 19 Waddell Wilson	.10
❑ 20 Ricky Rudd's Car	.20
❑ 21 Mark Martin	1.00
❑ 22 Jack Roush	.10
❑ 23 Robin Pemberton	.10
❑ 24 Steve Hmiel	.10
❑ 25 Mark Martin's Car	.50
❑ 26 Rick Wilson	.20
❑ 27 Beth Bruce	.10
Ms. Winston	
❑ 28 Harry Hyde	.10
❑ 29 Rick Wilson's Car	.10
❑ 30 Bob Whitcomb	.10
❑ 31 Buddy Parrott	.10
❑ 32 Derrike Cope's Car	.10
❑ 33 Geoff Bodine	.20
❑ 34 Junior Johnson	.20
❑ 35 Tim Brewer	.10
❑ 36 Geoff Bodine's Car	.10
❑ 37 Hut Stricklin	.20
❑ 38A Bobby Allison ERR	.50
text mentions son-in-law	
❑ 38B Bobby Allison COR	.50
no son-in-law mentioned	
❑ 39 Hut Stricklin's Car	.10
❑ 40 Morgan Shepherd	.20
❑ 41 Walter Bud Moore	.10
❑ 42 Morgan Shepherd's Car	.10
❑ 43 Dale Jarrett	.75
❑ 44 Dale Jarrett's Car	.40
❑ 45 Junior Johnson	.20
❑ 46 Mike Beam	.10
❑ 47 Sterling Marlin's Car	.20
❑ 48 Mickey Gibbs	.10
❑ 49 Barry Dodson	.10
❑ 50 Ken Schrader	.20
❑ 51 Rick Hendrick	.10
❑ 52 Richard Broome	.10
❑ 53 Doug Williams	.10
❑ 54 Kyle Petty	.40
❑ 55 Ned Jarrett	.40
Dale Jarrett	
❑ 56 Cale Yarborough	.20
❑ 57 Terry Labonte	1.00
❑ 58 Chuck Rider	.10
❑ 59 Bill Ingle	.10
❑ 60 Michael Waltrip's Car	.10

Ken Schrader's Car	.10	.05
Jimmy Fennig	.10	.05
Harry Gant	.40	.18
Andy Petree	.10	.05
Richard Petty	.75	.35
Dale Inman	.10	.05
Robbie Loomis	.10	.05
Richard Petty's Car	.20	.09
Jimmy Means	.20	.09
Jimmy Means' Car	.10	.05
Dave Marcis	.20	.09
Dave Marcis' Car	.10	.05
Lake Speed	.20	.09
Geoff Bodine	.20	.09
George Bradshaw	.10	.05
Joe Ruttman	.20	.09
Butch Mock	.10	.05
Bob Rahilly	.10	.05
Joe Ruttman's Car	.10	.05
Terry Labonte	1.00	.45
Steve Loyd	.10	.05
Terry Labonte's Car	.50	.23
Jimmy Spencer	.20	.09
Travis Carter	.10	.05
Jimmy Spencer's Car	.10	.05
Bobby Hillin	.20	.09
Kyle Petty	.40	.18
Felix Sabates	.10	.05
Gary Nelson	.10	.05
Wally Dallenbach Jr.	.20	.09
Danny Glad	.10	.05
Paul Andrews	.10	.05
Alan Kulwicki	.75	.35
Alan Kulwicki's Car	.40	.18
Chad Little	.20	.09
Jeff Hammond	.10	.05
Kenny Bernstein	.20	.09
Brett Bodine's Car	.10	.05
Mark Martin	1.00	.45
Lake Speed's Car	.10	.05
Wayne Bumgarner	.10	.05
Brett Bodine	.20	.09
Ted Musgrave	.75	.35
Ted Musgrave's Car	.10	.05
Larry Pearson	.20	.09
Larry Hedrick	.10	.05
Robert Harrington	.10	.05
Len Wood	.10	.05
Eddie Wood	.10	.05
Leonard Wood	.10	.05
Buddy Baker	.20	.09
Dick Moroso	.10	.05
Dick Moroso David Ifft	.10	.05
J.D. McDuffie	.40	.18
Stanley Smith	.10	.05
Eddie Bierschwale	.10	.05
Darrell Waltrip	.20	.09
Darrell Waltrip w/Car	.20	.09
Darrell Waltrip's Car	.10	.05
Chuck Little Alfred Allen	.10	.05
Greg Sacks	.20	.09
Junie Donlavey	.10	.05
Leo Jackson	.10	.05
Bill Stavola	.10	.05
Renee White Ms. Winston	.10	.05
Geoff Bodine	.20	.09
Ken Schrader	.20	.09
Ricky Rudd	.40	.18
Harry Gant	.40	.18
Richard Petty	.75	.35
Bobby Hamilton's Car	.10	.05
Felix Sabates Gary Nelson	.10	.05
Alan Kulwicki	.75	.35
Alan Kulwicki Army Car	.75	.35
Winston Showcar	.10	.05
Greg Sacks Navy Car	.20	.09
Mickey Gibbs Air Force Car	.20	.09
Buddy Baker Marines Car	.20	.09
Dave Marcis Coast Guard Car	.20	.09
T. Wayne Robertson	.10	.05
Ricky Rudd	.40	.18
Brett Bodine	.20	.09
A Phil Parsons ERR text reads Due to Health Problems...	.50	.23
B Phil Parsons COR text omits Due to Health Problems...	.50	.23
8 Bobby Allison ERR AUTO	80.00	36.00
Winston Cup HOLO/5000	80.00	36.00

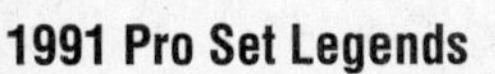

1991 Pro Set Legends

et produced this 37-card set as an insert into its Winston Cup Racing packs.The cards seemed to

have been produced in the same quantities as the regular issue and are often sold together as a set. Donnie Allison's card (#L11) contains an error that was later corrected.

	MINT	NRMT
COMPLETE SET (37)	5.00	2.20
COMMON CARD (L1-L37)	.20	.09

❑ L1 Dick Brooks	.20	.09
❑ L2 Buck Baker	.30	.14
❑ L3 Fred Lorenzen	.30	.14
❑ L4 Ned Jarrett	.30	.14
❑ L5 Dick Hutcherson	.20	.09
❑ L6 Marilyn Green	.20	.09
❑ L7 Harold Kinder	.20	.09
❑ L8 Coo Coo Marlin	.20	.09
❑ L9 Ralph Seagraves	.20	.09
❑ L10 Paul Bud Moore	.20	.09
❑ L11A Donnie Allison ERR text reads BGN crew chief	.40	.18
❑ L11B Donnie Allison COR text reads WC crew chief	.40	.18
❑ L12 Glen Wood	.20	.09
❑ L13 Marvin Panch	.30	.14
❑ L14 Cale Yarborough	.30	.14
❑ L15 Neil Castles (Soapy)	.20	.09
❑ L16 Maurice Petty	.30	.14
❑ L17 Junior Johnson	.30	.14
❑ L18 Tim Flock	.30	.14
❑ L19 Smokey Yunick	.20	.09
❑ L20 Larry Frank	.30	.14
❑ L21 Cotton Owens	.20	.09
❑ L22 Ralph Moody Jr.	.20	.09
❑ L23 Bob Welborn	.20	.09
❑ L24 Neil Bonnett	.75	.35
❑ L25 Edwin Matthews (Banjo)	.20	.09
❑ L26 Sam McQuagg	.20	.09
❑ L27 Jim Paschal	.20	.09
❑ L28 David Pearson	.30	.14
❑ L29 Tom Pistone	.30	.14
❑ L30 Jack Smith	.20	.09
❑ L31 Bobby Allison	.40	.18
❑ L32 Charles Ellington	.20	.09
❑ L33 Paul Goldsmith	.30	.14
❑ L34 Pete Hamilton	.20	.09
❑ L35 Rex White	.20	.09
❑ L36 Elmo Langley	.20	.09
❑ L37 Benny Parsons	.30	.14

1991 Pro Set Petty Family

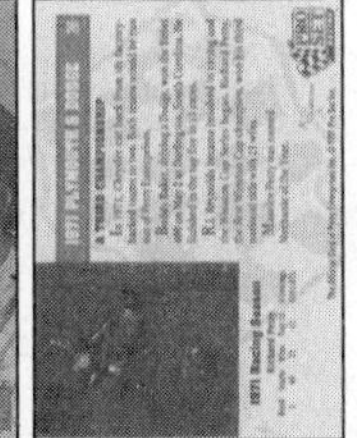

Pro Set produced this 50-card set in factory set form. It highlights the careers of Richard and the rest of the Petty racing family. The set was released again in 1992 as part of a special Petty Gift Pack containing a custom card album.

	MINT	NRMT
COMPLETE SET (50)	4.00	1.80
COMMON CARD (1-50)	.10	.05

❑ 1 Maurice Petty Art Richard Petty ART Lee Petty ART	.40	.18
❑ 2 1949 Reaper Shed	.10	.05
❑ 3 Lee Petty's Car 1949	.10	.05
❑ 4 Lee Petty's Car 1949	.10	.05
❑ 5 Lee Petty w/Car 1950	.15	.07
❑ 6 Lee Petty's Car 1951	.10	.05
❑ 7 Lee Petty's Car 1952	.10	.05
❑ 8 Lee Petty's Car 1953	.10	.05
❑ 9 Lee Petty Richard Petty Maurice Petty 1954	.40	.18
❑ 10 Lee Petty's Car 1955	.10	.05
❑ 11 Lee Petty's Car 1956	.10	.05
❑ 12 Lee Petty's Car 1957	.10	.05
❑ 13 Richard Petty 1958	.40	.18
❑ 14 Lee Petty's Car Johnny Beauchamp's Car	.10	.05
❑ 15 Lee Petty Richard Petty Maurice Petty 1960	.40	.18
❑ 16 Richard Petty's Car 1961	.15	.07
❑ 17 Richard Petty 1962	.40	.18
❑ 18 Richard Petty's Car Lee Petty's Car 1963	.15	.07
❑ 19 Richard Petty's Car 1964	.15	.07
❑ 20 Richard Petty's Car 1965	.15	.07
❑ 21 Richard Petty's Car 1966	.15	.07
❑ 22 Richard Petty 1967	.40	.18
❑ 23 Richard Petty's Car 1968	.15	.07
❑ 24 Richard Petty's Car 1969	.15	.07
❑ 25 Maurice Petty Art	.40	.18
❑ 26 Maurice Petty Buddy Baker	.10	.05
❑ 27 Richard Petty's Car 1972	.15	.07
❑ 29 Maurice Petty 1974	.10	.05
❑ 31 Richard Petty's Transporter	.10	.05
❑ 32 Richard Petty's Car 1977	.15	.07
❑ 33 Richard Petty's Car 1978	.15	.07
❑ 34 Richard Petty ART Kyle Petty	.40	.18
❑ 35 Richard Petty's Car Kyle Petty's Car	.15	.07
❑ 36 Richard Petty's Car Kyle Petty's Car	.15	.07
❑ 38 Richard Petty's Car 1983	.15	.07
❑ 39 Kyle Petty's Car 1984	.10	.05
❑ 40 Dick Brooks' Car	.10	.05
❑ 41 Richard Petty's Car 1986	.15	.07
❑ 42 Richard Petty's Car 1987	.15	.07
❑ 43 Richard Petty's Car 1989	.15	.07
❑ 44 Petty Enterprises	.10	.05
❑ 45 Lee Petty	.15	.07
❑ 46 Maurice Petty	.10	.05
❑ 47 Richard Petty	.40	.18
❑ 48 Kyle Petty	.25	.11
❑ 49 Richard Petty Maurice Petty	.40	.18
❑ 50 Richard Petty Museum	.10	.05

1992 Pro Set

This was Pro Set's second NASCAR release. The set features star drivers, cars and crew members of the top Winston Cup teams from the previous season. Six cards containing errors were corrected in a later printing and a 32-card Legends insert was also included with the release. The Club only factory set, of which 6,000 were made, contained the corrected cards.. Cards were packaged 12 per foil pack with 36 packs per box. A special hologram card featuring a Dale Earnhardt Winston Cup Champion logo (numbered of 5000) was produced and randomly distributed through packs. The card originally had a white border, but was later changed to black creating the variation.

	MINT	NRMT
COMPLETE SET (248)	14.00	6.25
COMP. FACTORY SET (280)	18.00	8.00
COMMON CARD (1-248)	.10	.05
COMMON DRIVER (1-248)	.20	.09

❑ 1 Dale Earnhardt	2.00	.90
❑ 2 Alan Kulwicki	.75	.35
❑ 3 Steve Grissom	.20	.09
❑ 4 Jimmy Hensley	.20	.09
❑ 5 Tommy Houston	.20	.09
❑ 6 Bobby Labonte	.60	.25
❑ 7 Joe Nemechek	.20	.09
❑ 8 Robert Pressley	.20	.09

❑ 9 Kenny Wallace .20 .09
❑ 10 Mike Wallace .20 .09
❑ 11 Rick Mast's Transporter .10 .05
❑ 12 Rusty Wallace's Transporter .50 .23
❑ 13 Geoff Bodine .20 .09
❑ 14 Ricky Rudd's Transporter .20 .09
❑ 15 Alan Kulwicki's Transporter .20 .09
❑ 16 Derrike Cope's Transporter .10 .05
❑ 17 Harry Gant's Transporter .20 .09
❑ 18 Kyle Petty's Transporter .20 .09
❑ 19 Dave Marcis' Transporter .20 .09
❑ 20 Ernie Irvan w/Pit Crew .40 .18
❑ 21 Terry Labonte's Transporter .50 .23
❑ 22 Jimmy Spencer's Transporter .10 .05
❑ 23 Michael Waltrip .20 .09
❑ 24 Dale Jarrett .75 .35
❑ 25 Derrike Cope's Car .10 .05
❑ 26 Kirk Shelmerdine .10 .05
❑ 27 Mike Wallace's Car .10 .05
❑ 28 Terry Labonte 1.00 .45
❑ 29 Joe Ruttman .20 .09
❑ 30 Kyle Petty .40 .18
❑ 31 Ricky Craven 1.00 .45
❑ 32 Clifford Allison .40 .18
❑ 33 Shawna Robinson .20 .09
❑ 34 Dorsey Schroeder .20 .09
❑ 35 Terry Labonte 1.00 .45
❑ 36 Phil Parsons' Car .10 .05
❑ 37 Jimmy Means' Car .10 .05
❑ 38 Dave Marcis' Car .20 .09
❑ 39 Richard Childress .10 .05
❑ 40 Hut Stricklin's Transporter .10 .05
❑ 41 Davey Allison's Transporter .40 .18
❑ 42 Rick Mast .20 .09
❑ 43 Richard Petty .60 .25
❑ 44 Kyle Petty .40 .18
❑ 45 Richard Petty .60 .25
❑ 46 Chad Little's Transporter .10 .05
❑ 47 Jimmy Means .20 .09
❑ 48 Dave Marcis .40 .18
❑ 49 Harry Gant .40 .18
❑ 50 Lake Speed .20 .09
❑ 51 Jimmy Spencer .20 .09
❑ 52 Bobby Hillin .20 .09
❑ 53 Chad Little .20 .09
❑ 54 Eddie Bierschwale .20 .09
❑ 55 Jack Sprague .20 .09
❑ 56 Dick Trickle w/Car .10 .05
❑ 57 Charlie Glotzbach .20 .09
❑ 58 Phil Barkdoll .20 .09
❑ 59 Dale Earnhardt 's Car 1.00 .45
❑ 60 Ernie Irvan .40 .18
❑ 61 Mark Martin's Car .50 .23
❑ 62 Geoff Bodine's Car .10 .05
❑ 63 Bobby Hamilton's Car .10 .05
❑ 64A Dorsey Schroeder's Car ERR .30 .14
crew chief Junior Dunlavey
❑ 64B Dorsey Schroeder's Car COR .50 .23
crew chief Junie Dunlavey
❑ 65 Jimmy Spencer's Car .10 .05
❑ 66 Geoff Bodine .20 .09
❑ 67A Hut Stricklin .30 .14
pictured in Chevy hat
❑ 67B Hut Stricklin .50 .23
pictured without Chevy hat
❑ 68 Mickey Gibbs .20 .09
❑ 69 Wally Dallenbach Jr. .20 .09
❑ 70 Ted Musgrave .20 .09
❑ 71 Mark Martin 1.00 .45
❑ 72 Larry Pearson .20 .09
❑ 73 Greg Sacks .20 .09
❑ 74 Phil Parsons .20 .09
❑ 75 Rick Wilson .20 .09
❑ 76 Dick Trickle's Car .10 .05
❑ 77 Greg Sacks' Car .10 .05
❑ 78 Ted Musgrave's Car .10 .05
❑ 79 Junior Johnson .20 .09
❑ 80 Tony Glover .10 .05
❑ 81 Tim Brewer .10 .05
❑ 82 Sterling Marlin .40 .18
❑ 83 Jeff Hammond .10 .05
❑ 84 Leonard Wood .10 .05
❑ 85 Andy Petree .10 .05
❑ 86 Robin Pemberton .10 .05
❑ 87 Robbie Loomis .20 .09
❑ 88 Buddy Baker .20 .09
❑ 89 J.D.McDuffie w/Car .20 .09
❑ 90 Steve Hmiel .10 .05
❑ 91 Jimmy Makar .10 .05
❑ 92 Michael Waltrip's Transporter .10 .05
❑ 93 Darrell Waltrip .40 .18
❑ 94 Ricky Rudd .40 .18
❑ 95 Ernie Irvan .40 .18
❑ 96 Mark Martin 1.00 .45
❑ 97 Darrell Waltrip .40 .18
❑ 98 Ken Schrader .20 .09
❑ 99 Rusty Wallace 1.00 .45
❑ 100 Alan Kulwicki .75 .35

❑ 101 Geoff Bodine .20 .09
❑ 102 Michael Waltrip .20 .09
❑ 103 Hut Stricklin .20 .09
❑ 104 Ken Schrader .20 .09
❑ 105 Dale Jarrett .75 .35
❑ 106 Jim Sauter .20 .09
❑ 107 Rusty Wallace's Car .50 .23
❑ 108 Ernie Irvan's Car .20 .09
❑ 109 Ricky Rudd's Car .20 .09
❑ 110 Hut Stricklin's Car .10 .05
❑ 111 Michael Waltrip's Car .10 .05
❑ 112 Harry Gant's Car .20 .09
❑ 113 Kyle Petty's Car .20 .09
❑ 114 Richard Petty's Car .20 .09
❑ 115 Rusty Wallace 1.00 .45
❑ 116 Terry Labonte's Car .50 .23
❑ 117 Stanley Smith .10 .05
❑ 118 Eddie Dickerson .10 .05
❑ 119 Doug Williams .10 .05
❑ 120 Donnie Wingo .10 .05
❑ 121 Steve Loyd .10 .05
❑ 122 David Ifft .10 .05
❑ 123 Dick Trickle's Transporter .10 .05
❑ 124 Richard Petty's Transporter .20 .09
❑ 125 Ward Burton .20 .09
❑ 126 Morgan Shepherd .20 .09
❑ 127 Todd Bodine .20 .09
❑ 128 Jeff Gordon 2.50 1.10
❑ 129 Bill Ingle .10 .05
❑ 130A Waddell Wilson ERR .30 .14
reads joined WC in 1979
❑ 130B Waddell Wilson COR .50 .23
reads joined WC in 1963
❑ 131 Doug Richert .10 .05
❑ 132 Dale Inman .10 .05
❑ 133 Ricky Rudd .40 .18
❑ 134 Morgan Shepherd .20 .09
❑ 135 Jeff Burton .40 .18
❑ 136 Tommy Ellis .10 .05
❑ 137 Allen Bestwick .10 .05
❑ 138 Barry Dodson .10 .05
❑ 139 Bobby Hamilton's Trans. .10 .05
❑ 140 Beth Bruce .10 .05
Ms.Winston
❑ 141 Bill Venturini .20 .09
❑ 142 Bob Johnson .10 .05
❑ 143 Bob Rahilly .10 .05
❑ 144 Bobby Allison .40 .18
❑ 145 Bobby Dotter .20 .09
❑ 146 Brett Bodine .20 .09
❑ 147 Buddy Parrott .10 .05
❑ 148 Butch Miller .20 .09
❑ 149 Cale Yarborough .20 .09
❑ 150 Rick Mast's Car .10 .05
❑ 151 Cecil Gordon .10 .05
❑ 152 Alan Kulwicki's Car .40 .18
❑ 153 Chad Little .20 .09
❑ 154 Dick Trickle's Car .10 .05
❑ 155 Ted Musgrave's Car .10 .05
❑ 156 Brett Bodine's Car .10 .05
❑ 157 Chuck Bown .20 .09
❑ 158 Chad Little's Car .10 .05
❑ 159 Chuck Rider .10 .05
❑ 160 Morgan Shepherd's Car .10 .05
❑ 161 Dale Earnhardt 2.00 .90
❑ 162 Sterling Marlin's Car .20 .09
❑ 163 Danny Myers .10 .05
❑ 164A David Fuge ERR .30 .14
wrong photo, wearing mustache
❑ 164B David Fuge COR .50 .23
correct photo, wearing beard
❑ 165 Ken Schrader's Car .10 .05
❑ 166 Dave Rezendes .20 .09
❑ 167 David Evans .10 .05
❑ 168 Dick Brooks .10 .05
❑ 169A Felix Sabates ERR .30 .14
back reads car #43
❑ 169B Felix Sabates COR .50 .23
back reads car #42
❑ 170 Gene Roberts .10 .05
❑ 171 Jack Pennington .10 .05
❑ 172 Dale Earnhardt's Transporter 1.00 .45
❑ 173 Ken Wilson .20 .09
❑ 174 Sterling Marlin's Transporter .20 .09
❑ 175 Renee White .10 .05
Ms.Winston
❑ 176 Rodney Combs .20 .09
❑ 177 Sterling Marlin .40 .18
❑ 178 Michael Waltrip's Car .10 .05
❑ 179 Winston Kelley .10 .05
❑ 180 Brett Bodine .20 .09
❑ 181 Wally Dallenbach Jr.'s Car .10 .05
❑ 182 Dale Earnhardt 2.00 .90
❑ 183 Davey Allison 1.00 .45
❑ 184 Mark Martin's Transporter .50 .23
❑ 185 Donnie Richeson .10 .05
❑ 186 Eddie Wood .10 .05
Len Wood

❑ 187 Eli Gold .10
❑ 188 Red Farmer .10
Tommy Allison Jr
❑ 189 Gary Nelson .10
❑ 190 Harry Gant .40
❑ 191 Jack Ingram .10
❑ 192 Jay Smith .10
❑ 193 Phil Parsons' Transporter .10
❑ 194 Joey Knuckles .10
Ryan Pemberton
❑ 195 L.D. Ottinger .10
❑ 196 Mark Cronquist .10
❑ 197 Elton Sawyer .20
Patty Moise
❑ 198 Mike Beam .10
❑ 199 Neil Bonnett .50
❑ 200 Butch Mock .10
Bob Rahilly
Dick Trickle's Car
❑ 201 Paul Andrews .10
❑ 202 Ernie Irvan's Transporter .20
❑ 203 Robert Yates .10
❑ 204 Richard Broome .10
❑ 205 Wally Dallenbach Jr.'s Trans. .10
❑ 206 Tracy Leslie .20
❑ 207 Will Lind .10
❑ 208 Barney Hall .10
❑ 209 Darrell Waltrip's Car .20
❑ 210 Danny Lawrence .10
❑ 211 Davey Allison 1.00
❑ 212 Dennis Connor .10
❑ 213 Dick Rahilly .10
❑ 214 Gary DeHart .10
❑ 215 Neil Bonnett .20
Buddy Baker
Mike Joy
Announcers
❑ 216 James Hylton .20
❑ 217 Jimmy Fennig .10
❑ 218 Jimmy Horton .20
❑ 219 Keith Almond .10
❑ 220 Marc Reno .10
❑ 221 Shelton Pittman .10
❑ 222 Brett Bodine's Transporter .10
❑ 223 Davey Allison w/Crew .75
❑ 224 Dale Earnhardt w/Crew 1.00
❑ 225 Geoff Bodine's Transporter .10
❑ 226 Walter Smith .10
❑ 227 NASCAR Softball Team .10
❑ 228 Troy Beebe .10
❑ 229 Davey Allison 's Car .40
❑ 230 David Green .20
❑ 231 Dewey Livengood .10
❑ 232 Ed Berrier .10
❑ 233 Eddie Lanier .10
❑ 234 Irv Hoerr .10
❑ 235 Jim Phillips .10
❑ 236 Larry McReynolds .10
❑ 237 Joe Moore .10
❑ 238 Jimmy Means' Transporter .10
❑ 239 David Smith .10
❑ 240 Morgan Shepherd's Pit Crew .10
❑ 241 Harry Gant DOY .40
❑ 242 Mark Martin Busch Pole .50
❑ 243 Larry McReynolds .10
❑ 244 Tom Peck .20
❑ 245 Darrell Waltrip's Transporter .20
❑ 246 Travis Carter .10
❑ 247 Morgan Shepherd's Trans. .10
❑ 248A Walter Bud Moore ERR .30
Paul on front
❑ 248B Walter Bud Moore COR .50
Walter on front
❑ NNO Dale Earnhardt HOLO 100.00
5000 White
❑ NNO Dale Earnhardt HOLO 80.00
5000 Black

1992 Pro Set Legends

Pro Set produced this 32-card set as an insert i 1992 Winston Cup Racing packs.The cards seer have been produced in the same quantities as the and are often sold together as a set. Dick ɜrson's card (#L4) contains a wrong photo error ɑs later corrected.

	MINT	NRMT
‿ETE SET (32)	5.00	2.20
ON CARD (L1-L32)	.20	.09
uck Baker	.30	.14
ɾed Lorenzen	.30	.14
ed Jarrett	.30	.14
Dick Hutcherson ERR photo of Johnny Rutherford	.40	.18
Dick Hutcherson COR correct photo	.40	.18
oo Coo Marlin	.20	.09
aul Bud Moore	.20	.09
onnie Allison	.30	.14
ˡarvin Panch	.20	.09
eil Castles (Soapy)	.20	.09
Maurice Petty	.30	.14
Tim Flock	.20	.09
Smokey Yunick	.20	.09
Larry Frank	.20	.09
Cotton Owens	.20	.09
Ralph Moody Jr.	.20	.09
Bob Welborn	.20	.09
Marilyn Green	.20	.09
Edwin Matthews (Banjo)	.20	.09
Sam McQuagg	.20	.09
Jim Paschal	.20	.09
David Pearson	.30	.14
Tom Pistone	.20	.09
Jack Smith	.20	.09
Charles Ellington	.20	.09
Pete Hamilton	.20	.09
Rex White	.20	.09
Elmo Langley	.20	.09
Benny Parsons	.30	.14
Harold Kinder	.20	.09
Cale Yarborough	.30	.14
Junior Johnson	.30	.14
Bobby Allison	.50	.23

92 Pro Set Maxwell House

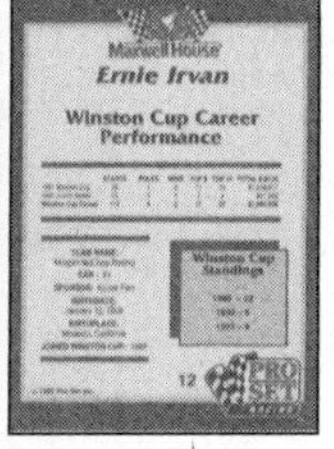

produced this 30-card set for Maxwell House. The ʋere distributed in six-card packs through Maxwell filter packs. There were two different title cards e in those packs. An offer to obtain a complete set) with 2 proofs of purchase or $15.00 without the ʼas also included in the promotion. The set features ; from the top NASCAR teams with a special sis on Sterling Marlin and the Maxwell House Team. The first 100 people who responded to the offer received a special set of cards autographed ing Marlin or Junior Johnson. Autograph cards are nly found in the $35 - $ 60 range.

	MINT	NRMT
ETE SET (30)	8.00	3.60
)N CARD (1-30)	.25	.11
e Card	.25	.11
rling Marlin	.50	.23
rling Marlin	.50	.23
ior Johnson	.25	.11
rling Marlin's Car	.25	.11
rling Marlin's Transporter	.25	.11
e Beam	.25	.11
rling Marlin's Car	.25	.11
ky Rudd	.50	.23
ɑvey Allison	1.00	.45
ɑrry Gant	.50	.23
nie Irvan	.50	.23
ark Martin	1.00	.45
ɑrrell Waltrip	.50	.23
·n Schrader	.25	.11
ısty Wallace	1.00	.45
organ Shepherd	.25	.11
an Kulwicki	.60	.25
ɞoff Bodine	.25	.11
chael Waltrip	.25	.11
ıt Stricklin	.25	.11

Card	MINT	NRMT
❑ 22 Dale Jarrett	.75	.35
❑ 23 Terry Labonte	1.00	.45
❑ 24 Brett Bodine	.25	.11
❑ 25 Richard Petty	.50	.23
❑ 26 Kyle Petty	.50	.23
❑ 27 Jimmy Spencer	.25	.11
❑ 28 Rick Mast	.25	.11
❑ 29 Wally Dallenbach Jr.	.25	.11
❑ 30 Sterling Marlin w/Car	.50	.23

1992 Pro Set Racing Club

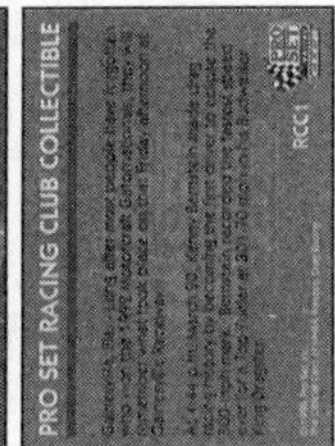

Cards from this set were issued over the course of the 1992 and 1993 race seasons and distributed to members of the Pro Set Racing Club. The cards include an RCC prefix on the numbers and feature drivers and events from both NASCAR Winston Cup and NHRA racing. Finish Line's Racing Club also distributed the cards in complete set form.

	MINT	NRMT
COMPLETE SET (8)	15.00	6.75
COMMON CARD (RCC1-RCC8)	1.25	.55
❑ 1 Kenny Bernstein's Car 301.70 MPH	2.00	.90
❑ 2 Charlotte Motor Speedway One Hot Night	1.25	.55
❑ 3 Clifford Allison	3.00	1.35
❑ 4 Clifford Allison In Memorium	3.00	1.35
❑ 5 Joe Amato Cruz Pedregon Warren Johnson 1992 Champions	2.00	.90
❑ 6 Richard Petty's Car The King's Last Race	2.00	.90
❑ 7 Fastest NHRA Drivers Pat Austin Kenny Bernstein Doug Herbert Don Prudhomme Joe Amato Scott Kalitta Rance McDaniel	1.25	.55
❑ 8 The Winston 1993	1.25	.55

1992 Pro Set Rudy Farms

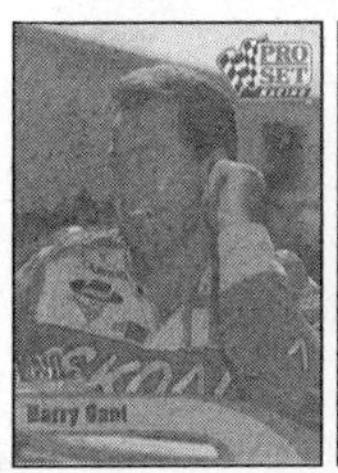

Pro Set produced this 20-card set for Rudy Farms stores. The cards were distributed in Rudy Farms Sandwiches via a 3-card cello packs. The set features cards from the regular issue Pro Set release that have been re-numbered. The five card Legends series is considered part of the 20-card regular set. The Legends cards are numbered 1-5. We have added the L prefix to make it easier to read. An album was also produced for distribution with complete sets. The 5 card Legends set was also available through a proofs-of-purchase mail-in offer from R.B Rice sausage.

	MINT	NRMT
COMPLETE SET (20)	30.00	13.50
COMMON CARD (1-15)	1.00	.45
COMMON LEGENDS (L1-L5)	1.00	.45
R.B. RICE SET (5)	7.00	3.10
❑ 1 Ricky Rudd	2.00	.90
❑ 2 Davey Allison	2.00	.90
❑ 3 Harry Gant	2.00	.90
❑ 4 Ernie Irvan	2.00	.90
❑ 5 Mark Martin	2.50	1.10
❑ 6 Sterling Marlin	2.00	.90
❑ 7 Darrell Waltrip	2.00	.90
❑ 8 Ken Schrader	1.00	.45
❑ 9 Rusty Wallace	2.50	1.10
❑ 10 Morgan Shepherd	1.00	.45
❑ 11 Alan Kulwicki	1.50	.70
❑ 12 Geoff Bodine	1.00	.45
❑ 13 Michael Waltrip	1.00	.45
❑ 14 Kyle Petty	2.00	.90
❑ 15 Richard Petty	2.50	1.10
❑ L1 Ned Jarrett	1.00	.45
❑ L2 David Pearson	1.00	.45
❑ L3 Cale Yarborough	2.00	.90
❑ L4 Junior Johnson	1.00	.45
❑ L5 Bobby Allison	2.00	.90

1992 Pro Set Tic Tac Hut Stricklin

Pro Set produced this 6-card set for Tic Tac. The cards were distributed in 2-card cello packs through Tic Tac four packs. The set focuses on Hut Stricklin and the associate sponsored Tic Tac Racing Team.

	MINT	NRMT
COMPLETE SET (6)	4.00	1.80
COMMON CARD (1-6)	.50	.23
❑ 1 Hut Stricklin	1.00	.45
❑ 2 Bobby Allison	1.00	.45
❑ 3 Jimmy Fennig	.50	.23
❑ 4 Keith Almond	.50	.23
❑ 5 Hut Stricklin's Car	.50	.23
❑ 6 Hut Stricklin	1.00	.45

1994 Quality Care Glidden/Speed

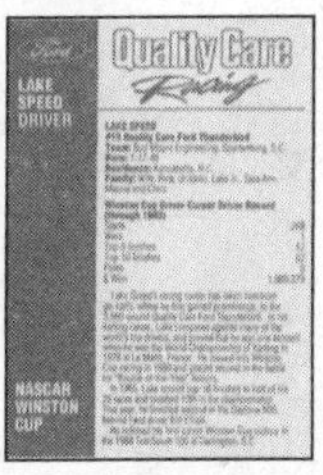

Ford produced this set as a continuation of their Motorcraft Racing issues released previously. Unlike the red colored Motorcraft cards, this set is designed primarily in blue to follow the paint scheme of the Quality Care Racing Teams. Lake Speed and Bob Glidden are the two featured drivers. The cards are unnumbered and listed alphabetically below.

	MINT	NRMT
COMPLETE SET (10)	6.00	2.70
COMMON CARD	.50	.23
COMMON DRIVER	1.00	.45
❑ 1 Bob Glidden	1.00	.45
❑ 2 Bob Glidden's Car	.50	.23
❑ 3 Bob Glidden's Car	.50	.23
❑ 4 Walter Bud Moore	.50	.23
❑ 5 Lake Speed's Pit Crew	.50	.23
❑ 6 Lake Speed	1.00	.45
❑ 7 Lake Speed's Car	.50	.23
❑ 8 Lake Speed's Car	.50	.23
❑ 9 Lake Speed's Car Bob Glidden's Car	.50	.23
❑ 10 Cover Card	.50	.23

1997 Race Sharks

This 45-card set is another uniquely themed set from Wheels. The cards feature the top names in racing. The cards are printed on 36 point paper. Each card has a wave like background and is stamped in silver foil. The cards were packaged three cards per pack, 24 packs per box and 16 boxes per case. There were a total of 1,250 numbered cases. The first 375 cases off the press had the first bite logo stamped on all the cards in those cases.

	MINT	NRMT
COMPLETE SET (45)	12.00	5.50
COMMON CARD (1-45)	.10	.05
COMMON DRIVER (1-45)	.20	.09
FIRST BITE COMP. SET (45)	15.00	6.75

*FIRST BITE CARDS: .5X TO 1.25X BASIC CARDS

❑ 1 Dale Earnhardt	2.00	.90
❑ 2 Jeff Gordon	2.00	.90
❑ 3 Dale Jarrett	.75	.35
❑ 4 Terry Labonte	1.00	.45
❑ 5 Rusty Wallace	1.00	.45
❑ 6 Mark Martin	1.00	.45
❑ 7 Sterling Marlin	.40	.18
❑ 8 Bill Elliott	1.00	.45
❑ 9 Bobby Labonte	.75	.35
❑ 10 Bobby Hamilton	.20	.09
❑ 11 Darrell Waltrip	.40	.18
❑ 12 Michael Waltrip	.20	.09
❑ 13 Mike Wallace	.20	.09
❑ 14 Kyle Petty	.40	.18
❑ 15 Ken Schrader	.20	.09
❑ 16 Ricky Craven	.20	.09
❑ 17 Derrike Cope	.20	.09
❑ 18 Jeff Burton	.40	.18
❑ 19 Ward Burton	.20	.09
❑ 20 Robert Pressley	.20	.09
❑ 21 Joe Nemechek	.20	.09
❑ 22 Brett Bodine	.20	.09
❑ 23 Jimmy Spencer	.20	.09
❑ 24 Chad Little	.20	.09
❑ 25 Bobby Labonte	.75	.35
❑ 26 Terry Labonte	1.00	.45
❑ 27 Mark Martin	1.00	.45
❑ 28 Jeff Green	.20	.09
❑ 29 David Green	.20	.09
❑ 30 Dale Jarrett	.75	.35
❑ 31 Joe Gibbs	.20	.09
❑ 32 Richard Childress	.10	.05
❑ 33 Bobby Allison	.20	.09
❑ 34 Dale Jarrett	.75	.35
❑ 35 Jeff Gordon	2.00	.90
❑ 36 Jeff Gordon	2.00	.90
❑ 37 Rusty Wallace	1.00	.45
❑ 38 Sterling Marlin	.40	.18
❑ 39 Rusty Wallace	1.00	.45
❑ 40 Jeff Gordon	2.00	.90
❑ 41 Dale Jarrett	.75	.35
❑ 42 Rusty Wallace	1.00	.45
❑ 43 Jeff Gordon	2.00	.90
❑ 44 Checklist	.10	.05
❑ 45 Checklist	.10	.05

1997 Race Sharks Great White Parallel

This 45-card set was made available through a letter redemption program. The sets leftover from this promotion were closed out through a hobby mail order company.

	MINT	NRMT
COMPLETE SET (45)	50.00	22.00
COMMON CARD (1-45)	.60	.25
COMMON DRIVER (1-45)	1.20	.55

*GREAT WHITE CARDS: 3X TO 6X BASIC CARDS

1997 Race Sharks Hammerhead

This 45-card set is a parallel to the base Race Sharks set. The cards are die-cut in a hammerhead shape to keep with the theme. There were 1,350 of each card produced and odds of pulling one out of a pack were one in eight packs. There is also a first bite version of the Hammerhead parallel. These cards were inserted one in eight first bite packs.

	MINT	NRMT
COMPLETE SET (45)	80.00	36.00
COMMON CARD (1-45)	.50	.23
COMMON DRIVER (1-45)	1.00	.45

*HAMMERHEAD CARDS: 2X TO 5X BASIC CARDS

FIRST BITE COMP. SET (45)	100.00	45.00

*FB CARDS: .5X TO 1.25X HAMMERHEAD CARDS

1997 Race Sharks Tiger Shark

This 45-card set is the toughest level parallel in the Race Sharks brand. The Tiger Shark cards were double foil stamped and micro-etched. There is 675 of each card available. The odds of pulling a Tiger Shark card were one in 16 packs. This is the same odds to pull a Tiger Shark First Bite card from a First Bite pack.

	MINT	NRMT
COMPLETE SET (45)	150.00	70.00
COMMON CARD (1-45)	.75	.35
COMMON DRIVER (1-45)	1.50	.70

*TIGER SHARK CARDS: 3X TO 8X BASIC CARDS

FIRST BITE COMP. SET (45)	200.00	90.00

*FIRST BITE CARDS: .5X TO 1.25X TIGER SHARK CARDS

1997 Race Sharks Great White

This 10-card insert set features the dominant drivers on the NASCAR circuit. Each card also features a real Shark's tooth embedded in the card. The odds of pulling one of these cards is one in 96 packs. The First Bite versions of the Great White cards featured white sharks teeth as opposed to gray colored sharks teeth on the regular Whites.

	MINT	
COMPLETE SET (10)	300.00	1
COMMON CARD (1-10)	6.00	

*SINGLES: 12X TO 30X BASE CARD HI

COMP. FIRST BITE (10)	500.00	2

*FIRST BITE CARDS: 15X TO 40X BASIC CARDS

❑ GW1 Dale Earnhardt	90.00
❑ GW2 Jeff Gordon	90.00
❑ GW3 Terry Labonte	50.00
❑ GW4 Dale Jarrett	40.00
❑ GW5 Rusty Wallace	50.00
❑ GW6 Mark Martin	50.00
❑ GW7 Bobby Labonte	20.00
❑ GW8 Bill Elliott	50.00
❑ GW9 Sterling Marlin	12.00
❑ GW10 Ricky Craven	6.00

1997 Race Sharks Previe First Bite Shark Attack

This 10-card set was issued via a box topper in Jewels Elite boxes. Wheels had their distributors their unsold inventory of Crown Jewels Elite box repackaged them with one of these Preview Fir Shark Attack cards. This was to help the deale through of the Crown Jewels Elite product.

	MINT
COMPLETE SET (10)	25.00
COMMON CARD (1-10)	.75

*SINGLES: 1.25X TO 3X BASE CARD HI

❑ 1 Jeff Burton	1.50
❑ 2 Ward Burton	.75
❑ 3 Dale Earnhardt	15.00
❑ 4 Jeff Gordon	15.00
❑ 5 Dale Jarrett	8.00
❑ 6 Terry Labonte	10.00
❑ 7 Sterling Marlin	1.50
❑ 8 Kyle Petty	1.50
❑ 9 Rusty Wallace	10.00
❑ 10 Darrell Waltrip	1.50

1997 Race Sharks Shark Attack

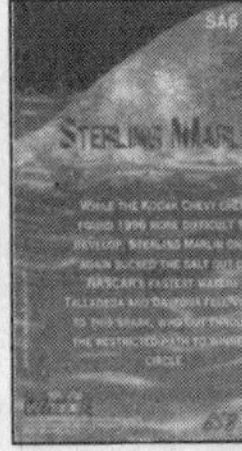

Just when you thought it was safe to go back in favorite hobby store. That was the slogan Wheels promote their Race Sharks product. The 10-carc Attack set featured micro-etched cards and a sir embossed shark's tooth. The cards were randomly one in 48 packs.

	MINT
COMPLETE SET (10)	120.00
COMMON CARD (1-10)	3.00

*SINGLES: 6X TO 15X BASE CARD HI

COMP. FIRST BITE SET(10)	150.00

*FB CARDS: 8X TO 20X SHARK ATTACK CARDS

❑ SA1 Dale Earnhardt	30.00
❑ SA2 Jeff Gordon	30.00
❑ SA3 Dale Jarrett	12.00
❑ SA4 Rusty Wallace	15.00

Terry Labonte 15.00 6.75
Sterling Marlin 6.00 2.70
Michael Waltrip 3.00 1.35
Kyle Petty 6.00 2.70
Ward Burton 3.00 1.35
0 Jeff Burton 6.00 2.70

1997 Race Sharks Shark Tooth Signatures

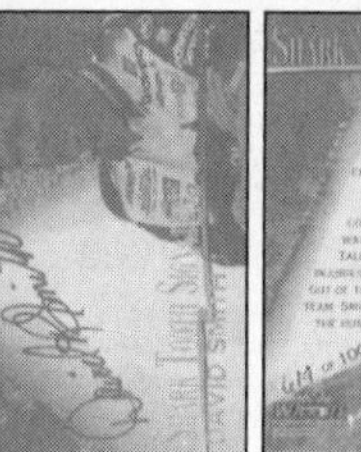

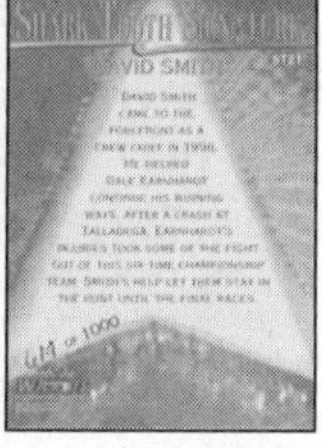

5-card set features autographs of Winston Cup and Grand National drivers, crew chiefs, owners and racing personalities. The cards were inserted one packs.

	MINT	NRMT
LETE SET (25)	700.00	325.00
ON CARD (1-25)	6.00	2.70
ON DRIVER (1-25)	15.00	6.75
. FIRST BITE SET(25)	1000.00	450.00

RDS: .75X TO 1.25X SHARK TOOTH SIGNATURE

Dale Earnhardt	200.00	90.00
Jeff Gordon	200.00	90.00
Dale Jarrett	60.00	27.00
Terry Labonte	80.00	36.00
Sterling Marlin	30.00	13.50
Bill Elliott	80.00	36.00
Ricky Craven	15.00	6.75
Robert Pressley	15.00	6.75
Jeff Burton	30.00	13.50
Ward Burton	15.00	6.75
Bobby Labonte	50.00	22.00
Joe Nemechek	15.00	6.75
Chad Little	15.00	6.75
David Green	15.00	6.75
Jeff Green	15.00	6.75
Joe Gibbs	8.00	3.60
Todd Parrott	6.00	2.70
Jeff Hammond	6.00	2.70
Charlie Pressley	6.00	2.70
Joey Knuckles	6.00	2.70
David Smith	6.00	2.70
Brad Parrott	6.00	2.70
Eddie Dickerson	6.00	2.70
Randy Dorton	6.00	2.70
Jimmy Johnson	6.00	2.70

1996 Racer's Choice

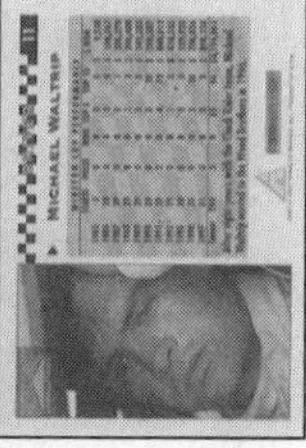

0-card set was the first time Pinnacle issued a set he Racer's Choice brand name. The black bordered eature top Winston Cup stars and their cars. The were packaged eight cards per pack; 36 packs per d 20 boxes per case. Suggested retail price on a as 99 cents. Also randomly inserted in the bottom by boxes was a 5" X 7" Jeff Gordon 1995 onship card. The card features the dufex printing ogy and could be found one in every three boxes. ed at the bottom of the base set listing.

	MINT	NRMT
ETE SET (110)	10.00	4.50
N CARD (1-110)	.10	.05
N DRIVER (1-110)	.20	.09

Mast	.20	.09
❑ 2 Rusty Wallace	.75	.35
❑ 3 Dale Earnhardt	1.50	.70
❑ 4 Sterling Marlin	.40	.18
❑ 5 Terry Labonte	.75	.35
❑ 6 Mark Martin	.75	.35
❑ 7 Ward Burton	.20	.09
❑ 8 Joe Nemechek	.20	.09
❑ 9 Jeff Gordon	1.50	.70
❑ 10 Ted Musgrave	.20	.09
❑ 11 Michael Waltrip	.20	.09
❑ 12 Johnny Benson, Jr.	.20	.09
❑ 13 Bill Elliott	.75	.35
❑ 14 Bobby Labonte	.60	.25
❑ 15 Ricky Rudd	.40	.18
❑ 16 Dale Jarrett	.60	.25
❑ 17 Bobby Hamilton	.20	.09
❑ 18 Ken Schrader	.20	.09
❑ 19 Derrike Cope	.20	.09
❑ 20 Brett Bodine	.20	.09
❑ 21 Darrell Waltrip	.40	.18
❑ 22 John Andretti	.20	.09
❑ 23 Jeremy Mayfield	.50	.23
❑ 24 Ernie Irvan	.40	.18
❑ 25 Lake Speed	.20	.09
❑ 26 Rusty Wallace's Car	.40	.18
❑ 27 Dale Earnhardt's Car	.75	.35
❑ 28 Sterling Marlin's Car	.20	.09
❑ 29 Terry Labonte's Car	.40	.18
❑ 30 Mark Martin's Car	.40	.18
❑ 31 Jimmy Spencer's Car	.10	.05
❑ 32 Dale Jarrett's Car	.40	.18
❑ 33 Ricky Rudd's Car	.20	.09
❑ 34 Derrike Cope's Car	.10	.05
❑ 35 Ward Burton's Car	.10	.05
❑ 36 Ted Musgrave's Car	.10	.05
❑ 37 Darrell Waltrip's Car	.20	.09
❑ 38 Bobby Labonte's Car	.40	.18
❑ 39 Michael Waltrip w/Car	.20	.09
❑ 40 Jeff Gordon's Car	.75	.35
❑ 41 Ernie Irvan's Car	.20	.09
❑ 42 Johnny Benson, Jr.'s Car	.10	.05
❑ 43 Brett Bodine's Car	.10	.05
❑ 44 Ricky Craven's Car	.10	.05
❑ 45 Bobby Hamilton's Car	.10	.05
❑ 46 Morgan Shepherd's Car	.10	.05
❑ 47 Joe Nemechek's Car	.10	.05
❑ 48 Bill Elliott's Car	.40	.18
❑ 49 Jeremy Mayfield's Car	.40	.18
❑ 50 John Andretti's Car	.10	.05
❑ 51 Jeff Gordon WCC	.75	.35
❑ 52 Jeff Gordon WCC	.75	.35
❑ 53 Jeff Gordon WCC	.75	.35
❑ 54 Jeff Gordon WCC	.75	.35
❑ 55 Jeff Gordon WCC Danielle Randall Jim Brochhausen	.75	.35
❑ 56 Dale Earnhardt I Don Hawk	.75	.35
❑ 57 Dale Earnhardt I	.75	.35
❑ 58 Dale Earnhardt I	.75	.35
❑ 59 Dale Earnhardt I	.75	.35
❑ 60 Dale Earnhardt I	.75	.35
❑ 61 Ted Musgrave HC	.10	.05
❑ 62 Ted Musgrave HC Howard Comstock	.10	.05
❑ 63 Ted Musgrave HC Brittany Musgrave	.10	.05
❑ 64 Ted Musgrave HC	.10	.05
❑ 65 Ted Musgrave HC	.10	.05
❑ 66 Bobby Labonte OF	.40	.18
❑ 67 Bobby Labonte OF	.40	.18
❑ 68 Bobby Labonte OF Donna Labonte	.40	.18
❑ 69 Bobby Labonte OF	.40	.18
❑ 70 Bobby Labonte OF	.40	.18
❑ 71 Sterling Marlin PH	.20	.09
❑ 72 Sterling Marlin PH Clifton Marlin Paula Marlin Sutherlin Marlin Steadman Marlin	.20	.09
❑ 73 Sterling Marlin PH	.20	.09
❑ 74 Sterling Marlin PH Tony Glover	.20	.09
❑ 75 Sterling Marlin PH	.20	.09
❑ 76 John Andretti's Car	.10	.05
❑ 77 Joe Nemechek's Car	.10	.05
❑ 78 Michael Waltrip's Car	.10	.05
❑ 79 Doyle Ford	.10	.05
❑ 80 Jimmy Cox	.10	.05
❑ 81 Elmo Langley	.10	.05
❑ 82 Rusty Wallace RW	.40	.18
❑ 83 Jeff Gordon RW	.75	.35
❑ 84 Dale Earnhardt RW	.75	.35
❑ 85 Mark Martin RW	.40	.18
❑ 86 Mark Martin RW	.40	.18
❑ 87 Ward Burton RW Tabitha Burton Sarah Burton Jeb Burton	.10	.05
❑ 88 Ricky Rudd RW Linda Rudd	.20	.09
❑ 89 Dale Earnhardt RW	.75	.35
❑ 90 Jeff Gordon BC	.75	.35
❑ 91 Dale Jarrett BC	.40	.18
❑ 92 Dale Earnhardt BC	.75	.35
❑ 93 Mark Martin BC	.40	.18
❑ 94 Bobby Labonte BC	.40	.18
❑ 95 Terry Labonte BC	.40	.18
❑ 96 Ricky Rudd BC	.20	.09
❑ 97 Ken Schrader BC	.10	.05
❑ 98 Bill Elliott BC	.40	.18
❑ 99 Sterling Marlin BC	.20	.09
❑ 100 John Andretti BC	.10	.05
❑ 101 Rick Mast BC	.10	.05
❑ 102 Ted Musgrave BC	.10	.05
❑ 103 David Green BC	.10	.05
❑ 104 Hut Stricklin BC	.10	.05
❑ 105 Darrell Waltrip BC	.20	.09
❑ 106 Johnny Benson Jr. R	.10	.05
❑ 107 Johnny Benson Jr. R	.10	.05
❑ 108 Johnny Benson Jr. R	.10	.05
❑ 109 Mark Martin CL	.40	.18
❑ 110 Jeff Gordon CL	.75	.35
❑ J52 Jeff Gordon 5 X 7	6.00	2.70

1996 Racer's Choice Artist's Proof

The 110-card Artist's Proof set is a parallel to the base set. Each card features copper foil and an Artist's Proof logo to differentiate them from the base cards. The cards were seeded one per 35 regular packs and one per 17 jumbo packs.

	MINT	NRMT
COMPLETE SET (110)	250.00	110.00
COMMON CARD (1-110)	2.50	1.10
COMMON DRIVER (1-110)	5.00	2.20

ARTIST'S PROOF CARDS: 10X TO X BASIC CARDS

1996 Racer's Choice Speedway Collection

The 110-card Speedway Collection set is a parallel to the base set. The cards feature silver foil and a Speedway Collection logo to differentiate them from the base cards. The cards were inserted one per six regular packs and one per three jumbo packs.

	MINT	NRMT
COMPLETE SET (110)	40.00	18.00
COMMON CARD (1-110)	.40	.18
COMMON DRIVER (1-110)	.80	.35

SPEEDWAY COL. CARDS: 2X TO X BASIC CARDS

1996 Racer's Choice Top Ten

This 10-card insert set features the drivers who finished in the Top Ten in the 1995 Winston Cup points standings. The cards were printed on foil board and use micro-etched highlights. Top Ten cards were randomly inserted in packs at a rate of one in 69 regular packs and of one in 35 jumbo packs.

	MINT	NRMT
COMPLETE SET (10)	100.00	45.00
COMMON CARD (1-10)	2.50	1.10

*SINGLES: 8X TO 20X BASE CARD HI

❑ 1 Jeff Gordon	25.00	11.00
❑ 2 Dale Earnhardt	25.00	11.00
❑ 3 Sterling Marlin	5.00	2.20
❑ 4 Mark Martin	12.00	5.50
❑ 5 Rusty Wallace	12.00	5.50
❑ 6 Terry Labonte	12.00	5.50
❑ 7 Ted Musgrave	2.50	1.10
❑ 8 Bill Elliott	12.00	5.50
❑ 9 Ricky Rudd	5.00	2.20
❑ 10 Bobby Labonte	8.00	3.60

1996 Racer's Choice Up Close with Dale Earnhardt

This 7-card insert set could be found in hobby only packs. The cards feature Winston Cup great Dale Earnhardt. The cards were randomly inserted in hobby packs at a rate of one in 31.

	MINT	NRMT
COMPLETE SET (7)	30.00	13.50
DALE EARNHARDT CARD (1-7)	5.00	2.20

1996 Racer's Choice Up Close with Jeff Gordon

This 7-card insert set features 1995 Winston Cup Champion Jeff Gordon.The cards were seeded in retail packs at a rate of one in 31.

	MINT	NRMT
COMPLETE SET (7)	30.00	13.50
JEFF GORDON CARD (1-7)	5.00	2.20

1996 Racer's Choice Sundrop

One card was inserted in each specially marked 12-packs of Sundrop citrus soda. The cards come in an opaque wrapper attached to the cardboard packaging of the 12-packs. There were signed copies of each of the three cards also randomly inserted in the soft drink packages. The autographed cards were not certified in any way and are otherwise indistinguishable from the unsigned regular cards. Many dealers have left the signed cards in the opaque wrappers to distinguish the origin of the card. Autographed cards without the wrapper are commonly found for $25-$50. Ones found in the wrapper are commonly found for $75-150.

	MINT	NRMT
COMPLETE SET (3)	15.00	6.75
COMMON CARD (SD1-SD3)	5.00	2.20
❑ SD1 Dale Earnhardt	5.00	2.20
❑ SD2 Dale Earnhardt	5.00	2.20
❑ SD3 Dale Earnhardt	5.00	2.20

1997 Racer's Choice

This 106-card set was prodcued by Pinnacle Brands. The white bordered cards feature the top Winston Cup stars and their cars. Cards were distributed in eight card packs with 36 pack in a box. The packs carried a suggested retail price of $.99.

	MINT	NRMT
COMPLETE SET (106)	12.00	5.50
COMMON CARD (1-106)	.10	.05
COMMON DRIVER (1-106)	.20	.09
CAR/SUBSET CARDS HALF VALUE		
❑ 1 Morgan Shepherd	.20	.09
❑ 2 Rusty Wallace	.75	.35
❑ 3 Dale Earnhardt	1.50	.70
❑ 4 Sterling Marlin	.40	.18
❑ 5 Terry Labonte	.75	.35
❑ 6 Mark Martin	.75	.35
❑ 7 Geoff Bodine	.20	.09
❑ 8 Hut Stricklin	.20	.09
❑ 9 Chad Little	.20	.09
❑ 10 Ricky Rudd	.40	.18
❑ 11 Brett Bodine	.20	.09
❑ 12 Derrike Cope	.20	.09
❑ 13 Jeremy Mayfield	.50	.23
❑ 14 Robby Gordon	.20	.09
❑ 15 Steve Grissom	.20	.09
❑ 16 Ted Musgrave	.20	.09
❑ 17 Darrell Waltrip	.40	.18
❑ 18 Bobby Labonte	.60	.25
❑ 19 John Andretti	.20	.09
❑ 20 Bobby Hamilton	.20	.09
❑ 21 Michael Waltrip	.20	.09
❑ 22 Ward Burton	.20	.09
❑ 23 Jimmy Spencer	.20	.09
❑ 24 Jeff Gordon	1.50	.70
❑ 25 Ricky Craven	.20	.09
❑ 26 Kyle Petty	.40	.18
❑ 27 Dale Earnhardt	1.50	.70
❑ 28 Ernie Irvan	.40	.18
❑ 29 Joe Nemechek	.20	.09
❑ 30 Johnny Benson	.20	.09
❑ 31 Mike Skinner	.20	.09
❑ 32 Dale Jarrett	.60	.25
❑ 33 Ken Schrader	.20	.09
❑ 34 Bill Elliott	.75	.35
❑ 35 David Green	.20	.09
❑ 36 Morgan Shepherd's Car	.10	.05
❑ 37 Rusty Wallace's Car	.40	.18
❑ 38 Dale Earnhardt's Car	.75	.35
❑ 39 Sterling Marlin's Car	.20	.09
❑ 40 Terry Labonte's Car	.40	.18
❑ 41 Mark Martin's Car	.40	.18
❑ 42 Geoff Bodine's Car	.10	.05
❑ 43 Hut Stricklin's Car	.10	.05
❑ 44 Chad Little's Car	.10	.05
❑ 45 Ricky Rudd's Car	.20	.09
❑ 46 Brett Bodine's Car	.10	.05
❑ 47 Derrike Cope's Car	.10	.05
❑ 48 Jeremy Mayfield's Car	.25	.11
❑ 49 Robby Gordon's Car	.10	.05
❑ 50 Steve Grissom's Car	.10	.05
❑ 51 Ted Musgrave's Car	.10	.05
❑ 52 Darrell Waltrip's Car	.20	.09
❑ 53 Bobby Labonte's Car	.40	.18
❑ 54 John Andretti's Car	.10	.05
❑ 55 Bobby Hamilton's Car	.10	.05
❑ 56 Michael Waltrip's Car	.10	.05
❑ 57 Ward Burton's Car	.10	.05
❑ 58 Jimmy Spencer's Car	.10	.05
❑ 59 Geoff Bodine's Car	.10	.05
❑ 60 Ricky Craven's Car	.10	.05
❑ 61 Kyle Petty's Car	.20	.09
❑ 62 Dale Earnhardt's Car	.75	.35
❑ 63 Ernie Irvan's Car	.20	.09
❑ 64 Joe Nemechek's Car	.10	.05
❑ 65 Johnny Benson's Car	.10	.05
❑ 66 Mike Skinner's Car	.10	.05
❑ 67 Dale Jarrett's Car	.40	.18
❑ 68 Ken Schrader's Car	.10	.05
❑ 69 Bill Elliott's Car	.40	.18
❑ 70 David Green's Car	.10	.05
❑ 71 Gary Nelson SS	.10	.05
❑ 72 Robert Yates SS	.10	.05
❑ 73 Robin Pemberton SS	.10	.05
❑ 74 Kyle Petty SS	.20	.09
❑ 75 Geoff Bodine SS	.10	.05
❑ 76 Earl Barban SS	.10	.05
❑ 77 Jeremy Mayfield SS	.40	.18
❑ 78 Steve Grissom SS	.10	.05
❑ 79 Mike Skinner SS	.10	.05
❑ 80 Richard Childress SS	.10	.05
❑ 81 Chocolate Meyers SS	.10	.05
❑ 82 Ward Burton SS	.10	.05
❑ 83 Chad Little SS	.10	.05
❑ 84 Buddy Parrott SS	.10	.05
❑ 85 Jimmy Cox SS	.10	.05
❑ 86 Richard Petty SS	.20	.09
❑ 87 Mike Skinner R	.10	.05
❑ 88 David Green R	.10	.05
❑ 89 Robby Gordon R	.10	.05
❑ 90 Dale Earnhardt TR	.75	.35
❑ 91 Rusty Wallace TR	.40	.18
❑ 92 Sterling Marlin TR	.20	
❑ 93 Terry Labonte TR	.40	
❑ 94 Mark Martin TR	.40	
❑ 95 Ricky Rudd TR	.20	
❑ 96 Ted Musgrave TR	.10	
❑ 97 Johnny Benson TR	.10	
❑ 98 Bobby Labonte TR	.40	
❑ 99 Bobby Hamilton TR	.10	
❑ 100 Michael Waltrip TR	.10	
❑ 101 Ward Burton TR	.10	
❑ 102 Ricky Craven TR	.10	
❑ 103 Ernie Irvan TR	.20	
❑ 104 Dale Earnhardt TR	.75	
❑ 105 Dale Jarrett TR	.40	
❑ 106 Dale Earnhardt CL	.75	

1997 Racer's Choice Showcase Series

The 106-card Showcase Series is a parallel to the set. The cards feature silver foil to differentiate them the base cards. The cards were randomly insert packs at a ratio of 1:7.

	MINT
COMPLETE SET (106)	80.00
COMMON CARD (1-106)	.60
COMMON DRIVER (1-106)	1.25

*SHOWCASE CARDS: 2.5X TO 6X BASIC CARDS

1997 Racer's Choice Busch Clash

This 14-card insert highlights those NASCAR drive have appeared in the Busch Clash. The cards randomly inserted in hobby packs at a ratio of 1:47 magazine packs at a ratio of 1:23.

	MINT
COMPLETE SET (14)	150.00
COMMON CARD (1-14)	3.00
*SINGLES: 8X TO 20X BASE CARD HI	
❑ 1 Dale Earnhardt	40.00
❑ 2 Terry Labonte	25.00
❑ 3 Johnny Benson	10.00
❑ 4 Ward Burton	10.00
❑ 5 Mark Martin	25.00
❑ 6 Ricky Craven	3.00
❑ 7 Ernie Irvan	6.00
❑ 8 Jeff Gordon	40.00
❑ 9 Ted Musgrave	3.00
❑ 10 Jeremy Mayfield	10.00
❑ 11 Dale Earnhardt	40.00
❑ 12 Dale Jarrett	20.00
❑ 13 Bobby Labonte	15.00
❑ 14 Rusty Wallace	25.00

1997 Racer's Choice Chevy Madness

This 6-card set is the continuation of the set that in 1997 Action Packed and ended in 1997 Pinna cards were randomly inserted in hobby packs at a 1:17 and in magazine packs at a ratio of 1:8.

	MINT	NRMT
LETE SET (6)	25.00	11.00
1ON CARD (7-12)	1.00	.45
LES: 2.5X TO 6X BASE CARD HI		
ff Gordon	15.00	6.75
ıle Earnhardt	15.00	6.75
cky Craven	1.00	.45
Robby Gordon	1.00	.45
eff Green	1.00	.45
'erry Labonte	8.00	3.60

1997 Racer's Choice High Octane

5-card set features the top 15 drivers from the n Cup circuit.The cards were randomly inserted in packs at a ratio of 1:23 and in magazine packs at a 1:12.

	MINT	NRMT
.ETE SET (15)	100.00	45.00
ON CARD (1-15)	2.00	.90
.ES: 8X TO 20X BASE CARD HI		
'ry Labonte	15.00	6.75
e Earnhardt	25.00	11.00
f Gordon	25.00	11.00
e Jarrett	12.00	5.50
rk Martin	15.00	6.75
sty Wallace	15.00	6.75
Elliott	15.00	6.75
oby Labonte	8.00	3.60
ie Irvan	4.00	1.80
/le Petty	4.00	1.80
cky Rudd	4.00	1.80
hnny Benson	2.00	.90
ard Burton	2.00	.90
d Musgrave	2.00	.90
ıle Earnhardt	25.00	11.00

1997 Racer's Choice h Octane Glow in the Dark

card set is a parallel of the regular High Octane an be differentiated from the regular cards by the the border of the card glows in the dark. The ere randomly inserted in hobby packs at a ratio of in magazine packs at a ratio of 1:35.

	MINT	NRMT
ETE SET (15)	200.00	90.00
N CARD (1-15)	4.00	1.80

1991 Racing Concepts Shawna Robinson

e-card set features one of the most popular rivers ever to race NASCAR, Shawna Robinson. was distributed through Sparky's and were sold with cards 1-6 and a Sparky's coupon that e redeemed for one of the cards, 7-9, with .

	MINT	NRMT
TE SET (9)	10.00	4.50
N CARD (1-9)	1.00	.45

❑ 1 Cover Card	.50	.23
❑ 2 Shawna Robinson	1.00	.45
❑ 3 Shawna Robinson	1.00	.45
❑ 4 Shawna Robinson	1.00	.45
❑ 5 Shawna Robinson	1.00	.45
❑ 6 Shawna Robinson Dwight Huffman Dennis Combs	1.00	.45
❑ 7 Shawna Robinson	1.00	.45
❑ 8 Shawna Robinson David Pearson	1.00	.45
❑ 9 Shawna Robinson	1.00	.45

1992 Redline Graphics Short Track

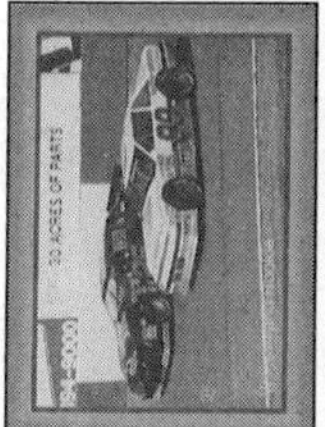
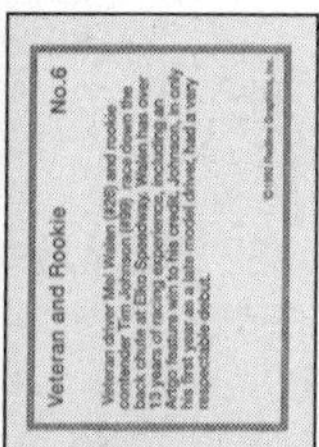

Redline Graphics produced this set featuring race action scenes from various short track races. The cards primarily picture exciting crashes caught by the photographer.

	MINT	NRMT
COMPLETE SET (30)	10.00	4.50
COMMON CARD (1-30)	.35	.16
❑ 1 Cover Card Mark Lamoreaux's Car Conrad Morgan's Car	.35	.16
❑ 2 Late Model Sandwich Tom Carlson's Car Conrad Morgan's Car Jason Keller's Car	.35	.16
❑ 3 Elko Speedway Brian Johnson's Car Bret Berg's Car	.35	.16
❑ 4 Window Shot #1 M.G.Gajewski's Car Al Schill's Car	.35	.16
❑ 5 Window Shot #2 M.G.Gajewski's Car Al Schill's Car	.35	.16
❑ 6 Veteran and Rookie Mel Walen's Car Tim Johnson's Car	.35	.16
❑ 7 Lift Off Mark Lamoreaux's Car Conrad Morgan's Car	.35	.16
❑ 8 Orbit Mark Lamoreaux's Car Conrad Morgan's Car	.35	.16
❑ 9 Landing Mark Lamoreaux's Car Conrad Morgan's Car	.35	.16
❑ 10 Aftermath Mark Lamoreaux's Car	.35	.16
❑ 11 Inside Move Dennis Barta's Car Tom Gille's Car	.35	.16
❑ 12 Three Deep Tom Karnish's Car Gary Petrash's Car Loren Petrash's Car	.35	.16
❑ 13 Roof Dance Tom Karnish's Car Gary Petrash's Car Loren Petrash's Car	.35	.16
❑ 14 The Ride Continues Tom Karnish's Car Gary Petrash's Car Loren Petrash's Car	.35	.16
❑ 15 Finally Over Tom Karnish's Car Gary Petrash's Car Loren Petrash's Car Steve Murgic's Car	.35	.16
❑ 16 Miraculous Tom Karnish's Car Gary Petrash's Car Loren Petrash's Car	.35	.16
❑ 17 High Speed Wipeout Loren Petrash's Car	.35	.16
❑ 18 Front Stretch Mishap Bruce Lee's Car Mike Mohn's Car	.35	.16
❑ 19 Prelude to Defeat Don Jenkins' Car Pete Moore's Car	.35	.16
❑ 20 Oh No! Rich Bickle's Car Don Jenkins' Car Pete Moore's Car	.60	.25
❑ 21 Fabulous Race Rich Bickle's Car Mike Garvey's Car	.60	.25
❑ 22 Raceway Park Doug Balombini's Car Christian Elder's Car	.35	.16
❑ 23 Champion Mike Tuma's Car Steve Fredrickson's Car	.35	.16
❑ 24 Hobby Crash Danny Hron's Car	.35	.16
❑ 25 Show Car Mike Mohn w/Car	.50	.23
❑ 26 Parking Lot multi-car crash	.35	.16
❑ 27 Ouch! Ken Reiser's Car	.35	.16
❑ 28 Father and Son Steve Murgic's Car Mike Murgic's Car	.50	.23
❑ 29 Infamous Turn Four Robbie Reiser's Car	.35	.16
❑ 30 Checklist Card	.35	.16

1992 Redline Racing Harry Gant

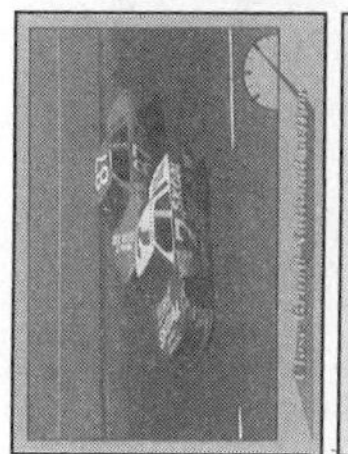
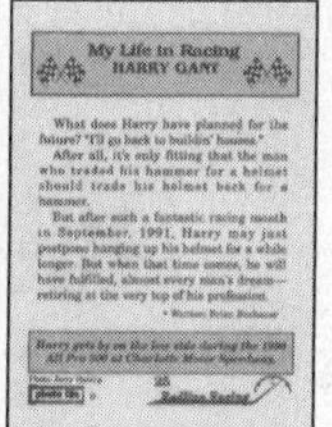

This set is one of four issues produced in 1992 by Redline Racing entitled My Life in Racing. The set focuses on the life of Harry Gant with text written in story form on the cardbacks. The four driver sets were packaged together in factory set form 24-sets per display box. Each set includes a colorful factory box and was limited to a production run of 25,000.

	MINT	NRMT
COMPLETE SET (30)	8.00	3.60
COMMON CARD (1-30)	.30	.14

1992 Redline Racing Rob Moroso

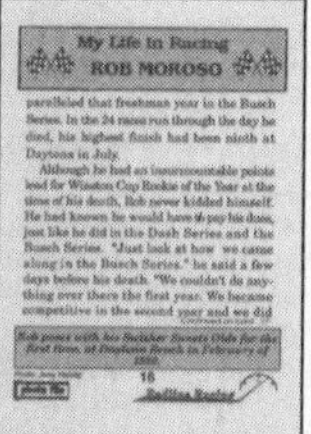

This set is one of four issues produced in 1992 by Redline Racing entitled My Life in Racing. The set focuses on the life and tragic death of Rob Moroso with text written in story form on the cardbacks. The four driver sets were packaged together in factory set form 24-sets per display box. Each set includes a colorful factory set box was limited to a production run of 25,000.

	MINT	NRMT
COMPLETE SET (30)	8.00	3.60
COMMON CARD (1-30)	.30	.14

1992 Redline Racing Ken Schrader

This set is one of four issues produced in 1992 by Redline Racing entitled My Life in Racing. The set focuses on the

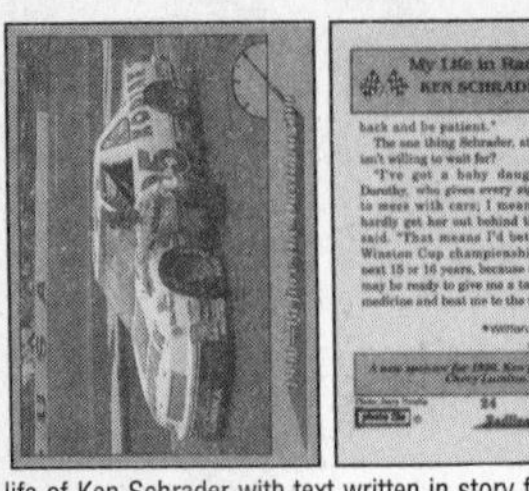

life of Ken Schrader with text written in story form on the cardbacks. The four driver sets were packaged together in factory set form 24-sets per display box. Each set includes a colorful factory box and was limited to a production run of 25,000.

	MINT	NRMT
COMPLETE SET (30)	7.00	3.10
COMMON CARD (1-30)	.25	.11

1992 Redline Racing Cale Yarborough

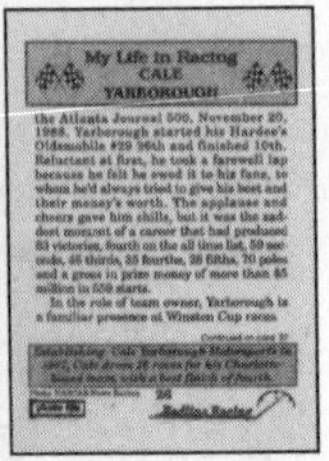

This set is one of four issues produced in 1992 by Redline Racing entitled My Life in Racing. The set focuses on the life of Cale Yarborough with text written in story form on the cardbacks. The four sets were packaged together in factory set form 24-sets per display box. Each set includes a colorful factory box and was limited to a production run of 25,000.

	MINT	NRMT
COMPLETE SET (30)	7.00	3.10
COMMON CARD (1-30)	.25	.11

1992 Redline Standups

Redline Racing and Photo File of New York produced this unique set in 1992. Each card could be folded in such a way as to stand-up independently. The cards were packed one per foil pack (48-packs per box) and contain a full bleed color photo on the front. Another photo and brief driver stats are on the cardback with the set name and die cut photo of the driver's car on the stand-up support piece. Uncut sheets of the 36-card set have also been made available.

	MINT	NRMT
COMPLETE SET (36)	10.00	4.50
COMMON CARD	.20	.09

Card	MINT	NRMT
❑ 1 Rick Mast	.20	.09
❑ 2 Dave Marcis	.20	.09
❑ 3 Richard Petty	.60	.25
❑ 4 Bobby Labonte	.75	.35
❑ 5 Jimmy Means	.20	.09
❑ 6 Mark Martin	1.00	.45
❑ 7 Alan Kulwicki	.60	.25
❑ 8 Rick Wilson	.20	.09
❑ 9 Bill Elliott	1.00	.45
❑ 10 Derrike Cope	.20	.09
❑ 11 Geoff Bodine	.20	.09
❑ 12 Jack Ingram	.20	.09
❑ 13 Dick Trickle	.20	.09
❑ 14 Jeff Burton	.40	.18
❑ 15 Morgan Shepherd	.20	.09
❑ 16 Tom Peck	.20	.09
❑ 17 Darrell Waltrip	.40	.18
❑ 18 Jimmy Spencer	.20	.09
❑ 19 Chad Little	.20	.09
❑ 20 Bobby Hillin	.20	.09
❑ 21 Dale Jarrett	.75	.35
❑ 22 Sterling Marlin	.40	.18
❑ 23 Bobby Hamilton	.20	.09
❑ 24 Kyle Petty	.40	.18
❑ 25 Ken Schrader	.20	.09
❑ 26 Brett Bodine	.20	.09
❑ 27 Chuck Bown	.20	.09
❑ 28 Kenny Wallace	.20	.09
❑ 29 Joe Nemechek	.20	.09
❑ 30 Terry Labonte	1.00	.45
❑ 31 Steve Grissom	.20	.09
❑ 32 Jimmy Hensley	.20	.09
❑ 33 Harry Gant	.40	.18
❑ 34 Harry Gant	.40	.18
❑ 35 Bobby Labonte	.75	.35
❑ 36 Doyle Ford	.20	.09

1992 RSS Motorsports Haulers

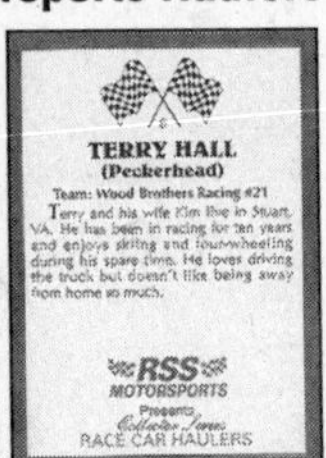

TERRY HALL
(Peckerhead)
Team: Wood Brothers Racing #21
RSS MOTORSPORTS
Presents
Collector Series
RACE CAR HAULERS

RSS Motorsports released these cards in complete set form. They feature transporter drivers for top NASCAR race teams. Jerry Schweitz is included in the set twice with the second card bearing a "promotional card" logo on the cardback. The checklist card contains two misnumbered cards.

	MINT	NRMT
COMPLETE (30)	3.00	1.35
COMMON CARD (1-30)	.10	.05

Card	MINT	NRMT
❑ 1 Richard Bostick Jr.	.10	.05
❑ 2 Jerry Seabolt	.10	.05
❑ 3 Ken J. Hartley	.10	.05
❑ 4 George R. Colwell	.10	.05
❑ 5 Carroll Hoss Berry	.10	.05
❑ 6 Terry Hall	.10	.05
❑ 7 Robin Metdepenningen	.10	.05
❑ 8 Buster Auton	.10	.05
❑ 9 Henry Benfield	.10	.05
❑ 10 Gale W. Wilson	.10	.05
❑ 11 Peter Jellen	.10	.05
❑ 12 Tommy Rigsbee	.10	.05
❑ 13 Harold Hughes	.10	.05
❑ 14 Gene Starnes	.10	.05
❑ 15 Bill McCarthy	.10	.05
❑ 16 Bryan Dorsey	.10	.05
❑ 17 Dennis Ritchie	.10	.05
❑ 18 Joe Lewis	.10	.05
❑ 19 Mike Powell	.10	.05
❑ 20 Steve Foster	.10	.05
❑ 21 Jerry Schweitz	.10	.05
❑ 22 Ted Harrison	.10	.05
❑ 23 Norman Koshimizu	.10	.05
❑ 24 Charlie Hyde	.10	.05
❑ 25 Mike Culbertson	.10	.05
❑ 26 Jim Baldwin	.10	.05
❑ 27 Bart Creasman	.10	.05
❑ 28 Jerry Schweitz Promo	.10	.05
❑ 29 Checklist Card UER cards 26 and 28 misnumbered	.10	.05
❑ 30 Cover Card	.10	.05

1997 SB Motorsports

This 100-card set captures the top names in Winston Cup racing, including drivers, owners, crew chiefs, crew members and announcers. Each card carries complete updated stats through the 1996 racing season. The cards were packaged six per pack with 36 packs per box and 16 boxes per case. SB stands for manufactuer Score Board.

	MINT	NRMT
COMPLETE SET (100)	10.00	4.50
COMMON CARD (1-100)	.10	.05
COMMON DRIVER (1-100)	.20	.09

Card	MINT	NRMT
❑ 1 Dale Earnhardt	1.50	.70

Card	MINT
❑ 2 Jeff Gordon	1.50
❑ 3 Terry Labonte	.75
❑ 4 Dale Jarrett	.60
❑ 5 Robby Gordon	.20
❑ 6 Mark Martin	.75
❑ 7 Ricky Rudd	.40
❑ 8 Richard Petty	.50
❑ 9 Ken Schrader	.20
❑ 10 Ernie Irvan	.40
❑ 11 Sterling Marlin	.40
❑ 12 Bobby Labonte	.60
❑ 13 Ted Musgrave	.20
❑ 14 Bobby Hamilton	.20
❑ 15 Jimmy Spencer	.20
❑ 16 Michael Waltrip	.20
❑ 17 Jeff Burton	.40
❑ 18 Rick Mast	.20
❑ 19 Geoff Bodine	.20
❑ 20 Ricky Craven	.20
❑ 21 Morgan Shepherd	.20
❑ 22 Johnny Benson	.20
❑ 23 Jeremy Mayfield	.50
❑ 24 Wally Dallenbach	.20
❑ 25 Brett Bodine	.20
❑ 26 Larry Hedrick	.10
❑ 27 Ned Jarrett	.20
❑ 28 Darrell Waltrip	.40
❑ 29 Hut Stricklin	.20
❑ 30 Richard Petty	.50
❑ 31 Kyle Petty	.40
❑ 32 Robert Yates	.10
❑ 33 Mike Skinner	.20
❑ 34 Robin Pemberton	.10
❑ 35 Ray Evernham	.20
❑ 36 Larry McReynolds	.10
❑ 37 Mike Wallace	.20
❑ 38 Steve Park	1.50
❑ 39 Steve Grissom	.20
❑ 40 Dale Jarrett	.60
❑ 41 Dale Earnhardt	1.50
❑ 42 Mark Martin	.75
❑ 43 Ricky Rudd	.40
❑ 44 Wood Brothers	.10
❑ 45 Robby Gordon's Car	.10
❑ 46 Rusty Wallace's Car	.40
❑ 47 Dale Earnhardt's Car	.75
❑ 48 Sterling Marlin's Car	.20
❑ 49 Mark Martin's Car	.40
❑ 50 Dale Earnhardt's Car CL	.75
❑ 51 Bobby Labonte's Car	.40
❑ 52 Michael Waltrip's Car	.10
❑ 53 Ernie Irvan's Car	.20
❑ 54 Darrell Waltrip's Car	.20
❑ 55 Dale Jarrett's Car	.40
❑ 56 Dave Rezendes	.20
❑ 57 Sterling Marlin	.40
❑ 58 Ken Schrader	.20
❑ 59 Richard Childress	.10
❑ 60 Wood Brothers	.10
❑ 61 Tony Glover	.10
❑ 62 Steve Hmiel	.10
❑ 63 The Rainbow Warriors	.40
❑ 64 Steve Grissom	.20
❑ 65 Larry McClure	.10
❑ 66 Ernie Irvan	.40
❑ 67 Jerry Punch	.10
❑ 68 Shelton Pittman	.10
❑ 69 Jack Roush UER Roush Racing	.10
❑ 70 Geoff Bodine	.20
❑ 71 Robert Pressley	.20
❑ 72 John Andretti	.20
❑ 73 Ward Burton	.20
❑ 74 Dick Trickle	.20
❑ 75 Dave Marcis	.40
❑ 76 Kenny Wallace	.20
❑ 77 Todd Bodine	.20
❑ 78 Gary DeHart	.10
❑ 79 Ron Hornaday	.20
❑ 80 David Green	.20
❑ 81 Randy Dorton	.10
❑ 82 Kellogg's Crew	.40
❑ 83 Johnny Benson	.20

eremy Mayfield	.50	.23
/ike Skinner	.20	.09
25 Hendrick Team	.10	.05
obby Labonte	.60	.25
immy Johnson	.10	.05
immy Spencer	.20	.09
/ichael Waltrip	.20	.09
/lorgan Shepherd	.20	.09
ale Earnhardt	1.50	.70
ale Jarrett	.60	.25
ick Hendrick	.10	.05
lark Martin	.75	.35
icky Rudd	.40	.18
rnie Irvan	.40	.18
terling Marlin	.40	.18
yle Petty	.40	.18
Sterling Marlin's Car CL	.20	.09

1997 SB Motorsports Autographs

o five drivers from the Winston Cup circuit have igned these insert cards. The cards were inserted 576 Packs. Each card was sequentially numbered.

	MINT	NRMT
.ETE SET (5)	700.00	325.00
ON CARD (AU1-AU5)	30.00	13.50
Dale Earnhardt	300.00	135.00
Jeff Gordon	300.00	135.00
Terry Labonte	90.00	40.00
Dale Jarrett	75.00	34.00
Robby Gordon	30.00	13.50

1997 SB Motorsports Race Chat

-card insert set features quotes on the backs of rd from drivers, owners, and crew chiefs about the eatured on the card. The quotes give insight as to ey feel about racing and their competitors. The ere seeded one in 35 packs.

	MINT	NRMT
ETE SET (10)	60.00	27.00
)N CARD (RC1-RC10)	2.50	1.10
ES: 6X TO 15X BASE CARD HI		
)ale Earnhardt	25.00	11.00
?icky Craven	2.50	1.10
:rnie Irvan	5.00	2.20
)ale Jarrett	8.00	3.60
Sterling Marlin	5.00	2.20
/lark Martin	12.00	5.50
ohnny Benson	2.50	1.10
?icky Rudd	5.00	2.20
?obby Labonte	6.00	2.70
Kyle Petty	5.00	2.20

1997 SB Motorsports W.C. Rewind

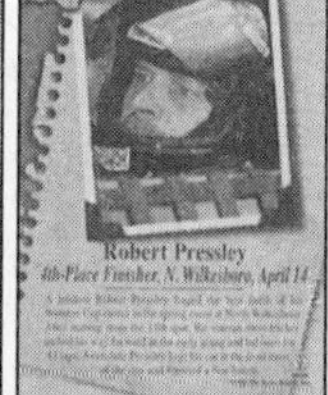

card insert set commemorates something from the Winston Cup events in 1996. The cards were y inserted in packs at a rate of one in 8 packs.

	MINT	NRMT
COMPLETE SET (31)	60.00	27.00
COMMON CARDS (WC1-WC31)	1.00	.45
*SINGLES: 2X TO 5X BASE CARD HI		
❑ WC2 Dale Earnhardt's Car	5.00	2.20
❑ WC3 Ted Musgrave	1.00	.45
❑ WC4 Johnny Benson	1.00	.45
❑ WC5 Ward Burton	1.00	.45
❑ WC6 Mark Martin	5.00	2.20
❑ WC7 Robert Pressley	1.00	.45
❑ WC8 Ricky Craven	1.00	.45
❑ WC9 Sterling Marlin	2.00	.90
❑ WC10 Wally Dallenbach	1.00	.45
❑ WC11 Dale Jarrett	3.00	1.35
❑ WC12 Bobby Labonte	2.50	1.10
❑ WC13 Geoff Bodine	1.00	.45
❑ WC14 Bobby Hamilton	1.00	.45
❑ WC15 Dave Marcis	2.00	.90
❑ WC16 Ernie Irvan	2.00	.90
❑ WC17 Ricky Rudd	2.00	.90
❑ WC18 Jeremy Mayfield	1.50	.70
❑ WC19 Dale Jarrett	3.00	1.35
❑ WC20 Dale Earnhardt's Car	5.00	2.20
❑ WC21 Jeff Burton	2.00	.90
❑ WC22 Mark Martin	5.00	2.20
❑ WC23 Hut Stricklin	1.00	.45
❑ WC24 Ernie Irvan	2.00	.90
❑ WC25 Bobby Labonte	2.50	1.10
❑ WC26 Bobby Hamilton	1.00	.45
❑ WC27 Ted Musgrave	1.00	.45
❑ WC28 Ricky Craven	1.00	.45
❑ WC29 Ricky Rudd	2.00	.90
❑ WC30 Bobby Hamilton	1.00	.45
❑ WC31 Terry Labonte's Car/1996	6.00	2.70

1997 Score Board IQ

This set contains 50 cards and is distributed in 2-card packs, with 30 packs in each box. The IQ notation is used by Score Board stands for "Insert Quality".

	MINT	NRMT
COMPLETE SET (50)	25.00	11.00
COMMON CARD (1-50)	.15	.07
COMMON DRIVER (1-50)	.30	.14
❑ 1 Dale Earnhardt	3.00	1.35
❑ 2 Jeff Gordon	3.00	1.35
❑ 3 Terry Labonte	1.50	.70
❑ 4 Dale Jarrett	1.25	.55
❑ 5 Michael Waltrip	.30	.14
❑ 6 Mark Martin	1.50	.70
❑ 7 Dale Jarrett	1.25	.55
❑ 8 Bobby Labonte	1.25	.55
❑ 9 Robby Gordon	.30	.14
❑ 10 Rick Mast	.30	.14
❑ 11 Geoff Bodine	.30	.14
❑ 12 Sterling Marlin	.60	.25
❑ 13 Jeff Burton	.60	.25
❑ 14 Ward Burton	.30	.14
❑ 15 Darrell Waltrip	.60	.25
❑ 16 Ken Schrader	.30	.14
❑ 17 Kyle Petty	.60	.25
❑ 18 Bobby Hamilton	.30	.14
❑ 19 Ernie Irvan	.60	.25
❑ 20 Steve Grissom	.30	.14
❑ 21 Ted Musgrave	.30	.14
❑ 22 Jeremy Mayfield	1.00	.45
❑ 23 Ricky Rudd	.60	.25
❑ 24 Ricky Craven	.30	.14
❑ 25 Hut Stricklin	.30	.14
❑ 26 Jeff Gordon	3.00	1.35
❑ 27 Dale Earnhardt	3.00	1.35
❑ 28 Dale Jarrett	1.25	.55
❑ 29 Terry Labonte	1.50	.70
❑ 30 Richard Childress	.30	.14
❑ 31 Rick Hendrick	.30	.14
❑ 32 Richard Petty	.75	.35
❑ 33 Robert Yates	.15	.07
❑ 34 Joe Gibbs	.30	.14
❑ 35 Ray Evernham	.60	.25
❑ 36 Larry McReynolds	.15	.07
❑ 37 Jeff Gordon	3.00	1.35
❑ 38 Dale Earnhardt	3.00	1.35
❑ 39 Rusty Wallace's Car	.75	.35
❑ 40 Dale Earnhardt's Car	1.50	.70
❑ 41 Sterling Marlin's Car	.30	.14
❑ 42 Mark Martin's Car	.75	.35
❑ 43 Bobby Labonte's Car	.60	.25
❑ 44 Michael Waltrip's Car	.15	.07
❑ 45 Jeff Gordon's Car	1.50	.70
❑ 46 Ernie Irvan's Car	.30	.14
❑ 47 Robby Gordon's Car	.15	.07
❑ 48 Bobby Hamilton's Car	.15	.07
❑ 49 Dale Jarrett's Car	.60	.25
❑ 50 Terry Labonte Jeff Gordon Ricky Craven	1.50	.70

1997 Score Board IQ $10 Phone Cards

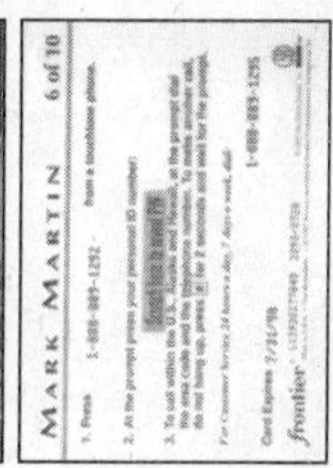

These cards feature a foil-stamped design and each card carries $10 of phone time. They are inserted one per ten packs.

	MINT	NRMT
COMPLETE SET (10)	25.00	11.00
COMMON CARD (PC1-PC10)	.75	.35
*SINGLES: 1.25X TO 3X BASE CARD HI		
❑ PC1 Dale Earnhardt	15.00	6.75
❑ PC2 Rusty Wallace's Car	2.00	.90
❑ PC3 Bobby Labonte	6.00	2.70
❑ PC4 Dale Earnhardt's Car	8.00	3.60
❑ PC5 Sterling Marlin	6.00	2.70
❑ PC6 Mark Martin	8.00	3.60
❑ PC7 Michael Waltrip	.75	.35
❑ PC8 Dale Jarrett	6.00	2.70
❑ PC9 Ricky Rudd	6.00	2.70
❑ PC10 Ernie Irvan	6.00	2.70

1997 Score Board IQ Remarques

These cards features the original artwork of renowed artist Sam Bass. Ten of his more famous artworks were reprinted on canvas stock in order to create these cards. These cards are numbered from 101 to 570 and are autographed by Bass. These cards are inserted one per 65 packs.

	MINT	NRMT
COMPLETE SET (10)	300.00	135.00
COMMON CARD (SB1-SB10)	8.00	3.60
*SINGLES: 10X TO 25X BASE CARD HI		
❑ SB1 Dale Earnhardt	150.00	70.00
❑ SB2 Jeff Gordon	150.00	70.00
❑ SB3 Richard Childress	8.00	3.60
❑ SB4 Ernie Irvan	15.00	6.75
❑ SB5 Rusty Wallace's Car	15.00	6.75
❑ SB6 Darrell Waltrip	15.00	6.75
❑ SB7 Richard Petty	50.00	22.00
❑ SB8 Bobby Labonte	40.00	18.00
❑ SB9 Alan Kulwicki	60.00	27.00
❑ SB10 Terry Labonte	75.00	34.00

1997 Score Board IQ Remarques Sam Bass Finished

These cards are the same as the previosuly listed set with the exception that these cards contain hand-drawn sketchings by Bass. These cards are numbered from 1 to 100 and are inserted one per 358 packs.

	MINT	NRMT
COMPLETE SET (10)	1200.00	550.00
COMMON CARD (SB1-SB10)	50.00	22.00

1995 Select

This 150-card set is the first racing set produced from manufacturer Pinnacle. The cards came eight cards per pack, 24 packs per box and 24 boxes per case. There were 2,950 numbered cases produced. The set features six topical subsets: Owners (73-90), Crew Chief (91-108), In the Blood (109-117), Young Stars (118-128), Idols (129-134), Pole Sitters (135-136). In the original set the only card with ties to Dale Earnhardt was card #41, a picture of his car. In the middle of 1995 Dale signed a spokesperson agreement with Pinnacle. Pinnacle then issued a special Select #151 card Dale to complete the set. This card was distributed to dealers that ordered the Select product. The card is not part of the regular set price. Also randomly inserted in the bottom of the boxes were a Jeff Gordon Jumbo and a Jumbo Geoff Bodine Magic Motion card. These two cards are priced at the bottom of the listing.

	MINT	NRMT
COMPLETE SET (150)	20.00	9.00
COMMON CARD (1-150)	.10	.05
COMMON DRIVER (1-150)	.20	.09
❑ 1 Loy Allen Jr.	.20	.09
❑ 2 John Andretti	.20	.09
❑ 3 Brett Bodine	.20	.09
❑ 4 Geoff Bodine	.20	.09
❑ 5 Todd Bodine	.20	.09
❑ 6 Jeff Burton	.40	.18
❑ 7 Ward Burton	.20	.09
❑ 8 Derrike Cope	.20	.09
❑ 9 Wally Dallenbach Jr.	.20	.09
❑ 10 Dave Marcis	.40	.18
❑ 11 Harry Gant	.40	.18
❑ 12 Jeff Gordon	2.50	1.10
❑ 13 Steve Grissom	.20	.09
❑ 14 Bobby Hamilton	.20	.09
❑ 15 Ernie Irvan	.40	.18
❑ 16 Dale Jarrett	1.00	.45
❑ 17 Bobby Labonte	1.00	.45
❑ 18 Terry Labonte	1.25	.55
❑ 19 Sterling Marlin	.40	.18
❑ 20 Mark Martin	1.25	.55
❑ 21 Rick Mast	.20	.09
❑ 22 Ted Musgrave	.20	.09
❑ 23 Joe Nemechek	.20	.09
❑ 24 Kyle Petty	.40	.18
❑ 25 Ricky Rudd	.40	.18
❑ 26 Greg Sacks	.20	.09
❑ 27 Ken Schrader	.20	.09
❑ 28 Morgan Shepherd	.20	.09
❑ 29 Lake Speed	.20	.09
❑ 30 Jimmy Spencer	.20	.09
❑ 31 Hut Stricklin	.20	.09
❑ 32 Kenny Wallace	.20	.09
❑ 33 Mike Wallace	.20	.09
❑ 34 Rusty Wallace	1.25	.55
❑ 35 Darrell Waltrip	.40	.18
❑ 36 Michael Waltrip	.20	.09
❑ 37 Morgan Shepherd's Car	.10	.05
❑ 38 Jeff Gordon's Car	1.25	.55
❑ 39 Geoff Bodine's Car	.10	.05
❑ 40 Ted Musgrave's Car	.10	.05
❑ 41 Dale Earnhardt's Car	1.25	.55
❑ 42 Dale Jarrett's Car	.50	.23
❑ 43 Terry Labonte's Car	.60	.25
❑ 44 Sterling Marlin's Car	.20	.09
❑ 45 Ken Schrader's Car	.10	.05
❑ 46 Kyle Petty's Car	.20	.09
❑ 47 Rusty Wallace's Car	.60	.25
❑ 48 Michael Waltrip's Car	.10	.05
❑ 49 Brett Bodine's Car	.10	.05
❑ 50 Lake Speed's Car	.10	.05
❑ 51 Ernie Irvan's Car	.20	.09
❑ 52 Ricky Rudd's Car	.20	.09
❑ 53 Mark Martin's Car	.60	.25
❑ 54 Darrell Waltrip's Car	.20	.09
❑ 55 Johnny Benson Jr.	.20	.09
❑ 56 Jim Bown	.20	.09
❑ 57 Ricky Craven	.20	.09
❑ 58 Bobby Dotter	.20	.09
❑ 59 Tim Fedewa	.20	.09
❑ 60 David Green	.20	.09
❑ 61 Tommy Houston	.20	.09
❑ 62 Jason Keller	.20	.09
❑ 63 Randy LaJoie	.20	.09
❑ 64 Tracy Leslie	.20	.09
❑ 65 Chad Little	.20	.09
❑ 66 Mark Martin	1.25	.55
❑ 67 Mike McLaughlin	.20	.09
❑ 68 Larry Pearson	.20	.09
❑ 69 Robert Pressley	.20	.09
❑ 70 Elton Sawyer	.20	.09
❑ 71 Dennis Setzer	.20	.09
❑ 72 Kenny Wallace	.20	.09
❑ 73 Richard Petty OWN	.50	.23
❑ 74 Leo Jackson OWN	.10	.05
❑ 75 Bobby Allison OWN	.20	.09
❑ 76 Richard Childress OWN	.10	.05
❑ 77 Geoff Bodine OWN	.20	.09
❑ 78 Joe Gibbs OWN	.20	.09
❑ 79 Kenny Bernstein OWN	.20	.09
❑ 80 Bill Davis OWN	.10	.05
❑ 81 Cale Yarborough OWN	.20	.09
❑ 82 Rick Hendrick OWN	.10	.05
❑ 83 Roger Penske OWN Don Miller OWN	.10	.05
❑ 84 Chuck Rider OWN	.10	.05
❑ 85 Ricky Rudd OWN	.40	.18
❑ 86 Jack Roush OWN	.10	.05
❑ 87 Felix Sabates OWN	.10	.05
❑ 88 Darrell Waltrip OWN	.40	.18
❑ 89 Glen Wood OWN Eddie Wood OWN Len Wood OWN	.10	.05
❑ 90 Robert Yates OWN	.10	.05
❑ 91 Paul Andrews	.10	.05
❑ 92 Ray Evernham	.10	.05
❑ 93 Jeff Hammond	.10	.05
❑ 94 Steve Hmiel	.10	.05
❑ 95 Ken Howes	.10	.05
❑ 96 Jimmy Makar	.10	.05
❑ 97 Larry McReynolds	.10	.05
❑ 98 Buddy Parrott	.10	.05
❑ 99 Leonard Wood	.10	.05
❑ 100 Andy Petree	.10	.05
❑ 101 Jimmy Fennig	.10	.05
❑ 102 Mike Beam	.10	.05
❑ 103 Tony Glover	.10	.05
❑ 104 Doug Hewitt	.10	.05
❑ 105 Donnie Richeson	.10	.05
❑ 106 Bill Ingle	.10	.05
❑ 107 Donnie Wingo	.10	.05
❑ 108 Robin Pemberton	.10	.05
❑ 109 Richard Petty IB Kyle Petty IB	.40	.18
❑ 110 Geoff Bodine IB Todd Bodine IB Brett Bodine IB	.20	.09
❑ 111 Rusty Wallace IB Kenny Wallace IB Mike Wallace IB	.75	.35
❑ 112 Davey Allison IB Bobby Allison IB	.60	.25
❑ 113 Darrell Waltrip IB Michael Waltrip IB	.40	.18
❑ 114 Bobby Labonte IB Terry Labonte IB	.60	.25
❑ 115 Dale Jarrett IB Ned Jarrett IB	.60	.25
❑ 116 David Pearson IB Larry Pearson IB	.20	.09
❑ 117 Jeff Burton IB Ward Burton IB	.40	.18
❑ 118 Jeff Gordon YS	1.50	.70
❑ 119 Jeff Burton YS	.40	.18
❑ 120 Loy Allen Jr. YS	.20	.09
❑ 121 Todd Bodine YS	.20	.09
❑ 122 John Andretti YS	.20	.09
❑ 123 Joe Nemechek YS	.20	.09
❑ 124 Kenny Wallace YS	.20	.09
❑ 125 Bobby Labonte YS	.60	.25
❑ 126 Ricky Craven YS	.20	.09
❑ 127 Johnny Benson YS	.20	.09
❑ 128 Chad Little YS	.20	
❑ 129 Richard Petty I Mark Martin I	.60	
❑ 130 David Pearson I Ken Schrader I	.20	
❑ 131 Bobby Allison I Kyle Petty I	.40	
❑ 132 Cale Yarborough I Ricky Rudd I	.40	
❑ 133 Junior Johnson I Darrell Waltrip I	.40	
❑ 134 Alan Kulwicki I Geoff Bodine I	.75	
❑ 135 Ernie Irvan PS	.40	
❑ 136 Geoff Bodine PS	.20	
❑ 137 Ted Musgrave PS	.20	
❑ 138 Ricky Rudd PS	.40	
❑ 139 Chuck Bown PS	.20	
❑ 140 Rusty Wallace PS	.75	
❑ 141 Jeff Gordon PS	1.50	
❑ 142 Rick Mast PS	.20	
❑ 143 Mark Martin PS	.75	
❑ 144 Loy Allen Jr. PS	.20	
❑ 145 Harry Gant PS	.40	
❑ 146 Jimmy Spencer PS	.20	
❑ 147 Checklist	.10	
❑ 148 Checklist	.10	
❑ 149 Checklist	.10	
❑ 150 Checklist	.10	
❑ 151S Dale Earnhardt Dealer Mail Out	8.00	
❑ NNO Jeff Gordon YS Jumbo	15.00	
❑ NNO G.Bodine Magic Motion	6.00	

1995 Select Flat Out

This 150-card set is a parallel to the base set. The feature all foil Gold Rush printing and have a Flat O on the back to differentiate them from the base car Out cards were randomly inserted at a rate of o three packs. Pinnacle also released a Flat Out ver the Dale Earnhardt card mentioned in the base se (#151). This card is not included in the complete se

	MINT
COMPLETE SET (150)	120.00
COMMON CARD (1-150)	.75
COMMON DRIVER (1-150)	1.50
*STARS: 4X TO 7X BASIC CARDS	
DALE EARNHARDT (151S)	20.00

1995 Select Dream Machi

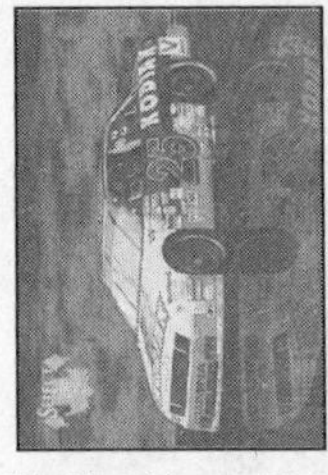

This 12-card insert set features of the top Wins Driver's cars. The cards are printed on an all-fo and use Dufex technology. Dream Machine car randomly inserted one per 48 packs.

	MINT
COMPLETE SET (12)	150.00
COMMON CARD (DM1-DM12)	5.00
*SINGLES: 8X TO 20X BASE CARD HI	
❑ DM1 Geoff Bodine's Car	5.00
❑ DM2 Rusty Wallace's Car	30.00
❑ DM3 Mark Martin's Car	30.00
❑ DM4 Ken Schrader's Car	5.00
❑ DM5 Ricky Rudd's Car	10.00
❑ DM6 Morgan Shepherd's Car	5.00

7 Ernie Irvan's Car	10.00	4.50
3 Jeff Gordon's Car	70.00	32.00
9 Michael Waltrip's Car	5.00	2.20
10 Darrell Waltrip's Car	10.00	4.50
11 Kyle Petty's Car	10.00	4.50
12 Terry Labonte's Car	30.00	13.50

1995 Select Skills

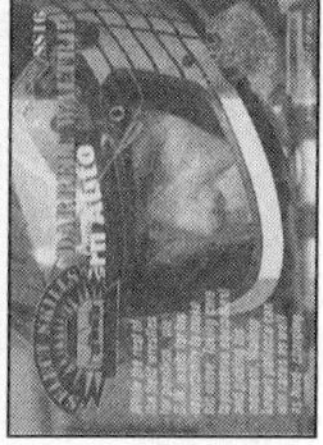

of Winston Cup racing's top drivers are featured in 3-card insert set. The cards feature all-foil, Gold printing technology and were randomly seeded one packs.

	MINT	NRMT
LETE SET (18)	80.00	36.00
'ON CARD (SS1-SS18)	2.00	.90
LES: 3X TO 8X BASE CARD HI		
Rusty Wallace	15.00	6.75
Mark Martin	15.00	6.75
Jeff Gordon	30.00	13.50
Ernie Irvan	4.00	1.80
Terry Labonte	15.00	6.75
Ricky Rudd	4.00	1.80
Kyle Petty	4.00	1.80
Ken Schrader	2.00	.90
Morgan Shepherd	2.00	.90
) Geoff Bodine	2.00	.90
Ted Musgrave	2.00	.90
2 Michael Waltrip	2.00	.90
3 John Andretti	2.00	.90
4 Todd Bodine	2.00	.90
5 Sterling Marlin	4.00	1.80
5 Darrell Waltrip	4.00	1.80
7 Jimmy Spencer	2.00	.90
3 Harry Gant	4.00	1.80

1994 SkyBox

7-card set is the first NASCAR issue by cturer SkyBox. The cards are oversized 4 1/2" X 2 d feature some of the top names in Winston Cup The set includes a Anatomy of a Pit Stop subset . Card #27 the SkyBox Winston Cup car that Dick drove in a few races, was redeemable for a card of 4 Brickyard 400 Winner. You could send that card $1.50 and receive a card of Jeff Gordon holding kyard 400 trophy. This card is not included in the e.

	MINT	NRMT
ETE FACT.SET (27)	8.00	3.60
N CARD (1-26)	.20	.09
N DRIVER (1-26)	.40	.18
e Earnhardt	2.50	1.10
rell Waltrip's Car	.40	.18
e Irvan's Car	.75	.35
Gordon's Car	2.00	.90
y Labonte's Car	1.00	.45
y Dallenbach Jr.'s Car	.20	.09
Petty's Car	.40	.18
e Speed's Car	.20	.09
k Martin's Car	1.00	.45
rgan Shepherd's Car	.20	.09
ky Rudd's Car	.40	.18
sty Wallace's Car	1.00	.45
rling Marlin's Car	.60	.25
❑ 14 Anatomy of a Pit Stop	.20	.09
❑ 15 Anatomy of a Pit Stop	.20	.09
❑ 16 Anatomy of a Pit Stop	.20	.09
❑ 17 Anatomy of a Pit Stop	.20	.09
❑ 18 Bare Frame	.20	.09
❑ 19 Chevy Engine	.20	.09
❑ 20 Jacked up Body	.20	.09
❑ 21 Finished Body	.20	.09
❑ 22 Sanding Body	.20	.09
❑ 23 Finished Race Car	.20	.09
❑ 24 Geoff Bodine's Car Todd Bodine's Car	.20	.09
❑ 25 Darrell Waltrip's Car Michael Waltrip's Car	.40	.18
❑ 26 John Andretti's Cars	.20	.09
❑ NNO Dick Trickle's Car Exchange Card Expired	.50	.23
❑ NNO Jeff Gordon Exchanged Card Redemption	5.00	2.20

1997 SkyBox Profile

This 80-card set was Fleer/Skybox's first NASCAR release under the SkyBox brand name. The product was highlighted by a autographed card redemption program. Cards were distributed in five card packs with 24 packs per box and 6 or 12 boxes per case. The packs carried a suggested retail price of $4.99.

	MINT	NRMT
COMPLETE SET (80)	20.00	9.00
COMMON CARD (1-80)	.15	.07
COMMON DRIVER (1-80)	.30	.14
❑ 1 John Andretti	.30	.14
❑ 2 Johnny Benson	.30	.14
❑ 3 Derrike Cope	.30	.14
❑ 4 Ricky Craven	.30	.14
❑ 5 Dale Earnhardt	3.00	1.35
❑ 6 Bill Elliott	1.50	.70
❑ 7 Jeff Gordon	3.00	1.35
❑ 8 Robby Gordon	.30	.14
❑ 9 Steve Grissom	.30	.14
❑ 10 David Green	.30	.14
❑ 11 Bobby Hamilton	.30	.14
❑ 12 Bobby Hillin	.30	.14
❑ 13 Ernie Irvan	.60	.25
❑ 14 Dale Jarrett	1.25	.55
❑ 15 Bobby Labonte	1.25	.55
❑ 16 Terry Labonte	1.50	.70
❑ 17 Dave Marcis	.60	.25
❑ 18 Sterling Marlin	.60	.25
❑ 19 Mark Martin	1.50	.70
❑ 20 Rick Mast	.30	.14
❑ 21 Jeremy Mayfield	1.00	.45
❑ 22 Ted Musgrave	.30	.14
❑ 23 Joe Nemechek	.30	.14
❑ 24 Ricky Rudd	.60	.25
❑ 25 Ken Schrader	.30	.14
❑ 26 Morgan Shepherd	.30	.14
❑ 27 Hut Stricklin	.30	.14
❑ 28 Dick Trickle	.30	.14
❑ 29 Kenny Wallace	.30	.14
❑ 30 Rusty Wallace	1.50	.70
❑ 31 Michael Waltrip	.30	.14
❑ 32 Richard Childress OWN	.15	.07
❑ 33 Richard Petty OWN	.60	.25
❑ 34 Rick Hendrick OWN	.15	.07
❑ 35 Robert Yates OWN	.15	.07
❑ 36 Joe Gibbs OWN	.30	.14
❑ 37 Cale Yarborough OWN	.15	.07
❑ 38 Jack Roush OWN	.15	.07
❑ 39 Ray Evernham CC	.60	.25
❑ 40 Larry McReynolds CC	.15	.07
❑ 41 Gary DeHart CC	.15	.07
❑ 42 Todd Parrott CC	.15	.07
❑ 43 Marc Reno CC	.15	.07
❑ 44 Steve Hmiel MG CC	.15	.07
❑ 45 Robin Pemberton CC	.15	.07
❑ 46 Todd Bodine	.30	.14
❑ 47 Jason Keller	.30	.14
❑ 48 Randy LaJoie	.30	.14
❑ 49 Phil Parsons	.30	.14
❑ 50 Steve Park	3.00	1.35
❑ 51 Buckshot Jones	.30	.14
❑ 52 Jeff Fuller	.30	.14
❑ 53 Tracy Leslie	.30	.14
❑ 54 Elton Sawyer	.30	.14
❑ 55 Jeff Green	.30	.14
❑ 56 Mike McLaughlin	.30	.14
❑ 57 Ron Barfield	.30	.14
❑ 58 Glen Allen Jr.	.30	.14
❑ 59 Kevin Lepage	.30	.14
❑ 60 Rodney Combs	.30	.14
❑ 61 Tim Fedewa	.30	.14
❑ 62 Rusty Wallace's Car	.75	.35
❑ 63 Dale Earnhardt's Car	1.50	.70
❑ 64 Sterling Marlin's Car	.30	.14
❑ 65 Terry Labonte's Car	.75	.35
❑ 66 Mark Martin's Car	.75	.35
❑ 67 Ricky Rudd's Car	.30	.14
❑ 68 Bobby Labonte's Car	.60	.25
❑ 69 Michael Waltrip's Car	.15	.07
❑ 70 Jeff Gordon's Car	1.50	.70
❑ 71 Ernie Irvan's Car	.30	.14
❑ 72 Ken Schrader's Car	.15	.07
❑ 73 Derrike Cope's Car	.15	.07
❑ 74 Jeremy Mayfield's Car	.60	.25
❑ 75 Robby Gordon's Car	.15	.07
❑ 76 Bobby Hamilton's Car	.15	.07
❑ 77 Dale Jarrett's Car	.60	.25
❑ 78 Bill Elliott's Car	.75	.35
❑ 79 David Green's Car	.15	.07
❑ 80 Checklist	.15	.07
❑ D1 Jeff Gordon Daytona	100.00	45.00

1997 SkyBox Profile Autograph

This 47-card insert set contains autograph redemption cards from each driver in this set. 11,100 cards total were set aside to be redemmed in this program. Each Winston Cup and Busch driver signed 200 cards, with the exception of Randy LaJoie who signed 500. The cards were randomly inserted in packs at a ratio of 1:24.

	MINT	NRMT
COMPLETE SET (47)	1600.00	700.00
COMMON CARD	15.00	6.75
❑ 1 John Andretti	15.00	6.75
❑ 2 Johnny Benson	15.00	6.75
❑ 3 Derrike Cope	15.00	6.75
❑ 4 Ricky Craven	15.00	6.75
❑ 5 Dale Earnhardt	300.00	135.00
❑ 6 Bill Elliott	90.00	40.00
❑ 7 Jeff Gordon	300.00	135.00
❑ 8 Robby Gordon	15.00	6.75
❑ 9 Steve Grissom	15.00	6.75
❑ 10 David Green	15.00	6.75
❑ 11 Bobby Hamilton	15.00	6.75
❑ 12 Bobby Hillin	15.00	6.75
❑ 13 Ernie Irvan	30.00	13.50
❑ 14 Dale Jarrett	75.00	34.00
❑ 15 Bobby Labonte	75.00	34.00
❑ 16 Terry Labonte	90.00	40.00
❑ 17 Dave Marcis	15.00	6.75
❑ 18 Sterling Marlin	30.00	13.50
❑ 19 Mark Martin	90.00	40.00
❑ 20 Rick Mast	15.00	6.75
❑ 21 Jeremy Mayfield	60.00	27.00
❑ 22 Ted Musgrave	15.00	6.75
❑ 23 Joe Nemechek	15.00	6.75
❑ 24 Ricky Rudd	30.00	13.50
❑ 25 Ken Schrader	15.00	6.75
❑ 26 Morgan Shepherd	15.00	6.75
❑ 27 Hut Stricklin	15.00	6.75
❑ 28 Dick Trickle	15.00	6.75
❑ 29 Kenny Wallace	15.00	6.75
❑ 30 Rusty Wallace	90.00	40.00
❑ 31 Michael Waltrip	15.00	6.75
❑ 46 Todd Bodine	15.00	6.75
❑ 47 Jason Keller	15.00	6.75
❑ 48 Randy LaJoie	15.00	6.75
❑ 49 Phil Parsons	15.00	6.75
❑ 50 Steve Park	50.00	22.00
❑ 51 Buckshot Jones	30.00	13.50
❑ 52 Jeff Fuller	15.00	6.75
❑ 53 Tracy Leslie	15.00	6.75
❑ 54 Elton Sawyer	15.00	6.75
❑ 55 Jeff Green	15.00	6.75
❑ 56 Mike McLaughlin	15.00	6.75
❑ 57 Ron Barfield	15.00	6.75
❑ 58 Glen Allen	15.00	6.75
❑ 59 Kevin Lepage	15.00	6.75
❑ 60 Rodney Combs	15.00	6.75
❑ 61 Tim Fedewa	15.00	6.75

1997 SkyBox Profile Break Out

This 9-card insert set features young drivers who could become stars in NASCAR. The cards were randomly inserted in packs at a ratio of 1:4.

	MINT	NRMT
COMPLETE SET (9)	15.00	6.75
COMMON CARD (B1-B9)	.75	.35
*SINGLES: 1.25X TO 3X BASE CARD HI		

	MINT	NRMT
❑ B1 Jeff Gordon	10.00	4.50
❑ B2 Robby Gordon	.75	.35
❑ B3 Ron Barfield	.75	.35
❑ B4 Johnny Benson	.75	.35
❑ B5 Steve Park	5.00	2.20
❑ B6 Ricky Craven	.75	.35
❑ B7 Bobby Labonte	3.00	1.35
❑ B8 Jeremy Mayfield	2.00	.90
❑ B9 David Green	.75	.35

1997 SkyBox Profile Pace Setters

This 9-card insert set covers those drivers who performances have secured their spots in the record books. The cards were randomly inserted in packs at a ratio of 1:10.

	MINT	NRMT
COMPLETE SET (9)	60.00	27.00
COMMON CARD (E1-E9)	1.50	.70
*SINGLES: 2X TO 5X BASE CARD HI		

	MINT	NRMT
❑ E1 Dale Earnhardt	20.00	9.00
❑ E2 Terry Labonte	10.00	4.50
❑ E3 Bill Elliott	10.00	4.50
❑ E4 Ricky Rudd	3.00	1.35
❑ E5 Jeff Gordon	20.00	9.00
❑ E6 Dale Jarrett	8.00	3.60
❑ E7 Michael Waltrip	1.50	.70
❑ E8 Rusty Wallace	10.00	4.50
❑ E9 Mark Martin	10.00	4.50

1997 SkyBox Profile Team

This 9-card set features the strongest teams in NASCAR. Each card front pictures the driver, crew chief and car owner. The cards were randomly inserted in packs at a ratio of 1:100.

	MINT	NRMT
COMPLETE SET (9)	400.00	180.00
COMMON CARD (T1-T9)	20.00	9.00
*SINGLES: 12X TO 30X BASE CARD HI		

	MINT	NRMT
❑ T1 Terry Labonte	75.00	34.00
❑ T2 Jeff Gordon	125.00	55.00
❑ T3 Dale Jarrett	60.00	27.00
❑ T4 Dale Earnhardt	125.00	55.00
❑ T5 Mark Martin	75.00	34.00
❑ T6 Ricky Rudd	20.00	9.00
❑ T7 Ernie Irvan	20.00	9.00
❑ T8 Bill Elliott	75.00	34.00
❑ T9 Rusty Wallace	75.00	34.00

1992 Slim Jim Bobby Labonte

Produced for and distributed by Slim Jim, the Bobby Labonte set includes 27 car and driver cards with one cover/checklist card and one bi-fold autograph card. The autograph card (#13) is not signed but is a bi-fold card intended to be large enough unfolded for the driver to

sign. The back of the checklist card included an offer to purchase additional sets at $5 each with 5 proofs of purchases from Slim Jim products. Regardless, the Slim Jim Bobby Labonte set is thought to be one of the toughest individual driver card sets to find.

	MINT	NRMT
COMPLETE SET (29)	35.00	16.00
COMMON CARD (1-29)	1.00	.45

	MINT	NRMT
❑ 1 Cover/Checklist Card	1.00	.45
❑ 2 Bobby Labonte's Car	1.00	.45
❑ 3 Bobby Labonte	3.00	1.35
❑ 4 Bobby Labonte's Car	1.00	.45
❑ 5 Bob Labonte Sr.	1.00	.45
❑ 6 Bobby Labonte's Car	1.00	.45
❑ 7 Bobby Labonte	3.00	1.35
Terry Labonte		
❑ 8 Bobby Labonte	3.00	1.35
❑ 9 Bobby Labonte in Pits	1.00	.45
❑ 10 Bobby Labonte's Car	1.00	.45
❑ 11 Bobby Labonte	3.00	1.35
❑ 12 Bobby Labonte's Car	1.00	.45
❑ 13 Bobby Labonte Auto.Card	1.00	.45
Bi-Fold Card		
❑ 14 Bobby Labonte in Pits	1.00	.45
❑ 15 Bobby Labonte	3.00	1.35
❑ 16 Bobby Labonte's Car	1.00	.45
Steve Grissom's Car		
Dale Earnhardt's Car		
❑ 17 Bobby Labonte	3.00	1.35
❑ 18 Bobby Labonte in Pits	1.00	.45
❑ 19 Bobby Labonte's Car	1.00	.45
❑ 20 Bobby Labonte's Car	1.00	.45
Chad Little's Car		
❑ 21 Bobby Labonte	3.00	1.35
❑ 22 Bobby Labonte's Car	1.00	.45
❑ 23 Bobby Labonte	1.00	.45
Donna Labonte		
❑ 24 Bobby Labonte	1.00	.45
Bob Labonte Sr.		
❑ 25 Bobby Labonte	3.00	1.35
❑ 26 Bobby Labonte's Car	1.00	.45
❑ 27 Bobby Labonte's Car	1.00	.45
❑ 28 Bobby Labonte w/Car	1.00	.45
❑ 29 Bobby Labonte w/Car	1.00	.45

1994 Slim Jim David Green

Similar to the 1992 set, the 1994 release was produced for and distributed by Slim Jim. New driver David Green is the set's focus that includes 16 driver and car cards with one checklist card and one bi-fold autograph card. The autograph card (#48) is not signed but is a bi-fold card intended to be large enough unfolded for the driver to sign. Cards from the Slim Jim David Green set are numbered consecutively after the 1992 Bobby Labonte set.

	MINT	NRMT
COMPLETE SET (18)	12.00	5.50
COMMON CARD (31-48)	.50	.23

	MINT	NRMT
❑ 31 Checklist Card	.50	.23
❑ 32 David Green	1.00	.45
❑ 33 David Green in Pits	.50	.23
❑ 34 David Green	1.00	.45
❑ 35 David Green	1.00	.45
❑ 36 David Green Action	.50	.23
❑ 37 David Green's Car	.50	.23
❑ 38 David Green	1.00	
❑ 39 Eddie Lowery	.50	
❑ 40 Curt Clouttier	.50	
❑ 41 Charlie Smith	.50	
❑ 42 David Green	1.00	
❑ 43 David Green	.50	
Steve Grissom		
❑ 44 David Green's Car	.50	
❑ 45 David Green	1.00	
❑ 46 David Green	.50	
❑ 47 David Green's Car	.50	
Hermie Sadler's Car		
❑ 48 David Green Bi-Fold	1.00	

1995 SP

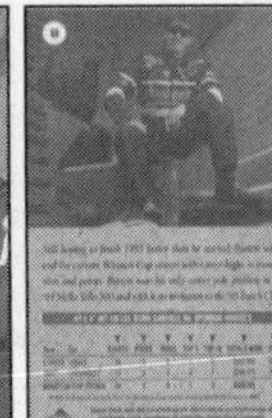

This 150-card set is the inaugural SP brand issue Upper Deck. The set is made up of seven sub-sets Contenders (1-30), Drivers (31-74), Cars (75- Premier Prospects (117-120), Owners (121-135 Crew Chiefs (136-150). The product came seven per pack, 32 packs per box and six boxes per cas original suggested retail price per pack was $3.99 a product was available only through hobby outlets. time it was announced that SP Racing was the produced SP product across the 5 major sports tha that brand. Also, SP was delayed a month from its c release date so that it could include a special Come Hologram insert card of Ernie Irvan and Michael J The Comebacks card could be found one per 192 pa

	MINT
COMPLETE SET (150)	25.00
COMMON CARD (1-150)	.15
COMMON DRIVER (1-150)	.30

	MINT
❑ 1 Rick Mast CC	.30
❑ 2 Rusty Wallace CC	1.50
❑ 3 Sterling Marlin CC	.60
❑ 4 Terry Labonte CC	1.50
❑ 5 Mark Martin CC	1.50
❑ 6 Geoff Bodine CC	.30
❑ 7 Jeff Burton CC	.60
❑ 8 Lake Speed CC	.30
❑ 9 Ricky Rudd CC	.60
❑ 10 Brett Bodine CC	.30
❑ 11 Derrike Cope CC	.30
❑ 12 Bobby Hamilton CC	.30
❑ 13 Ted Musgrave CC	.30
❑ 14 Darrell Waltrip CC	.60
❑ 15 Bobby Labonte CC	1.25
❑ 16 Morgan Shepherd CC	.30
❑ 17 Joe Nemechek CC	.30
❑ 18 Jeff Gordon CC	3.00
❑ 19 Ken Schrader CC	.30
❑ 20 Hut Stricklin CC	.30
❑ 21 Dale Jarrett CC	1.00
❑ 22 Steve Grissom CC	.30
❑ 23 Michael Waltrip CC	.30
❑ 24 Ward Burton CC	.30
❑ 25 Todd Bodine CC	.30
❑ 26 Robert Pressley CC	.30
❑ 27 Bill Elliott CC	1.50
❑ 28 John Andretti CC	.30
❑ 29 Ricky Craven CC	.30
❑ 30 Kyle Petty CC	.60
❑ 31 Rick Mast	.30
❑ 32 Rusty Wallace	1.50
❑ 33 Rusty Wallace	1.50
❑ 34 Sterling Marlin	.60
❑ 35 Sterling Marlin	.60
❑ 36 Terry Labonte	1.50
❑ 37 Mark Martin	1.50
❑ 38 Mark Martin	1.50
❑ 39 Geoff Bodine	.30
❑ 40 Jeff Burton	.60
❑ 41 Lake Speed	.30
❑ 42 Ricky Rudd	.60
❑ 43 Brett Bodine	.30
❑ 44 Derrike Cope	.30
❑ 45 Bobby Hamilton	.30
❑ 46 Dick Trickle	.30
❑ 47 Ted Musgrave	.30

ˈarrell Waltrip	.60	.25
obby Labonte	1.25	.55
ˈlorgan Shepherd	.30	.14
huck Bown	.30	.14
ɜff Purvis	.30	.14
immy Hensley	.30	.14
immy Spencer	.30	.14
ɜff Gordon	3.00	1.35
ɜff Gordon	3.00	1.35
en Schrader	.30	.14
ut Stricklin	.30	.14
andy LaJoie	.30	.14
ale Jarrett	1.25	.55
teve Grissom	.30	.14
ichael Waltrip	.30	.14
ˈard Burton	.30	.14
odd Bodine	.30	.14
obert Pressley	.30	.14
eremy Mayfield	1.00	.45
ike Wallace	.30	.14
ll Elliott	1.50	.70
ohn Andretti	.30	.14
ıad Little	.30	.14
e Nemechek	.30	.14
ave Marcis	.60	.25
cky Craven	.30	.14
yle Petty	.60	.25
ck Mast's Car	.15	.07
ısty Wallace's Car	.75	.35
ısty Wallace's Car	.75	.35
erling Marlin's Car	.30	.14
rry Labonte's Car	.75	.35
ark Martin's Car	.75	.35
eoff Bodine's Car	.15	.07
ff Burton's Car	.30	.14
ke Speed's Car	.15	.07
cky Rudd's Car	.30	.14
ett Bodine's Car	.15	.07
errike Cope's Car	.15	.07
bby Hamilton's Car	.15	.07
ck Trickle's Car	.15	.07
d Musgrave's Car	.15	.07
rrell Waltrip's Car	.30	.14
bby Labonte's Car	.60	.25
organ Shepherd's Car	.15	.07
ad Little's Car	.15	.07
f Purvis' Car	.15	.07
nmy Hensley's Car	.15	.07
nmy Spencer's Car	.15	.07
f Gordon's Car	1.50	.70
n Schrader's Car	.15	.07
t Stricklin's Car	.15	.07
ɜff Gordon's Car	1.50	.70
ale Jarrett's Car	.60	.25
teve Grissom's Car	.15	.07
ichael Waltrip's Car	.15	.07
ˈard Burton's Car	.15	.07
odd Bodine's Car	.15	.07
obert Pressley's Car	.15	.07
eremy Mayfield's Car	.50	.23
ike Wallace's Car	.15	.07
ll Elliott's Car	.75	.35
ll Elliott's Car	.75	.35
ohn Andretti's Car	.15	.07
enny Wallace's Car	.15	.07
e Nemechek's Car	.15	.07
ave Marcis's Car	.30	.14
cky Craven's Car	.15	.07
yle Petty's Car	.30	.14
cky Craven PP	.30	.14
obert Pressley PP	.30	.14
andy LaJoie PP	.30	.14
avy Jones PP	.30	.14
ck Hendrick OWN	.15	.07
ck Roush OWN	.15	.07
oger Penske OWN	.75	.35
ısty Wallace		
e Gibbs OWN	.30	.14
lix Sabates OWN	.15	.07
obby Allison OWN	.30	.14
chard Petty OWN	.75	.35
ıle Yarborough OWN	.30	.14
obert Yates OWN	.15	.07
arrell Waltrip OWN	.60	.25
l Elliott OWN	1.50	.70
eoff Bodine OWN	.30	.14
nior Johnson OWN	.30	.14
cky Rudd OWN	.60	.25
en Wood OWN	.15	.07
obin Pemberton	.15	.07
eve Hmiel	.15	.07
rry McReynolds	.15	.07
obbie Loomis	.15	.07
y Evernham	.60	.25
ward Comstock	.15	.07
ry DeHart	.15	.07
ul Andrews	.15	.07
l Ingle	.15	.07

❑ 145 Jimmy Makar	.15	.07
❑ 146 Barry Dodson	.15	.07
❑ 147 Jimmy Fennig	.15	.07
❑ 148 Leonard Wood	.15	.07
❑ 149 Pete Peterson	.15	.07
❑ 150 Ken Howes	.15	.07
❑ CB1 Ernie Irvan HOLO Michael Jordan	90.00	40.00

1995 SP Die Cut

This 150-card set is a parallel to the regular SP set. Each card is a die cut replica of the base cards. There was one die cut card per pack.

	MINT	NRMT
COMPLETE SET (150)	75.00	34.00
COMMON CARD (1-150)	.50	.23
COMMON DRIVER (1-150)	1.00	.45
*DIE CUT STARS: 1.25X TO 3X BASIC CARDS		

1995 SP Back-To-Back

This three-card insert set features the only three drivers to win back-to-back Daytona 500's. The cards feature a forward and reverse image on holographic board. Richard Petty won the event seven times including '73 and '74. Cale Yarborough was a four time winner including '83 and '84. Sterling Marlin's made the set for his '94 and '95 trips to the winner's circle. The cards were randomly inserted at a ratio of 1:81 packs.

	MINT	NRMT
COMPLETE SET (3)	30.00	13.50
COMMON CARD (BB1-BB3)	10.00	4.50
❑ BB1 Richard Petty	20.00	9.00
❑ BB2 Cale Yarborough	10.00	4.50
❑ BB3 Sterling Marlin	20.00	9.00

1995 SP Speed Merchants

The 30-card set uses HoloView technology to feature the top drivers and up and coming stars in Winston Cup racing. The cards were seeded one per five packs. There was also a die cut parallel version of the Speed Merchant cards. The die cut cards were randomly inserted one per 74 packs.

	MINT	NRMT
COMPLETE SET (30)	100.00	45.00
COMMON CARD (SM1-SM30)	1.50	.70
*SINGLES: 2X TO 5X BASE CARD HI		
COMPLETE DIE CUT SET (30)	500.00	220.00
*DIE CUTS: 10X TO 25X BASIC CARDS		
❑ SM1 Kyle Petty	3.00	1.35
❑ SM2 Rusty Wallace	8.00	3.60
❑ SM3 Bill Elliott	8.00	3.60
❑ SM4 Sterling Marlin	3.00	1.35
❑ SM5 Terry Labonte	8.00	3.60
❑ SM6 Mark Martin	8.00	3.60
❑ SM7 Geoff Bodine	1.50	.70
❑ SM8 Jeff Burton	3.00	1.35
❑ SM9 Steve Grissom	1.50	.70
❑ SM10 Ricky Rudd	3.00	1.35
❑ SM11 Brett Bodine	1.50	.70
❑ SM12 Derrike Cope	1.50	.70
❑ SM13 Ward Burton	1.50	.70
❑ SM14 Mike Wallace	1.50	.70
❑ SM15 Robert Pressley	1.50	.70
❑ SM16 Ted Musgrave	1.50	.70
❑ SM17 Darrell Waltrip	3.00	1.35
❑ SM18 Bobby Labonte	4.00	1.80
❑ SM19 Ricky Craven	1.50	.70
❑ SM20 Davy Jones	1.50	.70
❑ SM21 Morgan Shepherd	1.50	.70
❑ SM22 Randy LaJoie	1.50	.70
❑ SM23 Jeremy Mayfield	2.50	1.10
❑ SM24 Jeff Gordon	20.00	9.00
❑ SM25 Ken Schrader	1.50	.70
❑ SM26 Todd Bodine	1.50	.70
❑ SM27 John Andretti	1.50	.70
❑ SM28 Dale Jarrett	6.00	2.70
❑ SM29 Greg Sacks	1.50	.70
❑ SM30 Michael Waltrip	1.50	.70

1996 SP

The 1996 SP hobby set was issued in one series totalling 84 cards. The set contains the topical subsets: Driver Cards (1-42), Cup Contenders (43-74) and RPM (75-84). The 7-card packs retailed for $4.39 each. There were 20 packs per box and 12 boxes per case. The product was distributed through hobby channels only. Also, included as an insert in packs was a card titled Driving Aces. The card is a double sided card with Dale Earnhardt on one side and Jeff Gordon on the other. Their photo is boarded by a Ace playing card. This card was inserted in packs at a rate of one in 257 and is priced at the bottom of this set.

	MINT	NRMT
COMPLETE SET (84)	25.00	11.00
COMMON CARD (1-84)	.15	.07
COMMON DRIVER (1-84)	.30	.14
❑ 1 Rick Mast	.30	.14
❑ 2 Rusty Wallace	1.50	.70
❑ 3 Dale Earnhardt	3.00	1.35
❑ 4 Sterling Marlin	.60	.25
❑ 5 Terry Labonte	1.50	.70
❑ 6 Mark Martin	1.50	.70
❑ 7 Geoff Bodine	.30	.14
❑ 8 Hut Stricklin	.30	.14
❑ 9 Lake Speed	.30	.14
❑ 10 Ricky Rudd	.60	.25
❑ 11 Brett Bodine	.30	.14
❑ 12 Derrike Cope	.30	.14
❑ 13 Bill Elliott	1.50	.70
❑ 14 Bobby Hamilton	.30	.14
❑ 15 Wally Dallenbach	.30	.14
❑ 16 Ted Musgrave	.30	.14
❑ 17 Darrell Waltrip	.60	.25
❑ 18 Bobby Labonte	1.25	.55
❑ 19 Loy Allen	.15	.07
❑ 20 Morgan Shepherd	.30	.14
❑ 21 Michael Waltrip	.30	.14
❑ 22 Ward Burton	.30	.14
❑ 23 Jimmy Spencer	.30	.14
❑ 24 Jeff Gordon	3.00	1.35
❑ 25 Ken Schrader	.30	.14
❑ 26 Kyle Petty	.60	.25
❑ 27 Bobby Hillin	.30	.14
❑ 28 Ernie Irvan	.60	.25
❑ 29 Steve Grissom	.30	.14
❑ 30 Johnny Benson	.30	.14
❑ 31 Dave Marcis	.60	.25
❑ 32 Jeremy Mayfield	1.00	.45
❑ 33 Robert Pressley	.30	.14
❑ 34 Jeff Burton	.60	.25
❑ 35 Joe Nemechek	.30	.14
❑ 36 Dale Jarrett	1.25	.55
❑ 37 John Andretti	.30	.14
❑ 38 Kenny Wallace	.30	.14
❑ 39 Mike Wallace	.30	.14
❑ 40 Dick Trickle	.30	.14
❑ 41 Ricky Craven	.30	.14
❑ 42 Chad Little	.30	.14
❑ 43 Jeff Gordon CC	3.00	1.35
❑ 44 Sterling Marlin CC	.60	.25
❑ 45 Mark Martin CC	1.50	.70
❑ 46 Rusty Wallace CC	1.50	.70
❑ 47 Terry Labonte CC	1.50	.70

❑ 48 Ted Musgrave CC	.30	.14
❑ 49 Bill Elliott CC	1.50	.70
❑ 50 Ricky Rudd CC	.60	.25
❑ 51 Bobby Labonte CC	1.25	.55
❑ 52 Morgan Shepherd CC	.30	.14
❑ 53 Michael Waltrip CC	.30	.14
❑ 54 Dale Jarrett CC	1.25	.55
❑ 55 Bobby Hamilton CC	.30	.14
❑ 56 Derrike Cope CC	.30	.14
❑ 57 Geoff Bodine CC	.30	.14
❑ 58 Ken Schrader CC	.30	.14
❑ 59 John Andretti CC	.30	.14
❑ 60 Darrell Waltrip CC	.60	.25
❑ 61 Brett Bodine CC	.30	.14
❑ 62 Kenny Wallace CC	.30	.14
❑ 63 Ward Burton CC	.30	.14
❑ 64 Lake Speed CC	.30	.14
❑ 65 Ricky Craven CC	.30	.14
❑ 66 Jimmy Spencer CC	.30	.14
❑ 67 Steve Grissom CC	.30	.14
❑ 68 Joe Nemechek CC	.30	.14
❑ 69 Ernie Irvan CC	.60	.25
❑ 70 Kyle Petty CC	.60	.25
❑ 71 Johnny Benson CC	.30	.14
❑ 72 Jeff Burton CC	.60	.25
❑ 73 Dave Marcis CC	.60	.25
❑ 74 Jeremy Mayfield CC	1.00	.45
❑ 75 Michael Waltrip RPM	.30	.14
❑ 76 Dale Jarrett RPM	1.25	.55
❑ 77 Johnny Benson RPM	.30	.14
❑ 78 Ricky Craven RPM	.30	.14
❑ 79 Rusty Wallace RPM	1.50	.70
❑ 80 Jeff Gordon RPM	3.00	1.35
❑ 81 Terry Labonte RPM	1.50	.70
❑ 82 Sterling Marlin RPM	.60	.25
❑ 83 Mark Martin RPM	1.50	.70
❑ 84 Ernie Irvan RPM	.60	.25
❑ KR1 Dale Earnhardt Jeff Gordon Aces	120.00	55.00

1996 SP Driving Force

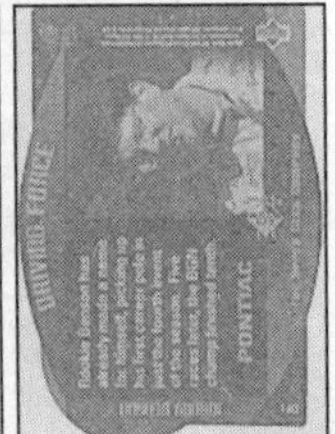

Randomly inserted in packs at a rate of one in 30, this 10-card set featues the top up and coming drivers on the NASCAR circuit. The die-cut cards incorporate a driver's photo and a picture of the driver's helmet on the front.

	MINT	NRMT
COMPLETE SET (10)	50.00	22.00
COMMON CARD (DF1-DF10)	3.00	1.35
*SINGLES: 4X TO 10X BASE CARD HI		
❑ DF1 Johnny Benson	3.00	1.35
❑ DF2 Jeremy Mayfield	8.00	3.60
❑ DF3 Brett Bodine	3.00	1.35
❑ DF4 Robert Pressley	3.00	1.35
❑ DF5 Jeff Burton	6.00	2.70
❑ DF6 Ricky Craven	3.00	1.35
❑ DF7 Wally Dallenbach	3.00	1.35
❑ DF8 Bobby Labonte	10.00	4.50
❑ DF9 Kenny Wallace	3.00	1.35
❑ DF10 Bobby Hamilton	3.00	1.35

1996 SP Holoview Maximum Effects

This 25-card insert set features holoview printing technology to bring your favorite driver to life. The cards put the driver's photo in motion. The cards were randomly inserted one in six packs. There is also a parallel die-cut version of this set. The cards were inserted one in 73 packs and are priced using the mulitplier line in the header.

	MINT	NRMT
COMPLETE SET (25)	100.00	45.00
COMMON CARD (ME1-ME25)	2.00	.90
*SINGLES: 6X TO 15X BASE CARD HI		
COMP. DIE-CUT SET (25)	500.00	220.00
*DIE-CUT CARDS: 25X TO 60X BASIC CARDS		
❑ ME1 Jeff Gordon	25.00	11.00
❑ ME2 Rusty Wallace	12.00	5.50
❑ ME3 Dale Earnhardt	25.00	11.00
❑ ME4 Sterling Marlin	4.00	1.80
❑ ME5 Terry Labonte	12.00	5.50
❑ ME6 Mark Martin	12.00	5.50
❑ ME7 Geoff Bodine	2.00	.90
❑ ME8 Johnny Benson	2.00	.90
❑ ME9 Derrike Cope	2.00	.90
❑ ME10 Ricky Rudd	4.00	1.80
❑ ME11 Ricky Craven	2.00	.90
❑ ME12 John Andretti	2.00	.90
❑ ME13 Ken Schrader	2.00	.90
❑ ME14 Ernie Irvan	4.00	1.80
❑ ME15 Steve Grissom	2.00	.90
❑ ME16 Ted Musgrave	2.00	.90
❑ ME17 Darrell Waltrip	4.00	1.80
❑ ME18 Bobby Labonte	6.00	2.70
❑ ME19 Kyle Petty	4.00	1.80
❑ ME20 Bobby Hamilton	2.00	.90
❑ ME21 Kenny Wallace	2.00	.90
❑ ME22 Dale Jarrett	10.00	4.50
❑ ME23 Bill Elliott	12.00	5.50
❑ ME24 Jeremy Mayfield	5.00	2.20
❑ ME25 Jeff Burton	4.00	1.80

1996 SP Racing Legends

This cross brand insert set features the final five cards from the 25 card series. The cards were randomly inserted in packs at a rate of one in 15.

	MINT	NRMT
COMPLETE SET (5)	40.00	18.00
COMMON CARD (RL21-RL25)	1.00	.45
*SINGLES: 2.5X TO 6X BASE CARD HI		
❑ RL21 Rusty Wallace	10.00	4.50
❑ RL22 Bill Elliott	10.00	4.50
❑ RL23 Mark Martin	10.00	4.50
❑ RL24 Jeff Gordon	20.00	9.00
❑ RL25 Header	1.00	.45

1996 SP Richard Petty/STP 25th Anniversary

Randomly inserted in packs at a rate of one in 47, this nine-card set provides a historical perspective on the 25 year relationship between two of the biggest names in racing. The cards use and intricate die-cut process to make them unique.

	MINT	NRMT
COMPLETE SET (9)	100.00	45.00
COM.R.PETTY CARD (RP1-RP9)	12.00	5.50

1997 SP

This 126-card set was produced by Upper Deck. It was distributed in packs in three tiers. The cards are designated by flags on their borders. The single flag cards are randomly inserted in packs at a ratio of 6:1. The double flag cards are randomly inserted in packs at a ratio of 1:3. The triple flag cards are randomly inserted in packs at a ratio of 1:7. The double flag and triple flag tiers contain 21 cards each. Cards were distributed in seven card packs with 20 packs per box and 12 boxes per cases. 1,000 cases of this product was produced.

	MINT	NRMT
COMPLETE SET (126)	300.00	135.00

COMP. SINGLE FLAG SET (84)	15.00
COMP. DOUBLE FLAG SET (21)	50.00
COMP. TRIPLE FLAG SET (21)	235.00
COMMON SINGLE FLAG	.15
COMMON DRIVER SINGLE FLAG	.30
COMMON DOUBLE FLAG	.75
COMMON DRIVER DOUBLE FLAG	1.50
COMMON TRIPLE FLAG	1.50
COMMON DRIVER TRIPLE FLAG	3.00
❑ 1 Morgan Shepherd	.30
❑ 2 Rusty Wallace	1.50
❑ 3 Dale Earnhardt 3F	30.00
❑ 4 Sterling Marlin	.60
❑ 5 Terry Labonte	1.50
❑ 6 Mark Martin 2F	8.00
❑ 7 Geoff Bodine	.30
❑ 8 Hut Stricklin	.30
❑ 9 Lake Speed	.30
❑ 10 Ricky Rudd	.60
❑ 11 Brett Bodine	.30
❑ 12 Dale Jarrett	1.25
❑ 13 Bill Elliott	1.50
❑ 14 Bobby Hamilton	.30
❑ 15 Wally Dallenbach	.30
❑ 16 Ted Musgrave	.30
❑ 17 Darrell Waltrip 3F	6.00
❑ 18 Bobby Labonte	1.25
❑ 19 Loy Allen	.30
❑ 20 Rick Mast	.30
❑ 21 Michael Waltrip 2F	1.50
❑ 22 Ward Burton 2F	1.50
❑ 23 Jimmy Spencer	.30
❑ 24 Jeff Gordon 3F	30.00
❑ 25 Ricky Craven 3F	3.00
❑ 26 Kyle Petty	.60
❑ 27 Bobby Hillin	.30
❑ 28 Ernie Irvan	.60
❑ 29 Robert Pressley	.30
❑ 30 Johnny Benson 2F	1.50
❑ 31 Dave Marcis	.60
❑ 32 Jeremy Mayfield	1.00
❑ 33 Ken Schrader 2F	1.50
❑ 34 Jeff Burton	.60
❑ 35 Chad Little	.30
❑ 36 Derrike Cope	.30
❑ 37 John Andretti	.30
❑ 38 Kenny Wallace	.30
❑ 39 Dick Trickle	.30
❑ 40 David Green 3F	3.00
❑ 41 Mike Wallace	.30
❑ 42 Joe Nemechek	.30
❑ 43 Morgan Shepherd's Car	.15
❑ 44 Rusty Wallace's Car	.75
❑ 45 Dale Earnhardt's Car 3F	15.00
❑ 46 Sterling Marlin's Car	.30
❑ 47 Terry Labonte's Car 2F	4.00
❑ 48 Mark Martin's Car	.75
❑ 49 Geoff Bodine's Car	.15
❑ 50 Hut Stricklin's Car	.15
❑ 51 Lake Speed's Car	.15
❑ 52 Ricky Rudd's Car 2F	1.50
❑ 53 Brett Bodine's Car	.15
❑ 54 Dale Jarrett's Car	.60
❑ 55 Bill Elliott's Car 3F	7.50
❑ 56 Bobby Hamilton's Car 2F	.75
❑ 57 Wally Dallenbach's Car	.15
❑ 58 Ted Musgrave's Car	.15
❑ 59 Darrell Waltrip's Car	.30
❑ 60 Bobby Labonte's Car	.60
❑ 61 Loy Allen's Car	.15
❑ 62 Rick Mast's Car	.15
❑ 63 Michael Waltrip's Car	.15
❑ 64 Ward Burton's Car	.15
❑ 65 Jimmy Spencer's Car 2F	.75
❑ 66 Jeff Gordon's Car	1.50
❑ 67 Ricky Craven's Car	.15
❑ 68 Kyle Petty's Car 3F	3.00
❑ 69 Bobby Hillin's Car	.15
❑ 70 Ernie Irvan's Car	.15
❑ 71 Robert Pressley's Car 3F	1.50
❑ 72 Johnny Benson's Car	.15
❑ 73 Dave Marcis's Car	.30

eremy Mayfield's Car	.50	.23
en Schrader's Car	.15	.07
eff Burton's Car	.30	.14
had Little's Car	.15	.07
errike Cope's Car 2F	.75	.35
ohn Andretti's Car	.15	.07
enny Wallace's Car	.15	.07
ick Trickle's Car	.15	.07
avid Green's Car 3F	1.50	.70
ike Wallace	.30	.14
oe Nemechek	.30	.14
usty Wallace 3F	15.00	6.75
terling Marlin 2F	3.00	1.35
erry Labonte 3F	15.00	6.75
ark Martin 2F	8.00	3.60
eoff Bodine	.30	.14
ake Speed	.30	.14
icky Rudd 3F	6.00	2.70
ale Jarrett 2F	6.00	2.70
ill Elliott 2F	8.00	3.60
obby Hamilton	.30	.14
ally Dallenbach	.30	.14
ed Musgrave	.30	.14
arrell Waltrip	.60	.25
obby Labonte 2F	6.00	2.70
ichael Waltrip	.30	.14
Ward Burton	.30	.14
Jimmy Spencer	.30	.14
Jeff Gordon 2F	15.00	6.75
Ricky Craven	.30	.14
Kyle Petty 3F	6.00	2.70
Ernie Irvan 2F	3.00	1.35
Johnny Benson	.30	.14
Jeremy Mayfield	1.00	.45
Ken Schrader 3F	3.00	1.35
Jeff Burton	.60	.25
Derrike Cope	.30	.14
John Andretti	.30	.14
Kenny Wallace	.30	.14
Rusty Wallace 3F	15.00	6.75
Sterling Marlin	.60	.25
erry Labonte 3F	15.00	6.75
Mark Martin 3F	15.00	6.75
Ricky Rudd 2F	3.00	1.35
Dale Jarrett 3F	12.00	5.50
Bill Elliott	1.50	.70
Bobby Labonte 2F	6.00	2.70
immy Spencer 2F	1.50	.70
eff Gordon 3F	30.00	13.50
Kyle Petty	.60	.25
rnie Irvan 3F	6.00	2.70
Ricky Craven 2F	1.50	.70
en Schrader	.30	.14

1997 SP Super Series

5-card insert set is a three tiered parallel of the . These cards are diecut and have red borders to iate them from the base set. The single flag cards domly inserted in packs at a ratio of 1:5. The ag cards are randomly inserted in packs at a ratio The triple flag cards are randomly inserted in a ratio of 1:240. The double flag and triple flag tains 21 cards each.

	MINT	NRMT
TE SET (126)	2400.00	1100.00
SINGLE FLAG SET (84)	150.00	70.00
OUBLE FLAG SET (21)	250.00	110.00
RIPLE FLAG SET (21)	2000.00	900.00
N SINGLE FLAG	1.50	.70
N DRIVER SINGLE FLAG	3.00	1.35
N DOUBLE FLAG	4.00	1.80
N DRIVER DOUBLE FLAG	8.00	3.60
N TRIPLE FLAG	15.00	6.75
N DRIVER TRIPLE FLAG	30.00	13.50

gan Shepherd	3.00	1.35
y Wallace	15.00	6.75
Earnhardt 3F	300.00	135.00
ing Marlin	6.00	2.70
Labonte	15.00	6.75
Martin 2F	40.00	18.00

❑ 7 Geoff Bodine	3.00	1.35
❑ 8 Hut Stricklin	3.00	1.35
❑ 9 Lake Speed	3.00	1.35
❑ 10 Ricky Rudd	6.00	2.70
❑ 11 Brett Bodine	3.00	1.35
❑ 12 Dale Jarrett	12.00	5.50
❑ 13 Bill Elliott	15.00	6.75
❑ 14 Bobby Hamilton	3.00	1.35
❑ 15 Wally Dallenbach	3.00	1.35
❑ 16 Ted Musgrave	3.00	1.35
❑ 17 Darrell Waltrip 3F	60.00	27.00
❑ 18 Bobby Labonte	12.00	5.50
❑ 19 Loy Allen	3.00	1.35
❑ 20 Rick Mast	3.00	1.35
❑ 21 Michael Waltrip 2F	8.00	3.60
❑ 22 Ward Burton 2F	8.00	3.60
❑ 23 Jimmy Spencer	3.00	1.35
❑ 24 Jeff Gordon 3F	300.00	135.00
❑ 25 Ricky Craven 3F	30.00	13.50
❑ 26 Kyle Petty	6.00	2.70
❑ 27 Bobby Hillin	3.00	1.35
❑ 28 Ernie Irvan	6.00	2.70
❑ 29 Robert Pressley	3.00	1.35
❑ 30 Johnny Benson 2F	8.00	3.60
❑ 31 Dave Marcis	6.00	2.70
❑ 32 Jeremy Mayfield	10.00	4.50
❑ 33 Ken Schrader 2F	8.00	3.60
❑ 34 Jeff Burton	6.00	2.70
❑ 35 Chad Little	3.00	1.35
❑ 36 Derrike Cope	3.00	1.35
❑ 37 John Andretti	3.00	1.35
❑ 38 Kenny Wallace	3.00	1.35
❑ 39 Dick Trickle	3.00	1.35
❑ 40 David Green 3F	30.00	13.50
❑ 41 Mike Wallace	3.00	1.35
❑ 42 Joe Nemechek	3.00	1.35
❑ 43 Morgan Shepherd's Car	1.50	.70
❑ 44 Rusty Wallace's Car	7.50	3.40
❑ 45 Dale Earnhardt's Car 3F	125.00	55.00
❑ 46 Sterling Marlin's Car	3.00	1.35
❑ 47 Terry Labonte's Car 2F	20.00	9.00
❑ 48 Mark Martin's Car	7.50	3.40
❑ 49 Geoff Bodine's Car	1.50	.70
❑ 50 Hut Stricklin's Car	1.50	.70
❑ 51 Lake Speed's Car	1.50	.70
❑ 52 Ricky Rudd's Car 2F	8.00	3.60
❑ 53 Brett Bodine's Car	1.50	.70
❑ 54 Dale Jarrett's Car	6.00	2.70
❑ 55 Bill Elliott's Car 3F	75.00	34.00
❑ 56 Bobby Hamilton's Car 2F	4.00	1.80
❑ 57 Wally Dallenbach's Car	1.50	.70
❑ 58 Ted Musgrave's Car	1.50	.70
❑ 59 Darrell Waltrip's Car	3.00	1.35
❑ 60 Bobby Labonte's Car	6.00	2.70
❑ 61 Loy Allen's Car	1.50	.70
❑ 62 Rick Mast's Car	1.50	.70
❑ 63 Michael Waltrip's Car	1.50	.70
❑ 64 Ward Burton's Car	1.50	.70
❑ 65 Jimmy Spencer's Car 2F	4.00	1.80
❑ 66 Jeff Gordon's Car	15.00	6.75
❑ 67 Ricky Craven's Car	1.50	.70
❑ 68 Kyle Petty's Car 3F	30.00	13.50
❑ 69 Bobby Hillin's Car	1.50	.70
❑ 70 Ernie Irvan's Car	3.00	1.35
❑ 71 Robert Pressley's Car 3F	15.00	6.75
❑ 72 Johnny Benson's Car	1.50	.70
❑ 73 Dave Marcis's Car	3.00	1.35
❑ 74 Jeremy Mayfield's Car	4.50	2.00
❑ 75 Ken Schrader's Car	1.50	.70
❑ 76 Jeff Burton's Car	3.00	1.35
❑ 77 Chad Little's Car	1.50	.70
❑ 78 Derrike Cope's Car 2F	4.00	1.80
❑ 79 John Andretti's Car	1.50	.70
❑ 80 Kenny Wallace's Car	1.50	.70
❑ 81 Dick Trickle's Car	1.50	.70
❑ 82 David Green's Car 3F	15.00	6.75
❑ 83 Mike Wallace	3.00	1.35
❑ 84 Joe Nemechek	3.00	1.35
❑ 85 Rusty Wallace 3F	150.00	70.00
❑ 86 Sterling Marlin 2F	15.00	6.75
❑ 87 Terry Labonte 3F	150.00	70.00
❑ 88 Mark Martin 2F	40.00	18.00
❑ 89 Geoff Bodine	3.00	1.35
❑ 90 Lake Speed	3.00	1.35
❑ 91 Ricky Rudd 3F	60.00	27.00
❑ 92 Dale Jarrett 2F	30.00	13.50
❑ 93 Bill Elliott 2F	40.00	18.00
❑ 94 Bobby Hamilton	3.00	1.35
❑ 95 Wally Dallenbach	3.00	1.35
❑ 96 Ted Musgrave	3.00	1.35
❑ 97 Darrell Waltrip	6.00	2.70
❑ 98 Bobby Labonte 2F	30.00	13.50
❑ 99 Michael Waltrip	3.00	1.35
❑ 100 Ward Burton	3.00	1.35
❑ 101 Jimmy Spencer	3.00	1.35
❑ 102 Jeff Gordon 2F	75.00	34.00
❑ 103 Ricky Craven	3.00	1.35
❑ 104 Kyle Petty 3F	60.00	27.00
❑ 105 Ernie Irvan 2F	15.00	6.75
❑ 106 Johnny Benson	3.00	1.35
❑ 107 Jeremy Mayfield	10.00	4.50
❑ 108 Ken Schrader 3F	30.00	13.50
❑ 109 Jeff Burton	6.00	2.70
❑ 110 Derrike Cope	3.00	1.35
❑ 111 John Andretti	3.00	1.35
❑ 112 Kenny Wallace	3.00	1.35
❑ 113 Rusty Wallace 3F	150.00	70.00
❑ 114 Sterling Marlin	6.00	2.70
❑ 115 Terry Labonte 3F	150.00	70.00
❑ 116 Mark Martin 3F	150.00	70.00
❑ 117 Ricky Rudd 2F	15.00	6.75
❑ 118 Dale Jarrett 3F	125.00	55.00
❑ 119 Bill Elliott	15.00	6.75
❑ 120 Bobby Labonte 2F	30.00	13.50
❑ 121 Jimmy Spencer 2F	4.00	1.80
❑ 122 Jeff Gordon 3F	300.00	135.00
❑ 123 Kyle Petty	6.00	2.70
❑ 124 Ernie Irvan 3F	60.00	27.00
❑ 125 Ricky Craven 2F	8.00	3.60
❑ 126 Ken Schrader	3.00	1.35

1997 SP Race Film

This 10-card insert set features film technology to capture race moments on the cards. Each card is hand numbered 1 of 400. The cards were randomly inserted in packs at a ratio of 1:63.

	MINT	NRMT
COMPLETE SET (10)	400.00	180.00
COMMON CARD (RD1-RD10)	20.00	9.00
*SINGLES: 12X TO 30X BASE CARD HI		

❑ RD1 Jeff Gordon	150.00	70.00
❑ RD2 Rusty Wallace	80.00	36.00
❑ RD3 Dale Earnhardt	150.00	70.00
❑ RD4 Sterling Marlin	20.00	9.00
❑ RD5 Terry Labonte	80.00	36.00
❑ RD6 Mark Martin	80.00	36.00
❑ RD7 Dale Jarrett	60.00	27.00
❑ RD8 Ernie Irvan	20.00	9.00
❑ RD9 Bill Elliott	80.00	36.00
❑ RD10 Ricky Rudd	20.00	9.00

1997 SP SPx Force Autographs

This 4-card set features Upper Deck's holoview technology. Each of the four drivers signed 100 cards each. The cards were randomly inserted in packs at a ratio of 1:480.

	MINT	NRMT
COMPLETE SET (4)	750.00	350.00
COMMON CARD (SF1-SF4)	100.00	45.00

❑ SF1 Jeff Gordon	400.00	180.00
❑ SF2 Rusty Wallace	150.00	70.00
❑ SF3 Ricky Craven	100.00	45.00
❑ SF4 Terry Labonte	150.00	70.00

1998 SP Authentic

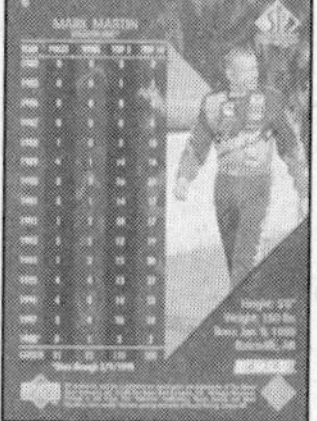

The 1998 SP Authentic set was issued in one series totalling 84 cards. The 5-card packs retail for a suggested price of $4.99 each. The set contains the topical subset: Victory Lap (69-84).

	MINT	NRMT
COMPLETE SET (84)	30.00	13.50
COMMON CARD (1-84)	.20	.09
COMMON DRIVER (1-84)	.40	.18
❑ 1 Jeremy Mayfield	1.25	.55
❑ 2 Rusty Wallace	2.00	.90
❑ 3 Dale Earnhardt	4.00	1.80
❑ 4 Bobby Hamilton	.40	.18
❑ 5 Terry Labonte	2.00	.90
❑ 6 Mark Martin	2.00	.90
❑ 7 Geoff Bodine	.40	.18
❑ 8 Hut Stricklin	.40	.18
❑ 9 Jeff Burton	.75	.35
❑ 10 Ricky Rudd	.75	.35
❑ 11 Johnny Benson	.40	.18
❑ 12 Dale Jarrett	1.50	.70
❑ 13 Jerry Nadeau	.40	.18
❑ 14 Steve Park	1.50	.70
❑ 15 Bill Elliott	2.00	.90
❑ 16 Ted Musgrave	.40	.18
❑ 17 Darrell Waltrip	.75	.35
❑ 18 Bobby Labonte	1.50	.70
❑ 19 Todd Bodine	.40	.18
❑ 20 Kyle Petty	.75	.35
❑ 21 Michael Waltrip	.40	.18
❑ 22 Ken Schrader	.40	.18
❑ 23 Jimmy Spencer	.40	.18
❑ 24 Jeff Gordon	4.00	1.80
❑ 25 Ricky Craven	.40	.18
❑ 26 John Andretti	.40	.18
❑ 27 Sterling Marlin	.75	.35
❑ 28 Kenny Irwin	1.25	.55
❑ 29 Mike Skinner	.40	.18
❑ 30 Derrike Cope	.40	.18
❑ 31 Ernie Irvan	.75	.35
❑ 32 Joe Nemechek	.40	.18
❑ 33 Kenny Wallace	.40	.18
❑ 34 Ward Burton	.40	.18
❑ 35 Jeremy Mayfield's Car	.60	.25
❑ 36 Rusty Wallace's Car	1.00	.45
❑ 37 Dale Earnhardt's Car	2.00	.90
❑ 38 Bobby Hamilton's Car	.20	.09
❑ 39 Terry Labonte's Car	1.00	.45
❑ 40 Mark Martin's Car	1.00	.45
❑ 41 Geoff Bodine's Car	.20	.09
❑ 42 Hut Stricklin's Car	.20	.09
❑ 43 Jeff Burton's Car	.40	.18
❑ 44 Ricky Rudd's Car	.40	.18
❑ 45 Johnny Benson's Car	.20	.09
❑ 46 Dale Jarrett's Car	.75	.35
❑ 47 Jerry Nadeau's Car	.20	.09
❑ 48 Steve Park's Car	.75	.35
❑ 49 Bill Elliott's Car	1.00	.45
❑ 50 Ted Musgrave's Car	.20	.09
❑ 51 Darrell Waltrip's Car	.40	.18
❑ 52 Bobby Labonte's Car	.75	.35
❑ 53 Todd Bodine's Càr	.20	.09
❑ 54 Kyle Petty's Car	.40	.18
❑ 55 Michael Waltrip's Car	.20	.09
❑ 56 Ken Schrader's Car	.20	.09
❑ 57 Jimmy Spencer's Car	.20	.09
❑ 58 Jeff Gordon's Car	2.00	.90
❑ 59 Ricky Craven's Car	.20	.09
❑ 60 John Andretti's Car	.20	.09
❑ 61 Sterling Marlin's Car	.40	.18
❑ 62 Kenny Irwin's Car	.60	.25
❑ 63 Mike Skinner's Car	.20	.09
❑ 64 Derrike Cope's Car	.20	.09
❑ 65 Ernie Irvan's Car	.40	.18
❑ 66 Joe Nemechek's Car	.20	.09
❑ 67 Kenny Wallace's Car	.20	.09
❑ 68 Ward Burton's Car	.20	.09
❑ 69 Darrell Waltrip	.75	.35
❑ 70 Rusty Wallace	2.00	.90
❑ 71 Bill Elliott	2.00	.90
❑ 72 Jeff Gordon	4.00	1.80
❑ 73 Geoff Bodine	.40	.18
❑ 74 Terry Labonte	2.00	.90
❑ 75 Mark Martin	2.00	.90
❑ 76 Ricky Rudd	.75	.35
❑ 77 Ernie Irvan	.75	.35
❑ 78 Dale Jarrett	1.50	.70
❑ 79 Kyle Petty	.75	.35
❑ 80 Sterling Marlin	.75	.35
❑ 81 Dave Marcis	.75	.35
❑ 82 Bobby Labonte	1.00	.45
❑ 83 Ken Schrader	.40	.18
❑ 84 Jimmy Spencer	.40	.18

1998 SP Authentic Behind the Wheel

Randomly inserted in packs at a rate of one in 4, this is the first of a three-tiered insert set that features 20 of the top NASCAR Winston Cup drivers, with each level boasting its own special insert ratio and foil treatment. Level 1 features a silver foil.

	MINT	NRMT
COMPLETE SET (20)	50.00	22.00
COMMON CARD (BW1-BW20)	1.00	.45
*SINGLES: 1X TO 2.5X BASE CARD HI		
❑ BW1 Jeff Gordon	10.00	4.50
❑ BW2 Dale Jarrett	4.00	1.80
❑ BW3 Mark Martin	5.00	2.20
❑ BW4 Jeff Burton	2.00	.90
❑ BW5 Terry Labonte	5.00	2.20
❑ BW6 Bobby Labonte	2.50	1.10
❑ BW7 Bill Elliott	5.00	2.20
❑ BW8 Rusty Wallace	5.00	2.20
❑ BW9 Ken Schrader	1.00	.45
❑ BW10 Johnny Benson	1.00	.45
❑ BW11 Ted Musgrave	1.00	.45
❑ BW12 Jeremy Mayfield	3.00	1.35
❑ BW13 Ernie Irvan	2.00	.90
❑ BW14 Kyle Petty	2.00	.90
❑ BW15 Bobby Hamilton	1.00	.45
❑ BW16 Ricky Rudd	2.00	.90
❑ BW17 Michael Waltrip	1.00	.45
❑ BW18 Ricky Craven	1.00	.45
❑ BW19 Kenny Irwin	3.00	1.35
❑ BW20 Steve Park	4.00	1.80

1998 SP Authentic Behind the Wheel Level 2

Randomly inserted in packs at a rate of one in 12, this is the second of a three-tiered insert set that features 20 of the top NASCAR Winston Cup drivers, with each level boasting its own special insert ratio and foil treatment. Level 2 features a gold foil.

	MINT	NRMT
COMPLETE SET (20)	100.00	45.00
COMMON CARD (BW1-BW20)	1.50	.70

1998 SP Authentic Behind the Wheel Level 3

Sequentially numbered to 100, this is the third of a three-tiered insert set that features 20 of the top NASCAR Winston Cup drivers, with each level boasting its own special insert ratio and foil treatment. Level 3 features a special die-cut, gold foil.

	MINT	NRMT
COMPLETE SET (20)	1200.00	550.00
COMMON CARD (BW1-BW20)	15.00	6.75

1998 SP Authentic Mark of a Legend

Randomly inserted in packs at a rate of one in 168, this 5-card insert set features autographs from all-time NASCAR greats including: Richard Petty, David Pearson, Benny Parsons, Ned Jarrett and Cale Yarborough.

	MINT	NRMT
COMPLETE SET (5)	250.00	110.00
COMMON CARD (M1-M5)	50.00	22.00
❑ M1 Richard Petty Redemption	75.00	34.00
❑ M2 David Pearson	50.00	
❑ M3 Benny Parsons	50.00	
❑ M4 Ned Jarrett	50.00	
❑ M5 Cale Yarborough	50.00	

1998 SP Authentic Sign of the Times Level 1

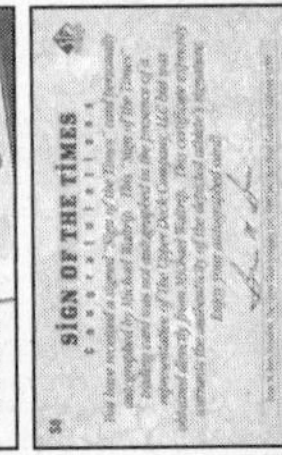

Randomly inserted in packs at a rate of one in 24, the first of a two-tiered insert set that contains autog from today's top NASCAR stars including Jeff Go Mark Martin and Rusty Wallace. Level 1 features blu

	MINT
COMPLETE SET (10)	250.00
COMMON CARD (S1-S10)	12.00
❑ S1 Rusty Wallace Redemption	60.00
❑ S2 Ted Musgrave Redemption	12.00
❑ S3 Ricky Craven Redemption	25.00
❑ S4 Sterling Marlin	25.00
❑ S5 John Andretti	12.00
❑ S6 Michael Waltrip	12.00
❑ S7 Darrell Waltrip	25.00
❑ S8 Jeremy Mayfield	40.00
❑ S9 Kenny Irwin Redemption	30.00
❑ S10 Bobby Hamilton	12.00

1998 SP Authentic Sign of the Times Level 2

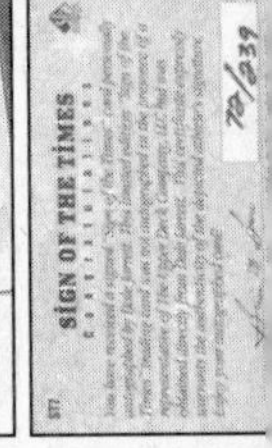

Randomly inserted in packs at a rate of one in 96 the second of a two-tiered insert set that co autographs from today's top NASCAR stars includ Gordon, Mark Martin and Rusty Wallace. Level 2 red foil.

	MINT
COMPLETE SET (10)	800.00
COMMON CARD (ST1-ST10)	40.00
❑ ST1 Jeff Gordon Redemption	250.00
❑ ST2 Ernie Irvan	40.00
❑ ST3 Dale Earnhardt	250.00
❑ ST4 Kyle Petty Redemption	40.00
❑ ST5 Terry Labonte	125.00
❑ ST6 Mark Martin	100.00
❑ ST7 Dale Jarrett	80.00
❑ ST8 Jeff Burton	40.00
❑ ST9 Bobby Labonte	40.00
❑ ST10 Ricky Rudd	40.00

1998 SP Authentic Traditi

Randomly inserted in packs at a rate of one in 28 card insert set features the ultimate signature each one highlights two authentic autographs: on NASCAR legend, and one from a current superstar.

	MINT
COMPLETE SET (5)	1200.00
COMMON CARD (T1-T5)	150.00
❑ T1 R.Petty/D.Earnhardt Redemption	400.00
❑ T2 D.Pearson/J.Gordon Red.	350.00

.Parsons/T.Labonte	200.00	90.00
.Jarrett/D.Jarrett	175.00	80.00
.Yarborough/R.Wallace	150.00	70.00

1996 SPx

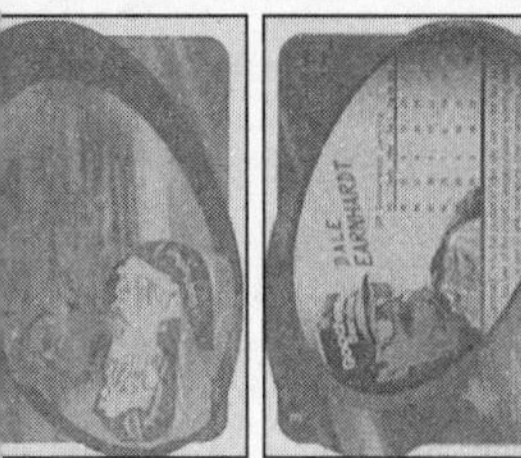

the inagural racing issue of Upper Deck's popular rand. The 25-card set features holoview technology ve a die cut design. The one-card packs retailed for each. The were 28 packs per box and 12 boxes per Randomly inserted in packs were special cards of Labonte and Jeff Gordon. The Terry Labonte card emorated his record breaking 514 consecutive These cards were seeded one in 47 packs. The Jeff n card was a tribute to the hottest young star in His card was seeded one in 71 packs. There were utograph cards of both drivers. The Terry Labonte d in packs was actually an autograph redemption his card was available one in 395 packs. The Jeff n card was an autographed version of the tribute nd was also seeded one in 395 packs. There was Jeff Gordon Sample card that was issued as a

	MINT	NRMT
.ETE SET (25)	60.00	27.00
ON CARD (1-25)	1.00	.45

f Gordon	10.00	4.50
sty Wallace	5.00	2.20
le Earnhardt	10.00	4.50
erling Marlin	2.00	.90
ry Labonte	5.00	2.20
rk Martin	5.00	2.20
f Burton	2.00	.90
bby Hamilton	1.00	.45
ke Speed	1.00	.45
icky Rudd	2.00	.90
rett Bodine	1.00	.45
errike Cope	1.00	.45
eremy Mayfield	3.00	1.35
icky Craven	1.00	.45
ohnny Benson	1.00	.45
ed Musgrave	1.00	.45
arrell Waltrip	2.00	.90
obby Labonte	4.00	1.80
teve Grissom	1.00	.45
yle Petty	2.00	.90
ichael Waltrip	1.00	.45
rnie Irvan	2.00	.90
ale Jarrett	4.00	1.80
ill Elliott	5.00	2.20
en Schrader	1.00	.45
erry Labonte Commemorative	30.00	13.50
Terry Labonte Commemorative AUTO	150.00	70.00
eff Gordon Tribute	40.00	18.00
Jeff Gordon Tribute AUTO	250.00	110.00

1996 SPx Gold

5-card set is a parallel to the base SPx set. The eautre a gold foil stamping and could be pulled one n packs.

	MINT	NRMT
.ETE SET (25)	150.00	70.00
ON CARD (1-25)	2.50	1.10

CARDS: 1.25X TO 2.5X BASIC CARDS

1996 SPx Elite

mly inserted in packs at a rate of one in 23, this rd set features some of the top names in racing. rds use the same holoview technology as the base rds.

	MINT	NRMT
ETE SET (5)	80.00	36.00
ON CARD (E1-E5)	8.00	3.60

.ES: 1.5X TO 4X BASE CARD HI

eff Gordon	50.00	22.00

❑ E2 Dale Jarrett	18.00	8.00
❑ E3 Terry Labonte	25.00	11.00
❑ E4 Rusty Wallace	25.00	11.00
❑ E5 Ernie Irvan	8.00	3.60

1997 SPx

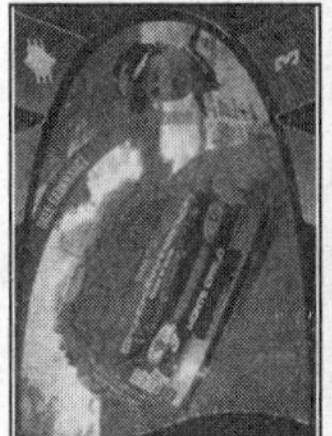

This 25-card set features the top names from the Winston Cup circuit. It is important to note that a significant percentage of base cards that were pulled from packs contain minor surface foil damage on the left side on each card. This has made the supply of Mint cards very small. Cards were distributed in three cards packs with 18 packs per box and 12 boxes per case. The packs carried a suggested retail price of $4.99.

	MINT	NRMT
COMPLETE SET (25)	30.00	13.50
COMMON CARD (1-25)	.50	.23

❑ 1 Robby Gordon	.50	.23
❑ 2 Rusty Wallace	2.50	1.10
❑ 3 Dale Earnhardt	5.00	2.20
❑ 4 Sterling Marlin	1.00	.45
❑ 5 Terry Labonte	2.50	1.10
❑ 6 Mark Martin	2.50	1.10
❑ 7 Geoff Bodine	.50	.23
❑ 8 Dale Jarrett	2.00	.90
❑ 9 Ernie Irvan	1.00	.45
❑ 10 Ricky Rudd	1.00	.45
❑ 11 Mike Skinner	.50	.23
❑ 12 Johnny Benson	.50	.23
❑ 13 Kyle Petty	1.00	.45
❑ 14 John Andretti	.50	.23
❑ 15 Jeff Burton	1.00	.45
❑ 16 Ted Musgrave	.50	.23
❑ 17 Darrell Waltrip	1.00	.45
❑ 18 Bobby Labonte	2.00	.90
❑ 19 Bobby Hamilton	.50	.23
❑ 20 Bill Elliott	2.50	1.10
❑ 21 Michael Waltrip	.50	.23
❑ 22 Ken Schrader	.50	.23
❑ 23 Jimmy Spencer	.50	.23
❑ 24 Jeff Gordon	5.00	2.20
❑ 25 Ricky Craven	.50	.23

1997 SPx Blue

This 25-card insert set is a parallel of the base set. These cards differ from the base cards in that the car number in the bottom right corner of the card is in blue foil rather than grey foil. The cards were randomly inserted in packs at a ratio of 1:1.

	MINT	NRMT
COMPLETE SET (25)	50.00	22.00
COMMON CARD (1-25)	.75	.35

*BLUE CARDS: .75X TO X BASIC CARDS

1997 SPx Gold

This 25-card insert set is a parallel of the base set. These cards differ from the base cards in that the car number in the bottom right corner of the card is in gold foil rather than grey foil. The cards were randomly inserted in packs at a ratio of 1:75.

	MINT	NRMT
COMPLETE SET (25)	600.00	275.00
COMMON CARD (1-25)	10.00	4.50

*GOLD CARDS: 15X TO X BASIC CARDS

1997 SPx Silver

This 25-card insert set is a parallel of the base set. These cards differ from the base cards in that the car number in the bottom right corner of the card is in silver foil rather than grey foil. The cards were randomly inserted in packs at a ratio of 1:5.

	MINT	NRMT
COMPLETE SET (25)	100.00	45.00
COMMON CARD (1-25)	1.50	.70

*SILVER CARDS: 1.5X TO X BASIC CARDS

1997 SPx SpeedView Autographs

This 10-card insert set features the top driver on the Winston Cup Circuit. Each card is autographed and has three photos of the driver on the front of the card. The cards were randomly inserted in packs at a ratio of 1:175.

	MINT	NRMT
COMPLETE SET (10)	800.00	350.00
COMMON CARD (SV1-SV10)	50.00	22.00

❑ SV1 Jeff Gordon	250.00	110.00
❑ SV2 Rusty Wallace	100.00	45.00
❑ SV3 Bill Elliott	100.00	45.00
❑ SV4 Sterling Marlin	50.00	22.00
❑ SV5 Terry Labonte	100.00	45.00
❑ SV6 Mark Martin	100.00	45.00
❑ SV7 Dale Jarrett	75.00	34.00
❑ SV8 Ernie Irvan	50.00	22.00
❑ SV9 Bobby Labonte	75.00	34.00
❑ SV10 Ricky Rudd	50.00	22.00

1997 SPx Tag Team

This 5-car insert set features the top pairs of teammates in NASCAR. The cards were randomly inserted in packs at a ratio of 1:55.

	MINT	NRMT
COMPLETE SET (5)	120.00	55.00
COMMON CARD (T1-T5)	15.00	6.75

❑ TT1 Terry Labonte Jeff Gordon	50.00	22.00
❑ TT2 Dale Jarrett Ernie Irvan	25.00	11.00
❑ TT3 Mark Martin Jeff Burton	25.00	11.00
❑ TT4 Jeff Gordon Ricky Craven	40.00	18.00
❑ TT5 Richard Petty Kyle Petty	15.00	6.75

1997 SPx Tag Team Autographs

This 5-card insert set is a parallel of the base Tag team set. Each card from this set is signed by both drivers featured on the card. The cards were randomly inserted in packs at a ratio of 1:2,500.

	MINT	NRMT
COMPLETE SET (5)	1300.00	575.00
COMMON CARD (T1-T5)	150.00	70.00

❑ TA1 Terry Labonte Jeff Gordon	400.00	180.00
❑ TA2 Dale Jarrett Ernie Irvan	225.00	100.00
❑ TA3 Mark Martin Jeff Burton	300.00	135.00
❑ TA4 Jeff Gordon Ricky Craven	325.00	145.00
❑ TA5 Richard Petty Kyle Petty	150.00	70.00

1996 Speedflix

The 1996 Speedflix Racing set was issued in one series totalling 87 cards. The set includes the following subsets: Black Lighting (51-54), Champion In Motion (55-62), Back on Track (63-66), Relentless Opponent (67-70), Championship Form (71-74), and Million Dollar Bill (75-78). The cards use lenticular animation to bring movement to every card. The cards were packaged 5 cards per pack in both hobby and retail packs. Jumbo packs had eight cards per pack.

	MINT	NRMT
COMPLETE SET (87)	12.00	5.50
COMMON CARD (1-87)	.10	.05
COMMON DRIVER (1-87)	.20	.09

❑ 1 Rusty Wallace	.75	.35
❑ 2 Sterling Marlin	.40	.18
❑ 3 Terry Labonte	.75	.35
❑ 4 Bill Elliott	.75	.35
❑ 5 John Andretti	.20	.09
❑ 6 Bobby Hamilton	.20	.09
❑ 7 Darrell Waltrip	.40	.18
❑ 8 Michael Waltrip	.20	.09
❑ 9 Jeff Gordon	1.50	.70
❑ 10 Dale Jarrett	.60	.25
❑ 11 Johnny Benson Jr.	.20	.09
❑ 12 Rick Mast	.20	.09
❑ 13 Geoff Bodine	.20	.09
❑ 14 Ward Burton	.20	.09
❑ 15 Kenny Wallace	.20	.09
❑ 16 Jeff Gordon	1.50	.70
❑ 17 Dale Earnhardt	1.50	.70
❑ 18 Rusty Wallace	.75	.35
❑ 19 Sterling Marlin	.40	.18
❑ 20 Mark Martin	.75	.35
❑ 21 Ricky Rudd	.40	.18
❑ 22 Darrell Waltrip	.40	.18
❑ 23 Bobby Labonte	.60	.25
❑ 24 Dale Jarrett	.60	.25
❑ 25 Ricky Craven	.20	.09
❑ 26 Johnny Benson Jr.	.20	.09
❑ 27 Joe Nemechek	.20	.09
❑ 28 Ernie Irvan	.40	.18
❑ 29 Jeff Burton	.40	.18
❑ 30 Terry Labonte	.75	.35
❑ 31 Bobby Hillin Jr.	.20	.09
❑ 32 John Andretti	.20	.09
❑ 33 Mike Wallace	.20	.09
❑ 34 Kyle Petty	.40	.18
❑ 35 Lake Speed	.20	.09
❑ 36 Rusty Wallace in Pits	.40	.18
❑ 37 Dale Earnhardt in Pits	.75	.35
❑ 38 Sterling Marlin in Pits	.20	.09
❑ 39 Terry Labonte in Pits	.40	.18
❑ 40 Mark Martin in Pits	.40	.18
❑ 41 Ricky Rudd in Pits	.20	.09
❑ 42 Bill Elliott in Pits	.40	.18
❑ 43 Ernie Irvan in Pits	.20	.09
❑ 44 Jeff Gordon in Pits	.75	.35
❑ 45 Bobby Labonte in Pits	.40	.18
❑ 46 Terry Labonte DT	.40	.18
❑ 47 Dale Jarrett DT	.40	.18
❑ 48 Michael Waltrip DT	.10	.05
❑ 49 Kenny Wallace DT	.10	.05
❑ 50 Mark Martin DT	.40	.18
❑ 51 Dale Earnhardt	.75	.35
❑ 52 Dale Earnhardt	.75	.35
❑ 53 Dale Earnhardt	.75	.35
❑ 54 Dale Earnhardt	.75	.35
❑ 55 Jeff Gordon	.75	.35
❑ 56 Jeff Gordon	.75	.35
❑ 57 Jeff Gordon	.75	.35
❑ 58 Jeff Gordon	.75	.35
❑ 59 Jeff Gordon	.75	.35
❑ 60 Jeff Gordon	.75	.35
❑ 61 Jeff Gordon	.75	.35
❑ 62 Jeff Gordon	.75	.35
❑ 63 Ernie Irvan	.20	.09
❑ 64 Ernie Irvan	.20	.09
❑ 65 Ernie Irvan	.20	.09
❑ 66 Ernie Irvan	.20	.09
❑ 67 Mark Martin	.40	.18
❑ 68 Mark Martin	.40	.18
❑ 69 Mark Martin	.40	.18
❑ 70 Mark Martin	.40	.18
❑ 71 Rusty Wallace	.40	.18
❑ 72 Rusty Wallace	.40	.18
❑ 73 Rusty Wallace	.40	.18
❑ 74 Rusty Wallace	.40	.18
❑ 75 Bill Elliott	.40	.18
❑ 76 Bill Elliott	.40	.18
❑ 77 Bill Elliott	.40	.18
❑ 78 Bill Elliott	.40	.18
❑ 79 Ricky Rudd	.20	.09
❑ 80 Ricky Rudd	.20	.09
❑ 81 Ricky Rudd	.20	.09
❑ 82 Ricky Rudd	.20	.09
❑ 83 Dale Earnhardt W	.75	.35
❑ 84 Jeff Gordon W	.75	.35
❑ 85 Dale Earnhardt W	.75	.35
❑ 86 Jeff Gordon CL	.75	.35
❑ 87 Mark Martin CL	.40	.18

1996 Speedflix Artist Proof's

This 87-card set is a parallel to the base Speedflix set. The cards feature a gold foil Artist Proof stamp on the front of each card to differentiate them from the base set. Odds of pulling an Artist Proof card is one in 24 packs.

	MINT	NRMT
COMPLETE SET (87)	250.00	110.00
COMMON CARD (1-87)	2.00	.90

*ARTIST PROOF CARDS: 15X TO X BASIC CARDS

1996 Speedflix Clear Shots

This 12-card insert set features almost clear lenticular technology. If you mixed an accetate card with lenticualr technology a Clear Shots card is what you would get. The cards were inserted in jumbo packs at a rate of one in 31.

	MINT	NRMT
COMPLETE SET (12)	150.00	70.00
COMMON CARD (1-12)	3.00	1.35

*SINGLES: 8X TO 20X BASE CARD HI

❑ 1 Dale Earnhardt	35.00	16.00
❑ 2 Jeff Gordon	35.00	16.00
❑ 3 Sterling Marlin	6.00	2.70
❑ 4 Rusty Wallace	18.00	8.00
❑ 5 Bobby Labonte	12.00	5.50
❑ 6 Terry Labonte	18.00	8.00
❑ 7 Dale Jarrett	16.00	7.25
❑ 8 Mark Martin	18.00	8.00
❑ 9 Bill Elliott	18.00	8.00
❑ 10 Ernie Irvan	6.00	2.70
❑ 11 Ted Musgrave	3.00	1.35
❑ 12 Johnny Benson Jr.	3.00	1.35

1996 Speedflix In Motion

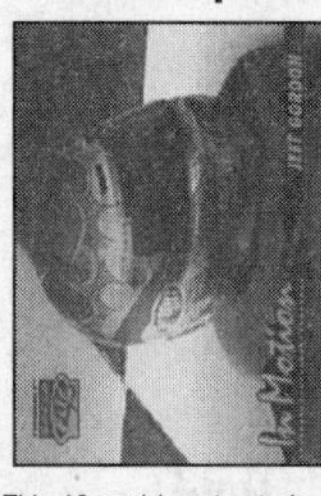

This 10-card insert set shows off the helmets of the top drivers on the Winston Cup circuit. The helmets are featured in multi-phase lenticular animation. In Motion cards were seeded one in 48 packs.

	MINT	NRMT
COMPLETE SET (10)	80.00	36.00
COMMON CARD (1-10)	2.00	

*SINGLES: 5X TO 12X BASE CARD HI

❑ 1 Dale Earnhardt's Helmet	25.00
❑ 2 Jeff Gordon's Helmet	25.00
❑ 3 Sterling Marlin's Helmet	4.00
❑ 4 Rusty Wallace's Helmet	14.00
❑ 5 Geoff Bodine's Helmet	2.00
❑ 6 Terry Labonte's Helmet	14.00
❑ 7 Darrell Waltrip's Helmet	4.00
❑ 8 Mark Martin's Helmet	14.00
❑ 9 Ted Musgrave's Helmet	2.00
❑ 10 Bill Elliott's Helmet	14.00

1996 Speedflix ProMotio

This 12-card insert set allows collectors to se favorites on the move. The cards use multi-lenticular animation to show drivers getting in and their cards. ProMotion cards were randomly insert per nine packs.

	MINT
COMPLETE SET (12)	50.00
COMMON CARD (1-12)	1.25

*SINGLES: 3X TO 8X BASE CARD HI

❑ 1 Dale Earnhardt	12.00
❑ 2 Jeff Gordon	12.00
❑ 3 Sterling Marlin	2.50
❑ 4 Rusty Wallace	6.00
❑ 5 Michael Waltrip	1.25
❑ 6 Terry Labonte	6.00
❑ 7 Dale Jarrett	4.00
❑ 8 Mark Martin	6.00
❑ 9 Bill Elliott	6.00
❑ 10 Darrell Waltrip	2.50
❑ 11 Bobby Hamilton	1.25
❑ 12 Johnny Benson Jr.	1.25

1991 Sports Legends Bobby Allison

K&M Cards produced this set honoring Bobby All part of a continuing Sports Legends card series. was issued in factory set form in an oversiz numbered as series three. The cards in each seri very similar with just the driver's name on the card

	MINT
COMPLETE SET (30)	5.00
COMMON CARD (BA1-BA30)	.20

1991 Sports Legends Donnie Allison

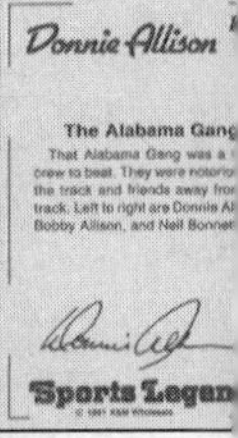

K&M Cards produced this set honoring Donnie All part of a continuing Sports Legends card series. was issued in factory set form in an oversiz numbered as series four. The cards in each seri very similar with just the driver's name on the car The Donnie Allison cards were printed with a red b

	MINT
COMPLETE SET (30)	5.00
COMMON CARD (DA1-DA30)	.20

1991 Sports Legends Neil Bonnett

Cards produced this set honoring Neil Bonnett as f a continuing Sports Legends card series. The set ssued in factory set form in an oversized box ered as series five. The cards in each series look imilar with just the driver's name on the cardfronts. eil Bonnett cards were printed with a red border.

	MINT	NRMT
LETE SET (30)	5.00	2.20
ION CARD (NB1-NB30)	.20	.09

1991 Sports Legends Harry Hyde

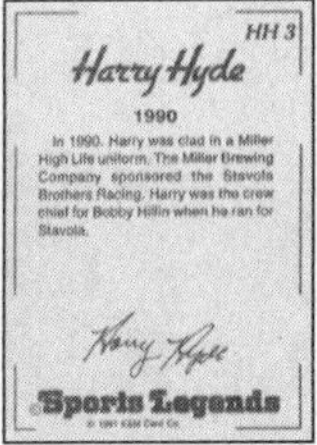

Cards produced this set honoring Harry Hyde as f a continuing Sports Legends card series. The set ssued in factory set form in an oversized box ered as series eight. The cards in each series look imilar with just the driver's name on the cardfronts. arry Hyde cards were printed with a red border.

	MINT	NRMT
LETE SET (30)	5.00	2.20
ION CARD (HH1-HH30)	.20	.09

1991 Sports Legends Dale Jarrett

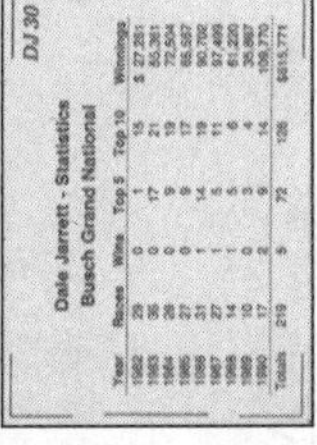

Cards produced this set honoring Dale Jarrett as a continuing Sports Legends card series. The set ssued in factory set form in an oversized box ered as series ten. The cards in each series look milar with just the driver's name on the cardfronts. ale Jarrett cards were printed with a dark blue

	MINT	NRMT
LETE SET (30)	6.00	2.70
ION CARD (DJ1-DJ30)	.20	.09

1991 Sports Legends Ned Jarrett

Cards produced this set honoring Ned Jarrett as the a continuing Sports Legends card series. The set ssued in factory set form in an oversized box ered as series one. The cards in each series look

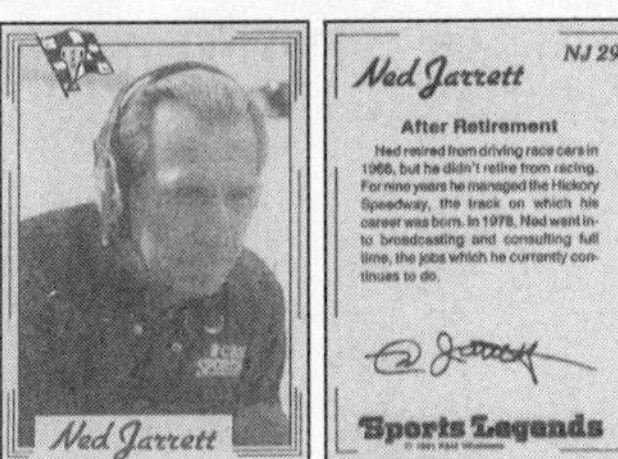

very similar with just the driver's name on the cardfronts. The Ned Jarrett cards were printed with a yellow border.

	MINT	NRMT
COMPLETE SET (30)	5.00	2.20
COMMON CARD (NJ1-NJ30)	.20	.09

1991 Sports Legends Rob Moroso

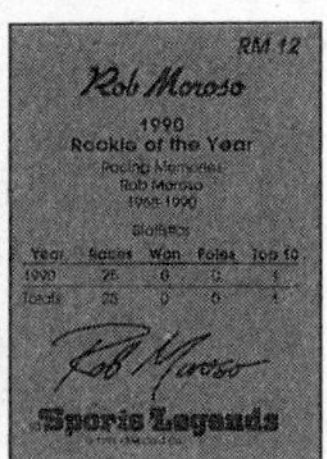

K&M Cards produced this set honoring Rob Moroso as part of a continuing Sports Legends card series. The set was issued in factory set form in an oversized box numbered as series six. The Rob Moroso cards were printed with a different design than most other Sports Legends sets. The cards feature Moroso's name in a black and gold strip running across the bottom of the cardfront. A special art print card portraying Moroso was inserted into 3,000 of the sets.

	MINT	NRMT
COMPLETE SET (30)	5.00	2.20
COMMON CARD (RM1-RM30)	.20	.09

1991 Sports Legends Phil Parsons

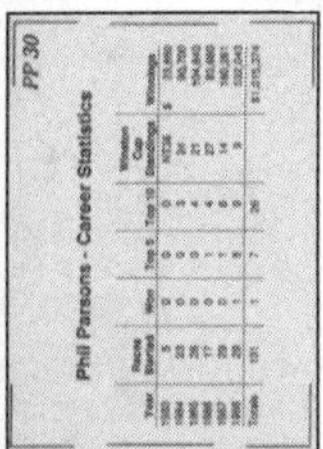

K&M Cards produced this set honoring Phil Parsons as part of a continuing Sports Legends card series. The set was issued in factory set form in an oversized box numbered as series nine. The cards in each series look very similar with just the driver's name on the cardfronts. The Phil Parsons cards were printed with a red border.

	MINT	NRMT
COMPLETE SET (30)	5.00	2.20
COMMON CARD (PP1-PP30)	.20	.09

1991 Sports Legends Wendell Scott

K&M Cards produced this set honoring Wendell Scott as part of a continuing Sports Legends card series. The set was issued in factory set form in an oversized box numbered as series thirteen. The cards in each series look very similar with just the driver's name on the cardfronts. The Wendell Scott cards were printed with a yellow border.

	MINT	NRMT
COMPLETE SET (30)	5.00	2.20
COMMON CARD (WS1-WS30)	.20	.09

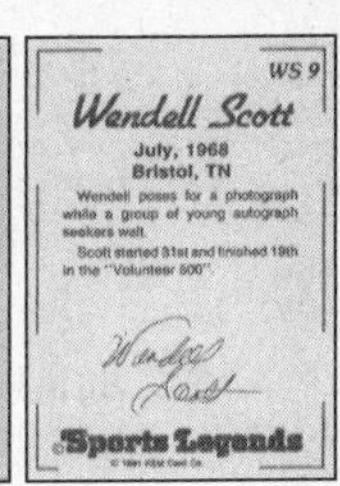

1991 Sports Legends Hut Stricklin

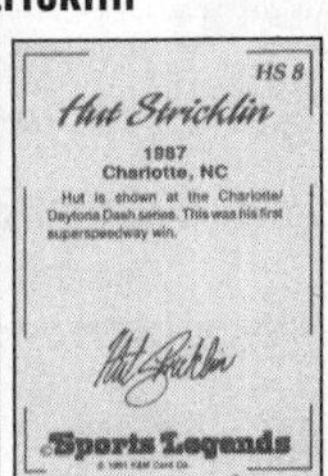

K&M Cards produced this set honoring Hut Stricklin as part of a continuing Sports Legends card series. The set was issued in factory set form in an oversized box numbered as series twelve. The Hut Stricklin cards were printed with a different design than most other Sports Legends sets. The cards feature Stricklin's name in a white and blue strip running across the bottom of the cardfront.

	MINT	NRMT
COMPLETE SET (30)	5.00	2.20
COMMON CARD (HS1-HS30)	.20	.09

1991 Sports Legends Herb Thomas

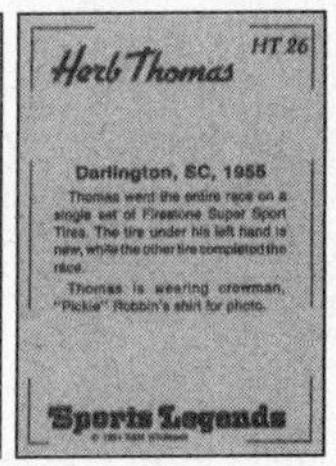

K&M Cards produced this set honoring Herb Thomas as the second in a continuing Sports Legends card series. The set was issued in factory set form in an oversized box numbered as series two. The cards in each series look very similar with just the driver's name on the cardfronts. The Herb Thomas cards were printed with a light blue border.

	MINT	NRMT
COMPLETE SET (30)	5.00	2.20
COMMON CARD (HT1-HT30)	.20	.09

1991 Sports Legends Cale Yarborough

K&M Cards produced this set honoring Cale Yarborough

as part of a continuing Sports Legends card series. The set was issued in factory set form in an oversized box numbered as series eleven. The cards in each series look very similar with just the driver's name on the cardfronts. The Cale Yarborough cards were printed with an orange border.

	MINT	NRMT
COMPLETE SET (30)	5.00	2.20
COMMON CARD (CY1-CY30)	.20	.09

1992 Sports Legends Buck Baker

K&M Cards produced this set honoring Buck Baker as part of a continuing Sports Legends card series. The set was issued in factory set form in an oversized box numbered as series fifteen. The Buck Baker cards were printed with a design featuring his name in a red strip running across the bottom of the card front.

	MINT	NRMT
COMPLETE SET (30)	5.00	2.20
COMMON CARD (BB1-BB30)	.20	.09

1992 Sports Legends Alan Kulwicki

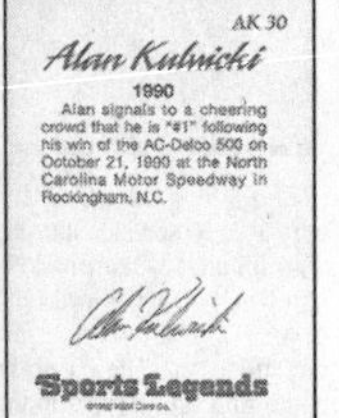

K&M Cards produced this set honoring Alan Kulwicki as part of a continuing Sports Legends card series. The set was issued in factory set form in an oversized box numbered as series seven. The cards in each series look very similar with just the driver's name on the cardfronts. The Alan Kulwicki cards were printed with an orange border.

	MINT	NRMT
COMPLETE SET (30)	10.00	4.50
COMMON CARD (AK1-AK30)	.50	.23

1992 Sports Legends Fred Lorenzen

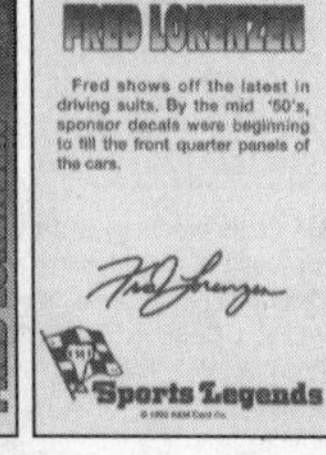

Produced in 1992 by K&M Cards, this Fred Lorenzen commemorative set was issued in factory set form. The cardfronts feature a photo of Lorenzen with backs containing text relating to the photo. The cards are numbered on back inside an outline of a trophy and checkered flag.

	MINT	NRMT
COMPLETE SET (16)	4.00	1.80
COMMON CARD (1-16)	.25	.11

1992 Sports Legends Rusty Wallace

K&M Cards produced this set honoring Rusty Wallace as part of a continuing Sports Legends card series. The set was issued in factory set form in an oversized box numbered as series fourteen. The cards in each series look very similar with just the driver's name on the cardfronts.

	MINT	NRMT
COMPLETE SET (30)	7.00	3.10
COMMON CARD (1-30)	.25	.11

1985 SportStars Photo-Graphics Stickers

SportStars Photo-Graphics Inc. produced this set on sticker card stock. The backs are blank and the fronts feature both a driver and car photo. They look very similar to the 1986 SportStars release, but are much smaller, measuring approximately 2" by 3."

	MINT	NRMT
COMPLETE SET (8)	80.00	36.00
COMMON CARD	8.00	3.60
❑ NNO Mario Andretti	12.00	5.50
❑ NNO A.J.Foyt	12.00	5.50
❑ NNO David Pearson ERR Daivd on Front	10.00	4.50
❑ NNO David Pearson COR David on Front	10.00	4.50
❑ NNO Richard Petty	15.00	6.75
❑ NNO Al Unser Sr.	8.00	3.60
❑ NNO Darrell Waltrip	15.00	6.75
❑ NNO Cale Yarborough	8.00	3.60

1986 SportStars Photo-Graphics

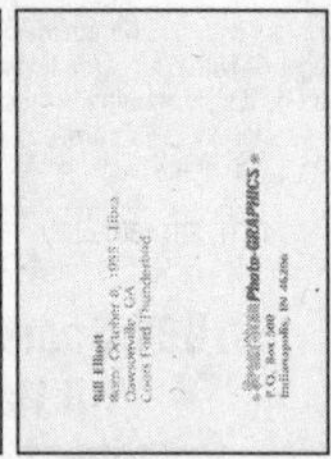

This 13-card set was produced by SportStars, Inc. The cards are a little larger than standard size, measuring 2 3/4" X 3 1/2". The cards have a white border and picture both the driver and his car. The backs contain only driver name, birth date and place, hometown and current car. The also have a "SportStars Photo-GRAPHICS" copyright on the back. Four of the cards appear to be in shorter supply than the others: Bodine, Earnhardt, Gant, and Richmond. All the cards are unnumbered and appear below numbered in alphabetical order. The list represents the 13 known regular versions. Some variations of these cards exist.

	MINT	NRMT
COMPLETE SET (13)	900.00	400.00
COMMON CARD	20.00	9.00
❑ 1 Bobby Allison	20.00	9.00
❑ 2 Geoff Bodine SP	125.00	55.00
❑ 3 Neil Bonnett	75.00	34.00
❑ 4 Dale Earnhardt SP	250.00	110.00
❑ 5 Bill Elliott	30.00	13.50
❑ 6 A.J. Foyt Stock Car	30.00	13.50
❑ 7 A.J. Foyt Indy Car	50.00	22.00
❑ 8 Harry Gant SP	100.00	45.00
❑ 9 Terry Labonte	75.00	34.00
❑ 10 Richard Petty	50.00	22.00
❑ 11 Tim Richmond SP	150.00	70.00
❑ 12 Darrell Waltrip	20.00	9.00
❑ 13 Cale Yarborough	20.00	9.00

1992 SportStars Racing Collectibles

This 16-card set features four top drivers from the mid to late '70's. Card #1 was inserted loosely in Racing

Collectibles magazines and given to dealers who so magazine. The other cards came as a stitched in ins the magazines.

	MINT
COMPLETE SET (16)	10.00
COMMON CARD (1-16)	.75
❑ 1 Joe Weatherly	.75
❑ 2 Joe Weatherly	.75
❑ 3 Joe Weatherly	.75
❑ 4 Joe Weatherly	.75
❑ 5 Dave Marcis	.75
❑ 6 Dave Marcis	.75
❑ 7 Dave Marcis	.75
❑ 8 Dave Marcis	.75
❑ 9 Mark Donohue	.75
❑ 10 Mark Donohue	.75
❑ 11 Mark Donohue	.75
❑ 12 Mark Donohue	.75
❑ 13 Janet Guthrie	.75
❑ 14 Janet Guthrie	.75
❑ 15 Janet Guthrie	.75
❑ 16 Janet Guthrie	.75

1993 Stove Top

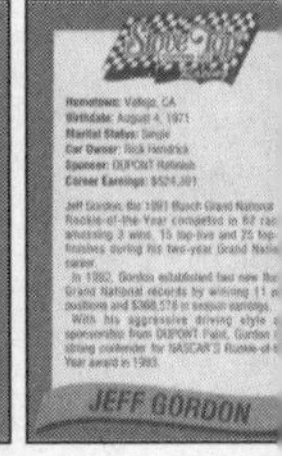

Issued in two different three-card packs in Stov Stuffing packages, the cards feature an artist's ren of a NASCAR driver on the cardfronts. Cardbacks i a driver career summary and stats. The card unnumbered and listed below alphabetically.

	MINT
COMPLETE SET (6)	6.00
COMMON CARD	.60
❑ 1 Jeff Gordon	2.50
❑ 2 Bobby Hamilton	.60
❑ 3 Bobby Labonte	.75
❑ 4 Kenny Wallace	.60
❑ 5 Rusty Wallace	1.25
❑ 6 Michael Waltrip	.75

1972 STP

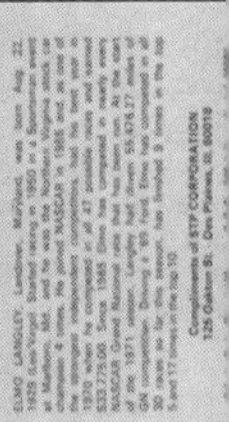

STP Corporation produced and distributed these ca a promotion in 1972. These are some of the e known NASCAR cards and, thus, are highly sough by collectors. Cards were printed on white stock wi lettering on the cardbacks which contain the STP and address. Photos are full-bleed and the car unnumbered.

	NRMT
COMPLETE SET (11)	800.00

ION CARD	60.00	27.00
obby Allison	100.00	45.00
uddy Baker	75.00	34.00
chard Brooks	60.00	27.00
narlie Glotzbach	60.00	27.00
mes Hylton	60.00	27.00
mo Langley	60.00	27.00
ed Lorenzen	75.00	34.00
ed Lorenzen w/Car	75.00	34.00
ave Marcis	75.00	34.00
Benny Parsons	75.00	34.00
Richard Petty	125.00	55.00

1991 STP Richard Petty

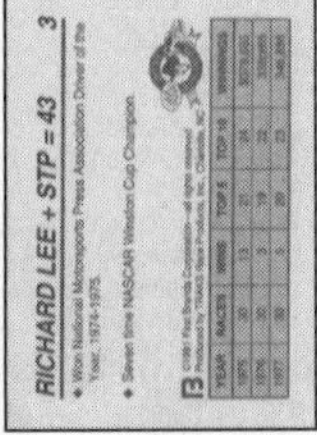

nine cards from the Richard Petty 20th anniversary raks produced this 10-card issue for First Brands and STP. A cover/checklist card was added as the card in the set.

	MINT	NRMT
LETE SET (10)	10.00	4.50
ION CARD (1-10)	1.00	.45
chard Petty A Winning Combination	1.50	.70
chard Petty's Car The Racer's Edge	1.00	.45
chard Petty Richard Lee + STP = 43	1.50	.70
chard Petty's Car Kyle Petty in Pits Son of a Gun!	1.00	.45
chard Petty's Car Pre-flight Checklist	1.00	.45
chard Petty The Fan's Choice	1.50	.70
chard Petty's Car Greased Lightning	1.00	.45
chard Petty w/Car Happy Anniversary	1.50	.70
chard Petty The King	1.50	.70
Checklist	1.00	.45

1992 STP Daytona 500

et produced this 10-card set for First Brands (STP). et commemorates Richard Petty's final entry in the na 500. It was made available through redeeming oof-of-purchase from any STP product.

	MINT	NRMT
LETE SET (10)	10.00	4.50
ION CARD (1-9)	1.00	.45
chard Petty	1.25	.55
chard Petty in Car	1.25	.55
een Flag race action	1.00	.45
chard Petty's Car	1.25	.55
chard Petty in Pits	1.25	.55
aytona 500 Fans	1.00	.45
chard Petty in Pits	1.00	.45
avey Allison	1.50	.70
chard Petty	1.25	.55
Checklist	.50	.23

1996 STP 25th Anniversary

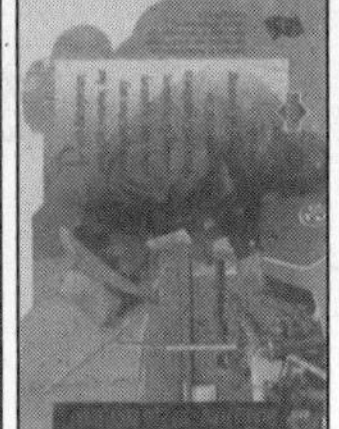

Cards were distributed through a mail in offer on cases of STP. The six-card set features a cover card and five cards with the different paint schemes that Bobby Hamilton, driver of the Richard Petty's STP pontiac, ran under during the 1996 Winston Cup season.

	MINT	NRMT
COMPLETE SET (6)	5.00	2.20
COMMON CAR CARD	1.00	.45
❏ NNO Bobby Hamilton's Car All Blue '72	1.00	.45
❏ NNO Bobby Hamilton's Car '72 Paint	1.00	.45
❏ NNO Bobby Hamilton's Car '79 Paint	1.00	.45
❏ NNO Bobby Hamilton's Car '84 Paint	1.00	.45
❏ NNO Bobby Hamilton's Silver Car	1.00	.45
❏ NNO Cover Card	.25	.11

1991 Superior Racing Metals

This 12-card set features some of the best names in Winston Cup racing. The cards were sold through mail and through Superior Performance's dealer network. The cards feature the were the first metal cards ever produced to feature a Winston Cup driver. The cards are unnumbered and listed below in alphabetical order.

	MINT	NRMT
COMPLETE SET (12)	150.00	70.00
COMMON CARD	10.00	4.50
❏ 1 Derrike Cope	10.00	4.50
❏ 2 Bill Elliott	15.00	6.75
❏ 3 Harry Gant	12.00	5.50
❏ 4 Bobby Hamilton	10.00	4.50
❏ 5 Ernie Irvan	15.00	6.75
❏ 6 Sterling Marlin	15.00	6.75
❏ 7 Mark Martin	16.00	7.25
❏ 8 Phil Parsons	10.00	4.50
❏ 9 Kyle Petty	12.00	5.50
❏ 10 Richard Petty	15.00	6.75
❏ 11 Ken Schrader	10.00	4.50
❏ 12 Darrell Waltrip	12.00	5.50

1991 Texas World Speedway

This 10-card set was released by Texas World Speedway in conjunction with the reopening of the track in 1991. The cards feature a turquoise-blue border and some of the top names in racing. The Tim Richmond card was one of the first produced after his death in 1988 and was the best selling card in the set. There were a reported 50,000 sets produced.

	MINT	NRMT
COMPLETE SET (10)	3.00	1.35
COMMON CARD (1-10)	.25	.11
❏ 1 Benny Parsons	.25	.11
❏ 2 Buddy Baker	.25	.11
❏ 3 Bobby Isaac	.25	.11
❏ 4 Cale Yarborough	.25	.11
❏ 5 Richard Petty	.50	.23
❏ 6 Tim Richmond	.50	.23
❏ 7 Richard Petty Bill France	.50	.23
❏ 8 Cale Yarborough	.25	.11
❏ 9 Darrell Waltrip	.25	.11
❏ NNO Cover Card	.25	.11

1989-90 TG Racing Masters of Racing

The 1989-90 Masters of Racing set was produced and distributed by TG Racing which used its extensive photo files to produce a history of stock car racing on cards. The 1989 issue (#1-152) was broken down into four series of 38-cards each, with each series featuring a different colored border. The set was sold by series (originally $7.95 each) directly to the card hobby. Part two (#153-262) of the Masters of Racing was released in the summer of 1990 under the title White Gold. The 1990 set was sold in complete factory set form only, not by series. A special Masters of Racing album was produced as well to house the cards.

	MINT	NRMT
COMPLETE SET (262)	150.00	70.00
COMPLETE SERIES 1 (152)	130.00	57.50
COMPLETE SERIES 2 (110)	20.00	9.00
COMMON CARD (1-152)	.50	.23
COMMON DRIVER (1-152)	.75	.35
COMMON WHITE GOLD (153-262)	.20	.09
COMMON WG DRIVER (153-262)	.30	.14
❏ 1 Cover Card Gun Gray 1-38	.50	.23
❏ 2 Red Byron	.75	.35
❏ 3 Red Byron's Car First Champion	.50	.23
❏ 4 Starting Lineup 1963 Atlanta 500	.50	.23
❏ 5 Speedy Thompson	.75	.35
❏ 6 Speedy Thompson Darlington 1956	.50	.23
❏ 7 Buck Baker	1.50	.70
❏ 8 Buck Baker w/Car	1.50	.70
❏ 9 Buck Baker Speedy Thompson Carl Kiekhaefer 300 and 300B	1.50	.70
❏ 10 Henley Gray	.75	.35
❏ 11 Henley Gray's Car	.50	.23
❏ 12 Ralph Earnhardt	2.50	1.10
❏ 13 The Wreck 1960 Modified-Sportsman 250	.50	.23
❏ 14 Paul Goldsmith	1.50	.70
❏ 15 Paul Goldsmith w/Car	1.50	.70
❏ 16 Bill Seifert	.75	.35
❏ 17 Bill Seifert w/Car	.75	.35
❏ 18 Edwin Matthews w/Car	.75	.35
❏ 19 Edwin Matthews w/Car	.75	.35
❏ 20 Johnny Thompson w/Car	.75	.35
❏ 21 Johnny Thompson w/Car Jacksonville 1950	.75	.35
❏ 22 Glenn Roberts(Fireball)	4.00	1.80
❏ 23 Glenn Roberts(Fireball) w/Car	4.00	1.80
❏ 24 Glenn Roberts(Fireball) In Action	4.00	1.80
❏ 25 Lennie Pond	.75	.35
❏ 26 Lennie Pond w/Car	.75	.35
❏ 27 David Pearson's Car Junior Johnson's Car Ned Jarrett's Car Marvin Panch's Car Fireball Roberts' Car 256 Wins	.75	.35
❏ 28 Sam McQuagg	.75	.35
❏ 29 Sam McQuagg w/Car	.75	.35
❏ 30 Gober Sosebee	.75	.35
❏ 31 Gober Sosebee's Car On The Beach	.50	.23
❏ 32 Larry Frank	1.50	.70
❏ 33 Larry Frank w/Car	1.50	.70
❏ 34 Eddie Pagan	.75	.35
❏ 35 Curtis Crider	.75	.35
❏ 36 Curtis Crider w/Car	.75	.35
❏ 37 Tiny Lund's Car Fireball Roberts' Cars Bristol 1963	.75	.35
❏ 38 Checklist Cards 1-38	.50	.23
❏ 39 Cover Card Red Fox 39-76 David Pearson's Car Earl Brooks' Car	.50	.23
❏ 40 Lloyd Dane	.75	.35
❏ 41 David Pearson w/Car	1.50	.70
❏ 42 David Pearson w/Car Champion 1968-69	1.50	.70
❏ 43 David Pearson Pearson 1976	1.50	.70
❏ 44 Roy Tyner's Car	.50	.23
❏ 45 David Ezell	.75	.35
❏ 46 Lee Roy Yarborough	1.50	.70
❏ 47 Lee Roy Yarborough w/Car Big Track Champ	1.50	.70
❏ 48 Marshall Teague	.75	.35
❏ 49 Night Time 1964 Columbia 200	.50	.23
❏ 50 Jabe Thomas	.75	.35
❏ 51 Dirt Track 1963 Orange Speedway	.50	.23
❏ 52 Billy Carden	.75	.35
❏ 53 Billy Carden's Car Birmingham Fairgrounds	.50	.23

❑ 54 Ed Samples .75 .35
❑ 55 Ed Samples' Car .50 .23
Greensboro 1947
❑ 56 Jack Smith w/Car .75 .35
❑ 57 Jack Smith w/Car .75 .35
Red Fox
❑ 58 Ralph Moody Jr. w/Car .75 .35
❑ 59 David Pearson's Car 2.50 1.10
Richard Petty's Car
Junior Johnson's Car
Hillsboro 1964
❑ 60 David Pearson 1.50 .70
Goat Power
❑ 61 Tiny Lund 1.50 .70
❑ 62 Tiny Lund w/Car 1.50 .70
55 lb. Fish Story
❑ 63 Tiny Lund w/Car 1.50 .70
Tiny Wins the Big One
❑ 64 Marvin Panch 1.50 .70
❑ 65 The 5 Heroes .50 .23
1963 Daytona
❑ 66 Wilkesboro 1962 .50 .23
❑ 67 Marvin Panch w/Car 1.50 .70
Ford in '64
❑ 68 Cotton Owens .75 .35
❑ 69 Cotton Owens w/Car .75 .35
❑ 70 Tommy Gale w/Car .75 .35
❑ 71 Tiny Lund 4.00 1.80
Marty Robbins
The Hat
❑ 72 Jack Smith's Car .50 .23
Cotton Owens' Car
Red Fox Edges Cotton
❑ 73 Johnny Allen 1.50 .70
❑ 74 Johnny Allen w/Car 1.50 .70
❑ 75 Lee Roy Yarborough 3.00 1.35
Junior Johnson
Herb Nab
Victory Lane
❑ 76 Checklist .50 .23
Cards 39-76 with Cotton Owens
❑ 77 Cover Card .50 .23
Sky Blue 77-114 with Junior Johnson
❑ 78 Walter Ballard .75 .35
❑ 79 Walter Ballard's Car .50 .23
❑ 80 Darel Dieringer .75 .35
❑ 81 Darel Dieringer's Car .50 .23
❑ 82 Ray Erickson .75 .35
❑ 83 Ray Erickson w/Car .75 .35
Pioneer
❑ 84 Dick Hutcherson w/Car .75 .35
❑ 85 Dick Hutcherson's Car .50 .23
❑ 86 Ramo Stott .75 .35
❑ 87 Ramo Stott w/Car .75 .35
❑ 88 Don White .75 .35
❑ 89 Don White's Car .50 .23
❑ 90 Dick Hutcherson .75 .35
Ramo Stott
Don White
Keokuk, Iowa
❑ 91 Glen Wood .75 .35
❑ 92 Rex White w/Car .75 .35
❑ 93 Rex White's Car .50 .23
❑ 94 Jimmie Lewallen .75 .35
❑ 95 Jimmie Lewallen w/Car .50 .23
❑ 96 Darel Dieringer 3.00 1.35
Junior Johnson
❑ 97 Banks Simpson .75 .35
❑ 98 Paul Lewis w/Car .75 .35
❑ 99 Glen Wood's Car .75 .35
Rex White's Car
Winston-Salem 1961
❑ 100 Junior Johnson 3.00 1.35
❑ 101 Junior Johnson's Car 1.50 .70
Darlington 1965
❑ 102 Junior Johnson w/Car 3.00 1.35
❑ 103 Joe Millikan .75 .35
❑ 104 Junior Johnson 3.00 1.35
Ray Fox
Cheat 'N Eat
❑ 105 Bobby Myers .75 .35
Billy Myers
❑ 106 Reino Tulonen w/Car .75 .35
❑ 107 World 600 1963 .50 .23
❑ 108 Coo Coo Marlin 1.50 .70
❑ 109 Coo Coo Marlin w/Car 1.50 .70
❑ 110 Bobby Myers .75 .35
❑ 111 Billy Myers .75 .35
❑ 112 Billy Myers .75 .35
Bowman Gray Stadium
❑ 113 Bobby Myers .75 .35
❑ 114 Checklist .50 .23
Cards 77-114
❑ 115 Cover Card .50 .23
Burnt Orange 115-152
Bobby Isaac's Car
Tiny Lund's car
❑ 116 Buddy Arrington .75 .35
❑ 117 Buddy Arrington's Car .50 .23
❑ 118 Bill Blair w/Car .75 .35
❑ 119 Bill Blair w/Car .75 .35
❑ 120 Earl Brooks w/Car .75 .35
❑ 121 Earl Brooks w/Car .75 .35
❑ 122 Charlie Glotzbach .75 .35
❑ 123 Charlie Glotzbach w/Car .75 .35
Famous Chevy
❑ 124 Charlie Glotzbach w/Car .75 .35
❑ 125 Gene Cline w/Car .75 .35
❑ 126 Nelson Stacy .75 .35
❑ 127 Nelson Stacy w/Car .75 .35
❑ 128 Jim Reed .75 .35
❑ 129 Jim Reed w/Car .75 .35
❑ 130 Charlie Glotzbach w/Car .75 .35
❑ 131 Bobby Isaac's Car .75 .35
❑ 132 Neil Castles' Car .50 .23
❑ 133 Buddy Arrington's Car .50 .23
❑ 134 Fireball Roberts in Pits 1.50 .70
Quick Stop
❑ 135 Neil Castles .75 .35
❑ 136 Neil Castles' Car .50 .23
❑ 137 Red Farmer .75 .35
❑ 138 Red Farmer's Car .50 .23
❑ 139 Big Winner .75 .35
Fred Lorenzen's Car
1964 Martinsville
❑ 140 Pete Hamilton .75 .35
❑ 141 Pete Hamilton w/Car .50 .23
❑ 142 Gwyn Staley .75 .35
❑ 143 Fred Lorenzen 1.50 .70
Fred and Donna
❑ 144 Gwyn Staley .75 .35
Enoch Staley
Charlie Combs
North Wilkesboro
❑ 145 Bobby Isaac w/Car 1.50 .70
❑ 146 G.C. Spencer .75 .35
❑ 147 Bob Derrington .75 .35
❑ 148 Earl Brooks' Car .50 .23
Lorenzen's Car
Nelson Stacy's Car
The Pack
❑ 149 Fred Lorenzen 1.50 .70
❑ 150 Fred Lorenzen w/Car 1.50 .70
❑ 151 Fred Lorenzen w/Car 1.50 .70
❑ 152 Checklist .50 .23
Cards 115-152
❑ 153 Cover Card .20 .09
White Gold 153-262
Red Byron's Car
❑ 154 Bob Flock .30 .14
❑ 155 Bob Flock's Car .20 .09
Red Byron's Car
Whitewalls
❑ 156 Fonty Flock .50 .23
❑ 157 Fonty Flock's Car .30 .14
1947 Champion
❑ 158 Tim Flock .50 .23
❑ 159 Tim Flock w/Car .50 .23
Automatic
❑ 160 Fonty Flock .50 .23
Tim Flock
Bob Flock
Carl Flock
❑ 161 James Hylton .30 .14
❑ 162 James Hylton's Car .20 .09
❑ 163 James Hylton w/Car .30 .14
Rookie Sensation
❑ 164 Perk Brown .30 .14
❑ 165 Perk Brown's Car .20 .09
❑ 166 Joe Frasson .30 .14
❑ 167 Joe Frasson's Car .20 .09
❑ 168 Jack Handle w/Car .30 .14
❑ 169 Louise Smith .50 .23
❑ 170 Louise Smith .50 .23
First Lady
❑ 171 Lee Petty 1.00 .45
Louise Smith
Janet Guthrie
Lella Lombardi
Christine Beckers
Racers All
❑ 172 Marshall Teague .50 .23
Interior
❑ 173 Marshall Teague w/Car .50 .23
Exterior
❑ 174 George Follmer .30 .14
❑ 175 George Follmer's Car .20 .09
Special Breed
❑ 176 George Follmer w/Car .30 .14
Hawk Ford
❑ 177 Bob Wellborn's Car .20 .09
Rex White's Car
Jim Reed's Car
Champions
❑ 178 Bob Burcham w/Car .30 .14
❑ 179 Tommy Moon .30 .14
❑ 180 Wendell Scott 1.00
❑ 181 Wendell Scott's Car .50
Independent
❑ 182 Wendell Scott's Car .50
David Pearson's Car
Late Win
❑ 183 Dick Linder .30
❑ 184 Larry Shurter .30
❑ 185 Johnny Halford .30
❑ 186 Johnny Halford's Car .20
High Pockets
❑ 187 Jim Paschal's Car .20
Fonty Flock's Car
Joe Eubanks' Car
Rough Day
❑ 188 Butch Lindley .30
❑ 189 Butch Lindley's Car .20
LMS Whiz
❑ 190 Checklist .20
Cards 153-190
❑ 191 Donnie Allison 1.00
❑ 192 Donnie Allison's Car .50
Banner Year
❑ 193 Donnie Allison's Car .50
Heartbreaker
❑ 194 Bob Welborn .30
❑ 195 Hershel McGriff .30
❑ 196 Hershel McGriff .30
❑ 197 Hershel McGriff's Car .20
The Comeback
❑ 198 Roscoe Pappy Hough .30
❑ 199 Roscoe Pappy Hough's Car .20
Double Dip
❑ 200 Ned Jarrett .75
❑ 201 Ned Jarrett w/Car .75
14-Lap Winner
❑ 202 Ned Jarrett w/Car .75
No Cigar
❑ 203 Ned Jarrett w/Car .75
Barely Lived
❑ 204 Joe Eubanks .30
❑ 205 Joe Eubanks' Car .20
That North Turn
❑ 206 Richard Brickhouse .30
❑ 207 Richard Brickhouse's Car .20
'70 Superbird
❑ 208 Tom Pistone .50
❑ 209 Tom Pistone's Car .30
Go-Go-Go
❑ 210 Buddy Shuman .30
❑ 211 Marshall Teague .30
Bob Flock
Ed Samples
Buddy Shuman
The Inlaw
❑ 212 Jody Ridley .30
❑ 213 Jody Ridley's Car .20
Unbelievable
❑ 214 Lee Petty 1.00
❑ 215 Lee Petty's Car .50
Deflated
❑ 216 Maurice Petty .50
❑ 217 Maurice Petty .50
Mickey Who?
❑ 218 Al Holbert .30
❑ 219 Al Holbert's Car .20
Top Rookie
❑ 220 Dick Brooks .30
❑ 221 Dick Brooks' Car .20
Pete Hamilton's Car
Last Race
❑ 222 Dick Brooks' Car .20
High Hopes
❑ 223 Dick Rathmann w/Car .30
❑ 224 Dick Rathmann's Car .20
Last to First
❑ 225 Jim Vandiver .30
❑ 226 Jim Vandiver's Car .20
Man On Move
❑ 227 Gene White .30
❑ 228 Checklist .20
Cards 191-228
Skyboxes 1953
❑ 229 Dick May .30
❑ 230 Dick May's Car .20
D.D. Dandy
❑ 231 Herb Thomas .50
❑ 232 Herb Thomas .50
Marshall Teague
The Secret?
❑ 233 Donald Thomas .30
❑ 234 Fans' Race .20
1950 North Wilkesboro
❑ 235 Jim Paschal .30
❑ 236 Jim Paschal w/Car .30
Pontiac Sweep
❑ 237 Jim Paschal w/Car .30
Richard Petty Power

Jim Paschal's Car .20 .09
69 Javelin
Frank Mundy .30 .14
Frank Mundy .30 .14
The Rebel
Frankie Schneider .30 .14
Joe Lee Johnson .30 .14
Joe Lee Johnson w/Car .30 .14
Tradersville
Dink Widenhouse .30 .14
Dink Widenhouse's Car .20 .09
Dink's Dilemma
Dave Marcis .75 .35
Dave Marcis' Car .30 .14
Flying High
Bill Rexford .30 .14
Bill Rexford w/Car .30 .14
1950 Champ
Cale Yarborough .75 .35
Cale Yarborough .75 .35
Cale Yarborough w/Car .75 .35
Ford In 1962
Cale Yarborough w/Car .75 .35
New Shoes
Cale Yarborough w/Car .75 .35
Old Yeller
Cale Yarborough's Car .30 .14
1981 Buick
Elmo Langley .50 .23
Elmo Langley's Car .30 .14
Green Machine
Ray Hendrick .30 .14
Ray Hendrick .30 .14
Perk Brown
Rivals
Ron Bouchard .30 .14
Ron Bouchard w/Car .30 .14
Lucky 13
Checklist .20 .09
Cards 229-262
Dave Marcis
Red, White, Blue

1991 TG Racing Tiny Lund

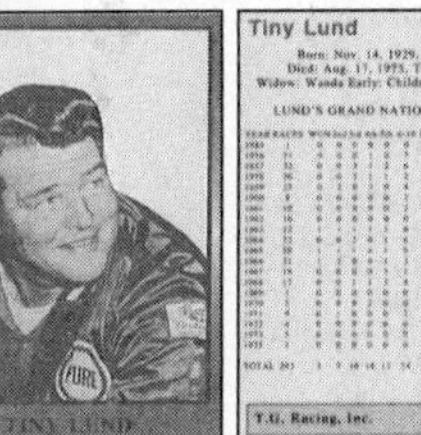

acing released this 55-card set highlighting the of Tiny Lund. The cards were sold in complete set Reportedly 20,000 sets were produced.

MINT NRMT
'LETE SET (55) 10.00 4.50
ION CARD (1-55) .20 .09

ny Lund .20 .09
Art Cover
ny Lund .20 .09
Statistics
ny Lund .20 .09
A Boy & His Dog
ny Lund .20 .09
Stylish in '50s
ny Lund .20 .09
Biker First
ny Lund's Car .20 .09
Hometown Hero
ny Lund's Car .20 .09
Blurry Win
ny Lund .20 .09
Trackside Wedding
ny Lund's Car .20 .09
Brushy Mountain
Tiny Lund w/Car .20 .09
For A Friend
Tiny Lund .30 .14
Tom Pistone
Laurel & Hardy
Tiny Lund w/Car .20 .09
Fish Camp Chevy
Tiny Lund .20 .09
The Fish Camp
Tiny Lund .20 .09
Louis Vogt
Legend Signs On
Tiny Lund .20 .09
Record Catch
❑ 16 Tiny Lund's Car .30 .14
Fred Lorenzen's Car
Tiny and Fred
❑ 17 Tiny Lund w/Car .20 .09
Cinderfella
❑ 18 Tiny Lund .30 .14
Fireball Roberts
Ned Jarrett
Fred Lorenzen
The Big Four
❑ 19 Carnegie Medal .20 .09
❑ 20 Tiny Lund .20 .09
They Knew Him
❑ 21 Tiny Lund .20 .09
Tiny Lund Day
❑ 22 Tiny Lund .20 .09
Atlanta Victory
❑ 23 Tiny Lund .20 .09
Miss Firebird
❑ 24 Tiny Lund's Car .20 .09
Tom Pistone's Car
Serious Racing
❑ 25 Tiny Lund .20 .09
Dick Hutcherson
Cale Yarborough
Ned Jarrett
Buddy Baker
Buck Baker
Playboy Bunny
❑ 26 Tiny Lund .30 .14
Buddy Baker
Brooks Robinson
Favorite Player
❑ 27 Tiny Lund's Car .30 .14
Fred Lorenzen's Car
Slippin', Slidin'
❑ 28 Tiny Lund's Car .20 .09
Hard Charger
❑ 29 Tiny Lund .20 .09
Movie Premiere
❑ 30 Tiny Lund .20 .09
Ride of Her Life
❑ 31 Tiny Lund .20 .09
Baby Alligator
❑ 32 Tiny Lund .30 .14
Buddy Baker
Paul Bud Moore
The Quartet
❑ 33 Tiny Lund .20 .09
Wanda's Wedding
❑ 34 Tiny Lund .20 .09
His Pets
❑ 35 Tiny Lund .20 .09
Buck Baker
Pretty Ladies
❑ 36 Tiny Lund's Car .20 .09
Talladega 1969
❑ 37 Tiny Lund .30 .14
Tom Pistone
Bill France Sr.
France Serves
❑ 38 Tiny Lund .20 .09
Seiichi Suzuki
Big In Japan
❑ 39 Tiny Lund .20 .09
Sushi and Saki
❑ 40 Tiny Lund .20 .09
Joan Crawford
❑ 41 Tiny Lund .20 .09
Wrecking Crew
❑ 42 Tiny Lund .20 .09
Bob Baskowitz
Mountain Dew
❑ 43 Tiny Lund .20 .09
A New Seat
❑ 44 Tiny Lund .20 .09
Santa Claus
❑ 45 Tiny Lund .20 .09
Kids Loved Him
❑ 46 Tiny Lund .30 .14
Andy Granatelli
STP's Andy
❑ 47 Tiny Lund .20 .09
Another Trophy
❑ 48 Tiny Lund .30 .14
President Richard Nixon
❑ 49 Tiny Lund w/Car .20 .09
Two Loves
❑ 50 Tiny Lund .20 .09
Proud Man
❑ 51 Tiny Lund .75 .35
Marty Robbins
❑ 52 Tiny Lund .20 .09
Canadian Tribute
❑ 53 1976 Marquee .20 .09
❑ 54 The Batter's Box .20 .09
June 1, 1991
❑ 55 Tiny Lund's Car .20 .09
Checklist back

1991 TG Racing David Pearson

T.G.Racing released this six-card set highlighting the career of David Pearson. The cards were sold in complete set form.

MINT NRMT
COMPLETE SET (6) 30.00 13.50
COMMON CARD (1-6) 4.00 1.80

❑ 1 David Pearson 4.00 1.80
❑ 2 David Pearson 4.00 1.80
❑ 3 David Pearson 4.00 1.80
❑ 4 David Pearson 4.00 1.80
❑ 5 David Pearson 10.00 4.50
Richard Petty
❑ 6 David Pearson 4.00 1.80

1991 TG Racing Wendell Scott

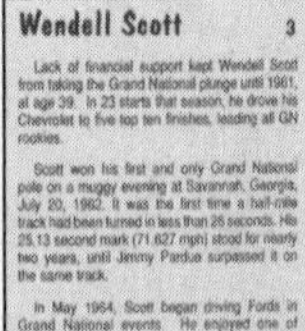
Wendell Scott 3

Lack of financial support kept Wendell Scott from taking the Grand National plunge until 1961, at age 39. In 23 starts that season, he drove his Chevrolet to five top ten finishes, leading all GN rookies.

Scott won his first and only Grand National pole on a muggy evening at Savannah, Georgia, July 20, 1962. It was the first time a half-mile track had been turned in less than 26 seconds. His 25.13 second mark (71.627 mph) stood for nearly two years, until Jimmy Pardue surpassed it on the same track.

In May 1964, Scott began driving Fords in Grand National events. He enjoyed one of his finest seasons on the track in 1966 with 34 finishes in 45 starts, including 16 top tens and three top fives. His annual winnings peaked in 1969 at over $27,000.

© 1991 T.G. RACING, INC.

T.G.Racing released this six-card set highlighting the career of Wendell Scott. The cards were sold in complete set form.

MINT NRMT
COMPLETE SET (6) 10.00 4.50
COMMON CARD (1-6) 1.50 .70

❑ 1 Wendell Scott Art 2.00 .90
❑ 2 Wendell Scott's Car 1.50 .70
The Sportsman Ranks
❑ 3 Wendell Scott 2.00 .90
The Pioneer
❑ 4 Wendell Scott's Car 1.50 .70
David Pearson's Car
Grand National Heat
❑ 5 Wendell Scott 2.00 .90
Priorities
❑ 6 Wendell Scott 2.00 .90
The Veteran

1991-92 TG Racing Masters of Racing Update

TG Racing reprinted the original Masters of Racing set in this "Update" form. This set was released in complete factory set form in a colorful box. Three cards were added to the original set and all cards contain a blue border as opposed to the various border colors of the original cards. Although the cards are marked 1991 on the copyright line, they are considered a 1992 release. Four promo cards were produced to promote the set. They are not considered part of the complete set price.

MINT NRMT
COMPLETE SET (265) 25.00 11.00
COMMON CARD (1-265) .05 .02
COMMON DRIVER (1-265) .10 .05

❑ 1 Cover Card .05 .02
Gun Gray 1-38
❑ 2 Red Byron .10 .05
❑ 3 Red Byron's Car .05 .02
First Champion
❑ 4 Starting Lineup .05 .02
1963 Atlanta 500
❑ 5 Speedy Thompson .10 .05
❑ 6 Speedy Thompson .05 .02
Darlington 1956
❑ 7 Buck Baker .20 .09
❑ 8 Buck Baker w/Car .20 .09
❑ 9 Buck Baker .20 .09
Speedy Thompson
Carl Kiekhaefer
300 and 300B
❑ 10 Henley Gray .10 .05
❑ 11 Henley Gray's Car .05 .02
❑ 12 Ralph Earnhardt .40 .18
❑ 13 The Wreck .05 .02
1960 Modified-Sportsman 250
❑ 14 Paul Goldsmith .20 .09

❑ 15 Paul Goldsmith w/Car .20 .09
❑ 16 Bill Seifert .10 .05
❑ 17 Bill Seifert w/Car .10 .05
❑ 18 Edwin Matthews w/Car .10 .05
❑ 19 Edwin Matthews w/Car .10 .05
❑ 20 Johnny Thompson w/Car .10 .05
❑ 21 Johnny Thompson w/Car .10 .05
Jacksonville 1950
❑ 22 Glenn Roberts(Fireball) .75 .35
❑ 23 Glenn Roberts(Fireball) w/Car .75 .35
❑ 24 Glenn Roberts(Fireball) .75 .35
In Action
❑ 25 Lennie Pond .10 .05
❑ 26 Lennie Pond w/Car .10 .05
❑ 27 David Pearson's Car .10 .05
Junior Johnson's Car
Ned Jarrett's Car
Marvin Panch's Car
Fireball Roberts' Car
256 Wins
❑ 28 Sam McQuagg .10 .05
❑ 29 Sam McQuagg w/Car .10 .05
❑ 30 Gober Sosebee .10 .05
❑ 31 Gober Sosebee's Car .05 .02
On The Beach
❑ 32 Larry Frank .20 .09
❑ 33 Larry Frank w/Car .20 .09
❑ 34 Eddie Pagan .10 .05
❑ 35 Curtis Crider .10 .05
❑ 36 Curtis Crider w/Car .10 .05
❑ 37 Tiny Lund's Car .10 .05
Fireball Roberts' Cars
Bristol 1963
❑ 38 Checklist .05 .02
Cards 1-38
❑ 39 Cover Card .05 .02
Red Fox 39-76
David Pearson's Car
Earl Brooks' Car
❑ 40 Lloyd Dane .10 .05
❑ 41 David Pearson w/Car .20 .09
❑ 42 David Pearson w/Car .20 .09
Champion 1968-69
❑ 43 David Pearson .20 .09
Pearson 1976
❑ 44 Roy Tyner's Car .05 .02
❑ 45 David Ezell .10 .05
❑ 46 Lee Roy Yarborough .20 .09
❑ 47 Lee Roy Yarborough w/Car .20 .09
Big Track Champ
❑ 48 Marshall Teague .10 .05
❑ 49 Night Time .05 .02
1964 Columbia 200
❑ 50 Jabe Thomas .10 .05
❑ 51 Dirt Track .05 .02
1963 Orange Speedway
❑ 52 Billy Carden .10 .05
❑ 53 Billy Carden's Car .05 .02
Birmingham Fairgrounds
❑ 54 Ed Samples .10 .05
❑ 55 Ed Samples' Car .05 .02
Greensboro 1947
❑ 56 Jack Smith w/Car .10 .05
❑ 57 Jack Smith w/Car .10 .05
Red Fox
❑ 58 Ralph Moody Jr. w/Car .10 .05
❑ 59 David Pearson's Car .40 .18
Richard Petty's Car
Junior Johnson's Car
Hillsboro 1964
❑ 60 David Pearson .20 .09
Goat Power
❑ 61 Tiny Lund .20 .09
❑ 62 Tiny Lund w/Car .20 .09
55 lb. Fish Story
❑ 63 Tiny Lund w/Car .20 .09
Tiny Wins the Big One
❑ 64 Marvin Panch .20 .09
❑ 65 The 5 Heroes .05 .02
1963 Daytona
❑ 66 Wilkesboro 1962 .05 .02
❑ 67 Marvin Panch w/Car .20 .09
Ford in '64
❑ 68 Cotton Owens .10 .05
❑ 69 Cotton Owens w/Car .10 .05
❑ 70 Tommy Gale w/Car .10 .05
❑ 71 Tiny Lund .75 .35
Marty Robbins
The Hat
❑ 72 Jack Smith's Car .05 .02
Cotton Owens' Car
Red Fox Edges Cotton
❑ 73 Johnny Allen .20 .09
❑ 74 Johnny Allen w/Car .20 .09
❑ 75 Lee Roy Yarborough .60 .25
Junior Johnson
Herb Nab
Victory Lane

❑ 76 Checklist .05 .02
Cards 39-76 with Cotton Owens
❑ 77 Cover Card .05 .02
Sky Blue 77-114 with Junior Johnson
❑ 78 Walter Ballard .10 .05
❑ 79 Walter Ballard's Car .05 .02
❑ 80 Darel Dieringer .10 .05
❑ 81 Darel Dieringer's Car .05 .02
❑ 82 Ray Erickson .10 .05
❑ 83 Ray Erickson w/Car .10 .05
Pioneer
❑ 84 Dick Hutcherson w/Car .10 .05
❑ 85 Dick Hutcherson's Car .05 .02
❑ 86 Ramo Stott .10 .05
❑ 87 Ramo Stott w/Car .10 .05
❑ 88 Don White .10 .05
❑ 89 Don White's Car .05 .02
❑ 90 Dick Hutcherson .10 .05
Ramo Stott
Don White
Keokuk, Iowa
❑ 91 Glen Wood .10 .05
❑ 92 Rex White w/Car .10 .05
❑ 93 Rex White's Car .05 .02
❑ 94 Jimmie Lewallen .10 .05
❑ 95 Jimmie Lewallen w/Car .05 .02
❑ 96 Darel Dieringer .60 .25
Junior Johnson
❑ 97 Banks Simpson .10 .05
❑ 98 Paul Lewis w/Car .10 .05
❑ 99 Glen Wood's Car .10 .05
Rex White's Car
Winston-Salem 1961
❑ 100 Junior Johnson .60 .25
❑ 101 Junior Johnson's Car .20 .09
Darlington 1965
❑ 102 Junior Johnson w/Car .60 .25
❑ 103 Joe Millikan .10 .05
❑ 104 Junior Johnson .60 .25
Ray Fox
Cheat 'N Eat
❑ 105 Bobby Myers .10 .05
Billy Myers
❑ 106 Reino Tulonen w/Car .10 .05
❑ 107 World 600 1963 .05 .02
❑ 108 Coo Coo Marlin .20 .09
❑ 109 Coo Coo Marlin w/Car .20 .09
❑ 110 Ray Fox .10 .05
❑ 111 Billy Myers .10 .05
❑ 112 Billy Myers .10 .05
Bowman Gray Stadium
❑ 113 Ray Fox .10 .05
❑ 114 Checklist .05 .02
Cards 77-114
❑ 115 Cover Card .05 .02
Burnt Orange 115-152
Bobby Isaac's Car
Tiny Lund's car
❑ 116 Buddy Arrington .10 .05
❑ 117 Buddy Arrington's Car .05 .02
❑ 118 Bill Blair w/Car .10 .05
❑ 119 Bill Blair w/Car .10 .05
❑ 120 Earl Brooks w/Car .10 .05
❑ 121 Earl Brooks w/Car .10 .05
❑ 122 Charlie Glotzbach .10 .05
❑ 123 Charlie Glotzbach w/Car .10 .05
Famous Chevy
❑ 124 Charlie Glotzbach w/Car .10 .05
❑ 125 Gene Cline w/Car .10 .05
❑ 126 Nelson Stacy .10 .05
❑ 127 Nelson Stacy w/Car .10 .05
❑ 128 Jim Reed .10 .05
❑ 129 Jim Reed w/Car .10 .05
❑ 130 Charlie Glotzbach w/Car .10 .05
❑ 131 Bobby Isaac's Car .10 .05
❑ 132 Neil Castles' Car .05 .02
❑ 133 Buddy Arrington's Car .05 .02
❑ 134 Fireball Roberts in Pits .20 .09
Quick Stop
❑ 135 Neil Castles .10 .05
❑ 136 Neil Castles' Car .05 .02
❑ 137 Red Farmer .10 .05
❑ 138 Red Farmer's Car .05 .02
❑ 139 Big Winner .10 .05
Fred Lorenzen's Car
1964 Martinsville
❑ 140 Pete Hamilton .10 .05
❑ 141 Pete Hamilton w/Car .05 .02
❑ 142 Gwyn Staley .10 .05
❑ 143 Fred Lorenzen .20 .09
Fred and Donna
❑ 144 Gwyn Staley .10 .05
Enoch Staley
Charlie Combs
North Wilkesboro
❑ 145 Bobby Isaac w/Car .20 .09
❑ 146 G.C. Spencer .10 .05
❑ 147 Bob Derrington .10 .05

❑ 148 Earl Brooks' Car .05
Lorenzen's Car
Nelson Stacy's Car
The Pack
❑ 149 Fred Lorenzen .20
❑ 150 Fred Lorenzen w/Car .20
❑ 151 Fred Lorenzen w/Car .20
❑ 152 Checklist .05
Cards 115-152
❑ 153 Cover Card .05
White Gold 153-262
Red Byron's Car
❑ 154 Bob Flock .10
❑ 155 Bob Flock's Car .05
Red Byron's Car
Whitewalls
❑ 156 Fonty Flock .20
❑ 157 Fonty Flock's Car .10
1947 Champion
❑ 158 Tim Flock .20
❑ 159 Tim Flock w/Car .20
Automatic
❑ 160 Fonty Flock .20
Tim Flock
Bob Flock
Carl Flock
❑ 161 James Hylton .10
❑ 162 James Hylton's Car .05
❑ 163 James Hylton w/Car .10
Rookie Sensation
❑ 164 Perk Brown .10
❑ 165 Perk Brown's Car .05
❑ 166 Joe Frasson .10
❑ 167 Joe Frasson's Car .05
❑ 168 Jack Handle w/Car .10
❑ 169 Louise Smith .20
❑ 170 Louise Smith .20
First Lady
❑ 171 Lee Petty .40
Louise Smith
Janet Guthrie
Lella Lombardi
Christine Beckers
Racers All
❑ 172 Frank Warren .20
❑ 173 Frank Warren's Car .20
❑ 174 George Follmer .10
❑ 175 George Follmer's Car .05
Special Breed
❑ 176 George Follmer w/Car .10
Hawk Ford
❑ 177 Bob Wellborn's Car .05
Rex White's Car
Jim Reed's Car
Champions
❑ 178 Bob Burcham w/Car .10
❑ 179 Tommy Moon .10
❑ 180 Wendell Scott .40
❑ 181 Wendell Scott's Car .20
Independent
❑ 182 Wendell Scott's Car .20
David Pearson's Car
Late Win
❑ 183 Dick Linder .10
❑ 184 Larry Shurter .10
❑ 185 Johnny Halford .10
❑ 186 Johnny Halford's Car .05
High Pockets
❑ 187 Jim Paschal's Car .05
Fonty Flock's Car
Joe Eubanks' Car
Rough Day
❑ 188 Butch Lindley .10
❑ 189 Butch Lindley's Car .05
LMS Whiz
❑ 190 Checklist .05
Cards 153-190
❑ 191 Donnie Allison .40
❑ 192 Donnie Allison's Car .20
Banner Year
❑ 193 Donnie Allison's Car .20
Heartbreaker
❑ 194 Bob Welborn .10
❑ 195 Hershel McGriff .10
❑ 196 Hershel McGriff .10
❑ 197 Hershel McGriff's Car .05
The Comeback
❑ 198 Roscoe Pappy Hough .10
❑ 199 Roscoe Pappy Hough's Car .05
Double Dip
❑ 200 Ned Jarrett .60
❑ 201 Ned Jarrett w/Car .60
14-Lap Winner
❑ 202 Ned Jarrett w/Car .60
No Cigar
❑ 203 Ned Jarrett w/Car .60
Barely Lived
❑ 204 Joe Eubanks .10

Joe Eubanks' Car	.05	.02
That North Turn		
Richard Brickhouse	.10	.05
Richard Brickhouse's Car	.05	.02
'70 Superbird		
Tom Pistone	.20	.09
Tom Pistone's Car	.10	.05
Go-Go-Go		
Buddy Shuman	.10	.05
Marshall Teague	.10	.05
Bob Flock		
Ed Samples		
Buddy Shuman		
The Inlaw		
Jody Ridley	.10	.05
Jody Ridley's Car	.05	.02
Unbelievable		
Lee Petty	.40	.18
Lee Petty's Car	.20	.09
Deflated		
Maurice Petty	.20	.09
Maurice Petty	.20	.09
Mickey Who?		
Al Holbert	.10	.05
Al Holbert's Car	.05	.02
Top Rookie		
Dick Brooks	.10	.05
Dick Brooks' Car	.05	.02
Pete Hamilton's Car		
Last Race		
Dick Brooks' Car	.05	.02
High Hopes		
Dick Rathmann w/Car	.10	.05
Dick Rathmann's Car	.05	.02
Last to First		
Jim Vandiver	.10	.05
Jim Vandiver's Car	.05	.02
Man On Move		
Gene White	.10	.05
Checklist	.05	.02
Cards 191-228		
Skyboxes 1953		
Dick May	.10	.05
Dick May's Car	.05	.02
D.D. Dandy		
Herb Thomas	.20	.09
Herb Thomas	.20	.09
Marshall Teague		
The Secret?		
Donald Thomas	.10	.05
Fans' Race	.05	.02
1950 North Wilkesboro		
Jim Paschal	.10	.05
Jim Paschal w/Car	.10	.05
Pontiac Sweep		
Jim Paschal w/Car	.10	.05
Richard Petty Power		
Jim Paschal's Car	.05	.02
'69 Javelin		
Frank Mundy	.10	.05
Frank Mundy	.10	.05
The Rebel		
Frankie Schneider	.10	.05
Joe Lee Johnson	.10	.05
Joe Lee Johnson w/Car	.10	.05
Tradersville		
Dink Widenhouse	.10	.05
Dink Widenhouse's Car	.05	.02
Dink's Dilemma		
Dave Marcis	.60	.25
Dave Marcis' Car	.10	.05
Flying High		
Bill Rexford	.10	.05
Bill Rexford w/Car	.10	.05
1950 Champ		
Cale Yarborough	.75	.35
Cale Yarborough	.75	.35
Cale Yarborough w/Car	.75	.35
Ford In 1962		
Cale Yarborough w/Car	.75	.35
New Shoes		
Cale Yarborough w/Car	.75	.35
Old Yeller		
Cale Yarborough's Car	.10	.05
1981 Buick		
Elmo Langley	.20	.09
Elmo Langley's Car	.10	.05
Green Machine		
Ray Hendrick	.10	.05
Ray Hendrick	.10	.05
Perk Brown		
Rivals		
Ron Bouchard	.10	.05
Ron Bouchard w/Car	.10	.05
Lucky 13		
Bobby Myers	.10	.05
Bobby Myers	.10	.05
Darlington		

❑ 264 Checklist	.05	.02
Cards 229-262		
Dave Marcis		
Red, White, Blue		
❑ 265 Tommy Moon w/Car	.10	.05

1994 Tide Ricky Rudd

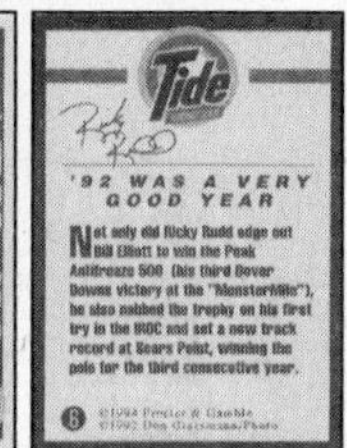

Proctor and Gamble produced and released this set featuring Ricky Rudd and the Tide Racing Team. The ten-card set was given away wherever the Tide showcar was on display during the 1995 Winston Cup season and was released in complete set form.

	MINT	NRMT
COMPLETE SET (10)	8.00	3.60
COMMON CARD (1-10)	.75	.35
❑ 1 Ricky Rudd w/Car	.75	.35
❑ 2 Ricky Rudd's Car	.75	.35
❑ 3 Ricky Rudd	1.00	.45
❑ 4 Ricky Rudd	.75	.35
Bill Ingle		
❑ 5 Ricky Rudd in Pits	.75	.35
❑ 6 Ricky Rudd	1.00	.45
❑ 7 Ricky Rudd's Transporter	.75	.35
❑ 8 Ricky Rudd	.75	.35
Linda Rudd		
❑ 9 Ricky Rudd	.75	.35
Linda Rudd		
❑ 10 Ricky Rudd	.75	.35
Linda Rudd		

1991 Tiger Tom Pistone

This is a 15 card set consisting of 3 color and 12 black and white cards were produced by "If Its Racing". The set covers Tom's career from 1954 to his victory in a legends race at Hickory Speedway in 1987.

	MINT	NRMT
COMPLETE SET (15)	4.00	1.80
COMMON CARD (1-15)	.25	.11
❑ 1 Tom Pistone	.25	.11
❑ 2 Tom Pistone	.25	.11
❑ 3 Tom Pistone	.25	.11
❑ 4 Tom Pistone	.25	.11
❑ 5 Tom Pistone	.25	.11
❑ 6 Tom Pistone	.25	.11
❑ 7 Tom Pistone	.40	.18
Andy Granatelli		
❑ 8 Tom Pistone	.25	.11
❑ 9 Tom Pistone	.25	.11
❑ 10 Tom Pistone	.25	.11
❑ 11 Tom Pistone	.25	.11
❑ 12 Tom Pistone	.25	.11
❑ 13 Tom Pistone	.40	.18
Richard Petty		
❑ 14 Tom Pistone	.40	.18
Tiny Lund		
❑ 15 Tom Pistone	.25	.11

1991 Track Pack Yesterday's Heroes

This 48-card set features some of the greatest names to ever run the NASCAR circuit. The set includes David Pearson, Ned Jarrett and Benny Parsons to name a few. The cards are listed in alphabetical order.

	MINT	NRMT
COMPLETE SET (48)	15.00	6.75
COMMON CARD (1-48)	.25	.11
❑ 1 Cover Card	.25	.11
❑ 2 Bill Blair	.25	.11
❑ 3 Neil Bonnett	1.00	.45
❑ 4 Dick Brooks	.25	.11
❑ 5 Neil Castles	.25	.11
❑ 6 Neil Castles	.25	.11
❑ 7 Richard Childress	.50	.23
❑ 8 Lloyd Dane	.25	.11
❑ 9 Tim Flock	.50	.23
❑ 10 Larry Frank	.50	.23
❑ 11 Dick Hutcherson	.25	.11
❑ 12 Ned Jarrett	.50	.23
❑ 13 JoeLee Johnson	.25	.11
❑ 14 Elmo Langley	.25	.11
❑ 15 Jimmie Lewallen	.25	.11
❑ 16 Fred Lorenzen	1.00	.45
❑ 17 CooCoo Marlin	.25	.11
❑ 18 Banjo Matthews	.25	.11
❑ 19 Banjo Matthews	.25	.11
❑ 20 Sam McQuagg	.25	.11
❑ 21 Ralph Moody	.25	.11
❑ 22 Ralph Moody	.25	.11
❑ 23 Bud Moore	.25	.11
❑ 24 Frank Mundy	.25	.11
❑ 25 Benny Parsons	.50	.23
❑ 26 Jim Paschal	.25	.11
❑ 27 David Pearson	.50	.23
❑ 28 David Pearson	.50	.23
❑ 29 Tom Pistone	.50	.23
❑ 30 Dick Rathmann	.25	.11
❑ 31 Jim Reed	.25	.11
❑ 32 Bill Rexford	.25	.11
❑ 33 Jim Roper	.25	.11
❑ 34 Jack Smith	.25	.11
❑ 35 Jack Smith	.25	.11
❑ 36 Louise Smith	.50	.23
❑ 37 G.C. Spencer	.25	.11
❑ 38 G.C. Spencer	.25	.11
❑ 39 Herb Thomas	.50	.23
❑ 40 Bob Welborn	.25	.11
❑ 41 Bob Welborn	.25	.11
❑ 42 Rex White	.25	.11
❑ 43 Glen Wood	.25	.11
❑ 44 Glen Wood	.25	.11
❑ 45 Cale Yarborough	1.00	.45
❑ 46 Cale Yarborough	1.00	.45
❑ 47 Smokey Yunick	.25	.11
❑ 48 Checklist Card	.25	.11

1991 Traks

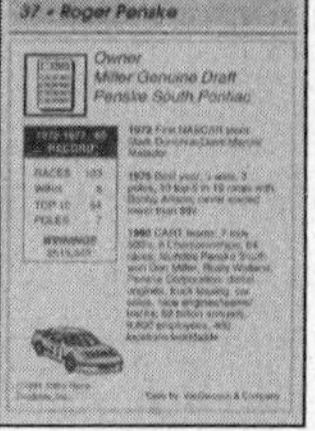

In addition to a 200-card factory set, the premier edition Traks set was distributed in 15-card packs with 30 packs per box in late 1991. The set features the top Busch and Winston Cup drivers along with owners and other racing team members. Traks also included the first regular issue card of Jeff Gordon (#1). The set was available in a factory wooden box version. These were distributed through some of the television shopping channels. 1,000 sets were produced and sell for $25 - $35.

	MINT	NRMT
COMPLETE SET (200)	14.00	6.25
COMPLETE FACT.SET (200)	16.00	7.25
COMMON CARD (1-200)	.10	.05
COMMON DRIVER (1-200)	.20	.09
❑ 1 Jeff Gordon	10.00	4.50
❑ 2 Rusty Wallace	1.00	.45
❑ 3A Dale Earnhardt	2.00	.90
Trademark reads "...than Sports Image, Inc is ..."		
❑ 3B Dale Earnhardt	2.00	.90
Trademark reads"...than Sports Image, Inc. at racing venues..."		
❑ 4 Ernie Irvan	.40	.18
❑ 5 Ricky Rudd	.40	.18
❑ 6 Mark Martin	1.00	.45
❑ 7 Alan Kulwicki	.75	.35
❑ 8 Rick Wilson	.20	.09
❑ 9 Troy Beebe	.10	.05
❑ 10 Ernie Irvan w/Car	.40	.18
❑ 11 Larry McClure	.10	.05
Ed McClure		
Teddy McClure		
Jerry McClure		
❑ 12 Hut Stricklin	.20	.09
❑ 13 High Speed Chaos	.10	.05
❑ 14 Bobby Hillin	.20	.09
❑ 15 Morgan Shepherd	.20	.09
❑ 16 Eddie Lanier	.10	.05
❑ 17 Jeff Hammond	.10	.05
❑ 18 Mike Wallace	.20	.09

❑ 19 Chad Little .20 .09
❑ 20 Bobby Hillin .20 .09
❑ 21 Dale Jarrett .75 .35
❑ 22 Sterling Marlin .40 .18
❑ 23 Danny Myers .10 .05
❑ 24 Barry Dodson .10 .05
❑ 25 Ken Schrader .20 .09
❑ 26 Neil Bonnett .50 .23
❑ 27A Mike Colyer .30 .14
Traks car logo on back
❑ 27B Mike Colyer .30 .14
Traks car logo on back is removed
❑ 28 Davey Allison 1.00 .45
❑ 29 Phil Parsons .20 .09
❑ 30 Michael Waltrip .20 .09
❑ 31 Steve Grissom .20 .09
❑ 32 Dale Jarrett .75 .35
❑ 33 Harry Gant .40 .18
❑ 34 Todd Bodine .20 .09
❑ 35 Chuck Rider .10 .05
❑ 36 Kenny Wallace .20 .09
❑ 37 Roger Penske .10 .05
❑ 38 Jimmy Makar .10 .05
❑ 39 Don Miller .10 .05
❑ 40 Felix Sabates .10 .05
❑ 41 Kyle Petty's Transporter .10 .05
❑ 42 Kyle Petty .40 .18
❑ 43 Richard Petty .75 .35
❑ 44 Dale Inman .10 .05
❑ 45 Bob Bilby .10 .05
❑ 46 Robert Yates .10 .05
❑ 47 Kyle Petty .40 .18
❑ 48 Sprague Turner .10 .05
❑ 49 Doug Richert .10 .05
❑ 50 Mark Martin 1.00 .45
❑ 51 Mike McLaughlin .20 .09
❑ 52 Butch Miller .20 .09
❑ 53 Harold Elliott .10 .05
❑ 54 Richard Childress .10 .05
❑ 55 Ted Musgrave w/Car .40 .18
❑ 56 Tommy Ellis .10 .05
❑ 57 Kirk Shelmerdine .10 .05
❑ 58 Larry McClure .10 .05
❑ 59 Robert Pressley .20 .09
❑ 60 Tim Morgan .10 .05
❑ 61 Dick Trickle .20 .09
❑ 62 Leonard Wood .10 .05
❑ 63 Chuck Bown .20 .09
❑ 64 Glen Wood .10 .05
❑ 65 Steve Loyd .10 .05
❑ 66 Cale Yarborough .20 .09
❑ 67 Jimmy Johnson .10 .05
Rick Hendrick
❑ 68 Ricky Rudd's Car .20 .09
❑ 69 Travis Carter .10 .05
❑ 70 Tony Glover .10 .05
❑ 71 Dave Marcis .40 .18
❑ 72 Waddell Wilson .10 .05
❑ 73 Alan Kulwicki's Car .40 .18
❑ 74 Jimmy Fennig .10 .05
❑ 75 Michael Waltrip .20 .09
❑ 76 Ken Wilson .10 .05
❑ 77 David Smith .10 .05
❑ 78 Junior Johnson .20 .09
❑ 79 Dave Rezendes .10 .05
❑ 80 Tony Furr .10 .05
❑ 81 Ted Conder .10 .05
❑ 82 Mike Beam .10 .05
❑ 83 Walter Bud Moore .10 .05
❑ 84 Terry Labonte 1.00 .45
❑ 85 Richard Petty w/Car .40 .18
❑ 86 Donnie Wingo .10 .05
❑ 87 Joe Nemechek .20 .09
❑ 88 Elton Sawyer .20 .09
Patty Moise
❑ 89 Doug Williams .10 .05
❑ 90 Jimmy Martin .10 .05
❑ 91 Richard Broome .10 .05
❑ 92 Greg Moore .10 .05
❑ 93 Hank Jones .10 .05
❑ 94 Terry Labonte 1.00 .45
❑ 95 Will Lind .10 .05
❑ 96 Tom Peck .20 .09
❑ 97 Morgan Shepherd .20 .09
❑ 98 Jimmy Spencer .20 .09
❑ 99 Leo Jackson .10 .05
❑ 100 Max Helton .10 .05
❑ 101 Bruce Roney .10 .05
❑ 102 Keith Almond .10 .05
❑ 103A Dale Earnhardt 2.00 .90
Trademark reads "...than Sports Image, Inc is ..."
❑ 103B Dale Earnhardt 2.00 .90
Trademark reads"...than Sports Image, Inc. at racing venues..."
❑ 104 Bob Tomlinson .10 .05
❑ 105 Benny Ertel .10 .05
❑ 106 Tommy Houston .20 .09
❑ 107 Cecil Gordon .10 .05
❑ 108 David Green .20 .09
❑ 109 Robin Pemberton .10 .05
❑ 110 David Green's Car .10 .05
❑ 111 John Mulloy .10 .05
❑ 112 Harry Gant .40 .18
❑ 113 Ed Whitaker .10 .05
❑ 114 Bobby Moody .10 .05
❑ 115 Steve Hmiel .10 .05
❑ 116 Red Farmer .10 .05
❑ 117 Eddie Jones .10 .05
❑ 118 Bill Stavola .10 .05
Mickey Stavola
❑ 119 David Ifft .10 .05
❑ 120 Dick Moroso .10 .05
❑ 121 Eddie Wood .10 .05
❑ 122 Len Wood .10 .05
❑ 123 Lou LaRosa .10 .05
❑ 124 Rusty Wallace 1.00 .45
❑ 125 Rob Moroso .40 .18
❑ 126 Ned Jarrett .20 .09
❑ 127 Tom Higgins .10 .05
❑ 128 Frank Edwards .10 .05
❑ 129 Steve Waid .10 .05
❑ 130 Steve Waid .10 .05
❑ 131A Jim Phillips .30 .14
Name in black type on front
❑ 131B Jim Phillips .30 .14
Name in white type on front
❑ 132 John Ervin .10 .05
❑ 133A Winston Kelley .30 .14
last name "Kelly" on back of card
name in black type on front
❑ 133B Winston Kelley .30 .14
last name spelled correct on back
name in white type on front
❑ 134A Allen Bestwick .30 .14
Name in black type on front
❑ 134B Allen Bestwick .30 .14
Name in white type on front
❑ 135A Dick Brooks .30 .14
Name in black type on front
❑ 135B Dick Brooks .30 .14
Name in white type on front
❑ 136 Ricky Rudd Winner .20 .09
❑ 137A Eli Gold .30 .14
Name in black type on front
❑ 137B Eli Gold .30 .14
Name in white type on front
❑ 138 Joe Hendrick (Papa) .10 .05
❑ 139 Barney Hall .10 .05
❑ 140 Tim Brewer .10 .05
❑ 141 George Bradshaw .10 .05
❑ 142 John Wilson .10 .05
❑ 143 Robbie Loomis .10 .05
❑ 144 Benny Parsons .20 .09
❑ 145 Jack Steele .10 .05
❑ 146 Gary Nelson .10 .05
❑ 147 Ed Brasefield .10 .05
❑ 148 Lake Speed .20 .09
❑ 149 Bill Brodrick .10 .05
❑ 150 Robert Black .10 .05
❑ 151 Carl Hill .10 .05
❑ 152 Jimmy Means .20 .09
❑ 153 Mark Garrow .10 .05
❑ 154 Lynda Petty .10 .05
❑ 155 D.K. Ulrich .10 .05
❑ 156 Davey Allison 1.00 .45
❑ 157 Jimmy Cox .10 .05
❑ 158 Clyde Booth .10 .05
❑ 159 John Kernan .10 .05
❑ 160 Marlin Wright .10 .05
❑ 161 Scott Houston .10 .05
❑ 162 Wayne Bumgarner .10 .05
❑ 163 Jeff Hensley .10 .05
❑ 164 Bill Davis .10 .05
❑ 165 Bob Jenkins .10 .05
❑ 166 Scott Cluka .10 .05
❑ 167 Sterling Marlin .40 .18
❑ 168 Tommy Allison .20 .09
❑ 169 Hubert Hensley .10 .05
❑ 170 Steve Bird .10 .05
❑ 171 John Hall .10 .05
❑ 172A L.D. Ottinger ERR .30 .14
❑ 172B L.D. Ottinger COR .30 .14
❑ 173 Kyle Petty .40 .18
Felix Sabates
Gary Nelson
❑ 174 Andy Petree .10 .05
❑ 175 Joe Moore .10 .05
❑ 176 Shelton Pittman .10 .05
❑ 177 Ricky Pearson .10 .05
❑ 178 Ed Berrier .10 .05
❑ 179 Rusty Wallace 1.00 .45
❑ 180 Richard Yates .10 .05
❑ 181 Frank Cicci .10 .05
Scott Welliver
❑ 182 Clyde McLeod .10 .05
❑ 183 A.G. Dillard .10 .05
❑ 184 Larry McReynolds .10
❑ 185 Joey Knuckles .10
❑ 186A Teresa Earnhardt .75
Trademark reads "...than Sports Image, Inc is
❑ 186B Teresa Earnhardt .75
Trademark reads"...than Sports Image, Inc. at racing venues..."
❑ 187 Rick Hendrick .10
❑ 188 Jerry Punch .10
❑ 189A Tim Petty .30
Team colors in the borders are blue and red
❑ 189B Tim Petty .30
Team colors are orange and yellow
❑ 190A Dale Earnhardt 2.00
Trademark reads "...than Sports Image, Inc is
❑ 190B Dale Earnhardt 2.00
Trademark reads"...than Sports Image, Inc. at racing venues..."
❑ 191 Checklist #1 .10
❑ 192 Checklist #2 .10
❑ 193 Checklist #3 .10
❑ 194 Checklist #4 .10
❑ 195 Checklist #5 .10
❑ 196 Checklist #6 .10
❑ 197 Checklist #7 .10
❑ 198 Checklist #8 .10
❑ 199 Patriotic Statement .10
❑ 200 Richard Petty .75
The King

1991 Traks Mello Yello Kyle Petty

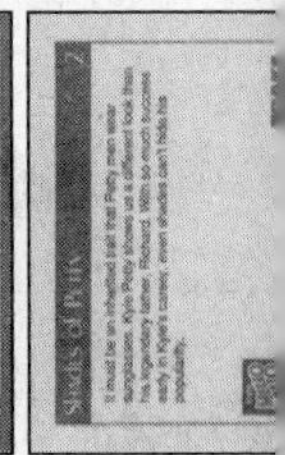

Traks issued a special set to commemorate Kyle Pe the Mello Yello race team in 1991. A cover/checklis (#13) was also included.

	MINT
COMPLETE SET (13)	10.00
COMMON CARD (1-13)	1.00

1991 Traks Mom-n-Pop's Biscuits Dale Earnhardt

In conjunction with Traks, Mom-n-Pop's produc set for distribution in its microwavable sandwich p in 1991. The cards were cello packed with one c one cover card per pack. Dale Earnhardt is the f driver due to Mom-n-Pop's associate sponsorshi RCR racing team. The "Biscuits" cards look very si the "Ham" cards produced the same year. A numb 20,000) uncut sheet version of the 6-cards w produced and offered through packs of 1993 Mom-n-Pop's cards at $20.00 for the pair of Bis Ham sheets.

	MINT
COMPLETE SET (6)	12.00
COMMON CARD (1-6)	2.00

❑ 1 Dale Earnhardt 2.00
Richard Childress
❑ 2 Dale Earnhardt 2.00
❑ 3 Dale Earnhardt's Car 2.00
❑ 4 Dale Earnhardt 2.00
❑ 5 Dale Earnhardt's Car 2.00
❑ 6 Dale Earnhardt in Pits 2.00

91 Traks Mom-n-Pop's Ham Dale Earnhardt

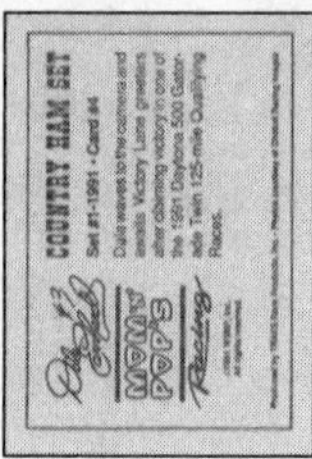

ıjunction with Traks, Mom-n-Pop's produced this ˑ distribution in its country ham products in 1991. ırds were cello packed with one card and one cover er pack. Dale Earnhardt is the featured driver due to n-Pop's associate sponsorship of the RCR racing The "Ham" cards look very similar to the "Biscuit" produced the same year. A numbered (of 20,000) sheet version of the 6-cards was also produced and d through packs of 1993 Wheels Mom-n-Pop's at $20.00 for the pair of Biscuit and Ham sheets.

	MINT	NRMT
LETE SET (6)	12.00	5.50
1ON CARD (1-6)	2.00	.90
ale Earnhardt	2.00	.90
Richard Childress		
ale Earnhardt w/Crew	2.00	.90
ale Earnhardt	2.00	.90
ale Earnhardt	2.00	.90
ale Earnhardt	2.00	.90
ale Earnhardt's Car	2.00	.90

1991 Traks Richard Petty

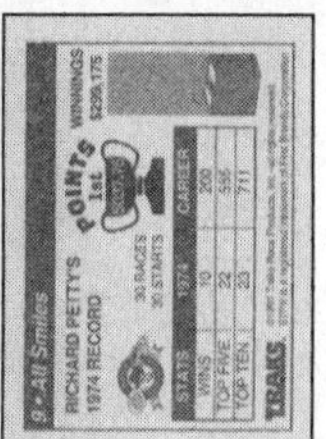

chard Petty 20th anniversary set was Traks' first card release. The issue chronicles Petty's life in and was distributed in 12-card packs. It was also ıted as a factory set. Cards 1-25 were packaged in ca model of Petty's 1972 Plymouth and cards 26- e packaged in a replica model of his 1991 Pontiac.

	MINT	NRMT
LETE SET (50)	8.00	3.60
LETE FACT.SET (50)	10.00	4.50
ON CARD (1-50)	.30	.14
chard Petty	.50	.23
chard Petty's Car	.30	.14
chard Petty's Car	.30	.14
chard Petty w/Car	.30	.14
chard Petty's Car	.30	.14
hard Petty w/Car	.30	.14
Gang's all Here		
chard Petty's Car	.30	.14
Under Cover		
chard Petty w/Car	.30	.14
Race Day		
hard Petty	.50	.23
All Smiles		
ichard Petty in Pits	.30	.14
The Treatment		
chard Petty w/Car	.30	.14
On Top of the World		
chard Petty's Car	.30	.14
Leading the Way		
ichard Petty's Car	.30	.14
Winner's Circle		
ichard Petty	.50	.23
The Beard		
ichard Petty's Car	.30	.14
What a Following		
chard Petty's Car	.30	.14
True Colors		
chard Petty's Car	.30	.14
And Petty's Away		
18 Richard Petty	.30	.14
Through the Years		
19 Richard Petty	.50	.23
The King		
20 Richard Petty's Car	.30	.14
STP Pontiacs		
21 Richard Petty w/Car	.30	.14
Southern Pride		
22 Richard Petty's Car	.30	.14
Dale Earnhardt's Car		
Darrell Waltrip's Car		
Lead Draft		
23 Richard Petty in Pits	.30	.14
Under the Gun		
24 Richard Petty's Car	.30	.14
The High Line		
25 Richard Petty's Car	.30	.14
Memories		
26 Richard Petty's Car	.30	.14
Round the Bend		
27 Richard Petty	.50	.23
Famous Smile		
28 Richard Petty's Car	.30	.14
Battle Scarred		
29 Richard Petty	.50	.23
Man of Miles		
30 Richard Petty in Pits	.30	.14
Team Work		
31 Richard Petty's Car	.30	.14
Sunday Drive		
32 Richard Petty w/Car	.30	.14
It's Getting Heavy		
33 Richard Petty in Pits	.30	.14
Wilkesboro Bash		
34 Richard Petty's Car	.30	.14
Line Drive		
35 Richard Petty's Car	.30	.14
Waiting for The King		
36 Richard Petty	.30	.14
Thanks for the Memories		
37 Richard Petty w/Car	.30	.14
Suited Up		
38 Richard Petty in Pits	.30	.14
Every Second Counts		
39 Richard Petty	.30	.14
The King's Office		
40 Richard Petty's Car	.30	.14
Famous 43		
41 Richard Petty w/Car	.30	.14
The High Bank		
42 Richard Petty in Pits	.30	.14
Pit Action		
43 Richard Petty	.50	.23
Happy Anniversary		
44 Richard Petty	.50	.23
Long Rider		
45 Richard Petty's Car	.30	.14
Tools of the Trade		
46 Richard Petty	.30	.14
In Appreciation		
47 Richard Petty	.50	.23
Most Photographed		
48 Richard Petty	.50	.23
Fan's Choice		
49 Richard Petty w/Car	.30	.14
Traditions		
50 Richard Petty w/Car	.30	.14
Profile of the King		

1992 Traks

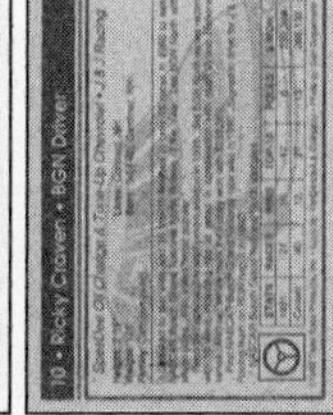

In addition to a 200-card factory set, the 1992 Traks set was distributed in 12-card packs with 30 packs per box. The set features the top Busch and Winston Cup drivers along with owners and other racing team members. Variations on several cards exist with the versions differing according to either pack or factory set distribution. Traks also included randomly packed autographed insert cards.

	MINT	NRMT
COMPLETE SET (200)	12.00	5.50
COMPLETE FACT.SET (200)	15.00	6.75
COMMON CARD (1-200)	.10	.05
COMMON DRIVER (1-200)	.20	.09
1 Rick Mast	.20	.09
2 Rusty Wallace	1.00	.45
3 Dale Earnhardt	2.00	.90
4 Ernie Irvan	.40	.18
5 Ricky Rudd	.40	.18
6 Mark Martin	1.00	.45
7 Alan Kulwicki	.60	.25
8 Rick Wilson	.20	.09
9 Phil Parsons	.20	.09
10 Ricky Craven	1.00	.45
11 Bobby Labonte	.60	.25
12 Hut Stricklin	.20	.09
13 Sam Bass	.10	.05
14 Bobby Allison	.40	.18
15 Rusty Wallace	1.00	.45
Mike Wallace		
Kenny Wallace		
16 Race Stoppers	.10	.05
17 Darrell Waltrip	.40	.18
18 Dale Jarrett	.75	.35
19 Cale Yarborough	.40	.18
20 Doyle Ford	.10	.05
21 Morgan Shepherd	.20	.09
22 Sterling Marlin	.40	.18
23 Kenny Wallace	.10	.05
Barry Dodson		
24 Kenny Wallace	.20	.09
25 Ken Schrader	.20	.09
26 Brett Bodine	.20	.09
27 Ward Burton	.20	.09
28 Davey Allison	1.00	.45
29A Andy Hillenburg	.20	.09
red stripe under name on back		
29B Andy Hillenburg	.20	.09
green stripe under name on back		
30 Michael Waltrip	.20	.09
31 Steve Grissom	.20	.09
32 Dale Jarrett	.75	.35
33 Harry Gant	.40	.18
34 Todd Bodine	.20	.09
35 Robert Yates	.10	.05
36 Kenny Wallace	.20	.09
37 Roger Penske	.10	.05
38 Mark Martin	1.00	.45
39 Don Miller	.10	.05
40 Chany Sabates	.10	.05
Felix Sabates		
41 Troy Beebe	.10	.05
42 Kyle Petty	.40	.18
43 Richard Petty	.60	.25
44 Bobby Labonte	.60	.25
45 Butch Miller	.20	.09
46 Chuck Rider	.10	.05
47 Dale Inman	.10	.05
48 Jack Sprague	.20	.09
49 Doug Richert	.10	.05
50 Jimmy Makar	.10	.05
51 Mike McLaughlin	.20	.09
52 Jimmy Means	.20	.09
53 Waddell Wilson	.10	.05
54 Richard Childress	.10	.05
55 Ted Musgrave	.20	.09
56 Darrell Waltrip	.40	.18
57 Kirk Shelmerdine	.10	.05
58 Larry McClure	.10	.05
59 Robert Pressley	.20	.09
60 Dale Earnhardt in Pits	1.00	.45
61 Dick Trickle	.20	.09
62 Leonard Wood	.10	.05
63 Chuck Bown	.20	.09
64 Elmo Langley	.10	.05
65 Barry Dodson	.10	.05
66 Chad Little	.20	.09
67 Elton Sawyer	.20	.09
68 Ed McClure	.10	.05
69A Kyle Petty	.40	.18
no green stripe under name on back		
69B Kyle Petty	.40	.18
green stripe under name on back		
70 Tony Glover	.10	.05
71 Dave Marcis	.40	.18
72A Rusty Wallace	1.00	.45
Eddie Dickerson		
title on back in white letters		
72B Rusty Wallace	1.00	.45
Eddie Dickerson		
title on back in black letters		
73 Alan Kulwicki	.75	.35
74 Jimmy Fennig	.10	.05
75 Michael Waltrip	.20	.09
76 Ken Wilson	.20	.09
77 David Smith	.10	.05
78 Junior Johnson	.20	.09
79 Dave Rezendes	.20	.09

❏ 80 Bruce Roney	.10	.05
❏ 81 Eddie Lanier	.10	.05
❏ 82 Mike Beam	.10	.05
❏ 83 Walter Bud Moore	.10	.05
❏ 84 Terry Labonte	1.00	.45
❏ 85 Richard Petty	.60	.25
❏ 86 Donnie Wingo	.10	.05
❏ 87 Joe Nemechek	.20	.09
❏ 88 Greg Moore	.10	.05
❏ 89 Doug Williams	.10	.05
❏ 90 Jimmy Martin	.10	.05
❏ 91 Richard Broome	.10	.05
❏ 92 Hut Stricklin	.20	.09
Bobby Allison		
❏ 93 Hank Jones	.10	.05
❏ 94 Terry Labonte	1.00	.45
❏ 95 Will Lind	.10	.05
❏ 96 Tom Peck	.20	.09
❏ 97 Morgan Shepherd	.20	.09
❏ 98 Jimmy Spencer	.20	.09
❏ 99 Jeff Burton	.60	.25
❏ 100 Max Helton	.10	.05
❏ 101 Jeff Gordon	2.50	1.10
❏ 102 Keith Almond	.10	.05
❏ 103 Dale Earnhardt	2.00	.90
❏ 104 Ernie Irvan	.40	.18
❏ 105 Greg Wilson	.10	.05
❏ 106 Tommy Houston	.20	.09
❏ 107 Ed Whitaker	.10	.05
❏ 108 David Green	.20	.09
❏ 109 Robin Pemberton	.10	.05
❏ 110 Mike Colyer	.10	.05
❏ 111 Jerry McClure	.10	.05
❏ 112 Cecil Gordon	.10	.05
❏ 113A Jimmy Johnson	.10	.05
name on back in white letters		
❏ 113B Jimmy Johnson	.10	.05
name on back in black letters		
❏ 114 Neil Bonnett	.50	.23
❏ 115 Steve Hmiel	.10	.05
❏ 116 Charles Farmer	.10	.05
❏ 117 Eddie Jones	.10	.05
❏ 118 Mickey Stavola	.10	.05
Bill Stavola		
❏ 119 Leo Jackson	.10	.05
❏ 120 Dick Moroso	.10	.05
❏ 121 Eddie Wood	.10	.05
❏ 122 Len Wood	.10	.05
❏ 123 Lou LaRosa	.10	.05
❏ 124A Rusty Wallace	1.00	.45
name on back in white letters		
❏ 124B Rusty Wallace	1.00	.45
name on back in black letters		
❏ 125 Bobby Hillin	.20	.09
❏ 126 Ned Jarrett	.20	.09
❏ 127 Ken Schrader	.20	.09
❏ 128 Travis Carter	.10	.05
❏ 129 Frank Edwards	.10	.05
❏ 130 Tom Higgins	.10	.05
Steve Waid		
❏ 131 Jim Phillips	.10	.05
Winston Kelley		
Dick Brooks		
❏ 132 John Ervin	.10	.05
❏ 133A Harry Gant	.40	.18
no line on back		
❏ 133B Harry Gant	.40	.18
red line on back		
❏ 133C Harry Gant	.40	.18
black line on back		
❏ 134 Allen Bestwick	.10	.05
❏ 135 Barney Hall	.10	.05
❏ 136 Ricky Rudd	.20	.09
Rick Hendrick		
❏ 137 Eli Gold	.10	.05
❏ 138 Joe Hendrick (Papa)	.10	.05
❏ 139 John Wilson	.10	.05
❏ 140 Tim Brewer	.10	.05
❏ 141 George Bradshaw	.10	.05
❏ 142 Kyle Petty	.40	.18
❏ 143 Robbie Loomis	.20	.09
❏ 144 Benny Parsons	.20	.09
❏ 145 Danny Myers	.10	.05
❏ 146 Harry Gant	.40	.18
Ed Whitaker		
❏ 147 Jeff Hammond	.10	.05
❏ 148 Donnie Richeson	.10	.05
❏ 149 Bill Brodrick	.10	.05
❏ 150 Robert Black	.10	.05
❏ 151 Carl Hill	.10	.05
❏ 152 Mike Wallace	.20	.09
❏ 153 Mark Garrow	.10	.05
❏ 154 Lynda Petty	.10	.05
❏ 155A Ted Musgrave ERR	.10	.05
D.K.Ulrich		
Mugrave on front		
❏ 155B Ted Musgrave COR	.10	.05
D.K.Ulrich		
Musgrave on front		
❏ 156 Davey Allison	.75	.35
❏ 157 Jimmy Cox	.10	.05
❏ 158 Clyde Booth	.10	.05
❏ 159 Bob Bilby	.10	.05
❏ 160 Marlin Wright	.10	.05
❏ 161 Gary Nelson	.10	.05
❏ 162 Jake Elder	.10	.05
❏ 163 Jeff Hensley	.10	.05
❏ 164 Bill Davis	.10	.05
❏ 165 Tracy Leslie	.20	.09
❏ 166 Tommy Ellis	.10	.05
❏ 167 Sterling Marlin	.40	.18
❏ 168 Tony Eury	.10	.05
❏ 169 Teddy McClure	.10	.05
❏ 170 Steve Bird	.10	.05
❏ 171A Paul Andrews	.10	.05
name on back in white letters		
❏ 171B Paul Andrews	.10	.05
name on back in black letters		
❏ 172 Brad Parrott	.10	.05
❏ 173A Eddie Dickerson	.10	.05
name on back in white letters		
❏ 173B Eddie Dickerson	.10	.05
name on back in black letters		
❏ 174 Andy Petree	.10	.05
❏ 175 Dale Earnhardt w/Crew	1.00	.45
❏ 176A Shelton Pittman	.10	.05
name on back in white letters		
❏ 176B Shelton Pittman	.10	.05
name on back in black letters		
❏ 177 Ricky Pearson	.10	.05
Robert Pressley		
❏ 178 Ed Berrier	.10	.05
❏ 179A Rusty Wallace	1.00	.45
name on back in white letters		
❏ 179B Rusty Wallace	1.00	.45
name on back in black letters		
❏ 180 Richard Yates	.10	.05
❏ 181 Scott Welliver	.10	.05
Frank Cicci		
❏ 182 Clyde McLeod	.10	.05
❏ 183 A.G. Dillard	.20	.09
❏ 184 Larry McReynolds	.10	.05
❏ 185 Joey Knuckles	.10	.05
❏ 186 Rodney Combs	.20	.09
❏ 187 Rick Hendrick	.10	.05
❏ 188 Jerry Punch	.10	.05
❏ 189 Tim Morgan	.10	.05
❏ 190 Dale Earnhardt	2.00	.90
❏ 191 Sterling Marlin	.20	.09
Darrell Waltrip Crash		
❏ 192 Safe and Sure	.10	.05
checklist back		
❏ 193 Dale Earnhardt's Car	1.00	.45
checklist back		
❏ 194 Rick Mast's Car	.10	.05
checklist back		
❏ 195 Follow the Signs	.10	.05
checklist back		
❏ 196 Kyle Petty's Car	.20	.09
checklist back		
❏ 197 Thread the Needle	.10	.05
checklist back		
❏ 198 Darrell Waltrip's Car	.20	.09
checklist back		
❏ 199 Rick Wilson's Car	.10	.05
checklist back		
❏ 200 Richard Petty	.50	.23
Lynda Petty		

1992 Traks Autographs

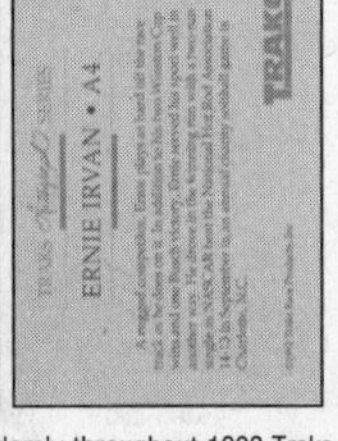

This set was distributed randomly throughout 1992 Traks packs. A maximum of 5000 cards were signed by each driver and many cards can be found, as well, without signatures. The Ricky Rudd card is considered a short print signed due to the seemingly large number of available copies unsigned. Unsigned cards typically sell for a fraction of autographed issues. The set is highlighted by a dually signed Dale Earnhardt and Richard Petty card (#A1).

	MINT
COMPLETE SET (10)	400.00
COMMON CARD (A1-A9)	12.00
❏ A1 Dale Earnhardt	200.00
Richard Petty	
❏ A2 Rusty Wallace	50.00
❏ A3 Harry Gant	25.00
❏ A4 Ernie Irvan	30.00
❏ A5 Ricky Rudd SP	40.00
❏ A6 Kyle Petty	30.00
❏ A7 Jeff Gordon	100.00
❏ A8 Bobby Labonte	30.00
❏ A9 Benny Parsons	12.00

1992 Traks Alliance Robert Pressley

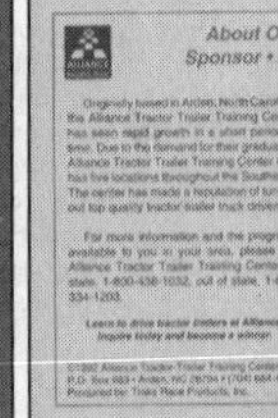

The 1992 Traks Alliance Racing Team Robert Press[ley] is very similar to the 1993-94 Alliance Robert Pr[essley] and Dennis Setzer issues. The Traks version includ[es] Traks logo on the cardfronts along with a black bord[er].

	MINT
COMPLETE SET (12)	8.00
COMMON CARD (1-12)	.60
❏ 1 Cover/Checklist Card	.60
❏ 2 Robert Pressley	.60
Victory Circle	
❏ 3 Robert Pressley's Transporter	.60
❏ 4 Robert Pressley's Transporter	.60
❏ 5 Robert Pressley's Cars	.60
❏ 6 Robert Pressley	1.50
❏ 7 Robert Pressley's Car	.60
❏ 8 Robert Pressley's Car	.60
❏ 9 Robert Pressley's Pit Crew	.60
❏ 10 Robert Pressley	1.50
❏ 11 Ricky Pearson	.60
❏ 12 Robert Pressley's Transporter	.60

1992 Traks ASA

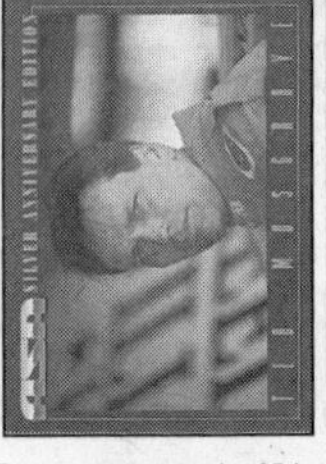

To commemorate the 25th anniversary of the Am[erican] Speed Association, Traks released a special 5[1-card] boxed set featuring many past greats of the ASA cir[cuit as] well as then current drivers.

	MINT
COMPLETE SET (51)	5.00
COMMON DRIVER (1-50)	.20
❏ 1 Josh DuVall	.20
❏ 2 Glenn Allen Jr.	.20
❏ 3 Mike Eddy Crew	.20
❏ 4 Mike Eddy	.20
❏ 5 Pat Schauer	.20
❏ 6 Tim Fedewa	.40
❏ 7 Tom Jones	.20
❏ 8 Tony Raines	.20
❏ 9 Jay Sauter	.20
❏ 10 Jeff Neal	.20
❏ 11 Terry Baldry	.20
❏ 12 Dennis Lampman	.20
❏ 13 Rusty Wallace w/Car	1.00
❏ 14 Johnny Benson Jr.	.50
❏ 15 Bob Senneker Crew	.20
❏ 16 Bob Senneker	.20

)ean South	.20	.09
John Wilson	.20	.09
3ruce VanderLaan	.20	.09
)ave Jackson	.20	.09
Chris Weiss	.20	.09
Tim Fedewa	.40	.18
3utch Fedewa	.20	.09
Gary St. Amant	.20	.09
3ud St. Amant	.20	.09
)ave Jackson	.20	.09
Glenn Allen Sr.	.20	.09
Tom Harrington Car	.20	.09
)ennis Vogel Car	.20	.09
Field of Dreams	.20	.09
Mario Caputo (Chip)	.20	.09
Kenny Wallace	.40	.18
)ick Trickle	.40	.18
3utch Miller	.20	.09
Scott Hansen	.20	.09
Alan Kulwicki w/Car	.75	.35
Jim Sauter Car	.20	.09
3obby Allison w/Car	.20	.09
)avey Allison w/Car	1.00	.45
Jimmy Fennig	.20	.09
Mark Martin	1.25	.55
)arrell Waltrip w/Car	.50	.23
Harold Fair Sr.	.20	.09
Kenny Adams	.20	.09
Kent Stauffer	.20	.09
)ave Taylor	.20	.09
Terry Baker	.20	.09
Howie Lettow	.20	.09
Harold Alan Fair Jr.	.20	.09
Ted Musgrave	.40	.18
) Souvenir Order Form Card	.20	.09

1992 Traks Baby Ruth Jeff Gordon

e first of two years, Traks released a special set ing the Baby Ruth sponsored Busch Series race n 1992 with Jeff Gordon as the focus. Gordon is ed on two cards with the others devoted to his car ew.

	MINT	NRMT
LETE SET (4)	10.00	4.50
ION CARD (1-4)	1.00	.45
ff Gordon	4.00	1.80
ff Gordon	4.00	1.80
ff Gordon's Car	1.00	.45
ff Gordon's Crew	1.00	.45

1992 Traks Country Star Racing

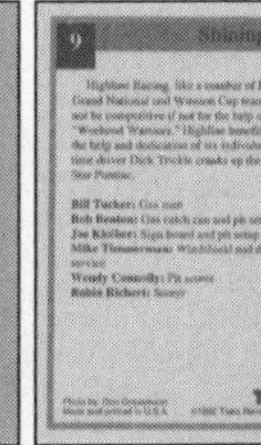

3-card set features Dick Trickle and the #2 Country ponsored car he drove on the Busch Grand National . The set was released both as a subset to the y Star Collection set and as an individual set.

	MINT	NRMT
LETE SET (13)	6.00	2.70
ON CARD (1-12)	.50	.23
ck Trickle	.75	.35

❑ 2 Dick Trickle	.75	.35
❑ 3 Ted Conder	.50	.23
❑ 4 Dick Trickle Ken Schrader	.75	.35
❑ 5 Mark Connolly	.50	.23
❑ 6 Dick Trickle	.75	.35
❑ 7 Danny Dias	.50	.23
❑ 8 Dick Trickle	.75	.35
❑ 9 Bill Tucker Bob Benton Joe Kloiber Mike Timmerman Wendy Connolly Robin Richert	.50	.23
❑ 10 Dick Trickle	.75	.35
❑ 11 Brian Grinstead	.50	.23
❑ 12 Ad Card	.50	.23
❑ NNO Checklist Card	.50	.23

1992 Traks Goody's

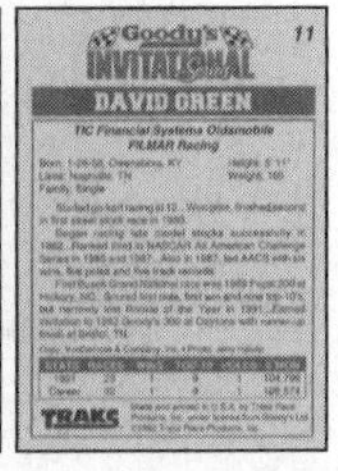

Drivers of the 1992 Goody's 300 are featured on this 25-card Traks release. The set was distributed in its own box through hobby outlets and includes most of the top drivers of 1992.

	MINT	NRMT
COMPLETE SET (25)	10.00	4.50
COMMON DRIVER (1-25)	.25	.11
❑ 1 Bobby Labonte	1.00	.45
❑ 2 Kenny Wallace	.25	.11
❑ 3 Robert Pressley	.25	.11
❑ 4 Chuck Bown	.25	.11
❑ 5 Jimmy Hensley	.25	.11
❑ 6 Todd Bodine	.25	.11
❑ 7 Tommy Houston	.25	.11
❑ 8 Steve Grissom	.25	.11
❑ 9 Jeff Gordon	2.50	1.10
❑ 10 Jeff Burton	.50	.23
❑ 11 David Green	.25	.11
❑ 12 Tracy Leslie	.25	.11
❑ 13 Butch Miller	.25	.11
❑ 14 Dave Rezendes	.25	.11
❑ 15 Ward Burton	.25	.11
❑ 16 Ed Berrier	.25	.11
❑ 17 Harry Gant	.50	.23
❑ 18 Dale Jarrett	1.00	.45
❑ 19 Dale Earnhardt	2.50	1.10
❑ 20 Ernie Irvan	.50	.23
❑ 21 Davey Allison	1.00	.45
❑ 22 Morgan Shepherd	.25	.11
❑ 23 Michael Waltrip	.25	.11
❑ 24 Ken Schrader	.25	.11
❑ 25 Richard Petty	.75	.35

1992 Traks Kodak Ernie Irvan

The Kodak Film Racing team and Ernie Irvan were the focus of this 25-card Traks release. The cards were distributed in specially marked 2-packs of Kodak Gold Plus film, as well as in complete factory sets. Five cards (#1,6,11,16,21,25) were also produced with gold foil embossing on the card fronts for distribution in the factory sets. An offer for uncut press sheets featuring the five gold cards was also included. Many of the cards are very similar to ones included in the Ernie Irvan team set also issued in 1992.

	MINT	NRMT
COMPLETE SET (25)	25.00	11.00
COMMON CARD (1-25)	1.00	.45
❑ 1A Ernie Irvan Richard Petty	2.50	1.10
❑ 1B Ernie Irvan Gold Richard Petty	4.00	1.80
❑ 2 Teddy McClure	1.00	.45
❑ 3 Tim Morgan	1.00	.45
❑ 4 Robert Larkins	1.00	.45
❑ 5 Shelton Pittman	1.00	.45
❑ 6A Ernie Irvan	2.50	1.10
❑ 6B Ernie Irvan Gold	4.00	1.80
❑ 7 Larry McClure	1.00	.45
❑ 8 Jerry McClure	1.00	.45
❑ 9 Tony Glover	1.00	.45
❑ 10 Clint Ballard	1.00	.45
❑ 11A Ernie Irvan's Car	1.00	.45
❑ 11B Ernie Irvan's Car Gold	2.00	.90
❑ 12 Jerry Puckett	1.00	.45
❑ 13 Ernie Irvan's Car	1.00	.45
❑ 14 Zeke Lester	1.00	.45
❑ 15 Randall Helbert	1.00	.45
❑ 16A Ernie Irvan	2.50	1.10
❑ 16B Ernie Irvan Gold	4.00	1.80
❑ 17 Bill Marsh	1.00	.45
❑ 18 Johnny Townsend	1.00	.45
❑ 19 Teddy McClure Larry McClure Tim Morgan Jerry McClure Ed McClure	1.00	.45
❑ 20 Ernie Irvan w/Crew Win at the Glen	1.00	.45
❑ 21A Ernie Irvan in Pits	2.50	1.10
❑ 21B Ernie Irvan in Pits Gold	4.00	1.80
❑ 22 George Gardner	1.00	.45
❑ 23 Power Builders	1.00	.45
❑ 24 Ed McClure	1.00	.45
❑ 25 Ernie Irvan w/Car Checklist	1.00	.45

1992 Traks Mom-n-Pop's Ham Dale Earnhardt

Produced by Traks, Mom-n-Pop's distributed this set in its country ham products in 1992. The cards were cello packed with one card and one cover card per pack. Dale Earnhardt is the featured driver due to Mom-n-Pop's associate sponsorship of the RCR racing team. A special "Pig" card (5000 made) was produced as well and randomly inserted in packs. The card was printed with a gold foil border and features a ghosted holographic image of Earnhardt's signature to prevent counterfeiting. Mom-n-Pop's Ham Christmas packaging distributed in North and South Carolina included the special card. A numbered (of 20,000) uncut sheet version of the 6-cards was also produced and offered through packs of 1993 Wheels Mom-n-Pop's cards.

	MINT	NRMT
COMPLETE SET (6)	20.00	9.00
COMMON CARD (1-6)	4.00	1.80
❑ 1 Dale Earnhardt w/Crew	4.00	1.80
❑ 2 Dale Earnhardt's Car	4.00	1.80
❑ 3 Dale Earnhardt Richard Childress	4.00	1.80
❑ 4 Dale Earnhardt in Pits	4.00	1.80
❑ 5 Dale Earnhardt	5.00	2.20
❑ 6 Dale Earnhardt	5.00	2.20
❑ NNO Dale Earnhardt with Thunder the pig	30.00	13.50

1992 Traks Benny Parsons

Benny Parsons and his career in racing is the focus of this 50-card release distributed to the hobby in 1992. 25,000 sets were printed and individually serial numbered with a certificate included with each boxed set.

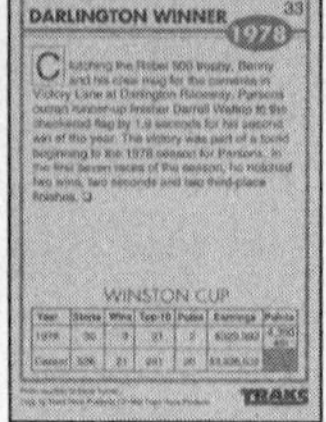

	MINT	NRMT
COMPLETE SET (50)	5.00	2.20
COMMON CARD (1-50)	.20	.09

1992 Traks Racing Machines

Traks produced the Racing Machines series to highlight the cars, rigs and race action of NASCAR racing. The 100-card set was distributed in 12-card packs. Cases were numbered up to a maximum of 2500 10-box cases with 36 packs per box. A special 20-card bonus set was also inserted two cards per pack as well as one set per Racing Machines factory set. Four prototype cards were issued for the release, but are not considered part of the complete set.

	MINT	NRMT
COMPLETE SET (100)	20.00	9.00
COMMON CARD (1-100)	.10	.05
❑ 1 Dale Earnhardt's Transporter	1.00	.45
❑ 2 Rusty Wallace's Car	.50	.23
❑ 3 Dale Earnhardt's Car	1.00	.45
❑ 4 Ernie Irvan's Car	.20	.09
❑ 5 Ricky Rudd's Car Ken Schrader's Car	.20	.09
❑ 6 Mark Martin's Car	.50	.23
❑ 7 Alan Kulwicki in Pits	.30	.14
❑ 8 Dick Trickle's Car	.10	.05
❑ 9 Dale Earnhardt's Car Ricky Rudd's Car Harry Gant's Car	1.00	.45
❑ 10 Ernie Irvan's Transporter	.20	.09
❑ 11 Rick Mast's Car	.10	.05
❑ 12 Hut Stricklin's Car	.10	.05
❑ 13 Kyle Petty's Car Pre-Race Check Off	.20	.09
❑ 14 Sterling Marlin's Car	.20	.09
❑ 15 Geoff Bodine's Transporter	.10	.05
❑ 16 Wally Dallenbach Jr.'s Car	.10	.05
❑ 17 Darrell Waltrip in Pits	.20	.09
❑ 18 Richard Petty's Transp.	.20	.09
❑ 19 Richard Petty in Pits	.50	.23
❑ 20 Ken Schrader's Transp.	.10	.05
❑ 21 Morgan Shepherd in Pits	.10	.05
❑ 22 Sterling Marlin's Car	.20	.09
❑ 23 Darrell Waltrip's Transp.	.20	.09
❑ 24 Rusty Wallace w/Truck	.50	.23
❑ 25 Ken Schrader's Car	.10	.05
❑ 26 Bobby Hamilton's Transporter	.10	.05
❑ 27 Round and Round Martinsville Speedway	.10	.05
❑ 28 Davey Allison's Car	.30	.14
❑ 29 Harry Gant's Transporter	.20	.09
❑ 30 Michael Waltrip's Car	.10	.05
❑ 31 Steve Grissom Roddenberry Car	.10	.05
❑ 32 Steve Grissom Channellock Car	.10	.05
❑ 33 Harry Gant in Pits	.30	.14
❑ 34 Dale Earnhardt's Car Davey Allison's Car	1.00	.45
❑ 35 Davey Allison's Transporter	.30	.14
❑ 36 Michael Waltrip's Car Under Cover	.10	.05
❑ 37 Darrell Waltrip's Car Pre Race Preparation	.20	.09
❑ 38 Hut Stricklin In Pits UER	.10	.05
❑ 40 Jeff Gordon's Car Davey Allison's Car	1.00	.45
❑ 41 Sterling Marlin in Pits	.30	.14
❑ 42 Kyle Petty's Car	.20	.09
❑ 43 Richard Petty's Car	.30	.14
❑ 44 Dale Earnhardt's Car Ricky Rudd's Car	1.00	.45
❑ 45 Sterling Marlin in Pits	.30	.14
❑ 46 Kyle Petty's Transporter	.20	.09
❑ 47 Rick Mast's Car	.10	.05
❑ 48 Ken Schrader in Pits	.20	.09
❑ 49 Morgan Shepherd's Trans.	.10	.05
❑ 50 Brett Bodine w/Car	.20	.09
❑ 51 Alan Kulwicki 's Car	.30	.14
❑ 52 Wally Dallenbach Jr. in Pits	.10	.05
❑ 53 Mark Martin's Transporter	.50	.23
❑ 54 Dale Earnhardt in Pits	1.00	.45
❑ 55 Richard Petty's Transporter Line Forms Here	.20	.09
❑ 56 Pre-Race Pageantry Multi-Car Starting Grid	.10	.05
❑ 57 Bobby Labonte in Pits	.75	.35
❑ 58 Ricky Rudd's Car Rusty Wallace's Car	.20	.09
❑ 59 Robert Pressley's Car	.10	.05
❑ 60 Bobby Labonte's Car Harry Gant's Car	.30	.14
❑ 61 Rick Mast's Transporter	.10	.05
❑ 62 Lightning Fast Race Action	.10	.05
❑ 63 Chuck Bown's Car	.10	.05
❑ 64 Rusty Wallace's Motorhome	.50	.23
❑ 65 Davey Allison's Car Michael Waltrip's Car	.30	.14
❑ 66 Ted Musgrave's Transporter	.10	.05
❑ 67 Bobby Hamilton in Pits	.20	.09
❑ 68 Bobby Hamilton's Car	.10	.05
❑ 69 Ernie Irvan in Pits	.30	.14
❑ 70 Lake Speed Crash	.10	.05
❑ 71 Dave Marcis' Car	.20	.09
❑ 72 Michael Waltrip's Transporter	.10	.05
❑ 73 Mark Martin in PIts	1.00	.45
❑ 74 Sterling Marlin's Transporter	.20	.09
❑ 75 Harry Gant's Car Brett Bodine's Car	.10	.05
❑ 76 Mark Martin in PIts	1.00	.45
❑ 77 Alan Kulwicki's Transporter	.30	.14
❑ 78 Rusty Wallace in Pits	1.00	.45
❑ 79 Dick Trickle's Transporter	.10	.05
❑ 80 Richard Petty Action	.30	.14
❑ 81 Rusty Wallace's Transporter	.50	.23
❑ 82 Terry Labonte w/Car	1.00	.45
❑ 83 Michael Waltrip's Car	.10	.05
❑ 84 Dale Earnhardt Morgan Shepherd Hut Stricklin Cars	1.50	.70
❑ 85 Jimmy Hensley's Transporter	.10	.05
❑ 86 Terry Labonte's Transporter	.50	.23
❑ 87 Kyle Petty's Car	.20	.09
❑ 88 Wally Dallenbach Jr.'s Trans.	.10	.05
❑ 89 Dale Earnhardt in Pits	1.50	.70
❑ 90 Jimmy Hensley's Car	.10	.05
❑ 91 Dale Earnhardt's Car Tommy Houston's Car	1.00	.45
❑ 92 Sterling Marlin's Car Ricky Rudd's Car	.20	.09
❑ 93 Davey Allison's Car Morgan Shepherd's Car	.30	.14
❑ 94 Terry Labonte Crash	.50	.23
❑ 95 Ernie Irvan in Pits	.20	.09
❑ 96 Derrike Cope's Transporter	.10	.05
❑ 97 Richard Petty in Pits checklist back	.30	.14
❑ 98 Bobby Labonte's Car Terry Labonte's Car Rusty Wallace's Car Ernie Irvan's Car Freight Train checklist back	.30	.14
❑ 99 Davey Allison's Car checklist back	.30	.14
❑ 100 Dale Earnhardt's Car Richard Petty's Car checklist back	1.00	.45

1992 Traks Racing Machines Bonus

Inserted two per pack in 1992 Traks Racing Machines packs and one complete set per regular factory set, the cards feature top drivers in the style of regular issue 1992 Traks cards.

	MINT	NRMT
COMPLETE SET (20)	5.00	2.20
COMMON CARD (1B-20B)	.05	.02
COMMON DRIVER (1B-20B)	.10	.05

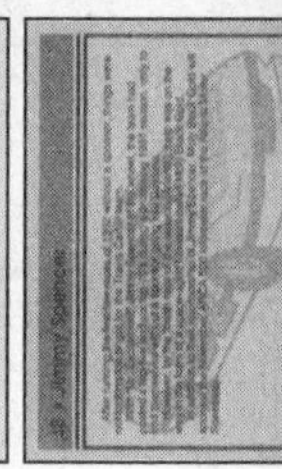

	MINT
❑ 1B Charlotte Under Lights	.05
❑ 2B Barry Dodson	.05
❑ 3B Dale Earnhardt's Car	.75
❑ 4B Jimmy Spencer	.10
❑ 5B Gary DeHart	.05
❑ 6B Steve Loyd	.05
❑ 7B Harry Gant MAC Team	.05
❑ 8B Dick Trickle	.10
❑ 9B Bobby Dotter's Car	.05
❑ 10B Ricky Craven	.60
❑ 11B Junior Johnson	.05
❑ 12B Joe Nemechek w/Car	.10
❑ 13B Terry Labonte w/Car	.50
❑ 14B Kenny Wallace	.10
❑ 15B Jimmy Hensley	.10
❑ 16B Mark Martin's Car Wally Dallenbach Jr.'s Car	.20
❑ 17B Mike Wallace	.10
❑ 18B Jeff Burton Ward Burton	.10
❑ 19B Tom Peck w/Car	.10
❑ 20B Jeff Gordon Baby Boomer	2.50

1992 Traks Team Sets

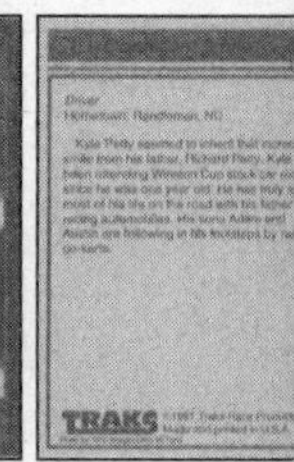

This 200-card release was actually distributed as separate 25-card team sets. Cards from the eigh were consecutively numbered though to form a cor set of 200. Each team set was sold in a cardboard style pack shaped like that team's race car.

	MINT
COMPLETE SET (200)	40.00
COMPLETE EARNHARDT (25)	8.00
COMPLETE D.ALLISON (25)	6.00
COMPLETE K.PETTY (25)	5.00
COMPLETE M.WALTRIP (25)	5.00
COMPLETE IRVAN (25)	6.00
COMPLETE D.WALTRIP (25)	5.00
COMPLETE STRICKLIN (25)	5.00
COMPLETE R.PETTY (25)	5.00
COMMON CARD (1-200)	.30
COMMON DRIVER (1-200)	.60
❑ 1 Dale Earnhardt's Car Driving Force	.60
❑ 2 Dale Earnhardt	1.00
❑ 3 Dale Earnhardt's Car Davey Allison's Car Familiar Position	.60
❑ 4 Dale Earnhardt's Car Flying Aces	.60
❑ 5 Kirk Shelmerdine	.30
❑ 6 David Smith	.30
❑ 7 Will Lind	.30
❑ 8 Danny Myers	.30
❑ 9 Hank Jones	.30
❑ 10 Eddie Lanier	.30
❑ 11 Danny Lawrence	.30
❑ 12 Cecil Gordon	.30
❑ 13 Dale Earnhardt Richard Childress Winning Combo	.60
❑ 14 Richard Childress	.30
❑ 15 Dale Earnhardt w/crew Party Time	.60
❑ 16 Dale Earnhardt's Cars Childress Promotions	1.00
❑ 17 Dale Earnhardt	1.00

Family Tradition
ale Earnhardt 1.00 .45
Cool Customer
ale Earnhardt's Car .60 .25
New Names
ale Earnhardt's Car .60 .25
Inspection Time
ale Earnhardt 1.00 .45
Friends of the Forest
ale Earnhardt's Planes .60 .25
Air Goodwrench
ale Earnhardt 1.00 .45
1991 Busch Clash
ale Earnhardt's Cars .60 .25
Arsenal
ale Earnhardt's Car .60 .25
Checklist
avey Allison .75 .35
obert Yates .30 .14
avey Allison's Car .60 .25
Star Power
avey Allison in Pits .60 .25
Controlled Frenzy
yan Pemberton .30 .14
ichard Yates .30 .14
arry McReynolds .30 .14
ary Beveridge .30 .14
oey Knuckles .30 .14
ommy Allison .30 .14
ike Bumgarner .30 .14
erry Throneburg .30 .14
ric Horn .30 .14
il Kerley .30 .14
aymond Fox III .30 .14
orman Koshimizu .30 .14
avey Allison .75 .35
Five-Time Winner
otor Minds .30 .14
Engine Builders
avey Allison .75 .35
Fantastic Phoenix
ames Lewter .30 .14
ernon Hubbard .30 .14
evin Barbee .30 .14
oug Yates .30 .14
avey Allison .75 .35
Larry McReynolds
Robert Yates
Triple Threats
avey Allison w/crew .75 .35
Checklist
yle Petty .60 .25
Confident Smile
elix Sabates .30 .14
elix Sabates .30 .14
Success Story
ary Nelson .30 .14
yle Petty .60 .25
Rocky Top
ohn Wilson .30 .14
arry Barnes Jr. .30 .14
erry Windell .30 .14
arry Cook .30 .14
cott Palmer .30 .14
harles Lane .30 .14
ichard Bostick .30 .14
arl Ramey .30 .14
Doug Hess
Machine Shop
cott Grant .30 .14
Jerry Brady
Cylinder Specialists
im Sutton .30 .14
teve Knipe .30 .14
ick Seidenspinner .30 .14
onnie Richeson .30 .14
im Long .30 .14
ike Ford .30 .14
en Sherrill .30 .14
lenn Funderburke .30 .14
ick Brakefield .30 .14
yle Petty .60 .25
Lean on Me
yle Petty's Car .60 .25
Checklist
ichael Waltrip .60 .25
ichael Waltrip .30 .14
Chuck Rider
Strategy Session
huck Rider .30 .14
ichael Waltrip's Car .30 .14
Bahari Racing
owrance Harry .30 .14
ichmond Gage .30 .14
ichael Waltrip in Pits .60 .25
Seconds Count
ill Ingle .30 .14
ngine Room .30 .14

Michael Waltrip's Engine Builders
❑ 85 Mark Cronquist .30 .14
❑ 86 Mike Windsor .30 .14
Jeff Rumple
Body By Bahari
❑ 87 Jon Leibensperger .30 .14
❑ 88 Jeff Dixon .30 .14
Paul Chencutt
Bryan Smith
Custom Made
❑ 89 Jeff Dixon .30 .14
❑ 90 Assembly Room .30 .14
Michael Waltrip's Crew
❑ 91 Barry Swift .30 .14
❑ 92 Ray Hall .30 .14
❑ 93 Tim Lancaster .30 .14
❑ 94 Tommy Rigsbee .30 .14
❑ 95 Michael Waltrip .60 .25
Game Face
❑ 96 Ronnie Silver .30 .14
❑ 97 Jeff Chandler .30 .14
❑ 98 BGN Team .30 .14
with Ronnie Silver
❑ 99 Michael Waltrip's Transporter .30 .14
❑ 100 Michael Waltrip's Car .30 .14
Checklist
❑ 101 Dale Earnhardt's Car .60 .25
Davey Allison's Car
Ernie Irvan's Car
Bobby Labonte's Car
Kyle Petty's Car
5 Laps From Victory
❑ 102 Ernie Irvan's Car .60 .25
Kodak Film Chevrolet
❑ 103 Tim Morgan .30 .14
❑ 104 Larry McClure .30 .14
❑ 105 Teddy McClure .30 .14
❑ 106 Ed McClure .30 .14
❑ 107 Shelton Pittman .30 .14
❑ 108 Ernie Irvan .75 .35
❑ 109 Ernie Irvan's Car .60 .25
Beat the Clock
❑ 110 Johnny Townsend .30 .14
❑ 111 Tony Glover .30 .14
❑ 112 Jerry McClure .30 .14
❑ 113 Zeke Lester .30 .14
❑ 114 Bill Marsh .30 .14
❑ 115 Randall Helbert .30 .14
❑ 116 Clint Ballard .30 .14
❑ 117 Robert Latonis .30 .14
❑ 118 George Gardner .30 .14
❑ 119 Ernie Irvan .75 .35
'91 Daytona 500
❑ 120 Teddy MClure .30 .14
Larry McClure
Tim Morgan
Jerry McClure
Ed McClure
❑ 121 Ernie Irvan's Car .60 .25
Morgan/McClure Racing Shop
❑ 122 Power Builders .30 .14
with Runt Pittman
❑ 123 Jerry Puckett .30 .14
❑ 124 Ernie Irvan w/crew .75 .35
Win at The Glen
❑ 125 Ernie Irvan w/Car .75 .35
Checklist
❑ 126 Western Auto Store .30 .14
❑ 127 Darrell Waltrip .60 .25
Winning Smile
❑ 128 Joe Carver Sr. .30 .14
❑ 129 Jeff Hammond .30 .14
❑ 130 Darrell Waltrip's Car .60 .25
Strong Finisher
❑ 131 Bobby Waltrip .30 .14
❑ 132 Clifford Smith .30 .14
❑ 133 Keith Sawyer .30 .14
❑ 134 Doug Richert .30 .14
❑ 135 Jake Elder .30 .14
❑ 136 Carolyn Waltrip .30 .14
❑ 137 Ronnie Hoover .30 .14
❑ 138 Darrell Waltrip in Pits .60 .25
Jacked Up
❑ 139 Billy Hodges .30 .14
❑ 140 Scott Mercer .30 .14
David Menear
Support Staff
❑ 141 Lisa Sigmon .30 .14
❑ 142 Darrell Waltrip .60 .25
❑ 143 Jeff Hammond .30 .14
Standing Tall
❑ 144 Bob Sutton .30 .14
❑ 145 Gregg Buchanan .30 .14
❑ 146 Tom McCrimmon .30 .14
❑ 147 Robbie Hancock .30 .14
Greg Carpenter
Body Men
❑ 148 Glen Skillman .30 .14

Joe Parlato
Built to Last
❑ 149 Ron McLeod .30 .14
Danny Shull
Tide Connections
❑ 150 Darrell Waltrip's Transporter .30 .14
Checklist
❑ 151 Hut Stricklin .30 .14
Race Ready
❑ 152 Hut Stricklin .60 .25
❑ 153 Hut Stricklin's Car .30 .14
❑ 154 Hut Stricklin in Pits .30 .14
Full Service
❑ 155 Hut Stricklin's Transporter .30 .14
Mike Culbertson
Big Rig
❑ 156 Keith Armond .30 .14
❑ 157 Jimmy Fennig .30 .14
❑ 158 Carolyn Freeman .30 .14
❑ 159 Brad Parrott .30 .14
❑ 160 Mike Basinger .30 .14
❑ 161 Glen Bobo .30 .14
❑ 162 Chris Meade .30 .14
❑ 163 Mike Boling .30 .14
❑ 164 Mike Culbertson .30 .14
❑ 165 Tom Bagen .30 .14
❑ 166 Tracie Honeycutt .30 .14
Lou Ann Kropp
Front Office
❑ 167 Kenny Freeman .30 .14
Glen Bobo
Paint and Body Shop
❑ 168 Horsepower .30 .14
Engine Builders
❑ 169 C.B.Lee .30 .14
Mike Basinger
Square One
❑ 170 Bobby Allison's Car .30 .14
❑ 171 Bob Bilby .30 .14
❑ 172 Nathan Sams .30 .14
❑ 173 Frank Plessinger .30 .14
❑ 174 Tom Kincaid .30 .14
❑ 175 Bobby Allison .60 .25
Checklist
❑ 176 Richard Petty .75 .35
❑ 177 Mike Cheek .30 .14
❑ 178 Roger Pierce .30 .14
❑ 179 Johnny Cline .30 .14
Jeff Chamberlain
The Royal Colors
❑ 180 Wade Thornburg .30 .14
Buddy Pugh
Stafford Wood
Jimmy Walker
Taking Shape
❑ 181 Dale Inman .30 .14
❑ 182 Ken Perkins .30 .14
❑ 183 Petty Power .30 .14
Engine Builders
❑ 184 Richard Petty w/Crew .75 .35
Home Team
❑ 185 Richard Petty w/Crew .75 .35
Away Team
❑ 186 Robbie Loomis .60 .25
❑ 187 Martha Bonkemeyer .30 .14
❑ 188 Kerry Lawrence .30 .14
❑ 189 From the Ground Up .30 .14
Fabricators
❑ 190 Wade Thomburg .30 .14
❑ 191 Stafford Wood .30 .14
❑ 192 Lynda Petty .30 .14
❑ 193 Bob Riffle .30 .14
❑ 194 David Walker .30 .14
❑ 195 Louise Loftin .60 .25
with Richard Petty
❑ 196 Randy Cox .30 .14
❑ 197 Lance Hill .30 .14
❑ 198 Jimmy Martin .30 .14
❑ 199 Richie Barsz .30 .14
❑ 200 Richard Petty .75 .35
The King
Checklist

1993 Traks

The 1993 Traks set was released in 12-card packs with 30 packs per box. The set is divided into two series, although released together in packs. The series two Silver cards (last 50-cards) were much more difficult to pull from packs than series one, thus the difference in value. 1993 marked the first year of the now traditional Traks First Run parallel issue set. The 1-150 First Runs were packaged two cards per pack.

	MINT	NRMT
COMPLETE SET (200)	40.00	18.00
COMPLETE REG.SET (150)	10.00	4.50
COMPLETE SILVER SET (50)	30.00	13.50

COMMON CARD (1-150) .10 .05
COMMON CARD (151-200) .30 .14
COMMON DRIVER (1-150) .20 .09
COMMON DRIVER (151-200) .60 .25

❑ 1 Rick Mast's Car .10 .05
❑ 2 Rusty Wallace Win .50 .23
❑ 3 Terry Labonte's Car .50 .23
❑ 4 Ernie Irvan's Car .20 .09
❑ 5 Neil Bonnett .50 .23
❑ 6 Mark Martin 1.00 .45
❑ 7 Alan Kulwicki .75 .35
❑ 8 Sterling Marlin's Car .20 .09
❑ 9 Mike Wallace .20 .09
❑ 10 Tommy Allison .10 .05
❑ 11 Mike Beam .10 .05
❑ 12 Jimmy Spencer .20 .09
❑ 13 Dick Trickle .20 .09
❑ 14 Terry Labonte 1.00 .45
❑ 15 Four Wide .10 .05
Talladega Speedway
❑ 16 Wally Dallenbach, Jr. .20 .09
❑ 17 Benny Parsons .20 .09
❑ 18 Dale Jarrett's Car .40 .18
❑ 19 Tom Peck .20 .09
❑ 20 Bobby Hamilton's Car .10 .05
❑ 21 Morgan Shepherd .20 .09
❑ 22 Bobby Labonte .60 .25
❑ 23 Troy Selburg .10 .05
❑ 24 Jeff Gordon's Car 1.00 .45
❑ 25 Rusty Wallace's Car .50 .23
checklist
❑ 26 Brett Bodine .20 .09
❑ 27 Alan Kulwicki Early Ride .40 .18
❑ 28 Davey Allison 1.00 .45
❑ 29 Buddy Parrott .10 .05
❑ 30 Michael Waltrip .20 .09
❑ 31 Steve Grissom's Car .10 .05
❑ 32 Mark Martin's Car .50 .23
Ken Schrader's Car
❑ 33 Harry Gant .40 .18
❑ 34 Todd Bodine's Car .10 .05
❑ 35 Shawna Robinson .20 .09
❑ 36 Kenny Bernstein .20 .09
❑ 37 Jeff Burton .20 .09
❑ 38 Len Wood .10 .05
❑ 39 Jeff Gordon 2.00 .90
❑ 40 Bobby Hillin .20 .09
❑ 41 Phil Parsons' Car .10 .05
❑ 42 Ward Burton .20 .09
❑ 43 Goodwrench 500 .10 .05
Rockingham
❑ 44 Rick Wilson .20 .09
❑ 45 Joe Nemechek .20 .09
❑ 46 Al Unser Jr.'s Car .40 .18
❑ 47 Ken Schrader .20 .09
❑ 48 Pete Wright .10 .05
❑ 49 Robert Yates .10 .05
❑ 50 Dale Inman .10 .05
checklist
❑ 51 Steve Hmiel .10 .05
❑ 52 Jimmy Means's Car .10 .05
❑ 53 Bruce Roney .10 .05
❑ 54 Tim Fedewa .20 .09
❑ 55 Ted Musgrave .20 .09
❑ 56 Mark Martin's Car .50 .23
❑ 57 Jason Keller's Car .10 .05
❑ 58 Rusty Wallace 1.00 .45
❑ 59 Bill Stavola .10 .05
Mickey Stavola
❑ 60 Mark Martin's Busch Car .50 .23
❑ 61 Tim Brewer .10 .05
❑ 62 Donnie Richeson .10 .05
❑ 63 Chuck Bown .20 .09
❑ 64 Larry Hedrick .10 .05
❑ 65 Joe Nemechek .20 .09
Ricky Craven
Todd Bodine
❑ 66 Gary DeHart .10 .05
❑ 67 Mark Martin 1.00 .45
❑ 68 Greg Sacks' Car .10 .05
❑ 69 Davey Allison 1.00 .45
Robert Yates
❑ 70 Harry Gant's Car .10 .05
❑ 71 Walter Bud Moore .10 .05
❑ 72 Andy Hillenburg .20 .09
❑ 73 Ray Evernham .20 .09
❑ 74 Sterling Marlin .40 .18
❑ 75 Checklist #3 .10 .05
❑ 76 Ned Jarrett .20 .09
❑ 77 Miller 400 .10 .05
Michigan International
❑ 78 Mark Martin's Car .50 .23
❑ 79 Glen Wood .10 .05
Leonard Wood
❑ 80 Hermie Sadler .20 .09
❑ 81 Jerry Glanville .20 .09
❑ 82 Alan Kulwicki First Win .40 .18
❑ 83 Lake Speed's Car .10 .05
❑ 84 Al Unser Jr. .40 .18
❑ 85 Ward Burton .20 .09
Todd Bodine
❑ 86 Larry McReynolds .10 .05
❑ 87 Greg Sacks .20 .09
❑ 88 Ken Schrader's Car .10 .05
❑ 89 Ken Howes .10 .05
❑ 90 Bobby Hillin's Car .10 .05
❑ 91 Don Miller .10 .05
❑ 92 Joe Ruttman .20 .09
❑ 93 Bill Brodrick .10 .05
❑ 94 David Green .20 .09
❑ 95 Joey Knuckles .10 .05
❑ 96 Derrike Cope .20 .09
❑ 97 Bill Davis .10 .05
❑ 98 Derrike Cope's Car .10 .05
❑ 99 Ricky Craven .40 .18
❑ 100 Davey Allison 1.00 .45
❑ 101 Junior Johnson .20 .09
❑ 102 Carl Hill .10 .05
❑ 103 Dick Trickle's Car .10 .05
❑ 104 Dave Marcis .20 .09
❑ 105 Larry Pearson's Car .10 .05
❑ 106 Rick Mast .20 .09
❑ 107 Eli Gold .10 .05
❑ 108 D.K. Ulrich .10 .05
❑ 109 Mark Martin's Car .50 .23
❑ 110 Hanes 500 .10 .05
Martinsville
❑ 111 Jimmy Johnson .10 .05
❑ 112 Buster Auton .10 .05
❑ 113 Waddell Wilson .10 .05
❑ 114 Eddie Wood .10 .05
❑ 115 Clyde McLeod .10 .05
❑ 116 Rick Hendrick .10 .05
❑ 117 Bobby Dotter's Car .10 .05
❑ 118 Jimmy Hensley .20 .09
❑ 119 Jerry McClure .10 .05
Tim Morgan
Larry McClure
Ed McClure
Teddy McClure
❑ 120 Dave Rezendes .10 .05
❑ 121 Jack Sprague's Car .10 .05
❑ 122 Tony Glover .10 .05
❑ 123 Cale Yarborough .20 .09
❑ 124 Jimmy Means .20 .09
❑ 125 Michael Waltrip's Trans. .10 .05
checklist
❑ 126 Roy Payne .10 .05
❑ 127 Davey Allison 1.00 .45
❑ 128 Davey Allison's Car .50 .23
❑ 129 Doug Richert .10 .05
❑ 130 Robert Pressley .20 .09
❑ 131 Ken Wilson .10 .05
❑ 132 Motorcraft 500 .10 .05
Atlanta Motorspeedway
❑ 133 Jay Luckwaldt .10 .05
❑ 134 Donnie Wingo .10 .05
❑ 135 Billy Hagan .10 .05
❑ 136 Ricky Rudd's Car .20 .09
The Winston
❑ 137 Jack Roush .10 .05
❑ 138 Joe Gibbs .20 .09
❑ 139 Robbie Loomis .10 .05
❑ 140 Jimmy Fennig .10 .05
❑ 141 Chuck Rider .10 .05
❑ 142 Alan Kulwicki On Pole .40 .18
❑ 143 Red Farmer .10 .05
❑ 144 Jim Bown .10 .05
❑ 145 Rusty Wallace in Pits .50 .23
❑ 146 Ricky Pearson .10 .05
❑ 147 Coca Cola 600 .10 .05
Charlotte Motorspeedway
❑ 148 Pam Rimer .10 .05
Valli Elliott
Lisa Shrowder
❑ 149 Bobby Allison .20 .09
❑ 150 Checklist #6 .10 .05
❑ 151 Jeff Gordon 6.00 2.70
❑ 152 Sterling Marlin 1.25 .55
❑ 153 Jeff Burton .60 .25
❑ 154 Jimmy Spencer .60
❑ 155 Ted Musgrave .60
❑ 156 Ricky Craven 1.25
❑ 157 Harry Gant 1.25
❑ 158 Tracy Leslie .30
❑ 159 Wally Dallenbach, Jr. .60
❑ 160 Jack Sprague .30
❑ 161 Mark Martin 3.00
❑ 162 Shawna Robinson .60
❑ 163 Tommy Houston .60
❑ 164 Rusty Wallace 3.00
❑ 165 Chuck Bown .60
❑ 166 Joe Nemechek .60
❑ 167 Ken Schrader .60
❑ 168 Rick Hendrick .30
❑ 169 Larry Pearson .60
❑ 170 Rick Mast .60
❑ 171 Robert Yates .30
❑ 172 Hermie Sadler .60
❑ 173 Morgan Shepherd .60
❑ 174 Mike Wallace .60
❑ 175 Tom Peck .30
checklist
❑ 176 Bobby Labonte .60
❑ 177 Lake Speed .60
❑ 178 Davey Allison 2.50
Bobby Allison
❑ 179 Derrike Cope .60
❑ 180 Walter Bud Moore .30
❑ 181 Rusty Wallace 3.00
❑ 182 Ward Burton .60
❑ 183 Bobby Dotter .30
❑ 184 Terry Labonte 3.00
❑ 185 Todd Bodine .60
❑ 186 Michael Waltrip .60
❑ 187 Roy Payne .30
❑ 188 Junior Johnson .60
❑ 189 Jack Roush .30
❑ 190 Davey Allison 3.00
❑ 191 David Green .60
❑ 192 Greg Sacks .60
❑ 193 Steve Grissom .60
❑ 194 Robert Pressley .60
❑ 195 Dick Trickle .60
❑ 196 Alan Kulwicki MEM 2.50
The Champ
❑ 197 Al Unser Jr. 1.25
❑ 198 Brett Bodine .60
❑ 199 Chuck Rider .30
❑ 200 Davey Allison 3.00

1993 Traks First Run

First Run cards were issued for the first time in 19[…] inserted two per pack in regular issue Traks. The two Silver cards were much tougher to pull than one. The cards can be distinguished from regular cards by the inclusion of a "First Run" logo on the fronts, otherwise they're identical to the regular release. Many of the First Run single cards are […] below using a multiplier of the regular issue cards.

MINT
COMPLETE SET (200) 120.00
COMPLETE REG.SET (150) 25.00
COMPLETE SILVER SET (50) 100.00
COMMON CARD (1-150) .20
COMMON CARD (151-200) 4.00
COMMON DRIVER (1-150) .40
COMMON DRIVER (151-200) 8.00
*STARS 1-150: 1.5X TO 3X BASIC CARDS
*STARS 151-200: 2X TO 4X BASIC CARDS

1993 Traks Kodak Ernie Irv[…]

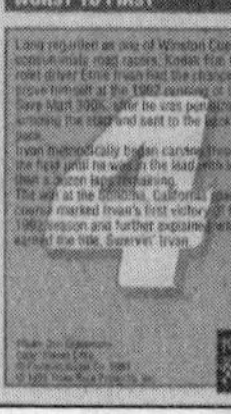

Once again, in 1993, Traks released a commemora[…] featuring the Kodak Film Racing Team and driver Irvan. The cards are oversized (3-3/4" by 5-1/4") design very similar to the 1992 set. All six cards issued with gold foil borders in a cardboard facto[…] type package. Reportedly 4,000 of these sets produced and most of them were given away at K[…] hospitality tent at Daytona.

	MINT	NRMT
LETE FACTORY SET (6)	16.00	7.25
ION CARD (1-6)	2.00	.90

	MINT	NRMT
nie Irvan w/Car	4.00	1.80
Man and Machine		
side Out	2.00	.90
nie Irvan w/Crew	4.00	1.80
Beat the Heat		
nie Irvan in Pits	2.00	.90
Bird's Eye View		
nie Irvan	4.00	1.80
Worst to First		
nie Irvan's Car	2.00	.90
200 mph in NYC		

93 Traks Preferred Collector

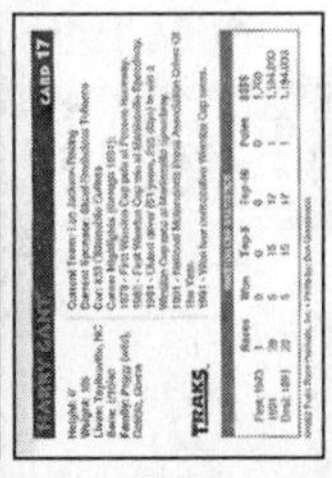

0-card set was made available thru the Traks Club. ards feature some of the top drivers in NASCAR on Cup racing. The backs list stats for the driver's and the 1992 season. President George Bush is ed on card #15 with Richard Petty.

	MINT	NRMT
LETE SET (20)	15.00	6.75
ION CARD (1-20)	.50	.23

	MINT	NRMT
chael Waltrip	.50	.23
ett Bodine	.50	.23
rry Labonte	1.50	.70
le Petty	.60	.25
an Kulwicki	1.25	.55
ark Martin	1.50	.70
organ Shepherd	.50	.23
rrell Waltrip	.60	.25
ut Stricklin	.50	.23
usty Wallace	1.50	.70
en Schrader	.50	.23
ale Jarrett	1.00	.45
rnie Irvan	1.25	.55
ichard Petty	1.00	.45
George Bush		
ichard Petty	1.00	.45
arry Gant	.60	.25
immy Hensley	.50	.23
ick Trickle	.50	.23
avey Allison	1.50	.70

1993 Traks Trivia

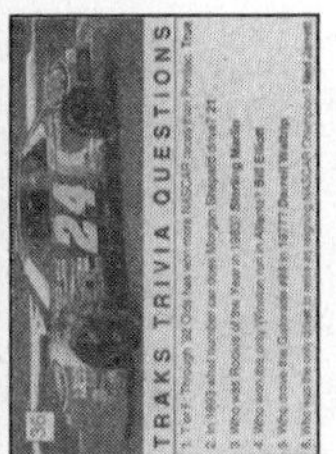

93 Traks Trivia set was released to retail outlets in er type packaging in complete set form. The 50- contain photos of NASCAR drivers on front with photos on back along with six racing trivia ons.

	MINT	NRMT
LETE SET (50)	10.00	4.50
ON CARD (1-50)	.15	.07

	MINT	NRMT
ark Martin	.50	.23
f Gordon	1.50	.70
sty Wallace	.50	.23
vey Allison	.50	.23
f Purvis	.15	.07
ark Martin	.50	.23
mmy Hensley	.15	.07
erling Marlin	.30	.14

	MINT	NRMT
❑ 9 Alan Kulwicki	.50	.23
❑ 10 Davey Allison's Helmet	.30	.14
❑ 11 Rusty Wallace	.50	.23
❑ 12 Jimmy Spencer	.15	.07
❑ 13 Joe Nemechek	.15	.07
❑ 14 Terry Labonte	.30	.14
❑ 15 Harry Gant	.15	.07
❑ 16 Wally Dallenbach Jr.	.15	.07
❑ 17 Al Unser Jr.	.30	.14
❑ 18 Davey Allison	.50	.23
Bobby Allison		
❑ 19 Mark Martin	.50	.23
❑ 20 Lake Speed	.15	.07
❑ 21 Morgan Shepherd	.15	.07
❑ 22 Bobby Labonte	.15	.07
❑ 23 Mark Martin	.50	.23
❑ 24 Jeff Gordon	1.50	.70
❑ 25 Ken Schrader	.15	.07
❑ 26 Brett Bodine	.15	.07
❑ 27 Morgan Shepherd's Car	.15	.07
❑ 28 Davey Allison	.50	.23
❑ 29 Rusty Wallace	.50	.23
❑ 30 Michael Waltrip	.15	.07
❑ 31 Bobby Labonte	.15	.07
❑ 32 Mark Martin	.50	.23
❑ 33 Harry Gant	.15	.07
❑ 34 Davey Allison w/Crew	.50	.23
❑ 35 Alan Kulwicki	.50	.23
❑ 36 Jeff Gordon	1.50	.70
❑ 37 Mark Martin	.50	.23
❑ 38 Jeff Gordon's Car	.60	.25
❑ 39 Rusty Wallace	.50	.23
❑ 40 Davey Allison	.50	.23
Jerry Glanville		
❑ 41 Mark Martin	.50	.23
❑ 42 Dave Marcis	.15	.07
❑ 43 Ken Schrader	.15	.07
❑ 44 Greg Sacks	.15	.07
❑ 45 Jeff Gordon	1.50	.70
❑ 46 Bobby Hillin	.15	.07
❑ 47 Ted Musgrave	.15	.07
❑ 48 Bobby Allison	.15	.07
❑ 49 Derrike Cope	.15	.07
❑ 50 Rick Mast	.15	.07

1994 Traks

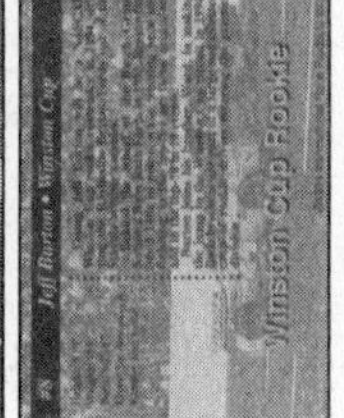

1994 Traks was released in two series of 100-cards each through 12-card packs. Boxes contained 30-packs. Series one cards were produced with gold foil layering while series two included silver foil. There were a couple of uncorrected error cards in the second series. The Ned Jarrett card was supposed to be number 134 but all of them were issued with the number 123 on the back. Also, the Tracy Leslie card was supposed to be number 148 but all of them were issued with the number 127 on the back. That means there are two different number 123's and two different number 127's. Club only factory sets were also produced with a 5-card Cartoons insert set per factory issue. A First Run factory set (400 sets made) was produced for sale to Club members at $35.00 as well that included a Cartoons set autographed by the card's artist.

	MINT	NRMT
COMPLETE SET (200)	20.00	9.00
COMPLETE SERIES 1 (100)	10.00	4.50
COMPLETE SERIES 2 (100)	10.00	4.50
COMMON CARD (1-200)	.10	.05
COMMON DRIVER (1-200)	.20	.09

	MINT	NRMT
❑ 1 Rick Mast	.20	.09
❑ 2 Rusty Wallace	1.00	.45
❑ 3 Sterling Marlin	.40	.18
❑ 4 Ward Burton's Car	.10	.05
❑ 5 Terry Labonte	1.00	.45
❑ 6 Mark Martin	1.00	.45
❑ 7 Alan Kulwicki	.75	.35
❑ 8 Jeff Burton	.40	.18
❑ 9 Mike Wallace	.20	.09
❑ 10 Jeff Gordon's Car	1.00	.45
❑ 11 Junior Johnson	.20	.09
❑ 12 Bobby Allison	.20	.09
❑ 13 Dale Jarrett	.75	.35
❑ 14 Sterling Marlin's Car	.20	.09
❑ 15 Lake Speed	.20	.09
❑ 16 Ted Musgrave	.20	.09
❑ 17 Ricky Rudd	.40	.18
❑ 18 Joe Gibbs	.20	.09
❑ 19 Davey Allison	1.00	.45
❑ 20 Buddy Parrott	.10	.05
❑ 21 Morgan Shepherd	.20	.09
❑ 22 Bobby Labonte	.60	.25
❑ 23 Ken Schrader	.20	.09
❑ 24 Jeff Gordon	2.00	.90
❑ 25 Neil Bonnett	.20	.09
Checklist #1		
❑ 26 Brett Bodine	.20	.09
❑ 27 Larry McReynolds	.10	.05
❑ 28 Ernie Irvan	.40	.18
❑ 29 Neil Bonnett	.50	.23
❑ 30 Michael Waltrip	.20	.09
❑ 31 Steve Grissom	.20	.09
❑ 32 Bruce Roney	.10	.05
❑ 33 Harry Gant	.40	.18
❑ 34 Derrike Cope	.20	.09
❑ 35 Shawna Robinson	.20	.09
❑ 36 Jeff Gordon	2.00	.90
❑ 37 Mark Martin's Car	.50	.23
❑ 38 Jimmy Hensley	.20	.09
❑ 39 Ricky Craven	.20	.09
❑ 40 Robert Yates	.10	.05
❑ 41 Dennis Setzer	.20	.09
❑ 42 Kenny Bernstein	.20	.09
❑ 43 Wally Dallenbach, Jr.	.20	.09
❑ 44 David Green	.20	.09
❑ 45 Ernie Irvan	.40	.18
❑ 46 Sterling Marlin	.40	.18
❑ 47 Joe Bessey	.20	.09
❑ 48 Bobby Labonte	.60	.25
❑ 49 Michael Waltrip's Car	.10	.05
❑ 50 Neil Bonnett	.20	.09
Checklist #2		
❑ 51 Morgan Shepherd's Car	.10	.05
❑ 52 Jimmy Means	.20	.09
❑ 53 Loy Allen Jr.'s Car	.10	.05
❑ 54 Steve Hmiel	.10	.05
❑ 55 Ricky Rudd	.40	.18
❑ 56 Jimmy Spencer	.20	.09
❑ 57 Roger Penske	.10	.05
❑ 58 Ken Schrader	.20	.09
❑ 59 Bobby Labonte's Car	.40	.18
❑ 60 Mark Martin	1.00	.45
❑ 61 Derrike Cope's Car	.10	.05
❑ 62 Rusty Wallace	1.00	.45
❑ 63 Chuck Bown	.20	.09
❑ 64 Cale Yarborough	.20	.09
❑ 65 Dale Jarrett	.75	.35
❑ 66 Ernie Irvan	.40	.18
❑ 67 Todd Bodine	.20	.09
❑ 68 Loy Allen Jr.	.20	.09
❑ 69 Morgan Shepherd	.20	.09
❑ 70 Terry Labonte's Car	.50	.23
❑ 71 Dave Marcis	.40	.18
❑ 72 Rusty Wallace's Car	.50	.23
❑ 73 Harry Gant	.40	.18
❑ 74 Bobby Dotter	.20	.09
❑ 75 Ken Schrader's Car	.10	.05
Brett Bodine's Car		
Checklist #3		
❑ 76 Robert Pressley	.20	.09
❑ 77 Leo Jackson	.10	.05
❑ 78 Brett Bodine	.20	.09
❑ 79 Ward Burton	.20	.09
❑ 80 Rusty Wallace	1.00	.45
❑ 81 Andy Hillenburg	.20	.09
❑ 82 Mark Martin	1.00	.45
❑ 83 Ray Evernham	.40	.18
❑ 84 Ricky Rudd's Car	.20	.09
❑ 85 Joe Nemechek	.20	.09
❑ 86 Jeff Gordon	2.00	.90
❑ 87 Ken Wilson	.10	.05
❑ 88 Carl Hill	.10	.05
❑ 89 Hermie Sadler	.20	.09
BGN Rookie of the Year		
❑ 90 Bobby Hillin	.20	.09
❑ 91 Ernie Irvan	.40	.18
❑ 92 Larry Pearson	.20	.09
❑ 93 Kenny Wallace	.20	.09
❑ 94 Ernie Irvan's Car	.20	.09
❑ 95 Jack Roush	.10	.05
❑ 96 Terry Labonte	1.00	.45
❑ 97 Greg Sacks	.20	.09
❑ 98 Jimmy Makar	.10	.05
❑ 99 Harry Gant	.40	.18
❑ 100 Mark Martin's Car	.50	.23
Checklist #4		
❑ 101 Ernie Irvan	.40	.18
❑ 102 Rusty Wallace	1.00	.45
❑ 103 Dale Jarrett	.75	.35
❑ 104 Mike McLaughlin	.20	.09
❑ 105 Billy Hagan	.10	.05

❑ 106 Jeff Gordon	2.00	.90
❑ 107 Jeremy Mayfield	2.00	.90
❑ 108 Dale Jarrett's Car	.40	.18
❑ 109 Sterling Marlin's Car	.20	.09
❑ 110 John Andretti	.20	.09
❑ 111 Kyle Petty	.40	.18
❑ 112 Sterling Marlin's Car	.20	.09
❑ 113 Mark Martin	1.00	.45
❑ 114 Bobby Allison	.20	.09
❑ 115 Jimmy Hensley	.20	.09
❑ 116 Harry Gant	.40	.18
❑ 117 Mike Beam	.10	.05
❑ 118 Terry Labonte	1.00	.45
❑ 119 Eddie Wood	.10	.05
❑ 120 Rodney Combs	.20	.09
❑ 121 Morgan Shepherd	.20	.09
❑ 122 Mike Wallace's Car	.10	.05
❑ 123 Bobby Labonte	.60	.25
❑ 124 Gary DeHart	.10	.05
❑ 125 Ricky Rudd's Car Checklist #5	.20	.09
❑ 126 Sterling Marlin	.40	.18
❑ 127 Ward Burton	.20	.09
❑ 128 Chuck Bown	.20	.09
❑ 129 Elton Sawyer	.20	.09
❑ 130 Ricky Rudd	.40	.18
❑ 131 Ken Schrader	.20	.09
❑ 132 Jimmy Fennig	.10	.05
❑ 133 Brett Bodine	.20	.09
❑ 134 Ned Jarrett UER Numbered 123	.10	.05
❑ 135 Ernie Irvan	.40	.18
❑ 136 Larry Hedrick	.10	.05
❑ 137 Kyle Petty	.40	.18
❑ 138 Todd Bodine's Car	.10	.05
❑ 139 Todd Bodine	.20	.09
❑ 140 Harry Gant's BGN Car	.20	.09
❑ 141 Bobby Allison	.20	.09
❑ 142 Charley Pressley	.10	.05
❑ 143 Loy Allen Jr.	.20	.09
❑ 144 Mark Martin	1.00	.45
❑ 145 Lake Speed's Car	.10	.05
❑ 146 Dale Jarrett	.75	.35
❑ 147 Dave Marcis	.40	.18
❑ 148 Tracy Leslie UER Numbered 127	.20	.09
❑ 149 Lake Speed	.20	.09
❑ 150 Ernie Irvan's Car Checklist #6	.20	.09
❑ 151 Ted Musgrave	.20	.09
❑ 152 Terry Labonte	1.00	.45
❑ 153 Len Wood	.10	.05
❑ 154 Michael Waltrip	.20	.09
❑ 155 Tim Fedewa	.20	.09
❑ 156 Glen Wood Leonard Wood	.10	.05
❑ 157 Rusty Wallace	1.00	.45
❑ 158 Tony Glover	.10	.05
❑ 159 Steve Grissom	.20	.09
❑ 160 Ernie Irvan's Car	.20	.09
❑ 161 Jeff Burton	.40	.18
❑ 162 Buster Auton	.10	.05
❑ 163 Ernie Irvan	.40	.18
❑ 164 Jim Bown	.20	.09
❑ 165 Derrike Cope	.20	.09
❑ 166 Harry Gant	.40	.18
❑ 167 Ken Howes	.10	.05
❑ 168 Ken Schrader's BGN Car	.10	.05
❑ 169 Robbie Loomis	.20	.09
❑ 170 Mike Wallace	.20	.09
❑ 171 Jeff Gordon	2.00	.90
❑ 172 Richard Jackson	.10	.05
❑ 173 Rick Mast	.20	.09
❑ 174 Jason Keller	.20	.09
❑ 175 Race Action Checklist #7	.10	.05
❑ 176 Mark Martin	1.00	.45
❑ 177 Greg Sacks	.20	.09
❑ 178 Elmo Langley	.10	.05
❑ 179 Doug Richert	.10	.05
❑ 180 Dick Trickle	.20	.09
❑ 181 Donnie Richeson	.10	.05
❑ 182 Sterling Marlin	.40	.18
❑ 183 Joe Nemechek	.20	.09
❑ 184 Kenny Wallace	.20	.09
❑ 185 Kyle Petty	.40	.18
❑ 186 Wally Dallenbach Jr.	.20	.09
❑ 187 Rusty Wallace's Car	.50	.23
❑ 188 Morgan Shepherd	.20	.09
❑ 189 Waddell Wilson	.10	.05
❑ 190 Ricky Craven's BGN Car	.20	.09
❑ 191 Ricky Rudd	.40	.18
❑ 192 Donnie Wingo	.10	.05
❑ 193 Rusty Wallace	1.00	.45
❑ 194 Chuck Bown's Car	.10	.05
❑ 195 Robert Pressley	.20	.09
❑ 196 Troy Selberg	.10	.05
❑ 197 Ted Musgrave's Car	.10	.05
❑ 198 Ernie Irvan	.40	.18
❑ 199 Benny Parsons	.20	.09
❑ 200 Jeff Gordon in Pits Checklist #8	1.00	.45

1994 Traks First Run

Packaged one per 1994 Traks foil pack, First Run is a parallel set to the regular Traks issue. The cards can be distinguished only by the presence of the "First Run" Traks logo. 400 factory First Run sets were also produced and offered to Traks Club members. Each factory set included a Cartoons insert set signed by artist Bill Stanford.

	MINT	NRMT
COMPLETE SET (200)	50.00	22.00
COMPLETE SERIES 1 (100)	25.00	11.00
COMPLETE SERIES 2 (100)	25.00	11.00
COMMON CARD (1-200)	.15	.07
COMMON DRIVER (1-200)	.25	.11

*FIRST RUN CARDS: 1.25X TO 2.5X BASIC CARDS

1994 Traks Autographs

Randomly inserted in both series one and two packs, these inserts are a specially designed card with each signed by the featured driver. A 13th card (cover/checklist card) was also inserted. A maximum of 3500 of each card was signed.

	MINT	NRMT
COMPLETE SET (13)	150.00	70.00
COMMON AUTO (A1-A12)	12.00	5.50
❑ A1 Todd Bodine	12.00	5.50
❑ A2 Jeff Burton Ward Burton	25.00	11.00
❑ A3 Harry Gant	20.00	9.00
❑ A4 Jeff Gordon	75.00	34.00
❑ A5 Steve Grissom	12.00	5.50
❑ A6 Ernie Irvan	25.00	11.00
❑ A7 Sterling Marlin	25.00	11.00
❑ A8 Mark Martin	40.00	18.00
❑ A9 Joe Nemechek	12.00	5.50
❑ A10 Robert Pressley	12.00	5.50
❑ A11 Ken Schrader	12.00	5.50
❑ A12 Rusty Wallace	40.00	18.00
❑ NNO Cover Card Checklist back	12.00	5.50

1994 Traks Winners

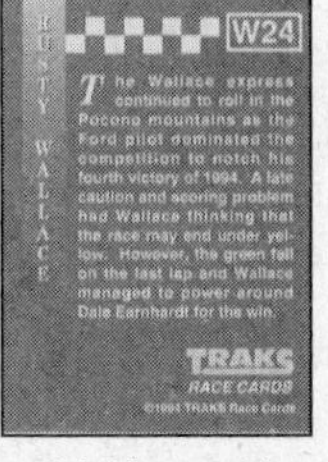

The Traks Winners cards are a Holofoil stamped issue randomly inserted in series two packs of 1994 Traks racing. The cards feature early 1994 race winners that also had cards in Traks series one.

	MINT	NRMT
COMPLETE SET (25)	30.00	13.50
COMMON DRIVER (W1-W25)	.60	.25

*SINGLES: .75X TO 2X BASE CARD HI

❑ W1 Sterling Marlin	1.25	.55
❑ W2 Rusty Wallace		
❑ W3 Ernie Irvan		
❑ W4 Ernie Irvan		
❑ W5 Terry Labonte		
❑ W6 Rusty Wallace		
❑ W7 Ernie Irvan		
❑ W8 Jeff Gordon		
❑ W9 Rusty Wallace		
❑ W10 Terry Labonte		
❑ W11 Joe Nemechek	.60	
❑ W12 Harry Gant	.60	
❑ W13 Terry Labonte		
❑ W14 Mark Martin		
❑ W15 Ricky Craven	1.25	
❑ W16 David Green	.60	
❑ W17 Hermie Sadler	.60	
❑ W18 Derrike Cope	.60	
❑ W19 Ricky Craven	1.25	
❑ W20 Mike Wallace	.60	
❑ W21 Jeff Gordon		
❑ W22 Jeff Gordon		
❑ W23 Ken Schrader	.60	
❑ W24 Rusty Wallace		
❑ W25 Elton Sawyer	.60	

1994 Traks Auto Value

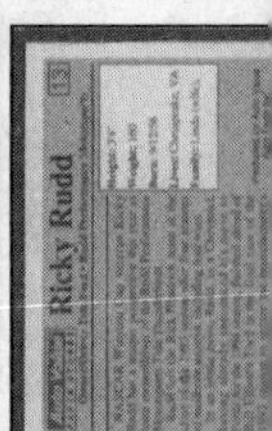

In conjunction with Auto Value stores, Traks issued featuring 50 NASCAR drivers and racing personalitie one cover/checklist card. The cards were releas packs and were free with the purchase of a specific purchase or purchase of certain items. The packs also be purchased outright. Reportedly, 84,456 of sets were produced.

	MINT
COMPLETE SET (51)	10.00
COMMON CARD (1-50)	.25
❑ 1 Sterling Marlin	.40
❑ 2 Brett Bodine	.25
❑ 3 Robert Pressley	.25
❑ 4 Ted Musgrave	.25
❑ 5 Harry Gant	.40
❑ 6 Ward Burton	.25
❑ 7 Michael Waltrip	.25
❑ 8 Jimmy Spencer	.25
❑ 9 Dale Jarrett	.50
❑ 10 Jack Roush	.25
❑ 11 Steve Grissom	.25
❑ 12 Morgan Shepherd	.25
❑ 13 Ricky Rudd	.40
❑ 14 Chuck Bown	.25
❑ 15 Neil Bonnett	.50
❑ 16 Rick Hendrick	.25
❑ 17 Lake Speed	.25
❑ 18 Todd Bodine	.25
❑ 19 Jeff Burton	.25
❑ 20 Greg Sacks	.25
❑ 21 Rusty Wallace	1.00
❑ 22 Rick Mast	.25
❑ 23 Loy Allen Jr.	.25
❑ 24 Chuck Rider	.25
❑ 25 Jeff Gordon	2.50
❑ 26 Bobby Hillin	.25
❑ 27 Bobby Labonte	.40
❑ 28 Dick Trickle	.25
❑ 29 Terry Labonte	1.00
❑ 30 Joe Nemechek	.25
❑ 31 Wally Dallenbach Jr.	.25
❑ 32 Bobby Allison	.25
❑ 33 Mark Martin	1.00
❑ 34 Alan Kulwicki	.60
❑ 35 Jimmy Hensley	.25
❑ 36 Walter Bud Moore	.25
❑ 37 Davey Allison	.75
❑ 38 Dave Marcis	.25
❑ 39 Derrike Cope	.25
❑ 40 Ned Jarrett	.25
❑ 41 Ken Schrader	.25
❑ 42 Junior Johnson	.25
❑ 43 Ernie Irvan	.60
❑ 44 Jimmy Means	.25
❑ 45 Robert Yates	.25
❑ 46 Roger Penske	.25
❑ 47 Joe Gibbs	.25
❑ 48 Derrike Cope's Car Ted Musgrave's Car	.25
❑ 49 Rusty Wallace's Car Ken Schrader's Car	.25

	MINT	NRMT
icky Rudd's Car Nose to Tail	.25	.11
Checklist Card	.25	.11

1994 Traks Cartoons

aks Cartoons set was produced for and distributed 994 Traks factory sets and First Run factory sets to Traks Club members. The cards are oversized easure approximately 8" X 10". First Run factory cluded a numbered Cartoons set signed the card's Bill Stanford.

	MINT	NRMT
ETE SET (5)	15.00	6.75
ON CARD (C1-C5)	2.00	.90
lark Martin	3.50	1.55
usty Wallace	3.50	1.55
terling Marlin	2.50	1.10
yle Petty	2.00	.90
eff Gordon	5.00	2.20

4 Traks Preferred Collector

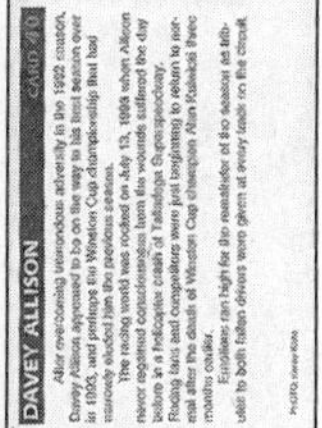

the second 20-card set made available only to club members. The cards continue in numbering he 1993 series left off. The cards feature some of drivers in NASCAR Winston Cup racing. The backs stats for the driver's career and the 1993 season. t two cards in the set are tributes to Davey Allison n Kulwicki.

	MINT	NRMT
ETE SET (20)	15.00	6.75
ON CARD (21-40)	.30	.14
usty Wallace	1.25	.55
arry Gant	.50	.23
erling Marlin	.50	.23
ark Martin	1.25	.55
d Musgrave	.30	.14
reg Sacks	.30	.14
en Schrader	.30	.14
organ Shepherd	.30	.14
ike Speed	.30	.14
mmy Spencer	.30	.14
ck Trickle	.30	.14
rry Labonte	1.25	.55
ff Gordon	2.50	1.10
nie Irvan	1.00	.45
obby Labonte	.50	.23
ett Bodine	.30	.14
il Bonnett	.50	.23
errike Cope	.30	.14
an Kulwicki	1.00	.45
avey Allison	1.50	.70

994 Traks Hermie Sadler

roduced this individual set to commemorate the ginia is for Lovers Racing Team. The cards were ted primarily through souvenir trailers and feature ermie Sadler.

	MINT	NRMT
ETE SET (10)	3.00	1.35
ON CARD (1-10)	.30	.14
mie Sadler	.60	.25

	MINT	NRMT
❑ 2 Don Beverley	.30	.14
❑ 3 Hermie Sadler's Car	.30	.14
❑ 4 Hermie Sadler	.60	.25
❑ 5 Bobby King	.30	.14
❑ 6 Hermie Sadler's Car	.30	.14
❑ 7 Hermie Sadler	.60	.25
❑ 8 Hermie Sadler w/Crew	.30	.14
❑ 9 Hermie Sadler BGN ROY	.30	.14
❑ 10 Hermie Sadler's Transporter	.30	.14

1995 Traks

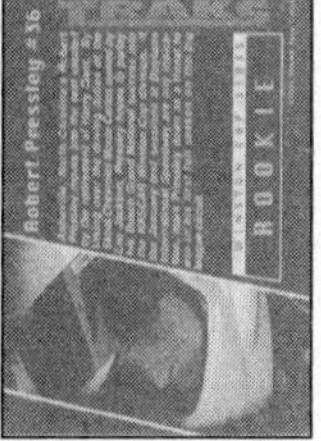

1995 Traks was released in one single series set of 75-cards through 12-card packs. Boxes contained 36-packs and production was limited to 2500 20-box cases. Dale Earnhardt was included in the set for the first time since 1992. The cards were released with an autographed Richard Petty promo card inserted along with other inserts: First Run parallel, Behind the Scenes, On the Rise, Race Scapes, Racing Machines, Series Stars and Challengers. Each insert set was also produced with a First Run parallel version. The Racing Machines and Series Stars First Run parallels were only available as part of the prizes for winners of the Challengers interactive game. A random insert in packs was a autographed Richard Petty card. The cards were inserted at a rate of one in 600 packs.

	MINT	NRMT
COMPLETE SET (75)	10.00	4.50
COMMON CARD (1-75)	.10	.05
COMP.RACE SCAPES SET (10)	3.00	1.35
❑ 1 Geoff Bodine	.10	.05
❑ 2 John Andretti	.10	.05
❑ 3 Harry Gant	.30	.14
❑ 4 Jeff Gordon	1.50	.70
❑ 5 Bobby Labonte	.60	.25
❑ 6 Sterling Marlin	.20	.09
❑ 7 Johnny Benson Jr.	.10	.05
❑ 8 Ward Burton	.10	.05
❑ 9 Ernie Irvan	.20	.09
❑ 10 Steve Grissom	.10	.05
❑ 11 Dennis Setzer	.10	.05
❑ 12 Greg Sacks	.10	.05
❑ 13 Rusty Wallace	.75	.35
❑ 14 Brett Bodine	.10	.05
❑ 15 Loy Allen Jr.	.10	.05
❑ 16 Ted Musgrave	.10	.05
❑ 17 Jeremy Mayfield	.50	.23
❑ 18 Dale Jarrett	.60	.25
❑ 19 Steve Kinser	.10	.05
❑ 20 Chad Little	.10	.05
❑ 21 Dave Marcis	.20	.09
❑ 22 Kyle Petty	.20	.09
❑ 23 Ricky Rudd	.20	.09
❑ 24 Hermie Sadler	.10	.05
❑ 25 Mike Wallace	.10	.05
❑ 26 Jeff Gordon	1.50	.70
❑ 27 Dale Earnhardt	1.50	.70
❑ 28 Ricky Craven	.10	.05
❑ 29 David Green	.10	.05
❑ 30 Mark Martin	.75	.35
❑ 31 Rick Mast	.10	.05
❑ 32 Joe Nemechek	.10	.05
❑ 33 Todd Bodine	.10	.05
❑ 34 Kyle Petty	.20	.09
❑ 35 Tommy Houston	.10	.05
❑ 36 Robert Pressley	.10	.05
❑ 37 Morgan Shepherd	.10	.05
❑ 38 Dick Trickle	.10	.05
❑ 39 Jeff Burton	.20	.09
❑ 40 Geoff Bodine	.10	.05
❑ 41 Terry Labonte	.75	.35
❑ 42 Ken Schrader	.10	.05
❑ 43 Dale Jarrett	.60	.25
❑ 44 Kenny Wallace	.10	.05
❑ 45 Bobby Hamilton	.10	.05
❑ 46 Rusty Wallace	.75	.35
❑ 47 Brett Bodine	.10	.05
❑ 48 Mark Martin	.75	.35
❑ 49 Michael Waltrip	.10	.05
❑ 50 Ward Burton	.10	.05
❑ 51 Kyle Petty	.20	.09
❑ 52 Jeff Gordon	1.50	.70
❑ 53 Mark Martin	.75	.35
❑ 54 Geoff Bodine	.10	.05
❑ 55 Ken Schrader	.10	.05
❑ 56 Jeff Burton	.20	.09
❑ 57 Randy LaJoie	.10	.05
❑ 58 Jeff Gordon	1.50	.70
❑ 59 Ernie Irvan	.20	.09
❑ 60 Dale Jarrett	.60	.25
❑ 61 Terry Labonte	.75	.35
❑ 62 Mark Martin	.75	.35
❑ 63 Ricky Rudd	.20	.09
❑ 64 Ken Schrader	.10	.05
❑ 65 Morgan Shepherd	.10	.05
❑ 66 Rusty Wallace	.75	.35
❑ 67 Derrike Cope	.10	.05
❑ 68 Jeff Gordon	1.50	.70
❑ 69 Michael Waltrip	.10	.05
❑ 70 Todd Bodine	.10	.05
❑ 71 Sterling Marlin	.20	.09
❑ 72 Sterling Marlin	.20	.09
❑ 73 Ricky Rudd	.20	.09
❑ 74 Ernie Irvan	.20	.09
❑ 75 Rusty Wallace	.75	.35
❑ NNO Richard Petty Autograph	100.00	45.00

1995 Traks First Run

Packaged one per 1995 Traks foil pack, First Run is a parallel set to the regular Traks issue. The cards can be distinguished only by the presence of the "First Run" Traks logo on the cardfront. Each card in the regular set, as well as all insert sets were produced with a First Run parallel. First Run versions of Racing Machines and Series Stars inserts were only available as prizes in the Challengers interactive contest.

	MINT	NRMT
COMPLETE SET (75)	30.00	13.50
COMMON CARD (1-75)	.20	.09

*FIRST RUN STARS: 1.5X TO 3X BASIC CARDS

1995 Traks Behind The Scenes

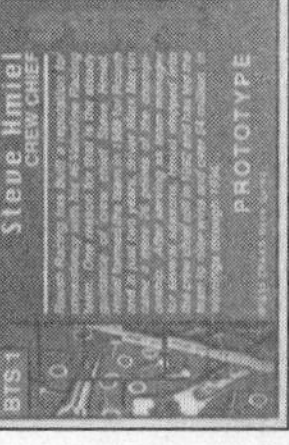

Behind the Scenes was produced by Traks as an insert in its 1995 Traks packs. The cards focus on non-drivers that make the sport of racing run. A parallel First Run version of each card was also produced. Wrapper stated odds of pulling a Behind the Scenes card is approximately two per pack.

	MINT	NRMT
COMPLETE SET (25)	4.00	1.80

COMMON CARD (BTS1-BTS25)	.25	.11
COMP. FIRST RUN (25)	12.00	5.50
*FIRST RUNS: 1.25X TO 3X BASIC CARDS		

❑ BTS1 Steve Hmiel	.25	.11
❑ BTS2 Rick Hendrick	.25	.11
❑ BTS3 Joe Gibbs	.25	.11
❑ BTS4 Chuck Rider	.25	.11
❑ BTS5 Buddy Parrott	.25	.11
❑ BTS6 Jack Roush	.25	.11
❑ BTS7 Larry McReynolds	.25	.11
❑ BTS8 Roger Penske	.25	.11
❑ BTS9 Robbie Loomis	.25	.11
❑ BTS10 Glen Wood Leonard Wood	.25	.11
❑ BTS11 Paul Andrews	.25	.11
❑ BTS12 Robert Yates	.25	.11
❑ BTS13 Cale Yarborough	.25	.11
❑ BTS14 Jimmy Johnson	.25	.11
❑ BTS15 Tony Glover	.25	.11
❑ BTS16 Ray Evernham	.25	.11
❑ BTS17 Eddie Wood	.25	.11
❑ BTS18 Andy Petree	.25	.11
❑ BTS19 Carl Hill	.25	.11
❑ BTS20 Richard Jackson	.25	.11
❑ BTS21 Bruce Roney	.25	.11
❑ BTS22 Junior Johnson	.25	.11
❑ BTS23 Leo Jackson	.25	.11
❑ BTS24 Len Wood	.25	.11
❑ BTS25 Kenny Bernstein	.25	.11

1995 Traks Challengers

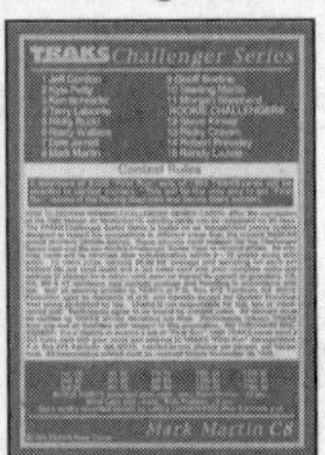

Challengers is a 15-card interactive game randomly packed in 1995 Traks packs. Production was limited to less than 2000 of each card and the top prize was a complete First Run set of all 1995 Traks cards. Contest winners were required to redeem the cards of both the top Challenger and Rookie Challenger points drivers according to Traks' point rating system. Jeff Gordon was the Challengers winner and the Rookie Challengers winner was Ricky Craven. The original expiration date of November 1995 was extended to April 15, 1996.

	MINT	NRMT
COMPLETE SET (15)	80.00	36.00
COMMON CARD (C1-C15)	2.00	.90
*SINGLES: 5X TO 12X BASE CARD HI		
COMP. FIRST RUN PRIZE SET	200.00	90.00
*FIRST RUNS: 6X TO 15X BASIC CARDS		

❑ C1 Jeff Gordon Winner Card	70.00	32.00
❑ C2 Kyle Petty	4.00	1.80
❑ C3 Ken Schrader	2.00	.90
❑ C4 Terry Labonte	16.00	7.25
❑ C5 Ricky Rudd	4.00	1.80
❑ C6 Rusty Wallace	16.00	7.25
❑ C7 Dale Jarrett	14.00	6.25
❑ C8 Mark Martin	16.00	7.25
❑ C9 Geoff Bodine	2.00	.90
❑ C10 Sterling Marlin	4.00	1.80
❑ C11 Morgan Shepherd	2.00	.90
❑ C12 Steve Kinser	2.00	.90
❑ C13 Ricky Craven Winner Card	20.00	9.00
❑ C14 Robert Pressley	2.00	.90
❑ C15 Randy LaJoie	2.00	.90

1995 Traks On The Rise

On the Rise inserts focus on the top future stars of the Winston Cup and Busch racing circuits. The cards were packed approximately one per pack in 1995 Traks. A First Run parallel of each card was also randomly issued through packs. Jeff Burton's card was also released as a prototype.

	MINT	NRMT
COMPLETE SET (20)	5.00	2.20
COMMON CARD (OTR1-OTR20)	.25	.11
COMP. FIRST RUN (20)	12.00	5.50
*FIRST RUNS: 1X TO 2.5X BASIC CARDS		

❑ OTR1 Johnny Benson Jr.	.25	.11
❑ OTR2 Steve Kinser	.25	.11
❑ OTR3 Mike Wallace	.25	.11
❑ OTR4 Larry Pearson	.25	.11
❑ OTR5 Bobby Dotter	.25	.11
❑ OTR6 Dennis Setzer	.25	.11
❑ OTR7 David Green	.25	.11
❑ OTR8 Steve Grissom	.25	.11
❑ OTR9 Hermie Sadler	.25	.11
❑ OTR10 Mike McLaughlin	.25	.11
❑ OTR11 Joe Nemechek	.25	.11
❑ OTR12 John Andretti	.25	.11
❑ OTR13 Ted Musgrave	.25	.11
❑ OTR14 Jeff Burton	.40	.18
❑ OTR15 Ward Burton	.25	.11
❑ OTR16 Kenny Wallace	.25	.11
❑ OTR17 Ricky Craven	.25	.11
❑ OTR18 Robert Pressley	.25	.11
❑ OTR19 Chad Little	.25	.11
❑ OTR20 Bobby Labonte	.40	.18

1995 Traks Racing Machines

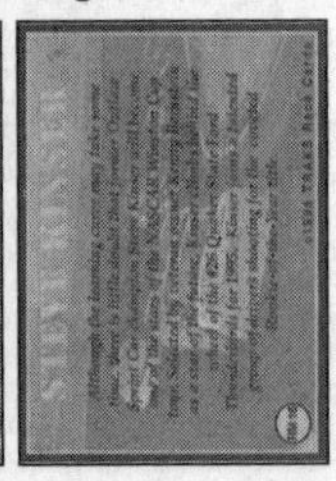

Traks Racing Machines inserts feature top Winston Cup cars printed on prism foil card stock. The cards were inserted at the wrapper stated rate of approximately 1:30 packs. A First Run parallel of each card was also produced as a prize to winners of the Challengers interactive contest.

	MINT	NRMT
COMPLETE SET (20)	60.00	27.00
COMMON CARD (RM1-RM20)	2.00	.90
*SINGLES: 5X TO 12X BASE CARD HI		
COMP.FIRST RUN SET (20)	100.00	45.00
*FIRST RUNS: 3X TO 8X BASIC CARDS		

❑ RM1 Todd Bodine	2.00	.90
❑ RM2 Sterling Marlin	4.00	1.80
❑ RM3 Geoff Bodine	2.00	.90
❑ RM4 Bobby Hamilton	2.00	.90
❑ RM5 Ricky Rudd	4.00	1.80
❑ RM6 Terry Labonte	12.00	5.50
❑ RM7 Jeff Gordon	30.00	13.50
❑ RM8 Morgan Shepherd	2.00	.90
❑ RM9 Mark Martin	15.00	6.75
❑ RM10 Rusty Wallace	15.00	6.75
❑ RM11 Rick Mast	2.00	.90
❑ RM12 Dale Jarrett	10.00	4.50
❑ RM13 Dick Trickle	2.00	.90
❑ RM14 Ken Schrader	2.00	.90
❑ RM15 Michael Waltrip	2.00	.90
❑ RM16 Steve Kinser	2.00	.90
❑ RM17 Ted Musgrave	2.00	.90
❑ RM18 Kyle Petty	4.00	1.80
❑ RM19 Jeff Burton	4.00	1.80
❑ RM20 Bobby Labonte	8.00	3.60

1995 Traks Series Stars

Traks Series Stars inserts feature top Winston Cup drivers printed on foil card stock. Each card was covered with a removable static cling "fan" sticker to protect the cardfront. The cards were inserted at the wrapper stated rate of approximately 1:30 packs. A First Run parallel of each card was also produced and available only as a prize to winners of the Challengers interactive contest.

	MINT
COMPLETE SET (20)	80.00
COMMON CARD (SS1-SS20)	1.50
*SINGLES: 4X TO 10X BASE CARD HI	
COMP. FIRST RUN SET (20)	175.00
*FIRST RUNS: 3X TO 8X BASIC CARDS	

❑ SS1 Ken Schrader	1.50
❑ SS2 Terry Labonte	16.00
❑ SS3 Morgan Shepherd	1.50
❑ SS4 Rusty Wallace	16.00
❑ SS5 Mark Martin	16.00
❑ SS6 Derrike Cope	1.50
❑ SS7 Sterling Marlin	3.00
❑ SS8 Jeff Gordon	40.00
❑ SS9 Harry Gant	3.00
❑ SS10 Geoff Bodine	1.50
❑ SS11 Ernie Irvan	3.00
❑ SS12 Brett Bodine	1.50
❑ SS13 Michael Waltrip	1.50
❑ SS14 Dick Trickle	1.50
❑ SS15 Ted Musgrave	1.50
❑ SS16 Ricky Rudd	3.00
❑ SS17 Kyle Petty	3.00
❑ SS18 Rick Mast	1.50
❑ SS19 Dale Earnhardt	40.00
❑ SS20 Dale Jarrett	14.00

1995 Traks Auto Value

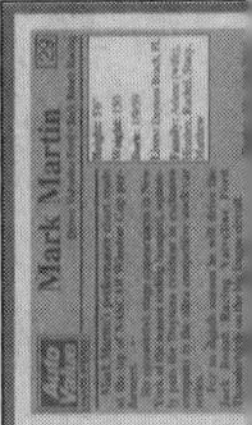

In conjunction with Auto Value stores, Traks issue featuring 50 NASCAR drivers and racing personali the second straight year. The cards were dist through Auto Value stores in cello packs.

	MINT
COMPLETE SET (51)	15.00
COMMON CARD (1-50)	.30

❑ 1 Jeff Gordon	2.00
❑ 2 Steve Grissom	.30
❑ 3 Randy LaJoie	.30
❑ 4 Junior Johnson	.30
❑ 5 Jeff Burton	.50
❑ 6 Geoff Bodine	.30
❑ 7 Kyle Petty	.50
❑ 8 Robert Pressley	.30
❑ 9 Greg Sacks	.30
❑ 10 Morgan Shepherd	.30
❑ 11 John Andretti	.30
❑ 12 Paul Andrews	.30
❑ 13 Brett Bodine	.30
❑ 14 Steve Hmiel	.30
❑ 15 Ernie Irvan	.50
❑ 16 Joe Gibbs	.30
❑ 17 Ray Evernham	.30
❑ 18 Ricky Craven	.30
❑ 19 Derrike Cope	.30
❑ 20 Ward Burton	.30
❑ 21 Todd Bodine	.30
❑ 22 Bobby Hamilton	.30
❑ 23 Rick Hendrick	.30
❑ 24 Dale Jarrett	.75
❑ 25 Bobby Labonte	.75
❑ 26 Steve Kinser	.30
❑ 27 Dave Marcis	.50
❑ 28 Sterling Marlin	.50
❑ 29 Mark Martin	1.00
❑ 30 Rick Mast	.30

eremy Mayfield	.60	.25
ʼichael Waltrip	.30	.14
ʼed Musgrave	.30	.14
ʼobert Yates	.30	.14
ale Yarborough	.30	.14
uddy Parrott	.30	.14
ʼike Wallace	.30	.14
oe Nemechek	.30	.14
arry McReynolds	.30	.14
ʼoger Penske	.30	.14
ʼick Trickle	.30	.14
,enny Wallace	.30	.14
ack Roush	.30	.14
,en Schrader	.30	.14
ʼusty Wallace	1.00	.45
,enny Bernstein	.30	.14
erry Labonte	1.00	.45
ace Action	.30	.14
ace Action	.30	.14
ace Aciton	.30	.14
Checklist	.30	.14

995 Traks 5th Anniversary

ntroduced a new premium brand, Visions, under me of 5th Anniversary in 1995. The release was ıted in 8-card packs with 24-packs per box. Each ontained eight boxes of Traks 5th Anniversary s and four boxes of Visons Elite. Reportedly, tion was limited to 1000 cases. Visions Elite is a Gold foil parallel set of the regular 5th rsary Visions cards. Insert sets include Clear ders and Retrospective.

	MINT	NRMT
ETE SET (80)	10.00	4.50
ON CARD (1-80)	.10	.05
ON DRIVER (1-80)	.20	.09
rk Martin	1.00	.45
ve Grissom	.20	.09
e Earnhardt	2.00	.90
f Gordon	2.00	.90
ky Rudd	.40	.18
off Bodine	.20	.09
rling Marlin	.40	.18
nny Benson Jr.	.20	.09
sty Wallace	1.00	.45
hn Andretti	.20	.09
errike Cope	.20	.09
nie Irvan	.40	.18
d Musgrave	.20	.09
ad Little	.20	.09
le Petty	.40	.18
ett Bodine	.20	.09
cky Craven	.40	.18
vid Green	.20	.09
rry Labonte	1.00	.45
le Jarrett	.75	.35
ard Burton	.20	.09
ke Wallace	.20	.09
organ Shepherd	.20	.09
bert Pressley	.20	.09
dd Bodine	.20	.09
e Nemechek	.20	.09
ck Mast	.20	.09
n Schrader	.20	.09
nny Wallace	.20	.09
f Burton	.40	.18
chael Waltrip	.20	.09
ck Trickle	.20	.09
bby Labonte	.75	.35
bby Hamilton	.20	.09
t Stricklin	.20	.09
rling Marlin	.40	.18
cky Rudd	.40	.18
f Gordon	2.00	.90
rry Labonte	1.00	.45
rk Martin	1.00	.45
e Jarrett	.75	.35
sty Wallace	1.00	.45
dd Bodine's Car	.10	.05
rling Marlin's Car	.20	.09

❑ 45 Geoff Bodine's Car	.10	.05
❑ 46 Bobby Hamilton's Car	.10	.05
❑ 47 Ricky Rudd's Car	.20	.09
❑ 48 Terry Labonte's Car	.50	.23
❑ 49 Jeff Gordon's Car	1.00	.45
❑ 50 Morgan Shepherd's Car	.10	.05
❑ 51 Mark Martin's Car	.50	.23
❑ 52 Rusty Wallace's Car	.50	.23
❑ 53 Michael Waltrip's Car	.20	.09
❑ 54 Dale Jarrett's Car	.40	.18
❑ 55 Dick Trickle's Car	.10	.05
❑ 56 Rick Mast's Car	.10	.05
❑ 57 Ricky Craven's Car	.10	.05
❑ 58 Joe Nemechek's Car	.10	.05
❑ 59 Ted Musgrave's Car	.10	.05
❑ 60 Kyle Petty's Car	.20	.09
❑ 61 Jeff Burton's Car	.20	.09
❑ 62 Bobby Hamilton's Car	.10	.05
❑ 63 Steve Grissom's Car	.10	.05
❑ 64 Robert Pressley's Car	.10	.05
❑ 65 Jack Roush	.10	.05
❑ 66 Steve Hmiel	.10	.05
❑ 67 Robert Yates	.10	.05
❑ 68 Gary DeHart	.10	.05
❑ 69 Cale Yarborough	.20	.09
❑ 70 Larry McClure	.10	.05
❑ 71 Robin Pemberton	.10	.05
❑ 72 Ed McClure	.10	.05
❑ 73 Larry McReynolds	.10	.05
❑ 74 Andy Petree	.10	.05
❑ 75 Joe Gibbs	.20	.09
❑ 76 Tony Glover	.10	.05
❑ 77 Rick Hendrick	.10	.05
❑ 78 Jimmy Makar	.10	.05
❑ 79 Paul Andrews	.10	.05
❑ 80 Ray Evernham	.10	.05

1995 Traks 5th Anniversary Gold

This 80-card set is a parallel to the base Traks 5th Anniversary set. The cards feature a gold foil stamping and came in the blue Anniversary packs. Each 12 box case of Traks 5th Anniversary came with four boxes of Anniversary Gold and eight boxes of the base Anniversary product.

	MINT	NRMT
COMPLETE SET (80)	30.00	13.50
COMMON CARDS (1-80)	.30	.14
COMMON DRIVERS (1-80)	.40	.18

*GOLD CARDS: 1X TO 1.5X BASIC CARDS

1995 Traks 5th Anniversary Clear Contenders

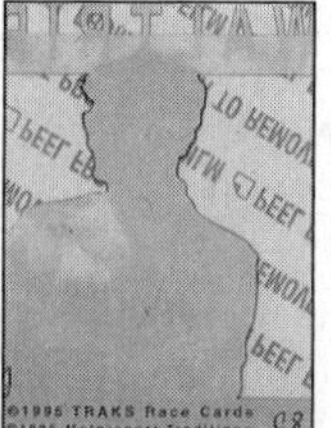

Clear Contenders were randomly inserted in packs of Traks 5th Anniversary Visions Elite. Wrapper stated insertion ratio is 1:3 packs. The cards feature 10 of the top NASCAR drivers on clear plastic card stock.

	MINT	NRMT
COMPLETE SET (10)	25.00	11.00
COMMON CARD (C1-C10)	.75	.35

*SINGLES: 1.5X TO 4X BASE CARD HI

❑ C1 Dale Earnhardt	10.00	4.50
❑ C2 Mark Martin	5.00	2.20
❑ C3 Jeff Gordon	10.00	4.50
❑ C4 Sterling Marlin	1.50	.70
❑ C5 Ted Musgrave	.75	.35
❑ C6 Rusty Wallace	5.00	2.20
❑ C7 Bobby Labonte	3.00	1.35
❑ C8 Michael Waltrip	.75	.35
❑ C9 Terry Labonte	5.00	2.20
❑ C10 Morgan Shepherd	.75	.35

1995 Traks 5th Anniversary Retrospective

Retrospective cards were randomly inserted in 1995 Traks

5th Anniversary Visions packs only. Wrapper stated insertion ratio is 1:3 packs. The 15-cards were printed on holofoil prism card stock and feature a photo of the driver's first Traks card on the back.

	MINT	NRMT
COMPLETE SET (15)	15.00	6.75
COMMON CARD (R1-R15)	.40	.18

*SINGLES: .75X TO 2X BASE CARD HI

❑ R1 Mark Martin	3.00	1.35
❑ R2 Dale Earnhardt	6.00	2.70
❑ R3 Jeff Gordon	6.00	2.70
❑ R4 Ricky Rudd	.75	.35
❑ R5 Sterling Marlin	.75	.35
❑ R6 Rusty Wallace	3.00	1.35
❑ R7 Dale Jarrett	2.50	1.10
❑ R8 Terry Labonte	3.00	1.35
❑ R9 Kyle Petty	.75	.35
❑ R10 Ken Schrader	.40	.18
❑ R11 Ernie Irvan	.75	.35
❑ R12 Geoff Bodine	.40	.18
❑ R13 Morgan Shepherd	.40	.18
❑ R14 Cale Yarborough	.40	.18
❑ R15 Richard Petty	2.50	1.10

1995 Traks 5th Anniversary Uncommon Enlarged Cards

This 10-card set features the top drivers in Winston Cup. The cards are a jumbo sized card (3"X5") and were inserted in the bottom of Anniversary boxes at a rate of one per three boxes. There was also a Gold parallel version of the jumbo cards. The cards were inserted at a rate of one per case. There were 100 of each gold card made.

	MINT	NRMT
COMPLETE SET (10)	20.00	9.00
COMMON CARD (E1-E10)	.60	.25

*SINGLES: 1.25X TO 3X BASE CARD HI
ONE PER BOX

❑ E1 Jeff Gordon	15.00	6.75
❑ E2 Terry Labonte	8.00	3.60
❑ E3 Rusty Wallace	8.00	3.60
❑ E4 Morgan Shepherd	.60	.25
❑ E5 Ted Musgrave	.60	.25
❑ E6 Dale Earnhardt	15.00	6.75
❑ E7 Sterling Marlin	1.25	.55
❑ E8 Michael Waltrip	.60	.25
❑ E9 Bobby Labonte	6.00	2.70
❑ E10 Mark Martin	8.00	3.60

1995 Traks Valvoline

Traks produced this set for Valvoline in celebration of 100-years of auto racing. The cards were available in factory set form directly from Valvoline with the purchase of a case of oil or any Valvoline oil change. Each set was packaged in a tin replica Mark Martin race car and offered for sale at $12.95. The black-bordered cards feature an art rendering of a great race car from racing's past with one representative car from each year.

	MINT	NRMT
COMPLETE SET (101)	18.00	8.00
COMMON CARD (1-100)	.15	.07

Card		
❑ 1 J.Frank Duryea's Car Duryea Motor Wagon	.15	.07
❑ 2 A.L.Riker's Car	.15	.07
❑ 3 Bollee Jamin	.15	.07
❑ 4 George Heath's Car	.15	.07
❑ 5 Camille Jenatzy's Car	.15	.07
❑ 6 Fernand Charron's Car	.15	.07
❑ 7 Henri Fournier's Car	.15	.07
❑ 8 Barney Oldfield's Car	.15	.07
❑ 9 H.T.Thomas' Car	.15	.07
❑ 10 George Heath's Car	.15	.07
❑ 11 B.F.Dingley's Car	.15	.07
❑ 12 Joseph Tracy's Car	.15	.07
❑ 13 Scipion Borghese's Car	.15	.07
❑ 14 Louis Wagner's Car	.15	.07
❑ 15 Carl Fisher's Car	.15	.07
❑ 16 Bob Burman's Car	.15	.07
❑ 17 Ray Harroun's Car	.15	.07
❑ 18 Joe Dawson's Car	.15	.07
❑ 19 Jules Goux's Car	.15	.07
❑ 20 Rene Thomas' Car	.15	.07
❑ 21 Ralph dePalma's Car	.15	.07
❑ 22 Dario Resta's Car	.15	.07
❑ 23 WWI Ambulance The War Years	.15	.07
❑ 24 Dodge 4 Staff Car The War Years	.15	.07
❑ 25 Albert Guyot's Car	.15	.07
❑ 26 Gaston Chevrolet's Car	.15	.07
❑ 27 Tommy Milton's Car	.15	.07
❑ 28 Jimmy Murphy's Car	.15	.07
❑ 29 Albert Guyot's Car	.15	.07
❑ 30 Jean Chassagne's Car	.15	.07
❑ 31 Dave Lewis' Car	.15	.07
❑ 32 Jules Goux's Car	.15	.07
❑ 33 Robert Benoist's Car	.15	.07
❑ 34 Louis Meyer's Car	.15	.07
❑ 35 Ray Keech's Car	.15	.07
❑ 36 Billy Arnold's Car	.15	.07
❑ 37 Lou Schneider's Car	.15	.07
❑ 38 Fred Frame's Car	.15	.07
❑ 39 Henry Birkin's Car	.15	.07
❑ 40 Bill Cummings' Car	.15	.07
❑ 41 Malcolm Campbell's Car	.15	.07
❑ 42 Louis Meyer's Car	.15	.07
❑ 43 Bernd Rosemeyer's Car	.15	.07
❑ 44 Louis Meyer's Car	.15	.07
❑ 45 Wilbur Shaw's Car	.15	.07
❑ 46 Ted Horn's Car	.15	.07
❑ 47 Floyd Davis' Car Mauri Rose's Car	.15	.07
❑ 48 Daimler Dingo The War Years	.15	.07
❑ 49 Willys Jeep The War Years	.15	.07
❑ 50 Red Ball Express The War Years	.15	.07
❑ 51 M-4 Sherman Tank The War Years	.15	.07
❑ 52 George Robson's Car	.15	.07
❑ 53 Mauri Rose's Car	.15	.07
❑ 54 Johnny Mauro's Car	.15	.07
❑ 55 Red Byron's Car	.15	.07
❑ 56 Johnnie Parsons' Car	.15	.07
❑ 57 Lee Walerd's Car	.15	.07
❑ 58 Alberto Ascari's Car	.15	.07
❑ 59 Bill Vukovich's Car	.15	.07
❑ 60 Lee Petty's Car	.25	.11
❑ 61 Bob Sweikert's Car	.15	.07
❑ 62 Fireball Roberts' Car	.25	.11
❑ 63 Juan Manuel Fangio's Car	.15	.07
❑ 64 Jimmy Bryan's Car	.15	.07
❑ 65 Lee Petty's Car	.25	.11
❑ 66 Jim Rathmann's Car	.15	.07
❑ 67 A.J.Foyt's Car	.50	.23
❑ 68 Joe Weatherly's Car	.15	.07
❑ 69 Parnelli Jones' Car	.25	.11
❑ 70 Ken Miles' Car	.15	.07
❑ 71 Jim Clark's Car	.15	.07
❑ 72 Don Garlits' Car	.25	.11
❑ 73 Richard Petty's Car	.75	.35
❑ 74 David Pearson's Car	.25	.11
❑ 75 Mario Andretti's Car	.50	.23
❑ 76 Ferrari 512S Roadster	.15	.07
❑ 77 Don Garlits' Car	.25	.11
❑ 78 Ronnie Sox's Car	.15	.07
❑ 79 Gordon Johncock's Car	.25	.11
❑ 80 Don Prudhomme's Car	.25	.11
❑ 81 Bobby Allison's Car	.15	.07
❑ 82 Buddy Baker's Car	.25	.11
❑ 83 A.J.Foyt's Car	.50	.23
❑ 84 Tom Sneva's Car	.25	.11
❑ 85 Richard Petty's Car	.75	.35
❑ 86 Benny Parsons' Car	.25	.11
❑ 87 Bobby Unser's Car	.15	.07
❑ 88 Gordon Johncock's Car	.25	.11
❑ 89 Cale Yarborough's Car	.25	.11
❑ 90 Joe Amato's Car	.15	.07
❑ 91 Ron Bouchard's Car	.15	.07
❑ 92 Shirley Muldowney's Car	.50	.23
❑ 93 Al Unser's Car	.50	.23
❑ 94 Neil Bonnett's Car	.50	.23
❑ 95 Ken Schrader's Car	.25	.11
❑ 96 Bobby Rahal's Car	.25	.11
❑ 97 Rusty Wallace's Car	1.00	.45
❑ 98 Al Unser Jr.'s Car	.50	.23
❑ 99 Mark Martin's Car	1.00	.45
❑ 100 Jeff Gordon's Car	2.00	.90
❑ NNO Cover Card Checklist	.15	.07

1996 Traks Review and Preview

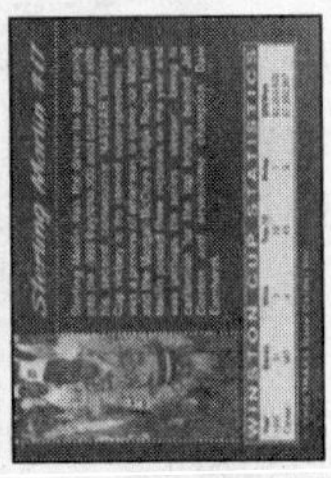

This 50-card set features top drivers from the Winston Cup circuit. The cards use gold foil stamping and UV coating. The product was packaged 12 boxes per case, 24 packs per box and eight cards per pack.

	MINT	NRMT
COMPLETE SET (50)	8.00	3.60
COMMON CARD (1-50)	.20	.09

Card	MINT	NRMT
❑ 1 Sterling Marlin	.40	.18
❑ 2 Bobby Hamilton	.20	.09
❑ 3 Ted Musgrave	.20	.09
❑ 4 Robert Pressley	.20	.09
❑ 5 Mark Martin	.75	.35
❑ 6 Dale Jarrett	.60	.25
❑ 7 Joe Nemechek	.20	.09
❑ 8 Kyle Petty	.40	.18
❑ 9 Ward Burton	.20	.09
❑ 10 Ernie Irvan	.40	.18
❑ 11 Mark Martin	.75	.35
❑ 12 Kyle Petty	.40	.18
❑ 13 Johnny Benson	.20	.09
❑ 14 Ward Burton	.20	.09
❑ 15 Jeff Gordon	1.50	.70
❑ 16 John Andretti	.20	.09
❑ 17 Sterling Marlin	.40	.18
❑ 18 Ted Musgrave	.20	.09
❑ 19 Ernie Irvan	.40	.18
❑ 20 Jeff Burton	.40	.18
❑ 21 Ricky Craven	.20	.09
❑ 22 Dale Jarrett	.60	.25
❑ 23 Morgan Shepherd	.20	.09
❑ 24 Ken Schrader	.20	.09
❑ 25 Robert Pressley	.20	.09
❑ 26 Bobby Hamilton	.20	.09
❑ 27 Geoff Bodine	.20	.09
❑ 28 Michael Waltrip	.20	.09
❑ 29 Joe Nemechek	.20	.09
❑ 30 Steve Grissom	.20	.09
❑ 31 Morgan Shepherd	.20	.09
❑ 32 Sterling Marlin	.40	.18
❑ 33 Hut Stricklin	.20	.09
❑ 34 Rick Mast	.20	.09
❑ 35 Kyle Petty	.40	.18
❑ 36 Mark Martin	.75	.35
❑ 37 Dale Earnhardt	1.50	.70
❑ 38 Derrike Cope	.20	.09
❑ 39 Dale Jarrett	.60	.25
❑ 40 Brett Bodine	.20	.09
❑ 41 Ernie Irvan	.40	.18
❑ 42 Ken Schrader	.20	.09
❑ 43 Ted Musgrave	.20	.09
❑ 44 Ernie Irvan	.40	.18
❑ 45 Geoff Bodine	.20	.09
❑ 46 Mike Wallace	.20	.09
❑ 47 Checklist I Dale Jarrett's Car on front -	.40	.18
❑ 48 Checklist II Ernie Irvan's Car on front	.20	.09
❑ 49 Checklist III Mike Wallace Jeff Burton's Cars on front	.20	.09
❑ 50 Checklist IV Geoff Bodine's Car on front	.20	.09

1996 Traks Review and Preview First R

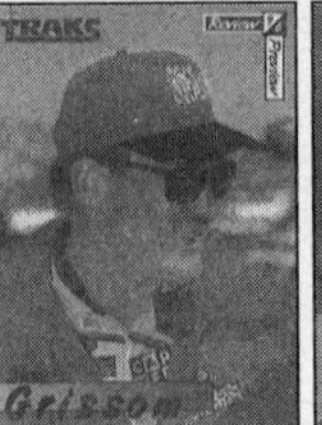

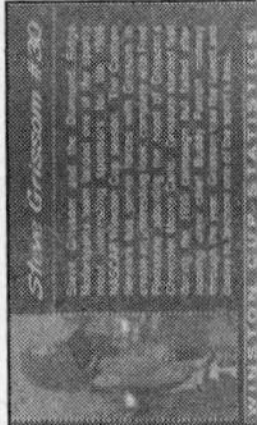

This 50-card set is a parallel to the base set. The feature a First Run on the front of each card in the l right hand corner. The first run cards were insert per pack.

	MINT
COMPLETE SET (50)	20.00
COMMON CARD (1-50)	.15

*FIRST RUN CARDS: 1.5X TO 3X BASIC CARDS

1996 Traks Review and Preview Magn

This 50-card parallel set features the top Winstc circuit drivers. The cards are a parallel to the base and are printed on magnet stock. Two magnet card inserted in every box. They were not found in packs

	MINT
COMPLETE SET (50)	80.00
COMMON CARD (1-50)	1.50

*STARS: 4X TO 10X BASIC CARDS

1996 Traks Review and Preview Liquid Gold

Inserted at a rate of one per 24 packs, the Liqui cards feature top names in Winston Cup racing. Th have vibrant colors and gold accents.

	MINT
COMPLETE SET (20)	50.00
COMMON CARD (LG1-LG20)	1.50

*SINGLES: 3X TO 8X BASE CARD HI

Card	MINT
❑ LG1 Dale Jarrett	10.00
❑ LG2 Ernie Irvan	3.00
❑ LG3 Mark Martin	12.00
❑ LG4 Jeff Burton	3.00
❑ LG5 Bobby Hamilton	1.50
❑ LG6 Morgan Shepherd	1.50
❑ LG7 John Andretti	1.50
❑ LG8 Steve Grissom	1.50
❑ LG9 Rick Mast	1.50
❑ LG10 Mike Wallace	1.50
❑ LG11 Derrike Cope	1.50
❑ LG12 Robert Pressley	1.50
❑ LG13 Ward Burton	1.50
❑ LG14 Kyle Petty	3.00
❑ LG15 Ricky Craven	1.50
❑ LG16 Sterling Marlin	3.00
❑ LG17 Geoff Bodine	1.50
❑ LG18 Jeff Gordon	25.00
❑ LG19 Brett Bodine	1.50
❑ LG20 Ted Musgrave	1.50

1996 Traks Review and Preview Triple-Chase

This 20-card insert set is the base set that features drivers in Winston Cup. The cards were inserted pack. There are two parallel versions: Gold and The Gold cards feature gold foil stamping and are at a rate of one per three packs. The Holofoil cards holofoil highlights and were inserted one per 48 pa

	MINT
COMPLETE SET (20)	5.00
COMMON CARD (TC1-TC20)	.10
COMMON DRIVER (TC1-TC20)	.20
COMPLETE GOLD SET (20)	8.00
COMMON GOLD (TC1-TC20)	.15

*GOLD CARDS: .6X TO 1.5X BASE TRIPLE CHASE

	MINT
COMPLETE HOLO.SET (20)	80.00
COMMON HOLO. (TC1-TC20)	1.50

*HOLOFOILS 6X TO 15X BASE TRIPLE CHASE

Card	MINT
❑ TC1 Sterling Marlin	.40
❑ TC2 Ted Musgrave	.10

Mark Martin 1.00 .45
Morgan Shepherd .10 .05
Michael Waltrip .10 .05
Dale Jarrett .75 .35
Bobby Hamilton .10 .05
Todd Bodine .10 .05
Geoff Bodine .10 .05
) Kyle Petty .40 .18
1 Ernie Irvan .40 .18
2 Steve Grissom .10 .05
3 Robert Pressley .10 .05
4 Ricky Craven .10 .05
5 Kodak Racing .10 .05
6 Valvoline Racing .40 .18
7 Havoline Racing .40 .18
3 Coors Light Racing .10 .05
9 Family Channel Racing .10 .05
) Quality Care Racing .40 .18

1996 Ultra

00-card set is the first NASCAR set produced by The set was distributed in 10-card packs with a sted retail of $2.49 each. The set contains the ng topical subsets: Busch Drivers (120-139), Car s (140-148), Award Winners (149-156), Road s (157-166) and Race Action (167-200).

	MINT	NRMT
ETE SET (200)	20.00	9.00
ON CARD (1-200)	.10	.05
ON DRIVER (1-200)	.20	.09

' Gordon 2.00 .90
' Gordon 2.00 .90
' Gordon's Car 1.00 .45
' Evernham .10 .05
e Earnhardt 2.00 .90
e Earnhardt 2.00 .90
e Earnhardt's Car 1.00 .45
y Petree .10 .05
'k Martin 1.00 .45
ark Martin 1.00 .45
ark Martin's Car .50 .23
eve Hmiel .10 .05
erling Marlin .40 .18
erling Marlin .40 .18
erling Marlin's Car .20 .09
ny Glover .10 .05
sty Wallace 1.00 .45
sty Wallace 1.00 .45
sty Wallace's Car .50 .23
bin Pemberton .10 .05
rry Labonte 1.00 .45
rry Labonte 1.00 .45
rry Labonte's Car .50 .23
ry DeHart .10 .05
d Musgrave .20 .09
d Musgrave .20 .09
d Musgrave's Car .10 .05
ward Comstock .10 .05
bby Labonte .75 .35
bby Labonte .75 .35
bby Labonte's Car .40 .18
mmy Makar .10 .05
Elliott 1.00 .45
Elliott 1.00 .45
Elliott's Car .50 .23
ke Beam .10 .05
ky Rudd .40 .18
ky Rudd .40 .18
ky Rudd's Car .20 .09
Ingle .10 .05
bby Hamilton .20 .09
bby Hamilton .20 .09
bby Hamilton's Car .10 .05
hael Waltrip .20 .09
hael Waltrip .20 .09
hael Waltrip's Car .10 .05
e Jarrett .75 .35
e Jarrett .75 .35
e Jarrett's Car .40 .18
rgan Shepherd .20 .09

❑ 51 Morgan Shepherd .20 .09
❑ 52 Morgan Shepherd's Car .10 .05
❑ 53 Derrike Cope .20 .09
❑ 54 Derrike Cope .20 .09
❑ 55 Derrike Cope's Car .10 .05
❑ 56 Geoff Bodine .20 .09
❑ 57 Geoff Bodine .20 .09
❑ 58 Geoff Bodine's Car .10 .05
❑ 59 Ken Schrader .20 .09
❑ 60 Ken Schrader .20 .09
❑ 61 Ken Schrader's Car .10 .05
❑ 62 John Andretti .20 .09
❑ 63 John Andretti .20 .09
❑ 64 John Andretti's Car .10 .05
❑ 65 Tim Brewer .10 .05
❑ 66 Brett Bodine .20 .09
❑ 67 Brett Bodine .20 .09
❑ 68 Brett Bodine's Car .10 .05
❑ 69 Rick Mast .20 .09
❑ 70 Rick Mast .20 .09
❑ 71 Rick Mast's Car .10 .05
❑ 72 Ward Burton .20 .09
❑ 73 Ward Burton .20 .09
❑ 74 Ward Burton's Car .10 .05
❑ 75 Lake Speed .20 .09
❑ 76 Lake Speed .20 .09
❑ 77 Lake Speed's Car .10 .05
❑ 78 Ricky Craven .20 .09
❑ 79 Ricky Craven .20 .09
❑ 80 Ricky Craven's Car .10 .05
❑ 81 Dick Trickle .20 .09
❑ 82 Dick Trickle .20 .09
❑ 83 Dick Trickle's Car .10 .05
❑ 84 Steve Grissom .20 .09
❑ 85 Steve Grissom .20 .09
❑ 86 Steve Grissom's Car .10 .05
❑ 87 Jimmy Spencer .20 .09
❑ 88 Jimmy Spencer .20 .09
❑ 89 Jimmy Spencer's Car .10 .05
❑ 90 Kyle Petty .40 .18
❑ 91 Kyle Petty .40 .18
❑ 92 Kyle Petty's Car .20 .09
❑ 93 Robert Pressley .20 .09
❑ 94 Robert Pressley .20 .09
❑ 95 Robert Pressley's Car .10 .05
❑ 96 Joe Nemechek .20 .09
❑ 97 Joe Nemechek .20 .09
❑ 98 Joe Nemechek's Car .10 .05
❑ 99 Jeremy Mayfield .60 .25
❑ 100 Jeremy Mayfield .60 .25
❑ 101 Jeremy Mayfield's Car .30 .14
❑ 102 Jeff Burton .40 .18
❑ 103 Jeff Burton .40 .18
❑ 104 Jeff Burton's Car .20 .09
❑ 105 Todd Bodine .20 .09
❑ 106 Todd Bodine .20 .09
❑ 107 Todd Bodine's Car .10 .05
❑ 108 Mike Wallace .20 .09
❑ 109 Mike Wallace .20 .09
❑ 110 Mike Wallace's Car .10 .05
❑ 111 Dave Marcis .40 .18
❑ 112 Dave Marcis .40 .18
❑ 113 Dave Marcis' Car .20 .09
❑ 114 Hut Stricklin .20 .09
❑ 115 Hut Stricklin .20 .09
❑ 116 Hut Stricklin's Car .10 .05
❑ 117 Ernie Irvan .40 .18
❑ 118 Ernie Irvan .40 .18
❑ 119 Ernie Irvan's Car .20 .09
❑ 120 Johnny Benson, Jr. .20 .09
❑ 121 Johnny Benson, Jr.'s Car .10 .05
❑ 122 Chad Little .20 .09
❑ 123 Chad Little's Car .10 .05
❑ 124 Mike McLaughlin .20 .09
❑ 125 Mike McLaughlin's Car .10 .05
❑ 126 Jeff Green .20 .09
❑ 127 Jeff Green's Car .10 .05
❑ 128 Jason Keller .20 .09
❑ 129 Jason Keller's Car .10 .05
❑ 130 Larry Pearson .20 .09
❑ 131 Larry Pearson's Car .10 .05
❑ 132 Phil Parsons .20 .09
❑ 133 Phil Parsons' Car .10 .05
❑ 134 Tim Fedewa .20 .09
❑ 135 Tim Fedewa's Car .10 .05
❑ 136 Elton Sawyer .20 .09
❑ 137 Elton Sawyer's Car .10 .05
❑ 138 Patty Moise .20 .09
❑ 139 Patty Moise's Car .10 .05
❑ 140 Rick Hendrick .10 .05
❑ 141 Richard Childress .10 .05
❑ 142 Jack Roush .10 .05
❑ 143 Larry McClure .10 .05
❑ 144 Roger Penske .10 .05
❑ 145 Joe Gibbs .20 .09
❑ 146 Richard Petty .50 .23
❑ 147 Bobby Allison .20 .09
❑ 148 Glen Wood .10 .05
❑ 149 Ricky Craven A .20 .09
❑ 150 Andy Petree A .10 .05
❑ 151 Ray Evernham A .10 .05
❑ 152 Jeff Gordon A 1.00 .45
❑ 153 Johnny Benson, Jr. A .20 .09
❑ 154 Chad Little A .20 .09
❑ 155 Bill Elliott A .50 .23
❑ 156 Ernie Irvan A .40 .18
❑ 157 Jeff Gordon's Helmet 1.00 .45
❑ 158 Geoff Bodine's Helmet .10 .05
❑ 159 Ted Musgrave's Helmet .10 .05
❑ 160 Derrike Cope's Helmet .10 .05
❑ 161 Rusty Wallace's Helmet .50 .23
❑ 162 Kyle Petty's Helmet .20 .09
❑ 163 Morgan Shepherd's Helmet .10 .05
❑ 164 Ricky Rudd's Helmet .20 .09
❑ 165 Mark Martin's Helmet .50 .23
❑ 166 Bobby Labonte's Helmet .40 .18
❑ 167 Daytona 500 Race Action .10 .05
❑ 168 Jeff Gordon's Car RW 1.00 .45
❑ 169 Terry Labonte RW .50 .23
❑ 170 Jeff Gordon RW 1.00 .45
Bobby Labonte
Terry Labonte
❑ 171 Bobby Labonte's Car RW .40 .18
❑ 172 Jeff Gordon RW 1.00 .45
Brooke Gordon
❑ 173 Dale Earnhardt RW 1.00 .45
❑ 174 Rusty Wallace's Car RW .50 .23
❑ 175 Dale Earnhardt's Car RW 1.00 .45
❑ 176 Dale Earnhardt 1.00 .45
Mark Martin's Car
❑ 177 Bobby Labonte's Car RW .40 .18
❑ 178 Kyle Petty RW .20 .09
❑ 179 UAW GM Teamwork 500 .10 .05
Race Action
❑ 180 Bobby Labonte RW .40 .18
❑ 181 Jeff Gordon's Car 1.00 .45
Race Action
❑ 182 Jeff Gordon's Car 1.00 .45
Race Action
❑ 183 Dale Jarrett RW .40 .18
❑ 184 Ken Schrader's Car RW .10 .05
❑ 185 Dale Earnhardt 1.00 .45
Teresa Earnhardt
❑ 186 Mark Martin's Car RW .50 .23
❑ 187 Dale Earnhart's Car RW 1.00 .45
❑ 188 Terry Labonte's Car RW .50 .23
❑ 189 Mountain Dew Southern 500 .10 .05
Darlington Race Action
❑ 190 Rusty Wallace's Car RW .50 .23
❑ 191 Jeff Gordon in Pits RW 1.00 .45
❑ 192 Dale Earnhardt RW 1.00 .45
❑ 193 Mark Martin RW .50 .23
❑ 194 Joe Nemechek's Car .10 .05
Race Action
❑ 195 Ward Burton RW .20 .09
❑ 196 Ricky Rudd RW .40 .18
❑ 197 Dale Earnhardt in Pits RW 1.00 .45
❑ 198 David Green w/Car .20 .09
❑ 199 Sterling Marlin .20 .09
Paula Marlin
Steadman Marlin
Sutherlin Marlin RW
❑ 200 Dale Earnhardt's Car 1.00 .45
Jeff Gordon's Car
Rusty Wallace's Car
Jimmy Spencer's Car
Ken Schrader's Car
Winston Select Race Action
❑ NNO Checklist #1 .10 .05
❑ NNO Checklist #2 .10 .05

1996 Ultra Autographs

This 37-card insert set features the top drivers on the Winston Cup circuit. The autographed cards have a front and back design that looks like a card in the regular set but the front of the card has a silver foil seal stating "Mark of Authenticity" in a circle surrounding the Ultra logo. The Ultra logo is also different than the one used on the regular card fronts. The back has the words " Certified

Autograph Card" and carries no number. An autograph redemption card was inserted one per 24 packs. This redemption card would have to be sent in to Fleer to obtain the actual autograph card. The cards have no numbers but are listed with numbers and in alphabetical order below. The autograph redemptions expired on 12/31/96.

	MINT	NRMT
COMPLETE SET (37)	1000.00	450.00
COMMON CARD	12.00	5.50
❑ 1 John Andretti	12.00	5.50
❑ 2 Johnny Benson	12.00	5.50
❑ 3 Brett Bodine	12.00	5.50
❑ 4 Geoff Bodine	12.00	5.50
❑ 5 Todd Bodine	12.00	5.50
❑ 6 Ward Burton	12.00	5.50
❑ 7 Derrike Cope	12.00	5.50
❑ 8 Ricky Craven	12.00	5.50
❑ 9 Dale Earnhardt	250.00	110.00
❑ 10 Bill Elliott	75.00	34.00
❑ 11 Jeff Gordon	200.00	90.00
❑ 12 Ernie Irvan	25.00	11.00
❑ 13 Dale Jarrett	50.00	22.00
❑ 14 Jason Keller	12.00	5.50
❑ 15 Bobby Labonte	50.00	22.00
❑ 16 Terry Labonte	75.00	34.00
❑ 17 Chad Little	12.00	5.50
❑ 18 Dave Marcis	12.00	5.50
❑ 19 Sterling Marlin	25.00	11.00
❑ 20 Mark Martin	75.00	34.00
❑ 21 Rick Mast	12.00	5.50
❑ 22 Jeremy Mayfield	40.00	18.00
❑ 23 Mike McLaughlin	12.00	5.50
❑ 24 Patty Moise	12.00	5.50
❑ 25 Ted Musgrave	12.00	5.50
❑ 26 Joe Nemechek	12.00	5.50
❑ 27 Kyle Petty	25.00	11.00
❑ 28 Richard Petty	35.00	16.00
❑ 29 Ricky Rudd	25.00	11.00
❑ 30 Elton Sawyer	12.00	5.50
❑ 31 Ken Schrader	12.00	5.50
❑ 32 Morgan Shepherd	12.00	5.50
❑ 33 Lake Speed	12.00	5.50
❑ 34 Jimmy Spencer	12.00	5.50
❑ 35 Dick Trickle	12.00	5.50
❑ 36 Rusty Wallace	75.00	34.00
❑ 37 Michael Waltrip	12.00	5.50

1996 Ultra Champions Club

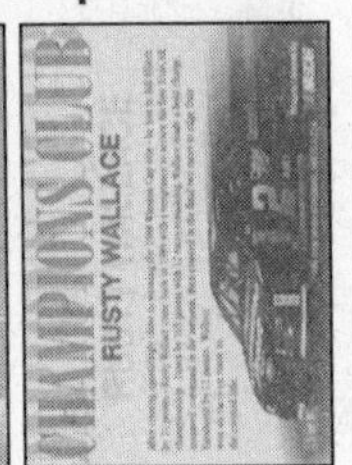

Randomly inserted in packs at a rate of one in six, this five-card set feature some of the former NASCAR Winston Cup Champions. The cards are printed on silver foil board and show both a picture of the driver and the current car they were driving.

	MINT	NRMT
COMPLETE SET (5)	10.00	4.50
COMMON CARD (1-5)	2.00	.90
*SINGLES: .75X TO 2X BASE CARD HI		
❑ 1 Rusty Wallace	2.00	.90
❑ 2 Dale Earnhardt	5.00	2.20
❑ 3 Bill Elliott	2.00	.90
❑ 4 Terry Labonte	2.00	.90
❑ 5 Jeff Gordon	5.00	2.20

1996 Ultra Flair Preview

This 10-card insert set pinpoints NASCAR's top drivers of '95 in a preview of Fleer's super-premium Flair product line. Randomly inserted in packs at a rate of one in 12 packs, each of these cards features 100% etched foil processing.

	MINT	NRMT
COMPLETE SET (10)	60.00	27.00
COMMON CARD (1-10)	1.25	.55
*SINGLES: 2.5X TO 6X BASE CARD HI		
❑ 1 Jeff Gordon	20.00	9.00
❑ 2 Dale Earnhardt	20.00	9.00
❑ 3 Sterling Marlin	2.50	1.10

❑ 4 Mark Martin	10.00	4.50
❑ 5 Rusty Wallace	10.00	4.50
❑ 6 Terry Labonte	10.00	4.50
❑ 7 Ted Musgrave	1.25	.55
❑ 8 Bill Elliott	10.00	4.50
❑ 9 Ricky Rudd	2.50	1.10
❑ 10 Bobby Labonte	2.50	1.10

1996 Ultra Golden Memories

This nine-card insert set highlights the '95 season's most memorable moments. The silver foil board the cards are printed on uses a checkered flag type background behind every front photo. The cards were randomly inserted in packs at a rate of one in six.

	MINT	NRMT
COMPLETE SET (9)	12.00	5.50
COMMON CARD (1-9)	.60	.25
*SINGLES: 1.25X TO 3X BASE CARD HI		
❑ 1 Ernie Irvan	1.25	.55
❑ 2 Ward Burton	.60	.25
❑ 3 Sterling Marlin	1.25	.55
❑ 4 Dale Earnhardt	6.00	2.70
❑ 5 Ken Schrader	.60	.25
❑ 6 Terry Labonte	3.00	1.35
❑ 7 Bobby Labonte	1.50	.70
❑ 8 Terry Labonte	3.00	1.35
❑ 9 John Andretti	.60	.25

1996 Ultra Season Crowns

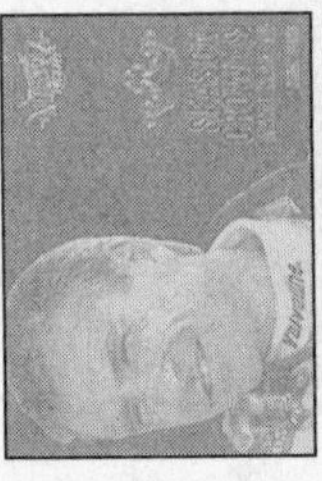

Randomly inserted in packs at a rate of one in four, this 15-card insert set features statistical leaders in areas such as wins, poles, most laps led and top 5 finishers from '95.

	MINT	NRMT
COMPLETE SET (15)	30.00	13.50
COMMON CARD (1-15)	.50	.23
*SINGLES: 1X TO 2.5X BASE CARD HI		
❑ 1 Terry Labonte	2.50	1.10
❑ 2 Jeff Gordon	5.00	2.20
❑ 3 Dale Earnhardt	5.00	2.20
❑ 4 Jeff Gordon	5.00	2.20
❑ 5 Dale Earnhardt	5.00	2.20
❑ 6 Mark Martin	2.50	1.10
❑ 7 Jeff Gordon	5.00	2.20
❑ 8 Mark Martin	2.50	1.10
❑ 9 Dale Earnhardt	5.00	2.20
❑ 10 Jeff Gordon	5.00	2.20
❑ 11 Jeff Gordon	5.00	2.20
❑ 12 Dale Earnhardt's Car Jeff Gordon's Car	2.50	1.10

❑ 13 Chad Little	.50
❑ 14 David Green	.50
❑ 15 Dale Earnhardt	5.00

1996 Ultra Thunder & Lightning

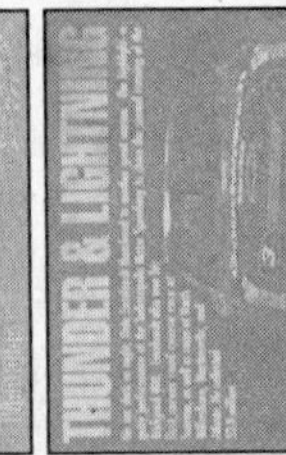

This 10-card insert set features teams generating th on the tracks and lightning in the pits. The carc multi-colored foil backgrounds to bring out the co NASCAR Winston Cup cars. The cards could be fou rate of one per four packs.

	MINT
COMPLETE SET (10)	12.00
COMMON CARD (1-10)	.30
*SINGLES: .6X TO 1.5X BASE CARD HI	
❑ 1 Brett Bodine's Car	.30
❑ 2 Brett Bodine's Car	.30
❑ 3 Jeff Gordon's Car	4.00
❑ 4 Jeff Gordon's Car	4.00
❑ 5 Dale Earnhardt's Car	4.00
❑ 6 Dale Earnhardt's Car	4.00
❑ 7 Sterling Marlin's Car	.60
❑ 8 Sterling Marlin's Car	.60
❑ 9 Bobby Labonte's Car	1.50
❑ 10 Bobby Labonte's Car	1.50

1996 Ultra Update

The 1996 Ultra Update set was issued in one totalling 100 cards. The 10-card packs retail fo each. The set contains the topical subsets: N Winston Cup Drivers (1-33), NASCAR Busch National Drivers (34-43), Hot Start (44-46), N Winston Cup Cars (47-79), Precious Metals (80- Fresh Start (84-98). The cards feature a large Ul in gold foil as the backdrop. The set updates the fi issue of 1996 by providing shots of driver chan sponsor changes. There were 24 packs per box boxes per case.

	MINT
COMPLETE SET (100)	12.00
COMMON CARD (1-100)	.10
COMMON DRIVER (1-100)	.20
❑ 1 John Andretti	.20
❑ 2 Johnny Benson Jr.	.20
❑ 3 Brett Bodine	.20
❑ 4 Geoff Bodine	.20
❑ 5 Jeff Burton	.40
❑ 6 Ward Burton	.20
❑ 7 Derrike Cope	.20
❑ 8 Ricky Craven	.20
❑ 9 Wally Dallenbach Jr.	.20
❑ 10 Dale Earnhardt	2.00
❑ 11 Bill Elliott	1.00
❑ 12 Jeff Gordon	2.00
❑ 13 Steve Grissom	.20
❑ 14 Bobby Hamilton	.20
❑ 15 Ernie Irvan	.40
❑ 16 Dale Jarrett	.75
❑ 17 Bobby Labonte	.75
❑ 18 Terry Labonte	1.00
❑ 19 Dave Marcis	.40
❑ 20 Sterling Marlin	.40

Mark Martin	1.00	.45
Rick Mast	.20	.09
Jeremy Mayfield	.60	.25
Ted Musgrave	.20	.09
Joe Nemechek	.20	.09
Kyle Petty	.40	.18
Robert Pressley	.20	.09
Ricky Rudd	.40	.18
Ken Schrader	.20	.09
Hut Stricklin	.20	.09
Kenny Wallace	.20	.09
Rusty Wallace	1.00	.45
Michael Waltrip	.20	.09
Glenn Allen Jr.	.20	.09
Rodney Combs	.20	.09
David Green	.20	.09
Randy LaJoie	.20	.09
had Little	.20	.09
urtis Markham	.20	.09
Mike McLaughlin	.20	.09
Patty Moise	.20	.09
hil Parsons	.20	.09
eff Purvis	.20	.09
Dale Jarrett HS	.40	.18
Dale Earnhardt HS	.75	.35
eff Gordon HS	.75	.35
ohn Andretti's Car	.10	.05
Johnny Benson's Car	.10	.05
rett Bodine's Car	.10	.05
eoff Bodine's Car	.10	.05
Jeff Burton's Car	.20	.09
Ward Burton's Car	.10	.05
errike Cope's Car	.10	.05
icky Craven's Car	.10	.05
Wally Dallenbach's Car	.10	.05
ale Earnhardt's Car	.75	.35
ill Elliott's Car	.40	.18
eff Gordon's Car	.75	.35
teve Grissom's Car	.10	.05
obby Hamilton's Car	.10	.05
rnie Irvan's Car	.20	.09
ale Jarrett's Car	.40	.18
obby Labonte's Car	.40	.18
erry Labonte's Car	.40	.18
ave Marcis' Car	.20	.09
terling Marlin's Car	.20	.09
Mark Martin's Car	.40	.18
ick Mast's Car	.10	.05
eremy Mayfield's Car	.40	.18
ed Musgrave's Car	.10	.05
oe Nemechek's Car	.10	.05
yle Petty's Car	.20	.09
obert Pressley's Car	.10	.05
icky Rudd's Car	.20	.09
en Schrader's Car	.10	.05
ut Stricklin's Car	.10	.05
enny Wallace's Car	.10	.05
usty Wallace's Car	.40	.18
chael Waltrip's Car	.10	.05
ale Earnhardt	1.00	.45
Olympic Car		
erry Labonte	.50	.23
ronman Car		
obby Hamilton	.10	.05
25th Anniversary		
ett Bodine	.10	.05
Gold Car		
ally Dallenbach	.10	.05
Jimmy Means		
ff Burton	.20	.09
Buddy Parrott		
le Jarrett	.40	.18
Todd Parrott		
t Stricklin	.10	.05
Philippe Lopez		
chael Waltrip	.10	.05
ddie Wood		
eonard Wood		
Shepherd	.10	.05
5 Team		
Remington Arms		
nny Wallace	.20	.09
nie Irvan	.40	.18
ck Mast	.20	.09
off Bodine	.20	.09
cky Rudd	.20	.09
Richard Broome		
ett Bodine	.10	.05
Ronnie Richeson		
le Earnhardt	1.00	.45
David Smith		
eve Grissom	.10	.05
Bill Ingle		
nny Benson	.20	.09
ecklist (1-100)	.10	.05
hecklist (inserts)	.10	.05

1996 Ultra Update Autographs

This 12-card insert set features the top names in NASCAR. The cards found in packs were redemption cards. These cards could be sent in to receive an autographed card of the driver who appeared on the front of the card. The redemption cards were seeded one in 100 packs.

	MINT	NRMT
COMPLETE SET (12)	800.00	350.00
COMMON CARD	12.00	5.50
❑ 1 Ricky Craven	12.00	5.50
❑ 2 Dale Earnhardt	250.00	110.00
❑ 3 Bill Elliott	70.00	32.00
❑ 4 Jeff Gordon	200.00	90.00
❑ 5 Ernie Irvan	25.00	11.00
❑ 6 Dale Jarrett	60.00	27.00
❑ 7 Bobby Labonte	60.00	27.00
❑ 8 Terry Labonte	70.00	32.00
❑ 9 Sterling Marlin	25.00	11.00
❑ 10 Mark Martin	70.00	32.00
❑ 11 Ted Musgrave	12.00	5.50
❑ 12 Rusty Wallace	70.00	32.00

1996 Ultra Update Proven Power

Randomly inserted in packs at a rate of one in 72, this 15-card set uses a reflective graphic design and 100 percent foil treatments to showcase the point leaders from the 1995 and 1996 seasons.

	MINT	NRMT
COMPLETE SET (15)	200.00	90.00
COMMON CARD (1-15)	5.00	2.20
*SINGLES: 10X TO 25X BASE CARD HI		
❑ 1 Ricky Craven	5.00	2.20
❑ 2 Dale Earnhardt	60.00	27.00
❑ 3 Bill Elliott	25.00	11.00
❑ 4 Jeff Gordon	60.00	27.00
❑ 5 Bobby Hamilton	5.00	2.20
❑ 6 Dale Jarrett	15.00	6.75
❑ 7 Bobby Labonte	10.00	4.50
❑ 8 Terry Labonte	25.00	11.00
❑ 9 Sterling Marlin	10.00	4.50
❑ 10 Mark Martin	25.00	11.00
❑ 11 Jeremy Mayfield	8.00	3.60
❑ 12 Ted Musgrave	5.00	2.20
❑ 13 Ricky Rudd	10.00	4.50
❑ 14 Ken Schrader	5.00	2.20
❑ 15 Rusty Wallace	25.00	11.00

1996 Ultra Update Rising Star

Randomly inserted in packs at a rate of one in four, this five-card set focuses on the newest drivers on the Winston Cup circuit. The cards use gold foil and thermo-embossed black ink to make the card have a tire like texture.

	MINT	NRMT
COMPLETE SET (5)	5.00	2.20
COMMON CARD (1-5)	1.00	.45
❑ 1 John Andretti	1.00	.45
❑ 2 Johnny Benson Jr.	1.00	.45
❑ 3 Jeff Burton	2.00	.90
❑ 4 Ricky Craven	1.00	.45
❑ 5 Jeremy Mayfield	2.00	.90

1996 Ultra Update Winner

Randomly inserted in packs at a rate of one in three, this 18-card set honors at least one winner from every track in the 1995 season. The cards feature a portrait of the winning driver on the front with track info and dates on the back.

	MINT	NRMT
COMPLETE SET (18)	25.00	11.00
COMMON CARD (1-18)	.40	.18
*SINGLES: .75X TO 2X BASE CARD HI		
❑ 1 Jeff Gordon	4.00	1.80
❑ 2 Terry Labonte	2.00	.90
❑ 3 Bobby Labonte	1.00	.45
❑ 4 Jeff Gordon	4.00	1.80
❑ 5 Sterling Marlin	.75	.35
❑ 6 Kyle Petty	.75	.35
❑ 7 Dale Earnhardt	4.00	1.80
❑ 8 Rusty Wallace	2.00	.90
❑ 9 Bobby Labonte	1.00	.45
❑ 10 Jeff Gordon	4.00	1.80
❑ 11 Mark Martin	2.00	.90
❑ 12 Ricky Rudd	.75	.35
❑ 13 Dale Jarrett	1.50	.70
❑ 14 Terry Labonte	2.00	.90
❑ 15 Ward Burton	.40	.18
❑ 16 Dale Earnhardt	4.00	1.80
❑ 17 Sterling Marlin	.75	.35
❑ 18 Mark Martin	2.00	.90

1996 Ultra Boxed Set

This 15-card set was issued by Fleer. The set comes in a grey and black checkered box and features the top names in Winston Cup racing. The sets were primarily sold through retail mail order catalogs.

	MINT	NRMT
COMPLETE SET (15)	15.00	6.75
COMMON CARD (1-15)	.50	.23
❑ 1 Jeff Gordon	4.00	1.80
❑ 2 Dale Earnhardt	4.00	1.80
❑ 3 Sterling Marlin	1.00	.45
❑ 4 Mark Martin	2.00	.90
❑ 5 Rusty Wallace	2.00	.90
❑ 6 Terry Labonte	2.00	.90
❑ 7 Ted Musgrave	.50	.23
❑ 8 Bill Elliott	2.00	.90
❑ 9 Ricky Rudd	1.00	.45
❑ 10 Bobby Labonte	1.50	.70
❑ 11 Morgan Shepherd	.50	.23
❑ 12 Michael Waltrip	.50	.23
❑ 13 Dale Jarrett	1.50	.70
❑ 14 Bobby Hamilton	.50	.23
❑ 15 Derrike Cope	.50	.23

1997 Ultra

This 100-card set features the same popular design Fleer used for the Baseball and Football Ultra lines. The cards use full-bleed photography with UV coating and foil stamping along with the driver's name written in script across the front of each card. The card contains an image of each driver and a still shot of his car superimposed over an action photo of the vehicle. There were 3,000 cases produced. The cards were packaged nine cards per pack, 24 packs per box and six boxes per case. There were three specially themed insert cards. Card #C1 is Terry Labonte, NASCAR Winston Cup Champion. The card was inserted at a rate of one in 180 packs. 500 of these cards were inserted into packs that carried an autograph redemption. Card # P1 is Bill Elliott, 1996 Most Popular Driver. This card was seeded one in 12 packs. Also, Johnny Benson, NASCAR Rookie of the Year, appears on card # R1. The Benson cards were randomly inserted one in 72 packs.

	MINT	NRMT
COMPLETE SET (100)	15.00	6.75
COMMON CARD (1-100)	.10	.05
COMMON DRIVER (1-100)	.20	.09

❑ 1 John Andretti	.20	.09
❑ 2 Johnny Benson	.20	.09
❑ 3 Brett Bodine	.20	.09
❑ 4 Geoff Bodine	.20	.09
❑ 5 Jeff Burton	.40	.18
❑ 6 Ward Burton	.20	.09
❑ 7 Derrike Cope	.20	.09
❑ 8 Ricky Craven	.20	.09
❑ 9 Wally Dallenbach	.20	.09
❑ 10 Dale Earnhardt	2.00	.90
❑ 11 Bill Elliott	1.00	.45
❑ 12 Jeff Gordon	2.00	.90
❑ 13 Bobby Hamilton	.20	.09
❑ 14 Bobby Hillin	.20	.09
❑ 15 Ernie Irvan	.40	.18
❑ 16 Dale Jarrett	.75	.35
❑ 17 Bobby Labonte	.75	.35
❑ 18 Terry Labonte	1.00	.45
❑ 19 Dave Marcis	.40	.18
❑ 20 Sterling Marlin	.40	.18
❑ 21 Mark Martin	1.00	.45
❑ 22 Rick Mast	.20	.09
❑ 23 Jeremy Mayfield	.60	.25
❑ 24 Ted Musgrave	.20	.09
❑ 25 Joe Nemechek	.20	.09
❑ 26 Kyle Petty	.40	.18
❑ 27 Robert Pressley	.20	.09
❑ 28 Ricky Rudd	.40	.18
❑ 29 Ken Schrader	.20	.09
❑ 30 Morgan Shepherd	.20	.09
❑ 31 Lake Speed	.20	.09
❑ 32 Jimmy Spencer	.20	.09
❑ 33 Hut Stricklin	.20	.09
❑ 34 Dick Trickle	.20	.09
❑ 35 Kenny Wallace	.20	.09
❑ 36 Rusty Wallace	1.00	.45
❑ 37 Michael Waltrip	.20	.09
❑ 38 Robby Gordon's Car	.10	.05
❑ 39 Terry Labonte's Car	.50	.23
❑ 40 Dale Jarrett's Car	.40	.18
❑ 41 Jeff Gordon's Car	1.00	.45
❑ 42 Mark Martin's Car	.50	.23
❑ 43 Dale Earnhardt's Car	1.00	.45
❑ 44 Ricky Rudd's Car	.20	.09
❑ 45 Sterling Marlin's Car	.20	.09
❑ 46 Rusty Wallace's Car	.50	.23
❑ 47 Bobby Hamilton's Car	.10	.05
❑ 48 Bill Elliott's Car	.50	.23
❑ 49 Bobby Labonte's Car	.40	.18
❑ 50 Jeremy Mayfield's Car	.40	.18
❑ 51 Johnny Benson's Car	.10	.05
❑ 52 Ted Musgrave's Car	.10	.05
❑ 53 Ricky Craven's Car	.10	.05
❑ 54 Ernie Irvan's Car	.20	.09
❑ 55 Michael Waltrip's Car	.10	.05
❑ 56 Jeff Burton's Car	.20	.09
❑ 57 Jimmy Spencer's Car	.10	.05
❑ 58 Bobby Allison	.20	.09
❑ 59 Richard Childress	.10	.05
❑ 60 Joe Gibbs	.20	.09
❑ 61 Rick Hendrick	.10	.05
❑ 62 Richard Petty	.50	.23
❑ 63 Jack Roush	.10	.05
❑ 64 Robert Yates	.10	.05
❑ 65 Cale Yarborough	.20	.09
❑ 66 Steve Hmiel	.10	.05
❑ 67 Mike Beam	.10	.05
❑ 68 David Smith	.10	.05
❑ 69 Eddie Wood Len Wood	.10	.05
❑ 70 Ray Evernham	.40	.18
❑ 71 Todd Parrott	.10	.05
❑ 72 Larry McReynolds	.10	.05
❑ 73 Tech Talk - Tires	.10	.05
❑ 74 Tech Talk - Fuel Cell	.10	.05
❑ 75 Tech Talk - Roof Flaps	.10	.05
❑ 76 Tech Talk - Motor	.10	.05
❑ 77 Tech Talk - Seat	.10	.05
❑ 78 Tech Talk - Rear Spoiler	.10	.05
❑ 79 Tech Talk - Generator	.10	.05
❑ 80 Tech Talk - Jack Stob	.10	.05
❑ 81 Tech Talk - Track Bar Hole	.10	.05
❑ 82 Todd Bodine	.20	.09
❑ 83 David Green	.20	.09
❑ 84 Jeff Green	.20	.09
❑ 85 Jason Keller	.20	.09
❑ 86 Randy LaJoie	.20	.09
❑ 87 Chad Little	.20	.09
❑ 88 Curtis Markham	.20	.09
❑ 89 Phil Parsons	.20	.09
❑ 90 Larry Pearson	.20	.09
❑ 91 Jeff Purvis	.20	.09
❑ 92 Mike McLaughlin	.20	.09
❑ 93 Patty Moise	.20	.09
❑ 94 Glenn Allen	.20	.09
❑ 95 Kevin Lepage	.20	.09
❑ 96 Rodney Combs	.20	.09
❑ 97 Tim Fedewa	.20	.09
❑ 98 Dennis Setzer	.20	.09
❑ 99 Checklist	.10	.05
❑ 100 Checklist	.10	.05
❑ C1 Terry Labonte	30.00	13.50
❑ C1A Terry Labonte Autograph	150.00	70.00
❑ P1 Bill Elliott	3.00	1.35
❑ R1 Johnny Benson	6.00	2.70

1997 Ultra AKA

This 10-card insert set captures the personalities of racing's very best drivers. The cards were randomly seeded one in 24 packs.

	MINT	NRMT
COMPLETE SET (10)	120.00	55.00
COMMON CARD (A1-A10)	2.50	1.10
*SINGLES: 5X TO 12X BASE CARD HI		

❑ A1 Dale Earnhardt	40.00	18.00
❑ A2 Jeff Gordon	40.00	18.00
❑ A3 Terry Labonte	20.00	9.00
❑ A4 Dale Jarrett	15.00	6.75
❑ A5 Bill Elliott	20.00	9.00
❑ A6 Mark Martin	20.00	9.00
❑ A7 Bobby Labonte	8.00	3.60
❑ A8 Ernie Irvan	5.00	2.20
❑ A9 Rusty Wallace	20.00	9.00
❑ A10 Ricky Craven	2.50	1.10

1997 Ultra Inside/Out

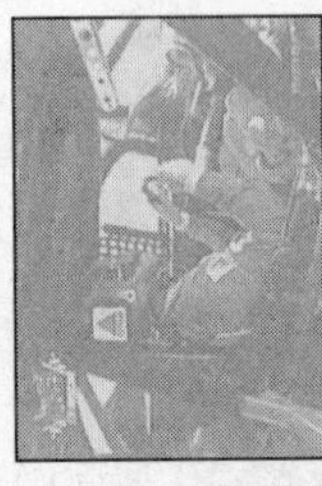

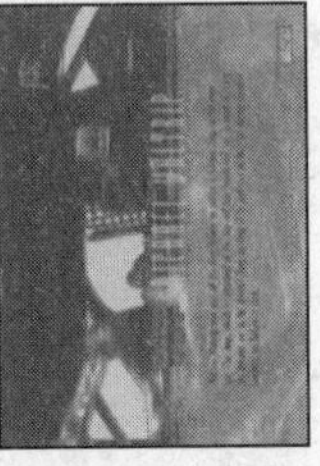

This 15-card set uses laser-cut technology to bring the action inside the car to life. The cards feature top names in NASCAR and were inserted one in six packs.

	MINT	NRMT
COMPLETE SET (15)	100.00	45.00
COMMON CARD (DC1-DC15)	1.50	.70
*SINGLES: 2.5X TO 6X BASE CARD HI		

❑ DC1 Dale Earnhardt	15.00	6.75
❑ DC2 Jeff Gordon	15.00	6.75
❑ DC3 Terry Labonte	8.00	3.60
❑ DC4 Dale Jarrett	6.00	2.70
❑ DC5 Bill Elliott	8.00	3.60
❑ DC6 Sterling Marlin	3.00	1.35
❑ DC7 Mark Martin	8.00	3.60
❑ DC8 Ernie Irvan	3.00	1.35
❑ DC9 Rusty Wallace	8.00	3.60
❑ DC10 Johnny Benson	1.50	
❑ DC11 Ricky Rudd	3.00	
❑ DC12 Bobby Labonte	4.00	
❑ DC13 Ricky Craven	1.50	
❑ DC14 Bobby Hamilton	1.50	
❑ DC15 Michael Waltrip	1.50	

1997 Ultra Shoney's

This 16-card set was offered through a special pro at Shoney's resturants. These cards maintain the design of the 1997 Ultra cards with the exception Shoney's logo on the top part of the card back.

	MINT
COMPLETE SET (16)	12.00
COMMON CARD (1-16)	.50

❑ 1 Johnny Benson	.50
❑ 2 Ward Burton	.50
❑ 3 Dale Earnhardt	3.00
❑ 4 Jeff Gordon	3.00
❑ 5 Bobby Hamilton	.50
❑ 6 Dale Jarrett	1.25
❑ 7 Bobby Labonte	1.25
❑ 8 Terry Labonte	1.50
❑ 9 Sterling Marlin	.75
❑ 10 Mark Martin	1.50
❑ 11 Ted Musgrave	.50
❑ 12 Ricky Rudd	.75
❑ 13 Michael Waltrip	.50
❑ 14 Hut Stricklin	.50
❑ 15 Richard Petty	1.00
❑ 16 Randy Lajoie	.50

1997 Ultra Update

This 97-card set was the second Ultra NASCAR se in 1997. The cards were distributed in nine car with 24 packs per box and 6 and 12 boxes per ca packs carried a suggested retail price of $2.49.

	MINT
COMPLETE SET (97)	15.00
COMMON CARD (1-97)	.10
COMMON DRIVER (1-97)	.20

❑ 1 Jeff Gordon	2.00
❑ 2 Dale Earnhardt	2.00
❑ 3 Dale Jarrett	.75
❑ 4 Mark Martin	1.00
❑ 5 Terry Labonte	1.00
❑ 6 Bill Elliott	1.00
❑ 7 Rusty Wallace	1.00
❑ 8 Ernie Irvan	.40
❑ 9 Sterling Marlin	.40
❑ 10 Bobby Hamilton	.20
❑ 11 Bobby Labonte	.75
❑ 12 John Andretti	.20
❑ 13 Robby Gordon	.20
❑ 14 Ken Schrader	.20
❑ 15 Michael Waltrip	.20
❑ 16 Ted Musgrave	.20
❑ 17 Ricky Rudd	.40
❑ 18 Johnny Benson	.20
❑ 19 Jeremy Mayfield	.60
❑ 20 Derrike Cope	.20
❑ 21 Ricky Craven	.20
❑ 22 Steve Grissom	.20

ick Mast	.20	.09
ick Trickle	.20	.09
enny Wallace	.20	.09
ut Stricklin	.20	.09
oe Nemechek	.20	.09
avid Green	.20	.09
organ Shepherd	.20	.09
obby Hillin	.20	.09
lenn Jarrett	.10	.05
ed Jarrett	.20	.09
enny Parsons	.10	.05
r. Jerry Punch	.10	.05
ave Despain	.10	.05
ill Weber	.10	.05
en Squire	.10	.05
ack Arute	.10	.05
arry McReynolds	.10	.05
ay Evernham	.40	.18
ike Beam	.10	.05
ary DeHart	.10	.05
mmy Fennig	.10	.05
arc Reno	.10	.05
oe Gibbs	.40	.18
ale Yarborough	.10	.05
ichard Petty	.50	.23
ndy Petree	.10	.05
ick Hendrick	.10	.05
ichard Childress	.10	.05
obert Yates	.10	.05
ack Roush	.10	.05
on Barfield	.10	.05
odd Bodine	.20	.09
m Fedewa	.20	.09
eff Fuller	.20	.09
eff Green	.20	.09
ason Keller	.20	.09
andy LaJoie	.20	.09
acy Leslie	.20	.09
evin Lepage	.20	.09
ike McLaughlin	.20	.09
eve Park	2.00	.90
il Parsons	.20	.09
ton Sawyer	.20	.09
enn Allen	.20	.09
ech Talk Helmet	.10	.05
ech Talk Front Grille	.10	.05
ech Talk Ground Clearance	.10	.05
ech Talk Air Filters	.10	.05
ech Talk Springs	.10	.05
ech Talk Dashboard	.10	.05
ech Talk Fuel Fillers	.10	.05
ech Talk Gloves	.10	.05
ech Talk War Wagon	.10	.05
usty Wallace's Car	.50	.23
ale Earnhardt's Car	1.00	.45
erling Marlin's Car	.40	.18
rry Labonte's Car	.50	.23
ark Martin's Car	.50	.23
ut Stricklin's Car	.10	.05
cky Rudd's Car	.40	.18
d Musgrave's Car	.10	.05
bby Labonte's Car	.40	.18
chael Waltrip's Car	.10	.05
ff Gordon's Car	1.00	.45
cky Craven's Car	.10	.05
nie Irvan's Car	.40	.18
hnny Benson's Car	.10	.05
n Schrader's Car	.10	.05
remy Mayfield's Car	.40	.18
eve Grissom's Car	.10	.05
bby Hamilton's Car	.10	.05
le Jarrett's Car	.40	.18
l Elliott's Car	.50	.23
ecklist	.10	.05
ecklist	.10	.05

7 Ultra Update Autograph

-card insert set contains autograph redemption om each driver in the base set. The cards were ly inserted in packs at a ratio of 1:25. The ion cards expired on 5/1/98.

	MINT	NRMT
ETE SET (44)	1200.00	550.00
N CARD	15.00	6.75

Gordon	175.00	80.00
Earnhardt	175.00	80.00
Jarrett	50.00	22.00
k Martin	60.00	27.00
y Labonte	60.00	27.00
Elliott	60.00	27.00
y Wallace	60.00	27.00
e Irvan	30.00	13.50
ing Marlin	30.00	13.50
bby Hamilton	15.00	6.75
bby Labonte	50.00	22.00
❑ 12 John Andretti	15.00	6.75
❑ 13 Robby Gordon	15.00	6.75
❑ 14 Ken Schrader	15.00	6.75
❑ 15 Michael Waltrip	15.00	6.75
❑ 16 Ted Musgrave	15.00	6.75
❑ 17 Ricky Rudd	30.00	13.50
❑ 18 Johnny Benson	15.00	6.75
❑ 19 Jeremy Mayfield	40.00	18.00
❑ 20 Derrike Cope	15.00	6.75
❑ 21 Ricky Craven	15.00	6.75
❑ 22 Steve Grissom	15.00	6.75
❑ 23 Rick Mast	15.00	6.75
❑ 24 Dick Trickle	15.00	6.75
❑ 25 Kenny Wallace	15.00	6.75
❑ 26 Hut Stricklin	15.00	6.75
❑ 27 Joe Nemechek	15.00	6.75
❑ 28 David Green	15.00	6.75
❑ 29 Morgan Shepherd	15.00	6.75
❑ 30 Bobby Hillin	15.00	6.75
❑ 53 Ron Barfield	15.00	6.75
❑ 54 Todd Bodine	15.00	6.75
❑ 55 Tim Fedewa	15.00	6.75
❑ 56 Jeff Fuller	15.00	6.75
❑ 57 Jeff Green	15.00	6.75
❑ 58 Jason Keller	15.00	6.75
❑ 59 Randy LaJoie	15.00	6.75
❑ 60 Tracy Leslie	15.00	6.75
❑ 61 Kevin Lepage	15.00	6.75
❑ 62 Mike McLaughlin	15.00	6.75
❑ 63 Steve Park	50.00	22.00
❑ 64 Phil Parsons	15.00	6.75
❑ 65 Elton Sawyer	15.00	6.75
❑ 66 Glenn Allen	15.00	6.75

1997 Ultra Update Double Trouble

This 8-card insert set features eight of the top drivers on both the Winston Cup and Busch circuits. The cards were randomly inserted in packs at a ratio of 1:4.

	MINT	NRMT
COMPLETE SET (9)	10.00	4.50
COMMON CARD (DT1-DT9)	.75	.35
*SINGLES: 1.5X TO 4X BASE CARD HI		

❑ DT1 Mark Martin	5.00	2.20
❑ DT2 Dick Trickle	.75	.35
❑ DT3 Bobby Labonte	2.50	1.10
❑ DT4 Ricky Craven	.75	.35
❑ DT5 Michael Waltrip	.75	.35
❑ DT6 Dale Jarrett	4.00	1.80
❑ DT7 Terry Labonte	5.00	2.20
❑ DT8 Joe Nemechek	.75	.35

1997 Ultra Update Driver View

This 10-card insert set offers an up-close view with laser cut cards into the window net of some of the top Winston Cup stars. The cards were randomly inserted in packs at a ratio of 1:8.

	MINT	NRMT
COMPLETE SET (10)	40.00	18.00
COMMON CARD (DV1-DV10)	1.25	.55
*SINGLES: 2.5X TO 6X BASE CARD HI		

❑ D1 Jeff Gordon	16.00	7.25
❑ D2 Dale Jarrett	8.00	3.60
❑ D3 Bill Elliott	10.00	4.50
❑ D4 Bobby Labonte	5.00	2.20
❑ D5 Sterling Marlin	2.50	1.10
❑ D6 Dale Earnhardt	16.00	7.25
❑ D7 Mark Martin	10.00	4.50
❑ D8 Terry Labonte	10.00	4.50
❑ D9 Ricky Rudd	2.50	1.10
❑ D10 Bobby Hamilton	1.25	.55

1997 Ultra Update Elite Seats

This 10-card set features ten of the top drivers on the Winston Cup circuit on special 40-point stock cards. The cards were randomly inserted in packs at a ratio of 1:12.

	MINT	NRMT
COMPLETE SET (10)	60.00	27.00
COMMON CARD (ES1-ES10)	1.50	.70
SEMISTARS	3.00	1.35
*SINGLES: 3X TO 8X BASE CARD HI		

❑ E1 Jeff Gordon	25.00	11.00
❑ E2 Dale Earnhardt	25.00	11.00
❑ E3 Bill Elliott	15.00	6.75
❑ E4 Ernie Irvan	3.00	1.35
❑ E5 Ricky Rudd	3.00	1.35
❑ E6 Dale Jarrett	12.00	5.50
❑ E7 Terry Labonte	15.00	6.75
❑ E8 Mark Martin	15.00	6.75
❑ E9 Rusty Wallace	15.00	6.75
❑ E10 Ricky Craven	1.50	.70

1983 UNO Racing

This 30-card promotional set features UNO sponsored cars from 1980-83 and the drivers who drove them. The cards usually have a photo of the driver standing next to the UNO car on the front of the card. The back of the card has the UNO logo and looks like a card from an UNO card game. The sets were originally distributed via give aways.

	MINT	NRMT
COMPLETE SET (30)	250.00	110.00
COMMON CARD (1-30)	4.00	1.80

❑ 1 Tim Richmond	6.00	2.70
❑ 2 Neil Bonnett	15.00	6.75
❑ 3 Tim Richmond	6.00	2.70
❑ 4 Lake Speed	4.00	1.80
❑ 5 D.K. Ulrich	4.00	1.80
❑ 6 Tim Richmond	6.00	2.70
❑ 7 Buddy Baker Ron Bouchard	4.00	1.80
❑ 8 Tim Richmond	6.00	2.70
❑ 9 Tim Richmond	6.00	2.70
❑ 10 Tim Richmond	6.00	2.70
❑ 11 Buddy Baker	4.00	1.80
❑ 12 Tim Richmond	6.00	2.70
❑ 13 Kyle Petty	6.00	2.70
❑ 14 Lake Speed	4.00	1.80
❑ 15 Tim Richmond	6.00	2.70
❑ 16 Kyle Petty	6.00	2.70
❑ 17 Tim Richmond	6.00	2.70
❑ 18 Tim Richmond	6.00	2.70
❑ 19 Kyle Petty	6.00	2.70
❑ 20 Buddy Baker	4.00	1.80
❑ 21 Buddy Baker	4.00	1.80
❑ 22 Tim Richmond	6.00	2.70
❑ 23 Richard Petty	30.00	13.50
❑ 24 Tim Richmond	6.00	2.70
❑ 25 Buddy Baker	4.00	1.80
❑ 26 Tim Richmond	6.00	2.70
❑ 27 Dale Earnhardt	75.00	34.00
❑ 28 Darrell Waltrip	15.00	6.75
❑ 29 Bobby Allison	15.00	6.75
❑ 30 Buddy Baker	4.00	1.80

1995 Upper Deck

Issued in two series over the first half of 1995, Upper Deck released both products through 10-card packs with 36-packs per box. Both series included several insert sets including the popular Predictor redemption cards and one Silver or Gold parallel card in every pack. Series one

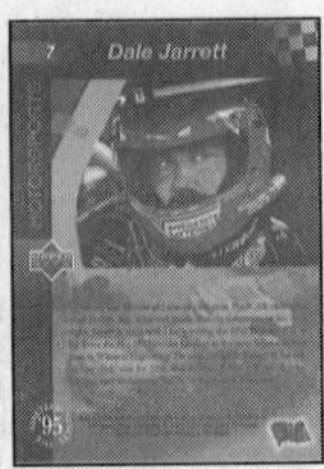

hobby packs featured a Jeff Gordon Salute card randomly inserted (1:108 packs) and the retail version a Sterling Marlin Salute (1:108 packs). A special Sterling Marlin Back-to-Back Salute card was randomly seeded in series two retail packs (1:108). As with most Upper Deck issues, subsets abound. Series one included Championship Pit Crew, Star Rookies, Images of '95 and Next in Line. Series two featured New for '95, Did You Know, Speedway Legends and more Star Rookies.

	MINT	NRMT
COMPLETE SET (300)	35.00	16.00
COMP.SERIES 1 SET (150)	20.00	9.00
COMP.SERIES 2 SET (150)	15.00	6.75
COMMON CARD (1-300)	.10	.05
COMMON DRIVER (1-300)	.20	.09

❑ 1 Rusty Wallace	1.00	.45
❑ 2 Jeff Gordon	2.00	.90
❑ 3 Bill Elliott	1.00	.45
❑ 4 Kyle Petty	.40	.18
❑ 5 Darrell Waltrip	.40	.18
❑ 6 Ernie Irvan	.40	.18
❑ 7 Dale Jarrett	.75	.35
❑ 8 Mark Martin	1.00	.45
❑ 9 Michael Waltrip	.20	.09
❑ 10 Rick Mast	.20	.09
❑ 11 Sterling Marlin	.40	.18
❑ 12 Chad Little	.20	.09
❑ 13 Geoff Bodine	.20	.09
❑ 14 Ricky Rudd	.40	.18
❑ 15 Lake Speed	.20	.09
❑ 16 Ted Musgrave	.20	.09
❑ 17 Morgan Shepherd	.20	.09
❑ 18 Bobby Labonte	.75	.35
❑ 19 Ken Schrader	.20	.09
❑ 20 Brett Bodine	.20	.09
❑ 21 Jimmy Spencer	.20	.09
❑ 22 Harry Gant	.40	.18
❑ 23 Dick Trickle	.20	.09
❑ 24 Derrike Cope	.20	.09
❑ 25 Kenny Wallace	.20	.09
❑ 26 Jeff Burton	.20	.09
❑ 27 Chuck Bown	.20	.09
❑ 28 John Andretti	.20	.09
❑ 29 Loy Allen Jr.	.20	.09
❑ 30 Hut Stricklin	.20	.09
❑ 31 Steve Grissom	.20	.09
❑ 32 Ward Burton	.20	.09
❑ 33 Robert Pressley	.20	.09
❑ 34 Joe Nemechek	.20	.09
❑ 35 Wally Dallenbach Jr.	.20	.09
❑ 36 Jeff Purvis	.20	.09
❑ 37 Terry Labonte	1.00	.45
❑ 38 Jimmy Hensley	.20	.09
❑ 39 Dave Marcis	.40	.18
❑ 40 Todd Bodine	.20	.09
❑ 41 Greg Sacks	.20	.09
❑ 42 Mike Wallace	.20	.09
❑ 43 Jeremy Mayfield	.60	.25
❑ 44 Rusty Wallace with Car	1.00	.45
❑ 45 Jeff Gordon with Car	2.00	.90
❑ 46 Bill Elliott with Car	1.00	.45
❑ 47 Kyle Petty with Car	.40	.18
❑ 48 Darrell Waltrip with Car	.40	.18
❑ 49 Ernie Irvan with Car	.40	.18
❑ 50 Dale Jarrett with Car	.75	.35
❑ 51 Mark Martin with Car	1.00	.45
❑ 52 Michael Waltrip with Car	.20	.09
❑ 53 Rick Mast with Car	.20	.09
❑ 54 Sterling Marlin with Car	.40	.18
❑ 55 Chad Little with Car	.20	.09
❑ 56 Geoff Bodine with Car	.20	.09
❑ 57 Ricky Rudd with Car	.40	.18
❑ 58 Lake Speed with Car	.20	.09
❑ 59 Ted Musgrave with Car	.20	.09
❑ 60 Morgan Shepherd with Car	.20	.09
❑ 61 Bobby Labonte with Car	.75	.35
❑ 62 Ken Schrader with Car	.20	.09
❑ 63 Brett Bodine with Car	.20	.09
❑ 64 Jimmy Spencer with Car	.20	.09
❑ 65 Harry Gant with Car	.40	.18
❑ 66 Dick Trickle with Car	.20	.09
❑ 67 Jeremy Mayfield with Car	.60	.25
❑ 68 Kenny Wallace with Car	.20	.09
❑ 69 Rusty Wallace's Car	.50	.23
❑ 70 Jeff Gordon's Car	1.00	.45
❑ 71 Bill Elliott's Car	.50	.23
❑ 72 Kyle Petty's Car	.20	.09
❑ 73 Darrell Waltrip's Car	.20	.09
❑ 74 Ernie Irvan's Car	.20	.09
❑ 75 Dale Jarrett's Car	.40	.18
❑ 76 Mark Martin's Car	.50	.23
❑ 77 Michael Waltrip's Car	.10	.05
❑ 78 Rick Mast's Car	.10	.05
❑ 79 Sterling Marlin's Car	.20	.09
❑ 80 Chad Little's Car	.10	.05
❑ 81 Geoff Bodine's Car	.10	.05
❑ 82 Ricky Rudd's Car	.20	.09
❑ 83 Lake Speed's Car	.10	.05
❑ 84 Ted Musgrave's Car	.10	.05
❑ 85 Morgan Shepherd's Car	.10	.05
❑ 86 Bobby Labonte's Car	.40	.18
❑ 87 Ken Schrader's Car	.10	.05
❑ 88 Brett Bodine's Car	.10	.05
❑ 89 Jimmy Spencer's Car	.10	.05
❑ 90 Harry Gant's Car	.20	.09
❑ 91 Dick Trickle's Car	.10	.05
❑ 92 Derrike Cope's Car	.10	.05
❑ 93 Kenny Wallace's Car	.10	.05
❑ 94 Jeff Burton's Car	.20	.09
❑ 95 Chuck Bown's Car	.10	.05
❑ 96 John Andretti's Car	.10	.05
❑ 97 Loy Allen Jr.'s Car	.10	.05
❑ 98 Hut Stricklin's Car	.10	.05
❑ 99 Steve Grissom's Car	.10	.05
❑ 100 Ward Burton's Car	.10	.05
❑ 101 Robert Pressley's Car	.10	.05
❑ 102 Joe Nemechek's Car	.10	.05
❑ 103 Wally Dallenbach Jr.'s Car	.10	.05
❑ 104 Jeff Purvis' Car	.10	.05
❑ 105 Terry Labonte's Car	.50	.23
❑ 106 Jimmy Hensley's Car	.10	.05
❑ 107 Dave Marcis' Car	.20	.09
❑ 108 Todd Bodine's Car	.10	.05
❑ 109 Greg Sacks' Car	.10	.05
❑ 110 Mike Wallace's Car	.10	.05
❑ 111 Jeremy Mayfield's Car	.40	.18
❑ 112 Rick Mast's Car NIL	.10	.05
❑ 113 Sterling Marlin's Car NIL	.20	.09
❑ 114 Bobby Labonte's Car NIL	.40	.18
❑ 115 Geoff Bodine NIL	.20	.09
❑ 116 Ricky Rudd's Car NIL	.20	.09
❑ 117 Lake Speed's Car NIL	.10	.05
❑ 118 Ted Musgrave's Car NIL	.10	.05
❑ 119 Morgan Shepherd's Car NIL	.10	.05
❑ 120 Ward Burton's Car NIL	.10	.05
❑ 121 Ken Schrader's Car NIL	.10	.05
❑ 122 Brett Bodine's Car NIL	.10	.05
❑ 123 Jimmy Spencer's Car NIL	.10	.05
❑ 124 Dick Trickle's Car NIL	.10	.05
❑ 125 Derrike Cope's Car NIL	.10	.05
❑ 126 Kenny Wallace NIL	.20	.09
❑ 127 John Andretti	.20	.09
❑ 128 Ward Burton	.20	.09
❑ 129 Steve Grissom	.20	.09
❑ 130 Jeremy Mayfield	.60	.25
❑ 131 Jeff Burton	.40	.18
❑ 132 Joe Nemechek	.20	.09
❑ 133 Michael Jordan CPC	5.00	2.20
❑ 134 Reggie Jackson CPC	.75	.35
❑ 135 Joe Montana CPC	2.00	.90
❑ 136 Ken Griffey Jr. CPC	3.00	1.35
❑ 137 Rusty Wallace's Car	.50	.23
❑ 138 Jeff Gordon's Car	1.00	.45
❑ 139 Bill Elliott's Car	.50	.23
❑ 140 Kyle Petty's Car	.20	.09
❑ 141 Darrell Waltrip's Car	.20	.09
❑ 142 Ernie Irvan's Car	.20	.09
❑ 143 Dale Jarrett's Car	.40	.18
❑ 144 Mark Martin's Car	.50	.23
❑ 145 Michael Waltrip's Car	.10	.05
❑ 146 Ford Engine	.10	.05
❑ 147 Chevy Engine	.10	.05
❑ 148 Pontiac Engine	.10	.05
❑ 149 Rusty Wallace CL	.50	.23
❑ 150 Rusty Wallace CL	.50	.23
❑ 151 Richard Petty SL	.40	.18
❑ 152 Cale Yarborough SL	.20	.09
❑ 153 Junior Johnson SL	.20	.09
❑ 154 Harry Gant SL	.20	.09
❑ 155 Bobby Allison SL	.20	.09
❑ 156 David Pearson SL	.20	.09
❑ 157 Ned Jarrett SL	.20	.09
❑ 158 Glen Wood SL	.10	.05
❑ 159 Benny Parsons SL	.20	.09
❑ 160 Smokey Yunick SL	.10	.05
❑ 161 Rusty Wallace DYK	.50	.23
❑ 162 Terry Labonte DYK	.50	.23
❑ 163 Jeff Gordon DYK	1.00	.45
❑ 164 Mark Martin DYK	.50	.23
❑ 165 Dale Jarrett DYK	.40	.18
❑ 166 Geoff Bodine DYK	.20	
❑ 167 Ricky Rudd DYK	.40	
❑ 168 Jeff Burton DYK	.20	
❑ 169 Sterling Marlin DYK	.40	
❑ 170 Darrell Waltrip DYK	.40	
❑ 171 Bobby Labonte DYK	.40	
❑ 172 Ken Schrader DYK	.20	
❑ 173 Kyle Petty DYK	.40	
❑ 174 John Andretti DYK	.20	
❑ 175 Ted Musgrave DYK	.20	
❑ 176 Randy LaJoie SR	.20	
❑ 177 Steve Kinser SR	.20	
❑ 178 Robert Pressley SR	.20	
❑ 179 Ricky Craven SR	.40	
❑ 180 Davy Jones SR	.20	
❑ 181 Rick Mast	.20	
❑ 182 Rusty Wallace	1.00	
❑ 183 Rusty Wallace	1.00	
❑ 184 Sterling Marlin	.40	
❑ 185 Terry Labonte	1.00	
❑ 186 Terry Labonte	1.00	
❑ 187 Mark Martin	1.00	
❑ 188 Mark Martin	1.00	
❑ 189 Geoff Bodine	.20	
❑ 190 Jeff Burton	.40	
❑ 191 Lake Speed	.20	
❑ 192 Ricky Rudd	.40	
❑ 193 Brett Bodine	.20	
❑ 194 Derrike Cope	.20	
❑ 195 Dick Trickle	.20	
❑ 196 Ted Musgrave	.20	
❑ 197 Darrell Waltrip	.40	
❑ 198 Bobby Labonte	.75	
❑ 199 Morgan Shepherd	.20	
❑ 200 Randy LaJoie	.20	
❑ 201 Jimmy Spencer	.20	
❑ 202 Jeff Gordon	2.00	
❑ 203 Ken Schrader	.20	
❑ 204 Steve Kinser	.20	
❑ 205 Loy Allen Jr.	.20	
❑ 206 Dale Jarrett	.75	
❑ 207 Ernie Irvan	.40	
❑ 208 Steve Grissom	.20	
❑ 209 Michael Waltrip	.20	
❑ 210 Ward Burton	.20	
❑ 211 Jimmy Hensley	.20	
❑ 212 Robert Pressley	.20	
❑ 213 John Andretti	.20	
❑ 214 Greg Sacks	.20	
❑ 215 Ricky Craven	.20	
❑ 216 Kyle Petty	.40	
❑ 217 Jeff Purvis	.20	
❑ 218 Gary Bradberry	.20	
❑ 219 Dave Marcis	.40	
❑ 220 Todd Bodine	.20	
❑ 221 Davy Jones	.20	
❑ 222 Kenny Wallace	.20	
❑ 223 Joe Nemechek	.20	
❑ 224 Mike Wallace	.20	
❑ 225 Bill Elliott	1.00	
❑ 226 Chad Little	.20	
❑ 227 Jeremy Mayfield	.60	
❑ 228 Rick Mast SD	.20	
❑ 229 Rusty Wallace SD	.50	
❑ 230 Sterling Marlin SD	.40	
❑ 231 Terry Labonte SD	.50	
❑ 232 Mark Martin SD	.50	
❑ 233 Geoff Bodine SD	.20	
❑ 234 Jeff Burton SD	.40	
❑ 235 Lake Speed SD	.20	
❑ 236 Ricky Rudd SD	.40	
❑ 237 Brett Bodine SD	.20	
❑ 238 Derrike Cope SD	.20	
❑ 239 Dick Trickle SD	.20	
❑ 240 Ted Musgrave SD	.20	
❑ 241 Darrell Waltrip SD	.40	
❑ 242 Bobby Labonte SD	.40	
❑ 243 Morgan Shepherd SD	.20	
❑ 244 Randy LaJoie SD	.20	
❑ 245 Jimmy Spencer SD	.20	
❑ 246 Jeff Gordon SD	1.00	
❑ 247 Ken Schrader SD	.20	
❑ 248 Steve Kinser SD	.20	
❑ 249 Loy Allen Jr. SD	.20	
❑ 250 Dale Jarrett SD	.40	
❑ 251 Steve Grissom SD	.20	
❑ 252 Michael Waltrip SD	.20	
❑ 253 Ward Burton SD	.20	
❑ 254 Jimmy Hensley SD	.20	
❑ 255 Robert Pressley SD	.20	
❑ 256 John Andretti SD	.20	
❑ 257 Greg Sacks SD	.20	
❑ 258 Ricky Craven SD	.40	
❑ 259 Kyle Petty SD	.40	
❑ 260 Gary Bradberry SD	.20	
❑ 261 Dave Marcis SD	.20	
❑ 262 Todd Bodine SD	.20	
❑ 263 Davy Jones SD	.20	

Kenny Wallace SD	.20	.09
Joe Nemechek SD	.20	.09
Mike Wallace SD	.20	.09
Bill Elliott SD	.50	.23
Chad Little SD	.20	.09
Jeremy Mayfield SD	.20	.09
Rusty Wallace's Car	.50	.23
Sterling Marlin's Car	.20	.09
Terry Labonte's Car	.50	.23
Geoff Bodine's Car	.10	.05
Jeff Burton's Car	.20	.09
Brett Bodine's Car	.10	.05
Dick Trickle's Car	.10	.05
Ted Musgrave's Car	.10	.05
Darrell Waltrip's Car	.20	.09
Bobby Labonte's Car	.20	.09
Randy LaJoie's Car	.10	.05
Jeff Gordon's Car	1.00	.45
Ken Schrader's Car	.10	.05
Steve Kinser's Car	.10	.05
Loy Allen Jr.'s Car	.10	.05
Dale Jarrett's Car	.40	.18
Steve Grissom's Car	.10	.05
Jimmy Hensley's Car	.10	.05
Robert Pressley's Car	.10	.05
John Andretti's Car	.10	.05
Greg Sacks' Car	.10	.05
Ricky Craven's Car	.20	.09
Kyle Petty's Car	.20	.09
Jeff Purvis' Car	.10	.05
Gary Bradberry's Car	.10	.05
Dave Marcis' Car	.20	.09
Davy Jones' Car	.10	.05
Kenny Wallace's Car	.10	.05
Joe Nemechek's Car	.10	.05
Bill Elliott's Car	.50	.23
Checklist (151-300)	.10	.05
Sterling Marlin Salute	12.00	5.50
Jeff Gordon Salute	30.00	13.50
Sterling Marlin BB Salute	12.00	5.50

1995 Upper Deck Gold Signature/Electric Gold

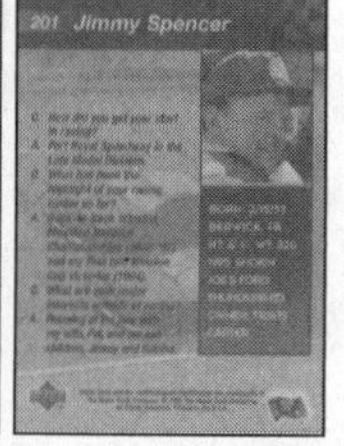

rallel cards were produced for both series of 1995 eck -- Gold Signature for series one and Electric series two. The parallel versions look very similar gular issue Upper Deck cards with the addition of gold foil facsimile signature or the word "Electric" foil on the card fronts. The Gold cards were y inserted at the wrapper stated rate of 1:35 packs r series.

	MINT	NRMT
TE GOLD SET (300)	1250.00	550.00
OLD SIG.SET (150)	750.00	350.00
LE.GOLD SET (150)	600.00	275.00
N CARD (1-300)	4.00	1.80
N DRIVER (1-300)	8.00	3.60

CARDS: 8X TO 20X BASIC CARDS

1995 Upper Deck Silver Signature/Electric Silver

rallel cards were produced for both series of per Deck -- Silver Signature for series one and Electric Silver for series two. The parallel versions look very similar to the regular issue Upper Deck cards with the addition of either a silver foil facsimile signature or the word "Electric" in refractive silver foil on the card fronts. The Silver cards were inserted at the wrapper stated rate of one per hobby or retail pack for either series and two per magazine distributor pack.

	MINT	NRMT
COMPLETE SILVER SET (300)	80.00	36.00
COMP.SILVER SIG.SET (150)	50.00	22.00
COMP.ELEC. SILV. SET (150)	30.00	13.50
COMMON CARD (1-300)	.20	.09
COMMON DRIVER (1-300)	.40	.18

*SILVER CARDS: 2X TO 3.5X BASIC CARDS

1995 Upper Deck Autographs

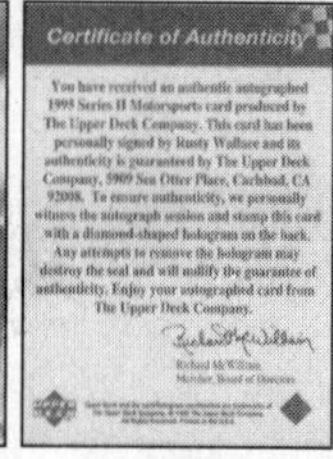

Randomly inserted in series two 1995 Upper Deck, the Autograph inserts were seeded approximately 1:300 packs. Reportedly, over 5000 total cards were signed for inclusion in packs.

	MINT	NRMT
COMPLETE SET (30)	1200.00	550.00
COMMON CARDS	30.00	13.50
❑ 181 Rick Mast	30.00	13.50
❑ 182 Rusty Wallace	100.00	45.00
❑ 186 Terry Labonte	100.00	45.00
❑ 187 Mark Martin	100.00	45.00
❑ 189 Geoff Bodine	30.00	13.50
❑ 190 Jeff Burton	50.00	22.00
❑ 191 Lake Speed	30.00	13.50
❑ 195 Dick Trickle	30.00	13.50
❑ 196 Ted Musgrave	30.00	13.50
❑ 197 Darrell Waltrip	50.00	22.00
❑ 199 Morgan Shepherd	30.00	13.50
❑ 201 Jimmy Spencer	30.00	13.50
❑ 202 Jeff Gordon	300.00	135.00
❑ 205 Loy Allen Jr.	30.00	13.50
❑ 206 Dale Jarrett	75.00	34.00
❑ 207 Ernie Irvan	50.00	22.00
❑ 208 Steve Grissom	30.00	13.50
❑ 209 Michael Waltrip	30.00	13.50
❑ 210 Ward Burton	30.00	13.50
❑ 212 Robert Pressley	30.00	13.50
❑ 213 John Andretti	30.00	13.50
❑ 214 Greg Sacks	30.00	13.50
❑ 215 Ricky Craven	30.00	13.50
❑ 216 Kyle Petty	50.00	22.00
❑ 219 Dave Marcis	30.00	13.50
❑ 220 Todd Bodine	30.00	13.50
❑ 222 Kenny Wallace	30.00	13.50
❑ 223 Joe Nemechek	30.00	13.50
❑ 224 Mike Wallace	30.00	13.50
❑ 225 Bill Elliott	100.00	45.00

1995 Upper Deck Illustrations

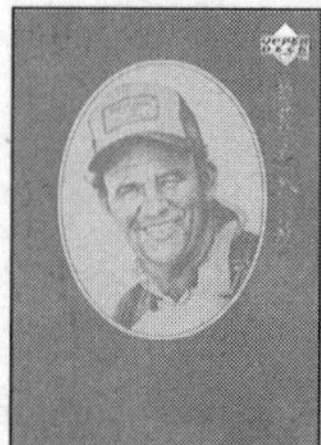

Illustrations cards were randomly inserted in Upper Deck series two hobby packs at the rate of 1:15 packs. The cards feauture portraits of ten legendary drivers painted by noted artists Jeanne Barnes and Jim Aukland.

	MINT	NRMT
COMPLETE SET (10)	30.00	13.50
COMMON CARD (I1-I10)	1.25	.55

*SINGLES: 2.5X TO 6X BASE CARD HI

❑ I1 Smokey Yunick	1.25	.55
❑ I2 Bobby Allison	2.50	1.10
❑ I3 Junior Johnson	1.25	.55
❑ I4 Cale Yarborough	2.50	1.10
❑ I5 David Pearson	1.25	.55
❑ I6 Benny Parsons	1.25	.55
❑ I7 Ned Jarrett	1.25	.55
❑ I8 Bill Elliott	8.00	3.60
❑ I9 Jeff Gordon	16.00	7.25
❑ I10 Rusty Wallace	8.00	3.60

1995 Upper Deck Oversized

Upper Deck issued the Oversized box inserts in two 5-card series. The cards could be found packaged one per at the bottom of each foil box of either series one or two 1995 Upper Deck. The cards are essentially an enlarged (5" X 7") version of a regular issue Upper Deck card. Complete series of 5-cards were offered on some Upper Deck packs in exchange for 15 wrappers and $3 per series.

	MINT	NRMT
COMPLETE SET (10)	30.00	13.50
COMMON CARD (OS1-OS10)	1.00	.45

*SINGLES: 2.5X TO 6X BASE CARD HI

❑ OS1 Rusty Wallace	5.00	2.20
❑ OS2 Kyle Petty	1.00	.45
❑ OS3 Jeff Gordon	12.00	5.50
❑ OS4 Mark Martin	5.00	2.20
❑ OS5 Ernie Irvan	1.00	.45
❑ OS6 Ken Schrader	1.00	.45
❑ OS7 Bill Elliott	5.00	2.20
❑ OS8 Geoff Bodine	1.00	.45
❑ OS9 Ricky Rudd	1.00	.45
❑ OS10 Terry Labonte	5.00	2.20

1995 Upper Deck Predictor Race Winners

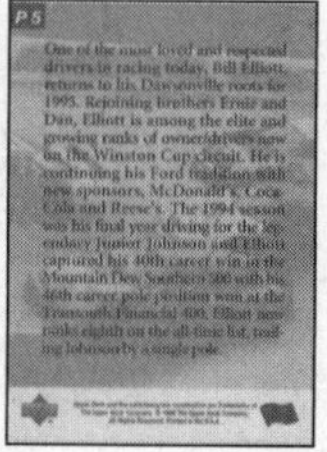

Upper Deck included its popular Predictor redemption cards in both series racing products. Series one packs included randomly inserted (1:18 packs) Predictor Race Winners cards. If the featured driver won any of the 31 Winston Cup races of 1995, the card (along with $3) could be exchanged for a special parallel set. A longshot card was included to cover races that none of the nine other driver cards won. The winning cards are designated below and often carry a slight premium since they were exchangeable. The parallel prize cards differ only on the cardbacks. Each prize card has a short driver biography as opposed to contest rules.The redemption game expired 2/1/96. Upper Deck produced a special Predictor Race Winner set for both the 1995 Daytona 500 and Coca-Cola 600 at Charlotte. The cards feature a gold foil stamp with the race date and use the same rules as the regular issue Predictor cards, except that the featured driver would have to win that specific race. The longshot wound up being the winning card for both races. Cards from these two versions typically sell for the same price as regular issue Predictors.

	MINT	NRMT
COMPLETE SET (10)	60.00	27.00
COMMON CARD (P1-P10)	1.50	.70

*SINGLES: 2.5X TO 6X BASE CARD HI

COMP. WIN PRIZE SET (10)	20.00	9.00

*PRIZE CARDS: 1X TO 2X BASIC CARDS

❑ P1 Rusty Wallace WIN	8.00	3.60
❑ P2 Mark Martin WIN	8.00	3.60
❑ P3 Ricky Rudd	7.00	3.10
❑ P4 Jeff Gordon WIN	15.00	6.75
❑ P5 Bill Elliott	8.00	3.60
❑ P6 Geoff Bodine	1.50	.70
❑ P7 Dale Jarrett WIN	5.00	2.20
❑ P8 Terry Labonte WIN	8.00	3.60
❑ P9 Jimmy Spencer	1.50	.70
❑ P10 Long Shot WIN	7.00	3.10

1995 Upper Deck Predictor Series Points

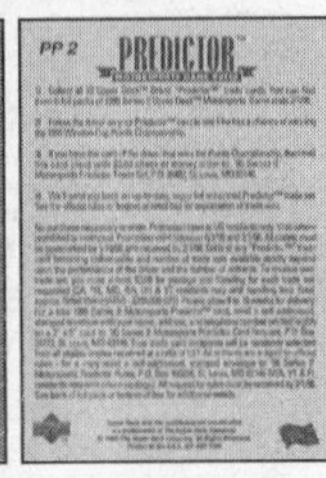

Upper Deck included its popular Predictor redemption cards in both series one and two racing products. Series two packs included randomly inserted (1:17 packs) Predictor Series Points cards. If the featured driver won the 1995 Winston Cup Points Championship, the card (along with $3) could be exchanged for a special parallel set. A longshot card was included to cover drivers not featured on individual cards. The winning card, Jeff Gordon, is designated below and often carries a slight premium since it was the only exchangeable card for the contest. The parallel prize cards differ only on the cardbacks. Each prize card has a short driver biography as opposed to contest rules.The redemption game expired 2/1/96.

	MINT	NRMT
COMPLETE SET (10)	30.00	13.50
COMMON CARD (PP1-PP10)	1.00	.45
*SINGLES: 2X TO 5X BASE CARD HI		
COMP. WIN PRIZE SET (10)	20.00	9.00
*PRIZE CARDS: 1X TO 2.5X BASE CARDS		

	MINT	NRMT
❑ PP1 Rusty Wallace	5.00	2.20
❑ PP2 Sterling Marlin	2.00	.90
❑ PP3 Terry Labonte	5.00	2.20
❑ PP4 Mark Martin	5.00	2.20
❑ PP5 Bobby Labonte	2.00	.90
❑ PP6 Jeff Gordon Winner Card	12.00	5.50
❑ PP7 Dale Jarrett	2.00	.90
❑ PP8 Kyle Petty	2.00	.90
❑ PP9 Bill Elliott	5.00	2.20
❑ PP10 Long Shot	1.00	.45

1996 Upper Deck

The 1996 Upper Deck set totals 150 cards. This is the second year of Upper Deck Motorsports. The set features the following topical subsets: Drivers (1-40), Scrapbook (41-80), Precision Performers (81-120) and The History Book (121-150). The product was available through both hobby and retail channels. There were 12 boxes per case with each box containing 28 packs. 10 cards came per pack and had a suggested retail of $1.99. In addition to numerous insert sets, Upper Deck produced two special Jeff Gordon single card inserts highlighting his championship 1995 season. Each of the cards features a die-cut design and light F/X printing. The cards were randomly inserted at the rate of 1:108 packs.

	MINT	NRMT
COMPLETE SET (150)	15.00	6.75
COMMON CARD (1-150)	.10	.05
COMMON DRIVER (1-150)	.20	.09

	MINT	NRMT
❑ 1 Rick Mast	.20	.09
❑ 2 Rusty Wallace	1.00	.45
❑ 3 Sterling Marlin	.40	.18
❑ 4 Terry Labonte	1.00	.45
❑ 5 Mark Martin	1.00	.45
❑ 6 Geoff Bodine	.20	.09
❑ 7 Jeff Burton	.40	.18
❑ 8 Lake Speed	.20	.09
❑ 9 Ricky Rudd	.40	.18
❑ 10 Brett Bodine	.20	.09
❑ 11 Derrike Cope	.20	.09
❑ 12 Bobby Hamilton	.20	.09
❑ 13 Dick Trickle	.20	.09
❑ 14 Ted Musgrave	.20	.09
❑ 15 Darrell Waltrip	.40	.18
❑ 16 Bobby Labonte	.75	.35
❑ 17 Morgan Shepherd	.20	.09
❑ 18 Chad Little	.20	.09
❑ 19 Jeff Purvis	.20	.09
❑ 20 Loy Allen Jr.	.20	.09
❑ 21 Jimmy Spencer	.20	.09
❑ 22 Jeff Gordon	2.00	.90
❑ 23 Ken Schrader	.20	.09
❑ 24 Hut Stricklin	.20	.09
❑ 25 Ernie Irvan	.40	.18
❑ 26 Dale Jarrett	.75	.35
❑ 27 Steve Grissom	.20	.09
❑ 28 Michael Waltrip	.20	.09
❑ 29 Ward Burton	.20	.09
❑ 30 Todd Bodine	.20	.09
❑ 31 Robert Pressley	.20	.09
❑ 32 Jeremy Mayfield	.60	.25
❑ 33 Mike Wallace	.20	.09
❑ 34 Bill Elliott	1.00	.45
❑ 35 John Andretti	.20	.09
❑ 36 Kenny Wallace	.20	.09
❑ 37 Joe Nemechek	.20	.09
❑ 38 Dave Marcis	.40	.18
❑ 39 Ricky Craven	.20	.09
❑ 40 Kyle Petty SB	.20	.09
❑ 41 Rick Mast SB	.10	.05
❑ 42 Rusty Wallace SB	.50	.23
❑ 43 Sterling Marlin SB	.20	.09
❑ 44 Terry Labonte SB	.50	.23
❑ 45 Mark Martin SB	.50	.23
❑ 46 Geoff Bodine SB	.10	.05
❑ 47 Jeff Burton SB	.20	.09
❑ 48 Lake Speed SB	.10	.05
❑ 49 Ricky Rudd SB	.20	.09
❑ 50 Brett Bodine SB	.10	.05
❑ 51 Derrike Cope SB	.10	.05
❑ 52 Bobby Hamilton SB	.10	.05
❑ 53 Dick Trickle SB	.10	.05
❑ 54 Ted Musgrave SB	.10	.05
❑ 55 Darrell Waltrip SB	.20	.09
❑ 56 Bobby Labonte SB	.40	.18
❑ 57 Morgan Shepherd SB	.10	.05
❑ 58 Ernie Irvan SB	.20	.09
❑ 59 Ernie Irvan SB	.20	.09
❑ 60 Ernie Irvan SB	.20	.09
❑ 61 Jimmy Spencer SB	.10	.05
❑ 62 Jeremy Mayfield SB	.40	.18
❑ 63 Mike Wallace SB	.10	.05
❑ 64 Ken Schrader SB	.10	.05
❑ 65 Hut Stricklin SB	.10	.05
❑ 66 Dale Jarrett SB	.40	.18
❑ 67 Steve Grissom SB	.10	.05
❑ 68 Michael Waltrip SB	.10	.05
❑ 69 Ward Burton SB	.10	.05
❑ 70 Todd Bodine SB	.10	.05
❑ 71 Robert Pressley SB	.10	.05
❑ 72 Jeff Gordon SB	1.00	.45
❑ 73 Jeff Gordon SB	1.00	.45
❑ 74 Bill Elliott SB	.50	.23
❑ 75 John Andretti SB	.10	.05
❑ 76 Kenny Wallace SB	.10	.05
❑ 77 Joe Nemechek SB	.10	.05
❑ 78 Dave Marcis SB	.20	.09
❑ 79 Ricky Craven SB	.10	.05
❑ 80 Kyle Petty PP	.20	.09
❑ 81 Rick Mast PP	.10	.05
❑ 82 Rusty Wallace PP	.50	.23
❑ 83 Sterling Marlin PP	.20	.09
❑ 84 Terry Labonte PP	.50	.23
❑ 85 Mark Martin PP	.50	.23
❑ 86 Geoff Bodine PP	.10	.05
❑ 87 Jeff Burton PP	.20	.09
❑ 88 Lake Speed PP	.10	.05
❑ 89 Ricky Rudd PP	.20	.09
❑ 90 Brett Bodine PP	.10	.05
❑ 91 Derrike Cope PP	.10	.05
❑ 92 Bobby Hamilton PP	.10	.05
❑ 93 Dick Trickle PP	.10	.05
❑ 94 Ted Musgrave PP	.10	.05
❑ 95 Darrell Waltrip PP	.20	.09
❑ 96 Bobby Labonte PP	.40	.18
❑ 97 Morgan Shepherd PP	.10	.05
❑ 98 Jeff Gordon PP	1.00	.45
❑ 99 Mark Martin PP	.50	.23
❑ 100 Michael Waltrip PP	.10	.05
❑ 101 Jimmy Spencer PP	.10	.05
❑ 102 Jeff Gordon PP	1.00	.45
❑ 103 Ken Schrader PP	.10	.05
❑ 104 Hut Stricklin PP	.10	.05
❑ 105 Ernie Irvan PP	.20	.09
❑ 106 Dale Jarrett PP	.40	.18
❑ 107 Steve Grissom PP	.10	.05
❑ 108 Michael Waltrip PP	.10	
❑ 109 Ward Burton PP	.10	
❑ 110 Todd Bodine PP	.10	
❑ 111 Robert Pressley PP	.10	
❑ 112 Jeremy Mayfield PP	.40	
❑ 113 Mike Wallace PP	.10	
❑ 114 Bill Elliott PP	.50	
❑ 115 John Andretti PP	.10	
❑ 116 Kenny Wallace PP	.10	
❑ 117 Joe Nemechek PP	.10	
❑ 118 Dave Marcis PP	.20	
❑ 119 Ricky Craven PP	.10	
❑ 120 Kyle Petty HB	.20	
❑ 121 Rick Hendrick HB	.10	
❑ 122 Jack Roush HB	.10	
❑ 123 Roger Penske HB	.10	
❑ 124 Joe Gibbs HB	.20	
❑ 125 Felix Sabates HB	.10	
❑ 126 Bobby Allison HB	.20	
❑ 127 Richard Petty HB	.40	
❑ 128 Cale Yarborough HB	.20	
❑ 129 Robert Yates HB	.10	
❑ 130 Darrell Waltrip HB	.20	
❑ 131 Bill Elliott HB	.50	
❑ 132 Geoff Bodine HB	.10	
❑ 133 Sterling Marlin HB	.20	
❑ 134 Ricky Rudd HB	.20	
❑ 135 Dave Marcis HB	.20	
❑ 136 Rusty Wallace HB	.50	
❑ 137 Ernie Irvan HB	.20	
❑ 138 Jeff Gordon HB	1.00	
❑ 139 Richard Petty HB	.40	
❑ 140 Ned Jarrett HB	.20	
❑ 141 Benny Parsons HB	.20	
❑ 142 Rusty Wallace HB	.50	
❑ 143 Jeff Burton HB	.20	
❑ 144 Smokey Yunick HB	.10	
❑ 145 Junior Johnson HB	.20	
❑ 146 Ken Schrader HB	.20	
❑ 147 Harry Gant HB	.20	
❑ 148 Rusty Wallace HB	.50	
❑ 149 Kyle Petty HB	.20	
❑ 150 Jeff Gordon HB	1.00	
❑ C1 Jeff Gordon Tribute	40.00	

1996 Upper Deck All-Pr

This 10-card set features the members of the Upp All-Pro team. The cards could be found on aver per every 36 packs of 1996 Upper Deck series one

	MINT
COMPLETE SET (10)	60.00
COMMON CARD (AP1-AP10)	1.25
COMMON DRIVER (AP1-AP10)	2.50
*SINGLES: 5X TO 12X BASE CARD HI	

	MINT
❑ AP1 Jeff Gordon	25.00
❑ AP2 Terry Labonte	14.00
❑ AP3 Ray Evernham	1.25
❑ AP4 Rick Hendrick	1.25
❑ AP5 Rusty Wallace	14.00
❑ AP6 Robin Pemberton	1.25
❑ AP7 Mark Martin	14.00
❑ AP8 Ted Musgrave	2.50
❑ AP9 Steve Hmiel	1.25
❑ AP10 Jack Roush	1.25

1996 Upper Deck Predic Poles

This 10-card interactive game set features nin plus one Longshot card. The object to the gam find a card for a driver who won any of the positions for a 1996 race. If you had a winning ca redeemable for a special version of all 1 Predictors. The cards came only in retail packs at one per 12 packs. The expiration date to redeem cards was 2/1/97. The redemption set was a 10 featuring the same fronts as the game ca difference is on the back. The cards are numbe RP10 just like the game cards but instead of hav

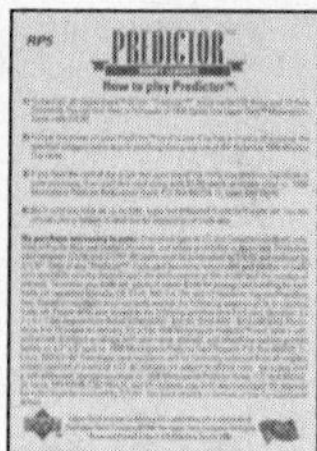

Predictor" game rules each card has a brief bio on
rticular driver.

	MINT	NRMT
LETE SET (10)	25.00	11.00
ON CARD (RP1-RP10)	.75	.35
LES: 2X TO 5X BASE CARD HI		
MPTION SET (10)	15.00	6.75
CARDS: 1X TO 2.5X BASE PREDICTOR CARDS		
Jeff Gordon WIN	12.00	5.50
Mark Martin WIN	8.00	3.60
Rusty Wallace	5.00	2.20
Ernie Irvan	1.50	.70
Bobby Labonte	3.00	1.35
Bill Elliott	6.00	2.70
Sterling Marlin	1.50	.70
Ricky Rudd	1.50	.70
Rick Mast	.75	.35
) Longshot WIN	.75	.35

996 Upper Deck Predictor Wins

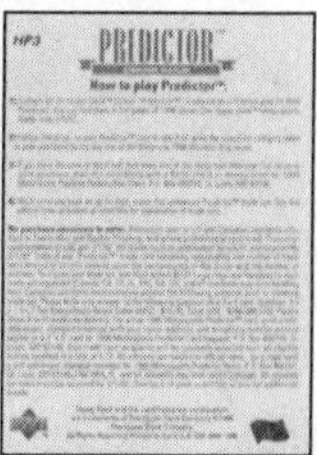

-card interactive game set features nine drivers e Longshot card. The object to the game was to card for a driver who won any of the 31 races in you had a winning card it was redeemable for a version of all 10 Hobby Predictors. The cards nly in hobby packs at a rate of one per 12 packs. ning cards expired for redemption on 2/1/97. The tion set was a 10-card set featuring the same s the game cards. The difference is on the back. ds are numbered HP1-HP10 just like the game ut instead of having "How to play Predictor" game ch card has a brief bio on that particular driver.

	MINT	NRMT
ETE SET (10)	30.00	13.50
N CARD (HP10-HP10)	.75	.35
ES: 2X TO 5X BASE CARD HI		
REDEMPTION SET (10)	15.00	6.75
ARDS: 1X TO 2.5X BASE PREDICTOR CARDS		
eff Gordon WIN	12.00	5.50
Rusty Wallace WIN	8.00	3.60
Sterling Marlin WIN	6.00	2.70
Bobby Labonte	3.00	1.35
Mark Martin	5.00	2.20
Ricky Rudd	1.50	.70
erry Labonte WIN	8.00	3.60
yle Petty	1.50	.70
ale Jarrett WIN	8.00	3.60
Longshot WIN	.75	.35

1996 Upper Deck Racing Legends

card set salutes the legends of racing as well as l future legends. The set was available across es in 1996. The cards are randomly inserted one acks.

	MINT	NRMT
TE SET (10)	25.00	11.00
RD (RCL1-RCL10)	2.50	1.10
Richard Petty	6.00	2.70

	MINT	NRMT
❑ RLC2 Cale Yarborough	5.00	2.20
❑ RLC3 Bobby Allison	2.50	1.10
❑ RLC4 Ned Jarrett	2.50	1.10
❑ RLC5 Dave Marcis	5.00	2.20
❑ RLC6 Junior Johnson	5.00	2.20
❑ RLC7 David Pearson	5.00	2.20
❑ RLC8 Harry Gant	5.00	2.20
❑ RLC9 Darrell Waltrip	5.00	2.20
❑ RLC10 Cover Card	2.50	1.10

1996 Upper Deck Virtual Velocity

This 15-card die-cut set features some of the top drivers in Winston Cup racing. The cards are die cut and feature light F/X processing. The cards were inserted at a rate of one per six packs. A parallel gold version was done of each card and was inserted at a rate of one per 72 packs.

	MINT	NRMT
COMPLETE SILVER SET (15)	30.00	13.50
COMMON CARD (VV1-VV15)	.75	.35
*SINGLES: 1.5X TO 4X BASE CARD HI		
COMPLETE GOLD SET (15)	150.00	70.00
GOLD CARDS: 6X TO 15X BASIC CARDS		
❑ VV1 Jeff Gordon	10.00	4.50
❑ VV2 Rusty Wallace	5.00	2.20
❑ VV3 Geoff Bodine	.75	.35
❑ VV4 Sterling Marlin	1.50	.70
❑ VV5 Terry Labonte		
❑ VV6 Mark Martin	5.00	2.20
❑ VV7 Bill Elliott		
❑ VV8 Darrell Waltrip	1.50	.70
❑ VV9 Ted Musgrave	.75	.35
❑ VV10 Ricky Rudd	1.50	.70
❑ VV11 Morgan Shepherd	.75	.35
❑ VV12 John Andretti	.75	.35
❑ VV13 Bobby Labonte	1.50	.70
❑ VV14 Michael Waltrip	.75	.35
❑ VV15 Kyle Petty	1.50	.70

1996 Upper Deck Jeff Gordon Profiles

This 20-card set features highlights from Jeff Gordon's racing career. The cards are 5" X 7" and were available through special retail outlets as well as hobby shops.

	MINT	NRMT
COMPLETE SET (20)	15.00	6.75
COMMON CARD (1-20)	1.00	.45

1998 Upper Deck Diamond Vision

This 15-card set focuses on 15 of the top driver in NASCAR utilizing motion technology. The Jeff Gordon Reeltime card was randomly inserted in packs at a ratio of 1:500. Cards were distirbuted in one card packs with 16 packs per box and 12 boxes per case. The packs carried a suggested retail price of $7.99.

	MINT	NRMT
COMPLETE SET (15)	75.00	34.00
COMMON CARD (1-15)	1.50	.70
❑ 1 Jeff Gordon	15.00	6.75
❑ 2 Rusty Wallace	8.00	3.60
❑ 3 Dale Earnhardt	15.00	6.75
❑ 4 Sterling Marlin	3.00	1.35
❑ 5 Terry Labonte	8.00	3.60
❑ 6 Mark Martin	8.00	3.60
❑ 7 Dale Jarrett	6.00	2.70
❑ 8 Bill Elliott	8.00	3.60
❑ 9 Ernie Irvin	3.00	1.35
❑ 10 Ricky Rudd	3.00	1.35
❑ 11 Jeff Burton	3.00	1.35
❑ 12 Ricky Craven	3.00	1.35
❑ 13 Bobby Labonte	6.00	2.70
❑ 14 Kyle Petty	3.00	1.35
❑ 15 Robby Gordon	1.50	.70
❑ RT1 Jeff Gordon	100.00	45.00

1998 Upper Deck Diamond Vision Signature Moves

This 15-card insert set is a parallel to the base set. This set features facsimile signatures on each card. The cards were randomly inserted in packs at a ratio of 1:3.

	MINT	NRMT
COMPLETE SET (15)	200.00	90.00
COMMON CARD (1-15)	5.00	2.20

1998 Upper Deck Diamond Vision Vision of a Champion

This 4-card insert set features four past Winston Cup champions. The cards were randomly inserted in packs at a ratio of 1:40.

	MINT	NRMT
COMPLETE SET (4)	175.00	80.00
COMMON CARD (VC1-VC4)	40.00	18.00
*SINGLES: 2X TO 5X BASE CARD HI		
❑ VC1 Rusty Wallace	40.00	18.00
❑ VC2 Dale Earnhardt	75.00	34.00
❑ VC3 Jeff Gordon	40.00	18.00
❑ VC4 Terry Labonte	40.00	18.00

1997 Upper Deck Hot Wheels

This 5-card set was produced by Upper Deck and made available by Toys 'R Us through a special point-of-purchase offer that would enable a collector to get the set of cards after buying $5.00 worth of Hot Wheels products.

	MINT	NRMT
COMPLETE SET (5)	5.00	2.20
COMMON CARD (HW1 - HW5)	1.00	.45
❑ HW1 Kyle Petty	1.50	.70
❑ HW2 Kyle Petty's Car	1.00	.45
❑ HW3 Kyle Petty's Car	1.00	.45
❑ HW4 Kyle Petty	1.50	.70
❑ HW5 Kyle Petty's Car	1.00	.45

1996 Upper Deck Road To The Cup

The 1996 Upper Deck Road To The Cup set was issued in one series totalling 150 cards. The 12-card packs had a suggested retail of $1.99 each. The set contains the topical subsets: Drivers (RC1-RC50), Screamin' Steel (RC51-RC90), Changin' Gears (RC91-RC120), Award Winner (RC121-RC135), Truckin' 96 (RC136-RC145) and Role Models (RC146-RC150). It is the first Upper Deck set to include Dale Earnhardt. In honor getting Dale inked Upper Deck went back and made a #301 card for its 1995 Upper Deck set. The card was seeded one in 95 packs. Also, they produced a Dale Earnhardt Tribute Card. This card was randomly inserted one in 190 packs. There is

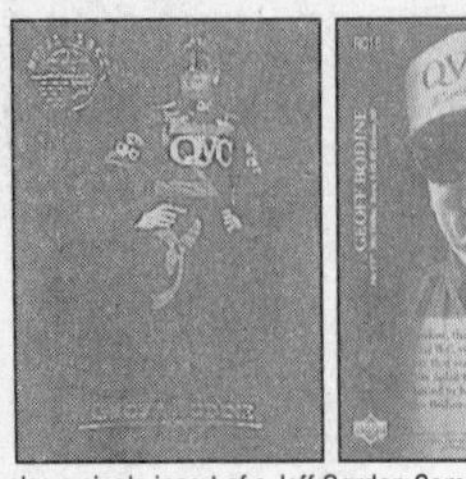

also a single insert of a Jeff Gordon Commemorative card. This card was inserted one in 72 packs and features 2-D technology.

	MINT	NRMT
COMPLETE SET (150)	20.00	9.00
COMMON CARD (RC1-RC150)	.10	.05
COMMON DRIVER (RC1-RC150)	.20	.09

	MINT	NRMT
❑ RC1 Jeff Gordon	2.00	.90
❑ RC2 Sterling Marlin	.40	.18
❑ RC3 Mark Martin	1.00	.45
❑ RC4 Rusty Wallace	1.00	.45
❑ RC5 Terry Labonte	1.00	.45
❑ RC6 Ted Musgrave	.20	.09
❑ RC7 Bill Elliott	1.00	.45
❑ RC8 Ricky Rudd	.40	.18
❑ RC9 Bobby Labonte	.75	.35
❑ RC10 Morgan Shepherd	.20	.09
❑ RC11 Michael Waltrip	.20	.09
❑ RC12 Dale Jarrett	.75	.35
❑ RC13 Bobby Hamilton	.20	.09
❑ RC14 Derrike Cope	.20	.09
❑ RC15 Geoff Bodine	.20	.09
❑ RC16 Ken Schrader	.20	.09
❑ RC17 John Andretti	.20	.09
❑ RC18 Darrell Waltrip	.40	.18
❑ RC19 Brett Bodine	.20	.09
❑ RC20 Kenny Wallace	.20	.09
❑ RC21 Ward Burton	.20	.09
❑ RC22 Lake Speed	.20	.09
❑ RC23 Ricky Craven	.20	.09
❑ RC24 Jimmy Spencer	.20	.09
❑ RC25 Steve Grissom	.20	.09
❑ RC26 Joe Nemechek	.20	.09
❑ RC27 Ernie Irvan	.40	.18
❑ RC28 Kyle Petty	.40	.18
❑ RC29 Johnny Benson	.20	.09
❑ RC30 Jeff Burton	.40	.18
❑ RC31 Mike Wallace	.20	.09
❑ RC32 Dave Marcis	.40	.18
❑ RC33 Hut Stricklin	.20	.09
❑ RC34 Bobby Hillin	.20	.09
❑ RC35 Elton Sawyer	.20	.09
❑ RC36 Loy Allen	.20	.09
❑ RC37 Rick Mast	.20	.09
❑ RC38 Jeff Purvis	.20	.09
❑ RC39 Robert Pressley	.20	.09
❑ RC40 Wally Dallenbach	.20	.09
❑ RC41 Jeremy Mayfield	.60	.25
❑ RC42 Dale Earnhardt	2.00	.90
❑ RC43 Chad Little	.20	.09
❑ RC44 Mike McLaughlin	.20	.09
❑ RC45 Jason Keller	.20	.09
❑ RC46 Randy LaJoie	.20	.09
❑ RC47 Tim Fedewa	.20	.09
❑ RC48 Jeff Fuller	.20	.09
❑ RC49 David Green	.20	.09
❑ RC50 Patty Moise	.20	.09
❑ RC51 Jeff Gordon's Car	1.00	.45
❑ RC52 Mark Martin's Car	.50	.23
❑ RC53 Rusty Wallace's Car	.50	.23
❑ RC54 Terry Labonte's Car	.50	.23
❑ RC55 Ted Musgrave's Car	.10	.05
❑ RC56 Bill Elliott's Car	.50	.23
❑ RC57 Ricky Rudd's Car	.20	.09
❑ RC58 Bobby Labonte's Car	.40	.18
❑ RC59 Morgan Shepherd's Car	.10	.05
❑ RC60 Michael Waltrip's Car	.10	.05
❑ RC61 Dale Jarrett's Car	.40	.18
❑ RC62 Bobby Hamilton's Car	.10	.05
❑ RC63 Derrike Cope's Car	.10	.05
❑ RC64 Geoff Bodine's Car	.10	.05
❑ RC65 Ken Schrader's Car	.10	.05
❑ RC66 John Andretti's Car	.10	.05
❑ RC67 Darrell Waltrip's Car	.20	.09
❑ RC68 Brett Bodine's Car	.10	.05
❑ RC69 Rick Mast's Car	.10	.05
❑ RC70 Ward Burton's Car	.10	.05
❑ RC71 Lake Speed's Car	.10	.05
❑ RC72 Ricky Craven's Car	.10	.05
❑ RC73 Jimmy Spencer's Car	.10	.05
❑ RC74 Chad Little's Car	.10	.05
❑ RC75 Joe Nemechek's Car	.10	.05
❑ RC76 Robert Pressley's Car	.10	.05
❑ RC77 Kyle Petty's Car	.20	.09
❑ RC78 Jeremy Mayfield's Car	.40	.18
❑ RC79 Jeff Burton's Car	.20	.09
❑ RC80 Mike Wallace's Car	.10	.05
❑ RC81 Dave Marcis's Car	.20	.09
❑ RC82 Hut Stricklin's Car	.10	.05
❑ RC83 Bobby Hillin's Car	.10	.05
❑ RC84 Elton Sawyer's Car	.10	.05
❑ RC85 Loy Allen's Car	.10	.05
❑ RC86 Kenny Wallace's Car	.10	.05
❑ RC87 Jeff Purvis's Car	.10	.05
❑ RC88 Ernie Irvan's Car	.20	.09
❑ RC89 Wally Dallenbach's Car	.10	.05
❑ RC90 Johnny Benson's Car	.10	.05
❑ RC91 Mark Martin	1.00	.45
❑ RC92 Rusty Wallace	1.00	.45
❑ RC93 Ricky Rudd	.40	.18
❑ RC94 Bobby Labonte	.75	.35
❑ RC95 Morgan Shepherd	.20	.09
❑ RC96 Michael Waltrip	.20	.09
❑ RC97 Dale Jarrett	.75	.35
❑ RC98 Bobby Hamilton	.20	.09
❑ RC99 Geoff Bodine	.20	.09
❑ RC100 Ken Schrader	.20	.09
❑ RC101 Darrell Waltrip	.40	.18
❑ RC102 Brett Bodine	.20	.09
❑ RC103 Rick Mast	.20	.09
❑ RC104 Ward Burton	.20	.09
❑ RC105 Lake Speed	.20	.09
❑ RC106 Jimmy Spencer	.20	.09
❑ RC107 Steve Grissom	.20	.09
❑ RC108 Joe Nemechek	.20	.09
❑ RC109 Robert Pressley	.20	.09
❑ RC110 Kyle Petty	.40	.18
❑ RC111 Jeremy Mayfield	.60	.25
❑ RC112 Jeff Burton	.40	.18
❑ RC113 Mike Wallace	.20	.09
❑ RC114 Dave Marcis	.40	.18
❑ RC115 Hut Stricklin	.20	.09
❑ RC116 Dick Trickle	.20	.09
❑ RC117 Loy Allen	.20	.09
❑ RC118 Kenny Wallace	.20	.09
❑ RC119 Wally Dallenbach	.20	.09
❑ RC120 Johnny Benson	.20	.09
❑ RC121 Jeff Gordon	2.00	.90
❑ RC122 Rick Hendrick	.10	.05
❑ RC123 Ray Evernham	.10	.05
❑ RC124 Jeff Gordon	2.00	.90
❑ RC125 Sterling Marlin	.40	.18
❑ RC126 Mark Martin	1.00	.45
❑ RC127 Rusty Wallace	1.00	.45
❑ RC128 Terry Labonte	1.00	.45
❑ RC129 Ted Musgrave	.20	.09
❑ RC130 Bill Elliott	1.00	.45
❑ RC131 Ricky Rudd	.40	.18
❑ RC132 Bobby Labonte	.75	.35
❑ RC133 Ricky Craven	.20	.09
❑ RC134 Bobby Hamilton	.20	.09
❑ RC135 Johnny Benson	.20	.09
❑ RC136 Ernie Irvan	.40	.18
❑ RC137 Geoff Bodine	.20	.09
❑ RC138 Geoff Bodine	.20	.09
❑ RC139 Todd Bodine	.20	.09
❑ RC140 Jimmy Hensley	.20	.09
❑ RC141 Darrell Waltrip	.40	.18
❑ RC142 Kenny Wallace	.20	.09
❑ RC143 Derrike Cope	.20	.09
❑ RC144 Ted Musgrave	.20	.09
❑ RC145 Mike Wallace	.20	.09
❑ RC146 Ricky Craven	.20	.09
❑ RC147 Jeff Burton	.20	.09
❑ RC148 Jeff Gordon	2.00	.90
❑ RC149 Jimmy Hensley	.20	.09
❑ RC150 Bobby Hamilton	.20	.09
❑ 301 Dale Earnhardt	25.00	11.00
❑ DE1 Dale Earnhardt	50.00	22.00
❑ JG1 Jeff Gordon	40.00	18.00

1996 Upper Deck Road To The Cup Autographs

Randomly inserted in hobby packs only at a rate of one in 16, this 29-card insert set features authentic signatures from the hottest motorsports drivers. Card # H7 was supposed to be Bill Elliott. Due to a crash at Talladega on April 28, 1996, Bill was unable to sign his cards and was dropped from the set.

	MINT	NRMT
COMPLETE SET (29)	700.00	325.00
COMMON CARD (H1-H30)	15.00	6.75

	MINT	NRMT
❑ H1 Jeff Gordon	250.00	110.00
❑ H2 Sterling Marlin	30.00	13.50
❑ H3 Mark Martin	75.00	34.00
❑ H4 Rusty Wallace	75.00	34.00
❑ H5 Terry Labonte	75.00	
❑ H6 Ted Musgrave	15.00	
❑ H8 Ricky Rudd	30.00	
❑ H9 Bobby Labonte	60.00	
❑ H10 Morgan Shepherd	15.00	
❑ H11 Michael Waltrip	15.00	
❑ H12 Dale Jarrett	60.00	
❑ H13 Bobby Hamilton	15.00	
❑ H14 Derrike Cope	15.00	
❑ H15 Geoff Bodine	15.00	
❑ H16 Ken Schrader	15.00	
❑ H17 John Andretti	15.00	
❑ H18 Darrell Waltrip	30.00	
❑ H19 Brett Bodine	15.00	
❑ H20 Kenny Wallace	15.00	
❑ H21 Ward Burton	15.00	
❑ H22 Lake Speed	15.00	
❑ H23 Ricky Craven	15.00	
❑ H24 Jimmy Spencer	15.00	
❑ H25 Steve Grissom	15.00	
❑ H26 Joe Nemechek	15.00	
❑ H27 Ernie Irvan	30.00	
❑ H28 Kyle Petty	30.00	
❑ H29 Johnny Benson	15.00	
❑ H30 Jeff Burton	30.00	

1996 Upper Deck Road To The Cup Diary of a Champion

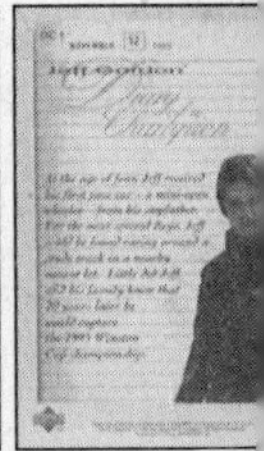

Randomly inserted in packs at a rate of one in 6, card insert set captures moments of "a day in the Jeff Gordon" both on and off the track.

	MINT
COMPLETE SET (10)	15.00
COMMON JEFF GORDON (DC1-DC10)	2.00

1996 Upper Deck Road To The Cup Game F

This 10-card insert set was available only in spec packs. The cards were inserted one per special ret

	MINT
COMPLETE SET (10)	10.00
COMMON CARD (GF1-GF10)	.75

*SINGLES: .75X TO 2X BASE CARD HI

	MINT
❑ GF1 Jeff Gordon	4.00
❑ GF2 Rusty Wallace	2.00
❑ GF3 Ernie Irvan	.75
❑ GF4 Dale Jarrett	1.50
❑ GF5 Terry Labonte	1.50
❑ GF6 Mark Martin	2.00
❑ GF7 Kyle Petty	.75
❑ GF8 Bobby Labonte	.75
❑ GF9 Bill Elliott	2.00
❑ GF10 Ricky Rudd	.75

1996 Upper Deck Road To The Cup Jumb

This five-card set was available through a redemption offer. The cards measure 5" X 7" an of the top names in Winston Cup.

	MINT	NRMT
LETE SET (5)	7.00	3.10
ON CARD (WC1-WC5)	1.00	.45
Jeff Gordon	3.00	1.35
Rusty Wallace	1.50	.70
Ernie Irvan	1.00	.45
Dale Jarrett	1.00	.45
Bill Elliott	1.50	.70

1996 Upper Deck Road To The Cup Leaders of the Pack

mly inserted in packs at a rate of one in 35, this rd insert set features the top motorsports drivers ing to miles and/or laps led.

	MINT	NRMT
LETE SET (5)	40.00	18.00
ON CARD (LP1-LP5)	4.00	1.80
LES: 4X TO 10X BASE CARD HI		
Jeff Gordon	20.00	9.00
Rusty Wallace	15.00	6.75
Ernie Irvan	8.00	3.60
Dale Jarrett	4.00	1.80
Terry Labonte		

1996 Upper Deck Road To The Cup Predictor Points

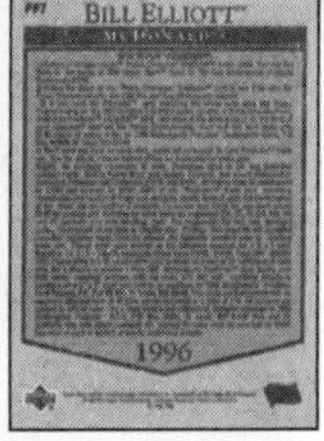

nly inserted in packs at a rate of one in 22. In this d insert set, the Terry Labonte card was the winning nd was redeemable for a special Championship Redemption set.

	MINT	NRMT
LETE SET (10)	30.00	13.50
ON CARD (PP1-PP10)	1.00	.45
LES: 2X TO 5X BASE CARD HI		
CARDS: 1.25X TO 3X BASE CARD HI		
Jeff Gordon	12.00	5.50
Sterling Marlin	2.00	.90
Mark Martin	4.00	1.80
Rusty Wallace	4.00	1.80
Terry Labonte WIN exp	15.00	6.75
Ted Musgrave	1.00	.45
Bill Elliott	4.00	1.80
Dale Jarrett	4.00	1.80
Bobby Labonte	2.00	.90
Longshot	1.00	.45

1996 Upper Deck Road To The Cup edictor Points Redemption

)-card set is the redemption for the winning Terry e card from the Predictor Points game. The cards gold micro-etched foil boarders coupled with

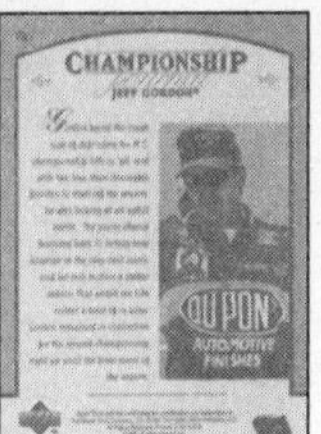

silver micro-etched backgrounds. The drivers photo is impossed on top of this silver background. Dale Earnhardt takes the place of the longshot card from the Predictor game.

	MINT	NRMT
COMPLETE SET (10)	20.00	9.00
COMMON CARD (PR1-PR10)	.50	.23
❑ PR1 Jeff Gordon	4.00	1.80
❑ PR2 Sterling Marlin	1.00	.45
❑ PR3 Mark Martin	2.00	.90
❑ PR4 Rusty Wallace	2.00	.90
❑ PR5 Terry Labonte	2.00	.90
❑ PR6 Ted Musgrave	.50	.23
❑ PR7 Bill Elliott	2.00	.90
❑ PR8 Dale Jarrett	1.50	.70
❑ PR9 Bobby Labonte	1.50	.70
❑ PR10 Dale Earnhardt	4.00	1.80

1996 Upper Deck Road To The Cup Predictor Top 3

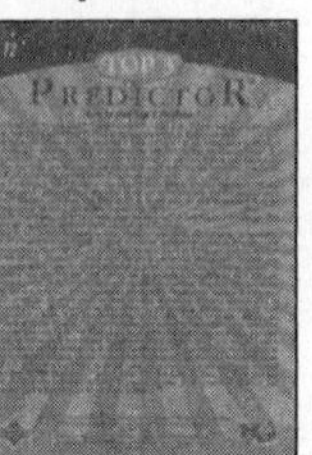

Randomly inserted in packs at a rate of one in 22. In this 10-card insert set, if the drivers whose helmets are pictured on the card finish in first, second and third in any order of any race in the 1996 season, that card is redeemable for a special 15-card set.

	MINT	NRMT
COMPLETE SET (10)	60.00	27.00
COMMON CARD (T1-T10)	2.00	.90
❑ T1 Jeff Gordon Rusty Wallace Terry Labonte	4.00	1.80
❑ T2 Terry Labonte Dale Jarrett Sterling Marlin	4.00	1.80
❑ T3 Jeff Gordon Ernie Irvan Longshot WIN	2.00	.90
❑ T4 Rusty Wallace Darrell Waltrip Longshot	4.00	1.80
❑ T5 Mark Martin Rusty Wallace Bobby Labonte	4.00	1.80
❑ T6 Sterling Marlin Jeff Gordon Longshot WIN	15.00	6.75
❑ T7 Jeff Gordon Mark Martin Johnny Benson		
❑ T8 Ricky Rudd Mark Martin Bill Elliott	4.00	1.80
❑ T9 Mark Martin Ted Musgrave Longshot	2.00	.90
❑ T10 Rusty Wallace Terry Labonte Kyle Petty	4.00	1.80

1996 Upper Deck Road To The Cup Predictor Top 3 Redemption

This 15-card set is the redemption prize for any of the winning Top 3 Predictor game cards. The cards feature individual drivers unlike the game which featured three driver's helmets per card. The cards are done in gold foil and have a portrait shot of the driver impossed over the top of the foil.

	MINT	NRMT
COMPLETE SET (15)	20.00	9.00
COMMON CARD (R1-R15)	.50	.23
❑ R1 Jeff Gordon	4.00	1.80
❑ R2 Rusty Wallace	2.00	.90
❑ R3 Ernie Irvan	1.50	.70
❑ R4 Sterling Marlin	1.00	.45
❑ R5 Terry Labonte	2.00	.90
❑ R6 Mark Martin	2.00	.90
❑ R7 Darrell Waltrip	1.00	.45
❑ R8 Bobby Labonte	1.50	.70
❑ R9 Dale Jarrett	1.50	.70
❑ R10 Ricky Rudd	1.00	.45
❑ R11 Bill Elliott	2.00	.90
❑ R12 Ted Musgrave	.50	.23
❑ R13 Kyle Petty	1.00	.45
❑ R14 Johnny Benson	.50	.23
❑ R15 Longshot	.50	.23

1996 Upper Deck Road To The Cup Racing Legends

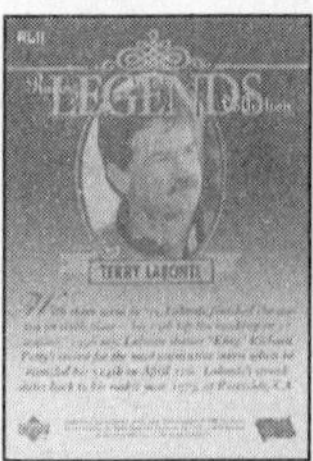

Randomly inserted in packs at a rate of one in 23, this 10-card insert set is a cross-brand chase set featuring active and retired motorsport drivers. The first ten cards from the Racing Legends series were inserted in 1996 Upper Deck.

	MINT	NRMT
COMPLETE SET (10)	50.00	22.00
COMMON CARD (RL11-RL20)	2.50	1.10
*SINGLES: 5X TO 12X BASE CARD HI		
❑ RL11 Terry Labonte	12.00	5.50
❑ RL12 Bobby Labonte	6.00	2.70
❑ RL13 Sterling Marlin	5.00	2.20
❑ RL14 Ernie Irvan	5.00	2.20
❑ RL15 Dale Jarrett	10.00	4.50
❑ RL16 Kyle Petty	5.00	2.20
❑ RL17 Geoff Bodine	2.50	1.10
❑ RL18 Ricky Rudd	5.00	2.20
❑ RL19 Ken Schrader	2.50	1.10
❑ RL20 Header	2.50	1.10

1997 Upper Deck Road To The Cup

This 150-card set features six topical subsets: Heroes of the Hardtop (1-45), Power Plants (46-89), Inside Track (90-104), Haulin' (105-120), Alternators (121-142), and Thunder Struck(143-150). Cards were distributed in ten

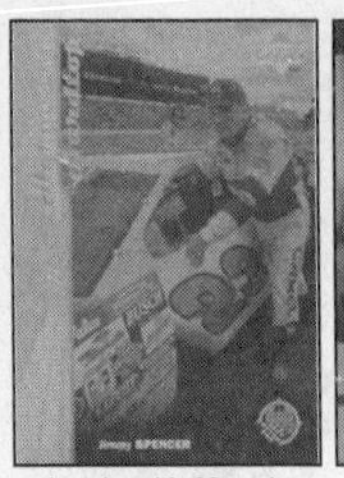
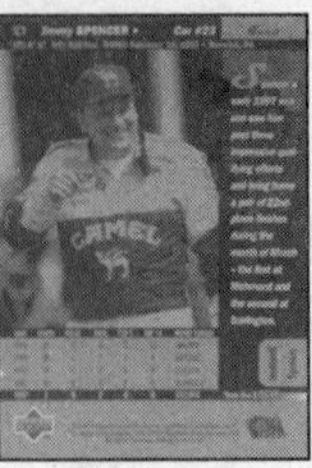

card packs with 28 packs per box and 12 boxes per case. The packs carried a suggested retail price of $2.49.

	MINT	NRMT
COMPLETE SET (150)	20.00	9.00
COMMON CARD (1-150)	.10	.05
COMMON DRIVER (1-150)	.20	.09

❑ 1 Terry Labonte	1.00	.45
❑ 2 Jeff Gordon	2.00	.90
❑ 3 Dale Jarrett	.75	.35
❑ 4 Dale Earnhardt	2.00	.90
❑ 5 Mark Martin	1.00	.45
❑ 6 Ricky Rudd	.40	.18
❑ 7 Rusty Wallace	1.00	.45
❑ 8 Sterling Marlin	.40	.18
❑ 9 Bobby Hamilton	.20	.09
❑ 10 Ernie Irvan	.40	.18
❑ 11 Bobby Labonte	.75	.35
❑ 12 Bill Elliott	1.00	.45
❑ 13 Kyle Petty	.40	.18
❑ 14 Ken Schrader	.20	.09
❑ 15 Jeff Burton	.40	.18
❑ 16 Michael Waltrip	.20	.09
❑ 17 Jimmy Spencer	.20	.09
❑ 18 Ted Musgrave	.20	.09
❑ 19 Geoff Bodine	.20	.09
❑ 20 Rick Mast	.20	.09
❑ 21 Morgan Shepherd	.20	.09
❑ 22 Ricky Craven	.20	.09
❑ 23 Johnny Benson	.20	.09
❑ 24 Hut Stricklin	.20	.09
❑ 25 Lake Speed	.20	.09
❑ 26 Brett Bodine	.20	.09
❑ 27 Wally Dallenbach	.20	.09
❑ 28 Jeremy Mayfield	.60	.25
❑ 29 Kenny Wallace	.20	.09
❑ 30 Darrell Waltrip	.40	.18
❑ 31 John Andretti	.20	.09
❑ 32 Robert Pressley	.20	.09
❑ 33 Ward Burton	.20	.09
❑ 34 Joe Nemechek	.20	.09
❑ 35 Derrike Cope	.20	.09
❑ 36 Dick Trickle	.20	.09
❑ 37 Dave Marcis	.40	.18
❑ 38 Steve Grissom	.20	.09
❑ 39 Mike Wallace	.20	.09
❑ 40 Chad Little	.20	.09
❑ 41 Gary Bradberry	.20	.09
❑ 42 David Green	.20	.09
❑ 43 Bobby Hillin	.20	.09
❑ 44 Terry Labonte's Car	.50	.23
❑ 45 Jeff Gordon's Car	1.00	.45
❑ 46 Dale Jarrett's Car	.40	.18
❑ 47 Mark Martin's Car	.50	.23
❑ 48 Ricky Rudd's Car	.20	.09
❑ 49 Rusty Wallace's Car	.50	.23
❑ 50 Sterling Marlin's Car	.20	.09
❑ 51 Bobby Hamilton's Car	.10	.05
❑ 52 Ernie Irvan's Car	.20	.09
❑ 53 Bobby Labonte's Car	.40	.18
❑ 54 Bill Elliott's Car	.50	.23
❑ 55 Kyle Petty's Car	.20	.09
❑ 56 Ken Schrader's Car	.10	.05
❑ 57 Jeff Burton's Car	.20	.09
❑ 58 Michael Waltrip's Car	.10	.05
❑ 59 Jimmy Spencer's Car	.10	.05
❑ 60 Ted Musgrave's Car	.10	.05
❑ 61 Geoff Bodine's Car	.10	.05
❑ 62 Rick Mast's Car	.10	.05
❑ 63 Morgan Shepherd's Car	.10	.05
❑ 64 Ricky Craven's Car	.10	.05
❑ 65 Johnny Benson's Car	.10	.05
❑ 66 Hut Stricklin's Car	.10	.05
❑ 67 Lake Speed's Car	.10	.05
❑ 68 Brett Bodine's Car	.10	.05
❑ 69 Wally Dallenbach's Car	.10	.05
❑ 70 Jeremy Mayfield's Car	.40	.18
❑ 71 Kenny Wallace's Car	.10	.05
❑ 72 Darrell Waltrip's Car	.20	.09
❑ 73 John Andretti's Car	.10	.05
❑ 74 Robert Pressley's Car	.10	.05
❑ 75 Ward Burton's Car	.10	.05
❑ 76 Joe Nemechek's Car	.10	.05
❑ 77 Derrike Cope's Car	.10	.05
❑ 78 Dick Trickle's Car	.10	.05
❑ 79 Dave Marcis's Car	.20	.09
❑ 80 Steve Grissom's Car	.10	.05
❑ 81 Mike Wallace's Car	.10	.05
❑ 82 Chad Little's Car	.10	.05
❑ 83 Gary Bradberry's Car	.10	.05
❑ 84 David Green's Car	.10	.05
❑ 85 Bobby Hillin's Car	.10	.05
❑ 86 Terry Labonte	1.00	.45
❑ 87 Jeff Gordon	2.00	.90
❑ 88 Dale Jarrett	.75	.35
❑ 89 Mark Martin	1.00	.45
❑ 90 Ricky Rudd	.40	.18
❑ 91 Rusty Wallace	1.00	.45
❑ 92 Sterling Marlin	.40	.18
❑ 93 Bobby Hamilton	.20	.09
❑ 94 Ernie Irvan	.40	.18
❑ 95 Bobby Labonte	.75	.35
❑ 96 Bill Elliott	1.00	.45
❑ 97 Kyle Petty	.40	.18
❑ 98 Ken Schrader	.20	.09
❑ 99 Jeff Burton	.40	.18
❑ 100 Ted Musgrave	.20	.09
❑ 101 Ricky Craven	.20	.09
❑ 102 Johnny Benson	.20	.09
❑ 103 Darrell Waltrip	.40	.18
❑ 104 John Andretti	.20	.09
❑ 105 Derrike Cope	.20	.09
❑ 106 Terry Labonte's Transporter	.50	.23
❑ 107 Jeff Gordon's Transporter	1.00	.45
❑ 108 Dale Jarrett's Transporter	.40	.18
❑ 109 Jeff Burton's Transporter	.20	.09
❑ 110 Ricky Rudd's Transporter	.20	.09
❑ 111 Sterling Marlin's Transporter	.20	.09
❑ 112 Rick Mast's Transporter	.10	.05
❑ 113 Michael Waltrip's Transpoter	.10	.05
❑ 114 Ken Schrader's Transporter	.10	.05
❑ 115 Steve Grissom's Transporter	.10	.05
❑ 116 Kyle Petty's Transporter	.20	.09
❑ 117 Darrell Waltrip's Transporter	.20	.09
❑ 118 Bobby Labonte's Transporter	.40	.18
❑ 119 Bill Elliott's Transporter	.50	.23
❑ 120 Chad Little's Transporter	.10	.05
❑ 121 Dale Earnhardt's Transporter	1.00	.45
❑ 122 Brett Bodine's Transporter	.10	.05
❑ 123 Geoff Bodine's Transporter	.10	.05
❑ 124 Rusty Wallace	1.00	.45
❑ 125 Sterling Marlin	.40	.18
❑ 126 Bobby Hamilton	.20	.09
❑ 127 Ernie Irvan	.40	.18
❑ 128 Bobby Labonte	.75	.35
❑ 129 Kyle Petty	.40	.18
❑ 130 Ken Schrader	.20	.09
❑ 131 Ted Musgrave	.20	.09
❑ 132 Rick Mast	.20	.09
❑ 133 Morgan Shepherd	.20	.09
❑ 134 Ricky Craven	.20	.09
❑ 135 Hut Stricklin	.20	.09
❑ 136 Lake Speed	.20	.09
❑ 137 Brett Bodine	.20	.09
❑ 138 Wally Dallenbach	.20	.09
❑ 139 Darrell Waltrip	.40	.18
❑ 140 Robert Pressley	.20	.09
❑ 141 Joe Nemechek	.20	.09
❑ 142 Derrike Cope	.20	.09
❑ 143 Steve Grissom	.20	.09
❑ 144 Mike Wallace	.20	.09
❑ 145 Chad Little	.20	.09
❑ 146 David Green	.20	.09
❑ 147 Mark Martin	1.00	.45
❑ 148 Ricky Rudd	.40	.18
❑ 149 Gary Bradberry	.20	.09
❑ 150 John Andretti	.20	.09

1997 Upper Deck Road To The Cup Cup Quest

This 10-card insert set features the top stars from the Winston Cup circuit. Each card in this set of serial numbered 1 of 5,000.

	MINT
COMPLETE SET (10)	60.00
COMMON CARD (CQ1-CQ10)	1.50
*SINGLES: 2.5X TO 6X BASE CARD HI	

❑ CQ1 Terry Labonte	20.00
❑ CQ2 Jeff Gordon	40.00
❑ CQ3 Dale Earnhardt	40.00
❑ CQ4 Dale Jarrett	15.00
❑ CQ5 Rusty Wallace	20.00
❑ CQ6 Ernie Irvan	3.00
❑ CQ7 Mark Martin	20.00
❑ CQ8 Sterling Marlin	3.00
❑ CQ9 Bobby Hamilton	1.50
❑ CQ10 Ricky Rudd	3.00

1997 Upper Deck Road To The Cup Cup Quest Checkered

This 10-card insert set is a parallel of the base(Gree Quest set. Each card features a diecut design checkered border around the drivers' pictures. Eac is hand numbered of 100.

	MINT
COMPLETE SET (10)	1500.00
COMMON CARD (CQ1-CQ10)	35.00

1997 Upper Deck Road To The Cup Cup Quest White

This 10-card insert set is a parallel of the base(Gree Quest set. Each card is individually numbered of 1,0

	MINT
COMPLETE SET (10)	120.00
COMMON CARD (CQ1-CQ10)	3.00

1997 Upper Deck Road To The Cup Million Dollar Memoirs

This 20-card set features five of top driver on the W Cup circuit. Each driver has four cards in the s cards were randomly inserted in packs at a ratio of

	MINT
COMPLETE SET (20)	150.00
COMMON CARD (MM1-MM20)	8.00
*SINGLES: 4X TO 10X BASE CARD HI	

❑ MM1 Terry Labonte	10.00
❑ MM2 Terry Labonte	10.00
❑ MM3 Terry Labonte	10.00
❑ MM4 Terry Labonte	10.00
❑ MM5 Jeff Gordon	20.00
❑ MM6 Jeff Gordon	20.00
❑ MM7 Jeff Gordon	20.00
❑ MM8 Rusty Wallace	10.00
❑ MM9 Rusty Wallace	10.00
❑ MM10 Rusty Wallace	10.00
❑ MM11 Rusty Wallace	10.00

2 Rusty Wallace	10.00	4.50
3 Dale Jarrett	8.00	3.60
4 Dale Jarrett	8.00	3.60
5 Dale Jarrett	8.00	3.60
6 Dale Jarrett	8.00	3.60
7 Bill Elliott	10.00	4.50
8 Bill Elliott	10.00	4.50
9 Bill Elliott	10.00	4.50
:0 Bill Elliott	10.00	4.50

1997 Upper Deck Road To The Cup Million Dollar Memoirs Autographs

)-card set is a parallel to the base Million Dollar rs set. Each card in this set is autographed. The vere randomly inserted in packs at a ratio of 1:109.

	MINT	NRMT
.ETE SET (20)	1200.00	550.00
ON CARD (MM1-MM20)	60.00	27.00
Terry Labonte	80.00	36.00
: Terry Labonte	80.00	36.00
Terry Labonte	80.00	36.00
Terry Labonte	80.00	36.00
Jeff Gordon	150.00	70.00
Jeff Gordon	150.00	70.00
' Jeff Gordon	150.00	70.00
Rusty Wallace	80.00	36.00
Rusty Wallace	80.00	36.00
0 Rusty Wallace	80.00	36.00
1 Rusty Wallace	80.00	36.00
2 Rusty Wallace	80.00	36.00
3 Dale Jarrett	60.00	27.00
4 Dale Jarrett	60.00	27.00
5 Dale Jarrett	60.00	27.00
6 Dale Jarrett	60.00	27.00
7 Bill Elliott	80.00	36.00
8 Bill Elliott	80.00	36.00
9 Bill Elliott	80.00	36.00
:0 Bill Elliott	80.00	36.00

1997 Upper Deck Road To The Cup Piece of the Action

·card set features pieces of a driver's seat, safety s and window net incorporated into a trading card. ·ds were seeded one in 1,117 packs.

	MINT	NRMT
.ETE SET (9)	1500.00	700.00
ON CARD (1-9)	125.00	55.00
f Gordon Seat Cover	300.00	135.00
f Gordon Shoulder Harness	300.00	135.00
f Gordon Window Net	300.00	135.00
le Jarrett Seat Cover	125.00	55.00
le Jarrett Shoulder Harness	125.00	55.00
le Jarrett Window Net	125.00	55.00
sty Wallace Seat Cover	150.00	70.00
sty Wallace Shoulder Harness	150.00	70.00
sty Wallace Window Net	150.00	70.00

1997 Upper Deck Road To The Cup Predictor Plus

·-card set features a scratch-off redemption game ve collectors three chances to win. Each card has scratch off areas that correspond to Starting n, Laps Led, and Finish Position. There are three of prizes available for the winning cards. The cards winners in one area could be redemmed for a cel that driver. The cards that are winners in two areas could be redemmed for a complete set of die-cut cel cards. The cards that are winners in all three areas could be redemmed for a complete set of cel cards and a complete base set of 1997 Upper Deck Road to the Cup. The prices below are for unscratched cards. These cards expired on 1/30/98. The cards were randomly inserted in packs at a ratio of 1:11.

	MINT	NRMT
COMPLETE SET (30)	100.00	45.00
COMMON CARD (+1-+30)	.75	.35

*SINGLES: 1.5X TO 4X BASE CARD HI

❑ +1 Terry Labonte	5.00	2.20
❑ +2 Jeff Gordon	8.00	3.60
❑ +3 Dale Jarrett	4.00	1.80
❑ +4 Sterling Marlin WIN	3.00	1.35
❑ +5 Ricky Craven	.75	.35
❑ +6 Ernie Irvan WIN	3.00	1.35
❑ +7 Rusty Wallace	5.00	2.20
❑ +8 Mark Martin	5.00	2.20
❑ +9 Terry Labonte	5.00	2.20
❑ +10 Bill Elliott	5.00	2.20
❑ +11 Jeff Gordon WIN	10.00	4.50
❑ +12 Geoff Bodine WIN 3	3.00	1.35
❑ +13 Dale Jarrett WIN	5.00	2.20
❑ +14 Rusty Wallace	5.00	2.20
❑ +15 Jeremy Mayfield	1.25	.55
❑ +16 Mark Martin	5.00	2.20
❑ +17 Ken Schrader WIN	3.00	1.35
❑ +18 Jimmy Spencer WIN	3.00	1.35
❑ +19 Ted Musgrave	.75	.35
❑ +20 Darrell Waltrip	1.50	.70
❑ +21 Jeff Burton	1.50	.70
❑ +22 Ward Burton WIN	3.00	1.35
❑ +23 Ricky Rudd WIN	3.00	1.35
❑ +24 Johnny Benson WIN	3.00	1.35
❑ +25 Kyle Petty WIN	3.00	1.35
❑ +26 Bobby Hamilton WIN 3	3.00	1.35
❑ +27 Terry Labonte	5.00	2.20
❑ +28 Jeff Gordon	8.00	3.60
❑ +29 Bobby Labonte WIN 2	3.00	1.35
❑ +30 Bill Elliott WIN	6.00	2.70

1997 Upper Deck Road To The Cup Predictor Plus Redemed Cels

This 30-card set is a parallel of the base Predictor set. This set was sent to those collectors who redemed either the Geoff Bodine card or the Bobby Hamilton.

	MINT	NRMT
COMPLETE SET (30)	200.00	90.00
COMMON CARD (+1-+30)	2.50	1.10

*NON-WIN CEL CARDS: 1.5X TO 3X BASIC PREDICTOR 2.50....1.10
*WIN CEL CARDS: 1X TO 2X BASIC PREDICTOR 2.50....1.10

1997 Upper Deck Road To The Cup Predictor Plus Redemed Die-Cut Cels

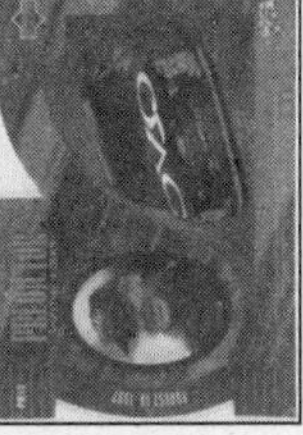

This 30-card set is a parallel of the base Predictor set. This set was sent to those collectors who redemed either the Bobby Labonte.

	MINT	NRMT
COMPLETE SET (30)	300.00	135.00
COMMON CARD (+1-+30)	4.00	1.80

1997 Upper Deck Road To The Cup Premiere Position

This 48-card card insert set showcases drivers who won the pole in one of 24 races in the 1996 season and early 1997 season. Each card features a diecut. The cards were randomly inserted in packs at a ratio of 1:5.

	MINT	NRMT
COMPLETE SET (48)	150.00	70.00
COMMON CARD (PP1-PP48)	.75	.35

*SINGLES: 1.5X TO 4X BASE CARD HI

❑ PP1 Terry Labonte	4.00	1.80
❑ PP2 Jeff Gordon	8.00	3.60
❑ PP3 Johnny Benson	.75	.35
❑ PP4 Dale Earnhardt	8.00	3.60
❑ PP5 Terry Labonte	4.00	1.80
❑ PP6 Terry Labonte	4.00	1.80
❑ PP7 Ricky Craven	.75	.35
❑ PP8 Rusty Wallace	4.00	1.80
❑ PP9 Ernie Irvan	1.50	.70
❑ PP10 Sterling Marlin	1.50	.70
❑ PP11 Jeff Gordon	8.00	3.60
❑ PP12 Jeff Gordon	8.00	3.60
❑ PP13 Bobby Hamilton	.75	.35
❑ PP14 Rusty Wallace	4.00	1.80
❑ PP15 Ricky Craven	.75	.35
❑ PP16 Ernie Irvan	1.50	.70
❑ PP17 Mark Martin	4.00	1.80
❑ PP18 Rusty Wallace	4.00	1.80
❑ PP19 Jeremy Mayfield	1.50	.70
❑ PP20 Jeff Gordon	8.00	3.60
❑ PP21 Jeff Gordon	8.00	3.60
❑ PP22 Dale Jarrett	3.00	1.35
❑ PP23 Jeff Burton	1.50	.70
❑ PP24 Dale Jarrett	3.00	1.35
❑ PP25 Mark Martin	4.00	1.80
❑ PP26 Rusty Wallace	4.00	1.80
❑ PP27 Dale Jarrett	3.00	1.35
❑ PP28 Jeff Gordon	8.00	3.60
❑ PP29 Mark Martin	4.00	1.80
❑ PP30 Ernie Irvan	1.50	.70
❑ PP31 Bobby Hamilton	.75	.35
❑ PP32 Jeff Gordon	8.00	3.60
❑ PP33 Bobby Labonte	2.00	.90
❑ PP34 Terry Labonte	4.00	1.80
❑ PP35 Dale Jarrett	3.00	1.35
❑ PP36 Ricky Rudd	1.50	.70
❑ PP37 Bobby Labonte	2.00	.90
❑ PP38 Bobby Hamilton	.75	.35
❑ PP39 Bobby Labonte	2.00	.90
❑ PP40 Bobby Labonte	2.00	.90
❑ PP41 Mark Martin	4.00	1.80
❑ PP42 Jeff Gordon	8.00	3.60
❑ PP43 Terry Labonte	4.00	1.80
❑ PP44 Rusty Wallace	4.00	1.80
❑ PP45 Dale Jarrett	3.00	1.35
❑ PP46 Dale Jarrett	3.00	1.35
❑ PP47 Dale Jarrett	3.00	1.35
❑ PP48 Jeff Burton	1.50	.70

1998 Upper Deck Road To The Cup

The 1998 Upper Deck Road to the Cup set consists of 120 standard size cards. The fronts feature full bleed photos of the driver or the driver's car. A silver band lines the left side of the card where bothe the driver's name and Upper Deck logo are found. The set contains the subsets: Taurus Time (46-60), Days of Daytona (61-75), Young Guns (76-

85), Viva Las Vegas (86-100), Double Barrel (101-115), and Checklists (116-120).

	MINT	NRMT
COMPLETE SET (120)	35.00	16.00
COMMON CARD (1-120)	.10	.05
COMMON DRIVER (1-120)	.20	.09

	MINT	NRMT
❑ 1 Kevin Lepage	.20	.09
❑ 2 Rusty Wallace	2.00	.90
❑ 3 Dale Earnhardt	4.00	1.80
❑ 4 Bobby Hamilton's Car	.10	.05
❑ 5 Terry Labonte	2.00	.90
❑ 6 Mark Martin's Car	1.00	.45
❑ 7 Geoff Bodine's Car	.10	.05
❑ 8 Hut Stricklin	.20	.09
❑ 9 Jeff Burton's Car	.20	.09
❑ 10 Ricky Rudd	.50	.23
❑ 11 Brett Bodine's Car	.10	.05
❑ 12 Jeremy Mayfield	1.25	.55
❑ 13 Jerry Nadeau	.20	.09
❑ 14 Loy Allen's Car	.10	.05
❑ 15 Bill Elliott's Car	1.00	.45
❑ 16 Jeff Green	.20	.09
❑ 17 Darrell Waltrip	.50	.23
❑ 18 Bobby Labonte's Car	.75	.35
❑ 19 David Green	.20	.09
❑ 20 Dale Jarrett	1.50	.70
❑ 21 Michael Waltrip	.20	.09
❑ 22 Ward Burton	.20	.09
❑ 23 Jimmy Spencer	.20	.09
❑ 24 Jeff Gordon	4.00	1.80
❑ 25 Randy LaJoie's Car	.10	.05
❑ 26 Johnny Benson	.20	.09
❑ 27 Gary Bradberry	.20	.09
❑ 28 Kenny Irwin	1.25	.55
❑ 29 Dave Marcis	.50	.23
❑ 30 Derrike Cope	.20	.09
❑ 31 Mike Skinner	.20	.09
❑ 32 Ron Hornaday	.20	.09
❑ 33 Ken Schrader	.20	.09
❑ 34 Rick Mast	.20	.09
❑ 35 Todd Bodine	.20	.09
❑ 36 Ernie Irvan	.50	.23
❑ 37 Dick Trickle's Car	.10	.05
❑ 38 Robert Pressley	.20	.09
❑ 39 Wally Dallenbach	.20	.09
❑ 40 Sterling Marlin's Car	.20	.09
❑ 41 Steve Grissom	.20	.09
❑ 42 Joe Nemechek's Car	.10	.05
❑ 43 John Andretti	.20	.09
❑ 44 Kyle Petty's Car	.20	.09
❑ 45 Kenny Wallace	.10	.05
❑ 46 Rusty Wallace's Car	1.00	.45
❑ 47 Mark Martin's Car	1.00	.45
❑ 48 Geoff Bodine's Car	.10	.05
❑ 49 Ricky Rudd's Car	.20	.09
❑ 50 Jeremy Mayfield's Car	.60	.25
❑ 51 Jerry Nadeau's Car	.10	.05
❑ 52 Chad Little's Car	.10	.05
❑ 53 Michael Waltrip's Car	.10	.05
❑ 54 Jimmy Spencer's Car	.10	.05
❑ 55 Johnny Benson's Car	.10	.05
❑ 56 Kenny Irwin's Car	.60	.25
❑ 57 Kenny Wallace's Car	.10	.05
❑ 58 Dale Jarrett's Car	.75	.35
❑ 59 Bill Elliott's Car	1.00	.45
❑ 60 Jeff Burton's Car	.20	.09
❑ 61 NASCAR Gold Car	.10	.05
❑ 62 Jimmy Spencer's Car	.10	.05
❑ 63 Rusty Wallace's Car	1.00	.45
❑ 64 Jeremy Mayfield	1.25	.55
❑ 65 Geoff Bodine's Car	.10	.05
❑ 66 Jeff Gordon	4.00	1.80
❑ 67 John Andretti	.20	.09
❑ 68 Bobby/Terry Labonte	1.50	.70
❑ 69 Terry Labonte's Car	1.00	.45
❑ 70 Bobby Labonte's Car	.75	.35
❑ 71 Chad Little's Car	.10	.05
❑ 72 Sterling Marlin's Car	.20	.09
❑ 73 Dave Marcis' Car	.20	.09
❑ 74 Jerry Nadeau's Car	.10	.05
❑ 75 Dale Earnhardt	4.00	1.80
❑ 76 Kenny Irwin	1.25	.55
❑ 77 Jerry Nadeau's Car	.10	.05
❑ 78 Todd Bodine	.20	.09
❑ 79 Johnny Benson's Car	.10	.05
❑ 80 John Andretti	.20	.09
❑ 81 Jeremy Mayfield	1.25	.55
❑ 82 Kevin Lepage	.20	.09
❑ 83 Dale Earnhardt Jr.'s Car	1.50	.70
❑ 84 Randy LaJoie	.20	.09
❑ 85 Mike Skinner's Car	.10	.05
❑ 86 Rusty Wallace's Car	1.00	.45
❑ 87 Ernie Irvan's Car	.20	.09
❑ 88 Jeff Gordon's Car	2.00	.90
❑ 89 Jeff Burton	.50	.23
❑ 90 Dale Jarrett's Car	.75	.35
❑ 91 Bill Elliott's Car	1.00	.45
❑ 92 Jeremy Mayfield's Car	.60	.25
❑ 93 Johnny Benson's Car	.10	.05
❑ 94 Dale Earnhardt Jr.'s Car VL	1.50	.70
❑ 95 Kyle Petty's Car	.20	.09
❑ 96 Rick Mast's Car	.10	.05
❑ 97 Terry Labonte's Car	1.00	.45
❑ 98 Ricky Rudd	.50	.23
❑ 99 Chad Little's Car	.10	.05
❑ 100 Mark Martin's Car	1.00	.45
❑ 101 Mark Martin	2.00	.90
❑ 102 Dale Jarrett	1.50	.70
❑ 103 Joe Nemechek	.20	.09
❑ 104 Dave Marcis	.50	.23
❑ 105 Hermie Sadler	.20	.09
❑ 106 Michael Waltrip	.20	.09
❑ 107 Dick Trickle	.20	.09
❑ 108 Jeff Burton	.50	.23
❑ 109 Derrike Cope	.20	.09
❑ 110 John Andretti	.20	.09
❑ 111 Mike Wallace	.20	.09
❑ 112 Robert Pressley	.20	.09
❑ 113 Elliott Sadler	.20	.09
❑ 114 Randy LaJoie	.20	.09
❑ 115 Tony Stewart	2.50	1.10
❑ 116 Checklist (1-50)	.10	.05
❑ 117 Checklist (51-100)	.10	.05
❑ 118 Checklist (101-AN25)	.10	.05
❑ 119 Checklist (AN26-CS18)	.10	.05
❑ 120 Checklist (CQ1-W5)	.10	.05

1998 Upper Deck Road To The Cup 50th Anniversary

Randomly inserted in packs at a rate of one 4, this 50-card insert set, highlights the top names in NASCAR from the past 50 years. The card fronts feature color photography surrounded by a blue border.

	MINT	NRMT
COMPLETE SET (50)	50.00	22.00
COMMON CARD (AN1 - AN50)	.40	.18
COMMON DRIVER (AN1 - AN50)	.75	.35

*SINGLES: .75X TO 2X BASE CARD HI

	MINT	NRMT
❑ AN1 Bill France Sr.	.75	.35
❑ AN2 Daytona Beach	.40	.18
❑ AN3 Jim Roper's Car	.40	.18
❑ AN4 Tim Flock	.75	.35
❑ AN5 Hudson Hornet	.40	.18
❑ AN6 Fireball Roberts	1.50	.70
❑ AN7 Smokey Yunick	.75	.35
❑ AN8 Buck Baker	1.50	.70
❑ AN9 Ned Jarrett	1.50	.70
❑ AN10 Richard Petty	1.50	.70
❑ AN11 Junior Johnson	1.50	.70
❑ AN12 David Pearson	1.50	.70
❑ AN13 Ned Jarrett	1.50	.70
❑ AN14 Richard Petty	1.50	.70
❑ AN15 Ford Turino	.40	.18
❑ AN16 Buddy Baker's Car	.75	.35
❑ AN17 Richard Petty's Car	.75	.35
❑ AN18 David Pearson	1.50	.70
❑ AN19 Winston Show Car	.40	.18
❑ AN20 Bobby Allison	1.50	.70
❑ AN21 Richard Petty	1.50	.70
❑ AN22 Benny Parsons	1.50	.70
❑ AN23 NASCAR Silver Anniversary	.40	
❑ AN24 Junior Johnson	1.50	
❑ AN25 Cale Yarborough	1.50	
❑ AN26 David Pearson	1.50	
❑ AN27 Richard Petty	1.50	
❑ AN28 Bobby Allison's Car	.75	
❑ AN29 Rusty Wallace's Car	2.00	
❑ AN30 Darrell Waltrip's Car	.75	
❑ AN31 Bobby Hillin's Car	.40	
❑ AN32 Cale Yarborough's Car	.75	
❑ AN33 Benny Parsons's Car	.75	
❑ AN34 Ernie Irvan's Car	.75	
❑ AN35 Darrell Waltrip	1.50	
❑ AN36 Richard Petty's Car	.75	
❑ AN37 Bill Elliott's Car	2.00	
❑ AN38 Davey Allison	3.00	
❑ AN39 Davey Allison/Bobby Allison	1.50	
❑ AN40 Rusty Wallace	4.00	
❑ AN41 Richard Petty	1.50	
❑ AN42 Alan Kulwicki	2.50	
❑ AN43 Jeff Gordon	8.00	
❑ AN44 Terry Labonte	4.00	
❑ AN45 Terry Labonte	4.00	
❑ AN46 Suzuka Speedway	.40	
❑ AN47 Jeff Gordon	8.00	
❑ AN48 Jeremy Mayfield's Car	1.25	
❑ AN49 Dale Earnhardt	8.00	
❑ AN50 Las Vegas Speedway	.40	

1998 Upper Deck Road To The Cup 50th Anniversary Autograp

Randomly inserted in hobby packs only, this 1 insert set is limited and hand-numbered to 50. Eac offers an autograph from a top name in NASCAF year history. The card fronts feature color photo surrounded by a blue border.

	MINT
COMPLETE SET (10)	1200.00
COMMON CARD	50.00

	MINT
❑ AN13 Ned Jarrett	50.00
❑ AN14 Richard Petty	75.00
❑ AN18 David Pearson	50.00
❑ AN25 Cale Yarborough	50.00
❑ AN35 Darrell Waltrip	60.00
❑ AN39 Bobby Allison	50.00
❑ AN40 Rusty Wallace	150.00
❑ AN44 Terry Labonte	150.00
❑ AN47 Jeff Gordon Redemption	350.00
❑ AN49 Dale Earnhardt Redemption	350.00

1998 Upper Deck Road To The Cup Cover St

Randomly inserted in packs at a rate of one in 11, t card insert set features hand-picked photos and ir prose from the editors of Tuff Stuff magazine and V Cup Scene.

	MINT
COMPLETE SET (16)	40.00
COMMON CARD (CS1 - CS16)	.75

*SINGLES: .75X TO 2X BASE CARD HI

	MINT
❑ CS1 Ernie Irvan	1.50
❑ CS2 Terry Labonte	4.00
❑ CS3 Darrell Waltrip	1.50
❑ CS4 Kyle Petty	1.50
❑ CS5 Rusty Wallace	4.00
❑ CS6 Alan Kulwicki	3.00
❑ CS7 Bill Elliott	4.00
❑ CS8 Jeff Gordon	8.00
❑ CS9 WC Grand National Scene	.75
❑ CS10 Dale Earnhardt	8.00
❑ CS11 Ernie Irvan	1.50
❑ CS12 Rusty Wallace	4.00
❑ CS13 Jeff Gordon	8.00
❑ CS14 Indianapolis Motor Speedway	.75

	MINT	NRMT
5 Gordon/Labonte/Craven	4.00	1.80
6 J.Gordon/D.Waltrip	4.00	1.80

1998 Upper Deck Road To The Cup Cup Quest Turn 1

ntially numbered to 4,000, this is the first tier of a ered insert set focused on the top ten drivers ding for this year's Winston Cup title.

	MINT	NRMT
LETE SET (10)	60.00	27.00
ON CARD (CQ1 - CQ10)	4.00	1.80
LES: 1X TO 2.5X BASE CARD HI		
Jeff Gordon's Car	20.00	9.00
Rusty Wallace's Car	10.00	4.50
Kenny Irwin's Car	6.00	2.70
Jeremy Mayfield's Car	6.00	2.70
Terry Labonte's Car	10.00	4.50
Mark Martin's Car	10.00	4.50
Bobby Labonte's Car	8.00	3.60
Dale Jarrett's Car	8.00	3.60
Jeff Burton's Car	4.00	1.80
0 Ernie Irvan's Car	4.00	1.80

1998 Upper Deck Road To The Cup Cup Quest Turn 2

ntially numbered to 2,000, this is the second tier of tiered insert set focused on the top ten drivers ding for this year's Winston Cup title.

	MINT	NRMT
LETE SET (10)	90.00	40.00
ON CARD (CQ1 - CQ10)	6.00	2.70

1998 Upper Deck Road To The Cup Cup Quest Turn 3

ntially numbered to 1,000, this is the third tier of a ered insert set focused on the top ten drivers ding for this year's Winston Cup title.

	MINT	NRMT
LETE SET (10)	150.00	70.00
ON CARD (CQ1 - CQ10)	10.00	4.50

1998 Upper Deck Road To The Cup Cup Quest Turn 4

ntially numbered to 100, this is the fourth tier of a ered insert set focused on the top ten drivers ding for this year's Winston Cup title.

	MINT	NRMT
LETE SET (10)	600.00	275.00
ON CARD (CQ1 - CQ10)	40.00	18.00

1998 Upper Deck Road To The Cup Cup Quest Victory Lane

ually numbered 1 of 1, this is the fifth and final tier ve-tiered insert set focused on the top ten drivers ding for this year's Winston Cup title. Due to the y of this set, only a checklist is provided.

	MINT	NRMT
Jeff Gordon's Car		
Rusty Wallace's Car		
Kenny Irwin's Car		
❑ CQ4 Jeremy Mayfield's Car		
❑ CQ5 Terry Labonte's Car		
❑ CQ6 Mark Martin's Car		
❑ CQ7 Bobby Labonte's Car		
❑ CQ8 Dale Jarrett's Car		
❑ CQ9 Jeff Burton's Car		
❑ CQ10 Ernie Irvan's Car		

1998 Upper Deck Road To The Cup Winning Material

Randomly inserted in packs at a rate of one in 999, this 5-card insert set sports special cards with authentic race-used pieces of the engine, along with an actual piece of a driver's race-worn fire suit.

	MINT	NRMT
COMPLETE SET (5)	800.00	350.00
COMMON CARD (W1-W5)	125.00	55.00
❑ W3 Dale Jarrett	225.00	100.00
❑ W4 Bobby Labonte	200.00	90.00
❑ W5 Jeff Burton	125.00	55.00

1997 Upper Deck Victory Circle

The 1997 Upper Deck set was issued in one series totalling 120 cards. The set contains the topical subsets: Driver (1-50), Momentum (51-100) Local Legends (101-115) and Track Facts (116-120). The cards were packaged 10 cards per pack, 28 packs per box and 12 boxes per case. Each pack carried a suggested retail price of $2.49.

	MINT	NRMT
COMPLETE SET (120)	20.00	9.00
COMMON CARD (1-120)	.10	.05
COMMON DRIVER (1-120)	.20	.09
❑ 1 Rick Mast	.20	.09
❑ 2 Rusty Wallace	1.00	.45
❑ 3 Dale Earnhardt	2.00	.90
❑ 4 Sterling Marlin	.40	.18
❑ 5 Terry Labonte	1.00	.45
❑ 6 Mark Martin	1.00	.45
❑ 7 Geoff Bodine	.20	.09
❑ 8 Hut Stricklin	.20	.09
❑ 9 Lake Speed	.20	.09
❑ 10 Ricky Rudd	.40	.18
❑ 11 Brett Bodine	.20	.09
❑ 12 Derrike Cope	.20	.09
❑ 13 Bill Elliott	1.00	.45
❑ 14 Bobby Hamilton	.20	.09
❑ 15 Wally Dallenbach	.20	.09
❑ 16 Ted Musgrave	.20	.09
❑ 17 Darrell Waltrip	.40	.18
❑ 18 Bobby Labonte	.75	.35
❑ 19 Loy Allen	.20	.09
❑ 20 Morgan Shepherd	.20	.09
❑ 21 Michael Waltrip	.20	.09
❑ 22 Ward Burton	.20	.09
❑ 23 Jimmy Spencer	.20	.09
❑ 24 Jeff Gordon	2.00	.90
❑ 25 Ken Schrader	.20	.09
❑ 26 Kyle Petty	.40	.18
❑ 27 Bobby Hillin	.20	.09
❑ 28 Ernie Irvan	.40	.18
❑ 29 Jeff Purvis	.20	.09
❑ 30 Johnny Benson	.20	.09
❑ 31 Dave Marcis	.40	.18
❑ 32 Jeremy Mayfield	.60	.25
❑ 33 Robert Pressley	.20	.09
❑ 34 Jeff Burton	.40	.18
❑ 35 Joe Nemechek	.20	.09
❑ 36 Dale Jarrett	.75	.35
❑ 37 John Andretti	.20	.09
❑ 38 Kenny Wallace	.20	.09
❑ 39 Elton Sawyer	.20	.09
❑ 40 Dick Trickle	.20	.09
❑ 41 Ricky Craven	.20	.09
❑ 42 Chad Little	.20	.09
❑ 43 Todd Bodine	.20	.09
❑ 44 David Green	.20	.09
❑ 45 Randy LaJoie	.20	.09
❑ 46 Larry Pearson	.20	.09
❑ 47 Jason Keller	.20	.09
❑ 48 Hermie Sadler	.20	.09
❑ 49 Mike McLaughlin	.20	.09
❑ 50 Tim Fedewa	.20	.09
❑ 51 Rick Mast's Car	.10	.05
❑ 52 Rusty Wallace's Car	.50	.23
❑ 53 Ricky Craven's Car	.10	.05
❑ 54 Sterling Marlin's Car	.20	.09
❑ 55 Terry Labonte's Car	.50	.23
❑ 56 Mark Martin's Car	.50	.23
❑ 57 Geoff Bodine's Car	.10	.05
❑ 58 Hut Stricklin's Car	.10	.05
❑ 59 Lake Speed's Car	.10	.05
❑ 60 Ricky Rudd's Car	.20	.09
❑ 61 Brett Bodine's Car	.10	.05
❑ 62 Derrike Cope's Car	.10	.05
❑ 63 Bill Elliott's Car	.50	.23
❑ 64 Bobby Hamilton's Car	.10	.05
❑ 65 Wally Dallenbach's Car	.10	.05
❑ 66 Ted Musgrave's Car	.10	.05
❑ 67 Darrell Waltrip's Car	.20	.09
❑ 68 Bobby Labonte's Car	.40	.18
❑ 69 Loy Allen's Car	.10	.05
❑ 70 Morgan Shepherd's Car	.10	.05
❑ 71 Michael Waltrip's Car	.10	.05
❑ 72 Ward Burton's Car	.10	.05
❑ 73 Jimmy Spencer's Car	.10	.05
❑ 74 Jeff Gordon's Car	1.00	.45
❑ 75 Ken Schrader's Car	.10	.05
❑ 76 Kyle Petty's Car	.20	.09
❑ 77 Bobby Hillin's Car	.10	.05
❑ 78 Ernie Irvan's Car	.20	.09
❑ 79 Jeff Purvis's Car	.10	.05
❑ 80 Johnny Benson's Car	.10	.05
❑ 81 Dave Marcis's Car	.20	.09
❑ 82 Jeremy Mayfield's Car	.40	.18
❑ 83 Robert Pressley's Car	.10	.05
❑ 84 Jeff Burton's Car	.20	.09
❑ 85 Joe Nemechek's Car	.10	.05
❑ 86 Dale Jarrett's Car	.40	.18
❑ 87 John Andretti's Car	.10	.05
❑ 88 Kenny Wallace's Car	.10	.05
❑ 89 Elton Sawyer's Car	.40	.18
❑ 90 Dick Trickle's Car	.10	.05
❑ 91 Chad Little's Car	.10	.05
❑ 92 Todd Bodine's Car	.10	.05
❑ 93 David Green's Car	.10	.05
❑ 94 Randy LaJoie's Car	.10	.05
❑ 95 Larry Pearson's Car	.10	.05
❑ 96 Jason Keller's Car	.10	.05
❑ 97 Hermie Sadler's Car	.10	.05
❑ 98 Mike McLaughlin's Car	.10	.05
❑ 99 Tim Fedewa's Car	.10	.05
❑ 100 Patty Moise's Car	.10	.05
❑ 101 Dale Jarrett	.75	.35
❑ 102 Ricky Rudd	.40	.18
❑ 103 Rusty Wallace	1.00	.45
❑ 104 Sterling Marlin	.40	.18
❑ 105 Geoff Bodine	.20	.09
❑ 106 John Andretti	.20	.09
❑ 107 Jeremy Mayfield	.60	.25
❑ 108 Terry Labonte	1.00	.45
❑ 109 Mark Martin	1.00	.45
❑ 110 Derrike Cope	.20	.09
❑ 111 Jeff Gordon	2.00	.90
❑ 112 Ricky Craven	.20	.09
❑ 113 Ted Musgrave	.20	.09
❑ 114 Joe Nemechek	.20	.09
❑ 115 Bill Elliott	1.00	.45
❑ 116 Kenny Wallace	.20	.09
❑ 117 Darrell Waltrip	.40	.18
❑ 118 Bobby Labonte	.75	.35
❑ 119 North Wilkesboro Speedway	.10	.05
❑ 120 North Wilkesboro Speedway	.10	.05

1997 Upper Deck Victory Circle Piece of the Action

This 9-card set features pieces of a driver's gloves, shoes, and uniform incorporated into a trading card. The cards were seeded one in 699 packs.

	MINT	NRMT
COMPLETE SET (9)	1500.00	700.00
COMMON CARD (FS1 - FS9)	100.00	45.00
❑ FS1 Jeff Gordon Fire Suit	300.00	135.00
❑ FS2 Jeff Gordon Glove	250.00	110.00

	MINT	NRMT
❑ FS3 Jeff Gordon Shoe	200.00	90.00
❑ FS4 Rusty Wallace Fire Suit	200.00	90.00
❑ FS5 Rusty Wallace Glove	150.00	70.00
❑ FS6 Rusty Wallace Shoe	120.00	55.00
❑ FS7 Dale Jarrett Fire Suit	150.00	70.00
❑ FS8 Dale Jarrett Glove	120.00	55.00
❑ FS9 Dale Jarrett Shoe	100.00	45.00

1997 Upper Deck Victory Circle Championship Reflections

Randomly inserted in packs at a rate of one in 4, this 10-card set highlights the top ten finishers in the point standings for the 1996 Winston Cup season.

	MINT	NRMT
COMPLETE SET (10)	25.00	11.00
COMMON CARD (CR1-CR10)	.60	.25
*SINGLES: 1.25X TO 3X BASE CARD HI		
❑ CR1 Terry Labonte	4.00	1.80
❑ CR2 Jeff Gordon	8.00	3.60
❑ CR3 Dale Jarrett	3.00	1.35
❑ CR4 Dale Earnhardt	8.00	3.60
❑ CR5 Mark Martin	4.00	1.80
❑ CR6 Ricky Rudd	2.50	1.10
❑ CR7 Rusty Wallace	4.00	1.80
❑ CR8 Sterling Marlin	2.50	1.10
❑ CR9 Bobby Hamilton	.60	.25
❑ CR10 Ernie Irvan	3.00	1.35

1997 Upper Deck Victory Circle Crowning Achievement

Randomly inserted in packs at a rate of one in 35, this five-card set takes a look back at Terry Labonte's record breaking season. The cards used a double die-cut design.

	MINT	NRMT
COMPLETE SET (5)	40.00	18.00
TERRY LABONTE CARD (CA1-CA5)	10.00	4.50

1997 Upper Deck Victory Circle Driver's Seat

Randomly inserted in packs at a rate of one in 69, this 10-card set takes cel technology and applies it to racing cards. The cards are best are like looking at slides and are best viewed when held up to light.

	MINT	NRMT
COMPLETE SET (10)	200.00	90.00
COMMON CARD (DS1-DS10)	4.00	1.80
*SINGLES: 8X TO 20X BASE CARD HI		
❑ DS1 Dale Earnhardt	40.00	18.00

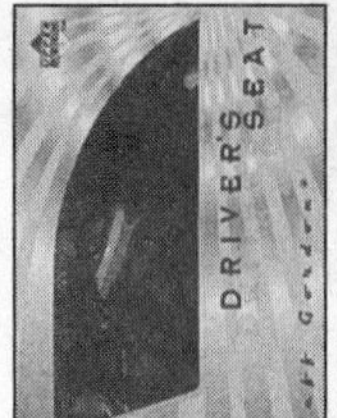

	MINT	NRMT
❑ DS2 Jeff Gordon	40.00	18.00
❑ DS3 Terry Labonte	20.00	9.00
❑ DS4 Ken Schrader	4.00	1.80
❑ DS5 Sterling Marlin	8.00	3.60
❑ DS6 Mark Martin	20.00	9.00
❑ DS7 Rusty Wallace	20.00	9.00
❑ DS8 Bobby Labonte	10.00	4.50
❑ DS9 Ernie Irvan	8.00	3.60
❑ DS10 Dale Jarrett	16.00	7.25

1997 Upper Deck Victory Circle Generation Excitement

This five-card set highlights some of the up and coming stars of NASCAR's Winston Cup circuit. The cards were inserted one in 11 packs.

	MINT	NRMT
COMPLETE SET (5)	15.00	6.75
COMMON CARD (GE1-GE5)	1.00	.45
*SINGLES: 2X TO 5X BASE CARD HI		
❑ GE1 Jeff Gordon	16.00	7.25
❑ GE2 Bobby Hamilton	1.00	.45
❑ GE3 Johnny Benson	1.00	.45
❑ GE4 Ricky Craven	1.00	.45
❑ GE5 Bobby Labonte	5.00	2.20

1997 Upper Deck Victory Circle Predictor

This 10-card is an interactive predictor game. Each card has a specific goal stamped on the front. If that driver accomplishes that goal anytime during the 1997 Winston Cup season that card may be redeemed for a 10 card prize set. These cards expired on 2/1/98. The predictor cards were inserted one per 21 packs.

	MINT	NRMT
COMPLETE SET (10)	50.00	22.00
COMMON CARD (PE1-PE10)	1.50	.70
*SINGLES: 3X TO 8X BASE CARD HI		
❑ PE1 Jeff Gordon WIN	25.00	11.00
❑ PE2 Rusty Wallace WIN	15.00	6.75
❑ PE3 Dale Jarrett WIN	15.00	6.75
❑ PE4 Sterling Marlin	1.50	.70
❑ PE5 Terry Labonte	8.00	3.60
❑ PE6 Mark Martin WIN	15.00	6.75
❑ PE7 Bobby Labonte WIN	8.00	3.60
❑ PE8 Ernie Irvan WIN	8.00	3.60
❑ PE9 Bill Elliott	8.00	3.60
❑ PE10 Ricky Rudd	1.50	.70

1997 Upper Deck Victory Circle Predictor Winner Cels

This ten-card set consists of the redemption cards available from redeemimg "winner" cards from the base Predictor set.

	MINT	NRMT
COMPLETE SET (10)	120.00	55.00
COMMON CARD (PH1 - PH10)	6.00	
❑ PH1 Jeff Gordon	40.00	
❑ PH2 Rusty Wallace	20.00	
❑ PH3 Dale Jarrett	15.00	
❑ PH6 Mark Martin	20.00	
❑ PH7 Bobby Labonte	15.00	
❑ PH8 Ernie Irvan	6.00	
❑ PH10 Ricky Rudd	6.00	

1997 Upper Deck Victory Circle Victory Lap

Randomly inserted in packs at a rate of one in 10 10-card set is a hobby only insert. The cards featu cut technology and a checkered flag design. Each drivers in this set visited victory lane in 1996. The were inserted one per 109 packs.

	MINT
COMPLETE SET (10)	300.00
COMMON CARD (VL1-VL10)	8.00
*SINGLES: 15X TO 40X BASE CARD HI	
❑ VL1 Dale Earnhardt	100.00
❑ VL2 Jeff Gordon	100.00
❑ VL3 Bobby Labonte	15.00
❑ VL4 Dale Jarrett	50.00
❑ VL5 Ernie Irvan	15.00
❑ VL6 Sterling Marlin	15.00
❑ VL7 Ricky Rudd	15.00
❑ VL8 Geoff Bodine	8.00
❑ VL9 Bobby Hamilton	8.00
❑ VL10 Rusty Wallace	60.00

1998 Upper Deck Victory Circle

The 1998 Upper Deck Victory Circle set was issued series totalling 135 cards. The set contains the t subsets: Season Highlights (91-105), Freeze Frame 120), and Hard Chargers (121-135).

	MINT
COMPLETE SET (150)	40.00
COMMON CARD (1-150)	.10
COMMON DRIVER (1-150)	.20
❑ 1 Morgan Shepherd	.20
❑ 2 Rusty Wallace	2.00
❑ 3 Dale Earnhardt	4.00
❑ 4 Sterling Marlin	.50
❑ 5 Terry Labonte	2.00
❑ 6 Mark Martin	2.00
❑ 7 Geoff Bodine	.20
❑ 8 Hut Stricklin	.20
❑ 9 Lake Speed	.20
❑ 10 Ricky Rudd	.50
❑ 11 Brett Bodine	.20
❑ 12 Dale Jarrett	1.50
❑ 13 Bill Elliott	2.00
❑ 14 Dick Trickle	.20
❑ 15 Wally Dallenbach	.20
❑ 16 Ted Musgrave	.20
❑ 17 Darrell Waltrip	.50
❑ 18 Bobby Labonte	1.50
❑ 19 Gary Bradberry	.20
❑ 20 Rick Mast	.20
❑ 21 Michael Waltrip	.20
❑ 22 Ward Burton	.20
❑ 23 Jimmy Spencer	.20
❑ 24 Jeff Gordon	4.00
❑ 25 Ricky Craven	.20
❑ 26 Chad Little	.20
❑ 27 Kenny Wallace	.20
❑ 28 Ernie Irvan	.50
❑ 29 Steve Park	1.50
❑ 30 Johnny Benson	.20
❑ 31 Mike Skinner	.20
❑ 32 Mike Wallace	.20
❑ 33 Ken Schrader	.20
❑ 34 Jeff Burton	.50

avid Green .20 .09
errike Cope .20 .09
eremy Mayfield 1.25 .55
ave Marcis .50 .23
ohn Andretti .20 .09
obby Gordon .20 .09
teve Grissom .20 .09
oe Nemechek .20 .09
obby Hamilton .20 .09
yle Petty .50 .23
enny Irwin 1.25 .55
organ Shepherd's Car .10 .05
usty Wallace's Car 1.00 .45
ale Earnhardt's Car 2.00 .90
terling Marlin's Car .20 .09
erry Labonte's Car 1.00 .45
ark Martin's Car 1.00 .45
eoff Bodine's Car .10 .05
ut Stricklin's Car .10 .05
ake Speed's Car .10 .05
icky Rudd's Car .20 .09
ett Bodine's Car .10 .05
ale Jarrett's Car .75 .35
ll Elliott's Car 1.00 .45
ick Trickle's Car .10 .05
ally Dallenbach's Car .10 .05
ed Musgrave's Car .10 .05
arrell Waltrip's Car .50 .23
obby Labonte's Car .75 .35
ary Bradberry's Car .10 .05
ick Mast's Car .10 .05
ichael Waltrip's Car .10 .05
ard Burton's Car .10 .05
mmy Spencer's Car .10 .05
eff Gordon's Car 2.00 .90
icky Craven's Car .10 .05
had Little's Car .10 .05
enny Wallace's Car .10 .05
rnie Irvan's Car .20 .09
teve Park's Car .75 .35
ohnny Benson's Car .10 .05
ike Skinner's Car .10 .05
ike Wallace's Car .10 .05
en Schrader's Car .10 .05
eff Burton's Car .20 .09
avid Green's Car .10 .05
errike Cope's Car .10 .05
eremy Mayfield's Car .60 .25
ave Marcis's Car .20 .09
ohn Andretti's Car .10 .05
obby Gordon's Car .10 .05
teve Grissom's Car .10 .05
oe Nemechek's Car .10 .05
obby Hamilton's Car .10 .05
yle Petty's Car .20 .09
enny Irwin's Car .60 .25
ike Skinner .20 .09
eff Gordon 2.00 .90
Terry Labonte
Ricky Craven
eff Gordon 4.00 1.80
obby Gordon .20 .09
ale Jarrett 1.50 .70
eff Burton .50 .23
ark Martin 2.00 .90
ark Martin 2.00 .90
oe Nemechek .20 .09
Jeff Gordon 4.00 1.80
Mike Skinner .20 .09
John Andretti .20 .09
Ricky Rudd .50 .23
Todd Bodine .20 .09
Jeff Gordon 4.00 1.80
Mark Martin 2.00 .90
Geoff Bodine .20 .09
Kenny Irwin 1.25 .55
Dave Marcis .50 .23
Rusty Wallace 2.00 .90
Ricky Rudd .50 .23
Bobby Labonte 1.50 .70
Ernie Irvan .50 .23
Kenny Wallace .20 .09
Mike Skinner .20 .09
Dale Jarrett 1.50 .70
Mark Martin 2.00 .90
Terry Labonte 2.00 .90
Jeff Gordon 4.00 1.80
Jeff Gordon 4.00 1.80
Derrike Cope .20 .09
Jeremy Mayfield 1.25 .55
Robby Gordon .20 .09
Ricky Craven .20 .09
Ernie Irvan .50 .23
Terry Labonte 2.00 .90
Johnny Benson .20 .09
Mike Skinner .20 .09
Kyle Petty .50 .23
Wally Dallenbach .20 .09

❑ 131 Rick Mast .20 .09
❑ 132 Morgan Shepherd .20 .09
❑ 133 Michael Waltrip .20 .09
❑ 134 Ted Musgrave .20 .09
❑ 135 Ricky Rudd .50 .23
❑ 136 Ricky Craven .20 .09
❑ 137 Geoff Bodine .20 .09
❑ 138 Morgan Shepherd .20 .09
❑ 139 Ted Musgrave .20 .09
❑ 140 Mark Martin 2.00 .90
❑ 141 Darrell Waltrip .50 .23
❑ 142 Rusty Wallace 2.00 .90
❑ 143 Jeff Burton .50 .23
❑ 144 Bill Elliott 2.00 .90
❑ 145 Ricky Rudd .50 .23
❑ 146 Terry Labonte 2.00 .90
❑ 147 Bobby Labonte 1.50 .70
❑ 148 Steve Grissom .20 .09
❑ 149 Dale Jarrett 1.50 .70
❑ 150 Ernie Irvan .50 .23

1998 Upper Deck Victory Circle 32 Days of Speed

Randomly inserted in packs at the rate of one in four, this 32-card set features color photos of one of the drivers from each of the 32 NASCAR Winston Cup races.

MINT NRMT
COMPLETE SET (32) 40.00 18.00
COMMON CARD (D1-D32) .60 .25
*SINGLES: .6X TO 1.5X BASE CARD HI

❑ D1 Mike Skinner .60 .25
❑ D2 Jeff Gordon 6.00 2.70
❑ D3 Rusty Wallace 3.00 1.35
❑ D4 Robby Gordon .60 .25
❑ D5 Dale Jarrett 2.50 1.10
❑ D6 Jeff Burton 1.25 .55
❑ D7 Rusty Wallace 3.00 1.35
❑ D8 Kenny Wallace .60 .25
❑ D9 Mark Martin 3.00 1.35
❑ D10 Mark Martin 3.00 1.35
❑ D11 Jeff Gordon 6.00 2.70
❑ D12 Ricky Rudd 1.25 .55
❑ D13 Bobby Hamilton .60 .25
❑ D14 Ernie Irvan 1.25 .55
❑ D15 Joe Nemechek .60 .25
❑ D16 John Andretti .60 .25
❑ D17 Ken Schrader .60 .25
❑ D18 Dale Jarrett 2.50 1.10
❑ D19 Ricky Rudd 1.25 .55
❑ D20 Todd Bodine .60 .25
❑ D21 Johnny Benson .60 .25
❑ D22 Kenny Wallace .60 .25
❑ D23 Bobby Labonte 2.50 1.10
❑ D24 Bill Elliott 3.00 1.35
❑ D25 Ken Schrader .60 .25
❑ D26 Mark Martin 3.00 1.35
❑ D27 Ward Burton .60 .25
❑ D28 Bobby Labonte 2.50 1.10
❑ D29 Terry Labonte 3.00 1.35
❑ D30 Bobby Hamilton .60 .25
❑ D31 Bobby Hamilton .60 .25
❑ D32 Jeff Gordon 6.00 2.70

1998 Upper Deck Victory Circle 32 Days of Speed Gold

Randomly inserted in packs, this 32-card set is a Gold Light F/X parallel version of the regular Days of Speed set. Each card is crash numbered 1 of 97.

MINT NRMT
COMPLETE SET (32) 1200.00 550.00
COMMON CARD (D1-D32) 15.00 6.75

1998 Upper Deck Victory Circle Autographs

Randomly inserted in packs, this five-card set features autographed color photos of favorite NASCAR Winston Cup drivers printed on unique die-cut cards and individually hand-numbered to 250.

MINT NRMT
COMPLETE SET (5) 550.00 250.00
COMMON CARD (AG1-AG5) 60.00 27.00

❑ AG1 Jeff Gordon 250.00 110.00
❑ AG2 Jeff Burton 60.00 27.00
❑ AG3 Dale Jarrett 100.00 45.00
❑ AG4 Mark Martin 125.00 55.00
❑ AG5 Terry Labonte 125.00 55.00

1998 Upper Deck Victory Circle Piece of the Engine

Randomly inserted in packs at the rate of one in 999, this five-card set features color photos of drivers with an actual race-used piece of the engine from the top cars in NASCAR contained in the card.

MINT NRMT
COMPLETE SET (5) 600.00 275.00
COMMON CARD (PE1-PE5) 100.00 45.00

❑ PE1 Darrell Waltrip 100.00 45.00
❑ PE2 Rusty Wallace 175.00 80.00
❑ PE3 Dale Jarrett 150.00 70.00
❑ PE4 Ernie Irvan 125.00 55.00
❑ PE5 Bobby Labonte 150.00 70.00

1998 Upper Deck Victory Circle Point Leaders

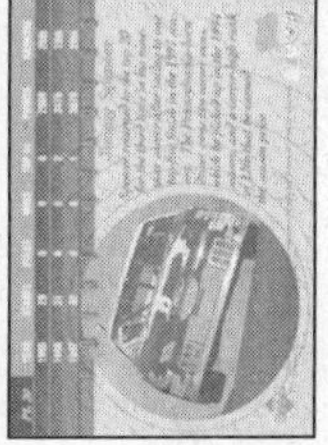

Randomly inserted in packs at the rate of one in 13, this 20-card set features color photos of drivers who finished in the top 20 in the final point standings for the season.

MINT NRMT
COMPLETE SET (20) 100.00 45.00
COMMON CARD (PL1-PL20) 2.00 .90
*SINGLES: 2X TO 5X BASE CARD HI

❑ PL1 Jeff Gordon 20.00 9.00
❑ PL2 Dale Jarrett 8.00 3.60
❑ PL3 Mark Martin 10.00 4.50
❑ PL4 Jeff Burton 4.00 1.80
❑ PL5 Dale Earnhardt 20.00 9.00
❑ PL6 Terry Labonte 10.00 4.50
❑ PL7 Bobby Labonte 8.00 3.60
❑ PL8 Bill Elliott 10.00 4.50
❑ PL9 Rusty Wallace 10.00 4.50
❑ PL10 Ken Schrader 2.00 .90
❑ PL11 Johnny Benson 2.00 .90
❑ PL12 Ted Musgrave 2.00 .90
❑ PL13 Jeremy Mayfield 6.00 2.70
❑ PL14 Ernie Irvan 4.00 1.80
❑ PL15 Kyle Petty 4.00 1.80
❑ PL16 Bobby Hamilton 2.00 .90
❑ PL17 Ricky Rudd 4.00 1.80
❑ PL18 Michael Waltrip 2.00 .90
❑ PL19 Ricky Craven 2.00 .90
❑ PL20 Jimmy Spencer 2.00 .90

1998 Upper Deck Victory Circle Predictor Plus

Randomly inserted in packs at the rate of one in 23, this 20-card set features scratch-off game cards which enabled the collector to win prizes if the driver pictured on the card achieved the goals displayed after scratching off the special cars on the card.

MINT NRMT
COMPLETE SET (20) 60.00 27.00

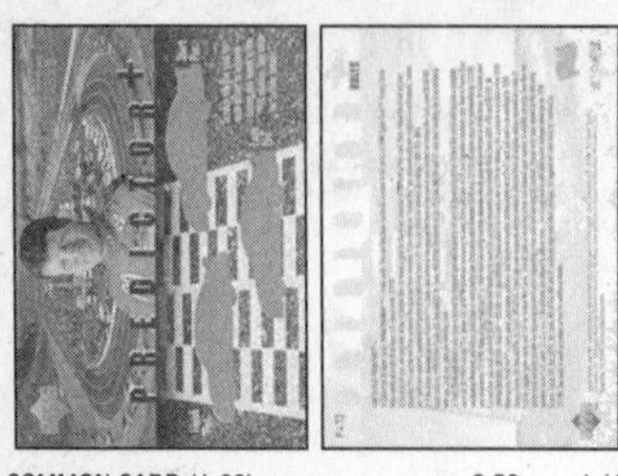

COMMON CARD (1-20)	2.50	1.10
*SINGLES: 2.5X TO 6X BASE CARD HI		
❑ 1 Ernie Irvan	2.50	1.10
❑ 2 Rusty Wallace	2.50	1.10
❑ 3 Dale Jarrett	2.50	1.10
❑ 4 Sterling Marlin	2.50	1.10
❑ 5 Terry Labonte	2.50	1.10
❑ 6 Mark Martin	2.50	1.10
❑ 7 Geoff Bodine	2.50	1.10
❑ 8 Hut Stricklin	2.50	1.10
❑ 9 Lake Speed	2.50	1.10
❑ 10 Ricky Rudd	2.50	1.10
❑ 11 Brett Bodine	2.50	1.10
❑ 12 Bill Elliott	2.50	1.10
❑ 13 Kyle Petty	2.50	1.10
❑ 14 Jeff Burton	2.50	1.10
❑ 15 Jeremy Mayfield	2.50	1.10
❑ 16 Ricky Craven	2.50	1.10
❑ 17 Ted Musgrave	2.50	1.10
❑ 18 Bobby Labonte	2.50	1.10
❑ 19 Mike Skinner	2.50	1.10
❑ 20 Johnny Benson	2.50	1.10

1998 Upper Deck Victory Circle Predictor Plus Cel Redemption

These cards were available from redeeming winning cards from the Predictor Plus set. Complete sets were available from "Instant Win" cards that were inserted at a ratio of 1 in 69 packs.

	MINT	NRMT
COMPLETE SET (20)	90.00	40.00
COMMON CARD (1-20)	4.00	1.80

1998 Upper Deck Victory Circle Sparks of Brilliance

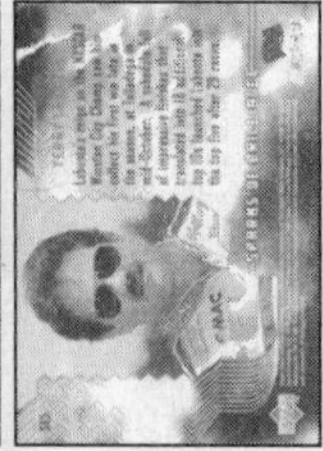

Randomly inserted in packs at the rate of one in 84, this ten-card set features color photos of top drivers with their unbelievable accomplishments on the track during the 1997 season.

	MINT	NRMT
COMPLETE SET (10)	300.00	135.00
COMMON CARD (SB1-SB10)	15.00	6.75
*SINGLES: 10X TO 20X BASE CARD HI		
❑ SB1 Jeff Gordon	80.00	36.00
❑ SB2 Rusty Wallace	40.00	18.00
❑ SB3 Dale Earnhardt	80.00	36.00
❑ SB4 Ernie Irvan	15.00	6.75
❑ SB5 Terry Labonte	40.00	18.00
❑ SB6 Mark Martin	40.00	18.00
❑ SB7 Bobby Labonte	30.00	13.50
❑ SB8 Ricky Rudd	15.00	6.75
❑ SB9 Dale Jarrett	30.00	13.50
❑ SB10 Jeff Burton	15.00	6.75

1995 US Air Greg Sacks

US Air produced and distributed this set featuring Greg Sacks and the US Air Racing Team. The five black bordered cards are not numbered and listed below alphabetically.

	MINT	NRMT
COMPLETE SET (5)	5.00	2.20
COMMON CARD	1.00	.45
❑ 1 Tony Furr	1.00	.45
❑ 2 Greg Sacks' Car	1.00	.45
❑ 3 Greg Sacks in Pits	1.00	.45
❑ 4 Greg Sacks UER birthdate incorrect	1.50	.70
❑ 5 D.K. Ulrich	1.00	.45

1992 U.S. Playing Card

This set is actually a deck of playing cards featuring the Junior Johnson Race Team and driver Bill Elliott. While the majority of the cards from the set show only a playing card design, a few include photos of Johnson and Elliott. The card's backs feature Bill Elliott's car.

	MINT	NRMT
COMPLETE SET (56)	3.00	1.35
COMMON CARD (1-56)	.05	.02
BILL ELLIOTT CARDS	.50	.23

1994 VIP

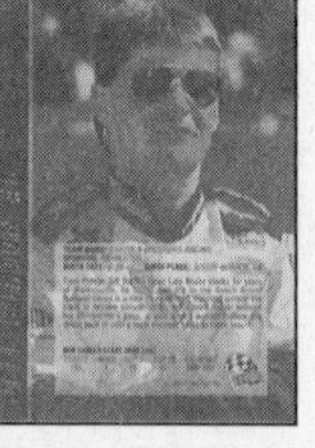

This 100-card set was the first issued by card maker Press Pass under the VIP brand name. The cards are printed on 24-point stock and are foil stamped on both sides. There are four topical subsets: Portraits (73-81), Alabama Gang (82-84), Heroes of Racing (85-90), Master Mechanics (91-99). The Portraits subset features nine water color paintings for racing artist Jeanne Barnes. There were reported 3,500 cases made. Each case contained 20 boxes, with 36 packs per box and 6 cards per pack.

	MINT
COMPLETE SET (100)	15.00
COMMON CARD (1-100)	.15
COMMON DRIVER (1-100)	.30
❑ 1 Loy Allen Jr.	.30
❑ 2 Brett Bodine	.30
❑ 3 Geoff Bodine	.30
❑ 4 Todd Bodine	.30
❑ 5 Chuck Bown	.30
❑ 6 Jeff Burton	.60
❑ 7 Ward Burton	.30
❑ 8 Derrike Cope	.30
❑ 9 Wally Dallenbach Jr.	.30
❑ 10 Dale Earnhardt	2.50
❑ 11 Harry Gant	.60
❑ 12 Jeff Gordon	2.50
❑ 13 Steve Grissom	.30
❑ 14 Bobby Hamilton	.30
❑ 15 Jimmy Hensley	.30
❑ 16 Ernie Irvan	.60
❑ 17 Dale Jarrett	1.00
❑ 18 Bobby Labonte	.75
❑ 19 Terry Labonte	1.25
❑ 20 Sterling Marlin	.60
❑ 21 Mark Martin	1.25
❑ 22 Rick Mast	.30
❑ 23 Ted Musgrave	.30
❑ 24 Joe Nemechek	.30
❑ 25 Kyle Petty	.60
❑ 26 Ricky Rudd	.60
❑ 27 Greg Sacks	.30
❑ 28 Ken Schrader	.30
❑ 29 Morgan Shepherd	.30
❑ 30 Lake Speed	.30
❑ 31 Jimmy Spencer	.30
❑ 32 Hut Stricklin	.30
❑ 33 Mike Wallace	.30
❑ 34 Rusty Wallace	1.25
❑ 35 Darrell Waltrip	.60
❑ 36 Michael Waltrip	.30
❑ 37 Morgan Shepherd w/Car	.15
❑ 38 Jeff Gordon w/Car	1.25
❑ 39 Geoff Bodine w/Car	.15
❑ 40 Ted Musgrave w/Car	.15
❑ 41 Derrike Cope w/Car	.15
❑ 42 Dale Earnhardt w/Car	1.25
❑ 43 Dale Jarrett w/Car	.50
❑ 44 Terry Labonte w/Car	.60
❑ 45 Ken Schrader w/Car	.15
❑ 46 Bobby Labonte w/Car	.50
❑ 47 Kyle Petty w/Car	.30
❑ 48 Rusty Wallace 's Car	.60
❑ 49 Michael Waltrip w/Car	.15
❑ 50 Brett Bodine w/Car	.15
❑ 51 Ernie Irvan w/Car	.30
❑ 52 Ricky Rudd w/Car	.30
❑ 53 Mark Martin w/Car	.60
❑ 54 Darrell Waltrip w/Car	.30
❑ 55 Johnny Benson Jr.	.30
❑ 56 Ricky Craven	.30
❑ 57 Bobby Dotter	.30
❑ 58 David Green	.30
❑ 59 Tracy Leslie	.30
❑ 60 Chad Little	.30
❑ 61 Mike McLaughlin	.30
❑ 62 Larry Pearson	.30
❑ 63 Tom Peck	.30
❑ 64 Robert Pressley	.30
❑ 65 Dennis Setzer	.30
❑ 66 Kenny Wallace	.30
❑ 67 Tom Peck's Car	.15
❑ 68 Bobby Dotter w/Car	.15
❑ 69 Ricky Craven w/Car	.15
❑ 70 Mike McLaughlin w/Car	.15
❑ 71 David Green w/Car	.15
❑ 72 Hermie Sadler's Car	.15
❑ 73 Harry Gant ART	.30
❑ 74 Jeff Gordon ART	1.25
❑ 75 Ernie Irvan ART	.30
❑ 76 Dale Jarrett ART	.50
❑ 77 Sterling Marlin ART	.30
❑ 78 Mark Martin ART	.60
❑ 79 Kyle Petty ART	.30
❑ 80 Morgan Shepherd ART	.15
❑ 81 Rusty Wallace ART	.60
❑ 82 Bobby Allison RF	.30
❑ 83 Donnie Allison RF	.30
❑ 84 Red Farmer RF	.15
❑ 85 Ned Jarrett HR	.15
❑ 86 Junior Johnson HR	.30
❑ 87 Ralph Moody HR	.15
❑ 88 Benny Parsons HR	.30
❑ 89 Wendell Scott HR	.30
❑ 90 Cale Yarborough HR	.30
❑ 91 Paul Andrews MM	.15
❑ 92 Barry Dodson MM	.15
❑ 93 Jeff Hammond MM	.15

	MINT	NRMT
:eve Hmiel MM	.15	.07
mmy Makar MM	.15	.07
ırry McReynolds MM	.15	.07
ıddy Parrott MM	.15	.07
obin Pemberton MM	.15	.07
ndy Petree MM	.15	.07
Checklist	.15	.07

1994 VIP Driver's Choice

e-card insert set features the drivers, as chosen by ers, as the most likely to win the 1994 Winston ampionship. The cards were seeded one per eight

	MINT	NRMT
ETE SET (9)	30.00	13.50
ON CARD (DC1-DC9)	1.25	.55
'ARS	2.50	1.10
ES: 2X TO 5X BASE CARD HI		
Dale Earnhardt	1.25	.55
Ernie Irvan	1.25	.55
Dale Jarrett	1.25	.55
Sterling Marlin	1.25	.55
Mark Martin	1.25	.55
Kyle Petty	1.25	.55
Ken Schrader	1.25	.55
Morgan Shepherd	1.25	.55
Rusty Wallace	1.25	.55

1994 VIP Exchange 24K

ven-card set was originally inserted in packs of VIP demption game. Inserted at a rate of one per 240 was a redemption card that had a driver's facsimile e in a gold foil stamping across the front. There ly 1,500 of each of the seven redemption cards. emption card was then used to receive a 24K Gold re card. The prices below are for the 24K Gold e cards and not the redemption card.

	MINT	NRMT
ETE SET (7)	200.00	90.00
N CARD (EC1-EC7)	20.00	9.00
ES: 12X TO 30X BASE CARD HI		
ale Earnhardt	80.00	36.00
arry Gant	20.00	9.00
eff Gordon	80.00	36.00
rnie Irvan	30.00	13.50
lark Martin	40.00	18.00
yle Petty	20.00	9.00
usty Wallace	40.00	18.00
Super Exchange Card Expired	2.00	.90

994 VIP Member's Only

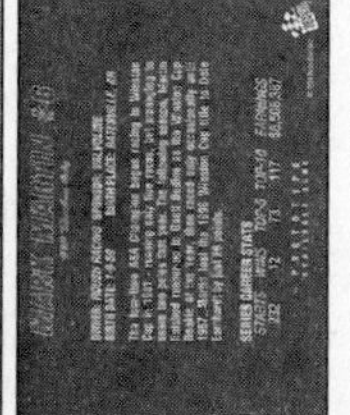

ı these two cards do not carry the VIP logo, they ıe same design as the 1994 VIP set. They were ıted directly to participants of Press Pass' r's Only collecting club. The cards are ered and carry a blue foil Member's Only logo.

	MINT	NRMT
TE SET (2)	10.00	4.50
N CARD	4.00	1.80
ieoff Bodine	4.00	1.80
Aark Martin	6.00	2.70

1995 VIP

This 64-card set represents the second year for the VIP brand. The cards feature top personalities from NASCAR racing. Each card is gold-foil stamped and is printed on 24-point stock.There are four topical subsets: Heroes of Racing (46-50), Track Dominators (51-54), Master Mechanics (55-59), SuperTruck (60-63). The cards came packed six cards per pack. There were 24 packs per box and 16 boxes per case.

	MINT	NRMT
COMPLETE SET (64)	15.00	6.75
COMMON CARD (1-64)	.15	.07
COMMON DRIVER (1-64)	.30	.14
❑ 1 John Andretti	.30	.14
❑ 2 Brett Bodine	.30	.14
❑ 3 Geoff Bodine	.30	.14
❑ 4 Todd Bodine	.30	.14
❑ 5 Jeff Burton	.60	.25
❑ 6 Ward Burton	.30	.14
❑ 7 Derrike Cope	.30	.14
❑ 8 Ricky Craven	.30	.14
❑ 9 Dale Earnhardt	3.00	1.35
❑ 10 Bill Elliott	1.50	.70
❑ 11 Jeff Gordon	3.00	1.35
❑ 12 Steve Grissom	.30	.14
❑ 13 Bobby Hamilton	.30	.14
❑ 14 Dale Jarrett	1.50	.70
❑ 15 Bobby Labonte	1.25	.55
❑ 16 Terry Labonte	1.50	.70
❑ 17 Randy LaJoie	.30	.14
❑ 18 Sterling Marlin	.60	.25
❑ 19 Mark Martin	1.50	.70
❑ 20 Ted Musgrave	.30	.14
❑ 21 Joe Nemechek	.30	.14
❑ 22 Kyle Petty	.60	.25
❑ 23 Robert Pressley	.30	.14
❑ 24 Ricky Rudd	.60	.25
❑ 25 Ken Schrader	.30	.14
❑ 26 Morgan Shepherd	.30	.14
❑ 27 Dick Trickle	.30	.14
❑ 28 Rusty Wallace	1.50	.70
❑ 29 Darrell Waltrip	.60	.25
❑ 30 Michael Waltrip	.30	.14
❑ 31 Jeff Gordon	3.00	1.35
❑ 32 Sterling Marlin	.60	.25
❑ 33 Mark Martin	1.50	.70
❑ 34 Kyle Petty	.60	.25
❑ 35 Ricky Rudd	.60	.25
❑ 36 Ken Schrader	.30	.14
❑ 37 Johnny Benson Jr.	.30	.14
❑ 38 Rodney Combs	.30	.14
❑ 39 Bobby Dotter	.30	.14
❑ 40 David Green	.30	.14
❑ 41 Chad Little	.30	.14
❑ 42 Mike McLaughlin	.30	.14
❑ 43 Larry Pearson	.30	.14
❑ 44 Dennis Setzer	.30	.14
❑ 45 Kenny Wallace	.30	.14
❑ 46 Bobby Allison HR	.30	.14
❑ 47 Ernie Irvan HR	.60	.25
❑ 48 Elmo Langley HR	.15	.07
❑ 49 Richard Petty HR	.75	.35
❑ 50 Tim Richmond HR	.60	.25
❑ 51 Bill Elliott TD	.75	.35
❑ 52 Sterling Marlin TD	.60	.25
❑ 53 Mark Martin TD	1.50	.70
❑ 54 Darrell Waltrip TD	.60	.25
❑ 55 Jeff Andrews MM	.15	.07
❑ 56 Danny Glad MM	.15	.07
❑ 57 Charlie Siegars MM	.15	.07
❑ 58 Rick Wetzel MM	.15	.07
❑ 59 Gregg Wilson MM	.15	.07
❑ 60 Geoff Bodine's Truck	.15	.07
❑ 61 Jeff Gordon's Truck	.75	.35
❑ 62 Ken Schrader's Truck	.15	.07
❑ 63 Mike Skinner's Truck	.15	.07
❑ 64 Checklist	.15	.07

1995 VIP Emerald Proofs

This 64-card set is a parallel of the base set. The cards feature a emerald color foil stamping and are number of 380. The cards were randomly inserted at a rate of one per 32 packs.

	MINT	NRMT
COMPLETE SET (64)	750.00	350.00
COMMON CARD (1-64)	8.00	3.60
COMMON DRIVER (1-64)	15.00	6.75

*EMERALDS STARS: 10X TO 25X BASIC CARDS

1995 VIP Red Hot/Cool Blue

This 64-card set is a parallel of the base set. The retail cards feature a blue foil stamping, while the hobby only cards feature a red foil stamping. Cool Blue cards were available one per pack in Retail packs. Red Hot cards were available one per pack in Hobby packs. The prices below reflect either parallel version.

	MINT	NRMT
COMPLETE SET (64)	40.00	18.00
COMMON CARD (1-64)	.30	.14
COMMON DRIVER (1-64)	.60	.25

*REDS/BLUES: 2.5X TO 4X BASIC CARDS

1995 VIP Autographs

This 24-card insert set consist of autographed regular VIP cards. The only way to tell the difference in one of these cards and one signed at a show or a track, is that the ones from packs don't have the UV coating. Press Pass does this intentionally to make them easier for the drivers to sign and to differentiate the insert cards. There were more than 30,000 signed cards inserted in the VIP packs at a rate of one per 24 packs. Each card was not signed in equal quantities.

	MINT	NRMT
COMPLETE SET (24)	500.00	220.00
COMMON CARD	10.00	4.50
COMMON DRIVER	20.00	9.00
❑ 7 Derrike Cope	20.00	9.00
❑ 8 Ricky Craven	20.00	9.00
❑ 11 Jeff Gordon	200.00	90.00
❑ 13 Bobby Hamilton	20.00	9.00
❑ 18 Sterling Marlin	20.00	9.00
❑ 19 Mark Martin	60.00	27.00
❑ 20 Ted Musgrave	20.00	9.00
❑ 22 Kyle Petty	40.00	18.00
❑ 25 Ken Schrader	20.00	9.00
❑ 37 Johnny Benson	20.00	9.00
❑ 38 Rodney Combs	20.00	9.00
❑ 39 Bobby Dotter	20.00	9.00
❑ 40 David Green	20.00	9.00
❑ 41 Chad Little	20.00	9.00
❑ 42 Mike McLaughlin	20.00	9.00
❑ 43 Larry Pearson	20.00	9.00
❑ 44 Dennis Setzer	20.00	9.00
❑ 45 Kenny Wallace	20.00	9.00
❑ 47 Ernie Irvan HR	20.00	9.00
❑ 55 Jeff Andrews MM	10.00	4.50
❑ 56 Danny Glad MM	10.00	4.50
❑ 57 Charlie Siegars MM	10.00	4.50
❑ 58 Rick Wetzel MM	10.00	4.50
❑ 59 Gregg Wilson MM	10.00	4.50

1995 VIP Fan's Choice

This nine-card insert set features the top nine Winston Cup drivers as voted by the Press Pass VIP Club members. The cards are printed on either gold or silver foil board. Fan's Choice Silver cards could be found at a rate of one per six packs. Gold cards were packed at the rate of 1:30 packs.

	MINT	NRMT
COMPLETE SILVER SET (9)	40.00	18.00
COMMON CARD (FC1-FC9)	1.00	.45
*SINGLES: 1.25X TO 3X BASE CARD HI		
COMPLETE GOLD SET (9)	120.00	55.00
*GOLD CARDS: 3X TO 8X SILVERS		
❑ FC1 Dale Earnhardt	12.00	5.50
❑ FC2 Bill Elliott	6.00	2.70
❑ FC3 Jeff Gordon	12.00	5.50
❑ FC4 Terry Labonte	6.00	2.70
❑ FC5 Sterling Marlin	6.00	2.70
❑ FC6 Mark Martin	6.00	2.70
❑ FC7 Ricky Rudd	6.00	2.70
❑ FC8 Ken Schrader	1.00	.45
❑ FC9 Rusty Wallace	6.00	2.70

1995 VIP Helmets

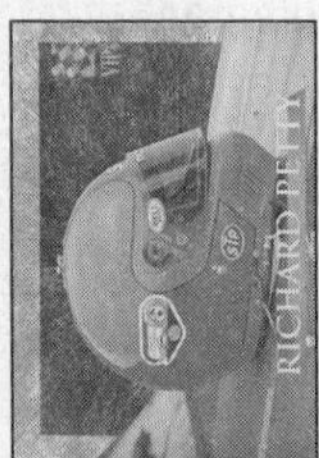

This nine-card insert set uses Nitrokrome technology along with etched foil printed on silver or gold foil to bring out the color in some of the best Winston Cup drivers' helmets. The Silver cards were randomly inserted in packs at a rate of one per 18 with Gold cards packed at 1:90.

	MINT	NRMT
COMPLETE SILVER SET (9)	60.00	27.00
COMMON CARD (H1-H9)	3.00	1.35
*SINGLES: 4X TO 10X BASE CARD HI		
COMPLETE GOLD SET (9)	150.00	70.00
*GOLD CARDS: 12X TO 30X SILVERS		
❑ H1 Geoff Bodine	3.00	1.35
❑ H2 Jeff Burton	6.00	2.70
❑ H3 Derrike Cope	3.00	1.35
❑ H4 Jeff Gordon	30.00	13.50
❑ H5 Kyle Petty	6.00	2.70
❑ H6 Ricky Rudd	6.00	2.70
❑ H7 Richard Petty 1960's	14.00	6.25
❑ H8 Richard Petty 1980's	14.00	6.25
❑ H9 Richard Petty 1990's	14.00	6.25

1995 VIP Reflections

This five-card insert set features the artwork of Jeanne Barnes. The card fronts show a portrait of the driver as if you were looking at him from head on. The card backs show a portrait of the driver as if you were standing behind him. The cards are printed on both silver and gold foil board with Silver cards inserted at a rate of one per 72 packs. Gold cards were packaged 1:360 packs.

	MINT	NRMT
COMPLETE SILVER SET (5)	100.00	45.00
COMMON CARD (R1-R5)	10.00	4.50
*SINGLES: 6X TO 15X BASE CARD HI		
COMPLETE GOLD SET (5)	250.00	110.00
*GOLD CARDS: 15X TO 40X SILVERS		
❑ R1 Ricky Craven	10.00	4.50
❑ R2 Jeff Gordon	60.00	27.00
❑ R3 Sterling Marlin	10.00	4.50
❑ R4 Mark Martin	30.00	13.50
❑ R5 Rusty Wallace	30.00	13.50

1996 VIP

The 1996 V.I.P. set was issued in one series totalling 54 cards. The cards are packaged six cards per pack, 24 packs per box and 16 boxes per case. Each card is printed on 24 point board and has foil stamping and UV coating.

	MINT	NRMT
COMPLETE SET (54)	12.00	5.50
COMMON CARD (1-54)	.15	.07
COMMON DRIVER (1-54)	.30	.14
❑ 1 John Andretti	.30	.14
❑ 2 Johnny Benson	.30	.14
❑ 3 Geoff Bodine	.30	.14
❑ 4 Jeff Burton	.60	.25
❑ 5 Ward Burton	.30	.14
❑ 6 Ricky Craven	.30	.14
❑ 7 Wally Dallenbach	.30	.14
❑ 8 Dale Earnhardt	2.50	1.10
❑ 9 Bill Elliott	1.25	.55
❑ 10 Jeff Gordon	2.50	1.10
❑ 11 Bobby Hamilton	.30	.14
❑ 12 Ernie Irvan	.60	.25
❑ 13 Dale Jarrett	1.00	.45
❑ 14 Bobby Labonte	1.00	.45
❑ 15 Terry Labonte	1.25	.55
❑ 16 Sterling Marlin	.60	.25
❑ 17 Mark Martin	1.25	.55
❑ 18 Jeremy Mayfield	.75	.35
❑ 19 Ted Musgrave	.30	.14
❑ 20 Joe Nemechek	.30	.14
❑ 21 Kyle Petty	.60	.25
❑ 22 Robert Pressley	.30	.14
❑ 23 Ricky Rudd	.60	.25
❑ 24 Ken Schrader	.30	.14
❑ 25 Morgan Shepherd	.30	.14
❑ 26 Mike Skinner	.30	.14
❑ 27 Rusty Wallace	1.25	.55
❑ 28 Darrell Waltrip	.60	.25
❑ 29 Michael Waltrip	.30	.14
❑ 30 Jeff Gordon	2.50	1.10
❑ 31 Mark Martin	1.25	.55
❑ 32 David Green	.30	.14
❑ 33 Jeff Green	.30	.14
❑ 34 Jason Keller	.30	.14
❑ 35 Chad Little	.30	.14
❑ 36 Mike McLaughlin	.30	.14
❑ 37 Jeff Gordon's Car	1.25	.55
❑ 38 Dale Earnhardt's Car	1.25	.55
❑ 39 Bill Elliott's Car	.60	.25
❑ 40 Rusty Wallace's Car	.60	.25
❑ 41 Dale Jarrett's Car	.50	.23
❑ 42 Bobby Hamilton's Car	.15	.07
❑ 43 Ernie Irvan's Car	.30	.14
❑ 44 Ricky Rudd's Car	.30	.14
❑ 45 Mark Martin's Car	.50	.23
❑ 46 Ray Evernham	.60	.25
❑ 47 Steve Hmiel	.15	.07
❑ 48 Larry McReynolds	.15	.07
❑ 49 David Smith	.15	.07
❑ 50 Jeff Andrews	.15	.07
❑ 51 Danny Glad	.15	.07
❑ 52 Charlie Siegars	.15	.07
❑ 53 Rick Wetzel	.15	
❑ 54 Checklist	.15	

1996 VIP Emerald Proofs

This 54-card set is a parallel to the base V.I.P. se[t] cards feature a metallic green foil stamping to differ[entiate] them. There are 380 of each of the 54 cards and the[y] inserted at a rate of one per 40 packs.

	MINT
COMPLETE SET (54)	450.00
COMMON CARD (1-54)	4.00
COMMON DRIVER (1-54)	8.00
STARS: 10X to 25X BASIC CARDS	

1996 VIP Torquers

This 54-card set is a parallel to the base V.I.P. s[et] cards feature blue foil stamping and could be pull[ed at a] rate of one per pack.

	MINT
COMPLETE SET (54)	25.00
COMMON CARD (1-54)	.25
*TORQUER CARDS: 1.5X TO X BASIC CARDS	

1996 VIP Autographs

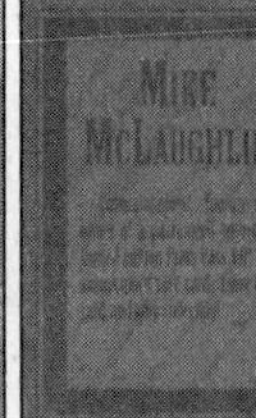

This 26-card set features desirable autograph[s of] NASCAR's biggest stars. More than 25,000 auto[graphs] were inserted in packs of V.I.P. The autograph car[ds were] inserted at a rate of one per 24 packs.

	MINT
COMPLETE SET (26)	700.00
COMMON CARD (1-26)	8.00
COMMON DRIVER (1-26)	15.00
❑ 1 Jeff Andrews	8.00
❑ 2 Johnny Benson	15.00
❑ 3 Geoff Bodine	15.00
❑ 4 Jeff Burton	30.00
❑ 5 Ricky Craven	15.00
❑ 6 Dale Earnhardt	200.00
❑ 7 Danny Glad	8.00
❑ 8 Jeff Gordon	200.00
❑ 9 David Green	15.00
❑ 10 Jeff Green	15.00
❑ 11 Steve Hmiel	8.00
❑ 12 Ernie Irvan	30.00
❑ 13 Jason Keller	15.00
❑ 14 Bobby Labonte	50.00
❑ 15 Chad Little	15.00
❑ 16 Jeremy Mayfield	40.00
❑ 17 Mike McLaughlin	15.00
❑ 18 Ted Musgrave	15.00
❑ 19 Joe Nemechek	15.00
❑ 20 Robert Pressley	15.00
❑ 21 Charlie Siegars	8.00
❑ 22 Mike Skinner	15.00
❑ 23 David Smith	8.00
❑ 24 Rusty Wallace	70.00
❑ 25 Michael Waltrip	15.00
❑ 26 Rick Wetzel	8.00

1996 VIP Dale Earnhard[t] Fire Suit

mly inserted in packs at a rate of one in 384, this ard set incorporates a piece of Dale Earnhardt's m in each card. There were four different color ons Gold foil 1:512, Silver foil 1:384 in Wal-mart acks, Blue foil 1:2,048, and Green 1:6,144. Cards ning multi-color pieces of cloth carry a 25% m over those that do not.

	MINT	NRMT
GOLD FOIL SET (2)	500.00	220.00
FOIL CARD (DE1-DE2)	250.00	110.00
OIL CARD (DE1-DE2)	400.00	180.00
FOIL CARD (DE1-DE2)	500.00	220.00
R FOIL CARD (DE1-DE2)	400.00	180.00
Dale Earnhardt	250.00	110.00
Dale Earnhardt	250.00	110.00

1996 VIP Head Gear

mly inserted in packs at a rate of one in 16, this ard set features today's top Winston Cup talent with elmets in an all-foil design. There was also a die-cut n of each Head Gear card and they were inserted at of one in 96 packs.

	MINT	NRMT
LETE SET (9)	80.00	36.00
ON CARD (HG1-HG9)	2.00	.90
LES: 3X TO 8X BASE CARD HI		
LETE DIE CUT SET (9)	200.00	90.00
T CARDS: 6X TO 15X BASIC CARDS		
Ricky Craven	2.00	.90
Dale Earnhardt	25.00	11.00
Jeff Gordon	25.00	11.00
Ernie Irvan	4.00	1.80
Mark Martin	15.00	6.75
Ricky Rudd	4.00	1.80
Rusty Wallace	15.00	6.75
Darrell Waltrip	4.00	1.80
Michael Waltrip	2.00	.90

6 VIP Sam Bass Top Flight

nly inserted in packs at a rate of one in 48, this rd set features art work from reknowned racing am Bass. The cards come with a silver foil boarder. s also a gold foil version inserted at a rate of one in cks.

	MINT	NRMT
LETE SET (5)	100.00	45.00
ON CARD (SB1-SB5)	20.00	9.00
LES: 6X TO 15X BASE CARD HI		
LETE GOLD SET (5)	200.00	90.00
CARDS: 12X TO 30X BASIC CARDS		
Dale Earnhardt	50.00	22.00
Bill Elliott	20.00	9.00
Terry Labonte	20.00	9.00
Mark Martin	20.00	9.00
Rusty Wallace	20.00	9.00

1996 VIP War Paint

nly inserted in packs at a rate of one in 12, this 18-t features the Winston Cup cars with wildest paint xed with all-foil NitroKrome technology.

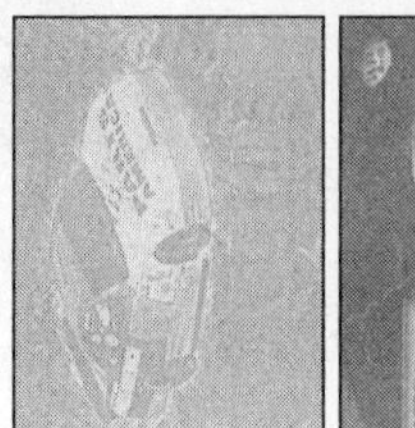

	MINT	NRMT
COMPLETE SET (18)	80.00	36.00
COMMON CARD (WP1-WP18)	2.00	.90
*SINGLES: 3X TO 8X BASE CARD HI		
COMPLETE GOLD SET (18)	150.00	70.00
GOLD CARDS: 6X TO 15X BASIC CARDS		
❑ WP1 Rusty Wallace's Car	12.00	5.50
❑ WP2 Dale Earnhardt's Car	25.00	11.00
❑ WP3 Sterling Marlin's Car	4.00	1.80
❑ WP4 Terry Labonte's Car	12.00	5.50
❑ WP5 Mark Martin's Car	12.00	5.50
❑ WP6 Ricky Rudd's Car	4.00	1.80
❑ WP7 Ted Musgrave's Car	2.00	.90
❑ WP8 Darrell Waltrip's Car	4.00	1.80
❑ WP9 Bobby Labonte's Car	8.00	3.60
❑ WP10 Michael Waltrip's Car	2.00	.90
❑ WP11 Ward Burton's Car	2.00	.90
❑ WP12 Jeff Gordon's Car	25.00	11.00
❑ WP13 Ernie Irvan's Car	4.00	1.80
❑ WP14 Ricky Craven's Car	2.00	.90
❑ WP15 Kyle Petty's Car	4.00	1.80
❑ WP16 Bobby Hamilton's Car	2.00	.90
❑ WP17 Dale Jarrett's Car	10.00	4.50
❑ WP18 Bill Elliott's Car	12.00	5.50

1997 VIP

This 50-card set features stars from the top three NASCAR divisions (Winston Cup, Busch Grand National and Truck racing) and was distributed in seven-card packs with a suggested retail price of $3.99. The set was printed on extra thick 24 pt. Card stock with two different foil stampings on the front.

	MINT	NRMT
COMPLETE SET (50)	15.00	6.75
COMMON CARD (1-50)	.15	.07
COMMON DRIVER (1-50)	.30	.14
❑ 1 Johnny Benson	.30	.14
❑ 2 Geoff Bodine	.30	.14
❑ 3 Jeff Burton	.60	.25
❑ 4 Ward Burton	.30	.14
❑ 5 Ricky Craven	.30	.14
❑ 6 Dale Earnhardt	3.00	1.35
❑ 7 Bill Elliott	1.50	.70
❑ 8 Jeff Gordon	3.00	1.35
❑ 9 Robby Gordon	.30	.14
❑ 10 Bobby Hamilton	.30	.14
❑ 11 Ernie Irvan	.60	.25
❑ 12 Dale Jarrett	1.25	.55
❑ 13 Bobby Labonte	1.25	.55
❑ 14 Terry Labonte	1.50	.70
❑ 15 Sterling Marlin	.60	.25
❑ 16 Mark Martin	1.50	.70
❑ 17 Ted Musgrave	.30	.14
❑ 18 Joe Nemechek	.30	.14
❑ 19 Kyle Petty	.60	.25
❑ 20 Ricky Rudd	.60	.25
❑ 21 Ken Schrader	.30	.14
❑ 22 Mike Skinner	.30	.14
❑ 23 Rusty Wallace	1.50	.70
❑ 24 Darrell Waltrip	.60	.25
❑ 25 Michael Waltrip	.30	.14
❑ 26 David Green	.30	.14
❑ 27 Chad Little	.30	.14
❑ 28 Todd Bodine	.30	.14
❑ 29 Tim Fedewa	.30	.14
❑ 30 Jeff Fuller	.30	.14
❑ 31 Jeff Green	.30	.14
❑ 32 Jason Keller	.30	.14
❑ 33 Randy LaJoie	.30	.14
❑ 34 Kevin Lepage	.30	.14
❑ 35 Mark Martin	1.50	.70
❑ 36 Mike McLaughlin	.30	.14
❑ 37 Rich Bickle	.30	.14
❑ 38 Mike Bliss	.30	.14
❑ 39 Rick Carelli	.30	.14
❑ 40 Ron Hornaday	.30	.14
❑ 41 Kenny Irwin	2.00	.90
❑ 42 Tammy Jo Kirk	.30	.14
❑ 43 Butch Miller	.30	.14
❑ 44 Joe Ruttman	.30	.14
❑ 45 Jack Sprague	.30	.14
❑ 46 Jeff Burton	.60	.25
❑ 47 Dale Jarrett	1.25	.55
❑ 48 Mark Martin	1.50	.70
❑ 49 Bruton Smith Eddie Gossage	.15	.07
❑ 50 Checklist	.15	.07

1997 VIP Explosives

This 50-card set is parallel to the regular base set and is similar in design. The difference is found in the state of the art technology used in etching and in the foil board it is printed on.

	MINT	NRMT
COMPLETE SET (50)	30.00	13.50
COMMON CARD (1-50)	.30	.14
COMMON DRIVER (1-50)	.60	.25
*EXPLOSIVE CARDS: .75X TO 2X BASIC CARDS		

1997 VIP Oil Slicks

Randomly inserted in hobby only packs at the rate of one in 64, this 50-card set is a custom made foil parallel version of the regular base VIP set. Only 100 of each card was produced and are individually numbered.

	MINT	NRMT
COMPLETE SET (50)	600.00	275.00
COMMON CARD (1-50)	8.00	3.60
COMMON DRIVER (1-50)	15.00	6.75
*OIL SLICKS: 15X TO 40X BASIC CARDS		

1997 VIP Head Gear

Randomly inserted in packs at the rate of one in 16, this nine-card set features the hottest drivers and driver helmets on the Winston Cup circuit and are printed on cards with an all foil NitroKrome embossed design.

	MINT	NRMT
COMPLETE SET (9)	50.00	22.00
COMMON CARD (HG1-HG9)	1.50	.70
*SINGLES: 2X TO 5X BASE CARD HI		
❑ HG1 Dale Earnhardt	20.00	9.00
❑ HG2 Bill Elliott	10.00	4.50
❑ HG3 Jeff Gordon	20.00	9.00
❑ HG4 Ernie Irvan	3.00	1.35
❑ HG5 Mark Martin	10.00	4.50
❑ HG6 Kyle Petty	3.00	1.35
❑ HG7 Ricky Rudd	3.00	1.35
❑ HG8 Rusty Wallace	10.00	4.50
❑ HG9 Michael Waltrip	1.50	.70

1997 VIP Head Gear Die Cut

Randomly inserted in packs at the rate of one in 40, this nine-card set is a parallel die cut version of the regular Head Gear insert set.

	MINT	NRMT
COMPLETE SET (9)	75.00	34.00
COMMON CARD (HG1-HG9)	2.25	1.00

1997 VIP Knights of Thunder

Randomly inserted in packs at the rate of one in 30, this six-card set features original artworks of leading drivers by number one Race Artist, Sam Bass.

	MINT	NRMT
COMPLETE SET (6)	80.00	36.00
COMMON CARD (KT1-KT6)	5.00	2.20

*SINGLES: 3X TO 8X BASE CARD HI

	MINT	NRMT
❑ KT1 Dale Earnhardt	30.00	13.50
❑ KT2 Jeff Gordon	30.00	13.50
❑ KT3 Dale Jarrett	12.00	5.50
❑ KT4 Bobby Labonte	6.00	2.70
❑ KT5 Terry Labonte	16.00	7.25
❑ KT6 Rusty Wallace	16.00	7.25

1997 VIP Knights of Thunder Gold

Randomly inserted in packs at the rate of one in 120, this six-card set is a parallel gold foil version of the regular Knights of Thunder insert set.

	MINT	NRMT
COMPLETE SET (6)	200.00	90.00
COMMON CARD (KT1-KT6)	7.50	3.40

1997 VIP Precious Metal

Randomly inserted in packs at the rate of one in 384, this set features color photos on authentic race-used sheet metal from top drivers and incorporated into a thick laminated card. Each card is individually numbered to 500 and comes with a certificate of authenticity. Cards with multi-color pieces of sheet metal carry a 25% premium over those that do not.

	MINT	NRMT
COMPLETE SET (5)	900.00	400.00
COMMON CARD (SM1-SM5)	120.00	55.00

MULTI-COLOR METAL: .75X TO 1.25X

	MINT	NRMT
❑ SM1 Jeff Gordon	350.00	160.00
❑ SM2 Bobby Labonte	150.00	70.00
❑ SM3 Bill Elliott	200.00	90.00
❑ SM4 Terry Labonte	200.00	90.00
❑ SM5 Rusty Wallace	200.00	90.00

1997 VIP Ring of Honor

Randomly inserted in packs at the rate of one in 10, this 12-card set features color photos of top NASCAR tracks and drivers who have tamed them. The set is printed on thick card stock and clear acetate.

	MINT	NRMT
COMPLETE SET (12)	40.00	18.00
COMMON CARD (1-12)	.75	.35

*SINGLES: 1.25X TO 3X BASE CARD HI

	MINT	NRMT
❑ RH1 Rusty Wallace's Car	8.00	3.60
❑ RH2 Dale Earnhardt's Car	15.00	6.75
❑ RH3 Sterling Marlin's Car	1.50	.70
❑ RH4 Terry Labonte's Car	8.00	3.60
❑ RH5 Mark Martin's Car	8.00	3.60
❑ RH6 Ricky Rudd's Car	1.50	.70
❑ RH7 Bobby Labonte's Car	4.00	1.80
❑ RH8 Jeff Gordon's Car	15.00	6.75
❑ RH9 Ernie Irvan's Car	1.50	.70
❑ RH10 Bobby Hamilton's Car	.75	.35
❑ RH11 Dale Jarrett's Car	6.00	2.70
❑ RH12 Bill Elliott's Car	8.00	3.60

1997 VIP Ring of Honor Die Cut

Randomly inserted in packs at the rate of one in 30, this 12-card set is a die cut parallel version of the regular Ring of Honor set.

	MINT	NRMT
COMPLETE SET (12)	60.00	27.00
COMMON CARD (1-12)	1.25	.55

1998 VIP

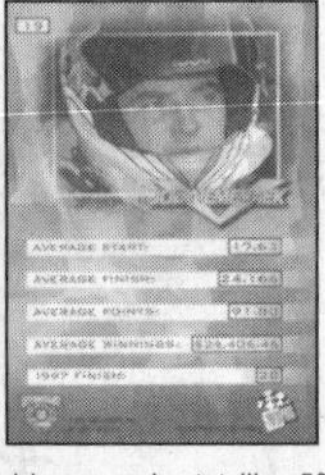

The 1998 VIP set was issued in one series totalling 50 cards. The card fronts feature full bleed color photography with two channels of etched foil stamping. The set contains the topical subsets: Winston Drivers (1-27), Busch Drivers (28-36), Winston Cars (37-46), and Las Vegas Motor Speedway (47-50).

	MINT	NRMT
COMPLETE SET (50)	30.00	13.50
COMMON CARD (1-50)	.15	.07
COMMON DRIVER (1-50)	.30	.14

	MINT	NRMT
❑ 1 John Andretti	.30	.14
❑ 2 Johnny Benson	.30	.14
❑ 3 Geoff Bodine	.30	.14
❑ 4 Jeff Burton	.60	.25
❑ 5 Ward Burton	.30	.14
❑ 6 Dale Earnhardt	3.00	1.35
❑ 7 Bill Elliott	1.50	.70
❑ 8 Jeff Gordon	3.00	1.35
❑ 9 Bobby Hamilton	.30	.14
❑ 10 Ernie Irvan	.60	.25
❑ 11 Kenny Irwin	1.00	.45
❑ 12 Dale Jarrett	1.25	.55
❑ 13 Bobby Labonte	1.25	.55
❑ 14 Terry Labonte	1.50	.70
❑ 15 Sterling Marlin	.60	.25
❑ 16 Mark Martin	1.50	.70
❑ 17 Jeremy Mayfield	1.00	.45
❑ 18 Ted Musgrave	.30	.14
❑ 19 Joe Nemechek	.30	.14
❑ 20 Steve Park	1.25	.55
❑ 21 Robert Pressley	.30	.14
❑ 22 Ricky Rudd	.60	.25
❑ 23 Ken Schrader	.30	.14
❑ 24 Mike Skinner	.30	.14
❑ 25 Jimmy Spencer	.30	.14
❑ 26 Rusty Wallace	1.50	.70
❑ 27 Michael Waltrip	.30	.14
❑ 28 Dale Earnhardt Jr.	4.00	1.80
❑ 29 Tim Fedewa	.30	.14
❑ 30 Jason Keller	.30	.14
❑ 31 Randy LaJoie	.30	.14
❑ 32 Mark Martin	1.50	.70
❑ 33 Mike McLaughlin	.30	.14
❑ 34 Elliott Sadler	.30	.14
❑ 35 Hermie Sadler	.30	.14
❑ 36 Tony Stewart	2.00	.90
❑ 37 Jeff Burton's Car	.30	.14
❑ 38 Dale Earnhardt's Car	1.50	.70
❑ 39 Bill Elliott's Car	.75	.35
❑ 40 Jeff Gordon's Car	1.50	.70
❑ 41 Dale Jarrett's Car	.60	.25
❑ 42 Bobby Labonte's Car	.60	.25
❑ 43 Terry Labonte's Car	.75	.35
❑ 44 Chad Little's Car	.15	.07
❑ 45 Mark Martin's Car	.75	
❑ 46 Rusty Wallace's Car	.75	
❑ 47 Mark Martin	1.50	
❑ 48 Dale Jarrett	1.25	
❑ 49 Roush Racing	.15	
❑ 50 Mark Martin CL	1.50	

1998 VIP Explosives

Randomly inserted one in every pack, this parallel base set is etched using a special custom die and p on a unifoil board.

	MINT
COMPLETE SET (50)	60.00
COMMON CARD (1-50)	.50
COMMON DRIVER (1-50)	1.00

1998 VIP Driving Force

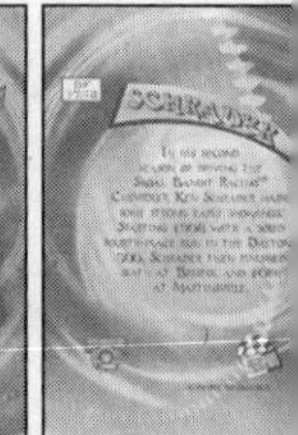

Randomly inserted in packs at a rate of one in 10, th card insert set features NASCAR's stock cars prin all-foil cards.

	MINT
COMPLETE SET (18)	50.00
COMMON CARD (DF1 - DF18)	1.00

*SINGLES: 1.25X TO 3X BASE CARD HI

	MINT
❑ DF1 John Andretti's Car	1.00
❑ DF2 Johnny Benson's Car	1.00
❑ DF3 Jeff Burton's Car	2.00
❑ DF4 Ward Burton's Car	1.00
❑ DF5 Dale Earnhardt's Car	10.00
❑ DF6 Bill Elliott's Car	5.00
❑ DF7 Jeff Gordon's Car	10.00
❑ DF8 Bobby Hamilton's Car	1.00
❑ DF9 Kenny Irwin's Car	3.00
❑ DF10 Dale Jarrett's Car	4.00
❑ DF11 Bobby Labonte's Car	4.00
❑ DF12 Terry Labonte's Car	5.00
❑ DF13 Sterling Marlin's Car	2.00
❑ DF14 Mark Martin's Car	5.00
❑ DF15 Jeremy Mayfield's Car	3.00
❑ DF16 Ricky Rudd's Car	2.00
❑ DF17 Ken Schrader's Car	1.00
❑ DF18 Rusty Wallace's Car	5.00

1998 VIP Driving Force Die

Randomly inserted in packs at a rate of one in 3 special 18-card die-cut version features NASCAR's cars printed on all-foil cards.

	MINT
COMPLETE SET (18)	100.00
COMMON CARD (DF1 - DF18)	2.00

1998 VIP Head Gear

Randomly inserted in packs at a rate of one in 16, card insert set was printed on all-foil and cus sculptured to resemble a driver's helmet.

	MINT
COMPLETE SET (9)	40.00
COMMON CARD (HG1 - HG9)	2.00

*SINGLES: 1.25X TO 3X BASE CARD HI

	MINT
❑ HG1 Jeff Burton	2.00
❑ HG2 Dale Earnhardt	10.00

	MINT	NRMT
Bill Elliott	5.00	2.20
Jeff Gordon	10.00	4.50
Dale Jarrett	4.00	1.80
Bobby Labonte	4.00	1.80
Terry Labonte	5.00	2.20
Mark Martin	5.00	2.20
Rusty Wallace	5.00	2.20

998 VIP Head Gear Diecut

mly inserted in packs at a rate of one in 40, this 9-
ısert set was printed on all-foil, specially die-cut,
stomed sculptured to resemble a driver's helmet.

	MINT	NRMT
ʟETE SET (9)	60.00	27.00
'ON CARD (HG1 - HG9)	5.00	2.20

1998 VIP Lap Leader

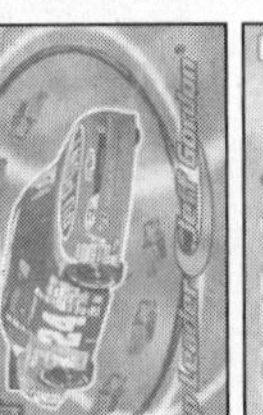
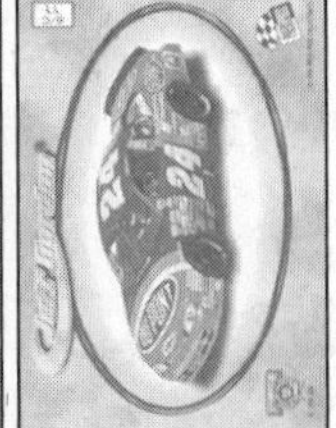

ˉnly inserted in packs at a rate of one in 20, this 9-
nsert features the top NASCAR rides on micro-
sed, super thick all-foil board.

	MINT	NRMT
ʟETE SET (9)	40.00	18.00
ON CARD (LL1 - LL9)	2.00	.90
ʟES: 1.25X TO 3X BASE CARD HI		

	MINT	NRMT
Jeff Burton's Car	2.00	.90
Dale Earnhardt's Car	10.00	4.50
Jeff Gordon's Car	10.00	4.50
Dale Jarrett's Car	4.00	1.80
Bobby Labonte's Car	4.00	1.80
Terry Labonte's Car	5.00	2.20
Mark Martin's Car	5.00	2.20
Jeremy Mayfield's Car	3.00	1.35
Rusty Wallace's Car	5.00	2.20

98 VIP Lap Leader Acetate

ˉnly inserted in packs at a rate of one in 60, this 9-
ısert features the top NASCAR rides on an acetate
tock card with double etched foil stamping.

	MINT	NRMT
ʟETE SET (9)	60.00	27.00
ON CARD (LL1 - LL9)	4.00	1.80

998 VIP NASCAR Country

ˉnly inserted in packs at a rate of one in 10, this 9-
sert helps celebrate NASCAR's 50th Anniversary.
rds feature the top NASCAR Winston Cup drivers
up with today's top country music.

	MINT	NRMT
ʟETE SET (9)	40.00	18.00
ON CARD (NC1 - NC9)	2.00	.90
ʟES: 1.25X TO 3X BASE CARD HI		

	MINT	NRMT
Dale Earnhardt	10.00	4.50
Bill Elliott	5.00	2.20
Jeff Gordon	10.00	4.50
Dale Jarrett	4.00	1.80
Bobby Labonte	4.00	1.80
Terry Labonte	5.00	2.20
Mark Martin	5.00	2.20
Ricky Rudd	2.00	.90
Rusty Wallace	5.00	2.20

1998 VIP NASCAR Country Diecut

Randomly inserted in packs at a rate of one in 30, this 9-card insert also helps celebrate NASCAR's 50th Anniversary. The special die-cut cards feature the top NASCAR Winston Cup drivers teamed up with today's top country music.

	MINT	NRMT
COMPLETE SET (9)	80.00	36.00
COMMON CARD (NC1 - NC9)	4.00	1.80

1998 VIP Triple Gear "Sheet Metal"

Randomly inserted in packs at a rate of one in 384, this 9-card insert set offers race-used sheet metal from the top NASCAR Winston Cup teams. Cards with multi-color pieces of sheet metal carry a 25% premium over those that do not. These cards are numbered to 225.

	MINT	NRMT
COMPLETE SET (9)	1000.00	450.00
COMMON CARD (TGS1 - TGS9)	50.00	22.00

	MINT	NRMT
❑ TGS1 Rusty Wallace	120.00	55.00
❑ TGS2 Dale Earnhardt	225.00	100.00
❑ TGS3 Terry Labonte	120.00	55.00
❑ TGS4 Mark Martin	120.00	55.00
❑ TGS5 Bobby Labonte	100.00	45.00
❑ TGS6 Jeff Gordon	225.00	100.00
❑ TGS7 Mike Skinner	50.00	22.00
❑ TGS8 Dale Jarrett	100.00	45.00
❑ TGS9 Jeff Burton	75.00	34.00

1996 Viper

This 78-card set features many of the top names in Winston Cup. The cards use the theme of the snake with the Viper logo appearing in the top left hand corner of each card. Cards are printed on 24-point stock. There are both hobby and retail boxes of Viper. Each box contains 24 packs with five cards per pack. Each card in the first 325 cases printed carried a special First Strike logo. These first strike cards are parallel to the base set. The first strike cards were packaged separately in specially marked boxes and packs.

	MINT	NRMT
COMPLETE SET (78)	15.00	6.75
COMMON CARD (1-78)	.10	.05
COMMON DRIVER (1-78)	.20	.09
FIRST STRIKE COMP. SET (78)	30.00	13.50
*FIRST STRIKE CARDS: .75X TO 2X BASIC CARDS		
COMP. RED COBRA SET (78)	80.00	36.00
*RED COBRA CARDS: 2X TO 4X BASIC CARDS		

	MINT	NRMT
❑ 1 Dale Earnhardt	2.00	.90
❑ 2 Jeff Gordon	2.00	.90
❑ 3 Sterling Marlin	.40	.18
❑ 4 Mark Martin	1.00	.45
❑ 5 Terry Labonte	1.00	.45
❑ 6 Rusty Wallace	1.00	.45
❑ 7 Bill Elliott	1.00	.45
❑ 8 Bobby Labonte	.75	.35
❑ 9 Ward Burton	.20	.09
❑ 10 Bobby Hamilton	.20	.09
❑ 11 Dale Jarrett	.75	.35
❑ 12 Ted Musgrave	.20	.09
❑ 13 Darrell Waltrip	.40	.18
❑ 14 Kyle Petty	.40	.18
❑ 15 Ken Schrader	.20	.09
❑ 16 Michael Waltrip	.20	.09
❑ 17 Derrike Cope	.20	.09
❑ 18 Jeff Burton	.20	.09
❑ 19 Ricky Craven	.40	.18
❑ 20 Steve Grissom	.20	.09
❑ 21 Robert Pressley	.20	.09
❑ 22 Joe Nemechek	.20	.09
❑ 23 Jeremy Mayfield	.60	.25
❑ 24 Mike Wallace	.20	.09
❑ 25 Johnny Benson	.20	.09
❑ 26 Jimmy Spencer	.20	.09
❑ 27 Tony Glover	.10	.05
❑ 28 Steve Hmiel	.10	.05
❑ 29 Mike Beam	.10	.05
❑ 30 Larry McReynolds	.10	.05
❑ 31 Robin Pemberton	.10	.05
❑ 32 Jimmy Makar	.10	.05
❑ 33 Richard Childress	.10	.05
❑ 34 Joe Gibbs	.20	.09
❑ 35 Jack Roush	.10	.05
❑ 36 Roger Penske	.10	.05
❑ 37 Mark Martin	1.00	.45
❑ 38 Bobby Labonte	.75	.35
❑ 39 Terry Labonte	1.00	.45
❑ 40 Jeff Gordon	2.00	.90
❑ 41 Rusty Wallace	1.00	.45
❑ 42 Jeff Gordon	2.00	.90
❑ 43 Dale Earnhardt	2.00	.90
❑ 44 Mark Martin	1.00	.45
❑ 45 Mark Martin	1.00	.45
❑ 46 Ward Burton	.20	.09
❑ 47 Chad Little	.20	.09
❑ 48 Mike McLaughlin	.20	.09
❑ 49 Jason Keller	.20	.09
❑ 50 David Green	.20	.09
❑ 51 Larry Pearson	.20	.09
❑ 52 Jeff Fuller	.20	.09
❑ 53 David Green	.20	.09
❑ 54 Hermie Sadler	.20	.09
❑ 55 Bobby Dotter	.20	.09
❑ 56 Terry Labonte	1.00	.45
❑ 57 Mark Martin	1.00	.45
❑ 58 Dale Jarrett	.75	.35
❑ 59 Michael Waltrip	.20	.09
❑ 60 Joe Nemechek	.20	.09
❑ 61 Ken Schrader	.20	.09
❑ 62 Mike Wallace	.20	.09
❑ 63 Randy Porter	.20	.09
❑ 64 Mike Skinner	.20	.09
❑ 65 Joe Ruttman	.20	.09
❑ 66 Ron Hornaday	.20	.09
❑ 67 Butch Miller	.20	.09
❑ 68 Rick Carelli	.20	.09
❑ 69 Bill Sedgwick	.20	.09
❑ 70 Tobey Butler	.20	.09
❑ 71 Steve Portenga	.20	.09
❑ 72 Bob Keselowski	.20	.09
❑ 73 Ken Schrader	.20	.09
❑ 74 Johnny Benson	.20	.09
❑ 75 Mike Chase	.20	.09
❑ 76 Checklist	.10	.05
❑ 77 Checklist	.10	.05
❑ 78 Cover Card	.10	.05

1996 Viper Black Mamba

This 78-card set is a hobby only parallel version of the base Viper set. The Black Mamba cards feature a black foil stamping to differentiate them from the base cards. The cards were randomly seeded in hobby packs at a rate of one per 13 packs. The cards are sequentially numbered of 499. There was also a special Black Mamba #R3 Dale Earnhardt card randomly inserted in packs.

	MINT	NRMT
COMPLETE SET (78)	350.00	160.00
COMMON CARD (1-78)	2.50	1.10
COMMON DRIVER (1-78)	5.00	2.20
BLACK MAMBA CARDS: 10X TO 25X BASIC CARDS		
D.EARN.R3 BLK MBA INSERT	75.00	34.00
COMP. FS SET (78)	700.00	325.00
*FS CARDS: .75X TO 2X REG.BLACK MAMBA		

1996 Viper Copperhead

This 78-card set is a parallel of the base Viper set. The cards feature a copper foil stamping and were randomly inserted at a rate of one in seven packs. Each Copperhead card is die cut and sequentially numbered of 1,399.

	MINT	NRMT
COMPLETE SET (78)	150.00	70.00
COMMON CARD (1-78)	1.25	.55
COMMON DRIVER (1-78)	2.50	1.10
*COPPERHEAD CARDS: 3X TO 8X HI COLUMN		
COMP.FIRST STRIKE SET (78)	300.00	135.00
*FS CARDS: .75X TO 2X REG.COPPERHEAD CARDS		

1996 Viper Green Mamba

This 78-card set is retail only parallel to the base Viper set. The cards are randomly inserted in retail only packs at a rate of one per 13 packs. The cards feature green foil stamping and are sequentially numbered of 349.

	MINT	NRMT
COMPLETE SET (78)	400.00	180.00
COMMON CARD (1-78)	3.00	1.35

COMMON DRIVER (1-78)	6.00	2.70
*GREEN MAMBA CARDS: 12X TO 30X BASIC CARDS		
D.EARNHARDT R3 G.MAMBA INSERT	75.00	34.00

1996 Viper Busch Clash

This 16-card set features drivers who captured a pole in 1995. The cards have many of the drivers holding the traditional Busch Pole plaque. The cards were inserted at a rate of one in eight packs. There was also a First Strike version available in First Strike boxes at a rate of one in eight packs

	MINT	NRMT
COMPLETE SET (16)	60.00	27.00
COMMON CARDS (B1-B16)	1.50	.70
*SINGLES: 3X TO 8X BASE CARD HI		
COMP. FIRST STRIKE SET (16)	100.00	45.00
*FIRST STRIKE CARDS: 5X TO 12X BASIC CARDS		
❑ B1 Terry Labonte	10.00	4.50
❑ B2 John Andretti	1.50	.70
❑ B3 Hut Stricklin	1.50	.70
❑ B4 David Green	1.50	.70
❑ B5 Jeff Gordon	20.00	9.00
❑ B6 Darrell Waltrip	3.00	1.35
❑ B7 Dale Jarrett	8.00	3.60
❑ B8 Sterling Marlin	3.00	1.35
❑ B9 Rick Mast	1.50	.70
❑ B10 Dave Marcis	3.00	1.35
❑ B11 Mark Martin	10.00	4.50
❑ B12 Ken Schrader	1.50	.70
❑ B13 Ted Musgrave	1.50	.70
❑ B14 Dale Earnhardt	20.00	9.00
❑ B15 Bobby Labonte	3.00	1.35
❑ B16 Bill Elliott	10.00	4.50

1996 Viper Cobra

This 10-card insert set ten of the top 15 finishers in the 1995 Winston Cup points race. The cards are randomly inserted one per 48 packs. The First Strike version has the same odds in First Strike boxes.

	MINT	NRMT
COMPLETE SET (10)	100.00	45.00
COMMON CARD (C1-C10)	3.00	1.35
*SINGLES: 6X TO 15X BASE CARD HI		
COMP. FIRST STRIKE SET (10)	150.00	70.00
*FS COBRA CARDS: 10X TO 25X BASIC CARDS		
❑ C1 Dale Earnhardt	35.00	16.00
❑ C2 Jeff Gordon	35.00	16.00
❑ C3 Bobby Labonte	10.00	4.50
❑ C4 Mark Martin	15.00	6.75
❑ C5 Sterling Marlin	6.00	2.70
❑ C6 Rusty Wallace	15.00	6.75
❑ C7 Terry Labonte	15.00	6.75
❑ C8 Bill Elliott	15.00	6.75
❑ C9 Bobby Hamilton	3.00	1.35
❑ C10 Dale Jarrett	12.00	5.50

1996 Viper Dale Earnhardt

This set was available through a redemption of a winning viper venom card. The set features seven time Winston Cup Champion Dale Earnhardt and comes in a simulated snake skin case.

	MINT	NRMT
COMPLETE SET (3)	60.00	27.00
COMMON CARD	20.00	9.00
❑ 1 Dale Earnhardt	20.00	9.00
❑ 2 Dale Earnhardt	20.00	9.00
❑ 3 Dale Earnhardt	20.00	9.00

1996 Viper Diamondback

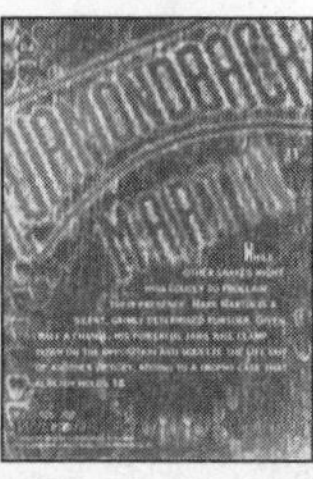

This eight-card insert set features a patch of simulated rattlesnake skin next to the picture of the driver on the fronts of the cards. The cards are randomly inserted in packs one per 72 packs. Each card is sequentially numbered of 1,499. The First Strike version were cards inserted into specially marked boxes of Viper First Strike. The cards are a parallel to the base cards.

	MINT	NRMT
COMPLETE SET (8)	150.00	70.00
COMMON CARD (D1-D8)	15.00	6.75
*SINGLES: 8X TO 20X BASE CARD HI		
COMP. FIRST STRIKE SET (8)	200.00	90.00
*FS DIAMONDBACK CARDS: 12X TO 30X BASIC CARDS		
❑ D1 Jeff Gordon	60.00	27.00
❑ D2 Dale Earnhardt	60.00	27.00
❑ D3 Bobby Labonte	12.00	5.50
❑ D4 Mark Martin	25.00	11.00
❑ D5 Terry Labonte	25.00	11.00
❑ D6 Rusty Wallace	25.00	11.00
❑ D7 Sterling Marlin	20.00	9.00
❑ D8 Bill Elliott	25.00	11.00

1996 Viper Diamondback Authentic

This eight-card insert set features authentic diamondback rattlesnake skin attached to each card. The cards are inserted at a rate of one per 120 packs and are sequentially numbered of 749. There is also a parallel First Strike version that is available in specially marked Viper First Strike boxes.

	MINT	NRMT
COMPLETE SET (8)	400.00	180.00
COMMON CARD (DA1-DA8)	40.00	18.00
COMP. FIRST STRIKE SET (8)	600.00	275.00
COMP.CALIFORNIA SET (8)	800.00	350.00
❑ DA1 Jeff Gordon	150.00	70.00
❑ DA2 Dale Earnhardt	150.00	70.00
❑ DA3 Sterling Marlin	40.00	18.00
❑ DA4 Bobby Labonte	50.00	22.00
❑ DA5 Rusty Wallace	70.00	32.00
❑ DA6 Terry Labonte	70.00	32.00
❑ DA7 Mark Martin	70.00	32.00
❑ DA8 Bill Elliott	70.00	32.00

1996 Viper King Cobra

This 10-card set is a jumbo sized parallel to the Viper Cobra insert set. The cards measure 3" X 5" and were inserted into boxes of Viper at a rate of one per three boxes. Each card is sequentially numbered of 699. The First Strike version is a parallel to the base cards and comes in specially marked Viper First Strike boxes.

	MINT	NRMT
COMPLETE SET (10)	150.00	70.00
COMMON CARDS (KC1-KC10)	3.00	1.35
*SINGLES: 6X TO 15X BASE CARD HI		
COMP. FIRST STRIKE SET (10)	200.00	90.00
*FS KING COBRA CARDS: 8X TO 20X BASIC CARDS		
❑ KC1 Dale Earnhardt	60.00	27.00
❑ KC2 Jeff Gordon	60.00	27.00
❑ KC3 Dale Jarrett	18.00	8.00
❑ KC4 Bill Elliott	25.00	11.00
❑ KC5 Terry Labonte	25.00	11.00
❑ KC6 Bobby Hamilton	3.00	1.35
❑ KC7 Rusty Wallace	25.00	11.00
❑ KC8 Mark Martin	25.00	11.00
❑ KC9 Bobby Labonte	12.00	
❑ KC10 Sterling Marlin	6.00	

1996 Viper Cobra Dale Earnhardt Mom-n-Pop's

This three-card set was available directly from M Pop's. The cards are similar to the three card Vipe Earnhardt redemption set except these cards are cards. The cards come in a simulated snake ski with red crushed velvet on the inside.

	MINT
COMPLETE SET (3)	35.00
COMMON CARD (1-3)	12.00
❑ 1 Dale Earnhardt	12.00
❑ 2 Dale Earnhardt	12.00
❑ 3 Dale Earnhardt	12.00

1997 Viper

This 82-card set features many of the top nar Winston Cup. The cards use the theme of the snak the Viper logo appearing in the top left hand cor each card. There are both hobby and retail boxes of Each hobby box contains 24 packs with six car pack. Each retail box contains 30 packs with five ca pack. There were 200 Eastern cases and 1,000 W cases produced. The difference in these cases Diamondback Authentic cards. The Eastern cases c cards that were not produced from Western Diamor skin. Each 16-box hobby case contains 12 regular and four First Strike boxes. Each card in the First boxes carried a special First Strike logo. These first cards are parallel to the base and parallel sets.

	MINT
COMPLETE SET (82)	20.00
COMMON CARD (1-82)	.10
COMMON DRIVER (1-82)	.20
CAR CARDS HALF VALUE	
COMP. FIRST STRIKE SET (82)	30.00
*FIRST STRIKE CARDS: .5X TO 1.25X BASIC CARD	
❑ 1 Jeff Gordon	2.00
❑ 2 Dale Jarrett	.75
❑ 3 Terry Labonte	1.00
❑ 4 Mark Martin	1.00
❑ 5 Rusty Wallace	1.00
❑ 6 Bobby Labonte	.75
❑ 7 Sterling Marlin	.40
❑ 8 Jeff Burton	.40
❑ 9 Ted Musgrave	.20
❑ 10 Michael Waltrip	.20
❑ 11 David Green	.20
❑ 12 Ricky Craven	.20
❑ 13 Johnny Benson	.20
❑ 14 Jeremy Mayfield	.60
❑ 15 Bobby Hamilton	.20
❑ 16 Kyle Petty	.40
❑ 17 Darrell Waltrip	.40
❑ 18 Wally Dallenbach	.20
❑ 19 Bill Elliott	1.00
❑ 20 Robert Pressley	.20
❑ 21 Joe Nemechek	.20
❑ 22 Derrike Cope	.20
❑ 23 Ward Burton	.20
❑ 24 Chad Little	.20
❑ 25 Mike Skinner	.20
❑ 26 Brett Bodine	.20
❑ 27 Hut Stricklin	.20
❑ 28 Dave Marcis	.40
❑ 29 Ken Schrader	.20
❑ 30 Steve Grissom	.20
❑ 31 Robby Gordon	.20
❑ 32 Kenny Wallace	.20
❑ 33 Bobby Hillin, Jr.	.20
❑ 34 Jimmy Spencer	.20
❑ 35 Dick Trickle	.20
❑ 36 John Andretti	.20
❑ 37 Steve Park	2.00

‹eff Burton	.40	.18
‹ichael Waltrip	.20	.09
‹ale Jarrett	.75	.35
‹ike McLaughlin	.20	.09
‹odd Bodine	.20	.09
‹obby Labonte	.75	.35
‹eff Fuller	.20	.09
‹yle Petty	.40	.18
‹ason Keller	.20	.09
‹ark Martin	1.00	.45
‹andy Lajoie	.20	.09
‹oe Nemechek	.20	.09
‹lenn Allen	.20	.09
‹eff Gordon	2.00	.90
‹usty Wallace	1.00	.45
‹ale Jarrett	.75	.35
‹eff Burton	.40	.18
‹ale Jarrett	.75	.35
‹eff Hammond	.10	.05
‹ndy Petree	.10	.05
‹obbie Loomis	.10	.05
‹ike Beam	.10	.05
‹uddy Parrott	.10	.05
‹oger Penske	.10	.05
‹ill Davis	.10	.05
‹ravis Carter	.10	.05
‹huck Rider	.10	.05
‹elix Sabates	.10	.05
‹arry Hedrick	.10	.05
‹usty Wallace's Car	.50	.23
‹ale Earnhardt's Car	1.00	.45
‹erry Labonte's Car	.50	.23
‹ark Martin's Car	.50	.23
‹rett Bodine's Car	.10	.05
‹obby Labonte's Car	.40	.18
‹immy Spencer's Car	.10	.05
‹eff Gordon's Car	1.00	.45
‹ike Skinner's Car	.10	.05
‹obby Gordon's Car	.10	.05
‹ally Dallenbach's Car	.10	.05
‹yle Petty's Car	.20	.09
‹ale Jarrett's Car	.40	.18
‹ill Elliott's Car	.50	.23
‹hecklist	.10	.05
‹hecklist	.10	.05

1997 Viper Black Racer

‹2-card insert set is a parallel to the base Viper set. ‹eatures cards that are horizontal and have the Black ‹ logo. The First Strike version of these cards were ‹ed into specially marked boxes of Viper First Strike. ‹ards were randomly inserted hobby packs, First ‹ packs and retial packs at a ratio of 1:5

	MINT	NRMT
‹LETE SET (82)	120.00	55.00
‹ON CARD (1-82)	.75	.35
‹ON DRIVER (1-82)	1.50	.70
‹K RACERS: 3X TO 8X BASIC CARDS		
‹. FIRST STRIKE SET (82)	150.00	70.00
‹T STRIKE CARDS: .5X TO 1.25X BLACK RACER ‹S		

1997 Viper Anaconda

‹13-card insert set features oversized cards ‹iting the top stars of the Winston Cup circuit. The ‹ were randomly inserted a chiptoppers at a ratio of ‹r two hobby boxes.

	MINT	NRMT
‹LETE SET (13)	100.00	45.00
‹ON CARD (A1-A13)	3.00	1.35
‹LES: 6X TO 15X BASE CARD HI		
‹erry Labonte	25.00	11.00
‹eff Gordon	40.00	18.00
‹ale Jarrett	20.00	9.00
‹obby Labonte	12.00	5.50
‹ale Earnhardt	40.00	18.00
‹usty Wallace	25.00	11.00
‹arrell Waltrip	6.00	2.70
‹oe Nemechek	3.00	1.35
❑ A9 Jeremy Mayfield	8.00	3.60
❑ A10 Bill Elliott	25.00	11.00
❑ A11 Jeff Burton	6.00	2.70
❑ A12 Mark Martin	25.00	11.00
❑ A13 Kyle Petty	6.00	2.70

1997 Viper Cobra

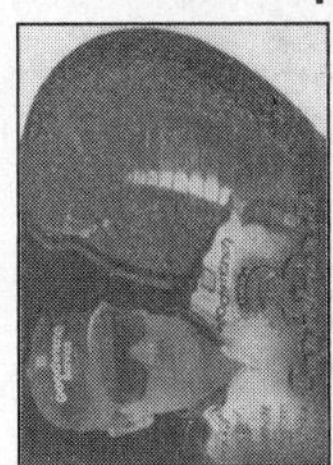

This 10-card insert set is highlights by micro-etchedcards that are diecut. The cards were randomly inserted in hobby packs at a ratio of 1:24.

	MINT	NRMT
COMPLETE SET (10)	80.00	36.00
COMMON CARD (C1-C10)	5.00	2.20
*SINGLES: 5X TO 12X BASE CARD HI		
COMP. FIRST STRIKE SET (10)	100.00	45.00
*FIRST STIKRE CARDS: 6X TO 15X BASIC CARDS		
❑ C1 Dale Earnhardt	25.00	11.00
❑ C2 Jeff Gordon	25.00	11.00
❑ C3 Bobby Labonte	6.00	2.70
❑ C4 Terry Labonte	15.00	6.75
❑ C5 Rusty Wallace	15.00	6.75
❑ C6 Bill Elliott	15.00	6.75
❑ C7 Sterling Marlin	5.00	2.20
❑ C8 Mark Martin	15.00	6.75
❑ C9 Dale Jarrett	12.00	5.50
❑ C10 Kyle Petty	5.00	2.20

1997 Viper Diamondback

The 10-card insert set features a patch of simulated rattlesnake skin next to the picture of the driver on the fronts of the cards. The First Strike version of these cards were inserted into specially marked boxes of Viper First Strike. The cards were randomly inserted in hobby and First Strike packs at a ratio of 1:48 and inserted in retail packs at a ratio of 1:30.

	MINT	NRMT
COMPLETE SET (10)	120.00	55.00
COMMON CARD (DB1-DB10)	3.00	1.35
*SINGLES: 6X TO 15X BASE CARD HI		
COMP. FIRST STRIKE SET (10)	150.00	70.00
*FIRST STRIKE CARDS: 8X TO 20X BASIC CARDS		
❑ DB1 Jeff Gordon	50.00	22.00
❑ DB2 Dale Jarrett	25.00	11.00
❑ DB3 Bobby Labonte	15.00	6.75
❑ DB4 Rusty Wallace	30.00	13.50
❑ DB5 Bill Elliott	30.00	13.50
❑ DB6 Jeff Burton	6.00	2.70
❑ DB7 Mark Martin	30.00	13.50
❑ DB8 Dale Earnhardt	50.00	22.00
❑ DB9 Mike Skinner	3.00	1.35
❑ DB10 Robby Gordon	3.00	1.35

1997 Viper Diamondback Authentic

This 10-card insert set features authentic diamondback rattlesnake skin attached to each card. The First Strike version of these cards were inserted into specially marked boxes of Viper First Strike. There are four different versions of each card: Western, Eastern, Western First Strike and Eastern First Strike. The cards were randomly inserted in hobby and First Strike packs at a ratio of 1:96 and inserted in retail packs at a ratio of 1:90.

	MINT	NRMT
COMPLETE SET (10)	300.00	135.00
COMMON CARD (DBA1-DBA10)	8.00	3.60
*SINGLES: 15X TO 40X BASE CARD HI		
COMP. FIRST STRIKE SET (10)	400.00	180.00
COMP. EASTERN SET (10)	500.00	220.00
COMP. EASTERN FS SET (10)	600.00	275.00
❑ DBA1 Jeff Gordon	125.00	55.00
❑ DBA2 Dale Jarrett	60.00	27.00
❑ DBA3 Bobby Labonte	50.00	22.00
❑ DBA4 Rusty Wallace	75.00	34.00
❑ DBA5 Bill Elliott	75.00	34.00
❑ DBA6 Jeff Burton	15.00	6.75
❑ DBA7 Mark Martin	75.00	34.00
❑ DBA8 Dale Earnhardt	125.00	55.00
❑ DBA9 Mike Skinner	8.00	3.60
❑ DBA10 Robby Gordon	8.00	3.60

1997 Viper King Cobra

This 10-card insert set features oversized, die-cut cards portraiting the top stars of the Winston Cup circuit. The cards were randomly inserted a chiptoppers at a ratio of one per two First Strike boxes.

	MINT	NRMT
COMPLETE SET (10)	150.00	70.00
COMMON CARD (KC1-KC10)	6.00	2.70
*SINGLES: 6X TO 15X BASE CARD HI		
❑ KC1 Dale Earnhardt	50.00	22.00
❑ KC2 Jeff Gordon	50.00	22.00
❑ KC3 Bobby Labonte	12.00	5.50
❑ KC4 Terry Labonte	30.00	13.50
❑ KC5 Rusty Wallace	30.00	13.50
❑ KC6 Bill Elliott	30.00	13.50
❑ KC7 Sterling Marlin	6.00	2.70
❑ KC8 Mark Martin	30.00	13.50
❑ KC9 Dale Jarrett	25.00	11.00
❑ KC10 Kyle Petty	6.00	2.70

1997 Viper Sidewinder

This 16-card insert set features stars from Winston Cup series on die-cut cards. The First Strike version of these cards were inserted into specially marked boxes of Viper First Strike. The cards were randomly inserted in hobby, First Strike and retail packs at a ratio of 1:6.

	MINT	NRMT
COMPLETE SET (16)	40.00	18.00
COMMON CARD (S1-S16)	1.25	.55
*SINGLES: 2.5X TO 6X BASE CARD HI		
COMP. FIRST STRIKE SET (10)	50.00	22.00
*FIRST STRIKE CARDS: 3X TO 8X BASIC CARDS		
❑ S1 Terry Labonte	10.00	4.50
❑ S2 Jeff Gordon	16.00	7.25
❑ S3 Johnny Benson	1.25	.55
❑ S4 Ward Burton	1.25	.55
❑ S5 Bobby Hamilton	1.25	.55
❑ S6 Ricky Craven	1.25	.55
❑ S7 Michael Waltrip	1.25	.55
❑ S8 Bobby Labonte	5.00	2.20
❑ S9 Dale Jarrett	8.00	3.60
❑ S10 Bill Elliott	10.00	4.50
❑ S11 Rusty Wallace	10.00	4.50
❑ S12 Jimmy Spencer	1.25	.55
❑ S13 Sterling Marlin	2.50	1.10
❑ S14 Kyle Petty	2.50	1.10
❑ S15 Ken Schrader	1.25	.55
❑ S16 Robby Gordon	1.25	.55

1997 Viper Snake Eyes

This 12-card insert set features stars from Winston Cup series on horizontal cards. The First Strike version of these cards were inserted into specially marked boxes of Viper First Strike. The cards were randomly inserted in hobby, First Strike and retail packs at a ratio of 1:12.

	MINT	NRMT
COMPLETE SET (12)	60.00	27.00
COMMON CARD (SE1-SE12)	1.50	.70
*SINGLES: 3X TO 8X BASE CARD HI		
COMP. FIRST STRIKE SET (12)	80.00	36.00
*FIRST STIRKE CARDS: 4X TO 10X BASIC CARDS		
❑ SE1 Dale Earnhardt	20.00	9.00
❑ SE2 Jeff Gordon	20.00	9.00
❑ SE3 Dale Jarrett	10.00	4.50
❑ SE4 Bobby Labonte	6.00	2.70
❑ SE5 Jimmy Spencer	1.50	.70
❑ SE6 Bill Elliott	12.00	5.50
❑ SE7 Terry Labonte	12.00	5.50
❑ SE8 Rusty Wallace	12.00	5.50
❑ SE9 Jeff Burton	3.00	1.35
❑ SE10 Mark Martin	12.00	5.50
❑ SE11 Brett Bodine	1.50	.70
❑ SE12 Sterling Marlin	3.00	1.35

1992 Wheels Kyle Petty

This 14-card set features Kyle Petty and the Mello Yello team. The cards were packaged in a rack display blister with the Title Card appearing on the front of the package. There were 30,000 silver foil stamped sets made. The original suggested retail was $12. Each of the card backs featured artwork from Sam Bass. There was a gold parallel version of the set that was produced in a quantity of 12,000. The gold version originally retailed for $15.

	MINT	NRMT
COMPLETE SILVER SET (14)	6.00	2.70
COMMON CARD (1-14)	.75	.35
*GOLD CARDS: 1X TO X SILVERS		
❑ 1 Title Card	.75	.35
❑ 2 Kyle Petty	1.00	.45
❑ 3 Felix Sabates	.75	.35
❑ 4 Robin Pemberton	.75	.35
❑ 5 Kyle Petty's Car	.75	.35
❑ 6 Kyle Petty	1.00	.45
❑ 7 Kyle Petty	1.00	.45
❑ 8 Kyle Petty	1.00	.45
❑ 9 Kyle Petty	1.00	.45
❑ 10 Kyle Petty in Pits	.75	.35
❑ 11 Kyle Petty's Car	.75	.35
❑ 12 Kyle Petty's Car	.75	.35
❑ 13 Kyle Petty	1.00	.45
❑ 14 Kyle Petty's Car Art	.75	.35

1992 Wheels Special Tribute to Dale Earnhardt

This single Dale Earnhardt holographic card comes in a snap-it deluxe card holder. It is packaged in a blister pack along with a AuthenTicket. The are four different versions; silver, gold, platinum and gold autographed. In each version the AuthenTicket is serial numbered. The color variations seem to sale for about the same price with none carrying a distinct premium over the other. The autographed version seems to carry 2X to 4X premium over the other versions.

	MINT	NRMT
COMPLETE SET (1)	3.00	1.35
❑ 1 Dale Earnhardt	3.00	1.35

1992 Wheels Special Tribute to Bill Elliott

This single Bill Elliott holographic card comes in a snap-it deluxe card holder. It is packaged in a blister pack along with a AuthenTicket. The are three different versions; silver, gold, and platinum. In each version the AuthenTicket is serial numbered. The color variations seem to sale for about the same price with none carrying a distinct premium over the other.

	MINT	NRMT
COMPLETE SET	3.00	1.35
❑ 1 Bill Elliott	3.00	1.35

1992 Wheels Special Tribute to Harry Gant

This single Harry Gant holographic card comes in a snap-it deluxe card holder. It is packaged in a blister pack along with a AuthenTicket. The are four different versions; silver, gold, platinum and silver autographed. In each version the AuthenTicket is serial numbered. The color variations seem to sale for about the same price with none carrying a distinct premium over the other. The autographed version seems to carry 2X to 4X premium over the other versions.

	MINT	NRMT
COMPLETE SET (1)	3.00	1.35
❑ 1 Harry Gant	3.00	1.35

1992 Wheels Rusty Wallace

This 14-card set features Rusty Wallace and the Miller Genuine Draft team. The cards were packaged in a rack display blister with the Title Card appearing on the front of the package. There were 35,000 silver foil stamped sets made. The original suggested retail was $12. Each of the card backs featured artwork from Tim Bruce. There was a gold parallel version of the set that was produced in a quantity of 15,000. The gold set orignally retailed for $15.

	MINT	NRMT
COMPLETE SILVER SET (14)	8.00	3.60
COMMON CARD (1-14)	.75	.35
*GOLD CARDS: 1X TO X SILVERS		
❑ 1 Title Card	1.00	.45
❑ 2 Rusty Wallace	1.25	.55
❑ 3 Roger Penske	.75	.35
❑ 4 Buddy Parrott	.75	.35
❑ 5 Rusty Wallace's Car	.75	.35
❑ 6 Rusty Wallace	1.25	.55
❑ 7 Bill Wilburn	.75	.35
❑ 8 Rusty Wallace w/Crew	.75	.35
❑ 9 Rusty Wallace Mike Wallace Kenny Wallace	1.25	.55
❑ 10 Rusty Wallace	1.25	.55
❑ 11 Rusty Wallace	1.25	.55
❑ 12 Rusty Wallace	1.25	.55
❑ 13 Rusty Wallace	1.25	.55
❑ 14 Rusty Wallace Art	.75	.35

1993 Wheels Mom-n-Pop's Dale Earnhardt

The 1993 Dale Earnhardt Mom-n-Pop's set was produced by Wheels and features photos of Dale's wins during the first half of 1993. The cards were packed one card and one cover card per cello pack in various ham, biscuit and sandwich products. A coupon was included as well offering complete sets and uncut sheets of previous year's sets.

	MINT	NRMT
COMPLETE SET (6)	12.00	5.50
COMMON CARD (1-6)	2.00	.90

	MINT
❑ 1 Dale Earnhardt Daytona	2.00
❑ 2 Dale Earnhardt Daytona	2.00
❑ 3 Dale Earnhardt Darlington	2.00
❑ 4 Dale Earnhardt Charlotte	2.00
❑ 5 Dale Earnhardt Charlotte	2.00
❑ 6 Dale Earnhardt Dover	2.00

1993 Wheels Rookie Thund

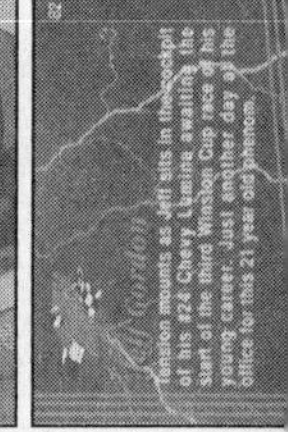

This 100-card set features Rookie of the Year drivers 1958-1993. The cards were printed on 24-pt stoc feature UV coating. The cards were packaged eigh per pack, 30 packs per box and 20 boxes per case.

	MINT
COMPLETE SET (100)	10.00
COMMON CARD (1-100)	.05
COMMON DRIVER (1-100)	.10
❑ 1 Shorty Rollins	.05
❑ 2 Richard Petty	.30
❑ 3 David Pearson	.10
❑ 4 Woodie Wilson	.05
❑ 5 Tom Cox	.05
❑ 6 Billy Wade	.05
❑ 7 Doug Cooper	.05
❑ 8 Sam McQuagg	.05
❑ 9 James Hylton	.05
❑ 10 Donnie Allison	.10
❑ 11 Dick Brooks	.05
❑ 12 Bill Dennis	.05
❑ 13 Walter Ballard	.05
❑ 14 Larry Smith	.05
❑ 15 Lennie Pond	.05
❑ 16 Earl Ross	.05
❑ 17 Bruce Hill	.05
❑ 18 Skip Manning	.05
❑ 19 Ricky Rudd	.20
❑ 20 Ronnie Thomas	.05
❑ 21 Jody Ridley	.10
❑ 22 Ron Bouchard	.05
❑ 23 Geoff Bodine	.10
❑ 24 Sterling Marlin	.20
❑ 25 Rusty Wallace	.50
❑ 26 Ken Schrader	.10
❑ 27 Alan Kulwicki	.30
❑ 28 Davey Allison	.50
❑ 29 Ken Bouchard	.10
❑ 30 Dick Trickle	.10
❑ 31 Jimmy Hensley	.10
❑ 32 Jeff Gordon	1.00
❑ 33 Bobby Labonte	.30
❑ 34 Kenny Wallace	.10
❑ 35 Rich Bickle	.10
❑ 36 Joe Nemechek	.10
❑ 37 Jeff Gordon	1.00
❑ 38 Ricky Craven	.20
❑ 39 Hermie Sadler	.10
❑ 40 Tim Fedewa	.10
❑ 41 Joe Bessey	.10
❑ 42 Roy Payne	.05
❑ 43 Nathan Buttke	.05
❑ 44 Ricky Rudd	.20

	MINT	NRMT
eoff Bodine	.10	.05
usty Wallace	.50	.23
en Schrader	.10	.05
lan Kulwicki	.50	.23
avey Allison	.50	.23
eff Gordon	1.00	.45
eff Gordon	1.00	.45
obby Labonte	.30	.14
enny Wallace	.10	.05
enny Wallace	.10	.05
ick Brooks	.05	.02
avey Allison	.50	.23
lan Kulwicki	.30	.14
lan Kulwicki	.40	.18
lan Kulwicki	.40	.18
usty Wallace's Car	.30	.14
ichard Petty	.30	.14
eff Gordon w/Car	1.00	.45
enny Wallace	.10	.05
obby Labonte	.30	.14
usty Wallace	.50	.23
usty Wallace	.50	.23
usty Wallace	.50	.23
usty Wallace	.50	.23
ermie Sadler	.10	.05
eff Gordon	1.00	.45
eff Gordon	1.00	.45
obby Labonte	.30	.14
obby Labonte	.30	.14
enny Wallace	.10	.05
enny Wallace	.10	.05
icky Craven	.20	.09
oe Nemechek	.10	.05
obby Labonte	.30	.14
ichard Petty	.30	.14
ichard Petty	.30	.14
obby Labonte	.30	.14
eff Gordon	1.00	.45
enny Wallace	.10	.05
avey Allison	.50	.23
avey Allison	.50	.23
lan Kulwicki	.50	.23
usty Wallace	.50	.23
icky Rudd	.20	.09
icky Rudd	.20	.09
usty Wallace	.50	.23
eoff Bodine	.10	.05
obby Labonte	.30	.14
eff Gordon's Car	.60	.25
obby Labonte in Pits	.10	.05
ichard Petty's Car	.20	.09
David Pearson's Car		
ichard Petty	.30	.14
eff Gordon	1.00	.45
eff Gordon	1.00	.45
Ken Schrader		
ichard Petty	.30	.14
Davey Allison	.50	.23

1993 Wheels Rookie Thunder Platinum

00-card set is a parallel to the base set. The cards e a platinum foil stamping to differentiate them from se cards. There was one platinum card per pack.

	MINT	NRMT
LETE SET (100)	50.00	22.00
ON CARD (1-100)	.15	.07
ON DRIVER (1-100)	.30	.14
S: 3X TO 5X BASIC CARDS		

1993 Wheels Rookie Thunder SPs

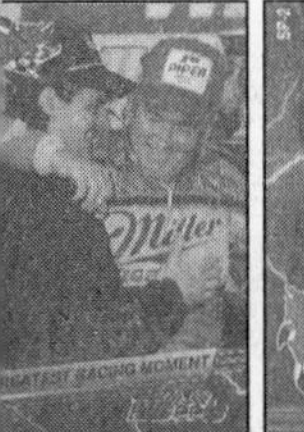
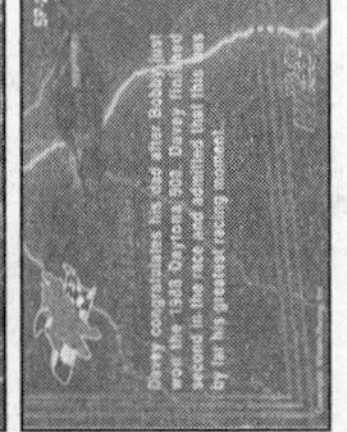

even-card insert set features some of the top names CAR history. The cards are similar in design to the et cards but with the only visable difference being bottom front of the cards is a lighting strike ound instead of the blue marblized background of the regular cards. The SP cards could be found one per box.

	MINT	NRMT
COMPLETE SET (7)	30.00	13.50
COMMON CARD (SP1-SP7)	5.00	2.20
❑ SP1 Terry Labonte	5.00	2.20
❑ SP2 Davey Allison	8.00	3.60
Bobby Allison		
❑ SP3 Davey Allison	8.00	3.60
❑ SP4 Alan Kulwicki	5.00	2.20
❑ SP5 Alan Kulwicki	5.00	2.20
❑ SP6 Richard Petty	5.00	2.20
❑ SP7 Richard Petty	5.00	2.20

1994 Wheels Harry Gant

This 80-card set pays tribute to racing great Harry Gant. The cards are a retrospective of Harry's career, plus the last 15 cards in the set are of other racing personalities holding a sign "I love Harry." The cards were packaged six cards per pack, 24 packs per box and 20 boxes per case. There were 1,500 cases produced. Randomly inserted in boxes were a 4" X 6" Signature card and a 4" X 6" Signature Hologram card. There were 3,300 of the Signature card produced and 1,000 of the Signature Hologram card produced. The odds of finding the Signature card was one in nine boxes. The odds of finding the Signature Hologram card was one in 30 boxes. Five promo cards were produced as well (#P1-P5).

	MINT	NRMT
COMPLETE SET (80)	10.00	4.50
COMMON CARD (1-80)	.20	.09
COMMON GANT (1-80)	.25	.11
❑ 1 Harry Gant	.25	.11
Baby Harry		
❑ 2 Harry Gant	.25	.11
Third Grade		
❑ 3 Harry Gant	.25	.11
High School Years		
❑ 4 Harry Gant	.25	.11
High School Years		
❑ 5 Harry Gant	.25	.11
High School Years		
❑ 6 Harry Gant	.25	.11
High School Years		
❑ 7 Harry Gant's Bike	.20	.09
First Harley '54		
❑ 8 Harry Gant's Car	.20	.09
First Race Car '65		
❑ 9 Harry Gant	.25	.11
First Race in Daytona		
❑ 10 Harry Gant	.25	.11
'64 Chevelle		
❑ 11 Harry Gant	.25	.11
Money Man		
❑ 12 Harry Gant	.25	.11
Dick Trickle		
Two Champions		
❑ 13 Harry Gant	.25	.11
Feature Winner		
❑ 14 Harry Gant	.25	.11
Weigh-In		
❑ 15 Harry Gant	.25	.11
First Trophy		
❑ 16 Harry Gant	.25	.11
'73 Track Champion		
❑ 17 Harry Gant	.25	.11
Fillin' Up		
❑ 18 Harry Gant	.25	.11
Harry's Steak Place		
❑ 19 Harry Gant	.25	.11
'79 Rookie On The Pole		
❑ 20 Harry Gant	.25	.11
'81 All Smiles		
❑ 21 Harry Gant	.25	.11
Ned Jarrett		
'82 Cool Harry		
❑ 22 Harry Gant	.25	.11
Peggy Gant		
❑ 23 Harry Gant	.25	.11
'83 Ready To Roll		
❑ 24 Harry Gant	.25	.11
Hal Needham		
Burt Reynolds		
Three Amigos		
❑ 25 Harry Gant	.25	.11
Hal Needham		
West Coast Bandits		
❑ 26 Harry Gant	.25	.11
Hal Needham		
Clowning Around		
❑ 27 Harry Gant	.25	.11
Rolling In The Dough		
❑ 28 Harry Gant	.25	.11
Buckling In		
❑ 29 Harry Gant w/Car	.20	.09
Bandit On Tour		
❑ 30 Harry Gant	.25	.11
Donna Gant		
Debbie Gant		
Harry's Girls		
❑ 31 Harry Gant	.25	.11
Peggy Gant		
❑ 32 Harry Gant	.25	.11
Harry's Classics		
❑ 33 Harry Gant	.25	.11
Virginia National Bank		
❑ 34 Harry Gant	.25	.11
National 500		
❑ 35 Harry Gant	.25	.11
TranSouth 500		
❑ 36 Harry Gant	.25	.11
Peggy Gant		
Like Cola 500		
❑ 37 Harry Gant	.25	.11
Southern 500		
❑ 38 Harry Gant	.25	.11
Delaware 500		
❑ 39 Harry Gant	.25	.11
Sovran Bank 500		
❑ 40 Harry Gant	.25	.11
Delaware 500		
❑ 41 Harry Gant	.25	.11
Peggy Gant		
Holly Farms 400		
❑ 42 Harry Gant	.25	.11
TranSouth 500		
❑ 43 Harry Gant	.25	.11
Miller Genuine Draft		
❑ 44 Harry Gant	.25	.11
Winston 500		
❑ 45 Harry Gant	.25	.11
Heinz Southern 500		
❑ 46 Harry Gant	.25	.11
Miller Genuine Draft		
❑ 47 Harry Gant	.25	.11
Peak 500		
❑ 48 Harry Gant	.25	.11
Peggy Gant		
Goody's 500		
❑ 49 Harry Gant	.25	.11
Bud 500		
❑ 50 Harry Gant	.25	.11
Champion 400		
❑ 51 Harry Gant	.25	.11
Life Begins at 51		
❑ 52 Harry Gant	.25	.11
Family Affair		
❑ 53 Harry Gant	.25	.11
New Face On Tour		
❑ 54 Harry Gant	.25	.11
All-American Boy		
❑ 55 Harry Gant	.25	.11
Bandit On The Loose		
❑ 56 Harry Gant	.25	.11
Handsome Harry		
❑ 57 Harry Gant	.25	.11
High Price of Success		
❑ 58 Harry Gant	.25	.11
'85 IROC Champion		
❑ 59 Harry Gant	.25	.11
'91 Myers' Brothers Award		
❑ 60 Harry Gant	.25	.11
'91 NMPA Driver of		
❑ 61 Harry Gant	.25	.11
Remembering		
❑ 62 Harry Gant	.25	.11
Winding Down		
❑ 63 Harry Gant	.25	.11
Leader of the Pack		
❑ 64 Harry Gant	.25	.11
Phoenix Bound		
❑ 65 Harry Gant	.25	.11
A Fond Farewell		
❑ 66 Jeff Gordon	2.00	.90
❑ 67 Ernie Irvan	.40	.18
❑ 68 Sterling Marlin	.40	.18
❑ 69 Derrike Cope	.20	.09

❑ 70 Bobby Labonte	.60	.25
❑ 71 Larry Hedrick	.20	.09
❑ 72 Benny Parsons	.20	.09
❑ 73 Rusty Wallace	1.00	.45
❑ 74 Mark Martin	1.00	.45
❑ 75 Kyle Petty	.25	.11
❑ 76 Ray Cooper	.20	.09
❑ 77 Andy Petree	.20	.09
❑ 78 Eddie Masencup	.20	.09
❑ 79 Brian Buchauer	.20	.09
❑ 80 Johnny Hayes	.20	.09
❑ HGS1 Harry Gant 4x6 AUTO 3300 produced	15.00	6.75
❑ NNO Harry Gant 4x6 HOLO 1000 produced	15.00	6.75

1994 Wheels Harry Gant Gold

This 80-card set is a parallel to the base Wheels Harry Gant set. The cards feature gold foil stamping and were inserted one per pack.

	MINT	NRMT
COMPLETE GOLD SET (80)	30.00	13.50
COMMON CARD (1-80)	.30	.14
COMMON GANT (1-80)	.45	.20

*GOLD CARDS: 1.5X TO X BASIC CARDS

1994 Wheels Harry Gant Down On The Farm

This five-card insert set gives a close look at Harry on his farm in Taylorsville, North Carolina. The cards are randomly inserted at a rate of one per box.

	MINT	NRMT
COMPLETE SET (5)	12.00	5.50
COMMON CARD (SP1-SP5)	3.00	1.35
❑ SP1 Harry Gant with horse Red	3.00	1.35
❑ SP2 Harry Gant	3.00	1.35
❑ SP3 Harry Gant Eddie Masencup	3.00	1.35
❑ SP4 Harry Gant On Tractor	3.00	1.35
❑ SP5 Harry Gant Hauling Rocks	3.00	1.35

1996 Wheels Dale Earnhardt Mom-n-Pop's

This three-card set features seven-time Winston Cup champion Dale Earnhardt. The cards were produced by Wheels and were inserted in to Mom-n-Pop's products.

	MINT	NRMT
COMPLETE SET (3)	15.00	6.75
COMMON CARD (MPC1-MPC3)	5.00	2.20
❑ MPC1 Dale Earnhardt	5.00	2.20
❑ MPC2 Dale Earnhardt	5.00	2.20
❑ MPC3 Dale Earnhardt	5.00	2.20

1998 Wheels

The 1998 Wheels set was issued in one series totalling 100 cards. The set contains the topical subsets: NASCAR

Winston Cup Drivers (1-30), NASCAR Winston Cup Cars (31-45), NASCAR Busch Series Drivers (46-59), NASCAR Busch Series Cars (60-63), NASCAR Craftsman Truck Series Drivers (64-68), NASCAR Winston Cup Crew Chiefs (69-75), NASCAR Winston Cup Owners (76-81), Daytona 500 Winners (82-90), and Team Members (91-100).

	MINT	NRMT
COMPLETE SET (100)	20.00	9.00
COMMON CARD (1-100)	.10	.05
COMMON DRIVER (1-100)	.20	.09
❑ 1 John Andretti	.20	.09
❑ 2 Johnny Benson	.20	.09
❑ 3 Geoff Bodine	.20	.09
❑ 4 Todd Bodine	.20	.09
❑ 5 Jeff Burton	.40	.18
❑ 6 Ward Burton	.20	.09
❑ 7 Ricky Craven	.20	.09
❑ 8 Wally Dallenbach	.20	.09
❑ 9 Dale Earnhardt	2.00	.90
❑ 10 Bill Elliott	1.00	.45
❑ 11 Jeff Gordon	2.00	.90
❑ 12 David Green	.20	.09
❑ 13 Bobby Hamilton	.20	.09
❑ 14 Ernie Irvan	.40	.18
❑ 15 Kenny Irwin	.60	.25
❑ 16 Dale Jarrett	.75	.35
❑ 17 Bobby Labonte	.75	.35
❑ 18 Terry Labonte	1.00	.45
❑ 19 Sterling Marlin	.40	.18
❑ 20 Mark Martin	1.00	.45
❑ 21 Jeremy Mayfield	.60	.25
❑ 22 Ted Musgrave	.20	.09
❑ 23 Joe Nemechek	.20	.09
❑ 24 Steve Park	.75	.35
❑ 25 Ricky Rudd	.40	.18
❑ 26 Ken Schrader	.20	.09
❑ 27 Mike Skinner	.20	.09
❑ 28 Jimmy Spencer	.20	.09
❑ 29 Rusty Wallace	1.00	.45
❑ 30 Michael Waltrip	.20	.09
❑ 31 John Andretti's Car	.10	.05
❑ 32 Johnny Benson's Car	.10	.05
❑ 33 Jeff Burton's Car	.20	.09
❑ 34 Dale Earnhardt's Car	1.00	.45
❑ 35 Bill Elliott's Car	.50	.23
❑ 36 Jeff Gordon's Car	1.00	.45
❑ 37 Kenny Irwin's Car	.30	.14
❑ 38 Dale Jarrett's Car	.40	.18
❑ 39 Bobby Labonte's Car	.40	.18
❑ 40 Terry Labonte's Car	.50	.23
❑ 41 Sterling Marlin's Car	.20	.09
❑ 42 Mark Martin's Car	.50	.23
❑ 43 Jeremy Mayfield's Car	.30	.14
❑ 44 Ricky Rudd's Car	.20	.09
❑ 45 Rusty Wallace's Car	.50	.23
❑ 46 Jeff Burton	.40	.18
❑ 47 Dale Earnhardt,Jr.	3.00	1.35
❑ 48 Tim Fedewa	.20	.09
❑ 49 Dale Jarrett	.75	.35
❑ 50 Jason Jarrett	.20	.09
❑ 51 Jason Keller	.20	.09
❑ 52 Randy LaJoie	.20	.09
❑ 53 Mark Martin	1.00	.45
❑ 54 Mike McLaughlin	.20	.09
❑ 55 Joe Nemechek	.20	.09
❑ 56 Elliott Sadler	.20	.09
❑ 57 Hermie Sadler	.20	.09
❑ 58 Tony Stewart	1.50	.70
❑ 59 Michael Waltrip	.20	.09
❑ 60 Dale Earnhardt Jr.'s Car	1.50	.70
❑ 61 Randy LaJoie's Car	.10	.05
❑ 62 Elliott Sadler's Car	.10	.05
❑ 63 Tony Stewart's Car	.40	.18
❑ 64 Rich Bickle	.20	.09
❑ 65 Mike Bliss	.20	.09
❑ 66 Ron Hornaday	.20	.09
❑ 67 Joe Ruttman	.20	.09
❑ 68 Jack Sprague	.20	.09
❑ 69 Ray Evernham	.20	.09
❑ 70 Jimmy Fenning	.10	.05
❑ 71 Andy Graves	.10	.05
❑ 72 Jimmy Makar	.10	.05
❑ 73 Larry McReynolds	.10	
❑ 74 Todd Parrott	.10	
❑ 75 Robin Pemberton	.10	
❑ 76 Richard Childress	.10	
❑ 77 Bill Elliott	1.00	
❑ 78 Joe Gibbs	.20	
❑ 79 John Hendrick	.10	
❑ 80 Jack Roush	.20	
❑ 81 Ricky Rudd	.40	
❑ 82 Geoff Bodine	.20	
❑ 83 Dale Earnhardt	2.00	
❑ 84 Bill Elliott	1.00	
❑ 85 Jeff Gordon	2.00	
❑ 86 Ernie Irvan	.40	
❑ 87 Dale Jarrett	.75	
❑ 88 Fred Lorenzen	.20	
❑ 89 Sterling Marlin	.40	
❑ 90 Richard Petty	.40	
❑ 91 Craig Lund	.10	
❑ 92 Chocolate Myers	.10	
❑ 93 Jack Lewis	.10	
❑ 94 Steve Muse	.10	
❑ 95 Jerry Hailey	.10	
❑ 96 Mike Moore	.10	
❑ 97 David Rogers	.10	
❑ 98 Larry McReynolds	.10	
❑ 99 Dale Earnhardt's Car	1.00	
❑ 100 Checklist	.10	
❑ 0 Mark Martin Las Vegas	75.00	

1998 Wheels 50th Annivers

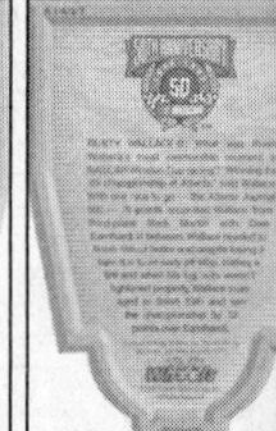

Randomly inserted in packs at a rate of one in 2, th card insert set celebrates NASCAR's 50th annive This "set within a set" shows off the most talented c and their cars in NASCAR Winston Cup racing. Eac is intricately die-cut and includes a customized r etched foil treatment.

	MINT
COMPLETE SET (27)	30.00
COMMON CARD (A1-A27)	.30
COMMON DRIVER (A1-A27)	.60

*SINGLES: 1.25X TO 3X BASE CARD HI

❑ A1 Johnny Benson	.60
❑ A2 Jeff Burton	1.25
❑ A3 Dale Earnhardt	6.00
❑ A4 Bill Elliott	3.00
❑ A5 Jeff Gordon	6.00
❑ A6 Kenny Irwin	2.00
❑ A7 Dale Jarrett	2.50
❑ A8 Bobby Labonte	2.50
❑ A9 Terry Labonte	3.00
❑ A10 Sterling Marlin	1.25
❑ A11 Mark Martin	3.00
❑ A12 Ricky Rudd	1.25
❑ A13 Jimmy Spencer	.30
❑ A14 Rusty Wallace	3.00
❑ A15 Michael Waltrip	.30
❑ A16 Johnny Benson's Car	.30
❑ A17 Jeff Burton's Car	.60
❑ A18 Dale Earnhardt's Car	3.00
❑ A19 Bill Elliott's Car	1.50
❑ A20 Jeff Gordon's Car	3.00
❑ A21 Kenny Irwin's Car	1.00
❑ A22 Dale Jarrett's Car	1.25
❑ A23 Bobby Labonte's Car	1.25
❑ A24 Terry Labonte's Car	1.50
❑ A25 Sterling Marlin's Car	.60
❑ A26 Mark Martin's Car	1.50
❑ A27 Rusty Wallace's Car	1.50

1998 Wheels Autographs

Randomly inserted in packs at a rate of one in 24 14-card insert set features autographs from top NA drivers and aspiring rookies. No more thar individually numbered and autographed cards per d

	MINT
COMPLETE SET (14)	800.00
COMMON CARD (1-14)	15.00

ale Earnhardt	200.00	90.00
ff Gordon	200.00	90.00
ale Jarrett	75.00	34.00
rry Labonte	90.00	40.00
obby Labonte	75.00	34.00
mmy Spencer	15.00	6.75
ff Burton	30.00	13.50
eoff Bodine	15.00	6.75
ichael Waltrip	15.00	6.75
Ricky Craven	30.00	13.50
Ricky Rudd	30.00	13.50
Mike Skinner	15.00	6.75
Kenny Irwin	40.00	18.00
Johnny Benson	15.00	6.75

998 Wheels Custom Shop Redemption

omly inserted in packs at the rate of one in 192, nption cards for this five-card set allowed the tor to customize his own card by selecting one of fronts and three backs for each card. The collector eceived his custom-made card by return mail with osen front and back selection.

	MINT	NRMT
LETE SET (3)	200.00	90.00
ION CARD	50.00	22.00
LES: 30X TO 60X BASE CARD HI		
J Dale Jarrett	50.00	22.00
G Jeff Gordon	125.00	55.00
W Rusty Wallace	60.00	27.00

998 Wheels Double Take

mly inserted in packs at a rate of one in 72, this 9- nsert set is a first-time offer that features technology lows you to change the exposure of the card front. n your favorite NASCAR Winston Cup driver ally transform into his NASCAR ride.

	MINT	NRMT
LETE SET (9)	250.00	110.00
ION CARD (E1-E9)	12.00	5.50
LES: 12X TO 30X BASE CARD HI		
eff Burton	12.00	5.50
Dale Earnhardt	60.00	27.00
Bill Elliott	30.00	13.50
Jeff Gordon	60.00	27.00
ale Jarrett	25.00	11.00
Bobby Labonte	25.00	11.00
Terry Labonte	30.00	13.50
Mark Martin	30.00	13.50
Rusty Wallace	30.00	13.50

1998 Wheels Golden

00-card set is a parallel of regular base set. Each serial numbered to 50. These cards were randomly d into hobby packs at a ratio of 1 per 68 packs.

	MINT	NRMT
LETE SET (100)	750.00	350.00
ION CARD (1-100)	5.00	2.20
ION DRIVER (1-100)	10.00	4.50

998 Wheels Green Flags

mly inserted in packs at a rate of one in 8, this 18- nsert set showcases NASCAR's fiercest cars in an , all-foil, emerald green foil set.

	MINT	NRMT
LETE SET (18)	60.00	27.00
ON CARD (GF1-GF18)	1.25	.55
LES: 2.5X TO 6X BASE CARD HI		
John Andretti's Car	1.25	.55
Johnny Benson's Car	1.25	.55
Jeff Burton's Car	2.50	1.10
Dale Earnhardt's Car	12.00	5.50
Bill Elliott's Car	6.00	2.70

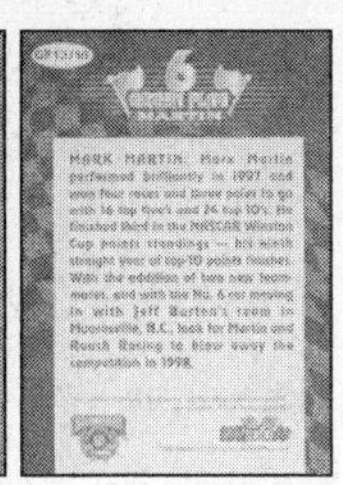

❑ GF6 Jeff Gordon's Car	12.00	5.50
❑ GF7 Bobby Hamilton's Car	1.25	.55
❑ GF8 Kenny Irwin's Car	4.00	1.80
❑ GF9 Dale Jarrett's Car	5.00	2.20
❑ GF10 Bobby Labonte's Car	5.00	2.20
❑ GF11 Terry Labonte's Car	6.00	2.70
❑ GF12 Sterling Marlin's Car	2.50	1.10
❑ GF13 Mark Martin's Car	6.00	2.70
❑ GF14 Ricky Rudd's Car	2.50	1.10
❑ GF15 Mike Skinner's Car	1.25	.55
❑ GF16 Jimmy Spencer's Car	1.25	.55
❑ GF17 Rusty Wallace's Car	6.00	2.70
❑ GF18 Michael Waltrip's Car	1.25	.55

1998 Wheels Jackpot

Randomly inserted in packs at a rate of one in 12, this 9-card insert set recognizes NASCAR's Winston Cup's biggest winners over the past five years on embossed all-foil technology.

	MINT	NRMT
COMPLETE SET (9)	40.00	18.00
COMMON CARD (J1-J9)	2.50	1.10
*SINGLES: 2.5X TO 6X BASE CARD HI		
❑ J1 Dale Earnhardt	12.00	5.50
❑ J2 Bill Elliott	6.00	2.70
❑ J3 Jeff Gordon	12.00	5.50
❑ J4 Dale Jarrett	5.00	2.20
❑ J5 Bobby Labonte	5.00	2.20
❑ J6 Terry Labonte	6.00	2.70
❑ J7 Jeremy Mayfield	4.00	1.80
❑ J8 Ricky Rudd	2.50	1.10
❑ J9 Rusty Wallace	6.00	2.70

1991 Winner's Choice New England Drivers

Winner's Choice, Inc. produced this set in 1991 featuring popular New England area drivers of various race circuits. The black-bordered cards look very similar to 1991 Winner's Choice Modifieds cards and include a color driver or car photo surrounded by a checkered flag frame. The cards were packaged and sold in complete factory set form.

	MINT	NRMT
COMPLETE SET (120)	10.00	4.50
COMMON CARD (1-120)	.10	.05
COMMON DRIVER (1-120)	.20	.09
❑ 1 Cover Card	.10	.05
❑ 2 Tony Hirschman	.20	.09
❑ 3 Mike Hirschman's Car	.10	.05
❑ 4 Mike Rowe	.20	.09
❑ 5 Mike Rowe's Car	.10	.05
❑ 6 Steve Knowlton	.20	.09
❑ 7 Steve Knowlton's Car	.10	.05
❑ 8 Bobby Dragon	.20	.09
❑ 9 Bobby Dragon's Car	.10	.05
❑ 10 Tony Sylvester	.20	.09
❑ 11 Tony Sylvester's Car	.10	.05
❑ 12 Dave Dion	.20	.09
❑ 13 Dave Dion's Car	.10	.05
❑ 14 Mike Weeden	.20	.09
❑ 15 Mike Weeden's Car	.10	.05
❑ 16 Bobby Gahan	.20	.09
❑ 17 Bobby Gahan's Car	.10	.05
❑ 18 Dean Ferri	.20	.09
❑ 19 Dean Ferri's Car	.10	.05
❑ 20 Lloyd Gillie	.20	.09
❑ 21 Lloyd Gillie's Car	.10	.05
❑ 22 Joey Kourafas	.20	.09
❑ 23 Joey Kourafas' Car	.10	.05
❑ 24 Jimmy Field	.20	.09
❑ 25 Jimmy Field's Car	.10	.05
❑ 26 Mike Johnson	.20	.09
❑ 27 Mike Johnson's Car	.10	.05
❑ 28 Dick McCabe	.20	.09
❑ 29 Dick McCabe's Car	.10	.05
❑ 30 Rick Miller	.20	.09
❑ 31 Rick Miller's Car	.10	.05
❑ 32 Joe Bessey	.40	.18
❑ 33 Joe Bessey's Car	.20	.09
❑ 34 Donny Ling Jr.	.20	.09
❑ 35 Donny Ling Jr.'s Car	.10	.05
❑ 36 Jamie Aube	.20	.09
❑ 37 Jamie Aube's Car	.10	.05
❑ 38 Ron Lamell Jr.	.20	.09
❑ 39 Ron Lamell Jr.'s Car	.10	.05
❑ 40 Checklist Card	.10	.05
❑ 41 Mike Maietta	.20	.09
❑ 42 Mike Maietta's Car	.10	.05
❑ 43 Tom Bolles	.20	.09
❑ 44 Tom Bolles' Car	.10	.05
❑ 45 Tom Rowe	.20	.09
❑ 46 Tom Rowe's Car	.10	.05
❑ 47 Kelly Moore	.20	.09
❑ 48 Kelly Moore's Car	.10	.05
❑ 49 Bobby Gada	.20	.09
❑ 50 Bobby Gada's Car	.10	.05
❑ 51 Pete Rondeau	.20	.09
❑ 52 Pete Rondeau's Car	.10	.05
❑ 53 Dale Shaw	.20	.09
❑ 54 Dale Shaw's Car	.10	.05
❑ 55 Mike Olsen	.20	.09
❑ 56 Mike Olsen's Car	.10	.05
❑ 57 Bob Randall	.20	.09
❑ 58 Bob Randall's Car	.10	.05
❑ 59 Billy Clark	.20	.09
❑ 60 Billy Clark's Car	.10	.05
❑ 61 Tracy Gordon	.20	.09
❑ 62 Tracy Gordon's Car	.10	.05
❑ 63 Paul Richardson	.20	.09
❑ 64 Paul Richardson's Car	.10	.05
❑ 65 Glenn Cusack	.20	.09
❑ 66 Glenn Cusack's Car	.10	.05
❑ 67 Barney McRae	.20	.09
❑ 68 Barney McRae's Car	.10	.05
❑ 69 Pete Fiandaca	.20	.09
❑ 70 Pete Fiandaca's Car	.10	.05
❑ 71 Jeff Spraker	.20	.09
❑ 72 Jeff Spraker's Car	.10	.05
❑ 73 Stub Fadden	.20	.09
❑ 74 Stub Fadden's Car	.10	.05
❑ 75 Bruce Haley	.20	.09
❑ 76 Bruce Haley's Car	.10	.05
❑ 77 Pete Silva	.20	.09
❑ 78 Pete Silva's Car	.10	.05
❑ 79 Paul Johnson	.20	.09
❑ 80 Paul Johnson's Car	.10	.05
❑ 81 Checklist Card	.10	.05
❑ 82 Dave Davis	.20	.09
❑ 83 Dave Davis' Car	.10	.05
❑ 84 Jimmy Burns	.20	.09
❑ 85 Jimmy Burns' Car	.10	.05
❑ 86 Bub Bilodeau	.20	.09
❑ 87 Bub Bilodeau's Car	.10	.05
❑ 88 Dave Darveau	.20	.09
❑ 89 Dave Darveau's Car	.10	.05
❑ 90 Glenn Sullivan	.20	.09
❑ 91 Glenn Sullivan's Car	.10	.05
❑ 92 Ricky Harrison	.20	.09
❑ 93 Ricky Harrison's Car	.10	.05
❑ 94 Billy Holbrook	.20	.09
❑ 95 Billy Holbrook's Car	.10	.05
❑ 96 John Marsh	.20	.09
❑ 97 John Marsh's Car	.10	.05
❑ 98 Ricky Craven	2.00	.90
❑ 99 Ricky Craven's Car	1.00	.45

❑ 100 Mike Stefanik	.40	.18
❑ 101 Mike Stefanik's Car	.20	.09
❑ 102 Bob Brunell	.20	.09
❑ 103 Bob Brunell's Car	.10	.05
❑ 104 Al Hammond	.20	.09
❑ 105 Al Hammond's Car	.10	.05
❑ 106 Babe Branscombe	.20	.09
❑ 107 Babe Branscombe's Car	.10	.05
❑ 108 Jeff Zuideman	.20	.09
❑ 109 Jeff Zuideman's Car	.10	.05
❑ 110 Jeff Barry	.20	.09
❑ 111 Jeff Barry's Car	.10	.05
❑ 112 Jerry Marquis	.20	.09
❑ 113 Jerry Marquis' Car	.10	.05
❑ 114 Art Tappen	.20	.09
❑ 115 Art Tappen's Car	.10	.05
❑ 116 Mike Rowe	.20	.09
Tom Rowe		
Father and Son		
❑ 117 Mike Maietta	.20	.09
Mike Maietta Jr.		
Father and Son		
❑ 118 Bentley Warren	.20	.09
❑ 119 Bentley Warren's Car	.10	.05
❑ 120 Checklist Card	.10	.05

1991 Winner's Choice Ricky Craven

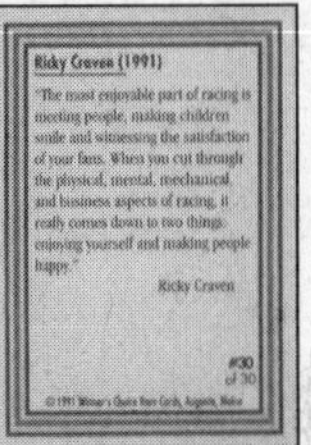

One of Winner's Choice's first card sets, this issue focuses on the career of up-and-coming driver Ricky Craven. The cards were released in complete factory set form with Craven pictured on the set box. A contest entry card was included with each set exchangeable for a chance to win Ricky Craven's 1990 Rookie of the Year driver's suit.

	MINT	NRMT
COMPLETE FACT.SET (31)	20.00	9.00
COMMON CARD (1-30)	.75	.35
❑ 1 Ricky Craven	1.00	.45
Boyhood photo		
❑ 2 Ricky Craven w/Car	1.00	.45
❑ 3 Ricky Craven w/Car	1.00	.45
❑ 4 Ricky Craven w/Car	1.00	.45
❑ 5 Ricky Craven's Car	.75	.35
Early Disappointments		
❑ 6 Ricky Craven	1.00	.45
❑ 7 Ricky Craven w/Car	1.00	.45
❑ 8 Ricky Craven w/Car	1.00	.45
❑ 9 Ricky Craven's Car	.75	.35
❑ 10 Ricky Craven's Car	.75	.35
❑ 11 Ricky Craven w/Car	1.00	.45
❑ 12 Ricky Craven's Car	.75	.35
❑ 13 Ricky Craven	1.00	.45
❑ 14 Ricky Craven w/Car	1.00	.45
❑ 15 Ricky Craven	1.00	.45
❑ 16 Ricky Craven	1.00	.45
Cathleen Craven		
❑ 17 Richard Petty	1.50	.70
Ricky Craven		
❑ 18 Ricky Craven	1.00	.45
❑ 19 Ricky Craven's Car	.75	.35
Chuck Bown's Car		
❑ 20 Ricky Craven	1.00	.45
❑ 21 Ricky Craven	1.00	.45
❑ 22 Ricky Craven	1.00	.45
Cathleen Craven		
❑ 23 Ricky Craven	1.00	.45
❑ 24 Ricky Craven w/Crew	1.00	.45
❑ 25 Ricky Craven	1.00	.45
❑ 26 Ricky Craven's Car	.75	.35
❑ 27 Ricky Craven's Car	.75	.35
❑ 28 Ricky Craven	1.00	.45
❑ 29 Ricky Craven	1.00	.45
❑ 30 Ricky Craven	1.00	.45
❑ NNO Contest Entry Card	.75	.35

1992 Winner's Choice Busch

Winner's Choice released a full 150-card set featuring the

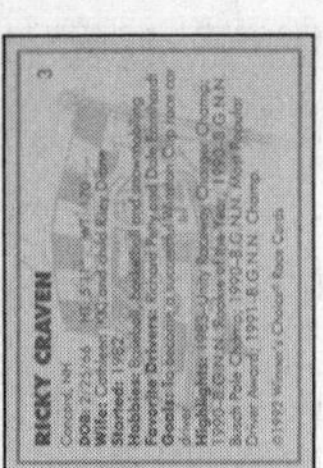

top drivers of the Winston Cup Busch Series. The cards were distributed in factory set form, as well as through 12-card foil packs. Randomly inserted autographed cards were included in some foil packs.

	MINT	NRMT
COMPLETE SET (150)	22.00	10.00
COMPLETE FACT.SET (150)	25.00	11.00
COMMON CARD (1-150)	.10	.05
COMMON DRIVER (1-150)	.25	.11
❑ 1 Cover Card	.10	.05
❑ 2 Ricky Craven	1.00	.45
❑ 3 Ricky Craven	1.00	.45
❑ 4 Ricky Craven's Car	.75	.35
❑ 5 Dick McCabe	.25	.11
❑ 6 Dick McCabe's Car	.10	.05
❑ 7 Billy Clark	.25	.11
❑ 8 Billy Clark's Car	.10	.05
❑ 9 Jamie Aube	.25	.11
❑ 10 Jamie Aube's Car	.10	.05
❑ 11 Kelly Moore	.25	.11
❑ 12 Kelly Moore's Car	.10	.05
❑ 13 Joey Kourafas	.25	.11
❑ 14 Joey Kourafas' Car	.10	.05
❑ 15 Tony Hirschman	.25	.11
❑ 16 Tony Hirschman's Car	.10	.05
❑ 17 Tony Hirschman	.25	.11
❑ 18 Stub Fadden	.25	.11
❑ 19 Stub Fadden's Car	.10	.05
❑ 20 Mike Rowe	.25	.11
❑ 21 Mike Rowe's Car	.10	.05
❑ 22 Dale Shaw	.25	.11
❑ 23 Dale Shaw's Car	.10	.05
❑ 24 Dave Dion	.25	.11
❑ 25 Dave Dion's Car	.10	.05
❑ 26 Joe Bessey	.50	.23
❑ 27 Joe Bessey's Car	.25	.11
❑ 28 Bobby Gada	.25	.11
❑ 29 Bobby Gada's Car	.10	.05
❑ 30 Jeff Barry	.25	.11
❑ 31 Jeff Barry's Car	.10	.05
❑ 32 Ken Bouchard	.50	.23
❑ 33 Peter Daniels	.25	.11
❑ 34 Peter Daniels' Car	.10	.05
❑ 35 Barney McRae	.25	.11
❑ 36 Barney McRae's Car	.10	.05
❑ 37 Mike Olsen	.25	.11
❑ 38 Mike Olsen's Car	.10	.05
❑ 39 Bob Brunell	.25	.11
❑ 40 Bob Brunell's Car	.10	.05
❑ 41 Donny Ling Jr.	.25	.11
❑ 42 Donny Ling Jr.'s Car	.10	.05
❑ 43 Dean Ferri	.25	.11
❑ 44 Dean Ferri's Car	.10	.05
❑ 45 Jeff Spraker	.25	.11
❑ 46 Jeff Spraker's Car	.10	.05
❑ 47 Rick Miller	.25	.11
❑ 48 Rick Miller's Car	.10	.05
❑ 49 Lloyd Gillie	.25	.11
❑ 50 Lloyd Gillie's Car	.10	.05
❑ 51 Checklist Card	.10	.05
❑ 52 Curtis Markham	.50	.23
❑ 53 Curtis Markham's Car	.25	.11
❑ 54 Ron Lamell	.25	.11
❑ 55 Ron Lamell's Car	.10	.05
❑ 56 Bobby Dragon	.25	.11
❑ 57 Bobby Dragon's Car	.10	.05
❑ 58 Mike Weeden	.25	.11
❑ 59 Mike Weeden's Car	.10	.05
❑ 60 Babe Branscombe	.25	.11
❑ 61 Babe Branscombe's Car	.10	.05
❑ 62 Kenny Wallace	.75	.35
❑ 63 Kenny Wallace's Car	.75	.35
❑ 64 Robert Pressley	.75	.35
❑ 65 Robert Pressley's Car	.75	.35
❑ 66 Chuck Bown	.75	.35
❑ 67 Chuck Bown's Car	.50	.23
❑ 68 Joe Nemechek	.75	.35
❑ 69 Joe Nemechek's Car	.75	.35
❑ 70 Todd Bodine	.75	.35
❑ 71 Todd Bodine's Car	.50	.23
❑ 72 Tom Peck	.25	.11
❑ 73 Tom Peck's Car	.10	.05
❑ 74 Steve Grissom	.75	
❑ 75 Steve Grissom's Car	.75	
❑ 76 Jeff Gordon	3.00	
❑ 77 Jeff Gordon's Car	2.00	
❑ 78 Jeff Burton	1.00	
❑ 79 Jeff Burton's Car	.75	
❑ 80 David Green	.75	
❑ 81 David Green's Car	.75	
❑ 82 Butch Miller	.25	
❑ 83 Butch Miller's Car	.10	
❑ 84 Dave Rezendes	.25	
❑ 85 Dave Rezendes' Car	.10	
❑ 86 Ward Burton	.75	
❑ 87 Ward Burton's Car	.75	
❑ 88 Ed Berrier	.25	
❑ 89 Ed Berrier's Car	.10	
❑ 90 Troy Beebe	.25	
❑ 91 Troy Beebe's Car	.10	
❑ 92 Ed Ferree	.25	
❑ 93 Ed Ferree's Car	.10	
❑ 94 Jim Bown	.25	
❑ 95 Jim Bown's Car	.10	
❑ 96 Tony Siscone	.25	
❑ 97 Tony Siscone's Car	.10	
❑ 98 Shawna Robinson	.75	
❑ 99 Shawna Robinson's Car	.75	
❑ 100 Checklist Card	.10	
❑ 101 Mike Maietta	.25	
❑ 102 Mike Maietta's Car	.10	
❑ 103 Tracy Gordon	.25	
❑ 104 Tracy Gordon's Car	.10	
❑ 105 Tony Papale	.25	
❑ 106 Tony Papale's Car	.10	
❑ 107 Jerry Marquis	.25	
❑ 108 Jerry Marquis' Car	.10	
❑ 109 Dave St. Clair	.25	
❑ 110 Dave St. Clair's Car	.10	
❑ 111 Steve Nelson	.25	
❑ 112 Steve Nelson's Car	.10	
❑ 113 Glenn Cusack	.25	
❑ 114 Glenn Cusack's Car	.10	
❑ 115 Jeff Zuideman	.25	
❑ 116 Jeff Zuideman's Car	.10	
❑ 117 Ed Carroll	.25	
❑ 118 Ed Carroll's Car	.10	
❑ 119 Tom Rosati	.25	
❑ 120 Tom Rosati's Car	.10	
❑ 121 Jim McCallum	.25	
❑ 122 Jim McCallum's Car	.10	
❑ 123 Eddy Carroll Jr.	.25	
❑ 124 Eddy Carroll Jr.'s Car	.10	
❑ 125 Bob Randall	.25	
❑ 126 Bob Randall's Car	.10	
❑ 127 Pete Fiandaca	.25	
❑ 128 Pete Fiandaca's Car	.10	
❑ 129 Bobby Gahan	.25	
❑ 130 Bobby Gahan's Car	.10	
❑ 131 Scott Bachand	.25	
❑ 132 Scott Bachand's Car	.10	
❑ 133 Tom Bolles	.25	
❑ 134 Tom Bolles' Car	.10	
❑ 135 Pete Silva	.25	
❑ 136 Pete Silva's Car	.10	
❑ 137 Jimmy Field	.25	
❑ 138 Jimmy Field's Car	.10	
❑ 139 Tony Sylvester	.25	
❑ 140 Tony Sylvester's Car	.10	
❑ 141 Mike Johnson	.25	
❑ 142 Mike Johnson's Car	.10	
❑ 143 Mike Maietta Jr.	.25	
❑ 144 Mike Maietta Jr.'s Car	.10	
❑ 145 Jimmy Hensley	.25	
❑ 146 Jimmy Hensley's Car	.10	
❑ 147 Sam Ard	.25	
❑ 148 Sam Ard's Car	.10	
❑ 149 Mike Greenwell	.25	
❑ 150 Checklist Card	.10	

1992 Winner's Choice Busch Autographs

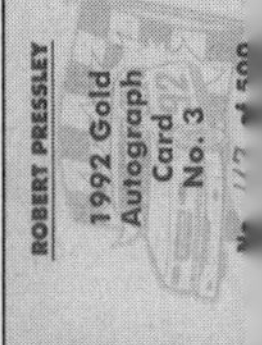

These four-cards were randomly inserted in

r's Choice Busch foil packs. Gold borders and Gold pen signatures highlight the cardfronts. Reportedly, f each card was autographed. The cards are nbered and arranged below alphabetically.

	MINT	NRMT
LETE SET (4)	180.00	80.00
ION AUTOGRAPH	45.00	20.00
nuck Bown/500	45.00	20.00
cky Craven/500	60.00	27.00
obert Pressley/500	60.00	27.00
enny Wallace/500	60.00	27.00

92 Winner's Choice Mainiac

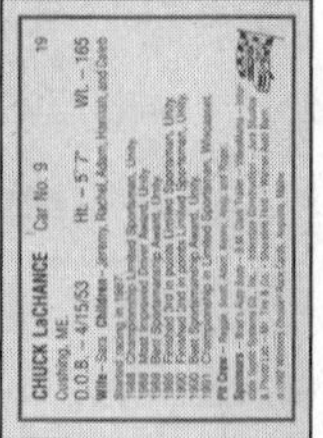

r's Choice Race Cards produced this set in 1992 ing drivers from various tracks in Maine. The onts include a black and white driver photo inside a on colored border. The 50-cards were sold in ete set form through Winner's Choice and area

	MINT	NRMT
LETE SET (50)	7.00	3.10
ION CARD (1-50)	.15	.07
over Card	.15	.07
eve Reny	.15	.07
ul Pierce	.15	.07
lph Hanson	.15	.07
ly Penfold	.15	.07
n Gray	.15	.07
mmy Burns	.15	.07
ary LeBlanc	.15	.07
ug Ripley	.15	.07
ob Libby	.15	.07
teve Chicoine	.15	.07
enny Wright	.15	.07
ark Cyr	.15	.07
arry Babb	.15	.07
avid Wilcox	.15	.07
teve Blood	.15	.07
orest Peaslee	.15	.07
amie Peaslee	.15	.07
huck LaChance	.15	.07
teve Nelson	.15	.07
ary Smith	.15	.07
erry Babb	.15	.07
ob Young	.15	.07
ay Penfold	.15	.07
ndy Santerie	.15	.07
ave McLaughlin	.15	.07
on Lizotte	.15	.07
ike Kimball	.15	.07
enji Rowe	.15	.07
ohn Phippen Jr.	.15	.07
asey Nash	.15	.07
oe Bowser	.15	.07
ene Wasson Jr.	.15	.07
ary Bellefleur Jr.	.15	.07
ck Belisle	.15	.07
ary Martin	.15	.07
oyd Poland	.15	.07
oe Belanger	.15	.07
ndy Lude	.15	.07
on Benjamin	.15	.07
ania Schafer	.15	.07
obby Babb	.15	.07
rad Hammond	.15	.07
en Beasley	.15	.07
anny Grover	.15	.07
uster Grover	.15	.07
ark Billings	.15	.07
aine Grover	.15	.07
abe Gaboury	.15	.07
hecklist Card	.15	.07
lankbacked		

1989 Winners Circle

the most sought after stock car racing sets, the inners Circle set was primarily distributed to kids of a drug awareness program in North Carolina.

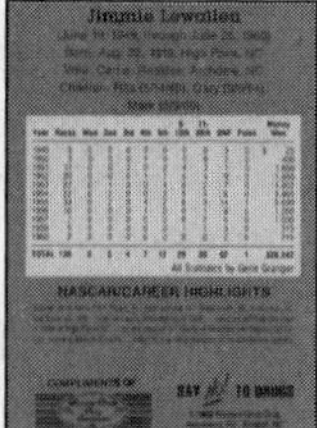

The cards were also given out at many race tracks including the Richmond International Speedway in February, 1989. The 45 black-bordered cards feature star drivers from the early days of NASCAR. The checklist was intended to be card #13, but is actually numbered "A." Reportedly only 150 of the 1A card of Lee Petty were produced. The set price doesn't include this card. A card album to house the set was also made available. Counterfeits have also been reported.

	MINT	NRMT
COMPLETE SET (45)	700.00	325.00
COMMON CARD (1-45)	10.00	4.50
COMMON DRIVER (1-45)	15.00	6.75
❑ 1A Lee Petty without NASCAR on back	500.00	220.00
❑ 1B Lee Petty with NASCAR on back	40.00	18.00
❑ 2 Fred Lorenzen	50.00	22.00
❑ 3 Tom Pistone	20.00	9.00
❑ 4 Tiny Lund	30.00	13.50
❑ 5 Paul Goldsmith	20.00	9.00
❑ 6 Dick Hutcherson	15.00	6.75
❑ 7 Louise Smith	20.00	9.00
❑ 8 Charlie Glotzbach	15.00	6.75
❑ 9 Bob Welborn	15.00	6.75
❑ 10 Bob Flock	15.00	6.75
❑ 11 Fonty Flock	20.00	9.00
❑ 12 Tim Flock	20.00	9.00
❑ 13 Checklist Card actually numbered A	10.00	4.50
❑ 14 Ethel Mobley	20.00	9.00
❑ 15 Cotton Owens	15.00	6.75
❑ 16 David Pearson	20.00	9.00
❑ 17 Glen Wood	20.00	9.00
❑ 18 Bobby Isaac	30.00	13.50
❑ 19 Joe Lee Johnson	15.00	6.75
❑ 20 G.C. Spencer	15.00	6.75
❑ 21 Jack Smith	15.00	6.75
❑ 22 Frank Mundy	15.00	6.75
❑ 23 Bill Rexford	15.00	6.75
❑ 24 Dick Rathmann	15.00	6.75
❑ 25 Bill Blair	15.00	6.75
❑ 26 Darel Dieringer	15.00	6.75
❑ 27 Speedy Thompson	15.00	6.75
❑ 28 Donald Thomas	15.00	6.75
❑ 29 Marvin Panch	20.00	9.00
❑ 30 Buddy Shuman	15.00	6.75
❑ 31 Neil Castles	15.00	6.75
❑ 32 Buck Baker	20.00	9.00
❑ 33 Curtis Turner	20.00	9.00
❑ 34 Larry Frank	20.00	9.00
❑ 35 Lee Roy Yarborough	20.00	9.00
❑ 36 Ralph Liguori	15.00	6.75
❑ 37 Wendell Scott	40.00	18.00
❑ 38 Jim Paschal	15.00	6.75
❑ 39 Johnny Allen	20.00	9.00
❑ 40 Jimmie Lewallen	15.00	6.75
❑ 41 Maurice Petty	20.00	9.00
❑ 42 Nelson Stacy	15.00	6.75
❑ 43 Glenn Roberts(Fireball)	30.00	13.50
❑ 44 Edwin Matthews (Banjo)	15.00	6.75
❑ 45 Pete Hamilton	15.00	6.75

1995 WSMP Dale Earnhardt The Next Generation

This 4-card set features Dale Earnhardt and three of his kids Kerry, Kelly, and Dale Jr. The cards were distributed by Western Steer and are 3-D. There are three regular size cards and one Jumbo sized card. 2,500 sets were produced. There is also a black binder that was available to hold all four of the cards. The cards were available through the WSMP restaurants, Sports Image souvenir trailers and mail order.

	MINT	NRMT
COMPLETE SET (4)	25.00	11.00
COMMON CARD (1-3)	6.00	2.70
❑ 1 Dale Earnhardt Kerry Earnhardt	6.00	2.70
❑ 2 Dale Earnhardt Kelley Earnhardt	6.00	2.70
❑ 3 Dale Earnhardt Dale Earnhardt Jr.	6.00	2.70
❑ NNO Dale Earnhardt Kerry Earnhardt Kelley Earnhardt Dale Earnhardt Jr. 5"x7" Blank back	8.00	3.60

1995 Zenith

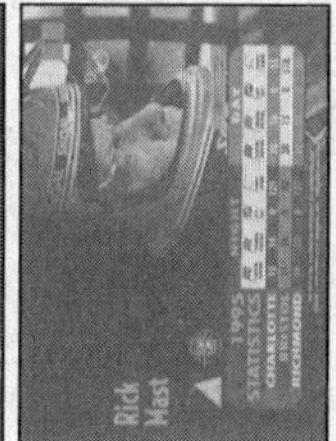

This is the inaugural set of Pinnacle's Zenith Racing brand. The 83-card set consists of five different subsets: Hot Guns (1-33), Mean Rides (34-58), End of the Day (59-68), Joe Gibbs Racing (69-75), and Championship Quest (78-83). The product came six cards per pack, with 24 packs per box and 16 boxes per case. The suggested retail price of a pack was $3.99.

	MINT	NRMT
COMPLETE SET (83)	20.00	9.00
COMMON CARD (1-83)	.15	.07
COMMON DRIVER (1-83)	.30	.14
❑ 1 Rick Mast HG	.30	.14
❑ 2 Rusty Wallace HG	1.50	.70
❑ 3 Dale Earnhardt HG	3.00	1.35
❑ 4 Sterling Marlin HG	.60	.25
❑ 5 Hut Stricklin HG	.30	.14
❑ 6 Mark Martin HG	1.50	.70
❑ 7 Geoff Bodine HG	.30	.14
❑ 8 Jeff Burton HG	.60	.25
❑ 9 Lake Speed HG	.30	.14
❑ 10 Ricky Rudd HG	.60	.25
❑ 11 Brett Bodine HG	.30	.14
❑ 12 Derrike Cope HG	.30	.14
❑ 13 Jeremy Mayfield HG	1.00	.45
❑ 14 Joe Nemechek HG	.30	.14
❑ 15 Dick Trickle HG	.30	.14
❑ 16 Ted Musgrave HG	.30	.14
❑ 17 Darrell Waltrip HG	.60	.25
❑ 18 Bobby Labonte HG	1.25	.55
❑ 19 Bobby Hillin HG	.30	.14
❑ 20 Morgan Shepherd HG	.30	.14
❑ 21 Kenny Wallace HG	.30	.14
❑ 22 Jimmy Spencer HG	.30	.14
❑ 23 Jeff Gordon HG	3.00	1.35
❑ 24 Ken Schrader HG	.30	.14
❑ 25 Terry Labonte HG	1.50	.70
❑ 26 Todd Bodine HG	.30	.14
❑ 27 Dale Jarrett HG	1.00	.45
❑ 28 Steve Grissom HG	.30	.14
❑ 29 Michael Waltrip HG	.30	.14
❑ 30 Bobby Hamilton HG	.30	.14
❑ 31 Robert Pressley HG	.30	.14
❑ 32 Ricky Craven HG	.30	.14
❑ 33 John Andretti HG	.30	.14
❑ 34 Rick Mast's Transporter	.15	.07
❑ 35 Rusty Wallace's Transporter	.75	.35
❑ 36 Dale Earnhardt's Transporter	1.50	.70
❑ 37 Sterling Marlin's Transporter	.30	.14
❑ 38 Terry Labonte's Transporter	.75	.35
❑ 39 Mark Martin's Transporter	.75	.35
❑ 40 Geoff Bodine's Transporter	.15	.07
❑ 41 Jeremy Mayfield's Trans.	.50	.23
❑ 42 Ricky Rudd's Transporter	.30	.14
❑ 43 Brett Bodine's Transporter	.15	.07
❑ 44 Jimmy Spencer's Transporter	.15	.07

❑ 45 Dick Trickle's Transporter	.15	.07
❑ 46 Ted Musgrave's Transporter	.15	.07
❑ 47 Darrell Waltrip's Transporter	.30	.14
❑ 48 Bobby Labonte's Transporter	.60	.25
❑ 49 Morgan Shepherd's Trans.	.15	.07
❑ 50 Bill Elliott's Transporter	.75	.35
❑ 51 Jeff Gordon's Transporter	1.50	.70
❑ 52 Robert Pressley's Transporter	.15	.07
❑ 53 Dale Jarrett's Transporter	.60	.25
❑ 54 Michael Waltrip's Transporter	.15	.07
❑ 55 Jeff Burton's Transporter	.30	.14
❑ 56 John Andretti's Transporter	.15	.07
❑ 57 Kyle Petty's Transporter	.30	.14
❑ 58 Bobby Hamilton's Transporter	.15	.07
❑ 59 Kenny Wallace EOD	.30	.14
❑ 60 John Andretti EOD	.30	.14
❑ 61 Ted Musgrave EOD	.30	.14
❑ 62 Jimmy Spencer EOD	.30	.14
❑ 63 Bobby Labonte EOD	1.25	.55
❑ 64 Jeff Gordon EOD	3.00	1.35
❑ 65 Robert Pressley EOD	.30	.14
❑ 66 Bobby Hillin EOD	.30	.14
❑ 67 Bobby Hamilton EOD	.30	.14
❑ 68 Brett Bodine EOD	.30	.14
❑ 69 Cruz Pedregon JG	.30	.14
❑ 70 Cruz Pedregon JG	.30	.14
❑ 71 Cory McClenathan JG	.30	.14
❑ 72 Cory McClenathan JG	.30	.14
❑ 73 Jim Yates JG	.15	.07
❑ 74 Jim Yates JG	.15	.07
❑ 75 Bobby Labonte JG	1.25	.55
❑ 76 Dale Earnhardt Checklist	1.50	.70
❑ 77 Jeff Gordon Checklist	1.50	.70
❑ 78 Jeff Gordon CQ	3.00	1.35
❑ 79 Jeff Gordon CQ	3.00	1.35
❑ 80 Jeff Gordon CQ	3.00	1.35
❑ 81 Jeff Gordon CQ	3.00	1.35
❑ 82 Jeff Gordon CQ	3.00	1.35
❑ 83 Jeff Gordon CQ	3.00	1.35

1995 Zenith Helmets

The 10 cards in this set were randomly inserted in Zenith Racing at a rate of one per 72 packs. The cards feature the helmets of some of Winston Cup's top drivers captured in all-foil Dufex printing technology.

	MINT	NRMT
COMPLETE SET (10)	300.00	135.00
COMMON CARD (1-10)	8.00	3.60
*SINGLES: 10X TO 25X BASE CARD HI		
❑ 1 Dale Earnhardt	120.00	55.00
❑ 2 Rusty Wallace	70.00	32.00
❑ 3 Jeff Gordon	120.00	55.00
❑ 4 Mark Martin	70.00	32.00
❑ 5 Bill Elliott	70.00	32.00
❑ 6 Bobby Labonte	20.00	9.00
❑ 7 Sterling Marlin	15.00	6.75
❑ 8 Ted Musgrave	8.00	3.60
❑ 9 Terry Labonte	60.00	27.00
❑ 10 Ricky Rudd	15.00	6.75

1995 Zenith Tribute

This two-card insert set pays tribute to racing superstars: Dale Earnhardt and Jeff Gordon. The cards were inserted at a rate of one per 120 packs. The cards use all-foil Dufex printing technology to picture these two racing greats.

	MINT	NRMT
COMPLETE SET (2)	80.00	36.00
COMMON CARD (1-2)	50.00	22.00
*SINGLES: 8X TO 20X BASE CARD HI		
❑ 1 Dale Earnhardt	80.00	36.00
❑ 2 Jeff Gordon	80.00	36.00

1995 Zenith Winston Winners

This 25-card set is a retrospective look at the winners of the first 25 Winston Cup races of the 1995 season. The cards feature all-gold foil card stock and could be found at a rate of one in six packs of Zenith Racing.

	MINT	NRMT
COMPLETE SET (25)	120.00	55.00
COMMON CARD (1-25)	2.50	1.10
*SINGLES: 1.5X TO 4X BASE CARD HI		
❑ 1 Sterling Marlin	2.50	1.10
❑ 2 Jeff Gordon	12.00	5.50
❑ 3 Terry Labonte	6.00	2.70
❑ 4 Jeff Gordon Ray Evernham	12.00	5.50
❑ 5 Sterling Marlin	2.50	1.10
❑ 6 Jeff Gordon	12.00	5.50
❑ 7 Dale Earnhardt	12.00	5.50
❑ 8 Rusty Wallace	6.00	2.70
❑ 9 Mark Martin	6.00	2.70
❑ 10 Dale Earnhardt Teresa Earnhardt	12.00	5.50
❑ 11 Bobby Labonte	4.00	1.80
❑ 12 Kyle Petty	2.50	1.10
❑ 13 Terry Labonte	6.00	2.70
❑ 14 Bobby Labonte	4.00	1.80
❑ 15 Jeff Gordon	12.00	5.50
❑ 16 Jeff Gordon	12.00	5.50
❑ 17 Dale Jarrett	4.00	1.80
❑ 18 Sterling Marlin Paula Marlin Sutherlin Marlin	2.50	1.10
❑ 19 Dale Earnhardt	12.00	5.50
❑ 20 Mark Martin	6.00	2.70
❑ 21 Bobby Labonte Donna Labonte Tyler Labonte	4.00	1.80
❑ 22 Terry Labonte	6.00	2.70
❑ 23 Jeff Gordon	12.00	5.50
❑ 24 Dale Earnhardt	12.00	5.50
❑ 25 Jeff Gordon Brooke Gordon	12.00	5.50

1995 Zenith Z-Team

This 12 card set features the top Winston Cup drivers. The full body driver's photo is located on a Z-Team pedestal with a prismatic and metallic background that contains various colors. The Z-Team cards were inserted at a rate of one per 48 packs in Zenith Racing.

	MINT	NRMT
COMPLETE SET (12)	200.00	90.00
COMMON CARD (1-12)	6.00	2.70
*SINGLES: 8X TO 20X BASE CARD HI		
❑ 1 Dale Earnhardt	90.00	40.00
❑ 2 Jeff Gordon	90.00	
❑ 3 Bobby Labonte	15.00	
❑ 4 Terry Labonte	50.00	
❑ 5 Sterling Marlin	12.00	
❑ 6 Ken Schrader	6.00	
❑ 7 Michael Waltrip	6.00	
❑ 8 Ricky Rudd	12.00	
❑ 9 Ted Musgrave	6.00	
❑ 10 Morgan Shepherd	6.00	
❑ 11 Rusty Wallace	50.00	
❑ 12 Mark Martin	50.00	

1996 Zenith

This 100-card set is the first issue of the Zenith bra Pinnacle. The set is made up of 10 different subse includes the top drivers for NASCAR racing. T subsets include Road Pilots (1-34), Heavenly Vie 49), Sunrise (50-64), Black by Design (65-68), T (69,70), Rookie of the Year (71,72), Championship (73-80), Trilogy (81-85), Robert Yates Racing (8 and Winners (91-98). The cards are packaged six per pack, 24 packs per box and 16 boxes per Suggested retail price for a pack was $3.99.

	MINT
COMPLETE SET (100)	30.00
COMMON CARD (1-100)	.15
COMMON DRIVER (1-100)	.30
❑ 1 Dale Earnhardt RP	3.00
❑ 2 Jeff Gordon RP	3.00
❑ 3 Sterling Marlin RP	.60
❑ 4 Terry Labonte RP	1.50
❑ 5 Ricky Rudd RP	.60
❑ 6 Mark Martin RP	1.50
❑ 7 Bill Elliott RP	1.50
❑ 8 Ernie Irvan RP	.60
❑ 9 Rusty Wallace RP	1.50
❑ 10 Dale Jarrett RP	1.25
❑ 11 Geoff Bodine RP	.30
❑ 12 Derrike Cope RP	.30
❑ 13 Michael Waltrip RP	.30
❑ 14 Brett Bodine RP	.30
❑ 15 Ted Musgrave RP	.30
❑ 16 Hut Stricklin RP	.30
❑ 17 Rick Mast RP	.30
❑ 18 Darrell Waltrip RP	.60
❑ 19 Bobby Labonte RP	1.25
❑ 20 Jeff Burton RP	.60
❑ 21 Jeremy Mayfield RP	1.00
❑ 22 Ken Schrader RP	.30
❑ 23 Johnny Benson RP	.30
❑ 24 Lake Speed RP	.30
❑ 25 John Andretti RP	.30
❑ 26 Robert Pressley RP	.30
❑ 27 Kyle Petty RP	.60
❑ 28 Ricky Craven RP	.60
❑ 29 Bobby Hamilton RP	.30
❑ 30 Joe Nemechek RP	.30
❑ 31 Morgan Shepherd RP	.30
❑ 32 Bobby Hillin RP	.30
❑ 33 Jimmy Spencer RP	.30
❑ 34 Ward Burton RP	.30
❑ 35 Dale Earnhardt's Car HV	1.50
❑ 36 Jeff Gordon's Car HV	1.50
❑ 37 Sterling Marlin's Car HV	.30
❑ 38 Mark Martin's Car HV	.75
❑ 39 Terry Labonte's Car HV	.75
❑ 40 Bobby Labonte's Car HV	.60
❑ 41 Darrell Waltrip's Car HV	.30
❑ 42 Ernie Irvan's Car HV	.30
❑ 43 Dale Jarrett's Car HV	.60
❑ 44 Bobby Hamilton's Car HV	.15
❑ 45 Bill Elliott's Car HV	.75
❑ 46 Joe Nemechek's Car HV	.15
❑ 47 Ted Musgrave's Car HV	.15
❑ 48 Kyle Petty's Car HV	.30
❑ 49 Michael Waltrip's Car HV	.15
❑ 50 Dale Earnhardt S	1.50
❑ 51 Jeff Gordon S	1.50
❑ 52 Mark Martin S	.75
❑ 53 Ricky Rudd S	.30

Card	MINT	NRMT
Terry Labonte S	.75	.35
Kyle Petty S	.30	.14
Bobby Hillin S	.15	.07
Ted Musgrave S	.15	.07
Ken Schrader S	.15	.07
John Andretti S	.15	.07
Dale Jarrett S	.60	.25
Johnny Benson S	.15	.07
Michael Waltrip S	.15	.07
Bobby Labonte S	.60	.25
Ernie Irvan S	.30	.14
Dale Earnhardt BD	1.50	.70
Dale Earnhardt BD	1.50	.70
Dale Earnhardt BD	1.50	.70
Dale Earnhardt BD	1.50	.70
Dale Earnhardt T	1.50	.70
Terry Labonte T	.75	.35
Ricky Craven ROY	.15	.07
Ricky Craven ROY	.15	.07
Jeff Gordon CS	1.50	.70
Jeff Gordon CS	1.50	.70
Jeff Gordon CS	1.50	.70
Jeff Gordon CS	1.50	.70
Jeff Gordon CS	1.50	.70
Jeff Gordon CS	1.50	.70
Jeff Gordon CS	1.50	.70
Jeff Gordon CS	1.50	.70
Kenny Wallace TRI	.15	.07
Kenny Wallace TRI	.15	.07
Kenny Wallace TRI	.15	.07
Kenny Wallace TRI	.15	.07
Kenny Wallace TRI	.15	.07
Robert Yates RYR	.15	.07
rnie Irvan RYR	.30	.14
arry McReynolds RYR	.15	.07
ale Jarrett RYR	.60	.25
odd Parrott RYR	.15	.07
eff Gordon W	1.50	.70
eff Gordon W	1.50	.70
erry Labonte W	.75	.35
usty Wallace W	.75	.35
terling Marlin W	.30	.14
usty Wallace W	.75	.35
ale Jarrett W	.60	.25
eff Gordon Brooke Gordon W	1.50	.70
eff Gordon CL	1.50	.70
Bill Elliott CL	.75	.35

1996 Zenith Artists Proof

00-card set is a parallel to the base set. The set s the base cards printed on Gold Rainbow holofoil. rds were randomly seeded in packs at a rate of

	MINT	NRMT
ETE SET (100)	600.00	275.00
ON CARD (1-100)	3.00	1.35
ON DRIVER (1-100)	6.00	2.70

STS PROOF CARDS: 8X TO 20X BASIC CARDS

96 Zenith Champion Salute

-card insert set pays tribute to the past 25 years of R Winston Cup racing. Each card features a photo drivers championship ring. The rings include a real d chip mounted on the surface of the card. The were randomly inserted 1:90.

	MINT	NRMT
ETE SET (26)	800.00	350.00
ON CARD (1-26)	4.00	1.80
ON DRIVER (1-26)	8.00	3.60

ES: 10X TO 25X BASE CARD HI

Card	MINT	NRMT
Gordon	120.00	55.00
e Earnhardt	120.00	55.00
e Earnhardt	120.00	55.00
n Kulwicki	50.00	22.00
e Earnhardt	120.00	55.00
e Earnhardt	120.00	55.00
sty Wallace	60.00	27.00
Elliott	60.00	27.00
e Earnhardt	120.00	55.00
ale Earnhardt	120.00	55.00
arrell Waltrip	15.00	6.75
rry Labonte	60.00	27.00
bby Allison	8.00	3.60
arrell Waltrip	15.00	6.75
arrell Waltrip	15.00	6.75
ale Earnhardt	120.00	55.00
chard Petty	45.00	20.00
le Yarborough	8.00	3.60
le Yarborough	8.00	3.60
le Yarborough	8.00	3.60
chard Petty	45.00	20.00
chard Petty	45.00	20.00
nny Parsons	8.00	3.60

Card	MINT	NRMT
❑ 24 Richard Petty	45.00	20.00
❑ 25 Richard Petty	45.00	20.00
❑ 26 Richard Childress	4.00	1.80

1996 Zenith Highlights

This 15-card insert set features top drivers in Winston Cup racing. The cards are die-cut, foil stamped and randomly seeded 1:11 packs.

	MINT	NRMT
COMPLETE SET (15)	80.00	36.00
COMMON CARD (1-15)	1.25	.55

*SINGLES: 1.5X TO 4X BASE CARD HI

Card	MINT	NRMT
❑ 1 Dale Earnhardt	15.00	6.75
❑ 2 Jeff Gordon	15.00	6.75
❑ 3 Sterling Marlin	2.50	1.10
❑ 4 Mark Martin	8.00	3.60
❑ 5 Ricky Rudd	2.50	1.10
❑ 6 Darrell Waltrip	2.50	1.10
❑ 7 Geoff Bodine	1.25	.55
❑ 8 Bobby Labonte	5.00	2.20
❑ 9 Terry Labonte	8.00	3.60
❑ 10 Michael Waltrip	1.25	.55
❑ 11 Ken Schrader	1.25	.55
❑ 12 Jimmy Spencer	1.25	.55
❑ 13 Kyle Petty	2.50	1.10
❑ 14 Ernie Irvan	2.50	1.10
❑ 15 Bill Elliott	8.00	3.60

1996 Zenith Seven Wonders

This single card insert features Dale Earnhardt. The chase card honors Dale's 1994 Winston Cup Championship and is not a part of the Championship Salute set. There were 94 of this card produced and randomly inserted in packs at a rate of 1:6,025. Each of the cards is hand numbered.

	MINT	NRMT
COMPLETE SET (1)	500.00	220.00
❑ 1 Dale Earnhardt	500.00	220.00

1986 Ace Drag

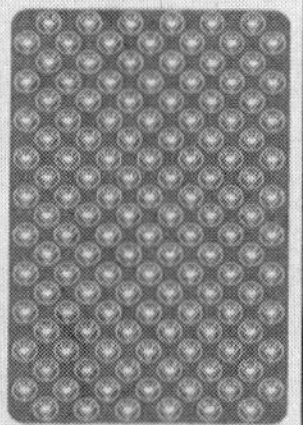

This set was made in West Germany for the British company Ace. The cards are actually part of a Trump card game featuring drag racing photos on the cardfront with a playing card back and rounded corners. The playing card deck contains 32-cards with one cover/rule card. Drivers are not specifically indentified on the cards, but are included below as noted.

	MINT	NRMT
COMPLETE SET (33)	10.00	4.50
COMMON CARD	.30	.14

Card	MINT	NRMT
❑ A1 Funny Car	.30	.14
❑ A2 Funny Car	.30	.14
❑ A3 Funny Car	.30	.14
❑ A4 Funny Car Tom Hoover	.50	.23
❑ B1 Stock Car Bob Glidden	.50	.23
❑ B2 Stock Car	.30	.14
❑ B3 Stock Car	.30	.14
❑ B4 GT Dragster Roy Johnson	.50	.23
❑ C1 Sling Shot	.30	.14
❑ C2 Sling Shot	.30	.14
❑ C3 Sling Shot	.30	.14
❑ C4 Sling Shot	.30	.14
❑ D1 Top Alcohol	.30	.14
❑ D2 Top Alcohol	.30	.14
❑ D3 Top Alcohol	.30	.14
❑ D4 Top Alcohol Tom Hoover	.50	.23
❑ E1 Sportsman Pro	.30	.14
❑ E2 Sportsman Pro	.30	.14
❑ E3 Sportsman Pro	.30	.14
❑ E4 Sportsman Pro	.30	.14
❑ F1 Top Fuel Funny Car	.30	.14
❑ F2 Top Fuel Funny Car Raymond Beadle	.50	.23
❑ F3 Top Fuel Funny Car	.30	.14
❑ F4 Top Fuel Funny Car	.30	.14
❑ G1 Dragster Truck	.30	.14
❑ G2 Dragster Truck	.30	.14
❑ G3 Dragster Truck	.30	.14
❑ G4 Dragster Truck	.30	.14
❑ H1 Dragster Truck	.30	.14
❑ H2 Dragster Truck	.30	.14
❑ H3 Dragster Truck	.30	.14
❑ H4 Dragster Truck	.30	.14
❑ NNO Cover Card Game rules on back	.30	.14

1994 Action Packed NHRA

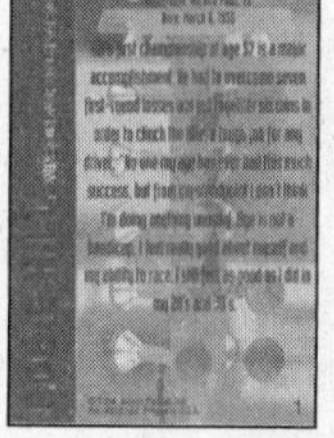

Action Packed expanded their auto racing card line in 1994 with their first set featuring popular drivers of NHRA. The card fronts feature a ghosted white background with gold lettering for the driver's name. Packaging included 6-card packs and 24-pack boxes with popular driver's photos on the wrapper fronts. 24Kt. Gold insert cards were randomly distributed in packs.

	MINT	NRMT
COMPLETE SET (42)	22.00	10.00
COMPLETE FACT.SET (42)	24.00	11.00
COMMON CARD (1-42)	.50	.23

Card	MINT	NRMT
❑ 1 Eddie Hill	1.50	.70
❑ 2 Scott Kalitta	.75	.35
❑ 3 Kenny Bernstein	1.50	.70
❑ 4 Mike Dunn	.50	.23
❑ 5 Rance McDaniel	.50	.23
❑ 6 Cory McClenathan	.75	.35
❑ 7 Joe Amato	.75	.35
❑ 8 Ed McCulloch	.50	.23
❑ 9 Doug Herbert	.50	.23
❑ 10 Tommy Johnson Jr.	.50	.23
❑ 11 Eddie Hill's Car	.75	.35
❑ 12 Scott Kalitta's Car	.50	.23
❑ 13 Kenny Bernstein's Car	.75	.35
❑ 14 Mike Dunn's Car	.50	.23
❑ 15 Rance McDaniel's Car	.50	.23
❑ 16 Cory McClenathan's Car	.50	.23
❑ 17 Joe Amato's Car	.50	.23
❑ 18 Ed McCulloch's Car	.50	.23
❑ 19 Doug Herbert's Car	.50	.23
❑ 20 Tommy Johnson Jr.'s Car	.50	.23
❑ 21 John Force	3.00	1.35
❑ 22 Chuck Etchells	.50	.23
❑ 23 Cruz Pedregon	.75	.35
❑ 24 Al Hofmann	.50	.23
❑ 25 Tom Hoover	.50	.23
❑ 26 Warren Johnson	.50	.23
❑ 27 Kurt Johnson	.50	.23
❑ 28 Scott Geoffrion	.50	.23
❑ 29 Larry Morgan	.50	.23
❑ 30 Mark Pawuk	.50	.23
❑ 31 Tom McEwen	.50	.23
❑ 32 Shirley Muldowney	1.50	.70
❑ 33 Darrell Gwynn	.50	.23
❑ 34 Don Garlits	1.50	.70
❑ 35 Bob Glidden's Car	.50	.23
❑ 36 Don Prudhomme	1.50	.70
❑ 37 Cory McClenathan's Car	.50	.23
❑ 38 Pat Austin's Car	.50	.23
❑ 39 John Force's Car	3.00	1.35

❑ 40 Jim Epler's Car	.50	.23
❑ 41 Warren Johnson's Car	.50	.23
❑ 42 Warren Johnson's Car	.50	.23

1994 Action Packed NHRA 24K Gold

Randomly inserted in 1994 Action Packed Drag racing packs, each card includes the now standard 24Kt. Gold logo on the card front. These Gold cards are essentially parallel versions of the corresponding driver's regular issue. Wrapper stated odds for pulling a 24K Gold card are 1:96.

	MINT	NRMT
COMPLETE SET (6)	200.00	90.00
COMMON CARD (31G-36G)	30.00	13.50
❑ 31G Tom McEwen	30.00	13.50
❑ 32G Shirley Muldowney	45.00	20.00
❑ 33G Darrell Gwynn	30.00	13.50
❑ 34G Don Garlits	45.00	20.00
❑ 35G Bob Glidden's Car	30.00	13.50
❑ 36G Don Prudhomme	40.00	18.00

1994 Action Packed Winston Drag Racing 24K Gold

This three-card set was produced by Action Packed and distributed through the Winston Cup Catalog and by Action Packed dealers. The cards were printed using Action Packed's 24K Gold process and feature NHRA stars John Force, Eddie Hill, and Warren Johnson.

	MINT	NRMT
COMPLETE SET (3)	30.00	13.50
COMMON CARD (1-3)	8.00	3.60
❑ 1 John Force	15.00	6.75
❑ 2 Eddie Hill	10.00	4.50
❑ 3 Warren Johnson	8.00	3.60

1995 Action Packed NHRA

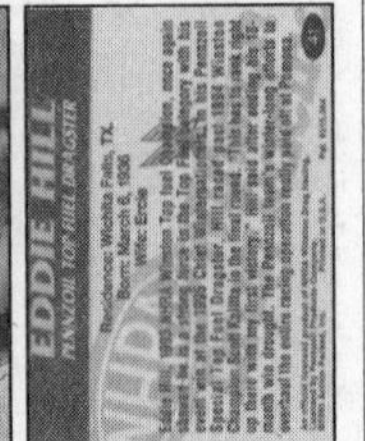

The 1995 Action Packed NHRA set was one of the first racing sets to be released after Action Packed became a Pinnacle brand. The set focuses on the top stars of NHRA with subsets on three of the more popular drivers: Joe Amato, Kenny Bernstein, and John Force. The standard packaging of 6-cards per pack and 24-packs per box was used with a four-tier insert card program: Silver Streak parallel, Autographs, Junior Dragster Champs, and 24K Gold.

	MINT	NRMT
COMPLETE SET (42)	15.00	6.75
COMMON CARD (1-42)	.40	.18
COMMON DRIVER (1-42)	.50	.23
❑ 1 Scott Kalitta's Car	.40	.18
❑ 2 Larry Dixon's Car	.40	.18
❑ 3 Cory McClenathan's Car	.50	.23
❑ 4 Connie Kalitta's Car	.50	.23
❑ 5 Joe Amato's Car	.40	.18
❑ 6 Kenny Bernstein's Car	.75	.35
❑ 7 Mike Dunn's Car	.40	.18
❑ 8 Pat Austin's Car	.40	.18
❑ 9 Tommy Johnson Jr.'s Car	.40	.18
❑ 10 Shelly Anderson's Car	.40	.18
❑ 11 John Force's Car	1.50	.70
❑ 12 Cruz Pedregon's Car	.50	.23
❑ 13 Al Hofmann's Car	.40	.18
❑ 14 Chuck Etchells's Car	.40	.18
❑ 15 K.C. Spurlock's Car	.40	.18
❑ 16 Gordie Bonin's Car	.40	.18
❑ 17 Jim Epler's Car	.40	.18
❑ 18 Dean Skuza's Car	.40	.18
❑ 19 Gary Bolger's Car	.40	.18
❑ 20 Kenji Okazaki's Car	.40	.18
❑ 21 Darrell Alderman's Car	.40	.18
❑ 22 Scott Geoffrion's Car	.40	.18
❑ 23 Warren Johnson's Car	.40	.18
❑ 24 Jim Yates' Car	.40	.18
❑ 25 Kurt Johnson's Car	.40	.18
❑ 26 Joe Amato	.75	.35
❑ 27 Joe Amato's Car	.50	.23
❑ 28 Joe Amato's Car	.50	.23
❑ 29 Joe Amato	.75	.35
❑ 30 Kenny Bernstein	1.50	.70
❑ 31 Kenny Bernstein's Car	.75	.35
❑ 32 Kenny Bernstein's Car	.75	.35
❑ 33 Kenny Bernstein's Car	.75	.35
❑ 34 Kenny Bernstein's Car	.75	.35
❑ 35 Kenny Bernstein's Car	.75	.35
❑ 36 John Force	2.50	1.10
❑ 37 John Force's Car	1.50	.70
❑ 38 John Force's Car	1.50	.70
❑ 39 John Force's Car	1.50	.70
❑ 40 John Force's Car	1.50	.70
❑ 41 Eddie Hill	.75	.35
❑ 42 Joe Gibbs	.75	.35

1995 Action Packed NHRA Silver Streak

Action Packed introduced a Pinnacle Brands tradition to its 1995 NHRA set with the addition of a full parallel set -- Silver Streak. The cards were randomly inserted in 1995 Action Packed NHRA packs at the rate of approximately one card every six foil packs. The cards were printed with a silver foil background on the driver photo and the Silver Streak logo on the card back.

	MINT	NRMT
COMPLETE SET (42)	100.00	45.00
COMMON CARD (1-42)	1.50	.70
COMMON DRIVER (1-42)	2.00	.90

*SILVER STARS: 3X TO 5X BASIC CARDS

1995 Action Packed NHRA Autographs

This 16-card insert set features the top drivers in the NHRA signatures. Each card is hand numbered of 500. The Kenny Bernstein and John Force cards were numbered of 125. The cards were availble one per 24 packs.

	MINT	NRMT
COMPLETE SET (16)	700.00	325.00
COMMON CARD	30.00	13.50
❑ 1 Scott Kalitta	30.00	13.50
❑ 2 Larry Dixon	30.00	13.50
❑ 3 Cory McClenathan	40.00	18.00
❑ 6 K.Bernstein/125	150.00	70.00
❑ 7 Mike Dunn	30.00	13.50
❑ 9 Tommy Johnson	30.00	13.50
❑ 10 Shelly Anderson	30.00	13.50
❑ 11 John Force/125	175.00	80.00
❑ 12 Cruz Pedregon	40.00	18.00
❑ 13 Al Hofmann	30.00	13.50
❑ 21 Darrell Alderman	30.00	13.50
❑ 22 Scott Geoffrion	30.00	13.50
❑ 23 Warren Johnson	30.00	13.50
❑ 24 Jim Yates	30.00	13.50
❑ 25 Kurt Johnson	30.00	13.50
❑ 41 Eddie Hill	40.00	18.00

1995 Action Packed NHRA 24K Gold

Randomly inserted in 1995 Action Packed NHRA packs, each card includes the standard 24Kt. Gold logo on the card front. These Gold cards are essentially parallel versions of the Kenny Bernstein and John Force subset cards. Wrapper stated odds for pulling a 24K Gold card are 1:96.

	MINT	NRMT
COMPLETE SET (10)	250.00	110.00
COMMON CARD (30-40)	25.00	11.00
❑ 30 Kenny Bernstein	25.00	11.00
❑ 31 Kenny Bernstein	25.00	11.00
❑ 32 Kenny Bernstein	25.00	11.00
❑ 33 Kenny Bernstein	25.00	11.00
❑ 34 Kenny Bernstein	25.00	11.00
❑ 35 Kenny Bernstein	25.00	11.00
❑ 36 John Force	40.00	18.00
❑ 37 John Force	40.00	18.00
❑ 38 John Force	40.00	18.00
❑ 39 John Force	40.00	18.00
❑ 40 John Force	40.00	18.00

1995 Action Packed NHRA Jr. Dragster Champs

Randomly inserted in 1995 Action Packed NHRA p this set provides a preview of future NHRA hopef Junior National Championship winners. Cards packed approximately one per 48 foil packs.

	MINT
COMPLETE SET (8)	30.00
COMMON CARD (1-8)	4.00
❑ 1 Richard Thompson	4.00
❑ 2 Chris Bear	4.00
❑ 3 Richard Coury Jr.	4.00
❑ 4 Jamie Lynn Innes	4.00
❑ 5 James Antonnette	4.00
❑ 6 Barrie Wagers	4.00
❑ 7 Michelle Banach	4.00
❑ 8 Mark Lowry	4.00

1990 Big Time Drag

This 21-card set features some of drag racings popular cars. There is everything from Tom Ho Showtime Funny Car to Roger Gustin's Jet Funn There were 1,500 sets produced. The cards are below in alphabetical order

	MINT
COMPLETE SET (21)	30.00
COMMON CARD	1.50
❑ 1 Bob Bealieu	1.50
❑ 2 Charles Carpenter's Car	1.50
❑ 3 Jim Druer	1.50
❑ 4 Artie Farmer	1.50
❑ 5 Gordy Foust's Car	1.50
❑ 6 Roger Gustin's Car	1.50
❑ 7 Al Hanna's Car	1.50
❑ 8 Tom Hoover's Car	2.00
❑ 9 Tom Jacobson's Car	1.50
❑ 10 Donnie Little	1.50
❑ 11 Jeff Littleton's Car	1.50
❑ 12 Jerry Moreland's Car	1.50
❑ 13 Rocky Pirrone	1.50
❑ 14 Dick Rosberg	1.50
❑ 15 Lou Sattelmaier's Car	1.50
❑ 16 Paul Strommen's Car	1.50
❑ 17 Ken Thurm's Car	1.50
❑ 18 William Townes	1.50
❑ 19 Roy Trevino's Car	1.50
❑ 20 Rob Vandergriff	1.50
❑ 21 Norm Wizner's Car	1.50

1990 Big Time Drag Sticke

This 21-card sticker set is a parallel to the 1990 Bi Drag set. The same photos were used in each set were 500 sticker sets produced.

	MINT
COMPLETE SET (21)	75.00
COMMON STICKER	4.00
❑ 1 Bob Bealieu	4.00
❑ 2 Charles Carpenter's Car	4.00
❑ 3 Jim Druer	4.00
❑ 4 Artie Farmer	4.00
❑ 5 Gordy Foust's Car	4.00
❑ 6 Roger Gustin's Car	4.00
❑ 7 Al Hanna's Car	4.00
❑ 8 Tom Hoover's Car	5.00
❑ 9 Tom Jacobson's Car	4.00
❑ 10 Donnie Little	4.00
❑ 11 Jeff Littleton's Car	4.00
❑ 12 Jerry Moreland's Car	4.00
❑ 13 Rocky Pirrone	4.00
❑ 14 Dick Rosberg	4.00
❑ 15 Lou Sattelmaier's Car	4.00
❑ 16 Paul Strommen's Car	4.00
❑ 17 Ken Thurm's Car	4.00
❑ 18 William Townes	4.00
❑ 19 Roy Trevino's Car	4.00

	MINT	NRMT
Rob Vandergriff	4.00	1.80
Norm Wizner's Car	4.00	1.80

1991 Big Time Drag

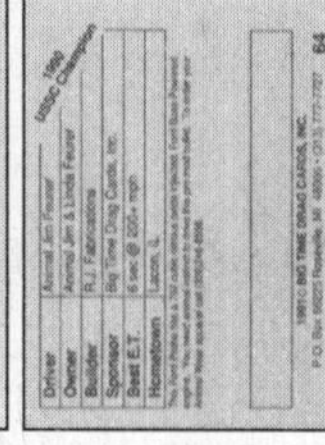

'ime Drag Cards, Inc. of Roseville, Michigan ced this 96-card set in complete factory set form. 'st 24-cards highlight the careers of Don Garlits and Day. The final card is an unnumbered cover card.

	MINT	NRMT
'LETE SET (96)	25.00	11.00
ION CARD (1-95)	.30	.14
on Garlits in Car	.60	.25
on Garlits in Car	.60	.25
on Garlits' Car	.60	.25
on Garlits' Car	.60	.25
on Garlits' Car	.60	.25
on Garlits' Car	.60	.25
on Garlits' Car	.60	.25
on Garlits' Car	.60	.25
on Garlits' Car	.60	.25
Don Garlits' Car	.60	.25
Don Garlits' Car	.60	.25
Don Garlits' Car	.60	.25
Norm Day Cover Card	.30	.14
Norm Day's Car	.30	.14
Norm Day's Car	.30	.14
Norm Day's Car	.30	.14
Norm Day's Car	.30	.14
Norm Day	.50	.23
Norm Day's Car	.30	.14
Norm Day W/Crew	.50	.23
Don Garlits' Car	.60	.25
Norm Day's Car	.30	.14
Norm Day's Car	.30	.14
Norm Day's Car	.30	.14
'om Hoover's Car	.50	.23
'erry Caminito's Car	.30	.14
Vyatt Radke's Car	.30	.14
'ruz Pedregon's Car	.60	.25
Vayne Torkelson's Car	.30	.14
Vhit Bazemore's Car	.30	.14
ruce Larson's Car	.30	.14
oe Amato's Car	.60	.25
arol Burkett	.30	.14
oe Amato's Car	.60	.25
ella Woods w/Car	.30	.14
ella Woods' Car	.30	.14
l Dapozzo's Car	.30	.14
ichard Hartman's Car	.30	.14
ichard Hartman	.30	.14
ruce Larson's Car	.30	.14
ob Vansciver's Car	.30	.14
erry Caminito's Car	.30	.14
Wyatt Radke's Car		
Vayne Bailey's Car	.30	.14
om Hoover's Car	.50	.23
Bruce Larson's Car		
m Feurer's Car	.30	.14
m Feurer's Car	.30	.14
lake Wiggins' Car	.30	.14
andy Moore	.30	.14
andy Moore's Car	.30	.14
arolyn Melendy's Car	.30	.14
onny Leonard's Motor	.30	.14
Vally Bell's Car	.30	.14
ary Grahner's Car	.30	.14
ill Kulhmann's Car	.30	.14
om Jacobson's Car	.30	.14
en Thurm's Car	.30	.14
Hanna's Car	.30	.14
onnie Little's Car	.30	.14
ou Sattelmaier's Car	.30	.14
ordy Foust's Car	.30	.14
harles Carpenter's Car	.30	.14
om Hoover's Car	.50	.23
oy Trevino's Car	.30	.14
m Feurer w/Car	.30	.14
aul Strommen's Car	.30	.14
oger Gustin's Car	.30	.14
ack Joyce's Car	.30	.14
erry Moreland's Car	.30	.14
❏ 69 Jeff Littleton's Car	.30	.14
❏ 70 Norm Wizner's Car	.30	.14
❏ 71 Kenneth Tripp Jr.'s Car	.30	.14
❏ 72 Tim McAmis' Car	.30	.14
❏ 73 Tom McEwen's Car	.50	.23
❏ 74 Tom McEwen's Car	.50	.23
❏ 75 Tom Hoover's Car	.50	.23
❏ 76 Ken Karsten Jr.'s Car	.30	.14
❏ 77 Johnny West's Car	.30	.14
❏ 78 Brian Gahm's Car	.30	.14
❏ 79 Wally Bell's Car	.30	.14
❏ 80 Roger Gustin's Car	.30	.14
❏ 81 Bob Bunker's Car	.30	.14
❏ 82 Terry Leggett's Car	.30	.14
❏ 83 Mike Ashley's Car	.30	.14
❏ 84 Al Hanna's Car	.30	.14
❏ 85 Whit Bazemore's Car	.30	.14
❏ 86 Wally Bell's Car	.30	.14
❏ 87 Aggi Hendriks' Car	.30	.14
❏ 88 Bruce Larson's Car	.30	.14
❏ 89 Darrell Amberson's Car	.30	.14
❏ 90 Bob Vansciver's Car	.30	.14
❏ 91 John H. Rocca's Car	.30	.14
❏ 92 Wayne Bailey	.30	.14
❏ 93 K.S. Pittman's Car	.30	.14
❏ 94 Jack Ostrander's Car	.30	.14
❏ 95 Rob Vandergriff's Car	.30	.14
❏ NNO Cover Card	.30	.14

1993-97 Bunny Burkett

This nine-card set features Bunny and the cars she has driven through the years. This set is distributed by her team through trackside souvneir sales and autoshow sales.

	MINT	NRMT
COMPLETE SET (9)	9.00	4.00
COMMON CARD (1-9)	1.00	.45
❏ 1 Bunny Burkett/1993	1.00	.45
❏ 2 Bunny Burkett/1993	1.00	.45
❏ 3 Bunny Burkett/1994	1.00	.45
❏ 4 Bunny Burkett/1995	1.00	.45
❏ 5 Bunny Burkett/1995	1.00	.45
❏ 6 Bunny Burkett/1996	1.00	.45
❏ 7 Bunny Burkett/1996	1.00	.45
❏ 8 Bunny Burkett/1997	1.00	.45
❏ 9 Bunny Burkett/1997	1.00	.45

1994 Card Dynamics Joe Amato

This three-card set features the five-time Winston Top Fuel Champion. The cards are made of polished aluminum and come in a display box. There were 10,000 sets made. Each set comes with a certificate of authenticity .

	MINT	NRMT
COMPLETE SET (3)	12.00	5.50
COMMON CARD	5.00	2.20

1994 Card Dynamics Kenny Bernstein

This three-card set features the "King of Speed." The cards are made of polished aluminum and come in a display box. There were 10,000 sets made. Each set comes with a certificate of authenticity .

	MINT	NRMT
COMPLETE SET (3)	12.00	5.50
COMMON CARD	5.00	2.20

1994 Card Dynamics Eddie Hill

This three-card set features the 1994 Winston Top Fuel Champion. The cards are made of polished aluminum and come in a display box. There were 10,000 sets made. Each set comes with a certificate of authenticity .

	MINT	NRMT
COMPLETE SET (3)	12.00	5.50
COMMON CARD	5.00	2.20

1994 Card Dynamics Don Prudhomme

This three-card set features drag racing legend Don "The Snake" Prudhomme. The cards are made of polished aluminum and come in a display box. There were 10,000 sets made. Each set comes with a certificate of authenticity .

	MINT	NRMT
COMPLETE SET (3)	12.00	5.50
COMMON CARD	5.00	2.20

1989 Checkered Flag IHRA

Checkered Flag Inc. produced sets in 1989 and 1990 featuring drivers and cars of the International Hot Rod Association. The cards were sold in complete factory set form. The 1989 set features black borders and horizontally oriented car cards with a few individual driver cars. The final card, number 100, is a checklist.

	MINT	NRMT
COMPLETE SET (100)	25.00	11.00
COMMON CARD (1-100)	.30	.14
❏ 1 Richard Holcomb's Car	.30	.14
❏ 2 Richard Holcomb's Car	.30	.14
❏ 3 Usif Lawson's Car	.30	.14
❏ 4 Scott Weis' Car	.30	.14
❏ 5 Butch Kernodle's Car	.30	.14
❏ 6 Paul Hall's Car	.30	.14
❏ 7 Bogie Kell's Car	.30	.14
❏ 8 Kurt Neighbor's Car	.30	.14
❏ 9 Gary Rettell's Car	.30	.14
❏ 10 Steve Litton's Car	.30	.14
❏ 11 Melinda Green's Car	.30	.14
❏ 12 Don DeFluiter's Car	.30	.14
❏ 13 Mark Thomas' Car	.30	.14
❏ 14 Gary Rettell's Car	.30	.14
❏ 15 Bob Gilbertson's Car	.30	.14
❏ 16 Greg Moss	.50	.23
❏ 17 Dan Nimmo's Car	.30	.14
❏ 18 Phil Sebring's Car	.30	.14
❏ 19 Dennis Ramey	.50	.23
❏ 20 Dennis Ramey's Car	.30	.14
❏ 21 Ted Osborne's Car	.30	.14
❏ 22 Mark Osborne's Car	.30	.14
❏ 23 Garley Daniels' Car	.30	.14
❏ 24 Danny Estep's Car	.30	.14
❏ 25 Tim Freeman's Car	.30	.14
❏ 26 George Supinski's Car	.30	.14
❏ 27 Dave Northrop's Car	.30	.14
❏ 28 Jerry Taylor's Car	.30	.14
❏ 29 Mike Davis' Car	.30	.14
❏ 30 Jim Yates' Car	.30	.14
❏ 31 Harold Denton	.50	.23
❏ 32 Harold Denton's Car	.30	.14
❏ 33 Ed Dixon's Car	.30	.14
❏ 34 Ed Dixon	.50	.23
❏ 35 Terry Adams	.50	.23
❏ 36 Terry Adams' Car	.30	.14
❏ 37 Harold Robinson's Car	.30	.14
❏ 38 Larry Morgan's Car	.30	.14
❏ 39 Tim Nabors' Car	.30	.14
❏ 40 Steve Schmidt's Car	.30	.14
❏ 41 Neil Moyer's Car	.30	.14
❏ 42 Joe Sway's Car	.30	.14
❏ 43 John Noble's Car	.30	.14
❏ 44 John Noble's Car	.30	.14
❏ 45 Shirl Greer's Car	.30	.14
❏ 46 Shirl Greer's Car	.30	.14
❏ 47 Dave Miller's Car	.30	.14
❏ 48 Dave Miller's Car	.30	.14
❏ 49 Billy Ewing's Car	.30	.14
❏ 50 Clay Broadwater's Car	.30	.14
❏ 51 Gary Litton's Car	.30	.14
❏ 52 Keith Jackson's Car	.30	.14
❏ 53 Whit Bazemore	.50	.23
❏ 54 Craig Cain's Car	.30	.14
❏ 55 Esua Speed's Car	.30	.14
❏ 56 Ed Hoover's Car	.30	.14
❏ 57 Ed Hoover's Car	.30	.14
❏ 58 Kenneth Tripp Jr.'s Car	.30	.14
❏ 59 Kenneth Tripp Sr.'s Car	.30	.14
❏ 60 Billy DeWitt's Car	.30	.14
❏ 61 Billy DeWitt	.50	.23
❏ 62 Scotty Cannon's Car	.30	.14
❏ 63 Scotty Cannon	.50	.23
❏ 64 Michael Martin	.50	.23
❏ 65 Michael Martin's Car	.30	.14
❏ 66 Gordy Hmiel's Car	.30	.14
❏ 67 Gordy Hmiel's Car	.30	.14
❏ 68 Sam Snyder's Car	.30	.14
❏ 69 Terry Housley's Car	.30	.14
❏ 70 Jim Ray's Car	.30	.14

❑ 71 John Ieppert's Car	.30	.14
❑ 72 Frankie Foster's Car	.30	.14
❑ 73 Buddy McGowan's Car	.30	.14
❑ 74 Brian Gahm's Car	.30	.14
❑ 75 Bob Dickson's Car	.30	.14
❑ 76 Walter Henry's Car	.30	.14
❑ 77 Gene Fryer's Car	.30	.14
❑ 78 Terry Leggett's Car	.30	.14
❑ 79 Blake Wiggins' Car	.30	.14
❑ 80 Tim Nabors' Car	.30	.14
❑ 81 Ernest Wrenn's Car	.30	.14
❑ 82 Donnie Little's Car	.30	.14
❑ 83 Mike Ashley's Car	.30	.14
❑ 84 Ron Miller's Car	.30	.14
❑ 85 Danny Bastianelli's Car	.30	.14
❑ 86 Tracy Eddins' Car	.30	.14
❑ 87 Kurt Neighbor's Car	.30	.14
❑ 88 Greg Moss' Car	.30	.14
❑ 89 Greg Moss' Car	.30	.14
❑ 90 Bogie Kell's Car	.30	.14
❑ 91 Jerry Gulley's Car	.30	.14
❑ 92 Ernest Wrenn's Car	.30	.14
❑ 93 Don DeFluiter	.50	.23
❑ 94 Blake Wiggins	.50	.23
❑ 95 Barry Shirley's Car	.30	.14
❑ 96 Ken Regenthal's Car UER	.30	.14
❑ 97 Donnie Little's Car	.30	.14
❑ 98 Rick Hord's Car	.30	.14
❑ 99 Ricky Bowie's Car	.30	.14
❑ 100 Checklist Card	.30	.14

1990 Checkered Flag IHRA

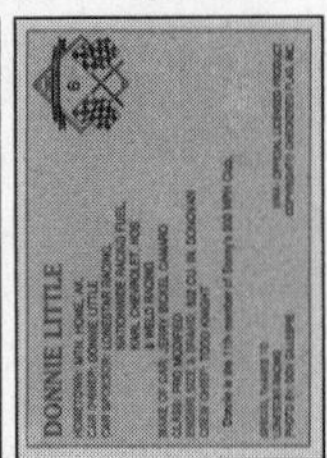

Checkered Flag Race Cards Inc. produced sets in 1989 and 1990 featuring drivers and cars of the International Hot Rod Association. The cards were sold in complete factory set form. The 1990 set features white borders and horizontally oriented car cards. The final card, #100, is a checklist. An unnumbered cover card was produced as well featuring an order form to purchase additional sets at $17.50 each.

	MINT	NRMT
COMPLETE SET (101)	12.00	5.50
COMMON CARD (1-100)	.15	.07
❑ 1 Mike Ashley's Car	.15	.07
❑ 2 Ronnie Sox's Car	.30	.14
❑ 3 Scotty Cannon's Car	.30	.14
❑ 4 Jeff Littleton's Car	.15	.07
❑ 5 Gordy Foust's Car	.15	.07
❑ 6 Donnie Little's Car	.15	.07
❑ 7 Rob Vandergriff's Car	.15	.07
❑ 8 Terry Leggett's Car	.15	.07
❑ 9 Ken Regenthal's Car	.15	.07
❑ 10 Ed Hoover's Car	.15	.07
❑ 11 Stanley Barker's Car	.15	.07
❑ 12 Tim McAmis' Car	.15	.07
❑ 13 Sam Snyder's Car	.15	.07
❑ 14 Brian Gahm's Car	.15	.07
❑ 15 Blake Wiggins' Car	.15	.07
❑ 16 Ken Karsten Jr.'s Car	.15	.07
❑ 17 Eddie Harris' Car	.15	.07
❑ 18 Carolyn Melendy's Car	.15	.07
❑ 19 Stuart Norman's Car	.15	.07
❑ 20 Terry Leggett's Car	.15	.07
❑ 21 Ron Iannotti's Car	.15	.07
❑ 22 Michael Martin's Car	.15	.07
❑ 23 Jeff Ensslin's Car	.15	.07
❑ 24 Tim McAmis' Car	.15	.07
❑ 25 Al Billes' Car	.15	.07
❑ 26 Gordy Hmiel's Car	.15	.07
❑ 27 Manny DeJesus' Car	.15	.07
❑ 28 Brian Gahm's Car	.15	.07
❑ 29 Ray Ervin's Car	.15	.07
❑ 30 Wally Stroupe's Car	.15	.07
❑ 31 Chuck VanVallis' Car	.15	.07
❑ 32 Ken Karsten Jr.'s Car	.15	.07
❑ 33 Ed Hoover's Car	.15	.07
❑ 34 Ronnie Sox w/Car	.50	.23
❑ 35 Scotty Cannon's Car	.30	.14
❑ 36 Rob Vandergriff's Car	.15	.07
❑ 37 Mike Ashley's Car	.15	.07
❑ 38 Gordy Foust's Car	.15	.07
❑ 39 Blake Wiggins' Car	.15	.07
❑ 40 Ken Regenthal's Car	.15	.07
❑ 41 Tracy Eddins' Car	.15	.07
❑ 42 Steve Litton's Car	.15	.07
❑ 43 Mark Thomas' Car	.15	.07
❑ 44 Johnny West's Car	.15	.07
❑ 45 Jerry Gulley's Car	.15	.07
❑ 46 Bob Gilbertson's Car	.15	.07
❑ 47 Dan Nimmo's Car	.15	.07
❑ 48 Ronnie Midyette's Car	.15	.07
❑ 49 Phil Sebring's Car	.15	.07
❑ 50 Art Hendey's Car	.15	.07
❑ 51 Bogie Kell's Car	.15	.07
❑ 52 Greg Moss' Car	.15	.07
❑ 53 Gary Litton's Car	.15	.07
❑ 54 Ricky Bowie's Car	.15	.07
❑ 55 Frank Kramberger's Car	.15	.07
❑ 56 Keith Jackson's Car	.15	.07
❑ 57 Clay Broadwater's Car	.15	.07
❑ 58 Tommy Mauney's Car	.15	.07
❑ 59 Ed Dixon's Car	.15	.07
❑ 60 David Drongowski's Car	.15	.07
❑ 61 Carlton Phillips' Car	.15	.07
❑ 62 Harold Denton's Car	.15	.07
❑ 63 Charlie Garrett's Car	.15	.07
❑ 64 Joe Sway's Car	.15	.07
❑ 65 Tim Nabors' Car	.15	.07
❑ 66 Tommy Mauney's Car	.15	.07
❑ 67 Terry Adams' Car	.15	.07
❑ 68 Harold Denton's Car	.15	.07
❑ 69 Terry Housley's Car	.15	.07
❑ 70 Doug Kirk's Car	.15	.07
❑ 71 Ed Dixon's Car	.15	.07
❑ 72 Terry Walters' Car	.15	.07
❑ 73 Neil Moyer's Car	.15	.07
❑ 74 Harold Robinson's Car	.15	.07
❑ 75 Jack Revelle's Car	.15	.07
❑ 76 Don Kohler's Car	.15	.07
❑ 77 Michael Brotherton's Car	.30	.14
❑ 78 Richard Holcomb's Car	.15	.07
❑ 79 Wayne Bailey's Car	.15	.07
❑ 80 Fred Farndon's Car	.15	.07
❑ 81 Chris Karamesines' Car	.30	.14
❑ 82 John Carey's Car	.15	.07
❑ 83 Melvin Eaves' Car	.15	.07
❑ 84 Carroll Smoot's Car	.15	.07
❑ 85 Gene Fryer's Car	.15	.07
❑ 86 Craig Cain's Car	.15	.07
❑ 87 Joe Groves' Car	.15	.07
❑ 88 Ron Miller's Car	.15	.07
❑ 89 Buddy McGowan's Car	.15	.07
❑ 90 Randy Daniels' Car	.15	.07
❑ 91 Mark Osborne's Car	.15	.07
❑ 92 Tim Freeman's Car	.15	.07
❑ 93 Ted Osborne's Car	.15	.07
❑ 94 Danny Estep's Car	.15	.07
❑ 95 Bruce Abbott's Car	.15	.07
❑ 96 Aggi Hendriks' Car	.15	.07
❑ 97 Tim Butler's Car	.15	.07
❑ 98 Bob Vansciver's Car	.15	.07
❑ 99 Usif Lawson's Car	.15	.07
❑ 100 Checklist Card	.15	.07
❑ NNO Cover Card	.20	.09
complete set order form on back		

1965 Donruss Spec Sheet

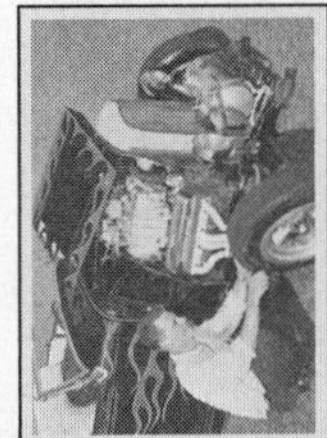

Donruss produced this 66-card set sponsored by Hot Rod magazine for distribution in gum wax packs. The cards primarily feature top cars from a wide variety of drag racing and show events, but also cover road racing and IndyCar. The most noteworthy card, #49, features Bobby Unser and his Pikes Peak Hill Climb championship.

	NRMT	VG-E
COMPLETE SET (66)	250.00	110.00
COMMON CARD (1-66)	4.00	1.80
❑ 1 Bill Burke's Car	6.00	2.70
Mel Chastain's Car		
Bonneville Streamliner		
❑ 2 Fred Larson's Car	4.00	1.80
Ready to Go		
❑ 3 Sam Parriott's Car	4.00	
Blown Ford Engine		
❑ 4 Jack Lufkin's Car	6.00	
Triple Threat 'Vette		
❑ 5 1925 T-Roadster	4.00	
❑ 6 Show Winner	4.00	
❑ 7 Agelesss Street Rod	4.00	
❑ 8 315 Horsepower	4.00	
❑ 9 Bob Summers' Car	4.00	
Bill Summers' Car		
700 Horsepower		
❑ 10 Hot Rod Fever	4.00	
❑ 11 East African Safari	4.00	
❑ 12 Beauty and Comfort	4.00	
❑ 13 Record Runs	4.00	
❑ 14 Ted Wingate's Car	4.00	
Pair Duces		
❑ 15 Six Pots	4.00	
❑ 16 Howard Peck's Car	6.00	
'64 Buick Mill		
❑ 17 What a Machine	4.00	
❑ 18 Al Eckstrand's Car	6.00	
Dodge Super Stock		
❑ 19 Kurtis Roadster	4.00	
❑ 20 World's Fastest	4.00	
❑ 21 Super Super Stock	4.00	
❑ 22 Hot Rod Dictionary	4.00	
❑ 23 Well Dressed Mill	4.00	
❑ 24 Custom Pick-Up	4.00	
❑ 25 Bob-Tailed T	4.00	
❑ 26 Jess Van Deventer's Car	4.00	
Fiery Chevy		
❑ 27 Offy Engine	4.00	
❑ 28 334 Cubic Inches	4.00	
❑ 29 Jack Williams' Car	4.00	
Points Champion		
❑ 30 Abandoned	4.00	
❑ 31 Salt Flats	4.00	
❑ 32 LeRoi Tex Smith's Car	4.00	
Experimental Roadster		
❑ 33 Modified Sport Car	4.00	
❑ 34 Instant Roadster	4.00	
❑ 35 1923 Dodge	4.00	
❑ 36 L.A. Roadsters	4.00	
❑ 37 Howard Brown's Car	4.00	
137 Quarter		
❑ 38 A Real Winner	4.00	
❑ 39 Steve LaBonge's Car	4.00	
Crusing Model A		
❑ 40 Mark 27	4.00	
❑ 41 Owners Pride	4.00	
❑ 42 Roman Red	4.00	
❑ 43 Tom McMullen's Car	4.00	
Flamed Roadster		
❑ 44 Hot Rod Dictionary	4.00	
❑ 45 Detailed Custom	4.00	
❑ 46 306 Streamliner	4.00	
❑ 47 The Wedge	4.00	
❑ 48 The Oakland Lational	4.00	
❑ 49 Bobby Unser's Car	8.00	
Hill Climb Champ		
❑ 50 Tony Nancy's Car	4.00	
Off the Line		
❑ 51 Hot Rod Dictionary	4.00	
❑ 52 Bob Herda's Car	4.00	
Record Holder		
❑ 53 Bobby Unser w/Car	8.00	
Pikes Peak Champ		
❑ 54 National Championship	4.00	
❑ 55 Hot Rod Dictionary	4.00	
❑ 56 John Mazmanian's Car	4.00	
Boss		
❑ 57 1964 Indianapolis 500	4.00	
❑ 58 Hot Rod Dictionary	4.00	
❑ 59 Connie Kalitta's Car	6.00	
Nitro Loaded		
❑ 60 Off the Line	4.00	
❑ 61 Chuck Griffith's Car	4.00	
Starlighter		
❑ 62 National Drags	4.00	
❑ 63 '35 Custom	4.00	
❑ 64 Tom Spaulding's Car	4.00	
Going Cart		
❑ 65 Hot Rod Dictionary	4.00	
❑ 66 Hot Rod Dictionary	4.00	

1993 Finish Line NHRA

For the first time Finish Line produced their own c with this 1993 NHRA release. The set feature drivers, cars and crew members of the top NHRA of the previous season. The cards were packaged foil pack with 36 packs per box and 25-cards per pack. Insert sets included a 17-card Speedways iss a 9-card Autographs set.

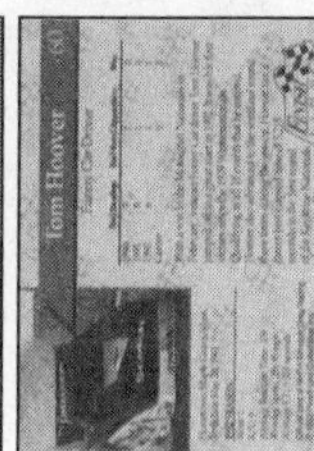

	MINT	NRMT
LETE SET (133)	10.00	4.50
ON CARD (1-133)	.05	.02
ON DRIVER (1-133)	.10	.05
e Amato	.20	.09
e Amato	.20	.09
e Amato's Car	.10	.05
elly Anderson	.20	.09
le Armstrong	.10	.05
t Austin	.10	.05
t Austin's Car	.05	.02
lt Austin	.10	.05
Pat Austin		
e Beard	.10	.05
enny Bernstein	.60	.25
enny Bernstein's Car	.20	.09
enny Bernstein	.60	.25
m Brissette	.10	.05
ichael Brotherton	.10	.05
ichael Brotherton's Car	.05	.02
uzzy Carter	.10	.05
es Cerny	.10	.05
annielle DePorter	.10	.05
arrell Gwynn	.20	.09
m Head	.10	.05
oug Herbert	.10	.05
ddie Hill	.60	.25
ddie Hill	.60	.25
ddie Hill's Car	.20	.09
ommy Johnson Jr.	.20	.09
ommy Johnson Sr.	.20	.09
Tommy Johnson Jr.		
Wendy Johnson		
m LaHaie	.10	.05
ory McClenathan	.60	.25
ory McClenathan	.60	.25
ory McClenathan's Car	.20	.09
McCulloch	.10	.05
McCulloch's Car	.05	.02
hn Medlen	.10	.05
ck Ostrander	.10	.05
n Prock	.10	.05
on Prudhomme	.60	.25
on Prudhomme's Car	.20	.09
n Richards	.10	.05
Segrini	.10	.05
ne Snow	.20	.09
n Veney	.10	.05
m Anderson	.10	.05
hit Bazemore	.10	.05
ry Bolger	.10	.05
rry Caminito	.10	.05
stin Coil	.10	.05
ry Densham	.10	.05
uck Etchells	.10	.05
uck Etchells' Car	.05	.02
n Epler	.10	.05
ry Evans	.10	.05
rnie Fedderly	.10	.05
hn Force	.60	.25
hn Force	.60	.25
hn Force's Car	.60	.25
chard Hartman	.10	.05
Hofmann	.20	.09
Hofmann	.20	.09
Hofmann's Car	.10	.05
m Hoover	.20	.09
m Hoover's Car	.10	.05
rdon Mineo	.10	.05
ke Green	.10	.05
rk Oswald	.10	.05
uz Pedregon	.60	.25
uz Pedregon	.60	.25
uz Pedregon's Car	.20	.09
Schultz	.10	.05
nny West	.10	.05
l Worsham	.10	.05
uck Worsham	.10	.05
ce Allen	.10	.05
ce Allen's Car	.05	.02
eg Anderson	.10	.05
urt Johnson		

❑ 75 Don Beverley	.10	.05
❑ 76 Gary Brown	.10	.05
❑ 77 Kenny Delco	.10	.05
❑ 78 Jerry Eckman	.10	.05
❑ 79 Jerry Eckman	.10	.05
❑ 80 Jerry Eckman's Car	.05	.02
❑ 81 Alban Gauthier's Car	.05	.02
❑ 82 Scott Geoffrion	.10	.05
❑ 83 Scott Geoffrion	.10	.05
❑ 84 Scott Geoffrion's Car	.05	.02
❑ 85 Bob Glidden	.20	.09
❑ 86 Bob Glidden's Car	.10	.05
❑ 87 Etta Glidden W/Crew	.20	.09
❑ 88 Jerry Haas	.10	.05
❑ 89 Dave Hutchens	.10	.05
Mike Sullivan		
❑ 90 Frank Iaconio	.10	.05
❑ 91 Bill Jenkins	.10	.05
❑ 92 Warren Johnson	.20	.09
❑ 93 Warren Johnson	.20	.09
❑ 94 Warren Johnson's Car	.10	.05
❑ 95 Joe Lepone Jr.	.10	.05
❑ 96 Larry Morgan	.10	.05
❑ 97 Larry Morgan's Car	.05	.02
❑ 98 Bill Orndorff	.10	.05
❑ 99 Mark Pawuk	.10	.05
❑ 100 Paul Rebeschi Jr.	.10	.05
❑ 101 David Reher	.10	.05
Buddy Morrison		
❑ 102 Gordie Rivera	.10	.05
❑ 103 Tom Roberts	.10	.05
❑ 104 Harry Scribner	.10	.05
❑ 105 Rickie Smith	.10	.05
❑ 106 Jim Yates	.10	.05
❑ 107 James Bernard w/Bike	.05	.02
❑ 108 Bryon Hines	.10	.05
❑ 109 Steve Johnson w/Bike	.05	.02
❑ 110 John Mafaro	.10	.05
❑ 111 John Myers	.10	.05
❑ 112 David Schultz	.10	.05
❑ 113 John Smith w/Bike	.05	.02
❑ 114 Blaine Johnson	.10	.05
❑ 115 Bob Newberry	.10	.05
❑ 116 Steve Johns	.10	.05
❑ 117 Greg Stanfield	.10	.05
❑ 118 Chad Guilford	.10	.05
❑ 119 Edmond Richardson	.10	.05
❑ 120 Jeg Coughlin Jr.	.10	.05
❑ 121 Pat Austin's Car	.05	.02
❑ 122 Bill Barney	.10	.05
❑ 123 Anthony Bartone's Car	.05	.02
❑ 124 David Nickens	.10	.05
❑ 125 Buster Couch	.10	.05
❑ 126 Steve Evans	.10	.05
❑ 127 Bob Frey	.10	.05
❑ 128 Dave McClelland	.10	.05
❑ 129 Larry Minor	.10	.05
❑ 130 Wally Parks	.10	.05
❑ 131 Shirley Muldowney	.60	.25
❑ 132 Del Worsham's Car	.05	.02
❑ 133 Larry Meyer	.10	.05

1993 Finish Line NHRA Autographs

Finish Line produced this nine-card set with each card individually signed by the featured driver. The cards were randomly inserted in 1993 Finish Line foil and jumbo packs.

	MINT	NRMT
COMPLETE SET (9)	180.00	80.00
COMMON AUTO (1-9)	16.00	7.25
❑ 1 Joe Amato	20.00	9.00
❑ 2 Cory McClenathan	20.00	9.00
❑ 3 Kenny Bernstein	30.00	13.50
❑ 4 Cruz Pedregon	20.00	9.00
❑ 5 John Force	50.00	22.00
❑ 6 Al Hofmann	16.00	7.25
❑ 7 Warren Johnson	20.00	9.00
❑ 8 Scott Geoffrion	16.00	7.25
❑ 9 Jerry Eckman	16.00	7.25

1993 Finish Line NHRA Speedways

NHRA race tracks are the focus of this 17-card insert set produced by Finish Line. The cards were randomly packed in 1993 Finish Line NHRA foil and jumbo packs.

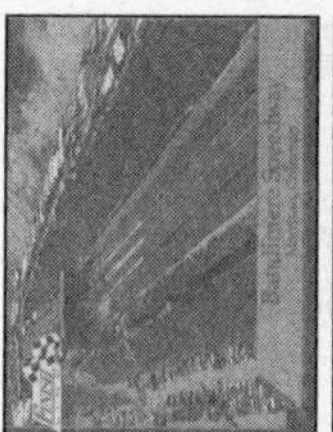

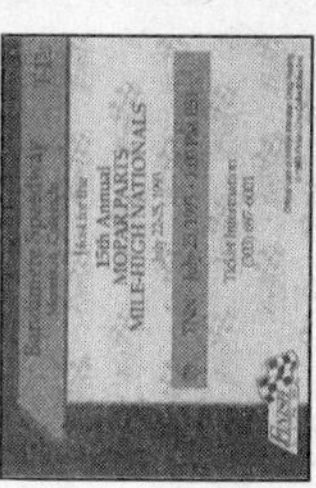

	MINT	NRMT
COMPLETE SET (17)	3.00	1.35
COMMON CARD (T1-T17)	.20	.09
❑ T1 Pomona Raceway	.20	.09
❑ T2 Firebird International	.20	.09
❑ T3 Houston Raceway Park	.20	.09
❑ T4 Gainesville Raceway	.20	.09
❑ T5 Rockingham Dragway	.20	.09
❑ T6 Atlanta Dragway	.20	.09
❑ T7 Memphis International	.20	.09
❑ T8 Old Bridge Township	.20	.09
❑ T9 National Trail Raceway	.20	.09
❑ T10 Saniar Int'l Dragway	.20	.09
❑ T11 Bandimere Speedway	.20	.09
❑ T12 Sears Point Int'l	.20	.09
❑ T13 Seattle International	.20	.09
❑ T14 Brainerd Int'l Raceway	.20	.09
❑ T15 Indianapolis Raceway	.20	.09
❑ T16 Maple Grove Raceway	.20	.09
❑ T17 Texas Motorplex	.20	.09

1970 Fleer Dragstrips

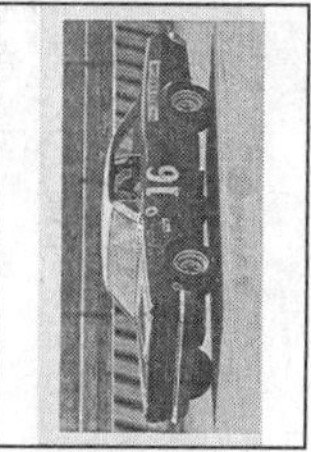

Fleer produced this 10-card set primarily as backers for their Dragstrips stickers. With each 5-cent wax pack, collector's received one of these cards and a group of automotive stickers. The cards are oversized (approximately 2-1/2" by 4-1/2") and blankbacked as are the sticker sheets. The black and white cards feature uncaptioned photos of top racers with an emphasis on Andy Granatelli and the STP IndyCar race team. We've assigned card numbers according to alphabetical order.

	NRMT	VG-E
COMPLETE SET (10)	250.00	110.00
COMMON CARD	25.00	11.00
STICKER INSERTS	10.00	4.50
❑ 1 Darel Dierenger's Car	25.00	11.00
❑ 2 Don Garlits' Car	100.00	45.00
❑ 3 Andy Granatelli	35.00	16.00
❑ 4 Dan Gurney's Car	35.00	16.00
❑ 5 Graham Hill's Car	35.00	16.00
❑ 6 Parnelli Jones' Car	50.00	22.00
Andy Granatelli		
❑ 7 Joe Leonard's Car	25.00	11.00
❑ 8 Joe Leonard's Car	25.00	11.00
Andy Granatelli		
❑ 9 Ken Miles' Car	25.00	11.00
Lloyd Ruby's Car		
MK II Ford		
❑ 10 Art Pollard's Car	25.00	11.00

1971 Fleer AHRA Drag Champs

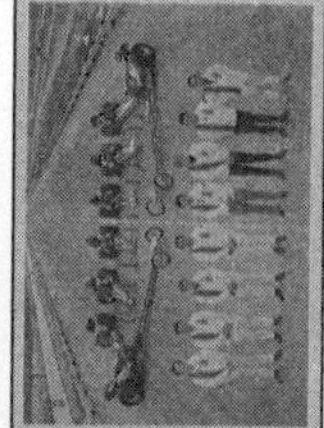

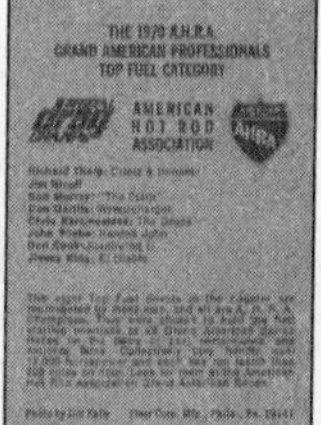

This is the first of three consecutive sets Fleer released featuring stars of AHRA drag racing. Wax packs contained five-cards and one stick of gum. There were three different wrappers produced, each featuring a different drag racer. Although virtually all of the 63-cards feature racing cars in action, three cards were devoted to the top champions in each drag racing category. An American and Canadian version was produced with the American cards printed on white card stock and are unnumbered. The Canadian set was numbered (listed below in that order) and printed on a cream colored paper stock.

	NRMT	VG-E
COMPLETE SET (63)	300.00	135.00
COMMON CARD (1-63)	5.00	2.20
AMERICAN/CANADIAN SAME VALUE		
❑ 1 Arlen Vanke's Car	5.00	2.20
❑ 2 John Wiebe's Car	6.00	2.70
❑ 3 Terry Hedrick's Car	5.00	2.20
❑ 4 Steve Carbone's Car	5.00	2.20
❑ 5 Leroy Goldstein's Car	5.00	2.20
❑ 6 Pat Foster's Car	5.00	2.20
❑ 7 Don Schumacher's Car	5.00	2.20
❑ 8 Don Gay's Car Roy Gay's Car	6.00	2.70
❑ 9 Dick Harrell's Car	5.00	2.20
❑ 10 Bill Jenkins' Car	5.00	2.20
❑ 11 Kenny Safford's Car	5.00	2.20
❑ 12 John Elliot's Car	5.00	2.20
❑ 13 Pat Minick's Car	5.00	2.20
❑ 14 Arnie Behling's Car	5.00	2.20
❑ 15 Gene Snow's Car	6.00	2.70
❑ 16 Jay Howell's Car	5.00	2.20
❑ 17 Norm Tanner's Car	5.00	2.20
❑ 18 Don Garlits' Car	6.00	2.70
❑ 19 Ray Alley's Car	5.00	2.20
❑ 20 K.S. Pittman's Car	5.00	2.20
❑ 21 Ed Miller's Car	5.00	2.20
❑ 22 Funny Car Champs Jay Howell Tom McEwen Danny Ongais Leroy Goldstein Gene Snow Mart Higgenbotham	6.00	2.70
❑ 23 Chris Karamesines' Car	6.00	2.70
❑ 24 Super Stock Champs Dick Harrell Ed Miller Don Nicholson Bill Hielscher Dave Lyall Herb McCandless	6.00	2.70
❑ 25 Jim Nicoll's Car	6.00	2.70
❑ 26 Dick Landy's Car	5.00	2.20
❑ 27 Shirley Shahan's Car	5.00	2.20
❑ 28 John McFadde's Car	5.00	2.20
❑ 29 Leonard Hughes' Car	5.00	2.20
❑ 30 Eddie Schartman's Car	5.00	2.20
❑ 31 Ed Terry's Car	5.00	2.20
❑ 32 Hubert Platt's Car	5.00	2.20
❑ 33 Gary Kimball's Car	5.00	2.20
❑ 34 Gary Watson's Car	5.00	2.20
❑ 35 Rich Siroonian's Car	5.00	2.20
❑ 36 Richard Tharp's Car	5.00	2.20
❑ 37 Jake Johnston's Car	5.00	2.20
❑ 38 Ronnie Sox's Car	6.00	2.70
❑ 39 Charles Therwanger's Car	5.00	2.20
❑ 40 Don Grotheer's Car	5.00	2.20
❑ 41 Pete Robinson's Car	5.00	2.20
❑ 42 Ron O'Donnell's Car	5.00	2.20
❑ 43 Dick Loehr's Car	5.00	2.20
❑ 44 Tom Hoover's Car	6.00	2.70
❑ 45 Dale Young's Car	5.00	2.20
❑ 46 Warren Gunter's Car	5.00	2.20
❑ 47 Bruce Larson's Car	5.00	2.20
❑ 48 Paula Murphy's Car	5.00	2.20
❑ 49 Bob Murray's Car	5.00	2.20
❑ 50 Jim Liberman's Car	5.00	2.20
❑ 51 Sam Auxier Jr.'s Car	5.00	2.20
❑ 52 Duane Ong's Car	5.00	2.20
❑ 53 Preston Davis' Car	5.00	2.20
❑ 54 Top Fuel Champs Richard Tharp Jim Nicoll Bob Murray Don Garlits Chris Karamesines John Wiebe Don Cook Jimmy King	6.00	2.70
❑ 55 Jimmy King's Car	5.00	2.20
❑ 56 Ron Martin's Car	5.00	2.20
❑ 57 Jerry Mallicoat's Car Tom Chamblis' Car	5.00	2.20
❑ 58 Jerry Miller's Car	5.00	2.20
❑ 59 Tommy Ivo's Car	5.00	2.20
❑ 60 Bill Hielscher's Car	5.00	2.20
❑ 61 Tony Nancy's Car	5.00	2.20
❑ 62 Fritz Callier's Car	5.00	2.20
❑ 63 Don Nicholson's Car	5.00	2.20

1971 Fleer Stick Shift

Similar to the 1970 Dragstrips release, Fleer Stick Shift cards were issued primarily as backers for Stick Shift race stickers. With each 10-cent wax pack, collector's received one of these cards and a group of race stickers. The cards are oversized (approximately 2-1/2" by 4-1/2") and blankbacked as are the sticker sheets. The black and white cards feature captioned photos of cars and racers. Although only eight cards can be confirmed, the set is thought to consist of ten cards. Any additions to this list are appreciated.

	NRMT	VG-E
COMPLETE SET (8)	700.00	325.00
COMMON CARD	80.00	36.00
STICKER INSERTS	10.00	4.50
❑ 1 Kelly Brown's Dragster The Unsinkable Kelly Brown	80.00	36.00
❑ 2 Dragster at Lion's Drag Strip	80.00	36.00
❑ 3 Plymouth Superbird	80.00	36.00
❑ 4 Plymouth GTX	80.00	36.00
❑ 5 Dan Ongais Drving the Winningest Funny Car ever	110.00	50.00
❑ 6 Don Burns A real crowd pleaser The VW Bug	80.00	36.00
❑ 7 Don Prudhomme	150.00	70.00
❑ 8 Chris Karamesines	125.00	55.00

1972 Fleer AHRA Drag Nationals

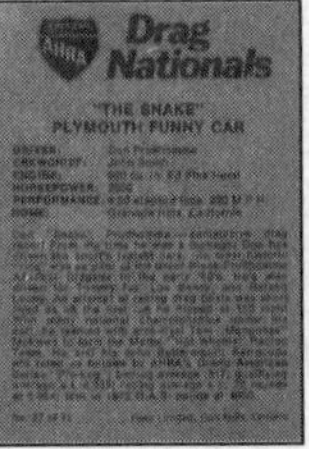

For the second consecutive year, Fleer released a set featuring stars of AHRA drag racing. Wax packs contained five-cards and one stick of gum and the set size was increased to 70-cards. There is some speculation that based on the odd set size, some cards may have been printed in shorter supply than others. Again, most of the cards feature drag racing cars in action, but a larger number (versus the 1971 set) were devoted to top drivers as well. An American and Canadian version was produced with the American cards printed on white card stock, while the Canadian set was printed on a cream colored paper stock.

	NRMT	VG-E
COMPLETE SET (70)	400.00	180.00
COMMON CARD (1-70)	6.00	2.70
AMERICAN/CANADIAN SAME VALUE		
❑ 1 Don Garlits' Car	10.00	4.50
❑ 2 Don Garlits	12.00	5.50
❑ 3 Don Garlits' Car	10.00	4.50
❑ 4 Phil Schofield's Car	6.00	2.70
❑ 5 Charlie Thurwanger's Car	6.00	2.70
❑ 6 Bill Leavitt's Car	6.00	2.70
❑ 7 Fritz Callier's Car	6.00	2.70
❑ 8 Richard Tharp's Car	8.00	3.60
❑ 9 John Wiebe's Car	6.00	2.70
❑ 10 Steve Carbone	6.00	2.70
❑ 11 Kenny Sanford's Car	6.00	2.70
❑ 12 Jim Hayter's Car	6.00	2.70
❑ 13 Herb McCandless' Car	6.00	2.70
❑ 14 Don Grotheer's Car	6.00	2.70
❑ 15 Mike Fons' Car	6.00	2.70
❑ 16 Ronnie Sox's Car	10.00	4.50
❑ 17 Joe Rundle's Car	6.00	2.70
❑ 18 Bill Jenkins' Car	6.00	2.70
❑ 19 Dick Landy's Car	6.00	2.70
❑ 20 Don Carlton's Car	6.00	2.70
❑ 21 Mart Higginbotham	6.00	2.70
❑ 22 Gene Snow	10.00	4.50
❑ 23 Butch Maas' Car	6.00	2.70
❑ 24 Dale Pulde's Car Mickey Thompson's Car	8.00	3.60
❑ 25 Gary Watson's Car	6.00	2.70
❑ 26 Tom McEwen	10.00	
❑ 27 Don Prudhomme	12.00	
❑ 28 Gary Cochran	6.00	
❑ 29 Tom Hoover	10.00	
❑ 30 Gene Snow's Car	8.00	
❑ 31 Steve Carbone's Car	6.00	
❑ 32 John Paxton's Car	6.00	
❑ 33 John Wiebe	6.00	
❑ 34 Dennis Baca's Car	6.00	
❑ 35 Tripp Shumake's Car	6.00	
❑ 36 Mart Higginbotham's Car	6.00	
❑ 37 Chris Karamesines	10.00	
❑ 38 Gary Cochran's Car	6.00	
❑ 39 Don Cook's Car	6.00	
❑ 40 Vic Brown's Car	6.00	
❑ 41 Chris Karamesines' Car	8.00	
❑ 42 Ronnie Sox Buddy Martin	10.00	
❑ 43 Tom Hoover's Car	8.00	
❑ 44 Gary Burgin's Car	6.00	
❑ 45 John Lombardo's Car	6.00	
❑ 46 Don Prudhomme's Car	10.00	
❑ 47 Tom McEwen's Car	8.00	
❑ 48 Leroy Goldstein's Car	6.00	
❑ 49 Russell Long's Car	6.00	
❑ 50 Don Moody's Car	6.00	
❑ 51 Don Schumacher's Car	6.00	
❑ 52 Doug Rose's Car	6.00	
❑ 53 Larry Christopherson's Car	6.00	
❑ 54 Tom Grove's Car	6.00	
❑ 55 Jim Dunn's Car	6.00	
❑ 56 Jim King's Car	6.00	
❑ 57 Butch Leal's Car	6.00	
❑ 58 Bill Jenkins' Car	6.00	
❑ 59 Don Moody's Car	6.00	
❑ 60 Clare Sanders' Car	6.00	
❑ 61 Jim Nicoll's Car	6.00	
❑ 62 Cecil Lankford's Car	6.00	
❑ 63 Jim Walther's Car	6.00	
❑ 64 Ralph Gould's Car	6.00	
❑ 65 Dale Pulde's Car Mickey Thompson's Car	8.00	
❑ 66 Dave Beebe's Car	6.00	
❑ 67 Joe Lee's Car	6.00	
❑ 68 Doug Rose's Car	6.00	
❑ 69 Dale Pulde's Car Mickey Thompson's Car	8.00	
❑ 70 Gary Watson's Car	6.00	

1973 Fleer AHRA Race US

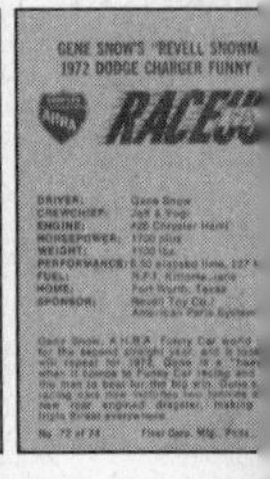

Race USA was Fleer's final AHRA release. Wax again contained five-cards and one stick of gum a different wrappers were produced. The set size ag increased to 74-cards. There is some speculati based on the odd set size, some cards may hav printed in shorter supply than others. Many of th feature drag racing cars in action, but several focus top drivers as well.

	NRMT
COMPLETE SET (74)	400.00
COMMON CARD (1-74)	6.00
❑ 1 Tom McEwen	8.00
❑ 2 Tom McEwen's Car	8.00
❑ 3 Tom McEwen's Car	8.00
❑ 4 Don Prudhomme's Car	8.00
❑ 5 Don Prudhomme's Car	8.00
❑ 6 Don Prudhomme's Car	8.00
❑ 7 Mike Randall's Car	6.00
❑ 8 Bill Leavitt's Car	6.00
❑ 9 Richard Tharp's Car	6.00
❑ 10 Bob Lambeck's Car	6.00
❑ 11 Butch Leal's Car	6.00
❑ 12 Dick Landy	6.00
❑ 13 Dick Landy's Car	6.00
❑ 14 Gary Kimball's Car Larry Kimballs' Car	6.00
❑ 15 Tom Hoover's Car	8.00
❑ 16 Tom Hoover w/Car	8.00
❑ 17 Don Nicholson's Car	6.00
❑ 18 Ken Holthe's Car	6.00

)on Grotheer's Car	6.00	2.70
:ddie Shartman's Car	6.00	2.70
Vayne Gapp's Car	6.00	2.70
(eyy Brown's Car	6.00	2.70
:ogo Eads' Car	6.00	2.70
ene Dunlap's Car	6.00	2.70
/lart Higginbotham's Car	6.00	2.70
iteve Carbone's Car	6.00	2.70
on Cook's Car	6.00	2.70
ary Cochran's Car	6.00	2.70
1ike Burkart's Car	6.00	2.70
om Akin's Car	6.00	2.70
on Garlits DOY	8.00	3.60
arry Christopherson w/car	6.00	2.70
arry Christopherson's Car	6.00	2.70
onnie Sox's Car	8.00	3.60
onnie Sox	8.00	3.60
Buddy Martin		
on Schumacher's Car	6.00	2.70
oe Satmary's Car	6.00	2.70
oe Satmary's Car	6.00	2.70
cott Shafiroff's Car	6.00	2.70
at Foster's Car	6.00	2.70
hris Karamesines' Car	8.00	3.60
ave Russell's Car	6.00	2.70
wig Zigler	6.00	2.70
onnie Martin's Car	8.00	3.60
lickey Thompson w/Car	6.00	2.70
ale Pulde's Car	6.00	2.70
enry Harrison's Car	6.00	2.70
d McCulloch's Car	8.00	3.60
d McCulloch's Car	8.00	3.60
ohn Wiebe	8.00	3.60
ary Watson's Car	6.00	2.70
rlen Vanke's Car	6.00	2.70
uane Jacobsen's Car	6.00	2.70
onnie Runyon's Car	6.00	2.70
erry Baker's Car	6.00	2.70
arrie Poole's Car	6.00	2.70
obby Yowell's Car	6.00	2.70
on Garlits' Car	8.00	3.60
on Garlits' Car	8.00	3.60
on Garlits' Car	8.00	3.60
eg Coughlin's Car	6.00	2.70
like Sullivan's Car	6.00	2.70
on Petrie's Car	6.00	2.70
ob Riffle's Car	6.00	2.70
ave Hough's Car	6.00	2.70
he Mob Dragster	6.00	2.70
he Mob Dragster	6.00	2.70
eb Allen's Car	6.00	2.70
m Nicoll's Car	8.00	3.60
d Sigmon's Car	6.00	2.70
ene Snow	8.00	3.60
ene Snow's Car	8.00	3.60
ake Johnston's Car	6.00	2.70
hip Woodall's Car	6.00	2.70

1989 Mega Drag

romotions Inc. of Florida released this set in mid- aturing the top names in drag racing. The cards ld in factory set form directly from Mega at the price of $19.95 plus $3 shipping. A series two set nned but never materialized.

	MINT	NRMT
ETE SET (110)	225.00	100.00
ON CARD (1-110)	2.25	1.00
ON DRIVER (1-110)	2.50	1.10
rell Gwynn	3.00	1.35
rell Gwynn's Car	2.50	1.10
ie Hill	4.00	1.80
ie Hill's Car	4.00	1.80
ie Hill's Car	4.00	1.80
Amato	4.00	1.80
Amato's Car	2.50	1.10
e Dunn	2.50	1.10
e Dunn's Car	2.25	1.00
orris Johnson Jr.	2.50	1.10
orris Johnson Jr.'s Car	2.25	1.00
McCulloch	2.50	1.10
❑ 13 Ed McCulloch's Car	2.25	1.00
❑ 14 Mike Troxel	2.50	1.10
❑ 15 Mike Troxel's Car	2.25	1.00
❑ 16 Dale Pulde	3.00	1.35
❑ 17 Jerry Haas	2.50	1.10
❑ 18 Jerry Haas' Car	2.25	1.00
❑ 19 Bruce Allen	2.50	1.10
❑ 20 Bruce Allen's Car	2.25	1.00
❑ 21 Shirley Muldowney	4.00	1.80
❑ 22 Shirley Muldowney's Car	4.00	1.80
❑ 23 Bill Kuhlman	2.50	1.10
❑ 24 Bill Kuhlman's Car	2.25	1.00
❑ 25 Rickie Smith	2.50	1.10
❑ 26 Rickie Smith's Car	2.25	1.00
❑ 27 Jim Feurer's Car	2.25	1.00
❑ 28 Denny Lucas	2.50	1.10
❑ 29 Denny Lucas' Car	2.25	1.00
❑ 30 Bruce Larson	2.50	1.10
❑ 31 Bruce Larson's Car	2.25	1.00
❑ 32 Tony Christian	2.50	1.10
❑ 33 Tony Christian's Car	2.25	1.00
❑ 34 John Martin	2.50	1.10
❑ 35 John Martin's Car	2.25	1.00
❑ 36 Frank Bradley	2.50	1.10
❑ 37 Frank Bradley's Car	2.25	1.00
❑ 38 Gary Ormsby	2.50	1.10
❑ 39 Gary Ormsby's Car	2.25	1.00
❑ 40 Kenny Koretsky	2.50	1.10
❑ 41 Kenny Koretsky's Car	2.25	1.00
❑ 42 Scott Geoffrion	2.50	1.10
❑ 43 Scott Geoffrion's Car	2.25	1.00
❑ 44 Earl Whiting	2.50	1.10
❑ 45 Earl Whiting's Car	2.25	1.00
❑ 46 Jerry Caminito	2.50	1.10
❑ 47 Jerry Caminito's Car	2.25	1.00
❑ 48 Darrell Alderman	3.00	1.35
❑ 49 Darrell Alderman's Car	2.50	1.10
❑ 50 Roland Leong	2.50	1.10
❑ 51 Roland Leong's Car	2.25	1.00
❑ 52 Gordie Rivera	2.50	1.10
❑ 53 Gordie Rivera's Car	2.25	1.00
❑ 54 R.C. Sherman's Car	2.25	1.00
❑ 55 Frank Manzo	2.50	1.10
❑ 56 Frank Manzo's Car	2.25	1.00
❑ 57 Frank Iaconio	2.50	1.10
❑ 58 Frank Iaconio's Car	2.25	1.00
❑ 59 Don Campanello	2.50	1.10
❑ 60 Don Campanello's Car	2.25	1.00
❑ 61 Bob Newberry's Car	2.25	1.00
❑ 62 Nick Nikolis	2.50	1.10
❑ 63 Nick Nikolis' Car	2.25	1.00
❑ 64 John Speelman's Car	2.25	1.00
❑ 65 Chuck Etchells	3.00	1.35
❑ 66 Chuck Etchells' Car	2.50	1.10
❑ 67 Paul Smith	2.50	1.10
❑ 68 Paul Smith's Car	2.25	1.00
❑ 69 Mark Pawuk	2.50	1.10
❑ 70 Mark Pawuk's Car	2.25	1.00
❑ 71 Arnie Karp	2.50	1.10
❑ 72 Arnie Karp's Car	2.25	1.00
❑ 73 Frank Sanchez	2.50	1.10
❑ 74 Frank Sanchez's Car	2.25	1.00
❑ 75 Lori Johns	3.00	1.35
❑ 76 Lori Johns' Car	2.50	1.10
❑ 77 Bubba Sewell's Car	2.25	1.00
❑ 78 Della Woods	2.50	1.10
❑ 79 Della Woods' Car	2.25	1.00
❑ 80 Brian Raymer's Car	2.25	1.00
❑ 81 Tim Grose	2.50	1.10
❑ 82 Tim Grose's Car	2.25	1.00
❑ 83 Tom Conway's Car	2.25	1.00
❑ 84 Darrell Amberson	2.50	1.10
❑ 85 Darrell Amberson's Car	2.25	1.00
❑ 86 Jim Head	2.50	1.10
❑ 87 Jim Head's Car	2.25	1.00
❑ 88 Doc Halladay	2.50	1.10
❑ 89 Doc Halladay's Car	2.25	1.00
❑ 90 Dal Denton's Car	2.25	1.00
❑ 91 Dick LaHaie	2.50	1.10
❑ 92 Dick LaHaie's Car	2.25	1.00
❑ 93 Don Coonce	2.50	1.10
❑ 94 Don Coonce's Car	2.25	1.00
❑ 95 Jerry Eckman	2.50	1.10
❑ 96 Jerry Eckman's Car	2.25	1.00
❑ 97 Harold Lewelling's Car	2.25	1.00
❑ 98 Domenic Santucci Sr.'s Car	2.25	1.00
❑ 99 Al Hanna's Car	2.25	1.00
❑ 100 Gene Snow	3.00	1.35
❑ 101 Gene Snow's Car	2.50	1.10
❑ 102 Joe Lepone Jr.	2.50	1.10
❑ 103 Joe Lepone Jr.'s Car	2.25	1.00
❑ 104 Hank Enders	2.50	1.10
❑ 105 Hank Enders' Car	2.25	1.00
❑ 106 Lee Dean's Car	2.25	1.00
❑ 107 Dennis Piranio's Car	2.25	1.00
❑ 108 Don Garlits	4.00	1.80
❑ 109 Don Garlits' Car	4.00	1.80
❑ 110 Checklist	2.25	1.00

1991 Pro Set NHRA

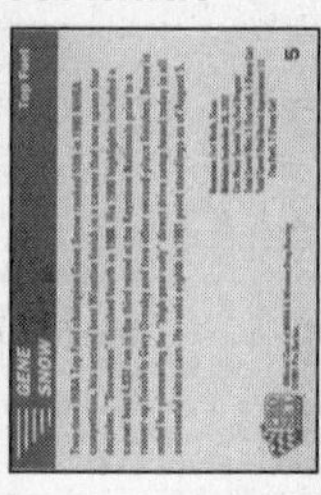

This was Pro Set's first NHRA release in a run of sets produced by the company from 1991-1993. The set features star drivers, cars and crew members of the top NHRA teams. The cards were packaged 10 per foil pack with 36 packs per box. Signed cards of Don Garlits, number 105, that were UV coated and autographed in silver ink were also randomly inserted.

	MINT	NRMT
COMPLETE SET (130)	12.00	5.50
COMMON CARD (1-130)	.10	.05
COMMON DRIVER (1-130)	.15	.07
❑ 1 Joe Amato	1.00	.45
❑ 2 Gary Ormsby	.15	.07
❑ 3 Dick LaHaie	.15	.07
❑ 4 Lori Johns	.25	.11
❑ 5 Gene Snow	.25	.11
❑ 6 Eddie Hill	1.00	.45
❑ 7 Frank Bradley	.15	.07
❑ 8 Kenny Bernstein	1.00	.45
❑ 9 Frank Hawley	.15	.07
❑ 10 Shirley Muldowney	1.00	.45
❑ 11 Chris Karamesines	.25	.11
❑ 12 Jim Head	.15	.07
❑ 13 Don Prudhomme	.25	.11
❑ 14 Tommy Johnson Jr.	.25	.11
❑ 15 Michael Brotherton	.15	.07
❑ 16 Darrell Gwynn	.25	.11
❑ 17 John Force	1.50	.70
❑ 18 Ed McCulloch	.15	.07
❑ 19 Bruce Larson	.15	.07
❑ 20 Mark Oswald	.15	.07
❑ 21 Jim White	.15	.07
❑ 22 K.C. Spurlock	.15	.07
❑ 23 Tom Hoover	.25	.11
❑ 24 Richard Hartman	.15	.07
❑ 25 Scott Kalitta	1.00	.45
❑ 26 Jerry Caminito	.15	.07
❑ 27 Al Hofmann	.15	.07
❑ 28 Glenn Mikres	.15	.07
❑ 29 Chuck Etchells	.15	.07
❑ 30 John Myers	.15	.07
❑ 31 Paula Martin	.15	.07
❑ 32 Mike Dunn	.15	.07
❑ 33 Connie Kalitta	.25	.11
❑ 34 Darrell Alderman	.15	.07
❑ 35 Bob Glidden	.25	.11
❑ 36 Jerry Eckman	.15	.07
❑ 37 Larry Morgan	.15	.07
❑ 38 Warren Johnson	.25	.11
❑ 39 Rickie Smith	.15	.07
❑ 40 Mark Pawuk	.15	.07
❑ 41 Bruce Allen	.15	.07
❑ 42 Joe Lepone Jr.	.15	.07
❑ 43 Kenny Delco	.15	.07
❑ 44 Scott Geoffrion	.15	.07
❑ 45 Gordie Rivera	.15	.07
❑ 46 Jerry Haas	.15	.07
❑ 47 Buddy Ingersoll	.15	.07
❑ 48 Jim Yates	.15	.07
❑ 49 Butch Leal	.15	.07
❑ 50 Joe Amato's Car	.15	.07
❑ 51 Gary Ormsby's Car	.10	.05
❑ 52 Dick LaHaie's Car	.10	.05
❑ 53 Lori Johns' Car	.10	.05
❑ 54 Gene Snow's Car	.15	.07
❑ 55 Eddie Hill's Car	.25	.11
❑ 56 Frank Bradley's Car	.10	.05
❑ 57 Kenny Bernstein's Car	.25	.11
❑ 58 Frank Hawley's Car	.10	.05
❑ 59 Shirley Muldowney's Car	.25	.11
❑ 60 Chris Karamesines' Car	.15	.07
❑ 61 Jim Head's Car	.10	.05
❑ 62 Don Prudhomme's Car	.15	.07
❑ 63 Tommy Johnson Jr.'s Car	.15	.07
❑ 64 Michael Brotherton's Car	.10	.05
❑ 65 Darrell Gwynn's Car	.15	.07
❑ 66 John Force's Car	1.00	.45
❑ 67 Ed McCulloch's Car	.10	.05
❑ 68 Bruce Larson's Car	.10	.05

❑ 69 Mark Oswald's Car .10 .05
❑ 70 Jim White's Car .10 .05
❑ 71 K.C. Spurlock's Car .10 .05
❑ 72 Tom Hoover's Car .15 .07
❑ 73 Richard Hartman's Car .10 .05
❑ 74 Scott Kalitta's Car .10 .05
❑ 75 Jerry Caminito's Car .10 .05
❑ 76 Al Hofmann's Car .10 .05
❑ 77 Glenn Mikres' Car .10 .05
❑ 78 Chuck Etchells' Car .10 .05
❑ 79 Whit Bazemore's Car .10 .05
❑ 80 Paula Martin's Car .10 .05
❑ 81 David Schultz .10 .05
❑ 82 Darrell Alderman's Car .10 .05
❑ 83 Bob Glidden's Car .15 .07
❑ 84 Jerry Eckman's Car .10 .05
❑ 85 Larry Morgan's Car .10 .05
❑ 86 Warren Johnson's Car .25 .11
❑ 87 Rickie Smith's Car .10 .05
❑ 88 Mark Pawuk's Car .10 .05
❑ 89 Bruce Allen's Car .10 .05
❑ 90 Joe Lepone Jr.'s Car .10 .05
❑ 91 Kenny Delco's Car .10 .05
❑ 92 Scott Geoffrion's Car .10 .05
❑ 93 Gordie Rivera's Car .10 .05
❑ 94 Jerry Haas' Car .10 .05
❑ 95 Buddy Ingersoll's Car .10 .05
❑ 96 Jim Yates' Car .10 .05
❑ 97 Butch Leal's Car .10 .05
❑ 98 Buster Couch .15 .07
❑ 99 Fuzzy Carter .15 .07
❑ 100 Austin Coil .15 .07
❑ 101 Tim Richards .15 .07
❑ 102 Bob Glidden Family .15 .07
❑ 103 Kenny Bernstein Funny Car .25 .11
❑ 104 Don Prudhomme Funny Car .25 .11
❑ 105 Don Garlits 1.00 .45
❑ 106 Dale Armstrong .15 .07
❑ 107 Tom McEwen .25 .11
❑ 108 Dave McClelland .15 .07
❑ 109 Steve Evans .15 .07
❑ 110 Bob Frey .15 .07
❑ 111 Deb Brittsan Miss Winston .15 .07
❑ 112 Safety Safari .10 .05
❑ 113 Gary Densham .15 .07
❑ 114 Frank Iaconio .15 .07
❑ 115 Don Beverly .15 .07
❑ 116 Lee Beard .15 .07
❑ 117 Wyatt Radke .15 .07
❑ 118 John Medlen .15 .07
❑ 119 Gary Brown .15 .07
❑ 120 Bernie Fedderly .15 .07
❑ 121 Rahn Tobler .15 .07
❑ 122 Del Worsham .15 .07
❑ 123 Kim LaHaie .15 .07
❑ 124 Larry Meyer .15 .07
❑ 125 Freddie Neely .15 .07
❑ 126 Dan Pastorini .25 .11
❑ 127 Bill Jenkins .15 .07
❑ 128 Wally Parks .15 .07
❑ 129 Connie Kalitta's Car .15 .07
❑ 130 Whit Bazemore .15 .07
❑ AU105 Don Garlits AUTO 60.00 27.00

1992 Pro Set NHRA

This was Pro Set's second NHRA release. The set features star drivers, cars and crew members of the top NHRA teams of the previous season. The cards were packaged 12 per foil pack with 36 packs per box. 1,500 factory sets were also produced for distribution to Pro Set Racing Club members. A special hologram card featuring a Pro Set Racing logo (numbered of 5000) was produced and randomly distributed through packs. The card originally had a white border, but was later changed to black creating a variation.

	MINT	NRMT
COMPLETE SET (200)	12.00	5.50
COMPLETE FACT. SET (200)	14.00	6.25
COMMON CARD (1-200)	.05	.02
COMMON DRIVER (1-200)	.10	.05

❑ 1 Joe Amato .20 .09
❑ 2 Kenny Bernstein .60 .25
❑ 3 Don Prudhomme .60 .25
❑ 4 Frank Hawley .05 .02
❑ 5 Eddie Hill .60 .25
❑ 6 Tom McEwen .20 .09
❑ 7 Gene Snow .20 .09
❑ 8 Dick LaHaie .10 .05
❑ 9 Cory McClenathan .20 .09
❑ 10 Jim Head .10 .05
❑ 11 Tommy Johnson Jr. .20 .09
❑ 12 Pat Austin .20 .09
❑ 13 Scott Kalitta .60 .25
❑ 14 Cruz Pedregon .60 .25
❑ 15 Doug Herbert .20 .09
❑ 16 Gary Ormsby .20 .09
❑ 17 Paula Martin 's Car .05 .02
❑ 18 Frank Bradley .10 .05
❑ 19 Jack Ostrander .10 .05
❑ 20 Jim Dunn .10 .05
❑ 21 Connie Kalitta .60 .25
❑ 22 Pat Dakin .10 .05
❑ 23 Jim Murphy's Car .05 .02
❑ 24 Bobby Baldwin .10 .05
❑ 25 Kenny Koretsky .05 .02
❑ 26 Russ Collins .05 .02
❑ 27 Shirley Muldowney .60 .25
❑ 28 Kim LaHaie .05 .02
❑ 29 Gene Snow .60 .25
❑ 30 Eddie Hill .60 .25
❑ 31 Don Prudhomme .60 .25
❑ 32 Kenny Bernstein .60 .25
❑ 33 Joe Amato .60 .25
❑ 34 Del Worsham .10 .05
❑ 35 John Force 1.00 .45
❑ 36 Tom Gilbertson .05 .02
❑ 37 Gary Ritter .05 .02
❑ 38 Johnny West .05 .02
❑ 39 Mark Sievers .05 .02
❑ 40 Jim Epler .10 .05
❑ 41 Ron Sutherland .05 .02
❑ 42 Wyatt Radke .10 .05
❑ 43 Freddie Neely .10 .05
❑ 44 Gordon Mineo .10 .05
❑ 45 Paula Martin .10 .05
❑ 46 Glenn Mikres .05 .02
❑ 47 John Force 1.00 .45
❑ 48 Jim White .10 .05
❑ 49 Ed McCulloch .20 .09
❑ 50 Mark Oswald .10 .05
❑ 51 Al Hofmann .20 .09
❑ 52 Tom Hoover .20 .09
❑ 53 Richard Hartman .10 .05
❑ 54 Jerry Caminito .10 .05
❑ 55 Chuck Etchells .20 .09
❑ 56 Gary Densham .10 .05
❑ 57 Whit Bazemore .05 .02
❑ 58 Gary Bolger .10 .05
❑ 59 Jim Murphy .05 .02
❑ 60 Al Hofmann .20 .09
❑ 61 Del Worsham .10 .05
❑ 62 Mark Oswald .10 .05
❑ 63 Ed McCulloch .20 .09
❑ 64 Mike Dunn .10 .05
❑ 65 Warren Johnson .20 .09
❑ 66 Larry Morgan .10 .05
❑ 67 Scott Geoffrion .10 .05
❑ 68 Bob Glidden .60 .25
❑ 69 Jerry Eckman .10 .05
❑ 70 Bruce Allen .10 .05
❑ 71 Jim Yates .20 .09
❑ 72 Rickie Smith .10 .05
❑ 73 Butch Leal .10 .05
❑ 74 Joe Lepone Jr. .10 .05
❑ 75 Gary Brown .05 .02
❑ 76 Harry Scribner .05 .02
❑ 77 Paul Rebeschi Jr. .05 .02
❑ 78 Joseph Folgore .05 .02
❑ 79 Steve Schmidt .10 .05
❑ 80 Brad Klein .05 .02
❑ 81 Gordie Rivera .10 .05
❑ 82 Don Beverly .05 .02
❑ 83 Jerry Haas .05 .02
❑ 84 Frank Iaconio .10 .05
❑ 85 Vincent Khoury .05 .02
❑ 86 Kenny Delco .05 .02
❑ 87 Ray Franks .10 .05
❑ 88 Daryl Thompson .05 .02
❑ 89 Mark Pawuk .10 .05
❑ 90 Jerry Eckman .10 .05
❑ 91 Bob Glidden .60 .25
❑ 92 Scott Geoffrion .10 .05
❑ 93 Larry Morgan .10 .05
❑ 94 Warren Johnson .20 .09
❑ 95 Buddy Ingersoll .05 .02
❑ 96 Steve Johnson W/Bike .10 .05
❑ 97 Paul Gast's Bike .05 .02
❑ 98 James Bernard's Bike .05 .02
❑ 99 John Myers' Bike .20
❑ 100 David Schultz's Bike .20
❑ 101 Joe Amato's Car .20
❑ 102 Kenny Bernstein's Car .20
❑ 103 Don Prudhomme's Car .20
❑ 104 Michael Brotherton's Car .05
❑ 105 Eddie Hill's Car .20
❑ 106 Tom McEwen's Car .05
❑ 107 Gene Snow's Car .05
❑ 108 Kim LaHaie's Car .05
❑ 109 Cory McClenathan's Car .05
❑ 110 Jim Head's Car .05
❑ 111 Tommy Johnson Jr.'s Car .05
❑ 112 Pat Austin's Car .05
❑ 113 Scott Kalitta's Car .20
❑ 114 Ed McCulloch's Car .05
❑ 115 Doug Herbert's Car .05
❑ 116 Frank Bradley's Car .05
❑ 117 John Force's Car 1.00
❑ 118 Cruz Pedregon's Car .20
❑ 119 Mark Oswald's Car .05
❑ 120 Del Worsham's Car .05
❑ 121 Al Hofmann's Car .05
❑ 122 Tom Hoover's Car .05
❑ 123 Richard Hartman's Car .05
❑ 124 Jerry Caminito's Car .05
❑ 125 Chuck Etchells' Car .05
❑ 126 Gary Densham's Car .05
❑ 127 Whit Bazemore's Car .05
❑ 128 Gary Bolger's Car .05
❑ 129 Gordon Mineo's Car .05
❑ 130 Freddie Neely's Car .05
❑ 131 Jerry Haas' Car .05
❑ 132 Joe Lepone Jr.'s Car .05
❑ 133 Gordie Rivera's Car .05
❑ 134 Gary Brown's Car .05
❑ 135 Harry Scribner's Car .05
❑ 136 Warren Johnson's Car .05
❑ 137 Larry Morgan's Car .05
❑ 138 Scott Geoffrion's Car .05
❑ 139 Rickie Smith's Car .05
❑ 140 Bob Glidden's Car .20
❑ 141 Frank Iaconio's Car .05
❑ 142 Jerry Eckman's Car .05
❑ 143 Jim Yates' Car .05
❑ 144 Bruce Allen's Car .05
❑ 145 Mark Pawuk's Car .05
❑ 146 Kenny Delco's Car .05
❑ 147 Kurt Johnson .05
❑ 148 Mike Sullivan .05
Dave Hutchens
❑ 149 Tom Anderson .05
❑ 150 Bernie Fedderly .05
❑ 151 John Davis .05
❑ 152 Fuzzy Carter .05
❑ 153 Dale Armstrong .05
❑ 154 Tim Richards .05
❑ 155 Ken Veney .05
❑ 156 Jim Prock .05
❑ 157 Austin Coil .05
❑ 158 Chuck Worsham .05
❑ 159 Richard Hartman .05
Ray Strasser
❑ 160 Tom Roberts .05
❑ 161 George Hoover .05
❑ 162 Bill Schultz .05
❑ 163 Larry Meyer .05
❑ 164 John Medlen .05
❑ 165 Walt Austin .05
❑ 166 Greg Anderson .05
❑ 167 Rusty Glidden .05
Etta Glidden
❑ 168 Bill Orndorff .05
❑ 169 Dave Butner .05
❑ 170 Buddy Morrison .05
David Reher
❑ 171 Rich Purdy .05
❑ 172 Morris Johnson Jr. .05
❑ 173 Lee Beard .05
❑ 174 Rahn Tobler .05
❑ 175 Dannielle DePorter .05
❑ 176 Chris Karamesines .05
❑ 177 Michael Brotherton .05
❑ 178 Bill Jenkins .05
❑ 179 Darrell Gwynn .20
❑ 180 Larry Minor .05
❑ 181 Buster Couch .05
❑ 182 Don Garlits .60
❑ 183 Dave McClelland .05
❑ 184 Steve Evans .05
❑ 185 Bob Frey .05
❑ 186 Brock Yates .05
❑ 187 Wally Parks .05
❑ 188 John Mullin .05
❑ 189 NHRA Softball Team .05
❑ 190 Safety Safari .05
❑ 191 Deb Brittsan Miss Winston .05
❑ 192 Gary Evans .05

Jim Brissette	.05	.02
Blaine Johnson's Car	.05	.02
Pat Austin's Car	.05	.02
David Nickens' Car	.05	.02
Jeff Taylor's Car	.05	.02
John Calvert's Car	.05	.02
John Asta's Car	.05	.02
Scott Richardson's Car	.05	.02
Trophy HOLO White	200.00	90.00
Trophy HOLO Black	200.00	90.00

92 Pro Set Kenny Bernstein

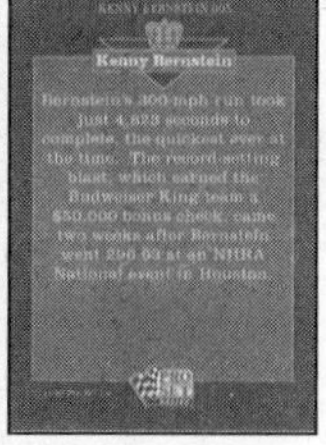

t produced this set to highlight the careers of Bernstein and his crew. The cards were primarily ted through Bernstein's souvenir outlets

	MINT	NRMT
ETE SET (7)	4.00	1.80
ON CARD (1-6)	.60	.25
nny Bernstein	1.00	.45
ny Bernstein w/Crew	.60	.25
e Armstrong	.60	.25
s Cerny	.60	.25
nny Bernstein	1.00	.45
nny Bernstein's Car	.60	.25
Cover Card	.30	.14

1965 Topps Hot Rods

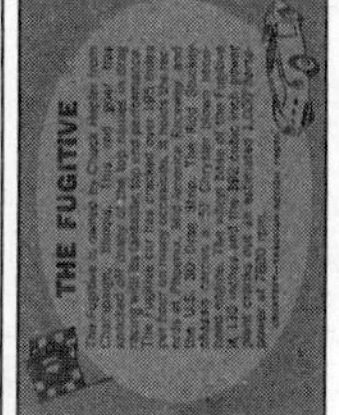

roduced this 66-card set for distribution in 5-cent x packs. The cards feature a wide range of cars ot rods and racers to custom and dream cars. ifferent cardback variations exist. All 66-cards oduced on gray card stock, while only 44 different xist with white backs. The 22-card yellow back s seem to be the toughest to find. They reportedly o included in a board game distributed in the late hat also included cards from Topps' 1967 football 1968 baseball card sets.

	NRMT	VG-E
ETE SET (66)	325.00	200.00
ACKS (1-66)	5.00	3.00
er Marauder	5.00	3.00
Breed T.V. Car	5.00	3.00
enet 29	5.00	3.00
Deuce	5.00	3.00
us 11	5.00	3.00
iolet	5.00	3.00
ster	5.00	3.00
Tangerine	5.00	3.00
Po Po	5.00	3.00
Beauty	5.00	3.00
ister ~T~	5.00	3.00
AK 400	5.00	3.00
SC 210	5.00	3.00
Capitola	5.00	3.00
of Riley T.V. Car	5.00	3.00
Pumkin	5.00	3.00
stang	5.00	3.00
ura	5.00	3.00
C Dream Truck	5.00	3.00
Thunderbird	5.00	3.00
ed Flame	5.00	3.00
Woody	5.00	3.00
Woody	5.00	3.00
❑ 24 Turbo-Sonic	5.00	3.00
❑ 25 Drag ~T~	5.00	3.00
❑ 26 Flaky ~T~	5.00	3.00
❑ 27 Black Beauty	5.00	3.00
❑ 28 Ruby ~T~	5.00	3.00
❑ 29 Bimimi Wagon	5.00	3.00
❑ 30 Cyclops	5.00	3.00
❑ 31 Emperor	5.00	3.00
❑ 32 Cosma Ray	5.00	3.00
❑ 33 Lemans Cadillac	5.00	3.00
❑ 34 Beatnik Bandit	5.00	3.00
❑ 35 Rotar	5.00	3.00
❑ 36 Silhouette	5.00	3.00
❑ 37 Roanoke Valley Special	5.00	3.00
❑ 38 Beach Baron	5.00	3.00
❑ 39 Show Boat	5.00	3.00
❑ 40 The Mysterion	5.00	3.00
❑ 41 Chuck Hepler's Car The Fugitive	5.00	3.00
❑ 42 Willy Mack's Car The Snapper	5.00	3.00
❑ 43 Rose Gennuso's Car Flaming Special	5.00	3.00
❑ 44 Weekly Norman's Car The Lightning Rod	6.00	3.60
❑ 45 Kamakai One	5.00	3.00
❑ 46 Little Old Bucket	5.00	3.00
❑ 47 Golden Rod	5.00	3.00
❑ 48 John Albright's Car Bo Weevil	6.00	3.60
❑ 49 Devil Cart	5.00	3.00
❑ 50 Funnel Master	5.00	3.00
❑ 51 Jim Nelson's Car Dode Martin's Car Modified Dart	6.00	3.60
❑ 52 Gary Cagle's Car Newhouse Special	6.00	3.60
❑ 53 The Riviera	5.00	3.00
❑ 54 The Undertaker	5.00	3.00
❑ 55 The Rushin' Roulette	5.00	3.00
❑ 56 T-Bird	5.00	3.00
❑ 57 Eddie Hill's Car Texas Terror	8.00	4.80
❑ 58 Li'l Coffin	5.00	3.00
❑ 59 The Honey	5.00	3.00
❑ 60 Dode Martin's Car The Drag Master	6.00	3.60
❑ 61 The Blazer	5.00	3.00
❑ 62 The Streamline	5.00	3.00
❑ 63 The Strip Star	5.00	3.00
❑ 64 Angelo Giampetroni's Car Li'l Billy	5.00	3.00
❑ 65 The Wild Dream	5.00	3.00
❑ 66 The Road Blazer	5.00	3.00

1983 A&S Racing Indy

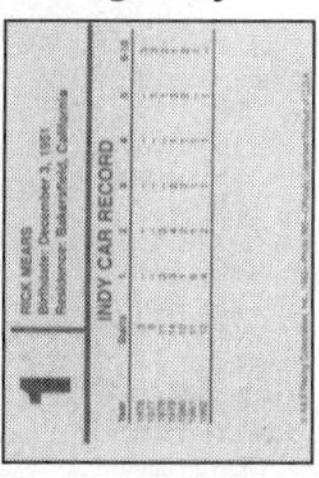

A&S Racing Collectables produced IndyCar sets from 1983-87. The 1983 set featured 51-cards sold in complete set form and includes the first card of driver Al Unser Jr. There was no card number 13 produced -- the checklist card was unnumbered and blankbacked.

	MINT	NRMT
COMPLETE SET (51)	30.00	13.50
COMMON CARD (1-51)	.40	.18
❑ 1 Rick Mears	2.00	.90
❑ 2 Dennis Firestone	.40	.18
❑ 3 Chip Mead	.40	.18
❑ 4 Chris Kneifel	.40	.18
❑ 5 Chip Ganassi	.40	.18
❑ 6 Howdy Holmes	.40	.18
❑ 7 Steve Krisloff UER	.40	.18
❑ 8 Pancho Carter	.40	.18
❑ 9 Chet Fillip	.40	.18
❑ 10 Phil Caliva	.40	.18
❑ 11 Geoff Brabham	.40	.18
❑ 12 Jerry Sneva	.40	.18
❑ 14 Herm Johnson	.40	.18
❑ 15 Spike Gehlhausen	.40	.18
❑ 16 Steve Chassey	.40	.18
❑ 17 Pete Halsmer	.40	.18
❑ 18 Kevin Cogan	.40	.18
❑ 19 Teo Fabi	.40	.18
❑ 20 Greg Leffler	.40	.18
❑ 21 Johnny Rutherford	2.00	.90
❑ 22 Tony Bettenhausen	.40	.18
❑ 23 Tom Frantz	.40	.18
❑ 24 George Snider	.40	.18
❑ 25 Michael Chandler	.40	.18
❑ 26 Danny Sullivan	.75	.35
❑ 27 Doug Heveron	.40	.18
❑ 28 Roger Mears	.40	.18
❑ 29 Josele Garza	.40	.18
❑ 30 Mike Mosley	.40	.18
❑ 31 Scott Brayton	.75	.35
❑ 32 Jerry Karl	.40	.18
❑ 33 Mario Andretti	3.00	1.35
❑ 34 Bobby Rahal	.75	.35
❑ 35 Gordon Smiley	.40	.18
❑ 36 Derek Daly	.40	.18
❑ 37 Phil Krueger	.40	.18
❑ 38 John Mahler	.40	.18
❑ 39 Bill Alsup	.40	.18
❑ 40 John Paul Jr.	.40	.18
❑ 41 Jim Buick	.40	.18
❑ 42 Jim Hickman	.40	.18
❑ 43 Al Unser Jr.	2.00	.90
❑ 44 Hector Rebaque	.40	.18
❑ 45 Bill Tempero	.40	.18
❑ 46 Dick Ferguson	.40	.18
❑ 47 Tom Sneva	.75	.35
❑ 48 Al Unser	2.00	.90
❑ 49 Gordon Johncock	.75	.35
❑ 50 Dick Simon	.40	.18
❑ 51 Gary Bettenhausen	.40	.18
❑ NNO Checklist	.40	.18

1984 A&S Racing Indy

The 1984 A&S Racing Indy set features 50 of the top drivers on the IndyCar circuit, along with one checklist card (#13). An offer to purchase 1983 complete sets for $8.50 was included on the checklist card. The cards are very similar in appearance to the other A&S Indy sets produced from 1983-87.

	MINT	NRMT
COMPLETE SET (51)	30.00	13.50
COMMON CARD (1-51)	.40	.18
❑ 1 Al Unser	1.50	.70
❑ 2 Phil Krueger	.40	.18
❑ 3 Howdy Holmes	.40	.18
❑ 4 Roger Mears	.40	.18
❑ 5 Johnny Rutherford	1.50	.70
❑ 6 Michael Chandler	.40	.18
❑ 7 Pancho Carter	.40	.18
❑ 8 Dick Ferguson	.40	.18
❑ 9 Phil Caliva	.40	.18
❑ 10 Rick Mears	1.50	.70
❑ 11 Pete Halsmer	.40	.18
❑ 12 Derek Daly	.40	.18
❑ 13 Checklist	.40	.18
❑ 14 Steve Chassey	.40	.18
❑ 15 Josele Garza	.40	.18
❑ 16 Mario Andretti	2.00	.90
❑ 17 Chris Kneifel	.40	.18
❑ 18 Al Loquasto	.40	.18
❑ 19 Dennis Firestone	.40	.18
❑ 20 Teo Fabi	.40	.18
❑ 21 George Snider	.40	.18
❑ 22 Patrick Bedard	.40	.18
❑ 23 Gary Bettenhausen	.40	.18
❑ 24 Dick Simon	.40	.18
❑ 25 Tom Sneva	.75	.35
❑ 26 Herm Johnson	.40	.18
❑ 27 Scott Brayton	.75	.35
❑ 28 Bill Tempero	.40	.18
❑ 29 Danny Ongais	.40	.18
❑ 30 John Paul Jr.	.40	.18
❑ 31 Tom Bagley	.40	.18
❑ 32 Gordon Johncock	.75	.35
❑ 33 Desire Wilson	.40	.18
❑ 34 Greg Leffler	.40	.18

❑ 35 Chip Ganassi	.40	.18
❑ 36 Michael Andretti	1.50	.70
❑ 37 Doug Heveron	.40	.18
❑ 38 Steve Krisloff	.40	.18
❑ 39 Geoff Brabham	.40	.18
❑ 40 Bill Alsup	.40	.18
❑ 41 Kevin Cogan	.40	.18
❑ 42 Chuck Ciprich	.40	.18
❑ 43 Mike Mosley	.40	.18
❑ 44 Chip Mead	.40	.18
❑ 45 Tony Bettenhausen	.40	.18
❑ 46 Jerry Karl	.40	.18
❑ 47 Al Unser Jr.	1.50	.70
❑ 48 Chet Fillip	.40	.18
❑ 49 Bill Vukovich Jr.	.40	.18
❑ 50 Bobby Rahal	1.50	.70
❑ 51 Tom Bigelow	.40	.18

1985 A&S Racing Indy

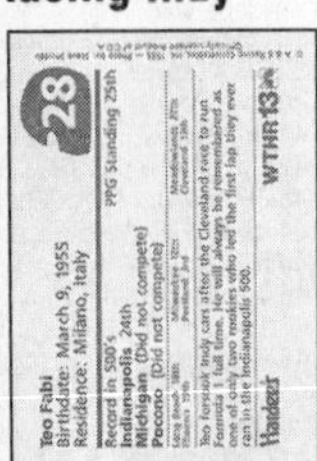

The top IndyCar drivers are featured on cards from the 1985 A&S Racing Indy set. The set was originally released in complete set form only. A checklist card, number 13, was produced along with an unnumbered card featuring announcer Don Hein. The checklist card features an offer to purchase 1983-1985 complete sets directly from A&S. An autographed uncut card sheet was offered to collectors as well at a cost of $110. The Jacques Villeneuve card in this set is the uncle of the 1995 PPG series winner.

	MINT	NRMT
COMPLETE SET (52)	30.00	13.50
COMMON CARD (1-51)	.40	.18

❑ 1 Mario Andretti	2.00	.90
❑ 2 Roberto Guerrero	.60	.25
❑ 3 Derek Daly	.40	.18
❑ 4 John Paul Jr.	.40	.18
❑ 5 Chet Fillip	.40	.18
❑ 6 Al Holbert	.40	.18
❑ 7 Stan Fox	.40	.18
❑ 8 Steve Chassey	.40	.18
❑ 9 Chip Ganassi	.40	.18
❑ 10 Mike Mosley	.40	.18
❑ 11 Michael Chandler	.40	.18
❑ 12 Bobby Rahal	1.25	.55
❑ 13 Checklist	.40	.18
❑ 14 Johnny Parsons Jr.	.40	.18
❑ 15 Howdy Holmes	.40	.18
❑ 16 Geoff Brabham	.40	.18
❑ 17 Pete Halsmer	.40	.18
❑ 18 Dick Ferguson	.40	.18
❑ 19 Gary Bettenhausen	.40	.18
❑ 20 Gordon Johncock	.60	.25
❑ 21 Roger Mears	.40	.18
❑ 22 Ed Pimm	.40	.18
❑ 23 Emerson Fittipaldi	.60	.25
❑ 24 Al Unser Jr.	1.25	.55
❑ 25 Rick Mears	1.25	.55
❑ 26 Bill Alsup	.40	.18
❑ 27 Spike Gehlhausen	.40	.18
❑ 28 Teo Fabi	.40	.18
❑ 29 Herm Johnson	.40	.18
❑ 30 Tom Sneva	.60	.25
❑ 31 Dick Simon	.40	.18
❑ 32 Tom Gloy	.40	.18
❑ 33 Dale Coyne	.40	.18
❑ 34 Patrick Bedard	.40	.18
❑ 35 Al Unser	1.25	.55
❑ 36 Jerry Karl	.40	.18
❑ 37 Chris Kneifel	.40	.18
❑ 38 George Snider	.40	.18
❑ 39 Tony Bettenhausen	.40	.18
❑ 40 Johnny Rutherford	1.25	.55
❑ 41 Scott Brayton	.60	.25
❑ 42 Michael Andretti	1.25	.55
❑ 43 Randy Lewis	.40	.18
❑ 44 Phil Krueger	.40	.18
❑ 45 Pancho Carter	.40	.18
❑ 46 Dennis Firestone	.40	.18
❑ 47 Kevin Cogan	.40	.18
❑ 48 Jacques Villeneuve	.40	.18
❑ 49 Arie Luyendyk	.60	.25
❑ 50 Mario Andretti Michael Andretti	1.25	.55
❑ 51 Al Unser Al Unser Jr.	1.25	.55
❑ NNO Don Hein	.40	.18

1986 A&S Racing Indy

A&S Racing released this 50-card set in complete set form. The cards feature the top IndyCar personalities and very closely resemble the other Indy sets released by the company between 1983-87. The last card in the set features a checklist and an offer to purchase 1983-1986 complete sets directly from A&S. An autographed uncut card sheet was again offered to collectors as well at a cost of $110.

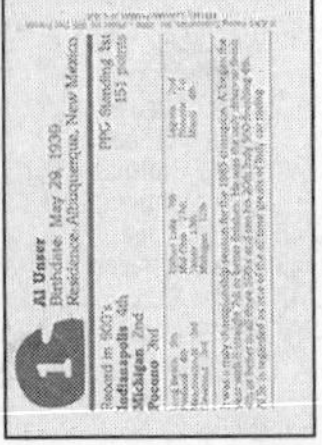

	MINT	NRMT
COMPLETE SET (50)	30.00	13.50
COMMON CARD (1-50)	.40	.18

❑ 1 Al Unser	1.25	.55
❑ 2 Mario Andretti	2.00	.90
❑ 3 Spike Gehlhausen	.40	.18
❑ 4 Josele Garza	.40	.18
❑ 5 Emerson Fittipaldi	.60	.25
❑ 6 Ed Pimm	.40	.18
❑ 7 Dale Coyne	.40	.18
❑ 8 Roberto Guerrero	.40	.18
❑ 9 Pancho Carter	.40	.18
❑ 10 Al Unser Jr.	1.25	.55
❑ 11 Pete Halsmer	.40	.18
❑ 12 George Snider	.40	.18
❑ 13 Gasoline Alley	.40	.18
❑ 14 Michael Roe	.40	.18
❑ 15 Dick Simon	.40	.18
❑ 16 Johnny Rutherford	1.25	.55
❑ 17 Steve Chassey	.40	.18
❑ 18 Geoff Brabham	.40	.18
❑ 19 Tom Bigelow	.40	.18
❑ 20 Herm Johnson	.40	.18
❑ 21 Arie Luyendyk	.60	.25
❑ 22 Chet Fillip	.40	.18
❑ 23 John Paul Jr.	.40	.18
❑ 24 Chip Ganassi	.40	.18
❑ 25 Scott Brayton	.60	.25
❑ 26 Phil Krueger	.40	.18
❑ 27 Kevin Cogan	.40	.18
❑ 28 Johnny Parsons Jr.	.40	.18
❑ 29 Dennis Firestone	.40	.18
❑ 30 Bobby Rahal	1.25	.55
❑ 31 Jim Crawford	.40	.18
❑ 32 Tom Sneva	.60	.25
❑ 33 Derek Daly	.40	.18
❑ 34 Dick Ferguson	.40	.18
❑ 35 Gordon Johncock	.60	.25
❑ 36 Scott Brayton Pancho Carter	.60	.25
❑ 37 Arie Luyendyk ROY	.60	.25
❑ 38 Danny Sullivan T10	.40	.18
❑ 39 Emerson Fittipaldi T10	.40	.18
❑ 40 Rick Mears T10	.60	.25
❑ 41 Jacques Villeneuve	.40	.18
❑ 42 Rupert Keegan	.40	.18
❑ 43 Michael Andretti	1.25	.55
❑ 44 Howdy Holmes	.40	.18
❑ 45 Rick Mears	1.25	.55
❑ 46 Tony Bettenhausen	.40	.18
❑ 47 Gary Bettenhausen	.40	.18
❑ 48 Raul Boesel	.40	.18
❑ 49 Danny Sullivan	.60	.25
❑ 50 Checklist	.40	.18

1987 A&S Racing Indy

A&S Racing released this 50-card set in complete set form. The cards feature the top IndyCar personalities and very closely resemble the other Indy sets released by the company between 1983-87. Card number 13 features a checklist along with an offer to purchase 1983-1987 complete sets directly from A&S. Fifty uncut card sheets

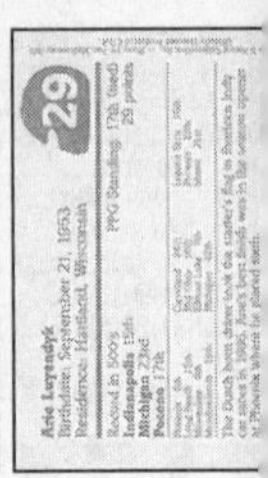

signed by all drivers were again offered to collecto cost of $110.

	MINT
COMPLETE SET (50)	25.00
COMMON CARD (1-50)	.40

❑ 1 Bobby Rahal	1.00
❑ 2 Mario Andretti Tom Carnegie	1.00
❑ 3 Steve Chassey	.40
❑ 4 Tom Sneva	.60
❑ 5 Geoff Brabham	.40
❑ 6 Emerson Fittipaldi	.60
❑ 7 Dale Coyne	.40
❑ 8 Gary Bettenhausen	.40
❑ 9 Al Unser	1.00
❑ 10 Rick Mears' Record	.60
❑ 11 Roberto Moreno	.40
❑ 12 Scott Brayton	.60
❑ 13 Checklist	.40
❑ 14 A.J. Foyt	1.00
❑ 15 Phil Krueger	.40
❑ 16 Jan Lammers	.40
❑ 17 Ed Pimm	.40
❑ 18 Michael Andretti w/Car	1.00
❑ 19 George Snider	.40
❑ 20 Mario Andretti w/Car	1.50
❑ 21 Spike Gehlhausen	.40
❑ 22 Johnny Rutherford	1.00
❑ 23 Mike Nish	.40
❑ 24 Kevin Cogan	.40
❑ 25 Josele Garza	.40
❑ 26 Tony Bettenhausen	.40
❑ 27 Rick Miaskiewicz	.40
❑ 28 Pancho Carter	.40
❑ 29 Arie Luyendyk	.60
❑ 30 Al Unser Jr.	1.00
❑ 31 Dennis Firestone	.40
❑ 32 Raul Boesel	.40
❑ 33 Dominic Dobson	.40
❑ 34 Danny Sullivan	.60
❑ 35 Derek Daly	.40
❑ 36 Ian Ashley	.40
❑ 37 Randy Lewis	.40
❑ 38 Jim Crawford	.40
❑ 39 Rick Mears	1.00
❑ 40 Johnny Parsons Jr.	.40
❑ 41 Dick Simon	.40
❑ 42 Jacques Villeneuve	.40
❑ 43 Roberto Guerrero	.60
❑ 44 Desire Wilson	.40
❑ 45 Danny Sullivan Rick Mears Michael Andretti	.60
❑ 46 Dominic Dobson ROY	.40
❑ 47 Bobby Rahal Winner	.60
❑ 48 Mario Andretti Winner	1.00
❑ 49 Johnny Rutherford Winner	.60
❑ 50 Tony Bettenhausen Gary Bettenhausen	.40

1986 Ace Formula One

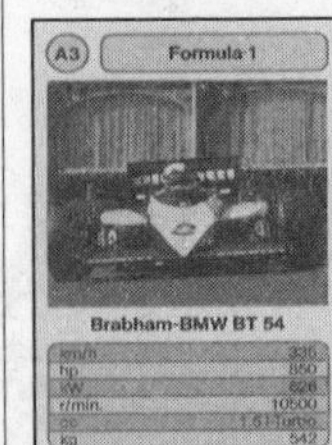

This set was made in West Germany for the company Ace. The cards actually resemble a playing cards with Formula One driver photo cardfront with a red playing card type back. The unnumbered and listed below alphabetically. A of the set was also produced entitled Top Ass. s no price difference between the two versions.

	MINT	NRMT
.ETE SET (33)	6.00	2.70
ON CARD	.20	.09
lfa Romeo 185T	.20	.09
rrows BMW A8	.20	.09
rabham BMW BT54	.20	.09
errari 156/85	.20	.09
igier Renault JS25	.20	.09
'cLaren TAG/Porsche	.20	.09
sella Alfa Romeo FA1F	.20	.09
enault RE60	.20	.09
otus Renault 97T	.20	.09
inardi Motori Moderni M185	.20	.09
AM Hart 03	.20	.09
pirit Hart 101B	.20	.09
oleman Hart	.20	.09
yrrell Cosworth 012	.20	.09
Villiams Honda FW10	.20	.09
akspeed 841	.20	.09
lfa Romeo 184T	.20	.09
rrows BMW A7	.20	.09
TS BMW D7	.20	.09
rabham BMW BT53	.20	.09
rrari 126C4	.20	.09
gier Renault JS23	.20	.09
AM Hart 02	.20	.09
'illiams Honda FW09B	.20	.09
otus Renault 95T	.20	.09
lcLaren TAG/Porsche	.20	.09
enault RE50	.20	.09
oleman Hart TG184	.20	.09
rabham BMW BT52B	.20	.09
otus Renault 94T	.20	.09
enault RE40	.20	.09
errari 126C3	.20	.09
Cover Card	.20	.09

1986 Ace Indy

et was made in West Germany for the British ny Ace. The cards are actually part of a Trump card eaturing IndyCar photos on the cardfront with a card back and rounded corners. The playing card ontains 32-cards with one cover/rule card. Drivers t specifically indentified on the cards, but are d below as noted.

	MINT	NRMT
.ETE SET (33)	8.00	3.60
ON CARD	.20	.09
mway Special	.60	.25
Scott Brayton		
ennzoil Special	.60	.25
Rick Mears		
'aco Special	1.00	.45
Michael Andretti		
'lmore Special	.75	.35
A.J.Foyt		
ving Well Special	.60	.25
Arie Luyendyk		
tersport March	.40	.18
Jim Ward		
udweiser Lola	.60	.25
Bobby Rahal		
yd's Valpack March	.40	.18
Rich Vogler		
cheid Tyre Special Buick	.40	.18
Derek Daly		
'P Special	.20	.09
eedol Special	.40	.18
Mike Mosley		
unoco Special	.40	.18
Gary Bettenhausen		
islone Special	.20	.09
'P Eagle Special	.40	.18
Wally Dallenbach Sr.		
cLaren Special	.40	.18
Gordon Johncock		
'ynn's Special Offy	.40	.18

	MINT	NRMT
Sam Sessions		
❑ E1 Lightning Special	.20	.09
❑ E2 Thermo King Special	.20	.09
❑ E3 A.J.Foyt Gilmore Special	.75	.35
A.J.Foyt's Car		
❑ E4 Eagle Chevrolet	.20	.09
❑ F1 True Value Special	.20	.09
❑ F2 Valvoline Special	.20	.09
❑ F3 Advan Special	.20	.09
❑ F4 Valvoline Spirit Honda	.20	.09
❑ G1 Lacatop Special	.20	.09
❑ G2 Vermont March Special	.20	.09
❑ G3 Gilmore Karco Special	1.00	.45
Michael Andretti		
❑ G4 Marlboro BRM Special	.20	.09
❑ H1 Nova Indy 47	.20	.09
❑ H2 Indy Midget	.20	.09
Mel Kenyon		
❑ H3 Indy Midget	.20	.09
❑ H4 Clubmann Indy Stocker	.20	.09
❑ NNO Cover Card	.20	.09
Game rules on back		

1987 Ace Formula One

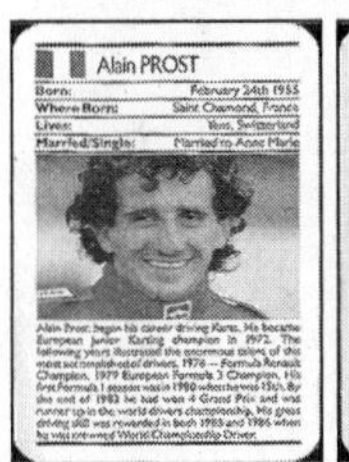

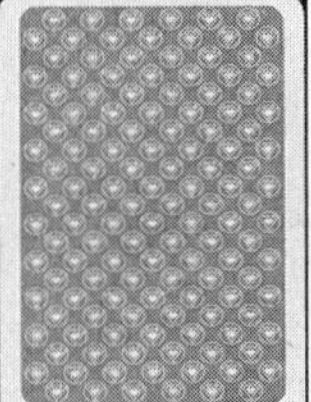

This set was made in West Germany for the British company Ace. The cards actually resemble a deck of playing cards with Formula One driver photos on the cardfront with a blue playing card type back. The set contains 32 individual driver cards with one cover card picturing Alain Prost. The cards are unnumbered and listed below alphabetically.

	MINT	NRMT
COMPLETE SET (33)	8.00	3.60
COMMON CARD	.20	.09
❑ 1 Michele Alboreto	.20	.09
❑ 2 Philippe Alliot	.20	.09
❑ 3 Rene Arnoux	.20	.09
❑ 4 Allen Berg	.20	.09
❑ 5 Gerhard Berger	.40	.18
❑ 6 Thierry Boutsen	.20	.09
❑ 7 Martin Brundle	.20	.09
❑ 8 Alex Caffi	.20	.09
❑ 9 Ivan Capelli	.20	.09
❑ 10 Eddie Cheever	.20	.09
❑ 11 Christian Danner	.20	.09
❑ 12 Andrea deCesaris	.20	.09
❑ 13 Johnny Dumfries	.20	.09
❑ 14 Teo Fabi	.20	.09
❑ 15 Piercarlo Ghinzani	.20	.09
❑ 16 Stefan Johansson	.20	.09
❑ 17 Alan Jones	.20	.09
❑ 18 Jacques Laffite	.20	.09
❑ 19 Nigel Mansell	.60	.25
❑ 20 Satoro Nakajma	.20	.09
❑ 21 Alessandro Nannini	.20	.09
❑ 22 Jonathan Palmer	.20	.09
❑ 23 Riccardo Patrese	.40	.18
❑ 24 Nelson Piquet	.40	.18
❑ 25 Alain Prost	.40	.18
❑ 26 Keke Rosberg	.40	.18
❑ 27 Huub Rothengatter	.20	.09
❑ 28 Ayrton Senna	1.00	.45
❑ 29 Philippe Streiff	.20	.09
❑ 30 Marc Surer	.20	.09
❑ 31 Patrick Tambay	.20	.09
❑ 32 Derek Warwick	.20	.09
❑ 33 Cover Card	.20	.09
Alain Prost		

1991 All World Indy

All World, in cooperation with A&S Racing, produced an IndyCar set in both 1991 and '92. The 1991 issue contained 100-cards featuring individual driver cards, race by race highlight cards of the previous season and All-Time Greats and Past Champion subset cards. Foil packs contained 9-cards and factory sets were produced. Signed cards from this set were randomly inserted in 1992 All World packs, although they have no distinguishing characteristics to differentiate them from regular issue

cards. An offer to purchase past A&S Racing sets was also included in packs.

	MINT	NRMT
COMPLETE SET (100)	4.00	1.80
COMP.FACT.SET (100)	5.00	2.20
COMMON CARD (1-100)	.05	.02
❑ 1 Al Unser Jr.	.20	.09
❑ 2 Bill Vukovich III	.05	.02
❑ 3 Tero Palmroth	.05	.02
❑ 4 John Andretti	.10	.05
❑ 5 Mario Andretti	.50	.23
❑ 6 Tony Bettenhausen	.05	.02
❑ 7 Tom Sneva	.10	.05
❑ 8 Willy T. Ribbs	.05	.02
❑ 9 Bobby Rahal	.10	.05
❑ 10 Danny Sullivan	.10	.05
❑ 11 Buddy Lazier	.05	.02
❑ 12 Stan Fox	.05	.02
❑ 13 Checklist 1 UER	.05	.02
❑ 14 Dean Hall	.05	.02
❑ 15 Arie Luyendyk	.10	.05
❑ 16 Eddie Cheever	.05	.02
❑ 17 Scott Goodyear	.05	.02
❑ 18 Jon Beekhuis	.05	.02
❑ 19 Jeff Wood	.05	.02
❑ 20 Emerson Fittipaldi	.10	.05
❑ 21 Pancho Carter W/Family	.05	.02
❑ 22 Mike Groff	.05	.02
❑ 23 Rocky Moran	.05	.02
❑ 24 Roberto Guerrero	.10	.05
❑ 25 Michael Andretti	.20	.09
❑ 26 Didier Theys	.05	.02
❑ 27 Geoff Brabham	.05	.02
❑ 28 Randy Lewis	.05	.02
❑ 29 Michael Greenfield	.05	.02
❑ 30 Rick Mears	.20	.09
❑ 31 Gary Bettenhausen	.05	.02
❑ 32 Raul Boesel	.05	.02
❑ 33 Michael Andretti	.20	.09
John Andretti		
❑ 34 Dominic Dobson	.05	.02
❑ 35 Al Unser	.20	.09
❑ 36 Kevin Cogan	.05	.02
❑ 37 Wally Dallenbach Jr.	.05	.02
❑ 38 Jim Crawford	.05	.02
❑ 39 Scott Brayton	.10	.05
❑ 40 Hiro Matsushita	.05	.02
❑ 41 Jeff Andretti	.05	.02
❑ 42 '90 Indy Standings	.05	.02
❑ 43 Emerson Fittipaldi Win	.10	.05
❑ 44 Arie Luyendyk Win	.10	.05
❑ 45 Al Unser Jr. WIN	.20	.09
❑ 46 Eddie Cheever ROY	.05	.02
❑ 47 Guido Dacco	.05	.02
❑ 48 Tony Bettenhausen	.05	.02
Gary Bettenhausen		
❑ 49 Steve Chassey	.05	.02
❑ 50 Derek Daly	.05	.02
❑ 51 Scott Pruett	.05	.02
❑ 52 Phil Krueger	.05	.02
❑ 53 Bernard Jourdain	.05	.02
❑ 54 Johnny Rutherford	.10	.05
❑ 55 Ludwig Heimrath Jr.	.05	.02
❑ 56 Scott Atchison	.05	.02
❑ 57 John Jones	.05	.02
❑ 58 Scott Harrington	.05	.02
❑ 59 Davy Jones	.05	.02
❑ 60 Steve Saleen	.05	.02
❑ 61 Gordon Johncock	.05	.02
❑ 62 Dale Coyne	.05	.02
❑ 63 Bill Vukovich III	.05	.02
❑ 64 Bernard Jourdain	.05	.02
Scott Pruett		
❑ 65 Emerson Fittipaldi WIN	.10	.05
❑ 66 Michael Andretti WIN	.20	.09
❑ 67 Danny Sullivan WIN	.10	.05
❑ 68 Jim Hurtubise	.05	.02
❑ 69 Sheldon Kinser	.05	.02
❑ 70 Al Holbert	.05	.02
❑ 71 Sam Hanks ATG	.05	.02
❑ 72 Duane Carter Sr. ATG	.05	.02
❑ 73 Tony Bettenhausen Sr. ATG	.05	.02

❑ 74 Rick Mears Winner	.20	.09
❑ 75 Al Unser Jr. Bobby Rahal	.20	.09
❑ 76 Checklist 2 UER	.05	.02
❑ 77 '90 Phoenix Race	.05	.02
❑ 78 '90 Long Beach Race	.05	.02
❑ 79 '90 Indy 500 Mile Race	.05	.02
❑ 80 '90 Wilwaukee Race	.05	.02
❑ 81 '90 Detroit Race	.05	.02
❑ 82 '90 Portland Race	.05	.02
❑ 83 '90 Cleveland Race	.05	.02
❑ 84 '90 Meadowlands Race	.05	.02
❑ 85 '90 Toronto Race	.05	.02
❑ 86 '90 Michigan 500 Race	.05	.02
❑ 87 '90 Denver Race	.05	.02
❑ 88 '90 Vancouver Race	.05	.02
❑ 89 '90 Mid Ohio Race	.05	.02
❑ 90 '90 Elkhart Lake Race	.05	.02
❑ 91 '90 Nazareth Race	.05	.02
❑ 92 '90 Laguna Seca Race	.05	.02
❑ 93 Johnny Rutherford PPGC	.10	.05
❑ 94 Rick Mears PPGC	.20	.09
❑ 95 Al Unser PPGC	.10	.05
❑ 96 Mario Andretti PPGC	.30	.14
❑ 97 Bobby Rahal PPGC	.10	.05
❑ 99 Emerson Fittipaldi PPGC	.10	.05
❑ 100 Al Unser Jr. PPGC	.20	.09

1992 All World Indy

All World, in cooperation with A&S Racing, produced an IndyCar set in both 1991 and '92. The 1992 issue again contained 100-cards featuring individual driver cards and Where are They Now, Careers, and All-Time Greats subset cards. Foil packs contained 9-cards and factory sets were produced as well. Autographed cards from the 1991 All World Indy set were randomly seeded throughout the run of 1992 packs. Reportedly, 100 cards were signed by 40 different drivers. The cards cannot otherwise be distinguished from regular issue 1991 cards and, therefore, generally do not carry a significant premium over other signed cards. An offer to purchase uncut sheets of the set for $19.95 was included on the wrapper.

	MINT	NRMT
COMPLETE SET (100)	4.00	1.80
COMP.FACT.SET (100)	5.00	2.20
COMMON CARD (1-100)	.05	.02

❑ 1 Michael Andretti	.25	.11
❑ 2 Mike Groff	.05	.02
❑ 3 Dean Hall	.05	.02
❑ 4 Gary Bettenhausen	.05	.02
❑ 5 Willy T. Ribbs	.05	.02
❑ 6 Scott Pruett	.05	.02
❑ 7 Scott Goodyear	.05	.02
❑ 8 Bobby Rahal	.25	.11
❑ 9 Eddie Cheever	.05	.02
❑ 10 Phil Krueger	.05	.02
❑ 11 Arie Luyendyk	.15	.07
❑ 12 Michael Greenfield	.05	.02
❑ 13 Checklist	.05	.02
❑ 14 Stan Fox	.05	.02
❑ 15 John Andretti	.15	.07
❑ 16 Guido Dacco	.05	.02
❑ 17 Kevin Cogan	.05	.02
❑ 18 Danny Sullivan	.15	.07
❑ 19 Mark Dismore	.05	.02
❑ 20 Emerson Fittipaldi	.15	.07
❑ 21 Al Unser Jr.	.25	.11
❑ 22 Didier Theys	.05	.02
❑ 23 Geoff Brabham	.05	.02
❑ 24 Buddy Lazier	.05	.02
❑ 25 Mario Andretti	.50	.23
❑ 26 Dale Coyne	.05	.02
❑ 27 Roberto Guerrero	.05	.02
❑ 28 Dominic Dobson	.05	.02
❑ 29 Johnny Parsons Jr.	.05	.02
❑ 30 Al Unser	.15	.07
❑ 31 Tony Bettenhausen	.05	.02
❑ 32 Scott Brayton	.15	.07
❑ 33 Gordon Johncock	.15	.07
❑ 34 Tero Palmroth	.05	.02
❑ 35 Dennis Vitolo	.05	.02
❑ 36 Bernard Jourdain	.05	.02
❑ 37 Hiro Matsushita	.05	.02
❑ 38 Ted Prappas	.05	.02
❑ 39 Jeff Wood	.05	.02
❑ 40 Jeff Andretti	.05	.02
❑ 41 Rick Mears	.25	.11
❑ 42 Pancho Carter	.05	.02
❑ 43 Jim Crawford	.05	.02
❑ 44 Randy Lewis	.05	.02
❑ 45 Buddy Lazier Bob Lazier	.05	.02
❑ 46 Michael Andretti	.25	.11
❑ 47 Jeff Andretti	.05	.02
❑ 48 John Andretti	.15	.07
❑ 49 Mario Andretti Michael Andretti John Andretti Jeff Andretti The Andretti Family	.40	.18
❑ 50 Mario Andretti Michael Andretti John Andretti The Andretti Trifecta	.40	.18
❑ 51 Norman Schwartzkopf Pancho Carter Johnny Rutherford Al Unser Sr.	.15	.07
❑ 52 Rich Vogler	.05	.02
❑ 53 Al Loquasto	.05	.02
❑ 54 Checklist	.05	.02
❑ 55 Rodger Ward ATG	.05	.02
❑ 56 Louis Meyer ATG	.05	.02
❑ 57 Wally Dallenbach Sr. ATG	.05	.02
❑ 58 Johnnie Parsons ATG	.05	.02
❑ 59 Troy Ruttman ATG	.05	.02
❑ 60 Parnelli Jones ATG	.05	.02
❑ 61 Eddie Sachs ATG	.05	.02
❑ 62 Johnny Boyd ATG	.05	.02
❑ 63 Lloyd Ruby ATG	.05	.02
❑ 64 Bill Vukovich Jr. ATG	.05	.02
❑ 65 George Snider	.05	.02
❑ 66 Gene Hartley	.05	.02
❑ 67 Howdy Holmes	.05	.02
❑ 68 Lee Kunzman	.05	.02
❑ 69 Larry Rice	.05	.02
❑ 70 Mario Andretti C	.40	.18
❑ 71 Arie Luyendyk C	.05	.02
❑ 72 Gordon Johncock C	.15	.07
❑ 73 Scott Goodyear C	.05	.02
❑ 74 Pancho Carter C	.05	.02
❑ 75 Jim Crawford C	.05	.02
❑ 76 John Andretti C	.15	.07
❑ 77 Johnny Rutherford C	.15	.07
❑ 78 Danny Sullivan C	.15	.07
❑ 79 Michael Andretti C	.25	.11
❑ 80 Emerson Fittipaldi C	.15	.07
❑ 81 Bobby Rahal C	.15	.07
❑ 82 Steve Chassey C	.05	.02
❑ 83 Checklist	.05	.02
❑ 84 Al Unser Jr.	.25	.11
❑ 85 Roberto Guerrero	.05	.02
❑ 86 Eddie Cheever	.05	.02
❑ 87 Tom Sneva	.05	.02
❑ 88 Scott Pruett	.05	.02
❑ 89 Phil Krueger	.05	.02
❑ 90 Rick Mears	.15	.07
❑ 91 Al Unser	.15	.07
❑ 92 Tony Bettenhausen	.05	.02
❑ 93 Dominic Dobson	.05	.02
❑ 94 Scott Brayton	.15	.07
❑ 95 Randy Lewis	.05	.02
❑ 96 Geoff Brabham	.05	.02
❑ 97 Mike Groff	.05	.02
❑ 98 Gary Bettenhausen	.05	.02
❑ 99 Didier Theys	.05	.02
❑ 100 Kevin Cogan	.05	.02

1911 American Tobacco Auto Drivers

This 25-card set was produced for The American Tobacco Company. Each card includes a small ad for either Hassan or Mecca Cigarettes on the cardback. All 25 cards were produced with both ad back variations. The cards measure 2 1/2 x 1 3/4 and came with square corners. The cards are unnumbered and feature top race car drivers of the day from both North America and Europe representing all types of auto racing events. They were packaged one card per 10 cigarette pack and two per 20 cigarette pack. The cards were inserted in cigarette packs starting on March 27th, 1911 and ending on March 31st, 1911. Special thanks to Jon Hardgrove for providing much of this information.

	NRMT	VG-E
COMPLETE SET (25)	800.00	475.00
COMMON CARD	25.00	

❑ 1 David Bruce-Brown	25.00
❑ 2 Bob Burman	25.00
❑ 3 Louis Chevrolet	50.00
❑ 4 Walter Christie	25.00
❑ 5 Demoget	25.00
❑ 6 Ralph dePalma	50.00
❑ 7 Bert Dingley	25.00
❑ 8 Arthur Duray	25.00
❑ 9 Henri Fournier	25.00
❑ 10 Harry E. Grant	25.00
❑ 11 Victor Hemery	25.00
❑ 12 Camille Jenatzy UER	25.00
❑ 13 Vincenzo Lancia	25.00
❑ 14 Herbert Lyttle	25.00
❑ 15 Fred Marriott	25.00
❑ 16 Harry Mitchner	25.00
❑ 17 R. Mulford	25.00
❑ 18 Felice Nazarro	25.00
❑ 19 Barney Oldfield	50.00
❑ 20 George H. Robertson	25.00
❑ 21 Joe Seymour	25.00
❑ 22 Lewis P. Strang	25.00
❑ 23 Francois Szisz	25.00
❑ 24 Joseph Tracy UER Misspelled Tracey	25.00
❑ 25 Louis Wagner	25.00

1980 Avalon Hill USAC Race Game

This 33-card set was part of a board game. The feature the Indy drivers who raced in the Indianapolis 500. An interesting note is the appeara NASCAR Winston Cup driver Tim Richmond. He fi 9th in the race. The cards are numbered in order of in the race.

	MINT
COMPLETE SET (33)	125.00
COMMON CARD (1-33)	3.00

❑ 1 Johnny Rutherford	6.00
❑ 2 Tom Sneva	4.00
❑ 3 Gary Bettenhausen	4.00
❑ 4 Gordon Johncock	4.00
❑ 5 Rick Mears	4.00
❑ 6 Pancho Carter	4.00
❑ 7 Danny Ongais	4.00
❑ 8 Tom Bigelow	3.00
❑ 9 Tim Richmond	8.00
❑ 10 Greg Leffler	3.00
❑ 11 Billy Engelhart	3.00
❑ 12 Billy Vukovich	3.00
❑ 13 Don Whittington	3.00
❑ 14 A.J.Foyt	8.00
❑ 15 George Snider	3.00
❑ 16 Dennis Firestone	3.00
❑ 17 Jerry Sneva	3.00
❑ 18 Hurley Haywood	3.00
❑ 19 Bobby Unser	4.00
❑ 20 Mario Andretti	10.00
❑ 21 Jerry Karl	3.00
❑ 22 Dick Simon	3.00
❑ 23 Roger Rager	3.00
❑ 24 Jim McElreath	3.00
❑ 25 Gordon Smiley	3.00
❑ 26 Johnny Parsons	3.00
❑ 27 Al Unser	6.00
❑ 28 Tom Bagley	3.00
❑ 29 Spike Gehlhausen	3.00
❑ 30 Bill Ehittington	3.00
❑ 31 Dick Ferguson	3.00
❑ 32 Mike Mosley	3.00
❑ 33 Larry Cannon	3.00

1986 BOSCH Indy

Bosch Spark Plugs produced this set featurir IndyCar drivers. Each card is unnumbered and feat driver photo and car photo on the cardfront. Card contain driver career information and stats.

	MINT
COMPLETE SET (8)	275.00
COMMON CARD	25.00

❑ 1 Mario Andretti	60.00
❑ 2 Emerson Fittipaldi	30.00
❑ 3 Bruno Giacomelli	25.00
❑ 4 Howdy Holmes	25.00
❑ 5 Rick Mears	30.00
❑ 6 Danny Sullivan	30.00
❑ 7 Al Unser, Jr.	60.00
❑ 8 Al Unser, Sr.	40.00

1991 Carms Formula One

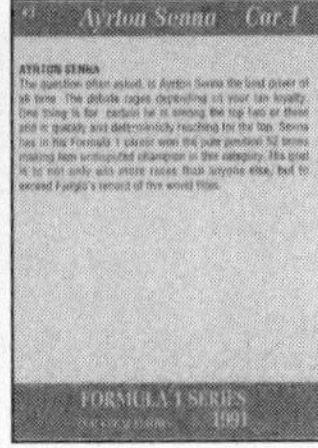

Sports Cards of Nova Scotia produced this set ng the top drivers of Formula One racing. Most ; have three cards: a portrait, a car photo, and a photo in his car. The last card in the set is a cover omplete with ordering information for additional Cards were sold in factory set form with Ayrton s car featured on the box.

	MINT	NRMT
LETE SET (105)	25.00	11.00
ON CARD (1-105)	.25	.11
ON DRIVER (1-105)	.50	.23
rton Senna	4.00	1.80
rton Senna's Car	3.00	1.35
rton Senna	4.00	1.80
rhard Berger	.75	.35
rhard Berger's Car	.50	.23
rhard Berger	.75	.35
turo Nakajima	.50	.23
turo Nakajima's Car	.25	.11
turo Nakajima	.50	.23
tefano Modena	.50	.23
tefano Modena's Car	.25	.11
tefano Modena	.50	.23
igel Mansell	2.00	.90
igel Mansell's Car	.75	.35
igel Mansell	2.00	.90
iccardo Patrese	.75	.35
iccardo Patrese's Car	.50	.23
iccardo Patrese	.75	.35
lartin Brundle	.50	.23
lartin Brundle's Car	.25	.11
lartin Brundle	.50	.23
lark Blundell	.50	.23
lark Blundell's Car	.25	.11
lark Blundell	.50	.23
lichele Alboreto	.50	.23
lichele Alboreto's Car	.25	.11
lichele Alboreto	.50	.23
lex Caffi	.50	.23
lex Caffi's Car	.25	.11
lex Caffi	.50	.23
lika Hakkinen	.50	.23
lika Hakkinen's Car	.25	.11
lika Hakkinen	.50	.23
ulian Bailey	.50	.23
ulian Bailey's Car	.25	.11
ulian Bailey	.50	.23
livier Grouillard	.50	.23
livier Grouillard's Car	.25	.11
livier Grouillard	.50	.23
lauricio Gugelmin	.50	.23
lauricio Gugelmin's Car	.25	.11
lauricio Gugelmin	.50	.23
an Capelli	.50	.23
an Capelli's Car	.25	.11
an Capelli	.50	.23
abriele Tarquini	.50	.23
abriele Tarquini's Car	.25	.11
abriele Tarquini	.50	.23
tefan Johansson	.75	.35
tefan Johansson's Car	.50	.23
tefan Johansson	.75	.35
oberto Moreno	.50	.23
oberto Moreno's Car	.25	.11
oberto Moreno	.50	.23
elson Piquet	.50	.23
elson Piquet's Car	.25	.11
elson Piquet	.50	.23
manuele Pirro	.50	.23
manuele Pirro's Car	.25	.11
manuele Pirro	.50	.23
J. Lehto	.50	.23
J. Lehto's Car	.25	.11
J. Lehto	.50	.23
ierluigi Martini	.50	.23
ierluigi Martini's Car	.25	.11
ierluigi Martini	.50	.23
ianni Morbidelli	.50	.23
ianni Morbidelli's Car	.25	.11
❑ 69 Gianni Morbidelli	.50	.23
❑ 70 Thierry Boutsen	.50	.23
❑ 71 Thierry Boutsen's Car	.25	.11
❑ 72 Thierry Boutsen	.50	.23
❑ 73 Erik Comas	.50	.23
❑ 74 Erik Comas' Car	.25	.11
❑ 75 Erik Comas	.50	.23
❑ 76 Alain Prost	.75	.35
❑ 77 Alain Prost's Car	.50	.23
❑ 78 Alain Prost	.75	.35
❑ 79 Jean Alesi	.50	.23
❑ 80 Jean Alesi's Car	.25	.11
❑ 81 Jean Alesi	.50	.23
❑ 82 Eric Bernard	.50	.23
❑ 83 Eric Bernard's Car	.25	.11
❑ 84 Eric Bernard	.50	.23
❑ 85 Aguri Suzuki	.50	.23
❑ 86 Aguri Suzuki's Car	.25	.11
❑ 87 Aguri Suzuki	.50	.23
❑ 88 Pedro Matos Chaves	.50	.23
❑ 89 Pedro Matos Chaves' Car	.25	.11
❑ 90 Bertrand Gachot	.50	.23
❑ 91 Bertrand Gachot's Car	.25	.11
❑ 92 Bertrand Gachot	.50	.23
❑ 93 Andrea deCesaris	.50	.23
❑ 94 Andrea deCesaris' Car	.25	.11
❑ 95 Andrea deCesaris	.50	.23
❑ 96 Nicola Larini	.50	.23
❑ 97 Nicola Larini's Car	.25	.11
❑ 98 Nicola Larini	.50	.23
❑ 99 Eric Van de Poele	.50	.23
❑ 100 Eric Van de Poele's Car	.25	.11
❑ 101 Mario Andretti	2.00	.90
❑ 102 Mario Andretti's Car	.75	.35
❑ 103 Gilles Villeneuve	2.00	.90
❑ 104 Gilles Villeneuve's Car	.75	.35
❑ 105 Cover Card	.25	.11

1997 CART Schedule Cards

The backs of these cards contain the 1997 CART schedule. It is unknown if this is a complete set. The card are unnumbered and appear in alphabetical order.

	MINT	NRMT
COMPLETE SET (6)	3.00	1.35
COMMON CARD	.50	.23
❑ 1 Michael Andretti	1.00	.45
❑ 2 Mark Blundell	.50	.23
❑ 3 Gil De Ferran	.60	.25
❑ 4 Christian Fittipaldi	.60	.25
❑ 5 Max Papis	.50	.23
❑ 6 Jimmy Vasser	.75	.35

1939 Churchman's Kings of Speed

This European tobacco issue is part of a bigger 50 card set. The set was issued by Imperial Tobacco Company and carries the theme speed. There were 13 car cards as part of the set. Other subsets were Aviators, Motorcycle racers, Bicycle racers, Boatsmen, Winter Olympians and Summer Olympians. The cards measure 1 3/8" X 2 5/8" and feature artwork of the drivers for card fronts. The backs give a bio of the driver pictured.

	NRMT	VG-E
COMPLETE SET (13)	35.00	21.00
COMMON CARDS	3.00	1.80
❑ 11 Captain G.E.T. Eyston	3.00	1.80
❑ 12 John Cobb	3.00	1.80
❑ 13 Major A.T.G. Gardner	3.00	1.80
❑ 14 Ab Jenkins	3.00	1.80
❑ 15 Birabongse Bira Prince of Siam	3.00	1.80
❑ 16 Rudolf Caracciola	3.00	1.80
❑ 17 Charlie Dodson	3.00	1.80
❑ 18 Louis Gerard	3.00	1.80
❑ 19 Percy Maclure	3.00	1.80
❑ 20 Raymond Mays	3.00	1.80
❑ 21 Tazio Nuvolari	3.00	1.80
❑ 22 Richard Seaman	3.00	1.80
❑ 23 J.P. Wakefield	3.00	1.80

1992 Collect-A-Card Andretti Racing

This Collect-A-Card set highlights the racing careers of Andretti family members Mario, Michael, Jeff and John. The cards were issued in 10-card packs as well as complete factory sets. Packs included randomly inserted 24K Gold autograph cards (250 of each made) of each of the four drivers. Factory sets included a special Hologram card featuring the CART/PPG IndyCar World Series Championship trophy.

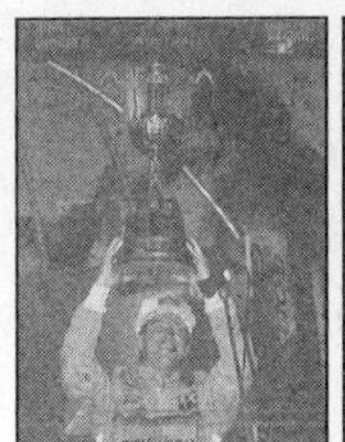

	MINT	NRMT
COMP.FACTORY SET (101)	5.00	2.20
COMPLETE SET (100)	4.00	1.80
COMMON CARD (1-100)	.05	.02
COMMON MARIO CARD (1-100)	.10	.05
❑ 1 Checklist Card	.05	.02
❑ 2 Mario Andretti's Car 1961 Lebanon Valley	.10	.05
❑ 3 Mario Andretti's Car 1967 Daytona Beach	.10	.05
❑ 4 Mario Andretti	.10	.05
❑ 5 Mario Andretti's Car 1965 Terre Haute	.10	.05
❑ 6 Mario Andretti's Car 1965 Indianapolis	.10	.05
❑ 7 Jeff Andretti	.05	.02
❑ 8 John Andretti	.05	.02
❑ 9 Mario Andretti's Car 1963 Allentown	.10	.05
❑ 10 Mario Andretti in Car	.10	.05
❑ 11 Mario Andretti's Car 1966 Indiana State FG	.10	.05
❑ 12 Mario Andretti in Car 1965 Indianapolis	.10	.05
❑ 13 Mario Andretti Aldo Andretti 1956 Langhorne	.10	.05
❑ 14 Mario Andretti in Car 1966 Indianapolis	.10	.05
❑ 15 Mario Andretti	.10	.05
❑ 16 Mario Andretti's Car 1967 Daytona Beach	.10	.05
❑ 17 Mario Andretti's Car 1967 Sebring	.10	.05
❑ 18 Mario Andretti's Car 1971 South Africa	.10	.05
❑ 19 Mario Andretti's Car 1967 St. Jovite	.10	.05
❑ 20 Mario Andretti's Car 1967 Riverside	.10	.05
❑ 21 Mario Andretti's Car 1972 Watkins Glen	.10	.05
❑ 22 Mario Andretti's Car 1967 Trenton	.10	.05
❑ 23 Mario Andretti's Car 1964 Allentown	.10	.05
❑ 24 Mario Andretti in Car 1964 Trenton	.10	.05
❑ 25 Mario Andretti's Car 1967 Indianapolis	.10	.05
❑ 26 John Andretti's Car 1990 Indianapolis	.05	.02
❑ 27 John Andretti's Car 1988 Indianapolis	.05	.02
❑ 28 John Andretti's Car 1987 Elkhart Lake	.05	.02
❑ 29 John Andretti's Car 1989 Daytona	.05	.02
❑ 30 John Andretti	.05	.02
❑ 31 John Andretti	.05	.02
❑ 32 John Andretti Car Michael Andretti Car Mario Andretti Car 1988 LeMans	.05	.02
❑ 33 John Andretti's Car 1988 Indianapolis	.05	.02
❑ 34 John Andretti's Car 1982 Dorney Park	.05	.02
❑ 35 John Andretti in Car	.05	.02
❑ 36 John Andretti's Car 1987 Mid-Ohio	.05	.02
❑ 37 John Andretti's Car 1988 Melbourne	.05	.02
❑ 38 John Andretti's Car 1989 Nuremberg	.05	.02
❑ 39 John Andretti	.05	.02
❑ 40 John Andretti's Car 1991 Milwaukee	.05	.02
❑ 41 Mario Andretti's Car A.J. Foyt's Car 1991 Indianapolis	.10	.05
❑ 42 Michael Andretti	.10	.05

Mario Andretti
Al Unser Jr.
❑ 43 Michael Andretti .... .10 .05
Mario Andretti
1991 Portland
❑ 44 Michael Andretti .... .10 .05
❑ 45 Michael Andretti's Car .... .05 .02
1991 Laguna Seca
❑ 46 Michael Andretti's Car .... .05 .02
1990 Portland
❑ 47 Michael Andretti .... .10 .05
❑ 48 Michael Andretti's Car .... .05 .02
1989 Cleveland
❑ 49 Michael Andretti's Car .... .05 .02
1988 Laguna Seca
❑ 50 Michael Andretti's Car .... .05 .02
1988 Laguna Seca
❑ 51 Mario Andretti's Car .... .10 .05
1969 Nazareth
❑ 52 Mario Andretti's Car .... .10 .05
1986 Phoenix
❑ 53 Mario Andretti's Car .... .10 .05
1986 Cleveland
❑ 54 Michael Andretti's Car .... .05 .02
1986 Cleveland
❑ 55 Mario Andretti............................ .10 .05
❑ 56 Mario Andretti's Car .... .10 .05
1988 Nazareth
❑ 57 Mario Andretti............................ .10 .05
❑ 58 Michael Andretti's Car .... .05 .02
1987 Michigan
❑ 59 Mario Andretti's Car .... .10 .05
1987 Long Beach
❑ 60 Mario Andretti............................ .10 .05
❑ 61 Mario Andretti's Car .... .10 .05
1984 Mid-Ohio
❑ 62 Mario Andretti's Car .... .10 .05
1984 Michigan
❑ 63 Michael Andretti's Car .... .05 .02
1984 Indianapolis
❑ 64 Michael Andretti's Car .... .05 .02
1990 Meadowlands
❑ 65 Mario Andretti's Car .... .10 .05
1969 Sebring
❑ 66 Jeff Andretti.............................. .05 .02
❑ 67 Michael Andretti's Car .... .05 .02
1991 Milwaukee
❑ 68 Michael Andretti .... .05 .02
Carl Haas
❑ 69 Mario Andretti............................ .10 .05
Michael Andretti
Jeff Andretti
1969 Nazareth
❑ 70 Mario Andretti's Car .... .10 .05
1978 Long Beach
❑ 71 Mario Andretti............................ .10 .05
❑ 72 Mario Andretti's Car .... .10 .05
Dan Gurney's Car
Gordon Johncock's Car
1969 Indianapolis
❑ 73 Mario Andretti's Car .... .10 .05
1966 LeMans
❑ 74 Jeff Andretti's Car...................... .05 .02
1991 Long Beach
❑ 75 Mario Andretti's Car .... .10 .05
Jeff Andretti's Car
John Andretti's Car
Michael Andretti's Car
❑ 76 Mario Andretti............................ .10 .05
Michael Andretti
Jeff Andretti
❑ 77 Michael Andretti in Pits.............. .05 .02
1991 Indianapolis
❑ 78 Mario Andretti............................ .10 .05
A.J. Foyt
Rick Mears
❑ 79 Michael Andretti .... .10 .05
❑ 80 Mario Andretti's Car .... .10 .05
1987 Elkhart Lake
❑ 81 Mario Andretti in Car .... .10 .05
1988 Cleveland
❑ 82 Jeff Andretti's Car...................... .05 .02
1991 Queensland
❑ 83 Mario Andretti's Transporter ...... .10 .05
❑ 84 Jeff Andretti.............................. .05 .02
❑ 85 Michael Andretti .... .05 .02
Paul Newman
❑ 86 1990 Indianapolis........................ .05 .02
❑ 87 Jeff Andretti.............................. .05 .02
❑ 88 Michael Andretti Car .... .10 .05
Mario Andretti Car
1984 Daytona
❑ 89 Mario Andretti's Car .... .10 .05
1977 Sweden
❑ 90 Mario Andretti............................ .10 .05
❑ 91 Michael Andretti Car .... .05 .02
Jeff Andretti Car
Mario Andretti Car
1991 Daytona
❑ 92 Jeff Andretti's Car...................... .05 .02
1985 Cleveland
❑ 93 Mario Andretti............................ .10 .05
Jeff Andretti in Car
1986 Mid-Ohio
❑ 94 Jeff Andretti's Car...................... .05 .02
1987 Phoenix
❑ 95 Jeff Andretti's Car...................... .05 .02
1988 Phoenix
❑ 96 Mario Andretti Collage .... .10 .05
35 Years of Racing
❑ 97 Mario Andretti............................ .10 .05
Michael Andretti
Jeff Andretti
1969 Indianapolis
❑ 98 Mario Andretti............................ .10 .05
❑ 99 Michael Andretti .... .10 .05
❑ 100 Checklist Card.......................... .05 .02
❑ NNO PPG Cup HOLO .... 1.00 .45

1987 Formula One Italian

This set was produced in Italy in 1987 and features popular drivers of the Formula One circuit. The cards are unnumbered, oversized (2-3/4" by 4") and have rounded corners. A 1987 yearly calendar makes up the cardback, while cardfronts typically show two small driver photos along with an F1 car shot. The cards are listed below alphabetically according to the alphabetized pair of drivers featured.

	MINT	NRMT
COMPLETE SET (16)	20.00	9.00
COMMON CARD	1.00	.45

❑ 1 Michele Alboreto.......................... 1.50 .70
Stefan Johansson
❑ 2 Rene Arnoux............................... 1.00 .45
Jacques Laffite
❑ 3 Gerhard Berger........................... 1.50 .70
Teo Fabi
❑ 4 Thierry Boutsen .... 1.00 .45
Marc Surer
❑ 5 Martin Brundle............................ 1.50 .70
Eddie Cheever
❑ 6 Ivan Capeli.................................. 1.00 .45
Christian Danner
❑ 7 Elio DeAngelis............................. 1.50 .70
Riccardo Patrese
❑ 8 Andrea DeCesais.......................... 1.00 .45
Alessandro Nannini
❑ 9 Johnny Dumfries.......................... 3.00 1.35
Ayrton Senna
❑ 10 Alan Jones................................. 1.50 .70
Patrick Tambay
❑ 11 Nigel Mansell............................. 2.00 .90
Nelson Piguet
❑ 12 Jonathan Palmer......................... 1.00 .45
❑ 13 Alain Prost................................. 1.50 .70
❑ 14 Alain Prost................................. 1.50 .70
Keke Rosberg
❑ 15 Checklist Card w/drivers............ 1.00 .45
❑ 16 Cover Card w/cars .... 1.00 .45

1988 Heraclio Fournier Formula One

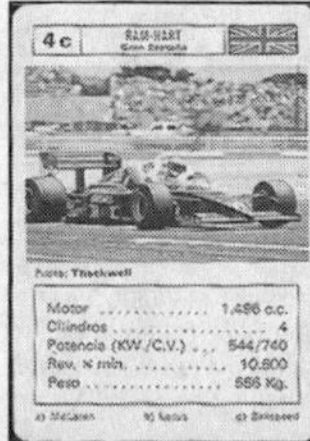

This set of 34-cards are pieces of a card game pro
in Spain. They contain a typical playing card back,
small size (2-1/4" by 3-1/2) and feature Grand Prix c
on the cardfront. All text is in Spanish and the car
numbered similarly to other playing card decks.

	MINT
COMPLETE SET (34)	10.00
COMMON CARD	.20

❑ 1A Rosenberg's Car........................ .20
❑ 1B Riccardo Patrese's Car .... .50
❑ 1C Rene Arnoux's Car .... .20
❑ 1D Martin Brundle's Car .... .30
❑ 2A Michele Alboreto's Car .... .30
❑ 2B Alan Jones' Car .... .20
❑ 2C Patrick Tambay's Car .... .20
❑ 2D Thierry Boutsen's Car.................. .30
❑ 3A Stefan Johansson's Car............... .30
❑ 3B Pierluigi Martini's Car................. .30
❑ 3C Piercarlo Ghinzani's Car .... .20
❑ 3D Gerhard Berger's Car .... .50
❑ 4A Alain Prost's Car......................... .50
❑ 4B Ayrton Senna's Car..................... 1.00
❑ 4C Thackwell's Car .... .20
❑ 4D Jonathan Palmer's Car................ .20
❑ 5A Emerson Fittipaldi's Car .... .50
❑ 5B Rick Mears' Car.......................... .50
❑ 5C Al Unser Jr.'s Car .... .75
❑ 5D Mauricio Gugelmin's Car............ .30
❑ 6A Kaiser's Car................................ .20
❑ 6B Thackwell's Car .... .20
❑ 6C Philippe Streiff's Car.................. .20
❑ 6D Raphanel's Car............................ .20
❑ 7A Morin's Car .... .20
❑ 7B Huysmann's Car.......................... .20
❑ 7C Nicola Larini's Car....................... .20
❑ 7D Trolle's Car................................. .20
❑ 8A Stefano Modena's Car .... .20
❑ 8B Yannick Dalmas' Car .... .20
❑ 8C Artztet's Car............................... .20
❑ 8D Birne's Car .... .20
❑ NNO Cover Card .... .20
Rene Arnoux's Car

1992 Golden Era Grand Pri
The Early Years

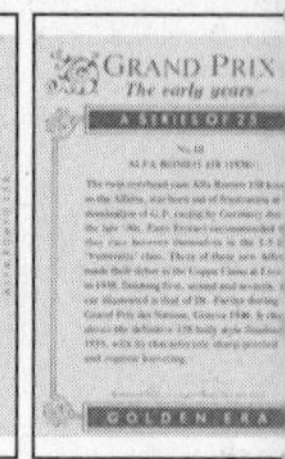

This 25-card set was produced by Rainbow Pr
Loughton Essex England. The cards feature illustr
by British artist Robert R. Wisdom. The cards de
colorful selection of the most thrilling and spect
racing cars to ever grace the Grand Prix circuits
World, driven by the famous and legendary drivers
day.

	MINT
COMPLETE SET (25)	10.00
COMMON CARD (1-25)	.50

❑ 1 Jimmy Murphy's Car..................... .50
❑ 2 Antonio Ascari's Car..................... .50
❑ 3 Bugatti Type 35B.......................... .50
❑ 4 Robert Benoist's Car..................... .50
❑ 5 Auto Union A-Type....................... .50
❑ 6 Alfa Romeo Tipo B........................ .50
❑ 7 Von Brauchitsch's Car .... .50
❑ 8 Raymond Mays' Car .... .50
❑ 9 Mercedes W125 .... .50
❑ 10 Giuseppe Farina's Car.................. .50
❑ 11 Tazio Nuvolari's Car.................... .50
❑ 12 Mercedes W163 .... .50
❑ 13 Peter Whitehead's Car .... .50
❑ 14 Giuseppe Farina's Car.................. .50
❑ 15 Juan Manuel Fangio's Car .... .50
❑ 16 Alberto Ascari's Car..................... .50
❑ 17 Juan Manuel Fangio's Car .... .50
❑ 18 Alberto Ascari's Car..................... .50
❑ 19 Stirling Moss' Car......................... 1.00
❑ 20 Stirling Moss' Car......................... 1.00
❑ 21 Stirling Moss' Car......................... 1.00
❑ 22 Mike Hawthorn's Car.................... .50
❑ 23 Jack Brabham's Car...................... .50

hil Hill's Car	.50	.23
m Clark's Car	.50	.23
Cover Card	.25	.11

1978-79 Grand Prix

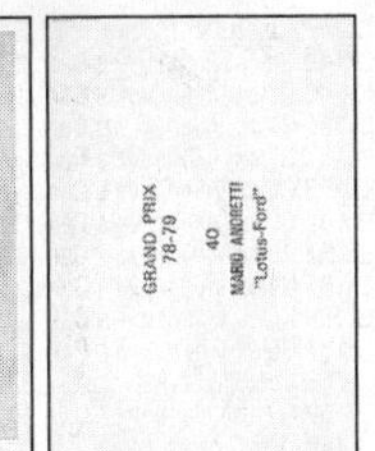

78-79 Grand Prix set was produced with an album ed to house the 240-card set. The album is written in French. The card fronts feature a color photo of Grand Prix driver, while the backs include the card r and, on most, a short card title.

	NRMT	VG-E
LETE SET (240)	125.00	55.00
ON CARD (1-240)	.30	.14
ON DRIVER (1-240)	.50	.23
ario Andretti	5.00	2.20
uno Giacomelli	.50	.23
n Lammers	.50	.23
dier Pironi	.50	.23
Jean Pierre Jaussaud		
Unser	5.00	2.20
arkku Alen	.50	.23
ny Carello	.50	.23
ario Andretti	5.00	2.20
ario Andretti's Car	2.00	.90
arlos Reutemann's Car	.30	.14
idier Pironi's Car	.30	.14
ames Hunt's Car	.30	.14
iki Lauda's Car	.50	.23
lario Andretti's Car	2.00	.90
illes Villeneuve's Car	.50	.23
rturo Merzario's Car	.30	.14
ean Pierre Jarier's Car	.30	.14
merson Fittipaldi	3.00	1.35
arlos Reutemann's Car	.30	.14
merson Fittipaldi's Car	1.00	.45
iki Lauda's Car	.50	.23
rand Prix Action	.30	.14
illes Villeneuve's Car	.50	.23
onnie Peterson's Car	.30	.14
lan Jones' Car	.50	.23
ddie Cheever's Car	.50	.23
acques Laffite's Car	.30	.14
onnie Peterson	.50	.23
atrick Depailler's Car	.30	.14
iccardo Patrese's Car	.50	.23
ean Pierre Jabouille's Car	.30	.14
ohn Watson's Car	.30	.14
idier Pironi's Car	.30	.14
ddie Cheever's Car	.50	.23
arlos Reutemann's Car	.30	.14
olf Stommelen's Car	.30	.14
ene Arnoux's Car	.30	.14
arlos Reutemann	.50	.23
arlos Reutemann's Car	.30	.14
lario Andretti's Car	2.00	.90
lan Jones' Car	.50	.23
atrick Depailler's Car	.30	.14
lay Regazzoni's Car	.50	.23
Gilles Villeneuve's Car		
ody Scheckter's Car	.30	.14
ans Stuck's Car	.30	.14
amberto Leoni's Car	.30	.14
acques Laffite's Car	.30	.14
Riccardo Patrese's Car		
atrick Depailler	.50	.23
rand Prix Action	.30	.14
iki Lauda's Car	.50	.23
arlos Reutemann's Car	.30	.14
atrick Tambay's Car	.30	.14
idier Pironi	.50	.23
Riccardo Patrese		
ohn Watson's Car	.30	.14
ean Pierre Jabouille's Car	.30	.14
lario Andretti's Car	2.00	.90
Volf-Ford	.30	.14
lario Andretti	5.00	2.20
lario Andretti's Car	2.00	.90
lan Jones' Car	.50	.23
arlos Reutemann's Car	.30	.14
illes Villeneuve's Car	.50	.23
❑ 63 Bruno Giacomelli's Car	.30	.14
❑ 64 Didier Pironi's Car	.30	.14
Rene Arnoux's Car		
Rolf Stommelen's Car		
❑ 65 Rene Arnoux' Car	.30	.14
❑ 66 Brett Lunger's Car	.30	.14
❑ 67 Jochen Mass' Car	.30	.14
❑ 68 Mario Andretti's Car	2.00	.90
❑ 69 Jacques Laffite's Car	.30	.14
❑ 70 Jody Scheckter's Car	.30	.14
❑ 71 James Hunt's Car	.30	.14
❑ 72 Jacques Laffite	.50	.23
❑ 73 Ronnie Peterson's Car	.30	.14
❑ 74 John Watson's Car	.30	.14
❑ 75 Hector Rebaque's Car	.30	.14
❑ 76 Emilio Villota's Car	.30	.14
❑ 77 Rupert Keegan's Car	.30	.14
❑ 78 Niki Lauda	1.00	.45
❑ 79 Niki Lauda's Car	.50	.23
❑ 80 Mario Andretti's Car	2.00	.90
❑ 81 Riccardo Patrese's Car	.50	.23
❑ 82 Patrick Tambay's Car	.30	.14
❑ 83 Mario Andretti's Car	2.00	.90
❑ 84 Ronnie Peterson's Car	.30	.14
❑ 85 Geoff Brabham's Car	.50	.23
❑ 86 Clay Regazzoni's Car	.30	.14
❑ 87 Grand Prix Action	.30	.14
❑ 88 Mario Andretti's Car	2.00	.90
❑ 89 Ronnie Peterson's Car	.30	.14
❑ 90 James Hunt's Car	.30	.14
❑ 91 Riccardo Patrese's Car	.50	.23
❑ 92 Niki Lauda's Car	.50	.23
❑ 93 James Hunt's Car	.30	.14
❑ 94 Jody Scheckter's Car	.30	.14
❑ 95 Jacques Laffite's Car	.30	.14
❑ 96 Alan Jones' Car	.50	.23
❑ 97 Carlos Reutemann's Car	.30	.14
❑ 98 Carlos Reutemann	.50	.23
❑ 99 Carlos Reutemann's Car	.30	.14
❑ 100 Niki Lauda's Car	.50	.23
❑ 101 Mario Andretti's Car	2.00	.90
❑ 102 Patrick Depailler's Car	.30	.14
❑ 103 Alan Jones' Car	.50	.23
❑ 104 Grand Prix Action	.30	.14
❑ 105 Hans Stuck's Car	.30	.14
❑ 106 Patrick Tambay's Car	.30	.14
❑ 107 Bruno Giacomelli's Car	.30	.14
❑ 108 Mario Andretti's Car	2.00	.90
❑ 109 Jody Scheckter's Car	.30	.14
❑ 110 Jody Scheckter	.50	.23
❑ 111 Jacques Laffite's Car	.30	.14
❑ 112 Harald Ertl	.50	.23
❑ 113 Emerson Fittipaldi's Car	1.00	.45
❑ 114 Didier Pironi	1.00	.45
Emerson Fittipaldi		
❑ 115 Keke Rosberg's Car	.50	.23
❑ 116 John Watson's Car	.30	.14
❑ 117 Gilles Villeneuve's Car	.50	.23
❑ 118 Ronnie Peterson's Car	.30	.14
❑ 119 Patrick Depailler's Car	.50	.23
Niki Lauda's Car		
❑ 120 Vittorio Brambilla's Car	.30	.14
❑ 121 Mario Andretti's Car	2.00	.90
❑ 122 Niki Lauda's Car	.50	.23
❑ 123 Gilles Villeneuve's Car	.50	.23
Patrick Depailler's Car		
Hans Stuck's Car		
❑ 124 Nelson Piquet's Car	.50	.23
❑ 125 Carlos Reutemann's Car	.30	.14
❑ 126 Jean Pierre Jabouille's Car	.30	.14
❑ 127 Derek Daly's Car	.30	.14
❑ 128 Mario Andretti	5.00	2.20
❑ 129 John Watson's Car	.30	.14
❑ 130 Jean Pierre Jabouille's Car	.30	.14
❑ 131 Michael Bleekemolen's Car	.30	.14
❑ 132 Gilles Villeneuve's Car	.50	.23
❑ 133 Emerson Fittipaldi's Car	1.00	.45
❑ 134 Patrick Tambay's Car	.30	.14
❑ 135 James Hunt's Car	.30	.14
❑ 136 Jochen Mass' Car	.30	.14
❑ 137 Derek Daly's Car	.30	.14
❑ 138 John Watson	.50	.23
❑ 139 Niki Lauda's Car	.50	.23
❑ 140 Mario Andretti's Car	2.00	.90
❑ 141 Ronnie Peterson's Car	.30	.14
❑ 142 Ronnie Peterson	.50	.23
❑ 143 John Watson's Car	.30	.14
❑ 144 Gilles Villeneuve's Car	.50	.23
❑ 145 Patrick Tambay's Car	.30	.14
❑ 146 Vittorio Brambilla's Car	.30	.14
❑ 147 Nelson Piquet's Car	.50	.23
❑ 148 Carlos Reutemann's Car	.30	.14
❑ 149 Carlos Reutemann	.50	.23
❑ 150 Alan Jones' Car	.50	.23
❑ 151 Jean Pierre Jabouille's Car	.30	.14
❑ 152 Jean Pierre Jarier's Car	.30	.14
❑ 153 James Hunt's Car	.30	.14
❑ 154 Patrick Tambay's Car	.30	.14
❑ 155 Clay Regazzoni	1.00	.45
Emerson Fittipaldi		
❑ 156 Rene Arnoux's Car	.30	.14
❑ 157 Bobby Rahal's Car	.75	.35
❑ 158 Gilles Villeneuve's Car	.50	.23
❑ 159 Gilles Villeneuve	.50	.23
❑ 160 Jody Scheckter's Car	.30	.14
❑ 161 Jean Pierre Jarier's Car	.30	.14
❑ 162 Riccardo Patrese's Car	.50	.23
❑ 163 Grand Prix Action	.30	.14
❑ 164 Grand Prix Action	.30	.14
❑ 165 Derek Daly's Car	.30	.14
❑ 166 Nelson Piquet's Car	.50	.23
❑ 167 Keke Rosberg's Car	.50	.23
❑ 168 Bruno Giacomelli's Car	.30	.14
❑ 169 Marc Surer's Car	.30	.14
❑ 170 March-BMW	.30	.14
❑ 171 Derek Daly's Car	.30	.14
❑ 172 Piero Necchi's Car	.30	.14
❑ 173 Alex Dias Ribeiro's Car	.30	.14
❑ 174 Keke Rosberg's Car	.50	.23
❑ 175 Jan Lammers' Car	.30	.14
❑ 176 Anders Olofsson's Car	.30	.14
❑ 177 Patrick Gaillard's Car	.30	.14
❑ 178 Nelson Piquet's Car	.50	.23
❑ 179 Derek Warwick's Car	.30	.14
❑ 180 Alain Prost's Car	.75	.35
❑ 181 Chico Serra's Car	.30	.14
❑ 182 Umberto Grano's Car	.30	.14
❑ 183 Armin Hahne's Car	.30	.14
❑ 184 Clemens Schickentanz's Car	.30	.14
Hans Heyer's Car		
❑ 185 Carlo Facetti's Car	.30	.14
Martini Finotto's Car		
❑ 186 Willi Bergmeistr's Car	.30	.14
Jorg Siegrst's Car		
❑ 187 Gordon Spice's Car	.30	.14
Teddy Pilette's Car		
❑ 188 Helmut Bauer's Car	.30	.14
❑ 189 Hezemans' Car	.30	.14
Ludwig's Car		
❑ 190 Bob Wollek's Car	.30	.14
Henri Pescarolo's Car		
❑ 191 Eddie Cheever's Car	.50	.23
Giorgio Francia's Car		
❑ 192 Tomaso Pantera's Car	.30	.14
❑ 193 Hans Heyer's Car	.30	.14
❑ 194 Harald Ertl's Car	.30	.14
❑ 195 Rolf Stommelen's Car	.30	.14
❑ 196 Didier Pironi's Car	.30	.14
Jean Pierre Jaussaud's Car		
❑ 197 Didier Pironi	.50	.23
❑ 198 Bob Wollek's Car	.30	.14
Jurgen Barth's Car		
❑ 199 Patrick Depailler's Car	.30	.14
Jean Pierre Jabouille's Car		
❑ 200 Renault Alpine A442A	.30	.14
❑ 201 Porsche 936	.30	.14
❑ 202 Rolf Stommelen's Car	.30	.14
Manfred Schurti's Car		
❑ 203 Redman's Car	.30	.14
❑ 204 Jacques Laffite's Car	.30	.14
Vern Schuppan's Car		
❑ 205 Grand Prix 78-79	.30	.14
❑ 206 512 Berlinetta Boxer	.30	.14
❑ 207 Pironi Jaussaud's Car	.30	.14
❑ 208 Al Unser	5.00	2.20
❑ 209 Al Unser's Car	2.00	.90
❑ 210 Grand Prix 78-79	.30	.14
❑ 211 Tom Sneva's Car	.75	.35
❑ 212 Bobby Unser's Car	1.00	.45
Wally Dallenbach Sr.'s Car		
❑ 213 Janet Guthrie's Car	1.50	.70
❑ 214 Mario Andretti's Car	2.00	.90
❑ 215 Martin Schanche's Car	.30	.14
❑ 216 Andreas Bentza's Car	.30	.14
❑ 217 Ake Anderson's Car	.30	.14
❑ 218 Grand Prix 78-79	.30	.14
❑ 219 Jos Fassbender's Car	.30	.14
❑ 220 Antero Laine's Car	.30	.14
❑ 221 Franz Wurz's Car	.30	.14
❑ 222 Jean Pierre Nicolas' Car	.30	.14
❑ 223 Jean Ragnotti's Car	.30	.14
❑ 224 Markku Alen's Car	.30	.14
❑ 225 Hannu Nikkola's Car	.30	.14
❑ 226 Anders Kullang's Car	.30	.14
❑ 227 Jean Pierre Nicolas' Car	.30	.14
❑ 228 Vic Preston's Car	.30	.14
❑ 229 Datsun 160J	.30	.14
❑ 230 Toyota Celica	.30	.14
❑ 231 Pentti Airikkala's Car	.30	.14
❑ 232 Bjorn Waldegaard's Car	.30	.14
❑ 233 Tony Pond's Car	.30	.14
❑ 234 Tony Carello's Car	.30	.14
❑ 235 Gilbert Staepelaere's Car	.30	.14
❑ 236 Franz Wittmann's Car	.30	.14
❑ 237 Roger Clark's Car	.30	.14
❑ 238 Michel Mouton's Car	.30	.14

❑ 239 Bernard Darniche's Car	.30	.14
❑ 240 Antonio Zanini's Car	.30	.14

1992 Grid Formula One

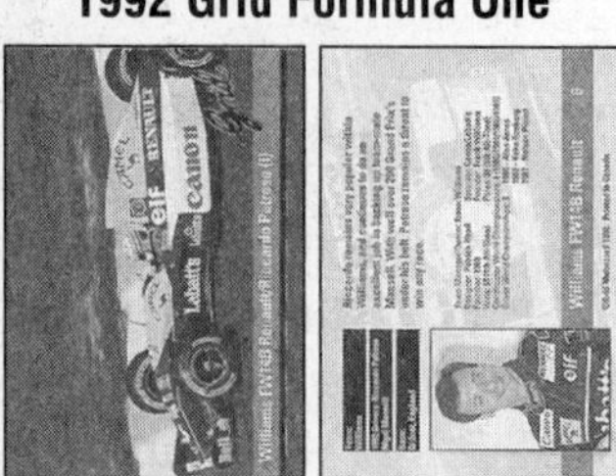

Released in foil packs and complete factory set form, this 200-card issue features top Formula One drivers and machines. The cards were produced with gold foil layering on the cardfronts and heavy UV coating. The set is highlighted by a large number of Ayrton Senna cards.

	MINT	NRMT
COMPLETE SET (200)	7.00	3.10
COMPLETE FACT.SET (200)	7.00	3.10
COMMON CARD (1-200)	.05	.02
COMMON DRIVER (1-200)	.10	.05

❑ 1 Ayrton Senna's Car	.25	.11
❑ 2 Gerhard Berger's Car	.10	.05
❑ 3 Olivier Grouillard's Car	.05	.02
❑ 4 Andrea deCesaris' Car	.05	.02
❑ 5 Nigel Mansell's Car	.15	.07
❑ 6 Riccardo Patrese's Car	.05	.02
❑ 7 Eric van de Poele's Car	.05	.02
❑ 8 Damon Hill's Car	.15	.07
❑ 9 Giovanna Amati's Car	.05	.02
❑ 10 Michele Alboreto's Car	.05	.02
❑ 11 Aguri Suzuki's Car	.05	.02
❑ 12 Mika Hakkinen's Car	.05	.02
❑ 13 Johnny Herbert's Car	.05	.02
❑ 14 Andrea Chiesa's Car	.05	.02
❑ 15 Gabriele Tarquini's Car	.05	.02
❑ 16 Karl Wendlinger's Car	.05	.02
❑ 17 Paul Belmondo's Car	.05	.02
❑ 18 Michael Schumacher's Car	.15	.07
❑ 19 Martin Brundle's Car	.05	.02
❑ 20 J.J. Lehto's Car	.05	.02
❑ 21 Pierluigi Martini's Car	.05	.02
❑ 22 Christian Fittipaldi's Car	.05	.02
❑ 23 Gianni Morbidelli's Car	.05	.02
❑ 24 Thierry Boutsen's Car	.05	.02
❑ 25 Erik Comas' Car	.05	.02
❑ 26 Jean Alesi's Car	.10	.05
❑ 27 Ivan Capelli's Car	.05	.02
❑ 28 Ukyo Katayama's Car	.05	.02
❑ 29 Bertrand Gachot's Car	.05	.02
❑ 30 Stefano Modena's Car	.05	.02
❑ 31 Mauricio Gugelmin's Car	.05	.02
❑ 32 Roberto Moreno's Car	.05	.02
❑ 33 Perry McCarthy's Car	.05	.02
❑ 34 Ayrton Senna	.30	.14
❑ 35 Gerhard Berger	.25	.11
❑ 36 Olivier Grouillard	.10	.05
❑ 37 Andrea deCesaris	.10	.05
❑ 38 Nigel Mansell	.25	.11
❑ 39 Riccardo Patrese	.15	.07
❑ 40 Eric van de Poele	.10	.05
❑ 41 Damon Hill	.25	.11
❑ 42 Giovanna Amati	.10	.05
❑ 43 Michele Alboreto	.10	.05
❑ 44 Aguri Suzuki	.10	.05
❑ 45 Mika Hakkinen	.10	.05
❑ 46 Johnny Herbert	.10	.05
❑ 47 Andrea Chiesa	.10	.05
❑ 48 Gabriele Tarquini	.10	.05
❑ 49 Karl Wendlinger	.10	.05
❑ 50 Paul Belmondo	.10	.05
❑ 51 Michael Schumacher	.25	.11
❑ 52 Martin Brundle	.10	.05
❑ 53 J.J. Lehto	.10	.05
❑ 54 Pierluigi Martini	.10	.05
❑ 55 Christian Fittipaldi	.10	.05
❑ 56 Gianni Morbidelli	.10	.05
❑ 57 Thierry Boutsen	.10	.05
❑ 58 Erik Comas	.10	.05
❑ 59 Jean Alesi	.15	.07
❑ 60 Ivan Capelli	.10	.05
❑ 61 Bertrand Gachot	.10	.05
❑ 62 Ukyo Katayama	.10	.05
❑ 63 Stefano Modena	.10	.05
❑ 64 Mauricio Gugelmin	.10	.05
❑ 65 Roberto Moreno	.10	.05
❑ 66 Perry McCarthy	.10	.05
❑ 67 Ayrton Senna	.30	.14
❑ 68 Gerhard Berger	.25	.11
❑ 69 Olivier Grouillard	.10	.05
❑ 70 Andrea deCesaris	.10	.05
❑ 71 Nigel Mansell	.25	.11
❑ 72 Riccardo Patrese	.15	.07
❑ 73 Eric van de Poele	.10	.05
❑ 74 Damon Hill	.25	.11
❑ 75 Giovanna Amati	.10	.05
❑ 76 Michele Alboreto	.10	.05
❑ 77 Aguri Suzuki	.10	.05
❑ 78 Mika Hakkinen	.10	.05
❑ 79 Johnny Herbert	.10	.05
❑ 80 Andrea Chiesa	.10	.05
❑ 81 Gabriele Tarquini	.10	.05
❑ 82 Karl Wendlinger	.10	.05
❑ 83 Paul Belmondo	.10	.05
❑ 84 Michael Schumacher	.25	.11
❑ 85 Martin Brundle	.10	.05
❑ 86 J.J. Lehto	.10	.05
❑ 87 Pierluigi Martini	.10	.05
❑ 88 Christian Fittipaldi	.10	.05
❑ 89 Gianni Morbidelli	.10	.05
❑ 90 Thierry Boutsen	.10	.05
❑ 91 Erik Comas	.10	.05
❑ 92 Jean Alesi	.15	.07
❑ 93 Ivan Capelli	.10	.05
❑ 94 Bertrand Gachot	.10	.05
❑ 95 Ukyo Katayama	.10	.05
❑ 96 Stefano Modena	.10	.05
❑ 97 Mauricio Gugelmin	.10	.05
❑ 98 Roberto Moreno	.10	.05
❑ 99 Perry McCarthy	.10	.05
❑ 100 Ayrton Senna Alain Prost Nelson Piquet	.15	.07
❑ 101 Ayrton Senna Winner	.25	.11
❑ 102 Ayrton Senna Gerhard Berger J.J.Lehto	.15	.07
❑ 103 Jean Alesi Ayrton Senna Nigel Mansell	.15	.07
❑ 104 Nelson Piquet Stefano Modena Riccardo Patrese	.10	.05
❑ 105 Ayrton Senna Riccardo Patrese Nigel Mansell	.15	.07
❑ 106 Nigel Mansell Alain Prost Ayrton Senna	.15	.07
❑ 107 Nigel Mansell Gerhard Berger Alain Prost	.15	.07
❑ 108 Riccardo Patrese Nigel Mansell Jean Alesi	.15	.07
❑ 109 Ayrton Senna Nigel Mansell Riccardo Patrese	.15	.07
❑ 110 Ayrton Senna Win	.25	.11
❑ 111 Nigel Mansell Ayrton Senna Alain Prost	.15	.07
❑ 112 Riccardo Patrese Win	.10	.05
❑ 113 Nigel Mansell Alain Prost Riccardo Patrese	.15	.07
❑ 114 Gerhard Berger Ayrton Senna Riccardo Patrese	.15	.07
❑ 115 Ayrton Senna Win	.25	.11
❑ 116 South Africa Race Track	.05	.02
❑ 117 Mexico Race Track	.05	.02
❑ 118 Brazil Race Track	.05	.02
❑ 119 Spain Race Track	.05	.02
❑ 120 San Marino Race Track	.05	.02
❑ 121 Monaco Race Track	.05	.02
❑ 122 Canada Race Track	.05	.02
❑ 123 France Race Track	.05	.02
❑ 124 England Race Track	.05	.02
❑ 125 Germany Race Track	.05	.02
❑ 126 Hungary Race Track	.05	.02
❑ 127 Belgium Race Track	.05	.02
❑ 128 Italy Race Track	.05	.02
❑ 129 Portugal Race Track	.05	.02
❑ 130 Japan Race Track	.05	.02
❑ 131 Australia Race Track	.05	.02
❑ 132 Frank Williams	.05	.02
❑ 133 Don Dennis	.05	.02
❑ 134 Tom Walkinshaw	.05	.02
❑ 135 Luca di Montezemolo	.05	.02
❑ 136 Gerard Larrousse	.05	.02
❑ 137 Eddie Jordan	.05	.02
❑ 138 Giancarlo Minardi	.05	.02
❑ 139 Charlie Moody	.05	.02
❑ 140 Ken Tyrrell	.05	.02
❑ 141 Peter Collins	.05	
❑ 142 Jackie Oliver	.05	
❑ 143 Guy Ligier	.05	
❑ 144 Andrea Sasetti	.05	
❑ 145 Dennis Nursey	.05	
❑ 146 Gabriele Rumi	.05	
❑ 147 Gianpaola Dallara	.05	
❑ 148 Gilles Villeneuve's Car	.10	
❑ 149 Gilles Villeneuve's Car	.10	
❑ 150 Gilles Villeneuve's Car	.10	
❑ 151 Gilles Villeneuve's Car	.10	
❑ 152 Gilles Villeneuve's Car	.10	
❑ 152 Gilles Villeneuve's Car	.10	
❑ 154 Gilles Villeneuve's Car	.10	
❑ 155 Gilles Villeneuve's Car	.10	
❑ 156 Gilles Villeneuve's Car	.10	
❑ 157 Gilles Villeneuve's Car	.10	
❑ 158 Checklist Card	.05	
❑ 159 Gilles Villeneuve	.15	
❑ 160 Davy Jones	.10	
❑ 161 Mark Blundell	.10	
❑ 162 Al Unser Jr.	.25	
❑ 163 David Coulthard	.15	
❑ 164 Rubens Barrichello	.10	
❑ 165 Alan McNish	.10	
❑ 166 Checklist Card	.05	
❑ 167 Paul Tracy	.15	
❑ 168 Emanuelle Naspetti	.10	
❑ 169 Alessandro Zanardi	.10	
❑ 170 Eddie Irvine	.10	
❑ 171 Antonio Tamburini	.10	
❑ 172 Jacques Villeneuve	.25	
❑ 173 Jordi Gene	.10	
❑ 174 Michael Bartels	.10	
❑ 175 Jimmy Vasser	.10	
❑ 176 Eric Bachelart	.10	
❑ 177 Robby Gordon	.15	
❑ 178 Alberto Ascari	.10	
❑ 179 Alberto Ascari's Car	.05	
❑ 180 Graham Hill	.10	
❑ 181 Graham Hill's Car	.05	
❑ 182 Emerson Fittipaldi	.15	
❑ 183 Emerson Fittipaldi's Car	.05	
❑ 184 Keke Rosberg	.15	
❑ 185 1982 Ferrari	.05	
❑ 186 Ayrton Senna	.30	
❑ 187 Ayrton Senna's Car	.25	
❑ 188 Ayrton Senna	.30	
❑ 189 Ayrton Senna's Car	.25	
❑ 190 Alain Prost	.15	
❑ 191 Jordan's First Points	.05	
❑ 192 Nigel Mansell's Car	.15	
❑ 193 Bertrand Gachot's Car	.05	
❑ 194 Michael Schumacher	.25	
❑ 195 Nelson Piquet's Car	.05	
❑ 196 J.P.Balestre	.10	
❑ 197 Alain Prost	.15	
❑ 198 Nigel Mansell Crash	.10	
❑ 199 Saturo Nakajima	.10	
❑ 200 Michael Andretti's Car	.15	

1960 Hawes Wax Indy

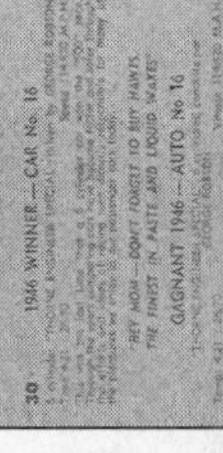

Although often considered to be one of the first Am auto racing card sets, the 50-card Hawes Wax issu printed by Parkhurst in Canada for distribution in Wax products. This set features 39 cards portrayin 500 race winners from 1911-1959; 11 cards fea race action scenes, and one card featuring the P University Marching Band. Cardbacks are printed i English and French. It's interesting to note that ca lists the winners of the Parkhurst Zip Gum H Contest originally offered on the backs of 19 Parkhurst hockey cards. Oversized ve (approximately 3" by 4") of six cards exist featuri fronts of 12 Hawes Wax (#9/26/29/31/33/35/37/38/39/40/43/44) placed ba back. Reportedly, the six cards were part of a produced in Canada that also included additional ca non-racing subjects. These six cards are val approximately $20.00 each.

	NRMT	VG-E
ETE SET (50)	600.00	350.00
N CARD (1-50)	15.00	9.00
Harroun	15.00	9.00
Dawson	15.00	9.00
s Goux	15.00	9.00
e Thomas	15.00	9.00
ph dePalma	25.00	15.00
io Resta	15.00	9.00
vard Wilcox	15.00	9.00
ton Chevrolet	25.00	15.00
nmy Milton	15.00	9.00
nmy Murphy	15.00	9.00
mmy Milton	15.00	9.00
L.Corum	15.00	9.00
oe Boyer		
ter DePaolo	15.00	9.00
ank Lockhart	15.00	9.00
orge Souders	15.00	9.00
uis Meyer	15.00	9.00
y Keech	15.00	9.00
lly Arnold	15.00	9.00
uis Schneider	15.00	9.00
ed Frame	15.00	9.00
uis Meyer	15.00	9.00
l Cummings	15.00	9.00
lly Petillo	15.00	9.00
uis Meyer	15.00	9.00
lbur Shaw	15.00	9.00
yd Roberts	15.00	9.00
ilbur Shaw	15.00	9.00
rdue University Band	15.00	9.00
auri Rose	15.00	9.00
loyd Davis		
Rose pictured)		
orge Robson	15.00	9.00
auri Rose	15.00	9.00
dger Ward VL	25.00	15.00
l Holland	15.00	9.00
hnnie Parsons	25.00	15.00
e Wallard	15.00	9.00
oy Ruttman	15.00	9.00
l Vukovich	25.00	15.00
art of Parade Lap	15.00	9.00
ace action		
b Sweikert	15.00	9.00
t Flaherty	15.00	9.00
m Hanks	15.00	9.00
nmy Bryan	15.00	9.00
dger Ward	25.00	15.00
ny Bettenhausen in Pits	25.00	15.00
dger Ward w/wife	25.00	15.00
e Borg-Warner Trophy	15.00	9.00
ain Gate of IMS	15.00	9.00
S Museum	15.00	9.00
ul Russo in Pits	15.00	9.00
rade Lap	15.00	9.00

ack lists winners of Zip Gum Hockey Contest

92 Hi-Tech Mario Andretti

produced this set in 1992, but actually released it 1993. The cards were distributed in factory set a tin box package. The set commemorates the reer of Mario Andretti and was limited to 100,000 sets. A #52 card was also produced (5000 made) 00 signed copies randomly inserted in some sets. It is not considered part of the complete set

	MINT	NRMT
ETE FACTORY SET (51)	20.00	9.00
N CARD (1-51)	.50	.23
rio Andretti	.75	.35
rio Andretti	.50	.23
Aldo Andretti		
rio Andretti's Car	.50	.23
White Hudson		
rio Andretti's Car	.50	.23
Fuel Activator Special		
rio Andretti in Car	.50	.23
❑ 6 Mario Andretti	.50	.23
Ed Mataka		
Bill Mataka		
❑ 7 Mario Andretti in Car	.50	.23
❑ 8 Mario Andretti in Car	.50	.23
❑ 9 Mario Andretti in Car	.50	.23
❑ 10 Mario Andretti in Car	.50	.23
❑ 11 Mario Andretti in Car	.50	.23
❑ 12 Mario Andretti	.75	.35
❑ 13 Mario Andretti	.75	.35
❑ 14 Mario Andretti in Car	.50	.23
❑ 15 Mario Andretti's Car	.50	.23
A.J.Foyt's Car		
❑ 16 Mario Andretti	.50	.23
Clint Brawner		
❑ 17 Mario Andretti	.50	.23
Chuck Rodee		
❑ 18 Mario Andretti in Car	.50	.23
❑ 19 Mario Andretti	.75	.35
❑ 20 Mario Andretti's Car	.50	.23
❑ 21 Mario Andretti in Car	.50	.23
❑ 22 Mario Andretti	.75	.35
❑ 23 Mario Andretti w/Car	.50	.23
❑ 24 Mario Andretti in Car	.50	.23
❑ 25 Mario Andretti's Car	.50	.23
❑ 26 Mario Andretti	.75	.35
❑ 27 Mario Andretti in Car	.50	.23
❑ 28 Mario Andretti in Car	.50	.23
❑ 29 Mario Andretti in Car	.50	.23
❑ 30 Mario Andretti	.50	.23
Jackie Ickx		
❑ 31 Mario Andretti in Car	.50	.23
❑ 32 Mario Andretti in Car	.50	.23
❑ 33 Mario Andretti in Car	.50	.23
❑ 34 Mario Andretti	.75	.35
❑ 35 Mario Andretti in Car	.50	.23
❑ 36 Mario Andretti	.75	.35
❑ 37 Mario Andretti in Car	.50	.23
❑ 38 Mario Andretti's Car	.50	.23
❑ 39 Mario Andretti's Car	.50	.23
❑ 40 Mario Andretti	.75	.35
❑ 41 Mario Andretti in Car	.50	.23
❑ 42 Mario Andretti's Car	.50	.23
❑ 43 Mario Andretti's Car	.50	.23
❑ 44 Mario Andretti	.75	.35
Michael Andretti		
❑ 45 Mario Andretti	.75	.35
❑ 46 Mario Andretti	.75	.35
Al Unser Jr.		
Tom Sneva		
❑ 47 Mario Andretti	.75	.35
❑ 48 Mario Andretti	.75	.35
❑ 49 Mario Andretti's Car	.50	.23
A.J.Foyt's Car		
Rick Mears' Car		
❑ 50 Mario Andretti's Car	.50	.23
❑ 51 Checklist Card	.50	.23
❑ 52 Mario Andretti Signature Card	2.00	.90
Unsigned		

1993 Hi-Tech Indy

Hi-Tech produced this set featuring drivers of the 1992 Indianapolis 500. The cards were released in 10-card packs with 36-packs per box. Reportedly, production was limited to 4000 cases. Cards from the Checkered Flag Finishers set were randomly inserted into packs.

	MINT	NRMT
COMPLETE SET (81)	10.00	4.50
COMMON CARD (1-81)	.15	.07
❑ 1 Roberto Guerrero	.25	.11
❑ 2 Eddie Cheever	.15	.07
❑ 3 Mario Andretti	.40	.18
❑ 4 Arie Luyendyk	.25	.11
❑ 5 Gary Bettenhausen	.25	.11
❑ 6 Michael Andretti	.60	.25
❑ 7 Scott Brayton	.15	.07
❑ 8 Danny Sullivan	.25	.11
❑ 9 Rick Mears	.40	.18
❑ 10 Bobby Rahal	.25	.11
❑ 11 Emerson Fittipaldi	.40	.18
❑ 12 Al Unser Jr.	.40	.18
❑ 13 Stan Fox	.15	.07
❑ 14 John Andretti	.40	.18
❑ 15 Eric Bachelart	.15	.07
❑ 16 Philippe Gache	.15	.07
❑ 17 Scott Pruett	.15	.07
❑ 18 John Paul Jr.	.15	.07
❑ 19 Paul Tracy	.25	.11
❑ 20 Jeff Andretti	.40	.18
❑ 21 Jim Crawford	.15	.07
❑ 22 Al Unser	.25	.11
❑ 23 A.J. Foyt	.40	.18
❑ 24 Buddy Lazier	.15	.07
❑ 25 Raul Boesel	.15	.07
❑ 26 Brian Bonner	.15	.07
❑ 27 Lyn St. James	.25	.11
❑ 28 Jimmy Vasser	.15	.07
❑ 29 Dominic Dobson	.15	.07
❑ 30 Tom Sneva	.25	.11
❑ 31 Gordon Johncock	.25	.11
❑ 32 Ted Prappas	.15	.07
❑ 33 Scott Goodyear	.15	.07
❑ 34 Al Unser Jr.	.40	.18
Indy Champ		
❑ 35 Roberto Guerrero	.25	.11
Pole Win		
❑ 36 Al Unser Jr.	.40	.18
❑ 37 Scott Goodyear	.15	.07
❑ 38 Al Unser	.25	.11
❑ 39 Eddie Cheever	.15	.07
❑ 40 Danny Sullivan	.25	.11
❑ 41 Bobby Rahal	.25	.11
❑ 42 Raul Boesel	.15	.07
❑ 43 John Andretti	.40	.18
❑ 44 A.J. Foyt	.40	.18
❑ 45 John Paul Jr.	.15	.07
❑ 46 Lyn St. James	.25	.11
❑ 47 Dominic Dobson	.15	.07
❑ 48 Michael Andretti	.60	.25
❑ 49 Buddy Lazier	.15	.07
❑ 50 Arie Luyendyk	.25	.11
❑ 51 Ted Prappas	.15	.07
❑ 52 Gary Bettenhausen	.25	.11
❑ 53 Jeff Andretti	.40	.18
❑ 54 Brian Bonner	.15	.07
❑ 55 Paul Tracy	.25	.11
❑ 56 Jimmy Vasser	.15	.07
❑ 57 Scott Brayton	.15	.07
❑ 58 Mario Andretti	.40	.18
❑ 59 Emerson Fittipaldi	.40	.18
❑ 60 Jim Crawford	.15	.07
❑ 61 Rick Mears	.40	.18
❑ 62 Stan Fox	.15	.07
❑ 63 Philippe Gache	.15	.07
❑ 64 Gordon Johncock	.25	.11
❑ 65 Scott Pruett	.15	.07
❑ 66 Tom Sneva	.25	.11
❑ 67 Eric Bachelart	.15	.07
❑ 68 Roberto Guerrero	.25	.11
❑ 69 1992 Pace Car	.15	.07
❑ 70 Roberto Guerrero	.15	.07
Eddie Cheever		
Mario Andretti		
❑ 71 Mario Andretti's Car	.15	.07
Michael Andretti's Car		
❑ 72 Al Unser Jr.'s Car	.15	.07
❑ 73 Race Start	.15	.07
❑ 74 Pit Crew Practice	.15	.07
❑ 75 Tom Sneva's Car	.15	.07
Jimmy Vasser's Car		
❑ 76 Nelson Piquet's Car	.15	.07
❑ 77 Gordon Johncock's Car	.15	.07
❑ 78 Protective Coverings	.15	.07
Pit Row		
❑ 79 Eric Bachelart's Car	.15	.07
❑ 80 Race Accidents	.15	.07
❑ 81 Checklist Card	.15	.07

1993 Hi-Tech Indy Checkered Flag Finishers

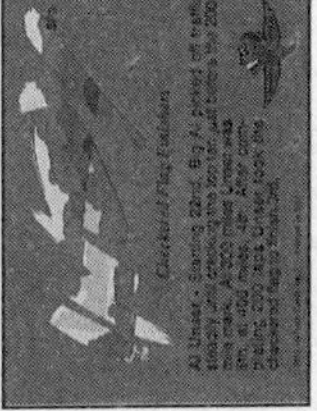

Randomly inserted in 1993 Hi-Tech Indy packs, these 12-

cards feature top drivers printed on holographic foil card stock.

	MINT	NRMT
COMPLETE SET (12)	30.00	13.50
COMMON CARD (SP1-SP12)	2.00	.90
❑ SP1 Al Unser Jr.	3.00	1.35
❑ SP2 Scott Goodyear	2.00	.90
❑ SP3 Al Unser	3.00	1.35
❑ SP4 Eddie Cheever	2.00	.90
❑ SP5 Danny Sullivan	3.00	1.35
❑ SP6 Bobby Rahal	3.00	1.35
❑ SP7 Raul Boesel	2.00	.90
❑ SP8 John Andretti	3.00	1.35
❑ SP9 A.J. Foyt	3.00	1.35
❑ SP10 John Paul Jr.	2.00	.90
❑ SP11 Lyn St. James	2.00	.90
❑ SP12 Dominic Dobson	2.00	.90

1994 Hi-Tech Indy

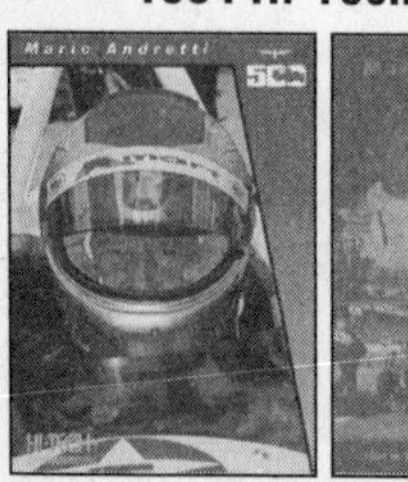

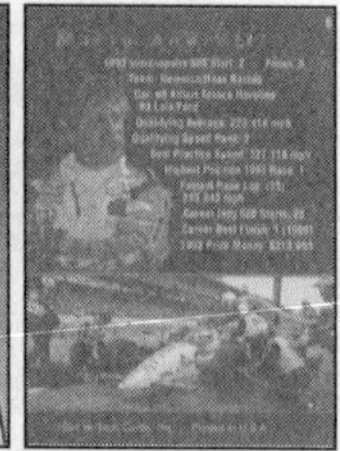

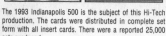

The 1993 Indianapolis 500 is the subject of this Hi-Tech production. The cards were distributed in complete set form with all insert cards. There were a reported 25,000 sets produced.

	MINT	NRMT
COMPLETE SET (51)	8.00	3.60
COMMON CARD (1-51)	.15	.07
❑ 1 Cover Card Emerson Fittipaldi	.15	.07
❑ 2 Emerson Fittipaldi	.40	.18
❑ 3 Arie Luyendyk's Car	.15	.07
❑ 4 Nigel Mansell	.50	.23
❑ 5 Raul Boesel's Car	.15	.07
❑ 6 Mario Andretti	.40	.18
❑ 7 Scott Brayton's Car	.15	.07
❑ 8 Scott Goodyear	.15	.07
❑ 9 Al Unser Jr.	.40	.18
❑ 10 Teo Fabi's Car	.15	.07
❑ 11 John Andretti	.40	.18
❑ 12 Stefan Johansson	.15	.07
❑ 13 Al Unser	.40	.18
❑ 14 Jimmy Vasser	.15	.07
❑ 15 Kevin Cogan	.15	.07
❑ 16 Davy Jones	.15	.07
❑ 17 Eddie Cheever in Pits	.15	.07
❑ 18 Gary Bettenhausen	.25	.11
❑ 19 Hiro Matsushita's Car	.15	.07
❑ 20 Stephan Gregoire in Pits	.15	.07
❑ 21 Tony Bettenhausen's Car	.15	.07
❑ 22 Willy T. Ribbs	.15	.07
❑ 23 Didier Theys' Car	.15	.07
❑ 24 Dominic Dobson	.15	.07
❑ 25 Jim Crawford	.15	.07
❑ 26 Lyn St. James	.40	.18
❑ 27 Geoff Brabham's Car	.15	.07
❑ 28 Robby Gordon's Car	.15	.07
❑ 29 Roberto Guerrero	.15	.07
❑ 30 Jeff Andretti's Car	.15	.07
❑ 31 Paul Tracy	.25	.11
❑ 32 Stan Fox in Pits	.15	.07
❑ 33 Nelson Piquet	.15	.07
❑ 34 Danny Sullivan	.25	.11
❑ 35 Mark Smith	.15	.07
❑ 36 Bobby Rahal	.40	.18
❑ 37 Stephan Gregoire Nelson Piquet Robby Gordon Stefan Johansson Nigel Mansell 1993 Rookies	.15	.07
❑ 38 A.J. Foyt's Car Foyt Salute	.25	.11
❑ 39 Arie Luyendyk Pole Win	.15	.07
❑ 40 Arie Luyendyk Mario Andretti Raul Boesel	.40	.18
❑ 41 The Staring Grid	.15	.07
❑ 42 Arie Luyendyk's Car Mario Andretti's Car Raul Boesel's Car Pace Lap	.15	.07
❑ 43 The Start Indy 500	.15	.07
❑ 44 Pit Action	.15	.07
❑ 45 Nigel Mansell in Pits	.15	.07
❑ 46 Jeff Andretti's Car Roberto Guerrero's Car Crash	.15	.07
❑ 47 Emerson Fittipaldi's Car Checkered Flag	.15	.07
❑ 48 Emerson Fittipaldi Winner	.15	.07
❑ 49 Rick Mears Brian Armenoff Race Rick Contest	.15	.07
❑ 50 Brian Armenoff	.15	.07
❑ 51 Checklist Card	.15	.07

1994 Hi-Tech Indy Championship Drivers

Inserted one set per 1994 Hi-Tech Indy factory set, these cards feature top IndyCar drivers with extensive biographical information on the cardback.

	MINT	NRMT
COMPLETE SET (36)	15.00	6.75
COMMON CARD (CD1-CD36)	.50	.23
❑ CD1 Jeff Andretti	.50	.23
❑ CD2 John Andretti	.75	.35
❑ CD3 Mario Andretti	.75	.35
❑ CD4 Michael Andretti	.75	.35
❑ CD5 Ross Bentley	.50	.23
❑ CD6 Gary Bettenhausen	.50	.23
❑ CD7 Raul Boesel	.50	.23
❑ CD8 Scott Brayton	.50	.23
❑ CD9 Robbie Buhl	.50	.23
❑ CD10 Eddie Cheever	.50	.23
❑ CD11 Jim Crawford	.50	.23
❑ CD12 Dominic Dobson	.50	.23
❑ CD13 Emerson Fittipaldi	.75	.35
❑ CD14 A.J. Foyt	.75	.35
❑ CD15 Stan Fox	.50	.23
❑ CD16 Scott Goodyear	.50	.23
❑ CD17 Mike Groff	.50	.23
❑ CD18 Roberto Guerrero	.50	.23
❑ CD19 Stefan Johansson	.50	.23
❑ CD20 Gordon Johncock	.50	.23
❑ CD21 Buddy Lazier	.50	.23
❑ CD22 Arie Luyendyk	.50	.23
❑ CD23 Rick Mears	.75	.35
❑ CD24 Johnny Parsons Jr.	.50	.23
❑ CD25 Ted Prappas	.50	.23
❑ CD26 Scott Pruett	.50	.23
❑ CD27 Bobby Rahal	.75	.35
❑ CD28 Johnny Rutherford	.75	.35
❑ CD29 Lyn St. James	.75	.35
❑ CD30 Mark Smith	.50	.23
❑ CD31 Tom Sneva	.50	.23
❑ CD32 Danny Sullivan	.75	.35
❑ CD33 Didier Theys	.50	.23
❑ CD34 Paul Tracy	.75	.35
❑ CD35 Al Unser Jr.	.50	.23
❑ CD36 Jimmy Vasser	.50	.23

1994 Hi-Tech Indy A.J. Foyt

A.J.Foyt is the focus of this Hi-Tech issue. The cards were inserted one set per 1994 Hi-Tech Indy factory set and highlight Foyt's first and last races, as well as h wins at IMS.

	MINT
COMPLETE SET (6)	5.00
COMMON CARD (AJ1-AJ6)	1.00
❑ AJ1 A.J.Foyt	1.00
❑ AJ2 A.J.Foyt	1.00
❑ AJ3 A.J.Foyt	1.00
❑ AJ4 A.J.Foyt	1.00
❑ AJ5 A.J.Foyt	1.00
❑ AJ6 A.J.Foyt	1.00

1994 Hi-Tech Indy Rick Me

Rick Mears is the focus of this Hi-Tech issue. The were inserted one set per 1994 Hi-Tech factory s highlight Mears' first and last races, as well as h wins at IMS.

	MINT
COMPLETE SET (6)	5.00
COMMON CARD (RM1-RM6)	1.00
❑ RM1 Rick Mears	1.00
❑ RM2 Rick Mears	1.00
❑ RM3 Rick Mears	1.00
❑ RM4 Rick Mears	1.00
❑ RM5 Rick Mears	1.00
❑ RM6 Rick Mears	1.00

1995 Hi-Tech Indy Championship Drivers

This 11-card set features some of the top drivers IndyCar circuit. The sets were sold in complete set Indianapolis Motor Speedway. They were also available to Hi-Tech Club members.

	MINT
COMPLETE SET (11)	15.00
COMMON CARD (CD1-CD11)	.75
❑ CD1 Al Unser Jr.	2.00
❑ CD2 Eddie Cheever	.75
❑ CD3 Emerson Fittipaldi	2.00
❑ CD4 Scott Pruett	.75
❑ CD5 Raul Boesel	.75
❑ CD6 Paul Tracy	1.25
❑ CD7 Jacques Villeneuve	2.00
❑ CD8 Michael Andretti	2.00
❑ CD9 Danny Sullivan	1.25
❑ CD10 Paul Newman	2.00
❑ CD11 Mario Andretti	2.00

1997 Hi-Tech IRL

This set commemorates the first season of th Racing League. The set comes in a box that cont 94 cards and a Dodge Viper Pace Car die-cast. The different sets within the box. The 37-card ba features drivers from the IRL circuit. The 20-car 500 set features the 80th Anniversary of the Ind There was also a 10-card Disney 200 set, a nin Phoenix set, a eight-card tribute to Scott Brayton eight-card set featuring the Dodge Viper. This p

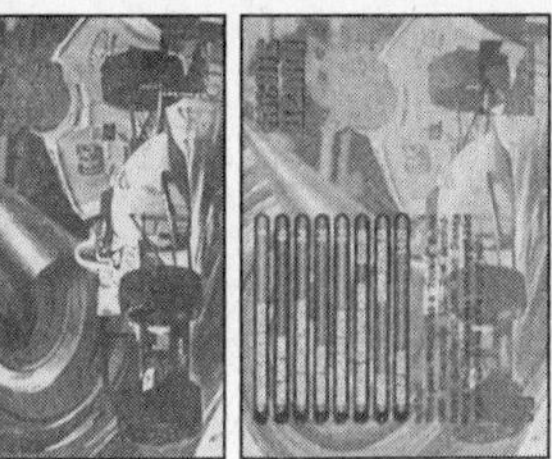

·sed out through retail outlets only a few months release to the hobby.

	MINT	NRMT
ETE SET (94)	20.00	9.00
' (38)	10.00	4.50
IDY 500 SET (20)	6.00	2.70
X/DISNEY SET (20)	4.00	1.80
BRAYTON (8)	1.25	.55
'ACE CAR (8)	.40	.18

	MINT	NRMT
Cover Card	.20	.09
·tt Sharp	.30	.14
z Calkins	.30	.14
)bie Buhl	.30	.14
nie Hearn	.30	.14
)erto Guerrero	.30	.14
e Groff	.30	.14
· Luyendyk	.30	.14
y Stewart	.40	.18
ivey Hamilton	.20	.09
hnny O'Connell	.20	.09
chele Alboreto	.20	.09
n St.James	.40	.18
ephan Gregoire	.20	.09
iddy Lazier	.30	.14
hn Paul Jr.	.20	.09
die Cheever	.20	.09
hnny Parsons	.20	.09
ott Brayton	.40	.18
vid Kudrave	.20	.09
chel Jourdain	.20	.09
n Guthrie	.20	.09
rmin Velez	.20	.09
seo Salazar	.20	.09
hnny Unser	.20	.09
an Wattles	.20	.09
vy Jones	.30	.14
ul Durant	.20	.09
ssandro Zampedri	.20	.09
nny Ongais	.20	.09
deshi Matsuda	.20	.09
ott Harrington	.20	.09
cin Gardner	.20	.09
rk Dismore	.20	.09
e Gosek	.20	.09
ad Murphey	.20	.09
rco Greco	.20	.09
Checklist	.20	.09

1991 K-Mart

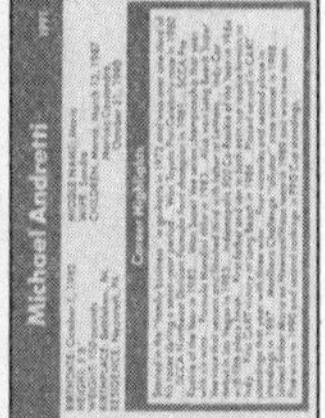

)roduced and distributed this two card set in 1991 ; the K-Mart/Texaco Havoline sponsored IndyCar 'eam.

	MINT	NRMT
ETE SET (2)	3.00	1.35
N CARD	1.00	.45

	MINT	NRMT
o Andretti	2.00	.90
nael Andretti	1.00	.45

1992 K-Mart

· card set was produced and distributed by K-Mart n 1992. It features the K-Mart/Texaco Havoline ed IndyCar Racing Team.

	MINT	NRMT
COMPLETE SET (2)	3.00	1.35
COMMON CARD	1.00	.45

	MINT	NRMT
❑ 1 Mario Andretti	2.00	.90
❑ 2 Michael Andretti	1.00	.45

1993 K-Mart

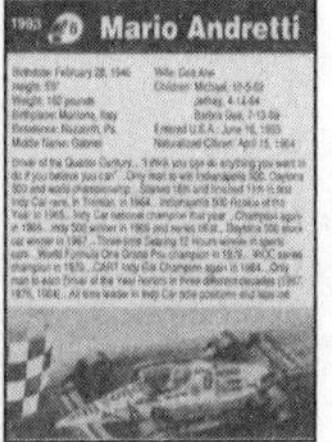

K-Mart produced and distributed this two card set in 1992 featuring the K-Mart/Texaco Havoline sponsored IndyCar Racing Team. The cards are distinguishable by the silver border.

	MINT	NRMT
COMPLETE SET (2)	3.00	1.35
COMMON CARD	1.00	.45

	MINT	NRMT
❑ 1 Mario Andretti	2.00	.90
❑ 2 Nigel Mansell	1.00	.45

1994 K-Mart

Silver and black borders help distinguish the fourth K-Mart issue from the previous three releases. It again features the K-Mart/Texaco Havoline sponsored IndyCar Racing Team headlined by Mario Andretti.

	MINT	NRMT
COMPLETE SET (2)	3.00	1.35
COMMON CARD	1.00	.45

	MINT	NRMT
❑ 1 Mario Andretti	2.00	.90
❑ 2 Nigel Mansell	1.00	.45

1991 Langenberg American IndyCar Series

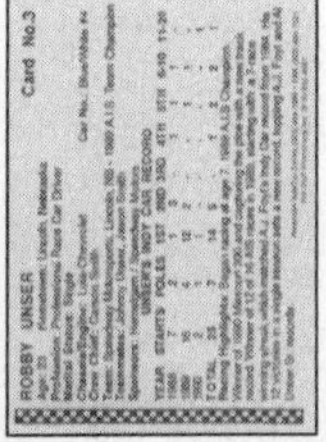

Langenberg Racing produced this set entitled 1991 Hot Stuff. The set features then present and past drivers of the American IndyCar Series. The set features the only Unser to run at the IRL's 1996 Indy 500, Johnny. The set also includes Rodger Ward, the winner of the 1959 and 1962 Indy 500.

	MINT	NRMT
COMPLETE SET (18)	10.00	4.50
COMMON CARD (1-18)	.35	.16

	MINT	NRMT
❑ 1 Cover Card Bill Tempero's Car	.35	.16
❑ 2 Bill Tempero	.50	.23
❑ 3 Robby Unser in Car	.75	.35
❑ 4 Johnny Unser	.75	.35
❑ 5 Jimmy Santos	.50	.23
❑ 6 Rick Sutherland	.50	.23
❑ 7 Jim Buick	.50	.23
❑ 8 Eddie Miller	.50	.23
❑ 9 Bob Tankersley	.50	.23
❑ 10 Bill Hansen	.50	.23
❑ 11 Rocco Desimone	.50	.23
❑ 12 Don Johnson	.50	.23
❑ 13 Ken Petrie	.50	.23
❑ 14 Kevin Whitesides	.50	.23
❑ 15 Ken Petrie's Car Eddie Miller's Car	.50	.23
❑ 16 Todd Snyder's Car Robby Unser's Car	.75	.35
❑ 17 Rodger Ward	.75	.35
❑ 18 Checklist Card 1991 Schedule on back	.35	.16

1991 Legends of Indy

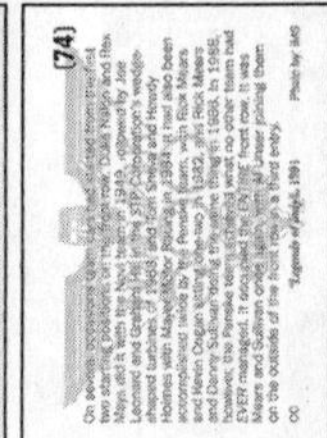

The first of two Legends of Indy sets was produced in 1991 by Collegiate Collection of Kentucky to celebrate the 75th Indy 500. The cards were distributed in complete set form and features past and present stars of the IndyCar circuit. An album to house the cards was also produced and originally sold for $8.95 plus $2.50 shipping.

	MINT	NRMT
COMPLETE SET (100)	15.00	6.75
COMMON CARD (1-100)	.10	.05
COMMON DRIVER (1-100)	.15	.07

	MINT	NRMT
❑ 1 The Start	.10	.05
❑ 2 Largest Starting Field 1933 field	.10	.05
❑ 3 Norman Batten	.10	.05
❑ 4 Parnelli Jones' Car A Turbine Almost Wins	.15	.07
❑ 5 Paul Russo's Car Fageol's Twin Coach Special	.10	.05
❑ 6 Eddie Sachs' Car A.J.Foyt's Car The Sachs/Foyt Duel	.10	.05
❑ 7 Transporters	.10	.05
❑ 8 Bill Holland's Car Mauri Rose's Car Holland and the EZY sign	.10	.05
❑ 9 Carl Graham Fisher Arthur Newby Frank Wheeler James Allison The Track Founders	.10	.05
❑ 10 New Garage Area	.10	.05
❑ 11 The Brick Surface	.10	.05
❑ 12 Jim Clark's Car Rear-Engine Almost Wins	.10	.05
❑ 13 First Rear Engine to Start 1939 Rear-Engine Car	.10	.05
❑ 14 Ralph dePalma in Pits	.10	.05
❑ 15 Mary Fendrich Hulman	.10	.05
❑ 16 Pete DePaolo	.15	.07
❑ 17 Johnnie Parsons' Car	.10	.05
❑ 18 Lee Wallard Cinderella Man	.15	.07
❑ 19 Arie Luyendyk's Car Fastest 500	.30	.14
❑ 20 Sam Hanks' Car Wins with an Experiment	.10	.05
❑ 21 Pre-500 Garage Area	.10	.05

❑ 22 The 1911 Front Row .10 .05
❑ 23 First Pace Car .10 .05
1911 race
❑ 24 Pit Stop .10 .05
3 Bud Car
❑ 25 Jules Goux w/Car .15 .07
❑ 26 Economical Maxwell .10 .05
❑ 27 Tony Hulman .10 .05
Luke Walton
❑ 28 Freddie Agabashian's Car .10 .05
A Diesel On The Pole
❑ 29 Tommy Milton .15 .07
Louis Meyer
Presentation Pace Car
❑ 30 Wilbur Shaw .15 .07
❑ 31 Rick Mears' Car .30 .14
Rick's Records
❑ 32 Eddie Rickenbacker .15 .07
Tony Hulman
❑ 33 Lou Moore's Car .10 .05
❑ 34 Dale Evans' Car .10 .05
❑ 35 Duke Nalon's Crash .15 .07
Duke's Lucky Escape
❑ 36 Tangled Start .10 .05
❑ 37 Wilbur Shaw's Crash .15 .07
Shaw Clears the Wall
❑ 38 Early Effort By Ford .10 .05
❑ 39 Rick Mears' Car .30 .14
Gordon Johncock's Car
The Closest Finish
❑ 40 Sampson Special .10 .05
❑ 41 Chester Gardner's Car .10 .05
Fuel Consumption
❑ 42 Jack Brabham's Car .10 .05
❑ 43 Parnelli Jones w/Crew .30 .14
The First 150
❑ 44 Billy Devore's Car .10 .05
The Six-Wheeler
❑ 45 Joe Leonard's Car .15 .07
Turbine Almost Wins
❑ 46 Bobby Unser w/Car .50 .23
❑ 47 Chester Miller w/Car .15 .07
A Hopped-Up Model T
❑ 48 Danny Sullivan's Car .30 .14
❑ 49 Speedway's First Event .10 .05
❑ 50 Motorcycles .10 .05
❑ 51 Bobby Rahal's Car .30 .14
Rick Mears' Car
Kevin Cogan's Car
The Closest Finish
❑ 52 The Stutz Team .10 .05
❑ 53 Chet Miller's Car .10 .05
❑ 54 Garage Fire .10 .05
❑ 55 Bobby Johns' Car .10 .05
Smokey's Sidecar
❑ 56 Brick to Asphalt .10 .05
❑ 57 Jim Clark's Car .15 .07
Rear-Engine Win
❑ 58 New Tower & Pit Lane .10 .05
❑ 59 Al Unser Jr.'s Car 1.00 .45
Emerson Fittipaldi's Car
Emmo And Little Al
❑ 60 Dave Lewis' Car .10 .05
500's First Front Drive
❑ 61 Streamliners .10 .05
❑ 62 Tom Sneva w/Crew .30 .14
❑ 63 Studebakers .10 .05
❑ 64 Old Victory Lane .10 .05
❑ 65 Tony Hulman .50 .23
A.J.Foyt
Lap Of Honor
❑ 66 Janet Guthrie w/Car .50 .23
❑ 67 The 1923 Lineup .10 .05
❑ 68 Emerson Fittipaldi w/Car .75 .35
Winning A Million
❑ 69 Balloons .10 .05
❑ 70 Bobby Unser's Car .30 .14
Winning In The Rain
❑ 71 Al Unser's Car .50 .23
Upset Winner
❑ 72 Troy Ruttman's Car .10 .05
❑ 73 Louis Schwitzer's Car .10 .05
Speedway's First Race
❑ 74 Rick Mears' Car .50 .23
Danny Sullivan's Car
Al Unser's Car
The '88 Front Row
❑ 75 Ralph dePalma w/Car .15 .07
dePalma Pushes Home
❑ 76 Bill Vukovich's Car .15 .07
Jimmy Bryan's Car
Vuky Laps the Field
❑ 77 Drivers' Meeting .10 .05
❑ 78 The Pagoda .10 .05
❑ 79 The Old Front Gate .10 .05
❑ 80 Tom Sneva's Car .30 .14
Garage Doors
❑ 81 Aerial View, 1922 .10 .05
❑ 82 Aerial View Today .10 .05
❑ 83 Jimmy Murphy's Car .15 .07
First Winner from the Pole
❑ 84 Hall Of Fame Museum .10 .05
❑ 85 Jim Rathmann's Car .15 .07
Rodger Ward's Car
Rathmann/Ward Duel
❑ 86 Mario Andretti 1.00 .45
Andy Granatelli
Mario Wins For Andy
❑ 87 Ray Harroun's Car .10 .05
The Marmon Wasp
❑ 88 Johnny Rutherford's Car .30 .14
Three For JR
❑ 89 Paul Russo's Car .10 .05
The Novi
❑ 90 Bleak Days .10 .05
❑ 91 A Winter's Scene .10 .05
❑ 92 Fact Card .10 .05
❑ 93 Fact Card .10 .05
❑ 94 Fact Card .10 .05
❑ 95 Fact Card .10 .05
❑ 96 Fact Card .10 .05
❑ 97 Fact Card .10 .05
❑ 98 Fact Card .10 .05
❑ 99 Fact Card .10 .05
❑ 100 Cover Card .10 .05
1991 Winner card offer on back

1992 Legends of Indy

The last of two Legends of Indy sets was produced in 1992 by G.S.S. of Indiana to celebrate the Indy 500. The cards were distributed in 10-card packs and feature past and present stars of the IndyCar circuit. Factory sets numbered of 25,000 were wrapped in a blister type packaging. An album to house the cards was also produced and offered for sale, along with the 1991 card album, for $9.95 plus $2.50 shipping. The coupon for the album offer also contained an offer to purchase complete sets of the 1991 series at $14.95 plus $3.50 shipping.

	MINT	NRMT
COMPLETE SET (100)	10.00	4.50
COMMON CARD (1-100)	.10	.05
COMMON DRIVER (1-100)	.15	.07

❑ 1 Rick Mears .25 .11
Four Time Winner
❑ 2 Rick Mears' Car .15 .07
❑ 3 Michael Andretti's Car .25 .11
❑ 4 Arie Luyendyk's Car .15 .07
❑ 5 Al Unser Jr.'s Car .25 .11
❑ 6 John Andretti's Car .15 .07
❑ 7 Gordon Johncock's Car .10 .05
❑ 8 Mario Andretti's Car .30 .14
❑ 9 Stan Fox's Car .10 .05
❑ 10 Tony Bettenhausen in Pits .10 .05
❑ 11 Danny Sullivan's Car .10 .05
❑ 12 Emerson Fittipaldi's Car .15 .07
❑ 13 Scott Pruett's Car .10 .05
❑ 14 Dominic Dobson's Car .10 .05
❑ 15 Randy Lewis's Car .10 .05
❑ 16 Jeff Andretti's Car .10 .05
❑ 17 Hiro Matsushita's Car .10 .05
❑ 18 Scott Brayton's Car .10 .05
❑ 19 Bernard Jourdain's Car .10 .05
❑ 20 Bobby Rahal in Pits .15 .07
❑ 21 Geoff Brabham's Car .10 .05
❑ 22 Pancho Carter's Car .10 .05
❑ 23 Gary Bettenhausen's Car .10 .05
❑ 24 Tero Palmroth's Car .10 .05
❑ 25 Mike Groff's Car .10 .05
❑ 26 John Paul Jr.'s Car .10 .05
❑ 27 Jim Crawford's Car .10 .05
❑ 28 Scott Goodyear's Car .10 .05
❑ 29 A.J. Foyt Jr.'s Car .25 .11
❑ 30 Kevin Cogan's Car .10 .05
❑ 31 Roberto Guerrero's Car .10 .05
❑ 32 Eddie Cheever's Car .10 .05
❑ 33 Willy T. Ribbs's Car .10 .05
❑ 34 Buddy Lazier's Car .10 .05
❑ 35 Hiro Matsushita's Car .10 .05
❑ 36 Willy T. Ribbs .10
❑ 37 Arie Luyendyk .15
with Dan Quayle
Special Visitor
❑ 38 Danny Sullivan's Car .10
❑ 39 1991 Pace Car .10
❑ 40 John Andretti's Car .15
Scott Pruett's Car
Gordon Johncock's Car
Race Action
❑ 41 The General .10
Norman Schwarzkopf
❑ 42 Rick Mears' Car .15
Michael Andretti's Car
❑ 43 Rick Mears' Car .15
A.J.Foyt's Car
Mario Andretti's Car
Illustrious Front Row
❑ 44 Rick Mears' Car .15
Checker for Mears
❑ 45 1991 Start .10
❑ 46 A.J.Foyt's Car .15
Ovation for A.J.
❑ 47 1980 Pace Car .10
❑ 48 1981 Pace Car .10
❑ 49 1982 Pace Car .10
❑ 50 1983 Pace Car .10
❑ 51 1984 Pace Car .10
❑ 52 1985 Pace Car .10
❑ 53 1986 Pace Car .10
❑ 54 1987 Pace Car .10
❑ 55 1988 Pace Car .10
❑ 56 1989 Pace Car .10
❑ 57 A.J.Foyt w/Car .25
Tony George
A.J.Foyt 's 34TH
❑ 58 Mario Andretti's Car .25
Dihedral Wings
❑ 59 Hall of Fame Museum .10
❑ 60 Alberto Ascari's Car .10
Ferrari At Indy
❑ 61 Janet Guthrie .15
Dick Simon
Janet Qualifies
❑ 62 Al Unser's Car .15
Yard of Bricks
❑ 63 1968 Pace Lap .10
❑ 64 A.J.Foyt's Car .25
Johnny Rutherford's Car
Two Tough Texans
❑ 65 Yellow Flag .10
❑ 66 How They Line Up .10
❑ 67 Pre-Race Laps .10
❑ 68 1969 Start .10
❑ 69 Mario Andretti's Car .25
Mario's Backup Wins
❑ 70 Joe Leonard in Pits .10
with Andy Granatelli
Leonard Pit Stop
❑ 71 Parnelli Jones' Car .10
Don Branson's Car
Jim Hurtubise's Car
1963 Front Row
❑ 72 Al Unser's Car .15
Victory Lane is Moved
❑ 73 Tommy Milton .10
Harry Stutz
Howdy Wilcox
with cars
HCS Specials
❑ 74 Chet Miller's Car .10
Front Drive Novis
❑ 75 Peter Revson w/Car .10
Revson's Upset
❑ 76 Danny Sullivan's Car .15
Mario Andretti's Car
❑ 77 Lloyd Ruby in Pits .10
❑ 78 Tom Sneva's Car .10
Al Unser's Car
Al Unser Jr.'s Car
Sneva's Dilemma
❑ 79 Eddie Sachs .10
Eddie and His Wheel
❑ 80 Dan Gurney's Car .10
Dan and Mickey's Debut
❑ 81 Mark Donohue's Car .10
❑ 82 Duane Carter Sr.'s Car .10
Low-Profile Tires
❑ 83 Balloons .10
❑ 84 Tom Sneva's Car .10
Danny Ongais' Car
Rick Mears' Car
200 MPH Front Row
❑ 85 Pit Stops .10
❑ 86 Pat Flaherty .10
Winning in a T-Shirt
❑ 87 Victory Circle .10
❑ 88 Mike Mosley's Car .10

Tom Sneva's Car		
Tom Bigelow's Car		
Scott Brayton's Car		
Turn One Parking		
obby Rahal	.25	.11
Victory Circle Baby		
ordon Johncock w/Car	.15	.07
'77 Heatbreak		
oger McCluskey's Car	.10	.05
Aerodynamic Experiment		
arnelli Jones in Pits	.15	.07
Andy Granatelli		
Parnelli and the Turbine		
911 Lineup	.10	.05
ill Cheesbourg's Car	.10	.05
Twin Porsche		
obby Rahal's Car	.15	.07
Kevin Cogan's Car		
Race to the Checker		
ony Bettenhausen	.10	.05
Paul Russo		
Relief Drivers		
arnelli Jones' Car	.10	.05
Famous Smokestack		
ld Main Entrance	.10	.05
am Hanks	.10	.05
Jimmy Bryan Car		
1957/58 Winner		
Checklist Card	.10	.05
lichael Andretti's Car	2.00	.90
Prototype Card		

1992 Limited Appeal Formula One

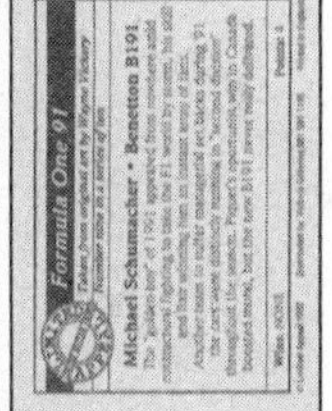

' ten of the top 1991 Formula One drivers are the d subject of this set produced by Limited Appeal of d. The cardfronts include a color photo in an ve white ghosted-out border. The backs include nformation from the 1991 season and carry a 1992 opyright line. The unnumbered cards are listed alphabetically and were released as a complete set Mansell featured on set wrapper).

	MINT	NRMT
ETE SET (10)	10.00	4.50
ON CARD (1-10)	.75	.35
rk Blundell	.75	.35
n Capelli	.75	.35
k Comas	.75	.35
drea deCesaris	.75	.35
ka Hakkinen	.75	.35
el Mansell	1.50	.70
fano Modena	.75	.35
in Prost	1.00	.45
chael Schumacher	2.00	.90
yrton Senna	2.50	1.10

1962 Marhoefer Indy

fer Meats of Muncie Indiana distributed this Indy in 1962 through its various meat products. The eature top IndyCar drivers in black and white As is common with most issues distributed with oducts, the cards were produced with a wax film g and are often found with product stains. The unnumbered cards are oversized (approximately 4" by 5-1/4") and contain rounded corners.

	NRMT	VG-E
COMPLETE SET (16)	500.00	220.00
COMMON CARD	30.00	13.50
❑ 1 Chuck Arnold	30.00	13.50
❑ 2 Don Branson	30.00	13.50
❑ 3 Bob Christie	30.00	13.50
❑ 4 Don Davis	30.00	13.50
❑ 5 A.J.Foyt	60.00	27.00
❑ 6 Elmer George	30.00	13.50
❑ 7 Cliff Griffith	30.00	13.50
❑ 8 Gene Hartley	30.00	13.50
❑ 9 Roger McCluskey	30.00	13.50
❑ 10 Dick Rathmann	30.00	13.50
❑ 11 Lloyd Ruby	30.00	13.50
❑ 12 Eddie Sachs	30.00	13.50
❑ 13 Len Sutton	30.00	13.50
❑ 14 Jack Turner	30.00	13.50
❑ 15 Rodger Ward	35.00	16.00
❑ 16 Wayne Weiler	30.00	13.50

1993 Maxx Williams Racing

This 100-card set was produced by Maxx and features present and past drivers of the Williams Formula One racing team. It was sold through Club Maxx for $14.95 per set.

	MINT	NRMT
COMPLETE SET (100)	18.00	8.00
COMMON CARD (1-100)	.10	.05
COMMON DRIVER (1-100)	.20	.09
❑ 1 Nigel Mansell	.60	.25
❑ 2 Riccardo Patrese	.30	.14
❑ 3 Alain Prost	.30	.14
❑ 4 Damon Hill	.30	.14
❑ 5 Mark Blundell	.20	.09
❑ 6 Thierry Boutsen	.20	.09
❑ 7 Jean-Louis Schlesser	.20	.09
❑ 8 Martin Brundle	.20	.09
❑ 9 Jonathan Palmer	.20	.09
❑ 10 Jacques Laffite	.20	.09
❑ 11 Keke Rosberg	.20	.09
❑ 12 Nelson Piquet	.30	.14
❑ 13 Derek Daly	.20	.09
❑ 14 Carlos Reutemann	.30	.14
❑ 15 Mario Andretti	.60	.25
❑ 16 Alan Jones	.30	.14
❑ 17 Clay Regazzoni	.20	.09
❑ 18 The Helmets	.10	.05
❑ 19 Frank Williams	.20	.09
❑ 20 Patrick Head	.20	.09
❑ 21 Adrian Newey	.20	.09
❑ 22 David Brown	.20	.09
❑ 23 The Conference Centre	.10	.05
❑ 24 The Trophies	.10	.05
❑ 25 The Crash Test	.10	.05
❑ 26 Clay Regazzoni's Car	.10	.05
❑ 27 Alan Jones' Car	.20	.09
❑ 28 Alan Jones' Car	.20	.09
❑ 29 Alan Jones' Car	.20	.09
❑ 30 Alan Jones' Car	.20	.09
❑ 31 Alan Jones' Car	.20	.09
❑ 32 Alan Jones' Car	.20	.09
❑ 33 Alan Jones' Car	.20	.09
❑ 34 Alan Jones' Car	.20	.09
❑ 35 Alan Jones	.30	.14
Jackie Stewart		
❑ 36 Alan Jones' Car	.20	.09
❑ 37 Alan Jones	.30	.14
❑ 38 Alan Jones' Car	.20	.09
❑ 39 Carlos Reutemann's Car	.20	.09
❑ 40 Carlos Reutemann's Car	.20	.09
❑ 41 Alan Jones' Car	.20	.09
❑ 42 Keke Rosberg's Car	.10	.05
❑ 43 Keke Rosberg's Car	.10	.05
❑ 44 Keke Rosberg's Car	.10	.05
❑ 45 Keke Rosberg's Car	.10	.05
❑ 46 Keke Rosberg's Car	.10	.05
❑ 47 Keke Rosberg's Car	.10	.05
❑ 48 Nigel Mansell's Car	.30	.14
❑ 49 Nigel Mansell	.60	.25
❑ 50 Nigel Mansell	.60	.25
❑ 51 Nelson Piquet's Car	.20	.09
❑ 52 Nigel Mansell's Car	.30	.14
❑ 53 Nigel Mansell's Car	.30	.14
❑ 54 Nigel Mansell's Car	.30	.14
❑ 55 Nigel Mansell's Car	.30	.14
❑ 56 Nigel Mansell's Car	.30	.14
❑ 57 Nigel Mansell's Car	.30	.14
❑ 58 Nelson Piquet's Car	.20	.09
❑ 59 Nigel Mansell's Car	.30	.14
❑ 60 Nigel Mansell's Car	.30	.14
❑ 61 Nigel Mansell's Car	.30	.14
❑ 62 Nigel Mansell	.60	.25
❑ 63 Nelson Piquet's Car	.20	.09
❑ 64 Nelson Piquet's Car	.20	.09
❑ 65 Nigel Mansell's Car	.30	.14
❑ 66 Nelson Piquet's Car	.20	.09
❑ 67 Nigel Mansell	.60	.25
❑ 68 Nigel Mansell's Car	.30	.14
❑ 69 Nelson Piquet's Car	.20	.09
❑ 70 Nigel Mansell's Car	.30	.14
❑ 71 Thierry Boutsen's Car	.10	.05
❑ 72 Thierry Boutsen	.30	.14
Riccardo Patrese		
❑ 73 Riccardo Patrese's Car	.20	.09
❑ 74 Thierry Boutsen's Car	.10	.05
❑ 75 Riccardo Patrese's Car	.20	.09
❑ 76 Nigel Mansell's Car	.30	.14
❑ 77 Nigel Mansell's Car	.30	.14
❑ 78 Nigel Mansell's Car	.30	.14
❑ 79 Nigel Mansell's Car	.30	.14
❑ 80 Riccardo Patrese's Car	.20	.09
❑ 81 Nigel Mansell's Car	.30	.14
❑ 82 Nigel Mansell's Car	.30	.14
❑ 83 Nigel Mansell's Car	.30	.14
❑ 84 Nigel Mansell's Car	.30	.14
❑ 85 Nigel Mansell's Car	.30	.14
❑ 86 Nigel Mansell's Car	.30	.14
❑ 87 Riccardo Patrese's Car	.20	.09
❑ 88 Nigel Mansell's Car	.30	.14
❑ 89 Nigel Mansell's Car	.30	.14
❑ 90 Nigel Mansell's Car	.30	.14
❑ 91 Nigel Mansell's Car	.30	.14
❑ 92 Nigel Mansell's Car	.30	.14
❑ 93 Keke Rosberg's Car	.10	.05
❑ 94 Alan Jones' Car	.20	.09
❑ 95 Alan Jones' Car	.20	.09
❑ 96 Nigel Mansell's Car	.30	.14
❑ 97 Ford Cosworth DFV	.10	.05
❑ 98 Honda V6	.10	.05
❑ 99 Judd V8	.10	.05
❑ 100 Renault V10	.10	.05

1971 Mobil The Story of Grand Prix Motor Racing

This 36-card set highlights some of the great drivers and their cars from 1906 to 1969. Famous names like Ralph de Palma and Jackie Stewart are depicted on the fronts of the cards via artist renderings. The set was sponsored by Mobil and issued in Europe.

	MINT	NRMT
COMPLETE SET (36)	25.00	11.00
COMMON CARD (1-36)	.75	.35
❑ 1 Szisz Renault's Car	.75	.35
❑ 2 Felice Nazzaro's Car	.75	.35
❑ 3 C.Lautenschlager's Car	.75	.35
❑ 4 Georges Boillot's Car	.75	.35
❑ 5 C.Lautenschlager's Car	.75	.35
❑ 6 Ralph de Palma's Car	1.50	.70
❑ 7 Jimmy Murphy's Car	.75	.35
❑ 8 P. Bordino's Car	.75	.35
❑ 9 H.Segrave's Car	.75	.35
❑ 10 G.Campari's Car	.75	.35
❑ 11 M.Costantini's Car	.75	.35
❑ 12 R.Benoist's Car	.75	.35
❑ 13 Rene Dreyfus' Car	.75	.35
❑ 14 Sir Henry Birkin's Car	.75	.35
❑ 15 Luigi Fagioli's Car	.75	.35

❑ 16 Tazio Nuvolari's Car	.75	.35
❑ 17 R.Carraciola's Car	.75	.35
❑ 18 Tazio Nuvolari's Car	.75	.35
❑ 19 B.Rosemeyer's Car	.75	.35
❑ 20 Richard Seaman's Car	.75	.35
❑ 21 Louis Chiron's Car	.75	.35
❑ 22 Jean Pierre Wimille's Car	.75	.35
❑ 23 Baron de Graffenried's Car	.75	.35
❑ 24 Giuseppe Farina's Car	.75	.35
❑ 25 Alberto Ascari's Car	.75	.35
❑ 26 Mike Hawthorn's Car	.75	.35
❑ 27 Juan Manuel Fangio's Car	1.00	.45
❑ 28 Tony Brooks's Car	.75	.35
❑ 29 Peter Collins' Car	.75	.35
❑ 30 Juan Manuel Fangio's Car	1.00	.45
❑ 31 Stirling Moss' Car	1.00	.45
❑ 32 Mike Hawthorn's Car	.75	.35
❑ 33 Jack Brabham's Car	.75	.35
❑ 34 Graham Hill's Car	1.00	.45
❑ 35 Jim Clark's Car	.75	.35
❑ 36 Jackie Stewart's Car	1.50	.70

1973 Nabisco Sugar Daddy Speedway Collection

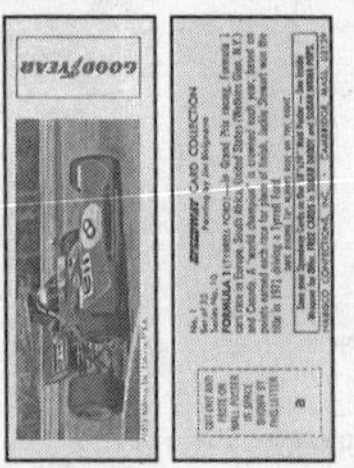

Cards from the Speedway Collection set were inserted into Sugar Daddy and Sugar Mama candies in 1973. A wall poster was also produced that was used by collectors to mount their card sets using the adhesive on the cardbacks.The cards themselves are small (approximately 1" by 2-3/4") and feature art renderings of cars from various auto racing circuits along with a racing sponsor logo on the right side of the cardfront. The sponsor logos were to be cut out and mounted separately to the poster. A few of the cards pertain to a particular driver as noted below. There were also six 5" X 7" premiums also issued with the set. The premium cards were available in the bottom of the Sugar Daddy's boxes. They were printed on text-weight paper and carry a value of approximately $30 - $50 each.

	NRMT	VG-E
COMPLETE SET (25)	700.00	425.00
COMMON CARD (1-25)	25.00	15.00
❑ 1 Jackie Stewart's Car Formula 1	50.00	30.00
❑ 2 Peter Revson's Car Can-Am	25.00	15.00
❑ 3 Mark Donohue's Car AMC Javelin Trans-Am	25.00	15.00
❑ 4 Mario Andretti's Car Jackie Ickx's Car Ferrari 312P IMC	60.00	36.00
❑ 5 Porsche 917 IMC	25.00	15.00
❑ 6 Al Unser's Car Championship	75.00	45.00
❑ 7 A.J.Foyt's Car Stock Car	100.00	60.00
❑ 8 Renault Alpine Rally	25.00	15.00
❑ 9 Ford Bronco Off-Road	25.00	15.00
❑ 10 Datsun 510 2-5 Challenge	25.00	15.00
❑ 11 Ferrari Daytona IMC	25.00	15.00
❑ 12 Volkswagon Bug Off-Road	25.00	15.00
❑ 13 Don Garlits' Car Fuel Dragster	60.00	36.00
❑ 14 Ed McCulloch's Car Funny Car	40.00	24.00
❑ 15 Bill Jenkins' Car Pro Stock Eliminator	25.00	15.00
❑ 16 Fiat Abarth 3000 Hill Climb	25.00	15.00
❑ 17 Corvette A-Production	25.00	15.00
❑ 18 John Morton's Car Datsun 240Z C-Production	25.00	15.00
❑ 19 MK1 Sprite H-Production	25.00	15.00
❑ 20 Blue Flame Land Speed Record	25.00	15.00
❑ 21 Goldenrod Land Speed Record	25.00	15.00
❑ 22 Gary Bettenhausen's Car Sprint Car USAC Sprint	40.00	24.00
❑ 23 David Hobbs' Car McLaren M10B Formula 5000	40.00	24.00
❑ 24 Mach 71 Ford Formula B	25.00	15.00
❑ 25 Lynx-VW Formula Vee	25.00	15.00

1931 Ogden's Motor Races

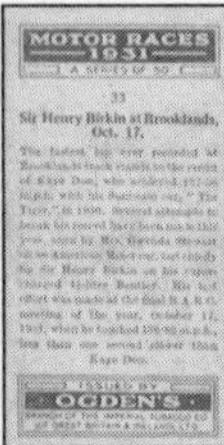

This 50-card series features artist renderings of cars and motorcycles at various racing events in 1931. The cards were produced for Imperial Tobacco Company of Great Britain & Ireland's Ogden cigarettes branch. The cards measure 1 3/8" X 2 5/8". The fronts of the cards depict cars or motorcycles in race action. "Ogden's Cigarettes" and the title and date of the event are on the front of every card. The card backs state at the top "Motor Races 1931" and "A series of 50". This dating gives the specific year all the racing events featured were run. The latest event featured is October 17, 1931, which in turn leads us to believe that the cards were probably not produced or issued until 1932. The cards backs also feature a brief story on the event featured on that card. The bottom of the card backs state "Issued by Ogden's." The series is broken into two groups, automobile races and motorcycle races. Cards 1-33 are the automobile races and cards 34-50 feature the motorcycle races.

	NRMT	VG-E
COMPLETE SET (50)	400.00	240.00
COMMON CARD (1-50)	8.00	4.80
❑ 1 Sir Malcom Campbell Blue Bird, Daytona, Feb 5	12.00	7.25
❑ 2 Swedish Winter Grand Prix Feb. 23	8.00	4.80
❑ 3 Argentine National Grand Prix March	8.00	4.80
❑ 4 Tunis Grand Prix, March 29	8.00	4.80
❑ 5 Austriailian Grand Prix, March	8.00	4.80
❑ 6 The Italian, 1000 Miles Race April 11-12	8.00	4.80
❑ 7 Monaco Grand Prix, April 20	8.00	4.80
❑ 8 The Double Twelve Race Brooklands, May 8-9	8.00	4.80
❑ 10 Grand Prix, Casablanca May 17	8.00	4.80
❑ 11 Italian Grand Prix, Monza May 24	8.00	4.80
❑ 12 The 500 Miles Race Indianapolis, May 30	8.00	4.80
❑ 13 Ernesto Maserati Royal Prix de Roma, June 7	8.00	4.80
❑ 14 Grand Prix d'Endurance LeMans, June 12-13	8.00	4.80
❑ 15 Grand Prix, Automobile Club de France, June 21	8.00	4.80
❑ 16 Southport 100 Mile Race June 27	8.00	4.80
❑ 17 Junior Car Club, High-Speed Trial, July 4	8.00	4.80
❑ 18 Belgian 24-Hours Race July 4-5	8.00	4.80
❑ 19 Irish Grand Prix, Saorstat Cup July 5	8.00	4.80
❑ 20 Irish Grand Prix, Eireann Cup July 6	8.00	4.80
❑ 21 Shelsley Walsh Hill Climb July 11	8.00	4.80
❑ 22 Belgian Grand Prix, July 12	8.00	4.80
❑ 23 Sand Race, Skegness, July 18	8.00	4.80
❑ 24 The German Grand Prix July 19	8.00	4.80
❑ 25 Relay Race, Brooklands July 25	8.00	4.80
❑ 26 Circuit de Dieppe (1500 cc. class), July 26	8.00	4.80
❑ 27 Circuit de Dieppe (over 1500 cc. class), July 26	8.00	4.80
❑ 28 Mile Record, Brooklands August 8	8.00	4.80
❑ 30 Mont Ventoux Hill Climb August 30	8.00	4.80
❑ 31 Monza Grand Prix, Sept. 6	8.00	
❑ 32 Circuit des Routes pavees Sept 13	8.00	
❑ 33 Sir Henry Birkin at Brooklands, Oct. 17	8.00	
❑ 34 The 100-Miles Sand Race Southport, May 9	8.00	
❑ 35 The Austrian Tourist Trophy May 10	8.00	
❑ 36 Junior Motorcycle Tourist Trophy, June 15	8.00	
❑ 37 Lightweight Motorcycle Tourist Trophy, June 17	8.00	
❑ 38 Senior Motorcycle Tourist Trophy, June 19	8.00	
❑ 40 F.I.C.M. Grand Prix (250cc and 500cc Classes), June 28	8.00	
❑ 41 German Grand Prix (500cc class), July 5	8.00	
❑ 42 Dutch Motorcycle Tourist Trophy, July 11	8.00	
❑ 43 Italian Tourist Trophy, July 12	8.00	
❑ 44 Phoenix Park Road Races July 18	8.00	
❑ 45 Belgian Grand Prix, July 19	8.00	
❑ 46 The Dieppe Grand Prix, July	8.00	
❑ 47 Ulster Grand Prix, Sept. 5	8.00	
❑ 48 Swedish Grand Prix, Sept. 6	8.00	
❑ 49 Manx Junior Grand Prix Sept. 8	8.00	
❑ 50 Manx Senior Grand Prix Sept. 10	8.00	

1962 Petpro Limited Gran Prix Racing Cars

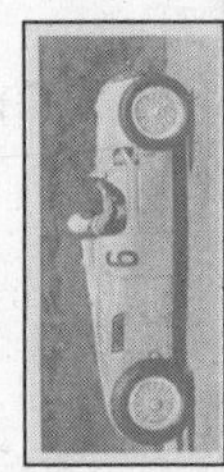

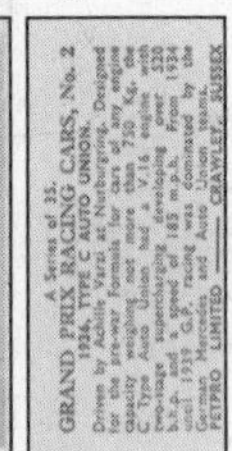

This 35-card set was issued by Petpro Limited of C Sussex England. The cards featue artist paintings o of the top Grand Prix cards than raced between 19 1961. The cards measure 2 1/2" X 1 1/8".

	MINT
COMPLETE SET (35)	30.00
COMMON CARD (1-35)	1.00
❑ 1 Tony Brook's Car	1.00
❑ 2 Achille Varzi's Car	1.00
❑ 3 W.F. Moss' Car	1.00
❑ 4 Tony Rolt's Car	1.00
❑ 5 B. Bira's Car	1.00
❑ 6 Reg Parnell's Car	1.00
❑ 7 Louis Rosier's Car	1.00
❑ 8 Guiseppe Farina's Car	1.00
❑ 9 Guiseppe Farina's Car	1.00
❑ 10 Arthur Dobson's Car	1.00
❑ 11 Joe Kelly's Car	1.00
❑ 12 Peter Whitehead's Car	1.00
❑ 13 Frolian Gonzales' Car	1.00
❑ 14 International Racing Flags	1.00
❑ 15 Lance Macklin's Car	1.00
❑ 16 Mike Hawthorn's Car	1.00
❑ 17 Juan Manuel Fangio's Car	1.50
❑ 18 Ken Wharton's Car	1.00
❑ 19 Tony Rolt's Car	1.00
❑ 20 Jack Brabham's Car	1.00
❑ 21 John Surtees' Car	1.00
❑ 22 Albert Ascari's Car	1.00
❑ 23 Jean Behra's Car	1.00
❑ 24 Karl Kling's Car	1.00
❑ 25 Stirling Moss' Car	2.00
❑ 26 Jean Behra's Car	1.00
❑ 27 Archie Scot Brown's Car	1.00
❑ 28 Froilan Gonzales' Car	1.00
❑ 29 Chuck Daigh's Car	1.00
❑ 30 Jack Brabham's Car	1.00
❑ 31 Jimmy Clark's Car	1.00
❑ 32 Phil Hill's Car	1.00
❑ 33 Joachim Bonnier's Car	1.00
❑ 34 Graham Hill's Car	1.50
❑ 35 Stirling Moss' Car	2.00

91 Pro Tracs Formula One

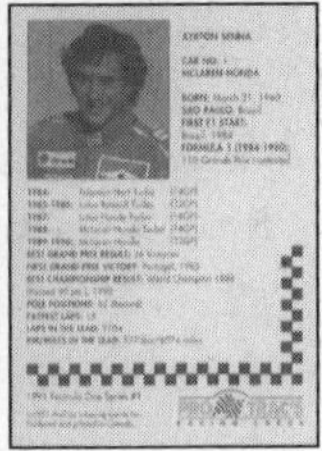

ian based Pro Tracs produced this 1991 issue ıg on Formula One drivers and top F1 teams. The were distributed in 10-card packs with 36-packs per he set is sometimes called Vroom, the name ıed on foil boxes.

	MINT	NRMT
LETE SET (200)	10.00	4.50
ON CARD (1-200)	.05	.02
ON DRIVER (1-200)	.10	.05

rton Senna	.60	.25
rton Senna's Car	.40	.18
rhard Berger	.20	.09
rhard Berger's Car	.10	.05
turo Nakajima	.10	.05
turo Nakajima's Car	.05	.02
efano Modena	.10	.05
efano Modena's Car	.05	.02
gel Mansell	.40	.18
igel Mansell's Car	.20	.09
iccardo Patrese	.20	.09
iccardo Patrese's Car	.10	.05
lartin Brundle	.10	.05
lartin Brundle's Car	.05	.02
lartin Brundle's Car	.05	.02
lark Blundell	.10	.05
lark Blundell's Car	.05	.02
lark Blundell's Car	.05	.02
lichele Alboreto	.10	.05
lichele Alboreto's Car	.05	.02
lichele Alboreto's Car	.05	.02
lex Caffi	.10	.05
lex Caffi's Car	.05	.02
tefan Johansson	.20	.09
tefan Johansson's Car	.10	.05
lika Hakkinen	.10	.05
lika Hakkinen's Car	.05	.02
ulian Bailey	.10	.05
ulian Bailey's Car	.05	.02
ohnny Herbert	.10	.05
ohnny Herbert's Car	.05	.02
livier Grouillard	.10	.05
livier Grouillard's Car	.05	.02
livier Grouillard's Car	.05	.02
lauricio Gugelmin	.10	.05
lauricio Gugelmin's Car	.05	.02
an Capelli	.10	.05
an Capelli's Car	.05	.02
abriele Tarquini	.10	.05
abriele Tarquini's Car	.05	.02
tefan Johansson	.20	.09
tefan Johansson's Car	.10	.05
abrizio Barbazza	.10	.05
abrizio Barbazza's Car	.05	.02
oberto Moreno	.10	.05
oberto Moreno's Car	.05	.02
oberto Moreno's Car	.05	.02
elson Piquet	.20	.09
elson Piquet's Car	.10	.05
elson Piquet's Car	.10	.05
manuele Pirro	.10	.05
manuele Pirro's Car	.05	.02
J. Lehto	.10	.05
J. Lehto's Car	.05	.02
ierluigi Martini	.10	.05
ierluigi Martini's Car	.05	.02
ianni Morbidelli	.10	.05
ianni Morbidelli's Car	.05	.02
hierry Boutsen	.10	.05
hierry Boutsen's Car	.05	.02
rik Comas	.10	.05
rik Comas' Car	.05	.02
lain Prost	.20	.09
lain Prost's Car	.10	.05
ean Alesi	.10	.05
ean Alesi's Car	.05	.02
ric Bernard	.10	.05
ric Bernard's Car	.05	.02
guri Suzuki	.10	.05
guri Suzuki's Car	.05	.02
❑ 71 Pedro Matos Chaves	.10	.05
❑ 72 Pedro Matos Chaves' Car	.05	.02
❑ 73 Bertrand Gachot	.10	.05
❑ 74 Bertrand Gachot's Car	.05	.02
❑ 75 Andrea deCesaris	.10	.05
❑ 76 Andrea deCesaris' Car	.05	.02
❑ 77 Nicola Larini	.10	.05
❑ 78 Nicola Larini's Car	.05	.02
❑ 79 Eric Van de Poele	.10	.05
❑ 80 Eric Van de Poele's Car	.05	.02
❑ 81 USA Race Track	.05	.02
❑ 82 Brazil Race Track	.05	.02
❑ 83 San Marino Race Track	.05	.02
❑ 84 Monaco Race Track	.05	.02
❑ 85 Canada Race Track	.05	.02
❑ 86 Mexico Race Track	.05	.02
❑ 87 France Race Track	.05	.02
❑ 88 Great Britain Track	.05	.02
❑ 89 Germany Race Track	.05	.02
❑ 90 Hungary Race Track	.05	.02
❑ 91 Belgium Race Track	.05	.02
❑ 92 Italy Race Track	.05	.02
❑ 93 Portugal Race Track	.05	.02
❑ 94 Spain Race Track	.05	.02
❑ 95 Japan Race Track	.05	.02
❑ 96 Australia Race Track	.05	.02
❑ 97 Ayrton Senna's Car	.40	.18
❑ 98 Ayrton Senna's Car	.40	.18
❑ 99 Ayrton Senna's Car	.40	.18
❑ 100 Ayrton Senna's Car	.40	.18
❑ 101 Ayrton Senna's Car	.40	.18
❑ 102 Ayrton Senna's Car	.40	.18
❑ 103 Ayrton Senna's Car	.40	.18
❑ 104 Ayrton Senna's Car	.40	.18
❑ 105 Ayrton Senna's Car	.40	.18
❑ 106 Ayrton Senna	.60	.25
❑ 107 Ayrton Senna	.60	.25
❑ 108 Alain Prost	.20	.09
❑ 109 Alain Prost's Car	.10	.05
❑ 110 Alain Prost's Car	.10	.05
❑ 111 Alain Prost's Car	.10	.05
❑ 112 Alain Prost's Car	.10	.05
❑ 113 Alain Prost's Car	.10	.05
❑ 114 Alain Prost's Car	.10	.05
❑ 115 Alain Prost's Car	.10	.05
❑ 116 Alain Prost's Car	.10	.05
❑ 117 Alain Prost's Car	.10	.05
❑ 118 Alain Prost	.20	.09
❑ 119 Alain Prost's Car	.10	.05
❑ 120 Alain Prost	.20	.09
❑ 121 Nigel Mansell's Car	.20	.09
❑ 122 Nigel Mansell's Car	.20	.09
❑ 123 Nigel Mansell's Car	.20	.09
❑ 124 Nigel Mansell's Car	.20	.09
❑ 125 Nigel Mansell's Car	.20	.09
❑ 126 Nigel Mansell's Car	.20	.09
❑ 127 Nigel Mansell's Car	.20	.09
❑ 128 Nigel Mansell's Car	.20	.09
❑ 129 Nigel Mansell's Car	.20	.09
❑ 130 Nigel Mansell's Car	.20	.09
❑ 131 Nigel Mansell	.40	.18
❑ 132 Porsche Engine	.05	.02
❑ 133 Yamaha Engine	.05	.02
❑ 134 Lamborghini Engine	.05	.02
❑ 135 Honda Engine	.05	.02
❑ 136 Ferrari Engine	.05	.02
❑ 137 Ford Engine	.05	.02
❑ 138 Renault Engine	.05	.02
❑ 139 Ilmor Engine	.05	.02
❑ 140 Judd Engine	.05	.02
❑ 141 Judd Engine	.05	.02
❑ 142 Honda Engine	.05	.02
❑ 143 Ford Engine	.05	.02
❑ 144 Ayrton Senna's Car	.40	.18
❑ 145 Alain Prost	.20	.09
❑ 146 Nelson Piquet	.20	.09
❑ 147 Ayrton Senna's Car	.40	.18
❑ 148 Ayrton Senna	.60	.25
❑ 149 Riccardo Patrese's Car	.10	.05
❑ 150 Gerhard Berger's Car	.10	.05
❑ 151 Ayrton Senna	.60	.25
❑ 152 Ayrton Senna's Car	.40	.18
❑ 153 San Marino	.05	.02
❑ 154 Ayrton Senna's Car	.40	.18
❑ 155 Monaco	.05	.02
❑ 156 Monaco	.05	.02
❑ 157 Nelson Piquet's Car	.10	.05
❑ 158 Nigel Mansell's Car	.20	.09
❑ 159 Nelson Piquet's Car	.10	.05
❑ 160 French Grand Prix	.05	.02
❑ 161 Aguri Suzuki Eric Bernard	.10	.05
❑ 162 Riccardo Patrese Alain Prost	.20	.09
❑ 163 Great Britain Grand Prix	.05	.02
❑ 164 Silverstone GB	.05	.02
❑ 165 Ayrton Senna's Car Nigell Mansell's Car	.40	.18
❑ 166 Ayrton Senna	.60	.25
❑ 167 Hockenheim GER	.05	.02
❑ 168 Start GER	.05	.02
❑ 169 Thierry Boutsen	.10	.05
❑ 170 Thierry Boutsen's Car	.05	.02
❑ 171 Martin Donnelly's Car	.05	.02
❑ 172 Ayrton Senna Gerhard Berger	.40	.18
❑ 173 Start HUN	.05	.02
❑ 174 View BEL	.05	.02
❑ 175 Ferrari ITA	.05	.02
❑ 176 Start ITA	.05	.02
❑ 177 Monza ITA	.05	.02
❑ 178 Race Grid POR	.05	.02
❑ 179 Nigel Mansell's Car	.20	.09
❑ 180 Nigel Mansell	.40	.18
❑ 181 Alain Prost	.20	.09
❑ 182 Alain Prost's Car	.10	.05
❑ 183 SPA	.05	.02
❑ 184 Nelson Piquet	.20	.09
❑ 185 Roberto Moreno Nelson Piquet	.20	.09
❑ 186 Johnny Herbert's Car	.05	.02
❑ 187 Nelson Piquet	.20	.09
❑ 188 Stag Hotel AUS	.05	.02
❑ 189 Yannick Dalmas' Car	.05	.02
❑ 190 Jody Scheckter	.10	.05
❑ 191 Keke Rosberg's Car	.05	.02
❑ 192 Niki Lauda	.20	.09
❑ 193 Colin Chapman Nigel Mansell	.20	.09
❑ 194 Patrick Tambay's Car	.05	.02
❑ 195 John Watson	.10	.05
❑ 196 Gilles Villeneuve's Car	.20	.09
❑ 197 Gilles Villeneuve's Car	.20	.09
❑ 198 Alain Prost's Car	.10	.05
❑ 199 Checklist	.05	.02
❑ 200 Checklist	.05	.02

1995 SkyBox Indy 500

This 108-card set was the first Indy set produced by SkyBox. The oversized cards 2 1/2" X 4 1/2" feature the top names in Indy Car racing. There are two topical subsets within the set: Qualifying Position (19-51) and Finishing Position (73-105). There was also a special 1994 Indy Champion insert of Al Unser Jr. The card was randomly inserted at a rate of one per 44 packs. A special Jacques Villeneuve Indy 500 Winner mail away card was produced as well. Both cards are priced at the bottom of the set listing but not included in the set price.

	MINT	NRMT
COMPLETE SET (108)	18.00	8.00
COMMON CARD (1-108)	.25	.11
❑ 1 Cover Card Checklist Back	.25	.11
❑ 2 IMS Speedway World's Greatest Race Course	.25	.11
❑ 3 Borg-Warner Trophy	.25	.11
❑ 4 IMS Speedway A New Look for the Speedway	.25	.11
❑ 5 Paul Tracy's Car Penske PC23 Chassis	.25	.11
❑ 6 Robby Gordon's Car Lola T94/00 Chassis	.25	.11
❑ 7 Michael Andretti's Car Reynard 941 Chassis	.50	.23
❑ 8 Paul Tracy Al Unser Emerson Fittipaldi's Car Penske Racing Teams	.40	.18
❑ 9 Stefan Johansson State-of-the-Art Helmets	.25	.11
❑ 10 Bryan Herta A.J.Foyt	.50	.23
❑ 11 Emerson Fittipaldi w/Car	.50	.23
❑ 12 Mario Andretti w/Car Pole Run	.75	.35
❑ 13 Jacques Villeneuve Fastest Rookie Qualifier	.75	.35
❑ 14 Al Unser Jr.	.50	.23

Roger Penske		
With Crew		
❑ 15 Al Unser Sr.	.50	.23
Retires		
❑ 16 Johnny Rutherford in Car	.40	.18
❑ 17 Bobby Rahal in Car	.40	.18
❑ 18 Emerson Fittipaldi	.50	.23
Raul Boesel		
Al Unser Jr.		
❑ 19 Al Unser Jr. in Car	.50	.23
❑ 20 Raul Boesel	.25	.11
❑ 21 Emerson Fittipaldi	.50	.23
❑ 22 Jacques Villeneuve in Car	.50	.23
❑ 23 Michael Andretti in Car	.50	.23
❑ 24 Lyn St. James	.25	.11
❑ 25 Nigel Mansell	.40	.18
❑ 26 Arie Luyendyk	.40	.18
❑ 27 Mario Andretti in Car	.50	.23
❑ 28 John Andretti	.40	.18
❑ 29 Eddie Cheever	.25	.11
❑ 30 Dominic Dobson	.25	.11
❑ 31 Stan Fox	.25	.11
❑ 32 Hideshi Matsuda	.25	.11
❑ 33 Dennis Vitolo	.25	.11
❑ 34 Jimmy Vasser	.25	.11
❑ 35 Scott Sharp	.40	.18
❑ 36 Hiro Matsushita	.25	.11
❑ 37 Robby Gordon	.40	.18
❑ 38 Roberto Guerrero	.40	.18
❑ 39 Brian Till	.25	.11
❑ 40 Bryan Herta	.25	.11
❑ 41 Scott Brayton	.25	.11
❑ 42 Teo Fabi	.40	.18
❑ 43 Paul Tracy	.40	.18
❑ 44 Adrian Fernandez	.25	.11
❑ 45 Stefan Johansson	.25	.11
❑ 46 Bobby Rahal	.40	.18
❑ 47 Mauricio Gugelmin	.25	.11
❑ 48 John Paul Jr.	.25	.11
❑ 49 Mike Groff	.25	.11
❑ 50 Marco Greco	.25	.11
❑ 51 Scott Goodyear	.25	.11
❑ 52 Al Unser Jr.	.50	.23
MVP for the Month of May		
❑ 53 Jim Nabors	.25	.11
Back Home Again		
❑ 54 Robby Gordon	.40	.18
Roberto Guerrero		
Bryan Till		
Ready To Roll		
❑ 55 IMS Speedway	.25	.11
The Greatest Spectacle in Racing		
❑ 56 IMS Speedway	.25	.11
Showtime		
❑ 57 IMS Speedway	.25	.11
The 78th Edition		
❑ 58 Dennis Vitolo's Car	.25	.11
❑ 59 Mario Andretti in Pits	.50	.23
❑ 60 Mike Groff's Car	.25	.11
Dominic Dobson's Car		
❑ 61 Adrian Fernandez's Car	.25	.11
❑ 62 Jacques Villeneuve's Car	.50	.23
Takes the Lead		
❑ 63 Robby Gordon's Car	.25	.11
Raul Boesel's Car		
Wheel-to-Wheel		
❑ 64 Hideshi Matsuda's Car	.25	.11
Hits the Wall		
❑ 65 Dennis Vitolo's Car	.25	.11
Nigel Mansell's Car		
Tangle in Turn Three		
❑ 66 Emerson Fittipaldi's Car	.40	.18
Pull's Away		
❑ 67 Emerson Fittipaldi's Car	.40	.18
Emmo's Day Comes to an End		
❑ 68 Stan Fox's Car	.25	.11
Brings Out Final caution		
❑ 69 Al Unser Jr.'s Car	.50	.23
Salute to the New Champion		
❑ 70 Al Unser Jr. in Car	.50	.23
Heads to Victory Lane		
❑ 71 Al Unser Jr. WIN	.50	.23
Number Two for the Record Books		
❑ 72 Al Unser Jr. WIN	.50	.23
❑ 73 Al Unser Jr.	.50	.23
❑ 74 Jacques Villeneuve	.50	.23
❑ 75 Bobby Rahal	.40	.18
❑ 76 Jimmy Vasser	.25	.11
❑ 77 Robby Gordon	.40	.18
❑ 78 Michael Andretti	.75	.35
❑ 79 Teo Fabi	.40	.18
❑ 80 Eddie Cheever	.25	.11
❑ 81 Bryan Herta	.25	.11
❑ 82 John Andretti	.40	.18
❑ 83 Mauricio Gugelmin	.25	.11
❑ 84 Brian Till	.25	.11
❑ 85 Stan Fox	.25	.11
❑ 86 Hiro Matsushita	.25	.11
❑ 87 Stefan Johansson	.25	.11
❑ 88 Scott Sharp	.40	.18
❑ 89 Emerson Fittipaldi	.50	.23
❑ 90 Arie Luyendyk	.40	.18
❑ 91 Lyn St.James	.25	.11
❑ 92 Scott Brayton	.40	.18
❑ 93 Raul Boesel	.25	.11
❑ 94 Nigel Mansell	.40	.18
❑ 95 Paul Tracy	.40	.18
❑ 96 Hideshi Matsuda	.25	.11
❑ 97 John Paul Jr.	.25	.11
❑ 98 Dennis Vitolo	.25	.11
❑ 99 Marco Greco	.25	.11
❑ 100 Adrian Fernandez	.25	.11
❑ 101 Dominic Dobson	.25	.11
❑ 102 Scott Goodyear	.25	.11
❑ 103 Mike Groff	.25	.11
❑ 104 Mario Andretti	.75	.35
❑ 105 Roberto Guerrero	.40	.18
❑ 106 Al Unser Jr.	.50	.23
❑ 107 Mario Andretti	.75	.35
❑ 108 Al Unser Jr.	.50	.23
1994 Indianapolis		
❑ FIN1 Jacques Villeneuve WIN	2.00	.90
❑ NNO Al Unser Jr. Champion	2.00	.90

1995 SkyBox Indy 500 Heir to Indy

This six-card insert set features some of the best of the youngest drivers on the Indy circuit. The cards were printed on silver foil board and were inserted at a rate of one per 29 packs.

	MINT	NRMT
COMPLETE SET (6)	30.00	13.50
COMMON CARD (1-6)	5.00	2.20
❑ 1 Raul Boesel	5.00	2.20
❑ 2 Jimmy Vasser	5.00	2.20
❑ 3 Robby Gordon	7.00	3.10
❑ 4 Michael Andretti	8.00	3.60
❑ 5 Paul Tracy	7.00	3.10
❑ 6 Jacques Villeneuve	10.00	4.50

1995 SkyBox Indy 500 Past Champs

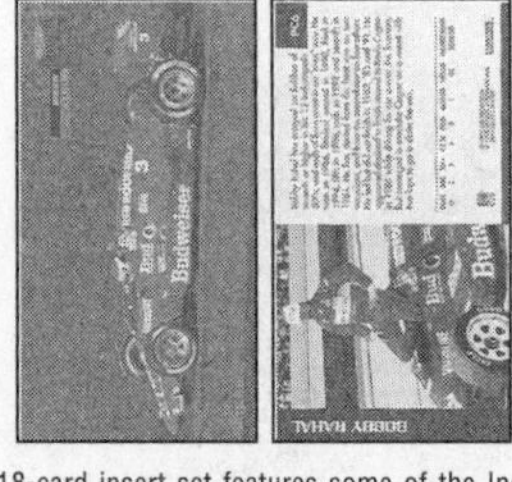

This 18-card insert set features some of the Indy 500 winners since 1962. The cards were printed on silver foil board and were inserted randomly at a rate of one per 10 packs.

	MINT	NRMT
COMPLETE SET (18)	35.00	16.00
COMMON CARD (1-18)	2.00	.90
❑ 1 Al Unser Jr.	4.00	1.80
❑ 2 Emerson Fittipaldi	4.00	1.80
❑ 3 Rick Mears	4.00	1.80
❑ 4 Arie Luyendyk	2.00	.90
❑ 5 Al Unser	3.00	1.35
❑ 6 Bobby Rahal	3.00	1.35
❑ 7 Danny Sullivan	2.00	.90
❑ 8 Tom Sneva	2.00	.90
❑ 9 Gordon Johncock	2.00	.90
❑ 10 Bobby Unser	3.00	1.35
❑ 11 Johnny Rutherford	3.00	
❑ 12 Mark Donahue	2.00	
❑ 13 Mario Andretti	4.00	
❑ 14 A.J. Foyt	4.00	
❑ 15 Graham Hill	2.00	
❑ 16 Jim Clark	2.00	
❑ 17 Parnelli Jones	2.00	
❑ 18 Rodger Ward	2.00	

1996 SkyBox Indy 500

The 1996 SkyBox Indy set was issued in a single 10 series. The cards feature the drivers of the 1995 Inc The cards were standard size for the first time in S racing cards history. There are four topical subsets the set: Qualifying Position (10-42), Indy 500 Car C (50-54), Finishing Position (55-87), Anatomy Modern Indy Car (91-99).

	MINT
COMPLETE SET (100)	18.00
COMMON CARD (1-100)	.20
COMMON DRIVER (1-100)	.25
❑ 1 Christian Fittipaldi	.25
❑ 2 Firestone's Return	.20
❑ 3 Honda's Comeback	.20
❑ 4 Dick Simon	.25
Lyn St.James	
❑ 5 Scott Brayton	.25
❑ 6 Qualifying Highlights	.20
❑ 7 Scott Brayton w/Crew	.25
❑ 8 Al Unser, Jr.	1.50
❑ 9 Emerson Fittipaldi	.40
❑ 10 Scott Brayton's Car	.20
❑ 11 Arie Luyendyk's Car	.20
❑ 12 Scott Goodyear's Car	.20
❑ 13 Michael Andretti's Car	.25
❑ 14 Jacques Villeneuve's Car	.40
❑ 15 Mauricio Gugelmin's Car	.20
❑ 16 Robby Gordon's Car	.25
❑ 17 Scott Pruett's Car	.20
❑ 18 Jimmy Vasser's Car	.20
❑ 19 Hiro Matsushita's Car	.20
❑ 20 Stan Fox's Car	.20
❑ 21 Andre Ribeiro's Car	.20
❑ 22 Roberto Guerrero's Car	.20
❑ 23 Eddie Cheever's Car	.20
❑ 24 Teo Fabi's Car	.20
❑ 25 Paul Tracy's Car	.25
❑ 26 Alessandro Zampedri's Car	.20
❑ 27 Danny Sullivan's Car	.20
❑ 28 Gil de Ferran's Car	.20
❑ 29 Hideshi Matsuda's Car	.20
❑ 30 Bobby Rahal's Car	.25
❑ 31 Raul Boesel's Car	.20
❑ 32 Buddy Lazier's Car	.20
❑ 33 Eliseo Salazar's Car	.20
❑ 34 Adrian Fernandez's Car	.20
❑ 35 Eric Bachelart's Car	.20
❑ 36 Christian Fittipaldi's Car	.20
❑ 37 Lyn St. James's Car	.25
❑ 38 Carlos Guerrero's Car	.20
❑ 39 Scott Sharp's Car	.20
❑ 40 Stefan Johansson's Car	.20
❑ 41 Davy Jones's Car	.20
❑ 42 Bryan Herta's Car	.20
❑ 43 Robby Gordon in Pits	.25
❑ 44 Green Flag	.20
❑ 45 Stan Fox's Car	.20
❑ 46 Scott Goodyear's Car	.20
Arie Luyendyk's Car	
❑ 47 Scott Goodyear's Car	.20
❑ 48 Checkered Flag	.20
❑ 49 Jacques Villeneuve	.75
❑ 50 Joe Montana	1.00
Chip Ganassi	
❑ 51 Roger Penske	.20
❑ 52 Paul Newman	.25
Carl Haas	
❑ 53 A.J. Foyt	.40
❑ 54 Walter Payton	.50
Dale Coyne	

acques Villeneuve	.75	.35
hristian Fittipaldi	.25	.11
obby Rahal	.40	.18
liseo Salazar	.25	.11
obby Gordon	.40	.18
lauricio Gugelmin	.25	.11
rie Luyendyk	.25	.11
eo Fabi	.25	.11
anny Sullivan	.25	.11
iro Matsushita	.25	.11
lessandro Zampedri	.25	.11
oberto Guerrero	.25	.11
ryan Herta	.25	.11
cott Goodyear	.25	.11
lideshi Matsuda	.25	.11
tefan Johansson	.25	.11
cott Brayton	.25	.11
ndre Ribeiro	.25	.11
cott Pruett	.25	.11
aul Boesel	.25	.11
drian Fernandez	.25	.11
immy Vasser	.25	.11
avy Jones	.25	.11
aul Tracy	.40	.18
lichael Andretti	.50	.23
cott Sharp	.25	.11
uddy Lazier	.25	.11
ric Bachelart	.25	.11
il de Ferran	.25	.11
tan Fox	.25	.11
ddie Cheever	.25	.11
yn St. James	.40	.18
arlos Guerrero	.25	.11
acques Villeneuve w/Crew	.50	.23
lauricio Gugelmin	.25	.11
cott Goodyear	.25	.11
eel the 500 - Tires/Gas	.20	.09
eel the 500 - Suspension	.20	.09
eel the 500 - Cockplt	.20	.09
eel the 500 - Engine	.20	.09
eel the 500 - Rear End	.20	.09
eel the 500 - Hauler	.20	.09
eel the 500 - Ground Effects	.20	.09
eel the 500 - Noise Piece	.20	.09
eel the 500 - IMS	.20	.09
Checklist	.20	.09

1996 SkyBox Indy 500 Champions Collection

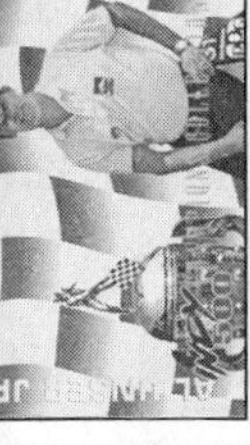
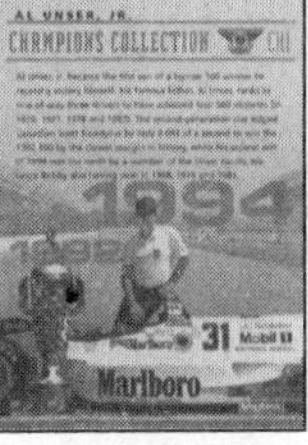

mly inserted in packs at a rate of one in five, this ard insert set features six former Indy 500 oions. The cards printed on silver foil board offers es of the past champions standing next to the Borg-r Trophy on the fronts of the cards and sitting in the winning car they drove on the backs.

	MINT	NRMT
LETE SET (6)	16.00	7.25
ION CARD (1-6)	2.00	.90
Unser, Jr.	6.00	2.70
merson Fittipaldi	2.50	1.10
obby Rahal	2.50	1.10
ie Luyendyk	2.00	.90
anny Sullivan	2.00	.90
cques Villeneuve	5.00	2.20

1996 SkyBox Indy 500 Rookies of the Year

ine-card insert set features the Indy 500 Rookies of ear from 1987-94. This includes the Co-Rookies of ear in 1989, Bernard Jourdain and Scott Pruett. The feature gold foil stamping and are die cut. Rookie of ear cards could be found at a rate of one per three

	MINT	NRMT
LETE SET (9)	16.00	7.25
ION CARD (1-9)	1.00	.45

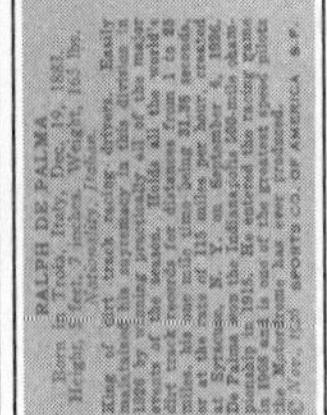

❑ 1 Fabrizio Barbazza	1.00	.45
❑ 2 Billy Vukovich III	1.00	.45
❑ 3 Bernard Jourdain	1.00	.45
❑ 4 Scott Pruett	1.00	.45
❑ 5 Eddie Cheever	1.00	.45
❑ 6 Jeff Andretti	2.00	.90
❑ 7 Lyn St. James	2.00	.90
❑ 8 Nigel Mansell	4.00	1.80
❑ 9 Jacques Villeneuve	4.00	1.80

1926 Sports Company of America Racing

This eight-card racing set was issued by Spalding Sporting Goods in 1926. The racing cards are just part of a larger mulit-sport set. The cards measure 1 1/2 x 2 1/4. The front features a glossy finished black and white framed photograph of the driver with his name and sport below the picture. The backs carry a detailed biography of the driver's achievements. Also on the back is the copyright date, Nov. 1926, and the Sports Co. of America S.F. title. The cards came in a glassine envelope along with a coupon for Spalding Sporting Goods. The front of the coupon reads "Sport-Scrip" "Value Ten Cents". The back of the coupon detailed how the coupon could be redeemed for ten cents worth of Spalding Sporting Goods.

	NRMT	VG-E
COMPLETE SET (8)	325.00	200.00
COMMON CARD (1-8)	40.00	24.00
❑ 1 Earl Cooper	40.00	24.00
❑ 2 Ralph De Palma	60.00	36.00
❑ 3 Ralph De Palo	40.00	24.00
❑ 4 Harry Hartz	40.00	24.00
❑ 5 Benny Hill	40.00	24.00
❑ 6 Bob McDonough	40.00	24.00
❑ 7 Tommy Milton	40.00	24.00
❑ 8 Barney Oldfield	60.00	36.00

1954 Stark and Wetzel Indy Winners

Stark and Wetzel Meats produced and distributed these cards in 1954. The issue features past winners of the Indy 500 and their cars. Since the cards were distributed in packages of meat products, they were produced with a wax covering that is often found stained making Near Mint copies especially tough to find. The cards are blankbacked and have lightly perforated edges. The cards are unnumbered and listed below in order of winning year.

	NRMT	VG-E
COMPLETE SET (37)	900.00	550.00
COMMON CARD	30.00	18.00
❑ 1911 Ray Harroun	30.00	18.00
❑ 1912 Joe Dawson	30.00	18.00
❑ 1913 Jules Goux	30.00	18.00
❑ 1914 Rene Thomas	30.00	18.00
❑ 1915 Ralph DePalma	40.00	24.00
❑ 1916 Dario Resta	30.00	18.00
❑ 1919 Howard Wilcox	30.00	18.00
❑ 1920 Gaston Chevrolet	40.00	24.00
❑ 1921 Tommy Milton	30.00	18.00
❑ 1922 Jimmy Murphy	30.00	18.00
❑ 1923 Tommy Milton	30.00	18.00
❑ 1924 Joe Boyer L.L.Corum	30.00	18.00
❑ 1925 Peter DePaolo	30.00	18.00
❑ 1926 Frank Lockhart	30.00	18.00
❑ 1927 George Souders	30.00	18.00
❑ 1928 Louis Meyer	30.00	18.00
❑ 1929 Ray Keech	30.00	18.00
❑ 1930 Billy Arnold	30.00	18.00
❑ 1931 Louis Schneider	30.00	18.00
❑ 1932 Fred Frame	30.00	18.00
❑ 1933 Louis Meyer	30.00	18.00
❑ 1934 Bill Cummings	30.00	18.00
❑ 1935 Kelly Petillo	30.00	18.00
❑ 1936 Louis Meyer	30.00	18.00
❑ 1937 Wilbur Shaw	40.00	24.00
❑ 1938 Floyd Roberts	30.00	18.00
❑ 1939 Wilbur Shaw	40.00	24.00
❑ 1940 Wilbur Shaw	40.00	24.00
❑ 1941 Floyd Davis Mauri Rose	40.00	24.00
❑ 1946 George Robson	30.00	18.00
❑ 1947 Mauri Rose	40.00	24.00
❑ 1948 Mauri Rose	40.00	24.00
❑ 1949 Bill Holland	30.00	18.00
❑ 1950 Johnnie Parsons	40.00	24.00
❑ 1951 Lee Wallard	30.00	18.00
❑ 1952 Troy Ruttman	30.00	18.00
❑ 1953 Bill Vukovich	30.00	18.00

1966 Strombecker

These cards were presumably made in Europe by the Strombecker Corporation. There are 12 known unnumbered cards with each featuring a type of race car from various manufacturers. The cardfronts include a gold or yellow border, a color photo of the car and the flag of the manufacturer's home country. The backs are blue and include detailed stats on the featured car.

	NRMT	VG-E
COMPLETE SET (12)	300.00	180.00
COMMON CARD	25.00	15.00
❑ 1 BRM Formula One	25.00	15.00
❑ 2 Cobra	25.00	15.00
❑ 3 Cooper Formula One	25.00	15.00
❑ 4 Ferrari Formula One	25.00	15.00
❑ 5 Ferrari GTO	25.00	15.00
❑ 6 Ford GT	25.00	15.00
❑ 7 Jaguar D-Type	25.00	15.00
❑ 8 Jaguar XK-E	25.00	15.00
❑ 9 Lotus 19	25.00	15.00
❑ 10 Lotus 38	25.00	15.00
❑ 11 Plymouth Barracuda	25.00	15.00
❑ 12 Porsche 904	25.00	15.00

1911 Turkey Red Automobile Series

This 50-card set features most of the race cars from the early 1900's. The cards were made in New York City and released in the Turkish cigarette brand from the American Tobacco Company. The cards measure 2" X 2 5/8" and came one per pack or box. Many of the card backs talk about the 1910 Vanderbilt Cup and therefore it has been determined that the set was issued either in late 1910 or in 1911. There is a possibility that the set was released over a period of years from 1909-1911. The set was reprinted by Bowman in 1953 and called Antique Autos. The reprint cards have 3-D backs that required the wearing of 3-D glasses for reading.

	NRMT	VG-E
COMPLETE SET (50)	600.00	350.00
COMMON CARDS	15.00	9.00
❑ 1 Acme Racer	15.00	9.00
❑ 2 Alco Racer	15.00	9.00
❑ 3 Apperson Racer	15.00	9.00
❑ 4 Baker Electric Racer	15.00	9.00
❑ 5 Benz Racer	15.00	9.00
❑ 6 Buick Racer	15.00	9.00
❑ 7 Cadillac Racer	15.00	9.00
❑ 8 Chadwick Racer	15.00	9.00
❑ 9 Chalmers-Detroit Racer	15.00	9.00
❑ 10 Corbin Racer	15.00	9.00
❑ 11 De Dietrcih Racer	15.00	9.00
❑ 12 Fiat Racer	15.00	9.00
❑ 13 Ford Racer	15.00	9.00
❑ 14 Franklin Racer	15.00	9.00
❑ 15 Gaeth Racer	15.00	9.00
❑ 16 Haynes Racer	15.00	9.00
❑ 17 Hotchkiss Racer	15.00	9.00
❑ 18 Hudson Racer	15.00	9.00
❑ 19 Isotta Racer	15.00	9.00
❑ 20 Knox Racer	15.00	9.00
❑ 21 Lancia Racer	15.00	9.00
❑ 22 Locomobile Racer	15.00	9.00
❑ 23 Lozier Racer	15.00	9.00
❑ 24 Matheson Racer	15.00	9.00
❑ 25 Maxwell Racer	15.00	9.00
❑ 26 Mercedes Racer	15.00	9.00
❑ 27 Mitchell Racer	15.00	9.00
❑ 28 Moline Racer	15.00	9.00
❑ 29 National Racer	15.00	9.00
❑ 30 Oldsmobile Racer	15.00	9.00
❑ 31 Packard Racer	15.00	9.00
❑ 32 Palmer-Singer Racer	15.00	9.00
❑ 33 Panhard Racer	15.00	9.00
❑ 34 Peerless Racer	15.00	9.00
❑ 35 Pierce-Arrow Racer	15.00	9.00
❑ 36 Pope-Hartford Racer	15.00	9.00
❑ 37 Premier Racer	15.00	9.00
❑ 38 Pullman Racer	15.00	9.00
❑ 39 Rainier Racer	15.00	9.00
❑ 40 Rambler Racer	15.00	9.00
❑ 41 Renault Racer	15.00	9.00
❑ 42 Reo Racer	15.00	9.00
❑ 43 Simplex Racer	15.00	9.00
❑ 44 Stearns Racer	15.00	9.00
❑ 45 Stevens-Duryea Racer	15.00	9.00
❑ 46 Stoddard-Dayton Racer	15.00	9.00
❑ 47 Studebaker Racer	15.00	9.00
❑ 48 Thomas Racer	15.00	9.00
❑ 49 White Racer	15.00	9.00
❑ 50 Winton Racer	15.00	9.00

1930 Wills' Cigarettes

This eight-card European tobacco issue is part of a bigger 50 card set. The cards were produced by Imperial Tobacco Company of Great Britain and Ireland. The set features all types of transportation vehicles. The cards measure 1 3/8" X 2 5/8" and feature artwork of the vehicles for card fronts. The backs give a bio of the car pictured.

	NRMT	VG-E
COMPLETE SET (8)	30.00	18.00
COMMON CARD (23-30)	4.00	2.40
❑ 23 Malcom Campbell	6.00	3.60
❑ 24 Sir Henry Seagrave	4.00	2.40
❑ 25 Captain Henry Birkin	4.00	2.40
❑ 26 Mrs. Victor Bruce	4.00	2.40
❑ 27 Boris Ivanonski	4.00	2.40
❑ 28 Kay Don	4.00	2.40
❑ 29 Rudolf Carcciola	4.00	2.40
❑ 30 Sv. Holbrook	4.00	2.40

1938 Wills' Cigarettes

This European tobacco issue is part of a bigger 50 card set. The set is titled Speed and features all types of transportation vehicles. The cards measure 1 3/8" X 2 5/8" and feature artwork of the vehicles for card fronts. The backs give a bio of the car pictured.

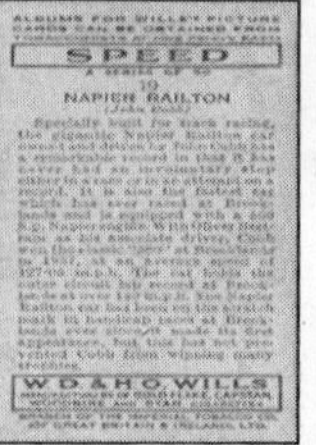

	NRMT	VG-E
COMPLETE SET (8)	20.00	12.00
COMMON CARDS	3.00	1.80
❑ 16 Captain G.E.T. Eyston	3.00	1.80
❑ 17 Malcom Campbell	3.00	1.80
❑ 18 Ab Jenkins	3.00	1.80
❑ 19 John Cobb	3.00	1.80
❑ 20 Major Goldie Gardner	3.00	1.80
❑ 21 Raymond Mays	3.00	1.80
❑ 22 Rudolf Caracciola	3.00	1.80
❑ 23 Bernt Rosemeyer	3.00	1.80

1991 Bull Ring

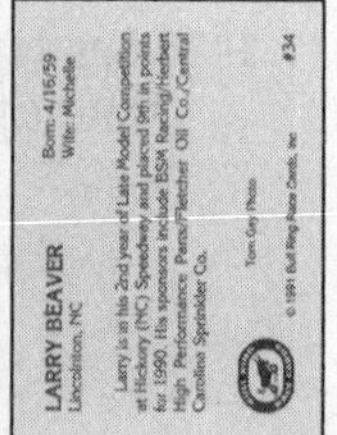

Bull Ring Race Cards produced this set in 1991 featuring popular drivers of short track competition. The cards include a color driver photo on the cardfront and a driver career summary on the back. Butch Lindley, Card number 1 is a memorial card.

	MINT	NRMT
COMPLETE SET (144)	12.00	5.50
COMMON CARD (1-144)	.10	.05
❑ 1 Butch Lindley	.10	.05
❑ 2 Jerry Goodwin	.10	.05
❑ 3 Todd Massey	.10	.05
❑ 4 Bobby Gill	.10	.05
❑ 5 Rich Bickle	.20	.09
❑ 6 Freddie Query	.10	.05
❑ 7 Mike Garvey	.10	.05
❑ 8 Jay Fogelman	.10	.05
❑ 9 Andy Thurman	.10	.05
❑ 10 Beano Francis	.10	.05
❑ 11 David Smith	.10	.05
❑ 12 Karen Schulz	.10	.05
❑ 13 Jerry McCart	.10	.05
❑ 14 Rick Crawford	.10	.05
❑ 15 Mark Day	.10	.05
❑ 16 Hal Goodson	.10	.05
❑ 17 Jerry Allen VanHorn	.10	.05
❑ 18 Joe Frasson	.10	.05
❑ 19 Kevin Smith	.10	.05
❑ 20 Sammy Pegram	.10	.05
❑ 21 Donnie York	.10	.05
❑ 22 Doug Noe	.10	.05
❑ 23 Dickie Linville	.10	.05
❑ 24 Granny Tatroe's Car	.10	.05
❑ 25 Mike Cope	.10	.05
❑ 26 Robby Faggart	.10	.05
❑ 27 James Trammell	.10	.05
❑ 28 Billy Bigley, Jr.	.10	.05
❑ 29 Mitchell Barrett	.10	.05
❑ 30 Scott Kilby	.10	.05
❑ 31 Brian Pack	.10	.05
❑ 32 Randy Porter	.10	.05
❑ 33 Jimmy McClain	.10	.05
❑ 34 Larry Beaver	.10	.05
❑ 35 Robby Johnson	.10	.05
❑ 36 David Russell	.10	.05
❑ 37 Larry Raines	.10	.05
❑ 38 Steve Walker	.10	.05
❑ 39 Stephen Grimes	.10	.05
❑ 40 Dale Fischlein	.10	.05
❑ 41 Max Prestwood, Jr.	.10	.05
❑ 42 Tres Wilson	.10	.05
❑ 43 Jerry Williams	.10	.05
❑ 44 Larry Caudill	.20	.09
❑ 45 Phil Gann	.10	.05
❑ 46 Danny Blevins	.10	.05
❑ 47 Ronnie Payne	.20	.09
❑ 48 Mike Miller	.10	.05
❑ 49 Debbie Lunsford	.10	.05
❑ 50 John Gerstner II	.10	.05
❑ 51 Chrissy Oliver	.10	
❑ 52 Scotty Lovelady	.10	
❑ 53 Duke Southard	.10	
❑ 54 Bob Pressley	.10	
❑ 55 Debris Brown	.10	
❑ 56 Robert Powell	.10	
❑ 57 Jason Keller	.20	
❑ 58 John Kelly	.10	
❑ 59 Robert Pressley	.50	
❑ 60 Don Carlton	.10	
❑ 61 Mike Pressley	.20	
❑ 62 Smiley Rich	.10	
❑ 63 Mark Miner	.10	
❑ 64 John Earl Barton	.10	
❑ 65 Rodger Gentry	.10	
❑ 66 Wesley Mills	.10	
❑ 67 Joey Sims	.10	
❑ 68 Lloyd Slagle	.10	
❑ 69 Sidney Minton	.10	
❑ 70 Ronnie Davidson	.10	
❑ 71 Donnie Bishop	.10	
❑ 72 Johnny Cochran	.10	
❑ 73 Scott Sutherland	.10	
❑ 74 Jack Sprague	.20	
❑ 75 Robert Huffman	.10	
❑ 76 Tim Roberts	.10	
❑ 77 Ted Hodgdon	.10	
❑ 78 Gary Bradberry	.20	
❑ 79 Steve Holzhausen	.10	
❑ 80 Danny Shortt	.10	
❑ 81 Lee Faulk	.10	
❑ 82 Barry Beggarly	.10	
❑ 83 Rodney Howard	.10	
❑ 84 Kevin Evans	.10	
❑ 85 Greg Hendrix	.10	
❑ 86 Tim Gordon	.10	
❑ 87 Danny Slack	.10	
❑ 88 Chris Mullinax	.10	
❑ 89 Brian Butler	.10	
❑ 90 Randy Couch	.10	
❑ 91 Dennis Setzer	.20	
❑ 92 Dick Anderson	.10	
❑ 93 Junior Niedecken	.10	
❑ 94 Gary Nix	.10	
❑ 95 Terry Davis	.10	
❑ 96 Charlie Stokes	.10	
❑ 97 Marty Ward	.10	
❑ 98 Jody Ridley	.10	
❑ 99 Chris Diamond	.10	
❑ 100 Tom Usry	.10	
❑ 101 Robin Hayes	.10	
❑ 102 Johnny Reynolds	.10	
❑ 103 Shelton McNair, Jr.	.10	
❑ 104 Grump Wills	.10	
❑ 105 Jeff Agnew	.10	
❑ 106 Ronald Walls	.10	
❑ 107 Eddie Hanks	.10	
❑ 108 Mickey York	.10	
❑ 109 Larry Ogle	.10	
❑ 110 Jacky Workman	.10	
❑ 111 Tuck Trentham	.10	
❑ 112 Richard Landreth, Jr.	.10	
❑ 113 David Rogers	.10	
❑ 114 Mike Harmon	.10	
❑ 115 Toby Porter	.10	
❑ 116 Stacy Compton	.25	
❑ 117 Ricky Vaughn	.10	
❑ 118 Tommy Grimes	.10	
❑ 119 Mike McSwain	.10	
❑ 120 Roy Chatham	.10	
❑ 121 Johnny Rumley	.10	
❑ 122 Doug Strickland	.10	
❑ 123 Tommy Ruff	.10	
❑ 124 Jeff Williams	.10	
❑ 125 Mike Love	.10	
❑ 126 A.J. Sanders	.10	
❑ 127 Dallas Wilcox	.10	
❑ 128 Dennis Crump	.10	
❑ 129 Kevin Barrett	.10	
❑ 130 Mike Toemmes	.10	
❑ 131 Gene Pack	.10	
❑ 132 Robbie Ferguson	.10	
❑ 133 Buddy Vance	.10	
❑ 134 Ralph Carnes	.10	
❑ 135 Rick Lambert	.10	
❑ 136 Bart Ingram	.10	
❑ 137 Pete Orr	.10	
❑ 138 Shawna Robinson	1.00	
❑ 139 Mike Porter	.10	
❑ 140 Scott Green	.10	
❑ 141 Darrell Holman	.10	
❑ 142 Jeff Finley	.10	
❑ 143 Junior Franks	.10	
❑ 144 Jabe Jones	.10	

1992 Bull Ring

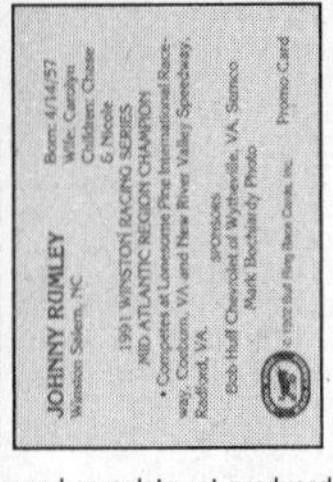

00-card set was the second complete set produced ll Ring Race Cards. The 1992 features popular s of short track competition. The cards include a driver photo on the cardfront with a blue border and er career summary and biographical information on ck.

	MINT	NRMT
LETE SET (200)	25.00	11.00
ION CARD (1-200)	.10	.05

ecklist Card	.10	.05
rry Goodwin	.10	.05
ano Francis	.10	.05
ward Jordan	.10	.05
ckie Bickle	.40	.18
acy Compton	.25	.11
ike Garvey	.10	.05
y Fogelman	.10	.05
J. Johnson	.10	.05
had Chaffin	.10	.05
avid Rogers	.10	.05
aren Schulz	.10	.05
erry McCart	.10	.05
ick Crawford	.10	.05
lay Brown	.10	.05
al Goodson	.10	.05
erry A. Van Horn	.10	.05
oe Frasson	.10	.05
cotty Lovelady	.10	.05
allas Wilcox	.10	.05
ammy Pegram	.10	.05
oug Noe	.10	.05
rad Sorenson	.10	.05
ike Harmon	.10	.05
ike Cope	.40	.18
uck Trentham	.10	.05
anny Fair	.10	.05
illy Bigley, Jr.	.10	.05
hris Mullinax	.10	.05
ike Love	.10	.05
ary Balough	.10	.05
andy Porter	.10	.05
immy McClain	.10	.05
cott Green	.10	.05
esley Mills	.10	.05
avid Russell	.10	.05
arry Raines	.10	.05
ete Orr	.10	.05
obert Huffman	.10	.05
hrissy Oliver Checklist back	.10	.05
ax Prestwood, Jr.	.10	.05
res Wilson	.10	.05
ike Borghi	.10	.05
arry Caudill	.40	.18
uke Southard	.10	.05
ade Buttrey	.10	.05
hil Warren	.10	.05
ack Sprague	.40	.18
ebbie Lunsford	.10	.05
ike Buffkin	.10	.05
eff Purvis	.50	.23
ammy Kirk	.10	.05
harlie Ragan, Jr.	.10	.05
ob Pressley	.10	.05
ebris Brown	.10	.05
obert Powell	.10	.05
ason Keller	.50	.23
eff Agnew	.10	.05
obert Pressley	.50	.23
alph Carnes	.10	.05
im Steele	.50	.23
uckshot Jones	.50	.23
huck Abell	.10	.05
ohn Earl Barton	.10	.05
obert Hester	.10	.05
reddie Query	.10	.05
odney Howard	.10	.05
ark Day	.10	.05
idney Minton	.10	.05
❑ 70 Granny Tatroe	.10	.05
❑ 71 Donnie Bishop	.10	.05
❑ 72 Eddie Mercer	.10	.05
❑ 73 John Livinston, Jr.	.10	.05
❑ 74 Wayne Willard	.10	.05
❑ 75 Bobby Brack	.10	.05
❑ 76 Dennis Schoenfeld	.10	.05
❑ 77 Johnny Chapman	.10	.05
❑ 78 Gary Bradberry	.40	.18
❑ 79 Robby Faggart	.10	.05
❑ 80 Randy Porter Checklist back	.10	.05
❑ 81 Mike Pressley	.10	.05
❑ 82 Barry Beggarly	.25	.11
❑ 83 Bubba Gale	.10	.05
❑ 84 Sean Graham	.10	.05
❑ 85 Joe Winchell	.10	.05
❑ 86 Bubba Adams	.10	.05
❑ 87 Ron Barfield	.40	.18
❑ 88 Mike McCrary, Jr.	.10	.05
❑ 89 Steve Walker	.10	.05
❑ 90 Stan Eads	.10	.05
❑ 91 Todd Massey	.10	.05
❑ 92 Dick Anderson	.10	.05
❑ 93 Junior Niedecken	.10	.05
❑ 94 Johnny Reynolds	.10	.05
❑ 95 Robert Elliott	.10	.05
❑ 96 Jack Cook	.10	.05
❑ 97 Marty Ward	.10	.05
❑ 98 Jody Ridley	.40	.18
❑ 99 Charlie Stokes	.10	.05
❑ 100 Chrissy Oliver	.10	.05
❑ 101 Eddie Perry	.10	.05
❑ 102 Claude Gwin, Jr.	.10	.05
❑ 103 Shelton McNair, Jr.	.10	.05
❑ 104 Charles Powell III	.10	.05
❑ 105 Jeff Agnew	.10	.05
❑ 106 P.B. Crowell III	.10	.05
❑ 107 Eddie Hanks	.10	.05
❑ 108 Tink Reedy	.10	.05
❑ 109 Larry Ogle	.10	.05
❑ 110 David Showers	.10	.05
❑ 111 David Rogers	.10	.05
❑ 112 Danny Sikes	.10	.05
❑ 113 Charlie Brown	.10	.05
❑ 114 Roy Hendrick	.10	.05
❑ 115 Randy Bynum	.10	.05
❑ 116 Mike Howell	.10	.05
❑ 117 Mark Miner	.10	.05
❑ 118 Danny Shortt	.10	.05
❑ 119 Kevin Smith	.10	.05
❑ 120 Larry Caudill Checklist back	.25	.11
❑ 121 Johnny Rumley	.25	.11
❑ 122 Mickey York	.10	.05
❑ 123 Dickie Linville	.10	.05
❑ 124 A.W. Kirby, Jr.	.10	.05
❑ 125 Mike Love	.10	.05
❑ 126 Gary Nix	.10	.05
❑ 127 Jeff Burkett	.10	.05
❑ 128 Rick Lambert	.10	.05
❑ 129 Marc Kinley	.10	.05
❑ 130 Mardy Lindley	.10	.05
❑ 131 Mitchell Barrett	.10	.05
❑ 132 Robbie Ferguson	.10	.05
❑ 133 Rodney Combs, Jr.	.40	.18
❑ 134 Ned Combs	.10	.05
❑ 135 Terry Davis	.10	.05
❑ 136 Bobby Knox	.10	.05
❑ 137 Richard Hargrove	.10	.05
❑ 138 Curtis Markham	.25	.11
❑ 139 Stephen Grimes	.10	.05
❑ 140 Penn Crim, Jr.	.10	.05
❑ 141 Brian Butler	.10	.05
❑ 142 Terry Lee	.10	.05
❑ 143 David Bonnett	.40	.18
❑ 144 Lloyd Slagle	.10	.05
❑ 145 Greg Motes	.10	.05
❑ 146 Don Carlton	.10	.05
❑ 147 David Smith	.10	.05
❑ 148 Darrell Holman	.10	.05
❑ 149 Orvil Reedy	.10	.05
❑ 150 Craig Gower	.10	.05
❑ 151 Bill Posey	.10	.05
❑ 152 Phil Gann	.10	.05
❑ 153 Bugs Hairfield	.10	.05
❑ 154 Ronnie Thomas	.10	.05
❑ 155 Dennis Southerlin	.10	.05
❑ 156 Brian King	.10	.05
❑ 157 Ed Meredith	.10	.05
❑ 158 Andy Houston	.10	.05
❑ 159 Ronnie Roach	.10	.05
❑ 160 Checklist Card	.10	.05
❑ 161 Elton Sawyer	.50	.23
❑ 162 Danny Blevins	.10	.05
❑ 163 Greg Marlowe	.10	.05
❑ 164 Mike Reynolds	.10	.05
❑ 165 Tommy Spangler	.10	.05
❑ 166 Dennis Setzer	.50	.23
❑ 167 Jabe Jones	.10	.05
❑ 168 Jacky Workman	.10	.05
❑ 169 Jimmy Cope	.10	.05
❑ 170 Mike Dillon	.25	.11
❑ 171 Bobby Gill	.10	.05
❑ 172 Chris Diamond	.10	.05
❑ 173 Scott Kilby	.10	.05
❑ 174 Pete Hughes	.10	.05
❑ 175 Donnie York	.10	.05
❑ 176 Junior Franks	.10	.05
❑ 177 Ron Young	.10	.05
❑ 178 Tom Usry	.10	.05
❑ 179 Greg Hendrix	.10	.05
❑ 180 Toby Porter	.10	.05
❑ 181 Mike Hovis	.10	.05
❑ 182 Richard Landreth, Jr.	.10	.05
❑ 183 Kevin Barrett	.10	.05
❑ 184 Marty Houston	.10	.05
❑ 185 G.C. Campbell	.10	.05
❑ 186 Tony Ponder	.10	.05
❑ 187 Danny Slack	.10	.05
❑ 188 Michael McSwain	.10	.05
❑ 189 Kevin Evans	.10	.05
❑ 190 Tim Roberts	.10	.05
❑ 191 Greg Cecil	.10	.05
❑ 192 A.J. Sanders	.10	.05
❑ 193 Richard Starkey	.10	.05
❑ 194 Hal Perry	.10	.05
❑ 195 Dennis Crump	.10	.05
❑ 196 Rob Underwood	.10	.05
❑ 197 Donn Fenn	.10	.05
❑ 198 Mark Cox	.10	.05
❑ 199 Lee Tissot	.10	.05
❑ 200 Butch Lindley	.10	.05

1992 Corter Selinsgrove and Clinton County Speedways

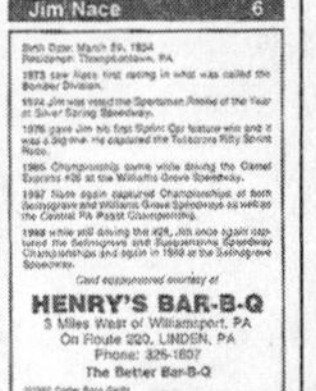

Corter Race Cards produced this set commemorating drivers of the Pennsylvania Selinsgrove and Clinton County Speedways. Sets were packaged in a plastic case and each was individually numbered of 1,200.

	MINT	NRMT
COMPLETE SET (36)	14.00	6.25
COMMON CARD (1-36)	.35	.16

❑ 1 David Corter's Car	.35	.16
❑ 2 Steve Campbell's Car	.35	.16
❑ 3 Lenny Krautheim's Car	.35	.16
❑ 4 Dale Schweikart's Car	.35	.16
❑ 5 Barry Knouse's Car	.35	.16
❑ 6 Jim Nace	.50	.23
❑ 7 Dennis Hahn	.50	.23
❑ 8 Richard Jensen's Car	.35	.16
❑ 9 Bill Glenn's Car	.35	.16
❑ 10 George Fultz's Car	.35	.16
❑ 11 Todd Shaffer	.50	.23
❑ 12 Craig Lindsey's Car	.35	.16
❑ 13 Penrose Kester's Car	.35	.16
❑ 14 Eric Hons' Car	.35	.16
❑ 15 Luke Hoffner's Car	.35	.16
❑ 16 Jim Stine w/Car	.50	.23
❑ 17 Alan Cole's Car	.35	.16
❑ 18 Fred Rahmer's Car	.35	.16
❑ 19 Ed Shafer's Car	.35	.16
❑ 20 Steve Byers' Car	.35	.16
❑ 21 Donald Schick, Jr.'s Car	.35	.16
❑ 22 Dustin Hoffman w/Car	.50	.23
❑ 23 James Gearhart	.50	.23
❑ 24 Wesley Matthews w/Car	.50	.23
❑ 25 John Hafer's Car	.35	.16
❑ 26 Glenn Fitzcharles' Car	.35	.16
❑ 27 Arthur Probst, Jr.	.50	.23
❑ 28 Scott Barrett's Car	.35	.16
❑ 29 Franklin Benfer's Car	.35	.16
❑ 30 Dwayne Wasson	.50	.23
❑ 31 Jerry Hollenbach w/Car	.50	.23
❑ 32 Chuck Reinert, Jr.'s Car	.35	.16
❑ 33 David Matthews w/Car	.50	.23
❑ 34 Robby Smith's Car	.35	.16

❑ 35 C.W. Smith's Car	.35	.16
❑ 36 Robin Johnson	.50	.23

1993 Corter Selinsgrove and Clinton County Speedways

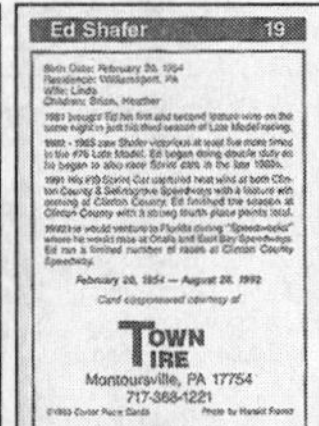

This 36-card set is the second edition from Corter Race Cards. The sets feature drivers and their cars that raced at the Pennsylvania speedway. There were 1,000 sets produced. Each set comes in a snap it case and has a cover card with the number of 1,000 that each particular set is. An uncut sheet of the set was given to each of the drivers that appeared in the set.

	MINT	NRMT
COMPLETE SET (36)	12.00	5.50
COMMON CARD (1-36)	.35	.16
❑ 1 Richie Jensen	.35	.16
❑ 2 Steve Campbell	.35	.16
❑ 3 Lenny Krautheim III	.35	.16
❑ 4 Dale Schweikart	.35	.16
❑ 5 Dwayne Wasson	.50	.23
❑ 6 Jim Nace	.50	.23
❑ 7 Dustin Hoffman	.50	.23
❑ 8 Chuck Reinert Jr.	.35	.16
❑ 9 Boyd Toner Sr.	.35	.16
❑ 10 George Fultz	.35	.16
❑ 11 Jim Stine	.50	.23
❑ 12 Craig Lindsey	.35	.16
❑ 13 David Brouse Sr.	.35	.16
❑ 14 Eric Hons	.35	.16
❑ 15 Luke Hoffner	.35	.16
❑ 16 Vern Wasson	.35	.16
❑ 17 Alan Cole	.35	.16
❑ 18 James Gearhart	.50	.23
❑ 19 Ed Shafer In Memory	.50	.23
❑ 20 Pen Kester's Car	.35	.16
❑ 21 Don Schick Jr.	.35	.16
❑ 22 Timothy Bowmaster	.35	.16
❑ 23 Larry Bair	.35	.16
❑ 24 Bob Bertasavage	.35	.16
❑ 25 John Hafer's Car	.35	.16
❑ 26 Glenn Fitzcharles	.50	.23
❑ 27 Wayne Peeling	.35	.16
❑ 28 Dave Lundgren	.35	.16
❑ 29 Bill Crawford	.35	.16
❑ 30 Grover Graham	.35	.16
❑ 31 Loren Armes	.35	.16
❑ 32 Edward Overdorf	.35	.16
❑ 33 Ron Kramer	.35	.16
❑ 34 Robby Smith	.35	.16
❑ 35 Joey Borich	.35	.16
❑ 36 Christa Koch Ms.Selinsgrove	.35	.16

1991 Dirt Trax

Volunteer racing produced this set in two series. Each series was released in its own plastic factory set box. The cards were printed on thin stock and carry blue borders and yellow cardbacks.

	MINT	NRMT
COMPLETE SET (72)	15.00	6.75
COMPLETE SERIES 1 (36)	7.50	3.40
COMPLETE SERIES 2 (36)	7.50	3.40
COMMON CARD (1-72)	.20	.09
❑ 1 Buck Simmons	.20	.09
❑ 2 Herman Goddard	.20	.09
❑ 3 H.E. Vinegard	.20	.09
❑ 4 Billy Moyer Jr.'s Car UER Moyers on front	.20	.09
❑ 5 Rodney Combs	.50	.23
❑ 6 Bob Pierce	.20	.09
❑ 7 Jack Boggs	.50	.23
❑ 8 Jack Pennington	.20	.09
❑ 9 Ronnie Johnson	.20	.09
❑ 10 Hot Rod LaMance	.20	.09
❑ 11 Scott Bloomquist	.50	.23
❑ 12 Donnie Moran	.20	.09
❑ 13 Eddie Carrier's Car	.20	.09
❑ 14 Ed Basey	.20	.09
❑ 15 Dale McDowell	.20	.09
❑ 16 Ed Gibbons	.20	.09
❑ 17 Mike Balzano	.20	.09
❑ 18 John Gill's Car	.20	.09
❑ 19 Jack Trammell	.20	.09
❑ 20 Skip Arp	.20	.09
❑ 21 David Bilbrey	.20	.09
❑ 22 James Cline	.20	.09
❑ 23 Wade Knowles	.20	.09
❑ 24 Joe Meadows' Car	.20	.09
❑ 25 Gary Hall's Car	.20	.09
❑ 26 Bob Cowen	.20	.09
❑ 27 Bob Wearing, Jr.	.30	.14
❑ 28 Rusty Goddard	.20	.09
❑ 29 Scott Sexton	.20	.09
❑ 30 Steve Francis	.20	.09
❑ 31 Billy Ogle, Jr.	.20	.09
❑ 32 Barry Hurt	.20	.09
❑ 33 Mark Vineyard	.20	.09
❑ 34 Bobby Thomas's Car	.20	.09
❑ 35 John Mason's Car	.20	.09
❑ 36 Cover Card Checklist 1-36	.20	.09
❑ 37 Buck Simmons	.20	.09
❑ 38 Jerry Inmon Mississippi Flyer	.20	.09
❑ 39 Billy Moyer	.20	.09
❑ 40 Mike Head	.20	.09
❑ 41 Stan Massey	.20	.09
❑ 42 Mike Duvall Flintstone Flyer	.20	.09
❑ 43 Jack Pennington	.20	.09
❑ 44 Jeff Purvis	.50	.23
❑ 45 Eddie Pace	.20	.09
❑ 46 Bill Ingram	.20	.09
❑ 47 Hot Rod LaMance	.20	.09
❑ 48 Ricky Weeks' Car	.20	.09
❑ 49 Lynn Geisler	.20	.09
❑ 50 Kevin Claycomb	.20	.09
❑ 51 Nathan Durboraw	.20	.09
❑ 52 Doug McCammon	.20	.09
❑ 53 Ed Basey	.20	.09
❑ 54 C.J. Rayburn	.20	.09
❑ 55 Bobby Thomas	.20	.09
❑ 56 Gary Stuhler	.20	.09
❑ 57 Davey Johnson	.30	.14
❑ 58 Clay Kelley	.20	.09
❑ 59 Chub Frank	.20	.09
❑ 60 Tom Rients	.20	.09
❑ 61 Todd Andrews	.20	.09
❑ 62 Paul Croft's Car	.20	.09
❑ 63 Wendall Wallace	.20	.09
❑ 64 Tom Helfrich w/Car	.20	.09
❑ 65 John Jones	.20	.09
❑ 66 Tony Cardin w/Car	.20	.09
❑ 67 Dion Deason's Car	.20	.09
❑ 68 Marty Calloway	.20	.09
❑ 69 Mark Gansmann	.20	.09
❑ 70 Jeff Treece	.20	.09
❑ 71 Darrell Lanigan	.20	.09
❑ 72 Cover Card Checklist 37-72	.20	.09

1992 Dirt Trax

Volunteer Racing Promotions produced this set featuring popular drivers of the Dirt Track Series. The blue bordered cards were sold in complete factory set form as well as through 10-card cello wrappers called wax pax. There were four Gold cards also produced (1000 of each) as a random insert in packs.

	MINT	NRMT
COMPLETE SET (100)	12.00	5.50
COMMON CARD (1-100)	.15	.07
❑ 1 Cover/Checklist Card	.15	.07
❑ 2 Freddy Smith	.15	.07
❑ 3 Jerry Inmon	.15	.07
❑ 4 Delmas Conley	.15	.07
❑ 5 Herman Goddard	.15	.07
❑ 6 Tom Nesbitt	.15	
❑ 7 Larry Moore	.15	
❑ 8 Billy Moyer	.15	
❑ 9 Mike Head	.15	
❑ 10 Bob Pierce	.15	
❑ 11 Rodney Combs	.40	
❑ 12 Jack Boggs	.25	
❑ 13 Mike Duvall	.15	
❑ 14 Ronnie Johnson	.15	
❑ 15 Rick Aukland	.15	
❑ 16 Steve Kosiski	.15	
❑ 17 Scott Bloomquist	.40	
❑ 18 Bill Ingram	.15	
❑ 19 Rod LaMance	.15	
❑ 20 Donnie Moran	.25	
❑ 21 Ed Basey	.15	
❑ 22 Pete Parker	.15	
❑ 23 Delbert Smith	.15	
❑ 24 Nathan Durboraw	.15	
❑ 25 Rex Richey	.15	
❑ 26 Bill Ogle Sr.	.15	
❑ 27 Mike Balzano	.15	
❑ 28 Tom Rients	.15	
❑ 29 John Gill	.15	
❑ 30 Skip Arp	.15	
❑ 31 David Bilbrey	.15	
❑ 32 Clay Kelley	.15	
❑ 33 Chub Frank	.15	
❑ 34 Todd Andrews	.15	
❑ 35 Wade Knowles	.15	
❑ 36 Bill Frye	.15	
❑ 37 Kevin Weaver	.15	
❑ 38 Joe Meadows	.15	
❑ 39 John Booper Bare	.15	
❑ 40 Ron Davies	.15	
❑ 41 Gary Hall	.15	
❑ 42 John Jones	.15	
❑ 43 Dick Barton	.15	
❑ 44 Andy Dill	.15	
❑ 45 Steve Francis	.25	
❑ 46 Davey Johnson	.15	
❑ 47 Billy Ogle Jr.	.15	
❑ 48 Troy Green	.15	
❑ 49 Gary Green	.15	
❑ 50 Jake Lowry	.15	
❑ 51 Checklist Card	.15	
❑ 52 Ronnie Johnson Jack Boggs Scott Bloomquist	.25	
❑ 53 Roger Bagwell	.15	
❑ 54 Randy Boggs	.15	
❑ 55 Denny Bonebrake	.15	
❑ 56 Marty Calloway	.15	
❑ 57 Tony Cardin	.15	
❑ 58 Perry County Speedway	.15	
❑ 59 Gene Chupp	.15	
❑ 60 Kevin Claycomb	.15	
❑ 61 Phil Coltrane	.15	
❑ 62 Tootle Estes	.15	
❑ 63 Red Farmer	.40	
❑ 64 Mark Gansmann	.15	
❑ 65 Lynn Geisler	.15	
❑ 66 Ed Gibbons	.15	
❑ 67 Matt Gilardi	.15	
❑ 68 Rusty Goddard	.15	
❑ 69 Tom Helfrich	.15	
❑ 70 Doug Ingalls	.15	
❑ 71 Joe Kosiski	.15	
❑ 72 Darrell Lanigan	.15	
❑ 73 Freddie Lee	.15	
❑ 74 Tiny Lund	.40	
❑ 75 John Mason	.15	
❑ 76 Stan Massey	.15	
❑ 77 Larry McDaniels	.15	
❑ 78 Dale McDowell	.15	
❑ 79 Ben Miley	.15	
❑ 80 Buddy Morris	.15	
❑ 81 David Moyer	.15	
❑ 82 Eddie Pace	.15	
❑ 83 Jack Pennington	.15	
❑ 84 C.J. Rayburn	.15	
❑ 85 Scott Sexton	.15	
❑ 86 Steve Shaver	.15	
❑ 87 Buck Simmons	.25	
❑ 88 Jeff Smith	.15	
❑ 89 Steve Smith	.25	
❑ 90 Steve Smith	.25	
❑ 91 Gary Stuhler	.15	
❑ 92 Charlie Swartz	.15	
❑ 93 Bobby Thomas	.15	
❑ 94 Jack Trammell	.15	
❑ 95 Carl Trimmer	.15	
❑ 96 Wendall Wallace	.15	
❑ 97 Bob Wearing Jr. Bob Wearing Sr.	.15	
❑ 98 Ricky Weeks	.15	
❑ 99 Johnny Williams	.15	
❑ 100 Ivan Russell	.15	

1991 DK IMCA Dirt Track

3-card set features Dirt Track drivers from the IMCA The cards were issued in complete set form.

	MINT	NRMT
LETE SET (53)	8.00	3.60
ON CARD (1-53)	.20	.09
ecklist Card	.20	.09
rry Gallaher	.20	.09
eve Watts	.20	.09
nny Breuer	.20	.09
rt Daughters	.20	.09
ke Carr	.20	.09
lly Shryock	.20	.09
d Dralle	.20	.09
ott Strothman	.20	.09
ay Johnson	.20	.09
usty Patterson	.20	.09
evin Cale	.20	.09
on Jackson	.20	.09
erry Ryan	.20	.09
/ade Russell	.20	.09
teve Sutliff	.20	.09
rian Birkhofer	.20	.09
erry Pilcher	.20	.09
ynn Richard	.20	.09
ony Stewart	.20	.09
teve Hennies	.20	.09
eff Johnson	.20	.09
avid Birkhofer	.20	.09
like Fitzpatrick	.20	.09
ollie Frink	.20	.09
ob Jennings	.20	.09
like Smith	.20	.09
rank Springsteen	.20	.09
on Wood	.20	.09
urt Stewart	.20	.09
teve Fraise	.20	.09
urt Martin	.20	.09
ay Guss, Jr.	.20	.09
ary Webb	.20	.09
onny Smyser	.20	.09
es Verly	.20	.09
arry Walker	.20	.09
reg Kastli	.20	.09
on Boyse	.20	.09
eff Alkey	.20	.09
ick Wendling	.20	.09
an Forsyth	.20	.09
yan Wanner	.20	.09
y Johnson	.20	.09
oug Hopkins	.20	.09
raig Jacobs	.20	.09
obby Greiner Jr.	.20	.09
ohnny Johnson	.20	.09
arrel DeFrance	.20	.09
arty Gall	.20	.09
andy Krampe	.20	.09
ed Pallister	.20	.09
ob LeKander	.20	.09

1991 Hav-A-Tampa

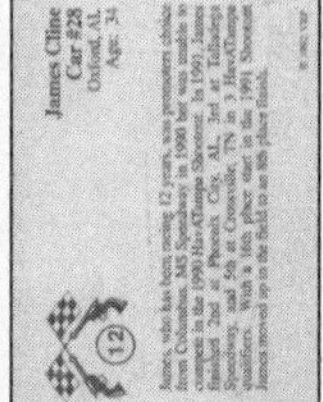

ed by Volunteer Racing, this 28-card set features and cars of the Hav-A-Tampa series. The cards black borders with color photos and were ted in complete set form. The cover/checklist card umbered, but was intended to be card #1.

	MINT	NRMT
ETE SET (28)	6.00	2.70
ON CARD (1-28)	.25	.11
ver Card Checklist Unnumbered	.25	.11
24 Drivers Team Photo	.25	.11
Ingram	.25	.11
y Reaid Jimmy Mosteller 1991 Champion	.25	.11
❑ 5 Tony Reaid	.25	.11
❑ 6 Rex Richey	.25	.11
❑ 7 Rodney Combs Sr.	.40	.18
❑ 8 Phil Coltrane	.25	.11
❑ 9 Wade Knowles	.25	.11
❑ 10 Mike Head	.25	.11
❑ 11 Ed Basey	.25	.11
❑ 12 James Cline	.25	.11
❑ 13 Bobby Thomas	.25	.11
❑ 14 Granger Howell's Car UER name misspelled Grainger	.25	.11
❑ 15 Ronnie Johnson's Car	.25	.11
❑ 16 Derrick Rainey	.25	.11
❑ 17 Wayne Echols' Car	.25	.11
❑ 18 Freddie Lee's Car	.25	.11
❑ 19 Wayne McCullough	.25	.11
❑ 20 Jeff Stansberry	.25	.11
❑ 21 Bill Ingram's Car	.25	.11
❑ 22 Steve Nicholson	.25	.11
❑ 23 John Jones	.25	.11
❑ 24 David Moyer's Car	.25	.11
❑ 25 Stan Massey	.25	.11
❑ 26 Skip Arp	.25	.11
❑ 27 Jody Summerville	.25	.11
❑ 28 Buddy Morris w/Car	.25	.11

1992 Hav-A-Tampa

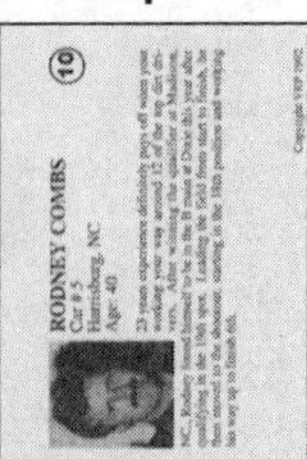

Volunteer Racing Promotions produced this set featuring drivers of the Hav-A-Tampa Series. The cards include the top 24 drivers of the series along with a checklist card and were sold in complete set form.

	MINT	NRMT
COMPLETE SET (28)	8.00	3.60
COMMON CARD (1-28)	.30	.14
❑ 1 Cover/Checklist Card	.30	.14
❑ 2 Top 24 Group	.30	.14
❑ 3 Jimmy Mosteller	.30	.14
❑ 4 Red Farmer Capitol Sports Radio	.30	.14
❑ 5 Buddy Morris	.30	.14
❑ 6 Ronnie Johnson's Car	.30	.14
❑ 7 Phil Coltrane's Car	.30	.14
❑ 8 Rex Richey's Car	.30	.14
❑ 9 Wade Knowles' Car	.30	.14
❑ 10 Rodney Combs' Car	.30	.14
❑ 11 Bobby Turner's Car	.30	.14
❑ 12 Dale McDowell's Car	.30	.14
❑ 13 Mike Head's Car	.30	.14
❑ 14 Stan Massey w/car	.30	.14
❑ 15 Tony Reaid's Car	.30	.14
❑ 16 Freddie Lee's Car	.30	.14
❑ 17 Ricky Williams' Car	.30	.14
❑ 18 Jody Summerville's Car	.30	.14
❑ 19 David Chancy's Car	.30	.14
❑ 20 Greg Knight's Car	.30	.14
❑ 21 Bobby Thomas' Car	.30	.14
❑ 22 Rodney Martin's Car	.30	.14
❑ 23 Granger Howell's Car	.30	.14
❑ 24 Buckshot Miles' Car	.30	.14
❑ 25 Wayne Echols' Car	.30	.14
❑ 26 Buster Goss' Car	.30	.14
❑ 27 John Jones' Car	.30	.14
❑ 28 Ed Basey's Car	.30	.14

1995 Hav-A-Tampa

REX RICHEY, of Ringgold, GA, has qualified for the SHOOTOUT feature 4 years in a row finishing 2nd in '91, and 4th in '92.

Speed Graphics produced this set featuring drivers of the Hav-A-Tampa Series. The cards include the top personalities of the series along with a checklist card and were sold in complete set form.

	MINT	NRMT
COMPLETE SET (42)	15.00	6.75
COMMON CARD (1-42)	.40	.18
❑ 1 Cover Card	.40	.18
❑ 2 Bill Frye	.40	.18
❑ 3 Drivers Meeting 1994 Shootout	.40	.18
❑ 4 Jeff Smith	.40	.18
❑ 5 Ronnie Johnson	.40	.18
❑ 6 Jack Boggs	.75	.35
❑ 7 Dale McDowell	.40	.18
❑ 8 Clint Smith	.40	.18
❑ 9 Rodney Martin	.40	.18
❑ 10 Dixie Speedway	.40	.18
❑ 11 Freddy Smith	.40	.18
❑ 12 Jeff Smith	.40	.18
❑ 13 Larry Moore	.40	.18
❑ 14 David Gibson	.40	.18
❑ 15 Danny McClure	.40	.18
❑ 16 Kenny Morrow	.40	.18
❑ 17 C.S.Fitzgerald	.40	.18
❑ 18 DeWayne Johnson	.40	.18
❑ 19 Kenny Merchant	.40	.18
❑ 20 Bill Ogle Jr.	.40	.18
❑ 21 Johnny Virden	.40	.18
❑ 22 Bobby Thomas	.40	.18
❑ 23 Gar Dickson	.40	.18
❑ 24 Mike Carter	.40	.18
❑ 25 Wendall Wallace	.40	.18
❑ 26 Rex Richey	.40	.18
❑ 27 Tony Reaid	.40	.18
❑ 28 Earl Pearson Jr.	.40	.18
❑ 29 Rick Aukland	.40	.18
❑ 30 Donnie Moran UER Donnnie on front	.40	.18
❑ 31 Billy Moyer	.40	.18
❑ 32 Curtis Gattis	.40	.18
❑ 33 Frank Ingram	.40	.18
❑ 34 Marshall Green	.40	.18
❑ 35 Mark Miner	.40	.18
❑ 36 Ray Cook	.40	.18
❑ 37 Stan Massey	.40	.18
❑ 38 Rod LaMance	.40	.18
❑ 39 Mike Duvall	.40	.18
❑ 40 Bill Ingram	.40	.18
❑ 41 Jimmy Mosteller Founder	.40	.18
❑ 42 HAT Officials Nick Masters David Roberts Jim Harrah Checklist back	.40	.18

1991 JAGS

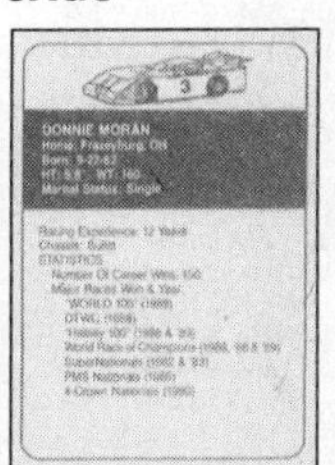

JAGS Race Cards produced this set featuring top drivers of Dirt Late Model competition. This was the first of four sets and featured a light gray card border.

	MINT	NRMT
COMPLETE SET (50)	12.00	5.50
COMMON CARD (1-50)	.20	.09
❑ 1 Scott Bloomquist	.50	.23
❑ 2 Jack Boggs' Car	.30	.14
❑ 3 Donnie Moran's Car	.20	.09
❑ 4 Mike Duvall	.30	.14
❑ 5 Gene Chupp's Car	.20	.09
❑ 6 Gary Stuhler's Car	.20	.09
❑ 7 Ronnie Johnson's Car	.20	.09
❑ 8 John Gill	.30	.14
❑ 9 James Cline's Car	.20	.09
❑ 10 C.J. Rayburn's Car	.20	.09
❑ 11 Jim Curry	.30	.14
❑ 12 Mike Balzano's Car	.20	.09
❑ 13 Rex Richey's Car	.20	.09
❑ 14 Kris Patterson	.30	.14
❑ 15 Tony Cardin	.30	.14

Card	MINT	NRMT
❑ 16 Eddie Carrier	.30	.14
❑ 17 Mike Head's Car	.20	.09
❑ 18 John Provenzano	.30	.14
❑ 19 Bill Frye's Car	.20	.09
❑ 20 Steve Francis	.50	.23
❑ 21 Randy Boggs' Car	.20	.09
❑ 22 Roger Long	.30	.14
❑ 23 Daryl Key	.30	.14
❑ 24 Bob Pohlman	.30	.14
❑ 25 Scott Bloomquist's Car	.50	.23
❑ 26 Johnny Stokes' Car	.20	.09
❑ 27 Steve Barnett	.30	.14
❑ 28 Rex McCroskey	.30	.14
❑ 29 Mitch Johnson	.30	.14
❑ 30 Wade Knowles	.30	.14
❑ 31 Darrell Mooneyham	.30	.14
❑ 32 John Mason's Car	.20	.09
❑ 33 Ken Essary's Car	.20	.09
❑ 34 Wendall Wallace	.30	.14
❑ 35 Leslie Essary	.30	.14
❑ 36 Rodney Franklin	.30	.14
❑ 37 Jerry Inmon	.30	.14
❑ 38 Tom Rients	.30	.14
❑ 39 Earl Pepper Newby	.30	.14
❑ 40 Bob Wearing Jr.	.30	.14
❑ 41 Dale McDowell	.30	.14
❑ 42 John Booper Bare	.30	.14
❑ 43 Buck Simmons' Car	.20	.09
❑ 44 Steve Kosiski's Car	.20	.09
❑ 45 John Jones' Car	.20	.09
❑ 46 Hot Rod LaMance's Car	.20	.09
❑ 47 Ricky Weeks' Car	.20	.09
❑ 48 Billy Scott	.30	.14
❑ 49 Ed Basey's Car	.20	.09
❑ 50 Bob Pierce	.30	.14

1992 JAGS

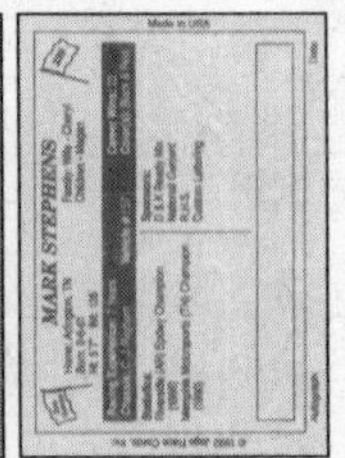

JAGS Race Cards produced this set featuring top drivers of Dirt Late Model competition. This was the second of four sets released by JAGS and featured a light blue card border. The set was distributed in two seperate series.

	MINT	NRMT
COMPLETE SET (256)	30.00	13.50
COMPLETE SERIES 1 (128)	15.00	6.75
COMPLETE SERIES 2 (128)	15.00	6.75
COMMON CARD	.10	.05

Card	MINT	NRMT
❑ 1 Skip Arp	.20	.09
❑ 2 Rick Aukland	.10	.05
❑ 3 Doug Ault	.10	.05
❑ 4 Mark Banal	.10	.05
❑ 5 Dick Barton	.10	.05
❑ 6 Shannon Bearden	.10	.05
❑ 7 Mike Bechelli	.10	.05
❑ 8 Jim Bernheisel	.10	.05
❑ 9 Scott Bloomquist	.35	.16
❑ 10 Jack Boggs	.35	.16
❑ 11 Johnny Bone Jr.	.10	.05
❑ 12 Mike Brown	.10	.05
❑ 13 Tony Cardin	.10	.05
❑ 14 Darrell Carpenter	.10	.05
❑ 15 Denny Chamberlain	.10	.05
❑ 16 Kevin Claycomb	.10	.05
❑ 17 Mike Clonce	.10	.05
❑ 18 Phil Coltrane	.10	.05
❑ 19 Paul Croft	.10	.05
❑ 20 Randy Dunn	.10	.05
❑ 21 Hank Edwards	.10	.05
❑ 22 Rick Egersdorf	.10	.05
❑ 23 Terry English	.10	.05
❑ 24 Dennis Erb	.10	.05
❑ 25 Ken Essary	.10	.05
❑ 26 Rocky Estes	.10	.05
❑ 27 Danny Felker	.10	.05
❑ 28 Ed Ferree	.10	.05
❑ 29 Jeff Floyd	.10	.05
❑ 30 Chub Frank	.10	.05
❑ 31 Rollie Frink	.10	.05
❑ 32 Bill Frye	.10	.05
❑ 33 Lynn Geisler	.10	.05
❑ 34 Ed Gibbons	.10	.05
❑ 35 Herman Goddard	.10	.05
❑ 36 Gary Green	.10	.05
❑ 37 Marshall Green	.10	.05
❑ 38 Kevin Gundaker	.10	.05
❑ 39 Phil Hall	.10	.05
❑ 40 Paul Harris	.10	.05
❑ 41 Mike Head	.10	.05
❑ 42 Tom Helfrich	.10	.05
❑ 43 Jack Hewitt	.20	.09
❑ 44 Brian Hickman	.10	.05
❑ 45 Bob Hill	.10	.05
❑ 46 Don Hobbs	.10	.05
❑ 47 Bruce Hogue	.10	.05
❑ 48 J.D. Howard	.10	.05
❑ 49 Charlie Hughes	.10	.05
❑ 50 Sam Hurd	.10	.05
❑ 51 Doug Ingalls	.10	.05
❑ 52 Bill Ingram	.10	.05
❑ 53 Mike Jewell	.10	.05
❑ 54 Johnny Johnson	.10	.05
❑ 55 Ronnie Johnson	.10	.05
❑ 56 Harvey Jones Jr.	.10	.05
❑ 57 Gary Keeling	.10	.05
❑ 58 Ed Kosiski	.10	.05
❑ 59 Steve Kosiski	.10	.05
❑ 60 Willy Kraft	.10	.05
❑ 61 Ted Lackey	.10	.05
❑ 62 Larry Lambeth	.10	.05
❑ 63 Steve Landrum	.10	.05
❑ 64 Darrell Lanigan	.10	.05
❑ 65 Jerry Lark	.10	.05
❑ 66 John Lawhorn	.10	.05
❑ 67 Tommy Lawwell	.10	.05
❑ 68 Rick Lebow	.10	.05
❑ 69 Mike Luna	.10	.05
❑ 70 Donald Marsh	.10	.05
❑ 71 Bill Martin	.10	.05
❑ 72 Stan Massey	.10	.05
❑ 73 Doug McCammon	.10	.05
❑ 74 Gary McPherson	.10	.05
❑ 75 Audie McWilliams	.10	.05
❑ 76 Joe Meadows	.10	.05
❑ 77 Buckshot Miles	.10	.05
❑ 78 Brett Miller	.10	.05
❑ 79 Larry Moore	.10	.05
❑ 80 Donnie Moran	.10	.05
❑ 81 David Moyer	.10	.05
❑ 82 Tom Nesbitt	.10	.05
❑ 83 Bill Ogle	.10	.05
❑ 84 Don O'Neal	.10	.05
❑ 85 Eddie Pace	.10	.05
❑ 86 Pete Parker	.10	.05
❑ 87 Bob Pierce	.10	.05
❑ 88 Ronnie Poche	.10	.05
❑ 89 Al Purkey	.10	.05
❑ 90 Jim Rarick	.10	.05
❑ 91 Frank Reaber	.10	.05
❑ 92 Tony Reaid	.10	.05
❑ 93 Joe Rice	.10	.05
❑ 94 Rex Richey	.10	.05
❑ 95 Eddie Rickman	.10	.05
❑ 96 Jerry Robertson	.10	.05
❑ 97 Jeff Robinson	.10	.05
❑ 98 Steve Russell	.10	.05
❑ 99 Doug Sanders	.10	.05
❑ 100 Charlie Schaffer	.10	.05
❑ 101 Ken Schrader	1.50	.70
❑ 102 Frank Seder	.10	.05
❑ 103 Randy Sellars	.10	.05
❑ 104 Scott Sexton	.10	.05
❑ 105 Paul Shafer	.10	.05
❑ 106 Steve Shaver	.10	.05
❑ 107 Clint Smith	.10	.05
❑ 108 Delbert Smith	.10	.05
❑ 109 Earl Smith	.10	.05
❑ 110 Steve Smith	.20	.09
❑ 111 Gibby Steinhaus	.10	.05
❑ 112 Charlie Swartz	.10	.05
❑ 113 Dick Taylor	.10	.05
❑ 114 Bobby Thomas	.10	.05
❑ 115 Jack Trammell	.20	.09
❑ 116 John Utsman	.10	.05
❑ 117 Troy VanderVeen	.10	.05
❑ 118 H.E. Vineyard	.10	.05
❑ 119 Wendall Wallace	.10	.05
❑ 120 Bob Wearing Jr.	.10	.05
❑ 121 Kevin Weaver	.10	.05
❑ 122 Gary Webb	.10	.05
❑ 123 Doug Wiggs	.10	.05
❑ 124 Rick Williams	.10	.05
❑ 125 Randy Woodling	.10	.05
❑ 126 Jeff Aikey's Car	.10	.05
❑ 127 Tony Albright's Car	.10	.05
❑ 128 Chris Anderson's Car	.10	.05
❑ 129 Todd Anderson's Car	.10	.05
❑ 130 Todd Andrews' Car	.10	.05
❑ 131 Brian Ater	.20	.09
❑ 132 Steve Baker	.20	.09
❑ 133 Mike Balzano's Car	.10	.05
❑ 134 Jr. Banks	.20	
❑ 135 John Booper Bare's Car	.10	
❑ 136 Joe Barnett	.20	
❑ 137 Steve Barnett	.20	
❑ 138 Ed Basey's Car	.10	
❑ 139 Dave Bilbrey's Car	.10	
❑ 140 Randy Boggs' Car	.10	
❑ 141 Don Bohlander's Car	.10	
❑ 142 Denny Bonebrake's Car	.10	
❑ 143 Mike Bowers' Car	.10	
❑ 144 Jay Brinkley	.20	
❑ 145 Randy Carte	.20	
❑ 146 David Chancy	.20	
❑ 147 Gene Chupp	.20	
❑ 148 Jimmy Clifton's Car	.10	
❑ 149 Tory Collins' Car	.10	
❑ 150 Delmas Conley's Car	.10	
❑ 151 Rick Corbin's Car	.10	
❑ 152 Jim Curry's Car	.10	
❑ 153 Jim Donofrio's Car	.10	
❑ 154 Nelson Dowd's Car	.10	
❑ 155 Bryan Dunaway	.20	
❑ 156 Mike Duvall's Car	.10	
❑ 157 Rick Eckert	.20	
❑ 158 Leslie Essary	.20	
❑ 159 Don Eyerly's Car	.10	
❑ 160 Lee Fleetwood	.20	
❑ 161 Randy Floyd	.20	
❑ 162 Steve Francis' Car	.20	
❑ 163 Rodney Franklin	.20	
❑ 164 Andy Fries	.20	
❑ 165 Andy Genzman's Car	.10	
❑ 166 John Gill's Car	.10	
❑ 167 Ray Godsey's Car	.10	
❑ 168 Barry Goodman's Car	.10	
❑ 169 Gary Gorby	.20	
❑ 170 Troy Green's Car	.10	
❑ 171 Phil Gregory's Car	.10	
❑ 172 Don Gross' Car	.10	
❑ 173 Johnny Schuler's Car	.10	
❑ 174 Dave Hoffman's Car	.10	
❑ 175 Dewayne Hughes' Car	.10	
❑ 176 Mike Hurlbert's Car	.10	
❑ 177 Ricky Idom's Car	.10	
❑ 178 Ricky Ingalls	.20	
❑ 179 Jerry Inmon	.20	
❑ 180 Tony Izzo Jr.	.20	
❑ 181 Mitch Johnson's Car	.10	
❑ 182 John Jones' Car	.10	
❑ 183 (Big) Jim Kelly's Car	.10	
❑ 184 Daryl Key's Car	.10	
❑ 185 Terry King's Car	.10	
❑ 186 Wade Knowles's Car	.10	
❑ 187 Joe Kosiski's Car	.10	
❑ 188 Hot Rod LaMance's Car	.10	
❑ 189 Freddie Lee's Car	.10	
❑ 190 Junior Lemmings	.20	
❑ 191 Joe Littlejohn's Car	.10	
❑ 192 Roger Long's Car	.10	
❑ 193 B.K. Luna	.20	
❑ 194 Garry Mahoney	.20	
❑ 195 Donnie Marcoullier Jr.	.20	
❑ 196 Bill Mason's Car	.10	
❑ 197 John Mason's Car	.10	
❑ 198 Lance Matthees' Car	.10	
❑ 199 Rex McCroskey's Car	.10	
❑ 200 Dale McDowell's Car	.10	
❑ 201 Ben Miley	.20	
❑ 202 Matt Miller	.20	
❑ 203 Matt Mitchell	.20	
❑ 204 Darrell Mooneyham	.20	
❑ 205 Bill Morgan	.20	
❑ 206 Mike Mullvain	.20	
❑ 207 Terry Muskrat's Car	.10	
❑ 208 Earl "Pepper" Newby	.20	
❑ 209 Bobby Joe Nicely's Car	.10	
❑ 210 Mike Norris' Car	.10	
❑ 211 Keith Nosbisch's Car	.10	
❑ 212 Jimmy Nowlin	.20	
❑ 213 Chuck Nutzmann's Car	.10	
❑ 214 Mike Nutzmann's Car	.10	
❑ 215 Lee Olibas's Car	.10	
❑ 216 Jim O'Conner	.20	
❑ 217 Marty O'Neal	.20	
❑ 218 Skip Pannell's Car	.10	
❑ 219 Kris Patterson's Car	.10	
❑ 220 Terry Phillips	.20	
❑ 221 Bob Pohlman Jr.'s Car	.10	
❑ 222 John Provenzano	.20	
❑ 223 C.J. Rayburn	.20	
❑ 224 Jerry Rice	.20	
❑ 225 Tom Rients	.20	
❑ 226 Kevin Roderick's Car	.10	
❑ 227 Todd Rust's Car	.10	
❑ 228 Ed Sans Jr.'s Car	.10	
❑ 229 Eric Sayre's Car	.10	
❑ 230 Darwin Scarlett's Car	.10	
❑ 231 Billy Scott	.20	

	MINT	NRMT
Russ Sell's Car	.10	.05
Steve Shute's Car	.10	.05
Buck Simmons' Car	.10	.05
Lavon Sloan's Car	.10	.05
Buddy Smith's Car	.10	.05
Sonny Smyser	.20	.09
Tommy Snell's Car	.10	.05
Mark Stevens	.20	.09
Johnny Stokes	.20	.09
Jim Tyron's Car	.10	.05
Wren Turner	.20	.09
Johnny Virdon's Car	.10	.05
Mike Walker's Car	.10	.05
Bob Wearing Jr.'s Car	.10	.05
Ricky Weeks' Car	.10	.05
Jimmie White	.20	.09
Dill Whittymore	.20	.09
Sam Williams' Car	.10	.05
Charlie Williamson's Car	.10	.05
Cover Card Checklist 126-167	.10	.05
Cover Card Checklist 85-125	.10	.05
Cover Card Checklist 43-84	.10	.05
Cover Card Checklist 1-42	.10	.05
Cover Card Checklist 168-209	.10	.05
Cover Card Checklist 210-250	.10	.05

1993 JAGS

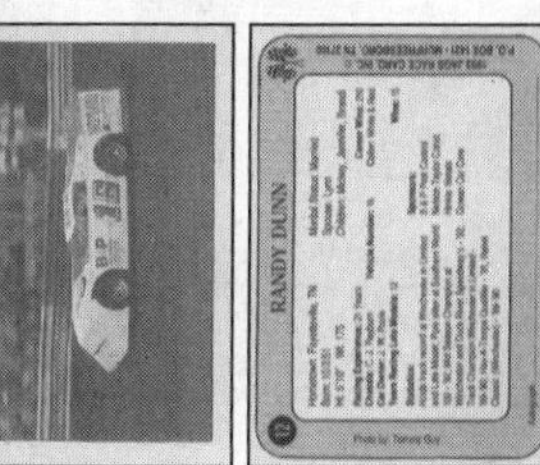

lace Cards produced this set featuring top drivers Late Model competition. This was the third of four eased by JAGS and featured a light tan border.

	MINT	NRMT
ETE SET (52)	12.00	5.50
ON CARD (1-51)	.25	.11
ny Albright	.25	.11
n Amacher	.25	.11
ott Bloomquist	.50	.23
e Boland	.25	.11
my Burwell	.25	.11
ty Calloway	.25	.11
ndall Chupp	.25	.11
in Coffey	.25	.11
Dickson	.25	.11
Dixon	.25	.11
trick Duggan	.25	.11
andy Dunn	.25	.11
nmy Edwards Jr.	.25	.11
ul Feistritzer	.25	.11
ike Freeman	.25	.11
ed F. Flatt	.25	.11
hn Gill	.25	.11
ay Guss Jr.	.25	.11
ly Hicks	.25	.11
nt Hicks	.25	.11
sey Huffman	.25	.11
nny Huskey	.25	.11
l Ingram	.25	.11
ank Ingram	.25	.11
lly Kraft	.25	.11
rrell Lanigan	.25	.11
K. Luna	.25	.11
ke Luna	.25	.11
ry Mann	.25	.11
ark DIRT Martin	.25	.11
le McDowell	.25	.11
onty Miller	.25	.11
ny W. Moody	.25	.11
nnie Moran	.25	.11
ly Moyer	.25	.11
n Nosbisch	.25	.11
l Palmer	.25	.11
te Parker	.25	.11
eve D. Russell	.25	.11
ug Sanders	.25	.11
ndy Sellars	.25	.11
rry Shannon	.25	.11

	MINT	NRMT
❑ 43 Clint Smith	.25	.11
❑ 44 Freddy Smith	.35	.16
❑ 45 Jeff Smith	.25	.11
❑ 46 Josh Tarter	.25	.11
❑ 47 John A. Utsman	.25	.11
❑ 48 Jeff Walker	.25	.11
❑ 49 Kevin Weaver	.25	.11
❑ 50 Randy Weaver	.25	.11
❑ 51 Cover Card Checklist	.25	.11
❑ NNO Jennifer Dunn Miss JAGS	.25	.11

1994 JAGS

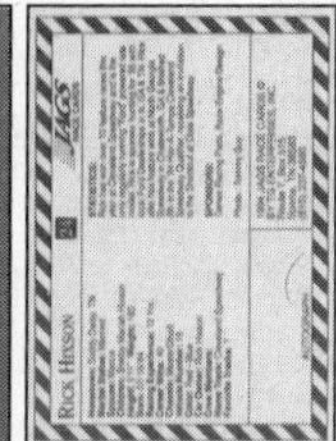

JAGS Race Cards produced this set featuring top drivers of Dirt Late Model competition. This was the last of four sets released by JAGS and featured a purple border.

	MINT	NRMT
COMPLETE SET (63)	12.00	5.50
COMMON CARD (1-63)	.20	.09
❑ 1 Tony Albright	.20	.09
❑ 2 Brian Ater	.20	.09
❑ 3 Steve Barnett	.20	.09
❑ 4 Wade Beaty	.20	.09
❑ 5 Eddie Benfield	.20	.09
❑ 6 Scott Bloomquist	.50	.23
❑ 7 Jackie Boggs Jr.	.20	.09
❑ 8 Rudy Boutwell	.20	.09
❑ 9 Jay Brinkley	.20	.09
❑ 10 Dave Burks	.20	.09
❑ 11 Ronnie Caldwell	.20	.09
❑ 12 Buster Cardwell	.20	.09
❑ 13 Randall Carte	.20	.09
❑ 14 Kevin Coffey	.20	.09
❑ 15 Ray Cook	.20	.09
❑ 16 Billy Drake	.20	.09
❑ 17 Patrick Duggan	.20	.09
❑ 18 Bryan Dunaway	.20	.09
❑ 19 Rick Eckert	.20	.09
❑ 20 Terry English	.20	.09
❑ 21 Wayne Fielden	.20	.09
❑ 22 Steve Francis	.30	.14
❑ 23 Billy Hicks	.20	.09
❑ 24 Rick Hixson	.20	.09
❑ 25 Larry Isley	.20	.09
❑ 26 Travis Johnson	.20	.09
❑ 27 Gary Keeling	.20	.09
❑ 28 Kenny LeCroy	.20	.09
❑ 29 Jr. Lemmings	.20	.09
❑ 30 Roger Long	.20	.09
❑ 31 Keith Longmire	.20	.09
❑ 32 Mike Luna	.20	.09
❑ 33 Gary Mabe	.20	.09
❑ 34 Tom Maddox	.20	.09
❑ 35 Robby Mason	.20	.09
❑ 36 Gary May	.20	.09
❑ 37 Jimmy McCormick	.20	.09
❑ 38 Dale McDowell	.20	.09
❑ 39 Gary McPherson	.20	.09
❑ 40 Byron L. Michael	.20	.09
❑ 41 Donnie Moran	.20	.09
❑ 42 Mike Mullvain	.20	.09
❑ 43 Billy Ogle Jr.	.20	.09
❑ 44 Carnell Parker	.20	.09
❑ 45 Jamie Perry	.20	.09
❑ 46 Bob Pierce	.20	.09
❑ 47 Phillip Richardson	.20	.09
❑ 48 Bobby Richey Jr.	.20	.09
❑ 49 Rick Rogers	.20	.09
❑ 50 Joe Ross Jr.	.20	.09
❑ 51 Randy Sellars	.20	.09
❑ 52 Scott Sexton	.20	.09
❑ 53 J.R. Shickel	.20	.09
❑ 54 Freddy Smith	.20	.09
❑ 55 Jeff Smith	.20	.09
❑ 56 Dick Taylor	.20	.09
❑ 57 Paul Tims	.20	.09
❑ 58 Mike Tinker	.20	.09
❑ 59 Leroy Vann	.20	.09
❑ 60 Kevin Weaver	.20	.09
❑ 61 Neil P. Welch	.20	.09
❑ 62 Rick Williams	.20	.09
❑ 63 Cover Card Checklist	.20	.09

1995 JSK Iceman

JSK Collectable Promotions produced this 27-card set featuring drivers of the Iceman Super Car Series. The cards are numbered according to the driver's car number and were distributed through souvenir stands at series' tracks. Set production was limited to 4000 sets that had an original cost of $12.50. Uncut sheets (52 made) were distributed for the set as well at a cost of $17.

	MINT	NRMT
COMPLETE SET (27)	14.00	6.25
COMMON CARD	.50	.23
❑ 1 Dennis Berry's Car	.75	.35
❑ 4 Scott Baker's Car	.50	.23
❑ 6 Tom Fedewa's Car	.50	.23
❑ 7 Jason Mignogna's Car	.50	.23
❑ 9 Matt Hutter's Car	.50	.23
❑ 10 Stan Perry's Car	.50	.23
❑ 13 Jerry Cook's Car	.50	.23
❑ 15 Kenny Phillips' Car	.50	.23
❑ 20 Ed Hage's Car	.50	.23
❑ 21 Dan Morse's Car	.50	.23
❑ 24 Dave Kuhlman's Car	.50	.23
❑ 32 Dennis Strickland's Car	.50	.23
❑ 48 Kenny Howard's Car	.50	.23
❑ 56 Chase Howe w/Car	.50	.23
❑ 65 Tim Ice's Car	1.00	.45
❑ 69 Ron Allen's Car	.50	.23
❑ 70 Fred Campbell's Car	.75	.35
❑ 72 Scott Hantz's Car	.50	.23
❑ 77 Kenny Sword's Car	.50	.23
❑ 81 Gary Camelot's Car	.50	.23
❑ 83 Bob Sibila's Car	.50	.23
❑ 90 Tim Curry's Car	.50	.23
❑ 97 Steve Sauve's Car	.50	.23
❑ 99 John Sawatsky's Car	.50	.23
❑ 0 Chuck Roumell's Car	.75	.35
❑ NNO Cover Card set order form on back	.50	.23
❑ NNO Schedule Card	.50	.23

1995 JSK Iceman Past Champions

JSK Collectable Promotions produced this 7-card set featuring past champs of the Iceman Super Car Series. Six cards focus on the champion drivers and cars, along with one cover card. The cards are numbered according to the driver's car number. Set production was limited to 4000 sets that had an original cost of $5. Uncut sheets (52 made) were distributed for the set as well at a cost of $7.

	MINT	NRMT
COMPLETE SET (7)	7.50	3.40
COMMON CARD	1.00	.45
❑ 40 Bruce Vanderlaan's Car	1.00	.45
❑ 51/52 Dennis Berry's Car Butch Miller's Car	1.00	.45
❑ 61 Dennis Berry w/Car	1.00	.45
❑ 65 Tim Ice w/Car	2.00	.90

Card	MINT	NRMT
❑ 70 Fred Campbell's Car	1.00	.45
❑ 0 Chuck Roumell's Car	1.00	.45
❑ NNO Cover Card set order form on back	1.00	.45

1995 JSK S.O.D. Sprints

JSK Collectable Promotions produced this 24-card set featuring drivers of the S.O.D. Sprints series. The cards are numbered according to the driver's car number and were distributed through souvenir stands at series' tracks. Set production was limited to 4000 sets that had an original cost of $10. Uncut sheets (52 made) were distributed for the set as well at a cost of $15.

	MINT	NRMT
COMPLETE SET (24)	12.00	5.50
COMMON CARD	.50	.23
❑ 1 Scott Seaton's Car	.50	.23
❑ 2 Mike Katz's Car	.50	.23
❑ 3S Brian Tyler's Car	.50	.23
❑ 5 Steve VanNote's Car	.50	.23
❑ 6 Jeff Bloom's Car	.50	.23
❑ 10 Ron Koehler's Car	.50	.23
❑ 16 Mike Mouch's Car	.50	.23
❑ 20 Bill Tyler's Car	.50	.23
❑ 21 Rocky Fisher's Car	.50	.23
❑ 22R Jay Sherston's Car	.50	.23
❑ 35 Ryan Katz's Car	.50	.23
❑ 37 Hank Lower's Car	.50	.23
❑ 42 Gary Fedewa's Car	.50	.23
❑ 43 Dan Osburn's Car	.50	.23
❑ 44J Bill Jacoby's Car	.50	.23
❑ 47 Bob Clark's Car	.50	.23
❑ 49 Lisa Ward's Car	.50	.23
❑ 72 Pat York's Car	.50	.23
❑ 77B Steve Burch's Car	.50	.23
❑ 77T John Turner's Car	.50	.23
❑ 83 Wayne Landon's Car	.50	.23
❑ NNO John Boy Hotchkiss numbered JB	.50	.23
❑ NNO Schedule Card	.50	.23
❑ NNO Cover Card set order form on back	.50	.23

1990 K&W Dirt Track

K&W Race Cards produced a series of sets featuring drivers of DIRT Modifieds sold through local area tracks. A percentage of set sales proceeds went to the DIRT driver's injury fund. This 42-card set was the first edition in the series and was printed with color photos surrounded by a black border on the cardfront. Cardbacks were printed in black and white. Reportedly, 2,500 sets were produced and 500 of each card were made available to the drivers. The remaining 2,000 sets were then distributed. The unnumbered cards are listed below alphabetically.

	MINT	NRMT
COMPLETE SET (42)	10.00	4.50
COMMON CARD (1-42)	.25	.11
❑ 1 Steve Ay	.25	.11
❑ 2 Johnny Bennett Jr.	.25	.11
❑ 3 Dave Bently	.25	.11
❑ 4 Frances Blauvelt	.25	.11
❑ 5 Billy Brennen	.25	.11
❑ 6 Ed Brown Jr.	.25	.11
❑ 7 Hal Browning	.25	.11
❑ 8 Barry Buckhart	.25	.11
❑ 9 Tom Capie	.25	.11
❑ 10 Darryl Carman	.25	.11
❑ 11 Richard Cass	.25	.11
❑ 12 Chic Cossaboone	.25	.11
❑ 13 Brian Donley	.25	.11
❑ 14 Joe Edwards	.25	.11
❑ 15 Rick Elliott	.25	.11
❑ 16 Butch Glisson	.25	.11
❑ 17 Garry Gollub	.25	.11
❑ 18 Newt Hartman	.25	.11
❑ 19 Frank Hayes	.25	.11
❑ 20 Jim Horton Sr.	.35	.16
❑ 21 Jimmy Horton	.50	.23
❑ 22 James Jackson	.25	.11
❑ 23 Bucky Kell	.25	.11
❑ 24 Robbie Keller	.25	.11
❑ 25 Bear Kelly	.25	.11
❑ 26 Ron Keys	.25	.11
❑ 27 Roger Laureno	.25	.11
❑ 28 John Leach	.25	.11
❑ 29 Mick MacNeir	.25	.11
❑ 30 Jimmy Martin	.25	.11
❑ 31 Ernie Miles Jr.	.25	.11
❑ 32 Jamie Mills	.25	.11
❑ 33 Brad Nash	.25	.11
❑ 34 Fred Orchard Jr.	.25	.11
❑ 35 Bobby Parks	.25	.11
❑ 36 Richie Pratt	.25	.11
❑ 37 Scott Pursell	.25	.11
❑ 38 Erwin Schlenger	.25	.11
❑ 39 Glenn Smith	.25	.11
❑ 40 Paul Weaver	.25	.11
❑ 41 Wayne Weaver	.25	.11
❑ 42 Edward Zehner	.25	.11

1991 K&W Dirt Track

This set of 50-cards featuring top Northeast DIRT Track drivers was produced and distributed by K&W Race Cards. The black bordered cards include 49-drivers and one cover/checklist card and were released in complete set form. A percentage of set sales proceeds went to the DIRT driver's injury fund. Reportedly, 2,500 sets were produced and 500 of each card were made available to the drivers. The remaining 2,000 were then distributed.

	MINT	NRMT
COMPLETE SET (50)	12.00	5.50
COMMON CARD (1-50)	.25	.11
❑ 1 Brett Hearn	.25	.11
❑ 2 Billy Pauch	.25	.11
❑ 3 Doug Hoffman	.25	.11
❑ 4 Scott Irwin	.25	.11
❑ 5 Johnny Betts	.25	.11
❑ 6 Chip Slocum	.25	.11
❑ 7 Fred Brightbill	.25	.11
❑ 8 Glenn Smith	.25	.11
❑ 9 Rick Elliott	.25	.11
❑ 10 John Leach	.25	.11
❑ 11 Jamie Mills	.25	.11
❑ 12 Wayne Weaver	.25	.11
❑ 13 Ron Keys	.25	.11
❑ 14 Newt Hartman	.25	.11
❑ 15 Garry Gollub	.25	.11
❑ 16 Mark Kenyon	.25	.11
❑ 17 Jimmy Chester	.25	.11
❑ 18 Sam Martz	.25	.11
❑ 19 John Pinter	.25	.11
❑ 20 Bobby Wilkins	.25	.11
❑ 21 Hal Browning	.25	.11
❑ 22 Donnie Wetmore	.25	.11
❑ 23 Tom Capie	.25	.11
❑ 24 Bucky Kell	.25	.11
❑ 25 Chic Cossaboone	.25	.11
❑ 26 Randy Glenski	.25	.11
❑ 27 Roger Laureno	.25	.11
❑ 28 Dave Adams	.25	.11
❑ 29 Bobby Parks	.25	.11
❑ 30 Pete Visconti	.25	.11
❑ 31 Ronnie Tobias	.25	
❑ 32 Richie Pratt	.25	
❑ 33 Frank Cozze	.25	
❑ 34 Jack Johnson	.25	
❑ 35 Jimmy Horton	.50	
❑ 36 Toby Tobias Jr.	.25	
❑ 37 Scott Pursell	.25	
❑ 38 Kenny Tremont	.25	
❑ 39 Steve Paine	.25	
❑ 40 Billy Decker	.25	
❑ 41 Whitey Kidd Jr.	.25	
❑ 42 Tom Peck	.35	
❑ 43 Ernie Miles Jr.	.25	
❑ 44 Bill Tanner	.25	
❑ 45 Fred Orchard	.25	
❑ 46 Bob Lineman	.25	
❑ 47 Deron Rust	.25	
❑ 48 Gary Bruckler	.25	
❑ 49 Craig Von Dohren	.25	
❑ 50 Cover Card Checklist	.25	

1991 K&W URC Sprints

This set of 43-cards featuring top drivers of the Racing Club Sprint Car series was produce distributed by K&W Race Cards. The blue borderec include 41-drivers, one cover/checklist card and a Miss URC. Reportedly 2,500 sets were produced a of each card were made available to the driver remaining 2,000 sets were then distributed.

	MINT
COMPLETE SET (43)	15.00
COMMON CARD (1-43)	.35
❑ 1 Glenn Fitzcharles	.35
❑ 2 Bruce Thompson	.35
❑ 3 Jimmy Martin	.35
❑ 4 Billy Ellis	.35
❑ 5 Lou Cicconi Jr.	.50
❑ 6 Stew Brown	.35
❑ 7 Sam Gangemi	.35
❑ 8 Mike Conway	.35
❑ 9 Todd Rittenhouse	.35
❑ 10 Mike Wells	.35
❑ 11 Wayne Rice	.35
❑ 12 Dave McGough	.35
❑ 13 Dan Nerl	.35
❑ 14 Tom Wanner	.35
❑ 15 Bob Kellar	.35
❑ 16 Tim Higgins	.35
❑ 17 Bruce Bowen	.35
❑ 18 Mares Stellfox	.35
❑ 19 Kramer Williamson	.35
❑ 20 Jerry Dinnen	.35
❑ 21 Ray Winiecki Jr.	.35
❑ 22 Tony Smolenyak	.35
❑ 23 Billy Hughes	.35
❑ 24 Bob Swavely	.35
❑ 25 Fran Hogue	.35
❑ 26 Gary Hieber	.35
❑ 27 John Jenkins	.35
❑ 28 Jim Baker	.35
❑ 29 Jon Holmquist Jr.	.35
❑ 30 Lance Dewease	.35
❑ 31 Midge Miller	.35
❑ 32 Dave McGough	.35
❑ 33 Mike Haggenbottom	.35
❑ 34 Bob Fisher Jr.	.35
❑ 35 Jon Eldreth	.35
❑ 36 Rich Bates	.35
❑ 37 Don Souders Jr.	.35
❑ 38 Larry Winchell	.35
❑ 39 Greg Coverdale	.35
❑ 40 Ralph Stettenbauer	.35
❑ 41 Glenn Fitzcharles	.35
❑ 42 Kolleen Reimel Miss URC	.35
❑ 43 Cover Card Checklist	.35

1992 K&W Dirt Track

Race Cards produced a series of sets featuring s of DIRT Modifieds sold through local area tracks. centage of set sales proceeds went to the DIRT 's injury fund. This 65-card set was printed with photos surrounded by an orange-red border on the ont. Cardbacks were printed in black and white. of each card were produced and 500 of those cards made available to the drivers. The remaining 2,000 ere then distributed.

	MINT	NRMT
LETE SET (65)	10.00	4.50
ION CARD (1-65)	.15	.07
lly Pauch	.15	.07
ɔug Hoffman	.15	.07
ett Hearn	.15	.07
ɔb McCreadie	.15	.07
mmy Horton	.50	.23
ck Johnson	.15	.07
by Tobias Jr.	.15	.07
onnie Tobias	.15	.07
eve Paine	.15	.07
enny Tremont	.15	.07
illy Decker	.15	.07
ick Elliott	.15	.07
obby Wilkins	.15	.07
om Hager	.15	.07
evin Collins	.15	.07
avid Lape	.15	.07
.D. Coville	.15	.07
uane Howard	.15	.07
rank Cozze	.15	.07
on Keys	.15	.07
ohn Leach	.15	.07
oger Laureno	.15	.07
ave Adams	.15	.07
hic Cossaboone	.15	.07
mmy Chester	.15	.07
arry Gollub	.15	.07
lenn Smith	.15	.07
amie Mills	.15	.07
Vayne Weaver	.15	.07
ohn Pinter	.15	.07
andy Glenski	.15	.07
uck Ward	.15	.07
ichie Pratt	.15	.07
.J. Bunting, III	.15	.07
eron Rust	.15	.07
obby Sapp	.15	.07
reg Humlhanz	.15	.07
d Brown, Jr.	.15	.07
avid Hill	.15	.07
ohn Bennett, Jr.	.15	.07
andy Adams	.15	.07
ete Visconti	.15	.07
cott Pursell	.15	.07
hip Slocum	.15	.07
om Capie	.15	.07
hitey Kidd, Jr.	.15	.07
nie Miles, Jr.	.15	.07
ll Tanner	.15	.07
obby Parks	.15	.07
raig Von Dohren	.15	.07
om Mayberry	.15	.07
ennis Bailey	.15	.07
ff Strunk	.15	.07
ck Schaffer	.15	.07
ck Follweiler	.15	.07
om Carberry	.15	.07
ed Dmuchowski	.15	.07
eve Bottcher	.15	.07
e Plazek	.15	.07
nokey Warren	.15	.07
ay Swinehart	.15	.07
ucky Kell	.15	.07
ewt Hartman	.15	.07
am Martz	.15	.07
hecklist Card	.15	.07

1994 K&W Dirt Track

K&W Race Cards produced a series of sets featuring drivers of DIRT Modifieds sold through local area tracks. A percentage of set sales proceeds went to the local driver's injury fund. This 40-card set was printed with color photos surrounded by a blue border on the cardfront. Cardbacks were printed in black and white. Reportedly, 2,500 sets were produced and 500 of each card were made available to the drivers. The remaining 2,000 sets were then distributed.

	MINT	NRMT
COMPLETE SET (40)	12.00	5.50
COMMON CARD (1-40)	.30	.14
❑ 1 Brett Hearn	.30	.14
❑ 2 Doug Hoffman	.30	.14
❑ 3 Bob McCreadie	.30	.14
❑ 4 Bobby Wilkins	.30	.14
❑ 5 Billy Pauch	.30	.14
❑ 6 Mitch Gibbs	.30	.14
❑ 7 Toby Tobias, Jr.	.30	.14
❑ 8 Kenny Tremont	.30	.14
❑ 9 Rick Elliott	.30	.14
❑ 10 Duane Howard	.30	.14
❑ 11 Jimmy Horton	.50	.23
❑ 12 Kevin Collins	.30	.14
❑ 13 Steve Paine	.30	.14
❑ 14 Pete Visconti	.30	.14
❑ 15 Jack Johnson	.30	.14
❑ 16 Craig Von Dohren	.30	.14
❑ 17 Billy Decker	.30	.14
❑ 18 Randy Glenski	.30	.14
❑ 19 Frank Cozze	.30	.14
❑ 20 Ray Swinehart	.30	.14
❑ 21 Roger Laureno	.30	.14
❑ 22 David Lape	.30	.14
❑ 23 Tom Mayberry	.30	.14
❑ 24 Ron Keys	.30	.14
❑ 25 Ronnie Tobias	.30	.14
❑ 26 Fred Dmuchowski	.30	.14
❑ 27 John Leach	.30	.14
❑ 28 Joe Plazek	.30	.14
❑ 29 Bucky Kell	.30	.14
❑ 30 Jamie Mills	.30	.14
❑ 31 Tom Hager	.30	.14
❑ 32 Dave Adams	.30	.14
❑ 33 Bobby Sapp	.30	.14
❑ 34 Jimmy Chester	.30	.14
❑ 35 Greg Humlhanz	.30	.14
❑ 36 Deron Rust	.30	.14
❑ 37 Chip Slocum	.30	.14
❑ 38 Rick Schaffer	.30	.14
❑ 39 Jeff Strunk	.30	.14
❑ 40 Cover/Checklist Card	.30	.14

1995 K&W Dirt Track

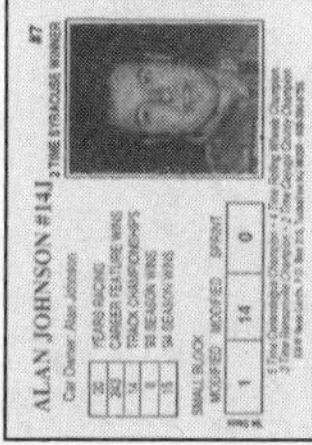

K&W Race Cards produced a series of sets featuring drivers of DIRT Modifieds sold through local area tracks. A percentage of set sales proceeds went to the local driver's injury fund. This 42-card set was printed with color photos surrounded by a white border on the cardfront. Cardbacks were printed in black and white. Reportedly, 2,500 sets were produced and 500 of each card were made available to the drivers. The remaining 2,000 sets were then distributed.

	MINT	NRMT
COMPLETE SET (42)	12.00	5.50
COMMON CARD (1-42)	.30	.14
❑ 1 Bob McCreadie	.30	.14
❑ 2 Dale Planck	.30	.14
❑ 3 Brett Hearn	.30	.14
❑ 4 Doug Hoffman	.30	.14
❑ 5 Rick Elliott	.30	.14
❑ 6 Mitch Gibbs	.30	.14
❑ 7 Alan Johnson	.30	.14
❑ 8 Jack Johnson	.30	.14
❑ 9 Danny Johnson	.50	.23
❑ 10 Bobby Wilkins	.30	.14
❑ 11 Joe Plazek	.30	.14
❑ 12 Billy Pauch	.30	.14
❑ 13 Jimmy Horton	.75	.35
❑ 14 Kenny Tremont	.30	.14
❑ 15 Craig Von Dohren	.30	.14
❑ 16 Frank Cozze	.30	.14
❑ 17 Garry Gollub	.30	.14
❑ 18 Meme DeSantis	.30	.14
❑ 19 Steve Paine	.30	.14
❑ 20 Billy Decker	.30	.14
❑ 21 Jimmy Chester	.30	.14
❑ 22 Wade Hendrickson	.30	.14
❑ 23 Billy Pauch	.30	.14
❑ 24 H.J. Bunting, III	.30	.14
❑ 25 David Lape	.30	.14
❑ 26 Dave Adams	.30	.14
❑ 27 Pete Visconti	.30	.14
❑ 28 Sammy Beavers	.30	.14
❑ 29 Ron Keys	.30	.14
❑ 30 Norman Short Jr.	.30	.14
❑ 31 Fred Dmuchowski	.30	.14
❑ 32 Randy Glenski	.30	.14
❑ 33 Tom Hager	.30	.14
❑ 34 Roger Laureno	.30	.14
❑ 35 John Leach	.30	.14
❑ 36 Greg Humlhanz	.30	.14
❑ 37 Jamie Mills	.30	.14
❑ 38 Mike Sena	.30	.14
❑ 39 Deron Rust	.30	.14
❑ 40 John Wyers	.30	.14
❑ 41 Wayne Weaver	.30	.14
❑ 42 Cover/Checklist Card	.30	.14

1990 Langenberg Rockford Speedway/Hot Stuff

M.B. Langenberg produced this set in 1990 under the title Hot Stuff. The cards feature drivers of various circuits that raced at the Rockford (Illinois) Speedway. As with most Langenberg sets, the cards feature a checkered flag design and black and white cardbacks. The card numbering is unusual in that it begins with 1001 and ends with 1045. We've shortened the numbering in the listings as reflected below.

	MINT	NRMT
COMPLETE SET (45)	8.00	3.60
COMMON CARD (1-45)	.20	.09
❑ 1 John Ganley	.20	.09
❑ 2 Jim Rieger	.20	.09
❑ 3 Mark Higby	.20	.09
❑ 4 Gary Anderson	.20	.09
❑ 5 Tom Cormack	.20	.09
❑ 6 Bob Torkelson	.20	.09
❑ 7 Walter Reitz	.20	.09
❑ 8 Bobby Wilberg	.20	.09
❑ 9 Curt Tillman	.20	.09
❑ 10 John Knaus	.20	.09
❑ 11 Bobby Davis	.20	.09
❑ 12 Steve Erickson	.20	.09
❑ 13 Dale Cox	.20	.09
❑ 14 Dave Cox	.20	.09
❑ 15 Gary Loos	.20	.09
❑ 16 Bob Parisot	.20	.09
❑ 17 Jim Reynolds	.20	.09
❑ 18 Dave Wagner	.20	.09
❑ 19 Terry Rahl	.20	.09
❑ 20 Dennis Miller	.20	.09
❑ 21 Larry Schuler	.20	.09
❑ 22 Bart Reinen	.20	.09
❑ 23 Jeff Watson	.20	.09
❑ 24 Bill McCoy	.20	.09
❑ 25 Nolan McBride	.20	.09
❑ 26 Dave Nelson	.20	.09
❑ 27 Brad Wagner	.20	.09
❑ 28 Dave Foltz	.20	.09
❑ 29 Mark Hartline	.20	.09
❑ 30 B.J.Sparkman	.20	.09
❑ 31 Jon Reynolds	.20	.09
❑ 32 Tom Gille	.20	.09
❑ 33 Bryan Young	.20	.09
❑ 34 Bobby LaPier	.20	.09

Card	MINT	NRMT
❑ 35 Todd Aldrich	.20	.09
❑ 36 Mike Lloyd	.20	.09
❑ 37 Don Russell	.20	.09
❑ 38 Dana Czach	.20	.09
❑ 39 Bruce Tucker	.20	.09
❑ 40 Tim Loos	.20	.09
❑ 41 Steve Gray	.20	.09
❑ 42 Dan Johnson	.20	.09
❑ 43 Murt Dunn	.20	.09
❑ 44 Jerry Gille	.20	.09
❑ 45 Al Sheppard	.20	.09

1991 Langenberg Rockford Speedway

This 66-card set features various drivers who raced at the Rockford (Illinois) Speedway. The set was produced by M.B. Langenberg. It was the second consecutive year a Rockford Speedway set was issued.

	MINT	NRMT
COMPLETE SET (66)	10.00	4.50
COMMON CARD (1-66)	.20	.09
❑ 1 Curt Tillman	.20	.09
❑ 2 Ricky Bilderback	.20	.09
❑ 3 Jerry Gille	.20	.09
❑ 4 Scott Dolliver	.20	.09
❑ 5 Tom Gille	.20	.09
❑ 6 Jim Reynolds	.20	.09
❑ 7 Kurt Danko	.20	.09
❑ 8 Don Russell	.20	.09
❑ 9 Bruce Devoy	.20	.09
❑ 10 Brian Johnson	.20	.09
❑ 11 Robert Parisot	.20	.09
❑ 12 Murt Dunn	.20	.09
❑ 13 Dennis Miller	.20	.09
❑ 14 Tom Graves	.20	.09
❑ 15 Daryl Luepkes	.20	.09
❑ 16 Ron Smykay	.20	.09
❑ 17 Bobby Hacker	.20	.09
❑ 18 Roy Crettol	.20	.09
❑ 19 Jeff Taber	.20	.09
❑ 20 Dave Lapier	.20	.09
❑ 21 Ricky Bilderback	.20	.09
Dennis Miller		
John Knaus		
❑ 22 Allan Merfeld	.20	.09
❑ 23 Dale Yardley	.20	.09
❑ 24 Mike Lloyd	.20	.09
❑ 25 Jeff Watson	.20	.09
❑ 26 John Knaus	.20	.09
❑ 27 Bill McCoy	.20	.09
❑ 28 Scott Lawver	.20	.09
Tom Schneider		
Doug Fermanich		
❑ 29 George Compo	.20	.09
❑ 30 Mike O'Leary	.20	.09
❑ 31 Gene Hill	.20	.09
❑ 32 Rodney Gilley	.20	.09
❑ 33 Brad Wagner	.20	.09
❑ 34 Bob Miller	.20	.09
❑ 35 Doug Fermanich	.20	.09
❑ 36 Darrell Williams	.20	.09
❑ 37 Scott Bryden	.20	.09
❑ 38 Mike Martindale	.20	.09
❑ 39 Mike Loos	.20	.09
❑ 40 Alan Sheppard	.20	.09
❑ 41 Mark Magee	.20	.09
❑ 42 Gary Head	.20	.09
❑ 43 Bobby Wilberg	.20	.09
❑ 44 B.J. Sparkman	.20	.09
❑ 45 Nolan McBride	.20	.09
❑ 46 Elmo Deery	.20	.09
❑ 47 Thomas Powell	.20	.09
❑ 48 Todd Aldrich	.20	.09
❑ 49 Jim Sanders	.20	.09
❑ 50 Dave Lee	.20	.09
❑ 51 Dale Cox	.20	.09
❑ 52 Patrick Rossmann	.20	.09
❑ 53 Derrick Spack	.20	.09
❑ 54 Lon Ritz	.20	.09
❑ 55 Jerry Ahlquist	.20	.09
❑ 56 Dave Wagner	.20	.09
❑ 57 Stan Burdick	.20	.09
❑ 58 Dana Czach	.20	.09
❑ 59 Larry O'Brien	.20	.09
❑ 60 Bobby Wilberg	.30	.14
Gary Head		
Brad Wagner		
Kurt Danko		
❑ 61 Rockford Speedway	.20	.09
❑ 62 Rockford Speedway	.20	.09
❑ 63 Rockford Speedway	.20	.09
❑ 64 Dave Wagner	.20	.09
Bill McCoy		
Bruce Devoy		
Richard Sanders		
Robert Parisot		
❑ 65 Scott Tripp	.20	.09
Brian Steward		
Tom Ragner Sr.		
❑ 66 Checklist Card	.20	.09

1991 Langenberg Seekonk Speedway

M.B. Langenberg produced this set of 29 cards. The cards feature various drivers who have raced at Seekonk Speedway. This set was done in conjunction with the tracks 45th anniversary.

	MINT	NRMT
COMPLETE SET (29)	8.00	3.60
COMMON CARD (1-29)	.30	.14
❑ 1 Vinny Annarummo	.30	.14
❑ 2 Ray Lee	.30	.14
❑ 3 Dick Houlihan	.30	.14
❑ 4 Rick Martin	.30	.14
❑ 5 Jimmy Wilkins	.30	.14
❑ 6 Joey Cerullo	.30	.14
❑ 7 Len Ellis	.30	.14
❑ 8 Jimmy Kuhn	.30	.14
❑ 9 John Tripp	.30	.14
❑ 10 David Berghman	.30	.14
❑ 11 Don Dionne	.30	.14
❑ 12 Carl Stevens	.30	.14
❑ 13 Wayne Dion	.30	.14
❑ 14 Tony Kias, Jr.	.30	.14
❑ 15 Fred Astle, Jr.	.30	.14
❑ 16 Jim McCallum	.30	.14
❑ 17 Bruce Taylor	.30	.14
❑ 18 Jeff Mecure	.30	.14
❑ 19 Manny Dias	.30	.14
❑ 20 Bob Stockel	.30	.14
❑ 21 Mike Santiano	.30	.14
❑ 22 Richard Hanatow	.30	.14
❑ 23 Bobby Tripp	.30	.14
❑ 24 Jim Proulx	.30	.14
❑ 25 D.Anthony Venditti	.30	.14
❑ 26 Jimmy Kuhn	.30	.14
❑ 27 Seekonk Speedway	.30	.14
❑ 28 Checklist 1-29	.30	.14
❑ 29 Cover Card	.30	.14

1992 Langenberg Rockford Speedway

This was the third consecutive year M.B. Langerberg produced a Rockford Speedway set. The cards features various drivers who have run at the track. The 61-card set is listed in alphabetical order.

	MINT	NRMT
COMPLETE SET (61)	12.00	5.50
COMMON CARD (1-61)	.25	.11
❑ 1 Jerry Ahlquist	.25	.11
❑ 2 Ricky Bilderback	.25	.11
❑ 3 Ricky Bilderback	.25	.11
❑ 4 George Bohn	.25	.11
❑ 5 Scotty Bryden	.25	.11
❑ 6 Stan Burdick	.25	.11
❑ 7 George Compo	.25	.11
❑ 8 Kurt Danko	.25	.11
❑ 9 Joe Darnell	.25	.11
❑ 10 Jack Deery	.25	.11
❑ 11 Steve DeMarb	.25	.11
❑ 12 Steve DeMarb	.25	.11
❑ 13 Scott Dolliver	.25	.11
❑ 14 Dave Ebrecht	.25	.11
❑ 15 Jerry Eckel	.25	.11
❑ 16 John Ganley	.25	.11
❑ 17 John Ganley	.25	.11
❑ 18 Jerry Gille	.25	.11
❑ 19 Tom Gille	.25	.11
❑ 20 Tom Gille	.25	.11
❑ 21 Rodney Gilley	.25	.11
❑ 22 Tom Graves	.25	.11
❑ 23 Bobby Hacker	.25	.11
❑ 24 Gary Head	.25	.11
❑ 25 Gary Head	.25	.11
❑ 26 Brian Johnson	.25	.11
❑ 27 Ron Johnson	.25	.11
❑ 28 John Knaus	.25	.11
❑ 29 John Knaus	.25	.11
❑ 30 Tom Kurth	.25	.11
❑ 31 Ritchie Lane	.25	.11
❑ 32 Marty Langenberg	.25	.11
❑ 33 Mike Lloyd	.25	.11
❑ 34 Daryl Luepkes	.25	.11
❑ 35 Mark Magee	.25	.11
❑ 36 Billy McCoy	.25	.11
❑ 37 Gary Meisman	.25	
❑ 38 Bob Miller	.25	
❑ 39 James Nuelle	.25	
❑ 40 Al Papini, III	.25	
❑ 41 Bob Parisot	.25	
❑ 42 Tom Powell	.25	
❑ 43 Jim Reynolds	.25	
❑ 44 John Robinson	.25	
❑ 45 Stephan Rubeck	.25	
❑ 46 Andi Rushiti	.25	
❑ 47 Kevin Smith	.25	
❑ 48 B.J. Sparkman	.25	
❑ 49 B.J. Sparkman	.25	
❑ 50 George Sparkman	.25	
❑ 51 Jeff Taber	.25	
❑ 52 Brad Wagner	.25	
❑ 53 Brad Wagner	.25	
❑ 54 David Wagner	.25	
❑ 55 Rob Wagner	.25	
❑ 56 Howie Ware	.25	
❑ 57 Jeff Watson	.25	
❑ 58 Jeff Watson	.25	
❑ 59 Bobby Wilberg	.25	
❑ 60 Bobby Wilberg	.25	
❑ 61 Darrell Williams	.25	

1992 Racing Legends Spri

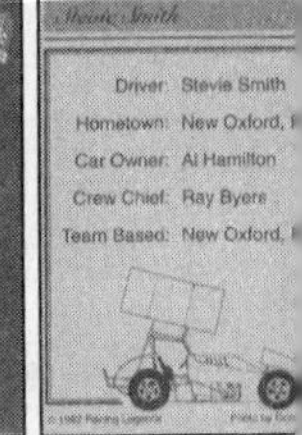

Driver: Stevie Smith
Hometown: New Oxford,
Car Owner: Al Hamilton
Crew Chief: Ray Byers
Team Based: New Oxford,

Racing Legends produced this set in 1992 to highli stars of Sprint Car racing. The 30-card set was relea factory set form with a certificate numbering it ar the production run of 10,000 sets.

	MINT
COMPLETE SET (30)	12.00
COMMON CARD (1-30)	.30
❑ 1 Steve Kinser w/Car	.50
❑ 2 Sammy Swindell w/Car	.50
❑ 3 Sammy Swindell	.50
❑ 4 Johnny Herrera's Car	.30
❑ 5 Johnny Herrera	.50
❑ 6 Steve Beitler's Car	.30
❑ 7 Steve Beitler	.30
❑ 8 Joe Gaerte's Car	.30
❑ 9 Mark Kinser's Car	.30
❑ 10 Mark Kinser	.50
❑ 11 Dave Blaney's Car	.50
❑ 12 Bobby Fletcher's Car	.30
❑ 13 Stevie Smith's Car	.30
❑ 14 Stevie Smith Jr.	.50
❑ 15 Steve Stambaugh's Car	.30
❑ 16 Kenny Jacobs' Car	.30
❑ 17 Fred Rahmer's Car	.30
❑ 18 Glenn Fitzcharles' Car	.30
❑ 19 Jim Carr's Car	.30
❑ 20 Joey Kuhn's Car	.30
❑ 21 Bobby Weaver's Car	.30
❑ 22 Paul Lotier's Car	.30
❑ 23 Cris Eash's Car	.30
❑ 24 Johnny Mackison Jr.'s Car	.30
❑ 25 Bobby Allen's Car	.30
❑ 26 Me Me DeSantis' Car	.30
❑ 27 Randy Wolfe's Car	.30
❑ 28 Bobby Davis Jr.'s Car	.30
❑ 29 Donnie Krietz Jr.'s Car	.30
❑ 30 Brent Kaeding's Car	.50

1992 STARS Modifieds

Short Track Auto Racing Stars (STARS) released card set in 1992. The cards were sold in comp form and feature photos of top drivers of the modifieds series.

	MINT
COMPLETE SET (48)	15.00
COMMON CARD (1-47)	.35
❑ 1 Blaine Aber	.35
❑ 2 Dub Barnhouse	.35
❑ 3 Mike Balzano w/Car	.35
❑ 4 Bob Adams, Jr.	.35

‹ Barton	.35	.16
›oper Bare	.35	.16
ıdy Bond	.35	.16
ːck Boggs	.50	.23
ırry Bond	.35	.16
'odd Andrews	.35	.16
im Gentry	.35	.16
‹eith Berner	.35	.16
3ob Cowen	.35	.16
im Curry	.35	.16
›arrell Lanigan w/Car	.35	.16
?odney Franklin	.35	.16
›lathan Durboraw w/Car	.35	.16
?on Davies	.35	.16
)enny Chamberlain	.35	.16
⁄lark Banal	.35	.16
⁄like Duvall	.35	.16
;hub Frank	.35	.16
²aul Davis	.35	.16
⁞.A. Malcuit	.35	.16
)avey Johnson w/Car	.35	.16
?ocky Hodges	.35	.16
im Hitt	.35	.16
ynn Geisler	.35	.16
›on Gross	.35	.16
›ob Wearing, Jr. w/Car	.35	.16
›ary Stuhler w/Car	.35	.16
reddy Smith	.35	.16
›uck Simmons	.35	.16
›teve Shaver w/Car	.35	.16
›arold Redman	.35	.16
›ob Pierce	.35	.16
›ark Myers	.35	.16
›onnie Moran	.35	.16
›illy Moyer w/Car	.35	.16
ohn Mason	.35	.16
;huck Maloney	.35	.16
:d Gibbons	.35	.16
›teve Francis	.35	.16
'utch McGill w/Car	.35	.16
:odney Combs Hillbilly 100 Winner	.75	.35
arry Moore w/Car	.35	.16
oe Meadows' Car	.35	.16
Cover Card Checklist	.35	.16

1994 STARS Modifieds

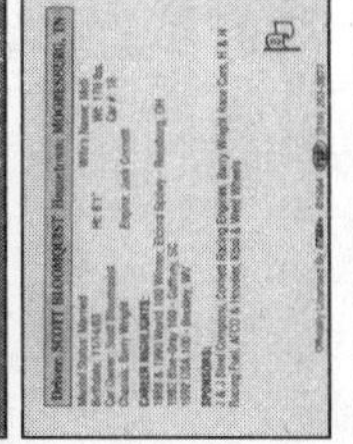

ſrack Auto Racing Stars (STARS) licensed this 54-ːet released in 1994. The cards were sold in ːte set form and feature action photos of top drivers STARS modifieds series.

	MINT	NRMT
ːETE SET (54)	12.00	5.50
ON CARD (1-53)	.25	.11
ːvey Johnson	.25	.11
ːdd Andrews	.25	.11
ːn Armbruster	.25	.11
ːk Aukland	.25	.11
ːke Balzano	.25	.11
ːn Booper Bare	.25	.11
ːve Barnett	.25	.11
ːott Bloomquist	.50	.23
ːry Bond	.25	.11
ːenny Bonebrake	.25	.11
ːevin Claycomb	.25	.11

❑ 12 D.J. Cline	.25	.11
❑ 13 Delmas Conley	.25	.11
❑ 14 R.J. Conley	.25	.11
❑ 15 Rod Conley	.25	.11
❑ 16 Ron Davies	.25	.11
❑ 17 Nathan Durboraw	.25	.11
❑ 18 Mike Duvall	.25	.11
❑ 19 Terry Eaglin	.25	.11
❑ 20 Rick Eckert	.25	.11
❑ 21 Vince Fanello	.25	.11
❑ 22 Steve Francis	.40	.18
❑ 23 Chub Frank	.25	.11
❑ 24 Ed Gibbons	.25	.11
❑ 25 Ed Griffin	.25	.11
❑ 26 Don Gross	.25	.11
❑ 27 Doug Hall	.25	.11
❑ 28 Mike Harrison	.25	.11
❑ 29 Scott Hartley	.25	.11
❑ 30 Bart Hartman	.25	.11
❑ 31 Billy Hicks	.25	.11
❑ 32 Tim Hitt	.25	.11
❑ 33 Bruce Hordusky	.25	.11
❑ 34 Bubby James	.25	.11
❑ 35 Tony Izzo Jr.	.25	.11
❑ 36 Darrell Lanigan	.25	.11
❑ 37 John Mason	.25	.11
❑ 38 Donnie Moran	.25	.11
❑ 39 Billy Moyer	.25	.11
❑ 40 Don O'Neal	.25	.11
❑ 41 Bob Pierce	.25	.11
❑ 42 Dick Potts	.25	.11
❑ 43 C.J. Rayburn	.25	.11
❑ 44 Brian Ruhlman	.25	.11
❑ 45 Steve Shaver	.25	.11
❑ 46 Eddie Smith	.25	.11
❑ 47 Freddy Smith	.25	.11
❑ 48 Michael Smith	.25	.11
❑ 49 Gary Stuhler	.25	.11
❑ 50 Kevin Weaver	.25	.11
❑ 51 Greg Williams	.25	.11
❑ 52 Rick Workman	.25	.11
❑ 53 Ricky Weeks	.25	.11
❑ NNO Checklist/Cover Card	.25	.11

1992 Traks Dirt

The 1992 Traks Dirt set features 15 numbered DIRT modified driver cards and one unnumbered cover/checklist card. The set was distributed by Traks through hobby channels.

	MINT	NRMT
COMPLETE SET (16)	4.00	1.80
COMMON CARD (1-15)	.30	.14
❑ 1 Dave Lape	.30	.14
❑ 2 Jack Johnson	.30	.14
❑ 3 Alan Johnson	.30	.14
❑ 4 Jeff Trombley	.30	.14
❑ 5 Brett Hearn	.30	.14
❑ 6 Steve Paine	.30	.14
❑ 7 Jeff Heotzler	.30	.14
❑ 8 Joe Plazek	.30	.14
❑ 9 Dick Larkin	.30	.14
❑ 10 Billy Decker	.30	.14
❑ 11 Frank Cozze	.30	.14
❑ 12 Bob McCreadie	.30	.14
❑ 13 Kenny Tremont	.30	.14
❑ 14 Doug Hoffman	.30	.14
❑ 15 Danny Johnson	.30	.14
❑ NNO Checklist Card	.30	.14

1992 Volunteer Racing East Alabama Speedway

This 20-card set feautres some of the top drivers that have run dirt cars at East Alabama Speedway. The set was produced by Volunteer racing and includes drivers like Buck Simmons, Jack Boggs and Scott Bloomquist. Also, included are a couple of cards of Busch Grand National regular Jeff Purvis.

	MINT	NRMT
COMPLETE SET (20)	6.00	2.70
COMMON CARD (1-20)	.25	.11
❑ 1 Checklist Card	.25	.11
❑ 2 Bobby Thomas	.25	.11
❑ 3 Bud Lunsford	.25	.11
❑ 4 Charlie Hughes	.25	.11
❑ 5 Buck Simmons	.30	.14
❑ 6 Billy Thomas	.25	.11
❑ 7 Don Hester	.25	.11
❑ 8 Tom Helfrich	.25	.11
❑ 9 Larry Moore	.25	.11
❑ 10 Jeff Purvis	.50	.23
❑ 11 Jeff Purvis	.50	.23
❑ 12 Buddy Boutwell	.25	.11
❑ 13 Jeff Purvis	.50	.23
❑ 14 Jack Boggs	.30	.14
❑ 15 Billy Moyer	.30	.14
❑ 16 Freddy Smith	.30	.14
❑ 17 Bobby Thomas	.25	.11
❑ 18 Scott Bloomquist	.30	.14
❑ 19 Jimmy Thomas	.30	.14
❑ 20 Parade Lap	.25	.11

1992 Volunteer Racing Lernersville Speedway I

This 72-card set features some of the top sprint car drivers to have raced at Lernersville Speedway. This is the first of a two set series produced by Volunteer Racing. The set includes such notables as Brad Doty and an unnumbered promo card of Dale and Lou Blaney.

	MINT	NRMT
COMPLETE SET (72)	8.00	3.60
COMMON CARD (1-71)	.15	.07
❑ 1 Checklist Card (1-36)	.15	.07
❑ 2 Checklist Card (37-72)	.15	.07
❑ 3 Jim Andrews	.15	.07
❑ 4 Johnny Axe	.15	.07
❑ 5 Bob Axe	.15	.07
❑ 6 Johnny Beaber	.15	.07
❑ 7 Johnny Beaber	.15	.07
❑ 8 Lou Blaney	.15	.07
❑ 9 Lou Blaney	.15	.07
❑ 10 John Braymer	.15	.07
❑ 11 John Britsky	.15	.07
❑ 12 Paul Brown	.15	.07
❑ 13 Mark Cassella	.15	.07
❑ 14 Ron Davies	.15	.07
❑ 15 Brad Doty	.25	.11
❑ 16 Bill Emig	.15	.07
❑ 17 Ernie Gardina	.15	.07
❑ 18 Lou Gentile	.15	.07
❑ 19 Lou Gentile	.15	.07
❑ 20 Dale Hafer	.15	.07
❑ 21 Dave Hess	.15	.07
❑ 22 Dave Hoffman	.15	.07
❑ 23 Dave Hoffman	.15	.07
❑ 24 Chuck Kennedy	.15	.07
❑ 25 Denny Keppel	.15	.07
❑ 26 Bob Kirchner	.15	.07
❑ 27 Mark Lezanic	.15	.07
❑ 28 Rick Majors	.15	.07
❑ 29 Jerry Matus	.15	.07
❑ 30 Chuck McDowell	.15	.07
❑ 31 Kevin McKinney	.15	.07
❑ 32 Ben Miley	.15	.07
❑ 33 Ben Miley	.15	.07
❑ 34 Jim Minton	.15	.07
❑ 35 Brian Muehlman	.15	.07
❑ 36 Carl Murdick	.15	.07
❑ 37 Bill Nobles	.15	.07
❑ 38 Mike Norris	.15	.07
❑ 39 Gary Pease	.15	.07
❑ 40 Dave Pegher	.15	.07
❑ 41 Barry Peters	.15	.07
❑ 42 Tom Phillips	.15	.07
❑ 43 Frank Raiti	.15	.07
❑ 44 Craig Rankin	.15	.07
❑ 45 L.B. Roenigk	.15	.07
❑ 46 Terry Rosenberger	.15	.07
❑ 47 Deek Scott	.15	.07
❑ 48 Herb Scott	.15	.07
❑ 49 Jack Sodeman	.15	.07
❑ 50 Ralph Spithaler, Jr.	.15	.07
❑ 51 Al Stivenson	.15	.07
❑ 52 Rod Stockdale	.15	.07
❑ 53 Rick Strong	.15	.07
❑ 54 Tom Sturgis	.15	.07
❑ 55 Mike Sutton	.15	.07
❑ 56 Dick Swartzlander	.15	.07
❑ 57 Mel Swartzlander	.15	.07
❑ 58 Dave Thompson	.15	.07
❑ 59 Tom Valasek	.15	.07

	MINT	NRMT
❑ 60 Blackie Watt	.15	.07
❑ 61 Blackie Watt	.15	.07
❑ 62 Blackie Watt	.15	.07
❑ 63 Bob Wearing	.15	.07
❑ 64 Bob Wearing	.15	.07
❑ 65 Bob Wearing	.15	.07
❑ 66 Bob Wearing	.15	.07
❑ 67 Don Wigton	.15	.07
❑ 68 Ted Wise	.15	.07
❑ 69 Russ Woolsey	.15	.07
❑ 70 Helen Martin	.15	.07
❑ 71 Don Martin	.15	.07
❑ NNO Dale Blaney Lou Blaney Promo card	.25	.11

1992 Volunteer Racing Lernersville Speedway 2

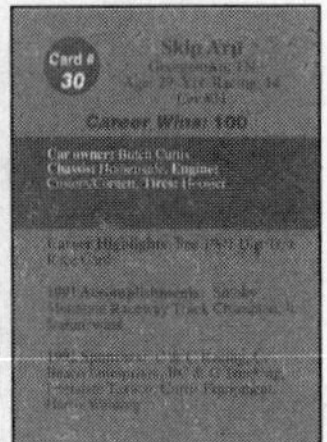

This is the second set of the Lernersville Speedway cards produced by Volunteer Racing. The 72-card set features various sprint car drivers to have raced at Lernersville Speedway. The set includes a card of the 1995 World of Outlaw champion, Dave Blaney.

	MINT	NRMT
COMPLETE SET (72)	8.00	3.60
COMMON CARD (1-71)	.15	.07

❑ 1 Checklist Card 1	.15	.07
❑ 2 Checklist Card 2	.15	.07
❑ 3 Earl Bauman	.15	.07
❑ 4 Johnny Beaber	.15	.07
❑ 5 Rodney Beltz	.15	.07
❑ 6 Rodney Beltz	.15	.07
❑ 7 Helene Bertges	.15	.07
❑ 8 Dave Blaney	.25	.11
❑ 9 Lou Blaney	.15	.07
❑ 10 Lou Blaney	.15	.07
❑ 11 Lou Blaney	.15	.07
❑ 12 Tony Burke	.15	.07
❑ 13 Ben Bussard	.15	.07
❑ 14 Tim Campbell	.15	.07
❑ 15 Marty Edwards	.15	.07
❑ 16 Bob Felmlee	.15	.07
❑ 17 Rick Ferkel	.15	.07
❑ 18 Bucky Fleming	.15	.07
❑ 19 George Frederick	.15	.07
❑ 20 Lynn Geisler	.15	.07
❑ 21 Lou Gentile	.15	.07
❑ 22 Lou Gentile	.15	.07
❑ 23 Rod George	.15	.07
❑ 24 Bob Graham	.15	.07
❑ 25 Mark Harvanek	.15	.07
❑ 26 Mark Hein	.15	.07
❑ 27 Gary Henry	.15	.07
❑ 28 Dave Hess	.15	.07
❑ 29 Dave Hoffman	.15	.07
❑ 30 Callen Hull	.15	.07
❑ 31 Tom Jarrett	.15	.07
❑ 32 Chuck Kennedy	.15	.07
❑ 33 Bud Kunkel	.15	.07
❑ 34 Ed Lynch, Sr.	.15	.07
❑ 35 Jean Lynch	.15	.07
❑ 36 Ed Lynch, Jr.	.15	.07
❑ 37 Don Luffy	.15	.07
❑ 38 Ed Lynch, Jr.	.15	.07
❑ 39 Ed Lynch, Sr.	.15	.07
❑ 40 Lynn Geisler	.15	.07
❑ 41 Bob Wearing	.15	.07
❑ 42 Ben Miley	.15	.07
❑ 43 Art Malies	.15	.07
❑ 44 Angelo Mariani	.15	.07
❑ 45 Don Martin	.15	.07
❑ 46 Jerry Matus	.15	.07
❑ 47 Brian Muehlman	.15	.07
❑ 48 Glenn Noland	.15	.07
❑ 49 Gary Pease	.15	.07
❑ 50 Dave Pegher	.15	.07
❑ 51 Barry Peters	.15	.07
❑ 52 Andy Phillips	.15	.07
❑ 53 Tom Phillips	.15	.07
❑ 54 Joe Pitkavish	.15	.07
❑ 55 Ralph Quarterson	.15	.07
❑ 56 Ralph Quarterson	.15	.07
❑ 57 Ralph Quarterson	.15	.07
❑ 58 Tommy Quarterson	.15	.07
❑ 59 Craig Rankin	.15	.07
❑ 60 Donny Roenigk	.15	.07
❑ 61 Dave Rupp	.15	.07
❑ 62 Barb Smith Ron Smith	.15	.07
❑ 63 Jack Sodeman	.15	.07
❑ 64 Bill Steinbach	.15	.07
❑ 65 William VanGuilder	.15	.07
❑ 66 Chuck Ward	.15	.07
❑ 67 Blackie Watt	.15	.07
❑ 68 Blackie Watt	.15	.07
❑ 69 Blackie Watt	.15	.07
❑ 70 Bob Wearing	.15	.07
❑ 71 Bobby Wearing	.15	.07
❑ NNO Bucky Ogle Promo Card	.25	.11

1991 Winner's Choice Modifieds

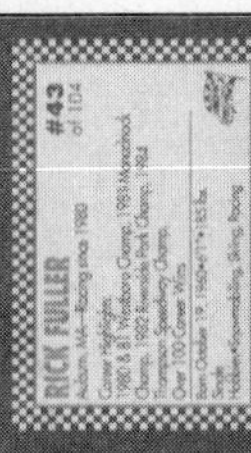

Winner's Choice, Inc. produced this set in 1991 featuring popular Modified car drivers with 14-cards devoted to the late Richie Evans. The black-bordered cards look very similar to 1991 Winner's Choice New England cards and include a color driver or car photo surrounded by a checkered flag frame. The cards were packaged and sold in complete factory set form.

	MINT	NRMT
COMPLETE SET (104)	10.00	4.50
COMMON CARD (1-104)	.10	.05
COMMON DRIVER (1-104)	.20	.09

❑ 1 Cover Card	.10	.05
❑ 2 Carl Pasteryak	.20	.09
❑ 3 Carl Pasteryak's Car	.10	.05
❑ 4 Tony Ferrante Jr.	.20	.09
❑ 5 Tony Ferrante Jr.'s Car	.10	.05
❑ 6 Tim Arre	.20	.09
❑ 7 Tim Arre's Car	.10	.05
❑ 8 Johnny Bush	.20	.09
❑ 9 Johnny Bush's Car	.10	.05
❑ 10 Jan Leaty	.20	.09
❑ 11 Jan Leaty's Car	.10	.05
❑ 12 Bob Park	.20	.09
❑ 13 Bob Park's Car	.10	.05
❑ 14 Richie Gallup	.20	.09
❑ 15 Richie Gallup's Car	.10	.05
❑ 16 Doug Heveron	.20	.09
❑ 17 Doug Heveron's Car	.10	.05
❑ 18 Jeff Fuller	.20	.09
❑ 19 Jeff Fuller's Car	.10	.05
❑ 20 Charlie Rudolph	.20	.09
❑ 21 Charlie Rudolph's Car	.10	.05
❑ 22 Satch Worley	.20	.09
❑ 23 Satch Worley's Car	.10	.05
❑ 24 George Brunnhoelzl	.20	.09
❑ 25 George Brunnhoelzl's Car	.10	.05
❑ 26 Randy Hedger	.20	.09
❑ 27 Randy Hedger's Car	.10	.05
❑ 28 S.J. Evonsion	.20	.09
❑ 29 S.J. Evonsion's Car	.10	.05
❑ 30 Mike Ewanitsko	.20	.09
❑ 31 Mike Ewanitsko's Car	.10	.05
❑ 32 Wayne Anderson	.20	.09
❑ 33 Wayne Anderson's Car	.10	.05
❑ 34 Steve Park	1.00	.45
❑ 35 Checklist Card	.10	.05
❑ 36 Steve Park's Car	.50	.23
❑ 37 Tom Bolles	.20	.09
❑ 38 Tom Bolles' Car	.10	.05
❑ 39 Ed Kennedy	.20	.09
❑ 40 Ed Kennedy's Car	.10	.05
❑ 41 Jerry Marquis	.20	.09
❑ 42 Jerry Marquis' Car	.10	.05
❑ 43 Rick Fuller	.20	.09
❑ 44 Rick Fuller's Car	.10	.05
❑ 45 Stan Greger	.20	
❑ 46 Stan Greger's Car	.10	
❑ 47 Dan Avery	.20	
❑ 48 Dan Avery's Car	.10	
❑ 49 Charlie Pasteryak	.20	
❑ 50 Charlie Pasteryak's Car	.10	
❑ 51 Bruce D'Alessandro	.20	
❑ 52 Bruce D'Alessandro's Car	.10	
❑ 53 Jamie Tomaino	.20	
❑ 54 Jamie Tomaino's Car	.10	
❑ 55 Bruce Haley	.20	
❑ 56 Bruce Haley's Car	.10	
❑ 57 Gary Drew	.20	
❑ 58 Gary Drew's Car	.10	
❑ 59 Mike Stefanik	.75	
❑ 60 Mike Stefanik's Car	.20	
❑ 61 Willie Elliott	.20	
❑ 62 Willie Elliott's Car	.10	
❑ 63 Kirby Monteith	.20	
❑ 64 Kirby Monteith's Car	.10	
❑ 65 George Kent	.20	
❑ 66 George Kent's Car	.10	
❑ 67 John Preston	.20	
❑ 68 John Preston's Car	.10	
❑ 69 Reggie Ruggiero	.20	
❑ 70 Checklist Card	.10	
❑ 71 Reggie Ruggiero's Car	.10	
❑ 72 Pete Rondeau	.20	
❑ 73 Pete Rondeau's Car	.10	
❑ 74 Tom Baldwin	.20	
❑ 75 Tom Baldwin's Car	.10	
❑ 76 Greg Tomaino	.20	
❑ 77 Greg Tomaino's Car	.10	
❑ 78 Ted Christopher	.20	
❑ 79 Ted Christopher's Car	.10	
❑ 80 Bo Gunning	.20	
❑ 81 Bo Gunning's Car	.10	
❑ 82 Bob Potter	.20	
❑ 83 Bob Potter's Car	.10	
❑ 84 Tony Hirschman	.20	
❑ 85 Tony Hirschman's Car	.10	
❑ 86 Steve Chowansky	.20	
❑ 87 Steve Chowansky's Car	.10	
❑ 88 Mike Christopher	.20	
❑ 89 Mike Christopher's Car	.10	
❑ 90 Richie Evans	.40	
❑ 91 Richie Evans' Car One of His First Cars	.20	
❑ 92 Richie Evans' Car One of Many Early Wins	.20	
❑ 93 Richie Evans w/Car 1973 at Stafford	.40	
❑ 94 Richie Evans' Car Modified Madness	.20	
❑ 95 Richie Evans w/Car Daytona Inter.Speedway	.40	
❑ 96 Richie Evans w/Car Another of Many Wins	.40	
❑ 97 Richie Evans' Car Supermodified	.20	
❑ 98 Richie Evans May 6, 1983	.40	
❑ 99 Richie Evans' Car 1983 at Martinsville	.20	
❑ 100 Richie Evans w/Car 1985 Thompson Ice Breaker	.40	
❑ 101 Richie Evans w/Car 1985 Spring Sizzler	.40	
❑ 102 Richie Evans 1985 Thompson Speedway	.40	
❑ 103 Richie Evans 1985	.40	
❑ 104 Checklist Card	.10	

1987 World of Outlaws

This marked the first year of World of Outlaws facto produced by James International Art, Inc. The car skip numbered and include two different numbe Steve Kinser cards. The set is most famous for inc the first card of Jeff Gordon. While the card sets 1987-90 look very similar, the 1987 set c ıtiated by the driver's name appearing in a blue box cardfront.

	MINT	NRMT
.ETE SET (49)	40.00	18.00
ON CARD	.40	.18
teve Kinser 1987 Race Highlights	5.00	2.20
teve Kinser Summary of 1987 Stats	5.00	2.20
ıd Doty	1.50	.70
bby Davis Jr.	.40	.18
: Haudenschild	2.00	.90
n Shuman	.40	.18
nny Smith	.40	.18
ınny Herrera	.40	.18
s Eash	.40	.18
raig Keel	.40	.18
ich Bubak	.40	.18
ammy Swindell	2.00	.90
ee Brewer Jr.	.40	.18
obby Allen	.40	.18
mmy Sills	.40	.18
m Gee	.40	.18
ave Blaney	1.50	.70
reg Wooley	.40	.18
ommie Estes Jr.	.40	.18
enny Jacobs	.40	.18
eith Kauffman	.40	.18
ocky Hodges	.40	.18
ealand McSpadden	.40	.18
arrell Hanestad	.40	.18
ick Ungar	.40	.18
ickey Hood	.40	.18
ony Armstrong	.40	.18
hane Carson	.40	.18
teve Siegel	.40	.18
erry Gray	.40	.18
ndy Hillenburg	1.50	.70
oey Allen	.40	.18
teve Kent	.40	.18
rent Kaeding	1.00	.45
tevie Smith Jr.	1.50	.70
ack Hewitt	1.00	.45
erry McCarl	.40	.18
teve Butler	.40	.18
eff Swindell	1.50	.70
huck Gurney	.40	.18
ed Lee	.40	.18
ichard Griffin	.40	.18
oe Gaerte	.40	.18
obby Fletcher	.40	.18
ason McMillen	.40	.18
andy Smith	.40	.18
m Green	.40	.18
eff Gordon	30.00	13.50
Cover Card Checklist	.40	.18

1988 World of Outlaws

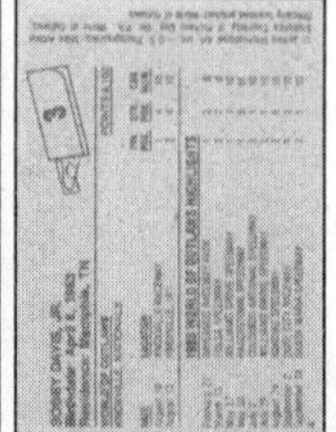

International Art again produced a World of ; set in 1988. The cards were released in factory n only and are skip numbered. The set includes ards of popular drivers Jeff Gordon and Steve Two unnumbered driver cards were part of the set as an unnumbered checklist card. While the card m 1987-90 look very similar, the 1988 set can be tiated by the driver's name appearing in a red box ardfront.

	MINT	NRMT
ETE SET (48)	25.00	11.00
ON CARD	.30	.14
ve Kinser	4.00	1.80
ımy Swindell	1.50	.70
by Davis Jr.	.30	.14
e Blaney	1.00	.45
k Kinser	.60	.25
y Hillenburg	.60	.25
Eash	.30	.14
Haudenschild	1.50	.70

❑ 10 Danny Smith	.30	.14
❑ 11 Greg Wooley	.30	.14
❑ 12 Bobby Allen	.30	.14
❑ 13 Jeff Swindell	.60	.25
❑ 14 Johnny Herrera	.30	.14
❑ 15 Brad Doty	1.00	.45
❑ 16 Jimmy Sills	.30	.14
❑ 17 Joey Allen	.30	.14
❑ 18 Lee Brewer Jr.	.30	.14
❑ 19 Craig Keel	.30	.14
❑ 20 Tony Armstrong	.30	.14
❑ 21 Kenny Jacobs	.30	.14
❑ 22 Tommie Estes Jr.	.30	.14
❑ 23 Jack Hewitt	.60	.25
❑ 24 Tim Green	.30	.14
❑ 25 Rich Bubak	.30	.14
❑ 26 Joe Gaerte	.30	.14
❑ 27 Robbie Stanley	.30	.14
❑ 28 Terry McCarl	.30	.14
❑ 29 Donnie Kretiz Jr.	.30	.14
❑ 30 Steve Siegel	.30	.14
❑ 31 Steve Kent	.30	.14
❑ 32 Keith Kauffman	.30	.14
❑ 33 Rick Ungar	.30	.14
❑ 34 Rocky Hodges	.30	.14
❑ 35 Tim Gee	.30	.14
❑ 36 Steve Butler	.30	.14
❑ 38 Randy Wolfe	.30	.14
❑ 39 Ron Shuman	.30	.14
❑ 40 Jim Carr	.30	.14
❑ 41 Chuck Miller	.30	.14
❑ 43 Danny Burton	.30	.14
❑ 45 Gary Dunkle	.30	.14
❑ 46 Rickey Hood	.30	.14
❑ 48 Lealand McSpadden	.30	.14
❑ 50 Chuck Gurney	.30	.14
❑ 54 Jeff Gordon	20.00	9.00
❑ NNO Cover Card Checklist	.30	.14
❑ NNO Max Dumesny	.30	.14
❑ NNO Brent Kaeding	.60	.25

1989 World of Outlaws

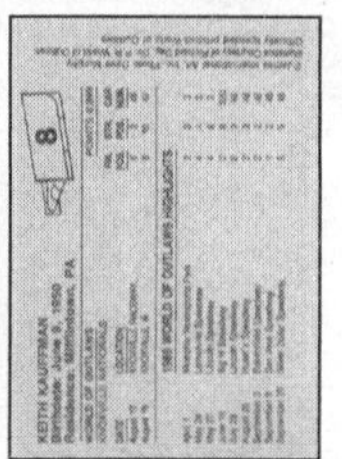

For the third year, James International Art produced a World of Outlaws set in 1989. The cards were released in factory set form only with a 32-card standard sized set and a 13-card postcard sized set together. Although packaged together, the two sets are often considered independent issues and, therefore, listed separately. The 32-card set is again skip-numbered and includes several unnumbered cards as well. The numbered cards are listed according to 1989 final points standings. While the card sets from 1987-90 look very similar, the 1989 set can be differentiated by the driver's name appearing in a yellow box on the cardfront.

	MINT	NRMT
COMPLETE SET (32)	20.00	9.00
COMMON CARD	.30	.14
❑ 1 Bobby Davis Jr.	.30	.14
❑ 2 Jeff Swindell	1.00	.45
❑ 3 Cris Eash	.30	.14
❑ 4 Tim Green	.30	.14
❑ 5 Joe Gaerte	.30	.14
❑ 6 Jac Haudenschild	2.00	.90
❑ 7 Andy Hillenburg	1.00	.45
❑ 8 Keith Kauffman	.30	.14
❑ 9 Doug Wolfgang	1.00	.45
❑ 10 Steve Siegel	.30	.14
❑ 11 Craig Keel	.30	.14
❑ 13 Steve Beitler	.30	.14
❑ 14 Jack Hewitt	.60	.25
❑ 15 Bobby Allen	.30	.14
❑ 16 Johnny Herrera	.30	.14
❑ 17 Dave Blaney	1.50	.70
❑ 19 Kenny Jacobs	.30	.14
❑ 20 Danny Smith	.30	.14
❑ 21 Brent Kaeding	.30	.14
❑ 25 Joey Allen	.30	.14
❑ 29 Danny Lasoski	.60	.25
❑ 31 Rickey Hood	.30	.14

❑ 33 Mark Kinser	1.50	.70
❑ 34 Steve Kinser	6.00	2.70
❑ 35 Frankie Kerr	.60	.25
❑ 38 Tommie Estes Jr.	.30	.14
❑ 64 Ron Shuman	.30	.14
❑ 65 Rich Vogler	.30	.14
❑ NNO Cover Card Checklist	.30	.14
❑ NNO Wayne C. Helland	.30	.14
❑ NNO Lealand McSpadden	.30	.14
❑ NNO Jimmy Sills	.30	.14

1989 World of Outlaws Postcards

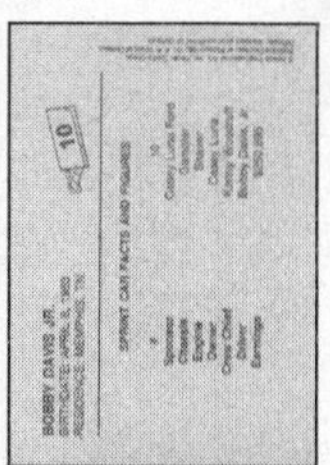

This 13-card set was included as an insert into 1989 World of Outlaws factory sets. The cards are oversized (3-1/2" by 5") and numbered according to the featured car's number.

	MINT	NRMT
COMPLETE SET (13)	8.00	3.60
COMMON CARD	.60	.25
❑ 2 Andy Hillenburg's Car	2.00	.90
❑ 2S Steve Siegel's Car	.60	.25
❑ 4 Tim Green Let's Do It Car 4	.60	.25
❑ 7TW Joe Gaerte's Car	.60	.25
❑ 8D Doug Wolfgang's Car	2.00	.90
❑ 10 Bobby Davis Jr.'s Car	1.25	.55
❑ 11X Jeff Swindell's Car	2.00	.90
❑ 14 Tim Green's Car	.60	.25
❑ 17E Cris Eash's Car	.60	.25
❑ 48 Keith Kauffman's Car	.60	.25
❑ 77 Pit Action	.60	.25
❑ NNO Jim Kingwell	.60	.25
❑ NNO Transporter Hauler	.60	.25

1990 World of Outlaws

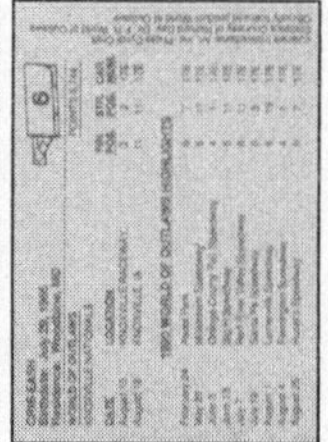

For the fourth year, James International Art produced a World of Outlaws set. The cards were released in factory set form only with a 36-card standard sized set and a 10-card postcard sized set together. Although packaged together, the two sets are often considered independent issues and, therefore, listed separately. The 36-card set is again skip-numbered and includes the first card of popular driver Sammy Swindell. Two unnumbered cards were produced as well. The numbered cards are listed according to 1990 final points standings. While the card sets from 1987-90 look very similar, the 1990 set can be differentiated by the driver's name appearing in an orange box on the cardfront.

	MINT	NRMT
COMPLETE SET (36)	16.00	7.25
COMMON CARD	.30	.14
❑ 1 Steve Kinser	5.00	2.20
❑ 2 Doug Wolfgang	1.00	.45
❑ 3 Joe Gaerte	.30	.14
❑ 4 Bobby Davis Jr.	.30	.14
❑ 5 Stevie Smith Jr.	1.00	.45
❑ 6 Cris Eash	.30	.14
❑ 7 Dave Blaney	1.50	.70
❑ 8 Keith Kauffman	.30	.14

❑ 9 Steve Beitler .30 .14
❑ 10 Sammy Swindell 2.00 .90
❑ 11 Johnny Herrera .30 .14
❑ 12 Mark Kinser .60 .25
❑ 13 Bobby Allen .30 .14
❑ 14 Jac Haudenschild 2.00 .90
❑ 16 Danny Lasoski .30 .14
❑ 17 Kenny Jacobs .30 .14
❑ 18 Jeff Swindell .60 .25
❑ 19 Andy Hillenburg .60 .25
❑ 20 Danny Smith .30 .14
❑ 21 Brent Kaeding .60 .25
❑ 22 Jim Carr .30 .14
❑ 23 Lee Brewer Jr. .30 .14
❑ 28 Jack Hewitt .60 .25
❑ 30 Tim Green .30 .14
❑ 31 Jimmy Sills .30 .14
❑ 34 Rickey Hood .30 .14
❑ 40 Mike Peters .30 .14
❑ 41 Joey Kuhn .30 .14
❑ 42 Steve Smith Sr. .30 .14
❑ 43 Craig Keel .30 .14
❑ 46 Ed Lynch Jr. .30 .14
❑ 49 Rick Ferkel .30 .14
❑ 50 Rick Ungar .30 .14
❑ NNO J.W. Hunt .30 .14
❑ NNO Cover Card .30 .14
Checklist

1990 World of Outlaws Postcards

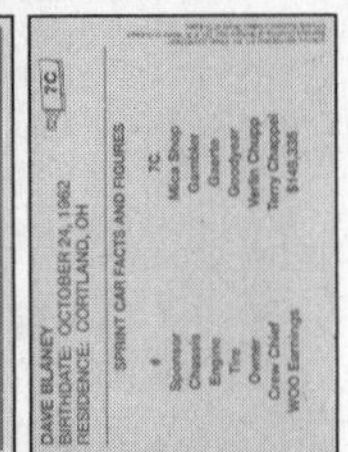

This 13-card set was included as an insert into 1990 World of Outlaws factory sets. The cards are oversized (3-1/2" by 5") and are numbered according to the featured car's number.

	MINT	NRMT
COMPLETE SET (10)	8.00	3.60
COMMON CARD	.60	.25

❑ 1 Sammy Swindell 2.50 1.10
❑ 1A Bobby Allen .60 .25
❑ 7C Dave Blaney's Car 1.50 .70
❑ 8 Doug Wolfgang's Car 1.50 .70
❑ 10 Bobby Davis Jr.'s Car .60 .25
❑ 11 Steve Kinser's Car 3.00 1.35
❑ 23S Frankie Kerr's Car 1.00 .45
❑ 69 Brent Kaeding's Car 1.00 .45
❑ 77 Stevie Smith Jr.'s Car 1.00 .45
❑ NNO Only the Best Go Four .60 .25

1991 World of Outlaws

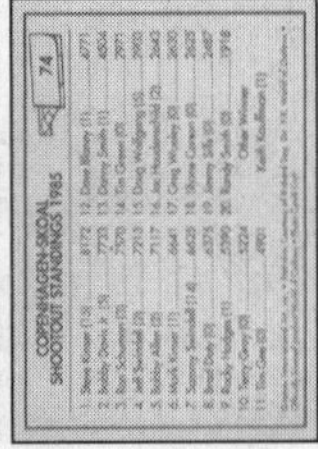

James International Art produced the largest World of Outlaws set to date in 1991. The cards were released in 10-card foil pack form with a 114-card regular set and four Most Wanted insert cards. The cards were redesigned from previous issues and contain a yellow border. Production and packaging problems resulted in a reportedly shorter print run for the 1991 set. Cards numbered 112-114 are considered in shorter supply. A Steve Kinser Promo card was released as well and is not considered part of the regular set.

	MINT	NRMT
COMPLETE SET (114)	40.00	18.00
COMMON CARD (1-114)	.30	.14

❑ 1 Checklist .30 .14
❑ 2 Steve Kinser 3.00 1.35
❑ 3 Mark Kinser 1.50 .70
❑ 4 Joe Gaerte .30 .14
❑ 5 Stevie Smith Jr. 1.00 .45
❑ 6 Dave Blaney 1.50 .70
❑ 7 Johnny Herrera .30 .14
❑ 8 Steve Beitler .30 .14
❑ 9 Jim Carr .30 .14
❑ 10 Checklist .30 .14
❑ 11 Sammy Swindell 2.00 .90
❑ 12 Gary Cameron II .30 .14
❑ 13 Bobby Davis Jr. .30 .14
❑ 14 Bobby Allen .30 .14
❑ 15 Danny Lasoski .30 .14
❑ 16 Doug Wolfgang 1.00 .45
❑ 17 Greg Hodnett .30 .14
❑ 18 Keith Kauffman .30 .14
❑ 19 Jac Haudenschild 2.00 .90
❑ 20 Jeff Swindell 1.00 .45
❑ 21 Craig Keel .30 .14
❑ 22 Gary Wright .30 .14
❑ 23 Dale Laakso .30 .14
❑ 24 Terry Gray .30 .14
❑ 25 Kenny Jacobs .30 .14
❑ 26 Aaron Berryhill .30 .14
❑ 27 Danny Smith .30 .14
❑ 28 Mike Peters .30 .14
❑ 29 Cris Eash .30 .14
❑ 30 Brent Kaeding .60 .25
❑ 31 Ronnie Day .30 .14
❑ 32 Donnie Kreitz Jr. .30 .14
❑ 33 Frankie Kerr .60 .25
❑ 34 Terry McCarl .30 .14
❑ 35 Jimmy Sills .30 .14
❑ 36 Steve Kent .30 .14
❑ 37 Tommie Estes Jr. .30 .14
❑ 38 Dan Hamilton .30 .14
❑ 39 Darrell Hanestad .30 .14
❑ 40 Paul McMahan .30 .14
❑ 41 Jason McMillen .30 .14
❑ 42 Toni Lutar .30 .14
❑ 43 Tim Green .30 .14
❑ 44 Greg DeCaires IV .30 .14
❑ 45 Ricky Stenhouse .30 .14
❑ 46 Bobby Fletcher .30 .14
❑ 47 Paul Lotier .30 .14
❑ 48 Shane Carson .30 .14
❑ 49 Steve Siegel .30 .14
❑ 50 Rich Bubak .30 .14
❑ 51 Bobby McMahan .30 .14
❑ 52 Chuck Miller .30 .14
❑ 53 Lealand McSpadden .30 .14
❑ 54 Dennis Rodriguez .30 .14
❑ 55 Rickie Gaunt .30 .14
❑ 56 Lee Brewer Jr. .30 .14
❑ 57 Rick Hirst .30 .14
❑ 58 Rickey Hood .30 .14
❑ 59 Jason Earls .30 .14
❑ 60 Ron Shuman .30 .14
❑ 61 Checklist .30 .14
❑ 62 Ted Johnson .30 .14
❑ 63 Dion Appleby .30 .14
❑ 64 Tom Basinger .30 .14
❑ 65 Dale Blaney .30 .14
❑ 66 Billy Boat .30 .14
❑ 67 Greg Brown .30 .14
❑ 68 Steve Butler .30 .14
❑ 69 Dan Dietrich .30 .14
❑ 70 Checklist .30 .14
❑ 71 Kevin Doty .30 .14
❑ 72 Kenny French .30 .14
❑ 73 Rick Haas .30 .14
❑ 74 Jack Hewitt .60 .25
❑ 75 Larry Hillerod .30 .14
❑ 76 Rocky Hodges .30 .14
❑ 77 Sparky Howard .30 .14
❑ 78 Chris Ikard .30 .14
❑ 79 Howard Kaeding .30 .14
❑ 80 Todd Kane .30 .14
❑ 81 Dave Kelly .30 .14
❑ 82 Kelly Kinser .30 .14
❑ 83 Joey Kuhn .30 .14
❑ 84 Nick Losasso .30 .14
❑ 85 Ed Lynch Jr. .30 .14
❑ 86 Rick Martin .30 .14
❑ 87 Fred Rahmer .30 .14
❑ 88 Nick Rescino .30 .14
❑ 89 Tommy Scott .30 .14
❑ 90 Todd Shaffer .30 .14
❑ 91 Terry Shepherd .30 .14
❑ 92 Steve Smith Sr. .30 .14
❑ 93 Steve Stambaugh .30 .14
❑ 94 Jason Statler .30 .14
❑ 95 Mitch Sue .30 .14
❑ 96 Bobby Weaver .30 .14
❑ 97 Max Dumesny .30 .14
❑ 98 Melinda Dumesny .30 .14
❑ 99 Skip Jackson .30
❑ 100 Jamie Moyle .30
❑ 101 Steve Kinser's Car 2.50
❑ 102 Mark Kinser's Car .30
❑ 103 Joe Gaerte .30
❑ 104 Dave Blaney's Car .60
❑ 105 Johnny Herrera's Car .30
❑ 106 Steve Beitler's Car .30
❑ 107 Sammy Swindell's Car 2.00
❑ 108 Bobby Davis Jr.'s Car .30
❑ 109 Greg Hodnett's Car .30
❑ 110 Gary Wright's Car .30
❑ 111 Terry Gray's Car .30
❑ 112 Aaron Berryhill's Car SP 3.00
❑ 113 Frankie Kerr's Car SP 3.00
❑ 114 Jimmy Sills' Car SP 2.50
❑ P1 Steve Kinser Promo 5.00

1991 World of Outlaws Most Wanted

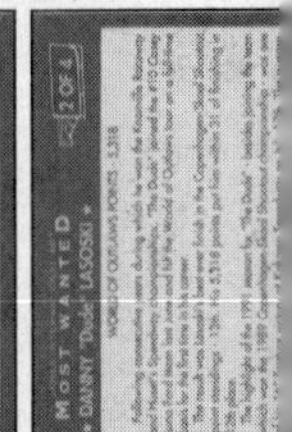

This six-card Most Wanted set was issued in bo packs of 1991 World of Outlaws and in complete se The four driver cards were released through pack and then re-issued as a complete set with the cov checklist cards. The card design is very similar to Most Wanted sets, but can be distinguished by the color of black.

	MINT
COMPLETE SET (6)	10.00
COMMON CARD (1-4)	1.50

❑ 1 Stevie Smith Jr. 2.00
❑ 2 Danny Lasoski 3.00
❑ 3 Jimmy Sills 1.50
❑ 4 Bobby Davis Jr. 2.00
❑ NNO Cover Card .75
World of Outlaws logo and complete set offe
❑ NNO Checklist Card .75

1992 World of Outlaws Most Wanted

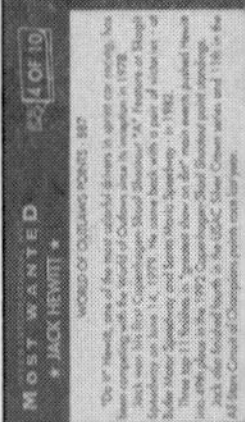

James International Art produced only 12-card Wanted set in 1992. The card design is very sir other Most Wanted sets, but can be distinguished border color of Maroon. The cover card describes as Most Wanted series two.

	MINT
COMPLETE SET (12)	10.00
COMMON CARD (1-10)	.75

❑ 1 Jac Haudenschild 1.50
❑ 2 Johnny Herrera .75
❑ 3 Steve Beitler .75
❑ 4 Jack Hewitt .75
❑ 5 Sammy Swindell 2.00
❑ 6 Jim Carr .75
❑ 7 Danny Smith .75
❑ 8 Keith Kauffman .75
❑ 9 Dale Blaney .75
❑ 10 Andy Hillenburg .75
❑ NNO Cover Card .60
World of Outlaws logo and complete set offe
❑ NNO Checklist Card .60

1993 World of Outlaws Most Wanted

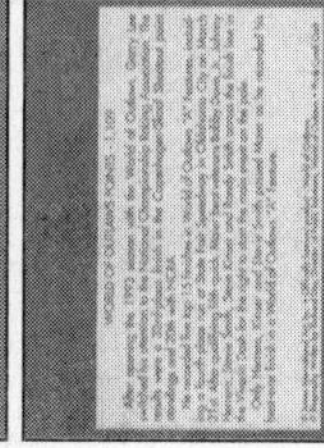

International Art produced only a 12-card Most set in 1993. The card design is very similar to ost Wanted sets, but can be distinguished by the color of blue. The cover card describes the set as anted series three.

	MINT	NRMT
ETE SET (12)	10.00	4.50
)N CARD (1-10)	.75	.35
'e Blaney	2.00	.90
ny Jacobs	1.25	.55
ig Keel	.75	.35
Gaerte	.75	.35
Lynch Jr.	.75	.35
nmie Estes Jr.	.75	.35
Eash	.75	.35
ry Lee Maier	.75	.35
y Cameron II	.75	.35
vin Huntley	.75	.35
Cover Card	.60	.25
Vorld of Outlaws logo and complete set offer		
Checklist Card	.60	.25
omplete set/sheet offer on back		

1994 World of Outlaws

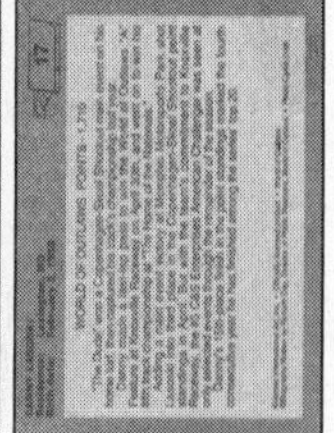

two year hiatus, James International once again d a regular issue World of Outlaws set in 1994, as a Most Wanted set. The cards were re-designed ude 50 to the set released in a factory set box.

	MINT	NRMT
ETE SET (50)	20.00	9.00
N CARD (1-50)	.30	.14
cklist	.30	.14
e Kinser	2.50	1.10
Blaney	1.00	.45
ie Smith Jr.	.75	.35
ny Jacobs	.30	.14
y Hillenburg	.60	.25
Haudenschild	1.50	.70
Hodnett	.60	.25
nny Herrera	.30	.14
hard Day	.30	.14
ve Beitler	.30	.14
ig Keel	.30	.14
f Swindell	.60	.25
rk Kinser	1.00	.45
on Berryhill	.30	.14
Gaerte	.30	.14
nny Lasoski	.60	.25
ry McCarl	.30	.14
bby Davis Jr.	.30	.14
Lynch Jr.	.30	.14
bby Allen	.30	.14
nnie Kreitz Jr.	.30	.14
th Kauffman	.30	.14
nny Smith	.30	.14
y Wright	.30	.14
nny Mackison Jr.	.30	.14
Carr	.30	.14
ndy Smith	.30	.14
ry Lee Maier	.30	.14
❑ 30 Steve Kent	.30	.14
❑ 31 Max Dumesny	.30	.14
❑ 32 Jimmy Sills	.30	.14
❑ 33 Gary Cameron II	.30	.14
❑ 34 Kevin Huntley	.30	.14
❑ 35 Rocky Hodges	.30	.14
❑ 36 Brent Kaeding	.60	.25
❑ 37 Frankie Kerr	.60	.25
❑ 38 Tim Green	.30	.14
❑ 39 Fred Rahmer	.60	.25
❑ 40 Steve Smith Sr.	.60	.25
❑ 41 Brad Noffsinger	.30	.14
❑ 42 Randy Hannagan	.30	.14
❑ 43 Garry Rush	.30	.14
❑ 44 Jason McMillen	.30	.14
❑ 45 Todd Kane	.30	.14
❑ 46 Dale Blaney	.30	.14
❑ 47 Rusty McClure	.30	.14
❑ 48 Kevin Pylant	.30	.14
❑ 49 Rod Henderson	.30	.14
❑ 50 Ron Shuman	.30	.14

1994 World of Outlaws Most Wanted

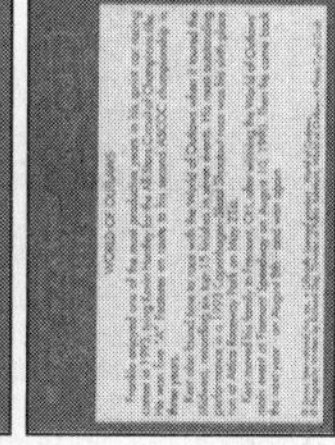

James International Art this 12-card Most Wanted set in 1994. The card design is very similar to other Most Wanted sets, but can be distinguished by the border color of brown. The cover card describes the set as Most Wanted series four and includes an offer to purchase complete sets or uncut sheets from previous year's sets.

	MINT	NRMT
COMPLETE SET (12)	10.00	4.50
COMMON CARD (1-10)	.75	.35
❑ 1 Steve Kinser	2.50	1.10
❑ 2 Greg Hodnett	.75	.35
❑ 3 Mark Kinser	1.50	.70
❑ 4 Frankie Kerr	1.00	.45
❑ 5 Aaron Berryhill	.75	.35
❑ 6 Terry McCarl	.75	.35
❑ 7 Jeff Swindell	1.00	.45
❑ 8 Brent Kaeding	1.00	.45
❑ 9 Lance Dewease	.75	.35
❑ 10 Steve Kent	.75	.35
❑ NNO Cover Card	.60	.25
offer for complete sets/sheets on back		
❑ NNO Checklist Card	.60	.25
offer for complete sets/sheets on back		

1990-97 Action Packed Promos

The first cards Action Packed did for racing was the four card Indy promo set. The next promo card series released by Action Packed was for their first racing product. Kyle Petty was the feature of the three-card series. The 1993 Alan Kulwicki and Davey Allison 24K Gold card came in a black box. The word Prototype is on the back of most Action Packed promos. 1994 saw two Kyle Petty's released for series one, four promos released for series two and four more for series three. The three card series in 1996 were distributed as a set in its own cello wrapper to hobby dealers and media. There are two Action Packed NHRA promos, Eddie Hill '95 and John Force '96.

	MINT	NRMT
❑ 1990 Emerson Fittipaldi	75.00	34.00
Card number 1		
❑ 1990 Mario Andretti	125.00	55.00
Card number 6		
❑ 1990 Rick Mears	75.00	34.00
Card number 22		
❑ 1990 Pancho Carter	60.00	27.00
Card Number 23		
❑ 1992 Kyle Petty's Car	12.00	5.50
Card Number 101		
❑ 1992 Kyle Petty	16.00	7.25
Card Number 102		
❑ 1992 Kyle Petty's Car	12.00	5.50
Card Number 103		
❑ 1993 Bobby Allison	25.00	11.00
Card Numbered BA1		
❑ 1993 Dale Earnhardt	60.00	27.00
Card Numbered DE1		
❑ 1993 Jeff Gordon	60.00	27.00
Card Numbered JG1		
❑ 1993 Dale Jarrett	25.00	11.00
Card Numbered DJ1		
❑ 1993 Alan Kulwicki	40.00	18.00
Card Numbered AK1		
❑ 1993 Alan Kulwicki	20.00	9.00
Davey Allison		
Card Numbered AKDA		
❑ 1993 Alan Kulwicki	75.00	34.00
Davey Allison		
24K Gold		
Card Numbered AKDAG		
❑ 1994 Dale Earnhardt	15.00	6.75
Card Numbered 2R941		
❑ 1994 Jeff Gordon	15.00	6.75
Card Numbered 2R942		
❑ 1994 Jeff Gordon 24K Gold	200.00	90.00
Card Numbered 2R942G		
❑ 1994 Kyle Petty	6.00	2.70
Card Numbered 2R943		
❑ 1994 Kyle Petty 24K Gold	80.00	36.00
Card Numbered 2R943G		
❑ 1994 Dale Jarrett	6.00	2.70
Card Numbered 2R944		
❑ 1994 Rusty Wallace's Car	8.00	3.60
Card Numbered 2R945		
❑ 1994 Ricky Rudd	5.00	2.20
Card Numbered 3R941		
❑ 1994 Richard Childress	4.00	1.80
Card Numbered 3R942		
❑ 1994 Mark Martin	6.00	2.70
Card Numbered 3R943		
❑ 1994 Jeff Gordon	12.00	5.50
Card Numbered 3R94S		
❑ 1994 Kyle Petty's Car	4.00	1.80
Card Numbered KP1		
❑ 1994 Kyle Petty	5.00	2.20
Card Numbered KP2		
❑ 1994 Eddie Hill NHRA	4.00	1.80
Card Numbered P1		
❑ 1995 Bobby Labonte	3.00	1.35
Action Packed Country		
Card Numbered 46		
❑ 1995 Jeff Gordon	6.00	2.70
AP Country Team Rainbow		
❑ 1995 Bill Elliott 24K Gold	25.00	11.00
AP Preview		
Card Numbered P1		
❑ 1995 Ricky Craven 24K Gold	15.00	6.75
AP Preview		
Card Numbered P2		
❑ 1995 Steve Kinser 24K Gold	15.00	6.75
AP Preview		
Card Numbered P3		
❑ 1995 Dale Earnhardt	15.00	6.75
Race For Eight		
Card Numbered DE2		
❑ 1995 John Force's Car NHRA	5.00	2.20
Card Numbered 11		
❑ 1996 Mark Martin	1.00	.45
AP Credentials		
Card Numbered 23		
❑ 1996 Kenny Wallace	.50	.23
AP Credentials		
Card Numbered 97		
❑ 1996 Jeff Gordon	2.00	.90
Leader of the Pack		
Card Numbered 5		
❑ 1997 Jeff Gordon		
Card Numbered 8		

1995-96 Classic Promos

The $1000 Dale Earnhardt sample phone card is the highlight of the Classic released promos. Jeff Gordon and Dale Earnhardt are the only ones to have a Classic promo.

	MINT	NRMT
❑ 1995 Dale Earnhardt	20.00	9.00
Assets $1000 Phone Card		
❑ 1995 Jeff Gordon	15.00	6.75
Images		
❑ 1996 Dale Earnhardt	8.00	3.60
Assets		
❑ 1996 Dale Earnhardt	8.00	3.60
Classic		

1993-96 Finish Line Promos

Finish Line released promos for both their NASCAR and NHRA lines. The also were the ones to release the Dale

Earnhardt Fan Club card in 1995. Their most recent promos are from their Phone Paks and Phone Paks 2 lines.

	MINT	NRMT
❑ 1993 Davey Allison Card Numbered P1	10.00	4.50
❑ 1993 Jeff Gordon Card Numbered P2	16.00	7.25
❑ 1993 Terry Labonte Bobby Labonte Card Numbered P3	8.00	3.60
❑ 1993 Scott Geoffrion NHRA	1.50	.70
❑ 1993 Cory McClenathan's Car NHRA	1.50	.70
❑ 1993 Cruz Pedregon NHRA	2.00	.90
❑ 1993 Cover Card NHRA	.30	.14
❑ 1994 Harry Gant Card Numbered P1	2.00	.90
❑ 1994 Mark Martin Card Numbered P2	3.00	1.35
❑ 1994 Rusty Wallace Card Numbered P3	3.00	1.35
❑ 1994 Jeff Gordon's Car Finish Line Gold	8.00	3.60
❑ 1994 Terry Labonte Finish Line Gold	6.00	2.70
❑ 1994 Cover Card Finish Line Gold	.30	.14
❑ 1995 Dale Earnhardt Finish Line Dale Earnhardt Card Numbered HP1	10.00	4.50
❑ 1995 Dale Earnhardt Finish Line Dale Earnhardt Card Numbered RP1	10.00	4.50
❑ 1995 Dale Earnhardt Dale Earnhardt Fan Club Card Numbered CE1	5.00	2.20
❑ 1996 Mark Martin Phone Paks	8.00	3.60
❑ 1996 Jeff Gordon Phone Paks 2 One Call Each Numbered of 1000	10.00	4.50

1996-97 Fleer Promos

Fleer began producing racing cards in 1996. There first series was Ultra. They released two different variations of the Jeff Gordon Ultra sheet that year. The tougher version features blue foil stamping and has February 1996 and First Ever Print Run on the Ultra cover card on the sheet. The '96 Ultra Update and '97 Ultra promos feature a double wide card. One half has the card and the other half has the information about the set.

	MINT	NRMT
❑ 1996 Jeff Gordon Flair	10.00	4.50
❑ 1996 Jeff Gordon Ultra Sheet with Blue Foil	5.00	2.20
❑ 1996 Jeff Gordon Ultra Sheet with Silver Foil	3.00	1.35
❑ 1996 Ernie Irvan Ultra Update	4.00	1.80
❑ 1997 Mark Martin Ultra Card Numbered S1	4.00	1.80

1992-95 Hi-Tech Promos

Hi-Tech did promos for their Indy car and NASCAR sets. Many of the promos were consecutively numbered and are often collected in sets.

	MINT	NRMT
❑ 1992 Mario Andretti Mario Andretti set	2.00	.90
❑ 1992 Mario Andretti Card Numbered 1	20.00	9.00
❑ 1992 Al Unser Jr.'s Car Card Numbered 2	8.00	3.60
❑ 1992 Michael Andretti Card Numbered 3	15.00	6.75
❑ 1992 Paul Newman Card Numbered 4	20.00	9.00
❑ 1992 Cover Card Card Numbered 5	2.00	.90
❑ 1992 Scott Goodyear Card Numbered 6	8.00	3.60
❑ 1993 Danny Sullivan Card Numbered P1	3.00	1.35
❑ 1993 Scott Goodyear Card Numbered P2	3.00	1.35
❑ 1993 Eddie Cheever's Car Card Numbered P3	2.00	.90
❑ 1993 Bobby Rahal's Car Foil Card Numbered P4	3.00	1.35
❑ 1993 Eddie Cheever's Car Foil Card Numbered P5	2.00	.90
❑ 1993 Al Unser's Car Foil Card Numbered P6	4.00	1.80
❑ 1993 Rusty Wallace's Car Tire Test Card Numbered P1	4.00	1.80
❑ 1993 Davey Allison's Car Tire Test Card Numbered P2	4.00	1.80
❑ 1994 Nigel Mansell's Car Card Numbered P1/3	2.00	.90
❑ 1994 Mario Andretti's Car Card Numbered P2/3	2.00	.90
❑ 1994 Mario Andrett Championship Driver Card Number P3/3	5.00	2.20
❑ 1994 Richard Petty Card Numbered 1/3	4.00	1.80
❑ 1994 Jeff Gordon's Car Card Numbered 2/3	8.00	3.60
❑ 1994 Kyle Petty's Car Card Numbered 3/3	3.00	1.35
❑ 1995 Mario Andretti Championship Driver Card Numbered P1/1	5.00	2.20
❑ 1995 Mark Martin's Car Card Numbered P1	4.00	1.80
❑ 1995 Ernie Irvan Card Numbered P2	3.00	1.35
❑ 1995 Dale Earnhardt Top Ten Card Numbered P3	8.00	3.60

1991-97 Maxx Promos

Bill Elliott was exclusive to Maxx from 1988-94, so it is understandable why the promo cards for each of their sets from 1991-94 featured Bill. Starting in 1995, many of the promo cards had two versions a gold foil and a red foil. The gold foil versions were distributed through hobby dealers, media and show appearances. The red foil versions were distributed to Maxx Club members.

	MINT	NRMT
❑ 1991 Bill Elliott	75.00	34.00
❑ 1992 Bill Elliott Black	20.00	9.00
❑ 1992 Bill Elliott Red	20.00	9.00
❑ 1993 Bill Elliott Green	5.00	2.20
❑ 1993 Bill Elliott Premier Plus	12.00	5.50
❑ 1993 Bill Elliott Premier Series	10.00	4.50
❑ 1994 Bill Elliott Card Numbered 11	5.00	2.20
❑ 1994 Bill Elliott Fan Club	10.00	4.50
❑ 1994 Jeff Gordon Card Numbered 24	8.00	3.60
❑ 1994 Ted Musgrave Series 2	2.00	.90
❑ 1994 Bill Elliott Premier Plus	8.00	3.60
❑ 1994 Bill Elliott Premier Series Card Numbered 11	8.00	3.60
❑ 1995 Jeff Gordon's Car Gold Foil	2.50	1.10
❑ 1995 Jeff Gordon's Car Red Foil Maxx Club issue	5.00	2.20
❑ 1995 Ricky Rudd Series 2	1.50	.70
❑ 1995 Mark Martin Steve Hmiel Sheet handed out at St.Louis National	4.00	1.80
❑ 1995 Ted Musgrave's Car Medallion	3.00	1.35
❑ 1995 Darrell Waltrip Premier Plus	1.50	.70
❑ 1995 Jeff Burton Premier Series Gold Foil	1.00	.45
❑ 1995 Jeff Burton Premier Series Red Foil Club	4.00	1.80
❑ 1996 Sterling Marlin	2.00	.90
❑ 1996 Dale Jarrett Four Card Sheet handed out at Anaheim National	4.00	1.80
❑ 1996 Terry Labonte Signed and Sealed	6.00	2.70
❑ 1996 Bobby Labonte Odyssey	2.00	.90
❑ 1996 Ricky Craven Premier Series Gold Foil	2.00	.90
❑ 1996 Ricky Craven Premier Series Red Foil Club	4.00	1.80
❑ 1997 Rusty Wallace 1997 Maxx Numbered R2		
❑ 1998 J.Gordon Maxximum (S24)		

1991-92 Miscellaneous Stc Car Promos

The following is a list of promo cards from variou mainstream Stock Car sets. On the continuation line set the promo card is from.

	MINT
❑ 1991 Rob Moroso Sports Legends Rob Moroso	2.00
❑ 1991 Phil Parsons Sports Legends Phil Parsons	2.00
❑ 1991 Harry Gant CM Handsome Harry	2.00
❑ 1991 Dale Jarrett Sports Legends Dale Jarrett	2.00
❑ 1991 Cale Yarborough Sports Legends Cale Yarborough	2.00
❑ 1991 Harry Hyde Sports Legends Harry Hyde	2.00
❑ 1991 Bobby Allison Donnie Allison Neil Bonnett Sports Legends Donnie Allison has red boarder	1.00
❑ 1991 Herb Thomas Sports Legends Herb Thomas	2.00
❑ 1991 Bobby Allison Donnie Allison Neil Bonnett Sports Legends Bobby Allison has yellow boarder	1.00
❑ 1991 Tom Pistone Tiger Tom Pistone	1.00
❑ 1991 Tiny Lund TG Racing Tiny Lund 55	1.00
❑ 1991 Hut Stricklin Sports Legends Hut Stricklin	2.00
❑ 1992 Buck Baker Sports Legends Buck Baker	2.00
❑ 1992 Alan Kulwicki Sports Legends Alan Kulwicki	2.00
❑ 1992 Rusty Wallace Sports Legends Rusty Wallace	2.00
❑ 1992 Charlie Owens TG Racing Masters of Racing	2.50
❑ 1992 Larry Frank TG Racing Masters of Racing	2.50
❑ 1992 Ken Schrader Redline Racing	2.00
❑ 1992 Charlie Glotzbach TG Racing Masters of Racing	2.50
❑ 1992 Donald Thomas TG Racing Masters of Racing	2.50
❑ 1992 Jeff Gordon Limited Edition 4	4.00
❑ 1992 Cale Yarborough Redline Racing	2.00
❑ 1992 Rick Wilson Bikers of the Racing Scene	3.00
❑ 1992 Harry Gant Limited Edition 1	2.50
❑ 1992 Harry Gant Redline Racing	2.00
❑ 1992 Kenny Wallace Jimmy Hensley Tommy Houston Chuck Bown Limited Edition 2	2.00
❑ 1992 Rob Moroso Redline Racing	2.00
❑ 1992 Jerry Glanville Limited Edition 3	2.00

1995-98 Pinnacle Prom

The 1995 Select Dream Machine promo of Jeff G consistently on promo collectors want list. The Allison Zenith Champion Salute is numbered differ what the actual card in the set is numbered.

	MINT
❑ 1995 Jeff Gordon Select Card Numbered 12	5.00
❑ 1995 Kyle Petty Select Card Numbered 24	1.50
❑ 1995 Loy Allen Select Card Number 128	1.50
❑ 1995 Geoff Bodine Select Card Number 136	1.00
❑ 1995 Jeff Gordon's Car	16.00

Select Dream Machines
Card Numbered DM8
Dale Earnhardt 8.00 3.60
Zenith
Card Numbered 132
Ted Musgrave 5.00 2.20
Zenith Helmets
Card Numbered 8
Sterling Marlin 5.00 2.20
Team Pinnacle
Card Numbered 8
Jeff Gordon 5.00 2.20
Racer's Choice
Sterling Marlin 2.00 .90
Racer's Choice
Card Numbered 99
Dale Earnhardt 5.00 2.20
Racer's Choice Top 10
Card Numbered 2
Dale Jarrett 4.00 1.80
Speedflix
Bobby Allison 5.00 2.20
Zenith Championship Salute
Card Numbered 12
Ricky Rudd
Pinnacle Totally Certified
Card Numbered 10
Mark Martin
Pinnacle Certified
Card Numbered 6
Dale Earnhardt
Pinnacle Spellbound
Card Numbered 3
Bill Elliott 5.00 2.20
Pinnacle Precision
Card Numbered 00
Dale Jarrett
Pinnacle Mint
Terry Labonte
Racer's Choice
Card Numbered 5
Mark Martin
Pinnacle Mint with coin
Mark Martin
Pinnacle Mint without coin

94-98 Press Pass Promos

ass first started doing promo cards with the 1994 XL set. There were two variations of the '94 XL Rusty Wallace. One has his name at the top on t of the card and the other has his name at the Press Pass also released many of their promo rectly to their club members. This is the only way f these cards are released. The '95 VIP promo ome in both gold and red foil versions. The M-romo cards were numbered #/4 but there were e different versions released.

MINT NRMT
Kyle Petty 8.00 3.60
ptima XL
ard Numbered 1
Rusty Wallace 8.00 3.60
ptima XL with Name at Top
ard Numbered 2
Rusty Wallace 8.00 3.60
ptima XL with Name at the bottom
ard Numbered 2
Jeff Gordon 8.00 3.60
ptima XL
ard Numbered 3
Geoff Bodine 8.00 3.60
IP Members Only
Harry Gant 3.00 1.35
IP
Jeff Gordon's Car 6.00 2.70
IP
Ernie Irvan 3.00 1.35
IP
Mark Martin 10.00 4.50
IP Members Only
Rusty Wallace 5.00 2.20
IP
Kyle Petty 2.00 .90
ard Numbered 1
Terry Labonte's Car 2.00 .90
ard Numbered 2
Jeff Gordon 4.00 1.80
ard Numbered 3
Kyle Petty 2.50 1.10
emium
Jeff Burton 2.50 1.10
ptima XL
ard Numbered 1/3
Darrell Waltrip 3.00 1.35
ptima XL
ard Numbered 2/3

❑ 1995 Mark Martin 5.00 2.20
Optima XL
Card Numbered 3
❑ 1995 Dale Jarrett 1.00 .45
VIP with Gold foil
Card Numbered 1
❑ 1995 Dale Jarrett 3.00 1.35
VIP with Red foil
Card Numbered 1
❑ 1995 Bobby Labonte 1.00 .45
VIP with Gold foil
Card Numbered 2
❑ 1995 Bobby Labonte 3.00 1.35
VIP with Red foil
Card Numbered 2
❑ 1995 Michael Waltrip .60 .25
VIP with Gold foil
Card Numbered 3
❑ 1995 Michael Waltrip 2.00 .90
VIP with Red foil
Card Numbered 3
❑ 1995 Bill Elliott 1.00 .45
VIP with Gold foil
Card Numbered 4
❑ 1995 Bill Elliott 3.00 1.35
VIP with Red foil
Card Numbered 4
❑ 1995 VIP Red Foil Versions 1.5X TO 3X
❑ 1996 Jeff Gordon 6.00 2.70
Focused
Card Numbered 1
❑ 1996 Terry Labonte 2.00 .90
Card Numbered 2
❑ 1996 Bobby Labonte 3.00 1.35
Premium
❑ 1996 Jeff Gordon 5.00 2.20
M-Force Blue tint
Card Numbered 1/4
❑ 1996 Jeff Gordon 5.00 2.20
M-Force Green tint
Card Numbered 2/4
❑ 1996 Jeff Gordon 5.00 2.20
M-Force Silver tint
Card Numbered 3/4
❑ 1996 Bobby Labonte 5.00 2.20
Gold Foil
handed out at the
National Convention in Anaheim
❑ 1996 Bobby Labonte 10.00 4.50
Red Foil
handed out at the
National Convention in Anaheim
❑ 1996 Mark Martin 5.00 2.20
VIP
❑ 1996 Kyle Petty 6.00 2.70
VIP Members Only
❑ 1997 Bobby Labonte
Actionvision
❑ 1997 Dale Jarrett 3.00 1.35
Card Numbered 1
❑ 1997 Bobby Labonte National
❑ 1997 Jeff Gordon 5.00 2.20
Premium
Card Numbered 1
❑ 1997 Dale Jarrett 8.00 3.60
Premium Members Only
Card Numbered 2
❑ 1997 Ernie Irvan 8.00 3.60
Premium Members Only
Card Numbered 3
❑ 1997 Dale Jarrett
VIP
Card numbered 1
❑ 1997 Dale Jarrett
VIP Explosive
Card numbered 2
❑ 1998 Jeff Gordon
Premium
Card Numbered 1
❑ 1998 Jeff Gordon
Stealth
Card Numbered 1
❑ 1998 Mark Martin
Press Pass Members Only
Card numbered 3
❑ 1998 Dale Jarrett
Press Pass Shockers
Card numbered 3
❑ 1998 Jeff Gordon
Press Pass
Card numbered 3
❑ 1998 Jeremy Mayfield
VIP
Card Numbered 1
❑ 1999 Dale Earnhardt Jr.
Press Pass
Card Numbered 3
❑ 1999 Jeff Gordon
Press Pass
Card Numbered 3

1991-94 Pro Set Promos

Pro Set released promos for its NASCAR and NHRA lines.

	MINT	NRMT
❑ 1991 Bobby Allison	2.00	.90
❑ 1991 Hut Stricklin	.50	.23
❑ 1991 Hut Stricklin's Car	.35	.16
❑ 1991 Lee Petty's Car Petty Family	.75	.35
❑ 1991 Maurice Petty Petty Family	.75	.35
❑ 1991 Richard Petty Petty Family	1.50	.70
❑ 1991 Kenny Bernstein's Car NHRA	1.50	.70
❑ 1991 John Force's Car NHRA	2.00	.90
❑ 1991 Bob Glidden NHRA	1.00	.45
❑ 1991 Lori Johns NHRA	1.00	.45
❑ 1991 Cover Card NHRA	.30	.14
❑ 1992 Dale Earnhardt	2.00	.90
❑ 1992 Sterling Marlin	1.00	.45
❑ 1992 Morgan Shepherd	.75	.35
❑ 1992 Joe Amato's Car NHRA	1.00	.45
❑ 1992 John Force's Car NHRA	2.00	.90
❑ 1992 Warren Johnson NHRA	1.00	.45
❑ 1992 Cover Card NHRA	.30	.14
❑ 1994 Harry Gant Power Preview Card Numbered 16	1.00	.45
❑ 1994 Dale Earnhardt Power Card Numbered DB1	6.00	2.70
❑ 1994 Jeff Gordon Power	6.00	2.70
❑ 1994 Ernie Irvan Power Card Numbered PW1	3.00	1.35

1995-97 SkyBox Promo

The promos from the 1995 SkyBox Indy set were distributed via hobby and media. The cards featured two of the most popular drivers at that time.

	MINT	NRMT
❑ 1995 Al Unser Jr.'s Car	2.00	.90
❑ 1995 Jacques Villeneuve	2.00	.90
❑ 1997 J.Gordon ProFiles	5.00	2.20

1991-96 Traks Promos

Traks released numerous promos for their 1991 and 1992 sets. The 1995 Mark Martin 5th Anniversary card was given out at the St.Louis National and is labeled of 4,000.

	MINT	NRMT
❑ 1991 Ernie Irvan	10.00	4.50
❑ 1991 Mark Martin	10.00	4.50
❑ 1991 Kyle Petty	6.00	2.70
❑ 1991 Richard Petty The King	8.00	3.60
❑ 1991 Richard Petty Lee Petty	8.00	3.60
❑ 1991 Richard Petty	8.00	3.60
❑ 1992 Benny Parsons	8.00	3.60
❑ 1992 Kyle Petty	10.00	4.50
❑ 1992 Richard Petty	12.00	5.50
❑ 1992 Rusty Wallace	15.00	6.75
❑ 1992 Dale Earnhardt Transporter Racing Machines Card Numbered P1	8.00	3.60
❑ 1992 Bobby Hamilton's Transporter Racing Machines Card Numbered P26	3.00	1.35
❑ 1992 Alan Kulwicki's Transporter Racing Machines Card Numbered P51	6.00	2.70
❑ 1992 Mark Martin's Car Racing Machines Card Numbered P76	6.00	2.70
❑ 1993 Jeff Gordon	8.00	3.60
❑ 1993 Rusty Wallace	5.00	2.20
❑ 1994 Mark Martin Top 10	5.00	2.20
❑ 1994 Ernie Irvan's Car Series 2	3.00	1.35
❑ 1995 Jeff Gordon Traks First Run Card Numbered 26	3.00	1.35
❑ 1995 Steve Hmiel Behind the Scenes Card Numbered BTS1	1.00	.45
❑ 1995 Jeff Burton On the Rise Card Numbered OTR14	1.00	.45
❑ 1995 Mark Martin	6.00	2.70

5th Anniversary
handed out at the St.Louis National

❑ 1995 Ray Evernham 1.00 .45
5th Anniversary
❑ 1995 Sterling Marlin's Car 1.00 .45
5th Anniversary
❑ 1995 Mark Martin 3.00 1.35
5th Anniversary
❑ 1996 Sterling Marlin 2.00 .90
❑ 1996 Mark Martin's Car 2.00 .90

1995-97 Upper Deck Promos

The first promo card of Rusty Wallace distributed in many places. Interestingly it was an insert in Atlanta Motor Speedway Hooter's 500 race programs in November of 1994. This was the event that Upper Deck made their announcement that they were going into motorsports trading cards.

MINT NRMT

❑ 1995 Rusty Wallace 2.00 .90
Series 1
Card Numbered PR1
❑ 1995 Rusty Wallace 2.00 .90
Series 2
Card Numbered PR2
❑ 1995 Rusty Wallace 2.00 .90
Card Numbered RW1
❑ 1996 Jeff Gordon 2.50 1.10
Card Numbered JG1
❑ 1996 Jeff Gordon 5.00 2.20
SP Card Numbered JG1
❑ 1996 Jeff Gordon 8.00 3.60
SPx Card Numbered 1
❑ 1997 Jeff Gordon
SP
Card Numbered S24
❑ 1998 Rusty Wallace SP (SPA2)

1993-98 Wheels Promos

Wheels has done many promos for most of their sets. The promo cards are generally released through hobby and media outlets. Recently their promo cards have included a version of each of the parallel sets in their products.

MINT NRMT

❑ 1993 Davey Allison 5.00 2.20
Rookie Thunder
❑ 1993 Jeff Gordon 8.00 3.60
Rookie Thunder
❑ 1993 Bobby Labonte 1.50 .70
Rookie Thunder
❑ 1993 Richard Petty 1.50 .70
Rookie Thunder
❑ 1993 Kenny Wallace 1.00 .45
Rookie Thunder
❑ 1994 Jeff Gordon 8.00 3.60
High Gear with Silver foil
❑ 1994 Jeff Gordon 16.00 7.25
High Gear with Gold foil
❑ 1994 Kyle Petty 4.00 1.80
High Gear with Silver foil
❑ 1994 Kyle Petty 8.00 3.60
High Gear with Gold foil
❑ 1994 Rusty Wallace 6.00 2.70
High Gear with Silver foil
❑ 1994 Rusty Wallace 12.00 5.50
High Gear with Gold foil
❑ 1994 High Gear Gold Cards 1.25X TO 2X
❑ 1994 Harry Gant 5.00 2.20
Harry Gant set
There are five different
❑ 1994 Jeff Gordon 10.00 4.50
Harry Gant set
❑ 1995 Jeff Gordon 35.00 16.00
Crown Jewels Diamond
Card Numbered P1
❑ 1995 Jeff Gordon 25.00 11.00
Crown Jewels Emerald
Card Numbered P1
❑ 1995 Jeff Gordon 10.00 4.50
Crown Jewels Ruby
Card Numbered P1
❑ 1995 Rusty Wallace 4.00 1.80
High Gear
Card Numbered P1
❑ 1995 Jeff Gordon 6.00 2.70
High Gear
Card Numbered P2
❑ 1995 Mark Martin 4.00 1.80
High Gear
Card Numbered 3
❑ 1996 Bobby Labonte 5.00 2.20
Viper
Card Numbered P1
❑ 1996 Rusty Wallace 8.00 3.60
Viper
Card Numbered P2
❑ 1996 Jeff Gordon 15.00 6.75
Viper
Card Numbered P3
❑ 1996 Bobby Labonte 5.00 2.20
Crown Jewels Elite
Card Numbered PC1
❑ 1996 Bobby Labonte 5.00 2.20
Crown Jewels Elite
Card Numbered PD1
❑ 1996 Bobby Labonte 5.00 2.20
Crown Jewels Elite
Card Numbered PE1
❑ 1996 Bobby Labonte 5.00 2.20
Crown Jewels Elite
Card Numbered PS1
❑ 1997 Jeff Gordon 8.00 3.60
Race Sharks
Card Numbered P1
❑ 1997 Jeff Gordon 8.00 3.60
Predator Red Wolf 1st Slash
Card Numbered P2
❑ 1997 Jeff Gordon 8.00 3.60
Predator
Card Numbered P1
❑ 1997 Jeff Gordon 8.00 3.60
Predator 1st Slash
Card Numbered P1
❑ 1997 Jeff Gordon 8.00 3.60
Predator Red Wolf
Card Numbered P2
❑ 1997 Jeff Gordon 8.00 3.60
Predator Black Wolf
Card Numbered P3
❑ 1997 Jeff Gordon 8.00 3.60
Predator Black Wolf 1st Slash
Card Numbered P3
❑ 1997 Mark Martin
Jurassic Park
Card Numbered P1
❑ 1998 B.Labonte
High Gear
Card Numbered 1
❑ 1998 M.Martin
Wheels
Card Numbered 1

1993-94 Ameritech

This phone company released the two card Smokey Yunick in quantities of 1000. The Richard Petty card was released in a quantity of 5000. The Richard Petty card used to commonly appear in ads for Ameritech phone cards.

MINT NRMT

❑ 1/94 $10 Richard Petty /5000 30.00 13.50
❑ 11/93 $5 S.Yunick (2 cards)/1000 75.00 34.00

1993-96 Collector's Advantage

This is the distributing agent for many different phone card companies. They have released cards for Planet Telecom, InterNet, Mecury Marketing, and Speed Call.

MINT NRMT

❑ 10/95 $6 All-Pro Bump.to B 14.00 6.25
300 /4000
❑ 10/95 $6 All-Pro Bump.to B 70.00 32.00
300 Jumbo/400
❑ 3/96 $10 Busch Lite 300/4000 15.00 6.75
❑ 5/95 $6 Coca-Cola 600 /4000 15.00 6.75
❑ 5/95 $6 Coca-Cola 600 90.00 40.00
Jumbo/400
❑ 2/96 $5 Goodwrench 200&400 14.00 6.25
/4000
❑ 3/96 $6 Hoosier 300 /4000 15.00 6.75
❑ 11/93 $5 Hooters 500 /1000 45.00 20.00
❑ 4/95 $6 LugNut /4000 14.00 6.25
❑ 11/95 $5 NAPA 500 /4000 14.00 6.25
❑ 3/95 $6 Purolator 500 /2500 14.00 6.25
❑ 5/95 $6 Red Dog 300 Inagural 15.00 6.75
/4000
❑ 5/95 $6 Red Dog 300 Inagural 80.00 36.00
Jumbo/400
❑ 10/95 $6 UAW-GM 500 14.00 6.25
/4000
❑ 10/95 $6 UAW-GM 500 70.00 32.00
Jumbo/400

1994-95 Finish Line Special Calling Cards

These two cards both celebrate 25th anniversaries. Both the Motor Racing Network and Talladega Motor Speedway had their 25th in 1994.

MINT

❑ 2/94 $10 MRN 25th Anv./5000 14.00
❑ 4/94 $10 Talladega 25th Anv./550 18.00

1994 Finish Line Calling Ca

These cards were issued in see through envelope cards were the first phone cards released by Finish There was 5,000 of each series one card produce 1,800 of each series two card. Also, Finish Line available a gold version of the Bill Elliott and the Irvan.

MINT

COMPLETE SER.1 SET (5) 90.00
COMPLETE SER.2 SET (10) 150.00
COMMON CARD (1-5) 14.00
COMMON CARD (6-15) 14.00
1,800 SERIES TWO CARDS PRODUCED
BILL ELLIOTT GOLD /600 40.00
ERNIE IRVAN GOLD /600 40.00

❑ 1 Bill Elliott 18.00
❑ 2 Jeff Gordon 25.00
❑ 3 Bobby Labonte 14.00
❑ 4 Sterling Marlin 18.00
❑ 5 Rusty Wallace 18.00
❑ 6 Geoff Bodine 14.00
❑ 7 Bill Elliott 18.00
❑ 8 Jeff Gordon 25.00
❑ 9 Ernie Irvan 18.00
❑ 10 Dale Jarrett 14.00
❑ 11 Mark Martin 18.00
❑ 12 Kyle Petty 14.00
❑ 13 Ricky Rudd 14.00
❑ 14 Rusty Wallace 18.00
❑ 15 Darrell Waltrip 14.00

1995 Finish Line Card of the Month

These cards were available through the Finish Line Club. The cards were printed in quantities of 1500 e

MINT

COMPLETE SET (4) 75.00
COMMON CARD 15.00

❑ 1 Jeff Gordon/1500 25.00
❑ 2 Sterling Marlin/1500 15.00
❑ 3 Mark Martin/1500 18.00
❑ 4 Rusty Wallace/1500 18.00

1995 Finish Line Platinu 5 Unit Phone Cards

There were 500 of each of the cards in this seri cards could be bought in different unit denominat 10, 25, and 60. The cards were sold through the Line Racing Club.

MINT

COMPLETE SET (4) 30.00
COMMON CARD
COMP. 10 UNIT SET (4) 50.00
*10 UNIT CARDS: 1X TO 1.5X 5 UNIT CARDS
COMP. 25 UNIT SET (4) 80.00
*25 UNIT CARDS: 2X TO 3X 5 UNIT CARDS
COMP. 60 UNIT SET (4) 200.00
*60 UNIT CARDS: 5X TO 7X 5 UNIT CARDS

❑ NNO Jeff Gordon 14.00
❑ NNO Mark Martin 8.00
❑ NNO Ricky Rudd 5.00
❑ NNO Rusty Wallace 8.00

1996 Finish Line Diamor Collection Phone Cards

This series of cards was sold through mass retail cards come in a black fold out case and each ca freatures a replica diamond.

MINT

COMPLETE SET (8) 40.00
COMMON CARD (1-8) 5.00

❑ 1 Jeff Gordon 10.00
❑ 2 Bill Elliott 6.00
❑ 3 Dale Jarrett 5.00
❑ 4 Ernie Irvan 5.00
❑ 5 Mark Martin 6.00
❑ 6 Ricky Rudd 5.00
❑ 7 Terry Labonte 6.00
❑ 8 Rusty Wallace 6.00

96 Finish Line Phone Pak

as the first set of phone cards in a pack. Each card
d a $2 phone value. Therre were 9,500 of each
ed. The cards were packaged three cards per pack,
ks per box and 16 boxes per case. There were 800
produced. Every case, box and phone card was
ually numbered.There was also a parallel set of $2
re cards. These cards were inserted one per pack
000 of each card was produced. Due to the
ptcy of Finish Line, the phone time on these cards
valid.

	MINT	NRMT
LETE SET (40)	20.00	9.00
ON CARD	.50	.23
ON DRIVER	.75	.35
LETE 2.00 SIG. SET (40)	40.00	18.00
SIG. CARDS: 1.25X TO 2X BASIC CARDS		
nn Andretti	.75	.35
ett Bodine	.75	.35
off Bodine	.75	.35
dd Bodine	.75	.35
f Burton	.75	.35
rd Burton	.75	.35
rrike Cope	.75	.35
ky Craven	1.00	.45
Elliott	1.50	.70
ll Elliott's Car	1.25	.55
eff Gordon	3.00	1.35
eff Gordon's Car	2.00	.90
teve Grissom	.75	.35
obby Hamilton	.75	.35
nie Irvan	1.25	.55
nie Irvan's Car	.75	.35
ale Jarrett	1.25	.55
obby Labonte	1.00	.45
obby Labonte's Car	.75	.35
erry Labonte	1.50	.70
erry Labonte's Car	1.25	.55
terling Marlin	1.00	.45
terling Marlin's Car	.75	.35
ark Martin	1.50	.70
ark Martin's Car	1.25	.55
ed Musgrave	.75	.35
oe Nemechek	.75	.35
yle Petty	1.00	.45
cky Rudd	.75	.35
cky Rudd's Car	.50	.23
en Schrader	.75	.35
organ Shepherd	.75	.35
ut Stricklin	.75	.35
ck Trickle	.75	.35
ike Wallace	.75	.35
usty Wallace	1.50	.70
usty Wallace's Car	1.00	.45
ichael Waltrip	.75	.35
arrell Waltrip	.75	.35
arrell Waltrip's Car	.50	.23

1996 Finish Line Phone Pak $5 Cards

sert series of 24 cards features $5 in phone time
There were 570 of each of the cards produced and
of pulling one from a pack was 1:15. Due to the
ptcy of Finish Line, the phone time on these cards
valid.

	MINT	NRMT
ETE SET (24)	60.00	27.00
ON CARD	2.00	.90
n Andretti	2.00	.90
tt Bodine	2.00	.90
ff Bodine	2.00	.90
Burton	2.00	.90
rd Burton	2.00	.90
ky Craven	2.50	1.10
rike Cope	2.00	.90
Elliott	4.00	1.80
Gordon	6.00	2.70
obby Hamilton	2.00	.90
nie Irvan	2.50	1.10
ale Jarrett	3.00	1.35
obby Labonte	2.50	1.10
rry Labonte	4.00	1.80
erling Marlin	2.50	1.10
ark Martin	4.00	1.80
d Musgrave	2.00	.90
le Petty	2.50	1.10
cky Rudd	2.50	1.10
n Schrader	2.00	.90
organ Shepherd	2.00	.90
usty Wallace	4.00	1.80
❑ 23 Michael Waltrip	2.00	.90
❑ 24 Darrell Waltrip	2.50	1.10

1996 Finish Line Phone Pak $10 Cards

There were 570 of each of the $10 cards. The cards were inserted at a rate of one in 30 packs. Due to the bankruptcy of Finish Line, the phone time on these cards is not valid.

	MINT	NRMT
COMPLETE SET (12)	75.00	34.00
COMMON CARD	3.00	1.35
❑ 1 Geoff Bodine	3.00	1.35
❑ 2 Bill Elliott	5.00	2.20
❑ 3 Jeff Gordon	8.00	3.60
❑ 4 Ernie Irvan	4.50	2.00
❑ 5 Bobby Labonte	4.50	2.00
❑ 6 Terry Labonte	5.00	2.20
❑ 7 Sterling Marlin	4.50	2.00
❑ 8 Mark Martin	5.00	2.20
❑ 9 Ricky Rudd	4.00	1.80
❑ 10 Ken Schrader	3.00	1.35
❑ 11 Rusty Wallace	5.00	2.20
❑ 12 Darrell Waltrip	4.00	1.80

1996 Finish Line Phone Pak $50 Cards

This series of insert phone cards features $50 in phone time value. The cards were inserted at a rate of one in 60 packs. Due to the bankruptcy of Finish Line, the phone time on these cards is not valid.

	MINT	NRMT
COMPLETE SET (8)	120.00	55.00
COMMON CARD	10.00	4.50
❑ 1 Bill Elliott	70.00	32.00
❑ 2 Jeff Gordon	80.00	36.00
❑ 3 Ernie Irvan	60.00	27.00
❑ 4 Bobby Labonte	10.00	4.50
❑ 5 Terry Labonte	20.00	9.00
❑ 6 Mark Martin	20.00	9.00
❑ 7 Ricky Rudd	10.00	4.50
❑ 8 Rusty Wallace	20.00	9.00

1996 Finish Line Phone Pak $100 Cards

There were 280 of each of the $100 phone cards. The cards were inserted one in 120 packs. Due to the bankruptcy of Finish Line, the phone time on these cards is not valid.

	MINT	NRMT
COMPLETE SET (6)	125.00	55.00
COMMON CARD	10.00	4.50
❑ 1 Bill Elliott	25.00	11.00
❑ 2 Jeff Gordon	50.00	22.00
❑ 3 Ernie Irvan	10.00	4.50
❑ 4 Terry Labonte	25.00	11.00
❑ 5 Mark Martin	25.00	11.00
❑ 6 Rusty Wallace	25.00	11.00

1996 Finish Line Save Mart Phone Cards

This set of three phone cards was distributed at the Save Mart's in the Sonoma, California area in conjunction with the Save Mart Supermarkets 300. They were used as a promotion to get people to come in to the stores. Due to the bankruptcy of Finish Line, the phone time on these cards is not valid.

	MINT	NRMT
COMPLETE SET (3)	10.00	4.50
COMMON CARD	2.00	.90
❑ 1 Geoff Bodine/2650	4.00	1.80
❑ 2 Ernie Irvan/2650	5.00	2.20
❑ 3 Save-Mart Car/2650	2.00	.90

1997 Finish Line Phone Pak II One Call

This was the second consecutive year for Finish Line Phone Paks. Each pack contained three cards. Each of the one call cards carried a five minutes in calling time. Each card is individually numbered. There was also a special Wild Card insert card. The card could be used for a random amount of phone time. When calling to collect your prize you would find out what denomination between 5 and 60 minutes you received. The Wild Card was inserted one in 15 packs. Each one call card was numbered of 7,950 and each Wild card was numbered of 4,180. The cares were packaged three cards per pack, 15 packs per box and 16 boxes per case. Due to the bankruptcy of Finish Line, the phone time on these cards is not valid.

	MINT	NRMT
COMPLETE SET (37)	15.00	6.75
COMMON CARD (1-37)	.25	.11
❑ 1 Jeff Gordon	2.50	1.10
❑ 2 Bill Elliott	1.50	.70
❑ 3 Mark Martin	1.50	.70
❑ 4 Rusty Wallace	1.50	.70
❑ 5 Terry Labonte	1.50	.70
❑ 6 Ernie Irvan	.50	.23
❑ 7 Ricky Rudd	.50	.23
❑ 8 Bobby Labonte	.50	.23
❑ 9 Sterling Marlin	.50	.23
❑ 10 Darrell Waltrip	.50	.23
❑ 11 Ted Musgrave	.25	.11
❑ 12 Dale Jarrett	1.25	.55
❑ 13 Ricky Craven	.50	.23
❑ 14 Jeremy Mayfield	.25	.11
❑ 15 Eli Gold	.25	.11
❑ 16 Michael Waltrip	.25	.11
❑ 17 Jimmy Spencer	.25	.11
❑ 18 Brett Bodine	.25	.11
❑ 19 Geoff Bodine	.25	.11
❑ 20 John Andretti	.25	.11
❑ 21 Ken Schrader	.25	.11
❑ 22 Bobby Hamilton	.25	.11
❑ 23 Derrike Cope	.25	.11
❑ 24 Ward Burton	.25	.11
❑ 25 Joe Nemechek	.25	.11
❑ 26 Kenny Wallace	.25	.11
❑ 27 Mike Wallace	.25	.11
❑ 28 Morgan Shepherd	.25	.11
❑ 29 Rick Hendrick	.25	.11
❑ 30 Jack Roush	.25	.11
❑ 31 Larry McClure	.25	.11
❑ 32 Felix Sabates	.25	.11
❑ 33 Joe Gibbs	.50	.23
❑ 34 Robert Yates	.25	.11
❑ 35 Chuck Rider	.25	.11
❑ 36 Len Wood Eddie Wood Michael Waltrip	.25	.11
❑ 37 Bill Elliott	1.50	.70
❑ 38 Wild Card	.25	.11

1997 Finish Line Phone Pak II $5

This 28-card insert set featured many of the top names in Winston Cup racing. The cards were worth $5 in phone time. Each card was numbered of 500. The cards were randomly inserted in packs at a rate of one in 7.5. Due to the bankruptcy of Finish Line, the phone time on these cards is not valid.

	MINT	NRMT
COMPLETE SET (28)	150.00	70.00
COMMON CARD (39-66)	.75	.35
❑ 39 Jeff Gordon	3.00	1.35
❑ 40 Bill Elliott	1.75	.80
❑ 41 Mark Martin	1.75	.80
❑ 42 Rusty Wallace	1.75	.80
❑ 43 Terry Labonte	1.75	.80
❑ 44 Ernie Irvan	1.50	.70
❑ 45 Ricky Rudd	1.50	.70
❑ 46 Bobby Labonte	1.50	.70
❑ 47 Sterling Marlin	1.50	.70
❑ 48 Darrell Waltrip	1.50	.70
❑ 49 Ted Musgrave	.75	.35
❑ 50 Dale Jarrett	.75	.35
❑ 51 Ricky Craven	1.50	.70
❑ 52 Jeremy Mayfield	.75	.35
❑ 53 Eli Gold	.75	.35
❑ 54 Michael Waltrip	.75	.35
❑ 55 Jimmy Spencer	.75	.35
❑ 56 Brett Bodine	.75	.35
❑ 57 Geoff Bodine	.75	.35
❑ 58 John Andretti	.75	.35
❑ 59 Ken Schrader	.75	.35
❑ 60 Bobby Hamilton	.75	.35
❑ 61 Derrike Cope	.75	.35
❑ 62 Ward Burton	.75	.35
❑ 63 Joe Nemechek	.75	.35
❑ 64 Kenny Wallace	.75	.35
❑ 65 Michael Waltrip	.75	.35
❑ 66 Morgan Shepherd	.75	.35

1997 Finish Line Phone Pak II $10

Each card in this series was numbered of 360. The cards were inserted one in 15 packs. Due to the bankruptcy of Finish Line, the phone time on these cards is not valid.

	MINT	NRMT
COMPLETE SET (20)	50.00	22.00
COMMON CARD (67-86)	.60	.25
❑ 67 Rusty Wallace's Car	4.00	1.80
❑ 68 Sterling Marlin's Car	.60	.25
❑ 69 Terry Labonte's Car	4.00	1.80
❑ 70 Mark Martin's Car	4.00	1.80
❑ 71 Geoff Bodine's Car	.60	.25
❑ 72 Ricky Rudd's Car	.60	.25
❑ 73 Brett Bodine's Car	.60	.25
❑ 74 Ted Musgrave's Car	.60	.25
❑ 75 Darrell Waltrip's Car	.60	.25
❑ 76 Bobby Labonte's Car	.60	.25
❑ 77 Michael Waltrip's Car	.60	.25
❑ 78 Ward Burton's Car	.60	.25
❑ 79 Jimmy Spencer's Car	.60	.25
❑ 80 Jeff Gordon's Car	4.00	1.80
❑ 81 Ricky Craven's Car	.60	.25
❑ 82 Ernie Irvan's Car	.60	.25
❑ 83 Johnny Benson's Car	.60	.25
❑ 84 Kyle Petty's Car	.60	.25
❑ 85 Dale Jarrett's Car	4.00	1.80
❑ 86 Bill Elliott's Car	4.00	1.80

1997 Finish Line Phone Pak II $50

The cards in this series were inserted at a rate of one in 60 packs.Due to the bankruptcy of Finish Line, the phone time on these cards is not valid.

	MINT	NRMT
COMPLETE SET (8)	60.00	27.00
COMMON CARD (87-94)	8.00	3.60
❑ 87 Jeff Gordon	20.00	9.00
❑ 88 Bill Elliott	12.00	5.50
❑ 89 Mark Martin	12.00	5.50
❑ 90 Rusty Wallace	12.00	5.50
❑ 91 Terry Labonte	12.00	5.50
❑ 92 Ernie Irvan	8.00	3.60
❑ 93 Ricky Rudd	8.00	3.60
❑ 94 Bobby Labonte	8.00	3.60

1997 Finish Line Phone Pak II $100

The cards in this series were inserted at a rate of one in 240 packs. Due to the bankruptcy of Finish Line, the phone time on these cards is not valid.

	MINT	NRMT
COMPLETE SET (6)	90.00	40.00
COMMON CARD (95-100)	10.00	4.50
❑ 95 Jeff Gordon	25.00	11.00
❑ 96 Bill Elliott	15.00	6.75
❑ 97 Mark Martin	15.00	6.75
❑ 98 Rusty Wallace	15.00	6.75
❑ 99 Terry Labonte	15.00	6.75
❑ 100 Ernie Irvan	10.00	4.50

1995 Upper Deck Phone Card Sets

These two sets were sold to hobby and retail outlets. The cards were sold in complete set form with each card in the set carrying five minutes in phone time.

	MINT	NRMT
5M Jeff Gordon (5)	25.00	11.00
5M Rusty Wallace (5)	20.00	9.00

1991-97 Kellogg's Cereal Boxes

CF= Corn Flakes
FF=Frosted Flakes
FMW= Frosted Mini-Wheats
HCCF= Honey Crunch Corn Flakes
RB= Raisin Bran

	MINT	NRMT
❑ 1991 CF #41 Yellow Car	30.00	13.50
❑ 1992 CF #41 Yellow Car w/G.Sacks.	30.00	13.50
❑ 1992 CF Richard Petty	30.00	13.50
❑ 1993 CF #14	30.00	13.50
❑ 1993 RB w/T.Labonte on back	40.00	18.00
❑ 1994 CF #5 busting through front ...	25.00	11.00
❑ 1994 CF #5 crew during stop	30.00	13.50
❑ 1994 CF D.Earnhardt '93 WC Champ	40.00	18.00
❑ 1994 CF T.Labonte	30.00	13.50
❑ 1994 FMW Jeff Gordon	25.00	11.00
❑ 1994 FMW Jeff Gordon Bass Artwork		13.50
❑ 1995 CF #5 at finish line	15.00	
❑ 1995 CF Victory Lap T.Labonte/D.Waltrip		6.75
❑ 1995 CF Corny in Labonte uniform..	10.00	
❑ 1995 CF D.Earnhardt '94 WC Champ		9.00
❑ 1995 CF T.Labonte w/N.Wilks Trophy		6.75
❑ 1995 FF Bill Elliott and #94 car	15.00	
❑ 1995 FF Tony the Tiger in racing uniform		4.50
❑ 1995 FMW D.Earnhardt/J.Gordon ...	20.00	
❑ 1995 FMW J.Gordon #24 at Indy	18.00	
❑ 1995 FMW J.Gordon victory lane Indy		8.00
❑ 1995 Pop Tarts w/T.Labonte and #5	8.00	
❑ 1995 RB D.Waltrip/M.Waltrip	15.00	
❑ 1996 CF T.Labonte Ironman	15.00	
❑ 1996 CF T.Labonte Ironman car	15.00	
❑ 1996 CF T.Labonte/R.Petty	20.00	
❑ 1996 CF J.Gordon '95 WC Champ...	25.00	
❑ 1996 FF D.Earnhardt and Tony the Tiger		6.75
❑ 1996 FMW J.Gordon and Pit Champs		9.00
❑ 1996 FMW MBNA car	15.00	
❑ 1996 RB Bill Elliott/J.Gibbs	15.00	
❑ 1997 CF T.Labonte Sam Bass Art	15.00	
❑ 1997 FMV D.Earnhardt in helmet	20.00	
❑ 1997 FF T.Labonte w/Tony	12.00	
❑ 1997 D.Jarrett wearing helmet	15.00	
❑ 1997 CF Team Monte Carlo T.L./J.G.		9.00
❑ 1997 CF/FMW/RB Top Four Drivers.	20.00	
❑ 1997 CF/HCCF T.Labonte value pack		6.75
❑ 1997 Eggo Waffels J.Gordon	10.00	
❑ 1997 Eggo Waffels T.Labonte	8.00	
❑ 1997 FMW Bite Size Jeff Gordon	15.00	
❑ 1997 FMW Team Monte Carlo T.L./J.G.		9.00
❑ 1997 RB N.Jarrett/D.Jarrett	15.00	
❑ 1997 RB T.Labonte/G.DeHart	15.00	
❑ 1998 CF T.Labonte car cut-out	8.00	
❑ 1998 FMW J.Gordon '97 WC champ		6.75
❑ 1998 CF T.Labonte/R. Byron	8.00	
❑ 1998 CF NASCAR 50th Ann.	5.00	

Die Cast Price Guide

1993-1998 Action Racing Collectables 1:16 Pit Wagon Banks

These 1:16 scale replicas of Pit Wagons were produced by Action Racing Collectibles. ARC began producing them in 1994 and they are a coin bank. The teams in Winston Cup racing have these Pit Wagons in which they tote from the garage area to the pits.

	Lo	Hi
2 Rusty Wallace Ford Motorsports	25.00	40.00
2 Rusty Wallace Miller Genuine Draft	30.00	50.00
2 Rusty Wallace Miller Lite 1997	40.00	60.00
2 Rusty Wallace Miller Lite 1998	35.00	60.00
3 Dale Earnhardt Goodwrench	45.00	70.00
3 Dale Earnhardt Goodwrench 1996	40.00	65.00
3 Dale Earnhardt Goodwrench 7-Time Champion	45.00	70.00
3 Dale Earnhardt Goodwrench Plus Bass Pro	45.00	70.00
3 Dale Earnhardt Wheaties	45.00	70.00
11 Bill Elliott Budweiser	20.00	40.00
16 Ted Musgrave Family Channel	15.00	30.00
18 Dale Jarrett Interstate Batteries	15.00	30.00
24 Jeff Gordon DuPont	60.00	100.00
24 Jeff Gordon DuPont '96	40.00	65.00
24 Jeff Gordon Lost World	35.00	60.00
28 Davey Allison Havoline	35.00	50.00
28 Davey Allison Havoline Mac Tools	35.00	50.00
28 Ernie Irvan Havoline	30.00	45.00
28 Ernie Irvan Mac Tools	20.00	35.00
28 Kenny Irwin Havoline Joker	35.00	60.00
30 Michael Waltrip Pennzoil	15.00	30.00
41 Joe Nemechek Meineke	15.00	30.00
42 Kyle Petty Mello Yello	15.00	30.00
51 Neil Bonnett Country Time	35.00	60.00
88 Dale Jarrett Quality Care Batman	35.00	60.00
94 Bill Elliott Mac Tonight	35.00	60.00
94 Bill Elliott McDonald's	20.00	35.00

1998-1999 Action Racing Collectables 1:18

These 1:18 scale cars were distributed by Action through their distributor network.

	Lo	Hi
3 Dale Earnhardt Goodwrench Plus Daytona	60.00	100.00
3 Dale Earnhardt Goowrench Silver	80.00	130.00
3 Dale Earnhardt Wheaties	70.00	100.00
31 Dale Earnhardt Jr. Sikkens	75.00	125.00
31 Dale Earnhardt Jr. Wrangler	75.00	125.00

1993-1995 Action Racing Collectables 1:24

These 1:24 scale replicas were produced by Action Racing Collectibles. Most pieces were packaged in a blue box and have the Action Racing Collectibles logo or the Racing Collectibles Inc. logo on the box.

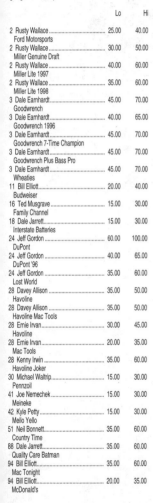

	Lo	Hi
1 Rick Mast Skoal Acrylic Case	40.00	60.00
1 Winston Show Car	40.00	60.00
2 Ricky Craven DuPont	50.00	90.00
2 Dale Earnhardt Wrangler 1981 Pontiac	150.00	250.00
2/43 Dale Earnhardt Richard Petty 7 and 7 Special	125.00	200.00
3 Richard Childress Black Gold	30.00	45.00
3 Dale Earnhardt Goodwrench 1995 Monte Carlo Black Windows Promo	60.00	100.00
3 Dale Earnhardt Goodwrench 1995 Monte Carlo Brickyard Special	60.00	100.00
3 Dale Earnhardt Goodwrench 1995 Monte Carlo Promo	60.00	100.00
3 Dale Earnhardt Wrangler 1981 Pontiac	125.00	200.00
3 Dale Earnhardt Wrangler 1985 Monte Carlo	125.00	200.00
3 Jeff Green Goodwrench	25.00	45.00
3/24 Dale Earnhardt Jeff Gordon Brickyard Special	75.00	125.00
4 Sterling Marlin Kodak	20.00	40.00
6 Mark Martin Valvoline 1995 Brickyard Special	60.00	100.00
6 Mark Martin Valvoline	50.00	90.00
7 Geoff Bodine Exide	20.00	40.00
7 Alan Kulwicki Hooter's	40.00	70.00
7 Alan Kulwicki Zerex	35.00	60.00
11 Bill Elliott Budweiser	70.00	120.00
11 Darrell Waltrip Budweiser 1984 Monte Carlo	30.00	50.00
11 Darrell Waltrip Mountain Dew	35.00	60.00
12 Neil Bonnett Budweiser 1984 Monte Carlo	30.00	50.00
15 Lake Speed Quality Care	12.50	25.00
16 Ted Musgrave Primestar	30.00	45.00
28 Ernie Irvan Havoline	25.00	40.00
41 Joe Nemechek Meineke	15.00	30.00
42 Kyle Petty Coors Light	35.00	60.00
42 Kyle Petty Mello Yello	50.00	90.00
94 Bill Elliott McDonald's	30.00	45.00
98 Derrike Cope Fingerhut	12.50	25.00

1996 Action Racing Collectables 1:24

These 1:24 scale replicas were produced by Action Racing Collectibles. Most pieces were packaged in a blue box and have the Action Racing Collectibles logo or the Racing Collectibles Inc. logo on the box.

	Lo	Hi
2 Mark Martin Miller ASA '85	35.00	60.00
2 Rusty Wallace Miller Genuine Draft	50.00	90.00
2 Rusty Wallace Miller Genuine Draft Silver Anniversary	50.00	80.00
3 Dale Earnhardt AC-Delco	35.00	60.00
3 Dale Earnhardt Goodwrench 1996 Monte Carlo	30.00	60.00
3 Dale Earnhardt Olympic Car	30.00	60.00
3 Dale Earnhardt Olympic Food City Promo	50.00	100.00
3 Dale Earnhardt Olympic Goodwrench Box	40.00	80.00
3 Dale Earnhardt Olympic Green Box	50.00	100.00
3 Dale Earnhardt Olympic Green Box No Trademark on Hood of Car	45.00	90.00
3 Dale Earnhardt Olympic with Mom-n-Pop's decal	50.00	100.00
3 Dale Earnhardt Olympic Sports Image	30.00	60.00
10 Ricky Rudd Tide	30.00	50.00
14 Jeff Green Racing For Kids	25.00	50.00
15 Dale Earnhardt Wrangler	60.00	110.00
18 Bobby Labonte Interstate Batteries 1996	30.00	60.00
21 Michael Waltrip Citgo	25.00	50.00
29 No Driver Association Scooby-Doo	30.00	60.00
31 Mike Skinner Snap-On	70.00	110.00
31 Mike Skinner Snap-On Promo	75.00	125.00
42 Kyle Petty Coors Light 1996	35.00	60.00
43 Bobby Hamilton STP Silver car with Clear Windows	60.00	100.00
43 Bobby Hamilton 5 Car set with Clear Windows	150.00	300.00
57 Jason Keller Halloween Havoc	25.00	50.00
88 Ernie Irvan Havoline	20.00	50.00
88 Dale Jarrett Quality Care	30.00	60.00
98 Jeremy Mayfield RCA	35.00	60.00

1997 Action Racing Collectables 1:24

These 1:24 scale replicas were produced by Action Racing Collectibles. Most pieces were packaged in a blue box and have the Action Racing Collectibles logo or the Racing Collectibles Inc. logo on the box.

	Lo	Hi
00 Buckshot Jones Aqua Fresh	35.00	55.00
2 Rusty Wallace Miller Lite	35.00	60.00
2 Rusty Wallace Miller Lite Japan	35.00	60.00
3 Dale Earnhardt Goodwrench Brickyard Special	35.00	60.00
3 Dale Earnhardt Wheaties	60.00	100.00
3 Dale Earnhardt Wheaties Mail-In	30.00	50.00
3 Dale Earnhardt Wheaties Snap-On	70.00	100.00
3 Dale Earnhardt Wheaties Sports Image	40.00	60.00
4 Sterling Marlin Kodak Mac Tools	40.00	60.00
6 Mark Martin Valvoline	35.00	60.00
6 Mark Martin Valvoline Mac Tools	40.00	75.00
8 Hut Stricklin Circuit City	30.00	45.00
10 Phil Parsons Channellock	30.00	45.00
11 Brett Bodine Close Call	30.00	45.00
12 Kenny Wallace Gray Bar	30.00	50.00
14 Steve Park Burger King	80.00	120.00
18 Bobby Labonte Interstate Batteries	30.00	50.00
18 Bobby Labonte Interstate Batteries Hall of Fame	25.00	50.00
18 Bobby Labonte Interstate Batteries Mac Tools	35.00	60.00
22 Ward Burton MBNA	30.00	45.00
23 Jimmy Spencer Camel	50.00	90.00
24 Jeff Gordon DuPont	35.00	60.00
24 Jeff Gordon DuPont Brickyard Special	35.00	60.00
24 Jeff Gordon DuPont Mac Tools	40.00	75.00
24 Jeff Gordon DuPont Premier Promo	70.00	120.00
24 Jeff Gordon DuPont Premier Sports Image	40.00	60.00
24 Jeff Gordon Lost World Sports Image	40.00	65.00
27 Kenny Irwin Action	35.00	70.00
27 Kenny Irwin Tonka	35.00	60.00
29 Jeff Green Tom & Jerry	35.00	55.00
30 Jonny Benson Pennzoil	25.00	40.00
31 Mike Skinner Lowe's	35.00	55.00
37 Mike Green Timber Wolf	30.00	45.00
42 Joe Nemechek Bell South	30.00	45.00
46 Wally Dallenbach First Union	30.00	50.00
75 Rick Mast Remington	30.00	45.00
75 Rick Mast Remington Camo	30.00	50.00
88 Dale Jarrett Quality Care	30.00	50.00
88 Dale Jarrett Quality Care Brickyard Special	35.00	50.00
88 Dale Jarrett Quality Care Mac Tools	35.00	65.00
94 Bill Elliott Mac Tonight	35.00	60.00
99 Jeff Burton Exide	30.00	50.00

1998 Action Racing Collectables 1:24

These 1:24 scale replicas were produced by Action Racing Collectibles. Most pieces were packaged in a blue box and have the Action Racing Collectibles logo or the Racing Collectibles Inc. logo on the box.

	Lo	Hi
00 Buckshot Jones Alka Seltzer	40.00	70.00
1 Dale Earnhardt Jr. Coke	60.00	90.00
1 Jeff Gordon Baby Ruth	50.00	80.00
1 Steve Park Pennzoil	90.00	150.00
1 Steve Park Pennzoil Indy	45.00	80.00
1 Darrell Waltrip Pennzoil	50.00	90.00
2 Rusty Wallace Adventures of Rusty	40.00	70.00
2 Rusty Wallace Miller Lite	40.00	70.00
2 Rusty Wallace Miller Lite Elvis	45.00	70.00
2 Rusty Wallace Miller Lite TCB	45.00	70.00
3 Dale Earnhardt Coke	60.00	90.00
3 Dale Earnhardt Goodwrench Plus	40.00	70.00
3 Dale Earnhardt Goodwrench Plus Bass Pro	50.00	90.00
3 Dale Earnhardt Goodwrench Plus Daytona	40.00	70.00
3 Dale Earnhardt Jr. AC Delco	125.00	200.00
4 Bobby Hamilton Kodak	35.00	60.00
5 Terry Labonte Blasted Fruit Loops	50.00	80.00
5 Terry Labonte Kellogg's	40.00	75.00
5 Terry Labonte Kellogg's Corny	45.00	75.00
5 Terry Labonte Kellogg's Ironman	50.00	90.00
8 Dale Earnhardt 10,000 RPM '78 Dodge	50.00	80.00
8 Hut Stricklin Circuit City	35.00	60.00
9 Jerry Nadeau Power Puff	45.00	75.00
9 Jerry Nadeau Zombie Island	40.00	70.00

	Lo	Hi
9 Lake Speed Birthday Cake	45.00	70.00
9 Lake Speed Huckleberry Hound	40.00	70.00
10 Ricky Rudd Tide Give Kids the World	35.00	60.00
10 Ricky Rudd Tide	35.00	60.00
12 Jeremy Mayfield Mobil 1	45.00	75.00
12 Jimmy Spencer Zippo	100.00	150.00
14 Patty Moise Rhodes	40.00	65.00
18 Bobby Labonte Interstate Batteries	40.00	70.00
18 Bobby Labonte Interstate Batteries Hot Rod	35.00	65.00
18 Bobby Labonte Interstate Batteries Small Soldiers	50.00	80.00
21 Michael Waltrip Citgo	35.00	60.00
21 Michael Waltrip Woody Woodpecker	40.00	70.00
22 Ward Burton MBNA	35.00	60.00
23 Jimmy Spencer No Bull	50.00	100.00
24 Jeff Gordon DuPont	45.00	80.00
24 Jeff Gordon DuPont Brickyard Winner	40.00	70.00
24 Jeff Gordon DuPont Chromalusion	60.00	110.00
24 Jeff Gordon DuPont Chromalusion Mac Tools	70.00	120.00
24 Jeff Gordon DuPont Mac Tools	60.00	100.00
24 Jeff Gordon DuPont No Bull	50.00	80.00
28 Kenny Irwin Havoline	40.00	65.00
28 Kenny Irwin Havoline Joker	45.00	65.00
30 Derrike Cope Gumout	35.00	60.00
31 Dale Earnhardt Jr. Sikkens	100.00	175.00
31 Dale Earnhardt Jr. Wrangler	125.00	200.00
31 Mike Skinner Lowe's	35.00	60.00
31 Mike Skinner Lowe's Special Olympics	40.00	65.00
32 Dale Jarrett White Rain	40.00	70.00
33 Tim Fedewa Kleenex	60.00	90.00
33 Ken Schrader Skoal	40.00	65.00
34 Mike McLaughlin Goulds	60.00	90.00
35 Todd Bodine Tabasco	40.00	70.00
35 Todd Bodine Tabasco Red	35.00	70.00
36 Ernie Irvan M&Ms	70.00	100.00
36 Ernie Irvan Skittles	35.00	60.00
36 Ernie Irvan Wildberry Skittles	35.00	60.00
40 Sterling Marlin Coors Light	40.00	70.00
41 Steve Grissom Kodiak	40.00	70.00
42 Joe Nemechek Bell South	35.00	60.00
42 Marty Robbins 1974 Dodge	35.00	60.00
44 Tony Stewart Shell	40.00	70.00
44 Tony Stewart Shell Small Soldiers	50.00	80.00
50 Ricky Craven Budweiser	75.00	125.00
50 No Driver Association Bud Louie	50.00	90.00
72 Mike Dillon Detroit Gasket	35.00	60.00
81 Kenny Wallace Square D	35.00	60.00
81 Kenny Wallace Square D Lightning	35.00	60.00
88 Dale Jarrett Quality Care	40.00	70.00
88 Dale Jarrett Quality Care Batman	45.00	70.00
90 Dale Trickle Heilig-Meyers	40.00	65.00
96 David Green Caterpillar	40.00	60.00
98 Greg Sacks Thorn Apple Valley	35.00	60.00
98 Greg Sacks Thorn Apple Valley Go Grill Crazy	35.00	60.00
300 Darrall Waltrip Flock Special	60.00	90.00
K2 Dale Earnhardt Dayvault's	45.00	90.00

1993-1995 Action Racing Collectables 1:24 Banks

These cars were produced by Action Racing Collectibles. Each car has a slot in the back window for a coin bank. Most banks have blacked in windows. This is the easiest way to tell banks apart from a regular car.

	Lo	Hi
2 Mark Martin Miller 1984 ASA	25.00	50.00
2 Rusty Wallace Ford Motorsports	100.00	175.00
2 Rusty Wallace Miller Geniune Draft	35.00	55.00
3 Dale Earnhardt Goodwrench 1988 Monte Carlo	400.00	550.00
3 Dale Earnhardt Goodwrench 1994 Lumina	125.00	200.00
3 Dale Earnhardt Goodwrench 1995 Monte Carlo with headlights	90.00	150.00
3 Dale Earnhardt Goodwrench 1995 Monte Carlo without headlights	100.00	175.00
3 Dale Earnhardt Goodwrench 1995 Monte Carlo Sports Image	30.00	50.00
3 Dale Earnhardt Goodwrench Silver Car Black Wheels	250.00	350.00
3 Dale Earnhardt Goodwrench Silver Car Red Wheels	250.00	350.00
3 Dale Earnhardt Wrangler 1984 Monte Carlo	175.00	300.00
5 Terry Labonte Kellogg's	300.00	400.00
6 Mark Martin Folgers	35.00	60.00
6 Mark Martin Valvoline 1995	30.00	45.00
7 Alan Kulwicki Hooters AK Racing	60.00	100.00
8 Kenny Wallace Red Dog Beer	35.00	50.00
11 Bill Elliott Budweiser	50.00	90.00
11 Darrell Waltrip Budweiser 1986 Monte Carlo	35.00	60.00
12 Neil Bonnett Budweiser 1986 Monte Carlo	45.00	75.00
16 Ted Musgrave Family Channel	125.00	200.00
21 Buddy Baker Valvoline	25.00	45.00
21 Neil Bonnett Hodgdon	25.00	45.00
21 David Pearson Chattanooga Chew	25.00	45.00
22 Bobby Allison Miller Beer Acrylic Case	30.00	50.00
24 Jeff Gordon DuPont 1995 Champion	20.00	50.00
24 Jeff Gordon DuPont 1995 Monte Carlo	50.00	90.00
25 Tim Richmond Folgers Monte Carlo Fastback	30.00	50.00
25 Ken Schrader Budweiser	30.00	50.00
27 Rusty Wallace Kodiak	75.00	125.00
28 Ernie Irvan Havoline Employee Special	100.00	175.00
28 Ernie Irvan Havoline Retail Special	20.00	35.00
28 Dale Jarrett Havoline	20.00	40.00
35 Alan Kulwicki Quincy's Steakhouse	30.00	50.00
51 Neil Bonnett Country Time	70.00	110.00
75 Buddy Baker Valvoline	25.00	40.00
88 Darrell Waltrip Gatorade Oldsmobile	60.00	100.00
94 Bill Elliott McDonald's	25.00	50.00
94 Bill Elliott McDonald's Thuderbat	80.00	120.00
95 David Green Busch Beer	25.00	50.00

1996 Action Racing Collectables 1:24 Banks

These cars were produced by Action Racing Collectibles. Each car has a slot in the back window for a coin bank. Most banks have blacked in windows. This is the easiest way to tell banks apart from a regular car.

	Lo	Hi
2 Mark Martin Miller 1985 ASA	30.00	60.00
2 Rusty Wallace Miller Genuine Draft 1996	35.00	70.00
3 Richard Childress CRC Chemical	30.00	50.00
3 Dale Earnhardt Olympic	40.00	80.00
5 Terry Labonte Kellogg's Silver Car	75.00	150.00
5 Terry Labonte Kellogg's Japan	40.00	80.00
6 Mark Martin Valvoline 1996	30.00	60.00
7 Geoff Bodine QVC	25.00	50.00
10 Ricky Rudd Tide 1996	30.00	60.00
11 Brett Bodine Lowe's	20.00	40.00
21 Michael Waltrip Citgo Star Trek	25.00	50.00
24 Jeff Gordon DuPont 1996 Monte Carlo with Quaker State decal	35.00	60.00
29 Steve Grissom Cartoon Network	25.00	50.00
29 Steve Grissom WCW	25.00	50.00
29 No Driver Association Scooby-Doo	30.00	50.00
42 Robby Gordon Tonka	30.00	50.00
42 Kyle Petty Coors Light Black Paint Scheme	35.00	60.00
43 Bobby Hamilton STP Silver 25th Anniversary	200.00	300.00
43 Bobby Hamilton STP Silver car	50.00	100.00
43 Bobby Hamilton STP 5 car set	175.00	300.00
88 Ernie Irvan Havoline	35.00	60.00

1997 Action Racing Collectables 1:24 Banks

These cars were produced by Action Racing Collectibles. Each car has a slot in the back window for a coin bank. Most banks have blacked in windows. This is the easiest way to tell banks apart from a regular car.

	Lo	Hi
1 Hermie Sadler Dewalt	35.00	60.00
2 Rusty Wallace Miller Lite Texas Motor Speedway	40.00	65.00
3 Dale Earnhardt AC Delco	30.00	60.00
3 Dale Earnhardt Goodwrench	40.00	70.00
3 Dale Earnhardt Goodwrench Plus	35.00	60.00
3 Dale Earnhardt Lowes Food	35.00	60.00
3 Dale Earnhardt Wheaties Snap-On	70.00	100.00
3 Dale Earnhardt Wrangler 1984 Monte Carlo Daytona	35.00	60.00
3 Steve Park AC Delco	50.00	90.00
3 Ricky Rudd Piedmont	35.00	55.00
4 Sterling Marlin Kodak	30.00	50.00
9 Jeff Burton Track Gear	30.00	45.00
10 Ricky Rudd Tide	30.00	50.00
17 Darrell Waltrip Parts America 7 Car Bank set	175.00	300.00
17 Darrell Waltrip Parts America	30.00	50.00
22 Ward Burton MBNA	25.00	40.00
22 Ward Burton MBNA Gold	30.00	45.00
24 Jeff Gordon DuPont Million Dollar Date	45.00	75.00
24 Jeff Gordon DuPont Million Dollar Date Mac Tools	45.00	80.00
24 Jeff Gordon DuPont Chroma Premier	60.00	100.00
24 Jeff Gordon Lost World	50.00	80.00
25 Ricky Craven Budweiser	35.00	65.00
26 Rich Bickle KFC	35.00	50.00
27 Kenny Irwin G.I. Joe	35.00	60.00
27 Rusty Wallace Miller Genuine Draft 1990 Grand Prix	35.00	60.00
29 Elliott Sadler Phillips 66	35.00	60.00
32 Dale Jarrett White Rain	35.00	50.00
33 Kenny Schrader Skoal	35.00	55.00
36 Todd Bodine Stanley Tools	30.00	45.00
36 Derrike Cope Skittles	30.00	45.00
37 Jeremy Mayfield Kmart	30.00	45.00
40 Robby Gordon Coors Light	35.00	55.00
41 Steve Grissom Kodiak	35.00	55.00
60 Mark Martin Winn Dixie	35.00	60.00
71 Dave Marcis Realtree	35.00	55.00
71 Dave Marcis Realtree Making of Champions	35.00	55.00
81 Kenny Wallace Square D	30.00	45.00
94 Bill Elliott McDonald's	45.00	80.00
96 David Green Caterpillar	30.00	50.00

1998 Action Racing Collectables 1:24 Banks

These cars were produced by Action Racing Collectibles. Each car has a slot in the back window for a coin bank. Most banks have blacked in windows. This is the easiest way to tell banks apart from a regular car.

	Lo	Hi
1 Dale Earnhardt Jr. Coke	45.00	90.00
1 Steve Park Pennzoil	75.00	125.00
1 Darrell Waltrip Pennzoil	45.00	80.00
2 Rusty Wallace Miller Lite	50.00	80.00
2 Rusty Wallace Miller Lite Elvis	45.00	80.00
3 Dale Earnhardt Coke	45.00	90.00
3 Dale Earnhardt Goodwrench Plus w/Coke	40.00	75.00
3 Dale Earnhardt Goodwrench Plus w/o Coke	90.00	150.00
3 Dale Earnhardt Goodwrench Plus Bass Pro	50.00	90.00
3 Dale Earnhardt Goodwrench Plus Daytona	40.00	70.00
3 Dale Earnhardt Jr. AC Delco	125.00	200.00
3 Dale Earnhardt Jr. AC Delco Snap-On	125.00	200.00
4 Bobby Hamilton Kodak	40.00	70.00
5 Terry Labonte Blasted Fruit Loops	40.00	70.00
5 Terry Labonte Kellogg's	50.00	80.00
5 Terry Labonte Kellogg's Corny	45.00	70.00
5 Terry Labonte Kellogg's Ironman	45.00	80.00
8 Dale Earnhardt 10,000 RPM 1975 Dodge	45.00	80.00
8 Hut Stricklin Circuit City	35.00	60.00
9 Lake Speed Birthday Cake	40.00	70.00
9 Lake Speed Huckleberry Hound	40.00	70.00
10 Ricky Rudd Tide	35.00	70.00
12 Jeremy Mayfield Mobil 1	40.00	70.00
12 Jimmy Spencer Zippo	125.00	200.00
14 Patty Moise Rhodes	40.00	70.00
18 Bobby Labonte Interstate Batteries Hot Rod	40.00	70.00
18 Bobby Labonte Interstate Batteries Small Soldiers	40.00	70.00
23 Jimmy Spencer No Bull	60.00	100.00
24 Jeff Gordon DuPont	40.00	70.00
24 Jeff Gordon DuPont Chromalusion	65.00	100.00
24 Jeff Gordon DuPont No Bull	60.00	90.00
28 Kenny Irwin Havoline Joker	45.00	70.00
31 Dale Earnhardt Jr. Sikkens	125.00	200.00
31 Dale Earnhardt Jr. Wrangler	150.00	225.00
31 Mike Skinner Lowe's	35.00	70.00
31 Mike Skinner Lowe's Special Olympics	35.00	70.00
33 Tim Fedewa Kleenex	50.00	80.00
34 Mike McLaughlin Goulds	50.00	80.00
35 Todd Bodine Tabasco	40.00	75.00
35 Todd Bodine Tabasco Red	40.00	70.00
36 Ernie Irvan M&Ms Mac Tools	60.00	90.00
41 Steve Grissom Kodiak	40.00	75.00
42 Joe Nemechek Bell South	40.00	70.00
44 Tony Stewart Shell	40.00	70.00
44 Tony Stewart Shell Small Soldiers	40.00	70.00
50 Ricky Craven Budweiser	90.00	150.00
50 Ricky Craven Budweiser Mac Tools	90.00	150.00
50 No Driver Association Bud Louie	60.00	100.00
88 Dale Jarrett Quality Care	35.00	70.00
88 Dale Jarrett Quality Care Batman	40.00	70.00
300 Darrell Waltrip Tim Flock Special	50.00	90.00
K2 Dale Earnhardt Dayvault's	40.00	80.00

1998 Action Racing Collectables 1:32

These 1:32 scale cars debuted in 1998. These cars were sold through GM and Ford dealerships as well as through various TV outlets.

	Lo	Hi
3 Dale Earnhardt	25.00	50.00
Goodwrench Plus Bass Pro		
3 Dale Earnhardt	25.00	50.00
Goodwrench Plus Daytona		
3 Dale Earnhardt Jr.	40.00	75.00
AC Delco		
24 Jeff Gordon	25.00	50.00
DuPont		
28 Kenny Irwin	25.00	50.00
Havoline Joker		
88 Dale Jarrett	25.00	50.00
Quality Care Batman		

1993-1995 Action Racing Collectables 1:64

These 1:64 scale cars feature the top cars in NASCAR racing. Since 1995, most of the cars are now produced with the Platinum Series label. Some of the Platinum Series cars comes with a SkyBox card. In most cases, the SkyBox card was specifically made for those Platinum Series pieces and was not distributed in any other method. Action now produces their own cards for inclusion with the die-cast pieces.

	Lo	Hi
2 Ricky Craven	4.00	8.00
DuPont Platinum Series		
2 Dale Earnhardt	20.00	35.00
Wrangler Platinum Series		
2 Mark Martin	6.00	12.00
Miller 1985 ASA		
2 Rusty Wallace	5.00	9.00
Ford Motorsports Platinum Series		
2 Rusty Wallace	8.00	18.00
Miller Geniune Draft Platinum Series		
Acrylic display case		
2 Rusty Wallace	5.00	10.00
Pontiac Excitement		
AC Racing Promo		
2 Rusty Wallace	6.00	10.00
Pontiac Excitement		
Delco Remy Promo		
2/43 Dale Earnhardt	10.00	20.00
Richard Petty		
7 and 7 Special		
3 Richard Childress	5.00	10.00
Black Gold Platinum Series		
3 Dale Earnhardt	7.00	14.00
Goodwrench		
AC Racing Promo		
3 Dale Earnhardt	25.00	40.00
Goodwrench 1988 Monte Carlo		
Platinum Series		
3 Dale Earnhardt	15.00	25.00
Goodwrench 1994 Lumina		
Platinum Series		
3 Dale Earnhardt	10.00	20.00
Goodwrench 1995 Monte Carlo		
Brickyard Special		
3 Dale Earnhardt	9.00	18.00
Goodwrench 1995 Monte Carlo		
Platinum Series		
3 Dale Earnhardt	25.00	50.00
Goodwrench Silver Car		
Blister without card package		
3 Dale Earnhardt	25.00	40.00
Goodwrench Silver Car		
Platinum Series		
3 Dale Earnhardt	10.00	20.00
Goodwrench Silver Car		
Race World Promo		
3 Dale Earnhardt	10.00	20.00
Wrangler 1984 Monte Carlo		
Platinum Series		
3 Jeff Green	5.00	10.00
Goodwrench Platinum Series		
3/24 Dale Earnhardt	15.00	25.00
Jeff Gordon		
Dual package Brickyard Special		
3/24 Dale Earnhardt	12.00	22.00
Jeff Gordon		
Dual package Kellogg's Promo		
4 Ernie Irvan	5.00	9.00
Kodak		
AC Racing Promo		
4 Ernie Irvan	5.00	8.00
Kodak		
Delco Remy Promo		
4 Sterling Marlin	5.00	10.00
Kodak 1994 Lumina		
Platinum Series		
4 Sterling Marlin	7.00	14.00
Kodak 1995 Monte Carlo		
Platinum Series		
5 Terry Labonte	4.00	8.00
Kellogg's Platinum Series		
5/24 Terry Labonte	12.00	24.00
Jeff Gordon		
Dual package Kellogg's Promo		
6 Tommy Houston	4.00	8.00
Roses		
6 Mark Martin	12.50	25.00
Folgers Platinum Series		
6 Mark Martin	6.00	12.00
Valvoline Brickyard Special		
Blister package		
6 Mark Martin	6.00	12.00
Valvoline Brickyard Special		
Platinum Series		
6 Mark Martin	5.00	10.00
Valvoline Platinum Series		
6 Mark Martin	5.00	8.00
Valvoline		
Valvoline Team Promo		
7 Geoff Bodine	4.00	8.00
Exide Platinum Series		
7 Alan Kulwicki	7.50	15.00
Army		
7 Alan Kulwicki	5.00	10.00
Hooter's 1992 Ford Thunderbird		
7 Alan Kulwicki	5.00	10.00
Hooter's AK Racing		
7 Alan Kulwicki	6.00	10.00
Zerex Camaro ASA		
Platinum Series		
7 Alan Kulwicki	6.00	12.00
Zerex Silver		
8 Dale Earnhardt	6.00	12.00
1985 Camaro ASA		
Platinum Series		
10 Ricky Rudd	6.00	10.00
Tide Blister package		
11 Bill Elliott	7.50	15.00
Budweiser Platinum Series		
11 Darrell Waltrip	5.00	10.00
Budweiser Platinum Series		
11 Darrell Waltrip	7.50	15.00
Mountain Dew		
11 Darrell Waltrip	5.00	10.00
Pepsi Camaro ASA		
Platinum Series		
12 Neil Bonnett	6.00	12.00
Budweiser Platinum Series		
15 Dale Earnhardt	25.00	40.00
Wrangler 1982 Thunderbird		
15 Lake Speed	4.00	8.00
Quality Car Platinum Series		
16 Wally Dallenbach	4.00	8.00
Roush Racing		
Valvoline Team Promo		
16 Ted Musgrave	4.00	8.00
Family Channel Platinum Series		
17 Darrell Waltrip	6.00	12.00
Superflo Camaro Platinum Series		
17 Darrell Waltrip	5.00	10.00
Tide Camaro Platinum Series		
17 Darrell Waltrip	5.00	9.00
Western Auto		
AC Racing Promo		
17 Darrell Waltrip	5.00	8.00
Western Auto		
Delco Remy Promo		
17 Darrell Waltrip	6.00	10.00
Western Auto 1995 Monte Carlo		
Platinum Series		
18 Bobby Labonte	5.00	10.00
Interstate Batteries		
21 Neil Bonnett	6.00	10.00
Hodgdon Platinum Series		
22 Bobby Allison	8.00	18.00
Miller Beer Platinum Series		
in acrylic case		
23 Jimmy Spencer	18.00	30.00
Smokin' Joe's Platinum Series		
in acrylic case		
24 Jeff Gordon	7.00	14.00
DuPont		
AC Racing Promo		
24 Jeff Gordon	6.00	12.00
DuPont 1994 Lumina		
Platinum Series		
24 Jeff Gordon	6.00	12.00
DuPont 1995 Champion		
24 Jeff Gordon	7.00	14.00
DuPont 1995 Monte Carlo		
Platinum Series		
24 Jeff Gordon	7.00	14.00
DuPont		
Valvoline Team Promo		
25 Tim Richmond	5.00	10.00
Folgers Monte Carlo Fastback		
25 Ken Schrader	6.00	12.00
Budweiser Platinum Series		
25 Ken Schrader	5.00	9.00
GMAC		
AC Racing Promo		
25 Ken Schrader	5.00	8.00
GMAC		
Valvoline Team Promo		
26 Sammy Swindell	4.00	8.00
Bull Hannah Promo		
27 Tim Richmond	5.00	10.00
Old Milwaukee Beer		
Platinum Series		
28 Ernie Irvan	6.00	12.00
Havoline Platinum Series		
28 Dale Jarrett	5.00	10.00
Havoline Platinum Series		
35 Shawna Robinson	6.00	12.00
Polaroid		
36 Todd Bodine	5.00	10.00
Stanley Platinum Series		
40 Kenny Wallace	5.00	9.00

	Lo	Hi
Dirt Devil		
AC Racing Promo		
41 Phil Parsons	5.00	9.00
AC Racing		
41 Joe Nemechek	4.00	8.00
Meineke Platinum Series		
42 Kyle Petty	8.00	18.00
Coors Light Platinum Series		
in Acrylic case		
42 Kyle Petty	5.00	9.00
Mello Yello		
AC Racing Promo		
42 Kyle Petty	4.00	8.00
Mello Yello Platinum Series		
46 Al Unser Jr.	5.00	10.00
Valvoline		
Valvoline Team Promo		
51 Neil Bonnett	6.00	12.00
Country Time Platinum Series		
52 Ken Schrader	5.00	10.00
AC Delco Platinum Series		
88 Darrell Waltrip	5.00	10.00
Gatorade Platinum Sieries		
93 Thunderbird Prototype	4.00	8.00
93 Lumina Prototype	4.00	8.00
93 Pontiac Prototype	4.00	8.00
94 Casey Elliott	5.00	10.00
Racing Collectibles Inc.		
94 Bill Elliott	5.00	10.00
McDonald's 1995 Platinum Series		
94 Bill Elliott	7.50	15.00
Thunderbat Platinum Series		
95 David Green	5.00	10.00
Busch Platinum Series		
98 Derrike Cope	4.00	8.00
Fingerhut Platinum Series		

1996 Action Racing Collectables 1:64

Most of these 1:64 scale cards were issued as part of the Platinum Series. Cars with alcohol and/or tobacco sponsorship are packaged in acrylic cases.

	Lo	Hi
2 Rusty Wallace	6.00	15.00
Miller Genuine Draft Silver		
3 Dale Earnhardt	7.50	15.00
Goodwrench		
3 Dale Earnhardt	7.00	12.00
AC-Delco		
3 Dale Earnhardt	6.00	12.00
Goodwrench		
Blister with card package		
3 Dale Earnhardt	10.00	20.00
Olympic Hood Open Car		
3 Dale Earnhardt	7.50	15.00
Olympic Car		
Blister with card package		
3 Dale Earnhardt	15.00	30.00
Olympic Hood Open in Green Box		
3 Dale Earnhardt	100.00	175.00
16-car set		
5 Terry Labonte	7.50	15.00
Kellogg's Iron Man		
5 Terry Labonte	6.00	12.00
Kellogg's Japan		
6 Mark Martin	5.00	10.00
Valvoline		
7 Geoff Bodine	4.00	8.00
Exide		
10 Ricky Rudd	4.00	8.00
Tide		
11 Brett Bodine	4.00	8.00
Lowe's		
14 Jeff Green	5.00	10.00
Racing For Kids		
21 Michael Waltrip	5.00	10.00
Citgo		
21 Michael Waltrip	5.00	12.00
Citgo Star Trek		
22 Ward Burton	5.00	10.00
MBNA		
24 Jeff Gordon	6.00	12.00
DuPont Monte Carlo		
24 Jeff Gordon	5.00	10.00
DuPont Monte Carlo		
Blister package		
27 Rusty Wallace		
Kodiak		
28 Davey Allison	6.00	12.00
Vinyl Tech 1987		
28 Ernie Irvan	5.00	10.00
Havoline		
29 Steve Grissom	5.00	10.00
Cartoon Network		
29 Steve Grissom	5.00	10.00
WCW		
29 No Driver Association	5.00	10.00
Scooby-Doo		
30 Johnny Benson	5.00	10.00
Pennzoil		
42 Kyle Petty	6.00	12.00
Coors Light		
42 Kyle Petty	6.00	12.00
Coors Light Black Paint Scheme		
43 Bobby Hamilton	10.00	20.00
STP Silver 25th Anniversary		
57 Jason Keller	5.00	10.00
Halloween Havoc		
88 Ernie Irvan	5.00	10.00
Havoline		
88 Dale Jarrett	5.00	10.00
Quality Care		
94 Bill Elliott	5.00	10.00
McDonald's		
96 David Green	4.00	8.00
Caterpillar		

1997 Action Racing Collectables 1:64

Most of these 1:64 scale cards were issued as part of the Platinum Series. Cars with alcohol and/or tobacco sponsorship are packaged in acrylic cases.

	Lo	Hi
00 Buckshot Jones	5.00	10.00
Aqua Fresh		
2 Rusty Wallace	6.00	12.00
Miller Lite		
2 Rusty Wallace	7.50	15.00
Miller Lite Japan		
2 Rusty Wallace	7.50	15.00
Miller Lite		
Texas Motor Speedway		
3 Dale Earnhardt	7.00	12.00
AC Delco		
3 Dale Earnhardt	6.00	10.00
AC Delco		
Black Window Blister Pack		
3 Dale Earnhardt	7.00	12.00
Goodwrench		
3 Dale Earnhardt	6.00	10.00
Goodwrench Brickyard Special		
3 Dale Earnhardt	7.50	12.00
Goodwrench Plus		
3 Dale Earnhardt	7.50	15.00
Goodwrench Plus Box		
3 Dale Earnhardt	7.50	15.00
Wheaties		
3 Dale Earnhardt	6.00	12.00
Wheaties		
Black Window Blister Pack		
3 Dale Earnhardt	7.50	15.00
Wheaties Hood Open		
Sports Image		
3 Dale Earnhardt	6.00	12.00
Wheaties Mail-In		
3 Steve Park	7.50	15.00
AC Delco		
3 Ricky Rudd	5.00	10.00
Piedmont		
4 Sterling Marlin	5.00	10.00
Kodak		
6 Mark Martin	5.00	10.00
Valvoline		
8 Hut Stricklin	5.00	10.00
Circuit City		
9 Jeff Burton	5.00	10.00
Track Gear		
10 Ricky Rudd	5.00	10.00
Tide		
11 Brett Bodine	5.00	10.00
Close Call		
12 Kenny Wallace	5.00	10.00
Gray Bar		
14 Steve Park	7.50	15.00
Burger King		
17 Darrell Waltrip	45.00	70.00
Parts America 7 Car set		
18 Bobby Labonte	5.00	10.00
Interstate Batteries		
18 Bobby Labonte	6.00	12.00
Interstate Batteries Hall of Fame		
22 Ward Burton	5.00	10.00
MBNA		
22 Ward Burton	5.00	10.00
MBNA Gold		
23 Jimmy Spencer	12.50	25.00
Camel		
24 Jeff Gordon	6.00	12.00
DuPont		
24 Jeff Gordon	5.00	10.00
DuPont Bickyard Special		
24 Jeff Gordon	6.00	12.00
DuPont Million Dollar Date		
24 Jeff Gordon	5.00	10.00
DuPont Million Dollar Date		
Black Window		
24 Jeff Gordon	10.00	20.00
DuPont Chroma Premier		
24 Jeff Gordon	7.50	15.00
Lost World		
24 Jeff Gordon	6.00	12.00
Lost World		
Black Window Blister Pack		
24 Jeff Gordon	7.50	15.00
Lost World		
Hood Open Sports Image		
25 Ricky Craven	7.50	15.00
Budweiser		
26 Rich Bickle	5.00	10.00
KFC		

	Lo	Hi
27 Kenny Irwin G.I. Joe	6.00	12.00
27 Kenny Irwin Tonka	6.00	12.00
27 Rusty Wallace Miller Genuine Draft 1990 Grand Prix	12.00	20.00
29 Jeff Green Tom & Jerry	5.00	10.00
29 Elliot Sadler Phillips 66	6.00	12.00
31 Mike Skinner Lowe's	6.00	12.00
31 Mike Skinner Lowe's Blister Pack	5.00	10.00
31 Mike Skinner Lowe's Japan	6.00	12.00
36 Todd Bodine Stanley Tools	5.00	10.00
36 Derrike Cope Skittles	5.00	10.00
37 Mark Green Timber Wolf	5.00	10.00
37 Jeremy Mayfield Kmart	6.00	12.00
40 Robby Gordon Coors Light	7.50	15.00
41 Steve Grissom Kodiak	7.50	15.00
46 Wally Dallenbach First Union	5.00	10.00
60 Mark Martin Winn Dixie	6.00	12.00
71 Dave Marcis Realtree	5.00	10.00
75 Rick Mast Remington	5.00	10.00
75 Rick Mast Remington Camo	5.00	10.00
77 Bobby Hillin Jasper	5.00	10.00
81 Kenny Wallace Square D	5.00	10.00
88 Dale Jarrett Quality Care	5.00	10.00
88 Dale Jarrett Quality Care Brickyard Special	5.00	10.00
94 Bill Elliott McDonald's	6.00	12.00
94 Bill Elliott Mac Tonight	5.00	10.00
96 David Green Caterpillar	5.00	10.00
99 Jeff Burton Exide	5.00	10.00

1998 Action Racing Collectables 1:64

Most of these 1:64 scale cards were issued as part of the Platinum Series. Cars with alcohol and/or tobacco sponsorship are packaged in acrylic cases.

	Lo	Hi
00 Buckshot Jones Alka Seltzer	6.00	12.00
1 Dale Earnhardt Jr. Coke	12.00	20.00
1 Steve Park Pennzoil	7.50	15.00
1 Darrell Waltrip Pennzoil	7.00	12.00
2 Rusty Wallace Adventures of Rusty	9.00	18.00
2 Rusty Wallace Miller Lite	9.00	18.00
2 Rusty Wallace Miller Lite Elvis	9.00	18.00
2 Rusty Wallace Miller Lite TCB	9.00	18.00
2/12 Rusty Wallace/Jeremy Mayfield on Pit Wall Base	7.50	15.00
3 Dale Earnhardt Coke	12.00	20.00
3 Dale Earnhardt Goodwrench Plus	7.00	12.00
3 Dale Earnhardt Goodwrench Plus Blister Pack	6.00	10.00
3 Dale Earnhardt Goodwrench Plus Daytona	7.00	12.00
3 Dale Earnhardt Goodwrench Plus Bass Pro	9.00	18.00
3 Dale Earnhardt Jr. AC Delco	15.00	25.00
3 Dale Earnhardt Jr. AC Delco Blister Pack	12.00	20.00
4 Bobby Hamilton Kodak	5.00	10.00
5 Terry Labonte Blasted Fruit Loops	7.50	15.00
5 Terry Labonte Kellogg's	6.00	12.00
5 Terry Labonte Kellogg's Corny	6.00	12.00
5 Terry Labonte Kellogg's Ironman	6.00	12.00
8 Dale Earnhardt 10,000 RPM 1978 Dodge	6.00	12.00
8 Hut Stricklin Circuit City	5.00	10.00
9 Jerry Nadeau Power Puff	6.00	12.00
9 Jerry Nadeau Zombie Island	6.00	12.00
9 Lake Speed Birthday Cake	6.00	12.00
9 Lake Speed Huckleberry Hound	6.00	12.00
10 Ricky Rudd Give Kids the World	5.00	10.00
10 Ricky Rudd Tide	5.00	10.00
14 Patty Moise Rhodes Xena	6.00	15.00
18 Bobby Labonte Interstate Batteries Hot Rod	5.00	10.00
18 Bobby Labonte Interstate Batteries Small Soldiers	5.00	10.00
18 Bobby Labonte Interstate Batteries	5.00	10.00
22 Ward Burton MBNA	5.00	10.00
23 Jimmy Spencer No Bull	10.00	20.00
24 Jeff Gordon DuPont	7.00	12.00
24 Jeff Gordon DuPont Brickyard Winner	7.00	12.00
24 Jeff Gordon DuPont Chromalusion	15.00	30.00
24 Jeff Gordon DuPont No Bull	7.00	12.00
28 Kenny Irwin Havoline	6.00	12.00
28 Kenny Irwin Havoline Joker	7.50	15.00
30 Derrike Cope Gumout	5.00	10.00
31 Dale Earnhardt Jr. Sikkens	15.00	25.00
31 Dale Earnhardt Wrangler	18.00	30.00
31 Mike Skinner Lowe's	5.00	10.00
31 Mike Skinner Lowe's Special Olympic	5.00	10.00
32 Dale Jarrett White Rain	6.00	12.00
35 Todd Bodine Tabasco Orange	6.00	12.00
35 Todd Bodine Tabasco Red	6.00	12.00
36 Ernie Irvan M&Ms	6.00	12.00
36 Ernie Irvan Skittles	6.00	12.00
36 Ernie Irvan Wildberry Skittles	6.00	12.00
40 Sterling Marlin Coors Light	6.00	15.00
41 Steve Grissom Kodiak	7.50	15.00
42 Joe Nemechek Bell South		
44 Tony Stewart Shell	6.00	12.00
44 Tony Stewart Shell Small Soldiers	6.00	12.00
50 Ricky Craven Budweiser	7.50	15.00
50 NDA Bud Louie	6.00	12.00
72 Mike Dillon Detroit Gasket	6.00	12.00
75 Rick Mast Remington	6.00	12.00
81 Kenny Wallace Square D	6.00	12.00
81 Kenny Wallace Square D Lightning	6.00	12.00
88 Dale Jarrett Quality Care	6.00	12.00
88 Dale Jarrett Quality Care Batman	7.50	15.00
90 Dick Trickle Heilig-Meyers	5.00	10.00
96 David Green Caterpillar	5.00	10.00
300 Darrell Waltrip Flock Speical	6.00	12.00
K2 Dale Earnhardt Dayvault's	7.50	15.00

1995-1996 Action Racing Collectables SuperTrucks 1:64

These pieces are 1:64 scale replicas of the SuperTrucks that

race in the NASCAR SuperTruck Series.

	Lo	Hi
3 Mike Skinner Goodwrench	6.00	12.00
3 Mike Skinner Goodwrench 1996	5.00	10.00
6 Rick Carelli Total Petroleum	4.00	8.00
7 Geoff Bodine Exide	4.00	8.00
16 Ron Hornaday Action	5.00	10.00
16 Ron Hornaday NAPA	5.00	10.00
16 Ron Hornaday Papa John's Pizza	8.00	16.00
24 Scott Lagasse DuPont	6.00	12.00
24 Jack Sprague Quaker State	5.00	10.00
28 Ernie Irvan NAPA	4.00	8.00
52 Ken Schrader AC Delco	4.00	8.00
71 Kenji Momota Action Racing Collectables	4.00	8.00
84 Joe Ruttman Mac Tools	4.00	8.00
98 Butch Miller Raybestos	4.00	8.00

1993-1995 Action/RCCA 1:24

These 1:24 scale pieces were distributed through Action's Racing Collectibles Club of America. The pieces are 1:24 replicas of the cars that have raced in NASCAR.

	Lo	Hi
1 Rick Mast Skoal	40.00	70.00
2 Rusty Wallace Ford Motorsports	40.00	80.00
2 Rusty Wallace Miller Genuine Draft 1995 Thunderbird	35.00	60.00
2/43 Dale Earnhardt Richard Petty 7 and 7 Special	100.00	175.00
3 Dale Earnhardt Goodwrench 1988 Monte Carlo Fast Back	350.00	500.00
3 Dale Earnhardt Goodwrench 1994 Lumina	125.00	225.00
3 Dale Earnhardt Goodwrench 1995 Monte Carlo	90.00	150.00
3 Dale Earnhardt Goodwrench Silver Car Black Wheels	700.00	1000.00
3 Dale Earnhardt Goodwrench Silver Car Red Wheels	550.00	800.00
3 Dale Earnhardt Wrangler 1984 Monte Carlo	200.00	300.00
3 Dale Earnhardt Wrangler 1987 Monte Carlo	300.00	450.00
6 Mark Martin Folgers	175.00	300.00
9 Ted Musgrave Action Racing Collectables	30.00	45.00
10 Ricky Rudd Tide	40.00	65.00
11 Brett Bodine Lowe's	25.00	40.00
18 Dale Jarrett Interstate Batteries	75.00	125.00
23 Jimmy Spencer Smokin' Joe's	200.00	325.00
24 Jeff Gordon DuPont 1995 Monte Carlo	150.00	250.00
25 Tim Richmond Folgers Monte Carlo Fastback	35.00	50.00
25 Ken Schrader Budweiser	35.00	60.00
26 Hut Stricklin Quaker State	20.00	40.00
28 Dale Jarrett Havoline	25.00	50.00
30 Michael Waltrip Pennzoil	60.00	100.00
42 Kyle Petty Coors Light Pumpkin Special	125.00	200.00
51 Neil Bonnett Country Time	150.00	250.00
94 Bill Elliott McDonald's 1995	30.00	50.00
94 Bill Elliott McDonald's Thunderbat	125.00	200.00
95 David Green Busch Beer	30.00	50.00

1996 Action/RCCA 1:24

These 1:24 scale pieces were distributed through Action's Racing Collectibles Club of America. The pieces are 1:24 replicas of the cars that have raced in NASCAR.

	Lo	Hi
2 Rusty Wallace Miller Genuine Draft	40.00	70.00
3 Richard Childress CRC Chemical	30.00	60.00
5 Terry Labonte Kellogg's Silver car	100.00	175.00
5 Terry Labonte Kellogg's Japan	50.00	80.00
6 Mark Martin Valvoline Thunderbird	35.00	60.00
17 Darrell Waltrip Parts America	35.00	60.00
17 Darrell Waltrip Tide	40.00	80.00
21 Neil Bonnett Hodgdon	25.00	60.00
21 Michael Waltrip Citgo Star Trek	25.00	60.00
22 Bobby Allison Miller Beer	35.00	60.00
24 Jeff Gordon DuPont Monte Carlo	40.00	70.00
27 Rusty Wallace Kodiak	70.00	100.00
29 Steve Grissom Cartoon Network	25.00	60.00
29 Steve Grissom WCW	25.00	60.00
33 Robert Pressley Skoal	35.00	60.00
42 Robby Gordon Tonka	30.00	60.00
42 Kyle Petty Coors Light Black Paint Scheme	40.00	65.00
43 Bobby Hamilton STP Silver car with Black Windows	60.00	100.00
43 Bobby Hamilton STP 5 car set with Black Windows	150.00	250.00

1997 Action/RCCA 1:24

These 1:24 scale pieces were distributed through Action's Racing Collectibles Club of America. The pieces are 1:24 replicas of the cars that have raced in NASCAR.

	Lo	Hi
2 Rusty Wallace Miller Lite Texas Motor Speedway	60.00	100.00
3 Dale Earnhardt AC Delco	50.00	80.00
3 Dale Earnhardt Goodwrench	150.00	250.00
3 Dale Earnhardt Goodwrench Plus	50.00	80.00
3 Dale Earnhardt Lowes Food	60.00	110.00
3 Dale Earnhardt Wrangler 1984 Monte Carlo Daytona	70.00	110.00
3 Steve Park AC Delco	100.00	175.00
3 Ricky Rudd Piedmont	40.00	65.00
4 Sterling Marlin Kodak	25.00	60.00
9 Jeff Burton Track Gear	40.00	75.00
17 Darrell Waltrip Parts America 7 Car set	200.00	300.00
17 Darrel Waltrip Parts America Chrome	75.00	150.00
22 Ward Burton MBNA	35.00	50.00
22 Ward Burton MBNA Gold	25.00	50.00
24 Jeff Gordon DuPont Million Dollar Date	50.00	75.00
24 Jeff Gordon DuPont ChromaPremier	90.00	150.00
24 Jeff Gordon Lost World	60.00	100.00
25 Ricky Craven Budweiser	45.00	70.00
26 Rich Bickle KFC	35.00	50.00
27 Kenny Irwin Action	40.00	70.00
27 Kenny Irwin G.I. Joe	40.00	65.00
27 Rusty Wallace Miller Genuine Draft 1990 Grand Prix	45.00	70.00
29 Elliott Sadler Phillips 66	25.00	60.00
31 Mike Skinner Lowe's Japan	30.00	60.00
32 Dale Jarrett White Rain	25.00	60.00
33 Ken Schrader Skoal	50.00	90.00
36 Todd Bodine Stanley Tools	35.00	50.00
36 Derrike Cope Skittles	25.00	50.00
37 Jeremy Mayfield Kmart	50.00	80.00
40 Robby Gordon Coors Light	40.00	65.00
41 Steve Grissom Kodiak	30.00	60.00
60 Mark Martin Winn Dixie	40.00	80.00
71 Dave Marcis Realtree	40.00	70.00
71 Dave Marcis Realtree Making of Champions	25.00	60.00
81 Kenny Wallace Square D	20.00	50.00
94 Bill Elliott McDonald's	40.00	70.00
96 David Green Caterpillar	25.00	50.00
97 Chad Little John Deere	40.00	60.00
97 Chad Little John Deere 160th Anniversary	40.00	65.00

1993-1995 Action/RCCA 1:24 Banks

These cars were produced by Action and distributed through the club (RCCA). Each car has a slot in the back window for a coin bank. Most banks have blacked in windows.

	Lo	Hi
1 Winston Show Car	40.00	60.00
2 Dale Earnhardt Wrangler 1981 Pontiac	100.00	175.00
3 Richard Childress Black Gold	35.00	50.00
3 Dale Earnhardt Goodwrench 1994 Lumina	100.00	175.00
3 Dale Earnhardt Wrangler 1981 Pontiac	90.00	150.00
3 Dale Earnhardt Wrangler 1985 Monte Carlo	150.00	250.00
3 Dale Earnhardt Wrangler 1987 Monte Carlo	200.00	300.00
3 Jeff Green	30.00	50.00

	Lo	Hi
Goodwrench		
4 Sterling Marlin	30.00	50.00
Kodak		
6 Mark Martin	30.00	50.00
Valvoline 1995		
6 Mark Martin	40.00	70.00
Valvoline Brickyard Special		
7 Alan Kulwicki	100.00	150.00
Hooters		
7 Alan Kulwicki	60.00	100.00
Zerex		
11 Darrell Waltrip	35.00	55.00
Budweiser 1986 Monte Carlo		
11 Darrell Waltrip	30.00	50.00
Mountain Dew		
12 Neil Bonnett	40.00	75.00
Budweiser 1986 Monte Carlo		
15 Dale Earnhardt	90.00	150.00
Wrangler 1982 Thunder Bird		
16 Ted Musgrave	35.00	60.00
Primestar		
25 Ken Schrader	45.00	60.00
Budweiser		
28 Ernie Irvan	30.00	45.00
Havoline		
42 Kyle Petty	35.00	55.00
Coors Light '95		
88 Darrell Waltrip	60.00	100.00
Gatorade Monte Carlo		

1996 Action/RCCA 1:24 Banks

These cars were produced by Action and distributed through the club (RCCA). Each car has a slot in the back window for a coin bank. All banks have blacked in windows.

	Lo	Hi
2 Rusty Wallace	35.00	60.00
Miller Genuine Draft		
2 Rusty Wallace	30.00	60.00
Miller Genuine Draft Silver Anniversary Car		
3 Dale Earnhardt	45.00	80.00
AC-Delco		
3 Dale Earnhardt	40.00	70.00
Goodwrench		
7 Geoff Bodine	20.00	50.00
Exide		
11 Darrell Waltrip	35.00	60.00
Budweiser 1984 Monte Carlo		
12 Neil Bonnett	40.00	75.00
Budweiser 1984 Monte Carlo		
14 Jeff Green	25.00	60.00
Racing For Kids		
17 Darrell Waltrip	25.00	50.00
Western Auto		
18 Bobby Labonte	25.00	50.00
Interstate Batteries		
21 Michael Waltrip	25.00	50.00
Citgo		
28 Ernie Irvan	25.00	50.00
Havoline		
30 Johnny Benson	25.00	60.00
Pennzoil		
31 Mike Skinner	50.00	80.00
Lowe's		
31 Mike Skinner	75.00	125.00
Snap-On		
42 Kyle Petty	40.00	65.00
Coors Light		
57 Jason Keller	30.00	50.00
Halloween Havoc		
88 Ernie Irvan	35.00	60.00
Havoline		
88 Dale Jarrett	35.00	60.00
Quality Care		
94 Bill Elliott	35.00	60.00
McDonald's		

1997 Action/RCCA 1:24 Banks

These cars were produced by Action and distributed through the club (RCCA). Each car has a slot in the back window for a coin bank. All banks have blacked in windows.

	Lo	Hi
00 Buckshot Jones	40.00	60.00
Aqua Fresh		
2 Rusty Wallace	45.00	70.00
Miller Lite		
2 Rusty Wallace	45.00	65.00
Miller Lite Japan		
3 Dale Earnhardt	25.00	60.00
Goodwrench Plus		
3 Dale Earnhardt	80.00	120.00
Wheaties		
6 Mark Martin	35.00	60.00
Valvoline		
10 Phill Parsons	30.00	50.00
Channellock		
11 Brett Bodine	35.00	60.00
Close Call		
12 Kenny Wallace	25.00	60.00
Gray Bar		
14 Steve Park	60.00	100.00
Burger King		
18 Bobby Labonte	25.00	50.00
Interstate Batteries		
18 Bobby Labonte	25.00	50.00
Interstate Batteries Hall of Fame		
23 Jimmy Spencer	100.00	175.00
Camel		
24 Jeff Gordon	90.00	150.00
DuPont		
27 Kenny Irwin	40.00	65.00
Nerf		
27 Kenny Irwin	40.00	65.00
Tonka		
37 Mark Green	35.00	60.00
Timber Wolf		
42 Joe Nemechek	35.00	60.00
Bell South		
46 Wally Dallenbach	25.00	60.00
First Union		
75 Rick Mast	35.00	60.00
Remington		
75 Rick Mast	35.00	60.00
Remington Camo		
88 Dale Jarrett	25.00	60.00
Quality Care		
94 Bill Elliott	50.00	80.00
Mac Tonight		
97 Chad Little	40.00	60.00
John Deere		
97 Chad Little	40.00	60.00
John Deere 160th Anniversary		
99 Jeff Burton	45.00	70.00
Exide		

1998 Action/RCCA 1:24 Banks

These cars were produced by Action and distributed through the club (RCCA). Each car has a slot in the back window for a coin bank. All banks have clear windows.

	Lo	Hi
1 Jeff Gordon	75.00	125.00
Baby Ruth		
1 Steve Park	100.00	175.00
Pennzoil		
1 Darrell Waltrip	60.00	100.00
Pennzoil		
2 Rusty Wallace	50.00	80.00
Adventures of Rusty		
2 Rusty Wallace	45.00	80.00
Miller Lite		
2 Rusty Wallace	45.00	80.00
Miller Lite Elvis		
2 Rusty Wallace	50.00	80.00
Miller Lite TCB		
3 Dale Earnhardt	60.00	100.00
Coke		
3 Dale Earnhardt	40.00	80.00
Goodwrench Plus		
3 Dale Earnhardt	70.00	120.00
Goodwrench Plus Bass Pro		
3 Dale Earnhardt	50.00	90.00
Goodwrench Plus Daytona		
3 Dale Earnhardt Jr.	200.00	300.00
AC Delco		
4 Bobby Hamilton	35.00	70.00
Kodak		
5 Terry Labonte	50.00	80.00
Blasted Fruit Loops		
5 Terry Labonte	50.00	90.00
Kellogg's		
5 Terry Labonte	65.00	100.00
Kellogg's Corny		
5 Terry Labonte	50.00	90.00
Kellogg's Ironman		
8 Dale Earnhardt	40.00	80.00
10,000 RPM 1978 Dodge		
8 Hut Stricklin	35.00	70.00
Circuit City		
9 Jerry Nadeau	40.00	80.00
Zombie Island		
9 Lake Speed	50.00	80.00
Birthday Cake		
9 Lake Speed	40.00	80.00
Huckleberry Hound		
10 Ricky Rudd	35.00	70.00
Tide		
12 Jeremy Mayfield	55.00	80.00
Mobil 1		
12 Jimmy Spener	150.00	225.00
Zippo		
14 Patty Moise	50.00	80.00
Rhodes Xena		
18 Bobby Labonte	40.00	75.00
Interstate Batteries		
18 Bobby Labonte	40.00	80.00
Interstate Batteries Small Soldiers		
23 Jimmy Spencer	90.00	150.00
No Bull		
24 Jeff Gordon	40.00	80.00
DuPont		
24 Jeff Gordon	90.00	150.00
DuPont Chromalusion		
28 Kenny Irwin	40.00	80.00
Havoline		
28 Kenny Irwin	45.00	90.00
Havoline Joker		
31 Dale Earnhardt Jr.	150.00	250.00
Sikkens		
31 Dale Earnhardt Jr.	175.00	250.00
Wrangler		
31 Mike Skinner	40.00	70.00
Lowe's		
31 Mike Skinner	40.00	80.00
Lowe's Special Olympic		
32 Dale Jarrett	40.00	70.00
White Rain		
33 Tim Fedewa	60.00	100.00
Kleenex		
34 Mike McLaughlin	60.00	100.00
Goulds		
35 Todd Bodine	40.00	80.00
Tabasco		
36 Ernie Irvan	70.00	110.00
M&Ms		
36 Ernie Irvan	40.00	70.00
Skittles		
36 Ernie Irvan	40.00	70.00
Wildberry Skittles		
41 Steve Grissom	50.00	85.00
Kodiak		
42 Joe Nemechek	40.00	70.00
Bell South		
44 Tony Stewart	40.00	70.00
Shell Small Soldiers		
50 Ricky Craven	90.00	150.00
Budweiser		
50 No Driver Association	50.00	80.00
Bud Louie		
81 Kenny Wallace	40.00	70.00
Square D		
81 Kenny Wallace	40.00	75.00
Square D Lightning		
88 Dale Jarrett	40.00	75.00
Quality Care		
88 Dale Jarrett	45.00	80.00

Quality Care Batman
90 Dick Trickle........ 40.00 80.00
Heilig-Meyers
96 David Green........ 40.00 70.00
Caterpillar
98 Greg Sacks........ 40.00 70.00
Thorn Apple Valley
300 Darrell Waltrip........ 60.00 100.00
Flock Special
K2 Dale Earnhardt........ 40.00 80.00
Dayvault's

1997 Action/RCCA 1:24 Elite

This series consists of upgraded versions of their standard production cars. It was started in 1997. The cars from this series contain serial number plates on the undercarriage at the end of the car.

	Lo	Hi
00 Buckshot Jones Aqua Fresh	90.00	150.00
2 Rusty Wallace Miller Lite Texas Motor Speedway	90.00	150.00
2 Rusty Wallace Miller Lite	90.00	150.00
3 Dale Earnhardt AC Delco	40.00	100.00
3 Dale Earnhardt Goodwrench	275.00	400.00
3 Dale Earnhardt Goodwrench Plus	100.00	175.00
3 Dale Earnhardt Wheaties Gold number plate	175.00	250.00
3 Dale Earnhardt Wheaties Pewter number plate	125.00	200.00
3 Steve Park AC Delco	125.00	200.00
4 Sterling Marlin Kodak	40.00	100.00
6 Mark Martin/ Valvoline	60.00	150.00
9 Jeff Burton Track Gear	40.00	100.00
10 Ricky Rudd Tide	60.00	150.00
14 Steve Park Burger King	150.00	250.00
17 Darrell Waltrip Parts America	50.00	120.00
17 Darrell Waltrip Parts America Chrome	125.00	175.00
18 Bobby Labonte Interstate Batteries	60.00	150.00
22 Ward Burton MBNA Gold	90.00	150.00
24 Jeff Gordon Dupont	175.00	300.00
24 Jeff Gordon Dupont Million Dollar Date	50.00	120.00
24 Jeff Gordon Dupont Premier	175.00	300.00
24 Jeff Gordon Lost World	125.00	250.00
25 Ricky Craven Budweiser	90.00	150.00
29 Jeff Green Tom & Jerry	40.00	100.00
29 Elliot Sadler Phillips 66	40.00	100.00
29 No Driver Associated Scooby-Doo	90.00	150.00
31 Mike Skinner Lowe's	100.00	175.00
31 M.Skinner Lowe's Japan	40.00	100.00
32 Dale Jarrett White Rain	100.00	175.00
36 Todd Bodine Stanley	90.00	150.00
36 Derrike Cope Skittles	40.00	100.00
37 Mark Green Timber Wolf	90.00	150.00
37 Jeremy Mayfield Kmart	90.00	150.00
46 Wally Dallenbach First Union	40.00	100.00
60 Mark Martin Winn Dixie	40.00	100.00
88 Dale Jarrett Ford Credit	60.00	150.00
94 Bill Elliott McDonald's	100.00	175.00
94 Bill Elliott Mac Tonight	40.00	100.00
96 David Green Caterpillar	40.00	100.00
97 Chad Little John Deere	40.00	100.00
97 Chad Little John Deere 160th Anniversary.	60.00	150.00
99 Jeff Burton Exide	100.00	150.00

1998 Action/RCCA 1:24 Elite

This series was consists of upgraded versions of their standard production cars. The cars from this series contain serial number plates on the undercarriage at the end of the car.

	Lo	Hi
1 Dale Earnhardt Jr. Coke	125.00	225.00
1 Steve Park Pennzoil	150.00	250.00
1 Steve Park Pennzoil Indy	100.00	175.00
1 Darrell Waltrip Pennzoil	100.00	175.00
2 Rusty Wallace Adventures of Rusty	75.00	150.00
2 Rusty Wallace Miller Lite	75.00	150.00
2 Rusty Wallace Miller Lite Elvis	75.00	150.00
3 Dale Earnhardt Coke	125.00	200.00
3 Dale Earnhardt Goodwrench Plus	100.00	200.00
3 Dale Earnhardt Goodwrench Plus Bass Pro	100.00	175.00
3 Dale Earnhardt Goodwrench Plus Daytona	90.00	150.00
3 Dale Earnhardt Goodwrench Silver	125.00	200.00
3 Dale Earnhardt Jr. AC Delco	300.00	500.00
4 Bobby Hamilton Kodak	75.00	150.00
5 Terry Labonte Blasted Fruit Loops	100.00	175.00
5 Terry Labonte Kellogg's	90.00	150.00
5 Terry Labonte Kellogg's Corny	150.00	225.00
5 Terry Labonte Kellogg's Ironman	90.00	150.00
8 Dale Earnhardt 10,000 RPM 1978 Dodge	75.00	150.00
8 Hut Stricklin Circuit City	80.00	150.00
9 Jerry Nadeau Zombie Island	90.00	150.00
9 Lake Speed Birthday Cake	75.00	150.00
9 Lake Speed Hucklerberry Hound	100.00	175.00
10 Ricky Rudd Tide	75.00	150.00
12 Jeremy Mayfield Mobil 1	90.00	150.00
12 Jimmy Spencer Zippo	200.00	350.00
14 Patty Moise Rhodes	100.00	175.00
18 Bobby Labonte Interstate Batteries Small Soldiers	75.00	150.00
23 Jimmy Spencer No Bull	150.00	225.00
24 Jeff Gordon DuPont	150.00	225.00
24 Jeff Gordon DuPont Chromalusion	150.00	300.00
28 Kenny Irwin Havoline	90.00	150.00
28 Kenny Irwin Havoline Joker	90.00	150.00
31 Dale Earnhardt Jr. Sikkens	150.00	250.00
31 Mike Skinner Lowe's	75.00	150.00
31 Mike Skinner Lowe's Special Olympics	100.00	175.00
33 Tim Fedewa Kleenex	100.00	175.00
34 Mike McLaughlin Goulds	100.00	175.00
35 Todd Bodine Tabasco	80.00	150.00
36 Ernie Irvan M&Ms	100.00	175.00
36 Ernie Irvan Skittles	90.00	150.00
36 Ernie Irvan Wildberry Skittles	80.00	150.00
41 Steve Grissom Kodiak	90.00	150.00
44 Tony Stewart Shell	90.00	150.00
44 Tony Stewart Shell Small Soldiers	50.00	120.00
50 Ricky Craven Budweiser	125.00	200.00
50 No Driver Association Bud Louie	100.00	175.00
81 Kenny Wallace Square D	90.00	150.00
81 Kenny Wallace Square D Lightning	90.00	150.00
88 Dale Jarrett Quality Care	90.00	150.00
88 Dale Jarrett Quality Care Batman	90.00	150.00
88 Dale Jarrett Quality Care No Bull	90.00	150.00
96 David Green Caterpillar	90.00	150.00
98 Greg Sacks Thorn Apple Valley	75.00	150.00
300 Darrell Waltrip Tim Flock Special	125.00	200.00
K2 Dale Earnhardt Dayvault's	50.00	120.00

1995-1996 Action/RCCA SuperTrucks 1:24

The top SuperTruck driver's trucks are featured in these die-cast pieces. Most pieces were distributed either through the Action Dealer Network or Action's Racing Collectibles Club of America. Some were made available through both outlets. There are two versions of most trucks, a bank and a regular version. The banks have a slot in the truck bed for the coin.

	Lo	Hi
3 Mike Skinner Goodwrench	25.00	40.00
3 Mike Skinner Goodwrench Bank	35.00	50.00
3 Mike Skinner Goodwrench 1996	20.00	40.00
3 Mike Skinner Goodwrench 1996 Bank	40.00	60.00
6 Rick Carelli Total Petroleum	30.00	45.00
6 Rick Carelli Total Petroleum Bank	30.00	45.00
7 Geoff Bodine Exide	30.00	45.00
7 Geoff Bodine Exide Bank	30.00	45.00
16 Ron Hornaday	20.00	40.00

Action
16 Ron Hornaday 20.00 40.00
Action Bank
16 Ron Hornaday 20.00 40.00
NAPA
16 Ron Hornaday 20.00 40.00
NAPA Bank
16 Ron Hornaday 35.00 60.00
NAPA Gold
16 Ron Hornaday 35.00 60.00
NAPA Gold B
16 Ron Hornaday 30.00 45.00
Papa John's
16 Ron Hornaday 30.00 45.00
Papa John's Bank
24 Jack Sprague 20.00 40.00
Quaker State
24 Jack Sprague 20.00 40.00
Quaker State Bank
24 Scott Lagasse 30.00 45.00
DuPont
24 Scott Lagasse 30.00 45.00
DuPont Bank
28 Ernie Irvan 30.00 45.00
NAPA
28 Ernie Irvan 35.00 50.00
NAPA Bank
52 Ken Schrader 25.00 40.00
AC Delco
52 Ken Schrader 30.00 45.00
AC Delco Bank
71 Kenji Momota 25.00 40.00
Action Racing Collectables
71 Kenji Momota 30.00 45.00
Action Racing Collectables Bank
80 Joe Ruttman 30.00 60.00
JR's Garage
84 Joe Ruttman 25.00 40.00
Mac Tools
84 Joe Ruttman 30.00 45.00
Mac Tools Bank
98 Butch Miller 30.00 45.00
Raybestos Bank

1998 Action/RCCA 1:32 Gold

These 1:32 scale cars were distributed by Action through RCCA.

	Lo	Hi
1 Steve Park Pennzoil	50.00	75.00
2 Rusty Wallace Miller Lite	50.00	75.00
3 Dale Earnhardt Goodwrench Plus Bass Pro	50.00	75.00
3 Dale Earnhardt Jr. AC Delco	50.00	90.00
5 Terry Labonte Kellogg's	50.00	75.00
12 Jeremy Mayfield Mobil 1	50.00	75.00
18 Bobby Labonte Interstate Batteries	50.00	75.00
23 Jimmy Spencer No Bull	50.00	75.00
24 Jeff Gordon DuPont	50.00	75.00
28 Kenny Irwin Havoline	50.00	75.00
36 Ernie Irvan M&Ms	50.00	75.00
88 Dale Jarrett Quality Care	50.00	75.00

1993-1995 Action/RCCA 1:64

These were the 1:64 scale cars that were made by Action and distributed through the club (RCCA). The most popular versions seem to be the hood open cars. Many of the first cars distributed throught the club were made for Action by Revell.

	Lo	Hi
1 Jeff Gordon Baby Ruth Revell	40.00	60.00
1 Winston Cup Car Platinum Series in acrylic case	10.00	20.00
2 Mark Martin Miller Acrylic	7.50	15.00
2 Rusty Wallace Miller Genuine Draft Club Only	9.00	18.00
2 Rusty Wallace Miller Genuine Draft 1995 Hood Open in acrylic case	7.50	15.00
2 Rusty Wallace Pontiac Excitement Revell	4.00	8.00
3 Dale Earnhardt Goodwrench Club Only	15.00	30.00
3 Dale Earnhardt Goodwrench 1994 Lumina Hood Open	15.00	30.00
3 Dale Earnhardt Goodwrench 1994 Lumina	9.00	18.00
3 Dale Earnhardt Goodwrench 1995 Monte Carlo Hood Open	12.50	25.00
3 Dale Earnhardt Goodwrench Silver Car Hood Open	70.00	100.00
3 Dale Earnhardt Wrangler 1981 Pontiac	15.00	30.00
3 Dale Earnhardt Wrangler 1985 Monte Carlo Notchback	15.00	30.00
3 Dale Earnhardt Wrangler 1987 Monte Carlo Fastback	20.00	40.00
3 Dale Earnhardt Jr. Mom-n-Pop's	25.00	40.00
5 Terry Labonte Kellogg's 1994 Lum	15.00	30.00
5 Terry Labonte Kellogg's Hood Open	6.00	12.00
5 Ricky Rudd Tide Revell Promo	3.00	6.00
6 Mark Martin Folgers Promo	15.00	25.00
6 Mark Martin Stroh's Light 2 car combo	25.00	50.00
6 Mark Martin Valvoline Hood Open Brickyard Special	8.00	16.00
6 Mark Martin Valvoline 1995 Thunderbird Hood Open	7.50	15.00
6 Mark Martin Valvoline Revell	3.00	6.00
7 Alan Kulwicki Hooters Hood Open	12.50	25.00
7 Alan Kulwicki Zerex	12.50	25.00
8 Kerry Earnhardt Mom-n-Pop's	10.00	20.00
9 Bill Elliott Melling Club Only	5.00	10.00
10 Derrike Cope Purolator Revell	3.00	6.00
10 Ricky Rudd Tide Hood Open	5.00	10.00
11 Brett Bodine Lowe's Hood Open	6.00	12.00
11 Bill Elliott Budweiser Hood Open	7.50	15.00
11 Darrell Waltrip Budweiser 1985 Monte Carlo	7.50	15.00
12 Neil Bonnett Budweiser 1985 Monte Carlo	7.50	15.00
12 Hut Stricklin Raybestos Revell	2.00	5.00
15 Dale Earnhardt Wrangler Revell	15.00	30.00
15 No Driver Association Motorcraft Revell	2.00	5.00
15 Lake Speed Quality Care Hood Open	7.50	15.00
16 Ted Musgrave Family Channel Hood Open	7.50	15.00
17 Darrell Waltrip Superflo Camaro	6.00	15.00
17 Darrell Waltrip Western Auto Revell Club Only	7.50	15.00
17 Darrell Waltrip Western Auto 1994 Lumina Hood Open	6.00	12.00
17 Darrell Waltrip Western Auto 1995 Monte Carlo Hood Open	7.50	15.00
18 Dale Jarrett Interstate Batteries Hood Open	6.00	12.00
18 Dale Jarrett Interstate Batteries Revell	2.00	5.00
21 David Pearson Chattanooga Chew 1985 Monte Carlo	7.50	15.00
21 David Pearson Pearson Racing	4.00	7.00
21 Morgan Shepherd Cheerwine Morema	5.00	10.00
21 Morgan Shepherd Citgo REV	2.00	5.00
22 Sterling Marlin Maxwell House Revell	2.00	5.00
23 Jimmy Spencer Smokin' Joe's Hood Open	25.00	40.00
24 Jeff Gordon DuPont 1993 Lumina	30.00	50.00
24 Jeff Gordon DuPont 1994 Lumina Hood Open	18.00	30.00
24 Jeff Gordon DuPont 1995 Monte Carlo Hood Open	10.00	20.00
25 Ricky Craven 1991 BGN Champion Promo	7.50	15.00
25 Tim Richmond	10.00	20.00
25 Ken Schrader Budweiser Hood Open	7.50	15.00
25 Bill Venturini Rain X Revell	2.00	5.00
26 Brett Bodine Quaker State Revell	2.00	5.00
26 Steve Kinser Quaker State Hood Open	6.00	15.00
27 Tim Richmond Old Milwaukee Hood Open	7.50	15.00
28 Davey Allison Havoline Club Only	10.00	20.00
28 Davey Allison Mac Tools Promo	12.50	25.00
28 Davey Allison Havoline Hood Open	9.00	18.00

Black Gold paint scheme
28 Davey Allison 9.00 18.00
Havoline Hood Open
Black Orange paint scheme
28 Dale Jarrett 6.00 15.00
Havoline Hood Open
30 Michael Waltrip 6.00 12.00
Pennzoil Hood Open
30 Michael Waltrip 2.00 5.00
Pennzoil Revell
35 Alan Kulwicki 15.00 25.00
Qunicy's
36 Kenny Wallace 2.00 5.00
Cox Lumber Revell
36 Kenny Wallace 2.00 5.00
Dirt Devil Revell
38 Kelley Earnhardt 7.50 15.00
Mom-n-Pop's
42 Kyle Petty 7.50 15.00
Coors Light Hood Open
42 Kyle Petty 30.00 50.00
Coors Light Pumpkin Special
Hood Open
42 Kyle Petty 6.00 12.00
Mello Yello Hood Open
42 Kyle Petty 2.00 5.00
Mello Yello Revell
43 Richard Petty 2.00 5.00
STP Revell
44 Larry Caudill 2.00 5.00
Army Revell
51 Neil Bonnett 10.00 20.00
Country Time
63 Chuck Bown 6.00 12.00
Nescafe Promo
66 Jimmy Hensley 2.00 5.00
TropArtic Revell
68 Bobby Hamilton 2.00 5.00
Country Time Revell
87 Joe Nemechek 2.00 5.00
Texas Pete Revell
88 Darrell Waltrip 7.50 15.00
Gatorade
89 Jimmy Sauter 2.00 5.00
Evinrude Revell
90 Bobby Hillin 6.00 12.00
Heilig-Meyers Promo
92 Circle Track Show Car Promo 6.00 12.00
93 Casey Elliott 5.00 12.00
Hood Open
93 Mike Wallace 2.00 5.00
No Sponsor Revell
94 Bill Elliott 7.50 15.00
McDonald's Hood Open
94 Bill Elliott 15.00 30.00
McDonald's Thunderbat
Hood Open
95 David Green 7.50 15.00
Busch Beer Hood Open
98 Derrike Cope 6.00 12.00
Fingerhut Hood Open
99 Ricky Craven 2.00 5.00
DuPont Revell

1996 Action/RCCA 1:64

These were the 1:64 scale cars that were made by Action and distributed through the club (RCCA). All cars have open hoods. These cars are packaged in boxes in contrast to their ARC counterparts.

Lo Hi
2 Rusty Wallace 7.50 15.00
Miller Genuine Draft
2 Rusty Wallace 10.00 20.00
Miller Genuine Draft Silver car
in Acrylic Case
3 Richard Childress 6.00 15.00
CRC Chemical
3 Dale Earnhardt 12.50 25.00
AC Delco
3 Dale Earnhardt 15.00 30.00
Goodwrench
4 Sterling Marlin 6.00 15.00
Kodak
5 Terry Labonte 12.50 25.00
Kellogg's Ironman
5 Terry Labonte 10.00 20.00
Kellogg's Japan
6 Mark Martin 7.50 15.00
Valvoline
7 Geoff Bodine 6.00 12.00
Exide
14 Jeff Green 6.00 12.00
Racing For Kids
18 Bobby Labonte 7.50 15.00
Interstate Batteries
21 Michael Waltrip 7.50 15.00
Citgo Star Trek
24 Jeff Gordon 10.00 20.00
DuPont
27 Rusty Wallace 15.00 25.00
Kodiak
packaged in acrylic case
28 Ernie Irvan 6.00 15.00
Havoline
29 Steve Grissom 7.50 15.00
Cartoon Network
29 No Driver Association 7.50 15.00
Scooby-Doo
30 Johnny Benson 6.00 15.00
Pennzoil
42 Kyle Petty 9.00 18.00
Coors Light
42 Kyle Petty 12.50 25.00
Coors Light Black Paint Scheme
In Acrylic Case
43 Bobby Hamilton 9.00 18.00
STP Silver car
43 Bobby Hamilton 50.00 80.00
STP 5 car set
57 Jason Keller 7.50 15.00
Halloween Havoc
88 Ernie Irvan 7.50 15.00
Havoline
88 Dale Jarrett 7.50 15.00
Quality Care
94 Bill Elliott 7.50 15.00
McDonald's

1997 Action/RCCA 1:64

These were the 1:64 scale cars that were made by Action and distributed through the club (RCCA). All cars have open hoods. These cars are packaged in boxes in contrast to their ARC counterparts.

Lo Hi
00 Buckshot Jones 7.50 15.00
Aqua Fresh
2 Rusty Wallace 7.50 15.00
Miller Lite
2 Rusty Wallace 9.00 18.00
Miller Lite Japan
2 Rusty Wallace 9.00 18.00
Miller Lite Texas Motor Speedway
3 Dale Earnhardt 12.50 25.00
AC Delco
3 Dale Earnhardt 12.50 25.00
Goodwrench
3 Dale Earnhardt 12.50 25.00
Goodwrench Plus
3 Dale Earnhardt 15.00 30.00
Wheaties
3 Steve Park 15.00 30.00
AC Delco
4 Sterling Marlin 6.00 12.00
Kodak
6 Mark Martin 7.50 15.00
Valvoline
9 Jeff Burton 7.50 15.00
Track Gear
10 Ricky Rudd 6.00 12.00
Tide
11 Brett Bodine 6.00 12.00
Close Call
12 Kenny Wallace 6.00 12.00
Gray Bar
14 Steve Park 15.00 30.00
Burger King
17 Darrell Waltrip 50.00 80.00
Parts America 7 Car set
17 Darrell Waltrip 12.50 25.00
Parts America Chrome
18 Bobby Labonte 7.50 15.00
Interstate Batteries
18 Bobby Labonte 6.00 15.00
Interstate Batteries Hall of Fame
22 Ward Burton 6.00 12.00
MBNA
22 Ward Burton 6.00 12.00
MBNA Gold
23 Jimmy Spencer 15.00 30.00
Camel
24 Jeff Gordon 12.50 25.00
DuPont
24 Jeff Gordon 12.50 25.00
DuPont Million Dollar Date
24 Jeff Gordon 15.00 30.00
DuPont ChromaPremier
24 Jeff Gordon 12.50 25.00
Lost World
25 Ricky Craven 9.00 18.00
Budweiser
26 Rich Bickle 6.00 12.00
KFC
27 Kenny Irwin 6.00 15.00
G.I. Joe
27 Kenny Irwin 9.00 18.00
Tonka
29 Jeff Green 6.00 12.00
Tom & Jerry
29 Elliott Sadler 6.00 12.00
Phillips 66
31 Mike Skinner 6.00 12.00
Lowe's
31 Mike Skinner 6.00 12.00
Lowe's Japan
32 Dale Jarrett 6.00 15.00
White Rain
36 Derrike Cope 6.00 12.00
Skittles
37 Mark Green 6.00 12.00
Timber Wolf
37 Jeremy Mayfield 7.50 15.00
Kmart
41 Steve Grissom 6.00 15.00
Kodiak
46 Wally Dallenbach 6.00 12.00
First Union
60 Mark Martin 7.50 15.00
Winn Dixie
71 Dave Marcis 6.00 12.00
Realtree
75 Rick Mast 6.00 12.00
Remington
75 Rick Mast 6.00 12.00
Remington Camo
77 Bobby Hillin 6.00 12.00
Jasper
81 Kenny Wallace 6.00 12.00
Square D
88 Dale Jarrett 6.00 15.00
Quality Care
94 Bill Elliott 7.50 15.00
McDonald's
94 Bill Elliott 7.50 15.00
Mac Tonight
96 David Green 6.00 12.00
Caterpillar
97 Chad Little 6.00 12.00
John Deere
97 Chad Little 6.00 12.00
John Deere 160th Anniversary

1998 Action/RCCA 1:64

These were the 1:64 scale cars that were made by Action and distributed through the club (RCCA). All cars have open hoods. These cars are packaged in boxes in contrast to their ARC counterparts.

Lo Hi
1 Dale Earnhardt Jr. 15.00 30.00
Coke
1 Jeff Gordon 20.00 35.00
Baby Ruth
1 Steve Park 18.00 30.00
Pennzoil
2 Rusty Wallace 10.00 20.00
Adventures of Rusty

2 Rusty Wallace Miller Lite	10.00	20.00
2 Rusty Wallace Miller Lite Elvis	10.00	20.00
2 Rusty Wallace Miller Lite TCB	10.00	20.00
3 Dale Earnhardt Coke	15.00	30.00
3 Dale Earnhardt Goodwrench Plus	12.50	25.00
3 Dale Earnhardt Goodwrench Plus Bass Pro	20.00	35.00
3 Dale Earnhardt Jr. AC Delco	30.00	40.00
4 Bobby Hamilton Kodak	7.50	15.00
5 Terry Labonte Blasted Fruit Loops	10.00	20.00
5 Terry Labonte Kellogg's	9.00	18.00
5 Terry Labonte Kellogg's Corny	9.00	18.00
5 Terry Labonte Kellogg's Ironman	9.00	18.00
8 Dale Earnhardt RPM 1978 Dodge	7.50	15.00
8 Hut Stricklin Circuit City	6.00	15.00
9 Lake Speed Birthday Cake	7.50	15.00
9 Lake Speed Huckleberry Hound	7.50	15.00
10 Ricky Rudd Tide	7.50	15.00
18 Bobby Labonte Interstate Batteries	7.50	15.00
18 Bobby Labonte Interstate Batteries Hot Rod	7.50	15.00
18 Bobby Labonte Interstate Batteries Small Soldiers	7.50	15.00
24 Jeff Gordon DuPont	10.00	20.00
24 Jeff Gordon DuPont Chromalusion	25.00	40.00
24 Jeff Gordon DuPont No Bull	15.00	25.00
28 Kenny Irwin Havoline	9.00	18.00
28 Kenny Irwin Havoline Joker	9.00	18.00
31 Dale Earnhardt Jr. Sikkens	20.00	35.00
31 Mike Skinner Lowe's	7.50	15.00
31 Mike Skinner Lowe's Special Olympics	7.50	15.00
32 Dale Jarrett White Rain	7.50	15.00
35 Todd Bodine Tabasco Orange	7.50	15.00
35 Todd Bodine Tabasco Red	7.50	15.00
36 Ernie Irvan Skittles	7.50	15.00
41 Steve Grissom Kodiak	10.00	20.00
44 Tony Stewart Shell	7.50	15.00
44 Tony Stewart Shell Small Soldiers	7.50	15.00
50 Ricky Craven Budweiser	10.00	20.00
81 Kenny Wallace Square D	7.50	15.00
88 Dale Jarrett Quality Care	9.00	18.00
88 Dale Jarrett Quality Care Batman	9.00	18.00
90 Dick Trickle Heilig-Meyers	7.50	15.00
98 Greg Sacks Thorn Apple Valley	7.50	15.00
300 Darrell Waltrip Tim Flock Special	9.00	18.00
K2 Dale Earnhardt Dayvault's	9.00	18.00

Action/RCCA 1:64 1991 Oldsmobile Series

This series consist of 1991 Oldsmobile 1:64 scale replicas. Included is a 2 car set of Rob Moroso plus two single cars of the 1990 Winston Cup Rookie of the Year.

	Lo	Hi
20/25 Rob Moroso Swisher Sweet 2 car set	15.00	30.00
22 Ed Berrier Greased Lightning	4.00	8.00
22 Rob Moroso Moroso Racing	3.00	6.00
22 Rob Moroso Prestone	3.00	6.00
33 Harry Gant Skoal with Mug	15.00	25.00
44 Bobby Labonte Penrose	4.00	8.00
44 Sterling Marlin Piedmont	5.00	10.00
73 Phil Barkdoll XR-1	4.00	8.00
88 Buddy Baker Red Baron	4.00	8.00
91 Clifford Allison Mac Tools	10.00	20.00
93 Christmas Car Promo	7.50	15.00

Action/RCCA 1:64 1983-86 T-Bird Series

The 1:64 die cast cars that appear in this series are replicas of Thunderbirds that were driven between 1983-1986. The series has one of the few die cast of Kyle Petty's 7-Eleven. The series also has Dale Earnhardt in a Ford Thunderbird.

	Lo	Hi
7 Kyle Petty 7-Eleven	4.00	8.00
9 Bill Elliott Melling	7.50	15.00
15 Dale Earnhardt Wrangler	18.00	35.00
15 Ricky Rudd Motorcraft	3.00	6.00
21 Buddy Baker Valvoline with V on deck lid	3.00	6.00
21 Buddy Baker Valvoline with Valvoline on deck lid	10.00	20.00
21 David Pearson Black Bumper	10.00	20.00
21 David Pearson Brown Bumper	4.00	8.00
22 Bobby Allison Gold Wheels	9.00	18.00
22 Bobby Allison Silver Wheels	7.50	15.00
28 Davey Allison Havoline	10.00	20.00
28 Cale Yarborough Hardee's	3.00	6.00
35 Alan Kulwicki Quincy's Steakhouse	25.00	50.00
35 David May Hanover Printing	3.00	6.00
57 Jody Ridley Nationwise	3.00	6.00
64 Rodney Combs Sunny King with Small Numbers	4.00	8.00
64 Rodney Combs Sunny King with Big Numbers	3.00	6.00
67 Buddy Arrington Arrington Racing	3.00	6.00
70 J.D.McDuffie Lockhart	4.00	8.00
71 Dave Marcis Shoney's	3.00	6.00
90 Junie Donlavey Chameleon	3.00	6.00
90 Ken Schrader Red Baron	3.00	6.00
90 Ken Schrader Sunny King	3.00	6.00
NNO Lumina Primer hood open	6.00	10.00
NNO Pontiac Primer hood open	6.00	10.00

1993-1998 Ertl 1:18

Some of the newer pieces are often sold in 2-car sets and 3-car sets. Many of the 1:18 scale cars are commonly refered to as American Muscle. This is due to the fact that the packaging many of the cars came in said American Muscle on the box. Ertl no longer produces a line of 1:18 scale cars to be distributed by themselves but does contract work for those companies that would like to add 1:18 scales to their product lines.

	Lo	Hi
1 Davey Allison Lancaster	35.00	60.00
1 Jeff Gordon Baby Ruth	90.00	120.00
1 Rick Mast Hooter's	35.00	60.00
1/33 Rick Mast Skoal 2 car set	80.00	140.00
2 Rusty Wallace Miller Genuine Draft	100.00	160.00
2 Rusty Wallace Miller Silver car	40.00	60.00
3 Dale Earnhardt Goodwrench '93 Lumina	40.00	60.00
3 Dale Earnhardt Goodwrench '95 Monte Carlo	45.00	75.00
3 Dale Earnhardt Goodwrench 7-Time	45.00	75.00
3 Dale Earnhardt Goodwrench Silver Car	100.00	150.00
3/43 Dale Earnhardt Richard Petty 7-time Champions	75.00	110.00
3 Jeff Green Goodwrench Buck Fever	30.00	45.00
3 Mike Skinner Goodwrench	30.00	45.00
4 Ernie Irvan Kodak	30.00	45.00
4 Sterling Marlin Kodak '95 Monte Carlo	35.00	60.00
4 Sterling Marlin Kodak 1997 Monte Carlo	30.00	45.00
4/4 Sterling Marlin Jeff Purvis Kodak Funsaver	90.00	150.00
4 Dennis Sensiba Lane Automotive	30.00	50.00
5 Terry Labonte Honey Crunch distributed by GMP	100.00	175.00
5 Terry Labonte Kellogg's	30.00	45.00
5 Terry Labonte Kellogg's Silver car	40.00	70.00
6 Mark Martin Valvoline	30.00	45.00
6 Mark Martin Valvoline 1996	30.00	45.00
6 Mark Martin Valvoline 1997	30.00	60.00
7 Geoff Bodine Exide GMP	45.00	65.00
7/33/54 Harry Gant Manheim 3 Car set	150.00	200.00
7 Geoff Bodine QVC	30.00	45.00
7 Alan Kulwicki Army Buck Fever	65.00	100.00
7 Alan Kulwicki Hooters Buck Fever	70.00	110.00
7 Alan Kulwicki Zerex Buck Fever	65.00	100.00
7 Gary St.Amant Wynn's ASA	45.00	65.00
8 Jeff Burton Raybestos	20.00	35.00
8 Bobby Dotter Lubteck ASA	45.00	60.00
8 Kenny Wallace Red Dog	40.00	60.00
8 Kenny Wallace Red Dog Bank	45.00	75.00

9 Lake Speed	40.00	60.00
SPAM		
10 Derrike Cope	60.00	90.00
Purolator		
10 Ricky Rudd	45.00	65.00
Tide GMP		
11 Brett Bodine	30.00	75.00
Lowe's		
11 Bill Elliott	25.00	40.00
Budweiser		
12 Jimmy Spencer	125.00	200.00
Meineke		
White Rose Collectibles Bank		
14 John Andretti	25.00	40.00
Kanawha		
15 Geoff Bodine	75.00	125.00
Motorcraft		
16 Chad Chaffin	30.00	50.00
31W Insulation		
16 Ted Musgrave	30.00	45.00
Primestar		
17 Bill Sedgwick	30.00	50.00
Die Hard Super Truck		
17 Darrell Waltrip	30.00	45.00
Parts America		
17 Darrell Waltrip	30.00	50.00
Western Auto		
18 Dale Jarrett	25.00	40.00
Interstate Batteries		
20 Bobby Hamilton	75.00	125.00
Fina Lube Bank		
21 Bobby Bowsher	45.00	70.00
Quality Farm		
21 Doug George	30.00	45.00
Ortho Super Truck		
21 Morgan Shepherd	45.00	70.00
Cheerwine		
21 Michael Waltrip	50.00	70.00
Citgo		
23 Davey Allison	30.00	60.00
Miller American Bank		
23 Davey Allison	30.00	60.00
Miller High Life Bank		
23 Chad Little	90.00	150.00
John Deere		
23 Chad Little	350.00	600.00
John Deere Autographed		
23 Jimmy Spencer	90.00	150.00
Smokin' Joe's		
24 Jeff Gordon	45.00	75.00
DuPont '94 Lumina		
24 Jeff Gordon	45.00	75.00
DuPont '95 Buck Fever		
24 Jeff Gordon	45.00	75.00
DuPont '95 GMP		
24 Jeff Gordon	500.00	600.00
DuPont		
White Rose Collectibles Bank		
24 Jeff Gordon	80.00	140.00
DuPont		
White Rose Collectibles Bank		
No serial number on bottom		
24 Jack Sprague	30.00	50.00
Quaker State Super Truck		
25 Ken Schrader	25.00	40.00
Budweiser		
25 R.Craven/Bud Pre. Series	60.00	100.00
26 Steve Kinser	70.00	110.00
Quaker State Hood Open		
27 Tim Richmond	30.00	50.00
Old Milwaukee		
27 Rusty Wallace	50.00	75.00
Kodiak		
27 Rusty Wallace	45.00	75.00
Miller Genuine Draft		
28 Davey Allison	30.00	50.00
Havoline		
28 Davey Allison	45.00	70.00
Havoline Black and Gold Paint Scheme		
28 Davey Allison	45.00	70.00
Havoline Black and White Paint Scheme		
28 Dale Jarrett	35.00	50.00
Havoline		
28 Ernie Irvan	40.00	70.00
Havoline		
30 Johnny Benson	30.00	50.00
Pennzoil		
30 Michael Waltrip	20.00	35.00
Pennzoil		
32 Dale Jarrett	40.00	65.00
Mac Tools		
33 Harry Gant	100.00	175.00
Skoal 2 car set		
33 Brad Loney	35.00	60.00
Winnebago		
33 Brad Loney	35.00	60.00
Winnebago 1996		
33 Robert Pressley	40.00	75.00
Skoal		
36 Derrike Cope	30.00	50.00
Skittles		
37 Jeremy Mayfield	35.00	60.00
Kmart		
distributed by GMP		
37 J.Mayfield/Kmart Pre. Series	50.00	90.00
41 Ricky Craven	45.00	70.00
Kodiak GMP		
42 Andy Hillenburg	50.00	75.00
Budget Gourmet Promo Bank		
42 Kyle Petty	45.00	65.00
Coors Light GMP		
42 Kyle Petty	30.00	75.00
Coors Light WRC		
42 Kyle Petty	25.00	40.00
Mello Yello		
43 John Andretti	45.00	70.00
STP		
43 Rodney Combs	55.00	85.00
French's		
43 Rodney Combs	45.00	80.00
Hulk Hogan		
43 Bobby Hamilton	125.00	250.00
STP 5-car set		
43 Bobby Hamilton	35.00	60.00
STP Silver		
43 Richard Petty	30.00	45.00
STP		
43 Richard Petty	35.00	65.00
STP 7-Time Champion		
43 Robert Pressley	55.00	85.00
French's		
44 David Green	50.00	75.00
Slim Jim		
52 Butch Miller	35.00	50.00
Liberty Ford		
52 Ken Schrader	35.00	60.00
AC Delco GMP Bank		
52 Ken Schrader	30.00	50.00
AC Delco Super Truck		
52 Ken Schrader	30.00	50.00
AC Delco 1995		
59 Andy Belmont	40.00	60.00
Dr. Die Cast		
59 Chad Chaffin	30.00	45.00
Dr. Die Cast		
59 Robert Pressley	250.00	325.00
Alliance		
59 Dennis Setzer	40.00	60.00
Alliance '95		
2500 produced		
59 Dennis Setzer	50.00	75.00
Alliance		
5000 produced		
59 Dennis Setzer	150.00	225.00
Alliance 2 car set		
60 Mark Martin	45.00	70.00
Winn Dixie GMP		
71 Dave Marcis	45.00	70.00
Olive Garden		
75 Todd Bodine	45.00	70.00
Factory Stores		
84 Benny Senneker	60.00	90.00
Lane Automotive		
87 Joe Nemechek	45.00	65.00
Burger King GMP		
87 Joe Nemechek	140.00	200.00
Dentyne		
White Rose Collectibles Bank		
88 Dale Jarrett	30.00	45.00
Quality Care		
90 Ernie Irvan	35.00	60.00
Bulls Eye		
90 Michael Waltrip	30.00	50.00
Heilig-Meyers		
94 Ron Barfield	40.00	65.00
New Holland		
94 Bill Elliott	30.00	45.00
McDonald's		
94 Bill Elliott	30.00	45.00
McDonald's 1996		
94 Bill Elliott	35.00	60.00
McDonald's 1997		
94 B.Elliott/MT Prestige Series	60.00	90.00
94 Bill Elliott	30.00	45.00
McDonald's Thunderbat		
95 David Green	150.00	200.00
Busch 2 car set		
95 David Green	45.00	80.00
Caterpillar Bank		
95 Tim Richmond	30.00	45.00
Old Milwaukee		
96 David Green	35.00	60.00
Caterpillar GMP		
96 D.Green/Cater. Pres. Series	50.00	90.00
97 Chad Little	100.00	140.00
John Deere		
Autographed Box		
98 Jeremy Mayfield	30.00	45.00
Fingerhut		
99 Dick Trickle	30.00	50.00
Articat		

Funstuf Pit Row 1:43

These 1:43 scale cars were distributed through retail outlets. The series features a Jeff Gordon Baby Ruth BGN car.

	Lo	Hi
1 Jeff Gordon	15.00	30.00
Baby Ruth		
6 Mark Martin	2.50	5.00
Valvoline		
11 Bill Elliott	2.50	5.00
Amoco		
12 Hut Stricklin	2.50	5.00
Raybestos		
16 Wally Dallenbach Jr.	3.00	6.00
Roush Racing		
18 Dale Jarrett	2.50	5.00
Interstate Batteries		
21 Morgan Shepherd	2.50	5.00
Citgo		
22 Sterling Marlin	2.50	5.00

	Lo	Hi
Maxwell House		
33 Harry Gant	2.50	5.00
Leo Jackson Motors		
41 Greg Sacks	3.00	6.00
Kellogg's		
49 Stan Smith	2.50	5.00
Ameritron Batteries		
66 Jimmy Hensley	2.50	5.00
TropArtic		
66 Chad Little	2.50	5.00
TropArtic		
75 Joe Ruttman	2.50	5.00
Dinner Bell		
83 Jeff McClure	3.00	6.00
Collector's World		
98 Jimmy Spencer	2.50	5.00
Moly Black Gold		

Funstuf Pit Row 1:64

This series of 1:64 cars was produced by Pit Row and distributed through retail outlets. The series features a Jeff Gordon Baby Ruth BGN car. Also in the series includes a variation of the #94 Terry Labonte car. Another variation in the series is some of the cars that come with a Winston Decal and without a Winston Decal.

	Lo	Hi
1 Jeff Gordon	12.00	20.00
Baby Ruth		
11 Bill Elliott	1.00	3.00
Amoco on the Deck Lid		
11 Bill Elliott	1.00	3.00
Amoco on the Hood		
11 No Driver Association	1.00	3.00
Baby Ruth		
12 Ken Schultz	2.00	5.00
Piggly Wiggly		
15 Morgan Shepherd	1.00	3.00
Motorcraft		
15 Morgan Shepherd	3.00	7.00
Motorcraft		
with Winston Decal on Fender		
15 No Driver Association	1.00	3.00
Motorcraft		
18 Dale Jarrett	1.00	3.00
Interstate Batteries		
18 No Driver Association	1.00	3.00
Interstate Batteries		
20 Michael Waltrip	2.00	5.00
Orkin		
21 Dale Jarrett	1.00	3.00
Citgo		
21 Dale Jarrett	3.00	7.00
Citgo		
with Winston Decal on Fender		
21 Morgan Shepherd	1.00	3.00
Citgo		
23 Eddie Bierschwale	2.00	5.00
AutoFinders		
27 Ward Burton	2.00	5.00
Gaultney		
27 Jeff McClure	2.00	5.00
Race For Life		
41 Greg Sacks	2.00	5.00
Kellogg's		
43 Richard Petty	1.00	3.00
STP		
43 Richard Petty	3.00	7.00
STP		
with Winston Decal on Fender		
49 Stan Smith	3.00	7.00
Ameritron Batteries		
66 Jimmy Hensley	1.00	3.00
TropArtic		
66 Chad Little	1.00	3.00
TropArtic		
66 Lake Speed	1.00	3.00
TropArtic		
75 No Driver Association	1.00	3.00
Dinner Bell		
75 Joe Ruttman	1.00	3.00
Dinner Bell		
83 Jeff McClure	2.00	5.00
Collector's World		
94 Terry Labonte	1.00	3.00
Sunoco		
94 Terry Labonte	2.00	5.00
Sunoco with Busch decal		

1998 Hot Wheels Pro Racing 1:43

These 1:43 scale cars were produced by Hot Wheels and marks there introduction in the NASCAR market. These cars were distributed through hobby, retail and trackside outlets.

	Lo	Hi
5 Terry Labonte	6.00	15.00
Kellogg's		
6 Mark Martin	6.00	15.00
Valvoline		
10 Ricky Rudd	6.00	15.00
Tide		
12 Jeremy Mayfield	6.00	15.00
Mobil 1		
35 Todd Bodine	6.00	15.00
Tabasco		
36 Ernie Irvan	6.00	15.00
Skittles		
43 John Andretti	6.00	15.00
STP		
44 Kyle Petty	6.00	15.00
Hot Wheels		

1997 Hot Wheels Collector Edition/Speedway Edition 1:64

This series of 1:64 cars marks Hot Wheels second mass-market venture into NASCAR. These cars are the upgraded versions of those cars available in the Pro Racing series.

	Lo	Hi
4 Sterling Marlin	3.00	6.00
Kodak		
5 Terry Labonte	3.00	6.00
Kellogg's		
6 Mark Martin	3.00	6.00
Valvoline		
7 Geoff Bodine	3.00	6.00
QVC		
10 Ricky Rudd	3.00	6.00
Tide		
16 Ted Musgrave	3.00	6.00
Primestar		
21 Michael Waltrip	3.00	6.00
Citgo		
28 Ernie Irvan	3.00	6.00
Havoline		
30 Johnny Benson	3.00	6.00
Penzoil		
37 Jeremy Mayfield	3.00	6.00
Kmart		
43 Bobby Hamilton	3.00	6.00
STP		
44 Kyle Petty	3.00	6.00
Hot Wheels		
91 Mike Wallace	3.00	6.00
Spam		
94 Bill Elliott	3.00	6.00
McDonald's		
96 David Green	3.00	6.00
Caterpillar		
98 John Andretti	3.00	6.00
RCA		
99 Jeff Burton	3.00	6.00
Exide		

1998 Hot Wheels Pit Crew 1:64

These 1:64 scale cars were produced by Hot Wheels and marks there introduction in the NASCAR market. They are packaged in blister packs with their corresponding pit wagon. The gold cars from this series are valued the same as the standard cars. These cars were distributed through hobby, retail and trackside outlets.

	Lo	Hi
5 Terry Labonte	4.00	8.00
Kellogg's		
6 Mark Martin	4.00	8.00
Valvoline		
10 Ricky Rudd	4.00	8.00
Tide		
12 Jeremy Mayfield	4.00	8.00
Mobil 1		
33 Tim Fedewa	4.00	8.00
Kleenex		
36 Matt Hutter	4.00	8.00
Stanley		
43 Bobby Hamilton	4.00	8.00
STP		
44 Kyle Petty	4.00	8.00
Hot Wheels		
94 Bill Elliott	4.00	8.00
McDonald's		
97 Chad Little	4.00	8.00
John Deere		

1997 Hot Wheels Pro Racing 1:64

This series of 1:64 cars marks Hot Wheels first mass-market venture into NASCAR. These cars are packaged with cardboard backing shaped like a number one.

	Lo	Hi
4 Sterling Marlin	1.50	4.00
Kodak		
5 Terry Labonte	1.50	4.00
Kellogg's		
6 Mark Martin	1.50	4.00
Valvoline		
7 Geoff Bodine	1.50	4.00
QVC		
10 Ricky Rudd	1.50	4.00
Tide		
16 Ted Musgrave	1.50	4.00
Primestar		
21 Michael Waltrip	1.50	4.00
Citgo		
28 Ernie Irvan	1.50	4.00
Havoline		
28 Erine Irvan	20.00	30.00
Hot Wheels Super Truck		
30 Johnny Benson	1.50	4.00
Penzoil		
37 Jeremy Mayfield	1.50	4.00
Kmart		
43 Bobby Hamilton	1.50	4.00
STP		
44 Kyle Petty	1.50	4.00
Hot Wheels		
44 Kyle Petty	10.00	25.00
Hot Wheels Blue Box		
91 Mike Wallace	1.50	4.00
Spam		
94 Bill Elliott	1.50	4.00
McDonald's		
96 David Green	1.50	4.00
Caterpillar		
98 John Andretti	1.50	4.00
RCA		
99 Jeff Burton	1.50	4.00
Exide		

1998 Hot Wheels Test Track 1:64

These 1:64 scale cars were produced by Hot Wheels and marks there introduction in the NASCAR market. They are packaged in blister packs and have primer coating as most test cars do. These cars were distributed through hobby and retail.

	Lo	Hi
4 Bobby Hamilton Kodak	2.50	5.00
6 Mark Martin Valvoline	2.50	5.00
10 Ricky Rudd Tide	2.50	5.00
28 Kenny Irwin Havoline	2.50	5.00
43 John Andretti STP	2.50	5.00
44 Kyle Petty Hot Wheels	2.50	5.00
99 Jeff Burton Exide	2.50	5.00

1998 Hot Wheels Track Edition 1:64

These 1:64 scale cars were produced by Hot Wheels and marks there introduction in the NASCAR market. They are packaged in black boxes. These cars were distributed through hobby and trackside outlets.

	Lo	Hi
4 Bobby Hamilton Kodak	8.00	20.00
5 Terry Labonte Kellogg's	10.00	20.00
6 Mark Martin Eagle One	12.00	30.00
6 Mark Martin Synpower	10.00	20.00
6 Mark Martin Valvoline	10.00	20.00
10 Ricky Rudd Tide	8.00	20.00
12 Jeremy Mayfield Mobil 1	10.00	20.00
13 Jerry Nadeau First Plus	8.00	20.00
26 Johnny Benson Cheerios	8.00	20.00
30 Derrike Cope Gumout	8.00	20.00
35 Todd Bodine Tabasco	8.00	20.00
36 Ernie Irvan Skittles	8.00	20.00
40 Sterling Marlin Sabco	8.00	20.00
42 Joe Nemechek Bell South	8.00	20.00
43 John Andretti Players Inc.	10.00	20.00
43 John Andretti STP	8.00	20.00
44 Kyle Petty Blues Brothers 2000	10.00	25.00
44 Kyle Petty Hot Wheels	8.00	20.00
44 Kyle Petty Players Inc.	10.00	25.00
50 Ricky Craven Hendrick	8.00	20.00
50 No Driver Association Boy Scouts	8.00	20.00
90 Dick Trickle Heilig-Meyers	8.00	20.00
94 Bill Elliott McDonald's	10.00	20.00

1990-1992 Matchbox White Rose 1:64 Super Stars Series 1

The was the first series of NASCAR replica cars distributed by White Rose. The cars were produced by Matchbox. They come in either a blister package, a box or a polybag.

	Lo	Hi
1 Jeff Gordon Baby Ruth Orange Lettering '92 BX	10.00	20.00
1 Jeff Gordon Baby Ruth Red Lettering '92 BX	6.00	12.00
2 Rusty Wallace Penske '92 BL	2.00	5.00
3 Dale Earnhardt GM '90 BX	28.00	50.00
3 Dale Earnhardt GM Parts '91 BX	15.00	30.00
3 Dale Earnhardt Goodwrench '92 BL	6.00	12.00
3 Dale Earnhardt Mom-n-Pop's '92 polly bag	5.00	10.00
4 Ernie Irvan Kodak '92 BL	2.00	5.00
7 Harry Gant Mac Tools '92 BX	4.00	8.00
7 Jimmy Hensley White Rose Collectibles '92 BX	4.00	8.00
7 Alan Kulwicki Hooters '92 BL	15.00	25.00
7 Alan Kulwicki Hooters Naturally Fresh '92 BL	10.00	16.00
8 Jeff Burton TIC Financial '92 BX	1.50	4.00
8 Dick Trickle Snicker's '92 BL	1.50	4.00
9 No Driver Association Melling '92 BL	1.50	4.00
10 Derrike Cope Purolator '92 BL	1.50	4.00
10 Ernie Irvan Mac Tools '91 BX	10.00	20.00
11 Bill Elliott Amoco '92 BL	1.50	4.00
12 Hut Stricklin Raybestos '92 BL	1.50	4.00
15 No Driver Association Motorcraft '92 BL	1.50	4.00
15 Morgan Shepherd Motorcraft '92 BL	1.50	4.00
18 Dale Jarrett Interstate Batteries '92 BL	1.50	4.00
22 Sterling Marlin Maxwell House '92 BL	1.50	4.00
26 Brett Bodine Quaker State '92 BL	1.50	4.00
28 Davey Allison Havoline '92 BL	7.50	15.00
28 Davey Allison Havoline Mac Tools '92 BL	7.50	15.00
29 No Driver Association Matchbox Racing White Rose Collectibles '92 BX	2.50	5.00
29 Phil Parsons Parsons Racing '92 BX	10.00	20.00
30 Michael Waltrip Pennzoil '92 BL	1.50	4.00
41 James Smith White House Apple Juice '92 BL	2.00	5.00
42 Kyle Petty Mello Yello '92 BL	1.50	4.00
43 Richard Petty STP '92 BL	1.50	4.00
44 Bobby Labonte Penrose '92 BX	4.00	8.00
44 Bobby Labonte Slim Jim '92 BX	4.00	8.00
48 James Hylton Valtrol '92 BL	1.50	4.00
49 Ed Feree Fergaed Racing '92 BX	1.50	4.00
55 Ted Musgrave Jasper Engines		
66 Chad Little Phillips 66 red car '92 BL	1.50	4.00
66 No Driver Association Phillips 66 black car '92 BL	1.50	4.00
68 Bobby Hamilton Country Time '92 BL	1.50	4.00
87 Joe Nemechek Texas Pete '92 BX	1.50	4.00
89 Jim Sauter Evinrude '92 BL	1.50	4.00
92 No Driver Association White Rose Collectibles '92 BL	25.00	35.00
92 Hut Stricklin Stanley Tools '92 BX	2.00	4.00

1993 Matchbox White Rose 1:64 Super Stars Series 1

This series features six Jimmy Hensley cars honoring many of the sponsors of the number 7 car. Each piece either comes in a blister package or a box. The year is on the end of each of the box packages.

	Lo	Hi
1 Rodney Combs Luxaire BL	10.00	18.00
1 Rodney Combs Goody's BX	9.00	16.00
6 Mark Martin Valvoline BX	3.00	5.00
7 Jimmy Hensley Bobsled BX	5.00	9.00
7 Jimmy Hensley Bojangles BL	5.00	9.00
7 Jimmy Hensley Cellular One BX	5.00	9.00
7 Jimmy Hensley Family Channel BX	5.00	9.00
7 Jimmy Hensley Hanes BX	5.00	9.00
7 Jimmy Hensley Matchbox BX	5.00	9.00
8 Jeff Burton TIC Financal BX	1.50	4.00
8 Jeff Burton Baby Ruth BX	1.50	4.00
8 Sterling Marlin Raybestos BL	1.50	4.00
8 Bobby Dotter Dewalt BX	1.50	4.00
9 Michael Wallace FDP Brakes BX	1.50	4.00
12 Jimmy Spencer Meineke BL	1.50	4.00
14 Terry Labonte MW Windows BX	1.50	4.00
21 Morgan Shepherd Citgo BL	1.50	4.00
22 Bobby Labonte Maxwell House BL	1.50	4.00
24 Jeff Gordon DuPont BL	6.00	10.00
25 Hermie Sadler VA is for Lovers BX	1.50	4.00
28 Davey Allison Havoline BL	10.00	18.00
29 Phil Parsons Matchbox BL	1.50	4.00
31 Bobby Hillin Team Ireland BL	1.50	4.00
32 Jimmy Horton Active Racing BL	1.50	4.00
32 Dale Jarrett Pic-N-Pay BX	1.50	4.00
40 Kenny Wallace Dirt Devil BL	1.50	4.00
41 Phil Parsons Manheim BL	1.50	4.00
48 Sterling Marlin Cappio BX	1.50	4.00
69 James Sparker WFE Challenge BL	6.00	12.00
71 Dave Marcis Enick's Catering BL	1.50	4.00
83 Lake Speed Purex	1.50	4.00
87 Joe Nemechek	1.50	4.00

Dentyne		
93 No Driver Association	20.00	35.00
White Rose Collectibles BL		
93 No Driver Association	4.00	8.00
American Zoom poly bag		
94 Terry Labonte	1.50	4.00
Sunoco BL		
98 Derrike Cope	1.50	4.00
Bojangles BL		
98 Jimmy Spencer	1.50	4.00
Moly Black Gold BL		
99 Ricky Craven	1.50	4.00
DuPont BX		

1994 Matchbox White Rose 1:64 Super Stars Series 2

This is considered the second Super Stars Series distributed by White Rose Collectibles. There were speical cars issued that featured Future Cup Stars and drivers who won Super Star Awards. The boxes for the Future Cup Stars' cars is different from the regular Series 2 boxes. The Super Star Awards cars come in a jewelry type box and the car is gold.

	Lo	Hi
0 Jeff Burton	5.00	9.00
TIC Financial		
Future Cup Stars '94 BX		
2 Ricky Craven	2.00	4.00
DuPont BX		
2 Rusty Wallace	3.00	5.00
Ford Motorsports BX		
3 Dale Earnhardt	18.00	30.00
Gold Lumina		
Super Star Awards		
4 Sterling Marlin	2.00	4.00
Kodak BX		
4 Sterling Marlin	2.00	4.00
Kodak FunSaver BX		
5 Terry Labonte	2.00	4.00
Kellogg's BX		
6 Mark Martin	2.00	4.00
Valvoline BX		
7 Geoff Bodine	4.00	8.00
Exide BX		
7 Harry Gant	2.00	4.00
Manheim BX		
8 Jeff Burton	2.00	4.00
Raybestos BX		
12 Derrike Cope	2.00	4.00
Straight Arrow BX		
15 Lake Speed	2.00	4.00
Quality Care BX		
16 Ted Musgrave	2.00	4.00
Family Channel BX		
17 Darrell Waltrip	2.00	4.00
Western Auto BX		
19 Loy Allen	2.00	4.00
Hooters BX		
23 Hut Stricklin	12.00	20.00
Smokin' Joe's BX		
24 Jeff Gordon	4.00	8.00
DuPont BX		
26 Brett Bodine	2.00	4.00
Quaker State BX		
29 Phil Parsons	12.00	20.00
Baltimore CFL BL		
29 Phil Parsons	2.00	4.00
Matchbox White Rose Collectibles BX		
30 Michael Waltrip	2.00	4.00
Pennzoil BX		
32 Dale Jarrett	2.00	4.00
Pic-N-Pay BX		
33 Harry Gant	14.00	22.00
Gold Lumina		
Super Star Awards		
34 Mike McLaughlin	2.00	4.00
Fiddle Faddle BL		
37 Loy Allen	4.00	8.00
Naturally Fresh		
Future Cup Stars '94 BX		
40 Bobby Hamilton	2.00	4.00
Kendall BX		
41 Joe Nemechek	2.00	4.00
Meineke BX		
43 Rodney Combs	4.00	8.00
Black Flag BX		
43 Rodney Combs	15.00	25.00
French's Black Flag BL		
43 Rodney Combs	4.00	8.00
French's BX		
46 Shawna Robinson	7.50	15.00
Polaroid BL		
52 Ken Schrader	2.00	4.00
AC Delco BX		
55 Jimmy Hensley	7.50	15.00
Petron Plus BL		
60 Mark Martin	5.00	10.00
Winn Dixie BX		
66 Michael Wallace	4.00	8.00
Duron Paint		
Future Cup Stars '94 BX		
75 Todd Bodine	2.00	4.00
Factory Stores of America BX		
87 Joe Nemechek	4.00	8.00
Cintas		
Future Cup Stars '94 BX		
92 Larry Pearson	2.00	4.00
Stanley Tools BX		
94 No Driver Association	15.00	25.00
Matchbox White Rose Collectibles BL		
94 No Driver Association	4.00	8.00
Series 2 preview BX		
98 Derrike Cope	2.00	4.00
Fingerhut BX		

1995 Matchbox White Rose 1:64 Super Stars Series 2

This is the continuation of the second Super Stars Series. The boxes the cars come each of the year on the end of them. The Super Star Awards cars again come in a special box and are gold.

	Lo	Hi
1 Hermie Sadler	3.00	5.00
DeWalt		
2 Ricky Craven	3.00	5.00
DuPont		
3 Dale Earnhardt	18.00	30.00
Gold 7-Time Champion		
Super Star Awards		
3 Dale Earnhardt	4.00	8.00
Goodwrench		
5 Terry Labonte	3.00	5.00
Kellogg's		
6 Mark Martin	3.00	5.00
Valvoline		
7 Geoff Bodine	3.00	5.00
Exide		
8 Jeff Burton	3.00	5.00
Raybestos		
8 Jeff Burton	10.00	18.00
Raybestos		
Super Star Awards		
8 Bobby Dotter	3.00	5.00
Hyde Tools		
11 Brett Bodine	3.00	5.00
Lowe's		
12 Derrike Cope	3.00	5.00
Straight Arrow		
18 Bobby Labonte	3.00	5.00
Interstate Batteries		
24 Jeff Gordon	4.00	8.00
DuPont		
24 York	6.00	10.00
Cobra Promo		
25 Ken Schrader	8.00	16.00
Budweiser in Acrylic Case		
26 Steve Kinser	3.00	5.00
Quaker State		
28 Dale Jarrett	3.00	5.00
Havoline		
40 Patty Moise	3.00	5.00
Dial Purex		
42 Kyle Petty	7.50	15.00
Coors Light in Acrylic Case		
57 Jason Keller	3.00	5.00
Budget Gourmet		
71 Kevin Lepage	3.00	5.00
Vermont Teddy Bear		
72 Tracy Leslie	3.00	5.00
Detroit Gasket		
74 Johnny Benson Jr.	3.00	5.00
Lipton Tea		
87 Joe Nemechek	7.50	15.00
Bell South		
87 Joe Nemechek	3.00	5.00
Burger King		
90 Michael Wallace	3.00	5.00
Heilig-Meyers		
94 Bill Elliott	10.00	18.00
Gold Thunderbird		
Super Star Awards		
94 Bill Elliott	3.00	5.00
McDonald's		
94 Bill Elliott	8.00	16.00
McDonald's Thunderbat		
95 John Tanner	3.00	5.00
Caterpillar		
99 Phil Parsons	3.00	5.00
Luxaire		

1995 Matchbox White Rose 1:64 SuperTrucks

This is the first series of SuperTrucks that White Rose Collectibles distributed.

	Lo	Hi
1 Mike Chase	3.00	5.00
Sears Diehard		
3 Mike Skinner	3.00	5.00
Goodwrench		
6 Rick Carelli	3.00	5.00
Total		
24 Scott Lagasse	3.00	5.00
DuPont		

1996 Matchbox White Rose 1:64 Super Stars

This series of 1:64 replicas features four Super Star Awards cars. The cars are gold in color and feature winners of the SuperTruck series, the Winston Cup Rookie of the Year and the Busch Grand National winner.

	Lo	Hi
4 Sterling Marlin Kodak	3.00	5.00
5 Terry Labonte Kellogg's	3.00	6.00
6 Mark Martin Valvoline	3.00	5.00
9 Lake Speed SPAM	3.00	5.00
10 Ricky Rudd Tide	3.00	5.00
12 Derrike Cope Badcock Promo	5.00	10.00
15 Wally Dallenbach Hayes Promo	5.00	10.00
16 Ted Musgrave Family Channel	3.00	5.00
21 Michael Waltrip Citgo	3.00	5.00
22 Ward Burton MBNA	3.00	5.00
24 Jeff Gordon DuPont SSA	15.00	25.00
24 Jeff Gordon DuPont	4.00	8.00
34 Mike McLaughlin Royal Oak	3.00	5.00
37 John Andretti K-Mart	3.00	5.00
40 Tim Fedewa Kleenex	3.00	5.00
41 Ricky Craven Gold Monte Carlo Super Star Awards	10.00	18.00
41 Ricky Craven Kodiak	3.00	5.00
43 Rodney Combs Lance's	3.00	5.00
74 Johnny Benson Jr. Gold Super Star Awards	10.00	18.00
87 Joe Nemechek Bell South Promo	5.00	10.00
87 Joe Nemechek Burger King	3.00	5.00
88 Dale Jarrett Quality Care	3.00	5.00
94 Ron Barfield New Holland	3.00	5.00
94 Bill Elliott McDonald's	3.00	5.00
95 David Green Caterpiller	3.00	5.00
99 Jeff Burton Exide	3.00	5.00

1996 Matchbox White Rose 1:64 SuperTrucks

This is the second series of SuperTrucks that White Rose distributed.

	Lo	Hi
0 Rick Eckart Rayvest Promo	4.00	8.00
2 Mike Bliss ASE	3.00	5.00
3 Mike Skinner Gold Super Star Awards	10.00	18.00
10 Phil Parsons Channellock	3.00	5.00
21 Toby Butler Ortho	3.00	5.00
24 Jack Sprague Quaker State	3.00	5.00

1997 Matchbox White Rose 1:64 Super Stars

This series of 1:64 replicas features two Super Star Awards cars and three other cars packaged in glass bottles. The most unique car from this series is that of Rick Mast which is packaged in a glass replica of a shotgun shell.

	Lo	Hi
2 Rusty Wallace Miller Lite packaged in a bottle	50.00	75.00
5 Terry Labonte Kellogg's	4.00	6.00
5 Terry Labonte Kellogg's SSA Gold	15.00	25.00
25 Ricky Craven Budweiser packaged in a bottle	40.00	60.00
36 Derrike Cope Skittles	3.00	5.00
40 Robby Gordon Coors Light packaged in a bottle	40.00	60.00
74 Randy Lajoie Fina	3.00	5.00
74 Randy Lajoie Fina SSA Gold	10.00	20.00
75 Rick Mast Remington packaged in a shotgun shell	35.00	50.00
88 Kevin Lepage Hype	3.00	5.00
94 Bill Elliott McDonald's	3.00	5.00
95 David Green Caterpillar	3.00	5.00

1996 Press Pass 1:24

Card manufactuer Press Pass ventured into die-cast with these two pieces. Each piece is a boxed set containing a 1:24 bank produced by Action, a 1:64 hood opened car produced by Action, and one Burning Rubber card produced by Press Pass. Each of the pieces were done in a quantity of 1,996.

	Lo	Hi
2 Rusty Wallace Miller Silver car	100.00	170.00
5 Terry Labonte Kellogg's Silver car	100.00	170.00

Raceway Replicas 1:24

This manufacturer of high end 1:24 scale die cast replicas has produced this series of four cars. The cars are sold directly to the public usually through ads in racing publications.

	Lo	Hi
4 Sterling Marlin Kodak 1996	105.00	130.00
6 Mark Martin Valvoline 1994	105.00	130.00
11 Bill Elliott Budweiser 1992	105.00	130.00
27 Hut Stricklin McDonald's 1993	105.00	130.00
28 Davey Allison Havoline 1993	105.00	130.00
96 David Green Caterpillar 1997	105.00	130.00

1995-1996 Racing Champions 1:18

This series of 1:18 scale cars were the first entries into the 1:18 scale size by manufacturer Racing Champions. The cars were sold through retail outlets and through hobby shops.

	Lo	Hi
2 Ricky Craven DuPont	15.00	30.00
2 Rusty Wallace MGD	15.00	30.00
4 Sterling Marlin Kodak	15.00	30.00
5 Terry Labonte Bayer	15.00	30.00
9 Joe Bessey Delco Remy	15.00	30.00
15 Wally Dallenbach Hayes Modems	20.00	40.00
16 Ted Musgrave Primestar	15.00	30.00
17 Darrell Waltrip Western Auto	15.00	30.00
18 Bobby Labonte Interstate Batteries	15.00	30.00
22 Ward Burton MBNA	15.00	30.00
24 Jeff Gordon DuPont	20.00	40.00
24 Jeff Gordon DuPont Signature Series	20.00	40.00
25 Ken Schrader Budweiser	15.00	30.00
25 Ken Schrader Budweiser Hood Open	25.00	50.00
25 Ken Schrader Budweiser Hood Open Chrome	200.00	400.00
29 Steve Grissom Cartoon Network	15.00	30.00
30 Johnny Benson Pennzoil	15.00	30.00
31 Mike Skinner Realtree Hood Open	50.00	90.00
34 Mike McLaughlin Royal Oak	15.00	30.00
43 Bobby Hamilton STP Silver car	20.00	35.00
43 Bobby Hamilton STP 5 car set	90.00	180.00
47 Jeff Fuller Sunoco	15.00	30.00
51 Chuck Bown Lucks	15.00	30.00
52 Ken Schrader AC Delco	15.00	30.00
57 Jim Bown Matco	20.00	40.00
57 Jason Keller Halloween Havoc	15.00	30.00
57 Jason Keller Slim Jim	15.00	30.00
74 Johnny Benson Lipton Tea	15.00	30.00
87 Joe Nemechek Burger King	15.00	30.00
88 Dale Jarrett Quality Care	15.00	30.00
94 Bill Elliott McDonald's Monopoly	15.00	30.00
97 Chad Little Sterling Cowboy	15.00	30.00

1996 Racing Champions SuperTrucks 1:18

This is a 1:18 scale series of SuperTrucks. The Mike Skinner piece is available both in a hood open version and the regular hood sealed version.

	Lo	Hi
2 Mike Bliss ASE	15.00	30.00
3 Mike Skinner Goodwrench	25.00	40.00
3 Mike Skinner Goodwrench Hood Open	30.00	45.00
6 Rick Carelli Total	15.00	30.00
7 Geoff Bodine QVC	15.00	30.00

	Lo	Hi
9 Joe Bessey New Hampshire Speedway	15.00	30.00
14 Butch Gilliland Stroppe	15.00	30.00
17 Bill Sedgwick Die Hard	15.00	30.00
17 Darrell Waltrip Western Auto	25.00	40.00
20 Walker Evans Dana	15.00	30.00
21 Doug George Ortho	15.00	30.00
24 Jack Sprague Quaker State	15.00	30.00
29 Bob Keselowski Winnebago	15.00	30.00
30 Jimmy Hensley Mopar	15.00	30.00
35 Bill Venturini Rain X	15.00	30.00
43 Rich Bickle Cummins	15.00	30.00
52 Ken Schrader AC Delco	25.00	40.00
75 Bobby Gill Spears	15.00	30.00
83 Steve Portenga Coffee Critic	15.00	30.00
98 Butch Miller Raybestos	15.00	30.00

1997 Racing Champions 1:18

This series of cars is highlighted by the Premier Gold cars. These cars were distributed through hobby outlets. There are 166 of each of the gold cars.

	Lo	Hi
2 Rusty Wallace Miller Lite Gold	200.00	400.00
2 Rusty Wallace Miller Lite Hobby	30.00	60.00
6 Mark Martin Valvoline Gold	200.00	400.00
6 Mark Martin Valvoline Hobby	30.00	60.00
10 Ricky Rudd Tide Gold	175.00	350.00
10 Ricky Rudd Tide Hobby	25.00	50.00
17 Darrell Waltrip Parts America Chrome	35.00	60.00
18 Bobby Labonte Interstate Batteries Gold	175.00	350.00
18 Bobby Labonte Interstate Batteries Hobby	25.00	50.00
36 Derrike Cope Skittles Gold	175.00	350.00
36 Derrike Cope Skittles Hobby	25.00	50.00
75 Rick Mast Remington Gold	175.00	350.00
75 Rick Mast Remington Hobby	25.00	50.00
94 Bill Elliott McDonald's Gold	200.00	400.00
94 Bill Elliott McDonald's Hobby	30.00	60.00
96 David Green Caterpillar Promo	25.00	40.00

1997 Racing Champions SuperTrucks 1:18

This is the series edition of 1:18 SuperTrucks released by Racing Champions.

	Lo	Hi
2 Mike Bliss Team ASE	15.00	30.00
07 Tammy Jo Kirk Loveable	15.00	30.00
15 Mike Cope Penrose	15.00	30.00
18 Mike Dokken Dana	15.00	30.00
24 Jack Sprague Quaker State	15.00	30.00
44 Boris Said Federated Auto	15.00	30.00
66 Bryan Reffner Carlin	15.00	30.00
75 Dan Press Spears	15.00	30.00
80 Joe Ruttman LCI	15.00	30.00
87 Joe Nemechek BellSouth	15.00	30.00

1998 Racing Champions 1:18 Gold Hood Open

This is a special series produced by Racing Champions to celebrate NASCAR's 50th anniversary. Each car is a limited edition of 1,998. Each car is also plated in gold chrome and contains a serial number on its chassis.

	Lo	Hi
4 Bobby Hamilton Kodak	30.00	60.00
5 Terry Labonte Kellogg's	60.00	100.00
30 Derrike Cope Gumout	30.00	60.00
33 Ken Schrader Petree	30.00	60.00
35 Todd Bodine Tabasco	30.00	60.00
36 Ernie Irvan Skittles	40.00	80.00

1991-1992 Racing Champions 1:24

This series of 1:24 cars features some of the most expensive and toughest to find die cast pieces. The pieces were packaged in a black box and were distributed through retail outlets and hobby shops. The Kenny Wallace Dirt Devil car and the Cox Lumber car are the two toughest to come by.

	Lo	Hi
1 Jeff Gordon Baby Ruth	600.00	1000.00
1 Rick Mast Majik Market	25.00	40.00
2 Rusty Wallace AC Delco	25.00	40.00
2 Rusty Wallace Pontiac Excitement	25.00	40.00
3 Dale Earnhardt Goodwrench with Fender Stickers	10.00	22.00
3 Dale Earnhardt Goodwrench with Tampo Decals	15.00	30.00
4 Ernie Irvan Kodak	8.00	20.00
5 Ricky Rudd Tide	8.00	20.00
6 Mark Martin Valvoline	12.50	25.00
7 Harry Gant Morema	30.00	50.00
7 No Driver Association Easy Off	30.00	50.00
7 No Driver Association French's	35.00	60.00
7 No Driver Association Gulf Lite	35.00	60.00
7 Jimmy Hensley Bojangles	30.00	50.00
7 Tommy Kendall Family Channel	30.00	50.00
7 Alan Kulwicki Hooters	90.00	150.00
9 J.Bessey/AC Delco	350.00	600.00
9 Bill Elliott Melling	20.00	40.00
10 Derrike Cope Purolator	8.00	20.00
11 Bill Elliott Amoco	10.00	22.00
15 Geoff Bodine Motorcraft	8.00	20.00
15 Morgan Shepherd Motorcraft	8.00	20.00
16 Wally Dallenbach Jr. Roush Racing	35.00	60.00
17 Darrell Waltrip Western Auto with Fender Stickers	8.00	20.00
17 Darrell Waltrip Western Auto with Tampo Decals	12.50	25.00
18 Dale Jarrett Interstate Batteries	12.50	25.00
18 Greg Trammell Melling	8.00	20.00
21 Dale Jarrett Citgo	8.00	20.00
21 Morgan Shepherd Citgo	8.00	20.00
22 Sterling Marlin Maxwell House	8.00	20.00
25 Ken Schrader No Sponsor with Large K on roof	15.00	30.00
25 Ken Schrader No Sponsor	8.00	20.00
25 Bill Venturini Rain X	300.00	500.00
28 Davey Allison Havoline	15.00	30.00
30 Michael Waltrip Pennzoil	8.00	20.00
33 Harry Gant No Sponsor Oldsmobile	20.00	40.00
33 Harry Gant No Sponsor Chevrolet	15.00	30.00
36 Kenny Wallace Cox Lumber	150.00	300.00
36 Kenny Wallace Dirt Devil	250.00	400.00
42 Bobby Hillin Mello Yello	20.00	40.00
42 Kyle Petty Mello Yello	15.00	30.00
43 Richard Petty STP with Blue Wheels	15.00	25.00
49 Stanley Smith Ameritron Batteries	250.00	400.00
51 No Driver Association Racing Champions	90.00	160.00
55 T.Musgrave/Jasper	600.00	1000.00
59 Andy Belmont FDP Brakes	300.00	500.00
60 Mark Martin Winn Dixie with Red Numbers	125.00	200.00
60 Mark Martin Winn Dixie with White Numbers	60.00	100.00
63 Chuck Bown Nescafe	500.00	800.00
66 Jimmy Hensley TropArtic	10.00	22.00
66 Chad Little TropArtic	10.00	22.00
66 No Driver Association TropArtic Red Car	12.50	25.00
66 Cale Yarborough TropArtic	10.00	20.00
68 Bobby Hamilton Country Time	15.00	30.00
70 J.D. McDuffie Son's Auto	8.00	20.00
71 Dave Marcis Big Apple Market	8.00	20.00
75 Butch Miller Food Country	250.00	400.00
83 Lake Speed Purex	125.00	175.00
87 Joe Nemechek Texas Pete	250.00	400.00
94 Terry Labonte Sunoco	15.00	30.00
94 Terry Labonte Sunoco Arrow on decal points at tire	20.00	40.00

1993 Racing Champions 1:24

These 1:24 scale cars come in a Red box and feature some of the top names in racing.

	Lo	Hi
2 Davey Allison	50.00	80.00
True Value IROC car		
2 Rusty Wallace	15.00	25.00
Pontiac Excitement		
3 Dale Earnhardt	12.00	22.00
Goodwrench		
Goodyear in White		
3 Dale Earnhardt	12.00	22.00
Goodwrench		
Goodyear in Yellow		
3 Dale Earnhardt	12.00	22.00
Goodwrench		
Mom-n-Pop's		
4 Ernie Irvan	8.00	20.00
Kodak Gold Film		
4 Ernie Irvan	8.00	20.00
Kodak Gold Film Plus		
5 Ricky Rudd	8.00	20.00
Tide Exxon		
5 Ricky Rudd	8.00	20.00
Tide Valvoline		
6 Mark Martin	12.00	22.00
Valvoline		
7 Alan Kulwicki	40.00	75.00
Hooters		
8 Sterling Marlin	8.00	20.00
Raybestos		
8 Sterling Marlin	12.00	22.00
Raybestos Douglas Batteries		
10 Bill Elliott	12.00	22.00
True Value IROC car		
11 Bill Elliott	12.00	20.00
Amoco		
12 Jimmy Spencer	8.00	20.00
Meineke		
14 Terry Labonte	75.00	125.00
Kellogg's		
15 Geoff Bodine	8.00	20.00
Motorcraft		
17 Darrell Waltrip	8.00	20.00
Western Auto		
18 Dale Jarrett	12.00	20.00
Interstate Batteries		
21 Morgan Shepherd	8.00	20.00
Citgo		
Red Pillar Post		
21 Morgan Shepherd	8.00	20.00
Citgo		
Tri-color Pillar Post		
22 Bobby Labonte	20.00	35.00
Maxwell House		
24 Jeff Gordon	30.00	60.00
DuPont		
25 Ken Schrader	20.00	40.00
No Sponsor		
26 Brett Bodine	8.00	20.00
Quaker State		
27 Hut Sticklin	8.00	20.00
McDonald's		
28 Davey Allison	15.00	30.00
Havoline		
Black and Gold paint scheme		
28 Davey Allison	20.00	35.00
Havoline		
Black and White paint scheme		
30 Michael Waltrip	17.50	35.00
Pennzoil		
42 Kyle Petty	15.00	30.00
Mello Yello		
44 Rick Wilson	8.00	20.00
STP		
49 Stanley Smith	75.00	125.00
Ameritron Batteries		
59 Andy Belmont	60.00	100.00
FDP Brakes		
60 Mark Martin	12.00	22.00
Winn Dixie		
75 No Driver Association	15.00	25.00
Auto Value		
75 No Driver Association	8.00	20.00
Factory Stores		
87 Joe Nemechek	8.00	20.00
Dentyne		
98 Derrike Cope	12.50	25.00
Bojangles		

1994 Racing Champions 1:24

These 1:24 scale cars were mostly available in red boxes but some could be found in black boxes. The cars were distributed through both hobby and retail outlets.

	Lo	Hi
0 D.McCabe	12.00	20.00
Fisher Snow Plows		
1 Rick Mast	8.00	16.00
Percision Products		
2 Ricky Craven	8.00	16.00
DuPont		
2 Rusty Wallace	10.00	20.00
Ford Motorsports		
Black Ford Oval		
2 Rusty Wallace	10.00	20.00
Ford Motorsports		
Blue Ford Oval		
3 Dale Earnhardt	12.00	24.00
Goodwrench		
4 Sterling Marlin	8.00	16.00
Kodak		
5 Terry Labonte	15.00	25.00
Kellogg's		
6 Mark Martin	10.00	18.00
Valvoline Reese's		
7 Geoff Bodine	8.00	16.00
Exide		
7 Harry Gant	15.00	25.00
Manheim		
7 Alan Kulwicki	20.00	35.00
Zerex		
8 Jeff Burton	8.00	16.00
Raybestos		
with Goodyear tires		
8 Jeff Burton	8.00	16.00
Raybestos		
with Hoosier tires		
8 Kenny Wallace	10.00	20.00
TIC Financial		
12 Clifford Allison	18.00	30.00
Sports Image		
14 John Andretti	15.00	25.00
Kanawha		
14 Terry Labonte	25.00	40.00
MW Windows		
15 Lake Speed	8.00	16.00
Quality Care		
16 Chad Chaffin	10.00	18.00
Dr. Die Cast		
16 Ted Musgrave	10.00	18.00
Family Channel		
17 Darrell Waltrip	8.00	16.00
Western Auto		
18 Dale Jarrett	9.00	18.00
Interstate Batteries		
19 Loy Allen	8.00	16.00
Hooters		
20 Bobby Hillin	10.00	20.00
Fina		
20 Randy LaJoie	12.00	22.00
Fina		
21 Morgan Shepherd	8.00	16.00
Citgo		
22 Bobby Labonte	12.00	20.00
Maxwell House		
23 Chad Little	8.00	16.00
Bayer		
23 Hut Stricklin	20.00	35.00
Smokin' Joe's		
24 Jeff Gordon	35.00	60.00
Coca-Cola Winner		
24 Jeff Gordon	35.00	60.00
DuPont		
Brickyard Special Purple Box		
24 Jeff Gordon	12.00	24.00
DuPont		
24 Jeff Gordon	12.00	24.00
DuPont Snickers		
25 Ken Schrader	25.00	40.00
GMAC		
26 Brett Bodine	8.00	16.00
Quaker State		
27 Jimmy Spencer	8.00	16.00
McDonald's		
28 Ernie Irvan	12.00	22.00
Havoline		
30 Michael Waltrip	8.00	16.00
Pennzoil		
31 Steve Grissom	10.00	20.00
Channellock		
31 Tom Peck	8.00	16.00
Channellock		
33 Harry Gant	10.00	18.00
No Sponsor		
33 Harry Gant	10.00	18.00
Leo Jackson Motorsports		
33 Harry Gant	20.00	35.00
Manheim Auctions		
33 Bobby Labonte	8.00	16.00
Dentyne		
34 Mike McLaughlin	10.00	20.00
Fiddle Faddle		
35 Shawna Robinson	10.00	20.00
Polaroid Captiva		
38 Elton Sawyer	8.00	16.00
Ford Credit		
40 Bobby Hamilton	8.00	16.00
Kendall		
42 Kyle Petty	10.00	20.00
Mello Yello		
44 David Green	10.00	20.00
Slim Jim		
44 Bobby Hillin	8.00	16.00
Buss Fuses		
46 Shawna Robinson	10.00	20.00
Polaroid		
52 Ken Schrader	10.00	20.00
AC Delco		
54 Robert Pressley	10.00	20.00
Manheim		
59 Andy Belmont	10.00	20.00
Metal Arrester		
59 Dennis Setzer	18.00	30.00
Alliance		
60 Mark Martin	15.00	25.00
Winn Dixie		

	Lo	Hi
63 Jim Bown Lysol	8.00	16.00
70 J.D. McDuffie Son's Auto	8.00	16.00
75 Todd Bodine Factory Stores of America	8.00	16.00
79 David Rezendes Lipton Tea	10.00	20.00
83 Sherry Blakley Ramses	15.00	30.00
92 Larry Pearson Stanley Tools	8.00	16.00
94 No Driver Association Auto Value	15.00	25.00
94 No Driver Association Brickyard 400 Purple Box	15.00	30.00
97 Joe Bessey Johnson	8.00	16.00
98 Derrike Cope Fingerhut	9.00	18.00

1995 Racing Champions 1:24 Previews

This is the first time Racing Champions did a preview series for its 1:24 scale series. The cars were a preview of some of the cars that raced in the 1995 season.

	Lo	Hi
2 Rusty Wallace Ford Motorsports	10.00	18.00
6 Mark Martin Valvoline	10.00	18.00
7 Geoff Bodine Exide with Goodyear tires	9.00	18.00
7 Geoff Bodine Exide with Hoosier tires	9.00	18.00
10 Ricky Rudd Tide	9.00	18.00
57 Jason Keller Budget Gourmet	9.00	18.00
63 Curtis Markham Lysol	9.00	18.00
94 Bill Elliott McDonald's	10.00	18.00
98 Jeremy Mayfield Fingerhut	9.00	18.00

1995 Racing Champions 1:24

This series of 1:24 cars features both Winston Cup cars and Busch Grand National cars. Featured in the series is Bill Elliott's Thunderbat car. The car was a promotion done inconjunction with the movie Batman Forever.

	Lo	Hi
2 Ricky Craven DuPont	10.00	20.00
2 Rusty Wallace Ford Motorsports	10.00	20.00
4 Sterling Marlin Kodak	9.00	18.00
4 Jeff Purvis Kodak Fun Saver	9.00	18.00
5 Terry Labonte Kellogg's	10.00	20.00
6 Tommy Houston Red Devil	9.00	18.00
6 Mark Martin Valvoline	9.00	18.00
7 Geoff Bodine Exide	9.00	18.00
7 Stevie Reeves Clabber Girl	9.00	18.00
8 Jeff Burton Raybestos	9.00	18.00
8 Kenny Wallace Red Dog	12.50	25.00
8 Bobby Dotter Hyde Tools	10.00	20.00
10 Ricky Rudd Tide	9.00	18.00
12 Derrike Cope Mane N' Tail	9.00	18.00
15 Dick Trickle Quality Care	9.00	18.00
16 Ted Musgrave Family Channel	9.00	18.00
17 Darrell Waltrip Western Auto	9.00	18.00
18 Bobby Labonte Interstate Batteries	10.00	20.00
21 Morgan Shepherd Citgo	9.00	18.00
23 Chad Little Bayer	10.00	20.00
24 Jeff Gordon DuPont	15.00	30.00
24 Jeff Gordon DuPont Signature Series	10.00	20.00
24 Jeff Gordon DuPont Signature Series Hood Open	12.50	25.00
25 Johnny Rumley Big Johnson	10.00	20.00
25 Ken Schrader Budweiser	10.00	20.00
26 Steve Kinser Quaker State	12.00	24.00
27 Loy Allen Hooters	9.00	18.00
28 Dale Jarrett Havoline	9.00	18.00
29 Steve Grissom Meineke	9.00	18.00
34 Mike McLaughlin French's	9.00	18.00
37 John Andretti K-Mart	10.00	20.00
38 Elton Sawyer Red Carpet Lease	9.00	18.00
40 Patty Moise Dial Purex	10.00	20.00
41 Ricky Craven Larry Hedrick	9.00	18.00
44 David Green Slim Jim	9.00	18.00
44 Jeff Purvis Jackaroo	9.00	18.00
51 Jim Bown Luck's	10.00	20.00
60 Mark Martin Winn Dixie	10.00	20.00
71 Kevin Lepage Vermont Teddy Bear	9.00	18.00
71 Dave Marcis Olive Garden	12.50	25.00
75 Todd Bodine Factory Stores of America	9.00	18.00
81 Kenny Wallace TIC Financial	9.00	18.00
87 Joe Nemechek Burger King	9.00	18.00
88 Ernie Irvan Havoline	15.00	25.00
90 Mike Wallace Heilig-Meyers	9.00	18.00
94 Bill Elliott McDonald's	9.00	18.00
94 Bill Elliott McDonald's Thunderbat	12.00	24.00

1995 Racing Champions SuperTrucks 1:24

This 1:24 scale series is representitive of the many different trucks that raced in the inaugural SuperTruck series. There are many different variation with with sponsors or paint schemes throughout the series.

	Lo	Hi
1 P.J.Jones Sears Diehard Chevrolet	10.00	20.00
1 P.J.Jones Vessells Ford	15.00	25.00
2 David Ashley Southern California Ford	9.00	18.00
3 Mike Skinner Goodwrench	10.00	20.00
6 Mike Bliss Ultra Wheels	9.00	18.00
6 Butch Gilliland Ultra Wheels	9.00	18.00
6 Rick Carelli Total Petroleum	9.00	18.00
7 Geoff Bodine Exide	9.00	18.00
7 Geoff Bodine Exide Salsa	9.00	18.00
7 David Rezendes Exide	9.00	18.00
8 Mike Bliss Ultra Wheels	9.00	18.00
10 Stan Fox Made for You	9.00	18.00
12 Randy MacCachren Venable	9.00	18.00
18 Johnny Benson Hella Lights	9.00	18.00
21 Toby Butler Ortho with Green Nose piece	9.00	18.00
21 Toby Butler Ortho with Yellow Nose piece	9.00	18.00
23 T.J.Clark ASE with Blue scheme	9.00	18.00
23 T.J.Clark ASE with White scheme	9.00	18.00
24 Jeff Gordon DuPont Signature Series	10.00	20.00
24 Scott Lagasse DuPont	10.00	20.00
24 Scott Lagasse DuPont Bank	12.00	22.00
37 Bob Strait Target Expediting	9.00	18.00
38 Sammy Swindell Channellock	9.00	18.00
51 Kerry Teague Rosenblum Racing	9.00	18.00
52 Ken Schrader AC Delco	9.00	18.00
54 Steve McEachern McEachern Racing	9.00	18.00
61 Todd Bodine Roush Racing	9.00	18.00
75 Bill Sedgwick Spears Motorsports	9.00	18.00
83 Steve Portenga Coffee Critic	9.00	18.00
95 No Driver Association Brickyard 400 Special	10.00	20.00
95 No Driver Association Brickyard 400 Special Bank	15.00	25.00
98 Butch Miller Raybestos	9.00	18.00

1996 Racing Champions 1:24 Previews

This series of 1:24 die cast replicas featured a preview at some of the new paint jobs to run in the 1996 season. The Terry Labonte Bayer car is one of the first for this new car.

	Lo	Hi
2 Ricky Craven DuPont	8.00	18.00
4 Sterling Marlin Kodak	8.00	18.00
5 Terry Labonte Kellogg's	8.00	18.00
5 Terry Labonte Bayer	8.00	18.00
6 Mark Martin Valvoline	8.00	18.00
7 Stevie Reeves Clabber Girl	8.00	18.00
9 Joe Bessey Delco Remy	8.00	18.00
9 Lake Speed SPAM	8.00	18.00
10 Ricky Rudd Tide	8.00	18.00

	Lo	Hi
11 Brett Bodine Lowe's	8.00	18.00
12 Derrike Cope Mane N' Tail	8.00	18.00
14 Patty Moise Dial Purex	8.00	18.00
16 Ted Musgrave Family Channel	8.00	18.00
17 Darrell Waltrip Western Auto	8.00	18.00
18 Bobby Labonte Interstate Batteries	8.00	18.00
22 Ward Burton MBNA	8.00	18.00
24 Jeff Gordon DuPont	8.00	20.00
30 Johnny Benson Pennzoil	8.00	18.00
40 Tim Fedewa Kleenex	8.00	18.00
41 Ricky Craven Kodiak	8.00	18.00
47 Jeff Fuller Sunoco	8.00	18.00
51 Chuck Bown Lucks	8.00	18.00
52 Ken Schrader AC Delco	8.00	18.00
57 Jason Keller Slim Jim	8.00	18.00
74 Johnny Benson Lipton Tea	8.00	18.00
87 Joe Nemechek Burger King	8.00	18.00
90 Mike Wallace Heilig-Meyers	8.00	18.00
94 Bill Elliott McDonald's	8.00	18.00

1996 Racing Champions 1:24

The 1:24 scale cars that appear in this series are replicas of many of the cars that ran in the 1996 season. The Rusty Wallace Miller Genuine Draft car is one of the few times that Racing Champions has offered a collectible die cast with a beer logo.

	Lo	Hi
1 Rick Mast Hooter's	15.00	30.00
1 Rick Mast Hooter's Hood Open	18.00	30.00
2 Ricky Craven DuPont	9.00	18.00
2 Ricky Craven DuPont Hood Open	15.00	25.00
2 Rusty Wallace Miller Genuine Draft	18.00	30.00
2 Rusty Wallace Miller Genuine Draft Hood Open	25.00	40.00
2 Rusty Wallace Penske Racing	12.50	25.00
3 Mike Skinner Goodwrench	12.50	25.00
4 Sterling Marlin Kodak Back to Back Special	12.50	25.00
5 Terry Labonte Bayer Hood Open	15.00	25.00
5 Terry Labonte Kellogg's	10.00	20.00
5 Terry Labonte Kellogg's Hood Open	25.00	35.00
5 Terry Labonte Kellogg's Silver car	25.00	40.00
5 Terry Labonte Kellogg's Silver Hood Open	25.00	40.00
6 Tommy Houston Suburban Propane	9.00	18.00
6 Mark Martin Valvoline	9.00	18.00
6 Mark Martin Valvoline Hood Open	25.00	35.00
7 Geoff Bodine QVC	9.00	18.00
8 Hut Stricklin Circuit City	9.00	18.00
9 Joe Bessey Delco Remy	9.00	18.00
9 Joe Bessey Delco Remy Hood Open	15.00	25.00
9 Lake Speed SPAM	10.00	20.00
10 Ricky Rudd Tide	9.00	18.00
11 Brett Bodine Lowe's	9.00	18.00
11 Brett Bodine Lowe's Hood Open	15.00	25.00
11 Brett Bodine Lowe's 50th Anniversary Paint Scheme	25.00	40.00
11 Brett Bodine Lowe's 50th Anniversary Paint Scheme Hood Open	15.00	25.00
14 Patty Moise Purex	10.00	20.00
15 Wally Dallenbach Hayes Modems	30.00	50.00
15 Wally Dallenbach Hayes Modems Hood Open	20.00	35.00
16 Ted Musgrave Primestar	9.00	18.00
17 Darrell Waltrip Parts America	9.00	18.00
18 Bobby Labonte Interstate Bat.	9.00	18.00
19 Loy Allen Healthsource	15.00	25.00
21 Michael Waltrip Citgo	9.00	18.00
21 Michael Waltrip Citgo Hood Open	15.00	30.00
22 Ward Burton MBNA	9.00	18.00
23 Chad Little John Deere	18.00	30.00
23 Chad Little John Deere Hood Open	25.00	40.00
23 Chad Little John Deere in a John Deere Box	25.00	40.00
24 Jeff Gordon DuPont	12.50	25.00
24 Jeff Gordon DuPont 1995 Champion	15.00	30.00
24 Jeff Gordon DuPont 1995 Champion Hood Open	20.00	35.00
25 Ken Schrader Budweiser	25.00	40.00
25 Ken Schrader Budweiser Chrome	150.00	300.00
25 Ken Schrader Hendrick Motorsports	9.00	18.00
28 Ernie Irvan Havoline	9.00	18.00
28 Ernie Irvan Havoline Hood Open	15.00	30.00
29 Steve Grissom Cartoon Network	10.00	20.00
29 Steve Grissom Cartoon Network Hood Open	12.50	25.00
29 Steve Grissom WCW	10.00	20.00
29 Steve Grissom WCW Hood Open	12.50	25.00
29 No Driver Association Scooby-Doo in Scooby Box	12.00	24.00
29 No Driver Association WCW Sting	9.00	18.00
30 Johnny Benson Pennzoil	9.00	18.00
30 Johnny Benson Pennzoil Hood Open	30.00	50.00
31 Mike Skinner Realtree	70.00	100.00
31 Mike Skinner Realtree Hood Open	40.00	70.00
34 Mike McLaughlin Royal Oak	9.00	18.00
37 John Andretti K-Mart	9.00	18.00
38 Dennis Setzer Lipton	9.00	18.00
40 Tim Fedewa Kleenex	9.00	18.00
40 Jim Sauter First Union	12.00	20.00
41 Ricky Craven Hedrick Racing	9.00	18.00
41 Ricky Craven Kodiak in Acrylic case	20.00	50.00
41 Ricky Craven Manheim	9.00	18.00
43 Bobby Hamilton STP 5 car set	60.00	100.00
43 Bobby Hamilton STP 5 car trailer set	75.00	150.00
43 Bobby Hamilton STP Silver car	12.50	25.00
44 Bobby Labonte Shell	15.00	30.00
47 Jeff Fuller Sunoco Hood Open	15.00	25.00
51 Jim Bown Lucks Hood Open	15.00	25.00
52 Ken Schrader AC Delco	9.00	18.00
52 Ken Schrader AC Delco Hood Open	15.00	25.00
57 Jason Keller Halloween Havoc	9.00	18.00
57 Jason Keller Slim Jim Hood Open	15.00	30.00
60 Mark Martin Winn Dixie	10.00	20.00
60 Mark Martin Winn Dixie Hood Open	25.00	35.00
63 Curtis Markham Lysol	9.00	18.00
74 Johnny Benson Lipton Tea 1995 BGN Champion	10.00	20.00
74 Johnny Benson Lipton Tea 1995 BGN Champion Hood Open	15.00	30.00
75 Morgan Shepherd Remington	15.00	30.00
75 Morgan Shepherd Remington Hood Open	20.00	35.00
77 Bobby Hillin Jasper Engines	9.00	18.00
81 Kenny Wallace Square D	9.00	18.00
87 Joe Nemechek Burger King	30.00	60.00
88 Dale Jarrett Quality Care	9.00	18.00
88 Dale Jarrett Quality Care Hood Open	15.00	30.00
90 Mike Wallace Duron	9.00	18.00
94 Ron Barfield New Holland	9.00	18.00
94 Bill Elliott McDonald's	9.00	18.00
94 Bill Elliott McDonald's Hood Open	15.00	30.00
94 Bill Elliott McDonald's Monopoly	10.00	20.00
94 Bill Elliott McDonald's Monopoly Hood Open	15.00	30.00
96 David Green Busch Chrome	150.00	250.00
96 David Green Busch Hobby	20.00	35.00
97 Chad Little Sterling Cowboy	9.00	18.00
99 Glenn Allen Luxaire	9.00	18.00
99 Jeff Burton Exide	9.00	18.00

1996 Racing Champions SuperTrucks 1:24

Racing Champions continued there line of 1:24 SuperTrucks in 1996. This series features many of the circuit's first-time drivers.

	Lo	Hi
2 Mike Bliss ASE	9.00	18.00

2 Mike Bliss Super Wheels	9.00	18.00
6 Rick Carelli Chesrown	9.00	18.00
7 Geoff Bodine QVC	9.00	18.00
14 Butch Gilliland Stropps	9.00	18.00
17 Bill Sedgwick Die Hard	9.00	18.00
19 Lance Norlock Maclanerg-Duncan	9.00	18.00
20 Walker Evans Dana	9.00	18.00
21 Doug George Ortho	9.00	18.00
24 Jack Sprague Quaker State	9.00	18.00
29 Bob Keselowski Winnebago	9.00	18.00
30 Jimmy Hensley Mopar	9.00	18.00
34 Bob Brevak Concor	9.00	18.00
43 Rich Bickle Cummins	9.00	18.00
44 Bryan Reffner 1-800-Collect	9.00	18.00
52 Ken Schrader AC Delco	9.00	18.00
57 Robbie Pyle Aisyn	9.00	18.00
75 Bobby Gill Spears	9.00	18.00
78 Mike Chase Petron Plus	9.00	18.00
83 Steve Portenga Coffee Critic	9.00	18.00
98 Butch Miller Raybestos	9.00	18.00

1997 Racing Champions 1:24 Previews

This series of 1:24 die cast replicas featured a preview at some of the new paint jobs to run in the 1997 season. The Rick Mast Remington car and the Robert Pressley Scooby Doo car features two of the numerous driver changes for the 97 Winston Cup season.

	Lo	Hi
4 Sterling Marlin Kodak	8.00	16.00
5 Terry Labonte Kellogg's	8.00	16.00
6 Mark Martin Valvoline	8.00	16.00
10 Ricky Rudd Tide	8.00	16.00
18 Bobby Labonte Interstate Batteries	8.00	16.00
21 Michael Waltrip Citgo	8.00	16.00
24 Jeff Gordon DuPont	8.00	16.00
28 Ernie Irvan Havoline	8.00	16.00
29 Robert Pressley Scooby-Doo	8.00	16.00
30 Johnny Benson Pennzoil	8.00	16.00
75 Rick Mast Remington	8.00	16.00
94 Bill Elliott McDonald's	8.00	16.00

1997 Racing Champions 1:24

The 1:24 scale cars that appear in this series are replicas of many of the cars that ran in the 1996 season. The series is higlighted by the Terry Labonte Kellogg's car commenerating his 1996 Winston Cup Championship. This car is available in two variations: standard and hood open. The Lake Speed University of Nebraska car is believed to be in short supply becuase of the dissolved team sponsorship. It is also believed to be available in a red tampo and black tampo.

	Lo	Hi
00 Buckshot Jones Aqua-Fresh	10.00	20.00
1 Hermie Sadler DeWalt	8.00	16.00
1 Morgan Shepherd Crusin' America	8.00	16.00
1 Morgan Shepherd R&L Carriers	10.00	20.00
2 Ricky Craven Raybestos	8.00	16.00
2 Rusty Wallace Miller Lite distributed by Matco	35.00	60.00
2 Rusty Wallace Penske	8.00	16.00
4 Sterling Marlin Kodak	8.00	16.00
5 Terry Labonte Bayer	9.00	18.00
5 Terry Labonte Kellogg's	9.00	18.00
5 Terry Labonte Kellogg's 1996 Champion	15.00	25.00
5 Terry Labonte Kellogg's 1996 Champion Hood Open	25.00	40.00
5 Terry Labonte Tony the Tiger	10.00	25.00
6 Tommy Houston Suburban Propane	8.00	16.00
6 Mark Martin Valvoline	8.00	16.00
7 Geoff Bodine QVC	8.00	16.00
7 Geoff Bodine QVC Gold Rush	12.50	25.00
8 Hut Stricklin Circuit City	8.00	16.00
9 Lake Speed University of Nebraska	40.00	80.00
9 Joe Bessey Power Team	8.00	16.00
9 Jeff Burton Track Gear	8.00	16.00
10 Ricky Rudd Tide	8.00	16.00
10 Phil Parsons Channellock	8.00	16.00
11 Brett Bodine Close Call	8.00	16.00
11 Jimmy Foster Speedvision	9.00	18.00
16 Ted Musgrave Primestar	8.00	16.00
17 Darrell Waltrip Parts America	9.00	18.00
17 Darrell Waltrip Parts America Chrome	12.50	25.00
17 Darrell Waltrip Parts America Chrome Promo	15.00	25.00
18 Bobby Labonte Interstate Batt.	8.00	16.00
19 Gary Bradberry CSR	8.00	16.00
21 Michael Waltrip Citgo	8.00	16.00
24 Jeff Gordon DuPont	12.50	25.00
25 Ricky Craven Bud Lizard	15.00	30.00
25 Ricky Craven Bud Lizard 3-car set	50.00	75.00
25 Ricky Craven Hendrick	8.00	16.00
28 Ernie Irvan Havoline	8.00	16.00
28 Ernie Irvan Havoline 10th Anniversary	9.00	18.00
29 Jeff Green Tom and Jerry	8.00	16.00
29 Robert Pressley Cartoon Network	8.00	16.00
29 Elliott Sadler Phillips 66	12.50	25.00
30 Johnny Benson Pennzoil	8.00	16.00
32 Dale Jarrett Gillette	8.00	16.00
32 Dale Jarrett White Rain	8.00	16.00
33 Ken Schrader Petree Racing	8.00	16.00
34 Mike McLaughlin Royal Oak	8.00	16.00
36 Todd Bodine Stanley Tools	8.00	16.00
36 Derrike Cope Skittles	8.00	16.00
37 Jeremy Mayfield K-Mart	8.00	16.00
38 Elton Sawyer Barbasol	8.00	16.00
40 Robby Gordon Sabco Racing	8.00	16.00
41 Steve Grissom Hedrick	8.00	16.00
42 Joe Nemechek Bell South	8.00	16.00
46 Wally Dallenbach First Union	8.00	16.00
47 Jeff Fuller Sunoco	8.00	16.00
49 Kyle Petty nWo	15.00	30.00
57 Jason Keller Slim Jim	8.00	16.00
60 Mark Martin Winn-Dixie Promo	15.00	35.00
72 Mike Dillon Detroit Gasket	8.00	16.00
74 Randy LaJoie Fina	8.00	16.00
74 Randy LaJoie Fina 1996 Busch Champion	20.00	35.00
75 Rick Mast Remington	8.00	16.00
75 Rick Mast Remington Camo	8.00	16.00
75 Rick Mast Remington Stren	8.00	16.00
87 Joe Nemechek Bell South	8.00	16.00
88 Kevin Lepage Hype	8.00	16.00

	Lo	Hi
90 Dick Trickle, Heilig-Meyers	8.00	16.00
91 Mike Wallace, Spam	8.00	16.00
94 Bill Elliott, McDonald's	8.00	16.00
94 Ron Barfield, New Holland	8.00	16.00
94 Bill Elliott, Mac Tonight	9.00	18.00
94 Bill Elliott, Mac Tonight 3-car set	50.00	80.00
96 David Green, Caterpillar	8.00	16.00
96 David Green, Caterpillar Promo	12.00	20.00
97 No Driver Association, Brickyard 500	12.00	20.00
97 Chad Little, John Deere	8.00	16.00
97 Chad Little, John Deere Promo	12.00	20.00
99 Jeff Burton, Exide	8.00	16.00
99 Glenn Allen, Luxaire	8.00	16.00

1997 Racing Champions 1:24 Stock Rods

These 1:24 scale cars are replicas of vintage stock rods with NASCAR paint schemes. Cars are listed by issue number instead of car number.

	Lo	Hi
1 Darrell Waltrip, Parts America	8.00	20.00
2 Sterling Marlin, Kodak	8.00	20.00
3 Steve Grissom, Hedrick	8.00	20.00
4 Ken Schrader, Petree	8.00	20.00
5 Dennis Setzer, Lance	8.00	20.00
6 Ricky Craven, Hendrick	8.00	20.00
7 Ricky Rudd, Tide	8.00	20.00
8 Rusty Wallace, Penske	8.00	20.00
9 Rick Mast, Remington	8.00	20.00
10 Terry Labonte, Spooky Loops	25.00	40.00
11 Bill Elliott, MacTonight	10.00	25.00
12 Bobby Hamilton, Kodak	8.00	20.00
13 Terry Labonte, Spooky Loops	10.00	25.00
14 Terry Labonte, Kellogg's	10.00	25.00

1997 Racing Champions SuperTrucks 1:24

Racing Champions continued there line of 1:24 SuperTrucks in 1997. This series features many of the circuit's first-time drivers and Winston Cup regulars.

	Lo	Hi
1 Michael Waltrip, MW Windows	8.00	16.00
2 Mike Bliss, Team ASE	8.00	16.00
4 Bill Elliott, Team ASE	8.00	16.00
6 Rick Carelli, ReMax	8.00	16.00
7 Tammy Kirk, Loveable	8.00	16.00
15 Mike Cope, Penrose	8.00	16.00
15 Mike Colabacci, VISA	8.00	16.00
18 Johnny Benson, Pennzoil	8.00	16.00
18 Mark Dokken, Dana	8.00	16.00
19 Tony Raines, Pennzoil	8.00	16.00
24 Jack Sprague, Quaker State	8.00	16.00
29 Bob Keslowski, Mopar	8.00	16.00
35 Dave Rezendes, Ortho	8.00	16.00
49 Rodney Combs, Lance	8.00	16.00
52 Toby Butler, Purolator	8.00	16.00
66 Bryan Reffner, Carlin	8.00	16.00
75 Dan Press, Spears	8.00	16.00
80 Joe Ruttman, LCI	8.00	16.00
86 Stacy Compton, Valvoline	8.00	16.00
87 Joe Nemechek, Bell South	8.00	16.00
92 Mark Kinser, Rotary	8.00	16.00
98 Kenny Irwin, Raybestos	10.00	25.00
99 Chuck Bown, Exide	8.00	16.00
99 Jeff Burton, Exide	8.00	16.00
99 Mark Martin, Exide	8.00	16.00

1998 Racing Champions 1:24

The 1:24 scale cars that appear in this series are replicas of many of the cars that ran in the 1998 season. The Mark Martin Kosei car is one of the cars that highlights this series.

	Lo	Hi
00 Buckshot Jones, Aquafresh	8.00	16.00
00 Buckshot Jones, Bayer	8.00	16.00
4 Bobby Hamilton, Kodak	8.00	16.00
5 Terry Labonte, Blasted Fruit Loops	10.00	20.00
5 Terry Labonte, Kellogg's	10.00	20.00
5 Terry Labonte, Kellogg's Corny	10.00	20.00
6 Joe Bessey, Power Team	8.00	16.00
6 Mark Martin, Eagle One	10.00	20.00
6 Mark Martin, Kosei	75.00	125.00
6 Mark Martin, Synpower	15.00	30.00
6 Mark Martin, Valvoline	9.00	18.00
7 Geoff Bodine, Phillips	12.50	25.00
8 Hut Stricklin, Circuit City	8.00	16.00
9 Jeff Burton, Track Gear	8.00	16.00
9 Lake Speed, Birthday Cake	9.00	18.00
9 Lake Speed, Huckleberry Hound	10.00	20.00
10 Ricky Rudd, Give Kids The World	8.00	16.00
10 Ricky Rudd, Tide	8.00	16.00
11 Brett Bodine, Paychex	8.00	16.00
13 Jerry Nadeau, First Plus	10.00	20.00
16 Ted Musgrave, Primestar	8.00	16.00
17 Matt Kenseth, Lycos	25.00	40.00
17 Darrell Waltrip, Builders' Square	10.00	20.00
20 Bliase Alexander, Rescue Engine	8.00	16.00
21 Michael Waltrip, Citgo	8.00	16.00
23 Jimmy Spencer, No Bull	75.00	125.00
26 Johnny Benson, Betty Crocker	10.00	20.00
26 Johnny Benson, Cheerios	10.00	20.00
28 Kenny Irwin, Havoline	20.00	35.00
29 Hermie Sadler, Dewalt	8.00	16.00
30 Derrick Cope, Gumout	8.00	16.00
30 Mike Cope, Slim Jim	8.00	16.00
33 Ken Schrader, Petree	8.00	16.00
35 Todd Bodine, Tabasco	8.00	16.00
36 Ernie Irvan, M&M's	10.00	25.00
36 Ernie Irvan, Skittles	8.00	16.00
36 Ernie Irvan, Wildberry Skittles	8.00	16.00
40 Sterling Marlin, Sabco	8.00	16.00
41 Steve Grissom, Hedrick	8.00	16.00
42 Joe Nemechek, Bell South	8.00	16.00
46 Wally Dallenbach, First Union	8.00	16.00
50 Ricky Craven, Hendrick	8.00	16.00
50 NDA/Dr. Pepper	8.00	16.00
59 Robert Pressley, Kingsford	8.00	16.00
66 Elliott Sadler, Phillips 66	8.00	16.00
72 Mike Dillon, Detroit Gasket	8.00	16.00
75 Rick Mast, Remington	8.00	16.00
78 Gary Bradberry, Pilot	8.00	16.00
87 Joe Nemechek, Bell South	12.50	25.00
88 Kevin Schwantz, Ryder	8.00	16.00
90 Dick Trickle, Heilig-Meyers	8.00	16.00
94 Bill Elliott, Happy Meal	8.00	16.00
94 Bill Elliott, McDonald's	8.00	16.00
94 Bill Elliott, Mac Tonight	8.00	16.00
96 David Green, Caterpiller	8.00	16.00
96 David Green, Caterpillar P	15.00	25.00
98 Greg Sacks, Thorn Apple Valley	8.00	16.00
99 Glenn Allen, Luxaire	8.00	16.00
99 Jeff Burton, Exide	8.00	16.00
300 Darrell Waltrip, Tim Flock Special	8.00	16.00

1998 Racing Champions 1:24 Gold

This is a special series produced by Racing Champions to celebrate NASCAR's 50th anniversary. It parallels the regular 1998 1:24 scale series. Each car is a limited edition of 2,500. Each car is also plated in gold chrome and contains a serial number on its chassis.

	Lo	Hi
00 Buskshot Jones Alka Seltzer	15.00	40.00
00 Buckshot Jones Bayer	15.00	40.00
00 Buckshot Jones Aquafresh	15.00	40.00
2 Ron Barfield New Holland	15.00	40.00
4 Bobby Hamilton Kodak	15.00	40.00
5 Terry Labonte Blasted Fruit Loops	45.00	90.00
5 Terry Labonte Kellogg's	45.00	90.00
5 Terry Labonte Kellogg's Corny	45.00	90.00
6 Joe Bessey Power Team	12.00	30.00
6 Mark Martin Eagle One	45.00	90.00
6 Mark Martin Syntec	45.00	90.00
6 Mark Martin Valvoline	45.00	90.00
8 Hut Stricklin Circuit City	12.00	30.00
9 Jeff Burton Track Gear	15.00	40.00
9 Jerry Nadeau Zombie Island	15.00	40.00
9 Lake Speed Birthday Cake	15.00	40.00
9 Lake Speed Huckleberry Hound	15.00	40.00
10 Phil Parsons Duralube	12.00	30.00
10 Ricky Rudd Tide	15.00	40.00
11 Brett Bodine Paychex	15.00	40.00
13 Jerry Nadeau First Plus	25.00	60.00
14 Patty Moise Rhodes	12.00	30.00
16 Ted Musgrave Primestar	15.00	40.00
17 Matt Kenseth Lycos	25.00	50.00
17 Darrell Waltrip Builders' Square	20.00	50.00
19 Tony Raines Yellow	12.00	30.00
20 Blasé Alexander Rescue Engine	12.00	30.00
21 Michael Waltrip Citgo	15.00	40.00
23 Lance Hooper WCW	12.00	30.00
23 Jimmy Spencer No Bull	90.00	150.00
26 Johnny Benson Cheerios	20.00	50.00
28 Kenny Irwin Havoline Mac Tools	75.00	125.00
29 Hermie Sadler Dewalt	12.00	30.00
30 Derike Cope Gumout	12.00	30.00
30 Mike Cope Slim Jim	12.00	30.00
33 Ken Schrader Petree	15.00	40.00
34 Mike McLaughlin Goulds	12.00	30.00
35 Todd Bodine Tabasco	15.00	40.00
36 Matt Hutter Stanley	12.00	30.00
36 Ernie Irvan M&M's	25.00	60.00
36 Ernie Irvan Skittles	15.00	40.00
36 Ernie Irvan Wildberry Skittles	20.00	50.00
40 Rick Fuller Channellock	12.00	30.00
40 Kevin Lepage Channellock	12.00	30.00
40 Sterling Marlin Sabco	15.00	40.00
41 Steve Grissom Hedrick	15.00	40.00
42 Joe Nemechek Bell South	15.00	40.00
46 Wally Dallenbach First Union	15.00	40.00
47 Andy Santerre Monroe	15.00	40.00
50 Ricky Craven Hendrick	20.00	50.00
50 No Driver Association 50th Anniversary	20.00	50.00
59 Robert Pressley Kingsford	12.00	30.00
60 Mark Martin Winn Dixie	40.00	80.00
64 Dike Trickle Schneider	15.00	40.00
66 Eliott Sadler Phillips 66	15.00	40.00
72 Mike Dillon Detroit Gasket	12.00	30.00
75 Rick Mast Remington	12.00	30.00
77 Robert Pressley Jasper	12.00	30.00
78 Gary Bradberry Pilot	12.00	30.00
87 Joe Nemechek Bell South	12.00	30.00
88 Kevin Schwantz Ryder	12.00	30.00
90 Dick Trickle Helig-Meyers	12.00	30.00
94 Bill Elliott Happy Meal	45.00	90.00
94 Bill Elliott McDonald's	45.00	90.00
96 David Green Caterpiller	12.00	30.00
97 Chad Little John Deere P	70.00	100.00
98 Greg Sacks Thorn Apple Valley	12.00	30.00
99 Glen Allen Luxaire	12.00	30.00
99 Jeff Burton Exide	15.00	40.00
300 Darrell Waltrip Flock Special	20.00	50.00
400 No Driver Association Brickyard 400	15.00	40.00

1998 Racing Champions 1:24 Gold Hood Open

This is a special series produced by Racing Champions to celebrate NASCAR's 50th anniversary. It parallels the regular 1998 1:24 scale series. Each car is a limited edition of 1,998. Each car is also plated in gold chrome and contains a serial number on its chassis.

	Lo	Hi
4 Bobby Hamilton Kodak	20.00	50.00
5 Terry Labonte Blasted Fruit Loops	50.00	100.00
5 Terry Labonte Kellogg's	50.00	100.00
5 Terry Labonte Kellogg's Corny	50.00	100.00
6 Joe Bessey Power Team	15.00	40.00
6 Mark Martin Syntec	50.00	100.00
6 Mark Martin Valvoline	50.00	100.00
8 Hut Stricklin Circuit City	15.00	40.00
9 Lake Speed Huckleberry Hound	20.00	50.00
10 Ricky Rudd Tide	20.00	50.00
11 Brett Bodine Paychex	15.00	40.00
16 Ted Musgrave Primestar	15.00	40.00
17 Darrell Waltrip Builders' Square	25.00	60.00
19 Tony Raines Yellow	15.00	40.00
21 Michael Waltrip Goodwill Games	15.00	40.00
30 Derrike Cope Gumout	15.00	40.00
33 Ken Schrader Petree	20.00	50.00
35 Todd Bodine Tabasco	20.00	50.00
36 Ernie Irvan Skittles	20.00	50.00
36 Ernie Irvan Wildberry Skittles	25.00	60.00
40 Sterling Marlin Sabco	20.00	50.00
50 Ricky Craven Hendrick	20.00	50.00
77 Robert Pressley Jasper	15.00	40.00
78 Gary Bradberry Pilot	15.00	40.00
90 Dick Trickle Heilig-Meyers	15.00	40.00
94 Bill Elliott Happy Meal	50.00	100.00
94 Bill Elliott McDonald's	50.00	100.00
98 Greg Sacks Thorn Apple Valley	15.00	40.00
99 Jeff Burton Exide	20.00	50.00
400 No Driver Association Brickyard 400	20.00	50.00

1998 Racing Champions 1:24 Reflections of Gold

This is a special series produced by Racing Champions to celebrate NASCAR's 50th anniversary. It parallels the regular 1998 1:24 scale series. Each car is a limited edition of 4,998. Each car is also plated in gold chrome and contains a serial number on its chassis.

	Lo	Hi
00 Buckshot Jones Aqua Fresh	15.00	30.00
4 Bobby Hamilton Kodak	15.00	30.00
5 Terry Labonte Kellogg's	30.00	60.00
6 Joe Bessey Power Team	15.00	30.00
6 Mark Martin Valvoline	30.00	60.00
8 Hut Stricklin Circuit City	15.00	30.00
9 Lake Speed Huckleberry Hound	15.00	30.00
10 Phill Parsons Duralube	15.00	30.00
10 Ricky Rudd Tide	20.00	40.00
11 Brett Bodine Paychex	15.00	30.00
13 Jerry Nadeau First Plus	15.00	30.00
16 Ted Musgrave Primestar	15.00	30.00
20 Blasé Alexander@{ Rescue Engine	15.00	30.00
21 Micheal Waltrip	15.00	30.00

Citgo		
23 Lance Hooper	15.00	30.00
WCW		
26 Johnny Benson	20.00	40.00
Cheerios		
29 Hermie Sadler	15.00	30.00
Dewalt		
30 Derrike Cope	15.00	30.00
Gumout		
33 Tim Fedewa	15.00	30.00
Kleenex		
33 Ken Schrader	20.00	40.00
Petree		
34 Mike McLaughlin	15.00	30.00
Goulds		
35 Todd Bodine	20.00	40.00
Tabasco		
36 Ernie Irvan	25.00	50.00
Skittles		
40 Sterling Marlin	20.00	40.00
Sabco		
41 Steve Grissom	15.00	30.00
Hedrick		
42 Joe Nemechek	15.00	30.00
Bell South		
46 Wally Dallenbach	15.00	30.00
First Union		
47 Andy Santerre	15.00	30.00
Monroe		
59 Robert Pressley	15.00	30.00
Kingsford		
60 Mark Martin	30.00	60.00
Winn Dixie		
63 Tracy Leslie	15.00	30.00
Lysol		
64 Dike Trickle	15.00	30.00
Scheinder		
72 Mike Dillon	15.00	30.00
Detroit Gasket		
74 Randy Lajoie	15.00	30.00
Fina		
75 Rick Mast	15.00	30.00
Remington		
90 Dick Trickle	20.00	40.00
Heilig-Meyers		
94 Bill Elliott	30.00	60.00
McDonald's		
99 Jeff Burton	25.00	50.00
Exide		

1998 Racing Champions 1:24 Signature Series

This is a special series produced by Racing Champions to celebrate NASCAR's 50th anniversary. It parallels the regular 1998 1:24 scale series. Each car is a packaged in a decorative box with the driver's facsimile autograph on the front.

	Lo	Hi
5 Terry Labonte	10.00	20.00
Kellogg's		
6 Mark Martin	10.00	20.00
Valvoline		
9 Jeff Burton	10.00	20.00
Track Gear		
9 Lake Speed	10.00	20.00
Huckleberry Hound		
10 Phill Parsons	10.00	20.00
Duralube		
10 Ricky Rudd	10.00	20.00
Tide		
11 Brett Bodine	10.00	20.00
Paychex		
13 Jerry Nadeau	10.00	20.00
First Plus		
16 Ted Musgrave	10.00	20.00
Primestar		
26 Johnny Benson	10.00	20.00
Cheerios		
30 Derrike Cope	10.00	20.00
Gumout		
33 Ken Schrader	10.00	20.00
Petree		
35 Todd Bodine	10.00	20.00
Tabasco		
36 Ernie Irvan	10.00	20.00
Skittles		
50 Ricky Craven	10.00	20.00
Hendrick		
75 Rick Mast	10.00	20.00
Remington		
94 Bill Elliott	10.00	20.00
McDonald's		
98 Greg Sacks	10.00	20.00
Thorn Apple Valley		

1998 Racing Champions 1:24 Stock Rods

These 1:24 scale cars are replicas of vintage stock rods with NASCAR paint schemes. Cars are listed by issue number instead of car number.

	Lo	Hi
15 Jeff Green	8.00	20.00
Cartoon Network		
16 Kevin Schwantz	8.00	20.00
Ryder		
17 Glen Allen	8.00	20.00
Luxaire		
18 Jeff Burton	8.00	20.00
Exide		
19 Michael Waltrip	8.00	20.00
Citgo		
20 Robert Pressley	8.00	20.00
Kingsford		
21 Kevin Schwantz	8.00	20.00
Ryder		
22 Ken Schrader	8.00	20.00
Petree		
23 Dick Trickle	8.00	20.00
Heilig-Meyers		
24 Joe Bessey	8.00	20.00
Power Team		
25 Glen Allen	8.00	20.00
Luxaire		
26 Jerry Nadeau	8.00	20.00
First Plus		
27 Hut Stricklin	8.00	20.00
Circuit City		
28 Terry Labonte	10.00	25.00
Kellogg's		
29 Wally Dallenbach	8.00	20.00
First Union		
30 Joe Nemechek	8.00	20.00
Bell South		
31 Robert Pressley	8.00	20.00
Kingsford		
32 Hut Stricklin	8.00	20.00
Circuit City		
33 Elliot Sadler	8.00	20.00
Phillips 66		
34 Hermie Sadler	8.00	20.00
Dewalt		
35 Steve Grissom	10.00	25.00
Hedrick Gold		
36 Lake Speed	8.00	20.00
Huckleberry Hound		
37 Bill Elliott	25.00	50.00
McDonald's Gold		
38 Michael Waltrip	8.00	20.00
Citgo		
39 Jeff Burton	8.00	20.00
Track Gear		
40 Mark Martin	10.00	25.00
Valvoline		
41 Bill Elliott	10.00	25.00
McDonald's		
42 Jeff Burton	12.00	30.00
Exide Gold		
43 Jerry Nadeau	10.00	25.00
First Plus Gold		
44 Jeff Burton	8.00	20.00
Exide		
45 Rick Fuller	8.00	20.00
Channellock		
46 Ted Musgrave	8.00	20.00
Primestar		
47 Ricky Craven	8.00	20.00
Hendrick		
48 Terry Labonte	25.00	50.00
Kellogg's Gold		
49 Hut Stricklin	10.00	25.00
Circuit City Gold		
50 NDA	8.00	20.00
NASCAR 50th Anniversary		
51 Wally Dallenbach	8.00	20.00
First Union		
52 Terry Labonte	10.00	25.00
Kellogg's Corny		
53 Elliot Sadler	8.00	20.00
Phillips 66		
54 Bill Elliott	25.00	50.00
McDonald's Gold		
55 Steve Grissom	10.00	25.00
Hedrick Gold		
56 Terry Labonte	10.00	25.00
Kellogg's		
57 Bobby Hamilton	8.00	20.00
Kodak		
58 Bill Elliott	25.00	50.00
McDonald's Gold		
59 Mark Martin	10.00	25.00
Valvoline		
60 Hut Stricklin	10.00	25.00
Circuit City Gold		
61 Ricky Rudd	8.00	20.00
Tide		
62 Johnny Benson	8.00	20.00
Cheerios		
63 Ricky Craven	12.00	30.00
Hendrick Gold		
64 Michael Waltrip	8.00	20.00
Citgo		
65 Hermie Sadler	8.00	20.00
Dewalt		
66 Ken Schrader	8.00	20.00
Petree		
67 Bill Elliott	25.00	50.00
McDonald's Gold		
68 Joe Nemechek	10.00	25.00
Bell South Gold		
69 Bill Elliott	10.00	25.00
McDonald's		
70 Steve Grissom	8.00	20.00
Hedrick		
71 Mark Martin	10.00	25.00
Valvoline		
72 Ken Schrader	8.00	20.00
Petree		
73 Michael Waltrip	10.00	25.00
Citgo Gold		

1998 Racing Champions 1:24 Stock Rods Reflections of Gold

These 1:24 scale cars are replicas of vintage stock rods with NASCAR paint schemes and gold plating. Cars are listed by issue number instead of car number.

	Lo	Hi
CARS ARE LISTED BY ISSUE NUMBER		
1 Bill Elliott	30.00	60.00
McDonald's		
2 Todd Bodine	15.00	30.00
Tabasco		
3 Terry Labonte	30.00	60.00
Kellogg's		
4 Bobby Hamilton	15.00	30.00
Kodak		
5 Mark Martin	30.00	60.00
Valvoline		
6 Jeff Burton	20.00	40.00
Exide		
7 Ernie Irvan	20.00	40.00
Skittles		
8 Ted Musgrave	15.00	30.00
Primestar		
9 Terry Labonte	30.00	60.00
Kellogg's		
10 Ken Schrader	15.00	30.00
Petree		
11 Dick Trickle	15.00	30.00
Scheinder		
12 Michael Waltrip	15.00	30.00
Citgo		

1998 Racing Champions Authentics 1:24

These 1:24 scale cars marks the first in a series by Racing Champions. These cars were distributed through hobby and trackside outlets. Each car is packaged in a special black snap case.

	Lo	Hi
6 Mark Martin Eagle One	45.00	70.00
6 Mark Martin Synpower	45.00	70.00
6 Mark Martin Valvoline	45.00	70.00
16 Kevin Lepage Primestar	45.00	70.00
26 Johnny Benson Betty Crocker	45.00	70.00
26 Johnny Benson Cheerios	45.00	70.00
26 Johnny Benson Trix	45.00	70.00
97 Chad Little John Deere	45.00	70.00
99 Jeff Burton Exide	45.00	70.00

1998 Racing Champions SuperTrucks 1:24

Racing Champions continued there line of 1:24 SuperTrucks in 1998. This series features many of the circuit's first-time drivers and Winston Cup regulars.

	Lo	Hi
2 Mike Bliss Team ASE	8.00	16.00
6 Rick Carelli Remax	8.00	16.00
18 No Driver Association Dana	8.00	16.00
29 Bob Keselowski Mopar	8.00	16.00
31 Tony Roper Concor Tools	8.00	16.00
35 Ron Barfield Ortho	8.00	16.00
44 Boris Said Federated	8.00	16.00
52 Mike Wallace Pure One	8.00	16.00
66 Bryan Reffner Carlin	8.00	16.00
84 Wayne Anderson Porter Cable	8.00	16.00
86 Stacy Compton RC Cola	8.00	16.00
87 Joe Nemechek BellSouth	8.00	16.00
90 Lance Norick National Hockey League	8.00	16.00
94 Bill Elliott Team ASE	8.00	16.00

1998 Racing Champions SuperTrucks 1:24 Gold

This is a special series produced by Racing Champions to celebrate NASCAR's 50th anniversary. It parallels the regular 1998 1:24 scale series. Each truck is a limited edition of 2,500. Each truck is also plated in gold chrome and contains a serial number on its chassis.

	Lo	Hi
2 Mike Bliss Team ASE	10.00	25.00
6 Rick Carelli Remax	10.00	25.00
29 Bob Keselowski Mopar	10.00	25.00
66 Bryan Reffner Carlin	10.00	25.00
86 Stacy Compton RC Cola	10.00	25.00

1992-1994 Racing Champions 1:24 Banks

These 1:24 scale cars feature banks in each car. There is usually a slot in the back window to slip your money into. The cars, as with most die cast banks, have blacked in windows.

	Lo	Hi
0 D.McCabe Fisher Snow Plows	18.00	30.00
1 Rick Mast Precision Products	12.00	22.00
2 Ward Burton Hardee's	12.00	22.00
2 Ricky Craven DuPont	15.00	25.00
2 Rusty Wallace Ford Motorsports	20.00	35.00
2 Rusty Wallace Pontiac Excitement	150.00	250.00
3 Dale Earnhardt Goodwrench BGN car	20.00	40.00
3 Dale Earnhardt Goodwrench with numbered box	25.00	45.00
3 Dale Earnhardt Goodwrench with unnumbered box	20.00	40.00
3 Dale Earnhardt Goodwrench wtih Snap On	20.00	40.00
3 Dale Earnhardt Mom-n-Pop's	25.00	45.00
4 Ernie Irvan Kodak	20.00	32.00
4 Sterling Marlin Kodak	16.00	25.00
4 Sterling Marlin Kodak Fun Saver	16.00	25.00
5 Terry Labonte Kellogg's	20.00	35.00
5 Ricky Rudd Tide	12.00	22.00
6 Mark Martin Valvoline	18.00	30.00
6 Mark Martin Valvoline Reese's	16.00	25.00
7 Geoff Bodine Exide	16.00	25.00
7 Harry Gant Black Flag	30.00	45.00
7 Harry Gant Easy Off	30.00	45.00
7 Harry Gant French's	30.00	45.00
7 Harry Gant Gulf Lite	30.00	45.00
7 Harry Gant Manheim	30.00	45.00
7 Harry Gant Morema	30.00	45.00
7 Harry Gant Woolite	30.00	45.00
7 Jimmy Hensley Bojangles	16.00	25.00
7 Tommy Kendall Family Channel	18.00	30.00
7 Alan Kulwicki Army	40.00	65.00
7 Alan Kulwicki Hooters	150.00	250.00
7 Alan Kulwicki Zerex	60.00	90.00
8 Sterling Marlin Raybestos	12.00	22.00
8 Kenny Wallace TIC Financial	20.00	32.00
10 Ricky Rudd Tide	20.00	32.00
10 Jimmy Spencer Kleenex	60.00	100.00
11 Bill Elliott Amoco	25.00	40.00
11 Bill Elliott Budweiser	30.00	50.00
11 Bill Elliott Budweiser Hardy Boys car	25.00	40.00
12 Clifford Allison Sports Image	25.00	40.00
12 Jimmy Spencer Meineke	40.00	65.00
14 John Andretti Kanawha	18.00	30.00
14 Terry Labonte MW Windows	20.00	35.00
15 Geoff Bodine Motorcraft	12.00	22.00
15 Lake Speed Quality Care	12.00	22.00
16 Chad Chaffin Dr. Die Cast	16.00	25.00
16 Ted Musgrave Family Channel	16.00	25.00
17 Darrell Waltrip Tide Orange paint scheme	30.00	50.00
17 Darrell Waltrip Tide Primer gray car	20.00	40.00
17 Darrell Waltrip Western Auto	90.00	150.00
18 Dale Jarrett Interstate Batteries	15.00	30.00
20 Randy LaJoie Fina	20.00	32.00
20 Joe Ruttman Fina	22.00	35.00
20 Joe Ruttman Fina 520 made	25.00	40.00
21 Morgan Shepherd Cheerwine	18.00	30.00
21 Morgan Shepherd Citgo	12.00	22.00
22 Bobby Labonte Maxwell House	12.00	22.00
23 Chad Little Bayer	12.00	22.00
24 Jeff Gordon DuPont	30.00	55.00
24 Jeff Gordon DuPont Brickyard Special	70.00	100.00
24 Jeff Gordon DuPont Coca-Cola 600 Winner	100.00	175.00
24 Jeff Gordon DuPont Snickers	20.00	40.00
25 Hermie Sadler Virginia is for Lovers	12.00	22.00
26 Brett Bodine Quaker State	12.00	22.00
27 Hut Stricklin McDonald's	18.00	30.00
28 Davey Allison Havoline	50.00	80.00
28 Davey Allison Havoline with Black and Gold paint scheme	75.00	125.00
28 Davey Allison Havoline with Black and White paint scheme	30.00	50.00
28 Davey Allison Mac Tools	75.00	125.00
28 Ernie Irvan Havoline	25.00	40.00
28 Ernie Irvan Mac Tools	25.00	40.00
30 Michael Waltrip Pennzoil	12.00	22.00
31 Steve Grissom Channellock	12.00	22.00
31 Tom Peck Channellock	12.00	22.00
33 Harry Gant Farewell Tour	20.00	32.00
33 Harry Gant Leo Jackson	16.00	25.00
33 Harry Gant Manheim Auctions	50.00	75.00
33 Harry Gant Manheim Auctions Autographed	75.00	125.00
33 Bobby Labonte Dentyne	16.00	25.00
34 Mike McLaughlin Fiddle Faddle	12.00	22.00
35 Shawna Robinson	18.00	30.00

	Lo	Hi
Polaroid Captiva		
38 Elton Sawyer	16.00	25.00
Ford Credit		
41 Ernie Irvan	25.00	40.00
Mac Tools		
42 Kyle Petty	18.00	30.00
Mello Yello		
43 Rodney Combs	12.00	22.00
French's		
43 Wally Dallenbach Jr.	12.00	22.00
STP		
43 Richard Petty	30.00	50.00
STP		
44 David Green	20.00	32.00
Slim Jim		
44 Bobby Hillin	16.00	25.00
Buss Fuses		
44 Rick Wilson	16.00	25.00
STP		
46 Shawna Robinson	18.00	30.00
Polaroid		
51 No Driver Association	60.00	100.00
Racing Champions		
52 Ken Schrader	16.00	25.00
AC Delco		
52 Ken Schrader	22.00	35.00
Morema		
54 Robert Pressley	22.00	35.00
Manheim Auctions		
55 Ted Musgrave	30.00	50.00
US Air		
59 Andy Belmont	20.00	32.00
Metal Arrester		
59 Robert Pressley	45.00	70.00
Alliance		
59 Dennis Setzer	30.00	45.00
Alliance		
60 Mark Martin	45.00	75.00
Winn Dixie of 5000		
60 Mark Martin	20.00	35.00
Winn Dixie of 10,000		
63 Jim Bown	12.00	22.00
Lysol		
70 J.D. McDuffie	12.50	25.00
Son's Auto		
71 Dave Marcis	30.00	45.00
Earnhardt Chevrolet		
75 Todd Bodine	12.00	22.00
Factory Stores		
77 Greg Sacks	20.00	32.00
US Air		
83 Sherry Blakely	18.00	30.00
Ramses		
87 Joe Nemechek	16.00	25.00
Dentyne		
92 Larry Pearson	12.00	22.00
Stanley Tools		
93 No Driver Associations	100.00	175.00
Racing Champions		
94 No Driver Association	20.00	32.00
Brickyard 400 Special		
97 Joe Bessey	18.00	30.00
Auto Palace		
97 Joe Bessey	18.00	30.00
Johnson AC Delco		
98 Derrike Cope	20.00	35.00
Bojangles Black car		
98 Derrike Cope	20.00	35.00
Bojangles Yellow car		
98 Jody Ridley	25.00	40.00
Ford Motorsports		

1995 Racing Champions 1:24 Banks

This series of 1:24 cars offers the collector the option to use them as bank. Each car has a slot in the rear window or in some cases the deck lid.

	Lo	Hi
2 Rusty Wallace	16.00	25.00
Ford Motorsports		
4 Sterling Marlin	16.00	25.00
Kodak		
5 Terry Labonte	16.00	25.00
Kellogg's		
6 Mark Martin	16.00	25.00
Valvoline		
7 Geoff Bodine	16.00	25.00
Exide		
8 Jeff Burton	16.00	25.00
Raybestos		
8 Kenny Wallace	20.00	35.00
Red Dog Hood Open		
12 Derrike Cope	16.00	25.00
Straight Arrow		
16 Ted Musgrave	16.00	25.00
Family Channel		
24 Jeff Gordon	18.00	30.00
DuPont		
24 Jeff Gordon	15.00	30.00
DuPont Signature Series Hood Open		
25 Ken Schrader	16.00	25.00
Budweiser		
25 Ken Schrader	20.00	32.00
Budweiser Hood Open		
27 Loy Allen	16.00	25.00
Hooters		
28 Dale Jarrett	22.00	35.00
Havoline Hood Open		
32 Dale Jarrett	20.00	32.00
Mac Tools		
37 John Andretti	22.00	35.00
K-Mart Hood Open		
44 David Green	16.00	25.00
Slim Jim		
59 Dennis Setzer	20.00	32.00
Alliance		
60 Mark Martin	20.00	35.00
Winn Dixie		
74 Johnny Benson	25.00	40.00
Lipton Tea Hood Open		
88 Ernie Irvan	25.00	40.00
Texaco Hood Open		
94 Bill Elliott	20.00	32.00
McDonald's		
94 Bill Elliott	25.00	40.00
McDonald's Thunderbat		

1996 Racing Champions 1:24 Banks

This series of 1:24 cars offers the collector the option to use them as bank. Each car has a slot in the rear window or in some cases the deck lid. These banks have blacked in windows.

	Lo	Hi
6 Mark Martin	16.00	25.00
Valvoline		
23 Chad Little	25.00	40.00
John Deere		
29 Steve Grissom	15.00	30.00
Cartoon Network		
32 Dale Jarrett	17.50	35.00
Band-Aid		
47 Jeff Fuller	16.00	25.00
Sunoco		
51 Chuck Bown	16.00	25.00
Lucks		
94 Bill Elliott	16.00	25.00
McDonald's		
94 Bill Elliott	15.00	30.00
McDonald's Monopoly		

1996 Racing Champions 1:24 Chrome Banks

These chrome banks were produced in quantites of 166 for each bank. This series is also highlighted two different beer diecast programs: The Ken Schrader Budweiser banks and the David Green Busch banks

	Lo	Hi
2 Rusty Wallace	250.00	400.00
Penske Chrome		
4 Sterling Marlin	200.00	350.00
Kodak		
5 Terry Labonte	500.00	800.00
Kellogg's Silver Hood Open		
6 Mark Martin	250.00	400.00
Valvoline Chrome		
10 Ricky Rudd	200.00	350.00
Tide Chrome		
17 Darrell Waltrip	200.00	350.00
Parts America Chrome		
18 Bobby Labonte	200.00	350.00
Interstate Batteries Chrome		
24 Jeff Gordon	700.00	1100.00
DuPont		
25 Ken Schrader	200.00	400.00
Budweiser		
29 Steve Grissom	200.00	350.00
Cartoon Network Chrome		
29 No Driver Association	200.00	350.00
Scooby-Doo Chrome		
37 John Andretti	150.00	300.00
Kmart		
88 Dale Jarrett	250.00	400.00
Quality Care		
94 Bill Elliott	250.00	400.00
McDonald's		
96 David Green	150.00	250.00
Busch Chrome		

1996 Racing Champions 1:24 Hobby Banks

These 1:24 scale banks were distributed with the chrome banks through hobby outlets.

	Lo	Hi
2 Rusty Wallace	20.00	40.00
Penske Hobby		
4 Sterling Marlin	20.00	40.00
Kodak Hobby		
5 Terry Labonte	20.00	40.00
Kellogg's Hobby		
6 Mark Martin	20.00	40.00

	Lo	Hi
Valvoline Hobby		
10 Ricky Rudd	20.00	40.00
Tide Hobby		
11 Brett Bodine	20.00	40.00
Lowe's 50th Anniversary Hobby		
17 Darrell Waltrip	20.00	40.00
Parts America Hobby		
18 Bobby Labonte	20.00	40.00
Interstate Batteries Hobby		
24 Jeff Gordon	20.00	40.00
DuPont Hobby		
25 Ken Schrader/Bud Olympic	25.00	50.00
29 Steve Grissom	20.00	40.00
Cartoon Hobby		
29 No Driver Association	20.00	40.00
Scooby-Doo Hobby		
37 John Andretti	20.00	40.00
K-Mart Hobby		
88 Dale Jarrett	20.00	40.00
Quality Care Hobby		
94 Bill Elliott	20.00	40.00
McDonald's Hobby		
96 David Green	20.00	40.00
Busch Hobby		

1996 Racing Champions 1:24 Hood Open Banks

These 1:24 scale banks have open hood and were distributed through hobby and retail outlets.

	Lo	Hi
2 Rusty Wallace	20.00	35.00
Miller Genuine Draft Hood Open		
5 Terry Labonte	20.00	35.00
Kellogg's Silver Hood Open		
21 Michael Waltrip	20.00	35.00
Citgo Hood Open		
23 Chad Little	30.00	50.00
John Deere Hood Open		
25 Ken Schrader	20.00	35.00
Budweiser Hood Open		
60 Mark Martin	25.00	40.00
Winn Dixe Hood Open		
75 Morgan Shepherd	20.00	35.00
Remington Hood Open		
88 Dale Jarrett	20.00	35.00
Quality Care Hood Open		
94 Bill Elliott	20.00	35.00
McDonald's Monopoly Hood Open		

1997 Racing Champions 1:24 Banks

This series of 1:24 cars offers the collector the option to use them as bank. Each car has a slot in the rear window or in some cases the deck lid. These banks have blacked in windows. he Mark Martin Winn Dixie bank was offered solely through Winn Dixie. There are 166 of each of the Terry Labonte Kellogg's Champions Chrome bank.

	Lo	Hi
2 Rusty Wallace	35.00	60.00
Miller Lite Matco		
2 Rusty Wallace	100.00	200.00
Miller Lite Matco Chrome		
5 Terry Labonte	30.00	45.00
Kellogg's 1996 Champion		
5 Terry Labonte	300.00	450.00
Kellogg's Champion Chrome		
28 Ernie Irvan	25.00	40.00
Havoline		
10th Anniversary paint scheme		
28 Ernie Irvan	200.00	300.00
Havoline		
10th Anniversary paint scheme Chrome		
60 Mark Martin	25.00	40.00
Winn Dixie		
94 Bill Elliott	35.00	50.00
Mac Tonight		
96 David Green	25.00	40.00
Caterpillar Promo		

1997 Racing Champions 1:24 Gold Banks

These were 166 of each of these 1:24 scale banks produced. There were distributed through hobby outlets.

	Lo	Hi
2 Rusty Wallace	200.00	350.00
Miller Lite Gold		
6 Mark Martin	200.00	350.00
Valvoline Gold		
10 Ricky Rudd	175.00	300.00
Tide Gold		
18 Bobby Labonte	175.00	300.00
Interstate Batteries Gold		
36 Derrike Cope	175.00	300.00
Skittles Gold		
75 Rick Mast	175.00	300.00
Remington Gold		
94 Bill Elliott	200.00	350.00
McDonald's Gold		

1997 Racing Champions 1:24 Hobby Banks

These 1:24 scale banks were distributed through hobby outlets.

	Lo	Hi
2 Rusty Wallace	20.00	40.00
Miller Lite Hobby		
6 Mark Martin	20.00	40.00
Valvoline Hobby		
10 Ricky Rudd	20.00	40.00
Tide Hobby		
18 Bobby Labonte	20.00	40.00
Interstate Batteries Hobby		
36 Derrike Cope	20.00	40.00
Skittles Hobby		
75 Rick Mast	20.00	40.00
Remington Hobby		
94 Bill Elliott	20.00	40.00
McDonald's Hobby		

1997 Racing Champions 1:24 Hood Open Banks

These 1:24 scale banks were distributed through retail outlets and have open hoods.

	Lo	Hi
5 Terry Labonte	20.00	35.00
Kellogg's Hood Open		
6 Mark Martin	20.00	35.00
Valvoline Hood Open		
10 Ricky Rudd	20.00	35.00
Tide Hood Open		
28 Ernie Irvan	20.00	35.00
Havoline Hood Open		
29 Robert Pressley	20.00	35.00
Scooby-Doo Hood Open		
36 Derrike Cope	20.00	35.00
Skittles Hood Open		
75 Rick Mast	20.00	35.00
Remington Hood Open		
94 Bill Elliott	20.00	35.00
McDonald's Hood Open		
96 David Green	20.00	35.00
Caterpillar Hood Open		
97 Chad Little	20.00	35.00
John Deere Hood Open		

1998 Racing Champions 1:24 Driver's Choice Banks

These 1:24 scale banks were distributed through trackside and hobby outlets.

	Lo	Hi
5 Terry Labonte	30.00	50.00
Kellogg's		
6 Mark Martin	30.00	50.00
Valvoline		
10 Ricky Rudd	30.00	45.00
Tide		
94 Bill Elliott	30.00	50.00
McDonald's		

1998 Racing Champions 1:24 Gold Banks

This is a special series produced by Racing Champions to celebrate NASCAR's 50th anniversary. It parallels the regular 1998 1:24 scale series. Each bank is a limited edition of 2,500. Each car is also plated in gold chrome and contains a serial number on its chassis.

	Lo	Hi
9 Lake Speed	25.00	60.00
Huckleberry Hound		
11 Brett Bodine	25.00	60.00
Paychex		
26 Johnny Benson	30.00	75.00
Cheerios		
94 Bill Elliott	60.00	100.00
McDonald's		
99 Jeff Burton	25.00	60.00
Exide		

1998 Racing Champions 1:24 Gold Hood Open Banks

This is a special series produced by Racing Champions to celebrate NASCAR's 50th anniversary. It parallels the regular 1998 1:24 scale series. Each car is a limited edition of 1,998. Each car is also plated in gold chrome and contains a serial number on its chassis.

	Lo	Hi
5 Terry Labonte	30.00	50.00
Blasted Fruit Loops		
5 Terry Labonte	30.00	50.00
Kellogg's Corny		
6 Mark Martin	30.00	50.00
Eagle One		
6 Mark Martin	30.00	50.00
Synpower		
6 Mark Martin	30.00	50.00
Valvoline		
10 Ricky Rudd	25.00	40.00
Tide		
36 Ernie Irvan	25.00	40.00
M&M		
36 Ernie Irvan	25.00	40.00
Skittles		
36 Ernie Irvan	25.00	40.00
Wildberry Skittles		
99 Jeff Burton	25.00	40.00
Exide		

1998 Racing Champions Authentics 1:24 Banks

These 1:24 scale cars marks the first in a series by Racing Champions. These banks were distributed through hobby and trackside outlets. Each bank is packaged in a special black snap case.

	Lo	Hi
6 Mark Martin Eagle One	50.00	80.00
6 Mark Martin Synpower	50.00	80.00
6 Mark Martin Valvoline	50.00	80.00
16 Kevin Lepage Primestar	50.00	80.00
26 Johnny Benson Betty Crocker	50.00	80.00
26 Johnny Benson Betty Crocker	50.00	80.00
26 Johnny Benson Cheerios	50.00	80.00
26 Johnny Benson Trix	50.00	80.00
97 Chad Little John Deere	50.00	80.00
99 Jeff Burton Exide	50.00	80.00

1991 Racing Champions 1:43

This was the first 1:43 scale size series from Racing Champions. Included in the sets are racing greats like Richard Petty, Mark Martin, Cale Yarborough, Bill Elliott and Rusty Wallace

	Lo	Hi
2 Rusty Wallace Pontiac Excitement	5.00	12.00
4 Ernie Irvan Kodak	3.00	6.00
6 Mark Martin Valvoline	5.00	12.00
9 Bill Elliott Melling	5.00	12.00
11 Geoff Bodine No Sponsor	3.00	6.00
15 Morgan Shepherd Motorcraft	3.00	6.00
18 Greg Trammell Melling	3.00	6.00
21 Dale Jarrett Citgo	5.00	12.00
22 Sterling Marlin Maxwell House	3.00	6.00
25 Ken Schrader No Sponsor	3.00	6.00
36 Kenny Wallace Cox Lumber	3.00	6.00
42 Kyle Petty Mello Yello	3.00	6.00
43 Richard Petty STP	3.00	6.00
66 Cale Yarborough TropArtic	3.00	6.00
70 J.D. McDuffie Son's Auto	4.00	10.00
72 Ken Bouchard ADAP	3.00	6.00
89 Jimmy Sauter Evinrude	3.00	6.00

1992 Racing Champions 1:43

This series of 1:43 scale cars was issued in black boxes. They were distributed through both hobby stores and retail outlets.

	Lo	Hi
1 J.Gordon/Baby Ruth	45.00	75.00
1 Rick Mast Majik Market	3.00	6.00
3 Dale Earnhardt Goodwrench	5.00	12.00
5 Ricky Rudd Tide	4.00	8.00
7 Alan Kulwicki Hooters	20.00	35.00
11 Bill Elliott Amoco	5.00	10.00
17 Darrell Waltrip Western Auto	4.00	8.00
17 Darrell Waltrip Western Auto Promo	4.00	8.00
18 Dale Jarrett Interstate Batteries	5.00	10.00
28 Davey Allison Havoline	10.00	20.00
30 Michael Waltrip Pennzoil	3.00	8.00
33 H.Gant/NS	15.00	30.00
66 Chad Little TropArtic	3.00	8.00
72 Ken Bouchard Auto Palace	3.00	6.00

1993 Racing Champions 1:43

This series of 1:43 cars features all the top names in racing. Racing Champions did a primer edition for each of the car makes that were running in NASCAR in 1993.

	Lo	Hi
2 Rusty Wallace Pontiac Excitement	4.00	8.00
3 D.Earnhardt Goodwrench	6.00	12.00
4 Ernie Irvan Kodak	3.00	6.00
5 Ricky Rudd Tide	3.00	6.00
6 Mark Martin Valvoline	4.00	8.00
7 Alan Kulwicki Hooters in Box	12.00	20.00
8 Sterling Marlin Raybestos	12.00	20.00
11 Bill Elliott Amoco	4.00	8.00
14 Terry Labonte Kellogg's	4.00	8.00
15 Geoff Bodine Motorcraft	3.00	6.00
17 Darrell Waltrip Western Auto	3.00	6.00
21 Morgan Shepherd Citgo	3.00	6.00
24 Jeff Gordon DuPont	6.00	12.00
25 Bill Venturini Rain X	6.00	12.00
26 Brett Bodine Quaker State	3.00	6.00
27 Hut Stricklin McDonald's	3.00	6.00
28 Davey Allison Havoline	6.00	12.00
33 Harry Gant No Sponsor	3.00	6.00
42 Kyle Petty Mello Yello	3.00	6.00
44 Rick Wilson STP	3.00	6.00
51 No Driver Association Chevrolet with Primer paint	6.00	12.00
51 No Driver Association Ford with Primer paint	6.00	12.00
51 No Driver Association Pontiac with Primer paint	6.00	12.00
59 Andy Belmont FDP Brakes	6.00	12.00
60 Mark Martin Winn Dixie	5.00	10.00

1993 Racing Champions Premier 1:43

This is the first year that Racing Champions did a Premier series for its 1:43 scale size.

	Lo	Hi
2 Ward Burton Hardee's	10.00	18.00
3 Dale Earnhardt Goodwrench	25.00	40.00
5 Ricky Rudd Tide	8.00	16.00
6 Mark Martin Valvoline	9.00	18.00
7 Alan Kulwicki Hooters	45.00	75.00
8 Sterling Marlin Raybestos	8.00	16.00
11 Bill Elliott Amoco	9.00	18.00
11 Bill Elliott Budweiser	12.00	22.00
17 Darrell Waltrip Western Auto	8.00	16.00
24 Jeff Gordon DuPont	25.00	40.00
27 Hut Stricklin McDonald's	8.00	16.00
28 Davey Allison Havoline	20.00	35.00
28 Davey Allison Havoline with Black and White paint scheme	15.00	30.00
28 Ernie Irvan Havoline	15.00	30.00
33 Harry Gant No Sponsor	8.00	16.00
42 Kyle Petty Mello Yello	8.00	16.00
59 Robert Pressley Alliance	25.00	45.00
60 Mark Martin Winn Dixie	15.00	25.00
97 Joe Bessey AC Delco	10.00	20.00
98 Derrike Cope Bojangles by RCCC	40.00	75.00

1994 Racing Champions 1:43

This was the last year that Racing Champions did a full size 1:43 scale series. The most popular piece in the series is a special Jeff Gordon Coca-Cola 600 winner car.

	Lo	Hi
1 Rick Mast Precision Products	2.00	5.00
4 Sterling Marlin Kodak	2.00	5.00
5 Terry Labonte Kellogg's	3.00	6.00
10 Ricky Rudd Tide	2.00	5.00
19 Loy Allen Hooter's	2.00	5.00
24 Jeff Gordon DuPont	4.00	10.00
24 Jeff Gordon DuPont Coca-Cola 600 Winner	15.00	25.00
26 Brett Bodine Quaker State	2.00	5.00
33 Harry Gant Farewell Tour	8.00	16.00
33 Harry Gant Leo Jackson	2.00	5.00
42 Kyle Petty Mello Yello	2.00	5.00
60 Mark Martin Winn Dixie	4.00	10.00

1994 Racing Champions Premier 1:43

This was the second year that Racing Champions did a 1:43 Premier series. Highlighting the series are two Alan Kulwicki cars (Zerex and Army).

	Lo	Hi
1 Rick Mast Precision Products	8.00	16.00
2 Rusty Wallace Ford Motorsports	10.00	18.00
3 Dale Earnhardt Goodwrench	12.00	22.00
4 Sterling Marlin Kodak	8.00	16.00
5 Terry Labonte Kellogg's	10.00	20.00
6 Mark Martin Valvoline	12.00	18.00
7 Harry Gant Manheim	15.00	25.00
7 Jimmy Hensley Bojangles	12.00	20.00
7 Tommy Kendall Family Channel	12.00	20.00
7 Alan Kulwicki Army	15.00	25.00
7 Alan Kulwicki Zerex	15.00	25.00
12 Clifford Allison Sports Image	12.00	20.00
15 Lake Speed Quality Care	8.00	16.00
16 Ted Musgrave Family Channel	8.00	16.00
21 Morgan Shepherd Cheerwine	10.00	18.00
22 Bobby Labonte Maxwell House	9.00	18.00
24 Jeff Gordon DuPont Snickers	15.00	25.00
25 Ken Schrader GMAC	8.00	16.00
26 Brett Bodine Quaker State	8.00	16.00
28 Ernie Irvan Havoline	12.00	20.00
28 Ernie Irvan Mac Tools	15.00	25.00
30 Michael Waltrip Pennzoil	8.00	16.00
33 Harry Gant Farewell Tour	10.00	18.00
33 Harry Gant Leo Jackson Motorsports	8.00	16.00
59 Dennis Setzer Alliance	12.00	20.00
60 Mark Martin Winn Dixie	12.00	20.00
77 Greg Sacks US Air	12.00	20.00

1995 Racing Champions Premier 1:43

In 1995, Racing Champions only produce 1:43 size cars for special circumstances. The Jeff Gordon was a salute to the inaugural Brickyard Winner and the Mark Martin was done as a promo. The Martin piece was available through Winn Dixie stores.

	Lo	Hi
24 Jeff Gordon Brickyard Win	40.00	70.00
60 Mark Martin Winn Dixie	10.00	20.00

1989 Racing Champions 1:64 Flat Bottom

This was the first series of NASCAR die cast cars produced by Racing Champions. The series is commonly refered to as flat bottoms because the blister package the car came in was flat across the bottom. In all subsequent years there was a bubble across the bottom to help the package freely stand up.

	Lo	Hi
3 Dale Earnhardt Goodwrench	90.00	150.00
9 Bill Elliott Motorcraft Melling Ford	50.00	90.00
16 Larry Pearson No Sponsor	30.00	50.00
28 Davey Allison Havoline	60.00	100.00
30 Michael Waltrip Country Time	35.00	60.00
94 Sterling Marlin Sunoco	35.00	60.00

1990 Racing Champions 1:64

This was the first full series of 1:64 scale cars produced by Racing Champions. Many of the cars came with rubber tires as opposed to plastic. Cars with rubber tires usually carry a $5.00 to $10.00 premium. The cars used many different body styles.

	Lo	Hi
1 Terry Labonte Oldsmobile	15.00	30.00
3 Dale Earnhardt Goodwrench	70.00	120.00
3 Dale Earnhardt GM Performance Parts	20.00	40.00
9 Bill Elliott Orange and Blue Stripe No Melling on the car	100.00	150.00
9 Bill Elliott Orange and Blue Stripe with Melling on the car	15.00	30.00
9 Bill Elliott Red and Blue Stripe with Melling on the car	30.00	50.00
10 Derrike Cope Lumina	60.00	100.00
14 A.J.Foyt Buick	60.00	100.00
14 A.J.Foyt Lumina	60.00	100.00
14 A.J.Foyt Old Pontiac body style	25.00	50.00
14 A.J.Foyt Oldsmobile	18.00	35.00
14 A.J.Foyt Pontiac	18.00	35.00
15 Morgan Shepherd Red and White color scheme	12.50	25.00
15 Morgan Shepherd Red and Cream color scheme	15.00	30.00
16 Larry Pearson Buick with White Bumper	75.00	125.00
16 Larry Pearson Buick with Brown Bumper Name in script	18.00	35.00
16 Larry Pearson Buick with Brown Bumper Name in print	10.00	20.00
16 Larry Pearson Lumina with Brown Bumper	50.00	90.00
16 Larry Pearson Old Pontiac with Brown Bumper	50.00	90.00
16 Larry Pearson Oldsmobile with Brown Bumper	50.00	90.00
16 Larry Pearson Pontiac with Brown Bumper	10.00	20.00
20 Rob Moroso Red Stripe	15.00	30.00
21 Neil Bonnett Citgo	12.50	25.00
26 Kenny Bernstein Buick	8.00	16.00
26 Kenny Bernstein Lumina	25.00	50.00
26 Kenny Bernstein Old Pontiac body style	25.00	50.00
26 Kenny Bernstein Oldsmobile	20.00	40.00
27 Rusty Wallace Old Pontiac Miller Genuine Draft	50.00	90.00
27 Rusty Wallace Oldsmobile	60.00	100.00
27 Rusty Wallace Pontiac Miller Genuine Draft	30.00	60.00
27 Rusty Wallace Pontiac Miller	30.00	60.00
27 Rusty Wallace Pontiac with Silver Decals	40.00	80.00
28 Davey Allison Black and White paint scheme	60.00	100.00
28 Davey Allison Black and Gold paint scheme	25.00	50.00
30 Michael Waltrip Country Time	35.00	70.00
30 Michael Waltrip Maxwell House	12.50	25.00
33 Harry Gant Pontiac	15.00	30.00
42 Kyle Petty Buick with Blue and White paint	75.00	125.00
42 Kyle Petty Lumina with Blue and White paint	75.00	125.00
42 Kyle Petty Old Pontiac with Blue and White paint	30.00	60.00
42 Kyle Petty Oldsmobile with Blue and White paint	50.00	100.00
42 Kyle Petty Sabco on the deck lid	15.00	30.00
42 Kyle Petty without Sabco on the deck lid Blue and Pink paint scheme	15.00	30.00
43 Richard Petty Pontiac	20.00	40.00
94 Sterling Marlin Buick	50.00	90.00
94 Sterling Marlin Lumina	40.00	75.00
94 Sterling Marlin Old Pontiac	50.00	90.00
94 Sterling Marlin Oldsmobile	10.00	20.00

1991 Racing Champions 1:64

This series of 1:64 scale Racing Champion cars has many different package variations. There were three variations that most of the pieces came in. One has Dale Earnhardt on the back of the package (abbreviated EB in the listing). Another has Richard Petty on the back of the package (abbreviated PB). Finally a third variation comes with NASCAR Properties on the stand the car sits on. Again many different body styles were used.

	Lo	Hi
1 Terry Labonte Oldsmobile EB	7.50	15.00
1 Terry Labonte Oldsmobile NP	18.00	35.00
1 Terry Labonte Oldsmobile PB	7.50	15.00
1 Rick Mast Buick PB	3.00	6.00
1 Rick Mast Oldsmobile PB	2.00	5.00
2 Rusty Wallace Pontiac EB	7.50	15.00
2 Rusty Wallace Pontiac PB	5.00	10.00
3 Dale Earnhardt Lumina EB	20.00	40.00
3 Dale Earnhardt Lumina NP	40.00	70.00
3 Dale Earnhardt Lumina PB	12.50	25.00
4 Ernie Irvan/PB Kodak PB	2.00	5.00

5 Jay Fogleman	Lumina PB	2.00	5.00
9 Bill Elliott	Ford PB	2.00	5.00
9 Bill Elliott	Ford EB Car is 1/2 blue	12.50	25.00
9 Bill Elliott	Ford EB Car is 3/4 blue	7.50	15.00
9 Bill Elliott	Old Ford body style EB Orange and White paint scheme	10.00	20.00
9 Bill Elliott	Old Ford body style NP Orange and White paint scheme	18.00	35.00
10 Derrike Cope	Purolator EB with 2 rows of checkers	3.00	6.00
10 Derrike Cope	Purolator EB with 3 rows of checkers	12.50	25.00
10 Derrike Cope	Purolator PB with 2 rows of checkers	2.00	5.00
10 Derrike Cope	Purolator PB with 3 rows of checkers	7.50	15.00
11 Geoff Bodine	Ford EB	2.00	5.00
11 Geoff Bodine	Ford PB	2.00	5.00
12 Bobby Allison	Buick PB	2.00	5.00
12 Hut Stricklin	Buick PB	2.00	5.00
12 Hut Stricklin	Lumina PB	2.00	5.00
14 A.J.Foyt	Buick PB	10.00	20.00
14 A.J.Foyt	Oldsmobile EB	10.00	20.00
14 A.J.Foyt	Oldsmobile NP	18.00	35.00
14 A.J.Foyt	Oldsmobile PB	5.00	10.00
15 Morgan Shepherd	Ford with Red paint scheme EB	5.00	10.00
15 Morgan Shepherd	Ford EB with Red and White paint scheme	7.50	15.00
15 Morgan Shepherd	Ford PB	2.00	5.00
15 Morgan Shepherd	Old Ford EB	5.00	10.00
15 Morgan Shepherd	Old Ford NP	12.50	25.00
16 Larry Pearson	Buick EB	3.00	6.00
16 Larry Pearson	Buick NP	12.50	25.00
16 Larry Pearson	Buick PB	2.00	5.00
16 Larry Pearson	Lumina PB	12.50	25.00
18 Greg Trammel	Ford Melling PB	2.00	5.00
20 Rob Moroso	Oldsmobile EB	10.00	20.00
20 Rob Moroso	Oldsmobile with STP decal NP	25.00	50.00
21 Neil Bonnett	Oldsmobile Ford EB	12.50	25.00
21 Neil Bonnett	Old Ford NP	25.00	50.00
21 Dale Jarrett	Ford EB	3.00	6.00
21 Dale Jarrett	Ford PB	2.00	5.00
22 Sterling Marlin	Ford with Black wheels PB	2.00	5.00
22 Sterling Marlin	Ford with Silver Wheels PB	10.00	20.00
25 Ken Schrader	Lumina PB	2.00	5.00
26 Kenny Bernstein	Buick EB	3.00	6.00
26 Kenny Bernstein	Buick Quaker State NP	10.00	20.00
26 Kenny Bernstein	Buick PB	2.00	5.00
26 Kenny Bernstein	Oldsmobile PB	5.00	10.00
26 Brett Bodine	Buick Quaker State PB	2.00	5.00
26 Brett Bodine	Lumina PB	2.00	5.00
27 Rusty Wallace	Pontiac Miller Genuine Draft EB	30.00	60.00
27 Rusty Wallace	Pontiac Miller Genuine Draft NP	50.00	90.00
27 Rusty Wallace	Pontiac no MGD EB	15.00	30.00
27 Rusty Wallace	Pontiac Miller EB	20.00	40.00
28 Davey Allison	Ford EB	20.00	40.00
28 Davey Allison	Ford PB	18.00	35.00
28 Davey Allison	Old Ford EB	20.00	40.00
28 Davey Allison	Old Ford NP	50.00	90.00
28 Davey Allison	Old Ford PB	15.00	30.00
30 Michael Waltrip	Pontiac Country Time EB	12.50	25.00
30 Michael Waltrip	Pontiac Pennzoil EB with STP decal	6.00	12.00
30 Michael Waltrip	Pontiac Pennzoil EB without STP decal	6.00	12.00
30 Michael Waltrip	Pontiac NP	20.00	40.00
30 Michael Waltrip	Pontiac PB	2.00	5.00
33 Harry Gant	Buick PB	10.00	20.00
33 Harry Gant	Oldsmobile EB	7.50	15.00
33 Harry Gant	Oldsmobile PB	6.00	12.00
33 Harry Gant	Pontiac EB	7.50	15.00
33 Harry Gant	Pontiac NP	20.00	45.00
34 Todd Bodine	Lumina Welco	2.00	5.00
36 Kenny Wallace	Pontiac Cox Lumber	2.00	5.00
42 Kyle Petty	Pontiac Peak EB	7.50	15.00
42 Kyle Petty	Pontiac Peak NB	18.00	35.00
42 Kyle Petty	Pontiac Peak PB	10.00	20.00
42 Kyle Petty	Pontiac Mello Yello PB	2.00	5.00
43 Richard Petty	Pontiac EB	7.50	15.00
43 Richard Petty	Pontiac NP	25.00	50.00
43 Richard Petty	Pontiac PB	2.00	5.00
52 Jimmy Means	Pontiac PB	2.00	5.00
59 Robert Pressley	Alliance	2.00	5.00
66 Cale Yarborough	Pontiac PB	2.00	5.00
68 Bobby Hamilton	Oldsmobile PB	2.00	5.00
68 Bobby Hamilton	Buick PB	10.00	20.00
70 J.D. McDuffie	Son's Auto	2.00	5.00
71 Dave Marcis	Lumina PB	2.00	5.00
72 Ken Bouchard	Pontiac ADAP PB	10.00	20.00
72 Tracy Leslie	Oldsmobile Detroit Gaskets PB	2.00	5.00
89 Jimmy Sauter	Pontiac PB	2.00	5.00
89 Jimmy Sauter	Pontiac Day Glow PB	5.00	10.00
94 Terry Labonte	Buick PB	5.00	10.00
94 Terry Labonte	Oldsmobile PB	2.00	5.00
94 Sterling Marlin	Oldsmobile EB	5.00	10.00
94 Sterling Marlin	Oldsmobile NP	12.50	25.00
96 Tom Peck	Lumina PB	18.00	35.00
96 Tom Peck	Oldsmobile PB	2.00	5.00

1992 Racing Champions 1:64

Every piece in this series either has a Petty back or a copyright list on the back. This was Jeff Gordon's first appearance in a Racing Champions die cast series.

		Lo	Hi
1 Jeff Gordon	Baby Ruth	25.00	50.00
1 Rick Mast	Majik Market	1.00	3.00
2 Rusty Wallace	Pontiac Excitement	2.00	5.00
3 Dale Earnhardt	Goodwrench	4.00	8.00
4 Ernie Irvan	Kodak	1.50	4.00
5 Jay Fogleman	Inn Keeper	1.00	3.00
5 Ricky Rudd	Tide	1.00	3.00
6 Mark Martin	Valvoline	2.00	5.00
7 Harry Gant	Mac Tools	7.50	15.00
7 Alan Kulwicki	Hooter's	10.00	20.00
8 Bobby Dotter	Team R	1.00	3.00
9 Joe Bessey	AC Delco	2.00	5.00
9 Bill Elliott	Melling	1.50	4.00
9 Chad Little	Melling Performance	2.00	5.00
10 Derrike Cope	Purolator Adam's Mark	2.00	5.00
10 Derrike Cope	Purolator with name in Blue	2.00	5.00
10 Derrike Cope	Purolator with name in White	7.50	15.00
10 Sterling Marlin	Maxwell House	4.00	8.00
11 Geoff Bodine	No Sponsor	2.00	5.00
11 Bill Elliott	Amoco	1.50	4.00
12 Bobby Allison	No Sponsor	1.00	3.00
12 Hut Stricklin	Raybestos	1.00	3.00
14 A.J.Foyt	No Sponsor	7.50	15.00
15 Geoff Bodine	Motorcraft	1.00	3.00
16 Wally Dallenbach Jr.	Roush Racing	7.50	15.00
17 Darrell Waltrip	Western Auto	1.00	3.00
18 Dale Jarrett	Interstate Batteries	2.00	5.00
18 Greg Trammell	Melling	1.00	3.00
19 Chad Little	Tyson	1.00	3.00
20 Mike Wallace	First Aide	4.00	8.00
21 Dale Jarrett	Citgo	2.00	5.00
21 Morgan Shepherd	Citgo	1.00	3.00
22 Sterling Marlin	Maxwell House	1.00	3.00
25 Ken Schrader	Hendrick Motorsports	2.00	5.00

	Lo	Hi
25 Bill Venturini	2.00	5.00
Amoco Rain X		
26 Brett Bodine	1.00	3.00
Quaker State		
28 Davey Allison	7.50	15.00
Havoline		
28 Bobby Hillin	3.00	6.00
Havoline		
30 Michael Waltrip	1.00	3.00
Pennzoil		
31 Bobby Hillin	2.00	5.00
Team Ireland		
33 Harry Gant	2.00	5.00
No Sponsor		
34 Todd Bodine	2.00	5.00
Welco Quick Stop		
36 Kenny Wallace	2.00	5.00
Cox Lumber		
36 Kenny Wallace	3.00	6.00
Dirt Devil		
42 Bobby Hillin	4.00	8.00
Mello Yello		
42 Kyle Petty	1.00	3.00
Mello Yello		
43 Richard Petty	1.00	3.00
STP with Black wheels		
43 Richard Petty	1.00	3.00
STP with Blue wheels		
44 Bill Caudill	2.00	5.00
Army		
49 Stanley Smith	5.00	10.00
Ameritron		
55 Ted Musgrave	5.00	10.00
Jasper Engines		
56 Jerry Glanville	3.00	6.00
Atlanta Falcons		
59 Andy Belmont	3.00	6.00
FDP Brakes		
60 Mark Martin	3.00	6.00
Winn Dixie		
63 Chuck Bown	2.00	5.00
Nescafe		
66 Jimmy Hensley	1.00	3.00
TropArtic		
66 Chad Little	1.00	3.00
TropArtic		
66 Cale Yarborough	2.00	5.00
TropArtic Ford		
66 Cale Yarborough	1.00	3.00
TropArtic Pontiac		
68 Bobby Hamilton	1.00	3.00
Country Time		
70 J.D. McDuffie	1.00	3.00
Son's Auto		
71 Dave Marcis	1.00	3.00
Big Apple Market		
72 Ken Bouchard	4.00	8.00
ADAP		
72 Tracy Leslie	1.00	3.00
Detroit Gasket		
75 Butch Miller	2.00	5.00
Food Country		
83 Lake Speed	3.00	6.00
Purex		
87 Joe Nemechek	2.00	5.00
Texas Pete		
89 Jimmy Sauter	1.00	3.00
Evinrude		
94 Terry Labonte	5.00	10.00
Sunoco with Blue bumper		
94 Terry Labonte	5.00	10.00
Suncoo with Yellow bumper		
96 Tom Peck	1.00	3.00
Thomas Brothers		

1992 Racing Champions Premier 1:64

This 5-piece series was the first time Racing Champions did a Premier Series. Each piece comes in a black shadow box and the number of quantity produced is on the front of the box.

	Lo	Hi
3 Dale Earnhardt	18.00	30.00
Goodwrench		
11 Bill Elliott	7.50	15.00
Amoco		
17 Darrell Waltrip	6.00	14.00
Western Auto		
28 Davey Allison	18.00	30.00
Havoline		
43 Richard Petty	10.00	20.00
STP		

1993 Racing Champions 1:64

This series of 1:64 scale cars features the top names in racing. The cars came in a blister pack and were sold through both hobby and retail outlets.

	Lo	Hi
0 D.McCabe	2.00	4.00
Fisher Snow Plows		
2 Rusty Wallace	2.00	5.00
Pontiac Excitement		
3 Dale Earnhardt	6.00	10.00
Goodwrench		
3 Dale Earnhardt	4.00	10.00
Goodwrench Mom-n-Pop's		
4 Ernie Irvan	2.00	5.00
Kodak		
5 Ricky Rudd	2.00	4.00
Tide		
6 Mark Martin	5.00	10.00
Valvoline		
7 Alan Kulwicki	7.50	15.00
Hooters		
8 Sterling Marlin	2.00	4.00
Raybestos		
11 Bill Elliott	2.00	5.00
Amoco		
12 Jimmy Spencer	2.00	4.00
Meineke		
14 Terry Labote	6.00	12.00
Kellogg's		
15 Geoff Bodine	2.00	4.00
Motorcraft		
17 Darrell Waltrip	2.00	4.00
Western Auto		
18 Dale Jarrett	2.00	5.00
Interstate Batteries		
21 Morgan Shepherd	2.00	4.00
Citgo		
22 Bobby Labonte	2.00	4.00
Maxwell House		
24 Jeff Gordon	15.00	30.00
DuPont		
25 Ken Schrader	5.00	10.00
Kodiak		
25 Bill Venturini	3.00	6.00
Rain X		
26 Brett Bodine	2.00	4.00
Quaker State		
27 Hut Stricklin	2.00	4.00
McDonald's		
28 Davey Allison	5.00	10.00
Havoline		
28 Davey Allison	6.00	12.00
Havoline		
with Black and White paint scheme		
28 Ernie Irvan	5.00	10.00
Havoline		
33 Harry Gant	2.00	4.00
No Sponsor Lumina		
33 Harry Gant	2.00	4.00
No Sponsor Oldsmobile		
42 Kyle Petty	2.00	4.00
Mello Yello		
44 Rick Wilson	2.00	4.00
STP		
59 Andy Belmont	4.00	8.00
FDP Brakes		
59 Robert Pressley	4.00	8.00
Alliance		
60 Mark Martin	4.00	8.00
Winn Dixie		
71 Dave Marcis	2.00	4.00
STG		
75 Butch Mock	2.00	4.00
Factory Stores of America		
87 Joe Nemechek	2.00	4.00
Dentyne		
98 Derrike Cope	2.00	4.00
Bojangles		

1993 Racing Champions Premier 1:64

This was the second year of the 1:64 scale Premier series. The series is highlighted by the Alan Kulwicki Hooters car and the three different Champion Forever Davey Allison pieces.

	Lo	Hi
1 Rodney Combs	5.00	10.00
Jebco Clocks		
2 Ward Burton	7.00	14.00
Hardee's		
02 Frank Kimmel	7.50	15.00
Harley Davidson		
2 Rusty Wallace	3.00	7.00
Pontiac Excitement		
3 Dale Earnhardt	12.50	25.00
Goodwrench		
3 D.Earnhardt	7.50	15.00
Dale Earnhardt Inc.		
4 Ernie Irvan	3.00	6.00
Kodak		

	Lo	Hi
4 Jeff Purvis	7.50	15.00
Kodak		
5 Ricky Rudd	3.00	6.00
Tide		
6 Mark Martin	3.00	7.00
Valvoline		
6 Mark Martin	7.00	14.00
Valvoline		
Four in a Row Promo		
6 Mike Stefanik	5.00	10.00
Valvoline Auto Palace		
7 Jimmy Hensley	15.00	30.00
Alan Kulwicki Racing		
7 Alan Kulwicki	20.00	40.00
Hooter's		
7 Alan Kulwicki	12.50	25.00
Zerex		
8 Sterling Marlin	3.00	6.00
Raybestos		
11 Bill Elliott	8.00	20.00
Budweiser Promo		
12 Jimmy Spencer	3.00	6.00
Meineke		
14 Terry Labonte	7.50	15.00
Kellogg's		
15 Geoff Bodine	3.00	6.00
Motorcraft		
18 Dale Jarrett	4.00	8.00
Interstate Batteries		
21 Morgan Shepherd	3.00	6.00
Citgo		
24 Jeff Gordon	10.00	20.00
DuPont		
26 Brett Bodine	3.00	6.00
Quaker State		
27 Hut Stricklin	3.00	6.00
McDonald's		
27 Hut Stricklin	3.00	6.00
Mr. Pibb		
28 Davey Allison	10.00	20.00
Havoline with Black paint scheme		
28 Davey Allison	7.50	15.00
Havoline with Champion Forever card and Black and Gold paint scheme		
28 Davey Allison	10.00	20.00
Havoline with Champion Forever card and Black and Orange paint scheme		
28 Davey Allison	10.00	20.00
Havoline with Champion Forever card and Black and White paint scheme		
28 Ernie Irvan	10.00	20.00
Havoline		
31 Neil Bonnett	25.00	50.00
Mom-n-Pop's		
33 Harry Gant	3.00	6.00
No Sponsor		
41 Ernie Irvan	7.50	15.00
Mac Tools		
42 Kyle Petty	3.00	6.00
Mello Yello		
44 Jimmy Hensley	6.00	12.00
STP		
59 Robert Pressley	8.00	20.00
Alliance		
59 Dennis Setzer	7.50	15.00
Alliance		
60 Mark Martin	10.00	20.00
Winn Dixie		
87 Joe Nemechek	3.00	6.00
Dentyne		
97 Joe Bessey	3.00	6.00
Auto Palace		
98 Derrike Cope	5.00	10.00
Bojangles with Black paint scheme		
98 Derrike Cope	5.00	10.00
Bojangles with Yellow paint scheme		

Racing Champions 1:64 1993 PVC Box

Almost each die cast in this series was done for a special occassion. Each piece comes a clear PVC box. The box has the drivers name, what the occassion is and the quantity produced in gold foil on top of it.

	Lo	Hi
3 Dale Earnhardt	7.50	15.00
Back in Black		
3 Dale Earnhardt	7.50	15.00
Darlington WIn		
3 Dale Earnhardt	7.50	15.00
Busch Clash Win		
3 Dale Earnhardt	7.50	15.00
Twin 125 Win		
4 Ernie Irvan	5.00	10.00
Kodak Talladega Win		
7 Harry Gant	4.00	8.00
Morema		
7 Jimmy Hensley	5.00	10.00
Hanes		
7 Jimmy Hensley	5.00	10.00
Purolator		
8 Sterling Marlin	5.00	10.00
Raybestos		
12 David Bonnett	4.00	8.00
Plasti-Kote		
18 Dale Jarrett	4.00	8.00
Interstate Batteries		
21 Morgan Shepherd	4.00	8.00
Cheerwine		
24 Jeff Gordon	15.00	30.00
DuPont		
24 Jeff Gordon	15.00	30.00
DuPont Fan Club		
24 Jeff Gordon	12.50	25.00
DuPont Daytona		
24 Jeff Gordon	12.50	25.00
DuPont Twin 125 Win		
27 Hut Stricklin	4.00	8.00
McDonald's All-American		
27 Hut Stricklin	10.00	20.00
McDonald's Daytona		
27 Hut Stricklin	25.00	50.00
McDonald's 250 produced		
27 Hut Stricklin	4.00	8.00
McDonald's Taylorsville		
28 Alan Kulwicki	20.00	40.00
Hardee's		
28 Davey Allison	10.00	20.00
Havoline		
28 Ernie Irvan	10.00	20.00
Havoline		
28 Ernie Irvan	10.00	20.00
Havoline Charlotte		
40 Kenny Wallace	12.50	25.00
Dirt Devil		
42 Kyle Petty	10.00	20.00
Mello Yello		
44 David Green	10.00	20.00
Slim Jim		
44 Rick Wilson	10.00	20.00
STP		
46 Al Unser Jr.	12.50	25.00
Valvoline		
51 No Driver Association	20.00	40.00
Pontiac Racing Champions		
51 No Driver Association	20.00	40.00
Lumina Racing Champions		
51 No Driver Association	20.00	40.00
Thunderbird Racing Champions		
51 No Driver Association	20.00	40.00
Racing Champions Mascot		
52 Ken Schrader	5.00	10.00
Morema		
56 Ernie Irvan	12.50	25.00
Earnhardt Chevrolet		
59 Robert Pressley	10.00	20.00
Alliance Fan Club		
59 Robert Pressley	18.00	35.00
Alliance September 1993		
59 Robert Pressley	10.00	20.00
Alliance Pressley		
60 Mark Martin	7.50	15.00
Winn Dixie		
68 Bobby Hamilton	40.00	75.00
Country Time		
89 Jeff McClure	4.00	8.00
Bero Motors		
93 No Driver Association	7.50	15.00
Budweiser 500		
93 No Driver Association	7.50	15.00
Food City 500		
93 No Driver Association	7.50	15.00
Slick 50 300		
93 No Driver Association	7.50	15.00
Racing Champions Club Car		

1994 Racing Champions 1:64

These 1:64 scale pieces were mainly packaged in a red blister pack and distributed through hobby shops and retail outlets. The highlight to the series is the Jeff Gordon Brickyard peice.

	Lo	Hi
00 Johnny Rumley	3.00	6.00
Big Dog Coal		
1 Rick Mast	2.00	4.00
Precision Products		
2 Ricky Craven	2.00	4.00
DuPont		
2 Rusty Wallace	2.00	5.00
Ford Motorsports		
2 Rusty Wallace	4.00	8.00
Ford Motorsports with no Blue		
4 Sterling Marlin	2.00	4.00
Kodak		
5 Terry Labonte	3.00	6.00
Kellogg's		
6 Mark Martin	2.00	5.00
Valvoline		
7 Geoff Bodine	2.00	4.00
Exide		
7 Harry Gant	4.00	8.00
Manheim		
8 Jeff Burton	4.00	8.00
Raybestos		
8 Kenny Wallace	2.00	4.00
TIC Financial		
10 Ricky Rudd	2.00	4.00
Tide		
12 Clifford Allison	5.00	10.00

	Lo	Hi
Sports Image		
14 John Andretti	2.00	4.00
Kanawaha		
15 Lake Speed	2.00	4.00
Quality Care		
16 Ted Musgrave	2.00	4.00
Family Channel		
17 Darrell Waltrip	2.00	4.00
Western Auto		
18 Dale Jarrett	5.00	10.00
Interstate Batteries		
19 Loy Allen	2.00	4.00
Hooters		
20 Randy LaJoie	2.00	4.00
Fina		
21 Morgan Shepherd	2.00	4.00
Citgo		
22 Bobby Labonte	4.00	8.00
Maxwell House		
23 Hut Stricklin	5.00	10.00
Smokin' Joe's in PVC box		
24 Jeff Gordon	3.00	6.00
DuPont		
24 Jeff Gordon	7.50	15.00
DuPont Brickyard special		
25 Hermie Sadler	2.00	4.00
Virginia is for Lovers		
25 Ken Schrader	2.00	4.00
GMAC		
26 Brett Bodine	2.00	4.00
Quaker State		
27 Jimmy Spencer	2.00	4.00
McDonald's		
28 Ernie Irvan	2.00	5.00
Havoline		
30 Michael Waltrip	2.00	4.00
Pennzoil		
31 Tom Peck	3.00	6.00
Channellock		
33 Harry Gant	20.00	40.00
No Sponsor		
38 Elton Sawyer	2.00	4.00
Ford Credit		
40 Bobby Hamilton	2.00	4.00
Kendall		
42 Kyle Petty	2.00	4.00
Mello Yello		
44 Bobby Hillin	2.00	4.00
Buss Fuses		
46 Shawna Robinson	2.00	4.00
Polaroid		
52 Ken Schrader	3.00	6.00
AC Delco		
54 Robert Pressley	2.00	4.00
Manheim		
60 Mark Martin	4.00	8.00
Winn Dixie		
63 Jim Bown	2.00	4.00
Lysol		
75 Todd Bodine	2.00	4.00
Factory Stores of America		
83 Sherry Blakely	2.00	4.00
Ramses		
92 Larry Pearson	2.00	4.00
Stanley Tools		
94 No Driver Association	3.00	6.00
Brickyard 400 special		
97 Joe Bessey	2.00	4.00
Johnson		
98 Derrike Cope	2.00	4.00
Fingerhut		

1994 Racing Champions 1:64 Hobby

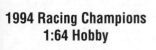

This series was distributed through hobby channels. Each peice came in a yellow box.

	Lo	Hi
1 Rick Mast	1.50	4.00
Precision Products		
2 Ricky Craven	1.50	4.00
DuPont		
2 Rusty Wallace	2.00	5.00
Ford Motorsports		
4 Sterling Marlin	1.50	4.00
Kodak		
4 Sterling Marlin	1.50	4.00
Kodak Funsaver		
5 Terry Labonte	3.00	6.00
Kellogg's		
6 Mark Martin	4.00	8.00
Valvoline		
7 Geoff Bodine	1.50	4.00
Exide		
8 Jeff Burton	1.50	4.00
Raybestos		
14 Terry Labonte	5.00	10.00
MW Windows		
15 Lake Speed	1.50	4.00
Quality Care		
16 Ted Musgrave	1.50	4.00
Family Channel		
17 Darrell Waltrip	3.00	6.00
Western Auto		
18 Dale Jarrett	4.00	8.00
Interstate Batteries		
19 Loy Allen	1.50	4.00
Hooter's		
22 Brett Bodine	1.50	4.00
Maxwell House		
23 Chad Little	1.50	4.00
Bayer		
24 Jeff Gordon	7.50	15.00
DuPont		
25 Hermie Sadler	1.50	4.00
Virginia is for Lovers		
26 Brett Bodine	1.50	4.00
Quaker State		
27 Jimmy Spencer	1.50	4.00
McDonald's		
30 Michael Waltrip	1.50	4.00
Pennzoil		
31 Tom Peck	1.50	4.00
Channellock		
33 Harry Gant	1.50	4.00
No Sponsor		
34 Mike McLaughlin	1.50	4.00
Fiddle Faddle		
38 Elton Sawyer	1.50	4.00
Ford Credit		
40 Bobby Hamilton	1.50	4.00
Kendall		
42 Kyle Petty	1.50	4.00
Mello Yello		
46 Shawna Robinson	1.50	4.00
Polaroid		
63 Jim Bown	1.50	4.00
Lysol		
75 Todd Bodine	1.50	4.00
Factory Stores of America		
92 Larry Pearson	1.50	4.00
Stanley Tools		
94 No Driver Association	3.00	6.00
Brickyard 400		
98 Derrike Cope	1.50	4.00
Fingerhut		

1994 Racing Champions Premier 1:64

This series of 1:64 Premier series was issued by Racing Champions through retail outlets and hobby dealers. The pieces come in a black shadow box and have the quantity produced stamped in gold on the front of the box.

	Lo	Hi
0 D.McCabe	5.00	10.00
Fisher Snow Plows		
1 Davey Allison	10.00	20.00
Lancaster		
2 Ricky Craven	3.00	6.00
DuPont		
2 Rusty Wallace	5.00	10.00
Miller Genuine Draft		
2 Rusty Wallace	10.00	20.00
Mac Tools		
3 Dale Earnhardt	10.00	20.00
Goodwrench		
4 Sterling Marlin	3.00	6.00
Kodak		
4 Sterling Marlin	5.00	10.00
Kodak Funsaver		
5 Terry Labonte	5.00	10.00
Kellogg's		
6 Mark Martin	3.00	6.00
Valvoline		
6 Mark Martin	7.00	14.00
Valvoline		
four in a row special		
7 Geoff Bodine	3.00	6.00
Exide		
7 Harry Gant	7.50	15.00
Manheim		
7 Alan Kulwicki	15.00	30.00
Army		
8 Jeff Burton	3.00	6.00
Raybestos		
8 Kenny Wallace	5.00	10.00
TIC Financial		

12 Clifford Allison Sports Image	7.50	15.00
15 Lake Speed Quality Care	3.00	6.00
16 Chad Chaffin 31W Insulation	6.00	12.00
16 Ted Musgrave Family Channel	3.00	6.00
18 Dale Jarrett Interstate Batteries	5.00	10.00
19 Loy Allen Hooters	3.00	6.00
20 Randy LaJoie Fina	3.00	6.00
21 Johnny Benson Berger	7.50	15.00
24 Jeff Gordon DuPont	15.00	30.00
24 Jeff Gordon DuPont 1993 Rookie of the Year	8.00	16.00
25 Hernie Sadler Virgina is for Lovers	6.00	12.00
25 Ken Schrader Kodiak	3.00	6.00
26 Brett Bodine Quaker State	3.00	6.00
27 Jimmy Spencer McDonald's	3.00	6.00
28 Ernie Irvan Mac Tools in Yellow box	9.00	18.00
31 Steve Grissom Channellock	6.00	12.00
33 Bobby Labonte Dentyne	20.00	40.00
34 Mike McLaughlin Fiddle Faddle	3.00	6.00
35 Shawna Robinson Polaroid Captiva	7.50	15.00
40 Bobby Hamilton Kendall	3.00	6.00
43 Rodney Combs French's	7.50	15.00
43 Wally Dallenbach Jr. STP	7.50	15.00
46 Shawna Robinson Polaroid	5.00	10.00
54 Robert Pressley Alliance	6.00	12.00
59 Andy Belmont Metal Arrester	5.00	10.00
59 Dennis Setzer Alliance 2000 produced	12.50	25.00
59 Dennis Setzer Alliance	6.00	12.00
60 Mark Martin Winn Dixie	7.50	15.00
70 J.D. McDuffie Son's Auto	7.50	15.00
71 Dave Marcis Earnhardt Chevrolet	7.50	15.00
75 Todd Bodine Factory Stores of America	3.00	6.00
77 Greg Sacks US Air Jasper Engines	7.50	15.00
85 Jimmy Sauter Rheem AC	5.00	10.00
89 Jeff McClure FSU Seminoles	5.00	10.00
98 Jody Ridley Ford Motorsports	3.00	6.00

1994 Racing Champions Premier 1:64 Brickyard 400

This series was issued in conjunction with the first Brickyard 400. The boxes are easily distinguishable due to their purple color. The Jeff Gordon pieces is the most popular due to his winning of the first Brickyard 400.

	Lo	Hi
3 Dale Earnhardt Goodwrench	20.00	35.00
6 Mark Martin Valvoline	5.00	10.00
18 Dale Jarrett Interstate Batteries	5.00	10.00
21 Morgan Shepherd Citgo	4.00	7.00
24 Jeff Gordon DuPont	40.00	75.00
26 Brett Bodine Quaker State	4.00	7.00
27 Jimmy Spencer McDonald's	4.00	7.00
30 Michael Waltrip Pennzoil	4.00	7.00
42 Kyle Petty Mello Yello	4.00	7.00

1994 Racing Champions 1:64 To the Maxx 1

This was the first series issued by Racing Champions that included MAXX Premier Plus card.

	Lo	Hi
2 Rusty Wallace Ford Motorsports	4.00	8.00
4 Sterling Marlin Kodak	4.00	7.00
5 Terry Labonte Kellogg's	4.00	8.00
6 Mark Martin Valvoline	4.00	8.00
16 Ted Musgrave Family Channel	4.00	7.00
24 Jeff Gordon DuPont	6.00	12.00
28 Ernie Irvan Havoline	4.00	8.00
42 Kyle Petty Mello Yello	4.00	7.00

1995 Racing Champions 1:64 Previews

This series of 1:64 replica cars was a Preview to many of the cars that raced in the 1995 season. The Geoff Bodine car came with either Hoosier or Goodyear tires.

	Lo	Hi
1 Rick Mast Precision Products	2.00	4.00
2 Ricky Craven DuPont	2.00	4.00
2 Rusty Wallace Ford Motorsports	2.00	5.00
4 Sterling Marlin Kodak	2.00	4.00
6 Mark Martin Valvoline	2.00	4.00
7 Geoff Bodine Exide with Goodyear tires	2.00	4.00
7 Geoff Bodine Exide with Hoosier tires	2.00	4.00
10 Ricky Rudd Tide	2.00	4.00
14 Terry Labonte MW Windows	2.00	5.00
16 Ted Musgrave Family Channel	2.00	4.00
21 Morgan Shepherd Citgo	2.00	4.00
23 Chad Little Bayer	2.00	4.00
24 Jeff Gordon DuPont	2.50	6.00
25 Kirk Shelmerdine Big Johnson	3.00	6.00
26 Steve Kinser Quaker State	2.00	4.00
28 Dale Jarrett Havoline	2.00	4.00
30 Michael Waltrip Pennzoil	2.00	4.00
38 Elton Sawyer Ford Credit	2.00	4.00
40 Bobby Hamilton Kendall	2.00	4.00
40 Patty Moise Dial Purex	2.00	4.00
52 Ken Schrader AC Delco	2.00	4.00
57 Jason Keller Budget Gourmet	2.00	4.00
63 Curtis Markham Lysol	2.00	4.00
75 Todd Bodine Factory Stores of America	2.00	4.00
92 Larry Pearson Stanley Tools	2.00	4.00
94 Bill Elliott McDonald's	2.00	4.00
98 Jeremy Mayfield Fingerhut	2.00	4.00

1995 Racing Champions 1:64

This is the regular issued of the 1:64 scale 1995 Racing Champions series. The Bobby Labonte car comes with and wthout roof flaps. This was one of the first cars to incorporate the new NASCAR safety feature into a die cast.

	Lo	Hi
1 Rick Mast Precision	2.00	4.00
2 Ricky Craven DuPont	3.00	6.00
2 Rusty Wallace Ford Motorsports	2.00	5.00
4 Sterling Marlin Kodak	2.00	4.00
4 Jeff Purvis Kodak Funsaver	2.00	4.00
5 Terry Labonte Kellogg's	2.00	5.00

	Lo	Hi
6 Tommy Houston Red Devil	2.00	4.00
6 Mark Martin Valvoline	2.00	5.00
7 Geoff Bodine Exide	2.00	4.00
7 Stevie Reeves Clabber Girl	2.00	4.00
8 Jeff Burton Raybestos with Blue numbers	2.00	4.00
8 Jeff Burton Raybestos	2.00	4.00
8 Kenny Wallace Red Dog	4.00	8.00
8 Bobby Dotter Hyde Tools	2.00	4.00
10 Ricky Rudd Tide	2.00	4.00
12 Derrike Cope Straight Arrow	2.00	4.00
14 Terry Labonte MW Windows	5.00	10.00
15 Jack Nadeau Buss Fuses	2.00	4.00
15 Dick Trickle Ford Quality	2.00	4.00
16 Stub Fadden NAPA	2.00	4.00
16 Ted Musgrave Family Channel	2.00	4.00
17 Darrell Waltrip Western Auto	2.00	4.00
18 Bobby Labonte Interstate Batteries with roof flaps	3.00	6.00
18 Bobby Labonte Interstate Batteries without roof flaps	2.00	4.00
21 Morgan Shepherd Citgo	2.00	4.00
22 Randy LaJoie MBNA	2.50	5.00
23 Chad Little Bayer	2.00	4.00
24 Jeff Gordon DuPont	5.00	10.00
24 Jeff Gordon DuPont Coca-Cola	7.50	15.00
24 Jeff Gordon DuPont Signature Series	5.00	10.00
24 Jeff Gordon DuPont Signature Series combo with SuperTruck	7.50	15.00
25 Johnny Rumley Big Johnson	2.00	4.00
25 Ken Schrader Hendrick	2.00	4.00
25 Kirk Shelmerdine Big Johnson	2.00	4.00
26 Steve Kinser Quaker State	2.00	4.00
27 Loy Allen Hooters	2.00	4.00
28 Dale Jarrett Havoline	2.00	5.00
29 Steve Grissom Meineke	2.00	4.00
30 Michael Waltrip Pennzoil	2.00	4.00
34 Mike McLaughlin French's	2.00	4.00
37 John Andretti K-Mart	2.00	4.00
40 Patty Moise Dial Purex	2.00	4.00
41 Ricky Craven Hedrick	2.00	4.00
44 David Green Slim Jim	2.00	4.00
44 Jeff Purvis Jackaroo	2.00	4.00
47 Jeff Fuller Sunoco	2.00	4.00
51 Jim Bown Luck's	2.00	4.00
52 Ken Schrader AC Delco	2.00	4.00
57 Jason Keller Budget Gourmet	2.00	4.00
60 Mark Martin Winn Dixie	2.00	5.00
71 Kevin Lepage Vermont Teddy Bear	2.00	4.00
71 Dave Marcis Olive Garden	4.00	8.00
75 Todd Bodine Factory Stores of America	2.00	4.00
81 Kenny Wallace TIC Financial	2.00	4.00
82 Derrike Cope FDP Brakes	2.00	4.00
87 Joe Nemechek Burger King	2.00	4.00
90 Mike Wallace Heilig-Meyers	2.00	4.00
92 Larry Pearson Stanley Tools	2.00	4.00
94 Bill Elliott McDonald's	4.00	8.00
94 Bill Elliott McDonald's Thunderbat	5.00	10.00
99 Phil Parsons Luxaire	2.00	4.00

1995 Racing Champions 1:64 Matched Serial Numbers

This series features cards and die cast whose serial numbers match. The cars come in a black blister pack with a card. The card has a gold border and features the driver of the car.

	Lo	Hi
2 Rusty Wallace Ford	4.00	7.00
5 Terry Labonte Kellogg's	4.00	7.00
6 Mark Martin Valvoline	4.00	7.00
7 Geoff Bodine Exide	3.00	6.00
18 Bobby Labonte Interstate Batteries	4.00	7.00
24 Jeff Gordon DuPont	12.50	25.00

1995 Racing Champions Premier 1:64

This is the 1995 series of the 1:64 Premier pieces. The cars are again packaged in a black shadow box and feature a gold foil number on the front of the box that states how many peices were made. The cars were distributed through both hobby and retail.

	Lo	Hi
2 Rusty Wallace Ford Motorsports	3.50	7.00
4 Sterling Marlin Kodak	3.00	6.00
6 Mark Martin Valvoline	3.50	7.00
8 J.Burton/Raybestos	5.00	10.00
18 Bobby Labonte Interstate Batteries	3.00	6.00
24 Jeff Gordon DuPont	15.00	30.00
25 Ken Schrader Budweiser	3.50	7.00
26 Steve Kinser Quaker State	3.00	6.00
27 Loy Allen Hooters	3.00	6.00
28 Dale Jarrett Havoline	3.00	6.00
40 Bobby Hamilton Kendall	3.00	6.00
40 Patty Moise Dial Purex	3.00	6.00
59 Dennis Setzer Alliance	3.00	6.00
60 Mark Martin Winn Dixie	5.00	10.00
75 Todd Bodine Factory Stores of America	3.00	6.00
81 Kenny Wallace TIC Financial	3.00	6.00
94 Bill Elliott McDonald's	10.00	20.00

1995 Racing Champions 1:64 To the Maxx 2-5

These pieces represent the second through fifth series of Racing Champions To the Maxx line. Each package includes a Maxx Premier Plus card that is only available with the die cast piece and was not inserted in any packs of the Premier Plus product.

	Lo	Hi
2 Rusty Wallace Ford Motorsports	4.00	8.00
4 Sterling Marlin Kodak	4.00	7.00
4 Jeff Purvis Kodak	4.00	7.00
6 Tommy Houston Dirt Devil	4.00	7.00
6 Mark Martin Valvoline	4.00	8.00
7 Geoff Bodine Exide	4.00	7.00
7 Stevie Reeves Clabber Girl	4.00	7.00
8 Jeff Burton Raybestos	4.00	7.00
10 Ricky Rudd Tide	4.00	7.00
12 Derrike Cope Mane N Tail	4.00	7.00
14 Terry Labonte MW Windows	4.00	7.00
15 Dick Trickle Quality Car	4.00	7.00
17 Darrell Waltrip Western Auto	4.00	7.00
18 Bobby Labonte Interstate Batteries	4.00	8.00
21 Morgan Shepherd Citgo	4.00	7.00
22 Randy LaJoie MBNA	4.00	7.00
23 Chad Little Bayer	4.00	7.00
24 Jeff Gordon DuPont	5.00	10.00
26 Steve Kinser Quaker State	4.00	7.00
28 Dale Jarrett Havoline	4.00	8.00
29 Steve Grissom Meineke	4.00	7.00
34 Mike McLaughlin French's	4.00	7.00
38 Elton Sawyer Ford Credit	4.00	7.00
44 David Green Slim JIm	4.00	7.00
44 Jeff Purvis Jackaroo	4.00	7.00
52 Ken Schrader AC Delco	4.00	7.00
57 Jason Keller Budget Gourmet	4.00	7.00
75 Todd Bodine Factory Stores of America	4.00	7.00
81 Kenny Wallace TIC Financial	4.00	7.00
90 Mike Wallace Heilig-Meyers	4.00	7.00
92 Larry Pearson Stanley Tools	4.00	7.00
94 Bill Elliott McDonald's	4.00	8.00

1995 Racing Champions SuperTrucks 1:64

This series of 1:64 SuperTrucks is a good sample of many of the trucks that competed in the first SuperTruck series. There are numerous variations in the series.

	Lo	Hi
1 P.J.Jones Sears Diehard	3.50	6.00
1 P.J.Jones Vessells Ford	5.00	10.00
1 Richmond Night Race Special	9.00	18.00
2 David Ashley Southern California Ford	3.00	6.00
3 Mike Skinner Goodwrench	3.50	6.00
6 Mike Bliss Ultra Wheels	3.00	6.00
6 Butch Gilliland Ultra Wheels	3.00	6.00
6 Rick Carelli Total Petroleum	3.00	6.00
7 Geoff Bodine Exide	3.00	6.00
7 Geoff Bodine Exide Salsa	3.00	6.00
7 David Rezendes Exide	3.00	6.00
8 Mike Bliss Ultra Wheels	3.00	6.00
8 C.Huartson AC Delco	3.00	6.00
10 Stan Fox Made for You	3.00	6.00
12 Randy MacCachren Venable	3.00	6.00
18 Johnny Benson Hella Lights	3.00	6.00
21 Tobey Butler Ortho with Green Nose	3.00	6.00
21 Tobey Butler Ortho with Yellow Nose	3.00	6.00
23 T.J.Clark ASE with Blue paint scheme	3.00	6.00
23 T.J.Clark ASE with White paint scheme	3.00	6.00
24 No Driver Association DuPont Gordon Signature Series	3.00	6.00
24 No Driver Association DuPont with Gordon on the card	4.00	8.00
37 Bob Strait Target Expediting	3.00	6.00
38 Sammy Swindell Channellock with White Goodyear on tires	3.00	6.00
38 Sammy Swindell Channellock with Yellow Goodyear on tires	3.00	6.00
51 Kerry Teague Rosenblum Racing	3.00	6.00
52 Ken Schrader AC Delco	3.00	6.00
54 Steve McEachern McEachern Racing	3.00	6.00
61 Todd Bodine Roush Racing	3.00	6.00
75 Bill Sedgwick Spears Motorsports	3.00	6.00
83 Steve Portenga Coffee Critic	3.00	6.00
95 No Driver Association Brickyard 400 special	2.00	4.00
98 Butch Miller Raybestos	3.00	6.00

1995 Racing Champions SuperTrucks 1:64 Matched Serial Numbers

This series featues trucks and cards wtih matching serial numbers. The truck has a serial number stamp on the bottom of it. The card has a black serial number stamped on the front of it. The truck sits on a stand that also has a serial number that matches

	Lo	Hi
1 Mike Chase Sears Diehard	4.00	7.00
3 Mike Skinner Goodwrench	4.00	7.00
6 Rick Carelli Total Petroleum	4.00	7.00
24 Scott Lagasse DuPont	4.00	7.00
75 Bill Sedgwick Spears Motorsports	4.00	7.00
98 Butch Miller Raybestos	4.00	7.00

1995 Racing Champions SuperTrucks 1:64 To the Maxx 1

This is the first series of SuperTruck To the Maxx pieces. Each piece is packaged in a red blister pack and comes with a Crown Chrome accetate card.

	Lo	Hi
1 P.J.Jones Sears Diehard	4.00	7.00
3 Mike Skinner Goodwrench	4.00	8.00
6 Rick Carelli Total Petroleum	4.00	7.00
7 Geoff Bodine Exide	4.00	7.00
21 Tobey Butler Ortho	4.00	7.00
24 Jeff Gordon DuPont	5.00	10.00
38 Sammy Swindell Channellock	4.00	7.00
98 Butch Miller Raybestos	4.00	7.00

1996 Racing Champions 1:64 Previews

This series features some of the new paint schemes and driver changes for the 1996 season. The cars again come in a red blister with the word preview appearing below the year in the upper right hand corner.

	Lo	Hi
2 Ricky Craven DuPont	2.00	4.00
4 Sterling Marlin Kodak	2.00	4.00
5 Terry Labonte Kellogg's	2.00	4.00
6 Mark Martin Valvoline	2.00	4.00
7 Stevie Reeves Clabber Girl	2.00	4.00
9 Joe Bessey Delco Remy	2.00	4.00
9 Lake Speed SPAM	2.00	4.00
10 Ricky Rudd Tide	2.00	4.00
11 Brett Bodine Lowe's	2.00	4.00
12 Derrike Cope Mane N' Tail	2.00	4.00
14 Patty Moise Dial Purex	2.00	4.00
16 Ted Musgrave Family Channel	2.00	4.00
17 Darrell Waltrip Western Auto	2.00	4.00
18 Bobby Labonte Interstate Batteries	2.00	4.00
22 Ward Burton MBNA	2.00	4.00
24 Jeff Gordon DuPont	3.00	6.00
30 Johnny Benson Pennzoil	2.00	4.00
40 Tim Fedewa Kleenex	2.00	4.00
41 Ricky Craven Kodiak	2.00	4.00
47 Jeff Fuller Sunoco	2.00	4.00
52 Ken Schrader AC Delco	2.00	4.00
57 Jason Keller Slim Jim	2.00	4.00
74 Johnny Benson Lipton Tea	2.00	4.00
87 Joe Nemechek Burger King	2.00	4.00
90 Mike Wallace Heilig-Meyers	2.00	4.00
94 Bill Elliott McDonald's	2.00	4.00

1996 Racing Champions 1:64

This set features some unique pieces that Racing Champions had never issued before. Some piece came with a metal and plastic medallion in the blister package with the car. The Rusty Wallace was also available in both the Penske Racing and the MGD car.

	Lo	Hi
1 Rick Mast Hooter's		
2 Ricky Craven DuPont	2.00	4.00
2 Rusty Wallace Miller Genuine Draft	8.00	15.00
2 Rusty Wallace Penske Racing	2.00	4.00
4 Sterling Marlin Kodak	2.00	4.00
5 Terry Labonte Kellogg's	2.00	4.00
5 Terry Labonte Kellogg's with Iron Man card	5.00	10.00
5 Terry Labonte Kellogg's Silver car	4.00	8.00
6 Mark Martin Valvoline	2.00	4.00
6 Tommy Houston Suburban Propane	2.00	4.00
6 Mark Martin Valvoline Dura Blend	2.00	4.00
6 Mark Martin Roush Box Promo	7.00	12.00
7 Geoff Bodine QVC	2.00	4.00
8 Hut Stricklin Circuit City	2.00	4.00
10 Phil Parsons Channellock	2.00	4.00
10 Ricky Rudd Tide	2.00	4.00
11 Brett Bodine Lowe's	2.00	4.00
11 Brett Bodine Lowe's 50th Anniversary	3.00	6.00
12 Derrike Cope Badcock	2.00	4.00
12 Michael Waltrip MW Windows	3.00	6.00
14 Patty Moise Dial Purex	2.00	4.00
16 Ted Musgrave Family Channel	2.00	4.00
17 Darrell Waltrip Parts America	2.00	4.00
18 Bobby Labonte Interstate Batteries	2.00	4.00
19 Loy Allen Healthsource	2.00	4.00

21 Michael Waltrip	2.00	4.00
Citgo		
22 Ward Burton	2.00	4.00
MBNA		
23 Chad Little	3.00	6.00
John Deere		
23 Chad Little	6.00	12.00
John Deere Promo		
24 Jeff Gordon	3.00	6.00
DuPont		
28 Ernie Irvan	2.00	4.00
Havoline		
29 Steve Grissom	3.00	6.00
Cartoon Network		
29 Steve Grissom	2.00	4.00
WCW		
29 No Driver Association	3.00	6.00
Scooby-Doo		
29 No Driver Association	2.00	4.00
WCW Sting		
30 Johnny Benson	2.00	4.00
Pennzoil		
31 Mike Skinner	10.00	20.00
Realtree		
32 Dale Jarrett	3.00	6.00
Band-Aid Promo		
34 Mike McLaughlin	2.00	4.00
Royal Oak		
37 John Andretti	2.00	4.00
K-Mart		
38 Dennis Setzer	2.00	4.00
Lipton Tea		
40 Tim Fedewa	2.00	4.00
Kleenex		
40 Jim Sauter	3.00	6.00
First Union		
41 Ricky Craven	2.00	4.00
Hedrick Motorsports		
41 Ricky Craven	2.00	4.00
Manheim		
43 Rodney Combs	2.00	4.00
Lance		
43 Bobby Hamilton	60.00	100.00
25th Anniversary 5 car set		
43 Bobby Hamilton	15.00	30.00
5-car 25th Anniversary		
43 Bobby Hamilton	30.00	50.00
5-car 25th Anniversary Hood Open		
43 Bobby Hamilton	3.00	6.00
STP Anniversary 1972 Red and Blue paint scheme		
43 Bobby Hamilton	3.00	6.00
STP Anniversary 1972 Blue paint scheme		
43 Bobby Hamilton	3.00	6.00
STP Anniversary 1979 Red and Blue paint scheme		
43 Bobby Hamilton	3.00	6.00
STP Anniversary 1984 Blue and Red paint scheme		
43 Bobby Hamilton	3.00	6.00
STP Anniversary 1996 Silver car		
43 Bobby Hamilton	9.00	18.00
STP Anniversary 1996 Silver car in Red and Blue Box		
44 Bobby Labonte	5.00	10.00
Shell		
47 Jeff Fuller	2.00	4.00
Sunoco		
51 Jim Bown	2.00	4.00
Lucks		
57 Jim Bown	5.00	10.00
Matco Tools		
57 Jason Keller	2.00	4.00
Halloween Havoc		
57 Jason Keller	2.00	4.00
Slim Jim		
58 Mike Cope	2.00	4.00
Penrose		
60 Mark Martin	4.00	8.00
Winn Dixie Promo		
61 Mike Olsen	3.00	6.00
Little Trees		
63 Curtis Markham	2.00	4.00
Lysol		
74 Randy LaJoie	2.00	4.00
Fina		
75 Morgan Shepherd	4.00	8.00
Remington		
81 Kenny Wallace	2.00	4.00
TIC Financial		
87 Joe Nemechek	3.00	6.00
Bell South		
87 Joe Nemechek	2.00	4.00
Burger King		
88 Dale Jarrett	2.00	4.00
Quality Care		
90 Mike Wallace	2.00	4.00
Duron		
92 David Pearson	2.00	4.00
Stanley Tools		
94 Ron Barfield	2.00	4.00
New Holland		
94 Bill Elliott	2.00	4.00
McDonald's		
94 Bill Elliott	2.00	4.00
McDonald's Monopoly		
94 Bill Elliott	40.00	70.00
10-Time Most Popular Driver Silver car		
94 Harry Gant	3.00	6.00
McDonald's		
96 David Green	5.00	10.00
Busch		
96 Stevie Reeves	2.00	4.00
Clabber Girl		
97 Chad Little	2.00	4.00
Sterling Cowboy		
99 Glenn Allen	2.00	4.00
Luxaire		
99 Jeff Burton	2.00	4.00
Exide		

1996 Racing Champions 1:64 Hobby Only

These pieces were released through Hobby outlets. The car come in a different box than the mainstream series.

	Lo	Hi
4 Sterling Marlin	3.00	6.00
Kodak		
6 Mark Martin	3.00	6.00
Valvoline		
18 Bobby Labonte	3.00	6.00
Interstate Batteries		
24 Jeff Gordon	3.00	6.00
DuPont		
47 Jeff Fuller	3.00	6.00
Sunoco		
81 Kenny Wallace	3.00	6.00
Square D		

1996 Racing Champions 1:64 Premier with Medallion

These pieces are the same as the standard Racing Champions 1:64 1996 pieces with the exception of the packaging. Each car is packaged with a medallion instead of a card.

	Lo	Hi
1 Hermie Sadler	4.00	8.00
DeWalt		
2 Ricky Craven	4.00	8.00
DuPont		
2 Ricky Craven	5.00	10.00
DuPont Hood Open		
2 Rusty Wallace	6.00	12.00
Miller Genuine Draft Hood Open In Miller Package		
3 Mike Skinner	4.00	8.00
Goodwrench		
4 Sterling Marlin	4.00	8.00
Kodak		
5 Terry Labonte	5.00	10.00
Bayer Hood Open		
5 Terry Labonte	5.00	10.00
Kellogg's Silver car Hood Open		
6 Mark Martin	5.00	10.00
Valvoline Dura Blend Hood Open		
7 Geoff Bodine	4.00	8.00
QVC		
10 Ricky Rudd	5.00	10.00
Tide Hood Open		
11 Brett Bodine	4.00	8.00
Lowe's		
15 Wally Dallenbach	10.00	20.00
Hayes Modems		
16 Ted Musgrave	4.00	8.00
Family Channel		
18 Bobby Labonte	4.00	8.00
Interstate Batteries		
18 Bobby Labonte	5.00	10.00
Interstate Batteries Hood Open		
22 Ward Burton	4.00	8.00
MBNA		
23 Chad Little	5.00	10.00
John Deere Hood Open		
23 Chad Little	8.00	16.00
John Deere Hood Open Promo		
24 Jeff Gordon	6.00	12.00
DuPont		
24 Jeff Gordon	7.50	15.00
DuPont Hood Open		
24 Jeff Gordon	6.00	12.00
DuPont 1995 Champion Hood Open		
25 Ken Schrader	6.00	12.00
Budweiser		
25 Ken Schrader	50.00	90.00
Budweiser Silver		
25 Ken Schrader	4.00	8.00
Hendrick		
28 Ernie Irvan	5.00	10.00
Havoline Hood Open		
29 Steve Grissom	5.00	10.00
Cartoon Network		
29 Steve Grissom	6.00	12.00
Cartoon Network Hood Open		
29 Steve Grissom	25.00	50.00
Cartoon Network 5-car set		
29 No Driver Association	4.00	8.00
Scooby-Doo		
29 No Driver Association	4.00	8.00
Shaggy		
30 Johnny Benson	4.00	8.00
Pennzoil		
31 Mike Skinner	20.00	35.00
Realtree		
34 Mike McLaughlin	4.00	8.00
Royal Oak		
37 John Andretti	4.00	8.00
K-Mart		
41 Ricky Craven	4.00	8.00
Hedrick		
43 Bobby Hamilton	6.00	12.00
STP Hood Open		
43 Bobby Hamilton	6.00	12.00
STP Silver Hood Open		
43 Bobby Hamilton	30.00	55.00
STP 5-car set		
44 Bobby Labonte	10.00	20.00
Shell		
52 Ken Schrader	4.00	8.00
AC Delco		
52 Ken Schrader	5.00	10.00
AC Delco Hood Open		
57 Chuck Bown	5.00	10.00
Matco		
71 Dave Marcis	10.00	20.00
Prodigy		
74 Johnny Benson	4.00	8.00
Lipton Tea		
87 Joe Nemechek	9.00	18.00
Burger King		
88 Dale Jarrett	4.00	8.00
Quality Care		
92 Larry Pearson	4.00	8.00
Stanley Tools		
94 Bill Elliott	5.00	10.00
McDonald's Hood Open		
94 Bill Elliott	5.00	10.00
McDonald's Monopoly Hood Open		
96 David Green	5.00	10.00
Busch		
97 Chad Little	4.00	8.00
Sterling Cowboy		

1996 Racing Champions 1:64 Silver Chase

Each of these 1:64 scale Silver cars were done in a quantity of 1,996. These cars were randomly inserted in the cases that were shipped to retail outlets.

	Lo	Hi
1 Rick Mast Hooter's	30.00	50.00
2 Rusty Wallace Miller Genuine Draft	45.00	80.00
4 Sterling Marlin Kodak	35.00	60.00
5 Terry Labonte Kellogg's	75.00	125.00
6 Mark Martin Valvoline	45.00	80.00
10 Ricky Rudd Tide	30.00	50.00
17 Darrell Waltrip Parts America	30.00	50.00
18 Bobby Labonte Interstate Batteries	35.00	60.00
24 Jeff Gordon DuPont	90.00	150.00
28 Ernie Irvan Havoline	40.00	75.00
88 Dale Jarrett Quality Care	45.00	80.00
94 Bill Elliott McDonald's	40.00	80.00

1996 Racing Champions SuperTrucks 1:64

Racing Champions continued there line of 1:24 SuperTrucks in 1996. This series features many of the circuit's first-time drivers.

	Lo	Hi
2 Mike Bliss Team ASE	2.00	4.00
3 Mike Skinner Goodwrench	2.00	4.00
5 Darrell Waltrip Die Hard	2.00	4.00
6 Rick Carelli Chesrown	2.00	4.00
6 Rick Carelli Total	2.00	4.00
9 Joe Bessey New Hampshire Speedway	2.00	4.00
14 Butch Gilliland Stroppe	2.00	4.00
17 Bill Sedgwick Die Hard	2.00	4.00
17 Darrell Waltrip Western Auto	2.00	4.00
19 Lance Norick Macklanburg-Duncan	2.00	4.00
20 Walker Evans Dana	2.00	4.00
21 Doug George Ortho	2.00	4.00
24 Jack Sprague Quaker State	2.00	4.00
29 Bob Keselowski Winnebago	2.00	4.00
30 Jimmy Hensley Mopar	2.00	4.00
52 Ken Schrader AC Delco	2.00	4.00
57 Robbie Pyne Aisyn	2.00	4.00
75 Bobby Gill Spears	2.00	4.00
78 Mike Chase Petron Plus	2.00	4.00
80 Joe Ruttman J.R.Garage	2.00	4.00
83 Steve Portenga Coffee Critic	2.00	4.00
98 Butch Miller Raybestos	2.00	4.00

1997 Racing Champions 1:64 Previews

This series of 1:64 die cast replicas featured a preview at some of the new paint jobs to run in the 1997 season. The Rick Mast Remington car and the Robert Pressley Scooby Doo car features two of the numerous driver changes for the 97 Winston Cup season.

	Lo	Hi
4 Sterling Marlin Kodak	2.00	4.00
5 Terry Labonte Kellogg's	2.00	4.00
6 Mark Martin Valvoline	2.00	4.00
18 Bobby Labonte Interstate Batteries	2.00	4.00
21 Michael Waltrip Citgo	2.00	4.00
24 Jeff Gordon DuPont	2.00	4.00
28 Ernie Irvan Havoline	2.00	4.00
29 Robert Pressley Scooby-Doo	2.00	4.00
30 Johnny Benson Pennzoil	2.00	4.00
75 Rick Mast Remington	2.00	4.00
94 Bill Elliott McDonald's	2.00	4.00
99 Jeff Burton Exide	2.00	4.00

1997 Racing Champions 1:64 Premier Preview with Medallion

This is the first time Racing Champions has issued a Premier Preview car. Each car comes with a medallion like the standard Premier cars.

	Lo	Hi
4 Sterling Marlin Kodak	3.00	6.00
5 Terry Labonte Kellogg's	4.00	8.00
6 Mark Martin Valvoline	3.00	6.00
18 Bobby Labonte Interstate Batteries	3.00	6.00
24 Jeff Gordon DuPont	4.00	8.00
29 Robert Pressley Scooby-Doo	3.00	6.00
94 Bill Elliott McDonald's	3.00	6.00

1997 Racing Champions 1:64

The 1:64 scale cars that appear in this series are replicas of many of the cars that ran in the 1997 season. The series is higlighted by the Terry Labonte Kellogg's car commenerating his 1996 Winston Cup Championship. This car is available in two variations: standard and hood open.

	Lo	Hi
00 Buckshot Jones Aqua-Fresh	3.00	6.00
1 Hermie Sadler DeWalt	2.00	4.00
1 Morgan Shepherd R& L Carriers	2.00	4.00
2 Ricky Craven Raybestos	2.00	4.00
2 Rusty Wallace Miller Lite Matco	5.00	10.00
2 Rusty Wallace Penske Racing	2.00	4.00
4 Sterling Marlin Kodak	2.00	4.00
5 Terry Labonte Bayer	2.00	4.00
5 Terry Labonte Kellogg's 1996 Champion	3.00	8.00
5 Terry Labonte Kellogg's 2-car set	12.00	20.00
5 Terry Labonte Tony the Tiger	3.00	6.00
6 Joe Bessey Power Team	2.00	4.00
6 Mark Martin Valvoline	2.00	4.00
7 Geoff Bodine QVC	2.00	4.00
7 Geoff Bodine QVC Gold Rush	3.00	6.00
8 Hut Stricklin Circuit City	2.00	4.00
9 Joe Bessey Power Team	2.00	4.00
9 Jeff Burton Track Gear	2.00	4.00
10 Phil Parsons Channellock	2.00	4.00
10 Ricky Rudd Tide	2.00	4.00
11 Jimmy Foster Speedvision	2.00	4.00
11 Brett Bodine Close Call	2.00	4.00
16 Ted Musgrave Primestar	2.00	4.00
17 Darrell Waltrip Parts America	2.00	4.00
17 Darrell Waltrip Parts America Chrome	3.00	8.00
18 Bobby Labonte Interstate Batteries	2.00	4.00
19 Gary Bradberry CSR	2.00	4.00
21 Michael Waltrip Citgo	2.00	4.00
24 Jeff Gordon DuPont	4.00	8.00
25 Ricky Craven Bud Lizard	6.00	12.00
25 Ricky Craven Hendrick	2.00	4.00
28 Ernie Irvan Havoline	2.00	4.00
28 Erine Irvan Havoline 10th Anniversary	2.00	5.00
29 Robert Pressley Cartoon Network	2.00	4.00
29 Jeff Green Tom and Jerry	2.00	4.00
29 Elliott Sadler Phillips 66	2.00	4.00
30 Johnny Benson Pennzoil	2.00	4.00
32 Dale Jarrett White Rain	2.00	4.00
33 Ken Schrader Petree Racing	2.00	4.00
34 Mike McLaughlin Royal Oak	2.00	4.00
36 Todd Bodine Stanley Tools	2.00	4.00
36 Derrike Cope Skittles	2.00	4.00
37 Jeremy Mayfield K-Mart	2.00	4.00
38 Elton Sawyer Barbasol	2.00	4.00
40 Tim Fedewa Kleenex	2.00	4.00
40 Robby Gordon Sabco Racing	2.00	4.00
41 Steve Grissom Hedrick	2.00	4.00
42 Joe Nemechek Bell South	2.00	4.00
43 Rodney Combs Lance	2.00	4.00
43 Dennis Setzer	2.00	4.00

Lance
46 Wally Dallenbach 2.00 4.00
First Union
47 Jeff Fuller 2.00 4.00
Sunoco
49 Kyle Petty 4.00 8.00
nWo
57 Jason Keller 2.00 4.00
Slim Jim
60 Mark Martin 4.00 8.00
Winn Dixie
72 Mike Dillon 2.00 4.00
Detriot Gasket
74 Randy Lajoie 4.00 8.00
Fina Promo
74 Randy LaJoie 2.00 4.00
Fina
75 Rick Mast 2.00 4.00
Remington
75 Rick Mast 2.00 4.00
Remington Camo
75 Rick Mast 2.00 4.00
Remington Stren
88 Kevin LePage 2.00 4.00
Hype
90 Dick Trickle 2.00 4.00
Heilig-Meyers
91 Mike Wallace 2.00 4.00
Spam
94 Ron Barfield 2.00 4.00
New Holland
94 Bill Elliott 2.00 4.00
McDonald's
94 Bill Elliott 2.00 4.00
Mac Tonight
96 David Green 2.00 4.00
Caterpillar
96 David Green 4.00 8.00
Caterpillar Promo
97 No Driver Association 3.00 6.00
Brickyard 500
97 No Driver Association 10.00 18.00
www.racingchamps.com
97 Chad Little 2.00 4.00
John Deere
97 Chad Little 4.00 8.00
John Deere Promo
98 No Driver Association 3.00 6.00
EA Sports
99 Glenn Allen 2.00 4.00
Luxaire
99 Jeff Burton 2.00 4.00
Exide

1997 Racing Champions 1:64 Gold

These 1:64 scale cars were distributed through hobby outlets.

Lo Hi
2 Rusty Wallace 60.00 100.00
Miller Lite
6 Mark Martin 60.00 100.00
Valvoline
10 Ricky Rudd 40.00 80.00
Tide
18 Bobby Labonte 40.00 80.00
Interstate Batteries
36 Derrike Cope 40.00 80.00
Skittles
75 Rick Mast/ 40.00 80.00
Remington
94 Bill Elliott 60.00 100.00
McDonald's

1997 Racing Champions 1:64 Hobby

These 1:64 scale cars were distributed through hobby outlets.

Lo Hi
2 Rusty Wallace 4.00 8.00
Miller Lite
6 Mark Martin 4.00 8.00
Valvoline
10 Ricky Rudd 4.00 8.00
Tide
18 Bobby Labonte 4.00 8.00
Interstate Batteries
36 Derrike Cope 4.00 8.00
Skittles
75 Rick Mast 4.00 8.00
Remington
94 Bill Elliott 4.00 8.00
McDonald's

1997 Racing Champions 1:64 Pinnacle Series

This marks the second time Racing Champions have teamed up with a card manufacturer to product a line of diecast car with trading cards. Each car is boxed in similar packaging as the standard cars, but are Pinnacle cards are featured in place of racing Champions generic cards.

Lo Hi
4 Sterling Marlin 4.00 8.00
Kodak
5 Terry Labonte 5.00 10.00
Kellogg's
6 Mark Martin 4.00 8.00
Valvoline
7 Geoff Bodine 4.00 8.00
QVC
8 Hut Stricklin 4.00 8.00
Circuit City
10 Ricky Rudd 4.00 8.00
Tide
16 Ted Musgrave 4.00 8.00
Primestar
18 Bobby Labonte 4.00 8.00
Interstate Batteries
21 Michael Waltrip 4.00 8.00
Citgo
28 Ernie Irvan 4.00 8.00
Havoline
29 Robert Pressley 4.00 8.00
Cartoon Network
30 Johnny Benson 4.00 8.00
Pennzoil
36 Derrike Cope 4.00 8.00
Skittles
37 Jeremy Mayfield 4.00 8.00
K-Mart
75 Rick Mast 4.00 8.00
Remington
87 Joe Nemechek 4.00 8.00
BellSouth
94 Bill Elliott 4.00 8.00
McDonald's
96 David Green 4.00 8.00
Caterpillar
97 Chad Little 4.00 8.00
John Deere
99 Jeff Burton 4.00 8.00
Exide

1997 Racing Champions 1:64 Premier with Medallion

These pieces are the same as the standard Racing Champions 1:64 1997 pieces with the exception of the packaging. Each car is packaged with a medallion instead of a card. The Lake Speed/University of Nebraska car highlights this series.

Lo Hi
1 Morgan Shepherd 4.00 8.00
Crusin' America
2 Rusty Wallace 4.00 8.00
Penske
5 Terry Labonte 5.00 10.00
Tony the Tiger
6 Mark Martin 4.00 8.00
Valvoline
7 Geoff Bodine 4.00 8.00
QVC
8 Hut Stricklin 4.00 8.00
Circuit City
9 Lake Speed 15.00 30.00
University of Nebraska
10 Ricky Rudd 4.00 8.00
Tide
11 Brett Bodine 4.00 8.00
Close Call
16 Ted Musgrave 4.00 8.00
Primestar
17 Darrell Waltrip 4.00 8.00
Parts America
17 Darrell Waltrip 5.00 10.00
Parts America Chrome
18 Bobby Labonte 4.00 8.00
Interstate Batteries
21 Michael Waltrip 4.00 8.00
Citgo
28 Ernie Irvan 4.00 8.00
Havoline
28 Ernie Irvan 5.00 10.00
Havoline 10th Anniversary
29 Robert Pressley 4.00 8.00
Scooby-Doo
29 No Driver Assocation 4.00 8.00
Tom and Jerry
30 Johnny Benson 4.00 8.00
Pennzoil
36 Derrike Cope 4.00 8.00
Skittles
37 Jeremy Mayfield 4.00 8.00
Kmart
75 Rick Mast 4.00 8.00
Remington
75 Rick Mast 4.00 8.00
Remington Camo
75 Rick Mast 4.00 8.00
Remington Stren
94 Bill Elliott 4.00 8.00
Mac Tonight
96 David Green 4.00 8.00
Caterpillar
96 David Green 6.00 12.00
Caterpillar Promo
97 Chad Little 4.00 8.00
John Deere
97 Chad Little 6.00 12.00
John Deere Promo
99 Jeff Burton 4.00 8.00
Exide

1997 Racing Champions 1:64 Premier with Medallion Silver Chase

These 1:64 scale Silver Chase cars were limited in production to 997 of each car.

Lo Hi
5 Terry Labonte 90.00 150.00
Kellogg's
7 Geoff Bodine 40.00 75.00
QVC
10 Ricky Rudd 40.00 75.00
Tide
16 Ted Musgrave 40.00 75.00
Primestar
18 Bobby Labonte 50.00 90.00
Intertstate Batteries
28 Ernie Irvan 50.00 90.00
Havoline

1997 Racing Champions 1:64 Silver Chase

Each of these 1:64 scale Silver cars were done in a quantity of

1,997. These cars were randomly inserted in the cases that were shipped to retail outlets.

	Lo	Hi
5 Terry Labonte	75.00	125.00
Kellogg's 1996 Champion		
7 Geoff Bodine	30.00	50.00
QVC		
16 Ted Musgrave	30.00	50.00
Primestar		
21 Michael Waltrip	30.00	50.00
Citgo		
30 Johnny Benson	30.00	50.00
Pennzoil		
36 Derrike Cope	30.00	50.00
Skittles		
40 Robby Gordon	30.00	50.00
Sabco Racing		
42 Joe Nemechek	30.00	50.00
Bell South		
46 Wally Dallenbach	30.00	50.00
First Union		
75 Rick Mast	30.00	50.00
Remington		
96 David Green	30.00	50.00
Caterpillar		
97 Chad Little	30.00	50.00
John Deere		
99 Jeff Burton	35.00	60.00
Exide		

1997 Racing Champions 1:64 Stock Rods

These 1:64 scale cars are replicas of vintage stock rods with NASCAR paint schemes. Cars are listed by issue number instead of car number.

	Lo	Hi
1 Terry Labonte	6.00	15.00
Kellogg's		
2 Bill Elliott	5.00	12.00
McDonald's		
3 Mark Martin	5.00	12.00
Valvoline		
4 Robert Pressley	3.00	8.00
Scooby-Doo		
5 Ted Musgrave	3.00	8.00
Primestar		
6 Jeff Burton	3.00	8.00
Exide		
7 Bobby Labonte	3.00	8.00
Interstate Batteries		
8 Ricky Craven	3.00	8.00
Hendrick		
9 Darrell Waltrip	3.00	8.00
Parts America		
10 Rusty Wallace	50.00	100.00
Miller Lite		
11 Derrike Cope	2.00	6.00
Skittles		
12 Ricky Rudd	2.00	6.00
Tide		
13 Rick Mast	2.00	6.00
Remington		
14 Ricky Craven	2.00	6.00
Hendrick		
15 Jeff Green	2.00	6.00
Tom & Jerry		
16 Bill Elliott	3.00	8.00
Mac Tonight		
17 Mark Martin	3.00	8.00
Valvoline		
18 Rusty Wallace	3.00	8.00
Penske		
19 Ted Musgrave	2.00	6.00
Primestar		
20 Jeff Burton	2.00	6.00
Exide		
21 Darrell Waltrip	2.00	6.00
Parts America		
22 Ricky Rudd	2.00	6.00
Tide		
23 Rick Mast	2.00	6.00
Remington		
24 Steve Grissom	2.00	6.00
Hedrick		
25 Bill Elliott	3.00	8.00
Mac Tonight		
26 Glen Allen	2.00	6.00
Luxaire		
27 Dennis Setzer	2.00	6.00
Lance		
28 Bill Elliott	3.00	8.00
McDonald's		
29 Ricky Craven	2.00	6.00
Hendrick		
30 Sterling Marlin	2.00	6.00
Sabco		
31 Jeff Green	2.00	6.00
Cartoon Network		
32 Joe Nemechek	2.00	6.00
Bell South		
33 Ernie Irvan	2.00	6.00
Havoline		
34 Ricky Rudd	2.00	6.00
Tide		
35 Rusty Wallace	3.00	8.00
Penske		
36 Ernie Irvan	2.00	6.00
Havoline		
37 Mark Martin	3.00	8.00
Valvoline		
38 Terry Labonte	5.00	10.00
Spooky Loops		
39 Terry Labonte	5.00	10.00
Spooky Loops		
40 Derrike Cope	2.00	6.00
Skittles		
41 Steve Grissom	2.00	6.00
Hedrick		
42 Terry Labonte	30.00	50.00
Spooky Loops Chrome		
43 Terry Labonte	7.50	15.00
Spooky Loops		
44 Jeff Burton	2.00	6.00
Exide		
45 Bill Elliott	3.00	8.00
McDonald's		
46 Ted Musgrave	2.00	6.00
Primestar		
47 Mark Martin	3.00	8.00
Valvoline		
48 Ricky Rudd	2.00	6.00
Tide		
49 Glen Allen	2.00	6.00
Luxaire		
50 Terry Labonte	3.00	8.00
Spooky Loops		
51 Joe Bessey	2.00	6.00
Power Team		
52 Terry Labonte	3.00	8.00
Kellogg's		
53 Wally Dallenbach	2.00	6.00
First Union		
54 Ricky Craven	2.00	6.00
Hendrick		
55 Ricky Craven	2.00	6.00
Hendrick		

1997 Racing Champions SuperTrucks 1:64

Racing Champions continued there line of 1:64 SuperTrucks in 1997. This series features many of the circuit's first-time drivers and Winston Cup regulars.

	Lo	Hi
1 Michael Waltrip	2.00	4.00
MW Windows		
2 Mike Bliss	2.00	4.00
Team ASE		
4 Bill Elliott	2.00	4.00
Team ASE		
6 Rick Carelli	2.00	4.00
Remax		
7 Tammy Kirk	2.00	4.00
Loveable		
13 Mike Colabucci	2.00	4.00
Visa		
15 Mike Colabacci	2.00	4.00
VISA		
15 Mike Cope	2.00	4.00
Penrose		
18 Johnny Benson	2.00	4.00
Pennzoil		
18 Mike Dokken	2.00	4.00
Dana		
19 Tony Raines	2.00	4.00
Pennzoil		
20 Butch Miller	2.00	4.00
The Orleans		
23 T.J. Clark	2.00	4.00
CRG Motorsports		
24 Jack Sprague	2.00	4.00
Quaker State		
29 Bob Keslowski	2.00	4.00
Mopar		
35 Dave Rezendes	2.00	4.00
Ortho		
44 Boris Said	2.00	4.00
Federated Auto		
49 Rodney Combs	2.00	4.00
Lance		
52 Toby Butler	2.00	4.00
Purolater		
66 Bryan Reffner	2.00	4.00
Carlin		
75 Dan Press	2.00	4.00
Spears		
80 Joe Ruttman	2.00	4.00
LCI		
86 Stacy Compton	2.00	4.00
Valvoline		
87 Joe Nemechek	2.00	4.00
Bell South		
92 Mark Kinser	2.00	4.00
Rotary		
94 Ron Barfield	2.00	4.00
Super 8		
99 Chuck Bown	2.00	4.00
Exide		
99 Jeff Burton	2.00	4.00
Exide		
99 Mark Martin	2.00	4.00
Exide		

1998 Racing Champions 1:64

The 1:64 scale cars that appear in this series are replicas of many of the cars that ran in the 1997 season, but also many replicas are of the cars slated to appear in the 1998 season. The cars in this series are packaged in special blister packs that display the NASCAR 50th anniversary logo.

	Lo	Hi
00 Buckshot Jones	2.00	4.00
Aquafresh		
00 Buckshot Jones	2.00	4.00
Alka Seltzer		
4 Bobby Hamilton	2.00	4.00
Kodak		
4 Jeff Purvis	2.00	4.00
Lance		
5 Terry Labonte	2.00	5.00
Kellogg's		
5 Terry Labonte	2.00	5.00
Kellogg's Corny		
6 Joe Bessey	2.00	4.00
Power Team		
6 Mark Martin	2.00	4.00
Eagle One		
6 Mark Martin	18.00	30.00
Kosei		
6 Mark Martin	2.00	4.00
Valvoline		
8 Hut Stricklin	2.00	4.00
Circuit City		
9 Jeff Burton	2.00	4.00
Track Gear		
9 Lake Speed	2.00	4.00
Birthday Cake		
10 Ricky Rudd	2.00	4.00
Tide		
11 Brett Bodine	2.00	4.00
Paychex		
12 Jeremy Mayfield	2.00	4.00

Mobil One		
13 Jerry Nadeau	2.00	4.00
First Plus		
16 Ted Musgrave	2.00	4.00
Primestar		
17 Matt Kenseth	5.00	12.00
Lycos		
17 Darrell Waltrip	3.00	6.00
Speedblock		
19 Tony Raines	2.00	4.00
Yellow		
20 Blaise Alexander	2.00	4.00
Rescue Engine		
21 Michael Waltrip	2.00	4.00
Citgo		
21 Michael Waltrip	2.00	4.00
Goodwill Games		
23 Lance Hooper	2.00	4.00
WCW		
23 Jimmy Spencer	10.00	30.00
No Bull		
23 Jimmy Spencer	15.00	50.00
No Bull Gold		
26 Johnny Benson	2.00	4.00
Betty Crocker		
26 Johnny Benson	2.00	4.00
Cheerios		
29 Hermie Sadler	2.00	4.00
Dewalt		
30 Derrike Cope	2.00	4.00
Gumout		
30 Mike Cope	2.00	4.00
Slim Jim		
33 Tim Fedewa	2.00	4.00
Kleenex		
33 Ken Schrader	2.00	4.00
Petree		
35 Todd Bodine	2.00	4.00
Tabasco Orange		
36 Matt Hutter	2.00	4.00
Stanley		
36 Ernie Irvan	2.00	4.00
Skittles		
40 Kevin Lepage	2.00	4.00
Chanellock		
40 Sterling Marlin	10.00	25.00
Coors Light		
40 Sterling Marlin	15.00	40.00
Coors Light Gold		
40 Sterling Marlin	2.00	4.00
Sabco		
41 Steve Grissom	2.00	4.00
Hedrick		
42 Joe Nemechek	2.00	4.00
BellSouth		
46 Wally Dallenbach	2.00	4.00
First Union		
50 Ricky Craven	2.00	4.00
Hendrick		
59 Robert Pressley	2.00	4.00
Kingsford		
60 Mark Martin	2.00	4.00
Winn Dixie		
60 Mark Martin	3.00	8.00
Winn Dixie Promo		
64 Dick Trickle	2.00	4.00
Scheinder		
66 Elliot Sadler	2.00	4.00
Phillips 66		
74 Randy Lajoie#: Fina	2.00	4.00
75 Rick Mast	2.00	4.00
Remington		
78 Gary Bradberry	2.00	4.00
Pilot		
90 Dick Trickle	2.00	4.00
Helig Meyers		
94 Bill Elliott	2.00	4.00
McDonald's		
96 David Green	2.00	4.00
Caterpiller		
97 Chad Little	4.00	8.00
John Deere Promo		
99 Glen Allen	2.00	4.00
Luxaire		
99 Jeff Burton	2.00	4.00
Exide		
300 Darrell Waltrip	3.00	6.00
Flock Special		

1998 Racing Champions 1:64 Chrome Chase

Each of these 1:64 scale Chrome cars were done in a quantity of 5,050 for Winston Cup cars and 1,000 for Busch cars. These cars were randomly inserted in the cases that were shipped to retail outlets.

	Lo	Hi
00 Buckshot Jones	20.00	40.00
Alka Seltzer		
5 Terry Labonte	40.00	75.00
Kellogg's		
5 Terry Labonte	40.00	75.00
Kellogg's Corny		
6 Mark Martin	40.00	75.00
Eagle One		
6 Mark Martin	40.00	75.00
Valvoline		
8 Hut Stricklin	20.00	40.00
Circuit City		
9 Jeff Burton	25.00	50.00
Track Gear		
10 Ricky Rudd	25.00	50.00
Tide		
16 Ted Musgrave	20.00	40.00
Primestar		
20 Bliase Alexander	20.00	40.00
Rescue Engine		
23 Lance Hooper	20.00	40.00
WCW		
26 Johnny Benson	25.00	50.00
Cheerios		
33 Tim Fedewa	20.00	40.00
Kleenex		
34 Mike McLaughlin	20.00	40.00
Goulds		
35 Todd Bodine	20.00	40.00
Tabasco		
36 Matt Hutter	20.00	40.00
Stanley		
36 Ernie Irvan	25.00	50.00
Skittles		
38 Elton Sawyer	20.00	40.00
Barbasol		
40 Kevin Lepage	20.00	40.00
Channellock		
60 Mark Martin	40.00	75.00
Winn Dixie		
64 Dick Trickle	20.00	40.00
Schneider		
74 Randy Lajoie	20.00	40.00
Fina		
94 Bill Elliott	40.00	75.00
McDonald's		
99 Jeff Burton	25.00	50.00
Exide		

1998 Racing Champions 1:64 Gold with Medallion

This is a special series produced by Racing Champions to celebrate NASCAR's 50th anniversary. It parallels the regular 1998 1:64 scale series. Each car is a limited edition of 5,000. Each car is also plated in gold chrome and contains a serial number on its chassis. This series is packaged with medallion sponsor emblems in blister packs.

	Lo	Hi
00 Buckshot Jones	10.00	25.00
Aqua Fresh		
00 Buckshot Jones	10.00	25.00
Alka Seltzer		
2 Ron Barfield	8.00	20.00
New Holland		
4 Bobby Hamilton	10.00	25.00
Kodak		
4 Jeff Purvis	8.00	20.00
Lance		
5 Terry Labonte	20.00	50.00
Blasted Fruit Loops		
5 Terry Labonte	20.00	50.00
Kellogg's		
5 Terry Labonte	20.00	50.00
Kellogg's Corny		
6 Joe Bessey	8.00	20.00
Power Team		
6 Mark Martin	20.00	50.00
Eagle One		
6 Mark Martin	20.00	50.00
Syntec		
6 Mark Martin	20.00	50.00
Valvoline		
8 Hut Stricklin	8.00	20.00
Circuit City		
9 Jeff Burton	10.00	25.00
Track Gear		
9 Jerry Nadeau	10.00	25.00
Zombie Island		
9 Lake Speed	10.00	25.00
Birthday Cake		
9 Lake Speed	10.00	25.00
Huckleberry Hound		
10 Phill Parsons	8.00	20.00
Duralube		
10 Ricky Rudd	10.00	25.00
Tide		
11 Brett Bodine	10.00	25.00
Paychex		
13 Jerry Nadeua	12.00	30.00
First Plus		
14 Patty Moise	8.00	20.00
Rhodes		
16 Ted Musgrave	8.00	20.00
Primestar		
17 Matt Kenseth	20.00	50.00
Lycos.com		
19 Tony Raines	8.00	20.00
Yellow		
20 Bliase Alexander	8.00	20.00
Rescue Engine		
21 Michael Waltrip	8.00	20.00
Citgo		
23 Lance Hooper	8.00	20.00
WCW		
26 Johnny Benson	12.00	30.00
Cheerios		
29 Hermie Sadler	8.00	20.00
Dewalt		
30 Derrike Cope	8.00	20.00
Gumout		
30 Mike Cope	8.00	20.00
Slim Jim		
33 Tim Fedewa	8.00	20.00
Kleenex		
33 Ken Schrader	8.00	20.00
Petree		
34 Mike McLaughlin	8.00	20.00
Goulds		
35 Todd Bodine	10.00	25.00
Tabasco		
36 Matt Hutter	8.00	20.00
Stanley		
36 Ernie Irvan	15.00	40.00
M&Ms		
36 Ernie Irvan	10.00	25.00
Skittles		
36 Ernie Irvan	12.00	30.00
Wildberry Skittles		
38 Elton Sawyer	8.00	20.00
Barbasol		
40 Rick Fuller	8.00	20.00
Channellock		
40 Kevin Lepage	8.00	20.00
Channellock		
40 Sterling Marlin	10.00	25.00
Sabco		
41 Steve Grissom	10.00	25.00
Hedrick		
42 Joe Nemechek	8.00	20.00
BellSouth		
46 Wally Dallenbach	8.00	20.00
First Union		
50 Ricky Craven	12.00	30.00
Hendrick		
50 NDA	8.00	20.00
Dr.Pepper		
59 Robert Pressley	8.00	20.00
Kingsford		
60 Mark Martin	20.00	50.00
Winn Dixie		
63 Tracy Leslie	8.00	20.00

Lysol		
64 Dick Trickle	8.00	20.00
Schneider		
66 Elliot Sadler	10.00	25.00
Phillips 66		
72 Mike Dillon	8.00	20.00
Detroit Gasket		
74 Randy Lajoie	8.00	20.00
Fina		
75 Rick Mast	8.00	20.00
Remington		
78 Gary Bradberry	8.00	20.00
Pilot		
87 Joe Nemecheck	8.00	20.00
BellSouth		
88 Kevin Schwantz	8.00	20.00
Ryder		
90 Dick Trickle	10.00	25.00
Heilig-Meyers		
94 Bill Elliott	20.00	50.00
Happy Meal		
94 Bill Elliott	20.00	50.00
McDonald's		
96 David Green	8.00	20.00
Caterpillar		
97 Chad Little	30.00	75.00
John Deere Promo		
98 Greg Sacks	10.00	25.00
Thom Apple Valley		
99 Glen Allen	8.00	20.00
Luxaire		
99 Jeff Burton	10.00	25.00
Exide		
300 Darrell Waltrip	12.00	30.00
Flock Special		

1998 Racing Champions 1:64 Pinnacle Series

This marks the second year Racing Champions have teamed up with Pinnacle to product a line of diecast car with trading cards. Each car is boxed in similar packaging as the standard cars, but are Pinnacle cards are featured in place of Racing Champions generic cards.

	Lo	Hi
4 Bobby Hamilton	2.00	6.00
Kodak		
5 Terry Labonte	3.00	6.00
Kellogg's		
6 Mark Martin	3.00	6.00
Valvoline		
8 Hut Stricklin	2.00	6.00
Circuit City		
9 Jeff Burton	2.00	6.00
Track Gear		
10 Ricky Rudd	2.00	6.00
Tide		
21 Michael Waltrip	2.00	6.00
Citgo		
33 Tim Fedewa	2.00	6.00
Kleenex		
33 Ken Schrader	2.00	6.00
Petree Racing		
35 Todd Bodine	2.00	6.00
Tabasco		
36 Ernie Irvan	2.00	6.00
Skittles		
40 Sterling Marlin	2.00	6.00
Sabco Racing		
42 Joe Nemechek	2.00	6.00
Bell South		
46 Wally Dallenbach	2.00	6.00
First Union		
50 Ricky Craven	2.00	6.00
Hendrick		
74 Randy Lajoie	2.00	6.00
Fina		
75 Rick Mast	2.00	6.00
Remington		
90 Dick Trickle	2.00	6.00
Helig Meyers		
94 Bill Elliott	3.00	6.00
McDonald's		
96 David Green	2.00	6.00
Caterpiller		

1998 Racing Champions 1:64 Press Pass Series

This series is a continuation of the Pinnacle series that was stopped when Press Pass was purchased by Racing Champions. Each car is boxed in similar packaging as the standard cars, but are Press Pass cards are featured in place of Racing Champions generic cards.

	Lo	Hi
00 Buckshot Jones	2.00	6.00
Aqua Fresh		
4 Bobby Hamilton	2.00	6.00
Kodak		
5 Terry Labonte	3.00	6.00
Kellogg's		
6 Mark Martin	3.00	6.00
Eagle One		
6 Mark Martin	3.00	6.00
Valvoline		
9 Jeff Burton	2.00	6.00
Track Gear		
10 Ricky Rudd	2.00	6.00
Tide		
11 Brett Bodine	2.00	6.00
Paychex		
13 Jerry Nadeau	2.00	6.00
First Plus		
16 Ted Musgrave	2.00	6.00
Primestar		
17 Darrell Waltrip	2.00	6.00
Builders Square		
21 Michael Waltrip	2.00	6.00
Goodwill Games		
26 Johnny Benson	2.00	6.00
Cheerios		
30 Derrike Cope	2.00	6.00
Gumout		
33 Tim Fedewa	2.00	6.00
Kleenex		
33 Ken Schrader	2.00	6.00
Petree		
35 Todd Bodine	2.00	6.00
Tabasco		
36 Ernie Irvan	2.00	6.00
M&Ms		
40 Sterling Marlin	2.00	6.00
Sabco		
41 Steve Grissom	2.00	6.00
Hedrick		
42 Joe Nemechek	2.00	6.00
Bell South		
50 Ricky Craven	2.00	6.00
Hendrick		
59 Robert Presley	2.00	6.00
Kingsford		
60 Mark Martin	3.00	6.00
Winn Dixie		
66 Elliot Sadler	2.00	6.00
Phillips 66		
75 Rick Mast	2.00	6.00
Remington		
90 Dick Trickle	2.00	6.00
Heilig-Meyers		
94 Bill Elliott	3.00	6.00
McDonald's		
96 David Green	2.00	6.00
Caterpillar		
97 Chad Little	2.00	6.00
John Deere		
98 Greg Sacks	2.00	6.00
Thorn Apple Valley		
99 Jeff Burton	2.00	6.00
Exide		

1998 Racing Champions 1:64 Reflections of Gold

This is a special series produced by Racing Champions to celebrate NASCAR's 50th anniversary. It parallels the regular 1998 1:64 scale series. Each car is a limited edition of 9,998. Each car is also plated in gold chrome and contains a serial number on its chassis.

	Lo	Hi
00 Buckshot Jones	8.00	20.00
Aqua Fresh		
4 Bobby Hamilton	8.00	20.00
Kodak		
4 Jeff Purvis	8.00	20.00
Lance		
5 Terry Labonte	15.00	40.00
Kellogg's		
6 Joe Bessey	8.00	20.00
Power Team		
6 Mark Martin	15.00	40.00
Valvoline		
8 Hut Stricklin	8.00	20.00
Circuit City		
9 Jeff Burton	10.00	25.00
Track Gear		
9 Lake Speed	8.00	20.00
Huckleberry Hound		
10 Phill Parsons	8.00	20.00
Duralube		
10 Ricky Rudd	10.00	25.00
Tide		
11 Brett Bodine	8.00	20.00
Paychex		
13 Jerry Nadeau	10.00	25.00
First Plus		
16 Ted Musgrave	8.00	20.00
Primestar		
20 Bliase Alexnader	8.00	20.00
Rescue		
21 Michael Waltrip	8.00	20.00
Citgo		
26 Johnny Benson	10.00	25.00
Cheerios		
29 Hermie Sadler	8.00	20.00
Dewalt		
30 Derrike Cope	8.00	20.00
Gumout		
30 Mike Cope	8.00	20.00
Slim Jim		
33 Tim Fedewa	8.00	20.00
Kleenex		
33 Ken Schrader	8.00	20.00
Petree		
34 Mike McLaughlin	8.00	20.00
Goulds		
35 Todd Bodine	10.00	25.00
Tabasco		
36 Ernie Irvan	12.00	30.00
Skittles		
38 Elton Sawyer	8.00	20.00
Barbasol		
40 Sterling Marlin	8.00	20.00
Sabco		
41 Steve Grissom	8.00	20.00
Hedrick		
42 Joe Nemechek	8.00	20.00
Bell South		
46 Wally Dallenbach	8.00	20.00
First Union		
47 Andy Santerre	8.00	20.00
Monroe		
50 Ricky Craven	10.00	20.00
Hendrick		
59 Robert Pressley	8.00	20.00
Kingsford		
60 Mark Martin	15.00	40.00
Winn Dixie		
63 Tracy Leslie	8.00	20.00
Lysol		
75 Rick Mast	8.00	20.00
Remington		
77 Robert Pressley	8.00	20.00
Jasper		
90 Dick Trickle	8.00	20.00
Heilig-Meyers		
94 Bill Elliott	15.00	40.00
McDonald's		
98 Greg Sacks	10.00	25.00
Thorn Apple Valley		
99 Glen Allen	8.00	20.00
Luxaire		
99 Jeff Burton	10.00	25.00
Exide		

1998 Racing Champions 1:64 Signature Series

This is a special series produced by Racing Champions to celebrate NASCAR's 50th anniversary. It parallels the regular 1998 1:64 scale series. Each car is a packaged in a decorative box with the driver's facsimile autograph on the front.

	Lo	Hi
00 Buckshot Jones AquaFresh	2.00	6.00
4 Bobby Hamilton Kodak	2.00	6.00
5 Terry Labonte Kellogg's	3.00	6.00
6 Mark Martin Valvoline	3.00	6.00
8 Hut Stricklin Circuit City	2.00	6.00
9 Jeff Burton Track Gear	2.00	6.00
9 Lake Speed Hucklerberry Hound	2.00	6.00
10 Ricky Rudd Tide	2.00	6.00
11 Brett Bodine Paychex	2.00	6.00
13 Jerry Nadeau First Plus	2.00	6.00
21 Michael Waltrip Citgo	2.00	6.00
26 Johnny Benson Cheerios	2.00	6.00
30 Mike Cope Slim Jim	2.00	6.00
33 Ken Schrader Petree	2.00	6.00
35 Todd Bodine Tabasco	2.00	6.00
36 Ernie Irvan Skittles	2.00	6.00
38 Elton Sawyer Barbasol	2.00	6.00
40 Sterling Marlin Saboc	2.00	6.00
42 Joe Nemechek Bell South	2.00	6.00
46 Wally Dallenbach First Union	2.00	6.00
50 Ricky Craven Hendrick	2.00	6.00
59 Robert Pressley Kingsford	2.00	6.00
75 Rick Mast Remington	2.00	6.00
90 Dick Trickle Heilig-Meyers	2.00	6.00
94 Bill Elliott Happy Meal	3.00	6.00
94 Bill Elliott McDonald's	3.00	6.00
97 Chad Little John Deere	2.00	6.00
98 Greg Sacks Thorn Apple Valley	2.00	6.00
99 Jeff Burton Exide	2.00	6.00

1998 Racing Champions 1:64 Stock Rods

These 1:64 scale cars are replicas of vintage stock rods with NASCAR paint schemes. Cars are listed by issue number instead of car number.

	Lo	Hi
56 Terry Labonte Spooky Loops	3.00	8.00
57 Terry Labonte Kellogg's	3.00	8.00
58 Glen Allen Luxaire	2.00	6.00
59 Bobby Hamilton Kodak	2.00	6.00
60 Dick Trickle Heilig-Meyers	2.00	6.00
61 Robert Pressley Kingsford	2.00	6.00
62 Ted Musgrave Primestar	2.00	6.00
63 Hut Stricklin Circuit City	2.00	6.00
64 Kevin Schwantz Ryder	2.00	6.00
65 Michael Waltrip Citgo	2.00	6.00
66 Buckshot Jones Alka-Seltzer	2.00	6.00
67 Ken Schrader Petree	2.00	6.00
68 Bobby Hamilton Kodak	2.00	6.00
69 Hut Stricklin Circuit City	2.00	6.00
70 Terry Labonte Kellogg's	3.00	8.00
71 Rick Mast Remington	2.00	6.00
72 Joe Nemechek Bell South	2.00	6.00
73 Ricky Rudd Tide	2.00	6.00
74 Bill Elliott McDonald's	3.00	8.00
75 Ernie Irvan M&M	2.00	6.00
76 Terry Labonte Kellogg's	3.00	8.00
77 Michael Waltrip Citgo	2.00	6.00
78 Ricky Rudd Tide Gold	6.00	15.00
79 Bill Elliott McDonald's Gold	15.00	30.00
80 Bobby Hamilton Kodak Gold	6.00	15.00
81 Hut Stricklin Circuit City Gold	6.00	15.00
82 Mark Martin Valvoline	3.00	8.00
83 Ted Musgrave Primestar	2.00	6.00
84 Jeff Burton Exide	2.00	6.00
85 Mark Martin Winn Dixie	3.00	8.00
86 Jeff Burton Exide Gold	8.00	20.00
87 Bill Elliott McDonald's Gold	15.00	30.00
88 Todd Bodine Tabasco	2.00	6.00
89 Lake Speed Huckleberry Hound	2.00	6.00
90 Jeff Burton Exide	2.00	6.00
91 Bill Elliott McDonald's	3.00	8.00
92 Mark Martin Winn Dixie	3.00	8.00
93 Mark Martin Valvoline	3.00	8.00
94 Lake Speed Cartoon Network	2.00	6.00
95 Terry Labonte Kellogg's Corny	3.00	8.00
96 Terry Labonte Kellogg's Corny Gold	15.00	30.00
97 Jeff Burton Exide Gold	8.00	20.00
98 Rick Mast Remington	2.00	6.00
99 Terry Labonte Kellogg's	3.00	8.00
100 Joe Nemechek Bell South	2.00	6.00
101 Robert Pressley Kingsford	2.00	6.00
102 Bill Elliott McDonald's	3.00	8.00
103 Mark Martin Winn Dixie	3.00	8.00
104 Jeff Burton Exide Gold	8.00	20.00
105 Bobby Hamilton Kodak Gold	6.00	15.00
106 Terry Labonte Kellogg's	3.00	8.00
107 Bill Elliott McDonald's	3.00	8.00
108 Mark Martin Valvoline	3.00	8.00
109 Jeff Burton Track Gear	2.00	6.00
110 Ted Musgrave Primestar	2.00	6.00
111 Lake Speed Huckleberry Hound	2.00	6.00
112 Terry Labonte Kellogg's Corny Gold	15.00	30.00
113 Ricky Rudd Tide Gold	6.00	15.00
114 Bobby Hamilton Kodak	2.00	6.00
115 Ken Schrader Petree	2.00	6.00
116 Dick Trickle Heilig-Meyers	2.00	6.00
117 Todd Bodine Tabasco	2.00	6.00
118 Terry Labonte Kellogg's	3.00	8.00
119 Terry Labonte Kellogg's	3.00	8.00
120 Joe Nemechek Bell South	2.00	6.00
121 Kevin Schwartz Ryder	2.00	6.00
122 Robert Pressley Kingsford	2.00	6.00
123 Bill Elliott McDonald's	3.00	8.00
124 Mark Martin Valvoline	3.00	8.00
125 Michael Waltrip Citgo	2.00	6.00
126 Dick Trickle Heilig-Meyers	2.00	6.00
127 Ted Musgrave Primestar	2.00	6.00
128 Michael Waltrip Citgo	2.00	6.00
129 Bobby Hamilton Kodak	2.00	6.00
130 Bill Elliott McDonald's	3.00	8.00
131 Terry Labonte Kellogg's	3.00	8.00
132 Rick Mast Remington Gold	6.00	15.00
133 Robert Pressley Kingsford	2.00	6.00
134 Michael Waltrip Citgo	2.00	6.00
135 Ken Schrader Petree Gold	6.00	15.00
136 Mark Martin Valvoline	3.00	8.00
137 Jeff Burton Track Gear	2.00	6.00
138 Bill Elliott McDonald's	3.00	8.00
139 Terry Labonte Kellogg's Corny	3.00	8.00
140 Rick Mast Remington	2.00	6.00
141 Terry Labonte Blasted Fruit Loops	3.00	8.00
142 Michael Waltrip Citgo Gold	6.00	15.00
143 Terry Labonte Kellogg's Gold	15.00	30.00

1998 Racing Champions 1:64 Stock Rods Reflections of Gold

These 1:64 scale cars are replicas of vintage stock rods with NASCAR paint schemes and gold plating. Cars are listed by issue number instead of car number.

	Lo	Hi
1 Terry Labonte Kellogg's	15.00	40.00
2 Jerry Nadeau First Plus	8.00	20.00
3 Bobby Hamilton Kodak	8.00	20.00
4 Todd Bodine Tabasco	8.00	20.00
5 Mark Martin Valvoline	15.00	40.00
6 Bill Elliott McDonald's	15.00	40.00
7 Ted Musgrave Primestar	8.00	20.00
8 Jeff Burton Exide	10.00	25.00

1998 Racing Champions 1:64 Toys 'R Us Gold

This is a special series produced by Racing Champions to celebrate NASCAR's 50th anniversary. Each car is a limited edition of 19,998. Each car is also plated in gold chrome. These cars were distributed in Toys 'R Us stores.

	Lo	Hi
5 Terry Labonte Blasted Fruit Loops	8.00	20.00
5 Terry Labonte Kellogg's Corny	8.00	20.00
6 Joe Bessey Power Team	4.00	10.00
6 Mark Martin Eagle One	8.00	20.00
6 Mark Martin Valvoline	8.00	20.00
9 Jerry Nadeau Zombie Island	5.00	12.00
9 Lake Speed Birthday Cake	5.00	12.00
10 Phill Parsons Duralube	4.00	10.00
10 Ricky Rudd Give Kids The World	4.00	10.00
11 Brett Bodine Paychex	4.00	10.00
13 Jerry Nadeau First Plus	4.00	10.00
17 Matt Kenseth Lycos	5.00	12.00
17 Darrell Waltrip Builders' Square	5.00	12.00
19 Tony Raines Yellow	4.00	10.00
20 Blaise Alexander Rescue Engine	4.00	10.00
21 Michael Waltrip Goodwill Games	4.00	10.00
23 Lance Hooper WCW	4.00	10.00
26 Johnny Benson Betty Crocker	4.00	10.00
26 Johnny Benson Cheerios	4.00	10.00
33 Tim Fedewa Kleenex	4.00	10.00
33 Ken Schrader Petree	4.00	10.00
35 Todd Bodine Tabasco	5.00	12.00
36 Ernie Irvan Wildberry Skittles	6.00	15.00
42 Joe Nemechek Bell South	4.00	10.00
50 NDA Dr. Pepper	4.00	10.00
60 Mark Martin Winn Dixie	8.00	20.00
63 Tracy Leslie Lysol	4.00	10.00
64 Dick Trickle Scheinder	4.00	10.00
74 Randy Lajoie Fina	4.00	10.00
77 Robert Pressley Jasper	4.00	10.00
87 Joe Nemechek Bell South	4.00	10.00
94 Bill Elliott Happy Meal	8.00	20.00
98 Greg Sacks Thorn Apple Valley	4.00	10.00
99 Jeff Burton Exide	5.00	12.00
300 Darrell Waltrip Flock Special	5.00	12.00

1998 Racing Champions SuperTrucks 1:64

Racing Champions continued there line of 1:64 SuperTrucks in 1998. This series features many of the circuit's first-time drivers and Winston Cup regulars.

	Lo	Hi
2 Mike Bliss Team ASE	2.00	4.00
6 Rick Carelli Remax	2.00	4.00
18 No Driver Association Dana	2.00	4.00
19 Tony Raines Pennzoil	2.00	4.00
29 Bob Keselowski Mopar	2.00	4.00
31 Tony Roper Concor Tools	2.00	4.00
35 Ron Barfield Ortho	2.00	4.00
44 Boris Said Federated	2.00	4.00
52 Mike Wallace Pure One	2.00	4.00
66 Bryan Reffner Carlin	2.00	4.00
75 Kevin Harvick Spears	2.00	4.00
84 Wayne Anderson Porter Cable	2.00	4.00
86 Stacy Compton RC Cola	2.00	4.00
87 Joe Nemechek BellSouth	2.00	4.00
90 Lance Norick National Hockey League	2.00	4.00
94 Bill Elliott Team ASE	2.00	4.00

1998 Racing Champions SuperTrucks 1:64 Gold

This is a special series produced by Racing Champions to celebrate NASCAR's 50th anniversary. It parallels the regular 1998 1:24 scale series. Each truck is a limited edition of 5,000. Each truck is also plated in gold chrome and contains a serial number on its chassis.

	Lo	Hi
2 Mike Bliss Team ASE	8.00	20.00
6 Rick Carelli Remax	8.00	20.00
29 Bob Keselowski Mopar	8.00	20.00
66 Bryan Reffner Carlin	8.00	20.00
84 Wayne Anderson Porter Cable	8.00	20.00
86 Stacy Compton RC Cola	8.00	20.00

1997 Revell Club 1:18

These 1:18 scale cars were the from the same production run as the Collection cars. Each car distributed by the club has a serial number on the chassis. The boxes were uniquely colored to match the colors on the car.

	Lo	Hi
1 NDA Coca Cola 600	70.00	110.00
5 Terry Labonte Tony the Tiger	90.00	150.00
5 Terry Labonte Spooky Loops	90.00	150.00
23 Jimmy Spencer Camel	90.00	150.00
33 Ken Schrader Skoal	80.00	120.00
46 Wally Dallenbach Woody	80.00	120.00
97 Chad Little John Deere	90.00	150.00

1997 Revell Collection 1:18

This series marks Revell's first attempt to produce a 1:18 scale car. It was distributed to hobby dealers are part of Revell's Collection line.

	Lo	Hi
1 No Driver Association Coca Cola 600	50.00	75.00
2 Rusty Wallace Miller Lite	50.00	100.00
3 Dale Earnhardt Wheaties	100.00	160.00
4 Sterling Marlin Kodak	55.00	80.00
5 Terry Labonte Kellogg's	50.00	100.00
5 Terry Labonte Spooky Loops	55.00	110.00
5 Terry Labonte Tony the Tiger	55.00	110.00
6 Mark Martin Valvoline	50.00	80.00
10 Ricky Rudd Tide	50.00	80.00
18 Bobby Labonte Interstate Batteries	50.00	80.00
21 Michael Waltrip Citgo Top Dog paint scheme	50.00	75.00
23 Jimmy Spencer Camel	55.00	110.00
24 Jeff Gordon Lost World	100.00	160.00
25 Ricky Craven Bud Lizard	50.00	100.00
28 Ernie Irvan Havoline 10th Anniversary paint scheme	50.00	100.00
29 Jeff Green Scooby-Doo	40.00	80.00
29 Jeff Green Tom & Jerry	40.00	80.00
29 Steve Grissom Flintstones	40.00	80.00
33 Ken Schrader Skoal	40.00	90.00
35 Todd Bodine Tabasco	55.00	80.00
37 Jeremy Mayfield Kmart	50.00	80.00
40 Robby Gordon Coors Light	50.00	75.00
41 Steve Grissom Kodiak	40.00	80.00
43 Bobby Hamilton STP Goody's	50.00	80.00
46 Wally Dallenbach Woody Woodpecker	50.00	80.00
60 Mark Martin Winn Dixie	50.00	90.00
88 Dale Jarrett	50.00	90.00

	Lo	Hi
Ford Credit		
94 Bill Elliott	50.00	90.00
McDonald's		
94 Bill Elliott	50.00	90.00
Mac Tonight		
97 Chad Little	50.00	90.00
John Deere Autographed box		
97 No Driver Association	40.00	75.00
Texas Motor Speedway		

1998 Revell Club 1:18

These 1:18 scale cars were the from the same production run as the Collection cars. Each car distributed by the club has a serial number on the chassis. The boxes were uniquely colored to match the colors on the car.

	Lo	Hi
1 Dale Earnhardt Jr. Coke	90.00	150.00
1 Steve Park Pennzoil	110.00	200.00
1 Steve Park Pennzoil Indy	90.00	150.00
2 Rusty Wallace Adventures of Rusty	100.00	175.00
2 Rusty Wallace Miller Lite Elvis	90.00	150.00
3 Dale Earnhardt Coke	90.00	150.00
3 Dale Earnhardt Goodwrench Plus	100.00	175.00
3 Dale Earnhardt Goodwrench Plus Bass Pro	125.00	200.00
3 Dale Earnhardt Goodwrench Plus Daytona	125.00	200.00
3 Dale Earnhardt Jr. AC Delco	200.00	300.00
5 Terry Labonte Blasted Fruit Loops	90.00	150.00
5 Terry Labonte Kellogg's Corny	100.00	175.00
9 Lake Speed Birthday Cake	90.00	150.00
9 Lake Speed Huckleberry Hound	90.00	150.00
18 Bobby Labonte Interstate Batteries Hot Rod	90.00	150.00
18 Bobby Labonte Interstate Batteries Small Soldiers	90.00	150.00
23 Jimmy Spencer No Bull	125.00	200.00
24 Jeff Gordon DuPont	100.00	175.00
24 Jeff Gordon DuPont Chromalusion	150.00	225.00
28 Kenny Irwin Havoline	90.00	150.00
28 Kenny Irwin Havoline Joker	100.00	175.00
31 Mike Skinner Lowe's	90.00	150.00
35 Todd Bodine Tabasco	90.00	150.00
36 Ernie Irvan M&Ms	125.00	200.00
36 Ernie Irvan Wildberry Skittles	90.00	150.00
44 Tony Stewart Shell	90.00	150.00
44 Tony Stewart Shell Small Soldiers	90.00	150.00
50 Ricky Craven Budweiser	90.00	150.00
81 Kenny Wallace Square D Lightning	90.00	150.00
88 Dale Jarrett Quality Care	90.00	150.00
88 Dale Jarrett Quality Care Batman	100.00	175.00

1998 Revell Collection 1:18

This series marks Revell's second year producing a 1:18 scale car. It was distributed to hobby dealers are part of Revell's Collection line.

	Lo	Hi
1 Dale Earnhardt Jr. Coke	50.00	100.00
1 Steve Park Pennzoil	60.00	120.00
2 Rusty Wallace Adventures of Rusty	50.00	100.00
2 Rusty Wallace Miller Lite	50.00	100.00
2 Rusty Wallace Miller Lite Elvis	50.00	100.00
2 Rusty Wallace Miller Lite TCB	50.00	100.00
3 Dale Earnhardt Coke	50.00	100.00
3 Dale Earnhardt Goodwrench Plus	50.00	120.00
3 Dale Earnhardt Goodwrench Plus Bass Pro	60.00	120.00
3 Dale Earnhardt Goodwrench Plus Brickyard Special	50.00	120.00
3 Dale Earnhardt Jr. AC Delco		
5 Terry Labonte Blasted Fruit Loops	50.00	100.00
5 Terry Labonte Kellogg's Corny	50.00	100.00
9 Lake Speed Birthday Cake	40.00	80.00
9 Lake Speed Huckleberry Hound	40.00	80.00
18 Bobby Labonte Interstate Batteries Hot Rod	40.00	80.00
18 Bobby Labonte Interstate Batteries Small Soldiers	40.00	80.00
23 Jimmy Spencer No Bull	60.00	120.00
24 Jeff Gordon DuPont	50.00	120.00
24 Jeff Gordon DuPont Brickyard Special	50.00	100.00
24 Jeff Gordon DuPont Chromalusion	90.00	150.00
28 Kenny Irwin Havoline	50.00	100.00
31 Dale Earnhardt Jr. Wrangler	100.00	175.00
31 Mike Skinner Lowe's	40.00	80.00
35 Todd Bodine Tabasco	40.00	80.00
36 Ernie Irvan M&Ms	50.00	100.00
36 Ernie Irvan Wildberry Skittles	40.00	80.00
44 Tony Stewart Shell	40.00	80.00
46 Jeff Green First Union Devil Rays	40.00	80.00
50 Ricky Craven Budweiser	50.00	90.00
50 No Driver Association Bud Louie	50.00	100.00
81 Kenny Wallace Sqaure D Lightning	40.00	80.00
88 Dale Jarrett Quality Care	50.00	100.00

1993-1995 Revell 1:24

This set features many NASCAR's top drivers. Many of the pieces were issued through retail outlets but some were distributed through the drivers souvenir trailers.

	Lo	Hi
1 Jeff Gordon Baby Ruth produced for RCI	300.00	400.00
3 Dale Earnhardt Goodwrench Kellogg's Promo	15.00	30.00
3 Dale Earnhardt Goodwrench Black Wheels Sports Image car	12.50	25.00
3 Dale Earnhardt Goodwrench Silver Wheels	8.00	16.00
3 Dale Earnhardt Goodwrench 1994 Sports Image	12.50	25.00
3 Dale Earnhardt Goodwrench 6-Time Champion	15.00	30.00
4 Rick Wilson Kodak produced for GMP	12.50	25.00
6 Mark Martin Valvoline	10.00	18.00
7 Harry Gant Mac Tools produced by RCI	35.00	60.00
7 Harry Gant Morema	25.00	40.00
8 Dick Trickle Snickers	10.00	18.00
8 1/2 No Driver Association Racing For Kids	7.50	15.00
10 Derrike Cope Purolator	10.00	20.00
15 Geoff Bodine Ford Motorsports	18.00	35.00
17 Darrell Waltrip Western Auto	8.00	16.00
18 Dale Jarrett Interstate Batteries	10.00	18.00
21 Morgan Shepherd Cheerwine	12.50	25.00
21 Morgan Shepherd Citgo	12.00	20.00
22 Sterling Marlin Maxwell House	12.00	20.00
26 Brett Bodine Quaker State	10.00	18.00
28 Davey Allison Havoline	15.00	30.00
28 Davey Allison Mac Tools	30.00	50.00
28 Ernie Irvan Mac Tools	25.00	40.00
30 Michael Waltrip Pennzoil	10.00	18.00
32 Dale Jarrett Mac Tools	20.00	35.00
33 Harry Gant No Sponsor Farewell Tour	15.00	30.00
42 Kyle Petty Mello Yello	8.00	16.00
52 Ken Schrader No Sponsor Morema	20.00	30.00
57 No Driver Association Heinz 57	10.00	18.00
59 Robert Pressley Alliance produced RCI	30.00	55.00
60 Mark Martin Winn Dixie produced for GMP	25.00	40.00
66 No Driver Association Phillips 66 TropArtic	10.00	18.00
66 Dick Trickle Phillips 66 TropArtic	20.00	40.00
68 Bobby Hamilton Country Time	10.00	18.00
75 Joe Ruttman Dinner Bell	10.00	18.00
83 Lake Speed Purex produced for GMP	12.50	25.00
90 Bobby Hillin Heilig-Meyers	12.50	25.00
94 Terry Labonte Sunoco	10.00	18.00

1994 Revell 1:24 Hobby

These pieces were distributed through hobby outlets. Each piece came in a black and yellow box and had a few colors that matched the car. There were also a few promo cars done in this series.

	Lo	Hi
4 Sterling Marlin Kodak	10.00	20.00
5 Terry Labonte Kellogg's	10.00	20.00

7 Geoff Bodine Exide	10.00	20.00
15 Lake Speed Quality Care	10.00	20.00
24 Jeff Gordon DuPont	25.00	50.00
31 Ward Rurton Hardee's	15.00	25.00
41 Joe Nemechek Meineke	10.00	20.00
43 Wally Dallenbach Jr. STP	10.00	20.00

1995 Revell 1:24

These pieces were also a part of the continued growth of Revell's presence in the die cast market. The pieces were at the time updated with driver and sponsor changes. The boxes were uniquely colored to match the colors on the car.

	Lo	Hi
4 Sterling Marlin Kodak	10.00	20.00
6 Mark Martin Valvoline	12.00	20.00
7 Geoff Bodine Exide Promo	12.00	20.00
15 Dick Trickle Ford Quality Care	10.00	20.00
16 Ted Musgrave Family Channel	10.00	20.00
18 Bobby Labonte Interstate Batteries	10.00	20.00
21 Morgan Shepherd Citgo	10.00	20.00
23 Chad Little Bayer	10.00	20.00
24 Jeff Gordon DuPont	30.00	50.00
25 Ken Schrader Budweiser	12.00	20.00
26 Steve Kinser Quaker State	12.00	20.00
31 Ward Burton Hardee's Promo	12.00	20.00
32 Dale Jarrett Mac Tools Promo by American Minitures	12.00	20.00
44 David Green Slim Jim	10.00	20.00
71 Kevin Lepage Vermont Teddy Bear	10.00	20.00
71 Dave Marcis Olive Garden Promo	20.00	40.00
75 Todd Bodine Factory Stores of America	10.00	20.00
87 Joe Nemechek Burger King	12.00	24.00

1996 Revell 1:24

This series was distributed in retail outlets. These cars were packaged in colored boxes that matched the color schemes of the cars.

	Lo	Hi
2 Rusty Wallace Penske Motorsports	12.00	20.00
3 Dale Earnhardt Goodwrench	15.00	30.00
3 Dale Earnhardt Olympic car	15.00	30.00
4 Sterling Marlin Kodak	12.00	20.00
5 Terry Labonte Kellogg's	15.00	25.00
6 Mark Martin Valvoline	12.00	20.00
10 Ricky Rudd Tide	12.00	20.00
11 Brett Bodine Lowe's	12.00	20.00
16 Ron Hornaday Smith Wesson	30.00	50.00
16 Ted Musgrave Family Channel Primestar	12.00	20.00
17 Darrell Waltrip Parts America	12.00	20.00
18 Bobby Labonte Interstate Batteries	12.00	20.00
21 Michael Waltrip Citgo	12.00	20.00
24 Jeff Gordon DuPont	15.00	25.00
28 Ernie Irvan Havoline	12.00	20.00
37 John Andretti K-Mart	12.00	20.00
75 Morgan Shepherd Remington	14.00	22.00
75 Morgan Shepherd Remington Camouflage	15.00	25.00
75 Morgan Shepherd Stren	14.00	22.00
77 Bobby Hillin Jasper Engines	15.00	25.00
87 Joe Nemechek Burger King	12.00	20.00
88 Dale Jarrett Quality Care	14.00	22.00
99 Jeff Burton Exide	12.00	20.00

1996 Revell Collection 1:24

This series was produced for and distributed in hobby outlets. These cars have significant upgrades in comparision to the standard Revell 1:24 1996 pieces. Each car is packaged with a mounting base. The Terry Labonte Honey Crunch car has been the subject of market manipulation due to the sale of a large portion of the prodcution run to the general public before they were distributed to hobby distributors.

	Lo	Hi
2 Rusty Wallace MGD Silver	25.00	45.00
2 Rusty Wallace Penske	20.00	35.00
3 Dale Earnhardt Olympic	25.00	40.00
4 Sterling Marlin Kodak	20.00	35.00
5 Terry Labonte Honey Crunch	225.00	300.00
5 Terry Labonte Kellogg's	50.00	80.00
5 Terry Labonte Kellogg's Silver	60.00	90.00
6 Mark Martin Valvoline	20.00	35.00
8 Kenny Wallace Red Dog	25.00	40.00
10 Ricky Rudd Tide	25.00	40.00
11 Brett Bodine Lowe's 50th Anniversary	20.00	35.00
16 Ted Musgrave Primestar	20.00	35.00
17 Darrell Waltrip Parts America	20.00	35.00
18 Bobby Labonte Interstate Batteries	20.00	35.00
22 Rusty Wallace Miller Genuine Draft SuperTruck	25.00	40.00
22 Rusty Wallace Miller Genuine Draft Silver SuperTruck	30.00	50.00
23 Chad Little John Deere	40.00	60.00
23 Chad Little John Deere Autographed	60.00	90.00
23 Chad Little John Deere Bank	45.00	70.00
23 Chad Little John Deere Bank Autographed	65.00	100.00
24 Jeff Gordon DuPont	30.00	50.00
24 Jack Sprague Quaker State	20.00	35.00
25 Ken Schrader Budweiser	20.00	35.00
25 Ken Schrader Budweiser Olympic car	20.00	35.00
28 Ernie Irvan Havoline	20.00	35.00
30 Johnny Benson Pennzoil	20.00	35.00
37 Jeremy Mayfield K-Mart	20.00	35.00
52 Jack Sprague Pedigree	20.00	35.00
75 Morgan Shepherd Remington	20.00	35.00
75 Morgan Shepherd Remington Camouflage	30.00	50.00
75 Morgan Shepherd Stren	20.00	35.00
76 David Green Smith and Wesson	20.00	35.00
77 Bobby Hillin Jasper Engines	25.00	35.00
87 Joe Nemechek Burger King	20.00	35.00
88 Dale Jarrett Quality Care	20.00	35.00
99 Jeff Burton Exide	20.00	35.00

1997 Revell Club 1:24

These pieces were also a part of the continued growth of Revell's presence in the die cast market. In the last quarter of 1997, Revell formed a collector's club to which they distributed cars in this series. The actual cars themselves were the from the same production run as the Collection cars and banks. Each car distributed by the club has a serial number on the chassis. The boxes were uniquely colored to match the colors on the car.

	Lo	Hi
1 NDA Coca Cola 600	45.00	80.00
1 No Driver Association Revell Club	25.00	40.00
2 Rusty Wallace Miller Lite	60.00	100.00
5 Terry Labonte Kellogg's	90.00	150.00
5 Terry Labonte Spooky Loops	125.00	200.00
5 Terry Labonte Spooky Loops Bank	150.00	225.00
5 Terry Labonte Tony the Tiger	100.00	175.00
5 Terry Labonte Tony the Tiger Bank	125.00	200.00
18 Bobby Labonte Interstate Batteries Texas Motor Speedway	60.00	100.00
21 Michael Waltrip Citgo Top Dog paint scheme	55.00	90.00
23 Jimmy Spencer Camel	100.00	175.00
23 Jimmy Spencer No Bull	225.00	350.00
28 Ernie Irvan Havoline	70.00	110.00
28 Ernie Irvan Havoline 10th Anniversary paint scheme.	90.00	150.00
28 Ernie Irvan Havoline Bank 10th Anniversary paint scheme	100.00	175.00
33 Ken Schrader Skoal	60.00	100.00
37 Jeremy Mayfield K-Mart	55.00	90.00
40 Robby Gordon Coors Light	55.00	90.00
43 Bobby Hamilton STP Goody's	50.00	90.00
43 Jimmy Hensley Cummins Super Truck	50.00	90.00
46 Wally Dallenbach Woody	50.00	90.00
75 Rick Mast Remington	55.00	90.00
96 David Green Caterpillar	50.00	90.00

	Lo	Hi
97 Chad Little John Deere	60.00	100.00
97 Chad Little John Deere 160th Anniversary	60.00	100.00

1997 Revell Collection 1:24

This series is the continuation of the 1996 series. It signals Revell's expansion into the diecast market by its sheer number of cars in the series.

	Lo	Hi
2 Rusty Wallace Miller Suzuka	50.00	75.00
2 Rusty Wallace Miller Lite	35.00	50.00
2 Rusty Wallace Miller Lite Japan	35.00	50.00
2 Rusty Wallace Miller Lite Texas Motor Speedway	40.00	65.00
4 Sterling Marlin Kodak	30.00	45.00
5 Terry Labonte Kellogg's	40.00	65.00
5 Terry Labonte Kellogg's 1996 Champion	50.00	80.00
5 Terry Labonte Kellogg's distributed by Mac Tools	50.00	80.00
5 Terry Labonte Kellogg's Texas Motor Speedway	70.00	110.00
5 Terry Labonte Spooky Loops	90.00	150.00
5 Terry Labonte Tony the Tiger	90.00	150.00
6 Mark Martin Valvoline	35.00	50.00
7 Geoff Bodine QVC	30.00	45.00
8 Hut Stricklin Circuit City	30.00	45.00
10 Ricky Rudd Tide	30.00	45.00
11 Brett Bodine Close Call	30.00	45.00
15 Mike Colabacci VISA	30.00	45.00
16 Ted Musgrave Primestar	30.00	45.00
17 Rich Bickle Die Hard Super Truck	30.00	45.00
17 Darrell Waltrip Parts America	30.00	45.00
18 Bobby Labonte Interstate Batteries	30.00	45.00
18 Bobby Labonte Interstate Batteries Texas Motor Speedway	35.00	60.00
19 Tony Raines Pennoil Super Truck	30.00	45.00
21 Michael Waltrip Citgo Pearson paint scheme	30.00	45.00
21 Michael Waltrip Citgo Top Dog paint scheme	30.00	45.00
23 Jimmy Spencer Camel	60.00	100.00
23 Jimmy Spencer No Bull	225.00	350.00
25 Ricky Craven Budwesier	35.00	50.00
28 Ernie Irvan Havoline	35.00	50.00
28 Ernie Irvan Havoline 10th Anniversary paint scheme	50.00	90.00
29 Jeff Green Scooby-Doo	25.00	40.00
29 Steve Grissom Flintstones	25.00	40.00
29 Robert Pressley Tom & Jerry	25.00	40.00
30 Johnny Benson Pennzoil	30.00	45.00
32 Dale Jarrett White Rain	25.00	40.00
33 Ken Schrader Skoal	35.00	55.00
35 Todd Bodine Tabasco	25.00	40.00
36 Todd Bodine Stanley	25.00	40.00
36 Derrike Cope Skittles	25.00	40.00
37 David and Jeff Green Red Man Super Truck	25.00	40.00
37 Mark Green Timber Wolf	25.00	40.00
37 Jeremy Mayfield Kmart Kids Against Drugs	30.00	45.00
37 Jeremy Mayfield K-Mart Lady Luck	30.00	45.00
37 Jeremy Mayfield K-Mart RC Cola	30.00	45.00
40 Robby Gordon Coors Light	25.00	40.00
41 Steve Grissom Kodiak	25.00	40.00
42 Joe Nemechek BellSouth	30.00	45.00
43 Bobby Hamilton STP Goody's	25.00	40.00
43 Jimmy Hensley Cummins Super Truck	25.00	40.00
46 Wally Dallenbach Woody Woodpecker	30.00	45.00
55 Michael Waltrip Sealy	30.00	45.00
60 Mark Martin Winn Dixie	35.00	50.00
75 Rick Mast Remington	30.00	45.00
90 Dick Trickle Heilig-Meyers	30.00	45.00
91 Mike Wallace SPAM	30.00	45.00
94 Ron Barfield New Holland	25.00	40.00
94 Bill Elliott McDonald's	30.00	45.00
94 Bill Elliott Mac Tonight	35.00	50.00
96 David Green Caterpillar	30.00	45.00
97 Chad Little John Deere Autographed box	40.00	60.00
97 Chad Little John Deere 160th Anniversary paint scheme	45.00	70.00
97 No Driver Association California 500	25.00	40.00
97 No Driver Association Texas Motor Speedway	25.00	40.00
98 John Andretti RCA	30.00	45.00
99 Jeff Burton Exide	30.00	45.00
99 Jeff Burton Exide Texas Motor Speedway	35.00	60.00

1997 Revell Collection 1:24 Banks

This series marks Revell's first attempt to produce a 1:24 scale car bank. It was distributed to hobby dealers are part of Revell's Collection line.

	Lo	Hi
5 Terry Labonte Tony the Tiger	100.00	175.00
18 Bobby Labonte Interstate Batteries Texas Motor Speedway	90.00	150.00
28 Ernie Irvan Havoline	50.00	80.00
28 Ernie Irvan Havoline 10th Anniversary paint scheme	70.00	110.00
29 Jeff Green Scooby-Doo	50.00	80.00
35 Todd Bodine Tabasco	50.00	80.00
46 Wally Dallenbach Woody Woodpecker	50.00	80.00
46 Wally Dallenbach First Union	45.00	70.00
91 Mike Wallace Spam	50.00	80.00
97 Chad Little John Deere Autographed box	45.00	70.00
97 Chad Little John Deere Autographed box 160th Anniversary paint scheme	50.00	80.00
97 No Driver Association California 500	40.00	75.00

1997 Revell Hobby 1:24

This series, Revell Select, was produced to appease those collectors who wanted a upgraded production diecast without the upgrade price. The cars themselves appear to have similar production qualities as the Collection cars, but are lower priced and are packaged in black window boxes.

	Lo	Hi
2 Rusty Wallace Miller Lite	25.00	40.00
4 Sterling Marlin Kodak	20.00	35.00
5 Terry Labonte Kellogg's	20.00	35.00
5 Terry Labonte Kellogg's Texas Motor Speedway	20.00	35.00
5 Terry Labonte Spooky Loops	30.00	60.00
5 Terry Labonte Tony the Tiger	25.00	40.00
6 Mark Martin Valvoline	20.00	35.00
10 Ricky Rudd Tide	20.00	35.00
17 Darrell Waltrip Parts America	20.00	35.00
18 Bobby Labonte Interstate Batteries	15.00	30.00
18 Bobby Labonte Interstate Batteries Texas Motor Speedway	15.00	30.00
21 Michael Waltrip Citgo Top Dog paint scheme	20.00	35.00
25 Ricky Craven Budwiser Lizard	20.00	40.00
28 Ernie Irvan Havoline	20.00	35.00
28 Ernie Irvan Havoline 10th Anniversary paint scheme	25.00	40.00
29 Robert Pressley Scooby-Doo	15.00	30.00
29 Robert Pressley Tom & Jerry	15.00	30.00
33 Ken Schrader Skoal	25.00	40.00
36 Derrike Cope Skittles	20.00	35.00
37 Jeremy Mayfield Kmart Kids Against Drugs	20.00	35.00
40 Robby Gordon Coors Light	20.00	35.00
42 Joe Nemechek Bell South	20.00	35.00
46 Wally Dallenbach First Union Bank	30.00	50.00
46 Wally Dallenbach Woody Woodpecker	15.00	30.00
75 Rick Mast Remington	20.00	35.00
91 Mike Wallace Spam	20.00	35.00
94 Bill Elliott McDonald's	20.00	35.00
94 Bill Elliott	20.00	35.00

	Lo	Hi
Mac Tonight		
97 Chad Little	30.00	35.00
John Deere		
160th Anniversary paint scheme		
97 No Driver Association	15.00	30.00
Texas Motor Speedway		
99 Jeff Burton	20.00	35.00
Exide		

1997 Revell Retail 1:24

This series, Revell Racing, was produced for and distributed in the mass-market.

	Lo	Hi
CARS (4/10/16/21/91)	10.00	20.00
1 No Driver Association	10.00	20.00
Coca Cola 600		
1 No Driver Association	45.00	75.00
Mac Tools		
packaged in collectible tin		
2 Rusty Wallace	12.50	25.00
Penske		
4 Sterling Marlin	15.00	30.00
Kodak		
5 Terry Labonte	12.50	25.00
Kellogg's Texas Motor Speedway		
5 Terry Labonte	12.50	30.00
Spooky Loops		
5 Terry Labonte	15.00	30.00
Tony The Tiger		
packaged in Food City box		
6 Mark Martin	12.50	25.00
Valvoline		
10 Ricky Rudd	15.00	30.00
Tide		
16 Ted Musgrave	15.00	30.00
Primestar		
17 Darrell Waltrip	10.00	20.00
Parts America		
17 Darrell Waltrip	125.00	200.00
Parts America		
6 Car set		
21 Michael Waltrip	15.00	30.00
Citgo Top Dog paint scheme		
28 Ernie Irvan	12.50	25.00
Havoline		
10th Anniversary paint scheme		
29 Robert Pressley	10.00	20.00
Flintstones		
29 Robert Pressley	10.00	20.00
Scooby-Doo		
29 Robert Pressley	10.00	20.00
Tom & Jerry		
37 Jeremy Mayfield	12.50	25.00
Kmart		
37 Jeremy Mayfield	12.50	25.00
Kmart		
Kids Against Drugs		
88 Dale Jarrett	12.50	25.00
Quality Care		
91 Mike Wallace	15.00	30.00
Spam		
97 No Driver Association	10.00	20.00
California 500		
97 No Driver Association	10.00	20.00
Texas Motor Speedway		
99 Jeff Burton	12.50	25.00
Exide		

1998 Revell Club 1:24

These 1:24 scale cars were the from the same production run as the Collection cars. Each car distributed by the club has a serial number on the chassis. The boxes were uniquely colored to match the colors on the car.

	Lo	Hi
1 Dale Earnhardt Jr.	90.00	150.00
Coke		
1 Steve Park	125.00	200.00
Pennzoil		
1 Steve Park	75.00	125.00
Pennzoil Indy		
2 Rusty Wallace	60.00	120.00
Miller Lite		
2 Rusty Wallace	90.00	150.00
Adventures of Rusty		
2 Rusty Wallace	60.00	120.00
Miller Lite Elvis		
2 Rusty Wallace	75.00	125.00
Miller Lite TCB Bank		
3 Dale Earnhardt	90.00	150.00
Coke		
3 Dale Earnhardt	90.00	150.00
Goodwrench Plus		
3 Dale Earnhardt	90.00	150.00
Goodwrench Plus Bass Pro		
3 Dale Earnhardt	90.00	150.00
Goodwrench Plus Daytona		
3 Dale Earnhardt Jr.	175.00	300.00
AC Delco		
4 Bobby Hamilton	60.00	100.00
Kodak		
5 Terry Labonte	90.00	150.00
Blasted Fruit Loops		
5 Terry Labonte	60.00	100.00
Kellogg's		
5 Terry Labonte	90.00	150.00
Kellogg's Corny		
5 Terry Labonte	100.00	175.00
Kellogg's Corny Bank		
5 Terry Labonte	90.00	150.00
Kellogg's Ironman Bank		
12 Jeremy Mayfield	60.00	120.00
Mobil 1		
18 Bobby Labonte	60.00	120.00
Interstate Batteries Hot Rod		
18 Bobby Labonte	60.00	100.00
Interstate Batteries Small Soldiers		
21 Michael Waltrip	60.00	100.00
Citgo		
23 Jimmy Spencer	125.00	200.00
No Bull		
24 Jeff Gordon	125.00	200.00
DuPont Chromalusion		
24 Jeff Gordon	90.00	150.00
DuPont		
25 John Andretti	60.00	100.00
Budweiser		
28 Kenny Irwin	60.00	100.00
Havoline		
31 Mike Skinner	60.00	100.00
Lowe's		
31 Mike Skinner	60.00	100.00
Lowe's Special Olympics		
33 Ken Schrader	60.00	110.00
Skoal		
35 Todd Bodine	75.00	125.00
Tabasco		
36 Ernie Irvan	75.00	125.00
M&Ms		
36 Ernie Irvan	60.00	120.00
Wildberry Skittles		
40 Sterling Marlin	60.00	120.00
Coors Light		
41 Steve Grissom	60.00	100.00
Kodiak		
42 Joe Nemechek	60.00	100.00
Bell South		
44 Tony Stewart	60.00	100.00
Shell		
44 Tony Stewart	60.00	100.00
Shell Small Soldiers		
46 Wally Dallenbach	60.00	100.00
First Union		
46 Jeff Green	60.00	100.00
First Union Devil Rays		
50 Ricky Craven	75.00	125.00
Budweiser		
50 No Driver Association	75.00	125.00
Bud Louie		
74 Randy Lajoie	60.00	100.00
Fina		
75 Rick Mast	60.00	100.00
Remington		
81 Kenny Wallace	70.00	110.00
Square D Lightning		
88 Dale Jarrett	60.00	120.00
Quality Care		
88 Dale Jarrett	60.00	120.00
Quality Care Batman		
90 Dick Trickle	60.00	100.00
Heilig-Meyers		
96 David Green	60.00	100.00
Caterpillar		
98 Greg Sacks	60.00	100.00
Thorn Apple Valley		

1998 Revell Collection 1:24

This series was produced for and distributed in hobby outlets.

	Lo	Hi
1 Dale Earnhardt Jr.	45.00	75.00
Coke		
1 Steve Park	40.00	65.00
Pennzoil		
2 Rusty Wallace	35.00	60.00
Adventures of Rusty		
2 Rusty Wallace	35.00	60.00
Miller Lite		
2 Rusty Wallace	35.00	60.00
Miller Lite Elvis		
2 Rusty Wallace	35.00	60.00
Miller Lite TCB		
3 Dale Earnhardt	45.00	75.00
Coke		
3 Dale Earnhardt	45.00	70.00
Goodwrench Plus		
3 Dale Earnhardt	50.00	90.00
Goodwrench Plus Bass Pro		
3 Dale Earnhardt	40.00	65.00
Goodwrench Plus Brickyard Special		
3 Dale Earnhardt Jr.	75.00	125.00
AC Delco Dealer Issued		
3 Dale Earnhardt Jr.	75.00	125.00
AC Delco Trackside Issued		
4 Bobby Hamilton	25.00	40.00
Kodak		
5 Terry Labonte	40.00	65.00
Blasted Fruit Loops		
5 Terry Labonte	40.00	70.00
Kellogg's		
5 Terry Labonte	50.00	80.00
Kellogg's Corny		
8 Hut Stricklin	25.00	40.00
Circuit City		
9 Lake Speed	25.00	40.00
Birthday Cake		
9 Lake Speed	25.00	40.00
Huckleberry Hound		
12 Jeremy Mayfield	40.00	65.00
Mobil 1		
18 Bobby Labonte	30.00	50.00
Interstate Batteries		
18 Bobby Labonte	30.00	60.00
Interstate Batteries Hot Rod		
18 Bobby Labonte	30.00	60.00
Interstate Batteries Small Soldiers		
21 Michael Waltrip	25.00	40.00
Citgo		
24 Jeff Gordon	45.00	70.00
DuPont		
24 Jeff Gordon	40.00	65.00
DuPont Brickyard Special		
24 Jeff Gordon	60.00	100.00
DuPont Chromalusion		
25 John Andretti	25.00	40.00
Budweiser		
28 Kenny Irwin	30.00	60.00
Havoline		
28 Kenny Irwin	35.00	65.00
Havoline Joker		
31 Dale Earnhardt Jr	150.00	225.00
Wrangler		
31 Mike Skinner	25.00	40.00
Lowe's		
33 Ken Schrader	30.00	50.00
Skoal		
35 Todd Bodine	25.00	40.00
Tabasco		
36 Ernie Irvan	40.00	80.00
M&Ms		
36 Ernie Irvan	35.00	60.00
Wildberry Skittles		
40 Sterling Marlin	30.00	60.00
Coors Light		

	Lo	Hi
41 Steve Grissom Kodiak	25.00	40.00
42 Joe Nemechek Bell South	25.00	40.00
44 Tony Stewart Shell	25.00	40.00
44 Tony Stewart Shell Small Soldiers	25.00	40.00
46 Wally Dallenbach First Union	25.00	40.00
46 Jeff Green First Union Devil Rays	25.00	40.00
50 Ricky Craven Budweiser	30.00	60.00
50 No Driver Association Bud Louie	35.00	65.00
74 Randy Lajoie Fina	25.00	40.00
81 Kenny Wallace Square D Lightning	25.00	40.00
88 Dale Jarrett Quality Care	30.00	60.00
88 Dale Jarrett Quality Care Batman	30.00	60.00
90 Dick Trickle Heilig-Meyers	25.00	40.00
98 Greg Sacks Thorn Apple Valley	25.00	40.00

1998 Revell Collection 1:24 Banks

This series marks Revell's second attempt to produce a 1:24 scale car bank. It was distributed to hobby dealers are part of Revell's Collection line.

	Lo	Hi
2 Rusty Wallace Miller Lite	50.00	100.00
3 Dale Earnhardt Jr. Coke	70.00	120.00
5 Terry Labonte Kellogg's	50.00	100.00
5 Terry Labonte Kellogg's Corny	50.00	100.00
9 Lake Speed Hucklerberry Hound	40.00	80.00
31 Dale Earnhardt Jr. Wrangler	175.00	250.00
88 Dale Jarrett Quality Care Batman	50.00	100.00

1998 Revell Hobby 1:24

This series, Revell Select, was produced to appease those collectors who wanted a upgraded production diecast without the upgrade price. The cars themselves appear to have similar production qualities as the Collection cars, but are lower priced and are packaged in black window boxes.

	Lo	Hi
1 Steve Park Pennzoil	25.00	45.00
2 Rusty Wallace Adventures of Rusty	20.00	35.00
2 Rusty Wallace Miller Lite Elvis	20.00	35.00
3 Dale Earnhardt Goodwrench Plus	25.00	40.00
3 Dale Earnhardt Goodwrench Plus Bass Pro	25.00	45.00
3 Dale Earnhardt Jr. AC Delco	35.00	50.00
4 Bobby Hamilton Kodak	15.00	30.00
5 Terry Labonte Kellogg's	20.00	35.00
5 Terry Labonte Kellogg's Corny	25.00	40.00
8 Hut Stricklin Circuit City	15.00	30.00
9 Lake Speed Birthday Cake	15.00	30.00
9 Lake Speed Hucklerberry Hound	15.00	30.00
18 Bobby Labonte Interstate Batteries	15.00	30.00
18 Bobby Labonte Interstate Batteries Hot Rod	15.00	30.00
21 Michael Waltrip Citgo	15.00	30.00
23 Jimmy Spencer No Bull	30.00	45.00
24 Jeff Gordon DuPont	25.00	40.00
28 Kenny Irwin Havoline	20.00	35.00
31 Mike Skinner Lowe's	15.00	30.00
33 Ken Schrader Skoal	20.00	35.00
35 Todd Bodine Tabasco	15.00	30.00
36 Ernie Irvan M&Ms	20.00	40.00
36 Ernie Irvan Wildberry Skittles	15.00	30.00
44 Tony Stewart Shell	15.00	30.00
50 Ricky Craven Budweiser	20.00	40.00
50 NDA Bud Louie	15.00	30.00
77 Robert Pressley Jasper	15.00	30.00
81 Kenny Wallace Square D Lightning	15.00	30.00
88 Dale Jarrett Quality Care	20.00	35.00

1997 Revell Collection 1:43

This series marks Revell's first attempt to produce a 1:43 scale car. It was distributed to hobby dealers are part of Revell's Collection line.

	Lo	Hi
1 No Driver Association Coca-Cola 600	18.00	30.00
2 Rusty Wallace Miller Lite	20.00	35.00
5 Terry Labonte Spooky Loops	20.00	35.00
5 Terry Labonte Tony The Tiger	20.00	35.00
6 Mark Martin Valvoline	18.00	30.00
21 Michael Waltrip Citgo	10.00	25.00
21 Michael Waltrip Citgo Top Dog paint scheme	10.00	25.00
23 Jimmy Spencer Camel	20.00	35.00
25 Ricky Craven Budwesier	18.00	30.00
28 Ernie Irvan Havoline	18.00	30.00
28 Ernie Irvan Texaco 10th Anniversary paint scheme	20.00	35.00
29 Jeff Green Tom & Jerry	10.00	25.00
29 Robert Pressley Flintstones	10.00	25.00
29 Robert Pressley Scooby-Doo	10.00	25.00
30 Johnny Benson Pennzoil	18.00	30.00
33 Ken Schrader Skoal	12.00	30.00
36 Derrike Cope Skittles	18.00	30.00
37 Jeremy Mayfield Kmart Kids Against Drugs	18.00	30.00
41 Steve Grissom Kodiak	12.00	30.00
43 Bobby Hamilton STP	18.00	30.00
46 Wally Dallenbach Woody Woodpecker	18.00	30.00
88 Dale Jarrett Ford Credit	20.00	35.00
94 Bill Elliott Mac Tonight	20.00	35.00
96 David Green Caterpillar	18.00	30.00
97 Chad Little John Deere 160th Anniversary paint scheme	20.00	35.00
99 Jeff Burton Exide	18.00	30.00

1998 Revell Collection 1:43

This series marks Revell's second attempt to produce a 1:43 scale car. It was distributed to hobby dealers are part of Revell's Collection line.

	Lo	Hi
1 Dale Earnhardt Jr. Coke	20.00	35.00
1 Steve Park Pennzoil	25.00	40.00
1 Steve Park Pennzoil Indy	20.00	35.00
2 Rusty Wallace Adventures of Rusty	20.00	35.00
2 Rusty Wallace Miller Lite Elvis	20.00	35.00
3 Dale Earnhardt Coke	20.00	35.00
3 Dale Earnhardt Goodwrench Plus	25.00	40.00
3 Dale Earnhardt Goodwrench Plus Bass Pro	25.00	40.00
5 Terry Labonte Blasted Fruit Loops	20.00	35.00
5 Terry Labonte Kellogg's	20.00	40.00
5 Terry Labonte Kellogg's Corny	25.00	40.00
5 Terry Labonte Kellogg's Ironman	20.00	35.00
12 Jeremy Mayfield Mobil 1	20.00	35.00
18 Bobby Labonte Interstate Batteries	18.00	30.00
18 Bobby Labonte Interstate Batteries Hot Rod	18.00	30.00
18 Bobby Labonte Interstate Batteries Small Soldiers	18.00	30.00
23 Jimmy Spencer No Bull	25.00	40.00
24 Jeff Gordon DuPont	25.00	40.00
24 Jeff Gordon DuPont Chromalusion	25.00	50.00
28 Kennt Irwin Havoline	15.00	30.00
28 Kenny Irwin Havoline Joker	20.00	35.00
31 Dale Earnhardt Jr. Wrangler	35.00	60.00
31 Mike Skinner Lowe's	15.00	30.00
31 Mike Skinner Lowe's Special Olympics	15.00	30.00
33 Ken Schrader Skoal	15.00	30.00
36 Ernie Irvan M&Ms	25.00	40.00
36 Ernie Irvan Wildberry Skittles	15.00	30.00
41 Steve Grissom Kodiak	15.00	30.00
44 Tony Stewart Shell Small Soldiers	15.00	30.00
50 Ricky Craven Budweiser	20.00	35.00
50 No Driver Association Bud Louie	20.00	35.00
81 Kenny Wallace	15.00	30.00

	Lo	Hi
Square D		
81 Kenny Wallace	15.00	30.00
Square D Lightning		
88 Dale Jarrett	20.00	35.00
Quality Care		
88 Dale Jarrett	20.00	35.00
Quality Care Batman		

1996 Revell 1:64

This series was distributed in retail outlets. These cars were packaged in black blister packs.

	Lo	Hi
2 Rusty Wallace	5.00	10.00
Miller Genuine Draft Promo		
2 Rusty Wallace	4.00	8.00
Miller Genuine Draft Silver car		
2 Rusty Wallace	4.00	8.00
Penske Racing		
3 Dale Earnhardt	4.00	8.00
Goodwrench		
3 Dale Earnhardt	5.00	10.00
Olympic		
4 Sterling Marlin	3.00	6.00
Kodak		
5 Terry Labonte	3.00	6.00
Kellogg's		
6 Mark Martin	3.00	6.00
Valvoline		
9 Lake Speed	3.00	6.00
SPAM		
10 Ricky Rudd	3.00	6.00
Tide		
11 Brett Bodine	3.00	6.00
Lowe's		
16 Ron Hornaday	4.00	8.00
Smith and Wesson		
17 Darrell Waltrip	3.00	6.00
Parts America		
18 Bobby Labonte	3.00	6.00
Interstate Batteries		
21 Michael Waltrip	3.00	6.00
Citgo		
21 Michael Waltrip	5.00	10.00
Citgo with Eagle on deck lid		
24 Jack Sprague	3.00	6.00
Quaker State		
24 Jeff Gordon	3.00	6.00
DuPont		
28 Ernie Irvan	3.00	6.00
Havoline		
37 Jeremy Mayfield	3.00	6.00
K-Mart		
71 Dave Marcis	6.00	10.00
Olive Garden Promo		
75 Morgan Shepherd	3.00	6.00
Remington		
75 Morgan Shepherd	4.00	8.00
Remington Camouflage		
77 Bobby Hillin	3.00	6.00
Jasper Engines		
87 Joe Nemechek	4.00	8.00
Bell South		
99 Jeff Burton	3.00	6.00
Exide		

1996 Revell Collection 1:64

This series was produced for and distributed in hobby outlets. These cars have significant upgrades in comparision to the standard Revell 1:64 1996 pieces. Each car is packaged in a box which has the same color scheme as the car.

	Lo	Hi
2 Rusty Wallace	4.00	8.00
Miller Genuine Draft		
2 Rusty Wallace	6.00	12.00
Miller Genuine Draft Silver		
2 Rusty Wallace	15.00	25.00
Miller Genuine Draft 2 car set		
3 Dale Earnhardt	6.00	12.00
Olympic		
4 Sterling Marlin	4.00	8.00
Kodak		
5 Terry Labonte	30.00	50.00
Honey Crunch		
5 Terry Labonte	15.00	25.00
Kellogg's 2 car set		
6 Mark Martin	4.00	8.00
Valvoline		
6 Mark Martin	4.00	8.00
Valvoline Dura Blend		
10 Ricky Rudd	4.00	8.00
Tide		
11 Brett Bodine	4.00	8.00
Lowe's		
16 Ted Musgrave	4.00	8.00
Family Channel		
17 Darrell Waltrip	4.00	8.00
Parts America		
18 Bobby Labonte	4.00	8.00
Interstate Batteries		
23 Chad Little	5.00	10.00
John Deere		
25 Ken Schrader	4.00	8.00
Budweiser		
25 Ken Schrader	4.00	8.00
Budweiser Olympic		
28 Ernie Irvan	4.00	8.00
Havoline		
30 Johnny Benson	4.00	8.00
Pennzoil		
37 Jeremy Mayfield	4.00	8.00
K-Mart		
75 Morgan Shepherd	4.00	8.00
Remington		
75 Morgan Shepherd	5.00	10.00
Remington Camouflage		
75 Morgan Shepherd	4.00	8.00
Stren		
76 David Green	4.00	8.00
Smith and Wesson		
87 Joe Nemechek	4.00	8.00
Burger King		
88 Dale Jarrett	4.00	8.00
Quality Care		
99 Jeff Burton	4.00	8.00
Exide		

1997 Revell Collection 1:64

This series is the continuation of the 1996 series. It signals Revell's expansion into the diecast market by its sheer number of cars in the series.

	Lo	Hi
1 No Driver Association	5.00	10.00
Coca Cola 600		
2 Rusty Wallace	6.00	12.00
Miller Lite		
5 Terry Labonte	6.00	12.00
Kellogg's		
5 Terry Labonte	6.00	12.00
Kellogg's 1996 Champion		
5 Terry Labonte	6.00	12.00
Spooky Loops		
5/18 Bobby and Terry Labonte	20.00	35.00
Interstate Batteries and Kellogg's		
2-car Tin Set		
6/60 Mark Martin	20.00	35.00
Valvoline/Winn Dixie		
2 car set		
16 Ted Musgrave	5.00	10.00
Primestar		
23/97 Chad.Little	20.00	30.00
John Deere 2 car set		
Autogrpahed tin		
28 Ernie Irvan	20.00	30.00
Havoline 2 car set		
29 Robert Pressley	5.00	10.00
Tom & Jerry		
30 Johnny Benson	5.00	10.00
Pennzoil		
33 Ken Schrader	6.00	10.00
Skoal		
36 Derrike Cope	5.00	10.00
Skittles		
37 Jeremy Mayfield	5.00	10.00
K-Mart RC Cola		
40 Robby Gordon	5.00	10.00
Coors Light		
43 Bobby Hamilton	5.00	10.00
STP Goody's		
91 Mike Wallace	5.00	10.00
SPAM		
97 Chad Little	6.00	12.00
John Deere		
Autographed box		
97 Chad Little	20.00	30.00
John Deere 2 car set		
97 No Driver Association	5.00	10.00
California 500		
99 Jeff Burton	5.00	10.00
Exide		

1997 Revell Hobby 1:64

This series, Revell Select, was produced to appease those collectors who wanted a upgraded production diecast without the upgrade price. The cars themselves appear to have similar production qualities as the Collection cars, but are lower priced and are packaged in black window boxes.

	Lo	Hi
CARS (4/7/17/21/36/42/75/91)	4.00	8.00
2 Rusty Wallace	5.00	10.00
Miller Lite		
4 Sterling Marlin	4.00	8.00
Kodak		
5 Terry Labonte	4.00	8.00
Kellogg's		
5 Terry Labonte	5.00	10.00
Spooky Loops		
5 Terry Labonte	5.00	10.00
Tony the Tiger		
6 Mark Martin	4.00	8.00
Valvoline		
7 Geoff Bodine	4.00	8.00
QVC		
17 Darrell Waltrip	4.00	8.00
Parts America		
18 Mike Dokken	4.00	8.00
Dana Super Truck		
18 Bobby Labonte	4.00	8.00
Intertstate Batteries		
18 Bobby Labonte	4.00	8.00
Intertstate Batteries		
Texas Motor Speedway		
21 Michael Waltrip	4.00	8.00
Citgo Top Dog paint scheme		
28 Ernie Irvan	4.00	8.00
Havoline		
28 Ernie Irvan	4.00	8.00
Havoline		
10th Anniversary paint scheme		
29 Steve Grissom	4.00	8.00
Flintstones		
29 Bob Keselowski	4.00	8.00
Mopar		
29 Robert Pressley	4.00	8.00
Cartoon Network		
32 Dale Jarrett	4.00	8.00
White Rain		
33 Ken Schrader	4.00	8.00
Skoal		
36 Derrike Cope	4.00	8.00
Skittles		
37 Jeremy Mayfield	4.00	8.00
Kmart		
Kids Against Drugs		
42 Joe Nemechek	4.00	8.00
Bell South		
75 Rick Mast	4.00	8.00
Remington		
91 Mike Wallace	4.00	8.00
Spam		
97 No Driver Association	4.00	8.00
Texas Motor Speedway		
99 Jeff Burton	4.00	8.00
Exide		

1997 Revell Retail 1:64

This series, Revell Racing, was produced for and distributed in the mass-market.

	Lo	Hi
CARS (1/16/21/30/91)	3.00	6.00
1 No Driver Association	3.00	6.00
Coca Cola 600		
2 Rusty Wallace	3.00	6.00
Penske		
5 Terry Labonte	3.00	6.00
Kellogg's Texas Motor Speedway		
5 Terry Labonte	3.00	8.00
Spooky Loops		
16 Ted Musgrave	3.00	6.00
Primestar		
18 Bobby Labonte	3.00	6.00
Interstate Batteries		
Texas Motor Speedway		
18 Bobby Labonte	3.00	6.00
Interstate Batteries		
21 Micahel Waltrip	3.00	6.00
Citgo Top Dog paint scheme		
29 Robert Pressley	3.00	6.00
Cartoon Network		
29 Robert Pressley	3.00	6.00
Tom & Jerry		
30 Johnny Benson	3.00	6.00
Pennzoil		
37 Jeremy Mayfield	3.00	6.00
Kmart		
Kids Against Drugs		
37 Jeremy Mayfield	3.00	6.00
Kmart		
42 Joe Nemechek		
Bell South		
91 Mike Wallace	3.00	6.00
SPAM		
97 No Driver Association	3.00	6.00
California 500		
97 No Driver Association	3.00	6.00
Texas Motor Speedway		

1998 Revell Collection 1:64

This series was produced for and distributed in hobby outlets.

	Lo	Hi
1 Dale Earnhardt Jr.	10.00	20.00
Coke		
1 Steve Park	9.00	18.00
Pennzoil		
1 Steve Park	7.50	15.00
Pennzoil Indy		
2 Rusty Wallace	6.00	12.00
Adventures of Rusty		
2 Rusty Wallace	6.00	12.00
Miller Lite Elvis		
2 Rusty Wallace	6.00	12.00
Miller Lite TCB		
3 Dale Earnhardt	10.00	20.00
Coke		
3 Dale Earnhardt	6.00	12.00
Goodwrench Plus		
3 Dale Earnhardt	9.00	18.00
Goodwrench Plus Bass Pro		
3 Dale Earnhardt	6.00	12.00
Goodwrench Plus Brickyard Special		
3 Dale Earnhardt Jr.	15.00	30.00
AC Delco		
4 Bobby Hamilton	5.00	10.00
Kodak		
5 Terry Labonte	7.50	15.00
Blasted Fruit Loops		
5 Terry Labonte	6.00	12.00
Kellogg's		
5 Terry Labonte	7.50	15.00
Kellogg's Corny		
5 Terry Labonte	7.50	15.00
Kellogg's Ironman		
9 Lake Speed	5.00	10.00
Birthday Cake		
9 Lake Speed	5.00	10.00
Huckleberry Hound		
12 Jeremy Mayfield	6.00	12.00
Mobil 1		
18 Bobby Labonte	5.00	10.00
Interstate Batteries		
18 Bobby Labonte	5.00	10.00
Interstate Batteries Hot Rod		
18 Bobby Labonte	6.00	12.00
Interstate Batteries Small Soldiers		
23 Jimmy Spencer	7.50	15.00
No Bull		
24 Jeff Gordon	6.00	12.00
DuPont		
24 Jeff Gordon	6.00	12.00
DuPont Brickyard Special		
24 Jeff Gordon	15.00	30.00
DuPont Chromalusion		
25 John Andretti	6.00	12.00
Budweiser		
28 Kenny Irwin	6.00	12.00
Havoline		
28 Kenny Irwin	6.00	12.00
Havoline Joker		
31 Mike Skinner	5.00	10.00
Lowe's		
31 Mike Skinner	5.00	10.00
Lowe's Special Olympics		
33 Ken Schrader	6.00	12.00
Skoal		
36 Ernie Irvan	6.00	12.00
M&Ms		
36 Ernie Irvan	6.00	12.00
Wildberry Skittles		
41 Steve Grissom	5.00	10.00
Kodiak		
42 Joe Nemechek	5.00	10.00
Bell South		
44 Tony Stewart	5.00	10.00
Shell		
44 Tony Stewart	6.00	12.00
Shell Small Soldiers		
46 Wally Dallenbach	5.00	10.00
First Union		
46 Jeff Green	5.00	10.00
First union Devil Rays		
50 Ricky Craven	6.00	12.00
Budweiser		
50 No Driver Association	6.00	12.00
Bud Louie		
81 Kenny Wallace	5.00	10.00
Square D Lightning		
88 Dale Jarrett	6.00	12.00
Quality Care		
88 Dale Jarrett	7.50	15.00
Quality Care Batman		

1998 Revell Hobby 1:64

This series, Revell Select, was produced to appease those collectors who wanted a upgraded production diecast without the upgrade price. The cars themselves appear to have similar production qualities as the Collection cars, but are lower priced and are packaged in black window boxes.

	Lo	Hi
1 Steve Park	6.00	12.00
Pennzoil		
3 Dale Earnhardt Jr.	10.00	20.00
AC Delco		
4 Bobby Hamilton	4.00	8.00
Kodak		
5 Terry Labonte	5.00	10.00
Kellogg's Corny		
8 Hut Stricklin	4.00	8.00
Circuit City		
18 Bobby Labonte	4.00	8.00
Interstate Batteries		
23 Jimmy Spencer	6.00	12.00
No Bull		
24 Jeff Gordon	5.00	10.00
DuPont		
31 Mike Skinner	4.00	8.00
Lowe's		
33 Ken Schrader	4.00	10.00
Skoal		
36 Ernie Irvan	5.00	10.00
M&Ms		
50 No Driver Association	5.00	10.00
Bud Louie		
77 Robert Pressley	4.00	8.00
Jasper		
81 Kenny Wallace	4.00	8.00
Square D Lightning		

1997-1998 Winner's Circle 1:24

This series marks the teaming of Action Performance and Hasbro. This line of cars was produced for and distributed in the mass-market. It is highlighted by the Jeff Gordon Lifetime Series and the Dale Earnhardt lifetime Series.

	Lo	Hi
2 Rusty Wallace	12.00	30.00
Penske Elvis		
3 Dale Earnhardt	12.00	30.00
Goodwrench		
3 Dale Earnhardt	12.00	30.00
Goodwrench Plus		
3 Dale Earnhardt	15.00	35.00
Goodwrench Plus Bass Pro		
3 Dale Earnhardt	15.00	40.00
Goodwrench Silver		
3 Dale Earnhardt	20.00	40.00
Wheaties		
3 Jay Sauter	10.00	25.00
Goodwrench Super Truck		
3 Dale Earnhardt Jr.	15.00	30.00
AC Delco		
16 Ron Hornaday	10.00	25.00
Napa		
18 Bobby Labonte	10.00	25.00
Interstate Batteries		
18 Bobby Labonte	10.00	25.00
Interstate Batteries Small Soldiers		
22 Ward Burton	10.00	25.00
MBNA Gold		
24 Jeff Gordon	10.00	30.00
DuPont		
24 Jeff Gordon	15.00	40.00
DuPont Premier		
24 Jeff Gordon	15.00	40.00
Lost World		
28 Kenny Irwin	10.00	25.00
Havolline		
31 Mike Skinner	10.00	25.00
Lowe's		
44 Tony Stewart	10.00	25.00
Shell Small Soldiers		
81 Kenny Wallace	10.00	25.00
Square D		
88 Dale Jarrett	10.00	25.00
Quality Care		

1998 Winner's Circle 1:43

This series marks the teaming of Action Performance and Hasbro. This line of cars was produced for and distributed in the mass-market.

	Lo	Hi
2 Rusty Wallace	6.00	15.00
Miller Lite Elvis		
3 Dale Earnhardt	6.00	15.00
Goodwrench Plus		
3 Dale Earnhardt	8.00	20.00
Goodwrench Plus Bass Pro		
3 Dale Earnhardt Jr.	8.00	20.00
AC Delco		
12 Jeremy Mayfield	6.00	15.00
Mobil 1		
24 Jeff Gordon	6.00	15.00
DuPont		
28 Kenny Irwin	6.00	15.00
Havoline		
88 Dale Jarrett	6.00	15.00
Quality Care		

1997-1998 Winner's Circle 1:64

This series marks the teaming of Action Performance and Hasbro. This line of cars was produced for and distributed in the mass-market. It is highlighted by the Jeff Gordon Lifetime Series and the Dale Earnhardt lifetime Series.

	Lo	Hi
1 Jeff Gordon Baby Ruth	8.00	20.00
1 Jeff Gordon Carolina Ford	5.00	12.00
1 Steve Park Pennzoil	4.00	10.00
2 Mike Bliss Team ASE Super Truck	2.00	6.00
2 Rusty Wallace Penske Elvis	3.00	8.00
2 Dale Earnhardt Wrangler 1981 Pontiac	8.00	20.00
3 Dale Earnhardt AC Delco	6.00	15.00
3 Dale Earnhardt Goodwrench 1990 Lumina	8.00	20.00
3 Dale Earnhardt Goodwrench	5.00	12.00
3 Dale Earnhardt Goodwrench Camaro ASA	6.00	15.00
3 Dale Earnhardt Goodwrench Plus	3.00	8.00
3 Dale Earnhardt Goodwrench Plus Daytona	3.00	8.00
3 Dale Earnhardt Goodwrench Silver	12.00	30.00
3 Dale Earnhardt Lowes Food	4.00	10.00
3 Dale Earnhardt Wheaties	4.00	10.00
3 Dale Earnhardt Wrangler 1981 Thunder Bird	5.00	12.00
3 Dale Earnhardt Wrangler 1984 Monte Carlo	6.00	15.00
3 Dale Earnhardt Wrangler 1986 Momte Carlo	6.00	15.00
3 Dale Earnhardt Jr. AC Delco	6.00	15.00
3 Jay Sauter Goodwrench Super Truck	2.00	6.00
8 Dale Earnhardt 10,000 RPM Dodge	8.00	20.00
12 Jeremy Mayfield Mobil 1	2.00	6.00
15 Dale Earnhardt Wrangler 1982 TB	3.00	8.00
16 Jeff Gordon 1985 Pro Sprint	15.00	30.00
16 Ron Hornaday NAPA	2.00	6.00
18 Bobby Labonte Interstate Batteries	2.00	6.00
18 Bobby Labonte Interstates Batteries Small Soldiers	2.00	6.00
22 Ward Burton MBNA Gold	2.00	6.00
24 Jeff Gordon DuPont 1993 Lumina	5.00	12.00
24 Jeff Gordon DuPont 1994 Monte Carlo	6.00	15.00
24 Jeff Gordon DuPont	2.00	6.00
24 Jeff Gordon DuPont ChromaPremier	10.00	25.00
24 Jeff Gordon Lost World	5.00	12.00
27 Kenny Irwin Tonka	2.00	6.00
28 Kenny Irwin Havoline	2.00	6.00
31 Mike Skinner Lowe's	2.00	6.00
40 Jeff Gordon Challenger Sprint	20.00	40.00
44 Tony Stewart Shell Small Soldiers	2.00	6.00
81 Kenny Wallace Square D	2.00	6.00
88 Dale Jarrett Quality Care	2.00	6.00
98 Dale Earnhardt 1978 MC	15.00	30.00
K2 Dale Earnhardt Dayvault's	4.00	10.00

Action 1:24 Dually Trucks

The majority of these 1:24 scale die cast replicas are banks. A dually truck is a pick up truck with four rear wheels, two on each side. They were distributed through both Action's dealer network and the Racing Collectibles Club of America.

	Lo	Hi
2 Rusty Wallace Miller Genuine Draft Bank	40.00	65.00
2 Rusty Wallace Miller Genuine Draft 1996 Bank	40.00	65.00
2 Rusty Wallace Miller Genuine Draft Silver Bank	40.00	70.00
2 Rusty Wallace Miller Lite Bank	30.00	75.00
3 Dale Earnhardt Goodwrench	70.00	120.00
3 Dale Earnhardt Goodwrench Bank 7-Time Champion	70.00	120.00
3 Dale Earnhardt Goodwrench 1996 Bank	45.00	70.00
3 Dale Earnhardt Wheaties Bank	60.00	90.00
5 Terry Labonte Kellogg's Bank	45.00	70.00
5 Terry Labonte Kellogg's '96 Bank	50.00	80.00
6 Mark Martin Valvoline Bank	40.00	65.00
11 Bill Elliott Budweiser Bank	60.00	100.00
16 Ted Musgrave Family Channel Bank	25.00	40.00
17 Darrell Waltrip Parts America Chrome Bank	55.00	90.00
18 Dale Jarrett Interstate Batteries Bank	25.00	40.00
18 Bobby Labonte Interstate Batteries	25.00	50.00
21 Morgan Shepherd Cheerwine Bank	25.00	40.00
22 Bobby Labonte Maxwell House B	25.00	40.00
24 Jeff Gordon DuPont Bank	80.00	120.00
24 Jeff Gordon DuPont Coca-Cola Bank	80.00	120.00
24 Jeff Gordon DuPont 1996	45.00	70.00
24 Jeff Gordon DuPont 1998	45.00	70.00
28 Davey Allison Havoline	150.00	250.00
28 Dale Jarrett Havoline Bank	25.00	40.00
42 Kyle Petty Coors Light Bank Pink and Blue paint scheme	40.00	65.00
42 Kyle Petty Coors Light 1996 Bank	35.00	60.00
51 Neil Bonnett Country Time Bank	40.00	70.00
59 Dennis Setzer Alliance	25.00	40.00
88 Dale Jarrett Quality Care Bank	40.00	65.00
94 Bill Elliott McDonald's Bank	40.00	65.00
94 Bill Elliott Mac Tonight Bank	50.00	80.00
98 Derrike Cope Fingerhut Bank	25.00	40.00

Action 1:64 Dually w/Chaparral Trailer

This series of 1:64 scale dually replicas usually comes with a Chaparral show trailer. The entire package of the dually and show trailer is a replica of what most teams use to haul there show car around from event to event.

	Lo	Hi
2 Rusty Wallace Miller Genuine Draft	40.00	75.00
2 Rusty Wallace Miller Genuine Draft without the trailer	8.00	16.00
2 Rusty Wallace Miller Lite	35.00	60.00
3 Dale Earnhardt Goodwrench	80.00	130.00
3 Dale Earnhardt Goodwrench 1996	60.00	100.00
3 Dale Earnhardt Goodwrench without Trailer	15.00	25.00
3 Dale Earnhardt Goodwrench 1996 without the trailer	8.00	16.00
3 Dale Earnhardt Goodwrench Bass Pro	40.00	70.00
3 Dale Earnhardt Wheaties	40.00	70.00
3 Dale Earnhardt Wheaties without trailer	8.00	16.00
3 Dale Earnhardt's Kids Mom-n-Pop's	40.00	75.00
7 Geoff Bodine Exide	25.00	50.00
11 Bill Elliott Budweiser	35.00	60.00
17 Darrell Waltrip Parts America Chrome	30.00	60.00
18 Dale Jarrett Interstate Batteries	25.00	40.00
18 Dale Jarrett Interstate Batteries without Trailer	7.00	14.00
21 Morgan Shepherd Citgo	30.00	50.00
23 Jimmy Spencer Smokin' Joe's	40.00	70.00
24 Jeff Gordon DuPont	60.00	100.00
24 Jeff Gordon DuPont without Trailer	35.00	60.00
24 Jeff Gordon DuPont 1996 without the trailer	8.00	16.00
24 Jeff Gordon DuPont 1998	40.00	70.00
24 Jeff Gordon DuPont Chromalusion	50.00	80.00
28 Ernie Irvan Mac Tools	25.00	40.00
28 Dale Jarrett Havoline	25.00	40.00
28 Dale Jarrett Havoline without Trailer	12.50	25.00
30 Michael Waltrip Pennzoil without Trailer	7.00	14.00
42 Kyle Petty Coors Light	30.00	50.00
94 Bill Elliott McDonald's	30.00	50.00
94 Bill Elliott Mac Tonight	35.00	60.00

Action/RCCA Transporters 1:64

This series of 1:64 scale transporters were distributed through both the club and Action's dealer network. Action was also contracted to do many of the haulers distributed by the companies Peachstate and GMP.

	Lo	Hi
Davey Allison Havoline	50.00	80.00
Davey Allison Havoline RCCA	80.00	140.00

Davey Allison Mac Tools	60.00	100.00
Brett Bodine Lowe's	40.00	60.00
Neil Bonnett Country Time RCCA	60.00	100.00
Dale Earnhardt Goodwrench BGN Dale Earnhardt Inc.	60.00	110.00
Dale Earnhardt Goodwrench RCR	60.00	110.00
Dale Earnhardt RCCA Club Only with cars	100.00	150.00
Dale Earnhardt Wrangler 85	60.00	100.00
Dale Earnhardt Wrangler 87	60.00	100.00
Bill Elliott Bud 93	60.00	90.00
Bill Elliott Bud 94	60.00	90.00
Bill Elliott McDonald's	50.00	80.00
Bill Elliott Melling RCCA	60.00	90.00
Harry Gant Morema	50.00	80.00
Jeff Gordon Baby Ruth produced for Peachstate	100.00	150.00
Jeff Gordon DuPont produced for GMP	80.00	130.00
Ernie Irvan Kodak produced for Peachstate	40.00	75.00
Ernie Irvan Delco Remy Platinum Series	45.00	75.00
Dale Jarrett Havoline	30.00	60.00
Alan Kulwicki Zerex	50.00	90.00
Bobby Labonte Maxwell House produced for Peachstate	40.00	75.00
Bobby Labonte Penrose	25.00	50.00
Terry Labonte Kellogg's produced for Peachstate	40.00	75.00
Sterling Marlin Raybestos produced for Peachstate	30.00	55.00
Mark Martin Valvoline '93	60.00	90.00
Mark Martin Valvoline 95	50.00	80.00
Mark Martin Winn Dixie PS	45.00	80.00
Rob Moroso Swisher RCCA	45.00	75.00
Ted Musgrave Family Channel produced for Peachstate	40.00	75.00
No Driver Association TropArtic	25.00	50.00
Joe Nemechek Dentyne produced for Peachstate	35.00	60.00
Joe Nemechek Meineke Platinum Series	35.00	60.00
David Pearson Chattanooga Chew	30.00	75.00
Larry Pearson Stanley Tools produced for Peachstate	30.00	55.00
Kyle Petty Coors Light	50.00	90.00
Kyle Petty Mello Yello produced for Peachstate	35.00	60.00
Richard Petty STP RCCA	45.00	75.00
Robert Pressley Alliance	45.00	75.00
Robert Pressley Alliance Fan Club	60.00	90.00
David Rezendes KPR Racing	35.00	60.00
Tim Richmond Old Milwaukee	35.00	80.00
Shawna Robinson Polaroid	35.00	65.00
Ken Schrader Budweiser	40.00	90.00
Ken Schrader Kodiak	50.00	80.00
Morgan Shepherd Cheerwine	35.00	65.00
Jimmy Spencer Smokin' Joe's	75.00	125.00
Kenny Wallace Dirt Devil produced for Peachstate	30.00	55.00
Rusty Wallace Delco Remy Platinum Series	50.00	80.00
Rusty Wallace Miller	40.00	90.00
Darrell Waltrip Delco Remy Platinum Series	35.00	65.00
Darrell Waltrip Western Auto RCCA	45.00	75.00
2 Rusty Wallace Miller Genuine Draft Platinum Series	50.00	80.00
2/43 Dale Earnhardt Richard Petty 7 and 7 Champion special	50.00	90.00

Action/RCCA Transporters 1:96

This series of 1:96 scale transporters features some of the best drivers in Winston Cup over the last 20 years. This is the smallest size piece that Action makes.

	Lo	Hi
1 Rick Mast Skoal	15.00	30.00
2 Rusty Wallace Miller Geniune Draft	30.00	50.00
3 Dale Earnhardt Goodwrench	25.00	60.00
3 Dale Earnhardt Goodwrench '96	40.00	60.00
3 Dale Earnhardt Wrangler 85	45.00	70.00
3 Dale Earnhardt Wrangler 87	45.00	70.00
23 Jimmy Spencer Smokin' Joe's	50.00	80.00
24 Jeff Gordon DuPont	20.00	40.00
25 Ken Schrader Budweiser	25.00	40.00
27 Tim Richmond Old Milwaukee	25.00	40.00
28 Dale Jarrett Havoline	25.00	40.00
42 Kyle Petty Coors Light	25.00	40.00
94 Bill Elliott McDonald's	25.00	40.00

Brookfield Collectors Guild 1:24 Suburbans

Brookfield Collectors Guild decided to do something different and produced this series of 1:24 scale Suburbans. The Suburbans are decorated in team or special event colors and were distributed either through direct sales or hobby outlets.

	Lo	Hi
Johnny Benson Pennzoil '96	25.00	50.00
Brickyard 400 White paint scheme '94	15.00	30.00
Brickyard 400 Yellow paint scheme '94	125.00	200.00
Dale Earnhardt AC-Delco	25.00	50.00
Dale Earnhardt Brickyard Winner	25.00	40.00
Dale Earnhardt Goodwrench '92	75.00	120.00
Dale Earnhardt Goodwrench Silver '95	100.00	180.00
D.Earnhardt/Olympic	20.00	40.00
Dale Earnhardt 7-Time Champion '95	40.00	75.00
Dale Earnhardt Richard Petty 7-Time Champion 2 pack '95	60.00	85.00
Dale Earnhardt Richard Petty 7-Time Champion '95 paint scheme split half 3 half 43	25.00	40.00
Dale Earnhardt Richard Petty 7-Time Champion '95 paint scheme split half 3 half 43 tampos are reversed	60.00	100.00
John Force Castrol GTX '95	40.00	70.00
Jeff Gordon DuPont Rookie of the Year '93	20.00	40.00
Jeff Gordon DuPont '96	25.00	50.00
Jeff Gordon DuPonrt Silver '96	175.00	250.00
Terry Labonte Kellogg's '96	25.00	50.00
Terry Labonte Kellogg's Silver '96	175.00	250.00
Kyle Petty Mello Yello '95	17.50	35.00
Don Prudhomme Snake Farewell Tour '95	35.00	50.00
Ken Schrader Budweiser '96	25.00	50.00
Michael Waltrip Pennzoil '94	25.00	40.00

Ertl White Rose Transporters 1:64 Past and Present

This series produced by Ertl and distributed by White Rose features many of the greats from Past and Present. The 1:64 scale replicas features greats like Davey Allison, Dale Earnhardt and Richard Petty.

	Lo	Hi
Davey Allison Havoline	75.00	125.00
Geoff Bodine	35.00	60.00

Exide		
Neil Bonnett	35.00	70.00
Warner Hodgdon		
Derrike Cope	25.00	45.00
Bojangles		
Dale Earnhardt	90.00	160.00
Goodwrench		
Dale Earnhardt	90.00	160.00
Wrangler		
Jeff Gordon	60.00	100.00
DuPont		
Dale Jarrett	25.00	45.00
Interstate Batteries		
Junior Johnson	30.00	50.00
Mountain Dew		
Alan Kulwicki	90.00	150.00
Hooter's		
Alan Kulwicki	45.00	75.00
Zerex		
Terry Labonte	30.00	50.00
Kellogg's		
Sterling Marlin	30.00	50.00
Piedmont		
Ted Musgrave	25.00	45.00
Family Channel		
Phil Parsons	25.00	45.00
Manheim		
Kyle Petty	30.00	50.00
7-Eleven		
Kyle Petty	75.00	125.00
Richard Petty		
STP Combo		
Morgan Shepherd	25.00	45.00
Citgo		
Lake Speed	25.00	45.00
Quality Care		
Jimmy Spencer	25.00	45.00
Meineke		
Kenny Wallace	25.00	45.00
Dirt Devil		
Darrell Waltrip	25.00	45.00
Western Auto		
Cale Yarborough	30.00	50.00
Hardee's		

Ertl White Rose Transporters 1:64 BGN/Promos

This series features many of the BGN drivers from the early '90's and many special promo pieces that were contracted. The pieces were made by Ertl and distributed through White Rose Collectibles.

	Lo	Hi
Jeff Burton	30.00	50.00
Baby Ruth BGN		
Ricky Craven	30.00	50.00
DuPont Promo		
Bill Elliott	75.00	125.00
Budweiser		
in Wooden case Promo		
Harry Gant	30.00	50.00
Manheim BGN		
Jeff Gordon	45.00	75.00
Baby Ruth BGN		
Alan Kulwicki	100.00	160.00
'92 Winston Cup Champion Promo		
Joe Nemechek	25.00	45.00
Dentyne BGN		
Joe Nemechek	45.00	75.00
'92 BGN Champion Promo		
Phil Parsons	25.00	45.00
White Rose BGN		
Richard Petty	125.00	175.00
Petty Anniversary Tour Promo		
Ken Schrader	25.00	45.00
AC Delco BGN		
Stanley Smith	25.00	45.00
White House Apple Juice BGN		
Jack Sprague	25.00	45.00
Staff America BGN		
Hut Stricklin	35.00	60.00
Smokin' Joe's		
in plexiglass case		
Kenny Wallace	25.00	45.00
Dirt Devil BGN		

Matchbox White Rose Transporters 1:64 1997

This series of 1:64 scale replicas represents the first year White Rose switched to the 1:64 scale size. The transporters were produced by Matchbox and distributed by White Rose Collectibles.

	Lo	Hi
2 Rusty Wallace	45.00	60.00
Miller Lite		
in acrylic case		
5 Terry Labonte	45.00	60.00
Kellogg's		
in acrylic case		
33 Ken Schrader	40.00	60.00
Skoal		
in acrylic case		
94 Bill Elliott	45.00	60.00
McDonald's		
in acrylic case		
94 Bill Elliott	40.00	60.00
Mac Tonight		
in acrylic case		

Matchbox White Rose Transporters 1:80 1994 Super Star Series

This series of 1:80 scale replicas represents the first year White Rose switched to the 1:80 scale size. The transporters were produced by Matchbox and distributed by White Rose Collectibles.

	Lo	Hi
2 Ricky Craven	5.00	10.00
DuPont		
3 Dale Earnhardt	10.00	20.00
Goodwrench		
4 Sterling Marlin	5.00	10.00
Kodak		
5 Terry Labonte	5.00	10.00
Kellogg's		
7 Geoff Bodine	5.00	10.00
Exide		
7 Harry Gant	5.00	10.00
Manheim Auctions		
15 Lake Speed	5.00	10.00
Quality Care		
16 Ted Musgrave	5.00	10.00
Family Channel		
17 Darrell Waltrip	5.00	10.00
Western Auto		
19 Loy Allen	5.00	10.00
Hooters		
24 Jeff Gordon	10.00	20.00
DuPont		
29 Phil Parsons	5.00	10.00
White Rose		
32 Dale Jarrett	5.00	10.00
Pic-N-Pay Shoes		
40 Bobby Hamilton	5.00	10.00
Kendall		
41 Stanley Smith	5.00	10.00
White House Apple Juice		
41 Stanley Smith	12.00	18.00
White House Apple Juice		
Gold box		
43 Harry Gant	5.00	10.00
Black Flag French's		
46 Shawna Robinson	5.00	10.00
Polaroid		
52 Ken Schrader	5.00	10.00
AC Delco		
75 Todd Bodine	5.00	10.00
Factory Stores of America		
94 No Driver Association	5.00	10.00
White Rose Promo		
98 Derrike Cope	5.00	10.00
Fingerhut		

Matchbox White Rose Transporters 1:80 1995 Super Star Series

This series of 1:80 scale transporters features drivers from the Winston Cup, Busch and SuperTruck circuits. The series includes a special Ken Schrader Budweiser piece that comes in an acrylic case.

	Lo	Hi
1 P.J.Jones	5.00	10.00
Diehard		
1 Hermie Sadler	5.00	10.00
DeWalt		
2 Ricky Craven	5.00	10.00
DuPont		
3 Dale Earnhardt	8.00	16.00
Goodwrench		
3 Dale Earnhardt	10.00	20.00
Snap On		
3 Mike Skinner	5.00	10.00
Goodwrench		
4 Sterling Marlin	5.00	10.00
Kodak		
6 Rick Carelli	5.00	10.00
Total Petroleum		
6 Mark Martin	5.00	10.00
Valvoline		
8 Jeff Burton	5.00	10.00
Raybestos		
8 Bobby Dotter	5.00	10.00
Hyde Tools		
11 Brett Bodine	5.00	10.00
Lowe's		
12 Derrike Cope	5.00	10.00
Straight Arrow		
23 Jimmy Spencer	7.00	14.00
Smokin' Joe's		
24 Jeff Gordon	9.00	18.00
DuPont		
24 Scott Lagasse	5.00	10.00
DuPont		
25 Ken Schrader	12.00	24.00
Budweiser in acrylic case		
26 Steve Kinser	5.00	10.00
Quaker State		
28 Dale Jarrett	5.00	10.00
Havoline		
40 Patty Moise	6.00	12.00
Dial Purex		
42 Kyle Petty	12.00	24.00
Coors Light in acrylic case		
57 Jason Keller	5.00	10.00
Budget Gourmet		
60 Mark Martin	6.00	12.00
Winn Dixie		
71 Kevin Lepage	5.00	10.00
Vermont Teddy Bear		
72 Tracy Leslie	5.00	10.00
Detroit Gasket		
74 Johnny Benson	5.00	10.00
Lipton Tea		
87 Joe Nemechek	6.00	12.00
Burger King		
90 Mike Wallace	5.00	10.00
Heilig-Meyers		
94 Bill Elliott	8.00	12.00
McDonald's		
95 John Tanner	5.00	10.00
Caterpillar		
99 Phil Parsons	5.00	10.00
Luxaire		

Matchbox White Rose Transporters 1:80 1996 Super Star Series

These 1:80 scale transporters featured many of the new driver and color changes for 1996. The pieces are distributed through White Rose Collectibles and are produced by Matchbox.

	Lo	Hi
2 Mike Bliss ASE	6.00	12.00
9 Lake Speed SPAM	6.00	12.00
10 Phil Parsons Channellock	6.00	12.00
21 Michael Waltrip Citgo	6.00	12.00
22 Ward Burton MBNA	6.00	12.00
24 Jack Sprague Quaker State	6.00	12.00
24 Jeff Gordon DuPont	6.00	12.00
34 Mike McLaughlin Royal Oak	6.00	12.00
37 John Andretti K-Mart Little Casears	6.00	12.00
40 Tim Fedewa Kleenex	6.00	12.00
41 Ricky Craven Kodiak in acrylic case	12.00	20.00
43 Rodney Combs Lance	6.00	12.00
77 Bobby Hillin Jasper Engines	6.00	12.00
88 Dale Jarrett Quality Care	6.00	12.00
94 Bill Elliott McDonald's	6.00	12.00
95 David Green Caterpillar	6.00	12.00

Matchbox White Rose Transporters 1:80 1997 Super Star Series

These 1:80 scale transporters featured many of the new driver and color changes for 1997. The pieces are distributed through White Rose Collectibles and are produced by Matchbox. Each transpoter is packaged with a car.

	Lo	Hi
36 Derrike Cope Skittles	6.00	12.00
37 Mark Green Timber Wolf	6.00	12.00
74 Randy Lajoie Fina	6.00	12.00
96 David Green Caterpillar	6.00	12.00

Matchbox White Rose Transporters 1:87 1989-90 Super Star Series

This series of pieces represents some of the most valuable 1:87 scale die cast transporters available. The series features many greats from Winston Cup racing. The '89 pieces are difficult to come by.

	Lo	Hi
3 Dale Earnhardt Goodwrench '89	200.00	300.00
3 Dale Earnhardt Goodwrench '90	75.00	125.00
6 Mark Martin Folgers '90	90.00	150.00
9 Bill Elliott Melling '90	60.00	90.00
20 Rob Moroso Crown '90	40.00	75.00
21 Neil Bonnett Citgo '89	100.00	160.00
28 Cale Yarborough Hardee's '89	90.00	150.00
43 Richard Petty STP '89	250.00	350.00
43 Richard Petty STP '90	75.00	125.00
66 Dick Trickle TropArtic '90	35.00	60.00
94 Sterling Marlin Sunoco '90 name on cab	125.00	225.00
94 Sterling Marlin Sunoco '90 no name on cab	125.00	225.00

Matchbox White Rose Transporters 1:87 1991 Super Star Series

This series of 1:87 scale transporters features the top names in Winston Cup racing from '91. The peices are packaged in a red and black box and the year of the release is on the end of each box. The piece were distriubted by White Rose Collectibles.

	Lo	Hi
3 Dale Earnhardt Goodwrench	20.00	40.00
4 Ernie Irvan Kodak	10.00	18.00
6 Mark Martin Folgers with Ford cab	10.00	20.00
6 Mark Martin Folgers with Mack cab	15.00	30.00
9 Bill Elliott Melling with Ford cab	10.00	20.00
9 Bill Elliott Melling with Mack cab	20.00	40.00
10 Derrike Cope Purolator with Pink paint scheme	10.00	20.00
10 Derrike Cope Purolator with Red paint scheme	25.00	45.00
10 Ernie Irvan Mac Tools	15.00	30.00
17 Darrell Waltrip Western Auto	10.00	20.00
22 Sterling Marlin Maxwell House	8.00	16.00
25 Ken Schrader	8.00	16.00
28 Davey Allison Havoline Kenworth	40.00	75.00
42 Kyle Petty Mello Yello	10.00	18.00
43 Richard Petty STP 20th Anniversary	15.00	30.00
59 Robert Pressley Alliance	12.50	25.00
66 Lake Speed TropArtic	8.00	16.00
68 Bobby Hamilton Country Time	8.00	16.00

Matchbox White Rose Transporters 1:87 1992 Super Star Series

These pieces are a continuation in the Super Star Series produced by Matchbox and distibuted by White Rose Collectibles. Each peice is packaged in a red and black box and has the year of release stamped on the end of the box.

	Lo	Hi
1 Jeff Gordon Baby Ruth	10.00	20.00
2 Rusty Wallace Penske	6.00	12.00
3 Dale Earnhardt Goodwrench	12.50	25.00
7 Harry Gant Mac Tools	12.50	25.00
7 Alan Kulwicki Hooters	25.00	50.00
8 Dick Trickle Snickers	5.00	10.00
9 Bill Elliott Melling	6.00	12.00
12 Hut Stricklin Raybestos	5.00	10.00
15 Morgan Shepherd Motorcraft	5.00	10.00
18 Dale Jarrett Interstate Batteries	5.00	10.00
26 Brett Bodine Quaker State	5.00	10.00
28 Davey Allison Havoline Ford cab	15.00	30.00
30 Michael Waltrip Pennzoil	5.00	10.00
31 Bobby Hillin Team Ireland	5.00	10.00
43 Richard Petty STP	7.50	15.00
44 Bobby Labonte Slim Jim	6.00	12.00
49 Ed Ferree Fergaed Racing	5.00	10.00
55 Ted Musgrave Jasper Engines	6.00	12.00
72 Ken Bouchard ADAP	8.00	16.00
89 Jimmy Sauter Evinrude	5.00	10.00
92 Hut Stricklin Stanley Tools	5.00	10.00

Matchbox White Rose Transporters 1:87 1993 Super Star Series

This is the last series of 1:87 scale size transporters done by Matchbox White Rose Collectibles. The pieces were distributed through White Rose Collectibles.

	Lo	Hi
6 Mark Martin Valvoline	6.00	10.00
8 Jeff Burton TIC Financial	6.00	10.00
8 Jeff Burton Baby Ruth	6.00	10.00
8 Sterling Marlin Raybestos	6.00	10.00
8 Bobby Dotter DeWalt	6.00	10.00
12 Jimmy Spencer Meineke	6.00	10.00
14 Terry Labonte MW Windows	6.00	10.00
21 Morgan Shepherd Citgo	6.00	10.00
22 Bobby Labonte Maxwell House	6.00	10.00
24 Jeff Gordon DuPont	7.00	14.00
25 Hermie Sadler Virginia is for Lovers	6.00	10.00
28 Davey Allison Mac Tools	15.00	30.00
29 Phil Parsons Matchbox White Rose Collectibles	6.00	10.00
32 Jimmy Horton Active Racing	6.00	10.00
34 Todd Bodine Fiddle Faddle	6.00	10.00
40 Kenny Wallace Dirt Devil	10.00	18.00
41 Phil Parsons Manheim Auctions	6.00	10.00
48 Sterling Marlin	6.00	10.00

	Lo	Hi
Cappio		
59 Robert Pressley	12.50	25.00
Alliance		
75 Jack Sprague	6.00	10.00
Staff America		
83 Lake Speed	6.00	10.00
Purex		
87 Joe Nemechek	6.00	10.00
Dentyne		
94 Terry Labonte	6.00	10.00
Sunoco		
98 Derrike Cope	6.00	10.00
Bojangles		
98 Jimmy Spencer	6.00	10.00
Moly Black Gold		
99 Ricky Craven	6.00	10.00
DuPont		

Peachstate Transporters 1:64 1996

These transporters were produced by GMP and distributed by Peachstate.

	Lo	Hi
3 Dale Earnhardt	50.00	75.00
Goodwrench		
6 Mark Martin	45.00	60.00
Valvoline		
10 Ricky Rudd	45.00	60.00
Tide		
11 Steve Kinser	60.00	80.00
Quaker State		
18 Bobby Labonte	45.00	60.00
Interstate Batteries		
87 Joe Nemechek	45.00	60.00
Burger King		
94 Bill Elliott	45.00	60.00
McDonald's		

Press Pass Transporter 1:64 1996

This was the first die-cast piece issued by Press Pass. The transporter comes with a 1:64 car and a burning rubber card. The die-cast were produced for Press Pass by Action and were limited in quantity to 1,008.

	Lo	Hi
18 Bobby Labonte	90.00	150.00
Interstate Batteries		

Racing Champions Transporters 1:64 1991

This small series was the first group of transporters done by Racing Champions. They were packaged in a black box and distributed through retail and hobby outlets.

	Lo	Hi
2 Rusty Wallace	18.00	30.00
Penske Racing		
9 Bill Elliott	60.00	100.00
Melling with Red paint scheme		
11 Geoff Bodine	12.00	20.00
28 Davey Allison	30.00	50.00
Havoline		

Racing Champions Transporters 1:64 1992

This series of 1:64 scale transporters features many of the top names from both Winston Cup and Busch in 1992. The pieces were packaged in a black box and were distributed through hobby and retail outlets.

	Lo	Hi
1 Jeff Gordon	25.00	50.00
Baby Ruth		
1 Rick Mast	10.00	20.00
Majik Market		
2 Rusty Wallace	10.00	20.00
Penske		
3 Dale Earnhardt	12.50	25.00
Goodwrench		
4 Ernie Irvan	8.00	16.00
Kodak		
5 Jay Fogleman	7.50	15.00
Inn Keeper		
5 Ricky Rudd	7.50	15.00
Tide		
6 Mark Martin	8.00	16.00
Valvoline		
7 Alan Kulwicki	30.00	55.00
Hooters		
9 Bill Elliott	12.50	25.00
Melling with Blue paint scheme		
9 Chad Little	12.50	25.00
Melling		
9 Joe Bessey	7.50	15.00
Auto Palace		
10 Derrike Cope	7.50	15.00
Purolator		
11 Bill Elliott	8.00	16.00
Amoco		
12 Bobby Allison	7.50	15.00
Allison Motorsports		
12 Hut Stricklin	6.00	12.00
Raybestos		
14 A.J. Foyt	6.00	12.00
15 Geoff Bodine	6.00	12.00
Motorcraft		
16 Wally Dallenbach Jr.	10.00	20.00
Roush Racing		
17 Darrell Waltrip	6.00	12.00
Western Auto		
17 Darrell Waltrip	7.50	15.00
Western Auto Promo		
18 Dale Jarrett	6.00	12.00
Interstate Batteries		
20 Joe Ruttman	12.50	25.00
Fina		
21 Morgan Shepherd	7.50	15.00
Citgo		
22 Sterling Marlin	6.00	12.00
Maxwell House		
25 Ken Schrader	7.50	15.00
25 Bill Venturini	25.00	50.00
Rain X		
26 Brett Bodine	6.00	12.00
Quaker State		
28 Davey Allison	15.00	30.00
Havoline		
30 Michael Waltrip	6.00	12.00
Pennzoil		
33 Harry Gant	10.00	20.00
Food Lion		
36 Kenny Wallace	12.50	25.00
Dirt Devil		
42 Kyle Petty	6.00	12.00
Mello Yello		
43 Richard Petty	10.00	20.00
STP Fan Appreciation Tour		
43 Richard Petty	7.50	15.00
STP		
49 Stanley Smith	15.00	30.00
Ameritron Batteries		
59 Andy Belmont	15.00	30.00
FDP Brakes		
59 Robert Pressley	25.00	50.00
Alliance		
60 Mark Martin	15.00	30.00
Winn Dixie		
66 Cale Yarborough	6.00	12.00
TropArtic		
68 Bobby Hamilton	6.00	12.00
Country Time		
70 J.D. McDuffie	15.00	30.00
Son's Auto		
71 Dave Marcis	6.00	12.00
Big Apple Market		
72 Ken Bouchard	6.00	12.00
ADAP		
90 Wally Dallenbach Jr.	15.00	30.00
Ford Motorsports		
97 Terry Labonte	10.00	20.00
Sunoco		

Racing Champions Transporters 1:64 1993

This series of 1:64 transporters was issued in red boxes. The pieces feature the top names in racing. The Ricky Rudd piece in the series comes with two different paint schemes. Promo pieces were made of Dale Earnhardt, Darrell Waltrip and Hut Stricklin.

	Lo	Hi
1 Rick Mast	9.00	18.00
Majik Market		
2 Rusty Wallace	8.00	16.00
Penske		
3 Dale Earnhardt	10.00	20.00
Goodwrench		
3 Dale Earnhardt	10.00	20.00
Goodwrench Promo		
4 Ernie Irvan	8.00	16.00
Kodak		
5 Ricky Rudd	7.50	15.00
Tide with Orange paint scheme		
5 Ricky Rudd	8.00	16.00
Tide with White paint scheme		
6 Mark Martin	8.00	16.00
Valvoline		
7 Alan Kulwicki	25.00	50.00
Hooters		
8 Sterling Marlin	6.00	12.00
Raybestos		
11 Bill Elliott	8.00	16.00
Amoco		
12 Jimmy Spencer	6.00	12.00
Meineke		
14 Terry Labonte	8.00	16.00
Kellogg's		
15 Geoff Bodine	6.00	12.00
Motorcraft		
17 Darrell Waltrip	6.00	12.00
Western Auto		
17 Darrell Waltrip	7.50	15.00
Western Auto Promo		
18 Dale Jarrett	6.00	12.00
Interstate Batteries		
21 Morgan Shepherd	6.00	12.00
Citgo		
22 Bobby Labonte	6.00	12.00
Maxwell House		
24 Jeff Gordon	12.50	25.00
DuPont		
26 Brett Bodine	6.00	12.00
Quaker State		
27 Hut Stricklin	6.00	12.00
McDonald's		
27 Hut Stricklin	8.00	16.00
McDonald's Promo		
28 Davey Allison	12.50	25.00
Havoline		
30 Michael Waltrip	6.00	12.00
Pennzoil		
33 Harry Gant	7.50	15.00
Food Lion		
42 Kyle Petty	6.00	12.00
Mello Yello		
44 Rick Wilson	7.50	15.00
STP		
59 Andy Belmont	12.50	25.00
FDP Brakes		
60 Mark Martin	10.00	20.00
Winn Dixie		
75 Todd Bodine	6.00	12.00
Factory Stores of America		
87 Joe Nemcheck	6.00	12.00
Dentyne		
98 Derrike Cope	6.00	12.00
Bojangles		

Racing Champions Premier Transporters 1:64 1993

This was the first year Racing Champions did 1:64 scale Premier series peices. The pieces come in a black shadow box. Each box has a gold stamped quantity of production on the front.

	Lo	Hi
2 Rusty Wallace Ford Motorsports	20.00	35.00
3 Dale Earnhardt Goodwrench	30.00	55.00
4 Ernie Irvan Kodak	20.00	35.00
5 Ricky Rudd Tide	20.00	35.00
7 Alan Kulwicki Hooters	40.00	75.00
8 Sterling Marlin Raybestos	18.00	30.00
11 Bill Elliott Budweiser	20.00	35.00
24 Jeff Gordon DuPont	30.00	50.00
26 Brett Bodine Quaker State	18.00	30.00
27 Hut Stricklin McDonald's	18.00	30.00
28 Davey Allison Havoliine	30.00	55.00
28 Ernie Irvan Mac Tools	25.00	45.00
33 Harry Gant Chevrolet	18.00	30.00
42 Kyle Petty Mello Yello	18.00	30.00
51 No Driver Association Primer Ford cab	18.00	30.00
51 No Driver Association Primer paint scheme Kenworth	15.00	25.00
94 No Driver Association Brickyard 400 special	30.00	50.00

Racing Champions Transporters 1:64 1994

This series features transporters issued through both retail outlets and some issued through hobby outlets only. The pieces that were hobby only are easily identifiable by the yellow box they come in.

	Lo	Hi
Rick Mast Majik Market	6.00	12.00
Rick Mast Precision Products	6.00	12.00
2 Ricky Craven DuPont	6.00	12.00
2 Rusty Wallace Penske	7.50	15.00
2 Rusty Wallace Penske Yellow box hobby only	10.00	20.00
3 Dale Earnhardt Goodwrench Promo	9.00	18.00
4 Sterling Marlin Kodak	6.00	12.00
4 Sterling Marlin Kodak Yellow box hobby only	7.50	15.00
Terry Labonte Kellogg's	7.50	15.00
Terry Labonte Kellogg's Yellow box hobby only	10.00	20.00
Mark Martin Valvoline	7.50	15.00
Geoff Bodine Exide Batteries	6.00	12.00
Harry Gant Manheim Auctions	10.00	20.00
Jeff Burton Raybestos	6.00	12.00
Ricky Rudd Tide	6.00	12.00
11 Bill Elliott Amoco	6.00	12.00
15 Lake Speed Quality Care	6.00	12.00
16 Ted Musgrave Family Channel	6.00	12.00
17 Darrell Waltrip Western Auto	6.00	12.00
18 Dale Jarrett Interstate Batteries	6.00	12.00
18 Dale Jarrett Interstate Batteries Yellow box hobby only	10.00	20.00
19 Loy Allen Hooters	6.00	12.00
22 Bobby Labonte Maxwell House	6.00	12.00
24 Jeff Gordon DuPont	9.00	18.00
26 Brett Bodine Quaker State	6.00	12.00
27 Jimmy Spencer McDonald's	6.00	12.00
28 Ernie Irvan Havoline	7.50	15.00
30 Michael Waltrip Pennzoil	6.00	12.00
30 Michael Waltrip Pennzoil Yellow box hobby only	7.50	15.00
33 Harry Gant Leo Jackson	7.50	15.00
33 Harry Gant Leo Jackson Yellow box hobby only	8.00	16.00
40 Bobby Hamilton Kendall	6.00	12.00
41 Joe Nemechek Meineke	6.00	12.00
42 Kyle Petty Mello Yello	6.00	12.00
42 Kyle Petty Mello Yello Yellow box hobby only	7.50	15.00
52 Ken Schrader AC Delco	6.00	12.00
60 Mark Martin Winn Dixie	6.00	12.00
75 Todd Bodine Factory Stores of America	6.00	12.00
98 Derrike Cope Fingerhut	6.00	12.00

Racing Champions Premier Transporters 1:64 1994

This is a small series of 1:64 scale Premier transporters. It does however feature four of the best and most popular drivers in racing. The Jeff Gordon piece was a special made for the Winston Select.

	Lo	Hi
3 Dale Earnhardt Goodwrench	25.00	40.00
4 Sterling Marlin Kodak	18.00	30.00
24 Jeff Gordon DuPont Winston Select special	20.00	35.00
33 Harry Gant Farewell Tour	20.00	35.00

Racing Champions Transporters 1:64 1995 Previews

This series of 1:64 scale transporters was the first time Racing Champions produced preview peices for transporters. The series features drivers from both the Winston Cup and Busch circuits.

	Lo	Hi
2 Rusty Wallace Penske	7.00	14.00
7 Geoff Bodine Exide	7.00	14.00
10 Ricky Rudd Tide	7.00	14.00
14 Terry Labonte MW Windows	7.00	14.00
16 Ted Musgrave Family Channel	7.00	14.00
24 Jeff Gordon DuPont	8.00	16.00
27 Loy Allen Hooters	7.00	14.00
38 Elton Sawyer Red Carpet	7.00	14.00
40 Bobby Hamilton Kendall	7.00	14.00
57 Jason Keller Budget Gourmet	7.00	14.00

Racing Champions Transporters 1:64 1995

Many of the top names in Winston Cup and Busch are featured in this series. The pieces were distributed through both hobby and retail outlets. A special series of Jeff Gordon Signature Series die cast was issued in '95 and included a 1:64 transporter.

	Lo	Hi
2 Rusty Wallace Penske	7.00	14.00
5 Terry Labonte Kellogg's	7.00	14.00
6 Tommy Houston Red Devil	7.00	14.00
6 Mark Martin Valvoline	7.50	15.00
7 Geoff Bodine Exide	7.00	14.00

8 Jeff Burton	7.00	14.00
Raybestos		
8 Kenny Wallace	7.00	14.00
Red Dog		
10 Ricky Rudd	7.00	14.00
Tide		
12 Derrike Cope	7.00	14.00
Straight Arrow		
18 Bobby Labonte	7.00	14.00
Interstate Batteries		
23 Chad Little	7.00	14.00
Bayer		
24 Jeff Gordon	8.00	16.00
DuPont		
24 Jeff Gordon	10.00	18.00
DuPont Signature Series		
26 Steve Kinser	7.00	14.00
Quaker State		
27 Loy Allen	7.00	14.00
Hooter's		
28 Dale Jarrett	7.00	14.00
Ernie Irvan		
Havoline		
both signatures on trailer		
34 Mike McLaughlin	7.00	14.00
French's		
40 Patty Moise	7.00	14.00
Dial		
44 David Green	7.00	14.00
Slim Jim		
47 Jeff Fuller	7.00	14.00
Sunoco		
60 Mark Martin	8.00	16.00
Winn Dixie		
90 Mike Wallace	7.00	14.00
Heilig-Meyers		
94 Bill Elliott	7.50	15.00
McDonald's		
94 Bill Elliott	10.00	20.00
McDonald's Thunderbat		
99 Phil Parsons	7.00	14.00
Luxaire		

Racing Champions Premier Transporters 1:64 1995

This series of 1:64 scale transporters was higlighted by two beer special transporters. The Rusty Wallace Miller Genuine Draft transporter and the Kyle Petty Coors Light transporters both came in acrylic cases.

	Lo	Hi
2 Rusty Wallace	30.00	45.00
Miller Genuine Draft		
in acrylic case		
2 Rusty Wallace	30.00	40.00
Penske Bank		
8 Jeff Burton	12.00	20.00
Raybestos		
12 Derrike Cope	12.00	20.00
Straight Arrow		
26 Steve Kinser	12.00	20.00
Quaker State		
26 Steve Kinser	25.00	40.00
Quaker State Bank		
27 Loy Allen	12.00	20.00
Hooters		
40 Bobby Hamilton	12.00	20.00
Kendall		
40 Patty Moise	12.00	20.00
Dial		
42 Kyle Petty	30.00	45.00
Coors Light in acrylic case		
90 Mike Wallace	12.00	20.00
Heilig-Meyers		
94 Bill Elliott	12.00	20.00
McDonald's		

Racing Champions Transporters 1:64 1996 Previews

This series of transporters was issued in a red box and has the word preview appear below the year of release. The pieces feature both Winston Cup and Busch series drives.

	Lo	Hi
4 Sterling Marlin	7.00	14.00
Kodak		
5 Terry Labonte	7.00	14.00
Kellogg's		
6 Mark Martin	7.00	14.00
Valvoline		
11 Brett Bodine	7.00	14.00
Lowe's		
12 Derrike Cope	7.00	14.00
Mane N' Tail		
16 Ted Musgrave	7.00	14.00
Family Channel		
17 Darrell Waltrip	7.00	14.00
Western Auto		
47 Jeff Fuller	7.00	14.00
Sunoco		
57 Jason Keller	7.00	14.00
Slim Jim		
90 Mike Wallace	7.00	14.00
Heilig-Meyers		

Racing Champions Transporters 1:64 1996

These pieces were issued in three different variations. Transporters were issued with no cars, one car, and with two cars. Transporters with one or two cars carry a slight premium over those issued without cars. The Chad Little trasnporters were issued in standard Racing Champion packaging and in John Deere promotional boxes. The Ken Scharder transporters were issued as part of a special Budweiser program. The Ricky Craven transporter was produced for and distributed by his fan club. The Mark Martin Winn Dixie transporter was distributed in Winn Dixie stores primarily in the Southeast.

	Lo	Hi
1 Rick Mast	10.00	20.00
Hooter's		
1 Hermie Sadler	10.00	20.00
Dewalt		
2 Rusty Wallace	15.00	30.00
Miller Genuine Draft		
2 Rusty Wallace	10.00	20.00
Penske		
2 Rusty Wallace	12.50	25.00
Penske with one car or two cars		
3 Mike Skinner	12.50	25.00
Goodwrench with one truck or two trucks		
4 Sterling Marlin	12.50	25.00
Kodak with one or two cars		
5 Terry Labonte	15.00	30.00
Kellogg's with one car or two cars		
7 Geoff Bodine	10.00	20.00
QVC		
8 Hut Stricklin	10.00	20.00
Circuit City		
10 Ricky Rudd	12.50	25.00
Tide with one car or two cars		
11 Brett Bodine	10.00	20.00
Lowe's		
11 Brett Bodine	12.50	25.00
Lowe's with one car or two cars		
14 Patty Moise	12.50	25.00
Dial Purex with one car or two cars		
15 Wally Dallenbach	10.00	20.00
Hayes		
17 Darrell Waltrip	10.00	20.00
Parts America		
21 Michael Waltrip	12.50	25.00
Citgo with one car or two cars		
22 Ward Burton	10.00	20.00
MBNA		
23 Chad Little	10.00	20.00
John Deere		
23 Chad Little	15.00	25.00
John Deere Promo		
23 Chad Little	12.50	25.00
John Deere with one car or two cars		
23 Chad Little	20.00	35.00
John Deere with one car Promo		
24 Jeff Gordon	15.00	30.00
DuPont with one car or two cars		
25 Ken Scharder	20.00	40.00
Budweiser		
25 Ken Scharder	150.00	300.00
Budweiser Chrome		
28 Ernie Irvan	10.00	20.00
Havoline		
28 Ernie Irvan	12.50	25.00
Havoline with one car or two cars		
29 Steve Grissom	10.00	20.00
Cartoon Network		
29 Steve Grissom	12.50	25.00
Cartoon Network with one car or two cars		
29 Steve Grissom	10.00	20.00
WCW		
29 Steve Grissom	12.50	25.00
WCW with one car or two cars		
29 No Driver Association	12.50	25.00
Scooby-Doo woth one car or two		
30 Johhny Benson	10.00	20.00
Pennzoil		
32 Dale Jarrett	25.00	40.00
Band-Aid with one car or two cars		
37 John Andretti	15.00	25.00
K-Mart Promo		
41 Ricky Craven	20.00	40.00
Kodiak Fan Club		
43 Rodney Combs	10.00	20.00
Lance		
43 Bobby Hamilton	10.00	20.00
STP		
43 Bobby Hamilton	12.50	25.00
STP with one car or two cars		
44 Bobby Labonte	15.00	25.00
Shell		
47 Jeff Fuller	10.00	20.00
Sunoco		
60 Mark Martin	15.00	25.00
Winn Dixie		
60 Mark Martin	20.00	35.00
Winn Dixie with one car or two cars		
74 Randy Lajoie	10.00	20.00
Fina		
74 Johhny Benson	12.50	25.00

Lipton Tea with one car or two cars		
87 Joe Nemechek	10.00	20.00
Bell South		
87 Joe Nemechek	10.00	20.00
Burger King		
88 Dale Jarrett	10.00	20.00
Quality Care		
88 Dale Jarrett	12.50	25.00
Quality Care with one car or two cars		
94 Bill Elliott	10.00	20.00
McDonald's		
94 Bill Elliott	12.50	25.00
McDonald's with one car or two cars		
94 Bill Elliott	10.00	20.00
McDonald's Monopoly		
94 Bill Elliott	12.50	25.00
McDonald's Monopoly with one car or two cars		

Racing Champions Premier Transporters 1:64 1996

These pieces were issued with a premier car. They were distributed through both hobby and retail outlets. Theie suggested retail price is higher due to the inclusion of the premier cars.

	Lo	Hi
2 Rusty Wallace	15.00	30.00
Penske		
6 Mark Martin	15.00	30.00
Valvoline		
1 Brett Bodine	15.00	30.00
Lowe's		
24 Jeff Gordon	15.00	30.00
DuPont		
29 S.Grissom	15.00	30.00
WCW		
29 S.Grissom	15.00	30.00
Cartoon Network		
3 Bobby Hamilton	15.00	30.00
STP Silver		
8 Dale Jarrett	15.00	30.00
Quality Care		
4 Bill Elliott	15.00	30.00
McDonald's		

Racing Champions Transporters 1:64 1997 Previews

Many of the top drivers from the Winston Cup circuit are featured in this series. The pieces were distributed through both hobby and retail outlets.

	Lo	Hi
Sterling Marlin	12.00	20.00
Kodak		
Terry Labonte	12.00	20.00
Kellogg's		
Mark Martin	12.00	20.00
Valvoline		
Geoff Bodine	12.00	20.00
QVC		
Hut Stricklin	12.00	20.00
Circuit City		
4 Jeff Gordon	12.00	20.00
DuPont		
9 Robert Pressley	12.00	20.00
Scooby-Doo		
5 Rick Mast	10.00	20.00
Remington		

Racing Champions Transporters 1:64 1997

Like 1996, Racing Champions has distributed standard transporters in three different variations. These transporters come with one car, two cars, and/or wothout a car. This series features drivers from both the Winston Cup and Busch circuits.

	Lo	Hi
00 Buckshot Jones	10.00	20.00
Aquafresh		
00 Buckshot Jones	12.50	25.00
Aquafresh with one car or two cars		
1 Hermie Sadler	12.50	25.00
Dewalt with one car or two cars		
1 Hermie Sadler	10.00	20.00
Dewalt		
2 Ricky Craven	10.00	20.00
Raybestos		
2 Rusty Wallace	10.00	20.00
Penske		
4 Sterling Marlin	12.50	25.00
Kodak with one car or two		
4 Sterling Marlin	10.00	20.00
Kodak		
5 Terry Labonte	10.00	20.00
Kellogg's		
5 Terry Labonte	12.50	25.00
Kellogg's 1996 Winston Cup Champion		
6 Mark Martin	10.00	20.00
Valvoline		
6 Mark Martin	12.50	25.00
Valvoline with one car or two cars		
7 Geoff Bodine	10.00	20.00
QVC		
8 Hut Stricklin	10.00	20.00
Circuit City		
9 Jeff Burton	10.00	20.00
Track Gear		
10 Phil Parsons	10.00	20.00
Channellock		
10 Ricky Rudd	10.00	20.00
Tide		
10 Ricky Rudd	12.50	25.00
Tide with one car or two cars		
11 Brett Bodine	10.00	20.00
Close Call		
11 Brett Bodine	12.50	25.00
Close Call with one car or two cars		
11 Jimmy Foster	10.00	20.00
Speedvision		
11 Jimmy Foster	12.50	25.00
Speedvision with one car or two cars		
16 Ted Musgrave	10.00	20.00
Primestar		
17 Darrell Waltrip	10.00	20.00
Parts America		
17 Darrell Waltrip	12.50	25.00
Parts America with one car or two cars		
19 Gary Bradberry	10.00	20.00
CSR		
19 Gary Bradberry	12.50	25.00
CSR with one car or two cars		
21 Michael Waltrip	10.00	20.00
Citgo		
24 Jeff Gordon	12.50	25.00
DuPont		
25 Ricky Craven	20.00	35.00
Bud Lizard with one car		
28 Ernie Irvan	10.00	20.00
Havoline		
10th Anniversary paint scheme		
28 Ernie Irvan	12.50	25.00
Havoline with one car or two cars		
10th Anniversary paint scheme		
29 Jeff Green	12.50	25.00
Tom and Jerry with one or two cars		
29 No Driver Association	10.00	20.00
Tom & Jerry		
29 Robert Pressley	10.00	20.00
Cartoon Network		
30 Johnny Benson	10.00	20.00
Pennzoil		
32 Dale Jarrett	10.00	20.00
Gillette		
32 Dale Jarrett	12.50	25.00
Gillette with one or two cars		
32 Dale Jarrett	10.00	20.00
White Rain		
33 Tim Fedewa	10.00	20.00
Kleenex		
34 Mike McLaughlin	10.00	20.00
Royal Oak		
34 Mike McLaughlin	12.50	25.00
Royal Oak with one car or two cars		
36 Todd Bodine	10.00	20.00
Stanley		
36 Derrike Cope	10.00	20.00
Skittles		
38 Elton Sawyer	10.00	20.00
Barbasol		
38 Elton Sawyer	12.50	25.00
Barbasol with one or two cars		
40 Robby Gordon	10.00	20.00
Sabco Racing		
43 Dennis Setzer	10.00	20.00
Lance		
43 Rodney Combs	10.00	20.00
Lance		
46 Wally Dallenbach	10.00	20.00
First Union		
57 Jason Keller	10.00	20.00
Slim Jim		
60 Mark Martin	10.00	20.00
Winn Dixie		
60 Mark Martin	12.50	25.00
Winn Dixie Promo		
63 Tracy Leslie	10.00	20.00
Lysol		
72 Mike Dillon	10.00	20.00
Detroit Gasket		
74 Randy Lajoie	10.00	20.00
Fina		
74 Randy Lajoie	12.50	25.00
Fina with one or two cars		
75 Rick Mast	10.00	20.00
Remington		
75 Rick Mast	12.50	25.00
Remington with one or two cars		
88 Kevin Lepage	10.00	20.00
Hype		
88 Kevin Lepage	12.50	25.00
Hype with one or two cars		
90 Dick Trickle	10.00	20.00
Heilig-Meyers		
94 Ron Barfield	10.00	20.00
New Holland		
94 Ron Barfield	12.50	25.00
New Holland with one or two cars		
94 Bill Elliott	10.00	20.00
McDonald's		
96 David Green	10.00	20.00
Caterpillar		
96 David Green	15.00	25.00
Caterpillar Promo		
97 No Driver Association	12.00	20.00
Brickyard 400		
97 Chad Little	10.00	20.00
John Deere		
97 Chad Little	12.00	20.00
John Deere Promo with one car		
99 Jeff Burton	10.00	20.00
Exide		

Racing Champions Premier Transporters 1:64 1997

This is the second year that Racing Champions has produced premier transporters that are packaged with a premier car. This series is highlighted by the special 1996 Winston Cup Champion Terry Labonte Kellogg's transporter.

	Lo	Hi
5 Terry Labonte	20.00	35.00
Kellogg's		
29 Robert Pressley	15.00	30.00
Cartoon Network		
60 Mark Martin	20.00	35.00
Winn Dixie		

Racing Champions Transporters 1:64 1998

The 1:64 scale transpoters that appear in this series are replicas of many of the cars that ran in the 1997 season, but also many replicas are of the cars slated to appear in the 1998 season. The transporters in this series are packaged in special boxes that display the NASCAR 50th anniversary logo.

	Lo	Hi
00 Buckshot Jones Aqua Fresh	10.00	20.00
00 Buckshot Jones Aqua Fresh with car	10.00	25.00
4 Bobby Hamilton Kodak	10.00	20.00
4 Bobby Hamilton Kodak with Car	10.00	25.00
4 Jeff Purvis Lance	10.00	20.00
4 Jeff Purvis Lance with car	10.00	25.00
5 Terry Labonte Kellogg's	10.00	25.00
5 Terry Labonte Kellogg's with car	12.00	30.00
5 Terr Labonte Kellogg's Corny	10.00	25.00
5 Terry Labonte Kellogg's Corny with car	12.00	30.00
6 Joe Bessey Power Team	10.00	20.00
6 Joe Bessey Power Team with car	10.00	25.00
6 Mark Martin Eagle One	10.00	20.00
6 Mark Martin Eagle One with car	10.00	25.00
8 Hut Stricklin Circuit City	10.00	20.00
8 Hut Stricklin Circuit City with car	10.00	25.00
9 Lake Speed Birthday Cake	10.00	20.00
9 Lake Speed Birthday Cake with car	10.00	25.00
9 Lake Speed Huckleberry Hound	10.00	20.00
9 Lake Speed Huckleberry Hound with car	10.00	25.00
10 Ricky Rudd Tide	10.00	20.00
10 Ricky Rudd Tide with car	10.00	25.00
11 Brett Bodine Paychex		
13 Jerry Nadeau First Plus	10.00	20.00
13 Jerry Nadeau First Plus with car	10.00	25.00
21 Michael Waltrip Citgo with car	10.00	25.00
21 Michael Waltrip Citgo	10.00	20.00
21 Michael Waltrip Goodwill Games	10.00	20.00
21 Michael Waltrip Goodwill Games with car	10.00	25.00
30 Mike Cope Slim Jim	10.00	20.00
33 Ken Schrader Petree	10.00	20.00
35 Todd Bodine Tabasco	10.00	20.00
35 Todd Bodine Tabasco with car	10.00	25.00
36 Ernie Irvan M&Ms	15.00	30.00
36 Ernie Irvan M&Ms with car	15.00	35.00
36 Ernie Irvan Skittles	10.00	20.00
36 Ernie Irvan Skittles with car	10.00	25.00
40 Kevin Lepage Channellock	10.00	20.00
40 Sterling Marlin Sabco	10.00	20.00
40 Sterling Marlin Sabco with car	10.00	25.00
42 Joe Nemecheck BellSouth	10.00	20.00
46 Wally Dallenbach First Union	10.00	20.00
50 Ricky Craven Hendrick	10.00	20.00
50 Ricky Craven Hendrick with car	10.00	25.00
59 Robert Pressley Kingsford	10.00	20.00
59 Robert Pressley Kingsford with car	10.00	25.00
60 Mark Martin Winn Dixie	10.00	20.00
60 Mark Martin Winn Dixie with car	10.00	25.00
60 Mark Martin Winn Dixie Promo with car	20.00	40.00
66 Elliot Sadler Phillips 66	10.00	20.00
66 Elliot Sadler Phillips 66 with car	10.00	25.00
75 Rick Mast Remington	10.00	20.00
94 Bill Elliott Happy Meal with car	10.00	25.00
96 David Green Caterpillar Promo with car	15.00	25.00
97 Chad Little John Deere	10.00	20.00
99 Jeff Burton Exide	10.00	20.00
99 Jeff Burton Exide with car	10.00	25.00

Racing Champions Transporters 1:64 1998 Gold

This is a special series produced by Racing Champions to celebrate NASCAR's 50th anniversary. It parallels the regular 1998 1:64 scale series. Each car is a limited edition of 1,500. Each transpoter is also plated in gold chrome and contains a serial number on its chassis.

	Lo	Hi
00 Buckshot Jones Aquafresh	20.00	50.00
4 Bobby Hamilton Kodak	15.00	40.00
5 Terry Labonte Kellogg's	50.00	100.00
5 Terry Labonte Kellogg's Corny	50.00	100.00
6 Joe Bessey Power Team	50.00	100.00
6 Mark Martin Eagle One	50.00	100.00
6 Mark Martin Valvoline	50.00	100.00
8 Hut Stricklin Circuit City	15.00	40.00
9 Jerry Nadeau Zombie Island	20.00	50.00
9 Lake Speed Birthday Cake	20.00	50.00
9 Lake Speed Huckleberry Hound	20.00	50.00
10 Ricky Rudd Tide	20.00	50.00
11 Brett Bodine Paychex	15.00	40.00
13 Jerry Nadeau First Plus	20.00	50.00
16 Ted Musgrave Primestar	15.00	40.00
19 Tony Raines Yellow	15.00	40.00
21 Michael Waltrip Citgo	15.00	40.00
29 Hermie Sadler Phillips 66	15.00	40.00
30 Mike Cope Slim Jim	15.00	40.00
33 Tim Fedewa Kleenex	15.00	40.00
33 Ken Schrader Petree	15.00	40.00
35 Todd Bodine Tabasco	20.00	50.00
36 Ernie Irvan Skittles	20.00	50.00
36 Ernie Irvan M&Ms	40.00	80.00
40 Rick Fuller Channellock	15.00	40.00
40 Sterling Marlin Sabco	20.00	50.00
42 Joe Nemecheck BellSouth	15.00	40.00
46 Wally Dallenbach First Union	15.00	40.00
50 Ricky Craven Hendrick	15.00	40.00
59 Robert Pressley Kingsford	15.00	40.00
66 Elliot Sadler Phillips 66	15.00	40.00
74 Randy Lajoie Fina	15.00	40.00
75 Rick Mast Remington	15.00	40.00
78 Gary Bradberry Pilot	15.00	40.00
88 Kevin Schwantz Ryder	15.00	40.00
90 Dick Trickle Heilig-Meyers	15.00	40.00
94 Bill Elliott Happy Meal	50.00	100.00
94 Bill Elliott McDonald's	50.00	100.00
94 Bill Elliott Mac Tonight	50.00	100.00
97 Chad Little John Deere Promo	50.00	90.00

Racing Champions Transporters 1:87 1993-94

This is the first series Racing Champions did of 1:87 scale transporters. By 1994 Racing Champions was doing both a regular retail issue product and a hobby only product. The hobby only products come in a yellow box.

	Lo	Hi
1 Rick Mast Precision Products Yellow box hobby only	6.00	10.00
2 Rusty Wallace Penske Yellow box hobby only	7.00	12.00
2 Rusty Wallace Penske	4.00	8.00
3 Dale Earnhardt Goodwrench	6.00	12.00
4 Ernie Irvan Kodak	3.00	6.00
4 Sterling Marlin Kodak Yellow box hobby only	6.00	10.00
5 Terry Labonte Kellogg's Yellow box hobby only	6.00	10.00
5 Ricky Rudd Tide	3.00	6.00
6 Mark Martin Valvoline	3.00	6.00
6 Mark Martin Valvoline Yellow box hobby only	6.00	10.00
7 Harry Gant Manheim Auctions	5.00	10.00
7 Harry Gant Morema	4.00	8.00
7 Alan Kulwicki Hooters	10.00	20.00

	Lo	Hi
8 Jeff Burton Raybestos Yellow box hobby only	6.00	10.00
8 Sterling Marlin Raybestos	3.00	6.00
9 Chad Little IOF Hotline	3.00	6.00
11 Bill Elliott Amoco	3.00	6.00
12 Jimmy Spencer Meineke	3.00	6.00
14 Terry Labonte Kellogg's	3.00	6.00
15 Geoff Bodine Motorcraft	3.00	6.00
17 Darrell Walttrip Western Auto	3.00	6.00
18 Dale Jarrett Interstate Batteries	3.00	6.00
18 Dale Jarrett Interstate Batteries Yellow box hobby only	6.00	10.00
21 Morgan Shepherd Citgo	3.00	6.00
22 Bobby Labonte Maxwell House	3.00	6.00
24 Jeff Gordon DuPont	6.00	12.00
24 Jeff Gordon DuPont Yellow box hobby only	10.00	20.00
25 Ken Schrader	3.00	6.00
26 Brett Bodine Quaker State	3.00	6.00
26 Brett Bodine Quaker State Yellow box hobby only	6.00	10.00
27 Hut Stricklin McDonald's	3.00	6.00
28 Davey Allison Havoline	6.00	12.00
28 Davey Allison Havoline with Black and White paint scheme	7.00	14.00
30 Michael Waltrip Pennzoil	3.00	6.00
30 Michael Waltrip Pennzoil Yellow box hobby only	6.00	10.00
33 Harry Gant Food Lion	4.00	8.00
33 Harry Gant Leo Jackson Yellow box hobby only	6.00	10.00
33 Harry Gant Morema	6.00	12.00
35 Bill Venturini Amoco	10.00	20.00
42 Kyle Petty Mello Yello	3.00	6.00
42 Kyle Petty Mello Yello Yellow box hobby only	6.00	10.00
44 Rick Wilson STP	3.00	6.00
52 Ken Schrader AC Delco	3.00	6.00
52 Ken Schrader Morema	5.00	10.00
66 Cale Yarborough TropArtic	6.00	12.00
75 Todd Bodine Factory Stores of America Yellow box hobby only	6.00	10.00
87 Joe Nemechek Dentyne	3.00	6.00
98 Derrike Cope Bojangles	3.00	6.00

Racing Champions Premier Transporters 1:87 1993

This is the first year that Racing Champions did a 1:87 scale Premier transporter. The set features the most popular drivers from Winston Cup racing. Each piece comes in a black shadow box and has the number produced stamped on the front of that box.

	Lo	Hi
2 Ward Burton Hardee's	10.00	20.00
2 Rusty Wallace Penske	15.00	30.00
3 Dale Earnhardt Goodwrench	15.00	30.00
3 Dale Earnhardt Goodwrench Dale Earnhardt Inc.	15.00	30.00
4 Ernie Irvan Kodak	10.00	20.00
5 Ricky Rudd Tide	10.00	20.00
6 Mark Martin Valvoline	10.00	20.00
7 Alan Kulwicki Hooters	40.00	75.00
8 Sterling Marlin Raybestos	10.00	20.00
11 Bill Elliott Amoco	10.00	20.00
11 Bill Elliott Budweiser	18.00	35.00
12 Jimmy Spencer Meineke	10.00	20.00
14 Terry Labonte Kellogg's	10.00	20.00
15 Geoff Bodine Motorcraft	10.00	20.00
18 Dale Jarrett Interstate Batteries	10.00	20.00
21 Morgan Shepherd Citgo	10.00	20.00
22 Bobby Labonte Maxwell House	10.00	20.00
24 Jeff Gordon DuPont	15.00	25.00
27 Hut Stricklin McDonald's	10.00	20.00
28 Davey Allison Havoline Black paint scheme	18.00	35.00
28 Davey Allison Havoline with Black and White paint scheme	18.00	35.00
28 Ernie Irvan Havoline	15.00	25.00
33 Harry Gant Food Lion	10.00	20.00
42 Kyle Petty Mello Yello	10.00	20.00
44 David Green Slim Jim	10.00	20.00
44 Rick Wilson STP	10.00	20.00
51 No Driver Association Primer paint Ford	12.00	20.00
51 No Driver Association Primer paint Kenworth	12.00	20.00
59 Robert Pressley Alliance	15.00	30.00
60 Mark Martin Winn Dixie	25.00	40.00
87 Joe Nemechek Dentyne	10.00	20.00

Racing Champions Premier Transporters 1:87 1994

Racing Champions continued there line of 1:87 Premier transporters in 1994. The pieces were again packaged in a black shadow box and carry the number produced on the front of that box.

	Lo	Hi
2 Ward Burton Hardee's	12.00	20.00
3 Dale Earnhardt Goodwrench	15.00	25.00
4 Sterling Marlin Kodak	12.00	20.00
4 Sterling Marlin Kodak FunSaver	12.00	20.00
5 Terry Labonte Kellogg's	12.00	20.00
7 Geoff Bodine Exide	15.00	25.00
7 Harry Gant Manheim Auctions	15.00	25.00
8 Kenny Wallace TIC Financial	12.00	20.00
15 Lake Speed Quality Care	12.00	20.00
16 Ted Musgrave Family Channel	12.00	20.00
17 Darrell Waltrip Western Auto	15.00	25.00
19 Loy Allen Hooters	12.00	20.00
21 Morgan Shepherd Cheerwine	15.00	25.00
28 Ernie Irvan Havoline	15.00	25.00
28 Ernie Irvan Mac Tools	15.00	25.00
32 Dale Jarrett Shoe World	12.00	20.00
40 Bobby Hamilton Kendall	12.00	20.00
52 Ken Schrader AC Delco	15.00	25.00
60 Mark Martin Winn Dixie	15.00	25.00
94 No Driver Association Brickyard 400 special	18.00	35.00
98 Derrike Cope Fingerhut	12.00	20.00

Racing Champions Transporters 1:87 1995

These 1:87 scale pieces were produced by Racing Champions. They were distributed through both hobby and retail outlets. This series is highlighted by the Rusty Wallace transporter which was released in an acrylic case.

	Lo	Hi
2 Rusty Wallace Miller Genuine Draft in acrylic case	10.00	20.00
7 Geoff Bodine Exide	3.00	6.00
24 Jeff Gordon DuPont '95	4.00	8.00
26 Steve Kinser Quaker State	3.00	6.00
27 Loy Allen Hooters	3.00	6.00
28 Dale Jarrett Ernie Irvan Havoline both signatures on trailer	3.00	6.00
99 Phil Parsons Luxaire	3.00	6.00

Racing Champions Transporters 1:87 1996

This series was produced by Racing Champions. It is highlighted by the Kyle Petty transporter which was released in an acrylic case.

	Lo	Hi
1 Rick Mast Hooter's	3.00	6.00
1 Hermie Sadler Dewalt	3.00	6.00
2 Rusty Wallace Penske	3.00	6.00
4 Sterling Marlin Kodak	3.00	6.00
5 Terry Labonte Kellogg's	3.00	6.00
6 Mark Martin	3.00	6.00

	Lo	Hi
Valvoline		
7 Geoff Bodine	3.00	6.00
QVC		
8 Hut Stricklin	3.00	6.00
Circuit City		
10 Ricky Rudd	3.00	6.00
Tide		
11 Brett Bodine	3.00	6.00
Lowe's		
12 Michael Waltrip	3.00	6.00
MW Windows		
15 Wally Dallenbach	3.00	6.00
Hayes		
16 Ted Musgrave	3.00	6.00
Family Channel		
17 Darrell Waltrip	3.00	6.00
Parts America		
18 Bobby Labonte	3.00	6.00
Interstate Batteries		
21 Michael Waltrip	3.00	6.00
Citgo		
22 Ward Burton	3.00	6.00
MBNA		
23 Chad Little	5.00	10.00
John Deere		
24 Jeff Gordon	15.00	25.00
DuPont		
Premier Transporter		
29 No Driver Association	4.00	8.00
Scooby-Doo		
30 Johnny Benson	3.00	6.00
Pennzoil		
34 Mike McLaughlin	3.00	6.00
Royal Oak		
37 John Andretti	3.00	6.00
K-Mart		
40 Tim Fedewa	3.00	6.00
Kleenex		
40 Patty Moise	3.00	6.00
Dial Purex		
42 Kyle Petty	10.00	20.00
Coors Light in acrylic case		
43 Rodney Combs	3.00	6.00
Lance		
44 David Green	3.00	6.00
Slim Jim		
44 Bobby Labonte	4.00	8.00
Shell		
47 Jeff Fuller	3.00	6.00
Sunoco		
74 Randy Lajoie	3.00	6.00
Fina		
81 Kenny Wallace	3.00	6.00
TIC Financial		
87 Joe Nemechek	3.00	6.00
Burger King		
87 Joe Nemechek	3.00	6.00
Bell South		
90 Mike Wallace	3.00	6.00
Heilig-Meyers		
99 Glenn Allen, Jr.	3.00	6.00
Luxaire		

Racing Champions Preview Transporters 1:87 1997

This is the first year that Racing Champions has done a 1:87 scale Preview transporter. The set features the most popular drivers from Winston Cup racing.

	Lo	Hi
5 Terry Labonte	4.00	8.00
Kellogg's		
6 Mark Martin	3.00	6.00
Valvoline		
7 Geoff Bodine	3.00	6.00
QVC		
8 Hut Stricklin	3.00	6.00
Circuit City		
24 Jeff Gordon	4.00	8.00
DuPont		
29 Robert Pressley	3.00	6.00
Cartoon Network		

Racing Champions Transporters 1:87 1997

These 1:87 pieces were produced by Racing Champions. They were distributed through both hobby and retail outlets. This series features drivers from the Winston Cup and Busch circuits.

	Lo	Hi
1 Hermie Sadler	3.00	6.00
Dewalt		
2 Ricky Craven	3.00	6.00
Raybestos		
2 Rusty Wallace	3.00	6.00
Penske		
4 Sterling Marlin	3.00	6.00
Kodak		
5 Terry Labonte	3.00	6.00
Kellogg's		
6 Mark Martin	3.00	6.00
Valvoline		
7 Geoff Bodine	3.00	6.00
QVC		
8 Hut Stricklin	3.00	6.00
Circuit City		
9 Jeff Burton	3.00	6.00
Track Gear		
10 Phil Parsons	3.00	6.00
Channellock		
10 Ricky Rudd	3.00	6.00
Tide		
11 Brett Bodine	3.00	6.00
Close Call		
11 Jimmy Foster	3.00	6.00
Speedvision		
16 Ted Musgrave	3.00	6.00
Primestar		
17 Darrell Waltrip	3.00	6.00
Parts America		
18 Bobby Labonte	3.00	6.00
Interstate Batteries		
19 Gary Bradberry	3.00	6.00
CSR		
21 Michael Waltrip	3.00	6.00
Citgo		
24 Jeff Gordon	4.00	8.00
DuPont		
28 Ernie Irvan	3.00	6.00
Havoline 10th Anniversary paint scheme		
29 Robert Pressley	3.00	6.00
Cartoon Network		
29 Jeff Green	3.00	6.00
Tom & Jerry		
30 Johnny Benson	3.00	6.00
Pennzoil		
32 Dale Jarrett	3.00	6.00
Gillette		
32 Dale Jarrett	3.00	6.00
White Rain		
34 Mike McLaughlin	3.00	6.00
Royal Oak		
36 Todd Bodine	3.00	6.00
Stanley Tools		
36 Derrike Cope	3.00	6.00
Skittles		
37 Jeremy Mayfield	3.00	6.00
Kmart		
38 Elton Sawyer	3.00	6.00
Barbasol		
40 Robby Gordon	3.00	6.00
Sabco Racing		
43 Rodney Combs	3.00	6.00
Lance		
46 Wally Dallenbach	3.00	6.00
First Union		
57 Jason Keller	3.00	6.00
Slim Jim		
60 Mark Martin	3.00	6.00
Winn Dixie		
75 Rick Mast	3.00	6.00
Remington		
90 Dick Trickle	3.00	6.00
Heilig-Meyers		
94 R.Barfield/New Holland	3.00	6.00
94 Bill Elliott	3.00	6.00
McDonald's		
96 David Green	3.00	6.00
Caterpillar		
97 Chad Little	3.00	6.00
John Deere		
99 Jeff Burton	3.00	6.00
Exide		

Racing Champions Transporters 1:87 1998

These 1:87 pieces were produced by Racing Champions. They were distributed through both hobby and retail outlets. This series features drivers from the Winston Cup and Busch circuits.

	Lo	Hi
00 Buckshot Jones	3.00	6.00
Aqua Fresh		
4 Jeff Purvis	3.00	6.00
Lance		
4 Bobby Hamilton	3.00	6.00
Kodak		
5 Terry Labonte	3.00	6.00
Kellogg's		
6 Joe Bessey	3.00	6.00
Power Team		
6 Mark Martin	3.00	6.00
Valvoline		
8 Hut Stricklin	3.00	6.00
Circuit City		
9 Lake Speed	3.00	6.00
Birthday Cake		
9 Lake Speed	3.00	6.00
Huckleberry Hound		
10 Ricky Rudd	3.00	6.00
Tide		
11 Brett Bodine	3.00	6.00
Paychex		
13 Jerry Nadeau	3.00	6.00
First Plus		
21 Michael Waltrip	3.00	6.00
Citgo		
21 Michael Waltrip	3.00	6.00
Goodwill Games		
33 Ken Schrader	3.00	6.00
Petree		
35 Todd Bodine	3.00	6.00
Tabasco		
36 Ernie Irvan	3.00	6.00
M&Ms		
36 Ernie Irvan	3.00	6.00
Skittles		
40 Serling Marlin	3.00	6.00
Sabco		
42 Joe Nemecheck	3.00	6.00
BellSouth		
46 Wally Dallembach	3.00	6.00
First Union		
50 Ricky Craven	3.00	6.00
Hendrick		
59 Robert Pressley	3.00	6.00
Kingsford		
66 Elliot Sadler	3.00	6.00
Phillips 66		
75 Rick Mast	3.00	6.00
Remington		

Winross Transporters 1:64 1987-1990

Winross entered the transporter market in 1987. The pieces originally had a cost higher than the mass marketed pieces and were produced in short quantities. This makes for these pieces to be some of the most valuable transporters available on the market.

	Lo	Hi
Bill Elliott	125.00	225.00
Coors '90		
Bob Gerhart	175.00	300.00
ARCA '88		
Sterling Marlin	60.00	100.00
Sunoco '90		
Stanley Smith	90.00	150.00

	Lo	Hi
Hamilton Trucking '88		
Rick Wilson	200.00	350.00
Kodak Ford '87		
Rick Wilson	300.00	500.00
Kodak Mack '87		

Winross Transporters 1:64 1991

Winross continued there series of 1:64 transporters in 1991. They issued three different Bill Elliott transporters that year along with their first Richard Petty piece.

	Lo	Hi
Ken Bouchard	40.00	75.00
ADAP		
Bill Elliott	75.00	125.00
Coors Light		
Bill Elliott	50.00	100.00
Fan Club		
Bill Elliott	50.00	100.00
Museum with Blue Paint scheme		
T.Ellis	100.00	175.00
Polaroid		
Terry Labonte	90.00	160.00
Sunoco		
Richard Petty	100.00	175.00
STP		
Ken Schrader	50.00	90.00
Kodiak		

Winross Transporters 1:64 1992

Winross produced serveral special issue transporters in their 1992 series. Dale Earnhardt was the focus of two of these speicals having one produced for White Rose Collectibles and another one produced and packagaed in a wooden box.

	Lo	Hi
Junie Donlavey	50.00	90.00
Truxmore		
Bill Elliott	50.00	90.00
Fan Club		
Bill Elliott	50.00	90.00
Museum with red paint scheme		
Dale Earnhardt	90.00	150.00
Goodwrench		
produced for White Rose Collectibles		
Dale Earnhardt# Goodwrench	175.00	300.00
in Wooden box		
T.Ellis	50.00	90.00
Polaroid		
Bobby Hamilton	30.00	60.00
Country Time		
Terry Labonte	40.00	75.00
Sunoco		
Tiny Lund	40.00	75.00
Jeff McClure	50.00	90.00
Superior Performance		
J.D. McDuffie	40.00	75.00
Son's Auto		
Phil Parsons	50.00	90.00
Kyle Petty	50.00	90.00
Mello Yello		
Richard Petty	50.00	100.00
STP Fan Appreciation Tour		
Robert Pressley	90.00	180.00
Alliance		
Glenn (Fireball) Roberts	40.00	75.00
Darrell Waltrip	50.00	90.00
Western Auto		
Darrell Waltrip	75.00	125.00
Western Auto		
with Red paint scheme		

Winross Transporters 1:64 1993

This series of Winross transporters is highlighted by a piece of the late Alan Kulwicki. The series also includes the third year in a row that Winross produced a piece for the Bill Elliott Fan Club.

	Lo	Hi
Joe Bessey	25.00	50.00
AC Delco		
Bill Elliott	40.00	75.00
Fan Club		
Doyle Ford	40.00	75.00
NASCAR Flags		
Jeff Gordon	50.00	90.00
DuPont		
Steve Grissom	25.00	50.00
Channellock		
Dale Jarrett	30.00	60.00
Interstate Batteries		
Alan Kulwicki	75.00	140.00
Hooter's		
Sterling Marlin	30.00	60.00
Maxwell House		
Mark Martin	40.00	75.00
Valvoline		
Robert Pressley	50.00	90.00
Alliance		
Mike Stefanik	25.00	50.00
Auto Palace		
No Driver Association	75.00	125.00
Mcclure Racing Kodak		

Winross Transporters 1:64 1994

This series features a variation on the Davey Allison piece. The sponsors name was misspelled on the original pieces produced.

	Lo	Hi
Davey Allison	75.00	125.00
Havoline misspelled Error		
Davey Allison	60.00	100.00
Havoline Corrected		
Bill Elliott	40.00	75.00
Budweiser		
Harry Gant	50.00	90.00
Farewell Tour		
Goodyear Racing	25.00	50.00
Terry Labonte	40.00	75.00
Kellogg's		
Sterling Marlin	30.00	60.00
Kodak		
Michael Waltrip	30.00	60.00
Pennzoil		

Winross Transporters 1:64 1995

This was the first series of transporters released under Winross' new price structure. The series features Bill Elliott's new McDonald's colors and Dale Jarrett sporting the colors of Mac Tools, his Busch ride at the time.

	Lo	Hi
Geoff Bodine	35.00	60.00
Exide		
Bill Elliott	40.00	70.00
McDonald's		
Dale Jarrett	35.00	60.00
Mac Tools		
Kevin LePage	35.00	60.00
Vermont Teddy Bear		
DickTrickle	35.00	60.00
Quality Care		
Mike Wallace	35.00	60.00
Heilig-Meyers		

Winross Transporters 1:64 1996

This series features the first David Green Caterpillar transporter.

	Lo	Hi
Ward Burton	30.00	45.00
MBNA		
David Green	30.00	45.00
Caterpillar		
Ernie Irvan	45.00	60.00
Havoline		
Sterling Marlin	35.00	50.00
Kodak		
Michael Waltrip	35.00	50.00
Citgo		

1995-1998 Action/RCCA Dragsters 1:24

This series of dragsters started with the Mac Tools releases at the beginning of 1995. The first pieces all featured a Mac Tools logo and the most difficult of all the dragsters to find. The 1997 and 1998 RCCA upgrade pieces contain serial numbers on the chassis of each car.

	Lo	Hi
Joe Amato	30.00	60.00
Keystone 1996		
Joe Amato	30.00	60.00
Keystone 1997		
Joe Amato	40.00	70.00
Keystone 1997 Mac Tools		
Joe Amato	35.00	60.00
Tenneco		
Joe Amato	40.00	70.00
Tenneco Mac Tools		
Joe Amato	45.00	80.00
Tenneco RCCA		
Joe Amato	40.00	65.00
Valvoline		
Joe Amato	350.00	500.00
Valvoline Mac Tools		
Shelly Anderson	60.00	100.00
Parts America		
Shelly Anderson	30.00	60.00
Western Auto		
Mike Austin	30.00	80.00
Red Wing		
Pat Austin	30.00	60.00
Castrol Syntex		
Kenny Bernstein	50.00	90.00
Budweiser 1992 300 MPH		
Kenny Bernstein	60.00	100.00
Bud 1992 300 MPH Mac Tools		
Kenny Bernstein	90.00	150.00
Budweiser 1995		
Kenny Bernstein	200.00	300.00
Budweiser 1995 Mac Tools		
Kenny Bernstein	60.00	90.00
Budweiser 1996		
Kenny Bernstein	80.00	130.00
Budweiser 1996		
part of 3 car Mac Tools Champions set		
Kenny Bernstein	35.00	70.00
Budweiser 1997		
Kenny Bernstein	60.00	100.00
Budweiser 1997 Mac Tools		
Kenny Bernstein	70.00	110.00
Budweiser 1997 RCCA		
Kenny Bernstein	50.00	80.00
Budwiser 1998		
Kenny Bernstein	60.00	90.00
Budwiser 1998 Mac Tools		
Kenny Bernstein	60.00	100.00
Budweiser 1998 RCCA		
Kenny Bernstein	50.00	90.00
Bud Lizard 1998		
Kenny Bernstein	60.00	100.00
Bud Lizard 1998 Mac Tools		
Larry Dixon	200.00	300.00
Miller Genuine Draft		
Larry Dixon	75.00	125.00

Miller Genuine Draft 1996
Larry Dixon 50.00 100.00
Miller Genuine Draft
with Silver Paint scheme
Larry Dixon 45.00 80.00
Miller Lite
Larry Dixon 50.00 80.00
Miller Lite 1998
Mike Dunn 400.00 600.00
La Victoria Mac Tools
Mike Dunn 25.00 50.00
Mopar
Don Garlits 40.00 80.00
Kendall
Gator Nationals 350.00 500.00
Mac Tools 1995
Gator Nationals 90.00 160.00
Mac Tools 1996
Gator Nationals 60.00 100.00
Mac Tools 1997
Gator Nationals 50.00 90.00
Mac Tools 1998
Darrell Gwynn 40.00 80.00
Budweiser
Darrell Gwynn 90.00 150.00
Coors Light/Kendall
Darrell Gwynn 60.00 90.00
Coors Light/Quaker State
Darrell Gwynn 60.00 100.00
Mopar Mac Tools
Frank Hawley 45.00 75.00
Coors Light
Jim Head 35.00 60.00
Close Call
Jim Head 65.00 90.00
Close Call RCCA
Jim Head 300.00 400.00
Smokin' Joe's
Doug Herbert 35.00 60.00
Snap-On
Eddie Hill 65.00 100.00
Pennzoil Super Shops 1988
Eddie Hill 50.00 80.00
Pennzoil 1995
Eddie Hill 40.00 65.00
Pennzoil 1997
Eddie Hill 45.00 70.00
Pennzoil 1998
Blaine Johnson 125.00 175.00
Travers
Blue and Yellow paint scheme
Blaine Johnson 75.00 125.00
Travers
Red and White paint scheme
Tommy Johnson Jr. 30.00 60.00
Mopar
Connie Kalitta 25.00 50.00
American
Scott Kalitta 25.00 50.00
American
Scott Kalitta 50.00 90.00
American 1997 Mac Tools
Scott Kalitta 60.00 100.00
American 1997 RCCA
Chris Karamesines 30.00 60.00
The Greek
Cory McClenathan 60.00 90.00
MacAttack
Cory McClenathan 30.00 60.00
McDonald's 1995
Cory McClenathan 40.00 70.00
McDonald's 1997
Cory McClenathan 35.00 60.00
McDonald's 1998
Cory McClenathan 45.00 75.00
McDonald's 1998 RCCA
Cory McClenathan 30.00 60.00
McDonald's Olympic
Tom McEwen 30.00 80.00
Mobil
Matco Supernationals 1997 .... 60.00 100.00
Shirley Muldowney 1995 .... 80.00 110.00
Shirley Muldowney 40.00 100.00
Action 1996 RCCA
Shirley Muldowney 45.00 75.00
Action 1997
Shirley Muldowney 60.00 100.00
Action 1997 Mac Tools
Shirley Muldowney 60.00 100.00
Action 1997 RCCA
Shirley Muldowney 35.00 60.00
Otter Pops
Gary Ornsby 70.00 100.00
Castrol GTX
Cristen Powell 50.00 80.00
Reebok
Cristen Powell 40.00 80.00
Reebok Orange
Cristen Powell 60.00 100.00
Reebok RCCA
Cristen Powell 35.00 60.00
Royal Purple
Don Prudhomme 45.00 70.00
Pepsi Challenge
Don Prudhomme 55.00 90.00
Pepsi Challenge Mac Tools
Don Prudhomme 90.00 150.00
Skoal Bandit
Don Prudhomme 125.00 200.00
Snake First Strike
Don Prudhomme 200.00 300.00
Snake Mac Tools
B.Reichert 50.00 90.00
Bars Leak
Bruce Sarver 35.00 60.00
CarQuest
Gary Scelzi 60.00 100.00
Winston 1997
Gary Scelzi 65.00 100.00
Winston 1997 Mac Tools
Gary Scelzi 75.00 125.00
Winston 1997 RCCA
Gary Scelzi 55.00 90.00
Winston 1998
Gary Scelzi 65.00 100.00
Winston 1998 RCCA
A.Segrini 35.00 60.00
Spies Hecker
Bob Vandergriff 30.00 60.00
Jerzees 1995
Bob Vandergriff 35.00 70.00
Jerzees 1997
Bob Vandergriff 60.00 100.00
Jerzees 1997 Mac Tools

1997-1998 Action/RCCA Dragsters 1:64

This series started in 1997 and is highlight by two Blaine Johnson issues.

Lo Hi
Joe Amato 6.00 12.00
Keystone 1997
Joe Amato 6.00 12.00
Tenneco
Kenny Bernstein 15.00 25.00
Budweiser 1992 RCCA
Kenny Bernstein 6.00 15.00
Budweiser 1997
Kenny Bernstein 7.50 15.00
Budweiser 1998
Kenny Bernstein 10.00 20.00
Budweiser 1998 RCCA
Kenny Bernstein 6.00 15.00
Bud Louie 1998
Kenny Bernstein 10.00 20.00
Bud Louie 1998 RCCA
Larry Dixon 10.00 25.00
Miller Lite
packaged in acrylic case
Larry Dixon 15.00 25.00
Miller Lite 1998 Acrylic
Gator Nationals 10.00 20.00
Mac Tools 1997
Jim Head 6.00 12.00
Close Call
Eddie Hill 6.00 12.00
Pennzoil 1997
Blaine Johnson 7.50 15.00
Travers
Blue and Yellow paint scheme
Blaine Johnson 10.00 20.00
Travers Blue/Yellow RCCA
Blaine Johnson 6.00 12.00
Travers
Red and White paint scheme
Blane Johnson 15.00 25.00
Travers Red/White RCCA
Cory McClenathan 6.00 12.00
McDonalds 1997
Cory McClenathan 10.00 20.00
McDonald's 1997 RCCA
Cory McClenathan 6.00 12.00
McDonald's 1998
Cory McClenathan 10.00 20.00
McDonald's 1998 RCCA
Shirley Muldowney 6.00 12.00
Action 1997
Shirley Muldowney 6.00 12.00
Otter Pops 1991
Cristen Powell 6.00 12.00
Reebok
Cristen Powell 10.00 20.00
Reebok RCCA
Cristen Powell 6.00 12.00
Royal Purple
Gary Scelzi 9.00 18.00
Winston 1997
Gary Scelzi 9.00 18.00
Winston 1998
Gary Scelzi 10.00 20.00
Winston 1998 RCCA

1996-1998 Action/RCCA Funny Car 1:24

This series of Funny Cars is highlighted by the fifteen John Force issues and the Whit Bazemore Smokin' Joe's piece. The Gator Nationals pieces have also been very popular. The 1997 and 1998 RCCA upgrade pieces contain serial numbers on the chassis of each car.

	Lo	Hi
Randy Anderson	35.00	60.00
Parts America		
Pat Austin	30.00	50.00
Red Wing Shoes		
Whit Bazemore	35.00	60.00
Fast Orange 1995		
Whit Bazemore	35.00	60.00
Mobil 1 1993		
Whit Bazemore	40.00	70.00
Mobil 1 1995		
Whit Bazemore	50.00	80.00
Mobil 1 1995 RCCA		
Whit Bazemore	90.00	150.00
Smokin' Joe's		
Whit Bazemore	40.00	80.00
Winston		
Whit Bazemore	70.00	110.00
Winston 1997 RCCA		
Whit Bazemore	50.00	90.00
Winston 1998		
Whit Bazemore	70.00	120.00
Winston 1998 RCCA		
Raymond Beadle	40.00	65.00
Blue Max		
Kenny Bernstein	40.00	70.00
Budweiser Plymouth		
Kenny Bernstein	70.00	100.00
Budweiser 1988 Buick		
Kenny Berstein	70.00	100.00
Budweiser		
Kenny Bernstein	70.00	100.00
Chelsea King 1979 RCCA		
Ron Capps	55.00	90.00
Copenhagen		
Ron Capps	60.00	100.00
Copenhagen Mac Tools		
Gary Densham	25.00	50.00
NEC		
Mike Dunn	35.00	60.00
Pisano		
Jim Epler	25.00	50.00
Rug Doctor		
Chuck Etchells	35.00	60.00
Kendall		
John Force	35.00	60.00
Brute Force 1977		
Blue paint scheme		
John Force	35.00	60.00
Brute Force 1978		
Orange paint scheme		
John Force	45.00	90.00
Castrol GTX/Jolly Rancher		
Olds 1993		
John Force	70.00	120.00
Castrol GTX Flames 1994		
John Force	50.00	80.00
Castrol GTX 1996		
John Force	150.00	250.00
Castrol GTX Black 1996		
John Force	90.00	150.00
Castrol GTX Mac Tools 1996		
John Force	100.00	150.00
Castrol GTX 1996		
part of 3 car Mac Tools champions set		
John Force	40.00	65.00
Castrol GTX Driver of the Year 1997		
John Force	60.00	90.00
Castrol GTX Driver of the Year 1997 RCCA		
John Force	50.00	80.00
Castrol GTX Driver of the Year 1997 Mac Tools		
John Force	40.00	65.00
Castrol GTX Mustang 1997		
John Force	50.00	80.00
Castrol GTX Mustang 1997 Mac Tools		
John Force	65.00	100.00
Castrol GTX Mustang 1997 RCCA		
John Force	30.00	60.00
Castrol GTX Pontiac 1997		
John Force	60.00	90.00
Castrol GTX Pontiac 1997 RCCA		
John Force	50.00	80.00
Castrol GTX/Elvis 1998 RCCA		
John Force	60.00	90.00
Castrol GTX Elvis Mac Tools		
John Force	65.00	100.00
Castrol GTX Elvis RCCA		
John Force	45.00	80.00
Castrol GTX 1998		
John Force	55.00	90.00
Castrol GTX 1998 Mac Tools		
John Force	60.00	100.00
Castrol GTX 1998 RCCA		
John Force	50.00	90.00
Castrol GTX 7-Time Champ		
Gator Nationals	80.00	110.00
Mac Tools 1996		
Gator Nationals	60.00	90.00
Mac Tools 1997		
Gator Nationals Mac Tools 1998	50.00	90.00
Al Hoffman	40.00	65.00
GM Performance		
Al Hoffman	25.00	50.00
Parts America		
Tom Hoover	35.00	60.00
Pioneer		
Tom Hoover	35.00	60.00
Pioneer 1998		
Tom Hoover	40.00	70.00
Showtime 1975		
Bruce Larsen	35.00	70.00
Sentry		
Bruce Larsen	40.00	70.00
USA-1		
Bruce Larsen	55.00	90.00
USA-1 RCCA		
Ed McCulloch	40.00	100.00
Miller		
Ed McCulloch	30.00	60.00
Otter Pops		
Matco Supernationals 1997	60.00	100.00
Kenji Okazaki	35.00	60.00
Mooneyes 1996		
Kenji Okazaki	35.00	60.00
Mooneyes '97		
Cruz Pedregon	40.00	75.00
Interstate Batteries		
Cruz Pedregon	40.00	75.00
Interstate Batteries Small Soldiers		
Curz Pedregon	45.00	80.00
Interstate Batteries Small Soldiers RCCA		
Cruz Pedregon	50.00	85.00
Interstate Batteries Small Soldiers Mac Tools		
Cruz Pedregon	60.00	90.00
McDonald's 1996		
Cruz Pedregon	30.00	60.00
McDonald's 1997		
Cruz Pedregon	35.00	70.00
McDonald's 1997 RCCA		
Tony Pedregon	30.00	60.00
Castrol GTX		
Tony Pedregon	55.00	90.00
Castrol GTX RCCA		
Tony Pedregon	40.00	70.00
Castrol Selena		
Tony Pedregon	40.00	75.00
Castrol Syntec		
Tony Pedregon	45.00	80.00
Castrol Syntec RCCA		
Don Prudhomme	50.00	80.00
Army 1975		
Don Prudhomme	60.00	90.00
Army 1975 RCCA		
Don Prudhomme	45.00	70.00
Pepsi 1983		
Dean Skuza	50.00	90.00
Matco 1997		
Dean Skuza	50.00	90.00
Matco 1998		
Dean Skuza	50.00	90.00
Matco Texas 1998		
Jerry Toliver	50.00	80.00
Mad		
Jerry Toliver	50.00	80.00
Spy vs. Spy		
Jerry Toliver/Spy vs. Spy RCCA	60.00	90.00

1996-1998 Action/RCCA Funny Car 1:64

This series of Funny Cars is highlighted by the eleven John Force issues and the Whit Bazemore Smokin' Joe's piece. The Gator Nationals pieces have also been very popular.

	Lo	Hi
Randy Anderson	6.00	12.00
Parts America		
Pat Austin	6.00	12.00
Red Wing		
Whit Bazemore	6.00	12.00
Fast Orange 1995		
Whit Bazemore	6.00	12.00
Mobil 1 1995		
Whit Bazemore	6.00	15.00
Winston		
Whit Bazemore	12.50	25.00
Winston RCCA		
Whit Bazemore	9.00	18.00
Winston 1998		
Whit Bazemore	12.50	25.00
Winston 1998 RCCA		
Raymond Beadle	6.00	12.00
Blue Max		
Kenny Bernstein	12.50	25.00
Budweiser 1987 Buick RCCA		
Kenny Bernstein	6.00	12.00
Budweiser 1988		
Kenny Bernstein	8.00	16.00
Budweiser Plymouth		
Kenny Bernstein	8.00	16.00
Chelsea King 1979		
Ron Capps	10.00	20.00
Copenhagen		
Gary Densham	6.00	12.00
NEC		
Mike Dunn	6.00	12.00
Pisano		
Jim Epler	6.00	12.00
Rug Doctor		
John Force	8.00	16.00
Brute Force 1977		
Blue paint scheme		
John Force	12.50	25.00
Brute Force 1977 RCCA		
Blue paint scheme		
John Force	6.00	15.00
Brute Force Orange 1978		
John Force	6.00	15.00
Castrol GTX/Jolly Rancher Olds 1993		
John Force	9.00	18.00
Castrol GTX 1994		
John Force	9.00	18.00
Castrol GTX 1996		
John Force	15.00	25.00
Castrol GTX 1996		
Black paint scheme		
John Force	15.00	25.00
Castrol GTX 1996 Mac Tools		
Black paint scheme		
John Force	6.00	15.00
Castrol GTX Driver of the Year 1997		
John Force	15.00	30.00
Castrol GTX Driver of the Year 1997 RCCA		
John Force	9.00	18.00
Castrol GTX Mustang 1997		
John Force	9.00	18.00
Castrol GTX Pontiac 1997		
John Force	10.00	20.00
Castrol GTX Elvis		
John Force	12.50	25.00
Castrol GTX Elvis MT		
John Force	12.50	25.00
Castrol GTX Elvis RCCA		
John Force	7.50	15.00
Castrol GTX 1998		
John Force	10.00	20.00
Castrol GTX 1998 RCCA		
John Force	9.00	18.00
Castrol GTX 7-Time Champ		
Gator Nationals	12.50	25.00
Mac Tools 1997		
Al Hoffman	6.00	12.00
GM Performance		
Al Hoffman	6.00	12.00
Parts America		

	Lo	Hi
Tom Hoover Pioneer	6.00	12.00
Bruce Larsen Sentry	6.00	12.00
Bruce Larsen USA-1	6.00	12.00
Ed McCulloch Miller Acrylic	6.00	15.00
Ed McCulloch Otter Pops	6.00	12.00
Kenji Okazaki Mooneyes	6.00	12.00
Cruz Pedregon Interstate Batteries	6.00	12.00
Cruz Pedregon Interstate Batteries Small Soldiers	6.00	12.00
Cruz Pedregon Interstate Batteries Small Soldiers RCCA	7.50	15.00
Cruz Pedregon McDonald's	6.00	12.00
Tony Pedregon Castrol GTX	6.00	12.00
Tony Pedregon Castrol Selena	6.00	12.00
Tony Pedregon Castrol Syntec	6.00	12.00
Tony Pedregon Castrol Syntec RCCA	7.50	15.00
Don Prudhomme Army 1975	6.00	15.00
Don Prudhomme Pepsi 1983	6.00	12.00
Jerry Toliver Mad	6.00	12.00
Jerry Toliver/Spy vs. Spy	6.00	12.00

1997-1998 Action/RCCA Pro Stock 1:24

This series of cars marks the entry of Action into the Pro Stock division of the NHRA. The series is highlighted by the RCCA pieces in which each chassis is serial numbered. The RCCA pieces also contain more detail than there Action counterparts.

	Lo	Hi
Darrell Alderman Mopar 1997	30.00	60.00
Darrell Alderman Mopar Mac Tools	50.00	80.00
Darrell Alderman Mopar RCCA	40.00	80.00
Darrell Alderman Mopar 1998	35.00	60.00
Bruce Allen Slick 50	30.00	60.00
Bruce Allen Slick 50 RCCA	40.00	80.00
Jerry Eckman Pennzoil	30.00	60.00
Gator Nationals Mac Tools 1997	50.00	90.00
Gator Nationals Mac Tools '98	50.00	90.00
Scott Geoffion Mopar	30.00	60.00
Scott Geoffion Mopar Mac Tools	50.00	80.00
Scott Geoffion Mopar RCCA	40.00	80.00
Scott Geoffion Mopar 1998	35.00	60.00
Bob Glidden Quality Care	30.00	60.00
Bob Glidden Quality Care RCCA	40.00	80.00
Roy Hill Hill's Drag Racing School	30.00	60.00
Roy Hill Hill's Racing School RCCA	40.00	80.00
Allen Johnson Amoco	30.00	60.00
Kurt Johnson AC Delco	30.00	60.00
Kurt Johnson AC Delco RCCA	40.00	80.00
Warren Johnson GM Performance	30.00	60.00
Warren Johnson GM Performance RCCA	40.00	80.00
Warren Johnson GM Performance Parts 1995	40.00	70.00
Warren Johnson GM Performance Parts 1995 RCCA	50.00	85.00
Warren Johnson GM Plus	30.00	60.00
Warren Johnson GM Plus RCCA	40.00	80.00
Tom Martino Six Flags 1997	40.00	70.00
Tom Martino Six Flags 1998	40.00	70.00
Matco Supernationals 1997	55.00	90.00
Larry Morgan Raybestos	30.00	60.00
Larry Morgan Raybestos RCCA	40.00	80.00
Mark Pawuk Summit Racing	30.00	60.00
Mark Pawuk Summitt RCCA	40.00	80.00
Rickie Smith Carrier	30.00	60.00
Rickie Smith Carrier RCCA	40.00	80.00
Jim Yates McDonald's	30.00	60.00
Jim Yates McDonald's RCCA	40.00	80.00

1997-1998 Action/RCCA Pro Stock 1:64

This series of cars marks the entry of Action into the Pro Stock division of the NHRA. The series is highlighted by the RCCA pieces in which each chassis is serial numbered. The RCCA pieces also contain more detail than there Action counterparts.

	Lo	Hi
Bruce Allen Slick 50	6.00	12.00
Bruce Allen Slick 50 RCCA	10.00	20.00
Darrell Alderman Mopar	6.00	12.00
Darrell Alderman Mopar RCCA	10.00	20.00
Jerry Eckman Pennzoil	6.00	12.00
Gator Nationals Mac Tools 1997	12.50	25.00
Scott Geoffrion Mopar	6.00	12.00
Scott Geoffion Mopar RCCA	10.00	20.00
Bob Gliddoen Quality Care	6.00	12.00
Bob Gliddoen Quality Care RCCA	10.00	20.00
Allen Johnson Amoco	6.00	12.00
Kurt Johnson AC Delco	6.00	12.00
Warren Johnson GM Performance	6.00	12.00
Warren Johnson GM Performance RCCA	10.00	20.00
Warren Johnson GM Plus	6.00	12.00
Warren Johnson GM Plus RCCA	10.00	20.00
Larry Morgan Raybestos	6.00	12.00
Mark Pawuk Summit Racing	6.00	12.00
Rickie Smith Carrier	6.00	12.00
Rickie Smith Carrier RCCA	10.00	20.00
Jim Yates McDonald's	6.00	12.00
Jim Yates McDonald's RCCA	10.00	20.00

1995-1998 Action/RCCA NHRA Transporters 1:64

This series of die-cast pieces features the trucks and transporters that haul the cars from race to race. The first piece released in this series was the Gator Nationals promotional piece.

	Lo	Hi
Joe Amato Valvoline Mac Tools	50.00	90.00
John Force Castrol GTX Prevost Bus	40.00	70.00
John Force Castrol GTX Mac Tools	125.00	200.00
John Force Castrol GTX 1997 Mac Tools	70.00	100.00
Gator Nationals Mac Tools 1995	250.00	350.00
Gator Nationals Mac Tools 1996	70.00	110.00
Gator Nationals Mac Tools 1997	60.00	90.00
Bob Glidden Quality Care Mac Tools	70.00	110.00
Matco Supernationals 1997	60.00	100.00

1995 Racing Champions Dragsters 1:24

This was Racing Champions first 1:24 Dragster issue. Former Winston NHRA Top Fuel Champions Joe Amato and Eddie Hill are a couple of the featured drivers.

	Lo	Hi
Joe Amato Valvoline	20.00	40.00
Shelly Anderson Western Auto	25.00	40.00
Eddie Hill Pennzoil	25.00	40.00
Doug Herbert Snap On	25.00	40.00
Tommy Johnson Jr. Mopar	25.00	40.00
Cory McClenathan McDonald's	25.00	40.00

1996 Racing Champions Dragsters 1:24

This was the second year that Racing Champions released 1:24 scale Dragsters. The most expensive and desired piece in the series is that of Blaine Johnson.

	Lo	Hi
Joe Amato Valvoline	15.00	30.00
Shelly Anderson Parts America	15.00	30.00
B.Blair Fugowie! Lost Tribe	15.00	30.00
Ron Capps RPR	15.00	30.00
Chuck Etchells Kendall	15.00	30.00
R.Fuller Montana Express	15.00	30.00
Gator Nationals	15.00	30.00
S.Gorr Greer Motorsports	15.00	30.00
Rhonda Hartman Hartman Enterprises	15.00	30.00
Doug Herbert Snap On	15.00	30.00
Eddie Hill Pennzoil	15.00	30.00
Blaine Johnson Travers	25.00	50.00

	Lo	Hi
L.Jones	20.00	40.00
Matco		
Connie Kalitta	20.00	30.00
American		
Scott Kalitta	15.00	30.00
American		
Cory McClenathan	15.00	30.00
McDonald's		
Cory McClenathan	15.00	30.00
McDonald's Olympic		
Rance McDaniel	15.00	30.00
La Bac Systems		
Jack Ostrander	15.00	30.00
Vista Food		
Bruce Sarver	15.00	30.00
Carquest		
Bob Vandergriff	15.00	30.00
Jerzees		
Winter Nationals	15.00	30.00

1997 Racing Champions Dragsters 1:24

This was the third year that Racing Champions released 1:24 scale Dragsters. The most expensive and desired piece in the series is that of Blaine Johnson. All the other piece are priced sale for relatively the same price.

	Lo	Hi
Joe Amato	15.00	30.00
Keystone		
Shelly Anderson	15.00	30.00
Parts America		
Jim Epler	15.00	30.00
Rug Doctor		
Doug Foxworth	15.00	30.00
Havoc		
S.Gorr	15.00	30.00
Greer Motorsports		
Doug Grubnik	15.00	30.00
Geronimo		
Rhonda Hartman	15.00	30.00
Hartman Racing		
Jim Head	15.00	30.00
Close Call		
Doug Herbert	15.00	30.00
Snap On		
Eddie Hill	15.00	30.00
Pennzoil		
Eddie Hill	20.00	40.00
Pennzoil Matco		
Blaine Johnson	25.00	40.00
Travers		
Connie Kalitta	15.00	30.00
American		
Scott Kalitta	15.00	30.00
American		
Cory McClenathan	15.00	30.00
McDonald's		
Randy Parks	35.00	50.00
Fluke		
Cristen Powell	15.00	30.00
CP Racing		
Cristen Powell	15.00	35.00
Royal Purple		
Bruce Sarver	15.00	30.00
Carquest		
Tony Schumacher	15.00	30.00
Peek Brothers		
J.Shoemaker	15.00	30.00
American Eagle		
Paul Smith	15.00	30.00
Smith Racing School		
Bobby Taylor	15.00	30.00
Turner Racing		
Marshall Topping	15.00	30.00
Montana Express		
Bob Vandergriff	15.00	30.00
Jerzees		

1998 Racing Champions Dragsters 1:24

This was the fourth year that Racing Champions released 1:24 scale Dragsters.

	Lo	Hi
Jim Head	12.00	30.00
Close Call		
D.Herbert	12.00	30.00
Snap On		
L.Meirsch	12.00	30.00
Powermate		
Cristen Powell	12.00	30.00
Reebok		
P.Romaine	12.00	30.00
CarQuest		
Bob Vandergriff	12.00	30.00
Jerzees		

1996 Racing Champions Dragsters 1:64

This was the first isssue of a Racing Champions 1:64 scale Dragster. The series is lead by the Blaine Johnson Travers piece. There was also a four pack available. There are many different combination of Dragsters that could be found in those four packs.

	Lo	Hi
Joe Amato	4.00	10.00
Keystone		
Shelly Anderson	4.00	10.00
Parts America		
B.Blair	4.00	10.00
Fugowie! Lost Tribe		
Ron Capps	4.00	10.00
RPR		
R.Fuller	4.00	10.00
Montana Express		
S.Gorr	4.00	10.00
Greer Motorsports		
Rhonda Hartman	4.00	10.00
Hartman Enterprises		
Doug Herbert	4.00	10.00
Snap On		
Eddie Hill	4.00	10.00
Pennzoil		
Blaine Johnson	7.50	15.00
Travers		
L.Jones	6.00	12.00
Matco		
Connie Kalitta	4.00	10.00
American		
Scott Kalitta	4.00	10.00
American		
Cory McClenathan	4.00	10.00
McDonald's		
Cory McClenathan	4.00	10.00
McDonald's Olympic		
R.McDaniel	4.00	10.00
La Bac Systems		
Jack Ostrander	4.00	10.00
Vista Food		
Bruce Sarver	4.00	10.00
CarQuest		
U.S.Nationals	4.00	10.00
Bob Vandergriff	4.00	10.00
Jerzees		
4 Car Drag Set	18.00	25.00
There are numerous four car combinations		

1997 Racing Champions Dragsters 1:64

Racing Champions returned their 1:64 Dragster line in 1997. The series features former Winston NHRA Champions Joe Amato and Scott Kalitta.

	Lo	Hi
Joe Amato	4.00	10.00
Keystone		
Shelly Anderson	4.00	10.00
Parts America		
Jim Epler	4.00	10.00
Rug Doctor		
Spike Gorr	4.00	10.00
Greer Motorsports		
Doug Grubnik	4.00	10.00
Geronimo		
Rhonda Hartman	4.00	10.00
Hartman Racing		
Jim Head	4.00	10.00
Close Call		
Doug Herbert	4.00	10.00
Snap On		
Eddie Hill	6.00	12.00
Pennzoil Matco		
Connie Kallita	4.00	10.00
American		
Scott Kalitta	4.00	10.00
American		
Randy Parks	4.00	10.00
Fluke		
Cristen Powell	4.00	10.00
Powell Racing		
Bruce Sarver	4.00	10.00
Carquest		
Tony Schumacher	4.00	10.00
Peek Brothers		
John Shoemaker	4.00	10.00
American Eagle		
Paul Smith	4.00	10.00
Roy Smith Racing School		
Bobby Taylor	4.00	10.00
Turner Racing		
Marshall Topping	4.00	10.00
Montana Express		
Bob Vandergriff	4.00	10.00
Jerzees		

1995-1996 Racing Champions Funny Car 1:24

This is the first 1:24 scale Funny Car series to hit the market. Racing Champions distributed the pieces through both hobby and retail outlets. The cars come in a red and black box.

	Lo	Hi
Randy Anderson	15.00	30.00
Parts America		
Whit Bazemore	15.00	30.00
Mobil 1		
Gary Bolger	15.00	30.00
Creasy		
Jerry Caminito	15.00	30.00
Blue Thunder		
Gary Clapshaw	15.00	30.00
Fuelish Pleasure		
Jim Epler	15.00	30.00
Rug Doctor		
Gator Nationals	15.00	30.00
Al Hoffman	15.00	30.00
Parts America		
Tom Hoover	15.00	30.00
Pioneer		
Kenji Okazaki	15.00	30.00
Mooneyes		
Cruz Pedregon	15.00	30.00
McDonald's		
Tony Pedregon	15.00	30.00
Geronimo		
Wyatt Radke	15.00	30.00
Nitro Bandit		
T.Simpson	15.00	30.00
Simpson Racing		
Dean Skuza	20.00	40.00
Matco		
U.S. Nationals	15.00	30.00
T.Wilkerson	15.00	30.00
NAPA		
Winter Nationals	15.00	30.00
Del Worsham	15.00	30.00
Worsham Fink		

1997 Racing Champions Funny Car 1:24

This was the third year for Racing Champions to release the 1:24 scale Funny Car series. A couple of regulars on the Alcohol Funny Car circuit Randy Anderson and Tony Bartone are in the set. 1997 saw Randy Anderson move up to Top Fuel.

	Lo	Hi
Randy Anderson Parts America	15.00	30.00
Tony Bartone Bartone Racing	15.00	30.00
Tony Bartone Quaker State	15.00	30.00
Gary Bolger Creasy	15.00	30.00
Jim Dunn Mooneyes	15.00	30.00
Chuck Etchells Kendall	15.00	30.00
Rhonda Hartman Geronimo	15.00	30.00
Ray Higley Red Line Oil	15.00	30.00
Tom Hoover Pioneer	15.00	30.00
Frank Manzo Kendall	15.00	30.00
Vern Moats Mopar	15.00	30.00
Cruz Pedregon McDonald's	15.00	30.00
Joe Penland Penland Racing	15.00	30.00
John Powell Etterman Racing	15.00	30.00
Von Smith Atomic City Tools	15.00	30.00
Dean Skuza Matco 1994	20.00	40.00
Dean Skuza Matco 1994 Gold	125.00	250.00
Dean Skuza Matco 1997	20.00	40.00
Tim Wilkerson NAPA	15.00	30.00
Del Worsham CSK	15.00	30.00

1998 Racing Champions Funny Car 1:24

This was the fourth year for Racing Champions to release the 1:24 scale Funny Car series.

	Lo	Hi
Randy Anderson Parts America	12.00	30.00
B.Burkett Burkett-Mopar	12.00	30.00
J.Epler East Care	12.00	30.00
B.Fanning Udder Nonsense	12.00	30.00
Al Hoffman Hoffman Racing	12.00	30.00
Tom Hoover Pioneer	12.00	30.00
F.Manzo Kendall	12.00	30.00
Cruz Pedregon Interstate Batteries	12.00	30.00

1996 Racing Champions Funny Car 1:64

This was the first year that Racing Champions did a 1:64 scale Funny Car. The only Winston Nitro Funny Car champion in 90's beside John Force, Cruz Pedregon (1992) is in the series.

	Lo	Hi
Randy Anderson Parts America	4.00	10.00
Gary Bolger Creasy	4.00	10.00
Gary Clapshaw Fuelish Pleasure	4.00	10.00
Gary Densham NEC	4.00	10.00
Chuck Etchells Kendall	4.00	10.00
Al Hoffman Parts America	4.00	10.00
Tom Hoover Pioneer	4.00	10.00
V.Moates Mopar	4.00	10.00
Kenji Okazaki Mooneyes	4.00	10.00
Cruz Pedregon McDonald's	4.00	10.00
J.Penland Penland Racing	4.00	10.00
Wyatt Radke Nitro Bandit	4.00	10.00
Dean Skuza Matco	4.00	10.00
T.Wilkerson NAPA	4.00	10.00
Dale Worsham Worsham Fink	4.00	10.00
4 piece Funny Car set There are numerous combinations	18.00	25.00

1997 Racing Champions Funny Car 1:64

Long time Funny Car driver Bunny Burkett is one of the drivers to highlight this series. The cars feature drivers from both the Alcohol and Nitro Funny Car circuits.

	Lo	Hi
Randy Anderson Parts America	4.00	10.00
Tony Bartone Bartone Racing	4.00	10.00
Tony Bartone Quaker State	4.00	10.00
Gary Bolger Creasy	4.00	10.00
Bunny Burkett Burkett Racing	4.00	10.00
Jim Dunn Mooneyes	4.00	10.00
Chuck Etchells Kendall	4.00	10.00
Rhonda Hartman Geronimo	4.00	10.00
Ray Higley Red Line Oil	4.00	10.00
Tom Hoover Pioneer	4.00	10.00
Frank Manzo Kendall	4.00	10.00
Vern Moats Mopar	4.00	10.00
Cruz Pedregon McDonald's	4.00	10.00
Joe Penland Penland Racing	4.00	10.00
John Powell Etterman Racing	4.00	10.00
Von Smith Atomic City Tools	4.00	10.00
Dean Skuza Matco 1994	6.00	12.00
Dean Skuza Matco 1994 Gold	25.00	50.00
Dean Skuza Matco Four Pack	20.00	40.00
Tim Wilkerson NAPA	4.00	10.00
Del Worsham CSK	4.00	10.00

1997 Racing Champions Pro Stock 1:24

Racing Champions expanded its drag racing line to Pro Stockers with this release. The series features former Pro Stock Champions Warren Johnson and Jim Yates.

	Lo	Hi
Troy Coughlin Jeg's	15.00	30.00
Jerry Eckman CSK	15.00	30.00
Mike Edwards Winnebago	15.00	30.00
Ray Franks Franks-Haas	15.00	30.00
Vern Gaines Western Racing	15.00	30.00
Tommy Hammonds Hammonds Racing	15.00	30.00
Chuck Harris Go Racing.com	15.00	30.00
Kurt Johnson AC Delco	15.00	30.00
Warren Johnson GM Performance	15.00	30.00
G.Marnell Marnell Black	15.00	30.00
Tony Martino Martino Racing	15.00	30.00
Larry Morgan Raybestos	15.00	30.00
Mark Osborne MaMa Rosa	15.00	30.00
Mark Pawuk Summit	15.00	30.00
Steve Schmidt Dynagear	15.00	30.00
Mike Thomas Gumout	15.00	30.00
Jim Yates McDonald's	15.00	30.00

1998 Racing Champions Pro Stock 1:24

This was the second year for Racing Champions to release the 1:24 scale Pro Stock series.

	Lo	Hi
G.Marnell Tenneco	12.00	30.00
Tom Martino Six Flags	12.00	30.00
M.Pawuk Summit	12.00	30.00
M.Thomas Gumout	12.00	30.00
Jim Yates Peak-Split Fire	12.00	30.00

1997 Racing Champions Pro Stock 1:64

This was the first year Racing Champions released 1:64 scale series Pro Stock cars. The series is highlighted by the appearance of Warren Johnson and Jim Yates.

	Lo	Hi
Troy Coughlin Jeg's	5.00	10.00
Jerry Eckman CSK	5.00	10.00
Mike Edwards Winnebago	5.00	10.00
Ray Franks Franks-Haas	5.00	10.00
Vern Gaines Western Racing	5.00	10.00

	Lo	Hi
Tommy Hammonds Hammonds Racing	5.00	10.00
Chuck Harris Go Racing.com	5.00	10.00
Kurt Johnson AC Delco	5.00	10.00
Warren Johnson GM Performance	5.00	10.00
Greg Marnell Marnell Black	5.00	10.00
Tony Martino Martino Racing	5.00	10.00
Larry Morgan Raybestos	5.00	10.00
John Nobile Nobile Trucking	5.00	10.00
Mark Osborne MaMa Rosa	5.00	10.00
Mark Pawuk Summit	5.00	10.00
Steve Schmidt Dynagear	5.00	10.00
Mike Thomas Gumout	5.00	10.00
P.Williams Williams Racing	5.00	10.00
Jim Yates McDonald's	5.00	10.00

1998 Revell Dragsters 1:24

This series is the debut of the production of NHRA pieces by Revell.

	Lo	Hi
Joe Amato Tenneco	50.00	80.00
Eddie Hill Pennzoil	60.00	100.00

1998 Revell Pro Stock 1:24

This series is the debut of the production of NHRA pieces by Revell.

	Lo	Hi
Kirt Johnson AC Delco	15.00	50.00
Warren Johnson GM Performance	15.00	50.00

1997-1998 Winner's Circle Dragsters 1:24

This series marks the teaming of Action Performance and Hasbro. This line of cars was produced for and distributed in the mass-market.

	Lo	Hi
Larry Dixon/Don Prudhomme MBNA	10.00	25.00
Mike Dunn Mopar	10.00	25.00
Shirley Muldowney Action	10.00	25.00

1997-1998 Winner's Circle Dragsters 1:64

This series marks the teaming of Action Performance and Hasbro. This line of cars was produced for and distributed in the mass-market.

	Lo	Hi
Larry Dixon/Don Prudhomme MBNA	3.00	8.00
Mike Dunn Mopar	3.00	8.00
Shirley Muldowney Action	3.00	8.00

1997-1998 Winner's Circle Funny Car 1:24

This series marks the teaming of Action Performance and Hasbro. This line of cars was produced for and distributed in the mass-market. It is highlighted by the John Force Lifetime Series.

	Lo	Hi
Pat Austin Red Wing	10.00	25.00
John Force Castrol GTX	15.00	30.00
John Force Castrol GTX Black	15.00	30.00
John Force Castrol GTX Elvis	15.00	30.00

1997-1998 Winner's Circle Funny Car 1:64

This series marks the teaming of Action Performance and Hasbro. This line of cars was produced for and distributed in the mass-market. It is highlighted by the John Force Lifetime Series.

	Lo	Hi
Pat Austin Red Wing	3.00	8.00
John Force Castrol GTX	4.00	10.00
John Force Castrol GTX Black	4.00	10.00
John Force Castrol GTX Elvis	4.00	10.00

Onyx F1 1:18 1995

This was the first year for Onyx to do the 1:18 scale Formula 1 cars. The two teams represented were the Williams team and the Ferrari team. The Williams cars came with an umbrella. There was a variation on who is the sponsor on the umbrella.

	Lo	Hi
5 Damon Hill Rothmans	30.00	50.00
5 Damon Hill Rothmans with Renault Umbrella	30.00	50.00
6 David Coulthard Rothmans with Renault Umbrella	30.00	50.00
6 David Coulthard Rothmans with Rothmans Umbrella	30.00	50.00
27 Jean Alesi Ferrari	30.00	50.00
28 Gerhard Berger Ferrari	30.00	50.00

Onyx F1 1:18 1996

Onyx cut back in its 1996 1:18 line to only include the Williams team. The Jacques Villeneuve is one of his first Formula 1 die-cast pieces.

	Lo	Hi
5 Damon Hill Rothmans	30.00	50.00
6 Jacques Villeneuve Rothmans	30.00	50.00

Onyx F1 1:24 1992

This was the first year for Onyx to do 1:24 scale Formula 1 cars. Williams, Ligier and Ferrari were the three teams represented in the set.

	Lo	Hi
5 Nigel Mansel Canon	16.00	28.00
6 Ricardo Patrese Canon	15.00	25.00
25 Thierry Boutsen Gitanes	15.00	25.00
26 Erik Comas Gitanes	15.00	25.00
27 Jean Alesi Ferrari	15.00	25.00
28 Ivan Capelli Ferrari	15.00	25.00

Onyx F1 1:24 1993

This series of Formula 1 cars was cut down to just two teams Williams-Renault and Benetton-Ford.

	Lo	Hi
0 Damon Hill Canon	15.00	25.00
2 Alain Prost Canon	15.00	25.00
5 Micheal Schumacher Benetton	15.00	25.00
6 Ricardo Patrese Benetton	15.00	25.00

Onyx F1 1:24 1994

This series of 1:24 scale Formula 1 cars includes test cars for the Benetton-Ford team. The cars are done in the Mild Seven paint scheme. For the second year in a row only the Williams-Renault and Benetton-Ford teams are represented.

	Lo	Hi
0 Damon Hill Rothmans	15.00	25.00
2 David Coulthard Rothmans	15.00	25.00
2 Nigel Mansel Rothmans	16.00	28.00
2 Ayrton Senna Rothmans	20.00	35.00
5 Micheal Schumacher Benetton Bitburger	15.00	25.00
5 Micheal Schumacher Benetton Mild Seven	15.00	25.00
5 Micheal Schumacher Benetton Mild Seven Test car	15.00	25.00
6 Jas Verstappen Benetton Mild Seven Test car	15.00	25.00
6 Jas Verstappen Benetton Mild Seven	15.00	25.00
6 J.J.Lehto Benetton Mild Seven Test car	15.00	25.00
6 J.J.Lehto Benetton Mild Seven	15.00	25.00

Onyx F1 1:43 1988

This was the first year Onyx starting making 1:43 scale Formula 1 replicas. The key pieces in the set are Ayrton Senna and Alain Prost. Both of the pieces carry the popular Marlboro sponsorship.

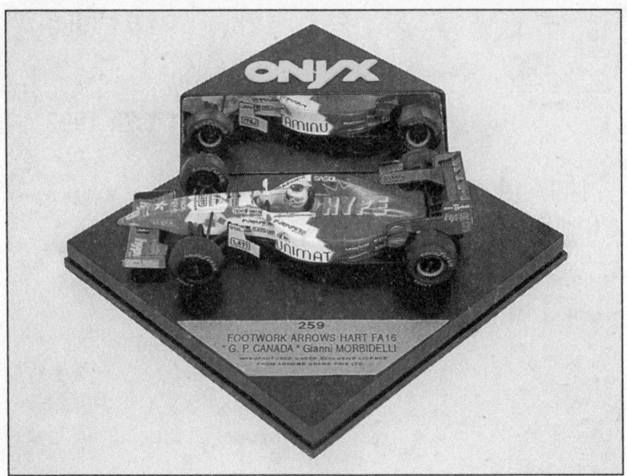

	Lo	Hi
1 Nelson Piquet	30.00	50.00
Camel		
1 Nelson Piquet	25.00	40.00
Coultaulds		
2 Saturo Nakajima	25.00	40.00
Camel		
2 Saturo Nakajima	20.00	35.00
Coultaulds		
11 Alain Prost	70.00	120.00
Marlboro		
12 Ayrton Senna	100.00	160.00
Marlboro		
19 Alessandro Nannini	25.00	40.00
Benetton		
20 Thierry Boutsen	25.00	40.00
Benetton		
27 Michele Albereto	25.00	40.00
Ferrari		
28 Gerhard Berger	25.00	40.00
Ferrari		

Onyx F1 1:43 1989

Nine different Formula 1 teams were represented in this series. The most popular cars for the second year in a row are the Ayrton Senna and Alain Prost with the Marlboro sponsorship. The Nelson Piquet and Saturo Nakajima cars carried another tobacco sponsor, Camel.

	Lo	Hi
1 Ayrton Senna	70.00	100.00
Marlboro		
2 Alain Prost	45.00	75.00
Marlboro		
5 Thierry Boutsen	18.00	30.00
Canon		
6 Ricardo Patrese	18.00	30.00
Canon		
11 Nelson Piquet	28.00	45.00
Camel		
12 Saturo Nakajima	25.00	40.00
Camel		
15 Maurico Gugelmin	18.00	30.00
Leyton House		
16 Ivan Capelli	18.00	30.00
Leyton House		
19 Alessandro Nannini	25.00	40.00
Benetton		
20 Emanuello Pirro	18.00	30.00
Benetton 7Up		
21 Alex Caffi	18.00	30.00
Marlboro Scuderi Itallia		
22 Andrea de Cesaris	18.00	30.00
Marlboro Scuderi Itallia		
23 Pierluigi Martin	18.00	30.00
SCM		
24 Sala Perez	18.00	30.00
SCM		
27 Nigel Mansel	25.00	40.00
Ferrari		
28 Gerhard Berger	18.00	30.00
Ferrari		
29 Michele Albereto	18.00	30.00
Camel BP Larrousse		
30 Philippe Alliot	18.00	30.00
Camel BP Larrousse		

Onyx F1 1:43 1990

Seven different Formula 1 teams were represented in this series. The Ayrton Senna is the most difficult to find but unlike previous years the car doesn't carry the Marlboro sponsorship.

	Lo	Hi
1 Alain Prost	14.00	22.00
Ferrari		
2 Nigel Mansel	16.00	24.00
Ferrari		
3 Saturo Nakajima	12.00	20.00
Epson		
4 Jean Alesi	12.00	20.00
Epson		
5 Thierry Boutsen	12.00	20.00
Canon		
6 Ricardo Patrese	12.00	20.00
Canon		
11 Derek Warick	14.00	22.00
Camel		
12 Martin Donnelly	14.00	22.00
Camel		
15 Maurcio Gugelmin	12.00	20.00
Leyton House		
16 Ivan Capelli	12.00	20.00
Leyton House		
19 Roberto Moreno	12.00	20.00
Riello		
19 Alessandro Nannini	12.00	20.00
Riello		
20 Nelson Piquet	12.00	20.00
Riello		
23 Pierluigi Martini	12.00	20.00
SCM		
24 Barilla Vittirio	12.00	20.00
SCM		
27 Ayrton Senna	25.00	35.00
Honda Shell		
28 Gerhard Berger	14.00	22.00
Honda Shell		
29 Eric Bernard	12.00	20.00
Toshiba ESPO		
30 Augri Suzuki	12.00	20.00
Toshiba ESPO		

Onyx F1 1:43 1991

The Michael Schumacher and Nelson Piquet cars in this series actually have multiple logos of a Camel on the car and not the printed word Camel. The Ayrton Senna and Gerhard Berger pieces are painted in the Marlboro colors but do not carry that actual sponsorship. It is also Michael Schumacher's first appearance in the Onyx 1:43 scale F1 cars.

	Lo	Hi
1 Ayrton Senna	25.00	35.00
2 Gerhard Berger	15.00	25.00
3 Saturo Nakajima	12.00	20.00
Braun Epson		
4 Stefano Modena	12.00	20.00
Braun Epson		
5 Nigel Mansel	20.00	30.00
Canon		
6 Ricardo Patrese	16.00	24.00
Canon		
11 Mika Hakkinen	12.00	20.00
Yellow Hat		
12 Johnny Herbert	12.00	20.00
Yellow Hat		
19 Micheal Schumacher	20.00	30.00
Camel Mobil1		
20 Nelson Piquet	14.00	22.00
Camel Mobil1		
27 Gianni Morbidelli	12.00	20.00
Ferrari		
27 Alain Prost	16.00	24.00
Ferrari		
28 Jean Alesi	14.00	24.00
Ferrari		
29 Eric Bernard	12.00	20.00
Toshiba Larrousse		
30 Aguri Suzuki	12.00	20.00
Toshiba Larrousse		
32 Alex Zanardi	12.00	20.00
Pepsi		
32 Bernard Gachot	12.00	20.00
7Up		
33 Andrea de Cesaris	12.00	20.00
7Up		

Onyx F1 1:43 1992

Noticeably absent from this series is Ayrton Senna. The series represents eight different Formula 1 teams.

	Lo	Hi
3 Olivier Grouillard	12.00	20.00
Calbee Tyrell		
4 Andrea de Cesaris	12.00	20.00
Calbee Tyrell		
5 Nigel Mansel	14.00	24.00
Canon		
6 Ricardo Patrese	12.00	20.00
Canon		
9 Michele Albereto	12.00	20.00
Footwork		
10 Aguri Suzuki	12.00	20.00
Footwork		
11 Mika Hakkinen	12.00	20.00
Hitachi		
12 Johnny Herbert	12.00	20.00
Hitachi		
19 Micheal Schumacher	20.00	35.00
Benetton		
20 Martin Brundle	12.00	20.00
Benetton		
25 Thierry Boutsen	12.00	20.00
ELF Renault		
26 Erik Comas	12.00	20.00
ELF Renault		
27 Jean Alesi	12.00	20.00
Ferrari		
28 Ivan Capelli	12.00	20.00
Ferrari		
32 Stefano Modena	12.00	20.00
Sasol		
33 Maurcio Gugelmin	12.00	20.00
Sasol		

Onyx F1 1:43 1993

Michael Andretti stayed in Formula 1 just long enough to get a die-cast made by Onyx in 1993. It was a horrible year for him in F1 and he left early to return to the Indy Car circuit. The car is in the Marlboro team colors but doesn't carry the sponsors name.

	Lo	Hi
0 Damon Hill	14.00	22.00
Canon		
2 Alain Prost	12.00	20.00
Canon		
3 Ukyo Katayama	12.00	20.00
Calbee Tyrell		
4 Andrea de Cesaris	12.00	20.00
Calbee Tyrell		
5 Nigel Mansel	35.00	50.00
K-Mart Benetton Back to Back		
Two car set		
5 Michael Schumacher	14.00	22.00
Benetton Camel Paint scheme		
5 Michael Schumacher	14.00	22.00
Benetton Mild Seven paint scheme		
5 Michael Schumacher	14.00	22.00
Kastle		
5 Michael Schumacher	14.00	22.00
Killer Loop		
5 Michael Schumacher	14.00	22.00
Nordica		
5 Michael Schumacher	14.00	22.00
Prince		
5 Michael Schumacher	14.00	22.00
Rollerblade		
6 J.J.Letho	12.00	20.00
Benetton		
6 Ricardo Patresse	12.00	20.00
Benetton		
6 Ricardo Patrese	12.00	20.00
Prince		
6 Ricardo Patrese	12.00	20.00
Rollerblade		
7 Michael Andretti	14.00	22.00
Shell		
8 Ayrton Senna	18.00	30.00
Shell		
11 Pedro Lamy	12.00	20.00
Castrol		
11 Alex Zanardi	12.00	20.00
Castrol		
12 Johnny Herbert	12.00	20.00
Castrol		
14 Ruebens Barrichello	12.00	20.00
Sasol		
15 Thierry Boutsen	12.00	20.00
Sasol		
27 Jean Alesi	12.00	20.00
Ferrari		
28 Gerhard Berger	12.00	20.00
Ferrari		
29 Karl Wenlinger	12.00	20.00
Liqui Moly		
30 J.J.Letho	12.00	20.00
Liqui Moly		

Onyx F1 1:43 1994

This series marks the first appearance of special race cars. There are three different Australian Grand Prix cars. Seven different teams were represented in this series.

	Lo	Hi
0 Damon Hill	14.00	22.00
Rothmans		
0 Damon Hill	14.00	22.00
Rothmans Australian Grand Prix		
0 Damon Hill	14.00	22.00
Rothmans Test car		
2 David Coulthard	14.00	22.00
Rothmans		
2 Nigel Mansell	14.00	22.00
Rothmans		
2 Ayrton Senna	28.00	40.00
Rothmans		
2 Ayrton Senna	20.00	35.00
Rothmans Test car		
3 Ukyo Katayama	12.00	20.00
Calbee		
4 Marc Blundell	12.00	20.00
Calbee		
5 Michael Schumacher	14.00	22.00
Benetton Mild Seven		
5 Damon Hill	14.00	22.00
Rothmans		
5 Michael Schumacher	14.00	22.00
Benetton Mild Seven		
Australian Grand Prix		
6 David Coulthard	12.00	20.00
Rothmans		
6 Johnny Herbert	12.00	20.00
Benetton Bitburger Mild Seven		
Australian Grand Prix		
6 J.J.Letho	12.00	20.00
Benetton Mild Seven		
6 Jos Verstappen	12.00	20.00
Benetton Mild Seven		
11 Pedro Lamy	12.00	20.00
Loctite		
12 Johnny Herbert	12.00	20.00
Loctite		
14 Ruebens Barrichello	12.00	20.00
Sasol		
15 Andrea de Cesaris	12.00	20.00
Sasol		
15 Eddie Irvine	12.00	20.00
Sasol		
25 Eric Bernard	12.00	20.00
ELF Renault		
25 Martin Brundle	12.00	20.00
Hugo Pratt Art		
26 Olivier Panis	12.00	20.00
ELF Renault		
27 Nicola Larini	12.00	20.00
Ferrari		
27 Jean Alesi	12.00	20.00
Ferrari 412 T1		
27 Jean Alesi	12.00	20.00
Ferrari 412 T1b		
28 Gerhard Berger	12.00	20.00
Ferrari		
28 Gerhard Berger	12.00	20.00
Ferrari 412 T1b		
29 Andrea de Cesaris	12.00	20.00
Broker 200th Grand Prix		
29 Andrea de Cesaris	12.00	20.00
Tissot		
29 Karl Wendlinger	12.00	20.00
Broker		
30 Hienz Harold Frentzen	12.00	20.00
Broker		
30 Hienz Harold Frentzen	12.00	20.00
Tissot		
33 Paul Belmondo	12.00	20.00
Ursus		
34 Gachot Bernard	12.00	20.00
Ursus		

Onyx F1 1:43 1995

Both Damon Hill and David Coulthard were represented with a regular and a Portugal Grand Prix car in this series. It was the last year that the Ferrari team was part of the set.

	Lo	Hi
3 Ukyo Katayama	12.00	20.00
Nokia		
3 Gabriel Tarquini	12.00	20.00
Nokia		
4 Mika Salo	12.00	20.00
Nokia		
5 Damon Hill	14.00	22.00
Rothmans		
5 Damon Hill	14.00	22.00
Rothmans Portugal Grand Prix		
6 David Coulthard	12.00	20.00
Rothmans Protugal Grand Prix		
6 David Coulthard	12.00	20.00
Rothmans		
9 Gianni Morbidelli	12.00	20.00
Hype		
9 Massimiliano Papis	12.00	20.00
Hype		
10 Taki Inoue	12.00	20.00
Hype		
16 Jean-Denis Deletraz	12.00	20.00
Ursus		
16 Giovanni Lavaggi	12.00	20.00
Ursus		
16 Bernard Gachot	12.00	20.00
Ursus		
17 Andrea Montermini	12.00	20.00
Ursus		
23 Pierluigi Martini	12.00	20.00
Lucchini		
24 Luca Badoer	12.00	20.00
Lucchini		
27 Jean Alesi	12.00	20.00
Ferrari		
28 Gerhard Berger	12.00	20.00
Ferrari		

Onyx F1 1:43 1996

Onyx retained only the Williams license and a few of the back marker teams for the 1996 series. All totaled five teams were represented in this set.

	Lo	Hi
5 Damon Hill	14.00	22.00
Rothmans French Grand Prix		
5 Jacques Villeneuve	14.00	22.00
Rothmans French Grand Prix		
16 Ricardo Rosset	12.00	20.00
Power Horse		
17 Ricardo Rosset	12.00	20.00
Phillips		
17 Jos Verstappen	12.00	20.00
Phillips		

	Lo	Hi
17 Jos Verstappen Power Horse	12.00	20.00
18 Ukyo Katayama Korean Air	12.00	20.00
19 Mika Salo Korean Air	12.00	20.00
20 Pedro Lamy Doimo	12.00	20.00
21 Giancarlo Fisichella Doimo	12.00	20.00
21 Tarso Marques Doimo	12.00	20.00
22 Luca Badeor Forti Yellow Paint scheme	12.00	20.00
22 Luca Badeor Shannon Green and White paint	12.00	20.00
23 Andre Montermini Forti Yellow Paint scheme	12.00	20.00
23 Andre Montermini Shannon Green and White paint	12.00	20.00

Onyx Indy 1:24 1993

This was the first year die-cast manufacturer Onyx began producing 1:24 scale indy cars. There were four cars featured.

	Lo	Hi
2 Scott Goodyear Mackenzie Financial	20.00	32.00
3 Al Unser Jr. Valvoline	22.00	35.00
5 Nigel Mansell K-Mart	20.00	32.00
6 Mario Andretti K-Mart	22.00	35.00

Onyx Indy 1:24 1994

The late Scott Brayton was one of the two 1:24 Indy cars released by Onyx in 1994.

	Lo	Hi
9 Raul Boesel Duracell	18.00	30.00
23 Scott Brayton Amway	18.00	30.00

Onyx Indy 1:43 1990

This was the first year Onyx began producing 1:43 scale Indy cars. The series is highlighted by Rick Mears and variations of the Emerson Fittipaldi and Danny Sullivan cars.

	Lo	Hi
1 Emerson Fittipaldi Marlboro w/black wheels	50.00	80.00
1 Emerson Fittipaldi Marlboro w/ silver wheels	25.00	40.00
2 Rick Mears Pennzoil	90.00	140.00
3 Michael Andretti K-Mart	20.00	35.00
4 Teo Fabi Quaker State	18.00	25.00
5 Al Unser Jr. Valvoline	25.00	40.00
6 Mario Andretti K-Mart	25.00	40.00
7 Danny Sullivan Marlboro w/o decals	25.00	40.00
7 Danny Sullivan Marlboro with decals	50.00	80.00
9 Tom Sneva RCA	18.00	25.00
11 Kevin Cogan Tuneup Masters	18.00	25.00
12 Randy Lewis AMP Oracle	18.00	25.00
14 A.J.Foyt Copenhagen	40.00	60.00
15 Jim Crawford Glidden	18.00	25.00
18 Bobby Rahal Kraco	18.00	25.00
19 Raul Boesel Budweiser	18.00	25.00
20 Roberto Guerrero Miller Genuine Draft	18.00	25.00
22 Scott Brayton Amway	25.00	40.00
25 Eddie Cheever Target	18.00	25.00
28 Scott Goodyear Mackenzie Financial	20.00	35.00
29 Panco Carter Hardee's	18.00	25.00
30 Arie Luyendyk Domino's	30.00	50.00
40 Al Unser Sr. Miller	18.00	25.00
41 John Andretti Foster's Quaker State	18.00	25.00
70 Didier Theys Tuneup Masters RCA	18.00	25.00
86 Dominic Dobson Texaco	18.00	25.00

Onyx Indy 1:43 1991

Three members of the Andretti family had cars in this series, Mario, Michael and John. The Kevin Cogan/Glidden car is one of the most difficult of all the Onyx Indy die-cast to find.

	Lo	Hi
2 Al Unser Jr. Valvoline	15.00	25.00
4 John Andretti Pennzoil	15.00	25.00
6 Mario Andretti K-Mart	25.00	40.00
9 Kevin Cogan Glidden	70.00	100.00
10 Michael Andretti K-Mart	15.00	25.00
51 Gary Bettenhausen Glidden	15.00	25.00

Onyx Indy 1:43 1992

This set is highlighted by the A.J.Foyt Copenhagen car. The series also has two beer sponsors Bud and Miller.

	Lo	Hi
10 Scott Pruett Budweiser	12.00	20.00
12 Bobby Rahal Miller Genuine Draft	12.00	20.00
14 A.J.Foyt Copenhagen	20.00	35.00
15 Scott Goodyear Mackenzie Financial	10.00	18.00
23 Scott Brayton Amway	12.00	20.00
27 Al Unser Sr. Conseco	12.00	20.00
36 Roberto Guerrero Quaker State	10.00	18.00

Onyx Indy 1:43 1993

This series marks the first appearance by Nigel Mansell in an Indy car.

	Lo	Hi
5 Nigel Mansell K-Mart	12.00	20.00
6 Arie Luyendyk Target	12.00	20.00
7 Danny Sullivan Molson	12.00	20.00
9 Raul Boesel Duracell	10.00	18.00
19 Robbie Buhl Mi-Jack	20.00	35.00
27 Geoff Brabham Glidden	20.00	40.00
29 Olivier Grouillard Eurosport	90.00	15.00
36 Roberto Guerrero Quaker State	10.00	18.00
39 Ross Bentley Rain-X	9.00	15.00

Onyx Indy 1:43 1994-95

This was the last year that Onyx made an entire line of 1:43 Indy cars. There was one 1995 piece, the number 60 Scott Brayton. It is priced below.

	Lo	Hi
1 Nigel Mansell K-Mart	9.00	15.00
5 Raul Boesell Duracell	9.00	15.00
6 Mario Andretti K-Mart	10.00	20.00
7 Adrian Fernandez Tecate	9.00	15.00
8 Michael Andretti Target	9.00	15.00
9 Robby Gordon Valvoline	9.00	15.00
11 Teo Fabi Pennzoil	9.00	15.00
18 Jimmy Vasser Conseco	9.00	15.00
21 Roberto Guerrero Interstate Batteries	9.00	15.00
27 Eddie Cheever Quaker State	9.00	15.00
60 Scott Brayton Quaker State 1995 Promo	30.00	50.00
88 Maurico Gugelmin Hollywood	9.00	15.00

Paul's Model Art Mini Champs F1 1:43 1992

This was the first year for Paul's Model Art to produced 1:43 scale Formula 1 die-cast. Three teams were represented.

	Lo	Hi
6 Ricardo Patrese Canon Williams	20.00	32.00
19 Michael Schumacher Benetton	28.00	40.00
20 Marc Brundle Benetton	15.00	25.00
27 Jean Alesi Ferrari	18.00	30.00
28 Ivan Capelli Ferrari	18.00	30.00

Paul's Model Art Mini Champs F1 1:43 1993

Damon Hill and Aryton Senna make their first Paul's Model Art 1:43 scale appearance in this series.

	Lo	Hi
0 Damon Hill Canon Williams	18.00	30.00
2 Alain Prost Canon Williams	15.00	25.00
5 Michael Schumacher Benetton	20.00	32.00
6 Ricardo Patrese Benetton	15.00	25.00
7 Michael Andretti McLaren	20.00	32.00

7 Mika Hakkinen.......... 15.00 25.00
McLaren
8 Ayrton Senna.......... 25.00 40.00
McLaren
27 Jean Alesi.......... 15.00 25.00
Ferrari
28 Gerhard Berger.......... 15.00 25.00
Ferrari
29 Karl Wendlinger.......... 15.00 25.00
Broker Sauber
30 Heinz Harldo Frentzen.......... 15.00 25.00
Liqui Moly Sauber
30 J.J. Lehto.......... 15.00 25.00
Liqui Moly Sauber

Paul's Model Art Mini Champs F1 1:43 1994

This was the first year that Paul's Model Art did special edition 1:43 cars. Michael Schumacher's F1 Championship car and Nigel Mansell's French Grand Prix car are among the most popular.

	Lo	Hi
0 Damon Hill.......... Rothmans Williams FW15	15.00	25.00
0 Damon Hill.......... Rothmans Williams FW16	15.00	25.00
0 Damon Hill.......... Rothmans Williams FW16 British Grand Prix	15.00	25.00
2 Nigel Mansell.......... Rothmans FW16 French Grand Prix	15.00	25.00
2 David Coulthard.......... Rothmans Williams	15.00	25.00
2 Ayrton Senna.......... Rothmans	22.00	35.00
3 Ukyo Katayama.......... Calbee Tyrell	14.00	35.00
4 Marc Blundell.......... Calbee Tyrell	14.00	22.00
5 Michael Schumacher.......... Benetton	15.00	25.00
5 Michael Schumacher.......... Benetton German Grand Prix	15.00	25.00
5 Michael Schumacher.......... Benetton Formula 1 Champion	15.00	25.00
6 Johnny Herbert.......... BITburger	14.00	22.00
6 J.J.Letho.......... Mild Seven	14.00	22.00
6 Jos Verstappen.......... Mild Seven	14.00	22.00
6 Jos Verstappen.......... Mild Seven German Grand Prix	14.00	22.00
7 Mika Hakkinen.......... McLaren	14.00	22.00
8 Martin Brundle.......... McLaren	15.00	25.00
27 Jean Alesi.......... Ferrari	15.00	25.00
27 N.Larini.......... Ferrari	14.00	22.00
28 Gerhard Berger.......... Ferrari	15.00	25.00
29 Andrea de Cesaris.......... Broker 200th Grand Prix	14.00	22.00
29 Andrea de Cesaris.......... Broker German Grand Prix	14.00	22.00
29 Karl Wendlinger.......... Broker Sauber	14.00	22.00
30 Heinz Harold Frentzen.......... Broker Sauber	14.00	22.00
31 David Brabham.......... MTV Ford	14.00	22.00
32 Roland Ratzenberger.......... MTV Ford	14.00	22.00

Paul's Model Art Mini Champs F1 1:43 1995

Ayrton Senna is noticeably absent from this set. The show car of Damon Hill and the Test car of David Coulthard are the special editions in this series.

	Lo	Hi
1 Michael Schumacher.......... Mild Seven B195	15.00	25.00
2 Johnny Herbert.......... Mild Seven B195	14.00	22.00
3 Ukyo Katayama.......... Calbee Tyrell	14.00	22.00
4 Mika Salo.......... Calbee Tyrell	14.00	22.00
5 Damon Hill.......... Rothmans FW16 Show car	15.00	25.00
5 Damon Hill.......... Rothmans Williams FW17	15.00	25.00
6 David Coulthard.......... Rothmans FW17	14.00	22.00
6 David Coulthard.......... Rothmans FW 16 Test car	14.00	22.00
7 Marc Blundell.......... McLaren	14.00	22.00
7 Nigel Mansell.......... McLaren	15.00	25.00
8 Mika Hakkinen.......... McLaren	14.00	22.00
11 M.Schiattarella.......... MTV Simtek Ford	14.00	22.00
12 Jos Verstappen.......... MTV Simtek Ford	14.00	22.00
14 Ruebens Barrichello.......... Peugeot Jordan	14.00	22.00
15 Eddie Irvine.......... Peugeot Jordan	14.00	22.00
25 Martin Brundle.......... Gitanes Ligier	14.00	22.00
25 Aguri Suzuki.......... Gitanes Ligier	14.00	22.00
26 Olivier Panis.......... Gitanes Ligier	14.00	22.00
27 Jean Alesi.......... Ferrari	15.00	25.00
28 Gerhard Berger.......... Ferrari	15.00	25.00
29 Bouillion.......... Red Bull Sauber	14.00	22.00
29 Karl Wendlinger.......... Red Bull Sauber	14.00	22.00
30 Heinz Harold Frentzen.......... Red Bull Sauber	14.00	22.00

Paul's Model Art Mini Champs F1 1:43 1996

Michael Schumacher has four different versions in this series. His first win in a Ferrari is commemorated as one of the special pieces.

	Lo	Hi
1 Michael Schumacher.......... Ferrari	15.00	25.00
1 Michael Schumacher.......... Ferrari 1st Win	15.00	25.00
1 Michael Schumacher.......... Ferrari High Nose	15.00	25.00
1 Michael Schumacher.......... Ferrari Launch car	15.00	25.00
2 Eddie Irvine.......... Ferrari	14.00	22.00
2 Eddie Irvine.......... Ferrari Launch car	14.00	22.00
3 Jean Alesi.......... Benetton Mild Seven	15.00	25.00
4 Gerhard Berger.......... Benetton Mild Seven	15.00	25.00
5 Damon Hill.......... Rothmans Williams FW18	15.00	25.00
5 Heinz Harold Frentzen.......... Rothmans Test car	14.00	22.00
6 Jacques Villenueve.......... Rothmans	15.00	25.00
6 Jacques Villenueve.......... Rothmans Test car	15.00	25.00
7 Mika Hakkinen.......... McLaren	14.00	22.00
8 David Coulthard.......... McLaren	14.00	22.00
9 Olivier Panis.......... Parmalat Ligier	14.00	22.00
10 Pedro Diniz.......... Parmalat Ligier	14.00	22.00
11 Ruebens Barrichello.......... Peugeot	14.00	22.00
11 Ruebens Barrichello.......... Peugeot Launch car	14.00	22.00
12 Martin Brundle.......... Peugeot	14.00	22.00
12 Martin Brundle.......... Peugeot Launch car	14.00	22.00
14 Johnny Herbert.......... Petronas Sauber	14.00	22.00
15 Heinz Harold Frentzen.......... Petronas Sauber	14.00	22.00
18 Ukyo Katayama.......... Korean Air Tyrrell	14.00	22.00
19 Mika Salo.......... Korean Air Tyrrell	14.00	22.00

Paul's Model Art Mini Champs Indy 1:43 1993

Each piece comes in both a road course and speedway version. This was the first year for Paul's Model Art to do 1:43 scale Indy cars.

	Lo	Hi
3 Al Unser Jr.......... Valvoline	14.00	22.00
4 Emerson Fittipaldi.......... Penske	12.00	20.00
5 Nigel Mansell.......... K-Mart	12.00	20.00
6 Mario Andretti.......... K-Mart	14.00	22.00
9 Raul Boesel.......... Duracell	12.00	20.00
12 Paul Tracy.......... Penske	12.00	20.00

Paul's Model Art Mini Champs Indy 1:43 1994 Speedway Edition

Each of these cars feature Road Course set up. Mario Andretti and Al Unser Jr. are among the most popular pieces in the set.

	Lo	Hi
2 Emerson Fittipaldi.......... Penske	12.00	20.00
3 Paul Tracy.......... Penske	12.00	20.00
6 Mario Andretti.......... K-Mart	14.00	22.00
7 Adrian Fernandez.......... Tecate	12.00	20.00
8 Michael Andretti.......... Target	12.00	20.00
16 Stefan Johansson.......... Alumax	12.00	20.00
19 Alessandro Zampedri.......... Mi-Jack	12.00	20.00
22 Hiro Matsushita.......... Panasonic	12.00	20.00
31 Al Unser Jr.......... Penske	14.00	22.00

Paul's Model Art Mini Champs Indy 1:43 1995 Road Course Edition

Each of these cars feature the Speedway set up. The Mario Andretti and Al Unser Jr. are among the most popular pieces in the set.

	Lo	Hi
15 Christian Fittipaldi Walker Racing	14.00	22.00
31 Andre Ribeiro LCI	14.00	22.00

Paul's Model Art Mini Champs Indy 1:43 1996 IRL Edition

Only two Indy cars were released from Paul's Model Art in 1995. Both cars feature Road Course set up.

	Lo	Hi
4 Richie Hearn Food 4 Less	14.00	22.00
12 Buzz Calkins Bradley	14.00	22.00
20 Tony Stewart Quaker State	14.00	22.00

Paul's Model Art Mini Champs Indy 1:43 1996 Road Course Edition

This was Paul's Model Art's first pass at making 1:43 Indy Racing League die-cast replicas.

	Lo	Hi
1 Nigel Mansell K-Mart	12.00	20.00
4 Bobby Rahal Miller Genuine Draft	12.00	20.00
6 Mario Andretti K-Mart	14.00	22.00
9 Robby Gordon Valvoline	12.00	20.00
19 Alessandro Zampedri Mi-Jack	12.00	20.00
23 Buddy Lazier Randy Owens	12.00	20.00
24 Willy T. Ribbs Walker Racing	12.00	20.00
28 Arie Luyendyyk Eurosports	12.00	20.00
31 Al Unser Jr. Penske	14.00	22.00
55 John Andretti Gillette	12.00	20.00

Racing Champions Indy Cars 1:24 1995

Racing Champions issued their 1995 Indy cars in two series. The red, white and blue boxes the pieces come states which series they are from.

	Lo	Hi
1 Nigel Mansel Texaco	10.00	20.00
2 Emerson Fittipaldi Penske Racing	10.00	20.00
3 Paul Tracy Penske	10.00	20.00
4 Bobby Rahal Rahal-Hogan	10.00	20.00
5 Raul Boesell Duracell	10.00	20.00
5 Nigel Mansel Texaco	10.00	20.00
6 Mario Andretti Texaco	10.00	20.00
7 Adrian Fernandez Tecate	10.00	20.00
8 Michael Andretti Target	10.00	20.00
8 Gil DeFarran Pennzoil	10.00	20.00
9 Robby Gordon Valvoline	10.00	20.00
10 Mike Groff Motorola	10.00	20.00
11 Teo Fabi Pennzoil	10.00	20.00
18 Jimmy Vasser Conseco	10.00	20.00
22 Hiro Matsushita Panasonic	10.00	20.00
24 Willy T. Ribbs Service Merchandise	10.00	20.00
28 Stefan Johansen Eurosports	10.00	20.00
31 Al Unser Jr. Penske Racing	10.00	20.00
90 Lynn St.James JC Penny's	12.00	22.00

Racing Champions Indy Cars 1:24 1995 Series 2

This is the second series of Indy cars from Racing Champions in 1995. The boxes state what series the cars are from.

	Lo	Hi
1 Al Unser Jr. Penske	10.00	20.00
2 Emerson Fittipaldi Penske	10.00	20.00
3 Paul Tracy K-Mart	10.00	20.00
4 Bryan Herta Target	10.00	20.00
5 Robby Gordon Valvoline	10.00	20.00
6 Michael Andretti K-Mart	10.00	20.00
7 Alex Salazar Crystal	10.00	20.00
8 Gil DeFerran Pennzoil	10.00	20.00
9 Bobby Rahal Honda	10.00	20.00
10 Adrian Fernandez Tecate	10.00	20.00
11 Raul Boesel Duracell	10.00	20.00
12 Jimmy Vasser Target	10.00	20.00
15 Christian Fittipaldi Telesena	10.00	20.00
17 Danny Sullivan VISA	10.00	20.00
18 Stefan Johansson Alumax	10.00	20.00
20 Scott Pruett Firestone	10.00	20.00
22 Roberto Guerrero	10.00	20.00
25 Hiro Matsushita Panasonic	10.00	20.00
31 Al Ribero LCI	10.00	20.00
34 Alex Sampadri	10.00	20.00
99 David Hall Subway	10.00	20.00

Racing Champions Indy Cars 1:24 1996

This 1:24 scale Indy car series was highlighted by the appearance of Michael Andretti and Robby Gordon. There is also an ex-Formula 1 driver Marc Blundell in the series.

	Lo	Hi
4 Alex Zanardi Target	10.00	20.00
5 Robby Gordon Valvoline	10.00	20.00
6 Michael Andretti Texaco	10.00	20.00
8 Gil DeFerran Pennzoil	10.00	20.00
12 Jimmy Vasser Target	10.00	20.00
15 Scott Goodyear Firestone	10.00	20.00
16 Stefan Johansson Alumax	10.00	20.00
19 Hiro Matsushita Panasonic	10.00	20.00
20 Scott Pruett Firestone	10.00	20.00
21 Marc Blundell VISA	10.00	20.00
22 M. Jourdain Herdez	10.00	20.00
31 Al Riberio LCI	10.00	20.00
49 Parker Johnstone Motorola	10.00	20.00

Racing Champions Indy Racing League 1:24 1996

This was Racing Champions first year to make Indy Racing League cars.

	Lo	Hi
5 Arie Luyendyk Bryant	12.00	22.00
12 Buzz Calkins Bradley	12.00	22.00
20 Tony Stewart Quaker State	12.00	22.00
45 Lyn St.James San Antonio	12.00	22.00
70 Davy Jones AC Delco	12.00	22.00
91 Buddy Lazier Delta Faucets	12.00	22.00

Racing Champions Indy Racing League 1:24 1997

Tony Stewart and Buddy Lazier are among the two most popular drivers in the Indy Racing League and are featured in this series.

	Lo	Hi
1 Scott Sharp Conseco	12.00	22.00
4 Davy Jones Monsoon	12.00	22.00
10 Mike Groff Byrd's Cafeteria	12.00	22.00
20 Tony Stewart Menards	12.00	22.00
21 Roberto Guerrero Pennzoil	12.00	22.00
91 Buddy Lazier Delco	12.00	22.00

Racing Champions Indy Cars Premier 1:43 1995

This series of 1:43 scale Indy Cars come in a red, white and blue Premier series box. The pieces do have a serial number on the back but unlike most Premier issues the number of quantity produced is not stated anywhere on the box.

	Lo	Hi
1 Nigel Mansel Texaco	7.00	12.00
2 Emerson Fittipaldi Penske Racing	7.00	12.00
3 Paul Tracy Penske	7.00	12.00
4 Bobby Rahal Rahal-Hogan	7.00	12.00
5 Raul Boesell Duracell	7.00	12.00
5 Nigel Mansel Texaco	7.00	12.00
6 Mario Andretti Texaco	7.00	12.00
7 Adrian Fernandez Tecate	7.00	12.00
8 Michael Andretti K-Mart	7.00	12.00
9 Robby Gordon Valvoline	7.00	12.00
11 Teo Fabi Pennzoil	7.00	12.00
18 Jimmy Vasser Conseco	7.00	12.00
31 Al Unser Jr. Penske Racing	7.00	12.00

Racing Champions Indy Cars 1:64 1995 Series 1

The Mario Andretti piece in this series has two variations. One is has the driver of the number six wearing a black helmet, while the other has the driver wearing a white helmet.

	Lo	Hi
1 Emerson Fittipaldi	2.00	4.00
1 Al Unser Jr. Valvoline	2.00	4.00
2 Rick Mears Pennzoil	2.00	4.00
3 Mario Andretti Havoline	2.00	4.00
4 Rick Mears Pennzoil	2.00	4.00
4 John Andretti Pennzoil	2.00	4.00
5 Michael Andretti Havoline	2.00	4.00
5 Al Unser Jr. Valvoline	2.00	4.00
6 Mario Andretti Havoline with Black Helmet	2.00	4.00
6 Mario Andretti Havoline with White Helmet	2.00	4.00
8 John Andretti Pennzoil	2.00	4.00
8 Scott Pruett Red Roof Inn	2.00	4.00
10 Derek Daly	2.00	4.00
14 A.J.Foyt	2.00	4.00
16 Tony Bettenhausen Amax	2.00	4.00
18 Bobby Rahal Kraco	2.00	4.00
21 Geoff Brabham Mac Tools	2.00	4.00
25 Al Unser Sr. Mobil	2.00	4.00
86 Barry Dobson Havoline	2.00	4.00

Racing Champions Indy Cars 1:64 1995-96 Series 2

This was the series two release of the Indy 1:64 scale cars. The cars were released in late 1995 and early 1996 and feature top drivers like Al Unser Jr., Michael Andretti and Bobby Rahal.

	Lo	Hi
1 Al Unser Jr. Penske	2.00	4.00
2 Emerson Fittipaldi Penske	2.00	4.00
3 Paul Tracy Penske	2.00	4.00
4 Bryan Herta Target	2.00	4.00
4 Alex Zanardi Target	2.00	4.00
5 Robby Gordon Valvoline	2.00	4.00
6 Michael Andretti K-Mart	2.00	4.00
7 Eliso Salazar Crystal	2.00	4.00
8 Gil DeFerran Pennzoil	2.00	4.00
9 Emerson Fittipaldi Mobil 1	2.00	4.00
9 Bobby Rahal Honda	2.00	4.00
10 Adrian Fernandez Tecate	2.00	4.00
11 Raul Boesel Duracell	2.00	4.00
12 Jimmy Vasser Target	2.00	4.00
15 Christian Fittipaldi Telesena	2.00	4.00
17 Danny Sullivan VISA	2.00	4.00
18 Stefan Johannsson Alumax	2.00	4.00
20 Scott Pruett Firestone	2.00	4.00
22 Roberto Guerrero	2.00	4.00
25 Hiro Matsushita Panasonic	2.00	4.00
31 Al Unser Jr.	2.00	4.00
31 Alberto Ribeiro LCI	2.00	4.00
34 Alex Zampadri	2.00	4.00
99 David Hall Subway	2.00	4.00

Racing Champions Indy Cars 1:64 1996

This series was the regular release in 1996 of 1:64 scale Indy cars. The series includes Michael Andretti and Jeff Krosnoff.

	Lo	Hi
2 Al Unser Jr. Penske	2.00	5.00
3 Paul Tracy Penske	2.00	5.00
4 Alex Zanardi Target	2.00	5.00
4 Richie Hearn Ralph's Foods	2.00	5.00
5 Robby Gordon Valvoline	2.00	5.00
6 Michael Andretti Texaco	2.00	5.00
8 Gil DeFerran Pennzoil	2.00	5.00
9 Emerson Fittipaldi Hogan-Penske	2.00	5.00
10 E.Lawson Delco	2.00	5.00
12 Jimmy Vasser Target	2.00	5.00
15 Scott Goodyear Firestone	2.00	5.00
16 Stefan Johansson Alumax	2.00	5.00
17 Maurcio Gugelmin Hollywood	2.00	5.00
19 Hiro Matsusuhita Panazonic	2.00	5.00
20 Scott Pruett Firestone	2.00	5.00
21 Marc Blundell VISA	2.00	5.00
22 M.Jourdain Herdez	2.00	5.00
25 Jeff Krosnoff Arciero Wines	2.00	5.00
28 Bryan Herta Shell Promo	2.00	5.00
31 Alberto Ribeiro LCI	2.00	5.00
49 Parker Johnstone Motorola	2.00	5.00

Racing Champions Indy Cars Premier 1:64 1995-96

This was the first series of Indy cars to be done in the Premium edition. The series includes such notables as Nigel Mansell, Mario Andretti, Michael Andretti and Al Unser Jr.

	Lo	Hi
1 Nigel Mansel Texaco	2.00	5.00
2 Emerson Fittipaldi Penske	2.00	5.00
3 Paul Tracy Penske	2.00	5.00
4 Bobby Rahal Honda	2.00	5.00
5 Nigel Mansel Texaco	2.00	5.00
6 Mario Andretti Texaco	2.00	5.00
7 Adrian Fernandez Tecate	2.00	5.00
8 Michael Andretti Target	2.00	5.00
9 Robby Gordon Valvoline	2.00	5.00
10 Mike Groff Motorola	2.00	5.00
11 Teo Fabi Pennzoil	2.00	5.00
18 Jimmy Vasser Conseco	2.00	5.00
22 Hiro Matsushita Panasonic	2.00	5.00
24 Willy T. Ribbs Service Merchandise	2.00	5.00
31 Al Unser Jr. Penske	2.00	5.00

Racing Champions Indy Racing League 1:64 1996

This series includes popular drivers Tony Stewart and Lyn St. James. The cars came in a red white and blue blister package and were sold through mass market retailers.

	Lo	Hi
2 Scott Brayton Glidden	2.00	5.00
3 Eddie Cheever Quaker State	2.00	5.00
4 Richie Hearn Food 4 Less	2.00	5.00
5 Arie Luyendyk Bryant	2.00	5.00

7 Elsio Salazar	2.00	5.00
Crystal		
11 Scott Sharp	2.00	5.00
Conseco		
12 Buzz Calkins	2.00	5.00
Bradley		
20 Tony Stewart	2.00	5.00
Quaker State		
21 Roberto Guerrero	2.00	5.00
Pennzoil		
60 Mike Groff	2.00	5.00
Valvoline		
70 Davy Jones	2.00	5.00
AC Delco		
90 Lyn St.James	2.00	5.00
Lifetime Channel		
91 Buddy Lazier	2.00	5.00
Delta Faucets		

Racing Champions Indy Racing League 1:64 1997

This was the first series of 1:64 Indy Racing League cars. The 1996 Indy 500 winner Buddy Lazier and fan favorite Tony Stewart are part of the set.

	Lo	Hi
1 Scott Sharp	2.00	5.00
Conseco		
4 Davy Jones	2.00	5.00
Monsoon		
10 Mike Groff	2.00	5.00
Byrd's Cafeteria		
20 Tony Stewart	2.00	5.00
Menards		
21 Roberto Guerrero	2.00	5.00
Pennzoil		
91 Buddy Lazier	2.00	5.00
Delco		

Tamiya F1 1:20 Collector's Club

These are some of the best detailed and most expensive Formula one die-cast pieces available. We have been unable to gather enough market information on the Ayrton Senna piece therefore it is not priced.

	Lo	Hi
5 Nigel Mansell	120.00	160.00
Canon 1992		
5 Michael Schumacher	120.00	160.00
Benetton 1993		
12 Mika Hakkinen	120.00	160.00
Castrol 1992		
12 Johnny Herbert	120.00	160.00
Castrol 1993		
12 Ayrton Senna		
McLaren		
28 Jean Alesi	120.00	160.00
Ferrari 1993		

1998 Action Sprint Cars 1:18 Xtreme Series

These 1:18 scale cars are part of the Action Racing Collectables Xtreme Series.

	Lo	Hi
7 Kevin Huntley	50.00	80.00
Peterbilt		
11 Steve Kinser	60.00	100.00
Quaker State		
19 Stevie Smith	50.00	80.00
Ingersoll-Rand		
22 Jac Haudenchild	50.00	80.00
Pennzoil		
23 Frankie Kerr	50.00	80.00
Shoff		
83 Danny Lasoski	50.00	80.00
Beefpackers		

1994-1998 Action Dirt Cars 1:24

This series of 1:24 scale dirt cars produced by Action features some of the top names from the dirt car circuit. Winston Cup regulars Ken Schrader and the late Davey Allison are included along with dirt car champion Scott Bloomquist.

	Lo	Hi
0 Freddy Smith	30.00	45.00
Christenberry '96		
0 Freddy Smith	35.00	50.00
Bazooka		
E1 Mark Balzano	30.00	45.00
J.D. Cals		
1 Rodney Combs	28.00	40.00
B4 Jack Boggs	28.00	40.00
Hawkeye Trucking		
5 Rodney Combs	28.00	40.00
Bull & Hannah		
5 Ronnie Johnson	30.00	45.00
1998		
5 Ronnie Johnson	28.00	40.00
Action		
6M Wendall Wallace	25.00	40.00
Rebco		
11 Bart Hartman	30.00	45.00
Pro Stocks		
12 Rick Aukland	30.00	45.00
1998		
B12 Kevin Weaver	30.00	45.00
Pizza Hut		
15 Steve Francis	28.00	40.00
18 Scott Bloomquist	30.00	50.00
1998		
18 Scott Bloomquist	40.00	60.00
18 Scott Bloomquist	40.00	60.00
Action RCCA '96		
21 Billy Moyer	28.00	40.00
21 Billy Moyer	30.00	45.00
Bazooka		
21 Billy Moyer	30.00	45.00
Bazooka 1998		
24 Rick Eckert	30.00	45.00
Raye-Vest		
25 Ken Schrader	20.00	35.00
Budweiser		
28 Jimmy Mars	28.00	40.00
Parker Store		
28 Davey Allison	40.00	60.00
Havoline		
30 Steve Shaver	28.00	40.00
Simonton		
41 Buck Simmons	25.00	35.00
66 Bob Frye	30.00	45.00
GRT		
75 Bart Hartman	30.00	45.00
Pennzoil		
75 John Gill	25.00	35.00
Mastersplit		
89 Steve Barnett	28.00	40.00
Rayburn		
99 Donnie Moran	30.00	45.00
99 Donnie Moran 1998	30.00	45.00

1994-1998 Action Dirt Cars 1:64

These 1:64 dirt cars were produced and distributed by Action Performance. The cars were available through both the dealer network and Action's Racing Collectibles Club of America.

	Lo	Hi
0 Freddy Smith	5.00	10.00
Bazooka with Blue paint scheme		
0 Freddy Smith	8.00	16.00
Bazooka with Orange paint scheme		
0 Freddy Smith	5.00	10.00
Christenberry '96		
1 Rodney Combs	5.00	10.00
E1 Mark Balzano	5.00	10.00
J.D. Cals		
F1 Mike Duvall	5.00	10.00
1 C.J.Rayburn	5.00	10.00
1 Charlie Swartz	5.00	10.00
1J Davey Johnson	5.00	10.00
B4 Jack Boggs	5.00	10.00
Hawkeye Trucking		
5 Rodney Combs	60.00	90.00
5 Rodney Combs	5.00	10.00
Bull & Hannah		
5 Ronnie Johnson	5.00	10.00
Action		
5 Ronnie Johnson	6.00	12.00
Hawkeye Trucking		
5 Ronnie Johnson 1998	5.00	10.00
6M Wendall Wallace	5.00	10.00
Rebco		
11 Bart Hartman	5.00	10.00
Pro-Shocks		
12 Rick Auckland 1998	5.00	10.00
B12 Kevin Weaver	5.00	10.00
Pizza Hut		
15 Steve Francis	5.00	10.00
15 Jeff Purvis	6.00	12.00
18 Scott Bloomquist	10.00	20.00
Ford Motorsports		
18 Scott Bloomquist	45.00	70.00
'94 car		
18 Scott Bloomquist	5.00	10.00
'95 car		
18 Scott Bloomquist	6.00	12.00
'96		
18 Scott Bloomquist	6.00	12.00
1998		
21 Jack Hewitt	30.00	45.00
blister package		
21 Jack Hewitt	6.00	12.00
box package		
21 Billy Moyer	60.00	90.00
21 Billy Moyer	5.00	10.00
1996		
21 Billy Moyer	6.00	10.00
Bazooka		
21 Billy Moyer	6.00	12.00
Bazooka 1998		
24 Rick Eckert	5.00	10.00
Raye-Vest		
25 Ken Schrader	6.00	10.00
Budweiser		
28 Davey Allison	9.00	18.00
Havoline		
28 Jimmy Mars	5.00	10.00
Parker Store		
30 Steve Shaver	5.00	10.00
Simonton		
32 Bob Pierce	5.00	10.00
Tall Cool One		
41 Buck Simmons	5.00	10.00
52 Ken Schrader	6.00	10.00
AC Delco		
52 Ken Schrader	6.00	10.00
Budweiser		
66 Bob Frye	6.00	10.00
GRT		
75 John Gill	5.00	10.00
Mastersplit		
75 Bart Hartman	6.00	12.00
Pennzoil		
89 Steve Barnett	5.00	10.00
Rayburn		
99 Donnie Moran	5.00	10.00

1995-1998 Action Sprint Cars 1:24

This series of 1:24 scale sprint cars feature some of the top names from the World of Outlaw circuit. Highlighting the series are former WoO champions Steve Kinser and Dave Blaney.

	Lo	Hi
1 Sammy Swindell	25.00	40.00

	Lo	Hi
Channellock		
1 Sammy Swindell	30.00	50.00
Channellock Silver		
1 Sammy Swindell	60.00	100.00
Hooters		
1 Sammy Swindell	25.00	40.00
Old Milwaukee		
1 Sammy Swindell	30.00	45.00
TMC 1993		
2 Andy Hillenburg	25.00	40.00
STP		
4 J.J.Yeley	30.00	45.00
Action Asphalt		
4 J.J.Yeley	30.00	45.00
Action Dirt		
5 Johnny Herrera	25.00	40.00
Jackpot		
5M Mark Kinser	30.00	50.00
Wirtgen		
7TW Jeff Swindell	25.00	40.00
Gold Eagle		
10 Dave Blaney	150.00	250.00
Viviran 2,500		
10 Dave Blaney	50.00	80.00
Viviran 4,500		
10 Dave Blaney	30.00	45.00
Vivarin 1997		
11 Steve Kinser	90.00	120.00
Quaker State		
11 Steve Kinser	100.00	150.00
Quaker State Mac Tools		
11 Steve Kinser	50.00	80.00
Valvoline		
11H Greg Hodnett	30.00	45.00
Selma		
18 Brad Doty	30.00	50.00
Coors Light Silver Bullet		
'86 Red and Silver Paint scheme		
18 Brad Doty	30.00	50.00
Coors Light Silver Bullet '87		
Blue and Silver Paint scheme		
19 Stevie Smith	30.00	45.00
19 Stivie Smith	30.00	50.00
Ingersoll-Rand		
20 Jeff Gordon	40.00	60.00
Hap's		
20 Tony Stewart	30.00	50.00
Triple Crown		
21 Lance Blevins	25.00	40.00
Citgo		
21 Fred Rahmer	100.00	175.00
Budweiser		
22 Jac Haudenchild	60.00	100.00
Pennzoil 1994		
22 Jac Haudenchild	35.00	60.00
Pennzoil 1996		
28D Brad Doty	40.00	75.00
Bower's		
38 Ken Schrader	40.00	70.00
Crawford		
40 Jeff Gordon	45.00	70.00
Stanton		
47 Johnny Herrera	30.00	50.00
Strange		
55 Tim Richmond	30.00	50.00
Elder Cadillac		
63 Jack Hewitt	40.00	65.00
J.W.Hunt		
69 Brent Kaeding	30.00	45.00
Pioneer Concrete		
69K Donny Kreitz	30.00	50.00
Kreitzer Excavating		
71M Stevie Smith	30.00	50.00
Ecowater		
75 Joey Saldana	30.00	50.00
Mopar		
77 Fred Rahmer	30.00	50.00
Manheim Auctions		

1998 Action Sprint Cars 1:50

These 1:50 scale cars debuted from Action this year.

	Lo	Hi
1 Sammy Swindell	6.00	12.00
Channellock		
5M Mark Kinser	6.00	12.00
Wirtgen		
7 Keven Huntley	6.00	12.00
Peterbilt		
23 Frankie Kerr	6.00	12.00
Shoff		
47 Johnny Herrera	6.00	12.00
Strange		
69K Donnie Kreitz	6.00	12.00
Kreitzer Excavating		

1995-1998 Action Sprint Cars 1:64

This series of 1:64 scale sprint cars feature some of the top names from the World of Outlaw circuit. Highlighting the series are former WoO champions Steve Kinser and Dave Blaney.

	Lo	Hi
1 Billy Pauch	5.00	10.00
Zemco		
1 Sammy Swindell	5.00	10.00
Channellock		
1 Sammy Swindell	5.00	10.00
TMC 1993		
2 Andy Hillenburg	5.00	10.00
STP 1997		
5 Steve Kinser	5.00	10.00
Maxim 1993		
7TW Jeff Swindell	5.00	10.00
Gold Eagle		
10 Dale Blaney	5.00	10.00
Vivarin 1997		
11 Steve Kinser	6.00	10.00
Quaker State		
19 Stevie Smith	5.00	10.00
19 Stevie Smith	5.00	10.00
Ingersoll-Rand		
22 Jac Haudenchild	5.00	10.00
Pennzoil		
40 Jeff Gordon	7.50	15.00
Stanton		
69K Donny Kreitz	5.00	10.00
Kreitzer Excavating		
77 Fred Rahmer	5.00	10.00
Manheim Auctions		

1996-1998 GMP Sprint Car 1:18

The first spring car piece released by GMP was the Steve Kinser. Upon release it was quickly one of the most popular pieces on the market. The Jeff Gordon and Jac Haudenschild pieces have also done well.

	Lo	Hi
1 Sammy Swindell	90.00	140.00
Channellock		
1 Sammy Swindell	80.00	120.00
Channellock		
25th Anniversary paint scheme		
1 Sammy Swindell	70.00	100.00
TMC		
5 Danny Lasoski	65.00	90.00
Jackpot Junction		
5M Mark Kinser	70.00	100.00
Wirtgen		
6 Jeff Gordon	140.00	200.00
Molds Unlimited		
7TW Jeff Swindell	70.00	100.00
Gold Eagle		
10 Dave Blaney	70.00	110.00
Vivarin		
11 Steve Kinser	250.00	350.00
Quaker State		
15 Donny Schatz	80.00	130.00
Petro Shopping Center		
18 Brad Doty	70.00	100.00
Coors Light		
22 Jac Haudenschild	90.00	150.00
Pennzoil		
47 Johnny Herrera	70.00	110.00
Strange		
69 Brent Kaeding	70.00	110.00
Pioneer Concrete		
96 El Dora Speedway	90.00	150.00
97 Knoxville Raceway	70.00	100.00

1996-1998 GMP Sprint Car 1:25

With the release of the Dale Blaney piece in early 1997, GMP started a whole new scale size for Sprint Cars. There were 4,404 of the All-Star Champion Dale Blaney's issued.

	Lo	Hi
1F Dean Jacobs	35.00	60.00
Frigidare		
1W Danny Lasoski	35.00	60.00
Con West		
2A Bobby Adamson	40.00	70.00
Johnny Lightning		
7TW Jeff Swindell	35.00	60.00
Gold Eagle		
11 Steve Kinser	50.00	90.00
Quaker State		
22 Jac Haudenchild	35.00	60.00
Pennzoil		
69 Brent Kaeding	35.00	60.00
Pioneer Concrete		
75 Joey Saldana	35.00	60.00
Mopar		
94 Dale Blaney	35.00	60.00
Hughes Axel		
97 Eldora Speedway	45.00	80.00

1994 Racing Champions Sprint Cars 1:24

This series of 1:24 Racing Champions sprint cars is a good cross section of all the different drivers that race sprints. The series features top names like Steve Kinser, Dave Blaney and Jac Haudenschild.

	Lo	Hi
0 Rick Ferkel	10.00	20.00
Kears		
0 Randy Smith	8.00	16.00
Bingo		
00 Jason Statler	8.00	16.00
Rios		
1 G.Brazier	12.00	22.00
O'Brein		
1 Sammy Swindell	20.00	35.00
Bull and Hannah		
1 Sammy Swindell	45.00	70.00
TMC		
1A Bobby Allen	60.00	100.00
Kriners		
2 Frankie Herr	10.00	20.00
Family Ford		
2 Frankie Herr	10.00	20.00
Rifes RV		
2 Andy Hillenburg	10.00	20.00
STP with Dark Blue paint scheme		
2 Andy Hillenburg	20.00	35.00
STP with Light Blue paint scheme		
2 Andy Hillenburg	18.00	32.00
STP with signature		
2 Gary Rush	10.00	20.00
Castrol		
2L Ed Lynch	10.00	20.00
U2 Rocky Hodges	10.00	20.00
United Express		
4A Greg Hodnett	10.00	20.00
Mid So Forklift		
4 Bobby Davis Jr.	8.00	16.00
Pro Shocks		
5 Max Dumesney	60.00	90.00
Valvoline		
5 Dennis Lasoski	30.00	50.00
7 Richard Griffin	8.00	16.00
Sanders		
7 Jimmy Sills	8.00	16.00
Berry B Racing		
7 S.Snellbaker	12.50	25.00
Rifes RV		
7TW Jeff Swindell	10.00	20.00
Gold Eagle		
8TW Greg Hodnett	8.00	16.00
Kele		
9TW Joe Gaerte	8.00	16.00
10 Dave Blaney	18.00	30.00
Vivarin		
11 Steve Kinser	15.00	25.00
Valvoline		
11 Ron Shuman	8.00	16.00
CH Enginering		
12 Fred Rahmer	15.00	30.00
Apple Chevrolet		
12X Danny Smith	10.00	20.00
Beaver Drill		
14 Tim Green	10.00	20.00
Swift Mete Finish		
14P Kevin Pylant	10.00	20.00
Taco Bravo		
18 Brad Doty	20.00	35.00
Shaver Racing		
21 Steve Beitler	8.00	16.00
Brownfield		
21 Lance Blevins	8.00	16.00
Citgo		
22 Jac Haudenschild	12.50	25.00
Pennzoil with Red numbers		
22 Jac Haudenschild	10.00	20.00
Pennzoil with Yellow numbers		
23S Frankie Kerr	10.00	20.00
Shoff Motorsports		
24 J.Stone	8.00	16.00
Weld Racing		
27 Terry McCarl	8.00	16.00
Westside Radiator		
29 Keith Kaufman	8.00	16.00
Weckerts Livestock		
45 Doug Wolfgang	10.00	20.00
Snap On		
45X Johnny Herrera	8.00	16.00
Herrera Motorsports		
47 Dennis Lasoski	15.00	25.00
Casey's		
49 Doug Wolfgang	25.00	40.00
Snap On		
55 Max Dumesy	12.00	22.00
Halletts Mats		
65 Jim Carr	8.00	16.00
Maxim		
66 Mike Peters	8.00	16.00
TropArtic		
69 Brent Kaeding	10.00	20.00
JW Hunt		
69 Brent Kaeding	8.00	16.00
High-Five Pizza		
69K Donnie Kreitz Jr.	12.00	22.00
Vollmer Patterns		
71M Kenny Jacobs	15.00	25.00
Beltline		
71M Kenny Jacobs	8.00	16.00
Eco Water		
77 J.Shepard	18.00	30.00
Mac Tools		
77 Stevie Smith	10.00	20.00
Hamilton		
77 Stevie Smith	20.00	35.00
Mac Tools		
97B Aaron Berryhill	10.00	20.00
Berryhill Racing		

1995 Racing Champions Sprint Cars 1:24

This was the second year that Racing Champions produced a 1:24 sprint car series. The series again included many of the big names from the World of Outlaw circuit.

	Lo	Hi
0 Danny Smith	7.00	14.00
0 Randy Smith	7.00	14.00
Bingo Casino		
1 Billy Pauch	8.00	16.00
Zemco		
1 Sammy Swindell	10.00	20.00
Bull and Hannah		
1 Sammy Swindell	10.00	20.00
Hooters		
2 Andy Hillenburg	8.00	16.00
STP		
2 Andy Hillenburg	9.00	18.00
STP Oil		
2J J.J.Yeley	7.00	14.00
4S Tommy Scott	9.00	18.00
Scott Performance		
5 Terry McCarl	10.00	20.00
CS Enterprises		
5M Mark Kinser	9.00	18.00
Wirtgen		
7TW Jeff Swindell	7.00	14.00
Gold Eagle		
8TW Greg Hodnett	8.00	16.00
with Red numbers		
8TW Greg Hodnett	15.00	25.00
with Yellow numbers		
9W Joe Gaerte	7.00	14.00
Two Winners		
9TW Gary Wright	7.00	14.00
Action Rent		
10 Dave Blaney	10.00	20.00
Vivarin		
11 Steve Kinser	10.00	20.00
Valvoline		
11 Ron Shuman	7.00	14.00
CH Enginering		
12 Fred Rahmer	9.00	18.00
Apple Chevrolet		
14P Kevin Pylant	8.00	16.00
Unicopy		
16 Jeff Gordon	8.00	16.00
JG Motorsports		
17E Cris Eash	8.00	16.00
Miller		
21 Steve Beitler	7.00	14.00
Brownfield		
21 Lance Blevins	7.00	14.00
Citgo		
21K L.Kennedy	7.00	14.00
CT Fleet		
21K L.Kennedy	7.00	14.00
Superior Custom		
22 Jac Haudenschild	10.00	20.00
Pennzoil		
23S Frankie Kerr	7.00	14.00
31 S.Blandford	7.00	14.00
Avenger		
47 Dennis Lasoski	7.00	14.00
Housby Trucking		
65 Jim Carr	7.00	14.00
Maxim		
66 Mike Peters	7.00	14.00
TropArtic		
69 Brent Keading	9.00	18.00
Motorola		
71M Kenny Jacobs	7.00	14.00
EcoWater		
71M Stevie Smith	7.00	14.00
EcoWater		
77 Joe Gaerte	15.00	30.00
Cornwell		
97B Aaron Berryhill	7.00	14.00

1996 Racing Champions Sprint Cars 1:24

For the thrid consecutive year Racing Champions produced 1:24 scale Sprint cars. The cars were primarily distributed through mass market retailiers. 1996 World of Outlaw Champion Mark Kinser is one of the highlights to the series.

	Lo	Hi
1X Randy Hannagan	8.00	16.00
Carrera		
5 Danny Lasoski	8.00	16.00
Jackpot Junction		
5M Mark Kinser	8.00	16.00
Wirtgen		
9W Gary Wright	8.00	16.00
10 Dave Blaney	8.00	16.00
Vivarin		
22 Jac Haudenschild	8.00	16.00
Pennzoil		
47 Johnny Herrera	8.00	16.00
69 Brent Kaeding	8.00	16.00
Motorola		
71M Stevie Smith	8.00	16.00
EcoWater		
83 Joey Saldana	8.00	16.00
Southwest Hide		
461 Lance Dewease	8.00	16.00
Dyer Masonary		

1997 Racing Champions Sprint Cars 1:24

This was the fourth year of production of the 1:24 scale Sprint cars by Racing Champions.

	Lo	Hi
1 Billy Pauch	12.00	20.00
Zemco		
1F Dean Jacobs	12.00	22.00
Frigidaire		
1J Marlon Jones	12.00	20.00
Energy Release		
1X Randy Hannigan	12.00	20.00
TRW		
2 Ron Shuman	12.00	20.00
Havoline		
2 Andy Hillenburg	12.00	20.00
STP		
2M Brent Kaeding	12.00	20.00
Pioneer		
3G Joe Gaerte	12.00	20.00
Gaerte Engines		
7TW Jeff Swindell	12.00	20.00
Gold Eagle		
8 Terry McCarl	12.00	20.00
Holbrook		
8R Stevie Reeves	12.00	20.00
D&B Racing		
9W Gary Wright	12.00	20.00
Action		
11H Greg Hodnet	12.00	20.00
Selma Shell		
12 Keith Kauffman	12.00	22.00

Apple Chevrolet		
15 Donny Schatz	12.00	20.00
Blue Beacon		
17E Chris Eash	12.00	20.00
Miller Brothers		
21L Lance Blevins	12.00	20.00
Citgo		
22 Jac Haudenchild	12.00	20.00
Pennzoil		
23S Frankie Kerr	12.00	20.00
Shoff Motorsports		
28 Brian Paulus	12.00	20.00
P&P Racing		
29 Tommy Estes	12.00	20.00
F&J Construction		
29 Brent Kaeding	12.00	20.00
BK Racing		
47 Johnny Herrera	12.00	20.00
Casey's		
69K Donnie Kreitz	12.00	20.00
Stockdale		
83 Paul McMahan	12.00	20.00
Beef Packers		
88 Todd Shaeffer	12.00	20.00
Turnbaugh		
92 Kenny Jacobs	12.00	20.00
Imperial		
94 Dale Blanney	12.00	20.00
Hughes		
461 Lance Dewease	12.00	20.00
Dyer Masonary		

1996 Racing Champions Sprint Cars 1:64

This series of 1:64 scale Sprint cars features some of the most talented drivers in the World of Outlaws series. 14-time Champion Steve Kinser and Winston Cup star Jeff Gordon are a couple of the highlights in the series.

	Lo	Hi
Sammy Swindell	2.00	5.00
Channellock		
W J.Shepard	2.00	5.00
Conn West		
X Randy Hannagan	2.00	5.00
Carrera		
Andy Hillenburg	2.00	5.00
STP		
S Tommy Scott	10.00	18.00
Scott Performance		
Danny Lasoski	2.00	5.00
Jackpot Junction		
M Mark Kinser	2.00	5.00
Wirtgen		
M Jim Carr	2.00	5.00
American Fire Extinguisher		
TW Jeff Swindell	2.00	5.00
Gold Eagle		
Gary Wright	2.00	5.00
TRW		
0 Dave Blaney	2.00	5.00
Vivarin		
1 Steve Kinser	4.00	8.00
Quaker State		
1H Greg Hodnett	2.00	5.00
Selma Shell		
6 Jeff Gordon	10.00	18.00
JG Motorsports		
1 Lance Blevins	2.00	5.00
Citgo		
2 Jac Haudenschild	2.00	5.00
Pennzoil Old number 22		
2 Jack Haudenschild	2.00	5.00
Pennzoil New number 22		
8D Brad Doty	2.00	5.00
Bower's Coal		
8D Brad Doty	10.00	18.00
Bower's Coal numbered of 5,000		
7 Johnny Herrera	2.00	5.00
Housby Trucks		
9 Brent Kaeding	2.00	5.00
Motorola		
9 Brent Kaeding	2.00	5.00
Pioneer Concrete		
1M Stevie Smith	2.00	5.00
EcoWater No red stripe		
71M Stevie Smith	2.00	5.00
EcoWater with Red stripe		
83 Joey Saldana	2.00	5.00
Beef Packers		
88 T.Shaffer	2.00	5.00
Leiby's Mobile Home		
94 Dale Blaney	2.00	5.00
Hughes Motorsports		
461 Lance Dewease	2.00	5.00
Dyer Masonry		

1997 Racing Champions Sprint Cars 1:64

This series of 1:64 Sprint cars by Racing Champions was primarily issued through mass market retailers.

	Lo	Hi
1 Billy Pauch	2.00	5.00
Zemco		
1F Dean Jacobs	2.00	5.00
Frigidaire		
1J Marlon Jones	2.00	5.00
Energy Release		
1X Randy Hannigan	2.00	5.00
TRW		
2 Andy Hillenburg	2.00	5.00
STP		
2 Ron Shuman	2.00	5.00
Havoline		
U2 Keith Kauffman	2.00	5.00
United Express		
2M Brent Kaeding	2.00	5.00
Pioneer		
3G Joe Gaerte	2.00	5.00
Gaerte Engines		
4S Tommy Scott	3.00	6.00
On Broadway		
7TW Jeff Swindell	2.00	5.00
Gold Eagle		
8 Terry McCarl	2.00	5.00
Holbrook		
8R Stevie Reeves	2.00	5.00
D&B Racing		
9W Gary Wright	2.00	5.00
Action		
11H Greg Hodnet	2.00	5.00
Selma Shell		
12 Keith Kauffman	2.00	5.00
Apple Chevrolet		
15 Donnie Schatz	2.00	5.00
Blue Beacon		
17E Chris Eash	2.00	5.00
Miller Brothers		
21L Lance Blevins	2.00	5.00
Citgo		
22 Jac Haudenchild	2.00	5.00
Pennzoil		
23S Frankie Kerr	2.00	5.00
Shoff Motorsports		
28 Brian Paulus	2.00	5.00
P&P Racing		
29 Brent Kaeding	2.00	5.00
BK Racing		
29 Tommy Estes	2.00	5.00
F&J Construction		
36 Joe Gaerte	2.00	5.00
Gaerte Engines		
47 Johnny Herrera	2.00	5.00
Casey's		
69K Donnie Kreitz	2.00	5.00
Stockdale		
83 Paul McMahan	2.00	5.00
Beef Packers		
88 Todd Shaeffer	2.00	5.00
Turnbaugh		
92 Kenny Jacobs	2.00	5.00
Imperial		
94 Dale Blanney	2.00	5.00
Hughes		
461 Lance Dewease	2.00	5.00
Dyer Masonry		

1998 Racing Champions Sprint Cars 1:64

This series of 1:64 Sprint cars by Racing Champions was primarily issued through mass market retailers.

	Lo	Hi
0 J.Statler	2.00	5.00
Rios Construction		
1 B.Pauch	2.00	5.00
Zemco		
1J M.Jones	2.00	5.00
Energy Release		
1W C.Dollansky	2.00	5.00
Conn West		
2M B.Kaeding	2.00	5.00
Pioneer		
3G J.Gaerte	2.00	5.00
Gaerte		
4J J.Shepard	2.00	5.00
York Excavating		
7 Kevin Huntley	2.00	5.00
Peterbilt		
9S S.Stewart	2.00	5.00
RC Cola		
11H G.Hodnet	2.00	5.00
Selma Shell		
11H G.Hodnett	2.00	5.00
Vivarin		
12S S.Carson	2.00	5.00
Helms Motorsports		
15 D.Schatz	2.00	5.00
Blue Beacon		
18 D.Hindi	2.00	5.00
Albuqueque		
23S Frankie Kerr	2.00	5.00
Shoff Motorsports		
24 T.McCarl	2.00	5.00
McCroskey		
28 B.Paulus	2.00	5.00
P&P Racing		
29 B.Kaeding	2.00	5.00
BK Motorsports		
29 T.Estes	2.00	5.00
F&J Construction		
35 T.Walker	2.00	5.00
Air Sep		
55 S.Jackson	2.00	5.00
Jensen Construction		
69K D.Kreitz	2.00	5.00
Stockdale		
88 T.Schaffer	2.00	5.00
Turnbaugh Oil		
461 L.DeWease	2.00	5.00
Dyer		
U2 K.Kauffman	2.00	5.00
United Express		

Racing Alphabetical Index

This alphabetical index presents all the cards issued for any particular driver (or person) included in the card sets listed in the Beckett Racing Price Guide. It will prove to be an invaluable tool for seasoned and novice collectors alike. Although this book was carefully compiled and proofread, it is inevitable that errors, misspellings, and inconsistencies may occur. Also, with winner circle type card photos, we have tried to identify and link at least the main figures on the card. If you should come across a card where we have not identified all persons on the card of if there are any errors that come to your attention, please send them to the author. These corrections will be incorporated into future editions of the racing alphabetical checklist.

How to Use the Alphabetical Checklist

The alphabetical checklist has been designed to be user friendly. The set code abbreviations used throughout are easily identified and memorized. The format adopted for card identification is explained below. However, the large number of card sets contained in this volume require that the reader first become familiar with how the abbreviations are organized. PLEASE READ THE FOLLOWING SECTION CAREFULLY BEFORE ATTEMPTING TO USE THE CHECKLIST.

The cards are listed alphabetically by the player's current last name. Where appropriate, nicknames (e.g. Glenn Fireball Roberts) are after the players first name and in parentheses. Different drivers with otherwise identical names are sometimes distinguished by additional information (e.g. Mark Martin and Mark DIRT Martin). The codes following the drivers' names are indented and give the card sets and card numbers in the sets in which the drivers appeared. The set codes are designed so that each code is distinctive for a particular card set.

The set code for each set name is done in a simple to use formula throughout the alphabetical checklist. The abbreviations are in a 3-3-1-1-1-1 pattern. What this means is that each set in the book as been abbreviated the first three letters of the first name of the set, the first three letters of the second name of the set, and the first letter of each name after that. Here is an example:

Allison, Clifford
93 ActPac-146
93 MaxTexDA-2

The first card is a 1993 Action Packed card #146. The first three letters of the first name (Action), and the first three letters of the second name (Packed) were used to create this abbreviation. The second card is a 1993 Maxx Texaco Davey Allison card #2. Again the first three letters of the first and second name of the set (Maxx Texaco) are used to give us the MaxTex part of the abbreviation. The first letter from each of the next two names (Davey Allison) is used to give us the last part of the abbreviation.

Depending on the particular card set, the set code abbreviations consist of from three to five distinctive elements:

a) Year of issue (listed in ascending chronological order);
b) Producer or sponsor;
c) Number on card;
d) Individual card descriptive prefixes or suffixes.

When two different producers issued cards for a driver in the same year, the cards are listed alphabetically according to the maker's name (e.g. 1992 Maxx precedes 1992 Traks).

The card number typically corresponds to the particular number on the card itself; in some instances, the card number also involves letter prefixes. For the most part, cards in unnumbered sets are usually entered alphabetically according to the driver's last name and assigned a number arbitrarily. In a few instances unnumbered cards are simply identified as if their card number were "NNO."

Lastly, the user of this checklist will notice that the cards of people from sports other than racing (as well as subjects not even from the world of sports) are contained in this checklist. This circumstance arose because of the many cross brand sets that manufacturers have done and the inclusion of many people that have appeared with a featured racing driver.

Abbott, Bruce
90CheFlal-95
Abell, Chuck
92BulRin-63
Aber, Blaine
92STAMod-1
Abernathy, Billy
94HigGeaPPT-G4
94HigGeaPPTG-4G
Adams, Bob Jr.
92STAMod-4
Adams, Bubba
92BulRin-86
Adams, Dave
91K&WDirT-28
92K&WDirT-23
94K&WDirT-32
95K&WDirT-26
Adams, Kenny
92TraASA-44
Adams, Landy
92K&WDirT-41
Adams, Terry
89CheFlal-35
89CheFlal-36
90CheFlal-67
Adams, Weldon
92SpoLegBB-BB20
Agabashian, Freddie
91LegInd-28
Agnew, Jeff
91BulRin-105
92BulRin-58
92BulRin-105
Ahlquist, Jerry
91LanRocS-55
92LanRocS-1
Aikey, Jeff
92JAG-126
Airikkala, Pentti
78GraPri-231
Akers, Wayne
92EriMaxTA-1
92EriMaxTA-2
Akin, Tom
73FleAHRRU-30
Alboreto, Michele
87AceForO-1
87ForOneI-1
88HerFouFO-2A
91CarForO-25
91CarForO-26
91CarForO-27
91ProTraFO-19
91ProTraFO-20
91ProTraFO-21
92GriForO-10
92GriForO-43
92GriForO-76
97Hi-IRL-12
97Hi-IRL'I5-I9
97Hi-IRLP-D7
Albright, John
65TopHotR-48
Albright, Tony
92JAG-127
93JAG-1
94JAG-1
Alderman, Darrell
89MegDra-48
89MegDra-49
91ProSetN-34
91ProSetN-82
95ActPacN-21
95ActPacNSS-21
Aldrich, Todd
90LanRocSHS-35
91LanRocS-48
Aldridge, Travis
92TraTeaS-122
Alen, Markku
78GraPri-6
78GraPri-224
Alesi, Jean
91CarForO-79
91CarForO-80
91CarForO-81
91ProTraFO-65
91ProTraFO-66
92GriForO-26
92GriForO-59
92GriForO-92
92GriForO-103
92GriForO-108
95FutFor1P-P2
Alexander, Mike
89Max-84
90Max-84
91Max-85
91MaxUpd-85
Alkey, Jeff
91DKIMCDT-40
Allen, Alfred
91ProSet-120
Allen, Bobby
87WorOut-14
88WorOut-12
89WorOut-15
90WorOut-13
90WorOutP-1A
91WorOut-14
92RacLegS-25
94WorOut-21
Allen, Bruce
89MegDra-19
89MegDra-20
91ProSetN-41
91ProSetN-89
92ProSetN-70
92ProSetN-144
93FinLinN-72
93FinLinN-73
Allen, Glenn Jr.
92TraASA-2
96Fla-37
96UltUpd-34
97Pre-43
97PreBlaWFS-43
97PreGri-43
97PreRedW-43
97SkyPro-58
97SkyProA-58
97Ult-94
97UltUpd-66
97UltUpdAR-66
97Viper-50
97ViperBlaR-50
99Pre-47
Allen, Glenn Sr.
92TraASA-27
99PrePas-47
Allen, Jeb
73FleAHRRU-68
Allen, Joey
87WorOut-34
88WorOut-17
89WorOut-25
Allen, Johnny
89Max-185
89TGRacMR-73
89TGRacMR-74
89WinCir-39
91TGRacMRU-73
91TGRacMRU-74
Allen, Ken
94LanARCF-10
94LanARCF-99
Allen, Loy Jr.
92LanARCF-36
93LanARCFP-PR1
94ActPac-56
94ActPac-87
94ActPac-106
94ActPac2G-41G
94DaySer3-32
94FinLin-76
94FinLin-77
94FinLinNSH-8
94FinLinS-76
94FinLinS-77
94HigGea-119
94HigGeaDO-119
94HigGeaDOG-119
94HigGeaG-119
94HigGeaRSA-RS6
94LanARCF-24
94Max-37
94Max-316
94MaxAut-7
94MaxAut-9
94MaxAut-37
94MaxMot-17
94MaxPreS-37
94MaxRooC'-7
94OptXL-61
94OptXLRH-61
94Pow-1
94Pow-26
94PowGol-1
94PowGol-26
94Tra-53
94Tra-68
94Tra-143
94TraAutV-23
94TraFirR-53
94TraFirR-68
94TraFirR-143
94VIP-1
95ActPacP-29
95FinLin-84
95FinLinPP-84
95FinLinSil-84
95HigGea-30
95HigGeaBC-BC1
95HigGeaBCG-BC1
95HigGeaDO-30
95HigGeaDOG-30
95HigGeaG-30
95Ima-19
95ImaGol-19
95Max-19
95Max-182
95MaxCroC-19
95MaxPreP-19
95MaxPreS-19
95MaxPreS-79
95MaxPreSU-1
95PrePas-1
95PrePasCC-1
95PrePasRH-1
95Sel-1
95Sel-120
95Sel-144
95SelFlaO-1
95SelFlaO-120
95SelFlaO-144
95SelPro-128
95Tra-15
95TraFirR-15
95UppDec-29
95UppDec-97
95UppDec-205
95UppDec-249
95UppDec-284
95UppDecA-205
95UppDecGSEG-29
95UppDecGSEG-97
95UppDecGSEG-205
95UppDecGSEG-249
95UppDecGSEG-284
95UppDecSSES-29
95UppDecSSES-97
95UppDecSSES-205
95UppDecSSES-249
95UppDecSSES-284
96ActPacC-43
96ActPacCSS-43
96Ass-12
96AutRac-37
96AutRacA-1
96AutRacCA-1
96MaxPre-19
96MaxPre-39
96SP-19
96UppDec-20
96UppDecRTTC-RC36
96UppDecRTTC-RC85
96UppDecRTTC-RC117
97ColCho-19
97ColCho-69
97ColChoUD5-UD38
97ColChoUD5-UD39
97JurPar-47
97JurParT-47
97SP-19
97SP-61
97SP SupS-19
97SP SupS-61
97UppDecVC-19
97UppDecVC-69
98UppDecRttC-14
Allen, Ron
95JSKIce-69
Alley, Ray
71FleAHRDC-19
Alligood, Teresa
91MaxBilETCM-37A
Alliott, Philippe
87AceForO-2
Allison, Bobby
72STP-1
83UNORac-29
86SpoPhoG-1
88MaxCha-7
88MaxCha-30
88MaxCha-94
89Max-12
89Max-141
89Max-180
90Max-12
90MaxHolF-HF26
91Max-27
91Max-175
91MaxWin2AF-13
91ProSet-38A
91ProSet-38B
91ProSet-AU38
91ProSetL-L31
91ProSetP-P1
91SpoLegBA-P1
91SpoLegBA-BA1
91SpoLegBA-BA2
91SpoLegBA-BA3
91SpoLegBA-BA4
91SpoLegBA-BA5
91SpoLegBA-BA6
91SpoLegBA-BA7
91SpoLegBA-BA8
91SpoLegBA-BA9
91SpoLegBA-BA10
91SpoLegBA-BA11
91SpoLegBA-BA12
91SpoLegBA-BA13
91SpoLegBA-BA14
91SpoLegBA-BA15
91SpoLegBA-BA16
91SpoLegBA-BA17
91SpoLegBA-BA18
91SpoLegBA-BA19
91SpoLegBA-BA20
91SpoLegBA-BA21
91SpoLegBA-BA22
91SpoLegBA-BA23
91SpoLegBA-BA24
91SpoLegBA-BA25
91SpoLegBA-BA26
91SpoLegBA-BA27
91SpoLegBA-BA28
91SpoLegBA-BA29
91SpoLegBA-BA30
91SpoLegDA-P1
91SpoLegDA-DA12
91SpoLegDA-DA16
91SpoLegDA-DA17
91SpoLegDA-DA20
91SpoLegDA-DA21
91SpoLegDA-DA22
91SpoLegDA-DA24
91SpoLegDA-DA27
91SpoLegNB-NB11
92ActPacAF-NNO
92MacTooWC-1
92MaxBla-114
92MaxRed-114
92MaxSamB-7
92MaxTexDA-19
92ProSet-144
92ProSetL-L32
92ProSetR-5
92ProSetRF-L5
92ProSetTTHS-2
92Tra-14
92Tra-92
92TraASA-38
92TraBenP-35
92TraTeaS-170
92TraTeaS-175
93ActPac-140
93ActPac-143
93ActPac-146
93ActPac-147
93ActPacDA-DA3
93ActPacP-BA1
93FinLin-113
93FinLinCS-20
93FinLinDA-4
93FinLinDA-5
93FinLinDA-10
93FinLinS-113
93Max-129
93MaxCluSBC-1
93MaxCluSBC-2
93MaxCluSBC-4
93MaxHou-17
93MaxPreP-116
93MaxPreP-188
93MaxPreS-129
93MaxTexDA-2
93MaxTexDA-11
93MaxWinM-3
93MaxWinM-5
93MaxWinM-6
93Pep400VL-1
93PrePasDA-4
93PrePasPre-23
93Tra-149
93Tra-178
93TraFirR-149
93TraFirR-178
93TraTri-18
93TraTri-48
93WheRooTS-SP2
94FinLin-132
94FinLinS-132
94HigGea-31
94HigGeaG-31
94HigGeaL-LS3
94Max-102
94MaxPreP-102
94MaxPreS-102
94Pow-74
94PowGol-74
94PrePas-73
94Tra-12
94Tra-114
94Tra-141
94TraAutV-32
94TraFirR-12
94TraFirR-114
94TraFirR-141
94VIP-82
95FinLin-12
95FinLinPP-12
95FinLinSil-12
95HigGea-38
95HigGeaDO-38
95HigGeaDOG-38
95HigGeaG-38
95MatWinCC-13
95Max-91
95MaxCroC-84
95MaxPreP-84
95MaxPreS-95
95MetImpWCC-6
95PrePas-124
95PrePasRH-124
95Sel-75
95Sel-112
95Sel-131
95SelFlaO-75
95SelFlaO-112
95SelFlaO-131
95SP-126
95SPDieC-126
95TraVal-81
95UppDec-155
95UppDecGSEG-155
95UppDecI-I2
95UppDecSSES-155
95VIP-46
95VIPCooB-46
95VIPEmeP-46
95VIPRedHCB-46
96ActPacC-77
96CroJewEDT-36
96CroJewEDTC-36
96CroJewEE-36
96CroJewEli-36
96CroJewES-36
96CroJewETC-36
96CroJewETCE-36
96CroJewETCS-36
96FinLin-25
96FinLinPriP-25
96FinLinS-25
96Fla-47
96M-F-16
96Max-73
96MaxPep5-1
96MaxPre-99
96MetImp2AWCC-13
96PrePas-82
96PrePasSco-82
96PrePasT-82
96Ult-147
96UppDec-126
96UppDecRL-RLC3
96ZenChaS-13
96ZenChaS-P12
97ActPacFA-3

97ActPacFAA-3
97ColCho-123
97ColChoUD5-UD24
97RacSha-33
97RacShaGWP-33
97RacShaH-33
97RacShaTS-33
97Ult-58
98Max10tA-21
98Max10tA-66
98Max10tA-92
98Max10tA-109
98Max10tABA-1
98Max10tACP-CP8
98Max10tACPDC-CP8
98PrePas-132
98PrePasPR-4B
98UppDecRTTC5A-AN20
98UppDecRTTC5A-AN28
98UppDecRTTC5AA-AN39
99PrePas-128

Allison, Clifford

92ActPacAF-NNO
92LanARCF-58
92LanARCF-NNO
92MaxBla-31
92MaxRed-31
92ProSet-32
92ProSetRC-3
92ProSetRC-4
93ActPac-142
93ActPac-146
93MaxTexDA-2

Allison, Davey

88MaxCha-5
88MaxCha-40
88MaxCha-49
88MaxCha-89
88MaxMyrB-47
89Max-28
89Max-113
89Max-119
89Max-124
89Max-127
89Max-159
89Max-162
89Max-180
89MaxCri-10
90Max-28A
90Max-28B
90Max-175
90MaxHolF-HF9
91Max-28
91Max-175
91Max-196
91MaxMcD-13
91MaxMot-2
91MaxMot-28
91MaxMot-30
91MaxRacFK-3
91MaxTheWA-1
91SpoLegDJ-DJ8
91SpoLegHS-HS7
91SunRacL-4
91Tra-28
91Tra-156
92ActPacAF-NNO
92CarDynDA-1
92CarDynDA-2
92CarDynDA-3
92CarDynDA-4
92CarDynDA-5
92CarDynGO-5
92CoyRoo-9
92DaySer1-1
92MacTooWC-2
92MaxBla-28
92MaxBla-190
92MaxBla-198
92MaxBla-273
92MaxBla-276
92MaxBla-278
92MaxBla-291
92MaxBla-292
92MaxMcD-1
92MaxMcD-3
92MaxMot-2
92MaxMot-37
92MaxMot-49
92MaxMot-50
92MaxRed-28
92MaxRed-190
92MaxRed-198
92MaxRed-273
92MaxRed-274
92MaxRed-276
92MaxRed-278
92MaxRed-291
92MaxRed-292
92MaxTexDA-1
92MaxTexDA-2
92MaxTexDA-5
92MaxTexDA-6
92MaxTexDA-7
92MaxTexDA-8
92MaxTexDA-10
92MaxTexDA-11
92MaxTexDA-12
92MaxTexDA-13
92MaxTexDA-14
92MaxTexDA-15
92MaxTexDA-16
92MaxTexDA-17
92MaxTexDA-18
92MaxTexDA-19
92MaxTexDA-20
92MaxTheW-1
92MaxTheW-21
92MaxTheW-41
92MaxTheW-42
92MaxTheW-48
92MaxTheW-50
92ProSet-41
92ProSet-183
92ProSet-211
92ProSet-223
92ProSet-229
92ProSetMH-10
92ProSetRF-2
92RPM-3
92STPDay5-8
92Tra-28
92Tra-156
92TraASA-39
92TraGoo-21
92TraRacM-28
92TraRacM-34
92TraRacM-35
92TraRacM-40
92TraRacM-65
92TraRacM-93
92TraRacM-99
92TraTeaS-3
92TraTeaS-26
92TraTeaS-28
92TraTeaS-29
92TraTeaS-42
92TraTeaS-44
92TraTeaS-49
92TraTeaS-50
92TraTeaS-101
93ActPac-5
93ActPac-21
93ActPac-43
93ActPac-79
93ActPac-80
93ActPac-97
93ActPac-98
93ActPac-140
93ActPac-144
93ActPac-146
93ActPac-AKDAG
93ActPac2G-4G
93ActPac2G-45G
93ActPac2G-46G
93ActPac2G-47G
93ActPac2G-48G
93ActPac2G-49G
93ActPac2G-50G
93ActPacDA-DA1
93ActPacDA-DA2
93ActPacDA-DA3
93ActPacDA-DA4
93ActPacDA-DA5
93ActPacDA-DA6
93FinLin-48
93FinLin-66
93FinLin-89
93FinLin-NNO
93FinLinCS-3
93FinLinCS-8
93FinLinCS-20
93FinLinDA-1
93FinLinDA-2
93FinLinDA-3
93FinLinDA-4
93FinLinDA-5
93FinLinDA-6
93FinLinDA-7
93FinLinDA-8
93FinLinDA-9
93FinLinDA-10
93FinLinDA-11
93FinLinDA-12
93FinLinDA-13
93FinLinDA-14
93FinLinDA-15
93FinLinP-P1
93FinLinS-48
93FinLinS-66
93FinLinS-89
93HiTecTT-3
93HiTecTT-P2
93Max-28
93Max-94
93Max-121
93Max-131
93Max-199
93Max-220
93Max-264
93Max-270
93Max-272
93Max-278
93Max-292
93MaxCluSBC-4
93MaxCluSBC-9
93MaxHou-3
93MaxHou-17
93MaxLowFS-3
93MaxMot-41
93MaxMot-42
93MaxMot-49
93MaxPreP-28
93MaxPreP-29
93MaxPreP-57
93MaxPreP-60
93MaxPreP-62
93MaxPreP-79
93MaxPreP-179
93MaxPreP-185
93MaxPreP-187
93MaxPreP-193
93MaxPreP-207
93MaxPrePJ-NNO
93MaxPreS-28
93MaxPreS-94
93MaxPreS-121
93MaxPreS-131
93MaxPreS-199
93MaxPreS-220
93MaxPreS-264
93MaxPreS-270
93MaxPreS-272
93MaxPreS-278
93MaxPreS-292
93MaxTexDA-1
93MaxTexDA-2
93MaxTexDA-5
93MaxTexDA-6
93MaxTexDA-7
93MaxTexDA-8
93MaxTexDA-9
93MaxTexDA-10
93MaxTexDA-11
93MaxTexDA-12
93MaxTexDA-13
93MaxTexDA-14
93MaxTexDA-15
93MaxTexDA-16
93MaxTexDA-17
93MaxTexDA-18
93MaxTexDA-19
93MaxTexDA-20
93MaxTexDA-AU1
93MaxTheW-9
93MaxTheW-29
93MotManC-1
93Pep400VL-2
93PrePasDA-1
93PrePasDA-2
93PrePasDA-3
93PrePasDA-4
93PrePasDA-5
93PrePasPre-1
93Tra-28
93Tra-69
93Tra-100
93Tra-127
93Tra-128
93Tra-178
93Tra-190
93Tra-200
93TraFirR-28
93TraFirR-69
93TraFirR-100
93TraFirR-127
93TraFirR-128
93TraFirR-178
93TraFirR-190
93TraFirR-200
93TraPreC-20
93TraTri-4
93TraTri-10
93TraTri-18
93TraTri-28
93TraTri-34
93TraTri-40
93WheRooT-28
93WheRooT-49
93WheRooT-56
93WheRooT-84
93WheRooT-85
93WheRooT-100
93WheRooTPla-28
93WheRooTPla-49
93WheRooTPla-56
93WheRooTPla-84
93WheRooTPla-85
93WheRooTPla-100
93WheRooTPro-P5
93WheRooTS-SP2
93WheRooTS-SP3
94ActPac-40
94ActPac2G-10G
94ActPacS2G-W7
94ActPacS2G-W8
94FinLinVL-VL1
94FinLinVL-VL16
94HigGea-77
94HigGea-100
94HigGeaG-77
94HigGeaG-100
94Max-28
94Max-53
94Max-203
94Max-209
94MaxPreP-28
94MaxPreP-31
94MaxPreP-58
94MaxPreP-69
94MaxPreP-168
94MaxPreS-28
94MaxPreS-53
94MaxPreS-262
94MaxPreS-268
94MaxPreSJ-11
94MaxRooY-9
94Pow-25
94PowGol-25
94PrePas-127
94PrePasRD-RD1
94Tra-19
94TraAutV-37
94TraFirR-19
94TraPreC-40
95FinLinCC6W-CC7
95Sel-112
95SelFlaO-112
98Max10tA-27
98Max10tA-72
98Max10tA-93
98Max10tA-113
98Max10tA-120
98Max10tA-121
98Max10tACotY-CY1
98PrePas-135
98UppDecRTTC5A-AN38
98UppDecRTTC5A-AN39

Allison, Deborah

92MaxBla-274
92MaxRed-274
92MaxTexDA-14

Allison, Donald

91SpoLegDA-DA5
91SpoLegHS-HS28
93ActPac-145

Allison, Donnie

89Max-184
89TGRacMR-191
89TGRacMR-192
89TGRacMR-193
91Max-117
91MaxUpd-117
91ProSetL-L11A
91ProSetL-L11B
91SpoLegBA-P1
91SpoLegDA-P1
91SpoLegDA-DA1
91SpoLegDA-DA2
91SpoLegDA-DA7
91SpoLegDA-DA8
91SpoLegDA-DA9
91SpoLegDA-DA10
91SpoLegDA-DA11
91SpoLegDA-DA12
91SpoLegDA-DA13
91SpoLegDA-DA14
91SpoLegDA-DA15
91SpoLegDA-DA16
91SpoLegDA-DA17
91SpoLegDA-DA18
91SpoLegDA-DA19
91SpoLegDA-DA20
91SpoLegDA-DA21
91SpoLegDA-DA22
91SpoLegDA-DA23
91SpoLegDA-DA24
91SpoLegDA-DA25
91SpoLegDA-DA26
91SpoLegDA-DA27
91SpoLegDA-DA28
91SpoLegDA-DA29
91SpoLegDA-DA30
91SpoLegNB-NB11
91TGRacMRU-191
91TGRacMRU-192
91TGRacMRU-193
92MaxBla-176
92MaxRed-176
92ProSetL-L7
93ActPac-141
93ActPac-143
93ActPac-145
93ActPac-148
93FinLin-63
93FinLinCS-24
93FinLinDA-10
93FinLinS-63
93WheRooT-10
93WheRooTPla-10
94Pep400VL-2
94PrePas-128
94VIP-83
98Max10tA-10
98Max10tA-55
98Max10tA-91

Allison, James

91LegInd-9

Allison, Judy

93ActPac-147
93ActPacDA-DA2
93MaxWinM-5

Allison, Katherine

93ActPac-140

Allison, Kenny

91SpoLegDA-DA3
91SpoLegHS-HS28
93ActPac-145

Allison, Krista

93ActPac-144

Allison, Liz

93ActPac-140
93ActPac-144

Allison, Pat

93ActPac-148

Allison, Robbie

93ActPac-144
93ActPacDA-DA4

Allison, Ronald

91SpoLegDA-DA4
93ActPac-145

Allison, Tommy

91Tra-168
92ProSet-188
92TraTeaS-35
93Tra-10
93TraFirR-10

Allman, Bud

91SpoLegNJ-NJ17

Almond, Earl

92TraTeaS-168

Almond, Jeff

92TraTeaS-168

Almond, Keith

91Tra-102
92ProSet-219
92ProSetTTHS-4
92Tra-102
92TraTeaS-168

Alsup, Bill

98Max-89
98Max-22
98Max-47
98Max-72
98Max-97
98Max10tA-41
98Max10tA-86
98Max10tAMP-P22
98MaxFieG-15
98MaxFieGTS-15
98MaxFieGTSA-15
98MaxFirC-F3
98MaxFouSGA-15
98MaxSwaP-SW6
98MaxYealRBS-42
98MaxYealRBS-76
98MaxYealRBS-124
98PrePasP-24
98PrePasP-42
98PrePasP-24
98PrePasP-42
98PrePasPS-PS14
98PrePasS-6
98PrePasSO-1
98PrePasSO-2
98PrePasSOD-1
98PrePasSOD-2
98SP Aut-26
98SP Aut-60
98SP AutSotTL1-S5
98UppDecRttC-43
98UppDecRttC-67
98UppDecRttC-80
98UppDecRttC-110
98UppDecVC-39
98UppDecVC-84
98UppDecVC-102
98UppDecVC3DoS-D16
98UppDecVC3DoSG-D16
98VIP-1
98VIPDriF-DF1
98VIPDriFD-DF1
98VIPExp-1
98Whe-1
98Whe-31
98WheGol-1
98WheGol-31
98WheGreF-GF1
99Pre-11
99PrePas-11
99PrePas-111
99PrePasCC-1
99UppDecVC-20
99UppDecVC-66
99UppDecVCIS-IS12
99UppDecVCNSS-JA
99UppDecVCSZ-SZ13
99UppDecVCTM-TM14
99UppDecVCUE-20
99UppDecVCUE-66
99WheHigG-11
99WheHigGAC-11
99WheHigGFG-11
99WheHigGM-11
99WheHigGS-GS11

Andretti, Mario
73NabSugDSC-4
77Spo-1009
77Spo-6513
77Spo-6716
77Spo-8112
78GraPri-1
78GraPri-8
78GraPri-9
78GraPri-14
78GraPri-40
78GraPri-56
78GraPri-58
78GraPri-59
78GraPri-68
78GraPri-80
78GraPri-83
78GraPri-88
78GraPri-101
78GraPri-108
78GraPri-121
78GraPri-128
78GraPri-140
78GraPri-214
80AvaHilURG-20
83A&SRacI-33
84A&SRacI-16
85A&SRacI-1
85A&SRacI-50
85SpoPhoGS-NNO
86A&SRacI-2
86BOSInd-1
87A&SRacI-2
87A&SRacI-20
87A&SRacI-48
90ActPacIP-6
91AllWorI-5
91AllWorI-96
91CarForO-101
91CarForO-102
91KMar-1
91LegInd-86
92AllWorI-25
92AllWorI-49
92AllWorI-50
92AllWorI-70
92ColACAR-2
92ColACAR-3
92ColACAR-4
92ColACAR-5
92ColACAR-6
92ColACAR-9
92ColACAR-10
92ColACAR-11
92ColACAR-12
92ColACAR-13
92ColACAR-14
92ColACAR-15
92ColACAR-16
92ColACAR-17
92ColACAR-18
92ColACAR-19
92ColACAR-20
92ColACAR-21
92ColACAR-22
92ColACAR-23
92ColACAR-24
92ColACAR-25
92ColACAR-32
92ColACAR-41
92ColACAR-42
92ColACAR-43
92ColACAR-51
92ColACAR-52
92ColACAR-53
92ColACAR-55
92ColACAR-56
92ColACAR-57
92ColACAR-59
92ColACAR-60
92ColACAR-61
92ColACAR-62
92ColACAR-65
92ColACAR-69
92ColACAR-70
92ColACAR-71
92ColACAR-72
92ColACAR-73
92ColACAR-75
92ColACAR-76
92ColACAR-78
92ColACAR-80
92ColACAR-81
92ColACAR-83
92ColACAR-86
92ColACAR-88
92ColACAR-89
92ColACAR-90
92ColACAR-91
92ColACAR-93
92ColACAR-96
92ColACAR-97
92ColACAR-98
92ColACAR-P1
92ColACAR-P2
92HiTecMA-1
92HiTecMA-2
92HiTecMA-3
92HiTecMA-4
92HiTecMA-5
92HiTecMA-6
92HiTecMA-7
92HiTecMA-8
92HiTecMA-9
92HiTecMA-10
92HiTecMA-11
92HiTecMA-12
92HiTecMA-13
92HiTecMA-14
92HiTecMA-15
92HiTecMA-16
92HiTecMA-17
92HiTecMA-18
92HiTecMA-19
92HiTecMA-20
92HiTecMA-21
92HiTecMA-22
92HiTecMA-23
92HiTecMA-24
92HiTecMA-25
92HiTecMA-26
92HiTecMA-27
92HiTecMA-28
92HiTecMA-29
92HiTecMA-30
92HiTecMA-31
92HiTecMA-32
92HiTecMA-33
92HiTecMA-34
92HiTecMA-35
92HiTecMA-36
92HiTecMA-37
92HiTecMA-38
92HiTecMA-39
92HiTecMA-40
92HiTecMA-41
92HiTecMA-42
92HiTecMA-43
92HiTecMA-44
92HiTecMA-45
92HiTecMA-46
92HiTecMA-47
92HiTecMA-48
92HiTecMA-49
92HiTecMA-50
92HiTecMA-52
92HiTecMA-P1
92HiTecP-1
92KMar-1
92LegInd-8
92LegInd-43
92LegInd-58
92LegInd-69
92LegInd-76
93HiTecI-3
93HiTecI-58
93HiTecI-70
93HiTecI-71
93KMar-1
93MaxWilR-15
94HiTecI-6
94HiTecI-40
94HiTecI-42
94HiTecICD-CD3
94HiTecIP-P2
94HiTecIP-P3
94KMar-1
95HiTecICD-CD11
95SkyInd5-12
95SkyInd5-27
95SkyInd5-59
95SkyInd5-104
95SkyInd5-107
95SkyInd5PC-13
95TraVal-75

Andretti, Michael
84A&SRacI-36
85A&SRacI-42
85A&SRacI-50
86A&SRacI-43
86AceInd-A3
86AceInd-G3
87A&SRacI-18
87A&SRacI-45
91AllWorI-25
91AllWorI-33
91AllWorI-66
91KMar-2
92AllWorI-1
92AllWorI-46
92AllWorI-49
92AllWorI-50
92AllWorI-79
92ColACAR-32
92ColACAR-42
92ColACAR-43
92ColACAR-44
92ColACAR-45
92ColACAR-46
92ColACAR-47
92ColACAR-48
92ColACAR-49
92ColACAR-50
92ColACAR-54
92ColACAR-58
92ColACAR-63
92ColACAR-64
92ColACAR-67
92ColACAR-68
92ColACAR-69
92ColACAR-75
92ColACAR-76
92ColACAR-77
92ColACAR-79
92ColACAR-85
92ColACAR-88
92ColACAR-91
92ColACAR-97
92ColACAR-99
92GriForO-200
92HiTecMA-44
92HiTecP-3
92KMar-2
92LegInd-3
92LegInd-42
92LegInd-P1
93HiTecI-6
93HiTecI-48
93HiTecI-71
94HiTecICD-CD4
95HiTecICD-CD8
95SkyInd5-7
95SkyInd5-23
95SkyInd5-78
95SkyInd5HI-4
96SkyInd5-13
96SkyInd5-79
97CARSchC-1

Andretti, Nancy
95FinLin-13
95FinLinPP-13
95FinLinSil-13

Andrew, Glenn
92EriMaxTA-52

Andrews, Darrell
91Max-207
92MaxAllPT-17
92MaxBla-243
92MaxRed-243
95MaxPreS-240

Andrews, Jeff
95VIP-55
95VIPAut-55
95VIPCooB-55
95VIPEmeP-55
95VIPRedHCB-55
96V.IAut-1
96VIP-50
96VIPEmeP-50
96VIPTor-50

Andrews, Jim
92VolRacLSI-3

Andrews, Paul
90Max-132
91Max-135
91MaxMot-24
91ProSet-92
92BikRacS-7
92MaxAllPT-26
92MaxBla-160
92MaxBla-249
92MaxMot-26
92MaxRed-160
92MaxRed-249
92ProSet-201
92Tra-171A
92Tra-171B
93FinLin-100
93FinLinCS-3
93FinLinS-100
93Max-142
93MaxPreP-127
93MaxPreS-142
94FinLinGT-TG9
94HigGea-137
94HigGeaDO-137
94HigGeaDOG-137
94HigGeaG-137
94Max-157
94MaxPreP-147
94MaxPreS-157
94PrePas-91
94VIP-91
95FinLin-36
95FinLinPP-36
95FinLinSil-36
95HigGea-47
95HigGeaDO-47
95HigGeaDOG-47
95HigGeaG-47
95Max-122
95MaxAut-122
95MaxCroC-126
95MaxPreP-126
95MaxPreS-150
95Sel-91
95SelFlaO-91
95SP-143
95SPDieC-143
95Tra5thA-79
95Tra5thAG-79
95TraAutV-12
95TraBehTS-BTS11
96AutRacA-3
96AutRacCA-3
96MaxPre-141
99Pre-71
99PrePas-71

Andrews, Todd
91DirTra-61
92DirTra-34
92JAG-130
92STAMod-10
94STAMod-2

Annarummo, Vinny
91LanSeeS-1
91LanStoCC-29

Anspaugh, David
91LanART-19

Antonnette, James
95ActPacNJDC-5

Appleby, Dion
91WorOut-63

Archer, Bobby
92EriMaxTA-3
92EriMaxTA-4

Archer, Tommy
92EriMaxTA-5
92EriMaxTA-6
95FinLinSRF-31
95FinLinSRF-40
95FinLinSRF-44
95FinLinSup-31
95FinLinSup-40
95FinLinSup-44
96MaxSup-ST2

Ard, Sam
92WinChoB-147
92WinChoB-148

Armbruster, Dan
94STAMod-3

Armenoff, Brian
94HiTecI-49
94HiTecI-50

Armes, Loren
93CorSelCCS-31

Armond, Keith
92TraTeaS-156

Armstrong, Dale
91ProSetN-106
92MacTooWC-3
92ProSetKB-3
92ProSetN-153
93FinLinN-5

Armstrong, Fred
94Pow-73
94PowGol-73

Armstrong, Mark
94HigGeaPPT-W33
94HigGeaPPTG-33W

Armstrong, Tony
87WorOut-29
88WorOut-20

Arnold, Billy
54StaWetIW-1930
60HawWaxI-18
95TraVal-36

Arnold, Chuck
62MarInd-1

Arnoux, Rene
78GraPri-37
78GraPri-64
78GraPri-65
78GraPri-156
87AceForO-3
87ForOneI-2
88HerFouFO-1C
88HerFouFO-NNO

Arp, Skip
91DirTra-20
91HavAT-26
92DirTra-30
92JAG-1

Arre, Tim
91WinChoM-6

Bazemore, Whit
89CheFlaI-53
91BigTimD-30
91BigTimD-85
91ProSetN-79
91ProSetN-130
92ProSetN-57
92ProSetN-127
93FinLinN-43
Beaber, Johnny
92VolRacLS2-4
92VolRacLSI-6
92VolRacLSI-7
Beadle, Raymond
86AceDra-F2
89Max-40
90Max-36
91Max-95
Bealieu, Bob
90BigTimD-1
90BigTimDS-1
Beam, Mike
89Max-81
90Max-53
91Max-45
91MaxMot-22
91ProSet-46
91Tra-82
92MaxBla-154
92MaxMot-27
92MaxRed-154
92ProSet-198
92ProSetMH-7
92Tra-82
93FinLin-80
93FinLinCS-14
93FinLinS-80
93Max-143
93MaxPreP-128
93MaxPreS-143
93Tra-11
93TraFirR-11
94FinLin-81
94FinLinS-81
94HigGea-42
94HigGeaG-42
94Max-135
94MaxPreP-128
94MaxPreS-135
94Tra-117
94TraFirR-117
95Max-120
95MaxAut-120
95MaxCroC-111
95MaxPreP-111
95MaxPreS-130
95MaxPreSU-9
95PrePas-91
95PrePasRH-91
95Sel-102
95SelFlaO-102
96Max-90
96MaxPre-151
96PrePas-81
96PrePasSco-81
96PrePasT-81
96Ult-36
96Viper-29
96ViperBlaM-29
96ViperCop-29
96ViperGreM-29
97PinPre-52
97PinPreBM-52
97PinPreGM-52
97PinPreP-TP10B
97PinPreSM-52
97PrePasAut-37
97Ult-67
97UltUpd-41
97Viper-59
97ViperBlaR-59
Bear, Chris
95ActPacNJDC-2
Beard, J.E.
92TraTeaS-122
Beard, Lee
91ProSetN-116
92ProSetN-173
93FinLinN-9
Bearden, Shannon
92JAG-6
Beasley, Ken
92WinChoM-44
Beaty, Dick
89Max-137
90Max-147
91Max-108
92MaxBla-206
92MaxRed-206
93Max-198
93MaxPreP-170
93MaxPreS-198
Beaty, Wade
94JAG-4
Beauchamp, Johnny
91ProSetPF-14
Beaudoin, Andre
92PacAmeCT-22
Beaver, Dennis
94HigGeaPPT-W20
94HigGeaPPTG-20W
Beaver, Larry
91BulRin-34
Beavers, Sammy
95K&WDirT-28
Bechelli, Mike
92JAG-7
Bechtel, Carolyn
94Max-296
95Max-88
95MaxCroC-85
95MaxPreP-85
95MaxPreS-96
96MaxPre-100
Bechtel, Gary
94Max-296
95Max-88
95MaxCroC-85
95MaxPreP-85
95MaxPreS-96
96MaxPre-86
Beckers, Christine
89TGRacMR-171
91TGRacMRU-171
Bedard, Patrick
84A&SRacI-22
85A&SRacI-34
Bedard, Yvon
92PacAmeCT-26
92PacAmeCT-45
92PacAmeCT-48
Beebe, Dave
72FleAHRDN-66
Beebe, Troy
91Tra-9
92MaxBla-90
92MaxRed-90
92ProSet-228
92Tra-41
92WinChoB-90
92WinChoB-91
93FinLin-139
93FinLinCS-17
93FinLinS-139
93Max-57
93MaxPreS-57
94Max-194
94MaxPreS-194
95FinLinSRF-12
95FinLinSRF-56
95FinLinSup-12
95FinLinSup-56
Beede, Dan
92PacAmeCT-8
92PacAmeCT-36
92PacAmeCT-38
Beekhuis, Jon
91AllWorl-18
Beggarly, Barry
91BulRin-82
92BulRin-82
94MaxPreS-251
94MaxPreS-254
95MaxPreS-253
Behling, Arnie
71FleAHRDC-14
Behra, Jean
62PetLimGPRC-23
62PetLimGPRC-26
77Spo-3121
Beitler, Steve
89WorOut-13
90WorOut-9
91WorOut-8
91WorOut-106
92RacLegS-6
92RacLegS-7
92WorOutMW-3
94WorOut-11
Belanger, Moe
92WinChoM-38
Belden, Mike
95OptXL-39
95OptXLCB-39
95OptXLDC-39
95OptXLRH-39
98PrePas-67
98PrePasOS-67
Belisle, Dick
92WinChoM-35
Bell, Wally
91BigTimD-52
91BigTimD-79
91BigTimD-86
Bellefleur, Gary Jr.
92WinChoM-34
Belmondo, Paul
92GriForO-17
92GriForO-50
92GriForO-83
Belmont, Andy
93Max-82
93MaxPreS-82
Beltoise, Jean Pierre
77Spo-2613
Beltz, Rodney
92VolRacLS2-5
92VolRacLS2-6
Benfer, Franklin
92CorSelCCS-29
Benfield, Eddie
94JAG-5
Benfield, Henry
91Max-218
92MaxAllPT-24
92MaxBla-247
92MaxRed-247
92RSSMotH-9
Benjamin, Ron
92WinChoM-40
Bennett, Gord
92PacAmeCT-23
92PacAmeCT-46
Bennett, John Jr.
90K&WDirT-2
92K&WDirT-40
Benoist, Robert
71MobTheSoGPMR-12
92GolEraGPTEY-4
95TraVal-33
Benson, Johnny Jr.
92TraASA-14
94Max-303
94VIP-55
95CroJew-56
95CroJewD-56
95CroJewE-56
95CroJewS-56
95FinLin-46
95FinLinPP-46
95FinLinSil-46
95HigGea-54
95HigGea-69
95HigGeaDO-54
95HigGeaDO-69
95HigGeaDOG-54
95HigGeaDOG-69
95HigGeaG-54
95HigGeaG-69
95LipTeaJBJ-NNO
95LipTeaJBJ-NNO
95LipTeaJBJ-NNO
95Max-155
95Max-201
95MaxAut-155
95MaxCroC-140
95MaxMed-BGN1
95MaxMedB-BGN1
95MaxPreP-140
95MaxPreS-171
95MaxPreS-256
95OptXL-25
95OptXLCB-25
95OptXLDC-25
95OptXLRH-25
95PrePas-55
95PrePas-113
95PrePas-139
95PrePasRH-55
95PrePasRH-113
95PrePasRH-139
95Sel-55
95Sel-127
95SelFlaO-55
95SelFlaO-127
95Tra-7
95Tra5thA-8
95Tra5thAG-8
95TraFirR-7
95TraOnTR-OTR1
95VIP-37
95VIPAut-37
95VIPCooB-37
95VIPEmeP-37
95VIPRedHCB-37
96ActPacC-54
96ActPacC-102
96ActPacCSS-54
96Ass-27
96AutRacA-4
96AutRacCA-4
96Cla-48
96ClaPriP-48
96ClaRacC-RC19
96ClaSil-48
96FinLin-58
96FinLin-70
96FinLin-98
96FinLinBGL-C13
96FinLinBGL-D15
96FinLinMM-MM10
96FinLinPriP-58
96FinLinPriP-70
96FinLinPriP-98
96FinLinS-58
96FinLinS-70
96FinLinS-98
96Fla-2
96Fla-58
96FlaCenS-1
96M-F-25
96Max-74
96MaxMadiA-30
96MaxMadiABR-BR12
96MaxOdyRA-RA12
96MaxPre-156
96MaxPre-258
96Pin-30
96Pin-53
96Pin-30
96Pin-53
96PinCutA-5
96PinPolP-20
96PinPolP-45
96PinPolP-61
96PinPolP-62
96PinPolP-63
96PinPolPLF-20
96PinPolPLF-45
96PinPolPLF-61
96PinPolPLF-62
96PinPolPLF-63
96PinWinCC-30
96PinWinCC-53
96PrePas-55
96PrePas-111
96PrePas-113
96PrePas&NC-55
96PrePasCC-37
96PrePasP-31
96PrePasP$10PC-1
96PrePasP$20PC-1
96PrePasP$5PC-1
96PrePasPCB-CB1
96PrePasPEP-31
96PrePasPH-31
96PrePasSco-55
96PrePasSco-111
96PrePasSco-113
96PrePasT-55
96PrePasT-111
96PrePasT-113
96RacCho-12
96RacCho-42
96RacCho-106
96RacCho-107
96RacCho-108
96RacChoAP-12
96RacChoAP-42
96RacChoAP-106
96RacChoAP-107
96RacChoAP-108
96RacChoSC-12
96RacChoSC-42
96RacChoSC-106
96RacChoSC-107
96RacChoSC-108
96SP-30
96SP-71
96SP-77
96SPDriF-DF1
96SpeArtP-11
96SpeArtP-26
96SpeCleS-12
96SpePro-12
96SpeRac-11
96SpeRac-26
96SPHoIME-ME8
96SPx-15
96SPxGol-15
96TraRevP-13
96TraRevPFR-13
96TraRevPM-13
96Ult-120
96Ult-121
96Ult-153
96UltAut-2
96UltUpd-2
96UltUpd-48
96UltUpd-98
96UltUpdRS-2
96UppDecRTTC-RC29
96UppDecRTTC-RC90
96UppDecRTTC-RC120
96UppDecRTTC-RC135
96UppDecRTTCAS-H29
96UppDecRTTCPT3-T7
96UppDecRTTCT3PR-R14
96V.IAut-2
96VIP-2
96VIPEmeP-2
96Viper-25
96Viper-74
96ViperBlaM-25
96ViperBlaM-74
96ViperCop-25
96ViperCop-74
96ViperGreM-25
96ViperGreM-74
96VIPTor-2
96Zen-23
96Zen-61
96ZenArtP-23
96ZenArtP-61
97ActPac-61
97ActPac-68
97ActPac-81
97ActPac2G-6
97ActPacFI-61
97ActPacFI-68
97ActPacFI-81
97ColCho-30
97ColCho-80
97ColCho-117
97ColChoC-CC33
97ColChoC-CC66
97ColChoS-S23
97ColChoS-S24
97ColChoSQ-SQ23
97ColChoTF-C1
97ColChoTF-J3
97ColChoUD5-UD62
97ColChoUD5-UD63
97FinLinPP2$10-83
97JurPar-13
97JurParR-R3
97JurParT-13
97Max-30
97Max-75
97MaxRoootY-MR9
97Pin-19
97Pin-48
97Pin-88
97PinArtP-19
97PinArtP-48
97PinArtP-88
97PinCer-12
97PinCer-46
97PinCerMB-12
97PinCerMB-46
97PinCerMG-12
97PinCerMG-46
97PinCerMR-12
97PinCerMR-46
97PinCerR-12
97PinCerR-46
97PinChe-3
97PinChe-6
97PinChe-9
97PinMin-12

92BulRin-5
92LanARCF-42
92LanARCF-59
92MaxBla-77
92MaxRed-77
92RedGraST-20
92RedGraST-21
93Max-84
93MaxPreS-84
93MaxWinM-2
93WheRooT-35
93WheRooTPla-35
94LanARCF-65
94Max-63
94Max-271
94MaxAut-63
94MaxMed-28
94MaxMot-21
94MaxPreS-63
94Pow-76
94PowGol-76
95HiTecB4-17
95HiTecB4-71
97VIP-37
97VIPExp-37
97VIPOilS-37
98HigGea-42
98HigGeaFG-42
98HigGeaM-42
98PrePas-50
98PrePasOS-50
98Whe-64
98WheGol-64
99Pre-57
99PrePas-57

Bierschwale, Don
91Max-151
92MaxBla-139
92MaxRed-139
93Max-141
93MaxPreS-141

Bierschwale, Eddie
88MaxCha-92
89Max-23
90Max-23
91Max-23
91ProSet-116
92LanARCF-49
92MaxBla-95
92MaxRed-95
92ProSet-54
93Max-23
93MaxPreS-23

Bigelow, Tom
80AvaHilURG-8
84A&SRacI-51
86A&SRacI-19
91LanARCHS-60
92LegInd-88
94LanARCF-54

Bigley Jr., Billy
91BulRin-28
92BulRin-28
92LanARCF-65
94LanARCF-41

Bilbrey, David
91DirTra-21
92DirTra-31
92JAG-139

Bilby, Bob
91Tra-45
92MaxBla-115
92MaxRed-115
92Tra-159
92TraTeaS-171
93Max-130
93MaxPreP-117
93MaxPreS-130
94Max-103
94MaxPreP-103
94MaxPreS-103

Bilderback, Ricky
91LanRocS-2
91LanRocS-21
92LanRocS-2
92LanRocS-3

Billes, Al
90CheFlaI-25

Billings, Mark
92WinChoM-47

Bilodeau, Bub
91WinChoNED-86
91WinChoNED-87

Bira, B
39ChuKinoS-15
62PetLimGPRC-5

Bird, Steve
91SpoLegRM-RM4
91Tra-170
92MaxBla-181
92MaxRed-181
92Tra-170

Birkhofer, Brian
91DKIMCDT-17

Birkhofer, David
91DKIMCDT-23

Birkin, Henry
30WilCig-25
71MobTheSoGPMR-14
95TraVal-39

Bishop, Donnie
91BulRin-71
92BulRin-71

Black, Robert
91Tra-150
92MaxBla-204
92MaxRed-204
92Tra-150

Blackstock, Roger
91LanARCHS-12
92LanARCF-32
94LanARCF-17

Blackwell, Teddy
94HigGeaPPT-G24
94HigGeaPPTG-24G

Blair, Bill
89TGRacMR-118
89TGRacMR-119
89WinCir-25
91TGRacMRU-118
91TGRacMRU-119
91TraPacYH-2

Blakely, Glen
91MaxBilETCM-25

Blaney, Dale
91WorOut-65
92VolRacLSI-NNO
92WorOutMW-9
94WorOut-46

Blaney, Dave
87WorOut-17
88WorOut-4
89WorOut-17
90WorOut-7
90WorOutP-7C
91WorOut-6
91WorOut-104
92RacLegS-11
92VolRacLS2-8
93WorOutMW-1
94WorOut-3

Blaney, Lou
92VolRacLS2-9
92VolRacLS2-10
92VolRacLS2-11
92VolRacLSI-8
92VolRacLSI-9
92VolRacLSI-NNO

Blanton, Chet
91LanARCHS-23

Blauvelt, Frances
90K&WDirT-4

Bleekemolen, Michael
78GraPri-131

Blevins, Danny
91BulRin-46
92BulRin-162

Bliss, Mike
95ActPacC-94
96MaxSup-ST1
96PrePas-64
96PrePasSco-64
96PrePasT-64
97PrePas-46
97PrePasL-46
97PrePasOS-46
97PrePasT-46
97VIP-38
97VIPExp-38
97VIPOilS-38
98PrePas-53
98PrePasOS-53
98Whe-65
98WheGol-65

Blood, Steve
92WinChoM-16

Bloom, Jeff
95JSKS.OS-6

Bloomquist, Scott
91DirTra-11
91JAG-1
91JAG-25
92DirTra-17
92DirTra-52
92JAG-9
92LanARCF-77
92VolRacEAS-18
93JAG-3
94JAG-6
94STAMod-8

Blundell, Mark
91CarForO-22
91CarForO-23
91CarForO-24
91ProTraFO-16
91ProTraFO-17
91ProTraFO-18
92GriForO-161
92LimAppFO-1
93MaxWilR-5
97CARSchC-2

Boat, Billy
91WorOut-66

Bobo, Glen
92MaxAllPT-46
92MaxBla-262
92MaxRed-262
92TraTeaS-161
92TraTeaS-167
93Max-254
93MaxPreS-254
95MaxPreS-241

Bodine, Brett
88MaxCha-59
89Max-15
89Max-202
89MaxCri-9
90Max-26
90MaxHolF-HF21
91Max-26
91Max-176
91MaxMcD-12
91MaxTheWA-2
91ProSet-98
91ProSet-102
91ProSet-142
92MaxBla-26
92MaxBla-191
92MaxMcD-26
92MaxMot-7
92MaxMot-42
92MaxRed-26
92MaxRed-191
92ProSet-146
92ProSet-156
92ProSet-180
92ProSet-222
92ProSetMH-24
92RedSta-26
92Tra-26
92TraRacM-50
92TraRacM-75
93ActPac-27
93ActPac-57
93ActPac-96
93ActPac-161
93ActPac-180
93ActPac2G-62G
93FinLin-6
93FinLin-108
93FinLin-125
93FinLinCS-7
93FinLinCS-21
93FinLinS-6
93FinLinS-108
93FinLinS-125
93Max-26
93MaxHou-12
93MaxHou-20
93MaxLowFS-5
93MaxMot-1
93MaxMot-21
93MaxPreP-26
93MaxPreS-26
93MaxRetJ-9
93MaxTheW-10
93MaxTheW-30
93PrePasPre-2
93Tra-26
93Tra-198
93TraFirR-26
93TraFirR-198
93TraPreC-2
93TraTri-26
94ActPac-20
94ActPac-75
94ActPac-132
94ActPac-139
94ActPac-205
94ActPac2G-29G
94FinLin-61
94FinLin-68
94FinLin-103
94FinLinG-23
94FinLinG-25
94FinLinG-82
94FinLinG-99
94FinLinGA-99
94FinLinGT-TG8
94FinLinS-61
94FinLinS-68
94FinLinS-103
94Hi-Bri4AP-6
94Hi-Bri4AP-32
94Hi-Bri4AP-41
94Hi-Bri4AP-54
94HigGea-93
94HigGea-126
94HigGeaDO-126
94HigGeaDOG-126
94HigGeaG-93
94HigGeaG-126
94HiTecB4-6
94HiTecB4-32
94HiTecB4-41
94HiTecB4-54
94Max-26
94Max-76
94Max-150
94MaxMed-2
94MaxMed-60
94MaxMot-8
94MaxPreP-26
94MaxPreP-57
94MaxPreP-76
94MaxPreS-26
94MaxPreS-76
94MaxPreS-150
94MaxTheS2-20
94OptXL-1
94OptXLRH-1
94Pow-55
94Pow-77
94Pow-144
94PowGol-55
94PowGol-77
94PowGol-144
94PrePas-1
94PrePas-36
94PrePasCC-CC1
94Tra-26
94Tra-75
94Tra-78
94Tra-133
94TraAutV-2
94TraFirR-26
94TraFirR-75
94TraFirR-78
94TraFirR-133
94TraPreC-36
94VIP-2
94VIP-50
95ActPacC-75
95ActPacCSS-75
95ActPacP-2
95ActPacS-7
95ActPacSSS-7
95Ass-5
95Ass1M$PC-3
95AssGolS-5
95CroJew-21
95CroJew-45
95CroJewD-21
95CroJewD-45
95CroJewE-21
95CroJewE-45
95CroJewS-21
95CroJewS-45
95FinLin-11
95FinLin-68
95FinLin-78
95FinLinCC6-5
95FinLinPP-11
95FinLinPP-68
95FinLinPP-78
95FinLinSil-11
95FinLinSil-68
95FinLinSil-78
95HigGea-20
95HigGeaDO-20
95HigGeaDOG-20
95HigGeaG-20
95HiTecB4-7
95HiTecB4-73
95HiTecB4TT-BY2
95Ima-11
95Ima-64
95ImaGol-11
95ImaGol-64
95Max-26
95Max-223
95Max-224
95MaxCroC-26
95MaxCroC-44
95MaxLicD-14
95MaxMed-10
95MaxMed-40
95MaxMedB-10
95MaxMedB-40
95MaxOveW-2
95MaxPreP-26
95MaxPreP-44
95MaxPrePTH-TH5
95MaxPreS-26
95MaxPreS-70
95OptXL-1
95OptXLCB-1
95OptXLDC-1
95OptXLRH-1
95PrePas-3
95PrePas-49
95PrePasCC-3
95PrePasPH-16
95PrePasPre-16
95PrePasPRH-16
95PrePasRH-3
95PrePasRH-49
95Sel-3
95Sel-49
95Sel-110
95SelFlaO-3
95SelFlaO-49
95SelFlaO-110
95SP-10
95SP-43
95SP-85
95SPDieC-10
95SPDieC-43
95SPDieC-85
95SPSpeM-SM11
95SPSpeMDC-SM11
95Tra-14
95Tra-47
95Tra5thA-16
95Tra5thAG-16
95TraAutV-13
95TraFirR-14
95TraFirR-47
95TraSerS-SS12
95UppDec-20
95UppDec-63
95UppDec-88
95UppDec-122
95UppDec-193
95UppDec-237
95UppDec-275
95UppDecGSEG-20
95UppDecGSEG-63
95UppDecGSEG-88
95UppDecGSEG-122
95UppDecGSEG-193
95UppDecGSEG-237
95UppDecGSEG-275
95UppDecSSES-20
95UppDecSSES-63
95UppDecSSES-88
95UppDecSSES-122
95UppDecSSES-193
95UppDecSSES-237
95UppDecSSES-275
95VIP-2
95VIPCooB-2
95VIPEmeP-2
95VIPRedHCB-2
95Zen-11
95Zen-43
95Zen-68
96ActPacC-39
96ActPacCSS-39
96Ass-39

95HiTecB4-53
95HiTecB4-74
95Ima-7
95Ima-53
95Ima-92
95ImaGol-7
95ImaGol-53
95ImaGol-92
95Max-7
95Max-73
95Max-99
95Max-112
95Max-133
95Max-177
95Max-212
95Max-213
95MaxAut-7
95MaxCroC-7
95MaxCroC-66
95MaxCroC-159
95MaxCroC-166
95MaxCroC-170
95MaxCroC-176
95MaxLicD-13
95MaxMed-6
95MaxMed-36
95MaxMedB-6
95MaxMedB-36
95MaxOveW-9
95MaxPreP-7
95MaxPreP-66
95MaxPreP-159
95MaxPreP-166
95MaxPreP-170
95MaxPreP-176
95MaxPrePRJ-1
95MaxPreS-7
95MaxPreS-66
95MaxPreS-274
95MaxPreS-281
95MaxPreS-285
95MaxPreS-291
95MaxStaU-1
95MaxStaU-2
95MaxSup-8
95OptXL-2
95OptXLCB-2
95OptXLDC-2
95OptXLRH-2
95PrePas-4
95PrePas-39
95PrePas-101
95PrePas-110
95PrePas-127
95PrePasCC-4
95PrePasCF-CF1
95PrePasPH-15
95PrePasPHP-HP1
95PrePasPPC-NNO
95PrePasPre-15
95PrePasPRH-15
95PrePasRD-RD2
95PrePasRH-4
95PrePasRH-39
95PrePasRH-101
95PrePasRH-110
95PrePasRH-127
95Sel-4
95Sel-39
95Sel-77
95Sel-110
95Sel-134
95Sel-136
95Sel-NNO
95SelDreM-DM1
95SelFlaO-4
95SelFlaO-39
95SelFlaO-77
95SelFlaO-110
95SelFlaO-134
95SelFlaO-136
95SelPro-136
95SelSki-SS10
95SP-6
95SP-39
95SP-81
95SP-132
95SPDieC-6
95SPDieC-39
95SPDieC-81
95SPDieC-132
95SPSpeM-SM7
95SPSpeMDC-SM7
95Tra-1
95Tra-40
95Tra-54
95Tra5thA-6
95Tra5thA-45
95Tra5thAG-6
95Tra5thAG-45
95Tra5thAR-R12
95TraAutV-6
95TraCha-C9
95TraFirR-1
95TraFirR-40
95TraFirR-54
95TraRacM-RM3
95TraSerS-SS10
95UppDec-13
95UppDec-56
95UppDec-81
95UppDec-115
95UppDec-166
95UppDec-189
95UppDec-233
95UppDec-273
95UppDecA-189
95UppDecGSEG-13
95UppDecGSEG-56
95UppDecGSEG-81
95UppDecGSEG-115
95UppDecGSEG-166
95UppDecGSEG-189
95UppDecGSEG-233
95UppDecGSEG-273
95UppDecO-OS8
95UppDecPRW-P6
95UppDecSSES-13
95UppDecSSES-56
95UppDecSSES-81
95UppDecSSES-115
95UppDecSSES-166
95UppDecSSES-189
95UppDecSSES-233
95UppDecSSES-273
95VIP-3
95VIP-60
95VIPCooB-3
95VIPCooB-60
95VIPEmeP-3
95VIPEmeP-60
95VIPHel-H1
95VIPHelG-H1
95VIPRedHCB-3
95VIPRedHCB-60
95Zen-7
95Zen-40
96ActPacC-49
96ActPacCSS-49
96Ass-4
96Ass$2PC-4
96AssComL-CL13
96AutRac-9
96AutRacA-6
96AutRacCA-6
96AutRacFR-2
96AutRacFR-3
96AutRacFR-4
96AutRacHP-HP20
96Cla-47
96ClaInn-IV9
96ClaMarMC-MC7
96ClaPriP-47
96ClaSil-47
96FinLin-30
96FinLin-59
96FinLinGS-GS9
96FinLinPP-4
96FinLinPP$10C-1
96FinLinPP$5C-3
96FinLinPP$S-3
96FinLinPriP-30
96FinLinPriP-59
96FinLinS-30
96FinLinS-59
96FinLinSMPC-1
96Fla-4
96Fla-60
96Kni-16
96KniBlaK-16
96KniQueRKP-16
96KniRoy-16
96KniWhiK-16
96Max-7
96Max-19
96MaxFamT-FT1
96MaxMadiA-7
96MaxMadiA-48
96MaxOdy-7
96MaxOdy-8
96MaxOveTW-OTW6
96MaxPep5-2
96MaxPre-7
96MaxPre-62
96Pin-7
96Pin-42
96Pin-7
96Pin-42
96PinCheF-14
96PinCutA-15
96PinPolP-7
96PinPolPLF-7
96PinWinCC-7
96PinWinCC-42
96PrePas-3
96PrePas-83
96PrePasCC-3
96PrePasP-16
96PrePasPEP-16
96PrePasPH-16
96PrePasSco-3
96PrePasSco-83
96PrePasT-3
96PrePasT-83
96SP-7
96SP-57
96SpeArtP-13
96SpeInM-5
96SpeRac-13
96SPHolME-ME7
96TraRev&PTCG-TC9
96TraRev&PTCH-TC9
96TraRevP-27
96TraRevP-45
96TraRevP-50
96TraRevPFR-27
96TraRevPFR-45
96TraRevPFR-50
96TraRevPLG-LG17
96TraRevPM-27
96TraRevPM-45
96TraRevPTC-TC9
96Ult-56
96Ult-57
96Ult-58
96Ult-158
96UltAut-4
96UltUpd-4
96UltUpd-50
96UltUpd-93
96UppDec-6
96UppDec-46
96UppDec-86
96UppDec-132
96UppDecRTTC-RC15
96UppDecRTTC-RC64
96UppDecRTTC-RC99
96UppDecRTTC-RC137
96UppDecRTTC-RC138
96UppDecRTTCAS-H15
96UppDecRTTCRL-RL17
96UppDecVV-VV3
96UppDecVVG-VV3
96V.IAut-3
96VIP-3
96VIPEmeP-3
96VIPTor-3
96Zen-11
96ZenArtP-11
96ZenHig-7
97ActPac-22
97ActPac-48
97ActPacFI-22
97ActPacFI-48
97AutRac-11
97AutRac-48
97AutRacA-4
97AutRacMS-KM11
97ColCho-7
97ColCho-57
97ColCho-152
97ColChoC-CC11
97ColChoC-CC44
97ColChoC-CC77
97ColChoSQ-SQ19
97ColChoSQ-SQ47
97ColChoTF-H3
97ColChoUD5-UD12
97ColChoUD5-UD13
97ColChoVC-VC6
97FinLinPP2-19
97FinLinPP2$10-71
97FinLinPP2$5-57
97Max-7
97Max-52
97Max-115
97Pin-7
97Pin-36
97PinArtP-7
97PinArtP-36
97PinCer-23
97PinCer-57
97PinCer-88
97PinCerMB-23
97PinCerMB-57
97PinCerMB-88
97PinCerMG-23
97PinCerMG-57
97PinCerMG-88
97PinCerMR-23
97PinCerMR-57
97PinCerMR-88
97PinCerR-23
97PinCerR-57
97PinCerR-88
97PinMin-16
97PinMin2GC-16
97PinMinB-16
97PinMinC-16
97PinMinG-16
97PinMinNC-16
97PinMinS-16
97PinPreP-7
97PinPreP-36
97PinTotCPB-23
97PinTotCPB-57
97PinTotCPB-88
97PinTotCPG-23
97PinTotCPG-57
97PinTotCPG-88
97PinTotCPR-23
97PinTotCPR-57
97PinTotCPR-88
97PinTroC-7
97PinTroC-36
97PrePas-16
97PrePas-103
97PrePasAut-15
97PrePasL-16
97PrePasL-103
97PrePasOS-16
97PrePasOS-103
97PrePasPA-15
97PrePasT-16
97PrePasT-103
97RacCho-7
97RacCho-42
97RacCho-59
97RacCho-75
97RacChoSS-7
97RacChoSS-42
97RacChoSS-59
97RacChoSS-75
97SBMot-19
97SBMot-70
97SBMotWR-WC13
97ScoBoal-11
97SP-7
97SP-49
97SP-89
97SP SupS-7
97SP SupS-49
97SP SupS-89
97SPX-7
97SPxBlu-7
97SPxGol-7
97SPxSil-7
97Ult-4
97UppDecRTTC-19
97UppDecRTTC-61
97UppDecRTTC-123
97UppDecRTTCPPlu-+12
97UDRTTCPPRC-+12
97UppDRTTCPPRDC-+12
97UppDecVC-7
97UppDecVC-57
97UppDecVC-105
97UppDecVCVL-VL8
97VIP-2
97VIPExp-2
97VIPOilS-2
98ColCho-7
98ColCho-43
98Max-7
98Max-37
98Max-7
98Max-32
98Max-57
98Max-82
98Max10tA-7
98Max10tA-52
98Max10tA-103
98Max10tABA-4
98Max10tAMP-P7
98MaxBatP-B9
98MaxFirC-F14
98MaxSwaP-SW7
98MaxYealRBS-19
98MaxYealRBS-109
98MaxYealRBS-125
98MaxYealRBS-137
98MaxYealRBS-157
98PrePas-16
98PrePas-116
98PrePasOS-16
98PrePasP-48
98PrePasP-48
98PrePasS-15
98SP Aut-7
98SP Aut-41
98SP Aut-73
98UppDecRttC-7
98UppDecRttC-48
98UppDecRttC-65
98UppDecVC-7
98UppDecVC-52
98UppDecVC-107
98UppDecVC-137
98UppDecVCPP-7
98UppDecVCPPCR-7
98VIP-3
98VIPExp-3
98Whe-3
98Whe-82
98WheAut-8
98WheGol-3
98WheGol-82
99Pre-27
99PrePas-27
99PrePas-127
99UppDecVC-10
99UppDecVC-55
99UppDecVCUE-10
99UppDecVCUE-55
99WheHigG-25
99WheHigG-56
99WheHigGAC-25
99WheHigGFG-25
99WheHigGFG-56
99WheHigGM-25
99WheHigGM-56
99WheHigGS-GS25

Bodine, Lynn

95FinLin-75
95FinLinPP-75
95FinLinSil-75

Bodine, Todd

91Max-203
91Tra-34
92MaxBla-35
92MaxRed-35
92ProSet-127
92Tra-34
92TraGoo-6
92WinChoB-70
92WinChoB-71
93FinLin-10
93FinLinCS-9
93FinLinS-10
93Max-34
93MaxMot-3
93MaxMot-23
93MaxPreP-34
93MaxPreS-34
93Tra-34
93Tra-65
93Tra-85
93Tra-185
93TraFirR-34
93TraFirR-65
93TraFirR-85
93TraFirR-185
94ActPac-91
94ActPac-134
94ActPac-141
94ActPac-205
94ActPac2G-45G
94FinLin-108
94FinLinBGN-BGN4
94FinLinNSH-2

94FinLinS-108
94Hi-Bri4AP-41
94Hi-Bri4AP-65
94HigGea-61
94HigGea-102
94HigGeaDO-102
94HigGeaDOG-102
94HigGeaG-61
94HigGeaG-102
94HiTecB4-41
94HiTecB4-65
94Max-73
94Max-75
94MaxMed-8
94MaxMot-9
94MaxPreP-73
94MaxPreP-75
94MaxPreS-73
94MaxPreS-75
94Pow-32
94Pow-134
94PowGol-32
94PowGol-134
94PrePas-55
94PrePas-68
94Sky-24
94Tra-67
94Tra-138
94Tra-139
94TraAut-A1
94TraAutV-18
94TraFirR-67
94TraFirR-138
94TraFirR-139
94VIP-4
95ActPacC-80
95ActPacCSS-80
95ActPacP-4
95ActPacS-20
95ActPacSSS-20
95Ass-25
95AssGolS-25
95FinLin-35
95FinLin-75
95FinLin-102
95FinLinCC6-25
95FinLinPP-35
95FinLinPP-75
95FinLinPP-102
95FinLinSil-35
95FinLinSil-75
95FinLinSil-102
95HigGea-22
95HigGeaDO-22
95HigGeaDOG-22
95HigGeaG-22
95HiTecB4-23
95HiTecB4-64
95HiTecB4TT-BY9
95Ima-75
95Ima-86
95ImaGol-75
95ImaGol-86
95Max-75
95Max-178
95MaxCroC-46
95MaxCroC-75
95MaxLicD-15
95MaxMed-26
95MaxMed-56
95MaxMedB-26
95MaxMedB-56
95MaxPreP-46
95MaxPreP-75
95MaxPreS-13
95MaxPreS-68
95MaxPreS-75
95OptXL-3
95OptXLCB-3
95OptXLDC-3
95OptXLRH-3
95PrePas-5
95PrePasCC-5
95PrePasPH-17
95PrePasPre-17
95PrePasPRH-17
95PrePasRH-5
95Sel-5
95Sel-110
95Sel-121
95SelFlaO-5
95SelFlaO-110
95SelFlaO-121
95SelSki-SS14
95SP-25
95SP-64
95SP-105
95SPDieC-25
95SPDieC-64
95SPDieC-105
95SPSpeM-SM26
95SPSpeMDC-SM26
95Tra-33
95Tra-70
95Tra5thA-25
95Tra5thA-43
95Tra5thAG-25
95Tra5thAG-43
95TraAutV-21
95TraFirR-33
95TraFirR-70
95TraRacM-RM1
95UppDec-40
95UppDec-108
95UppDec-220
95UppDec-262
95UppDecA-220
95UppDecGSEG-40
95UppDecGSEG-108
95UppDecGSEG-220
95UppDecGSEG-262
95UppDecSSES-40
95UppDecSSES-108
95UppDecSSES-220
95UppDecSSES-262
95VIP-4
95VIPCooB-4
95VIPEmeP-4
95VIPRedHCB-4
95Zen-26
96Ass-17
96AutRac-48
96AutRacA-7
96AutRacCA-7
96Cla-2
96ClaPriP-2
96ClaSil-2
96FinLin-48
96FinLin-71
96FinLinPP-3
96FinLinPP$S-4
96FinLinPriP-48
96FinLinPriP-71
96FinLinS-48
96FinLinS-71
96MaxFamT-FT1
96MaxOveTW-OTW10
96MaxPre-64
96MaxPre-75
96PrePas-4
96PrePasCC-4
96PrePasSco-4
96PrePasT-4
96TraRev&PTCG-TC8
96TraRev&PTCH-TC8
96TraRevPTC-TC8
96Ult-105
96Ult-106
96Ult-107
96UltAut-5
96UppDec-30
96UppDec-70
96UppDec-110
96UppDecRTTC-RC139
97AutRacA-5
97ColCho-43
97ColCho-92
97JurPar-26
97JurPar-39
97JurParC-C11
97JurParT-26
97JurParT-39
97PrePas-64
97PrePasAut-31
97PrePasL-64
97PrePasOS-64
97PrePasPA-31
97PrePasT-64
97SBMot-77
97SkyPro-46
97SkyProA-46
97Ult-82
97UltUpd-54
97UltUpdAR-54
97UppDecVC-43
97UppDecVC-92
97VIP-28
97Viper-42
97ViperBlaR-42
97VIPExp-28
97VIPOilS-28
98HigGea-38
98HigGea-56
98HigGeaFG-38
98HigGeaFG-56
98HigGeaM-38
98HigGeaM-56
98Max-19
98Max-49
98Max-79
98Max-17
98Max-42
98Max-67
98Max-92
98Max10tA-105
98Max10tAMP-P17
98MaxSwaP-SW17
98MaxYealRBS-97
98PrePas-38
98PrePas-60
98PrePasOS-38
98PrePasOS-60
98PrePasP-51
98PrePasP-51
98SP Aut-19
98SP Aut-53
98UppDecRttC-35
98UppDecRttC-78
98UppDecVC-104
98UppDecVC3DoS-D20
98UppDecVC3DoSG-D20
98Whe-4
98WheGol-4
Boesel, Raul
86A&SRacI-48
87A&SRacI-32
91AllWorl-32
93HiTecI-25
93HiTecI-42
93HiTecICFF-SP7
94HiTecI-5
94HiTecI-40
94HiTecI-42
94HiTecICD-CD7
95HiTecICD-CD5
95SkyInd5-18
95SkyInd5-20
95SkyInd5-63
95SkyInd5-93
95SkyInd5HI-1
96SkyInd5-31
96SkyInd5-74
Boggs, David
91LanARCHS-52
94LanARCF-82
Boggs, Jack
91DirTra-7
91JAG-2
92DirTra-12
92DirTra-52
92JAG-10
92STAMod-8
92VolRacEAS-14
95HavAT-6
Boggs, Jackie Jr.
94JAG-7
Boggs, Randy
91JAG-21
92DirTra-54
92JAG-140
Bohlander, Don
92JAG-141
Bohn, George
92LanRocS-4
Boillot, Georges
71MobTheSoGPMR-4
Boland, Mike
93JAG-4
Boles, Dick
93AllRobPDS-5
Boley, Steve
94MaxPreS-252
Bolger, Gary
92ProSetN-58
92ProSetN-128
93FinLinN-44
95ActPacN-19
95ActPacNSS-19
Boling, Mike
92TraTeaS-163
Bolles, Tom
91WinChoM-37
91WinChoM-38
91WinChoNED-43
91WinChoNED-44
92WinChoB-133
92WinChoB-134
Bond, Andy
92STAMod-7
Bond, Larry
92STAMod-9
94STAMod-9
Bone, Johnny Jr.
92JAG-11
Bonebrake, Denny
92DirTra-55
92JAG-142
94STAMod-10
Bonin, Gordie
94ActPacSJ-5
94ActPacSJ-6
95ActPacN-16
95ActPacNSS-16
Bonkemeyer, Martha
92TraTeaS-187
Bonner, Brian
93HiTecI-26
93HiTecI-54
Bonnett, David
91SpoLegNB-NB28
92BulRin-143
94ActPac-98
94Max-196
94MaxPreS-196
Bonnett, Neil
83UNORac-2
86SpoPhoG-3
88MaxCha-7
88MaxCha-20
88MaxCha-34
89Max-21
89Max-102
89Max-103
89Max-118
89Max-142
89Max-143
89MaxCri-14
90Max-21
90MaxHolF-HF10
91Max-36
91MaxRacFK-1
91ProSetL-L24
91SpoLegBA-P1
91SpoLegDA-P1
91SpoLegDA-DA16
91SpoLegDA-DA17
91SpoLegDA-DA21
91SpoLegNB-NB1
91SpoLegNB-NB2
91SpoLegNB-NB3
91SpoLegNB-NB4
91SpoLegNB-NB5
91SpoLegNB-NB6
91SpoLegNB-NB7
91SpoLegNB-NB8
91SpoLegNB-NB9
91SpoLegNB-NB10
91SpoLegNB-NB11
91SpoLegNB-NB12
91SpoLegNB-NB13
91SpoLegNB-NB14
91SpoLegNB-NB15
91SpoLegNB-NB16
91SpoLegNB-NB17
91SpoLegNB-NB18
91SpoLegNB-NB19
91SpoLegNB-NB20
91SpoLegNB-NB21
91SpoLegNB-NB22
91SpoLegNB-NB23
91SpoLegNB-NB24
91SpoLegNB-NB25
91SpoLegNB-NB26
91SpoLegNB-NB27
91SpoLegNB-NB28
91SpoLegNB-NB29
91SpoLegNB-NB30
91Tra-26
91TraPacYH-3
92MaxBla-222
92MaxRed-222
92MaxSamB-10
92ProSet-199
92ProSet-215
92Tra-114
93FinLin-119
93FinLinCS-3
93FinLinDA-10
93FinLinS-119
93Max-219
93MaxPreS-219
93Tra-5
93TraFirR-5
94ActPac-98
94ActPac-99
94ActPac-100
94ActPac-101
94ActPac-102
94ActPacCC-31
94DaySer3-26
94FinLin-57
94FinLinNB-1
94FinLinNB-2
94FinLinNB-3
94FinLinNB-4
94FinLinNB-5
94FinLinS-57
94HigGea-24
94HigGeaG-24
94Max-31
94MaxPreP-77
94MaxPreS-31
94Tra-25
94Tra-29
94Tra-50
94TraAutV-15
94TraFirR-25
94TraFirR-29
94TraFirR-50
94TraPreC-37
95TraVal-94
98Max10tA-44
98Max10tA-89
98Max10tA-115
98PrePas-140
Bonnier, Joakim
62PetLimGPRC-33
77Spo-7222
Booher, Joe
91LanARCHS-46
92LanARCF-97
Booth, Clyde
91Tra-158
92Tra-158
Bordino, P.
71MobTheSoGPMR-8
Borghese, Scipion
95TraVal-13
Borghi, Mike
92BulRin-43
Borich, Joey
93CorSelCCS-35
Bostick, Richard
92RSSMotH-1
92TraTeaS-62
Bottcher, Steve
92K&WDirT-58
Bouchard, Ken
88MaxCha-88
88MaxMyrB-88
89Max-1
89Max-10
90Max-124
91Max-13
91MaxUpd-13
92CoyRoo-10
92WinChoB-32
93WheRooT-29
93WheRooTPla-29
94Max-61
94MaxPreS-61
94MaxRooY-10
97MaxRoootY-MR1
Bouchard, Ron
83UNORac-7
89TGRacMR-260
89TGRacMR-261
91TGRacMRU-260
91TGRacMRU-261
92CoyRoo-3
93WheRooT-22
93WheRooTPla-22
95TraVal-91
Boutsen, Thierry
87AceForO-6
87ForOneI-4
88HerFouFO-2D
91CarForO-70
91CarForO-71
91CarForO-72

91ProTraFO-59
91ProTraFO-60
91ProTraFO-169
91ProTraFO-170
92GriForO-24
92GriForO-57
92GriForO-90
93MaxWilR-6
93MaxWilR-71
93MaxWilR-72
93MaxWilR-74

Boutwell, Buddy
92VolRacEAS-12

Boutwell, Rudy
94JAG-8

Bowen, Bruce
91K&WURCS-17

Bowers, Mike
92JAG-143

Bowie, Ricky
89CheFlal-99
90CheFlal-54

Bowmaster, Timothy
93CorSelCCS-22

Bown, Chuck
89Max-218
90Max-97A
90Max-97B
91Max-97
91Max-167
91MaxUpd-97
91Tra-63
91WinChoRC-19
92LimEdiCB-2
92LimEdiCB-3
92LimEdiCB-4
92LimEdiCB-5
92LimEdiCB-6
92LimEdiCB-7
92LimEdiCB-8
92LimEdiCB-9
92LimEdiCB-10
92LimEdiCB-11
92LimEdiCB-12
92LimEdiCB-13
92LimEdiCB-14
92LimEdiCB-15
92LimEdiP-2
92MaxBla-34
92MaxRed-34
92PacAmeCT-30
92ProSet-157
92RedSta-27
92Tra-63
92TraGoo-4
92TraRacM-63
92WinChoB-66
92WinChoB-67
92WinChoBA-1
93FinLin-30
93FinLinCS-11
93FinLinS-30
93Max-63
93MaxPreP-63
93MaxPreS-63
93Tra-63
93Tra-165
93TraFirR-63
93TraFirR-165
94DaySer3-31
94FinLin-147
94FinLinBGN-BGN9
94FinLinNSH-3
94FinLinS-147
94HigGea-60
94HigGea-112
94HigGeaDO-112
94HigGeaDOG-112
94HigGeaG-60
94HigGeaG-112
94Max-166
94Max-265
94MaxPreP-153
94MaxPreS-166
94Pow-33
94PowGol-33
94PrePas-56
94PrePas-69
94PrePasPro-PP1
94Tra-63
94Tra-128
94Tra-194
94TraAutV-14
94TraFirR-63
94TraFirR-128
94TraFirR-194
94VIP-5
95ActPacP-31
95Max-265
95Sel-139
95SelFlaO-139
95SP-51
95SPDieC-51
95UppDec-27
95UppDec-95
95UppDecGSEG-27
95UppDecGSEG-95
95UppDecSSES-27
95UppDecSSES-95
96MaxPre-32

Bown, Jim
89Max-41
90Max-41
91Max-57
91MaxUpd-57
92MaxBla-72
92MaxRed-72
92WinChoB-94
92WinChoB-95
93FinLin-65
93FinLinCS-29
93FinLinS-65
93Max-98
93MaxPreP-77
93MaxPreS-98
93Tra-144
93TraFirR-144
94HigGea-176
94HigGeaDO-176
94HigGeaDOG-176
94HigGeaG-176
94Max-186
94MaxPreS-186
94Tra-164
94TraFirR-164
95MaxPreS-174
95PrePas-56
95PrePasRH-56
95Sel-56
95SelFlaO-56
96MaxPre-173

Bowser, Joe
92WinChoM-32

Bowsher, Bobby
91LanARCHS-6
91LanARCHS-21
92LanARCF-2
92LanARCF-14
94LanARCF-4
94LanARCF-93

Boyd, Johnny
92AllWorl-62

Boyer, Joe
54StaWetIW-1924
60HawWaxI-12

Boys, Trevor
88MaxCha-24
89Max-95

Boyse, Ron
91DKIMCDT-39

Brabham, Geoff
78GraPri-85
83A&SRacI-11
84A&SRacI-39
85A&SRacI-16
86A&SRacI-18
87A&SRacI-5
91AllWorl-27
91IRO-9
92AllWorl-23
92AllWorl-96
92LegInd-21
94HiTecI-27

Brabham, Jack
62PetLimGPRC-20
62PetLimGPRC-30
71MobTheSoGPMR-33
77Spo-5719
91LegInd-42
92GolEraGPTEY-23
92MaxIMH-13

Brack, Bobby
92BulRin-75

Bradberry, Gary
91BulRin-78
92BulRin-78
94LanARCF-37
95UppDec-218
95UppDec-260
95UppDec-294
95UppDecGSEG-218
95UppDecGSEG-260
95UppDecGSEG-294
95UppDecSSES-218
95UppDecSSES-260
95UppDecSSES-294
97Max-19
97Max-64
97UppDecRTTC-41
97UppDecRTTC-83
97UppDecRTTC-149
98UppDecRttC-27
98UppDecVC-19
98UppDecVC-64

Bradley, Frank
89MegDra-36
89MegDra-37
91ProSetN-7
91ProSetN-56
92ProSetN-18
92ProSetN-116

Bradshaw, George
91ProSet-75
91Tra-141
92MaxBla-124
92MaxRed-124
92Tra-141
93FinLin-21
93FinLinCS-19
93FinLinS-21
93Max-127
93MaxPreP-114
93MaxPreS-127
94Max-118
94MaxPreS-118
94Pow-79
94PowGol-79
95MaxPreS-112

Brady, Jerry
92TraTeaS-64

Brakefield, Rick
92TraTeaS-73

Brambilla, Vittorio
77Spo-5602
77Spo-7113
78GraPri-120
78GraPri-146

Brandt, Mike
91MaxBilETCM-28

Brannan, Bob
96Kni-36
96KniBlaK-36
96KniQueRKP-36
96KniRoy-36
96KniWhiK-36
97PinPre-1
97PinPreBM-1
97PinPreGM-1
97PinPreSM-1

Branscombe, Babe
91LanStoCC-16
91WinChoNED-106
91WinChoNED-107
92WinChoB-60
92WinChoB-61

Branson, Don
62MarInd-2
92LegInd-71

Branz, Jerry
94HigGeaPPT-W21
94HigGeaPPTG-21W

Brasefield, Ed
91Tra-147

Brassfield, Darin
92EriMaxTA-74
92EriMaxTA-80
92EriMaxTA-81
92EriMaxTA-83
92EriMaxTA-85
92EriMaxTA-86
92EriMaxTA-88
92EriMaxTA-91
92EriMaxTA-93

Brauchitsch, Von
92GolEraGPTEY-7

Brawner, Clint
92HiTecMA-16

Braymer, John
92VolRacLSI-10

Brayton, Scott
83A&SRacI-31
84A&SRacI-27
85A&SRacI-41
86A&SRacI-25
86A&SRacI-36
86AceInd-A1
87A&SRacI-12
91AllWorl-39
92AllWorl-32
92AllWorl-94
92LegInd-18
92LegInd-88
93HiTecI-7
93HiTecI-57
94HiTecI-7
94HiTecICD-CD8
95SkyInd5-41
95SkyInd5-92
96SkyInd5-5
96SkyInd5-7
96SkyInd5-10
96SkyInd5-71
97Hi-IRL-19
97Hi-IRL'I5-I2
97Hi-IRLP-P3
97Hi-IRLP-P8
97Hi-IRLSB-BR1
97Hi-IRLSB-BR2
97Hi-IRLSB-BR3
97Hi-IRLSB-BR4
97Hi-IRLSB-BR5
97Hi-IRLSB-BR6
97Hi-IRLSB-BR7
97Hi-IRLSB-BR8

Brennen, Billy
90K&WDirT-5

Breuer, Danny
91DKIMCDT-4

Brevak, Bob
91LanARCHS-1
91LanARCHS-34
92LanARCF-6
92LanARCF-18
94LanARCF-6
94LanARCF-95
95MaxSup-16

Brewer Jr., Lee
87WorOut-13
88WorOut-18
90WorOut-23
91WorOut-56

Brewer, Glenn
91LanARCHS-10
92LanARCF-8
92LanARCF-20
94LanARCF-9
94LanARCF-98

Brewer, Tim
89Max-22
90Max-96
91Max-79
91MaxMot-27
91ProSet-35
91Tra-140
92MaxAllPT-15
92MaxBla-161
92MaxBla-241
92MaxMcD-10
92MaxMot-24
92MaxRed-161
92MaxRed-241
92ProSet-81
92Tra-140
93FinLin-175
93FinLinCS-18
93FinLinS-175
93Max-175
93MaxPreP-130
93MaxPreP-157
93MaxPreS-175
93Tra-61
93TraFirR-61
94Max-146
94MaxPreP-139
94MaxPreS-146
94Pow-49
94PowGol-49
96MaxPre-149
96Ult-65

Brickhouse, Richard
89TGRacMR-206
89TGRacMR-207
91TGRacMRU-206
91TGRacMRU-207

Brightbill, Fred
91K&WDirT-7

Brinkley, Jay
92JAG-144
94JAG-9

Brissette, Jim
92ProSetN-193
93FinLinN-13

Britsky, John
92VolRacLSI-11

Brittsan, Deb
91ProSetN-111
92ProSetN-191

Broadwater, Clay
89CheFlal-50
90CheFlal-57

Brodrick, Bill
91Tra-149
92Tra-149
93Tra-93
93TraFirR-93
96PrePas-110
96PrePasSco-110
96PrePasT-110

Brooks, Dick
72STP-3
89TGRacMR-220
89TGRacMR-221
89TGRacMR-222
90Max-165
91Max-223
91ProSetL-L1
91ProSetPF-40
91TGRacMRU-220
91TGRacMRU-221
91TGRacMRU-222
91Tra-135A
91Tra-135B
91TraPacYH-4
92BikRacS-28
92MaxBlaU-U20
92MaxRedU-U20
92ProSet-168
92Tra-131
93FinLin-34
93FinLinCS-1
93FinLinS-34
93Max-213
93MaxPreS-213
93WheRooT-11
93WheRooT-55
93WheRooTPla-11
93WheRooTPla-55
94MaxPreS-205
94Pow-72
94PowGol-72
94PrePas-110
95MaxCroC-102
95MaxPreP-102
95MaxPreS-120

Brooks, Earl
89TGRacMR-39
89TGRacMR-120
89TGRacMR-121
89TGRacMR-148
91TGRacMRU-39
91TGRacMRU-120
91TGRacMRU-121
91TGRacMRU-148

Brooks, Gary
92MaxAllPT-21
92MaxBla-245
92MaxRed-245
93Max-249
93MaxPreS-249
94HigGeaPPT-W11
94HigGeaPPTG-11W
94MaxPreS-237

Brooks, Ron
91MaxBilETCM-30

Brooks, Tony
62PetLimGPRC-1
71MobTheSoGPMR-28

Broome, Richard
90Max-68
91Max-144
91ProSet-52
91Tra-91
92MaxBla-156
92MaxRed-156
92ProSet-204
92Tra-91
94FinLin-146
94FinLinS-146
95Max-211
95MaxCroC-122

96AutRac-44
96AutRacA-9
96AutRacCA-9
96AutRacHP-HP5
96Cla-20
96Cla-44
96ClaPriP-20
96ClaPriP-44
96ClaSil-20
96ClaSil-44
96CroJewEADJ-DJ8
96CroJewEDT-24
96CroJewEDTC-24
96CroJewEDTDJA-DJ8
96CroJewEDTDJG-DJ8
96CroJewEE-24
96CroJewEGDJ-DJ8
96CroJewEli-24
96CroJewES-24
96CroJewESDJ-DJ8
96CroJewETC-24
96CroJewETCDJA-DJ8
96CroJewETCDJS-DJ8
96CroJewETCE-24
96CroJewETCGDJ-DJ8
96CroJewETCS-24
96FinLin-4
96FinLin-36
96FinLin-65
96FinLinPP-6
96FinLinPP$5C-5
96FinLinPP$S-6
96FinLinPriP-4
96FinLinPriP-36
96FinLinPriP-65
96FinLinS-4
96FinLinS-36
96FinLinS-65
96Fla-6
96Fla-62
96MaxFamT-FT2
96MaxMadiA-22
96MaxMadiA-36
96MaxMadiABR-BR9
96MaxOdy-22
96MaxOdy-36
96MaxOdyRA-RA9
96MaxPre-31
96MaxPre-54
96MaxPre-74
96Pin-22
96Pin-49
96Pin-22
96Pin-49
96PinPolP-22
96PinPolP-38
96PinPolPLF-22
96PinPolPLF-38
96PinWinCC-22
96PinWinCC-49
96PrePas-6
96PrePasCC-6
96PrePasP-21
96PrePasPEP-21
96PrePasPH-21
96PrePasSco-6
96PrePasT-6
96RacCho-7
96RacCho-35
96RacCho-87
96RacChoAP-7
96RacChoAP-35
96RacChoAP-87
96RacChoSC-7
96RacChoSC-35
96RacChoSC-87
96SP-22
96SP-63
96SpeArtP-14
96SpeRac-14
96TraRevP-9
96TraRevP-14
96TraRevPFR-9
96TraRevPFR-14
96TraRevPLG-LG13
96TraRevPM-9
96TraRevPM-14
96Ult-72
96Ult-73
96Ult-74
96Ult-195
96UltAut-6
96UltGolM-2
96UltUpd-6
96UltUpd-52
96UltUpdW-15
96UppDec-29
96UppDec-69
96UppDec-109
96UppDecRTTC-RC21
96UppDecRTTC-RC70
96UppDecRTTC-RC104
96UppDecRTTCAS-H21
96VIP-5
96VIPEmeP-5
96Viper-9
96Viper-46
96ViperBlaM-9
96ViperBlaM-46
96ViperCop-9
96ViperCop-46
96ViperGreM-9
96ViperGreM-46
96VIPTor-5
96VIPWarP-WP11
96VIPWarPG-WP11
96Zen-34
96ZenArtP-34
97ActPac-14
97ActPac-35
97ActPacFI-14
97ActPacFI-35
97ColCho-22
97ColCho-72
97ColChoC-CC26
97ColChoC-CC59
97ColChoS-S43
97ColChoSQ-SQ24
97ColChoUD5-UD44
97ColChoUD5-UD45
97FinLinPP2-24
97FinLinPP2$10-78
97FinLinPP2$5-62
97JurPar-23
97JurParC-C9
97JurParP-P6
97JurParT-23
97JurParTL-TL6
97Max-22
97Max-67
97Max-94
97Pin-22
97Pin-51
97PinArtP-22
97PinArtP-51
97PinCer-22
97PinCer-56
97PinCer-75
97PinCerMB-22
97PinCerMB-56
97PinCerMB-75
97PinCerMG-22
97PinCerMG-56
97PinCerMG-75
97PinCerMR-22
97PinCerMR-56
97PinCerMR-75
97PinCerR-22
97PinCerR-56
97PinCerR-75
97PinMin-19
97PinMin2GC-19
97PinMinB-19
97PinMinC-19
97PinMinG-19
97PinMinNC-19
97PinMinS-19
97PinPreP-22
97PinPreP-51
97PinTotCPB-22
97PinTotCPB-56
97PinTotCPB-75
97PinTotCPG-18
97PinTotCPG-22
97PinTotCPG-56
97PinTotCPG-75
97PinTotCPR-22
97PinTotCPR-56
97PinTotCPR-75
97PinTroC-22
97PinTroC-51
97Pre-24
97PreBlaWFS-24
97PreGri-24
97PrePas-28
97PrePasAut-39
97PrePasCC'-CC3
97PrePasL-28
97PrePasOS-28
97PrePasP-22
97PrePasPEP-22
97PrePasPM-22
97PrePasPOS-22
97PrePasT-28
97PreRedW-24
97RacCho-22
97RacCho-57
97RacCho-82
97RacCho-101
97RacChoBC-4
97RacChoHO-13
97RacChoHOGitD-13
97RacChoSS-22
97RacChoSS-57
97RacChoSS-82
97RacChoSS-101
97RacSha-19
97RacShaGWP-19
97RacShaH-19
97RacShaPFBSA-2
97RacShaSA-SA9
97RacShaSTS-ST10
97RacShaTS-19
97SBMot-73
97SBMotWR-WC5
97ScoBoaI-14
97SP-22
97SP-64
97SP-100
97SP SupS-22
97SP SupS-64
97SP SupS-100
97Ult-6
97UltSho-2
97UppDecRTTC-33
97UppDecRTTC-75
97UppDecRTTCPPlu-+22
97UDRTTCPPRC-+22
97UppDRTTCPPRDC-+22
97UppDecVC-22
97UppDecVC-72
97VIP-4
97Viper-23
97ViperBlaR-23
97ViperSid-S4
97VIPExp-4
97VIPOilS-4
98ColCho-22
98ColCho-58
98ColCho-78
98HigGea-21
98HigGeaA-3
98HigGeaFG-16
98HigGeaGJ-GJ11
98HigGeaM-16
98Max-86
98Max10tA-18
98Max10tA-63
98MaxYeaIRBS-4
98MaxYeaIRBS-65
98MaxYeaIRBS-80
98MaxYeaIRBS-132
98PrePas-17
98PrePasCC'-CC3
98PrePasOS-17
98PrePasP-49
98PrePasP-49
98PrePasPS-PS11
98PrePasS-ST15A
98PrePasS-16
98PrePasSO-7
98PrePasSO-8
98PrePasSOD-7
98PrePasSOD-8
98PrePasTorp-ST15B
98SP Aut-34
98SP Aut-68
98UppDecRttC-22
98UppDecVC-22
98UppDecVC-67
98UppDecVC3DoS-D27
98UppDecVC3DoSG-D27
98VIP-5
98VIPDriF-DF4
98VIPDriFD-DF4
98VIPExp-5
98Whe-6
98WheGol-6
99Pre-20
99Pre-81
99PrePas-20
99PrePas-81
99PrePas-120
99UppDecVC-11
99UppDecVC-74
99UppDecVCUE-11
99UppDecVCUE-74
99WheHigG-20
99WheHigG-55
99WheHigGAC-20
99WheHigGFG-20
99WheHigGFG-55
99WheHigGM-20
99WheHigGM-55
99WheHigGS-GS20

Burwell, Jimmy
93JAG-5

Bush, George
93TraPreC-15

Bush, Johnny
91WinChoM-8
91WinChoM-9

Bussard, Ben
92VolRacLS2-13

Butler, Brian
91BulRin-89
92BulRin-141

Butler, Steve
87WorOut-41
88WorOut-36
91WorOut-68

Butler, Tim
90CheFlaI-97

Butler, Tobey
95ActPacC-89
95FinLinSRF-18
95FinLinSRF-33
95FinLinSRF-52
95FinLinSSSS-SS6
95FinLinSup-18
95FinLinSup-33
95FinLinSup-52
95MaxSup-3
95MaxSup-17
96Viper-70
96ViperBlaM-70
96ViperCop-70
96ViperGreM-70

Butner, Dave
92ProSetN-169

Butner, Randy
92BikRacS-9

Buttke, Nathan
93WheRooT-43
93WheRooTPla-43
94Max-187
94MaxPreS-187

Buttrey, Wade
92BulRin-46

Byers, Steve
92CorSelCCS-20

Bynum, Randy
92BulRin-115

Byron, Red (Robert)
89TGRacMR-2
89TGRacMR-3
89TGRacMR-153
89TGRacMR-155
91GalPrePR-63
91GalPrePR-85
91GalPrePR-104
91TGRacMRU-2
91TGRacMRU-3
91TGRacMRU-153
91TGRacMRU-155
95TraVal-55
98PrePas-144

Cabana, Jean-Paul
92PacAmeCT-11
92PacAmeCT-49

Caffi, Alex
87AceForO-8
91CarForO-28
91CarForO-29
91CarForO-30
91ProTraFO-22
91ProTraFO-23

Cagle, Gary
65TopHotR-52

Cain, Craig
89CheFlaI-54
90CheFlaI-86

Caldwell, Ronnie
94JAG-11

Cale, Kevin
91DKIMCDT-12

Caliva, Phil
83A&SRacI-10
84A&SRacI-9

Calkins, Buzz
97Hi-IRL-3
97Hi-IRL'I5-I4
97Hi-IRLP-D3
97Hi-IRLP-D9
97Hi-IRLP-D10

Callier, Fritz
71FleAHRDC-62
72FleAHRDN-7

Calloway, Marty
91DirTra-68
92DirTra-56
93JAG-6

Calvert, John
92ProSetN-198

Camelot, Gary
95JSKIce-81

Cameron II, Gary
91WorOut-12
93WorOutMW-9
94WorOut-33

Caminito, Jerry
89MegDra-46
89MegDra-47
91BigTimD-26
91BigTimD-42
91ProSetN-26
91ProSetN-75
92ProSetN-54
92ProSetN-124
93FinLinN-45

Campanello, Don
89MegDra-59
89MegDra-60

Campari, G.
71MobTheSoGPMR-10

Campbell, Fred
95JSKIce-70
95JSKIcePC-70

Campbell, G.C.
92BulRin-185

Campbell, Malcolm
30WilCig-23
31OgdMotR-1
77Spo-2103
92MaxIMH-14
95TraVal-41

Campbell, Mark
94HigGeaPPT-W29
94HigGeaPPTG-29W

Campbell, Steve
92CorSelCCS-2
93CorSelCCS-2

Campbell, Tim
92VolRacLS2-14

Cannon, Larry
80AvaHilURG-33

Cannon, Scotty
89CheFlaI-62
89CheFlaI-63
90CheFlaI-3
90CheFlaI-35

Capelli, Ivan
87AceForO-9
87ForOneI-6
91CarForO-43
91CarForO-44
91CarForO-45
91ProTraFO-37
91ProTraFO-38
92GriForO-27
92GriForO-60
92GriForO-93
92LimAppFO-2

Capie, Tom
90K&WDirT-9
91K&WDirT-23
92K&WDirT-45

Caputo , Chip (Mario)
92TraASA-31

Caracciola, Rudolf
38WilCig-22
39ChuKinoS-16
71MobTheSoGPMR-17
77Spo-1002

Carberry, Tom
92K&WDirT-56

Carbone, Steve
71FleAHRDC-4
72FleAHRDN-10
72FleAHRDN-31

73FleAHRRU-26
Carcciola, Rudolf
30WilCig-29
Card, Play
97ColChoC-CC1
97ColChoC-CC2
97ColChoC-CC3
97ColChoC-CC4
97ColChoC-CC5
98PrePasCC'-CC20
99PrePasCC-20
Carden, Billy
89TGRacMR-52
89TGRacMR-53
91TGRacMRU-52
91TGRacMRU-53
Cardin, Tony
91DirTra-66
91JAG-15
92DirTra-57
92JAG-13
Cardwell, Buster
94JAG-12
Carelli, Rick
94Max-79
94MaxPreS-79
95ActPacC-90
95FinLinSCalC-2
95FinLinSChaC-CC3
95FinLinSRF-3
95FinLinSRF-68
95FinLinSRF-79
95FinLinSup-3
95FinLinSup-68
95FinLinSup-79
95FinLinSWHHS-HS3
95Ima-60
95ImaGol-60
95MaxSup-2
95MaxSup-5
95MaxSup-10
96PrePas-65
96PrePasSco-65
96PrePasT-65
96Viper-68
96ViperBlaM-68
96ViperCop-68
96ViperGreM-68
97PrePas-47
97PrePasL-47
97PrePasOS-47
97PrePasT-47
97VIP-39
97VIPExp-39
97VIPOilS-39
Carello, Tony
78GraPri-7
78GraPri-234
Carey, John
90CheFlal-82
Carlson, Steve
91LanART-28
Carlson, Tom
91LanART-18
92RedGraST-2
Carlton, Don
72FleAHRDN-20
91BulRin-60
92BulRin-146
Carman, Darryl
90K&WDirT-10
Carnegie, Tom
87A&SRacl-2
Carnes, Ralph
91BulRin-134
92BulRin-60
Carpenter, Charles
90BigTimD-2
90BigTimDS-2
91BigTimD-61
Carpenter, Darrell
92JAG-14
Carpenter, Greg
92TraTeaS-147
Carr, Jim
88WorOut-40
90WorOut-22
91WorOut-9
92RacLegS-19
92WorOutMW-6
94WorOut-27
Carr, Mike
91DKIMCDT-6
Carrier, Eddie
91DirTra-13
91JAG-16
Carrigan, Gene
94MaxTexEI-28
Carroll Jr., Eddy
92WinChoB-123
92WinChoB-124
Carroll, Ed
92WinChoB-117
92WinChoB-118
Carson, Shane
87WorOut-30
91WorOut-48
Carte, Randy
92JAG-145
94JAG-13
Carter Sr., Duane
91AllWorl-72
92LegInd-82
Carter, Fuzzy
91ProSetN-99
92ProSetN-152
93FinLinN-16
Carter, Hal
94HigGeaPPT-E16
94HigGeaPPTG-16E
Carter, Jimmy
92TraBenP-23
Carter, Mike
95HavAT-24
Carter, Pancho
80AvaHilURG-6
83A&SRacl-8
84A&SRacl-7
85A&SRacl-45
86A&SRacl-9
86A&SRacl-36
87A&SRacl-28
90ActPacIP-23
91AllWorl-21
92AllWorl-42
92AllWorl-51
92AllWorl-74
92LegInd-22
Carter, Travis
89Max-24
90Max-65
91Max-120
91ProSet-84
91Tra-69
92MaxBla-129
92MaxRed-129
92ProSet-246
92Tra-128
94FinLin-8
94FinLinS-8
94HigGea-146
94HigGeaDO-146
94HigGeaDOG-146
94HigGeaG-146
94Max-295
94MaxPreP-37
94Pow-52
94Pow-80
94PowGol-52
94PowGol-80
95CroJew-29
95CroJewD-29
95CroJewE-29
95CroJewS-29
95FinLin-85
95FinLinPP-85
95FinLinSil-85
95ImaOwnP-OP1
95Max-81
95Max-228
95MaxCroC-100
95MaxPreP-100
95MaxPreS-115
96CroJewEDT-35
96CroJewEDTC-35
96CroJewEE-35
96CroJewEli-35
96CroJewES-35
96CroJewETC-35
96CroJewETCE-35
96CroJewETCS-35
96Kni-35
96KniBlaK-35
96KniQueRKP-35
96KniRoy-35
96KniWhiK-35
96Max-72
96MaxPre-112
97JurPar-58
97JurParT-58
97Viper-63
97ViperBlaR-63
Carver Sr., Joe
92TraTeaS-128
Carver, Terron
91MaxBilETCM-15
Case, Ricky
93AllRobPDS-3
Caspers, Spook
92BikRacS-4
Cass, Richard
90K&WDirT-11
Cassella, Mark
92VolRacLSI-13
Castles, Soapy (Neil)
89TGRacMR-132
89TGRacMR-135
89TGRacMR-136
89WinCir-31
91ProSetL-L15
91TGRacMRU-132
91TGRacMRU-135
91TGRacMRU-136
91TraPacYH-5
91TraPacYH-6
92ProSetL-L9
Caudill, Larry
91BulRin-44
92BulRin-44
92BulRin-120
92JusRacLC-1
92JusRacLC-2
92JusRacLC-3
92JusRacLC-4
92JusRacLC-5
92JusRacLC-6
92JusRacLC-7
92JusRacLC-8
92JusRacLC-9
92JusRacLC-10
92JusRacLC-11
92JusRacLC-12
92JusRacLC-13
92JusRacLC-14
92JusRacLC-15
92JusRacLC-16
92JusRacLC-17
92JusRacLC-18
92JusRacLC-19
92JusRacLC-20
92JusRacLC-21
92JusRacLC-22
92JusRacLC-23
92JusRacLC-24
92JusRacLC-25
92JusRacLC-26
92JusRacLC-27
92JusRacLC-28
92JusRacLC-29
92JusRacLC-30
Caver, Greg
94LanARCF-66
Cecil, Greg
92BulRin-191
Cerny, Wes
92ProSetKB-4
93FinLinN-17
Cerullo, Joey
91LanSeeS-6
Cevert, Francois
77Spo-5621
Chaffin, Chad
92BulRin-10
Chamberlain, Denny
92JAG-15
92STAMod-19
Chamberlain, Jeff
92TraTeaS-179
Chamblis, Tom
71FleAHRDC-57
Champion, Cliff
89Max-93
90Max-24
91Max-67
Chancy, David
92HavAT-19
92JAG-146
Chandler, Jeff
92TraTeaS-97
Chandler, Michael
83A&SRacl-25
84A&SRacl-6
85A&SRacl-11
Chaplin, Mike
92MaxBla-210
92MaxRed-210
93Max-236
93MaxPreS-236
94MaxPreS-225
Chapman, Colin
77Spo-6812
91ProTraFO-193
Chapman, Johnny
92BulRin-77
Charron, Fernand
95TraVal-6
Chase, Mike
92MaxBla-14
92MaxRed-14
94MaxMed-39
94MaxMed-51
95ActPacC-95
95MaxSup-14
96Viper-75
96ViperBlaM-75
96ViperCop-75
96ViperGreM-75
Chassagne, Jean
95TraVal-30
Chassey, Steve
83A&SRacl-16
84A&SRacl-14
85A&SRacl-8
86A&SRacl-17
87A&SRacl-3
91AllWorl-49
92AllWorl-82
Chastain, Mel
65DonSpeS-1
Chastain, Roger
94HigGeaPPT-G25
94HigGeaPPTG-25G
Chatham, Roy
91BulRin-120
Chaves, Pedro Matos
91CarForO-88
91CarForO-89
91ProTraFO-71
91ProTraFO-72
Cheek, Mike
92TraTeaS-177
92TraTeaS-189
Cheesbourg, Bill
92LegInd-94
Cheever, Eddie
78GraPri-26
78GraPri-34
78GraPri-191
87AceForO-10
87ForOneI-5
91AllWorl-16
91AllWorl-46
92AllWorl-9
92AllWorl-86
92LegInd-32
93HiTecl-2
93HiTecl-39
93HiTecl-70
93HiTeclCFF-SP4
93HiTeclP-P3
93HiTeclP-P5
94HiTecl-17
94HiTeclCD-CD10
95HiTeclCD-CD2
95SkyInd5-29
95SkyInd5-80
96SkyInd5-23
96SkyInd5-85
96SkyInd5RY-5
97Hi-IRL-17
Chencutt, Paul
92TraTeaS-88
Chester, Jimmy
91K&WDirT-17
92K&WDirT-25
94K&WDirT-34
95K&WDirT-21
Chester, Ted
91GalPrePR-102
Chevrolet, Gaston
54StaWetIW-1920
60HawWaxI-8
95TraVal-26
Chevrolet, Louis
11AmeTobAD-3
Chicoine, Steve
92WinChoM-11
Chiesa, Andrea
92GriForO-14
92GriForO-47
92GriForO-80
Childress, Richard
88MaxCha-29
89Max-87
90Max-45
90Max-193
91Max-54
91MaxRacFK-2
91MaxUpd-54
91Tra-54
91TraMomPBDE-1
91TraMomPHDE-1
91TraPacYH-7
92BikRacS-3
92BikRacS-31
92MaxBla-102
92MaxBla-289
92MaxMcD-5
92MaxRed-102
92MaxRed-289
92ProSet-39
92Tra-54
92TraMomPHDE-3
92TraTeaS-13
92TraTeaS-14
93Max-110
93MaxPreP-99
93MaxPreS-110
93MaxWinM-6
94ActPac-177
94ActPacP-3R942
94ActPacRCR-RCR1
94HigGea-33
94HigGeaG-33
94HigGeaPPT-E1
94HigGeaPPT-E4
94HigGeaPPT-E17
94HigGeaPPTG-1E
94HigGeaPPTG-4E
94HigGeaPPTG-17E
94Max-84
94MaxPreP-84
94MaxPreS-84
94OptXL-47
94OptXLRH-47
94Pow-6
94Pow-66
94Pow-81
94PowGol-6
94PowGol-66
94PowGol-81
95ActPacSDESS-2
95ActPacSTTH-5
95FinLinSRF-30
95FinLinSRF-57
95FinLinSSSS-SS2
95FinLinSup-30
95FinLinSup-57
95HigGea-31
95HigGeaDO-31
95HigGeaDOG-31
95HigGeaG-31
95ImaOwnP-OP2
95Max-35
95MaxChaC-9
95MetImpCDE-E1
95PrePas-82
95PrePasRH-82
95Sel-76
95SelFlaO-76
96ActPacC-63
96ActPacC-71
96Ass-13
96AutRac-5
96AutRacA-10
96AutRacCA-10
96ClaImaP-RP5
96Fla-48
96Kni-44
96KniBlaK-44
96KniQueRKP-44
96KniRoy-44
96KniWhiK-44
96PinPolP-87
96PinPolPLF-87
96Ult-141
96Viper-33
96ViperBlaM-33
96ViperCop-33
96ViperGreM-33

94PowGol-136
94PowPre-2
94PowPre-30
94PrePas-3
94PrePas-37
94PrePas-138
94PrePasCC-CC3
94Tra-34
94Tra-61
94Tra-165
94TraAutV-39
94TraAutV-48
94TraFirR-34
94TraFirR-61
94TraFirR-165
94TraPreC-38
94TraWin-W18
94VIP-8
94VIP-41
94WheHarG-69
94WheHarGG-69
95ActPacC-74
95ActPacC2CC-5
95ActPacCSS-74
95ActPacP-6
95ActPacS-8
95ActPacS-66
95ActPacS-67
95ActPacS-68
95ActPacS-69
95ActPacS-70
95ActPacSSS-8
95ActPacSSS-66
95ActPacSSS-67
95ActPacSSS-68
95ActPacSSS-69
95ActPacSSS-70
95CroJew-24
95CroJew-44
95CroJewD-24
95CroJewD-44
95CroJewE-24
95CroJewE-44
95CroJewS-24
95CroJewS-44
95FinLin-62
95FinLin-119
95FinLinPP-62
95FinLinPP-119
95FinLinSil-62
95FinLinSil-119
95HigGea-26
95HigGeaDO-26
95HigGeaDOG-26
95HigGeaG-26
95HiTecB4-37
95HiTecB4-82
95Ima-12
95Ima-74
95ImaGol-12
95ImaGol-74
95Max-12
95Max-144
95MaxCroC-12
95MaxMed-11
95MaxMed-41
95MaxMedB-11
95MaxMedB-41
95MaxMedORA-OTR9
95MaxPreP-12
95MaxPreS-12
95MaxPreS-249
95OptXL-4
95OptXLCB-4
95OptXLDC-4
95OptXLRH-4
95PrePas-8
95PrePasCC-8
95PrePasRH-8
95Sel-8
95SelFlaO-8
95SP-11
95SP-44
95SP-86
95SPDieC-11
95SPDieC-44
95SPDieC-86
95SPSpeM-SM12
95SPSpeMDC-SM12
95Tra-67
95Tra5thA-11
95Tra5thAG-11
95TraAutV-19
95TraFirR-67
95TraSerS-SS6
95UppDec-24
95UppDec-92
95UppDec-125
95UppDec-194
95UppDec-238
95UppDecGSEG-24
95UppDecGSEG-92
95UppDecGSEG-125
95UppDecGSEG-194
95UppDecGSEG-238
95UppDecSSES-24
95UppDecSSES-92
95UppDecSSES-125
95UppDecSSES-194
95UppDecSSES-238
95VIP-7
95VIPAut-7
95VIPCooB-7
95VIPEmeP-7
95VIPHel-H3
95VIPHelG-H3
95VIPPro-4
95VIPRedHCB-7
95Zen-12
96ActPacC-34
96ActPacCSS-34
96CroJewEDT-16
96CroJewEDT-51
96CroJewEDT-59
96CroJewEDTC-16
96CroJewEDTC-51
96CroJewEDTC-59
96CroJewEE-16
96CroJewEE-51
96CroJewEE-59
96CroJewEli-16
96CroJewEli-59
96CroJewES-16
96CroJewES-51
96CroJewES-59
96CroJewETC-16
96CroJewETC-51
96CroJewETC-59
96CroJewETCE-16
96CroJewETCE-51
96CroJewETCE-59
96CroJewETCS-16
96CroJewETCS-51
96CroJewETCS-59
96FinLin-6
96FinLin-21
96FinLin-54
96FinLinMM-MM9
96FinLinPP-7
96FinLinPP$5C-7
96FinLinPP$S-7
96FinLinPriP-6
96FinLinPriP-21
96FinLinPriP-54
96FinLinS-6
96FinLinS-21
96FinLinS-54
96Fla-7
96Fla-63
96Kni-14
96KniBlaK-14
96KniQueRKP-14
96KniRoy-14
96KniWhiK-14
96Max-12
96Max-45
96MaxMadiA-12
96MaxMadiA-45
96MaxMadiABR-BR1
96MaxOdy-12
96MaxOdy-45
96MaxOdyRA-RA1
96MaxOveTW-OTW4
96MaxPep5-4
96MaxPre-12
96MaxPre-67
96MaxSup-ST6
96Pin-12
96Pin-44
96Pin-12
96Pin-44
96PinPolP-33
96PinPolPLF-33
96PinWinCC-12
96PinWinCC-44
96PrePas-7
96PrePas-45
96PrePas-84
96PrePasCC-7
96PrePasP-15
96PrePasPEP-15
96PrePasPH-15
96PrePasSco-7
96PrePasSco-45
96PrePasSco-84
96PrePasT-7
96PrePasT-45
96PrePasT-84
96RacCho-19
96RacCho-34
96RacChoAP-19
96RacChoAP-34
96RacChoSC-19
96RacChoSC-34
96SP-12
96SP-56
96SPHolME-ME9
96SPx-12
96SPxGol-12
96TraRevP-38
96TraRevPFR-38
96TraRevPLG-LG11
96TraRevPM-38
96Ult-53
96Ult-54
96Ult-55
96Ult-160
96UltAut-7
96UltBoxS-15
96UltUpd-7
96UltUpd-53
96UltUpd-97
96UppDec-11
96UppDec-51
96UppDec-91
96UppDecRTTC-RC14
96UppDecRTTC-RC63
96UppDecRTTC-RC143
96UppDecRTTCAS-H14
96Viper-17
96ViperBlaM-17
96ViperCop-17
96ViperGreM-17
96Zen-12
96ZenArtP-12
97ColCho-12
97ColCho-62
97ColChoC-CC39
97ColChoC-CC72
97ColChoS-S14
97ColChoSQ-SQ6
97ColChoUD5-UD22
97ColChoUD5-UD23
97FinLinPP2-23
97FinLinPP2$5-61
97JurPar-22
97JurParT-22
97Max-36
97Max-81
97Max-109
97Pin-12
97Pin-41
97PinArtP-12
97PinArtP-41
97PinPreP-12
97PinPreP-41
97PinTroC-12
97PinTroC-41
97Pre-23
97PreBlaWFS-23
97PreGri-23
97PrePas-133
97PrePasL-133
97PrePasOS-133
97PrePasT-133
97PreRedW-23
97RacCho-12
97RacCho-47
97RacChoSS-12
97RacChoSS-47
97RacSha-17
97RacShaGWP-17
97RacShaH-17
97RacShaTS-17
97SkyPro-3
97SkyPro-73
97SkyProA-3
97SP-36
97SP-78
97SP-110
97SP SupS-36
97SP SupS-78
97SP SupS-110
97Ult-7
97UltUpd-20
97UltUpdAR-20
97UppDecRTTC-35
97UppDecRTTC-77
97UppDecRTTC-105
97UppDecRTTC-142
97UppDecVC-12
97UppDecVC-62
97UppDecVC-110
97Viper-22
97ViperBlaR-22
98ColCho-36
98ColCho-72
98HigGeaFG-57
98HigGeaM-57
98Max-30
98Max-60
98MaxSwaP-SW5
98MaxYealRBS-63
98MaxYealRBS-68
98SP Aut-30
98SP Aut-64
98UppDecRttC-30
98UppDecRttC-109
98UppDecVC-36
98UppDecVC-81
98UppDecVC-121
99Pre-91
99PrePas-91
99UppDecVC-2
99UppDecVC-61
99UppDecVCUE-2
99UppDecVCUE-61

Cope, Jimmy
92BulRin-169

Cope, Mike
91BulRin-25
92BulRin-25
97PrePas-120
97PrePasL-120
97PrePasOS-120
97PrePasT-120

Corbin, Rick
92JAG-151

Cormack, Tom
90LanRocSHS-5

Correll, P.B.
91PioStoCR-4

Corter, David
92CorSelCCS-1

Corum, L.L.
54StaWetIW-1924
60HawWaxI-12

Cossaboone, Chic
90K&WDirT-12
91K&WDirT-25
92K&WDirT-24

Costantini, M.
71MobTheSoGPMR-11

Couch, Buster
91ProSetN-98
92ProSetN-181
93FinLinN-125

Couch, Larry
91LanARCHS-53

Couch, Randy
91BulRin-90

Coughlin Jr., Jeg
73FleAHRRU-61
93FinLinN-120

Coulthard, David
92GriForO-163

Coury, Richard Jr.
95ActPacNJDC-3

Coverdale, Greg
91K&WURCS-39

Coville, C.D.
92K&WDirT-17

Cowart, Delma
94LanARCF-80

Cowart, Robbie
92LanARCF-107

Cowen, Bob
91DirTra-26
92STAMod-13

Cox, Dale
90LanRocSHS-13
91LanRocS-51

Cox, Dave
90LanRocSHS-14

Cox, Jimmy
91Max-107
91Tra-157
92BikRacS-10
92MaxBla-212
92MaxRed-212
92Tra-157
93Max-228
93MaxPreS-228
94MaxPreS-222
95MaxPreS-220
96MaxPre-221
96RacCho-80
96RacChoAP-80
96RacChoSC-80
97RacCho-85
97RacChoSS-85

Cox, Marion
91GalPrePR-54

Cox, Mark
92BulRin-198

Cox, Randy
92TraTeaS-183
92TraTeaS-196

Cox, Tom
93WheRooT-5
93WheRooTPla-5

Coyle, Bobby
94LanARCF-84

Coyne, Dale
85A&SRacI-33
86A&SRacI-7
87A&SRacI-7
91AllWorI-62
92AllWorI-26
96SkyInd5-54

Cozze, Frank
91K&WDirT-33
92K&WDirT-19
92TraDir-11
94K&WDirT-19
95K&WDirT-16

Cragen, Charlie
93Max-222
93MaxPreS-222
94MaxPreS-254
95MaxPreS-253

Craven, Cathleen
91WinChoRC-16
91WinChoRC-22

Craven, Ricky
91WinChoNED-98
91WinChoNED-99
91WinChoRC-1
91WinChoRC-2
91WinChoRC-3
91WinChoRC-4
91WinChoRC-5
91WinChoRC-6
91WinChoRC-7
91WinChoRC-8
91WinChoRC-9
91WinChoRC-10
91WinChoRC-11
91WinChoRC-12
91WinChoRC-13
91WinChoRC-14
91WinChoRC-15
91WinChoRC-16
91WinChoRC-17
91WinChoRC-18
91WinChoRC-19
91WinChoRC-20
91WinChoRC-21
91WinChoRC-22
91WinChoRC-23
91WinChoRC-24
91WinChoRC-25
91WinChoRC-26
91WinChoRC-27
91WinChoRC-28
91WinChoRC-29
91WinChoRC-30
92MaxBla-88
92MaxRed-88
92PacAmeCT-29
92ProSet-31
92Tra-10
92TraRacMB-10B
92WinChoB-2
92WinChoB-3
92WinChoB-4
92WinChoBA-2
93FinLin-60
93FinLinCS-16
93FinLinS-60

93Max-99
93Max-196
93MaxPreP-73
93MaxPreP-177
93MaxPreS-99
93MaxPreS-196
93Tra-65
93Tra-99
93Tra-156
93TraFirR-65
93TraFirR-99
93TraFirR-156
93WheRooT-38
93WheRooT-76
93WheRooTPla-38
93WheRooTPla-76
94FinLinBGN-BGN8
94FinLinG-44
94FinLinGA-44
94HigGea-47
94HigGeaG-47
94Max-164
94MaxPreP-151
94MaxPreS-164
94PrePas-58
94PrePas-67
94PrePasPro-PP3
94Tra-39
94Tra-190
94TraFirR-39
94TraFirR-190
94TraWin-W15
94TraWin-W19
94VIP-56
94VIP-69
95ActPacC-79
95ActPacCSS-79
95ActPacP-26
95ActPacPP2G-P2
95ActPacS-30
95ActPacSSS-30
95Ass-10
95AssGolS-10
95FinLin-41
95FinLin-120
95FinLinCC6-10
95FinLinPP-41
95FinLinPP-120
95FinLinSil-41
95FinLinSil-120
95HigGea-52
95HigGeaDO-52
95HigGeaDOG-52
95HigGeaG-52
95Ima-41
95Ima-95
95ImaGol-41
95ImaGol-95
95Max-151
95Max-248
95Max-249
95Max-250
95Max-251
95MaxAut-151
95MaxCroC-9
95MaxCroC-52
95MaxCroC-132
95MaxMed-HTH1
95MaxMed-HTH2
95MaxMedB-HTH1
95MaxMedB-HTH2
95MaxPreP-9
95MaxPreP-52
95MaxPreP-132
95MaxPreS-9
95MaxPreS-52
95MaxPreS-161
95MaxPreS-162
95MaxPreSU-10
95MaxTop52-TOP1
95OptXL-5
95OptXLCB-5
95OptXLDC-5
95OptXLRH-5
95OptXLS-XLS1
95PrePas-57
95PrePas-76
95PrePas-140
95PrePasPH-25
95PrePasPre-25
95PrePasPRH-25
95PrePasRH-57
95PrePasRH-76
95PrePasRH-140
95Sel-57
95Sel-126
95SelFlaO-57
95SelFlaO-126
95SP-29
95SP-73
95SP-115
95SP-117
95SPDieC-29
95SPDieC-73
95SPDieC-115
95SPDieC-117
95SPSpeM-SM19
95SPSpeMDC-SM19
95Tra-28
95Tra5thA-17
95Tra5thA-57
95Tra5thAG-17
95Tra5thAG-57
95TraAutV-18
95TraCha-C13
95TraFirR-28
95TraOnTR-OTR17
95UppDec-179
95UppDec-215
95UppDec-258
95UppDec-291
95UppDecA-215
95UppDecGSEG-179
95UppDecGSEG-215
95UppDecGSEG-258
95UppDecGSEG-291
95UppDecSSES-179
95UppDecSSES-215
95UppDecSSES-258
95UppDecSSES-291
95VIP-8
95VIPAut-8
95VIPCooB-8
95VIPEmeP-8
95VIPRedHCB-8
95VIPRef-R1
95VIPRefG-R1
95Zen-32
96ActPacC-103
96Ass-40
96Ass$1000CCIPC-3
96Ass$100CCIPC-18
96Ass$2PC-8
96AssComL-CL8
96AutRac-46
96AutRacA-11
96AutRacCA-11
96AutRacFR-10
96AutRacFR-11
96AutRacFR-12
96AutRacHP-HP8
96Cla-45
96ClaPriP-45
96ClaSil-45
96CroJewEDitR-DR3
96CroJewEDitRC-DR3
96CroJewEDitRS-DR3
96CroJewEDT-18
96CroJewEDT-49
96CroJewEDTC-18
96CroJewEDTC-49
96CroJewEDTCSA-CS7
96CroJewEE-18
96CroJewEE-49
96CroJewEli-18
96CroJewEli-49
96CroJewERCSG-CS7
96CroJewERCSP-CS7
96CroJewES-18
96CroJewES-49
96CroJewETC-18
96CroJewETC-49
96CroJewETCE-18
96CroJewETCE-49
96CroJewETCS-18
96CroJewETCS-49
96FinLin-31
96FinLin-76
96FinLinGS-GS16
96FinLinPP-8
96FinLinPP$5C-6
96FinLinPP$S-8
96FinLinPriP-31
96FinLinPriP-76
96FinLinS-31
96FinLinS-76
96Fla-8
96Fla-64
96FlaAut-1
96FlaPowP-1
96M-F-28
96M-F-29
96M-FSil-S12
96Max-41
96Max-56
96MaxMadiA-41
96MaxMadiA-56
96MaxMadiA-78
96MaxMadiA-79
96MaxMadiABR-BR4
96MaxOdy-41
96MaxOdy-56
96MaxOdy-78
96MaxOdy-79
96MaxOdyRA-RA4
96MaxPre-41
96MaxPre-51
96MaxPre-170
96MaxPre-182
96MaxPre-260
96MaxPreSS-SL6
96MaxSamBR-5
96MaxSamBR-6
96Pin-32
96Pin-56
96Pin-32
96Pin-56
96PinCheF-12
96PinCutA-11
96PinPolP-47
96PinPolPCS-15
96PinPolPLF-47
96PinWinCC-32
96PinWinCC-56
96PrePas-8
96PrePas-44
96PrePas-91
96PrePas&NC-8
96PrePasCC-8
96PrePasP-22
96PrePasP-38
96PrePasP$10PC-2
96PrePasP$20PC-2
96PrePasP$5PC-2
96PrePasPCB-CB2
96PrePasPEP-22
96PrePasPEP-38
96PrePasPH-22
96PrePasPH-38
96PrePasSco-8
96PrePasSco-44
96PrePasSco-91
96PrePasT-8
96PrePasT-44
96PrePasT-91
96RacCho-44
96RacChoAP-44
96RacChoSC-44
96SP-41
96SP-65
96SP-78
96SPDriF-DF6
96SpeArtP-25
96SpeRac-25
96SPHolME-ME11
96SPx-14
96SPxGol-14
96TraRev&PTCG-TC14
96TraRev&PTCH-TC14
96TraRevP-21
96TraRevPFR-21
96TraRevPLG-LG15
96TraRevPM-21
96TraRevPTC-TC14
96Ult-78
96Ult-79
96Ult-80
96Ult-149
96UltAut-8
96UltUpd-8
96UltUpd-54
96UltUpdA-1
96UltUpdPP-1
96UltUpdRS-4
96UppDec-39
96UppDec-79
96UppDec-119
96UppDecRTTC-RC23
96UppDecRTTC-RC72
96UppDecRTTC-RC133
96UppDecRTTC-RC146
96UppDecRTTCAS-H23
96V.IAut-5
96VIP-6
96VIPEmeP-6
96Viper-19
96ViperBlaM-19
96ViperCop-19
96ViperGreM-19
96VIPHeaG-HG1
96VIPHeaGD-HG1
96VIPTor-6
96VIPWarP-WP14
96VIPWarPG-WP14
96Zen-28
96Zen-71
96Zen-72
96ZenArtP-28
96ZenArtP-71
96ZenArtP-72
97Act-6
97ActPac-25
97ActPac-51
97ActPacFI-25
97ActPacFI-51
97ActPacRT-9
97AutRac-24
97AutRac-43
97AutRacA-8
97AutRacMS-KM24
97ColCho-41
97ColCho-53
97ColCho-115
97ColCho-146
97ColChoC-CC28
97ColChoC-CC61
97ColChoS-S15
97ColChoS-S16
97ColChoSQ-SQ11
97ColChoTF-C2
97ColChoTF-I1
97ColChoUD5-UD85
97ColChoUD5-UD86
97FinLinPP2-13
97FinLinPP2$10-81
97FinLinPP2$5-51
97JurPar-12
97JurParR-R6
97JurParT-12
97Max-25
97Max-70
97Max-99
97MaxRoootY-MR8
97Pin-25
97Pin-54
97PinArtP-25
97PinArtP-54
97PinCer-25
97PinCerMB-25
97PinCerMG-25
97PinCerMR-25
97PinCerR-25
97PinPor-12
97PinPor-32
97PinPre-74
97PinPreBM-74
97PinPreGM-74
97PinPreP-25
97PinPreP-54
97PinPreSM-74
97PinTotCPB-25
97PinTotCPB-59
97PinTotCPG-25
97PinTotCPG-59
97PinTotCPR-25
97PinTotCPR-59
97PinTroC-25
97PinTroC-54
97Pre-13
97PreBlaWFS-13
97PreGri-13
97PrePas-19
97PrePas-41
97PrePas-66
97PrePas-83
97PrePasAut-16
97PrePasCC'-CC4
97PrePasL-19
97PrePasL-41
97PrePasL-66
97PrePasL-83
97PrePasOS-19
97PrePasOS-41
97PrePasOS-66
97PrePasOS-83
97PrePasP-16
97PrePasPCB-CB1
97PrePasPCBD-CB1
97PrePasPEP-16
97PrePasPM-16
97PrePasPOS-16
97PrePasT-19
97PrePasT-41
97PrePasT-66
97PrePasT-83
97PreRedW-13
97RacCho-25
97RacCho-60
97RacCho-102
97RacChoBC-6
97RacChoCM-9
97RacChoSS-25
97RacChoSS-60
97RacChoSS-102
97RacSha-16
97RacShaGW-GW10
97RacShaGWP-16
97RacShaH-16
97RacShaSTS-ST7
97RacShaTS-16
97SBMot-20
97SBMot-86
97SBMotRC-RC2
97SBMotWR-WC8
97SBMotWR-WC28
97ScoBoal-24
97ScoBoal-50
97SkyPro-4
97SkyProA-4
97SkyProBO-B6
97SP-25
97SP-67
97SP-103
97SP-125
97SP SPxFA-SF3
97SP SupS-25
97SP SupS-67
97SP SupS-103
97SP SupS-125
97SPX-25
97SPxBlu-25
97SPxGol-25
97SPxSil-25
97SPXTagT-TT4
97SPxTagTA-TA4
97Ult-8
97Ult-53
97UltAKA-A10
97UltDouT-DT4
97UltEliS-E10
97UltIns-DC13
97UltUpd-21
97UltUpd-87
97UltUpdAR-21
97UppDecRTTC-22
97UppDecRTTC-64
97UppDecRTTC-101
97UppDecRTTC-134
97UppDecRTTCPP-PP7
97UppDecRTTCPP-PP15
97UppDecRTTCPPlu-+5
97UDRTTCPPRC-+5
97UppDRTTCPPRDC-+5
97UppDecVC-41
97UppDecVC-53
97UppDecVC-112
97UppDecVCGE-GE4
97VIP-5
97Viper-12
97ViperBlaR-12
97ViperSid-S6
97VIPExp-5
97VIPOilS-5
98ColCho-25
98ColCho-61
98ColCho-77
98ColCho-90
98HigGea-19
98HigGeaA-4
98HigGeaFG-17
98HigGeaGJ-GJ26
98HigGeaM-17
98Max-25
98Max-55
98Max-82
98MaxSwaP-SW25
98MaxTea-TW3
98MaxYealRBS-3
98MaxYealRBS-5
98MaxYealRBS-10

98MaxYeaIRBS-40
98MaxYeaIRBS-133
98PrePas-18
98PrePas-47
98PrePasA-10
98PrePasCC'-CC4
98PrePasOS-18
98PrePasOS-47
98PrePasP-46
98PrePasP-46
98PrePasPFC-FC17
98PrePasPFCR-FC17
98PrePasS-17
98SP Aut-25
98SP Aut-59
98SP AutBtW-BW18
98SP AutBtWL2-BW18
98SP AutBtWL3-BW18
98SP AutSotTL1-S3
98UppDecDV-12
98UppDecDVSM-12
98UppDecRTTCCS-CS15
98UppDecVC-25
98UppDecVC-70
98UppDecVC-92
98UppDecVC-124
98UppDecVC-136
98UppDecVCPL-PL19
98UppDecVCPP-16
98UppDecVCPPCR-16
98Whe-7
98WheAut-10
98WheGol-7

Crawford, Angela
94HigGeaPPT-W15
94HigGeaPPTG-15W

Crawford, Billy
93CorSelCCS-29

Crawford, Jim
86A&SRacI-31
87A&SRacI-38
91AllWorI-38
92AllWorI-43
92AllWorI-75
92LegInd-27
92MacTooWC-7
93HiTecI-21
93HiTecI-60
94HiTecI-25
94HiTecICD-CD11

Crawford, Rick
91BulRin-14
92BulRin-14

Creasman, Bart
92RSSMotH-27

Crettol, Roy
91LanRocS-18

Crider, Curtis
89TGRacMR-35
89TGRacMR-36
91PioStoCR-5
91TGRacMRU-35
91TGRacMRU-36

Crim, Penn Jr.
92BulRin-140

Croft, Paul
91DirTra-62
92JAG-19

Cronquist, Mark
92ProSet-196
92TraTeaS-85

Crouch, Robbie
92PacAmeCT-2
92PacAmeCT-35

Crowell, P.B. III
92BulRin-106

Crump, Dennis
91BulRin-128
92BulRin-195

Culbertson, Mike
92RSSMotH-25
92TraTeaS-155
92TraTeaS-164

Culler, Danny
92BikRacS-11
92BikRacS-31

Cummings, Bill
54StaWetIW-1934
60HawWaxI-22
95TraVal-40

Curley, Tom
92PacAmeCT-34

Curry, Jim
91JAG-11
92JAG-152
92STAMod-14

Curry, Tim
95JSKIce-90

Cusack, Glenn
91WinChoNED-65
91WinChoNED-66
92WinChoB-113
92WinChoB-114

Cyr, Mark
92WinChoM-13

Cywinski, Kevin
91LanART-25

Czach, Dana
90LanRocSHS-38
91LanRocS-58

D'Alessandro, Bruce
91WinChoM-51
91WinChoM-52

Dacco, Guido
91AllWorI-47
92AllWorI-16

Daigh, Chuck
62PetLimGPRC-29

Dakin, Pat
92ProSetN-22

Dallara, Gianpaola
92GriForO-147

Dallenbach Jr., Wally
91AllWorI-37
91MaxMot-3
91MaxMot-31
91MaxMot-40
91ProSet-90
92MaxBla-16
92MaxMot-10
92MaxMot-45
92MaxRed-16
92ProSet-69
92ProSet-181
92ProSet-205
92ProSetMH-29
92TraRacM-16
92TraRacM-52
92TraRacM-88
92TraRacMB-16B
93ActPac-65
93ActPac-66
93ActPac-113
93ActPac-114
93ActPac-170
93ActPac2G-52G
93FinLin-13
93FinLin-43
93FinLinCS-10
93FinLinS-13
93FinLinS-43
93Max-16
93MaxMot-5
93MaxMot-25
93MaxPreP-16
93MaxPreS-16
93Tra-16
93Tra-159
93TraFirR-16
93TraFirR-159
93TraTri-16
94ActPac-22
94ActPac-120
94ActPac-144
94FinLin-3
94FinLin-89
94FinLin-150
94FinLinG-20
94FinLinS-3
94FinLinS-89
94FinLinS-150
94HigGea-18
94HigGea-103
94HigGeaDO-103
94HigGeaDOG-103
94HigGeaG-18
94HigGeaG-103
94Max-16
94Max-80
94Max-268
94MaxMed-22
94MaxMed-59
94MaxPreP-16
94MaxPreP-80
94MaxPreS-16
94MaxPreS-80
94MaxTheS2-22
94Pow-83
94Pow-147
94PowGol-83
94PowGol-147
94PowPre-3
94PowPre-21
94PrePas-4
94PrePasCC-CC4
94Sky-6
94Tra-43
94Tra-186
94TraAutV-31
94TraFirR-43
94TraFirR-186
94VIP-9
95HiTecB4-20
95HiTecB4-43
95Max-45
95Sel-9
95SelFlaO-9
95UppDec-35
95UppDec-103
95UppDecGSEG-35
95UppDecGSEG-103
95UppDecSSES-35
95UppDecSSES-103
96Fla-9
96Fla-65
96Pin-15
96Pin-15
96PinWinCC-15
96PrePasP-30
96PrePasPEP-30
96PrePasPH-30
96SP-15
96SPDriF-DF7
96UltUpd-9
96UltUpd-55
96UltUpd-84
96UppDecRTTC-RC40
96UppDecRTTC-RC89
96UppDecRTTC-RC119
96VIP-7
96VIPEmeP-7
96VIPTor-7
97ColCho-15
97ColCho-65
97ColChoC-CC19
97ColChoC-CC52
97ColChoS-S44
97ColChoS-S45
97ColChoUD5-UD30
97ColChoUD5-UD31
97Pre-29
97PreBlaWFS-29
97PreGri-29
97PrePas-132
97PrePasAut-23
97PrePasL-132
97PrePasOS-132
97PrePasP-18
97PrePasPA-23
97PrePasPEP-18
97PrePasPM-18
97PrePasPOS-18
97PrePasT-132
97PreRedW-29
97SBMot-24
97SBMotWR-WC10
97SP-15
97SP-57
97SP-95
97SP SupS-15
97SP SupS-57
97SP SupS-95
97Ult-9
97UppDecRTTC-27
97UppDecRTTC-69
97UppDecRTTC-138
97UppDecVC-15
97UppDecVC-65
97Viper-18
97ViperBlaR-18
98ColCho-15
98ColCho-51
98HigGeaA-5

Dallenbach Sr., Wally
86AceInd-D2
92AllWorI-57

Dalmas, Yannick
88HerFouFO-8B
91ProTraFO-189

Dalrymple, Mike
91MaxBilETCM-16

Dalton, Wayne
92MaxAllPT-44
92MaxBla-261
92MaxRed-261

Daly, Derek
78GraPri-127
78GraPri-137
78GraPri-165
78GraPri-171
83A&SRacI-36
84A&SRacI-12
85A&SRacI-3
86A&SRacI-33
86AceInd-C1
87A&SRacI-35
91AllWorI-50
93MaxWilR-13

Dane, Lloyd
89TGRacMR-40
91TGRacMRU-40
91TraPacYH-8

Daniels, Garley
89CheFlaI-23

Daniels, Peter
92WinChoB-33
92WinChoB-34

Daniels, Randy
90CheFlaI-90

Danko, Kurt
91LanRocS-7
91LanRocS-60
92LanRocS-8

Danner, Christian
87AceForO-11
87ForOneI-6

Dapozzo, Al
91BigTimD-37

Darnell, Joe
92LanRocS-9

Darniche, Bernard
78GraPri-239

Darveau, Dave
91WinChoNED-88
91WinChoNED-89

Daughters, Curt
91DKIMCDT-5

Davidson, Ronnie
91BulRin-70

Davies, Ron
92DirTra-40
92STAMod-18
92VolRacLSI-14
94STAMod-16

Davis Jr., Bobby
87WorOut-3
88WorOut-3
89WorOut-1
89WorOutP-10
90LanRocSHS-11
90WorOut-4
90WorOutP-10
91WorOut-13
91WorOut-108
91WorOutMW-4
92RacLegS-28
94WorOut-19

Davis, Bill
91Tra-164
92Tra-164
93FinLin-98
93FinLinCS-8
93FinLinS-98
93Max-135
93MaxPreP-121
93MaxPreS-135
93Tra-97
93TraFirR-97
94HigGea-34
94HigGeaG-34
94Max-109
94MaxPreP-109
94MaxPreS-109
94Pow-84
94PowGol-84
94PrePas-76
95Max-78
95Max-194
95MaxCroC-91
95MaxPreP-91
95MaxPreS-103
95Sel-80
95SelFlaO-80
96MaxPre-116
97Viper-62
97ViperBlaR-62

Davis, Dave
91WinChoNED-82
91WinChoNED-83

Davis, Don
62MarInd-4

Davis, Floyd
54StaWetIW-1941
60HawWaxI-29
95TraVal-47

Davis, Jeff
92EriMaxTA-53

Davis, John
92ProSetN-151

Davis, Mike
89CheFlaI-29
91LanARCHS-26
92LanARCF-68

Davis, Paul
92STAMod-23

Davis, Preston
71FleAHRDC-53

Davis, Terry
91BulRin-95
92BulRin-135

Dawson, Dennis
92BikRacS-12

Dawson, Joe
54StaWetIW-1912
60HawWaxI-2
95TraVal-18

Day, Mark
91BulRin-15
92BulRin-68

Day, Norm
91BigTimD-13
91BigTimD-14
91BigTimD-15
91BigTimD-16
91BigTimD-17
91BigTimD-18
91BigTimD-19
91BigTimD-20
91BigTimD-22
91BigTimD-23
91BigTimD-24

Day, Richard
94WorOut-10

Day, Ronnie
91WorOut-31

de Ferran, Gil
96SkyInd5-28
96SkyInd5-83
97CARSchC-3

de Graffenried, Baron
71MobTheSoGPMR-23

De Palo, Ralph
26SpoComoAR-3

Dean, Lee
89MegDra-106

DeAngelis, Elio
87ForOneI-7

Deason, Dion
91DirTra-67

DeCaires IV, Greg
91WorOut-44

deCesaris, Andrea
87AceForO-12
87ForOneI-8
91CarForO-93
91CarForO-94
91CarForO-95
91ProTraFO-75
91ProTraFO-76
92GriForO-4
92GriForO-37
92GriForO-70
92LimAppFO-4

Decker, Billy
91K&WDirT-40
92K&WDirT-11
92TraDir-10
94K&WDirT-17
95K&WDirT-20

Deery, Elmo
91LanRocS-46

Deery, Jack
92LanRocS-10

DeFluiter, Don
89CheFlaI-12
89CheFlaI-93

DeFrance, Darrel
91DKIMCDT-49

DeHart, Brian
95MaxPreS-218

92PacAmeCT-3
92PacAmeCT-47
Dragon, Bobby
91WinChoNED-8
91WinChoNED-9
92WinChoB-56
92WinChoB-57
Drake, Billy
94JAG-16
Dralle, Red
91DKIMCDT-8
Drew, Gary
91WinChoM-57
91WinChoM-58
Dreyfus, Rene
71MobTheSoGPMR-13
Drongowski, David
90CheFlal-60
Druer, Jim
90BigTimD-3
90BigTimDS-3
Dubay, Lonnie
98PrePas-77
98PrePasOS-77
Duggan, Patrick
93JAG-11
94JAG-17
Dumesny, Max
88WorOut-NNO
91WorOut-97
94WorOut-31
Dumesny, Melinda
91WorOut-98
Dumfries, Johnny
87AceForO-13
87ForOnel-9
Dunaway, Bryan
92JAG-155
94JAG-18
Dunkle, Gary
88WorOut-45
Dunlap, Gene
73FleAHRRU-24
Dunn, Darrell
92MaxAllPT-36
92MaxBla-255
92MaxRed-255
Dunn, Jennifer
93JAG-NNO
Dunn, Jim
72FleAHRDN-55
92ProSetN-20
Dunn, Mike
89MegDra-8
89MegDra-9
91ProSetN-32
92MacTooWC-8
92ProSetN-64
94ActPacN-4
94ActPacN-14
95ActPacN-7
95ActPacNSS-7
Dunn, Murt
90LanRocSHS-43
91LanRocS-12
Dunn, Randy
92JAG-20
93JAG-12
Dunnaway, Glenn
91GalPrePR-82
Durant, Paul
97Hi-IRL-28
Duray, Arthur
11AmeTobAD-8
Durboraw, Nathan
91DirTra-51
92DirTra-24
92STAMod-17
94STAMod-17
Durchman, Eric
94HigGeaPPT-W26
94HigGeaPPTG-26W
Duryea, J.Frank
95TraVal-1
DuVall, Josh
92TraASA-1
Duvall, Mike
91DirTra-42
91JAG-4
92DirTra-13
92JAG-156
92STAMod-21
94STAMod-18
95HavAT-39
Ead, Cogo
73FleAHRRU-23
Eads, Stan
92BulRin-90
Eaglin, Terry
94STAMod-19
Earls, Jason
91WorOut-59
Earnhardt Jr., Dale
93Max-274
93MaxPreP-189
93MaxPreS-274
94HigGea-180
94HigGea-183
94HigGeaDO-180
94HigGeaDO-183
94HigGeaDOG-180
94HigGeaDOG-183
94HigGeaG-180
94HigGeaG-183
94OptXL-46
94OptXLRH-46
95ActPacSDE-SD3
95WSMDalETNG-3
95WSMDalETNG-NNO
98PrePas-46
98PrePasOS-46
98PrePasP-12
98PrePasP-12
98PrePasS-39
98PrePasSS-3
98PrePasSSD-3
98Whe-47
Earnhardt, Dale
83UNORac-27
86SpoPhoG-4
88MaxCha-9
88MaxCha-13
88MaxCha-17
88MaxCha-38
88MaxCha-45
88MaxCha-49
88MaxCha-54
88MaxCha-84
88MaxCha-87
89Max-3
89Max-60
89Max-102
89Max-108
89Max-121
89Max-144
89Max-148
89Max-160
89MaxCri-6
90ACRacPW-3
90Max-3
90Max-116
90Max-179
90Max-183
90Max-191
90Max-195
90MaxHolF-HF1
91ACRac-1
91HicMotS-6
91HicMotS-10
91IRO-12
91Max-3
91Max-173
91Max-174
91Max-178
91Max-179
91Max-184
91Max-185
91Max-187
91Max-191
91Max-192
91Max-198
91Max-200
91Max-220
91MaxMcD-1A
91MaxMcD-1B
91MaxMcD-30
91MaxRacFK-1
91MaxTheWA-5
91MaxUpd-3
91MaxUpd-200
91MaxUpd-220
91MaxWin2AF-10
91MaxWin2AF-16
91MaxWin2AF-17
91MaxWin2AF-20
91SpoLegPP-PP18
91SunRacL-3
91Tra-3A
91Tra-3B
91Tra-103A
91Tra-103B
91Tra-190A
91Tra-190B
91TraMomPBDE-1
91TraMomPBDE-2
91TraMomPBDE-3
91TraMomPBDE-4
91TraMomPBDE-5
91TraMomPBDE-6
91TraMomPHDE-1
91TraMomPHDE-2
91TraMomPHDE-3
91TraMomPHDE-4
91TraMomPHDE-5
91TraMomPHDE-6
91TraRicP-22
92-CarDynBTBS-1
92ACRacP-1
92MaxAllPT-1
92MaxBla-3
92MaxBla-203
92MaxBla-231
92MaxBla-265
92MaxBla-271
92MaxBla-281
92MaxBla-289
92MaxBla-294
92MaxMcD-1
92MaxMcD-2
92MaxRed-3
92MaxRed-203
92MaxRed-231
92MaxRed-265
92MaxRed-271
92MaxRed-281
92MaxRed-289
92MaxRed-294
92MaxTexDA-12
92MaxTheW-14
92MaxTheW-34
92ProSet-1
92ProSet-59
92ProSet-161
92ProSet-172
92ProSet-182
92ProSet-224
92ProSet-NNO
92ProSet-NNO
92ProSetP-P1
92RPM-1
92SpoLegAK-AK11
92Tra-3
92Tra-60
92Tra-103
92Tra-175
92Tra-190
92Tra-193
92TraAut-A1
92TraGoo-19
92TraMomPHDE-1
92TraMomPHDE-2
92TraMomPHDE-3
92TraMomPHDE-4
92TraMomPHDE-5
92TraMomPHDE-6
92TraMomPHDE-NNO
92TraRacM-1
92TraRacM-3
92TraRacM-9
92TraRacM-34
92TraRacM-44
92TraRacM-54
92TraRacM-84
92TraRacM-89
92TraRacM-91
92TraRacM-100
92TraRacM-P1
92TraRacMB-3B
92TraTeaS-1
92TraTeaS-2
92TraTeaS-3
92TraTeaS-4
92TraTeaS-13
92TraTeaS-15
92TraTeaS-16
92TraTeaS-17
92TraTeaS-18
92TraTeaS-19
92TraTeaS-20
92TraTeaS-21
92TraTeaS-22
92TraTeaS-23
92TraTeaS-24
92TraTeaS-25
92TraTeaS-101
92WheSpeTtDE-1
93ACRacF-3
93ActPac-88
93ActPac-89
93ActPac-94
93ActPac-95
93ActPac-120
93ActPac-121
93ActPac-122
93ActPac-123
93ActPac-124
93ActPac-125
93ActPac-126
93ActPac-127
93ActPac-138
93ActPac-139
93ActPac-171
93ActPac-198
93ActPac-202
93ActPac-207
93ActPac2G-18G
93ActPac2G-19G
93ActPac2G-20G
93ActPac2G-21G
93ActPac2G-22G
93ActPac2G-23G
93ActPac2G-24G
93ActPac2G-25G
93ActPac2G-37G
93ActPac2G-38G
93ActPac2G-53G
93ActPacP-DE1
93CarDynDEP-3
93CarDynGO-8
93CarDynNSC-2
93CarDynQC-8
93DaySer2RW-12
93HiTecTT-1
93Max-3
93Max-56
93Max-274
93MaxPreP-3
93MaxPreP-56
93MaxPreP-189
93MaxPrePJ-NNO
93MaxPreS-3
93MaxPreS-56
93MaxPreS-274
93MaxTheW-1
93MaxTheW-21
93MaxTheW-49
93MaxTheW-50
93MaxTheW-51
93WheMomPDE-1
93WheMomPDE-2
93WheMomPDE-3
93WheMomPDE-4
93WheMomPDE-5
93WheMomPDE-6
94ActPac-1
94ActPac-8
94ActPac-32
94ActPac-41
94ActPac-68
94ActPac-99
94ActPac-104
94ActPac-126
94ActPac-179
94ActPac-180
94ActPac-187
94ActPac2G-2G
94ActPac2G-11G
94ActPac2G-22G
94ActPac2G-179G
94ActPac2G-180G
94ActPac2G-187G
94ActPacC-2
94ActPacCC-21
94ActPacCC-22
94ActPacCC-23
94ActPacCC-24
94ActPacCC-25
94ActPacCC-26
94ActPacCC-27
94ActPacCC-28
94ActPacCC-29
94ActPacCC-30
94ActPacCC-31
94ActPacCC-32
94ActPacCC-33
94ActPacCC-34
94ActPacCC-35
94ActPacCC-36
94ActPacCC-37
94ActPacCC-38
94ActPacCC-39
94ActPacCC-40
94ActPacCC-41
94ActPacCC-42
94ActPacCC2G-22G
94ActPacCC2G-28G
94ActPacCC2G-30G
94ActPacCC2G-32G
94ActPacCC2G-39G
94ActPacCC2G-41G
94ActPacCC2G-42G
94ActPacP-2R941
94ActPacRCR-RCR2
94ActPacRCR-RCR3
94ActPacRCR-RCR4
94ActPacRCR-RCR5
94ActPacRCR-RCR6
94ActPacS2G-W3
94ActPacS2G-W6
94ActPacS2G-W9
94CarDynDEDE-1
94CarDynDEDE-2
94CarDynDEDE-3
94CarDynDEDE-4
94CarDynDEDE-5
94CarDynDEDE-6
94Hi-Bri4AP-9
94Hi-Bri4AP-38
94HigGea-1
94HigGea-79
94HigGea-85
94HigGea-92
94HigGea-186
94HigGea-188
94HigGeaD-D3
94HigGeaDO-186
94HigGeaDO-188
94HigGeaDOG-186
94HigGeaDOG-188
94HigGeaG-1
94HigGeaG-79
94HigGeaG-85
94HigGeaG-92
94HigGeaG-186
94HigGeaG-188
94HigGeaMG-MG1
94HigGeaMG-MG1S
94HigGeaMG-SMG1
94HigGeaPPT-E3
94HigGeaPPT-E4
94HigGeaPPT-E5
94HigGeaPPT-E18
94HigGeaPPT-E19
94HigGeaPPT-E20
94HigGeaPPT-E21
94HigGeaPPTG-3E
94HigGeaPPTG-4E
94HigGeaPPTG-5E
94HigGeaPPTG-18E
94HigGeaPPTG-19E
94HigGeaPPTG-20E
94HigGeaRTU-104
94HigGeaRTUP-104
94HigMinV-1B
94HigMinV-1G
94HigMinV-1S
94HiTecB4-9
94HiTecB4-38
94Max-3
94Max-23
94Max-211
94Max-218
94Max-219
94Max-222
94Max-224
94Max-225
94Max-238
94Max-334
94Max-335
94MaxMed-46
94MaxMed-99SP
94MaxPreP-3
94MaxPreP-23
94MaxPreP-165
94MaxPreP-170
94MaxPreP-177
94MaxPreP-178
94MaxPreP-181
94MaxPreP-183
94MaxPreP-184

96M-F-4
96M-F-45
96M-FBla-B3
96M-FBla-B4
96M-FSheM-M2
96M-FSil-S2
96M-FSil-S3
96Max-3
96MaxOdyM-MM1
96MaxPre-3
96MaxPre-73
96MaxPre-262
96MetImp-1
96MetImp2AWCC-10
96MetImp2AWCC-16
96MetImp2AWCC-17
96MetImp2AWCC-20
96MetImp2AWCC-21
96MetImp2AWCC-23
96MetImp2AWCC-24
96MetImpWCTF-4
96Pin-3
96Pin-38
96Pin-91
96Pin-3
96Pin-38
96Pin-91
96PinCheF-3
96PinPolP-3
96PinPolP-27
96PinPolP-56
96PinPolP-57
96PinPolP-58
96PinPolP-59
96PinPolP-60
96PinPolP-72
96PinPolPCS-3
96PinPolPLF-3
96PinPolPLF-27
96PinPolPLF-56
96PinPolPLF-57
96PinPolPLF-58
96PinPolPLF-59
96PinPolPLF-60
96PinPolPLF-72
96PinPolPNL-3
96PinPolPNLG-3
96PinTeaP-3
96PinTeaP-11
96PinWinCC-3
96PinWinCC-38
96PinWinCC-91
96PrePas-9
96PrePas-40
96PrePas&NC-9
96PrePasBR-BR3
96PrePasCC-9
96PrePasFoc-F1
96PrePasFQS-FQS1A
96PrePasFQS-FQS1B
96PrePasP-2
96PrePasP-35
96PrePasPBRI-BR5
96PrePasPCB-CB3
96PrePasPEP-2
96PrePasPEP-35
96PrePasPH-2
96PrePasPH-35
96PrePasPHP-HP1
96PrePasSco-9
96PrePasSco-40
96PrePasT-9
96PrePasT-40
96RacCho-3
96RacCho-27
96RacCho-56
96RacCho-57
96RacCho-58
96RacCho-59
96RacCho-60
96RacCho-84
96RacCho-89
96RacCho-92
96RacCho-P1
96RacChoAP-3
96RacChoAP-27
96RacChoAP-56
96RacChoAP-57
96RacChoAP-58
96RacChoAP-59
96RacChoAP-60
96RacChoAP-84
96RacChoAP-89
96RacChoAP-92
96RacChoS-SD1
96RacChoS-SD2
96RacChoS-SD3
96RacChoSC-3
96RacChoSC-27
96RacChoSC-56
96RacChoSC-57
96RacChoSC-58
96RacChoSC-59
96RacChoSC-60
96RacChoSC-84
96RacChoSC-89
96RacChoSC-92
96RacChoTT-2
96RacChoUCDE-1
96RacChoUCDE-2
96RacChoUCDE-3
96RacChoUCDE-4
96RacChoUCDE-5
96RacChoUCDE-6
96RacChoUCDE-7
96SP-3
96SP-KR1
96SpeArtP-17
96SpeArtP-37
96SpeArtP-51
96SpeArtP-52
96SpeArtP-53
96SpeArtP-54
96SpeArtP-83
96SpeArtP-85
96SpeCleS-1
96SpeInM-1
96SpePro-1
96SpeRac-17
96SpeRac-37
96SpeRac-51
96SpeRac-52
96SpeRac-53
96SpeRac-54
96SpeRac-83
96SpeRac-85
96SPHolME-ME3
96SPKinotR-K1
96SPx-3
96SPxGol-3
96TraRevP-37
96TraRevPFR-37
96TraRevPM-37
96Ult-5
96Ult-6
96Ult-7
96Ult-173
96Ult-175
96Ult-176
96Ult-185
96Ult-187
96Ult-192
96Ult-197
96Ult-200
96UltAut-9
96UltBoxS-2
96UltChaC-2
96UltFlaP-2
96UltGolM-4
96UltSeaC-3
96UltSeaC-5
96UltSeaC-9
96UltSeaC-12
96UltSeaC-15
96UltThu&L-5
96UltThu&L-6
96UltUpd-10
96UltUpd-45
96UltUpd-56
96UltUpd-96
96UltUpdA-2
96UltUpdPP-2
96UltUpdW-7
96UltUpdW-16
96UppDecRTTC-RC42
96UppDecRTTC-301
96UppDecRTTC-DE1
96UppDecRTTCDEM-301
96UppDecRttCDEW-DE1
96UppDRTTCPPR-PR10
96V.IAut-6
96VIP-8
96VIP-38
96VIPDalEAFS-DE1
96VIPDalEAFS-DE2
96VipDalEM-1
96VipDalEM-2
96VipDalEM-3
96VIPEmeP-8
96VIPEmeP-38
96Viper-1
96Viper-43
96ViperBlaM-1
96ViperBlaM-43
96ViperBusC-B14
96ViperCob-C1
96ViperCop-1
96ViperCop-43
96ViperDalE-1
96ViperDalE-2
96ViperDalE-3
96ViperDia-D2
96ViperDiaA-DA2
96ViperGreM-1
96ViperGreM-43
96ViperKinC-KC1
96VIPHeaG-HG2
96VIPHeaGD-HG2
96VIPSamBTF-SB1
96VIPSamBTFG-SB1
96VIPTor-8
96VIPTor-38
96VIPWarP-WP2
96VIPWarPG-WP2
96WheDalEM-MPC1
96WheDalEM-MPC2
96WheDalEM-MPC3
96Zen-1
96Zen-35
96Zen-50
96Zen-65
96Zen-66
96Zen-67
96Zen-68
96Zen-69
96ZenArtP-1
96ZenArtP-35
96ZenArtP-50
96ZenArtP-65
96ZenArtP-66
96ZenArtP-67
96ZenArtP-68
96ZenArtP-69
96ZenChaS-2
96ZenChaS-3
96ZenChaS-5
96ZenChaS-6
96ZenChaS-9
96ZenChaS-10
96ZenChaS-16
96ZenHig-1
96ZenSevW-1
97Act-3
97Act-8
97ActPac-3
97ActPac-45
97ActPac-84
97ActPac2G-2
97ActPacCM-1
97ActPacFA-6
97ActPacFI-3
97ActPacFI-45
97ActPacFI-84
97ActPacRT-2
97ActPreM-6
97AutRac-1
97AutRac-36
97AutRac-47
97AutRac-49
97AutRacA-12
97AutRacMS-KM1
97ColCho-3
97ColChoSQ-SQ26
97ColChoUD5-UD1
97ColChoVC-VC2
97JurParC-C1
97JurParP-P1
97JurParTL-TL8
97JurParTR-TR5
97Max-3
97Max-48
97Pin-3
97Pin-32
97Pin-66
97Pin-68
97Pin-69
97Pin-70
97Pin-82
97Pin-84
97Pin-91
97Pin-95
97Pin-96
97PinArtP-3
97PinArtP-32
97PinArtP-66
97PinArtP-68
97PinArtP-69
97PinArtP-70
97PinArtP-82
97PinArtP-84
97PinArtP-91
97PinArtP-95
97PinCer-3
97PinCer-37
97PinCer-76
97PinCer-93
97PinCerCGT-1
97PinCerCT-1
97PinCerE-E1
97PinCerEE-E1
97PinCerEP-E1
97PinCerMB-3
97PinCerMB-37
97PinCerMB-76
97PinCerMB-93
97PinCerMG-3
97PinCerMG-37
97PinCerMG-76
97PinCerMG-93
97PinCerMR-3
97PinCerMR-37
97PinCerMR-76
97PinCerMR-93
97PinCerR-3
97PinCerR-37
97PinCerR-76
97PinCerR-93
97PinCheM-13
97PinMin-21
97PinMin2GC-21
97PinMinB-21
97PinMinC-21
97PinMinG-21
97PinMinNC-21
97PinMinS-21
97PinPor-3
97PinPor-23
97PinPre-15
97PinPre-18
97PinPreBM-15
97PinPreBM-18
97PinPreGM-15
97PinPreGM-18
97PinPreP-3
97PinPreP-32
97PinPreP-66
97PinPreP-68
97PinPreP-69
97PinPreP-70
97PinPreP-82
97PinPreP-84
97PinPreP-91
97PinPreP-95
97PinPreP-96
97PinPreP-S3-S
97PinPreP-CM13
97PinPreP-TP3A
97PinPreSM-15
97PinPreSM-18
97PinSpe-3-S
97PinSpeA-3-S
97PinTeaP-3
97PinTotCPB-3
97PinTotCPB-37
97PinTotCPB-76
97PinTotCPB-93
97PinTotCPG-3
97PinTotCPG-37
97PinTotCPG-76
97PinTotCPG-93
97PinTotCPR-3
97PinTotCPR-37
97PinTotCPR-76
97PinTotCPR-93
97PinTroC-3
97PinTroC-32
97PinTroC-66
97PinTroC-68
97PinTroC-69
97PinTroC-70
97PinTroC-82
97PinTroC-84
97PinTroC-91
97PinTroC-95
97PinTroC-96
97Pre-3
97PreAmeE-AE1
97PreBlaWFS-3
97PreEyeotT-ET1
97PreGat-GB1
97PreGatA-GBA1
97PreGolE-GE1
97PreGri-3
97PrePas-4
97PrePas-32
97PrePas-56
97PrePas-95
97PrePasAut-4
97PrePasBB-BB4
97PrePasBR-BR2
97PrePasCC'-CC5
97PrePasCleC-C1
97PrePasL-4
97PrePasL-32
97PrePasL-56
97PrePasL-95
97PrePasOS-4
97PrePasOS-32
97PrePasOS-56
97PrePasOS-95
97PrePasP-4
97PrePasP-29
97PrePasPA-4
97PrePasPCB-CB2
97PrePasPCBD-CB2
97PrePasPDB-DB1
97PrePasPEP-4
97PrePasPEP-29
97PrePasPLL-LL1
97PrePasPM-4
97PrePasPM-29
97PrePasPOS-4
97PrePasPOS-29
97PrePasT-4
97PrePasT-32
97PrePasT-56
97PrePasT-95
97PrePasVL-VL1A
97PrePasVL-VL1B
97PreRedW-3
97RacCho-3
97RacCho-27
97RacCho-38
97RacCho-62
97RacCho-90
97RacCho-104
97RacCho-106
97RacChoBC-1
97RacChoBC-11
97RacChoCM-8
97RacChoHO-2
97RacChoHO-15
97RacChoHOGitD-2
97RacChoHOGitD-15
97RacChoSS-3
97RacChoSS-27
97RacChoSS-38
97RacChoSS-62
97RacChoSS-90
97RacChoSS-104
97RacChoSS-106
97RacSha-1
97RacShaGW-GW1
97RacShaGWP-1
97RacShaH-1
97RacShaPFBSA-3
97RacShaSA-SA1
97RacShaSTS-ST1
97RacShaTS-1
97SBMot-1
97SBMot-41
97SBMot-47
97SBMot-50
97SBMot-92
97SBMotAC-AU1
97SBMotRC-RC1
97SBMotWR-WC2
97SBMotWR-WC20
97ScoBoal-1
97ScoBoal-27
97ScoBoal-38
97ScoBoal-40
97ScoBoal$PC-PC1
97ScoBoal$PC-PC4
97ScoBoalR-SB1
97ScoBoaRSBF-SB1
97SkyPro-5
97SkyPro-63
97SkyProA-5
97SkyProPS-E1

90MaxBilEVC-E1
90MaxBilEVC-E2
90MaxBilEVC-E3
90MaxBilEVC-E4
90MaxHolF-HF2
91IRO-5
91Max-9
91Max-50
91Max-193
91Max-P1
91MaxBilETCM-5
91MaxBilETCM-7
91MaxBilETCM-11
91MaxBilETCM-20
91MaxBilETCM-39
91MaxMcD-4A
91MaxMcD-4B
91MaxMcD-30
91MaxMot-1
91MaxMot-29
91MaxRacFK-1
91MaxRacFK-2
91MaxTheWA-6
91MaxUpd-9
91MaxUpd-50
91MaxWin2AF-18
91SunRacL-9
91SupRacM-2
92CarDynGO-9
92MaxBla-11
92MaxBla-100
92MaxBla-279
92MaxCra-NNO
92MaxMcD-1
92MaxMcD-4
92MaxMot-1
92MaxMot-36
92MaxMot-49
92MaxMot-50
92MaxRed-11
92MaxRed-100
92MaxRed-279
92MaxRed-P1
92MaxSamB-8
92MaxTheW-5
92MaxTheW-25
92RedSta-9
92WheSpeTtBE-1
93CarDynGO-2
93CarDynQC-4
93HiTecTT-9
93Max-11
93Max-13
93Max-37
93Max-94
93Max-193
93Max-265
93Max-266
93Max-267
93Max-268
93Max-293
93Max-P1
93MaxLowFS-2
93MaxMot-6
93MaxMot-26
93MaxMot-47
93MaxPreP-11
93MaxPreP-13
93MaxPreP-29
93MaxPreP-37
93MaxPreP-175
93MaxPreP-180
93MaxPreP-181
93MaxPreP-182
93MaxPreP-183
93MaxPreP-208
93MaxPreP-P1
93MaxPreS-11
93MaxPreS-13
93MaxPreS-37
93MaxPreS-94
93MaxPreS-193
93MaxPreS-265
93MaxPreS-266
93MaxPreS-267
93MaxPreS-268
93MaxPreS-293
93MaxRetJ-7
93MaxTheW-14
93MaxTheW-34
93MotManC-3
94ActPac-48
94ActPac-138
94ActPac2G-18G

94ActPacC-3
94ActPacS2G-W2
94FinLin-1
94FinLin-7
94Hi-Bri4AP-10
94Hi-Bri4AP-15
94Hi-Bri4AP-44
94HigMinV-2B
94HigMinV-2S
94HiTecB4-10
94HiTecB4-15
94HiTecB4-44
94Max-11
94Max-54
94Max-202
94Max-241
94Max-P1
94Max-P2
94MaxAut-9
94MaxAut-11
94MaxMed-3
94MaxMed-64
94MaxMot-4
94MaxPreP-9
94MaxPreP-11
94MaxPreP-54
94MaxPreP-P1
94MaxPreS-11
94MaxPreS-54
94MaxPreS-261
94MaxPreS-P1
94MaxPreSJ-1
94MaxTheS2-8
94Pow-57
94PowGol-57
95ActPacC-3
95ActPacC-24
95ActPacC-72
95ActPacC2T-11
95ActPacCSS-3
95ActPacCSS-24
95ActPacCSS-72
95ActPacM-MM2
95ActPacMBE-MC1
95ActPacMBE-MC3
95ActPacMBE-MC4
95ActPacMBE-MC5
95ActPacMBE-MC6
95ActPacMBE-MC7
95ActPacMBE-MC8
95ActPacMBE-MC9
95ActPacMBE-MC10
95ActPacMBE-MC11
95ActPacMBE-MC12
95ActPacMBE-MC13
95ActPacMBE-MC14
95ActPacMBE-MC15
95ActPacMBE-MC16
95ActPacMBE-MC17
95ActPacMBE-MC18
95ActPacMBE-MG19
95ActPacMBE-MG20
95ActPacMBE-MG21
95ActPacP-8
95ActPacP-34
95ActPacP-49
95ActPacP-68
95ActPacP-69
95ActPacP2G-1G
95ActPacPBE-BE1
95ActPacPBE-BE2
95ActPacPBE-BE3
95ActPacPBE-BE4
95ActPacPBE-BE5
95ActPacPBE-BE6
95ActPacPBE-BEFC1
95ActPacPP2G-P1
95ActPacS-22
95ActPacS-36
95ActPacS-82
95ActPacS-83
95ActPacS-84
95ActPacS-85
95ActPacSSS-22
95ActPacSSS-36
95ActPacSSS-82
95ActPacSSS-83
95CroJew-15
95CroJew-35
95CroJew-65
95CroJewD-15
95CroJewD-35
95CroJewD-65
95CroJewDJ-DJ3

95CroJewDJD-DJ3
95CroJewDJE-DJ3
95CroJewE-15
95CroJewE-35
95CroJewE-65
95CroJewS-15
95CroJewS-35
95CroJewS-65
95CroJewSG-SG7
95HigGea-13
95HigGea-80
95HigGea-92
95HigGea-100
95HigGeaBC-BC4
95HigGeaBCG-BC4
95HigGeaDO-13
95HigGeaDO-80
95HigGeaDO-92
95HigGeaDO-100
95HigGeaDOG-13
95HigGeaDOG-80
95HigGeaDOG-92
95HigGeaDOG-100
95HigGeaG-13
95HigGeaG-80
95HigGeaG-92
95HigGeaG-100
95HiTecB4-6
95HiTecB4-63
95HiTecB4TT-BY3
95MatWinCC-18
95Max-11
95Max-119
95Max-221
95Max-222
95MaxBilEBC-1
95MaxBilEBC-2
95MaxBilEBC-3
95MaxBilEBC-4
95MaxBilEBC-5
95MaxBilEBC-6
95MaxBilEBC-7
95MaxBilEBC-8
95MaxBilEBC-9
95MaxBilEBC-10
95MaxBilEBC-NNO
95MaxCroC-11
95MaxCroC-51
95MaxCroC-172
95MaxMed-30
95MaxMed-60
95MaxMedB-30
95MaxMedB-60
95MaxMedORA-OTR5
95MaxOveW-8
95MaxPreP-11
95MaxPreP-51
95MaxPreP-172
95MaxPrePP-PS9
95MaxPreS-11
95MaxPreS-51
95MaxPreS-260
95MaxPreS-287
95MetImpWCC-8
95OptXL-7
95OptXL-44
95OptXL-55
95OptXLCB-7
95OptXLCB-44
95OptXLCB-55
95OptXLDC-7
95OptXLDC-44
95OptXLDC-55
95OptXLRH-7
95OptXLRH-44
95OptXLRH-55
95OptXLS-XLS3
95SP-27
95SP-68
95SP-109
95SP-110
95SP-131
95SPDieC-27
95SPDieC-68
95SPDieC-109
95SPDieC-110
95SPDieC-131
95SPSpeM-SM3
95SPSpeMDC-SM3
95UppDec-3
95UppDec-46
95UppDec-71
95UppDec-139
95UppDec-225

95UppDec-267
95UppDec-299
95UppDecA-225
95UppDecGSEG-3
95UppDecGSEG-46
95UppDecGSEG-71
95UppDecGSEG-139
95UppDecGSEG-225
95UppDecGSEG-267
95UppDecGSEG-299
95UppDecI-I8
95UppDecO-OS7
95UppDecPRW-P5
95UppDecPSP-PP9
95UppDecSSES-3
95UppDecSSES-46
95UppDecSSES-71
95UppDecSSES-139
95UppDecSSES-225
95UppDecSSES-267
95UppDecSSES-299
95VIP-10
95VIP-51
95VIPCooB-10
95VIPCooB-51
95VIPEmeP-10
95VIPEmeP-51
95VIPFanC-FC2
95VIPFanCG-FC2
95VIPRedHCB-10
95VIPRedHCB-51
95Zen-50
95ZenHel-5
96ActPacC-27
96ActPacC-81
96ActPacC-91
96ActPacC-101
96ActPacCO-4
96ActPacCSS-27
96ActPacM-1
96ActPacM-11
96ActPacM-21
96ActPacM-22
96ActPacM-23
96ActPacM-24
96ActPacM-25
96ActPacM-26
96ActPacM-27
96ActPacM-28
96ActPacM-NNO
96Ass$2PC-14
96Ass$5PC-5
96AutRacKotC$PC-KC4
96AutRacKotC$PC-KC7
96CroJewEADJ-DJ4
96CroJewEBotC-BC5
96CroJewEDT-7
96CroJewEDT-61
96CroJewEDTBoC-BC5
96CroJewEDTC-7
96CroJewEDTC-61
96CroJewEDTCSA-CS4
96CroJewEDTDJA-DJ4
96CroJewEDTDJG-DJ4
96CroJewEE-7
96CroJewEE-61
96CroJewEGDJ-DJ4
96CroJewEli-7
96CroJewEli-61
96CroJewERCSG-CS4
96CroJewERCSP-CS4
96CroJewES-7
96CroJewES-61
96CroJewESDJ-DJ4
96CroJewETC-7
96CroJewETC-61
96CroJewETCBoC-BC5
96CroJewETCDJA-DJ4
96CroJewETCDJS-DJ4
96CroJewETCE-7
96CroJewETCE-61
96CroJewETCGDJ-DJ4
96CroJewETCS-7
96CroJewETCS-61
96FinLin-40
96FinLin-42
96FinLin-77
96FinLinBGL-C10
96FinLinBGL-D11
96FinLinBGL-SG2
96FinLinBGL-JPC1
96FinLinDCPC-2
96FinLinGS-GS6
96FinLinMM-MM8

96FinLinMPXR-NNO
96FinLinPP-9
96FinLinPP-10
96FinLinPP$100C-1
96FinLinPP$10C-2
96FinLinPP$1kC-K2
96FinLinPP$50C-1
96FinLinPP$5C-8
96FinLinPP$S-9
96FinLinPP$S-10
96FinLinPriP-40
96FinLinPriP-42
96FinLinPriP-77
96FinLinS-40
96FinLinS-42
96FinLinS-77
96Fla-11
96Fla-67
96FlaAut-3
96FlaCenS-3
96FlaHotN-2
96FlaPowP-3
96Kni-11
96KniBlaK-11
96KniFirK-FK9
96KniKniRT-KT7
96KniProC-PC5
96KniQueRKP-11
96KniRoy-11
96KniWhiK-11
96M-F-35
96M-F-36
96M-F-43
96M-FBla-B11
96M-FSheM-M6
96M-FSil-S17
96Max-32
96Max-94
96MaxMadiA-32
96MaxMadiA-94
96MaxMadiABR-BR3
96MaxOdy-32
96MaxOdy-94
96MaxOdyM-MM9
96MaxOdyRA-RA3
96MaxPre-50
96MaxPre-94
96MaxPre-261
96MaxPreSS-SL1
96MetImp-3
96MetImp2AWCC-18
96Pin-27
96Pin-27
96PinBilB-1
96PinBilB-2
96PinCheF-9
96PinCutA-2
96PinDriSC-1
96PinPolP-14
96PinPolPCS-13
96PinPolPLF-14
96PinPolPNL-11
96PinPolPNLG-11
96PinTeaP-7
96PinWinCC-27
96PrePas-10
96PrePas-46
96PrePas-81
96PrePas-85
96PrePas-92
96PrePasBR-BR6
96PrePasCC-10
96PrePasFoc-F2
96PrePasFQS-FQS2A
96PrePasFQS-FQS2B
96PrePasP-8
96PrePasP-39
96PrePasP$10PC-3
96PrePasP$20PC-3
96PrePasP$5PC-3
96PrePasPCB-CB4
96PrePasPEP-8
96PrePasPEP-39
96PrePasPH-8
96PrePasPH-39
96PrePasPHP-HP2
96PrePasSco-10
96PrePasSco-46
96PrePasSco-81
96PrePasSco-85
96PrePasSco-92
96PrePasT-10
96PrePasT-46
96PrePasT-81

96PrePasT-85
96PrePasT-92
96RacCho-13
96RacCho-48
96RacCho-98
96RacChoAP-13
96RacChoAP-48
96RacChoAP-98
96RacChoSC-13
96RacChoSC-48
96RacChoSC-98
96RacChoTT-8
96SP-13
96SP-49
96SpeArtP-4
96SpeArtP-42
96SpeArtP-75
96SpeArtP-76
96SpeArtP-77
96SpeArtP-78
96SpeCleS-9
96SpeInM-10
96SpePro-9
96SpeRac-4
96SpeRac-42
96SpeRac-75
96SpeRac-76
96SpeRac-77
96SpeRac-78
96SPHolME-ME23
96SPRacLC-RL22
96SPx-24
96SPxGol-24
96Ult-33
96Ult-34
96Ult-35
96Ult-155
96UltAut-10
96UltBoxS-8
96UltChaC-3
96UltFlaP-8
96UltUpd-11
96UltUpd-57
96UltUpd-80
96UltUpdA-3
96UltUpdPP-3
96UppDec-34
96UppDec-74
96UppDec-114
96UppDec-131
96UppDecPP-RP6
96UppDecRTTC-RC7
96UppDecRTTC-RC56
96UppDecRTTC-RC130
96UppDecRTTCGF-GF9
96UppDecRTTCJ-WC5
96UppDecRTTCPPoi-PP7
96UppDRTTCPPR-PR7
96UppDecRTTCPT3-T8
96UppDecRTTCT3PR-R11
96UppDecVV-VV7
96VIP-9
96VIP-39
96VIPEmeP-9
96VIPEmeP-39
96Viper-7
96ViperBlaM-7
96ViperBusC-B16
96ViperCob-C8
96ViperCop-7
96ViperDia-D8
96ViperDiaA-DA8
96ViperGreM-7
96ViperKinC-KC4
96VIPSamBTF-SB2
96VIPSamBTFG-SB2
96VIPTor-9
96VIPTor-39
96VIPWarP-WP18
96VIPWarPG-WP18
96Zen-7
96Zen-45
96Zen-100
96ZenArtP-7
96ZenArtP-45
96ZenArtP-100
96ZenChaS-8
96ZenHig-15
97Act-12
97ActPac-11
97ActPac-32
97ActPac-58
97ActPac-64
97ActPacFA-12
97ActPacFI-11
97ActPacFI-32
97ActPacFI-58
97ActPacFI-64
97ActPacRT-13
97ColCho-13
97ColCho-63
97ColCho-111
97ColCho-148
97ColChoC-CC17
97ColChoC-CC50
97ColChoC-CC83
97ColChoS-S5
97ColChoS-S6
97ColChoSQ-SQ38
97ColChoSQ-SQ42
97ColChoUD5-UD25
97ColChoUD5-UD26
97ColChoVC-VC4
97FinLinPP2-2
97FinLinPP2-37
97FinLinPP2$10-86
97FinLinPP2$100-96
97FinLinPP2$5-40
97FinLinPP2$50-88
97JurPar-19
97JurParC-C6
97JurParR-R10
97JurParT-19
97JurParTL-TL5
97JurParTR-TR10
97Max-13
97Max-58
97Max-95
97Max-96
97Max-118
97MaxChaTC-C10
97MaxChatCG-C10
97Pin-8
97Pin-37
97Pin-63
97PinArtP-8
97PinArtP-37
97PinArtP-63
97PinCer-7
97PinCer-41
97PinCer-81
97PinCerCGT-8
97PinCerCT-8
97PinCerMB-7
97PinCerMB-41
97PinCerMB-81
97PinCerMG-7
97PinCerMG-41
97PinCerMG-81
97PinCerMR-7
97PinCerMR-41
97PinCerMR-81
97PinCerR-7
97PinCerR-41
97PinCerR-81
97PinMin-17
97PinMin-29
97PinMin2GC-17
97PinMin2GC-29
97PinMinB-17
97PinMinB-29
97PinMinC-17
97PinMinC-29
97PinMinG-17
97PinMinG-29
97PinMinNC-17
97PinMinNC-29
97PinMinS-17
97PinMinS-29
97PinPor-6
97PinPor-26
97PinPor-45
97PinPre-47
97PinPre-48
97PinPre-49
97PinPre-50
97PinPre-51
97PinPre-53
97PinPre-54
97PinPreBM-47
97PinPreBM-48
97PinPreBM-49
97PinPreBM-50
97PinPreBM-51
97PinPreBM-53
97PinPreBM-54
97PinPreGM-47
97PinPreGM-48
97PinPreGM-49
97PinPreGM-50
97PinPreGM-51
97PinPreGM-53
97PinPreGM-54
97PinPreP-8
97PinPreP-37
97PinPreP-63
97PinPreP-S11-N
97PinPreP-TP10A
97PinPreSM-47
97PinPreSM-48
97PinPreSM-49
97PinPreSM-50
97PinPreSM-51
97PinPreSM-53
97PinPreSM-54
97PinSpe-11-N
97PinSpeA-11-N
97PinTeaP-10
97PinTotCPB-7
97PinTotCPB-41
97PinTotCPB-81
97PinTotCPG-7
97PinTotCPG-41
97PinTotCPG-81
97PinTotCPR-7
97PinTotCPR-41
97PinTotCPR-81
97PinTroC-8
97PinTroC-37
97PinTroC-63
97Pre-20
97Pre-64
97PreAmeE-AE9
97PreBlaWFS-20
97PreBlaWFS-64
97PreGat-GB10
97PreGatA-GBA10
97PreGolE-GE9
97PreGri-20
97PreGri-64
97PrePas-26
97PrePas-45
97PrePas-130
97PrePasAut-20
97PrePasCC'-CC6
97PrePasL-26
97PrePasL-45
97PrePasL-130
97PrePasOS-26
97PrePasOS-45
97PrePasOS-130
97PrePasP-21
97PrePasP-36
97PrePasP-37
97PrePasPCB-CB3
97PrePasPCBD-CB3
97PrePasPEP-21
97PrePasPEP-36
97PrePasPEP-37
97PrePasPLL-LL2
97PrePasPM-21
97PrePasPM-36
97PrePasPM-37
97PrePasPOS-21
97PrePasPOS-36
97PrePasPOS-37
97PrePasT-26
97PrePasT-45
97PrePasT-130
97PreRedW-20
97PreRedW-64
97RacCho-34
97RacCho-69
97RacChoHO-7
97RacChoHOGitD-7
97RacChoSS-34
97RacChoSS-69
97RacSha-8
97RacShaGW-GW8
97RacShaGWP-8
97RacShaH-8
97RacShaSTS-ST6
97RacShaTS-8
97ScoBoal$PC-PC7
97SkyPro-6
97SkyPro-78
97SkyProA-6
97SkyProPS-E3
97SkyProT-T8
97SP-13
97SP-55
97SP-93
97SP-119
97SP SupS-13
97SP SupS-55
97SP SupS-93
97SP SupS-119
97SPX-20
97SPxBlu-20
97SPxGol-20
97SPxSil-20
97SPXSpeA-SV3
97Ult-11
97Ult-48
97Ult-P1
97UltAKA-A5
97UltDriV-D3
97UltEliS-E3
97UltIns-DC5
97UltUpd-6
97UltUpd-95
97UltUpdAR-6
97UltWinCMPD-P1
97UppDecRTTC-12
97UppDecRTTC-54
97UppDecRTTC-96
97UppDecRTTC-119
97UppDecRTTCGF-RD9
97UDRTTCMDM-MM17
97UDRTTCMDM-MM18
97UDRTTCMDM-MM19
97UDRTTCMDM-MM20
97UDRTTCMDMA-MM17
97UDRTTCMDMA-MM18
97UDRTTCMDMA-MM19
97UDRTTCMDMA-MM20
97UppDecRTTCPPlu-+10
97UppDecRTTCPPlu-+30
97UDRTTCPPRC-+10
97UDRTTCPPRC-+30
97UppDRTTCPPRDC-+10
97UppDRTTCPPRDC-+30
97UppDecVC-13
97UppDecVC-63
97UppDecVC-115
97UppDecVCP-PE9
97UppDecVCPC-PH9
97VIP-7
97Viper-19
97Viper-80
97ViperAna-A10
97ViperBlaR-19
97ViperBlaR-80
97ViperCob-C6
97ViperDia-DB5
97ViperDiaA-DBA5
97ViperKinC-KC6
97ViperSid-S10
97ViperSnaE-SE6
97VIPExp-7
97VIPHeaGD-HG2
97VIPHigG-HG2
97VIPOilS-7
97VIPRinoH-RH12
97VIPRinoHDC-RH12
97VIPSheM-SM3
98ColCho-13
98ColCho-49
98ColCho-109
98HigGea-8
98HigGea-35
98HigGea-71
98HigGeaA-7
98HigGeaFG-22
98HigGeaFG-35
98HigGeaFG-71
98HigGeaGJ-GJ16
98HigGeaHG-HG8
98HigGeaM-22
98HigGeaM-35
98HigGeaM-71
98HigGeaMaM-MM8
98HigGeaMaM-C-8
98HigGeaPG-PG8
98HigGeaTT-TT8
98Max-15
98Max-45
98Max-62
98Max-98
98Max-19
98Max-44
98Max-69
98Max-94
98Max10tA-14
98Max10tA-59
98Max10tA-117
98Max10tA-121
98Max10tACP-CP6
98Max10tACPDC-CP6
98Max10tAMP-P19
98MaxBatP-B4
98MaxFirC-F5
98MaxFocOAC-FC9
98MaxMakOACC-FC9
98MaxYealRBS-44
98MaxYealRBS-70
98MaxYealRBS-90
98MaxYealRBS-104
98MaxYealRBS-117
98MaxYealRBS-149
98MaxYealRBS-AW4
98MaxYealRBS-PO8
98MayAutS-11
98PinMin-7
98PinMin-19
98PinMinB-7
98PinMinB-19
98PinMinBC-7
98PinMinBC-19
98PinMinBPPC-7
98PinMinBPPC-19
98PinMinGMT-7
98PinMinGMT-19
98PinMinGPC-7
98PinMinGPC-19
98PinMinGPPC-7
98PinMinGPPC-19
98PinMinNC-7
98PinMinNC-19
98PinMinSGC-7
98PinMinSGC-19
98PinMinSMT-7
98PinMinSMT-19
98PinMinSPPC-7
98PinMinSPPC-19
98PinMinSSC-7
98PinMinSSC-19
98PrePas-23
98PrePas-36
98PrePas-107
98PrePasCC'-CC6
98PrePasGS-22
98PrePasOS-23
98PrePasOS-36
98PrePasP-26
98PrePasP-35
98PrePasP-26
98PrePasP-35
98PrePasPFC-FC13
98PrePasPFC-FC26
98PrePasPFCR-FC13
98PrePasPFCR-FC26
98PrePasPS-PS17
98PrePasPSH-SH11
98PrePasS-ST8A
98PrePasS-22
98PrePasS-7
98PrePasS-8
98PrePasSF-7
98PrePasSF-8
98PrePasSFT-2
98PrePasSFTD-2
98PrePasSO-11
98PrePasSO-12
98PrePasSOD-11
98PrePasSOD-12
98PrePasSS-4
98PrePasSSD-4
98PrePasTorp-ST8B
98SP Aut-15
98SP Aut-49
98SP Aut-71
98SP AutBtW-BW7
98SP AutBtWL2-BW7
98SP AutBtWL3-BW7
98UppDecDV-8
98UppDecDVSM-8
98UppDecRttC-15
98UppDecRttC-59
98UppDecRttC-91
98UppDecRTTC5A-AN37
98UppDecRTTCCS-CS7
98UppDecVC-13
98UppDecVC-58
98UppDecVC-144
98UppDecVC3DoS-D24
98UppDecVC3DoSG-D24
98UppDecVCPL-PL8
98UppDecVCPP-12
98UppDecVCPPCR-12

92MaxRed-255
94MaxPreS-250
95MaxPreS-235
Ford, Doyle
91Max-104
92MaxBla-207
92MaxRed-207
92RedSta-36
92Tra-20
93Max-231
93MaxPreS-231
94MaxPreS-227
95MaxPreS-225
96MaxPre-226
96Pin-83
96Pin-83
96PinWinCC-83
96RacCho-79
96RacChoAP-79
96RacChoSC-79
Ford, Hank
89TGRacMR-176
Ford, Mike
92TraTeaS-70
Forrest, Renee
94HigGeaPPT-G14
94HigGeaPPTG-14G
Forsyth, Dan
91DKIMCDT-42
Forte, Donald
92PacAmeCT-24
Foster, Frankie
89CheFlal-72
Foster, Pat
71FleAHRDC-6
Foster, Steve
92RSSMotH-20
94MaxTexEl-31
Fournier, Henri
11AmeTobAD-9
95TraVal-7
Foust, Gordy
90BigTimD-5
90BigTimDS-5
90CheFlal-5
90CheFlal-38
91BigTimD-60
Fox III, Raymond
92TraTeaS-40
94MaxPreS-239
94MaxTexEl-32
95MaxPreS-237
Fox, Glenn
92EriMaxTA-45
92EriMaxTA-46
Fox, Ray Sr.
89TGRacMR-104
91TGRacMRU-104
91TGRacMRU-110
91TGRacMRU-113
92SpoLegFL-13
Fox, Red
89TGRacMR-57
89TGRacMR-72
91TGRacMRU-57
Fox, Stan
85A&SRacl-7
91AllWorl-12
92AllWorl-14
92LanARCF-53
92Legind-9
93HiTecl-13
93HiTecl-62
94HiTecl-32
94HiTeclCD-CD15
95Skylnd5-31
95Skylnd5-68
95Skylnd5-85
96Skylnd5-20
96Skylnd5-45
96Skylnd5-84
Foyt, A.J.
62MarInd-5
73NabSugDSC-7
77Spo-1917
77Spo-4501
80AvaHilURG-14
85SpoPhoGS-NNO
86AceInd-A4
86AceInd-E3
86SpoPhoG-6
86SpoPhoG-7
87A&SRacl-14
90Max-14
91Legind-6
91Legind-65
91Max-14
91MaxRacFK-3
92ColACAR-41
92ColACAR-78
92HiTecMA-15
92HiTecMA-49
92Legind-29
92Legind-43
92Legind-46
92Legind-57
92Legind-64
92MaxBla-141
92MaxRed-141
93HiTecl-23
93HiTecl-44
93HiTeclCFF-SP9
94HiTecl-38
94HiTeclAF-AJ1
94HiTeclAF-AJ2
94HiTeclAF-AJ3
94HiTeclAF-AJ4
94HiTeclAF-AJ5
94HiTeclAF-AJ6
94HiTeclCD-CD14
94MaxMed-29
94MaxMed-68
94Pep400VL-3
95Skylnd5-10
95Skylnd5PC-14
95TraVal-67
95TraVal-83
96Skylnd5-53
97Hi-IRL'I5-I7
98PrePas-143
Foyt, Jerry
94LanARCF-29
Fraise, Steve
91DKIMCDT-31
91LanStoCC-2
Frame, Fred
54StaWetIW-1932
60HawWaxI-20
95TraVal-38
France, Bill Jr.
91TexWorS-7
France, Bill Sr.
91TGRacTL-37
98UppDecRTTC5A-AN1
Francia, Giorgio
78GraPri-191
Francis, Beano
91BulRin-10
92BulRin-3
Francis, Steve
91DirTra-30
91JAG-20
92DirTra-45
92JAG-162
92STAMod-43
94JAG-22
94STAMod-22
Frank, Chub
91DirTra-59
92DirTra-33
92JAG-30
92STAMod-22
94STAMod-23
Frank, Larry
89TGRacMR-32
89TGRacMR-33
89WinCir-34
91GalPrePR-65
91ProSetL-L20
91TGRacMRU-32
91TGRacMRU-33
91TGRacMRU-P1
91TraPacYH-10
92ProSetL-L13
Franklin, Rodney
91JAG-36
92JAG-163
92STAMod-16
Franks, Junior
91BulRin-143
92BulRin-176
Franks, Ray
92ProSetN-87
Frantz, Tom
83A&SRacl-23
Frasson, Joe
89TGRacMR-166
89TGRacMR-167
91BulRin-18
91TGRacMRU-166
91TGRacMRU-167
92BulRin-18
Frazier, Ellis
94HigGeaPPT-G10
94HigGeaPPTG-10G
Frederick, George
92VolRacLS2-19
Fredrickson, Steve
92RedGraST-23
Freeman, Carolyn
92TraTeaS-158
Freeman, Kenny
92TraTeaS-167
Freeman, Mike
93JAG-15
Freeman, Tim
89CheFlal-25
90CheFlal-92
Freeze, Jamie
94HigGeaPPT-W24
94HigGeaPPTG-24W
French, Kenny
91WorOut-72
Frey, Bob
91ProSetN-110
92ProSetN-185
93FinLinN-127
Fries, Andy
92JAG-164
Frink, Rollie
91DKIMCDT-25
92JAG-31
Fry, Mike
91LanARCHS-4
92LanARCF-60
Fryar, Freddy
91PioStoCR-4
94Max-288
95Max-134
Frye, Bill
91JAG-19
92DirTra-36
92JAG-32
95HavAT-2
Fryer, Gene
89CheFlal-77
90CheFlal-85
Fuge, David
92MaxBla-125
92MaxRed-125
92ProSet-164A
92ProSet-164B
93FinLin-102
93FinLinCS-10
93FinLinS-102
93Max-167
93MaxPreP-150
93MaxPreS-167
94Max-120
94MaxPreS-120
95MaxPreS-114
Fuller, Jeff
91WinChoM-18
91WinChoM-19
95Max-261
96MaxMadiA-62
96MaxMadiA-72
96MaxMadiA-73
96MaxOdy-72
96MaxOdy-73
96MaxPre-165
96MaxPre-243
96MaxPre-257
96PrePas-57
96PrePasSco-57
96PrePasT-57
96UppDecRTTC-RC48
96Viper-52
96ViperBlaM-52
96ViperCop-52
96ViperGreM-52
97JurPar-41
97JurParT-41
97Pre-35
97PreBlaWFS-35
97PreGri-35
97PrePas-67
97PrePasAut-30
97PrePasL-67
97PrePasOS-67
97PrePasPA-30
97PrePasT-67
97PreRedW-35
97SkyPro-52
97SkyProA-52
97UltUpd-56
97UltUpdAR-56
97VIP-30
97Viper-44
97ViperBlaR-44
97VIPExp-30
97VIPOilS-30
Fuller, Rick
91WinChoM-43
91WinChoM-44
Fultz, George
92CorSelCCS-10
93CorSelCCS-10
Funderburke, Glenn
92TraTeaS-72
Furr, Tony
91Tra-80
94Max-293
95Max-131
95Max-198
95MaxAut-131
95MaxPreS-147
95USAirGS-1
Gaboury, Gabe
92WinChoM-49
Gache, Philippe
93HiTecl-16
93HiTecl-63
Gachot, Bertrand
91CarForO-90
91CarForO-91
91CarForO-92
91ProTraFO-73
91ProTraFO-74
92GriForO-29
92GriForO-61
92GriForO-94
92GriForO-193
Gada, Bobby
91WinChoNED-49
91WinChoNED-50
92WinChoB-28
92WinChoB-29
Gaddis, Mark
91MaxBilETCM-33
Gaerte, Joe
87WorOut-47
88WorOut-26
89WorOut-5
89WorOutP-7TW
90WorOut-3
91WorOut-4
91WorOut-103
92RacLegS-8
93WorOutMW-4
94WorOut-16
Gage, Richmond
92TraTeaS-81
Gahan, Bobby
91WinChoNED-16
91WinChoNED-17
92WinChoB-129
92WinChoB-130
Gahm, Brian
89CheFlal-74
90CheFlal-14
90CheFlal-28
91BigTimD-78
Gaillard, Patrick
78GraPri-177
Gajewski, M.G.
91LanART-31
92RedGraST-4
92RedGraST-5
Gale, Bubba
92BulRin-83
Gale, Tommy
89TGRacMR-70
91TGRacMRU-70
Gall, Marty
91DKIMCDT-50
Gallaher, Terry
91DKIMCDT-2
Gallup, Richie
91WinChoM-14
91WinChoM-15
Ganassi, Chip
83A&SRacl-5
84A&SRacl-35
85A&SRacl-9
86A&SRacl-24
96Skylnd5-50
Gangemi, Sam
91K&WURCS-7
Ganley, John
90LanRocSHS-1
92LanRocS-16
92LanRocS-17
Gann, Phil
91BulRin-45
92BulRin-152
Gansmann, Mark
92DirTra-64
Gant, Debbie
94WheHarG-30
94WheHarGG-30
Gant, Donna
94WheHarG-30
94WheHarGG-30
Gant, Harry
86SpoPhoG-8
89Max-33
89Max-111
89MaxCri-16
90Max-33
90Max-171
90MaxHolF-HF7
91CMHanH-1
91CMHanH-2
91CMHanH-3
91CMHanH-4
91CMHanH-5
91CMHanH-6
91CMHanH-7
91CMHanH-8
91CMHanH-9
91CMHanH-10
91CMHanH-11
91CMHanH-12
91CMHanH-13
91CMHanH-14
91CMHanH-P1
91HicMotS-6
91Max-33
91Max-183
91MaxMcD-17
91MaxTheWA-7
91MaxUpd-33
91ProSet-63
91ProSet-129
91SunRacL-8
91SupRacM-3
91Tra-33
91Tra-112
92-CarDynBTBS-2
92BikRacS-33
92CarDynGO-2
92CarDynHG-1
92CarDynHG-2
92CarDynHG-3
92CarDynHG-4
92CarDynHG-5
92LimEdiHG-1
92LimEdiHG-2
92LimEdiHG-3
92LimEdiHG-4
92LimEdiHG-5
92LimEdiHG-6
92LimEdiHG-7
92LimEdiHG-8
92LimEdiHG-9
92LimEdiHG-10
92LimEdiHG-11
92LimEdiHG-12
92LimEdiHG-13
92LimEdiHG-14
92LimEdiHG-15
92LimEdiP-1
92MacTooWC-9
92MaxAllPT-2
92MaxBla-33
92MaxBla-201
92MaxBla-232
92MaxBla-272
92MaxBla-285
92MaxBla-286
92MaxBla-287
92MaxBla-288
92MaxCra-NNO
92MaxMcD-12
92MaxRed-33
92MaxRed-201
92MaxRed-232
92MaxRed-272
92MaxRed-285

94Max-201
94Max-327
94Max-328
94Max-335
94Max-P3
94MaxAut-24
94MaxMed-1
94MaxMed-46
94MaxMed-47
94MaxMed-48
94MaxMed-49
94MaxMed-50
94MaxMed-52
94MaxMed-53
94MaxMed-56
94MaxPreP-13
94MaxPreP-24
94MaxPreP-46
94MaxPreP-65
94MaxPreS-13
94MaxPreS-24
94MaxPreS-65
94MaxPreS-260
94MaxPreSJ-8
94MaxRacC-1
94MaxRooY-16
94MaxTheS2-14
94MWWin-1
94MWWin-5
94OptXL-6
94OptXL-26
94OptXL-38
94OptXL-56
94OptXL-62
94OptXL-CC1
94OptXLP-3
94OptXLRH-6
94OptXLRH-26
94OptXLRH-38
94OptXLRH-56
94OptXLRH-62
94Pow-5
94Pow-89
94Pow-90
94Pow-132
94Pow-P2
94PowGol-5
94PowGol-89
94PowGol-90
94PowGol-132
94PowPre-12
94PowPre-22
94PowPro-P2
94PrePas-7
94PrePas-40
94PrePas-124
94PrePasA-NNO
94PrePasCC-CC7
94PrePasH-H2
94PrePasRD-RD7
94Sky-4
94Sky-NNO
94Tra-10
94Tra-24
94Tra-36
94Tra-86
94Tra-106
94Tra-171
94Tra-200
94TraAut-A4
94TraAutV-25
94TraCar-C5
94TraFirR-10
94TraFirR-24
94TraFirR-36
94TraFirR-86
94TraFirR-106
94TraFirR-171
94TraFirR-200
94TraPreC-33
94TraWin-W8
94TraWin-W21
94TraWin-W22
94VIP-12
94VIP-38
94VIP-74
94VIP-P1
94VIPExc2-EC3
94WheHarG-66
94WheHarGG-66
95ActPacC-6
95ActPacC-14
95ActPacC-22
95ActPacC-50
95ActPacC-51
95ActPacC-63
95ActPacC-99
95ActPacC-P1
95ActPacC2T-1
95ActPacC2T-2
95ActPacC2T-3
95ActPacCSS-6
95ActPacCSS-14
95ActPacCSS-22
95ActPacCSS-50
95ActPacCSS-51
95ActPacCSS-63
95ActPacCTR-1
95ActPacCTR-2
95ActPacCTR-3
95ActPacCTR-5
95ActPacCTR-6
95ActPacCTR-7
95ActPacCTR-8
95ActPacCTR-9
95ActPacCTR-10
95ActPacCTR-11
95ActPacCTR-12
95ActPacCTR-P1
95ActPacHM-1
95ActPacM-MM4
95ActPacP-9
95ActPacP-36
95ActPacP-50
95ActPacP-66
95ActPacP-70
95ActPacP2G-2G
95ActPacS-24
95ActPacS-40
95ActPacS-47
95ActPacS-49
95ActPacS-51
95ActPacS-60
95ActPacS-61
95ActPacS-62
95ActPacS-63
95ActPacS-64
95ActPacS-65
95ActPacS-86
95ActPacS2G-2G
95ActPacS2G-4G
95ActPacS2G-6G
95ActPacS2G-19G
95ActPacS2G-20G
95ActPacSSS-24
95ActPacSSS-40
95ActPacSSS-47
95ActPacSSS-49
95ActPacSSS-51
95ActPacSSS-60
95ActPacSSS-61
95ActPacSSS-62
95ActPacSSS-63
95ActPacSSS-64
95ActPacSSS-65
95ActPacSSS-86
95ActPacSTTH-1
95Ass-3
95Ass-31
95Ass-49
95Ass10PC-3
95Ass$5$25PC-4
95Ass1M$PC-9
95AssCocC6DC-3
95AssGolS-3
95AssGolS-31
95AssGolS-49
95AssImaP-RI4
95CroJew-2
95CroJew-68
95CroJew-73
95CroJew-75
95CroJew-77
95CroJew-P1
95CroJew-DT1
95CroJewD-2
95CroJewD-68
95CroJewD-73
95CroJewD-75
95CroJewD-77
95CroJewD-P1
95CroJewDJ-DJ1
95CroJewDJD-DJ1
95CroJewDJE-DJ1
95CroJewDT-DT1
95CroJewE-2
95CroJewE-68
95CroJewE-73
95CroJewE-75
95CroJewE-77
95CroJewE-P1
95CroJewPS-P1R
95CroJewPS-P1E
95CroJewPS-P1D
95CroJewS-2
95CroJewS-68
95CroJewS-73
95CroJewS-75
95CroJewS-77
95CroJewSG-SG1
95FinLin-24
95FinLin-53
95FinLin-67
95FinLin-105
95FinLinCC6-3
95FinLinCC6-31
95FinLinCC6-49
95FinLinCC6DC-C3
95FinLinCC6W-CC10
95FinLinCotM-1
95FinLinGS-GS1
95FinLinP5U-NNO
95FinLinPP-24
95FinLinPP-53
95FinLinPP-67
95FinLinPP-105
95FinLinSC-SC7
95FinLinSD-SD7
95FinLinSil-24
95FinLinSil-53
95FinLinSil-67
95FinLinSil-105
95FinLinSRF-17
95FinLinSSSS-SS1
95FinLinSup-17
95HigGea-6
95HigGea-78
95HigGea-91
95HigGea-98
95HigGeaBC-BC7
95HigGeaBCG-BC7
95HigGeaDO-6
95HigGeaDO-78
95HigGeaDO-91
95HigGeaDO-98
95HigGeaDOG-6
95HigGeaDOG-78
95HigGeaDOG-91
95HigGeaDOG-98
95HigGeaG-6
95HigGeaG-78
95HigGeaG-91
95HigGeaG-98
95HigGeaP-P2
95HiTecB4-3
95HiTecB4-40
95HiTecB4-53
95HiTecB4-88
95HiTecB4-89
95HiTecB4-P1
95HiTecB4-NNO
95HiTecB4-NNO
95HiTecB4TT-BY1
95Ima-24
95Ima-48
95Ima-72
95Ima-99
95Ima-P1
95ImaDri-D2
95ImaGol-24
95ImaGol-48
95ImaGol-72
95ImaGol-99
95ImaHarC-HC8
95ImaOwnP-OP5
95ImaRacRJG-JG1
95ImaRacRJG-JG2
95ImaRacRJG-JG3
95ImaRacRJG-JG4
95ImaRacRJG-JG5
95ImaRacRJG-JG6
95ImaRacRJG-JG7
95ImaRacRJG-JG8
95ImaRacRJG-JG9
95ImaRacRJG-JG10
95Max-3
95Max-24
95Max-72
95Max-80
95Max-105
95Max-139
95Max-169
95Max-236
95Max-237
95Max-P1
95MaxAut-24
95MaxCroC-24
95MaxCroC-64
95MaxCroC-147
95MaxCroC-158
95MaxCroC-160
95MaxCroC-168
95MaxMed-17
95MaxMed-47
95MaxMedB-17
95MaxMedB-47
95MaxMedJGP-1
95MaxMedJGP-2
95MaxMedJGP-3
95MaxMedJGP-4
95MaxMedJGP-5
95MaxMedJGP-6
95MaxMedJGP-7
95MaxMedJGP-8
95MaxMedJGP-9
95MaxMedORA-OTR2
95MaxOveW-1
95MaxPreP-24
95MaxPreP-64
95MaxPreP-147
95MaxPreP-158
95MaxPreP-160
95MaxPreP-168
95MaxPrePP-PS7
95MaxPreS-3
95MaxPreS-24
95MaxPreS-64
95MaxPreS-257
95MaxPreS-262
95MaxPreS-273
95MaxPreS-275
95MaxPreS-283
95OptXL-8
95OptXL-31
95OptXL-50
95OptXL-56
95OptXLCB-8
95OptXLCB-31
95OptXLCB-50
95OptXLCB-56
95OptXLDC-8
95OptXLDC-31
95OptXLDC-50
95OptXLDC-56
95OptXLJX-1
95OptXLJX-2
95OptXLJX-3
95OptXLJX-4
95OptXLRH-8
95OptXLRH-31
95OptXLRH-50
95OptXLRH-56
95OptXLS-XLS4
95PrePas-10
95PrePas-38
95PrePas-102
95PrePas-129
95PrePas-136
95PrePasCC-10
95PrePasCCR-CCR3
95PrePasCCR-CCR4
95PrePasCF-CF3
95PrePasPH-8
95PrePasPH-33
95PrePasPHP-HP3
95PrePasPPC-NNO
95PrePasPre-8
95PrePasPre-33
95PrePasPRH-8
95PrePasPRH-33
95PrePasPro-3
95PrePasRD-RD4
95PrePasRH-10
95PrePasRH-38
95PrePasRH-102
95PrePasRH-129
95PrePasRH-136
95Sel-12
95Sel-38
95Sel-118
95Sel-141
95Sel-NNO
95SelDreM-DM8
95SelFlaO-12
95SelFlaO-38
95SelFlaO-118
95SelFlaO-141
95SelPro-12
95SelPro-DM8
95SelSki-SS3
95SP-18
95SP-55
95SP-56
95SP-97
95SP-100
95SP-P1
95SPDieC-18
95SPDieC-55
95SPDieC-56
95SPDieC-97
95SPDieC-100
95SPSpeM-SM24
95SPSpeMDC-SM24
95Tra-4
95Tra-26
95Tra-52
95Tra-58
95Tra-68
95Tra-P1
95Tra5thA-4
95Tra5thA-30
95Tra5thA-49
95Tra5thACC-C3
95Tra5thAG-4
95Tra5thAG-38
95Tra5thAG-49
95Tra5thAR-R3
95Tra5thAUEC-E1
95TraAutV-1
95TraCha-C1
95TraFirR-4
95TraFirR-26
95TraFirR-52
95TraFirR-58
95TraFirR-68
95TraRacM-RM7
95TraSerS-SS8
95TraVal-100
95UppDec-2
95UppDec-45
95UppDec-70
95UppDec-138
95UppDec-163
95UppDec-202
95UppDec-246
95UppDec-281
95UppDec-UD2
95UppDecA-202
95UppDecGSEG-2
95UppDecGSEG-45
95UppDecGSEG-70
95UppDecGSEG-138
95UppDecGSEG-163
95UppDecGSEG-202
95UppDecGSEG-246
95UppDecGSEG-281
95UppDecI-I9
95UppDecO-OS3
95UppDecPRW-P4
95UppDecPSP-PP6
95UppDecSSES-2
95UppDecSSES-45
95UppDecSSES-70
95UppDecSSES-138
95UppDecSSES-163
95UppDecSSES-202
95UppDecSSES-246
95UppDecSSES-281
95VIP-11
95VIP-31
95VIP-61
95VIPAut-11
95VIPCooB-11
95VIPCooB-31
95VIPCooB-61
95VIPEmeP-11
95VIPEmeP-31
95VIPEmeP-61
95VIPFanC-FC3
95VIPFanCG-FC3
95VIPHel-H4
95VIPHelG-H4
95VIPRedHCB-11
95VIPRedHCB-31
95VIPRedHCB-61
95VIPRef-R2
95VIPRefG-R2
95Zen-23
95Zen-51
95Zen-64

95Zen-77
95Zen-78
95Zen-79
95Zen-80
95Zen-81
95Zen-82
95Zen-83
95ZenHel-3
95ZenTri-2
95ZenWinW-2
95ZenWinW-4
95ZenWinW-6
95ZenWinW-15
95ZenWinW-16
95ZenWinW-23
95ZenWinW-25
95ZenZT-2
96ActPacC-1
96ActPacC-2
96ActPacC-3
96ActPacC-4
96ActPacC-5
96ActPacC-20
96ActPacC-99
96ActPacC-105
96ActPacCFS-4
96ActPacCO-2
96ActPacCP-5
96ActPacCSS-1
96ActPacCSS-2
96ActPacCSS-3
96ActPacCSS-4
96ActPacCSS-5
96ActPacCSS-20
96ActPacLotP-5
96ActPacLotP-6
96ActPacLotP-7
96ActPacLotP-8
96ActPacM-3
96ActPacM-13
96Ass-2
96Ass$100CCIPC-2
96AutRac-2
96AutRacA-16
96AutRacCA-16
96ClaWinCC-J1
96ClaWinCC-J2
96ClaWinCC-J3
96ClaWinCC-J4
96ClaWinCC-J5
96CroJewEADJ-DJ1
96CroJewEBotC-BC2
96CroJewEDT-2
96CroJewEDT-28
96CroJewEDT-29
96CroJewEDT-30
96CroJewEDTBoC-BC2
96CroJewEDTC-2
96CroJewEDTC-28
96CroJewEDTC-29
96CroJewEDTC-30
96CroJewEDTCSA-CS2
96CroJewEDTDJA-DJ1
96CroJewEDTDJG-DJ1
96CroJewEE-2
96CroJewEE-28
96CroJewEE-29
96CroJewEE-30
96CroJewEGDJ-DJ1
96CroJewEli-2
96CroJewEli-28
96CroJewEli-29
96CroJewEli-30
96CroJewERCSG-CS2
96CroJewERCSP-CS2
96CroJewES-2
96CroJewES-28
96CroJewES-29
96CroJewES-30
96CroJewESDJ-DJ1
96CroJewETC-2
96CroJewETC-28
96CroJewETC-29
96CroJewETC-30
96CroJewETCBoC-BC2
96CroJewETCDJA-DJ1
96CroJewETCDJS-DJ1
96CroJewETCE-2
96CroJewETCE-28
96CroJewETCE-29
96CroJewETCE-30
96CroJewETCGDJ-DJ1
96CroJewETCS-2
96CroJewETCS-28
96CroJewETCS-29
96CroJewETCS-30
96FinLin-1
96FinLin-87
96FinLin-95
96FinLinBGL-C1
96FinLinBGL-D1
96FinLinBGL-SG1
96FinLinBGL-JPC2
96FinLinDCPC-1
96FinLinGS-GS1
96FinLinMM-MM1
96FinLinMPXR-NNO
96FinLinPP-11
96FinLinPP-12
96FinLinPP$100C-2
96FinLinPP$10C-3
96FinLinPP$1kC-K1
96FinLinPP$50C-2
96FinLinPP$5C-9
96FinLinPP$S-11
96FinLinPP$S-12
96FinLinPriP-1
96FinLinPriP-87
96FinLinPriP-95
96FinLinRTTT-JG1
96FinLinRTTT-JG2
96FinLinRTTT-JG3
96FinLinRTTT-JG4
96FinLinRTTT-JG5
96FinLinRTTT-JG6
96FinLinRTTT-JG7
96FinLinRTTT-JG8
96FinLinRTTT-JG9
96FinLinRTTT-JG10
96FinLinS-1
96FinLinS-87
96FinLinS-95
96Fla-12
96Fla-68
96Fla-99
96Fla-P1
96FlaAut-4
96FlaCenS-4
96FlaHotN-3
96FlaPowP-4
96Kni-2
96Kni-21
96Kni-30
96Kni-31
96KniBlaK-2
96KniBlaK-21
96KniBlaK-30
96KniBlaK-31
96KniFirK-FK3
96KniKniRT-KT1
96KniProC-PC6
96KniQueRKP-2
96KniQueRKP-21
96KniQueRKP-30
96KniQueRKP-31
96KniRoy-2
96KniRoy-21
96KniRoy-30
96KniRoy-31
96KniWhiK-2
96KniWhiK-21
96KniWhiK-30
96KniWhiK-31
96M-F-19
96M-F-20
96M-F-40
96M-F-P1
96M-F-P2
96M-F-P3
96M-FBla-B7
96M-FBla-B8
96M-FBla-B12
96M-FSheM-M5
96M-FSil-S10
96M-FSil-S14
96Max-24
96Max-88
96MaxAut-24
96MaxChaC-1
96MaxChaC-2
96MaxChaC-3
96MaxChaC-4
96MaxChaC-5
96MaxChaC-6
96MaxChaC-7
96MaxChaC-8
96MaxChaC-9
96MaxChaC-10
96MaxChaC-11
96MaxChaC-12
96MaxChaC-13
96MaxChaC-14
96MaxMadiA-24
96MaxOdy-24
96MaxOdyM-MM6
96MaxPre-24
96MaxPre-296
96MaxSamBR-1
96MaxSamBR-2
96MetImp-1
96MetImp-2
96MetImp-3
96MetImp-4
96MetImp-5
96MetImp2AWCC-25
96MetImpJGWCC-1
96MetImpJGWCC-2
96MetImpJGWCC-3
96MetImpJGWCC-4
96MetImpJGWCC-5
96MetImpJGWCC-6
96MetImpJGWCC-7
96MetImpJGWCC-8
96MetImpJGWCC-9
96MetImpJGWCC-10
96MetImpWCTF-2
96Pin-24
96Pin-51
96Pin-66
96Pin-67
96Pin-68
96Pin-69
96Pin-70
96Pin-71
96Pin-72
96Pin-73
96Pin-85
96Pin-92
96Pin-95
96Pin-24
96Pin-51
96Pin-66
96Pin-67
96Pin-68
96Pin-69
96Pin-70
96Pin-71
96Pin-72
96Pin-73
96Pin-85
96Pin-92
96Pin-95
96PinCheF-1
96PinCutA-1
96PinPolP-24
96PinPolP-40
96PinPolP-51
96PinPolP-52
96PinPolP-53
96PinPolP-54
96PinPolP-55
96PinPolP-68
96PinPolP-69
96PinPolP-73
96PinPolPCS-1
96PinPolPLF-24
96PinPolPLF-40
96PinPolPLF-51
96PinPolPLF-52
96PinPolPLF-53
96PinPolPLF-54
96PinPolPLF-55
96PinPolPLF-68
96PinPolPLF-69
96PinPolPLF-73
96PinPolPNL-1
96PinPolPNLG-1
96PinTeaP-1
96PinTeaP-10
96PinWinCC-24
96PinWinCC-51
96PinWinCC-66
96PinWinCC-67
96PinWinCC-68
96PinWinCC-69
96PinWinCC-70
96PinWinCC-71
96PinWinCC-72
96PinWinCC-73
96PinWinCC-85
96PinWinCC-92
96PinWinCC-95
96PrePas-11
96PrePas-38
96PrePas-78
96PrePas-93
96PrePas-100
96PrePas-111
96PrePas-O
96PrePas-P1
96PrePas&NC-11
96PrePas&NC-38
96PrePasBR-BR2
96PrePasCC-11
96PrePasCF-CF1
96PrePasFoc-F3
96PrePasFQS-FQS3A
96PrePasFQS-FQS3B
96PrePasJGC-0
96PrePasP-1
96PrePasP-34
96PrePasPBRI-BR1
96PrePasPCB-CB5
96PrePasPEP-1
96PrePasPEP-34
96PrePasPH-1
96PrePasPH-34
96PrePasPHP-HP3
96PrePasSco-11
96PrePasSco-38
96PrePasSco-78
96PrePasSco-93
96PrePasSco-100
96PrePasSco-111
96PrePasT-11
96PrePasT-38
96PrePasT-78
96PrePasT-93
96PrePasT-100
96PrePasT-111
96RacCho-9
96RacCho-40
96RacCho-51
96RacCho-52
96RacCho-53
96RacCho-54
96RacCho-55
96RacCho-83
96RacCho-90
96RacCho-110
96RacCho-J52
96RacCho-P2
96RacChoAP-9
96RacChoAP-40
96RacChoAP-51
96RacChoAP-52
96RacChoAP-53
96RacChoAP-54
96RacChoAP-55
96RacChoAP-83
96RacChoAP-90
96RacChoAP-110
96RacChoSC-9
96RacChoSC-40
96RacChoSC-51
96RacChoSC-52
96RacChoSC-53
96RacChoSC-54
96RacChoSC-55
96RacChoSC-83
96RacChoSC-90
96RacChoSC-110
96RacChoTT-1
96RacChoUCJG-1
96RacChoUCJG-2
96RacChoUCJG-3
96RacChoUCJG-4
96RacChoUCJG-5
96RacChoUCJG-6
96RacChoUCJG-7
96SP-24
96SP-43
96SP-80
96SP-KR1
96SpeArtP-9
96SpeArtP-16
96SpeArtP-44
96SpeArtP-55
96SpeArtP-56
96SpeArtP-57
96SpeArtP-58
96SpeArtP-59
96SpeArtP-60
96SpeArtP-61
96SpeArtP-62
96SpeArtP-84
96SpeArtP-86
96SpeCleS-2
96SpeInM-2
96SpePro-2
96SpeRac-9
96SpeRac-16
96SpeRac-44
96SpeRac-55
96SpeRac-56
96SpeRac-57
96SpeRac-58
96SpeRac-59
96SpeRac-60
96SpeRac-61
96SpeRac-62
96SpeRac-84
96SpeRac-86
96SPHolME-ME1
96SPKinotR-K1
96SPRacLC-RL24
96SPx-1
96SPx-T1
96SPx-T1A
96SPx-S1
96SPxEli-E1
96SPxGol-1
96SPxTriC-T1
96TraRevP-15
96TraRevPFR-15
96TraRevPLG-LG18
96TraRevPM-15
96Ult-1
96Ult-2
96Ult-3
96Ult-152
96Ult-157
96Ult-168
96Ult-170
96Ult-172
96Ult-181
96Ult-182
96Ult-191
96Ult-200
96Ult-P1
96UltAut-11
96UltBoxS-1
96UltChaC-5
96UltFlaP-1
96UltSeaC-2
96UltSeaC-4
96UltSeaC-7
96UltSeaC-10
96UltSeaC-11
96UltSeaC-12
96UltThu&L-3
96UltThu&L-4
96UltUpd-12
96UltUpd-46
96UltUpd-58
96UltUpdA-4
96UltUpdPP-4
96UltUpdW-1
96UltUpdW-4
96UltUpdW-10
96UppDec-22
96UppDec-72
96UppDec-73
96UppDec-98
96UppDec-102
96UppDec-138
96UppDec-150
96UppDec-C1
96UppDec-C2
96UppDec-P1
96UppDecAP-AP1
96UppDecJGP-1
96UppDecJGP-2
96UppDecJGP-3
96UppDecJGP-4
96UppDecJGP-5
96UppDecJGP-6
96UppDecJGP-7
96UppDecJGP-8
96UppDecJGP-9
96UppDecJGP-10
96UppDecJGP-11
96UppDecJGP-12
96UppDecJGP-13
96UppDecJGP-14
96UppDecJGP-15
96UppDecJGP-16
96UppDecJGP-17
96UppDecJGP-18
96UppDecJGP-19

96UppDecJGP-20
96UppDecPP-RP1
96UppDecPW-HP1
96UppDecRTTC-RC1
96UppDecRTTC-RC51
96UppDecRTTC-RC121
96UppDecRTTC-RC124
96UppDecRTTC-RC148
96UppDecRTTC-JG1
96UppDecRTTCAS-H1
96UppDecRTTCDC-DC1
96UppDecRTTCDC-DC2
96UppDecRTTCDC-DC3
96UppDecRTTCDC-DC4
96UppDecRTTCDC-DC5
96UppDecRTTCDC-DC6
96UppDecRTTCDC-DC7
96UppDecRTTCDC-DC8
96UppDecRTTCDC-DC9
96UppDecRTTCDC-DC10
96UppDecRTTCGF-GF1
96UppDecRTTCJ-WC1
96UppDecRTTCJG2D-JG1
96UppDecRTTCLP-LP1
96UppDecRTTCPPoi-PP1
96UppDRTTCPPR-PR1
96UppDecRTTCPT3-T1
96UppDecRTTCPT3-T3
96UppDecRTTCPT3-T6
96UppDecRTTCPT3-T7
96UppDecRTTCT3PR-R1
96UppDecVV-VV1
96UppDecVVG-VV1
96V.IAut-8
96VIP-10
96VIP-30
96VIP-37
96VIPEmeP-10
96VIPEmeP-30
96VIPEmeP-37
96Viper-2
96Viper-40
96Viper-42
96ViperBlaM-2
96ViperBlaM-40
96ViperBlaM-42
96ViperBusC-B5
96ViperCob-C2
96ViperCop-2
96ViperCop-40
96ViperCop-42
96ViperDia-D1
96ViperDiaA-DA1
96ViperGreM-2
96ViperGreM-40
96ViperGreM-42
96ViperKinC-KC2
96VIPHeaG-HG3
96VIPHeaGD-HG3
96VipPro-P3
96VIPTor-10
96VIPTor-30
96VIPTor-37
96VIPWarP-WP12
96VIPWarPG-WP12
96Zen-2
96Zen-36
96Zen-51
96Zen-73
96Zen-74
96Zen-75
96Zen-76
96Zen-77
96Zen-78
96Zen-79
96Zen-80
96Zen-91
96Zen-92
96Zen-98
96Zen-99
96ZenArtP-2
96ZenArtP-36
96ZenArtP-51
96ZenArtP-73
96ZenArtP-74
96ZenArtP-75
96ZenArtP-76
96ZenArtP-77
96ZenArtP-78
96ZenArtP-79
96ZenArtP-80
96ZenArtP-91
96ZenArtP-92
96ZenArtP-98
96ZenArtP-99
96ZenChaS-1
96ZenHig-2
97Act-2
97Act-5
97Act-6
97Act-10
97ActPac-8
97ActPac-29
97ActPac2G-3
97ActPacCM-4
97ActPacFA-8
97ActPacFI-8
97ActPacFI-29
97ActPacRT-3
97AutRac-4
97AutRacA-16
97AutRacMS-KM4
97AutRacTtCF-TF1
97ColCho-24
97ColCho-74
97ColCho-101
97ColCho-127
97ColCho-128
97ColCho-129
97ColCho-154
97ColCho-NNO
97ColCho-NNO
97ColChoS-S47
97ColChoS-S48
97ColChoSQ-SQ36
97ColChoSQ-SQ41
97ColChoTF-F1
97ColChoTF-G2
97ColChoTF-G3
97ColChoUD5-UD48
97ColChoUD5-UD49
97ColChoVC-VC9
97FinLinPP2-1
97FinLinPP2$10-80
97FinLinPP2$100-95
97FinLinPP2$5-39
97FinLinPP2$50-87
97JurPar-1
97JurPar-48
97JurPar-51
97JurParC-C2
97JurParP-P2
97JurParR-R2
97JurParT-1
97JurParT-48
97JurParT-51
97JurParTL-TL1
97JurParTR-TR2
97Max-24
97Max-69
97MaxChaTC-C1
97MaxChatCG-C1
97MaxRoootY-MR6
97Pin-24
97Pin-53
97PinArtP-24
97PinArtP-53
97PinCer-24
97PinCer-58
97PinCer-74
97PinCer-89
97PinCerCGT-2
97PinCerCT-2
97PinCerE-E2
97PinCerEE-E2
97PinCerEP-E2
97PinCerMB-24
97PinCerMB-58
97PinCerMB-74
97PinCerMB-89
97PinCerMG-24
97PinCerMG-58
97PinCerMG-74
97PinCerMG-89
97PinCerMR-24
97PinCerMR-58
97PinCerMR-74
97PinCerMR-89
97PinCerR-24
97PinCerR-58
97PinCerR-74
97PinCerR-89
97PinCheM-15
97PinMin-2
97PinMin-24
97PinMin2GC-2
97PinMin2GC-24
97PinMinB-2
97PinMinB-24
97PinMinC-2
97PinMinC-24
97PinMinG-2
97PinMinG-24
97PinMinNC-2
97PinMinNC-24
97PinMinS-2
97PinMinS-24
97PinPor-1
97PinPor-21
97PinPre-3
97PinPre-4
97PinPre-5
97PinPre-6
97PinPre-8
97PinPre-9
97PinPreBM-3
97PinPreBM-4
97PinPreBM-6
97PinPreBM-9
97PinPreGM-3
97PinPreGM-4
97PinPreGM-6
97PinPreGM-9
97PinPreP-24
97PinPreP-53
97PinPreP-S6-R
97PinPreP-CM15
97PinPreP-TP1A
97PinPreSM-3
97PinPreSM-4
97PinPreSM-6
97PinPreSM-9
97PinSpe-6-R
97PinSpeA-6-R
97PinTeaP-1
97PinTotCPB-24
97PinTotCPB-58
97PinTotCPB-74
97PinTotCPB-89
97PinTotCPG-24
97PinTotCPG-58
97PinTotCPG-74
97PinTotCPG-89
97PinTotCPR-24
97PinTotCPR-58
97PinTotCPR-74
97PinTotCPR-89
97PinTroC-24
97PinTroC-53
97Pre-1
97Pre-44
97PreAmeE-AE2
97PreBlaWFS-1
97PreBlaWFS-44
97PreEyeotT-ET2
97PreGat-GB2
97PreGatA-GBA2
97PreGolE-GE2
97PreGri-1
97PreGri-44
97PrePas-2
97PrePas-39
97PrePas-57
97PrePas-96
97PrePas-104
97PrePas-105
97PrePas-134
97PrePas-135
97PrePas-136
97PrePas-137
97PrePas-138
97PrePas-SB1
97PrePasAut-2
97PrePasBB-BB2
97PrePasBR-BR5
97PrePasCC'-CC7
97PrePasCleC-C2
97PrePasL-2
97PrePasL-39
97PrePasL-57
97PrePasL-96
97PrePasL-104
97PrePasL-105
97PrePasL-134
97PrePasL-135
97PrePasL-136
97PrePasL-137
97PrePasL-138
97PrePasOS-2
97PrePasOS-39
97PrePasOS-57
97PrePasOS-96
97PrePasOS-104
97PrePasOS-105
97PrePasOS-134
97PrePasOS-135
97PrePasOS-136
97PrePasOS-137
97PrePasOS-138
97PrePasP-2
97PrePasP-33
97PrePasP-38
97PrePasPA-2
97PrePasPCB-CB4
97PrePasPCBD-CB4
97PrePasPDB-DB2
97PrePasPEP-2
97PrePasPEP-33
97PrePasPEP-38
97PrePasPLL-LL3
97PrePasPM-2
97PrePasPM-33
97PrePasPM-38
97PrePasPOS-2
97PrePasPOS-27
97PrePasPOS-33
97PrePasPOS-38
97PrePasT-2
97PrePasT-39
97PrePasT-57
97PrePasT-96
97PrePasT-104
97PrePasT-105
97PrePasT-134
97PrePasT-135
97PrePasT-136
97PrePasT-137
97PrePasT-138
97PrePasVL-VL2A
97PrePasVL-VL2B
97PreRedW-1
97PreRedW-44
97RacCho-24
97RacChoBC-8
97RacChoCM-7
97RacChoHO-3
97RacChoHOGitD-3
97RacChoSS-24
97RacSha-2
97RacSha-35
97RacSha-36
97RacSha-40
97RacSha-43
97RacShaGW-GW2
97RacShaGWP-2
97RacShaGWP-35
97RacShaGWP-36
97RacShaGWP-40
97RacShaGWP-43
97RacShaH-2
97RacShaH-35
97RacShaH-36
97RacShaH-40
97RacShaH-43
97RacShaPFBSA-4
97RacShaSA-SA2
97RacShaSTS-ST2
97RacShaTS-2
97RacShaTS-35
97RacShaTS-36
97RacShaTS-40
97RacShaTS-43
97SBMot-2
97SBMot-63
97SBMotAC-AU2
97ScoBoal-2
97ScoBoal-26
97ScoBoal-37
97ScoBoal-45
97ScoBoal-50
97ScoBoalR-SB2
97ScoBoaRSBF-SB2
97SkyPro-7
97SkyPro-70
97SkyProA-7
97SkyProBO-B1
97SkyProPS-E5
97SkyProT-T2
97SP-24
97SP-66
97SP-102
97SP-122
97SP SPxFA-SF1
97SP SupS-24
97SP SupS-66
97SP SupS-102
97SP SupS-122
97SPX-24
97SPxBlu-24
97SPxGol-24
97SPxSil-24
97SPXSpeA-SV1
97SPXTagT-TT1
97SPXTagT-TT4
97SPxTagTA-TA1
97SPxTagTA-TA4
97Ult-12
97Ult-41
97UltAKA-A2
97UltDriV-D1
97UltEliS-E1
97UltIns-DC2
97UltSho-4
97UltUpd-1
97UltUpd-86
97UltUpdAR-1
97UppDecRTTC-2
97UppDecRTTC-45
97UppDecRTTC-87
97UppDecRTTC-107
97UppDecRTTCCQ-CQ2
97UDRTTCCQC-CQ2
97UppDecRTTCGF-RD1
97UDRTTCMDM-MM5
97UDRTTCMDM-MM6
97UDRTTCMDM-MM7
97UDRTTCMDMA-MM5
97UDRTTCMDMA-MM6
97UDRTTCMDMA-MM7
97UppDecRTTCPotA-1
97UppDecRTTCPotA-2
97UppDecRTTCPotA-3
97UppDecRTTCPP-PP2
97UppDecRTTCPP-PP11
97UppDecRTTCPP-PP12
97UppDecRTTCPP-PP20
97UppDecRTTCPP-PP21
97UppDecRTTCPP-PP28
97UppDecRTTCPP-PP32
97UppDecRTTCPP-PP42
97UppDecRTTCPPlu-+2
97UppDecRTTCPPlu-+11
97UppDecRTTCPPlu-+28
97UDRTTCPPRC-+2
97UDRTTCPPRC-+11
97UDRTTCPPRC-+28
97UppDRTTCPPRDC-+2
97UppDRTTCPPRDC-+11
97UppDRTTCPPRDC-+28
97UppDecRTTCQW-CQ2
97UppDecVC-24
97UppDecVC-74
97UppDecVC-111
97UppDecVCAPotA-FS1
97UppDecVCAPotA-FS2
97UppDecVCAPotA-FS3
97UppDecVCCR-CR2
97UppDecVCDS-DS2
97UppDecVCGE-GE1
97UppDecVCP-PE1
97UppDecVCPC-PH1
97UppDecVCVL-VL2
97VIP-8
97Viper-1
97Viper-51
97Viper-74
97ViperAna-A2
97ViperBlaR-1
97ViperBlaR-51
97ViperBlaR-74
97ViperCob-C2
97ViperDia-DB1
97ViperDiaA-DBA1
97ViperKinC-KC2
97ViperSid-S2
97ViperSnaE-SE2
97VIPExp-8
97VIPHeaGD-HG3
97VIPHigG-HG3
97VIPOilS-8
97VIPRinoH-RH8
97VIPRinoHDC-RH8
97VIPSamB-KT2
97VIPSamBG-KT2
97VIPSheM-SM1
98ColCho-24
98ColCho-60
98ColCho-88
98ColCho-98
98HigGea-1

98HigGea-33
98HigGea-50
98HigGea-69
98HigGeaA-8
98HigGeaFG-1
98HigGeaFG-33
98HigGeaFG-50
98HigGeaFG-69
98HigGeaGJ-GJ12
98HigGeaHG-HG5
98HigGeaM-1
98HigGeaM-33
98HigGeaM-50
98HigGeaM-69
98HigGeaMaM-MM1
98HigGeaMaM-C-1
98HigGeaPG-PG3
98HigGeaTT-TT1
98Max-24
98Max-54
98Max-64
98Max-91
98Max-24
98Max-49
98Max-74
98Max-99
98Max10tA-24
98Max10tA-69
98Max10tA-124
98Max10tA-125
98Max10tA-126
98Max10tABA-20
98Max10tABA-21
98Max10tABA-22
98Max10tABA-23
98Max10tABA-24
98Max10tACotY-CY5
98Max10tACotY-CY10
98Max10tACP-CP1
98Max10tACPDC-CP1
98Max10tAMP-P24
98MaxBatP-B5
98MaxFieG-3
98MaxFieGTS-3
98MaxFieGTSA-3
98MaxFirC-F1
98MaxFocOAC-FC1
98MaxFouSGA-3
98MaxMakOACC-FC1
98MaxTea-TW1
98MaxYealRBS-1
98MaxYealRBS-5
98MaxYealRBS-6
98MaxYealRBS-29
98MaxYealRBS-31
98MaxYealRBS-36
98MaxYealRBS-51
98MaxYealRBS-52
98MaxYealRBS-61
98MaxYealRBS-71
98MaxYealRBS-96
98MaxYealRBS-111
98MaxYealRBS-121
98MaxYealRBS-130
98MaxYealRBS-AW1
98MaxYealRBS-PO1
98MayAutS-30
98PinMin-1
98PinMin-13
98PinMin-27
98PinMinB-1
98PinMinB-13
98PinMinB-27
98PinMinBC-1
98PinMinBC-13
98PinMinBC-03
98PinMinBPPC-1
98PinMinBPPC-13
98PinMinBPPC-03
98PinMinCM-1
98PinMinCM-2
98PinMinCMC-1A
98PinMinCMC-1B
98PinMinCMC-2A
98PinMinCMC-2B'
98PinMinGMT-1
98PinMinGMT-13
98PinMinGMT-27
98PinMinGPC-1
98PinMinGPC-13
98PinMinGPC-27
98PinMinGPPC-1
98PinMinGPPC-13
98PinMinGPPC-27

98PinMinNC-1
98PinMinNC-13
98PinMinNC-27
98PinMinSGC-1
98PinMinSGC-13
98PinMinSGC-27
98PinMinSMT-1
98PinMinSMT-13
98PinMinSMT-27
98PinMinSPPC-1
98PinMinSPPC-13
98PinMinSPPC-27
98PinMinSSC-1
98PinMinSSC-13
98PinMinSSC-27
98PrePas-1
98PrePas-34
98PrePas-101
98PrePas-0
98PrePasA-2
98PrePasCC'-CC7
98PrePasGS-1
98PrePasOC-OC3
98PrePasOS-1
98PrePasOS-34
98PrePasP-21
98PrePasP-28
98PrePasP-21
98PrePasP-28
98PrePasPFC-FC1
98PrePasPFC-FC24
98PrePasPFCR-FC1
98PrePasPFCR-FC24
98PrePasPR-1B
98PrePasPR-6A
98PrePasPS-PS12
98PrePasPSH-SH7
98PrePasPTGF-TGF6
98PrePasS-ST2A
98PrePasS-1
98PrePasS-10
98PrePasS-11
98PrePasS-47
98PrePasS-0
98PrePasS-0
98PrePasS-0
98PrePasSA-5
98PrePasSA-7
98PrePasSF-10
98PrePasSF-11
98PrePasSF-47
98PrePasSF-0
98PrePasSFT-3
98PrePasSFTD-3
98PrePasSO-13
98PrePasSO-47
98PrePasSOD-13
98PrePasSOD-14
98PrePasSRG-G6
98PrePasSS-5
98PrePasSSD-5
98PrePasTG3R-STG6
98PrePasTGBR-TG6
98PrePasTorp-ST2B
98SP Aut-24
98SP Aut-58
98SP Aut-72
98SP AutBtW-BW1
98SP AutBtWL2-BW1
98SP AutBtWL3-BW1
98SP AutSotTL2-ST1
98SP AutT-T2
98UppDecDV-1
98UppDecDV-RT1
98UppDecDVSM-1
98UppDecDVSM-RT1
98UppDecDVVoaC-VC3
98UppDecRttC-24
98UppDecRttC-66
98UppDecRttC-88
98UppDecRTTC5A-AN43
98UppDecRTTC5A-AN47
98UppDecRTTC5AA-AN47
98UDRTTCCQT1-CQ1
98UDRTTCCQT2-CQ1
98UDRTTCCQT3-CQ1
98UDRTTCCQT4-CQ1
98UppDRTTCCQVL-CQ1
98UppDecRTTCCS-CS8
98UppDecRTTCCS-CS15
98UppDecRTTCCS-CS16
98UppDecVC-24
98UppDecVC-69

98UppDecVC-92
98UppDecVC-93
98UppDecVC-100
98UppDecVC-105
98UppDecVC-119
98UppDecVC-120
98UppDecVC3DoS-D2
98UppDecVC3DoS-D11
98UppDecVC3DoS-D32
98UppDecVC3DoSG-D2
98UppDecVC3DoSG-D11
98UppDecVC3DoSG-D32
98UppDecVCA-AG1
98UppDecVCPL-PL1
98UppDecVCSoB-SB1
98VIP-8
98VIP-40
98VIPDriF-DF7
98VIPDriFD-DF7
98VIPExp-8
98VIPExp-40
98VIPHeaG-HG4
98VIPHeaGD-HG4
98VIPLapL-LL3
98VIPLapLA-LL3
98VIPNASC-NC3
98VIPNASCD-NC3
98VIPTriG"M-TGS6
98Whe-11
98Whe-36
98Whe-85
98Whe50tA-A5
98Whe50tA-A20
98WheAut-2
98WheCusS-CSJG
98WheDouT-E4
98WheGol-11
98WheGol-36
98WheGol-85
98WheGreF-GF6
98WheJac-J3
99Pre-1
99Pre-28
99Pre-79
99Pre-99
99PrePas-1
99PrePas-28
99PrePas-79
99PrePas-99
99PrePas-101
99PrePasBR-BR7
99PrePasCC-11B
99PrePasCC-6
99PrePasOC-6
99PrePasPS-12
99PrePasS-11A
99PrePasTG"i1R-TG3
99UppDecVC-3
99UppDecVC-41
99UppDecVC-76
99UppDecVC-80
99UppDecVC-84
99UppDecVCIS-IS1
99UppDecVCNSS-JG
99UppDecVCSZ-SZ3
99UppDecVCTM-TM1
99UppDecVCUE-3
99UppDecVCUE-41
99UppDecVCUE-76
99UppDecVCUE-80
99UppDecVCUE-84
99UppDecVCVC-V8
99WheHigG-1
99WheHigG-33
99WheHigG-46
99WheHigG-54
99WheHigG-58
99WheHigG-69
99WheHigG-72
99WheHigGAC-1
99WheHigGCS-CSJG
99WheHigGFC-FC1/5
99WheHigGFG-1
99WheHigGFG-33
99WheHigGFG-46
99WheHigGFG-54
99WheHigGFG-58
99WheHigGFG-69
99WheHigGFG-72
99WheHigGHS-HS1/6
99WheHigGM-MM1B/9
99WheHigGM-1
99WheHigGM-33
99WheHigGM-46

99WheHigGM-54
99WheHigGM-58
99WheHigGM-69
99WheHigGM-72
99WheHigGM&M-MM1A/9
99WheHigGS-GS1
99WheHigGTT-TT1/8

Gordon, Robby
92GriForO-177
94HiTecI-28
94HiTecI-37
95Ima-14
95Ima-85
95ImaDri-D12
95ImaGol-14
95ImaGol-85
95SkyInd5-6
95SkyInd5-37
95SkyInd5-54
95SkyInd5-63
95SkyInd5-77
95SkyInd5HI-3
96SkyInd5-16
96SkyInd5-43
96SkyInd5-59
97ActPac-26
97ActPac-52
97ActPac-75
97ActPacFI-26
97ActPacFI-52
97ActPacFI-75
97AutRac-9
97AutRac-32
97AutRacA-17
97AutRacMS-KM9
97ColChoC-CC38
97ColChoC-CC71
97ColChoSQ-SQ25
97ColChoSQ-SQ49
97JurPar-30
97JurParR-R16
97JurParT-30
97JurParTL-TL10
97Max-40
97Max-85
97Max-92
97Pin-14
97Pin-43
97PinArtP-14
97PinArtP-43
97PinCer-11
97PinCer-45
97PinCer-79
97PinCerMB-11
97PinCerMB-45
97PinCerMB-79
97PinCerMG-11
97PinCerMG-45
97PinCerMG-79
97PinCerMR-11
97PinCerMR-45
97PinCerMR-79
97PinCerR-11
97PinCerR-45
97PinCerR-79
97PinPreP-14
97PinPreP-43
97PinTotCPB-11
97PinTotCPB-45
97PinTotCPB-79
97PinTotCPG-11
97PinTotCPG-45
97PinTotCPG-79
97PinTotCPR-11
97PinTotCPR-45
97PinTotCPR-79
97PinTroC-14
97PinTroC-43
97Pre-33
97PreBlaWFS-33
97PreGri-33
97PrePas-91
97PrePas-128
97PrePasAut-24
97PrePasAut-27A
97PrePasL-91
97PrePasL-128
97PrePasOS-91
97PrePasOS-128
97PrePasP-26
97PrePasP-27
97PrePasPA-24
97PrePasPEP-26

97PrePasPEP-27
97PrePasPM-26
97PrePasPOS-26
97PrePasPOS-27
97PrePasT-91
97PrePasT-128
97PreRedW-33
97RacCho-14
97RacCho-49
97RacCho-89
97RacChoCM-10
97RacChoSS-14
97RacChoSS-49
97RacChoSS-89
97SBMot-5
97SBMot-45
97SBMotAC-AU5
97ScoBoal-9
97ScoBoal-47
97SkyPro-8
97SkyPro-75
97SkyProA-8
97SkyProBO-B2
97SPX-1
97SPxBlu-1
97SPxGol-1
97SPxSil-1
97Ult-38
97UltUpd-13
97UltUpdAR-13
97VIP-9
97Viper-31
97Viper-76
97ViperBlaR-31
97ViperBlaR-76
97ViperDia-DB10
97ViperDiaA-DBA10
97ViperSid-S16
97VIPExp-9
97VIPOilS-9
98ColCho-35
98ColCho-71
98ColCho-74
98MaxYealRBS-17
98MaxYealRBS-100
98MaxYealRBS-129
98UppDecDV-15
98UppDecDVSM-15
98UppDecVC-40
98UppDecVC-85
98UppDecVC-94
98UppDecVC-123
98UppDecVC3DoS-D4
98UppDecVC3DoSG-D4

Gordon, Tim
91BulRin-86

Gordon, Tracy
91WinChoNED-61
91WinChoNED-62
92WinChoB-103
92WinChoB-104

Gosek, Joe
97Hi-IRL-35

Goss, Buster
92HavAT-26

Gossage, Eddie
97VIP-49
97VIPExp-49
97VIPOilS-49

Gould, Ralph
72FleAHRDN-64

Goux, Jules
54StaWetIW-1913
60HawWaxI-3
91LegInd-25
95TraVal-19
95TraVal-32

Gowen, Matt
91SpoLegHT-HT13

Gower, Craig
92BulRin-150

Graham, Bob
92VolRacLS2-24

Graham, Grover
93CorSelCCS-30

Graham, Sean
92BulRin-84

Grahner, Gary
91BigTimD-53

Granatelli, Andy
70FleDra-3
70FleDra-6
70FleDra-8
91LegInd-86

97Hi-IRL-14
97Hi-IRLP-D6
Gregory, Phil
92JAG-171
Greiner, Bobby Jr.
91DKIMCDT-47
Gress, Monte
91LanART-17
Griffey Jr., Ken
95UppDec-136
95UppDecGSEG-136
95UppDecSSES-136
Griffin, Ed
94STAMod-25
Griffin, Richard
87WorOut-45
Griffith, Chuck
65DonSpeS-61
Griffith, Cliff
62MarInd-7
Grimes, Stephen
91BulRin-39
92BulRin-139
Grimes, Tommy
91BulRin-118
Grinstead, Brian
92TraCouSR-11
Grissom, Kyle
94ActPac-147
Grissom, Steve
89Max-204
90Max-142
91Max-161
91Tra-31
92-CarDynBTBS-4
92MaxBla-58
92MaxRed-58
92ProSet-3
92RedSta-31
92SliJimBL-16
92Tra-31
92TraGoo-8
92TraRacM-31
92TraRacM-32
92WinChoB-74
92WinChoB-75
93FinLin-130
93FinLinCS-12
93FinLinS-130
93Max-31
93MaxPreP-31
93MaxPreS-31
93Tra-31
93Tra-193
93TraFirR-31
93TraFirR-193
94ActPac-53
94ActPac-122
94ActPac-147
94FinLin-30
94FinLinBGN-BGN10
94FinLinNSH-6
94FinLinS-30
94HigGea-67
94HigGea-72
94HigGea-129
94HigGeaDO-129
94HigGeaDOG-129
94HigGeaG-67
94HigGeaG-72
94HigGeaG-129
94HigGeaRSA-RS1
94Max-163
94Max-197
94MaxAut-2
94MaxAut-163
94MaxPreP-61
94MaxPreP-150
94MaxPreS-163
94MaxPreS-256
94MaxRooC'-2
94OptXL-7
94OptXL-55
94OptXLRH-7
94OptXLRH-55
94Pow-28
94PowGol-28
94PrePas-61
94PrePas-64
94PrePas-125
94PrePasPro-PP4
94SliJimDG-43
94Tra-31
94Tra-159
94TraAut-A5
94TraAutV-11
94TraFirR-31
94TraFirR-159
94VIP-13
95ActPacC-73
95ActPacCSS-73
95ActPacP-10
95ActPacS-29
95ActPacSSS-29
95CarDynAP-1
95CroJew-23
95CroJewD-23
95CroJewE-23
95CroJewS-23
95FinLin-48
95FinLin-109
95FinLinPP-48
95FinLinPP-109
95FinLinSil-48
95FinLinSil-109
95HigGea-25
95HigGeaDO-25
95HigGeaDOG-25
95HigGeaG-25
95Ima-29
95Ima-79
95ImaGol-29
95ImaGol-79
95Max-29
95Max-183
95MaxCroC-29
95MaxMedORA-OTR4
95MaxPreP-29
95MaxPrePSTP-PRE3
95MaxPrePTH-TH3
95MaxPreS-29
95OptXL-9
95OptXLCB-9
95OptXLDC-9
95OptXLRH-9
95PrePas-11
95PrePasCC-11
95PrePasPH-23
95PrePasPre-23
95PrePasPRH-23
95PrePasRH-11
95Sel-13
95SelFlaO-13
95SP-22
95SP-61
95SP-102
95SPDieC-22
95SPDieC-61
95SPDieC-102
95SPSpeM-SM9
95SPSpeMDC-SM9
95Tra-10
95Tra5thA-2
95Tra5thA-63
95Tra5thAG-2
95Tra5thAG-63
95TraAutV-2
95TraFirR-10
95TraOnTR-OTR8
95UppDec-31
95UppDec-99
95UppDec-129
95UppDec-208
95UppDec-251
95UppDec-286
95UppDecA-208
95UppDecGSEG-31
95UppDecGSEG-99
95UppDecGSEG-129
95UppDecGSEG-208
95UppDecGSEG-251
95UppDecGSEG-286
95UppDecSSES-31
95UppDecSSES-99
95UppDecSSES-129
95UppDecSSES-208
95UppDecSSES-251
95UppDecSSES-286
95VIP-12
95VIPCooB-12
95VIPEmeP-12
95VIPRedHCB-12
95Zen-28
96CroJewEDitR-DR2
96CroJewEDitRC-DR2
96CroJewEDitRS-DR2
96CroJewEDT-19
96CroJewEDT-66
96CroJewEDT-75
96CroJewEDTC-19
96CroJewEDTC-66
96CroJewEDTC-75
96CroJewEE-19
96CroJewEE-66
96CroJewEE-75
96CroJewEli-19
96CroJewEli-66
96CroJewEli-75
96CroJewES-19
96CroJewES-66
96CroJewES-75
96CroJewETC-19
96CroJewETC-66
96CroJewETC-75
96CroJewETCE-19
96CroJewETCE-66
96CroJewETCE-75
96CroJewETCS-19
96CroJewETCS-66
96CroJewETCS-75
96FinLin-7
96FinLin-53
96FinLinPP-13
96FinLinPP$S-13
96FinLinPriP-7
96FinLinPriP-53
96FinLinS-7
96FinLinS-53
96Fla-13
96Fla-69
96M-F-24
96Max-29
96Max-46
96MaxMadiA-67
96MaxMadiA-91
96MaxMadiA-92
96MaxOdy-29
96MaxOdy-46
96MaxOdy-66
96MaxOdy-67
96MaxOdy-91
96MaxOdy-92
96MaxOdyOTRA-OTRA1
96MaxOdyOTRA-OTRA5
96MaxPre-29
96MaxPre-69
96MaxPre-186
96MaxPre-187
96PrePas-12
96PrePasCC-12
96PrePasP-23
96PrePasPEP-23
96PrePasPH-23
96PrePasSco-12
96PrePasT-12
96SP-29
96SP-67
96SPHolME-ME15
96SPx-19
96SPxGol-19
96TraRev&PTCG-TC12
96TraRev&PTCH-TC12
96TraRevP-30
96TraRevPFR-30
96TraRevPLG-LG8
96TraRevPM-30
96TraRevPTC-TC12
96Ult-84
96Ult-85
96Ult-86
96UltUpd-13
96UltUpd-59
96UppDec-27
96UppDec-67
96UppDec-107
96UppDecRTTC-RC25
96UppDecRTTC-RC107
96UppDecRTTCAS-H25
96Viper-20
96ViperBlaM-20
96ViperCop-20
96ViperGreM-20
97ActPacCM-6
97ActPacRT-12
97AutRac-20
97AutRacA-19
97AutRacMS-KM20
97ColChoC-CC23
97ColChoC-CC56
97ColChoC-CC89
97ColChoSQ-SQ12
97JurPar-29
97JurParT-29
97Max-41
97Max-86
97Pin-15
97Pin-44
97PinArtP-15
97PinArtP-44
97PinCer-16
97PinCer-50
97PinCerMB-16
97PinCerMB-50
97PinCerMG-16
97PinCerMG-50
97PinCerMR-16
97PinCerMR-50
97PinCerR-16
97PinCerR-50
97PinPor-50
97PinPreP-15
97PinPreP-44
97PinTotCPB-16
97PinTotCPB-50
97PinTotCPG-16
97PinTotCPG-50
97PinTotCPR-16
97PinTotCPR-50
97PinTroC-15
97PinTroC-44
97PrePas-127
97PrePasL-127
97PrePasOS-127
97PrePasT-127
97RacCho-15
97RacCho-50
97RacCho-78
97RacChoSS-15
97RacChoSS-50
97RacChoSS-78
97SBMot-39
97SBMot-64
97ScoBoaI-20
97SkyPro-9
97SkyProA-9
97UltUpd-22
97UltUpd-92
97UltUpdAR-22
97UppDecRTTC-38
97UppDecRTTC-80
97UppDecRTTC-115
97UppDecRTTC-143
97Viper-30
97ViperBlaR-30
98ColCho-19
98ColCho-55
98ColCho-80
98Max-83
98Max10tA-37
98Max10tA-82
98MaxYealRBS-20
98MaxYealRBS-28
98MaxYealRBS-98
98MaxYealRBS-108
98UppDecRttC-41
98UppDecVC-41
98UppDecVC-86
98UppDecVC-148
99UppDecVC-37
99UppDecVCUE-37
Groff, Mike
91AllWorI-22
92AllWorI-2
92AllWorI-97
92LegInd-25
94HiTecICD-CD17
95SkyInd5-49
95SkyInd5-60
95SkyInd5-103
97Hi-IRL-7
97Hi-IRLP-D4
Grose, Tim
89MegDra-81
89MegDra-82
Gross, Don
92JAG-172
92STAMod-29
94STAMod-26
Grotheer, Don
71FleAHRDC-40
72FleAHRDN-14
73FleAHRRU-19
Grouillard, Olivier
91CarForO-37
91CarForO-38
91CarForO-39
91ProTraFO-32
91ProTraFO-33
91ProTraFO-34
92GriForO-3
92GriForO-36
92GriForO-69
Grove, Tom
72FleAHRDN-54
Grover, Buster
92WinChoM-46
Grover, Danny
92WinChoM-45
Grover, Elaine
92WinChoM-48
Groves, Joe
90CheFlaI-87
Guerrero, Carlos
96SkyInd5-38
96SkyInd5-87
Guerrero, Roberto
85A&SRacI-2
86A&SRacI-8
87A&SRacI-43
91AllWorI-24
92AllWorI-27
92AllWorI-85
92LegInd-31
93HiTecI-1
93HiTecI-35
93HiTecI-68
93HiTecI-70
94HiTecI-29
94HiTecI-46
94HiTecICD-CD18
95SkyInd5-38
95SkyInd5-54
95SkyInd5-105
96SkyInd5-22
96SkyInd5-66
97Hi-IRL-6
97Hi-IRL'I5-I18
97Hi-IRLP-P7
Gugelmin, Mauricio
88HerFouFO-5D
91CarForO-40
91CarForO-41
91CarForO-42
91ProTraFO-35
91ProTraFO-36
92GriForO-31
92GriForO-64
92GriForO-97
95SkyInd5-47
95SkyInd5-83
96SkyInd5-15
96SkyInd5-60
96SkyInd5-89
Guide, Joe Jr.
91GalPrePR-33
91GalPrePR-58
91GalPrePR-74
Guilford, Chad
93FinLinN-118
Guithues, Tom
91LanStoCC-17
Gulley, Jerry
89CheFlaI-91
90CheFlaI-45
Gundaker, Kevin
92JAG-38
Gunning, Bo
91WinChoM-80
91WinChoM-81
Gunter, Warren
71FleAHRDC-46
Gurney, Chuck
87WorOut-43
88WorOut-50
Gurney, Dan
70FleDra-4
92ColACAR-72
92LegInd-80
92MaxIMH-18
Guss, Ray Jr.
91DKIMCDT-33
93JAG-18
96MaxPre-212
96PrePas-108
96PrePasSco-108
96PrePasT-108
Gustin, Roger
90BigTimD-6
90BigTimDS-6
91BigTimD-66

91BigTimD-80
Guthrie, Janet
77Spo-1803
78GraPri-213
89TGRacMR-171
91LegInd-66
91TGRacMRU-171
92LegInd-61
92SpoRacC-13
92SpoRacC-14
92SpoRacC-15
92SpoRacC-16
Guthrie, Jim
97Hi-IRL-22
Guy, Jay
94HigGeaPPT-G9
94HigGeaPPTG-9G
Guyot, Albert
95TraVal-25
95TraVal-29
Gwin, Claude Jr.
92BulRin-102
Gwynn, Darrell
89MegDra-1
89MegDra-2
91ProSetN-16
91ProSetN-65
92MacTooWC-10
92ProSetN-179
93FinLinN-19
94ActPacN-33
94ActPacN2G-33G
Gwynn, Jerry
92MacTooWC-11
Haas, Carl
92ColACAR-68
96ActPacC-83
96MaxPre-102
96SkyInd5-52
Haas, Jerry
89MegDra-17
89MegDra-18
91ProSetN-46
91ProSetN-94
92ProSetN-83
92ProSetN-131
93FinLinN-88
Haas, Rick
91WorOut-73
Hacker, Bobby
91LanRocS-17
92LanRocS-23
Hafer, Dale
92VolRacLSI-20
Hafer, John
92CorSelCCS-25
93CorSelCCS-25
Hagan, Billy
89Max-173
90Max-135
91Max-55
92MaxBla-119
92MaxRed-119
93FinLin-146
93FinLinCS-5
93FinLinS-146
93MaxPreP-95
93Tra-135
93TraFirR-135
94HigGea-145
94HigGeaDO-145
94HigGeaDOG-145
94HigGeaG-145
94Max-108
94MaxPreP-108
94MaxPreS-108
94Tra-105
94TraFirR-105
Hage, Ed
95JSKIce-20
Hagen, Billy
93Max-106
93MaxPreS-106
Hager, Tom
92K&WDirT-14
94K&WDirT-31
95K&WDirT-33
Haggenbottom, Mike
91K&WURCS-33
Hahn, Dennis
92CorSelCCS-7
Hahne, Armin
78GraPri-183
Hailey, Jerry
98Whe-95
98WheGol-95
Hairfield, Bugs
92BulRin-153
Hakkinen, Mika
91CarForO-31
91CarForO-32
91CarForO-33
91ProTraFO-26
91ProTraFO-27
92GriForO-12
92GriForO-45
92GriForO-78
92LimAppFO-5
Hale, Mike
94ActPacSJ-7
94ActPacSJ-8
Haley, Bruce
91WinChoM-55
91WinChoM-56
91WinChoNED-75
91WinChoNED-76
Halford, Johnny
89TGRacMR-185
89TGRacMR-186
91TGRacMRU-185
91TGRacMRU-186
Hall, Barney
90Max-163
91Max-226
91SpoLegNJ-NJ28
91Tra-139
92MaxBlaU-U23
92MaxRedU-U23
92ProSet-208
92Tra-135
93FinLin-87
93FinLinCS-2
93FinLinS-87
93Max-200
93MaxPreS-200
94FinLin-6
94FinLinS-6
94MaxPreS-197
94Pow-71
94PowGol-71
94PrePas-112
95MaxPreS-194
96MaxPre-193
Hall, David
92LanARCF-45
94LanARCF-47
Hall, Dean
91AllWorl-14
92AllWorl-3
Hall, Doug
94STAMod-27
Hall, Gary
91DirTra-25
92DirTra-41
Hall, John
91Tra-171
92BikRacS-16
Hall, Paul
89CheFlal-6
Hall, Phil
92JAG-39
Hall, Ray
92TraTeaS-92
Hall, Terry
92RSSMotH-6
Halladay, Doc
89MegDra-88
89MegDra-89
Halsmer, Pete
83A&SRacl-17
84A&SRacl-11
85A&SRacl-17
86A&SRacl-11
Ham, Robert
94LanARCF-8
94LanARCF-97
Hamby, Wayne
91MaxBilETCM-35
Hamilton, Bill
93MaxMot-27
Hamilton, Bobby
90Max-151
91Max-68
91MaxUpd-68
91ProSet-131
91SupRacM-4
92CoyRoo-13
92DaySer1-9
92MaxBla-68
92MaxBla-99
92MaxBla-197
92MaxBobH-1
92MaxBobH-2
92MaxBobH-3
92MaxBobH-4
92MaxBobH-5
92MaxBobH-6
92MaxBobH-7
92MaxBobH-8
92MaxBobH-9
92MaxBobH-10
92MaxBobH-11
92MaxBobH-12
92MaxBobH-13
92MaxBobH-14
92MaxBobH-15
92MaxBobH-16
92MaxCra-NNO
92MaxMcD-28
92MaxRed-68
92MaxRed-99
92MaxRed-197
92ProSet-63
92ProSet-139
92RedSta-23
92TraRacM-26
92TraRacM-67
92TraRacM-68
92TraRacM-P26
93FinLin-126
93FinLinCS-10
93FinLinS-126
93Max-68
93Max-97
93MaxLowFS-3
93MaxMot-7
93MaxPreP-35
93MaxPreP-68
93MaxPreS-68
93MaxPreS-97
93StoTop-2
93Tra-20
93TraFirR-20
94HigGea-120
94HigGeaDO-120
94HigGeaDOG-120
94HigGeaG-120
94HigGeaRTU-103
94HigGeaRTUP-103
94Max-20
94Max-272
94Max-280
94MaxMed-23
94MaxPreP-20
94MaxPreS-20
94MaxRooY-12
94Pow-91
94PowGol-91
94PrePas-8
94PrePas-39
94PrePasCC-CC8
94VIP-14
95ActPacC-66
95ActPacCSS-66
95ActPacS-45
95ActPacSSS-45
95Ass-28
95AssGolS-28
95FinLin-116
95FinLinCC6-28
95FinLinPP-116
95FinLinSil-116
95HiTecB4-30
95HiTecB4-49
95Ima-43
95Ima-83
95ImaGol-43
95ImaGol-83
95Max-40
95Max-185
95MaxCroC-40
95MaxCroC-54
95MaxMed-25
95MaxMed-55
95MaxMedB-25
95MaxMedB-55
95MaxPreP-40
95MaxPreP-54
95MaxPreS-40
95MaxPreS-213
95PrePas-12
95PrePas-130
95PrePasCC-12
95PrePasRH-12
95PrePasRH-130
95Sel-14
95SelFlaO-14
95SP-12
95SP-45
95SP-87
95SPDieC-12
95SPDieC-45
95SPDieC-87
95Tra-45
95Tra5thA-34
95Tra5thA-46
95Tra5thA-62
95Tra5thAG-34
95Tra5thAG-46
95TraAutV-22
95TraFirR-45
95TraRacM-RM4
95VIP-13
95VIPAut-13
95VIPCooB-13
95VIPEmeP-13
95VIPRedHCB-13
95Zen-30
95Zen-58
95Zen-67
96ActPacC-33
96ActPacC-59
96ActPacCFS-7
96ActPacCSS-33
96Ass-26
96Ass$1000CCIPC-14
96Ass$100CCIPC-19
96Ass$10PC-2
96Ass$2PC-21
96AssComL-CL16
96AutRac-50
96AutRacA-18
96AutRacCA-18
96AutRacHP-HP16
96Cla-34
96ClaPriP-34
96ClaSil-34
96CroJewEADJ-DJ6
96CroJewEDT-10
96CroJewEDTC-10
96CroJewEDTDJA-DJ6
96CroJewEDTDJG-DJ6
96CroJewEE-10
96CroJewEGDJ-DJ6
96CroJewEli-10
96CroJewES-10
96CroJewESDJ-DJ6
96CroJewETC-10
96CroJewETCDJA-DJ6
96CroJewETCDJS-DJ6
96CroJewETCE-10
96CroJewETCGDJ-DJ6
96CroJewETCS-10
96FinLin-19
96FinLin-49
96FinLinGS-GS10
96FinLinPP-14
96FinLinPP$5C-10
96FinLinPP$S-14
96FinLinPriP-19
96FinLinPriP-49
96FinLinS-19
96FinLinS-49
96Fla-14
96Fla-70
96FlaCenS-5
96M-F-26
96M-F-27
96M-FSil-S11
96Max-40
96Max-44
96MaxMadiA-39
96MaxMadiA-44
96MaxOdy-39
96MaxOdy-44
96MaxOdyM-MM7
96MaxPre-44
96MaxPreSS-SL5
96Pin-29
96Pin-58
96Pin-29
96Pin-58
96PinPolP-19
96PinPolP-43
96PinPolPCS-12
96PinPolPLF-19
96PinPolPLF-43
96PinWinCC-29
96PinWinCC-58
96PrePas-13
96PrePas-49
96PrePas-80
96PrePas&NC-13
96PrePasCC-13
96PrePasP-14
96PrePasP-42
96PrePasPEP-14
96PrePasPEP-42
96PrePasPH-14
96PrePasPH-42
96PrePasSco-13
96PrePasSco-49
96PrePasSco-80
96PrePasT-13
96PrePasT-49
96PrePasT-80
96RacCho-17
96RacCho-45
96RacChoAP-17
96RacChoAP-45
96RacChoSC-17
96RacChoSC-45
96SP-14
96SP-55
96SPDriF-DF10
96SpeArtP-6
96SpePro-11
96SpeRac-6
96SPHolME-ME20
96SPx-8
96SPxGol-8
96STP25tA-NNO
96STP25tA-NNO
96STP25tA-NNO
96STP25tA-NNO
96STP25tA-NNO
96TraRev&PTCG-TC7
96TraRev&PTCH-TC7
96TraRevP-2
96TraRevP-26
96TraRevPFR-2
96TraRevPFR-26
96TraRevPLG-LG5
96TraRevPM-2
96TraRevPM-26
96TraRevPTC-TC7
96Ult-41
96Ult-42
96Ult-43
96UltBoxS-14
96UltUpd-14
96UltUpd-60
96UltUpd-82
96UltUpdPP-5
96UppDec-12
96UppDec-52
96UppDec-92
96UppDecRTTC-RC13
96UppDecRTTC-RC62
96UppDecRTTC-RC98
96UppDecRTTC-RC134
96UppDecRTTC-RC150
96UppDecRTTCAS-H13
96VIP-11
96VIP-42
96VIPEmeP-11
96VIPEmeP-42
96Viper-10
96ViperBlaM-10
96ViperCob-C9
96ViperCop-10
96ViperGreM-10
96ViperKinC-KC6
96VIPTor-11
96VIPTor-42
96VIPWarP-WP16
96VIPWarPG-WP16
96Zen-29
96Zen-44
96ZenArtP-29
96ZenArtP-44
97ActPac-1
97ActPac-49
97ActPac-86
97ActPac2G-12
97ActPacFI-1
97ActPacFI-49
97ActPacFI-86
97AutRac-18
97AutRac-33

96SkyInd5-67
Hesketh, Lord
77Spo-8322
Hess, Ben
89Max-209
90Max-77A
90Max-77B
91LanARCHS-40
91Max-76
92LanARCF-7
92LanARCF-19
92LanARCF-103
92MaxBlaU-U8
92MaxRedU-U8
Hess, Dave
92VolRacLS2-28
92VolRacLSI-21
Hess, Doug
92TraTeaS-63
Hester, Allen
94HigGeaPPT-G8
94HigGeaPPTG-8G
Hester, Don
92VolRacEAS-7
Hester, Robert
92BulRin-65
Heuser, Rick
94LanARCF-35
Heveron, Doug
83A&SRacI-27
84A&SRacI-37
91WinChoM-16
91WinChoM-17
95MaxPreS-178
96MaxPre-177
96MaxPre-246
Hewitt, Doug
93FinLin-116
93FinLinCS-8
93FinLinS-116
93Max-165
93MaxPreP-148
93MaxPreS-165
94ActPac-66
94FinLin-33
94FinLinS-33
94HigGea-136
94HigGeaDO-136
94HigGeaDOG-136
94HigGeaG-136
94Max-144
94MaxPreP-137
94MaxPreS-144
94PrePas-96
95HigGea-49
95HigGeaDO-49
95HigGeaDOG-49
95HigGeaG-49
95Max-108
95MaxAut-108
95MaxCroC-120
95MaxPreP-120
95MaxPreS-139
95Sel-104
95SelFlaO-104
96AutRacA-19
96AutRacCA-19
96Max-82
96MaxPre-134
Hewitt, Jack
87WorOut-38
88WorOut-23
89WorOut-14
90WorOut-28
91WorOut-74
92JAG-43
92WorOutMW-4
Hewitt, Scott
92TraTeaS-168
Heyer, Hans
78GraPri-184
78GraPri-193
Hickman, Brian
92JAG-44
Hickman, Jim
83A&SRacI-42
Hicks, Billy
93JAG-19
94JAG-23
94STAMod-31
Hicks, Kent
93JAG-20
Hieber, Gary
91K&WURCS-26
Hielscher, Bill
71FleAHRDC-24
71FleAHRDC-60
Higby, Mark
90LanRocSHS-3
Higginbotham, Mart
71FleAHRDC-22
72FleAHRDN-21
72FleAHRDN-36
73FleAHRRU-25
Higgins, Tim
91K&WURCS-16
Higgins, Tom
91Tra-127
92Tra-130
Hildreth, Elton
92SpoLegBB-BB20
Hill, Benny
26SpoComoAR-5
Hill, Bob
92JAG-45
94LanARCF-49
Hill, Bruce
93WheRooT-17
93WheRooTPla-17
Hill, Carl
91Tra-151
92MaxBla-217
92MaxRed-217
92Tra-151
93Max-239
93MaxPreS-239
93Tra-102
93TraFirR-102
94MaxPreS-219
94Tra-88
94TraFirR-88
95MaxPreS-217
95TraBehTS-BTS19
96MaxPre-218
97ActPac-62
97ActPacFI-62
Hill, Chuck
91MaxBilETCM-24
Hill, Damon
92GriForO-8
92GriForO-41
92GriForO-74
93MaxWilR-4
Hill, David
92K&WDirT-39
Hill, Eddie
65TopHotR-57
89MegDra-3
89MegDra-4
89MegDra-5
91ProSetN-6
91ProSetN-55
92ProSetN-5
92ProSetN-30
92ProSetN-105
93FinLinN-22
93FinLinN-23
93FinLinN-24
94ActPacN-1
94ActPacN-11
94ActPacN-P1
94ActPacWDR2G-2
94CarDynEH-1
94CarDynEH-2
94CarDynEH-3
95ActPacN-41
95ActPacNSS-41
Hill, Gene
91LanRocS-31
Hill, Graham
62PetLimGPRC-34
70FleDra-5
71MobTheSoGPMR-34
77Spo-1201
92GriForO-180
92GriForO-181
95SkyInd5PC-15
Hill, Jerry
91LanARCHS-56
92LanARCF-29
93Max-89
93MaxPreS-89
94LanARCF-81
Hill, Lance
92TraTeaS-197
Hill, Mike
89Max-86
90Max-113
91Max-209
92MaxAllPT-27
92MaxBla-249
92MaxRed-249
93FinLin-81
93FinLinCS-15
93FinLinS-81
93Max-152
93MaxPreP-136
93MaxPreS-152
94ActPac-65
94FinLin-98
94FinLinS-98
94HigGea-41
94HigGeaG-41
94Max-136
94MaxPreP-129
94MaxPreS-136
95Max-132
95Max-199
95MaxAut-132
95MaxCroC-112
95MaxPreP-112
95MaxPreS-131
Hill, Phil
62PetLimGPRC-32
92GolEraGPTEY-24
Hill, Ray
93Max-230
93MaxPreS-230
94MaxPreS-218
95MaxPreS-216
96MaxPre-217
Hillenburg, Andy
87WorOut-33
88WorOut-6
89WorOut-7
89WorOutP-2
90WorOut-19
92LanARCF-71
92Tra-29A
92Tra-29B
92WorOutMW-10
93Tra-72
93TraFirR-72
94Max-99
94MaxPreS-99
94Tra-81
94TraFirR-81
94WorOut-6
96PrePas-101
96PrePasSco-101
96PrePasT-101
Hillerod, Larry
91WorOut-75
Hillin, Bobby Jr.
88MaxCha-52
89Max-8
89MaxCri-20
89MaxPre-NNO
90ACRacPW-6
90Max-8A
90Max-8B
90Max-172
90MaxHolF-HF28
91Max-99
91MaxMcD-19
91MaxTheWA-8
91ProSet-86
91Tra-14
91Tra-20
92MaxBla-53
92MaxRed-53
92ProSet-52
92RedSta-20
92Tra-125
93ActPac-174
93ActPac2G-56G
93FinLin-11
93FinLin-145
93FinLinCS-9
93FinLinS-11
93FinLinS-145
93Max-90
93MaxHou-30
93MaxMot-9
93MaxMot-29
93MaxPreP-84
93MaxPreS-90
93MaxTexDA-18
93Tra-40
93Tra-90
93TraFirR-40
93TraFirR-90
93TraTri-46
94ActPac-26
94FinLin-15
94FinLin-44
94FinLinS-15
94FinLinS-44
94Hi-Bri4AP-3
94Hi-Bri4AP-66
94HigGea-21
94HigGeaG-21
94HiTecB4-3
94HiTecB4-66
94Max-82
94Max-90
94MaxMed-20
94MaxMot-22
94MaxPreP-82
94MaxPreP-90
94MaxPreS-82
94MaxPreS-90
94PowPre-18
94PowPre-23
94PrePas-10
94PrePas-35
94PrePas-41
94PrePasCC-CC10
94Tra-90
94TraAutV-26
94TraFirR-90
95ActPacC2CC-1
95HiTecB4-33
95HiTecB4-50
95Max-144
95MaxMed-27
95MaxMed-57
95MaxMedB-27
95MaxMedB-57
95MaxPreS-44
95MaxPreS-193
95MaxPreSU-5
95Zen-19
95Zen-66
96ActPacC-53
96ActPacCSS-53
96Pin-20
96Pin-61
96Pin-20
96Pin-61
96PinPolP-48
96PinPolPLF-48
96PinWinCC-20
96PinWinCC-61
96SP-27
96SpeArtP-31
96SpeRac-31
96UppDecRTTC-RC34
96UppDecRTTC-RC83
96Zen-32
96Zen-56
96ZenArtP-32
96ZenArtP-56
97ColCho-27
97ColCho-77
97ColChoUD5-UD56
97ColChoUD5-UD57
97JurPar-32
97JurParT-32
97SkyPro-12
97SkyProA-12
97SP-27
97SP-69
97SP SupS-27
97SP SupS-69
97Ult-14
97UltUpd-30
97UltUpdAR-30
97UppDecRTTC-43
97UppDecRTTC-85
97UppDecVC-27
97UppDecVC-77
97Viper-33
97ViperBlaR-33
98UppDecRTTC5A-AN31
Hillman, Mike
94Max-290
95Max-143
95MaxAut-143
95MaxPreS-152
Hinchliff, Ed
92EriMaxTA-58
Hinds, Richard
91LanARCHS-42
Hines, Bryon
93FinLinN-108
Hipps, Mike
92TraTeaS-122
Hirschman, Mike
91WinChoNED-3
Hirschman, Tony
91WinChoM-84
91WinChoM-85
91WinChoNED-2
92WinChoB-15
92WinChoB-16
92WinChoB-17
97PrePas-118
97PrePasL-118
97PrePasOS-118
97PrePasT-118
Hirst, Rick
91WorOut-57
Hitt, Tim
92STAMod-27
94STAMod-32
Hixson, Rick
94JAG-24
Hmiel, Gordy
89CheFlaI-66
89CheFlaI-67
90CheFlaI-26
Hmiel, Steve
90Max-46
91Max-77
91ProSet-24
91Tra-115
92MaxBla-146
92MaxMot-28
92MaxRed-146
92ProSet-90
92Tra-115
93FinLin-153
93FinLinCS-27
93FinLinS-153
93Max-147
93Max-271
93MaxPreP-132
93MaxPreS-147
93MaxPreS-271
93Tra-51
93TraFirR-51
94ActPac-64
94FinLin-66
94FinLinGT-TG2
94FinLinS-66
94HigGea-46
94HigGeaG-46
94Max-128
94Max-200
94MaxPreP-53
94MaxPreP-121
94MaxPreS-128
94MaxPreS-235
94MaxPreS-259
94PrePas-97
94PrePas-120
94Tra-54
94TraFirR-54
94VIP-94
95ActPacC-58
95ActPacCSS-58
95FinLin-66
95FinLinPP-66
95FinLinSil-66
95HigGea-45
95HigGeaDO-45
95HigGeaDOG-45
95HigGeaG-45
95Ima-45
95ImaGol-45
95Max-101
95MaxAut-101
95MaxCroC-105
95MaxPreP-105
95MaxPreS-124
95PrePas-93
95PrePasRH-93
95Sel-94
95SelFlaO-94
95SP-137
95SPDieC-137
95Tra5thA-66
95Tra5thAG-66
95TraAutV-14
95TraBehTS-BTS1
95TraBehTS-P1
96AutRac-31
96AutRacA-20
96AutRacCA-20

92VolRacLS2-30
Hulman, Mary Fendrich
91LegInd-15
Hulman, Tony
91LegInd-27
91LegInd-32
91LegInd-65
92MaxIMH-19
Hulme, Denis
77Spo-2913
77Spo-4819
Humlhanz, Greg
92K&WDirT-37
94K&WDirT-35
95K&WDirT-36
Humphrey, Al
91LanStoCC-8
Huneycutt, Rick
92TraTeaS-168
Hunt, J.W.
90WorOut-NNO
Hunt, James
77Spo-521
78GraPri-12
78GraPri-71
78GraPri-90
78GraPri-93
78GraPri-135
78GraPri-153
Huntley, Kevin
93WorOutMW-10
94WorOut-34
Hurd, Sam
92JAG-50
Hurlbert, Kregg
91LanART-12
Hurlbert, Mike
92JAG-176
Hurt, Barry
91DirTra-32
Hurtubise, Jim
91AllWorl-68
92LegInd-71
Huskey, Sonny
93JAG-22
Huskins, Jerry
92BikRacS-9
Hussey, Chris
94HigGea-134
94HigGeaDO-134
94HigGeaDOG-134
94HigGeaG-134
94Max-289
95Max-124
95Max-193
95MaxAut-124
95MaxPreS-141
96MaxPre-154
Hutch, Dick
89TGRacMR-85
Hutchens, Dave
92ProSetN-148
93FinLinN-89
Hutcherson, Dick
89TGRacMR-84
89TGRacMR-90
89WinCir-6
91ProSetL-L5
91TGRacMRU-84
91TGRacMRU-85
91TGRacMRU-90
91TGRacTL-25
91TraPacYH-11
92ProSetL-L4A
92ProSetL-L4B
Hutio, David
95MaxTop52-TOP4
Hutter, Matt
95JSKIce-9
Hyde, Charlie
92RSSMotH-24
Hyde, Harry
89Max-14
90Max-141
91Max-38
91MaxMot-26
91ProSet-28
91SpoLegHH-P1
91SpoLegHH-HH1
91SpoLegHH-HH3
91SpoLegHH-HH5
91SpoLegHH-HH6
91SpoLegHH-HH8
91SpoLegHH-HH9
91SpoLegHH-HH10
91SpoLegHH-HH11
91SpoLegHH-HH12
91SpoLegHH-HH14
91SpoLegHH-HH16
91SpoLegHH-HH18
91SpoLegHH-HH19
91SpoLegHH-HH20
91SpoLegHH-HH21
91SpoLegHH-HH22
91SpoLegHH-HH23
91SpoLegHH-HH25
91SpoLegHH-HH26
91SpoLegHH-HH27
91SpoLegHH-HH28
91SpoLegHH-HH29
91SpoLegHH-HH30
92MaxBla-179
92MaxRed-179
93Max-183
93MaxPreP-163
93MaxPreS-183
94Max-156
94MaxPreS-156
94Pow-50
94PowGol-50
97ActPac-66
97ActPacFI-66
Hylton, Butch
98PrePas-79
98PrePasOS-79
Hylton, James
72STP-5
89TGRacMR-161
89TGRacMR-163
91Max-48
91TGRacMRU-161
91TGRacMRU-162
91TGRacMRU-163
92LanARCF-95
92MaxBla-48
92MaxRed-48
92ProSet-216
93Max-48
93MaxPreS-48
93WheRooT-9
93WheRooTPla-9
94LanARCF-52
94Max-46
94MaxPreS-46
94MaxRooY-1
Iaconio, Frank
89MegDra-57
89MegDra-58
91ProSetN-114
92ProSetN-84
92ProSetN-141
93FinLinN-90
Iannotti, Ron
90CheFlal-21
Ice, Tim
95JSKIce-65
95JSKIcePC-65
Icenhower, Ricky
93Max-223
93MaxPreS-223
Ickx, Jackie
73NabSugDSC-4
77Spo-603
92HiTecMA-30
Idom, Ricky
92JAG-177
Ieppert, John
89CheFlal-71
Ifft, David
91ProSet-113
91Tra-119
92MaxBla-174
92MaxRed-174
92ProSet-122
Ikard, Chris
91WorOut-78
Ingalls, Doug
92DirTra-70
92JAG-51
Ingalls, Ricky
92JAG-178
Ingersoll, Buddy
91ProSetN-47
91ProSetN-95
92ProSetN-95
Ingle, Bill
90Max-137A
90Max-137B
91Max-56
91ProSet-59
92MaxBla-162
92MaxRed-162
92ProSet-129
92TraTeaS-83
94FinLinGT-TG3
94HigGea-138
94HigGeaDO-138
94HigGeaDOG-138
94HigGeaG-138
94Max-286
94TidRicR-4
95CroJew-38
95CroJewD-38
95CroJewE-38
95CroJewS-38
95FinLin-99
95FinLinPP-99
95FinLinSil-99
95Max-106
95MaxAut-106
95MaxCroC-116
95MaxPreP-116
95MaxPreS-135
95PrePas-95
95PrePasRH-95
95Sel-106
95SelFlaO-106
95SP-144
95SPDieC-144
96CroJewEDT-40
96CroJewEDTC-40
96CroJewEE-40
96CroJewEli-40
96CroJewES-40
96CroJewETC-40
96CroJewETCE-40
96CroJewETCS-40
96FinLin-93
96FinLinPriP-93
96FinLinS-93
96Max-81
96MaxPre-130
96Ult-40
98PrePasS-30
98PrePasSF-30
Ingram, Bart
91BulRin-136
Ingram, Bill
91DirTra-46
91HavAT-3
91HavAT-21
92DirTra-18
92JAG-52
93JAG-23
95HavAT-40
Ingram, Frank
93JAG-24
95HavAT-33
Ingram, Jack
89Max-201
90Max-152
91HicMotS-5
91Max-138
92MaxBla-54
92MaxRed-54
92ProSet-191
92RedSta-12
98PrePas-148
Inman, Dale
89Max-76
90Max-64
91Max-162
91ProSet-66
91Tra-44
92MaxAllPT-NNO
92MaxBla-145
92MaxRed-145
92ProSet-132
92Tra-47
92TraTeaS-181
93FinLin-86
93FinLinCS-12
93FinLinS-86
93Max-182
93MaxPreP-162
93MaxPreS-182
93Tra-50
93TraFirR-50
94FinLin-95
94FinLinS-95
94Max-160
94MaxPreP-149
94MaxPreS-160
94Pow-48
94PowGol-48
95MaxPreS-157
96MaxPre-147
Inmon, Jerry
91DirTra-38
91JAG-37
92DirTra-3
92JAG-179
Innes, Jamie Lynn
95ActPacNJDC-4
Irvan, Ernie
88MaxCha-95
89Max-2
90Max-2
90MaxHolF-HF23
91ACRac-4
91Max-4
91Max-140
91Max-190
91MaxMcD-9
91MaxUpd-4
91ProSet-9
91ProSet-13
91ProSet-14
91SupRacM-5
91Tra-4
91Tra-10
91Tra-P1
92-CarDynBTBS-5
92ACDel-5
92ACRacP-2
92CarDynEl-1
92CarDynEl-2
92CarDynEl-3
92CarDynEl-4
92CarDynEl-5
92CarDynGO-7
92DaySer1-4
92MacTooWC-12
92MaxBla-4
92MaxBla-264
92MaxBla-282
92MaxMcD-13
92MaxRed-4
92MaxRed-264
92MaxRed-282
92MaxTheW-8
92MaxTheW-28
92ProSet-20
92ProSet-60
92ProSet-95
92ProSet-108
92ProSet-202
92ProSetMH-12
92ProSetRF-4
92Tra-4
92Tra-104
92TraAut-A4
92TraGoo-20
92TraKodEl-1A
92TraKodEl-1B
92TraKodEl-6A
92TraKodEl-6B
92TraKodEl-11A
92TraKodEl-11B
92TraKodEl-13
92TraKodEl-16A
92TraKodEl-16B
92TraKodEl-20
92TraKodEl-21A
92TraKodEl-21B
92TraKodEl-23
92TraKodEl-25
92TraRacM-4
92TraRacM-10
92TraRacM-69
92TraRacM-95
92TraRacM-98
92TraTeaS-101
92TraTeaS-102
92TraTeaS-108
92TraTeaS-109
92TraTeaS-119
92TraTeaS-121
92TraTeaS-124
92TraTeaS-125
93ACRacF-4
93ActPac-8
93ActPac-25
93ActPac-33
93ActPac-34
93ActPac-128
93ActPac-129
93ActPac-182
93ActPac-199
93ActPac-201
93ActPac2G-64G
93CarDynDEP-5
93CarDynNSC-1
93FinLin-40
93FinLin-68
93FinLin-124
93FinLinCS-2
93FinLinCS-24
93FinLinS-40
93FinLinS-68
93FinLinS-124
93HiTecTT-5
93Max-4
93Max-244
93Max-276
93Max-279
93Max-281
93MaxHou-9
93MaxPreP-4
93MaxPreP-67
93MaxPreP-191
93MaxPreP-194
93MaxPreP-196
93MaxPreS-4
93MaxPreS-244
93MaxPreS-276
93MaxPreS-279
93MaxPreS-281
93MaxTheW-3
93MaxTheW-23
93MaxTheW-41
93Pep400VL-4
93Tra-4
93TraFirR-4
93TraKodEl-1
93TraKodEl-3
93TraKodEl-4
93TraKodEl-5
93TraKodEl-6
93TraPreC-14
94ActPac-6
94ActPac-34
94ActPac-46
94ActPac-58
94ActPac-81
94ActPac-105
94ActPac-135
94ActPac-148
94ActPac-181
94ActPac-182
94ActPac-188
94ActPac-194
94ActPac-195
94ActPac-196
94ActPac-197
94ActPac-198
94ActPac2G-4G
94ActPac2G-16G
94ActPac2G-35G
94ActPac2G-181G
94ActPac2G-182G
94ActPac2G-188G
94ActPacC-6
94CarDynGO-3
94CarDynMM-1
94ErnIrvFC-1
94ErnIrvFC-2
94ErnIrvFC-3
94ErnIrvFC-4
94ErnIrvFC-5
94FinLin-10
94FinLin-31
94FinLin-52
94FinLin-112
94FinLin-9
94FinLinDH-2
94FinLinG-8
94FinLinG-43
94FinLinG-46
94FinLinG-80
94FinLinG-93
94FinLinG-NNO
94FinLinGA-80
94FinLinGCC-NNO
94FinLinGS-NNO
94FinLinGT-TG7
94FinLinS-10
94FinLinS-31
94FinLinS-52
94FinLinS-112

94FinLinVL-VL3
94FinLinVL-VL18
94HigGea-5
94HigGea-83
94HigGea-95
94HigGea-128
94HigGea-168
94HigGea-195
94HigGea-197
94HigGeaD-D4
94HigGeaDO-128
94HigGeaDO-168
94HigGeaDO-195
94HigGeaDO-197
94HigGeaDOG-128
94HigGeaDOG-168
94HigGeaDOG-195
94HigGeaDOG-197
94HigGeaG-5
94HigGeaG-83
94HigGeaG-95
94HigGeaG-128
94HigGeaG-168
94HigGeaG-195
94HigGeaG-197
94HigGeaMG-MG2
94HigMinV-4B
94HigMinV-4S
94Max-29
94Max-48
94Max-215
94Max-232
94Max-234
94Max-250
94Max-251
94Max-334
94Max-336
94MaxMed-16
94MaxMed-52
94MaxMed-61
94MaxMed-67
94MaxMot-1
94MaxPreP-29
94MaxPreP-48
94MaxPreP-174
94MaxPreP-191
94MaxPreP-193
94MaxPreS-29
94MaxPreS-48
94MaxPreS-274
94MaxPreS-291
94MaxPreS-293
94MaxPreSJ-2
94MaxRacC-2
94MaxTexEI-1
94MaxTexEI-4
94MaxTexEI-5
94MaxTexEI-6
94MaxTexEI-7
94MaxTexEI-9
94MaxTexEI-10
94MaxTexEI-11
94MaxTexEI-12
94MaxTexEI-14
94MaxTexEI-15
94MaxTexEI-16
94MaxTexEI-17
94MaxTexEI-18
94MaxTexEI-19
94MaxTexEI-20
94MaxTexEI-21
94MaxTexEI-22
94MaxTexEI-23
94MaxTexEI-24
94MaxTheS2-6
94OptXL-8
94OptXL-25
94OptXL-32
94OptXL-42
94OptXL-52
94OptXL-CC2
94OptXLDouC-DC2
94OptXLRH-8
94OptXLRH-25
94OptXLRH-32
94OptXLRH-42
94OptXLRH-52
94Pow-3
94Pow-18
94Pow-61
94Pow-95
94Pow-148
94Pow-P3
94PowGol-3
94PowGol-18
94PowGol-61
94PowGol-95
94PowGol-148
94PowPro-P3
94PrePas-11
94PrePas-53
94PrePasA-NNO
94PrePasCC-CC11
94PrePasCF-CF2
94PrePasH-H3
94PrePasRD-RD3
94Sky-3
94Tra-28
94Tra-45
94Tra-66
94Tra-91
94Tra-94
94Tra-101
94Tra-135
94Tra-150
94Tra-160
94Tra-163
94Tra-198
94Tra-P1
94TraAut-A6
94TraAutV-43
94TraFirR-28
94TraFirR-45
94TraFirR-66
94TraFirR-91
94TraFirR-94
94TraFirR-101
94TraFirR-135
94TraFirR-150
94TraFirR-160
94TraFirR-163
94TraFirR-198
94TraPreC-34
94TraWin-W3
94TraWin-W4
94TraWin-W7
94VIP-16
94VIP-51
94VIP-75
94VIP-P2
94VIPDriC-DC2
94VIPExc2-EC4
94WheHarG-67
94WheHarGG-67
95ActPacP-38
95ActPacP-51
95ActPacP-71
95ActPacP2G-3G
95ActPacS-71
95ActPacS-72
95ActPacS-73
95ActPacS-74
95ActPacS-75
95ActPacS2G-21G
95ActPacSSS-71
95ActPacSSS-72
95ActPacSSS-73
95ActPacSSS-74
95ActPacSSS-75
95Ass-18
95Ass-38
95Ass1M$PC-7
95AssGolS-18
95AssGolS-38
95CroJew-14
95CroJew-69
95CroJewD-14
95CroJewD-69
95CroJewDJ-DJ4
95CroJewDJD-DJ4
95CroJewDJE-DJ4
95CroJewE-14
95CroJewE-69
95CroJewS-14
95CroJewS-69
95CroJewSG-SG4
95FinLin-28
95FinLin-51
95FinLin-92
95FinLinCC6-18
95FinLinCC6-38
95FinLinPP-28
95FinLinPP-51
95FinLinPP-92
95FinLinSil-28
95FinLinSil-51
95FinLinSil-92
95HigGea-18
95HigGea-96
95HigGeaBC-BC5
95HigGeaBCG-BC5
95HigGeaDO-18
95HigGeaDO-96
95HigGeaDOG-18
95HigGeaDOG-96
95HigGeaG-18
95HigGeaG-96
95HiTecB4-16
95HiTecB4-79
95HiTecB4-86
95HiTecB4-P2
95HITecB4P-P2
95Ima-80
95Ima-82
95Ima-93
95ImaGol-80
95ImaGol-82
95ImaGol-93
95Max-28
95Max-34
95Max-38
95Max-46
95Max-68
95Max-163
95MaxCroC-28
95MaxCroC-150
95MaxCroC-151
95MaxCroC-157
95MaxPreP-28
95MaxPreP-150
95MaxPreP-151
95MaxPreP-157
95MaxPreS-18
95MaxPreS-28
95MaxPreS-184
95MaxPreS-265
95MaxPreS-266
95MaxPreS-272
95MaxPreSU-12
95MaxPreSU-13
95MaxPreSU-14
95MaxStaU-4
95OptXLS-XLS5
95PrePas-13
95PrePas-51
95PrePasCC-13
95PrePasCF-CF4
95PrePasPH-19
95PrePasPre-19
95PrePasPRH-19
95PrePasRD-RD5
95PrePasRH-13
95PrePasRH-51
95Sel-15
95Sel-51
95Sel-135
95SelDreM-DM7
95SelFlaO-15
95SelFlaO-51
95SelFlaO-135
95SelSki-SS4
95SP-CB1
95Tra-9
95Tra-59
95Tra-74
95Tra5thA-12
95Tra5thAG-12
95Tra5thAR-R11
95TraAutV-15
95TraFirR-9
95TraFirR-59
95TraFirR-74
95TraSerS-SS11
95UppDec-6
95UppDec-49
95UppDec-74
95UppDec-142
95UppDec-207
95UppDecA-207
95UppDecGSEG-6
95UppDecGSEG-49
95UppDecGSEG-74
95UppDecGSEG-142
95UppDecGSEG-207
95UppDecO-OS5
95UppDecSSES-6
95UppDecSSES-49
95UppDecSSES-74
95UppDecSSES-142
95UppDecSSES-207
95VIP-47
95VIPAut-47
95VIPCooB-47
95VIPEmeP-47
95VIPRedHCB-47
96ActPacC-18
96ActPacC-35
96ActPacCFS-6
96ActPacCSS-18
96ActPacCSS-35
96ActPacM-8
96ActPacM-18
96Ass-5
96Ass-33
96Ass-48
96Ass$1000CCIPC-13
96Ass$100CCIPC-7
96Ass$10PC-5
96Ass$2PC-6
96Ass$2PC-17
96Ass$2PC-25
96Ass$5PC-10
96AssComL-CL1
96AssRacD-RD7
96AutRac-30
96AutRacA-21
96AutRacCA-21
96AutRacFR-19
96AutRacFR-20
96AutRacFR-21
96AutRacFR-22
96AutRacFR-23
96AutRacFR-24
96AutRacFR-25
96AutRacFR-26
96AutRacFR-27
96AutRacFR-28
96AutRacFR-29
96AutRacFR-30
96AutRacFR-31
96AutRacHP-HP19
96AutRacKotC$PC-KC5
96Cla-37
96Cla-56
96ClaPriP-37
96ClaRacC-RC8
96ClaRacC-RC18
96ClaSil-37
96FinLin-13
96FinLin-33
96FinLin-92
96FinLinBGL-C6
96FinLinBGL-D7
96FinLinBGL-JPC3
96FinLinCB-EI1
96FinLinCB-EI2
96FinLinCB-EI3
96FinLinCB-EI4
96FinLinCB-EI5
96FinLinDCPC-4
96FinLinGS-GS13
96FinLinMM-MM6
96FinLinPP-15
96FinLinPP-16
96FinLinPP$100C-3
96FinLinPP$10C-4
96FinLinPP$50C-3
96FinLinPP$5C-11
96FinLinPP$S-15
96FinLinPP$S-16
96FinLinPriP-13
96FinLinPriP-33
96FinLinPriP-92
96FinLinS-13
96FinLinS-33
96FinLinS-92
96FinLinSMPC-2
96Fla-15
96Fla-71
96Fla-93
96FlaAut-5
96FlaHotN-4
96Kni-12
96KniBlaK-12
96KniKniRT-KT10
96KniQueRKP-12
96KniRoy-12
96KniWhiK-12
96M-F-22
96M-F-23
96M-F-44
96M-FBla-B9
96M-FSil-S18
96Max-98
96MaxMadiA-8
96MaxMadiA-28
96MaxMadiABR-BR2
96MaxOdy-28
96MaxOdy-48
96MaxOdyRA-RA2
96MaxPre-47
96MaxPre-88
96Pin-28
96Pin-52
96Pin-88
96Pin-28
96Pin-52
96Pin-88
96PinCheF-13
96PinCutA-4
96PinPolP-12
96PinPolP-41
96PinPolPCS-7
96PinPolPLF-12
96PinPolPLF-41
96PinPolPNL-7
96PinPolPNLG-7
96PinWinCC-28
96PinWinCC-52
96PinWinCC-88
96PrePas-14
96PrePas-51
96PrePas-67
96PrePas-86
96PrePas&NC-14
96PrePasCC-14
96PrePasFoc-F4
96PrePasP-29
96PrePasP-43
96PrePasPBRI-BR7
96PrePasPCB-CB6
96PrePasPEP-29
96PrePasPEP-43
96PrePasPH-29
96PrePasPH-43
96PrePasPHP-HP4
96PrePasSco-14
96PrePasSco-51
96PrePasSco-67
96PrePasSco-86
96PrePasT-14
96PrePasT-51
96PrePasT-67
96PrePasT-86
96RacCho-24
96RacCho-41
96RacChoAP-24
96RacChoAP-41
96RacChoSC-24
96RacChoSC-41
96SP-28
96SP-69
96SP-84
96SpeArtP-28
96SpeArtP-43
96SpeArtP-63
96SpeArtP-64
96SpeArtP-65
96SpeArtP-66
96SpeCleS-10
96SpeRac-28
96SpeRac-43
96SpeRac-63
96SpeRac-64
96SpeRac-65
96SpeRac-66
96SPHolME-ME14
96SPx-22
96SPxEli-E5
96SPxGol-22
96TraRev&PTCG-TC11
96TraRev&PTCG-TC17
96TraRev&PTCH-TC11
96TraRev&PTCH-TC17
96TraRevP-10
96TraRevP-19
96TraRevP-41
96TraRevP-44
96TraRevP-48
96TraRevPFR-10
96TraRevPFR-19
96TraRevPFR-41
96TraRevPFR-44
96TraRevPFR-48
96TraRevPLG-LG2
96TraRevPM-10
96TraRevPM-19
96TraRevPM-41
96TraRevPM-44
96TraRevPTC-TC11

96TraRevPTC-TC17
96Ult-117
96Ult-118
96Ult-119
96Ult-156
96UltAut-12
96UltGolM-1
96UltUpd-15
96UltUpd-61
96UltUpd-91
96UltUpd-P1
96UltUpdA-5
96UppDec-25
96UppDec-58
96UppDec-59
96UppDec-60
96UppDec-105
96UppDec-137
96UppDecPP-RP4
96UppDecRTTC-RC27
96UppDecRTTC-RC88
96UppDecRTTC-RC136
96UppDecRTTCAS-H27
96UppDecRTTCGF-GF3
96UppDecRTTCJ-WC3
96UppDecRTTCLP-LP3
96UppDecRTTCPT3-T3
96UppDecRTTCRL-RL14
96UppDecRTTCT3PR-R3
96V.IAut-12
96VIP-12
96VIP-43
96VIPEmeP-12
96VIPEmeP-43
96VIPHeaG-HG4
96VIPHeaGD-HG4
96VIPTor-12
96VIPTor-43
96VIPWarP-WP13
96VIPWarPG-WP13
96Zen-8
96Zen-42
96Zen-64
96Zen-87
96ZenArtP-8
96ZenArtP-42
96ZenArtP-64
96ZenArtP-87
96ZenHig-14
97ActPac-9
97ActPac-30
97ActPac-77
97ActPac-80
97ActPac2G-4
97ActPacFI-9
97ActPacFI-30
97ActPacFI-77
97ActPacFI-80
97ActPacRT-4
97ActPreM-8
97AutRac-19
97AutRac-31
97AutRac-42
97AutRacA-24
97AutRacMS-KM19
97ColCho-28
97ColCho-78
97ColCho-110
97ColChoC-CC31
97ColChoC-CC64
97ColChoS-S25
97ColChoSQ-SQ31
97ColChoTF-A2
97ColChoTF-I2
97ColChoUD5-UD58
97ColChoUD5-UD59
97ColChoVC-VC10
97FinLinPP2-6
97FinLinPP2$10-82
97FinLinPP2$100-100
97FinLinPP2$5-44
97FinLinPP2$50-92
97Max-28
97Max-73
97Max-102
97Max-120
97Pin-28
97Pin-57
97Pin-65
97Pin-80
97PinArtP-28
97PinArtP-57
97PinArtP-65
97PinArtP-80
97PinCer-19
97PinCer-53
97PinCer-87
97PinCerE-E10
97PinCerEE-E10
97PinCerEP-E10
97PinCerMB-19
97PinCerMB-53
97PinCerMB-87
97PinCerMG-19
97PinCerMG-53
97PinCerMG-87
97PinCerMR-19
97PinCerMR-53
97PinCerMR-87
97PinCerR-19
97PinCerR-53
97PinCerR-87
97PinMin-10
97PinMin-28
97PinMin2GC-10
97PinMin2GC-28
97PinMinB-10
97PinMinB-28
97PinMinC-10
97PinMinC-28
97PinMinG-10
97PinMinG-28
97PinMinNC-10
97PinMinNC-28
97PinMinS-10
97PinMinS-28
97PinPor-15
97PinPor-35
97PinPor-47
97PinPreP-28
97PinPreP-57
97PinPreP-65
97PinPreP-80
97PinPreP-S9-C
97PinSpe-9-C
97PinTotCPB-19
97PinTotCPB-53
97PinTotCPB-87
97PinTotCPG-19
97PinTotCPG-53
97PinTotCPG-87
97PinTotCPR-19
97PinTotCPR-53
97PinTotCPR-87
97PinTroC-28
97PinTroC-57
97PinTroC-65
97PinTroC-80
97PrePas-10
97PrePas-40
97PrePas-58
97PrePas-101
97PrePasBB-BB10
97PrePasBR-BR6
97PrePasCC'-CC9
97PrePasCleC-C3
97PrePasL-10
97PrePasL-40
97PrePasL-58
97PrePasL-101
97PrePasOS-10
97PrePasOS-40
97PrePasOS-58
97PrePasOS-101
97PrePasP-10
97PrePasP-39
97PrePasPCB-CB5
97PrePasPCBD-CB5
97PrePasPEP-10
97PrePasPEP-39
97PrePasPLL-LL4
97PrePasPM-10
97PrePasPM-39
97PrePasPOS-10
97PrePasPOS-39
97PrePasT-10
97PrePasT-40
97PrePasT-58
97PrePasT-101
97PrePasVL-VL3A
97PrePasVL-VL3B
97RacCho-28
97RacCho-63
97RacCho-103
97RacChoBC-7
97RacChoHO-9
97RacChoHOGitD-9
97RacChoSS-28
97RacChoSS-63
97RacChoSS-103
97SBMot-10
97SBMot-53
97SBMot-66
97SBMot-97
97SBMotRC-RC3
97SBMotWR-WC16
97SBMotWR-WC24
97ScoBoaI-19
97ScoBoaI-46
97ScoBoaI$PC-PC10
97ScoBoaIR-SB4
97ScoBoaRSBF-SB4
97SkyPro-13
97SkyPro-71
97SkyProA-13
97SkyProT-T7
97SP-28
97SP-70
97SP-105
97SP-124
97SP SupS-28
97SP SupS-70
97SP SupS-105
97SP SupS-124
97SPX-9
97SPxBlu-9
97SPxGol-9
97SPxSil-9
97SPXSpeA-SV8
97SPXTagT-TT2
97SPxTagTA-TA2
97Ult-15
97Ult-54
97UltAKA-A8
97UltEliS-E4
97UltIns-DC8
97UltUpd-8
97UltUpd-88
97UltUpdAR-8
97UppDecRTTC-10
97UppDecRTTC-52
97UppDecRTTC-94
97UppDecRTTC-127
97UppDecRTTCCQ-CQ6
97UDRTTCCQC-CQ6
97UppDecRTTCGF-RD8
97UppDecRTTCPP-PP9
97UppDecRTTCPP-PP16
97UppDecRTTCPP-PP30
97UppDecRTTCPPlu-+6
97UDRTTCPPRC-+6
97UppDRTTCPPRDC-+6
97UppDecRTTCQW-CQ6
97UppDecVC-28
97UppDecVC-78
97UppDecVCCR-CR10
97UppDecVCDS-DS9
97UppDecVCP-PE8
97UppDecVCPC-PH8
97UppDecVCVL-VL5
97VIP-11
97VIPExp-11
97VIPHeaGD-HG4
97VIPHigG-HG4
97VIPOilS-11
97VIPRinoH-RH9
97VIPRinoHDC-RH9
98ColCho-28
98ColCho-64
98HigGea-14
98HigGea-59
98HigGeaA-10
98HigGeaFG-27
98HigGeaFG-59
98HigGeaM-27
98HigGeaM-59
98Max-8
98Max-38
98Max-69
98Max-103
98Max-8
98Max-33
98Max-58
98Max-83
98Max10tA-32
98Max10tA-77
98Max10tABA-25
98Max10tAMP-P8
98MaxBatP-B10
98MaxFieG-11
98MaxFieGTS-11
98MaxFieGTSA-11
98MaxFirC-F13
98MaxFocOAC-FC14
98MaxFouSGA-11
98MaxMakOACC-FC14
98MaxSwaP-SW3
98MaxYealRBS-8
98MaxYealRBS-15
98MaxYealRBS-49
98MaxYealRBS-66
98MaxYealRBS-92
98MaxYealRBS-123
98MaxYealRBS-142
98MayAutS-08
98PinMin-30
98PinMinB-30
98PinMinBC-06
98PinMinBPPC-06
98PinMinGMT-30
98PinMinGPC-30
98PinMinGPPC-30
98PinMinNC-30
98PinMinSGC-30
98PinMinSMT-30
98PinMinSPPC-30
98PinMinSSC-30
98PrePas-10
98PrePas-55
98PrePas-150
98PrePasCC'-CC9
98PrePasOS-10
98PrePasOS-55
98PrePasP-41
98PrePasP-41
98PrePasPFC-FC10
98PrePasPFCR-FC10
98PrePasS-9
98PrePasSO-15
98PrePasSO-16
98PrePasSOD-15
98PrePasSOD-16
98SP Aut-31
98SP Aut-65
98SP Aut-77
98SP AutBtW-BW13
98SP AutBtWL2-BW13
98SP AutBtWL3-BW13
98SP AutSotTL2-ST2
98UppDecDV-9
98UppDecDVSM-9
98UppDecRttC-36
98UppDecRttC-87
98UppDecRTTC5A-AN34
98UDRTTCCQT1-CQ10
98UDRTTCCQT2-CQ10
98UDRTTCCQT3-CQ10
98UDRTTCCQT4-CQ10
98UppDRTTCCQVL-CQ10
98UppDecRTTCCS-CS1
98UppDecRTTCCS-CS11
98UppDecVC-28
98UppDecVC-73
98UppDecVC-113
98UppDecVC-125
98UppDecVC-150
98UppDecVC3DoS-D14
98UppDecVC3DoSG-D14
98UppDecVCPL-PL14
98UppDecVCPotE-PE4
98UppDecVCPP-1
98UppDecVCPPCR-1
98UppDecVCSoB-SB4
98VIP-10
98VIPExp-10
98Whe-14
98Whe-86
98WheGol-14
98WheGol-86
99Pre-12
99Pre-82
99Pre-96
99PrePas-12
99PrePas-82
99PrePas-96
99PrePas-112
99PrePasCC-14B
99PrePasCC-8
99PrePasPS-15
99PrePasS-14A
99UppDecVC-18
99UppDecVC-51
99UppDecVCIS-IS13
99UppDecVCNSS-EI
99UppDecVCSZ-SZ4
99UppDecVCTM-TM3
99UppDecVCUE-18
99UppDecVCUE-51
99WheHigG-12
99WheHigG-71
99WheHigGAC-12
99WheHigGFG-12
99WheHigGFG-71
99WheHigGM-12
99WheHigGM-71
99WheHigGS-GS12

Irvan, Jordan
94ActPac-105
94ActPac-194
95FinLin-51
95FinLinPP-51
95FinLinSil-51

Irvan, Kim
94ActPac-105
94ActPac-194
96ActPacC-87

Irvine, Eddie
92GriForO-170

Irwin, Kenny
97VIP-41
97VIPExp-41
97VIPOilS-41
98HigGea-60
98HigGeaFG-60
98HigGeaM-60
98Max-28
98Max-58
98Max-76
98Max-105
98Max-25
98Max-50
98Max-75
98Max-100
98Max10tA-28
98Max10tA-73
98Max10tAMP-P25
98MaxFieG-8
98MaxFieGTS-8
98MaxFieGTSA-8
98MaxFocOAC-FC15
98MaxFouSGA-8
98MaxMakOACC-FC15
98MaxSwaP-SW24
98MaxTea-TW10
98MaxYealRBS-120
98PrePas-56
98PrePasOS-56
98PrePasP-23
98PrePasP-54
98PrePasP-23
98PrePasP-54
98PrePasPFC-FC16
98PrePasPFCR-FC16
98PrePasPS-PS13
98PrePasPSH-SH8
98PrePasS-26
98PrePasS-13
98PrePasS-14
98PrePasS-46
98PrePasSA-3
98PrePasSF-13
98PrePasSF-14
98PrePasSF-46
98PrePasSS-7
98PrePasSSD-7
98SP Aut-28
98SP Aut-62
98SP AutBtW-BW19
98SP AutBtWL2-BW19
98SP AutBtWL3-BW19
98SP AutSotTL1-S9
98UppDecRttC-28
98UppDecRttC-56
98UppDecRttC-76
98UDRTTCCQT1-CQ3
98UDRTTCCQT2-CQ3
98UDRTTCCQT3-CQ3
98UDRTTCCQT4-CQ3
98UppDRTTCCQVL-CQ3
98UppDecVC-45
98UppDecVC-90
98UppDecVC-108
98VIP-11
98VIPDriF-DF9
98VIPDriFD-DF9
98VIPExp-11
98Whe-15
98Whe-37
98Whe50tA-A6
98Whe50tA-A21

95PrePasPre-14
95PrePasPRH-14
95PrePasRD-RD6
95PrePasRH-14
95PrePasRH-42
95Sel-16
95Sel-42
95Sel-115
95SelFlaO-16
95SelFlaO-42
95SelFlaO-115
95SP-21
95SP-60
95SP-101
95SPDieC-21
95SPDieC-60
95SPDieC-101
95SPSpeM-SM28
95SPSpeMDC-SM28
95Tra-18
95Tra-43
95Tra-60
95Tra5thA-20
95Tra5thA-41
95Tra5thA-54
95Tra5thAG-20
95Tra5thAG-41
95Tra5thAG-54
95Tra5thAR-R7
95TraAutV-24
95TraCha-C7
95TraFirR-18
95TraFirR-43
95TraFirR-60
95TraRacM-RM12
95TraSerS-SS20
95UppDec-7
95UppDec-50
95UppDec-75
95UppDec-143
95UppDec-165
95UppDec-206
95UppDec-250
95UppDec-285
95UppDecA-206
95UppDecGSEG-7
95UppDecGSEG-50
95UppDecGSEG-75
95UppDecGSEG-143
95UppDecGSEG-165
95UppDecGSEG-206
95UppDecGSEG-250
95UppDecGSEG-285
95UppDecPRW-P7
95UppDecPSP-PP7
95UppDecSSES-7
95UppDecSSES-50
95UppDecSSES-75
95UppDecSSES-143
95UppDecSSES-165
95UppDecSSES-206
95UppDecSSES-250
95UppDecSSES-285
95VIP-14
95VIPCooB-14
95VIPEmeP-14
95VIPPro-1
95VIPRedHCB-14
95Zen-27
95Zen-53
95ZenWinW-17
96ActPacC-16
96ActPacC-19
96ActPacC-32
96ActPacCFS-8
96ActPacCO-3
96ActPacCSS-16
96ActPacCSS-19
96ActPacCSS-32
96ActPacM-10
96ActPacM-20
96Ass-9
96Ass-42
96Ass$1000CCIPC-6
96Ass$100CCIPC-4
96Ass$2PC-5
96Ass$2PC-22
96AssComL-CL12
96AssRacD-RD8
96AutRac-15
96AutRacA-22
96AutRacCA-22
96AutRacFR-32
96AutRacFR-33
96AutRacFR-34
96AutRacFR-35
96AutRacFR-36
96AutRacFR-37
96AutRacFR-38
96AutRacFR-39
96AutRacHP-HP13
96AutRacKotC$PC-KC1
96Cla-33
96Cla-49
96Cla-57
96ClaMarMC-MC4
96ClaPriP-33
96ClaPriP-49
96ClaSil-33
96ClaSil-49
96CroJewEADJ-DJ2
96CroJewEDT-9
96CroJewEDT-26
96CroJewEDT-52
96CroJewEDT-62
96CroJewEDTC-9
96CroJewEDTC-26
96CroJewEDTC-52
96CroJewEDTC-62
96CroJewEDTCSA-CS9
96CroJewEDTDJA-DJ2
96CroJewEDTDJG-DJ2
96CroJewEE-9
96CroJewEE-26
96CroJewEE-52
96CroJewEE-62
96CroJewEGDJ-DJ2
96CroJewEli-9
96CroJewEli-26
96CroJewEli-52
96CroJewEli-62
96CroJewERCSG-CS9
96CroJewERCSP-CS9
96CroJewES-9
96CroJewES-26
96CroJewES-52
96CroJewES-62
96CroJewESDJ-DJ2
96CroJewETC-9
96CroJewETC-26
96CroJewETC-52
96CroJewETC-62
96CroJewETCDJA-DJ2
96CroJewETCDJS-DJ2
96CroJewETCE-9
96CroJewETCE-26
96CroJewETCE-52
96CroJewETCE-62
96CroJewETCGDJ-DJ2
96CroJewETCS-9
96CroJewETCS-26
96CroJewETCS-52
96CroJewETCS-62
96FinLin-43
96FinLin-90
96FinLin-100
96FinLinBGL-C11
96FinLinBGL-D14
96FinLinDCPC-3
96FinLinGS-GS14
96FinLinPP-17
96FinLinPP$5C-12
96FinLinPP$S-17
96FinLinPriP-43
96FinLinPriP-90
96FinLinPriP-100
96FinLinS-43
96FinLinS-90
96FinLinS-100
96Fla-16
96Fla-72
96Fla-93
96Fla-94
96FlaAut-6
96FlaHotN-5
96FlaPowP-5
96Kni-15
96Kni-32
96KniBlaK-15
96KniBlaK-32
96KniFirK-FK2
96KniQueRKP-15
96KniQueRKP-32
96KniRoy-15
96KniRoy-32
96KniWhiK-15
96KniWhiK-32
96M-F-33
96M-F-34
96M-FBla-B10
96Max-28
96Max-48
96Max-98
96MaxBanDJ-1
96MaxBanDJ-2
96MaxBanDJ-3
96MaxBanDJ-4
96MaxMadiA-40
96MaxMadiA-88
96MaxMadiA-96
96MaxMadiA-97
96MaxOdy-40
96MaxOdy-88
96MaxOdy-96
96MaxOdy-97
96MaxPre-28
96MaxPre-89
96MetImpWCTF-3
96Pin-13
96Pin-64
96Pin-13
96Pin-64
96PinCheF-8
96PinCutA-7
96PinPolP-13
96PinPolP-44
96PinPolP-67
96PinPolPCS-8
96PinPolPLF-13
96PinPolPLF-44
96PinPolPLF-67
96PinPolPNL-9
96PinPolPNLG-9
96PinTeaP-4
96PinTeaP-12
96PinWinCC-13
96PinWinCC-64
96PrePas-15
96PrePas-50
96PrePas-79
96PrePas-87
96PrePas-115
96PrePas&NC-15
96PrePas&NC-50
96PrePasCC-15
96PrePasFQS-FQS4A
96PrePasFQS-FQS4B
96PrePasP-13
96PrePasP-41
96PrePasP$10PC-4
96PrePasP$20PC-4
96PrePasP$5PC-4
96PrePasPBRI-BR3
96PrePasPCB-CB7
96PrePasPEP-13
96PrePasPEP-41
96PrePasPH-13
96PrePasPH-41
96PrePasSco-15
96PrePasSco-50
96PrePasSco-79
96PrePasSco-87
96PrePasSco-115
96PrePasT-15
96PrePasT-50
96PrePasT-79
96PrePasT-87
96PrePasT-115
96RacCho-16
96RacCho-32
96RacCho-91
96RacChoAP-16
96RacChoAP-32
96RacChoAP-91
96RacChoSC-16
96RacChoSC-32
96RacChoSC-91
96SP-36
96SP-54
96SP-76
96SpeArtP-10
96SpeArtP-24
96SpeArtP-47
96SpeCleS-7
96SpePro-7
96SpeRac-10
96SpeRac-24
96SpeRac-47
96SpeRac-P1
96SPHolME-ME22
96SPx-23
96SPxEli-E2
96SPxGol-23
96TraRev&PTCG-TC6
96TraRev&PTCG-TC20
96TraRev&PTCH-TC6
96TraRev&PTCH-TC20
96TraRevP-6
96TraRevP-22
96TraRevP-39
96TraRevP-47
96TraRevPFR-6
96TraRevPFR-22
96TraRevPFR-39
96TraRevPFR-47
96TraRevPLG-LG1
96TraRevPM-6
96TraRevPM-22
96TraRevPM-39
96TraRevPTC-TC6
96TraRevPTC-TC20
96Ult-47
96Ult-48
96Ult-49
96Ult-183
96UltAut-13
96UltBoxS-13
96UltUpd-16
96UltUpd-44
96UltUpd-62
96UltUpd-86
96UltUpdA-6
96UltUpdPP-6
96UltUpdW-13
96UppDec-26
96UppDec-66
96UppDec-106
96UppDecPW-HP9
96UppDecRTTC-RC12
96UppDecRTTC-RC61
96UppDecRTTC-RC97
96UppDecRTTCAS-H12
96UppDecRTTCGF-GF4
96UppDecRTTCJ-WC4
96UppDecRTTCLP-LP4
96UppDecRTTCPPoi-PP8
96UppDRTTCPPR-PR8
96UppDecRTTCPT3-T2
96UppDecRTTCRL-RL15
96UppDecRTTCT3PR-R9
96UppDecVVG-VV7
96VIP-13
96VIP-41
96VIPEmeP-13
96VIPEmeP-41
96Viper-11
96Viper-58
96ViperBlaM-11
96ViperBlaM-58
96ViperBusC-B7
96ViperCob-C10
96ViperCop-11
96ViperCop-58
96ViperGreM-11
96ViperGreM-58
96ViperKinC-KC3
96VIPTor-13
96VIPTor-41
96VIPWarP-WP17
96VIPWarPG-WP17
96Zen-10
96Zen-43
96Zen-60
96Zen-89
96Zen-97
96ZenArtP-10
96ZenArtP-43
96ZenArtP-60
96ZenArtP-89
96ZenArtP-97
97Act-4
97Act-11
97ActPac-13
97ActPac-34
97ActPac-54
97ActPac-63
97ActPac-72
97ActPac-78
97ActPac2G-8
97ActPacFA-10
97ActPacFI-13
97ActPacFI-34
97ActPacFI-54
97ActPacFI-63
97ActPacFI-72
97ActPacFI-78
97ActPacRT-10
97ActPreM-7
97AutRac-6
97AutRac-34
97AutRac-42
97AutRac-47
97AutRacA-25
97AutRacMS-KM6
97ColCho-36
97ColCho-86
97ColCho-109
97ColChoC-CC16
97ColChoC-CC49
97ColChoC-CC82
97ColChoS-S37
97ColChoS-S38
97ColChoSQ-SQ39
97ColChoSQ-SQ43
97ColChoTF-A1
97ColChoTF-A3
97ColChoTF-E2
97ColChoTF-I3
97ColChoUD5-UD75
97ColChoUD5-UD76
97FinLinPP2-12
97FinLinPP2$10-85
97FinLinPP2$5-50
97JurPar-2
97JurPar-37
97JurParC-C3
97JurParP-P9
97JurParR-R9
97JurParT-2
97JurParT-37
97JurParTL-TL2
97JurParTR-TR3
97Max-12
97Max-57
97Max-117
97MaxChaTC-C4
97MaxChatCG-C4
97Pin-27
97Pin-56
97Pin-60
97Pin-74
97Pin-89
97PinArtP-27
97PinArtP-56
97PinArtP-60
97PinArtP-74
97PinArtP-89
97PinCer-15
97PinCer-49
97PinCer-92
97PinCerCGT-9
97PinCerCT-9
97PinCerE-E9
97PinCerEE-E9
97PinCerEP-E9
97PinCerMB-15
97PinCerMB-49
97PinCerMB-92
97PinCerMG-15
97PinCerMG-49
97PinCerMG-92
97PinCerMR-15
97PinCerMR-49
97PinCerMR-92
97PinCerR-15
97PinCerR-49
97PinCerR-92
97PinMin-3
97PinMin-23
97PinMin2GC-3
97PinMin2GC-23
97PinMinB-3
97PinMinB-23
97PinMinC-3
97PinMinC-23
97PinMinG-3
97PinMinG-23
97PinMinNC-3
97PinMinNC-23
97PinMinS-3
97PinMinS-23
97PinPor-8
97PinPor-28
97PinPor-44
97PinPre-28
97PinPre-30
97PinPre-31
97PinPre-33
97PinPre-36
97PinPreBM-28

97PinPreBM-30
97PinPreBM-31
97PinPreBM-33
97PinPreBM-36
97PinPreGM-28
97PinPreGM-30
97PinPreGM-31
97PinPreGM-33
97PinPreGM-36
97PinPreP-27
97PinPreP-56
97PinPreP-60
97PinPreP-74
97PinPreP-89
97PinPreP-S2-A
97PinPreP-TP9A
97PinPreSM-28
97PinPreSM-30
97PinPreSM-31
97PinPreSM-33
97PinPreSM-36
97PinSpe-2-A
97PinSpeA-2-A
97PinTeaP-9
97PinTotCPB-15
97PinTotCPB-49
97PinTotCPB-92
97PinTotCPG-15
97PinTotCPG-49
97PinTotCPG-92
97PinTotCPR-15
97PinTotCPR-49
97PinTotCPR-92
97PinTroC-27
97PinTroC-56
97PinTroC-60
97PinTroC-74
97PinTroC-89
97Pre-4
97Pre-39
97PreAmeE-AE5
97PreBlaWFS-4
97PreBlaWFS-39
97PreEyeotT-ET5
97PreGat-GB4
97PreGatA-GBA4
97PreGolE-GE5
97PreGri-4
97PreGri-39
97PrePas-3
97PrePas-44
97PrePas-59
97PrePas-70
97PrePas-80
97PrePas-94
97PrePas-96
97PrePas-102
97PrePas-124
97PrePasAut-3
97PrePasBB-BB3
97PrePasBR-BR7
97PrePasCC'-CC10
97PrePasCleC-C4
97PrePasL-3
97PrePasL-44
97PrePasL-59
97PrePasL-70
97PrePasL-80
97PrePasL-94
97PrePasL-96
97PrePasL-102
97PrePasL-124
97PrePasOS-3
97PrePasOS-44
97PrePasOS-59
97PrePasOS-70
97PrePasOS-80
97PrePasOS-94
97PrePasOS-96
97PrePasOS-102
97PrePasOS-124
97PrePasP-3
97PrePasP-35
97PrePasP-40
97PrePasPCB-CB6
97PrePasPCBD-CB6
97PrePasPEP-3
97PrePasPEP-35
97PrePasPEP-40
97PrePasPLL-LL5
97PrePasPM-3
97PrePasPM-35
97PrePasPM-40
97PrePasPOS-3
97PrePasPOS-35
97PrePasPOS-40
97PrePasT-3
97PrePasT-44
97PrePasT-59
97PrePasT-70
97PrePasT-80
97PrePasT-94
97PrePasT-96
97PrePasT-102
97PrePasT-124
97PrePasVL-VL4A
97PrePasVL-VL4B
97PreRedW-4
97PreRedW-39
97RacCho-32
97RacCho-67
97RacCho-105
97RacChoBC-12
97RacChoHO-4
97RacChoHOGitD-4
97RacChoSS-32
97RacChoSS-67
97RacChoSS-105
97RacSha-3
97RacSha-30
97RacSha-34
97RacSha-41
97RacShaGW-GW4
97RacShaGWP-3
97RacShaGWP-30
97RacShaGWP-34
97RacShaGWP-41
97RacShaH-3
97RacShaH-30
97RacShaH-34
97RacShaH-41
97RacShaPFBSA-5
97RacShaSA-SA3
97RacShaSTS-ST3
97RacShaTS-3
97RacShaTS-30
97RacShaTS-34
97RacShaTS-41
97SBMot-4
97SBMot-40
97SBMot-55
97SBMot-93
97SBMotAC-AU4
97SBMotRC-RC4
97SBMotWR-WC1
97SBMotWR-WC11
97SBMotWR-WC19
97ScoBoal-4
97ScoBoal-7
97ScoBoal-28
97ScoBoal-49
97ScoBoal$PC-PC8
97SkyPro-14
97SkyPro-77
97SkyProA-14
97SkyProPS-E6
97SkyProT-T3
97SP-12
97SP-54
97SP-92
97SP-118
97SP SupS-12
97SP SupS-54
97SP SupS-92
97SP SupS-118
97SPX-8
97SPxBlu-8
97SPxGol-8
97SPxSil-8
97SPXSpeA-SV7
97SPxTagTA-TA2
97Ult-16
97Ult-40
97UltAKA-A4
97UltDouT-DT6
97UltDriV-D2
97UltEliS-E6
97UltIns-DC4
97UltSho-6
97UltUpd-3
97UltUpd-94
97UltUpdAR-3
97UppDecRTTC-3
97UppDecRTTC-46
97UppDecRTTC-88
97UppDecRTTC-108
97UppDecRTTCCQ-CQ4
97UDRTTCCQC-CQ4
97UppDecRTTCGF-RD7
97UDRTTCMDM-MM13
97UDRTTCMDM-MM14
97UDRTTCMDM-MM15
97UDRTTCMDM-MM16
97UDRTTCMDMA-MM13
97UDRTTCMDMA-MM14
97UDRTTCMDMA-MM15
97UDRTTCMDMA-MM16
97UppDecRTTCPotA-4
97UppDecRTTCPotA-5
97UppDecRTTCPotA-6
97UppDecRTTCPP-PP22
97UppDecRTTCPP-PP24
97UppDecRTTCPP-PP27
97UppDecRTTCPP-PP35
97UppDecRTTCPP-PP45
97UppDecRTTCPP-PP46
97UppDecRTTCPP-PP47
97UppDecRTTCPPlu-+3
97UppDecRTTCPPlu-+13
97UDRTTCPPRC-+3
97UDRTTCPPRC-+13
97UppDRTTCPPRDC-+3
97UppDRTTCPPRDC-+13
97UppDecRTTCQW-CQ4
97UppDecVC-36
97UppDecVC-86
97UppDecVC-101
97UppDecVCAPotA-FS7
97UppDecVCAPotA-FS8
97UppDecVCAPotA-FS9
97UppDecVCCR-CR3
97UppDecVCDS-DS10
97UppDecVCP-PE3
97UppDecVCPC-PH3
97UppDecVCVL-VL4
97VIP-12
97VIP-47
97Viper-2
97Viper-40
97Viper-53
97Viper-55
97Viper-79
97ViperAna-A3
97ViperBlaR-2
97ViperBlaR-40
97ViperBlaR-53
97ViperBlaR-55
97ViperBlaR-79
97ViperCob-C9
97ViperDia-DB2
97ViperDiaA-DBA2
97ViperKinC-KC9
97ViperSid-S9
97ViperSnaE-SE3
97VIPExp-12
97VIPExp-47
97VIPOilS-12
97VIPOilS-47
97VIPRinoH-RH11
97VIPRinoHDC-RH11
97VIPSamB-KT3
97VIPSamBG-KT3
98ColCho-12
98ColCho-48
98ColCho-92
98ColCho-101
98HigGea-2
98HigGea-34
98HigGea-54
98HigGeaA-11
98HigGeaFG-3
98HigGeaFG-34
98HigGeaFG-54
98HigGeaGJ-GJ15
98HigGeaHG-HG7
98HigGeaM-3
98HigGeaM-34
98HigGeaM-54
98HigGeaMaM-MM3
98HigGeaMaM-C-3
98HigGeaTT-TT2
98Max-12
98Max-42
98Max-70
98Max-92
98Max-11
98Max-36
98Max-61
98Max-86
98Max10tA-23
98Max10tA-68
98Max10tABA-26
98Max10tACotY-CY8
98Max10tAMP-P11
98MaxBatP-B11
98MaxFieG-5
98MaxFieGTS-5
98MaxFieGTSA-5
98MaxFirC-F10
98MaxFocOAC-FC2
98MaxFouSGA-5
98MaxMakOACC-FC2
98MaxTea-TW9
98MaxYealRBS-16
98MaxYealRBS-21
98MaxYealRBS-22
98MaxYealRBS-27
98MaxYealRBS-45
98MaxYealRBS-67
98MaxYealRBS-85
98MaxYealRBS-86
98MaxYealRBS-106
98MaxYealRBS-116
98MaxYealRBS-136
98MaxYealRBS-151
98MaxYealRBS-154
98MaxYealRBS-AW3
98MaxYealRBS-PO2
98MayAutS-10
98PinMin-5
98PinMin-15
98PinMin-28
98PinMinB-5
98PinMinB-15
98PinMinB-28
98PinMinBC-5
98PinMinBC-15
98PinMinBC-04
98PinMinBPPC-5
98PinMinBPPC-15
98PinMinBPPC-04
98PinMinGMT-5
98PinMinGMT-15
98PinMinGMT-28
98PinMinGPC-5
98PinMinGPC-15
98PinMinGPC-28
98PinMinGPPC-5
98PinMinGPPC-15
98PinMinGPPC-28
98PinMinNC-5
98PinMinNC-15
98PinMinNC-28
98PinMinSGC-5
98PinMinSGC-15
98PinMinSGC-28
98PinMinSMT-5
98PinMinSMT-15
98PinMinSMT-28
98PinMinSPPC-5
98PinMinSPPC-15
98PinMinSPPC-28
98PinMinSSC-5
98PinMinSSC-15
98PinMinSSC-28
98PrePas-3
98PrePas-35
98PrePas-45
98PrePas-103
98PrePasA-3
98PrePasCC'-CC10
98PrePasGS-2
98PrePasOC-OC4
98PrePasOS-3
98PrePasOS-35
98PrePasOS-45
98PrePasP-8
98PrePasP-25
98PrePasP-29
98PrePasP-8
98PrePasP-25
98PrePasP-29
98PrePasPFC-FC3
98PrePasPFC-FC25
98PrePasPFCR-FC3
98PrePasPFCR-FC25
98PrePasPR-5B
98PrePasPS-PS16
98PrePasPSH-SH10
98PrePasPTGF-TGF8
98PrePasS-ST4A
98PrePasS-2
98PrePasS-16
98PrePasS-17
98PrePasS-45
98PrePasSF-16
98PrePasSF-17
98PrePasSF-45
98PrePasSFT-4
98PrePasSFTD-4
98PrePasSO-17
98PrePasSO-18
98PrePasSOD-17
98PrePasSOD-18
98PrePasSRG-G7
98PrePasSS-8
98PrePasSSD-8
98PrePasTG3R-STG8
98PrePasTGBR-TG8
98PrePasTorp-ST4B
98SP Aut-12
98SP Aut-46
98SP Aut-78
98SP AutBtW-BW2
98SP AutBtWL2-BW2
98SP AutBtWL3-BW2
98SP AutSotTL2-ST7
98SP AutT-T4
98UppDecDV-7
98UppDecDVSM-7
98UppDecRttC-20
98UppDecRttC-58
98UppDecRttC-90
98UppDecRttC-102
98UDRTTCCQT1-CQ8
98UDRTTCCQT2-CQ8
98UDRTTCCQT3-CQ8
98UDRTTCCQT4-CQ8
98UppDRTTCCQVL-CQ8
98UppDecRTTCWM-W3
98UppDecVC-12
98UppDecVC-57
98UppDecVC-95
98UppDecVC-116
98UppDecVC-149
98UppDecVC3DoS-D5
98UppDecVC3DoS-D18
98UppDecVC3DoSG-D5
98UppDecVC3DoSG-D18
98UppDecVCA-AG3
98UppDecVCPL-PL2
98UppDecVCPotE-PE3
98UppDecVCPP-3
98UppDecVCPPCR-3
98UppDecVCSoB-SB9
98VIP-12
98VIP-41
98VIP-48
98VIPDriF-DF10
98VIPDriFD-DF10
98VIPExp-12
98VIPExp-41
98VIPExp-48
98VIPHeaG-HG5
98VIPHeaGD-HG5
98VIPLapL-LL4
98VIPLapLA-LL4
98VIPNASC-NC4
98VIPNASCD-NC4
98VIPTriG"M-TGS8
98Whe-16
98Whe-38
98Whe-49
98Whe-87
98Whe50tA-A7
98Whe50tA-A22
98WheAut-3
98WheCusS-CSDJ
98WheDouT-E5
98WheGol-16
98WheGol-38
98WheGol-87
98WheGreF-GF9
98WheJac-J4
99Pre-3
99Pre-30
99Pre-48
99Pre-87
99PrePas-3
99PrePas-30
99PrePas-48
99PrePas-87
99PrePas-103
99PrePasBR-BR5
99PrePasCC-1B
99PrePasCC-10
99PrePasOC-4
99PrePasPS-16
99PrePasS-1A
99PrePasTG"i1R-TG6

99UppDecVC-1
99UppDecVC-52
99UppDecVCIS-IS8
99UppDecVCMN-M3
99UppDecVCMNA-M3
99UppDecVCNSS-DJ
99UppDecVCSZ-SZ8
99UppDecVCTM-TM2
99UppDecVCUE-1
99UppDecVCUE-52
99UppDecVCVC-V6
99WheHigG-3
99WheHigG-34
99WheHigG-70
99WheHigGAC-4
99WheHigGFG-3
99WheHigGFG-34
99WheHigGFG-70
99WheHigGHS-HS6/6
99WheHigGM-MM3B/9
99WheHigGM-3
99WheHigGM-34
99WheHigGM-70
99WheHigGM&M-MM5A/9
99WheHigGS-GS3
99WheHigGTT-TT3/8

Jarrett, Glenn
91SpoLegNJ-NJ3
92MaxBlaU-U24
92MaxRedU-U24
93Max-203
93MaxPreS-203
94MaxPreS-214
95MaxPreS-208
96MaxPre-206
97UltUpd-31

Jarrett, Jason
98Whe-50
98WheGol-49
99Pre-42
99Pre-60
99Pre-98
99PrePas-42
99PrePas-60
99PrePas-98
99WheHigG-42
99WheHigGFG-42
99WheHigGM-42

Jarrett, Ned
89Max-200
89TGRacMR-27
89TGRacMR-200
89TGRacMR-201
89TGRacMR-202
89TGRacMR-203
90Max-155
90MaxHolF-HF30
91Max-227
91ProSet-55
91ProSetL-L4
91SpoLegDJ-DJ2
91SpoLegDJ-DJ5
91SpoLegDJ-DJ10
91SpoLegNJ-NJ1
91SpoLegNJ-NJ2
91SpoLegNJ-NJ3
91SpoLegNJ-NJ4
91SpoLegNJ-NJ5
91SpoLegNJ-NJ6
91SpoLegNJ-NJ7
91SpoLegNJ-NJ8
91SpoLegNJ-NJ9
91SpoLegNJ-NJ10
91SpoLegNJ-NJ11
91SpoLegNJ-NJ12
91SpoLegNJ-NJ13
91SpoLegNJ-NJ14
91SpoLegNJ-NJ15
91SpoLegNJ-NJ16
91SpoLegNJ-NJ17
91SpoLegNJ-NJ18
91SpoLegNJ-NJ19
91SpoLegNJ-NJ20
91SpoLegNJ-NJ21
91SpoLegNJ-NJ22
91SpoLegNJ-NJ23
91SpoLegNJ-NJ24
91SpoLegNJ-NJ25
91SpoLegNJ-NJ26
91SpoLegNJ-NJ27
91SpoLegNJ-NJ28
91SpoLegNJ-NJ29
91SpoLegNJ-NJ30
91TGRacMRU-27
91TGRacMRU-200
91TGRacMRU-201
91TGRacMRU-202
91TGRacMRU-203
91TGRacTL-18
91TGRacTL-25
91Tra-126
91TraPacYH-12
92MaxBla-221
92MaxIMH-20
92MaxRed-221
92MaxSamB-3
92ProSetL-L3
92ProSetR-1
92ProSetRF-L1
92Tra-126
93ActPac-165
93FinLin-177
93FinLinCS-18
93FinLinS-177
93Max-202
93MaxHou-22
93MaxPreS-202
93Tra-76
93TraFirR-76
94FinLin-9
94FinLinS-9
94HigGeaL-LS6
94MaxPreS-199
94PrePas-113
94Tra-134
94TraAutV-40
94TraFirR-134
94VIP-85
94WheHarG-21
94WheHarGG-21
95Sel-115
95SelFlaO-115
95UppDec-157
95UppDecGSEG-157
95UppDecI-I7
95UppDecSSES-157
96Ass-15
96AutRacA-23
96AutRacCA-23
96Cla-10
96ClaPriP-10
96ClaSil-10
96UppDec-140
96UppDecRL-RLC4
97ActPacFA-4
97ActPacFAA-4
97ColCho-124
97SBMot-27
97UltUpd-32
98HigGeaPG-PG7
98Max10tA-33
98Max10tA-78
98PrePas-124
98SP AutMoaL-M4
98SP AutT-T4
98UppDecRTTC5A-AN9
98UppDecRTTC5A-AN13
98UppDecRTTC5AA-AN13
99PrePas-130

Jarrett, Tom
92VolRacLS2-31

Jaussaud, Jean Pierre
78GraPri-4
78GraPri-196

Jaussaud, Pironi
78GraPri-207

Jellen, Peter
92RSSMotH-11

Jenatzy, Camille
11AmeTobAD-12
95TraVal-5

Jenkins, Ab
38WilCig-18
39ChuKinoS-14

Jenkins, Bill
71FleAHRDC-10
72FleAHRDN-18
72FleAHRDN-58
73NabSugDSC-15
91ProSetN-127
92ProSetN-178
93FinLinN-91

Jenkins, Bob
90Max-154
91Max-228
91Tra-165
92MaxBlaU-U25
92MaxRedU-U25
93Max-206
93MaxPreS-206
94Max-317
95Max-260
96MaxPre-204

Jenkins, Don
92RedGraST-19
92RedGraST-20

Jenkins, John
91K&WURCS-27

Jennings, Bob
91DKIMCDT-26

Jensen, Dave
91LanARCHS-24
92LanARCF-79
94LanARCF-32

Jensen, Richard
91LanStoCC-11
92CorSelCCS-8
93CorSelCCS-1

Jewell, Mike
92JAG-53

Joehnck, Fred
91LanStoCC-22

Johansson, Stefan
87AceForO-16
87ForOneI-1
88HerFouFO-3A
91CarForO-49
91CarForO-50
91CarForO-51
91ProTraFO-24
91ProTraFO-25
91ProTraFO-41
91ProTraFO-42
93MaxWinM-8
94HiTecI-12
94HiTecI-37
94HiTecICD-CD19
95SkyInd5-9
95SkyInd5-45
95SkyInd5-87
96SkyInd5-40
96SkyInd5-70

Johncock, Gordon
80AvaHilURG-4
83A&SRacI-49
84A&SRacI-32
85A&SRacI-20
86A&SRacI-35
86AceInd-D3
91AllWorI-61
91LegInd-39
92AllWorI-33
92AllWorI-72
92ColACAR-72
92LegInd-7
92LegInd-40
92LegInd-90
93HiTecI-31
93HiTecI-64
93HiTecI-77
94HiTecICD-CD20
95SkyInd5PC-9
95TraVal-79
95TraVal-88

Johns, Bobby
91GalPrePR-30
91LegInd-55

Johns, Lori
89MegDra-75
89MegDra-76
91ProSetN-4
91ProSetN-53
91ProSetNP-4
92MacTooWC-13

Johns, Steve
93FinLinN-116

Johnson, Alan
92TraDir-3
95K&WDirT-7

Johnson, Blaine
92ProSetN-194
93FinLinN-114

Johnson, Bob
91ProSet-3
92MaxBla-165
92MaxMot-34
92MaxRed-165
92ProSet-142
93Max-171
93MaxPreP-153
93MaxPreS-171
94Max-149
94MaxPreP-142
94MaxPreS-149

Johnson, Brian
91LanRocS-10
92LanRocS-26
92RedGraST-3

Johnson, C.J.
92BulRin-9

Johnson, Dan Stock
90LanRocSHS-42

Johnson, Danny Modified
92TraDir-15
95K&WDirT-9

Johnson, Davey
91DirTra-57
91Max-134
92DirTra-46
92STAMod-25
94STAMod-1

Johnson, Dean
94HigGeaPPT-G18
94HigGeaPPTG-18G

Johnson, DeWayne
95HavAT-18

Johnson, Don
91LanAmeIS-12

Johnson, Herm
83A&SRacI-14
84A&SRacI-26
85A&SRacI-29
86A&SRacI-20

Johnson, Jack
91K&WDirT-34
92K&WDirT-6
92TraDir-2
94K&WDirT-15
95K&WDirT-8

Johnson, Jay
91DKIMCDT-10
91DKIMCDT-44

Johnson, Jeff
91DKIMCDT-22

Johnson, Jimmy
91Tra-67
92Tra-113A
92Tra-113B
93FinLin-132
93FinLinCS-21
93FinLinS-132
93Tra-111
93TraFirR-111
94ActPacCC-12
94FinLin-136
94FinLinS-136
95ActPacHM-8
95FinLin-113
95FinLinPP-113
95FinLinSil-113
95TraBehTS-BTS14
97AutRacA-26
97PrePas-92
97PrePasL-92
97PrePasOS-92
97PrePasT-92
97RacShaSTS-ST25
97SBMot-88

Johnson, Joe Lee
89TGRacMR-242
89WinCir-19
91GalPrePR-101
91TraPacYH-13

Johnson, Johnny
91DKIMCDT-48
92JAG-54

Johnson, Junior
89Max-77
89Max-170
89Max-190
89TGRacMR-27
89TGRacMR-59
89TGRacMR-75
89TGRacMR-77
89TGRacMR-96
89TGRacMR-100
89TGRacMR-101
89TGRacMR-102
89TGRacMR-104
90Max-117
90MaxHolF-HF24
91GalPrePR-23
91GalPrePR-94
91Max-87
91MaxMot-16
91MaxRacFK-1
91PioStoCR-2
91ProSet-34
91ProSet-45
91ProSetL-L17
91TGRacMRU-27
91TGRacMRU-59
91TGRacMRU-75
91TGRacMRU-77
91TGRacMRU-96
91TGRacMRU-100
91TGRacMRU-101
91TGRacMRU-102
91TGRacMRU-104
91Tra-78
92MaxBla-109
92MaxIMH-21
92MaxMcD-7
92MaxMot-14
92MaxRed-109
92MaxSamB-9
92ProSet-79
92ProSetL-L31
92ProSetMH-4
92ProSetR-4
92ProSetRF-L4
92Tra-78
92TraRacMB-11B
93FinLin-18
93FinLin-172
93FinLinCS-4
93FinLinCS-17
93FinLinS-18
93FinLinS-172
93Max-100
93Max-267
93MaxPreP-89
93MaxPreP-183
93MaxPreS-100
93MaxPreS-267
93Tra-101
93Tra-188
93TraFirR-101
93TraFirR-188
94ActPac-169
94FinLin-49
94FinLinS-49
94HigGea-29
94HigGeaG-29
94Max-97
94MaxPreP-97
94MaxPreS-97
94Pow-14
94Pow-65
94Pow-97
94PowGol-14
94PowGol-65
94PowGol-97
94Tra-11
94TraAutV-42
94TraFirR-11
94VIP-86
95CroJew-30
95CroJewD-30
95CroJewE-30
95CroJewS-30
95FinLin-108
95FinLinPP-108
95FinLinSil-108
95HigGea-37
95HigGeaDO-37
95HigGeaDOG-37
95HigGeaG-37
95HigGeaL-L1
95ImaOwnP-OP6
95Max-76
95Max-225
95MaxCroC-73
95MaxCroC-172
95MaxPreP-73
95MaxPreP-172
95MaxPreS-92
95MaxPreS-287
95Sel-133
95SelFlaO-133
95SP-133
95SPDieC-133
95TraAutV-4
95TraBehTS-BTS22
95UppDec-153
95UppDecGSEG-153
95UppDecI-I3
95UppDecSSES-153
96Kni-34

89Max-103
89Max-114
89Max-127
89Max-168
89MaxCri-13
90Max-7
90MaxHolF-HF11
91Max-7
91Max-145
91Max-197
91MaxMcD-8
91MaxMot-7
91MaxMot-35
91MaxRacFK-3
91MaxTheWA-9
91MaxUpd-7
91ProSet-93
91ProSet-94
91ProSet-133
91ProSet-134
91Tra-7
91Tra-73
92-CarDynBTBS-6
92CarDynAK-1
92CarDynAK-2
92CarDynAK-3
92CarDynAK-4
92CarDynAK-5
92CarDynGO-10
92CoyRoo-8
92HooAlaK-1
92HooAlaK-2
92HooAlaK-3
92HooAlaK-4
92HooAlaK-5
92HooAlaK-6
92HooAlaK-7
92HooAlaK-8
92HooAlaK-9
92HooAlaK-10
92HooAlaK-11
92HooAlaK-12
92HooAlaK-13
92HooAlaK-14
92MaxBla-7
92MaxBla-284
92MaxMcD-20
92MaxMot-3
92MaxMot-38
92MaxMot-49
92MaxMot-50
92MaxRed-7
92MaxRed-284
92MaxTheW-7
92MaxTheW-27
92ProSet-2
92ProSet-15
92ProSet-100
92ProSet-152
92ProSetMH-18
92ProSetRF-11
92RedSta-7
92SpoLegAK-P1
92SpoLegAK-AK1
92SpoLegAK-AK2
92SpoLegAK-AK3
92SpoLegAK-AK4
92SpoLegAK-AK5
92SpoLegAK-AK6
92SpoLegAK-AK7
92SpoLegAK-AK8
92SpoLegAK-AK9
92SpoLegAK-AK10
92SpoLegAK-AK11
92SpoLegAK-AK12
92SpoLegAK-AK13
92SpoLegAK-AK14
92SpoLegAK-AK15
92SpoLegAK-AK16
92SpoLegAK-AK17
92SpoLegAK-AK18
92SpoLegAK-AK19
92SpoLegAK-AK20
92SpoLegAK-AK21
92SpoLegAK-AK22
92SpoLegAK-AK23
92SpoLegAK-AK24
92SpoLegAK-AK25
92SpoLegAK-AK26
92SpoLegAK-AK27
92SpoLegAK-AK28
92SpoLegAK-AK29
92SpoLegAK-AK30
92Tra-7
92Tra-73
92TraASA-36
92TraRacM-7
92TraRacM-51
92TraRacM-77
92TraRacM-P51
93ActPac-1
93ActPac-26
93ActPac-40
93ActPac-64
93ActPac-85
93ActPac-AKDA
93ActPac-AKDAG
93ActPac2G-1G
93ActPac2G-39G
93ActPac2G-40G
93ActPac2G-41G
93ActPac2G-42G
93ActPac2G-43G
93ActPac2G-44G
93ActPacAK-AK1
93ActPacAK-AK2
93ActPacAK-AK3
93ActPacAK-AK4
93ActPacAK-AK5
93ActPacAK-AK6
93ActPacP-AK1
93CarDynDEP-4
93CarDynGO-10
93CarDynQC-1
93FinLin-1
93FinLin-37
93FinLin-76
93FinLin-170
93FinLin-NNO
93FinLinCS-6
93FinLinCS-14
93FinLinCS-30
93FinLinS-1
93FinLinS-37
93FinLinS-76
93FinLinS-170
93Max-7
93Max-13
93Max-20
93Max-190
93Max-269
93Max-277
93Max-294
93MaxCluSBC-8
93MaxHou-2
93MaxMot-43
93MaxMot-44
93MaxMot-47
93MaxPreP-7
93MaxPreP-13
93MaxPreP-20
93MaxPreP-81
93MaxPreP-172
93MaxPreP-184
93MaxPreP-192
93MaxPrePJ-NNO
93MaxPreS-7
93MaxPreS-13
93MaxPreS-20
93MaxPreS-190
93MaxPreS-269
93MaxPreS-277
93MaxPreS-294
93MotManC-5
93PrePasPre-8
93PrePasPre-21
93Tra-7
93Tra-27
93Tra-82
93Tra-142
93Tra-196
93TraFirR-7
93TraFirR-27
93TraFirR-82
93TraFirR-142
93TraFirR-196
93TraPreC-5
93TraTri-9
93TraTri-35
93WheRooT-27
93WheRooT-48
93WheRooT-57
93WheRooT-58
93WheRooT-59
93WheRooT-86
93WheRooTPla-27
93WheRooTPla-48
93WheRooTPla-57
93WheRooTPla-58
93WheRooTPla-59
93WheRooTPla-86
93WheRooTS-SP4
93WheRooTS-SP5
94ActPac-29
94ActPacCC-34
94HigGea-100
94HigGeaG-100
94Max-7
94Max-125
94MaxPreP-7
94MaxPreP-49
94MaxPrePAK-1
94MaxPrePAK-2
94MaxPrePAK-3
94MaxPrePAK-4
94MaxPrePAK-5
94MaxPrePAK-6
94MaxPrePAK-7
94MaxPrePAK-8
94MaxPrePAK-9
94MaxPrePAK-10
94MaxPrePAK-11
94MaxPrePAK-12
94MaxPrePAK-13
94MaxPrePAK-14
94MaxPreS-7
94MaxPreS-125
94MaxPreSJ-7
94MaxRooY-8
94PrePas-130
94Tra-7
94TraAutV-34
94TraFirR-7
94TraPreC-39
95MatWinCC-22
95MetImpWCC-10
96MetImp2AWCC-22
96ZenChaS-4
97ScoBoaIR-SB9
97ScoBoaRSBF-SB9
98Max10tA-6
98Max10tA-51
98Max10tA-116
98Max10tACP-CP4
98Max10tACPDC-CP4
98PrePas-131
98UppDecRTTC5A-AN42
98UppDecRTTCCS-CS6

Kunkel, Bud
92VolRacLS2-33

Kunzman, Lee
92AllWorl-68

Kurth, Tom
92LanRocS-30

Laakso, Dale
91WorOut-23

LaBonge, Steve
65DonSpeS-39

Labonte, Bob
92MaxBla-180
92MaxRed-180
92SliJimBL-5
92SliJimBL-24
93Max-185
93MaxPreP-165
93MaxPreS-185

Labonte, Bobby
91Max-53
91MaxUpd-53
92-CarDynBTBS-7
92MacTooWC-14
92MaxBla-44
92MaxBla-91
92MaxRed-44
92MaxRed-91
92ProSet-6
92RedSta-4
92RedSta-35
92SliJimBL-2
92SliJimBL-3
92SliJimBL-4
92SliJimBL-6
92SliJimBL-7
92SliJimBL-8
92SliJimBL-9
92SliJimBL-10
92SliJimBL-11
92SliJimBL-12
92SliJimBL-13
92SliJimBL-14
92SliJimBL-15
92SliJimBL-16
92SliJimBL-17
92SliJimBL-18
92SliJimBL-19
92SliJimBL-20
92SliJimBL-21
92SliJimBL-22
92SliJimBL-23
92SliJimBL-24
92SliJimBL-25
92SliJimBL-26
92SliJimBL-27
92SliJimBL-28
92SliJimBL-29
92Tra-11
92Tra-44
92TraAut-A8
92TraGoo-1
92TraRacM-57
92TraRacM-60
92TraRacM-98
92TraTeaS-101
93ActPac-12
93ActPac-62
93ActPac-63
93ActPac-152
93ActPac-155
93ActPac-156
93ActPac-162
93ActPac-166
93ActPac-184
93ActPac2G-11G
93ActPac2G-12G
93ActPac2G-28G
93ActPac2G-31G
93ActPac2G-32G
93ActPac2G-66G
93FinLin-27
93FinLin-117
93FinLin-135
93FinLin-165
93FinLinCS-16
93FinLinCS-19
93FinLinCS-28
93FinLinP-P3
93FinLinS-27
93FinLinS-117
93FinLinS-135
93FinLinS-165
93Max-22
93Max-113
93Max-199
93MaxHou-1
93MaxHou-16
93MaxHou-24
93MaxLowFS-4
93MaxMot-11
93MaxMot-31
93MaxPreP-22
93MaxPreP-51
93MaxPreP-57
93MaxPreP-NNO
93MaxPreS-22
93MaxPreS-113
93MaxPreS-199
93MaxWinM-2
93PrePasPre-17
93PrePasPre-19
93PrePasPre-28
93StoTop-3
93Tra-22
93Tra-176
93TraFirR-22
93TraFirR-176
93TraTri-22
93TraTri-31
93WheRooT-33
93WheRooT-52
93WheRooT-64
93WheRooT-72
93WheRooT-73
93WheRooT-78
93WheRooT-81
93WheRooT-92
93WheRooT-94
93WheRooTPla-33
93WheRooTPla-52
93WheRooTPla-64
93WheRooTPla-72
93WheRooTPla-73
93WheRooTPla-78
93WheRooTPla-81
93WheRooTPla-92
93WheRooTPla-94
93WheRooTPro-P4
94ActPac-19
94ActPac-85
94ActPac-130
94ActPac-150
94ActPac2G-39G
94ActPacC-8
94CarDynGO-9
94DaySer3-34
94FinLin-26
94FinLin-63
94FinLin-128
94FinLin-3
94FinLinG-32
94FinLinS-26
94FinLinS-63
94FinLinS-128
94Hi-Bri4AP-12
94Hi-Bri4AP-51
94HigGea-13
94HigGea-96
94HigGea-177
94HigGeaDO-177
94HigGeaDOG-177
94HigGeaG-13
94HigGeaG-96
94HigGeaG-177
94HiTecB4-12
94HiTecB4-51
94Max-22
94Max-74
94Max-254
94Max-255
94MaxAut-22
94MaxMed-15
94MaxMed-57
94MaxPreP-22
94MaxPreP-74
94MaxPreS-22
94MaxPreS-74
94MaxRooY-15
94MaxTheS2-19
94MWWin-2
94MWWin-5
94Pow-98
94PowGol-98
94PrePas-13
94PrePas-44
94PrePasCC-CC13
94Tra-22
94Tra-48
94Tra-59
94Tra-123
94TraAutV-27
94TraFirR-22
94TraFirR-48
94TraFirR-59
94TraFirR-123
94TraPreC-35
94VIP-18
94VIP-46
94WheHarG-70
94WheHarGG-70
95ActPacC-1
95ActPacC-46
95ActPacC-49
95ActPacC-56
95ActPacC-68
95ActPacC-P2
95ActPacC2CC-7
95ActPacC2T-10
95ActPacCSS-1
95ActPacCSS-46
95ActPacCSS-49
95ActPacCSS-56
95ActPacCSS-68
95ActPacP-13
95ActPacS-11
95ActPacS-86
95ActPacSSS-11
95ActPacSSS-86
95Ass-12
95Ass1M$PC-2
95AssCocC6DC-4
95AssGolS-12
95CroJew-7
95CroJew-42
95CroJew-71
95CroJewD-7
95CroJewD-42
95CroJewD-71
95CroJewE-7
95CroJewE-42
95CroJewE-71
95CroJewS-7

95CroJewS-42
95CroJewS-71
95FinLin-91
95FinLin-103
95FinLinCC6-12
95FinLinPP-91
95FinLinPP-103
95FinLinSil-91
95FinLinSil-103
95HigGea-21
95HigGea-66
95HigGeaDO-21
95HigGeaDO-66
95HigGeaDOG-21
95HigGeaDOG-66
95HigGeaG-21
95HigGeaG-66
95HiTecB4-5
95HiTecB4-61
95Ima-18
95Ima-46
95Ima-81
95ImaDri-D3
95ImaGol-18
95ImaGol-46
95ImaGol-81
95ImaHarC-HC1
95Max-22
95Max-148
95Max-240
95Max-241
95Max-243
95MaxAut-22
95MaxCroC-22
95MaxCroC-36
95MaxMed-14
95MaxMed-44
95MaxMedB-14
95MaxMedB-44
95MaxMedORA-OTR7
95MaxPreP-22
95MaxPreP-36
95MaxPreS-22
95MaxPreS-36
95MaxPreS-213
95MaxPreS-296
95MaxTop52-TOP2
95OptXL-11
95OptXL-32
95OptXL-52
95OptXLCB-11
95OptXLCB-32
95OptXLCB-52
95OptXLDC-11
95OptXLDC-32
95OptXLDC-52
95OptXLRH-11
95OptXLRH-32
95OptXLRH-52
95OptXLS-XLS6
95PrePas-15
95PrePasCC-15
95PrePasPH-18
95PrePasPre-18
95PrePasPRH-18
95PrePasRH-15
95Sel-17
95Sel-114
95Sel-125
95SelFlaO-17
95SelFlaO-114
95SelFlaO-125
95SP-15
95SP-49
95SP-91
95SPDieC-15
95SPDieC-49
95SPDieC-91
95SPSpeM-SM18
95SPSpeMDC-SM18
95Tra-5
95Tra5thA-33
95Tra5thACC-C7
95Tra5thAG-33
95Tra5thAG-62
95Tra5thAUEC-E9
95TraAutV-25
95TraFirR-5
95TraOnTR-OTR20
95TraRacM-RM20
95UppDec-18
95UppDec-61
95UppDec-86
95UppDec-114
95UppDec-171
95UppDec-198
95UppDec-242
95UppDec-279
95UppDecGSEG-18
95UppDecGSEG-61
95UppDecGSEG-86
95UppDecGSEG-114
95UppDecGSEG-171
95UppDecGSEG-198
95UppDecGSEG-242
95UppDecGSEG-279
95UppDecPSP-PP5
95UppDecSSES-18
95UppDecSSES-61
95UppDecSSES-86
95UppDecSSES-114
95UppDecSSES-171
95UppDecSSES-198
95UppDecSSES-242
95UppDecSSES-279
95VIP-15
95VIPCooB-15
95VIPEmeP-15
95VIPPro-2
95VIPRedHCB-15
95Zen-18
95Zen-48
95Zen-63
95Zen-75
95ZenHel-6
95ZenWinW-11
95ZenWinW-14
95ZenWinW-21
95ZenZT-3
96ActPacC-29
96ActPacC-60
96ActPacC-98
96ActPacCSS-29
96ActPacM-6
96ActPacM-16
96Ass-20
96Ass$1000CCIPC-18
96Ass$100CCIPC-16
96AssComL-CL17
96AssRacD-RD5
96AutRac-43
96AutRacA-25
96AutRacCA-25
96AutRacFR-40
96AutRacFR-41
96AutRacFR-42
96AutRacFR-43
96AutRacFR-44
96AutRacFR-45
96AutRacFR-46
96AutRacFR-47
96AutRacHP-HP7
96Cla-43
96Cla-58
96ClaImaP-RP3
96ClaInn-IV12
96ClaMarMC-MC9
96ClaPriP-43
96ClaRacC-RC7
96ClaRacC-RC17
96ClaSil-43
96CroJewEADJ-DJ3
96CroJewEDT-8
96CroJewEDT-55
96CroJewEDT-64
96CroJewEDT-76
96CroJewEDTC-8
96CroJewEDTC-55
96CroJewEDTC-64
96CroJewEDTC-76
96CroJewEDTCSA-CS6
96CroJewEDTDJA-DJ3
96CroJewEDTDJG-DJ3
96CroJewEE-8
96CroJewEE-55
96CroJewEE-64
96CroJewEE-76
96CroJewEGDJ-DJ3
96CroJewEli-8
96CroJewEli-55
96CroJewEli-64
96CroJewEli-76
96CroJewERCSG-CS6
96CroJewERCSP-CS6
96CroJewES-8
96CroJewES-55
96CroJewES-64
96CroJewES-76
96CroJewESDJ-DJ3
96CroJewETC-8
96CroJewETC-55
96CroJewETC-64
96CroJewETC-76
96CroJewETCDJA-DJ3
96CroJewETCDJS-DJ3
96CroJewETCE-8
96CroJewETCE-55
96CroJewETCE-64
96CroJewETCE-76
96CroJewETCGDJ-DJ3
96CroJewETCS-8
96CroJewETCS-55
96CroJewETCS-64
96CroJewETCS-76
96FinLin-26
96FinLin-69
96FinLin-85
96FinLinBGL-C7
96FinLinBGL-D8
96FinLinGS-GS7
96FinLinMM-MM7
96FinLinPP-18
96FinLinPP-19
96FinLinPP$10C-5
96FinLinPP$50C-4
96FinLinPP$5C-13
96FinLinPP$S-18
96FinLinPP$S-19
96FinLinPriP-26
96FinLinPriP-69
96FinLinPriP-85
96FinLinS-26
96FinLinS-69
96FinLinS-85
96Fla-17
96Fla-73
96Fla-95
96FlaAut-7
96FlaCenS-6
96FlaHotN-6
96Kni-9
96Kni-26
96Kni-29
96KniBlaK-9
96KniBlaK-26
96KniBlaK-29
96KniFirK-FK5
96KniQueRKP-9
96KniQueRKP-26
96KniQueRKP-29
96KniRoy-9
96KniRoy-26
96KniRoy-29
96KniSanC-SC2
96KniWhiK-9
96KniWhiK-26
96KniWhiK-29
96M-F-17
96M-FSil-S9
96Max-18
96Max-22
96MaxFamT-FT3
96MaxMadiA-18
96MaxMadiA-29
96MaxMadiA-34
96MaxMadiA-90
96MaxMadiABR-BR7
96MaxOdy-18
96MaxOdy-34
96MaxOdy-P1
96MaxOdyRA-RA7
96MaxOveTW-OTW7
96MaxPre-18
96MaxPre-36
96MaxPreSS-SL3
96Pin-18
96Pin-47
96Pin-79
96Pin-81
96Pin-90
96Pin-18
96Pin-47
96Pin-79
96Pin-81
96Pin-90
96PinCheF-7
96PinCutA-9
96PinPolP-18
96PinPolP-36
96PinPolP-75
96PinPolPCS-11
96PinPolPLF-18
96PinPolPLF-36
96PinPolPLF-75
96PinPolPNL-15
96PinPolPNLG-15
96PinWinCC-18
96PinWinCC-47
96PinWinCC-79
96PinWinCC-81
96PinWinCC-90
96PrePas-16
96PrePas-41
96PrePas-77
96PrePas-94
96PrePas&NC-16
96PrePasCC-16
96PrePasCF-CF2
96PrePasFQS-FQS5A
96PrePasFQS-FQS5B
96PrePasP-10
96PrePasP-36
96PrePasP-P1
96PrePasP$10PC-5
96PrePasP$20PC-5
96PrePasP$5PC-5
96PrePasPCB-CB8
96PrePasPEP-10
96PrePasPEP-36
96PrePasPH-10
96PrePasPH-36
96PrePasPHP-HP5
96PrePasSco-16
96PrePasSco-41
96PrePasSco-77
96PrePasSco-94
96PrePasT-16
96PrePasT-41
96PrePasT-77
96PrePasT-94
96RacCho-14
96RacCho-38
96RacCho-66
96RacCho-67
96RacCho-68
96RacCho-69
96RacCho-70
96RacCho-94
96RacChoAP-14
96RacChoAP-38
96RacChoAP-66
96RacChoAP-67
96RacChoAP-68
96RacChoAP-69
96RacChoAP-70
96RacChoAP-94
96RacChoSC-14
96RacChoSC-38
96RacChoSC-66
96RacChoSC-67
96RacChoSC-68
96RacChoSC-69
96RacChoSC-70
96RacChoSC-94
96RacChoTT-10
96SP-18
96SP-51
96SPDriF-DF8
96SpeArtP-23
96SpeArtP-45
96SpeCleS-5
96SpeRac-23
96SpeRac-45
96SPHolME-ME18
96SPx-18
96SPxGol-18
96Ult-29
96Ult-30
96Ult-31
96Ult-166
96Ult-170
96Ult-171
96Ult-177
96Ult-180
96UltAut-15
96UltBoxS-10
96UltFlaP-10
96UltGolM-7
96UltThu&L-9
96UltThu&L-10
96UltUpd-17
96UltUpd-63
96UltUpdA-7
96UltUpdPP-7
96UltUpdW-3
96UltUpdW-9
96UppDec-16
96UppDec-56
96UppDec-96
96UppDecPP-RP5
96UppDecPW-HP4
96UppDecRTTC-RC9
96UppDecRTTC-RC58
96UppDecRTTC-RC94
96UppDecRTTC-RC132
96UppDecRTTCAS-H9
96UppDecRTTCGF-GF8
96UppDecRTTCPPoi-PP9
96UppDRTTCPPR-PR9
96UppDecRTTCPT3-T5
96UppDecRTTCRL-RL12
96UppDecRTTCT3PR-R8
96UppDecVV-VV13
96UppDecVVG-VV13
96V.IAut-14
96VIP-14
96VIPEmeP-14
96Viper-8
96Viper-38
96ViperBlaM-8
96ViperBlaM-38
96ViperBusC-B15
96ViperCob-C3
96ViperCop-8
96ViperCop-38
96ViperDia-D3
96ViperDiaA-DA4
96ViperGreM-8
96ViperGreM-38
96ViperKinC-KC9
96VipPro-P1
96VIPTor-14
96VIPWarP-WP9
96VIPWarPG-WP9
96Zen-19
96Zen-40
96Zen-63
96ZenArtP-19
96ZenArtP-40
96ZenArtP-63
96ZenHig-8
97ActPac-18
97ActPac-39
97ActPacFI-18
97ActPacFI-39
97ActPacIC-2
97AutRac-8
97AutRac-39
97AutRac-45
97AutRac-50
97AutRacA-28
97AutRacMS-KM8
97ColCho-18
97ColCho-68
97ColCho-113
97ColChoC-CC22
97ColChoC-CC55
97ColChoC-CC88
97ColChoS-S35
97ColChoS-S36
97ColChoSQ-SQ4
97ColChoSQ-SQ45
97ColChoUD5-UD36
97ColChoUD5-UD37
97FinLinPP2-8
97FinLinPP2$10-76
97FinLinPP2$5-46
97FinLinPP2$50-94
97JurPar-6
97JurParC-C4
97JurParP-P3
97JurParR-R8
97JurParT-6
97JurParTL-TL3
97JurParTR-TR4
97Max-18
97Max-63
97Max-93
97MaxChaTC-C6
97MaxChatCG-C6
97Pin-18
97Pin-47
97Pin-64
97Pin-77
97PinArtP-18
97PinArtP-47
97PinArtP-64
97PinArtP-77
97PinCer-18
97PinCer-52

97PinCer-77
97PinCer-97
97PinCerCGT-4
97PinCerCT-4
97PinCerE-E4
97PinCerEE-E4
97PinCerEP-E4
97PinCerMB-18
97PinCerMB-52
97PinCerMB-77
97PinCerMB-97
97PinCerMG-18
97PinCerMG-52
97PinCerMG-77
97PinCerMG-97
97PinCerMR-18
97PinCerMR-52
97PinCerMR-77
97PinCerMR-97
97PinCerR-18
97PinCerR-52
97PinCerR-77
97PinCerR-97
97PinHel-1
97PinHel-2
97PinHel-3
97PinHel-4
97PinHel-5
97PinHel-6
97PinHel-7
97PinHel-8
97PinHel-9
97PinHel-10
97PinMin-11
97PinMin-27
97PinMin2GC-11
97PinMin2GC-27
97PinMinB-11
97PinMinB-27
97PinMinC-11
97PinMinC-27
97PinMinG-11
97PinMinG-27
97PinMinNC-11
97PinMinNC-27
97PinMinS-11
97PinMinS-27
97PinPor-5
97PinPor-25
97PinPre-73
97PinPreBM-73
97PinPreGM-73
97PinPreP-18
97PinPreP-47
97PinPreP-64
97PinPreP-77
97PinPreP-H1
97PinPreP-H2
97PinPreP-H3
97PinPreP-H4
97PinPreP-H5
97PinPreP-H6
97PinPreP-H7
97PinPreP-H8
97PinPreP-H9
97PinPreP-H10
97PinPreP-S12-G
97PinPreP-TP7A
97PinPreSM-73
97PinSpe-12-G
97PinTeaP-7
97PinTotCPB-18
97PinTotCPB-52
97PinTotCPB-77
97PinTotCPB-97
97PinTotCPG-52
97PinTotCPG-77
97PinTotCPG-97
97PinTotCPR-18
97PinTotCPR-52
97PinTotCPR-77
97PinTotCPR-97
97PinTroC-18
97PinTroC-47
97PinTroC-64
97PinTroC-77
97Pre-12
97Pre-38
97Pre-47
97PreAmeE-AE8
97PreBlaWFS-12
97PreBlaWFS-38
97PreBlaWFS-47
97PreEyeotT-ET7
97PreGat-GB6
97PreGatA-GBA6
97PreGolE-GE8
97PreGri-12
97PreGri-38
97PreGri-47
97PrePas-11
97PrePas-37
97PrePas-81
97PrePas-109
97PrePasAut-10
97PrePasCC'-CC11
97PrePasCleC-C5
97PrePasL-11
97PrePasL-37
97PrePasL-81
97PrePasL-109
97PrePasOS-11
97PrePasOS-37
97PrePasOS-81
97PrePasOS-109
97PrePasP-11
97PrePasP-41
97PrePasPA-10
97PrePasPCB-CB7
97PrePasPCBD-CB7
97PrePasPEP-11
97PrePasPEP-41
97PrePasPLL-LL6
97PrePasPM-11
97PrePasPM-41
97PrePasPOS-11
97PrePasPOS-41
97PrePasT-11
97PrePasT-37
97PrePasT-81
97PrePasT-109
97PreRedW-12
97PreRedW-38
97PreRedW-47
97RacCho-18
97RacCho-53
97RacCho-98
97RacChoBC-13
97RacChoHO-8
97RacChoHOGitD-8
97RacChoSS-18
97RacChoSS-53
97RacChoSS-98
97RacSha-9
97RacSha-25
97RacShaGW-GW7
97RacShaGWP-9
97RacShaGWP-25
97RacShaH-9
97RacShaH-25
97RacShaSTS-ST11
97RacShaTS-9
97RacShaTS-25
97SBMot-12
97SBMot-51
97SBMot-87
97SBMotRC-RC9
97SBMotWR-WC12
97SBMotWR-WC25
97ScoBoal-8
97ScoBoal-43
97ScoBoal$PC-PC3
97ScoBoalR-SB8
97ScoBoaRSBF-SB8
97SkyPro-15
97SkyPro-68
97SkyProA-15
97SkyProBO-B7
97SP-18
97SP-60
97SP-98
97SP-120
97SP SupS-18
97SP SupS-60
97SP SupS-98
97SP SupS-120
97SPX-18
97SPxBlu-18
97SPxGol-18
97SPxSil-18
97SPXSpeA-SV9
97Ult-17
97Ult-49
97UltAKA-A7
97UltDouT-DT3
97UltDriV-D4
97UltIns-DC12
97UltSho-7
97UltUpd-11
97UltUpd-84
97UltUpdAR-11
97UppDecRTTC-11
97UppDecRTTC-53
97UppDecRTTC-95
97UppDecRTTC-118
97UppDecRTTC-128
97UppDecRTTCPP-PP33
97UppDecRTTCPP-PP37
97UppDecRTTCPP-PP39
97UppDecRTTCPP-PP40
97UppDecRTTCPPlu-+29
97UDRTTCPPRC-+29
97UppDRTTCPPRDC-+29
97UppDecVC-18
97UppDecVC-68
97UppDecVC-118
97UppDecVCDS-DS8
97UppDecVCGE-GE5
97UppDecVCP-PE7
97UppDecVCPC-PH7
97UppDecVCVL-VL3
97VIP-13
97Viper-6
97Viper-43
97Viper-72
97ViperAna-A4
97ViperBlaR-6
97ViperBlaR-43
97ViperBlaR-72
97ViperCob-C3
97ViperDia-DB3
97ViperDiaA-DBA3
97ViperKinC-KC3
97ViperSid-S8
97ViperSnaE-SE4
97VIPExp-13
97VIPOilS-13
97VIPRinoH-RH7
97VIPRinoHDC-RH7
97VIPSamB-KT4
97VIPSamBG-KT4
97VIPSheM-SM2
98ColCho-18
98ColCho-54
98ColCho-83
98ColCho-95
98HigGea-7
98HigGea-32
98HigGea-67
98HigGeaA-12
98HigGeaFG-11
98HigGeaFG-32
98HigGeaFG-67
98HigGeaGJ-GJ9
98HigGeaHG-HG6
98HigGeaM-11
98HigGeaM-32
98HigGeaM-67
98HigGeaMaM-MM6
98HigGeaMaM-C-6
98HigGeaTT-TT7
98Max-18
98Max-48
98Max-71
98Max-90
98Max-97
98Max-18
98Max-43
98Max-68
98Max-93
98Max10tA-17
98Max10tA-62
98Max10tA-107
98Max10tAMP-P18
98MaxBatP-B14
98MaxFieG-12
98MaxFieGTS-12
98MaxFieGTSA-12
98MaxFirC-F6
98MaxFocOAC-FC8
98MaxFouSGA-12
98MaxMakOACC-FC8
98MaxYealRBS-57
98MaxYealRBS-59
98MaxYealRBS-112
98MaxYealRBS-139
98MaxYealRBS-147
98MaxYealRBS-156
98MaxYealRBS-PO7
98PinMin-6
98PinMin-18
98PinMinB-6
98PinMinB-18
98PinMinBC-6
98PinMinBC-18
98PinMinBPPC-6
98PinMinBPPC-18
98PinMinGMT-6
98PinMinGMT-18
98PinMinGPC-6
98PinMinGPC-18
98PinMinGPPC-6
98PinMinGPPC-18
98PinMinNC-6
98PinMinNC-18
98PinMinSGC-6
98PinMinSGC-18
98PinMinSMT-6
98PinMinSMT-18
98PinMinSPPC-6
98PinMinSPPC-18
98PinMinSSC-6
98PinMinSSC-18
98PrePas-11
98PrePas-33
98PrePasA-6
98PrePasCC'-CC11
98PrePasGS-10
98PrePasOC-OC5
98PrePasOS-11
98PrePasOS-33
98PrePasP-20
98PrePasP-34
98PrePasP-20
98PrePasP-34
98PrePasPFC-FC9
98PrePasPFC-FC23
98PrePasPFCR-FC9
98PrePasPFCR-FC23
98PrePasPS-PS9
98PrePasPSH-SH6
98PrePasPTGF-TGF5
98PrePasS-ST9A
98PrePasS-10
98PrePasS-19
98PrePasS-20
98PrePasSF-19
98PrePasSF-20
98PrePasSFT-5
98PrePasSFTD-5
98PrePasSO-19
98PrePasSO-20
98PrePasSOD-19
98PrePasSOD-20
98PrePasSRG-G5
98PrePasSS-9
98PrePasSSD-9
98PrePasTG3R-STG5
98PrePasTGBR-TG5
98PrePasTorp-ST9B
98SP Aut-18
98SP Aut-52
98SP Aut-82
98SP AutBtW-BW6
98SP AutBtWL2-BW6
98SP AutBtWL3-BW6
98SP AutSotTL2-ST9
98UppDecDV-13
98UppDecDVSM-13
98UppDecRttC-18
98UppDecRttC-68
98UppDecRttC-70
98UDRTTCCQT1-CQ7
98UDRTTCCQT2-CQ7
98UDRTTCCQT3-CQ7
98UDRTTCCQT4-CQ7
98UppDRTTCCQVL-CQ7
98UppDecRTTCWM-W4
98UppDecVC-18
98UppDecVC-63
98UppDecVC-112
98UppDecVC-147
98UppDecVC3DoS-D23
98UppDecVC3DoS-D28
98UppDecVC3DoSG-D23
98UppDecVC3DoSG-D28
98UppDecVCPL-PL7
98UppDecVCPotE-PE5
98UppDecVCPP-18
98UppDecVCPPCR-18
98UppDecVCSoB-SB7
98VIP-13
98VIP-42
98VIPDriF-DF11
98VIPDriFD-DF11
98VIPExp-13
98VIPExp-42
98VIPHeaG-HG6
98VIPHeaGD-HG6
98VIPLapL-LL5
98VIPLapLA-LL5
98VIPNASC-NC5
98VIPNASCD-NC5
98VIPTriG"M-TGS5
98Whe-17
98Whe-39
98Whe50tA-A8
98Whe50tA-A23
98WheAut-5
98WheDouT-E6
98WheGol-17
98WheGol-39
98WheGreF-GF10
98WheJac-J5
99Pre-5
99Pre-17
99Pre-32
99Pre-83
99PrePas-5
99PrePas-17
99PrePas-32
99PrePas-83
99PrePas-105
99PrePasBR-BR3
99PrePasCC-2B
99PrePasCC-11
99PrePasOC-7
99PrePasPS-10
99PrePasS-2A
99PrePasTG'i1R-TG4
99UppDecVC-5
99UppDecVC-68
99UppDecVCIS-IS2
99UppDecVCMN-M2
99UppDecVCMNA-M2
99UppDecVCNSS-BL
99UppDecVCSZ-SZ1
99UppDecVCTM-TM11
99UppDecVCUE-5
99UppDecVCUE-68
99UppDecVCVC-V2
99WheHigG-5
99WheHigG-32
99WheHigG-66
99WheHigGAC-5
99WheHigGFG-5
99WheHigGFG-32
99WheHigGFG-66
99WheHigGM-MM6B/9
99WheHigGM-5
99WheHigGM-32
99WheHigGM-66
99WheHigGM&M-MM6A/9
99WheHigGS-GS5
99WheHigGTT-TT5/8

Labonte, Donna
92SliJimBL-23
95ZenWinW-21
96ActPacC-93
96RacCho-68
96RacChoAP-68
96RacChoSC-68

Labonte, Justin
94ActPac-151

Labonte, Terry
86SpoPhoG-9
88MaxCha-63
89Max-11
89Max-147
89Max-170
89MaxCri-7
90Max-1
90Max-181
90Max-185
90MaxHolF-HF12
91Max-94
91MaxMcD-15
91MaxTheWA-10
91MaxUpd-94
91MaxWin2AF-14
91ProSet-57
91ProSet-80
91ProSet-82
91Tra-84
91Tra-94
92-CarDynBTBS-8
92MaxBla-94
92MaxMcD-25
92MaxRed-94

92MaxTheW-10
92MaxTheW-30
92ProSet-21
92ProSet-28
92ProSet-35
92ProSet-116
92ProSetMH-23
92RedSta-30
92SliJimBL-7
92Tra-84
92Tra-94
92TraRacM-82
92TraRacM-86
92TraRacM-94
92TraRacM-98
92TraRacMB-13B
93ActPac-11
93ActPac-36
93ActPac-46
93ActPac-162
93ActPac-167
93ActPac-168
93ActPac-185
93ActPac2G-7G
93ActPac2G-67G
93FinLin-27
93FinLin-39
93FinLin-90
93FinLinCS-11
93FinLinCS-19
93FinLinCS-28
93FinLinP-P3
93FinLinS-27
93FinLinS-39
93FinLinS-90
93Max-14
93MaxHou-16
93MaxHou-29
93MaxLowFS-4
93MaxPreP-14
93MaxPreS-14
93MaxTheW-15
93MaxTheW-35
93Tra-3
93Tra-14
93Tra-184
93TraFirR-3
93TraFirR-14
93TraFirR-184
93TraPreC-3
93TraTri-14
93WheRooTS-SP1
94ActPac-18
94ActPac-78
94ActPac-110
94ActPac-151
94ActPac-184
94ActPac2G-32G
94ActPac2G-184G
94ActPacC-9
94ActPacS2G-W4
94FinLin-17
94FinLin-38
94FinLin-124
94FinLinG-29
94FinLinG-33
94FinLinG-47
94FinLinG-77
94FinLinG-P2
94FinLinGA-33
94FinLinS-17
94FinLinS-38
94FinLinS-124
94Hi-Bri4AP-22
94Hi-Bri4AP-39
94HigGea-12
94HigGea-105
94HigGea-165
94HigGeaDO-105
94HigGeaDO-165
94HigGeaDOG-105
94HigGeaDOG-165
94HigGeaG-12
94HigGeaG-105
94HigGeaG-165
94HigGeaMG-MG10
94HiTecB4-22
94HiTecB4-39
94Max-14
94Max-246
94Max-247
94Max-275
94MaxAut-14
94MaxMed-11
94MaxPreP-14
94MaxPreS-14
94MaxRacC-7
94MaxTheS2-18
94MWWin-3
94MWWin-5
94OptXL-10
94OptXL-39
94OptXLDouC-DC3
94OptXLRH-10
94OptXLRH-39
94Pow-40
94Pow-140
94PowGol-40
94PowGol-140
94PrePas-14
94PrePasCC-CC14
94Sky-5
94Tra-5
94Tra-70
94Tra-96
94Tra-118
94Tra-152
94TraAutV-29
94TraFirR-5
94TraFirR-70
94TraFirR-96
94TraFirR-118
94TraFirR-152
94TraPreC-32
94TraWin-W5
94TraWin-W10
94TraWin-W13
94VIP-19
94VIP-44
95ActPacC-19
95ActPacC-48
95ActPacC2CC-9
95ActPacCSS-19
95ActPacCSS-48
95ActPacHM-3
95ActPacP-14
95ActPacP-53
95ActPacP-65
95ActPacS-2
95ActPacS-34
95ActPacS-48
95ActPacS-86
95ActPacS2G-3G
95ActPacSSS-2
95ActPacSSS-34
95ActPacSSS-48
95ActPacSSS-86
95Ass-24
95Ass-40
95Ass$5$25PC-10
95Ass1M$PC-20
95AssCocC6DC-5
95AssGolS-24
95AssGolS-40
95CroJew-6
95CroJew-52
95CroJew-68
95CroJew-73
95CroJew-76
95CroJew-DT1
95CroJewD-6
95CroJewD-52
95CroJewD-68
95CroJewD-73
95CroJewD-76
95CroJewDJ-DJ3
95CroJewDJD-DJ3
95CroJewDJE-DJ3
95CroJewDT-DT1
95CroJewE-6
95CroJewE-52
95CroJewE-68
95CroJewE-73
95CroJewE-76
95CroJewS-6
95CroJewS-52
95CroJewS-68
95CroJewS-73
95CroJewS-76
95FinLin-5
95FinLin-69
95FinLin-97
95FinLinCC6-24
95FinLinCC6-40
95FinLinGS-GS5
95FinLinPP-5
95FinLinPP-69
95FinLinPP-97
95FinLinSC-SC6
95FinLinSCalC-7
95FinLinSChaC-CC2
95FinLinSD-SD6
95FinLinSil-5
95FinLinSil-69
95FinLinSil-97
95FinLinSRF-27
95FinLinSRF-55
95FinLinSRF-60
95FinLinSSSS-SS10
95FinLinSup-27
95FinLinSup-55
95FinLinSup-60
95HigGea-8
95HigGea-61
95HigGea-77
95HigGea-90
95HigGea-TLS1
95HigGeaD-D2
95HigGeaDO-8
95HigGeaDO-61
95HigGeaDO-77
95HigGeaDO-90
95HigGeaDOG-8
95HigGeaDOG-61
95HigGeaDOG-77
95HigGeaDOG-90
95HigGeaG-8
95HigGeaG-61
95HigGeaG-77
95HigGeaG-90
95HigGeaMD-MD2
95HiTecB4-19
95HiTecB4-47
95Ima-5
95Ima-55
95Ima-91
95ImaDri-D13
95ImaGol-5
95ImaGol-55
95ImaGol-91
95ImaHarC-HC10
95MatWinCC-14
95Max-5
95Max-58
95Max-123
95Max-139
95Max-142
95Max-173
95Max-230
95Max-231
95Max-232
95Max-233
95MaxAut-5
95MaxCroC-5
95MaxCroC-34
95MaxCroC-141
95MaxCroC-142
95MaxCroC-154
95MaxCroC-173
95MaxCroC-179
95MaxLicD-1
95MaxMed-4
95MaxMed-34
95MaxMedB-4
95MaxMedB-34
95MaxMedORA-OTR3
95MaxOveW-10
95MaxPreP-5
95MaxPreP-34
95MaxPreP-141
95MaxPreP-142
95MaxPreP-154
95MaxPreP-173
95MaxPreP-179
95MaxPrePP-PS6
95MaxPreS-5
95MaxPreS-34
95MaxPreS-187
95MaxPreS-188
95MaxPreS-249
95MaxPreS-269
95MaxPreS-288
95MaxPreS-294
95MetImpWCC-7
95MWWin-3
95MWWin-5
95OptXL-12
95OptXL-33
95OptXL-53
95OptXLCB-12
95OptXLCB-33
95OptXLCB-53
95OptXLDC-12
95OptXLDC-33
95OptXLDC-53
95OptXLRH-12
95OptXLRH-33
95OptXLRH-53
95OptXLS-XLS7
95PrePas-16
95PrePas-43
95PrePasCC-16
95PrePasCF-CF5
95PrePasPH-7
95PrePasPPC-NNO
95PrePasPre-7
95PrePasPRH-7
95PrePasPro-2
95PrePasRD-RD7
95PrePasRH-16
95PrePasRH-43
95Sel-18
95Sel-43
95Sel-114
95SelDreM-DM12
95SelFlaO-18
95SelFlaO-43
95SelFlaO-114
95SelSki-SS5
95SP-4
95SP-36
95SP-79
95SPDieC-4
95SPDieC-36
95SPDieC-79
95SPSpeM-SM5
95SPSpeMDC-SM5
95Tra-41
95Tra-61
95Tra5thA-19
95Tra5thA-39
95Tra5thA-48
95Tra5thACC-C9
95Tra5thAG-19
95Tra5thAG-39
95Tra5thAG-48
95Tra5thAR-R8
95Tra5thAUEC-E2
95TraAutV-47
95TraCha-C4
95TraFirR-41
95TraFirR-61
95TraFirR-71
95TraRacM-RM6
95TraSerS-SS2
95UppDec-37
95UppDec-105
95UppDec-162
95UppDec-185
95UppDec-186
95UppDec-231
95UppDec-272
95UppDecA-186
95UppDecGSEG-37
95UppDecGSEG-105
95UppDecGSEG-162
95UppDecGSEG-185
95UppDecGSEG-186
95UppDecGSEG-231
95UppDecGSEG-272
95UppDecO-OS10
95UppDecPRW-P8
95UppDecPSP-PP3
95UppDecSSES-37
95UppDecSSES-105
95UppDecSSES-162
95UppDecSSES-185
95UppDecSSES-186
95UppDecSSES-231
95UppDecSSES-272
95VIP-16
95VIPCooB-16
95VIPEmeP-16
95VIPFanC-FC4
95VIPFanCG-FC4
95VIPRedHCB-16
95Zen-25
95Zen-38
95ZenHel-9
95ZenWinW-3
95ZenWinW-13
95ZenWinW-22
95ZenZT-4
96ActPacC-25
96ActPacC-56
96ActPacCSS-25
96ActPacM-7
96ActPacM-17
96Ass-46
96AssComL-CL20
96AutRac-6
96AutRacA-26
96AutRacCA-26
96CroJewEADJ-DJ3
96CroJewEBotC-BC6
96CroJewEDT-3
96CroJewEDT-31
96CroJewEDT-63
96CroJewEDTBoC-BC6
96CroJewEDTC-3
96CroJewEDTC-31
96CroJewEDTC-63
96CroJewEDTCSA-CS5
96CroJewEDTDJA-DJ3
96CroJewEDTDJG-DJ3
96CroJewEE-3
96CroJewEE-31
96CroJewEE-63
96CroJewEGDJ-DJ3
96CroJewEli-3
96CroJewEli-31
96CroJewEli-63
96CroJewERCSG-CS5
96CroJewERCSP-CS5
96CroJewES-3
96CroJewES-31
96CroJewES-63
96CroJewESDJ-DJ3
96CroJewETC-3
96CroJewETC-31
96CroJewETC-63
96CroJewETCBoC-BC6
96CroJewETCDJA-DJ3
96CroJewETCDJS-DJ3
96CroJewETCE-3
96CroJewETCE-31
96CroJewETCE-63
96CroJewETCGDJ-DJ3
96CroJewETCS-3
96CroJewETCS-31
96CroJewETCS-63
96FinLin-5
96FinLin-74
96FinLin-78
96FinLinBGL-C4
96FinLinBGL-D5
96FinLinBGL-JPC4
96FinLinDCPC-7
96FinLinGS-GS5
96FinLinMM-MM5
96FinLinPP-20
96FinLinPP-21
96FinLinPP$100C-4
96FinLinPP$10C-6
96FinLinPP$50C-5
96FinLinPP$5C-14
96FinLinPP$S-20
96FinLinPP$S-21
96FinLinPriP-5
96FinLinPriP-74
96FinLinPriP-78
96FinLinS-5
96FinLinS-74
96FinLinS-78
96Fla-18
96Fla-74
96Fla-96
96FlaAut-8
96FlaCenS-7
96FlaHotN-7
96FlaPowP-6
96Kni-6
96Kni-28
96KniBlaK-6
96KniBlaK-28
96KniFirK-FK6
96KniKniRT-KT5
96KniProC-PC3
96KniQueRKP-6
96KniQueRKP-28
96KniRoy-6
96KniRoy-28
96KniWhiK-6
96KniWhiK-28
96M-F-7
96M-F-8
96M-FBla-B5
96M-FSheM-M3
96M-FSil-S5
96M-FSil-S6

96Max-5
96Max-35
96Max-P2
96MaxAut-5
96MaxFamT-FT3
96MaxMadiA-5
96MaxMadiA-35
96MaxMadiA-82
96MaxMadiA-83
96MaxOdy-5
96MaxOdy-35
96MaxOdy-82
96MaxOdy-83
96MaxOdyM-MM10
96MaxOveTW-OTW5
96MaxPre-5
96MaxPre-34
96MaxPre-185
96MaxPre-242
96MaxPreSS-SL4
96MetImp-4
96MetImp2AWCC-14
96MetImpWCTF-1
96Pin-5
96Pin-40
96Pin-5
96Pin-40
96PinCheF-5
96PinCutA-3
96PinPolP-5
96PinPolP-29
96PinPolP-79
96PinPolPCS-5
96PinPolPLF-5
96PinPolPLF-29
96PinPolPLF-79
96PinPolPNL-5
96PinPolPNLG-5
96PinTeaP-5
96PinWinCC-5
96PinWinCC-40
96PrePas-17
96PrePas-42
96PrePas-75
96PrePas-P2
96PrePas&NC-17
96PrePas&NC-42
96PrePasBR-BR4
96PrePasCC-17
96PrePasCF-CF3
96PrePasFoc-F5
96PrePasFQS-FQS6A
96PrePasFQS-FQS6B
96PrePasP-6
96PrePasP-37
96PrePasPCB-CB9
96PrePasPEP-6
96PrePasPEP-37
96PrePasPH-6
96PrePasPH-37
96PrePasSco-17
96PrePasSco-42
96PrePasSco-75
96PrePasT-17
96PrePasT-42
96PrePasT-75
96RacCho-5
96RacCho-29
96RacCho-95
96RacChoAP-5
96RacChoAP-29
96RacChoAP-95
96RacChoSC-5
96RacChoSC-29
96RacChoSC-95
96RacChoTT-6
96SP-5
96SP-47
96SP-81
96SpeArtP-3
96SpeArtP-30
96SpeArtP-39
96SpeArtP-46
96SpeCleS-6
96SpeInM-6
96SpePro-6
96SpeRac-3
96SpeRac-30
96SpeRac-39
96SpeRac-46
96SPHolME-ME5
96SPx-5
96SPx-C1
96SPx-C1A
96SPxComC-C1
96SPxEli-E3
96SPxGol-5
96Ult-21
96Ult-22
96Ult-23
96Ult-169
96Ult-170
96Ult-188
96UltAut-16
96UltBoxS-6
96UltChaC-4
96UltFlaP-6
96UltGolM-6
96UltGolM-8
96UltSeaC-1
96UltUpd-18
96UltUpd-64
96UltUpd-81
96UltUpdA-8
96UltUpdPP-8
96UltUpdW-2
96UltUpdW-14
96UppDec-4
96UppDec-44
96UppDec-84
96UppDecAP-AP2
96UppDecPW-HP7
96UppDecRTTC-RC5
96UppDecRTTC-RC54
96UppDecRTTC-RC128
96UppDecRTTCAS-H5
96UppDecRTTCGF-GF5
96UppDecRTTCLP-LP5
96UppDecRTTCPPoi-PP5
96UppDRTTCPPR-PR5
96UppDecRTTCPT3-T1
96UppDecRTTCPT3-T2
96UppDecRTTCPT3-T10
96UppDecRTTCRL-RL11
96UppDecRTTCT3PR-R5
96UppDecVV-VV5
96UppDecVVG-VV5
96VIP-15
96VIPEmeP-15
96Viper-5
96Viper-39
96Viper-56
96ViperBlaM-5
96ViperBlaM-39
96ViperBlaM-56
96ViperBusC-B1
96ViperCob-C7
96ViperCop-5
96ViperCop-39
96ViperCop-56
96ViperDia-D5
96ViperDiaA-DA6
96ViperGreM-5
96ViperGreM-39
96ViperGreM-56
96ViperKinC-KC5
96VIPSamBTF-SB3
96VIPSamBTFG-SB3
96VIPTor-15
96VIPWarP-WP4
96VIPWarPG-WP4
96Zen-4
96Zen-39
96Zen-54
96Zen-70
96Zen-93
96ZenArtP-4
96ZenArtP-39
96ZenArtP-54
96ZenArtP-70
96ZenArtP-93
96ZenChaS-12
96ZenHig-9
97Act-1
97Act-5
97Act-6
97Act-9
97ActPac-5
97ActPac-47
97ActPac-53
97ActPac-83
97ActPac2G-5
97ActPacFA-9
97ActPacFI-5
97ActPacFI-47
97ActPacFI-53
97ActPacFI-83
97ActPacIC-1
97ActPacIC-2
97ActPacRT-5
97AlkTerL-1
97AlkTerL-2
97AlkTerL-3
97AutRac-3
97AutRac-50
97AutRacA-27
97AutRacMS-KM3
97ColCho-5
97ColCho-55
97ColCho-104
97ColCho-130
97ColCho-131
97ColCho-132
97ColChoC-CC9
97ColChoS-S9
97ColChoS-S10
97ColChoSQ-SQ37
97ColChoTF-D1
97ColChoTF-D2
97ColChoTF-D3
97ColChoTF-F2
97ColChoTF-G1
97ColChoUD5-UD7
97ColChoUD5-UD8
97ColChoVC-VC7
97FinLinPP2-5
97FinLinPP2$10-69
97FinLinPP2$100-99
97FinLinPP2$5-43
97FinLinPP2$50-91
97JurPar-3
97JurPar-40
97JurParC-C7
97JurParP-P4
97JurParR-R1
97JurParT-3
97JurParT-40
97JurParTR-TR1
97Max-5
97Max-50
97Max-91
97Max-114
97MaxChaTC-C3
97MaxChatCG-C3
97Pin-5
97Pin-34
97Pin-59
97Pin-76
97Pin-93
97PinArtP-5
97PinArtP-34
97PinArtP-59
97PinArtP-76
97PinArtP-93
97PinCer-5
97PinCer-39
97PinCer-59
97PinCer-80
97PinCer-90
97PinCerCGT-5
97PinCerCT-5
97PinCerE-E5
97PinCerEE-E5
97PinCerEP-E5
97PinCerMB-5
97PinCerMB-39
97PinCerMB-59
97PinCerMB-80
97PinCerMB-90
97PinCerMG-5
97PinCerMG-39
97PinCerMG-59
97PinCerMG-80
97PinCerMG-90
97PinCerMR-5
97PinCerMR-39
97PinCerMR-59
97PinCerMR-80
97PinCerMR-90
97PinCerR-5
97PinCerR-39
97PinCerR-59
97PinCerR-80
97PinCerR-90
97PinMin-1
97PinMin-25
97PinMin2GC-1
97PinMin2GC-25
97PinMinB-1
97PinMinB-25
97PinMinC-1
97PinMinC-25
97PinMinG-1
97PinMinG-25
97PinMinNC-1
97PinMinNC-25
97PinMinS-1
97PinMinS-25
97PinPor-4
97PinPor-24
97PinPor-42
97PinPre-55
97PinPre-57
97PinPre-58
97PinPre-59
97PinPre-60
97PinPre-62
97PinPre-63
97PinPreBM-57
97PinPreBM-58
97PinPreBM-60
97PinPreBM-63
97PinPreGM-57
97PinPreGM-58
97PinPreGM-60
97PinPreGM-63
97PinPreP-5
97PinPreP-34
97PinPreP-59
97PinPreP-76
97PinPreP-93
97PinPreP-S1-N
97PinPreP-TP5A
97PinPreSM-57
97PinPreSM-58
97PinPreSM-60
97PinPreSM-63
97PinPreTL-55
97PinPreTL-57
97PinPreTL-58
97PinPreTL-59
97PinPreTL-60
97PinPreTL-62
97PinPreTL-63
97PinSpe-1-N
97PinSpeA-1-N
97PinTeaP-5
97PinTotCPB-5
97PinTotCPB-39
97PinTotCPB-80
97PinTotCPB-90
97PinTotCPG-5
97PinTotCPG-39
97PinTotCPG-80
97PinTotCPG-90
97PinTotCPR-5
97PinTotCPR-39
97PinTotCPR-80
97PinTotCPR-90
97PinTroC-5
97PinTroC-34
97PinTroC-59
97PinTroC-76
97PinTroC-93
97Pre-2
97Pre-45
97Pre-GD1
97Pre-SD1
97PreAmeE-AE4
97PreBlaWFS-2
97PreBlaWFS-45
97PreBlaWFS-GD1
97PreBlaWFS-SD1
97PreEyeotT-ET4
97PreGolE-GE4
97PreGri-2
97PreGri-45
97PrePas-1
97PrePas-34
97PrePas-60
97PrePas-72
97PrePas-82
97PrePas-97
97PrePas-106
97PrePas-110
97PrePas-0
97PrePasAut-1
97PrePasBB-BB1
97PrePasBR-BR3
97PrePasCC'-CC12
97PrePasCleC-C6
97PrePasL-1
97PrePasL-34
97PrePasL-60
97PrePasL-72
97PrePasL-82
97PrePasL-97
97PrePasL-106
97PrePasL-110
97PrePasOS-1
97PrePasOS-34
97PrePasOS-60
97PrePasOS-72
97PrePasOS-82
97PrePasOS-97
97PrePasOS-106
97PrePasOS-110
97PrePasP-1
97PrePasP-30
97PrePasPA-1
97PrePasPCB-CB8
97PrePasPCBD-CB8
97PrePasPDB-DB3
97PrePasPEP-1
97PrePasPEP-30
97PrePasPLL-LL7
97PrePasPM-1
97PrePasPM-30
97PrePasPOS-1
97PrePasPOS-30
97PrePasT-1
97PrePasT-34
97PrePasT-60
97PrePasT-72
97PrePasT-82
97PrePasT-97
97PrePasT-106
97PrePasT-110
97PrePasVL-VL5A
97PrePasVL-VL5B
97PreRedW-2
97PreRedW-45
97RacCho-5
97RacCho-40
97RacCho-93
97RacChoBC-2
97RacChoCM-12
97RacChoHO-1
97RacChoHOGitD-1
97RacChoSS-5
97RacChoSS-40
97RacChoSS-93
97RacSha-4
97RacSha-26
97RacShaGW-GW3
97RacShaGWP-4
97RacShaGWP-26
97RacShaH-4
97RacShaH-26
97RacShaPFBSA-6
97RacShaSA-SA5
97RacShaSTS-ST4
97RacShaTS-4
97RacShaTS-26
97SBMot-3
97SBMot-82
97SBMotAC-AU3
97SBMotWR-WC31
97ScoBoal-3
97ScoBoal-29
97ScoBoal-50
97ScoBoalR-SB10
97ScoBoaRSBF-SB10
97SkyPro-16
97SkyPro-65
97SkyProA-16
97SkyProPS-E2
97SkyProT-T1
97SP-5
97SP-47
97SP-87
97SP-115
97SP SPxFA-SF4
97SP SupS-5
97SP SupS-47
97SP SupS-87
97SP SupS-115
97SPX-5
97SPxBlu-5
97SPxGol-5
97SPxSil-5
97SPXSpeA-SV5
97SPXTagT-TT1
97SPxTagTA-TA1
97Ult-18
97Ult-39
97Ult-C1
97UltAKA-A3
97UltDouT-DT7
97UltDriV-D8

97UltEliS-E7
97UltIns-DC3
97UltSho-8
97UltUpd-5
97UltUpd-79
97UltUpdAR-5
97UltWinCC-C1
97UppDecRTTC-1
97UppDecRTTC-44
97UppDecRTTC-86
97UppDecRTTC-106
97UppDecRTTCCQ-CQ1
97UDRTTCCQC-CQ1
97UppDecRTTCGF-RD5
97UDRTTCMDM-MM1
97UDRTTCMDM-MM2
97UDRTTCMDM-MM3
97UDRTTCMDM-MM4
97UDRTTCMDMA-MM1
97UDRTTCMDMA-MM2
97UDRTTCMDMA-MM3
97UDRTTCMDMA-MM4
97UppDecRTTCPP-PP1
97UppDecRTTCPP-PP5
97UppDecRTTCPP-PP6
97UppDecRTTCPP-PP34
97UppDecRTTCPP-PP43
97UppDecRTTCPPlu-+1
97UppDecRTTCPPlu-+9
97UppDecRTTCPPlu-+27
97UDRTTCPPRC-+1
97UDRTTCPPRC-+9
97UDRTTCPPRC-+27
97UppDRTTCPPRDC-+1
97UppDRTTCPPRDC-+9
97UppDRTTCPPRDC-+27
97UppDecRTTCQW-CQ1
97UppDecVC-5
97UppDecVC-55
97UppDecVC-108
97UppDecVCCA-CA1
97UppDecVCCA-CA2
97UppDecVCCA-CA3
97UppDecVCCA-CA4
97UppDecVCCA-CA5
97UppDecVCCR-CR1
97UppDecVCDS-DS3
97UppDecVCP-PE5
97UppDecVCPC-PH5
97VIP-14
97Viper-3
97Viper-69
97ViperAna-A1
97ViperBlaR-3
97ViperBlaR-69
97ViperCob-C4
97ViperKinC-KC4
97ViperSid-S1
97ViperSnaE-SE7
97VIPExp-14
97VIPOilS-14
97VIPRinoH-RH4
97VIPRinoHDC-RH4
97VIPSamB-KT5
97VIPSamBG-KT5
97VIPSheM-SM4
98ColCho-5
98ColCho-41
98ColCho-89
98ColCho-100
98HigGea-6
98HigGea-30
98HigGea-65
98HigGeaA-13
98HigGeaFG-5
98HigGeaFG-30
98HigGeaFG-65
98HigGeaGJ-GJ4
98HigGeaHG-HG3
98HigGeaM-5
98HigGeaM-30
98HigGeaM-65
98HigGeaMaM-MM5
98HigGeaMaM-C-5
98HigGeaPG-PG4
98HigGeaTT-TT6
98Max-5
98Max-35
98Max-72
98Max-96
98Max-5
98Max-30
98Max-55
98Max-80
98Max10tA-4
98Max10tA-49
98Max10tA-106
98Max10tABA-27
98Max10tACP-CP2
98Max10tACPDC-CP2
98Max10tAMP-P5
98MaxBatP-B7
98MaxFieG-4
98MaxFieGTS-4
98MaxFieGTSA-4
98MaxFirC-F16
98MaxFocOAC-FC7
98MaxFouSGA-4
98MaxMakOACC-FC7
98MaxSwaP-SW2
98MaxTea-TW2
98MaxYealRBS-5
98MaxYealRBS-12
98MaxYealRBS-78
98MaxYealRBS-138
98MaxYealRBS-141
98MaxYealRBS-PO6
98MayAutS-12
98PinMin-4
98PinMin-16
98PinMinB-4
98PinMinB-16
98PinMinBC-4
98PinMinBC-16
98PinMinBPPC-4
98PinMinBPPC-16
98PinMinGMT-4
98PinMinGMT-16
98PinMinGPC-4
98PinMinGPC-16
98PinMinGPPC-4
98PinMinGPPC-16
98PinMinNC-4
98PinMinNC-16
98PinMinSGC-4
98PinMinSGC-16
98PinMinSMT-4
98PinMinSMT-16
98PinMinSPPC-4
98PinMinSPPC-16
98PinMinSSC-4
98PinMinSSC-16
98PrePas-5
98PrePas-30
98PrePas-108
98PrePasA-4
98PrePasCC'-CC12
98PrePasGS-4
98PrePasOC-OC6
98PrePasOS-5
98PrePasOS-30
98PrePasP-17
98PrePasP-33
98PrePasP-17
98PrePasP-33
98PrePasPFC-FC8
98PrePasPFC-FC21
98PrePasPFCR-FC8
98PrePasPFCR-FC21
98PrePasPS-PS4
98PrePasPSH-SH3
98PrePasPTGF-TGF3
98PrePasS-ST1A
98PrePasS-4
98PrePasS-22
98PrePasS-23
98PrePasS-48
98PrePasSF-22
98PrePasSF-23
98PrePasSF-48
98PrePasSFT-6
98PrePasSFTD-6
98PrePasSO-21
98PrePasSO-22
98PrePasSOD-21
98PrePasSOD-22
98PrePasSRG-G3
98PrePasSS-10
98PrePasSSD-10
98PrePasTG3R-STG3
98PrePasTGBR-TG3
98PrePasTorp-ST1B
98SP Aut-5
98SP Aut-39
98SP Aut-74
98SP AutBtW-BW5
98SP AutBtWL2-BW5
98SP AutBtWL3-BW5
98SP AutSotTL2-ST5
98SP AutT-T3
98UppDecDV-5
98UppDecDVSM-5
98UppDecDVVoaC-VC4
98UppDecRttC-5
98UppDecRttC-68
98UppDecRttC-69
98UppDecRttC-97
98UppDecRTTC5A-AN44
98UppDecRTTC5A-AN45
98UppDecRTTC5AA-AN44
98UDRTTCCQT1-CQ5
98UDRTTCCQT2-CQ5
98UDRTTCCQT3-CQ5
98UDRTTCCQT4-CQ5
98UppDRTTCCQVL-CQ5
98UppDecRTTCCS-CS2
98UppDecRTTCCS-CS15
98UppDecVC-5
98UppDecVC-50
98UppDecVC-92
98UppDecVC-118
98UppDecVC-126
98UppDecVC-146
98UppDecVC3DoS-D29
98UppDecVC3DoSG-D29
98UppDecVCA-AG5
98UppDecVCPL-PL6
98UppDecVCPP-5
98UppDecVCPPCR-5
98UppDecVCSoB-SB5
98VIP-14
98VIP-43
98VIPDriF-DF12
98VIPDriFD-DF12
98VIPExp-14
98VIPExp-43
98VIPHeaG-HG7
98VIPHeaGD-HG7
98VIPLapL-LL6
98VIPLapLA-LL6
98VIPNASC-NC6
98VIPNASCD-NC6
98VIPTriG"M-TGS3
98Whe-18
98Whe-40
98Whe50tA-A9
98Whe50tA-A24
98WheAut-4
98WheDouT-E7
98WheGol-18
98WheGol-40
98WheGreF-GF11
98WheJac-J6
99Pre-9
99Pre-36
99PrePas-9
99PrePas-36
99PrePas-109
99PrePasBR-BR1
99PrePasCC-13B
99PrePasCC-12
99PrePasOC-5
99PrePasPS-5
99PrePasS-13A
99PrePasTG"i1R-TG1
99UppDecVC-8
99UppDecVC-49
99UppDecVCIS-IS14
99UppDecVCNSS-TL
99UppDecVCSZ-SZ9
99UppDecVCTM-TM9
99UppDecVCUE-8
99UppDecVCUE-49
99UppDecVCVC-V3
99WheHigG-9
99WheHigG-30
99WheHigG-65
99WheHigGAC-9
99WheHigGCS-CSTL
99WheHigGFC-FC3/5
99WheHigGFG-9
99WheHigGFG-30
99WheHigGFG-65
99WheHigGHS-HS2/6
99WheHigGM-MM5B/9
99WheHigGM-9
99WheHigGM-30
99WheHigGM-65
99WheHigGM&M-MM9A/9
99WheHigGS-GS9

Labonte, Tyler
95ZenWinW-21

LaChance, Chuck
92WinChoM-19

Lackey, Larry
94MaxTexEI-42

Lackey, Ted
92JAG-61

Lackey, Terry
91LanStoCC-28

Laffite, Jacques
77Spo-3603
78GraPri-27
78GraPri-47
78GraPri-69
78GraPri-72
78GraPri-95
78GraPri-111
78GraPri-204
87AceForO-18
87ForOneI-2
93MaxWilR-10

Lagasse, Scott
95ActPacC-91
95ActPacC-93
95ActPacHM-4
95FinLinSRF-7
95FinLinSRF-45
95FinLinSRF-64
95FinLinSSSS-SS8
95FinLinSup-7
95FinLinSup-45
95FinLinSup-64
95Max-238
95Max-239
95MaxCroC-3
95MaxCroC-13
95MaxPreP-3
95MaxPreP-13
95MaxPreS-46
95MaxPreS-57
95MaxSup-4
95MaxSup-6

LaHaie, Dick
89MegDra-91
89MegDra-92
91ProSetN-3
91ProSetN-52
92ProSetN-8

LaHaie, Kim
91ProSetN-123
92ProSetN-28
92ProSetN-108
93FinLinN-27

Laine, Antero
78GraPri-220

LaJoie, Randy
92MaxBla-19
92MaxRed-19
94HigGea-63
94HigGeaG-63
94Max-190
94MaxMot-24
94MaxPreS-190
94Pow-36
94Pow-135
94PowGol-36
94PowGol-135
95ActPacS-28
95ActPacSSS-28
95Max-196
95MaxCroC-23
95MaxPreP-23
95MaxPreS-23
95PrePas-63
95PrePas-78
95PrePasPH-28
95PrePasPre-28
95PrePasPRH-28
95PrePasRH-63
95PrePasRH-78
95Sel-63
95SelFlaO-63
95SP-59
95SP-119
95SPDieC-59
95SPDieC-119
95SPSpeM-SM22
95SPSpeMDC-SM22
95Tra-57
95TraAutV-3
95TraCha-C15
95TraFirR-57
95UppDec-176
95UppDec-200
95UppDec-244
95UppDec-280
95UppDecGSEG-176
95UppDecGSEG-200
95UppDecGSEG-244
95UppDecGSEG-280
95UppDecSSES-176
95UppDecSSES-200
95UppDecSSES-244
95UppDecSSES-280
95VIP-17
95VIPCooB-17
95VIPEmeP-17
95VIPRedHCB-17
96AutRac-40
96AutRacA-27
96AutRacCA-27
96CroJewEDT-68
96CroJewEDTC-68
96CroJewEE-68
96CroJewEli-68
96CroJewES-68
96CroJewETC-68
96CroJewETCE-68
96CroJewETCS-68
96Fla-40
96MaxPre-22
96UltUpd-37
96UppDecRTTC-RC46
97ActPac-55
97ActPac-57
97ActPac2G-14
97ActPacFI-55
97ActPacFI-57
97AutRac-16
97AutRacA-29
97AutRacMS-KM16
97ColCho-45
97ColCho-94
97JurPar-45
97JurParT-45
97PinMin-20
97PinMin2GC-20
97PinMinB-20
97PinMinC-20
97PinMinG-20
97PinMinNC-20
97PinMinS-20
97Pre-34
97Pre-63
97PreBlaWFS-34
97PreBlaWFS-63
97PreGri-34
97PreGri-63
97PrePas-73
97PrePas-111
97PrePasAut-33
97PrePasL-73
97PrePasL-111
97PrePasOS-73
97PrePasOS-111
97PrePasPA-33
97PrePasT-73
97PrePasT-111
97PreRedW-34
97PreRedW-63
97SkyPro-48
97SkyProA-48
97Ult-86
97UltSho-16
97UltUpd-59
97UltUpdAR-59
97UppDecVC-45
97UppDecVC-94
97VIP-33
97Viper-48
97ViperBlaR-48
97VIPExp-33
97VIPOilS-33
98HigGea-37
98HigGeaFG-37
98HigGeaM-37
98PrePas-37
98PrePas-82
98PrePasOS-37
98PrePasOS-82
98PrePasP-1
98PrePasP-1
98PrePasS-33
98PrePasS-39
98PrePasSF-39
98UppDecRttC-25
98UppDecRttC-84
98UppDecRttC-114

98VIP-31
98VIPExp-31
98Whe-52
98Whe-61
98WheGol-52
98WheGol-61
99Pre-40
99PrePas-40
99WheHigG-40
99WheHigGFG-40
99WheHigGM-40
LaMance, Rod
91DirTra-10
91DirTra-47
91JAG-46
92DirTra-19
92JAG-188
95HavAT-38
Lambeck, Bob
73FleAHRRU-10
Lambert, Rick
91BulRin-135
92BulRin-128
Lambert, Tony
94HigGeaPPT-W31
94HigGeaPPTG-31W
Lambeth, Larry
92JAG-62
Lamell, Ron
91WinChoNED-38
91WinChoNED-39
92WinChoB-54
92WinChoB-55
Lammers, Jan
78GraPri-3
78GraPri-175
87A&SRacI-16
Lamoreaux, Mark
92RedGraST-1
92RedGraST-7
92RedGraST-8
92RedGraST-9
92RedGraST-10
Lampman, Dennis
91LanART-34
92TraASA-12
Lancaster, Tim
92TraTeaS-93
Lancia, Vincenzo
11AmeTobAD-13
Landon, Wayne
95JSKS.OS-83
Landreth, Richard Jr.
91BulRin-112
92BulRin-182
Landrum, Steve
92JAG-63
Landy, Dick
71FleAHRDC-26
72FleAHRDN-19
73FleAHRRU-12
73FleAHRRU-13
Lane , Rat (Charles)
92TraTeaS-61
Lane, Laura
94LanARCF-36
Lane, Ritchie
92LanRocS-31
Langenberg, Marty
92LanRocS-32
Langley, Elmo
72STP-6
89Max-203
89TGRacMR-256
89TGRacMR-257
90Max-149
91Max-105
91MaxMot-39
91ProSetL-L36
91TGRacMRU-256
91TGRacMRU-257
91TraPacYH-14
92MaxBla-215
92MaxRed-215
92ProSetL-L27
92RedRacKS-9
92Tra-64
93Max-233
93MaxPreS-233
94MaxPreS-229
94Tra-178
94TraFirR-178
95MaxPreS-227
95VIP-48
95VIPCooB-48
95VIPEmeP-48
95VIPRedHCB-48
96MaxPre-228
96Pin-82
96Pin-82
96PinWinCC-82
96RacCho-81
96RacChoAP-81
96RacChoSC-81
97ActPac-65
97ActPacFI-65
Lanier, Eddie
91Max-215
91Tra-16
92CleEngB-11
92MaxAllPT-9
92MaxBla-237
92MaxRed-237
92ProSet-233
92Tra-81
92TraTeaS-10
94ActPacRCR-RCR8
94HigGeaPPT-E9
94HigGeaPPTG-9E
Lanigan, Darrell
91DirTra-71
92DirTra-72
92JAG-64
92STAMod-15
93JAG-26
94STAMod-36
Lankford, Cecil
72FleAHRDN-62
Lankford, Fred
92TraTeaS-183
Lape, David
92K&WDirT-16
92TraDir-1
94K&WDirT-22
95K&WDirT-25
Laperle, Roger
92PacAmeCT-9
92PacAmeCT-38
92PacAmeCT-45
LaPier, Bobby
90LanRocSHS-34
Lapier, Dave
91LanRocS-20
Larini, Nicola
88HerFouFO-7C
91CarForO-96
91CarForO-97
91CarForO-98
91ProTraFO-77
91ProTraFO-78
Lark, Jerry
92JAG-65
Larkin, Dick
92TraDir-9
Larkins, Robert
92TraKodEI-4
LaRosa, Lou
91Tra-123
92CleEngB-8
92Tra-123
Larrousse, Gerard
92GriForO-136
Larson, Bruce
71FleAHRDC-47
89MegDra-30
89MegDra-31
91BigTimD-31
91BigTimD-40
91BigTimD-44
91BigTimD-88
91ProSetN-19
91ProSetN-68
Larson, Fred
65DonSpeS-2
Larson, Wayne
94LanARCF-55
Lasater, Richard
93FinLin-148
93FinLinCS-26
93FinLinS-148
93Max-51
93MaxPreS-51
94Max-182
94MaxPreS-182
Lasoski, Danny
89WorOut-29
90WorOut-16
91WorOut-15
91WorOutMW-2
94WorOut-17
Latonis, Robert
92TraTeaS-117
Lauda, Niki
77Spo-622
77Spo-824
77Spo-2207
77Spo-4412
77Spo-7415
78GraPri-13
78GraPri-21
78GraPri-50
78GraPri-78
78GraPri-79
78GraPri-92
78GraPri-100
78GraPri-119
78GraPri-122
78GraPri-139
91ProTraFO-192
Laureno, Roger
90K&WDirT-27
91K&WDirT-27
92K&WDirT-22
94K&WDirT-21
95K&WDirT-34
Lautenschlager, C.
71MobTheSoGPMR-3
71MobTheSoGPMR-5
Lawhorn, John
92JAG-66
Lawrence, Danny
91Max-208
92MaxAllPT-31
92MaxBla-252
92MaxRed-252
92ProSet-210
92TraTeaS-11
94ActPacRCR-RCR12
94HigGeaPPT-E8
94HigGeaPPTG-8E
94MaxPreS-249
95MaxPreS-247
Lawrence, Kerry
92TraTeaS-188
92TraTeaS-189
Lawson, Usif
89CheFlaI-3
90CheFlaI-99
Lawver, Scott
91LanRocS-28
Lawwell, Tommy
92JAG-67
Lazier, Bob
92AllWorI-45
Lazier, Buddy
91AllWorI-11
92AllWorI-24
92AllWorI-45
92LegInd-34
93HiTecI-24
93HiTecI-49
94HiTecICD-CD21
96SkyInd5-32
96SkyInd5-81
97Hi-IRL-15
97Hi-IRL'I5-I14
97Hi-IRL'I5-I19
97Hi-IRL'I5-I20
97Hi-IRLP-D6
Leach, John
90K&WDirT-28
91K&WDirT-10
92K&WDirT-21
94K&WDirT-27
95K&WDirT-35
Leal, Butch
72FleAHRDN-57
73FleAHRRU-11
91ProSetN-49
91ProSetN-97
92ProSetN-73
Leaty, Jan
91WinChoM-10
91WinChoM-11
Leavitt, Bill
72FleAHRDN-6
73FleAHRRU-8
LeBlanc, Mary
92WinChoM-8
Lebow, Rick
92JAG-68
Leclerc, Claude
92PacAmeCT-13
92PacAmeCT-43
LeCroy, Kenny
94JAG-28
Lee, Bruce
92RedGraST-18
Lee, C.B.
92TraTeaS-169
Lee, Dave
91LanRocS-50
Lee, Freddie
91HavAT-18
92DirTra-73
92HavAT-16
92JAG-189
Lee, Joe
72FleAHRDN-67
89TGRacMR-243
91TGRacMRU-242
91TGRacMRU-243
Lee, Ray
91LanSeeS-2
Lee, Ted
87WorOut-44
Lee, Terry
92BulRin-142
Leffler, Greg
80AvaHilURG-10
83A&SRacI-20
84A&SRacI-34
Leggett, Terry
89CheFlaI-78
90CheFlaI-8
90CheFlaI-20
91BigTimD-82
Lehto, J.J.
91CarForO-61
91CarForO-62
91CarForO-63
91ProTraFO-53
91ProTraFO-54
92GriForO-20
92GriForO-53
92GriForO-86
92GriForO-102
Leibensperger, Jon
92TraTeaS-87
Leighton, Brad
92PacAmeCT-6
92PacAmeCT-39
92PacAmeCT-43
LeKander, Bob
91DKIMCDT-53
Lemmings, Junior
92JAG-190
94JAG-29
Leonard, Joe
70FleDra-7
70FleDra-8
91LegInd-45
92LegInd-70
Leonard, Sonny
91BigTimD-51
Leong, Roland
89MegDra-50
89MegDra-51
Leoni, Lamberto
78GraPri-46
Lepage, Kevin
92PacAmeCT-4
94Max-302
95MaxPreS-180
96MaxPre-179
96MaxPre-247
97SkyPro-59
97SkyProA-59
97Ult-95
97UltUpd-61
97UltUpdAR-61
97VIP-34
97VIPExp-34
97VIPOilS-34
98Max10tA-26
98Max10tA-71
98PrePas-40
98PrePasOS-40
98PrePasS-36
98UppDecRttC-1
98UppDecRttC-82
99Pre-95
99PrePas-95
99UppDecVC-38
99UppDecVC-62
99UppDecVCUE-38
99UppDecVCUE-62
Lepone Jr., Joe
89MegDra-102
89MegDra-103
91ProSetN-42
91ProSetN-90
92ProSetN-74
92ProSetN-132
93FinLinN-95
Leras, Alexis
91MaxBilETCM-22
Leslie, Ben
98PrePas-74
98PrePasOS-74
Leslie, Tracy
91Max-116
92BikRacS-29
92MaxBla-64
92MaxRed-64
92ProSet-206
92Tra-165
92TraGoo-12
93FinLin-140
93FinLinCS-21
93FinLinS-140
93Max-72
93MaxPreP-72
93MaxPreS-72
93Tra-158
93TraFirR-158
94FinLinBGN-BGN7
94HigGea-57
94HigGeaG-57
94Max-173
94MaxPreP-159
94MaxPreS-173
94Tra-148
94TraFirR-148
94VIP-59
95MaxCroC-136
95MaxPreP-136
95MaxPreS-167
95PrePas-64
95PrePasRH-64
95Sel-64
95SelFlaO-64
96MaxPre-167
96MaxPre-248
97SkyPro-53
97SkyProA-53
97UltUpd-60
97UltUpdAR-60
Lester, Zeke
92TraKodEI-14
92TraTeaS-113
Letner, Danny
91GalPrePR-59
Lettow, Howie
92TraASA-48
Lewallen, Jimmie
89TGRacMR-94
89TGRacMR-95
89WinCir-40
91GalPrePR-29
91GalPrePR-32
91SpoLegHT-HT10
91TGRacMRU-94
91TGRacMRU-95
91TraPacYH-15
92HilG.HGTL-13
Lewelling, Harold
89MegDra-97
Lewis, Dave
91LegInd-60
95TraVal-31
Lewis, Jack
98Whe-93
98WheGol-93
Lewis, Joe
92RSSMotH-18
95MaxPreS-246
Lewis, Paul
89TGRacMR-98
91TGRacMRU-98
Lewis, Randy
85A&SRacI-43
87A&SRacI-37
91AllWorI-28
92AllWorI-44
92AllWorI-95
92LegInd-15
Lewter, James
89Max-20
90Max-107

91Max-211
92MaxAllPT-40
92MaxBla-258
92MaxRed-258
92TraTeaS-43
92TraTeaS-45
93Max-255
93MaxPreS-255
94MaxPreS-244
94MaxTexEl-43
95MaxPreS-242
Lezanic, Mark
92VolRacLSI-27
Libby, Bob
92WinChoM-10
Liberman, Jim
71FleAHRDC-50
Ligier, Guy
77Spo-8210
92GriForO-143
Liguori, Ralph
89WinCir-36
91SpoLegHT-HT10
91SpoLegHT-HT25
Lind, Will
89Max-36
90Max-108
91Max-212
91Tra-95
92BikRacS-8
92MaxAllPT-12
92MaxAllPT-28
92MaxBla-239
92MaxBla-250
92MaxRed-239
92MaxRed-250
92ProSet-207
92Tra-95
92TraTeaS-7
93FinLin-141
93FinLinCS-17
93FinLinS-141
94MaxPreS-247
96MaxOdy-90
Linder, Dick
89TGRacMR-183
91TGRacMRU-183
Lindley, Butch
89TGRacMR-188
89TGRacMR-189
91BulRin-1
91TGRacMRU-188
91TGRacMRU-189
92BulRin-200
Lindley, Les
92EriMaxTA-60
92EriMaxTA-75
92EriMaxTA-82
92EriMaxTA-84
92EriMaxTA-86
92EriMaxTA-91
Lindley, Mardy
92BulRin-130
Lindsey, Craig
92CorSelCCS-12
93CorSelCCS-12
Lineman, Bob
91K&WDirT-46
Ling Jr., Donny
91WinChoNED-34
91WinChoNED-35
92WinChoB-41
92WinChoB-42
Linville, Dickie
91BulRin-23
92BulRin-123
Little, Chad
89Max-90
90Max-120
91Max-19
91MaxMot-10
91MaxMot-38
91ProSet-95
91Tra-19
92MaxBla-66
92MaxBlaU-U10
92MaxMcD-32
92MaxMot-13
92MaxMot-48
92MaxRed-66
92MaxRedU-U10
92ProSet-46
92ProSet-53
92ProSet-153
92ProSet-158
92RedSta-19
92SliJimBL-20
92Tra-66
93Max-9
93MaxPreP-9
93MaxPreS-9
94HigGea-167
94HigGeaDO-167
94HigGeaDOG-167
94HigGeaG-167
94Max-19
94MaxPreS-19
94Pow-99
94PowGol-99
94VIP-60
95CroJew-57
95CroJew-67
95CroJew-GS1
95CroJewD-57
95CroJewD-67
95CroJewE-57
95CroJewE-67
95CroJewG3S-GS1
95CroJewS-57
95CroJewS-67
95FinLin-23
95FinLinPP-23
95FinLinSil-23
95HigGea-58
95HigGeaDO-58
95HigGeaDOG-58
95HigGeaG-58
95Max-152
95Max-208
95Max-269
95MaxAut-152
95MaxCroC-133
95MaxMed-BGN2
95MaxMedB-BGN2
95MaxPreP-133
95MaxPreS-163
95MaxPreS-164
95OptXL-29
95OptXLCB-29
95OptXLDC-29
95OptXLRH-29
95PrePas-65
95PrePas-74
95PrePasRH-65
95PrePasRH-74
95Sel-65
95Sel-128
95SelFlaO-65
95SelFlaO-128
95SP-70
95SP-93
95SPDieC-70
95SPDieC-93
95Tra-20
95Tra5thA-14
95Tra5thAG-14
95TraFirR-20
95TraOnTR-OTR19
95UppDec-12
95UppDec-55
95UppDec-80
95UppDec-226
95UppDec-268
95UppDecGSEG-12
95UppDecGSEG-55
95UppDecGSEG-80
95UppDecGSEG-226
95UppDecGSEG-268
95UppDecSSES-12
95UppDecSSES-55
95UppDecSSES-80
95UppDecSSES-226
95UppDecSSES-268
95VIP-41
95VIPAut-41
95VIPCooB-41
95VIPEmeP-41
95VIPRedHCB-41
96CroJewEDT-71
96CroJewEDTC-71
96CroJewEE-71
96CroJewEli-71
96CroJewES-71
96CroJewETC-71
96CroJewETCE-71
96CroJewETCS-71
96FinLin-47
96FinLinPriP-47
96FinLinS-47
96Fla-41
96Max-75
96MaxMadiA-68
96MaxMadiA-74
96MaxMadiABR-BR14
96MaxOdy-68
96MaxOdy-74
96MaxOdyRA-RA14
96MaxPre-157
96MaxPre-160
96MaxSup-ST5
96PrePas-60
96PrePasP-32
96PrePasPEP-32
96PrePasPH-32
96PrePasSco-60
96PrePasT-60
96SP-42
96Ult-122
96Ult-123
96Ult-154
96UltAut-17
96UltSeaC-13
96UltUpd-38
96UppDec-18
96UppDecRTTC-RC43
96UppDecRTTC-RC74
96V.IAut-15
96VIP-35
96VIPEmeP-35
96Viper-47
96ViperBlaM-47
96ViperCop-47
96ViperGreM-47
96VIPTor-35
97ActPac-21
97ActPac-42
97ActPacFI-21
97ActPacFI-42
97ColCho-42
97ColCho-91
97ColChoSQ-SQ8
97ColChoUD5-UD87
97ColChoUD5-UD88
97JurPar-24
97JurParT-24
97Max-26
97Max-71
97PinCer-31
97PinCer-65
97PinCer-83
97PinCerMB-31
97PinCerMB-65
97PinCerMB-83
97PinCerMG-31
97PinCerMG-65
97PinCerMG-83
97PinCerMR-31
97PinCerMR-65
97PinCerMR-83
97PinCerR-31
97PinCerR-65
97PinCerR-83
97PinPor-43
97PinTotCPB-31
97PinTotCPB-65
97PinTotCPB-83
97PinTotCPG-31
97PinTotCPG-65
97PinTotCPG-83
97PinTotCPR-31
97PinTotCPR-65
97PinTotCPR-83
97Pre-25
97PreBlaWFS-25
97PreGri-25
97PrePas-74
97PrePas-88
97PrePas-125
97PrePasAut-29
97PrePasL-74
97PrePasL-88
97PrePasL-125
97PrePasOS-74
97PrePasOS-88
97PrePasOS-125
97PrePasP-24
97PrePasPEP-24
97PrePasPM-24
97PrePasPOS-24
97PrePasT-74
97PrePasT-88
97PrePasT-125
97PreRedW-25
97RacCho-9
97RacCho-44
97RacCho-83
97RacChoSS-9
97RacChoSS-44
97RacChoSS-83
97RacSha-24
97RacShaGWP-24
97RacShaH-24
97RacShaSTS-ST13
97RacShaTS-24
97SP-35
97SP-77
97SP SupS-35
97SP SupS-77
97Ult-87
97UppDecRTTC-40
97UppDecRTTC-82
97UppDecRTTC-120
97UppDecRTTC-145
97UppDecVC-42
97UppDecVC-91
97VIP-27
97Viper-24
97ViperBlaR-24
97VIPExp-27
97VIPOilS-27
98ColCho-87
98Max-87
98Max-16
98Max-41
98Max-66
98Max-91
98Max10tA-2
98Max10tA-47
98Max10tAMP-P16
98MaxSwaP-SW20
98MaxTea-TW7
98MaxYealRBS-113
98MaxYealRBS-160
98PrePasS-53
98PrePasSF-53
98UppDecRttC-52
98UppDecRttC-71
98UppDecRttC-99
98UppDecVC-26
98UppDecVC-71
98VIP-44
98VIPExp-44
99PrePas-108
99UppDecVC-31
99UppDecVC-56
99UppDecVCUE-31
99UppDecVCUE-56
99WheHigGAC-21
Little, Chuck
91MaxMot-17
91ProSet-120
92MaxBla-132
92MaxRed-132
Little, David
92MaxAllPT-43
92MaxBla-260
92MaxRed-260
93Max-248
93MaxPreS-248
94HigGeaPPT-W31
94HigGeaPPTG-31W
Little, Donnie
89CheFlal-82
89CheFlal-97
90BigTimD-10
90BigTimDS-10
90CheFlal-6
91BigTimD-58
Littlejohn, Joe
91HicMotS-2
92JAG-191
Littleton, Jeff
90BigTimD-11
90BigTimDS-11
90CheFlal-4
91BigTimD-69
Litton, Gary
89CheFlal-51
90CheFlal-53
Litton, Steve
89CheFlal-10
90CheFlal-42
Livengood, Dewey
92MaxBla-164
92MaxRed-164
92ProSet-231
Livingston, Ed
91GalPrePR-105
Livinston, John Jr.
92BulRin-73
Lizotte, Jon
92WinChoM-27
Lloyd, Mike
90LanRocSHS-36
91LanRocS-24
92LanRocS-33
Lockhart, Frank
54StaWetIW-1926
60HawWaxI-14
Loehman, John
91LanART-20
Loehr, Dick
71FleAHRDC-43
Loftin, Louise
92TraTeaS-195
Lombardi, Lella
89TGRacMR-171
91TGRacMRU-171
Lombardo, John
72FleAHRDN-45
Long, Jim
92TraTeaS-69
94Max-285
95Max-126
95MaxAut-126
97PinPreP-TP8B
Long, Mike
94MaxTexEl-44
Long, Rod
91PioStoCR-1
91PioStoCR-6
Long, Roger
91JAG-22
92JAG-192
94JAG-30
Long, Russell
72FleAHRDN-49
Longmire, Keith
94JAG-31
Loomis, Robbie
91Max-131
91ProSet-67
91Tra-143
92MaxBla-173
92MaxRed-173
92ProSet-87
92Tra-143
92TraTeaS-186
93FinLin-129
93FinLinCS-19
93FinLinS-129
93Max-169
93MaxPreP-151
93MaxPreS-169
93Tra-139
93TraFirR-139
94FinLin-131
94FinLinS-131
94HigGea-143
94HigGeaDO-143
94HigGeaDOG-143
94HigGeaG-143
94Max-158
94MaxPreP-148
94MaxPreS-158
94Tra-169
94TraFirR-169
95CroJew-39
95CroJewD-39
95CroJewE-39
95CroJewS-39
95HigGea-46
95HigGeaDO-46
95HigGeaDOG-46
95HigGeaG-46
95Max-145
95MaxAut-145
95MaxCroC-127
95MaxPreP-127
95MaxPreS-151
95SP-139
95SPDieC-139
95TraBehTS-BTS9
96Max-83
96MaxPre-142
96PrePas-80
96PrePasSco-80
96PrePasT-80
97Viper-58
97ViperBlaR-58

95ActPacS-1
95ActPacS-33
95ActPacS-46
95ActPacS-50
95ActPacS-54
95ActPacS-55
95ActPacS-56
95ActPacS-57
95ActPacS-58
95ActPacS-59
95ActPacS2G-1G
95ActPacS2G-5G
95ActPacSSS-1
95ActPacSSS-33
95ActPacSSS-46
95ActPacSSS-50
95ActPacSSS-54
95ActPacSSS-55
95ActPacSSS-56
95ActPacSSS-57
95ActPacSSS-58
95ActPacSSS-59
95Ass-6
95Ass-8
95Ass-34
95Ass$5$25PC-1
95Ass1M$PC-19
95AssGolS-6
95AssGolS-8
95AssGolS-34
95CroJew-9
95CroJew-66
95CroJew-74
95CroJew-78
95CroJew-SM1
95CroJewD-9
95CroJewD-66
95CroJewD-74
95CroJewD-78
95CroJewD5BTBW-SM1
95CroJewE-9
95CroJewE-66
95CroJewE-74
95CroJewE-78
95CroJewS-9
95CroJewS-66
95CroJewS-74
95CroJewS-78
95FinLin-4
95FinLin-27
95FinLin-94
95FinLinCC6-6
95FinLinCC6-8
95FinLinCC6-34
95FinLinCotM-2
95FinLinGS-GS4
95FinLinPP-4
95FinLinPP-27
95FinLinPP-94
95FinLinSil-4
95FinLinSil-27
95FinLinSil-94
95HigGea-15
95HigGea-81
95HigGea-93
95HigGeaBC-BC14
95HigGeaBCG-BC14
95HigGeaDO-15
95HigGeaDO-81
95HigGeaDO-93
95HigGeaDOG-15
95HigGeaDOG-81
95HigGeaDOG-93
95HigGeaG-15
95HigGeaG-81
95HigGeaG-93
95HiTecB4-8
95HiTecB4-84
95Ima-4
95Ima-54
95Ima-84
95ImaDri-D4
95ImaGol-4
95ImaGol-54
95ImaGol-84
95ImaHarC-HC2
95Max-4
95Max-9
95Max-172
95MaxCroC-4
95MaxCroC-38
95MaxCroC-148
95MaxLicD-3
95MaxMed-3
95MaxMed-33
95MaxMedB-3
95MaxMedB-33
95MaxPreP-4
95MaxPreP-38
95MaxPreP-148
95MaxPreS-4
95MaxPreS-38
95MaxPreS-263
95MaxStaU-2
95OptXL-13
95OptXL-34
95OptXL-54
95OptXL-57
95OptXLCB-13
95OptXLCB-34
95OptXLCB-54
95OptXLCB-57
95OptXLDC-13
95OptXLDC-34
95OptXLDC-54
95OptXLDC-57
95OptXLRH-13
95OptXLRH-34
95OptXLRH-54
95OptXLRH-57
95OptXLS-XLS8
95PrePas-18
95PrePas-44
95PrePas-137
95PrePas-A18
95PrePasCC-18
95PrePasCCR-CCR1
95PrePasPH-12
95PrePasPH-36
95PrePasPPC-NNO
95PrePasPre-12
95PrePasPre-36
95PrePasPRH-12
95PrePasPRH-36
95PrePasRD-RD8
95PrePasRH-18
95PrePasRH-44
95PrePasRH-137
95Sel-19
95Sel-44
95SelFlaO-19
95SelFlaO-44
95SelSki-SS15
95SP-3
95SP-34
95SP-35
95SP-78
95SPBacTB-BB3
95SPDieC-3
95SPDieC-34
95SPDieC-35
95SPDieC-78
95SPSpeM-SM4
95SPSpeMDC-SM4
95Tra-6
95Tra-71
95Tra-72
95Tra5thA-7
95Tra5thA-36
95Tra5thA-44
95Tra5thACC-C4
95Tra5thAG-7
95Tra5thAG-36
95Tra5thAG-44
95Tra5thAR-R5
95Tra5thAUEC-E7
95TraAutV-28
95TraCha-C10
95TraFirR-6
95TraFirR-72
95TraRacM-RM2
95TraSerS-SS7
95UppDec-11
95UppDec-54
95UppDec-79
95UppDec-113
95UppDec-169
95UppDec-184
95UppDec-230
95UppDec-271
95UppDec-UD1
95UppDec-UD3
95UppDecGSEG-11
95UppDecGSEG-54
95UppDecGSEG-79
95UppDecGSEG-113
95UppDecGSEG-169
95UppDecGSEG-184
95UppDecGSEG-230
95UppDecGSEG-271
95UppDecPSP-PP2
95UppDecSSES-11
95UppDecSSES-54
95UppDecSSES-79
95UppDecSSES-113
95UppDecSSES-169
95UppDecSSES-184
95UppDecSSES-230
95UppDecSSES-271
95VIP-18
95VIP-32
95VIP-52
95VIPAut-18
95VIPCooB-18
95VIPCooB-32
95VIPCooB-52
95VIPEmeP-18
95VIPEmeP-32
95VIPEmeP-52
95VIPFanC-FC5
95VIPFanCG-FC5
95VIPRedHCB-18
95VIPRedHCB-32
95VIPRedHCB-52
95VIPRef-R3
95VIPRefG-R3
95Zen-4
95Zen-37
95ZenHel-7
95ZenWinW-1
95ZenWinW-5
95ZenWinW-18
95ZenZT-5
96ActPacC-22
96ActPacC-95
96ActPacCSS-22
96ActPacLotP-9
96ActPacLotP-10
96ActPacM-4
96ActPacM-14
96Ass-10
96Ass$1000CCIPC-19
96Ass$100CCIPC-8
96Ass$2PC-12
96AssComL-CL7
96AssRacD-RD4
96AutRac-13
96AutRacA-30
96AutRacCA-30
96AutRacFR-48
96AutRacFR-49
96AutRacFR-50
96AutRacFR-51
96AutRacFR-52
96AutRacFR-53
96AutRacFR-54
96AutRacFR-55
96AutRacFR-56
96AutRacFR-57
96AutRacFR-58
96AutRacHP-HP4
96AutRacKotC$PC-KC3
96Cla-1
96Cla-31
96Cla-52
96ClaImaP-RP1
96ClaInn-IV4
96ClaInn-IV11
96ClaMarMC-MC5
96ClaPriP-1
96ClaPriP-31
96ClaRacC-RC4
96ClaRacC-RC14
96ClaSil-1
96ClaSil-31
96CroJewEADJ-DJ2
96CroJewEDT-5
96CroJewEDT-33
96CroJewEDTC-5
96CroJewEDTC-33
96CroJewEDTCSA-CS8
96CroJewEE-5
96CroJewEE-33
96CroJewEli-5
96CroJewEli-33
96CroJewERCSG-CS8
96CroJewERCSP-CS8
96CroJewES-5
96CroJewES-33
96CroJewETC-5
96CroJewETC-33
96CroJewETCE-5
96CroJewETCE-33
96CroJewETCS-5
96CroJewETCS-33
96FinLin-23
96FinLin-41
96FinLin-62
96FinLinBGL-C3
96FinLinBGL-D4
96FinLinGS-GS2
96FinLinMM-MM4
96FinLinPP-22
96FinLinPP-23
96FinLinPP$10C-7
96FinLinPP$5C-15
96FinLinPP$S-22
96FinLinPP$S-23
96FinLinPriP-23
96FinLinPriP-41
96FinLinPriP-62
96FinLinS-23
96FinLinS-41
96FinLinS-62
96Fla-20
96Fla-76
96FlaAut-9
96FlaPowP-7
96Kni-3
96Kni-33
96KniBlaK-3
96KniBlaK-33
96KniFirK-FK10
96KniKniRT-KT6
96KniQueRKP-3
96KniQueRKP-33
96KniRoy-3
96KniRoy-33
96KniWhiK-3
96KniWhiK-33
96M-F-5
96M-F-6
96M-FSil-S4
96Max-4
96Max-P1
96MaxMadiA-4
96MaxMadiA-66
96MaxMadiABR-BR13
96MaxOdy-4
96MaxOdyM-MM5
96MaxOdyOTRA-OTRA3
96MaxOdyRA-RA13
96MaxPep5-5
96MaxPre-4
96MaxPre-61
96MaxSteMR-1
96Pin-4
96Pin-39
96Pin-74
96Pin-75
96Pin-76
96Pin-77
96Pin-87
96Pin-93
96Pin-4
96Pin-39
96Pin-74
96Pin-75
96Pin-76
96Pin-77
96Pin-87
96Pin-93
96PinCheF-4
96PinCutA-14
96PinPolP-4
96PinPolP-28
96PinPolP-64
96PinPolP-71
96PinPolP-76
96PinPolPCS-4
96PinPolPLF-4
96PinPolPLF-28
96PinPolPLF-64
96PinPolPLF-71
96PinPolPLF-76
96PinPolPNL-4
96PinPolPNLG-4
96PinTeaP-8
96PinTeaP-P8
96PinWinCC-4
96PinWinCC-39
96PinWinCC-74
96PinWinCC-75
96PinWinCC-76
96PinWinCC-77
96PinWinCC-87
96PinWinCC-93
96PrePas-19
96PrePas-43
96PrePas-74
96PrePas-88
96PrePas-95
96PrePas&NC-19
96PrePasBR-BR5
96PrePasCC-19
96PrePasCF-CF4
96PrePasFoc-F6
96PrePasFQS-FQS7A
96PrePasFQS-FQS7B
96PrePasP-3
96PrePasP$10PC-6
96PrePasP$20PC-6
96PrePasP$5PC-6
96PrePasPCB-CB10
96PrePasPEP-3
96PrePasPH-3
96PrePasSco-19
96PrePasSco-43
96PrePasSco-74
96PrePasSco-88
96PrePasSco-95
96PrePasT-19
96PrePasT-43
96PrePasT-74
96PrePasT-88
96PrePasT-95
96RacCho-4
96RacCho-28
96RacCho-71
96RacCho-72
96RacCho-73
96RacCho-74
96RacCho-75
96RacCho-99
96RacCho-P3
96RacChoAP-4
96RacChoAP-28
96RacChoAP-71
96RacChoAP-72
96RacChoAP-73
96RacChoAP-74
96RacChoAP-75
96RacChoAP-99
96RacChoSC-4
96RacChoSC-28
96RacChoSC-71
96RacChoSC-72
96RacChoSC-73
96RacChoSC-74
96RacChoSC-75
96RacChoSC-99
96RacChoTT-3
96SP-4
96SP-44
96SP-82
96SpeArtP-2
96SpeArtP-19
96SpeArtP-38
96SpeCleS-3
96SpeInM-3
96SpePro-3
96SpeRac-2
96SpeRac-19
96SpeRac-38
96SPHolME-ME4
96SPx-4
96SPxGol-4
96TraRev&PTCG-TC1
96TraRev&PTCG-TC15
96TraRev&PTCH-TC1
96TraRev&PTCH-TC15
96TraRevP-1
96TraRevP-17
96TraRevP-32
96TraRevP-P1
96TraRevPFR-1
96TraRevPFR-17
96TraRevPFR-32
96TraRevPLG-LG16
96TraRevPM-1
96TraRevPM-17
96TraRevPM-32
96TraRevPTC-TC1
96TraRevPTC-TC15
96Ult-13
96Ult-14
96Ult-15
96Ult-199
96UltAut-19
96UltBoxS-3

96UltFlaP-3
96UltGolM-3
96UltThu&L-7
96UltThu&L-8
96UltUpd-20
96UltUpd-66
96UltUpdA-9
96UltUpdPP-9
96UltUpdW-5
96UltUpdW-17
96UppDec-3
96UppDec-43
96UppDec-83
96UppDec-133
96UppDecPP-RP7
96UppDecPW-HP3
96UppDecRTTC-RC2
96UppDecRTTC-RC125
96UppDecRTTCAS-H2
96UppDecRTTCPPoi-PP2
96UppDRTTCPPR-PR2
96UppDecRTTCPT3-T2
96UppDecRTTCPT3-T6
96UppDecRTTCRL-RL13
96UppDecRTTCT3PR-R4
96UppDecVV-VV4
96UppDecVVG-VV4
96VIP-16
96VIPEmeP-16
96Viper-3
96ViperBlaM-3
96ViperBusC-B8
96ViperCob-C5
96ViperCop-3
96ViperDia-D7
96ViperDiaA-DA3
96ViperGreM-3
96ViperKinC-KC10
96VIPTor-16
96VIPWarP-WP3
96VIPWarPG-WP3
96Zen-3
96Zen-37
96Zen-95
96ZenArtP-3
96ZenArtP-37
96ZenArtP-95
96ZenHig-3
97ActPac-4
97ActPac-46
97ActPac-76
97ActPac2G-9
97ActPacCM-5
97ActPacFI-4
97ActPacFI-46
97ActPacFI-76
97ActPacRT-11
97AutRac-12
97AutRac-37
97AutRac-44
97AutRacA-31
97AutRacMS-KM12
97ColCho-4
97ColCho-54
97ColCho-103
97ColChoC-CC8
97ColChoC-CC42
97ColChoC-CC75
97ColChoS-S7
97ColChoS-S8
97ColChoSQ-SQ30
97ColChoUD5-UD5
97ColChoUD5-UD6
97FinLinPP2-9
97FinLinPP2$10-68
97FinLinPP2$5-47
97JurPar-7
97JurParC-C12
97JurParP-P7
97JurParR-R13
97JurParT-7
97Max-4
97Max-49
97Max-112
97Pin-4
97Pin-33
97Pin-71
97Pin-78
97PinArtP-4
97PinArtP-33
97PinArtP-71
97PinArtP-78
97PinCer-4
97PinCer-38
97PinCerMB-4
97PinCerMB-38
97PinCerMG-4
97PinCerMG-38
97PinCerMR-4
97PinCerMR-38
97PinCerR-4
97PinCerR-38
97PinChe-2
97PinChe-5
97PinChe-8
97PinMin-8
97PinMin2GC-8
97PinMinB-8
97PinMinC-8
97PinMinG-8
97PinMinNC-8
97PinMinS-8
97PinPre-19
97PinPre-21
97PinPre-22
97PinPre-23
97PinPre-24
97PinPre-26
97PinPre-27
97PinPreBM-19
97PinPreBM-21
97PinPreBM-22
97PinPreBM-24
97PinPreBM-27
97PinPreGM-19
97PinPreGM-21
97PinPreGM-22
97PinPreGM-24
97PinPreGM-27
97PinPreP-4
97PinPreP-33
97PinPreP-71
97PinPreP-78
97PinPreSM-19
97PinPreSM-21
97PinPreSM-22
97PinPreSM-24
97PinPreSM-27
97PinTotCPB-4
97PinTotCPB-38
97PinTotCPG-4
97PinTotCPG-38
97PinTotCPR-4
97PinTotCPR-38
97PinTroC-4
97PinTroC-33
97PinTroC-71
97PinTroC-78
97Pre-7
97PreAmeE-AE6
97PreBlaWFS-7
97PreEyeotT-ET8
97PreGat-GB8
97PreGatA-GBA8
97PreGolE-GE6
97PreGri-7
97PrePas-8
97PrePas-33
97PrePas-61
97PrePas-98
97PrePasAut-8
97PrePasBB-BB8
97PrePasCC'-CC13
97PrePasL-8
97PrePasL-33
97PrePasL-61
97PrePasL-98
97PrePasOS-8
97PrePasOS-33
97PrePasOS-61
97PrePasOS-98
97PrePasP-8
97PrePasP-42
97PrePasPCB-CB9
97PrePasPCBD-CB9
97PrePasPEP-8
97PrePasPEP-42
97PrePasPM-8
97PrePasPM-42
97PrePasPOS-8
97PrePasPOS-42
97PrePasT-8
97PrePasT-33
97PrePasT-61
97PrePasT-98
97PrePasVL-VL6A
97PrePasVL-VL6B
97PreRedW-7
97RacCho-4
97RacCho-39
97RacCho-92
97RacChoSS-4
97RacChoSS-39
97RacChoSS-92
97RacSha-7
97RacSha-38
97RacShaGW-GW9
97RacShaGWP-7
97RacShaGWP-38
97RacShaH-7
97RacShaH-38
97RacShaPFBSA-7
97RacShaSA-SA6
97RacShaSTS-ST5
97RacShaTS-7
97RacShaTS-38
97SBMot-11
97SBMot-48
97SBMot-57
97SBMot-98
97SBMot-100
97SBMotRC-RC5
97SBMotWR-WC9
97ScoBoal-12
97ScoBoal-41
97ScoBoal$PC-PC5
97SkyPro-18
97SkyPro-64
97SkyProA-18
97SP-4
97SP-46
97SP-86
97SP-114
97SP SupS-4
97SP SupS-46
97SP SupS-86
97SP SupS-114
97SPX-4
97SPxBlu-4
97SPxGol-4
97SPxSil-4
97SPXSpeA-SV4
97Ult-20
97Ult-45
97UltDriV-D5
97UltIns-DC6
97UltSho-9
97UltUpd-9
97UltUpd-78
97UltUpdAR-9
97UppDecRTTC-8
97UppDecRTTC-50
97UppDecRTTC-92
97UppDecRTTC-111
97UppDecRTTC-125
97UppDecRTTCCQ-CQ8
97UDRTTCCQC-CQ8
97UppDecRTTCGF-RD4
97UppDecRTTCPP-PP10
97UppDecRTTCPPlu-+4
97UDRTTCPPRC-+4
97UppDRTTCPPRDC-+4
97UppDecRTTCQW-CQ8
97UppDecVC-4
97UppDecVC-54
97UppDecVC-104
97UppDecVCCR-CR8
97UppDecVCDS-DS5
97UppDecVCP-PE4
97UppDecVCPC-PH4
97UppDecVCVL-VL6
97VIP-15
97Viper-7
97ViperBlaR-7
97ViperCob-C7
97ViperKinC-KC7
97ViperSid-S13
97ViperSnaE-SE12
97VIPExp-15
97VIPOilS-15
97VIPRinoH-RH3
97VIPRinoHDC-RH3
98ColCho-4
98ColCho-40
98HigGea-22
98HigGea-61
98HigGeaFG-8
98HigGeaGJ-GJ3
98HigGeaM-8
98Max-27
98Max-57
98Max10tA-36
98Max10tA-81
98Max10tAMP-P3
98MaxBatP-B13
98MaxFirC-F20
98MaxSwaP-SW14
98MaxYealRBS-148
98PrePas-8
98PrePas-57
98PrePasCC'-CC13
98PrePasOS-8
98PrePasOS-57
98PrePasP-50
98PrePasP-50
98PrePasPS-PS3
98PrePasPSH-SH9
98PrePasS-7
98PrePasS-56
98PrePasSF-56
98PrePasSO-23
98PrePasSO-24
98PrePasSOD-23
98PrePasSOD-24
98PrePasSS-11
98PrePasSSD-11
98SP Aut-27
98SP Aut-61
98SP Aut-80
98SP AutSotTL1-S4
98UppDecDV-4
98UppDecDVSM-4
98UppDecRttC-40
98UppDecRttC-72
98UppDecVC-4
98UppDecVC-49
98UppDecVCPP-4
98UppDecVCPPCR-4
98VIP-15
98VIPDriF-DF13
98VIPDriFD-DF13
98VIPExp-15
98Whe-19
98Whe-41
98Whe-89
98Whe50tA-A10
98Whe50tA-A25
98WheGol-19
98WheGol-41
98WheGol-89
98WheGreF-GF12
99Pre-14
99PrePas-14
99PrePas-114
99PrePasCC-16B
99PrePasCC-13
99PrePasS-16A
99UppDecVC-30
99UppDecVC-46
99UppDecVCTM-TM4
99UppDecVCUE-30
99UppDecVCUE-46
99WheHigG-14
99WheHigGAC-14
99WheHigGFG-14
99WheHigGM-14
99WheHigGS-GS14

Marlin, Sutherlin
95ZenWinW-18
96RacCho-72
96RacChoAP-72
96RacChoSC-72

Marlowe, Greg
92BulRin-163

Marquis, Jerry
91WinChoM-41
91WinChoM-42
91WinChoNED-112
91WinChoNED-113
92WinChoB-107
92WinChoB-108

Marriott, Fred
11AmeTobAD-15

Marsh, Bill
92TraKodEl-17
92TraTeaS-114

Marsh, Donald
92JAG-70

Marsh, John
91WinChoNED-96
91WinChoNED-97

Martin, Bill
92JAG-71

Martin, Buddy
72FleAHRDN-42
73FleAHRRU-34
73FleAHRRU-35

Martin, Cary
92WinChoM-36

Martin, Curt
91DKIMCDT-32

Martin, Dode
65TopHotR-51
65TopHotR-60

Martin, Don
92VolRacLS2-45
92VolRacLSI-71

Martin, Gil
93Max-176
93MaxBabRJB-NNO
93MaxPreS-176
94Max-310

Martin, Helen
92VolRacLSI-70

Martin, Jeff
91LanStoCC-13

Martin, Jimmy
90K&WDirT-30
91K&WURCS-3
91Tra-90
92Tra-90
92TraTeaS-198

Martin, John
89MegDra-34
89MegDra-35

Martin, Mark
88MaxCha-48
89Max-6
89Max-127
89MaxPre-NNO
90Max-6
90Max-185
90Max-195
90MaxHolF-HF8
91IRO-4
91Max-6
91Max-113
91Max-171
91Max-189
91Max-195
91MaxMcD-2A
91MaxMcD-2B
91MaxMcD-30
91MaxMot-5
91MaxMot-33
91MaxRacFK-1
91MaxTheWA-11
91MaxUpd-6
91ProSet-21
91ProSet-25
91ProSet-99
91SunRacL-6
91SupRacM-7
91Tra-6
91Tra-50
91Tra-P2
92-CarDynBTBS-9
92CarDynGO-6
92MacTooWC-15
92MaxAllPT-3
92MaxBla-6
92MaxBla-200
92MaxBla-233
92MaxBla-293
92MaxBlaU-U11
92MaxMcD-14
92MaxMot-5
92MaxMot-40
92MaxMot-49
92MaxMot-50
92MaxRed-6
92MaxRed-200
92MaxRed-233
92MaxRed-293
92MaxRedU-U11
92MaxTheW-17
92MaxTheW-37
92ProSet-61
92ProSet-71
92ProSet-96
92ProSet-184
92ProSet-242
92ProSetMH-13
92ProSetRF-5
92RedSta-6
92SpoLegAK-AK9
92SpoLegAK-AK11
92Tra-6
92Tra-38
92TraASA-41

92TraRacM-6
92TraRacM-53
92TraRacM-73
92TraRacM-76
92TraRacM-P76
92TraRacMB-16B
93ActPac-9
93ActPac-22
93ActPac-44
93ActPac-77
93ActPac-78
93ActPac-109
93ActPac-110
93ActPac-176
93ActPac2G-5G
93ActPac2G-58G
93CarDynDEP-8
93CarDynQC-10
93FinLin-12
93FinLin-133
93FinLin-164
93FinLinCS-5
93FinLinCS-11
93FinLinCS-27
93FinLinS-12
93FinLinS-133
93FinLinS-164
93HiTecTT-6
93Max-6
93Max-85
93Max-199
93Max-271
93Max-290
93MaxHou-6
93MaxMot-13
93MaxMot-33
93MaxMot-50
93MaxPreP-6
93MaxPreP-57
93MaxPreP-85
93MaxPreP-186
93MaxPreP-205
93MaxPreS-6
93MaxPreS-85
93MaxPreS-199
93MaxPreS-271
93MaxPreS-290
93MaxRetJ-5
93MaxTheW-2
93MaxTheW-22
93MotManC-7
93PrePasPre-10
93PrePasPre-34
93Tra-6
93Tra-32
93Tra-56
93Tra-60
93Tra-67
93Tra-78
93Tra-109
93Tra-161
93TraFirR-6
93TraFirR-32
93TraFirR-56
93TraFirR-60
93TraFirR-67
93TraFirR-78
93TraFirR-109
93TraFirR-161
93TraPreC-6
93TraTri-1
93TraTri-6
93TraTri-19
93TraTri-23
93TraTri-32
93TraTri-37
93TraTri-41
94ActPac-3
94ActPac-33
94ActPac-43
94ActPac-69
94ActPac-115
94ActPac-153
94ActPac-199
94ActPac-200
94ActPac-201
94ActPac-202
94ActPac-203
94ActPac2G-3G
94ActPac2G-13G
94ActPac2G-23G
94ActPacC-11
94ActPacP-3R944
94CarDynGO-8
94CarDynMM-2
94FinLin-7
94FinLin-85
94FinLin-99
94FinLin-126
94FinLin-11
94FinLinDH-4
94FinLinG-14
94FinLinG-48
94FinLinG-72
94FinLinG-79
94FinLinG-81
94FinLinGA-81
94FinLinGCC-NNO
94FinLinGS-NNO
94FinLinGT-TG2
94FinLinP-P2
94FinLinS-7
94FinLinS-85
94FinLinS-99
94FinLinS-126
94FinLinVL-VL5
94FinLinVL-VL14
94Hi-Bri4AP-14
94Hi-Bri4AP-19
94Hi-Bri4AP-27
94Hi-Bri4AP-29
94Hi-Bri4AP-31
94Hi-Bri4AP-40
94HigGea-3
94HigGea-89
94HigGea-106
94HigGea-175
94HigGea-189
94HigGea-190
94HigGea-191
94HigGea-192
94HigGea-199
94HigGea-MMS1
94HigGeaD-D1
94HigGeaD-D6
94HigGeaDO-106
94HigGeaDO-175
94HigGeaDO-189
94HigGeaDO-190
94HigGeaDO-191
94HigGeaDO-192
94HigGeaDO-199
94HigGeaDOG-106
94HigGeaDOG-175
94HigGeaDOG-189
94HigGeaDOG-190
94HigGeaDOG-191
94HigGeaDOG-192
94HigGeaDOG-199
94HigGeaG-3
94HigGeaG-89
94HigGeaG-106
94HigGeaG-175
94HigGeaG-189
94HigGeaG-190
94HigGeaG-191
94HigGeaG-192
94HigGeaG-199
94HigGeaMG-MG4
94HigMinV-5B
94HigMinV-5S
94HiTecB4-14
94HiTecB4-19
94HiTecB4-27
94HiTecB4-29
94HiTecB4-31
94HiTecB4-40
94Max-6
94Max-35
94Max-226
94Max-227
94Max-228
94Max-229
94Max-236
94Max-258
94Max-259
94MaxAut-6
94MaxAut-227
94MaxMed-33
94MaxMed-70
94MaxMot-3
94MaxPreP-6
94MaxPreP-35
94MaxPreP-185
94MaxPreP-186
94MaxPreP-187
94MaxPreP-188
94MaxPreP-195
94MaxPreS-6
94MaxPreS-35
94MaxPreS-285
94MaxPreS-286
94MaxPreS-287
94MaxPreS-288
94MaxPreS-295
94MaxPreSJ-4
94MaxRacC-4
94MaxTheS2-3
94OptXL-12
94OptXL-27
94OptXL-52
94OptXLDouC-DC5
94OptXLRH-12
94OptXLRH-27
94OptXLRH-52
94Pow-20
94Pow-44
94Pow-56
94Pow-62
94PowGol-20
94PowGol-44
94PowGol-56
94PowGol-62
94PowPre-15
94PowPre-19
94PrePas-17
94PrePas-32
94PrePas-54
94PrePas-121
94PrePas-141
94PrePasA-NNO
94PrePasCC-CC17
94PrePasCF-CF3
94PrePasH-H4
94PrePasRD-RD5
94Sky-9
94Tra-6
94Tra-37
94Tra-60
94Tra-82
94Tra-100
94Tra-113
94Tra-144
94Tra-176
94Tra-P2
94TraAut-A8
94TraAutV-33
94TraCar-C1
94TraFirR-6
94TraFirR-37
94TraFirR-60
94TraFirR-82
94TraFirR-100
94TraFirR-113
94TraFirR-144
94TraFirR-176
94TraPreC-24
94TraWin-W14
94VIP-21
94VIP-53
94VIP-78
94VIPDriC-DC5
94VIPExc2-EC5
94VIPMemO-NNO
94WheHarG-74
94WheHarGG-74
95ActPacC-44
95ActPacC-55
95ActPacC2T-4
95ActPacCSS-44
95ActPacCSS-55
95ActPacM-MM5
95ActPacP-15
95ActPacP-40
95ActPacP-55
95ActPacP-60
95ActPacP-72
95ActPacP2G-4G
95ActPacS-3
95ActPacS-35
95ActPacSSS-3
95ActPacSSS-35
95Ass-27
95Ass-41
95Ass-48
95Ass$5$25PC-7
95Ass1M$PC-13
95AssCocC6DC-8
95AssGolS-27
95AssGolS-41
95AssGolS-48
95CroJew-3
95CroJewD-3
95CroJewDJ-DJ4
95CroJewDJD-DJ4
95CroJewDJE-DJ4
95CroJewE-3
95CroJewS-3
95CroJewSG-SG6
95FinLin-6
95FinLin-54
95FinLin-79
95FinLinCC6-27
95FinLinCC6-41
95FinLinCC6-48
95FinLinCC6DC-C5
95FinLinCotM-3
95FinLinGS-GS6
95FinLinP5U-NNO
95FinLinPP-6
95FinLinPP-54
95FinLinPP-79
95FinLinSC-SC2
95FinLinSD-SD2
95FinLinSil-6
95FinLinSil-54
95FinLinSil-79
95HigGea-3
95HigGea-63
95HigGea-73
95HigGea-88
95HigGeaBC-BC10
95HigGeaBCG-BC10
95HigGeaDO-3
95HigGeaDO-63
95HigGeaDO-73
95HigGeaDO-88
95HigGeaDOG-3
95HigGeaDOG-63
95HigGeaDOG-73
95HigGeaDOG-88
95HigGeaG-3
95HigGeaG-63
95HigGeaG-73
95HigGeaG-88
95HigGeaP-P3
95HiTecB4-9
95HiTecB4-70
95HiTecB4P-P1
95Ima-6
95Ima-65
95Ima-88
95ImaDri-D5
95ImaGol-6
95ImaGol-65
95ImaGol-88
95ImaHarC-HC3
95Max-6
95Max-109
95Max-125
95Max-146
95Max-162
95Max-215
95MaxCroC-6
95MaxCroC-35
95MaxCroC-169
95MaxCroC-180
95MaxLicD-7
95MaxMed-5
95MaxMed-35
95MaxMedB-5
95MaxMedB-35
95MaxPreP-6
95MaxPreP-35
95MaxPreP-169
95MaxPreP-180
95MaxPrePP-PS1
95MaxPrePRJ-3
95MaxPreS-6
95MaxPreS-35
95MaxPreS-261
95MaxPreS-284
95MaxPreS-295
95OptXL-14
95OptXL-35
95OptXL-48
95OptXL-58
95OptXLCB-14
95OptXLCB-35
95OptXLCB-48
95OptXLCB-58
95OptXLDC-14
95OptXLDC-35
95OptXLDC-48
95OptXLDC-58
95OptXLP-XL3
95OptXLRH-14
95OptXLRH-35
95OptXLRH-48
95OptXLRH-58
95OptXLS-XLS9
95PrePas-19
95PrePas-53
95PrePas-66
95PrePas-104
95PrePas-116
95PrePasCC-19
95PrePasCF-CF6
95PrePasPH-2
95PrePasPH-30
95PrePasPHP-HP5
95PrePasPPC-NNO
95PrePasPre-2
95PrePasPre-30
95PrePasPRH-2
95PrePasPRH-30
95PrePasRD-RD9
95PrePasRH-19
95PrePasRH-53
95PrePasRH-66
95PrePasRH-104
95PrePasRH-116
95Sel-20
95Sel-53
95Sel-66
95Sel-129
95Sel-143
95SelDreM-DM3
95SelFlaO-20
95SelFlaO-53
95SelFlaO-66
95SelFlaO-129
95SelFlaO-143
95SelSki-SS2
95SP-5
95SP-37
95SP-38
95SP-80
95SPDieC-5
95SPDieC-37
95SPDieC-38
95SPDieC-80
95SPSpeM-SM6
95SPSpeMDC-SM6
95Tra-30
95Tra-48
95Tra-53
95Tra-62
95Tra5thA-1
95Tra5thA-40
95Tra5thA-51
95Tra5thA-P1
95Tra5thACC-C2
95Tra5thAG-1
95Tra5thAG-40
95Tra5thAG-51
95Tra5thAR-R1
95Tra5thAUEC-E10
95TraAutV-29
95TraCha-C8
95TraFirR-30
95TraFirR-48
95TraFirR-53
95TraFirR-62
95TraRacM-RM9
95TraSerS-SS5
95TraVal-99
95UppDec-8
95UppDec-51
95UppDec-76
95UppDec-144
95UppDec-164
95UppDec-187
95UppDec-188
95UppDec-232
95UppDecA-187
95UppDecGSEG-8
95UppDecGSEG-51
95UppDecGSEG-76
95UppDecGSEG-144
95UppDecGSEG-164
95UppDecGSEG-187
95UppDecGSEG-188
95UppDecGSEG-232
95UppDecO-OS4
95UppDecPRW-P2
95UppDecPSP-PP4
95UppDecSSES-8
95UppDecSSES-51
95UppDecSSES-76

95UppDecSSES-144
95UppDecSSES-164
95UppDecSSES-187
95UppDecSSES-188
95UppDecSSES-232
95VIP-19
95VIP-33
95VIP-53
95VIPAut-19
95VIPCooB-19
95VIPCooB-33
95VIPCooB-53
95VIPEmeP-19
95VIPEmeP-33
95VIPEmeP-53
95VIPFanC-FC6
95VIPFanCG-FC6
95VIPRedHCB-19
95VIPRedHCB-33
95VIPRedHCB-53
95VIPRef-R4
95VIPRefG-R4
95Zen-6
95Zen-39
95ZenHel-4
95ZenWinW-9
95ZenWinW-20
95ZenZT-12
96ActPacC-11
96ActPacC-12
96ActPacC-13
96ActPacC-14
96ActPacC-15
96ActPacC-23
96ActPacC-62
96ActPacCFS-3
96ActPacCP-23
96ActPacCSS-11
96ActPacCSS-12
96ActPacCSS-13
96ActPacCSS-14
96ActPacCSS-15
96ActPacCSS-23
96ActPacM-5
96ActPacM-15
96Ass-18
96Ass-29
96Ass-49
96Ass$1000CCIPC-10
96Ass$100CCIPC-11
96Ass$10PC-8
96Ass$2PC-9
96Ass$5PC-3
96AssComL-CL3
96AssRacD-RD6
96AutRac-20
96AutRac-24
96AutRacA-31
96AutRacCA-31
96AutRacFR-59
96AutRacFR-60
96AutRacFR-61
96AutRacFR-62
96AutRacFR-63
96AutRacFR-64
96AutRacFR-65
96AutRacFR-66
96AutRacFR-67
96AutRacFR-68
96AutRacFR-69
96AutRacFR-70
96AutRacFR-71
96AutRacHP-HP6
96AutRacKotC$PC-KC2
96Cla-14
96Cla-30
96Cla-51
96ClaImaP-RP2
96ClaInn-IV1
96ClaInn-IV6
96ClaMarMC-MC10
96ClaPriP-14
96ClaPriP-30
96ClaRacC-RC6
96ClaRacC-RC16
96ClaSil-14
96ClaSil-30
96CroJewEADJ-DJ4
96CroJewEDT-4
96CroJewEDT-53
96CroJewEDT-74
96CroJewEDTC-4
96CroJewEDTC-53
96CroJewEDTC-74
96CroJewEDTCSA-CS10
96CroJewEDTDJA-DJ4
96CroJewEDTDJG-DJ4
96CroJewEE-4
96CroJewEE-53
96CroJewEE-74
96CroJewEGDJ-DJ4
96CroJewEli-4
96CroJewEli-53
96CroJewEli-74
96CroJewERCSG-CS10
96CroJewERCSP-CS10
96CroJewES-4
96CroJewES-53
96CroJewES-74
96CroJewESDJ-DJ4
96CroJewETC-4
96CroJewETC-53
96CroJewETC-74
96CroJewETCDJA-DJ4
96CroJewETCDJS-DJ4
96CroJewETCE-4
96CroJewETCE-53
96CroJewETCE-74
96CroJewETCGDJ-DJ4
96CroJewETCS-4
96CroJewETCS-53
96CroJewETCS-74
96FinLin-8
96FinLin-9
96FinLin-60
96FinLinBGL-C5
96FinLinBGL-D6
96FinLinDCPC-5
96FinLinGS-GS3
96FinLinMM-MM2
96FinLinMPXR-NNO
96FinLinPP-24
96FinLinPP-25
96FinLinPP-P1
96FinLinPP$100C-5
96FinLinPP$10C-8
96FinLinPP$1kC-K3
96FinLinPP$50C-6
96FinLinPP$5C-16
96FinLinPP$S-24
96FinLinPP$S-25
96FinLinPriP-8
96FinLinPriP-9
96FinLinPriP-60
96FinLinS-8
96FinLinS-9
96FinLinS-60
96Fla-21
96Fla-77
96Fla-97
96FlaAut-10
96FlaCenS-8
96FlaHotN-8
96FlaPowP-8
96Kni-5
96Kni-24
96KniBlaK-5
96KniBlaK-24
96KniFirK-FK4
96KniKniRT-KT4
96KniQueRKP-5
96KniQueRKP-24
96KniRoy-5
96KniRoy-24
96KniSanC-SC4
96KniWhiK-5
96KniWhiK-24
96M-F-9
96M-F-10
96M-F-41
96M-FBla-B6
96M-FSheM-M4
96M-FSil-S15
96Max-6
96Max-54
96Max-70
96MaxMadiA-6
96MaxMadiA-54
96MaxOdy-6
96MaxOdy-54
96MaxPre-6
96MaxPre-35
96MaxPreSS-SL2
96MetImpWCTF-5
96Pin-6
96Pin-41
96Pin-96
96Pin-6
96Pin-41
96Pin-96
96PinCheF-6
96PinCutA-10
96PinPolP-6
96PinPolP-30
96PinPolP-77
96PinPolPCS-6
96PinPolPLF-6
96PinPolPLF-30
96PinPolPLF-77
96PinPolPNL-6
96PinPolPNLG-6
96PinTeaP-6
96PinWinCC-6
96PinWinCC-41
96PinWinCC-96
96PrePas-20
96PrePas-53
96PrePas-76
96PrePas-96
96PrePas&NC-20
96PrePas&NC-53
96PrePasBR-BR7
96PrePasCC-20
96PrePasCF-CF5
96PrePasFoc-F7
96PrePasFQS-FQS8A
96PrePasFQS-FQS8B
96PrePasP-4
96PrePasP-45
96PrePasP$10PC-7
96PrePasP$20PC-7
96PrePasP$5PC-7
96PrePasP$96PC-1
96PrePasPBRI-BR2
96PrePasPCB-CB11
96PrePasPEP-4
96PrePasPEP-45
96PrePasPH-4
96PrePasPH-45
96PrePasPHP-HP6
96PrePasSco-20
96PrePasSco-53
96PrePasSco-76
96PrePasSco-96
96PrePasT-20
96PrePasT-53
96PrePasT-76
96PrePasT-96
96RacCho-6
96RacCho-30
96RacCho-85
96RacCho-86
96RacCho-93
96RacCho-109
96RacChoAP-6
96RacChoAP-30
96RacChoAP-85
96RacChoAP-86
96RacChoAP-93
96RacChoAP-109
96RacChoSC-6
96RacChoSC-30
96RacChoSC-85
96RacChoSC-86
96RacChoSC-93
96RacChoSC-109
96RacChoTT-4
96SP-6
96SP-45
96SP-83
96SpeArtP-20
96SpeArtP-40
96SpeArtP-50
96SpeArtP-67
96SpeArtP-68
96SpeArtP-69
96SpeArtP-70
96SpeArtP-87
96SpeCleS-8
96SpeInM-8
96SpePro-8
96SpeRac-20
96SpeRac-40
96SpeRac-50
96SpeRac-67
96SpeRac-68
96SpeRac-69
96SpeRac-70
96SpeRac-87
96SPHolME-ME6
96SPRacLC-RL23
96SPx-6
96SPxGol-6
96TraRev&PTCG-TC3
96TraRev&PTCG-TC16
96TraRev&PTCH-TC3
96TraRev&PTCH-TC16
96TraRevP-5
96TraRevP-11
96TraRevP-36
96TraRevP-P2
96TraRevPFR-5
96TraRevPFR-11
96TraRevPFR-36
96TraRevPLG-LG3
96TraRevPM-5
96TraRevPM-11
96TraRevPM-36
96TraRevPTC-TC3
96TraRevPTC-TC16
96Ult-9
96Ult-10
96Ult-11
96Ult-165
96Ult-176
96Ult-186
96Ult-193
96UltAut-20
96UltBoxS-4
96UltFlaP-4
96UltSeaC-6
96UltSeaC-8
96UltUpd-21
96UltUpd-67
96UltUpdA-10
96UltUpdPP-10
96UltUpdW-11
96UltUpdW-18
96UppDec-5
96UppDec-45
96UppDec-85
96UppDec-99
96UppDecAP-AP7
96UppDecPP-RP2
96UppDecPW-HP5
96UppDecRTTC-RC3
96UppDecRTTC-RC52
96UppDecRTTC-RC91
96UppDecRTTC-RC126
96UppDecRTTCAS-H3
96UppDecRTTCGF-GF6
96UppDecRTTCPPoi-PP3
96UppDRTTCPPR-PR3
96UppDecRTTCPT3-T5
96UppDecRTTCPT3-T7
96UppDecRTTCPT3-T8
96UppDecRTTCPT3-T9
96UppDecRTTCT3PR-R6
96UppDecVV-VV6
96UppDecVVG-VV6
96VIP-17
96VIP-31
96VIP-45
96VIPEmeP-17
96VIPEmeP-31
96VIPEmeP-45
96Viper-4
96Viper-37
96Viper-44
96Viper-45
96Viper-57
96ViperBlaM-4
96ViperBlaM-37
96ViperBlaM-44
96ViperBlaM-45
96ViperBlaM-57
96ViperBusC-B11
96ViperCob-C4
96ViperCop-4
96ViperCop-37
96ViperCop-44
96ViperCop-45
96ViperCop-57
96ViperDia-D4
96ViperDiaA-DA7
96ViperGreM-4
96ViperGreM-37
96ViperGreM-44
96ViperGreM-45
96ViperGreM-57
96ViperKinC-KC8
96VIPHeaG-HG5
96VIPHeaGD-HG5
96VIPSamBTF-SB4
96VIPSamBTFG-SB4
96VIPTor-17
96VIPTor-31
96VIPTor-45
96VIPWarP-WP5
96VIPWarPG-WP5
96Zen-6
96Zen-38
96Zen-52
96ZenArtP-6
96ZenArtP-38
96ZenArtP-52
96ZenHig-4
97ActPac-6
97ActPac-27
97ActPac2G-11
97ActPacFA-11
97ActPacFI-6
97ActPacFI-27
97ActPacRT-1
97ActPreM-9
97AutRac-17
97AutRac-38
97AutRac-44
97AutRacA-33
97AutRacMS-KM17
97AutRacTtCF-TF2
97ColCho-6
97ColCho-56
97ColCho-105
97ColCho-136
97ColCho-137
97ColCho-138
97ColChoC-CC10
97ColChoC-CC43
97ColChoC-CC76
97ColChoS-S11
97ColChoS-S12
97ColChoSQ-SQ29
97ColChoSQ-SQ46
97ColChoTF-B3
97ColChoTF-J1
97ColChoUD5-UD9
97ColChoUD5-UD10
97ColChoVC-VC5
97FinLinPP2-3
97FinLinPP2$10-70
97FinLinPP2$100-97
97FinLinPP2$5-41
97FinLinPP2$50-89
97JurPar-4
97JurPar-44
97JurPar-49
97JurPar-50
97JurParC-C10
97JurParP-P8
97JurParT-4
97JurParT-44
97JurParT-49
97JurParT-50
97JurParTL-TL7
97Max-6
97Max-51
97Max-103
97Max-106
97MaxChaTC-C2
97MaxChatCG-C2
97Pin-6
97Pin-35
97Pin-61
97Pin-75
97Pin-90
97PinArtP-6
97PinArtP-35
97PinArtP-61
97PinArtP-75
97PinArtP-90
97PinCer-6
97PinCer-40
97PinCer-91
97PinCerCGT-7
97PinCerCT-7
97PinCerE-E7
97PinCerEE-E7
97PinCerEP-E7
97PinCerMB-6
97PinCerMB-40
97PinCerMB-91
97PinCerMG-6
97PinCerMG-40
97PinCerMG-91
97PinCerMR-6
97PinCerMR-40
97PinCerMR-91
97PinCerR-6
97PinCerR-40

96AutRacHP-HP3
96Cla-11
96ClaPriP-11
96ClaSil-11
96CroJewEDitR-DR5
96CroJewEDitRC-DR5
96CroJewEDitRS-DR5
96CroJewEDT-25
96CroJewEDTC-25
96CroJewEE-25
96CroJewEli-25
96CroJewES-25
96CroJewETC-25
96CroJewETCE-25
96CroJewETCS-25
96FinLin-14
96FinLinPriP-14
96FinLinS-14
96Fla-23
96Fla-79
96M-F-37
96MaxMadiA-26
96MaxMadiA-98
96MaxOdy-26
96MaxOdy-98
96MaxPre-20
96MaxPre-98
96Pin-35
96Pin-35
96PinPolPCS-9
96PinWinCC-35
96PrePas-22
96PrePas&NC-22
96PrePasCC-22
96PrePasP-27
96PrePasPEP-27
96PrePasPH-27
96PrePasSco-22
96PrePasT-22
96RacCho-23
96RacCho-49
96RacChoAP-23
96RacChoAP-49
96RacChoSC-23
96RacChoSC-49
96SP-32
96SP-74
96SPDriF-DF2
96SPHolME-ME24
96SPx-13
96SPxGol-13
96Ult-99
96Ult-100
96Ult-101
96UltAut-22
96UltUpd-23
96UltUpd-69
96UltUpdPP-11
96UltUpdRS-5
96UppDec-32
96UppDec-62
96UppDec-112
96UppDecRTTC-RC41
96UppDecRTTC-RC78
96UppDecRTTC-RC111
96V.IAut-16
96VIP-18
96VIPEmeP-18
96Viper-23
96ViperBlaM-23
96ViperCop-23
96ViperGreM-23
96VIPTor-18
96Zen-21
96ZenArtP-21
97ActPac-7
97ActPac-28
97ActPacFI-7
97ActPacFI-28
97AutRac-22
97AutRacA-35
97AutRacMS-KM22
97ColCho-32
97ColCho-82
97ColCho-118
97ColChoC-CC35
97ColChoC-CC68
97ColChoS-S39
97ColChoS-S40
97ColChoSQ-SQ28
97ColChoTF-C3
97ColChoUD5-UD66
97ColChoUD5-UD67
97FinLinPP2-14
97FinLinPP2$5-52
97JurPar-14
97JurParT-14
97JurParTR-TR9
97Max-37
97Max-82
97MaxChaTC-C9
97MaxChatCG-C9
97Pin-13
97Pin-42
97PinArtP-13
97PinArtP-42
97PinCer-8
97PinCer-42
97PinCer-72
97PinCer-73
97PinCerCGT-10
97PinCerCT-10
97PinCerMB-8
97PinCerMB-42
97PinCerMB-72
97PinCerMB-73
97PinCerMG-8
97PinCerMG-42
97PinCerMG-72
97PinCerMG-73
97PinCerMR-8
97PinCerMR-42
97PinCerMR-72
97PinCerMR-73
97PinCerR-8
97PinCerR-42
97PinCerR-72
97PinCerR-73
97PinPor-10
97PinPor-30
97PinPre-76
97PinPreBM-76
97PinPreGM-76
97PinPreP-13
97PinPreP-42
97PinPreSM-76
97PinTotCPB-8
97PinTotCPB-42
97PinTotCPB-72
97PinTotCPB-73
97PinTotCPG-8
97PinTotCPG-42
97PinTotCPG-72
97PinTotCPG-73
97PinTotCPR-8
97PinTotCPR-42
97PinTotCPR-72
97PinTotCPR-73
97PinTroC-13
97PinTroC-42
97Pre-15
97PreBlaWFS-15
97PreGri-15
97PrePas-22
97PrePas-87
97PrePasAut-18
97PrePasL-22
97PrePasL-87
97PrePasOS-22
97PrePasOS-87
97PrePasP-19
97PrePasPEP-19
97PrePasPM-19
97PrePasPOS-19
97PrePasT-22
97PrePasT-87
97PreRedW-15
97RacCho-13
97RacCho-48
97RacCho-77
97RacChoBC-10
97RacChoSS-13
97RacChoSS-48
97RacChoSS-77
97SBMot-23
97SBMot-84
97SBMotWR-WC18
97ScoBoaI-22
97SkyPro-21
97SkyPro-74
97SkyProA-21
97SkyProBO-B8
97SP-32
97SP-74
97SP-107
97SP SupS-32
97SP SupS-74
97SP SupS-107
97Ult-23
97Ult-50
97UltUpd-19
97UltUpd-91
97UltUpdAR-19
97UppDecRTTC-28
97UppDecRTTC-70
97UppDecRTTCPP-PP19
97UppDecRTTCPPlu-+15
97UDRTTCPPRC-+15
97UppDRTTCPPRDC-+15
97UppDecVC-32
97UppDecVC-82
97UppDecVC-107
97Viper-14
97ViperAna-A9
97ViperBlaR-14
98ColCho-32
98ColCho-68
98ColCho-79
98ColCho-107
98HigGea-13
98HigGeaA-15
98HigGeaFG-19
98HigGeaGJ-GJ25
98HigGeaM-19
98Max-1
98Max-31
98Max-81
98Max-12
98Max-37
98Max-62
98Max-87
98Max10tA-11
98Max10tA-56
98Max10tAMP-P12
98MaxFieG-2
98MaxFieGTS-2
98MaxFieGTSA-2
98MaxFirC-F9
98MaxFouSGA-2
98MaxSwaP-SW18
98MaxYealRBS-34
98PinMin-11
98PinMin-23
98PinMinB-11
98PinMinB-23
98PinMinBC-11
98PinMinBC-23
98PinMinBPPC-11
98PinMinBPPC-23
98PinMinGMT-11
98PinMinGMT-23
98PinMinGPC-11
98PinMinGPC-23
98PinMinGPPC-11
98PinMinGPPC-23
98PinMinNC-11
98PinMinNC-23
98PinMinSGC-11
98PinMinSGC-23
98PinMinSMT-11
98PinMinSMT-23
98PinMinSPPC-11
98PinMinSPPC-23
98PinMinSSC-11
98PinMinSSC-23
98PrePas-20
98PrePasOS-20
98PrePasP-40
98PrePasP-40
98PrePasS-49
98PrePasSA-1
98PrePasSF-49
98PrePasSO-27
98PrePasSO-28
98PrePasSOD-27
98PrePasSOD-28
98PrePasSS-13
98PrePasSSD-13
98SP Aut-1
98SP Aut-35
98SP AutBtW-BW12
98SP AutBtWL2-BW12
98SP AutBtWL3-BW12
98SP AutSotTL1-S8
98UppDecRttC-12
98UppDecRttC-50
98UppDecRttC-64
98UppDecRttC-81
98UppDecRttC-92
98UppDecRTTC5A-AN48
98UDRTTCCQT1-CQ4
98UDRTTCCQT2-CQ4
98UDRTTCCQT3-CQ4
98UDRTTCCQT4-CQ4
98UppDRTTCCQVL-CQ4
98UppDecRTTCWM-W2
98UppDecVC-37
98UppDecVC-82
98UppDecVC-122
98UppDecVCPL-PL13
98UppDecVCPP-15
98UppDecVCPPCR-15
98VIP-17
98VIPDriF-DF15
98VIPDriFD-DF15
98VIPExp-17
98VIPLapL-LL8
98VIPLapLA-LL8
98Whe-21
98Whe-43
98WheGol-21
98WheGol-43
98WheJac-J7
99Pre-6
99Pre-33
99Pre-90
99PrePas-6
99PrePas-33
99PrePas-90
99PrePas-106
99PrePasCC-4B
99PrePasCC-15
99PrePasOC-8
99PrePasPS-8
99PrePasS-4A
99UppDecVC-7
99UppDecVC-58
99UppDecVC-77
99UppDecVCIS-IS7
99UppDecVCNSS-JM
99UppDecVCSZ-SZ12
99UppDecVCTM-TM10
99UppDecVCUE-7
99UppDecVCUE-58
99UppDecVCUE-77
99UppDecVCVC-V7
99WheHigG-6
99WheHigGAC-6
99WheHigGFG-6
99WheHigGM-MM7B/9
99WheHigGM-6
99WheHigGS-GS6
99WheHigGTT-TT6/8

Mayne, Kenny
97AutRacA-36

Mays, Raymond
38WilCig-21
39ChuKinoS-20
92GolEraGPTEY-8

Mazmanian, John
65DonSpeS-56

McAmis, Tim
90CheFlaI-12
90CheFlaI-24
91BigTimD-72

McBride, Nolan
90LanRocSHS-25
91LanART-16
91LanRocS-45

McCabe, Dick
91WinChoNED-28
91WinChoNED-29
92WinChoB-5
92WinChoB-6

McCall, Buz
92EriMaxTA-96

McCallum, Jim
91LanSeeS-16
92WinChoB-121
92WinChoB-122

McCammon, Doug
91DirTra-52
92JAG-73

McCandless, Herb
71FleAHRDC-24
72FleAHRDN-13

McCarl, Terry
87WorOut-39
88WorOut-28
91WorOut-34
94WorOut-18
94WorOutMW-6

McCarson, Dennis
93AllRobPDS-10

McCart, Jerry
91BulRin-13
92BulRin-13

McCarthy, Bill
92RSSMotH-15
96PinPolP-99
96PinPolPLF-99

McCarthy, Perry
92GriForO-33
92GriForO-66
92GriForO-99

McClain, Jimmy
91BulRin-33
92BulRin-33

McClelland, Dave
91ProSetN-108
92ProSetN-183
93FinLinN-128

McClenathan, Cory
92ProSetN-9
92ProSetN-109
93FinLinN-28
93FinLinN-29
93FinLinN-30
93FinLinNA-2
93FinLinNP-2
94ActPacN-6
94ActPacN-16
94ActPacN-37
95ActPacN-3
95ActPacNSS-3
95Zen-71
95Zen-72

McClure, Danny
95HavAT-15

McClure, Ed
91Tra-11
92MaxBla-101
92MaxRed-101
92Tra-68
92TraKodEl-19
92TraKodEl-24
92TraTeaS-106
92TraTeaS-120
93Max-109
93MaxPreP-98
93MaxPreS-109
93Tra-119
93TraFirR-119
94Max-93
94MaxPreP-93
94MaxPreS-93
95MaxPreS-87
95Tra5thA-72
95Tra5thAG-72

McClure, Jeff
92LanARCF-38
92MaxBla-101
94LanARCF-57
94LanARCF-100
94LanARCF-P1

McClure, Jerry
91Tra-11
92MaxRed-101
92Tra-111
92TraKodEl-8
92TraKodEl-19
92TraTeaS-112
92TraTeaS-120
93Max-109
93MaxPreP-98
93MaxPreS-109
93Tra-119
93TraFirR-119
94Max-93
94MaxPreP-93
94MaxPreS-93
95MaxPreS-87

McClure, Larry
89Max-206
90Max-85A
90Max-85B
91Max-81
91ProSet-15
91Tra-11
91Tra-58
92MaxBla-106
92MaxRed-106
92Tra-58
92TraKodEl-7
92TraKodEl-19
92TraTeaS-104
92TraTeaS-120
93FinLin-152
93FinLinCS-20
93FinLinS-152

94JAG-42
Munari, David
92MaxAllPT-48
92MaxBla-263
92MaxRed-263
94HigGeaPPT-W22
94HigGeaPPTG-22W
94MaxPreS-243
Munari, Sandro
77Spo-7412
Mundy, Frank
89TGRacMR-239
89TGRacMR-240
89WinCir-22
91GalPrePR-38
91GalPrePR-44
91TGRacMRU-239
91TGRacMRU-240
91TraPacYH-24
Murdick, Carl
92VolRacLSI-36
Murgic, Mike
92RedGraST-28
Murgic, Steve
92RedGraST-15
92RedGraST-28
93Max-223
93MaxPreS-223
Murphey, Brad
97Hi-IRL-36
Murphy, Jim Drag
92ProSetN-23
92ProSetN-59
Murphy, Jimmy Indy
54StaWetIW-1922
60HawWaxI-10
71MobTheSoGPMR-7
91LegInd-83
92GolEraGPTEY-1
95TraVal-28
Murphy, Paula
71FleAHRDC-48
Murphy, Spud
91GalPrePR-101
Murray, Bob
71FleAHRDC-49
71FleAHRDC-54
Muse, Barry
95OptXL-42
95OptXLCB-42
95OptXLDC-42
95OptXLRH-42
98PrePas-66
98PrePasOS-66
Muse, Steve
98Whe-94
98WheGol-94
Musgrave, Brittany
94ActPac-155
96RacCho-63
96RacChoAP-63
96RacChoSC-63
Musgrave, Ted
91ProSet-103
91ProSet-104
91Tra-55
92MaxBla-55
92MaxBla-197
92MaxMcD-29
92MaxRed-55
92MaxRed-197
92ProSet-70
92ProSet-78
92ProSet-155
92Tra-55
92Tra-155A
92Tra-155B
92TraASA-50
92TraRacM-66
93FinLin-7
93FinLin-92
93FinLin-167
93FinLinCS-13
93FinLinCS-25
93FinLinS-7
93FinLinS-92
93FinLinS-167
93Max-55
93MaxMot-15
93MaxMot-35
93MaxPreP-55
93MaxPreS-55
93Tra-55
93Tra-155
93TraFirR-55
93TraFirR-155
93TraTri-47
94ActPac-89
94ActPac-114
94ActPac-155
94ActPac2G-43G
94FinLin-19
94FinLin-107
94FinLin-149
94FinLinG-18
94FinLinG-50
94FinLinG-55
94FinLinS-19
94FinLinS-107
94FinLinS-149
94Hi-Bri4AP-62
94HigGea-20
94HigGea-116
94HigGeaDO-116
94HigGeaDOG-116
94HigGeaG-20
94HigGeaG-116
94HiTecB4-62
94Max-55
94Max-266
94Max-276
94Max-P4
94MaxMed-12
94MaxMed-71
94MaxMot-6
94MaxPreP-55
94MaxPreS-55
94MaxRacC-8
94MaxTheS2-25
94Pow-106
94PowGol-106
94PowPre-4
94PowPre-20
94PrePas-20
94PrePasCC-CC20
94Tra-16
94Tra-151
94Tra-197
94TraAutV-4
94TraAutV-48
94TraFirR-16
94TraFirR-151
94TraFirR-197
94TraPreC-25
94VIP-23
94VIP-40
95ActPacC-64
95ActPacC2T-14
95ActPacCSS-64
95ActPacP-42
95ActPacS-9
95ActPacSSS-9
95Ass-23
95AssGolS-23
95CroJew-18
95CroJewD-18
95CroJewE-18
95CroJewS-18
95FinLin-16
95FinLin-72
95FinLinCC6-23
95FinLinGS-GS16
95FinLinPP-16
95FinLinPP-72
95FinLinSil-16
95FinLinSil-72
95HigGea-10
95HigGea-83
95HigGeaBC-BC3
95HigGeaBCG-BC3
95HigGeaDO-10
95HigGeaDO-83
95HigGeaDOG-10
95HigGeaDOG-83
95HigGeaG-10
95HigGeaG-83
95HiTecB4-35
95HiTecB4-65
95Ima-16
95Ima-61
95ImaGol-16
95ImaGol-61
95Max-16
95Max-168
95MaxAut-16
95MaxCroC-16
95MaxCroC-61
95MaxLicD-6
95MaxMed-12
95MaxMed-42
95MaxMed-P1
95MaxMedB-12
95MaxMedB-42
95MaxPreP-16
95MaxPreP-61
95MaxPrePTH-TH1
95MaxPreS-16
95MaxPreS-61
95OptXL-15
95OptXL-43
95OptXLCB-15
95OptXLCB-43
95OptXLDC-15
95OptXLDC-43
95OptXLRH-15
95OptXLRH-43
95OptXLS-XLS10
95PrePas-21
95PrePas-40
95PrePasCC-21
95PrePasPH-11
95PrePasPre-11
95PrePasPRH-11
95PrePasRH-21
95PrePasRH-40
95Sel-22
95Sel-40
95Sel-137
95SelFlaO-22
95SelFlaO-40
95SelFlaO-137
95SelSki-SS11
95SP-13
95SP-47
95SP-89
95SPDieC-13
95SPDieC-47
95SPDieC-89
95SPSpeM-SM16
95SPSpeMDC-SM16
95Tra-16
95Tra5thA-13
95Tra5thA-59
95Tra5thACC-C5
95Tra5thAG-13
95Tra5thAG-59
95Tra5thAUEC-E5
95TraAutV-33
95TraFirR-16
95TraOnTR-OTR13
95TraRacM-RM17
95TraSerS-SS15
95UppDec-16
95UppDec-59
95UppDec-84
95UppDec-118
95UppDec-175
95UppDec-196
95UppDec-240
95UppDec-277
95UppDecA-196
95UppDecGSEG-16
95UppDecGSEG-59
95UppDecGSEG-84
95UppDecGSEG-118
95UppDecGSEG-175
95UppDecGSEG-196
95UppDecGSEG-240
95UppDecGSEG-277
95UppDecSSES-16
95UppDecSSES-59
95UppDecSSES-84
95UppDecSSES-118
95UppDecSSES-175
95UppDecSSES-196
95UppDecSSES-240
95UppDecSSES-277
95VIP-20
95VIPAut-20
95VIPCooB-20
95VIPEmeP-20
95VIPRedHCB-20
95Zen-16
95Zen-46
95Zen-61
95Zen-P2
95ZenHel-8
95ZenZT-9
96ActPacC-26
96ActPacCFS-5
96ActPacCSS-26
96Ass-31
96Ass$1000CCIPC-15
96Ass$100CCIPC-13
96Ass$2PC-23
96Ass$5PC-8
96AssComL-CL9
96AutRac-16
96AutRacFR-72
96AutRacHP-HP11
96Cla-3
96Cla-42
96ClaInn-IV2
96ClaMarMC-MC1
96ClaPriP-3
96ClaPriP-42
96ClaSil-3
96ClaSil-42
96CroJewEDT-11
96CroJewEDTC-11
96CroJewEE-11
96CroJewEli-11
96CroJewES-11
96CroJewETC-11
96CroJewETCE-11
96CroJewETCS-11
96FinLin-2
96FinLin-57
96FinLinBGL-D12
96FinLinGS-GS8
96FinLinPP-26
96FinLinPP$5C-17
96FinLinPP$S-26
96FinLinPriP-2
96FinLinPriP-57
96FinLinS-2
96FinLinS-57
96Fla-24
96Fla-80
96FlaAut-11
96Kni-4
96KniBlaK-4
96KniQueRKP-4
96KniRoy-4
96KniWhiK-4
96M-F-13
96Max-16
96Max-63
96Max-97
96MaxMadiA-16
96MaxMadiA-63
96MaxOdy-16
96MaxOdy-63
96MaxPre-16
96MaxPre-58
96Pin-16
96Pin-45
96Pin-16
96Pin-45
96PinCutA-13
96PinPolP-34
96PinPolPLF-34
96PinWinCC-16
96PinWinCC-45
96PrePas-23
96PrePas-39
96PrePas&NC-23
96PrePasCC-23
96PrePasP-7
96PrePasPEP-7
96PrePasPH-7
96PrePasSco-23
96PrePasSco-39
96PrePasT-23
96PrePasT-39
96RacCho-10
96RacCho-36
96RacCho-61
96RacCho-62
96RacCho-63
96RacCho-64
96RacCho-65
96RacCho-102
96RacChoAP-10
96RacChoAP-36
96RacChoAP-61
96RacChoAP-62
96RacChoAP-63
96RacChoAP-64
96RacChoAP-65
96RacChoAP-102
96RacChoSC-10
96RacChoSC-36
96RacChoSC-61
96RacChoSC-62
96RacChoSC-63
96RacChoSC-64
96RacChoSC-65
96RacChoSC-102
96RacChoTT-7
96SP-16
96SP-48
96SpeCleS-11
96SpeInM-9
96SPHolME-ME16
96SPx-16
96SPxGol-16
96TraRev&PTCG-TC2
96TraRev&PTCG-TC19
96TraRev&PTCH-TC2
96TraRev&PTCH-TC19
96TraRevP-3
96TraRevP-18
96TraRevP-43
96TraRevPFR-3
96TraRevPFR-18
96TraRevPFR-43
96TraRevPLG-LG20
96TraRevPM-3
96TraRevPM-18
96TraRevPM-43
96TraRevPTC-TC2
96TraRevPTC-TC19
96Ult-25
96Ult-26
96Ult-27
96Ult-159
96UltAut-25
96UltBoxS-7
96UltFlaP-7
96UltUpd-24
96UltUpd-70
96UltUpdA-11
96UltUpdPP-12
96UppDec-14
96UppDec-54
96UppDec-94
96UppDecAP-AP8
96UppDecRTTC-RC6
96UppDecRTTC-RC55
96UppDecRTTC-RC129
96UppDecRTTC-RC144
96UppDecRTTCAS-H6
96UppDecRTTCPPoi-PP6
96UppDRTTCPPR-PR6
96UppDecRTTCPT3-T9
96UppDecRTTCT3PR-R12
96UppDecVV-VV9
96UppDecVVG-VV9
96V.IAut-18
96VIP-19
96VIPEmeP-19
96Viper-12
96ViperBlaM-12
96ViperBusC-B13
96ViperCop-12
96ViperGreM-12
96VIPTor-19
96VIPWarP-WP7
96VIPWarPG-WP7
96Zen-15
96Zen-47
96Zen-57
96ZenArtP-15
96ZenArtP-47
96ZenArtP-57
97ActPac-16
97ActPac-37
97ActPac2G-13
97ActPacFI-16
97ActPacFI-37
97AutRac-21
97AutRacA-38
97AutRacMS-KM21
97ColCho-16
97ColCho-66
97ColCho-107
97ColCho-139
97ColCho-140
97ColCho-141
97ColChoC-CC20
97ColChoC-CC53
97ColChoC-CC86
97ColChoS-S31
97ColChoS-S32
97ColChoSQ-SQ27
97ColChoSQ-SQ50
97ColChoTF-B1
97ColChoUD5-UD32
97ColChoUD5-UD33

92GriForO-142
Ollila, Nick
94HigGeaPPT-W14
94HigGeaPPTG-14W
Olofsson, Anders
78GraPri-176
Olsen, Mike
91WinChoNED-55
91WinChoNED-56
92WinChoB-37
92WinChoB-38
Olson, Randy
91LanStoCC-18
Ong, Duane
71FleAHRDC-52
Ongais, Danny
71FleAHRDC-22
80AvaHilURG-7
84A&SRacl-29
92LegInd-84
97Hi-IRL-30
97Hi-IRL'I5-I13
Orchard, Fred Jr.
90K&WDirT-34
91K&WDirT-45
Ormsby, Gary
89MegDra-38
89MegDra-39
91ProSetN-2
91ProSetN-51
92ProSetN-16
Orndorff, Bill
92ProSetN-168
93FinLinN-98
Orr, Pete
91BulRin-137
92BulRin-38
Orr, Phil
91GalPrePR-8
Osborn, Mark
92MaxAllPT-42
92MaxBla-259
92MaxRed-259
92TraTeaS-168
Osborne, Mark
89CheFlal-22
90CheFlal-91
Osborne, Ted
89CheFlal-21
90CheFlal-93
Osburn, Dan
95JSKS.OS-43
Osterlund, Rod
89Max-174
90Max-89
91Max-101
Ostrander, Jack
91BigTimD-94
92ProSetN-19
93FinLinN-34
Oswald, Mark
91ProSetN-20
91ProSetN-69
92ProSetN-50
92ProSetN-62
92ProSetN-119
93FinLinN-64
93MotDecC-6
Ottinger, L.D.
89Max-214
90Max-122
91Max-157
91Tra-172A
91Tra-172B
92ProSet-195
Otto, Roger
91LanARCHS-14
91LanStoCC-23
Otto, Ron
92LanARCF-99
Overdorf, Edward
93CorSelCCS-32
Owenby, Rocky
94HigGeaPPT-W23
94HigGeaPPTG-23W
Owens, Cotton
89TGRacMR-68
89TGRacMR-69
89TGRacMR-72
89TGRacMR-76
89WinCir-15
91GalPrePR-57
91GalPrePR-84
91ProSetL-L21
91TGRacMRU-68
91TGRacMRU-69
91TGRacMRU-72
91TGRacMRU-76
91TGRacMRU-P3
92ProSetL-L14
98PrePas-145
Owens, Wally
92EriMaxTA-43
Pace, Eddie
91DirTra-45
92DirTra-82
92JAG-85
Pack, Brian
91BulRin-31
Pack, Gene
91BulRin-131
Pagan, Eddie
89TGRacMR-34
91GalPrePR-51
91TGRacMRU-34
Paine, Steve
91K&WDirT-39
92K&WDirT-9
92TraDir-6
94K&WDirT-13
95K&WDirT-19
Pallister, Ted
91DKIMCDT-52
Palmer, Alan
91MaxBilETCM-17
Palmer, Bill
93JAG-37
Palmer, Charles
91MaxBilETCM-12
Palmer, Dan
91MaxBilETCM-36
Palmer, Jonathan
87AceForO-22
87ForOnel-12
88HerFouFO-4D
93MaxWilR-9
Palmer, Scott
92TraTeaS-60
Palmroth, Tero
91AllWorl-3
92AllWorl-34
92LegInd-24
Panch, Marvin
89Max-185
89Max-192
89TGRacMR-27
89TGRacMR-64
89TGRacMR-67
89WinCir-29
91GalPrePR-25
91GalPrePR-37
91GalPrePR-78
91ProSetL-L13
91TGRacMRU-27
91TGRacMRU-64
91TGRacMRU-67
92ProSetL-L8
95PrePas-122
95PrePasRH-122
98PrePas-147
Pannell, Skip
92JAG-218
Pantera, Tomaso
78GraPri-192
Panzarella, Frank
92EriMaxTA-62
Papale, Tony
92WinChoB-105
92WinChoB-106
Papathanassiou, Andy
95OptXL-41
95OptXLCB-41
95OptXLDC-41
95OptXLRH-41
Papini, Al III
92LanRocS-40
Papis, Max
97CARSchC-5
Parisot, Bob
90LanRocSHS-16
91LanRocS-11
91LanRocS-64
92LanRocS-41
Park, Bob
91WinChoM-12
91WinChoM-13
Park, Steve
91WinChoM-34
91WinChoM-36
97AutRac-14
97AutRacMS-KM14
97JurPar-35
97JurParT-35
97Pre-42
97PreBlaWFS-42
97PreGri-42
97PreRedW-42
97SBMot-38
97SkyPro-50
97SkyProA-50
97SkyProBO-B5
97UltUpd-63
97UltUpdAR-63
97Viper-37
97ViperBlaR-37
98HigGea-39
98HigGea-62
98HigGeaFG-39
98HigGeaFG-61
98HigGeaM-39
98HigGeaM-61
98Max-14
98Max-44
98Max-77
98Max-104
98MaxSwaP-SW1
98PrePas-44
98PrePas-58
98PrePasOS-44
98PrePasOS-58
98PrePasPFC-FC2
98PrePasPFCR-FC2
98PrePasS-27
98SP Aut-14
98SP Aut-48
98SP AutBtW-BW20
98SP AutBtWL2-BW20
98SP AutBtWL3-BW20
98UppDecVC-29
98UppDecVC-74
98VIP-20
98VIPExp-20
98Whe-24
98WheGol-24
99Pre-26
99PrePas-26
99PrePas-126
99PrePasPS-1
99UppDecVC-22
99UppDecVC-59
99UppDecVC-82
99UppDecVCNSS-SP
99UppDecVCSZ-SZ11
99UppDecVCUE-22
99UppDecVCUE-59
99UppDecVCUE-82
99WheHigG-27
99WheHigGFG-27
99WheHigGM-27
99WheHigGS-GS27
Parker, Carnell
94JAG-44
Parker, Pete
92DirTra-22
92JAG-86
93JAG-38
Parks, Bobby
90K&WDirT-35
91K&WDirT-29
92K&WDirT-49
Parks, Marc
94HigGeaPPT-G22
94HigGeaPPTG-22G
Parks, Raymond
91GalPrePR-98
Parks, Wally
91ProSetN-128
92ProSetN-187
93FinLinN-130
Parlato, Joe
92TraTeaS-148
Parnell, Reg
62PetLimGPRC-6
Parriott, Sam
65DonSpeS-3
Parrott, Brad
92Tra-172
92TraTeaS-159
94HigGeaPPT-W7
94HigGeaPPTG-7W
96AutRacA-38
96AutRacCA-38
97RacShaSTS-ST22
Parrott, Buddy
90Max-37
91Max-111
91ProSet-31
92MaxBla-167
92MaxRed-167
92ProSet-147
92WheRusW-4
92WheRusWG-4
93DaySer2RW-21
93DaySer2RW-23
93FinLin-79
93FinLinCS-21
93FinLinS-79
93Max-155
93MaxPreP-139
93MaxPreS-155
93Tra-29
93TraFirR-29
94ActPac-62
94FinLin-5
94FinLinGA-16
94FinLinGT-TG1
94FinLinS-5
94HigGea-39
94HigGeaG-39
94HigGeaPPT-W5
94HigGeaPPT-W34
94HigGeaPPTG-5W
94HigGeaPPTG-34W
94Max-127
94MaxPreP-120
94MaxPreS-127
94Pow-53
94PowGol-53
94PrePas-102
94Tra-20
94TraFirR-20
94VIP-97
95CroJew-40
95CroJewD-40
95CroJewE-40
95CroJewS-40
95FinLin-63
95FinLinPP-63
95FinLinSil-63
95Max-100
95MaxAut-100
95MaxCroC-104
95MaxPreP-104
95MaxPreS-123
95PrePas-97
95PrePasRH-97
95Sel-98
95SelFlaO-98
95TraAutV-36
95TraBehTS-BTS5
96AutRacA-39
96AutRacCA-39
96MaxPre-120
96UltUpd-85
97AutRacA-39
97RacCho-84
97RacChoSS-84
97Viper-60
97ViperBlaR-60
Parrott, Todd
89Max-32
92MaxAllPT-18
92MaxBla-243
92MaxRed-243
94HigGeaPPT-W6
94HigGeaPPTG-6W
94MaxPreS-242
96ActPacC-69
96AutRacA-40
96AutRacCA-40
96CroJewEDT-42
96CroJewEDT-52
96CroJewEDTC-42
96CroJewEDTC-52
96CroJewEE-42
96CroJewEE-52
96CroJewEli-42
96CroJewEli-52
96CroJewES-42
96CroJewES-52
96CroJewETC-42
96CroJewETC-52
96CroJewETCE-42
96CroJewETCE-52
96CroJewETCS-42
96CroJewETCS-52
96Fla-54
96MaxPre-155
96UltUpd-86
96Zen-90
96ZenArtP-90
97AutRacA-40
97PinPre-34
97PinPreBM-34
97PinPreGM-34
97PinPreP-TP9B
97PinPreSM-34
97Pre-50
97PreBlaWFS-50
97PreGri-50
97PreRedW-50
97RacShaSTS-ST17
97SkyPro-42
97Ult-71
98PrePas-98
98PrePasOS-98
98PrePasS-32
98PrePasS-18
98PrePasSF-18
98Whe-74
98WheGol-74
99Pre-67
99PrePas-67
Parsons Jr., Johnny
80AvaHilURG-26
85A&SRacl-14
86A&SRacl-28
87A&SRacl-40
92AllWorl-29
94HiTecICD-CD24
97Hi-IRL-18
97Hi-IRLP-D5
Parsons, Benny
72STP-10
88MaxCha-18
88MaxCha-35
88MaxCha-76
88MaxCha-94
89Max-131
90Max-156
90MaxHolF-HF29
91Max-231
91MaxWin2AF-3
91ProSetL-L37
91SpoLegPP-PP25
91TexWorS-1
91Tra-144
91TraPacYH-25
92MaxBlaU-U27
92MaxRedU-U27
92ProSetL-L28
92Tra-144
92Tra-P1
92TraAut-A9
92TraBenP-1
92TraBenP-2
92TraBenP-3
92TraBenP-4
92TraBenP-5
92TraBenP-6
92TraBenP-7
92TraBenP-8
92TraBenP-9
92TraBenP-10
92TraBenP-11
92TraBenP-12
92TraBenP-13
92TraBenP-14
92TraBenP-15
92TraBenP-16
92TraBenP-17
92TraBenP-18
92TraBenP-19
92TraBenP-20
92TraBenP-21
92TraBenP-22
92TraBenP-23
92TraBenP-24
92TraBenP-25
92TraBenP-26
92TraBenP-27
92TraBenP-28
92TraBenP-29
92TraBenP-30
92TraBenP-31
92TraBenP-32
92TraBenP-33
92TraBenP-34
92TraBenP-35
92TraBenP-36

92TraBenP-37
92TraBenP-38
92TraBenP-39
92TraBenP-40
92TraBenP-41
92TraBenP-42
92TraBenP-43
92TraBenP-44
92TraBenP-45
92TraBenP-46
92TraBenP-47
92TraBenP-48
92TraBenP-49
92TraBenP-50
93Max-207
93MaxPreS-207
93Tra-17
93TraFirR-17
94FinLin-120
94FinLinS-120
94HigGeaL-LS5
94MaxPreS-200
94PrePas-116
94Tra-199
94TraFirR-199
94VIP-88
94WheHarG-72
94WheHarGG-72
95MatWinCC-3
95MaxPreS-196
95MetImpWCC-2
95TraVal-86
95UppDec-159
95UppDecGSEG-159
95UppDecI-I6
95UppDecSSES-159
96MaxPre-195
96MetImp2AWCC-3
96UppDec-141
96ZenChaS-23
97ActPacFA-5
97ActPacFAA-5
97ColCho-122
97UltUpd-33
98Max10tA-42
98Max10tA-87
98Max10tA-111
98Max10tABA-29
98PrePas-125
98SP AutMoaL-M3
98SP AutT-T3
98UppDecRTTC5A-AN22
98UppDecRTTC5A-AN33
99PrePas-135

Parsons, Johnnie
54StaWetIW-1950
60HawWaxI-34
91LegInd-17
92AllWorI-58
95TraVal-56

Parsons, Phil
88MaxCha-26
88MaxMyrB-26
89Max-55
89Max-124
89Max-131
89Max-149
89MaxCri-18
90Max-4
90Max-194
90MaxHolF-HF19
91Max-61
91MaxTheWA-12
91ProSet-143A
91ProSet-143B
91SpoLegPP-P1
91SpoLegPP-PP1
91SpoLegPP-PP2
91SpoLegPP-PP3
91SpoLegPP-PP4
91SpoLegPP-PP5
91SpoLegPP-PP6
91SpoLegPP-PP7
91SpoLegPP-PP8
91SpoLegPP-PP9
91SpoLegPP-PP10
91SpoLegPP-PP11
91SpoLegPP-PP12
91SpoLegPP-PP13
91SpoLegPP-PP14
91SpoLegPP-PP15
91SpoLegPP-PP16
91SpoLegPP-PP17
91SpoLegPP-PP18
91SpoLegPP-PP19
91SpoLegPP-PP20
91SpoLegPP-PP21
91SpoLegPP-PP22
91SpoLegPP-PP23
91SpoLegPP-PP24
91SpoLegPP-PP25
91SpoLegPP-PP26
91SpoLegPP-PP27
91SpoLegPP-PP28
91SpoLegPP-PP29
91SpoLegPP-PP30
91SupRacM-8
91Tra-29
92MaxBla-9
92MaxRed-9
92ProSet-36
92ProSet-74
92ProSet-193
92Tra-9
93ACRacF-41
93FinLin-49
93FinLinCS-20
93FinLinS-49
93Max-41
93MaxPreP-41
93MaxPreS-41
93MaxRetJ-3
93Tra-41
93TraFirR-41
94Max-47
94Max-301
94MaxAut-47
94MaxPreP-47
94MaxPreS-47
95MaxPreS-183
96CroJewEDT-70
96CroJewEDTC-70
96CroJewEE-70
96CroJewEli-70
96CroJewES-70
96CroJewETC-70
96CroJewETCE-70
96CroJewETCS-70
96Fla-45
96MaxMadiA-65
96MaxMadiA-71
96MaxOdy-65
96MaxOdy-71
96MaxPre-181
96MaxPre-252
96Ult-132
96Ult-133
96UltUpd-42
97JurPar-42
97JurParT-42
97SkyPro-49
97SkyProA-49
97Ult-89
97UltUpd-64
97UltUpdAR-64
98HigGea-40

Paschal, Jim
89TGRacMR-187
89TGRacMR-235
89TGRacMR-236
89TGRacMR-238
89WinCir-38
91GalPrePR-64
91ProSetL-L27
91TGRacMRU-187
91TGRacMRU-235
91TGRacMRU-236
91TGRacMRU-237
91TGRacMRU-238
91TraPacYH-26
92ProSetL-L20

Pasteryak, Carl
91WinChoM-2
91WinChoM-3

Pasteryak, Charlie
91WinChoM-49
91WinChoM-50

Pastorini, Dan
91ProSetN-126

Patch, Bob
92EriMaxTA-63

Patrese, Riccardo
78GraPri-30
78GraPri-47
78GraPri-53
78GraPri-81
78GraPri-91
78GraPri-162
87AceForO-23
87ForOneI-7
88HerFouFO-1B
91CarForO-16
91CarForO-17
91CarForO-18
91ProTraFO-11
91ProTraFO-12
91ProTraFO-148
91ProTraFO-149
91ProTraFO-162
92GriForO-6
92GriForO-39
92GriForO-72
92GriForO-104
92GriForO-105
92GriForO-108
92GriForO-109
92GriForO-112
92GriForO-113
92GriForO-114
93MaxWilR-2
93MaxWilR-72
93MaxWilR-73
93MaxWilR-75
93MaxWilR-80
93MaxWilR-87

Patterson, Kris
91JAG-14
92JAG-219

Patterson, Pat
92MaxBlaU-U28
92MaxRedU-U28
95MaxPreS-209

Patterson, Rusty
91DKIMCDT-11

Pauch, Billy
91K&WDirT-2
92K&WDirT-1
94K&WDirT-5
95K&WDirT-12
95K&WDirT-23

Paul Jr., John
78GraPri-203
83A&SRacI-40
84A&SRacI-30
85A&SRacI-4
86A&SRacI-23
92LegInd-26
92MaxBla-70
92MaxRed-70
93HiTecI-18
93HiTecI-45
93HiTecICFF-SP10
95SkyInd5-48
95SkyInd5-97
97Hi-IRL-16

Paul, Donny
94LanARCF-46

Pawuk, Mark
89MegDra-69
89MegDra-70
91ProSetN-40
91ProSetN-88
92ProSetN-89
92ProSetN-145
93FinLinN-99
94ActPacN-30

Paxton, John
72FleAHRDN-32

Payne, Ronnie
91BulRin-47

Payne, Roy
91LanARCHS-16
92LanARCF-10
92LanARCF-22
93Tra-126
93Tra-187
93TraFirR-126
93TraFirR-187
93WheRooT-42
93WheRooTPla-42
94HigGea-54
94HigGeaG-54
94Max-183
94MaxPreS-183

Paysor, Dick
94HigGeaPPT-W4
94HigGeaPPTG-4W

Paysor, Stella
94HigGeaPPT-W16
94HigGeaPPTG-16W

Payton, Walter
96SkyInd5-54

Pearson, David
85SpoPhoGS-NNO
85SpoPhoGS-NNO
89Max-194
89Max-215
89TGRacMR-27
89TGRacMR-39
89TGRacMR-41
89TGRacMR-42
89TGRacMR-43
89TGRacMR-59
89TGRacMR-60
89TGRacMR-182
89WinCir-16
90Max-131
91Max-169
91ProSetL-L28
91RacConSR-8
91TGRacDP-1
91TGRacDP-2
91TGRacDP-3
91TGRacDP-4
91TGRacDP-5
91TGRacDP-6
91TGRacMRU-27
91TGRacMRU-39
91TGRacMRU-41
91TGRacMRU-42
91TGRacMRU-43
91TGRacMRU-59
91TGRacMRU-60
91TGRacMRU-182
91TGRacWS-4
91TraPacYH-27
91TraPacYH-28
92ProSetL-L21
92ProSetR-2
92ProSetRF-L2
93Pep400VL-5
93WheRooT-3
93WheRooT-95
93WheRooTPla-3
93WheRooTPla-95
94HigGeaL-LS2
94PrePas-133
95PrePas-125
95PrePasRH-125
95Sel-116
95Sel-130
95SelFlaO-116
95SelFlaO-130
95TraVal-74
95UppDec-156
95UppDecGSEG-156
95UppDecI-I5
95UppDecSSES-156
96M-F-32
96UppDecRL-RLC7
97PrePas-93
97PrePasL-93
97PrePasOS-93
97PrePasT-93
98Max10tA-20
98Max10tA-65
98PrePas-127
98PrePasPR-2A
98SP AutMoaL-M2
98SP AutT-T2
98UppDecRTTC5A-AN12
98UppDecRTTC5A-AN18
98UppDecRTTC5A-AN26
98UppDecRTTC5AA-AN18
99PrePas-131

Pearson, Earl Jr.
95HavAT-28

Pearson, Eddie
92MaxBla-185
92MaxBlaU-NNO
92MaxRed-185
92MaxRedU-NNO
93AllRobPDS-8

Pearson, Larry
88MaxCha-37
89Max-16
90Max-16
91Max-41
91ProSet-105
92JusRacLC-1
92MaxBla-41
92MaxRed-41
92ProSet-72
93Max-93
93MaxPreS-93
93Tra-105
93Tra-169
93TraFirR-105
93TraFirR-169
94HigGea-55
94HigGeaG-55
94Max-185
94Max-306
94MaxPreS-185
94Tra-92
94TraFirR-92
94VIP-62
95FinLin-71
95FinLinPP-71
95FinLinSil-71
95HigGea-59
95HigGeaDO-59
95HigGeaDOG-59
95HigGeaG-59
95Max-157
95MaxAut-157
95MaxCroC-137
95MaxMed-BGN5
95MaxMedB-BGN5
95MaxPreP-137
95MaxPreS-168
95OptXL-30
95OptXLCB-30
95OptXLDC-30
95OptXLRH-30
95PrePas-68
95PrePas-80
95PrePasRH-68
95PrePasRH-80
95Sel-68
95Sel-116
95SelFlaO-68
95SelFlaO-116
95TraOnTR-OTR4
95VIP-43
95VIPAut-43
95VIPCooB-43
95VIPEmeP-43
95VIPRedHCB-43
96MaxMadiA-60
96MaxMadiA-86
96MaxOdy-60
96MaxOdy-86
96MaxPre-168
96MaxPre-251
96PrePas-62
96PrePasSco-62
96PrePasT-62
96Ult-130
96Ult-131
96Viper-51
96ViperBlaM-51
96ViperCop-51
96ViperGreM-51
97ColCho-46
97ColCho-95
97PrePas-77
97PrePasL-77
97PrePasOS-77
97PrePasT-77
97Ult-90
97UppDecVC-46
97UppDecVC-95

Pearson, Ricky
91Max-149
91Tra-177
92MaxBla-183
92MaxRed-183
92Tra-177
92TraAllRP-11
93AllRobPDS-2
93CarDynARD-3
93Max-188
93MaxPreP-167
93MaxPreS-188
93Tra-146
93TraFirR-146
94Max-309

Pease, Gary
92VolRacLS2-49
92VolRacLSI-39

Peaslee, Forest
92WinChoM-17

Peaslee, Jamie
92WinChoM-18

Peck, Howard
65DonSpeS-16

Peck, Tom
91K&WDirT-42
91Max-204

91Tra-96
92MaxBla-74
92MaxRed-74
92ProSet-244
92RedSta-16
92Tra-96
92TraRacMB-19B
92WinChoB-72
92WinChoB-73
93FinLin-84
93FinLinCS-3
93FinLinS-84
93Max-19
93MaxPreP-19
93MaxPreS-19
93Tra-19
93Tra-175
93TraFirR-19
93TraFirR-175
94FinLinBGN-BGN6
94HigGea-58
94HigGeaG-58
94Max-174
94MaxPreP-161
94MaxPreS-174
94VIP-63
94VIP-67
Pedregon, Cruz
91BigTimD-28
92ProSetN-14
92ProSetN-118
92ProSetRC-5
93FinLinN-65
93FinLinN-66
93FinLinN-67
93FinLinNA-4
93FinLinNP-3
94ActPacN-23
95ActPacN-12
95ActPacNSS-12
95Zen-69
95Zen-70
Peeling, Wayne
93CorSelCCS-27
Peeples, Paul Jr.
95MaxPreS-254
Pegher, Dave
92VolRacLS2-50
92VolRacLSI-40
Pegram, Sammy
91BulRin-20
92BulRin-21
Pemberton, Randy
92MaxBlaU-U29
92MaxRedU-U29
93Max-216
93MaxPreS-216
94MaxPreS-209
95MaxPreS-203
96MaxPre-201
Pemberton, Robin
90Max-86
91Max-86
91Max-126
91MaxMot-20
91MaxUpd-126
91ProSet-23
91Tra-109
92MaxBla-153
92MaxRed-153
92ProSet-86
92Tra-109
92WheKylP-4
92WheKylPG-4
93FinLin-57
93FinLinCS-14
93FinLinS-57
93Max-146
93MaxPreP-131
93MaxPreS-146
94FinLin-72
94FinLinS-72
94Max-131
94MaxPreP-124
94MaxPreS-131
94PrePas-103
94VIP-98
95ActPacC-61
95ActPacCSS-61
95CroJew-36
95CroJewD-36
95CroJewE-36
95CroJewS-36
95Max-110
95Max-192
95MaxAut-110
95MaxCroC-107
95MaxPreP-107
95MaxPreS-126
95Sel-108
95SelFlaO-108
95SP-136
95SPDieC-136
95Tra5thA-71
95Tra5thAG-71
96AutRac-36
96AutRacA-41
96AutRacCA-41
96Cla-50
96ClaPriP-50
96ClaSil-50
96CroJewEDT-54
96CroJewEDTC-54
96CroJewEE-54
96CroJewEli-54
96CroJewES-54
96CroJewETC-54
96CroJewETCE-54
96CroJewETCS-54
96FinLin-81
96FinLinPriP-81
96FinLinS-81
96Fla-55
96Max-89
96MaxPre-123
96PrePas-73
96PrePasSco-73
96PrePasT-73
96Ult-20
96UppDecAP-AP6
96Viper-31
96ViperBlaM-31
96ViperCop-31
96ViperGreM-31
97ActPac-82
97ActPacFI-82
97AutRacA-41
97ColChoUD5-UD4
97PinPre-43
97PinPreBM-43
97PinPreGM-43
97PinPreP-TP2B
97PinPreSM-43
97Pre-52
97PreBlaWFS-52
97PreGri-52
97PreRedW-52
97RacCho-73
97RacChoSS-73
97SBMot-34
97SkyPro-45
98PrePas-99
98PrePasOS-99
98PrePasS-28
98PrePasS-33
98PrePasSF-33
98Whe-75
98WheGol-75
99Pre-66
99PrePas-66
Pemberton, Ryan
92ProSet-194
92TraTeaS-30
93Max-258
93MaxPreS-258
Penfold, Billy
92WinChoM-5
Penfold, Ray
92WinChoM-24
Penland, Jimmy
94HigGeaPPT-G7
94HigGeaPPTG-7G
Pennington, Jack
90Max-134
91DirTra-8
91DirTra-43
91Max-47
92DirTra-83
92ProSet-171
Penske, Roger
91ProSet-12
91Tra-37
92MaxBla-110
92MaxRed-110
92Tra-37
92WheRusW-3
92WheRusWG-3
93DaySer2RW-14
93FinLin-178
93FinLinCS-6
93FinLinS-178
93Max-111
93MaxPreP-100
93MaxPreS-111
94ActPac-168
94FinLin-96
94FinLinS-96
94HigGea-147
94HigGeaDO-147
94HigGeaDOG-147
94HigGeaG-147
94HigGeaPPT-W1
94HigGeaPPTG-1W
94Max-85
94MaxPreP-85
94MaxPreS-85
94Pow-7
94Pow-107
94Pow-124
94PowGol-7
94PowGol-107
94PowGol-124
94PrePas-82
94Tra-57
94TraAutV-46
94TraFirR-57
95HigGea-32
95HigGeaDO-32
95HigGeaDOG-32
95HigGeaG-32
95ImaOwnP-OP15
95Max-50
95MaxCroC-68
95MaxPreP-68
95MaxPreS-80
95PrePas-85
95PrePasRH-85
95Sel-83
95SelFlaO-83
95SkyInd5-14
95SP-123
95SPDieC-123
95TraAutV-40
95TraBehTS-BTS8
96ActPacC-70
96Max-55
96MaxPre-80
96PrePas-73
96PrePasSco-73
96PrePasT-73
96SkyInd5-51
96Ult-144
96UppDec-123
96Viper-36
96ViperBlaM-36
96ViperCop-36
96ViperGreM-36
97PinPre-38
97PinPreBM-38
97PinPreGM-38
97PinPreSM-38
97Viper-61
97ViperBlaR-61
Perkins, Ken
92TraTeaS-182
Perry, Eddie
92BulRin-101
Perry, Hal
92BulRin-194
Perry, Jamie
94JAG-45
Perry, Stan
95JSKIce-10
Pescarolo, Henri
78GraPri-190
Peters, Barry
92VolRacLS2-51
92VolRacLSI-41
Peters, Mike
90WorOut-40
91WorOut-28
Peterson, Pete
95Max-114
95MaxAut-114
95MaxCroC-117
95MaxPreP-117
95MaxPreS-136
95SP-149
95SPDieC-149
96MaxPre-131
Peterson, Ronnie
77Spo-6910
78GraPri-24
78GraPri-28
78GraPri-73
78GraPri-84
78GraPri-89
78GraPri-118
78GraPri-141
78GraPri-142
Peterson, Steve
96MaxPre-234
Petillo, Kelly
54StaWetIW-1935
60HawWaxI-23
Petrash, Gary
92RedGraST-12
92RedGraST-13
92RedGraST-14
92RedGraST-15
92RedGraST-16
Petrash, Loren
92RedGraST-12
92RedGraST-13
92RedGraST-14
92RedGraST-15
92RedGraST-16
92RedGraST-17
Petree, Andy
91Max-160
91ProSet-64
91SpoLegDJ-DJ26
91Tra-174
92MaxAllPT-11
92MaxBla-151
92MaxBla-239
92MaxRed-151
92MaxRed-239
92ProSet-85
92Tra-174
93FinLin-155
93FinLinCS-20
93FinLinS-155
93Max-154
93MaxPreP-138
93MaxPreS-154
94ActPacRCR-RCR7
94HigGea-38
94HigGeaG-38
94HigGeaPPT-E2
94HigGeaPPT-E5
94HigGeaPPTG-2E
94HigGeaPPTG-5E
94Max-126
94MaxPreP-119
94MaxPreS-126
94OptXL-49
94OptXLRH-49
94VIP-99
94WheHarG-77
94WheHarGG-77
95ActPacC-57
95ActPacCSS-57
95HigGea-41
95HigGeaDO-41
95HigGeaDOG-41
95HigGeaG-41
95Max-96
95Max-203
95MaxAut-96
95MaxCroC-103
95MaxPreP-103
95MaxPreS-122
95PrePas-98
95PrePasRH-98
95Sel-100
95SelFlaO-100
95Tra5thA-74
95Tra5thAG-74
95TraBehTS-BTS18
96Ass-30
96Kni-43
96KniBlaK-43
96KniQueRKP-43
96KniRoy-43
96KniWhiK-43
96Max-84
96MaxPre-119
96PinPolP-85
96PinPolPLF-85
96Ult-8
96Ult-150
97JurPar-57
97JurParT-57
97UltUpd-48
97Viper-57
97ViperBlaR-57
Petrie, Jon
73FleAHRRU-63
Petrie, Ken
91LanAmeIS-13
91LanAmeIS-15
Petty, Adam
99Pre-63
99PrePas-63
Petty, Austin
94ActPac-96
Petty, Kyle
83UNORac-13
83UNORac-16
83UNORac-19
89Max-42
89Max-220
89MaxCri-12
90Max-42
90Max-192
90MaxHolF-HF17
91ACRac-7
91Max-42
91Max-109
91Max-140
91Max-172
91MaxMcD-11
91MaxRacFK-2
91MaxTheWA-13
91MaxUpd-42
91ProSet-54
91ProSet-87
91ProSetPF-34
91ProSetPF-35
91ProSetPF-36
91ProSetPF-39
91ProSetPF-48
91STPRicP-4
91SupRacM-9
91Tra-41
91Tra-42
91Tra-47
91Tra-173
91Tra-P3
91TraMelYKP-1
91TraMelYKP-2
91TraMelYKP-3
91TraMelYKP-4
91TraMelYKP-5
91TraMelYKP-6
91TraMelYKP-8
91TraMelYKP-9
91TraMelYKP-10
91TraMelYKP-11
91TraMelYKP-12
92ACDel-3
92ACRacP-3
92ActPacKPP-101
92ActPacKPP-102
92ActPacKPP-103
92BikRacS-25
92CarDynGO-8
92CarDynKP-1
92CarDynKP-2
92CarDynKP-3
92CarDynKP-4
92CarDynKP-5
92MaxBla-42
92MaxBla-192
92MaxBla-266
92MaxMcD-35
92MaxRed-42
92MaxRed-192
92MaxRed-266
92MaxTheW-2
92MaxTheW-22
92MaxTheW-48
92ProSet-18
92ProSet-30
92ProSet-44
92ProSet-113
92ProSetMH-26
92ProSetRF-14
92RedSta-24
92RPM-2
92Tra-42
92Tra-69A
92Tra-69B
92Tra-142
92Tra-196
92Tra-P2
92TraAut-A6
92TraRacM-13
92TraRacM-42

92TraRacM-46
92TraRacM-87
92TraTeaS-51
92TraTeaS-55
92TraTeaS-74
92TraTeaS-75
92TraTeaS-101
92WheKylP-2
92WheKylP-5
92WheKylP-6
92WheKylP-7
92WheKylP-8
92WheKylP-9
92WheKylP-10
92WheKylP-11
92WheKylP-12
92WheKylP-13
92WheKylP-14
92WheKylPG-2
92WheKylPG-5
92WheKylPG-6
92WheKylPG-7
92WheKylPG-8
92WheKylPG-9
92WheKylPG-10
92WheKylPG-11
92WheKylPG-12
92WheKylPG-13
92WheKylPG-14
93ACRacF-42
93ActPac-2
93ActPac-13
93ActPac-14
93ActPac-23
93ActPac-42
93ActPac-91
93ActPac-99
93ActPac-100
93ActPac-160
93ActPac-186
93ActPac-P1KP
93ActPac-P2KP
93ActPac2G-3G
93ActPac2G-34G
93ActPac2G-68G
93CarDynGO-7
93CarDynQC-7
93FinLin-38
93FinLin-121
93FinLin-171
93FinLinCS-14
93FinLinCS-22
93FinLinS-38
93FinLinS-121
93FinLinS-171
93HiTecTT-7
93Max-42
93Max-61
93Max-74
93Max-282
93Max-291
93MaxHou-5
93MaxHou-18
93MaxLowFS-3
93MaxPreP-23
93MaxPreP-42
93MaxPreP-60
93MaxPreP-61
93MaxPreP-197
93MaxPreP-206
93MaxPreS-42
93MaxPreS-61
93MaxPreS-74
93MaxPreS-282
93MaxPreS-291
93MaxTheW-20
93MaxTheW-40
93PrePasPre-11
93PrePasPre-30
93TraPreC-4
94ActPac-5
94ActPac-37
94ActPac-44
94ActPac-45
94ActPac-82
94ActPac-92
94ActPac-92D
94ActPac-93
94ActPac-94
94ActPac-95
94ActPac-96
94ActPac-97
94ActPac-119
94ActPac-157
94ActPac-92D
94ActPac2G-7G
94ActPac2G-14G
94ActPac2G-15G
94ActPac2G-36G
94ActPacC-13
94ActPacP-2R943
94ActPacP-2R943
94ActPacP-KP1
94ActPacP-KP2
94FinLin-11
94FinLin-28
94FinLin-60
94FinLin-84
94FinLin-12
94FinLinDH-5
94FinLinG-7
94FinLinG-22
94FinLinG-58
94FinLinG-71
94FinLinG-85
94FinLinGCC-NNO
94FinLinGS-NNO
94FinLinS-11
94FinLinS-28
94FinLinS-60
94FinLinS-84
94FinLinVL-VL6
94FinLinVL-VL13
94Hi-Bri4AP-60
94HigGea-86
94HigGea-88
94HigGea-122
94HigGeaDO-122
94HigGeaDOG-122
94HigGeaG-86
94HigGeaG-88
94HigGeaG-122
94HigGeaMG-MG9
94HiTecB4-60
94HiTecB4P-3
94Max-39
94Max-42
94Max-205
94Max-220
94MaxAut-42
94MaxMed-24
94MaxMed-73
94MaxPreP-39
94MaxPreP-42
94MaxPreP-79
94MaxPreP-179
94MaxPreS-39
94MaxPreS-42
94MaxPreS-263
94MaxPreS-279
94MaxPreSJ-10
94MaxRacC-6
94MaxTheS2-5
94OptXL-14
94OptXL-28
94OptXLP-1
94OptXLRH-14
94OptXLRH-28
94Pow-22
94Pow-108
94Pow-109
94PowGol-22
94PowGol-108
94PowGol-109
94PowPre-14
94PowPre-26
94PrePas-21
94PrePas-46
94PrePasA-NNO
94PrePasCC-CC21
94PrePasH-H5
94PrePasRD-RD6
94Sky-7
94Tra-111
94Tra-137
94Tra-185
94TraCar-C4
94TraFirR-111
94TraFirR-137
94TraFirR-185
94VIP-25
94VIP-47
94VIP-79
94VIPDriC-DC6
94VIPExc2-EC6
94WheHarG-75
94WheHarGG-75
95ActPacC-47
95ActPacCSS-47
95ActPacP-16
95ActPacS-16
95ActPacSSS-16
95Ass-4
95Ass-32
95Ass$5$25PC-6
95Ass1M$PC-12
95AssGolS-4
95AssGolS-32
95CroJew-12
95CroJew-46
95CroJew-50
95CroJew-72
95CroJewD-12
95CroJewD-46
95CroJewD-50
95CroJewD-72
95CroJewDJ-DJ5
95CroJewDJD-DJ5
95CroJewDJE-DJ5
95CroJewE-12
95CroJewE-46
95CroJewE-50
95CroJewE-72
95CroJewS-12
95CroJewS-46
95CroJewS-50
95CroJewS-72
95FinLin-42
95FinLin-52
95FinLin-73
95FinLinCC6-4
95FinLinCC6-32
95FinLinCC6W-CC3
95FinLinGS-GS9
95FinLinPP-42
95FinLinPP-52
95FinLinPP-73
95FinLinSil-42
95FinLinSil-52
95FinLinSil-73
95HigGea-17
95HigGeaDO-17
95HigGeaDOG-17
95HigGeaG-17
95HiTecB4-34
95HiTecB4-52
95Ima-42
95Ima-76
95ImaDri-D6
95ImaGol-42
95ImaGol-76
95Max-42
95Max-171
95Max-234
95Max-235
95MaxAut-42
95MaxCroC-39
95MaxCroC-42
95MaxMed-24
95MaxMed-54
95MaxMedB-24
95MaxMedB-54
95MaxOveW-4
95MaxPreP-39
95MaxPreP-42
95MaxPreS-39
95MaxPreS-42
95MetImpKP-1
95MetImpKP-1
95MetImpKP-2
95MetImpKP-2
95MetImpKP-3
95MetImpKP-3
95MetImpKP-4
95MetImpKP-4
95MetImpKP-5
95MetImpKP-5
95MetImpKP-6
95MetImpKP-7
95MetImpKP-8
95MetImpKP-9
95MetImpKP-10
95OptXL-16
95OptXL-36
95OptXLCB-16
95OptXLCB-36
95OptXLDC-16
95OptXLDC-36
95OptXLRH-16
95OptXLRH-36
95OptXLS-XLS11
95PrePas-23
95PrePas-46
95PrePas-131
95PrePasCC-23
95PrePasPH-13
95PrePasPH-34
95PrePasPHP-HP6
95PrePasPPC-NNO
95PrePasPre-13
95PrePasPre-34
95PrePasPre-P1
95PrePasPRH-13
95PrePasPRH-34
95PrePasPro-1
95PrePasRH-23
95PrePasRH-46
95PrePasRH-131
95Sel-24
95Sel-46
95Sel-109
95Sel-131
95SelDreM-DM11
95SelFlaO-24
95SelFlaO-46
95SelFlaO-109
95SelFlaO-131
95SelPro-24
95SelSki-SS7
95SP-30
95SP-74
95SP-116
95SPDieC-30
95SPDieC-74
95SPDieC-116
95SPSpeM-SM1
95SPSpeMDC-SM1
95Tra-22
95Tra-34
95Tra-51
95Tra5thA-15
95Tra5thA-60
95Tra5thAG-15
95Tra5thAG-60
95Tra5thAR-R9
95TraAutV-7
95TraCha-C2
95TraFirR-22
95TraFirR-34
95TraFirR-51
95TraRacM-RM18
95TraSerS-SS17
95UppDec-4
95UppDec-47
95UppDec-72
95UppDec-140
95UppDec-173
95UppDec-216
95UppDec-259
95UppDec-292
95UppDecA-216
95UppDecGSEG-4
95UppDecGSEG-47
95UppDecGSEG-72
95UppDecGSEG-140
95UppDecGSEG-173
95UppDecGSEG-216
95UppDecGSEG-259
95UppDecGSEG-292
95UppDecO-OS2
95UppDecPSP-PP8
95UppDecSSES-4
95UppDecSSES-47
95UppDecSSES-72
95UppDecSSES-140
95UppDecSSES-173
95UppDecSSES-216
95UppDecSSES-259
95UppDecSSES-292
95VIP-22
95VIP-34
95VIPAut-22
95VIPCooB-22
95VIPCooB-34
95VIPEmeP-22
95VIPEmeP-34
95VIPHel-H5
95VIPHelG-H5
95VIPRedHCB-22
95VIPRedHCB-34
95Zen-57
95ZenWinW-12
96Ass-7
96Ass-41
96Ass$1000CCIPC-12
96Ass$100CCIPC-5
96Ass$10PC-7
96Ass$2PC-19
96Ass$5PC-12
96AssComL-CL2
96AutRac-3
96AutRacHP-HP2
96Cla-13
96Cla-59
96ClaInn-IV5
96ClaPriP-13
96ClaSil-13
96CroJewEDT-13
96CroJewEDT-58
96CroJewEDTC-13
96CroJewEDTC-58
96CroJewEE-13
96CroJewEE-58
96CroJewEli-13
96CroJewEli-58
96CroJewES-13
96CroJewES-58
96CroJewETC-13
96CroJewETC-58
96CroJewETCE-13
96CroJewETCE-58
96CroJewETCS-13
96CroJewETCS-58
96FinLin-20
96FinLin-86
96FinLinBGL-C8
96FinLinBGL-D9
96FinLinGS-GS18
96FinLinPP-28
96FinLinPP$5C-18
96FinLinPP$S-28
96FinLinPriP-20
96FinLinPriP-86
96FinLinS-20
96FinLinS-86
96Fla-26
96Fla-82
96Kni-18
96Kni-27
96KniBlaK-18
96KniBlaK-27
96KniQueRKP-18
96KniQueRKP-27
96KniRoy-18
96KniRoy-27
96KniWhiK-18
96KniWhiK-27
96M-F-30
96M-F-31
96M-FSil-S13
96Max-31
96Max-42
96MaxMadiA-31
96MaxMadiA-42
96MaxOdy-31
96MaxOdy-42
96MaxOdyM-MM8
96MaxOnTRA-OTRA1
96MaxOveTW-OTW2
96MaxPre-42
96MaxPre-72
96Pin-31
96Pin-57
96Pin-31
96Pin-57
96PinPolP-11
96PinPolP-42
96PinPolP-74
96PinPolPCS-14
96PinPolPLF-11
96PinPolPLF-42
96PinPolPLF-74
96PinWinCC-31
96PinWinCC-57
96PrePas-25
96PrePas-37
96PrePas-97
96PrePas&NC-25
96PrePasBR-BR1
96PrePasCC-25
96PrePasFoc-F8
96PrePasP-26
96PrePasP$10PC-8
96PrePasP$20PC-8
96PrePasP$5PC-8
96PrePasPEP-26
96PrePasPH-26
96PrePasSco-25
96PrePasSco-37
96PrePasSco-97

91TraRicP-34
91TraRicP-35
91TraRicP-36
91TraRicP-37
91TraRicP-38
91TraRicP-39
91TraRicP-40
91TraRicP-41
91TraRicP-42
91TraRicP-43
91TraRicP-44
91TraRicP-45
91TraRicP-46
91TraRicP-47
91TraRicP-48
91TraRicP-49
91TraRicP-50
91WinChoRC-17
92BikRacS-1
92FooLioRP-2
92FooLioRP-3
92FooLioRP-4
92FooLioRP-6
92FooLioRP-7
92FooLioRP-8
92FooLioRP-10
92FooLioRP-11
92FooLioRP-12
92FooLioRP-14
92FooLioRP-15
92FooLioRP-16
92FooLioRP-18
92FooLioRP-19
92FooLioRP-20
92FooLioRP-22
92FooLioRP-23
92FooLioRP-24
92FooLioRP-26
92FooLioRP-27
92FooLioRP-28
92FooLioRP-30
92FooLioRP-31
92FooLioRP-32
92FooLioRP-34
92FooLioRP-35
92FooLioRP-36
92FooLioRP-38
92FooLioRP-39
92FooLioRP-40
92FooLioRP-42
92FooLioRP-43
92FooLioRP-44
92FooLioRP-46
92FooLioRP-47
92FooLioRP-48
92FooLioRP-50
92FooLioRP-51
92FooLioRP-52
92FooLioRP-54
92FooLioRP-55
92FooLioRP-56
92FooLioRP-58
92FooLioRP-59
92FooLioRP-60
92FooLioRP-62
92FooLioRP-63
92FooLioRP-64
92FooLioRP-66
92FooLioRP-67
92FooLioRP-68
92FooLioRP-70
92FooLioRP-71
92FooLioRP-72
92FooLioRP-74
92FooLioRP-75
92FooLioRP-76
92FooLioRP-78
92FooLioRP-79
92FooLioRP-80
92FooLioRP-82
92FooLioRP-83
92FooLioRP-84
92FooLioRP-86
92FooLioRP-87
92FooLioRP-88
92FooLioRP-90
92FooLioRP-91
92FooLioRP-92
92FooLioRP-94
92FooLioRP-95
92FooLioRP-96
92FooLioRP-98
92FooLioRP-99
92FooLioRP-100
92FooLioRP-102
92FooLioRP-103
92FooLioRP-104
92FooLioRP-106
92FooLioRP-107
92FooLioRP-108
92FooLioRP-110
92FooLioRP-111
92FooLioRP-112
92FooLioRP-114
92FooLioRP-115
92FooLioRP-116
92FooLioRP-NNO
92MacTooWC-17
92MaxBla-43
92MaxIMH-36
92MaxMcD-30
92MaxRed-43
92MaxSamB-1
92MaxTheW-9
92MaxTheW-29
92PepRicP-1
92PepRicP-2
92PepRicP-3
92PepRicP-4
92PepRicP-5
92ProSet-43
92ProSet-45
92ProSet-114
92ProSet-124
92ProSetMH-25
92ProSetRC-6
92ProSetRF-15
92RedSta-3
92RPM-4
92STPDay5-1
92STPDay5-2
92STPDay5-4
92STPDay5-5
92STPDay5-7
92STPDay5-9
92Tra-43
92Tra-85
92Tra-200
92Tra-P3
92TraAut-A1
92TraBenP-28
92TraBenP-31
92TraBenP-39
92TraGoo-25
92TraKodEl-1A
92TraKodEl-1B
92TraRacM-18
92TraRacM-19
92TraRacM-43
92TraRacM-55
92TraRacM-80
92TraRacM-97
92TraRacM-100
92TraTeaS-176
92TraTeaS-184
92TraTeaS-185
92TraTeaS-195
92TraTeaS-200
93ActPac-10
93ActPac-31
93ActPac-50
93ActPac-51
93ActPac-52
93ActPac-53
93ActPac-54
93ActPac-70
93ActPac-71
93ActPac-72
93ActPac-75
93ActPac-76
93ActPac-81
93ActPac-82
93ActPac-92
93ActPac-160
93ActPac2G-13G
93ActPac2G-14G
93ActPac2G-15G
93ActPac2G-16G
93ActPac2G-17G
93ActPac2G-35G
93ActPacAK-AK3
93CarDynGO-1
93CarDynQC-3
93FinLin-61
93FinLin-85
93FinLin-114
93FinLinCS-12
93FinLinCS-27
93FinLinCS-29
93FinLinS-61
93FinLinS-85
93FinLinS-114
93Max-43
93Max-156
93Max-199
93Max-245
93MaxHou-15
93MaxHou-18
93MaxPreP-43
93MaxPreP-48
93MaxPreP-57
93MaxPreP-74
93MaxPreS-43
93MaxPreS-156
93MaxPreS-199
93MaxPreS-245
93TraPreC-15
93TraPreC-16
93WheRooT-2
93WheRooT-61
93WheRooT-79
93WheRooT-80
93WheRooT-95
93WheRooT-96
93WheRooT-99
93WheRooTPla-2
93WheRooTPla-61
93WheRooTPla-79
93WheRooTPla-80
93WheRooTPla-95
93WheRooTPla-96
93WheRooTPla-99
93WheRooTPro-P1
93WheRooTS-SP6
93WheRooTS-SP7
94ActPac-178
94FinLin-58
94FinLin-64
94FinLinG-83
94FinLinS-58
94FinLinS-64
94HigGea-28
94HigGeaG-28
94HigGeaL-LS4
94HigGeaP-P3
94HiTecB4P-1
94HiTecB4RP-1
94HiTecB4RP-2
94HiTecB4RP-3
94HiTecB4RP-4
94HiTecB4RP-5
94HiTecB4RP-6
94Max-43
94MaxPreP-43
94MaxPreS-43
94MaxPreSJ-6
94Pep400VL-1
94Pow-64
94Pow-110
94PowGol-64
94PowGol-110
95ActPacC-20
95ActPacCSS-20
95ActPacP-73
95ActPacP2G-5G
95Ass10PC-4
95Ass$5$25PC-8
95FinLin-43
95FinLin-104
95FinLinPP-43
95FinLinPP-104
95FinLinSil-43
95FinLinSil-104
95MatWinCC-1
95MatWinCC-2
95MatWinCC-4
95MatWinCC-5
95MatWinCC-9
95Max-43
95MaxCroC-43
95MaxPreP-43
95MaxPreS-43
95MaxStaU-6
95MetImpWCC-1
95PrePas-86
95PrePas-126
95PrePas-132
95PrePasPH-20
95PrePasPre-20
95PrePasPRH-20
95PrePasRH-86
95PrePasRH-126
95PrePasRH-132
95Sel-73
95Sel-109
95Sel-129
95SelFlaO-73
95SelFlaO-109
95SelFlaO-129
95SP-127
95SPBacTB-BB1
95SPDieC-127
95Tra-NNO
95Tra5thAR-R15
95TraVal-73
95TraVal-85
95UppDec-151
95UppDecGSEG-151
95UppDecSSES-151
95VIP-49
95VIPCooB-49
95VIPEmeP-49
95VIPHel-H7
95VIPHel-H8
95VIPHel-H9
95VIPHelG-H7
95VIPHelG-H8
95VIPHelG-H9
95VIPRedHCB-49
96ActPacC-78
96Ass-47
96AutRac-10
96AutRacFR-73
96AutRacFR-74
96AutRacFR-75
96AutRacFR-76
96Cla-12
96ClaPriP-12
96ClaSil-12
96CroJewEADJ-DJ6
96CroJewEDTDJA-DJ6
96CroJewEDTDJG-DJ6
96CroJewEGDJ-DJ6
96CroJewESDJ-DJ6
96CroJewETCDJA-DJ6
96CroJewETCDJS-DJ6
96CroJewETCGDJ-DJ6
96Fla-51
96M-F-14
96M-FSil-S8
96Max-43
96MaxMadiA-43
96MaxOdy-43
96MaxPre-43
96MaxPre-52
96MetImp2AWCC-1
96MetImp2AWCC-2
96MetImp2AWCC-4
96MetImp2AWCC-5
96MetImp2AWCC-9
96PrePas-80
96PrePas-89
96PrePasSco-80
96PrePasSco-89
96PrePasT-80
96PrePasT-89
96SPRicP2A-RP1
96SPRicP2A-RP2
96SPRicP2A-RP3
96SPRicP2A-RP4
96SPRicP2A-RP5
96SPRicP2A-RP6
96SPRicP2A-RP7
96SPRicP2A-RP8
96SPRicP2A-RP9
96Ult-146
96UltAut-28
96UppDec-127
96UppDec-139
96UppDecRL-RLC1
96ZenChaS-17
96ZenChaS-21
96ZenChaS-22
96ZenChaS-24
96ZenChaS-25
97ActPac-67
97ActPacFA-1
97ActPacFAA-1
97ActPacFI-67
97ColCho-126
97ColChoUD5-UD29
97PrePas-97
97PrePas-108
97PrePasL-97
97PrePasL-108
97PrePasOS-97
97PrePasOS-108
97PrePasT-97
97PrePasT-108
97RacCho-86
97RacChoSS-86
97SBMot-8
97SBMot-30
97ScoBoal-32
97ScoBoalR-SB7
97ScoBoaRSBF-SB7
97SkyPro-33
97SPXTagT-TT5
97Ult-62
97UltSho-15
97UltUpd-47
98HigGeaPG-PG2
98Max10tA-39
98Max10tA-84
98Max10tA-94
98Max10tA-108
98Max10tABA-39
98Max10tABA-40
98Max10tABA-41
98Max10tACotY-CY2
98Max10tACotY-CY6
98Max10tACP-CP9
98Max10tACPDC-CP9
98PrePas-134
98PrePasPR-2B
98SP AutMoaL-M1
98SP AutT-T1
98UppDecRTTC5A-AN10
98UppDecRTTC5A-AN14
98UppDecRTTC5A-AN17
98UppDecRTTC5A-AN21
98UppDecRTTC5A-AN27
98UppDecRTTC5A-AN36
98UppDecRTTC5A-AN41
98UppDecRTTC5AA-AN14
98Whe-90
98WheGol-90
99PrePas-132

Petty, Steve
92EriMaxTA-93

Petty, Tim
91Tra-189A
91Tra-189B

Pflum, Jeep
94LanARCF-21

Pharer, Larry
92SpoLegBB-BB12

Phillips, Andy
92VolRacLS2-52

Phillips, Carlton
90CheFlal-61

Phillips, Jim
90Max-40
91Max-232
91Tra-131A
91Tra-131B
92MaxBla-227
92MaxRed-227
92ProSet-235
92Tra-131
93FinLin-34
93FinLinCS-1
93FinLinS-34
93Max-210
93MaxPreS-210
94MaxPreS-207
94Pow-72
94PowGol-72
94PrePas-117
95MaxPreS-201
96MaxPre-199

Phillips, Kenny
95JSKIce-15

Phillips, Larry
92MaxBla-78
92MaxRed-78
93Max-221
93Max-225
93MaxPreS-221
93MaxPreS-225
94MaxPreS-253
95MaxPreS-254
96MaxPre-256

Phillips, Ronnie
94HigGeaPPT-W27
94HigGeaPPTG-27W

Phillips, Terry
92JAG-220

Phillips, Tom
92VolRacLS2-53

92VolRacLSI-42
hippen, John Jr.
92WinChoM-30
ickett, Greg
92EriMaxTA-29
92EriMaxTA-30
92EriMaxTA-73
92EriMaxTA-74
92EriMaxTA-76
ielsticker, Mark
92EriMaxTA-64
ierce, Bob
91DirTra-6
91JAG-50
92DirTra-10
92JAG-87
92STAMod-36
94JAG-46
94STAMod-41
Pierce, Paul
92WinChoM-3
Pierce, Roger
92TraTeaS-178
92TraTeaS-189
Pilcher, Jerry
91DKIMCDT-18
Pilette, Teddy
78GraPri-187
Pimm, Ed
85A&SRacI-22
86A&SRacI-6
87A&SRacI-17
Pinkham, Phil
92PacAmeCT-20
Pinter, John
91K&WDirT-19
92K&WDirT-30
Piquet, Nelson
78GraPri-124
78GraPri-147
78GraPri-166
78GraPri-178
87AceForO-24
87ForOneI-11
91CarForO-55
91CarForO-56
91CarForO-57
91ProTraFO-48
91ProTraFO-49
91ProTraFO-50
91ProTraFO-146
91ProTraFO-157
91ProTraFO-159
91ProTraFO-184
91ProTraFO-185
91ProTraFO-187
92GriForO-100
92GriForO-104
92GriForO-195
93HiTecI-76
93MaxWilR-12
93MaxWilR-51
93MaxWilR-58
93MaxWilR-63
93MaxWilR-64
93MaxWilR-66
93MaxWilR-69
94HiTecI-33
94HiTecI-37
Piranio, Dennis
89MegDra-107
Pironi, Didier
78GraPri-4
78GraPri-11
78GraPri-33
78GraPri-53
78GraPri-64
78GraPri-114
78GraPri-196
78GraPri-197
Pirro, Emanuele
91CarForO-58
91CarForO-59
91CarForO-60
91ProTraFO-51
91ProTraFO-52
Pirrone, Rocky
90BigTimD-13
90BigTimDS-13
Pistone, Tom
89TGRacMR-208
89TGRacMR-209
89WinCir-3
91ProSetL-L29
91TGRacMRU-208
91TGRacMRU-209
91TGRacTL-11
91TGRacTL-24
91TGRacTL-37
91TigTomP-1
91TigTomP-2
91TigTomP-3
91TigTomP-4
91TigTomP-5
91TigTomP-6
91TigTomP-7
91TigTomP-8
91TigTomP-9
91TigTomP-10
91TigTomP-11
91TigTomP-12
91TigTomP-13
91TigTomP-14
91TigTomP-15
91TraPacYH-29
92ProSetL-L22
Pitkavish, Joe
92VolRacLS2-54
Pittman, K.S.
71FleAHRDC-20
91BigTimD-93
Pittman, Shelton
91Tra-176
92CleEngB-12
92ProSet-221
92Tra-176A
92Tra-176B
92TraKodEl-5
92TraTeaS-107
92TraTeaS-122
93FinLin-131
93FinLinCS-23
93FinLinS-131
93Max-252
93MaxPreS-252
96AutRacA-42
96AutRacCA-42
96Cla-21
96ClaPriP-21
96ClaSil-21
97AutRacA-43
97PinPre-25
97PinPreBM-25
97PinPreGM-25
97PinPreSM-25
97SBMot-68
Planck, Dale
95K&WDirT-2
95MaxPreS-252
96MaxPre-209
96PrePas-107
96PrePasSco-107
96PrePasT-107
Platt, Hubert
71FleAHRDC-32
Plazek, Joe
92K&WDirT-59
92TraDir-8
94K&WDirT-28
95K&WDirT-11
Plessinger, Frank
92TraTeaS-173
Pletcher, Dave
88MaxCha-39
Poche, Ronnie
92JAG-88
Pohlman, Bob
91JAG-24
92JAG-221
Poland, Lloyd
92WinChoM-37
Pollard, Art
70FleDra-10
Pollard, Larry
88MaxCha-16
Pond, Lennie
89TGRacMR-25
89TGRacMR-26
91TGRacMRU-25
91TGRacMRU-26
93WheRooT-15
93WheRooTPla-15
95PrePas-123
95PrePasRH-123
Pond, Tony
78GraPri-233
Ponder, Tony
92BulRin-186
94MaxPreS-255
Poole, Barrie
73FleAHRRU-56
Poovey, Barry
94HigGeaPPT-W23
94HigGeaPPTG-23W
Portenga, Steve
95MaxSup-18
96Viper-71
96ViperBlaM-71
96ViperCop-71
96ViperGreM-71
99Pre-78
99PrePas-78
Porter, Mike
91BulRin-139
Porter, Randy
91BulRin-32
92BulRin-32
92BulRin-80
96Viper-63
96ViperBlaM-63
96ViperCop-63
96ViperGreM-63
Porter, Tim
92LanARCF-86
94LanARCF-70
Porter, Toby
91BulRin-115
92BulRin-180
95MaxTop52-TOP5
Porterfield, Andy
92EriMaxTA-65
Posey, Bill
92BulRin-151
Poston , Slick (Howard)
89Max-96
90Max-102
91Max-214
92MaxAllPT-34
92MaxBla-254
92MaxRed-254
93Max-261
93MaxPreS-261
95MaxPreS-248
Potter, Allen
92TraTeaS-122
Potter, Bob
91WinChoM-82
91WinChoM-83
Potter, Mike
93Max-77
93MaxPreS-77
Potts, Dick
94STAMod-42
Powell, Charles III
92BulRin-104
Powell, Mike
92RSSMotH-19
Powell, Robert
91BulRin-56
92BulRin-56
Powell, Thomas
91LanRocS-47
92LanRocS-42
Prappas, Ted
92AllWorl-38
93HiTecI-32
93HiTecI-51
94HiTecICD-CD25
Pratt, Richie
90K&WDirT-36
91K&WDirT-32
92K&WDirT-33
Presnell, Jim
94HigGeaPPT-G20
94HigGeaPPTG-20G
Pressley, Bob
91BulRin-54
92BulRin-54
Pressley, Charley
92MaxAllPT-20
92MaxBla-245
92MaxRed-245
94HigGea-43
94HigGeaG-43
94HigGeaPPT-G3
94HigGeaPPTG-3G
94Max-284
94Tra-142
94TraFirR-142
95HigGea-42
95HigGeaDO-42
95HigGeaDOG-42
95HigGeaG-42
95Max-140
95MaxAut-140
95MaxCroC-124
95MaxPreP-124
95MaxPreS-146
96AutRacA-43
96AutRacCA-43
96CroJewEDT-43
96CroJewEDT-49
96CroJewEDTC-43
96CroJewEDTC-49
96CroJewEE-43
96CroJewEE-49
96CroJewEli-43
96CroJewEli-49
96CroJewES-43
96CroJewES-49
96CroJewETC-43
96CroJewETC-49
96CroJewETCE-43
96CroJewETCE-49
96CroJewETCS-43
96CroJewETCS-49
96MaxPre-139
97RacShaSTS-ST19
Pressley, Mike
91BulRin-61
92BulRin-81
Pressley, Robert
91BulRin-59
91Max-147
91MaxUpd-147
91Tra-59
92-CarDynBTBS-10
92BulRin-59
92MaxBla-81
92MaxRed-81
92ProSet-8
92Tra-59
92Tra-177
92TraAllRP-2
92TraAllRP-3
92TraAllRP-4
92TraAllRP-5
92TraAllRP-6
92TraAllRP-7
92TraAllRP-8
92TraAllRP-9
92TraAllRP-10
92TraAllRP-12
92TraGoo-3
92TraRacM-59
92WinChoB-64
92WinChoB-65
92WinChoBA-3
93AllRobPDS-11A
93AllRobPDS-NNO
93CarDynARD-1
93CarDynARD-2
93CarDynRP-1
93CarDynRPP-1
93FinLin-28
93FinLinCS-4
93FinLinS-28
93Max-59
93MaxPreP-59
93MaxPreS-59
93Tra-130
93Tra-194
93TraFirR-130
93TraFirR-194
94FinLinBGN-BGN12
94FinLinG-17
94FinLinGA-17
94HigGea-50
94HigGea-113
94HigGeaDO-113
94HigGeaDOG-113
94HigGeaG-50
94HigGeaG-113
94HigGeaPPT-W19
94HigGeaPPTG-19W
94Max-170
94Max-307
94MaxAut-307
94MaxPreP-157
94MaxPreS-170
94Pow-34
94PowGol-34
94Tra-76
94Tra-195
94TraAut-A10
94TraAutV-3
94TraFirR-76
94TraFirR-195
94VIP-64
95ActPacC-81
95ActPacCSS-81
95ActPacP-28
95ActPacP-74
95ActPacP2G-6G
95ActPacS-18
95ActPacSSS-18
95Ass-11
95AssGolS-11
95FinLin-33
95FinLinCC6-11
95FinLinPP-33
95FinLinSil-33
95Ima-33
95Ima-57
95ImaGol-33
95ImaGol-57
95Max-154
95Max-214
95MaxAut-154
95MaxCroC-60
95MaxCroC-139
95MaxMed-HTH3
95MaxMed-HTH4
95MaxMedB-HTH3
95MaxMedB-HTH4
95MaxPreP-60
95MaxPreP-139
95MaxPreS-60
95MaxPreS-170
95MaxPreSU-11
95OptXL-17
95OptXLCB-17
95OptXLDC-17
95OptXLRH-17
95OptXLS-XLS12
95PrePas-69
95PrePasPH-27
95PrePasPre-27
95PrePasPRH-27
95PrePasRH-69
95Sel-69
95SelFlaO-69
95SP-26
95SP-65
95SP-106
95SP-118
95SPDieC-26
95SPDieC-65
95SPDieC-106
95SPDieC-118
95SPSpeM-SM15
95SPSpeMDC-SM15
95Tra-36
95Tra5thA-24
95Tra5thA-64
95Tra5thAG-24
95Tra5thAG-64
95TraAutV-8
95TraCha-C14
95TraFirR-36
95TraOnTR-OTR18
95UppDec-33
95UppDec-101
95UppDec-178
95UppDec-212
95UppDec-255
95UppDec-288
95UppDecA-212
95UppDecGSEG-33
95UppDecGSEG-101
95UppDecGSEG-178
95UppDecGSEG-212
95UppDecGSEG-255
95UppDecGSEG-288
95UppDecSSES-33
95UppDecSSES-101
95UppDecSSES-178
95UppDecSSES-212
95UppDecSSES-255
95UppDecSSES-288
95VIP-23
95VIPCooB-23
95VIPEmeP-23
95VIPRedHCB-23
95Zen-31
95Zen-52
95Zen-65
96ActPacC-48
96ActPacCSS-48
96Ass-21

96Ass$10PC-3
96Ass$5PC-14
96AutRac-14
96AutRacA-44
96AutRacCA-44
96AutRacFR-77
96AutRacHP-HP18
96Cla-9
96ClaInn-IV14
96ClaPriP-9
96ClaSil-9
96CroJewEDitR-DR4
96CroJewEDitRC-DR4
96CroJewEDitRS-DR4
96CroJewEDT-20
96CroJewEDTC-20
96CroJewEE-20
96CroJewEli-20
96CroJewES-20
96CroJewETC-20
96CroJewETCE-20
96CroJewETCS-20
96Fla-27
96Fla-83
96Max-33
96Max-57
96MaxMadiA-33
96MaxMadiA-57
96MaxOdy-33
96MaxOdy-57
96MaxOdyM-MM3
96MaxPre-33
96MaxPre-57
96MaxSamBR-7
96MaxSamBR-8
96Pin-33
96Pin-54
96Pin-33
96Pin-54
96PinCutA-12
96PinPolP-16
96PinPolP-46
96PinPolPLF-16
96PinPolPLF-46
96PinPolPNL-8
96PinPolPNLG-8
96PinWinCC-33
96PinWinCC-54
96PrePas-26
96PrePasCC-26
96PrePasP-25
96PrePasPEP-25
96PrePasPH-25
96PrePasSco-26
96PrePasT-26
96SP-33
96SPDriF-DF4
96TraRev&PTCG-TC13
96TraRev&PTCH-TC13
96TraRevP-4
96TraRevP-25
96TraRevPFR-4
96TraRevPFR-25
96TraRevPLG-LG12
96TraRevPM-4
96TraRevPM-25
96TraRevPTC-TC13
96Ult-93
96Ult-94
96Ult-95
96UltUpd-27
96UltUpd-73
96UppDec-31
96UppDec-71
96UppDec-111
96UppDecRTTC-RC39
96UppDecRTTC-RC76
96UppDecRTTC-RC109
96V.IAut-20
96VIP-22
96VIPEmeP-22
96Viper-21
96ViperBlaM-21
96ViperCop-21
96ViperGreM-21
96VIPTor-22
96Zen-26
96ZenArtP-26
97ActPac-20
97ActPac-41
97ActPacFI-20
97ActPacFI-41
97AutRac-29
97AutRacA-44
97AutRacMS-KM29
97ColCho-33
97ColCho-83
97ColChoUD5-UD69
97ColChoUD5-UD70
97JurPar-54
97JurParT-54
97Pre-21
97PreBlaWFS-21
97PreGri-21
97PrePas-27
97PrePasL-27
97PrePasOS-27
97PrePasT-27
97PreRedW-21
97RacSha-20
97RacShaGWP-20
97RacShaH-20
97RacShaSTS-ST8
97RacShaTS-20
97SBMot-71
97SBMotWR-WC7
97SP-29
97SP-71
97SP SupS-29
97SP SupS-71
97Ult-27
97UppDecRTTC-32
97UppDecRTTC-74
97UppDecRTTC-140
97UppDecVC-33
97UppDecVC-83
97Viper-20
97ViperBlaR-20
98HigGea-57
98Max10tA-38
98Max10tA-83
98MaxSwaP-SW10
98PrePasS-34
98UppDecRttC-38
98UppDecRttC-112
98VIP-21
98VIPExp-21
99Pre-25
99PrePas-25
99PrePas-125
99UppDecVC-36
99UppDecVC-73
99UppDecVCUE-36
99UppDecVCUE-73
99WheHigG-26
99WheHigGFG-26
99WheHigGM-26
99WheHigGS-GS26
Preston, John
91WinChoM-67
91WinChoM-68
Preston, Vic
78GraPri-228
Prestwood Jr., Max
91BulRin-41
91HicMotS-7
92BulRin-41
Priebe, Tim
92LanARCF-90
Pritchett, Swayne
91GalPrePR-48
Probst, Arthur Jr.
92CorSelCCS-27
Prock, Jim
92ProSetN-156
93FinLinN-35
Pronger, Bob
91GalPrePR-78
Prost, Alain
78GraPri-180
87AceForO-25
87AceForO-33
87ForOneI-13
87ForOneI-14
88HerFouFO-4A
91CarForO-76
91CarForO-77
91CarForO-78
91ProTraFO-63
91ProTraFO-64
91ProTraFO-108
91ProTraFO-109
91ProTraFO-110
91ProTraFO-111
91ProTraFO-112
91ProTraFO-113
91ProTraFO-114
91ProTraFO-115
91ProTraFO-116
91ProTraFO-117
91ProTraFO-118
91ProTraFO-119
91ProTraFO-120
91ProTraFO-145
91ProTraFO-162
91ProTraFO-181
91ProTraFO-182
91ProTraFO-198
92GriForO-100
92GriForO-106
92GriForO-107
92GriForO-111
92GriForO-113
92GriForO-190
92GriForO-197
92LimAppFO-8
93MaxWilR-3
Proulx, Jim
91LanSeeS-24
Provenzano, John
91JAG-18
92JAG-222
Prudhomme, Don
72FleAHRDN-27
72FleAHRDN-46
73FleAHRRU-4
73FleAHRRU-5
73FleAHRRU-6
91ProSetN-13
91ProSetN-62
91ProSetN-104
92MacTooWC-18
92ProSetN-3
92ProSetN-31
92ProSetN-103
92ProSetRC-7
92RPM-5
93FinLinN-36
93FinLinN-37
94ActPacN-36
94ActPacN2G-36G
94CarDynDP-1
94CarDynDP-2
94CarDynDP-3
95TraVal-80
Pruett, Scott
91AllWorI-51
91AllWorI-64
91IRO-7
92AllWorI-6
92AllWorI-88
92EriMaxTA-85
92LegInd-13
92LegInd-40
93HiTecI-17
93HiTecI-65
94HiTecICD-CD26
95HiTecICD-CD4
96SkyInd5-17
96SkyInd5-73
96SkyInd5RY-4
Pruitt, Alan
92LanARCF-43
94LanARCF-38
Pryce, Tom
77Spo-5217
Pryor, Richard
91SpoLegWS-WS21
Puckett, Jerry
92TraKodEI-12
92TraTeaS-123
Pugh, Buddy
92TraTeaS-180
Pugh, Diana
91MaxBilETCM-6
Pulde, Dale
72FleAHRDN-24
72FleAHRDN-65
72FleAHRDN-69
73FleAHRRU-46
89MegDra-16
Punch, Dr. (Jerry)
90Max-157
91Max-233
91Tra-188
92MaxBlaU-U30
92MaxRedU-U30
92Tra-188
93Max-208
93MaxPreS-208
94FinLin-100
94FinLinS-100
94MaxPreS-202
95MaxPreS-197
96Ass-23
96AutRacA-45
96AutRacCA-45
96MaxPre-196
97AutRacA-45
97SBMot-67
97UltUpd-34
Purdy, Rich
92ProSetN-171
Purkey, Al
92JAG-89
Pursell, Scott
90K&WDirT-37
91K&WDirT-37
92K&WDirT-43
Purvis, Jeff
91DirTra-44
91Max-51
92BulRin-51
92LanARCF-61
92MaxBla-51
92MaxRed-51
92VolRacEAS-10
92VolRacEAS-11
92VolRacEAS-13
93Max-35
93MaxPreS-35
93TraTri-5
94LanARCF-18
94Max-77
94Max-269
94MaxMed-32
94MaxPreS-77
95HiTecB4-27
95HiTecB4-69
95SP-52
95SP-94
95SPDieC-52
95SPDieC-94
95UppDec-36
95UppDec-104
95UppDec-217
95UppDec-293
95UppDecGSEG-36
95UppDecGSEG-104
95UppDecGSEG-217
95UppDecGSEG-293
95UppDecSSES-36
95UppDecSSES-104
95UppDecSSES-217
95UppDecSSES-293
96Fla-46
96MaxPre-45
96UltUpd-43
96UppDec-19
96UppDecRTTC-RC38
96UppDecRTTC-RC87
97ColCho-29
97ColCho-79
97ColChoUD5-UD60
97ColChoUD5-UD61
97Ult-91
97UppDecVC-29
97UppDecVC-79
Pylant, Kevin
94WorOut-48
Quarterson, Ralph
92VolRacLS2-55
92VolRacLS2-56
92VolRacLS2-57
Quarterson, Tommy
92VolRacLS2-58
Quayle, Dan
92LegInd-37
Query, Freddie
91BulRin-6
92BulRin-66
Radke, Wyatt
91BigTimD-27
91BigTimD-42
91ProSetN-117
92ProSetN-42
Ragan, Charlie Jr.
92BulRin-53
Ragan, Ken
88MaxCha-51
90Max-58
91LanARCHS-47
91Max-58
91MaxUpd-58
92LanARCF-104
Rager, Roger
80AvaHilURG-23
Ragner, Tom
91LanRocS-65
Ragnotti, Jean
78GraPri-223
Rahal, Bobby
78GraPri-157
83A&SRacI-34
84A&SRacI-50
85A&SRacI-12
86A&SRacI-30
86AceInd-B3
87A&SRacI-1
87A&SRacI-47
91AllWorI-9
91AllWorI-75
91AllWorI-97
91LegInd-51
92AllWorI-8
92AllWorI-81
92LegInd-20
92LegInd-89
92LegInd-95
93HiTecI-10
93HiTecI-41
93HiTecICFF-SP6
93HiTecIP-P4
94HiTecI-36
94HiTecICD-CD27
95SkyInd5-17
95SkyInd5-46
95SkyInd5-75
95SkyInd5PC-6
95TraVal-96
96SkyInd5-30
96SkyInd5-57
96SkyInd5CC-3
Rahilly, Bob
89Max-46
90Max-143
91Max-124
91ProSet-78
92MaxBla-122
92MaxRed-122
92ProSet-143
92ProSet-200
93Max-140
93MaxPreP-126
93MaxPreS-140
Rahilly, Dick
92ProSet-213
Rahl, Terry
90LanRocSHS-19
Rahmer, Fred
91WorOut-87
92CorSelCCS-18
92RacLegS-17
94WorOut-39
Raimer, Harry
97AutRacA-46
Raines, Larry
91BulRin-37
92BulRin-37
Raines, Tony
92TraASA-8
Rainey, Derrick
91HavAT-16
Raiti, Frank
92VolRacLSI-43
Ramey, Dennis
89CheFlaI-19
89CheFlaI-20
Ramey, Earl
92TraTeaS-63
Ramey, Nick
92TraTeaS-183
94MaxTexEI-45
Rampy, David
93MaxWinM-9
Randall, Bobby
91WinChoNED-57
91WinChoNED-58
92PacAmeCT-31
92WinChoB-125
92WinChoB-126
Randall, Danielle
96RacCho-55
96RacChoAP-55
96RacChoSC-55
Randall, Maurice
92LanARCF-105
Randall, Mike
73FleAHRRU-7
Ranier, Harry

88MaxCha-72
Rankin, Craig
92VolRacLS2-59
92VolRacLSI-44
Rarick, Jim
92JAG-90
Rasnake, Daryl
92TraTeaS-122
Rathmann, Dick
62MarInd-10
89TGRacMR-223
89TGRacMR-224
89WinCir-24
91GalPrePR-81
91TGRacMRU-223
91TGRacMRU-224
91TraPacYH-30
Rathmann, Jim
91LegInd-85
95TraVal-66
Raudman, Chris
97PrePas-119
97PrePasL-119
97PrePasOS-119
97PrePasT-119
Ray, Jim
89CheFlaI-70
Rayburn, C.J.
91DirTra-54
91JAG-10
92DirTra-84
92JAG-223
94STAMod-43
Raymer, Brian
89MegDra-80
Raymond, Lee
91LanARCHS-2
92LanARCF-39
Reaber, Frank
92JAG-91
Reagan, Ronald
91SpoLegNJ-NJ5
Reaid, Tony
91HavAT-4
91HavAT-5
92HavAT-15
92JAG-92
95HavAT-27
Reavis, Ronnie
92MaxAllPT-33
92MaxBla-253
92MaxRed-253
Rebaque, Hector
78GraPri-75
83A&SRacI-44
Rebeschi Jr., Paul
92ProSetN-77
93FinLinN-100
Redman, Brian
77Spo-8505
Redman, Harold
92STAMod-35
Reed, Jim
89TGRacMR-128
89TGRacMR-129
89TGRacMR-177
91GalPrePR-19
91GalPrePR-52
91TGRacMRU-128
91TGRacMRU-129
91TGRacMRU-177
91TraPacYH-31
Reedy, Orvil
92BulRin-149
Reedy, Tink
92BulRin-108
Reeves, Stevie
95CroJew-62
95CroJewD-62
95CroJewE-62
95CroJewS-62
95MaxPreS-182
Refner, Bryan
91LanART-8
91LanStoCC-21
Regazzoni, Clay
77Spo-401
77Spo-5218
78GraPri-43
78GraPri-86
78GraPri-155
93MaxWilR-17
93MaxWilR-26
Regenthal, Ken
89CheFlaI-96
90CheFlaI-9
90CheFlaI-40
Reher, David
92ProSetN-170
93FinLinN-101
Reimel, Kolleen
91K&WURCS-42
Reinen, Bart
90LanRocSHS-22
Reinert, Chuck Jr.
92CorSelCCS-32
93CorSelCCS-8
Reiser, Ken
92RedGraST-27
Reiser, Robbie
91LanART-2
92RedGraST-29
Reitz, Walter
90LanRocSHS-7
Ren, Rick
96MaxPre-150
Reno, Marc
92ProSet-220
97SkyPro-43
97UltUpd-44
Reny, Steve
92WinChoM-2
Rescino, Nick
91WorOut-88
Resta, Dario
54StaWetIW-1916
60HawWaxI-6
95TraVal-22
Rettell, Gary
89CheFlaI-9
89CheFlaI-14
Reutemann, Carlos
77Spo-5602
77Spo-6717
78GraPri-10
78GraPri-19
78GraPri-35
78GraPri-38
78GraPri-39
78GraPri-51
78GraPri-61
78GraPri-97
78GraPri-98
78GraPri-99
78GraPri-125
78GraPri-148
78GraPri-149
93MaxWilR-14
93MaxWilR-39
93MaxWilR-40
Revelle, Jack
90CheFlaI-75
Revson, Peter
73NabSugDSC-2
92LegInd-75
Rexford, Bill
89TGRacMR-248
89TGRacMR-249
89WinCir-23
91TGRacMRU-248
91TGRacMRU-249
91TraPacYH-32
Reynolds, Burt
94WheHarG-24
94WheHarGG-24
Reynolds, Jim
90LanRocSHS-17
91LanRocS-6
92LanRocS-43
Reynolds, Johnny
91BulRin-102
92BulRin-94
Reynolds, Jon
90LanRocSHS-31
Reynolds, Mike
92BulRin-164
Rezendes, Dave
91Max-133
91Tra-79
92MaxBla-38
92MaxRed-38
92ProSet-166
92Tra-79
92TraGoo-14
92WinChoB-84
92WinChoB-85
93Max-79
93MaxPreS-79
93Tra-120
93TraFirR-120
94Max-191
94MaxPreS-191
97AutRacA-47
97SBMot-56
Rhodes, Mickey
91GalPrePR-63
Ribbs, Willy T.
91AllWorI-8
92AllWorI-5
92LegInd-33
92LegInd-36
94HiTecI-22
Ribeiro, Alex Dias
78GraPri-173
Ribeiro, Andre
96SkyInd5-21
96SkyInd5-72
Rice, Jerry
92JAG-224
Rice, Joe
92JAG-93
Rice, Larry
92AllWorI-69
Rice, Wayne
91K&WURCS-11
Rich, Mike
91MaxBilETCM-32
Rich, Smiley
91BulRin-62
Richard, Lynn
91DKIMCDT-19
Richards, Brian
92EriMaxTA-66
Richards, Tim
91ProSetN-101
91SpoLegHH-HH6
91SpoLegHH-HH9
92ProSetN-154
93FinLinN-38
Richardson, Edmond
93FinLinN-119
Richardson, Paul
91WinChoNED-63
91WinChoNED-64
Richardson, Phillip
94JAG-47
Richardson, Scott
92ProSetN-200
Richert, Doug
90Max-82
91Max-165
91MaxUpd-165
91Tra-49
92MaxAllPT-14
92MaxBla-241
92MaxRed-241
92ProSet-131
92Tra-49
92TraTeaS-134
93FinLin-26
93FinLinCS-30
93FinLinS-26
93Max-172
93MaxPreP-154
93MaxPreS-172
93Tra-129
93TraFirR-129
94Max-153
94MaxPreP-145
94MaxPreS-153
94Tra-179
94TraFirR-179
95Max-141
95MaxAut-141
Richert, Robin
92TraCouSR-9
Richeson, Donnie
92MaxBla-187
92MaxMot-30
92MaxRed-187
92ProSet-185
92Tra-148
92TraTeaS-68
93FinLin-25
93FinLinCS-7
93FinLinS-25
93Max-158
93MaxPreP-141
93MaxPreS-158
93Tra-62
93TraFirR-62
94ActPac-63
94FinLin-97
94FinLinGT-TG8
94FinLinS-97
94HigGea-141
94HigGeaDO-141
94HigGeaDOG-141
94HigGeaG-141
94Max-147
94MaxPreP-140
94MaxPreS-147
94PrePas-104
94Tra-181
94TraFirR-181
95Max-128
95Max-197
95MaxAut-128
95MaxCroC-121
95MaxPreP-121
95MaxPreS-142
95Sel-105
95SelFlaO-105
96CroJewEDT-47
96CroJewEDT-50
96CroJewEDTC-47
96CroJewEDTC-50
96CroJewEE-47
96CroJewEli-47
96CroJewEli-50
96CroJewES-47
96CroJewES-50
96CroJewETC-47
96CroJewETC-50
96CroJewETCE-47
96CroJewETCE-50
96CroJewETCS-47
96CroJewETCS-50
96MaxPre-136
96UltUpd-95
Richey, Bobby Jr
94JAG-48
Richey, Rex
91HavAT-6
91JAG-13
92DirTra-25
92HavAT-8
92JAG-94
95HavAT-26
Richmond, Tim
80AvaHilURG-9
83UNORac-1
83UNORac-3
83UNORac-6
83UNORac-8
83UNORac-9
83UNORac-10
83UNORac-12
83UNORac-15
83UNORac-17
83UNORac-18
83UNORac-22
83UNORac-24
83UNORac-26
86SpoPhoG-11
91SpoLegHH-HH1
91SpoLegHH-HH2
91SpoLegHH-HH4
91SpoLegHH-HH10
91TexWorS-6
92MaxSamB-4
95VIP-50
95VIPCooB-50
95VIPEmeP-50
95VIPRedHCB-50
98PrePas-129
Richter, Les
89Max-136
90Max-146
91Max-102
92MaxBla-205
92MaxRed-205
93Max-229
93MaxPreS-229
94MaxPreS-216
Rickenbacker, Eddie
91LegInd-32
Rickman, Eddie
92JAG-95
Rider, Chuck
89Max-98
90Max-121
91Max-75
91ProSet-58
91Tra-35
92MaxBla-113
92MaxRed-113
92ProSet-159
92Tra-46
92TraTeaS-77
92TraTeaS-78
93FinLin-52
93FinLinCS-6
93FinLinS-52
93Max-126
93MaxPreP-113
93MaxPreS-126
93Tra-141
93Tra-199
93TraFirR-141
93TraFirR-199
94FinLin-59
94FinLinS-59
94HigGea-37
94HigGeaG-37
94Max-107
94MaxPreP-107
94MaxPreS-107
94Pow-111
94PowGol-111
94PrePas-83
94TraAutV-24
95Max-66
95MaxCroC-89
95MaxPreP-89
95MaxPreS-101
95PrePas-87
95PrePasRH-87
95Sel-84
95SelFlaO-84
95TraBehTS-BTS4
96AutRacA-46
96AutRacCA-46
96Max-67
96MaxPre-104
97FinLinPP2-35
97Viper-64
97ViperBlaR-64
Ridley, Jody
89TGRacMR-212
89TGRacMR-213
91BulRin-98
91TGRacMRU-212
91TGRacMRU-213
92BulRin-98
92CoyRoo-2
92CoyRoo-14
93WheRooT-21
93WheRooTPla-21
Rieger, Jim
90LanRocSHS-2
Rients, Tom
91DirTra-60
91JAG-38
91LanStoCC-5
92DirTra-28
92JAG-225
Riffle, Bob
73FleAHRRU-64
92TraTeaS-183
92TraTeaS-193
Rigsbee, Tommy
92BikRacS-20
92RSSMotH-12
92TraTeaS-94
Riker, A.L.
95TraVal-2
Rimer, Pam
93Tra-148
93TraFirR-148
Rindt, Jochen
77Spo-2509
77Spo-7906
Rinker, Michael
91MaxBilETCM-18
Ripley, Doug
92WinChoM-9
Ritch, Michael
93Max-224
93MaxPreS-224
Ritchie, Dennis
92RSSMotH-17
98PrePas-75
98PrePasOS-75
Rittenhouse, Todd
91K&WURCS-9
Ritter, Gary
92ProSetN-37
Ritz, Lon
91LanRocS-54

Rivera, Gordie
89MegDra-52
89MegDra-53
91ProSetN-45
91ProSetN-93
92ProSetN-81
92ProSetN-133
93FinLinN-102
Roach, Ronnie
92BulRin-159
Robbins, Marty
89TGRacMR-71
91TGRacMRU-71
91TGRacTL-51
Roberts, Dave
94HigGeaPPT-W32
94HigGeaPPTG-32W
Roberts, Floyd
54StaWetIW-1938
60HawWaxI-26
Roberts, Gene
92MaxBla-171
92MaxMot-35
92MaxRed-171
92ProSet-170
Roberts, Glenn Fireball
89Max-197
89TGRacMR-22
89TGRacMR-23
89TGRacMR-24
89TGRacMR-27
89TGRacMR-37
89TGRacMR-134
89WinCir-43
91GalPrePR-1
91GalPrePR-9
91GalPrePR-16
91GalPrePR-24
91GalPrePR-51
91GalPrePR-58
91GalPrePR-68
91GalPrePR-86
91GalPrePR-93
91TGRacMRU-22
91TGRacMRU-23
91TGRacMRU-24
91TGRacMRU-27
91TGRacMRU-37
91TGRacMRU-134
91TGRacTL-18
92MaxIMH-27
92MaxIMH-39
94PrePas-134
95TraVal-62
98PrePas-139
98UppDecRTTC5A-AN6
Roberts, Tim
91BulRin-76
92BulRin-190
Roberts, Tom
92ProSetN-160
93FinLinN-103
Robertson, George H.
11AmeTobAD-20
Robertson, Jerry
92JAG-96
Robertson, T. Wayne
91ProSet-140
Robinette, Scott
92MaxAllPT-16
92MaxBla-242
92MaxRed-242
Robinson, Brooks
91TGRacTL-26
Robinson, George
92EriMaxTA-31
92EriMaxTA-32
92EriMaxTA-75
92EriMaxTA-77
92EriMaxTA-82
Robinson, Harold
89CheFlaI-37
90CheFlaI-74
Robinson, Jeff
92JAG-97
Robinson, John
92LanRocS-44
Robinson, Pete
71FleAHRDC-41
Robinson, Scott
93Max-253
93MaxPreS-253
94HigGeaPPT-W9
94HigGeaPPTG-9W
Robinson, Shawna
90Max-118
91BulRin-138
91RacConSR-2
91RacConSR-3
91RacConSR-4
91RacConSR-5
91RacConSR-6
91RacConSR-7
91RacConSR-8
91RacConSR-9
92MaxBla-65
92MaxRed-65
92ProSet-33
92WinChoB-98
92WinChoB-99
93Max-78
93MaxPreP-78
93MaxPreS-78
93Tra-35
93Tra-162
93TraFirR-35
93TraFirR-162
94HigGea-62
94HigGea-169
94HigGeaDO-169
94HigGeaDOG-169
94HigGeaG-62
94HigGeaG-169
94Max-184
94Max-314
94MaxAut-184
94MaxPreS-184
94OptXL-60
94OptXLRH-60
94PrePas-63
94PrePas-70
94Tra-35
94TraFirR-35
95CarDynAP-2
95MaxPreS-185
Robson, George
54StaWetIW-1946
60HawWaxI-30
95TraVal-52
Rocca, John H.
91BigTimD-91
Rodee, Chuck
92HiTecMA-17
Roderick, Kevin
92JAG-226
Rodriguez, Dennis
91WorOut-54
Rodriguez, Pedro
77Spo-4022
Roe, Greg
94LanARCF-83
Roe, Michael
86A&SRacI-14
Roenigk, Donny
92VolRacLS2-60
Roenigk, L.B.
92VolRacLSI-45
Rogers, David
91BulRin-113
92BulRin-11
92BulRin-111
94HigGeaPPT-G6
94HigGeaPPTG-6G
95MaxPreS-250
95MaxPreS-251
98Whe-97
98WheGol-97
Rogers, Rick
94JAG-49
Rollins, Shorty
93WheRooT-1
93WheRooTPla-1
Rolt, Tony
62PetLimGPRC-4
62PetLimGPRC-19
Romeo, Chuck
92MaxBla-211
92MaxRed-211
93Max-232
93MaxPreS-232
94MaxPreS-220
Rondeau, Pete
91WinChoM-72
91WinChoM-73
91WinChoNED-51
91WinChoNED-52
Roney, Bruce
91Tra-101
92MaxBla-209
92MaxRed-209
92Tra-80
93Max-238
93MaxPreS-238
93Tra-53
93TraFirR-53
94MaxPreS-223
94Tra-32
94TraFirR-32
95MaxPreS-221
95TraBehTS-BTS21
96MaxPre-222
Roper, Jim
91TraPacYH-33
98UppDecRTTC5A-AN3
Rosati, Tom
92WinChoB-119
92WinChoB-120
Rosberg, Dick
90BigTimD-14
90BigTimDS-14
Rosberg, Keke
78GraPri-115
78GraPri-167
78GraPri-174
87AceForO-26
87ForOneI-14
91ProTraFO-191
92GriForO-184
93MaxWilR-11
93MaxWilR-42
93MaxWilR-43
93MaxWilR-44
93MaxWilR-45
93MaxWilR-46
93MaxWilR-47
93MaxWilR-93
Rose, Doug
72FleAHRDN-52
72FleAHRDN-68
Rose, Mauri
54StaWetIW-1941
54StaWetIW-1947
54StaWetIW-1948
60HawWaxI-29
60HawWaxI-31
91LegInd-8
95TraVal-47
95TraVal-53
Rosemeyer, Bernd
38WilCig-23
71MobTheSoGPMR-19
95TraVal-43
Rosenberger, Terry
92VolRacLSI-46
Rosier, Louis
62PetLimGPRC-7
Ross, Earl
93WheRooT-16
93WheRooTPla-16
Ross, Joe Jr.
94JAG-50
Rossmann, Patrick
91LanRocS-52
Rothengatter, Huub
87AceForO-27
Roumell, Chuck
95JSKIce-0
95JSKIcePC-0
Roush, Jack
89Max-134
90Max-54
91Max-60
91MaxMot-12
91ProSet-22
92MaxBla-108
92MaxMot-16
92MaxRed-108
93FinLin-17
93FinLinCS-5
93FinLinS-17
93Max-104
93Max-271
93MaxPreP-93
93MaxPreS-104
93MaxPreS-271
93Tra-137
93Tra-189
93TraFirR-137
93TraFirR-189
94ActPac-174
94FinLin-92
94FinLinG-61
94FinLinS-92
94HigGea-36
94HigGeaG-36
94Max-87
94MaxPreP-87
94MaxPreP-195
94MaxPreS-87
94Pow-8
94Pow-112
94PowGol-8
94PowGol-112
94PrePas-32
94PrePas-84
94Tra-95
94TraAutV-10
94TraFirR-95
95HigGea-33
95HigGeaDO-33
95HigGeaDOG-33
95HigGeaG-33
95ImaOwnP-OP8
95Max-61
95MaxCroC-70
95MaxPreP-70
95MaxPreS-82
95MaxPreS-284
95Sel-86
95SelFlaO-86
95SP-122
95SPDieC-122
95Tra5thA-65
95Tra5thAG-65
95TraAutV-43
95TraBehTS-BTS6
96ActPacC-74
96AutRac-49
96AutRacA-47
96AutRacCA-47
96Cla-5
96ClaPriP-5
96ClaSil-5
96FinLin-96
96FinLinPriP-96
96FinLinS-96
96Fla-52
96Max-65
96MaxPre-83
96PinPolP-91
96PinPolPLF-91
96PrePas-76
96PrePasSco-76
96PrePasT-76
96Ult-142
96UppDec-122
96UppDecAP-AP10
96Viper-35
96ViperBlaM-35
96ViperCop-35
96ViperGreM-35
97FinLinPP2-30
97SBMot-69
97SkyPro-38
97Ult-63
97UltUpd-52
98PrePasS-6
98PrePasSF-6
98Whe-80
98WheGol-80
Rowe, Benji
92WinChoM-29
Rowe, Mike
91WinChoNED-4
91WinChoNED-5
91WinChoNED-116
92WinChoB-20
92WinChoB-21
Rowe, Tom
91WinChoNED-45
91WinChoNED-46
91WinChoNED-116
Rowley, Ken
91LanARCHS-27
92LanARCF-87
94LanARCF-31
Roy, Travis
96ActPacC-103
Rubeck, Stephan
92LanRocS-45
Rubright, Craig
91LanARCHS-15
92LanARCF-28
92LanARCF-56
94LanARCF-16
Ruby, Lloyd
62MarInd-11
70FleDra-9
92AllWorI-63
92LegInd-77
Rudd, Linda
94ActPac-158
94TidRicR-8
94TidRicR-9
94TidRicR-10
96RacCho-88
96RacChoAP-88
96RacChoSC-88
Rudd, Ricky
88MaxCha-31
89Max-26
89Max-158
89MaxCri-11
90ACRacPW-5
90Max-5
90MaxHolF-HF13
91ACRac-5
91Max-5
91Max-188
91MaxMcD-7
91MaxRacFK-2
91MaxTheWA-14
91MaxUpd-5
91ProSet-17
91ProSet-20
91ProSet-128
91ProSet-141
91SunRacL-5
91Tra-5
91Tra-68
91Tra-136
92ACDel-2
92ACRacP-4
92CarDynRR-1
92CarDynRR-2
92CarDynRR-3
92CarDynRR-4
92CarDynRR-5
92MaxBla-5
92MaxBla-268
92MaxMcD-11
92MaxRed-5
92MaxRed-268
92MaxTheW-4
92MaxTheW-24
92ProSet-14
92ProSet-94
92ProSet-109
92ProSet-133
92ProSetMH-9
92ProSetRF-1
92Tra-5
92Tra-136
92TraAut-A5
92TraRacM-5
92TraRacM-9
92TraRacM-44
92TraRacM-58
92TraRacM-92
93FinLin-3
93FinLin-67
93FinLin-144
93FinLinCS-4
93FinLinCS-7
93FinLinCS-17
93FinLinS-3
93FinLinS-67
93FinLinS-144
93Max-5
93Max-150
93Max-197
93Max-287
93MaxHou-7
93MaxLowFS-1
93MaxPreP-5
93MaxPreP-88
93MaxPreP-169
93MaxPreP-202
93MaxPreS-5
93MaxPreS-150
93MaxPreS-197
93MaxPreS-287
93MaxTheW-16
93MaxTheW-36
93MotDecC-7
93Tra-136
93TraFirR-136
93WheRooT-19
93WheRooT-44
93WheRooT-88

93WheRooT-89
93WheRooTPla-19
93WheRooTPla-44
93WheRooTPla-88
93WheRooTPla-89
94ActPac-10
94ActPac-38
94ActPac-50
94ActPac-79
94ActPac-112
94ActPac-158
94ActPac-172
94ActPac2G-8G
94ActPac2G-20G
94ActPac2G-33G
94ActPacC-14
94ActPacP-3R941
94FinLin-65
94FinLin-73
94FinLin-91
94FinLin-135
94FinLin-13
94FinLinDH-6
94FinLinG-3
94FinLinG-34
94FinLinG-49
94FinLinG-57
94FinLinG-94
94FinLinGA-94
94FinLinGCC-NNO
94FinLinGT-TG3
94FinLinS-65
94FinLinS-73
94FinLinS-91
94FinLinS-135
94FinLinVL-VL8
94FinLinVL-VL11
94HigGea-8
94HigGea-87
94HigGea-155
94HigGeaDO-155
94HigGeaDOG-155
94HigGeaG-8
94HigGeaG-87
94HigGeaG-155
94HigGeaMG-MG8
94Max-5
94Max-59
94Max-221
94Max-281
94MaxAut-5
94MaxMed-10
94MaxMed-66
94MaxMed-72
94MaxMot-14
94MaxPreP-5
94MaxPreP-59
94MaxPreP-180
94MaxPreS-5
94MaxPreS-59
94MaxPreS-280
94MaxRooY-2
94MaxTheS2-10
94OptXL-15
94OptXL-33
94OptXL-53
94OptXLRH-15
94OptXLRH-33
94OptXLRH-53
94Pow-13
94Pow-23
94Pow-41
94PowGol-13
94PowGol-23
94PowGol-41
94PowPre-13
94Sky-11
94TidRicR-1
94TidRicR-2
94TidRicR-3
94TidRicR-4
94TidRicR-5
94TidRicR-6
94TidRicR-7
94TidRicR-8
94TidRicR-9
94TidRicR-10
94Tra-17
94Tra-55
94Tra-84
94Tra-125
94Tra-130
94Tra-191
94TraAutV-13
94TraAutV-50
94TraFirR-17
94TraFirR-55
94TraFirR-84
94TraFirR-125
94TraFirR-130
94TraFirR-191
94VIP-26
94VIP-52
95ActPacC-7
95ActPacC-16
95ActPacC-70
95ActPacC2T-12
95ActPacCSS-7
95ActPacCSS-16
95ActPacCSS-70
95ActPacP-17
95ActPacP-43
95ActPacP-56
95ActPacP-63
95ActPacP-75
95ActPacP2G-7G
95ActPacS-6
95ActPacS-37
95ActPacSSS-6
95ActPacSSS-37
95Ass-21
95Ass-39
95Ass10PC-1
95Ass1M$PC-17
95AssCocC6DC-9
95AssGolS-21
95AssGolS-39
95CroJew-5
95CroJew-32
95CroJew-49
95CroJewD-5
95CroJewD-32
95CroJewD-49
95CroJewDJ-DJ5
95CroJewDJD-DJ5
95CroJewDJE-DJ5
95CroJewE-5
95CroJewE-32
95CroJewE-49
95CroJewS-5
95CroJewS-32
95CroJewS-49
95CroJewSG-SG5
95FinLin-10
95FinLin-83
95FinLin-106
95FinLinCC6-21
95FinLinCC6-39
95FinLinGS-GS10
95FinLinP5U-NNO
95FinLinPP-10
95FinLinPP-83
95FinLinPP-106
95FinLinSC-SC4
95FinLinSD-SD4
95FinLinSil-10
95FinLinSil-83
95FinLinSil-106
95HigGea-4
95HigGea-35
95HigGea-75
95HigGea-89
95HigGeaBC-BC13
95HigGeaBCG-BC13
95HigGeaDO-4
95HigGeaDO-35
95HigGeaDO-75
95HigGeaDO-89
95HigGeaDOG-4
95HigGeaDOG-35
95HigGeaDOG-75
95HigGeaDOG-89
95HigGeaG-4
95HigGeaG-35
95HigGeaG-75
95HigGeaG-89
95Ima-10
95Ima-58
95Ima-89
95ImaDri-D7
95ImaGol-10
95ImaGol-58
95ImaGol-89
95ImaHarC-HC4
95ImaOwnP-OP9
95Max-10
95Max-95
95Max-166
95Max-204
95Max-205
95Max-P2
95MaxCroC-10
95MaxCroC-59
95MaxCroC-165
95MaxMed-9
95MaxMed-39
95MaxMedB-9
95MaxMedB-39
95MaxMedORA-OTR10
95MaxPreP-10
95MaxPreP-59
95MaxPreP-165
95MaxPrePP-PS4
95MaxPrePRJ-4
95MaxPreS-10
95MaxPreS-59
95MaxPreS-280
95OptXL-18
95OptXL-47
95OptXL-59
95OptXLCB-18
95OptXLCB-47
95OptXLCB-59
95OptXLDC-18
95OptXLDC-47
95OptXLDC-59
95OptXLRH-18
95OptXLRH-47
95OptXLRH-59
95OptXLS-XLS13
95PrePas-24
95PrePas-52
95PrePasCC-24
95PrePasPH-5
95PrePasPH-32
95PrePasPHP-HP7
95PrePasPre-5
95PrePasPre-32
95PrePasPRH-5
95PrePasPRH-32
95PrePasRD-RD10
95PrePasRH-24
95PrePasRH-52
95Sel-25
95Sel-52
95Sel-85
95Sel-132
95Sel-138
95SelDreM-DM5
95SelFlaO-25
95SelFlaO-52
95SelFlaO-85
95SelFlaO-132
95SelFlaO-138
95SelSki-SS6
95SP-9
95SP-42
95SP-84
95SP-134
95SPDieC-9
95SPDieC-42
95SPDieC-84
95SPDieC-134
95SPSpeM-SM10
95SPSpeMDC-SM10
95Tra-23
95Tra-63
95Tra-73
95Tra5thA-5
95Tra5thA-37
95Tra5thA-47
95Tra5thAG-5
95Tra5thAG-37
95Tra5thAG-47
95Tra5thAR-R4
95TraCha-C5
95TraFirR-23
95TraFirR-63
95TraFirR-73
95TraRacM-RM5
95TraSerS-SS16
95UppDec-14
95UppDec-57
95UppDec-82
95UppDec-116
95UppDec-167
95UppDec-192
95UppDec-236
95UppDecGSEG-14
95UppDecGSEG-57
95UppDecGSEG-82
95UppDecGSEG-116
95UppDecGSEG-167
95UppDecGSEG-192
95UppDecGSEG-236
95UppDecO-OS9
95UppDecPRW-P3
95UppDecSSES-14
95UppDecSSES-57
95UppDecSSES-82
95UppDecSSES-116
95UppDecSSES-167
95UppDecSSES-192
95UppDecSSES-236
95VIP-24
95VIP-35
95VIPCooB-24
95VIPCooB-35
95VIPEmeP-24
95VIPEmeP-35
95VIPFanC-FC7
95VIPFanCG-FC7
95VIPHel-H6
95VIPHelG-H6
95VIPRedHCB-24
95VIPRedHCB-35
95Zen-10
95Zen-42
95ZenHel-10
95ZenZT-8
96ActPacC-28
96ActPacC-76
96ActPacCSS-28
96Ass-3
96Ass-24
96Ass-50
96Ass$1000CCIPC-5
96Ass$100CCIPC-9
96Ass$10PC-10
96Ass$2PC-13
96Ass$5PC-1
96AssComL-CL11
96AssRacD-RD10
96AutRac-17
96AutRacA-48
96AutRacCA-48
96AutRacHP-HP10
96Cla-6
96Cla-55
96ClaImaP-RP4
96ClaInn-IV10
96ClaPriP-6
96ClaRacC-RC5
96ClaSil-6
96FinLin-10
96FinLin-52
96FinLin-80
96FinLinBGL-C9
96FinLinBGL-D10
96FinLinDCPC-6
96FinLinGS-GS17
96FinLinPP-29
96FinLinPP-30
96FinLinPP$10C-9
96FinLinPP$50C-7
96FinLinPP$5C-19
96FinLinPP$S-29
96FinLinPP$S-30
96FinLinPriP-10
96FinLinPriP-52
96FinLinPriP-80
96FinLinS-10
96FinLinS-52
96FinLinS-80
96Fla-28
96Fla-84
96FlaCenS-9
96FlaHotN-9
96FlaPowP-9
96Kni-10
96KniBlaK-10
96KniFirK-FK7
96KniQueRKP-10
96KniRoy-10
96KniWhiK-10
96M-F-11
96M-F-12
96M-FSil-S7
96Max-10
96Max-38
96MaxMadiA-10
96MaxMadiA-38
96MaxMadiABR-BR10
96MaxOdy-10
96MaxOdy-38
96MaxOdyRA-RA10
96MaxOveTW-OTW9
96MaxPre-10
96MaxPre-56
96Pin-10
96Pin-43
96Pin-10
96Pin-43
96PinCheF-10
96PinCutA-6
96PinPolP-10
96PinPolP-31
96PinPolP-80
96PinPolPCS-10
96PinPolPLF-10
96PinPolPLF-31
96PinPolPLF-80
96PinPolPNL-10
96PinPolPNLG-10
96PinTeaP-9
96PinWinCC-10
96PinWinCC-43
96PrePas-27
96PrePas-52
96PrePas-98
96PrePasCC-27
96PrePasFoc-F9
96PrePasFQS-FQS9A
96PrePasFQS-FQS9B
96PrePasP-9
96PrePasP-44
96PrePasPEP-9
96PrePasPEP-44
96PrePasPH-9
96PrePasPH-44
96PrePasPHP-HP7
96PrePasSco-27
96PrePasSco-52
96PrePasSco-98
96PrePasT-27
96PrePasT-52
96PrePasT-98
96RacCho-15
96RacCho-33
96RacCho-88
96RacCho-96
96RacChoAP-15
96RacChoAP-33
96RacChoAP-88
96RacChoAP-96
96RacChoSC-15
96RacChoSC-33
96RacChoSC-88
96RacChoSC-96
96RacChoTT-9
96SP-10
96SP-50
96SpeArtP-21
96SpeArtP-41
96SpeArtP-79
96SpeArtP-80
96SpeArtP-81
96SpeArtP-82
96SpeRac-21
96SpeRac-41
96SpeRac-79
96SpeRac-80
96SpeRac-81
96SpeRac-82
96SPHolME-ME10
96SPx-10
96SPxGol-10
96Ult-37
96Ult-38
96Ult-39
96Ult-164
96Ult-196
96UltAut-29
96UltBoxS-9
96UltFlaP-9
96UltUpd-28
96UltUpd-74
96UltUpd-94
96UltUpdPP-13
96UltUpdW-12
96UppDec-9
96UppDec-49
96UppDec-89
96UppDec-134
96UppDecPP-RP8
96UppDecPW-HP6
96UppDecRTTC-RC8
96UppDecRTTC-RC57
96UppDecRTTC-RC93
96UppDecRTTC-RC131

96UppDecRTTCAS-H8
96UppDecRTTCGF-GF10
96UppDecRTTCPT3-T8
96UppDecRTTCRL-RL18
96UppDecRTTCT3PR-R10
96UppDecVV-VV10
96UppDecVVG-VV10
96VIP-23
96VIP-44
96VIPEmeP-23
96VIPEmeP-44
96VIPHeaG-HG6
96VIPHeaGD-HG6
96VIPTor-23
96VIPTor-44
96VIPWarP-WP6
96VIPWarPG-WP6
96Zen-5
96Zen-53
96ZenArtP-5
96ZenArtP-53
96ZenHig-5
97ActPac-10
97ActPac-31
97ActPacFI-10
97ActPacFI-31
97ActPacRT-14
97AutRac-23
97AutRacMS-KM23
97ColCho-10
97ColCho-60
97ColCho-106
97ColCho-147
97ColChoC-CC14
97ColChoC-CC47
97ColChoC-CC80
97ColChoS-S19
97ColChoS-S20
97ColChoSQ-SQ32
97ColChoUD5-UD18
97ColChoUD5-UD19
97ColChoVC-VC8
97FinLinPP2-7
97FinLinPP2$10-72
97FinLinPP2$5-45
97FinLinPP2$50-93
97Max-10
97Max-55
97Max-110
97MaxChaTC-C7
97MaxChatCG-C7
97Pin-10
97Pin-39
97Pin-67
97PinArtP-10
97PinArtP-39
97PinArtP-67
97PinCer-10
97PinCer-44
97PinCer-94
97PinCerCGT-3
97PinCerCT-3
97PinCerE-E3
97PinCerEE-E3
97PinCerEP-E3
97PinCerMB-10
97PinCerMB-44
97PinCerMB-94
97PinCerMG-10
97PinCerMG-44
97PinCerMG-94
97PinCerMR-10
97PinCerMR-44
97PinCerMR-94
97PinCerR-10
97PinCerR-44
97PinCerR-94
97PinChe-1
97PinChe-4
97PinChe-7
97PinMin-6
97PinMin-22
97PinMin2GC-6
97PinMin2GC-22
97PinMinB-6
97PinMinB-22
97PinMinC-6
97PinMinC-22
97PinMinG-6
97PinMinG-22
97PinMinNC-6
97PinMinNC-22
97PinMinS-6
97PinMinS-22
97PinPor-7
97PinPor-27
97PinPre-64
97PinPre-65
97PinPre-66
97PinPre-67
97PinPre-68
97PinPre-69
97PinPre-70
97PinPre-71
97PinPre-72
97PinPreBM-64
97PinPreBM-65
97PinPreBM-66
97PinPreBM-67
97PinPreBM-68
97PinPreBM-69
97PinPreBM-70
97PinPreBM-71
97PinPreBM-72
97PinPreGM-64
97PinPreGM-65
97PinPreGM-66
97PinPreGM-67
97PinPreGM-68
97PinPreGM-69
97PinPreGM-70
97PinPreGM-71
97PinPreGM-72
97PinPreP-10
97PinPreP-39
97PinPreP-67
97PinPreP-S10-I
97PinPreP-TP8A
97PinPreSM-64
97PinPreSM-65
97PinPreSM-66
97PinPreSM-67
97PinPreSM-68
97PinPreSM-69
97PinPreSM-70
97PinPreSM-71
97PinPreSM-72
97PinSpe-10-I
97PinTeaP-8
97PinTotCPB-10
97PinTotCPB-44
97PinTotCPB-94
97PinTotCPG-10
97PinTotCPG-44
97PinTotCPG-94
97PinTotCPR-10
97PinTotCPR-44
97PinTotCPR-94
97PinTroC-10
97PinTroC-39
97PinTroC-67
97PrePas-6
97PrePas-36
97PrePas-107
97PrePasAut-6
97PrePasBB-BB6
97PrePasCC'-CC16
97PrePasCleC-C8
97PrePasL-6
97PrePasL-36
97PrePasL-107
97PrePasOS-6
97PrePasOS-36
97PrePasOS-107
97PrePasP-6
97PrePasP-32
97PrePasPCB-CB11
97PrePasPCBD-CB11
97PrePasPEP-6
97PrePasPEP-32
97PrePasPLL-LL10
97PrePasPM-6
97PrePasPM-32
97PrePasPOS-6
97PrePasPOS-32
97PrePasT-6
97PrePasT-36
97PrePasT-107
97PrePasVL-VL7A
97PrePasVL-VL7B
97RacCho-10
97RacCho-45
97RacCho-95
97RacChoHO-11
97RacChoHOGitD-11
97RacChoSS-10
97RacChoSS-45
97RacChoSS-95
97SBMot-7
97SBMot-43
97SBMot-96
97SBMotRC-RC8
97SBMotWR-WC17
97SBMotWR-WC29
97ScoBoal-23
97ScoBoal$PC-PC9
97SkyPro-24
97SkyPro-67
97SkyProA-24
97SkyProPS-E4
97SkyProT-T6
97SP-10
97SP-52
97SP-91
97SP-117
97SP SupS-10
97SP SupS-52
97SP SupS-91
97SP SupS-117
97SPX-10
97SPxBlu-10
97SPxGol-10
97SPxSil-10
97SPXSpeA-SV10
97Ult-28
97Ult-44
97UltDriV-D9
97UltEliS-E5
97UltIns-DC11
97UltSho-12
97UltUpd-17
97UltUpd-82
97UltUpdAR-17
97UppDecRTTC-6
97UppDecRTTC-48
97UppDecRTTC-90
97UppDecRTTC-110
97UppDecRTTC-148
97UppDecRTTCCQ-CQ10
97UDRTTCCQC-CQ10
97UppDecRTTCGF-RD10
97UppDecRTTCPP-PP36
97UppDecRTTCPPlu-+23
97UDRTTCPPRC-+23
97UppDRTTCPPRDC-+23
97UppDecRTTCQW-CQ10
97UppDecVC-10
97UppDecVC-60
97UppDecVC-102
97UppDecVCCR-CR6
97UppDecVCP-PE10
97UppDecVCPC-PH10
97UppDecVCVL-VL7
97VIP-20
97VIPExp-20
97VIPHeaGD-HG7
97VIPHigG-HG7
97VIPOilS-20
97VIPRinoH-RH6
97VIPRinoHDC-RH6
98ColCho-10
98ColCho-46
98ColCho-94
98ColCho-105
98HigGea-17
98HigGea-66
98HigGeaFG-6
98HigGeaFG-66
98HigGeaGJ-GJ6
98HigGeaM-6
98HigGeaM-66
98Max-10
98Max-40
98Max-74
98Max-10
98Max-35
98Max-60
98Max-85
98Max10tA-9
98Max10tA-54
98Max10tAMP-P10
98MaxBatP-B8
98MaxFirC-F11
98MaxYealRBS-14
98MaxYealRBS-56
98MaxYealRBS-73
98MaxYealRBS-91
98MaxYealRBS-99
98MayAutS-13
98PinMin-9
98PinMin-21
98PinMin-29
98PinMinB-9
98PinMinB-21
98PinMinB-29
98PinMinBC-9
98PinMinBC-21
98PinMinBC-05
98PinMinBPPC-9
98PinMinBPPC-21
98PinMinBPPC-05
98PinMinGMT-9
98PinMinGMT-21
98PinMinGMT-29
98PinMinGPC-9
98PinMinGPC-21
98PinMinGPC-29
98PinMinGPPC-9
98PinMinGPPC-21
98PinMinGPPC-29
98PinMinNC-9
98PinMinNC-21
98PinMinNC-29
98PinMinSGC-9
98PinMinSGC-21
98PinMinSGC-29
98PinMinSMT-9
98PinMinSMT-21
98PinMinSMT-29
98PinMinSPPC-9
98PinMinSPPC-21
98PinMinSPPC-29
98PinMinSSC-9
98PinMinSSC-21
98PinMinSSC-29
98PrePas-6
98PrePas-32
98PrePas-106
98PrePasA-11
98PrePasCC'-CC16
98PrePasOC-OC8
98PrePasOS-6
98PrePasOS-32
98PrePasP-19
98PrePasP-44
98PrePasP-19
98PrePasP-44
98PrePasPFC-FC7
98PrePasPFC-FC22
98PrePasPFCR-FC7
98PrePasPFCR-FC22
98PrePasPS-PS6
98PrePasPSH-SH5
98PrePasS-ST6A
98PrePasS-5
98PrePasS-28
98PrePasS-29
98PrePasSF-28
98PrePasSF-29
98PrePasSFT-8
98PrePasSFTD-8
98PrePasSO-29
98PrePasSO-30
98PrePasSOD-29
98PrePasSOD-30
98PrePasSS-15
98PrePasSSD-15
98PrePasTorp-ST6B
98SP Aut-10
98SP Aut-44
98SP Aut-76
98SP AutBtW-BW16
98SP AutBtWL2-BW16
98SP AutBtWL3-BW16
98SP AutSotTL2-ST10
98UppDecDV-10
98UppDecDVSM-10
98UppDecRttC-10
98UppDecRttC-49
98UppDecRttC-98
98UppDecVC-10
98UppDecVC-55
98UppDecVC-103
98UppDecVC-111
98UppDecVC-135
98UppDecVC-145
98UppDecVC3DoS-D12
98UppDecVC3DoS-D19
98UppDecVC3DoSG-D12
98UppDecVC3DoSG-D19
98UppDecVCPL-PL17
98UppDecVCPP-10
98UppDecVCPPCR-10
98UppDecVCSoB-SB8
98VIP-22
98VIPDriF-DF16
98VIPDriFD-DF16
98VIPExp-22
98VIPNASC-NC8
98VIPNASCD-NC8
98Whe-25
98Whe-44
98Whe-81
98Whe50tA-A12
98WheAut-11
98WheGol-25
98WheGol-44
98WheGol-81
98WheGreF-GF14
98WheJac-J8
99Pre-23
99PrePas-23
99PrePas-123
99PrePasBR-BR6
99PrePasCC-9B
99PrePasCC-16
99PrePasPS-7
99PrePasS-9A
99UppDecVC-4
99UppDecVC-67
99UppDecVCIS-IS11
99UppDecVCNSS-RR
99UppDecVCUE-4
99UppDecVCUE-67
99WheHigG-23
99WheHigGAC-23
99WheHigGFG-23
99WheHigGHS-HS4/6
99WheHigGM-23
99WheHigGS-GS23

Rudolph, Charlie
91WinChoM-20
91WinChoM-21

Ruff, Tommy
91BulRin-123

Ruggiero, Reggie
91WinChoM-69
91WinChoM-71

Ruhlman, Brian
94STAMod-44

Ruhlman, Randy
92EriMaxTA-33
92EriMaxTA-34

Rumi, Gabriele
92GriForO-146

Rumley, Johnny
91BulRin-121
92BulRin-121
92BulRin-P2

Rumple, Jeff
92TraTeaS-86

Rundle, Joe
72FleAHRDN-17

Runyon, Ronnie
73FleAHRRU-54

Rupp, Dave
92VolRacLS2-61

Rush Jr., Lonnie
93Max-81
93MaxPreS-81

Rush, Garry
94WorOut-43

Rushiti, Andi
92LanRocS-46

Russell, Dave Drag
73FleAHRRU-42

Russell, David Dirt
91BulRin-36
92BulRin-36

Russell, Don
90LanRocSHS-37
91LanRocS-8

Russell, Ivan
92DirTra-100

Russell, Steve
92JAG-98
93JAG-39

Russell, Wade
91DKIMCDT-15

Russo, Paul
60HawWaxI-49
91LegInd-5
91LegInd-89
92LegInd-96

Rust, Deron
91K&WDirT-47
92K&WDirT-35
94K&WDirT-36
95K&WDirT-39

Rust, Todd

92JAG-227
Rutherford, Johnny
80AvaHilURG-1
83A&SRacI-21
84A&SRacI-5
85A&SRacI-40
86A&SRacI-16
87A&SRacI-22
87A&SRacI-49
91AllWorI-54
91AllWorI-93
91LegInd-88
92AllWorI-51
92AllWorI-77
92LegInd-64
94HiTecICD-CD28
95SkyInd5-16
95SkyInd5PC-11
Ruttman, Joe
91ProSet-76
91ProSet-79
92MaxBla-75
92MaxRed-75
92ProSet-29
93Tra-92
93TraFirR-92
94Max-51
94MaxPreS-51
95FinLinSRF-14
95FinLinSRF-63
95FinLinSup-14
95FinLinSup-63
96MaxPre-78
96PrePas-69
96PrePasSco-69
96PrePasT-69
96Viper-65
96ViperBlaM-65
96ViperCop-65
96ViperGreM-65
97PrePas-50
97PrePasL-50
97PrePasOS-50
97PrePasT-50
97VIP-44
97VIPExp-44
97VIPOilS-44
98HigGea-44
98HigGeaFG-44
98HigGeaM-44
98PrePas-52
98PrePasOS-52
98Whe-67
98WheGol-67
99Pre-55
99PrePas-55
Ruttman, Troy
54StaWetIW-1952
60HawWaxI-36
91LegInd-72
92AllWorI-59
Ryan, Terry
91DKIMCDT-14
Rypien, Mark
95CroJew-67
95CroJewD-67
95CroJewE-67
95CroJewS-67
Sabates, Chany
92LimEdiKW-10
92LimEdiKW-12
92Tra-40
94FinLinG-56
95ImaOwnP-OP10
Sabates, Felix
89Max-39
90Max-55
91Max-78
91ProSet-88
91ProSet-132
91Tra-40
91Tra-173
92LimEdiKW-10
92MaxBla-134
92MaxRed-134
92ProSet-169A
92ProSet-169B
92Tra-40
92TraTeaS-52
92TraTeaS-53
92WheKylP-3
92WheKylPG-3
93FinLin-78
93FinLinCS-15
93FinLinS-78
93Max-103
93Max-282
93MaxPreP-92
93MaxPreS-103
93MaxPreS-282
94ActPac-176
94FinLin-142
94FinLinG-56
94FinLinS-142
94HigGea-32
94HigGeaG-32
94Max-89
94MaxPreP-89
94MaxPreS-89
94Pow-12
94Pow-113
94PowGol-12
94PowGol-113
94PrePas-85
95FinLin-40
95FinLinPP-40
95FinLinSil-40
95HigGea-39
95HigGeaDO-39
95HigGeaDOG-39
95HigGeaG-39
95ImaOwnP-OP10
95Max-37
95MaxCroC-76
95MaxPreP-76
95MaxPreS-84
95PrePas-88
95PrePasRH-88
95Sel-87
95SelFlaO-87
95SP-125
95SPDieC-125
96FinLin-91
96FinLinPriP-91
96FinLinS-91
96MaxPre-85
96UppDec-125
97FinLinPP2-32
97Viper-65
97ViperBlaR-65
Sachs, Eddie
62MarInd-12
91LegInd-6
92AllWorI-61
92LegInd-79
Sacks, Greg
88MaxCha-65
89Max-88
89MaxCri-1
89MaxCri-24
90Max-48
91Max-18
91ProSet-121
91ProSet-136
92MaxBla-47
92MaxBlaU-U1
92MaxCra-NNO
92MaxRed-47
92MaxRedU-U1
92ProSet-73
92ProSet-77
93Max-69
93MaxMot-16
93MaxMot-36
93MaxPreP-69
93MaxPreS-69
93Tra-68
93Tra-87
93Tra-192
93TraFirR-68
93TraFirR-87
93TraFirR-192
93TraTri-44
94ActPac-159
94FinLin-48
94FinLinS-48
94Hi-Bri4AP-21
94Hi-Bri4AP-24
94Hi-Bri4AP-63
94HigGea-130
94HigGeaDO-130
94HigGeaDOG-130
94HigGeaG-130
94HiTecB4-21
94HiTecB4-24
94HiTecB4-63
94Max-68
94Max-270
94Max-277
94MaxMed-17
94MaxMot-19
94MaxPreP-68
94MaxPreS-68
94OptXL-16
94OptXLRH-16
94Pep400VL-4
94Pow-114
94Pow-149
94PowGol-114
94PowGol-149
94Tra-97
94Tra-177
94TraAutV-20
94TraFirR-97
94TraFirR-177
94TraPreC-26
94VIP-27
95ActPacP-44
95HigGeaBC-BC15
95HigGeaBCG-BC15
95HiTecB4-12
95HiTecB4-68
95Max-77
95MaxCroC-77
95MaxPreP-77
95MaxPreS-77
95MaxPreSU-7
95PrePas-25
95PrePasCC-25
95PrePasPH-21
95PrePasPre-21
95PrePasPRH-21
95PrePasRH-25
95Sel-26
95SelFlaO-26
95SPSpeM-SM29
95SPSpeMDC-SM29
95Tra-12
95TraAutV-9
95TraFirR-12
95UppDec-41
95UppDec-109
95UppDec-214
95UppDec-257
95UppDec-290
95UppDecA-214
95UppDecGSEG-41
95UppDecGSEG-109
95UppDecGSEG-214
95UppDecGSEG-257
95UppDecGSEG-290
95UppDecSSES-41
95UppDecSSES-109
95UppDecSSES-214
95UppDecSSES-257
95UppDecSSES-290
95USAirGS-2
95USAirGS-3
95USAirGS-4
96Max-34
96MaxPre-40
97AutRacA-48
Sadler, Elliott
97Max-45
97Max-90
98HigGea-41
98HigGeaFG-41
98HigGeaM-41
98PrePas-48
98PrePasOS-48
98PrePasP-4
98PrePasP-4
98PrePasS-42
98PrePasSF-42
98UppDecRttC-113
98VIP-34
98VIPExp-34
98Whe-56
98Whe-62
98WheGol-56
98WheGol-62
99Pre-43
99Pre-59
99Pre-92
99PrePas-43
99PrePas-59
99PrePas-92
99UppDecVC-86
99UppDecVCNSS-ES
99UppDecVCUE-86
99WheHigG-43
99WheHigG-62
99WheHigGFG-43
99WheHigGFG-62
99WheHigGM-43
99WheHigGM-62
Sadler, Hermie
93Tra-80
93Tra-172
93TraFirR-80
93TraFirR-172
93WheRooT-39
93WheRooT-69
93WheRooTPla-39
93WheRooTPla-69
94FinLin-NNO
94FinLinBGN-BGN5
94FinLinG-78
94FinLinGA-78
94HigGea-59
94HigGea-74
94HigGeaG-59
94HigGeaG-74
94HigGeaRTU-101
94HigGeaRTUP-101
94Max-171
94Max-198
94MaxPreP-51
94MaxPreP-158
94MaxPreS-171
94MaxPreS-257
94PrePas-72
94SliJimDG-47
94Tra-89
94TraFirR-89
94TraHerS-1
94TraHerS-3
94TraHerS-4
94TraHerS-6
94TraHerS-7
94TraHerS-8
94TraHerS-9
94TraHerS-10
94TraWin-W17
94VIP-72
95CroJew-59
95CroJewD-59
95CroJewE-59
95CroJewS-59
95FinLin-45
95FinLinPP-45
95FinLinSil-45
95HigGea-56
95HigGeaDO-56
95HigGeaDOG-56
95HigGeaG-56
95Tra-24
95TraFirR-24
95TraOnTR-OTR9
96MaxMadiA-61
96MaxMadiA-69
96MaxOdy-61
96MaxOdy-69
96MaxPre-164
96MaxPre-244
96Viper-54
96ViperBlaM-54
96ViperCop-54
96ViperGreM-54
97ColCho-48
97ColCho-97
97UppDecVC-48
97UppDecVC-97
98PrePas-49
98PrePasOS-49
98PrePasP-11
98PrePasP-11
98PrePasS-43
98PrePasSF-43
98UppDecRttC-105
98VIP-35
98VIPExp-35
98Whe-57
98WheGol-57
99Pre-46
99PrePas-46
Safford, Kenny
71FleAHRDC-11
Sak, Don
92EriMaxTA-67
Salazar, Eliseo
96SkyInd5-33
96SkyInd5-58
97Hi-IRL-24
97Hi-IRL'I5-I10
Saleen, Steve
91AllWorI-60
Samples, Ed
89TGRacMR-54
89TGRacMR-55
89TGRacMR-211
91TGRacMRU-54
91TGRacMRU-55
91TGRacMRU-211
Sams, Nathan
92TraTeaS-172
Sanchez, Frank
89MegDra-73
89MegDra-74
Sanders, A.J.
91BulRin-126
92BulRin-192
Sanders, Clare
72FleAHRDN-60
Sanders, Doug
92JAG-99
93JAG-40
Sanders, Jim
91LanRocS-49
Sanders, R.
91LanRocS-64
Sands, Scotty
92LanARCF-51
94LanARCF-75
Sanford, Kenny
72FleAHRDN-11
Sans, Ed Jr.
92JAG-228
Santerie, Andy
92WinChoM-25
Santiano, Mike
91LanSeeS-21
Santos, Jimmy
91LanAmeIS-5
Santucci Sr., Domenic
89MegDra-98
Sapp, Bobby
92K&WDirT-36
94K&WDirT-33
Sasetti, Andrea
92GriForO-144
Satmary, Joe
73FleAHRRU-37
73FleAHRRU-38
Sattelmaier, Lou
90BigTimD-15
90BigTimDS-15
91BigTimD-59
Sauter, Jay
92TraASA-9
99Pre-56
99PrePas-56
Sauter, Jim
88MaxCha-93
89Max-31
90Max-31
91Max-31
92MaxBla-89
92MaxRed-89
92ProSet-106
92TraASA-37
93Max-95
93MaxPreP-58
93MaxPreS-95
94Max-58
94MaxPreS-58
Sauve, Steve
95JSKIce-97
Sawatsky, John
95JSKIce-99
Sawyer, Elton
89Max-175
90Max-61
91Max-92
91Tra-88
92BulRin-161
92MaxBla-60
92MaxRed-60
92ProSet-197
92Tra-67
94HigGea-171
94HigGeaDO-171
94HigGeaDOG-171
94HigGeaG-171
94Max-299
94Tra-129
94TraFirR-129
94TraWin-W25
95HigGea-57
95HigGeaDO-57

95HigGeaDOG-57
95HigGeaG-57
95Max-200
95MaxPreS-175
95MaxPreSU-2
95PrePas-70
95PrePas-141
95PrePasRH-70
95PrePasRH-141
95Sel-70
95SelFlaO-70
96AutRac-26
96AutRacA-49
96AutRacCA-49
96AutRacFR-78
96Cla-17
96ClaPriP-17
96ClaSil-17
96Max-61
96MaxPre-27
96MaxPre-46
96MaxPre-174
96MaxPre-253
96PrePas-63
96PrePasSco-63
96PrePasT-63
96Ult-136
96Ult-137
96UltAut-30
96UppDecRTTC-RC35
96UppDecRTTC-RC84
97ColCho-39
97ColCho-89
97ColChoUD5-UD81
97ColChoUD5-UD82
97SkyPro-54
97SkyProA-54
97UltUpd-65
97UltUpdAR-65
97UppDecVC-39
97UppDecVC-89
98Max10tA-15
98Max10tA-60
99Pre-41
99PrePas-41
99WheHigG-41
99WheHigGFG-41
99WheHigGM-41

Sawyer, Keith
92TraTeaS-133

Saylor, Connie
88MaxCha-85
89Max-99
90Max-99

Sayre, Eric
92JAG-229

Scarlett, Darwin
92JAG-230

Scelzi, Gary
98PrePas-91
98PrePasOS-91

Schacht, Bob
92LanARCF-44
92LanARCF-106
92MaxBlaU-U13
92MaxRedU-U13
93Max-91
93MaxPreP-86
93MaxPreS-91
94LanARCF-42
94Max-57
94MaxPreS-57

Schafer, Tania
92WinChoM-41

Schaffer, Charlie
92JAG-100

Schaffer, Rick
92K&WDirT-54
94K&WDirT-38

Schanche, Martin
78GraPri-215

Schartman, Eddie
71FleAHRDC-30

Schauer, Pat
92TraASA-5

Scheckter, Jody
77Spo-2122
77Spo-5119
77Spo-7323
78GraPri-44
78GraPri-70
78GraPri-94
78GraPri-109
78GraPri-110
78GraPri-160
91ProTraFO-190

Schick, Donald Jr.
92CorSelCCS-21
93CorSelCCS-21

Schickentanz, Clemens
78GraPri-184

Schiff, Danny
89Max-64
90Max-92

Schill, Al Jr.
91LanART-30

Schill, Al Sr.
91LanART-5
92RedGraST-4
92RedGraST-5

Schlager, Bo
94HigGeaPPT-W33
94HigGeaPPTG-33W

Schlenger, Erwin
90K&WDirT-38

Schlesser, Jean-Louis
93MaxWilR-7

Schmaling, Joe
94HigGeaPPT-G16
94HigGeaPPTG-16G

Schmidt, Steve
89CheFlaI-40
92ProSetN-79

Schneider, Frankie
89TGRacMR-241
91GalPrePR-71
91TGRacMRU-241

Schneider, Lou
54StaWetIW-1931
60HawWaxI-19
95TraVal-37

Schneider, Tom
91LanRocS-28

Schoenfeld, Dennis
92BulRin-76

Schofield, Phil
72FleAHRDN-4

Schrader, Ken
88MaxCha-74
88MaxCha-81
89Max-25
89Max-157
89MaxCri-3
90ACRacPW-4
90Max-25
90Max-183
90MaxHolF-HF5
91ACRac-6
91Max-25
91MaxMcD-10
91MaxRacFK-2
91MaxTheWA-15
91MaxUpd-25
91ProSet-50
91ProSet-61
91ProSet-127
91SpoLegHH-HH7
91SupRacM-11
91Tra-25
92ACDel-6
92ACRacP-5
92CoyRoo-7
92JAG-101
92MaxBla-25
92MaxBla-194
92MaxBla-267
92MaxBla-275
92MaxMcD-17
92MaxRed-25
92MaxRed-194
92MaxRed-267
92MaxRed-275
92MaxTheW-3
92MaxTheW-23
92ProSet-98
92ProSet-104
92ProSet-165
92ProSetMH-15
92ProSetRF-8
92RedRacKS-1
92RedRacKS-2
92RedRacKS-3
92RedRacKS-4
92RedRacKS-5
92RedRacKS-6
92RedRacKS-7
92RedRacKS-8
92RedRacKS-9
92RedRacKS-10
92RedRacKS-11
92RedRacKS-12
92RedRacKS-13
92RedRacKS-14
92RedRacKS-15
92RedRacKS-16
92RedRacKS-17
92RedRacKS-18
92RedRacKS-19
92RedRacKS-20
92RedRacKS-21
92RedRacKS-22
92RedRacKS-23
92RedRacKS-24
92RedRacKS-25
92RedRacKS-26
92RedRacKS-27
92RedRacKS-28
92RedRacKS-29
92RedRacKS-30
92RedRacKS-P1
92RedSta-25
92Tra-25
92Tra-127
92TraCouSR-4
92TraGoo-24
92TraRacM-5
92TraRacM-20
92TraRacM-25
92TraRacM-48
93ACRacF-25
93ActPac-18
93ActPac-19
93ActPac-20
93ActPac-134
93ActPac-135
93ActPac-187
93ActPac-203
93ActPac2G-69G
93FinLin-74
93FinLin-134
93FinLin-143
93FinLinCS-3
93FinLinCS-18
93FinLinS-74
93FinLinS-134
93FinLinS-143
93Max-25
93Max-186
93Max-194
93MaxHou-13
93MaxLowFS-5
93MaxPreP-25
93MaxPreP-32
93MaxPreP-171
93MaxPreS-25
93MaxPreS-186
93MaxPreS-194
93MaxRetJ-2
93MaxTheW-4
93MaxTheW-24
93MaxWinM-6
93MaxWinM-7
93PrePasPre-12
93Tra-32
93Tra-47
93Tra-88
93Tra-167
93TraFirR-32
93TraFirR-47
93TraFirR-88
93TraFirR-167
93TraPreC-12
93TraTri-25
93TraTri-43
93WheRooT-26
93WheRooT-47
93WheRooT-98
93WheRooTPla-26
93WheRooTPla-47
93WheRooTPla-98
94ActPac-9
94ActPac-49
94ActPac-74
94ActPac-117
94ActPac-160
94ActPac2G-19G
94ActPac2G-28G
94ActPacC-15
94CarDynGO-10
94FinLin-27
94FinLin-56
94FinLin-93
94FinLin-116
94FinLinDH-7
94FinLinG-19
94FinLinG-35
94FinLinG-76
94FinLinG-87
94FinLinGA-76
94FinLinS-27
94FinLinS-56
94FinLinS-93
94FinLinS-116
94Hi-Bri4AP-53
94HigGea-4
94HigGea-90
94HigGea-173
94HigGeaDO-173
94HigGeaDOG-173
94HigGeaG-4
94HigGeaG-90
94HigGeaG-173
94HigGeaMG-MG6
94HiTecB4-53
94LanARCF-43
94Max-25
94Max-56
94Max-256
94Max-257
94Max-326
94MaxAut-25
94MaxMed-6
94MaxPreP-25
94MaxPreP-56
94MaxPreS-25
94MaxPreS-56
94MaxRooY-7
94MaxTheS2-9
94MWWin-4
94MWWin-5
94OptXL-17
94OptXL-29
94OptXL-34
94OptXLRH-17
94OptXLRH-29
94OptXLRH-34
94Pow-115
94PowGol-115
94PowPre-11
94PrePas-22
94PrePas-43
94PrePas-119
94PrePas-142
94PrePasCC-CC22
94Tra-23
94Tra-58
94Tra-75
94Tra-131
94Tra-168
94TraAut-A11
94TraAutV-41
94TraAutV-49
94TraFirR-23
94TraFirR-58
94TraFirR-75
94TraFirR-131
94TraFirR-168
94TraPreC-27
94TraWin-W23
94VIP-28
94VIP-45
94VIPDriC-DC7
95ActPacC-71
95ActPacC-88
95ActPacC-97
95ActPacC-101
95ActPacC2T-13
95ActPacCSS-71
95ActPacHM-2
95ActPacP-18
95ActPacP-62
95ActPacP-76
95ActPacP2G-8G
95ActPacS-14
95ActPacS-42
95ActPacSSS-14
95ActPacSSS-42
95ActPacSTTH-6
95Ass-17
95Ass-37
95Ass$5$25PC-5
95Ass1M$PC-11
95AssGolS-17
95AssGolS-37
95CroJew-8
95CroJew-41
95CroJewD-8
95CroJewD-41
95CroJewE-8
95CroJewE-41
95CroJewS-8
95CroJewS-41
95FinLin-25
95FinLin-47
95FinLin-100
95FinLinCC6-17
95FinLinCC6-37
95FinLinGS-GS8
95FinLinPP-25
95FinLinPP-47
95FinLinPP-100
95FinLinSCalC-9
95FinLinSil-25
95FinLinSil-47
95FinLinSil-100
95FinLinSRF-6
95FinLinSRF-51
95FinLinSRF-70
95FinLinSRF-75
95FinLinSSSS-SS3
95FinLinSup-6
95FinLinSup-51
95FinLinSup-70
95FinLinSup-75
95HigGea-12
95HigGea-65
95HigGea-74
95HigGeaDO-12
95HigGeaDO-65
95HigGeaDO-74
95HigGeaDOG-12
95HigGeaDOG-65
95HigGeaDOG-74
95HigGeaG-12
95HigGeaG-65
95HigGeaG-74
95HiTecB4-21
95HiTecB4-53
95HiTecB4-60
95HiTecB4TT-BY7
95Ima-25
95Ima-52
95ImaDri-D9
95ImaGol-25
95ImaGol-52
95ImaHarC-HC5
95Max-25
95Max-139
95Max-164
95Max-252
95Max-253
95Max-254
95Max-255
95Max-256
95Max-257
95MaxAut-25
95MaxCroC-14
95MaxCroC-25
95MaxCroC-56
95MaxCroC-143
95MaxCroC-144
95MaxMed-18
95MaxMed-48
95MaxMedB-18
95MaxMedB-48
95MaxMedORA-OTR1
95MaxOveW-7
95MaxPreP-14
95MaxPreP-25
95MaxPreP-56
95MaxPreP-143
95MaxPreP-144
95MaxPrePP-PS3
95MaxPreS-25
95MaxPreS-56
95MaxPreS-102
95MaxPreS-189
95MaxPreS-190
95MaxSup-7
95OptXL-19
95OptXL-49
95OptXLCB-19
95OptXLCB-49
95OptXLDC-19
95OptXLDC-49
95OptXLRH-19
95OptXLRH-49
95OptXLS-XLS14
95PrePas-26
95PrePas-45

91SpoLegWS-WS1
91SpoLegWS-WS2
91SpoLegWS-WS3
91SpoLegWS-WS4
91SpoLegWS-WS5
91SpoLegWS-WS6
91SpoLegWS-WS7
91SpoLegWS-WS8
91SpoLegWS-WS9
91SpoLegWS-WS10
91SpoLegWS-WS11
91SpoLegWS-WS12
91SpoLegWS-WS13
91SpoLegWS-WS14
91SpoLegWS-WS15
91SpoLegWS-WS16
91SpoLegWS-WS17
91SpoLegWS-WS18
91SpoLegWS-WS19
91SpoLegWS-WS20
91SpoLegWS-WS21
91SpoLegWS-WS22
91SpoLegWS-WS23
91SpoLegWS-WS24
91SpoLegWS-WS25
91SpoLegWS-WS26
91SpoLegWS-WS27
91SpoLegWS-WS28
91SpoLegWS-WS29
91SpoLegWS-WS30
91TGRacMRU-180
91TGRacMRU-181
91TGRacMRU-182
91TGRacWS-1
91TGRacWS-2
91TGRacWS-3
91TGRacWS-4
91TGRacWS-5
91TGRacWS-6
94VIP-89

Scribner, Harry
92ProSetN-76
92ProSetN-135
93FinLinN-104

Seabolt, Jerry
91MaxBilETCM-13
92RSSMotH-2

Seabolt, Phil
91MaxBilETCM-29

Seagraves, Ralph
91ProSetL-L9

Seaman, Richard
39ChuKinoS-22
71MobTheSoGPMR-20

Seaton, Scott
95JSKS.OS-1

Seay, Lloyd
91GalPrePR-3
91GalPrePR-95

Seberg, Troy
93MaxPreP-159

Sebring, Phil
89CheFlaI-18
90CheFlaI-49

Seder, Frank
92JAG-102

Sedgewick, Bill
95FinLinSRF-21
95FinLinSup-21

Sedgwick, Bill
92MaxBla-56
92MaxRed-56
93Max-58
93MaxPreS-58
96PrePas-70
96PrePasSco-70
96PrePasT-70
96Viper-69
96ViperBlaM-69
96ViperCop-69
96ViperGreM-69
97PrePas-51
97PrePasL-51
97PrePasOS-51
97PrePasT-51

Seebold, Bill
95Ima-34
95ImaCirC-3
95ImaGol-34

Segrave, Sir Henry
30WilCig-24
71MobTheSoGPMR-9

Segrini, Al
93FinLinN-39

Seidenspinner, Dick
92TraTeaS-67

Seifert, Bill
89TGRacMR-16
89TGRacMR-17
91TGRacMRU-16
91TGRacMRU-17

Selberg, Troy
93Max-179
93MaxPreS-179
93Tra-23
94Max-159
94MaxPreS-159
94Tra-196
94TraFirR-196
95Max-130
95MaxAut-130
95MaxCroC-128
95MaxPreP-128
95MaxPreS-153
96MaxPre-143

Sell, Russ
92JAG-232

Sellars, Randy
92JAG-103
93JAG-41
94JAG-51

Sena, Mike
95K&WDirT-38

Senna, Ayrton
87AceForO-28
87ForOneI-9
88HerFouFO-4B
91CarForO-1
91CarForO-2
91CarForO-3
91ProTraFO-1
91ProTraFO-2
91ProTraFO-97
91ProTraFO-98
91ProTraFO-99
91ProTraFO-100
91ProTraFO-101
91ProTraFO-102
91ProTraFO-103
91ProTraFO-104
91ProTraFO-105
91ProTraFO-106
91ProTraFO-107
91ProTraFO-144
91ProTraFO-147
91ProTraFO-148
91ProTraFO-151
91ProTraFO-152
91ProTraFO-154
91ProTraFO-165
91ProTraFO-166
91ProTraFO-172
92GriForO-1
92GriForO-34
92GriForO-67
92GriForO-100
92GriForO-101
92GriForO-102
92GriForO-103
92GriForO-105
92GriForO-106
92GriForO-109
92GriForO-110
92GriForO-111
92GriForO-114
92GriForO-115
92GriForO-186
92GriForO-187
92GriForO-188
92GriForO-189
92LimAppFO-10

Senneker, Bob
92TraASA-15
92TraASA-16

Serra, Chico
78GraPri-181

Sessions, Sam
86AceInd-D4

Setzer, Berry
73FleAHRRU-40

Setzer, Dennis
91BulRin-91
91LanStoCC-19
92BulRin-166
92LanARCF-78
93AllRobPDS-11B
93AllRobPDS-NNO
94HigGea-174
94HigGeaDO-174
94HigGeaDOG-174
94HigGeaG-174
94Max-195
94MaxPreS-195
94Tra-41
94TraFirR-41
94VIP-65
95FinLin-88
95FinLinPP-88
95FinLinSil-88
95HigGea-53
95HigGeaDO-53
95HigGeaDOG-53
95HigGeaG-53
95Max-158
95MaxAut-158
95MaxCroC-138
95MaxPreP-138
95MaxPreS-169
95PrePas-71
95PrePas-73
95PrePas-142
95PrePasRH-71
95PrePasRH-73
95PrePasRH-142
95Sel-71
95SelFlaO-71
95Tra-11
95TraFirR-11
95TraOnTR-OTR6
95VIP-44
95VIPAut-44
95VIPCooB-44
95VIPEmeP-44
95VIPRedHCB-44
96MaxPre-169
96MaxPre-241
97Ult-98

Sewell, Bubba
89MegDra-77

Sexton, Scott
91DirTra-29
92DirTra-85
92JAG-104
94JAG-52

Seymour, Joe
11AmeTobAD-21

Shaak, Doug
91MaxBilETCM-19

Shafer, Craig
92EriMaxTA-68

Shafer, Ed
92CorSelCCS-19
93CorSelCCS-19

Shafer, Paul
92JAG-105

Shaffer, Todd
91WorOut-90
92CorSelCCS-11

Shafiroff, Scott
73FleAHRRU-39

Shahan, Shirley
71FleAHRDC-27

Shannon, Terry
93JAG-42

Sharp, Scott
92EriMaxTA-19
92EriMaxTA-20
92EriMaxTA-40
92EriMaxTA-42
92EriMaxTA-73
92EriMaxTA-75
92EriMaxTA-76
92EriMaxTA-77
92EriMaxTA-78
92EriMaxTA-80
92EriMaxTA-81
92EriMaxTA-83
92EriMaxTA-84
92EriMaxTA-85
92EriMaxTA-86
92EriMaxTA-88
92EriMaxTA-89
92EriMaxTA-90
92EriMaxTA-91
92EriMaxTA-92
92EriMaxTA-93
92EriMaxTA-95
92EriMaxTA-100
95SkyInd5-35
95SkyInd5-88
96SkyInd5-39
96SkyInd5-80
97Hi-IRL-2
97Hi-IRL'I5-I8

Shartman, Eddie
73FleAHRRU-20

Shaut, Dean
92TraTeaS-189

Shaver, Steve
92DirTra-86
92JAG-106
92STAMod-34
94STAMod-45

Shaw, Dale
91WinChoNED-53
91WinChoNED-54
92WinChoB-22
92WinChoB-23

Shaw, Wilbur
54StaWetIW-1937
54StaWetIW-1939
54StaWetIW-1940
60HawWaxI-25
60HawWaxI-27
77Spo-6511
91LegInd-30
91LegInd-37
92MaxIMH-28
95TraVal-45

Shear, Joe
91LanART-9
91LanART-33

Shelby, Carroll
92MaxIMH-29

Shelmerdine, Kirk
89Max-38
90Max-39A
90Max-39B
91Max-96
91Max-205
91Max-219
91Tra-57
92BikRacS-5
92MaxAllPT-5
92MaxAllPT-13
92MaxBla-148
92MaxBla-235
92MaxBla-240
92MaxMcD-8
92MaxRed-148
92MaxRed-235
92MaxRed-240
92ProSet-26
92Tra-57
92TraTeaS-5

Shepherd, Morgan
88MaxCha-25
89Max-75
89MaxCri-23
90Max-15
90Max-183
90MaxHolF-HF16
91HicMotS-6
91Max-15
91Max-199
91MaxMcD-5
91MaxMot-6
91MaxMot-34
91MaxTheWA-16
91MaxUpd-15
91MotRac-1
91MotRac-6
91MotRac-7
91ProSet-40
91ProSet-42
91Tra-15
91Tra-97
92DaySer1-8
92MaxBla-21
92MaxBla-147
92MaxMcD-19
92MaxMot-8
92MaxMot-43
92MaxRed-21
92MaxRed-147
92MaxTheW-19
92MaxTheW-39
92ProSet-126
92ProSet-134
92ProSet-160
92ProSet-240
92ProSet-247
92ProSetMH-17
92ProSetP-P3
92ProSetRF-10
92RedSta-15
92Tra-21
92Tra-97
92TraGoo-22
92TraRacM-21
92TraRacM-49
92TraRacM-84
92TraRacM-93
93ActPac-58
93ActPac-59
93ActPac-116
93ActPac-117
93ActPac-177
93ActPac2G-59G
93FinLin-47
93FinLin-91
93FinLin-156
93FinLinCS-4
93FinLinCS-16
93FinLinCS-25
93FinLinS-47
93FinLinS-91
93FinLinS-156
93Max-21
93MaxHou-11
93MaxLowFS-5
93MaxMot-17
93MaxMot-37
93MaxPreP-21
93MaxPreS-21
93MaxTheW-12
93MaxTheW-32
93MotDecC-8
93MotManC-8
93PrePasPre-13
93PrePasPre-24
93Tra-21
93Tra-173
93TraFirR-21
93TraFirR-173
93TraPreC-7
93TraTri-21
93TraTri-27
94ActPac-7
94ActPac-36
94ActPac-47
94ActPac-72
94ActPac-129
94ActPac-161
94ActPac2G-6G
94ActPac2G-17G
94ActPac2G-26G
94CarDynGO-7
94FinLin-37
94FinLin-42
94FinLin-80
94FinLin-122
94FinLinDH-8
94FinLinG-15
94FinLinG-27
94FinLinG-40
94FinLinG-69
94FinLinG-98
94FinLinGA-15
94FinLinGT-TG5
94FinLinS-37
94FinLinS-42
94FinLinS-80
94FinLinS-122
94FinLinVL-VL7
94FinLinVL-VL12
94Hi-Bri4AP-4
94Hi-Bri4AP-7
94Hi-Bri4AP-50
94HigGea-78
94HigGea-121
94HigGea-166
94HigGeaDO-121
94HigGeaDO-166
94HigGeaDOG-121
94HigGeaDOG-166
94HigGeaG-78
94HigGeaG-121
94HigGeaG-166
94HiTecB4-4
94HiTecB4-7
94HiTecB4-50
94Max-21
94Max-50
94Max-210
94Max-248
94Max-249
94MaxMed-9
94MaxMed-62
94MaxMot-13

94TraPreC-30
94VIP-31
95ActPacC-84
95ActPacCSS-84
95ActPacP-19
95ActPacP-45
95ActPacP-57
95ActPacS-13
95ActPacS-41
95ActPacSSS-13
95ActPacSSS-41
95CroJew-20
95CroJew-48
95CroJewD-20
95CroJewD-48
95CroJewE-20
95CroJewE-48
95CroJewS-20
95CroJewS-48
95FinLin-9
95FinLin-77
95FinLinPP-9
95FinLinPP-77
95FinLinSil-9
95FinLinSil-77
95HigGea-97
95HigGeaBC-BC11
95HigGeaBCG-BC11
95HigGeaDO-97
95HigGeaDOG-97
95HigGeaG-97
95HiTecB4-32
95HiTecB4-58
95Ima-23
95Ima-63
95ImaGol-23
95ImaGol-63
95Max-27
95Max-34
95Max-92
95Max-102
95Max-226
95Max-227
95MaxCroC-27
95MaxCroC-67
95MaxCroC-164
95MaxCroC-167
95MaxMed-16
95MaxMed-46
95MaxMedB-16
95MaxMedB-46
95MaxPreP-27
95MaxPreP-67
95MaxPreP-164
95MaxPreP-167
95MaxPrePSTP-PRE2
95MaxPrePTH-TH4
95MaxPreS-27
95MaxPreS-67
95MaxPreS-184
95MaxPreS-279
95MaxPreS-282
95PrePas-29
95PrePas-107
95PrePas-138
95PrePasCC-29
95PrePasCF-CF7
95PrePasRD-RD11
95PrePasRH-29
95PrePasRH-107
95PrePasRH-138
95Sel-30
95Sel-146
95SelFlaO-30
95SelFlaO-146
95SelSki-SS17
95SP-54
95SP-96
95SPDieC-54
95SPDieC-96
95UppDec-21
95UppDec-64
95UppDec-89
95UppDec-123
95UppDec-201
95UppDec-245
95UppDecA-201
95UppDecGSEG-21
95UppDecGSEG-64
95UppDecGSEG-89
95UppDecGSEG-123
95UppDecGSEG-201
95UppDecGSEG-245
95UppDecPRW-P9
95UppDecSSES-21
95UppDecSSES-64
95UppDecSSES-89
95UppDecSSES-123
95UppDecSSES-201
95UppDecSSES-245
95Zen-22
95Zen-44
95Zen-62
96ActPacC-45
96ActPacCSS-45
96Ass-11
96Ass$10PC-6
96Ass$2PC-3
96Ass$5PC-13
96AssComL-CL18
96AutRac-47
96AutRacA-54
96AutRacCA-54
96AutRacHP-HP15
96CroJewEDT-23
96CroJewEDTC-23
96CroJewEE-23
96CroJewEli-23
96CroJewES-23
96CroJewETC-23
96CroJewETCE-23
96CroJewETCS-23
96FinLin-32
96FinLin-45
96FinLin-94
96FinLinPriP-32
96FinLinPriP-45
96FinLinPriP-94
96FinLinS-32
96FinLinS-45
96FinLinS-94
96Fla-31
96Fla-87
96Max-14
96Max-23
96MaxMadiA-14
96MaxMadiA-23
96MaxOdy-14
96MaxOdy-23
96MaxOdyM-MM2
96MaxPre-23
96MaxPre-63
96Pin-23
96Pin-50
96Pin-23
96Pin-50
96PinPolP-23
96PinPolP-39
96PinPolPLF-23
96PinPolPLF-39
96PinPolPNL-14
96PinPolPNLG-14
96PinWinCC-23
96PinWinCC-50
96RacCho-31
96RacChoAP-31
96RacChoSC-31
96SP-23
96SP-66
96Ult-87
96Ult-88
96Ult-89
96Ult-200
96UltAut-34
96UppDec-21
96UppDec-61
96UppDec-101
96UppDecRTTC-RC24
96UppDecRTTC-RC73
96UppDecRTTC-RC106
96UppDecRTTCAS-H24
96Viper-26
96ViperBlaM-26
96ViperCop-26
96ViperGreM-26
96Zen-33
96ZenArtP-33
96ZenHig-12
97ActPac-12
97ActPac-33
97ActPacFI-12
97ActPacFI-33
97ColCho-23
97ColCho-73
97ColChoC-CC27
97ColChoC-CC60
97ColChoS-S46
97ColChoSQ-SQ2
97ColChoTF-E1
97ColChoUD5-UD46
97ColChoUD5-UD47
97FinLinPP2-17
97FinLinPP2$10-79
97FinLinPP2$5-55
97JurPar-33
97JurParC-C5
97JurParR-R12
97JurParT-33
97Max-23
97Max-68
97Pin-23
97Pin-52
97PinArtP-23
97PinArtP-52
97PinCer-26
97PinCer-60
97PinCerMB-26
97PinCerMB-60
97PinCerMG-26
97PinCerMG-60
97PinCerMR-26
97PinCerMR-60
97PinCerR-26
97PinCerR-60
97PinMin-14
97PinMin2GC-14
97PinMinB-14
97PinMinC-14
97PinMinG-14
97PinMinNC-14
97PinMinS-14
97PinPor-20
97PinPor-40
97PinPreP-23
97PinPreP-52
97PinTotCPB-26
97PinTotCPB-60
97PinTotCPG-26
97PinTotCPG-60
97PinTotCPR-26
97PinTotCPR-60
97PinTroC-23
97PinTroC-52
97Pre-27
97PreBlaWFS-27
97PreGri-27
97PreRedW-27
97RacCho-23
97RacCho-58
97RacChoSS-23
97RacChoSS-58
97RacSha-23
97RacShaGWP-23
97RacShaH-23
97RacShaTS-23
97SBMot-15
97SBMot-89
97SP-23
97SP-65
97SP-101
97SP-121
97SP SupS-23
97SP SupS-65
97SP SupS-101
97SP SupS-121
97SPX-23
97SPxBlu-23
97SPxGol-23
97SPxSil-23
97Ult-32
97Ult-57
97UppDecRTTC-17
97UppDecRTTC-59
97UppDecRTTCPPlu-+18
97UDRTTCPPRC-+18
97UppDRTTCPPRDC-+18
97UppDecVC-23
97UppDecVC-73
97Viper-34
97Viper-73
97ViperBlaR-34
97ViperBlaR-73
97ViperSid-S12
97ViperSnaE-SE5
98ColCho-23
98ColCho-59
98HigGea-20
98HigGeaFG-10
98HigGeaGJ-GJ19
98HigGeaM-10
98Max-23
98Max-53
98Max-61
98Max-23
98Max-48
98Max-73
98Max-98
98Max10tA-22
98Max10tA-67
98Max10tAMP-P23
98MaxFieG-14
98MaxFieGTS-14
98MaxFieGTSA-14
98MaxFirC-F2
98MaxFouSGA-14
98MaxSwaP-SW23
98MaxYeaIRBS-74
98PrePas-63
98PrePasGS-40
98PrePasOS-63
98PrePasP-47
98PrePasP-47
98PrePasS-40
98PrePasSO-33
98PrePasSO-34
98PrePasSOD-33
98PrePasSOD-34
98PrePasSS-16
98PrePasSSD-16
98SP Aut-23
98SP Aut-57
98SP Aut-84
98UppDecRttC-23
98UppDecRttC-54
98UppDecRttC-62
98UppDecVC-23
98UppDecVC-68
98UppDecVCPL-PL20
98VIP-25
98VIPExp-25
98Whe-28
98Whe50tA-A13
98WheAut-6
98WheGol-28
98WheGreF-GF16
99Pre-13
99PrePas-13
99PrePas-113
99WheHigG-13
99WheHigGAC-13
99WheHigGFG-13
99WheHigGM-MM8B/9
99WheHigGM-13
99WheHigGM&M-
MM8A/9
99WheHigGS-GS13
Spice, Gordon
78GraPri-187
Spithaler, Ralph Jr.
92VolRacLSI-50
Sprague, Jack
91BulRin-74
92BulRin-48
92MaxBla-80
92MaxRed-80
92ProSet-55
92Tra-48
93FinLin-160
93FinLinCS-26
93FinLinS-160
93Max-54
93MaxPreP-54
93MaxPreS-54
93Tra-121
93Tra-160
93TraFirR-121
93TraFirR-160
94Max-181
94MaxPreS-181
95FinLinSRF-16
95FinLinSRF-39
95FinLinSRF-48
95FinLinSup-16
95FinLinSup-39
95FinLinSup-48
97VIP-45
97VIPExp-45
97VIPOilS-45
98HigGea-43
98HigGeaFG-43
98HigGeaM-43
98PrePas-51
98PrePas-83
98PrePasOS-51
98PrePasOS-83
98Whe-68
98WheGol-68
99Pre-54
99PrePas-54
Spraker, Jeff
91WinChoNED-71
91WinChoNED-72
92WinChoB-45
92WinChoB-46
Springsteen, Frank
91DKIMCDT-28
Spurlock, K.C.
91ProSetN-22
91ProSetN-71
95ActPacN-15
95ActPacNSS-15
Squier, Ken
90Max-158
91Max-234
92MaxBla-228
92MaxRed-228
93Max-218
93MaxPreS-218
94MaxPreS-210
95MaxPreS-212
St. James, Lyn
93HiTecI-27
93HiTecI-46
93HiTecICFF-SP11
94HiTecI-26
94HiTecICD-CD29
95SkyInd5-24
95SkyInd5-91
96SkyInd5-4
96SkyInd5-37
96SkyInd5-86
96SkyInd5RY-7
97Hi-IRL-13
St.Amant, Bud
92TraASA-25
St.Amant, Gary
92TraASA-24
St.Clair, Dave
92WinChoB-109
92WinChoB-110
Stacy, Nelson
89TGRacMR-126
89TGRacMR-127
89TGRacMR-148
89WinCir-42
91TGRacMRU-126
91TGRacMRU-127
91TGRacMRU-148
Staepelaere, Gilbert
78GraPri-235
Stahl, Mark
88MaxCha-71
90Max-128
91Max-82
92MaxBla-82
92MaxRed-82
Staley, Enoch
89TGRacMR-144
91TGRacMRU-144
Staley, Gwyn
89TGRacMR-142
89TGRacMR-144
91GalPrePR-90
91TGRacMRU-142
91TGRacMRU-144
92SpoLegBB-BB26
Stambaugh, Steve
91WorOut-93
92RacLegS-15
Stanard, Scott
92TraTeaS-183
Standridge, Billy
89Max-212
90Max-140
91Max-114
94MaxRooC'-9
94Pow-37
94PowGol-37
95Max-144
95MaxPreS-47
95MaxPreS-193
Stanfield, Greg
93FinLinN-117
Stanley, Robbie
88WorOut-27
Stansberry, Jeff
91HavAT-20
Starkey, Richard
92BulRin-193
Starnes, Gene

92RSSMotH-14
Statler, Jason
91WorOut-94
Stauffer, Kent
92TraASA-45
Stavola, Bill
89Max-19
90Max-153
91Max-155
91ProSet-124
91Tra-118
92MaxBla-130
92MaxMot-20
92MaxRed-130
92Tra-118
93FinLin-50
93FinLinCS-11
93FinLinS-50
93Max-123
93MaxPreP-110
93MaxPreS-123
93Tra-59
93TraFirR-59
94HigGea-150
94HigGeaDO-150
94HigGeaDOG-150
94HigGeaG-150
94Max-104
94MaxPreP-104
94MaxPreS-104
94PrePas-86
95Max-82
95MaxCroC-86
95MaxPreP-86
95MaxPreS-97
96MaxPre-107
Stavola, Mickey
89Max-19
91Tra-118
92Tra-118
93Max-124
93MaxPreP-111
93MaxPreS-124
93Tra-59
93TraFirR-59
94HigGea-151
94HigGeaDO-151
94HigGeaDOG-151
94HigGeaG-151
94Max-105
94MaxPreP-105
94MaxPreS-105
94PrePas-86
95Max-84
95MaxCroC-87
95MaxPreP-87
95MaxPreS-99
Steele, Jack
91Tra-145
Steele, Tim
92BulRin-61
94LanARCF-2
94LanARCF-91
94LanARCF-P2
Stefanik, Mike
91WinChoM-59
91WinChoM-60
91WinChoNED-100
91WinChoNED-101
98PrePas-84
98PrePasOS-84
99Pre-75
99PrePas-75
Steinbach, Bill
92VolRacLS2-64
Steinhaus, Gibby
92JAG-111
Stellfox, Mares
91K&WURCS-18
Stenhouse, Ricky
91WorOut-45
Stephens, Dirk
94HigGea-172
94HigGeaDO-172
94HigGeaDOG-172
94HigGeaG-172
95MaxPreS-181
96MaxPre-249
Stettenbauer, Ralph
91K&WURCS-40
Stevens, Carl
91LanSeeS-12
Stevens, Jeff
92PacAmeCT-25
Stevens, Mark
92JAG-239
Steward, Brian
91LanRocS-65
Stewart, Jackie
71MobTheSoGPMR-36
73NabSugDSC-1
77Spo-1716
77Spo-2312
77Spo-3219
77Spo-5907
93MaxWilR-35
Stewart, Kurt
91DKIMCDT-30
Stewart, Tony
91DKIMCDT-20
97Hi-IRL-9
97Hi-IRLP-D3
97Hi-IRLP-P7
98PrePasP-5
98PrePasP-5
98PrePasS-21
98PrePasS-44
98PrePasSF-44
98UppDecRttC-115
98VIP-36
98VIPExp-36
98Whe-58
98Whe-63
98WheGol-58
98WheGol-63
99Pre-61
99Pre-94
99PrePas-61
99PrePas-94
99UppDecVC-88
99UppDecVCUE-88
99WheHigG-45
99WheHigG-61
99WheHigGFG-45
99WheHigGFG-61
99WheHigGM-45
99WheHigGM-61
Stine, Jim
92CorSelCCS-16
93CorSelCCS-11
Stivenson, Al
92VolRacLSI-51
Stockdale, Rod
92VolRacLSI-52
Stockel, Bob
91LanSeeS-20
Stokes, Charlie
91BulRin-96
92BulRin-99
Stokes, Johnny
91JAG-26
92JAG-240
Stommelen, Rolf
78GraPri-36
78GraPri-64
78GraPri-195
78GraPri-202
Stone, Andy
94LanARCF-48
Stott, Harold
92MaxAllPT-10
92MaxBla-238
92MaxRed-238
93Max-257
93MaxPreS-257
94MaxPreS-246
Stott, Ramo
89TGRacMR-86
89TGRacMR-87
89TGRacMR-90
91TGRacMRU-86
91TGRacMRU-87
91TGRacMRU-90
Stovall, Scott
91LanARCHS-5
Stradtman, John
94LanARCF-74
Strait, Bob
92LanARCF-23
94LanARCF-7
94LanARCF-96
95FinLinSRF-34
95FinLinSRF-67
95FinLinSup-34
95FinLinSup-67
95MaxSup-13
96PrePas-72
96PrePasSco-72
96PrePasT-72
Strang, Lewis P.
11AmeTobAD-22
Strasser, Ray
92ProSetN-159
Streiff, Philippe
87AceForO-29
88HerFouFO-6C
Strickland, Dennis
95JSKIce-32
Strickland, Doug
91BulRin-122
Stricklin, Hut
88MaxCha-28
89Max-57
90Max-57
91ACRac-9
91Max-12
91MaxMcD-28
91MaxUpd-12
91ProSet-37
91ProSet-39
91ProSetP-P2
91ProSetP-P3
91SpoLegDA-DA6
91SpoLegHS-P1
91SpoLegHS-HS1
91SpoLegHS-HS2
91SpoLegHS-HS3
91SpoLegHS-HS4
91SpoLegHS-HS5
91SpoLegHS-HS6
91SpoLegHS-HS7
91SpoLegHS-HS8
91SpoLegHS-HS9
91SpoLegHS-HS10
91SpoLegHS-HS11
91SpoLegHS-HS12
91SpoLegHS-HS13
91SpoLegHS-HS14
91SpoLegHS-HS15
91SpoLegHS-HS16
91SpoLegHS-HS17
91SpoLegHS-HS18
91SpoLegHS-HS19
91SpoLegHS-HS20
91SpoLegHS-HS21
91SpoLegHS-HS22
91SpoLegHS-HS23
91SpoLegHS-HS24
91SpoLegHS-HS25
91SpoLegHS-HS26
91SpoLegHS-HS27
91SpoLegHS-HS28
91SpoLegHS-HS29
91SpoLegHS-HS30
91Tra-12
92ACDel-8
92ACRacP-6
92DaySer1-6
92MacTooWC-1
92MaxBla-12
92MaxMcD-23
92MaxRed-12
92MaxTheW-20
92MaxTheW-40
92ProSet-40
92ProSet-67A
92ProSet-67B
92ProSet-103
92ProSet-110
92ProSetMH-21
92ProSetTTHS-1
92ProSetTTHS-5
92ProSetTTHS-6
92RPM-11
92Tra-12
92Tra-92
92TraRacM-12
92TraRacM-38
92TraRacM-84
92TraTeaS-151
92TraTeaS-152
92TraTeaS-153
92TraTeaS-154
92TraTeaS-155
93ActPac-69
93ActPac-149
93ActPac-159
93ActPac-189
93ActPac2G-71G
93FinLin-9
93FinLin-136
93FinLin-180
93FinLinCS-15
93FinLinCS-28
93FinLinDA-10
93FinLinS-9
93FinLinS-136
93FinLinS-180
93Max-27
93MaxHou-27
93MaxMot-20
93MaxMot-40
93MaxPreP-27
93MaxPreS-27
93TraPreC-10
94ActPac-24
94ActPac-84
94ActPac-116
94ActPac-164
94ActPac2G-38G
94ActPacSJ-1
94ActPacSJ-2
94CarDynGO-5
94DaySer3-35
94FinLin-12
94FinLin-35
94FinLin-127
94FinLinG-2
94FinLinG-5
94FinLinG-67
94FinLinG-73
94FinLinS-12
94FinLinS-35
94FinLinS-127
94HigGea-17
94HigGea-123
94HigGeaDO-123
94HigGeaDOG-123
94HigGeaG-17
94HigGeaG-123
94Max-27
94Max-263
94Max-274
94MaxMed-34
94MaxMot-16
94MaxPreP-27
94MaxPreP-38
94MaxPreS-27
94MaxTheS2-24
94OptXL-21
94OptXLRH-21
94Pow-119
94Pow-131
94PowGol-119
94PowGol-131
94PowPre-7
94PowPre-28
94PrePas-26
94PrePasCC-CC26
94VIP-32
95CroJew-47
95CroJewD-47
95CroJewE-47
95CroJewS-47
95HiTecB4-18
95HiTecB4-42
95HiTecB4-85
95Ima-26
95ImaGol-26
95Max-23
95Max-179
95Max-209
95Max-210
95MaxLicD-5
95MaxMed-19
95MaxMed-49
95MaxMedB-19
95MaxMedB-49
95MaxOveW-3
95MaxPreSU-3
95OptXL-21
95OptXLCB-21
95OptXLDC-21
95OptXLRH-21
95PrePas-30
95PrePasCC-30
95PrePasRH-30
95Sel-31
95SelFlaO-31
95SP-20
95SP-58
95SP-99
95SPDieC-20
95SPDieC-58
95SPDieC-99
95Tra5thA-35
95Tra5thAG-35
95UppDec-30
95UppDec-98
95UppDecGSEG-30
95UppDecGSEG-98
95UppDecSSES-30
95UppDecSSES-98
95Zen-5
96ActPacC-44
96ActPacCSS-44
96Ass-22
96AutRac-21
96AutRacA-55
96AutRacCA-55
96FinLin-16
96FinLin-73
96FinLinPP-33
96FinLinPP$S-33
96FinLinPriP-16
96FinLinPriP-73
96FinLinS-16
96FinLinS-73
96Fla-32
96Fla-88
96Max-26
96MaxPre-26
96Pin-8
96Pin-65
96Pin-8
96Pin-65
96PinPolP-8
96PinPolPLF-8
96PinWinCC-8
96PinWinCC-65
96PrePas-31
96PrePasCC-31
96PrePasSco-31
96PrePasT-31
96RacCho-104
96RacChoAP-104
96RacChoSC-104
96SP-8
96TraRevP-33
96TraRevPFR-33
96TraRevPM-33
96Ult-114
96Ult-115
96Ult-116
96UltUpd-30
96UltUpd-76
96UltUpd-87
96UppDec-24
96UppDec-65
96UppDec-104
96UppDecRTTC-RC33
96UppDecRTTC-RC82
96UppDecRTTC-RC115
96ViperBusC-B3
96Zen-16
96ZenArtP-16
97ActPac-60
97ActPacFI-60
97AutRac-25
97AutRacA-50
97AutRacMS-KM25
97ColCho-8
97ColCho-58
97ColChoC-CC12
97ColChoC-CC45
97ColChoC-CC78
97ColChoSQ-SQ9
97ColChoUD5-UD14
97ColChoUD5-UD15
97JurPar-27
97JurParT-27
97Max-8
97Max-53
97PinCer-33
97PinCer-67
97PinCerMB-33
97PinCerMB-67
97PinCerMG-33
97PinCerMG-67
97PinCerMR-33
97PinCerMR-67
97PinCerR-33
97PinCerR-67
97PinTotCPB-33
97PinTotCPB-67
97PinTotCPG-33
97PinTotCPG-67
97PinTotCPR-33
97PinTotCPR-67
97Pre-16

92PacAmeCT-41
Thompson, Speedy
89TGRacMR-5
89TGRacMR-6
89TGRacMR-9
89WinCir-27
91TGRacMRU-5
91TGRacMRU-6
91TGRacMRU-9
92SpoLegBB-BB9
Thornburg, Wade
92TraTeaS-180
Thousand, Jeff
94HigGeaPPT-W13
94HigGeaPPTG-13W
Throneburg, Terry
92TraTeaS-37
94MaxTexEl-47
Thurm, Ken
90BigTimD-17
90BigTimDS-17
91BigTimD-56
Thurman, Andy
91BulRin-9
Thurman, Joe
89Max-179
90Max-136
Thurwanger, Charlie
72FleAHRDN-5
Till, Brian
95SkyInd5-39
95SkyInd5-54
95SkyInd5-84
Tilley, Don
92BikRacS-31
Tillman, Carol
91GalPrePR-6
Tillman, Curt
90LanRocSHS-9
91LanRocS-1
Timmerman, Mike
92TraCouSR-9
Tims, Paul
94JAG-57
Tinker, Mike
94JAG-58
Tissot, Lee
92BulRin-199
Tobias, Ronnie
91K&WDirT-31
92K&WDirT-8
94K&WDirT-25
Tobias, Toby Jr.
91K&WDirT-36
92K&WDirT-7
94K&WDirT-7
Tobler, Rahn
91ProSetN-121
92ProSetN-174
Toemmes, Mike
91BulRin-130
Tomaino, Greg
91WinChoM-76
91WinChoM-77
Tomaino, Jamie
91WinChoM-53
91WinChoM-54
Tomlinson, Bob
91Tra-104
Toner, Boyd Sr.
93CorSelCCS-9
Torkelson, Bob
90LanRocSHS-6
Torkelson, Wayne
91BigTimD-29
Townes, William
90BigTimD-18
90BigTimDS-18
Townsend, Johnny
92TraKodEl-18
92TraTeaS-110
Tracy, Joseph
11AmeTobAD-24
95TraVal-12
Tracy, Paul
92GriForO-167
93HiTecI-19
93HiTecI-55
94HiTecI-31
94HiTecICD-CD34
95HiTecICD-CD6
95SkyInd5-5
95SkyInd5-8
95SkyInd5-43
95SkyInd5-95
95SkyInd5HI-5
96SkyInd5-25
96SkyInd5-78
Trammell, Gregory
91MaxBilETCM-34
Trammell, Jack
91DirTra-19
92DirTra-94
92JAG-115
Trammell, James
91BulRin-27
Trammell, Johnny
91MaxBilETCM-31
Treece, Jeff
91DirTra-70
Tremont, Kenny
91K&WDirT-38
92K&WDirT-10
92TraDir-13
94K&WDirT-8
95K&WDirT-14
Trentham, Tuck
91BulRin-111
92BulRin-26
Trevino, Roy
90BigTimD-19
90BigTimDS-19
91BigTimD-63
Trickle, Dick
90Max-66
90Max-150
91Max-66
91MaxMcD-22A
91MaxMcD-22B
91MaxTheWA-18
91MaxUpd-66
91Tra-61
92CoyRoo-11
92MaxBla-46
92MaxBlaU-U16
92MaxMcD-36
92MaxMot-9
92MaxMot-44
92MaxRed-46
92MaxRedU-U16
92ProSet-56
92ProSet-76
92ProSet-123
92ProSet-154
92ProSet-200
92RedSta-13
92Tra-61
92TraASA-33
92TraCouSR-1
92TraCouSR-2
92TraCouSR-4
92TraCouSR-6
92TraCouSR-8
92TraCouSR-10
92TraRacM-8
92TraRacM-79
92TraRacMB-8B
93FinLin-70
93FinLinCS-13
93FinLinS-70
93Max-75
93MaxPreP-75
93MaxPreS-75
93Tra-13
93Tra-103
93Tra-195
93TraFirR-13
93TraFirR-103
93TraFirR-195
93TraPreC-19
93WheRooT-30
93WheRooTPla-30
94ActPac-60
94HigGea-14
94HigGeaG-14
94Max-41
94Max-273
94MaxPreP-41
94MaxPreS-41
94MaxRooY-11
94Pow-120
94PowGol-120
94PrePas-50
94Sky-NNO
94Tra-180
94TraAutV-28
94TraFirR-180
94TraPreC-31
94WheHarG-12
94WheHarGG-12
95ActPacC-78
95ActPacCSS-78
95ActPacP-20
95ActPacS-27
95ActPacSSS-27
95Ass-14
95Ass1M$PC-1
95AssGolS-14
95FinLin-50
95FinLinCC6-14
95FinLinPP-50
95FinLinSil-50
95Ima-15
95Ima-69
95ImaGol-15
95ImaGol-69
95Max-32
95Max-184
95MaxCroC-32
95MaxCroC-58
95MaxLicD-4
95MaxPreP-32
95MaxPreP-58
95MaxPrePSTP-PRE5
95MaxPreS-32
95MaxPreS-58
95PrePas-31
95PrePasCC-31
95PrePasRH-31
95SP-46
95SP-88
95SPDieC-46
95SPDieC-88
95Tra-38
95Tra5thA-32
95Tra5thA-55
95Tra5thAG-32
95Tra5thAG-55
95TraAutV-41
95TraFirR-38
95TraRacM-RM13
95TraSerS-SS14
95UppDec-23
95UppDec-66
95UppDec-91
95UppDec-124
95UppDec-195
95UppDec-239
95UppDec-276
95UppDecA-195
95UppDecGSEG-23
95UppDecGSEG-66
95UppDecGSEG-91
95UppDecGSEG-124
95UppDecGSEG-195
95UppDecGSEG-239
95UppDecGSEG-276
95UppDecSSES-23
95UppDecSSES-66
95UppDecSSES-91
95UppDecSSES-124
95UppDecSSES-195
95UppDecSSES-239
95UppDecSSES-276
95VIP-27
95VIPCooB-27
95VIPEmeP-27
95VIPRedHCB-27
95Zen-15
95Zen-45
96Ass-36
96AutRac-38
96AutRacA-56
96AutRacCA-56
96Cla-4
96ClaPriP-4
96ClaSil-4
96FinLin-22
96FinLinPP-34
96FinLinPP$S-34
96FinLinPriP-22
96FinLinS-22
96Max-15
96MaxPre-15
96MaxPre-55
96PrePas-32
96PrePasCC-32
96PrePasSco-32
96PrePasT-32
96SP-40
96Ult-81
96Ult-82
96Ult-83
96UltAut-35
96UppDec-13
96UppDec-53
96UppDec-93
96UppDecRTTC-RC116
97AutRac-30
97AutRacA-51
97AutRacMS-KM30
97ColCho-40
97ColCho-90
97ColChoSQ-SQ13
97ColChoUD5-UD83
97ColChoUD5-UD84
97Max-14
97Max-59
97MaxRoootY-MR2
97SBMot-74
97SkyPro-28
97SkyProA-28
97SP-39
97SP-81
97SP SupS-39
97SP SupS-81
97Ult-34
97UltDouT-DT2
97UltUpd-24
97UltUpdAR-24
97UppDecRTTC-36
97UppDecRTTC-78
97UppDecVC-40
97UppDecVC-90
97Viper-35
97ViperBlaR-35
98MaxSwaP-SW22
98MaxYealRBS-114
98UppDecRttC-37
98UppDecRttC-107
98UppDecVC-14
98UppDecVC-59
99UppDecVC-32
99UppDecVCUE-32
Trimmer, Carl
92DirTra-95
Triplett, Steve
94HigGeaPPT-W25
94HigGeaPPTG-25W
Tripp Jr., Kenneth
89CheFlal-58
91BigTimD-71
Tripp Sr., Kenneth
89CheFlal-59
Tripp, Bobby
91LanSeeS-23
Tripp, John
91LanSeeS-9
Tripp, Perry
94LanARCF-72
Tripp, Scott
91LanRocS-65
Trombley, Jeff
92TraDir-4
Trower, Mike
95OptXL-40
95OptXLCB-40
95OptXLDC-40
95OptXLRH-40
98PrePas-68
98PrePasOS-68
Troxel, Mike
89MegDra-14
89MegDra-15
Tucker, Bill
92TraCouSR-9
Tucker, Bruce
90LanRocSHS-39
Tullius, Bob
90Max-44
91Max-110
Tulonen, Reino
89TGRacMR-106
91TGRacMRU-106
Tuma, Mike
92RedGraST-23
Turner, Bobby
92HavAT-11
Turner, Brad
94HigGeaPPT-G26
94HigGeaPPTG-26G
Turner, Curtis
89Max-188
89WinCir-33
91GalPrePR-9
91GalPrePR-15
91GalPrePR-21
91GalPrePR-49
91GalPrePR-69
91GalPrePR-91
91SpoLegNJ-NJ20
92HilG.HGTL-5
94PrePas-135
98PrePas-130
Turner, Jack
62MarInd-14
Turner, John
95JSKS.OS-77T
Turner, Melvin
91MaxBilETCM-2
Turner, Sprague
91Tra-48
Turner, Wren
92JAG-242
Tyler, Bill
95JSKS.OS-20
Tyler, Brian
95JSKS.OS-3S
Tyner, Roy
89TGRacMR-44
91TGRacMRU-44
Tyron, Jim
92JAG-241
Tyrrell, Ken
77Spo-8821
92GriForO-140
Ulrich, D.K.
83UNORac-5
91Max-156
91Tra-155
92MaxBla-127
92MaxRed-127
92Tra-155A
92Tra-155B
93Max-120
93MaxPreP-108
93MaxPreS-120
93Tra-108
93TraFirR-108
94Hi-Bri4AP-43
94HigGea-157
94HigGeaDO-157
94HigGeaDOG-157
94HigGeaG-157
94HiTecB4-43
94Max-113
94MaxPreP-113
94MaxPreS-113
95Max-79
95MaxCroC-94
95MaxPreP-94
95MaxPreS-107
95USAirGS-5
Underwood, Rob
92BulRin-196
Ungar, Rick
87WorOut-27
88WorOut-33
90WorOut-50
Unser Jr., Al
83A&SRacI-43
84A&SRacI-47
85A&SRacI-24
85A&SRacI-51
86A&SRacI-10
86BOSInd-7
87A&SRacI-30
88HerFouFO-5C
91AllWorI-1
91AllWorI-45
91AllWorI-75
91AllWorI-100
91IRO-6
91LegInd-59
92AllWorI-21
92AllWorI-84
92ColACAR-42
92GriForO-162
92HiTecMA-46
92LegInd-5
92LegInd-78
93HiTecI-12
93HiTecI-34
93HiTecI-36
93HiTecI-72
93HiTecICFF-SP1
93Max-46
93MaxPreP-46
93Tra-46
93Tra-84

93Tra-197
93TraFirR-46
93TraFirR-84
93TraFirR-197
93TraTri-17
94HiTecI-9
94HiTecICD-CD35
95AssImaP-RI2
95Ima-1
95Ima-49
95ImaCirC-1
95ImaDri-D14
95ImaGol-1
95ImaGol-49
95SkyInd5-8
95SkyInd5-14
95SkyInd5-18
95SkyInd5-19
95SkyInd5-52
95SkyInd5-69
95SkyInd5-70
95SkyInd5-71
95SkyInd5-72
95SkyInd5-73
95SkyInd5-106
95SkyInd5-108
95SkyInd5-NNO
95SkyInd5PC-1
96SkyInd5-8
96SkyInd5CC-1
Unser, Al
73NabSugDSC-6
78GraPri-5
78GraPri-208
78GraPri-209
80AvaHilURG-27
83A&SRacI-48
84A&SRacI-1
85A&SRacI-35
85A&SRacI-51
85SpoPhoGS-NNO
86A&SRacI-1
86BOSInd-8
87A&SRacI-9
91AllWorI-35
91AllWorI-95
91AllWorI-P1
91AllWorI-P2
91IRO-1
91LegInd-71
91LegInd-74
92AllWorI-30
92AllWorI-51
92AllWorI-91
92HiTecP-2
92LegInd-62
92LegInd-72
92LegInd-78
92RPM-6
93HiTecI-22
93HiTecI-38
93HiTecICFF-SP3
93HiTecIP-P6
93MaxPreS-46
94HiTecI-13
95HiTecICD-CD1
95SkyInd5-15
95SkyInd5PC-5
95TraVal-93
95TraVal-98
Unser, Bobby
65DonSpeS-49
65DonSpeS-53
77Spo-1604
78GraPri-212
80AvaHilURG-19
91LegInd-46
91LegInd-70
91SpoLegHH-HH13
92MaxIMH-30
95SkyInd5PC-10
95TraVal-87
Unser, Johnny
91LanAmeIS-4
97Hi-IRL-25
Unser, Robby
91LanAmeIS-3
91LanAmeIS-16
Usry, Tom
91BulRin-100
92BulRin-178
Utsman, John
92JAG-116
93JAG-47
Valasek, Tom
92VolRacLSI-59
Valentine, R.J.
92EriMaxTA-37
92EriMaxTA-38
Van de Poele, Eric
91CarForO-99
91CarForO-100
91ProTraFO-79
91ProTraFO-80
92GriForO-7
92GriForO-40
92GriForO-73
Van Deventer, Jess
65DonSpeS-26
Vance, Buddy
91BulRin-133
Vandergriff, Rob
90BigTimD-20
90BigTimDS-20
90CheFlaI-7
90CheFlaI-36
91BigTimD-95
VanderLaan, Bruce
92TraASA-19
95JSKIcePC-40
VanderLaan, Paul
94HigGeaPPT-W10
94HigGeaPPTG-10W
VanderVeen, Troy
92JAG-117
Vandiver, Jim
89TGRacMR-225
89TGRacMR-226
91TGRacMRU-225
91TGRacMRU-226
VanGuilder, William
92VolRacLS2-65
VanHorn, Jerry Allen
91BulRin-17
92BulRin-17
Vanke, Arlen
71FleAHRDC-1
73FleAHRRU-52
Vann, Leroy
94JAG-59
VanNote, Steve
95JSKS.OS-5
Vansciver, Bob
90CheFlaI-98
91BigTimD-41
91BigTimD-90
VanVallis, Chuck
90CheFlaI-31
Varzi, Achille
62PetLimGPRC-2
Vasser, Jimmy
92GriForO-175
93HiTecI-28
93HiTecI-56
93HiTecI-75
94HiTecI-14
94HiTecICD-CD36
95SkyInd5-34
95SkyInd5-76
95SkyInd5HI-2
96SkyInd5-18
96SkyInd5-76
97CARSchC-6
Vaughn, Ricky
91BulRin-117
Velez, Fermin
97Hi-IRL-23
Venable, Jim
95ActPacC-100
Veney, Ken
92ProSetN-155
93FinLinN-41
Venturini, Bill
91LanARCHS-25
91LanART-14
91Max-143
91ProSet-11
92LanARCF-1
92LanARCF-13
92LanARCF-37
92LanARCF-44
92MaxBla-61
92MaxRed-61
92ProSet-141
93Max-47
93MaxPreP-47
93MaxPreS-47
94LanARCF-68
94LanARCF-73
96PrePas-112
96PrePasSco-112
96PrePasT-112
Verly, Les
91DKIMCDT-36
Vess, Jerry
94HigGeaPPT-G23
94HigGeaPPTG-23G
Vessels, Frank
95ActPacSTTH-3
Viers, Ricky
94HigGeaPPT-G5
94HigGeaPPTG-5G
Villeneuve, Gilles
77Spo-7723
78GraPri-15
78GraPri-23
78GraPri-43
78GraPri-62
78GraPri-117
78GraPri-123
78GraPri-132
78GraPri-144
78GraPri-158
78GraPri-159
91CarForO-103
91CarForO-104
91ProTraFO-196
91ProTraFO-197
92GriForO-148
92GriForO-149
92GriForO-150
92GriForO-151
92GriForO-152
92GriForO-152
92GriForO-154
92GriForO-155
92GriForO-156
92GriForO-157
92GriForO-159
Villeneuve, Jacques (Gilles Brother)
85A&SRacI-48
86A&SRacI-41
87A&SRacI-42
92GriForO-172
Villeneuve, Jacques (Gilles Son)
95HiTecICD-CD7
95SkyInd5-13
95SkyInd5-22
95SkyInd5-62
95SkyInd5-74
95SkyInd5-FIN1
95SkyInd5HI-6
96SkyInd5-14
96SkyInd5-49
96SkyInd5-55
96SkyInd5-88
96SkyInd5CC-6
96SkyInd5RY-9
Villoresi, Gigi
77Spo-7711
Villota, Emilio
78GraPri-76
Vineyard, H.E.
91DirTra-3
92JAG-118
Vineyard, Mark
91DirTra-33
Virden, Johnny
92JAG-243
95HavAT-21
Visconti, Pete
91K&WDirT-30
92K&WDirT-42
94K&WDirT-14
95K&WDirT-27
Vitolo, Dennis
92AllWorI-35
95SkyInd5-33
95SkyInd5-58
95SkyInd5-65
95SkyInd5-98
Vogel, Dennis
92TraASA-29
Vogler, Rich
86AceInd-B4
89WorOut-65
92AllWorI-52
Vogt, Red
91GalPrePR-46
91TGRacTL-14
Von Dohren, Craig
91K&WDirT-49
92K&WDirT-50
94K&WDirT-16
95K&WDirT-15
Vukovich III, Bill
91AllWorI-2
91AllWorI-63
96SkyInd5RY-2
Vukovich Jr., Bill
80AvaHilURG-12
84A&SRacI-49
92AllWorI-64
Vukovich, Bill Sr.
54StaWetIW-1953
60HawWaxI-37
91LegInd-76
92MaxIMH-31
95TraVal-59
Wade, Billy
93WheRooT-6
93WheRooTPla-6
Wagers, Barrie
95ActPacNJDC-6
Wagner, Brad
90LanRocSHS-27
91LanRocS-33
91LanRocS-60
92LanRocS-52
92LanRocS-53
Wagner, Dave
90LanRocSHS-18
91LanRocS-56
91LanRocS-64
92LanRocS-54
Wagner, Louis
11AmeTobAD-25
95TraVal-14
Wagner, Rob
92LanRocS-55
Waid, Keith
91LanARCHS-20
92LanARCF-27
Waid, Steve
91Tra-129
91Tra-130
92Tra-130
Wakefield, J.P.
39ChuKinoS-23
Waldegaard, Bjorn
78GraPri-232
Waldrop, Jim
91MaxBilETCM-1
Walen, Mel
91LanStoCC-7
92RedGraST-6
94MaxPreS-253
96MaxPre-208
96PrePas-105
96PrePasSco-105
96PrePasT-105
Walerd, Lee
95TraVal-57
Walker, David
92TraTeaS-194
Walker, Harry
91DKIMCDT-37
Walker, Jeff
93JAG-48
Walker, Jimmy
92TraTeaS-180
Walker, Mike
92JAG-244
Walker, Steve
91BulRin-38
92BulRin-89
Walkinshaw, Tom
92GriForO-134
Wallace, Kenny
89Max-178
89Max-210
90Max-95
91Max-39
91MaxUpd-39
91Tra-36
92LimEdiKW-1
92LimEdiKW-2
92LimEdiKW-3
92LimEdiKW-4
92LimEdiKW-5
92LimEdiKW-6
92LimEdiKW-7
92LimEdiKW-8
92LimEdiKW-9
92LimEdiKW-10
92LimEdiKW-11
92LimEdiKW-12
92LimEdiKW-13
92LimEdiKW-14
92LimEdiKW-15
92LimEdiP-2
92MacTooWC-19
92MaxBla-24
92MaxBlaU-U17
92MaxRed-24
92MaxRedU-U17
92ProSet-9
92RedSta-28
92Tra-15
92Tra-23
92Tra-24
92Tra-36
92TraASA-32
92TraGoo-2
92TraRacMB-14B
92WheRusW-9
92WheRusWG-9
92WinChoB-62
92WinChoB-63
92WinChoBA-4
93ACRacF-40
93ActPac-35
93ActPac-60
93ActPac-63
93ActPac-101
93ActPac-102
93ActPac-151
93ActPac-154
93ActPac-156
93ActPac-163
93ActPac-178
93ActPac2G-9G
93ActPac2G-12G
93ActPac2G-27G
93ActPac2G-30G
93ActPac2G-32G
93ActPac2G-60G
93DaySer2RW-16
93FinLin-112
93FinLin-151
93FinLin-154
93FinLinCS-15
93FinLinCS-17
93FinLinCS-29
93FinLinS-112
93FinLinS-151
93FinLinS-154
93Max-40
93Max-177
93MaxHou-19
93MaxHou-24
93MaxHou-26
93MaxLowFS-1
93MaxPreP-40
93MaxPreP-82
93MaxPreP-NNO
93MaxPreS-40
93MaxPreS-177
93MaxWinM-2
93PrePasPre-17
93PrePasPre-20
93PrePasPre-25
93StoTop-4
93WheRooT-34
93WheRooT-53
93WheRooT-54
93WheRooT-63
93WheRooT-74
93WheRooT-75
93WheRooT-83
93WheRooTPla-34
93WheRooTPla-53
93WheRooTPla-54
93WheRooTPla-63
93WheRooTPla-74
93WheRooTPla-75
93WheRooTPla-83
93WheRooTPro-P3
94ActPac-23
94ActPac-204
94FinLin-18
94FinLinG-37
94FinLinGA-37
94FinLinS-18
94Hi-Bri4AP-11
94Hi-Bri4AP-26
94Hi-Bri4AP-59
94HigGea-16

97RacShaTS-13
97SBMot-37
97SP-41
97SP-83
97SP SupS-41
97SP SupS-83
97UppDecRTTC-39
97UppDecRTTC-81
97UppDecRTTC-144
98ColCho-85
98Max10tA-100
98UppDecRttC-111
98UppDecVC-32
98UppDecVC-77
99UppDecVC-39
99UppDecVCUE-39

Wallace, Rusty

88MaxCha-14
88MaxCha-62
89Max-27
89Max-54
89Max-114
89Max-125
89Max-127
89Max-152
89Max-154
89Max-165
89Max-166
89Max-167
89Max-169
89Max-210
89MaxCri-5
89MaxPre-NNO
90ACRacPW-1
90Max-27
90Max-168
90Max-187
90Max-190
90Max-196
90Max-197
90Max-198
90MaxHolF-HF4
91ACRac-2
91IRO-10
91Max-2
91Max-180
91Max-182
91MaxMcD-6
91MaxRacFK-3
91MaxTheWA-19
91MaxWin2AF-19
91ProSet-5
91ProSet-6
91ProSet-8
91SunRacL-2
91Tra-2
91Tra-124
91Tra-179
92ACDel-1
92ACRacP-7
92CarDynGO-4
92CarDynRW-1
92CarDynRW-2
92CarDynRW-3
92CarDynRW-4
92CarDynRW-5
92CoyRoo-6
92DaySer1-2
92MacTooWC-20
92MaxBla-2
92MaxBla-202
92MaxBla-269
92MaxBla-280
92MaxMcD-18
92MaxRed-2
92MaxRed-202
92MaxRed-269
92MaxRed-280
92MaxTheW-6
92MaxTheW-26
92MilGenDRW-NNO
92MilGenDRW-NNO
92MilGenDRW-NNO
92MilGenDRW-NNO
92MilGenDRW-NNO
92MilGenDRW-NNO
92ProSet-12
92ProSet-99
92ProSet-107
92ProSet-115
92ProSetMH-16
92ProSetRF-9
92RPM-8
92SpoLegRW-1
92SpoLegRW-2
92SpoLegRW-3
92SpoLegRW-4
92SpoLegRW-5
92SpoLegRW-6
92SpoLegRW-7
92SpoLegRW-8
92SpoLegRW-9
92SpoLegRW-10
92SpoLegRW-11
92SpoLegRW-12
92SpoLegRW-13
92SpoLegRW-14
92SpoLegRW-15
92SpoLegRW-16
92SpoLegRW-17
92SpoLegRW-18
92SpoLegRW-19
92SpoLegRW-20
92SpoLegRW-21
92SpoLegRW-22
92SpoLegRW-23
92SpoLegRW-24
92SpoLegRW-25
92SpoLegRW-26
92SpoLegRW-27
92SpoLegRW-28
92SpoLegRW-29
92SpoLegRW-30
92SpoLegRW-P1
92Tra-2
92Tra-15
92Tra-72A
92Tra-72B
92Tra-124A
92Tra-124B
92Tra-179A
92Tra-179B
92Tra-P4
92TraASA-13
92TraAut-A2
92TraRacM-2
92TraRacM-24
92TraRacM-58
92TraRacM-64
92TraRacM-78
92TraRacM-81
92TraRacM-98
92WheRusW-2
92WheRusW-5
92WheRusW-6
92WheRusW-8
92WheRusW-9
92WheRusW-10
92WheRusW-11
92WheRusW-12
92WheRusW-13
92WheRusW-14
92WheRusWG-2
92WheRusWG-5
92WheRusWG-6
92WheRusWG-8
92WheRusWG-9
92WheRusWG-10
92WheRusWG-11
92WheRusWG-12
92WheRusWG-13
92WheRusWG-14
93ACRacF-2
93ActPac-6
93ActPac-28
93ActPac-83
93ActPac-84
93ActPac-107
93ActPac-108
93ActPac-163
93ActPac-191
93ActPac-192
93ActPac-193
93ActPac-194
93ActPac-195
93ActPac-196
93ActPac-197
93CarDynDEP-2
93CarDynGO-3
93CarDynQC-5
93DaySer2RW-11
93DaySer2RW-12
93DaySer2RW-13
93DaySer2RW-14
93DaySer2RW-15
93DaySer2RW-16
93DaySer2RW-17
93DaySer2RW-18
93DaySer2RW-19
93DaySer2RW-20
93DaySer2RW-21
93DaySer2RW-22
93DaySer2RW-23
93DaySer2RW-24
93DaySer2RW-25
93FinLin-5
93FinLin-45
93FinLin-122
93FinLinCS-2
93FinLinCS-9
93FinLinCS-21
93FinLinS-5
93FinLinS-45
93FinLinS-122
93HiTecTT-4
93HiTecTT-P1
93Max-2
93Max-286
93MaxCluSBC-3
93MaxCluSBC-6
93MaxHou-10
93MaxHou-19
93MaxPreP-2
93MaxPreP-201
93MaxPreS-2
93MaxPreS-286
93MaxTexDA-8
93MaxTheW-8
93MaxTheW-28
93MilGenDRWPC-NNO
93MilGenDRWPC-NNO
93MilGenDRWPC-NNO
93MilGenDRWPC-NNO
93PrePasPre-15
93PrePasPre-22
93PrePasPre-31
93StoTop-5
93Tra-2
93Tra-25
93Tra-58
93Tra-145
93Tra-164
93Tra-181
93Tra-P2
93TraFirR-2
93TraFirR-25
93TraFirR-58
93TraFirR-145
93TraFirR-164
93TraFirR-181
93TraPreC-11
93TraTri-3
93TraTri-11
93TraTri-29
93TraTri-39
93WheRooT-25
93WheRooT-46
93WheRooT-60
93WheRooT-65
93WheRooT-66
93WheRooT-67
93WheRooT-68
93WheRooT-87
93WheRooT-90
93WheRooTPla-25
93WheRooTPla-46
93WheRooTPla-60
93WheRooTPla-65
93WheRooTPla-66
93WheRooTPla-67
93WheRooTPla-68
93WheRooTPla-87
93WheRooTPla-90
94ActPac-2
94ActPac-31
94ActPac-42
94ActPac-67
94ActPac-108
94ActPac-183
94ActPac-186
94ActPac-190
94ActPac-191
94ActPac-192
94ActPac-204
94ActPac-206
94ActPac2G-1G
94ActPac2G-12G
94ActPac2G-21G
94ActPac2G-183G
94ActPac2G-186G
94ActPac2G-190G
94ActPac2G-191G
94ActPac2G-192G
94ActPacC-16
94ActPacCC-37
94ActPacP-2R945
94ActPacS2G-W5
94CarDynGO-2
94CarDynMM-3
94DaySer3-27
94FinLin-29
94FinLin-74
94FinLin-90
94FinLin-104
94FinLin-5
94FinLin-14
94FinLinDH-10
94FinLinG-10
94FinLinG-16
94FinLinG-24
94FinLinG-59
94FinLinG-68
94FinLinGCC-NNO
94FinLinGS-NNO
94FinLinGT-TG1
94FinLinP-P3
94FinLinS-29
94FinLinS-74
94FinLinS-90
94FinLinS-104
94FinLinVL-VL9
94FinLinVL-VL10
94Hi-Bri4AP-2
94Hi-Bri4AP-28
94Hi-Bri4AP-37
94HigGea-2
94HigGea-70
94HigGea-71
94HigGea-76
94HigGea-80
94HigGea-81
94HigGea-82
94HigGea-91
94HigGea-187
94HigGea-193
94HigGea-194
94HigGea-196
94HigGea-198
94HigGea-200
94HigGeaD-D2
94HigGeaDO-187
94HigGeaDO-193
94HigGeaDO-194
94HigGeaDO-196
94HigGeaDO-198
94HigGeaDO-200
94HigGeaDOG-187
94HigGeaDOG-193
94HigGeaDOG-194
94HigGeaDOG-196
94HigGeaDOG-198
94HigGeaDOG-200
94HigGeaG-2
94HigGeaG-70
94HigGeaG-71
94HigGeaG-76
94HigGeaG-80
94HigGeaG-81
94HigGeaG-82
94HigGeaG-91
94HigGeaG-187
94HigGeaG-193
94HigGeaG-194
94HigGeaG-196
94HigGeaG-198
94HigGeaG-200
94HigGeaMG-MG3
94HigGeaP-P2
94HigGeaPPT-W2
94HigGeaPPT-W34
94HigGeaPPT-W35
94HigGeaPPT-W36
94HigGeaPPT-W37
94HigGeaPPT-W38
94HigGeaPPT-W39
94HigGeaPPT-W40
94HigGeaPPT-W41
94HigGeaPPTG-2W
94HigGeaPPTG-34W
94HigGeaPPTG-35W
94HigGeaPPTG-36W
94HigGeaPPTG-37W
94HigGeaPPTG-38W
94HigGeaPPTG-39W
94HigGeaPPTG-40W
94HigMinV-6B
94HigMinV-6S
94HiTecB4-2
94HiTecB4-28
94HiTecB4-37
94Max-2
94Max-34
94Max-199
94Max-206
94Max-208
94Max-212
94Max-213
94Max-214
94Max-223
94Max-230
94Max-231
94Max-233
94Max-235
94Max-237
94Max-322
94Max-335
94MaxMed-4
94MaxMed-69
94MaxMot-2
94MaxPreP-2
94MaxPreP-34
94MaxPreP-99
94MaxPreP-118
94MaxPreP-167
94MaxPreP-171
94MaxPreP-172
94MaxPreP-173
94MaxPreP-182
94MaxPreP-189
94MaxPreP-190
94MaxPreP-192
94MaxPreP-194
94MaxPreP-196
94MaxPreS-2
94MaxPreS-34
94MaxPreS-258
94MaxPreS-265
94MaxPreS-267
94MaxPreS-271
94MaxPreS-272
94MaxPreS-273
94MaxPreS-282
94MaxPreS-289
94MaxPreS-290
94MaxPreS-292
94MaxPreS-294
94MaxPreS-296
94MaxPreSJ-9
94MaxRacC-3
94MaxRooY-6
94MaxTheS2-2
94OptXL-22
94OptXL-30
94OptXL-35
94OptXL-40
94OptXL-51
94OptXL-52
94OptXLP-2A
94OptXLP-2B
94OptXLRH-22
94OptXLRH-30
94OptXLRH-35
94OptXLRH-40
94OptXLRH-51
94OptXLRH-52
94Pow-17
94Pow-39
94Pow-54
94Pow-63
94Pow-122
94Pow-123
94PowGol-17
94PowGol-39
94PowGol-54
94PowGol-63
94PowGol-122
94PowGol-123
94PowPre-8
94PrePas-28
94PrePas-31
94PrePas-47
94PrePas-118
94PrePas-123
94PrePas-144
94PrePasA-NNO
94PrePasCC-CC28
94PrePasCF-CF4
94PrePasH-H6
94PrePasRD-RD9
94Sky-12

94Tra-2
94Tra-62
94Tra-72
94Tra-80
94Tra-102
94Tra-157
94Tra-187
94Tra-193
94TraAut-A12
94TraAutV-21
94TraAutV-49
94TraCar-C2
94TraFirR-2
94TraFirR-62
94TraFirR-72
94TraFirR-80
94TraFirR-102
94TraFirR-157
94TraFirR-187
94TraFirR-193
94TraPreC-21
94TraWin-W2
94TraWin-W6
94TraWin-W9
94TraWin-W24
94VIP-34
94VIP-48
94VIP-81
94VIP-P4
94VIPDriC-DC9
94VIPExc2-EC7
94WheHarG-73
94WheHarGG-73
95ActPacC-12
95ActPacC-38
95ActPacC-39
95ActPacC-40
95ActPacC-41
95ActPacC-42
95ActPacC-43
95ActPacC2CC-3
95ActPacC2T-8
95ActPacCSS-12
95ActPacCSS-38
95ActPacCSS-39
95ActPacCSS-40
95ActPacCSS-41
95ActPacCSS-42
95ActPacCSS-43
95ActPacM-MM3
95ActPacP-23
95ActPacP-46
95ActPacP-58
95ActPacP-61
95ActPacP-77
95ActPacP2G-9G
95ActPacS-25
95ActPacS-32
95ActPacS-53
95ActPacS-76
95ActPacS-77
95ActPacS-78
95ActPacS-79
95ActPacS-80
95ActPacS-81
95ActPacS2G-8G
95ActPacS2G-17G
95ActPacS2G-18G
95ActPacSSS-25
95ActPacSSS-32
95ActPacSSS-53
95ActPacSSS-76
95ActPacSSS-77
95ActPacSSS-78
95ActPacSSS-79
95ActPacSSS-80
95ActPacSSS-81
95Ass-2
95Ass-30
95Ass-47
95Ass10PC-5
95Ass$5$25PC-9
95Ass1M$PC-18
95AssCocC6DC-2
95AssGolS-2
95AssGolS-30
95AssGolS-47
95CroJew-4
95CroJewD-4
95CroJewDJ-DJ2
95CroJewDJD-DJ2
95CroJewDJE-DJ2
95CroJewE-4
95CroJewS-4
95CroJewSG-SG2
95FinLin-2
95FinLin-34
95FinLin-70
95FinLinCC6-2
95FinLinCC6-30
95FinLinCC6-47
95FinLinCC6DC-C2
95FinLinCC6W-CC6
95FinLinCotM-4
95FinLinGS-GS2
95FinLinP5U-NNO
95FinLinPP-2
95FinLinPP-34
95FinLinPP-70
95FinLinSC-SC3
95FinLinSD-SD3
95FinLinSil-2
95FinLinSil-34
95FinLinSil-70
95HigGea-2
95HigGea-72
95HigGea-87
95HigGeaBC-BC6
95HigGeaBCG-BC6
95HigGeaD-D1
95HigGeaDO-2
95HigGeaDO-72
95HigGeaDO-87
95HigGeaDOG-2
95HigGeaDOG-72
95HigGeaDOG-87
95HigGeaG-2
95HigGeaG-72
95HigGeaG-87
95HigGeaMD-MD1
95HigGeaP-P1
95HiTecB4-11
95HiTecB4-83
95HiTecB4TT-BY4
95Ima-2
95Ima-66
95Ima-94
95ImaDri-D8
95ImaGol-2
95ImaGol-66
95ImaGol-94
95ImaHarC-HC6
95MatWinCC-19
95Max-2
95Max-13
95Max-51
95Max-60
95Max-83
95Max-87
95Max-89
95Max-115
95Max-127
95Max-129
95Max-161
95MaxCroC-2
95MaxCroC-37
95MaxCroC-149
95MaxCroC-153
95MaxCroC-155
95MaxCroC-161
95MaxCroC-162
95MaxCroC-163
95MaxCroC-171
95MaxCroC-174
95MaxCroC-175
95MaxMed-2
95MaxMed-32
95MaxMedB-2
95MaxMedB-32
95MaxPreP-2
95MaxPreP-37
95MaxPreP-149
95MaxPreP-153
95MaxPreP-155
95MaxPreP-161
95MaxPreP-162
95MaxPreP-163
95MaxPreP-171
95MaxPreP-174
95MaxPreP-175
95MaxPrePP-PS2
95MaxPrePRJ-6
95MaxPreS-2
95MaxPreS-37
95MaxPreS-264
95MaxPreS-268
95MaxPreS-270
95MaxPreS-276
95MaxPreS-277
95MaxPreS-278
95MaxPreS-286
95MaxPreS-289
95MaxPreS-290
95MaxStaU-5
95MetImpRW-1
95MetImpRW-2
95MetImpRW-3
95MetImpRW-4
95MetImpRW-5
95MetImpRW-1
95MetImpRW-2
95MetImpRW-3
95MetImpRW-4
95MetImpRW-5
95MetImpRW-6
95MetImpRW-7
95MetImpRW-8
95MetImpRW-9
95MetImpRW-10
95MetImpRW-11
95MetImpRW-12
95MetImpRW-13
95MetImpRW-14
95MetImpRW-15
95MetImpRW-16
95MetImpRW-17
95MetImpRW-18
95MetImpRW-19
95MetImpRW-20
95MetImpWCC-9
95OptXL-22
95OptXL-45
95OptXLCB-22
95OptXLCB-45
95OptXLDC-22
95OptXLDC-45
95OptXLRH-22
95OptXLRH-45
95OptXLS-XLS16
95PrePas-34
95PrePas-47
95PrePas-135
95PrePasCC-34
95PrePasCCR-CCR5
95PrePasCF-CF8
95PrePasPH-3
95PrePasPH-31
95PrePasPHP-HP9
95PrePasPre-3
95PrePasPre-31
95PrePasPRH-3
95PrePasPRH-31
95PrePasRD-RD12
95PrePasRH-34
95PrePasRH-47
95PrePasRH-135
95Sel-34
95Sel-47
95Sel-111
95Sel-140
95SelDreM-DM2
95SelFlaO-34
95SelFlaO-47
95SelFlaO-111
95SelFlaO-140
95SelSki-SS1
95SP-2
95SP-32
95SP-33
95SP-76
95SP-77
95SP-123
95SPDieC-2
95SPDieC-32
95SPDieC-33
95SPDieC-76
95SPDieC-77
95SPDieC-123
95SPSpeM-SM2
95SPSpeMDC-SM2
95Tra-13
95Tra-46
95Tra-66
95Tra-75
95Tra5thA-9
95Tra5thA-42
95Tra5thA-52
95Tra5thACC-C6
95Tra5thAG-9
95Tra5thAG-42
95Tra5thAG-52
95Tra5thAR-R6
95Tra5thAUEC-E3
95TraAutV-45
95TraCha-C6
95TraFirR-13
95TraFirR-46
95TraFirR-66
95TraFirR-75
95TraRacM-RM10
95TraSerS-SS4
95TraVal-97
95UppDec-1
95UppDec-44
95UppDec-69
95UppDec-137
95UppDec-149
95UppDec-150
95UppDec-161
95UppDec-182
95UppDec-183
95UppDec-229
95UppDec-270
95UppDec-RW1
95UppDec-PR1
95UppDec-PR2
95UppDecA-182
95UppDecGSEG-1
95UppDecGSEG-44
95UppDecGSEG-69
95UppDecGSEG-137
95UppDecGSEG-149
95UppDecGSEG-150
95UppDecGSEG-161
95UppDecGSEG-182
95UppDecGSEG-183
95UppDecGSEG-229
95UppDecGSEG-270
95UppDecI-I10
95UppDecO-OS1
95UppDecPRW-P1
95UppDecPSP-PP1
95UppDecSSES-1
95UppDecSSES-44
95UppDecSSES-69
95UppDecSSES-137
95UppDecSSES-149
95UppDecSSES-150
95UppDecSSES-161
95UppDecSSES-182
95UppDecSSES-183
95UppDecSSES-229
95UppDecSSES-270
95VIP-28
95VIPCooB-28
95VIPEmeP-28
95VIPFanC-FC9
95VIPFanCG-FC9
95VIPRedHCB-28
95VIPRef-R5
95VIPRefG-R5
95Zen-2
95Zen-35
95ZenHel-2
95ZenWinW-8
95ZenZT-11
96ActPacC-24
96ActPacC-55
96ActPacCSS-24
96Ass$1000CCIPC-17
96Ass$100CCIPC-10
96Ass$2PC-15
96AssRacD-RD2
96AutRac-7
96AutRacFR-80
96AutRacKotC$PC-KC9
96Cla-36
96ClaMarMC-MC8
96ClaPriP-36
96ClaRacC-RC2
96ClaRacC-RC12
96ClaSil-36
96CroJewEADJ-DJ7
96CroJewEBotC-BC3
96CroJewEDT-6
96CroJewEDT-32
96CroJewEDT-34
96CroJewEDT-54
96CroJewEDT-60
96CroJewEDTBoC-BC3
96CroJewEDTC-6
96CroJewEDTC-32
96CroJewEDTC-34
96CroJewEDTC-54
96CroJewEDTC-60
96CroJewEDTCSA-CS3
96CroJewEDTDJA-DJ2
96CroJewEDTDJA-DJ7
96CroJewEDTDJG-DJ2
96CroJewEDTDJG-DJ7
96CroJewEE-6
96CroJewEE-32
96CroJewEE-34
96CroJewEE-54
96CroJewEE-60
96CroJewEGDJ-DJ2
96CroJewEGDJ-DJ7
96CroJewEli-6
96CroJewEli-32
96CroJewEli-34
96CroJewEli-54
96CroJewEli-60
96CroJewERCSG-CS3
96CroJewERCSP-CS3
96CroJewES-6
96CroJewES-32
96CroJewES-34
96CroJewES-54
96CroJewES-60
96CroJewESDJ-DJ2
96CroJewESDJ-DJ7
96CroJewETC-6
96CroJewETC-32
96CroJewETC-34
96CroJewETC-54
96CroJewETC-60
96CroJewETCBoC-BC3
96CroJewETCDJA-DJ2
96CroJewETCDJA-DJ7
96CroJewETCDJS-DJ2
96CroJewETCDJS-DJ7
96CroJewETCE-6
96CroJewETCE-32
96CroJewETCE-34
96CroJewETCE-54
96CroJewETCE-60
96CroJewETCGDJ-DJ2
96CroJewETCGDJ-DJ7
96CroJewETCS-6
96CroJewETCS-32
96CroJewETCS-34
96CroJewETCS-54
96CroJewETCS-60
96FinLin-3
96FinLin-27
96FinLin-28
96FinLinBGL-C2
96FinLinBGL-D2
96FinLinDCPC-8
96FinLinGS-GS4
96FinLinMM-MM3
96FinLinMPXR-NNO
96FinLinPP-36
96FinLinPP-37
96FinLinPP$100C-6
96FinLinPP$10C-11
96FinLinPP$1kC-K4
96FinLinPP$50C-8
96FinLinPP$5C-22
96FinLinPP$S-36
96FinLinPP$S-37
96FinLinPriP-3
96FinLinPriP-27
96FinLinPriP-28
96FinLinS-3
96FinLinS-27
96FinLinS-28
96Fla-35
96Fla-91
96Fla-100
96FlaAut-12
96FlaCenS-10
96FlaHotN-10
96FlaPowP-10
96Kni-7
96Kni-23
96KniBlaK-7
96KniBlaK-23
96KniKniRT-KT8
96KniProC-PC4
96KniQueRKP-7
96KniQueRKP-23
96KniRoy-7
96KniRoy-23
96KniSanC-SC3
96KniWhiK-7
96KniWhiK-23
96M-F-1
96M-F-2
96M-F-42

96M-FBla-B1
96M-FBla-B2
96M-FSheM-M1
96M-FSil-S1
96M-FSil-S16
96Max-2
96Max-53
96MaxFamT-FT4
96MaxMadiA-2
96MaxMadiA-53
96MaxMadiABR-BR6
96MaxOdy-2
96MaxOdy-53
96MaxOdyRA-RA6
96MaxOnTRA-OTRA3
96MaxPre-2
96MaxPre-38
96MetImp-5
96MetImp2AWCC-19
96Pin-2
96Pin-37
96Pin-86
96Pin-89
96Pin-94
96Pin-2
96Pin-37
96Pin-86
96Pin-89
96Pin-94
96PinCheF-2
96PinCutA-8
96PinPolP-2
96PinPolP-26
96PinPolP-65
96PinPolP-70
96PinPolP-78
96PinPolPCS-2
96PinPolPLF-2
96PinPolPLF-26
96PinPolPLF-65
96PinPolPLF-70
96PinPolPLF-78
96PinPolPNL-2
96PinPolPNLG-2
96PinTeaP-2
96PinWinCC-2
96PinWinCC-37
96PinWinCC-86
96PinWinCC-89
96PinWinCC-94
96PrePas-34
96PrePas-47
96PrePas-73
96PrePas-99
96PrePas-119
96PrePas&NC-34
96PrePas&NC-47
96PrePasCC-34
96PrePasCF-CF6
96PrePasFoc-F10
96PrePasP-5
96PrePasP-40
96PrePasPBRI-BR6
96PrePasPCB-CB12
96PrePasPEP-5
96PrePasPEP-40
96PrePasPH-5
96PrePasPH-40
96PrePasPHP-HP8
96PrePasSco-34
96PrePasSco-47
96PrePasSco-73
96PrePasSco-99
96PrePasSco-119
96PrePasT-34
96PrePasT-47
96PrePasT-73
96PrePasT-99
96PrePasT-119
96RacCho-2
96RacCho-26
96RacCho-82
96RacChoAP-2
96RacChoAP-26
96RacChoAP-82
96RacChoSC-2
96RacChoSC-26
96RacChoSC-82
96RacChoTT-5
96SP-2
96SP-46
96SP-79
96SpeArtP-1
96SpeArtP-18
96SpeArtP-36
96SpeArtP-71
96SpeArtP-72
96SpeArtP-73
96SpeArtP-74
96SpeCleS-4
96SpeInM-4
96SpePro-4
96SpeRac-1
96SpeRac-18
96SpeRac-36
96SpeRac-71
96SpeRac-72
96SpeRac-73
96SpeRac-74
96SPHolME-ME2
96SPRacLC-RL21
96SPx-2
96SPxEli-E4
96SPxGol-2
96Ult-17
96Ult-18
96Ult-19
96Ult-161
96Ult-174
96Ult-190
96Ult-200
96UltAut-36
96UltBoxS-5
96UltChaC-1
96UltFlaP-5
96UltUpd-32
96UltUpd-78
96UltUpdA-12
96UltUpdPP-15
96UltUpdW-8
96UppDec-2
96UppDec-42
96UppDec-82
96UppDec-136
96UppDec-142
96UppDec-148
96UppDecAP-AP5
96UppDecPP-RP3
96UppDecPW-HP2
96UppDecRTTC-RC4
96UppDecRTTC-RC53
96UppDecRTTC-RC92
96UppDecRTTC-RC127
96UppDecRTTCAS-H4
96UppDecRTTCGF-GF2
96UppDecRTTCJ-WC2
96UppDecRTTCLP-LP2
96UppDecRTTCPPoi-PP4
96UppDRTTCPPR-PR4
96UppDecRTTCPT3-T1
96UppDecRTTCPT3-T4
96UppDecRTTCPT3-T5
96UppDecRTTCPT3-T10
96UppDecRTTCT3PR-R2
96UppDecVV-VV2
96UppDecVVG-VV2
96V.IAut-24
96VIP-27
96VIP-40
96VIPEmeP-27
96VIPEmeP-40
96Viper-6
96Viper-41
96ViperBlaM-6
96ViperBlaM-41
96ViperCob-C6
96ViperCop-6
96ViperCop-41
96ViperDia-D6
96ViperDiaA-DA5
96ViperGreM-6
96ViperGreM-41
96ViperKinC-KC7
96VIPHeaG-HG7
96VIPHeaGD-HG7
96VipPro-P2
96VIPSamBTF-SB5
96VIPSamBTFG-SB5
96VIPTor-27
96VIPTor-40
96VIPWarP-WP1
96VIPWarPG-WP1
96Zen-9
96Zen-94
96Zen-96
96ZenArtP-9
96ZenArtP-94
96ZenArtP-96
96ZenChaS-7
97Act-5
97Act-7
97ActPac-2
97ActPac-44
97ActPac-69
97ActPac-73
97ActPac2G-1
97ActPacFA-7
97ActPacFI-2
97ActPacFI-44
97ActPacFI-69
97ActPacFI-73
97AutRac-35
97AutRac-49
97ColCho-2
97ColCho-52
97ColCho-102
97ColCho-145
97ColCho-155
97ColChoC-CC7
97ColChoC-CC41
97ColChoC-CC74
97ColChoS-S3
97ColChoS-S4
97ColChoSQ-SQ34
97ColChoSQ-SQ48
97ColChoTF-H2
97ColChoTF-J2
97ColChoUD5-UD2
97ColChoUD5-UD3
97ColChoVC-VC3
97FinLinPP2-4
97FinLinPP2$10-67
97FinLinPP2$100-98
97FinLinPP2$5-42
97FinLinPP2$50-90
97JurPar-5
97JurParC-C8
97JurParP-P5
97JurParR-R11
97JurParT-5
97JurParTL-TL4
97JurParTR-TR6
97Max-2
97Max-47
97Max-98
97Max-101
97Max-107
97Pin-2
97Pin-31
97Pin-62
97Pin-73
97Pin-92
97PinArtP-2
97PinArtP-31
97PinArtP-62
97PinArtP-73
97PinArtP-92
97PinArtP-96
97PinCer-2
97PinCer-36
97PinCer-95
97PinCerCGT-6
97PinCerCT-6
97PinCerE-E6
97PinCerEE-E6
97PinCerEP-E6
97PinCerMB-2
97PinCerMB-36
97PinCerMB-95
97PinCerMG-2
97PinCerMG-36
97PinCerMG-95
97PinCerMR-2
97PinCerMR-36
97PinCerMR-95
97PinCerR-2
97PinCerR-36
97PinCerR-95
97PinMin-7
97PinMin2GC-7
97PinMinB-7
97PinMinC-7
97PinMinG-7
97PinMinNC-7
97PinMinS-7
97PinPor-18
97PinPor-38
97PinPre-37
97PinPre-39
97PinPre-40
97PinPre-41
97PinPre-42
97PinPre-44
97PinPre-45
97PinPreBM-37
97PinPreBM-39
97PinPreBM-40
97PinPreBM-41
97PinPreBM-42
97PinPreBM-44
97PinPreBM-45
97PinPreGM-37
97PinPreGM-39
97PinPreGM-40
97PinPreGM-41
97PinPreGM-42
97PinPreGM-44
97PinPreGM-45
97PinPreP-2
97PinPreP-31
97PinPreP-62
97PinPreP-73
97PinPreP-92
97PinPreP-S4-C
97PinPreP-TP2A
97PinPreSM-37
97PinPreSM-39
97PinPreSM-40
97PinPreSM-41
97PinPreSM-42
97PinPreSM-44
97PinPreSM-45
97PinSpe-4-C
97PinTeaP-2
97PinTotCPB-2
97PinTotCPB-36
97PinTotCPB-95
97PinTotCPG-2
97PinTotCPG-36
97PinTotCPG-95
97PinTotCPR-2
97PinTotCPR-36
97PinTotCPR-95
97PinTroC-2
97PinTroC-31
97PinTroC-62
97PinTroC-73
97PinTroC-92
97Pre-6
97PreAmeE-AE3
97PreBlaWFS-6
97PreEyeotT-ET3
97PreGat-GB5
97PreGatA-GBA5
97PreGolE-GE3
97PreGri-6
97PrePas-7
97PrePas-31
97PrePas-53
97PrePas-62
97PrePas-84
97PrePas-99
97PrePas-122
97PrePasAut-7
97PrePasBB-BB7
97PrePasBR-BR1
97PrePasCC'-CC18
97PrePasCleC-C9
97PrePasL-7
97PrePasL-31
97PrePasL-53
97PrePasL-62
97PrePasL-84
97PrePasL-99
97PrePasL-122
97PrePasOS-7
97PrePasOS-31
97PrePasOS-53
97PrePasOS-62
97PrePasOS-84
97PrePasOS-99
97PrePasOS-122
97PrePasP-7
97PrePasP-28
97PrePasP-44
97PrePasPCB-CB12
97PrePasPCBD-CB12
97PrePasPDB-DB4
97PrePasPEP-7
97PrePasPEP-28
97PrePasPEP-44
97PrePasPLL-LL11
97PrePasPM-7
97PrePasPM-28
97PrePasPM-44
97PrePasPOS-7
97PrePasPOS-28
97PrePasPOS-44
97PrePasT-7
97PrePasT-31
97PrePasT-53
97PrePasT-62
97PrePasT-84
97PrePasT-99
97PrePasT-122
97PrePasVL-VL8A
97PrePasVL-VL8B
97PreRedW-6
97RacCho-2
97RacCho-37
97RacCho-91
97RacChoBC-14
97RacChoHO-6
97RacChoHOGitD-6
97RacChoSS-2
97RacChoSS-37
97RacChoSS-91
97RacSha-5
97RacSha-37
97RacSha-39
97RacSha-42
97RacShaGW-GW5
97RacShaGWP-5
97RacShaGWP-37
97RacShaGWP-39
97RacShaGWP-42
97RacShaH-5
97RacShaH-37
97RacShaH-39
97RacShaH-42
97RacShaPFBSA-9
97RacShaSA-SA4
97RacShaTS-5
97RacShaTS-37
97RacShaTS-39
97RacShaTS-42
97SBMot-46
97ScoBoal-39
97ScoBoal$PC-PC2
97ScoBoalR-SB5
97ScoBoaRSBF-SB5
97SkyPro-30
97SkyPro-62
97SkyProA-30
97SkyProPS-E8
97SkyProT-T9
97SP-2
97SP-44
97SP-85
97SP-113
97SP SPxFA-SF2
97SP SupS-2
97SP SupS-44
97SP SupS-85
97SP SupS-113
97SPX-2
97SPxBlu-2
97SPxGol-2
97SPxSil-2
97SPXSpeA-SV2
97Ult-36
97Ult-46
97UltAKA-A9
97UltEliS-E9
97UltIns-DC9
97UltUpd-7
97UltUpd-76
97UltUpdAR-7
97UppDecRTTC-7
97UppDecRTTC-49
97UppDecRTTC-91
97UppDecRTTC-124
97UppDecRTTCCQ-CQ5
97UDRTTCCQC-CQ5
97UppDecRTTCGF-RD2
97UDRTTCMDM-MM8
97UDRTTCMDM-MM9
97UDRTTCMDM-MM10
97UDRTTCMDM-MM11
97UDRTTCMDM-MM12
97UDRTTCMDMA-MM8
97UDRTTCMDMA-MM9
97UDRTTCMDMA-MM10
97UDRTTCMDMA-MM11
97UDRTTCMDMA-MM12
97UppDecRTTCPotA-7
97UppDecRTTCPotA-8
97UppDecRTTCPotA-9
97UppDecRTTCPP-PP8
97UppDecRTTCPP-PP14

97UppDecRTTCPP-PP18
97UppDecRTTCPP-PP26
97UppDecRTTCPP-PP44
97UppDecRTTCPPlu-+7
97UppDecRTTCPPlu-+14
97UDRTTCPPRC-+7
97UDRTTCPPRC-+14
97UppDRTTCPPRDC-+7
97UppDRTTCPPRDC-+14
97UppDecRTTCQW-CQ5
97UppDecVC-2
97UppDecVC-52
97UppDecVC-103
97UppDecVCAPotA-FS4
97UppDecVCAPotA-FS5
97UppDecVCAPotA-FS6
97UppDecVCCR-CR7
97UppDecVCDS-DS7
97UppDecVCP-PE2
97UppDecVCPC-PH2
97UppDecVCVL-VL10
97VIP-23
97Viper-5
97Viper-52
97Viper-67
97ViperAna-A6
97ViperBlaR-5
97ViperBlaR-52
97ViperBlaR-67
97ViperCob-C5
97ViperDia-DB4
97ViperDiaA-DBA4
97ViperKinC-KC5
97ViperSid-S11
97ViperSnaE-SE8
97VIPExp-23
97VIPHeaGD-HG8
97VIPHigG-HG8
97VIPOilS-23
97VIPRinoH-RH1
97VIPRinoHDC-RH1
97VIPSamB-KT6
97VIPSamBG-KT6
97VIPSheM-SM5
98ColCho-2
98ColCho-38
98ColCho-93
98ColCho-111
98HigGea-9
98HigGea-28
98HigGeaFG-7
98HigGeaFG-28
98HigGeaGJ-GJ1
98HigGeaHG-HG1
98HigGeaM-7
98HigGeaM-28
98HigGeaMaM-MM9
98HigGeaMaM-C-9
98HigGeaPG-PG9
98Max-2
98Max-32
98Max-99
98Max-2
98Max-27
98Max-52
98Max-77
98Max10tA-1
98Max10tA-46
98Max10tA-101
98Max10tA-117
98Max10tA-118
98Max10tA-122
98Max10tA-123
98Max10tABA-45
98Max10tACotY-CY3
98Max10tACotY-CY7
98Max10tACP-CP5
98Max10tACPDC-CP5
98Max10tAMP-P2
98MaxBatP-B3
98MaxFieG-1
98MaxFieGTS-1
98MaxFieGTSA-1
98MaxFirC-F18
98MaxFocOAC-FC10
98MaxFouSGA-1
98MaxMakOACC-FC10
98MaxYeaIRBS-i1
98MaxYeaIRBS-32
98MaxYeaIRBS-39
98MaxYeaIRBS-84
98MaxYeaIRBS-103
98MaxYeaIRBS-135
98MaxYeaIRBS-PO9
98MayAutS-13
98PinMin-10
98PinMin-22
98PinMin-26
98PinMinB-10
98PinMinB-22
98PinMinB-26
98PinMinBC-10
98PinMinBC-22
98PinMinBC-02
98PinMinBPPC-10
98PinMinBPPC-22
98PinMinBPPC-02
98PinMinGMT-10
98PinMinGMT-22
98PinMinGMT-26
98PinMinGPC-10
98PinMinGPC-22
98PinMinGPC-26
98PinMinGPPC-10
98PinMinGPPC-22
98PinMinGPPC-26
98PinMinNC-10
98PinMinNC-22
98PinMinNC-26
98PinMinSGC-10
98PinMinSGC-22
98PinMinSGC-26
98PinMinSMT-10
98PinMinSMT-22
98PinMinSMT-26
98PinMinSPPC-10
98PinMinSPPC-22
98PinMinSPPC-26
98PinMinSSC-10
98PinMinSSC-22
98PinMinSSC-26
98PrePas-7
98PrePas-28
98PrePas-105
98PrePasA-8
98PrePasCC'-CC18
98PrePasOC-OC9
98PrePasOS-7
98PrePasOS-28
98PrePasP-14
98PrePasP-36
98PrePasP-14
98PrePasP-36
98PrePasPFC-FC6
98PrePasPFC-FC19
98PrePasPFCR-FC6
98PrePasPFCR-FC19
98PrePasPR-3B
98PrePasPS-PS1
98PrePasPSH-SH1
98PrePasPTGF-TGF1
98PrePasS-ST7A
98PrePasS-31
98PrePasS-32
98PrePasS-50
98PrePasSF-31
98PrePasSF-32
98PrePasSF-50
98PrePasSFT-9
98PrePasSFTD-9
98PrePasSO-35
98PrePasSO-36
98PrePasSOD-35
98PrePasSOD-36
98PrePasSRG-G1
98PrePasSS-17
98PrePasSSD-17
98PrePasTG3R-STG1
98PrePasTGBR-TG1
98PrePasTorp-ST7B
98SP Aut-2
98SP Aut-36
98SP Aut-70
98SP AutBtW-BW8
98SP AutBtWL2-BW8
98SP AutBtWL3-BW8
98SP AutSotTL1-S1
98SP AutT-T5
98UppDecDV-2
98UppDecDVSM-2
98UppDecDVVoaC-VC1
98UppDecRttC-2
98UppDecRttC-46
98UppDecRttC-63
98UppDecRttC-86
98UppDecRTTC5A-AN29
98UppDecRTTC5A-AN40
98UppDecRTTC5AA-AN40
98UDRTTCCQT1-CQ2
98UDRTTCCQT2-CQ2
98UDRTTCCQT3-CQ2
98UDRTTCCQT4-CQ2
98UppDRTTCCQVL-CQ2
98UppDecRTTCCS-CS5
98UppDecRTTCCS-CS12
98UppDecRTTCWM-W1
98UppDecVC-2
98UppDecVC-47
98UppDecVC-110
98UppDecVC-142
98UppDecVC3DoS-D3
98UppDecVC3DoS-D7
98UppDecVC3DoSG-D3
98UppDecVC3DoSG-D7
98UppDecVCPL-PL9
98UppDecVCPotE-PE2
98UppDecVCPP-2
98UppDecVCPPCR-2
98UppDecVCSoB-SB2
98VIP-26
98VIP-46
98VIPDriF-DF18
98VIPDriFD-DF18
98VIPExp-26
98VIPExp-46
98VIPHeaG-HG9
98VIPHeaGD-HG9
98VIPLapL-LL9
98VIPLapLA-LL9
98VIPNASC-NC9
98VIPNASCD-NC9
98VIPTriG"M-TGS1
98Whe-29
98Whe-45
98Whe50tA-A14
98Whe50tA-A27
98WheCusS-CSRW
98WheDouT-E9
98WheGol-29
98WheGol-45
98WheGreF-GF17
98WheJac-J9
99Pre-4
99Pre-31
99Pre-80
99PrePas-4
99PrePas-31
99PrePas-80
99PrePas-104
99PrePasBR-BR8
99PrePasCC-18B
99PrePasCC-19
99PrePasOC-9
99PrePasPS-2
99PrePasS-18A
99PrePasTG'i1R-TG5
99UppDecVC-9
99UppDecVC-42
99UppDecVC-78
99UppDecVC-81
99UppDecVC-89
99UppDecVCIS-IS4
99UppDecVCMN-M4
99UppDecVCMNA-M4
99UppDecVCNSS-RW
99UppDecVCSZ-SZ6
99UppDecVCTM-TM5
99UppDecVCUE-9
99UppDecVCUE-42
99UppDecVCUE-78
99UppDecVCUE-81
99UppDecVCUE-89
99UppDecVCVC-V9
99WheHigG-4
99WheHigG-28
99WheHigG-68
99WheHigGFC-FC4/5
99WheHigGFG-4
99WheHigGFG-28
99WheHigGFG-68
99WheHigGM-MM9B/9
99WheHigGM-4
99WheHigGM-28
99WheHigGM-68
99WheHigGS-GS4
99WheHigGTT-TT4/8

Wallace, Walter
91PioStoCR-4

Wallace, Wendall
91DirTra-63
91JAG-34
92DirTra-96
92JAG-119
95HavAT-25

Wallard, Lee
54StaWetIW-1951
60HawWaxI-35
91LegInd-18

Walls, Ronald
91BulRin-106

Walters, Terry
90CheFlal-72

Walther, Jim
72FleAHRDN-63

Walton, Luke
91LegInd-27

Waltrip, Bobby
92TraTeaS-131

Waltrip, Carolyn
92TraTeaS-136

Waltrip, Darrell
83UNORac-28
85SpoPhoGS-NNO
86SpoPhoG-12
88MaxCha-10
88MaxCha-27
88MaxCha-75
89Max-17
89Max-125
89Max-140
89Max-150
89Max-164
89MaxCri-2
90ACRacPW-2
90Max-17
90Max-50
90Max-100
90Max-167
90Max-168
90Max-174
90Max-177
90Max-178
90Max-185
90MaxHolF-HF3
91ACRac-3
91Max-17
91Max-150
91MaxMcD-20
91MaxRacFK-3
91MaxTheWA-20
91MaxUpd-17
91MaxUpd-150
91MaxWin2AF-12
91MaxWin2AF-12
91MaxWin2AF-15
91PioStoCR-4
91ProSet-117
91ProSet-118
91ProSet-119
91SunRacL-7
91SupRacM-12
91TexWorS-9
91TraRicP-22
92ACDel-4
92ACRacP-8
92CarDynDW-1
92CarDynDW-2
92CarDynDW-3
92CarDynDW-4
92CarDynDW-5
92CarDynGO-1
92MaxBla-17
92MaxBla-190
92MaxBla-195
92MaxBla-270
92MaxBla-277
92MaxCra-NNO
92MaxIMH-37
92MaxMcD-16
92MaxRed-17
92MaxRed-190
92MaxRed-195
92MaxRed-270
92MaxRed-277
92MaxTheW-11
92MaxTheW-31
92ProSet-93
92ProSet-97
92ProSet-209
92ProSet-245
92ProSetMH-14
92ProSetRF-7
92RedSta-17
92RPM-10
92Tra-17
92Tra-56
92Tra-191
92Tra-198
92TraASA-42
92TraRacM-17
92TraRacM-23
92TraRacM-37
92TraTeaS-127
92TraTeaS-130
92TraTeaS-138
92TraTeaS-142
92TraTeaS-150
93ACRacF-17
93ActPac-3
93ActPac-16
93ActPac-17
93ActPac-24
93ActPac-41
93ActPac-103
93ActPac-104
93ActPac-164
93ActPac-190
93ActPac2G-2G
93ActPac2G-72G
93FinLin-4
93FinLin-51
93FinLin-95
93FinLin-107
93FinLinCS-8
93FinLinCS-18
93FinLinCS-30
93FinLinS-4
93FinLinS-51
93FinLinS-95
93FinLinS-107
93HiTecTT-2
93Max-17
93Max-226
93Max-280
93Max-284
93Max-285
93MaxHou-8
93MaxHou-21
93MaxLowFS-2
93MaxPreP-17
93MaxPreP-65
93MaxPreP-195
93MaxPreP-199
93MaxPreP-200
93MaxPreS-17
93MaxPreS-226
93MaxPreS-280
93MaxPreS-284
93MaxPreS-285
93MaxRetJ-1
93MaxTheW-6
93MaxTheW-26
93TraPreC-9
94ActPac-13
94ActPac-70
94ActPac-100
94ActPac-127
94ActPac-166
94ActPac2G-24G
94ActPacC-17
94ActPacS2G-W1
94CarDynGO-6
94FinLin-40
94FinLin-102
94FinLin-129
94FinLin-15
94FinLinG-13
94FinLinG-30
94FinLinG-31
94FinLinG-64
94FinLinG-66
94FinLinGCC-NNO
94FinLinGT-TG10
94FinLinS-40
94FinLinS-102
94FinLinS-129
94Hi-Bri4AP-18
94Hi-Bri4AP-48
94HigGea-117
94HigGeaDO-117
94HigGeaDOG-117
94HigGeaG-117
94HigGeaMG-MG11
94HiTecB4-18
94HiTecB4-48
94Max-17
94Max-64
94MaxMed-5
94MaxPreP-17
94MaxPreP-64

94MaxPreS-17
94MaxPreS-64
94MaxPreSJ-5
94MaxTheS2-13
94OptXL-23
94OptXL-36
94OptXLRH-23
94OptXLRH-36
94Pow-46
94Pow-60
94Pow-69
94Pow-125
94Pow-150
94PowGol-46
94PowGol-60
94PowGol-69
94PowGol-125
94PowGol-150
94PowPre-9
94PrePas-29
94PrePas-33
94PrePas-87
94PrePasCC-CC29
94Sky-2
94Sky-25
94VIP-35
94VIP-54
95ActPacC-4
95ActPacC-18
95ActPacC-21
95ActPacC-32
95ActPacC-33
95ActPacC-34
95ActPacC-35
95ActPacC-36
95ActPacC-37
95ActPacCSS-4
95ActPacCSS-18
95ActPacCSS-21
95ActPacCSS-32
95ActPacCSS-33
95ActPacCSS-34
95ActPacCSS-35
95ActPacCSS-36
95ActPacCSS-37
95ActPacP-24
95ActPacP-67
95ActPacP-78
95ActPacP2G-10G
95ActPacS-10
95ActPacS-39
95ActPacSSS-10
95ActPacSSS-39
95Ass-7
95Ass-35
95Ass$5$25PC-3
95Ass1M$PC-6
95AssGolS-7
95AssGolS-35
95CroJew-10
95CroJew-33
95CroJew-51
95CroJew-64
95CroJewD-10
95CroJewD-33
95CroJewD-51
95CroJewD-64
95CroJewE-10
95CroJewE-33
95CroJewE-51
95CroJewE-64
95CroJewS-10
95CroJewS-33
95CroJewS-51
95CroJewS-64
95FinLin-3
95FinLin-17
95FinLin-58
95FinLinCC6-7
95FinLinCC6-35
95FinLinCC6W-CC1
95FinLinCC6W-CC4
95FinLinCC6W-CC5
95FinLinGS-GS12
95FinLinPP-3
95FinLinPP-17
95FinLinPP-58
95FinLinSC-SC8
95FinLinSD-SD8
95FinLinSil-3
95FinLinSil-17
95FinLinSil-58
95HigGea-7
95HigGea-79
95HigGeaDO-7
95HigGeaDO-79
95HigGeaDOG-7
95HigGeaDOG-79
95HigGeaG-7
95HigGeaG-79
95HiTecB4-25
95HiTecB4-78
95HiTecB4TT-BY6
95Ima-17
95Ima-47
95ImaDri-D15
95ImaGol-17
95ImaGol-47
95MatWinCC-11
95MatWinCC-12
95MatWinCC-15
95Max-17
95Max-174
95Max-206
95Max-207
95MaxCroC-17
95MaxCroC-63
95MaxLicD-12
95MaxMed-13
95MaxMed-43
95MaxMedB-13
95MaxMedB-43
95MaxOveW-5
95MaxPreP-17
95MaxPreP-63
95MaxPreP-P1
95MaxPrePP-PS8
95MaxPreS-17
95MaxPreS-63
95MetImpWCC-5
95OptXL-23
95OptXLCB-23
95OptXLDC-23
95OptXLP-XL2
95OptXLRH-23
95OptXLS-XLS17
95PrePas-35
95PrePas-54
95PrePas-108
95PrePasCC-35
95PrePasPH-9
95PrePasPre-9
95PrePasPRH-9
95PrePasRH-35
95PrePasRH-54
95PrePasRH-108
95Sel-35
95Sel-54
95Sel-88
95Sel-113
95Sel-133
95SelDreM-DM10
95SelFlaO-35
95SelFlaO-54
95SelFlaO-88
95SelFlaO-113
95SelFlaO-133
95SelSki-SS16
95SP-14
95SP-48
95SP-90
95SP-130
95SPDieC-14
95SPDieC-48
95SPDieC-90
95SPDieC-130
95SPSpeM-SM17
95SPSpeMDC-SM17
95UppDec-5
95UppDec-48
95UppDec-73
95UppDec-141
95UppDec-170
95UppDec-197
95UppDec-241
95UppDec-278
95UppDecA-197
95UppDecGSEG-5
95UppDecGSEG-48
95UppDecGSEG-73
95UppDecGSEG-141
95UppDecGSEG-170
95UppDecGSEG-197
95UppDecGSEG-241
95UppDecGSEG-278
95UppDecSSES-5
95UppDecSSES-48
95UppDecSSES-73
95UppDecSSES-141
95UppDecSSES-170
95UppDecSSES-197
95UppDecSSES-241
95UppDecSSES-278
95VIP-29
95VIP-54
95VIPCooB-29
95VIPCooB-54
95VIPEmeP-29
95VIPEmeP-54
95VIPRedHCB-29
95VIPRedHCB-54
95Zen-17
95Zen-47
96ActPacC-38
96ActPacC-61
96ActPacC-79
96ActPacC-90
96ActPacC-94
96ActPacCSS-38
96Ass-8
96Ass-43
96Ass$1000CCIPC-11
96Ass$100CCIPC-6
96Ass$2PC-11
96Ass$5PC-4
96AssComL-CL10
96AutRac-35
96AutRacA-59
96AutRacCA-59
96AutRacFR-81
96AutRacFR-82
96AutRacFR-83
96AutRacFR-84
96AutRacFR-85
96AutRacHP-HP17
96Cla-24
96Cla-60
96ClaPriP-24
96ClaRacC-RC15
96ClaSil-24
96CroJewEADJ-DJ5
96CroJewEBotC-BC4
96CroJewEDT-12
96CroJewEDTBoC-BC4
96CroJewEDTC-12
96CroJewEDTDJA-DJ5
96CroJewEDTDJG-DJ5
96CroJewEE-12
96CroJewEGDJ-DJ5
96CroJewEli-12
96CroJewES-12
96CroJewESDJ-DJ5
96CroJewETC-12
96CroJewETCBoC-BC4
96CroJewETCDJA-DJ5
96CroJewETCDJS-DJ5
96CroJewETCE-12
96CroJewETCGDJ-DJ5
96CroJewETCS-12
96FinLin-11
96FinLin-56
96FinLin-67
96FinLin-68
96FinLinBGL-C12
96FinLinBGL-D13
96FinLinGS-GS11
96FinLinPP-39
96FinLinPP-40
96FinLinPP$10C-12
96FinLinPP$5C-24
96FinLinPP$S-39
96FinLinPP$S-40
96FinLinPriP-11
96FinLinPriP-56
96FinLinPriP-67
96FinLinPriP-68
96FinLinS-11
96FinLinS-56
96FinLinS-67
96FinLinS-68
96Kni-17
96KniBlaK-17
96KniKniRT-KT3
96KniProC-PC1
96KniQueRKP-17
96KniRoy-17
96KniWhiK-17
96M-F-15
96Max-17
96Max-27
96MaxFamT-FT5
96MaxMadiA-17
96MaxMadiA-27
96MaxMadiABR-BR11
96MaxOdy-17
96MaxOdy-27
96MaxOdyRA-RA11
96MaxOnTRA-OTRA4
96MaxPep5-3
96MaxPre-17
96MaxPre-60
96MaxSup-ST8
96MetImp-2
96MetImp2AWCC-11
96MetImp2AWCC-12
96MetImp2AWCC-15
96Pin-17
96Pin-46
96Pin-17
96Pin-46
96PinCheF-15
96PinPolP-17
96PinPolP-35
96PinPolP-81
96PinPolPLF-17
96PinPolPLF-35
96PinPolPLF-81
96PinPolPNL-12
96PinPolPNLG-12
96PinWinCC-17
96PinWinCC-46
96PrePas-35
96PrePas-54
96PrePas-90
96PrePas&NC-35
96PrePasCC-35
96PrePasP-19
96PrePasPEP-19
96PrePasPH-19
96PrePasSco-35
96PrePasSco-54
96PrePasSco-90
96PrePasT-35
96PrePasT-54
96PrePasT-90
96RacCho-21
96RacCho-37
96RacCho-105
96RacChoAP-21
96RacChoAP-37
96RacChoAP-105
96RacChoSC-21
96RacChoSC-37
96RacChoSC-105
96SP-17
96SP-60
96SpeArtP-7
96SpeArtP-22
96SpeInM-7
96SpePro-10
96SpeRac-7
96SpeRac-22
96SPHolME-ME17
96SPx-17
96SPxGol-17
96UppDec-15
96UppDec-55
96UppDec-95
96UppDec-130
96UppDecRL-RLC9
96UppDecRTTC-RC18
96UppDecRTTC-RC67
96UppDecRTTC-RC101
96UppDecRTTC-RC141
96UppDecRTTCAS-H18
96UppDecRTTCPT3-T4
96UppDecRTTCT3PR-R7
96UppDecVV-VV8
96UppDecVVG-VV8
96VIP-28
96VIPEmeP-28
96Viper-13
96ViperBlaM-13
96ViperBusC-B6
96ViperCop-13
96ViperGreM-13
96VIPHeaG-HG8
96VIPHeaGD-HG8
96VIPTor-28
96VIPWarP-WP8
96VIPWarPG-WP8
96Zen-18
96Zen-41
96ZenArtP-18
96ZenArtP-41
96ZenChaS-11
96ZenChaS-14
96ZenChaS-15
96ZenHig-6
97ActPac-17
97ActPac-38
97ActPac-85
97ActPacCM-2
97ActPacFI-17
97ActPacFI-38
97ActPacFI-85
97ActPacRT-7
97AutRac-15
97AutRac-48
97AutRacA-54
97AutRacMS-KM15
97ColCho-17
97ColCho-67
97ColCho-119
97ColCho-151
97ColChoC-CC21
97ColChoC-CC54
97ColChoC-CC87
97ColChoS-S33
97ColChoS-S34
97ColChoSQ-SQ35
97ColChoUD5-UD34
97ColChoUD5-UD35
97ColChoVC-VC1
97FinLinPP2-10
97FinLinPP2$10-75
97FinLinPP2$5-48
97JurPar-17
97JurParT-17
97Max-17
97Max-62
97Max-119
97Pin-17
97Pin-46
97Pin-94
97PinArtP-17
97PinArtP-46
97PinArtP-94
97PinCer-17
97PinCer-51
97PinCer-69
97PinCer-70
97PinCer-71
97PinCerE-E8
97PinCerEE-E8
97PinCerEP-E8
97PinCerMB-17
97PinCerMB-51
97PinCerMB-69
97PinCerMB-70
97PinCerMB-71
97PinCerMG-17
97PinCerMG-51
97PinCerMG-69
97PinCerMG-70
97PinCerMG-71
97PinCerMR-17
97PinCerMR-51
97PinCerMR-69
97PinCerMR-70
97PinCerMR-71
97PinCerR-17
97PinCerR-51
97PinCerR-69
97PinCerR-70
97PinCerR-71
97PinMin-4
97PinMin2GC-4
97PinMinB-4
97PinMinC-4
97PinMinG-4
97PinMinNC-4
97PinMinS-4
97PinPreP-17
97PinPreP-46
97PinPreP-94
97PinPreP-TP4A
97PinTeaP-4
97PinTotCPB-17
97PinTotCPB-51
97PinTotCPB-69
97PinTotCPB-70
97PinTotCPB-71
97PinTotCPG-17
97PinTotCPG-51
97PinTotCPG-69
97PinTotCPG-70
97PinTotCPG-71
97PinTotCPR-17
97PinTotCPR-51
97PinTotCPR-69
97PinTotCPR-70
97PinTotCPR-71
97PinTroC-17
97PinTroC-46

96FinLin-15
96FinLin-34
96FinLin-61
96FinLinBGL-C14
96FinLinBGL-D16
96FinLinGS-GS12
96FinLinPP-38
96FinLinPP$5C-23
96FinLinPP$S-38
96FinLinPriP-15
96FinLinPriP-34
96FinLinPriP-61
96FinLinS-15
96FinLinS-34
96FinLinS-61
96Fla-36
96Fla-92
96Kni-19
96KniBlaK-19
96KniKniRT-KT9
96KniQueRKP-19
96KniRoy-19
96KniWhiK-19
96M-F-18
96Max-30
96Max-39
96MaxFamT-FT5
96MaxMadiA-21
96MaxMadiA-51
96MaxMadiA-80
96MaxMadiA-81
96MaxMadiABR-BR5
96MaxOdy-21
96MaxOdy-51
96MaxOdy-80
96MaxOdy-81
96MaxOdyOTRA-OTRA2
96MaxOdyRA-RA5
96MaxPre-30
96MaxPre-65
96MaxPre-190
96MaxPre-191
96Pin-21
96Pin-48
96Pin-21
96Pin-48
96PinCheF-11
96PinPolP-21
96PinPolP-37
96PinPolP-66
96PinPolPLF-21
96PinPolPLF-37
96PinPolPLF-66
96PinWinCC-21
96PinWinCC-48
96PrePas-36
96PrePas-48
96PrePas-118
96PrePas&NC-36
96PrePasCC-36
96PrePasP-12
96PrePasP-33
96PrePasP$10PC-9
96PrePasP$20PC-9
96PrePasP$5PC-9
96PrePasPEP-12
96PrePasPEP-33
96PrePasPH-12
96PrePasPH-33
96PrePasPHP-HP9
96PrePasSco-36
96PrePasSco-48
96PrePasSco-118
96PrePasT-36
96PrePasT-48
96PrePasT-118
96RacCho-11
96RacCho-39
96RacCho-78
96RacChoAP-11
96RacChoAP-39
96RacChoAP-78
96RacChoSC-11
96RacChoSC-39
96RacChoSC-78
96SP-21
96SP-53
96SP-75
96SpeArtP-8
96SpeArtP-48
96SpePro-5
96SpeRac-8
96SpeRac-48
96SPx-21
96SPxGol-21
96TraRev&PTCG-TC5
96TraRev&PTCH-TC5
96TraRevP-28
96TraRevPFR-28
96TraRevPM-28
96TraRevPTC-TC5
96Ult-44
96Ult-45
96Ult-46
96UltAut-37
96UltBoxS-12
96UltUpd-33
96UltUpd-79
96UltUpd-88
96UppDec-28
96UppDec-68
96UppDec-100
96UppDec-108
96UppDecRTTC-RC11
96UppDecRTTC-RC60
96UppDecRTTC-RC96
96UppDecRTTCAS-H11
96UppDecVV-VV14
96UppDecVVG-VV14
96V.IAut-25
96VIP-29
96VIPEmeP-29
96Viper-16
96Viper-59
96ViperBlaM-16
96ViperBlaM-59
96ViperCop-16
96ViperCop-59
96ViperGreM-16
96ViperGreM-59
96VIPHeaG-HG9
96VIPHeaGD-HG9
96VIPTor-29
96VIPWarP-WP10
96VIPWarPG-WP10
96Zen-13
96Zen-49
96Zen-62
96ZenArtP-13
96ZenArtP-49
96ZenArtP-62
96ZenHig-10
97ActPac-15
97ActPac-36
97ActPac-59
97ActPac-71
97ActPac-74
97ActPac2G-10
97ActPacFI-15
97ActPacFI-36
97ActPacFI-59
97ActPacFI-71
97ActPacFI-74
97AutRac-5
97AutRac-40
97AutRac-41
97AutRac-45
97AutRacA-55
97AutRacMS-KM5
97ColCho-21
97ColCho-71
97ColCho-108
97ColChoC-CC25
97ColChoC-CC58
97ColChoS-S41
97ColChoS-S42
97ColChoSQ-SQ22
97ColChoTF-E3
97ColChoUD5-UD42
97ColChoUD5-UD43
97FinLinPP2-16
97FinLinPP2-36
97FinLinPP2$10-77
97FinLinPP2$5-54
97FinLinPP2$5-65
97JurPar-10
97JurPar-36
97JurParR-R7
97JurParT-10
97JurParT-36
97Max-21
97Max-66
97Max-113
97MaxChaTC-C8
97MaxChatCG-C8
97Pin-21
97Pin-50
97Pin-83
97PinArtP-21
97PinArtP-50
97PinArtP-83
97PinCer-21
97PinCer-55
97PinCer-78
97PinCerMB-21
97PinCerMB-55
97PinCerMB-78
97PinCerMG-21
97PinCerMG-55
97PinCerMG-78
97PinCerMR-21
97PinCerMR-55
97PinCerMR-78
97PinCerR-21
97PinCerR-55
97PinCerR-78
97PinMin-13
97PinMin2GC-13
97PinMinB-13
97PinMinC-13
97PinMinG-13
97PinMinNC-13
97PinMinS-13
97PinPor-13
97PinPor-33
97PinPor-48
97PinPreP-21
97PinPreP-50
97PinPreP-83
97PinTotCPB-21
97PinTotCPB-55
97PinTotCPB-78
97PinTotCPG-21
97PinTotCPG-55
97PinTotCPG-78
97PinTotCPR-21
97PinTotCPR-55
97PinTotCPR-78
97PinTroC-21
97PinTroC-50
97PinTroC-83
97Pre-11
97Pre-40
97PreBlaWFS-11
97PreBlaWFS-40
97PreGri-11
97PreGri-40
97PrePas-14
97PrePas-38
97PrePas-63
97PrePas-78
97PrePas-79
97PrePas-93
97PrePas-100
97PrePas-123
97PrePasAut-13
97PrePasBR-BR4
97PrePasCC'-CC19
97PrePasCleC-C10
97PrePasL-14
97PrePasL-38
97PrePasL-63
97PrePasL-78
97PrePasL-79
97PrePasL-93
97PrePasL-100
97PrePasL-123
97PrePasOS-14
97PrePasOS-38
97PrePasOS-63
97PrePasOS-78
97PrePasOS-79
97PrePasOS-93
97PrePasOS-100
97PrePasOS-123
97PrePasP-14
97PrePasPA-13
97PrePasPDB-DB5
97PrePasPEP-14
97PrePasPLL-LL12
97PrePasPM-14
97PrePasPOS-14
97PrePasT-14
97PrePasT-38
97PrePasT-63
97PrePasT-78
97PrePasT-79
97PrePasT-93
97PrePasT-100
97PrePasT-123
97PrePasVL-VL9A
97PrePasVL-VL9B
97PreRedW-11
97PreRedW-40
97RacCho-21
97RacCho-56
97RacCho-100
97RacChoSS-21
97RacChoSS-56
97RacChoSS-100
97RacSha-12
97RacShaGWP-12
97RacShaH-12
97RacShaSA-SA7
97RacShaTS-12
97SBMot-16
97SBMot-52
97SBMot-90
97ScoBoal-5
97ScoBoal-44
97SkyPro-31
97SkyPro-69
97SkyProA-31
97SkyProPS-E7
97SP-21
97SP-63
97SP-99
97SP SupS-21
97SP SupS-63
97SP SupS-99
97SPX-21
97SPxBlu-21
97SPxGol-21
97SPxSil-21
97Ult-37
97Ult-55
97UltDouT-DT5
97UltIns-DC15
97UltSho-13
97UltUpd-15
97UltUpd-85
97UltUpdAR-15
97UppDecRTTC-16
97UppDecRTTC-58
97UppDecRTTC-113
97UppDecVC-21
97UppDecVC-71
97VIP-25
97Viper-10
97Viper-39
97ViperBlaR-10
97ViperBlaR-39
97ViperSid-S7
97VIPExp-25
97VIPHeaGD-HG9
97VIPHigG-HG9
97VIPOilS-25
98ColCho-21
98ColCho-57
98ColCho-106
98HigGea-18
98HigGea-68
98HigGeaA-22
98HigGeaFG-14
98HigGeaFG-68
98HigGeaGJ-GJ10
98HigGeaM-14
98HigGeaM-68
98Max-21
98Max-51
98Max-21
98Max-46
98Max-71
98Max-96
98Max10tA-19
98Max10tA-64
98Max10tA-99
98Max10tABA-47
98Max10tAMP-P21
98MaxFirC-F4
98MaxYealRBS-24
98MaxYealRBS-94
98PinMin-12
98PinMin-24
98PinMinB-12
98PinMinB-24
98PinMinBC-12
98PinMinBC-24
98PinMinBPPC-12
98PinMinBPPC-24
98PinMinGMT-12
98PinMinGMT-24
98PinMinGPC-12
98PinMinGPC-24
98PinMinGPPC-12
98PinMinGPPC-24
98PinMinNC-12
98PinMinNC-24
98PinMinSGC-12
98PinMinSGC-24
98PinMinSMT-12
98PinMinSMT-24
98PinMinSPPC-12
98PinMinSPPC-24
98PinMinSSC-12
98PinMinSSC-24
98PrePas-14
98PrePasA-9
98PrePasCC'-CC19
98PrePasGS-13
98PrePasOS-14
98PrePasP-7
98PrePasP-45
98PrePasP-7
98PrePasP-45
98PrePasPFC-FC12
98PrePasPFCR-FC12
98PrePasPS-PS10
98PrePasS-ST12A
98PrePasS-13
98PrePasS-34
98PrePasS-35
98PrePasSF-34
98PrePasSF-35
98PrePasSS-18
98PrePasSSD-18
98PrePasTorp-ST12B
98SP Aut-21
98SP Aut-55
98SP AutBtW-BW17
98SP AutBtWL2-BW17
98SP AutBtWL3-BW17
98SP AutSotTL1-S6
98UppDecRttC-21
98UppDecRttC-53
98UppDecRttC-106
98UppDecVC-21
98UppDecVC-66
98UppDecVC-133
98UppDecVCPL-PL18
98VIP-27
98VIPExp-27
98Whe-30
98Whe-59
98Whe50tA-A15
98WheAut-9
98WheGol-30
98WheGol-59
98WheGreF-GF18
99Pre-15
99Pre-51
99PrePas-15
99PrePas-51
99PrePas-115
99PrePasCC-10B
99PrePasPS-11
99PrePasS-10A
99UppDecVC-28
99UppDecVC-69
99UppDecVCNSS-MW
99UppDecVCUE-28
99UppDecVCUE-69
99WheHigG-15
99WheHigGAC-15
99WheHigGFG-15
99WheHigGM-15
99WheHigGS-GS15

Waltrip, Sarah
94ActPac-13
94ActPac-166

Waltrip, Stevie
94ActPac-166
95ActPacC-21
95ActPacCSS-21
96ActPacC-90

Wanner, Bryan
91DKIMCDT-43

Wanner, Tom
91K&WURCS-14

Ward, Buck
92K&WDirT-32

Ward, Chuck
92VolRacLS2-66

Ward, Jim
86AceInd-B2

Ward, Lisa
95JSKS.OS-49

Ward, Marty
91BulRin-97
92BulRin-97

Ward, Rodger
60HawWaxI-32
60HawWaxI-43
60HawWaxI-45
62MarInd-15

92MaxCra-NNO
92MaxRed-8
92ProSet-75
92RedSta-8
92Tra-8
92Tra-199
93ActPac-118
93ActPac-119
93FinLin-72
93FinLin-75
93FinLinCS-19
93FinLinCS-29
93FinLinS-72
93FinLinS-75
93Max-44
93MaxPreP-44
93MaxPreS-44
93Tra-44
93TraFirR-44
94ActPac-27
94Hi-Bri4AP-61
94HigGea-15
94HigGeaG-15
94HiTecB4-61
94Max-44
94MaxPreP-44
94MaxPreS-44

Wilson, Tres
91BulRin-42
92BulRin-42

Wilson, Waddell
89Max-89
90Max-87
91Max-84
91ProSet-19
91Tra-72
92BikRacS-26
92MaxBla-149
92MaxRed-149
92ProSet-130A
92ProSet-130B
92Tra-53
93FinLin-36
93FinLinCS-19
93FinLinS-36
93Tra-113
93TraFirR-113
94Max-152
94MaxPreP-144
94MaxPreS-152
94Tra-189
94TraFirR-189
95MaxPreS-156
96MaxPre-146

Wilson, Woodie
93WheRooT-4
93WheRooTPla-4

Wimille, Jean Pierre
71MobTheSoGPMR-22
77Spo-2314

Winchell, Joe
92BulRin-85

Winchell, Larry
91K&WURCS-38

Windell, Jerry
92TraTeaS-58

Windsor, Mike
92TraTeaS-86

Wingate, Mike
94HigGeaPPT-W24
94HigGeaPPTG-24W

Wingate, Ted
65DonSpeS-14

Wingo, Donnie
91Max-128
91MaxMot-21
91Tra-86
92MaxBla-159
92MaxMot-29
92MaxRed-159
92ProSet-120
92Tra-86
93FinLin-55
93FinLinCS-25
93FinLinS-55
93Max-159
93MaxPreP-142
93MaxPreS-159
93Tra-134
93TraFirR-134
94FinLin-47
94FinLinS-47
94Max-143
94MaxPreP-136
94MaxPreS-143
94PrePas-107
94Tra-192
94TraFirR-192
95Max-113
95MaxAut-113
95MaxCroC-119
95MaxPreP-119
95MaxPreS-138
95Sel-107
95SelFlaO-107
96CroJewEDT-44
96CroJewEDTC-44
96CroJewEE-44
96CroJewEli-44
96CroJewES-44
96CroJewETC-44
96CroJewETCE-44
96CroJewETCS-44
96MaxPre-133
97JurPar-55
97JurParT-55

Winiecki Jr., Ray
91K&WURCS-21

Wise, Ted
92VolRacLSI-68

Wittmann, Franz
78GraPri-236

Wizner, Norm
90BigTimD-21
90BigTimDS-21
91BigTimD-70

Wlodyka, Roland
89Max-63

Wolfe, Randy
88WorOut-38
92RacLegS-27

Wolfgang, Doug
89WorOut-9
89WorOutP-8D
90WorOut-2
90WorOutP-8
91WorOut-16

Wollek, Bob
78GraPri-190
78GraPri-198
91IRO-3

Wood, Don
91DKIMCDT-29

Wood, Eddie
90Max-110
91Max-159
91ProSet-109
91Tra-121
92MaxBla-116
92MaxMot-19
92MaxRed-116
92ProSet-186
92Tra-121
93FinLin-149
93FinLin-162
93FinLinCS-4
93FinLinCS-27
93FinLinS-149
93FinLinS-162
93Max-116
93MaxPreP-104
93MaxPreS-116
93Tra-114
93TraFirR-114
94ActPac-173
94FinLin-94
94FinLinS-94
94HigGea-152
94HigGeaDO-152
94HigGeaDOG-152
94HigGeaG-152
94Max-96
94MaxAut-96
94MaxPreP-96
94MaxPreS-96
94MaxPreS-238
94PrePas-88
94Tra-119
94TraFirR-119
95Max-54
95MaxCroC-82
95MaxPreP-82
95MaxPreS-91
95Sel-89
95SelFlaO-89
95TraBehTS-BTS17
96AutRacA-61
96AutRacCA-61
96CroJewEDT-45
96CroJewEDTC-45
96CroJewEE-45
96CroJewEli-45
96CroJewES-45
96CroJewETC-45
96CroJewETCE-45
96CroJewETCS-45
96Max-58
96MaxPre-105
96UltUpd-88
97AutRacA-56
97FinLinPP2-36
97PrePasAut-21
97Ult-69

Wood, Glen
89Max-199
89Max-213
89TGRacMR-91
89TGRacMR-99
89WinCir-17
90Max-139
91Max-159
91MaxMot-15
91ProSetL-L12
91TGRacMRU-91
91TGRacMRU-99
91Tra-64
91TraPacYH-43
91TraPacYH-44
92MaxBla-118
92MaxRed-118
93FinLin-19
93FinLin-162
93FinLinCS-4
93FinLinCS-16
93FinLinS-19
93FinLinS-162
93Max-114
93MaxPreP-102
93MaxPreS-114
93Tra-79
93TraFirR-79
94ActPac-27
94FinLin-83
94FinLinS-83
94HigGea-153
94HigGeaDO-153
94HigGeaDOG-153
94HigGeaG-153
94Max-94
94MaxAut-94
94MaxPreP-94
94MaxPreS-94
94Pow-10
94PowGol-10
94PrePas-88
94Tra-156
94TraFirR-156
95ImaCirC-9
95Max-52
95MaxCroC-80
95MaxPreP-80
95MaxPreS-88
95Sel-89
95SelFlaO-89
95SP-135
95SPDieC-135
95TraBehTS-BTS10
95UppDec-158
95UppDecGSEG-158
95UppDecSSES-158
96AutRac-28
96AutRacA-62
96AutRacCA-62
96Cla-27
96ClaPriP-27
96ClaSil-27
96Max-58
96MaxPre-92
96Ult-148
97ColCho-121
98PrePas-136
98PrePasS-36
98PrePasSF-36

Wood, Jeff
91AllWorl-19
92AllWorl-39

Wood, Jerry
91LanART-6

Wood, Kim
94ActPac-173
96AutRacA-63
96AutRacCA-63
96Max-58
96MaxPre-117

Wood, Len
91Max-159
91ProSet-108
91Tra-122
92MaxBla-117
92MaxRed-117
92ProSet-186
92Tra-122
93FinLin-162
93FinLin-176
93FinLinCS-4
93FinLinCS-25
93FinLinS-162
93FinLinS-176
93Max-115
93MaxPreP-103
93MaxPreS-115
93Tra-38
93TraFirR-38
94ActPac-173
94FinLin-94
94FinLinS-94
94HigGea-154
94HigGeaDO-154
94HigGeaDOG-154
94HigGeaG-154
94Max-95
94MaxAut-95
94MaxPreP-95
94MaxPreS-95
94PrePas-88
94Tra-153
94TraFirR-153
95Max-53
95MaxCroC-81
95MaxPreP-81
95MaxPreS-89
95Sel-89
95SelFlaO-89
95TraBehTS-BTS24
96AutRacA-64
96AutRacCA-64
96Cla-27
96ClaPriP-27
96ClaSil-27
96CroJewEDT-46
96CroJewEDTC-46
96CroJewEE-46
96CroJewEli-46
96CroJewES-46
96CroJewETC-46
96CroJewETCE-46
96CroJewETCS-46
96Max-58
96MaxPre-91
96UltUpd-88
97AutRacA-56
97FinLinPP2-36
97SBMot-44
97SBMot-60
97Ult-69

Wood, Leonard
89Max-56
89Max-199
90Max-74
91Max-88
91MaxMot-15
91MaxMot-25
91ProSet-110
91Tra-62
92MaxBla-170
92MaxMot-31
92MaxRed-170
92ProSet-84
92Tra-62
93FinLin-162
93FinLin-166
93FinLinCS-4
93FinLinCS-18
93FinLinS-162
93FinLinS-166
93Max-157
93MaxPreP-140
93MaxPreS-157
93Tra-79
93TraFirR-79
94FinLin-110
94FinLinGT-TG5
94FinLinS-110
94HigGea-142
94HigGeaDO-142
94HigGeaDOG-142
94HigGeaG-142
94Max-134
94MaxPreP-127
94MaxPreS-134
94Pow-47
94PowGol-47
94PrePas-108
94Tra-156
94TraFirR-156
95ImaCirC-9
95Max-104
95MaxAut-104
95MaxCroC-110
95MaxPreP-110
95MaxPreS-129
95PrePas-99
95PrePasRH-99
95Sel-99
95SelFlaO-99
95SP-148
95SPDieC-148
95TraBehTS-BTS10
96Max-79
96MaxPre-125

Wood, Stafford
92TraTeaS-180
92TraTeaS-191

Woodall, Chip
73FleAHRRU-74

Woodling, Randy
92JAG-125

Woodruff, Billy
89Max-53
94HigGeaPPT-W27
94HigGeaPPTG-27W

Woods, Bobby
92LanARCF-83

Woods, Della
89MegDra-78
89MegDra-79
91BigTimD-35
91BigTimD-36

Woods, Shaun
94HigGeaPPT-G13
94HigGeaPPTG-13G

Wooley, Greg
87WorOut-18
88WorOut-11

Woolsey, Russ
92VolRacLSI-69

Workman, Jacky
91BulRin-110
92BulRin-168

Workman, Rick
94STAMod-52

Worley, Satch
91WinChoM-22
91WinChoM-23

Worsham, Chuck
92ProSetN-158
93FinLinN-71

Worsham, Del
91ProSetN-122
92ProSetN-34
92ProSetN-61
92ProSetN-120
93FinLinN-70
93FinLinN-132

Wren, Mike
92LanARCF-48

Wrenn, Ernest
89CheFlaI-81
89CheFlaI-92

Wright, Gary
91WorOut-22
91WorOut-110
94WorOut-25

Wright, Kenny
92WinChoM-12

Wright, Marlin
91Tra-160
92Tra-160
93Max-242
93MaxPreS-242
94MaxPreS-224
95MaxPreS-222
96MaxPre-223

Wright, Pete
93FinLin-88
93FinLinCS-22
93FinLinS-88
93Max-149
93MaxPreP-134
93MaxPreS-149
93Tra-48
93TraFirR-48
94FinLin-41
94FinLinS-41
94HigGea-133

94HigGeaDO-133
94HigGeaDOG-133
94HigGeaG-133
94Max-145
94Max-294
94MaxPreP-138
94MaxPreS-145
94Pow-127
94PowGol-127
Wurz, Franz
78GraPri-221
Wyers, John
95K&WDirT-40
Yarborough, Cale
77Spo-2801
85SpoPhoGS-NNO
86SpoPhoG-13
88MaxCha-4
88MaxCha-90
89Max-37
89TGRacMR-250
89TGRacMR-251
89TGRacMR-252
89TGRacMR-253
89TGRacMR-254
89TGRacMR-255
90Max-18
90MaxHolF-HF25
91Max-32
91MaxMot-39
91MaxWin2AF-6
91MaxWin2AF-7
91MaxWin2AF-8
91ProSet-56
91ProSetL-L14
91SpoLegCY-P1
91SpoLegCY-CY1
91SpoLegCY-CY2
91SpoLegCY-CY3
91SpoLegCY-CY4
91SpoLegCY-CY5
91SpoLegCY-CY6
91SpoLegCY-CY7
91SpoLegCY-CY8
91SpoLegCY-CY9
91SpoLegCY-CY10
91SpoLegCY-CY11
91SpoLegCY-CY12
91SpoLegCY-CY13
91SpoLegCY-CY14
91SpoLegCY-CY15
91SpoLegCY-CY16
91SpoLegCY-CY17
91SpoLegCY-CY18
91SpoLegCY-CY19
91SpoLegCY-CY20
91SpoLegCY-CY21
91SpoLegCY-CY22
91SpoLegCY-CY23
91SpoLegCY-CY24
91SpoLegCY-CY25
91SpoLegCY-CY26
91SpoLegCY-CY27
91SpoLegCY-CY28
91SpoLegCY-CY29
91SpoLegCY-CY30
91SpoLegDJ-DJ17
91SpoLegNB-NB7
91SpoLegWS-WS14
91TexWorS-4
91TexWorS-8
91TGRacMRU-250
91TGRacMRU-251
91TGRacMRU-252
91TGRacMRU-253
91TGRacMRU-254
91TGRacMRU-255
91TGRacTL-25
91Tra-66
91TraPacYH-45
91TraPacYH-46
92MaxBla-135
92MaxMot-21
92MaxRed-135
92ProSet-149
92ProSetL-L30
92ProSetR-3
92ProSetRF-L3
92RedRacCY-1
92RedRacCY-2
92RedRacCY-3
92RedRacCY-4
92RedRacCY-5
92RedRacCY-6
92RedRacCY-7
92RedRacCY-8
92RedRacCY-9
92RedRacCY-10
92RedRacCY-11
92RedRacCY-12
92RedRacCY-13
92RedRacCY-14
92RedRacCY-15
92RedRacCY-16
92RedRacCY-17
92RedRacCY-18
92RedRacCY-19
92RedRacCY-20
92RedRacCY-21
92RedRacCY-22
92RedRacCY-23
92RedRacCY-24
92RedRacCY-25
92RedRacCY-26
92RedRacCY-27
92RedRacCY-28
92RedRacCY-29
92RedRacCY-30
92RedRacCY-P1
92Tra-19
92TraBenP-47
93FinLin-99
93FinLinCS-22
93FinLinS-99
93Max-136
93MaxPreP-122
93MaxPreS-136
93Tra-123
93TraFirR-123
94FinLin-143
94FinLinS-143
94HigGea-35
94HigGeaG-35
94HigGeaL-LS1
94Max-114
94MaxPreP-114
94MaxPreS-114
94Pep400VL-5
94Pow-128
94PowGol-128
94PrePas-89
94Tra-64
94TraFirR-64
94VIP-90
95HigGea-40
95HigGeaDO-40
95HigGeaDOG-40
95HigGeaG-40
95MatWinCC-6
95MatWinCC-7
95MatWinCC-8
95Max-67
95Max-264
95MaxCroC-95
95MaxPreP-95
95MaxPreS-108
95MetImpWCC-3
95PrePas-89
95PrePasRH-89
95Sel-81
95Sel-132
95SelFlaO-81
95SelFlaO-132
95SP-128
95SPBacTB-BB2
95SPDieC-128
95Tra5thA-69
95Tra5thAG-69
95Tra5thAR-R14
95TraAutV-35
95TraBehTS-BTS13
95TraVal-89
95UppDec-152
95UppDecGSEG-152
95UppDecI-I4
95UppDecSSES-152
96ActPacC-75
96CroJewEDT-39
96CroJewEDTC-39
96CroJewEE-39
96CroJewEli-39
96CroJewES-39
96CroJewETC-39
96CroJewETCE-39
96CroJewETCS-39
96M-F-39
96MaxPre-108
96MetImp2AWCC-6
96MetImp2AWCC-7
96MetImp2AWCC-8
96UppDec-128
96UppDecRL-RLC2
96ZenChaS-18
96ZenChaS-19
96ZenChaS-20
97ActPacFA-2
97ActPacFAA-2
97ColCho-125
97ColChoUD5-UD68
97SkyPro-37
97Ult-65
97UltUpd-46
98Max10tA-31
98Max10tA-76
98Max10tA-110
98Max10tABA-48
98Max10tACP-CP10
98Max10tACPDC-CP10
98PrePas-133
98PrePasPR-4A
98SP AutMoaL-M5
98SP AutT-T5
98UppDecRTTC5A-AN25
98UppDecRTTC5A-AN32
98UppDecRTTC5AA-AN25
99PrePas-133
Yarborough, Lee Roy
89TGRacMR-46
89TGRacMR-47
89TGRacMR-75
89WinCir-35
91TGRacMRU-46
91TGRacMRU-47
91TGRacMRU-75
98PrePas-141
Yardley, Dale
91LanRocS-23
Yates, Brock
92ProSetN-186
Yates, Doug
91GalPrePR-106
92TraTeaS-43
92TraTeaS-48
94MaxTexEI-48
Yates, Jim
89CheFlaI-30
91ProSetN-48
91ProSetN-96
92ProSetN-71
92ProSetN-143
93FinLinN-106
95ActPacN-24
95ActPacNSS-24
95Zen-73
95Zen-74
Yates, Richard
91Tra-180
92Tra-180
92TraTeaS-31
94MaxTexEI-49
Yates, Robert
89Max-176
90Max-126
91Max-35
91MaxMot-11
91Tra-46
92MaxBla-104
92MaxBla-278
92MaxBla-292
92MaxMcD-6
92MaxMot-15
92MaxRed-104
92MaxRed-278
92MaxRed-292
92MaxTexDA-3
92MaxTexDA-9
92MaxTexDA-14
92MaxTexDA-17
92MaxTexDA-18
92MaxTexDA-19
92ProSet-203
92Tra-35
92TraTeaS-27
92TraTeaS-49
93FinLin-158
93FinLinCS-23
93FinLinS-158
93Max-101
93Max-264
93Max-270
93Max-273
93Max-292
93MaxPreP-90
93MaxPreP-193
93MaxPreS-101
93MaxPreS-264
93MaxPreS-270
93MaxPreS-273
93MaxPreS-292
93MaxTexDA-3
93MaxTexDA-6
93MaxTexDA-10
93MaxTexDA-11
93MaxTexDA-14
93Tra-49
93Tra-69
93Tra-171
93TraFirR-49
93TraFirR-69
93TraFirR-171
94ActPac-170
94FinLin-119
94FinLinG-26
94FinLinS-119
94HigGea-26
94HigGeaG-26
94Max-117
94Max-232
94MaxPreP-117
94MaxPreP-191
94MaxPreS-117
94MaxPreS-241
94MaxPreS-291
94MaxTexEI-2
94MaxTexEI-13
94MaxTexEI-16
94MaxTexEI-17
94MaxTexEI-18
94MaxTexEI-20
94Pow-9
94Pow-129
94PowGol-9
94PowGol-129
94PrePas-90
94Tra-40
94TraAutV-45
94TraFirR-40
95FinLin-44
95FinLinPP-44
95FinLinSil-44
95HigGea-36
95HigGeaDO-36
95HigGeaDOG-36
95HigGeaG-36
95ImaOwnP-OP11
95Max-49
95MaxCroC-99
95MaxPreP-99
95MaxPreS-111
95MaxPreS-239
95PrePas-90
95PrePasRH-90
95Sel-90
95SelFlaO-90
95SP-129
95SPDieC-129
95Tra5thA-67
95Tra5thAG-67
95TraAutV-34
95TraBehTS-BTS12
96ActPacC-82
96Ass-35
96AutRac-39
96AutRacA-65
96AutRacCA-65
96Cla-23
96ClaPriP-23
96ClaSil-23
96CroJewEDT-37
96CroJewEDTC-37
96CroJewEE-37
96CroJewEli-37
96CroJewES-37
96CroJewETC-37
96CroJewETCE-37
96CroJewETCS-37
96FinLin-79
96FinLinPriP-79
96FinLinS-79
96Max-52
96MaxPre-111
96PinPolP-93
96PinPolPLF-93
96PrePas-79
96PrePasSco-79
96PrePasT-79
96UppDec-129
96Zen-86
96ZenArtP-86
97FinLinPP2-34
97PinPre-29
97PinPre-32
97PinPre-35
97PinPreBM-29
97PinPreBM-32
97PinPreBM-35
97PinPreGM-29
97PinPreGM-32
97PinPreGM-35
97PinPreSM-29
97PinPreSM-32
97PinPreSM-35
97Pre-61
97PreBlaWFS-61
97PreGri-61
97PreRedW-61
97RacCho-72
97RacChoSS-72
97SBMot-32
97ScoBoal-33
97SkyPro-35
97Ult-64
97UltUpd-51
98PrePasS-15
98PrePasSF-15
York, Donnie
91BulRin-21
92BulRin-175
York, Mickey
91BulRin-108
92BulRin-122
York, Pat
95JSKS.OS-72
Young, Bob
92WinChoM-23
Young, Bryan
90LanRocSHS-33
Young, Clay
92LanARCF-28
92LanARCF-76
Young, Dale
71FleAHRDC-45
Young, Ron
92BulRin-177
Youngblood, Kevin
92BikRacS-15
Yowell, Bobby
73FleAHRRU-57
Yunick, Smokey
89Max-182
91ProSetL-L19
91TraPacYH-47
92MaxIMH-32
92ProSetL-L12
95UppDec-160
95UppDecGSEG-160
95UppDecI-I1
95UppDecSSES-160
96UppDec-144
98UppDecRTTC5A-AN7
Zampedri, Alessandro
96SkyInd5-26
96SkyInd5-65
97Hi-IRL-29
97Hi-IRL'I5-I4
97Hi-IRL'I5-I17
Zamrzla, Jimmy
94HigGeaPPT-W28
94HigGeaPPTG-28W
Zanardi, Alessandro
92GriForO-169
Zanini, Antonio
78GraPri-240
Zardo, Bill Jr.
92PacAmeCT-16
Zardo, Bill Sr.
92PacAmeCT-12
92PacAmeCT-42
Zehner, Edward
90K&WDirT-42
Zeigler, John
91LanART-10
Zigler, Twig
73FleAHRRU-43
Zuideman, Jeff
91WinChoNED-108
91WinChoNED-109
92WinChoB-115
92WinChoB-116

Acknowledgments

When we started this Beckett Guide we were unsure what type of response we would get from dealers when we asked them to play a major role in our price gathering. Most were more than happy to lend a hand. Thanks again to all the contributors nationwide (listed below) as well as our staff here in Dallas.

Those who worked closely with us on this book have proven themselves invaluable. We would like to thank the following manufacturers -- Action Performance (Fred & Lisa Wagenhals and Melodee Volosin), Brookfield Collector's Guild (Terry Rubritz), Finish Line (Art West), Fleer/SkyBox (Rich Bradley and Jay Miller), Highland Mint (Timm Boyle), Hi-Tech (Ed Kelly and Kevin Roberts), Metallic Impressions (Connie Nelson) Peachstate/GMP (Tom Long and Mark Long), Pinnacle Brands (Laurie Goldberg), Press Pass (Victor Schaffer, Rod Ulrich and Bill Surdock), Racing Champions (Pete Hensler and Howard Schacter), Revell (Dick Nelson), Scoreboard/Classic (Brian Cahill), Upper Deck, Wheels (Danny Correll, Conrad Powell), White Rose Collectibles (Ron Slider and Jerry Graham), and WSMP (Dennis Punch). Finally we give a special acknowledgment to the late Dennis W. Eckes, "Mr. Sports Americana." The success of the Beckett Price Guides has always been a result of a team effort.

It is very difficult to be "accurate" -- one can only do one's best. But this job is especially difficult since we're shooting at a moving target. Prices are fluctuating all the time. Having a several full-time pricing experts has definitely proven to be better than just one, and I thank all of them for working together to provide you, our readers, with the most accurate prices possible.

Many people have provided price input, illustrative material, checklist verifications, errata, and/or background information. We should like to individually thank George Barnett (Hobby Maker), Dave Countryman (Diamond End Zone), Homer & Phyllis Frazier (Korner Fun & Games), Ed & Lynn Gaffney (North Coast Racing), David Giffert (Victory Lane Race Cards), Jon Hargrove (The Carburetor Shop), Bob Harmon & Dan Talbert (North State Race Cards), Greg Jeffries, Dean & Kathy Knight (Kathy's Kards), Luke Krisher & Anna Schreck (A&L Racing Collectibles), Norm LaBarge, Sandy Larson (Northern Likes Racing) Stewart Lehman (Lehman Racing Collectables) Mike Locotosh (North Coast Racing), Johnny Love (Win Racing), Gene Persinger (G n' G Sports Cards), Scott Polner (Collector's Choice), Marie Raucci (Lane Automotive), Brian Shepherd (Shepherd's Racing), Richard Schultz (Racing Around), Bill Spertzel (Cards Etc.), Danny West (Golden Legacy), Kevin & Trish Wheeler (Sport Cards, Etc.).

Every year we make active solicitations for expert input. We are particularly appreciative of help (however extensive or cursory) provided for this volume. We receive many inquiries, comments and questions regarding material within this book. In fact, each and every one is read and digested. Time constraints, however, prevent us from personally replying. But keep sharing your knowledge. Your letters and input are part of the "big picture" of hobby information we can pass along to readers in our books and magazines. Even though we cannot respond to each letter, you are making significant contributions to the hobby through your interest and comments.

The effort to continually refine and improve this book also involves a growing number of people and types of expertise on our home team. Our company boasts a substantial Sports Data Publishing team, which strengthens our ability to provide comprehensive analysis of the marketplace. Sports Data Publishing capably handled numerous technical details and provided able assistance in the preparation of this edition.

Our racing analyst played a major part in compiling this year's book, traveling thousands of miles during the past year to attend sports card shows, racing events and visit card shops around the United States and Canada. The Beckett racing specialist is Steven Judd (Price Guide Editor). His pricing analysis and careful proofreading were key contributions to the accuracy of this annual.

The effort was led by the Manager of Technical Services Dan Hitt. They were ably assisted by the rest of the Price Guide analysts: Pat Blandford, Mark Anderson, Rob Springs and Bill Sutherland.

The price gathering and analytical talents of this fine group of hobbyists have helped make our Beckett team stronger, while making this guide and its companion monthly Price Guide more widely recognized as the hobby's most reliable and relied upon sources of pricing information.

The Beckett Interactive Department, ably headed by Mark Harwell, played a critical role in technology. Working with software designed by assistant manager Eric Best, they spent countless hours programming, testing, and implementing it to simplify the handling of thousands of prices that must be checked and updated for each edition.

In the Production Department, Airey Baringer and Gean Paul Figari were responsible for the typesetting and for the card photos you see throughout the book.

David Yandry spent tireless hours on the phone attending to the wishes of our dealer advertisers. Once the ad specifications were delivered to our offices, Quentin Smith used his computer skills to turn raw copy into attractive display advertisements.

In the years since this guide debuted, Beckett Publications has grown beyond any rational expectation. A great many talented and hard working individuals have been instrumental in this growth and success. Our whole team is to be congratulated for what we together have accomplished. Our Beckett Publications team is led by President Jeff Amano, Executive Vice President Claire Backus, Division Vice Presidents Joe Galindo, Chuck Robison and Margaret Steele, Directors Rudy Klancnik and Beth Harwell. They are ably assisted by Pete Adauto, John Ayres, Joel Brown, Kaye Ball, Therese Bellar, Louise Bird, Bob Brown, Angie Calandro, Allen Christopherson, Randall Calvert, Susan Catka, Albert Chavez, Marty Click, Amy March, Aaron Derr, Ryan Duckworth, Mitchell Dyson, Eric Evans, Craig Ferris, Carol Fowler, Rosanna Gonzalez-Oleachea, Jenifer Grellhesl, Julie Grove, Barry Hacker, Tracy Hackler, Patti Harris, Joanna Hayden, Pepper Hastings, Doug Kale, Kevin King, Gayle Klancnik, Tom Layberger, Jane Ann Layton, Benedito Leme, Lori Lindsey, Stanley Lira, John Marshall, Mike McAllister, Matt McGuire, Omar Mediano, Sherry Monday, Mila Morante, Daniel Moscoso Jr., Allan Muir, Hugh Murphy, Mike Obert, Stacy Olivieri, Andrea Paul, Clark Palomino, Missy Patrello, Mike Pagel, Wendy Pallugna, Mike Payne, Tim Polzer, Bob Richardson, Wade Rugenstein, Susan Thompson, Christine Seibert, Dave Sliepka, Judi Smalling, Sheri Smith, Marcia Stoesz, Mark Stokes, Dawn Sturgeon, Margie Swoyer, Doree Tate, Jim Tereschuk, Ed Wornson, David Yandry, Bryan Winstead and Mark Zeske. The whole Beckett Publications team has my thanks for jobs well done. Thank you, everyone.

I also thank my family, especially my wife, Patti, and our daughters, Christina, Rebecca, and Melissa, for putting up with me again.

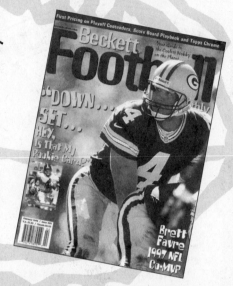